Peterson's Scholarships, Grants & Prizes 2018

PETERSON'S®

About Peterson's®

Peterson's® provides the accurate, dependable, high-quality education content and guidance you need to succeed. No matter where you are on your academic or professional path, you can rely on Peterson's publications and its online information at **www.petersons.com** for the most up-to-date education exploration data, expert test-prep tools, and top notch career success resources—everything you need to achieve your goals.

For more information, contact Peterson's, 3 Columbia Circle, Suite 205, Albany, NY 12203-5158; 800-338-3282 Ext. 54229; or visit us online at **www.petersons.com**.

ISBN 978-0-7689-4155-5

Printed in the United States of America

10 9 8 7 6 5 4 3 2 1   19 18 17

Twenty-second Edition

OTHER RECOMMENDED TITLES

Peterson's *The Best Scholarships for the Best Students*
Peterson's *The "C" Students Guide to Scholarships,* by Felecia Hatcher
Peterson's *How to Get Money for College: Go Beyond Federal Aid—Get Money from Your School and State*
Peterson's *Plan and Finance Your Family's College Dreams,* by John A. Hupalo and Peter Mazareas, Ph.D.

Contents

INDEXES

A Note from the Peterson's® Editors

Billions of dollars in financial aid are made available by private donors and governmental agencies to students and their families every year to help pay for college. Yet, to the average person, the task of finding financial aid awards in this huge network of scholarships, grants, and prizes appears to be nearly impossible.

For nearly forty years, Peterson's® has given students and parents the most comprehensive, up-to-date information on how to get their fair share of the financial aid pie. *Peterson's® Scholarships, Grants & Prizes* was created to help students and their families pinpoint those specific private financial aid programs that best match students' backgrounds, interests, talents, or abilities.

In *Peterson's® Scholarships, Grants & Prizes,* you will find nearly 3,500 award programs and resources that are providing financial awards to undergraduates in the 2017–18 academic year. Foundations, fraternal and ethnic organizations, community service clubs, churches and religious groups, philanthropies, companies and industry groups, labor unions and public employees' associations, veterans' groups, and trusts and bequests are all possible sources.

For those seeking to enter college, *Peterson's® Scholarships, Grants & Prizes* includes information needed to make financing a college education as seamless as possible.

The **How to Find an Award That's Right for You** section paints a complete picture of the financial aid landscape, discusses strategies for finding financial awards, provides important tips on how to avoid scholarship scams, and offers insight into how to make scholarship management organizations work for you.

Also found in **How to Find an Award That's Right for You** is the "How to Use This Guide" article, which describes how the nearly 3,500 awards in the guide are profiled, along with information on how to search for an award in one of eleven categories.

If you would like to compare awards quickly, refer to the **Quick-Reference Chart.** Here you can search through the "Scholarships, Grants & Prizes At-a-Glance" chart and select awards by the highest dollar amount.

In the **Profiles of Scholarships, Grants & Prizes** section you'll find updated award programs, along with information about award sponsors. The profile section is divided into three categories: *Academic Fields/Career Goals, Nonacademic/Noncareer Criteria,* and *Miscellaneous Criteria.* Each profile provides all of the need-to-know information about available scholarships, grants, and prizes.

Finally, the back of the book features thirteen **Indexes** listing scholarships, grants, and prizes based on award name; sponsor; academic fields/career goals; civic, professional, social, or union affiliation; corporate affiliation; employment/volunteer experience; impairment; military service; nationality or ethnic background; religious affiliation; residence; location of study; and talent/interest area.

Peterson's® publishes a full line of books—financial aid, career preparation, test prep, and education exploration. Peterson's® publications can be found at high school guidance offices, college libraries and career centers, and your local bookstore and library. Peterson's® books are also available at www.petersonsbooks.com. To search for scholarships online, check out www.petersons.com/college-search/scholarship-search.aspx.

We welcome any comments or suggestions you may have about this publication. Your feedback will help us make educational dreams possible for you—and others like you.

HOW TO FIND AN AWARD THAT'S RIGHT FOR YOU

All About Scholarships

Dr. Gary M. Bell
Former Academic Dean, Honors College, Texas Tech University

During the next four (or more) years you will spend your time earning your college baccalaureate degree, think of the learning task as your primary employment. It is helpful to think of a scholarship as part of the salary for undertaking your job of learning. One of your first inquiries as you examine a potential college setting is about the type of assistance it might provide given your interests, academic record, and personal history. Talk to a financial aid officer or a scholarship coordinator at the school. At most schools, these are special officers—people specifically employed to assist you in your quest for financial assistance. Virtually all schools also have brochures or publications and specific information on their website that show the scholarship opportunities at their institution. Take a close look at this scholarship information.

Also, high school counselors often have keen insight into resources available at colleges, especially for the schools in your area. These people are the key points of contact between institutions of higher education and you.

In general, it is not a good idea to use a private company that promises to provide you with a list of scholarships for which you might be eligible. Such lists are often very broad, and you can secure the same results by using available high school, university, web-based, and published information. The scholarship search you perform online will probably be more fruitful than what any private company can do for you.

What do we mean by the word "scholarship," anyway? In the very broadest sense, scholarships consist of outright grants of monetary assistance to eligible students to help them attend college. The money is applied to tuition or the cost of living while in school. Scholarships do not need to be repaid. They do, however, often carry stringent criteria for maintaining them, such as the achievement of a certain grade point average, the carrying of a given number of class hours, matriculation in a specific program, or membership in a designated group. Scholarships at many schools may be combined with college work-study programs, in which some work is also required. Often, scholarships are combined with other forms of financial aid so that collectively they provide you with a truly attractive financial aid package. This may include low-interest loan programs to make the school of your choice financially feasible.

Scholarships generally fall into three major categories: *need-based scholarships*, predicated on income; *merit-based scholarships*, based on your academic and sometimes extracurricular achievements; and *association-based scholarships*, which are dependent on as many different associations as you can imagine (for instance, your home county, your identification with a particular group, fraternal and religious organizations, or the company for which a parent may work). The range of reasons for which scholarships are given is almost infinite.

Most schools accommodate students who have financial need. The largest and best grant programs are the U.S. government-sponsored Federal Pell Grants and the Federal Supplemental Educational Opportunity Grants, which you might want to explore with your financial aid counselor. Also inquire about state-sponsored scholarship and grant programs.

Merit-based scholarships come from a variety of sources—the university, individual departments or colleges within the university, state scholarship programs, or special donors who want to assist worthy students. Remember this as you meet with your financial aid officer because he or she knows that different opportunities may be available for you as a petroleum engineering, agriculture, accounting, pre-veterinary, or performing arts major. Merit-based scholarships are typically designed to reward the highest performers on such precollege measures as standardized tests (the SAT® or ACT®) and high school grades. Because repeated performance on standardized tests often leads to higher scores, it may be financially advantageous for you to take these college admission tests several times.

Inquire about each of the three categories of scholarships. The association-based scholarships can sometimes be particularly helpful and quite surprising. Employers of parents, people from specific geographic locations, or organizations (churches, civic groups, unions, special interest clubs, and even family name associations) may provide assistance for college students. Campus scholarship literature is the key to unlocking the mysteries of association-based financial assistance (and the other two categories as well), but personal interviews with financial officers are also crucial.

There are several issues to keep in mind as you seek scholarship assistance. Probably the most important is to determine deadlines that apply to a scholarship for which you may be eligible. It's wise to begin your search early, so that your eligibility is not nullified by missing a published deadline. Most scholarship opportunities require that you complete an application form, and it is time well spent to make sure your answers are neat (if using a paper application), grammatically correct, and logical. Correct spelling is essential. Have someone proofread your application. Keep in mind that if applications require essays, fewer students typically take the time to complete these essays, and this gives those students who do so a better chance of winning that particular scholarship. Always be truthful in these applications, but at the same time provide the most positive self-portrayal to enhance your chances of being considered. Most merit-based and association-based scholarships are awarded competitively.

Finally, let the people who offer you assistance know whether you will accept their offer. Too many students simply assume that a scholarship offer means automatic acceptance. This is not the case! In most instances, you must send a letter of acknowledgement and acceptance. Virtually all schools have agreed that students must make up their minds about scholarship acceptance no later than May 1, but earlier deadlines may apply.

As you probably know, tuition at private schools is typically higher than tuition at state colleges and universities. Scholarships can narrow this gap. Many private institutions have a great deal of money to spend on scholarship assistance, so you may find that with a scholarship, going to a private college will cost no more than attending a state-supported college or university. **Note:** A substantial scholarship from a private school may still leave you with a very large annual bill to cover the difference between the scholarship amount and the actual cost of tuition, fees, and living expenses.

When you evaluate a scholarship, take into account your final out-of-pocket costs. Also consider the length of time for which the school extends scholarship support. Be cautious about schools that promise substantial assistance for the first year to get you there, but then provide little or nothing in subsequent years. The most attractive and meaningful scholarships are offered for four to five years. Do not abandon the scholarship search once you are enrolled at the school of your choice. Often, a number of additional scholarship opportunities are available for you once you're enrolled, especially as you prove your ability and interest in a given field.

It's Never Too Early to Look for College Scholarships

Many high school students make the mistake of thinking that their race to the top of the scholarship mountain begins during their senior year. Some have the forethought to begin their hunt for college money in their junior year. But even that may be too late. Rising costs of college tuition, the increasing number of people attending college for the first time, and the reduction in federal, state, and local grants for college goers have made paying for college without student loan debt a competitive sport. And only those who are prepared are coming out unscathed and debt free.

The importance of securing scholarships and grants to help pay for college cannot be overestimated. The nation is currently in the midst of a student-loan debt crisis that is crippling the earning power of millions of college graduates. If you need any further convincing to get serious about finding money for college other than student loans, check out these sobering statistics:*

- In recent years, college students borrowed more than $100 billion to pay for college, the highest amount of student borrowing ever.

- In 2015, the outstanding balance of student loan debt reached nearly $1.27 trillion (yes, that's with a "T"), surpassing credit card debt of $900 billion.

- Nearly every student who earns a four-year degree graduates with student loan debt, which currently averages about $33,300.

Student loan debt may be inevitable, but it doesn't have to be crippling. And the more money you can get that doesn't require repayment, the better your financial future will be once you do get your college degree. Here are some tips on how to get ahead of the college money rat race and come out a winner:

1. **Make a Family College Payment Plan.** While 70 percent of parents surveyed by an investment group said their students are so brilliant that they will win enormous amounts of scholarships to pay for college, the reality is paying for college without student loans doesn't happen by chance. Paying for college takes planning, and the sooner you begin the better off you'll be. But a student cannot plan for college payments alone. Parents must meet with their children to develop a college payment plan. In their discussions, they need to discuss all family college payment plan options, including parental tax credits, college saving accounts, trusts, savings bonds, and even stock options. At the meeting, parents and their children should do the following:

   - Calculate the real costs of attending college.
   - Decide who is going to pay and how much.
   - Develop a strategy to meet those payment commitments.

   Making a family college payment plan is an essential first step. The outcome of this plan gives students a clear scholarship money goal and provides an excellent starting point for your scholarship sojourn.

2. **Start scholarship research on day one.** While most scholarships and grants require you to be a junior or senior in high school, this does not preclude you from creating an application strategy the day you enter high school—or even before! In truth, the minute you decide to go to college you should start researching the best ways to pay for it. Talk to guidance counselors, do research online, learn what the scholarship requirements are, and develop a plan to apply when ready. By searching for scholarships as early as possible, you will be able to zero in on the ones that match with your skills, abilities, characteristics, and passions. In addition to finding scholarships, use this preliminary time to learn the scholarship rules. Build a checklist of all the accompanying documents you're going to need to accompany your scholarship application. Save items

---

* All statistics are derived from the Federal Reserve Bank of New York as well as its report "Grading Student Loans." https://www.federalreserve.gov/econresdata/notes/feds-notes/2015/how-much-student-debt-is-out-there-20150807.html.

that you think would work well in your personal statement or essay. Develop a list of people who could be references or write letters of recommendations. Organize, organize, organize—the more organized you are, the easier it will be to apply for multiple scholarships.

3. **Be Your Guidance Counselor's Best Friend.** Long the butt of jokes, guidance counselors are the most maligned members of a high school system. But they can be your best ally when it comes to securing scholarships and grants for college. Get to know your guidance counselor well. Offer your counselor a proactive strategy for getting money for college. Your guidance counselor is more apt to help you with planning your high school career if he or she knows you are serious about going to college.

4. **Rack up scholarships as you go along.** College savings bonds may seem like a blast from the 1950s, but believe it or not there are still essay, speech, and music contests all over the nation that offer them to winners. You can earn these types of rewards as well as cold hard cash at anytime—even before you even get into high school. Check out contests such as the Ayn Rand Institute's Anthem and Atlas Shrugged Essay Contests or the American Legion National High School Oratorical Contest. These are open to all high school-age students.

5. **Plan Your High School Years with College in Mind.** As you do your research on college scholarships, you will see that many have academic requirements. You need to start early on developing a course of study to help you hit those necessary academic marks. Few students wake up one day and score 31 on the ACT or start a charity out of the blue. So plan your classes, extracurricular events, and charity activities with college in mind. To be sure, you need to do what appeals to you, but keep in mind that every class you attend, every test you take, and every club you join can be an asset to your scholarship hunt. Be deliberate about your school choices, and start with the end goal in mind.

Filling out a scholarship application is the end, not the beginning of a long process to earn money for college. Fortunately, you can begin all the organization and planning necessary to secure scholarship money well before the scholarship is due. Do not wait. It's never too early to start your scholarship journey. The earlier you begin, the better your journey will be!

A Strategy for Finding Awards

Private scholarships and awards can be characterized by unpredictable, sometimes seemingly bizarre, criteria. Before you begin your award search, write a personal profile of yourself to help establish as many criteria as possible that might form a basis for your scholarship award. Here is a basic checklist of fifteen questions you should consider:

1. **What are your career goals?**

   Be both narrow and broad in your designations. If, for example, you aim to be a TV news reporter, you will find many awards specific to this field in the *TV/Radio Broadcasting* section. However, collegiate broadcasting courses are offered in departments or schools of communication. So, be sure that you consider *Communications* as a relevant section for your search. Consider *Journalism,* too, for the same reasons. Then look under other broadly inclusive but possibly relevant areas, such as *Trade/Technical Specialties.* Or check a related but different field, such as *Performing Arts.* Finally, look under marginally related basic academic fields, such as *Humanities, Social Sciences,* or *Political Science.* Peterson's makes every attempt to provide the best cross-reference aids, but the nuances of specific awards can be difficult to capture even with the most flexible cross-referencing systems. You will need to be broadly associative in your thinking to get the most out of this wealth of information.

   If you have no clear career goal, browsing the huge variety of academic/career awards may well spark new interest in a career path. Be open to imagining yourself filling different career roles that you previously may not have considered.

2. **In what academic fields might you major?**

   Your educational experiences or your sense about your personal talents or interests may have given you a good idea of what academic discipline you wish to pursue. Again, use both broad and narrow focuses in designing your search, and look at related subject fields. For example, if you want to major in history, check the *History* section, but be sure to check out *Social Sciences* and *Humanities* as well, and maybe *Area/Ethnic Studies. Education,* for example, could suggest the perfect scholarship for a future historian.

3. **In which jobs, industries, or occupations have your parents or other members of your immediate family been employed? What employment experiences do you have?**

   Individual companies, employee organizations, trade unions, government agencies, and industry associations frequently establish scholarships for workers, children of workers, or other relatives of workers from specific companies or industries. These awards might require that you stay in the same career field, but most are offered regardless of the field of study you wish to undertake. Also, if one of your parents is a public service employee, especially a firefighter or police officer, you have many relevant awards from which to choose.

4. **Do you have any hobbies or special interests? Have you ever been an officer or leader of a group? Do you possess special skills or talents? Have you won any competitions? Are you a good writer?**

   From gardening to clarinet playing, from caddying to playing basketball, your special interests can win awards for you from groups that wish to promote and/or reward these pursuits. Many scholarships are targeted to "student leaders," including sports team captains; yearbook or newspaper editors; student government officers; and club, organization, and community activists.

5. **Where do you live? Where have you lived? Where will you go to college?**

   Residence criteria are among the most common qualifications for scholarship aid. Local clubs and companies provide millions of dollars in scholarship aid to students who live in a particular state, province, region, or section of a state. This means that your residential identity puts you at the head of the line for these grants. State of residence can—depending on the sponsor's criteria—include the place of your official residence, the place you attend college, the place you were born, or anywhere you have lived for more than a year.

6. **What is your family's ethnic heritage?**

   Hundreds of scholarships have been endowed for students who can claim a particular nationality or racial or ethnic descent. Partial ethnic descent frequently qualifies, so don't be put off if you do not think of your identity as a specific "ethnic" entity. Awards are available for Colonial American,

English, Polish, Welsh, Scottish, European, and other backgrounds that students may not consider especially "ethnic." One is even available for descendants of the signers of the Declaration of Independence, whatever ethnicity that might have turned out to be some ten generations later.

7. **Do you have a physical disability?**
Many awards are available to individuals with physical disabilities. Of course, commonly recognized impairments of mobility, sight, communication, and hearing are recognized, but learning disabilities and chronic diseases, such as asthma and epilepsy, are also criteria for some awards.

8. **Do you currently or have you ever served in the Armed Forces? Did one of your parents serve in a war? Was one of your parents lost or disabled while serving in the Armed Forces?**
Hundreds of awards use these qualifications.

9. **Do you belong to a civic association, union, or religious organization? Do your parents belong to such groups?**
Hundreds of clubs and religious groups provide scholarship assistance to members or children of members.

10. **Are you male or female?**

11. **What is your age?**

12. **Do you qualify for need-based aid?**

13. **Did you graduate in the upper one-half, upper one-third, or upper one-quarter of your class?**

14. **Do you plan to attend a two-year college, a four-year college, or a trade/technical school?**

15. **In what academic year will you be entering?**

Be expansive when considering your possible qualifications. Although some awards may be small, you may qualify for more than one award—and these can add up to significant amounts in the end.

Who Wants to Be a College Scholarship Millionaire?

There are high school seniors around the country who are becoming rich beyond their wildest dreams even before stepping inside the hallowed halls of higher education. These college upstarts are not start-up kings and queens, á la Mark Zuckerberg of Facebook fame. But they may be just as innovative. They're a part of small, but growing, elite—the College Scholarship Millionaire Club.

The concept of earning a million dollars for college sounds like the premise of a television game show. And to be honest, such a goal remains incredibly lofty for some and downright impossible for others. But what was once a fantasy of every would-be college student is now fast becoming a reality for those willing to work incredibly hard to make it happen.

So just what is the College Scholarship Millionaire Club? It's a group of students who have won $1 million or more in scholarship commitments from universities and colleges and private scholarship funds. The definition should clue you in on at least one prerequisite for joining this club—you have to apply for scholarships—A LOT OF THEM. Still, a quick analysis of some college scholarship millionaires and how they secured their awards can offer any pre-college student great advice on how to get the most out of their scholarship application season.

While there is no sure-fire way to ensure that you earn big bucks in the college scholarship process—anyone promising that is just running a scam—there are steps you can take to increase your odds of having a big scholarship haul. Here are some valuable tips:

Make High-Achieving a Group Sport

More than a decade ago James Ralph Sparks, a calculus teacher at Whitehaven High School (WHS), in Memphis, Tennessee, wanted to find a way to get more of his students into college. Back in 2002, the public school located on Elvis Presley Blvd., wasn't exactly known for its academic aptitude. Back then, graduating seniors were bringing in less than $5 million in scholarship offers for the entire school. But Sparks felt the school could do better. So he created a competition. The 30+ club was the first weapon in the battle to get students more money for

college there was only one criterion for membership: a score of 30 or higher on the ACT. By encouraging students to score high on the national standardize test, Sparks ensured that his students would be in the running for top scholarships. Students who achieved entrance into the club had their scholarship offer letters and scores posted on bulletin boards in the school.

But Sparks wasn't finished. He created the Fortune 500 club, providing exclusive membership only to students who could achieve more than $100,000 in scholarships. The combination of the 30+ club and the Fortune 500 club helped to spur students to achieve. The WHS graduating senior class brought in more than $30 million in scholarship offers in 2010–11.

Apply, Apply, and Apply Again

Another facet of the Whitehaven High School's scholarship program was playing the odds. Anyone who has guided students through a college scholarship application understands that the process can become a numbers game. The more applications you complete, the better your chances of securing a scholarship. While the average high school student applies for two to three scholarships, WHS' millionaire club members applied for ten times that number—about thirty or forty.

Become a Super College Candidate

By now everyone applying to college knows you have to do more than get good grades to stand out. If you want to rise to the top of the scholarship heap, you're going to have to be extraordinary. You can't just volunteer at your local soup kitchen—that's a given. You might have to start your *own* soup kitchen to be considered above your peers. To be a part of the million-dollar scholarship club, you're going to have to go above and beyond to pull down that six-figure college gift.

So let's break down what it takes to be a million-dollar scholar:

- **Start early.** It's never too early to research scholarship opportunities as well as plan your scholarship strategy. Practice writing your personal statement, essay, interviewing skills, and so on to get yourself acquainted with the scholarship process.

- **Make applying a group sport.** Everyone loves a good competition, and it seems earning scholarship money is no exception. At Whitehaven High School, teachers publicly listed the scholarship earnings of students with more than $100,000. WHS also had a scoreboard in front of its school that highlighted scholarship amounts, not just football scores.

- **Don't forget the academics.** Many scholarships have an academic threshold, so you want to make sure to get above that to open more opportunities.

- **Keep Your Options Open.** There are critics who say that applying for scholarships you have no intention of using is not appropriate. But how do you know where you want to go until you figure out how to pay for it? Don't pigeon-hole yourself into one option. If you don't get your first-choice, you'll at least have something to fall back upon.

- **Be sincere.** You may think it's all about the numbers, but you become a million-dollar scholar through authenticity not fakery. Apply to scholarships that fit your passion, purpose, and educational prowess. And apply to schools you actually want to attend. Applying for scholarships and grants take time, and you don't want to waste it on pipe dreams.

Snap and Chat: Use Your Fingertips and Social Media to Pay for College

Felecia Hatcher
Author of *The C Student's Guide to Scholarships* and *Start Your Business on a Ramen Noodle Budget*

Snapchat, Vine, Instagram, Facebook, Twitter, Periscope—everyday a new social media platform is being launched to suck more of our precious time away. As a prospective college student trying to snag scholarship dollars, every second counts. But what if I told you that you don't have to sacrifice your time on social media and that you could find thousands of scholarship dollars and opportunities by using your cell phone and your thumbs!

It's said that over $1 billion in scholarships goes unawarded each year. You may think that this money is being hidden on purpose. I promise you that colleges and scholarship committees are not trying to hide the money from you; they are actually starting to use social media more and more to get the information directly to you. Currently, there are thousands of social media sites on the Internet, and these sites could possibly bring you one step closer to paying for college. Keep reading to find out how you can use social media and crowd funding sites to get creative with your search and not only think outside the box, but also think outside the application.

TWITTER™

Twitter allows you to get short messages of 140 characters or less in real time. The one thing that is great about Twitter is that it has a search bar that allows you to search for tweets from anyone or any entity that belongs to the social network. By using special keywords in the search bar, you should be able to find scholarship information the organization tweeted about and direct links to scholarship applications.

Go to the search bar in Twitter and type in the following keywords:

"Scholarship Deadline"
"Scholarship + [Your State]"
"Scholarship PDF"
"Scholarship Deadline http"

GOOGLE IT!

I jokingly tell people that I feel like I can rule the world with my iPhone, 2 safety pins, a rubber band, and Google. Need a restaurant recommendation? Google it! Need to research the best place to get school supplies for a project? Google it! Need to find money for your college education? Google it! Yes, believe it or not, it may be just that simple. But in order to not be bombarded with thousands of useless results, you must use the right keywords. Here is a short list of some keyword combinations that will yield some great results in your scholarship search.

You can use the same search terms previously used for your Twitter searches for Google as well as the following:

Scholarship+2018
Scholarship+2019
Scholarship + Deadline + Current Month
Scholarship + [your city/hometown]
Scholarship + [your race/ethnicity/religion]
Scholarship + [your talent]

You can also replace the word "scholarship" with "grant" or "fellowship".

CROWD FUNDING

So, you applied but didn't win that big $25,000 scholarship. Don't despair—put the power of your network of family, friends, and social media followers to work, and create your own scholarship through crowd funding! With crowd funding, you can get 5,000 strangers to donate $5 each, which equals $25,000 . . . right?

No, I'm not talking about standing on a busy corner and playing your guitar. The following websites allow you to reach out to your friends and family or total strangers; pitch your need through a profile, pictures, and compelling video; and creatively fundraise your way to funding your college education.

Paypal.com

Gofundme.com

YouCaring.com

blog.zerobound.com

Indiegogo.com

ScholarMatch.org

PeerBackers.com

TIPS TO HELP YOU MAXIMIZE YOUR CHANCES OF GETTING FUNDING

Tell a Compelling Story through Video: Writing an essay is one way to let your personality shine through, but nothing trumps seeing you! Use social media platforms like Instagram, Periscope, YouTube, and Vine to create short videos the showcase who you are and why you deserve the scholarships, and get as many people as you can to share them. Scholarship committees know that you need money, that's a given. But you want to captivate the committee with an exciting story that will keep them viewing and opening up their wallets with each word. Tell them who you are and what makes you and your needs different from other students. Most importantly, tell them why they should care enough to part with their money. Get Creative!

Create an exciting profile: Photos and video go a long way when you are creating profiles on crowd-funding sites or even on an application that asks for additional information. Take the time to capture great pictures that really let your personality show through. There are an increasing number of applications asking for video submissions. This is your time to shine, so take out your camera and start shooting testimonials from teachers, coaches, and guidance counselors raving about how fabulous you are instead of (or in addition to) submitting the traditional recommendation letter. Capture video when you are doing community service work, working at your part-time job, playing sports, or engaging in your hobbies. Remember photos and video paint the best picture and make the need *real.*

Tip: Use Pathrite.com to create a portfolio that not only showcases your education and your resume but also your talents and hobbies. Colleges and Scholarship committees are always searching for well-rounded students!

Don't be afraid to ask for help: Let me put it frankly: The truth is you only get what you ask for! Networks like Facebook®, Twitter™, LinkedIn, and YouCaring.com allow you to amplify your message, so put the message out there. If you don't ask for the help and let everyone know, then you can't expect anyone to assist you.

So, the next time your parents tell you to get off Facebook or Twitter or to put down your phone, tell them that you are tweeting or searching for scholarship dollars.

CLEAN UP YOUR ACT: SPRUCE UP YOUR INTERNET AND SOCIAL MEDIA PRESENCE

Social media is a huge part of today's social realm. There is a good chance that you probably communicate with your friends on Facebook and Twitter more then you do in person. While these social networks are great for connecting with friends and family, and even meeting new people, they can hurt your scholarship efforts if you are not careful. Having this information in mind, set aside some time before, or directly after, you mail out that first scholarship application to investigate and (if necessary) clean up your online presence.

Are you wondering why this is necessary? I bet you think that your Facebook page has nothing to do with your scholarship application. Well, if these are your thoughts, you are unfortunately very wrong. There's an excellent chance that a scholarship organization will spend time searching for you on the Internet. If you're shuddering at the thought of the scholarship committee members seeing anything on your page, I recommend you follow these tips for "scrubbing" your web reputation squeaky clean:

1. **Google yourself.**
   Search for every possible variation of your name on Google. If anything unbecoming pops up in the search results, do what you can to have it taken down.

2. **Check your social media sites.**
   This includes Facebook, LinkedIn, Twitter, Flickr, Instagram, Tumblr, WordPress, and so on. Make sure all the content on these sites is dignified and academic, meaning that it's serious and grammatically correct. It would be wise to include blog posts about social issues, quotes from famous people you admire, poetry you've written (not including dirty limericks), and so on. Your social media pages need to present you as being smart, mature, and hardworking. If it doesn't do those things, then clean up your page, and replace it with content that does. I am not saying that you have to be boring; just be cautious of how everything you post on the Internet *looks* because it's like a tattoo—once it is posted, it can not be erased.

3. **Web pages that can't be scrubbed should be hidden.**
   Try to use nicknames when creating your social profiles, and always use the highest privacy settings so that people must be approved in order to see the page. After doing these things, you should still log

out and check what information appears on your default profile page. If a picture that depicts you partying or anything else that would be unflattering to a scholarship committee appears, log back in and replace it with something else.

4. Take those videos off YouTube.
Do this right now. You know which ones I mean.

5. Remain vigilant.
Just because you cleaned up your web presence today doesn't mean it will be clean as a whistle next week. Be aware of what others are posting and tagging with your name. Some search engines even allow you to set up "alerts" to warn you every time your name shows up on the web. I would recommend using this to your full extent.

6. Check your voicemail.
This is of the utmost importance. If you have an inappropriate ring-back tone or voicemail greeting, you need to either replace it with something professional and appropriate, or kiss your scholarship chances goodbye.

ABOUT THE AUTHOR

Felecia Hatcher-Pearson is a trailblazing social entrepreneur with an authentic voice for change. For the past decade, Felecia has dedicated her life to inspiring a new generation of leaders through her conversational talks on entrepreneurship, college funding, and personal branding.

As an author and social entrepreneur, Felecia Hatcher-Pearson has been honored by the White House as a 2014 Champion of Change for STEM Access & Diversity, Black Enterprise Innovator of the Week, and featured *Essence Magazine* Tech Master. She has been featured on NBC's *Today Show*, MSNBC, The Cooking Channel, and Grio's "100 African American's Making History" for her very successful company, Feverish Ice Cream & Gourmet Pops, where she is former Chief Popsicle.

As a "C" student in high school, Felicia beat the odds and won over $100,000 in scholarships to attend college by getting creative. She used her experience and knack for personal marketability to start her first business called Urban Excellence as a freshman in college. She built and ran innovative college-prep programs for DeVry University and companies such as MECA, AMPS Institute, the YMCA, the TED Center, and the Urban League.

In 2008, after falling flat on her face while attempting to chase an ice cream truck in heels, Felecia started her own gourmet ice pops and dessert catering company, Feverish Pops. Felecia has presented engaging talks on Embracing Failure at Google London and Entrepreneurship and Managing Investor Relations at SXSW. She has spoken as part of the White House Young America Series, at Coca Cola's headquarters, and at TEDxMiami and TEDxJamaica. Felecia is also the author of three books, *Start Your Business on a Ramen Noodle Budget, The C Students Guide to Scholarships*, and *Focused*.

Aside from being a successful entrepreneur and author Felecia Hatcher-Pearson has dedicated her life to turning kids and young adults from undeserved communities into entrepreneurs and exposing them to careers and entrepreneurial opportunities in technology with her programs Code Fever and Black Tech Week initiatives that helps to increase tech entrepreneurship funding and training to underserved Florida communities.

Ask the Experts: College Scholarships

Here are some frequently asked scholarship-related questions of college planning and admissions experts. You may have some of the same questions too.

Q: When college representatives visit high schools, do they offer a certain amount of scholarships to students who may be interested in attending that institution?

College reps do visit many high schools on recruiting trips, usually in the early to mid-fall and sometimes in the late spring. Watch your guidance office bulletin board or school website to see when representatives from the colleges you might be interested in are visiting your school or a location near your home. Colleges do not offer a limited amount of scholarships based on where you go to high school. School representatives will discuss both need-based and, often, merit-based financial awards their college may provide. Scholarships might be available to students from your area for one reason or another, but, generally there aren't a specific number based on a particular high school. You should apply to the colleges in which you are interested, and apply for both need-based financial aid and possible additional merit (non-need-based) scholarships for which you might qualify.

Q: How do I get a scholarship through the PSAT/NMSQT®?

The "NMSQT" in "PSAT/NMSQT" stands for the National Merit Scholarship Qualifying Test. About 55,000 of the more than 1.3 million students taking that test each year will be selected as National Merit Commended Students. Going into senior year, in September, smaller proportions of students will be selected as Semifinalists, then Finalists, and, finally, Merit Scholars (who can earn $2,500 awards). See www.nationalmerit.org for more information on these programs.

Q: I am a 4.0 student and I'm in the National Honor Society. Do you know the level of difficulty of getting an NHS scholarship?

The National Honor Society (www.NHS.us) awards 200 scholarships of $1,000 each year. Your NHS chapter can nominate two students to compete for the scholarships, so the first hurdle is to get one of your chapter's nominations. It's pretty competitive after that, since some highly talented students across the country are in the pool for these merit-based awards. But go for it—you could be one of the lucky winners.

Q: What do I need to do to qualify for a merit scholarship?

It is important to research the colleges you are interested in and determine their merit scholarship criteria. For example, a school might state that it will guarantee a scholarship as long as the student has a certain grade point average, minimum SAT®/ACT® scores, and a specific rank in high school. It is critical to make an in-person appointment with an admissions representative to find out all of the details and requirements for obtaining any of the institution's scholarships. You can also search for merit-based scholarships online.

Q: What are some requirements for athletic scholarships?

The website ncaa.org is a good place to look into the differences between Division I, II, and III colleges and universities, and recruiting prospects. Division I and II schools (except the Ivies) offer athletic scholarships. Division III colleges do not. Minimum requirements for scholarships are actually quite low on the whole. However, particular colleges and universities have their own admission and scholarship requirements that you'll need to meet in order to be recruited and admitted.

As you begin the athletic recruiting process and talk with coaches, ask them about their college's recruiting and admission requirements, as well as typical scholarship packages for athletes. If you visit a school's campus on an "official visit," talk with other players about their recruiting experiences and scholarship packages. There are typically minimum college GPA and "reasonable academic progress" requirements that you must meet in order to maintain your eligibility to play college sports and keep your scholarship.

If you want to scope out some athletic scholarships, you can take a look through the scholarship search tool at Petersons.com and also in this book.

Q: Are grants better than scholarships?

Grants and scholarships are both "free money," in the sense that you don't need to repay them. Grants are usually need-based, while scholarships are based on merit of some kind, or they are a basic discounting of tuition. They are equal, though a hitch with scholarships is that sometimes you have to meet conditions, such as participation in a sport or another activity or maintaining a certain GPA, in order to renew the scholarship. Always read the fine print when evaluating scholarship offers to see how long they last, if they are annually renewable, and what the conditions are that are associated with them.

Q: Will my SAT® or ACT® score qualify me for a scholarship?

It's possible that a high score on these college admission tests will qualify you for a scholarship, though typically colleges like to see the score plus a certain GPA in combination for many of their merit-based scholarship opportunities. Sometimes colleges will elaborate on award criteria on their websites and in their informational materials, explaining that a certain SAT, or SAT/GPA, or GPA level will qualify all or a selection of students for certain levels of awards. Other times, it will be apparent that if your scores are in the top third or so of a college's range, you will likely qualify for a merit-based award (aka a discount on tuition) if that institution has a non-need-based aid program. Most do.

Winning the Scholarship with a Winning Essay

Who knew it was going to be this hard? You've already dealt with SO much: the SAT®, doing community service, excelling in your AP® class, etc. Convincing your parents that you will be fine 1,500 miles from home and that each and every one of those college application fees are, yes, absolutely necessary! You even learned calculus for goodness sake!

And now in front of you—yet, for right now, somehow out of reach—the golden ticket to make it all come true. Just 500 words (more or less) separate you from those hallowed halls: It's the scholarship essay.

IT HAS TO BE EASY, RIGHT?

Much as you may feel like, c'mon, I'm worth it, just give me the scholarship money, we all know it just doesn't work like that. Because you know what—lots of students are worth it! And lots of students are special, just like you! And where does that leave a scholarship selection committee in deciding to whom their money should be awarded? Yes, now you are catching on—they will pour over *everyone*'s scholarship essay.

So, first and foremost, write your scholarship essay in a way that makes it EASY for the scholarship-awarding committees to do their job! It's almost like a partnership—you show them (in 500 words, more or less) why YOU ARE THE MOST WORTHY RECIPIENT, and they say, thank you, you're right, here is a scholarship for you, and everyone wins! Easy, right?

SORRY—IT REALLY ISN'T THAT EASY

What? You are still sitting there in front of a blank computer screen with nary a thought or sentence? Understood. It's really not that easy. That, too, is part of the point.

No doubt that your GPA, SAT scores, volunteer efforts, leadership roles, and community service are immensely important, but again, you must remember that, during the process of selecting an award recipient, pretty much all the applicants are going to be stellar on some level. And so the scholarship-awarding committee uses your essay to see what sets you apart from the crowd. They are looking for a reason to select you over everyone else.

Your scholarship essay serves many purposes. You have to convince the scholarship-awarding committee you are able to do the following:

- Effectively communicate through the written word
- Substantiate your merit and unique qualities
- Follow directions and adhere to guidelines

A winning scholarship essay can mean up to tens of thousands of dollars for your college education, so let's get started on putting that money in YOUR hands!

EFFECTIVE WRITTEN COMMUNICATION

Be Passionate

Let's face it—you have already written lots of essays. And, we won't tell, but most were probably about topics that were as interesting to you as watching paint dry, right? But you plowed through them and even managed to get some good grades along the way. You may think about just "plowing through" your scholarship essay the same way—mustering up the same amount of excitement you feel when you have to watch old videos of your Aunt Monica on her summer camping trips. But that would be a huge mistake!

An important feature of all winning essays is that they are written on subjects about which the author is truly passionate. Think about it—it actually takes a good bit of effort to fake passion for a subject. But when you are genuinely enthusiastic about something, the words and thoughts flow much more easily, and your passion and energy naturally shine through in your writing. Therefore, when you are choosing your scholarship essay topic, be sure it is something about which you truly care and for which you can show affinity—keeping both you and your reader interested and intrigued!

Be Positive

You've probably heard the expression: "If you don't have anything nice to say, don't say anything at all." Try to steer clear of essays that are too critical, pessimistic, or antagonistic. This doesn't mean that your essay shouldn't acknowledge a serious problem or that everything has to have a happy ending. But it does mean that you should not just write about the negative. If you are writing about a problem, present solutions. If your story doesn't have a happy ending, write about what you learned from the experience and how you would do things differently if faced with a similar situation in the future. Your optimism is what makes the scholarship-awarding committee excited about giving you money to pursue your dreams. Use positive language and be proud to share yourself and your accomplishments. Everyone likes an uplifting story, and even scholarship judges want to feel your enthusiasm and zest for life.

Be Clear and Concise

Don't fall into the common essay-writing trap of using general statements instead of specific ones. All scholarship judges read at least one essay that starts with "Education is the key to success." And that means nothing to them. What does mean something is writing about how your tenth-grade English teacher opened your eyes to the understated beauty and simplicity of haiku—how less can be more—and how that then translated into you donating some of your old video games to a homeless shelter where you now volunteer once a month. That's powerful stuff! It's a very real story, clearly correlating education to a successful outcome. Focusing on a specific and concise example from your life helps readers relate to you and your experiences. It also guarantees you bonus points for originality!

Edit and Proofread and Then Edit and Proofread

There is an old saying: "Behind every good writer is an even better editor." Find people (friends, siblings, coaches, teachers, guidance counselors) to read your essay, provide feedback on how to make it better, and edit it for silly, sloppy mistakes. Some people will read your essay and find issues with your grammar. Others will read your essay and point out how one paragraph doesn't make sense in relation to another paragraph. Some people will tell you how to give more examples to better make your point. All of those people are giving you great information, and you need to take it all in and use it to your advantage! However, don't be overwhelmed by it, and don't let it become all about what everyone else thinks. It's your essay and your thoughts—the goal of editing and proofreading is to clean up the rough edges and make the entire essay shine!

And when you do get to that magical point where you think "DONE!"—instead, just put the essay aside for a few days. Come back to it with an open mind and read, edit, and proofread it one last time. Check it one last time

for spelling and grammar fumbles. Check it one last time for clarity and readability (reading it out loud helps!). Check it one last time to ensure it effectively communicates why you are absolutely the winning scholarship candidate!

YOUR UNIQUE QUALITIES

It's one thing to help out at the local library a few hours a week; it's a completely different thing if you took it upon yourself to suggest, recruit, organize, and lead a fundraising campaign to buy 10 new laptops for kids to use at the library!

And don't simply rattle off all your different group memberships. Write about things you did that demonstrate leadership and initiative within those groups. Did you recruit new members or offer to head up a committee? Did you find a way for the local news station to cover your event or reach out to another organization and collaborate on an activity? Think about your unique qualities and how you have used them to bring about change.

A SLICE OF YOUR LIFE

While one goal of your essay is surely to explain why you should win the scholarship money, an equally important goal is to reveal something about you, something that makes it easy to see why you should win. Notice we said to reveal "something" about you and not "everything" about you. Most likely, the rest of the scholarship application gathers quite a bit of information about you. The essay is where you need to hone in on just one aspect of your unique talents, one aspect of an experience, one aspect of reaching a goal. It's not about listing all your accomplishments in your essay (again, you probably did that on the application). It's about sharing a slice of your life—telling your story and giving your details about what makes YOU memorable.

YOUR ACCOMPLISHMENTS, LOUD AND PROUD

Your extracurricular activities illustrate your personal priorities and let the scholarship selection committee know what's important to you. Being able to elaborate on your accomplishments and awards within those activities certainly bolsters your chances of winning the scholarship. Again, though, be careful to not just repeat what is already on the application itself. Use your essay to focus on a specific accomplishment (or activity or talent or award) of which you are most proud.

Did your community suffer through severe flooding last spring? And did you organize a clothing drive for neighbors who were in need? How did that make you feel? What feedback did you get? How did it inspire your desire to become a climatologist?

Were school budget cuts going to mean the disbanding of some afterschool clubs? Did you work with teachers and parents to write a proposal to present to the school board, addressing how new funds could be raised in order to save the clubs? How did that make you feel? What feedback did you get? How did it inspire you to start a writing lab for junior high kids?

You have done great things—think about that one special accomplishment and paint the picture of how it has made you wiser, stronger, or more compassionate to the world around you. Share the details!

But Don't Go Overboard

A five-hanky story may translate into an Oscar-worthy movie, but rarely does it translate into winning a scholarship. If your main reason for applying for the scholarship is that you feel you deserve the money because of how much suffering you have been through, you need a better reason. Scholarship selection committees are not really interested in awarding money to people with problems; they want to award money to people who solve problems. While it's just fine to write about why you need the scholarship money to continue your education, it's not fine for your essay to simply be a laundry list of family tragedies and hardships.

So, instead of presenting a sob story, present how you have succeeded and what you have accomplished despite the hardships and challenges you faced. Remember that everyone has faced difficulties. What's unique about you is how YOU faced your difficulties and overcame them. That is what makes your essay significant and memorable.

FOLLOWING DIRECTIONS

Does Your Essay Really Answer the Question?

Have you ever been asked one question but felt like there was another question that was really being asked? Maybe your dad said something like, "Tell me about your new friend Logan." But what he really meant to ask you was, "Tell me about your new friend Logan. Do his lip rings and tattoos mean he's involved in things I don't want you involved in?"

The goal of every scholarship judge is to determine the best applicant out of a pool of applicants who are all rather similar. Pay attention and you'll find that the essay question is an alternate way for you to answer the real question the scholarship-awarding committee wants to ask. For instance, an organization giving an award to students who plan to study business might ask, "Why do you want to study business?" But their real underlying question is, "Why are you the best future business person to whom we should give our money?" If there is a scholarship for students who want to become doctors, you can bet that 99 percent of the students applying want to become doctors. And if you apply for that scholarship with an essay simply delving into your lifelong desire to be a potter, well, that doesn't make you unique, it makes you pretty much unqualified for that opportunity. Be sure to connect your personal skills, characteristics, and experiences with the objectives of the scholarship and its awarding organization.

Does Your Essay Theme Tie In?

Let's say that you are applying for a community service-based award and, on the application, you go ahead and list all the community service groups you belong to and all the awards you have won. But in your essay, you write about how homeless people should find a job instead of sitting on street corners begging for money. Hey—everyone is entitled to their opinion, but would you agree that there is some sort of disconnect between your application and your essay? And no doubt you have made the scholarship-awarding committee wonder the same thing.

So how do you ensure your essay doesn't create a conflicting message? You need to examine the theme of your essay and how it relates both to your application and the reason the scholarship exists in the first place. If the scholarship-funding organization seeks to give money to someone who wants a career in public relations and your essay focuses on how you are not really a "people person," well, you can see how that sends a mixed message to your reader.

Think about it this way: The theme of your essay should naturally flow around the overarching purpose or goal of the organization awarding the scholarship money. Once you have clarified this nugget, you can easily see if and how your words tie in to the organization's vision of whom their scholarship winner is.

Three More Pieces of Advice

1. **Follow the essay length guidelines closely.** You certainly don't want your essay disqualified simply because it was too long or too short!

2. **The deadline is the deadline.** A day late and you could certainly be more than a dollar short in terms of the award money that isn't going to be awarded to you if your application is not received by the due date. Begin the essay writing process well in advance of the scholarship deadline. Writing and editing and rewriting takes time so you should probably allow yourself at least 2 weeks to write your scholarship essay.

3. **Tell the truth.** No need to say anything further on that, right? Right.

Getting in the Minority Scholarship Mix

Did you know that a great duck call can win you scholarship money in the Chick and Sophie Major Memorial Duck Calling Contest?

Website: http://www.stuttgartarkansas.org/duck-festival/scholarship_contest.aspx

Perhaps duck-calling is not your calling but creativity with Duck® brand duct tape is. If so, the "Stuck at Prom" scholarship may be just for you—design promware for you and your date and win some moola!

Website: http://www.duckbrand.com/promotions/stuck-at-prom.aspx

How about this tall order? Tall Clubs International awards scholarships to men who are taller than 6'2" or women who are taller than 5'10".

Website: http://tallclubfoundation.org/scholarship program.html

Oh? Not necessarily the minority group you had in mind? That's OK because guess what? In this day and age, just about everyone is a minority of some sort. It all depends on a scholarship benefactor's definition of minority.

In the college realm, the word "minority" takes on a myriad of meanings. One definition of a minority that often springs to mind is of someone of an underrepresented ethnicity, such as Native Americans, African Americans, or Hispanic Americans. No question there. Similarly though, a minority can be someone pursuing an underrepresented college major, such as paranormal research. Think that all scholarships for minorities target United States–specific groups? Think again. For example, Canadian students, whether they plan to study at home or abroad, can qualify for scholarships for aboriginals. Getting the picture? The key is to use your own unique qualities as you search for scholarships. Think about your gender, your family's economic status, your religious background, and your geographic locale just to start the ball rolling. Once you broadly frame your search along those lines, you'll quickly see how easily you can qualify for a scholarship!

AM I REALLY A MINORITY?

No matter the source—federal, state, professional organization, private endowment, corporate donor, college, or university—they all offer minority scholarships, looking to create diversity and inclusion in an increasingly global marketplace.

It's more than probable that you fit into at least one of the ever-expanding minority scholarship categories—nearly everyone does—by some broadly based definition of minority. Some of the niche scholarship "minorities" have already been mentioned. Now let's take a look at some of the broader categories—one of which likely fits you!

African American Students

While African Americans make up a large U.S. minority group, they are still met with one of the biggest barriers to college enrollment—money. To combat that challenge, scholarships for African American students have grown over the years, with some of the best sources of funding found within partnerships between minority organizations and corporate sponsors.

As the nation's largest minority education organization, the United Negro College Fund (UNCF) provides operating funds for 38-member historically black colleges and universities (HBCUs), along with scholarships and internships for students at about 900 institutions. The UNCF has helped more than 400,000 students attend and graduate college with the more than $3.3 billion it has raised—more funds helping minorities attend college than any other entity outside of the U.S. government.

United Negro College Fund
8260 Willow Oaks Corporate Drive
P.O. Box 10444
Fairfax, VA 22031-8044
Phone: 800-331-2244
Website: www.uncf.org

Hispanic American Students

Fortunately, over the years, the U.S. government has contributed millions of dollars toward startup costs for the development of Hispanic universities and colleges and toward already established Hispanic universities and colleges. The effort has been paying off with dramatic increases in college enrollment by Hispanic American students. Scholarship programs for Hispanic American students look to increase the number of Hispanic students studying in subject areas most underrepresented by them, for instance, the sciences, engineering, math, and technology.

As the nation's leading Hispanic higher-education fund, the Hispanic Scholarship Fund (HSF) works to remove the barriers keeping many Hispanic American students from earning a college degree. Over the past 35 years, HSF has awarded more than $430 million in scholarships (over 150 types of scholarships) and supported a wide range of outreach and education programs for both college students and their families.

Hispanic Scholarship Fund
55 Second Street, Suite 1500
San Francisco, CA 94105
Phone: 877-HSF-INFO (877-473-4636)
E-mail: scholar1@hsf.net
Website: www.hsf.net

Asian American Students

Identifying yourself as Asian American means you probably consider yourself Cambodian, Hmong, Laotian, Malaysian, Okinawan, Tahitian, or Thai—just to name a few possibilities. As a somewhat smaller, yet growing, minority group, Asian Americans attend college more than any other minority group and tend to stay in college once they have enrolled. Excellent merit-based aid sources for Asian American students include cultural organizations, university departments such as law and journalism, and professional organizations.

The Asian & Pacific Islander American Scholarship Fund (APIASF), founded in 2003, has provided more than $50 million in scholarships to Asian and Pacific Islander Americans with financial need.

The Asian & Pacific Islander American
   Scholarship Fund
2025 M Street NW, Suite 610
Washington, DC 20036
Phone: 202-986-6892
Phone (toll-free): 877-808-7032
Fax: 202-530-0643
E-mail: info@apiasf.org
Website: http://www.apiasf.org/

Native American Students

Native American (inclusive of American Indians and Native Alaskans) students make up the smallest minority population on college campuses. As you explore scholarship opportunities for Native Americans, you may find that you'll need proof of your Native American status, which means your Certificate of Indian Blood (CIB), as well as belonging to a well-recognized tribe. If you are like most Native American descendants, though, you will probably not have this proof, as many tribes change names and have nonexistent documentation records. If somehow you do have a CIB and belong to a tribe, you may have an upper hand in qualifying for some more esoteric scholarship and grant programs.

American Indian College Fund

Located in Denver, Colorado, the mission of the American Indian College Fund (AICF) is threefold: to spread awareness of the Fund and of tribal colleges and universities; to raise college scholarship funds for American Indian students attending tribal and mainstream colleges; and to raise money for other needs and projects of the tribal schools.

The AICF awards approximately 5,000 college scholarships a year. Monies given to individual schools are used to award Tribal College Scholarships to candidates of each school's choosing. Other undergraduate scholarships are awarded directly from the AICF to American Indian students attending both tribal and mainstream colleges and universities.

The American Indian College Fund
8333 Greenwood Boulevard
Denver, CO 80221
Phone: 303-426-8900
Phone (toll-free): 800-776-3863
Website: www.collegefund.org

American Indian Graduate Center

Another large source of student scholarships and financial aid for Native Americans is the American Indian

Graduate Center (AIGC), which provides monies to both undergraduate and graduate students.

The mission of the AIGC is to improve the cultural and economic well-being of American Indians and Native Alaskans both individually and tribally. Their efforts focus on developing educated and forward-thinking leaders who will steer their communities into an era of prosperity, productivity, and self-reliance.

The AIGC, with the generous support of the Tommy Hilfiger Corporation Foundation, also administers the All Native American High School Academic Team, a program recognizing Native American/Alaska Native students who demonstrate superior success in academics, leadership, and American Indian community service.

As part of the AIGC's overall mission, this program promotes academic excellence and the pursuit of higher education among Native American and Alaska Native students, with the goal of preparing them for future roles as community leaders and role models. All of the students recognized by this program receive financial awards to pay for the cost of attending the college or university of their choice.

The American Graduate Center
3701 San Mateo Boulevard NE #200
Albuquerque, NM 87110
Phone: 505-881-4584
Website: www.aigcs.org/scholarships

Other Opportunities

In addition to the AICF and the AIGC, there are several other organizations that provide various student scholarships to Native Americans:

- **American Indian Science and Engineering Society (AISES):** With the goal of substantially increasing "the representation of American Indian and Alaskan Natives in engineering, science and other related technology disciplines," the AISES awards university scholarships to Native American undergraduate and graduate students pursuing degrees in various areas of engineering and science. (www.aises.org/scholarships)
- **Association on American Indian Affairs (AAIA):** Offers college scholarship opportunities to both undergraduate and graduate students demonstrating financial need. (https://www.indian-affairs.org/scholarships.html)

- **Indian Health Service (IHS):** As an arm of the U.S. Department of Health and Human Services, the IHS awards university scholarships to pay for the education and training of undergraduate, graduate, and doctoral students pursuing degrees in health-care related areas. (https://www.ihs.gov/scholarship/)
- **Intertribal Timber Council (ITC):** Dedicated to improving the management of natural resources that are important to Native American communities, the ITC sponsors a variety of different undergraduate scholarships and fellowship opportunities each year. (www.itcnet.org/about_us/scholarships.html)

Interracial Students

There is an interesting trend in minority scholarships where scholarship-funding organizations seek to include students of mixed heritage, blended cultures, and students whose ethnic backgrounds don't fit neatly into one particular category. Search for prizes tagged as "interracial scholarships," "multicultural scholarships," or "multiethnic scholarships."

Lesbian, Gay, Bisexual, and Transgender Students

Lesbian, gay, bisexual, and transgender (LGBT) students are recognized as a legitimate minority, and many colleges and organizations offer scholarships to this group. As an LGBT student, also be on the lookout for scholarship opportunities for sons and daughters of gay and lesbian parents, as well as friends and allies of the LGBT community.

Since its inception in 2001, the Point Foundation has invested more than $3 million in outstanding gay, lesbian, bisexual, and transgender students. An average Point Scholarship is about $13,600 and covers tuition, books, supplies, room and board, transportation, and living expenses.

Point Foundation
5055 Wilshire Boulevard, Suite 501
Los Angeles, CA 90036
Phone: 323-933-1234
Fax: 866-397-6468
E-mail: info@pointfoundation.org
Website: www.pointfoundation.org

EVERYONE NEEDS A GOOD RESOURCE

From specialized databases to award programs serving as umbrella organizations for numerous other organizations and awards, many resources are out there for criteria-based scholarships, all with one goal—to help you find the money you need to get you on your college path.

CHCI (Congressional Hispanic Caucus Institute)

CHCI provides a free, comprehensive list of scholarships, internships, and fellowships for Hispanic students.

> Congressional Hispanic Caucus Institute
> 1128 16th Street NW
> Washington, DC 20036
> *Phone:* 202-543-1771
> *Phone: (toll-free)* 800-EXCEL-DC (392-3532)
> *Fax:* 202-548-8799
> *Websites:* www.chci.org
>   www.chcinextopp.net

Gates Millennium Scholars

The Gates Millennium Scholars program was founded by a grant from the Bill and Melinda Gates Foundation with the intention of increasing the number of African Americans, Native Americans, Asian Americans, and Hispanic Americans enrolling in and completing undergraduate and graduate degree programs.

> Gates Millennium Scholars
> P.O. Box 10500
> Fairfax, VA 22031-8044
> *Phone (toll-free):* 877-690-4677
> *Website:* www.gmsp.org

GETTING CREATIVE WITH MINORITY SCHOLARSHIPS

Now that you are really thinking outside of the box, you may consider one or more of your outstanding features as the conduit to classifying yourself as a minority. And if you still need some more inspiration:

- Juniata College in Pennsylvania offers a scholarship for left-handed students.
- Little People of America offers a scholarship to adult students who are 4'10" or shorter.
- There are even scholarships for white males offered by The Former Majority Association for Equality, a nonprofit group in Texas.

Be creative and get in the mix! To which minority groups do *you* belong?

What to Do If You Don't Win a Scholarship, Grant, or Prize

More than 20 million students will enroll in the nation's colleges and universities this year, and you can bet nearly all of them will be vying for the more than $4 billion in private scholarship money that's available. In fact, 85 percent of all first-time undergraduate students attending a four-year college receive some type of financial aid—including scholarships, grants, awards, and student loans.

Yet, even though billions of dollars are out there for the grasping, the average scholarship award may just be a few thousand dollars. That's only going to put a minor dent in the over $20,000 annual price tag for in-state tuition, room, and board at a public four-year institution (over $40,000 for private). So, unless you started working as a toddler you're going to have to do something spectacular to avoid buckling under a mountain of student loan debt to get your degree.

Applying for grants and private scholarships is a given. But what if your living room table is filling up with denial letters? What do you do then? Well, the first thing is not to panic. There are plenty of ways to pay for college without going into an enormous amount of debt. Here are some tips and suggestions that will help you to formulate a back-up plan if, by some miracle, you miss out on the college scholarship lottery.

IF AT FIRST YOU DON'T SUCCEED

A rejection letter doesn't mean no, it really means, "Not right now." There is nothing wrong with applying for a private scholarship, fellowship or grant again, even if you've been rejected. Just think, you'll have a leg up on everyone who is coming to the competition cold, as you've been there before. Before you dust off your essay from last year and shove it into an envelope this year, be sure to contact the organization and ask for feedback.

Sure, some may not be willing to speak to you, but you won't lose any sleep by trying. Often the best advice comes from the unlikeliest places, and asking pointed, mature questions about why your first application failed can only serve you in your college money hunt. In addition, the counsel might help you to improve an application for another organization. So follow up on those

who've said no—you never know what kind of great tips and suggestions they will have for you. Here are some questions you may ask when you seek feedback:

- Did my application get rejected because of a procedural mistake? Did I mess up the application process? Did I meet the deadline? Were all my documents included?
- Was my personal statement/essay well done? How could it have been improved?
- Could you give me suggestions on how best to apply for your scholarship again?

Note: You, of course, can't do any of this if you waited until the last minute to fill out your scholarship application, so it pays to start your quest for college treasure early.

YOU CAN APPLY FOR SCHOLARSHIPS WHILE IN COLLEGE

Even if you've already started your college career with your scholarship coffers empty and your student loan debt toppling over, do not fret. You can still apply for grants, scholarships, and programs that do not require you go into debt while you're attending school. Many scholarships are not automatically renewed, and if students do not apply for them, there may be more cash for you. Create an application cycle for every year you attend school. You never know what opportunity you may be missing if you do not at least try to apply while attending school.

WORK NOW, NOT LATER

It used to be that flipping burgers at the local fast-food joint was the way most college students paid for college. And to be sure that option is still open. But the recent technology boom fueled by the monetization of the Internet has allowed even the youngest among us to become entrepreneurs. From teen-age search engine app maker Nick D'Alosio, who has raised capital from one of China's billionaires, to the pre-adolescent Mallory Kiveman, who invented a lollipop to cure the hiccups, the spirit of innovation runs deep among the young. Use technology to start your version of a lemonade stand, and you may make enough in your senior year to pay for college and beyond. Technology has allowed people to think better, smarter, and bigger than ever before. As you're working on that latest science project, think about ways to monetize it. It could be your ticket to a full-ride to college.

DON'T LEAVE MONEY ON THE TABLE

Did you know that only 1 in 10 undergraduate students receive a scholarship award? This isn't because there aren't enough scholarships available. On the contrary, millions of dollars in scholarship money go unclaimed because students do not apply for them.

Yes, that's right. College students, desperate to incur massive amounts of debts forget to apply for grants, miss deadlines and sloppily fill out scholarship applications to ensure they get rejected and leave money on the table. You, of course, would never do that. But some people will.

Do not be one of those people. Make sure you are taking advantage of all your opportunities to gain debt-free money for college. In addition to applying for private scholarships, make sure you go beyond the Federal Pell Grant. Remember, there are state grants, local grants, need-based grants, merit grants, and college university grants that are available for students. Be sure to check with your admitting institution to make sure you haven't overlooked grants—many of which are automatically offered to students regardless of income.

PRACTICE SOME ALTRUISM

Though it may seem to have gone the way of milkshakes and quaint small-town post offices, there are still some programs that will help pay for your college education as long as you commit to do public service. From Ameri-Corps, which defrays college costs for students who work for nonprofits or in high-need areas to the Public Service Loan Forgiveness Program, in which borrowers may qualify for forgiveness of the remaining balance of their Direct Loans after they make 120 qualifying payments on those loans while employed full time by certain public service employers, there are dozens of programs that will lower your college costs in exchange for public service. Even top-tier universities such as Harvard and Princeton

are offering free tuition (Harvard for just one year) for students who choose to work in public service careers. There are loan forgiveness programs for virtually every public service profession from state-appointed prosecutors, teachers, primary care doctors, and law enforcement officers; members of the armed forces; nurses and health-care workers; and even Peace Corps volunteers. But beware—the programs have strict guidelines; one misstep and you could end up footing the bill for your entire college dream. And, as always, consult your tax advisor as current law categorizes the loan amount that is forgiven as income.

Here are some contacts for programs that pay down college costs for volunteerism or public service:

AmeriCorps

More than 75,000 adults work with thousands of non-profits around the country providing tutoring, mentoring, housing management, and a host of other services to the disadvantaged through AmeriCorps. In exchange they receive money to pay for college or graduate school, or they obtain forgiveness on student loans plus a pay check.

AmeriCorps
1201 New York Avenue, NW
Washington, DC 20525
Phone: 202-606-5000
TTY: 800-833-3722 (toll-free)
Website: www.americorps.gov

National Health Service Corps

The National Health Service Corps awards scholarships to students who are pursuing careers in primary care. Students must be pursuing degrees in medicine, dentistry, nursing, and physician assistant studies.

National Health Corps
Phone: 800-221-9393 (toll-free)
Website: http://nhsc.hrsa.gov

Public Service Loan Forgiveness

Congress created the Public Service Loan Forgiveness Program in 2007 as an incentive for people to enter fields that focused on public service. The beneficial program offers qualified borrowers the opportunity to have their federal loans forgiven if they work in certain public service areas.

Website: www.studentaid.gov.

How to Use This Guide

The more than 3,800 award programs described in this book are organized into eleven broad categories that represent the major factors used to determine eligibility for scholarships, awards, and prizes. To build a basic list of awards available to you, look under the broad category or categories that fit your particular academic goals, skills, personal characteristics, or background. The categories are:

- Academic Fields/Career Goals
- Civic, Professional, Social, or Union Affiliation
- Corporate Affiliation
- Employment/Volunteer Experience
- Impairment
- Military Service
- Nationality or Ethnic Heritage
- Religious Affiliation
- Residence/Location of Study
- Talent/Interest Area
- Miscellaneous Criteria

The **Academic Fields/Career Goals** category is subdivided into 131 subject areas that are organized alphabetically by award sponsor. The **Military Service** category is subdivided alphabetically by branch of service. All other categories are organized A to Z by the name of the award sponsor.

Full descriptive profiles appear in only one location in the book. Cross-references to the name and page number of the full descriptive profile appear at other locations under the other relevant categories for the award. The full description appears in the first relevant location in the book and cross-references later locations, so you will always be redirected toward the front of the book.

Your major field of study and career goals have central importance in college planning. As a result, we have combined these into a single category and have given this category precedence over the others. The **Academic Fields/Career Goals** section appears first in the book. If an academic major or career area is a criterion for a scholarship, the description of this award will appear in this section.

Within the **Academic Fields/Career Goals** section, cross-references are only from and to other academic fields or career areas. You will be able to locate relevant awards from nonacademic or noncareer criteria through the indexes in the back of this book.

For example, the full descriptive profile of a scholarship for any type of engineering student who resides in Ohio might appear under *Aviation/Aerospace*, which is the first engineering category heading in the **Academic Fields/Career Goals** section. Cross-references to this first listing may occur from any other relevant engineering or technological academic field subject area, such as *Chemical Engineering, Civil Engineering, Electrical Engineering/Electronics, Engineering-Related Technologies, Engineering/Technology, Mechanical Engineering,* or *Nuclear Science.* There would not be a cross-reference from the *Residence* category. However, the name of the award will appear in the Residence index under Ohio.

Within the major category sections, descriptive profiles are organized alphabetically by the name of the sponsoring organization. If more than one award from the same organization appears in a particular section, the awards are listed alphabetically under the sponsor name, which appears only once, by the name of the first award.

HOW THE PROFILES ARE ORGANIZED

Here are the elements of a full profile:

Name of Sponsoring Organization

These appear alphabetically under the appropriate category. In most instances, acronyms are given as full names. However, occasionally a sponsor will refer to itself by an acronym. In these instances, we present the sponsor's name as an acronym.

World Wide Web Address

Award Name

Brief Textual Description of the Award

Academic Fields/Career Goals (only in the Academic Fields/Career Goals section of the book)

This is a list of all academic or career subject terms that are assigned to this award.

Award

Is it a scholarship? A prize for winning a competition? A forgivable loan? For what type and for what years of college can it be used? Is it renewable or is it for only one year?

Eligibility Requirements

Application Requirements

What information do you need to supply to be considered? What are the deadlines?

Contact

If provided by the sponsor, this element includes the name, mailing address, phone and fax numbers, and e-mail address of the person to contact for information about a specific award.

USING THE INDEXES

The alphabetical indexes in the back of the book are designed to aid your search. Two are name indexes. One lists scholarships alphabetically by academic fields and career goals. The other ten indexes supply access by nonacademic and noncareer criteria. The indexes give you the page number of the descriptions of relevant awards regardless of the part of the book in which they appear.

These are the indexes:

> **Award Name**
> **Sponsor**
> **Academic Fields/Career Goals**
> > [131 subject areas, from Academic Advising to Women's Studies]
>
> **Civic, Professional, Social, or Union Affiliation**
> **Corporate Affiliation**
> **Employment/Volunteer Experience**
> **Impairment**
> **Military Service**
> **Nationality or Ethnic Heritage**
> **Religious Affiliation**
> **Residence**
> **Location of Study**
> **Talent/Interest Area**

In general, when using the indexes, writing down the names and page numbers of the awards that you are interested in is an effective technique.

DATA COLLECTION PROCEDURES

Peterson's takes its responsibility to its readers as a provider of trustworthy information very seriously. Peterson's administered an electronic survey between December 2016 and April 2017 in order to update information from all programs listed within this guide. All collected data was updated between January and April 2017. Additional award program data was obtained between January 2012 and April 2017. Peterson's research staff makes every effort to verify unusual figures and resolve discrepancies. Nonetheless, errors and omissions are possible in a data collection endeavor of this scope. Also, facts and figures, such as number and amount of awards, can suddenly change, or awards can be discontinued by a sponsoring organization. Therefore, readers should verify data with the specific sponsoring agency responsible for administering these awards before applying.

CRITERIA FOR INCLUSION IN THIS BOOK

The programs listed in this book have the primary characteristics of legitimate scholarships: verifiable sponsor addresses and phone numbers, appropriate descriptive materials, and fees that, if required, are not exorbitant. Peterson's assumes that these fees are used to defray administrative expenses and are not major sources of income.

QUICK REFERENCE CHART

Scholarships, Grants & Prizes At-a-Glance

This chart lists award programs that indicate that their largest award provides $2000 or more. The awards are ranked in descending order on the basis of the dollar amount of the largest award. Because the award criteria in the Academic Fields/Career Goals and Nonacademic/Noncareer Criteria column may represent only some of the criteria or limitations that affect eligibility for the award, you should refer to the full description in the award profiles to ascertain all relevant details.

Award Name	Page Number	Highest Dollar Amount	Lowest Dollar Amount	Number of Awards	Academic Fields/Career Goals and Nonacademic/Noncareer Criteria
Regeneron Science Talent Search	883	$250,000	$25,000	40	Must be in high school.
U.S. Army ROTC Four-Year College Scholarship	645	$150,000	$9000	1,000–2,500	Military Service: Army; Army National Guard. Must be in high school.
Army (ROTC) Reserve Officers Training Corps Two-, Three-, Four-Year Campus-Based Scholarships	645	$120,000	$10,000	2,000–3,500	Military Service: Army. Limited to Asian/Pacific Islander students.
U.S. Army ROTC Guaranteed Reserve Forces Duty (GRFD), (ARNG/USAR) and Dedicated ARNG Scholarships	647	$120,000	$10,000	1,000–3,000	Military Service: Army National Guard.
Careers Through Culinary Arts Program Cooking Competition for Scholarships	229	$90,000	$1000	50–70	Culinary Arts; Hospitality Management. Residence: Arizona; California; Illinois; Maryland; New York; Pennsylvania; Virginia. Must be in high school.
SME Family Scholarship	309	$80,000	$5000	1–10	Engineering/Technology.
Intel International Science and Engineering Fair	883	$75,000	$500	1–600	Must be in high school.
Indian Health Service Health Professions Pre-graduate Scholarships	114	$63,500	$23,000	50–100	Applied Sciences; Biology; Health and Medical Sciences. Limited to American Indian/Alaska Native students.
Health Professions Preparatory Scholarship Program	152	$52,600	$13,250	25–50	Behavioral Science; Health and Medical Sciences; Nursing; Pharmacy; Psychology; Social Sciences. Limited to American Indian/Alaska Native students.
Tuition Exchange Scholarships	622	$52,140	$4190	7,000–9,000	Employment/Volunteer Experience: teaching/education.
U.S. Army ROTC Military Junior College (MJC) Scholarship	646	$52,000	$5600	110–150	Military Service: Army; Army National Guard.
Kentucky Transportation Cabinet Civil Engineering Scholarship Program	195	$51,200	$12,400	15–25	Civil Engineering. Residence: Kentucky. Studying in Kentucky.
Davidson Fellows Scholarship Program	113	$50,000	$10,000	15–20	Applied Sciences; Engineering/Technology; Literature/English/Writing; Mathematics; Music; Philosophy; Science, Technology, and Society.
Elks National Foundation Most Valuable Student Scholarship Contest	818	$50,000	$4000	500	Talent/Interest Area: leadership. Must be in high school.
Miss America Organization Competition Scholarships	822	$50,000	$2000	70	Talent/Interest Area: beauty pageant.

Award Name	Page Number	Highest Dollar Amount	Lowest Dollar Amount	Number of Awards	Academic Fields/Career Goals and Nonacademic/Noncareer Criteria
U.S. Army ROTC Four-Year Nursing Scholarship	449	$50,000	$5000	100	Nursing. Military Service: Army; Army National Guard.
Boettcher Foundation Scholarship	741	$40,000	$13,000	42	Residence: Colorado. Studying in Colorado. Talent/Interest Area: leadership. Must be in high school.
Mas Family Scholarship Award	165	$40,000	$8000	5–10	Business/Consumer Services; Chemical Engineering; Civil Engineering; Communications; Economics; Electrical Engineering/Electronics; Engineering-Related Technologies; International Studies; Journalism; Materials Science, Engineering, and Metallurgy; Mechanical Engineering. Limited to Hispanic students.
OhioLEADS! Scholarship	784	$40,000	$1500	200–250	Residence: Ohio. Studying in Ohio. Must be in high school.
Ron Brown Scholar Program	697	$40,000	$10,000	10–20	Talent/Interest Area: leadership. Must be in high school. Limited to Black (non-Hispanic) students.
U.S. Army ROTC Four-Year Historically Black College/ University Scholarship	645	$40,000	$9000	20–200	Military Service: Army; Army National Guard.
Science, Mathematics, and Research for Transformation Defense Scholarship for Service Program	110	$39,000	$22,000	200	Applied Sciences; Engineering-Related Technologies; Engineering/Technology; Mathematics; Physical Sciences.
Master's Scholarship Program	181	$32,000	$25,000	1–15	Chemical Engineering; Computer Science/Data Processing; Electrical Engineering/Electronics; Engineering/Technology; Materials Science, Engineering, and Metallurgy. Limited to American Indian/Alaska Native; Black (non-Hispanic); Hispanic students.
Baer Reintegration Scholarship	580	$30,000	$1000	20–30	Limited to students with schizophrenia, schizoaffective disorder or bipolar disorder.
Dependent Children Scholarship Program	619	$30,000	$3000	N/A	Residence: Tennessee. Studying in Tennessee.
The Frank M. and Gertrude R. Doyle Foundation, Inc.	857	$30,000	$500	N/A	Must be age 17–99.
Los Alamos Employees' Scholarship	769	$30,000	$1000	50	Residence: New Mexico.
National Security Agency Stokes Educational Scholarship Program	217	$30,000	$1000	15–20	Computer Science/Data Processing; Electrical Engineering/Electronics. Must be in high school.
St. Andrews Scholarship	698	$30,000	$20,000	2	Limited to students of Scottish heritage.
Voice of Democracy Program	837	$30,000	$1000	54	Talent/Interest Area: public speaking; writing. Must be in high school.
National FFA Collegiate Scholarship Program	550	$28,000	$300	1,700–1,800	Civic Affiliation: Future Farmers of America.
Florida Space Research Program	142	$25,000	$12,500	13–15	Aviation/Aerospace; Earth Science; Materials Science, Engineering, and Metallurgy; Mathematics; Mechanical Engineering. Residence: Florida. Studying in Florida.
Ford Opportunity Program	756	$25,000	$1000	30–50	Residence: California; Oregon. Studying in California; Oregon.

Award Name	Page Number	Highest Dollar Amount	Lowest Dollar Amount	Number of Awards	Academic Fields/Career Goals and Nonacademic/Noncareer Criteria
Ford ReStart Program	756	$25,000	$1000	45–46	Residence: California; Oregon. Studying in California; Oregon.
Ford Scholars Program	757	$25,000	$1000	100–120	Residence: California; Oregon. Studying in California; Oregon.
Horatio Alger Association Scholarship Programs	860	$25,000	$7000	1,009	Must be in high school.
Princess Grace Awards in Dance, Theater, and Film	327	$25,000	$5000	15–25	Filmmaking/Video; Performing Arts.
Young Entrepreneur Awards	829	$25,000	$2000	100	Talent/Interest Area: entrepreneurship. Must be in high school.
1B USD Worldwide Venture Capital	116	$20,000	$2000	1–20	Applied Sciences; Aviation/Aerospace; Business/Consumer Services; Campus Activities; Communications; Computer Science/Data Processing; Fashion Design; Filmmaking/Video; Industrial Design; Marketing; Materials Science, Engineering, and Metallurgy; Science, Technology, and Society. Nationality: Chinese; Japanese; Korean. Talent/Interest Area: Asian language; entrepreneurship; foreign language; international exchange; public speaking.
Atlas Shrugged Essay Contest	845	$20,000	$50	84	N/A
Coca-Cola Scholars Program	848	$20,000	$10,000	250	Must be in high school.
Gates Millennium Scholars Program	669	$20,000	$500	150	Talent/Interest Area: leadership. Limited to American Indian/Alaska Native students.
Jesse Brown Memorial Youth Scholarship Program	584	$20,000	$5000	8	Employment/Volunteer Experience: community service; helping handicapped.
Milton Fisher Scholarship for Innovation and Creativity	791	$20,000	$250	1–8	Residence: Alabama; Alaska; Arizona; Arkansas; California; Colorado; Connecticut; Delaware; District of Columbia; Florida; Georgia; Hawaii; Idaho; Illinois; Indiana; Iowa; Kansas; Kentucky; Louisiana; Maine; Maryland; Massachusetts; Michigan; Minnesota; Mississippi; Missouri; Montana; Nebraska; Nevada; New Hampshire; New Jersey; New Mexico; New York; North Carolina; North Dakota; Ohio; Oklahoma; Oregon; Pennsylvania; Rhode Island; South Carolina; South Dakota; Tennessee; Texas; Utah; Vermont; Virginia; Washington; West Virginia; Wisconsin; Wyoming. Studying in Alabama; Alaska; Arizona; Arkansas; California; Colorado; Connecticut; Delaware; District of Columbia; Florida; Georgia; Hawaii; Idaho; Illinois; Indiana; Iowa; Kansas; Kentucky; Louisiana; Maine; Maryland; Massachusetts; Michigan; Minnesota; Mississippi; Missouri; Montana; Nebraska; Nevada; New Hampshire; New Jersey; New Mexico; New York; North Carolina; North Dakota; Ohio; Oklahoma; Oregon; Pennsylvania; Rhode Island; South Carolina; South Dakota; Tennessee; Texas; Utah; Vermont; Virginia; Washington; West Virginia; Wisconsin; Wyoming.

Award Name	Page Number	Highest Dollar Amount	Lowest Dollar Amount	Number of Awards	Academic Fields/Career Goals and Nonacademic/Noncareer Criteria
Pride Foundation Scholarship Program	790	$20,000	$1000	85–125	Residence: Alaska; Idaho; Montana; Oregon; Washington. Talent/Interest Area: LGBT issues.
American Legion Department of Kansas High School Oratorical Contest	732	$18,000	$150	4	Residence: Kansas. Talent/Interest Area: public speaking. Must be in high school.
Stephen Phillips Memorial Scholarship Fund, Inc.	797	$18,000	$3000	130–140	Residence: Connecticut; Maine; Massachusetts; New Hampshire; Rhode Island; Vermont.
5 Strong Scholars Scholarship	666	$16,000	$10,000	25	Residence: Georgia. Studying in Georgia. Must be in high school. Limited to ethnic minority students.
Air Force ROTC College Scholarship	640	$15,000	$9000	2,000–4,000	Military Service: Air Force.
Applications International Corporation Impact Scholarship	463	$15,000	$10,000	4	Occupational Safety and Health.
Armenian Relief Society Undergraduate Scholarship	670	$15,000	$13,000	N/A	Nationality: Armenian.
Barnes Scholarship	798	$15,000	$1000	1–4	Residence: Florida. Must be in high school.
First in Family Scholarship	766	$15,000	$12,500	10	Residence: Alabama. Studying in Alabama. Must be in high school.
Life Lessons Scholarship Program	866	$15,000	$5000	20–50	N/A
National Beta Club Scholarship	550	$15,000	$1000	221	Civic Affiliation: National Beta Club. Must be in high school.
National Black MBA Association Graduate Scholarship Program	869	$15,000	$2500	10–25	N/A
ODKF General Scholarship Award	611	$15,000	$1450	30–50	Residence: Hawaii. Talent/Interest Area: athletics/sports.
Pennsylvania Institute of Certified Public Accountants Sophomore Scholarship	83	$15,000	$1000	60–85	Accounting. Residence: Pennsylvania. Studying in Pennsylvania.
Sallie Mae® Make College Happen Challenge	579	$15,000	$1000	10	N/A
Scholarship America Dream Award	880	$15,000	$5000	N/A	N/A

Award Name	Page Number	Highest Dollar Amount	Lowest Dollar Amount	Number of Awards	Academic Fields/Career Goals and Nonacademic/Noncareer Criteria
Scholarship for Students Pursuing a Business or STEM Degree	84	$15,000	$2500	35–120	Accounting; Advertising/Public Relations; Agribusiness; Agriculture; Animal/Veterinary Sciences; Applied Sciences; Archaeology; Architecture; Audiology; Aviation/Aerospace; Biology; Business/Consumer Services; Chemical Engineering; Civil Engineering; Computer Science/Data Processing; Dental Health/Services; Earth Science; Economics; Electrical Engineering/Electronics; Energy and Power Engineering; Engineering-Related Technologies; Engineering/Technology; Environmental Science; Finance; Food Science/Nutrition; Geography; Health Administration; Health and Medical Sciences; Health Information Management/Technology; Hospitality Management; Human Resources; Insurance and Actuarial Science; Marine Biology; Marine/Ocean Engineering; Marketing; Materials Science, Engineering, and Metallurgy; Mathematics; Mechanical Engineering; Meteorology/Atmospheric Science; Natural Sciences; Neurobiology; Nuclear Science; Nursing; Oceanography; Oncology; Optometry; Osteopathy; Pharmacy; Physical Sciences; Sports-Related/Exercise Science; Therapy/Rehabilitation. Residence: Tennessee.
The Soroptimist Live Your Dream: Education and Training Awards for Women	883	$15,000	$500	N/A	N/A
Texas 4-H Opportunity Scholarship	799	$15,000	$1500	225	Residence: Texas. Studying in Texas. Talent/Interest Area: animal/agricultural competition.
Tribal Priority Award	682	$15,000	$2500	1–5	Limited to American Indian/Alaska Native students.
Howard P. Rawlings Educational Excellence Awards Guaranteed Access Grant	771	$14,800	$400	1,000	Residence: Maryland. Studying in Maryland.
Educational Benefits for Children of Deceased Veterans	583	$14,421	$7479	N/A	Employment/Volunteer Experience: police/firefighting. Military Service: General. Residence: Delaware.
American Angus Auxiliary Scholarship	870	$14,000	$1000	10	Must be in high school.
North Dakota Scholars Program	783	$13,848	$6652	40–50	Residence: North Dakota. Studying in North Dakota. Must be in high school.
Safety Officers' Survivor Grant Program	604	$13,840	N/A	1–10	Employment/Volunteer Experience: police/firefighting. Residence: Minnesota. Studying in Minnesota.
Entitlement Cal Grant B	743	$13,665	$700	61,340	Residence: California. Studying in California.
Law Enforcement Personnel Dependents Scholarship	579	$13,665	$100	N/A	Employment/Volunteer Experience: police/firefighting. Residence: California. Studying in California.

Award Name	Page Number	Highest Dollar Amount	Lowest Dollar Amount	Number of Awards	Academic Fields/Career Goals and Nonacademic/Noncareer Criteria
National Space Grant College and Fellowship Program	114	$13,333	$1250	1–50	Applied Sciences; Aviation/Aerospace; Chemical Engineering; Civil Engineering; Computer Science/Data Processing; Earth Science; Engineering/Technology; Mathematics; Mechanical Engineering; Natural Sciences; Physical Sciences. Residence: Nevada. Studying in Nevada.
The Elizabeth Greenshields Foundation Grant	586	$13,000	$10,500	40–70	Talent/Interest Area: art.
Environmental Protection Scholarship	157	$13,000	$10,000	1–4	Biology; Chemical Engineering; Civil Engineering; Earth Science; Environmental Science; Hydrology; Mechanical Engineering; Natural Sciences. Residence: Kentucky. Studying in Kentucky.
GSBA Scholarship Fund	761	$13,000	$2000	40–45	Residence: Washington. Talent/Interest Area: LGBT issues.
National Honor Society Scholarships	550	$13,000	$1000	200	Civic Affiliation: National Honor Society. Must be in high school.
Law Enforcement Officers/Firemen Scholarship	604	$12,854	$2010	1–30	Employment/Volunteer Experience: police/firefighting. Residence: Mississippi. Studying in Mississippi.
Competitive Cal Grant A	743	$12,192	$5472	1,000–2,000	Residence: California. Studying in California.
Tuition Aid Grant	779	$12,190	$1012	N/A	Residence: New Jersey. Studying in New Jersey.
Airline Pilots Association Scholarship Program	528	$12,000	$1000	1–3	Civic Affiliation: Airline Pilots Association.
Herman O. West Foundation Scholarship Program	569	$12,000	$3000	1–14	Corporate Affiliation: West Pharmaceuticals. Must be in high school.
Humane Studies Fellowships	204	$12,000	$2000	140–180	Communications; Economics; History; Humanities; Law/Legal Services; Literature/English/Writing; Political Science; Social Sciences.
Kappa Alpha Theta Foundation Scholarship Program	547	$12,000	$1000	N/A	Civic Affiliation: Greek Organization.
Massachusetts AFL-CIO Scholarship	772	$12,000	$250	100–150	Residence: Massachusetts. Studying in Massachusetts. Must be in high school.
National Italian American Foundation Category II Scholarship	125	$12,000	$2500	N/A	Area/Ethnic Studies. Talent/Interest Area: Italian language.
Police Officers and Firefighters Survivors Education Assistance Program-Alabama	725	$12,000	$1600	15–30	Residence: Alabama. Studying in Alabama.
Sand Hill Scholars Program	795	$12,000	$1000	1–2	Residence: California. Must be in high school.
Kentucky National Guard Tuition Award	643	$11,500	$100	1,000–1,500	Military Service: Air Force National Guard; Army National Guard. Residence: Kentucky. Studying in Kentucky.
Minnesota State Grant Program	774	$11,334	$100	71,000–120,000	Residence: Minnesota. Studying in Minnesota.
Global Study Awards	885	$11,215	$11,215	1–9	N/A

Award Name	Page Number	Highest Dollar Amount	Lowest Dollar Amount	Number of Awards	Academic Fields/Career Goals and Nonacademic/Noncareer Criteria
SPIE Educational Scholarships in Optical Science and Engineering	114	$11,000	$2000	100–150	Applied Sciences; Chemical Engineering; Electrical Engineering/Electronics; Engineering-Related Technologies; Engineering/Technology; Materials Science, Engineering, and Metallurgy; Mechanical Engineering.
Frank O'Bannon Grant Program	797	$10,992	$200	N/A	Residence: Indiana. Studying in Indiana.
Vermont Incentive Grants	802	$10,800	$500	N/A	Residence: Vermont.
Academy of Nutrition and Dietetics Foundation Scholarship Program	330	$10,000	$500	200–250	Food Science/Nutrition. Civic Affiliation: American Dietetic Association.
AG Bell College Scholarship Program	628	$10,000	$2500	15–25	Disability: hearing impaired.
Air Traffic Control Association Scholarship	573	$10,000	$2000	7–12	Employment/Volunteer Experience: air traffic control. Talent/Interest Area: aviation.
Antibody Scholarship Program	500	$10,000	$5000	6	Science, Technology, and Society.
AREMA Graduate and Undergraduate Scholarships	191	$10,000	$1000	30–40	Civil Engineering; Computer Science/Data Processing; Construction Engineering/Management; Electrical Engineering/Electronics; Engineering-Related Technologies; Engineering/Technology; Mechanical Engineering.
Arkansas Governor's Scholars Program	737	$10,000	$4000	75–375	Residence: Arkansas. Studying in Arkansas. Must be in high school.
Buckingham Memorial Scholarship	573	$10,000	$2000	1–4	Employment/Volunteer Experience: air traffic control.
California Junior Miss Scholarship Program	742	$10,000	$500	25	Residence: California. Talent/Interest Area: beauty pageant; leadership; public speaking. Must be in high school.
Carmen V. D'Anna Memorial Scholarship of the Mars Supermarket Educational Fund	744	$10,000	N/A	1	Residence: Maryland. Studying in Maryland. Must be in high school.
Center for Architecture, Women's Auxiliary Eleanor Allwork Scholarship	120	$10,000	$4000	1–5	Architecture. Residence: New York. Studying in New York.
Christianson Grant	861	$10,000	$2500	8	N/A
CTIA Wireless Foundation Drive Smart Digital Short Contest	579	$10,000	$1000	6	N/A
Cystic Fibrosis Scholarship	629	$10,000	$1000	40–50	Disability: physically disabled.
DC Tuition Assistance Grant Program (DCTAG)	752	$10,000	$2500	5,999–6,000	Residence: District of Columbia.
Director's Scholarship Award	308	$10,000	$1000	1–5	Engineering/Technology. Talent/Interest Area: leadership.

Award Name	Page Number	Highest Dollar Amount	Lowest Dollar Amount	Number of Awards	Academic Fields/Career Goals and Nonacademic/Noncareer Criteria
Duck Brand Duct Tape "Stuck at Prom" Scholarship Contest	591	$10,000	$1000	1–11	Residence: Alabama; Alaska; Alberta; Arizona; Arkansas; British Columbia; California; Connecticut; Delaware; District of Columbia; Florida; Georgia; Guam; Hawaii; Idaho; Illinois; Indiana; Iowa; Kansas; Kentucky; Louisiana; Maine; Manitoba; Massachusetts; Michigan; Minnesota; Mississippi; Missouri; Montana; Nebraska; Nevada; New Brunswick; Newfoundland; New Hampshire; New Jersey; New Mexico; New York; North Carolina; North Dakota; Northwest Territories; Nova Scotia; Ohio; Oklahoma; Ontario; Oregon; Pennsylvania; Prince Edward Island; Puerto Rico; Rhode Island; Saskatchewan; South Carolina; South Dakota; Tennessee; Texas; Utah; Virginia; Washington; West Virginia; Wisconsin; Wyoming; Yukon. Must be in high school.
ESA Youth Scholarship Program	585	$10,000	$500	N/A	Employment/Volunteer Experience: police/firefighting. Must be in high school.
E. Wayne Kay Community College Scholarship Award	308	$10,000	$1000	1–20	Engineering/Technology; Trade/Technical Specialties.
Executive Women International Scholarship Program	854	$10,000	$1000	75–100	Must be in high school.
ExploraVision Science Competition	835	$10,000	$5000	N/A	Talent/Interest Area: science.
Federation of American Consumers and Travelers Educational Grant Program	542	$10,000	$250	4–10	Civic Affiliation: Federation of American Consumers and Travelers.
Federation of American Consumers and Travelers In-School Scholarship	855	$10,000	$2500	2	N/A
Federation of American Consumers and Travelers Second Chance Scholarship	855	$10,000	$2500	2	N/A
Gabriel A. Hartl Scholarship	136	$10,000	$2000	1–4	Aviation/Aerospace. Studying in Arkansas. Talent/Interest Area: aviation.
Harold Johnson Law Enforcement Scholarship	616	$10,000	$1000	1–5	Residence: California.
Hellenic Times Scholarship Fund	680	$10,000	$500	30–40	N/A
The Hirsch Family Scholarship	851	$10,000	$2000	N/A	N/A

Award Name	Page Number	Highest Dollar Amount	Lowest Dollar Amount	Number of Awards	Academic Fields/Career Goals and Nonacademic/Noncareer Criteria
Hispanic Engineer National Achievement Awards Corporation Scholarship Program	106	$10,000	$500	100–120	Animal/Veterinary Sciences; Architecture; Audiology; Aviation/Aerospace; Biology; Chemical Engineering; Civil Engineering; Computer Science/Data Processing; Construction Engineering/Management; Earth Science; Electrical Engineering/ Electronics; Energy and Power Engineering; Engineering-Related Technologies; Engineering/Technology; Entomology; Environmental Health; Environmental Science; Food Science/ Nutrition; Hydrology; Industrial Design; Marine Biology; Marine/Ocean Engineering; Materials Science, Engineering, and Metallurgy; Mathematics; Mechanical Engineering; Meteorology/ Atmospheric Science; Natural Resources; Natural Sciences; Neurobiology; Nuclear Science; Oceanography; Oncology; Optometry; Osteopathy; Paper and Pulp Engineering; Pharmacy; Physical Sciences; Statistics. Limited to Hispanic students.
HORIZONS Scholarship	426	$10,000	$500	5–6	Military and Defense Studies.
Illinois Restaurant Association Educational Foundation Scholarships	229	$10,000	$1000	50–70	Culinary Arts; Food Science/Nutrition; Food Service/Hospitality; Hospitality Management. Employment/Volunteer Experience: food service; hospitality/hotel administration/operations. Residence: Illinois.
James R. Hoffa Memorial Scholarship Fund	545	$10,000	$1000	1–100	Civic Affiliation: International Brotherhood of Teamsters. Must be in high school.
Janet L. Hoffmann Loan Assistance Repayment Program	254	$10,000	$1500	700	Education; Law/Legal Services; Nursing; Social Services; Therapy/Rehabilitation. Employment/Volunteer Experience: government/politics. Residence: Maryland. Studying in Maryland.
John Lennon Scholarships	814	$10,000	$5000	3	Talent/Interest Area: music.
Jules Cohen Scholarship	266	$10,000	$5000	1–13	Electrical Engineering/Electronics; Engineering-Related Technologies; Science, Technology, and Society. Studying in Alabama; Alaska; Arizona; Arkansas; California; Colorado; Connecticut; Delaware; District of Columbia; Florida; Georgia; Guam; Hawaii; Idaho; Illinois; Indiana; Iowa; Kansas; Kentucky; Louisiana; Maine; Maryland; Massachusetts; Michigan; Minnesota; Mississippi; Missouri; Montana; Nebraska; Nevada; New Hampshire; New Jersey; New Mexico; New York; North Carolina; North Dakota; Ohio; Oklahoma; Oregon; Pennsylvania; Puerto Rico; Rhode Island; South Carolina; South Dakota; Tennessee; Texas; Utah; Vermont; Virginia; Washington; West Virginia; Wisconsin; Wyoming.
J. Wood Platt Caddie Scholarship Trust	766	$10,000	$1000	N/A	Residence: Delaware; New Jersey; Pennsylvania.
Krishnan-Shah Family Scholarship	794	$10,000	$1000	1–5	Residence: California.

Award Name	Page Number	Highest Dollar Amount	Lowest Dollar Amount	Number of Awards	Academic Fields/Career Goals and Nonacademic/Noncareer Criteria
Latinos in Technology Scholarship	617	$10,000	$1000	1–100	Residence: California. Limited to Hispanic students.
Lawrence C. Fortier Memorial Scholarship	573	$10,000	$2000	1–5	Talent/Interest Area: aviation.
Lee-Jackson Educational Foundation Scholarship Competition	768	$10,000	$1000	27	Residence: Virginia. Talent/Interest Area: writing. Must be in high school.
Louie Family Foundation Scholarship	864	$10,000	$1000	25–35	N/A
MaleSense Pro Internet Marketing Scholarship	867	$10,000	$1000	1–10	N/A
Marine Corps Scholarship Foundation	566	$10,000	$1500	2,000–2,300	Civic Affiliation: American Legion or Auxiliary.
Medicus Student Exchange	701	$10,000	$2000	1–10	Talent/Interest Area: foreign language.
Nancy Lorraine Jensen Memorial Scholarship	189	$10,000	$2500	1–6	Chemical Engineering; Electrical Engineering/Electronics; Mechanical Engineering. Talent/Interest Area: science.
National Aviation Explorer Scholarships	141	$10,000	$3000	5	Aviation/Aerospace. Talent/Interest Area: aviation; leadership.
National Italian American Foundation Category I Scholarship	691	$10,000	$2500	40–45	N/A
Needham and Company September 11th Scholarship Fund	870	$10,000	$7000	8–15	N/A
PanHellenic Scholarship Awards	611	$10,000	$2500	40	N/A
Peninsula Regent Charitable Foundation Educational Grant Program	795	$10,000	$1000	1–30	Residence: California.
PFund Foundation Scholarship Program	789	$10,000	$2000	15–30	Residence: Iowa; Minnesota; North Dakota; South Dakota; Wisconsin. Studying in Iowa; Minnesota; North Dakota; South Dakota; Wisconsin.
Profile in Courage Essay Contest	863	$10,000	$500	7	Must be in high school.
Prompt's $20,000 Scholarship	614	$10,000	$2000	14	Must be in high school.
Ralph Hale and Martha L. Ruppert Educational Scholarship	795	$10,000	$1000	1–30	Residence: California.
Scholastic Art and Writing Awards	574	$10,000	$500	89	Must be in high school.
SHRM Foundation Student Scholarships	371	$10,000	$2500	44	Human Resources. Civic Affiliation: Society for Human Resource Management.
Sons of Italy Foundation's National Leadership Grant Competition	699	$10,000	$4000	9–10	N/A
Sons of Italy National Leadership Grants Competition Language Scholarship	339	$10,000	$4000	1	Foreign Language.
Spencer Educational Foundation Scholarship	375	$10,000	$5000	30–40	Insurance and Actuarial Science.
State Tuition Assistance	642	$10,000	N/A	1–200	Military Service: Air Force National Guard; Army National Guard. Studying in Delaware.
Swanson Scholarship	341	$10,000	$1000	1–10	Funeral Services/Mortuary Science. Residence: Nebraska.

Award Name	Page Number	Highest Dollar Amount	Lowest Dollar Amount	Number of Awards	Academic Fields/Career Goals and Nonacademic/Noncareer Criteria
Tailhook Educational Foundation Scholarship	649	$10,000	$2000	70	Military Service: Coast Guard; Marine Corps; Navy.
Technical Minority Scholarship	190	$10,000	$1000	128	Chemical Engineering; Computer Science/Data Processing; Electrical Engineering/Electronics; Engineering-Related Technologies; Engineering/Technology; Materials Science, Engineering, and Metallurgy; Mechanical Engineering; Physical Sciences. Limited to ethnic minority students.
Teletoon Animation Scholarship	131	$10,000	$5000	9	Arts; Filmmaking/Video. Residence: Alberta; British Columbia; Manitoba; New Brunswick; Newfoundland; Northwest Territories; Nova Scotia; Ontario; Prince Edward Island; Quebec; Saskatchewan.
Television Academy Foundation	619	$10,000	$2000	20–25	N/A
Theodore R. and Vivian M. Johnson Scholarship Program for Children of UPS Employees or UPS Retirees	571	$10,000	$1000	1–205	Corporate Affiliation: Universal American Financial Corporation. Residence: Florida. Studying in Florida.
UCB Family Epilepsy Scholarship	638	$10,000	$5000	32	Disability: physically disabled.
United States Society on Dams Scholarship Award	199	$10,000	$1000	1–4	Civil Engineering; Engineering/Technology; Environmental Science; Hydrology. Civic Affiliation: United States Society on Dams.
Vectorworks Design Scholarship	124	$10,000	$3000	15–18	Architecture; Arts; Civil Engineering; Construction Engineering/Management; Drafting; Engineering-Related Technologies; Engineering/Technology; Graphics/Graphic Arts/Printing; Industrial Design; Interior Design; Landscape Architecture; Urban and Regional Planning.
The Vegetarian Resource Group Scholarship	891	$10,000	$5000	N/A	Must be in high school.
The Walter A. Hunt, Jr. Scholarship	120	$10,000	$7500	1–2	Architecture. Residence: New York. Must be in high school.
Young American Creative Patriotic Art Awards Program	824	$10,000	$500	8	Talent/Interest Area: art. Must be in high school.
Canadian Nurses Foundation Scholarships	448	$9000	$1500	50–60	Nursing. Employment/Volunteer Experience: nursing. Nationality: Canadian.
Edward T. Conroy Memorial Scholarship Program	602	$9000	$7200	121	Employment/Volunteer Experience: police/firefighting. Military Service: General. Residence: Maryland. Studying in Maryland.
New Jersey Society of Certified Public Accountants High School Scholarship Program	82	$9000	$7000	20–25	Accounting. Residence: New Jersey. Must be in high school.
Delegate Scholarship Program-Maryland	770	$8650	$200	3,500	Residence: Maryland. Studying in Maryland.
Huang Leadership Development Scholarship	617	$8500	$1000	1–10	N/A

Award Name	Page Number	Highest Dollar Amount	Lowest Dollar Amount	Number of Awards	Academic Fields/Career Goals and Nonacademic/Noncareer Criteria
Undergraduate STEM Research Scholarships	114	$8500	$3000	1–35	Applied Sciences; Aviation/Aerospace; Biology; Chemical Engineering; Computer Science/Data Processing; Electrical Engineering/Electronics; Engineering-Related Technologies; Materials Science, Engineering, and Metallurgy; Mathematics; Mechanical Engineering; Physical Sciences; Science, Technology, and Society. Studying in Virginia.
CBC Spouses Education Scholarship	676	$8200	$500	250–350	Studying in Alabama; Alaska; Arizona; Arkansas; California; Colorado; Connecticut; Delaware; District of Columbia; Florida; Georgia; Guam; Hawaii; Idaho; Illinois; Indiana; Iowa; Kansas; Kentucky; Louisiana; Maine; Maryland; Massachusetts; Michigan; Minnesota; Mississippi; Missouri; Montana; Nebraska; Nevada; New Hampshire; New Jersey; New Mexico; New York; North Carolina; North Dakota; Ohio; Oklahoma; Oregon; Pennsylvania; Puerto Rico; Rhode Island; South Carolina; South Dakota; Tennessee; Texas; Utah; Vermont; Virginia; Washington; West Virginia; Wisconsin; Wyoming. Limited to Black (non-Hispanic) students.
Vermont Part-Time Student Grants	803	$8100	$250	N/A	Residence: Vermont.
AACE International Competitive Scholarship	118	$8000	$2000	10–20	Architecture; Aviation/Aerospace; Business/Consumer Services; Chemical Engineering; Civil Engineering; Construction Engineering/Management; Electrical Engineering/Electronics; Engineering-Related Technologies; Engineering/Technology; Mechanical Engineering.
AIFS-HACU Scholarships	669	$8000	$6000	1	Talent/Interest Area: international exchange. Limited to Hispanic students.
AQHF Racing Scholarships	536	$8000	$4000	1–5	Civic Affiliation: American Quarter Horse Association. Employment/Volunteer Experience: designated career field; harness racing.
California Wine Grape Growers Foundation Scholarship	742	$8000	$2000	6–7	Residence: California. Studying in California. Must be in high school.
Hispanic Metropolitan Chamber Scholarships	592	$8000	$2000	45–50	Residence: Oregon. Limited to Hispanic students.
Jewish Federation of Metropolitan Chicago Academic Scholarship Program	684	$8000	$1000	100–125	Religion: Jewish.
Jonathan Lax Scholarship for Gay Men	741	$8000	$4000	4–20	Residence: Pennsylvania. Studying in Pennsylvania.
Pat and Jim Host Scholarship	370	$8000	$2000	1	Hospitality Management; Travel/Tourism.
Texas Educational Opportunity Grant (TEOG)	799	$8000	N/A	N/A	Residence: Texas. Studying in Texas.
Toward EXcellence, Access, and Success (TEXAS) Grant	800	$8000	N/A	N/A	Residence: Texas. Studying in Texas.

Award Name	Page Number	Highest Dollar Amount	Lowest Dollar Amount	Number of Awards	Academic Fields/Career Goals and Nonacademic/Noncareer Criteria
Vocational Nurse & Licensed Vocational Nurse to Associate Degree Nursing Scholarship Program	453	$8000	$4000	N/A	Nursing. Residence: California.
Abby Sobrato Scholarship	616	$7500	$1000	20	Residence: California.
AGC Education and Research Foundation Undergraduate Scholarships	193	$7500	$2500	100–150	Civil Engineering; Construction Engineering/Management.
American Legion Department of Pennsylvania High School Oratorical Contest	735	$7500	$4000	3	Residence: Pennsylvania. Talent/Interest Area: public speaking. Must be in high school.
Civil Air Patrol Academic Scholarships	541	$7500	$1000	40	Civic Affiliation: Civil Air Patrol.
Epsilon Sigma Alpha Foundation Scholarships	678	$7500	$350	125–175	Limited to ethnic minority students.
E. Wayne Kay Scholarship	309	$7500	$2500	10–30	Engineering/Technology; Trade/Technical Specialties.
International Violoncello Competition	837	$7500	$2500	3	Talent/Interest Area: music.
Palmetto Fellows Scholarship Program	796	$7500	$6700	4,846	Residence: South Carolina. Studying in South Carolina. Must be in high school.
Paraprofessional Teacher Preparation Grant	255	$7500	$250	N/A	Education. Residence: Massachusetts.
TELACU Education Foundation	753	$7500	$500	350–600	Residence: California; Illinois; New York; Texas.
William Faulkner-William Wisdom Creative Writing Competition	416	$7500	$250	8	Mathematics. Employment/Volunteer Experience: human services. Talent/Interest Area: English language; writing.
Higher Education Legislative Plan (HELP)	775	$7344	$340	2,661	Residence: Mississippi. Studying in Mississippi.
Teaching Assistant Program in France	104	$7280	$1040	1,120	American Studies; Art History; Education; European Studies; Foreign Language; History; Humanities; International Studies; Literature/English/Writing; Political Science; Social Sciences. Talent/Interest Area: English language; foreign language; French language; international exchange.
Indiana National Guard Supplemental Grant	644	$7110	$20	503–925	Military Service: Air Force National Guard; Army National Guard. Residence: Indiana. Studying in Indiana.
Charles and Lucille King Family Foundation Scholarships	203	$7000	$3500	10–20	Communications; Filmmaking/Video; TV/Radio Broadcasting.
Colorado Masons Benevolent Fund Scholarships	581	$7000	$1000	6–10	Residence: Colorado. Studying in Colorado. Must be in high school.
Jane M. Klausman Women in Business Scholarships	171	$7000	$1000	30–32	Business/Consumer Services.
Myrtle and Earl Walker Scholarship Fund	287	$7000	$1000	1–25	Engineering-Related Technologies; Engineering/Technology; Mechanical Engineering.
Selby Scholar Program	805	$7000	$1000	40	Residence: Florida. Talent/Interest Area: leadership.

Award Name	Page Number	Highest Dollar Amount	Lowest Dollar Amount	Number of Awards	Academic Fields/Career Goals and Nonacademic/Noncareer Criteria
Senatorial Scholarships-Maryland	771	$7000	$400	7,000	Residence: Maryland. Studying in Maryland.
Women's jewelry association student scholarship	132	$7000	$500	5–12	Arts; Trade/Technical Specialties. Employment/Volunteer Experience: fine arts. Talent/Interest Area: art.
Taylor Opportunity Program for Students Honors Level	769	$6736	$836	9,661	Residence: Louisiana. Studying in Louisiana.
Armenian Students Association of America Inc. Scholarships	670	$6700	$3300	35	N/A
Charles W. Riley Fire and Emergency Medical Services Tuition Reimbursement Program	329	$6500	N/A	1–150	Fire Sciences; Health and Medical Sciences; Trade/Technical Specialties. Employment/Volunteer Experience: police/firefighting. Residence: Maryland. Studying in Maryland.
New Jersey World Trade Center Scholarship	779	$6500	N/A	N/A	Residence: New Jersey.
Pennsylvania Burglar and Fire Alarm Association Youth Scholarship Program	611	$6500	$500	6–8	Employment/Volunteer Experience: police/firefighting. Residence: Pennsylvania. Must be in high school.
Taylor Opportunity Program for Students Performance Level	769	$6336	$636	11,928	Residence: Louisiana. Studying in Louisiana.
AIA New Jersey Scholarship Program	118	$6000	$4000	1–2	Architecture. Residence: New Jersey. Studying in New Jersey. Talent/Interest Area: art.
American Legion Department of New York High School Oratorical Contest	734	$6000	$2000	N/A	Residence: New York. Talent/Interest Area: public speaking. Must be in high school.
American Meteorological Society Minority Scholarships	424	$6000	$3000	3	Meteorology/Atmospheric Science. Must be in high school. Limited to ethnic minority students.
Contemporary Record Society National Competition for Performing Artists	817	$6000	$2000	1	Talent/Interest Area: music/singing.
Don't Mess With Texas Scholarship Program	752	$6000	$2000	2–3	Residence: Texas. Studying in Texas. Must be in high school.
Foster Care to Success Scholarship Program	856	$6000	$1000	100	N/A
Friends of 440 Scholarship Fund, Inc.	757	$6000	$500	1–60	Residence: Florida.
GCSAA Scholars Competition	365	$6000	$500	N/A	Horticulture/Floriculture. Civic Affiliation: Golf Course Superintendents Association of America.
Golden Gate Restaurant Association Scholarship Foundation	229	$6000	$1000	9–15	Culinary Arts; Food Service/Hospitality; Hospitality Management. Residence: California.
Higher Education Scholarship Program	693	$6000	$50	60–72	Limited to American Indian/Alaska Native students.

Award Name	Page Number	Highest Dollar Amount	Lowest Dollar Amount	Number of Awards	Academic Fields/Career Goals and Nonacademic/Noncareer Criteria
International Foodservice Editorial Council Communications Scholarship	88	$6000	$250	1–8	Advertising/Public Relations; Communications; Culinary Arts; Food Science/Nutrition; Food Service/Hospitality; Graphics/Graphic Arts/Printing; Home Economics; Hospitality Management; Journalism; Literature/English/Writing; Marketing; Photojournalism/Photography. Talent/Interest Area: photography/photogrammetry/filmmaking; writing.
Jackie Robinson Scholarship	596	$6000	$6000	40–60	Employment/Volunteer Experience: community service. Talent/Interest Area: leadership. Must be in high school. Limited to ethnic minority students.
Jo Anne J. Trow Scholarships	841	$6000	$1000	1–36	N/A
Marion Huber Learning Through Listening Awards	548	$6000	$2000	6	Civic Affiliation: Learning Ally. Disability: learning disabled. Must be in high school.
Mary P. Oenslager Scholastic Achievement Awards	548	$6000	$1000	3–9	Civic Affiliation: Learning Ally. Disability: visually impaired.
Montana University System Honor Scholarship	777	$6000	$4000	200	Residence: Montana. Studying in Montana. Must be in high school.
National Competition for Composers' Recordings	817	$6000	$2000	1	Talent/Interest Area: music/singing.
Office and Professional Employees International Union Howard Coughlin Memorial Scholarship Fund	552	$6000	$2400	18	Civic Affiliation: Office and Professional Employees International Union.
Roadway Worker Memorial Scholarship Program	576	$6000	$5000	2–5	Employment/Volunteer Experience: construction; roadway work; transportation industry.
Society of Plastics Engineers Scholarship Program	182	$6000	$1000	35–40	Chemical Engineering; Electrical Engineering/Electronics; Engineering/Technology; Industrial Design; Materials Science, Engineering, and Metallurgy; Trade/Technical Specialties.
TELS - Tennessee HOPE Scholarship	620	$6000	$2000	N/A	Residence: Tennessee. Studying in Tennessee.
Texas Mutual Insurance Company Scholarship Program	622	$6000	$600	1–25	N/A
Twin Towers Orphan Fund	887	$6000	$1500	N/A	N/A
Taylor Opportunity Program for Students Opportunity Level	769	$5936	$436	24,633	Residence: Louisiana. Studying in Louisiana.
UNCF/Travelers Insurance Scholarship	170	$5850	$3000	N/A	Business/Consumer Services; Insurance and Actuarial Science. Residence: California; Colorado; Florida; Georgia; Illinois; Massachusetts; Missouri; North Carolina; Texas; Washington. Limited to Black (non-Hispanic) students.
Iowa Tuition Grant Program	765	$5650	$100	16,500–19,000	Residence: Iowa. Studying in Iowa.
Kansas Teacher Service Scholarship	254	$5514	$2206	N/A	Education. Residence: Kansas. Studying in Kansas.

Award Name	Page Number	Highest Dollar Amount	Lowest Dollar Amount	Number of Awards	Academic Fields/Career Goals and Nonacademic/Noncareer Criteria
Academic Scholars Program	872	$5500	$1800	N/A	Studying in Oklahoma. Must be in high school.
Marion A. and Eva S. Peeples Scholarships	455	$5500	$1000	5–20	Nursing. Residence: Indiana. Studying in Indiana.
Oregon Veterans' Education Aid	661	$5400	$3600	1–200	Military Service: General. Residence: Oregon. Studying in Oregon.
1-800-HANSONS Scholarship Program	572	$5000	$500	8	N/A
$5,000 Nitro College Scholarship	871	$5000	$1000	1–2	N/A
Academy of Motion Picture Arts and Sciences Student Academy Awards	325	$5000	$2000	3–15	Filmmaking/Video.
AIAA Foundation Undergraduate Scholarships	110	$5000	$500	7	Applied Sciences; Aviation/Aerospace; Electrical Engineering/Electronics; Engineering-Related Technologies; Engineering/Technology; Materials Science, Engineering, and Metallurgy; Mechanical Engineering; Physical Sciences; Science, Technology, and Society. Civic Affiliation: American Institute of Aeronautics and Astronautics.
Alabama Student Assistance Program	725	$5000	$300	3,500–4,500	Residence: Alabama. Studying in Alabama.
Albert E. Wischmeyer Memorial Scholarship Award	306	$5000	$1000	1–10	Engineering/Technology. Residence: New York. Studying in New York.
All-Ink.com College Scholarship Program	840	$5000	$1000	5–10	N/A
American Chemical Society Scholars Program	172	$5000	$1000	100–130	Chemical Engineering; Environmental Science; Materials Science, Engineering, and Metallurgy; Natural Sciences; Paper and Pulp Engineering; Trade/Technical Specialties. Limited to American Indian/Alaska Native; Black (non-Hispanic); Hispanic students.
AMPCUS Hallmark Scholarship	707	$5000	$2000	N/A	Must be in high school. Limited to Asian/Pacific Islander students.
AMS Freshman Undergraduate Scholarship	424	$5000	$2500	14	Meteorology/Atmospheric Science. Must be in high school.
Anchor Scholarship Foundation Program	664	$5000	$2000	35–43	Military Service: Navy.
Angus Foundation Scholarships	550	$5000	$250	75–90	Civic Affiliation: American Angus Association.
ARC of Washington Trust Fund Stipend Program	504	$5000	$4000	4–5	Special Education. Employment/Volunteer Experience: community service; helping handicapped; human services; physical therapy/rehabilitation; teaching/education. Residence: Alaska; Idaho; Oregon; Washington.
Armed Forces Communications and Electronics Association ROTC Scholarship Program	137	$5000	$2000	16	Aviation/Aerospace; Computer Science/Data Processing; Electrical Engineering/Electronics; Engineering-Related Technologies; Engineering/Technology; Materials Science, Engineering, and Metallurgy; Mathematics; Physical Sciences.

Award Name	Page Number	Highest Dollar Amount	Lowest Dollar Amount	Number of Awards	Academic Fields/Career Goals and Nonacademic/Noncareer Criteria
ARTBA-TDF Lanford Family Highway Workers Memorial Scholarship Program	576	$5000	$1000	N/A	Employment/Volunteer Experience: construction; roadway work.
Arthur and Gladys Cervenka Scholarship Award	306	$5000	$1000	1–10	Engineering/Technology.
Ashby B. Carter Memorial Scholarship Fund Founders Award	548	$5000	$2000	3	Civic Affiliation: National Alliance of Postal and Federal Employees. Must be in high school.
Associated General Contractors NYS Scholarship Program	194	$5000	$1500	15–25	Civil Engineering; Construction Engineering/Management; Surveying, Surveying Technology, Cartography, or Geographic Information Science; Transportation. Residence: New York.
Baltimore Ravens Scholarship Program	744	$5000	N/A	1–5	Residence: Maryland. Must be in high school.
BMI Student Composer Awards	127	$5000	$500	9–11	Arts; Music. Talent/Interest Area: music; music/singing.
Bruce Lee Scholarship	890	$5000	$2000	1	Must be in high school.
BURGER KING Scholars Program	847	$5000	$1000	N/A	Must be in high school.
Caterpillar Scholars Award Fund	306	$5000	$1000	1–15	Engineering/Technology.
Center for Architecture Design Scholarship	119	$5000	$2000	1–2	Architecture; Civil Engineering; Electrical Engineering/Electronics; Industrial Design; Interior Design; Landscape Architecture; Mechanical Engineering. Residence: New York. Studying in New York.
Chapter 198-Downriver Detroit Scholarship	307	$5000	$1000	1–5	Engineering/Technology; Industrial Design; Mechanical Engineering; Trade/Technical Specialties. Studying in Michigan.
Chapter 23-Quad Cities Iowa/Illinois Scholarship	307	$5000	$1000	5	Engineering/Technology. Studying in Illinois; Iowa.
Chapter 31-Tri City Scholarship	307	$5000	$1000	5	Engineering/Technology. Studying in Michigan.
Chapter 3-Peoria Endowed Scholarship	307	$5000	$1000	5	Engineering/Technology. Residence: Illinois. Studying in Illinois.
Chapter 4-Lawrence A. Wacker Memorial Scholarship	307	$5000	$1000	1–10	Engineering/Technology; Mechanical Engineering. Studying in Wisconsin.
Chapter 63-Portland James E. Morrow Scholarship	307	$5000	$1000	5	Engineering/Technology. Residence: Oregon; Washington. Studying in Oregon; Washington.
Chapter 63-Portland Uncle Bud Smith Scholarship	307	$5000	$1000	5	Engineering/Technology. Residence: Oregon; Washington. Studying in Oregon; Washington.
Chapter 67-Phoenix Scholarship	307	$5000	$1000	1–5	Engineering/Technology; Industrial Design; Mechanical Engineering; Trade/Technical Specialties. Studying in Arizona.
Chapter 6-Fairfield County Scholarship	308	$5000	$1000	4	Engineering/Technology.
Chapter 93-Albuquerque Scholarship	308	$5000	$1000	1–5	Engineering/Technology. Studying in New Mexico.
Clarence and Josephine Myers Scholarship	308	$5000	$1000	5	Engineering/Technology. Studying in Indiana.

Award Name	Page Number	Highest Dollar Amount	Lowest Dollar Amount	Number of Awards	Academic Fields/Career Goals and Nonacademic/Noncareer Criteria
Classic Scholarships	622	$5000	$2500	300–350	Residence: Alabama; Alaska; Arizona; Arkansas; California; Colorado; Connecticut; Delaware; Florida; Georgia; Hawaii; Idaho; Illinois; Indiana; Iowa; Kansas; Kentucky; Louisiana; Maine; Maryland; Massachusetts; Michigan; Minnesota; Mississippi; Missouri; Montana; Nebraska; Nevada; New Hampshire; New Jersey; New Mexico; New York; North Carolina; North Dakota; Ohio; Oklahoma; Oregon; Pennsylvania; Puerto Rico; Rhode Island; South Carolina; South Dakota; Tennessee; Texas; Utah; Vermont; Virginia; Washington; West Virginia; Wisconsin; Wyoming. Studying in Alabama; Alaska; Arizona; Arkansas; California; Colorado; Connecticut; Delaware; Florida; Georgia; Hawaii; Idaho; Illinois; Indiana; Iowa; Kansas; Kentucky; Louisiana; Maine; Maryland; Massachusetts; Michigan; Minnesota; Mississippi; Missouri; Montana; Nebraska; Nevada; New Hampshire; New Jersey; New Mexico; New York; North Carolina; North Dakota; Ohio; Oklahoma; Oregon; Pennsylvania; Puerto Rico; Rhode Island; South Carolina; South Dakota; Tennessee; Texas; Utah; Vermont; Virginia; Washington; West Virginia; Wisconsin; Wyoming.
Clinton J. Helton Manufacturing Scholarship Award Fund	308	$5000	$1000	1–5	Engineering/Technology; Trade/Technical Specialties. Studying in Colorado.
CollegeWeekLive.com Scholarship	816	$5000	$1000	1–15	Talent/Interest Area: writing.
Colorado Student Grant	746	$5000	$300	N/A	Residence: Colorado. Studying in Colorado.
Common Scholarship Application	793	$5000	$500	95–110	Residence: California.
Congressional Hispanic Caucus Institute Scholarship Awards	676	$5000	$1000	100–150	Limited to Hispanic students.
Connie and Robert T. Gunter Scholarship	308	$5000	$1000	1–5	Engineering/Technology. Studying in Georgia.
Course Hero $5,000 Monthly Scholarship	850	$5000	$1000	1	N/A
Crain Educational Grants Program	794	$5000	$1000	10	Residence: California. Must be in high school.
Culinary Trust Scholarship Program for Culinary Study and Research	229	$5000	$1000	21	Culinary Arts; Food Science/Nutrition; Food Service/Hospitality.
Darooge Family Scholarship for Construction Trades	222	$5000	$1000	1–5	Construction Engineering/Management. Residence: Michigan. Must be in high school.
Daughters of the Cincinnati Scholarship	851	$5000	$3000	4–5	Must be in high school.

Award Name	Page Number	Highest Dollar Amount	Lowest Dollar Amount	Number of Awards	Academic Fields/Career Goals and Nonacademic/Noncareer Criteria
Direct Energy Live Brighter Scholarship	584	$5000	$2500	3	Residence: Connecticut; Delaware; District of Columbia; Illinois; Indiana; Maryland; Massachusetts; Michigan; New Hampshire; New Jersey; New York; Ohio; Pennsylvania; Rhode Island; Texas. Studying in Connecticut; Delaware; District of Columbia; Illinois; Indiana; Maryland; Massachusetts; Michigan; New Hampshire; New Jersey; New York; Ohio; Pennsylvania; Rhode Island; Texas.
Donaldson D. Frizzell Scholarship	655	$5000	$1000	5–14	Military Service: General.
Doran/Blair Scholarships	543	$5000	$1000	1–20	Civic Affiliation: Fleet Reserve Association/Auxiliary. Military Service: Coast Guard.
Duke Energy Scholars Program	568	$5000	$1000	50	Corporate Affiliation: Duke Energy Corporation. Must be in high school.
EDSF Board of Directors Scholarships	342	$5000	$1000	1–40	Graphics/Graphic Arts/Printing.
Edward S. Roth Manufacturing Engineering Scholarship	308	$5000	$1000	1–10	Engineering/Technology. Studying in California; Florida; Illinois; Massachusetts; Minnesota; Ohio; Texas; Utah.
Elie Wiesel Prize in Ethics Essay Contest	818	$5000	$500	5	Talent/Interest Area: writing.
Environmental Litigation Group, P.C. Asbestos Scholarship	586	$5000	$2000	3	N/A
Eric J. Gennuso and LeRoy D. (Bud) Loy, Jr. Scholarship Program	173	$5000	$2500	1–3	Chemical Engineering; Civil Engineering; Construction Engineering/Management; Electrical Engineering/Electronics; Energy and Power Engineering; Engineering-Related Technologies; Engineering/Technology; Environmental Science; Marine/Ocean Engineering; Materials Science, Engineering, and Metallurgy; Mechanical Engineering; Surveying, Surveying Technology, Cartography, or Geographic Information Science; Transportation. Residence: Pennsylvania.
E. Wayne Kay Co-op Scholarship	309	$5000	$1000	1–10	Engineering/Technology.
Explosive Ordnance Disposal Memorial Scholarship	586	$5000	$1000	25–75	Employment/Volunteer Experience: explosive ordnance disposal. Military Service: General.
Federated Garden Clubs of Connecticut Inc. Scholarships	156	$5000	$1000	2–5	Biology; Horticulture/Floriculture; Landscape Architecture. Residence: Connecticut. Studying in Connecticut.
Federation of American Consumers and Travelers Trade/Technical School Scholarship	542	$5000	$1000	1–3	Civic Affiliation: Federation of American Consumers and Travelers.
Fleet Reserve Association Education Foundation Scholarships	649	$5000	$1000	1–10	Military Service: Coast Guard.
Foreclosure.com Scholarship Program	856	$5000	$1000	5	N/A
Fort Wayne Chapter 56 Scholarship	309	$5000	$1000	1–10	Engineering/Technology; Industrial Design; Mechanical Engineering; Trade/Technical Specialties. Studying in Indiana.

Award Name	Page Number	Highest Dollar Amount	Lowest Dollar Amount	Number of Awards	Academic Fields/Career Goals and Nonacademic/Noncareer Criteria
Foundation for Seacoast Health Scholarships	351	$5000	$1000	2–6	Health and Medical Sciences. Residence: Maine; New Hampshire.
Franz Stenzel M.D. and Kathryn Stenzel Scholarship Fund	354	$5000	$2000	70	Health and Medical Sciences; Nursing. Residence: Oregon.
Gene and John Athletic Fund Scholarship	833	$5000	$2500	1–3	Talent/Interest Area: athletics/sports; LGBT issues.
General John Ratay Educational Fund Grants	868	$5000	$4000	1–5	N/A
Georgia Engineering Foundation Scholarship Program	298	$5000	$1000	45	Engineering/Technology. Employment/ Volunteer Experience: community service. Residence: Georgia.
Geraldo Rivera Scholarship	384	$5000	$1000	N/A	Journalism; TV/Radio Broadcasting.
Girls Impact the World Scholarship Program	849	$5000	$1000	12	N/A
Gloria Barron Prize for Young Heroes	821	$5000	N/A	1–15	Talent/Interest Area: leadership.
Governor's Scholarship Program—Need/Merit Scholarship	749	$5000	$900	2,404	Residence: Connecticut. Studying in Connecticut.
Graco Inc. Scholarship Program	569	$5000	$3500	N/A	Corporate Affiliation: Graco, Inc..
Graduate and Professional Scholarship Program-Maryland	238	$5000	$1000	584	Dental Health/Services; Health and Medical Sciences; Law/Legal Services; Nursing; Social Services. Residence: Maryland. Studying in Maryland.
Great Falls Broadcasters Association Scholarship	524	$5000	$2000	1	TV/Radio Broadcasting. Residence: Montana. Studying in Montana.
Greenhouse Scholars	590	$5000	$1000	15–25	Employment/Volunteer Experience: community service. Residence: Colorado; Georgia; Illinois; North Carolina. Studying in Alabama; Alaska; Arizona; Arkansas; California; Colorado; Connecticut; Delaware; District of Columbia; Florida; Georgia; Hawaii; Idaho; Illinois; Indiana; Iowa; Kansas; Kentucky; Louisiana; Maine; Maryland; Michigan; Mississippi; Missouri; Montana; Nebraska; Nevada; New Hampshire; New Jersey; New Mexico; New York; North Carolina; North Dakota; Ohio; Oklahoma; Oregon; Pennsylvania; Rhode Island; South Carolina; South Dakota; Tennessee; Texas; Utah; Vermont; Virginia; Washington; West Virginia; Wisconsin; Wyoming. Talent/Interest Area: leadership. Must be in high school.
Guiliano Mazzetti Scholarship Award	309	$5000	$1000	1–10	Engineering/Technology.
Harry A. Applegate Scholarship	75	$5000	$1000	20–25	Accounting; Business/Consumer Services; Education; Fashion Design; Finance; Food Service/Hospitality; Hospitality Management; Marketing. Civic Affiliation: Distribution Ed Club or Future Business Leaders of America.
Harry Ludwig Scholarship Fund	636	$5000	$500	1–3	Disability: visually impaired.
Hazel Reed Baumeister Scholarship Program	616	$5000	$1000	1–15	Residence: California.

Award Name	Page Number	Highest Dollar Amount	Lowest Dollar Amount	Number of Awards	Academic Fields/Career Goals and Nonacademic/Noncareer Criteria
Herbert Hoover Uncommon Student Award	763	$5000	$1000	15	Residence: Iowa. Must be in high school.
Higher Education Success Stipend Program	802	$5000	$300	495–8,243	Residence: Utah. Studying in Utah.
Houston Symphony Ima Hogg Competition	430	$5000	$300	5	Music. Talent/Interest Area: music.
HSF/General College Scholarship Program	682	$5000	$500	2,200–5,000	Limited to Hispanic students.
IAAO Academic Partnership Program	861	$5000	$1000	1–5	N/A
IABA Scholarship	683	$5000	$3000	20–30	Limited to Black (non-Hispanic) students.
IFMA Foundation Scholarships	122	$5000	$1500	25–35	Architecture; Construction Engineering/Management; Engineering-Related Technologies; Engineering/Technology; Interior Design; Urban and Regional Planning.
Indiana Health Care Policy Institute Nursing Scholarship	454	$5000	$750	1–5	Nursing. Residence: Indiana. Studying in Illinois; Indiana; Kentucky; Michigan; Ohio.
Indian American Scholarship Fund	682	$5000	$500	3	Residence: Georgia. Must be in high school. Limited to Asian/Pacific Islander students.
Indiana Nursing Scholarship Fund	460	$5000	$200	490–690	Nursing. Residence: Indiana. Studying in Indiana.
Ingersoll Rand Scholarship	707	$5000	$2000	N/A	Must be in high school. Limited to Asian/Pacific Islander students.
ISA Educational Foundation Scholarships	282	$5000	$500	15	Engineering-Related Technologies.
ISF National Scholarship	108	$5000	$2000	1–40	Anthropology; Filmmaking/Video; History; International Studies; Journalism; Law Enforcement/Police Administration; Law/Legal Services; Near and Middle East Studies; TV/Radio Broadcasting. Religion: Muslim faith.
Jerry McDowell Fund	282	$5000	$1500	1–3	Engineering-Related Technologies; Engineering/Technology.
John Kimball Memorial Trust Scholarship Program for the Study of History	361	$5000	$300	3–10	History. Residence: Massachusetts. Studying in Massachusetts.
John L. Dales Scholarship Program	880	$5000	$1000	1–16	N/A
John M. Azarian Memorial Armenian Youth Scholarship Fund	684	$5000	$500	1–5	N/A
Joseph Shinoda Memorial Scholarship	366	$5000	$1000	8–15	Horticulture/Floriculture.
Judith McManus Price Scholarship	526	$5000	$2000	N/A	Urban and Regional Planning. Limited to American Indian/Alaska Native; Black (non-Hispanic); Hispanic students.
Juniper Networks Engineering Scholarship	794	$5000	$1000	1–10	Residence: California; Massachusetts; New Jersey; Ontario; Virginia. Must be in high school.
JVS Scholarship Program	684	$5000	$1000	125–200	Residence: California. Religion: Jewish.

Award Name	Page Number	Highest Dollar Amount	Lowest Dollar Amount	Number of Awards	Academic Fields/Career Goals and Nonacademic/Noncareer Criteria
Kappa Alpha Theta Foundation Non-Degree Educational Grant Program	546	$5000	$100	1	Civic Affiliation: Greek Organization.
Louis F. Wolf Jr. Memorial Scholarship	210	$5000	$1000	1	Communications; Electrical Engineering/Electronics; Engineering-Related Technologies; Engineering/Technology; Filmmaking/Video; Science, Technology, and Society; TV/Radio Broadcasting. Civic Affiliation: Society of Motion Picture and Television Engineers.
L. Ron Hubbard's Illustrators of the Future Contest	813	$5000	$500	12	Talent/Interest Area: art.
L. Ron Hubbard's Writers of the Future Contest	813	$5000	$500	12	Talent/Interest Area: writing.
Lucile B. Kaufman Women's Scholarship	309	$5000	$1000	1–5	Engineering/Technology.
Marie A. Calderilla Scholarship	795	$5000	$1000	1–30	Residence: California. Studying in California.
Marion Barr Stanfield Art Scholarship	131	$5000	$1500	5–8	Arts. Religion: Unitarian Universalist. Talent/Interest Area: art.
Mary McMillan Scholarship Award	249	$5000	$3000	1–6	Education; Health and Medical Sciences; Therapy/Rehabilitation. Employment/Volunteer Experience: physical therapy/rehabilitation.
Masonic Range Science Scholarship	94	$5000	$1000	1	Agribusiness; Agriculture; Animal/Veterinary Sciences; Environmental Science; Natural Resources.
Math, Engineering, Science, Business, Education, Computers Scholarships	162	$5000	$500	180	Business/Consumer Services; Computer Science/Data Processing; Education; Engineering/Technology; Humanities; Physical Sciences; Science, Technology, and Society; Social Sciences. Limited to American Indian/Alaska Native students.
Minority Teacher Incentive Grant Program	251	$5000	$2500	72	Education. Studying in Connecticut. Limited to ethnic minority students.
MOAA American Patriot Scholarship	868	$5000	$2500	1–60	N/A
NADONA Stephanie Carroll Memorial Scholarship	456	$5000	$1000	1–13	Nursing. Employment/Volunteer Experience: nursing.
Native American Leadership in Education (NALE)	163	$5000	$500	30	Business/Consumer Services; Education; Humanities; Physical Sciences; Science, Technology, and Society. Limited to American Indian/Alaska Native students.
New England Employee Benefits Council Scholarship Program	81	$5000	$1000	1–3	Accounting; Business/Consumer Services; Economics; Health Administration; Human Resources; Insurance and Actuarial Science; Law/Legal Services; Public Health; Public Policy and Administration. Residence: Connecticut; Maine; Massachusetts; New Hampshire; Rhode Island; Vermont. Studying in Connecticut; Maine; Massachusetts; New Hampshire; Rhode Island; Vermont.
New York State Tuition Assistance Program	781	$5000	$500	350,000–360,000	Residence: New York. Studying in New York.

Award Name	Page Number	Highest Dollar Amount	Lowest Dollar Amount	Number of Awards	Academic Fields/Career Goals and Nonacademic/Noncareer Criteria
NGWA Foundation's Len Assante Scholarship	244	$5000	$1000	1–15	Earth Science; Environmental Science; Hydrology.
Norm Manly—YMTA Maritime Educational Scholarships	402	$5000	$1000	6–7	Marine Biology; Marine/Ocean Engineering; Oceanography; Trade/Technical Specialties. Residence: Washington. Must be in high school.
North Carolina Association of CPAs Foundation Scholarships	81	$5000	$1000	50–60	Accounting. Residence: North Carolina. Studying in North Carolina.
North Carolina Education and Training Voucher Program	871	$5000	N/A	N/A	N/A
North Central Region 9 Scholarship	309	$5000	$1000	1–10	Engineering/Technology; Industrial Design; Mechanical Engineering; Trade/Technical Specialties. Studying in Iowa; Michigan; Minnesota; Nebraska; North Dakota; South Dakota; Wisconsin.
NSCS Scholar Abroad Scholarship	551	$5000	$2500	3	Civic Affiliation: National Society of Collegiate Scholars.
Outdoor Writers Association of America - Bodie McDowell Scholarship Award	207	$5000	$1000	2–6	Communications; Environmental Science; Filmmaking/Video; Journalism; Literature/English/Writing; Natural Resources; Photojournalism/Photography; TV/Radio Broadcasting. Talent/Interest Area: amateur radio; art; athletics/sports; photography/photogrammetry/filmmaking; writing.
Pellegrini Scholarship Grants	701	$5000	$500	50	Residence: Connecticut; Delaware; New Jersey; New York; Pennsylvania.
PepsiCo Hallmark Scholarships	707	$5000	$2000	1	Must be in high school. Limited to Asian/Pacific Islander students.
Peter and Alice Koomruian Armenian Education Fund	695	$5000	$1000	4–10	Nationality: Armenian.
PHCC Educational Foundation Scholarship Program	167	$5000	$2500	1–4	Business/Consumer Services; Engineering-Related Technologies; Engineering/Technology; Heating, Air-Conditioning, and Refrigeration Mechanics; Mechanical Engineering; Trade/Technical Specialties.
Plan New Hampshire Scholarship and Program	123	$5000	$1200	1–5	Architecture; Civil Engineering; Energy and Power Engineering; Engineering/Technology; Environmental Science; Historic Preservation and Conservation; Interior Design; Landscape Architecture; Mechanical Engineering; Natural Resources; Transportation; Urban and Regional Planning. Residence: New Hampshire.
Print and Graphics Scholarships Foundation	207	$5000	$1500	150–200	Communications; Graphics/Graphic Arts/Printing.
Promise of Nursing Scholarship	451	$5000	$1000	N/A	Nursing. Studying in California; Florida; Georgia; Illinois; Massachusetts; Michigan; New Jersey; Tennessee; Texas.
Regional and Restricted Scholarship Award Program	748	$5000	$2000	200–300	Residence: Connecticut.
Risk Management Association Foundation Scholarship Program	83	$5000	$2000	40	Accounting; Agriculture; Economics; Finance.
Samuel Robinson Award	721	$5000	$250	16	Religion: Presbyterian.

Award Name	Page Number	Highest Dollar Amount	Lowest Dollar Amount	Number of Awards	Academic Fields/Career Goals and Nonacademic/Noncareer Criteria
Scholarship Program for Sons & Daughters of Employees of Roseburg Forest Products Co.	568	$5000	$3000	30–47	Corporate Affiliation: Roseburg Forest Products.
Screen Actors Guild Foundation/ John L. Dales Scholarship Fund (Standard)	880	$5000	$1000	100–135	N/A
SEMA Memorial Scholarship Fund	85	$5000	$2000	50–60	Accounting; Advertising/Public Relations; Business/Consumer Services; Communications; Computer Science/Data Processing; Electrical Engineering/ Electronics; Engineering/Technology; Finance; Marketing; Mechanical Engineering; Trade/Technical Specialties; Transportation. Talent/Interest Area: automotive.
Sergeant Major Douglas R. Drum Memorial Scholarship	842	$5000	$1000	1–24	N/A
Sigma Delta Chi Scholarships	387	$5000	$3000	4–7	Journalism. Studying in District of Columbia; Maryland; Virginia.
Sigma Xi Grants-In-Aid of Research	101	$5000	$1000	400	Agriculture; Animal/Veterinary Sciences; Anthropology; Biology; Chemical Engineering; Civil Engineering; Computer Science/Data Processing; Earth Science; Electrical Engineering/Electronics; Energy and Power Engineering; Engineering/ Technology; Environmental Science; Geography; Health and Medical Sciences; Hydrology; Marine Biology; Marine/Ocean Engineering; Materials Science, Engineering, and Metallurgy; Mathematics; Mechanical Engineering; Meteorology/ Atmospheric Science; Natural Sciences; Nuclear Science; Physical Sciences; Psychology; Science, Technology, and Society; Social Sciences.
Society of Physics Students Leadership Scholarships	487	$5000	$2000	17–22	Physical Sciences. Civic Affiliation: Society of Physics Students.
TAC Foundation Scholarships	519	$5000	$2500	30–45	Transportation; Urban and Regional Planning. Nationality: Canadian. Residence: Alberta; British Columbia; Manitoba; New Brunswick; Newfoundland; Northwest Territories; Nova Scotia; Ontario; Prince Edward Island; Quebec; Saskatchewan; Yukon.
Taylor Michaels Scholarship Fund	601	$5000	$1000	N/A	Employment/Volunteer Experience: community service. Must be in high school. Limited to ethnic minority students.
Theta Delta Chi Educational Foundation Inc. Scholarship	886	$5000	$1000	15	N/A
TLMI 4 Year College Degree Scholarship Program	288	$5000	$2500	1–6	Engineering-Related Technologies; Flexography; Graphics/Graphic Arts/ Printing.

Award Name	Page Number	Highest Dollar Amount	Lowest Dollar Amount	Number of Awards	Academic Fields/Career Goals and Nonacademic/Noncareer Criteria
Tribal Business Management Program (TBM)	74	$5000	$500	35	Accounting; Business/Consumer Services; Computer Science/Data Processing; Economics; Electrical Engineering/ Electronics; Engineering-Related Technologies. Limited to American Indian/ Alaska Native students.
Truckload Carriers Association Scholarship Fund	168	$5000	$1500	18	Business/Consumer Services; Transportation. Employment/Volunteer Experience: transportation industry.
Two Ten Footwear Foundation Scholarship	622	$5000	$2500	300–350	Employment/Volunteer Experience: leather/ footwear industry. Residence: Alabama; Alaska; Arizona; Arkansas; California; Colorado; Connecticut; Delaware; Florida; Georgia; Hawaii; Idaho; Illinois; Indiana; Iowa; Kansas; Kentucky; Louisiana; Maine; Maryland; Massachusetts; Michigan; Minnesota; Mississippi; Missouri; Montana; Nebraska; Nevada; New Hampshire; New Jersey; New Mexico; New York; North Carolina; North Dakota; Ohio; Oklahoma; Ontario; Oregon; Pennsylvania; Puerto Rico; Rhode Island; South Carolina; South Dakota; Tennessee; Texas; Utah; Vermont; Virginia; Washington; West Virginia; Wisconsin; Wyoming. Studying in Alabama; Alaska; Arizona; Arkansas; California; Colorado; Connecticut; Delaware; Florida; Georgia; Hawaii; Idaho; Illinois; Indiana; Iowa; Kansas; Kentucky; Louisiana; Maine; Maryland; Massachusetts; Michigan; Minnesota; Mississippi; Missouri; Montana; Nebraska; Nevada; New Hampshire; New Jersey; New Mexico; New York; North Carolina; North Dakota; Ohio; Oklahoma; Oregon; Pennsylvania; Puerto Rico; Rhode Island; South Carolina; South Dakota; Tennessee; Texas; Utah; Vermont; Virginia; Washington; West Virginia; Wisconsin; Wyoming.
Udall Undergraduate Scholarship	868	$5000	N/A	50	N/A
UPS Hallmark Scholarships	707	$5000	$2000	N/A	Must be in high school. Limited to Asian/ Pacific Islander students.
Vermont Space Grant Consortium	96	$5000	$2500	6–9	Agribusiness; Applied Sciences; Aviation/ Aerospace; Biology; Civil Engineering; Computer Science/Data Processing; Earth Science; Electrical Engineering/ Electronics; Energy and Power Engineering; Engineering-Related Technologies; Engineering/Technology; Materials Science, Engineering, and Metallurgy; Mathematics; Mechanical Engineering; Physical Sciences; Science, Technology, and Society; Trade/Technical Specialties. Residence: Vermont. Studying in Vermont.

Award Name	Page Number	Highest Dollar Amount	Lowest Dollar Amount	Number of Awards	Academic Fields/Career Goals and Nonacademic/Noncareer Criteria
Vertical Flight Foundation Scholarship	134	$5000	$1500	10–19	Aviation/Aerospace; Electrical Engineering/Electronics; Engineering-Related Technologies; Engineering/Technology; Mechanical Engineering. Talent/Interest Area: aviation.
VSCPA Educational Foundation Accounting Scholarships	87	$5000	$1000	26	Accounting. Residence: Virginia. Studying in Virginia.
Warner Norcross and Judd LLP Scholarship for Students of Color	394	$5000	$1000	3	Law/Legal Services. Residence: Michigan. Studying in Michigan. Limited to ethnic minority students.
Washington Crossing Foundation Scholarship	489	$5000	$500	N/A	Political Science; Public Policy and Administration. Must be in high school.
Watson-Brown Foundation Scholarship	804	$5000	$3000	200	Residence: Georgia; South Carolina.
William E. Weisel Scholarship Fund	269	$5000	$1000	1–10	Electrical Engineering/Electronics; Engineering/Technology; Mechanical Engineering; Trade/Technical Specialties.
Wine Group Scholarships	881	$5000	$1000	1–10	N/A
WinWin Products, Inc. Scholarship	708	$5000	$2000		Must be in high school. Limited to Asian/Pacific Islander students.
Women in Defense HORIZONS-Michigan Scholarship	806	$5000	$1500	1–4	Residence: Michigan. Studying in Michigan.
Worldstudio AIGA Scholarships	133	$5000	$1000	10–25	Arts; Graphics/Graphic Arts/Printing.
Young Artist Competition	478	$5000	$500	8	Performing Arts. Residence: Illinois; Indiana; Iowa; Kansas; Manitoba; Michigan; Minnesota; Missouri; Nebraska; North Dakota; Ontario; South Dakota; Wisconsin. Talent/Interest Area: music.
Young Patriots Essay Contest	869	$5000	$2000	3	Must be in high school.
Youth Activity Fund	439	$5000	$500	10–30	Natural Sciences; Science, Technology, and Society.
Osage Nation Higher Education Scholarship	610	$4950	$150	1–1,200	Limited to American Indian/Alaska Native students.
ASCSA Summer Sessions Scholarships	108	$4900	$500	10–11	Anthropology; Archaeology; Architecture; Art History; Arts; Classics; Historic Preservation and Conservation; History; Humanities; Museum Studies; Philosophy; Religion/Theology.
Tuition Equalization Grant (TEG) Program	886	$4875	N/A	N/A	Studying in Texas.
Alaska Performance Scholarship	725	$4755	$500	N/A	Residence: Alaska. Studying in Alaska.
AIA West Virginia Scholarship	124	$4500	$3500	N/A	Architecture. Residence: West Virginia.
Arkansas Academic Challenge Scholarship Program	737	$4500	$1250	30,000–35,000	Residence: Arkansas. Studying in Arkansas.
Brook Hollow Golf Club Scholarship	851	$4500	$2000	N/A	Must be in high school.
Ernest Alan and Barbara Park Meyer Scholarship Fund	785	$4500	$1000	5	Residence: Oregon.
Glenn Miller Instrumental Scholarship	820	$4500	$1000	3	Talent/Interest Area: music/singing. Must be in high school.

Award Name	Page Number	Highest Dollar Amount	Lowest Dollar Amount	Number of Awards	Academic Fields/Career Goals and Nonacademic/Noncareer Criteria
Greater Washington Society of CPAs Scholarship	78	$4500	$2000	3–5	Accounting. Residence: District of Columbia. Studying in District of Columbia.
Hawaii Association of Broadcasters Scholarship	523	$4500	$500	20–30	TV/Radio Broadcasting.
Charley Wootan Grant Program	886	$4394	$1000	N/A	N/A
Pennsylvania State Grant Program	612	$4340	$200	N/A	Residence: Pennsylvania.
Nebraska Opportunity Grant	608	$4270	$100	N/A	Residence: Nebraska. Studying in Nebraska.
American Legion Department of Indiana High School Oratorical Contest	731	$4200	$200	4–8	Residence: Indiana. Talent/Interest Area: public speaking. Must be in high school.
Actuarial Diversity Scholarship	375	$4000	$1000	N/A	Insurance and Actuarial Science; Mathematics. Limited to ethnic minority students.
AFIO Undergraduate and Graduate Scholarships	103	$4000	$1000	10	American Studies; Aviation/Aerospace; Computer Science/Data Processing; Criminal Justice/Criminology; Foreign Language; History; International Studies; Law Enforcement/Police Administration; Military and Defense Studies; Natural Sciences; Near and Middle East Studies; Peace and Conflict Studies; Political Science; Public Policy and Administration.
Alexander and Maude Hadden Scholarship	627	$4000	$2500	96–108	Employment/Volunteer Experience: community service. Residence: Yukon.
American Legion Auxiliary Department of California Past Presidents' Parley Nursing Scholarships	445	$4000	$4000	1–2	Nursing. Military Service: General. Residence: California.
American Society for Enology and Viticulture Scholarships	97	$4000	$500	30	Agriculture; Chemical Engineering; Food Science/Nutrition; Horticulture/Floriculture.
American Society of Civil Engineers-Maine High School Scholarship	193	$4000	$1000	1–4	Civil Engineering. Residence: Maine. Must be in high school.
American Society of Naval Engineers Scholarship	110	$4000	$3000	8–14	Applied Sciences; Aviation/Aerospace; Civil Engineering; Electrical Engineering/Electronics; Energy and Power Engineering; Engineering/Technology; Marine/Ocean Engineering; Materials Science, Engineering, and Metallurgy; Mechanical Engineering; Nuclear Science; Physical Sciences.
Bridging Scholarship for Study Abroad in Japan	574	$4000	$2500	70–100	N/A
C.A.R. Scholarship Foundation Award	495	$4000	$2000	10–25	Real Estate. Residence: California. Studying in California.
College Now Greater Cleveland Adult Learner Program Scholarship	746	$4000	$500	250–450	Residence: Ohio.
Community Bankers Assoc. of IL Essay Contest	582	$4000	$500	13–26	Residence: Illinois. Must be in high school.
Elks Emergency Educational Grants	542	$4000	$1000	N/A	Civic Affiliation: Elks Club.

Award Name	Page Number	Highest Dollar Amount	Lowest Dollar Amount	Number of Awards	Academic Fields/Career Goals and Nonacademic/Noncareer Criteria
Fifth/Graduate Year Student Scholarship	80	$4000	$2000	16–25	Accounting. Studying in Michigan.
Fresh Start Scholarship	757	$4000	$1000	25–30	Residence: Delaware. Studying in Delaware.
General Henry H. Arnold Education Grant Program	639	$4000	$500	3,000	Military Service: Air Force; Air Force National Guard.
GMP Memorial Scholarship Program	543	$4000	$2000	10	Civic Affiliation: Glass, Molders, Pottery, Plastics and Allied Workers International Union. Must be in high school.
Governors' Scholarship for Foster Youth Program	746	$4000	$2000	30–50	Residence: Washington. Studying in Washington. Must be in high school.
Harvard Travellers Club Permanent Fund	859	$4000	$1000	1–4	N/A
Illinois CPA Society Accounting Scholarship Program	78	$4000	$500	12–35	Accounting. Residence: Illinois. Studying in Illinois.
John F. and Anna Lee Stacey Scholarship Fund	824	$4000	$1000	3–5	Talent/Interest Area: art.
Minority Student Summer Scholarship	118	$4000	$1500	2	Archaeology; Arts; Classics; Foreign Language; History. Limited to ethnic minority students.
Mississippi Press Association Education Foundation Scholarship	382	$4000	$1000	1	Journalism. Residence: Mississippi.
New Mexico Vietnam Veteran Scholarship	780	$4000	$3500	100	Residence: New Mexico. Studying in New Mexico.
New Mexico Wartime Veterans Scholarship	660	$4000	$3500	100	Military Service: General. Residence: New Mexico. Studying in New Mexico.
NGPA Education Fund, Inc.	145	$4000	$3000	3–4	Aviation/Aerospace. Employment/Volunteer Experience: community service. Talent/Interest Area: aviation; LGBT issues.
Part-Time Grant Program	797	$4000	$20	4,680–6,700	Residence: Indiana. Studying in Indiana.
Sikh Education Aid Fund	845	$4000	$400	N/A	N/A
South Florida Fair College Scholarship	797	$4000	$1000	10	Residence: Florida.
SSPI International Scholarships	147	$4000	$2500	1–4	Aviation/Aerospace; Communications; Law/Legal Services; Meteorology/Atmospheric Science; Military and Defense Studies.
Student-View Scholarship program	885	$4000	$500	13	Must be in high school.
Tennessee Step Up Scholarship	621	$4000	$2000	N/A	Residence: Tennessee. Studying in Tennessee.
Tennessee Student Assistance Award	621	$4000	$100	N/A	Residence: Tennessee. Studying in Tennessee.
Texas Gridiron Club Scholarships	212	$4000	$500	10–15	Communications; Journalism; Photojournalism/Photography; TV/Radio Broadcasting.
Union Plus Credit Card Scholarship Program	528	$4000	$500	N/A	Civic Affiliation: American Federation of State, County, and Municipal Employees.
Union Plus Education Foundation Scholarship Program	564	$4000	$500	100–120	Civic Affiliation: AFL-CIO.

Award Name	Page Number	Highest Dollar Amount	Lowest Dollar Amount	Number of Awards	Academic Fields/Career Goals and Nonacademic/Noncareer Criteria
Union Plus Scholarship Program	549	$4000	$500	3	Civic Affiliation: National Association of Letter Carriers. Must be in high school.
University Film and Video Association Carole Fielding Student Grants	327	$4000	$1000	5	Filmmaking/Video.
Veterans Education (VetEd) Reimbursement Grant	639	$4000	$1340	N/A	Disability: hearing impaired; learning disabled; physically disabled; visually impaired. Military Service: Air Force; Air Force National Guard; Army; Army National Guard; Coast Guard; General; Marine Corps; Navy. Residence: Wisconsin. Studying in Minnesota; Wisconsin.
Wenderoth Undergraduate Scholarship	555	$4000	$1750	1–4	Civic Affiliation: Phi Sigma Kappa.
William L. Cullison Scholarship	436	$4000	$2000	1–2	Natural Resources; Paper and Pulp Engineering.
WRI Foundation College Scholarship Program	200	$4000	$2000	2–5	Civil Engineering; Construction Engineering/Management.
Taylor Opportunity Program for Students Tech Level	770	$3985	$436	1,671	Residence: Louisiana. Studying in Louisiana.
Early Childhood Educators Scholarship Program	254	$3600	$150	N/A	Education.
American Council of the Blind Scholarships	574	$3500	$1000	16–20	Disability: visually impaired.
American Legion Auxiliary National President's Scholarship	651	$3500	$2500	15	Military Service: General. Must be in high school.
American Legion Department of Arkansas High School Oratorical Contest	730	$3500	$1250	4	Residence: Arkansas. Talent/Interest Area: public speaking. Must be in high school.
Annual Award Program	714	$3500	$800	3–5	Religion: Muslim faith.
Freedom Alliance Scholarship Fund	588	$3500	$500	250–325	N/A
National Defense Transportation Association, Scott Air Force Base-St. Louis Area Chapter Scholarship	777	$3500	$2000	6	Residence: Illinois; Missouri. Studying in Colorado; Illinois; Indiana; Iowa; Kansas; Michigan; Minnesota; Missouri; Montana; Nebraska; North Dakota; South Dakota; Wisconsin; Wyoming.
OAB Foundation Scholarship	207	$3500	$2500	4	Communications; Journalism; TV/Radio Broadcasting. Residence: Oregon.
Order Of The Golden Rule Foundation Awards of Excellence Scholarship Program	340	$3500	$2000	2	Funeral Services/Mortuary Science.
Robert Guthrie PKU Scholarship and Awards	635	$3500	$500	4–8	Disability: physically disabled.
Unmet NEED Grant Program	692	$3500	$1000	10–500	Residence: Pennsylvania. Limited to Black (non-Hispanic) students.
North Carolina National Guard Tuition Assistance Program	644	$3440	$100	N/A	Military Service: Air Force National Guard; Army National Guard. Residence: North Carolina. Studying in North Carolina.
Dolphin Scholarships	585	$3400	$2000	25–30	N/A
Peter Kong-Ming New Student Prize	883	$3350	$500	3	N/A

Award Name	Page Number	Highest Dollar Amount	Lowest Dollar Amount	Number of Awards	Academic Fields/Career Goals and Nonacademic/Noncareer Criteria
South Carolina Tuition Grants Program	617	$3200	$100	N/A	Residence: South Carolina. Studying in South Carolina.
Cal Grant C	743	$3168	$576	7,761	Residence: California. Studying in California.
Virginia Tuition Assistance Grant Program (Private Institutions)	803	$3100	$775	N/A	Residence: Virginia. Studying in Virginia.
2016 High School Senior Scholarship Essay Contest	853	$3000	$500	3	Must be in high school.
Adelante Fund Scholarships	160	$3000	$1000	30–52	Business/Consumer Services; Science, Technology, and Society. Studying in Arizona; California; Colorado; Florida; Illinois; New Mexico; New York; Texas. Talent/Interest Area: leadership. Limited to Hispanic students.
AH&LEF Annual Scholarship Grant Program	227	$3000	$500	N/A	Culinary Arts; Food Service/Hospitality; Hospitality Management; Recreation, Parks, Leisure Studies; Travel/Tourism.
AlaskAdvantage Education Grant	725	$3000	$500	N/A	Residence: Alaska. Studying in Alaska.
The Alexander Foundation Scholarship Program	727	$3000	$300	6–35	Residence: Colorado. Studying in Colorado. Talent/Interest Area: LGBT issues.
AMBUCS Scholars-Scholarships for Therapists	134	$3000	$500	275	Audiology; Therapy/Rehabilitation.
American Hotel & Lodging Educational Foundation Pepsi Scholarship	228	$3000	$500	N/A	Culinary Arts; Food Service/Hospitality; Hospitality Management; Recreation, Parks, Leisure Studies; Travel/Tourism. Residence: District of Columbia.
American Legion Department of Tennessee High School Oratorical Contest	735	$3000	$1000	1–3	Residence: Tennessee. Talent/Interest Area: public speaking. Must be in high school.
American Montessori Society Teacher Education Scholarship Fund	248	$3000	$1000	10–20	Education.
American Physical Society Corporate-Sponsored Scholarship for Minority Undergraduate Students Who Major in Physics	485	$3000	$2000	N/A	Physical Sciences. Limited to ethnic minority students.
American Water Ski Educational Foundation Scholarship	539	$3000	$1500	5	Civic Affiliation: USA Water Ski.
Arizona Nursery Association Foundation Scholarship	363	$3000	$500	12–16	Horticulture/Floriculture.
Astrid G. Cates and Myrtle Beinhauer Scholarship Funds	559	$3000	$1000	2–7	Civic Affiliation: Mutual Benefit Society.
A.T. Cross Scholarship	571	$3000	$1000	N/A	Corporate Affiliation: A.T. Cross. Residence: Rhode Island.
AWG Ethnic Minority Scholarship	241	$3000	$500	1–5	Earth Science; Education; Environmental Science; Gemology; Geography; Hydrology; Meteorology/Atmospheric Science; Museum Studies; Natural Resources; Natural Sciences; Oceanography; Physical Sciences. Limited to American Indian/Alaska Native; Black (non-Hispanic); Hispanic students.

Award Name	Page Number	Highest Dollar Amount	Lowest Dollar Amount	Number of Awards	Academic Fields/Career Goals and Nonacademic/Noncareer Criteria
Blackfeet Nation Higher Education Grant	672	$3000	$2800	180	Limited to American Indian/Alaska Native students.
Calcot-Seitz Scholarship	98	$3000	$500	1–30	Agriculture. Residence: Arizona; California; New Mexico; Texas.
Chief Master Sergeants of the Air Force Scholarship Program	640	$3000	$500	30	Military Service: Air Force; Air Force National Guard.
CollegeBound Foundation Last Dollar Grant	744	$3000	$500	40–70	Residence: Maryland. Must be in high school.
College Tuition Assistance Program	688	$3000	$2000	25–30	Residence: New Jersey; New York. Must be in high school. Limited to Hispanic students.
Developmental Disabilities Scholastic Achievement Scholarship for College Students who are Lutheran	236	$3000	$500	2–3	Dental Health/Services; Education; Health Administration; Health and Medical Sciences; Health Information Management/Technology; Humanities; Religion/Theology; Social Services; Special Education; Therapy/Rehabilitation. Religion: Lutheran.
DirectTextbook.com 2017 High School Senior Scholarship Essay Contest	853	$3000	$500	3	Must be in high school.
The Donaldson Company, Inc. Scholarship Program	568	$3000	$1000	N/A	Corporate Affiliation: Donaldson Company.
Edward J. and Virginia M. Routhier Nursing Scholarship	460	$3000	$500	N/A	Nursing. Studying in Rhode Island.
Freedom From Religion Foundation Michael Hakeem Memorial Ongoing College Essay Competition	714	$3000	$200	6–20	Talent/Interest Area: writing.
Freedom From Religion Foundation William J. Schulz Memorial College-bound High School Senior Essay Competition	714	$3000	$200	6–20	Talent/Interest Area: writing. Must be in high school.
GAPA Scholarships	820	$3000	$1000	3–5	Talent/Interest Area: leadership; LGBT issues.
George and Pearl Strickland Scholarship	747	$3000	$1000	1–25	Residence: Georgia. Studying in Georgia.
Hubertus W.V. Wellems Scholarship for Male Students	180	$3000	$2000	1	Chemical Engineering; Engineering-Related Technologies; Engineering/Technology; Physical Sciences. Civic Affiliation: National Association for the Advancement of Colored People. Limited to ethnic minority students.
Humana Foundation Scholarship Program	593	$3000	$1500	74–75	N/A
Idaho Opportunity Scholarship	763	$3000	N/A	700–2,000	Residence: Idaho. Studying in Idaho.
Illinois PTA Scholarship	253	$3000	$2000	2	Education. Residence: Illinois. Must be in high school.
John T. Riordan School for Professional Development	495	$3000	$2999	10–15	Real Estate.
Joseph S. Rumbaugh Historical Oration Contest	828	$3000	$1000	1–3	Talent/Interest Area: public speaking.

Award Name	Page Number	Highest Dollar Amount	Lowest Dollar Amount	Number of Awards	Academic Fields/Career Goals and Nonacademic/Noncareer Criteria
Kellogg Scholarship	185	$3000	$1000	3	Chemical Engineering; Mechanical Engineering. Civic Affiliation: Society of Women Engineers.
Kentucky Tuition Grant (KTG)	767	$3000	$200	10,000–12,500	Residence: Kentucky. Studying in Kentucky.
Kildee Scholarships	100	$3000	$1000	1–2	Agriculture; Animal/Veterinary Sciences.
Lone Star Rising Career Scholarship	242	$3000	N/A	1–2	Earth Science; Education; Environmental Science; Gemology; Hydrology; Meteorology/Atmospheric Science; Museum Studies; Natural Resources; Natural Sciences; Oceanography; Physical Sciences; Science, Technology, and Society. Employment/Volunteer Experience: physical or natural sciences.
Millie Brother Scholarship for Children of Deaf Adults	581	$3000	$1000	2–5	N/A
Minnesota GI Bill Program	774	$3000	$50	N/A	Residence: Minnesota. Studying in Minnesota.
Missouri Higher Education Academic Scholarship (Bright Flight)	776	$3000	$1000	N/A	Residence: Missouri. Studying in Missouri.
Moody Research Grants	104	$3000	$600	10–15	American Studies; History; International Studies; Military and Defense Studies; Museum Studies; Political Science.
MRCA Foundation Scholarship Program	122	$3000	$500	40	Architecture; Civil Engineering; Construction Engineering/Management; Drafting; Engineering/Technology; Industrial Design; Materials Science, Engineering, and Metallurgy; Trade/Technical Specialties. Employment/Volunteer Experience: construction.
National Asphalt Pavement Association Research and Education Foundation Scholarship Program	196	$3000	$500	50–150	Civil Engineering; Construction Engineering/Management.
National Federation of Paralegal Associates Inc. Thomson Reuters Scholarship	396	$3000	$2000	2	Law/Legal Services.
National High School Journalist of the Year/Sister Rita Jeanne Scholarships	863	$3000	$850	1–7	Must be in high school.
NMCRS Education Assistance Program	870	$3000	$500	1–300	N/A
Ohio American Legion Scholarships	535	$3000	$2000	15–18	Civic Affiliation: American Legion or Auxiliary. Military Service: General.
One Million Degrees Signature Fund Scholarship	785	$3000	$500	1–80	Residence: Illinois. Studying in Illinois.
OSCPA Educational Foundation Scholarship Program	82	$3000	$500	50–100	Accounting. Residence: Oregon. Studying in Oregon.
Overseas Press Club Foundation Scholar Awards	386	$3000	$2000	15	Journalism. Talent/Interest Area: writing.
Pennsylvania Masonic Youth Foundation Educational Endowment Fund Scholarships	554	$3000	$1000	25–75	Civic Affiliation: Freemasons.

Award Name	Page Number	Highest Dollar Amount	Lowest Dollar Amount	Number of Awards	Academic Fields/Career Goals and Nonacademic/Noncareer Criteria
Rama Scholarship for the American Dream	228	$3000	$1000	N/A	Culinary Arts; Food Service/Hospitality; Hospitality Management; Recreation, Parks, Leisure Studies; Travel/Tourism. Limited to ethnic minority students.
Roberta B. Willis Scholarship Program—Need-Based Grant	676	$3000	$650	N/A	Nationality: Ukrainian. Residence: Connecticut. Studying in Connecticut.
Rockefeller State Wildlife Scholarship	157	$3000	$2000	20–30	Biology; Marine Biology; Marine/Ocean Engineering; Natural Resources; Oceanography. Residence: Louisiana. Studying in Louisiana.
Roothbert Fund Inc. Scholarship	793	$3000	$2000	50–60	Residence: Connecticut; Delaware; District of Columbia; Maine; Maryland; Massachusetts; New Hampshire; New Jersey; New York; North Carolina; Ohio; Pennsylvania; Rhode Island; Virginia; West Virginia. Studying in Connecticut; Delaware; District of Columbia; Maryland; Massachusetts; New Hampshire; New Jersey; New York; Ohio; Pennsylvania; Rhode Island; Vermont; Virginia; West Virginia.
Scholarships for Education, Business and Religion	163	$3000	$500	N/A	Business/Consumer Services; Education; Religion/Theology. Residence: California.
Seol Bong Scholarship	637	$3000	$2000	21	Disability: learning disabled. Residence: Connecticut; Delaware; Maine; Massachusetts; New Hampshire; New Jersey; New York; Pennsylvania; Rhode Island; Vermont. Studying in Connecticut; Delaware; Maine; Massachusetts; New Hampshire; New Jersey; New York; Pennsylvania; Rhode Island; Vermont. Limited to Asian/Pacific Islander students.
Simplilearn Student Ambassador Scholarship	881	$3000	$1000	1–3	N/A
Society of Louisiana CPAs Scholarships	84	$3000	$500	N/A	Accounting. Residence: Louisiana. Studying in Louisiana.
Sonne Scholarship	453	$3000	$1000	2–4	Nursing. Residence: Illinois. Studying in Illinois.
Student Design Competition	108	$3000	$1000	6	Anthropology.
Tortoise Young Entrepreneurs Scholarship	801	$3000	$1000	3	Residence: Kansas; Missouri. Studying in Kansas; Missouri.
Traub-Dicker Rainbow Scholarship	618	$3000	$1000	3–4	Talent/Interest Area: LGBT issues.
Undergraduate Marketing Education Merit Scholarships	162	$3000	$500	7	Business/Consumer Services; Marketing. Studying in Maryland.
William P. Willis Scholarship	785	$3000	$2000	N/A	Residence: Oklahoma. Studying in Oklahoma.
Wisconsin Higher Education Grants (WHEG)	805	$3000	$250	N/A	Residence: Wisconsin. Studying in Wisconsin.
Women in Logistics Scholarship	170	$3000	$1000	1–3	Business/Consumer Services; Trade/Technical Specialties; Transportation. Civic Affiliation: Women in Logistics. Residence: California. Studying in California.
Women's Independence Scholarship Program	891	$3000	$500	350–500	N/A

Award Name	Page Number	Highest Dollar Amount	Lowest Dollar Amount	Number of Awards	Academic Fields/Career Goals and Nonacademic/Noncareer Criteria
Writer's Digest Annual Writing Competition	838	$3000	$100	501	Talent/Interest Area: writing.
Writer's Digest Self-Published Book Awards	838	$3000	$1000	45	Talent/Interest Area: writing.
Postsecondary Child Care Grant Program-Minnesota	775	$2800	$100	1–3,500	Residence: Minnesota. Studying in Minnesota.
Howard P. Rawlings Educational Excellence Awards Educational Assistance Grant	771	$2700	$400	15,000–30,000	Residence: Maryland. Studying in Maryland.
West Virginia Higher Education Grant Program	804	$2700	$300	18,000–21,000	Residence: West Virginia. Studying in Pennsylvania; West Virginia.
Florida Postsecondary Student Assistance Grant	755	$2610	$200	N/A	Residence: Florida. Studying in Florida.
Florida Private Student Assistance Grant	755	$2610	$200	N/A	Residence: Florida. Studying in Florida.
Florida Public Student Assistance Grant	755	$2610	$200	N/A	Residence: Florida. Studying in Florida.
Florida Student Assistance Grant-Career Education	755	$2610	$200	N/A	Residence: Florida. Studying in Florida.
NJ Student Tuition Assistance Reward Scholarship	779	$2600	$500	N/A	Residence: New Jersey. Studying in New Jersey.
Ohio College Opportunity Grant	609	$2592	$888	N/A	Residence: Ohio. Studying in Ohio; Pennsylvania.
ACES Education Fund Scholarship	841	$2500	$1500	5	N/A
Adult Students in Scholastic Transition	854	$2500	$250	100–150	N/A
Agnes Jones Jackson Scholarship	549	$2500	$1500	1	Civic Affiliation: National Association for the Advancement of Colored People. Limited to ethnic minority students.
AHIMA Foundation Student Merit Scholarship	357	$2500	$1000	1	Health Information Management/Technology. Civic Affiliation: American Health Information Management Association.
Alaska Geological Society Scholarship	240	$2500	$500	3–8	Earth Science. Studying in Alaska.
American Board of Funeral Service Education Scholarships	340	$2500	$500	5–15	Funeral Services/Mortuary Science.
American Legion Auxiliary Department of North Dakota National President's Scholarship	575	$2500	$1000	3	Employment/Volunteer Experience: community service. Military Service: General. Residence: North Dakota. Studying in North Dakota. Must be in high school.
American Legion Auxiliary Department of Oregon National President's Scholarship	729	$2500	$1000	3	Residence: Oregon. Must be in high school.
American Legion Auxiliary Department of Utah National President's Scholarship	530	$2500	$1000	15	Civic Affiliation: American Legion or Auxiliary. Military Service: General. Residence: Utah. Must be in high school.
American Legion Baseball Scholarship	809	$2500	$500	1–51	Talent/Interest Area: athletics/sports. Must be in high school.

Award Name	Page Number	Highest Dollar Amount	Lowest Dollar Amount	Number of Awards	Academic Fields/Career Goals and Nonacademic/Noncareer Criteria
American Legion Department of North Carolina High School Oratorical Contest	734	$2500	$1000	5	Residence: North Carolina. Talent/Interest Area: public speaking. Must be in high school.
American Legion Department of Washington Children and Youth Scholarships	536	$2500	$1500	2	Civic Affiliation: American Legion or Auxiliary. Residence: Washington. Must be in high school.
American-Scandinavian Foundation Translation Prize	399	$2500	$2000	2	Literature/English/Writing. Talent/Interest Area: Scandinavian language.
American Welding Society District Scholarship Program	277	$2500	$100	150–200	Engineering-Related Technologies; Trade/Technical Specialties.
ASCPA Educational Foundation Scholarship	73	$2500	$1500	34–38	Accounting. Residence: Alabama. Studying in Alabama.
Assured Life Association Endowment Scholarship Program	540	$2500	$500	65–75	Civic Affiliation: Woodmen of the World.
BIA Higher Education Grant	682	$2500	$50	1–150	Limited to American Indian/Alaska Native students.
Breakthrough to Nursing Scholarships for Racial/Ethnic Minorities	451	$2500	$1000	N/A	Nursing. Limited to ethnic minority students.
California Council of the Blind Scholarships	628	$2500	$375	20	Disability: visually impaired. Residence: California. Studying in California.
Career Journalism Scholarship	210	$2500	$1000	1–10	Communications; Journalism; Photojournalism/Photography; TV/Radio Broadcasting. Residence: Florida.
Clem Judd, Jr. Memorial Scholarship	368	$2500	$1000	2	Hospitality Management. Residence: Hawaii. Limited to Asian/Pacific Islander students.
Crohn's & Colitis Foundation of America Student Research Fellowship Awards	351	$2500	$2500	N/A	Health and Medical Sciences.
CrossLites Scholarship Award	817	$2500	$100	33	Talent/Interest Area: writing.
Distinguished Raven FAC Memorial Scholarship	678	$2500	$1000	10	Limited to Asian/Pacific Islander students.
E. Wayne Kay High School Scholarship	309	$2500	$1000	1–20	Engineering/Technology.
Feeding Tomorrow Undergraduate General Education Scholarships	332	$2500	$1000	N/A	Food Science/Nutrition.
Foundation for Accounting Education Scholarship	82	$2500	$500	1–60	Accounting. Residence: New York. Studying in New York.
Foundation of the National Student Nurses' Association Career Mobility Scholarship	451	$2500	$1000	N/A	Nursing.
Foundation of the National Student Nurses' Association General Scholarships	451	$2500	$1000	N/A	Nursing.
Foundation of the National Student Nurses' Association Specialty Scholarship	451	$2500	$1000	N/A	Nursing.

Award Name	Page Number	Highest Dollar Amount	Lowest Dollar Amount	Number of Awards	Academic Fields/Career Goals and Nonacademic/Noncareer Criteria
The Foundation of the Nebraska Society of Certified Public Accountants Fifth-Year Scholarship Awards	81	$2500	$1500	1–25	Accounting. Studying in Nebraska.
Friends of Bill Rutherford Education Fund	785	$2500	$1000	1–2	Residence: Oregon.
Fulfilling Our Dreams Scholarship Fund	698	$2500	$500	50–60	Residence: California. Studying in California. Limited to Hispanic students.
Graphic Communications Scholarship Fund of New England	343	$2500	$1350	16–35	Graphics/Graphic Arts/Printing. Residence: Connecticut; Maine; Massachusetts; New Hampshire; Rhode Island; Vermont.
HBCUConnect.com Minority Scholarship Program	680	$2500	$1000	1	Limited to ethnic minority students.
High School Scholarship	298	$2500	$1500	6	Engineering/Technology. Employment/Volunteer Experience: engineering/technology. Residence: Florida. Must be in high school.
Hopi Education Award	682	$2500	$50	1–400	Limited to American Indian/Alaska Native students.
Hungry To Lead Scholarship	232	$2500	$500	4	Culinary Arts; Food Science/Nutrition; Food Service/Hospitality.
Institute of Management Accountants Memorial Education Fund Scholarships	79	$2500	$1000	6–15	Accounting; Business/Consumer Services.
International Association of Fire Chiefs Foundation Scholarship Award	329	$2500	$500	20–30	Fire Sciences.
Jack and Jill of America Foundation Scholarship	704	$2500	$1500	N/A	Must be in high school. Limited to Black (non-Hispanic) students.
Jackson-Stricks Scholarship	633	$2500	$1500	1–2	Disability: physically disabled. Studying in New York.
Joseph S. Garske Collegiate Grant Program	544	$2500	$500	1–5	Civic Affiliation: Golf Course Superintendents Association of America. Must be in high school.
Kentucky Educational Excellence Scholarship (KEES)	767	$2500	$125	65,000–75,000	Residence: Kentucky. Studying in Kentucky.
Kentucky Society of Certified Public Accountants College Scholarship	79	$2500	$1000	23	Accounting. Residence: Kentucky. Studying in Kentucky.
Korean-American Scholarship Foundation Northeastern Region Scholarships	686	$2500	$1000	60	Studying in Connecticut; Maine; Massachusetts; New Hampshire; New Jersey; New York; Rhode Island; Vermont. Limited to Asian/Pacific Islander students.
LEAGUE Foundation Academic Scholarship	825	$2500	$1500	4–8	Talent/Interest Area: LGBT issues. Must be in high school.
Legislative Endowment Scholarships	780	$2500	$1000	1	Residence: New Mexico. Studying in New Mexico.
Lessans Family Scholarship	674	$2500	$1000	12–20	Residence: Maryland. Religion: Jewish.
Leveraging Educational Assistance Partnership	737	$2500	$100	N/A	Residence: Arizona. Studying in Arizona.
Literacy Grant Competition	544	$2500	$300	18	Civic Affiliation: Phi Kappa Phi.

Award Name	Page Number	Highest Dollar Amount	Lowest Dollar Amount	Number of Awards	Academic Fields/Career Goals and Nonacademic/Noncareer Criteria
Maine State Society Foundation Scholarship	601	$2500	$1000	5–10	Residence: Maine. Studying in Maine.
Making the Turn Against Parkinson's Scholarship	770	$2500	$1000	1–4	Residence: Michigan.
Massachusetts Gilbert Matching Student Grant Program	773	$2500	$200	N/A	Residence: Massachusetts. Studying in Massachusetts.
Minnesota Space Grant Consortium Scholarship Program	142	$2500	$500	20–40	Aviation/Aerospace; Computer Science/Data Processing; Earth Science; Electrical Engineering/Electronics; Engineering/Technology; Environmental Science; Mathematics; Mechanical Engineering; Meteorology/Atmospheric Science; Natural Sciences; Nuclear Science; Oceanography; Physical Sciences. Studying in Minnesota.
Minority Undergraduate Retention Grant-Wisconsin	708	$2500	$250	N/A	Residence: Wisconsin. Studying in Wisconsin. Limited to ethnic minority students.
Mississippi Eminent Scholars Grant	775	$2500	$1157	N/A	Residence: Mississippi. Studying in Mississippi.
Missouri Broadcasters Association Scholarship	524	$2500	$1000	3–5	TV/Radio Broadcasting. Residence: Missouri. Studying in Missouri.
Missouri Insurance Education Foundation Scholarship	375	$2500	$2000	6	Insurance and Actuarial Science. Residence: Missouri. Studying in Missouri.
NASA Idaho Space Grant Consortium Scholarship Program	157	$2500	$1000	1–15	Biology; Chemical Engineering; Civil Engineering; Computer Science/Data Processing; Earth Science; Electrical Engineering/Electronics; Geography; Materials Science, Engineering, and Metallurgy; Mathematics; Mechanical Engineering; Natural Sciences; Physical Sciences. Studying in Idaho.
National Federation of the Blind of Missouri Scholarship Program for Legally Blind Students	635	$2500	$500	1–3	Disability: visually impaired. Residence: Missouri. Studying in Missouri.
National Poultry and Food Distributors Association Scholarship Foundation	94	$2500	$2500	5	Agribusiness; Agriculture; Animal/Veterinary Sciences; Food Science/Nutrition; Food Service/Hospitality.
New Hampshire Society of Certified Public Accountants Scholarship Fund	81	$2500	$500	1–7	Accounting. Residence: New Hampshire.
New Jersey Association of Realtors Educational Foundation Scholarship Program	496	$2500	$1000	20–32	Real Estate. Civic Affiliation: New Jersey Association of Realtors. Residence: New Jersey. Must be in high school.
New Mexico Student Incentive Grant	780	$2500	$200	1	Residence: New Mexico. Studying in New Mexico.
New York Ramblers Scholarship for Student Athletes	618	$2500	$1000	1–2	Talent/Interest Area: athletics/sports; LGBT issues.
Noplag Scholarship Essay Contest	609	$2500	$300	3	N/A
Norma Ross Walter Scholarship	400	$2500	$1250	1–3	Literature/English/Writing. Residence: Nebraska. Must be in high school.
North Carolina Hispanic College Fund Scholarship	693	$2500	$500	N/A	Residence: North Carolina. Limited to Hispanic students.
Ohio Environmental Science & Engineering Scholarships	323	$2500	$1250	18	Environmental Science. Studying in Ohio.

Award Name	Page Number	Highest Dollar Amount	Lowest Dollar Amount	Number of Awards	Academic Fields/Career Goals and Nonacademic/Noncareer Criteria
Optimist International Oratorical Contest	830	$2500	$1000	90–115	Talent/Interest Area: public speaking.
Overseas Spouse Education Assistance Program	844	$2500	$500	N/A	N/A
Polish Heritage Scholarship	696	$2500	$1500	1–9	Residence: Maryland.
Raymond W. Miller, PE Scholarship	298	$2500	$1500	1	Engineering/Technology. Residence: Florida. Studying in Florida.
Richard B. Gassett, PE Scholarship	298	$2500	$1500	1	Engineering/Technology. Residence: Florida. Studying in Florida.
Robert P. Sheppard Leadership Award for NSHSS Members	552	$2500	$1000	5	Civic Affiliation: National Society of High School Scholars. Talent/Interest Area: leadership. Must be in high school.
Robert T. Kenney Scholarship Program at the American Savings Foundation	576	$2500	$1000	400	Residence: Connecticut.
Samuel Fletcher Tapman ASCE Student Chapter Scholarship	192	$2500	$2000	1–12	Civil Engineering. Civic Affiliation: American Society of Civil Engineers.
SCACPA Educational Fund Scholarships	84	$2500	$500	19–25	Accounting. Residence: South Carolina. Studying in South Carolina.
Scholarships for Orphans of Veterans	660	$2500	$1500	1–10	Military Service: General. Residence: New Hampshire. Studying in New Hampshire.
Simon Youth Foundation Community Scholarship Program	881	$2500	$1400	100–200	Must be in high school.
Society of Physics Students Outstanding Student in Research	487	$2500	$500	1–2	Physical Sciences. Civic Affiliation: Society of Physics Students.
South Carolina Need-Based Grants Program	796	$2500	$1250	1–26,730	Residence: South Carolina. Studying in South Carolina.
South Carolina Tourism and Hospitality Educational Foundation Scholarships	232	$2500	$750	5–16	Culinary Arts; Food Service/Hospitality; Hospitality Management. Residence: South Carolina. Studying in South Carolina.
Stella Blum Student Research Grant	125	$2500	$2000	1	Area/Ethnic Studies; Art History; Arts; Historic Preservation and Conservation; History; Home Economics; Museum Studies; Performing Arts. Civic Affiliation: Costume Society of America.
Steve Dearduff Scholarship	351	$2500	$1000	1–3	Health and Medical Sciences; Social Services. Residence: Georgia.
Sussman-Miller Educational Assistance Fund	727	$2500	$500	25–30	Residence: New Mexico.
Swiss Benevolent Society of Chicago Scholarships	701	$2500	$500	30	Residence: Illinois; Wisconsin.
Tennessee Society of CPA Scholarship	85	$2500	$250	120–130	Accounting. Residence: Tennessee.
Tilford Field Studies Scholarship	240	$2500	$500	4–5	Earth Science. Civic Affiliation: Association of Engineering Geologists.
Truman D. Picard Scholarship	93	$2500	$2000	15–30	Agribusiness; Agriculture; Environmental Science; Natural Resources. Limited to American Indian/Alaska Native students.
U.S. Scholarship Program	603	$2500	$600	100–150	N/A

Award Name	Page Number	Highest Dollar Amount	Lowest Dollar Amount	Number of Awards	Academic Fields/Career Goals and Nonacademic/Noncareer Criteria
WIFLE Scholarship	227	$2500	$1000	1–6	Criminal Justice/Criminology; Law Enforcement/Police Administration; Law/Legal Services; Social Sciences.
Women in Accounting Scholarship	77	$2500	$2500	3–4	Accounting. Residence: Massachusetts.
Women in Technology Scholarship (WITS)	220	$2500	$500	1–20	Computer Science/Data Processing; Earth Science; Engineering/Technology.
Writer's Digest Popular Fiction Awards	838	$2500	$500	7	Talent/Interest Area: writing.
Crush The CPA Exam Scholarship	75	$2295	$1000	1	Accounting.
South Dakota Retailers Association Scholarship Program	96	$2250	$500	10–15	Agribusiness.
Menominee Indian Tribe Adult Vocational Training Program	689	$2200	$100	50–70	Limited to American Indian/Alaska Native students.
Menominee Indian Tribe of Wisconsin Higher Education Grants	689	$2200	$100	136	Limited to American Indian/Alaska Native students.
Scholarship Incentive Program (ScIP)	751	$2200	$700	700–2,200	Residence: Delaware. Studying in Delaware; Pennsylvania.

PROFILES OF SCHOLARSHIPS, GRANTS & PRIZES

Academic Fields/Career Goals

ACCOUNTING

ALABAMA SOCIETY OF CERTIFIED PUBLIC ACCOUNTANTS

http://www.ascpa.org/

ASCPA EDUCATIONAL FOUNDATION SCHOLARSHIP

Scholarships available for students with a declared major in accounting. Must have completed intermediate accounting courses (I and II) with a 3.0 average in all accounting courses, and a 3.0 average overall. Available for fourth or fifth year of study. Must be U.S. citizen or hold permanent resident status. Must have one full year of study remaining. 300 word essay.

Academic Fields/Career Goals: Accounting.

Award: Scholarship for use in senior or graduate years; not renewable. *Number:* 34–38. *Amount:* $1500–$2500.

Eligibility Requirements: Applicant must be enrolled or expecting to enroll full-time at a four-year institution or university; resident of Alabama and studying in Alabama. Applicant must have 3.0 GPA or higher. Available to U.S. citizens.

Application Requirements: Application form, essay. *Deadline:* March 10.

Contact: Ms. Diane Christy, Vice President of Communications
Alabama Society of Certified Public Accountants
1041 Longfield Court
Montgomery, AL 36117
Phone: 334-386-5752
E-mail: dchristy@ascpa.org

ALASKA SOCIETY OF CERTIFIED PUBLIC ACCOUNTANTS

http://www.akcpa.org/

PAUL HAGELBARGER MEMORIAL FUND SCHOLARSHIP

Scholarships open to all junior, senior, and graduate students who are majoring in accounting and attending institutions in Alaska.

Academic Fields/Career Goals: Accounting.

Award: Scholarship for use in junior, senior, or graduate years; not renewable. *Number:* 2–3. *Amount:* $2000.

Eligibility Requirements: Applicant must be enrolled or expecting to enroll full-time at a four-year institution or university and studying in Alaska. Available to U.S. citizens.

Application Requirements: Application form, recommendations or references, resume, transcript. *Deadline:* November 15.

Contact: Linda Plimpton, Executive Director
Alaska Society of Certified Public Accountants
341 West Tudor Road, Suite 105
Anchorage, AK 99503
Phone: 907-562-4334
Fax: 907-562-4025
E-mail: akcpa@ak.net

AMERICAN INSTITUTE OF CERTIFIED PUBLIC ACCOUNTANTS

http://www.aicpa.org/

AICPA/ACCOUNTEMPS STUDENT SCHOLARSHIP

The AICPA/Accountemps Student Scholarship program provides financial assistance to outstanding accounting students who demonstrate the potential to become leaders in the CPA profession. Students must have maintained a minimum GPA of 3.0 and have completed at least 30 semester credit hours (or equivalent) with at least 6 semester hours (or equivalent) in accounting coursework. Students must be enrolled full-time for the upcoming academic year. Additionally, award recipients are required to perform 16 community service hours to advocate on behalf of the CPA profession. More details and information are available on the program website: http://thiswaytocpa.com/.

Academic Fields/Career Goals: Accounting.

Award: Scholarship for use in sophomore, junior, senior, or graduate years; not renewable. *Number:* up to 10. *Amount:* up to $2500.

Eligibility Requirements: Applicant must be enrolled or expecting to enroll full-time at a four-year institution or university. Applicant must have 3.0 GPA or higher. Available to U.S. citizens.

Application Requirements: Application form, application form may be submitted online (http://www.thiswaytocpa.com/), essay, recommendations or references, test scores, transcript. *Deadline:* April 1.

Contact: Samantha Mithell, Scholarship Programs Manager
American Institute of Certified Public Accountants
American Institute of CPAs
220 Leigh Farm Road
Durham, NC 27707
Phone: 919-402-2161
Fax: 919-419-4705
E-mail: scholarships@aicpa.org

SCHOLARSHIP FOR MINORITY ACCOUNTING STUDENTS

The AICPA Minority Scholarship awards outstanding minority students to encourage their selection of accounting as a major and their ultimate entry into the profession. Funding is provided by the AICPA Foundation, with contributions from the New Jersey Society of CPAs and Robert Half International. For four decades, this program has provided over $14.6 million in scholarships to approximately 8,000 accounting scholars. Additionally, award recipients are required to perform 16 community service hours to advocate on behalf of the CPA profession. More details and information is available on the program website: http://ThisWayToCPA.com/aicpascholarships.

Academic Fields/Career Goals: Accounting.

Award: Scholarship for use in sophomore, junior, senior, or graduate years; not renewable. *Number:* 67–110. *Amount:* up to $5000.

Eligibility Requirements: Applicant must be American Indian/Alaska Native, Asian/Pacific Islander, Black (non-Hispanic), Hispanic and enrolled or expecting to enroll full-time at a four-year institution or university. Applicant must have 3.0 GPA or higher. Available to U.S. citizens.

Application Requirements: Application form, application form may be submitted online (http://www.ThisWayToCPA.com/MinorityScholarship), copy of acceptance letter, essay, recommendations or references, test scores, transcript. *Deadline:* April 1.

Contact: Samantha Mitchell, Scholarship Programs Manager
American Institute of Certified Public Accountants (CPAs)
220 Leigh Farm Road
Durham, NC 27707
Phone: 919-402-2161
Fax: 919-419-4705
E-mail: scholarships@aicpa.org

AMERICAN SOCIETY OF WOMEN ACCOUNTANTS

http://www.afwa.org/

AMERICAN SOCIETY OF WOMEN ACCOUNTANTS UNDERGRADUATE SCHOLARSHIP

Scholarship awards are presented to students who have completed their sophomore year of college and are majoring in accounting or finance. Candidates will be reviewed on leadership, character, communication skills, scholastic average, and financial need.

Academic Fields/Career Goals: Accounting.

Award: Scholarship for use in junior, senior, or graduate years; not renewable.

Eligibility Requirements: Applicant must be enrolled or expecting to enroll full- or part-time at a four-year institution or university and must have an interest in leadership. Available to U.S. and non-U.S. citizens.

Application Requirements: Application form, essay, financial need analysis, recommendations or references, transcript. *Deadline:* varies.

Contact: Kristin Edwards, Administrator
Phone: 703-506-3265
Fax: 703-506-3266
E-mail: kedwards@aswa.org

ASSOCIATION OF CERTIFIED FRAUD EXAMINERS

http://www.acfe.com/

RITCHIE-JENNINGS MEMORIAL SCHOLARSHIP

Applicant must be an undergraduate or graduate student, currently enrolled full-time (12 semester hours undergraduate; 9 semester hours graduate, or equivalent) at an accredited four-year college or university (or equivalent) with a declared major or minor in accounting or criminal justice.

Academic Fields/Career Goals: Accounting; Criminal Justice/Criminology.

Award: Scholarship for use in freshman, sophomore, junior, or senior years; not renewable. *Number:* up to 30. *Amount:* $1000.

Eligibility Requirements: Applicant must be enrolled or expecting to enroll full-time at a four-year institution or university. Available to U.S. and non-U.S. citizens.

Application Requirements: Application form, essay, recommendations or references, transcript. *Deadline:* April 16.

Contact: Keely Miers, Scholarship Coordinator
Association of Certified Fraud Examiners
The Gregor Building, 716 West Avenue
Austin, TX 78701
Phone: 800-245-3321
Fax: 512-478-9297
E-mail: scholarships@acfe.com

AUTOMOTIVE WOMEN'S ALLIANCE FOUNDATION

http://www.awafoundation.org/index.php

AUTOMOTIVE WOMEN'S ALLIANCE FOUNDATION SCHOLARSHIPS

Scholarships are the root of our purpose in Automotive Women's Alliance Foundation (AWAF). As an active professional foundation dedicated to supporting the advancement of automotive professionals, AWAF strives to motivate current and future students studying an automotive related field. Scholarships are selected by the Scholarship Committee and awarded quarterly to the women that solicit passion and drive for the automotive industry. It is our hope that with these scholarships, we can lessen the burden on students and allow them to focus on gaining knowledge and development in automotive related fields and thus enhance their potential career path and the future of the industry. Scholarships are awarded to female, North American citizens, with a passion for a career or advancement in the automotive and its related industries. While AWAF members and family members are encouraged to apply for scholarships, we encourage applicants who are not affiliated with the organization to apply as well. In order to be eligible for a scholarship applicants should be already accepted to or enrolled in an accredited collegiate program, with a 3.0 or higher GPA.

Academic Fields/Career Goals: Accounting; Advertising/Public Relations; Business/Consumer Services; Chemical Engineering; Communications; Computer Science/Data Processing; Economics; Electrical Engineering/Electronics; Energy and Power Engineering; Engineering-Related Technologies; Engineering/Technology; Environmental Science; Finance; Graphics/Graphic Arts/Printing; Human Resources; Industrial Design; International Studies; Marketing; Materials Science, Engineering, and Metallurgy; Mathematics; Mechanical Engineering; Science, Technology, and Society; Statistics; Transportation.

Award: Scholarship for use in freshman, sophomore, junior, senior, graduate, or postgraduate years; not renewable. *Number:* 20–24. *Amount:* $2500.

Eligibility Requirements: Applicant must be Canadian, Mexican citizen; enrolled or expecting to enroll full- or part-time at a two-year or four-year institution or university; female and must have an interest in automotive. Applicant must have 3.0 GPA or higher. Available to U.S. and Canadian citizens.

Application Requirements: Application form. *Deadline:* continuous.

Contact: Administrator
E-mail: admin@awafoundation.org

BHW GROUP

https://thebhwgroup.com/

BHW WOMEN IN STEM SCHOLARSHIP

The Women In STEM Scholarship is available to undergraduate and graduate female students. You must be pursuing a degree in science, technology, engineering, or mathematics to be eligible for this award.

Academic Fields/Career Goals: Accounting; Applied Sciences; Archaeology; Architecture; Aviation/Aerospace; Behavioral Science; Biology; Chemical Engineering; Civil Engineering; Computer Science/Data Processing; Construction Engineering/Management; Dental Health/Services; Earth Science; Electrical Engineering/Electronics; Energy and Power Engineering; Engineering-Related Technologies; Engineering/Technology; Entomology; Environmental Health; Environmental Science; Food Science/Nutrition; Gemology; Geography; Health Administration; Health and Medical Sciences; Health Information Management/Technology; Heating, Air-Conditioning, and Refrigeration Mechanics; Horticulture/Floriculture; Hydrology; Industrial Design; Insurance and Actuarial Science; Landscape Architecture; Marine/Ocean Engineering; Materials Science, Engineering, and Metallurgy; Mathematics; Mechanical Engineering; Meteorology/Atmospheric Science; Military and Defense Studies; Natural Resources; Natural Sciences; Near and Middle East Studies; Neurobiology; Nuclear Science; Nursing; Occupational Safety and Health; Oceanography; Oncology; Optometry; Osteopathy; Paper and Pulp Engineering; Pharmacy; Physical Sciences; Psychology; Science, Technology, and Society; Social Sciences.

Award: Scholarship for use in freshman, sophomore, junior, senior, graduate, or postgraduate years; not renewable. *Number:* 1. *Amount:* $3000.

Eligibility Requirements: Applicant must be enrolled or expecting to enroll full-time at a two-year or four-year or technical institution or university and female. Available to U.S. and non-U.S. citizens.

Application Requirements: Essay. *Deadline:* April 15.

Contact: Mr. Paul Francis, Partner
BHW Group
6011 W. Courtyard Dr
Suite 410
Austin, TX 78730
Phone: 512-2200035
E-mail: scholarship@thebhwgroup.com

CATCHING THE DREAM

http://www.catchingthedream.org/

TRIBAL BUSINESS MANAGEMENT PROGRAM (TBM)

Renewable scholarships available for Native American and Alaska Native students to study business administration, economic development, and related subjects, with the goal to provide experts in business management to Native American tribes in the U.S. Must be at least one-quarter Native American from a federally recognized, state recognized, or terminated tribe. Must demonstrate high academic achievement, depth of character, leadership, seriousness of purpose, and service orientation.

Academic Fields/Career Goals: Accounting; Business/Consumer Services; Computer Science/Data Processing; Economics; Electrical Engineering/Electronics; Engineering-Related Technologies.

Award: Scholarship for use in freshman, sophomore, junior, senior, graduate, or postgraduate years; renewable. *Number:* 35. *Amount:* $500–$5000.

Eligibility Requirements: Applicant must be American Indian/Alaska Native and enrolled or expecting to enroll full-time at a four-year institution or university. Applicant must have 3.0 GPA or higher. Available to U.S. citizens.

Application Requirements: Application form, essay, financial need analysis, personal photograph.

Contact: Mary Frost, Recruiter
Catching the Dream
8200 Mountain Road, NE, Suite 203
Albuquerque, NM 87110
Phone: 505-262-2351
E-mail: nscholarsh@aol.com

COLORADO SOCIETY OF CERTIFIED PUBLIC ACCOUNTANTS EDUCATIONAL FOUNDATION

http://www.cocpa.org/

COLORADO COLLEGE AND UNIVERSITY SCHOLARSHIPS

Award available to declared accounting majors at Colorado colleges and universities with accredited accounting programs. Must have completed at least 8 semester hours of accounting courses. Overall GPA and accounting GPA must be at least 3.0. Must be Colorado resident.

Academic Fields/Career Goals: Accounting.

Award: Scholarship for use in junior, senior, graduate, or postgraduate years; not renewable. *Number:* 15–20. *Amount:* $2500.

Eligibility Requirements: Applicant must be enrolled or expecting to enroll full- or part-time at a four-year institution or university; resident of Colorado and studying in Colorado. Applicant must have 3.0 GPA or higher. Available to U.S. citizens.

Application Requirements: Application form, recommendations or references, transcript. *Deadline:* June 1.

Contact: Gena Mantz, Membership Coordinator
Phone: 303-741-8613
Fax: 303-773-6344
E-mail: gmantz@cocpa.org

CONNECTICUT SOCIETY OF CERTIFIED PUBLIC ACCOUNTANTS

http://www.ctcpas.org/

CT SOCIETY OF CPAS RISING SOPHOMORE ACCOUNTING SCHOLARSHIP

The Educational Trust Fund of the Connecticut Society of CPAs (CTCPA) has established this scholarship to assist Connecticut accounting majors entering into their sophomore year of study at a four-year college or university in financing their education.

Academic Fields/Career Goals: Accounting.

Award: Scholarship for use in sophomore year; not renewable. *Number:* 1–4. *Amount:* $1500.

Eligibility Requirements: Applicant must be enrolled or expecting to enroll full-time at a four-year institution or university; resident of Connecticut and studying in Connecticut. Applicant must have 3.0 GPA or higher. Available to U.S. citizens.

Application Requirements: Application form, driver's license, essay. *Deadline:* April 17.

Contact: Mrs. Jill Brightman, Program Coordinator
Connecticut Society of Certified Public Accountants
716 Brook Street, Suite 100
Rocky Hill, CT 06067
Phone: 860-258-0329
E-mail: jillb@ctcpas.org

EDUCATIONAL TRUST FUND OF THE CTCPA - CANDIDATE'S SCHOLARSHIP

Scholarship of $5000 that assists students in complying with the 150-hour requirement of the Connecticut State Board of Accountancy to sit for the Uniform Certified Public Accountant Examination. An overall GPA of 3.0.

Academic Fields/Career Goals: Accounting.

Award: Scholarship for use in senior or graduate years; not renewable. *Number:* 1. *Amount:* $5000.

Eligibility Requirements: Applicant must be enrolled or expecting to enroll full- or part-time at a four-year institution or university; resident of Connecticut and studying in Connecticut. Applicant must have 3.0 GPA or higher. Available to U.S. citizens.

Application Requirements: Application form, driver's license, essay. *Deadline:* April 17.

Contact: Mrs. Jill Brightman, Program Coordinator
Connecticut Society of Certified Public Accountants
716 Brook Street, Suite100
Rocky Hill, CT 06067
Phone: 860-258-0239
E-mail: jillb@ctcpas.org

CRUSH THE CPA EXAM

http://crushthecpaexam.com

CRUSH THE CPA EXAM SCHOLARSHIP

Crush The CPA Exam is very excited to tell you that we have created an annual scholarship program to help one accounting student become a Certified Public Accountant. The winner will receive $1,000 to pay for their CPA exam fees and also a complete CPA review course from Wiley CPAexcel worth $2,295.

Academic Fields/Career Goals: Accounting.

Award: Scholarship for use in junior, senior, or graduate years; not renewable. *Number:* 1. *Amount:* $1000–$2295.

Eligibility Requirements: Applicant must be enrolled or expecting to enroll full-time at a four-year institution or university. Applicant must have 3.0 GPA or higher. Available to U.S. and non-U.S. citizens.

Application Requirements: Application form, driver's license. *Deadline:* November 29.

Contact: Bryce Welker, CEO
Crush The CPA Exam
10505 Roselle St
San Diego, CA 92121
Phone: 858-858-888-9063
E-mail: crushthecpaexam@gmail.com

DECA (DISTRIBUTIVE EDUCATION CLUBS OF AMERICA)

http://www.deca.org/

HARRY A. APPLEGATE SCHOLARSHIP

Scholarship available to current DECA or Collegiate DECA members for undergraduate study in marketing education, marketing, entrepreneurship, finance, hospitality or management. Nonrenewable merit-based award for current DECA members based on DECA activities, grades, and leadership.

Academic Fields/Career Goals: Accounting; Business/Consumer Services; Education; Fashion Design; Finance; Food Service/Hospitality; Hospitality Management; Marketing.

Award: Scholarship for use in freshman, sophomore, junior, or senior years; not renewable. *Number:* 20–25. *Amount:* $1000–$5000.

Eligibility Requirements: Applicant must be enrolled or expecting to enroll full-time at a two-year or four-year institution or university. Applicant or parent of applicant must be member of Distribution Ed Club or Future Business Leaders of America. Available to U.S. and non-U.S. citizens.

Application Requirements: Application form, application form may be submitted online (http://www.deca.org/high-school-programs/scholarships/), copy of DECA chapter roster, recommendations or references, test scores, transcript. *Deadline:* January 16.

Contact: Kathy Onion, Corporate and External Affairs Assistant
DECA (Distributive Education Clubs of America)
1908 Association Drive
Reston, VA 20191
Phone: 703-860-5000 Ext. 248
Fax: 703-860-4013
E-mail: kathy_onion@deca.org

EDUCATIONAL FOUNDATION FOR WOMEN IN ACCOUNTING (EFWA)

http://www.efwa.org/

MICHELE L. MCDONALD SCHOLARSHIP

Individuals eligible for this award will be women who are returning to college from the workforce or after raising children. Scholarship recipients will be awarded $1000 to begin their studies in pursuit of a college degree in accounting.

Academic Fields/Career Goals: Accounting.

Award: Scholarship for use in freshman, sophomore, junior, or senior years; not renewable. *Amount:* $1000.

Eligibility Requirements: Applicant must be enrolled or expecting to enroll full- or part-time at a four-year institution or university and married female. Available to U.S. citizens.

Application Requirements: Application form, financial need analysis, transcript. *Deadline:* April 15.

Contact: Cynthia Hires, Foundation Administrator
    Phone: 610-407-9229
    Fax: 610-644-3713
    E-mail: info@efwa.org

ROWLING, DOLD & ASSOCIATES LLP SCHOLARSHIP

One year $1000 scholarship award for minority women enrolled in an accounting program at an accredited college or university. Women returning to school with undergraduate status; incoming, current, or reentry juniors or seniors; or minority women are all eligible.

Academic Fields/Career Goals: Accounting.

Award: Scholarship for use in junior, senior, or graduate years; not renewable. *Amount:* $1000.

Eligibility Requirements: Applicant must be American Indian/Alaska Native, Asian/Pacific Islander, Black (non-Hispanic), Hispanic; enrolled or expecting to enroll full- or part-time at a four-year institution or university and female. Available to U.S. citizens.

Application Requirements: Application form, financial need analysis, transcript. *Deadline:* April 15.

Contact: Cynthia Hires, Foundation Administrator
    Phone: 610-407-9229
    Fax: 610-644-3713
    E-mail: info@efwa.org

SEATTLE AMERICAN SOCIETY OF WOMEN ACCOUNTANTS CHAPTER SCHOLARSHIP

Scholarship for an amount up to $2000 to be awarded to a women attending an accredited school within the State of Washington. The scholarship will be renewable for one additional year upon satisfactory completion of course requirements. Must pursue a degree in accounting.

Academic Fields/Career Goals: Accounting.

Award: Scholarship for use in freshman, sophomore, junior, or senior years; renewable. *Amount:* up to $2000.

Eligibility Requirements: Applicant must be enrolled or expecting to enroll full- or part-time at a four-year institution or university; female and studying in Washington. Available to U.S. citizens.

Application Requirements: Application form, financial need analysis, transcript. *Deadline:* April 15.

Contact: Cynthia Hires, Foundation Administrator
    Phone: 610-407-9229
    Fax: 610-644-3713
    E-mail: info@efwa.org

WOMEN IN NEED SCHOLARSHIP

Scholarship provides financial assistance to female reentry students who wish to pursue a degree in accounting. Scholarship is available to incoming, current, or reentry juniors.

Academic Fields/Career Goals: Accounting.

Award: Scholarship for use in junior year; renewable. *Number:* 1. *Amount:* $2000.

Eligibility Requirements: Applicant must be enrolled or expecting to enroll full- or part-time at a four-year institution or university and female. Available to U.S. citizens.

Application Requirements: Application form, financial need analysis, transcript. *Deadline:* April 15.

Contact: Cynthia Hires, Foundation Administrator
    Phone: 610-407-9229
    Fax: 610-644-3713
    E-mail: info@efwa.org

WOMEN IN TRANSITION SCHOLARSHIP

Renewable award available to incoming or current freshmen and women returning to school with a freshman status. Scholarship value may be up to $16,000 over four years.

Academic Fields/Career Goals: Accounting.

Award: Scholarship for use in freshman year; renewable. *Number:* 1. *Amount:* up to $4000.

Eligibility Requirements: Applicant must be enrolled or expecting to enroll full- or part-time at a four-year institution or university and female. Available to U.S. citizens.

Application Requirements: Application form, financial need analysis, transcript. *Deadline:* April 15.

Contact: Cynthia Hires, Foundation Administrator
    Phone: 610-407-9229
    Fax: 610-644-3713
    E-mail: info@efwa.org

EDUCATIONAL FOUNDATION OF THE MASSACHUSETTS SOCIETY OF CERTIFIED PUBLIC ACCOUNTANTS

http://MSCPAonline.org

KATHLEEN M. PEABODY, CPA, MEMORIAL SCHOLARSHIP

Scholarship available for Massachusetts resident who has completed sophomore year. Must be accounting major with plans to seek an accounting career in Massachusetts. Must demonstrate academic excellence and financial need. Information on website at http://www.cpatrack.com.

Academic Fields/Career Goals: Accounting.

Award: Scholarship for use in junior or senior years; not renewable. *Number:* 1. *Amount:* $2500.

Eligibility Requirements: Applicant must be enrolled or expecting to enroll full-time at a four-year institution or university and resident of Massachusetts. Applicant must have 3.0 GPA or higher. Available to U.S. citizens.

Application Requirements: Application form, application form may be submitted online (http://ThisWayToCPA.com/MSCPA), essay, financial need analysis, recommendations or references, transcript. *Deadline:* April 1.

Contact: Barbara Iannoni, Senior Academic Specialist
    Educational Foundation of the Massachusetts Society of
        Certified Public Accountants
    105 Chauncy Street
    Boston, MA 02111
    Phone: 617-303-2415
    Fax: 617-556.4126
    E-mail: biannoni@mscpaonline.org

MSCPA FIRM SCHOLARSHIP

Scholarship to encourage individuals who have demonstrated academic excellence and financial need to pursue a career in public accounting in Massachusetts.

Academic Fields/Career Goals: Accounting.

Award: Scholarship for use in junior, senior, or graduate years; not renewable. *Number:* 12–16. *Amount:* $2500.

Eligibility Requirements: Applicant must be enrolled or expecting to enroll full-time at a four-year institution or university and resident of Massachusetts. Applicant must have 3.0 GPA or higher. Available to U.S. citizens.

Application Requirements: Application form, essay, financial need analysis, recommendations or references, transcript. *Deadline:* April 1.

Contact: Barbara Iannoni, Senior Academic Specialist
Educational Foundation of the Massachusetts Society of
Certified Public Accountants
105 Chauncy Street
Boston, MA 02111
Phone: 617-303-2415
Fax: 617-556.4126
E-mail: biannoni@mscpaonline.org

WOMEN IN ACCOUNTING SCHOLARSHIP

The purpose of these scholarships is to encourage women who have demonstrated academic excellence and financial need to pursue a career as a CPA in Massachusetts.

Academic Fields/Career Goals: Accounting.

Award: Scholarship for use in junior, senior, or graduate years; not renewable. *Number:* 3–4. *Amount:* $2500–$2500.

Eligibility Requirements: Applicant must be enrolled or expecting to enroll full-time at a four-year institution; female and resident of Massachusetts. Applicant must have 3.5 GPA or higher. Available to U.S. citizens.

Application Requirements: Application form, application form may be submitted online (http://ThisWayToCPA.com/MSCPA), essay, financial need analysis, transcript. *Deadline:* April 1.

Contact: Barbara Iannoni, Senior Academic Specialist
Educational Foundation of the Massachusetts Society of
Certified Public Accountants
105 Chauncy Street
Boston, MA 02111
Phone: 617-303-2415
Fax: 617-556.4126
E-mail: biannoni@mscpaonline.org

FLORIDA INSTITUTE OF CERTIFIED PUBLIC ACCOUNTANTS EDUCATIONAL FOUNDATION, INC.

http://www.ficpa.org/

I040K RUN/WALK SCHOLARSHIPS

Applicant(s) must be a citizen of the United States or hold permanent residency status and be a resident of Miami-Dade County, Broward County, Monroe County, or Palm Beach Count. The Lewis Davis scholarship is to be awarded to an African-American student. One scholarship is to be awarded to a minority student (may or not be African-American). One scholarship is to be awarded to a student based on need (may or not be African-American). See website for details.

Academic Fields/Career Goals: Accounting.

Award: Scholarship for use in senior or graduate years; not renewable. *Number:* up to 3. *Amount:* up to $3000.

Eligibility Requirements: Applicant must be Black (non-Hispanic); enrolled or expecting to enroll full-time at a four-year institution or university; resident of Florida and studying in Florida. Applicant must have 3.0 GPA or higher. Available to U.S. citizens.

Application Requirements: Application form, must be recommended by accounting faculty committee at Florida college or university attended, recommendations or references, transcript. *Deadline:* February 15.

Contact: Mrs. Betsy Wilson, Educational Foundation Assistant
Florida Institute of Certified Public Accountants Educational
Foundation, Inc.
325 West College Avenue, PO Box 5437
Tallahassee, FL 32314
Phone: 850-224-2727 Ext. 0
Fax: 850-222-8190
E-mail: wilsonb@ficpa.org

FICPA EDUCATIONAL FOUNDATION SCHOLARSHIPS

Scholarship for full-time or part-time (minimum of six credit hours), fourth- or fifth-year accounting major at participating Florida colleges or universities. Must be a member of the Florida Institute of CPAs, a Florida resident and plan to practice accounting in Florida. See website for list of institutions http://www1.ficpa.org/ficpa/Visitors/Careers/EdFoundation/Scholarships .

Academic Fields/Career Goals: Accounting.

Award: Scholarship for use in senior or graduate years; not renewable. *Number:* up to 63. *Amount:* $1000–$2000.

Eligibility Requirements: Applicant must be enrolled or expecting to enroll full- or part-time at a four-year institution or university; resident of Florida and studying in Florida. Applicant must have 3.0 GPA or higher. Available to U.S. citizens.

Application Requirements: Application form, must be recommended by faculty committee at school attended, recommendations or references, transcript. *Deadline:* April 15.

Contact: Mrs. Betsy Wilson, Educational Foundation Assistant
Florida Institute of Certified Public Accountants Educational
Foundation, Inc.
325 West College Avenue, PO Box 5437
Tallahassee, FL 32314
Phone: 850-224-2727 Ext. 0
Fax: 850-222-8190
E-mail: wilsonb@ficpa.org

FUKUNAGA SCHOLARSHIP FOUNDATION

http://fukunagascholarship.com

FUKUNAGA SCHOLARSHIP FOUNDATION

Renewable scholarships available only to U.S. citizens/Hawaii residents pursuing a business degree at the undergraduate level at an accredited institution. Minimum 3.0 GPA required.

Academic Fields/Career Goals: Accounting; Advertising/Public Relations; Business/Consumer Services; Economics; Finance; Hospitality Management; Human Resources; Marketing.

Award: Scholarship for use in freshman, sophomore, junior, or senior years; renewable. *Number:* 10–15. *Amount:* $4500.

Eligibility Requirements: Applicant must be enrolled or expecting to enroll full-time at a four-year institution or university and resident of Hawaii. Applicant must have 3.0 GPA or higher. Available to U.S. citizens.

Application Requirements: Application form, essay, financial need analysis, interview. *Deadline:* March 1.

Contact: Mrs. Sandy Wong, Foundation Director
Fukunaga Scholarship Foundation
PO Box 2788
Honolulu, HI 96803-2788
Phone: 808-564-1386
E-mail: sandy.wong@servco.com

GEORGIA GOVERNMENT FINANCE OFFICERS ASSOCIATION

http://www.ggfoa.org/

GGFOA ANNUAL COLLEGE SCHOLARSHIP

The scholarship recognizes outstanding performance in the study of public finance at the undergraduate and graduate level and encourages careers in state and local government. The GGFOA Scholarship is awarded to undergraduate or graduate students who meet the eligibility requirements and are preparing for a career in public finance. Must have nomination by the head of the applicable program (e.g., public administration, accounting, finance). Preference will be given to GGFOA members and employees of GGFOA governmental entities who are eligible for in-state tuition.

Academic Fields/Career Goals: Accounting; Business/Consumer Services; Finance; Public Policy and Administration.

Award: Scholarship for use in freshman, sophomore, junior, senior, or graduate years; not renewable. *Number:* 1–2. *Amount:* $1–$1500.

Eligibility Requirements: Applicant must be enrolled or expecting to enroll full- or part-time at a four-year institution or university; resident of Hawaii and studying in Georgia. Available to U.S. citizens.

Application Requirements: Application form, essay. *Deadline:* August 1.

Contact: Jennifer Fricks, Scholarship Selection Committee, GGFOA
Georgia Government Finance Officers Association
117 Putnam Drive
Eatonton, GA 31024
Phone: 706-485-1882
E-mail: jfricks@putnamcountyga.us

GOVERNMENT FINANCE OFFICERS ASSOCIATION

http://www.gfoa.org/

FRANK L. GREATHOUSE GOVERNMENT ACCOUNTING SCHOLARSHIP

Two scholarships awarded to undergraduate or graduate students enrolled full-time study, preparing for a career in state or local government finance. Submit resume. One-time award of $9000.

Academic Fields/Career Goals: Accounting.

Award: Scholarship for use in senior or graduate years; not renewable. *Number:* 2. *Amount:* $9000.

Eligibility Requirements: Applicant must be enrolled or expecting to enroll full-time at a four-year institution or university. Applicant must have 3.0 GPA or higher. Available to U.S. and Canadian citizens.

Application Requirements: Application form, essay. *Deadline:* February 19.

Contact: Mr. Robert Kotchen, Administrative Assistant
Government Finance Officers Association
203 North Lasalle Street
Suite 2700
Chicago, IL 60601
Phone: 312-977-9700
E-mail: rkotchen@gfoa.org

MINORITIES IN GOVERNMENT FINANCE SCHOLARSHIP

Awards upper-division undergraduate or graduate students of public administration, governmental accounting, finance, political science, economics, or business administration to recognize outstanding performance by minority students preparing for a career in state and local government finance.

Academic Fields/Career Goals: Accounting; Business/Consumer Services; Economics; Political Science; Public Policy and Administration.

Award: Scholarship for use in junior, senior, or graduate years; not renewable. *Number:* 1. *Amount:* $9000.

Eligibility Requirements: Applicant must be American Indian/Alaska Native, Asian/Pacific Islander, Black (non-Hispanic), Hispanic and enrolled or expecting to enroll full- or part-time at a four-year institution or university. Applicant must have 3.0 GPA or higher. Available to U.S. and Canadian citizens.

Application Requirements: Application form, essay. *Deadline:* February 19.

Contact: Mr. Robert Kotchen, Administrative Assistant
Government Finance Officers Association
203 North Lasalle Street
Suite 2700
Chicago, IL 60601
Phone: 312-977-9700
E-mail: rkotchen@gfoa.org

GREATER WASHINGTON SOCIETY OF CPAS

http://www.gwscpa.org/

GREATER WASHINGTON SOCIETY OF CPAS SCHOLARSHIP

Scholarship available to accounting students. School must offer an accounting degree that qualifies graduates to sit for the CPA exam (must meet the 150-hour rule). Minimum 3.0 GPA in major courses required. Application details on our website http://www.gwscpa.org.

Academic Fields/Career Goals: Accounting.

Award: Scholarship for use in junior, senior, or graduate years; not renewable. *Number:* 3–5. *Amount:* $2000–$4500.

Eligibility Requirements: Applicant must be enrolled or expecting to enroll full-time at a four-year institution or university; resident of District of Columbia and studying in District of Columbia. Applicant must have 3.0 GPA or higher. Available to U.S. citizens.

Application Requirements: Application form, essay, financial need analysis, recommendations or references, resume, transcript. *Deadline:* February 15.

Contact: Mr. Brian Calvary, Membership Director
Greater Washington Society of CPAs
1140 Connecticut Ave, NW
Suite 606
Washington, DC 20036
Phone: 202-601-0569
E-mail: info@gwscpa.org

HAWAII SOCIETY OF CERTIFIED PUBLIC ACCOUNTANTS

http://www.hscpa.org/

HSCPA SCHOLARSHIP PROGRAM FOR ACCOUNTING STUDENTS

Scholarship for Hawaii resident currently attending an accredited Hawaii college or university. Minimum 3.0 GPA required. Must be majoring, or concentrating, in accounting with the intention to sit for the CPA exam, and have completed an intermediate accounting course. Number of awards vary from year to year.

Academic Fields/Career Goals: Accounting.

Award: Scholarship for use in freshman, sophomore, junior, or senior years; not renewable. *Amount:* $500–$1500.

Eligibility Requirements: Applicant must be enrolled or expecting to enroll full-time at a four-year institution or university; resident of Hawaii and studying in Hawaii. Applicant must have 3.0 GPA or higher. Available to U.S. citizens.

Application Requirements: Application form, community service, recommendations or references, test scores, transcript. *Deadline:* January 31.

Contact: Kathy Castillo, Executive Director
Hawaii Society of Certified Public Accountants
900 Fort Street Mall, Suite 850
Honolulu, HI 96813
Phone: 808-537-9475
Fax: 808-537-3520
E-mail: info@hscpa.org

ILLINOIS CPA SOCIETY/CPA ENDOWMENT FUND OF ILLINOIS

http://www.icpas.org/

ILLINOIS CPA SOCIETY ACCOUNTING SCHOLARSHIP PROGRAM

The Illinois CPA Society has numerous scholarships available to support accounting students who are studying accounting and planning to become a CPA. Candidates must demonstrate a course of study which reflects a goal to sit for the CPA exam in Illinois. The scholarship program supports diversity of students, investing in their success and helping them to realize their dream of becoming CPAs. Scholarship recipients have studied at a variety of schools throughout the state, from large state universities to small private schools to community colleges. Some scholarships have supported students with their graduate studies, while others support a fifth year of undergraduate education.

Academic Fields/Career Goals: Accounting.

Award: Scholarship for use in junior, senior, graduate, or postgraduate years; not renewable. *Number:* 12–35. *Amount:* $500–$4000.

Eligibility Requirements: Applicant must be enrolled or expecting to enroll full- or part-time at a four-year institution or university; resident of Illinois and studying in Illinois. Applicant must have 3.0 GPA or higher. Available to U.S. citizens.

Application Requirements: Application form, essay. *Deadline:* April 1.

Contact: Ms. Devin Payne
E-mail: scholarship@icpas.org

INSTITUTE OF MANAGEMENT ACCOUNTANTS

https://www.imanet.org/students/scholarships-and-awards/scholarships?ssopc=1

INSTITUTE OF MANAGEMENT ACCOUNTANTS MEMORIAL EDUCATION FUND SCHOLARSHIPS

Scholarships for IMA undergraduate or graduate student members studying at accredited institutions in the U.S. and Puerto Rico. Must be pursuing a career in management accounting, financial management, or information technology, and have a minimum GPA of 3.0. Awards based on academic merit, IMA participation, strength of recommendations, and quality of written statements.

Academic Fields/Career Goals: Accounting; Business/Consumer Services.

Award: Scholarship for use in sophomore, junior, senior, or graduate years; not renewable. *Number:* 6–15. *Amount:* $1000–$2500.

Eligibility Requirements: Applicant must be enrolled or expecting to enroll full- or part-time at a two-year or four-year institution or university. Applicant must have 3.0 GPA or higher. Available to U.S. citizens.

Application Requirements: Application form, essay. *Deadline:* February 15.

Contact: Kerry Butkera, Research & Academic Relations Administrator
Institute of Management Accountants
IMA
10 Paragon Drive, Suite 1
Montvale, NJ 07628
Phone: 800-638-4427 Ext. 1546
E-mail: kbutkera@imanet.org

ROLF S. JAEHNIGEN FAMILY SCHOLARSHIP

A scholarship to recognize a student who is passionate not only about his/her business career, but about the arts as well. You must be a junior or senior accounting, finance or information systems major at an accredited business school.

Academic Fields/Career Goals: Accounting; Computer Science/Data Processing; Finance.

Award: Scholarship for use in junior or senior years; not renewable. *Amount:* $1000.

Eligibility Requirements: Applicant must be enrolled or expecting to enroll full- or part-time at a four-year institution or university. Available to U.S. citizens.

Application Requirements: *Deadline:* October 31.

Contact: Kerry Butkera, Research & Academic Relations Administrator
Institute of Management Accountants
IMA
10 Paragon Drive, Suite 1
Montvale, NJ 07628
Phone: 800-638-4427 Ext. 1546
E-mail: kbutkera@imanet.org

STUART CAMERON AND MARGARET MCLEOD MEMORIAL SCHOLARSHIP

Scholarships for IMA undergraduate or graduate student members studying at accredited institutions in the U.S. and Puerto Rico and carrying 12 credits per semester. Must be pursuing a career in management accounting, financial management, or information technology, and have a minimum GPA of 3.0. Awards based on academic merit, IMA participation, strength of recommendations, and quality of written statements.

Academic Fields/Career Goals: Accounting; Business/Consumer Services.

Award: Scholarship for use in junior, senior, or graduate years; not renewable. *Number:* 1. *Amount:* $5000.

Eligibility Requirements: Applicant must be enrolled or expecting to enroll full- or part-time at a two-year or four-year institution or university. Applicant must have 3.0 GPA or higher. Available to U.S. citizens.

Application Requirements: Application form, essay, resume, transcript. *Deadline:* February 15.

Contact: Kerry Butkera, Research & Academic Relations Administrator
Institute of Management Accountants
IMA
10 Paragon Drive, Suite 1
Montvale, NJ 07628
Phone: 800-638-4427 Ext. 1546
E-mail: kbutkera@imanet.org

INTERNAL AUDIT FOUNDATION

http://www.theiia.org/

ESTHER R. SAWYER RESEARCH AWARD

Awarded to a student entering or currently enrolled in an Internal Auditing Education Partnership (IAEP) program at an IIA-affiliated school. Awarded based on submission of an original manuscript on a specific topic related to modern internal auditing.

Academic Fields/Career Goals: Accounting.

Award: Prize for use in freshman, sophomore, junior, senior, or graduate years; not renewable. *Number:* 1. *Amount:* $5000.

Eligibility Requirements: Applicant must be enrolled or expecting to enroll full-time at a four-year institution or university. Available to U.S. and non-U.S. citizens.

Application Requirements: Application form, essay. *Deadline:* March 1.

Contact: Benjamin Bouchillon, Manager of Fundraising Operations
Phone: 407-937-1352
E-mail: foundation@theiia.org

KENTUCKY SOCIETY OF CERTIFIED PUBLIC ACCOUNTANTS

http://www.kycpa.org/

KENTUCKY SOCIETY OF CERTIFIED PUBLIC ACCOUNTANTS COLLEGE SCHOLARSHIP

Nonrenewable award for accounting majors at a Kentucky college or university. Must rank in upper third of class or have a minimum 3.0 GPA. Must be a Kentucky resident.

Academic Fields/Career Goals: Accounting.

Award: Scholarship for use in sophomore, junior, or senior years; not renewable. *Number:* up to 23. *Amount:* $1000–$2500.

Eligibility Requirements: Applicant must be enrolled or expecting to enroll full-time at a two-year or four-year institution or university; resident of Kentucky and studying in Kentucky. Applicant must have 3.0 GPA or higher. Available to U.S. and non-U.S. citizens.

Application Requirements: Application form, essay, recommendations or references, transcript. *Deadline:* January 31.

Contact: Becky Ackerman, Foundation Administrator
Phone: 502-266-5272
Fax: 502-261-9512
E-mail: backerman@kycpa.org

MARYLAND ASSOCIATION OF CERTIFIED PUBLIC ACCOUNTANTS EDUCATIONAL FOUNDATION

https://www.macpa.org/for-students/

MACPA EDUCATIONAL FOUNDATION SCHOLARSHIP AWARD

Award for Maryland residents who will have completed at least 60 credit hours at a Maryland college or university by the time of the award. Must have 3.0 GPA, demonstrate commitment to 150 semester hours of education, and intend to pursue a career as a certified public accountant. Number of awards varies. Must submit accounting department chairman's signature on required statement. Must be a student member with the Maryland Association of CPAs. U.S. citizenship required. See website at for further details. https://www.macpa.org/for-students/

Academic Fields/Career Goals: Accounting.

Award: Scholarship for use in junior, senior, or graduate years; renewable. *Number:* 10–12. *Amount:* $500–$1500.

Eligibility Requirements: Applicant must be enrolled or expecting to enroll full-time at a four-year institution or university; resident of Maryland and studying in Maryland. Applicant must have 3.0 GPA or higher. Available to U.S. citizens.

Application Requirements: Application form, financial need analysis. *Deadline:* April 15.

Contact: Margaret DeRoose, Staff Accountant
Maryland Association of Certified Public Accountants
Educational Foundation
901 Dulaney Valley Road
Suite 800
Towson, MD 21204
Phone: 443-632-2327
E-mail: margaret@macpa.org

MICHIGAN ASSOCIATION OF CPAS
http://www.michcpa.org/

FIFTH/GRADUATE YEAR STUDENT SCHOLARSHIP
Scholarship for a full-time student in senior year, or a student with a combination of education and employment (defined as a minimum of two classes per term and 20 hours per week of employment). Must be majoring in accounting, and a U.S. citizen.

Academic Fields/Career Goals: Accounting.

Award: Scholarship for use in senior year; not renewable. *Number:* 16–25. *Amount:* $2000–$4000.

Eligibility Requirements: Applicant must be enrolled or expecting to enroll full- or part-time at a four-year institution or university and studying in Michigan. Available to U.S. citizens.

Application Requirements: Application form, application form may be submitted online (http://www.mafonline.org), essay, financial need analysis, recommendations or references, transcript. *Deadline:* January 31.

Contact: MACPA Academic Services Specialist
Michigan Association of CPAs
5480 Corporate Drive, Suite 200
Troy, MI 48007-5068
Phone: 248-267-3700
Fax: 248-267-3737
E-mail: macpa@michcpa.org

MONTANA SOCIETY OF CERTIFIED PUBLIC ACCOUNTANTS
http://www.mscpa.org/

MONTANA SOCIETY OF CERTIFIED PUBLIC ACCOUNTANTS SCHOLARSHIP
Scholarship available to one student in each of the following five schools: Montana State University Billings, MSU Bozeman, Carroll College, Montana Tech and University of Montana. Must be: 1. Accounting Major 2. At least a junior standing with at least one semester of coursework remaining 3. Minimum GPA of 3.0 4. Graduate students eligible 5. Must be a student member of the MSCPA 6. Graduate of a Montana high school and currently a Montana resident. Two additional scholarships are awarded through our Endowment Fund and may be applied for through the Montana Community Foundation.

Academic Fields/Career Goals: Accounting.

Award: Scholarship for use in junior, senior, or graduate years; not renewable. *Number:* 7. *Amount:* $1000.

Eligibility Requirements: Applicant must be enrolled or expecting to enroll full-time at a four-year institution or university; resident of Montana and studying in Montana. Applicant must have 3.0 GPA or higher. Available to U.S. citizens.

Application Requirements: Application form, essay. *Deadline:* March 17.

Contact: Mrs. Margaret Herriges, Communications Director
Montana Society of Certified Public Accountants
1534 9th Avenue
Helena, MT 59601
Phone: 406-442-7301
E-mail: mscpa@mscpa.org

NATIONAL ASSOCIATION OF WATER COMPANIES-NEW JERSEY CHAPTER
http://www.nawc.org

NATIONAL ASSOCIATION OF WATER COMPANIES-NEW JERSEY CHAPTER SCHOLARSHIP
For college students interested in a career in the water utility industry or any related field. Must be U.S. citizen, five-year resident of New Jersey, high school senior or college student attending or enrolled in a New Jersey college or university. Must maintain a 3.0 GPA.

Academic Fields/Career Goals: Accounting; Advertising/Public Relations; Biology; Business/Consumer Services; Chemical Engineering; Civil Engineering; Communications; Computer Science/Data Processing; Construction Engineering/Management; Earth Science; Economics; Engineering-Related Technologies; Engineering/Technology; Environmental Science; Law/Legal Services; Natural Resources; Natural Sciences; Physical Sciences; Science, Technology, and Society; Trade/Technical Specialties.

Award: Scholarship for use in freshman, sophomore, junior, senior, or graduate years; not renewable. *Number:* 2. *Amount:* $2500.

Eligibility Requirements: Applicant must be enrolled or expecting to enroll full- or part-time at a two-year or four-year institution or university; resident of New Jersey and studying in New Jersey. Applicant must have 3.0 GPA or higher. Available to U.S. citizens.

Application Requirements: Application form, essay. *Deadline:* April 1.

Contact: Gail Brady, Scholarship Committee Chairperson
National Association of Water Companies-New Jersey Chapter
49 Howell Drive
Verona, NJ 07044
Phone: 973-669-5807
E-mail: gbradygbconsult@verizon.net

NATIONAL SOCIETY OF ACCOUNTANTS
http://www.nsacct.org/

NATIONAL SOCIETY OF ACCOUNTANTS SCHOLARSHIP
One-time award of $500 to $1000 available to undergraduate students. Applicants must maintain a 3.0 GPA and have declared a major in accounting. Must submit an appraisal form and transcripts in addition to application. Must be U.S. or Canadian citizen attending an accredited U.S. school.

Academic Fields/Career Goals: Accounting.

Award: Scholarship for use in freshman, sophomore, junior, or senior years; not renewable. *Number:* up to 40. *Amount:* $500–$1000.

Eligibility Requirements: Applicant must be enrolled or expecting to enroll full- or part-time at a two-year or four-year institution or university. Applicant must have 3.0 GPA or higher. Available to U.S. and Canadian citizens.

Application Requirements: Application form, appraisal form, financial need analysis, transcript. *Deadline:* March 10.

Contact: Susan Noell, Director of Education Programs
National Society of Accountants
1010 North Fairfax Street
Alexandria, VA 22314-1574
Phone: 703-549-6400 Ext. 1312
Fax: 703-549-2984 Ext. 1312
E-mail: snoell@nsacct.org

STANLEY H. STEARMAN SCHOLARSHIP
One award for accounting major who is a relative of an active, retired, or deceased member of National Society of Accountants. Must be citizen of the United States or Canada and attend school in the United States. Minimum GPA of 3.0 required. Not available for freshman year. Submit application, appraisal form, and letter of intent.

Academic Fields/Career Goals: Accounting.

Award: Scholarship for use in freshman, sophomore, junior, senior, or graduate years; renewable. *Number:* 1. *Amount:* up to $2000.

Eligibility Requirements: Applicant must be enrolled or expecting to enroll full- or part-time at a two-year or four-year institution or university. Applicant or parent of applicant must be member of National Society of Accountants. Applicant must have 3.0 GPA or higher. Available to U.S. and Canadian citizens.

Application Requirements: Application form, appraisal form, essay, financial need analysis, transcript. *Deadline:* March 10.

Contact: Sally Brasse, Director of Education Programs
National Society of Accountants
1010 North Fairfax Street
Alexandria, VA 22314-1574
Phone: 703-549-6400 Ext. 1307
Fax: 703-549-2984
E-mail: sbrasse@nsacct.org

NC CPA FOUNDATION INC.

http://www.ncacpa.org/ncacpa-foundation/

NORTH CAROLINA ASSOCIATION OF CPAS FOUNDATION SCHOLARSHIPS

Scholarship available for North Carolina residents enrolled in a program leading to a degree in accounting or its equivalent in a North Carolina college or university. Must have completed at least one college or university level accounting course and have completed at least 36 semester hours (or equivalent) by the start of the spring semester of the year of application. The applicant must be sponsored by one accounting faculty members. Application and information at http://csbapp.csb.uncw.edu/nccpa.

Academic Fields/Career Goals: Accounting.

Award: Scholarship for use in sophomore, junior, senior, or graduate years; not renewable. *Number:* 50–60. *Amount:* $1000–$5000.

Eligibility Requirements: Applicant must be enrolled or expecting to enroll full- or part-time at a two-year or four-year institution or university; resident of North Carolina and studying in North Carolina. Applicant must have 3.0 GPA or higher. Available to U.S. citizens.

Application Requirements: Application form, application form may be submitted online (http://www.ncacpa.org/Member_Connections/Students/Foundation.aspx), essay, transcript. *Deadline:* February 10.

Contact: Mr. Jim Ahler, Chief Executive Officer
NC CPA Foundation Inc.
PO Box 80188
Raleigh, NC 27623
Phone: 919-469-1040 Ext. 130
E-mail: jtahler@ncacpa.org

NEBRASKA SOCIETY OF CERTIFIED PUBLIC ACCOUNTANTS

http://www.nescpa.org/

THE FOUNDATION OF THE NEBRASKA SOCIETY OF CERTIFIED PUBLIC ACCOUNTANTS FIFTH-YEAR SCHOLARSHIP AWARDS

The scholarship is for accounting majors who have completed their junior year and are enrolled in a fifth-year (150-hour) program at a Nebraska college or university; accounting students who plan to sit for the CPA exam; accounting students who have the interest and capabilities of becoming a successful accountant and who are considering an accounting career in Nebraska. When candidates are reviewed, scholarship, personality, leadership and character should be considered by the accounting instructional staff at each college or university.

Academic Fields/Career Goals: Accounting.

Award: Scholarship for use in senior or graduate years; not renewable. *Number:* 1–25. *Amount:* $1500–$2500.

Eligibility Requirements: Applicant must be enrolled or expecting to enroll full-time at a four-year institution or university and studying in Nebraska. Available to U.S. citizens.

Application Requirements: Application form, letter(s) of recommendation, recommendations or references, resume, transcript. *Deadline:* April 1.

Contact: Trudy Meyer, Executive Vice President
Nebraska Society of Certified Public Accountants
635 South 14th Street
Lincoln, NE 68508
Phone: 402-476-8482
Fax: 402-476-8731
E-mail: tmeyer@nescpa.org

NEBRASKA SOCIETY OF CPAS GENERAL ACCOUNTING SCHOLARSHIP

Scholarship awards are presented to accounting students who have completed their junior year; accounting majors who plan to sit for the CPA exam; students who have the interest and capabilities of becoming a successful accountant and who are considering an accounting career in Nebraska are to be considered. Recipients need not necessarily have the highest scholastic average.

Academic Fields/Career Goals: Accounting.

Award: Scholarship for use in senior year; not renewable. *Number:* 30–40. *Amount:* $1000–$1500.

Eligibility Requirements: Applicant must be enrolled or expecting to enroll full-time at a four-year institution or university. Available to U.S. citizens.

Application Requirements: Application form, nomination letter. *Deadline:* August 1.

Contact: Trudy Meyer, Executive Vice President
Nebraska Society of Certified Public Accountants
635 South 14th Street
Lincoln, NE 68508
Phone: 402-476-8482
Fax: 402-476-8731
E-mail: tmeyer@nescpa.org

NEW ENGLAND EMPLOYEE BENEFITS COUNCIL

http://www.neebc.org/

NEW ENGLAND EMPLOYEE BENEFITS COUNCIL SCHOLARSHIP PROGRAM

Renewable award designed to encourage undergraduate or graduate students to pursue a course of study leading to a Bachelor's degree or higher in the employee benefits field. Must be a resident of/or studying in Maine, Massachusetts, New Hampshire, Rhode Island, Connecticut or Vermont. Must have demonstrated interest in the fields of employee benefits, human resources, business law.

Academic Fields/Career Goals: Accounting; Business/Consumer Services; Economics; Health Administration; Human Resources; Insurance and Actuarial Science; Law/Legal Services; Public Health; Public Policy and Administration.

Award: Scholarship for use in freshman, sophomore, junior, or senior years; renewable. *Number:* 1–3. *Amount:* $1000–$5000.

Eligibility Requirements: Applicant must be enrolled or expecting to enroll full- or part-time at a four-year institution or university; resident of Connecticut, Maine, Massachusetts, New Hampshire, Rhode Island, Vermont and studying in Connecticut, Maine, Massachusetts, New Hampshire, Rhode Island, Vermont. Available to U.S. citizens.

Application Requirements: Application form, essay, recommendations or references, transcript. *Deadline:* April 1.

Contact: Linda Viens, Manager of Operations and Member Services
New England Employee Benefits Council
NEEBC
240 Bear Hill Road
Waltham, MA 02451
Phone: 781-684-8700
Fax: 781-684-9200
E-mail: linda@neebc.org

NEW HAMPSHIRE SOCIETY OF CERTIFIED PUBLIC ACCOUNTANTS

http://www.nhscpa.org/

NEW HAMPSHIRE SOCIETY OF CERTIFIED PUBLIC ACCOUNTANTS SCHOLARSHIP FUND

Applicant must be a U.S. citizen, a New Hampshire resident, and an accounting or business major entering their senior year at an accredited four-year college or university; a graduate student pursuing a Master's degree in accounting or business in an accredited program; or those seeking the additional 30 hours of education to become eligible for a CPA license in New Hampshire. Must be recommended by a teacher or person responsible for the accounting or business program where the applicant is presently enrolled. Complete and return the application provided by the

New Hampshire Society of Certified Public Accountants by the due date. Must have at least 90 credits or have senior-standing. Must have taken at least 3 courses of upper level accounting courses which would exclude introductory financial and managerial classes or the first 6 credits in accounting courses.

Academic Fields/Career Goals: Accounting.

Award: Scholarship for use in senior or graduate years; not renewable. *Number:* 1–7. *Amount:* $500–$2500.

Eligibility Requirements: Applicant must be enrolled or expecting to enroll full-time at a four-year institution or university and resident of New Hampshire. Available to U.S. citizens.

Application Requirements: Application form, recommendations or references, transcript. *Deadline:* November 30.

Contact: Roberta Daly, CPE and Events Manager
Phone: 603-622-1999 Ext. 201

NEW JERSEY SOCIETY OF CERTIFIED PUBLIC ACCOUNTANTS

http://www.njscpa.org/

NEW JERSEY SOCIETY OF CERTIFIED PUBLIC ACCOUNTANTS COLLEGE SCHOLARSHIP PROGRAM

Award for college juniors or those entering an accounting-related graduate program. Must be a New Jersey resident attending a four-year New Jersey institution. Must be nominated by accounting department chair or submit application directly. Minimum 3.2 GPA required. Award values at $5,500

Academic Fields/Career Goals: Accounting.

Award: Scholarship for use in junior or senior years; not renewable. *Number:* 40–50. *Amount:* $5500.

Eligibility Requirements: Applicant must be enrolled or expecting to enroll full- or part-time at a four-year institution or university; resident of New Jersey and studying in New Jersey. Applicant must have 3.0 GPA or higher. Available to U.S. citizens.

Application Requirements: Application form, essay, interview, recommendations or references, resume, transcript. *Deadline:* January 12.

Contact: Ms. Lauren Matullo, Membership Coordinator, NextGen Outreach
New Jersey Society of Certified Public Accountants
425 Eagle Rock Avenue, Suite 100
Roseland, NJ 07068-1723
Phone: 973-226-4494 Ext. 241
Fax: 973-226-7425
E-mail: lmatullo@njscpa.org

NEW JERSEY SOCIETY OF CERTIFIED PUBLIC ACCOUNTANTS HIGH SCHOOL SCHOLARSHIP PROGRAM

Renewable scholarship of $7000 to $9000 for New Jersey high school seniors who wish to pursue a degree in accounting. Must be resident of New Jersey. Deadline is in December.

Academic Fields/Career Goals: Accounting.

Award: Scholarship for use in freshman, sophomore, junior, or senior years; renewable. *Number:* 20–25. *Amount:* $7000–$9000.

Eligibility Requirements: Applicant must be high school student; planning to enroll or expecting to enroll full-time at a four-year institution or university and resident of New Jersey. Applicant must have 3.0 GPA or higher. Available to U.S. citizens.

Application Requirements: Application form, application form may be submitted online (http://www.njscpa.org/scholarship), essay, interview, test scores, transcript. *Deadline:* December 27.

Contact: Ms. Lauren Matullo, Membership Coordinator, NextGen Outreach
New Jersey Society of Certified Public Accountants
425 Eagle Rock Avenue, Suite 100
Roseland, NJ 07068-1723
Phone: 973-226-4494 Ext. 241
Fax: 973-226-7425
E-mail: lmatullo@njscpa.org

NEW YORK STATE SOCIETY OF CERTIFIED PUBLIC ACCOUNTANTS FOUNDATION FOR ACCOUNTING EDUCATION

http://www.nysscpa.org/page/future-cpas/college-students

FOUNDATION FOR ACCOUNTING EDUCATION SCHOLARSHIP

Awards up to $500 to $2500 scholarships to college students to encourage them to pursue a career in accounting. Must be a New York resident studying in New York and maintaining a 3.0 GPA.

Academic Fields/Career Goals: Accounting.

Award: Scholarship for use in junior, senior, or graduate years; not renewable. *Number:* 1–60. *Amount:* $500–$2500.

Eligibility Requirements: Applicant must be enrolled or expecting to enroll full- or part-time at a four-year institution or university; resident of New York and studying in New York. Applicant must have 3.0 GPA or higher. Available to U.S. citizens.

Application Requirements: Application form, application form may be submitted online (http://www.nysscpa.org), essay, financial need analysis, recommendations or references, transcript. *Deadline:* April 1.

Contact: Ms. Lisa Axisa, Associate Director, Recruitment and Retention
New York State Society of Certified Public Accountants
Foundation for Accounting Education
3 Park Avenue, 18th Floor
New York, NY 10016
Phone: 212-719-8362
E-mail: laxisa@nysspca.org

OREGON ASSOCIATION OF PUBLIC ACCOUNTANTS SCHOLARSHIP FOUNDATION

http://www.oaia.net/

OAIA SCHOLARSHIP

Scholarships of $1000 to $2000 are awarded to full-time students. Must be a resident of the state of Oregon and major in accounting studies at an accredited school in the state of Oregon. The scholarship may be used for tuition, fees, books or other academic expenses incurred during the term.

Academic Fields/Career Goals: Accounting.

Award: Scholarship for use in freshman, sophomore, junior, or senior years; not renewable. *Number:* 5. *Amount:* $1000–$2000.

Eligibility Requirements: Applicant must be enrolled or expecting to enroll full-time at a two-year or four-year institution or university; resident of Oregon and studying in Oregon. Available to U.S. citizens.

Application Requirements: Application form, financial need analysis. *Deadline:* April 1.

Contact: Sue Robertson, Treasurer
Oregon Association of Public Accountants Scholarship Foundation
1804 NE 43rd Ave.
Portland, OR 97213
Phone: 503-282-7247
E-mail: srobertson4oaia@aol.com

OSCPA EDUCATIONAL FOUNDATION

http://www.orcpa.org/

OSCPA EDUCATIONAL FOUNDATION SCHOLARSHIP PROGRAM

One-time award for students majoring in accounting. Must attend an accredited Oregon college/university or community college on full-time basis. College students must have a minimum 3.2 GPA. Must be a U.S. citizen and Oregon resident.

Academic Fields/Career Goals: Accounting.

Award: Scholarship for use in freshman, sophomore, junior, senior, or graduate years; not renewable. *Number:* 50–100. *Amount:* $500–$3000.

Eligibility Requirements: Applicant must be enrolled or expecting to enroll full-time at a two-year or four-year or technical institution or university; resident of Oregon and studying in Oregon. Available to U.S. citizens.

Application Requirements: Application form, application form may be submitted online (https://app.smarterselect.com/programs/11479-The-Oscpa-Educational-Foundation), recommendations or references, transcript. *Deadline:* January 24.

Contact: Tonna Hollis, Senior Manager - Member Services & Professional Development
OSCPA Educational Foundation
PO Box 4555
Beaverton, OR 97076-4555
Phone: 503-641-7200 Ext. 29
Fax: 503-626-2942
E-mail: thollis@orcpa.org

PENNSYLVANIA INSTITUTE OF CERTIFIED PUBLIC ACCOUNTANTS

http://www.cpazone.org/

PENNSYLVANIA INSTITUTE OF CERTIFIED PUBLIC ACCOUNTANTS SOPHOMORE SCHOLARSHIP

To promote the accounting profession and CPA credential as an exciting and rewarding career path. Scholarship amounts range from $1000 to $15,000 and can be renewed annually until you graduate. Candidates must have completed a 36 credit hours and have a minimum 3.0 GPA.

Academic Fields/Career Goals: Accounting.

Award: Scholarship for use in sophomore, junior, senior, graduate, or postgraduate years; renewable. *Number:* 60–85. *Amount:* $1000–$15,000.

Eligibility Requirements: Applicant must be enrolled or expecting to enroll full-time at a four-year institution or university; resident of Pennsylvania and studying in Pennsylvania. Applicant must have 3.0 GPA or higher. Available to U.S. and non-U.S. citizens.

Application Requirements: Application form, essay, recommendations or references, resume, transcript. *Deadline:* March 10.

Contact: Scholarship Committee
Pennsylvania Institute of Certified Public Accountants
1650 Arch Street, 17th Floor
Philadelphia, PA 19103
E-mail: schools@picpa.org

RHODE ISLAND FOUNDATION

http://www.rifoundation.org/

CARL W. CHRISTIANSEN SCHOLARSHIP

$1000 scholarship for Rhode Island residents pursuing full-time study in accounting or related fields. Must maintain a minimum 3.0 GPA.

Academic Fields/Career Goals: Accounting.

Award: Scholarship for use in freshman, sophomore, junior, senior, or graduate years; not renewable. *Amount:* $1000.

Eligibility Requirements: Applicant must be enrolled or expecting to enroll full-time at a two-year or four-year institution or university and resident of Rhode Island. Applicant must have 3.0 GPA or higher. Available to U.S. citizens.

Application Requirements: Application form. *Deadline:* January 11.

Contact: Denise Jacobson
E-mail: djacobson@riscpa.org

CHERYL A. RUGGIERO SCHOLARSHIP

Award for female Rhode Island residents pursuing full-time study in public accounting. Must maintain a minimum 3.0 GPA.

Academic Fields/Career Goals: Accounting.

Award: Scholarship for use in freshman, sophomore, junior, senior, or graduate years; not renewable. *Amount:* $1000.

Eligibility Requirements: Applicant must be enrolled or expecting to enroll full-time at a two-year or four-year institution or university; female and resident of Rhode Island. Applicant must have 3.0 GPA or higher. Available to U.S. citizens.

Application Requirements: Application form, essay, interview, proof of U.S. citizenship, proof of RI residency, recommendations or references, transcript. *Deadline:* January 11.

Contact: Denise Jacobson
E-mail: djacobson@riscpa.org

RHODE ISLAND SOCIETY OF CERTIFIED PUBLIC ACCOUNTANTS

http://www.riscpa.org/

RHODE ISLAND SOCIETY OF CERTIFIED PUBLIC ACCOUNTANTS SCHOLARSHIP

Annual scholarship for graduates and undergraduates majoring in accounting, who are legal residents of Rhode Island and U.S. citizens. Must have interest in a career in public accounting, and submit one-page memo outlining that interest. Minimum GPA of 3.0 required. For more information, see website http://www.riscpa.org.

Academic Fields/Career Goals: Accounting.

Award: Scholarship for use in freshman, sophomore, junior, senior, or graduate years; not renewable.

Eligibility Requirements: Applicant must be enrolled or expecting to enroll full-time at a four-year institution or university and resident of Rhode Island. Applicant must have 3.0 GPA or higher. Available to U.S. citizens.

Application Requirements: Application form, recommendations or references, resume, test scores, transcript. *Deadline:* January 15.

Contact: Robert Mancini, Executive Director
Phone: 401-331-5720
Fax: 401-454-5780
E-mail: rmancini@riscpa.org

RISK MANAGEMENT ASSOCIATION FOUNDATION

www.scholarshipamerica.org

RISK MANAGEMENT ASSOCIATION FOUNDATION SCHOLARSHIP PROGRAM

40 awards of up to $5,000 are renewable up to two years or until a Bachelor's degree is earned, whichever occurs first. Renewal is contingent upon maintaining a 3.0 GPA, full-time enrollment, continuing to major in eligible field of study, maintaining free RMA student membership, and confirming desire to work in the banking industry. The Risk Management Association (RMA) Foundation scholarship program is awarding up to $200,000 in renewable scholarships ranging from $2,000 to $5,000 each, to current undergraduates interested in pursuing a career in the banking industry. To be eligible, students must be a citizen or permanent resident of the U.S. or Canada, have completed a minimum of two years of college and be pursuing a degree in accounting, business, finance, economics, banking or a related area of study. All applicants must be currently enrolled full-time at an accredited four-year college or university in the U.S. or Canada and have a minimum grade point average (GPA) of 3.0 on a 4.0 scale overall and within business core courses. Applicants do not have to be a current RMA member, but they must join (free) and remain a member to receive and renew their scholarship. Applicable majors: accounting, business, finance, economics, banking, or related area of study. Website: https://www.scholarsapply.org/rma/

Academic Fields/Career Goals: Accounting; Agriculture; Economics; Finance.

Award: Scholarship for use in junior or senior years; renewable. *Number:* 40. *Amount:* $2000–$5000.

Eligibility Requirements: Applicant must be enrolled or expecting to enroll full-time at a four-year institution. Applicant must have 3.0 GPA or higher. Available to U.S. and Canadian citizens.

Application Requirements: Application form. *Deadline:* November 13.

Contact: Program Manager
Risk Management Association Foundation
One Scholarship Way
Saint Peter, MN 56082
Phone: 800-537-4180
E-mail: rma@scholarshipamerica.org

SCARLETT FAMILY FOUNDATION SCHOLARSHIP PROGRAM

http://www.scarlettfoundation.org/

SCHOLARSHIP FOR STUDENTS PURSUING A BUSINESS OR STEM DEGREE

Each year, the Scarlett Family Foundation will award scholarships in varying amounts based on financial need and merit that is directly tied to the cost of the college the student attends. The minimum scholarship award is $2,500 per academic year. The maximum award is $15,000 per academic year. The scholarship is applied to tuition, books and fees. Scholarships are renewable awards for up to 4 years or until the recipient completes their undergraduate degree, whichever comes first. The scholarships are open to high school seniors and college freshmen, sophomores, and juniors who will graduate or have graduated from a public, independent or homeschool association high school in 40 Middle Tennessee counties. Also eligible are individuals who have obtained a GED.

Academic Fields/Career Goals: Accounting; Advertising/Public Relations; Agribusiness; Agriculture; Animal/Veterinary Sciences; Applied Sciences; Archaeology; Architecture; Audiology; Aviation/Aerospace; Biology; Business/Consumer Services; Chemical Engineering; Civil Engineering; Computer Science/Data Processing; Dental Health/Services; Earth Science; Economics; Electrical Engineering/Electronics; Energy and Power Engineering; Engineering-Related Technologies; Engineering/Technology; Environmental Science; Finance; Food Science/Nutrition; Geography; Health Administration; Health and Medical Sciences; Health Information Management/Technology; Hospitality Management; Human Resources; Insurance and Actuarial Science; Marine Biology; Marine/Ocean Engineering; Marketing; Materials Science, Engineering, and Metallurgy; Mathematics; Mechanical Engineering; Meteorology/Atmospheric Science; Natural Sciences; Neurobiology; Nuclear Science; Nursing; Oceanography; Oncology; Optometry; Osteopathy; Pharmacy; Physical Sciences; Sports-Related/Exercise Science; Therapy/Rehabilitation.

Award: Scholarship for use in freshman, sophomore, junior, or senior years; renewable. *Number:* 35–120. *Amount:* $2500–$15,000.

Eligibility Requirements: Applicant must be enrolled or expecting to enroll full-time at a four-year institution or university and resident of Tennessee. Applicant must have 2.5 GPA or higher. Available to U.S. citizens.

Application Requirements: Application form, driver's license, essay, financial need analysis. *Deadline:* December 15.

Contact: Tom Parrish, Chief Operating Officer
Scarlett Family Foundation Scholarship Program
4117 Hillsboro Pike
Suite 10255
Nashville, TN 37215
E-mail: TomParrish@ScarlettFoundation.org

SOCIETY OF AUTOMOTIVE ANALYSTS

http://saaauto.com/

SOCIETY OF AUTOMOTIVE ANALYSTS SCHOLARSHIP

A scholarship of $1500 awarded to students in economics, finance, business administration or marketing management. Minimum 3.0 GPA required. Must submit two letters of recommendation.

Academic Fields/Career Goals: Accounting; Business/Consumer Services; Economics.

Award: Scholarship for use in freshman, sophomore, junior, or senior years; not renewable. *Number:* 2. *Amount:* $1500.

Eligibility Requirements: Applicant must be enrolled or expecting to enroll full-time at a two-year or four-year or technical institution or university. Applicant must have 3.0 GPA or higher. Available to U.S. and non-U.S. citizens.

Application Requirements: Application form, recommendations or references, transcript. *Deadline:* June 1.

Contact: Lynne Hall, Awards and Scholarships
Phone: 313-240-4000
Fax: 313-240-8641

SOCIETY OF LOUISIANA CERTIFIED PUBLIC ACCOUNTANTS

http://www.lcpa.org/

SOCIETY OF LOUISIANA CPAS SCHOLARSHIPS

One-time award for accounting majors. Applicant must be a Louisiana resident attending a four-year college or university in Louisiana. For full-time undergraduates entering their junior or senior year, or full-time graduate students. Minimum 2.5 GPA required. Deadline varies. Must be U.S. citizen.

Academic Fields/Career Goals: Accounting.

Award: Scholarship for use in junior, senior, or graduate years; not renewable. *Amount:* $500–$3000.

Eligibility Requirements: Applicant must be enrolled or expecting to enroll full-time at a four-year institution or university; resident of Louisiana and studying in Louisiana. Applicant must have 2.5 GPA or higher. Available to U.S. citizens.

Application Requirements: Application form, essay, recommendations or references, transcript. *Deadline:* varies.

Contact: Lisa Richardson, Member Services Manager
Society of Louisiana Certified Public Accountants
2400 Veterans Boulevard, Suite 500
Kenner, LA 70062-4739
Phone: 504-904-1139
Fax: 504-469-7930
E-mail: lrichardson@lcpa.org

SOUTH CAROLINA ASSOCIATION OF CERTIFIED PUBLIC ACCOUNTANTS

http://www.scacpa.org

SCACPA EDUCATIONAL FUND SCHOLARSHIPS

These scholarships are awarded to South Carolina residents who are rising juniors or seniors majoring in accounting, or master's degree students at a South Carolina college or university. Applicants must have a GPA of no less than 3.25 overall and a GPA in accounting no less than 3.5 (on a 4.0 scale).

Academic Fields/Career Goals: Accounting.

Award: Scholarship for use in junior, senior, or graduate years; not renewable. *Number:* 19–25. *Amount:* $500–$2500.

Eligibility Requirements: Applicant must be enrolled or expecting to enroll full-time at a four-year institution or university; resident of South Carolina and studying in South Carolina. Applicant must have 3.0 GPA or higher. Available to U.S. citizens.

Application Requirements: Application form, essay, financial need analysis, recommendations or references, resume, transcript. *Deadline:* June 1.

Contact: Mrs. Maureen Taylor, Director of Marketing and Member Services
South Carolina Association of Certified Public Accountants
1300 12th Street, Suite D
Cayce, SC 29033
Phone: 803-791-4181 Ext. 105
Fax: 803-791-4196
E-mail: mtaylor@scacpa.org

SOUTH DAKOTA CPA SOCIETY

http://www.sdcpa.org/

5TH YEAR FULL TUITION SCHOLARSHIP

Scholarship pays for the full tuition up to $7,500 for a South Dakota student to attend an accredited South Dakota college or university. If awarded the scholarship, the student must become a member of the SD CPA Society, work for or be supervised by a member of the SD CPA Society for 2 years, and upon eligibility, must sit for a minimum of 4 parts of the CPA exam per year for two years or until completed.

Academic Fields/Career Goals: Accounting.

Award: Scholarship for use in senior or graduate years; not renewable. *Number:* 1–2. *Amount:* $7500.

Eligibility Requirements: Applicant must be enrolled or expecting to enroll full-time at a four-year institution or university and studying in

South Dakota. Applicant must have 3.0 GPA or higher. Available to U.S. citizens.

Application Requirements: Application form, essay. *Deadline:* April 30.

Contact: Laura Coome, Executive Director
South Dakota CPA Society
5024 S Bur Oak Pl #108
Sioux Falls, SD 57108
Phone: 605-334-3848
E-mail: laura@sdcpa.org

EXCELLENCE IN ACCOUNTING SCHOLARSHIP

Scholarships available for senior undergraduate and graduate students majoring in accounting. Must have completed 90 credit hours, demonstrated excellence in academics and leadership potential. Application available online at http://www.sdcpa.org.

Academic Fields/Career Goals: Accounting.

Award: Scholarship for use in senior or graduate years; not renewable. *Number:* 5–10. *Amount:* $1000.

Eligibility Requirements: Applicant must be enrolled or expecting to enroll full-time at a four-year institution or university and studying in South Dakota. Applicant must have 3.0 GPA or higher. Available to U.S. citizens.

Application Requirements: Application form. *Deadline:* April 30.

Contact: Laura Coome, Executive Director
South Dakota CPA Society
5024 S Bur Oak Pl #108
Sioux Falls, SD 57108
Phone: 605-334-3848
E-mail: laura@sdcpa.org

SPECIALTY EQUIPMENT MARKET ASSOCIATION

http://www.sema.org/

SEMA MEMORIAL SCHOLARSHIP FUND

Scholarships for college students pursuing careers in or related to the automotive industry. All applicants must be U.S. citizens who are currently attending U.S. institutions. Minimum 2.5 GPA required. For more information and to apply, please visit: http://www.SEMA.org/scholarships.

Academic Fields/Career Goals: Accounting; Advertising/Public Relations; Business/Consumer Services; Communications; Computer Science/Data Processing; Electrical Engineering/Electronics; Engineering/Technology; Finance; Marketing; Mechanical Engineering; Trade/Technical Specialties; Transportation.

Award: Scholarship for use in junior, senior, graduate, or postgraduate years; not renewable. *Number:* 50–60. *Amount:* $2000–$5000.

Eligibility Requirements: Applicant must be enrolled or expecting to enroll full-time at a two-year or four-year or technical institution or university and must have an interest in automotive. Applicant must have 2.5 GPA or higher. Available to U.S. citizens.

Application Requirements: Application form, essay. *Deadline:* March 1.

Contact: Ms. Juliet Marshall, Education Manager
Phone: 909-978-6655
Fax: 909-860-0184
E-mail: julietm@sema.org

TENNESSEE SOCIETY OF CPAS

http://www.tscpa.com/

TENNESSEE SOCIETY OF CPA SCHOLARSHIP

Scholarships are available only to full-time students who have completed introductory courses in accounting and/or students majoring in accounting. Applicants must be legal residents of Tennessee.

Academic Fields/Career Goals: Accounting.

Award: Scholarship for use in freshman, sophomore, junior, senior, or graduate years; not renewable. *Number:* 120–130. *Amount:* $250–$2500.

Eligibility Requirements: Applicant must be enrolled or expecting to enroll full-time at a four-year institution or university and resident of Tennessee. Available to U.S. citizens.

Application Requirements: Application form, financial need analysis, recommendations or references, transcript. *Deadline:* June 1.

Contact: Wendy Garvin, Member Services Manager
Phone: 615-377-3825
Fax: 390-377-3904
E-mail: wgarvin@tscpa.com

TKE EDUCATIONAL FOUNDATION

http://www.tke.org/

HARRY J. DONNELLY MEMORIAL SCHOLARSHIP

One-time award of $500 given to a member of Tau Kappa Epsilon pursuing an undergraduate degree in accounting or a graduate degree in law. Applicant should have demonstrated leadership ability within his chapter, campus, or community. Minimum 3.0 GPA required.

Academic Fields/Career Goals: Accounting; Law/Legal Services.

Award: Scholarship for use in sophomore, junior, senior, or graduate years; not renewable. *Number:* 1. *Amount:* $500.

Eligibility Requirements: Applicant must be enrolled or expecting to enroll full-time at a four-year institution or university; male and must have an interest in leadership. Applicant or parent of applicant must be member of Tau Kappa Epsilon. Applicant must have 3.0 GPA or higher. Available to U.S. and non-U.S. citizens.

Application Requirements: Application form, application form may be submitted online (http://www.tke.org/member_resources/scholarships/apply_online), essay, narrative summary of how TKE membership has benefited applicant, personal photograph, transcript. *Deadline:* March 15.

Contact: Offices of the Grand Chapter
TKE Educational Foundation
7439 Woodland Drive, Suite 100
Indianapolis, IN 46278
E-mail: tkeogc@tke.org

TRANSTUTORS

http://www.transtutors.com/scholarship

TRANSTUTORS SCHOLARSHIP 2015-16

Transtutors scholarship program wants to help students get aids for their studies. We really value good education for all. We have a very simple criteria of writing an essay on your college experience, how do you see it changing and what can be done so that you get best experience.

Academic Fields/Career Goals: Accounting; Biology; Chemical Engineering; Civil Engineering; Computer Science/Data Processing; Economics; Education; Electrical Engineering/Electronics; Energy and Power Engineering; Engineering-Related Technologies; Engineering/Technology; Environmental Health; Environmental Science; Finance; Industrial Design; Marketing; Mathematics; Mechanical Engineering; Statistics.

Award: Scholarship for use in freshman, sophomore, junior, senior, graduate, or postgraduate years; renewable. *Number:* 1. *Amount:* $10,000.

Eligibility Requirements: Applicant must be American Indian/Alaska Native, Asian/Pacific Islander, Black (non-Hispanic), Hispanic; age 18-30 and enrolled or expecting to enroll full- or part-time at a two-year or four-year institution or university. Available to U.S. and non-U.S. citizens.

Application Requirements: Essay, personal photograph. *Deadline:* June 30.

Contact: Aditya Singhal, Co-Founder
Transtutors
500startups
6th Floor Del Norte,
814 Mission Street
San Francisco, CA 94103
Phone: 415-619-1033
E-mail: aditya.singhal@transtutors.com

UNITED NEGRO COLLEGE FUND

http://www.uncf.org/

ANHEUSER-BUSCH LEGENDS OF THE CROWN SCHOLARSHIP PROGRAM

$5000 scholarship to a student leader entering their junior year of study at an accredited Historically Black College or University. Minimum 3.2 GPA required. Finalists must be available to attend a one-of-a-kind leadership seminar and community service project with Anheuser-Busch senior leaders in St. Louis, MO. Must have declared majors in the following disciplines: mechanical, electrical, industrial, or chemical engineering; computer science, chemistry, marketing, sales, accounting, finance, or supply chain and logistics. Preference to students with an interest in career within the Consumer Package Goods industry.

Academic Fields/Career Goals: Accounting; Chemical Engineering; Computer Science/Data Processing; Electrical Engineering/Electronics; Engineering/Technology; Finance; Marketing; Mechanical Engineering; Physical Sciences.

Award: Scholarship for use in junior year; not renewable. *Amount:* $5000.

Eligibility Requirements: Applicant must be Black (non-Hispanic); enrolled or expecting to enroll full-time at a four-year institution or university and must have an interest in leadership. Applicant must have 3.0 GPA or higher. Available to U.S. citizens.

Application Requirements: Application form, essay. *Deadline:* April 30.

Contact: Mary Williams, Director of Outreach and Recruitment
Phone: 800-331-2244

BASF/ALFRED CHISHOLM ENDOWED MEMORIAL SCHOLARSHIP

Scholarship of up to $2000 for a student who has a relative employed by the BASF Corporation. Must attend an historically black college or university and have minimum GPA of 3.0. Eligible majors include accounting, biology, business, chemistry, computer science, electrical engineering, engineering, finance, mathematics, supply chain management, and logistics.

Academic Fields/Career Goals: Accounting; Biology; Business/Consumer Services; Computer Science/Data Processing; Electrical Engineering/Electronics; Engineering/Technology; Finance; Mathematics; Physical Sciences.

Award: Scholarship for use in sophomore, junior, or senior years; not renewable.

Eligibility Requirements: Applicant must be Black (non-Hispanic) and enrolled or expecting to enroll full- or part-time at a four-year institution or university. Applicant must have 3.0 GPA or higher. Available to U.S. citizens.

Application Requirements: Application form, essay. *Deadline:* December 18.

Contact: Mary Williams, Director of Outreach and Recruitment
Phone: 800-331-2244

COLGATE-PALMOLIVE CORPORATE SCHOLARS PROGRAM

scholarship and internship opportunities to African American students attending HBCUs, and are planning to pursue a career in supply chain management, engineering, or sales. The program selects interns to work at Colgate-Palmolive's Commercial (Sales & Marketing) OR its Global Supply Chain Division. The internship program includes: participation in a 4-day professional development Student Leadership Conference (SLC) prior to the start of their internship; 10-Week Summer internship at Colgate-Palmolive; scholarship at the beginning of the fall semester, following their summer internship, of up to $5000 (based on need).

Academic Fields/Career Goals: Accounting; Business/Consumer Services; Chemical Engineering; Computer Science/Data Processing; Economics; Electrical Engineering/Electronics; Engineering/Technology; Mechanical Engineering; Statistics.

Award: Scholarship for use in sophomore or junior years.

Eligibility Requirements: Applicant must be Black (non-Hispanic) and enrolled or expecting to enroll at a four-year institution or university. Applicant must have 3.0 GPA or higher. Available to U.S. citizens.

Application Requirements: Application form, financial need analysis. *Deadline:* November 13.

Contact: Mary Williams, Director of Outreach and Recruitment
Phone: 800-331-2244

CVS PHARMACY, INC. BUSINESS SCHOLARSHIPS

$5000 scholarship for an undergraduate or graduate student studying business or business-related fields. Must attend an accredited four year undergraduate or Master's level program and be a U.S. citizen or permanent legal resident. Minimum 3.0 GPA required. Must have demonstrated unmet financial need.

Academic Fields/Career Goals: Accounting; Business/Consumer Services; Finance; Human Resources.

Award: Scholarship for use in freshman, sophomore, junior, senior, or graduate years; not renewable. *Amount:* $5000.

Eligibility Requirements: Applicant must be Black (non-Hispanic) and enrolled or expecting to enroll full-time at a four-year institution or university. Applicant must have 3.0 GPA or higher. Available to U.S. citizens.

Application Requirements: Application form, essay, financial need analysis. *Deadline:* March 31.

Contact: Mary Williams, Director of Outreach and Recruitment
Phone: 800-331-2244

NASCAR BLACK HISTORY MONTH AWARDS

Up to $10,000 scholarship for students in undergraduate or master's program. Must major in business-related disciplines, communications, engineering, information technology or public relations.

Academic Fields/Career Goals: Accounting; Business/Consumer Services; Communications; Computer Science/Data Processing; Engineering/Technology; Marketing.

Award: Scholarship for use in freshman, sophomore, junior, senior, or graduate years.

Eligibility Requirements: Applicant must be Black (non-Hispanic) and enrolled or expecting to enroll full-time at a four-year institution or university. Applicant must have 3.0 GPA or higher. Available to U.S. citizens.

Application Requirements: Application form. *Deadline:* January 27.

Contact: Mary Williams, Director of Outreach and Recruitment
Phone: 800-331-2244

NATIONAL BLACK MCDONALD'S OWNERS ASSOCIATION HOSPITALITY SCHOLARS PROGRAM

Scholarship of up to $5000 for a student majoring in restaurant/hotel/hospitality management, accounting, business, or marketing as full-time students at an accredited Historically Black College or University (HBCU) that have an interest in hospitality management. Minimum 2.8 GPA required. Dependents of either McDonald's executives or NBMOA owners are ineligible for this opportunity as are former recipients of the NBMOA scholarship.

Academic Fields/Career Goals: Accounting; Business/Consumer Services; Food Service/Hospitality; Hospitality Management; Marketing.

Award: Scholarship for use in freshman, sophomore, or junior years; not renewable.

Eligibility Requirements: Applicant must be Black (non-Hispanic) and enrolled or expecting to enroll full-time at a two-year or four-year institution or university. Applicant must have 2.5 GPA or higher. Available to U.S. citizens.

Application Requirements: Application form. *Deadline:* June 30.

Contact: Mary Williams, Director of Outreach and Recruitment
Phone: 800-331-2244

RICOH SCHOLARSHIP PROGRAM

Up to $2500 scholarship for a college junior at an HBCU who is majoring in accounting, business, business operations, computer engineering, computer science, finance, information technology, mechanical engineering, or marketing. Must be a U.S. citizen or permanent legal resident; demonstrate leadership abilities through participation in community service, extracurricular or other activities, and/or work history; have an unmet financial need and have a minimum 2.5 GPA.

Academic Fields/Career Goals: Accounting; Business/Consumer Services; Engineering/Technology; Finance; Marketing.

Award: Scholarship for use in junior year; renewable.

Eligibility Requirements: Applicant must be Black (non-Hispanic); enrolled or expecting to enroll full-time at a four-year institution or university and must have an interest in leadership. Applicant must have 2.5 GPA or higher. Available to U.S. citizens.

Application Requirements: Application form, financial need analysis. *Deadline:* July 7.

Contact: Mary Williams, Director of Outreach and Recruitment
Phone: 800-331-2244

SUEZ CORPORATE SCHOLARS PROGRAM

$5000 scholarship and paid internship. Applicant must be college sophomore or junior at the time of application. Major in Accounting, Business Administration, Civil Engineering, Communications, Computer Science, Electrical Engineering, English, Environmental Engineering, Environmental Science(s), Health & Safety (Select Environmental Science), Finance, Human Resources, Marketing, Mechanical Engineering, Political Science, Pre-law or Sociology.

Academic Fields/Career Goals: Accounting; Business/Consumer Services; Civil Engineering; Communications; Computer Science/Data Processing; Electrical Engineering/Electronics; Environmental Science; Finance; Human Resources; Law/Legal Services; Marketing; Mechanical Engineering; Political Science; Social Sciences.

Award: Scholarship for use in sophomore, junior, or senior years. *Amount:* $5000.

Eligibility Requirements: Applicant must be Black (non-Hispanic) and enrolled or expecting to enroll at a four-year institution or university. Applicant must have 3.0 GPA or higher. Available to U.S. citizens.

Application Requirements: Application form. *Deadline:* February 28.

Contact: Mary Williams, Director of Outreach and Recruitment
Phone: 800-331-2244

UNCF/KOCH SCHOLARS PROGRAM FOR UNDERGRADUATES

Scholarships of up to $5,000 each available to African-American high school students planning to attend HBCU colleges and universities on a full-time basis. Must major in accounting, business, economics, engineering, history, philosophy, or political science. Minimum 2.7 GPA required. Must be committed to learning about how entrepreneurship, innovation, and economics contribute to well-being through participation in an online community and Annual Summit.

Academic Fields/Career Goals: Accounting; Business/Consumer Services; Economics; Engineering/Technology; History; Philosophy; Political Science.

Award: Scholarship for use in freshman year; not renewable. *Number:* 200.

Eligibility Requirements: Applicant must be Black (non-Hispanic); high school student and planning to enroll or expecting to enroll full-time at a four-year institution or university. Applicant must have 2.5 GPA or higher. Available to U.S. citizens.

Application Requirements: Application form, financial need analysis. *Deadline:* April 1.

Contact: Mary Williams, Director of Outreach and Recruitment
Phone: 800-331-2244

VIRCHOW, KRAUSE & COMPANY, LLP

http://www.virchowkrause.com/

VIRCHOW, KRAUSE AND COMPANY SCHOLARSHIP

One-time scholarship for students enrolled either full-time or part-time in accredited colleges or universities of Wisconsin, majoring in accounting.

Academic Fields/Career Goals: Accounting.

Award: Scholarship for use in freshman, sophomore, junior, or senior years; not renewable. *Number:* up to 3. *Amount:* up to $1000.

Eligibility Requirements: Applicant must be enrolled or expecting to enroll full- or part-time at a two-year or four-year institution or university and studying in Wisconsin. Available to U.S. citizens.

Application Requirements: Application form, transcript. *Deadline:* varies.

Contact: Darbie Miller, Human Resources Coordinator
Virchow, Krause & Company, LLP
4600 American Parkway, PO Box 7398
Madison, WI 53707-7398
Phone: 608-240-2474
Fax: 608-249-1411
E-mail: dmiller@virchowkrause.com

VIRGINIA SOCIETY OF CERTIFIED PUBLIC ACCOUNTANTS EDUCATIONAL FOUNDATION

http://www.vscpa.com/

VSCPA EDUCATIONAL FOUNDATION ACCOUNTING SCHOLARSHIPS

All applicants must be U.S. citizens; successfully complete 3 credit hours of accounting prior to the fall semester; be currently enrolled in an accredited Virginia college or university with the intent to pursue a degree in accounting; and enrollment in an accredited Virginia college or university accounting program in the fall semester.

Academic Fields/Career Goals: Accounting.

Award: Scholarship for use in sophomore, junior, senior, graduate, or postgraduate years; not renewable. *Number:* up to 26. *Amount:* $1000–$5000.

Eligibility Requirements: Applicant must be enrolled or expecting to enroll full- or part-time at a two-year or four-year institution or university; resident of Virginia and studying in Virginia. Applicant must have 2.5 GPA or higher. Available to U.S. citizens.

Application Requirements: Application form, application form may be submitted online (http://www.vscpa.com/Scholarships), essay, recommendations or references, resume, transcript. *Deadline:* April 1.

Contact: Tracey Zink, Academic and Career Development Coordinator
Phone: 800-612-9427
E-mail: tzink@vscpa.com

WYOMING TRUCKING ASSOCIATION SCHOLARSHIP FUND TRUST

http://www.wytruck.org/

WYOMING TRUCKING ASSOCIATION SCHOLARSHIP TRUST FUND

To qualify, students must (1) be a graduate of a Wyoming high school; (2) plan to pursue a course of study which will lead to a career in the Highway Transportation Industry with the following approved courses of study: business management, computer skills, accounting, office procedures and management, safety, diesel mechanics and truck driving; (3) attend a Wyoming school (University, Community College or trade school) approved by the WTA Scholarship Committee.

Academic Fields/Career Goals: Accounting; Business/Consumer Services; Communications; Computer Science/Data Processing; Marketing; Trade/Technical Specialties; Transportation.

Award: Scholarship for use in freshman, sophomore, junior, or senior years; not renewable. *Number:* 4–8. *Amount:* $500–$1500.

Eligibility Requirements: Applicant must be enrolled or expecting to enroll full-time at a two-year or four-year or technical institution or university; resident of Wyoming and studying in Wyoming. Available to U.S. citizens.

Application Requirements: Application form, community service, essay, financial need analysis. *Deadline:* March 5.

Contact: Kathy Cundall, Administrative Assistant
Phone: 307-234-1579
E-mail: khcundall@aol.com

ADVERTISING/PUBLIC RELATIONS

ASIAN AMERICAN JOURNALISTS ASSOCIATION, SEATTLE CHAPTER

http://www.aajaseattle.org/

NORTHWEST JOURNALISTS OF COLOR SCHOLARSHIP

One-time award for Washington state high school and college students seeking careers in journalism. Awardees are also paired with a mentor, expected to join AAJA, and participate in AAJA activities. The program also offers "The Founder's Scholarship," which pays for registration and airfare so a student may attend the AAJA National Convention.

Academic Fields/Career Goals: Advertising/Public Relations; Communications; Filmmaking/Video; Journalism; Photojournalism/Photography; TV/Radio Broadcasting.

Award: Scholarship for use in freshman, sophomore, junior, or senior years; not renewable. *Number:* 1–5. *Amount:* $250–$1000.

Eligibility Requirements: Applicant must be of African, Arab, Chinese, Hispanic, Indian, Japanese, Korean, Lao/Hmong, Latin American/Caribbean, Lebanese, Mexican, Mongolian, Sub-Saharan African, Syrian, Turkish, Vietnamese, Yemeni heritage; American Indian/Alaska Native, Asian/Pacific Islander, Black (non-Hispanic); enrolled or expecting to enroll full- or part-time at a two-year or four-year or technical institution or university and resident of Washington. Applicant or parent of applicant must have employment or volunteer experience in journalism/broadcasting. Available to U.S. citizens.

Application Requirements: Application form, community service, essay, financial need analysis. *Deadline:* May 1.

Contact: Ms. Mai Hoang, AAJA Chapter Treasurer
Asian American Journalists Association, Seattle Chapter
Yakima Herald–Republic
114 North Fourth Street
Yakima, WA 98909
Phone: 509-577-7724
E-mail: mhoang@yakimaherald.com

AUTOMOTIVE WOMEN'S ALLIANCE FOUNDATION

http://www.awafoundation.org/index.php

AUTOMOTIVE WOMEN'S ALLIANCE FOUNDATION SCHOLARSHIPS
• See page 74

DIGITAL THIRD COAST INTERNET MARKETING

http://www.digitalthirdcoast.net/

DIGITAL MARKETING SCHOLARSHIP

In a 500+ word essay, share how you think digital marketing will develop in the next five to ten years, and what you think the industry will be like when you're out of school and working in the marketing industry. You may focus on how one aspect of digital marketing will change, or you can address how each branch of digital marketing will grow to interact with the others.

Academic Fields/Career Goals: Advertising/Public Relations; Business/Consumer Services; Marketing.

Award: Scholarship for use in freshman, sophomore, junior, or senior years; not renewable. *Number:* 1. *Amount:* $500.

Eligibility Requirements: Applicant must be enrolled or expecting to enroll full-time at a four-year institution. Applicant must have 2.5 GPA or higher. Available to U.S. citizens.

Application Requirements: Application form may be submitted online (http://www.digitalthirdcoast.net/blog/dtc-digital-marketing-scholarship), essay, personal photograph. *Deadline:* March 1.

Contact: Barry Dyke, Account Manager
Digital Third Coast Internet Marketing
2035 West Wabansia Avenue
Chicago, IL 60647
Phone: 773-897-0572
E-mail: bdyke@digitalthirdcoast.net

FUKUNAGA SCHOLARSHIP FOUNDATION

http://fukunagascholarship.com

FUKUNAGA SCHOLARSHIP FOUNDATION
• See page 77

INTERNATIONAL FOODSERVICE EDITORIAL COUNCIL

http://www.ifeconline.com/

INTERNATIONAL FOODSERVICE EDITORIAL COUNCIL COMMUNICATIONS SCHOLARSHIP

Applicant must be a full-time student enrolled in an accredited postsecondary educational institution working toward an associate, bachelor's, or master's degree. Must demonstrate financial need, academic achievement, service orientation, and writing ability. Must have background, education, and interests indicating preparedness for entering careers in editorial or public relations within the foodservice industry.

Academic Fields/Career Goals: Advertising/Public Relations; Communications; Culinary Arts; Food Science/Nutrition; Food Service/Hospitality; Graphics/Graphic Arts/Printing; Home Economics; Hospitality Management; Journalism; Literature/English/Writing; Marketing; Photojournalism/Photography.

Award: Scholarship for use in sophomore, junior, senior, graduate, or postgraduate years; not renewable. *Number:* 1–8. *Amount:* $250–$6000.

Eligibility Requirements: Applicant must be enrolled or expecting to enroll full-time at a two-year or four-year or technical institution or university and must have an interest in photography/photogrammetry/filmmaking or writing. Available to U.S. and non-U.S. citizens.

Application Requirements: Application form, essay. *Deadline:* March 15.

Contact: Carol Lally, Executive Director
International Foodservice Editorial Council
PO Box 491
Hyde Park, NY 12538-0491
Phone: 845-229-6973
E-mail: ifec@ifeconline.com

LAGRANT FOUNDATION

http://www.lagrantfoundation.org/

LAGRANT FOUNDATION SCHOLARSHIP FOR UNDERGRADUATES

Awards are for undergraduate minority students who are attending accredited four-year institutions and are pursuing careers in the fields of advertising, marketing, and public relations. Must have at least one year to complete his/her degree from the time the scholarships are awarded. The applicant must make a one-year commitment to maintain contact with TLF to receive professional guidance and academic support. Minimum 2.75 GPA required.

Academic Fields/Career Goals: Advertising/Public Relations; Business/Consumer Services; Communications.

Award: Scholarship for use in freshman, sophomore, junior, or senior years; renewable. *Amount:* $2500.

Eligibility Requirements: Applicant must be American Indian/Alaska Native, Asian/Pacific Islander, Black (non-Hispanic), Hispanic and enrolled or expecting to enroll full-time at a four-year institution or university. Available to U.S. citizens.

Application Requirements: Application form, essay, recommendations or references, resume, transcript. *Deadline:* February 28.

Contact: Program Manager
LAGRANT Foundation
600 Wilshire Boulevard, Suite 1520
Los Angeles, CA 90017
Phone: 323-469-8680
Fax: 323-469-8683

NATIONAL ACADEMY OF TELEVISION ARTS AND SCIENCES, MICHIGAN CHAPTER

http://natasmichigan.org

DR. LYNNE BOYLE/JOHN SCHIMPF UNDERGRADUATE SCHOLARSHIP

This scholarship is for tuition for undergraduate school. Only Michigan residents are eligible for the scholarship. The university or college attended does not have to be a Michigan institution. Work submitted must be that done by the student which is representative of the students ability. Scholarships are awarded on the basis of merit. Student must be enrolled in a undergraduate program of an accredited 4-year college or university for their Junior and Senior years of study.

Academic Fields/Career Goals: Advertising/Public Relations; Communications; Filmmaking/Video; Journalism; Performing Arts; TV/Radio Broadcasting.

Award: Scholarship for use in junior or senior years; not renewable. *Number:* 1. *Amount:* $5000.

Eligibility Requirements: Applicant must be enrolled or expecting to enroll full- or part-time at a four-year institution or university and resident of Michigan. Applicant must have 3.0 GPA or higher. Available to U.S. citizens.

Application Requirements: Application form, essay. *Deadline:* April 8.

Contact: Adm. Stacia Mottley, Executive Director
National Academy of Television Arts and Sciences, Michigan Chapter
24903 Lois Lane
Southfield, MI 48075
Phone: 248-827-0931
E-mail: smottley@comcast.net

NATIONAL ASSOCIATION OF WATER COMPANIES-NEW JERSEY CHAPTER

http://www.nawc.org

NATIONAL ASSOCIATION OF WATER COMPANIES-NEW JERSEY CHAPTER SCHOLARSHIP

• See page 80

NATIVE AMERICAN JOURNALISTS ASSOCIATION

http://www.naja.com/

NATIVE AMERICAN JOURNALISTS ASSOCIATION SCHOLARSHIPS

One-time award for undergraduate study leading to journalism career at accredited colleges and universities. Applicants must be current members of Native-American Journalists Association or may join at time of application. Applicants must have proof of tribal association. Send cover letter, letters of reference, and work samples with application. Financial need considered.

Academic Fields/Career Goals: Advertising/Public Relations; Journalism; Photojournalism/Photography.

Award: Scholarship for use in freshman, sophomore, junior, senior, or graduate years; renewable. *Number:* 1–10. *Amount:* $500–$2000.

Eligibility Requirements: Applicant must be American Indian/Alaska Native; enrolled or expecting to enroll full-time at a two-year or four-year institution or university and must have an interest in writing. Applicant or parent of applicant must be member of Native American Journalists Association. Available to U.S. and Canadian citizens.

Application Requirements: Application form, community service, essay, financial need analysis, interview, personal photograph, portfolio. *Deadline:* June 30.

Contact: Jeffrey Palmer, Education Director
Phone: 405-325-9008
Fax: 866-325-7565
E-mail: jeffrey.p.palmer@ou.edu

NEBRASKA PRESS ASSOCIATION

http://www.nebpress.com/

NEBRASKA PRESS ASSOCIATION FOUNDATION SCHOLARSHIP

Award for graduates of Nebraska high schools who have a minimum GPA of 2.5. Preference will be given to students who will be pursuing newspaper journalism education at Nebraska colleges or universities.

Academic Fields/Career Goals: Advertising/Public Relations; Graphics/Graphic Arts/Printing; Journalism; Photojournalism/Photography.

Award: Scholarship for use in freshman, sophomore, or junior years; not renewable. *Number:* 2–4. *Amount:* $2000.

Eligibility Requirements: Applicant must be enrolled or expecting to enroll full-time at a four-year institution or university; resident of Nebraska and studying in Nebraska. Applicant must have 2.5 GPA or higher. Available to U.S. citizens.

Application Requirements: Application form, application form may be submitted online (http://www.nebpress.com), essay, recommendations or references, up to 3 work samples, if available. *Deadline:* February 20.

Contact: Allen Beermann, Executive Director
Phone: 402-476-2851
Fax: 402-476-2942
E-mail: abeermann@nebpress.com

OHIO NEWSPAPERS FOUNDATION

http://www.ohionews.org

HAROLD K. DOUTHIT SCHOLARSHIP

$1500 scholarship for student enrolled as a sophomore, junior or senior at an Ohio college or university. Must be majoring in journalism, marketing, communications, or advertising. Minimum 3.0 GPA required.

Academic Fields/Career Goals: Advertising/Public Relations; Communications; Journalism; Marketing.

Award: Scholarship for use in sophomore, junior, or senior years; not renewable. *Number:* 1. *Amount:* $1500.

Eligibility Requirements: Applicant must be enrolled or expecting to enroll full-time at a four-year institution or university; resident of Ohio and studying in Ohio. Applicant must have 3.0 GPA or higher. Available to U.S. citizens.

Application Requirements: Application form, autobiography, financial need analysis. *Deadline:* March 31.

Contact: Ms. Ann Riggs, Secretary
Ohio Newspapers Foundation
1335 Dublin Road, Suite 216B
Columbus, OH 43215
Phone: 614-486-6677 Ext. 1010
E-mail: ariggs@ohionews.org

OHIO NEWSPAPERS FOUNDATION MINORITY SCHOLARSHIP

One scholarship for a minority high school senior in Ohio who plans to major in a field relevant to the newspaper industry, particularly journalism, advertising, marketing, or a communications degree program. Applicants must plan to enroll for fall classes at an accredited college or university within the United States. Must be African-American, Hispanic, Asian-American or American-Indian. A minimum high school GPA of 2.5 required.

Academic Fields/Career Goals: Advertising/Public Relations; Communications; Journalism; Marketing.

Award: Scholarship for use in freshman year; not renewable. *Number:* 1. *Amount:* $1500.

Eligibility Requirements: Applicant must be American Indian/Alaska Native, Asian/Pacific Islander, Black (non-Hispanic), Hispanic; high school student; planning to enroll or expecting to enroll full-time at a four-year institution or university and resident of Ohio. Applicant must have 2.5 GPA or higher. Available to U.S. citizens.

Application Requirements: Application form, autobiography. *Deadline:* March 31.

Contact: Ann Riggs, Secretary
Ohio Newspapers Foundation
1335 Dublin Road, Suite 216B
Columbus, OH 43215
Phone: 614-486-6677 Ext. 1010
E-mail: ariggs@ohionews.org

OHIO NEWSPAPERS FOUNDATION UNIVERSITY JOURNALISM SCHOLARSHIP

The Foundation will award 2 scholarships of $2,000 each for a student currently enrolled in an Ohio college or university and majoring in a field relevant to the newspaper industry, particularly journalism, advertising, marketing, or communications degree program. Preference will be given to students demonstrating a career commitment to newspaper journalism. A minimum GPA of 2.5 required.

Academic Fields/Career Goals: Advertising/Public Relations; Communications; Journalism; Marketing.

Award: Scholarship for use in sophomore, junior, or senior years; not renewable. *Number:* 2. *Amount:* $2000.

Eligibility Requirements: Applicant must be enrolled or expecting to enroll full-time at a four-year institution or university; resident of Ohio and studying in Ohio. Applicant must have 2.5 GPA or higher. Available to U.S. citizens.

Application Requirements: Application form, autobiography. *Deadline:* March 31.

Contact: Ann Riggs, Secretary
Ohio Newspapers Foundation
1335 Dublin Road, Suite 216B
Columbus, OH 43215
Phone: 614-486-6677 Ext. 1010
E-mail: ariggs@ohionews.org

ONWA ANNUAL SCHOLARSHIP

One-time scholarship. Applicant may be a male or female student enrolled as a junior or senior in an Ohio college or university and majoring in a field relevant to the newspaper industry, particularly journalism, advertising, marketing, or communications degree program. Must be U.S. citizen.

Academic Fields/Career Goals: Advertising/Public Relations; Communications; Journalism; Marketing.

Award: Scholarship for use in junior or senior years; not renewable. *Number:* 1. *Amount:* $2000.

Eligibility Requirements: Applicant must be enrolled or expecting to enroll full-time at a four-year institution or university; female; resident of Ohio and studying in Ohio. Applicant must have 2.5 GPA or higher. Available to U.S. citizens.

Application Requirements: Application form, essay, financial need analysis. *Deadline:* March 31.

Contact: Ann Riggs, Secretary
Ohio Newspapers Foundation
1335 Dublin Road, Suite 216B
Columbus, OH 43215
Phone: 614-486-6677 Ext. 1010
E-mail: ariggs@ohionews.org

PUBLIC RELATIONS STUDENT SOCIETY OF AMERICA

http://www.prssa.org/

PUBLIC RELATIONS SOCIETY OF AMERICA MULTICULTURAL AFFAIRS SCHOLARSHIP

Two, one-time $1500 awards for members of a principal minority group who are in their junior or senior year at an accredited four-year college or university. Must have at least a 3.0 GPA and be preparing for career in public relations or communications. Must be a full-time student and U.S. citizen.

Academic Fields/Career Goals: Advertising/Public Relations; Communications.

Award: Scholarship for use in freshman, sophomore, junior, or senior years; not renewable. *Number:* 2. *Amount:* $1500.

Eligibility Requirements: Applicant must be American Indian/Alaska Native, Asian/Pacific Islander, Black (non-Hispanic), Hispanic and enrolled or expecting to enroll full-time at a four-year institution or university. Applicant must have 3.0 GPA or higher. Available to U.S. citizens.

Application Requirements: Application form, essay, financial need analysis. *Deadline:* April 18.

Contact: Dora Tovar, Chair, Multicultural Communications Section
Public Relations Student Society of America
33 Maiden Lane, 11th Floor
New York, NY 10038-5150
Phone: 212-460-1476
E-mail: jeneen.garcia@prsa.org

RHODE ISLAND FOUNDATION

http://www.rifoundation.org/

J. D. EDSAL SCHOLARSHIP

Award to benefit Rhode Island residents studying advertising (public relations, marketing, graphic design, film, video, television, or broadcast production) with the expectation of pursuing a career in one of more of these fields. Applicants must be college undergraduates, sophomore or above.

Academic Fields/Career Goals: Advertising/Public Relations; Communications; Filmmaking/Video; Graphics/Graphic Arts/Printing; Marketing; TV/Radio Broadcasting.

Award: Scholarship for use in sophomore, junior, or senior years; renewable. *Amount:* $500–$1000.

Eligibility Requirements: Applicant must be enrolled or expecting to enroll full-time at a four-year institution or university and resident of Rhode Island. Available to U.S. citizens.

Application Requirements: Application form, essay, financial need analysis, recommendations or references, self-addressed stamped envelope with application, transcript.

Contact: Libby Monahan, Funds Administrator
Phone: 401-274-4564 Ext. 3117
E-mail: libbym@rifoundation.org

SCARLETT FAMILY FOUNDATION SCHOLARSHIP PROGRAM

http://www.scarlettfoundation.org/

SCHOLARSHIP FOR STUDENTS PURSUING A BUSINESS OR STEM DEGREE

• *See page 84*

SPECIALTY EQUIPMENT MARKET ASSOCIATION

http://www.sema.org/

SEMA MEMORIAL SCHOLARSHIP FUND

• *See page 85*

STRAIGHTFORWARD MEDIA

http://www.straightforwardmedia.com/

STRAIGHTFORWARD MEDIA BUSINESS SCHOOL SCHOLARSHIP

Scholarship of $500 for undergraduate and graduate students pursuing a business-related degree, including but not limited to economics, finance, marketing, and management. Students pursuing an online business degree are also eligible. Awarded four times per year. Deadlines: March 31, June 30, September 30, and December 31.

Academic Fields/Career Goals: Advertising/Public Relations; Business/Consumer Services; Economics; Finance; Marketing.

Award: Scholarship for use in freshman, sophomore, junior, senior, or graduate years; not renewable. *Number:* 4. *Amount:* $500.

Eligibility Requirements: Applicant must be enrolled or expecting to enroll full- or part-time at a two-year or four-year or technical institution or university. Available to U.S. and non-U.S. citizens.

Application Requirements: Essay. *Deadline:* varies.

Contact: Scholarship Committee
Phone: 605-348-3042

STRAIGHTFORWARD MEDIA MEDIA & COMMUNICATIONS SCHOLARSHIP

Scholarship of $500 available to students of media and communications. Must be majoring in programs such as journalism, broadcasting, advertising, speech, mass communications, or marketing. Awarded four times per year. Deadlines are March 31, June 30, September 30, and December 31. For more information, visit website at http://www.straightforwardmedia.com/media/form.php.

Academic Fields/Career Goals: Advertising/Public Relations; Communications; Journalism; Marketing; Photojournalism/Photography; TV/Radio Broadcasting.

Award: Scholarship for use in freshman, sophomore, junior, or senior years; not renewable. *Number:* 4. *Amount:* $500.

Eligibility Requirements: Applicant must be enrolled or expecting to enroll full- or part-time at a two-year or four-year or technical institution or university. Available to U.S. and non-U.S. citizens.

Application Requirements: Essay. *Deadline:* varies.

Contact: Scholarship Committee
Phone: 605-348-3042

TAMPA BAY TIMES FUND, INC.

http://www.tampabay.com/fund

TAMPA BAY TIMES FUND CAREER JOURNALISM SCHOLARSHIPS

Scholarship to high school seniors in the Tampa Bay Times' audience area who have a demonstrated interest in pursuing journalism/media major in college and career after graduation.

Academic Fields/Career Goals: Advertising/Public Relations; Communications; Journalism; Marketing; Photojournalism/Photography; TV/Radio Broadcasting.

Award: Scholarship for use in freshman, sophomore, junior, or senior years; renewable. *Number:* 3. *Amount:* $2500.

Eligibility Requirements: Applicant must be high school student; age 18–22; planning to enroll or expecting to enroll full-time at a four-year institution or university; single and resident of Florida. Applicant must have 3.0 GPA or higher. Available to U.S. citizens.

Application Requirements: Application form, essay, portfolio. *Deadline:* January 23.

Contact: Nancy Waclawek, Scholarship Administrator
Phone: 813-340-4125
E-mail: tbtschls@gmail.com

UNITED NEGRO COLLEGE FUND

http://www.uncf.org/

PROCTER & GAMBLE GENERAL SCHOLARSHIP

Up to $5000 scholarship for academically achieving undergraduate students at any accredited four-year colleges or universities within the United States. The scholarship is focused on majors in business, information technology and public relations.

Academic Fields/Career Goals: Advertising/Public Relations; Business/Consumer Services; Computer Science/Data Processing; Marketing.

Award: Scholarship for use in freshman, sophomore, junior, or senior years.

Eligibility Requirements: Applicant must be Black (non-Hispanic) and enrolled or expecting to enroll at a four-year institution. Applicant must have 3.0 GPA or higher. Available to U.S. citizens.

Application Requirements: Application form. *Deadline:* July 15.

Contact: Mary Williams, Director of Outreach and Recruitment
Phone: 800-331-2244

UNCF/ALLIANCE DATA SCHOLARSHIP AND INTERNSHIP PROGRAM

Up to $5000 scholarship, summer internship, stipend and travel expenses to the UNCF Student Leadership Conference. Applicant must be an under-represented minority college student enrolled at an accredited four-year college or university with preference given to students attending private or public historically black colleges and universities. Students residing in/or attending school near Plano, TX and Atlanta, GA will receive priority consideration for internships designated in those locations. Must be classified as sophomores (rising juniors) or juniors (rising seniors) at time of application and demonstrate unmet financial need.

Academic Fields/Career Goals: Advertising/Public Relations; Communications; Computer Science/Data Processing; Marketing.

Award: Scholarship for use in junior or senior years.

Eligibility Requirements: Applicant must be American Indian/Alaska Native, Asian/Pacific Islander, Black (non-Hispanic), Hispanic and enrolled or expecting to enroll at a four-year institution or university. Applicant must have 3.0 GPA or higher. Available to U.S. citizens.

Application Requirements: Application form, essay, financial need analysis. *Deadline:* January 20.

Contact: Mary Williams, Director of Outreach and Recruitment
Phone: 800-331-2244

AGRIBUSINESS

ABBIE SARGENT MEMORIAL SCHOLARSHIP INC.

http://www.nhfarmbureau.org/

ABBIE SARGENT MEMORIAL SCHOLARSHIP

Up to three awards between $400 and $700 will be provided to deserving New Hampshire residents, planning to attend an institution of higher learning. Must be a U.S. citizen.

Academic Fields/Career Goals: Agribusiness; Agriculture; Animal/Veterinary Sciences; Environmental Science; Home Economics; Horticulture/Floriculture.

Award: Scholarship for use in freshman, sophomore, junior, senior, graduate, or postgraduate years; not renewable. *Number:* 1–5. *Amount:* $400–$700.

Eligibility Requirements: Applicant must be enrolled or expecting to enroll full- or part-time at a two-year or four-year or technical institution or university and resident of New Hampshire. Applicant or parent of applicant must have employment or volunteer experience in agriculture. Available to U.S. citizens.

Application Requirements: Application form, driver's license, financial need analysis, personal photograph. *Deadline:* March 15.

Contact: Diane Clary, Administrator
Abbie Sargent Memorial Scholarship Inc.
Abbie Sargent Scholarship
295 Sheep Davis Road
Concord, NH 03301
Phone: 603-224-1934
E-mail: dianec@nhfarmbureau.org

CHS FOUNDATION

http://www.chsfoundation.org/

CHS FOUNDATION HIGH SCHOOL SCHOLARSHIPS

Scholarships available to graduating high school seniors who plan to enroll in an agricultural-related program of study in a two-year or four-year college or university. Student must be a U.S. citizen. For additional information and an application, see website http://www.chsfoundation.org.

Academic Fields/Career Goals: Agribusiness; Agriculture; Horticulture/Floriculture.

Award: Scholarship for use in freshman year; not renewable. *Number:* 50. *Amount:* $1000.

Eligibility Requirements: Applicant must be high school student and planning to enroll or expecting to enroll full- or part-time at a two-year or four-year or technical institution or university. Available to U.S. citizens.

Application Requirements: Application form, essay, recommendations or references, transcript. *Deadline:* April 1.

Contact: Scholarship Committee
Phone: 800-814-0506
E-mail: info@chsfoundation.org

CHS FOUNDATION TWO-YEAR COLLEGE SCHOLARSHIPS

Non-renewable scholarship available to first-year agricultural students at a two-year college. Must be studying an agricultural-related major; scholarship is intended for the second year of study. Must be a U.S. citizen. For additional information and application, see website http://www.chsfoundation.org.

Academic Fields/Career Goals: Agribusiness; Agriculture; Horticulture/Floriculture.

Award: Scholarship for use in sophomore year; not renewable. *Number:* 25. *Amount:* $1000.

Eligibility Requirements: Applicant must be enrolled or expecting to enroll full- or part-time at a two-year or technical institution. Available to U.S. citizens.

Application Requirements: Application form, essay, recommendations or references, transcript. *Deadline:* April 1.

Contact: Scholarship Committee
Phone: 800-814-0506
E-mail: info@chsfoundation.org

CHS FOUNDATION UNIVERSITY SCHOLARSHIPS

Renewable scholarship available for students in sophomore, junior, or senior year currently studying agriculture at select universities around the nation. Preference given to students interested in a career in or studying agricultural-based cooperatives and working towards a degree in agribusiness or production agriculture. Students apply to the School of Agriculture or Financial Aid Office at one of the participating universities and follow individual procedures and deadlines for that institution. For additional information and a list of participating universities, see website http://www.chsfoundation.org.

Academic Fields/Career Goals: Agribusiness; Agriculture.

Award: Scholarship for use in sophomore, junior, or senior years; not renewable. *Number:* up to 150. *Amount:* $1000.

Eligibility Requirements: Applicant must be enrolled or expecting to enroll full- or part-time at a four-year institution or university. Available to U.S. citizens.

Application Requirements: Application form, essay, recommendations or references, transcript.

Contact: Scholarship Committee
Phone: 800-814-0506
E-mail: info@chsfoundation.org

HOLSTEIN ASSOCIATION USA INC.

http://www.holsteinusa.com/

ROBERT H. RUMLER SCHOLARSHIP

Awards to encourage deserving and qualified persons with an established interest in the dairy field, who have demonstrated leadership qualities and managerial abilities to pursue a master's degree in business administration.

Academic Fields/Career Goals: Agribusiness; Business/Consumer Services.

Award: Scholarship for use in freshman, sophomore, junior, senior, or graduate years; not renewable. *Number:* 1. *Amount:* $3000.

Eligibility Requirements: Applicant must be enrolled or expecting to enroll full-time at an institution or university and must have an interest in leadership. Applicant must have 3.0 GPA or higher. Available to U.S. and non-U.S. citizens.

Application Requirements: Application form, essay, personal photograph, recommendations or references, transcript. *Deadline:* April 15.

Contact: John Meyer, Chief Executive Officer
Holstein Association USA Inc.
One Holstein Place, PO Box 808
Brattleboro, VT 05302-0808
Phone: 802-254-4551
Fax: 802-254-8251
E-mail: jmeyer@holstein.com

HORTICULTURAL RESEARCH INSTITUTE

http://www.hriresearch.org/

BRYAN A. CHAMPION MEMORIAL SCHOLARSHIP

On November 10, 2011, Bryan A. Champion, president of Herman Losely and Son, Inc. located in Perry, Ohio, passed away at the age of 47. Champion was diagnosed with cancer in 2007, and fought a courageous 4-year battle to try to beat the devastating disease. Champion was a 5th generation nurseryman with a passion for the nursery and landscape industry. During his career he was involved with local, state and national associations that represent the industry. He sought to advance the industry through sound leadership, volunteer participation, and peer-to-peer networking and education events. He was a Buckeye, and graduated from Ohio State University (OSU) in 1987. Champion understood the value of a quality education and the importance of industry research. During his career at Herman Losely and Son, Inc., he worked with OSU and the United States of America- Agricultural Research Service to successfully solve industry issues. In honor of Champion's legacy and dedication to the nursery and landscape industry, donations have been received from his peers to establish The Bryan A. Champion Memorial Scholarship Fund. Each year, Champion's legacy will be remembered when the fund provides a student scholarship to a deserving horticultural student. It is our hope that each recipient will show a similar passion for the industry as Champion exhibited throughout his life. Applicant must be enrolled in an accredited undergraduate or graduate: landscape, horticulture or related discipline at a two or four-year institution. Students in vocational agriculture programs will also be considered. Undergraduate: Applicant must have at least a sophomore standing in a four-year curriculum or senior standing in a two-year curriculum as of the fall semester of scholarship application year. Graduate: All applicants in graduate school regardless of year in school may apply.

Academic Fields/Career Goals: Agribusiness; Entomology; Horticulture/Floriculture; Landscape Architecture.

Award: Scholarship for use in sophomore, junior, senior, or graduate years; not renewable. *Number:* 1. *Amount:* $1000.

Eligibility Requirements: Applicant must be enrolled or expecting to enroll full-time at a two-year or four-year institution or university and studying in Ohio. Available to U.S. citizens.

Application Requirements: Application form, application form may be submitted online (http://americanhort.org/HRI/Scholarship/Scholarship_Programs/HRI/Scholarship/Scholarships.aspx?hkey=241f5ffb-ed35-4165-9169-8a3b0b5ccbbc), essay, financial need analysis, recommendations or references, resume, transcript. *Deadline:* May 31.

Contact: Teresa Jodon, Executive Director
Horticultural Research Institute
1200 G Street, NW
Suite 800
Washington, DC 20005
Phone: 202-695-2474
Fax: 888-761-7883
E-mail: scholarships@hriresearch.org

TIMOTHY AND PALMER W. BIGELOW JR, SCHOLARSHIP

Award for students who are enrolled in accredited undergraduate or graduate landscape/horticulture program. Must be resident of Connecticut, Maine, Massachusetts, New Hampshire, Rhode Island, or Vermont. Undergraduates must have a GPA of 2.25. Financial need, desire to work in nursery industry are factors. For more information, visit website http://www.hriresearch.org. Application must be completed on the HRI website.

Academic Fields/Career Goals: Agribusiness; Entomology; Horticulture/Floriculture; Landscape Architecture.

Award: Scholarship for use in junior or senior years; not renewable. *Number:* 1. *Amount:* $3000.

Eligibility Requirements: Applicant must be enrolled or expecting to enroll full-time at a four-year institution or university and resident of

Connecticut, Maine, Massachusetts, New Hampshire, Rhode Island, Vermont. Available to U.S. citizens.

Application Requirements: Application form, application form may be submitted online (http://americanhort.org/HRI/Scholarship/Scholarship_Programs/HRI/Scholarship/Scholarships.aspx?hkey=241f5ffb-ed35-4165-9169-8a3b0b5ccbbc), essay, financial need analysis, recommendations or references, resume, transcript. *Deadline:* May 31.

Contact: Ms. Teresa Jodon, Executive Director
Horticultural Research Institute
1200 G Street, NW, Suite 800
Washington, DC 20005
Phone: 202-695-2474
Fax: 888-761-7883
E-mail: scholarships@hriresearch.org

INTERTRIBAL TIMBER COUNCIL

http://www.itcnet.org/

TRUMAN D. PICARD SCHOLARSHIP

The program is dedicated to assisting Native American/Native-Alaskan youth seeking careers in natural resources. Graduating senior high school students and those currently attending institutions of higher education are encouraged to apply. A valid tribal/Alaska native corporation's enrollment card is required.

Academic Fields/Career Goals: Agribusiness; Agriculture; Environmental Science; Natural Resources.

Award: Scholarship for use in freshman, sophomore, junior, senior, or graduate years; not renewable. *Number:* 15–30. *Amount:* $2000–$2500.

Eligibility Requirements: Applicant must be American Indian/Alaska Native and enrolled or expecting to enroll full-time at a two-year or four-year institution or university. Available to U.S. citizens.

Application Requirements: Application form, essay. *Deadline:* January 18.

Contact: Laura Alvidrez, Education Committee
Intertribal Timber Council
1112 NE 21st Avenue, Suite 4
Portland, OR 97232-2114
Phone: 503-282-4296
E-mail: itc1@teleport.com

LES DAMES D'ESCOFFIER INTERNATIONAL, COLORADO CHAPTER

www.lesdamescolorado.org

LES DAMES D'ESCOFFIER INTERNATIONAL, COLORADO CHAPTER SCHOLARSHIP

Les Dames d'Escoffier International, Colorado Chapter, will award two $1,000 scholarships in 2017 to qualified female students in food-related fields and attending schools in Colorado. The awards are based on financial need, academic performance, and personal/professional accomplishments.

Academic Fields/Career Goals: Agribusiness; Agriculture; Culinary Arts; Food Science/Nutrition; Food Service/Hospitality; Home Economics.

Award: Scholarship for use in freshman, sophomore, junior, or senior years; not renewable. *Number:* 2. *Amount:* $1000.

Eligibility Requirements: Applicant must be enrolled or expecting to enroll full- or part-time at a two-year or four-year or technical institution or university; female and studying in Colorado.

Application Requirements: Essay, financial need analysis. *Deadline:* April 1.

Contact: Carol Fenster
Les Dames d'Escoffier International, Colorado Chapter
5397 E Mineral Circle
Centennial, CO 80122
Phone: 303-741-5408
E-mail: info@savorypalate.com

MAINE DEPARTMENT OF AGRICULTURE, FOOD AND RURAL RESOURCES

http://www.maine.gov/agriculture

MAINE RURAL REHABILITATION FUND SCHOLARSHIP PROGRAM

One-time scholarship open to Maine residents enrolled in or accepted by any school, college, or university. Must be full-time and demonstrate financial need. Those opting for a Maine institution given preference. Major must lead to an agricultural career. Minimum 3.0 GPA required.

Academic Fields/Career Goals: Agribusiness; Agriculture; Animal/Veterinary Sciences.

Award: Scholarship for use in freshman, sophomore, junior, senior, graduate, or postgraduate years; not renewable. *Number:* 10–20. *Amount:* $800–$2000.

Eligibility Requirements: Applicant must be enrolled or expecting to enroll full-time at a two-year or four-year or technical institution or university and resident of Maine. Applicant must have 3.0 GPA or higher. Available to U.S. citizens.

Application Requirements: Application form, driver's license, financial need analysis, transcript. *Deadline:* June 15.

Contact: Jane Aiudi, Director of Marketing
Phone: 207-287-7628
Fax: 207-287-5576
E-mail: jane.aiudi@maine.gov

NATIONAL CATTLEMEN'S FOUNDATION

http://www.nationalcattlemensfoundation.org/

CME BEEF INDUSTRY SCHOLARSHIP

Ten $1500 scholarships will be awarded to students who intend to pursue a career in the beef industry, including areas such as agricultural education, communications, production, or research. Must be enrolled as an undergraduate student in a four-year institution.

Academic Fields/Career Goals: Agribusiness; Agriculture; Communications.

Award: Scholarship for use in freshman, sophomore, junior, or senior years; not renewable. *Number:* 10. *Amount:* $1500.

Eligibility Requirements: Applicant must be enrolled or expecting to enroll full-time at a four-year institution or university. Available to U.S. citizens.

Application Requirements: Application form, essay, recommendations or references, transcript. *Deadline:* varies.

Contact: RoxAnn Johnson, Executive Director
Phone: 303-850-3388
Fax: 303-694-7372
E-mail: mcf@beef.org

NATIONAL DAIRY SHRINE

http://www.dairyshrine.org/

NATIONAL DAIRY SHRINE/MAURICE E. CORE SCHOLARSHIP

Available to college freshman who are majoring in a dairy/animal industry related field with interest in working in the dairy industry in the future. Scholarship is based on leadership abilities, volunteerism, activities and plans for the future.

Academic Fields/Career Goals: Agribusiness; Agriculture.

Award: Scholarship for use in sophomore year; not renewable. *Number:* 1–4. *Amount:* $1000.

Eligibility Requirements: Applicant must be enrolled or expecting to enroll full-time at a four-year institution or university. Applicant must have 2.5 GPA or higher. Available to U.S. citizens.

Application Requirements: Application form, personal photograph. *Deadline:* April 15.

Contact: Executive Director
E-mail: info@dairyshrine.org

NDS STUDENT RECOGNITION AWARD

Awards available to college seniors enrolled in dairy science courses. Applicants must be nominated by their college or university professor and must intend to continue in the dairy field. A college or university may nominate up to 2 applicants.

Academic Fields/Career Goals: Agribusiness; Agriculture; Animal/Veterinary Sciences; Food Science/Nutrition.

Award: Scholarship for use in senior year; not renewable. *Number:* 2–9. *Amount:* $1000–$2000.

Eligibility Requirements: Applicant must be enrolled or expecting to enroll full-time at a four-year institution or university. Applicant must have 3.0 GPA or higher. Available to U.S. and Canadian citizens.

Application Requirements: Application form, personal photograph. *Deadline:* April 15.

Contact: Executive Director
E-mail: info@dairyshrine.org

NATIONAL POULTRY AND FOOD DISTRIBUTORS ASSOCIATION

http://www.npfda.org/

NATIONAL POULTRY AND FOOD DISTRIBUTORS ASSOCIATION SCHOLARSHIP FOUNDATION

The scholarships are awarded to full-time students in their junior or senior years at a U.S. college pursuing degrees in poultry science, food science, Food Marketing, agricultural business, or other related areas of study pertaining to the poultry and food industries. Dietetics does not qualify. Must attend U.S. College or university full-time.

Academic Fields/Career Goals: Agribusiness; Agriculture; Animal/Veterinary Sciences; Food Science/Nutrition; Food Service/Hospitality.

Award: Scholarship for use in junior or senior years; not renewable. *Number:* 5. *Amount:* $2500–$2500.

Eligibility Requirements: Applicant must be enrolled or expecting to enroll full-time at a four-year institution or university. Available to U.S. and non-U.S. citizens.

Application Requirements: Application form, application form may be submitted online (http://www.npfda.org), essay, recommendations or references, transcript. *Deadline:* May 31.

Contact: Kristin McWhorter, Executive Director
National Poultry and Food Distributors Association
2014 Osborne Road
Saint Marys, GA 31558
Phone: 770-535-9901
Fax: 770-535-7385
E-mail: kkm@npfda.org

NEW YORK STATE ASSOCIATION OF AGRICULTURAL FAIRS

http://www.nyfairs.org/

NEW YORK STATE ASSOCIATION OF AGRICULTURAL FAIRS AND NEW YORK STATE SHOWPEOPLE'S ASSOCIATION ANNUAL SCHOLARSHIP

Scholarship of $1000 given to New York high school seniors and students attending college and planning to pursue, or already pursuing a degree in an agricultural field, a fair management related field or an outdoor amusement related field.

Academic Fields/Career Goals: Agribusiness; Agriculture.

Award: Scholarship for use in freshman, sophomore, junior, senior, or graduate years; not renewable. *Number:* 6. *Amount:* $1000.

Eligibility Requirements: Applicant must be enrolled or expecting to enroll full-time at a two-year or four-year institution or university and resident of New York. Available to U.S. citizens.

Application Requirements: Application form, essay, recommendations or references, transcript. *Deadline:* April 9.

Contact: Mark St. Jacques, President
Phone: 518-692-2464
E-mail: markwashfair@aol.com

OHIO FARMERS UNION

http://www.ohfarmersunion.org/

VIRGIL THOMPSON MEMORIAL SCHOLARSHIP CONTEST

Award available to members of Ohio Farmers Union who are enrolled as full-time college sophomores, juniors or seniors. Awards of $1000 to winner and $500 each to two runners-up.

Academic Fields/Career Goals: Agribusiness; Agriculture.

Award: Scholarship for use in sophomore, junior, or senior years; not renewable. *Number:* 1–3. *Amount:* $500–$1000.

Eligibility Requirements: Applicant must be enrolled or expecting to enroll full-time at a four-year institution or university and resident of Ohio. Applicant or parent of applicant must be member of Ohio Farmers Union. Available to U.S. citizens.

Application Requirements: Application form, entry in a contest, essay. *Deadline:* December 31.

Contact: Ms. Linda Borton, Executive Director
Ohio Farmers Union
PO Box 363
Ottawa, OH 45875
Phone: 419-523-5300
E-mail: lborton@ohfarmersunion.org

OREGON SHEEP GROWERS ASSOCIATION

www.sheeporegon.com

OREGON SHEEP GROWERS ASSOCIATION MEMORIAL SCHOLARSHIP

Award is for those individuals interested in agricultural sciences, pre-veterinary medicine, or an agriculture-related subject area that would be supportive of production agriculture, particularly in the state of Oregon.

Academic Fields/Career Goals: Agribusiness; Agriculture; Animal/Veterinary Sciences.

Award: Scholarship for use in sophomore, junior, or senior years; not renewable. *Number:* 1. *Amount:* $1000–$1500.

Eligibility Requirements: Applicant must be enrolled or expecting to enroll full-time at a four-year institution or university. Available to U.S. citizens.

Application Requirements: Application form, essay. *Deadline:* July 15.

Contact: Scholarship Committee
Oregon Sheep Growers Association
1270 Chemeketa St. NE
Salem, OR 97301
Phone: 503-364-5462
Fax: 503-585-1921
E-mail: info@sheeporegon.com

SCARLETT FAMILY FOUNDATION SCHOLARSHIP PROGRAM

http://www.scarlettfoundation.org/

SCHOLARSHIP FOR STUDENTS PURSUING A BUSINESS OR STEM DEGREE
• See page 84

SOCIETY FOR RANGE MANAGEMENT

http://www.rangelands.org/

MASONIC RANGE SCIENCE SCHOLARSHIP

Renewable award for undergraduate students pursuing degree in agribusiness, agriculture, animal/veterinary sciences, earth science, natural resources and range science. Must maintain minimum 2.5 GPA for eligibility. Award amount varies each year.

Academic Fields/Career Goals: Agribusiness; Agriculture; Animal/Veterinary Sciences; Environmental Science; Natural Resources.

Award: Scholarship for use in freshman or sophomore years; renewable. *Number:* 1. *Amount:* $1000–$5000.

Eligibility Requirements: Applicant must be enrolled or expecting to enroll full-time at a four-year institution or university. Applicant must have 2.5 GPA or higher. Available to U.S. citizens.

Application Requirements: Application form, essay. *Deadline:* January 6.

Contact: Vicky Trujillo, Office Services Manager
Society for Range Management
6901 South Pierce St STE 225
Littleton, CO 80128
Phone: 303-986-3309
E-mail: vtrujillo@rangelands.org

SOIL AND WATER CONSERVATION SOCIETY

http://www.swcs.org

DONALD A. WILLIAMS SCHOLARSHIP SOIL CONSERVATION SCHOLARSHIP

The scholarship provides financial assistance to members who are employed but wish to improve their technical or administrative competence in a conservation-related field. Applicants must be an SWCS member for at least 1 year and has completed at least one year of full-time employment in a natural resource conservation endeavor.

Academic Fields/Career Goals: Agribusiness; Agriculture; Biology; Earth Science; Environmental Science; Food Science/Nutrition; Hydrology; Natural Resources; Natural Sciences; Science, Technology, and Society.

Award: Scholarship for use in freshman, sophomore, junior, senior, graduate, or postgraduate years; not renewable. *Number:* 1–3. *Amount:* $700–$1000.

Eligibility Requirements: Applicant must be enrolled or expecting to enroll full- or part-time at a two-year or four-year or technical institution or university. Applicant or parent of applicant must be member of Soil and Water Conservation Society. Applicant or parent of applicant must have employment or volunteer experience in agriculture, environmental-related field. Available to U.S. and non-U.S. citizens.

Application Requirements: Application form, essay, recommendations or references. *Deadline:* February 13.

Contact: SWCS Scholarships Program Coordinator
Soil and Water Conservation Society
945 SW Ankeny Road
Ankeny, IA 50023-9723
Phone: 515-289-2331 Ext. 114
E-mail: scholarships@swcs.org

SOIL AND WATER CONSERVATION SOCIETY-MISSOURI SHOW-ME CHAPTER

http://www.moswcs.org/

MO SHOW-ME CHAPTER SWCS SCHOLARSHIP

The SWCS Scholarship provides financial assistance to students wishing to pursue studies with a natural resource conservation orientation at properly accredited colleges or universities. This scholarship is for students who attend/graduated from an approved program of study in Missouri. Applicants must major in a conservation or natural resource-related field. Due date is the Monday after Thanksgiving.

Academic Fields/Career Goals: Agribusiness; Agriculture; Biology; Earth Science; Environmental Health; Environmental Science; Hydrology; Natural Resources; Natural Sciences; Recreation, Parks, Leisure Studies; Surveying, Surveying Technology, Cartography, or Geographic Information Science.

Award: Scholarship for use in freshman, sophomore, junior, or senior years; not renewable. *Number:* 1. *Amount:* $2000.

Eligibility Requirements: Applicant must be enrolled or expecting to enroll full-time at a two-year or four-year institution or university and resident of Missouri. Available to U.S. citizens.

Application Requirements: Application form, essay.

Contact: Kim Worth
Soil and Water Conservation Society-Missouri Show-Me Chapter
7005 SE Ketchem Rd
Cameron, MO 64429
Phone: 816-632-0735
E-mail: worths@centurytel.net

SOIL AND WATER CONSERVATION SOCIETY-NEW JERSEY CHAPTER

http://www.geocities.com/njswcs

EDWARD R. HALL SCHOLARSHIP

Two $500 scholarships awarded annually to students attending a New Jersey accredited college or New Jersey residents attending any out-of-state college. Undergraduate students, with the exception of freshmen, are eligible. Must be enrolled in a curriculum related to natural resources. Other areas related to conservation may qualify.

Academic Fields/Career Goals: Agribusiness; Agriculture; Animal/Veterinary Sciences; Biology; Earth Science; Environmental Science; Horticulture/Floriculture; Natural Resources; Natural Sciences.

Award: Scholarship for use in sophomore, junior, or senior years; not renewable. *Number:* 2. *Amount:* $500.

Eligibility Requirements: Applicant must be enrolled or expecting to enroll full-time at a two-year or four-year institution or university and resident of New Jersey. Available to U.S. and non-U.S. citizens.

Application Requirements: Application form, essay, financial need analysis, list of clubs and organizations related to natural resources of which applicant is a member, recommendations or references, transcript. *Deadline:* April 15.

Contact: Fireman E. Bear Chapter, c/o USDA-NRCS
Soil and Water Conservation Society-New Jersey Chapter
220 Davidson Avenue, Fourth Floor
Somerset, NJ 08873
Phone: 732-932-9295
E-mail: njswcs@yahoo.com

SOUTH DAKOTA BOARD OF REGENTS

http://www.sdbor.edu/

SOUTH DAKOTA BOARD OF REGENTS BJUGSTAD SCHOLARSHIP

Scholarship for graduating North or South Dakota high school senior who is a Native American. Must demonstrate academic achievement, character and leadership abilities. Must submit proof of tribal enrollment. One-time award of $500. Must rank in upper half of class or have a minimum 2.5 GPA. Must be pursuing studies in agriculture, agribusiness, or natural resources.

Academic Fields/Career Goals: Agribusiness; Agriculture; Natural Resources.

Award: Scholarship for use in freshman year; not renewable. *Number:* 2. *Amount:* $500.

Eligibility Requirements: Applicant must be American Indian/Alaska Native; high school student; planning to enroll or expecting to enroll full-time at a four-year institution or university; resident of North Dakota, South Dakota and must have an interest in leadership. Applicant must have 2.5 GPA or higher. Available to U.S. citizens.

Application Requirements: Application form, proof of tribal enrollment, recommendations or references, transcript. *Deadline:* February 15.

Contact: Dr. Paul Turman, System Vice President for Research and Economic Development
South Dakota Board of Regents
301 East Capital Avenue, Suite 200
Pierre, SD 57501
Phone: 605-773-3455
Fax: 605-773-2422
E-mail: paul.turman@sdbor.edu

SOUTH DAKOTA RETAILERS ASSOCIATION

http://www.sdra.org

SOUTH DAKOTA RETAILERS ASSOCIATION SCHOLARSHIP PROGRAM

Scholarships for students studying for a career in retailing. See application for eligible fields of study. Applicants must have graduated from a South Dakota high school or be enrolled in postsecondary school in South Dakota. Must complete required number of college or vocational school prior to receiving award, or have work experience in lieu of education.

Academic Fields/Career Goals: Agribusiness.

Award: Scholarship for use in sophomore, junior, senior, graduate, or postgraduate years; not renewable. *Number:* 10–15. *Amount:* $500–$2250.

Eligibility Requirements: Applicant must be enrolled or expecting to enroll full- or part-time at a two-year or four-year or technical institution or university. Available to U.S. and non-U.S. citizens.

Application Requirements: Application form, essay. *Deadline:* April 17.

Contact: Donna Leslie, Communications Director
South Dakota Retailers Association
SDRA
PO Box 638
Pierre, SD 57501
Phone: 800-658-5545
Fax: 605-224-2059
E-mail: donna@sdra.org

VERMONT SPACE GRANT CONSORTIUM

http://www.cems.uvm.edu/vsgc

VERMONT SPACE GRANT CONSORTIUM

Applicant must be a U.S. citizen, Vermont resident, graduating senior in a Vermont high school, or current undergraduate with a minimum 3.0 GPA enrolled full-time for the following academic year in a degree program in a Vermont institution of higher education. Must plan to pursue a professional career which has direct relevance to the U.S. aerospace industry and the goals of NASA. Three awards will be given to students enrolled in the Burlington Technical College Aviation Technology Program.

Academic Fields/Career Goals: Agribusiness; Applied Sciences; Aviation/Aerospace; Biology; Civil Engineering; Computer Science/Data Processing; Earth Science; Electrical Engineering/Electronics; Energy and Power Engineering; Engineering-Related Technologies; Engineering/Technology; Materials Science, Engineering, and Metallurgy; Mathematics; Mechanical Engineering; Physical Sciences; Science, Technology, and Society; Trade/Technical Specialties.

Award: Scholarship for use in freshman, sophomore, junior, or senior years; not renewable. *Number:* 6–9. *Amount:* $2500–$5000.

Eligibility Requirements: Applicant must be enrolled or expecting to enroll full-time at a two-year or four-year or technical institution or university; resident of Vermont and studying in Vermont. Applicant must have 3.0 GPA or higher. Available to U.S. citizens.

Application Requirements: Application form, essay. *Deadline:* March 1.

Contact: Ms. Debra Fraser, Program Coordinator
Vermont Space Grant Consortium
University of Vermont -Vermont Space Grant Consortium
210 Colchester Avenue, Room 120
Burlington, VT 05405-0156
Phone: 802-656-1429
E-mail: dfraser1@uvm.edu

AGRICULTURE

ABBIE SARGENT MEMORIAL SCHOLARSHIP INC.

http://www.nhfarmbureau.org/

ABBIE SARGENT MEMORIAL SCHOLARSHIP
• *See page 91*

ALABAMA GOLF COURSE SUPERINTENDENTS ASSOCIATION

http://www.agcsa.org/

ALABAMA GOLF COURSE SUPERINTENDENT'S ASSOCIATION'S DONNIE ARTHUR MEMORIAL SCHOLARSHIP

One-time award for students majoring in agriculture with an emphasis on turf-grass management. Must have a minimum 2.0 GPA. Applicant must be a full-time student. High school students not considered. Award available to U.S. citizens.

Academic Fields/Career Goals: Agriculture; Horticulture/Floriculture.

Award: Scholarship for use in freshman, sophomore, junior, or senior years; not renewable. *Number:* 1. *Amount:* $2000.

Eligibility Requirements: Applicant must be enrolled or expecting to enroll full-time at a two-year or four-year institution or university. Applicant must have 2.5 GPA or higher. Available to U.S. citizens.

Application Requirements: Application form, essay, recommendations or references, transcript. *Deadline:* October 15.

Contact: Melanie Bonds, Secretary
Phone: 205-967-0397
E-mail: agcsa@charter.net

ALBERTA HERITAGE SCHOLARSHIP FUND

http://www.alis.alberta.ca/

ALBERTA BARLEY COMMISSION-EUGENE BOYKO MEMORIAL SCHOLARSHIP

Award of CAN$500 to recognize and encourage students entering the field of crop production and/or crop processing technology studies. Must be a Canadian citizen or landed immigrant attending an Alberta postsecondary institution. Students must be enrolled in the second or subsequent year of postsecondary study and taking courses that have an emphasis on crop production and/or crop processing technology. Awarded on basis of academic achievement. For additional information, see website http://alis.alberta.ca.

Academic Fields/Career Goals: Agriculture.

Award: Scholarship for use in sophomore, junior, or senior years; not renewable. *Number:* 1.

Eligibility Requirements: Applicant must be enrolled or expecting to enroll full-time at a four-year institution or university and resident of Alberta. Available to Canadian citizens.

Application Requirements: Application form, transcript. *Deadline:* August 1.

Contact: Scholarship Committee
Phone: 780-427-8640
E-mail: scholarships@gov.ab.ca

AMERICAN LEGION DEPARTMENT OF NORTH DAKOTA

http://www.ndlegion.org/

O. NESHEIM MEMORIAL SCHOLARSHIP

Must be a legal resident of North Dakota and a direct descendent (child, grandchild or great-grandchild) of a U.S. veteran who served honorably. Proof of service and lineage are required. Must have maintained a secondary school GPA of 2.75 or higher and be pursuing a degree in some phase of agriculture, human nutrition, or medicine (Medical

Doctor, PA, Dentistry, Dental Hygiene, Pharmacy or Chiropractic). Must be a high school senior or a previous Nesheim Scholarship recipient now attending an institution of higher education. The applicant must submit the completed application form and include and attach an original essay (500 to 750 words, typed, double spaced, 12 pt. font with 1" margins) to address the following issues: 1. What are your educational and career goals?, 2. How do you plan to accomplish those goals and what part will your education play in attaining those goals?, 3. Where do you plan to continue your education and why did you choose that institution?, 4. Briefly discuss your secondary education (coursework, extracurricular activities, sports, jobs, volunteerism, etc.) and how you feel they may or may not have helped you prepare for your choice of college, your life, and your career. Must provide proof of acceptance into a postsecondary institution in North Dakota that grants Associate or higher degrees. Include a high school transcript. Include 3 letters of reference, all from non-family members, and one of which must be from a U.S. veteran who served honorably. Provide proof of financial need from the educational institution to be attended

Academic Fields/Career Goals: Agriculture; Dental Health/Services; Food Science/Nutrition; Health Administration; Health and Medical Sciences; Pharmacy.

Award: Scholarship for use in senior year; not renewable.

Eligibility Requirements: Applicant must be high school student; age 17-18; planning to enroll or expecting to enroll full-time at a two-year or four-year or technical institution or university; single; resident of North Dakota and studying in North Dakota. Applicant must have 2.5 GPA or higher. Available to U.S. citizens. Applicant or parent must meet one or more of the following requirements: general military experience; retired from active duty; disabled or killed as a result of military service; prisoner of war; or missing in action.

Application Requirements: Application form, community service, essay, financial need analysis. *Deadline:* April 1.

Contact: Teri Bryant, Programs/Membership Coordinator
Phone: 701-293-3120
Fax: 701-293-9951
E-mail: programs@ndlegion.org

AMERICAN OIL CHEMISTS' SOCIETY

http://www.aocs.org/

AOCS BIOTECHNOLOGY STUDENT EXCELLENCE AWARD

Award to recognize an outstanding paper in the field of biotechnology presented by a student at the AOCS Annual Meeting and Expo. Graduate students presenting within the Biotechnology Division technical program are eligible for the award.

Academic Fields/Career Goals: Agriculture; Chemical Engineering; Food Science/Nutrition.

Award: Prize for use in junior, senior, or graduate years; not renewable. *Number:* 1–3. *Amount:* $100–$300.

Eligibility Requirements: Applicant must be enrolled or expecting to enroll full- or part-time at a four-year institution or university. Available to U.S. and non-U.S. citizens.

Application Requirements: Essay, extended abstract, recommendations or references. *Deadline:* February 1.

Contact: Barbara Semeraro, Area Manager, Membership
American Oil Chemists' Society
AOCS
PO Box 17190
Urbana, IL 61803
Phone: 217-693-4804
Fax: 217-693-4849
E-mail: awards@aocs.org

AMERICAN SOCIETY FOR ENOLOGY AND VITICULTURE

http://www.asev.org/

AMERICAN SOCIETY FOR ENOLOGY AND VITICULTURE SCHOLARSHIPS

One-time award for college juniors, seniors, and graduate students residing in North America and enrolled in a program studying viticulture, enology, or any field related to the wine and grape industry. Minimum 3.0 GPA for undergraduates; minimum 3.2 GPA for graduate students. Must be a resident of the United States, Canada, or Mexico.

Academic Fields/Career Goals: Agriculture; Chemical Engineering; Food Science/Nutrition; Horticulture/Floriculture.

Award: Scholarship for use in junior, senior, or graduate years; not renewable. *Number:* up to 30. *Amount:* $500–$4000.

Eligibility Requirements: Applicant must be enrolled or expecting to enroll full-time at a four-year institution or university. Applicant must have 3.0 GPA or higher. Available to U.S. and non-U.S. citizens.

Application Requirements: Application form, essay, financial need analysis, recommendations or references, transcript. *Deadline:* March 1.

Contact: Karli Kolb, Administrative Assistant
Phone: 530-753-3142
Fax: 530-753-3318
E-mail: society@asev.org

AMERICAN SOCIETY OF AGRICULTURAL AND BIOLOGICAL ENGINEERS

http://www.asabe.org/

WILLIAM J. ADAMS, JR. AND MARIJANE E. ADAMS SCHOLARSHIP

One-time award for a full-time U.S. or Canadian undergraduate who is a student member of the American Society of Agricultural Engineers and a declared major in biological or agricultural engineering. Must be at least a sophomore and have minimum 2.5 GPA. Must be interested in agricultural machinery product design or development. Application procedures can be found on http://www.asabe.org website.

Academic Fields/Career Goals: Agriculture; Biology.

Award: Scholarship for use in sophomore, junior, or senior years; not renewable. *Number:* 1. *Amount:* $1200.

Eligibility Requirements: Applicant must be enrolled or expecting to enroll full-time at a four-year institution or university. Applicant or parent of applicant must be member of Other Student Academic Clubs. Applicant must have 2.5 GPA or higher. Available to U.S. and Canadian citizens.

Application Requirements: Application form, essay, financial need analysis, recommendations or references, resume. *Deadline:* March 15.

Contact: Carol Flautt, Scholarship Program
American Society of Agricultural and Biological Engineers
2950 Niles Road
St. Joseph, MI 49085-9659
Phone: 269-932-7036
Fax: 269-429-3852
E-mail: flautt@asabe.org

AMERICAN SOCIETY OF AGRONOMY, CROP SCIENCE SOCIETY OF AMERICA, SOIL SCIENCE SOCIETY OF AMERICA

http://www.agronomy.org

J. FIELDING REED SCHOLARSHIP

Scholarship of $1000 to honor an outstanding undergraduate senior pursuing a career in soil or plant sciences. Must have GPA of 3.0, or above, and nominations should contain a history of community and campus leadership activities, specifically in agriculture. For more information on nomination and eligibility criteria, visit website https://www.agronomy.org/awards

Academic Fields/Career Goals: Agriculture; Earth Science; Entomology; Environmental Science; Natural Resources; Natural Sciences.

Award: Scholarship for use in senior year; not renewable. *Number:* 1. *Amount:* up to $1000.

Eligibility Requirements: Applicant must be enrolled or expecting to enroll full-time at a four-year institution or university and must have an interest in leadership. Applicant or parent of applicant must have employment or volunteer experience in community service. Applicant must have 3.0 GPA or higher. Available to U.S. and non-U.S. citizens.

Application Requirements: Application form, application form may be submitted online (http://www.agronomy.org/awards), letter of interest, recommendations or references, resume. *Deadline:* February 26.

Contact: Sara Uttech, Communications Manager
American Society of Agronomy, Crop Science Society of
America, Soil Science Society of America
5585 Guilford Road
Madison, WI 53711
Phone: 608-268-4948
Fax: 608-273-2021
E-mail: awards@sciencesocieties.org

ASSOCIATION ON AMERICAN INDIAN AFFAIRS, INC.

http://www.indian-affairs.org/

ELIZABETH AND SHERMAN ASCHE MEMORIAL SCHOLARSHIP FUND

Scholarship of up to $1500 available for undergraduate and graduate students seeking a Bachelor's or Master's degree in science or public health. Students must apply each year. Must be a Native American. See website for details http://www.indian-affairs.org. Must be seeking an Associate's degree or higher at an accredited school.

Academic Fields/Career Goals: Agriculture; Animal/Veterinary Sciences; Biology; Chemical Engineering; Dental Health/Services; Earth Science; Health and Medical Sciences; Marine Biology; Natural Sciences; Nursing; Physical Sciences; Public Health.

Award: Scholarship for use in freshman, sophomore, junior, senior, or graduate years; not renewable. *Number:* 6–8. *Amount:* up to $1500.

Eligibility Requirements: Applicant must be American Indian/Alaska Native and enrolled or expecting to enroll full-time at a two-year or four-year or technical institution or university. Available to U.S. citizens.

Application Requirements: Application form, essay, Tribal Enrollment. *Deadline:* June 1.

Contact: Lisa Wyzlic, Director of Scholarship Programs
Association on American Indian Affairs, Inc.
966 Hungerford Drive, Suite 12-B
Rockville, MD 20850
Phone: 240-314-7155
Fax: 240-314-7159
E-mail: lw.aaia@indian-affairs.org

CALCOT-SEITZ FOUNDATION

http://www.calcot.com/

CALCOT-SEITZ SCHOLARSHIP

Scholarship for young students from Arizona, New Mexico, Texas, and California who plan to attend a college or are attending a college offering at least a four-year degree in agriculture.

Academic Fields/Career Goals: Agriculture.

Award: Scholarship for use in freshman, sophomore, junior, senior, or graduate years; not renewable. *Number:* 1–30. *Amount:* $500–$3000.

Eligibility Requirements: Applicant must be enrolled or expecting to enroll full-time at a four-year institution or university and resident of Arizona, California, New Mexico, Texas. Available to U.S. and non-U.S. citizens.

Application Requirements: Application form, community service, essay, interview, personal photograph, recommendations or references, test scores, transcript. *Deadline:* March 31.

Contact: Marci Cunningham, Scholarship Committee
Calcot-Seitz Foundation
PO Box 259
Bakersfield, CA 93302
Phone: 661-327-5961
Fax: 661-861-9870
E-mail: mcunningham@calcot.com

CHS FOUNDATION

http://www.chsfoundation.org/

CHS FOUNDATION HIGH SCHOOL SCHOLARSHIPS
• *See page 91*

CHS FOUNDATION TWO-YEAR COLLEGE SCHOLARSHIPS
• *See page 92*

CHS FOUNDATION UNIVERSITY SCHOLARSHIPS
• *See page 92*

GARDEN CLUB OF AMERICA

http://www.gcamerica.org/

ELIZABETH GARDNER NORWEB SUMMER ENVIRONMENTAL STUDIES SCHOLARSHIP

Award for college students who wish to pursue summer studies doing field work, research, or classroom work in the environmental field following their freshman, sophomore, or junior years. Work may award academic credit but should be in addition to required courses.

Academic Fields/Career Goals: Agriculture; Earth Science; Environmental Science; Natural Resources.

Award: Scholarship for use in freshman, sophomore, or junior years; not renewable. *Number:* 1. *Amount:* $3000.

Eligibility Requirements: Applicant must be enrolled or expecting to enroll full-time at a four-year institution or university. Available to U.S. and non-U.S. citizens.

Application Requirements: Application form, essay. *Deadline:* February 10.

Contact: Scholarship Committee Administrator
Phone: 212-753-8287
E-mail: scholarshipapplications@gcamerica.org

INSTITUTE OF FOOD TECHNOLOGISTS

http://www.ift.org/

EVAN TUREK MEMORIAL SCHOLARSHIP

Applicant must be enrolled as a full-time junior who will be a senior Fall 2017 pursuing a food science degree at an IFT-approved undergraduate program for the 2016-2017 academic year. Major in food science, nutrition, agricultural engineering, biochemistry, chemical engineering, dairy science, food chemistry, food engineering, food packaging, non-thermal processing or related discipline. Applicant must demonstrate exceptional leadership experience. Applicant must be an IFTSA member at the time of application. Consideration for Kraft Heinz Internship will be conducted in October/ November

Academic Fields/Career Goals: Agriculture; Food Science/Nutrition.

Award: Scholarship for use in senior year. *Number:* 1. *Amount:* $1000.

Eligibility Requirements: Applicant must be enrolled or expecting to enroll full-time at a four-year institution or university. Applicant must have 3.5 GPA or higher. Available to U.S. and non-U.S. citizens.

Application Requirements: Application form, interview. *Deadline:* October 15.

Contact: IFT Foundation Coordinator
Institute of Food Technologists
525 West Van Buren, Suite 1000
Chicago, IL 60607
Phone: 312-782-8424
E-mail: info@ift.org

EVAN TUREK MEMORIAL SCHOLARSHIP AND INTERNSHIP

Applicant must be enrolled as a full-time rising sophomore, junior, or senior university student pursuing a food science degree at an IFT-approved undergraduate program. Major in agricultural engineering, biochemistry, chemical engineering, dairy science, food chemistry, food engineering, food packaging, non-thermal processing or related discipline. Applicant must demonstrate exceptional leadership experience. Applicant be a member of IFT at time of application. Mondel's International will conduct phone and video interviews for top candidates in November. Scholarship recipient will begin a (10-12 week) internship with Mondel's International beginning in mid-May/June.

Academic Fields/Career Goals: Agriculture; Food Science/Nutrition.

Award: Scholarship for use in sophomore, junior, or senior years. *Number:* 1. *Amount:* $1000.

Eligibility Requirements: Applicant must be enrolled or expecting to enroll at a four-year institution or university. Applicant must have 3.0 GPA or higher. Available to U.S. and non-U.S. citizens.

Application Requirements: Application form, interview. *Deadline:* October 15.

Contact: IFT Foundation Coordinator
Institute of Food Technologists
525 West Van Buren, Suite 1000
Chicago, IL 60607
Phone: 312-782-8424
E-mail: info@ift.org

KRAFT HEINZ RESEARCH SCHOLARSHIP

Applicant must be enrolled as a full-time junior who will be a senior Fall 2017 pursuing a food science degree at an IFT-approved undergraduate program. Majors include food science, nutrition, agricultural engineering, biochemistry, chemical engineering, dairy science, food chemistry, food engineering, food packaging, non-thermal processing or related discipline. Applicant must demonstrate exceptional leadership experience. Applicant must be an IFTSA member at the time of application. The scholarship recipient will also have the opportunity to be considered for an internship at Kraft Heinz in the summer

Academic Fields/Career Goals: Agriculture; Food Science/Nutrition.

Award: Scholarship for use in senior year. *Number:* 1. *Amount:* $1000.

Eligibility Requirements: Applicant must be enrolled or expecting to enroll full-time at a four-year institution or university. Applicant must have 3.5 GPA or higher. Available to U.S. and non-U.S. citizens.

Application Requirements: Application form, interview. *Deadline:* October 15.

Contact: IFT Foundation Coordinator
Institute of Food Technologists
525 West Van Buren, Suite 1000
Chicago, IL 60607
Phone: 312-782-8424
E-mail: info@ift.org

INTERTRIBAL TIMBER COUNCIL

http://www.itcnet.org/

TRUMAN D. PICARD SCHOLARSHIP
• *See page 93*

JAPANESE AMERICAN CITIZENS LEAGUE (JACL)

http://www.jacl.org/

NATIONAL JACL HEADQUARTERS SCHOLARSHIP

Scholarship offers over 30 awards to qualified students nationwide. Scholarships are provided to students at the entering freshman, undergraduate, graduate, law, financial need and creative & performing arts. All scholarships are one-time awards. Every applicant must be an active National JACL member at either an Individual or Student/Youth Level.

Academic Fields/Career Goals: Agriculture; Journalism; Law/Legal Services; Literature/English/Writing; Public Policy and Administration.

Award: Scholarship for use in freshman, sophomore, junior, senior, or graduate years; not renewable. *Number:* 30.

Eligibility Requirements: Applicant must be of Japanese heritage; Asian/Pacific Islander and enrolled or expecting to enroll full-time at a two-year or four-year institution or university. Available to U.S. and non-U.S. citizens.

Application Requirements: Application form, financial need analysis, recommendations or references, transcript. *Deadline:* varies.

Contact: Scholarship Committee
Phone: 415-921-5225
E-mail: jacl@jacl.org

THE LAND CONSERVANCY OF NEW JERSEY

http://tlc-nj.org/

RUSSELL W. MYERS SCHOLARSHIP

The scholarship program is administered by the Board of Trustees of The Land Conservancy of New Jersey and is awarded annually to deserving individuals who plan careers in environmental science, natural resource management, conservation, horticulture, park administration, or a related field. An applicant must be a student in good standing with at least 15 credits completed, have an academic average equivalent to a 3.0 or higher, be a resident of New Jersey and considering a career in New Jersey that is consistent with the goals of the Conservancy. Selected finalist will have to attend an interview with The Committee in early June.

Academic Fields/Career Goals: Agriculture; Environmental Science; Horticulture/Floriculture; Landscape Architecture; Marine Biology; Natural Resources; Recreation, Parks, Leisure Studies.

Award: Scholarship for use in freshman, sophomore, junior, senior, or graduate years; not renewable. *Amount:* up to $7500.

Eligibility Requirements: Applicant must be enrolled or expecting to enroll full-time at a four-year institution or university and resident of New Jersey. Applicant must have 3.0 GPA or higher. Available to U.S. citizens.

Application Requirements: Application form, essay, recommendations or references, resume, transcript. *Deadline:* April 1.

Contact: Scholarship Program
The Land Conservancy of New Jersey
19 Boonton Avenue
Boonton, NJ 07005
Phone: 973-541-1010

LES DAMES D'ESCOFFIER INTERNATIONAL, COLORADO CHAPTER

www.lesdamescolorado.org

LES DAMES D'ESCOFFIER INTERNATIONAL, COLORADO CHAPTER SCHOLARSHIP
• *See page 93*

MAINE DEPARTMENT OF AGRICULTURE, FOOD AND RURAL RESOURCES

http://www.maine.gov/agriculture

MAINE RURAL REHABILITATION FUND SCHOLARSHIP PROGRAM
• *See page 93*

NATIONAL CATTLEMEN'S FOUNDATION

http://www.nationalcattlemensfoundation.org/

CME BEEF INDUSTRY SCHOLARSHIP
• *See page 93*

NATIONAL COUNCIL OF STATE GARDEN CLUBS INC. SCHOLARSHIP

http://www.gardenclub.org/

NATIONAL COUNCIL OF STATE GARDEN CLUBS INC. SCHOLARSHIP

Scholarship to students for study in agriculture education, horticulture, floriculture, landscape design, botany, biology, plant pathology/science, forestry, agronomy, environmental concerns.

Academic Fields/Career Goals: Agriculture; Biology; Environmental Science; Horticulture/Floriculture.

Award: Scholarship for use in sophomore, junior, senior, or graduate years; not renewable. *Number:* 34. *Amount:* $3500.

Eligibility Requirements: Applicant must be enrolled or expecting to enroll full-time at a two-year or four-year institution or university. Applicant must have 3.0 GPA or higher. Available to U.S. citizens.

Application Requirements: Application form, financial need analysis, recommendations or references, transcript. *Deadline:* March 1.

Contact: Kathy Romine, National Headquarters
Phone: 314-776-7574 Ext. 15
Fax: 314-776-5108
E-mail: headquarters@gardenclub.org

NATIONAL DAIRY SHRINE

http://www.dairyshrine.org/

KILDEE SCHOLARSHIPS

Top 25 contestants in the three most recent national intercollegiate dairy cattle judging contests or the top ranking team members from the North American Intercollegiate Dairy Challenge are eligible to apply for two $3000 one-time scholarships for graduate study in the field related to dairy cattle production or vet school at the university of their choice. Also the top 25 contestants in the most recent National 4-H & National FFA Dairy Judging contests are eligible to apply for one $1000 scholarship for undergraduate study in the field related to dairy cattle production at the university of their choice.

Academic Fields/Career Goals: Agriculture; Animal/Veterinary Sciences.

Award: Scholarship for use in junior, senior, or postgraduate years; not renewable. *Number:* 1–2. *Amount:* $1000–$3000.

Eligibility Requirements: Applicant must be enrolled or expecting to enroll full-time at a four-year institution or university. Applicant must have 3.0 GPA or higher. Available to U.S. and Canadian citizens.

Application Requirements: Application form, personal photograph. *Deadline:* April 15.

Contact: Executive Director
National Dairy Shrine
PO Box 725
Denmark, WI 54208
Phone: 920-863-6333
E-mail: info@dairyshrine.org

KLUSSENDORF / MCKOWN SCHOLARSHIP

The scholarship will be granted to a student successfully completing the first, second or third years at a two-year or four-year college or university. To be eligible, students must major in a dairy science (animal science) curriculum with plans to enter the dairy cattle field as a breeder, owner, herdsperson, or fitter.

Academic Fields/Career Goals: Agriculture; Animal/Veterinary Sciences.

Award: Scholarship for use in freshman, sophomore, or junior years; not renewable. *Number:* 1–7. *Amount:* $1500.

Eligibility Requirements: Applicant must be enrolled or expecting to enroll full-time at a two-year or four-year institution or university. Available to U.S. and Canadian citizens.

Application Requirements: Application form, personal photograph. *Deadline:* April 15.

Contact: Executive Director
E-mail: info@dairyshrine.org

MARSHALL E. MCCULLOUGH-NATIONAL DAIRY SHRINE SCHOLARSHIPS

Scholarship for high school seniors planning to enter a four-year college or university with an intent to major in dairy/animal science with a communications emphasis, or agricultural journalism with a dairy/animal science emphasis.

Academic Fields/Career Goals: Agriculture; Communications; Journalism; TV/Radio Broadcasting.

Award: Scholarship for use in freshman year; not renewable. *Number:* 2. *Amount:* $1500–$2000.

Eligibility Requirements: Applicant must be high school student and planning to enroll or expecting to enroll full-time at a four-year institution or university. Applicant must have 3.0 GPA or higher. Available to U.S. citizens.

Application Requirements: Application form, personal photograph. *Deadline:* April 15.

Contact: Executive Director
E-mail: info@dairyshrine.org

NATIONAL DAIRY SHRINE/DAIRY MARKETING INC. MILK MARKETING SCHOLARSHIPS

One-time awards for undergraduate students pursuing careers in marketing of dairy products. Major areas can include: dairy science, animal science, agricultural economics, agricultural communications, agricultural education, general education, food and nutrition, home economics and journalism. For more information, visit website http://www.dairyshrine.org.

Academic Fields/Career Goals: Agriculture; Food Science/Nutrition; Marketing.

Award: Scholarship for use in sophomore or junior years; not renewable. *Number:* 5–9. *Amount:* $1000–$1500.

Eligibility Requirements: Applicant must be enrolled or expecting to enroll full-time at a four-year institution or university. Applicant must have 2.5 GPA or higher. Available to U.S. citizens.

Application Requirements: Application form, personal photograph. *Deadline:* April 15.

Contact: Executive Director
E-mail: info@dairyshrine.org

NATIONAL DAIRY SHRINE/IAGER DAIRY SCHOLARSHIP

$1000 annual scholarship to encourage qualified second-year dairy students in a two-year agricultural school to pursue careers in the dairy industry. Scholarships will be awarded based on academic standing, leadership ability, interest in the dairy industry, and plans for the future. Cumulative 2.5 GPA required.

Academic Fields/Career Goals: Agriculture.

Award: Scholarship for use in sophomore year; not renewable. *Number:* 1–2. *Amount:* $1000.

Eligibility Requirements: Applicant must be enrolled or expecting to enroll full-time at a two-year or technical institution. Applicant must have 2.5 GPA or higher. Available to U.S. citizens.

Application Requirements: Application form, personal photograph. *Deadline:* April 15.

Contact: Executive Director
E-mail: info@dairyshrine.org

NATIONAL DAIRY SHRINE/MAURICE E. CORE SCHOLARSHIP
• *See page 93*

NDS STUDENT RECOGNITION AWARD
• *See page 94*

NATIONAL GARDEN CLUBS INC.

http://www.gardenclub.org/

NATIONAL GARDEN CLUBS INC. SCHOLARSHIP PROGRAM

One-time award for full-time students in plant sciences, agriculture and related or allied subjects. Applicants must have at least a 3.25 GPA.

Academic Fields/Career Goals: Agriculture; Biology; Earth Science; Environmental Science; Horticulture/Floriculture; Landscape Architecture.

Award: Scholarship for use in junior, senior, or graduate years; not renewable. *Number:* 41. *Amount:* $4000.

Eligibility Requirements: Applicant must be enrolled or expecting to enroll full-time at a four-year institution or university. Available to U.S. citizens.

Application Requirements: Application form, financial need analysis, personal photograph. *Deadline:* February 1.

Contact: Sandra Robinson, Vice President for Scholarship
Phone: 606-878-7281
E-mail: sandyr@kayandkay.com

NATIONAL POULTRY AND FOOD DISTRIBUTORS ASSOCIATION

http://www.npfda.org/

NATIONAL POULTRY AND FOOD DISTRIBUTORS ASSOCIATION SCHOLARSHIP FOUNDATION
• *See page 94*

NEW YORK STATE ASSOCIATION OF AGRICULTURAL FAIRS

http://www.nyfairs.org/

NEW YORK STATE ASSOCIATION OF AGRICULTURAL FAIRS AND NEW YORK STATE SHOWPEOPLE'S ASSOCIATION ANNUAL SCHOLARSHIP
• *See page 94*

NEW YORK STATE GRANGE

http://www.nysgrange.org/

HOWARD F. DENISE SCHOLARSHIP
Awards for undergraduates under 21 years old to pursue studies in agriculture. Must be a New York resident with a minimum 3.0 GPA. One-time award of $1000.

Academic Fields/Career Goals: Agriculture.

Award: Scholarship for use in freshman, sophomore, junior, or senior years; not renewable. *Number:* 1–6. *Amount:* $1000.

Eligibility Requirements: Applicant must be enrolled or expecting to enroll full-time at a two-year or four-year institution and resident of New York. Applicant must have 3.0 GPA or higher. Available to U.S. citizens.

Application Requirements: Application form, financial need analysis. *Deadline:* April 15.

Contact: Scholarship Committee
New York State Grange
100 Grange Place
Cortland, NY 13045
Phone: 607-756-7553
E-mail: nysgrange@nysgrange.org

OHIO FARMERS UNION

http://www.ohfarmersunion.org/

JOSEPH FITCHER SCHOLARSHIP CONTEST
Scholarship available to member of Ohio Farmers Union who is a high school junior or senior, or enrolled as a college freshman. Participants are to submit an application obtained from OFU and a typed essay. Essay subject matter changes annually. Award of $1000 to winner and $250 to two runners-up.

Academic Fields/Career Goals: Agriculture.

Award: Scholarship for use in freshman year; not renewable. *Number:* 1–3. *Amount:* $250–$1000.

Eligibility Requirements: Applicant must be high school student; planning to enroll or expecting to enroll full-time at a four-year institution or university and resident of Ohio. Applicant or parent of applicant must be member of Ohio Farmers Union. Available to U.S. citizens.

Application Requirements: Application form, entry in a contest, essay. *Deadline:* December 31.

Contact: Ms. Linda Borton, Executive Director
Ohio Farmers Union
PO Box 363
Ottawa, OH 45875
Phone: 419-523-5300
E-mail: lborton@ohfarmersunion.org

VIRGIL THOMPSON MEMORIAL SCHOLARSHIP CONTEST
• *See page 94*

OREGON SHEEP GROWERS ASSOCIATION

www.sheeporegon.com

OREGON SHEEP GROWERS ASSOCIATION MEMORIAL SCHOLARSHIP
• *See page 94*

OREGON STUDENT ASSISTANCE COMMISSION

http://www.GetCollegeFunds.org/

OREGON HORTICULTURE SOCIETY SCHOLARSHIP
Award for college sophomore or above for fall term/semester in agriculture science or a related field, with a preference to those students majoring in horticulture. To be used at Oregon public and nonprofit colleges and universities only. Minimum 2.5 GPA preference.

Academic Fields/Career Goals: Agriculture.

Award: Scholarship for use in sophomore, junior, or senior years; not renewable.

Eligibility Requirements: Applicant must be enrolled or expecting to enroll full-time at a four-year institution or university and studying in Oregon. Applicant must have 2.5 GPA or higher. Available to U.S. citizens.

Application Requirements: Application form. *Deadline:* March 1.

Contact: Melissa Adams, Scholarship Processing Coordinator
Phone: 541-687-7409
E-mail: melissa.adams@hecc.oregon.gov

RISK MANAGEMENT ASSOCIATION FOUNDATION

www.scholarshipamerica.org

RISK MANAGEMENT ASSOCIATION FOUNDATION SCHOLARSHIP PROGRAM
• *See page 83*

SCARLETT FAMILY FOUNDATION SCHOLARSHIP PROGRAM

http://www.scarlettfoundation.org/

SCHOLARSHIP FOR STUDENTS PURSUING A BUSINESS OR STEM DEGREE
• *See page 84*

SIGMA XI, THE SCIENTIFIC RESEARCH SOCIETY

http://www.sigmaxi.org/

SIGMA XI GRANTS-IN-AID OF RESEARCH
Award to undergraduate and graduate students currently enrolled in degree seeking programs. Applications are accepted through an online form only. Deadlines for all application material are March 15 and October 11 annually and are available online two months prior to the deadline (January 15 and August 1 respectively).

Academic Fields/Career Goals: Agriculture; Animal/Veterinary Sciences; Anthropology; Biology; Chemical Engineering; Civil Engineering; Computer Science/Data Processing; Earth Science; Electrical Engineering/Electronics; Energy and Power Engineering; Engineering/Technology; Environmental Science; Geography; Health and Medical Sciences; Hydrology; Marine Biology; Marine/Ocean Engineering; Materials Science, Engineering, and Metallurgy; Mathematics; Mechanical Engineering; Meteorology/Atmospheric Science; Natural Sciences; Nuclear Science; Physical Sciences; Psychology; Science, Technology, and Society; Social Sciences.

Award: Grant for use in freshman, sophomore, junior, senior, or graduate years; not renewable. *Number:* 400. *Amount:* $1000–$5000.

Eligibility Requirements: Applicant must be enrolled or expecting to enroll full-time at a four-year institution or university. Available to U.S. and non-U.S. citizens.

Application Requirements: Application form.

Contact: Janelle Simmons, Manager of Programs
Sigma Xi, The Scientific Research Society
3200 Chapel Hill Nelson Hwy
P.O. Box 13975
Research Triangle Park, NC 27709
Phone: 800-243-6534 Ext. 206
E-mail: giar@sigmaxi.org

SOCIETY FOR RANGE MANAGEMENT

http://www.rangelands.org/

MASONIC RANGE SCIENCE SCHOLARSHIP
• *See page 94*

SOIL AND WATER CONSERVATION SOCIETY

http://www.swcs.org

DONALD A. WILLIAMS SCHOLARSHIP SOIL CONSERVATION SCHOLARSHIP
• *See page 95*

SOIL AND WATER CONSERVATION SOCIETY-MISSOURI SHOW-ME CHAPTER

http://www.moswcs.org/

MO SHOW-ME CHAPTER SWCS SCHOLARSHIP
• *See page 95*

SOIL AND WATER CONSERVATION SOCIETY-NEW JERSEY CHAPTER

http://www.geocities.com/njswcs

EDWARD R. HALL SCHOLARSHIP
• *See page 95*

SOUTH DAKOTA BOARD OF REGENTS

http://www.sdbor.edu/

SOUTH DAKOTA BOARD OF REGENTS BJUGSTAD SCHOLARSHIP
• *See page 95*

SOUTH FLORIDA FAIR AND PALM BEACH COUNTY EXPOSITIONS INC.

http://www.southfloridafair.com/

SOUTH FLORIDA FAIR AGRICULTURAL COLLEGE SCHOLARSHIP

Renewable award of $2000 for students pursuing a degree in agriculture. Must be a permanent resident of Florida.

Academic Fields/Career Goals: Agriculture.

Award: Scholarship for use in freshman, sophomore, junior, or senior years; renewable. *Number:* 2. *Amount:* $2000.

Eligibility Requirements: Applicant must be enrolled or expecting to enroll full- or part-time at a four-year institution or university and resident of Florida. Available to U.S. and non-U.S. citizens.

Application Requirements: Application form, community service, essay, recommendations or references, test scores, transcript. *Deadline:* October 15.

Contact: Agriculture Committee
South Florida Fair and Palm Beach County Expositions Inc.
PO Box 210367
West Palm Beach, FL 33421-0367
Phone: 561-790-5245

TAILOR MADE LAWNS

http://www.tailormadelawns.com

2017 TAILOR MADE LAWNS SCHOLARSHIP FUND

This $1,000 scholarship will be awarded to a student based on merit and passion for the enhancement of their local and global environment. Candidates will be evaluated according to letters of recommendation, academic records, and their passion for the environment. These qualifications will be demonstrated through faculty references, academic transcripts, SAT/ACT scores, and most importantly, a letter of intent written by the student. All eligible North Carolina students are encouraged to apply online or through the mail.

Academic Fields/Career Goals: Agriculture; Environmental Science; Nuclear Science; Physical Sciences.

Award: Scholarship for use in freshman, sophomore, junior, or senior years; not renewable. *Number:* 1. *Amount:* $1000.

Eligibility Requirements: Applicant must be enrolled or expecting to enroll full-time at a four-year institution or university; resident of North Carolina and studying in North Carolina. Applicant must have 3.0 GPA or higher. Available to U.S. citizens.

Application Requirements: Application form, essay. *Deadline:* May 31.

Contact: Damon Milotte, General Manager & VP
Tailor Made Lawns
1003 1st St W
Conover, NC 28613
Phone: 828-465-4070
E-mail: scholarship@tailormadelawns.com

TURF AND ORNAMENTAL COMMUNICATORS ASSOCIATION

http://www.toca.org/

TURF AND ORNAMENTAL COMMUNICATORS ASSOCIATION SCHOLARSHIP PROGRAM

One-time award for undergraduate students majoring or minoring in technical communications or in a green industry field such as horticulture, plant sciences, botany, or agronomy. The applicant must also demonstrate an interest in using this course of study in the field of communications. An overall GPA of 3.0 is required in major area of study.

Academic Fields/Career Goals: Agriculture; Communications; Horticulture/Floriculture.

Award: Scholarship for use in freshman, sophomore, junior, or senior years; not renewable. *Number:* 1. *Amount:* $2500.

Eligibility Requirements: Applicant must be enrolled or expecting to enroll full-time at a two-year or four-year institution or university. Applicant must have 3.0 GPA or higher. Available to U.S. and non-U.S. citizens.

Application Requirements: Application form, essay, portfolio, recommendations or references, resume, transcript. *Deadline:* March 1.

Contact: Den Gardner, Executive Director
Phone: 952-758-6340
E-mail: toca@gardnerandgardnercommunications.com

UNITED STATES DEPARTMENT OF AGRICULTURE

http://www.usda.gov/

USDA/1994 TRIBAL SCHOLARS PROGRAM

Scholarships for applicants attending 1994 Land Grant Tribal Colleges and Universities seeking careers in food, agriculture, and natural resource sciences, and/or other related disciplines. The program offers support for an Associate's degree (up to 2 Years of support) or Bachelor's of Science Degree (up to 4 Years of support).

Academic Fields/Career Goals: Agriculture; Food Science/Nutrition; Natural Resources.

Award: Scholarship for use in freshman, sophomore, junior, or senior years; renewable.

Eligibility Requirements: Applicant must be American Indian/Alaska Native and enrolled or expecting to enroll full- or part-time at an institution or university. Available to U.S. citizens.

Application Requirements: *Deadline:* February 1.

WILLIAM HELMS SCHOLARSHIP PROGRAM (WHSP)

The USDA APHIS is the agency responsible for safeguarding America's agricultural and natural resources from exotic plant and animal pests and diseases. APHIS' PPQ program deals specifically with plant health issues. Scholarship benefits include: financial aid while pursuing a degree; mentoring; paid work experience during school breaks; possible permanent employment upon graduation. Applicants must be enrolled in programs related to agriculture or the biological sciences and must maintain at least a 2.5 GPA.

Academic Fields/Career Goals: Agriculture; Biology.

Award: Scholarship for use in junior or senior years; renewable. *Number:* up to 5000.

Eligibility Requirements: Applicant must be enrolled or expecting to enroll full- or part-time at a four-year institution or university. Available to U.S. citizens.

Application Requirements: *Deadline:* March 1.

Contact: United States Department of Agriculture
Attention: HR/Recruitment
1400 Independence Avenue, SW, Room 1710
Washington, DC 20250
Phone: 202-690-4759

WASHINGTON ASSOCIATION OF WINE GRAPE GROWERS

http://www.wawgg.org/

WALTER J. CLORE SCHOLARSHIP

A scholarship of minimum $500 to a maximum $2000 is awarded to undergraduate and graduate students enrolled in areas of study pertaining to the wine industry. Scholarships will be given to students who are residents of the state of Washington. The number of awards vary each year.

Academic Fields/Career Goals: Agriculture; Food Science/Nutrition.

Award: Scholarship for use in freshman, sophomore, junior, senior, or graduate years; not renewable. *Number:* 6. *Amount:* $500–$2000.

Eligibility Requirements: Applicant must be enrolled or expecting to enroll full-time at a two-year or four-year institution or university and resident of Washington. Available to U.S. and non-U.S. citizens.

Application Requirements: Application form, essay, recommendations or references, resume, transcript. *Deadline:* November 30.

Contact: Vicky Scharlau, Executive Director
Phone: 509-782-8234
E-mail: vicky@501consultants.com

WOMEN GROCERS OF AMERICA

http://www.nationalgrocers.org/

MARY MACEY SCHOLARSHIP

Award for students intending to pursue a career in the independent sector of the grocery industry. One-time award for students who have completed freshman year. Submit statement and recommendation from sponsor in the grocery industry. Applicant should have a minimum 2.0 GPA.

Academic Fields/Career Goals: Agriculture; Business/Consumer Services; Food Service/Hospitality.

Award: Scholarship for use in sophomore, junior, senior, graduate, or postgraduate years; not renewable. *Number:* 2–7. *Amount:* $1000.

Eligibility Requirements: Applicant must be enrolled or expecting to enroll full-time at a two-year or four-year institution or university. Available to U.S. citizens.

Application Requirements: Application form, personal statement, recommendations or references, transcript. *Deadline:* May 15.

Contact: Kristen Comley, Director of Administration
Women Grocers of America
1005 North Glebe Road, Suite 250
Arlington, VA 22201-5758
Phone: 703-516-0700
Fax: 703-516-0115
E-mail: kcomley@nationalgrocers.org

AMERICAN STUDIES

AMERICAN FEDERATION OF STATE, COUNTY, AND MUNICIPAL EMPLOYEES

http://www.afscme.org/

AFSCME/UNCF UNION SCHOLARS PROGRAM

One-time award for a sophomore or junior majoring in ethnic studies, women's studies, labor studies, American studies, sociology, anthropology, history, political science, psychology, social work or economics. Must be African-American, Hispanic-American, Asian Pacific Islander, or American-Indian/Alaska Native. Minimum 2.5 GPA.

Academic Fields/Career Goals: American Studies; Anthropology; History; Political Science; Psychology; Social Sciences; Social Services; Women's Studies.

Award: Scholarship for use in sophomore or junior years; not renewable. *Number:* 10. *Amount:* up to $5000.

Eligibility Requirements: Applicant must be American Indian/Alaska Native, Asian/Pacific Islander, Black (non-Hispanic), Hispanic and enrolled or expecting to enroll full-time at a four-year institution or university. Applicant must have 2.5 GPA or higher. Available to U.S. citizens.

Application Requirements: Application form, essay, recommendations or references, transcript. *Deadline:* February 28.

Contact: Philip Allen, Scholarship Coordinator
Phone: 202-429-1250
Fax: 202-429-1293
E-mail: pallen@asscme.org

ASSOCIATION OF FORMER INTELLIGENCE OFFICERS

http://www.afio.com

AFIO UNDERGRADUATE AND GRADUATE SCHOLARSHIPS

The type of institution attended is less important than the clarity that the course of study being undertaken leads to a career in the U.S. Intelligence Community. So this covers law enforcement, foreign policy, intelligence analysis, counterterrorism, homeland security, foreign language mastery (Farsi, Tagalog, Pashto, Urdu, Mandarin, Arabic, Hindi, etc.—not Spanish or French), and related disciplines. Applicants seeking funding for law or medical school are placed in a third tier as a currently overabundant category inessential to current needs of the I.C. which already suffers from too many lawyers. Applicants must be a U.S. citizen studying at a U.S. Institution. Advanced knowledge and corroboration of claims of near-native performance in one of the mission-critical languages mentioned above puts applicants at top of consideration. Applicants going to online-only schools are acceptable but only institutions that are on a nationally accredited list maintained by the U.S. Dept. of Education. Costly, for-profit and non-profit institutions suspected of gaming the college-loan system, and those with no national accreditation or with fake, odd, bogus, or foreign accreditations, are not considered and cause a student application for support to be set aside.

Academic Fields/Career Goals: American Studies; Aviation/Aerospace; Computer Science/Data Processing; Criminal Justice/Criminology; Foreign Language; History; International Studies; Law Enforcement/Police Administration; Military and Defense Studies; Natural Sciences; Near and Middle East Studies; Peace and Conflict Studies; Political Science; Public Policy and Administration.

Award: Scholarship for use in junior, senior, graduate, or postgraduate years; not renewable. *Number:* 10. *Amount:* $1000–$4000.

Eligibility Requirements: Applicant must be age 19-35 and enrolled or expecting to enroll full-time at a two-year or four-year or technical institution or university. Available to U.S. citizens.

Application Requirements: Application form, essay, personal photograph. *Deadline:* July 1.

Contact: Mrs. Eileen Doughty, Director, AFIO Scholarship Program
Association of Former Intelligence Officers
7700 Leesburg Pike, Suite 324
Falls Church, VA 22043
Phone: 703-790-0320
E-mail: scholarships@afio.com

CULTURAL SERVICES OF THE FRENCH EMBASSY

http://www.frenchculture.org/

TEACHING ASSISTANT PROGRAM IN FRANCE

Grants support American students as they teach English for 7 months in the French school system. Monthly stipend of about 790 euros (net) supports recipient in the life-style of a typical French student. Must be U.S. citizen or a permanent resident (not a French citizen). Proficiency in French is required. May not have received a similar grant from the French government for the last three years. For additional information and application, visit website http://highereducation.frenchculture.org/teach-in-france.

Academic Fields/Career Goals: American Studies; Art History; Education; European Studies; Foreign Language; History; Humanities; International Studies; Literature/English/Writing; Political Science; Social Sciences.

Award: Grant for use in junior, senior, graduate, or postgraduate years; not renewable. *Number:* 1120. *Amount:* $1040–$7280.

Eligibility Requirements: Applicant must be age 20-30; enrolled or expecting to enroll full- or part-time at a four-year institution or university and must have an interest in English language, foreign language, French language, or international exchange. Available to U.S. citizens.

Application Requirements: Application form, application form may be submitted online, essay, passport, personal photograph, recommendations or references, transcript. *Fee:* $40. *Deadline:* January 15.

Contact: Ms. Carolyn Collins, Educational Affairs Program Officer
Cultural Services of the French Embassy
Embassy of France
4101 Reservoir Road, NW
Washington, DC 20007
Phone: 202-944-6011
Fax: 202-944-6268
E-mail: assistant.washington-amba@diplomatie.gouv.fr

THE GEORGIA TRUST FOR HISTORIC PRESERVATION

http://www.georgiatrust.org/

B. PHINIZY SPALDING, HUBERT B. OWENS, AND THE NATIONAL SOCIETY OF THE COLONIAL DAMES OF AMERICA IN THE STATE OF GEORGIA ACADEMIC SCHOLARSHIPS

The Georgia Trust annually awards two $1000 and two $1,500 scholarships to encourage the study of historic preservation and related fields. Recipients are chosen on the basis of leadership and academic achievement. Applicants must be residents of Georgia enrolled in an accredited Georgia institution.

Academic Fields/Career Goals: American Studies; Historic Preservation and Conservation; History; Landscape Architecture.

Award: Scholarship for use in sophomore, junior, senior, or graduate years; not renewable. *Number:* 4. *Amount:* $1000–$1500.

Eligibility Requirements: Applicant must be enrolled or expecting to enroll full-time at a four-year institution or university; resident of Georgia and studying in Georgia. Applicant must have 3.0 GPA or higher. Available to U.S. citizens.

Application Requirements: Application form, essay. *Deadline:* February 9.

Contact: Mr. Neale Nickels, Director of Preservation
The Georgia Trust for Historic Preservation
1516 Peachtree Street, NW
Atlanta, GA 30309
Phone: 404-885-7817
E-mail: nnickels@georgiatrust.org

THE LYNDON BAINES JOHNSON FOUNDATION

http://www.lbjlibrary.org/page/foundation/

MOODY RESEARCH GRANTS

Grants to defray travel and other expenses incurred while conducting research at LBJ Library. September 15 deadline for spring term (January 1 - August 31), March 15 deadline for fall term (June 1 - December 31). Must contact Archives regarding availability of material. Should state clearly how Library's holdings will contribute to completion of project.

Academic Fields/Career Goals: American Studies; History; International Studies; Military and Defense Studies; Museum Studies; Political Science.

Award: Grant for use in senior, graduate, or postgraduate years; not renewable. *Number:* 10–15. *Amount:* $600–$3000.

Eligibility Requirements: Applicant must be enrolled or expecting to enroll full- or part-time at an institution or university. Available to U.S. and non-U.S. citizens.

Application Requirements: Application form. *Deadline:* March 15.

Contact: Mrs. Samantha Stone, Deputy Director
Phone: 512-721-0265
Fax: 512-721-0220
E-mail: samantha@lbjfoundation.org

SOUTHERN BAPTIST HISTORICAL LIBRARY AND ARCHIVES

http://www.sbhla.org/

LYNN E. MAY JR. STUDY GRANT

Grants to assist researchers (graduate students, college and seminary professors, historians, and other writers) with travel and research costs related to research in the Southern Baptist Historical Library and Archives.

Academic Fields/Career Goals: American Studies; History; Religion/Theology; Women's Studies.

Award: Grant for use in freshman, sophomore, junior, senior, graduate, or postgraduate years; renewable. *Number:* 10–12. *Amount:* up to $750.

Eligibility Requirements: Applicant must be enrolled or expecting to enroll full- or part-time at a two-year or four-year institution or university. Available to U.S. and non-U.S. citizens.

Application Requirements: Application form, application form may be submitted online (http://www.sbhla.org/sg_info.htm), recommendations or references. *Deadline:* April 1.

Contact: Bill Sumners, Director
Southern Baptist Historical Library and Archives
901 Commerce Street, Suite 400
Nashville, TN 37203-3630
Phone: 615-244-0344
Fax: 615-782-4821
E-mail: bill@sbhla.org

ANIMAL/VETERINARY SCIENCES

ABBIE SARGENT MEMORIAL SCHOLARSHIP INC.

http://www.nhfarmbureau.org/

ABBIE SARGENT MEMORIAL SCHOLARSHIP
• *See page 91*

AMERICAN PHYSIOLOGICAL SOCIETY

http://www.the-aps.org

DAVID S. BRUCE AWARDS FOR EXCELLENCE IN UNDERGRADUATE RESEARCH

Award available for research in physiology. The student must be enrolled as an undergraduate student at the time of the application. The applicant must be the first author on a submitted abstract to the EB meeting and must be working with an APS member who attests that the student is deserving of the first authorship. Bruce Outstanding Undergraduate Abstract Awards ($100) are given to up to 30 students based on abstract, 1-page letter, and letter of recommendation. Those awardees then compete for Bruce Excellence in Undergraduate Research Awards ($400) by giving oral poster presentations.

Academic Fields/Career Goals: Animal/Veterinary Sciences; Biology; Environmental Science; Health and Medical Sciences; Marine Biology; Natural Sciences; Neurobiology; Sports-Related/Exercise Science.

Award: Prize for use in freshman, sophomore, junior, or senior years; not renewable. *Number:* 10–30. *Amount:* $100–$500.

Eligibility Requirements: Applicant must be enrolled or expecting to enroll full-time at a two-year or four-year institution or university. Available to U.S. and non-U.S. citizens.

Application Requirements: Application form, essay, first author abstract, recommendations or references. *Deadline:* January 12.

Contact: Melinda Lowy, Senior Program Manager, Higher Education Programs
American Physiological Society
9650 Rockville Pike
Bethesda, MD 20814
Phone: 301-634-7787
Fax: 301-634-7098
E-mail: mlowy@the-aps.org

AMERICAN QUARTER HORSE FOUNDATION (AQHF)

http://www.aqha.com/foundation

JAY PUMPHREY ANIMAL SCIENCES SCHOLARSHIP

Ideal candidate is an AQHA or AQHYA member from Texas with a rural farming and or ranching background who wishes to pursue a major in animal science or a large animal related degree from Tarleton State University or Texas A&M University.

Academic Fields/Career Goals: Animal/Veterinary Sciences.

Award: Scholarship for use in freshman, sophomore, junior, or senior years; renewable. *Number:* 1. *Amount:* $6000.

Eligibility Requirements: Applicant must be high school student; planning to enroll or expecting to enroll full-time at a four-year institution or university; resident of Texas and studying in Texas. Applicant or parent of applicant must be member of American Quarter Horse Association. Applicant or parent of applicant must have employment or volunteer experience in agriculture, farming. Applicant must have 3.0 GPA or higher. Available to U.S. citizens.

Application Requirements: Application form, financial need analysis. *Deadline:* December 1.

Contact: Scholarship Office
American Quarter Horse Foundation (AQHF)
2601 East Interstate 40
Amarillo, TX 79104
Phone: 806-378-5040
E-mail: foundation@aqha.org

APPALOOSA HORSE CLUB-APPALOOSA YOUTH PROGRAM

http://www.appaloosayouth.com/

LEW AND JOANN EKLUND EDUCATIONAL SCHOLARSHIP

One-time award for college juniors and seniors and graduate students studying a field related to the equine industry. Must be member or dependent of member of the Appaloosa Horse Club.

Academic Fields/Career Goals: Animal/Veterinary Sciences.

Award: Scholarship for use in junior, senior, or graduate years; not renewable. *Number:* 1. *Amount:* $2000.

Eligibility Requirements: Applicant must be enrolled or expecting to enroll full-time at a four-year institution or university. Applicant or parent of applicant must be member of Appaloosa Horse Club/Appaloosa Youth Association. Applicant must have 2.5 GPA or higher. Available to U.S. and non-U.S. citizens.

Application Requirements: Application form, entry in a contest, essay, personal photograph, recommendations or references, transcript. *Deadline:* June 1.

Contact: Anna Brown, AYF Coordinator
Appaloosa Horse Club-Appaloosa Youth Program
2720 West Pullman Road
Moscow, ID 83843
Phone: 208-882-5578 Ext. 264
Fax: 208-882-8150
E-mail: youth@appaloosa.com

ASSOCIATION ON AMERICAN INDIAN AFFAIRS, INC.

http://www.indian-affairs.org/

ELIZABETH AND SHERMAN ASCHE MEMORIAL SCHOLARSHIP FUND
• *See page 98*

AVACARE MEDICAL

https://avacaremedical.com

AVACARE MEDICAL SCHOLARSHIP

The AvaCare Medical Scholarship recognizes those who are working to better the lives of our customers, students who are pursuing a degree in the medical field, with a prize of $1000 toward college tuition. This scholarship is awarded annually to one submission that tells about an inspiring act of kindness. AvaCare Medical judges will choose five to ten finalists, whose work will then be posted on our website. Voting will be open on our website, and the scholarship winner will be chosen based on a combination of judges' scores and the number of votes.

Academic Fields/Career Goals: Animal/Veterinary Sciences; Behavioral Science; Cosmetology; Dental Health/Services; Food Science/Nutrition; Health Administration; Health and Medical Sciences; Health Information Management/Technology; Neurobiology; Nursing; Oncology; Optometry; Osteopathy; Pharmacy; Psychology; Public Health; Therapy/Rehabilitation.

Award: Scholarship for use in freshman, sophomore, junior, senior, graduate, or postgraduate years; not renewable. *Number:* 1. *Amount:* $1000.

Eligibility Requirements: Applicant must be enrolled or expecting to enroll full- or part-time at a two-year or four-year institution or university. Applicant must have 3.0 GPA or higher. Available to U.S. citizens.

Application Requirements: *Deadline:* December 15.

Contact: AvaCare Medical Judges
AvaCare Medical
1665 Corporate Road West
Lakewood, NJ 08701
Phone: 877-813-7799
E-mail: scholarship@avacaremedical.com

GREAT MINDS IN STEM

www.greatmindsinstem.org

HISPANIC ENGINEER NATIONAL ACHIEVEMENT AWARDS CORPORATION SCHOLARSHIP PROGRAM

Scholarships available to Hispanic students maintaining a 3.0 GPA. Must be studying science, technology, engineering or math related discipline. Health fields do not qualify.

Academic Fields/Career Goals: Animal/Veterinary Sciences; Architecture; Audiology; Aviation/Aerospace; Biology; Chemical Engineering; Civil Engineering; Computer Science/Data Processing; Construction Engineering/Management; Earth Science; Electrical Engineering/Electronics; Energy and Power Engineering; Engineering-Related Technologies; Engineering/Technology; Entomology; Environmental Health; Environmental Science; Food Science/Nutrition; Hydrology; Industrial Design; Marine Biology; Marine/Ocean Engineering; Materials Science, Engineering, and Metallurgy; Mathematics; Mechanical Engineering; Meteorology/Atmospheric Science; Natural Resources; Natural Sciences; Neurobiology; Nuclear Science; Oceanography; Oncology; Optometry; Osteopathy; Paper and Pulp Engineering; Pharmacy; Physical Sciences; Statistics.

Award: Scholarship for use in freshman, sophomore, junior, senior, or graduate years; not renewable. *Number:* 100–120. *Amount:* $500–$10,000.

Eligibility Requirements: Applicant must be of Hispanic heritage and enrolled or expecting to enroll full-time at a two-year or four-year institution or university. Applicant must have 3.0 GPA or higher. Available to U.S. and non-U.S. citizens.

Application Requirements: Application form, community service, essay, personal photograph. *Deadline:* April 30.

Contact: Dr. Gary Cruz
Great Minds in STEM
602 Monterey Pass Road
Monterey Park, CA 91754
Phone: 323-262-0997 Ext. 775
E-mail: scholars@greatmindsinstem.org

MAINE DEPARTMENT OF AGRICULTURE, FOOD AND RURAL RESOURCES

http://www.maine.gov/agriculture

MAINE RURAL REHABILITATION FUND SCHOLARSHIP PROGRAM

• *See page 93*

MEDICAL SCRUBS COLLECTION

http://medicalscrubscollection.com

MEDICAL SCRUBS COLLECTION SCHOLARSHIP

Medical Scrubs Collection is dedicated to recognizing the individuals who go above and beyond to help others every day. To show our appreciation for these hard working individuals, MSC has decided to Pay it Forward by creating an annual scholarship opportunity for students studying in any health or medical-related field. MSC's scholarship will provide each applicant with a chance to win $1000 towards their college tuition by answering one question: What Inspired You To Pursue A Career In Helping Others? The Medical Scrubs Collection Scholarship will be awarded to the applicant with the winning submission for the thousand dollar question. When the deadline has passed, Medical Scrubs Collection judges will choose five to ten submissions that best fit the criteria for the MSC Scholarship question: What inspired you to pursue a career in helping others? The submissions of these finalists will be posted on Medical Scrubs Collection's website, https://medicalscrubscollection.com/scholarship-program where voting will be open to the public. The final winner will be determined by a combination of judges' scores and the number of votes.

Academic Fields/Career Goals: Animal/Veterinary Sciences; Anthropology; Applied Sciences; Archaeology; Audiology; Behavioral Science; Biology; Chemical Engineering; Cosmetology; Dental Health/Services; Earth Science; Entomology; Food Science/Nutrition; Health Administration; Health and Medical Sciences; Health Information Management/Technology; Marine Biology; Materials Science, Engineering, and Metallurgy; Natural Sciences; Neurobiology; Nursing; Oncology; Optometry; Osteopathy; Pharmacy; Physical Sciences; Psychology; Public Health; Radiology; Therapy/Rehabilitation.

Award: Scholarship for use in freshman, sophomore, junior, senior, graduate, or postgraduate years; renewable. *Number:* 1. *Amount:* $1000.

Eligibility Requirements: Applicant must be enrolled or expecting to enroll full- or part-time at a two-year or four-year or technical institution or university. Applicant must have 3.0 GPA or higher. Available to U.S. citizens.

Application Requirements: Application form. *Deadline:* December 15.

Contact: Program Manager
Medical Scrubs Collection
1665 Corporate Road West
Lakewood, NJ 08701
Phone: 888-567-2782
E-mail: scholarships@medicalscrubscollection.com

NATIONAL DAIRY SHRINE

http://www.dairyshrine.org/

KILDEE SCHOLARSHIPS

• *See page 100*

KLUSSENDORF / MCKOWN SCHOLARSHIP

• *See page 100*

NDS STUDENT RECOGNITION AWARD

• *See page 94*

NATIONAL POULTRY AND FOOD DISTRIBUTORS ASSOCIATION

http://www.npfda.org/

NATIONAL POULTRY AND FOOD DISTRIBUTORS ASSOCIATION SCHOLARSHIP FOUNDATION

• *See page 94*

NEXTSTEPU

http://www.nextstepu.com/

$1,500 STEM SCHOLARSHIP

NextStepU.com will award one $1,500 scholarship to one randomly selected winner three times a year. Applicants must enter online at http://www.nextstepu.com/nextstep-scholarships. Winner must be enrolled in college within 3 years from the time the prize is awarded. 3 Awards: DEADLINE (1): January 31 DEADLINE (2): May 31 DEADLINE (3) September 30

Academic Fields/Career Goals: Animal/Veterinary Sciences; Anthropology; Applied Sciences; Architecture; Aviation/Aerospace; Behavioral Science; Biology; Chemical Engineering; Civil Engineering; Computer Science/Data Processing; Construction Engineering/Management; Earth Science; Electrical Engineering/Electronics; Energy and Power Engineering; Engineering-Related Technologies; Engineering/Technology; Environmental Health; Environmental Science; Food Science/Nutrition; Health and Medical Sciences; Health Information Management/Technology; Marine Biology; Marine/Ocean Engineering; Materials Science, Engineering, and Metallurgy; Mathematics; Mechanical Engineering; Meteorology/Atmospheric Science; Natural Sciences; Neurobiology; Nuclear Science; Nursing; Oceanography; Oncology; Optometry; Osteopathy; Paper and Pulp Engineering; Pharmacy; Physical Sciences; Radiology; Science, Technology, and Society; Sports-Related/Exercise Science; Statistics; Surveying, Surveying Technology, Cartography, or Geographic Information Science; Trade/Technical Specialties.

Award: Scholarship for use in freshman, sophomore, junior, senior, or graduate years; not renewable. *Number:* 2–3. *Amount:* $1500.

Eligibility Requirements: Applicant must be enrolled or expecting to enroll full- or part-time at a two-year or four-year or technical institution or university. Available to U.S. and Canadian citizens.

Application Requirements: Application form, essay. *Deadline:* continuous.

Contact: Web Department
E-mail: webcopy@nextstepu.com

OREGON SHEEP GROWERS ASSOCIATION

www.sheeporegon.com

OREGON SHEEP GROWERS ASSOCIATION MEMORIAL SCHOLARSHIP
• *See page 94*

OREGON STUDENT ASSISTANCE COMMISSION

http://www.GetCollegeFunds.org/

WESTERN VETERINARY SCHOLARSHIP

Award for students who will enroll as college juniors or above. Grad students attending veterinary school preferred. Must be majoring in veterinarian medicine or pre-vet studies with the intent of becoming a DMV. For study at four-year public or nonprofit colleges and universities. Automatically renewable if renewal criteria are met.

Academic Fields/Career Goals: Animal/Veterinary Sciences.

Award: Scholarship for use in junior, senior, or graduate years; renewable.

Eligibility Requirements: Applicant must be enrolled or expecting to enroll full-time at a four-year institution or university and resident of Oregon. Available to U.S. citizens.

Application Requirements: Application form, essay, financial need analysis. *Deadline:* March 1.

Contact: Melissa Adams, Scholarship Processing Coordinator
Phone: 541-687-7409
E-mail: melissa.adams@hecc.oregon.gov

PLATINUM EDUCATIONAL GROUP

www.platinumed.com

PLATINUM EDUCATIONAL GROUP SCHOLARSHIPS PROGRAM FOR EMS, NURSING, AND ALLIED HEALTH

Applicant must be attending a state approved or accredited EMS, Nursing, or Allied Health Program. Must provide a copy of student ID and state identification card, letter of recommendation form from program Instructor (form provided), and a brief essay (500 words maximum) on what interested you in your field and what your plans are upon graduating.

Academic Fields/Career Goals: Animal/Veterinary Sciences; Dental Health/Services; Health and Medical Sciences; Nursing; Pharmacy; Public Health; Radiology.

Award: Scholarship for use in freshman, sophomore, junior, senior, graduate, or postgraduate years; not renewable. *Number:* 3. *Amount:* $1000.

Eligibility Requirements: Applicant must be enrolled or expecting to enroll full- or part-time at a two-year or four-year or technical institution or university. Available to U.S. and non-U.S. citizens.

Application Requirements: Application form, driver's license, essay. *Deadline:* July 14.

Contact: Jeremy Johnson, Director of Marketing
Platinum Educational Group
4370 Chicago Dr SW
Ste B#205
Grandville, MI 49418
Phone: 616-818-7877 Ext. 2904
E-mail: jeremy@platinumed.com

SCARLETT FAMILY FOUNDATION SCHOLARSHIP PROGRAM

http://www.scarlettfoundation.org/

SCHOLARSHIP FOR STUDENTS PURSUING A BUSINESS OR STEM DEGREE
• *See page 84*

SIGMA XI, THE SCIENTIFIC RESEARCH SOCIETY

http://www.sigmaxi.org/

SIGMA XI GRANTS-IN-AID OF RESEARCH
• *See page 101*

SOCIETY FOR RANGE MANAGEMENT

http://www.rangelands.org/

MASONIC RANGE SCIENCE SCHOLARSHIP
• *See page 94*

SOIL AND WATER CONSERVATION SOCIETY-NEW JERSEY CHAPTER

http://www.geocities.com/njswcs

EDWARD R. HALL SCHOLARSHIP
• *See page 95*

STRAIGHTFORWARD MEDIA

http://www.straightforwardmedia.com/

STRAIGHTFORWARD MEDIA VOCATIONAL-TECHNICAL SCHOOL SCHOLARSHIP

Scholarship of $500 available to students enrolled in vocational and technical education programs. Awarded four times per year. Deadlines: November 30, February 28, May 31, and August 31. To apply, visit http://www.straightforwardmedia.com/votech/form.php.

Academic Fields/Career Goals: Animal/Veterinary Sciences; Cosmetology; Culinary Arts; Dental Health/Services; Fire Sciences; Heating, Air-Conditioning, and Refrigeration Mechanics; Pharmacy; Real Estate; Sports-Related/Exercise Science; Trade/Technical Specialties.

Award: Scholarship for use in freshman, sophomore, junior, or senior years; not renewable. *Number:* 4. *Amount:* $500.

Eligibility Requirements: Applicant must be enrolled or expecting to enroll full- or part-time at a two-year or four-year or technical institution or university. Available to U.S. and non-U.S. citizens.

Application Requirements: Essay. *Deadline:* varies.

Contact: Scholarship Committee
Phone: 605-348-3042

UNITED STATES DEPARTMENT OF AGRICULTURE

http://www.usda.gov/

SAUL T. WILSON, JR, SCHOLARSHIP PROGRAM (STWJS)

Undergraduate student applicants must have completed at least two years (60 semester or 90 quarter hours) of a 4-year pre-veterinary medicine or other biomedical science curriculum. Graduate student applicants must have completed not more than 1 year (18 semester or 27 quarter hours) of study in veterinary medicine. Awards up to $1000 per year for undergraduate studies, up to $5000 for graduate studies. Benefits include paid employment during summers and school breaks, full-time agency employment after graduation.

Academic Fields/Career Goals: Animal/Veterinary Sciences; Biology.

Award: Scholarship for use in junior, senior, or graduate years; renewable. *Amount:* up to $5000.

Eligibility Requirements: Applicant must be enrolled or expecting to enroll full-time at a four-year institution or university. Available to U.S. citizens.

Application Requirements: *Deadline:* March 1.

Contact: Saul T. Wilson, Jr. Scholarship
United States Department of Agriculture
USDA, APHIS, Human Resources Division/Office of Recruitment
1400 Independence Avenue, SW, Room 1710
Washington, DC 20250
Phone: 202-690-4759

WILSON ORNITHOLOGICAL SOCIETY

http://www.wilsonsociety.org/

GEORGE A. HALL/HAROLD F. MAYFIELD AWARD

One-time award for scientific research on birds. Available to independent researchers without access to funds or facilities at a college or university. Must be a nonprofessional to apply. Submit research proposal.

Academic Fields/Career Goals: Animal/Veterinary Sciences; Biology; Natural Resources.

Award: Grant for use in freshman, sophomore, junior, or senior years; not renewable. *Number:* 1. *Amount:* $1000.

Eligibility Requirements: Applicant must be enrolled or expecting to enroll full- or part-time at a four-year institution or university. Available to U.S. and non-U.S. citizens.

Application Requirements: Application form, proposal, recommendations or references. *Deadline:* February 1.

Contact: Dr. Carla Dove, Research Grants Coordinator
Phone: 202-633-0787
E-mail: dove@si.edu

PAUL A. STEWART AWARDS

One-time award for studies of bird movements based on banding, analysis of recoveries, and returns of banded birds, or research with an emphasis on economic ornithology. Submit research proposal.

Academic Fields/Career Goals: Animal/Veterinary Sciences; Biology; Natural Resources.

Award: Grant for use in freshman, sophomore, junior, or senior years; not renewable. *Number:* 1–4. *Amount:* up to $500.

Eligibility Requirements: Applicant must be enrolled or expecting to enroll full- or part-time at a four-year institution or university. Available to U.S. and non-U.S. citizens.

Application Requirements: Application form, proposal, recommendations or references. *Deadline:* February 1.

Contact: Dr. Carla Dove, Research Grants Coordinator
Phone: 202-633-0787
E-mail: dove@si.edu

ANTHROPOLOGY

AMERICAN FEDERATION OF STATE, COUNTY, AND MUNICIPAL EMPLOYEES

http://www.afscme.org/

AFSCME/UNCF UNION SCHOLARS PROGRAM
• See page 103

AMERICAN SCHOOL OF CLASSICAL STUDIES AT ATHENS

http://www.ascsa.edu.gr/

ASCSA SUMMER SESSIONS SCHOLARSHIPS

Funding for ASCSA Summer Sessions participants only. Awards for graduate students, high school teachers, and college teachers. One award (Charles Edwards for $500) at undergraduate level used only for participation in the ASCSA Summer Sessions. Six-week sessions in Greece are conducted to become acquainted with Greece and its antiquities. Funding cannot be used for home institution in U.S.

Academic Fields/Career Goals: Anthropology; Archaeology; Architecture; Art History; Arts; Classics; Historic Preservation and Conservation; History; Humanities; Museum Studies; Philosophy; Religion/Theology.

Award: Scholarship for use in senior or graduate years; not renewable. *Number:* 10–11. *Amount:* $500–$4900.

Eligibility Requirements: Applicant must be enrolled or expecting to enroll part-time at a four-year institution or university. Available to U.S. and non-U.S. citizens.

Application Requirements: Application form. *Fee:* $25. *Deadline:* January 15.

Contact: Chair, Committee on the Summer Sessions
American School of Classical Studies at Athens (ASCSA)
6-8 Charlton Street
Princeton, NJ 08540
Phone: 609-683-0800
E-mail: ssapplication@ascsa.org

INTERNATIONAL HOUSEWARES ASSOCIATION

www.housewares.org

STUDENT DESIGN COMPETITION

Industrial design students invent a new product and must submit user research, market research, concept drawings, exploded views and narrative.

Academic Fields/Career Goals: Anthropology.

Award: Prize for use in freshman, sophomore, junior, or senior years; not renewable. *Number:* 6. *Amount:* $1000–$3000.

Eligibility Requirements: Applicant must be enrolled or expecting to enroll full- or part-time at an institution or university. Available to U.S. and non-U.S. citizens.

Application Requirements: *Deadline:* December 15.

Contact: MS. Victoria Matranga, Design Programs Coordinator
International Housewares Association
6400 Shafer Court
Suite 650
Rosemont, IL 60302
Phone: 847-692-0136
Fax: 847-292-4200
E-mail: vmatranga@housewares.org

ISLAMIC SCHOLARSHIP FUND

http://islamicscholarshipfund.org/

ISF NATIONAL SCHOLARSHIP

ISF is a non profit 501 (c)(3) organization with the mission to improve the understanding and acceptance of Islam by supporting students and increasing Muslim American representation in the professions that influence public policy and public opinion through academic scholarships, film grants and networking opportunities. Award is available to both U.S. citizens and green card holders and may be renewed if reapplying. Minimum 3.0 GPA required.

Academic Fields/Career Goals: Anthropology; Filmmaking/Video; History; International Studies; Journalism; Law Enforcement/Police Administration; Law/Legal Services; Near and Middle East Studies; TV/Radio Broadcasting.

Award: Scholarship for use in sophomore, junior, senior, graduate, or postgraduate years; not renewable. *Number:* 1–40. *Amount:* $2000–$5000.

Eligibility Requirements: Applicant must be Muslim faith and enrolled or expecting to enroll full-time at a two-year or four-year institution or university. Applicant must have 3.0 GPA or higher. Available to U.S. citizens.

Application Requirements: Application form, essay. *Deadline:* March 21.

Contact: Ms. Somayeh Nikooei, Director of Operations
Islamic Scholarship Fund
540 Shattuck Avenue
Suite 706
Berkeley, CA 94704
Phone: 650-995-6782
E-mail: admin@islamicscholarshipfund.org

MEDICAL SCRUBS COLLECTION

http://medicalscrubscollection.com

MEDICAL SCRUBS COLLECTION SCHOLARSHIP
• *See page 106*

NEXTSTEPU

http://www.nextstepu.com/

$1,500 STEM SCHOLARSHIP
• *See page 106*

SIGMA XI, THE SCIENTIFIC RESEARCH SOCIETY

http://www.sigmaxi.org/

SIGMA XI GRANTS-IN-AID OF RESEARCH
• *See page 101*

THE SOCIETY FOR THE SCIENTIFIC STUDY OF SEXUALITY

http://www.sexscience.org/

THE SOCIETY FOR THE SCIENTIFIC STUDY OF SEXUALITY STUDENT RESEARCH GRANT

Award to support students doing scientific research related to sexuality. Purpose of research can be master's thesis or doctoral dissertation, but this is not a requirement. Must be enrolled in degree-granting program. Deadlines: February 1 and June 1. All applicants MUST be a member of the SSSS organization. A one-time award of $1000.

Academic Fields/Career Goals: Anthropology; Behavioral Science; Biology; Education; Health and Medical Sciences; Nursing; Psychology; Public Health; Religion/Theology; Social Sciences; Women's Studies.

Award: Grant for use in freshman, sophomore, junior, senior, or graduate years; not renewable. *Number:* 2. *Amount:* $1000.

Eligibility Requirements: Applicant must be enrolled or expecting to enroll full- or part-time at a four-year institution or university. Available to U.S. and non-U.S. citizens.

Application Requirements: Application form, essay.

Contact: Mandy Peters, Executive Director
The Society for the Scientific Study of Sexuality
881 Third Street, Suite B5
Whitehall, PA 18052
Phone: 610-443-3100
E-mail: thesociety@sexscience.org

APPLIED SCIENCES

AMERICAN CHEMICAL SOCIETY, RUBBER DIVISION

http://www.rubber.org/

AMERICAN CHEMICAL SOCIETY, RUBBER DIVISION UNDERGRADUATE SCHOLARSHIP

Candidate must be majoring in a technical discipline relevant to the rubber industry with a "B" or better overall academic average. Two scholarships are awarded to juniors and seniors enrolled in an accredited college or university in the United States, Canada, Mexico, India or Brazil.

Academic Fields/Career Goals: Applied Sciences; Aviation/Aerospace; Chemical Engineering; Electrical Engineering/Electronics; Energy and Power Engineering; Engineering-Related Technologies; Engineering/Technology; Materials Science, Engineering, and Metallurgy; Mechanical Engineering; Nuclear Science.

Award: Scholarship for use in junior or senior years; not renewable. *Number:* 3. *Amount:* $5000.

Eligibility Requirements: Applicant must be enrolled or expecting to enroll full-time at a four-year institution or university. Applicant must have 3.0 GPA or higher. Available to U.S. and non-U.S. citizens.

Application Requirements: Application form, essay, interview. *Deadline:* March 1.

Contact: Christie Robinson, Training and Development Director
American Chemical Society, Rubber Division
411 Wolf Ledges Pwky
Suite 201
Akron, OH 44311
Phone: 330-595-7602
E-mail: crobinson@rubber.org

AMERICAN INDIAN SCIENCE AND ENGINEERING SOCIETY

http://www.aises.org/

A.T. ANDERSON MEMORIAL SCHOLARSHIP PROGRAM

Award for full-time students majoring in Mathematics, Medical Sciences, Physical Science, Technology, Science, Engineering, or Natural Resources. Must be a member of the AISES and an enrolled member/citizen or a decedent of an enrolled member/citizen of a federally or state recognized American Indian Tribe or Alaskan Native Village (or be Native Hawaiian or decedent from a Native Hawaiian). Must have minimum 3.0 GPA.

Academic Fields/Career Goals: Applied Sciences; Biology; Business/Consumer Services; Chemical Engineering; Civil Engineering; Computer Science/Data Processing; Construction Engineering/Management; Dental Health/Services; Earth Science; Electrical Engineering/Electronics; Energy and Power Engineering; Engineering-Related Technologies; Engineering/Technology; Entomology; Environmental Health; Environmental Science; Food Science/Nutrition; Gemology; Geography; Health and Medical Sciences; Heating, Air-Conditioning, and Refrigeration Mechanics; Horticulture/Floriculture; Hydrology; Marine Biology; Marine/Ocean Engineering; Materials Science, Engineering, and Metallurgy; Mathematics; Mechanical Engineering; Meteorology/Atmospheric Science; Natural Resources; Natural Sciences; Neurobiology; Nuclear Science; Nursing; Occupational Safety and Health; Oceanography; Oncology; Optometry; Osteopathy; Paper and Pulp Engineering; Pharmacy; Physical Sciences; Radiology; Science, Technology, and Society; Social Sciences; Sports-Related/Exercise Science; Statistics; Surveying, Surveying Technology, Cartography, or Geographic Information Science; Therapy/Rehabilitation; Transportation.

Award: Scholarship for use in freshman, sophomore, junior, or graduate years; not renewable. *Amount:* $1000–$2000.

Eligibility Requirements: Applicant must be American Indian/Alaska Native and enrolled or expecting to enroll full-time at a two-year or four-year institution or university. Applicant must have 3.0 GPA or higher. Available to U.S. citizens.

Application Requirements: Application form, essay. *Deadline:* May 1.

Contact: Kyle Coulon, Program Officer
Phone: 720-552-6123 Ext. 108
E-mail: kcoulon@aises.org

AMERICAN INSTITUTE OF AERONAUTICS AND ASTRONAUTICS

http://www.aiaafoundation.org/

AIAA FOUNDATION UNDERGRADUATE SCHOLARSHIPS

Available to college students that will be sophomores, juniors, and seniors enrolled full-time in an accredited college/university. Must be AIAA student member to apply. Course of study must provide entry into some field of science or engineering encompassed by an AIAA technical committee. Minimum 3.3 GPA required.

Academic Fields/Career Goals: Applied Sciences; Aviation/Aerospace; Electrical Engineering/Electronics; Engineering-Related Technologies; Engineering/Technology; Materials Science, Engineering, and Metallurgy; Mechanical Engineering; Physical Sciences; Science, Technology, and Society.

Award: Scholarship for use in sophomore, junior, or senior years; not renewable. *Number:* 7. *Amount:* $500–$5000.

Eligibility Requirements: Applicant must be enrolled or expecting to enroll full-time at a two-year or four-year institution or university. Applicant or parent of applicant must be member of American Institute of Aeronautics and Astronautics. Applicant must have 3.5 GPA or higher. Available to U.S. and non-U.S. citizens.

Application Requirements: Application form, essay. *Deadline:* January 31.

Contact: Felicia Livingston
American Institute of Aeronautics and Astronautics
12700 Sunrise Valley Drive
Suite 200
Reston, VA 20191
Phone: 703-2647502
E-mail: felicial@aiaa.org

LEATRICE GREGORY PENDRAY SCHOLARSHIP

Available to female college students that will be sophomores, juniors, and seniors enrolled full-time in an accredited college/university. Must be AIAA student member to apply. Course of study must provide entry into some field of science or engineering encompassed by AIAA. Minimum 3.3 GPA required.

Academic Fields/Career Goals: Applied Sciences; Aviation/Aerospace; Electrical Engineering/Electronics; Engineering-Related Technologies; Engineering/Technology; Materials Science, Engineering, and Metallurgy; Mechanical Engineering; Physical Sciences; Science, Technology, and Society.

Award: Scholarship for use in sophomore, junior, or senior years; not renewable. *Number:* 1. *Amount:* $1250.

Eligibility Requirements: Applicant must be enrolled or expecting to enroll full-time at a two-year or four-year institution or university and female. Applicant or parent of applicant must be member of American Institute of Aeronautics and Astronautics. Applicant must have 3.5 GPA or higher. Available to U.S. and non-U.S. citizens.

Application Requirements: Application form, essay. *Deadline:* January 31.

Contact: Felicia Livingston, Foundation Program Coordinator
American Institute of Aeronautics and Astronautics
12700 Sunrise Valley Drive
Suite 200
Reston, VA 20191-5807
Phone: 703-264-7502
E-mail: felicial@aiaa.org

AMERICAN SOCIETY FOR ENGINEERING EDUCATION

http://www.asee.org/

SCIENCE, MATHEMATICS, AND RESEARCH FOR TRANSFORMATION DEFENSE SCHOLARSHIP FOR SERVICE PROGRAM

Award established by the Department of Defense to support the education, recruitment, and retention of undergraduate and graduate students in the fields of science, technology, engineering, and mathematics. Available only to full-time undergraduate or graduate students with 3.0 GPA or above.

Academic Fields/Career Goals: Applied Sciences; Engineering-Related Technologies; Engineering/Technology; Mathematics; Physical Sciences.

Award: Scholarship for use in sophomore, junior, or senior years; renewable. *Number:* 200. *Amount:* $22,000–$39,000.

Eligibility Requirements: Applicant must be enrolled or expecting to enroll full-time at a two-year or four-year institution or university. Applicant must have 3.0 GPA or higher. Available to U.S. citizens.

Application Requirements: Application form, essay, recommendations or references, transcript. *Deadline:* December 14.

Contact: Evan Gaines, Project Coordinator
American Society for Engineering Education
1818 North Street, NW, Suite 600
Washington, DC 20036
Phone: 202-331-3544
Fax: 202-265-8504
E-mail: smart@asee.org

AMERICAN SOCIETY OF NAVAL ENGINEERS

http://www.navalengineers.org/

AMERICAN SOCIETY OF NAVAL ENGINEERS SCHOLARSHIP

Award for naval engineering students or students in related disciplines in the final year of an undergraduate program or for one year of graduate study at an accredited institution. Must be full-time student and a U.S. citizen. Award of $3000 for undergraduates and $4000 for graduate students.

Academic Fields/Career Goals: Applied Sciences; Aviation/Aerospace; Civil Engineering; Electrical Engineering/Electronics; Energy and Power Engineering; Engineering/Technology; Marine/Ocean Engineering; Materials Science, Engineering, and Metallurgy; Mechanical Engineering; Nuclear Science; Physical Sciences.

Award: Scholarship for use in senior or graduate years; not renewable. *Number:* 8–14. *Amount:* $3000–$4000.

Eligibility Requirements: Applicant must be enrolled or expecting to enroll full-time at a four-year institution or university. Applicant must have 2.5 GPA or higher. Available to U.S. citizens.

Application Requirements: Application form, personal photograph. *Deadline:* February 15.

Contact: Erica Cox, Senior Manager for Education and Business
Development
American Society of Naval Engineers
1452 Duke St
Alexandria, VA 22314
Phone: 703-836-6727
Fax: 703-836-7491
E-mail: asnehq@navalengineers.org

ARMED FORCES COMMUNICATIONS AND ELECTRONICS ASSOCIATION, EDUCATIONAL FOUNDATION

http://www.afcea.org/site/?q=foundation/scholarships

STEM MAJORS SCHOLARSHIPS FOR UNDERGRADUATE STUDENTS

Scholarships of $5,000 for full-time students currently working toward a undergraduate degree in the following STEM majors related to the mission of AFCEA include: Biometry/Biometrics, Computer

Engineering, Computer Forensics Science, Computer Programming, Computer Science, Computer Systems, Cybersecurity, Electrical Engineering, Electronics Engineering, Geospatial Science, Information Science, Information Technology, Information Resource, Management, Intelligence, Mathematics, Network Engineering, Network Security, Operations, Research, Physics, Robotics Engineering, Robotics Technology, Statistics, Strategic Intelligence, and Telecommunications Engineering at an accredited college or university in the United States.

Academic Fields/Career Goals: Applied Sciences; Computer Science/Data Processing; Electrical Engineering/Electronics; Engineering-Related Technologies; Engineering/Technology; Materials Science, Engineering, and Metallurgy; Mathematics; Military and Defense Studies; Physical Sciences; Statistics.

Award: Scholarship for use in sophomore or junior years; not renewable. *Number:* 1–5. *Amount:* $5000.

Eligibility Requirements: Applicant must be enrolled or expecting to enroll full-time at a four-year institution or university. Applicant must have 3.0 GPA or higher. Available to U.S. citizens.

Application Requirements: Application form, community service, essay, financial need analysis. *Deadline:* April 22.

Contact: Mrs. Casmere Kistner, Scholarships, Awards and Grants
Armed Forces Communications and Electronics Association, Educational Foundation
4400 Fair Lakes Court
Fairfax, VA 22033
Phone: 703-631-6147
E-mail: edfoundation@afcea.org

STEM TEACHERS SCHOLARSHIP

The AFCEA Educational Foundation will offer scholarships of $5,000 to students actively pursuing an undergraduate degree, graduate degree or credential/licensure for the purpose of teaching STEM (Science, Technology, Engineering or Mathematics) subjects at a U.S. middle/intermediate or high school.

Academic Fields/Career Goals: Applied Sciences; Biology; Earth Science; Education; Engineering/Technology; Mathematics; Natural Sciences; Physical Sciences; Statistics.

Award: Scholarship for use in sophomore, junior, graduate, or postgraduate years; not renewable. *Number:* 5–25. *Amount:* $5000.

Eligibility Requirements: Applicant must be enrolled or expecting to enroll full-time at a four-year institution or university. Applicant must have 3.5 GPA or higher. Available to U.S. citizens.

Application Requirements: Application form, community service, essay, financial need analysis. *Deadline:* April 22.

Contact: Mrs. Casmere Kistner, Scholarships, Awards, and Grants
Armed Forces Communications and Electronics Association, Educational Foundation
4400 Fair Lakes Court
Fairfax, VA 22033
Phone: 703-631-6147
E-mail: edfoundation@afcea.org

VADM SAMUEL L. GRAVELY, JR, USN(RET.) MEMORIAL SCHOLARSHIP

Scholarships will be awarded to full-time students pursuing an undergraduate degree in a STEM major related to the mission of AFCEA include: Biometry/Biometrics, Computer Engineering, Computer Forensics Science, Computer Programming, Computer Science, Computer Systems, Cybersecurity, Electrical Engineering, Electronics Engineering, Geospatial Science, Information Science, Information Technology, Information Resource, Management, Intelligence, Mathematics, Network Engineering, Network Security, Operations, Research, Physics, Robotics Engineering, Robotics Technology, Statistics, Strategic Intelligence, and Telecommunications Engineering and currently enrolled in an accredited Historically Black College or University (HBCU) institution in the United States.

Academic Fields/Career Goals: Applied Sciences; Computer Science/Data Processing; Electrical Engineering/Electronics; Engineering-Related Technologies; Engineering/Technology; Materials Science, Engineering, and Metallurgy; Mathematics; Military and Defense Studies; Physical Sciences; Statistics.

Award: Scholarship for use in sophomore or junior years; not renewable. *Number:* 2–4. *Amount:* $5000.

Eligibility Requirements: Applicant must be Black (non-Hispanic) and enrolled or expecting to enroll full-time at a four-year institution or university. Applicant must have 3.0 GPA or higher. Available to U.S. citizens.

Application Requirements: Application form, community service, essay, financial need analysis. *Deadline:* April 22.

Contact: Mrs. Casmere Kistner, Scholarships, Awards and Grants
Armed Forces Communications and Electronics Association, Educational Foundation
4400 Fair Lakes Court
Fairfax, VA 22033
Phone: 703-631-6147
E-mail: edfoundation@afcea.org

ARRL FOUNDATION INC.

http://www.arrl.org/

CHARLES N. FISHER MEMORIAL SCHOLARSHIP

One-time award available to amateur radio operators in any class. Applicant must be majoring in electronics, communications, or a related field. Preference is given to residents of Arizona and Los Angeles, Orange County, San Diego, or Santa Barbara, California. Must attend a regionally accredited institution.

Academic Fields/Career Goals: Applied Sciences; Communications; Electrical Engineering/Electronics; Engineering/Technology.

Award: Scholarship for use in freshman, sophomore, junior, or senior years; not renewable. *Number:* 1. *Amount:* $1000.

Eligibility Requirements: Applicant must be enrolled or expecting to enroll full-time at a four-year institution or university; resident of Arizona, California and must have an interest in amateur radio. Available to U.S. citizens.

Application Requirements: Application form. *Deadline:* January 31.

Contact: Ms. Mary Hobart, Secretary
Phone: 860-594-0397
E-mail: k1mmh@arrl.org

MISSISSIPPI SCHOLARSHIP

Available to students pursuing a degree in electronics, communications, or related fields. Must be licensed in any class of amateur radio operators. Preference given to residents of Mississippi attending college in Mississippi. Must be under 30 years of age.

Academic Fields/Career Goals: Applied Sciences; Communications; Electrical Engineering/Electronics; Engineering/Technology.

Award: Scholarship for use in freshman, sophomore, junior, senior, or graduate years; not renewable. *Number:* 1. *Amount:* $500.

Eligibility Requirements: Applicant must be enrolled or expecting to enroll full-time at a four-year institution or university; resident of Mississippi; studying in Mississippi and must have an interest in amateur radio. Applicant or parent of applicant must be member of American Radio Relay League. Available to U.S. citizens.

Application Requirements: Application form. *Deadline:* January 31.

Contact: Ms. Mary Hobart, Secretary
Phone: 860-594-0397
E-mail: k1mmh@arrl.org

PAUL AND HELEN L. GRAUER SCHOLARSHIP

One award available to students licensed as amateur radio operators. Applicant must be majoring in electronics, communications, or a related field at the Baccalaureate level or higher. Preference given to residents of Iowa, Kansas, Missouri, and Nebraska or those attending institutions in Iowa, Kansas, Missouri, or Nebraska.

Academic Fields/Career Goals: Applied Sciences; Communications; Electrical Engineering/Electronics; Engineering/Technology.

Award: Scholarship for use in freshman, sophomore, junior, senior, or graduate years; not renewable. *Number:* 1. *Amount:* $1000.

Eligibility Requirements: Applicant must be enrolled or expecting to enroll full-time at a four-year institution or university; resident of Iowa, Kansas, Missouri, Nebraska; studying in Iowa, Kansas, Missouri, Nebraska and must have an interest in amateur radio. Available to U.S. citizens.

Application Requirements: Application form. *Deadline:* January 31.

Contact: Ms. Mary Hobart, Secretary
Phone: 860-594-0397
E-mail: k1mmh@arrl.org

WIFDR SCHOLARSHIP

One $1000 scholarship for a student with active General Class or higher Amateur Radio license who is studying at any accredited 4-year college or university. Must be studying science, math, engineering, or technology.

Academic Fields/Career Goals: Applied Sciences; Chemical Engineering; Civil Engineering; Electrical Engineering/Electronics; Energy and Power Engineering; Engineering/Technology; Environmental Science; Health and Medical Sciences; Marine/Ocean Engineering; Materials Science, Engineering, and Metallurgy; Mathematics; Mechanical Engineering; Natural Sciences; Nuclear Science; Paper and Pulp Engineering; Physical Sciences.

Award: Scholarship for use in freshman, sophomore, junior, or senior years; not renewable. *Number:* 1. *Amount:* $1000.

Eligibility Requirements: Applicant must be enrolled or expecting to enroll full- or part-time at a four-year institution or university and must have an interest in amateur radio. Available to U.S. citizens.

Application Requirements: Application form. *Deadline:* January 31.

Contact: Ms. Mary Hobart, Secretary
Phone: 860-594-0397
E-mail: k1mmh@arrl.org

ASSOCIATION FOR WOMEN GEOSCIENTISTS (AWG)

http://www.awg.org/

AWG UNDERGRADUATE EXCELLENCE IN PALEONTOLOGY AWARD

The Association for Women Geoscientists is pleased to announce the AWG Undergraduate Paleontology Award. The award, which consists of a $1000 cash prize and membership in the Paleontological Society and AWG for the tenure of the awardee's schooling, will be presented to an outstanding female undergraduate student pursuing a career in paleontology.

Academic Fields/Career Goals: Applied Sciences; Archaeology; Biology; Earth Science; Marine Biology; Natural Sciences.

Award: Scholarship for use in freshman, sophomore, junior, or senior years; not renewable. *Number:* 1. *Amount:* $1000.

Eligibility Requirements: Applicant must be enrolled or expecting to enroll full- or part-time at a two-year or four-year institution or university and female. Available to U.S. and non-U.S. citizens.

Application Requirements: Application form, essay. *Deadline:* April 15.

Contact: Dr. Erin Saupe, Co-Chair
E-mail: goldring@awg.org

ASSOCIATION OF CALIFORNIA WATER AGENCIES

http://www.acwa.com/

ASSOCIATION OF CALIFORNIA WATER AGENCIES SCHOLARSHIPS

Two $3500 awards available to juniors and seniors who are California residents attending California universities. Must be in a water-related field of study. Community college transfers are also eligible as long as they will hold junior class standing as of the fall.

Academic Fields/Career Goals: Applied Sciences; Biology; Civil Engineering; Environmental Science; Hydrology; Natural Resources; Natural Sciences; Surveying, Surveying Technology, Cartography, or Geographic Information Science.

Award: Scholarship for use in junior or senior years; not renewable. *Number:* 2. *Amount:* $3500.

Eligibility Requirements: Applicant must be enrolled or expecting to enroll full-time at a four-year institution or university; resident of California and studying in California. Available to U.S. citizens.

Application Requirements: Application form, essay. *Deadline:* March 1.

Contact: Marie Meade, Outreach Specialist
Association of California Water Agencies
901 K Street, Suite 100
Sacramento, CA 95814
Phone: 916-441-4545
E-mail: mariem@acwa.com

CLAIR A. HILL SCHOLARSHIP

Scholarship is administered by a different member agency each year and guidelines vary based on the administrator. Contact ACWA for current information. Applicants must be in a water-related field of study and must be a resident of California enrolled in a California four-year college or university.

Academic Fields/Career Goals: Applied Sciences; Biology; Civil Engineering; Environmental Science; Hydrology; Natural Resources; Natural Sciences; Surveying, Surveying Technology, Cartography, or Geographic Information Science.

Award: Scholarship for use in junior or senior years; not renewable. *Number:* 1. *Amount:* $5000.

Eligibility Requirements: Applicant must be enrolled or expecting to enroll full-time at a four-year institution or university; resident of California and studying in California. Available to U.S. citizens.

Application Requirements: Application form, essay. *Deadline:* February 1.

Contact: Marie Meade, Outreach Specialist
Association of California Water Agencies
910 K Street, Suite 100
Sacramento, CA 95814
Phone: 916-441-4545
E-mail: mariem@acwa.com

ASTRONAUT SCHOLARSHIP FOUNDATION

http://www.astronautscholarship.org/

ASTRONAUT SCHOLARSHIP FOUNDATION

Scholarship candidates must be nominated by the faculty members. Students may not apply directly for the scholarship. Must be U.S. citizens. Scholarship nominees must be engineering or natural or applied science students.

Academic Fields/Career Goals: Applied Sciences; Aviation/Aerospace; Biology; Chemical Engineering; Computer Science/Data Processing; Earth Science; Electrical Engineering/Electronics; Engineering-Related Technologies; Materials Science, Engineering, and Metallurgy; Mechanical Engineering; Meteorology/Atmospheric Science.

Award: Scholarship for use in sophomore, junior, senior, or graduate years; renewable. *Number:* 19. *Amount:* $10,000.

Eligibility Requirements: Applicant must be enrolled or expecting to enroll full-time at a four-year institution or university. Available to U.S. citizens.

Application Requirements: Financial need analysis, recommendations or references, transcript. *Deadline:* varies.

Contact: Linn LeBlanc, Executive Director
Astronaut Scholarship Foundation
6225 Vectorspace Boulevard
Titusville, FL 32780
Phone: 321-269-6101 Ext. 6176
Fax: 321-264-9176
E-mail: linnleblanc@astronautscholarship.org

BARRY GOLDWATER SCHOLARSHIP AND EXCELLENCE IN EDUCATION FOUNDATION

https://goldwater.scholarsapply.org

BARRY M. GOLDWATER SCHOLARSHIP AND EXCELLENCE IN EDUCATION PROGRAM

One-time award to college juniors and seniors who will pursue advanced degrees in mathematics, natural sciences, or engineering. Students planning to study medicine are eligible if they plan a career in research. Candidates must be nominated by their college or university. Minimum 3.0 GPA required. Nomination deadline: February 1.

Academic Fields/Career Goals: Applied Sciences; Biology; Chemical Engineering; Computer Science/Data Processing; Earth Science;

Electrical Engineering/Electronics; Energy and Power Engineering; Engineering-Related Technologies; Engineering/Technology; Entomology; Environmental Science; Hydrology; Marine Biology; Marine/Ocean Engineering; Materials Science, Engineering, and Metallurgy; Mathematics; Mechanical Engineering; Meteorology/Atmospheric Science; Natural Sciences; Neurobiology; Nuclear Science; Oceanography; Pharmacy; Physical Sciences.

Award: Scholarship for use in junior or senior years; renewable. *Number:* 300. *Amount:* $7500.

Eligibility Requirements: Applicant must be enrolled or expecting to enroll full-time at a two-year or four-year institution or university. Applicant must have 3.0 GPA or higher. Available to U.S. citizens.

Application Requirements: Application form, essay. *Deadline:* January 31.

Contact: Ms. Lucy Decher, Executive Administrator
Phone: 703-756-6012
Fax: 703-756-6015
E-mail: goldh2o@vacoxmail.com

BHW GROUP
https://thebhwgroup.com/

BHW WOMEN IN STEM SCHOLARSHIP
• *See page 74*

DAVIDSON INSTITUTE FOR TALENT DEVELOPMENT
http://www.davidsongifted.org/

DAVIDSON FELLOWS SCHOLARSHIP PROGRAM
One-time award to recognize outstanding achievements of young people. Must be 18 or younger as of October 1, 2018. Must have completed a significant piece of work in one of the following areas: science, technology, engineering, mathematics, humanities (music, literature or philosophy) or outside the box. Must be a U.S. citizen or a permanent resident.

Academic Fields/Career Goals: Applied Sciences; Engineering/Technology; Literature/English/Writing; Mathematics; Music; Philosophy; Science, Technology, and Society.

Award: Scholarship for use in freshman, sophomore, junior, senior, or graduate years; not renewable. *Number:* 15–20. *Amount:* $10,000–$50,000.

Eligibility Requirements: Applicant must be enrolled or expecting to enroll full- or part-time at a two-year or four-year or technical institution or university. Available to U.S. citizens.

Application Requirements: Application form, essay, portfolio. *Deadline:* February 14.

Contact: Tacie Moessner, Davidson Fellows Program Manager
Davidson Institute for Talent Development
9665 Gateway Drive, Suite B
Reno, NV 89521
Phone: 775-852-3483 Ext. 423
E-mail: davidsonfellows@davidsongifted.org

THE ELECTROCHEMICAL SOCIETY
http://www.electrochem.org/

H.H. DOW MEMORIAL STUDENT ACHIEVEMENT AWARD OF THE INDUSTRIAL ELECTROLYSIS AND ELECTROCHEMICAL ENGINEERING DIVISION OF THE ELECTROCHEMICAL SOCIETY INC.
Award to recognize promising young engineers and scientists in the field of electrochemical engineering and applied electrochemistry. Applicant must be enrolled or accepted for enrollment in a college or university as a graduate student. Must submit description of proposed research project and how it relates to the field of electrochemistry, a letter of recommendation from research supervisor, and biography or resume.

Academic Fields/Career Goals: Applied Sciences; Chemical Engineering; Electrical Engineering/Electronics; Energy and Power Engineering; Engineering-Related Technologies; Engineering/Technology; Physical Sciences.

Award: Prize for use in freshman, sophomore, junior, senior, or graduate years; not renewable. *Number:* 1. *Amount:* $1000.

Eligibility Requirements: Applicant must be enrolled or expecting to enroll full-time at a four-year institution or university. Available to U.S. and non-U.S. citizens.

Application Requirements: Abstract of research project, statement of relationship of the project to the field of electrochemical engineering or applied electrochemistry, application form, recommendations or references, resume, transcript. *Deadline:* September 15.

Contact: Ms. Marcelle Austin, Board Relations Specialist
The Electrochemical Society
65 S Main Street, Building D
Pennington, NJ 08534
Phone: 609-737-1902 Ext. 124
Fax: 609-737-2743
E-mail: marcelle.austin@electrochem.org

STUDENT RESEARCH AWARDS OF THE BATTERY DIVISION OF THE ELECTROCHEMICAL SOCIETY INC.
Award to recognize promising young engineers and scientists in the field of electrochemical power sources. Student must be enrolled or must have been accepted for enrollment at a college or university.

Academic Fields/Career Goals: Applied Sciences; Chemical Engineering; Electrical Engineering/Electronics; Energy and Power Engineering; Engineering-Related Technologies; Engineering/Technology; Materials Science, Engineering, and Metallurgy; Mechanical Engineering; Natural Sciences; Physical Sciences.

Award: Prize for use in freshman, sophomore, junior, senior, or graduate years; not renewable. *Number:* 1. *Amount:* $1000.

Eligibility Requirements: Applicant must be enrolled or expecting to enroll full-time at a four-year institution or university. Available to U.S. and non-U.S. citizens.

Application Requirements: Application form, recommendations or references, resume, transcript, written summary of research accomplished. *Deadline:* March 15.

Contact: Ms. Marcelle Austin, Board Relations Specialist
The Electrochemical Society
65 S Main Street, Building D
Pennington, NJ 08534
Phone: 609-737-1902 Ext. 124
Fax: 609-737-2743
E-mail: marcelle.austin@electrochem.org

FOUNDATION FOR SCIENCE AND DISABILITY
http://stemd.org/

GRANTS FOR DISABLED GRADUATE STUDENTS IN THE SCIENCES
Available to graduate students who are disabled. Awards are given for an assistive device or as financial support for scientific research. Undergraduate seniors may apply. One-time award. Electronic application is available.

Academic Fields/Career Goals: Applied Sciences; Biology; Chemical Engineering; Civil Engineering; Computer Science/Data Processing; Electrical Engineering/Electronics; Engineering/Technology; Health and Medical Sciences; Mechanical Engineering; Physical Sciences.

Award: Grant for use in senior or graduate years; not renewable. *Number:* 1–3. *Amount:* $1000.

Eligibility Requirements: Applicant must be hearing impaired, learning disabled, physically disabled, or visually impaired and enrolled or expecting to enroll full-time at an institution or university. Applicant must be hearing impaired, learning disabled, physically disabled, or visually impaired. Available to U.S. citizens.

Application Requirements: Application form, essay. *Deadline:* December 1.

Contact: Dr. Richard Mankin, Grants Committee Chair
Foundation for Science and Disability
503 NW 89th Street
Gainesville, FL 32607
Phone: 352-374-5774
E-mail: Richard.Mankin@ars.usda.gov

INDIAN HEALTH SERVICES, UNITED STATES DEPARTMENT OF HEALTH AND HUMAN SERVICES

http://www.ihs.gov/scholarship

INDIAN HEALTH SERVICE HEALTH PROFESSIONS PRE-GRADUATE SCHOLARSHIPS

Renewable scholarship for American Indian/Alaska Native students who are enrolled part-time or full-time in courses leading to a bachelor degree in the areas of pre-medicine, pre-dentistry, pre-optometry, or pre-podiatry. Minimum 2.0 GPA required to apply. Must intend to serve AI/AN people upon completion of professional healthcare education.

Academic Fields/Career Goals: Applied Sciences; Biology; Health and Medical Sciences.

Award: Scholarship for use in freshman, sophomore, junior, or senior years; renewable. *Number:* 50–100. *Amount:* $23,000–$63,500.

Eligibility Requirements: Applicant must be American Indian/Alaska Native and enrolled or expecting to enroll full- or part-time at a two-year or four-year or technical institution or university. Available to U.S. citizens.

Application Requirements: Application form, application form may be submitted online (http://www.ihs.gov/scholarship), essay, proof of AI/AN descent, curriculum for major, course curriculum verification, recommendations or references, transcript. *Deadline:* March 28.

Contact: Capt. Dawn Kelly, Branch Chief
Indian Health Services
United States Department of Health and Human Services
801 Thompson Avenue
Suite 450-A (TMP)
Rockville, MD 20852
Phone: 301-443-6197
Fax: 301-443-6048
E-mail: dawn.kelly@ihs.gov

INTERNATIONAL SOCIETY FOR OPTICAL ENGINEERING-SPIE

http://www.spie.org/scholarships

SPIE EDUCATIONAL SCHOLARSHIPS IN OPTICAL SCIENCE AND ENGINEERING

Scholarships for high school seniors, undergraduate and graduate students who are SPIE student member. High school students will receive a one-year complimentary student membership. Undergraduate and graduate students must be enrolled in an optics, photonics, imaging, optoelectronics program or related discipline for the full year. More details on eligibility and application requirements/forms can be found at http://spie.org/scholarships.

Academic Fields/Career Goals: Applied Sciences; Chemical Engineering; Electrical Engineering/Electronics; Engineering-Related Technologies; Engineering/Technology; Materials Science, Engineering, and Metallurgy; Mechanical Engineering.

Award: Scholarship for use in freshman, sophomore, junior, senior, or graduate years; not renewable. *Number:* 100–150. *Amount:* $2000–$11,000.

Eligibility Requirements: Applicant must be enrolled or expecting to enroll full- or part-time at a two-year or four-year or technical institution or university. Available to U.S. and non-U.S. citizens.

Application Requirements: Application form, essay, recommendations or references. *Deadline:* January 15.

Contact: Scholarship Committee
International Society for Optical Engineering-SPIE
PO Box 10
Bellingham, WA 98227-0010
Phone: 360-676-3290 Ext. 5452
Fax: 360-647-1445
E-mail: scholarships@spie.org

MEDICAL SCRUBS COLLECTION

http://medicalscrubscollection.com

MEDICAL SCRUBS COLLECTION SCHOLARSHIP

• See page 106

NASA'S VIRGINIA SPACE GRANT CONSORTIUM

http://www.vsgc.odu.edu/

COMMUNITY COLLEGE STEM SCHOLARSHIPS

This scholarship is designated for Virginia community college students studying STEM fields involving science, technology, engineering and math with aerospace relevance. Applicant must be U.S. citizen with a minimum GPA of 3.0 currently enrolled full-time with at least one semester of coursework (minimum of 12 credit hours) completed.

Academic Fields/Career Goals: Applied Sciences; Biology; Computer Science/Data Processing; Construction Engineering/Management; Drafting; Electrical Engineering/Electronics; Engineering/Technology; Environmental Science; Industrial Design; Materials Science, Engineering, and Metallurgy; Mathematics; Mechanical Engineering.

Award: Scholarship for use in sophomore year; not renewable. *Number:* 1–12. *Amount:* $2000–$2000.

Eligibility Requirements: Applicant must be enrolled or expecting to enroll full-time at a two-year institution and studying in Virginia. Applicant must have 3.0 GPA or higher. Available to U.S. citizens.

Application Requirements: Application form, essay, recommendations or references, resume, transcript. *Deadline:* March 17.

Contact: Mr. Chris Carter, Deputy Director
NASA's Virginia Space Grant Consortium
VSGC ODU, PHEC 600 Butler Farm Road
Hampton, VA 23666
Phone: 757-766-5210
Fax: 757-766-5205
E-mail: cxcarter@odu.edu

UNDERGRADUATE STEM RESEARCH SCHOLARSHIPS

Scholarships designated for undergraduate students pursuing any field of study with aerospace relevance. Must attend one of the five Virginia Space Grant colleges and universities. Must have minimum 3.0 GPA. Please refer to website for further details http://www.vsgc.odu.edu.

Academic Fields/Career Goals: Applied Sciences; Aviation/Aerospace; Biology; Chemical Engineering; Computer Science/Data Processing; Electrical Engineering/Electronics; Engineering-Related Technologies; Materials Science, Engineering, and Metallurgy; Mathematics; Mechanical Engineering; Physical Sciences; Science, Technology, and Society.

Award: Scholarship for use in junior or senior years; not renewable. *Number:* 1–35. *Amount:* $3000–$8500.

Eligibility Requirements: Applicant must be enrolled or expecting to enroll full-time at a four-year institution or university and studying in Virginia. Applicant must have 3.0 GPA or higher. Available to U.S. citizens.

Application Requirements: Application form, essay, recommendations or references, resume, transcript. *Deadline:* February 10.

Contact: Mr. Chris Carter, Deputy Director
NASA's Virginia Space Grant Consortium
VSGC PHEC 600 Butler Farm Road
Hampton, VA 23666
Phone: 757-766-5210
Fax: 757-766-5205

NEVADA NASA SPACE GRANT CONSORTIUM

http://www.nvspacegrant.org/

NATIONAL SPACE GRANT COLLEGE AND FELLOWSHIP PROGRAM

The grant provides graduate fellowships and undergraduate scholarship to qualified students majoring in science, technology, engineering, mathematics and science education. Must be a U.S. citizen (permanent residence status, green card or student visa is not accepted)and enrolled full-time in an accredited educational institution in the state of Nevada. Minimum 3.0 GPA required. Awardees cannot receive other federal training grants during the time they are receiving a Nevada NASA Space Grant award.

Academic Fields/Career Goals: Applied Sciences; Aviation/Aerospace; Chemical Engineering; Civil Engineering; Computer Science/Data Processing; Earth Science; Engineering/Technology; Mathematics; Mechanical Engineering; Natural Sciences; Physical Sciences.

Award: Scholarship for use in freshman, sophomore, junior, senior, or graduate years; not renewable. *Number:* 1–50. *Amount:* $1250–$13,333.

Eligibility Requirements: Applicant must be enrolled or expecting to enroll full-time at a two-year or four-year institution or university; resident of Nevada and studying in Nevada. Applicant must have 3.0 GPA or higher. Available to U.S. citizens.

Application Requirements: Application form, application form may be submitted online (http://www.nvspacegrant.org), essay, recommendations or references, research proposal, resume, transcript. *Deadline:* April 28.

Contact: Leone Thierman, Program Coordinator
Nevada NASA Space Grant Consortium
2601 Enterprise Road
Reno, NV 89512
Phone: 775-784-3476
Fax: 775-784-1127
E-mail: nvspacegrant@nshe.nevada.edu

NEXTSTEPU

http://www.nextstepu.com/

$1,500 STEM SCHOLARSHIP
• *See page 106*

OREGON STUDENT ASSISTANCE COMMISSION

http://www.GetCollegeFunds.org/

ANDY AITKENHEAD SCHOLARSHIP

Award for college sophomore or above for fall term/semester of undergraduate study. Must be studying science, mathematics, or engineering. Minimum 3.8 GPA and FAFSA are required.

Academic Fields/Career Goals: Applied Sciences; Earth Science; Engineering/Technology; Environmental Science; Health and Medical Sciences; Mathematics; Natural Sciences; Nuclear Science; Physical Sciences.

Award: Scholarship for use in sophomore, junior, or senior years; not renewable.

Eligibility Requirements: Applicant must be enrolled or expecting to enroll full- or part-time at a four-year institution or university. Applicant must have 3.5 GPA or higher. Available to U.S. citizens.

Application Requirements: Application form, essay, financial need analysis. *Deadline:* March 1.

Contact: Melissa Adams, Scholarship Processing Coordinator
Phone: 541-687-7409
E-mail: melissa.adams@hecc.oregon.gov

SEHAR SALEHA AHMAD AND ABRAHIM EKRAMULLAH ZAFAR FOUNDATION SCHOLARSHIP

Scholarship available to female graduating seniors of Oregon high schools (including GED recipients and home schooled students). Minimum 3.8 GPA. Must be a mathematics or science major at a 4-year public or nonprofit college or university. Scholarship is automatically renewable if renewal criteria met.

Academic Fields/Career Goals: Applied Sciences; Biology; Earth Science; Mathematics; Natural Sciences; Physical Sciences.

Award: Scholarship for use in freshman year; renewable.

Eligibility Requirements: Applicant must be high school student; planning to enroll or expecting to enroll full-time at a four-year institution or university; female and resident of Oregon. Available to U.S. citizens.

Application Requirements: Application form, financial need analysis. *Deadline:* March 1.

Contact: Melissa Adams, Scholarship Processing Coordinator
Phone: 541-687-7409
E-mail: melissa.adams@hecc.oregon.gov

SCARLETT FAMILY FOUNDATION SCHOLARSHIP PROGRAM

http://www.scarlettfoundation.org/

SCHOLARSHIP FOR STUDENTS PURSUING A BUSINESS OR STEM DEGREE
• *See page 84*

SINO-AMERICAN PHARMACEUTICAL PROFESSIONALS ASSOCIATION

http://www.sapaweb.org

SAPA SCHOLARSHIP AND EXCELLENCE IN EDUCATION PROGRAM

$1000 award for a high school senior who is planning to attend a full-time undergraduate program at an accredited four-year college/university with a major related to life sciences. Must have a minimum GPA of 3.3, a minimum SAT score of 2000 out of 2400 (or 1400 out of 1600 for new SAT) or ACT score of 30, and be a United States citizen or a legal resident alien.

Academic Fields/Career Goals: Applied Sciences.

Award: Scholarship for use in freshman year; not renewable. *Number:* 2. *Amount:* $1000.

Eligibility Requirements: Applicant must be high school student and planning to enroll or expecting to enroll full-time at a four-year institution or university. Available to U.S. citizens.

Application Requirements: Application form, essay. *Deadline:* June 30.

TKE EDUCATIONAL FOUNDATION

http://www.tke.org/

CARROL C. HALL MEMORIAL SCHOLARSHIP

One-time award of $400 given to a full-time undergraduate member of Tau Kappa Epsilon, who is earning a degree in education or science and has plans to become a teacher or pursue a profession in science. Applicant should have a demonstrated record of leadership within his chapter, on campus and in the community. Minimum 3.0 GPA required.

Academic Fields/Career Goals: Applied Sciences; Biology; Earth Science; Education; Meteorology/Atmospheric Science; Physical Sciences.

Award: Scholarship for use in sophomore, junior, or senior years; not renewable. *Number:* 1. *Amount:* $400.

Eligibility Requirements: Applicant must be enrolled or expecting to enroll full-time at a four-year institution or university; male and must have an interest in leadership. Applicant or parent of applicant must be member of Tau Kappa Epsilon. Applicant must have 3.0 GPA or higher. Available to U.S. and non-U.S. citizens.

Application Requirements: Application form, application form may be submitted online (http://www.tke.org/member_resources/scholarships/apply_online), essay, personal photograph, transcript. *Deadline:* March 15.

Contact: Offices of the Grand Chapter
TKE Educational Foundation
7439 Woodland Drive, Suite 100
Indianapolis, IN 46278
E-mail: tkeogc@tke.org

UNITED NEGRO COLLEGE FUND

http://www.uncf.org/

BLUE CROSS BLUE SHIELD OF ILLINOIS AND BLUE CROSS BLUE SHIELD OF TEXAS SCHOLARSHIP

Scholarship for residents of Texas or Illinois majoring in a STEM discipline. The scholarship is renewable over four years or graduation to students who meet the renewal criteria.

Academic Fields/Career Goals: Applied Sciences; Chemical Engineering; Computer Science/Data Processing; Electrical Engineering/Electronics; Engineering/Technology; Materials Science, Engineering, and Metallurgy; Mathematics; Mechanical Engineering; Physical Sciences.

Award: Scholarship for use in freshman, sophomore, junior, or senior years; renewable. *Amount:* $5000.

Eligibility Requirements: Applicant must be Black (non-Hispanic); enrolled or expecting to enroll full-time at a four-year institution or university and resident of Illinois, Texas. Applicant must have 3.0 GPA or higher. Available to U.S. citizens.

Application Requirements: Application form, essay. *Deadline:* June 24.

Contact: Mary Williams, Director of Outreach and Recruitment
Phone: 800-331-2244

PROCTER & GAMBLE STEM SCHOLARSHIP

Up to $5000 for academically achieving undergraduate students at accredited four-year colleges or universities within the United States. Focus on providing financial assistance to ensure students have access to quality education toward a successful career in the STEM industry.

Academic Fields/Career Goals: Applied Sciences; Chemical Engineering; Civil Engineering; Electrical Engineering/Electronics; Engineering-Related Technologies; Engineering/Technology; Materials Science, Engineering, and Metallurgy; Mathematics; Mechanical Engineering; Natural Sciences; Nuclear Science; Science, Technology, and Society.

Award: Scholarship for use in freshman, sophomore, junior, or senior years.

Eligibility Requirements: Applicant must be Black (non-Hispanic) and enrolled or expecting to enroll at a four-year institution or university. Applicant must have 3.0 GPA or higher. Available to U.S. citizens.

Application Requirements: Application form. *Deadline:* July 15.

Contact: Mary Williams, Director of Outreach and Recruitment
Phone: 800-331-2244

UNIVERSITIES SPACE RESEARCH ASSOCIATION

http://www.usra.edu/

UNIVERSITIES SPACE RESEARCH ASSOCIATION SCHOLARSHIP AWARD PROGRAM

Award for full-time undergraduate students who are within two years of earning a B.A. or B.S. by time award is received. Must be majoring in the physical sciences or engineering; which include, but are not limited to, aerospace engineering, astronomy, astrobiology, biophysics, chemical engineering, computer science, electrical engineering, geophysics, geology, mathematics, mechanical engineering, physics, and space science education. Must be U.S. citizen or permanent resident. Minimum 3.5 GPA required.

Academic Fields/Career Goals: Applied Sciences; Aviation/Aerospace; Chemical Engineering; Civil Engineering; Computer Science/Data Processing; Earth Science; Electrical Engineering/Electronics; Engineering/Technology; Materials Science, Engineering, and Metallurgy; Mathematics; Mechanical Engineering; Nuclear Science; Physical Sciences; Science, Technology, and Society.

Award: Scholarship for use in junior or senior years; not renewable. *Number:* 4. *Amount:* $4000.

Eligibility Requirements: Applicant must be enrolled or expecting to enroll full-time at a four-year institution or university. Applicant must have 3.5 GPA or higher. Available to U.S. citizens.

Application Requirements: Application form, essay. *Deadline:* August 11.

Contact: Dr. James Lochner, Director of University Relations
Universities Space Research Association
7178 Columbia Gateway Dr.
Columbia, MD 21046
Phone: 410-740-6253
E-mail: jlochner@usra.edu

VERMONT SPACE GRANT CONSORTIUM

http://www.cems.uvm.edu/vsgc

VERMONT SPACE GRANT CONSORTIUM

• See page 96

WHOMENTORS.COM, INC.

http://www.WHOmentors.com/

1B USD WORLDWIDE VENTURE CAPITAL

This is an open call for new creative ideas. Any unincorporated, workable nonexempt project proposals will be considered. 1. What is the nonexempt project idea? 2. Who conducts the nonexempt project? 3. When is the nonexempt project conducted? 4. Where is the nonexempt project conducted? 5. How does the nonexempt project further the 501(c)(3) exempt purposes of WHOmentors.com, Inc.? 6. What percentage of your total time is allocated to the nonexempt project? 7. How will the activity earn revenue beyond the startup grant?

Academic Fields/Career Goals: Applied Sciences; Aviation/Aerospace; Business/Consumer Services; Campus Activities; Communications; Computer Science/Data Processing; Fashion Design; Filmmaking/Video; Industrial Design; Marketing; Materials Science, Engineering, and Metallurgy; Science, Technology, and Society.

Award: Grant for use in freshman, sophomore, junior, senior, graduate, or postgraduate years; not renewable. *Number:* 1–20. *Amount:* $2000–$20,000.

Eligibility Requirements: Applicant must be of Chinese, Japanese, Korean heritage and Chinese, Japanese, Korean citizen; age 12-30; enrolled or expecting to enroll full- or part-time at a two-year or four-year or technical institution or university; single female and must have an interest in Asian language, entrepreneurship, foreign language, international exchange, or public speaking. Available to U.S. and non-U.S. citizens.

Application Requirements: Application form, application form may be submitted online (http://WHOmentors.com/startupgrantapplication), autobiography, community service, complete 10 week, 300 hour internship, driver's license, essay, financial need analysis, interview, personal photograph, portfolio, recommendations or references, resume, self-addressed stamped envelope with application, test scores, transcript. *Deadline:* continuous.

Contact: Rauhmel Fox, CEO
WHOmentors.com, Inc.
110 Pacific Avenue, Suite 250
San Francisco, CA 94111
Phone: 415-373-6767
E-mail: rauhmel@whomentors.com

ARCHAEOLOGY

AMERICAN SCHOOL OF CLASSICAL STUDIES AT ATHENS

http://www.ascsa.edu.gr/

ASCSA SUMMER SESSIONS SCHOLARSHIPS

• See page 108

ARCHAEOLOGICAL INSTITUTE OF AMERICA

http://www.archaeological.org/

JANE C. WALDBAUM ARCHAEOLOGICAL FIELD SCHOOL SCHOLARSHIP

Scholarship available to support participation in an archaeological excavation or survey project. Open to junior and senior undergraduates and first-year graduate students who are currently enrolled in a U.S. or Canadian college or university. Applicants cannot have previously participated in an archaeological excavation, and must be at least a junior at time of application. Applicants must be at least 18 years of age.

Academic Fields/Career Goals: Archaeology.

Award: Scholarship for use in junior, senior, or graduate years; not renewable. *Number:* 5–20. *Amount:* $1000.

Eligibility Requirements: Applicant must be enrolled or expecting to enroll full- or part-time at a four-year institution or university. Available to U.S. and non-U.S. citizens.

Application Requirements: Application form, essay. *Deadline:* March 1.

Contact: Laurel Sparks, Coordinator, Lecture and Fellowship
Phone: 617-358-4184
Fax: 617-353-6550
E-mail: lsparks@aia.bu.edu

ASSOCIATION FOR WOMEN GEOSCIENTISTS (AWG)

http://www.awg.org/

AWG MARIA LUISA CRAWFORD FIELD CAMP SCHOLARSHIP

The Crawford Scholarship encourages promising young women to pursue geoscience careers through attendance at field camp. Two $750 scholarships are awarded annually through a competitive process.

Academic Fields/Career Goals: Archaeology; Earth Science; Education; Energy and Power Engineering; Environmental Science; Gemology; Hydrology; Meteorology/Atmospheric Science; Natural Resources; Natural Sciences; Oceanography; Physical Sciences.

Award: Scholarship for use in freshman, sophomore, junior, or senior years; not renewable. *Number:* 2. *Amount:* $750.

Eligibility Requirements: Applicant must be enrolled or expecting to enroll full-time at a four-year institution or university and female. Applicant must have 3.0 GPA or higher. Available to U.S. citizens.

Application Requirements: Application form, essay. *Deadline:* February 14.

Contact: Sarah Hunt, Crawford Scholarship Coordinator
E-mail: crawford@awg.org

AWG SALT LAKE CHAPTER (SLC) RESEARCH SCHOLARSHIP

Offered by AWG's Salt Lake Chapter, this scholarship will help defray the costs of presenting geoscience research results at national, or regional, science conventions and meetings. It is awarded based upon the quality and importance of the research being conducted and reported.

Academic Fields/Career Goals: Archaeology; Earth Science; Education; Environmental Science; Geography; Hydrology; Meteorology/Atmospheric Science; Museum Studies; Natural Resources; Natural Sciences; Oceanography; Physical Sciences.

Award: Scholarship for use in freshman, sophomore, junior, senior, or graduate years; not renewable. *Number:* 1. *Amount:* $1–$1000.

Eligibility Requirements: Applicant must be enrolled or expecting to enroll full- or part-time at a two-year or four-year institution or university; female and studying in Utah. Applicant must have 3.0 GPA or higher. Available to U.S. citizens.

Application Requirements: Application form, letter from applicant summarizing research, purpose and importance of research, recommendations or references. *Deadline:* March 12.

Contact: Janae Wallace, AWG Salt Lake Chapter Scholarship
Coordinator
Association for Women Geoscientists (AWG)
AWG Salt Lake Chapter
PO Box 58691
Salt Lake City, UT 84152
Phone: 801-537-3387
E-mail: janaewallace@utah.gov

AWG UNDERGRADUATE EXCELLENCE IN PALEONTOLOGY AWARD

• *See page 112*

JANET CULLEN TANAKA GEOSCIENCES UNDERGRADUATE SCHOLARSHIP

This scholarship is for undergraduate women who are committed to completing a Bachelor's degree and pursuing a career or graduate work in the geosciences.

Academic Fields/Career Goals: Archaeology; Earth Science; Environmental Science; Hydrology; Meteorology/Atmospheric Science; Natural Resources; Natural Sciences; Oceanography; Physical Sciences.

Award: Scholarship for use in sophomore, junior, or senior years; not renewable. *Number:* 1–2. *Amount:* $1–$1500.

Eligibility Requirements: Applicant must be enrolled or expecting to enroll full-time at a two-year or four-year institution or university; female and studying in Oregon, Washington. Applicant must have 3.0 GPA or higher. Available to U.S. citizens.

Application Requirements: Essay, financial need analysis, recommendations or references, transcript. *Deadline:* December 15.

Contact: Jenny Saltonstall, AWG PNW Scholarship Chair
Association for Women Geoscientists (AWG)
AWG Pacific Northwest Chapter
PO Box 28391
Seattle, WA 98118
Phone: 425-827-7701
Fax: 425-827-5424
E-mail: scholarship@awg-ps.org

OSAGE CHAPTER UNDERGRADUATE SERVICE SCHOLARSHIP

This Service Scholarship provides an undergraduate student in the geosciences with funding for research, tuition or books. The recipient will be required to participate in two service events (e.g. AWG outreach activities) within a year following receipt of the award.

Academic Fields/Career Goals: Archaeology; Earth Science; Environmental Science; Gemology; Geography; Hydrology; Meteorology/Atmospheric Science; Museum Studies; Natural Resources; Oceanography; Physical Sciences.

Award: Scholarship for use in freshman, sophomore, junior, or senior years; not renewable. *Number:* 1. *Amount:* $500.

Eligibility Requirements: Applicant must be enrolled or expecting to enroll full-time at a four-year institution or university and studying in Kansas, Missouri, Nebraska. Available to U.S. citizens.

Application Requirements: Application form, personal statement, transcript. *Deadline:* April 15.

Contact: Sarah Morton, AWG Osage Chapter President
Association for Women Geoscientists (AWG)
University of Kansas
1475 Jayhawk Boulevard, Room 120
Lawrence, KS 66045
E-mail: awgosage@gmail.com

BHW GROUP

https://thebhwgroup.com/

BHW WOMEN IN STEM SCHOLARSHIP
• *See page 74*

MEDICAL SCRUBS COLLECTION

http://medicalscrubscollection.com

MEDICAL SCRUBS COLLECTION SCHOLARSHIP
• *See page 106*

SCARLETT FAMILY FOUNDATION SCHOLARSHIP PROGRAM

http://www.scarlettfoundation.org/

SCHOLARSHIP FOR STUDENTS PURSUING A BUSINESS OR STEM DEGREE
• *See page 84*

SOCIETY FOR CLASSICAL STUDIES

http://www.classicalstudies.org/

MINORITY STUDENT SUMMER SCHOLARSHIP

Award to minority undergraduate students for a scholarship to further an undergraduate's preparation for graduate work in classics or archaeology. Applicants should be current students of classics. Eligible proposals might include (but are not limited to) participation in summer programs or field schools in Italy, Greece, Egypt, or language training at institutions in the U.S, Canada, or Europe. Amount of the award will range from $1,500 to $4,000. Application must be supported by a member of the SCS.

Academic Fields/Career Goals: Archaeology; Arts; Classics; Foreign Language; History.

Award: Scholarship for use in freshman, sophomore, junior, or senior years; not renewable. *Number:* 2. *Amount:* $1500–$4000.

Eligibility Requirements: Applicant must be American Indian/Alaska Native, Asian/Pacific Islander, Black (non-Hispanic), Hispanic and enrolled or expecting to enroll full-time at a four-year institution or university. Available to U.S. and non-U.S. citizens.

Application Requirements: Application form, application form may be submitted online (http://www.classicalstudies.org), essay, financial need analysis, recommendations or references, transcript. *Deadline:* December 15.

Contact: Dr. Adam Blistein, Executive Director
Phone: 215-898-4975
Fax: 215-573-7874
E-mail: scsclassics@sas.upenn.edu

ARCHITECTURE

AACE INTERNATIONAL

http://www.aacei.org/

AACE INTERNATIONAL COMPETITIVE SCHOLARSHIP

AACE International scholarships are available in amounts ranging from $2000 to $8000. Specific awards will be determined based on overall scholarship and collegiate accomplishments. Applications are only available on line and are accepted from mid-December through February 7th. Applicants should attach an unofficial transcript in a PDF format to their application.

Academic Fields/Career Goals: Architecture; Aviation/Aerospace; Business/Consumer Services; Chemical Engineering; Civil Engineering; Construction Engineering/Management; Electrical Engineering/Electronics; Engineering-Related Technologies; Engineering/Technology; Mechanical Engineering.

Award: Scholarship for use in freshman, sophomore, junior, senior, or graduate years; not renewable. *Number:* 10–20. *Amount:* $2000–$8000.

Eligibility Requirements: Applicant must be enrolled or expecting to enroll full-time at a two-year or four-year institution or university. Applicant must have 3.0 GPA or higher. Available to U.S. and non-U.S. citizens.

Application Requirements: Application form, application form may be submitted online (http://www.aacei.org/awards/scholarships/application.shtml), essay, recommendations or references, transcript. *Deadline:* February 7.

Contact: Mr. John Hines, Manager, Education
AACE International
1265 Suncrest Towne Centre Drive
Morgantown, WV 26505-1876
Phone: 304-296-8444 Ext. 119
E-mail: jhines@aacei.org

AIA NEW JERSEY SCHOLARSHIP FOUNDATION, INC.

http://www.aia-nj.org/

AIA NEW JERSEY SCHOLARSHIP PROGRAM

Scholarship available to New Jersey residents or residents from other states attending school in New Jersey. Must be full-time student in an accredited architectural program at a School of Architecture and have completed one full year of study toward a first professional degree. Applicant must indicate interest in and commitment to pursuing an architectural career in New Jersey after graduation. See website for more information and application, http://www.aia-nj.org/about/scholarship.shtml.

Academic Fields/Career Goals: Architecture.

Award: Scholarship for use in sophomore, junior, senior, or graduate years; not renewable. *Number:* 1–2. *Amount:* $4000–$6000.

Eligibility Requirements: Applicant must be enrolled or expecting to enroll full-time at a four-year institution or university; resident of New Jersey; studying in New Jersey and must have an interest in art. Available to U.S. citizens.

Application Requirements: Application form, essay, financial need analysis, portfolio, recommendations are optional, self-addressed stamped envelope with application, transcript. *Fee:* $5. *Deadline:* June 15.

Contact: Ms. Cris Miseo, Secretary/Treasurer
AIA New Jersey Scholarship Foundation, Inc.
Cris Miseo and Associates, Architect
205 Mt. Pleasant Avenue
East Hanover, NH 07936
Phone: 973-768-1333
E-mail: miseoarchitect@yahoo.com

AMERICAN INSTITUTE OF ARCHITECTS

http://www.aia.org

AIA/F DIVERSITY ADVANCEMENT SCHOLARSHIP

The AIA/F Diversity Advancement Scholarship provides assistance to high school graduates, college freshmen, and community college students from a minority and/or financially disadvantaged background who intend to pursue a NAAB-accredited professional degree in Architecture. A professional degree is either a 5-year Bachelor of Architecture degree or a 4+2 pre-professional Bachelor degree followed by a Master of Architecture degree. At least two letters of recommendation are required from any of the following: an architect; an AIA component; a community design center representative; a guidance counselor or teacher; a director of a community, civic, or religious organization; or the dean, administrative head, or professor at a NAAB-accredited professional program. All applicants must be U.S. citizens. All applications must be submitted via the online portal.

Academic Fields/Career Goals: Architecture.

Award: Scholarship for use in freshman, sophomore, junior, senior, or graduate years; renewable. *Number:* 1–3. *Amount:* $5000.

Eligibility Requirements: Applicant must be American Indian/Alaska Native, Asian/Pacific Islander, Black (non-Hispanic), Hispanic and enrolled or expecting to enroll full-time at a two-year or four-year or technical institution or university. Applicant must have 3.0 GPA or higher. Available to U.S. citizens.

Application Requirements: Application form, essay, financial need analysis, portfolio. *Deadline:* January 25.

Contact: Jeffrey Ostrander, Manager, Diversity and Inclusion
American Institute of Architects
1735 New York Avenue, NW
Washington, DC 20006-5292
Phone: 202-626-7524
E-mail: divscholarship@aia.org

AMERICAN SCHOOL OF CLASSICAL STUDIES AT ATHENS

http://www.ascsa.edu.gr/

ASCSA SUMMER SESSIONS SCHOLARSHIPS
• *See page 108*

AMERICAN SOCIETY OF HEATING, REFRIGERATING, AND AIR CONDITIONING ENGINEERS, INC.

http://www.ashrae.org/

ASHRAE REGION IV BENNY BOOTLE SCHOLARSHIP

One-year scholarship available to an undergraduate engineering or architecture student enrolled full-time in a program accredited by ABET or NAAB and attending a school located within the geographic boundaries of ASHRAE Region IV (North Carolina, South Carolina, Georgia). See Website for application and additional information, http://www.ashrae.org.

Academic Fields/Career Goals: Architecture; Engineering/Technology.

Award: Scholarship for use in freshman, sophomore, junior, or senior years; not renewable. *Number:* 1. *Amount:* $5000.

Eligibility Requirements: Applicant must be enrolled or expecting to enroll full-time at a four-year institution or university and studying in Georgia, North Carolina, South Carolina. Applicant must have 3.0 GPA or higher. Available to U.S. and non-U.S. citizens.

Application Requirements: Application form, financial need analysis. *Deadline:* December 1.

Contact: Lois Benedict, Scholarship Administrator
Phone: 404-636-8400 Ext. 1120
E-mail: lbenedict@ashrae.org

ARCHITECTURAL PRECAST ASSOCIATION

http://www.archprecast.org

TOM CORY MEMORIAL SCHOLARSHIPS

One $2000 scholarship available to college upperclassmen, Master's, and doctoral students. Must be studying architecture and have a minimum 3.0 GPA.

Academic Fields/Career Goals: Architecture.

Award: Scholarship for use in junior, senior, graduate, or postgraduate years; not renewable. *Number:* 1. *Amount:* $2000.

Eligibility Requirements: Applicant must be enrolled or expecting to enroll full-time at a four-year institution or university. Applicant must have 3.0 GPA or higher. Available to U.S. and Canadian citizens.

Application Requirements: Application form. *Deadline:* March 31.

Contact: Mrs. Lisa Collier, Program Manager
Architectural Precast Association
325 John Knox Road
Suite L103
Tallahassee, FL 32303
Phone: 850-224-0711
E-mail: info@archprecast.org

ASSOCIATION FOR WOMEN IN ARCHITECTURE FOUNDATION

http://www.awa-la.org/

ASSOCIATION FOR WOMEN IN ARCHITECTURE FOUNDATION SCHOLARSHIP

Must be a California resident or attend school in California. Open to women only. Must major in architecture or a related design field (landscape architecture, urban and land planning, interior design and environmental design) and have completed 18 units in that major by the application date. Recipients may reapply. Applications and further details are available for download on Website http://www.awaplusd.org/scholarships.

Academic Fields/Career Goals: Architecture.

Award: Scholarship for use in sophomore, junior, senior, or graduate years; not renewable. *Number:* 2–5. *Amount:* $2500.

Eligibility Requirements: Applicant must be enrolled or expecting to enroll full-time at a four-year institution or university and female. Available to U.S. and non-U.S. citizens.

Application Requirements: Application form, portfolio. *Deadline:* April 12.

Contact: Ms. Lise Bornstein, Scholarship Chair
Association for Women in Architecture Foundation
AWAF Scholarships/ Association for Women in Architecture Foundation
1315 Storm Parkway
Torrance, CA 90501-5034
Phone: 310-534-8466
E-mail: scholarships@awaplusd.org

BHW GROUP

https://thebhwgroup.com/

BHW WOMEN IN STEM SCHOLARSHIP

• See page 74

BRASKEM ODEBRECHT

http://www.odebrechtaward.com

ODEBRECHT AWARD FOR SUSTAINABLE DEVELOPMENT

Award for undergraduate students in all engineering fields, architecture, building and construction management, and chemistry. By submitting a paper that outlines contributions to sustainability, students have an opportunity to win $65,000 in cash prizes for themselves, their faculty advisors and their universities. Ideas can be related to efficient, real-world uses of sustainable materials, new chemical and petrochemical processes or new building techniques. Must register at website to enter.

Academic Fields/Career Goals: Architecture; Chemical Engineering; Civil Engineering; Construction Engineering/Management; Electrical Engineering/Electronics; Energy and Power Engineering; Mechanical Engineering.

Award: Prize for use in freshman, sophomore, junior, or senior years; not renewable.

Eligibility Requirements: Applicant must be enrolled or expecting to enroll full- or part-time at a four-year institution or university. Available to U.S. citizens.

Application Requirements: Application form, application form may be submitted online, recommendations or references, university identification. *Deadline:* May 31.

CENTER FOR ARCHITECTURE

http://www.cfafoundation.org/scholarships

CENTER FOR ARCHITECTURE DESIGN SCHOLARSHIP

Merit-based scholarships that support deserving students studying architecture, design, engineering, planning or a related discipline in an accredited program within New York State.

Academic Fields/Career Goals: Architecture; Civil Engineering; Electrical Engineering/Electronics; Industrial Design; Interior Design; Landscape Architecture; Mechanical Engineering.

Award: Scholarship for use in freshman, sophomore, junior, senior, or graduate years; not renewable. *Number:* 1–2. *Amount:* $2000–$5000.

Eligibility Requirements: Applicant must be enrolled or expecting to enroll full-time at a two-year or four-year or technical institution or university; resident of New York and studying in New York. Available to U.S. citizens.

Application Requirements: Application form, essay, portfolio. *Deadline:* March 15.

Contact: Ms. Morgan Watson, Development Associate
Center for Architecture
Attention: CFA Design Scholarship
536 LaGuardia Place
New York, NY 10012
Phone: 212-358-6110
E-mail: scholarships@cfafoundation.org

CENTER FOR ARCHITECTURE, DOUGLAS HASKELL AWARD FOR STUDENT JOURNALS

Any journal (online or print) published by a school of architecture, landscape architecture or planning in the United States that is edited by students is eligible. The publication must have been produced in the current or previous school year.

Academic Fields/Career Goals: Architecture; Engineering/Technology; Landscape Architecture; Urban and Regional Planning.

Award: Prize for use in freshman, sophomore, junior, senior, or graduate years; not renewable. *Number:* 1–3. *Amount:* $1000–$2000.

Eligibility Requirements: Applicant must be enrolled or expecting to enroll full- or part-time at a two-year or four-year or technical institution or university and must have an interest in writing. Available to U.S. citizens.

Application Requirements: Application form, essay, portfolio. *Deadline:* May 1.

Contact: Ms. Morgan Watson, Development Associate
Center for Architecture
Attention: Haskell Award
536 LaGuardia Place
New York, NY 10012
Phone: 212-358-6110
E-mail: scholarships@cfafoundation.org

CENTER FOR ARCHITECTURE, WOMEN'S AUXILIARY ELEANOR ALLWORK SCHOLARSHIP

Students seeking their first degree in architecture from an NAAB accredited school within the State of New York are eligible. The Dean or Chair of the architectural school shall nominate up to three students from their respective college or university to apply. Nominated students will have a high level of academic performance and evidence of financial need. The financial need of each student shall be determined by the guidelines of the Financial Aid Officer of the school nominating the candidate. Students need not be U.S. citizens.

Academic Fields/Career Goals: Architecture.

Award: Scholarship for use in freshman, sophomore, junior, senior, or graduate years; not renewable. *Number:* 1–5. *Amount:* $4000–$10,000.

Eligibility Requirements: Applicant must be enrolled or expecting to enroll full-time at a four-year institution or university; resident of New York and studying in New York. Available to U.S. and non-U.S. citizens.

Application Requirements: Application form, portfolio. *Deadline:* March 15.

Contact: Ms. Morgan Watson, Development Associate
Center for Architecture
Attention: Allwork Scholarship
536 LaGuardia Place
New York, NY 10012
Phone: 212-358-6110
E-mail: scholarships@cfafoundation.org

THE WALTER A. HUNT, JR. SCHOLARSHIP

To promote and encourage the study of architecture by New York City public high school students through a two-year scholarship to supplement tuition and related costs during their freshman and sophomore years at Architecture School in the US.

Academic Fields/Career Goals: Architecture.

Award: Scholarship for use in freshman or sophomore years; not renewable. *Number:* 1–2. *Amount:* $7500–$10,000.

Eligibility Requirements: Applicant must be high school student; planning to enroll or expecting to enroll full-time at a four-year institution or university and resident of New York. Available to U.S. and non-U.S. citizens.

Application Requirements: Application form, essay, interview, portfolio. *Deadline:* May 15.

Contact: Ms. Morgan Watson, Development Associate
Center for Architecture
Attention: Walter A. Hunt, Jr. Scholarship
536 LaGuardia Place
NY, NY 10012
Phone: 212-358-6110
E-mail: scholarships@cfafoundation.org

CONGRESSIONAL BLACK CAUCUS FOUNDATION, INC.

http://www.cbcfinc.org/

CBC SPOUSES VISUAL ARTS SCHOLARSHIP

The CBC Spouses Visual Arts Scholarship was established in 2006. This program provides financial awards to students who have a passion for and plan on pursuing a career in the visual arts.

Academic Fields/Career Goals: Architecture; Arts; Fashion Design; Filmmaking/Video; Graphics/Graphic Arts/Printing.

Award: Scholarship for use in freshman, sophomore, junior, or senior years; not renewable. *Number:* 10. *Amount:* $3000.

Eligibility Requirements: Applicant must be enrolled or expecting to enroll full-time at a two-year or four-year institution or university and studying in Alabama, Alaska, Arizona, Arkansas, California, Colorado, Connecticut, Delaware, District of Columbia, Florida, Georgia, Guam, Hawaii, Idaho, Illinois, Indiana, Iowa, Kansas, Kentucky, Louisiana, Maine, Maryland, Massachusetts, Michigan, Minnesota, Mississippi, Missouri, Montana, Nebraska, Nevada, New Hampshire, New Jersey, New Mexico, New York, North Carolina, North Dakota, Ohio, Oklahoma, Oregon, Pennsylvania, Puerto Rico, Rhode Island, South Carolina, South Dakota, Tennessee, Texas, Utah, Vermont, Virginia, Washington, West Virginia, Wisconsin, Wyoming. Applicant must have 2.5 GPA or higher. Available to U.S. citizens.

Application Requirements: Application form, essay, financial need analysis, personal photograph. *Deadline:* April 21.

Contact: Ms. Katrina Finch, Program Administrator, Scholarships
Phone: 202-263-2800
E-mail: scholarships@cbcfinc.org

THE DALLAS FOUNDATION

http://www.dallasfoundation.org/

DALLAS CENTER FOR ARCHITECTURE FOUNDATION—HKS/JOHN HUMPHRIES SCHOLARSHIP

The scholarship must be used in the year it is awarded. If the funds are not used in this time period, they will be forfeited. The funds are intended to be used for college tuition towards a degree in architecture, and as such, will be routed directly to the appropriate college office for credit towards tuition. Must be a Dallas city resident.

Academic Fields/Career Goals: Architecture.

Award: Scholarship for use in freshman year; not renewable. *Amount:* $2000.

Eligibility Requirements: Applicant must be high school student; planning to enroll or expecting to enroll full-time at a four-year institution or university and resident of Texas.

Application Requirements: Application form, essay, portfolio, recommendations or references, transcript. *Deadline:* March 31.

Contact: Rachel Lasseter, Program Associate
Phone: 214-741-9898
E-mail: scholarships@dallasfoundation.org

WHITLEY PLACE SCHOLARSHIP

Established in 2009, the Whitley Place Scholarship seeks to provide aid to graduating seniors in Prosper ISD who plan to study civil engineering, construction science, construction management, architecture, landscape architecture, planning, public administration, mechanical engineering or other math/science related fields.

Academic Fields/Career Goals: Architecture; Civil Engineering; Engineering/Technology; Landscape Architecture; Mathematics; Mechanical Engineering; Physical Sciences; Public Policy and Administration.

Award: Scholarship for use in freshman, sophomore, junior, or senior years; renewable. *Amount:* $2500.

Eligibility Requirements: Applicant must be high school student; planning to enroll or expecting to enroll full-time at a two-year or four-year institution or university and resident of Texas. Applicant must have 3.0 GPA or higher.

Application Requirements: Application form, driver's license, financial need analysis, recommendations or references, resume, transcript. *Deadline:* March 31.

Contact: Rachel Lasseter, Program Associate
Phone: 214-741-9898
E-mail: scholarships@dallasfoundation.org

FLORIDA EDUCATIONAL FACILITIES PLANNERS' ASSOCIATION

http://www.fefpa.org/

FEFPA ASSISTANTSHIP

Renewable scholarship for full-time sophomores, juniors, seniors and graduate students enrolled in an accredited four-year Florida university or community college, majoring in facilities planning or a field related to facilities planning. Must be a resident of Florida with a 3.0 GPA.

Academic Fields/Career Goals: Architecture; Construction Engineering/Management.

Award: Scholarship for use in sophomore, junior, senior, or graduate years; renewable. *Number:* 2. *Amount:* $3000.

Eligibility Requirements: Applicant must be enrolled or expecting to enroll full-time at a four-year institution or university; resident of Florida and studying in Florida. Applicant must have 3.0 GPA or higher. Available to U.S. and non-U.S. citizens.

Application Requirements: Application form, essay, financial need analysis, recommendations or references, test scores, transcript. *Deadline:* June 1.

Contact: Robert Griffith, Selection Committee Chair
Phone: 305-348-4070 Ext. 4002
Fax: 305-341-3377
E-mail: griffith@fiu.edu

GARDEN CLUB OF AMERICA

http://www.gcamerica.org/

GCA AWARD IN DESERT STUDIES

One or more awards of $4,000 to promote the study of horticulture, conservation, botany, environmental science, and landscape design relating to the arid landscape. Open to graduate or advanced undergraduate students studying at an accredited U.S. university. Preference given to students wishing to gain practical field experience—specifically, planning and design for sustainability, rainwater harvesting and plant management, etc.—through structured internships at accredited botanical gardens and arboreta.

Academic Fields/Career Goals: Architecture; Environmental Science; Horticulture/Floriculture; Landscape Architecture; Natural Sciences.

Award: Prize for use in junior, senior, or graduate years; not renewable. *Number:* 1. *Amount:* $4000.

Eligibility Requirements: Applicant must be enrolled or expecting to enroll full-time at a four-year institution or university. Available to U.S. citizens.

Application Requirements: Application form. *Deadline:* January 15.

Contact: Kenny Zelov, Assistant Director of Horticulture
Desert Botanical Garden
Garden Club of America
1201 North Galvin Parkway
Phoenix, AZ 85008
Phone: 408-481-8162
E-mail: kzelov@dbg.org

THE GEORGIA TRUST FOR HISTORIC PRESERVATION

http://www.georgiatrust.org/

J. NEEL REID PRIZE

A $4000 fellowship is given to an architecture student, architecture intern or a recently-registered architect residing, studying or working in Georgia. Proposed projects should involve the study of an aspect of classic architecture.

Academic Fields/Career Goals: Architecture; Historic Preservation and Conservation; Landscape Architecture.

Award: Prize for use in sophomore, junior, senior, graduate, or postgraduate years; not renewable. *Number:* 1. *Amount:* $4000.

Eligibility Requirements: Applicant must be enrolled or expecting to enroll full- or part-time at a four-year institution or university and resident of Georgia. Available to U.S. and non-U.S. citizens.

Application Requirements: Application form, essay, portfolio. *Deadline:* February 9.

Contact: Mr. Neale Nickels, Director of Preservation
The Georgia Trust for Historic Preservation
1516 Peachtree Street, NW
Atlanta, GA 30309
Phone: 404-885-7817
E-mail: nnickels@georgiatrust.org

GREAT MINDS IN STEM

www.greatmindsinstem.org

HISPANIC ENGINEER NATIONAL ACHIEVEMENT AWARDS CORPORATION SCHOLARSHIP PROGRAM
• *See page 106*

HELLENIC UNIVERSITY CLUB OF PHILADELPHIA

http://www.hucphiladelphia.org/

DIMITRI J. VERVERELLI MEMORIAL SCHOLARSHIP FOR ARCHITECTURE AND/OR ENGINEERING

$2000 award for full-time student enrolled in an architecture or engineering degree program at an accredited four-year college or university. High school seniors accepted for enrollment in such a degree program may also apply. Must be a U.S. citizen of Greek descent and a resident of particular counties in NJ or PA.

Academic Fields/Career Goals: Architecture; Engineering/Technology.

Award: Scholarship for use in freshman, sophomore, junior, or senior years; not renewable. *Amount:* up to $2000.

Eligibility Requirements: Applicant must be of Greek heritage; enrolled or expecting to enroll full-time at a four-year institution or university and resident of New Jersey, Pennsylvania. Available to U.S. citizens.

Application Requirements: Application form, financial need analysis, transcript. *Deadline:* April 3.

Contact: Anna Hadgis, Scholarship Chairman
Phone: 610-613-4310
E-mail: www.hucphiladelphia.org

IFDA EDUCATIONAL FOUNDATION

http://www.ifdaef.org/

GREEN/SUSTAINABLE SCHOLARSHIP

The student applying for this scholarship is planning to become an educated participant in the green movement. Paying equal attention to both sustainability factors and design aesthetics, the student should be demonstrating creative use of green products and eco-friendly furnishings in class projects. The student is familiar with current information in the green/sustainable field, is applying this knowledge in class work and has a goal of seeking a future LEED accreditation.

Academic Fields/Career Goals: Architecture; Interior Design.

Award: Scholarship for use in sophomore, junior, or senior years; not renewable. *Number:* 1. *Amount:* $1500.

Eligibility Requirements: Applicant must be enrolled or expecting to enroll full- or part-time at a four-year or technical institution or university. Available to U.S. and non-U.S. citizens.

Application Requirements: Application form, essay. *Deadline:* March 31.

Contact: Earline Feldman, IFDA Director of Scholarships and Grants
IFDA Educational Foundation
112 Hidden Lake Circle
Canton, GA 30114
Phone: 770-378-7221
E-mail: ef.ifda@tapestries.org

ILLUMINATING ENGINEERING SOCIETY OF NORTH AMERICA

http://www.ies.org/

ROBERT W. THUNEN MEMORIAL SCHOLARSHIPS

One-time award for juniors, seniors, or graduate students enrolled at four-year colleges and universities in northern California, Nevada, Oregon, or Washington pursuing lighting career. Must submit statement describing proposed lighting course work or project and three recommendations, at least one from someone involved professionally or academically with lighting. Curriculum must be accredited by ABET, ACSA, or FIDER.

Academic Fields/Career Goals: Architecture; Engineering-Related Technologies; Engineering/Technology; Interior Design; Performing Arts; TV/Radio Broadcasting.

Award: Scholarship for use in junior, senior, or graduate years; not renewable. *Number:* 2. *Amount:* $2500.

Eligibility Requirements: Applicant must be enrolled or expecting to enroll full-time at a four-year institution or university and studying in California, Nevada, Oregon, Washington. Available to U.S. and non-U.S. citizens.

Application Requirements: Application form, recommendations or references, transcript. *Deadline:* April 1.

Contact: Phil Hall, Chairman
Phone: 510-864-0204
Fax: 510-248-5017
E-mail: mrcatisbac@aol.com

ILLUMINATING ENGINEERING SOCIETY OF NORTH AMERICA–GOLDEN GATE SECTION

http://www.iesgg.org/

ALAN LUCAS MEMORIAL EDUCATIONAL SCHOLARSHIP

Scholarship available to full-time student for pursuit of lighting education or research as part of undergraduate, graduate, or doctoral studies. Scholarships may be made by those who will be a junior, senior, or graduate student in an accredited four-year college or university located in Northern California. The scholarships to be awarded will be at least $1500.

Academic Fields/Career Goals: Architecture; Electrical Engineering/Electronics; Filmmaking/Video; Interior Design.

Award: Scholarship for use in junior, senior, or graduate years; not renewable. *Number:* 1. *Amount:* $1500.

Eligibility Requirements: Applicant must be enrolled or expecting to enroll full-time at a four-year institution or university and studying in California. Available to U.S. citizens.

Application Requirements: Application form, recommendations or references, statement of purpose, description of work in progress, scholar agreement form, transcript. *Deadline:* April 1.

Contact: Phil Hall, Scholarship Committee
Phone: 510-864-0204
Fax: 510-864-8511
E-mail: iesggthunenfund@aol.com

INTERNATIONAL FACILITY MANAGEMENT ASSOCIATION FOUNDATION

http://www.ifmafoundation.org/

IFMA FOUNDATION SCHOLARSHIPS

One-time scholarships of up to $5000 awarded to students currently enrolled in full-time facility management programs or related programs. Minimum 3.2 GPA required for undergraduates and 3.5 for graduate students.

Academic Fields/Career Goals: Architecture; Construction Engineering/Management; Engineering-Related Technologies; Engineering/Technology; Interior Design; Urban and Regional Planning.

Award: Scholarship for use in junior, senior, graduate, or postgraduate years; not renewable. *Number:* 25–35. *Amount:* $1500–$5000.

Eligibility Requirements: Applicant must be enrolled or expecting to enroll full-time at a four-year institution or university. Applicant must have 3.5 GPA or higher. Available to U.S. and non-U.S. citizens.

Application Requirements: Application form. *Deadline:* April 20.

Contact: Amy Arnold, Foundation Administrator
International Facility Management Association Foundation
800 Gessner
Suite 900
Houston, TX 77024
Phone: 713-623-4362
E-mail: amy.arnold@ifma.org

MIDWEST ROOFING CONTRACTORS ASSOCIATION

http://www.mrca.org/

MRCA FOUNDATION SCHOLARSHIP PROGRAM

Renewable scholarships for full-time students enrolled or intending to enroll in an accredited university, college, community college, or trade school. Applicant must be pursuing a curriculum leading to a career in the construction industry or related. Award amount ranges from $500 to $3000.

Academic Fields/Career Goals: Architecture; Civil Engineering; Construction Engineering/Management; Drafting; Engineering/Technology; Industrial Design; Materials Science, Engineering, and Metallurgy; Trade/Technical Specialties.

Award: Scholarship for use in freshman, sophomore, junior, or senior years; not renewable. *Number:* up to 40. *Amount:* $500–$3000.

Eligibility Requirements: Applicant must be enrolled or expecting to enroll full-time at a two-year or four-year or technical institution or university. Applicant or parent of applicant must have employment or volunteer experience in construction. Applicant must have 3.0 GPA or higher. Available to U.S. citizens.

Application Requirements: Application form, community service, essay, financial need analysis, recommendations or references, transcript. *Deadline:* June 20.

Contact: Ms. Peggy Doherty, Operations Manager
Midwest Roofing Contractors Association
4700 West Lake Avenue
Glenview, IL 60025
Phone: 847-375-6378
Fax: 847-375-6473

NATIONAL ASSOCIATION OF WOMEN IN CONSTRUCTION

http://www.nawic.org/

NAWIC UNDERGRADUATE SCHOLARSHIPS

One-time award for any student having at least one year of study remaining in a construction-related program leading to an Associate or higher degree. Awards range from $500 to $2000. Submit application and transcript of grades.

Academic Fields/Career Goals: Architecture; Civil Engineering; Drafting; Electrical Engineering/Electronics; Engineering-Related Technologies; Engineering/Technology; Interior Design; Landscape Architecture; Mechanical Engineering; Trade/Technical Specialties.

Award: Scholarship for use in sophomore or junior years; not renewable. *Number:* 40–50. *Amount:* $500–$2000.

Eligibility Requirements: Applicant must be enrolled or expecting to enroll full-time at a two-year or four-year or technical institution or university. Applicant must have 3.0 GPA or higher. Available to U.S. and Canadian citizens.

Application Requirements: Application form, essay, financial need analysis, interview, transcript. *Deadline:* March 15.

Contact: Scholarship Committee
National Association of Women in Construction
327 South Adams Street
Fort Worth, TX 76104
Phone: 817-877-5551
Fax: 817-877-0324

NEXTSTEPU

http://www.nextstepu.com/

$1,500 STEM SCHOLARSHIP
• *See page 106*

OREGON STUDENT ASSISTANCE COMMISSION

http://www.GetCollegeFunds.org/

HOME BUILDERS FOUNDATION JIM IRVINE STATEWIDE SCHOLARSHIP

One-time award for first-year freshmen or other undergraduates studying architecture, construction, engineering (civil, electrical, industrial, management), interior design/architecture, or landscape architecture. Must be enrolled at least half time. Minimum 3.0 GPA preferred.

Academic Fields/Career Goals: Architecture; Civil Engineering; Electrical Engineering/Electronics; Engineering/Technology; Interior Design; Landscape Architecture.

Award: Scholarship for use in freshman, sophomore, junior, or senior years; not renewable.

Eligibility Requirements: Applicant must be enrolled or expecting to enroll full- or part-time at a two-year or four-year institution or university and studying in Oregon. Applicant must have 3.0 GPA or higher. Available to U.S. citizens.

Application Requirements: Application form, essay, financial need analysis. *Deadline:* March 1.

Contact: Melissa Adams, Scholarship Processing Coordinator
Phone: 541-687-7409
E-mail: melissa.adams@hecc.oregon.gov

SOUTHERN OREGON CHAPTER OF THE AMERICAN INSTITUTE OF ARCHITECTS SCHOLARSHIP

Award available to graduates of (including GED and home-schooled students) Curry, Harney, Jackson, Josephine, Klamath, Lake, or Malheur County high schools. Must attend a four-year nonprofit college or university in the United States, and major in architecture. Preference given to students who have taken the SAT or ACT. Apply/compete for one additional year.

Academic Fields/Career Goals: Architecture.

Award: Scholarship for use in freshman, sophomore, junior, or senior years; not renewable.

Eligibility Requirements: Applicant must be enrolled or expecting to enroll full-time at a four-year institution or university and resident of Oregon. Available to U.S. citizens.

Application Requirements: Application form. *Deadline:* March 1.

Contact: Melissa Adams, Scholarship Processing Coordinator
Phone: 541-687-7409
E-mail: melissa.adams@hecc.oregon.gov

PLAN NEW HAMPSHIRE

www.plannh.org

PLAN NEW HAMPSHIRE SCHOLARSHIP AND PROGRAM

Plan NH, in partnership with the NH Charitable Foundation, offers scholarships and fellowships to students who call New Hampshire home and are studying a field related to planning, design or development of the built environment in an accredited school anywhere in the world. Applicants must have at least one semester of college or equivalent completed before application. Scholarships are available for colleges, universities and tech schools; fellowships are available for grad students of architecture. This is a competitive process for funding from several sources.

Academic Fields/Career Goals: Architecture; Civil Engineering; Energy and Power Engineering; Engineering/Technology; Environmental Science; Historic Preservation and Conservation; Interior Design; Landscape Architecture; Mechanical Engineering; Natural Resources; Transportation; Urban and Regional Planning.

Award: Scholarship for use in sophomore, junior, senior, graduate, or postgraduate years; not renewable. *Number:* 1–5. *Amount:* $1200–$5000.

Eligibility Requirements: Applicant must be enrolled or expecting to enroll full-time at a two-year or four-year or technical institution or university and resident of New Hampshire. Available to U.S. citizens.

Application Requirements: Application form, essay, interview, portfolio. *Fee:* $10. *Deadline:* April 12.

Contact: Robin LeBlanc, Executive Director
Plan New Hampshire
PO Box 1105
21 Daniel Street 2nd floor c/o GPI
Portsmouth, NH 03801
Phone: 603-452-7526
E-mail: r_leblanc@plannh.org

QUALITY BATH

www.qualitybath.com

QUALITYBATH.COM SCHOLARSHIP PROGRAM

Convey the beauty of humanity, e.g. a good deed you witnessed or envision, in a way that will inspire others. Original, unpublished content only. Submit one of the following: essay up to 1,500 words, image up to 8.5 x 11, with description, video up to 90 seconds long, in one of the following formats:.mov,.mp4,.m4v,.flv,.3gp,.avi,.wmv. Submissions containing grammatical or spelling errors, or any inappropriate language or content, may be disqualified. Save a digital copy in case we decide to publish your work. Must be U.S. citizen or permanent resident alien, high school senior or enrolled in accredited U.S. college or university; achieved minimum cumulative GPA of 3.0; currently pursuing a degree in the arts or design field. No professional or familial relation with QualityBath.com and its management. Email to scholarships@qualitybath.com or mail Scholarship Contest, c/o Quality Bath, 1144 East County Line Road, Unit 200, Lakewood, NJ 08701. Include submission, copy of transcript, your name, email address, phone number, degree you are pursuing, proof of citizenship/alien status. Deadline: March 1, 2017.

Academic Fields/Career Goals: Architecture; Art History; Arts; Fashion Design; Filmmaking/Video; Graphics/Graphic Arts/Printing; Interior Design; Landscape Architecture; Music; Performing Arts; Photojournalism/Photography.

Award: Prize for use in freshman, sophomore, junior, senior, or graduate years; not renewable. *Number:* 1. *Amount:* $1500.

Eligibility Requirements: Applicant must be enrolled or expecting to enroll full- or part-time at a two-year or four-year or technical institution or university. Applicant must have 3.0 GPA or higher. Available to U.S. citizens.

Application Requirements: Application form. *Deadline:* March 1.

Contact: Fay Friedman, Director of SEO/Marketing
Quality Bath
1144 East County Line Road
Lakewood, NJ 08701
Phone: 800-554-3210
E-mail: scholarships@qualitybath.com

RHODE ISLAND FOUNDATION

http://www.rifoundation.org/

NORTON E. SALK SCHOLARSHIP

Scholarship for a student enrolled in an accredited school in Rhode Island and pursuing the study of architecture. Must have completed at least one academic year and demonstrate financial need.

Academic Fields/Career Goals: Architecture.

Award: Scholarship for use in sophomore, junior, or senior years; not renewable.

Eligibility Requirements: Applicant must be enrolled or expecting to enroll full-time at a four-year institution or university and studying in Rhode Island. Available to U.S. citizens.

Application Requirements: Application form, essay, financial need analysis, letter of eligibility for financial aid, recommendations or references. *Deadline:* June 15.

Contact: Executive Director, Rhode Island AIA Architectural Forum
Phone: 401-272-6418
E-mail: execdir@aia-ri.org

SCARLETT FAMILY FOUNDATION SCHOLARSHIP PROGRAM

http://www.scarlettfoundation.org/

SCHOLARSHIP FOR STUDENTS PURSUING A BUSINESS OR STEM DEGREE

• See page 84

SUPPORT CREATIVITY

http://wesupportcreativity.org

SUPPORT CREATIVITY SCHOLARSHIP

The Support Creativity Scholarship is for (but not limited to) passionate designers, animators, editors, photographers, artists, illustrators, and painters, who wish to develop their skills at higher education institutions. The student must submit a project that illustrates their passion for their specific creative field in any medium. The student must also submit an essay describing their project as well as any financial hardships.

Academic Fields/Career Goals: Architecture; Art History; Arts; Communications; Culinary Arts; Drafting; Fashion Design; Filmmaking/Video; Graphics/Graphic Arts/Printing; Industrial Design; Interior Design; Landscape Architecture; Marketing; Photojournalism/Photography.

Award: Scholarship for use in freshman, sophomore, junior, senior, or graduate years; not renewable. *Number:* 3. *Amount:* $1000.

Eligibility Requirements: Applicant must be enrolled or expecting to enroll full-time at a two-year or four-year institution or university and studying in Connecticut, New Jersey, New York. Available to U.S. and non-U.S. citizens.

Application Requirements: Application form, essay. *Deadline:* May 1.

Contact: Steve Lucin, Founder
Support Creativity
244 West 54th Street, Suite 800
New York, NY 10019
E-mail: lucin@wesupportcreativity.org

TURNER CONSTRUCTION COMPANY

http://www.turnerconstruction.com/

YOUTHFORCE 2020 SCHOLARSHIP PROGRAM

The scholarship will be awarded to five graduating high school seniors from New York City schools and in the amount of $2000 per year; totaling $8000 after the completion of four years in college. As a scholarship recipient, students must maintain a 2.80 GPA and complete a four-year summer internship at Turner Construction that begins immediately following their first full year of college.

Academic Fields/Career Goals: Architecture; Civil Engineering; Construction Engineering/Management; Electrical Engineering/Electronics; Engineering-Related Technologies; Engineering/Technology; Interior Design; Landscape Architecture; Materials Science, Engineering, and Metallurgy; Mechanical Engineering.

Award: Scholarship for use in freshman, sophomore, junior, or senior years; renewable. *Number:* 5. *Amount:* $8000.

Eligibility Requirements: Applicant must be American Indian/Alaska Native, Asian/Pacific Islander, Black (non-Hispanic), Hispanic; high school student; planning to enroll or expecting to enroll full-time at a four-year institution or university; resident of New York and studying in New York. Applicant must have 3.0 GPA or higher. Available to U.S. citizens.

Application Requirements: Application form, community service, essay, financial need analysis, interview, personal photograph, recommendations or references, resume, test scores, transcript. *Deadline:* April 30.

Contact: Stephanie Burns, Community Affairs Director
Turner Construction Company
375 Hudson Street
6th Floor
New York, NY 10014
Phone: 212-229-6000 Ext. 6480
Fax: 212-229-6083
E-mail: yf2020@tcco.com

VECTORWORKS, INC.

http://www.vectorworks.net

VECTORWORKS DESIGN SCHOLARSHIP

Nemetschek Vectorworks is inviting talented students across all design disciplines to submit their best individual or group work to the Vectorworks Design Scholarship for the chance to win up to $10,000! Additionally, winners' schools receive free Vectorworks design software, as well as free in-person or virtual training for faculty and students. Submissions can be created in any software, and can even be a project previously completed for school. Entering is simple. Answer three short questions by August 31.

Academic Fields/Career Goals: Architecture; Arts; Civil Engineering; Construction Engineering/Management; Drafting; Engineering-Related Technologies; Engineering/Technology; Graphics/Graphic Arts/Printing; Industrial Design; Interior Design; Landscape Architecture; Urban and Regional Planning.

Award: Scholarship for use in freshman, sophomore, junior, senior, or graduate years; not renewable. *Number:* 15–18. *Amount:* $3000–$10,000.

Eligibility Requirements: Applicant must be enrolled or expecting to enroll full- or part-time at a two-year or four-year or technical institution or university. Available to U.S. and non-U.S. citizens.

Application Requirements: Application form, application form may be submitted online (http://www.vectorworks.net/scholarship/en), CAD or Drawn Design submission, entry in a contest. *Deadline:* August 31.

Contact: Marissa Diehl, Marketing Intern
Vectorworks, Inc.
7150 Riverwood Drive
Columbia, MD 21046
Phone: 443-542-0275 Ext. 275
E-mail: mdiehl97@vectorworks.net

WEST VIRGINIA SOCIETY OF ARCHITECTS/AIA

http://www.aiawv.org/

AIA WEST VIRGINIA SCHOLARSHIP

Award for a West Virginia resident who has completed at least their sixth semester of an NAAB-accredited undergraduate architectural program or accepted to a NAAB-accredited graduate architectural program by application deadline. Must submit resume and letter stating need, qualifications, and portfolio of work.

Academic Fields/Career Goals: Architecture.

Award: Scholarship for use in junior, senior, graduate, or postgraduate years; not renewable. *Amount:* $3500–$4500.

Eligibility Requirements: Applicant must be enrolled or expecting to enroll full-time at an institution or university and resident of West Virginia. Available to U.S. citizens.

Application Requirements: Application form, portfolio. *Deadline:* October 16.

Contact: William Yoke, Scholarship Committee Chair
West Virginia Society of Architects/AIA
P.O. Box 813
Charleston, WV 25323
Phone: 304-344-9872
E-mail: aiawv@aiawv.org

AREA/ETHNIC STUDIES

CANADIAN INSTITUTE OF UKRAINIAN STUDIES

http://www.cius.ca/

CANADIAN INSTITUTE OF UKRAINIAN STUDIES RESEARCH GRANTS

Grants for students who pursue Ukrainian and Ukrainian-Canadian studies in history, literature, language, education, social sciences, women's studies, law, and library sciences.

Academic Fields/Career Goals: Area/Ethnic Studies; Canadian Studies; European Studies.

Award: Grant for use in freshman, sophomore, junior, or senior years; renewable. *Number:* 1.

Eligibility Requirements: Applicant must be enrolled or expecting to enroll full-time at a four-year institution or university. Available to U.S. and non-U.S. citizens.

Application Requirements: Application form. *Deadline:* March 1.

Contact: Iryna Fedoriw, Administrative Assistant
Phone: 780-492-2972
E-mail: cius@ualberta.ca

LEO J. KRYSA UNDERGRADUATE SCHOLARSHIP

One-time award for a Canadian citizen or a landed immigrant to enter their final year of undergraduate study in pursuit of a degree with emphasis on Ukrainian and/or Ukrainian-Canadian studies in the disciplines of education, history, humanities, or social sciences. To be used at any Canadian university for an eight-month period of study. Dollar amount CAN$3500.

Academic Fields/Career Goals: Area/Ethnic Studies; Education; History; Humanities; Social Sciences.

Award: Scholarship for use in senior year; not renewable. *Number:* 1.

Eligibility Requirements: Applicant must be Canadian citizen; enrolled or expecting to enroll full-time at a four-year institution or university; resident of Alberta, British Columbia, Manitoba, New Brunswick, Newfoundland, Northwest Territories, Nova Scotia, Ontario, Prince Edward Island, Quebec, Saskatchewan, Yukon and studying in Alberta, British Columbia, Manitoba, New Brunswick, Newfoundland, Nova Scotia, Ontario, Prince Edward Island, Quebec, Saskatchewan.

Application Requirements: Application form, recommendations or references, transcript. *Deadline:* March 1.

Contact: Iryna Fedoriw, Administrative Assistant
Phone: 780-492-2972
E-mail: cius@ualberta.ca

COSTUME SOCIETY OF AMERICA

http://www.costumesocietyamerica.com/

ADELE FILENE STUDENT PRESENTER GRANT

Adele Filene Student Presenter Grants provide financial assistance to students who have been selected to present oral research papers or research exhibits at the CSA National Symposium. These grants of up to $500 and a day-of-presentation registration fee, funded by the CSA Endowment, are intended to encourage student participation in both the symposium and CSA.

Academic Fields/Career Goals: Area/Ethnic Studies; Art History; Arts; Historic Preservation and Conservation; History; Home Economics; Museum Studies; Performing Arts.

Award: Grant for use in freshman, sophomore, junior, senior, or graduate years; not renewable. *Number:* 1. *Amount:* $150–$500.

Eligibility Requirements: Applicant must be enrolled or expecting to enroll full- or part-time at a two-year or four-year or technical institution or university. Applicant or parent of applicant must be member of Costume Society of America. Available to U.S. and non-U.S. citizens.

Application Requirements: Application form, essay. *Deadline:* March 1.

Contact: Dennita Sewell
Costume Society of America
Phoenix Art Museum
1625 North Central Avenue
Phoenix, AZ 85004-1685
E-mail: Dennita.Sewell@phxart.org

STELLA BLUM STUDENT RESEARCH GRANT

The Stella Blum Student Research Grant is intended to assist the research of a current undergraduate or graduate student who is a member of the Costume Society of America and conducting original research in the field of North American costume. This $2,000 grant, funded by the CSA Endowment, is awarded annually to provide a student with financial assistance with research. An additional stipend of up to $500 and a day-of-presentation registration fee, also funded by the CSA Endowment, is awarded to allow the recipient to present the completed research at a CSA National Symposium.

Academic Fields/Career Goals: Area/Ethnic Studies; Art History; Arts; Historic Preservation and Conservation; History; Home Economics; Museum Studies; Performing Arts.

Award: Grant for use in freshman, sophomore, junior, senior, or graduate years; not renewable. *Number:* 1. *Amount:* $2000–$2500.

Eligibility Requirements: Applicant must be enrolled or expecting to enroll full- or part-time at a two-year or four-year or technical institution or university. Applicant or parent of applicant must be member of Costume Society of America. Available to U.S. and non-U.S. citizens.

Application Requirements: Application form, essay. *Deadline:* May 1.

Contact: Ann Wass
Costume Society of America
5903 60th Avenue
Riverdale, MD 20737
E-mail: annbwass@aol.com

KOSCIUSZKO FOUNDATION

http://www.thekf.org

YEAR ABROAD PROGRAM IN POLAND

Grants for upper division and graduate students who wish to study language and culture at the Center for Polish Language and Culture in the World, Jagiellonian University in Cracow, Poland. U.S. citizens who are undergraduate sophomores, juniors, seniors and graduate students may apply. Scholarship is given towards junior, senior or graduate year of studies. Graduate students receive priority. Must have letters of recommendation, personal statement, and transcript. Covers tuition fees and provides stipend for housing. Application fee: $50. Minimum 3.0 GPA required. Restricted to U.S. citizens.

Academic Fields/Career Goals: Area/Ethnic Studies; Foreign Language.

Award: Scholarship for use in junior, senior, or graduate years; not renewable. *Number:* 5–11. *Amount:* $900–$1800.

Eligibility Requirements: Applicant must be enrolled or expecting to enroll full-time at a four-year institution or university and must have an interest in Polish language. Applicant must have 3.0 GPA or higher. Available to U.S. citizens.

Application Requirements: Application form, application form may be submitted online (http://www.thekf.org/kf/scholarships/exchange-poland/year-abroad/), essay, interview, personal photograph, personal statement, recommendations or references, transcript. *Fee:* $50. *Deadline:* January 15.

Contact: Ms. Addy Tymczyszyn, Scholarship and Grant Officer for Americans
Kosciuszko Foundation
15 East 65th Street
New York, NY 10065
Phone: 212-734-2130 Ext. 210
E-mail: Addy@thekf.org

NATIONAL ITALIAN AMERICAN FOUNDATION

http://www.niaf.org/

NATIONAL ITALIAN AMERICAN FOUNDATION CATEGORY II SCHOLARSHIP

Award available to students majoring or minoring in Italian language, Italian Studies, Italian-American Studies or a related field who have outstanding potential and high academic achievements. Minimum 3.5 GPA required. Must be a U.S. citizen and be enrolled in an accredited institution of higher education. Application can only be submitted online. For further information, deadlines, and online application visit website http://www.niaf.org/scholarships/index.asp.

Academic Fields/Career Goals: Area/Ethnic Studies.

Award: Scholarship for use in freshman, sophomore, junior, senior, or graduate years; not renewable. *Amount:* $2500–$12,000.

Eligibility Requirements: Applicant must be enrolled or expecting to enroll full-time at a two-year or four-year institution or university and must have an interest in Italian language. Applicant must have 3.5 GPA or higher. Available to U.S. citizens.

Application Requirements: Application form, essay, recommendations or references, transcript. *Deadline:* March 6.

Contact: Serena Cantoni, Director, Culture and Education
National Italian American Foundation
The National Italian American Foundation
1860 19th Street, NW
Washington, DC 20009
Phone: 202-939-3107
E-mail: serena@niaf.org

NATIONAL SECURITY EDUCATION PROGRAM

http://www.iie.org/

NATIONAL SECURITY EDUCATION PROGRAM (NSEP) DAVID L. BOREN UNDERGRADUATE SCHOLARSHIPS

The Boren Scholarships provide funding to American undergraduate students for study abroad in regions critical to U.S. national interests. Emphasized world areas include Africa, Asia, Central and Eastern Europe, the NIS, Latin America and the Caribbean, and the Middle East. NSEP scholarship recipients incur a federal service agreement. Must be a U.S. citizen. Program must have a foreign language component.

Academic Fields/Career Goals: Area/Ethnic Studies; Business/Consumer Services; Economics; Engineering-Related Technologies; Environmental Science; Foreign Language; International Studies; Peace and Conflict Studies; Social Sciences.

Award: Scholarship for use in freshman, sophomore, junior, or senior years; not renewable. *Number:* 130–170. *Amount:* up to $20,000.

Eligibility Requirements: Applicant must be enrolled or expecting to enroll full- or part-time at a two-year or four-year institution or university. Available to U.S. citizens.

Application Requirements: Application form, application form may be submitted online (http://www.borenawards.org), campus review, essay, financial need analysis, recommendations or references, transcript. *Deadline:* February 5.

Contact: Boren Awards Program
Phone: 800-618-6737
E-mail: boren@iie.org

SONS OF NORWAY FOUNDATION

http://www.sonsofnorway.com/foundation

KING OLAV V NORWEGIAN-AMERICAN HERITAGE FUND

Scholarship available to American students interested in studying Norwegian heritage or modern Norway, or Norwegian students 18 or older interested in studying North American culture. Selection of applicants is based on a 500-word essay, educational and career goals, community service, work experience, and GPA. Must have minimum 3.0 GPA.

Academic Fields/Career Goals: Area/Ethnic Studies.

Award: Scholarship for use in freshman, sophomore, junior, or senior years; not renewable. *Number:* 4–8. *Amount:* $1000–$1500.

Eligibility Requirements: Applicant must be of Norwegian heritage and Norwegian citizen; age 18-30 and enrolled or expecting to enroll full-time at a two-year or four-year or technical institution or university. Applicant must have 3.0 GPA or higher. Available to U.S. and non-Canadian citizens.

Application Requirements: Application form, application form may be submitted online (http://www.sonsofnorway.com/foundation), community service, essay, recommendations or references, transcript. *Deadline:* March 1.

Contact: Scholarship Coordinator
Sons of Norway Foundation
1455 West Lake Street
Minneapolis, MN 55408-2666
Phone: 612-827-3611
Fax: 612-827-0658

STRAIGHTFORWARD MEDIA

http://www.straightforwardmedia.com/

STRAIGHTFORWARD MEDIA LIBERAL ARTS SCHOLARSHIP

Scholarship of $500 available exclusively to liberal arts students. Awarded four times per year. For more information, see web http://www.straightforwardmedia.com/liberal-arts/form.php.

Academic Fields/Career Goals: Area/Ethnic Studies; Art History; Classics; Economics; Foreign Language; History; Humanities; Literature/English/Writing; Philosophy; Political Science; Psychology; Social Sciences.

Award: Scholarship for use in freshman, sophomore, junior, or senior years; not renewable. *Number:* 4. *Amount:* $500.

Eligibility Requirements: Applicant must be enrolled or expecting to enroll full- or part-time at a two-year or four-year or technical institution or university. Available to U.S. and non-U.S. citizens.

Application Requirements: Essay. *Deadline:* varies.

Contact: Scholarship Committee
Phone: 605-348-3042

ART HISTORY

AMERICAN SCHOOL OF CLASSICAL STUDIES AT ATHENS

http://www.ascsa.edu.gr/

ASCSA SUMMER SESSIONS SCHOLARSHIPS
• See page 108

COSTUME SOCIETY OF AMERICA

http://www.costumesocietyamerica.com/

ADELE FILENE STUDENT PRESENTER GRANT
• See page 125

STELLA BLUM STUDENT RESEARCH GRANT
• See page 125

CULTURAL SERVICES OF THE FRENCH EMBASSY

http://www.frenchculture.org/

TEACHING ASSISTANT PROGRAM IN FRANCE
• See page 104

QUALITY BATH

www.qualitybath.com

QUALITYBATH.COM SCHOLARSHIP PROGRAM
• See page 123

ROBERT H. MOLLOHAN FAMILY CHARITABLE FOUNDATION, INC.

http://www.mollohanfoundation.org/

MARY OLIVE EDDY JONES ART SCHOLARSHIP

Scholarship awarded to a rising sophomore or junior seriously interested in pursuing an art-related degree. Applicant must be a West Virginia resident attending a West Virginia college or university.

Academic Fields/Career Goals: Art History; Arts; Graphics/Graphic Arts/Printing.

Award: Scholarship for use in sophomore or junior years; not renewable. *Number:* 1–3. *Amount:* up to $1000.

Eligibility Requirements: Applicant must be enrolled or expecting to enroll full- or part-time at a four-year institution or university; resident of West Virginia and studying in West Virginia. Available to U.S. citizens.

Application Requirements: Application form, essay, portfolio, recommendations or references, resume, transcript. *Deadline:* February 9.

Contact: Aime Shaffer, Program Manager
Robert H. Mollohan Family Charitable Foundation, Inc.
1000 Technology Drive, Suite 2000
Fairmont, WV 26554
Phone: 304-333-6783
Fax: 304-333-3900
E-mail: ashaffer@wvhtf.org

STRAIGHTFORWARD MEDIA

http://www.straightforwardmedia.com/

STRAIGHTFORWARD MEDIA LIBERAL ARTS SCHOLARSHIP
• *See page 126*

SUPPORT CREATIVITY

http://wesupportcreativity.org

SUPPORT CREATIVITY SCHOLARSHIP
• *See page 124*

UNITED NEGRO COLLEGE FUND

http://www.uncf.org/

CATHERINE W. PIERCE SCHOLARSHIP
Up to $5000 scholarship for full-time students at UNCF member colleges and universities majoring in the arts or history. Minimum 2.5 GPA required. Open to U.S. citizens, nationals and permanent residents.

Academic Fields/Career Goals: Art History; Arts; History.

Award: Scholarship for use in freshman, sophomore, junior, senior, or graduate years; not renewable.

Eligibility Requirements: Applicant must be American Indian/Alaska Native, Asian/Pacific Islander, Black (non-Hispanic), Hispanic and enrolled or expecting to enroll full-time at a four-year institution or university. Applicant must have 2.5 GPA or higher. Available to U.S. and non-U.S. citizens.

Application Requirements: Application form, essay. *Deadline:* July 29.

Contact: Mary Williams, Director of Outreach and Recruitment
Phone: 800-331-2244

ARTS

ALLIANCE FOR YOUNG ARTISTS AND WRITERS INC.

http://www.artandwriting.org/

SCHOLASTIC ART AND WRITING AWARDS-WRITING SECTION SCHOLARSHIP
Students currently enrolled in grades 7 to 12 who attend a public, private, parochial, or home school in the United States, U.S. territories, or U.S. sponsored schools abroad may apply.

Academic Fields/Career Goals: Arts; Literature/English/Writing.

Award: Scholarship for use in freshman year; not renewable.

Eligibility Requirements: Applicant must be high school student; planning to enroll or expecting to enroll full- or part-time at a four-year institution or university and must have an interest in writing. Available to U.S. and non-U.S. citizens.

Application Requirements: Application form, entry in a contest, essay, manuscript, portfolio, recommendations or references. *Deadline:* varies.

Contact: General Information
Alliance for Young Artists and Writers Inc.
557 Broadway
New York, NY 10012
Phone: 212-343-7700
E-mail: info@artandwriting.org

AMERICAN INSTITUTE OF POLISH CULTURE INC.

http://www.ampolinstitute.org/

HARRIET IRSAY SCHOLARSHIP GRANT
Merit-based $1000 scholarships for students studying communications, public relations, and/or journalism. All U.S. citizens may apply, but preference will be given to U.S. citizens of Polish heritage. Must submit three letters of recommendation on appropriate letterhead with application mailed directly to AIPC. For study in the United States only. Non-refundable fee of $10 will be collected.

Academic Fields/Career Goals: Arts; Communications; Education; Foreign Language; Journalism; Public Policy and Administration.

Award: Scholarship for use in freshman, sophomore, junior, senior, or graduate years; not renewable. *Number:* 10–15. *Amount:* $1000.

Eligibility Requirements: Applicant must be enrolled or expecting to enroll full-time at a two-year or four-year institution or university. Available to U.S. citizens.

Application Requirements: Application form, recommendations or references, resume, self-addressed stamped envelope with application, transcript. *Fee:* $10. *Deadline:* April 20.

Contact: Scholarship Committee
Phone: 305-864-2349
Fax: 305-865-5150
E-mail: info@ampolinstitute.org

AMERICAN SCHOOL OF CLASSICAL STUDIES AT ATHENS

http://www.ascsa.edu.gr/

ASCSA SUMMER SESSIONS SCHOLARSHIPS
• *See page 108*

BMI FOUNDATION, INC.

http://www.bmifoundation.org/

BMI STUDENT COMPOSER AWARDS
One-time awards for original compositions in the classical genre for young student composers who are under age 28 and citizens of the Western Hemisphere. Must submit application and original musical score. Online application available: bmifoundation.org/sca

Academic Fields/Career Goals: Arts; Music.

Award: Prize for use in freshman, sophomore, junior, senior, graduate, or postgraduate years; not renewable. *Number:* 9–11. *Amount:* $500–$5000.

Eligibility Requirements: Applicant must be enrolled or expecting to enroll full- or part-time at a two-year or four-year or technical institution or university and must have an interest in music or music/singing. Available to U.S. and non-U.S. citizens.

Application Requirements: Application form. *Deadline:* February 1.

Contact: Ms. Deirdre Chadwick, Director
BMI Foundation, Inc.
7 World Trade Center
250 Greenwich Street
New York, NY 10007-0030
Phone: 212-220-3103
E-mail: info@bmifoundation.org

BULKOFFICESUPPLY.COM

http://www.bulkofficesupply.com

OFFICE SUPPLY SCHOLARSHIP

If you have an interest in teaching, art or owning your own business you are eligible to apply for our scholarship program. The program is open to all high school students as well as College Freshmen and Sophomores.

Academic Fields/Career Goals: Arts; Business/Consumer Services; Education.

Award: Scholarship for use in freshman or sophomore years; not renewable. *Number:* 1. *Amount:* $1000.

Eligibility Requirements: Applicant must be enrolled or expecting to enroll full- or part-time at a two-year or four-year or technical institution or university. Available to U.S. and non-U.S. citizens.

Application Requirements: Application form may be submitted online(www.bulkofficesupply.com/scholarships-in-new-york), entry in a contest, essay. *Deadline:* February 1.

Contact: Mr. Harrison Blackhurst, Online Marketing Manager
BulkOfficeSupply.com
1614 Hereford Road
Hewlett, NY 11557
Phone: 800-658 -1488
E-mail: webteam.bulkofficesupply@gmail.com

COMMUNITY FOUNDATION FOR GREATER ATLANTA, INC.

http://cfgreateratlanta.org/

JAMES M. AND VIRGINIA M. SMYTH SCHOLARSHIP

Scholarship of $2000 annually for up to four years to students enrolled at an accredited college pursuing an undergraduate degree. Applicant should pursue a degree in the arts and sciences, human services, music or ministry.

Academic Fields/Career Goals: Arts; Humanities; Music; Natural Sciences; Physical Sciences; Religion/Theology.

Award: Scholarship for use in freshman, sophomore, junior, or senior years; renewable. *Number:* 4–15. *Amount:* $2000.

Eligibility Requirements: Applicant must be enrolled or expecting to enroll full-time at a four-year institution or university and resident of Georgia, Illinois, Mississippi, Missouri, Oklahoma, Tennessee, Texas. Applicant must have 3.0 GPA or higher. Available to U.S. citizens.

Application Requirements: Application form, driver's license, essay, financial need analysis. *Deadline:* February 15.

CONGRESSIONAL BLACK CAUCUS FOUNDATION, INC.

http://www.cbcfinc.org/

CBC SPOUSES VISUAL ARTS SCHOLARSHIP
• See page 120

COSTUME SOCIETY OF AMERICA

http://www.costumesocietyamerica.com/

ADELE FILENE STUDENT PRESENTER GRANT
• See page 125

STELLA BLUM STUDENT RESEARCH GRANT
• See page 125

FLORIDA PTA/PTSA

http://www.floridapta.org/

FLORIDA PTA/PTSA FINE ARTS SCHOLARSHIP

Renewable award of $1000 to a graduating Florida high school senior who plans to attend a fine arts program within the State of Florida. Must have a least a two-year attendance in a Florida PTA/PTSA high school. Minimum 3.0 GPA.

Academic Fields/Career Goals: Arts.

Award: Scholarship for use in freshman year; renewable. *Number:* 3. *Amount:* $1000.

Eligibility Requirements: Applicant must be high school student; planning to enroll or expecting to enroll full-time at a four-year institution or university; resident of Florida and studying in Florida. Applicant must have 3.0 GPA or higher. Available to U.S. citizens.

Application Requirements: Application form, essay, recommendations or references. *Deadline:* March 1.

Contact: Scholarship Chair, Scholarship Chair
Florida PTA/PTSA
1747 Orlando Central Parkway
Orlando, FL 32809
Phone: 407-855-7604
Fax: 407-240-9577
E-mail: scholarship@floridapta.org

GOLDEN KEY INTERNATIONAL HONOUR SOCIETY

http://www.goldenkey.org/

VISUAL AND PERFORMING ARTS ACHIEVEMENT AWARDS

Award of $500 will be given to winners in each of the following nine categories: painting, drawing, photography, sculpture, computer-generated art/graphic design/illustration, mixed media, instrumental performance, vocal performance, and dance.

Academic Fields/Career Goals: Arts; Graphics/Graphic Arts/Printing.

Award: Prize for use in freshman, sophomore, junior, senior, graduate, or postgraduate years; not renewable. *Number:* 9. *Amount:* $500.

Eligibility Requirements: Applicant must be enrolled or expecting to enroll full- or part-time at a four-year institution or university and must have an interest in art. Available to U.S. and non-U.S. citizens.

Application Requirements: Application form, artwork, cover letter, entry in a contest. *Deadline:* April 1.

Contact: Scholarship Program Administrators
Golden Key International Honour Society
PO Box 23737
Nashville, TN 37202
Phone: 800-377-2401

GRAND RAPIDS COMMUNITY FOUNDATION

http://www.grfoundation.org/

ARTS COUNCIL OF GREATER GRAND RAPIDS MINORITY SCHOLARSHIP

Scholarship is for students of color (African American, Asian, Hispanic, Native American, Pacific Islander) attending a non-profit public or private college/university majoring in Fine Arts including all visual and performing art forms. Must have financial need, be a Kent County resident, and have a minimum 2.5 GPA.

Academic Fields/Career Goals: Arts.

Award: Scholarship for use in freshman, sophomore, junior, or senior years; not renewable. *Number:* 1. *Amount:* $4500.

Eligibility Requirements: Applicant must be American Indian/Alaska Native, Asian/Pacific Islander, Black (non-Hispanic), Hispanic; enrolled or expecting to enroll full-time at a two-year or four-year institution or university and resident of Michigan. Applicant must have 2.5 GPA or higher. Available to U.S. citizens.

Application Requirements: Application form, application form may be submitted online (http://grfoundation.org), essay, financial need analysis, transcript. *Deadline:* April 1.

Contact: Ms. Ruth Bishop, Education Program Officer
Grand Rapids Community Foundation
185 Oakes SW
Grand Rapids, MI 49503
Phone: 616-454-1751 Ext. 103
E-mail: rbishop@grfoundation.org

IFDA EDUCATIONAL FOUNDATION
http://www.ifdaef.org/

RUTH CLARK FURNITURE DESIGN SCHOLARSHIP
Scholarship available to students studying design at an accredited college or design school with a focus on residential furniture design. Applicant must submit five examples of original designs, three of which must be residential furniture examples. (pdf format only), Include design examples with a short description of each illustration.

Academic Fields/Career Goals: Arts; Industrial Design; Interior Design.

Award: Scholarship for use in sophomore, junior, senior, or graduate years; not renewable. *Number:* 1. *Amount:* $3000.

Eligibility Requirements: Applicant must be enrolled or expecting to enroll full- or part-time at a four-year institution or university. Available to U.S. and non-U.S. citizens.

Application Requirements: Application form, essay, portfolio. *Deadline:* March 31.

Contact: Earline Feldman, Director of Scholarships and Grants
IFDA Educational Foundation
112 Hidden Lake Circle
Canton, GA 30114
Phone: 770-378-7221
E-mail: ef.ifda@tapestries.org

JACK J. ISGUR FOUNDATION
www.isgur.org

JACK J. ISGUR FOUNDATION SCHOLARSHIP
Awards scholarships to juniors, seniors, and graduate students with intentions of teaching the humanities in grades kindergarten through 8th grade, preferably in rural Missouri.

Academic Fields/Career Goals: Arts; Education; Humanities; Music.

Award: Scholarship for use in junior, senior, graduate, or postgraduate years; not renewable. *Number:* 5–100. *Amount:* $750–$1500.

Eligibility Requirements: Applicant must be Muslim faith and enrolled or expecting to enroll full- or part-time at a four-year institution or university. Available to U.S. and non-U.S. citizens.

Application Requirements: Application form, interview. *Deadline:* May 15.

Contact: Mr. Charles Jensen, Administrator, Jack J. Isgur Foundation
Jack J. Isgur Foundation
Stinson Leonard Street Law Firm
1201 Walnut Street, 29th Floor
Kansas City, MO 64106
Phone: 816-691-2760
E-mail: charles.jensen@stinson.com

NATIONAL ACADEMY OF TELEVISION ARTS AND SCIENCES
http://www.emmyonline.tv/

DOUGLAS W. MUMMERT SCHOLARSHIP
Awarded to a student pursuing a career in any aspect of the television industry, who has made a positive impact through community service.

Academic Fields/Career Goals: Arts; Communications; Filmmaking/Video; Journalism; Music; Performing Arts; Photojournalism/Photography; Public Policy and Administration; TV/Radio Broadcasting.

Award: Scholarship for use in freshman year; not renewable. *Number:* 1. *Amount:* $10,000.

Eligibility Requirements: Applicant must be high school student and planning to enroll or expecting to enroll full-time at a four-year institution. Available to U.S. citizens.

Application Requirements: Application form, community service, essay. *Deadline:* February 28.

Contact: Mr. Adam Sharp, Chair, Scholarship Committee
Phone: 212-586-8424
Fax: 212-246-8129
E-mail: scholarship@emmyonline.tv

NATIONAL OPERA ASSOCIATION
http://www.noa.org/

NOA VOCAL COMPETITION/LEGACY AWARD PROGRAM
Awards granted based on competitive audition to support study and career development. Singers compete in Scholarship and Artist Division. Legacy Awards are granted for study and career development in any opera-related career to those who further NOA's goal of increased minority participation in the profession.

Academic Fields/Career Goals: Arts; Performing Arts.

Award: Prize for use in freshman, sophomore, junior, senior, graduate, or postgraduate years; not renewable. *Number:* 3–8. *Amount:* $500–$2000.

Eligibility Requirements: Applicant must be age 18-24; enrolled or expecting to enroll full- or part-time at a two-year or four-year or technical institution or university and must have an interest in music or music/singing. Available to U.S. and non-U.S. citizens.

Application Requirements: Application form, audition tape/proposal, driver's license, entry in a contest, personal photograph, recommendations or references. *Fee:* $25. *Deadline:* October 15.

Contact: Robert Hansen, Executive Secretary
National Opera Association
2403 Russell Long Boulevard, PO Box 60869
Canyon, TX 79016-0001
Phone: 806-651-2857
Fax: 806-651-2958
E-mail: hansen@mail.wtamu.edu

ONLINE LOGO MAKER
http://onlinelogomaker.com

OLM MALALA YOUSAFZAI SCHOLARSHIP 2017-2018
Online Logo Maker is proud to announce its own Scholarship named after the great activist from the actual time: Malala Yousafzai, known for fighting for education. And from now on, we are going to provide an annual scholarship for minorities as an act for education. Acknowledging the difficulty that women face on a sexist society, the 2017–2018 scholarship will provide a $1000 scholarship to a woman. All women, from all over the world, who has 30 years old or more and want the opportunity to go back to school to start or continue interrupted studies in the Arts and Design field can apply. The OLM Malala Yousafzai Scholarship 2017–2018 application requires a 500–1000 words essay written in English about a challenge you have faced and how you overcame it. Fill out the online form including your essay and good luck! For more info, see website http://www.onlinelogomaker.com/scholarships-for-women

Academic Fields/Career Goals: Arts; Drafting; Industrial Design; Interior Design; Performing Arts.

Award: Scholarship for use in freshman, sophomore, junior, senior, graduate, or postgraduate years; not renewable. *Number:* 1. *Amount:* $1000.

Eligibility Requirements: Applicant must be Baha'i faith, Baptist, Brethren, Buddhist faith, Christian, Disciple of Christ, Eastern Orthodox, Episcopalian, Friends, Hindu faith, Jewish, Latter-day Saints, Lutheran, Methodist, Muslim faith, Pentecostal, Presbyterian, Protestant, Roman Catholic, Seventh-Day Adventist, Unitarian Universalist; of African, Albanian, Arab, Armenian, Arumanian/Ulacedo-Romanian, Australian, Belgian, Bulgarian, Canadian, Central European, Chinese, Croatian/Serbian, Cypriot, Danish, Dutch, Eastern European, English, European Union, Finnish, former Soviet Union, French, German, Greek, Haitian, Hispanic, Hungarian, Icelandic, Indian, Irish, Israeli, Italian, Japanese, Jewish, Korean, Lao/Hmong, Latin American/Caribbean, Latvian, Lebanese, Lithuanian, Mexican, Mongolian, New Zealander, Nicaraguan, Norwegian, Polish, Portuguese, Rumanian, Russian, Scandinavian, Scottish, Slavic/Czech, Spanish, Sub-Saharan African, Swedish, Swiss, Syrian, Turkish, Ukrainian, Vietnamese, Welsh, Yemeni heritage and African, Albanian, Arab, Armenian, Arumanian/Ulacedo-Romanian, Australian, Belgian, Bulgarian, Canadian, Central European, Chinese, Croatian/Serbian, Cypriot, Danish, Dutch, Eastern European, English, European Union, Finnish, former Soviet Union, French, German, Greek, Haitian, Hispanic, Hungarian, Icelandic, Indian, Irish, Israeli, Italian, Japanese, Jewish, Korean, Lao/Hmong, Latin American/Caribbean, Latvian, Lebanese, Lithuanian, Mexican, Mongolian, New Zealander, Nicaraguan, Norwegian, Polish, Portuguese,

Rumanian, Russian, Scandinavian, Scottish, Slavic/Czech, Spanish, Sub-Saharan African, Swedish, Swiss, Syrian, Turkish, Ukrainian, Vietnamese, Welsh, Yemeni citizen; American Indian/Alaska Native, Asian/Pacific Islander, Black (non-Hispanic); age 30-70; enrolled or expecting to enroll full- or part-time at a two-year or four-year or technical institution or university and female. Available to U.S. and non-U.S. citizens.

Application Requirements: Application form, essay. *Deadline:* December 1.

Contact: OLM Malala Yousafzai Scholarship
E-mail: scholarship@onlinelogomaker.com

OREGON STUDENT ASSISTANCE COMMISSION

http://www.GetCollegeFunds.org/

KERDRAGON SCHOLARSHIP

Scholarships for students who are graduates (including GED recipients) of Oregon high schools who have not yet attended college and are planning to study fine arts, graphic arts, or photography. Minimum GPA of 3.0 preferred for high school students, 2.75 GPA required for prior recipients. Semifinalists will be required to submit nonreturnable slides of photos of art samples or film/video of other artistic endeavors.

Academic Fields/Career Goals: Arts; Graphics/Graphic Arts/Printing; Photojournalism/Photography.

Award: Scholarship for use in freshman year; not renewable.

Eligibility Requirements: Applicant must be enrolled or expecting to enroll full- or part-time at a four-year institution or university. Available to U.S. citizens.

Application Requirements: Application form, portfolio. *Deadline:* March 1.

Contact: Melissa Adams, Scholarship Processing Coordinator
Phone: 541-687-7409
E-mail: melissa.adams@hecc.oregon.gov

KIRCHHOFF FAMILY FINE ARTS SCHOLARSHIP

Award available to students studying fine art or graphic art at an Oregon nonprofit college or university. Preference will be given to upper-level undergraduates and MFA students. Semifinalists may be asked to submit non-returnable slides or photos of art samples. Recipients may apply for one additional year of funding.

Academic Fields/Career Goals: Arts; Graphics/Graphic Arts/Printing.

Award: Scholarship for use in freshman, sophomore, junior, senior, or graduate years; not renewable.

Eligibility Requirements: Applicant must be enrolled or expecting to enroll full-time at a four-year institution or university and studying in Oregon. Available to U.S. citizens.

Application Requirements: Application form, portfolio. *Deadline:* March 1.

Contact: Melissa Adams, Scholarship Processing Coordinator
Phone: 541-687-7409
E-mail: melissa.adams@hecc.oregon.gov

TECHNICAL TRAINING FUND SCHOLARSHIP

Award is available to graduates (including GED recipients and home-schooled graduates) of Oregon high schools. Preference given to students who will enroll as a junior, senior, or graduate-level student for fall term/semester at a traditional four-year institution; then applicants at any class level enrolled at a special vocational/trade school. Applicants must demonstrate extraordinary technical or artistic potential in areas such as craftsmanship, manual skills, art, music, or culinary arts. Recipient must enroll at least half-time.

Academic Fields/Career Goals: Arts; Culinary Arts; Music; Trade/Technical Specialties.

Award: Scholarship for use in sophomore, junior, senior, or graduate years; not renewable.

Eligibility Requirements: Applicant must be enrolled or expecting to enroll full- or part-time at a four-year or technical institution or university and resident of Oregon. Available to U.S. citizens.

Application Requirements: Application form, essay. *Deadline:* March 1.

Contact: Melissa Adams, Scholarship Processing Coordinator
Phone: 541-687-7409
E-mail: melissa.adams@hecc.oregon.gov

P. BUCKLEY MOSS FOUNDATION FOR CHILDREN'S EDUCATION

www.mossfoundation.org

MOSS ENDOWED SCHOLARSHIP

The Moss Endowed Scholarship is an up-to-$1,000 financial award given annually to one high school senior with a verified financial need, a verified language-related learning difference, visual arts talent, acceptance to an accredited 4-year college or university and the intent to pursue a career in the visual arts field. Art classes must be taken each semester to continue the award renewal.

Academic Fields/Career Goals: Arts.

Award: Scholarship for use in freshman year; renewable. *Number:* 1. *Amount:* $1.

Eligibility Requirements: Applicant must be high school student; planning to enroll or expecting to enroll full-time at a four-year institution; resident of Alabama, Arizona, Arkansas, California, Colorado, Connecticut, Delaware, District of Columbia, Florida, Georgia, Hawaii, Idaho, Illinois, Indiana, Iowa, Kansas, Kentucky, Louisiana, Maine, Maryland, Massachusetts, Michigan, Minnesota, Mississippi, Missouri, Montana, Nebraska, Nevada, New Hampshire, New Jersey, New York, North Carolina, North Dakota, Ohio, Oklahoma, Oregon, Pennsylvania, Rhode Island, South Carolina, South Dakota, Tennessee, Texas, Utah, Vermont, Virginia, Washington, West Virginia, Wisconsin, Wyoming and must have an interest in art. Applicant must have 2.5 GPA or higher. Available to U.S. citizens.

Application Requirements: Application form, essay, financial need analysis, portfolio. *Deadline:* March 31.

POLISH ARTS CLUB OF BUFFALO SCHOLARSHIP FOUNDATION

http://www.pacb.bfn.org/

POLISH ARTS CLUB OF BUFFALO SCHOLARSHIP FOUNDATION TRUST

Provides educational scholarships to students of Polish background who are legal residents of New York. Must be enrolled at the junior level or above in an accredited college or university in NY during the upcoming year of application. Must be a U.S. citizen. For application and additional information, visit website http://www.pacb.bfn.org.

Academic Fields/Career Goals: Arts; Communications; Filmmaking/Video; Humanities; Music; Performing Arts; TV/Radio Broadcasting.

Award: Scholarship for use in junior, senior, graduate, or postgraduate years; not renewable. *Number:* 1–3. *Amount:* $1000.

Eligibility Requirements: Applicant must be of Polish heritage; enrolled or expecting to enroll full- or part-time at a four-year institution or university and resident of New York. Available to U.S. citizens.

Application Requirements: Application form, essay, interview, portfolio. *Deadline:* April 15.

Contact: Anne Flansburg, Selection Chair
Polish Arts Club of Buffalo Scholarship Foundation
24 Amherston Drive
Williamsville, NY 14221-7002
Phone: 716-863-3631
E-mail: anneflanswz@aol.com

QUALITY BATH

www.qualitybath.com

QUALITYBATH.COM SCHOLARSHIP PROGRAM

• See page 123

RHODE ISLAND FOUNDATION

http://www.rifoundation.org/

MJSA EDUCATION FOUNDATION JEWELRY SCHOLARSHIP

Scholarships ranging from $500 to $2000 are available for students enrolled in tool making, design, metals fabrication or other jewelry-related courses of study at colleges, universities or non-profit technical schools on the post-secondary level in the United States. Renewable up to four years if the student maintains good academic standing.

Academic Fields/Career Goals: Arts.

Award: Scholarship for use in freshman year; renewable. *Amount:* $500–$2000.

Eligibility Requirements: Applicant must be enrolled or expecting to enroll full-time at a two-year or four-year or technical institution or university and must have an interest in art. Available to U.S. citizens.

Application Requirements: Application form, essay, financial need analysis, self-addressed stamped envelope with application, transcript. *Deadline:* June 14.

Contact: Libby Monahan, Funds Administrator
Phone: 401-274-4564 Ext. 3117
E-mail: libbym@rifoundation.org

PATRICIA W. EDWARDS MEMORIAL ART SCHOLARSHIP

Award to further education of young Rhode Island artists (such as art lessons for high school students in two-dimensional art) and/or scholarships for Rhode Island art students (freshmen, sophomores, and juniors) at Rhode Island institutions.

Academic Fields/Career Goals: Arts.

Award: Scholarship for use in freshman year; not renewable. *Amount:* up to $425.

Eligibility Requirements: Applicant must be high school student; planning to enroll or expecting to enroll full- or part-time at a two-year or four-year institution or university; resident of Rhode Island and studying in Rhode Island. Available to U.S. citizens.

Application Requirements: Application form. *Deadline:* March 4.

Contact: Libby Monahan, Funds Administrator
Phone: 401-274-4564 Ext. 3117
E-mail: libbym@rifoundation.org

ROBERT H. MOLLOHAN FAMILY CHARITABLE FOUNDATION, INC.

http://www.mollohanfoundation.org/

MARY OLIVE EDDY JONES ART SCHOLARSHIP

• *See page 126*

SERVICE EMPLOYEES INTERNATIONAL UNION (SEIU)

http://www.seiu.org/

SEIU MOE FONER SCHOLARSHIP PROGRAM FOR VISUAL AND PERFORMING ARTS

Scholarship for students pursuing a degree or training full-time in the visual or performing arts. Scholarship funding must be applied to tuition at a two- or four-year college, university, or an accredited community college, technical or trade school in an arts-related field.

Academic Fields/Career Goals: Arts; Performing Arts.

Award: Scholarship for use in freshman, sophomore, junior, or senior years; not renewable. *Number:* 1. *Amount:* $5000.

Eligibility Requirements: Applicant must be enrolled or expecting to enroll full-time at a two-year or four-year or technical institution or university. Applicant or parent of applicant must be member of Service Employees International Union. Available to U.S. citizens.

Application Requirements: 6 copies of a single original creative work, application form, essay, transcript. *Deadline:* March 1.

Contact: c/o Scholarship Program Administrators, Inc.
Phone: 615-320-3149
Fax: 615-320-3151
E-mail: info@spaprog.com

SOCIETY FOR CLASSICAL STUDIES

http://www.classicalstudies.org/

MINORITY STUDENT SUMMER SCHOLARSHIP

• *See page 118*

STRAIGHTFORWARD MEDIA

http://www.straightforwardmedia.com/

STRAIGHTFORWARD MEDIA ART SCHOOL SCHOLARSHIP

Award of $500 for students pursuing a degree in any art-related field. May be used for full- or part-time study. Scholarship is awarded four times per year. Deadlines: November 30, February 28, May 31, and August 31. For more information, visit website http://www.straightforwardmedia.com/art/form.php.

Academic Fields/Career Goals: Arts.

Award: Scholarship for use in freshman, sophomore, junior, or senior years; not renewable. *Number:* 4. *Amount:* $500.

Eligibility Requirements: Applicant must be enrolled or expecting to enroll full- or part-time at a two-year or four-year or technical institution or university. Available to U.S. and non-U.S. citizens.

Application Requirements: Essay. *Deadline:* varies.

Contact: Scholarship Committee
Phone: 605-348-3042

SUPPORT CREATIVITY

http://wesupportcreativity.org

SUPPORT CREATIVITY SCHOLARSHIP

• *See page 124*

TELETOON

http://www.teletoon.com/

TELETOON ANIMATION SCHOLARSHIP

Scholarship competition created by TELETOON to encourage creative, original, and imaginative animation by supporting Canadians studying in the animation field or intending to pursue studies in animation. One-time award. Must submit portfolio.

Academic Fields/Career Goals: Arts; Filmmaking/Video.

Award: Scholarship for use in freshman, sophomore, junior, senior, graduate, or postgraduate years; not renewable. *Number:* 9. *Amount:* $5000–$10,000.

Eligibility Requirements: Applicant must be enrolled or expecting to enroll full-time at a two-year or four-year or technical institution or university and resident of Alberta, British Columbia, Manitoba, New Brunswick, Newfoundland, Northwest Territories, Nova Scotia, Ontario, Prince Edward Island, Quebec, Saskatchewan. Available to Canadian citizens.

Application Requirements: 5-minute film, application form, driver's license, essay, portfolio, transcript. *Deadline:* June 15.

Contact: Denise Vaughan, Senior Coordinator, Public Relations
Phone: 416-956-2060
Fax: 416-956-2070
E-mail: denisev@teletoon.com

UNITARIAN UNIVERSALIST ASSOCIATION

http://www.uua.org/

MARION BARR STANFIELD ART SCHOLARSHIP

Scholarship for graduate or undergraduate students preparing for a career in fine arts. Eligibility is limited to those in the study of painting, drawing, photography, and/or sculpture. Performing arts majors are not eligible. Applicants must be members of or affiliated with a Unitarian Universalist congregation.

Academic Fields/Career Goals: Arts.

Award: Scholarship for use in freshman, sophomore, junior, senior, or graduate years; not renewable. *Number:* 5–8. *Amount:* $1500–$5000.

Eligibility Requirements: Applicant must be Unitarian Universalist; enrolled or expecting to enroll full-time at a four-year institution or university and must have an interest in art. Available to U.S. citizens.

Application Requirements: Application form, essay, financial need analysis, portfolio. *Deadline:* March 1.

Contact: Ms. Hillary Goodridge, Program Director
  Phone: 617-971-9600
  Fax: 617-971-0029
  E-mail: uufp@aol.com

PAULY D'ORLANDO MEMORIAL ART SCHOLARSHIP

Scholarship for graduate or undergraduate students preparing for a career in fine arts. Student must be studying painting, drawing, photography, and/or sculpture. Performing arts majors are not eligible.

Academic Fields/Career Goals: Arts; Photojournalism/Photography.

Award: Scholarship for use in freshman, sophomore, junior, senior, or graduate years; not renewable.

Eligibility Requirements: Applicant must be Unitarian Universalist and enrolled or expecting to enroll full-time at a four-year institution or university. Available to U.S. citizens.

Application Requirements: Application form, essay, financial need analysis, list of works, personal tax information, recommendations or references. *Deadline:* varies.

Contact: Ms. Hillary Goodridge, Program Director
  Phone: 617-971-9600
  Fax: 617-971-0029
  E-mail: uufp@aol.com

STANFIELD AND D'ORLANDO ART SCHOLARSHIP

Scholarships for both Master's and undergraduate Unitarian Universalist students studying the fields of art and law.

Academic Fields/Career Goals: Arts; Law/Legal Services.

Award: Scholarship for use in freshman, sophomore, junior, senior, or graduate years; not renewable.

Eligibility Requirements: Applicant must be Unitarian Universalist and enrolled or expecting to enroll full- or part-time at a four-year institution or university. Available to U.S. citizens.

Application Requirements: Application form. *Deadline:* February 15.

Contact: Ms. Hillary Goodridge, Program Director
  Phone: 617-971-9600
  Fax: 617-971-0029
  E-mail: uufp@aol.com

UNITED NEGRO COLLEGE FUND

http://www.uncf.org/

CATHERINE W. PIERCE SCHOLARSHIP
• *See page 127*

OSSIE DAVIS ENDOWMENT SCHOLARSHIP PROGRAM

Need-based scholarship of up to $6800 for a high school senior planning to attend a four-year HBCU. Applicants must demonstrate the ability and desire to use artistic activism to proactively address the concerns of humanity. Eligible majors include African American studies, communications, fine arts, humanities, performing arts, political science, social sciences, and theater arts/drama. The scholarship is renewable for up to 4 years, provided that students continue to meet the scholarship criteria. Minimum 3.0 GPA required.

Academic Fields/Career Goals: Arts; Communications; Humanities; Performing Arts; Political Science; Social Sciences.

Award: Scholarship for use in freshman year; not renewable.

Eligibility Requirements: Applicant must be Black (non-Hispanic); high school student and planning to enroll or expecting to enroll full-time at a four-year institution or university. Applicant must have 3.0 GPA or higher. Available to U.S. citizens.

Application Requirements: Application form, essay, financial need analysis. *Deadline:* January 31.

Contact: Mary Williams, Director of Outreach and Recruitment
  Phone: 800-331-2244

RHYTHM NATION/JANET JACKSON SCHOLARSHIP

Up to $5000 award for students attending UNCF affiliated colleges and universities. Must be studying communications. Minimum 2.5 GPA required.

Academic Fields/Career Goals: Arts; Communications; Journalism; Music; Photojournalism/Photography; TV/Radio Broadcasting.

Award: Scholarship for use in freshman, sophomore, junior, senior, or graduate years; not renewable.

Eligibility Requirements: Applicant must be Black (non-Hispanic) and enrolled or expecting to enroll full- or part-time at a four-year institution or university. Applicant must have 2.5 GPA or higher. Available to U.S. citizens.

Application Requirements: Application form, essay. *Deadline:* October 31.

Contact: Mary Williams, Director of Outreach and Recruitment
  Phone: 800-331-2244

VECTORWORKS, INC.

http://www.vectorworks.net

VECTORWORKS DESIGN SCHOLARSHIP
• *See page 124*

WARNER BROS. ENTERTAINMENT

http://www.warnerbros.com/

WARNER BROS. ANIMATION/HANNA-BARBERA HONORSHIP

The Honorship will be awarded annually to a graduating high school senior enrolling in a college, university, or trade school to study animation. Applicants must have (1) a passion and talent for a career in animation; (2) a minimum GPA of 3.0 upon graduation; and (3) demonstrate financial need. Each cash scholarship will be for $10,000, disbursed annually in equal amounts over the course of enrollment. In addition, the winner will have the opportunity to receive (4) consecutive, paid summer internships at Warner Bros. Studios in Burbank while at university.

Academic Fields/Career Goals: Arts.

Award: Scholarship for use in freshman, sophomore, junior, or senior years; renewable. *Number:* 1. *Amount:* $10,000.

Eligibility Requirements: Applicant must be high school student and planning to enroll or expecting to enroll full- or part-time at a four-year or technical institution or university. Applicant must have 3.0 GPA or higher. Available to U.S. citizens.

Application Requirements: *Deadline:* March 1.

WOMEN'S JEWELRY ASSOCIATION

http://www.womensjewelryassociation.com

WOMEN'S JEWELRY ASSOCIATION STUDENT SCHOLARSHIP

This is a student scholarship for a woman studying in the jewelry, gem and watch fields.

Academic Fields/Career Goals: Arts; Trade/Technical Specialties.

Award: Scholarship for use in freshman, sophomore, junior, senior, graduate, or postgraduate years; renewable. *Number:* 5–12. *Amount:* $500–$7000.

Eligibility Requirements: Applicant must be enrolled or expecting to enroll full-time at a two-year or four-year or technical institution or university; female and must have an interest in art. Applicant or parent of applicant must have employment or volunteer experience in fine arts. Available to U.S. and non-U.S. citizens.

Application Requirements: Application form, essay, personal photograph, portfolio. *Fee:* $10. *Deadline:* April 1.

Contact: Jenny Calleri
  E-mail: Jennyo@tbirdjewels.com

WORLDSTUDIO FOUNDATION

http://www.aiga.org/

WORLDSTUDIO AIGA SCHOLARSHIPS

Scholarships available for minority and economically disadvantaged students who are pursuing degrees in the design/arts disciplines in colleges and universities in the United States.

Academic Fields/Career Goals: Arts; Graphics/Graphic Arts/Printing.

Award: Scholarship for use in freshman, sophomore, junior, senior, or graduate years; not renewable. *Number:* 10–25. *Amount:* $1000–$5000.

Eligibility Requirements: Applicant must be enrolled or expecting to enroll full-time at a two-year or four-year or technical institution or university. Available to U.S. citizens.

Application Requirements: Application form, application form may be submitted online (http://www.aiga.org/content.cfm/worldstudio-scholarship), essay, portfolio, recommendations or references, transcript. *Deadline:* April 1.

Contact: Tiia Schurig, Web Production Manager
Worldstudio Foundation
164 Fifth Avenue
New York, NY 10010
Phone: 212-807-1990
Fax: 212-807-1799
E-mail: scholarship@aiga.org

ASIAN STUDIES

MINISTRY OF EDUCATION, CULTURE, SPORTS, SCIENCE AND TECHNOLOGY

http://www.mext.go.jp/

JAPAN STUDIES SCHOLARSHIP

This is a one time non-renewable scholarship to engage in the study of the Japanese language or Japanese studies in Japan.

Academic Fields/Career Goals: Asian Studies.

Award: Scholarship for use in junior or senior years; not renewable. *Amount:* $15,600.

Eligibility Requirements: Applicant must be enrolled or expecting to enroll full-time at a four-year institution and must have an interest in Asian language. Available to U.S. citizens.

Application Requirements: Application form, interview, personal photograph.

UNITED NATIONS ASSOCIATION OF CONNECTICUT

http://www.unausa.org

UNITED NATIONS ASSOCIATION OF CONNECTICUT SCHOLARSHIP

Scholarship to encourage and support students with a demonstrated interest in promoting world peace through work in international relations and diplomatic service to cultivate an understanding of and support for the work of the UN in the United States. At least one award of $1000 will be made in the Spring of each year to assist the selected student with his or her college expenses. Applicants must be graduating seniors of a public high school in Connecticut. The scholarship is based on demonstrated academic excellence, evidence of engagement in international issues, progress in developing proficiency in a foreign language, commitment to social advancement as documented through community service or related activities, and participation in a Model UN or similar intercultural program. The e-mail application (postmarked not later than March 31) must be sent to UNACT.studentfund@gmail.com.

Academic Fields/Career Goals: Asian Studies; Foreign Language; Health and Medical Sciences; International Migration; International Studies; Natural Sciences; Near and Middle East Studies; Nuclear Science; Peace and Conflict Studies; Political Science; Women's Studies.

Award: Scholarship for use in freshman year; not renewable. *Number:* 1–3. *Amount:* $1000.

Eligibility Requirements: Applicant must be high school student; planning to enroll or expecting to enroll full-time at a two-year or four-year institution or university and resident of Connecticut. Available to U.S. and non-U.S. citizens.

Application Requirements: Application form, essay. *Deadline:* March 31.

Contact: Ms. Barbara Bacewicz
Phone: 860-9274333
E-mail: jjbaxer@icloud.com

AUDIOLOGY

AMERICAN LEGION AUXILIARY DEPARTMENT OF COLORADO

http://www.alacolorado.com

AMERICAN LEGION AUXILIARY DEPARTMENT OF COLORADO PAST PRESIDENTS' PARLEY HEALTH CARE PROFESSIONAL SCHOLARSHIPNURSES SCHOLARSHIP

Open to children, spouses, grandchildren, and great-grandchildren of American Legion veterans, and veterans who served in the armed forces during eligibility dates for membership in the American Legion. Must be Colorado residents who have been accepted by an accredited health care professional school in Colorado.

Academic Fields/Career Goals: Audiology; Dental Health/Services; Health Administration; Health and Medical Sciences; Health Information Management/Technology; Nursing; Oncology; Optometry; Osteopathy; Pharmacy; Therapy/Rehabilitation.

Award: Scholarship for use in freshman, sophomore, junior, senior, or graduate years; not renewable. *Number:* 3–5. *Amount:* $500–$1500.

Eligibility Requirements: Applicant must be enrolled or expecting to enroll full- or part-time at a two-year or four-year institution or university; resident of Colorado and studying in Colorado. Available to U.S. citizens.

Application Requirements: Application form, essay, financial need analysis. *Deadline:* March 15.

Contact: Rhonda Larkowski, Department Secretary and Treasurer
American Legion Auxiliary Department of Colorado
7465 East First Avenue, Suite D
Denver, CO 80230
Phone: 303-367-5388
E-mail: www.dept-sec@alacolorado.com

GREAT MINDS IN STEM

www.greatmindsinstem.org

HISPANIC ENGINEER NATIONAL ACHIEVEMENT AWARDS CORPORATION SCHOLARSHIP PROGRAM

• *See page 106*

MEDICAL SCRUBS COLLECTION

http://medicalscrubscollection.com

MEDICAL SCRUBS COLLECTION SCHOLARSHIP

• *See page 106*

NATIONAL AMBUCS INC.

http://www.ambucs.org/

AMBUCS SCHOLARS-SCHOLARSHIPS FOR THERAPISTS

Scholarships are open to students who are U.S. citizens at a junior level or above in college. Must be enrolled in an accredited program by the appropriate health therapy profession authority in physical therapy, occupational therapy, speech-language pathology, or audiology and must demonstrate a financial need. Application available on website at http://www.ambucs.org. Paper applications are not accepted.

Academic Fields/Career Goals: Audiology; Therapy/Rehabilitation.

Award: Scholarship for use in junior, senior, graduate, or postgraduate years; not renewable. *Number:* 275. *Amount:* $500–$3000.

Eligibility Requirements: Applicant must be enrolled or expecting to enroll full-time at a four-year institution or university. Available to U.S. citizens.

Application Requirements: Application form, enrollment certification form, essay, financial need analysis. *Deadline:* April 15.

Contact: Janice Blankenship, Scholarship Coordinator
National AMBUCS Inc.
PO Box 5127
High Point, NC 27262
Phone: 336-852-0052 Ext. 10
Fax: 336-852-6830
E-mail: janiceb@ambucs.org

NEW YORK STATE GRANGE

http://www.nysgrange.org/

CAROLINE KARK AWARD

Award available to a Grange member who is preparing for a career working with the deaf, or a deaf individual who is furthering his or her education beyond high school. The recipient must be a New York State resident. The award is based on funds available.

Academic Fields/Career Goals: Audiology.

Award: Scholarship for use in freshman year; not renewable. *Number:* 1.

Eligibility Requirements: Applicant must be hearing impaired; high school student; planning to enroll or expecting to enroll full- or part-time at a four-year institution or university and resident of New York. Applicant or parent of applicant must be member of Grange Association. Applicant must be hearing impaired. Available to U.S. citizens.

Application Requirements: Application form. *Deadline:* April 15.

Contact: Program Manager
New York State Grange
100 Grange Place
Cortland, NY 13045
Phone: 607-756-7553
E-mail: nysgrange@nysgrange.com

SCARLETT FAMILY FOUNDATION SCHOLARSHIP PROGRAM

http://www.scarlettfoundation.org/

SCHOLARSHIP FOR STUDENTS PURSUING A BUSINESS OR STEM DEGREE

• See page 84

AVIATION/AEROSPACE

AACE INTERNATIONAL

http://www.aacei.org/

AACE INTERNATIONAL COMPETITIVE SCHOLARSHIP

• See page 118

AHS INTERNATIONAL—THE VERTICAL FLIGHT TECHNICAL SOCIETY

http://www.vtol.org/

VERTICAL FLIGHT FOUNDATION SCHOLARSHIP

This award is available for undergraduate (must be at least a second semester freshman), graduate, or doctoral study in aerospace, electrical, or mechanical engineering. Applicants must demonstrate an interest in vertical flight technology through contribution to the vertical flight technical community such as technical papers presented at technical meetings, submission to technical journals, participating in aerospace engineering design competitions, etc. All students must attend for the entire year following acceptance of the scholarship.

Academic Fields/Career Goals: Aviation/Aerospace; Electrical Engineering/Electronics; Engineering-Related Technologies; Engineering/Technology; Mechanical Engineering.

Award: Scholarship for use in sophomore, junior, senior, graduate, or postgraduate years; not renewable. *Number:* 10–19. *Amount:* $1500–$5000.

Eligibility Requirements: Applicant must be enrolled or expecting to enroll full-time at a four-year institution or university and must have an interest in aviation. Applicant must have 3.5 GPA or higher. Available to U.S. and non-U.S. citizens.

Application Requirements: Application form, essay, recommendations or references, resume, transcript. *Deadline:* February 1.

Contact: Ms. Holly Cafferelli, VFF Scholarship Coordinator
AHS International—The Vertical Flight Technical Society
217 North Washington Street
Alexandria, VA 22314
Phone: 703-684-6777 Ext. 100
Fax: 703-739-9279
E-mail: hcafferelli@vtol.org

AIRCRAFT ELECTRONICS ASSOCIATION EDUCATIONAL FOUNDATION

http://www.aea.net/

CHUCK PEACOCK MEMORIAL SCHOLARSHIP

Scholarship of $1000 for high school seniors or college students who plan to attend or are attending an aviation management program in an accredited school. Minimum 2.5 GPA required.

Academic Fields/Career Goals: Aviation/Aerospace.

Award: Scholarship for use in freshman, sophomore, junior, or senior years; not renewable. *Number:* 1. *Amount:* $1000.

Eligibility Requirements: Applicant must be enrolled or expecting to enroll full- or part-time at a two-year or four-year or technical institution or university. Applicant must have 2.5 GPA or higher. Available to U.S. citizens.

Application Requirements: Application form, essay, transcript. *Deadline:* February 15.

Contact: Mike Adamson, Executive Director
Phone: 816-373-6565
E-mail: info@aea.net

DAVID ARVER MEMORIAL SCHOLARSHIP

Scholarship of $1000 available to high school seniors and college students who plan to or are attending an avionics or aircraft repair program in an accredited school. Restricted to use for study in the following states: Iowa, Illinois, Indiana, Kansas, Michigan, Minnesota, Mississippi, North Dakota, Nebraska, South Dakota, and Wisconsin. Minimum 2.5 GPA required.

Academic Fields/Career Goals: Aviation/Aerospace.

Award: Scholarship for use in freshman, sophomore, junior, or senior years; not renewable. *Number:* 1. *Amount:* $1000.

Eligibility Requirements: Applicant must be enrolled or expecting to enroll full- or part-time at a two-year or four-year or technical institution or university. Applicant must have 2.5 GPA or higher. Available to U.S. and non-U.S. citizens.

Application Requirements: Application form, essay, recommendations or references, test scores, transcript. *Deadline:* February 15.

Contact: Mike Adamson, Executive Director
Phone: 816-373-6565
E-mail: info@aea.net

DUTCH AND GINGER ARVER SCHOLARSHIP

Scholarship available to high school seniors or college students who plan to attend or are attending an avionics or aircraft repair program in an accredited school. Minimum 2.5 GPA required.

Academic Fields/Career Goals: Aviation/Aerospace; Trade/Technical Specialties.

Award: Scholarship for use in freshman, sophomore, junior, or senior years; not renewable. *Number:* 1. *Amount:* $1000.

Eligibility Requirements: Applicant must be enrolled or expecting to enroll full- or part-time at a two-year or four-year or technical institution or university. Applicant must have 2.5 GPA or higher. Available to U.S. citizens.

Application Requirements: Application form, essay, recommendations or references, test scores, transcript. *Deadline:* February 15.

Contact: Mike Adamson, Executive Director
Phone: 816-373-6565
E-mail: info@aea.net

FIELD AVIATION COMPANY INC. SCHOLARSHIP

Scholarship for high school seniors and college students who plan to or are attending an avionics or aircraft repair program in an accredited college/university. The educational institution must be located in Canada.

Academic Fields/Career Goals: Aviation/Aerospace.

Award: Scholarship for use in freshman, sophomore, junior, or senior years; not renewable. *Number:* 1. *Amount:* $1000.

Eligibility Requirements: Applicant must be enrolled or expecting to enroll full-time at a two-year or four-year or technical institution or university. Applicant must have 2.5 GPA or higher. Available to Canadian citizens.

Application Requirements: Application form, essay, recommendations or references, test scores, transcript. *Deadline:* February 15.

Contact: Mike Adamson, Executive Director
Phone: 816-373-6565
E-mail: info@aea.net

GARMIN-JERRY SMITH MEMORIAL SCHOLARSHIP

Scholarship available for high school, college, or vocational or technical school students who plan to attend or are attending an avionics or aircraft repair program in an accredited vocational or technical school. Minimum 2.5 GPA required.

Academic Fields/Career Goals: Aviation/Aerospace; Trade/Technical Specialties.

Award: Scholarship for use in freshman or sophomore years; not renewable. *Number:* 1. *Amount:* $1000.

Eligibility Requirements: Applicant must be enrolled or expecting to enroll full-time at a two-year or technical institution. Applicant must have 2.5 GPA or higher. Available to U.S. and non-U.S. citizens.

Application Requirements: Application form, community service, essay, transcript. *Deadline:* February 15.

Contact: Mike Adamson, Executive Director
Phone: 816-373-6565
E-mail: info@aea.net

GARMIN SCHOLARSHIP

Scholarship available to high school seniors and college students who plan to attend or are attending an avionics or aircraft repair program in an accredited school. Minimum 2.5 GPA required.

Academic Fields/Career Goals: Aviation/Aerospace; Trade/Technical Specialties.

Award: Scholarship for use in freshman, sophomore, junior, or senior years; not renewable. *Number:* 1. *Amount:* $2000.

Eligibility Requirements: Applicant must be enrolled or expecting to enroll full- or part-time at a two-year or four-year or technical institution or university. Applicant must have 2.5 GPA or higher. Available to U.S. citizens.

Application Requirements: Application form, essay, recommendations or references, test scores, transcript. *Deadline:* February 15.

Contact: Mike Adamson, Executive Director
Phone: 816-373-6565
E-mail: info@aea.net

JOHNNY DAVIS MEMORIAL SCHOLARSHIP

Scholarship of $1000 available to high school seniors and college students who plan to or are attending an avionics or aircraft repair program in an accredited school. Minimum 2.5 GPA required.

Academic Fields/Career Goals: Aviation/Aerospace.

Award: Scholarship for use in freshman, sophomore, junior, or senior years; not renewable. *Number:* 1. *Amount:* $1000.

Eligibility Requirements: Applicant must be enrolled or expecting to enroll full- or part-time at a two-year or four-year or technical institution or university. Applicant must have 2.5 GPA or higher. Available to U.S. citizens.

Application Requirements: Application form, essay, transcript. *Deadline:* February 15.

Contact: Mike Adamson, Executive Director
Phone: 816-373-6565
E-mail: info@aea.net

L-3 AVIONICS SYSTEMS SCHOLARSHIP

Scholarship of $2500 available to high school seniors and college students who plan to attend or are attending an avionics or aircraft repair program in an accredited school. Minimum 2.5 GPA required.

Academic Fields/Career Goals: Aviation/Aerospace.

Award: Scholarship for use in freshman, sophomore, junior, or senior years; not renewable. *Number:* 1. *Amount:* $2500.

Eligibility Requirements: Applicant must be enrolled or expecting to enroll full- or part-time at a two-year or four-year or technical institution or university. Applicant must have 2.5 GPA or higher. Available to U.S. citizens.

Application Requirements: Application form, essay, transcript. *Deadline:* February 15.

Contact: Mike Adamson, Executive Director
Phone: 816-373-6565
E-mail: info@aea.net

LEE TARBOX MEMORIAL SCHOLARSHIP

Scholarship available to high school seniors or college students who plan to attend or are attending an avionics or aircraft repair program in an accredited school.

Academic Fields/Career Goals: Aviation/Aerospace; Trade/Technical Specialties.

Award: Scholarship for use in freshman, sophomore, junior, or senior years; not renewable. *Number:* 1. *Amount:* $2500.

Eligibility Requirements: Applicant must be enrolled or expecting to enroll full- or part-time at a two-year or four-year or technical institution or university. Applicant must have 2.5 GPA or higher. Available to U.S. citizens.

Application Requirements: Application form, essay, recommendations or references, test scores, transcript. *Deadline:* February 15.

Contact: Mike Adamson, Executive Director
Phone: 816-373-6565
E-mail: info@aea.net

LOWELL GAYLOR MEMORIAL SCHOLARSHIP

Scholarship for high school seniors and college students who plan to attend or are attending an avionics or aircraft repair program in an accredited school. Minimum 2.5 GPA required.

Academic Fields/Career Goals: Aviation/Aerospace; Trade/Technical Specialties.

Award: Scholarship for use in freshman, sophomore, junior, or senior years; not renewable. *Number:* 1. *Amount:* $1000.

Eligibility Requirements: Applicant must be enrolled or expecting to enroll full- or part-time at a two-year or four-year or technical institution or university. Applicant must have 2.5 GPA or higher. Available to U.S. and non-U.S. citizens.

Application Requirements: Application form, essay, recommendations or references, test scores, transcript. *Deadline:* February 15.

Contact: Mike Adamson, Executive Director
Phone: 816-373-6565
E-mail: info@aea.net

MID-CONTINENT INSTRUMENT SCHOLARSHIP

Scholarship available to high school seniors or college students who plan to attend or are attending an avionics or aircraft repair program in an accredited school. Minimum 2.5 GPA required.

Academic Fields/Career Goals: Aviation/Aerospace; Trade/Technical Specialties.

Award: Scholarship for use in freshman, sophomore, junior, or senior years; not renewable. *Number:* 1. *Amount:* $1000.

Eligibility Requirements: Applicant must be enrolled or expecting to enroll full- or part-time at a two-year or four-year or technical institution or university. Applicant must have 2.5 GPA or higher. Available to U.S. citizens.

Application Requirements: Application form, essay, recommendations or references, test scores, transcript. *Deadline:* February 15.

Contact: Mike Adamson, Executive Director
Phone: 816-373-6565
E-mail: info@aea.net

MONTE R. MITCHELL GLOBAL SCHOLARSHIP

Scholarship of $1000 available to European students pursuing a degree in aviation maintenance technology, avionics, or aircraft repair at an accredited school located in Europe or the United States.

Academic Fields/Career Goals: Aviation/Aerospace.

Award: Scholarship for use in freshman, sophomore, junior, or senior years; not renewable. *Number:* 1. *Amount:* $1000.

Eligibility Requirements: Applicant must be enrolled or expecting to enroll full- or part-time at a two-year or four-year or technical institution or university. Applicant must have 2.5 GPA or higher. Available to citizens of countries other than the U.S. or Canada.

Application Requirements: Application form, essay, recommendations or references, transcript. *Deadline:* February 15.

Contact: Mike Adamson, Executive Director
Phone: 816-373-6565
E-mail: info@aea.net

AIRPORT MINORITY ADVISORY COUNCIL EDUCATIONAL AND SCHOLARSHIP PROGRAM

http://www.amac-org.com/

AMACESP STUDENT SCHOLARSHIPS

Applicant must be seeking a BS or BA with interest and desire to pursue a career in the aviation/airport industry and seeking a degree in Aviation, Business Administration, Accounting, Architecture, Engineering or Finance and admitted by an accredited school or university for the current school term in which you are applying for a scholarship. Demonstration of a cumulative 3.0 GPA and involvement in community activities and extracurricular activities. Applicants must be a U.S. citizen. A commitment to involvement in furthering the mission of the Airport Minority Advisory Council (AMAC) by participating in the AMAC Student Program. AMAC Member Scholarship Awards are offered to Airport Minority Advisory Council (AMAC) members, their spouses, and their children. The AMAC Aviation & Professional Development Committee grant four $2000 scholarships each year to a number of students who are enrolled in an aviation related program and have a grade point average 3.0 or higher.

Academic Fields/Career Goals: Aviation/Aerospace.

Award: Scholarship for use in sophomore, junior, or senior years; not renewable. *Number:* 1–3. *Amount:* $2000.

Eligibility Requirements: Applicant must be enrolled or expecting to enroll full-time at a four-year institution or university. Applicant must have 3.0 GPA or higher. Available to U.S. citizens.

Application Requirements: Application form, autobiography, essay, personal photograph, recommendations or references, transcript. *Deadline:* May 18.

Contact: Miss. Jennifer Ibe, AMACESP Intern
Airport Minority Advisory Council Educational and
Scholarship Program
2345 Crystal Drive, Suite 902
Arlington, VA 22202
Phone: 703-414-2622 Ext. 1
Fax: 703-414-2686
E-mail: gene.roth@amac-org.com

AIR TRAFFIC CONTROL ASSOCIATION INC.

http://www.atca.org/

GABRIEL A. HARTL SCHOLARSHIP

Awarded to students enrolled in an two-year or greater air traffic control program at an institution approved and/or listed by the FAA as supporting the FAA's college training initiative.

Academic Fields/Career Goals: Aviation/Aerospace.

Award: Scholarship for use in freshman, sophomore, junior, senior, graduate, or postgraduate years; not renewable. *Number:* 1–4. *Amount:* $2000–$10,000.

Eligibility Requirements: Applicant must be enrolled or expecting to enroll full-time at a two-year or four-year institution or university; studying in Arkansas and must have an interest in aviation. Available to U.S. and non-U.S. citizens.

Application Requirements: Application form, community service, essay, financial need analysis. *Deadline:* May 1.

Contact: Tim Wagner, Membership Manager
Air Traffic Control Association Inc.
1101 King Street
Suite 300
Alexandria, VA 22314
Phone: 703-299-2430 Ext. 314
Fax: 703-299-2437
E-mail: tim.wagner@atca.org

ALASKAN AVIATION SAFETY FOUNDATION

http://www.aasfonline.org

ALASKAN AVIATION SAFETY FOUNDATION MEMORIAL SCHOLARSHIP FUND

Scholarships for undergraduate or graduate study in aviation. Must be a resident of Alaska and a U.S. citizen. Write for deadlines and details.

Academic Fields/Career Goals: Aviation/Aerospace.

Award: Scholarship for use in freshman, sophomore, junior, senior, or graduate years; not renewable. *Number:* 1–3. *Amount:* $500–$750.

Eligibility Requirements: Applicant must be enrolled or expecting to enroll full- or part-time at a two-year or four-year or technical institution or university; resident of Alaska and must have an interest in aviation. Available to U.S. citizens.

Application Requirements: Application form, driver's license, financial need analysis, recommendations or references, test scores, transcript. *Deadline:* May 30.

Contact: Scholarship Committee
Alaskan Aviation Safety Foundation
c/o Aviation Technology Division UAA
2811 Merril Field Drive
Anchorage, AK 99501
Phone: 907-243-7237

AMERICAN ASSOCIATION OF AIRPORT EXECUTIVES-SOUTHWEST CHAPTER

http://www.swaaae.org/

SWAAAE ACADEMIC SCHOLARSHIPS

A scholarship of $1500 for students pursuing an undergraduate or graduate degree in airport management may apply annually for an academic scholarship. Applicant must attend a college in Arizona, California, Nevada, Utah, or Hawaii.

Academic Fields/Career Goals: Aviation/Aerospace.

Award: Scholarship for use in sophomore, junior, senior, or graduate years; not renewable. *Number:* 5. *Amount:* $500–$1500.

Eligibility Requirements: Applicant must be enrolled or expecting to enroll full- or part-time at a four-year institution or university and studying in Arizona, California, Hawaii, Nevada, Utah. Available to U.S. and non-U.S. citizens.

Application Requirements: Application form. *Deadline:* September 29.

Contact: Charles Mangum, Scholarship Committee
American Association of Airport Executives-Southwest
Chapter
8565 North Sand Dune Place
Tucson, AZ 85743
Phone: 520-682-9565
E-mail: cman2122@comcast.net

AMERICAN CHEMICAL SOCIETY, RUBBER DIVISION

http://www.rubber.org/

AMERICAN CHEMICAL SOCIETY, RUBBER DIVISION UNDERGRADUATE SCHOLARSHIP

• *See page 109*

AMERICAN INSTITUTE OF AERONAUTICS AND ASTRONAUTICS

http://www.aiaafoundation.org/

AIAA FOUNDATION UNDERGRADUATE SCHOLARSHIPS

• *See page 110*

LEATRICE GREGORY PENDRAY SCHOLARSHIP

• *See page 110*

AMERICAN SOCIETY OF NAVAL ENGINEERS

http://www.navalengineers.org/

AMERICAN SOCIETY OF NAVAL ENGINEERS SCHOLARSHIP

• *See page 110*

ARMED FORCES COMMUNICATIONS AND ELECTRONICS ASSOCIATION, EDUCATIONAL FOUNDATION

http://www.afcea.org/site/?q=foundation/scholarships

ARMED FORCES COMMUNICATIONS AND ELECTRONICS ASSOCIATION ROTC SCHOLARSHIP PROGRAM

Award for ROTC students in their sophomore or junior years enrolled in four-year accredited colleges or universities in the United States. Eligible C4I-related fields of study or majors that align with the mission statement of AFCEA Educational Foundation. The list of acceptable majors can be found on the website. Must exhibit academic excellence and potential to serve as an officer in the armed forces of the United States. Nominations are submitted by professors of military science, naval science, or aerospace studies.

Academic Fields/Career Goals: Aviation/Aerospace; Computer Science/Data Processing; Electrical Engineering/Electronics; Engineering-Related Technologies; Engineering/Technology; Materials Science, Engineering, and Metallurgy; Mathematics; Physical Sciences.

Award: Scholarship for use in sophomore or junior years; not renewable. *Number:* 16. *Amount:* $2000–$5000.

Eligibility Requirements: Applicant must be enrolled or expecting to enroll full-time at a four-year institution or university. Applicant must have 3.0 GPA or higher. Available to U.S. citizens.

Application Requirements: Application form, community service, financial need analysis. *Deadline:* February 17.

Contact: Mrs. Casmere Kistner, Scholarships, Awards and Grants
Armed Forces Communications and Electronics Association,
Educational Foundation
4400 Fair Lakes Court
Fairfax, VA 22015
Phone: 703-631-6147
E-mail: edfoundation@afcea.org

ASSOCIATION OF FORMER INTELLIGENCE OFFICERS

http://www.afio.com

AFIO UNDERGRADUATE AND GRADUATE SCHOLARSHIPS

• *See page 103*

ASTRONAUT SCHOLARSHIP FOUNDATION

http://www.astronautscholarship.org/

ASTRONAUT SCHOLARSHIP FOUNDATION

• *See page 112*

AVIATION COUNCIL OF PENNSYLVANIA

http://www.acpfly.com/

AVIATION COUNCIL OF PENNSYLVANIA SCHOLARSHIP PROGRAM

Sponsored by the Aviation Council of Pennsylvania Awards for Pennsylvania residents are available in the following categories: Aviation Technology, Aviation Management, and Aviation Pilot.

Academic Fields/Career Goals: Aviation/Aerospace.

Award: Scholarship for use in freshman, sophomore, junior, or senior years; not renewable. *Number:* 3–4. *Amount:* $500–$1000.

Eligibility Requirements: Applicant must be enrolled or expecting to enroll full- or part-time at a two-year or four-year or technical institution or university; resident of Pennsylvania; studying in Pennsylvania and must have an interest in aviation. Available to U.S. citizens.

Application Requirements: Application form, financial need analysis. *Deadline:* July 8.

Contact: Debra Bowman, Executive Director
Aviation Council of Pennsylvania
3915 Union Deposit Rd., #935
Harrisburg, PA 17109
Phone: 717-850-0227
E-mail: dbowman@acpfly.com

AVIATION DISTRIBUTORS AND MANUFACTURERS ASSOCIATION INTERNATIONAL

ADMA SCHOLARSHIP

Scholarship to provide assistance to students pursuing careers in the aviation field. Those enrolled in an accredited Aviation program may be eligible.

Academic Fields/Career Goals: Aviation/Aerospace.

Award: Scholarship for use in junior or senior years; not renewable. *Number:* 1. *Amount:* up to $2000.

Eligibility Requirements: Applicant must be enrolled or expecting to enroll full-time at a two-year or four-year institution or university and must have an interest in aviation. Applicant must have 3.0 GPA or higher. Available to U.S. citizens.

Application Requirements: Application form, essay, financial need analysis, recommendations or references, transcript. *Deadline:* March 28.

Contact: Scholarship Committee
Aviation Distributors and Manufacturers Association
International
100 North 20th Street, Fourth Floor
Philadelphia, PA 19103-1443
Phone: 215-564-3484
Fax: 215-963-9785
E-mail: adma@fernley.com

BHW GROUP

https://thebhwgroup.com/

BHW WOMEN IN STEM SCHOLARSHIP
• *See page 74*

CHARLIE WELLS MEMORIAL SCHOLARSHIP FUND

http://www.wellsscholarship.com/

CHARLIE WELLS MEMORIAL AVIATION SCHOLARSHIP

Scholarship(s) of varying amounts will be awarded each year when funds are available. The applicant must be a resident of the United States or one of its territories. Must be a full-time student majoring in an aviation-oriented curriculum.

Academic Fields/Career Goals: Aviation/Aerospace.

Award: Scholarship for use in freshman, sophomore, junior, senior, or graduate years; not renewable.

Eligibility Requirements: Applicant must be enrolled or expecting to enroll full-time at a four-year institution or university. Available to U.S. citizens.

Application Requirements: Application form, recommendations or references, transcript. *Deadline:* April 30.

Contact: Roger Thompson, Manager
Phone: 217-899-3263
E-mail: rog@wellsscholarship.com

CHICAGO AREA BUSINESS AVIATION ASSOCIATION

http://www.cabaa.com

CABAA/FLIGHTSAFETY CITATION EXCEL PROFESSIONAL PILOT TRAINING AWARD

The CABAA Education Foundation, along with FlightSafety, will award a 2017 applicant with advanced training to enhance the individual's progress toward a career in Business Aviation. The award will only be available for students who will have graduated with a pilot degree Spring 2017, or graduated Spring/Summer/Winter 2016. This year, the award will be a Citation Excel/XLS Series Course. With completion of this course the pilot will obtain skills to operate a Citation Excel/XLS as an SIC. The retail value of this award is approximately $22,200. CABAA and FlightSafety have teamed up to offer this award to promote professional development for a career in business Aviation. The winner will be notified by phone and presented the award at the annual CABAA Golf Classic held on August 7th, 2017. The recipient's presence is required at the time of award presentation. For more information about the course please visit resources.flightsafety.com. For information about CABAA membership, please visit www.cabaa.com.

Academic Fields/Career Goals: Aviation/Aerospace.

Award: Scholarship for use in senior year; not renewable. *Number:* 1. *Amount:* $22,000.

Eligibility Requirements: Applicant must be enrolled or expecting to enroll full- or part-time at a two-year or four-year or technical institution or university and resident of Illinois, Indiana, Iowa, Michigan, Missouri, Wisconsin. Applicant must have 3.0 GPA or higher. Available to U.S. citizens.

Application Requirements: Application form, essay, interview. *Deadline:* May 1.

Contact: Brian Zankowski
Lake Villa, IL 60046
Phone: 224-931-8064
E-mail: scholarships@cabaa.com

CABAA/FLIGHTSAFETY CORPORATE SCHEDULER AND DISPATCHER TRAINING AWARD

The CABAA Education Foundation, along with FlightSafety, will award a 2017 applicant a FlightSafety Corporate Scheduler/Dispatcher Initial. This approved course addresses the unique needs of individuals serving, or planning to serve as corporate aircraft schedulers/dispatchers. The course is designed to provide individuals with practical information, which will enable them to function as integral members of the corporate travel team. All subject matter is approached from a scheduler/dispatcher's perspective, using real-world examples and scenarios. CABAA and FlightSafety have teamed up to offer this award to promote professional development for a career in business aviation. The winner will be notified by phone and presented the award at the annual CABAA Golf Classic held on August 7th, 2017. The recipient's presence is required at the time of award presentation. For more information about the course visit resources.flightsafety.com

Academic Fields/Career Goals: Aviation/Aerospace.

Award: Scholarship for use in senior year; not renewable. *Number:* 1. *Amount:* $4000.

Eligibility Requirements: Applicant must be enrolled or expecting to enroll full- or part-time at a two-year or four-year or technical institution or university and resident of Illinois, Indiana, Iowa, Michigan, Missouri, Wisconsin. Applicant must have 3.0 GPA or higher. Available to U.S. citizens.

Application Requirements: Application form, essay. *Deadline:* May 1.

Contact: Brian Zankowski
Lake Villa, IL 60046
Phone: 224-931-8064
E-mail: scholarships@cabaa.com

CABAA/FLIGHTSAFETY MAINTENANCE PROFESSIONAL TRAINING AWARD

One recipient will be awarded the Citation Sovereign Maintenance Initial course. This course is designed to meet the training requirements of aviation maintenance professionals maintaining Citation Sovereign aircraft. The retail value of this award is approximately $18,000. The recipient of the award must be a college student who graduated with a degree in Aircraft Maintenance and holds a current A&P license. The winners will be notified by phone and presented the award at the annual CABAA Golf Classic held on August 7th, 2017. The recipient's presence is required at the time of award presentation at the award presentations. CABAA and FlightSafety have teamed up to offer these awards to promote continuing professional development during a business aviation career. These awards are established to encourage all to reach the highest level of achievement in their aviation studies and career. For more information on the course, visit http://resources.flightsafety.com

Academic Fields/Career Goals: Aviation/Aerospace.

Award: Scholarship for use in senior year; not renewable. *Number:* 1. *Amount:* $18,000.

Eligibility Requirements: Applicant must be enrolled or expecting to enroll full- or part-time at a two-year or four-year or technical institution or university and resident of Illinois, Indiana, Iowa, Michigan, Missouri, Wisconsin. Applicant or parent of applicant must have employment or volunteer experience in air traffic control. Applicant must have 2.5 GPA or higher. Available to U.S. citizens.

Application Requirements: Application form, essay. *Deadline:* May 1.

Contact: Brian Zankowski
Lake Villa, IL 60046
Phone: 224-931-8064
E-mail: scholarships@cabaa.com

CABAA MAINTENANCE COMMITTEE FINANCIAL AWARD

One scholarship will be awarded in the amount of $7500 to a student seeking a degree in aviation maintenance. This scholarship is open to both high school seniors graduating in 2017 and college level students. Scholarship funds will be paid to the student and college or university of which the recipient is enrolled. The scholarship funds are to be used to pay tuition or fees for aviation specific programs. CABAA and the CABAA Maintenance Committee offer this award to promote professional development for a career in business aviation maintenance. The winner will be notified by phone and presented the award at the annual CABAA Golf Classic held on August 7th, 2017. The recipient's presence is required at the time of the award presentation. For more information about CABAA, Including membership, please visit http://www.cabaa.com

Academic Fields/Career Goals: Aviation/Aerospace.

Award: Scholarship for use in freshman, sophomore, junior, or senior years; not renewable. *Number:* 1. *Amount:* $7500.

Eligibility Requirements: Applicant must be enrolled or expecting to enroll full- or part-time at a two-year or four-year or technical institution or university and resident of Illinois, Indiana, Iowa, Michigan, Missouri, Wisconsin. Applicant must have 2.5 GPA or higher. Available to U.S. citizens.

Application Requirements: Application form, essay. *Deadline:* May 1.

Contact: Brian Zankowski
Lake Villa, IL 60046
Phone: 224-931-8064
E-mail: scholarships@cabaa.com

CABAA SCHOLARSHIP

Up to four (4) scholarships will be awarded in the amount of $7500 per recipient. These scholarships are open to both high school seniors graduating in 2017 and college level students. Scholarship funds will be paid to the student and college or university of which the recipient is enrolled and are to be used to pay tuition or fees for aviation specific programs. CABAA offers this award to promote professional development for a career in business aviation. The winner will be notified by phone and presented the award at the annual CABAA Golf Classic held on August 7th, 2017. The recipient's presence is required at the time of award presentation. For more information about CABAA, including membership visit http://www.CABAA.com

Academic Fields/Career Goals: Aviation/Aerospace.

Award: Scholarship for use in freshman, sophomore, junior, or senior years; not renewable. *Number:* 4. *Amount:* $7500.

Eligibility Requirements: Applicant must be enrolled or expecting to enroll full- or part-time at a two-year or four-year or technical institution or university and resident of Illinois, Indiana, Iowa, Michigan, Missouri, Wisconsin. Applicant must have 3.0 GPA or higher. Available to U.S. citizens.

Application Requirements: Application form, essay. *Deadline:* May 1.

Contact: Brian Zankowski
Lake Villa, IL 60046
Phone: 224-931-8064
E-mail: scholarships@cabaa.com

KEN JOHNSON MEMORIAL SCHOLARSHIP

One scholarship will be awarded in the amount of $7500 to a 2017 graduating high school student seeking a degree in aviation. Scholarship funds will be paid to the student and college or university of which the recipient is enrolled and are to be used to pay tuition or fees for aviation specific programs. CABAA offers this award to promote professional development for a career in business aviation. The winner will be notified by phone and presented the award at the annual CABAA Golf Classic held on August 7th, 2017. Recipient presence is required at the time of award presentation. For more information about CABAA, including membership visit www.CABAA.com.

Academic Fields/Career Goals: Aviation/Aerospace.

Award: Scholarship for use in freshman year; not renewable. *Number:* 1. *Amount:* $7500.

Eligibility Requirements: Applicant must be high school student; planning to enroll or expecting to enroll full- or part-time at a two-year or four-year or technical institution or university and resident of Illinois, Indiana, Iowa, Michigan, Missouri, Wisconsin. Applicant must have 3.0 GPA or higher. Available to U.S. citizens.

Application Requirements: Application form, essay. *Deadline:* May 1.

Contact: Brian Zankowski
Lake Villa, IL 60046
Phone: 224-931-8064
E-mail: scholarships@cabaa.com

CIVIL AIR PATROL, USAF AUXILIARY

http://www.gocivilairpatrol.com/

MAJOR GENERAL LUCAS V. BEAU FLIGHT SCHOLARSHIPS SPONSORED BY THE ORDER OF DAEDALIANS

One-time scholarships for active cadets of the Civil Air Patrol who desire a career in military aviation. Award is to be used toward flight training for a private pilot license. Must be 15 1/2 to 18 1/2 years of age on April 1st of the year for which applying. Must be an active CAP cadet officer. Not open to the general public.

Academic Fields/Career Goals: Aviation/Aerospace.

Award: Scholarship for use in freshman year; not renewable. *Number:* 5. *Amount:* $2100.

Eligibility Requirements: Applicant must be high school student; planning to enroll or expecting to enroll full- or part-time at a four-year institution or university; single and must have an interest in aviation. Applicant or parent of applicant must be member of Civil Air Patrol. Available to U.S. citizens.

Application Requirements: Application form, essay, interview, personal photograph, recommendations or references, test scores, transcript. *Deadline:* March 1.

Contact: Kelly Easterly, Assistant Program Manager
Civil Air Patrol, USAF Auxiliary
105 South Hansell Street, Building 714
Maxwell Air Force Base, AL 36112-6332
Phone: 334-953-8640
Fax: 334-953-6699
E-mail: cpr@capnhq.gov

DAEDALIAN FOUNDATION

http://www.daedalians.org/

DAEDALIAN FOUNDATION MATCHING SCHOLARSHIP PROGRAM

Scholarship program, wherein the foundation matches amounts given by flights, or chapters of the Order of Daedalians, to deserving college and university students who are pursuing a career as a military aviator.

Academic Fields/Career Goals: Aviation/Aerospace.

Award: Scholarship for use in freshman, sophomore, junior, senior, or graduate years; not renewable. *Number:* 75–80. *Amount:* up to $2500.

Eligibility Requirements: Applicant must be enrolled or expecting to enroll full-time at a four-year institution or university. Available to U.S. citizens.

Application Requirements: Application form, flight/ROTC/CAP recommendation, personal photograph, test scores. *Deadline:* December 31.

Contact: Kristi Cavenaugh, Program Executive Secretary
Daedalian Foundation
55 Main Circle, Building 676
Randolph AFB, TX 78148
Phone: 210-945-2111
Fax: 210-945-2112
E-mail: kristi@daedalians.org

EAA AVIATION FOUNDATION, INC.

http://www.eaa.org/

HANSEN SCHOLARSHIP

Renewable scholarship of $1000 for a student enrolled in an accredited institution and pursuing a degree in aerospace engineering or aeronautical engineering. Student must be in good standing; financial need not a requirement. Must be an EAA member. Applications may be downloaded from the website http://www.youngeagles.org.

Academic Fields/Career Goals: Aviation/Aerospace.

Award: Scholarship for use in freshman, sophomore, junior, or senior years; not renewable. *Number:* up to 1. *Amount:* up to $1000.

Eligibility Requirements: Applicant must be enrolled or expecting to enroll full-time at a two-year or four-year or technical institution or university. Applicant or parent of applicant must be member of Experimental Aircraft Association. Available to U.S. and non-U.S. citizens.

Application Requirements: Application form. *Deadline:* February 28.

Contact: Jane Smith, Scholarship Coordinator
EAA Aviation Foundation, Inc.
PO Box 3086
Oshkosh, WI 54903-3086
Phone: 920-426-6823
Fax: 920-426-4873
E-mail: jsmith@eaa.org

PAYZER SCHOLARSHIP

Scholarship for a student accepted or enrolled in an accredited college, university, or postsecondary school with an emphasis on technical information. Awarded to an individual who is seeking a major and declares an intention to pursue a professional career in engineering, mathematics, or the physical/biological sciences. Visit http://www.youngeagles.org for criteria and to download official application. Must be an EAA member or recommended by an EAA member.

Academic Fields/Career Goals: Aviation/Aerospace; Biology; Engineering/Technology; Physical Sciences.

Award: Scholarship for use in freshman, sophomore, junior, or senior years; not renewable. *Number:* up to 1. *Amount:* up to $5000.

Eligibility Requirements: Applicant must be enrolled or expecting to enroll full-time at a two-year or four-year or technical institution or university. Applicant or parent of applicant must be member of Experimental Aircraft Association. Available to U.S. and non-U.S. citizens.

Application Requirements: Application form. *Deadline:* February 28.

Contact: Jane Smith, Scholarship Coordinator
EAA Aviation Foundation, Inc.
PO Box 3086
Oshkosh, WI 54903-3086
Phone: 920-426-6823
Fax: 920-426-4873
E-mail: jsmith@eaa.org

GENERAL AVIATION MANUFACTURERS ASSOCIATION

http://www.gama.aero/

EDWARD W. STIMPSON "AVIATION EXCELLENCE" AWARD

One-time scholarship award for students who are graduating from high school and have been accepted to attend aviation college or university in the upcoming year. See website at http://www.gama.aero for more details.

Academic Fields/Career Goals: Aviation/Aerospace.

Award: Scholarship for use in freshman year; not renewable. *Number:* 1. *Amount:* $500.

Eligibility Requirements: Applicant must be high school student; planning to enroll or expecting to enroll full-time at a four-year institution or university and must have an interest in aviation. Applicant must have 3.0 GPA or higher. Available to U.S. citizens.

Application Requirements: Application form, essay, recommendations or references, transcript. *Deadline:* April 28.

Contact: Katie Pribyl, Director, Communications
Phone: 202-393-1500
Fax: 202-842-4063
E-mail: kpribyl@gama.aero

HAROLD S. WOOD AWARD FOR EXCELLENCE

One-time scholarship award for an university student who is attending a National Intercollegiate Flying Association (NIFA) school. Must have completed at least one semester of coursework. See website at http://www.gama.aero for additional details.

Academic Fields/Career Goals: Aviation/Aerospace.

Award: Scholarship for use in freshman, sophomore, junior, or senior years; not renewable. *Number:* 1. *Amount:* $1000.

Eligibility Requirements: Applicant must be enrolled or expecting to enroll full-time at a four-year institution or university. Applicant must have 3.0 GPA or higher. Available to U.S. citizens.

Application Requirements: Application form, nomination, recommendations or references, transcript. *Deadline:* February 24.

Contact: Katie Pribyl, Director, Communications
Phone: 202-393-1500
Fax: 202-842-4063
E-mail: kpribyl@gama.aero

GRAND RAPIDS COMMUNITY FOUNDATION

http://www.grfoundation.org/

JOSHUA ESCH MITCHELL AVIATION SCHOLARSHIP

For students pursuing studies in the field of professional pilot with an emphasis on general aviation, flight engineer, or airway science. Applicant must be a U.S. citizens enrolled in a full- or part-time program at a college or university in the United States providing an accredited flight science curriculum. Applicant should have a minimum GPA of 2.75. A valid pilot's certificate (not to include a Student Certificate) is required. A letter of recommendation from a professional in the aviation field is required.

Academic Fields/Career Goals: Aviation/Aerospace.

Award: Scholarship for use in sophomore, junior, or senior years; not renewable. *Number:* 1–3. *Amount:* $1000.

Eligibility Requirements: Applicant must be enrolled or expecting to enroll full-time at a four-year institution and must have an interest in aviation. Applicant must have 2.5 GPA or higher. Available to U.S. citizens.

Application Requirements: Application form, application form may be submitted online (http://grfoundation.org), financial need analysis, recommendations or references, transcript, valid pilot's certificate required. *Deadline:* April 1.

Contact: Ms. Ruth Bishop, Education Program Officer
Grand Rapids Community Foundation
185 Oakes SW
Grand Rapids, MI 49503
Phone: 616-454-1751 Ext. 103
E-mail: rbishop@grfoundation.org

GREAT MINDS IN STEM

www.greatmindsinstem.org

HISPANIC ENGINEER NATIONAL ACHIEVEMENT AWARDS CORPORATION SCHOLARSHIP PROGRAM
• *See page 106*

ILLINOIS PILOTS ASSOCIATION

http://www.illinoispilots.com/

ILLINOIS PILOTS ASSOCIATION MEMORIAL SCHOLARSHIP

Recipient must be a resident of Illinois established in an Illinois postsecondary institution in a full-time aviation-related program. Applicants will be judged by the scholarship committee, and the award (usually $2000 annually) will be sent directly to the recipient's school. For further details visit website http://www.illinoispilots.com.

Academic Fields/Career Goals: Aviation/Aerospace.

Award: Scholarship for use in sophomore, junior, or senior years; not renewable. *Number:* 1. *Amount:* $500–$2000.

Eligibility Requirements: Applicant must be enrolled or expecting to enroll full-time at a two-year or four-year or technical institution or university; resident of Illinois; studying in Illinois and must have an interest in aviation. Available to U.S. citizens.

Application Requirements: Application form, essay, personal photograph, recommendations or references, transcript. *Deadline:* March 1.

Contact: Ruth Frantz, Scholarship Committee Chairman
Illinois Pilots Association
40W297 Apache Lane
Huntley, IL 60142
Phone: 847-669-3821
E-mail: landings8e@aol.com

INTERNATIONAL SOCIETY OF WOMEN AIRLINE PILOTS (ISA+21)

http://www.iswap.org/

INTERNATIONAL SOCIETY OF WOMEN AIRLINE PILOTS AIRLINE SCHOLARSHIPS

Scholarships are available to women who are pursuing careers as airline pilots. Applicants must demonstrate financial need. Must have an U.S. FAA Commercial Pilot Certificate with an Instrument Rating and First Class Medical Certificate. Must have flight time in a fixed wing aircraft commensurate with the rating sought.

Academic Fields/Career Goals: Aviation/Aerospace.

Award: Scholarship for use in freshman, sophomore, junior, or senior years; not renewable. *Number:* up to 5.

Eligibility Requirements: Applicant must be enrolled or expecting to enroll full-time at a four-year institution or university and female. Available to U.S. and non-U.S. citizens.

Application Requirements: Application form, driver's license, financial need analysis, income tax forms, logbook pages, pilot licenses, medical certificates, interview, personal photograph, recommendations or references, resume, transcript. *Deadline:* December 10.

Contact: Ms. Julie Clippard, Scholarship Chairwoman
    E-mail: scholarshipsponsor@iswap.org

INTERNATIONAL SOCIETY OF WOMEN AIRLINE PILOTS FINANCIAL SCHOLARSHIP

Scholarships are available to women who are pursuing careers as airline pilots. Must have flight time in a fixed wing aircraft commensurate with the rating sought. Must have flight time in a fixed wing aircraft commensurate with the rating sought.

Academic Fields/Career Goals: Aviation/Aerospace.

Award: Scholarship for use in freshman, sophomore, junior, or senior years; not renewable. *Number:* 1.

Eligibility Requirements: Applicant must be enrolled or expecting to enroll full-time at a four-year institution or university and female. Available to U.S. and non-U.S. citizens.

Application Requirements: Application form, copies of income tax forms, logbook pages, pilot licenses, medical certificates, driver's license, financial need analysis, interview, personal photograph, recommendations or references, resume, transcript. *Deadline:* December 10.

Contact: Ms. Julie Clippard, Scholarship Chairwoman
    E-mail: scholarshipsponsor@iswap.org

INTERNATIONAL SOCIETY OF WOMEN AIRLINE PILOTS FIORENZA DE BERNARDI MERIT SCHOLARSHIP

Financial award will aid those pilots endeavoring to fill some of the basic squares, i.e. a CFI, CFII, MEI or any international equivalents. Must have flight time in a fixed wing aircraft commensurate with the rating sought. Must have flight time in a fixed wing aircraft commensurate with the rating sought.

Academic Fields/Career Goals: Aviation/Aerospace.

Award: Scholarship for use in freshman, sophomore, junior, or senior years; not renewable. *Number:* 1.

Eligibility Requirements: Applicant must be enrolled or expecting to enroll full- or part-time at a four-year institution or university and female. Available to U.S. and non-U.S. citizens.

Application Requirements: Application form, copies of income tax forms, logbook pages, pilot licenses, medical certificates, driver's license, financial need analysis, interview, personal photograph, recommendations or references, resume, transcript. *Deadline:* December 10.

Contact: Ms. Julie Clippard, Scholarship Chairwoman
    E-mail: scholarshipsponsor@iswap.org

INTERNATIONAL SOCIETY OF WOMEN AIRLINE PILOTS GRACE MCADAMS HARRIS SCHOLARSHIP

Scholarship may fund any ISA scholarship if the applicant has demonstrated an exceptionally spirited and ingenious attitude under difficult circumstances in the field of aviation. Applicants must have an U.S. FAA Commercial Pilot Certificate with an Instrument Rating and

First Class Medical Certificate. Visit website http://www.iswap.org for more details.

Academic Fields/Career Goals: Aviation/Aerospace.

Award: Scholarship for use in freshman, sophomore, junior, or senior years; not renewable. *Number:* 1.

Eligibility Requirements: Applicant must be enrolled or expecting to enroll full-time at a four-year institution or university; female and must have an interest in aviation. Available to U.S. and non-U.S. citizens.

Application Requirements: Application form, copies of income tax forms, logbook pages, pilot licenses, medical certificates, driver's license, financial need analysis, interview, personal photograph, recommendations or references, transcript. *Deadline:* December 10.

Contact: Ms. Julie Clippard, Scholarship Chairwoman
    E-mail: scholarshipsponsor@iswap.org

INTERNATIONAL SOCIETY OF WOMEN AIRLINE PILOTS HOLLY MULLENS MEMORIAL SCHOLARSHIP

Financial award is reserved for that applicant who is a single mother. Applicants must have an U.S. FAA Commercial Pilot Certificate with an Instrument Rating and First Class Medical Certificate. Visit website, http://www.iswap.org, for more details.

Academic Fields/Career Goals: Aviation/Aerospace.

Award: Scholarship for use in freshman, sophomore, junior, or senior years; not renewable. *Number:* 1.

Eligibility Requirements: Applicant must be enrolled or expecting to enroll full-time at a four-year institution or university and single female. Available to U.S. and non-U.S. citizens.

Application Requirements: Application form, copies of income tax forms, logbook pages, pilot licenses, medical certificates, driver's license, financial need analysis, interview, recommendations or references, transcript. *Deadline:* December 10.

Contact: Ms. Julie Clippard, Scholarship Chairwoman
    E-mail: scholarshipsponsor@iswap.org

INTERNATIONAL SOCIETY OF WOMEN AIRLINE PILOTS NORTH CAROLINA FINANCIAL SCHOLARSHIP

Scholarships for a woman pilot from North Carolina interested in a career in the airline world. Must have flight time in a fixed wing aircraft commensurate with the rating sought. Must have flight time in a fixed wing aircraft commensurate with the rating sought.

Academic Fields/Career Goals: Aviation/Aerospace.

Award: Scholarship for use in freshman, sophomore, junior, or senior years; not renewable. *Number:* 1.

Eligibility Requirements: Applicant must be enrolled or expecting to enroll full-time at a four-year institution or university; female and resident of North Carolina. Available to U.S. and non-U.S. citizens.

Application Requirements: Application form, copies of income tax forms, logbook pages, pilot licenses, medical certificates, driver's license, financial need analysis, interview, personal photograph, recommendations or references, resume, transcript. *Deadline:* December 10.

Contact: Ms. Julie Clippard, Scholarship Chairwoman
    E-mail: scholarshipsponsor@iswap.org

LEARNING FOR LIFE/EXPLORING

http://www.learning-for-life.org/

NATIONAL AVIATION EXPLORER SCHOLARSHIPS

$3000-$10,000 scholarships for aviation Explorers pursuing a career in the aviation industry. The intent of these scholarships is to identify and reward those individuals who best exemplify the qualities that lead to success in the aviation industry. Must be participant of the Learning for Life Exploring program.

Academic Fields/Career Goals: Aviation/Aerospace.

Award: Scholarship for use in freshman, sophomore, junior, or senior years; not renewable. *Number:* 5. *Amount:* $3000–$10,000.

Eligibility Requirements: Applicant must be enrolled or expecting to enroll full- or part-time at a technical institution and must have an interest in aviation or leadership. Available to U.S. and non-U.S. citizens.

Application Requirements: Application form, essay, recommendations or references. *Deadline:* March 31.

Contact: Bill Taylor, Exploring Director
Learning for Life/Exploring
1325 West Walnut Hill Drive
Irving, TX 75038
Phone: 972-580-2241
Fax: 972-580-2137
E-mail: william.taylor@lflmail.org

MANUFACTURERS ASSOCIATION OF MAINE

http://www.mainemfg.com/

MAINE MANUFACTURING CAREER AND TRAINING FOUNDATION SCHOLARSHIP

Maine Manufacturing Career and Training Foundation offers scholarship awards to individuals seeking education in the manufacturing field of study. Any Maine student or worker can apply for tuition assistance at any Maine institute of higher learning. All applicants must be full-time students and maintain a minimum of a C average.

Academic Fields/Career Goals: Aviation/Aerospace; Engineering-Related Technologies; Engineering/Technology; Industrial Design; Marine/Ocean Engineering; Materials Science, Engineering, and Metallurgy; Mechanical Engineering; Trade/Technical Specialties.

Award: Scholarship for use in freshman, sophomore, junior, senior, graduate, or postgraduate years; not renewable. *Number:* 5–25. *Amount:* $650–$750.

Eligibility Requirements: Applicant must be enrolled or expecting to enroll full- or part-time at a two-year or four-year or technical institution or university; resident of Maine and studying in Maine. Available to U.S. citizens.

Application Requirements: Application form, essay. *Deadline:* April 30.

Contact: Marion Sprague, Outreach Communications Director
Manufacturers Association of Maine
101 Mcalister Farm Raod
Portland, ME 04103
Phone: 207-747-4406
E-mail: marion@mainemfg.com

NASA FLORIDA SPACE GRANT CONSORTIUM

http://www.floridaspacegrant.org/

FLORIDA SPACE RESEARCH PROGRAM

Grants for faculty researchers from Florida public and private universities and community colleges. One-time award for aerospace and technology research. Submit research proposal with budget.

Academic Fields/Career Goals: Aviation/Aerospace; Earth Science; Materials Science, Engineering, and Metallurgy; Mathematics; Mechanical Engineering.

Award: Grant for use in junior, senior, graduate, or postgraduate years; not renewable. *Number:* 13–15. *Amount:* $12,500–$25,000.

Eligibility Requirements: Applicant must be enrolled or expecting to enroll full- or part-time at a two-year or four-year institution or university; resident of Florida and studying in Florida. Available to U.S. citizens.

Application Requirements: Application form. *Deadline:* June 17.

Contact: Dr. Jaydeep Mukherjee, FSGC Director
NASA Florida Space Grant Consortium
PO Box 160650, 12354 Research Parkway, Room 218
Orlando, FL 32826
Phone: 407-823-6177
E-mail: fsgc@ucf.edu

NASA/MARYLAND SPACE GRANT CONSORTIUM

http://md.spacegrant.org/

NASA MARYLAND SPACE GRANT CONSORTIUM UNDERGRADUATE SCHOLARSHIPS

Scholarship for full-time student majoring in the biological and life sciences, chemistry, geological sciences, physics, astronomy, engineering, computer science, or other related fields. Must be a U.S. citizen and a Maryland resident. Enrollment in an affiliate institution of the Maryland Space Grant Consortium is necessary.

Academic Fields/Career Goals: Aviation/Aerospace; Biology; Chemical Engineering; Computer Science/Data Processing; Earth Science; Engineering/Technology; Environmental Science; Materials Science, Engineering, and Metallurgy; Mathematics; Physical Sciences.

Award: Scholarship for use in freshman, sophomore, junior, or senior years; not renewable. *Amount:* up to $1000.

Eligibility Requirements: Applicant must be enrolled or expecting to enroll full-time at a four-year institution or university; resident of Maryland and studying in Maryland. Applicant must have 3.0 GPA or higher. Available to U.S. citizens.

Application Requirements: Application form, essay, recommendations or references. *Deadline:* May 15.

Contact: Richard Henry, Director
Phone: 410-516-7350
Fax: 410-516-4109
E-mail: henry@jhu.edu

NASA MINNESOTA SPACE GRANT CONSORTIUM

http://www.aem.umn.edu/mnsgc

MINNESOTA SPACE GRANT CONSORTIUM SCHOLARSHIP PROGRAM

Scholarships for full-time undergraduates attending institutions belonging to the Minnesota Space Grant Consortium—institution list on the website. Preference given to students studying aerospace engineering, space science, and NASA-related math, science, or engineering fields. Minimum 3.0 GPA required. Must be U.S. citizen. For more details go to http://www.aem.umn.edu/mnsgc.

Academic Fields/Career Goals: Aviation/Aerospace; Computer Science/Data Processing; Earth Science; Electrical Engineering/Electronics; Engineering/Technology; Environmental Science; Mathematics; Mechanical Engineering; Meteorology/Atmospheric Science; Natural Sciences; Nuclear Science; Oceanography; Physical Sciences.

Award: Scholarship for use in freshman, sophomore, junior, or senior years; not renewable. *Number:* 20–40. *Amount:* $500–$2500.

Eligibility Requirements: Applicant must be enrolled or expecting to enroll full-time at a two-year or four-year institution or university and studying in Minnesota. Applicant must have 3.0 GPA or higher. Available to U.S. citizens.

Application Requirements: Application form. *Deadline:* continuous.

Contact: Minnesota Space Grant, Department of Aerospace Engineering
NASA Minnesota Space Grant Consortium
107 Akerman Hall, 110 Union Street, SE
Minneapolis, MN 55455
Phone: 612-626-9295
E-mail: mnsgc@umn.edu

NASA MONTANA SPACE GRANT CONSORTIUM

http://www.spacegrant.montana.edu/

MONTANA SPACE GRANT SCHOLARSHIP PROGRAM

Awards are made on a competitive basis to students enrolled in fields of study relevant to the aerospace sciences and engineering. Must be U.S. citizen enrolled as full-time student at a Montana Consortium campus.

Academic Fields/Career Goals: Aviation/Aerospace; Biology; Chemical Engineering; Civil Engineering; Computer Science/Data

Processing; Electrical Engineering/Electronics; Engineering/Technology; Mathematics; Mechanical Engineering.

Award: Scholarship for use in freshman, sophomore, junior, or senior years; not renewable. *Number:* 15–20. *Amount:* $1000–$2000.

Eligibility Requirements: Applicant must be enrolled or expecting to enroll full-time at a two-year or four-year institution or university and studying in Montana. Available to U.S. citizens.

Application Requirements: Application form, application form may be submitted online (http://spacegrant.montana.edu), essay, recommendations or references, transcript. *Deadline:* April 1.

Contact: Chris Harmon, Program Coordinator
    Phone: 406-994-4223
    Fax: 406-994-4452

NASA RHODE ISLAND SPACE GRANT CONSORTIUM

http://brown/initiatives/ri-space-grant

NASA RHODE ISLAND SPACE GRANT CONSORTIUM UNDERGRADUATE RESEARCH SCHOLARSHIP

Scholarship for undergraduate students for study and/or outreach related to NASA and space sciences, engineering and/or technology. Must attend a Rhode Island Space Grant Consortium participating school. Recipients are expected to devote a maximum of 4 hours per week in science education for K-12 children and teachers. See website for additional information http://www.spacegrant.brown.edu.

Academic Fields/Career Goals: Aviation/Aerospace; Engineering/Technology; Meteorology/Atmospheric Science.

Award: Scholarship for use in sophomore, junior, or senior years; not renewable. *Number:* up to 2. *Amount:* up to $4000.

Eligibility Requirements: Applicant must be enrolled or expecting to enroll full-time at a four-year institution or university and studying in Rhode Island. Applicant must have 3.0 GPA or higher. Available to U.S. citizens.

Application Requirements: Application form, essay, recommendations or references, resume, transcript. *Deadline:* varies.

Contact: Nancy Ciminelli, Program Manager
    NASA Rhode Island Space Grant Consortium
    Brown University
    Box 1846, Lincoln Field
    Providence, RI 02912
    Phone: 401-863-1151
    Fax: 401-863-3978
    E-mail: nancy_ciminelli@brown.edu

NASA RISGC SCIENCE EN ESPANOL SCHOLARSHIP FOR UNDERGRADUATE STUDENTS

Award for undergraduate students attending a Rhode Island Space Grant Consortium participating school and studying in any space-related field of science, math, engineering, or other field with applications in space study. Recipients are expected to devote a maximum of 8 hours per week in outreach activities, supporting ESL teachers with science instruction.

Academic Fields/Career Goals: Aviation/Aerospace; Engineering/Technology; Mathematics.

Award: Scholarship for use in sophomore, junior, or senior years; not renewable. *Number:* 2. *Amount:* up to $4000.

Eligibility Requirements: Applicant must be enrolled or expecting to enroll full-time at a four-year institution or university and studying in Rhode Island. Applicant must have 3.0 GPA or higher. Available to U.S. citizens.

Application Requirements: Application form, essay, resume, transcript. *Deadline:* varies.

Contact: Nancy Ciminelli, Program Manager
    NASA Rhode Island Space Grant Consortium
    Brown University
    Box 1846, Lincoln Field
    Providence, RI 02912
    Phone: 401-863-1151
    Fax: 401-863-3978
    E-mail: nancy_ciminelli@brown.edu

NASA RISGC SUMMER SCHOLARSHIP FOR UNDERGRADUATE STUDENTS

Scholarship for full-time summer study. Students are expected to devote 75 percent of their time to a research project with a faculty adviser and 25 percent to outreach activities in science education for K-12 students and teachers. Must attend a Rhode Island Space Grant Consortium participating school. See website for additional information http://www.spacegrant.brown.edu.

Academic Fields/Career Goals: Aviation/Aerospace; Education.

Award: Scholarship for use in sophomore, junior, or senior years; not renewable. *Number:* up to 2. *Amount:* up to $4000.

Eligibility Requirements: Applicant must be enrolled or expecting to enroll full-time at a four-year institution or university and studying in Rhode Island. Applicant must have 3.0 GPA or higher. Available to U.S. citizens.

Application Requirements: Application form, letter of interest, recommendations or references, resume. *Deadline:* varies.

Contact: Nancy Ciminelli, Program Manager
    NASA Rhode Island Space Grant Consortium
    Brown University
    Box 1846, Lincoln Field
    Providence, RI 02912
    Phone: 401-863-1151
    Fax: 401-863-3978
    E-mail: nancy_ciminelli@brown.edu

NASA SOUTH CAROLINA SPACE GRANT CONSORTIUM

http://www.cofc.edu/~scsgrant

UNDERGRADUATE RESEARCH AWARD PROGRAM

The undergraduate research program is designed to increase the number of highly trained scientists and engineers and enable undergraduate students to conduct NASA-related research. Awards: Research money awarded by the SC Space Grant Consortium will be administered as a stipend through the Financial Aid office on whose campus the Scholar is working. The full research stipend amount is $5000. Two types of Undergraduate Research stipends are available, each $5000. Up to $500 of the $5000 will be available for research related expenses, not including any application fees. The applicant may select which one they wish to apply for: (a) An academic year award given to students interested in conducting research on an aerospace- or space science-related topic during the academic calendar year or (b) A student may conduct aerospace or space science related research for 10 weeks in the summer. For details refer to website: http://spinner.cofc.edu/~scsgrant/scholar/undergraduate.html

Academic Fields/Career Goals: Aviation/Aerospace; Biology; Earth Science; Engineering-Related Technologies; Engineering/Technology.

Award: Grant for use in freshman, sophomore, junior, or senior years; not renewable. *Number:* 5–10. *Amount:* up to $5000.

Eligibility Requirements: Applicant must be enrolled or expecting to enroll full-time at a four-year institution or university and studying in South Carolina. Available to U.S. citizens.

Application Requirements: Application form, entry in a contest, essay, recommendations or references, research proposal, resume, transcript. *Deadline:* February 9.

Contact: Mrs. Tara Scozzaro, Program Manager
    NASA South Carolina Space Grant Consortium
    College of Charleston, 66 George Street
    Charleston, SC 29424
    Phone: 843-953-5463
    Fax: 843-953-5446
    E-mail: scozzarot@cofc.edu

NASA'S VIRGINIA SPACE GRANT CONSORTIUM

http://www.vsgc.odu.edu/

UNDERGRADUATE STEM RESEARCH SCHOLARSHIPS
• *See page 114*

NASA WISCONSIN SPACE GRANT CONSORTIUM

https://spacegrant.carthage.edu/

WISCONSIN SPACE GRANT CONSORTIUM UNDERGRADUATE SCHOLARSHIP PROGRAM

Scholarship of up to $2000 for a U.S. citizen enrolled full-time in, admitted to, or applying to any undergraduate program at a Wisconsin Space Grant Consortium college or university. Awards will be given to students with outstanding potential in programs of aerospace, space science, or other interdisciplinary space-related studies. Minimum 3.0 GPA required. Refer to website for more information https://spacegrant.carthage.edu/funding-programs/undergraduate/scholarship/.

Academic Fields/Career Goals: Aviation/Aerospace.

Award: Scholarship for use in freshman, sophomore, junior, or senior years; not renewable. *Number:* 15. *Amount:* $2000.

Eligibility Requirements: Applicant must be enrolled or expecting to enroll full-time at a two-year or four-year institution or university; resident of Wisconsin and studying in Wisconsin. Applicant must have 3.0 GPA or higher. Available to U.S. citizens.

Application Requirements: Application form, essay. *Deadline:* February 6.

Contact: Christine Thompson, Assistant Director
  Phone: 262-551-2120
  E-mail: cthompson2@carthage.edu

NATIONAL AIR TRANSPORTATION FOUNDATION

http://www.nata.aero

DAN L. MEISINGER, SR. MEMORIAL LEARN TO FLY SCHOLARSHIP

Scholarship established in the honor and memory of Dan L. Meisinger Sr., whose career in aviation spanned 63 years. He was founder of Executive Beechcraft, headquartered in Kansas City, Mo., and was twice named Beech Aircraft's Man of the Year. Purpose of fund is to provide an annual flight training scholarship to a qualified individual. For more information, visit website http://www.nata.aero/Scholarships/Dan-L.-Meisinger,-Sr.-Memorial-Scholarship.aspx.

Academic Fields/Career Goals: Aviation/Aerospace.

Award: Scholarship for use in freshman, sophomore, junior, or senior years; not renewable. *Number:* 1. *Amount:* $2500.

Eligibility Requirements: Applicant must be enrolled or expecting to enroll full-time at a two-year or four-year institution or university. Applicant must have 3.0 GPA or higher. Available to U.S. citizens.

Application Requirements: Application form, essay, recommendations or references, test scores, transcript. *Deadline:* November 28.

Contact: Ms. Elizabeth Nicholson, Manager, Safety 1st Programs
  Phone: 703-845-9000
  E-mail: safety1st@nata.aero

NATA BUSINESS SCHOLARSHIP

Scholarship available for education or training to establish a career in the business aviation industry. Applicable education includes any aviation-related two-year, four-year or graduate degree program at an accredited college or university. Must be 18 years of age or older, be nominated and endorsed by a representative of a regular or associate member company of the NATA. Applicable training includes any aviation maintenance program under the aegis of Part 147 or 65, any pilot certificate or rating under Part 61 or 141, and any aviation-related two-year, four-year or graduate degree program at an accredited college or university. Visit website for more information http://www.nata.aero/Scholarships/NATA-Business-Scholarship.aspx.

Academic Fields/Career Goals: Aviation/Aerospace.

Award: Scholarship for use in freshman, sophomore, junior, senior, graduate, or postgraduate years; not renewable. *Number:* 1. *Amount:* $2500.

Eligibility Requirements: Applicant must be enrolled or expecting to enroll full- or part-time at a two-year or four-year or technical institution or university. Available to U.S. citizens.

Application Requirements: Application form, essay, recommendations or references, resume, transcript. *Deadline:* December 26.

Contact: Ms. Elizabeth Nicholson, Manager, Safety 1st Programs
  Phone: 703-845-9000
  E-mail: safety1st@nata.aero

NAVIGATE YOUR FUTURE SCHOLARSHIP

$2500 scholarship for a high school senior planning a career in the general aviation field. Must be enrolled or accepted into an aviation-related program at an accredited college or university and be able to demonstrate an interest in pursuing a career in general aviation.

Academic Fields/Career Goals: Aviation/Aerospace.

Award: Scholarship for use in freshman year; not renewable. *Number:* 1. *Amount:* $2500.

Eligibility Requirements: Applicant must be high school student and planning to enroll or expecting to enroll full-time at a four-year institution or university. Applicant must have 3.0 GPA or higher. Available to U.S. citizens.

Application Requirements: Application form, essay, personal statement, recommendations or references, transcript. *Deadline:* June 29.

Contact: Ms. Elizabeth Nicholson, Manager, Safety 1st Programs
  Phone: 703-845-9000
  E-mail: safety1st@nata.aero

PIONEERS OF FLIGHT SCHOLARSHIP

Scholarship recipients will be notified in writing by the end of April. Interested students must complete the attached application and submit it along with a complete transcript of grades, a letter of recommendation, an essay on general aviation and a paper indicating career goals in general aviation postmarked no later than the last Friday in December. For more information, visit website http://www.nata.aero/Scholarships/Pioneers-of-Flight-Scholarship-Program.aspx

Academic Fields/Career Goals: Aviation/Aerospace.

Award: Scholarship for use in sophomore or junior years; not renewable. *Number:* 2. *Amount:* $1000.

Eligibility Requirements: Applicant must be enrolled or expecting to enroll full-time at a four-year institution or university. Applicant must have 3.0 GPA or higher. Available to U.S. citizens.

Application Requirements: Application form, essay, recommendations or references, test scores, transcript. *Deadline:* December 26.

Contact: Ms. Elizabeth Nicholson, Manager, Safety 1st Programs
  Phone: 703-845-9000
  E-mail: safety1st@nata.aero

RICHARD L. TAYLOR FLIGHT TRAINING SCHOLARSHIP

The Richard L. Taylor Flight Training Scholarship applicant must be enrolled in an accredited college/university, be enrolled in a flight program through the college/university with aspirations to become a pilot (general or commercial aviation), and have a private pilot's license (a copy must be included in application the packet). Must also have a GPA of 3.0 or greater. Show junior and senior grade point averages from high school if applying as an incoming freshman. Submit an essay about aviation, your goals and dreams and why you should receive this scholarship. Complete the official application.

Academic Fields/Career Goals: Aviation/Aerospace.

Award: Scholarship for use in freshman, sophomore, junior, or senior years; not renewable. *Number:* 1. *Amount:* $1500.

Eligibility Requirements: Applicant must be enrolled or expecting to enroll full- or part-time at a two-year or four-year institution or university. Applicant must have 3.0 GPA or higher. Available to U.S. citizens.

Application Requirements: Application form, essay, pilot's license, transcript. *Deadline:* March 29.

Contact: Ms. Elizabeth Nicholson, Manager, Safety 1st Programs
  Phone: 703-845-9000
  E-mail: safety1st@nata.aero

NATIONAL BUSINESS AVIATION ASSOCIATION INC.

http://www.nbaa.org/

AL CONKLIN AND BILL DE DECKER BUSINESS AVIATION MANAGEMENT SCHOLARSHIP

$5000 scholarship for students pursuing a career in business aviation management at NBAA and UAA institutions. Minimum 3.0 GPA required. Must be a U.S. citizen.

Academic Fields/Career Goals: Aviation/Aerospace.

Award: Scholarship for use in sophomore, junior, or senior years; not renewable. *Amount:* $5000.

Eligibility Requirements: Applicant must be enrolled or expecting to enroll full-time at a four-year institution or university. Applicant must have 3.0 GPA or higher. Available to U.S. citizens.

Application Requirements: Application form, essay. *Deadline:* June 31.

Contact: Tyler Austin, Project Manager, Professional Development
Phone: 202-783-9267
Fax: 202-331-8364
E-mail: taustin@nbaa.org

NBAA INTERNATIONAL OPERATORS SCHOLARSHIP

One-time $5000 scholarship offered to one or more recipients. Include with application 500-word essay explaining how this scholarship will help the applicant achieve their international aviation career goals, statement of the funds required to achieve these goals, and at least one professional letter of recommendation, preferably from an NBAA member company employee.

Academic Fields/Career Goals: Aviation/Aerospace.

Award: Scholarship for use in freshman, sophomore, junior, senior, or graduate years; not renewable. *Number:* 1. *Amount:* $5000.

Eligibility Requirements: Applicant must be enrolled or expecting to enroll full- or part-time at a two-year or four-year or technical institution or university. Applicant must have 3.0 GPA or higher. Available to U.S. and non-U.S. citizens.

Application Requirements: Application form, essay. *Deadline:* November 30.

Contact: Tyler Austin, Project Manager, Professional Development
Phone: 202-783-9267
Fax: 202-331-8364
E-mail: taustin@nbaa.org

NBAA JANICE K. BARDEN SCHOLARSHIP

One-time $1000 scholarships for students officially enrolled in NBAA/UAA programs. Must be U.S. citizen, officially enrolled in an aviation-related program with 3.0 minimum GPA. Include with application a 250-word essay describing the applicant's interest and goals for a career in the business aviation industry, and a letter of recommendation from member of aviation department faculty at institution where applicant is enrolled.

Academic Fields/Career Goals: Aviation/Aerospace.

Award: Scholarship for use in sophomore, junior, senior, graduate, or postgraduate years; not renewable. *Number:* 5. *Amount:* $1000.

Eligibility Requirements: Applicant must be enrolled or expecting to enroll full-time at a two-year or four-year institution or university. Applicant must have 3.0 GPA or higher. Available to U.S. citizens.

Application Requirements: Application form, essay. *Deadline:* October 30.

Contact: Tyler Austin, Project Manager, Professional Development
Phone: 202-783-9267
Fax: 202-331-8364
E-mail: taustin@nbaa.org

NBAA LAWRENCE GINOCCHIO AVIATION SCHOLARSHIP

One-time $4500 scholarship for students officially enrolled in NBAA/UAA programs. Must be officially enrolled in aviation-related program with 3.0 minimum GPA. Include with application a 500- to 1000-word essay describing interest in and goals for a career in the business aviation industry while demonstrating strength of character. Must also have two letters of recommendation, including one from member of aviation department faculty at institution where applicant is enrolled.

Academic Fields/Career Goals: Aviation/Aerospace.

Award: Scholarship for use in sophomore, junior, or senior years; not renewable. *Number:* 5. *Amount:* $4500.

Eligibility Requirements: Applicant must be enrolled or expecting to enroll full-time at a four-year institution or university. Applicant must have 3.0 GPA or higher. Available to U.S. and Canadian citizens.

Application Requirements: Application form, essay. *Deadline:* August 1.

Contact: Tyler Austin, Project Manager, Professional Development
Phone: 202-783-9267
Fax: 202-331-8364
E-mail: taustin@nbaa.org

NBAA WILLIAM M. FANNING MAINTENANCE SCHOLARSHIP

One-time award given to two students pursuing careers as maintenance technicians. One award will benefit a student who is currently enrolled in an accredited Airframe and Power-plant (A&P) program at an approved FAR Part 147 school. The second award will benefit an individual who is not currently enrolled but has been accepted into an A&P program. Include with application a 250-word essay describing applicant's interest in and goals for a career in the aviation maintenance field. A letter of recommendation from an NBAA Member Company representative is encouraged.

Academic Fields/Career Goals: Aviation/Aerospace.

Award: Scholarship for use in freshman, sophomore, junior, or senior years; not renewable. *Number:* 2. *Amount:* $2500.

Eligibility Requirements: Applicant must be enrolled or expecting to enroll full-time at a two-year or four-year or technical institution or university. Available to U.S. citizens.

Application Requirements: Application form, essay. *Deadline:* August 1.

Contact: Tyler Austin, Project Manager, Professional Development
Phone: 202-783-9267
Fax: 202-331-8364
E-mail: taustin@nbaa.org

NATIONAL GAY PILOTS ASSOCIATION EDUCATION FUND

http://www.ngpa.org/

NGPA EDUCATION FUND, INC.

Scholarship for candidates pursuing a career as a professional pilot. Funds cannot be used to pay for the basic private certificate; they must be applied towards advanced fight training at a government certified flight school or to college tuition if enrolled in an accredited aviation degree program. Applicants must provide evidence of their contribution to the gay and lesbian community.

Academic Fields/Career Goals: Aviation/Aerospace.

Award: Scholarship for use in freshman, sophomore, junior, or senior years; not renewable. *Number:* 3–4. *Amount:* $3000–$4000.

Eligibility Requirements: Applicant must be enrolled or expecting to enroll full- or part-time at a two-year or four-year or technical institution or university and must have an interest in aviation or LGBT issues. Applicant or parent of applicant must have employment or volunteer experience in community service. Available to U.S. and non-U.S. citizens.

Application Requirements: Application form, copies of the applicant's pilot certificate, medical certificate, recent logbook page, essay, recommendations or references, transcript. *Deadline:* March 31.

Contact: David Pettet, Executive Director
National Gay Pilots Association Education Fund
PO Box 11313
Norfolk, VA 23517
E-mail: ExecDir@ngpa.org

NEVADA NASA SPACE GRANT CONSORTIUM

http://www.nvspacegrant.org/

NATIONAL SPACE GRANT COLLEGE AND FELLOWSHIP PROGRAM

• *See page 114*

NEXTSTEPU

http://www.nextstepu.com/

$1,500 STEM SCHOLARSHIP

• *See page 106*

PALWAUKEE AIRPORT PILOTS ASSOCIATION

http://www.pwkpilots.org

PAPA SCHOLARSHIP & SAFETY FOUNDATION

Scholarship offered to Illinois residents who are attending accredited programs at Illinois institutions. Must be pursuing a course of study in an aviation-related program. Minimum GPA of 2.0. Applications available on website http://www.pwkpilots.org.

Academic Fields/Career Goals: Aviation/Aerospace.

Award: Scholarship for use in freshman, sophomore, junior, or senior years; not renewable. *Number:* 2. *Amount:* $1000.

Eligibility Requirements: Applicant must be enrolled or expecting to enroll full- or part-time at a two-year or four-year or technical institution or university; resident of Illinois; studying in Illinois and must have an interest in aviation. Applicant must have 2.5 GPA or higher. Available to U.S. citizens.

Application Requirements: Application form, driver's license, essay, personal photograph. *Deadline:* May 1.

Contact: Jason Simpson, Chairman, Scholarship Committee
Palwaukee Airport Pilots Association
1005 South Wolf Road Suite 106
Wheeling, IL 60090
Phone: 773-842-5088
E-mail: scholarship@pwkpilots.org

RHODE ISLAND PILOTS ASSOCIATION

http://www.ripilots.com/

RHODE ISLAND PILOTS ASSOCIATION SCHOLARSHIP

A scholarship open to Rhode Island residents to begin or advance a career in aviation. Must be age 16 or above.

Academic Fields/Career Goals: Aviation/Aerospace.

Award: Scholarship for use in freshman, sophomore, junior, or senior years; not renewable. *Number:* 2–4. *Amount:* $500–$1500.

Eligibility Requirements: Applicant must be enrolled or expecting to enroll full- or part-time at a two-year or four-year or technical institution; resident of Rhode Island and must have an interest in aviation. Available to U.S. citizens.

Application Requirements: Application form, essay, financial need analysis. *Deadline:* February 28.

Contact: Marilyn Biagetti, Scholarship Chair
Phone: 401-568-3497
E-mail: biagettim@aol.com

ROBERT H. MOLLOHAN FAMILY CHARITABLE FOUNDATION, INC.

http://www.mollohanfoundation.org/

MID-ATLANTIC AEROSPACE SCHOLARSHIP

The Mid-Atlantic Aerospace Complex Scholarship provides scholarship opportunities to students who wish to pursue one of the following aerospace programs offered at the Robert C. Byrd National Aerospace Education Center which awards degrees through Fairmont State University and Pierpont Community and Technical College: BS in Aviation Administration Management, BS in Aviation Administration-Professional Flight, BS in Aviation Maintenance Management, AAS in Airframe & Aerospace Electronics Technology, AAS in Aviation Maintenance Technology. The student must have at least a 2.5 GPA, and will be expected to remain actively involved in an aviation program upon receipt of the scholarship.

Academic Fields/Career Goals: Aviation/Aerospace.

Award: Scholarship for use in freshman, sophomore, junior, or senior years. *Amount:* $1000.

Eligibility Requirements: Applicant must be high school student; planning to enroll or expecting to enroll full-time at a four-year institution or university; resident of West Virginia and studying in West Virginia. Applicant must have 2.5 GPA or higher. Available to U.S. citizens.

Application Requirements: Application form, essay, recommendations or references, resume, test scores, transcript.

Contact: Aime Shaffer, Program Manager
Phone: 304-333-6783
E-mail: ashaffer@wvhtf.org

SCARLETT FAMILY FOUNDATION SCHOLARSHIP PROGRAM

http://www.scarlettfoundation.org/

SCHOLARSHIP FOR STUDENTS PURSUING A BUSINESS OR STEM DEGREE

• *See page 84*

SOCIETY OF AUTOMOTIVE ENGINEERS

http://www.sae.org/

BMW/SAE ENGINEERING SCHOLARSHIP

Scholarship is provided by BMW AG in recognition of its commitment to excellence in engineering. This scholarship is in support of the SAE Foundation to ensure an adequate supply of well-trained engineers for the future. One scholarship will be awarded at $1500 per year, renewable for four years. Must have a 3.75 GPA, rank in the 90th percentile in both math and critical reading on SAT or composite ACT scores. A 3.0 GPA must be maintained to renew the scholarship.

Academic Fields/Career Goals: Aviation/Aerospace; Chemical Engineering; Electrical Engineering/Electronics; Engineering-Related Technologies; Engineering/Technology; Mechanical Engineering.

Award: Scholarship for use in freshman year; renewable. *Number:* 1. *Amount:* $1500.

Eligibility Requirements: Applicant must be high school student and planning to enroll or expecting to enroll full-time at a four-year institution or university. Available to U.S. citizens.

Application Requirements: Application form, essay, test scores, transcript. *Deadline:* December 15.

Contact: Claudia Tremmelling, Scholarship Program Administrator
Phone: 208-388-2200
E-mail: ctremmelling@idahopower.com

EDWARD D. HENDRICKSON/SAE ENGINEERING SCHOLARSHIP

Scholarship of $4000 awarded at $1000 per year for four years. A 3.0 GPA and continued engineering enrollment must be maintained to renew the scholarship. Applicants must have a 3.75 GPA, rank in the 90th percentile in both math and critical reading on SAT or composite ACT scores, and pursue an engineering degree accredited by ABET.

Academic Fields/Career Goals: Aviation/Aerospace; Chemical Engineering; Electrical Engineering/Electronics; Engineering-Related Technologies; Engineering/Technology; Mechanical Engineering.

Award: Scholarship for use in freshman year; renewable. *Number:* 1. *Amount:* $1000.

Eligibility Requirements: Applicant must be high school student and planning to enroll or expecting to enroll full-time at a four-year institution or university. Available to U.S. citizens.

Application Requirements: Application form, essay, test scores, transcript. *Deadline:* December 15.

Contact: Connie Harnish, SAE Educational Relations
Society of Automotive Engineers
400 Commonwealth Drive
Warrendale, PA 15096-0001
Phone: 724-772-4047
Fax: 724-776-0890
E-mail: connie@sae.org

TMC/SAE DONALD D. DAWSON TECHNICAL SCHOLARSHIP

One scholarship of $1500 a year for up to four years. Minimum 3.0 GPA and continuing engineering enrollment must be maintained to remain qualified. High school seniors must have a 3.25 or higher GPA, SAT math 600 or above and critical reading 550 or above and/or an ACT composite score 27 or above. Transfer students from accredited four-year colleges/universities must have a 3.0 GPA. Students from postsecondary technical/vocational schools must have a 3.5 GPA.

Academic Fields/Career Goals: Aviation/Aerospace; Chemical Engineering; Electrical Engineering/Electronics; Engineering-Related Technologies; Engineering/Technology; Materials Science, Engineering, and Metallurgy; Mechanical Engineering.

Award: Scholarship for use in freshman, sophomore, junior, or senior years; renewable. *Number:* 1. *Amount:* $1500.

Eligibility Requirements: Applicant must be enrolled or expecting to enroll full-time at a two-year or four-year or technical institution or university. Available to U.S. citizens.

Application Requirements: Application form, essay, test scores, transcript. *Deadline:* December 15.

Contact: Connie Harnish, SAE Educational Relations
Society of Automotive Engineers
400 Commonwealth Drive
Warrendale, PA 15096-0001
Phone: 724-772-4047
Fax: 724-776-0890
E-mail: connie@sae.org

SOCIETY OF SATELLITE PROFESSIONALS INTERNATIONAL

http://www.sspi.org/

SSPI INTERNATIONAL SCHOLARSHIPS

Scholarship open to students majoring or planning to major in fields related to satellite communications. Selection is based on academic and leadership achievement, commitment to pursue education and career opportunities in the satellite industry or a field making direct use of satellite technology. Available to members of SSPI.

Academic Fields/Career Goals: Aviation/Aerospace; Communications; Law/Legal Services; Meteorology/Atmospheric Science; Military and Defense Studies.

Award: Scholarship for use in freshman, sophomore, junior, senior, or graduate years; not renewable. *Number:* 1–4. *Amount:* $2500–$4000.

Eligibility Requirements: Applicant must be enrolled or expecting to enroll full- or part-time at a two-year or four-year institution or university. Available to U.S. and non-U.S. citizens.

Application Requirements: Essay, financial need analysis. *Deadline:* April 15.

Contact: Ms. Tamara Bond-Williams, Membership Director
Society of Satellite Professionals International
250 Park Avenue, 7th Floor
New York, NY 10177
Phone: 212-809-5199 Ext. 103
Fax: 212-825-0075
E-mail: tbond-williams@sspi.org

TUSKEGEE AIRMEN SCHOLARSHIP FOUNDATION

http://www.taisf.org/

TUSKEGEE AIRMEN SCHOLARSHIP

Each year the Foundation grants scholarship awards to deserving young men and women. The number of available scholarship awards is directly related to income received from investments. The selection committee

uses academic achievement, extracurricular and community activities, relative financial need, recommendations, and two essays in order to competitively rank applicants.

Academic Fields/Career Goals: Aviation/Aerospace.

Award: Scholarship for use in freshman year; not renewable. *Number:* 40. *Amount:* $1500.

Eligibility Requirements: Applicant must be high school student and planning to enroll or expecting to enroll full-time at a two-year or four-year institution or university. Applicant must have 3.0 GPA or higher. Available to U.S. citizens.

Application Requirements: Application form, autobiography, community service, essay, financial need analysis, personal photograph. *Deadline:* January 26.

Contact: Mr. Errol Lewis
E-mail: lewisei@aol.com

UNIVERSITIES SPACE RESEARCH ASSOCIATION

http://www.usra.edu/

UNIVERSITIES SPACE RESEARCH ASSOCIATION SCHOLARSHIP AWARD PROGRAM

• *See page 116*

UNIVERSITY AVIATION ASSOCIATION

http://www.uaa.aero/

CAE SIMUFLITE CITATION TYPE RATING SCHOLARSHIP

Scholarship open to undergraduate seniors and post-Baccalaureate graduates of aviation degree programs up to two years after graduation. Must have a minimum 3.25 GPA. Students must attend, or must have graduated from, a University Aviation Association member institution. The application is posted at the University Aviation Association website at http://www.uaa.aero. There are extensive aviation flight certification and flight time requirements for this application so please consult the application directly for more details.

Academic Fields/Career Goals: Aviation/Aerospace.

Award: Scholarship for use in senior year; not renewable. *Number:* 6. *Amount:* $10,500.

Eligibility Requirements: Applicant must be enrolled or expecting to enroll full-time at a four-year institution or university and must have an interest in aviation. Available to U.S. citizens.

Application Requirements: Application form, essay, FAA first class medical certificate, recommendations or references, resume, transcript. *Deadline:* March 31.

Contact: Dr. David NewMyer, Professor and Department Chair, Aviation Management and Flight
University Aviation Association
Transportation Education Center, 545 North Airport Road
Southern Illinois University Carbondale
Murphysboro, IL 62966
Phone: 616-453-8898
Fax: 618-453-5230
E-mail: newmyer@siu.edu

CHICAGO AREA BUSINESS AVIATION ASSOCIATION SCHOLARSHIP

One-time awards of $2500 for U.S. citizens who are Illinois residents. Minimum GPA of 2.5. Priority given to Chicagoland residents followed by Illinois residents who are attending, or will attend, a postsecondary aviation degree program in such fields as Aerospace Engineering, Air Traffic Control, Aircraft Charter, Aircraft Maintenance, Aviation Administration/Management, Aviation Flight, Avionics/Aviation Electronics, etc. At least three letters of recommendation required; at least one of these must be from a person currently employed in the field of Business Aviation. The financial statement that is included in the CABAA Scholarship Application must be completed and attached to the application. Application is posted at the website of the University Aviation Association at http://www.uaa.aero.

Academic Fields/Career Goals: Aviation/Aerospace.

Award: Scholarship for use in freshman, sophomore, junior, senior, graduate, or postgraduate years; not renewable. *Number:* 8. *Amount:* $4000.

Eligibility Requirements: Applicant must be enrolled or expecting to enroll full-time at a two-year or four-year or technical institution or university and resident of Illinois. Applicant must have 2.5 GPA or higher. Available to U.S. citizens.

Application Requirements: Application form, essay, recommendations or references. *Deadline:* April 20.

Contact: Dr. David Newmyer, Department Chair, Aviation Management
 and Flight
 University Aviation Association
 Southern Illinois University at Carbondale, College of Applied
  Sciences and Arts
 1365 Douglas Drive
 Carbondale, IL 62901-6623
 Phone: 618-453-8898
 Fax: 618-453-7286
 E-mail: newmyer@siu.edu

JOSEPH FRASCA EXCELLENCE IN AVIATION SCHOLARSHIP

Established to encourage those who demonstrate the highest level of commitment to and achievement in aviation studies. Applicant must be a junior or senior currently enrolled in a University Aviation Association member institution. Must be FAA certified/qualified in either aviation maintenance or flight, have membership in at least one aviation organization (such as National Intercollegiate Flying Association flying team, Alpha Eta Rho, Warbirds of America, Experimental Aircraft Association, etc.), and be involved in aviation activities, projects, and events. Minimum 3.0 GPA required. Application is posted at http://www.uaa.aero and applications are due on the second Monday of April each year.

Academic Fields/Career Goals: Aviation/Aerospace.

Award: Scholarship for use in junior or senior years; not renewable. *Number:* 2. *Amount:* $2000.

Eligibility Requirements: Applicant must be enrolled or expecting to enroll full- or part-time at a four-year institution or university and must have an interest in aviation. Applicant must have 3.0 GPA or higher. Available to U.S. and non-U.S. citizens.

Application Requirements: Application form, essay, FAA certification as a pilot or mechanic or both, financial need analysis, recommendations or references, transcript. *Deadline:* April 10.

Contact: Dr. David Newmyer, Department Chair, Aviation Management
 and Flight
 University Aviation Association
 1365 Douglas Drive
 Carbondale, IL 62901-6623
 Phone: 618-453-8898
 Fax: 618-453-4850
 E-mail: newmyer@siu.edu

PAUL A. WHELAN AVIATION SCHOLARSHIP

One-time award of $2000 given to sophomore, junior, senior or graduate. Must be a U.S. citizen. Must be enrolled in University Aviation Association member institution. 2.5 GPA required. Current or past military service (active duty, reserves or national guard, FAA certification, membership in aviation-related association preferred. Application is posted at the University Aviation Association website at http://www.uaa.aero

Academic Fields/Career Goals: Aviation/Aerospace.

Award: Scholarship for use in sophomore, junior, senior, or graduate years; not renewable. *Number:* 1. *Amount:* $2000.

Eligibility Requirements: Applicant must be enrolled or expecting to enroll full-time at a two-year or four-year institution or university and must have an interest in aviation. Applicant must have 2.5 GPA or higher. Available to U.S. citizens.

Application Requirements: Application form, essay, FAA certification, recommendations or references, transcript. *Deadline:* May 15.

Contact: David Newmyer, Department Chair, Aviation Management and
 Flight
 University Aviation Association
 Southern Illinois University at Carbondale, College of Applied
  Sciences and Arts
 1365 Douglas Drive
 Carbondale, IL 62901-6623
 Phone: 618-453-8898
 Fax: 618-453-7268
 E-mail: newmyer@siu.edu

VERMONT SPACE GRANT CONSORTIUM

http://www.cems.uvm.edu/vsgc

VERMONT SPACE GRANT CONSORTIUM
• *See page 96*

VIRGINIA AVIATION AND SPACE EDUCATION FORUM

http://www.doav.virginia.gov/

JOHN R. LILLARD VIRGINIA AIRPORT OPERATORS COUNCIL SCHOLARSHIP PROGRAM

Scholarship of $3000 offered to high school seniors planning a career in the field of aviation. Must be enrolled or accepted into an aviation-related program at an accredited college. Minimum 3.75 unweighted GPA.

Academic Fields/Career Goals: Aviation/Aerospace.

Award: Scholarship for use in freshman year; not renewable. *Number:* 1. *Amount:* $3000.

Eligibility Requirements: Applicant must be high school student; planning to enroll or expecting to enroll full-time at a four-year institution or university and must have an interest in aviation. Available to U.S. and non-U.S. citizens.

Application Requirements: Application form, essay, financial need analysis, recommendations or references, transcript. *Deadline:* February 20.

Contact: Betty Wilson, Program Coordinator
 Phone: 804-236-3624
 Fax: 804-236-3636
 E-mail: betty.wilson@doav.virginia.gov

WILLARD G. PLENTL AVIATION SCHOLARSHIP PROGRAM

Scholarship of $1000 awarded to a high school senior who is planning an aviation career in a non-engineering area.

Academic Fields/Career Goals: Aviation/Aerospace.

Award: Scholarship for use in freshman year; not renewable. *Number:* 1. *Amount:* $1000.

Eligibility Requirements: Applicant must be high school student; planning to enroll or expecting to enroll full-time at a four-year institution or university and must have an interest in aviation. Applicant must have 3.5 GPA or higher. Available to U.S. and non-U.S. citizens.

Application Requirements: Application form, essay, financial need analysis, recommendations or references, transcript. *Deadline:* February 20.

Contact: Betty Wilson, Program Coordinator
 Virginia Aviation and Space Education Forum
 5702 Gulfstream Road
 Richmond, VA 23250-2422
 E-mail: betty.wilson@doav.virginia.gov

WHOMENTORS.COM, INC.

http://www.WHOmentors.com/

IB USD WORLDWIDE VENTURE CAPITAL
• *See page 116*

WOMEN IN AEROSPACE FOUNDATION

http://www.womeninaerospace.org/index.html

WIA FOUNDATION SCHOLARSHIP

The WIA Foundation is pleased to provide scholarships to women interested in a career in the aerospace field to pursue higher education degrees in engineering, math or science. One or more awards will be given each year to a rising junior or senior in college, to be applied during the upcoming academic year. To be eligible for the WIA Foundation Scholarship, an applicant must be interested in pursuing a career in the aerospace field and be a rising junior or senior working towards a Bachelor's degree in engineering, math or science. An applicant must have completed at least two and a half academic years of full-time college work at the time of application and must be currently enrolled in an accredited college or university in the United States or its territories, and plan to be enrolled in the subsequent academic year. Each applicant must have a college grade point average of at least 3.0 on a 4.0 scale. Applicants must be female of any nationality. Applications will be available on or about November 15 for the subsequent academic year

Academic Fields/Career Goals: Aviation/Aerospace; Engineering-Related Technologies; Engineering/Technology; Mathematics; Science, Technology, and Society.

Award: Scholarship for use in junior or senior years; not renewable. *Number:* 3. *Amount:* $2000.

Eligibility Requirements: Applicant must be enrolled or expecting to enroll full-time at an institution or university and female. Applicant must have 3.0 GPA or higher. Available to U.S. and non-U.S. citizens.

Application Requirements: Application form, essay. *Deadline:* June 21.

Contact: Ms. Torrie Nickerson, Program and Event Specialist
Women in Aerospace Foundation
204 E St NE
Washington, DC 20002
Phone: 202-547-0229
E-mail: tnickerson@womeninaerospace.org

WOMEN IN AVIATION, INTERNATIONAL

http://www.wai.org/

AIRBUS LEADERSHIP GRANT

One scholarship to a college sophomore or higher level student who is pursuing a degree in an aviation-related field. Must have a minimum GPA of 3.0 and must exhibit leadership potential. Must be a WAI member.

Academic Fields/Career Goals: Aviation/Aerospace.

Award: Scholarship for use in sophomore, junior, or senior years; not renewable. *Number:* 1. *Amount:* $5000.

Eligibility Requirements: Applicant must be enrolled or expecting to enroll full- or part-time at a four-year institution or university and must have an interest in leadership. Applicant or parent of applicant must be member of Women in Aviation, International. Applicant must have 3.0 GPA or higher. Available to U.S. and non-U.S. citizens.

Application Requirements: Application form, essay, recommendations or references, resume. *Deadline:* November 12.

Contact: Donna Wallace, Scholarships Committee
Women in Aviation, International
3647 State Route 503 South
West Alexandria, OH 45381
Phone: 937-839-4647
Fax: 937-839-4645
E-mail: dwallace@wai.org

BOEING COMPANY CAREER ENHANCEMENT SCHOLARSHIP

Scholarship is available for a woman who wishes to advance her career in aerospace industry in the fields of engineering, technology development or management. The award is to be used for educational purposes only and may not be applied toward flight hours. Applicants may be full-time or part-time employees currently in the aerospace industry or related field. Students pursuing aviation-related degrees that are at the junior level with a minimum GPA of 2.5 (on a 4.0 scale) are also eligible.

Academic Fields/Career Goals: Aviation/Aerospace.

Award: Scholarship for use in junior or senior years; not renewable. *Number:* 2. *Amount:* $2500.

Eligibility Requirements: Applicant must be enrolled or expecting to enroll full- or part-time at a four-year institution or university and female. Applicant or parent of applicant must be member of Women in Aviation, International. Available to U.S. and non-U.S. citizens.

Application Requirements: Application form, essay, recommendations or references, resume. *Deadline:* November 12.

Contact: Donna Wallace, Scholarships Committee
Women in Aviation, International
3647 State Route 503 South
West Alexandria, OH 45381
Phone: 937-839-4647
Fax: 937-839-4645
E-mail: dwallace@wai.org

DASSAULT FALCON JET CORPORATION SCHOLARSHIP

Scholarship of $1000 available for a woman pursuing an undergraduate or graduate degree in an aviation-related field. Applicant must be a U.S. citizen with fluency in English. Must have minimum 3.0 GPA or better (on a 4.0 scale) in her most recent year of schooling. Must be a member of WAI.

Academic Fields/Career Goals: Aviation/Aerospace.

Award: Scholarship for use in freshman, sophomore, junior, or senior years; not renewable. *Number:* 1. *Amount:* $1000.

Eligibility Requirements: Applicant must be enrolled or expecting to enroll full- or part-time at a four-year institution or university and female. Applicant or parent of applicant must be member of Women in Aviation, International. Applicant must have 3.0 GPA or higher. Available to U.S. citizens.

Application Requirements: Application form, essay, recommendations or references, resume. *Deadline:* November 12.

Contact: Donna Wallace, Scholarships Committee
Women in Aviation, International
3647 State Route 503 South
West Alexandria, OH 45381
Phone: 937-839-4647
Fax: 937-839-4645
E-mail: dwallace@wai.org

DELTA AIR LINES AIRCRAFT MAINTENANCE TECHNOLOGY SCHOLARSHIP

Scholarship of $5000 available to a student currently enrolled in an Aviation Maintenance Technician Program (A&P) or a degree in Aviation Maintenance Technology. Applicant must be a full-time student with a minimum of two semesters left (as of February March 2016, with a minimum GPA of 3.0 or better (on a 4.0 scale). Must be a member of WAI. Must be an U.S. citizen or eligible non-citizen.

Academic Fields/Career Goals: Aviation/Aerospace.

Award: Scholarship for use in freshman, sophomore, or junior years; not renewable. *Number:* 1. *Amount:* $5000.

Eligibility Requirements: Applicant must be enrolled or expecting to enroll full-time at a two-year or four-year or technical institution or university. Applicant or parent of applicant must be member of Women in Aviation, International. Applicant must have 3.0 GPA or higher. Available to U.S. and non-U.S. citizens.

Application Requirements: Application form, essay, recommendations or references, resume. *Deadline:* November 12.

Contact: Donna Wallace, Scholarships Committee
Women in Aviation, International
3647 State Route 503 South
West Alexandria, OH 45381
Phone: 937-839-4647
Fax: 937-839-4645
E-mail: dwallace@wai.org

DELTA AIR LINES ENGINEERING SCHOLARSHIP

Student must be currently enrolled in a Baccalaureate degree in Aerospace / Aeronautical, Electrical, or Mechanical Engineering. Applicants must be full-time students at the junior or senior level with a minimum of two semesters left (as of February 2016), with a cumulative GPA of 3.0 (on a 4.0 scale) or better. Must be a member of WAI and be U.S. citizen or eligible non-citizen.

Academic Fields/Career Goals: Aviation/Aerospace; Electrical Engineering/Electronics; Mechanical Engineering.

Award: Scholarship for use in junior or senior years; not renewable. *Number:* 1. *Amount:* $7000.

Eligibility Requirements: Applicant must be enrolled or expecting to enroll full-time at a four-year institution or university. Applicant or parent of applicant must be member of Women in Aviation, International. Applicant must have 3.0 GPA or higher. Available to U.S. and non-U.S. citizens.

Application Requirements: Application form, essay, recommendations or references, resume. *Deadline:* November 12.

Contact: Donna Wallace, Scholarships Committee
Women in Aviation, International
3647 State Route 503 South
West Alexandria, OH 45381
Phone: 937-839-4647
Fax: 937-839-4645
E-mail: dwallace@wai.org

DELTA AIR LINES MAINTENANCE MANAGEMENT/AVIATION BUSINESS MANAGEMENT SCHOLARSHIP

Scholarship to a student currently enrolled in an Associate or Baccalaureate degree in Aviation Maintenance Management or Aviation Business Management. Applicant must be a full-time college student, with a minimum of two semesters left (as of February 2016). Must have a minimum GPA of 3.0 (on a 4.0 scale) or better. Must be a member of WAI and be a U.S. citizen or eligible non-citizen.

Academic Fields/Career Goals: Aviation/Aerospace.

Award: Scholarship for use in freshman, sophomore, or junior years; not renewable. *Number:* 1. *Amount:* $5000.

Eligibility Requirements: Applicant must be enrolled or expecting to enroll full-time at a two-year or four-year institution or university. Applicant or parent of applicant must be member of Women in Aviation, International. Applicant must have 3.0 GPA or higher. Available to U.S. and non-U.S. citizens.

Application Requirements: Application form, essay, recommendations or references, resume. *Deadline:* November 12.

Contact: Donna Wallace, Scholarships Committee
Women in Aviation, International
3647 State Route 503 South
West Alexandria, OH 45381
Phone: 937-839-4647
Fax: 937-839-4645
E-mail: dwallace@wai.org

KEEP FLYING SCHOLARSHIP

One scholarship of up to $3000 will be awarded to an individual working on an instrument or multi engine rating, commercial or initial flight instructor certificate. Flight training must be completed within one year. Minimum requirements: private pilot certificate, 100 hours of flight time, and a copy of a current written test (with passing grade) for the certificate/rating sought. One letter of recommendation must be from a pilot that you have flown with. Finalist will only be interviewed at the annual Women in Aviation Conference. Must be a member of WAI.

Academic Fields/Career Goals: Aviation/Aerospace.

Award: Scholarship for use in freshman year; not renewable. *Number:* 1. *Amount:* $3000.

Eligibility Requirements: Applicant must be enrolled or expecting to enroll full- or part-time at a technical institution. Applicant or parent of applicant must be member of Women in Aviation, International. Available to U.S. and non-U.S. citizens.

Application Requirements: Application form, essay, recommendations or references, resume. *Deadline:* November 12.

Contact: Donna Wallace, Scholarships Committee
Women in Aviation, International
3647 State Route 503 South
West Alexandria, OH 45381
Phone: 937-839-4647
Fax: 937-839-4645
E-mail: dwallace@wai.org

WOMEN IN AVIATION, INTERNATIONAL ACHIEVEMENT AWARDS

One scholarships will be awarded to a full-time college or university student pursuing any type of aviation or aviation related career. A second scholarship will be awarded to an individual, not required to be a student, pursuing any type of aviation interest. Include in your essay how you plan to use the scholarship if awarded and what you have accomplished to date to reach your goals. Must be a member of WAI.

Academic Fields/Career Goals: Aviation/Aerospace.

Award: Scholarship for use in freshman, sophomore, junior, or senior years; not renewable. *Number:* 2. *Amount:* $1000.

Eligibility Requirements: Applicant must be enrolled or expecting to enroll full-time at a two-year or four-year institution or university. Applicant or parent of applicant must be member of Women in Aviation, International. Available to U.S. and non-U.S. citizens.

Application Requirements: Application form. *Deadline:* November 12.

Contact: Donna Wallace, Scholarships Committee
Women in Aviation, International
3647 State Route 503 South
West Alexandria, OH 45381
Phone: 937-839-4647
Fax: 937-839-4645
E-mail: dwallace@wai.org

WOMEN IN AVIATION, INTERNATIONAL MANAGEMENT SCHOLARSHIPS

This scholarship will be awarded to a woman in an aviation management field who has exemplified the traits of leadership, community spirit, and volunteerism. Scholarship can be used to attend a leadership-related course or seminar to raise the individual's level of management or establish a new aviation-related business. Must be a member of WAI.

Academic Fields/Career Goals: Aviation/Aerospace.

Award: Scholarship for use in freshman, sophomore, junior, or senior years; not renewable. *Number:* 1. *Amount:* $1000.

Eligibility Requirements: Applicant must be enrolled or expecting to enroll full- or part-time at a two-year or four-year or technical institution or university; female and must have an interest in leadership. Applicant or parent of applicant must be member of Women in Aviation, International. Available to U.S. and non-U.S. citizens.

Application Requirements: Application form. *Deadline:* November 12.

Contact: Donna Wallace, Scholarships Committee
Women in Aviation, International
3647 State Route 503 South
West Alexandria, OH 45381
Phone: 937-839-4647
Fax: 937-839-4645
E-mail: dwallace@wai.org

WOMEN IN CORPORATE AVIATION CAREER SCHOLARSHIPS

Scholarship will be given to a person pursuing professional development or career advancement in any job classification in corporate/business aviation. Applicants should be actively working toward their goal and show financial need. Award can be used toward a specific program of education, flight training, dispatcher training, or upgrades in aviation education, and so forth, but cannot include general business course work. If you are a pilot please submit copies of pilot licenses, medical and the last three pages of logbook with your application. Must be a member of WAI.

Academic Fields/Career Goals: Aviation/Aerospace.

Award: Scholarship for use in freshman, sophomore, junior, or senior years; not renewable. *Number:* 1. *Amount:* $2000.

Eligibility Requirements: Applicant must be enrolled or expecting to enroll full- or part-time at a two-year or four-year or technical institution or university and female. Applicant or parent of applicant must be member of Women in Aviation, International. Available to U.S. and non-U.S. citizens.

Application Requirements: Application form, essay, financial need analysis, recommendations or references, resume, transcript. *Deadline:* November 12.

Contact: Donna Wallace, Scholarships Committee
Women in Aviation, International
3647 State Route 503 South
West Alexandria, OH 45381
Phone: 937-839-4647
Fax: 937-839-4645
E-mail: dwallace@wai.org

WOMEN MILITARY AVIATORS DREAM OF FLIGHT SCHOLARSHIP

This will be awarded to a woman pursuing her flight ratings at an accredited institution or FAA Part 141 approved flight school. Must demonstrate persistence and determination to flight. Training must be completed within one year of the award and be a member of WAI.

Academic Fields/Career Goals: Aviation/Aerospace.

Award: Scholarship for use in freshman, sophomore, junior, or senior years; not renewable. *Number:* 1. *Amount:* $2000.

Eligibility Requirements: Applicant must be enrolled or expecting to enroll full- or part-time at a two-year or four-year or technical institution or university. Applicant or parent of applicant must be member of Women in Aviation, International. Available to U.S. and non-U.S. citizens.

Application Requirements: Application form, financial need analysis, recommendations or references, resume. *Deadline:* November 12.

Contact: Donna Wallace, Scholarships Committee
Women in Aviation, International
3647 State Route 503 South
West Alexandria, OH 45381
Phone: 937-839-4647
Fax: 937-839-4645
E-mail: dwallace@wai.org

WRIGHT CHAPTER, WOMEN IN AVIATION, INTERNATIONAL, ELISHA HALL MEMORIAL SCHOLARSHIP

Scholarship offered to a woman seeking to further the aviation career in flight training, aircraft scheduling or dispatch, aviation management, aviation maintenance, or avionics. Preference will be given to applicants from Cincinnati Ohio/Tri-State area, but all applicants will be considered based upon character, need, community involvement, and accomplishments. Must be a member of WAI, but does not have to be member of Cincinnati Chapter.

Academic Fields/Career Goals: Aviation/Aerospace.

Award: Scholarship for use in freshman, sophomore, junior, or senior years; not renewable. *Number:* 1. *Amount:* $1000.

Eligibility Requirements: Applicant must be enrolled or expecting to enroll full- or part-time at a two-year or four-year or technical institution or university and female. Applicant or parent of applicant must be member of Women in Aviation, International. Available to U.S. and non-U.S. citizens.

Application Requirements: Application form, essay, recommendations or references, resume. *Deadline:* November 12.

Contact: Donna Wallace, Scholarships Committee
Women in Aviation, International
3647 State Route 503 South
West Alexandria, OH 45381
Phone: 937-839-4647
Fax: 937-839-4645
E-mail: dwallace@wai.org

BEHAVIORAL SCIENCE

AVACARE MEDICAL

https://avacaremedical.com

AVACARE MEDICAL SCHOLARSHIP
• *See page 105*

BHW GROUP

https://thebhwgroup.com/

BHW WOMEN IN STEM SCHOLARSHIP
• *See page 74*

COMPHEALTH

http://www.comphealth.com

COMPHEALTH MEDICAL SCHOLARSHIP

We're offering a $5,000 scholarship to one medical student in the United States. The best video response to one of the topics below wins it all. Topics: How do you plan to make a difference in the lives of your patients? We get to know you so we can connect you with the just right job. How can you apply that mindset in your patient interactions? How do you find a balance between your job and your personal life to avoid getting burned out? Video requirements: video must be less than 2 minutes and answer one of the above questions. In addition to submitting your video to CompHealth, video must be posted to YouTube or Facebook, with a tag for @CompHealth. Entry deadline is August 1, 2017. Must be a U.S. citizen. The CompHealth Medical Scholarship is to be used exclusively for school tuition and related expenses. Minimum GPA of 3.0. The awarded recipient shall provide proof of admission and enrollment in an institution of higher education. Must be a full-time student attending (or planning to attend on a full-time basis) an accredited institution of higher education. If selected, please be prepared to provide an official statement of your current academic status. Your school's registrar will be able to provide you with documentation that proves your enrollment. Failure to include all required materials will result in immediate rejection of the application. The CompHealth Medical Scholarship recipient will be notified on or about August 15th. Completed applications must be submitted no later than August 1, 2017. Please send any questions to scholarship@comphealth.com.

Academic Fields/Career Goals: Behavioral Science; Biology; Chemical Engineering; Child and Family Studies; Dental Health/Services; Health Administration; Health and Medical Sciences; Natural Sciences; Neurobiology; Nuclear Science; Nursing; Occupational Safety and Health; Oncology; Optometry; Osteopathy; Pharmacy; Physical Sciences; Psychology; Public Health; Radiology; Science, Technology, and Society; Social Services; Sports-Related/Exercise Science; Therapy/Rehabilitation.

Award: Scholarship for use in freshman, sophomore, junior, senior, or graduate years; not renewable. *Number:* 1. *Amount:* $5000.

Eligibility Requirements: Applicant must be high school student and planning to enroll or expecting to enroll full-time at a four-year institution or university. Applicant or parent of applicant must have employment or volunteer experience in medicine (physician/surgeon), nursing, occupational health and safety, physical or natural sciences, physical therapy/rehabilitation. Applicant must have 3.0 GPA or higher. Available to U.S. citizens.

Application Requirements: *Deadline:* August 1.

Contact: Chase Johnson, Scholarship Coordinator
CompHealth
7259 Bingham Junction Blvd
Midvale, UT 84047
Phone: 801-9303370
E-mail: communications@comphealth.com

HEALTH PROFESSIONS EDUCATION FOUNDATION

http://www.healthprofessions.ca.gov/

ALLIED HEALTHCARE SCHOLARSHIP PROGRAM

One-time award available to students enrolled in, or accepted to California accredited allied health education programs. Scholarship worth up to $4000. Deadlines: check website http://oshpd.ca.gov/HPEF. Must be resident of California.

Academic Fields/Career Goals: Behavioral Science; Dental Health/Services; Health and Medical Sciences; Pharmacy; Psychology; Radiology; Social Services; Therapy/Rehabilitation.

Award: Scholarship for use in freshman, sophomore, junior, senior, graduate, or postgraduate years; not renewable. *Number:* 5–40. *Amount:* up to $4000.

Eligibility Requirements: Applicant must be enrolled or expecting to enroll full- or part-time at a two-year or four-year or technical institution or university; resident of California and studying in California. Available to U.S. citizens.

Application Requirements: Application form, application form may be submitted online (http://calreach.oshpd.ca.gov), community service, driver's license, financial need analysis, recommendations or references, Student Aid Report (SAR) or tax return with W2, transcript. *Deadline:* varies.

Contact: Meaghan Harrington, Program Officer
Health Professions Education Foundation
400 R Street
Sacramento, CA 95811
Phone: 800-773-1669
Fax: 916-324-6585
E-mail: HPEF-EMail@oshpd.ca.gov

INDIAN HEALTH SERVICES, UNITED STATES DEPARTMENT OF HEALTH AND HUMAN SERVICES

http://www.ihs.gov/scholarship

HEALTH PROFESSIONS PREPARATORY SCHOLARSHIP PROGRAM

Renewable scholarship for undergraduate American Indian/Alaska Native students enrolled part-time or full-time in programs related to health and allied health professions. Minimum 2.0 GPA required to apply. Applicant must demonstrate a desire to serve AI/AN people when their health or allied health profession education/ training is complete. The dollar amount and number of awards varies annually.

Academic Fields/Career Goals: Behavioral Science; Health and Medical Sciences; Nursing; Pharmacy; Psychology; Social Sciences.

Award: Scholarship for use in freshman, sophomore, junior, or senior years; renewable. *Number:* 25–50. *Amount:* $13,250–$52,600.

Eligibility Requirements: Applicant must be American Indian/Alaska Native and enrolled or expecting to enroll full- or part-time at a two-year or four-year or technical institution or university. Available to U.S. citizens.

Application Requirements: Application form, application form may be submitted online (http://www.ihs.gov/scholarship), essay, proof of AI/AN descent, curriculum for major, course curriculum verification, recommendations or references, transcript. *Deadline:* March 28.

Contact: Capt. Dawn Kelly, Branch Chief
Indian Health Services, United States Department of Health and Human Services
801 Thompson Avenue
Suite 450-A (TMP)
Rockville, MD 20852
Phone: 301-443-6197
Fax: 301-443-6048
E-mail: dawn.kelly@ihs.gov

KETAMINE CLINICS OF LOS ANGELES

http://www.ketamineclinics.com/

KETAMINE CLINICS OF LOS ANGELES SCHOLARSHIP PROGRAM

Students must be planning to enroll in medical school, or a degree program that leads to medical school, in the following academic year, or already be enrolled in a medical degree program and plan to return in the next academic year. The scholarship is available to all students ages 18 and over, at all levels from high school to graduate school.

Academic Fields/Career Goals: Behavioral Science; Biology; Health and Medical Sciences; Neurobiology; Nursing; Optometry; Psychology; Therapy/Rehabilitation.

Award: Scholarship for use in freshman, sophomore, junior, senior, graduate, or postgraduate years; renewable. *Number:* 1. *Amount:* $1000.

Eligibility Requirements: Applicant must be enrolled or expecting to enroll full-time at a two-year or four-year or technical institution or university. Available to U.S. and non-U.S. citizens.

Application Requirements: Essay. *Deadline:* December 1.

Contact: Mr. Sam Mandel, Chief Operating Officer
Ketamine Clinics of Los Angeles
11645 Wilshire Blvd. STE 852
Los Angeles, CA 90025
Phone: 310-270-0625
E-mail: scholarship@ketamineclinics.com

MEDICAL SCRUBS COLLECTION

http://medicalscrubscollection.com

MEDICAL SCRUBS COLLECTION SCHOLARSHIP
• *See page 106*

NATIONAL INSTITUTES OF HEALTH

http://www.nih.gov/

NIH UNDERGRADUATE SCHOLARSHIP PROGRAM FOR STUDENTS FROM DISADVANTAGED BACKGROUNDS

Award to student from a disadvantaged background is one who comes from a family with an annual income below a level based on low-income thresholds according to family size, as published by the U.S. Bureau of the Census. Must be enrolled full-time at a postsecondary institution and have a GPA of 3.3 or higher. Visit website https://www.training.nih.gov/programs/ugsp for more details.

Academic Fields/Career Goals: Behavioral Science; Biology; Health and Medical Sciences; Social Sciences.

Award: Scholarship for use in freshman, sophomore, junior, or senior years; renewable. *Number:* 10–15. *Amount:* $20,000.

Eligibility Requirements: Applicant must be enrolled or expecting to enroll full-time at a two-year or four-year institution or university. Applicant must have 3.5 GPA or higher. Available to U.S. citizens.

Application Requirements: Application form, essay, financial need analysis. *Deadline:* March 15.

Contact: Adrian Warren, Administrative Assistant
National Institutes of Health
Two Center Drive, Room 2W11A, MSC 0230
Bethesda, MD 20892-0230
Phone: 301-402-3831
E-mail: wardron@mail.nih.gov

NEXTSTEPU

http://www.nextstepu.com/

$1,500 STEM SCHOLARSHIP
• *See page 106*

THE SOCIETY FOR THE SCIENTIFIC STUDY OF SEXUALITY

http://www.sexscience.org/

THE SOCIETY FOR THE SCIENTIFIC STUDY OF SEXUALITY STUDENT RESEARCH GRANT
• *See page 109*

UNITED NEGRO COLLEGE FUND

http://www.uncf.org/

UNITED HEALTH FOUNDATION DIVERSE SCHOLARS INITIATIVE

Scholarship open to students attending one of the 37 UNCF member colleges or universities, planning to pursue a degree that will lead to a career in the primary care industry. Must be sophomores or juniors. Must major in one of the following academic areas, behavioral health, biochemistry, biological sciences, biology, biomedical research, biotechnical health, medicine, nursing, pharmacy, public health or radiology.

Academic Fields/Career Goals: Behavioral Science; Biology; Health and Medical Sciences; Nursing; Pharmacy; Public Health; Radiology.

Award: Scholarship for use in sophomore or junior years; renewable.

Eligibility Requirements: Applicant must be Black (non-Hispanic) and enrolled or expecting to enroll full-time at a four-year institution or university. Applicant must have 3.0 GPA or higher. Available to U.S. citizens.

Application Requirements: Application form, essay. *Deadline:* December 15.

Contact: Mary Williams, Director of Outreach and Recruitment
Phone: 800-331-2244

BIOLOGY

AIST FOUNDATION
http://www.aistfoundation.org/

ASSOCIATION FOR IRON AND STEEL TECHNOLOGY OHIO VALLEY CHAPTER SCHOLARSHIP
Scholarship of $1000 per year for up to four years provided that applicant continues to meet requirements and reapplies for scholarship. Applicant must be a dependent of Ohio Valley Chapter member, or student or Young Professional member. Must attend or plan to attend an accredited school full-time and pursue a degree in any technological field, including engineering, physics, computer sciences, chemistry or other fields approved by the scholarship committee.

Academic Fields/Career Goals: Biology; Computer Science/Data Processing; Electrical Engineering/Electronics; Engineering-Related Technologies; Engineering/Technology; Materials Science, Engineering, and Metallurgy; Physical Sciences.

Award: Scholarship for use in freshman, sophomore, junior, or senior years; not renewable. *Number:* 1–2. *Amount:* $1000.

Eligibility Requirements: Applicant must be enrolled or expecting to enroll full-time at a four-year institution or university. Applicant or parent of applicant must be member of Association for Iron and Steel Technology. Applicant must have 3.0 GPA or higher. Available to U.S. and non-U.S. citizens.

Application Requirements: Application form, essay, recommendations or references, resume, test scores, transcript. *Deadline:* March 31.

Contact: Jeff McKain, Scholarship Chairman
AIST Foundation
11451 Reading Road
Cincinnati, OH 45241
Phone: 724-776-6040
E-mail: jeff.mckain@xtek.com

ALBERTA HERITAGE SCHOLARSHIP FUND
http://www.alis.alberta.ca/

ABORIGINAL HEALTH CAREERS BURSARY
Award between CAN$2000 and CAN$11,000 for aboriginal students in Alberta, entering their second or subsequent year of postsecondary education in a health field. Must be Indian, Inuit, or Metis students who have been living in Alberta for at least the last three years, and are enrolled full-time at the technical, college, or university level. Students are selected on the basis of financial need, previous academic record, program of study, involvement in the aboriginal community, and experience in the health care field. For additional information and an application, visit website http://alis.alberta.ca.

Academic Fields/Career Goals: Biology; Dental Health/Services; Health Administration; Health and Medical Sciences; Nursing; Therapy/Rehabilitation.

Award: Scholarship for use in sophomore, junior, or senior years; not renewable.

Eligibility Requirements: Applicant must be Canadian citizen; American Indian/Alaska Native; enrolled or expecting to enroll full-time at a two-year or four-year or technical institution or university and resident of Alberta.

Application Requirements: Application form, essay, financial need analysis, proof of Aboriginal status, recommendations or references, transcript. *Deadline:* May 1.

Contact: Scholarship Committee
Phone: 780-427-8640
E-mail: scholarships@gov.ab.ca

AMERICAN ALPINE CLUB
https://americanalpineclub.org/

AAC RESEARCH GRANTS
AAC Research Grants support scientific endeavors in mountains and crags around the world. We fund projects that contribute vital knowledge of our climbing environment, enrich our understanding of global climber impacts and support and improve the health and sustainability of mountain environments and habitats. AAC Research Grants are powered by the Alliance for Sustainable Energy and supported by the following endowments: Lara-Karena Bitenieks Kellogg Memorial Fund, Scott Fischer Memorial Fund, Arthur K. Gilkey Memorial Fund, and the Bedayn Research Fund. In addition to their relevance, applications are considered in terms of their scientific or technical quality and merit; qualifications of the applicant; strength of the research framework; dissemination plans; merit of the investigation; and financial contribution the AAC grant would make to the total research budget. Application period is November 15 to January 15 each year. Grant recipient research reflects AAC's mission to support our shared passion for climbing and respect for the places we climb by contributing valuable information to our understanding of the world's mountain ecosystems. Each grant recipient becomes an AAC Researcher, sharing their experiences, lessons learned, and findings with fellow climbers and the research community

Academic Fields/Career Goals: Biology; Earth Science; Environmental Science; Geography; Hydrology; Materials Science, Engineering, and Metallurgy; Natural Resources; Natural Sciences; Physical Sciences; Public Health; Recreation, Parks, Leisure Studies.

Award: Grant for use in sophomore, junior, senior, graduate, or postgraduate years; not renewable. *Number:* 8–15. *Amount:* $800–$1500.

Eligibility Requirements: Applicant must be enrolled or expecting to enroll full- or part-time at a four-year institution or university. Available to U.S. and non-U.S. citizens.

Application Requirements: Application form. *Deadline:* January 15.

Contact: Maria Povec, Policy Director
Phone: 3033840110
E-mail: grants@americanalpineclub.org

AMERICAN ASSOCIATION OF BLOOD BANKS-SBB SCHOLARSHIP AWARDS
http://www.aabb.org/

AABB-FENWAL SCHOLARSHIP AWARD
Scholarship for an individual enrolled, accepted for enrollment in, or having recently completed a program leading to Specialist in Blood Banking certification in an AABB-accredited institution.

Academic Fields/Career Goals: Biology.

Award: Scholarship for use in freshman, sophomore, junior, senior, or graduate years; not renewable. *Number:* 2.

Eligibility Requirements: Applicant must be enrolled or expecting to enroll full- or part-time at an institution or university. Available to U.S. citizens.

Application Requirements: Application form. *Deadline:* June 1.

Contact: Scholarship Coordinator
E-mail: rsinger@aabb.org

AMERICAN INDIAN SCIENCE AND ENGINEERING SOCIETY
http://www.aises.org/

A.T. ANDERSON MEMORIAL SCHOLARSHIP PROGRAM
• See page 109

AMERICAN PHYSIOLOGICAL SOCIETY
http://www.the-aps.org

DAVID S. BRUCE AWARDS FOR EXCELLENCE IN UNDERGRADUATE RESEARCH
• See page 105

AMERICAN SOCIETY OF AGRICULTURAL AND BIOLOGICAL ENGINEERS

http://www.asabe.org/

WILLIAM J. ADAMS, JR. AND MARIJANE E. ADAMS SCHOLARSHIP
• *See page 97*

AMERICAN SOCIETY OF ICHTHYOLOGISTS AND HERPETOLOGISTS

http://www.asih.org/

GAIGE FUND AWARD

Funds are used to provide support to young herpetologists for museum or laboratory study, travel, fieldwork, or any other activity that will effectively enhance their professional careers and their contributions to the science of herpetology. Applicants must be members of ASIH and be enrolled for an advanced degree. Visit website at http://www.asih.org for additional information.

Academic Fields/Career Goals: Biology.

Award: Grant for use in freshman, sophomore, junior, senior, or graduate years; not renewable. *Number:* 5–10. *Amount:* $400–$1000.

Eligibility Requirements: Applicant must be enrolled or expecting to enroll full-time at a four-year institution or university. Applicant or parent of applicant must be member of American Society of Ichthyologists and Herpetologists. Available to U.S. and non-U.S. citizens.

Application Requirements: Application form, financial need analysis, recommendations or references. *Deadline:* March 1.

Contact: Maureen Donnelly, Secretary
          Phone: 305-348-1235
          Fax: 305-348-1986
          E-mail: asih@fiu.edu

RANEY FUND AWARD

Applications are solicited for grants awarded from the Raney Fund for ichthyology. Funds are used to provide support for young ichthyologists for museums or laboratory study, travel, fieldwork, or any activity that will effectively enhance their professional careers and their contributions to the sciences of ichthyology. Must be a member of ASIH and be enrolled for an advanced degree. Visit website at http://www.asih.org for additional information.

Academic Fields/Career Goals: Biology.

Award: Grant for use in freshman, sophomore, junior, senior, or graduate years; not renewable. *Number:* 5–10. *Amount:* $400–$1000.

Eligibility Requirements: Applicant must be enrolled or expecting to enroll full-time at a four-year institution or university. Applicant or parent of applicant must be member of American Society of Ichthyologists and Herpetologists. Available to U.S. and non-U.S. citizens.

Application Requirements: Application form, financial need analysis, recommendations or references. *Deadline:* March 1.

Contact: Maureen Donnelly, Secretary
          Phone: 305-348-1235
          Fax: 305-348-1986
          E-mail: asih@fiu.edu

ARMED FORCES COMMUNICATIONS AND ELECTRONICS ASSOCIATION, EDUCATIONAL FOUNDATION

http://www.afcea.org/site/?q=foundation/scholarships

STEM TEACHERS SCHOLARSHIP
• *See page 111*

ARRL FOUNDATION INC.

http://www.arrl.org/

YASME FOUNDATION SCHOLARSHIP

Multiple awards available to students who have been licensed for at least two years and currently hold a General Class or higher Amateur Radio license. Preference given to high school applicants ranked in top 5-10% of class and college students ranked in top 10% of class who are active in their local Amateur Radio club and community service activities. Must be studying sciences or engineering at an accredited four-year college or university. Previous awardees seeking renewal must submit a new application and transcript each year.

Academic Fields/Career Goals: Biology; Engineering-Related Technologies; Engineering/Technology; Natural Sciences; Science, Technology, and Society.

Award: Scholarship for use in freshman, sophomore, junior, or senior years; not renewable. *Amount:* $3000.

Eligibility Requirements: Applicant must be enrolled or expecting to enroll full- or part-time at a four-year institution or university and must have an interest in amateur radio. Applicant must have 3.5 GPA or higher. Available to U.S. citizens.

Application Requirements: Application form. *Deadline:* January 31.

Contact: Ms. Mary Hobart, Secretary
          Phone: 860-594-0397
          E-mail: k1mmh@arrl.org

ASSOCIATION FOR WOMEN GEOSCIENTISTS (AWG)

http://www.awg.org/

AWG UNDERGRADUATE EXCELLENCE IN PALEONTOLOGY AWARD
• *See page 112*

ASSOCIATION OF CALIFORNIA WATER AGENCIES

http://www.acwa.com/

ASSOCIATION OF CALIFORNIA WATER AGENCIES SCHOLARSHIPS
• *See page 112*

CLAIR A. HILL SCHOLARSHIP
• *See page 112*

ASSOCIATION ON AMERICAN INDIAN AFFAIRS, INC.

http://www.indian-affairs.org/

ELIZABETH AND SHERMAN ASCHE MEMORIAL SCHOLARSHIP FUND
• *See page 98*

ASTRONAUT SCHOLARSHIP FOUNDATION

http://www.astronautscholarship.org/

ASTRONAUT SCHOLARSHIP FOUNDATION
• *See page 112*

BARRY GOLDWATER SCHOLARSHIP AND EXCELLENCE IN EDUCATION FOUNDATION

https://goldwater.scholarsapply.org

BARRY M. GOLDWATER SCHOLARSHIP AND EXCELLENCE IN EDUCATION PROGRAM
• *See page 112*

BHW GROUP

https://thebhwgroup.com/

BHW WOMEN IN STEM SCHOLARSHIP
• *See page 74*

B.O.G. PEST CONTROL

http://www.bogpestcontrol.com/

B.O.G. PEST CONTROL SCHOLARSHIP FUND

B.O.G. Pest Control has established a merit-based scholarship fund for individuals seeking undergraduate or graduate level education in chemistry, chemical engineering, biology, environmental studies or related fields. The winner of the scholarship will be a person who demonstrates academic excellence, as well as a passion for the pursuit of further study in environmental education at an accredited college or university.

Academic Fields/Career Goals: Biology; Chemical Engineering; Earth Science; Environmental Science; Natural Resources; Natural Sciences.

Award: Scholarship for use in freshman, sophomore, junior, senior, or graduate years; not renewable. *Number:* 1. *Amount:* $1000.

Eligibility Requirements: Applicant must be enrolled or expecting to enroll full-time at a four-year institution or university. Available to U.S. citizens.

Application Requirements: Application form, essay. *Deadline:* March 15.

Contact: Angela Osborne
          B.O.G. Pest Control
          645 Central Ave E #200
          Edgewater, MD 21037
          Phone: 410-867-1002

BROWN AND CALDWELL

http://www.brownandcaldwell.com

ECKENFELDER SCHOLARSHIP

Dr. Wesley Eckenfelder, Jr.'s career as an environmental trailblazer spanned more than 50 years, during which time he trained thousands of graduate students and professionals in the science and art of industrial wastewater treatment. To honor his dedication to the environmental industry, we offer a $5,000 Dr. Wesley Eckenfelder, Jr. Scholarship to support students who are interested in pursuing a career in the environmental profession. Applicant must be a United States citizen or permanent resident; a full-time student enrolled in his/her junior, senior, or graduate program at an accredited college/university; must have declared a major in civil, chemical or environmental engineering, or one of the environmental sciences (e.g. geology, hydrogeology, ecology); must have a cumulative GPA of 3.0 or higher on a 4.0 scale (or equivalent on a 5.0 scale). All candidates must submit with a completed application; resume; an essay of 250 words minimum, "Tell us about a personal experience that influenced your decision to focus on environmental studies"; two written recommendations, with at least one from a university official (e.g. advisor, professor); and an official transcript of your academic record. Scholarship funds my only be used for university/college billed expenses such as tuition. We will be accepting 2017 applications starting at the end of March 2017. Applications will closed and materials must be postmarked by April 30th 2017 to be considered for our 2017 scholarships.

Academic Fields/Career Goals: Biology; Chemical Engineering; Civil Engineering; Construction Engineering/Management; Earth Science; Electrical Engineering/Electronics; Energy and Power Engineering; Engineering-Related Technologies; Engineering/Technology; Environmental Health; Environmental Science; Geography; Hydrology; Marine/Ocean Engineering; Mechanical Engineering; Meteorology/Atmospheric Science; Natural Resources; Natural Sciences; Oceanography; Paper and Pulp Engineering; Science, Technology, and Society; Surveying, Surveying Technology, Cartography, or Geographic Information Science.

Award: Scholarship for use in junior, senior, graduate, or postgraduate years; not renewable. *Number:* 1. *Amount:* $5000.

Eligibility Requirements: Applicant must be enrolled or expecting to enroll full-time at a four-year institution or university. Applicant must have 3.0 GPA or higher. Available to U.S. citizens.

Application Requirements: Application form, essay. *Deadline:* April 30.

Contact: BC Scholarships Committee
          Brown and Caldwell
          1527 Cole Boulevard
          Suite 300
          Lakewood, CO 80401
          E-mail: Scholarships@brwncald.com

MINORITY SCHOLARSHIP PROGRAM

At Brown and Caldwell, we value diversity in the workplace, supporting organizations like the National Society of Black Engineers and the Society for Hispanic Professional Engineers. We also offer a $5,000 Minority Scholarship to support students who identify as minorities and are interested in pursuing a career in the environmental profession. Applicant must be a United States citizen or permanent resident; a full-time student enrolled in his/her junior, senior, or graduate program at an accredited college/university; declared a major in civil, chemical, or environmental engineering or one of the environmental sciences (e.g. geology, hydrogeology, ecology); have a cumulative GPA of 3.0 or higher on a 4.0 scale (or equivalent on a 5.0 scale); identify as a member of a minority group (e.g. African American, Hispanic, Asian or Pacific American or Alaska Native). All candidates must submit with a completed application; resume; an essay of 250 words minimum, "Tell us about a personal experience that influenced your decision to focus on environmental studies"; two written recommendations, with at least one from a university official (e.g. advisor, professor); and an official transcript of your academic record. Scholarship funds my only be used for university/college billed expenses such as tuition. We will be accepting 2017 applications starting at the end of March 2017. Applications will closed and materials must be postmarked by April 30th 2017 to be considered for our 2017 scholarships

Academic Fields/Career Goals: Biology; Chemical Engineering; Civil Engineering; Construction Engineering/Management; Earth Science; Electrical Engineering/Electronics; Energy and Power Engineering; Engineering-Related Technologies; Engineering/Technology; Environmental Health; Environmental Science; Geography; Hydrology; Marine/Ocean Engineering; Materials Science, Engineering, and Metallurgy; Mechanical Engineering; Meteorology/Atmospheric Science; Natural Resources; Natural Sciences; Oceanography; Paper and Pulp Engineering; Surveying, Surveying Technology, Cartography, or Geographic Information Science.

Award: Scholarship for use in junior, senior, graduate, or postgraduate years; not renewable. *Number:* 1. *Amount:* $5000.

Eligibility Requirements: Applicant must be American Indian/Alaska Native, Asian/Pacific Islander, Black (non-Hispanic), Hispanic and enrolled or expecting to enroll full-time at a four-year institution or university. Applicant must have 3.0 GPA or higher. Available to U.S. citizens.

Application Requirements: Application form, essay. *Deadline:* April 30.

Contact: BC Scholarships Committee
          Brown and Caldwell
          1527 Cole Boulevard
          Suite 300
          Lakewood, CO 80401
          E-mail: scholarships@brwncald.com

COMPHEALTH

http://www.comphealth.com

COMPHEALTH MEDICAL SCHOLARSHIP
• *See page 151*

CUSHMAN FOUNDATION FOR FORAMINIFERAL RESEARCH

http://www.cushmanfoundation.org/index.php

LOEBLICH AND TAPPAN STUDENT RESEARCH AWARD

Research award given to both graduate and undergraduates interested in foraminiferal research. The maximum dollar value for the award is $2000.

Academic Fields/Career Goals: Biology; Marine Biology.

Award: Grant for use in freshman, sophomore, junior, senior, or graduate years; not renewable. *Number:* 1–57. *Amount:* $100–$2000.

Eligibility Requirements: Applicant must be enrolled or expecting to enroll full- or part-time at a four-year institution or university. Available to U.S. and non-U.S. citizens.

Application Requirements: Proposal for research, recommendations or references, resume. *Deadline:* September 15.

Contact: Jennifer Jett, Secretary and Treasurer
Cushman Foundation for Foraminiferal Research
MRC-121 Department of Paleobiology
PO Box 37012
Washington, DC 20013-7012
E-mail: jettje@si.edu

EAA AVIATION FOUNDATION, INC.

http://www.eaa.org/

PAYZER SCHOLARSHIP
• See page 140

THE EXPERT INSTITUTE

https://www.theexpertinstitute.com

ANNUAL HEALTHCARE AND LIFE SCIENCES SCHOLARSHIP

The scholarship is available to students who are interested in or are already pursuing an undergraduate or graduate-level degree in healthcare or the life sciences. Applicants must have a 3.0 GPA or higher, and must also submit a 1,000-2,000 word essay on how their specialized knowledge could be applied to improving the practice of law.

Academic Fields/Career Goals: Biology; Dental Health/Services; Health and Medical Sciences; Marine Biology; Neurobiology; Nursing; Oncology; Optometry; Public Health; Therapy/Rehabilitation.

Award: Scholarship for use in freshman, sophomore, junior, senior, or graduate years; not renewable. *Number:* 1. *Amount:* $1000.

Eligibility Requirements: Applicant must be enrolled or expecting to enroll full- or part-time at a two-year or four-year or technical institution or university. Applicant must have 3.0 GPA or higher. Available to U.S. and non-U.S. citizens.

Application Requirements: Essay. *Deadline:* December 31.

Contact: Mr. Joseph O'Neill, Senior Associate, Marketing
The Expert Institute
48 Wall Street
32nd Floor
New York, NY 10005
Phone: 646-216-2339
E-mail: joe@theexpertinstitute.com

FEDERATED GARDEN CLUBS OF CONNECTICUT

http://www.ctgardenclubs.org/

FEDERATED GARDEN CLUBS OF CONNECTICUT INC. SCHOLARSHIPS

One-time award for Connecticut residents entering his or her junior, senior, or graduate year at a Connecticut college or university and pursuing studies in gardening, landscaping, or biology. Minimum 3.0 GPA. Ph.D. candidates are not eligible.

Academic Fields/Career Goals: Biology; Horticulture/Floriculture; Landscape Architecture.

Award: Scholarship for use in junior, senior, or graduate years; not renewable. *Number:* 2–5. *Amount:* $1000–$5000.

Eligibility Requirements: Applicant must be enrolled or expecting to enroll full-time at a four-year institution or university; resident of Connecticut and studying in Connecticut. Applicant must have 3.0 GPA or higher. Available to U.S. citizens.

Application Requirements: Application form, driver's license, financial need analysis, recommendations or references, self-addressed stamped envelope with application, test scores, transcript. *Deadline:* July 1.

Contact: Barbara Bomblad, Office Manager
Phone: 203-488-5528
Fax: 203-488-5528 Ext. 51
E-mail: fgcctoff@hotmail.com

FOUNDATION FOR SCIENCE AND DISABILITY

http://stemd.org/

GRANTS FOR DISABLED GRADUATE STUDENTS IN THE SCIENCES
• See page 113

GREATER KANAWHA VALLEY FOUNDATION

http://www.tgkvf.org/

MATH AND SCIENCE SCHOLARSHIP

Renewable scholarship for students pursuing a degree in math, science, or engineering at any accredited college or university. For purposes of this fund, science shall include chemistry, physics, biology, and other scientific fields. Must be a resident of West Virginia.

Academic Fields/Career Goals: Biology; Engineering/Technology; Mathematics; Physical Sciences.

Award: Scholarship for use in freshman, sophomore, junior, or senior years; renewable. *Amount:* $1000.

Eligibility Requirements: Applicant must be enrolled or expecting to enroll full-time at a four-year institution or university and resident of West Virginia. Available to U.S. citizens.

Application Requirements: Application form, essay, recommendations or references, transcript. *Deadline:* January 15.

Contact: Susan Hoover, Scholarship Program Officer
Greater Kanawha Valley Foundation
900 Lee Street East, 16th Floor
Charleston, WV 25301
Phone: 304-346-3620
E-mail: shoover@tgkvf.org

GREAT MINDS IN STEM

www.greatmindsinstem.org

HISPANIC ENGINEER NATIONAL ACHIEVEMENT AWARDS CORPORATION SCHOLARSHIP PROGRAM
• See page 106

INDEPENDENT LABORATORIES INSTITUTE SCHOLARSHIP ALLIANCE

http://www.acil.org/

INDEPENDENT LABORATORIES INSTITUTE SCHOLARSHIP ALLIANCE

Scholarships are given to full-time undergraduate juniors or seniors, or graduate students majoring in the physical sciences: physics, chemistry, geology, engineering, biology or environmental science.

Academic Fields/Career Goals: Biology; Chemical Engineering; Civil Engineering; Earth Science; Electrical Engineering/Electronics; Engineering-Related Technologies; Engineering/Technology; Environmental Science; Fire Sciences; Materials Science, Engineering, and Metallurgy; Mechanical Engineering; Physical Sciences.

Award: Scholarship for use in freshman, sophomore, junior, senior, or graduate years; not renewable. *Number:* 1–2. *Amount:* $1000–$2000.

Eligibility Requirements: Applicant must be enrolled or expecting to enroll full-time at a four-year institution or university. Available to U.S. citizens.

Application Requirements: Application form, recommendations or references, resume, transcript. *Deadline:* April 7.

Contact: Janet Allen, Senior Administrator
Independent Laboratories Institute Scholarship Alliance
1629 K Street, NW, Suite 400
Washington, DC 20006-1633
Phone: 202-887-5872 Ext. 204
Fax: 202-887-0021
E-mail: jallen@acil.org

INDIAN HEALTH SERVICES, UNITED STATES DEPARTMENT OF HEALTH AND HUMAN SERVICES

http://www.ihs.gov/scholarship

INDIAN HEALTH SERVICE HEALTH PROFESSIONS PRE-GRADUATE SCHOLARSHIPS
• See page 114

KENTUCKY ENERGY AND ENVIRONMENT CABINET

http://dep.ky.gov

ENVIRONMENTAL PROTECTION SCHOLARSHIP

Renewable awards for college juniors, seniors, and graduate students for in-state tuition, fees, room and board, and a book allowance at a Kentucky public university. Minimum 3.0 GPA required. Must work full-time for the Kentucky Department for Environmental Protection upon graduation (six months for each semester of scholarship support received). Interview required. Program not generally appropriate for non-residents.

Academic Fields/Career Goals: Biology; Chemical Engineering; Civil Engineering; Earth Science; Environmental Science; Hydrology; Mechanical Engineering; Natural Sciences.

Award: Scholarship for use in junior, senior, or graduate years; renewable. *Number:* 1–4. *Amount:* $10,000–$13,000.

Eligibility Requirements: Applicant must be enrolled or expecting to enroll full-time at a four-year institution or university; resident of Kentucky and studying in Kentucky. Applicant must have 3.0 GPA or higher. Available to U.S. citizens.

Application Requirements: Application form, essay, interview. *Deadline:* February 15.

Contact: James Kipp, Scholarship Program Coordinator
Kentucky Energy and Environment Cabinet
233 Mining/Mineral Resources Building
Lexington, KY 40506-0107
Phone: 859-257-1299
E-mail: kipp@uky.edu

KETAMINE CLINICS OF LOS ANGELES

http://www.ketamineclinics.com/

KETAMINE CLINICS OF LOS ANGELES SCHOLARSHIP PROGRAM
• See page 152

LOUISIANA OFFICE OF STUDENT FINANCIAL ASSISTANCE

http://www.osfa.la.gov/

ROCKEFELLER STATE WILDLIFE SCHOLARSHIP

For college undergraduates with a minimum of 60 credit hours who are majoring in Forestry, Wildlife, or Marine Science, and for college graduate students who are majoring in Forestry, Wildlife, or Marine Science. College undergraduates must have a grade point average of at least 2.50 to apply. College graduate students must have a grade point average of at least 3.00 in order to apply. Renewable up to three years as an undergraduate and two years as a graduate student.

Academic Fields/Career Goals: Biology; Marine Biology; Marine/Ocean Engineering; Natural Resources; Oceanography.

Award: Scholarship for use in freshman, sophomore, junior, senior, graduate, or postgraduate years; renewable. *Number:* 20–30. *Amount:* $2000–$3000.

Eligibility Requirements: Applicant must be enrolled or expecting to enroll full-time at a four-year institution or university; resident of Louisiana and studying in Louisiana. Applicant must have 2.5 GPA or higher. Available to U.S. citizens.

Application Requirements: Application form, application form may be submitted online (http://www.osfa.la.gov for Rockefeller app), FAFSA, test scores, transcript. *Deadline:* July 1.

Contact: Bonnie Lavergne, Public Information
Louisiana Office of Student Financial Assistance
PO Box 91202
Baton Rouge, LA 70821-9202
Phone: 800-259-5626 Ext. 7714
Fax: 225-612-6508
E-mail: custserv@osfa.la.gov

MEDICAL SCRUBS COLLECTION

http://medicalscrubscollection.com

MEDICAL SCRUBS COLLECTION SCHOLARSHIP
• See page 106

NASA IDAHO SPACE GRANT CONSORTIUM

http://www.id.spacegrant.org/

NASA IDAHO SPACE GRANT CONSORTIUM SCHOLARSHIP PROGRAM

Applicants must attend an Idaho accredited institution and maintain a 3.0 GPA. Major/career interest in engineering, mathematics, science or secondary education in math or science. Applicants must be a U.S. citizen.

Academic Fields/Career Goals: Biology; Chemical Engineering; Civil Engineering; Computer Science/Data Processing; Earth Science; Electrical Engineering/Electronics; Geography; Materials Science, Engineering, and Metallurgy; Mathematics; Mechanical Engineering; Natural Sciences; Physical Sciences.

Award: Scholarship for use in freshman, sophomore, junior, or senior years; renewable. *Number:* 1–15. *Amount:* $1000–$2500.

Eligibility Requirements: Applicant must be enrolled or expecting to enroll full-time at a two-year or four-year institution or university and studying in Idaho. Applicant must have 3.0 GPA or higher. Available to U.S. citizens.

Application Requirements: Application form, application form may be submitted online (http://www.id.spacegrant.org/index.php?page=scholarships), essay, recommendations or references, resume, test scores, transcript. *Deadline:* March 1.

Contact: Becky Highfill, Program Manager
Phone: 208-885-6438
Fax: 208-885-1339
E-mail: bhighfill@uidaho.edu

NASA/MARYLAND SPACE GRANT CONSORTIUM

http://md.spacegrant.org/

NASA MARYLAND SPACE GRANT CONSORTIUM UNDERGRADUATE SCHOLARSHIPS
• See page 142

NASA MONTANA SPACE GRANT CONSORTIUM

http://www.spacegrant.montana.edu/

MONTANA SPACE GRANT SCHOLARSHIP PROGRAM
• *See page 142*

NASA SOUTH CAROLINA SPACE GRANT CONSORTIUM

http://www.cofc.edu/~scsgrant

UNDERGRADUATE RESEARCH AWARD PROGRAM
• *See page 143*

NASA'S VIRGINIA SPACE GRANT CONSORTIUM

http://www.vsgc.odu.edu/

COMMUNITY COLLEGE STEM SCHOLARSHIPS
• *See page 114*

UNDERGRADUATE STEM RESEARCH SCHOLARSHIPS
• *See page 114*

NATIONAL ASSOCIATION OF WATER COMPANIES-NEW JERSEY CHAPTER

http://www.nawc.org

NATIONAL ASSOCIATION OF WATER COMPANIES-NEW JERSEY CHAPTER SCHOLARSHIP
• *See page 80*

NATIONAL COUNCIL OF STATE GARDEN CLUBS INC. SCHOLARSHIP

http://www.gardenclub.org/

NATIONAL COUNCIL OF STATE GARDEN CLUBS INC. SCHOLARSHIP
• *See page 99*

NATIONAL GARDEN CLUBS INC.

http://www.gardenclub.org/

NATIONAL GARDEN CLUBS INC. SCHOLARSHIP PROGRAM
• *See page 100*

NATIONAL INSTITUTES OF HEALTH

http://www.nih.gov/

NIH UNDERGRADUATE SCHOLARSHIP PROGRAM FOR STUDENTS FROM DISADVANTAGED BACKGROUNDS
• *See page 152*

NEXTSTEPU

http://www.nextstepu.com/

$1,500 STEM SCHOLARSHIP
• *See page 106*

OREGON STUDENT ASSISTANCE COMMISSION

http://www.GetCollegeFunds.org/

ROBERTS SCHOLARSHIP
One-time award for graduates of Oregon public high schools attending four-year public and nonprofit colleges at least half-time. This award is not open to graduating high school seniors. Preference given to Oregon state residents majoring in the biological and chemical sciences and pursing careers in environmental toxicology and chemistry. Must have completed 1+ year of college-level science by the March scholarship deadline.

Academic Fields/Career Goals: Biology; Environmental Science; Natural Sciences.

Award: Scholarship for use in freshman, sophomore, junior, or senior years; not renewable.

Eligibility Requirements: Applicant must be enrolled or expecting to enroll full- or part-time at a four-year institution. Applicant must have 2.5 GPA or higher. Available to U.S. citizens.

Application Requirements: Application form. *Deadline:* March 1.

Contact: Melissa Adams, Scholarship Processing Coordinator
    Phone: 541-687-7409
    E-mail: melissa.adams@hecc.oregon.gov

SEHAR SALEHA AHMAD AND ABRAHIM EKRAMULLAH ZAFAR FOUNDATION SCHOLARSHIP
• *See page 115*

ROBERT H. MOLLOHAN FAMILY CHARITABLE FOUNDATION, INC.

http://www.mollohanfoundation.org/

HIGH TECHNOLOGY SCHOLARS PROGRAM
Scholarship for West Virginia students pursuing a technology-related career and residing in one of the following counties: Barbour, Brooke, Calhoun, Doddridge, Gilmer, Grant, Hancock, Harrison, Marion, Marshall, Mineral, Monongalia, Ohio, Pleasants, Preston, Ritchie, Taylor, Tucker, Tyler, Wetzel, Wood. Scholarship recipients become eligible for a paid internship with a West Virginia business. Students may also apply for debt-forgiveness loans up to $2000 per year.

Academic Fields/Career Goals: Biology; Chemical Engineering; Computer Science/Data Processing; Electrical Engineering/Electronics; Energy and Power Engineering; Engineering-Related Technologies; Engineering/Technology; Mechanical Engineering; Physical Sciences.

Award: Scholarship for use in freshman year; not renewable. *Number:* 1–60. *Amount:* $500–$2000.

Eligibility Requirements: Applicant must be high school student; planning to enroll or expecting to enroll full-time at a four-year institution or university and resident of West Virginia. Applicant must have 3.0 GPA or higher. Available to U.S. citizens.

Application Requirements: Application form, essay, recommendations or references, resume, test scores, transcript. *Deadline:* February 9.

Contact: Aime Shaffer, Program Manager
    Robert H. Mollohan Family Charitable Foundation, Inc.
    1000 Technology Drive, Suite 2000
    Fairmont, WV 26554
    Phone: 304-333-6783
    Fax: 304-333-3900
    E-mail: ashaffer@wvhtf.org

SCARLETT FAMILY FOUNDATION SCHOLARSHIP PROGRAM

http://www.scarlettfoundation.org/

SCHOLARSHIP FOR STUDENTS PURSUING A BUSINESS OR STEM DEGREE
• *See page 84*

SIGMA XI, THE SCIENTIFIC RESEARCH SOCIETY

http://www.sigmaxi.org/

SIGMA XI GRANTS-IN-AID OF RESEARCH
• *See page 101*

SOCIETY FOR INTEGRATIVE AND COMPARATIVE BIOLOGY

http://www.sicb.org/

LIBBIE H. HYMAN MEMORIAL SCHOLARSHIP

Scholarship provides assistance to students to take courses or to carry on research on invertebrates at a marine freshwater or terrestrial field station. For more information and/or an application see website, http://www.sicb.org.

Academic Fields/Career Goals: Biology; Marine Biology.

Award: Scholarship for use in senior year; not renewable. *Number:* 1. *Amount:* $750–$1200.

Eligibility Requirements: Applicant must be enrolled or expecting to enroll full- or part-time at a four-year institution or university. Available to U.S. and non-U.S. citizens.

Application Requirements: Application form, essay, financial need analysis, recommendations or references, transcript. *Deadline:* March 6.

Contact: Bruno Pernet, Chair, Scholarship Committee
Society for Integrative and Comparative Biology
California State University
Long Beach, CA 90840
Phone: 562-985-5378
Fax: 562-985-8878
E-mail: bpernet@csulb.edu

THE SOCIETY FOR THE SCIENTIFIC STUDY OF SEXUALITY

http://www.sexscience.org/

THE SOCIETY FOR THE SCIENTIFIC STUDY OF SEXUALITY STUDENT RESEARCH GRANT
• *See page 109*

SOCIETY OF TOXICOLOGY

http://www.toxicology.org/

UNDERGRADUATE DIVERSITY STUDENT AWARDS

The program provides travel support and registration for the SOT Undergraduate Program held every year in conjunction with the SOT Annual Meeting. The program introduces the discipline of toxicology and reviews steps to prepare for biomedical graduate school.

Academic Fields/Career Goals: Biology; Environmental Health; Environmental Science.

Award: Prize for use in sophomore or junior years; not renewable. *Number:* 25–33.

Eligibility Requirements: Applicant must be enrolled or expecting to enroll full-time at a two-year or four-year institution or university and must have an interest in science. Applicant must have 3.0 GPA or higher. Available to U.S. citizens.

Application Requirements: Application form, essay. *Deadline:* October 9.

Contact: Betty Eidemiller
Society of Toxicology
1821 Michael Faraday Drive
Suite 300
Reston, VA 20190
Phone: 703-438-3115 Ext. 1430
E-mail: bettye@toxicology.org

SOIL AND WATER CONSERVATION SOCIETY

http://www.swcs.org

DONALD A. WILLIAMS SCHOLARSHIP SOIL CONSERVATION SCHOLARSHIP
• *See page 95*

SOIL AND WATER CONSERVATION SOCIETY-MISSOURI SHOW-ME CHAPTER

http://www.moswcs.org/

MO SHOW-ME CHAPTER SWCS SCHOLARSHIP
• *See page 95*

SOIL AND WATER CONSERVATION SOCIETY-NEW JERSEY CHAPTER

http://www.geocities.com/njswcs

EDWARD R. HALL SCHOLARSHIP
• *See page 95*

TKE EDUCATIONAL FOUNDATION

http://www.tke.org/

CARROL C. HALL MEMORIAL SCHOLARSHIP
• *See page 115*

TRANSTUTORS

http://www.transtutors.com/scholarship

TRANSTUTORS SCHOLARSHIP 2015-16
• *See page 85*

UNITED NEGRO COLLEGE FUND

http://www.uncf.org/

BASF/ALFRED CHISHOLM ENDOWED MEMORIAL SCHOLARSHIP
• *See page 86*

UNCF STEM SCHOLARS PROGRAM

Tiered tuition scholarship for talented African-American high school students who aspire to earn STEM (science, technology, engineering and mathematics) degrees and pursue careers in STEM fields. $2,500 per academic year for freshmen and sophomores, $5,000 for juniors and seniors, and an additional $5,000 for students whose academic programs require a fifth year. Must have demonstrated unmet financial need.

Academic Fields/Career Goals: Biology; Civil Engineering; Computer Science/Data Processing; Construction Engineering/Management; Electrical Engineering/Electronics; Energy and Power Engineering; Engineering-Related Technologies; Engineering/Technology; Health and Medical Sciences; Materials Science, Engineering, and Metallurgy; Mathematics; Mechanical Engineering; Physical Sciences.

Award: Scholarship for use in freshman, sophomore, junior, or senior years; renewable. *Number:* 100.

Eligibility Requirements: Applicant must be Black (non-Hispanic) and enrolled or expecting to enroll at a four-year institution or university. Applicant must have 3.0 GPA or higher. Available to U.S. citizens.

Application Requirements: Application form, essay, financial need analysis. *Deadline:* February 23.

Contact: Mary Williams, Director of Outreach and Recruitment
Phone: 800-331-2244

UNITED HEALTH FOUNDATION DIVERSE SCHOLARS INITIATIVE
• *See page 152*

UNITED STATES DEPARTMENT OF AGRICULTURE

http://www.usda.gov/

SAUL T. WILSON, JR, SCHOLARSHIP PROGRAM (STWJS)
• *See page 107*

WILLIAM HELMS SCHOLARSHIP PROGRAM (WHSP)
• *See page 103*

VERMONT SPACE GRANT CONSORTIUM

http://www.cems.uvm.edu/vsgc

VERMONT SPACE GRANT CONSORTIUM
• *See page 96*

WILSON ORNITHOLOGICAL SOCIETY

http://www.wilsonsociety.org/

GEORGE A. HALL/HAROLD F. MAYFIELD AWARD
• *See page 108*

PAUL A. STEWART AWARDS
• *See page 108*

BUSINESS/CONSUMER SERVICES

280 GROUP

https://280group.com/contact/280-group-product-management-scholarship/

280 GROUP PRODUCT MANAGEMENT SCHOLARSHIP
The 280 Group is a strategic consulting partner to any business that needs a proven methodology to optimize Product Management and Product Marketing functions in their company. We're excited to be offering five $500 scholarships to students pursuing a Bachelor's or Master's degree in business, economics or a related field. Students who receive the scholarships will also get the chance to attend the 280 Group's one-day, How to be a Phenomenal Product Manager course, valued at $695. The scholarship is recurring and submissions must be received by November 15th of each calendar year, recipients will be notified by email the last week of December of that year.

Academic Fields/Career Goals: Business/Consumer Services; Economics; Marketing.

Award: Scholarship for use in freshman, sophomore, junior, senior, or graduate years; renewable. *Number:* 5. *Amount:* $500.

Eligibility Requirements: Applicant must be enrolled or expecting to enroll full- or part-time at a four-year institution or university. Applicant must have 2.5 GPA or higher. Available to U.S. and non-U.S. citizens.

Application Requirements: Application form, essay. *Deadline:* November 15.

AACE INTERNATIONAL

http://www.aacei.org/

AACE INTERNATIONAL COMPETITIVE SCHOLARSHIP
• *See page 118*

THE ACTUARIAL FOUNDATION

http://www.actuarialfoundation.org

ACTUARY OF TOMORROW—STUART A. ROBERTSON MEMORIAL SCHOLARSHIP
The Actuary of Tomorrow—Stuart A. Robertson Memorial Scholarship recognizes and encourages the academic achievements of undergraduate students pursuing a career in actuarial science. Applicants must be full-time students entering as a sophomore, junior or senior, must have a minimum cumulative GPA of 3.0 (on 4.0 scale) and must have successfully completed two actuarial exams. The Actuarial Foundation will provide an award of $9,000 for education expenses at any accredited U.S. educational institution.

Academic Fields/Career Goals: Business/Consumer Services; Economics; Finance; Insurance and Actuarial Science; Mathematics; Statistics.

Award: Scholarship for use in sophomore, junior, or senior years; not renewable. *Amount:* $9000.

Eligibility Requirements: Applicant must be enrolled or expecting to enroll full-time at a four-year institution. Applicant must have 3.0 GPA or higher. Available to U.S. and non-U.S. citizens.

Application Requirements: Application form, essay. *Deadline:* June 1.

Contact: Actuary of Tomorrow, Stuart A. Robertson Memorial
  Scholarship
  The Actuarial Foundation
  475 North Martingale Road, Suite 600
  Schaumburg, IL 60173
  Phone: 847-706-3535
  E-mail: scholarships@actfnd.org

ADELANTE! U.S. EDUCATION LEADERSHIP FUND

http://www.adelantefund.org/

ADELANTE FUND SCHOLARSHIPS
Awards are primarily created to enhance the leadership qualities of the recipients for transition into postgraduate education, business and/or corporate America. Financial need is a factor for these awards. Minimum 3.0 GPA is required for most scholarships. Main awards are available for colleges located in the states of California, New Mexico, Arizona, Texas, Florida, Illinois, and New York. Applicants should view website for all award criteria and for scholarship application forms.

Academic Fields/Career Goals: Business/Consumer Services; Science, Technology, and Society.

Award: Scholarship for use in sophomore, junior, or senior years; renewable. *Number:* 30–52. *Amount:* $1000–$3000.

Eligibility Requirements: Applicant must be of Hispanic heritage; enrolled or expecting to enroll full-time at a two-year or four-year institution or university; studying in Arizona, California, Colorado, Florida, Illinois, New Mexico, New York, Texas and must have an interest in leadership. Applicant must have 3.0 GPA or higher. Available to U.S. citizens.

Application Requirements: Application form, application form may be submitted online (http://www.adelantefund.org), essay, financial need analysis, personal photograph, recommendations or references, resume, transcript. *Deadline:* May 30.

Contact: Miss. Sarah Ramos, Assistant Director of Student Services
  Adelante! U.S. Education Leadership Fund
  8415 Datapoint Drive, Suite 400
  San Antonio, TX 78229
  Phone: 210-692-1971
  Fax: 210-692-1951
  E-mail: sramos@adelantefund.org

ALICE L. HALTOM EDUCATIONAL FUND

http://www.alhef.org/

ALICE L. HALTOM EDUCATIONAL FUND
Award for students pursuing a career in information and records management. Up to $1000 for those in an associate degree program, and up to $2000 for students in a baccalaureate or advanced degree program. Students must be citizens of the United States or Canada.

Academic Fields/Career Goals: Business/Consumer Services; Computer Science/Data Processing; Health Administration; Health Information Management/Technology; Library and Information Sciences.

Award: Scholarship for use in freshman, sophomore, junior, senior, graduate, or postgraduate years; not renewable. *Number:* 5–25. *Amount:* $1000–$2000.

Eligibility Requirements: Applicant must be Canadian citizen and enrolled or expecting to enroll full- or part-time at a two-year or four-year institution or university. Available to U.S. and Canadian citizens.

Application Requirements: Application form, essay. *Deadline:* May 1.

Contact: Executive Director
E-mail: contact@alhef.org

AMERICAN CONGRESS ON SURVEYING AND MAPPING

http://landsurveyorsunited.com/acsm

TRI-STATE SURVEYING AND PHOTOGRAMMETRY KRIS M. KUNZE MEMORIAL SCHOLARSHIP

One-time award of $1000 for students pursuing college-level courses in business administration or business management. Candidates, in order of priority, include professional land surveyors and certified photogrammetrists, land survey interns and students enrolled in a two- or four-year program in surveying and mapping. Must be ACSM member.

Academic Fields/Career Goals: Business/Consumer Services; Surveying, Surveying Technology, Cartography, or Geographic Information Science.

Award: Scholarship for use in freshman, sophomore, junior, or senior years; not renewable. *Number:* 1. *Amount:* $1000.

Eligibility Requirements: Applicant must be enrolled or expecting to enroll full- or part-time at a two-year or four-year institution or university. Applicant or parent of applicant must be member of American Congress on Surveying and Mapping. Available to U.S. citizens.

Application Requirements: Application form, essay, membership proof, recommendations or references, transcript. *Deadline:* October 1.

Contact: Ilse Genovese, Communications Director
American Congress on Surveying and Mapping
6 Montgomery Village Avenue, Suite 403
Gaithersburg, MD 20879
Phone: 240-632-9716 Ext. 113
Fax: 240-632-1321
E-mail: ilse.genovese@acsm.net

AMERICAN INDIAN SCIENCE AND ENGINEERING SOCIETY

http://www.aises.org/

A.T. ANDERSON MEMORIAL SCHOLARSHIP PROGRAM
• See page 109

AMERICAN PUBLIC TRANSPORTATION FOUNDATION

http://www.apta.com/

DAN REICHARD JR. SCHOLARSHIP

Scholarship for study towards a career in the business administration/management area of the transit industry. Must be sponsored by APTA member organization and complete internship with APTA member organization. Minimum GPA of 3.0 required.

Academic Fields/Career Goals: Business/Consumer Services; Transportation.

Award: Scholarship for use in sophomore, junior, senior, or graduate years; renewable. *Number:* 1. *Amount:* $2500.

Eligibility Requirements: Applicant must be enrolled or expecting to enroll full-time at a two-year or four-year institution or university. Applicant must have 3.0 GPA or higher. Available to U.S. and Canadian citizens.

Application Requirements: Application form, essay, financial need analysis, recommendations or references, transcript, verification of enrollment for the current semester, copy of fee schedule from the college/university. *Deadline:* June 16.

Contact: Pamela Boswell, Vice President of Program Management
American Public Transportation Foundation
1666 K Street, NW
Washington, DC 20006-1215
Phone: 202-496-4803
Fax: 202-496-2323
E-mail: pboswell@apta.com

AMERICAN WELDING SOCIETY

http://www.aws.org/

JAMES A. TURNER, JR. MEMORIAL SCHOLARSHIP

Award for a full-time student pursuing minimum four-year bachelor's degree in business that will lead to a management career in welding store operations or a welding distributorship. Applicant must be working in this field at least 10 hours per week. Submit verification of employment, a copy of proposed curriculum, and acceptance letter.

Academic Fields/Career Goals: Business/Consumer Services.

Award: Scholarship for use in freshman, sophomore, junior, or senior years; renewable.

Eligibility Requirements: Applicant must be enrolled or expecting to enroll full-time at a four-year institution or university. Available to U.S. citizens.

Application Requirements: Application form, financial need analysis. *Deadline:* February 15.

Contact: Vicki Pinsky, Associate Director, Foundation
American Welding Society
8669 NW 36 Street, Suite 130
Miami, FL 33166
Phone: 800-443-9353 Ext. 212
E-mail: vpinsky@aws.org

RICHARD J. SEIF TECHNICAL SALES AND MARKETING SCHOLARSHIP

Awarded to a college junior or senior, with a minimum 2.5 overall GPA. Applicant may be a citizen of the US or Canada, and attend a US or Canadian university. The recipient must be pursuing a bachelors degree in engineering or business with a sales or marketing emphasis. The annual award is $3,000.

Academic Fields/Career Goals: Business/Consumer Services; Engineering-Related Technologies; Engineering/Technology.

Award: Scholarship for use in junior or senior years; not renewable.

Eligibility Requirements: Applicant must be enrolled or expecting to enroll full- or part-time at a four-year institution or university. Applicant must have 3.5 GPA or higher. Available to U.S. and Canadian citizens.

Application Requirements: Application form, financial need analysis. *Deadline:* February 15.

Contact: Ms. Vicki Pinsky, Associate Director, Scholarships, AWS Foundation
American Welding Society
8669 NW 36 Street, #130
Miami, FL 33187
Phone: 305-443-9363 Ext. 212
E-mail: vpinsky@aws.org

AMERICAN WHOLESALE MARKETERS ASSOCIATION

http://www.awmanet.org/

RAY FOLEY MEMORIAL YOUTH EDUCATION FOUNDATION SCHOLARSHIP

Scholarship program annually offers two $5000 scholarships to deserving students. Awards are based on academic merit and a career interest in the candy/tobacco/ convenience-products wholesale industry. Must be employed by an AWMA wholesaler distributor member or be an immediate family member. Must be enrolled full-time in an undergraduate or graduate program. For details visit website http://www.awmanet.org/.

Academic Fields/Career Goals: Business/Consumer Services.

Award: Scholarship for use in freshman, sophomore, junior, senior, or graduate years; not renewable. *Number:* 2. *Amount:* $5000.

Eligibility Requirements: Applicant must be enrolled or expecting to enroll full-time at a four-year institution or university. Available to U.S. citizens.

Application Requirements: Application form, essay, recommendations or references. *Deadline:* May 21.

Contact: Kathy Trost, Manager of Education
American Wholesale Marketers Association
2750 Prosperity Avenue, Suite 530
Fairfax, VA 22031
Phone: 800-482-2962 Ext. 648
Fax: 703-573-5738
E-mail: kathyt@awmanet.org

ARRL FOUNDATION INC.

http://www.arrl.org/

WILSE MORGAN, WX7P, MEMORIAL ARRL NORTHWESTERN DIVISION SCHOLARSHIP

$1000 scholarship for a student with a General Class radio license or higher who is a resident in the ARRL Northwestern Division (Alaska, Idaho, Montana, Oregon or Washington). Must be studying engineering, medicine, science, or business. Preference given to applicants with 3.0 GPA or higher for the academic year immediately prior to application (high school or college).

Academic Fields/Career Goals: Business/Consumer Services; Engineering-Related Technologies; Engineering/Technology; Science, Technology, and Society.

Award: Scholarship for use in freshman, sophomore, junior, or senior years; not renewable. *Number:* 1. *Amount:* $1000.

Eligibility Requirements: Applicant must be enrolled or expecting to enroll full- or part-time at a two-year or four-year or technical institution or university; resident of Alaska, Idaho, Montana, Oregon, Washington and must have an interest in amateur radio. Applicant must have 3.0 GPA or higher. Available to U.S. citizens.

Application Requirements: Application form. *Deadline:* January 31.

Contact: Ms. Mary Hobart, Secretary
Phone: 860-594-0397
E-mail: k1mmh@arrl.org

ASSOCIATION FOR FOOD AND DRUG OFFICIALS

http://www.afdo.org/

ASSOCIATION FOR FOOD AND DRUG OFFICIALS SCHOLARSHIP FUND

A $1500 scholarship for students in their third or fourth year of college/university who have demonstrated a desire for a career in research, regulatory work, quality control, or teaching in an area related to some aspect of food, drugs, or consumer products safety. Minimum 3.0 GPA required in first two years of undergraduate study. For further information visit website http://www.afdo.org.

Academic Fields/Career Goals: Business/Consumer Services; Food Science/Nutrition.

Award: Scholarship for use in junior or senior years; not renewable. *Number:* 3–1500.

Eligibility Requirements: Applicant must be enrolled or expecting to enroll full-time at a four-year institution or university. Applicant must have 3.0 GPA or higher. Available to U.S. and non-U.S. citizens.

Application Requirements: Application form, essay. *Deadline:* February 1.

Contact: Krystal Reed, Association Manager
Association for Food and Drug Officials
2550 Kingston Road, Suite 311
York, PA 17402
Phone: 717-757-2888
E-mail: afdo@afdo.org

AUTOMOTIVE WOMEN'S ALLIANCE FOUNDATION

http://www.awafoundation.org/index.php

AUTOMOTIVE WOMEN'S ALLIANCE FOUNDATION SCHOLARSHIPS

• *See page 74*

BALTIMORE CHAPTER OF THE AMERICAN MARKETING ASSOCIATION

http://www.amabaltimore.org/

UNDERGRADUATE MARKETING EDUCATION MERIT SCHOLARSHIPS

Scholarship of $3000 awarded for first place, two $1000 second place, and four $500 third place awards for full-time students in marketing. Must be attending a 4-year college or university in Maryland with credits equivalent to the status of a junior or senior as of September. Minimum 3.0 GPA required.

Academic Fields/Career Goals: Business/Consumer Services; Marketing.

Award: Scholarship for use in sophomore or junior years; not renewable. *Number:* 7. *Amount:* $500–$3000.

Eligibility Requirements: Applicant must be enrolled or expecting to enroll full-time at a four-year institution or university and studying in Maryland. Applicant must have 3.0 GPA or higher. Available to U.S. and non-U.S. citizens.

Application Requirements: Application form, test scores. *Deadline:* February 16.

Contact: Marisa O'Brien, Scholarship Committee
Phone: 410-467-2529
E-mail: scholarship@amabaltimore.org

BULKOFFICESUPPLY.COM

http://www.bulkofficesupply.com

OFFICE SUPPLY SCHOLARSHIP

• *See page 128*

CATCHING THE DREAM

http://www.catchingthedream.org/

MATH, ENGINEERING, SCIENCE, BUSINESS, EDUCATION, COMPUTERS SCHOLARSHIPS

Renewable scholarships for Native American students planning to study math, engineering, science, business, education, and computers, or presently studying in these fields. Study of social science, humanities and liberal arts also funded. Scholarships are awarded on merit and on the basis of likelihood of recipient improving the lives of Native American people. Scholarships are available nationwide.

Academic Fields/Career Goals: Business/Consumer Services; Computer Science/Data Processing; Education; Engineering/Technology; Humanities; Physical Sciences; Science, Technology, and Society; Social Sciences.

Award: Scholarship for use in freshman, sophomore, junior, senior, graduate, or postgraduate years; renewable. *Number:* 180. *Amount:* $500–$5000.

Eligibility Requirements: Applicant must be American Indian/Alaska Native and enrolled or expecting to enroll full-time at a two-year or four-year institution or university. Applicant must have 3.0 GPA or higher. Available to U.S. citizens.

Application Requirements: Application form, essay, financial need analysis, personal photograph.

Contact: Mary Frost, Recruiter
Catching the Dream
8200 Mountain Road, NE, Suite 203
Albuquerque, NM 87110
Phone: 505-262-2351
E-mail: nscholarsh@aol.com

NATIVE AMERICAN LEADERSHIP IN EDUCATION (NALE)

Renewable scholarships available for Native American and Alaska Native students. Must be at least one-quarter Native American from a federally recognized, state recognized, or terminated tribe. Must be U.S. citizen. Must demonstrate high academic achievement, depth of character, leadership, seriousness of purpose, and service orientation.

Academic Fields/Career Goals: Business/Consumer Services; Education; Humanities; Physical Sciences; Science, Technology, and Society.

Award: Scholarship for use in freshman, sophomore, junior, senior, graduate, or postgraduate years; renewable. *Number:* 30. *Amount:* $500–$5000.

Eligibility Requirements: Applicant must be American Indian/Alaska Native and enrolled or expecting to enroll full-time at a four-year institution or university. Applicant must have 3.0 GPA or higher. Available to U.S. citizens.

Application Requirements: Application form, essay, financial need analysis, personal photograph.

Contact: Mary Frost, Recruiter
Catching the Dream
8200 Mountain Road, NE, Suite 203
Albuquerque, NM 87110
Phone: 505-262-2351
E-mail: nscholarsh@aol.com

TRIBAL BUSINESS MANAGEMENT PROGRAM (TBM)
• See page 74

CRUSH THE CPA EXAM

http://crushthecpaexam.com

CRUSH THE PMP SCHOLARSHIP PROGRAM

One Grand Prize Winner: A PMP Review Course from PM Training ($599 value) and a reimbursement of up to $555 for the exam fee and the PMI fee. This is an annual scholarship. Applicants must enter before May 31st, 2017, when the winner will be picked and announced.

Academic Fields/Career Goals: Business/Consumer Services.

Award: Scholarship for use in junior, senior, or graduate years; not renewable. *Number:* 1. *Amount:* $1000–$1154.

Eligibility Requirements: Applicant must be enrolled or expecting to enroll full- or part-time at a four-year institution or university. Applicant must have 3.0 GPA or higher. Available to U.S. and non-U.S. citizens.

Application Requirements: Application form, essay. *Deadline:* May 31.

Contact: Stephanie Murguia
E-mail: stephanie@crushempire.com

DECA (DISTRIBUTIVE EDUCATION CLUBS OF AMERICA)

http://www.deca.org/

HARRY A. APPLEGATE SCHOLARSHIP
• See page 75

DELTA SIGMA PI LEADERSHIP FOUNDATION

http://www.dspnet.org/

DELTA SIGMA PI UNDERGRADUATE SCHOLARSHIP

Applicant must be a member of Delta Sigma Pi in good standing with at least one full semester or quarter of college remaining in the fall following application.

Academic Fields/Career Goals: Business/Consumer Services.

Award: Scholarship for use in sophomore, junior, or senior years; not renewable. *Number:* 1–8. *Amount:* $1000–$1000.

Eligibility Requirements: Applicant must be enrolled or expecting to enroll full-time at a four-year institution or university. Applicant or parent of applicant must be member of Greek Organization. Available to U.S. and non-U.S. citizens.

Application Requirements: Application form, community service, description of fraternity, campus, community involvement, essay, financial need analysis, recommendations or references, transcript. *Deadline:* June 15.

Contact: Shanda Gray, Executive Vice President
Delta Sigma Pi Leadership Foundation
330 South Campus Avenue
Oxford, OH 45056
Phone: 513-523-1907
Fax: 513-523-7292
E-mail: foundation@dspnet.org

DIGITAL THIRD COAST INTERNET MARKETING

http://www.digitalthirdcoast.net/

DIGITAL MARKETING SCHOLARSHIP
• See page 88

EASTERN STAR-GRAND CHAPTER OF CALIFORNIA

http://www.oescal.org/

SCHOLARSHIPS FOR EDUCATION, BUSINESS AND RELIGION

Scholarship of $500 to $3000 awarded to students residing in California for post-secondary study. These scholarships are awarded for the study of business, education or religion.

Academic Fields/Career Goals: Business/Consumer Services; Education; Religion/Theology.

Award: Scholarship for use in freshman, sophomore, junior, or senior years; renewable. *Amount:* $500–$3000.

Eligibility Requirements: Applicant must be enrolled or expecting to enroll full-time at a two-year or four-year or technical institution or university and resident of California. Applicant must have 3.0 GPA or higher. Available to U.S. citizens.

Application Requirements: Application form, financial need analysis, personal photograph, proof of acceptance to college or university, recommendations or references, self-addressed stamped envelope with application, transcript. *Deadline:* March 8.

Contact: Maryann Barrios, Grand Secretary
Eastern Star-Grand Chapter of California
16960 Bastanchury Road, Suite E
Yorba Linda, CA 92886-1711
Phone: 714-986-2380
Fax: 714-986-2385
E-mail: gsecretary@oescal.org

ELECTRONIC DOCUMENT SYSTEMS FOUNDATION

http://www.edsf.org/

LYNDA BABOYIAN MEMORIAL SCHOLARSHIP

$2000 award for full-time students whose academic focus includes all document management and graphic communications careers. Minimum 3.0 GPA required.

Academic Fields/Career Goals: Business/Consumer Services; Computer Science/Data Processing; Graphics/Graphic Arts/Printing.

Award: Scholarship for use in freshman, sophomore, junior, or senior years; not renewable. *Number:* 1. *Amount:* $2000.

Eligibility Requirements: Applicant must be enrolled or expecting to enroll full-time at a two-year or four-year institution or university. Applicant must have 3.0 GPA or higher. Available to U.S. and non-U.S. citizens.

Application Requirements: Application form, community service, essay. *Deadline:* May 1.

Contact: Ms. Brenda Kai, Executive Director
Phone: 817-849-1145
E-mail: brenda.kai@edsf.org

FAMILY, CAREER AND COMMUNITY LEADERS OF AMERICA-TEXAS ASSOCIATION

http://www.texasfccla.org/

FCCLA REGIONAL SCHOLARSHIPS

One-time award for graduating high school seniors enrolled in full-time program in family and consumer sciences. Must be Texas resident and should study in Texas. Must have minimum GPA of 2.5.

Academic Fields/Career Goals: Business/Consumer Services; Home Economics.

Award: Scholarship for use in freshman year; not renewable. *Number:* up to 5. *Amount:* $1000.

Eligibility Requirements: Applicant must be high school student; planning to enroll or expecting to enroll full-time at a four-year institution or university; single; resident of Texas and studying in Texas. Applicant or parent of applicant must be member of Family, Career and Community Leaders of America. Applicant must have 2.5 GPA or higher. Available to U.S. citizens.

Application Requirements: Application form, essay, recommendations or references, test scores, transcript. *Deadline:* March 1.

Contact: Staff
Family, Career and Community Leaders of America-Texas Association
1107 West 45th Street
Austin, TX 78756
Phone: 512-306-0099
Fax: 512-442-7100
E-mail: fccla@texasfccla.org

FCCLA TEXAS FARM BUREAU SCHOLARSHIP

One-time award for a graduating high school senior enrolled in full-time program in family and consumer sciences. Must be a Texas resident and must study in Texas. Must have minimum GPA of 2.5. The award value is $5000.

Academic Fields/Career Goals: Business/Consumer Services; Home Economics.

Award: Scholarship for use in freshman year; not renewable. *Number:* 1. *Amount:* $1000.

Eligibility Requirements: Applicant must be high school student; planning to enroll or expecting to enroll full-time at a four-year institution or university; single; resident of Texas and studying in Texas. Applicant or parent of applicant must be member of Family, Career and Community Leaders of America. Applicant must have 2.5 GPA or higher. Available to U.S. citizens.

Application Requirements: Application form, driver's license, essay, recommendations or references, test scores, transcript. *Deadline:* March 1.

Contact: Staff
Family, Career and Community Leaders of America-Texas Association
1107 West 45th Street
Austin, TX 78756
Phone: 512-306-0099
Fax: 512-442-7100
E-mail: fccla@texasfccla.org

FUKUNAGA SCHOLARSHIP FOUNDATION

http://fukunagascholarship.com

FUKUNAGA SCHOLARSHIP FOUNDATION
• *See page 77*

GEORGIA GOVERNMENT FINANCE OFFICERS ASSOCIATION

http://www.ggfoa.org/

GGFOA ANNUAL COLLEGE SCHOLARSHIP
• *See page 77*

GLOBAL AUTOMOTIVE AFTERMARKET SYMPOSIUM

http://www.automotivescholarships.com/

AUTOMOTIVE AFTERMARKET SCHOLARSHIP CENTRAL

To receive a scholarship, applicants must be a high school graduate enrolled in a full time college-level program or an ASE/NATEF certified postsecondary automotive technical program, and planning a career in the automotive aftermarket.

Academic Fields/Career Goals: Business/Consumer Services; Engineering-Related Technologies; Marketing; Mechanical Engineering; Trade/Technical Specialties.

Award: Scholarship for use in freshman, sophomore, junior, senior, graduate, or postgraduate years; not renewable. *Amount:* $1000.

Eligibility Requirements: Applicant must be enrolled or expecting to enroll full-time at a two-year or four-year or technical institution or university and must have an interest in automotive. Available to U.S. and Canadian citizens.

Application Requirements: Application form, essay, personal photograph. *Deadline:* March 31.

Contact: Jennifer Hollar, Scholarship Committee Chairman
Global Automotive Aftermarket Symposium
PO Box 13966
Research Triangle Park, NC 27709-3966
Phone: 919-406-8811
E-mail: media@mema.org

GOLDEN KEY INTERNATIONAL HONOUR SOCIETY

http://www.goldenkey.org/

BUSINESS ACHIEVEMENT AWARD

Award to members who excel in the study of business. Applicants will be asked to respond to a problem posed by an honorary member within the discipline. The response will be in the form of a professional business report. One winner will receive a $1000 award. The second place winner will receive $750 and the third place winner will receive $500.

Academic Fields/Career Goals: Business/Consumer Services.

Award: Prize for use in freshman, sophomore, junior, senior, graduate, or postgraduate years; not renewable. *Number:* 3. *Amount:* $500–$1000.

Eligibility Requirements: Applicant must be enrolled or expecting to enroll full- or part-time at a four-year institution or university. Available to U.S. and non-U.S. citizens.

Application Requirements: Application form, business-related report, entry in a contest, essay, recommendations or references, transcript. *Deadline:* March 3.

Contact: Scholarship Program Administrators
Golden Key International Honour Society
PO Box 23737
Nashville, TN 37202-3737
Phone: 800-377-2401
E-mail: scholarships@goldenkey.org

GOVERNMENT FINANCE OFFICERS ASSOCIATION

http://www.gfoa.org/

MINORITIES IN GOVERNMENT FINANCE SCHOLARSHIP
• *See page 78*

GREATER KANAWHA VALLEY FOUNDATION

http://www.tgkvf.org/

WILLARD H. ERWIN JR. MEMORIAL SCHOLARSHIP FUND

Award of $600 for West Virginia residents who are starting their junior or senior year of undergraduate or graduate studies in a business or health-care finance degree program. Must be enrolled at a college in West Virginia. Scholarships are awarded on the basis of financial need and scholastic ability.

Academic Fields/Career Goals: Business/Consumer Services; Health Administration.

Award: Scholarship for use in junior, senior, or graduate years; renewable. *Number:* 1. *Amount:* $600.

Eligibility Requirements: Applicant must be enrolled or expecting to enroll full- or part-time at a four-year institution or university; resident of West Virginia and studying in West Virginia. Available to U.S. citizens.

Application Requirements: Application form, essay, financial need analysis, recommendations or references, self-addressed stamped envelope with application, test scores, transcript. *Deadline:* January 15.

Contact: Susan Hoover, Scholarship Program Officer
Greater Kanawha Valley Foundation
900 Lee Street East, 16th Floor
Charleston, WV 25301
Phone: 304-346-3620
E-mail: shoover@tgkvf.org

GREENPAL

GREENPAL BUSINESS SCHOLARSHIP

$2000 scholarship open to any high school senior, college freshman, or sophomore who owns and operates his/her own small business, or has put together a business plan to start a business while in college. The student must enter their freshman year at an accredited two- or four-year university, college or vocational/technical institute. Must be graduating high school senior or currently enrolled in a college of business with a 3.0 or higher GPA.

Academic Fields/Career Goals: Business/Consumer Services.

Award: Scholarship for use in freshman or sophomore years; not renewable. *Amount:* $2000.

Eligibility Requirements: Applicant must be enrolled or expecting to enroll full-time at a four-year or technical institution or university. Applicant must have 3.0 GPA or higher. Available to U.S. citizens.

Application Requirements: Application form, essay, recommendations or references, transcript. *Deadline:* February 28.

HOLSTEIN ASSOCIATION USA INC.

http://www.holsteinusa.com/

ROBERT H. RUMLER SCHOLARSHIP

• *See page 92*

IDAHO STATE BROADCASTERS ASSOCIATION

http://www.idahobroadcasters.org/

WAYNE C. CORNILS MEMORIAL SCHOLARSHIP

Scholarship for students enrolled in an Idaho school on a full-time basis. Must be majoring in a broadcasting related field. Must have minimum GPA of 2.0 if in the first two years of school or 2.5 in the last two years of school.

Academic Fields/Career Goals: Business/Consumer Services; Engineering/Technology; Journalism; TV/Radio Broadcasting.

Award: Scholarship for use in sophomore, junior, or senior years; not renewable. *Number:* 3. *Amount:* $1000.

Eligibility Requirements: Applicant must be enrolled or expecting to enroll full-time at a four-year institution or university; resident of Idaho and studying in Idaho. Applicant must have 2.5 GPA or higher. Available to U.S. citizens.

Application Requirements: Application form, essay, recommendations or references, transcript. *Deadline:* March 15.

Contact: Connie Searles, President and CEO
Idaho State Broadcasters Association
1674 Hill Road
Suite 3
Boise, ID 83702
Phone: 208-345-3072
Fax: 208-343-8046
E-mail: isba@qwestoffice.net

INSTITUTE FOR OPERATIONS RESEARCH AND THE MANAGEMENT SCIENCES

http://www.informs.org/

GEORGE NICHOLSON STUDENT PAPER COMPETITION

Honors outstanding papers in the field of operations research and the management sciences. Entrant must be student on or after the year of application. Research papers present original results and be written by student. Electronic submission of paper required.

Academic Fields/Career Goals: Business/Consumer Services.

Award: Prize for use in junior, senior, graduate, or postgraduate years; not renewable. *Number:* up to 6. *Amount:* $100–$600.

Eligibility Requirements: Applicant must be enrolled or expecting to enroll full- or part-time at a four-year institution or university. Available to U.S. and non-U.S. citizens.

Application Requirements: Application form, application form may be submitted online (https://www.informs.org/Recognize-Excellence/INFORMS-Prizes-Awards/George-Nicholson-Student-Paper-Competition/George-Nicholson-Student-Paper-Competition-Application-Process), entry in a contest, recommendations or references. *Deadline:* June 5.

Contact: Melissa Moore, Executive Director
Institute for Operations Research and the Management Sciences
5521 Research Park Drive
Catonsville, MD 21228
Phone: 443-757-3500
Fax: 443-757-2505
E-mail: informs@informs.org

INSTITUTE OF MANAGEMENT ACCOUNTANTS

https://www.imanet.org/students/scholarships-and-awards/scholarships?ssopc=1

INSTITUTE OF MANAGEMENT ACCOUNTANTS MEMORIAL EDUCATION FUND SCHOLARSHIPS

• *See page 79*

STUART CAMERON AND MARGARET MCLEOD MEMORIAL SCHOLARSHIP

• *See page 79*

JORGE MAS CANOSA FREEDOM FOUNDATION

http://masscholarships.org/

MAS FAMILY SCHOLARSHIP AWARD

Scholarship for Cuban American student who is a direct descendant of those who left Cuba or was born in Cuba. Minimum 3.5 GPA in college. Scholarships available only in the fields of engineering, business, international relations, economics, communications and journalism.

Academic Fields/Career Goals: Business/Consumer Services; Chemical Engineering; Civil Engineering; Communications; Economics; Electrical Engineering/Electronics; Engineering-Related Technologies;

International Studies; Journalism; Materials Science, Engineering, and Metallurgy; Mechanical Engineering.

Award: Scholarship for use in freshman, sophomore, junior, senior, or graduate years; renewable. *Number:* 5–10. *Amount:* $8000–$40,000.

Eligibility Requirements: Applicant must be of Latin American/Caribbean heritage; Hispanic and enrolled or expecting to enroll full-time at a two-year or four-year institution or university. Applicant must have 3.5 GPA or higher. Available to U.S. and non-U.S. citizens.

Application Requirements: Application form, essay, financial need analysis, proof of Cuban descent, recommendations or references, test scores, transcript. *Deadline:* April 15.

Contact: Mr. Daniel Lafuente, Mas Scholarship Coordinator
Jorge Mas Canosa Freedom Foundation
1312 SW 27th Avenue
Miami, FL 33145
Phone: 305-592-7768
E-mail: dlafuente@canf.org

LAGRANT FOUNDATION

http://www.lagrantfoundation.org/

LAGRANT FOUNDATION SCHOLARSHIP FOR UNDERGRADUATES
• *See page 88*

LEAGUE OF UNITED LATIN AMERICAN CITIZENS NATIONAL EDUCATIONAL SERVICE CENTERS INC.

http://www.lnesc.org/

GE/LULAC SCHOLARSHIP

The scholarship for business and engineering students offers outstanding minority or low-income students entering their sophomore year in pursuit of an undergraduate degree a renewable scholarship up to 3 years.

Academic Fields/Career Goals: Business/Consumer Services; Engineering/Technology.

Award: Scholarship for use in sophomore, junior, or senior years; renewable. *Number:* up to 9. *Amount:* up to $5000.

Eligibility Requirements: Applicant must be American Indian/Alaska Native, Asian/Pacific Islander, Black (non-Hispanic), Hispanic and enrolled or expecting to enroll full-time at a four-year institution or university. Applicant must have 3.0 GPA or higher. Available to U.S. citizens.

Application Requirements: Application form, personal statement with career goals, recommendations or references, transcript. *Deadline:* July 15.

Contact: Scholarship Administrator
League of United Latin American Citizens National
Educational Service Centers Inc.
2000 L Street, NW, Suite 610
Washington, DC 20036
Phone: 202-835-9646 Ext. 10
Fax: 202-835-9685

MAINE COMMUNITY FOUNDATION, INC.

http://www.mainecf.org/

PATRIOT EDUCATION SCHOLARSHIP FUND

Scholarship for graduating seniors or prior graduates of a Maine high school who are enrolling or enrolled in a college or university in Maine pursuing a degree in business as a full-or part-time student. Preference is given to applicants who have a demonstrated interest in personal and commercial insurance professions.

Academic Fields/Career Goals: Business/Consumer Services.

Award: Scholarship for use in freshman, sophomore, junior, or senior years; not renewable.

Eligibility Requirements: Applicant must be enrolled or expecting to enroll full- or part-time at a two-year or four-year institution or university and studying in Maine. Available to U.S. citizens.

Application Requirements: Application form. *Deadline:* June 1.

Contact: Ms. Amy Pollien, Grants Administration
Phone: 207-667-9735 Ext. 1109
E-mail: apollien@mainecf.org

NATIONAL ASSOCIATION OF WATER COMPANIES-NEW JERSEY CHAPTER

http://www.nawc.org

NATIONAL ASSOCIATION OF WATER COMPANIES-NEW JERSEY CHAPTER SCHOLARSHIP
• *See page 80*

NATIONAL SECURITY EDUCATION PROGRAM

http://www.iie.org/

NATIONAL SECURITY EDUCATION PROGRAM (NSEP) DAVID L. BOREN UNDERGRADUATE SCHOLARSHIPS
• *See page 126*

NEBRASKA DECA

http://www.nedeca.org/

NEBRASKA DECA LEADERSHIP SCHOLARSHIP

Awards applicants who intend to pursue a full-time two- or four-year course of study in a marketing or business-related field. Applicant must be active in DECA and involved in community service activities.

Academic Fields/Career Goals: Business/Consumer Services.

Award: Scholarship for use in freshman year; not renewable. *Number:* 2–9. *Amount:* $250–$1000.

Eligibility Requirements: Applicant must be high school student; planning to enroll or expecting to enroll full-time at a two-year or four-year or technical institution or university and resident of Nebraska. Applicant or parent of applicant must be member of Distribution Ed Club or Future Business Leaders of America. Applicant must have 2.5 GPA or higher. Available to U.S. citizens.

Application Requirements: Application form, DECA participation and accomplishment documents, essay, recommendations or references, resume, test scores, transcript. *Deadline:* February 1.

Contact: Scholarship Review Committee
Nebraska DECA
301 Centennial Mall South, PO Box 94987
Lincoln, NE 68509-4987
Phone: 402-471-4803
Fax: 402-471-0117
E-mail: nedeca@nedeca.org

NEW ENGLAND EMPLOYEE BENEFITS COUNCIL

http://www.neebc.org/

NEW ENGLAND EMPLOYEE BENEFITS COUNCIL SCHOLARSHIP PROGRAM
• *See page 81*

NEW ENGLAND WATER WORKS ASSOCIATION

http://www.newwa.org/

FRANCIS X. CROWLEY SCHOLARSHIP

Scholarships are awarded to eligible civil engineering, environmental and business management students on the basis of merit, character, and need. Preference given to those students whose programs are considered by a committee as beneficial to water works practice in New England. NEWWA student membership is required to receive a scholarship award. Applicants for scholarships should be residents or attend school in New England. (Maine, New Hampshire, Vermont, Massachusetts, Rhode Island and Connecticut).

Academic Fields/Career Goals: Business/Consumer Services; Civil Engineering; Environmental Science.

Award: Scholarship for use in freshman, sophomore, junior, senior, or graduate years; not renewable. *Number:* 1. *Amount:* up to $3000.

Eligibility Requirements: Applicant must be enrolled or expecting to enroll full-time at a four-year institution or university. Applicant or parent of applicant must be member of New England Water Works Association. Available to U.S. citizens.

Application Requirements: Application form, essay, recommendations or references, transcript. *Fee:* $25. *Deadline:* July 1.

Contact: Thomas MacElhaney, Chair, Scholarship Committee
Phone: 631-231-8100
Fax: 978-418-9156
E-mail: tmacelhaney@preloadinc.com

OREGON STUDENT ASSISTANCE COMMISSION

http://www.GetCollegeFunds.org/

FRED FIELDS SCHOLARSHIP

For students enrolled at least half-time in Oregon two-year public schools. Must be majoring in industrial mechanics/maintenance, industrial/mechanical engineering, manufacturing technology, business administration, commerce, entrepreneurship, management or career and technology (in order of preference). Automatically renewable if renewal criteria is met.

Academic Fields/Career Goals: Business/Consumer Services; Engineering-Related Technologies; Mechanical Engineering.

Award: Scholarship for use in freshman, sophomore, junior, or senior years; renewable.

Eligibility Requirements: Applicant must be enrolled or expecting to enroll full- or part-time at a two-year institution and studying in Oregon. Available to U.S. citizens.

Application Requirements: Application form, financial need analysis. *Deadline:* March 1.

Contact: Melissa Adams, Scholarship Processing Coordinator
Phone: 541-687-7409
E-mail: melissa.adams@hecc.oregon.gov

PLUMBING-HEATING-COOLING CONTRACTORS EDUCATION FOUNDATION

http://www.phccfoundation.org/scholarships

DELTA FAUCET COMPANY SCHOLARSHIP PROGRAM

Applicants must be sponsored by a member of the National Association of Plumbing-Heating-Cooling Contractors. Must pursue studies in a major related to the plumbing-heating-cooling industry. Visit website for additional information.

Academic Fields/Career Goals: Business/Consumer Services; Engineering-Related Technologies; Engineering/Technology; Heating, Air-Conditioning, and Refrigeration Mechanics; Mechanical Engineering; Trade/Technical Specialties.

Award: Scholarship for use in freshman, sophomore, junior, or senior years; not renewable. *Number:* 6. *Amount:* $2500.

Eligibility Requirements: Applicant must be enrolled or expecting to enroll full-time at a two-year or four-year or technical institution or university. Applicant must have 2.5 GPA or higher. Available to U.S. and Canadian citizens.

Application Requirements: Application form, community service, essay, interview. *Deadline:* May 1.

Contact: John Zink, Scholarship Coordinator
Phone: 800-533-7694
E-mail: scholarships@naphcc.org

PHCC EDUCATIONAL FOUNDATION NEED-BASED SCHOLARSHIP

Need-based scholarship worth $2500 to a student enrolled in an approved four-year PHCC apprenticeship program, or at an accredited two-year technical college, community college, or an accredited four-year college or university.

Academic Fields/Career Goals: Business/Consumer Services; Engineering-Related Technologies; Engineering/Technology; Heating, Air-Conditioning, and Refrigeration Mechanics; Mechanical Engineering; Trade/Technical Specialties.

Award: Scholarship for use in freshman, sophomore, junior, or senior years; renewable. *Number:* 1. *Amount:* $2500.

Eligibility Requirements: Applicant must be enrolled or expecting to enroll full-time at a two-year or four-year or technical institution or university. Applicant must have 2.5 GPA or higher. Available to U.S. and Canadian citizens.

Application Requirements: Application form, community service, essay, financial need analysis, interview. *Deadline:* May 1.

Contact: John Zink, Scholarship Coordinator
Phone: 800-533-7694
E-mail: scholarships@naphcc.org

PHCC EDUCATIONAL FOUNDATION SCHOLARSHIP PROGRAM

Applicants must be sponsored by a member of the National Association of Plumbing-Heating-Cooling Contractors. Must pursue studies in a major related to the plumbing-heating-cooling industry. Visit website for additional information.

Academic Fields/Career Goals: Business/Consumer Services; Engineering-Related Technologies; Engineering/Technology; Heating, Air-Conditioning, and Refrigeration Mechanics; Mechanical Engineering; Trade/Technical Specialties.

Award: Scholarship for use in freshman, sophomore, junior, or senior years; not renewable. *Number:* 1–4. *Amount:* $2500–$5000.

Eligibility Requirements: Applicant must be enrolled or expecting to enroll full-time at a two-year or four-year or technical institution or university. Applicant must have 2.5 GPA or higher. Available to U.S. and Canadian citizens.

Application Requirements: Application form, community service, essay, interview. *Deadline:* May 1.

Contact: John Zink, Scholarship Coordinator
Phone: 800-533-7694
E-mail: scholarships@naphcc.org

ROBERT H. MOLLOHAN FAMILY CHARITABLE FOUNDATION, INC.

http://www.mollohanfoundation.org/

TEAMING TO WIN BUSINESS SCHOLARSHIP

Scholarship for a rising college sophomore or junior pursuing a degree in business administration at a West Virginia college or university.

Academic Fields/Career Goals: Business/Consumer Services.

Award: Scholarship for use in sophomore or junior years; not renewable. *Number:* 2. *Amount:* up to $1000.

Eligibility Requirements: Applicant must be enrolled or expecting to enroll full- or part-time at a four-year institution or university; resident of West Virginia; studying in West Virginia and must have an interest in leadership. Applicant must have 3.0 GPA or higher. Available to U.S. citizens.

Application Requirements: Application form, essay, interview, recommendations or references, resume, test scores, transcript. *Deadline:* February 9.

Contact: Aime Shaffer, Program Manager
Robert H. Mollohan Family Charitable Foundation, Inc.
1000 Technology Drive, Suite 2000
Fairmont, WV 26554
Phone: 304-333-6783
Fax: 304-333-3900
E-mail: ashaffer@wvhtf.org

SALES PROFESSIONALS-USA

http://www.salesprofessionals-usa.com/

SALES PROFESSIONALS-USA SCHOLARSHIP

Scholarships are awarded to students furthering their degree or obtaining a degree in business or marketing. The scholarships are initiated and awarded by the individual Sales Pros Clubs (located in Colorado, Kansas and Missouri) and are not nationally awarded. A listing of local clubs can be found at http://www.salesprofessionals-usa.com.

Academic Fields/Career Goals: Business/Consumer Services.

Award: Scholarship for use in freshman, sophomore, junior, or senior years; not renewable. *Number:* 3–5. *Amount:* $600–$1000.

Eligibility Requirements: Applicant must be enrolled or expecting to enroll full- or part-time at a two-year or four-year institution or university; resident of Colorado, Indiana, Kansas and studying in Colorado, Kansas, Missouri. Applicant must have 3.0 GPA or higher. Available to U.S. citizens.

Application Requirements: Application form, essay. *Deadline:* varies.

Contact: Jay Berg, National President
Sales Professionals-USA
2870 North Speer Boulevard
Denver, CO 80001
Phone: 303-433-1051
E-mail: jberg@spacelogic.net

SCARLETT FAMILY FOUNDATION SCHOLARSHIP PROGRAM

http://www.scarlettfoundation.org/

SCHOLARSHIP FOR STUDENTS PURSUING A BUSINESS OR STEM DEGREE
• *See page 84*

SOCIETY OF AUTOMOTIVE ANALYSTS

http://saaauto.com/

SOCIETY OF AUTOMOTIVE ANALYSTS SCHOLARSHIP
• *See page 84*

SPECIALTY EQUIPMENT MARKET ASSOCIATION

http://www.sema.org/

SEMA MEMORIAL SCHOLARSHIP FUND
• *See page 85*

STRAIGHTFORWARD MEDIA

http://www.straightforwardmedia.com/

STRAIGHTFORWARD MEDIA BUSINESS SCHOOL SCHOLARSHIP
• *See page 90*

TED ROLLINS AND TXG CAPITAL

http://www.txgcapital.com/

TED ROLLINS ECO SCHOLARSHIP

Ted Rollins and TXG Capital award a $1,000 scholarship each year to one talented student who is majoring in a field related to sustainability. This money may be used to pay for tuition, books or living expenses.

Academic Fields/Career Goals: Business/Consumer Services; Environmental Health; Environmental Science; Natural Sciences.

Award: Scholarship for use in freshman, sophomore, junior, or senior years; not renewable. *Number:* 1. *Amount:* $1000.

Eligibility Requirements: Applicant must be enrolled or expecting to enroll full- or part-time at a two-year or four-year or technical institution or university. Available to U.S. and non-U.S. citizens.

Application Requirements: Application form, essay. *Deadline:* June 15.

Contact: Caroline Davis
Phone: 864-9184534
E-mail: caroline@tedrollinsecoscholars.com

TKE EDUCATIONAL FOUNDATION

http://www.tke.org/

JOHN C. FITZGERALD, JR. SCHOLARSHIP

One-time award of $300 given to an undergraduate member of Tau Kappa Epsilon who has demonstrated leadership ability within his chapter, campus, or community. Must be a full-time student in good standing with a GPA of 2.5 or higher and pursuing a degree in business administration. Preference will first be given to a member of Theta-Upsilon Chapter, but if there is no qualified applicant, the scholarship will be open to any other qualified Teke

Academic Fields/Career Goals: Business/Consumer Services.

Award: Scholarship for use in sophomore, junior, or senior years; not renewable. *Number:* 1. *Amount:* $300.

Eligibility Requirements: Applicant must be enrolled or expecting to enroll full-time at a four-year institution or university; male and must have an interest in leadership. Applicant or parent of applicant must be member of Tau Kappa Epsilon. Applicant must have 2.5 GPA or higher. Available to U.S. and non-U.S. citizens.

Application Requirements: Application form, application form may be submitted online (http://www.tke.org/member_resources/scholarships/apply_online), essay, personal photograph, transcript. *Deadline:* March 15.

Contact: Offices of the Grand Chapter
TKE Educational Foundation
7439 Woodland Drive, Suite 100
Indianapolis, IN 46278
E-mail: tkeogc@tke.org

TRUCKLOAD CARRIERS ASSOCIATION

http://www.truckload.org/

TRUCKLOAD CARRIERS ASSOCIATION SCHOLARSHIP FUND

This scholarship fund is for persons affiliated with the trucking industry and their families to pursue higher education. Special consideration will be given to applicants pursuing transportation or business degrees. Minimum 3.3 GPA required. For junior and senior undergraduate students at four-year college or university. Further information and application deadlines available at website http://www.truckload.org.

Academic Fields/Career Goals: Business/Consumer Services; Transportation.

Award: Scholarship for use in junior or senior years; not renewable. *Number:* 18. *Amount:* $1500–$5000.

Eligibility Requirements: Applicant must be enrolled or expecting to enroll full-time at a four-year institution or university. Applicant or parent of applicant must have employment or volunteer experience in transportation industry. Available to U.S. and Canadian citizens.

Application Requirements: Application form, course schedule including tuition and fees, essay, financial need analysis, transcript. *Deadline:* May 23.

Contact: Debbie Sparks, Vice President of Development
Phone: 703-838-1950
Fax: 703-836-6610
E-mail: tca@truckload.org

UNITED DAUGHTERS OF THE CONFEDERACY

http://www.hqudc.org/

WALTER REED SMITH SCHOLARSHIP

Award for full-time female undergraduate students who are descendant of a Confederate soldier, studying nutrition, home economics, nursing, business administration, or computer science in accredited college or university. Minimum 3.0 GPA required. Submit application and letter of endorsement from sponsoring chapter of the United Daughters of the Confederacy.

Academic Fields/Career Goals: Business/Consumer Services; Computer Science/Data Processing; Food Science/Nutrition; Home Economics; Nursing.

Award: Scholarship for use in freshman, sophomore, junior, or senior years; renewable. *Number:* 1–2. *Amount:* $800–$1000.

Eligibility Requirements: Applicant must be enrolled or expecting to enroll full-time at a four-year institution or university and female. Applicant or parent of applicant must be member of United Daughters of the Confederacy. Applicant must have 3.0 GPA or higher. Available to U.S. citizens.

Application Requirements: Application form, copy of applicant's birth certificate, copy of confederate ancestor's proof of service, essay, financial need analysis, personal photograph, recommendations or references, self-addressed stamped envelope with application, test scores, transcript. *Deadline:* March 15.

Contact: Ms. Jamie Davis, Second Vice President General
  Phone: 804-355-1636
  E-mail: hqudc@rcn.com

UNITED NEGRO COLLEGE FUND

http://www.uncf.org/

ASHLEY STEWART SCHOLARSHIP

Scholarship of up to $5000 to encourage minority female students to pursue a future career in the business of fashion. Must be a full-time sophomore or junior at a UNCF member school and majoring in a business field (business administration, marketing, finance, communications, or fashion merchandising). Minimum 3.3 GPA required.

Academic Fields/Career Goals: Business/Consumer Services; Communications; Finance; Marketing.

Award: Scholarship for use in sophomore, junior, or senior years; not renewable. *Number:* 2.

Eligibility Requirements: Applicant must be Black (non-Hispanic); enrolled or expecting to enroll full-time at a four-year institution or university and female. Applicant must have 3.0 GPA or higher. Available to U.S. and non-U.S. citizens.

Application Requirements: Application form, essay, financial need analysis. *Deadline:* May 22.

Contact: Mary Williams, Director of Outreach and Recruitment
  Phone: 800-331-2244

BASF/ALFRED CHISHOLM ENDOWED MEMORIAL SCHOLARSHIP
• *See page 86*

COLGATE–PALMOLIVE CORPORATE SCHOLARS PROGRAM
• *See page 86*

COOPER INDUSTRIES

Scholarship to support engineering and business students at accredited 4 year colleges and universities. Students must have a 2.75 GPA minimum.

Academic Fields/Career Goals: Business/Consumer Services; Engineering/Technology.

Award: Scholarship for use in freshman, sophomore, junior, or senior years.

Eligibility Requirements: Applicant must be Black (non-Hispanic) and enrolled or expecting to enroll at a four-year institution or university. Applicant must have 2.5 GPA or higher. Available to U.S. citizens.

Application Requirements: Application form. *Deadline:* March 6.

Contact: Mary Williams, Director of Outreach and Recruitment
  Phone: 800-331-2244

CVS PHARMACY, INC. BUSINESS SCHOLARSHIPS
• *See page 86*

DELL CORPORATE SCHOLARS PROGRAM

Scholarship of up to $4500 for a student majoring or having an academic focus in engineering, supply chain management, computer science, or information technology. Must be a minority student enrolled full-time at a U.S. located accredited four year institution as a junior during the application and interview process. Must possess a demonstrated unmet financial need as verified by their institution/college (for scholarship award) and have a minimum 3.0 GPA. All applicants for the UNCF/Dell Corporate Scholars Program may be considered for internship opportunities at Dell.

Academic Fields/Career Goals: Business/Consumer Services; Computer Science/Data Processing; Engineering/Technology.

Award: Scholarship for use in junior year; not renewable.

Eligibility Requirements: Applicant must be American Indian/Alaska Native, Asian/Pacific Islander, Black (non-Hispanic), Hispanic and enrolled or expecting to enroll full-time at a four-year institution or university. Applicant must have 3.0 GPA or higher. Available to U.S. citizens.

Application Requirements: Application form, essay. *Deadline:* October 2.

Contact: Mary Williams, Director of Outreach and Recruitment
  Phone: 800-331-2244

DELL CORPORATE SCHOLARS PROGRAM

Scholarship up to $4500 based on need. Students must major or have an academic focus in Supply Chain Management, Engineering, Electrical Engineering, Computer Science or Information Technology. Applicants may be considered for 10-week summer internship opportunities at Dell HQ in Round Rock, TX.

Academic Fields/Career Goals: Business/Consumer Services; Computer Science/Data Processing; Electrical Engineering/Electronics.

Award: Scholarship for use in junior year; not renewable.

Eligibility Requirements: Applicant must be American Indian/Alaska Native, Asian/Pacific Islander, Black (non-Hispanic), Hispanic and enrolled or expecting to enroll full-time at a four-year institution or university. Applicant must have 3.0 GPA or higher. Available to U.S. citizens.

Application Requirements: Application form, essay, financial need analysis, interview. *Deadline:* April 28.

Contact: Mary Williams, Director of Outreach and Recruitment
  Phone: 800-331-2244

LIBERTY MUTUAL SCHOLARSHIP

Up to $4500 scholarships to provide recognition of and financial assistance to outstanding students from UNCF member institutions who are business majors. Minimum 3.0 GPA required. Recipients are encouraged to apply for a summer internship with Liberty Mutual.

Academic Fields/Career Goals: Business/Consumer Services; Insurance and Actuarial Science.

Award: Scholarship for use in freshman, sophomore, junior, or senior years; not renewable.

Eligibility Requirements: Applicant must be Black (non-Hispanic) and enrolled or expecting to enroll full-time at a four-year institution or university. Applicant must have 3.0 GPA or higher. Available to U.S. citizens.

Application Requirements: Application form, financial need analysis. *Deadline:* June 30.

Contact: Mary Williams, Director of Outreach and Recruitment
  Phone: 800-331-2244

NASCAR BLACK HISTORY MONTH AWARDS
• *See page 86*

NATIONAL BLACK McDONALD'S OWNERS ASSOCIATION HOSPITALITY SCHOLARS PROGRAM
• *See page 86*

ORACLE CORPORATE SCHOLARS PROGRAM

African American student scholars who are majoring in computer science, computer engineering, mathematics, business, marketing, or human resources. Candidates must be a U.S. citizen, African American college student, have a minimum 3.0 GPA, and attend a four-year, accredited college or university located in the U.S. Successful candidates will be offered internships during the summer.

Academic Fields/Career Goals: Business/Consumer Services; Computer Science/Data Processing; Human Resources; Marketing; Mathematics.

Award: Scholarship for use in sophomore, junior, or senior years; not renewable.

Eligibility Requirements: Applicant must be Black (non-Hispanic) and enrolled or expecting to enroll full-time at a four-year institution or university. Applicant must have 3.0 GPA or higher. Available to U.S. citizens.

Application Requirements: Application form, essay, financial need analysis. *Deadline:* March 10.

Contact: Mary Williams, Director of Outreach and Recruitment
Phone: 800-331-2244

PROCTER & GAMBLE GENERAL SCHOLARSHIP
• *See page 91*

RICOH SCHOLARSHIP PROGRAM
• *See page 86*

SUEZ CORPORATE SCHOLARS PROGRAM
• *See page 87*

UNCF/ANTHEM CORPORATE SCHOLARS PROGRAM

Up $5000 scholarship for an underrepresented minority student that is a college sophomore and a resident of or enrolled in an accredited higher education institution in one of the following states: California, Virginia, Georgia, Indiana, Missouri, New York, or Ohio. Minimum 3.0 GPA required. Must major in business, communications, marketing, finance, health care administration, information systems, management information systems, computer technology or computer science and possess strong analytical problem solving, interpersonal, written and oral communication skills. Must be proficient in Microsoft Office Suite (Excel, Word, and Outlook) and social media platforms. All applicants for the UNCF/Anthem Corporate Scholars Program can apply and may be eligible for internship opportunities at the Anthem Corporation.

Academic Fields/Career Goals: Business/Consumer Services; Communications; Computer Science/Data Processing; Finance; Health Administration; Marketing.

Award: Scholarship for use in sophomore year; not renewable.

Eligibility Requirements: Applicant must be American Indian/Alaska Native, Asian/Pacific Islander, Black (non-Hispanic), Hispanic and enrolled or expecting to enroll full-time at a four-year institution or university. Applicant must have 3.0 GPA or higher. Available to U.S. citizens.

Application Requirements: Application form, essay, financial need analysis. *Deadline:* February 17.

Contact: Mary Williams, Director of Outreach and Recruitment
Phone: 800-331-2244

UNCF/CARNIVAL CORPORATE SCHOLARS PROGRAM

Up to $5000 scholarship and paid summer internship for minority college sophomores with an interest in pursuing a career in the hospitality industry and whose experience in their first two years of college demonstrates leadership and strategic and analytical ability. Minimum 2.75 GPA. Open to transfer students from community colleges that have been accepted into an accredited four-year college or university. Majoring in hospitality management and/or administration, tourism, culinary arts, business, finance, communications, marketing or other related field.

Academic Fields/Career Goals: Business/Consumer Services; Communications; Culinary Arts; Finance; Hospitality Management; Marketing; Travel/Tourism.

Award: Scholarship for use in sophomore year; renewable.

Eligibility Requirements: Applicant must be American Indian/Alaska Native, Asian/Pacific Islander, Black (non-Hispanic), Hispanic and enrolled or expecting to enroll full-time at a four-year institution or university. Applicant must have 2.5 GPA or higher. Available to U.S. citizens.

Application Requirements: Application form, essay. *Deadline:* January 22.

Contact: Mary Williams, Director of Outreach and Recruitment
Phone: 800-331-2244

UNCF/KOCH SCHOLARS PROGRAM FOR UNDERGRADUATES
• *See page 87*

UNCF/NISSAN SCHOLARSHIP

Scholarship for current college freshmen enrolled at any HBCU. Total award of $10,000 over 4 years ($2,500 per academic year) and an opportunity to participate in Nissan's Internship Program or enrichment opportunities. Must be majoring in engineering, business, marketing, information technology and/or finance. Minimum 3.0 GPA required.

Academic Fields/Career Goals: Business/Consumer Services; Engineering/Technology; Finance; Marketing.

Award: Scholarship for use in freshman, sophomore, junior, or senior years; not renewable. *Number:* 10. *Amount:* $2500.

Eligibility Requirements: Applicant must be Black (non-Hispanic); high school student and planning to enroll or expecting to enroll full-time at a four-year institution or university. Applicant must have 3.0 GPA or higher. Available to U.S. citizens.

Application Requirements: Application form, financial need analysis. *Deadline:* June 15.

Contact: Mary Williams, Director of Outreach and Recruitment
Phone: 800-331-2244

UNCF/TRAVELERS INSURANCE SCHOLARSHIP

Scholarship for African-American students with unmet financial need. Selected Scholars shall be expected to participate in Travelers-sponsored online and/or on site career readiness opportunities. Applicants must be pursuing a major in a business-related field, risk management or insurance and reside in California, Colorado, Florida, Georgia, Illinois, Massachusetts, Missouri, North Carolina, Texas or Washington.

Academic Fields/Career Goals: Business/Consumer Services; Insurance and Actuarial Science.

Award: Scholarship for use in sophomore, junior, or senior years. *Amount:* $3000–$5850.

Eligibility Requirements: Applicant must be Black (non-Hispanic); enrolled or expecting to enroll at a four-year institution or university and resident of California, Colorado, Florida, Georgia, Illinois, Massachusetts, Missouri, North Carolina, Texas, Washington. Applicant must have 3.0 GPA or higher. Available to U.S. citizens.

Application Requirements: Application form, essay, financial need analysis. *Deadline:* January 13.

Contact: Mary Williams, Director of Outreach and Recruitment
Phone: 800-331-2244

WHOMENTORS.COM, INC.
http://www.WHOmentors.com/

1B USD WORLDWIDE VENTURE CAPITAL
• *See page 116*

WOMEN GROCERS OF AMERICA
http://www.nationalgrocers.org/

MARY MACEY SCHOLARSHIP
• *See page 103*

WOMEN IN LOGISTICS, NORTHERN CALIFORNIA
http://www.womeninlogistics.org/

WOMEN IN LOGISTICS SCHOLARSHIP

Award for students (undergraduate/graduate, male/female) studying and eventually planning careers in logistics/supply chain management. Applicants must be enrolled in a degree program at an institution within the 9 counties comprising the San Francisco Bay Area and have at least one semester left, as this award goes directly to the institution towards tuition/fees. Deadlines typically fall on November 1st. While student need may considered, awards are based primarily on merit, work experience and demonstrated interest in the field.

Academic Fields/Career Goals: Business/Consumer Services; Trade/Technical Specialties; Transportation.

Award: Scholarship for use in freshman, sophomore, junior, senior, or graduate years; not renewable. *Number:* 1–3. *Amount:* $1000–$3000.

Eligibility Requirements: Applicant must be enrolled or expecting to enroll full- or part-time at a two-year or four-year institution or university; resident of California and studying in California. Applicant or parent of applicant must be member of Women in Logistics. Available to U.S. and non-U.S. citizens.

Application Requirements: Application form, essay. *Deadline:* November 1.

Contact: Dr. Susan Cholette, Scholarship Director
Phone: 415-405-2173
E-mail: cholette@sfsu.edu

WYOMING TRUCKING ASSOCIATION SCHOLARSHIP FUND TRUST

http://www.wytruck.org/

WYOMING TRUCKING ASSOCIATION SCHOLARSHIP TRUST FUND
• *See page 87*

Y'S MEN INTERNATIONAL

http://www.ysmen.org/

ALEXANDER SCHOLARSHIP LOAN FUND
The purpose of the fund is to promote the training of staff of the YMCA and/or those seeking to become members or staff of the YMCA. Deadlines are May 30 for fall semester and October 30 for spring semester.

Academic Fields/Career Goals: Business/Consumer Services; Child and Family Studies; Education; Human Resources; Social Sciences; Social Services; Sports-Related/Exercise Science.

Award: Scholarship for use in freshman, sophomore, junior, or senior years; renewable.

Eligibility Requirements: Applicant must be enrolled or expecting to enroll full- or part-time at a two-year or four-year institution or university. Available to U.S. citizens.

Application Requirements: Application form. *Fee:* $1. *Deadline:* varies.

Contact: Dean Currie, Area Service Director
Phone: 908-753-9493
Fax: 602-935-6322
E-mail: kidcurrie@adelphia.net

ZONTA INTERNATIONAL FOUNDATION

http://www.zonta.org/

JANE M. KLAUSMAN WOMEN IN BUSINESS SCHOLARSHIPS
Any woman undertaking a business and/or business-related program at an accredited university/college/institute, in at least the second year of an undergraduate program through the final year of a Masters program at the time the application is submitted, is eligible to apply. Applicants must contact their local Zonta club for deadlines.

Academic Fields/Career Goals: Business/Consumer Services.

Award: Scholarship for use in junior, senior, or graduate years; not renewable. *Number:* 30–32. *Amount:* $1000–$7000.

Eligibility Requirements: Applicant must be enrolled or expecting to enroll full-time at a four-year institution or university and female. Available to U.S. and non-U.S. citizens.

Application Requirements: Application form, essay.

Contact: Programs Department
Fax: 630-928-1559
E-mail: programs@zonta.org

CAMPUS ACTIVITIES

NATIONAL ASSOCIATION FOR CAMPUS ACTIVITIES

http://www.naca.org/

MARKLEY SCHOLARSHIP
Scholarship available to students who are strongly involved in the field of student activities and/or student activities employment, and who have

made significant contributions to NACA Central. Must be classified as a junior, senior or graduate student at a four-year school located in the NACA Central region, or a sophomore at a two-year school in the NACA Central region. Must have minimum 2.5 GPA.

Academic Fields/Career Goals: Campus Activities.

Award: Scholarship for use in sophomore, junior, senior, or graduate years; not renewable. *Number:* 1–2. *Amount:* $300.

Eligibility Requirements: Applicant must be enrolled or expecting to enroll full- or part-time at a two-year or four-year institution and studying in Arkansas, Colorado, Kansas, Louisiana, Missouri, New Mexico, Oklahoma, Texas. Applicant or parent of applicant must have employment or volunteer experience in community service. Applicant must have 2.5 GPA or higher. Available to U.S. citizens.

Application Requirements: Application form, autobiography, essay. *Deadline:* September 1.

Contact: Kayla Brennan, Education and Development Coordinator
Phone: 803-217-3471
Fax: 803-749-1047
E-mail: kaylab@naca.org

MULTICULTURAL SCHOLARSHIP PROGRAM
The Multicultural Scholarship Program is part of the NACA Foundation's affirmative action effort to increase the participation of ethnic minority individuals in the field of campus activities. The program is designed to provide economic assistance to qualified under-represented programmers, allowing them to attend NACA-sponsored training workshops, regional conferences and National Conventions. The awards are for registration only - travel is not included. Scholarships are NOT to be used for educational expenses, including tuition, books, fees or other related expenses. They are for the purpose of attending an NACA event. Scholarships will be given to applicants identified as African-American, Latina/Latino, Native-American, Asian-American or Pacific Islander ethnic minorities. A letter of recommendation affirming his/her ethnic minority status, his/her financial need, and that he/she will be in the campus activity field at least one year following the program for which a scholarship is being sought, should accompany applications.

Academic Fields/Career Goals: Campus Activities.

Award: Scholarship for use in freshman, sophomore, junior, senior, graduate, or postgraduate years; not renewable. *Number:* 1–3. *Amount:* $300.

Eligibility Requirements: Applicant must be American Indian/Alaska Native, Asian/Pacific Islander, Black (non-Hispanic), Hispanic; enrolled or expecting to enroll full- or part-time at a two-year or four-year institution or university and must have an interest in leadership. Available to U.S. citizens.

Application Requirements: Application form, essay, financial need analysis. *Deadline:* May 1.

Contact: Kayla Brennan, Education and Development Coordinator
Phone: 803-217-3471
Fax: 803-749-1047
E-mail: kaylab@naca.org

NATIONAL ASSOCIATION FOR CAMPUS ACTIVITIES MID ATLANTIC HIGHER EDUCATION RESEARCH SCHOLARSHIP
Scholarships will be given for research that will add to the college student personnel knowledge base, particularly campus activities, or address issues challenging student affairs practitioners as they relate to campus activities.

Academic Fields/Career Goals: Campus Activities; Education.

Award: Scholarship for use in freshman, sophomore, junior, senior, graduate, or postgraduate years; not renewable. *Number:* 1. *Amount:* $50–$500.

Eligibility Requirements: Applicant must be enrolled or expecting to enroll full- or part-time at a two-year or four-year institution or university and studying in Delaware, Maryland, New Jersey, New York, Pennsylvania. Available to U.S. citizens.

Application Requirements: Application form, autobiography, essay. *Deadline:* June 15.

Contact: Kayla Brennan, Education and Development Coordinator
Phone: 803-217-3471
Fax: 803-749-1047
E-mail: kaylab@naca.org

WHOMENTORS.COM, INC.

http://www.WHOmentors.com/

IB USD WORLDWIDE VENTURE CAPITAL
• *See page 116*

CANADIAN STUDIES

CANADIAN INSTITUTE OF UKRAINIAN STUDIES

http://www.cius.ca/

CANADIAN INSTITUTE OF UKRAINIAN STUDIES RESEARCH GRANTS
• *See page 124*

CHEMICAL ENGINEERING

AACE INTERNATIONAL

http://www.aacei.org/

AACE INTERNATIONAL COMPETITIVE SCHOLARSHIP
• *See page 118*

AIST FOUNDATION

http://www.aistfoundation.org/

ASSOCIATION FOR IRON AND STEEL TECHNOLOGY BENJAMIN F. FAIRLESS SCHOLARSHIP (AIME)

Scholarship for full-time students of metallurgy, materials science, chemical, mechanical, electrical, environmental, computer science, and industrial engineering. Students must have an interest in a career in the steel industry as demonstrated by an internship or related experience, or who have plans to pursue such experiences during college. Student may apply after first term of freshman year of college. Applications are accepted from 1 Sep through 31 Dec each year. Note: High school students do not qualify but are encouraged to learn about the steel industry and the career opportunities available therein, during their freshman year.

Academic Fields/Career Goals: Chemical Engineering; Electrical Engineering/Electronics; Engineering-Related Technologies; Materials Science, Engineering, and Metallurgy; Mechanical Engineering.

Award: Scholarship for use in sophomore, junior, or senior years; not renewable. *Number:* 2. *Amount:* $3000.

Eligibility Requirements: Applicant must be enrolled or expecting to enroll full-time at a four-year institution or university. Applicant must have 2.5 GPA or higher. Available to U.S. and non-U.S. citizens.

Application Requirements: Application form, essay, recommendations or references, resume, transcript. *Deadline:* December 31.

Contact: Lori Wharrey, AIST Manager, Board Services
AIST Foundation
186 Thorn Hill Road
Warrendale, PA 15086
Phone: 724-814-3044
E-mail: lwharrey@aist.org

ASSOCIATION FOR IRON AND STEEL TECHNOLOGY DAVID H. SAMSON CANADIAN SCHOLARSHIP

Scholarship for full-time students of metallurgy, materials science, chemical, mechanical, electrical, environmental, computer science, and industrial engineering. Students must have an interest in a career in the steel industry as demonstrated by an internship or related experience, or who have plans to pursue such experiences during college. Student may apply after first term of freshman year of college. Applications are accepted from 1 Sep through 31 Dec each year. Note: High school students do not qualify but are encouraged to learn about the steel industry and the career opportunities available therein, during their freshman year.

Academic Fields/Career Goals: Chemical Engineering; Civil Engineering; Electrical Engineering/Electronics; Engineering/Technology; Materials Science, Engineering, and Metallurgy.

Award: Scholarship for use in sophomore, junior, or senior years; not renewable. *Number:* 1. *Amount:* $3000.

Eligibility Requirements: Applicant must be Canadian citizen and enrolled or expecting to enroll full-time at a four-year institution or university. Applicant must have 2.5 GPA or higher.

Application Requirements: Application form, essay, recommendations or references, resume, transcript. *Deadline:* December 31.

Contact: Lori Wharrey, AIST Manager, Board Services
AIST Foundation
186 Thorn HIll Road
Warrendale, PA 15086
Phone: 724-814-3044
E-mail: lwharrey@aist.org

ASSOCIATION FOR IRON AND STEEL TECHNOLOGY WILLY KORF MEMORIAL SCHOLARSHIP

Scholarships are available for full-time students of metallurgy, chemical, materials science, mechanical, electrical, computer science, industrial and environmental engineering who have a genuine demonstrated interest in a career in the steel industry as demonstrated by an internship or related experience, or who have plans to pursue such experiences during college. Student may apply first during the freshman year of college. Applications are accepted 1 Sep through 31 Dec each year. Note: High school seniors are not eligible though are encouraged to learn and investigate the steel industry and the career opportunities available, during their freshman year.

Academic Fields/Career Goals: Chemical Engineering; Computer Science/Data Processing; Electrical Engineering/Electronics; Environmental Science; Industrial Design; Materials Science, Engineering, and Metallurgy; Mechanical Engineering.

Award: Scholarship for use in sophomore, junior, senior, or graduate years; not renewable. *Number:* 2. *Amount:* $3000.

Eligibility Requirements: Applicant must be enrolled or expecting to enroll full-time at a four-year institution or university. Applicant or parent of applicant must have employment or volunteer experience in engineering/technology. Applicant must have 2.5 GPA or higher. Available to U.S. and non-U.S. citizens.

Application Requirements: Application form, essay, recommendations or references, resume, transcript. *Deadline:* December 31.

Contact: Lori Wharrey, AIST Manager, Board Services
AIST Foundation
186 Thorn Hill Road
Warrendale, PA 15086
Phone: 724-814-3044 Ext. 621
E-mail: lwharrey@aist.org

AMERICAN CHEMICAL SOCIETY

http://www.acs.org/

AMERICAN CHEMICAL SOCIETY SCHOLARS PROGRAM

Renewable award for minority students pursuing studies in chemistry, biochemistry, chemical technology, chemical engineering, or chemical sciences. Must be U.S. citizen or permanent resident and have minimum 3.0 GPA. Must be Native American, African-American, or Hispanic.

Academic Fields/Career Goals: Chemical Engineering; Environmental Science; Materials Science, Engineering, and Metallurgy; Natural Sciences; Paper and Pulp Engineering; Trade/Technical Specialties.

Award: Scholarship for use in freshman, sophomore, or junior years; renewable. *Number:* 100–130. *Amount:* $1000–$5000.

Eligibility Requirements: Applicant must be American Indian/Alaska Native, Black (non-Hispanic), Hispanic and enrolled or expecting to enroll full-time at a two-year or four-year or technical institution or university. Applicant must have 3.0 GPA or higher. Available to U.S. citizens.

Application Requirements: Application form, financial need analysis. *Deadline:* March 1.

Contact: Dr. Racquel Jemison, Manager, ACS Scholars Program
American Chemical Society
1155 16th Street, NW
Washington, DC 20036
Phone: 202-872-6048
E-mail: scholars@acs.org

AMERICAN CHEMICAL SOCIETY, RUBBER DIVISION

http://www.rubber.org/

AMERICAN CHEMICAL SOCIETY, RUBBER DIVISION UNDERGRADUATE SCHOLARSHIP
• *See page 109*

AMERICAN COUNCIL OF ENGINEERING COMPANIES OF PENNSYLVANIA (ACEC/PA)

http://www.acecpa.org/

ERIC J. GENNUSO AND LEROY D. (BUD) LOY, JR. SCHOLARSHIP PROGRAM

Scholarship for full-time engineering students enrolled in accredited colleges or universities. Must be a Must be a United States Citizen. Must be a full-time sophomore or junior student as of the school year in which the scholarship is awarded, pursuing a bachelor degree in engineering or environmental sciences. Must meet at least one of these criteria: Attend a college or university located in Pennsylvania or be a Pennsylvania Resident. Up to three awards are granted annually.

Academic Fields/Career Goals: Chemical Engineering; Civil Engineering; Construction Engineering/Management; Electrical Engineering/Electronics; Energy and Power Engineering; Engineering-Related Technologies; Engineering/Technology; Environmental Science; Marine/Ocean Engineering; Materials Science, Engineering, and Metallurgy; Mechanical Engineering; Surveying, Surveying Technology, Cartography, or Geographic Information Science; Transportation.

Award: Scholarship for use in sophomore or junior years; not renewable. *Number:* 1–3. *Amount:* $2500–$5000.

Eligibility Requirements: Applicant must be enrolled or expecting to enroll full-time at a four-year institution or university and resident of Pennsylvania. Available to U.S. citizens.

Application Requirements: Application form, community service, essay. *Deadline:* May 15.

Contact: Jenna Earley, Director of Marketing
American Council of Engineering Companies of Pennsylvania (ACEC/PA)
800 N. 3rd Street
Suite 301
Harrisburg, PA 17102
Phone: 800-651-1946
E-mail: jearley@acecpa.org

AMERICAN INDIAN SCIENCE AND ENGINEERING SOCIETY

http://www.aises.org/

A.T. ANDERSON MEMORIAL SCHOLARSHIP PROGRAM
• *See page 109*

AMERICAN INSTITUTE OF CHEMICAL ENGINEERS

http://www.aiche.org/

CHEME-CAR NATIONAL LEVEL COMPETITION

Each student chapter region may send their first and second place winners to the design competition. Multiple entries from a single school may be permitted at the regional competitions, but only one entry per school is allowed at the national competition. Students majoring in chemical engineering can participate.

Academic Fields/Career Goals: Chemical Engineering.

Award: Prize for use in freshman, sophomore, junior, or senior years; not renewable. *Number:* up to 3. *Amount:* $200–$2000.

Eligibility Requirements: Applicant must be enrolled or expecting to enroll full-time at a four-year institution or university. Available to U.S. and non-U.S. citizens.

Application Requirements: Application form, entry in a contest, student chapter name, team contact, list of team members, title of entry, description of chemical reaction/drive system, list of chemicals to be used and estimated quantity needed. *Fee:* $100. *Deadline:* June 30.

Contact: Prof. David Dixon, Department of Chemistry and Chemical Engineering
American Institute of Chemical Engineers
South Dakota School of Mines and Technology
501 East Saint Joseph Street
Rapid City, SD 57701
Phone: 605-394-1235
Fax: 605-394-1232
E-mail: david.dixon@sdsmt.edu

DONALD F. AND MILDRED TOPP OTHMER FOUNDATION-NATIONAL SCHOLARSHIP AWARDS

Awards for 15 national AICHE student members, a scholarship of $1000. Awards are presented on the basis of academic achievement and involvement in student chapter activities. The student chapter advisor must make nominations. Only one nomination will be accepted from each AICHE student chapter or chemical engineering club.

Academic Fields/Career Goals: Chemical Engineering.

Award: Scholarship for use in freshman, sophomore, junior, senior, or graduate years; not renewable. *Number:* 15. *Amount:* $1000.

Eligibility Requirements: Applicant must be enrolled or expecting to enroll full-time at a four-year institution or university. Available to U.S. and non-U.S. citizens.

Application Requirements: Application form, essay, recommendations or references, statement of long-range career plans, transcript. *Deadline:* May 11.

Contact: AIChE Awards Administrator
American Institute of Chemical Engineers
Three Park Avenue
New York, NY 10016-5901
Phone: 212-591-7107
Fax: 212-591-8882
E-mail: awards@aiche.org

ENVIRONMENTAL DIVISION UNDERGRADUATE STUDENT PAPER AWARD

Cash prizes awarded to full-time undergraduate students who prepare the best original papers based on the results of research or an investigation related to the environment. The work must be performed during the student's undergraduate enrollment, and the paper must be submitted prior to or within six months of graduation. Student must be the sole author of the paper, but faculty guidance is encouraged. Student must be a member of the American Institute of Chemical Engineers Student Chapter.

Academic Fields/Career Goals: Chemical Engineering; Environmental Science.

Award: Prize for use in freshman, sophomore, junior, or senior years; not renewable. *Number:* 3. *Amount:* $100–$300.

Eligibility Requirements: Applicant must be enrolled or expecting to enroll full-time at a four-year institution or university. Available to U.S. and non-U.S. citizens.

Application Requirements: 5 copies of the nomination package, entry in a contest, essay, recommendations or references. *Deadline:* May 15.

Contact: Tapas Das, Environmental Division Awards Committee
American Institute of Chemical Engineers
125 Mandy Place, NE
Olympia, WA 98516
Phone: 360-456-0573
E-mail: shivaniki@comcast.net

JOHN J. MCKETTA UNDERGRADUATE SCHOLARSHIP

A $5000 scholarship will be awarded to a junior or senior student member of AICHE who is planning a career in the chemical engineering process industries. Must maintain a 3.0 GPA. Applicant should show leadership or activity in either the school's AICHE student chapter or other university sponsored campus activities. Must attend ABET-accredited school in the United States, Canada, or Mexico.

Academic Fields/Career Goals: Chemical Engineering.

Award: Scholarship for use in junior or senior years; not renewable. *Number:* 1. *Amount:* $5000.

Eligibility Requirements: Applicant must be enrolled or expecting to enroll full-time at a four-year institution or university and must have an interest in leadership. Applicant must have 3.0 GPA or higher. Available to U.S. and non-U.S. citizens.

Application Requirements: Application form, essay, recommendations or references. *Deadline:* May 25.

Contact: AIChE Awards Administrator
American Institute of Chemical Engineers
Three Park Avenue
New York, NY 10016
Phone: 212-591-7107
Fax: 212-591-8882
E-mail: awards@aiche.org

MINORITY AFFAIRS COMMITTEE AWARD FOR OUTSTANDING SCHOLASTIC ACHIEVEMENT

Award recognizing the outstanding achievements of a chemical engineering student who serves as a role model for minority students. Offers $1000 award and $500 travel allowance to attend AICHE meeting. Must be nominated.

Academic Fields/Career Goals: Chemical Engineering.

Award: Scholarship for use in freshman, sophomore, junior, senior, or graduate years; not renewable. *Number:* 1. *Amount:* $1500.

Eligibility Requirements: Applicant must be American Indian/Alaska Native, Asian/Pacific Islander, Black (non-Hispanic), Hispanic and enrolled or expecting to enroll full-time at a four-year institution or university. Applicant must have 3.0 GPA or higher. Available to U.S. and non-U.S. citizens.

Application Requirements: Application form. *Deadline:* May 15.

Contact: Dr. Emmanuel Dada, Scholarship Administrator
American Institute of Chemical Engineers
PO Box 8
Princeton, NJ 08543
Phone: 212-591-7107
E-mail: emmanuel_dada@fmc.com

MINORITY SCHOLARSHIP AWARDS FOR COLLEGE STUDENTS

Award for college undergraduates who are studying chemical engineering. Must be a member of a minority group that is underrepresented in chemical engineering. Must be an AICHE national student member at the time of application. Recipients of this scholarship are eligible to reapply.

Academic Fields/Career Goals: Chemical Engineering.

Award: Scholarship for use in freshman, sophomore, junior, or senior years; renewable. *Number:* up to 10. *Amount:* $1000.

Eligibility Requirements: Applicant must be American Indian/Alaska Native, Asian/Pacific Islander, Black (non-Hispanic), Hispanic and enrolled or expecting to enroll full-time at a two-year or four-year institution or university. Applicant must have 3.0 GPA or higher. Available to U.S. and non-U.S. citizens.

Application Requirements: Application form, career objective, essay, financial need analysis, recommendations or references, transcript. *Deadline:* May 15.

Contact: Dr. Emmanuel Dada, FMC Corporation
American Institute of Chemical Engineers
PO Box 8
Princeton, NJ 08543
Phone: 212-591-7107
E-mail: emmanuel_dada@fmc.com

MINORITY SCHOLARSHIP AWARDS FOR INCOMING COLLEGE FRESHMEN

Up to ten awards of $1000 for high school graduates who are members of a minority group that is underrepresented in chemical engineering.

Students must be high school seniors planning to enroll during the next academic year in a four-year college or university offering a science/engineering degree.

Academic Fields/Career Goals: Chemical Engineering.

Award: Scholarship for use in freshman year; not renewable. *Number:* up to 10. *Amount:* $1000.

Eligibility Requirements: Applicant must be American Indian/Alaska Native, Asian/Pacific Islander, Black (non-Hispanic), Hispanic; high school student and planning to enroll or expecting to enroll full-time at a four-year institution or university. Applicant must have 3.0 GPA or higher. Available to U.S. and non-U.S. citizens.

Application Requirements: Application form, confirmation of minority status, essay, financial need analysis, recommendations or references, transcript. *Deadline:* May 15.

Contact: Dr. Emmanuel Dada, Minority Affairs Committee
American Institute of Chemical Engineers
PO Box 8
Princeton, NJ 08543
Phone: 212-591-7107
E-mail: emmanuel_dada@fmc.com

NATIONAL STUDENT DESIGN COMPETITION-INDIVIDUAL

Three cash prizes for student contest problem that typifies a real, working, chemical engineering design situation. Competition statements are distributed online to student chapter advisors and department heads.

Academic Fields/Career Goals: Chemical Engineering.

Award: Prize for use in freshman, sophomore, junior, senior, or graduate years; not renewable. *Number:* 3. *Amount:* $200–$500.

Eligibility Requirements: Applicant must be enrolled or expecting to enroll full-time at a four-year institution or university. Available to U.S. and non-U.S. citizens.

Application Requirements: Entry in a contest, essay. *Deadline:* June 6.

Contact: AIChE Awards Administrator
American Institute of Chemical Engineers
Three Park Avenue
New York, NY 10016
Phone: 212-591-7107
Fax: 212-591-8882
E-mail: awards@aiche.org

NATIONAL STUDENT PAPER COMPETITION

First place winners from each of the nine regional student paper competitions present their prize-winning papers during the American Institute of Chemical Engineers meeting held in the current calendar year. First prize is $500, second prize is $300, and third prize is $200.

Academic Fields/Career Goals: Chemical Engineering.

Award: Prize for use in freshman, sophomore, junior, senior, or graduate years; not renewable. *Number:* 3. *Amount:* $200–$500.

Eligibility Requirements: Applicant must be enrolled or expecting to enroll full-time at a four-year institution or university. Available to U.S. and non-U.S. citizens.

Application Requirements: Entry in a contest, student paper. *Deadline:* varies.

Contact: AIChE Awards Administrator
American Institute of Chemical Engineers
Three Park Avenue
New York, NY 10016-5901
Phone: 212-591-7107
Fax: 212-591-8882
E-mail: awards@aiche.org

OUTSTANDING STUDENT CHAPTER ADVISOR AWARD

Award for service and leadership in guiding the activities of an AIChE student chapter in accordance with AIChE principles. Must be advisor of a chartered AIChE student chapter for at least the last three years. Award winners cannot be renominated.

Academic Fields/Career Goals: Chemical Engineering.

Award: Prize for use in freshman, sophomore, junior, or senior years; not renewable. *Number:* 1. *Amount:* up to $1000.

Eligibility Requirements: Applicant must be enrolled or expecting to enroll full-time at a four-year institution or university. Available to U.S. and non-U.S. citizens.

Application Requirements: 4 copies of the nomination, application form, recommendations or references. *Deadline:* June 1.

Contact: Marvin Borgmeyer, Scholarship Committee
American Institute of Chemical Engineers
PO Box 1607
Baton Rouge, LA 70821-1607
Phone: 225-977-6206
Fax: 225-977-6396

PROCESS DEVELOPMENT DIVISION STUDENT PAPER AWARD

Award presented to a full-time graduate or undergraduate student who prepares the best technical paper to describe the results of process development related studies within chemical engineering. Must be carried out while the student is enrolled at a university with an accredited chemical engineering program. Student must be the primary author. Paper must be suitable for publication in a refereed journal. Must be a member of AIChE.

Academic Fields/Career Goals: Chemical Engineering.

Award: Prize for use in freshman, sophomore, junior, senior, or graduate years; not renewable. *Number:* 1. *Amount:* $200.

Eligibility Requirements: Applicant must be enrolled or expecting to enroll full-time at a four-year institution or university. Available to U.S. and non-U.S. citizens.

Application Requirements: Original and five copies of the nomination form, recommendations or references. *Deadline:* June 15.

Contact: A.R. Cartolano, Awards Committee Chair
American Institute of Chemical Engineers
7201 Hamilton Boulevard
Allentown, PA 18195-1501
Phone: 610-481-4262
E-mail: cartolar@airproducts.com

REGIONAL STUDENT PAPER COMPETITION

Students present technical papers at the student regional conferences which are held during spring. Deadlines for regional conferences vary. First prize is $200, second prize is $100, and third prize is $50. First place winner from each region present their paper at the regional competition.

Academic Fields/Career Goals: Chemical Engineering.

Award: Prize for use in freshman, sophomore, junior, or senior years; not renewable. *Number:* 3. *Amount:* $50–$200.

Eligibility Requirements: Applicant must be enrolled or expecting to enroll full-time at a four-year institution or university. Available to U.S. and non-U.S. citizens.

Application Requirements: Entry in a contest, student paper. *Deadline:* varies.

Contact: AIChE Awards Administrator
American Institute of Chemical Engineers
Three Park Avenue
New York, NY 10016-5901
Phone: 212-591-7107
Fax: 212-591-8882
E-mail: awards@aiche.org

SAFETY AND CHEMICAL ENGINEERING EDUCATION (SACHE) STUDENT ESSAY AWARD FOR SAFETY

Awards individuals or a team submitting the best essays on the topic of chemical process safety. Essays may focus on process safety in education, relevance of safety in undergraduate education, or integrating safety principles into the undergraduate chemical engineering curriculum.

Academic Fields/Career Goals: Chemical Engineering.

Award: Prize for use in freshman, sophomore, junior, or senior years; not renewable. *Number:* up to 4. *Amount:* $500.

Eligibility Requirements: Applicant must be enrolled or expecting to enroll full-time at a four-year institution or university. Available to U.S. and non-U.S. citizens.

Application Requirements: Entry in a contest, essay. *Deadline:* June 5.

Contact: AIChE Awards Administrator
American Institute of Chemical Engineers
Three Park Avenue
New York, NY 10016
Phone: 212-591-7107
Fax: 212-591-8880
E-mail: awards@aiche.org

SAFETY AND HEALTH NATIONAL STUDENT DESIGN COMPETITION AWARD FOR SAFETY

Four $600 awards available for each of the teams or individuals who apply one or more of the following concepts of inherent safety in their designs: design the plant for easier and effective maintainability; design the plant with less waste; design the plant with special features that demonstrate inherent safety; include design concepts regarding the entire life cycle. The school must have a student chapter of AIChE.

Academic Fields/Career Goals: Chemical Engineering; Industrial Design.

Award: Prize for use in freshman, sophomore, junior, senior, or graduate years; not renewable. *Number:* 4. *Amount:* $600.

Eligibility Requirements: Applicant must be enrolled or expecting to enroll full- or part-time at a four-year institution or university. Available to U.S. and non-U.S. citizens.

Application Requirements: Application form, design. *Deadline:* June 6.

Contact: AIChE Awards Administrator
American Institute of Chemical Engineers
Three Park Avenue
New York, NY 10016
Phone: 212-591-7478
Fax: 212-591-8882
E-mail: awards@aiche.org

AMERICAN OIL CHEMISTS' SOCIETY

http://www.aocs.org/

AOCS ANALYTICAL DIVISION STUDENT AWARD

$250 prize, $500 travel funding and certificate to recognize an outstanding graduate student's presentation in the field of lipid analytical chemistry at the Society's annual meeting.

Academic Fields/Career Goals: Chemical Engineering; Food Science/Nutrition.

Award: Prize for use in junior, senior, or graduate years; not renewable. *Number:* 1–2. *Amount:* $250–$750.

Eligibility Requirements: Applicant must be enrolled or expecting to enroll full- or part-time at a four-year institution or university. Available to U.S. and non-U.S. citizens.

Application Requirements: Abstract, application form, essay, recommendations or references. *Deadline:* October 15.

Contact: Barbara Semeraro, Area Manager, Membership
American Oil Chemists' Society
AOCS
PO Box 17190
Urbana, IL 61803
Phone: 217-693-4804
Fax: 217-693-4849
E-mail: awards@aocs.org

AOCS BIOTECHNOLOGY STUDENT EXCELLENCE AWARD

• *See page 97*

AOCS PROCESSING DIVISION AWARDS

Award and certificate to recognize graduate students presenting an outstanding paper at the Society's annual meeting. All graduate students presenting a paper at any of the AOCS Annual Meeting Processing Division sessions are eligible for the award.

Academic Fields/Career Goals: Chemical Engineering; Food Science/Nutrition.

Award: Prize for use in junior, senior, or graduate years; not renewable. *Number:* 1. *Amount:* $1000.

Eligibility Requirements: Applicant must be enrolled or expecting to enroll full-time at a four-year institution or university. Available to U.S. and non-U.S. citizens.

Application Requirements: Essay, extended abstract, recommendations or references. *Deadline:* February 1.

Contact: Barbara Semeraro, Area Manager, Membership
American Oil Chemists' Society
AOCS
PO Box 17190
Urbana, IL 61803
Phone: 217-693-4804
Fax: 217-693-4849
E-mail: awards@aocs.org

AMERICAN PUBLIC POWER ASSOCIATION
http://publicpower.org/DEED

DEED EDUCATIONAL SCHOLARSHIP

This scholarship targets students who are pursuing a major that could lead to an electric utility career. Applicants must be sponsored by a DEED member utility and attend an accredited university/college full-time in the U.S. Email DEED@publicpower.org for access to the application. Application deadline: Feb. 15 and Oct. 15 annually.

Academic Fields/Career Goals: Chemical Engineering; Civil Engineering; Construction Engineering/Management; Electrical Engineering/Electronics; Energy and Power Engineering; Engineering-Related Technologies; Engineering/Technology; Environmental Science; Mechanical Engineering; Natural Resources.

Award: Scholarship for use in freshman, sophomore, junior, or senior years; not renewable. *Number:* 10. *Amount:* $2000.

Eligibility Requirements: Applicant must be enrolled or expecting to enroll full-time at a two-year or four-year or technical institution or university. Available to U.S. and non-U.S. citizens.

Application Requirements: Application form, essay. *Deadline:* continuous.

Contact: Richelle Dodds, DEED and Engineering Services Coordinator
E-mail: DEED@publicpower.org

DEED STUDENT INTERNSHIP

The Student Internships are paid and provide work experience at a DEED member electric utility. Applicants must be sponsored by a DEED member utility and attend an accredited university/college full-time in the U.S. Email DEED@publicpower.org for access to the application. Application deadline is Feb. 15 and Oct. 15 annually.

Academic Fields/Career Goals: Chemical Engineering; Civil Engineering; Construction Engineering/Management; Electrical Engineering/Electronics; Energy and Power Engineering; Engineering-Related Technologies; Engineering/Technology; Environmental Science; Mechanical Engineering; Natural Resources.

Award: Scholarship for use in freshman, sophomore, junior, senior, graduate, or postgraduate years; not renewable. *Number:* 10. *Amount:* $5000.

Eligibility Requirements: Applicant must be enrolled or expecting to enroll full-time at a two-year or four-year or technical institution or university. Available to U.S. and non-U.S. citizens.

Application Requirements: Application form. *Deadline:* continuous.

Contact: Richelle Dodds, DEED and Engineering Services Coordinator
E-mail: DEED@publicpower.org

DEED TECHNICAL DESIGN PROJECT

The Technical Design Project (TDP) provides funding to support students working on a technical project of interest to electric utilities. Applicants must attend an accredited university/college full-time in the U.S. Email DEED@publicpower.org for access to the application. Application deadline is Oct. 15 annually.

Academic Fields/Career Goals: Chemical Engineering; Civil Engineering; Construction Engineering/Management; Electrical Engineering/Electronics; Energy and Power Engineering; Engineering-Related Technologies; Engineering/Technology; Environmental Science; Mechanical Engineering; Natural Resources.

Award: Scholarship for use in junior, senior, or graduate years; not renewable. *Number:* 1. *Amount:* $8000.

Eligibility Requirements: Applicant must be enrolled or expecting to enroll full-time at a two-year or four-year or technical institution or university. Available to U.S. and non-U.S. citizens.

Application Requirements: Application form. *Deadline:* October 15.

Contact: Richelle Dodds, DEED and Engineering Services Coordinator
E-mail: DEED@publicpower.org

AMERICAN SOCIETY FOR ENOLOGY AND VITICULTURE
http://www.asev.org/

AMERICAN SOCIETY FOR ENOLOGY AND VITICULTURE SCHOLARSHIPS
• *See page 97*

AMERICAN SOCIETY OF CERTIFIED ENGINEERING TECHNICIANS
http://www.ascet.org/

KURT H. AND DONNA M. SCHULER SMALL GRANT

The small cash grant program was suggested by students and faculty advisors who recommended that several grants be awarded to deserving students and that these awards carry as few restrictions as possible. Each award shall be in the amount of $400 to be used to offset the cost of educational expenses as desired. Such grants may be awarded to one or more students each year. Must be either a student, certified, regular, registered or associate member of ASCET, or be a high school senior in the last five months of the academic year who will be enrolled in an Engineering Technology curriculum no later than six months following selection for award; and achieve passing grades in their present curriculum.

Academic Fields/Career Goals: Chemical Engineering; Civil Engineering; Construction Engineering/Management; Drafting; Electrical Engineering/Electronics; Energy and Power Engineering; Engineering-Related Technologies; Engineering/Technology; Fire Sciences; Landscape Architecture; Marine/Ocean Engineering; Materials Science, Engineering, and Metallurgy; Mechanical Engineering; Surveying, Surveying Technology, Cartography, or Geographic Information Science; Trade/Technical Specialties; Transportation.

Award: Grant for use in freshman, sophomore, junior, or senior years; not renewable. *Number:* 1–4. *Amount:* $400.

Eligibility Requirements: Applicant must be enrolled or expecting to enroll full- or part-time at a two-year or four-year or technical institution or university. Available to U.S. citizens.

Application Requirements: Application form. *Deadline:* April 1.

Contact: Mr. Larry Killer, General Manager
American Society of Certified Engineering Technicians
15621 W. 87th St Pkwy
#205
Lenexa, KS 66219
Phone: 773-242-7238
Fax: 913-890-1021
E-mail: office@ascet.org

AMERICAN SOCIETY OF HEATING, REFRIGERATING, AND AIR CONDITIONING ENGINEERS, INC.
http://www.ashrae.org/

ASHRAE REGION III BOGGARM SETTY SCHOLARSHIP

One $3,000 scholarship for an undergraduate pre-engineering or engineering student enrolled full time in a post-secondary educational institution within the geographic boundaries of ASHRAE Region III (Delaware, Maryland, Pennsylvania, Virginia, Washington, DC). Minimum 3.0 GPA required.

Academic Fields/Career Goals: Chemical Engineering; Construction Engineering/Management; Electrical Engineering/Electronics; Energy and Power Engineering; Engineering-Related Technologies; Engineering/Technology; Mechanical Engineering; Paper and Pulp Engineering.

Award: Scholarship for use in freshman, sophomore, junior, or senior years; not renewable. *Number:* 1. *Amount:* $3000.

Eligibility Requirements: Applicant must be enrolled or expecting to enroll full-time at a four-year institution or university and studying in

Delaware, District of Columbia, Maryland, Pennsylvania, Virginia. Applicant must have 3.0 GPA or higher. Available to U.S. citizens.

Application Requirements: Application form, financial need analysis. *Deadline:* December 1.

Contact: Lois Benedict, Scholarship Administrator
Phone: 404-636-8400 Ext. 1120
E-mail: lbenedict@ashrae.org

ARRL FOUNDATION INC.

http://www.arrl.org/

ALFRED E. FRIEND JR, W4CF, MEMORIAL SCHOLARSHIP

One $5000 scholarship for a student with active Amateur Radio license who is studying any field in engineering.

Academic Fields/Career Goals: Chemical Engineering; Civil Engineering; Construction Engineering/Management; Electrical Engineering/Electronics; Energy and Power Engineering; Engineering/Technology; Marine/Ocean Engineering; Materials Science, Engineering, and Metallurgy; Mechanical Engineering; Paper and Pulp Engineering.

Award: Scholarship for use in freshman, sophomore, junior, or senior years; not renewable. *Number:* 1. *Amount:* $5000.

Eligibility Requirements: Applicant must be enrolled or expecting to enroll full- or part-time at a two-year or four-year or technical institution or university and must have an interest in amateur radio. Available to U.S. citizens.

Application Requirements: Application form. *Deadline:* January 31.

Contact: Ms. Mary Hobart, Secretary
Phone: 860-594-0397
E-mail: k1mmh@arrl.org

GARY WAGNER, K3OMI, SCHOLARSHIP

One $1000 award available to student who possesses a novice class or higher amateur radio license and who is or will be attending a four-year college or university. Must be a U.S. citizen and resident of North Carolina, Virginia, West Virginia, Maryland, or Tennessee and studying toward a Bachelor of science degree in any field of engineering. Financial need must be demonstrated.

Academic Fields/Career Goals: Chemical Engineering; Civil Engineering; Construction Engineering/Management; Electrical Engineering/Electronics; Energy and Power Engineering; Engineering-Related Technologies; Engineering/Technology; Materials Science, Engineering, and Metallurgy; Mechanical Engineering.

Award: Scholarship for use in freshman, sophomore, junior, or senior years; not renewable. *Number:* 1. *Amount:* $1000.

Eligibility Requirements: Applicant must be enrolled or expecting to enroll full- or part-time at a four-year institution or university; resident of Maryland, North Carolina, Tennessee, Virginia, West Virginia and must have an interest in amateur radio. Available to U.S. citizens.

Application Requirements: Application form, financial need analysis. *Deadline:* January 31.

Contact: Ms. Mary Hobart, Secretary
Phone: 860-594-0397
E-mail: k1mmh@arrl.org

W1FDR SCHOLARSHIP
• *See page 112*

ASSOCIATION ON AMERICAN INDIAN AFFAIRS, INC.

http://www.indian-affairs.org/

ELIZABETH AND SHERMAN ASCHE MEMORIAL SCHOLARSHIP FUND
• *See page 98*

ASTRONAUT SCHOLARSHIP FOUNDATION

http://www.astronautscholarship.org/

ASTRONAUT SCHOLARSHIP FOUNDATION
• *See page 112*

AUTOMOTIVE WOMEN'S ALLIANCE FOUNDATION

http://www.awafoundation.org/index.php

AUTOMOTIVE WOMEN'S ALLIANCE FOUNDATION SCHOLARSHIPS
• *See page 74*

BARRY GOLDWATER SCHOLARSHIP AND EXCELLENCE IN EDUCATION FOUNDATION

https://goldwater.scholarsapply.org

BARRY M. GOLDWATER SCHOLARSHIP AND EXCELLENCE IN EDUCATION PROGRAM
• *See page 112*

BHW GROUP

https://thebhwgroup.com/

BHW WOMEN IN STEM SCHOLARSHIP
• *See page 74*

B.O.G. PEST CONTROL

http://www.bogpestcontrol.com/

B.O.G. PEST CONTROL SCHOLARSHIP FUND
• *See page 155*

BRASKEM ODEBRECHT

http://www.odebrechtaward.com

ODEBRECHT AWARD FOR SUSTAINABLE DEVELOPMENT
• *See page 119*

BROWN AND CALDWELL

http://www.brownandcaldwell.com

ECKENFELDER SCHOLARSHIP
• *See page 155*

MINORITY SCHOLARSHIP PROGRAM
• *See page 155*

COMPHEALTH

http://www.comphealth.com

COMPHEALTH MEDICAL SCHOLARSHIP
• *See page 151*

THE ELECTROCHEMICAL SOCIETY

http://www.electrochem.org/

H.H. DOW MEMORIAL STUDENT ACHIEVEMENT AWARD OF THE INDUSTRIAL ELECTROLYSIS AND

ELECTROCHEMICAL ENGINEERING DIVISION OF THE ELECTROCHEMICAL SOCIETY INC.
• *See page 113*

STUDENT RESEARCH AWARDS OF THE BATTERY DIVISION OF THE ELECTROCHEMICAL SOCIETY INC.
• *See page 113*

ENGINEERS' SOCIETY OF WESTERN PENNSYLVANIA

http://www.eswp.com/

JOSEPH A. LEVENDUSKY MEMORIAL SCHOLARSHIP

Scholarship of up to $7000 awarded to an undergraduate student in mechanical or chemical engineering. Must be accepted or enrolled in good standing as a student at an accredited institution.

Academic Fields/Career Goals: Chemical Engineering; Mechanical Engineering.

Award: Scholarship for use in sophomore, junior, or senior years; not renewable. *Number:* 1. *Amount:* $7000.

Eligibility Requirements: Applicant must be enrolled or expecting to enroll full-time at a four-year institution or university. Available to U.S. citizens.

Application Requirements: Application form, application form may be submitted online (http://www.eswp.com/water), essay, financial need analysis, recommendations or references, resume, transcript. *Deadline:* September 7.

Contact: Stephanie Mueller, Conference Manager
Engineers' Society of Western Pennsylvania
337 Fourth Avenue
Pittsburgh, PA 15222
Phone: 412-261-0710
Fax: 412-261-1606
E-mail: s.mueller@eswp.com

FABRICATORS AND MANUFACTURERS ASSOCIATION FOUNDATION

http://www.nutsandboltsfoundation.org/scholarships/

COLLEGE AND TRADE/TECHNICAL SCHOOL SCHOLARSHIPS

Nuts, Bolts & Thingamajigs®, The Foundation of the Fabricators & Manufacturers Association, Intl. (NBT) Through its manufacturing summer camps and scholarships, NBT is inspiring the next generation of manufacturers, inventors and entrepreneurs.

Academic Fields/Career Goals: Chemical Engineering; Civil Engineering; Electrical Engineering/Electronics; Engineering/Technology; Heating, Air-Conditioning, and Refrigeration Mechanics; Marine/Ocean Engineering; Materials Science, Engineering, and Metallurgy; Mechanical Engineering; Trade/Technical Specialties.

Award: Scholarship for use in freshman, sophomore, junior, or senior years; not renewable. *Amount:* $2500.

Eligibility Requirements: Applicant must be enrolled or expecting to enroll full-time at a technical institution or university. Applicant must have 2.5 GPA or higher. Available to U.S. and Canadian citizens.

Application Requirements: Application form, essay. *Deadline:* March 31.

FLORIDA ENGINEERING SOCIETY

http://www.fleng.org/scholarships.cfm

DAVID F. LUDOVICI SCHOLARSHIP

One-time scholarship of $1000 given to students in their junior or senior year in any Florida university engineering program, with at least 3.0 GPA. Applicants must be interested in civil, structural, or consulting engineering.

Academic Fields/Career Goals: Chemical Engineering; Civil Engineering; Construction Engineering/Management; Electrical Engineering/Electronics; Energy and Power Engineering; Engineering-Related Technologies; Engineering/Technology.

Award: Scholarship for use in junior or senior years; not renewable. *Number:* 1. *Amount:* $1000.

Eligibility Requirements: Applicant must be enrolled or expecting to enroll full-time at an institution or university; resident of Florida and studying in Florida. Applicant must have 3.0 GPA or higher. Available to U.S. citizens.

Application Requirements: Application form. *Deadline:* February 1.

Contact: Amanda Hudson, Director of Information Technology
Florida Engineering Society
125 South Gadsden Street
Tallahassee, FL 32301
Phone: 850-224-7121
E-mail: ahudson@fleng.org

FOUNDATION FOR SCIENCE AND DISABILITY

http://stemd.org/

GRANTS FOR DISABLED GRADUATE STUDENTS IN THE SCIENCES
• *See page 113*

GREATER KANAWHA VALLEY FOUNDATION

http://www.tgkvf.org/

STEVEN ENGINEERING SCHOLARSHIP

Renewable award for a West Virginia resident pursuing full-time postsecondary studies in engineering. Preference given to students at West Virginia University Institute of Technology or West Virginia University. Minimum 2.5 GPA required.

Academic Fields/Career Goals: Chemical Engineering; Construction Engineering/Management; Electrical Engineering/Electronics; Energy and Power Engineering; Engineering/Technology; Marine/Ocean Engineering; Materials Science, Engineering, and Metallurgy; Mechanical Engineering; Paper and Pulp Engineering.

Award: Scholarship for use in freshman, sophomore, junior, or senior years; renewable. *Amount:* $550.

Eligibility Requirements: Applicant must be enrolled or expecting to enroll full-time at a four-year institution or university and resident of West Virginia. Applicant must have 2.5 GPA or higher. Available to U.S. citizens.

Application Requirements: Application form, recommendations or references, transcript. *Deadline:* January 15.

Contact: Susan Hoover, Scholarship Program Officer
Greater Kanawha Valley Foundation
900 Lee Street East, 16th Floor
Charleston, WV 25301
Phone: 304-346-3620
E-mail: shoover@tgkvf.org

GREAT MINDS IN STEM

www.greatmindsinstem.org

HISPANIC ENGINEER NATIONAL ACHIEVEMENT AWARDS CORPORATION SCHOLARSHIP PROGRAM
• *See page 106*

INDEPENDENT LABORATORIES INSTITUTE SCHOLARSHIP ALLIANCE

http://www.acil.org/

INDEPENDENT LABORATORIES INSTITUTE SCHOLARSHIP ALLIANCE
• *See page 156*

INTERNATIONAL SOCIETY FOR OPTICAL ENGINEERING-SPIE

http://www.spie.org/scholarships

SPIE EDUCATIONAL SCHOLARSHIPS IN OPTICAL SCIENCE AND ENGINEERING
• *See page 114*

JORGE MAS CANOSA FREEDOM FOUNDATION

http://masscholarships.org/

MAS FAMILY SCHOLARSHIP AWARD
• *See page 165*

KENTUCKY ENERGY AND ENVIRONMENT CABINET

http://dep.ky.gov

ENVIRONMENTAL PROTECTION SCHOLARSHIP
• *See page 157*

LOS ANGELES COUNCIL OF BLACK PROFESSIONAL ENGINEERS

http://www.lablackengineers.org/

AL-BEN SCHOLARSHIP FOR ACADEMIC INCENTIVE

One-time scholarship for students enrolled full-time with scholastic achievements in the academic pursuits of engineering, math, computer or scientific studies. Must be from a minority group. Scholarship value is $500 to $1000. Two scholarships are granted annually. Preference given to residents of Southern California.

Academic Fields/Career Goals: Chemical Engineering; Civil Engineering; Computer Science/Data Processing; Electrical Engineering/Electronics; Engineering-Related Technologies; Engineering/Technology; Materials Science, Engineering, and Metallurgy; Mechanical Engineering; Physical Sciences.

Award: Scholarship for use in freshman, sophomore, junior, or senior years; not renewable. *Number:* 2. *Amount:* $500–$1000.

Eligibility Requirements: Applicant must be American Indian/Alaska Native, Asian/Pacific Islander, Black (non-Hispanic), Hispanic and enrolled or expecting to enroll full-time at a four-year institution or university. Available to U.S. citizens.

Application Requirements: Application form, essay, recommendations or references, transcript. *Deadline:* April 2.

Contact: Leroy Freelon, President
 Phone: 310-635-7734
 E-mail: lfreelonjr@aol.com

AL-BEN SCHOLARSHIP FOR PROFESSIONAL MERIT

One-time scholarship for students enrolled full-time with scholastic achievements in the academic pursuits of engineering, math, computer or scientific studies. Must be from a minority group. Scholarship value is $500 to $1000. Two scholarships are granted annually. Preference given to residents of Southern California.

Academic Fields/Career Goals: Chemical Engineering; Civil Engineering; Computer Science/Data Processing; Electrical Engineering/Electronics; Engineering-Related Technologies; Engineering/Technology; Materials Science, Engineering, and Metallurgy; Mechanical Engineering; Physical Sciences.

Award: Scholarship for use in freshman, sophomore, junior, or senior years; not renewable. *Number:* 2. *Amount:* $500–$1000.

Eligibility Requirements: Applicant must be American Indian/Alaska Native, Asian/Pacific Islander, Black (non-Hispanic), Hispanic and enrolled or expecting to enroll full-time at a four-year institution or university. Available to U.S. citizens.

Application Requirements: Application form, essay, recommendations or references, transcript. *Deadline:* April 2.

Contact: Leroy Freelon, President
 Phone: 310-635-7734
 E-mail: lfreelonjr@aol.com

AL-BEN SCHOLARSHIP FOR SCHOLASTIC ACHIEVEMENT

Scholarships for students enrolled full-time with scholastic achievements in the academic pursuits of engineering, math, computer or scientific studies. Must be from a minority group.

Academic Fields/Career Goals: Chemical Engineering; Civil Engineering; Computer Science/Data Processing; Electrical Engineering/Electronics; Engineering-Related Technologies; Engineering/Technology; Materials Science, Engineering, and Metallurgy; Mechanical Engineering; Physical Sciences.

Award: Scholarship for use in freshman, sophomore, junior, or senior years; not renewable. *Number:* 2. *Amount:* $500–$1000.

Eligibility Requirements: Applicant must be American Indian/Alaska Native, Asian/Pacific Islander, Black (non-Hispanic), Hispanic and enrolled or expecting to enroll full-time at a four-year institution or university. Available to U.S. citizens.

Application Requirements: Application form, essay, recommendations or references, transcript. *Deadline:* April 2.

Contact: Leroy Freelon, President
 Phone: 310-635-7734
 E-mail: lfreelonjr@aol.com

MEDICAL SCRUBS COLLECTION

http://medicalscrubscollection.com

MEDICAL SCRUBS COLLECTION SCHOLARSHIP
• *See page 106*

NASA IDAHO SPACE GRANT CONSORTIUM

http://www.id.spacegrant.org/

NASA IDAHO SPACE GRANT CONSORTIUM SCHOLARSHIP PROGRAM
• *See page 157*

NASA/MARYLAND SPACE GRANT CONSORTIUM

http://md.spacegrant.org/

NASA MARYLAND SPACE GRANT CONSORTIUM UNDERGRADUATE SCHOLARSHIPS
• *See page 142*

NASA MONTANA SPACE GRANT CONSORTIUM

http://www.spacegrant.montana.edu/

MONTANA SPACE GRANT SCHOLARSHIP PROGRAM
• *See page 142*

NASA'S VIRGINIA SPACE GRANT CONSORTIUM

http://www.vsgc.odu.edu/

UNDERGRADUATE STEM RESEARCH SCHOLARSHIPS
• *See page 114*

NATIONAL ASSOCIATION FOR THE ADVANCEMENT OF COLORED PEOPLE

http://www.naacp.org/

HUBERTUS W.V. WELLEMS SCHOLARSHIP FOR MALE STUDENTS

Scholarship for a male, full-time student, majoring in engineering, chemistry, physics, or mathematical sciences. Graduate student may be full- or part-time and have 2.5 minimum GPA. Graduating high school seniors and undergraduates must have 3.0 minimum GPA. Must demonstrate financial need. Undergraduate scholarship is $2000; and graduate scholarship is $3000.

Academic Fields/Career Goals: Chemical Engineering; Engineering-Related Technologies; Engineering/Technology; Physical Sciences.

Award: Scholarship for use in freshman, sophomore, junior, senior, or graduate years; not renewable. *Number:* 1. *Amount:* $2000–$3000.

Eligibility Requirements: Applicant must be American Indian/Alaska Native, Asian/Pacific Islander, Black (non-Hispanic), Hispanic; enrolled or expecting to enroll full- or part-time at a two-year or four-year institution or university and male. Applicant or parent of applicant must be member of National Association for the Advancement of Colored People. Applicant must have 3.0 GPA or higher. Available to U.S. citizens.

Application Requirements: Application form, financial need analysis, recommendations or references, transcript. *Deadline:* March 7.

Contact: Victor Goode, Attorney
Phone: 410-580-5760
E-mail: info@naacp.org

NATIONAL ASSOCIATION OF WATER COMPANIES-NEW JERSEY CHAPTER

http://www.nawc.org

NATIONAL ASSOCIATION OF WATER COMPANIES-NEW JERSEY CHAPTER SCHOLARSHIP

• See page 80

NATIONAL BOARD OF BOILER AND PRESSURE VESSEL INSPECTORS

http://www.nationalboard.org/

NATIONAL BOARD TECHNICAL SCHOLARSHIP

Two $6000 scholarships to selected students meeting eligibility standards, who are pursuing a Bachelor's degree in certain engineering or related studies. Must be a child, step-child, grandchild, or great-grandchild of a past or present National Board member (living or deceased), or of a past or present Commissioned Inspector (living or deceased), employed by a member jurisdiction, or of a past or present National Board employee (living or deceased).

Academic Fields/Career Goals: Chemical Engineering; Electrical Engineering/Electronics; Mechanical Engineering.

Award: Scholarship for use in freshman, sophomore, junior, or senior years; not renewable. *Number:* 2. *Amount:* $6000.

Eligibility Requirements: Applicant must be enrolled or expecting to enroll full-time at a four-year or technical institution or university. Applicant or parent of applicant must be member of National Board of Boiler and Pressure Vessel Inspectors. Applicant must have 3.0 GPA or higher. Available to U.S. and Canadian citizens.

Application Requirements: Application form, essay, recommendations or references, transcript. *Deadline:* February 28.

Contact: Donald Tanner, Executive Director
Phone: 614-888-8320
Fax: 614-888-0750
E-mail: dtanner@nationalboard.org

NATIONAL SOCIETY OF PROFESSIONAL ENGINEERS

http://www.nspe.org/

MAUREEN L. AND HOWARD N. BLITMAN, PE SCHOLARSHIP TO PROMOTE DIVERSITY IN ENGINEERING

Award of $5000 in two disbursements of $2500 to a high school senior from an ethnic minority who has been accepted into an ABET-accredited engineering program at a four-year college or university.

Academic Fields/Career Goals: Chemical Engineering; Civil Engineering; Electrical Engineering/Electronics; Engineering-Related Technologies; Engineering/Technology; Materials Science, Engineering, and Metallurgy; Mechanical Engineering.

Award: Scholarship for use in freshman year; not renewable. *Number:* 1. *Amount:* $5000.

Eligibility Requirements: Applicant must be American Indian/Alaska Native, Black (non-Hispanic), Hispanic; high school student and planning to enroll or expecting to enroll full-time at a four-year institution or university. Applicant must have 2.5 GPA or higher. Available to U.S. citizens.

Application Requirements: Application form, community service, essay, recommendations or references, test scores, transcript. *Deadline:* March 1.

Contact: Cindy Simpson, Director of Education
Phone: 703-684-2833
E-mail: csimpson@nspe.org

PAUL H. ROBBINS HONORARY SCHOLARSHIP

Awarded annually to a current engineering undergraduate student entering the junior year in an ABET-accredited engineering program and attending a college/university that participates in the NSPE Professional Engineers in Higher Education (PEHE) Sustaining University Program(SUP).

Academic Fields/Career Goals: Chemical Engineering; Civil Engineering; Electrical Engineering/Electronics; Engineering-Related Technologies; Engineering/Technology; Materials Science, Engineering, and Metallurgy; Mechanical Engineering.

Award: Scholarship for use in junior year; renewable. *Number:* 1. *Amount:* $5000.

Eligibility Requirements: Applicant must be enrolled or expecting to enroll full-time at a four-year institution or university. Applicant or parent of applicant must be member of National Society of Professional Engineers. Available to U.S. citizens.

Application Requirements: Application form, essay, recommendations or references, test scores, transcript. *Deadline:* March 1.

Contact: Cindy Simpson, Director of Education
Phone: 703-684-2833
E-mail: csimpson@nspe.org

PROFESSIONAL ENGINEERS IN INDUSTRY SCHOLARSHIP

Applicants must be sponsored by an NSPE/PEI member. Students must have completed a minimum of two semesters or three quarters of undergraduate engineering studies (or be enrolled in graduate study) accredited by ABET.

Academic Fields/Career Goals: Chemical Engineering; Civil Engineering; Electrical Engineering/Electronics; Engineering-Related Technologies; Engineering/Technology; Materials Science, Engineering, and Metallurgy; Mechanical Engineering.

Award: Scholarship for use in sophomore, junior, or senior years; not renewable. *Number:* 1. *Amount:* $2500.

Eligibility Requirements: Applicant must be enrolled or expecting to enroll full-time at a four-year institution or university. Applicant must have 3.5 GPA or higher. Available to U.S. citizens.

Application Requirements: Application form, community service, essay, recommendations or references, resume, transcript, work experience certificates. *Deadline:* April 1.

Contact: Erin Reyes, Practice Division Manager
National Society of Professional Engineers
1420 King Street
Alexandria, VA 22314
Phone: 703-684-2884
E-mail: egarcia@nspe.org

NEVADA NASA SPACE GRANT CONSORTIUM

http://www.nvspacegrant.org/

NATIONAL SPACE GRANT COLLEGE AND FELLOWSHIP PROGRAM
• See page 114

NEXTSTEPU

http://www.nextstepu.com/

$1,500 STEM SCHOLARSHIP
• See page 106

OREGON STUDENT ASSISTANCE COMMISSION

http://www.GetCollegeFunds.org/

SOCIETY OF AMERICAN MILITARY ENGINEERS PORTLAND POST SCHOLARSHIP

Award for a student who will enroll as college sophomore or above for fall term/semester in undergraduate study. Preference given to ROTC reservist, National Guard reservist, or prior service veteran. Must major in aeronautical, biomedical, chemical, civil, electrical, or mechanical engineering.

Academic Fields/Career Goals: Chemical Engineering; Civil Engineering; Electrical Engineering/Electronics; Engineering/Technology; Mechanical Engineering.

Award: Scholarship for use in sophomore, junior, or senior years; not renewable.

Eligibility Requirements: Applicant must be enrolled or expecting to enroll full-time at a four-year institution or university and resident of Oregon. Applicant must have 3.0 GPA or higher. Available to U.S. citizens.

Application Requirements: Application form, essay. *Deadline:* March 1.

Contact: Melissa Adams, Scholarship Processing Coordinator
Phone: 541-687-7409
E-mail: melissa.adams@hecc.oregon.gov

ROBERT H. MOLLOHAN FAMILY CHARITABLE FOUNDATION, INC.

http://www.mollohanfoundation.org/

HIGH TECHNOLOGY SCHOLARS PROGRAM
• See page 158

SCARLETT FAMILY FOUNDATION SCHOLARSHIP PROGRAM

http://www.scarlettfoundation.org/

SCHOLARSHIP FOR STUDENTS PURSUING A BUSINESS OR STEM DEGREE
• See page 84

SEMICONDUCTOR RESEARCH CORPORATION (SRC)

http://www.src.org/

MASTER'S SCHOLARSHIP PROGRAM

Scholarship given to women or members of an under represented minority category (African-American, Hispanic, Native American). Scholarships are for study in disciplines related to microelectronics at U.S.-based universities having research funded by the Semiconductor Research Corporation and require U.S. citizenship or permanent resident status.

Academic Fields/Career Goals: Chemical Engineering; Computer Science/Data Processing; Electrical Engineering/Electronics; Engineering/Technology; Materials Science, Engineering, and Metallurgy.

Award: Scholarship for use in senior or graduate years; renewable. *Number:* 1–15. *Amount:* $25,000–$32,000.

Eligibility Requirements: Applicant must be American Indian/Alaska Native, Black (non-Hispanic), Hispanic and enrolled or expecting to enroll full-time at a four-year institution or university. Applicant must have 3.0 GPA or higher. Available to U.S. citizens.

Application Requirements: Application form, recommendations or references, resume, test scores, transcript. *Deadline:* February 15.

Contact: Virginia Wiggins, Student Relations Manager
Phone: 919-941-9453
E-mail: students@src.org

SIGMA XI, THE SCIENTIFIC RESEARCH SOCIETY

http://www.sigmaxi.org/

SIGMA XI GRANTS-IN-AID OF RESEARCH
• See page 101

SOCIETY OF AUTOMOTIVE ENGINEERS

http://www.sae.org/

BMW/SAE ENGINEERING SCHOLARSHIP
• See page 146

EDWARD D. HENDRICKSON/SAE ENGINEERING SCHOLARSHIP
• See page 146

TMC/SAE DONALD D. DAWSON TECHNICAL SCHOLARSHIP
• See page 147

SOCIETY OF PLASTICS ENGINEERS FOUNDATION (SPE)

http://www.4spe.org/

FLEMING/BASZCAK SCHOLARSHIP

Award available for a full-time undergraduate student, with a demonstrated interest in the plastics industry. Must be a U.S. citizen and provide documentation of Mexican heritage.

Academic Fields/Career Goals: Chemical Engineering; Electrical Engineering/Electronics; Engineering/Technology; Industrial Design; Materials Science, Engineering, and Metallurgy; Trade/Technical Specialties.

Award: Scholarship for use in freshman, sophomore, junior, or senior years; not renewable. *Number:* 1. *Amount:* $2000.

Eligibility Requirements: Applicant must be of Mexican heritage; Hispanic and enrolled or expecting to enroll full-time at a two-year or four-year institution or university. Available to U.S. citizens.

Application Requirements: Application form, community service, essay, financial need analysis. *Deadline:* April 1.

Contact: Mr. Gene Havel, Scholarships Program Administrator
Society of Plastics Engineers Foundation (SPE)
6 Berkshire Blvd., Suite 306
Bethel, CT 06801-1065
Phone: 203-740-5457
E-mail: foundation@4spe.org

GULF COAST HURRICANE SCHOLARSHIP

One $6,000 scholarship for a student at a 4-year college. One $2,000 scholarship for a student at a 2-year junior college or technical institute. Must be a resident of and attending school in FL, AL, MS, LA or TX.

Academic Fields/Career Goals: Chemical Engineering; Engineering-Related Technologies; Engineering/Technology; Industrial Design; Materials Science, Engineering, and Metallurgy; Mechanical

Engineering; Science, Technology, and Society; Trade/Technical Specialties.

Award: Scholarship for use in freshman, sophomore, junior, or senior years; not renewable. *Number:* 1. *Amount:* $2000.

Eligibility Requirements: Applicant must be enrolled or expecting to enroll full-time at a two-year or four-year or technical institution or university; resident of Alabama, Florida, Louisiana, Mississippi, Texas and studying in Alabama, Florida, Louisiana, Mississippi, Texas. Available to U.S. citizens.

Application Requirements: Application form, community service, essay. *Deadline:* April 1.

Contact: Mr. Gene Havel, Scholarships Program Administrator
Society of Plastics Engineers Foundation (SPE)
6 Berkshire Blvd., Suite 306
Bethel, CT 06801-1065
Phone: 203-740-5457
E-mail: foundation@4spe.org

PLASTICS PIONEERS ASSOCIATION SCHOLARSHIPS

Scholarships available to undergraduate students who are committed to becoming "hands-on" workers in the plastics industry, such as plastics technicians or engineers. Must be a U.S. citizen.

Academic Fields/Career Goals: Chemical Engineering; Engineering/Technology.

Award: Scholarship for use in freshman, sophomore, junior, or senior years; renewable. *Amount:* $3000.

Eligibility Requirements: Applicant must be enrolled or expecting to enroll full-time at a two-year or four-year or technical institution or university. Available to U.S. citizens.

Application Requirements: Application form, essay, financial need analysis. *Deadline:* April 1.

Contact: Managing Director
Society of Plastics Engineers Foundation (SPE)
13 Church Hill Road
Newtown, CT 06470
Phone: 203-740-5447
E-mail: foundation@4spe.org

SOCIETY OF PLASTICS ENGINEERS SCHOLARSHIP PROGRAM

Scholarships awarded to full-time students who have demonstrated or expressed an interest in the plastics industry. Major or course of study must be beneficial to a career in the plastics industry.

Academic Fields/Career Goals: Chemical Engineering; Electrical Engineering/Electronics; Engineering/Technology; Industrial Design; Materials Science, Engineering, and Metallurgy; Trade/Technical Specialties.

Award: Scholarship for use in freshman, sophomore, junior, senior, or graduate years; not renewable. *Number:* 35–40. *Amount:* $1000–$6000.

Eligibility Requirements: Applicant must be enrolled or expecting to enroll full-time at a two-year or four-year or technical institution or university. Available to U.S. and non-U.S. citizens.

Application Requirements: Application form, community service, essay. *Deadline:* April 1.

Contact: Mr. Gene Havel, Scholarship Program Administrator
Society of Plastics Engineers Foundation (SPE)
6 Berkshire Boulevard, Suite 306
Bethel, CT 06801-1065
Phone: 203-740-5457
E-mail: foundation@4spe.org

SOCIETY OF WOMEN ENGINEERS

http://societyofwomenengineers.swe.org/

ADA I. PRESSMAN MEMORIAL SCHOLARSHIP

$5000 renewable scholarship for women pursuing ABET-accredited baccalaureate or graduate programs in preparation for careers in engineering, engineering technology, and computer science in the United States and Mexico. Must be a U.S. citizen and have a minimum 3.0 GPA.

Academic Fields/Career Goals: Chemical Engineering; Construction Engineering/Management; Electrical Engineering/Electronics; Energy and Power Engineering; Engineering/Technology; Marine/Ocean Engineering; Mechanical Engineering; Paper and Pulp Engineering.

Award: Scholarship for use in sophomore, junior, senior, or graduate years; renewable. *Number:* 9. *Amount:* $5000.

Eligibility Requirements: Applicant must be enrolled or expecting to enroll full-time at a four-year institution or university and female. Applicant must have 3.0 GPA or higher. Available to U.S. citizens.

Application Requirements: Application form. *Deadline:* February 15.

Contact: Scholarship Committee
Phone: 800-793-4636
E-mail: scholarships@swe.org

AMERICAN TRANSMISSION CO. SCHOLARSHIP

$1500 renewable scholarship for women pursuing ABET-accredited baccalaureate or graduate programs in preparation for careers in engineering, engineering technology, and computer science in the United States and Mexico. Must be a U.S. citizen and have a minimum 3.0 GPA. First choice college and home address must be in Illinois, Indiana, Iowa, Michigan, Minnesota, or Wisconsin.

Academic Fields/Career Goals: Chemical Engineering; Civil Engineering; Construction Engineering/Management; Electrical Engineering/Electronics; Energy and Power Engineering; Engineering/Technology; Marine/Ocean Engineering; Materials Science, Engineering, and Metallurgy; Mechanical Engineering; Paper and Pulp Engineering.

Award: Scholarship for use in sophomore, junior, or senior years; renewable. *Number:* 2. *Amount:* $1500.

Eligibility Requirements: Applicant must be enrolled or expecting to enroll full-time at a four-year institution or university; female; resident of Illinois, Indiana, Iowa, Michigan, Minnesota, Wisconsin and studying in Illinois, Indiana, Iowa, Michigan, Minnesota, Wisconsin. Applicant must have 3.0 GPA or higher. Available to U.S. citizens.

Application Requirements: Application form. *Deadline:* February 15.

Contact: Scholarship Committee
Phone: 800-793-4636
E-mail: scholarships@swe.org

ANNE MAUREEN WHITNEY BARROW MEMORIAL SCHOLARSHIP

$7000 award for women pursuing ABET-accredited baccalaureate programs in preparation for careers in engineering or engineering technology in the United States and Mexico. One award, renewable up to 5 years.

Academic Fields/Career Goals: Chemical Engineering; Construction Engineering/Management; Electrical Engineering/Electronics; Energy and Power Engineering; Engineering/Technology; Marine/Ocean Engineering; Mechanical Engineering; Paper and Pulp Engineering.

Award: Scholarship for use in freshman, sophomore, junior, or senior years; renewable. *Number:* 1. *Amount:* $7000.

Eligibility Requirements: Applicant must be enrolled or expecting to enroll full-time at a four-year institution or university and female. Available to U.S. citizens.

Application Requirements: Application form. *Deadline:* February 15.

Contact: Scholarship Committee
Phone: 800-793-4636
E-mail: scholarships@swe.org

ANNE SHEN SMITH ENDOWED SCHOLARSHIP

$1000 scholarship for women pursuing ABET-accredited Baccalaureate programs in preparation for careers in engineering, engineering technology, and computer science in the United States and Mexico. U.S. citizenship and minimum 3.0 GPA required; under-represented groups preferred. Must be studying at a California college or university.

Academic Fields/Career Goals: Chemical Engineering; Civil Engineering; Construction Engineering/Management; Electrical Engineering/Electronics; Energy and Power Engineering; Engineering/Technology; Marine/Ocean Engineering; Materials Science, Engineering, and Metallurgy; Mechanical Engineering; Paper and Pulp Engineering.

Award: Scholarship for use in sophomore, junior, or senior years; not renewable. *Number:* 1. *Amount:* $1000.

Eligibility Requirements: Applicant must be enrolled or expecting to enroll full-time at a four-year institution or university; female and studying in California. Applicant must have 3.0 GPA or higher. Available to U.S. citizens.

Application Requirements: Application form, essay. *Deadline:* February 15.

Contact: Scholarship Committee
Phone: 800-793-4636
E-mail: scholarships@swe.org

BAYER SCHOLARSHIP

$2500 scholarships available to women pursuing ABET-accredited Baccalaureate programs in preparation for careers in engineering, engineering technology, and computer science in the United States and Mexico. Under-represented, financial need, and veteran candidates preferred. Must attend a school in Pennsylvania or Texas. Minimum 3.0 GPA required.

Academic Fields/Career Goals: Chemical Engineering; Civil Engineering; Construction Engineering/Management; Electrical Engineering/Electronics; Energy and Power Engineering; Engineering/Technology; Marine/Ocean Engineering; Materials Science, Engineering, and Metallurgy; Mechanical Engineering; Paper and Pulp Engineering.

Award: Scholarship for use in sophomore, junior, or senior years; renewable. *Number:* 2. *Amount:* $2500.

Eligibility Requirements: Applicant must be enrolled or expecting to enroll full-time at a four-year institution or university; female and studying in Pennsylvania, Texas. Applicant must have 3.0 GPA or higher. Available to U.S. citizens.

Application Requirements: Application form, essay, financial need analysis. *Deadline:* February 15.

Contact: Scholarship Committee
Phone: 800-793-4636
E-mail: scholarships@swe.org

BETTY LOU BAILEY SWE REGION F SCHOLARSHIP

$1500 award for women pursuing ABET-accredited Baccalaureate or graduate programs in preparation for careers in engineering, engineering technology, and computer science in the United States and Mexico. U.S. citizenship, SWE membership, minimum 3.0 GPA, and financial need required. First choice is for the applicant to attend a college/university within the Region F boundaries of Connecticut, Maine, Massachusetts, New Hampshire, New York (upstate), Rhode Island, and Vermont. Second choice would be for the applicant's home address to be within the Region F boundaries.

Academic Fields/Career Goals: Chemical Engineering; Civil Engineering; Construction Engineering/Management; Electrical Engineering/Electronics; Energy and Power Engineering; Engineering/Technology; Marine/Ocean Engineering; Materials Science, Engineering, and Metallurgy; Mechanical Engineering; Paper and Pulp Engineering.

Award: Scholarship for use in sophomore, junior, senior, or graduate years; not renewable. *Number:* 1. *Amount:* $1500.

Eligibility Requirements: Applicant must be enrolled or expecting to enroll full-time at a four-year institution or university and female. Applicant or parent of applicant must be member of Society of Women Engineers. Applicant must have 3.0 GPA or higher. Available to U.S. citizens.

Application Requirements: Application form, financial need analysis. *Deadline:* February 15.

Contact: Scholarship Committee
Phone: 800-793-4636
E-mail: scholarships@swe.org

B.J. HARROD SCHOLARSHIP

Two $1500 scholarships for women pursuing ABET-accredited Baccalaureate or graduate programs in preparation for careers in engineering, engineering technology, and computer science in the United States and Mexico. Minimum 3.5 GPA required.

Academic Fields/Career Goals: Chemical Engineering; Civil Engineering; Construction Engineering/Management; Electrical Engineering/Electronics; Energy and Power Engineering; Engineering/Technology; Marine/Ocean Engineering; Materials Science, Engineering, and Metallurgy; Mechanical Engineering; Paper and Pulp Engineering.

Award: Scholarship for use in freshman year; not renewable. *Number:* 2. *Amount:* $1500.

Eligibility Requirements: Applicant must be enrolled or expecting to enroll full-time at a four-year institution or university and female. Applicant must have 3.5 GPA or higher. Available to U.S. citizens.

Application Requirements: Application form, essay. *Deadline:* May 15.

BK KRENZER MEMORIAL REENTRY SCHOLARSHIP

One $2500 award for women pursuing ABET-accredited Baccalaureate or graduate programs in preparation for careers in engineering, engineering technology, and computer science in the United States and Mexico. Must have been out of school and the engineering or technology workforce for a minimum of two years prior to beginning the current course of study. The student is not required to have prior engineering experience or education.

Academic Fields/Career Goals: Chemical Engineering; Construction Engineering/Management; Electrical Engineering/Electronics; Energy and Power Engineering; Engineering/Technology; Marine/Ocean Engineering; Materials Science, Engineering, and Metallurgy; Mechanical Engineering; Paper and Pulp Engineering.

Award: Scholarship for use in freshman, sophomore, junior, senior, or graduate years; not renewable. *Number:* 1. *Amount:* $2500.

Eligibility Requirements: Applicant must be enrolled or expecting to enroll full- or part-time at a four-year institution or university and female. Available to U.S. citizens.

Application Requirements: Application form. *Deadline:* February 15.

Contact: Scholarship Committee
Phone: 800-793-4636
E-mail: scholarships@swe.org

CAROL STEPHENS SWE REGION F SCHOLARSHIP

One $1250 scholarship for women pursuing ABET-accredited Baccalaureate or graduate programs in preparation for careers in engineering, engineering technology, and computer science in the United States and Mexico. Must attend a college/university within the Region F boundaries or home address must be within the Region F boundaries. U.S. citizenship, SWE membership and minimum 3.0 GPA required.

Academic Fields/Career Goals: Chemical Engineering; Civil Engineering; Construction Engineering/Management; Electrical Engineering/Electronics; Energy and Power Engineering; Engineering/Technology; Marine/Ocean Engineering; Materials Science, Engineering, and Metallurgy; Mechanical Engineering; Paper and Pulp Engineering.

Award: Scholarship for use in sophomore, junior, senior, or graduate years; not renewable. *Number:* 1. *Amount:* $1250.

Eligibility Requirements: Applicant must be enrolled or expecting to enroll full-time at a four-year institution or university and female. Applicant or parent of applicant must be member of Society of Women Engineers. Applicant must have 3.0 GPA or higher. Available to U.S. citizens.

Application Requirements: Application form, financial need analysis. *Deadline:* February 15.

Contact: Scholarship Committee
Phone: 800-793-4636
E-mail: scholarships@swe.org

CUMMINS SCHOLARSHIP

Two $2500 awards for women pursuing ABET-accredited Baccalaureate or graduate programs in preparation for careers in engineering, engineering technology, and computer science in the United States and Mexico. Preference given to under-represented groups and those willing to intern. Minimum 3.0 GPA required.

Academic Fields/Career Goals: Chemical Engineering; Computer Science/Data Processing; Electrical Engineering/Electronics; Engineering/Technology; Materials Science, Engineering, and Metallurgy; Mechanical Engineering.

Award: Scholarship for use in sophomore, junior, senior, or graduate years; not renewable. *Number:* 2. *Amount:* $2500.

Eligibility Requirements: Applicant must be enrolled or expecting to enroll full-time at a four-year institution or university and female. Applicant or parent of applicant must be member of Society of Women Engineers. Applicant must have 3.0 GPA or higher. Available to U.S. citizens.

Application Requirements: Application form. *Deadline:* February 15.

Contact: Scholarship Committee
Phone: 800-793-4636
E-mail: scholarships@swe.org

DR. IVY M. PARKER MEMORIAL SCHOLARSHIP

$1500 scholarship for a woman pursuing an ABET-accredited Baccalaureate program in preparation for a career in engineering, engineering technology, and computer science in the United States and Mexico. Must demonstrate financial need and have a minimum 3.0 GPA.

Academic Fields/Career Goals: Chemical Engineering; Civil Engineering; Construction Engineering/Management; Electrical Engineering/Electronics; Energy and Power Engineering; Engineering/Technology; Marine/Ocean Engineering; Materials Science, Engineering, and Metallurgy; Mechanical Engineering; Paper and Pulp Engineering.

Award: Scholarship for use in junior or senior years; renewable. *Number:* 1. *Amount:* $1500.

Eligibility Requirements: Applicant must be enrolled or expecting to enroll full-time at a four-year institution or university and female. Applicant or parent of applicant must be member of Society of Women Engineers. Applicant must have 3.0 GPA or higher. Available to U.S. citizens.

Application Requirements: Application form, financial need analysis. *Deadline:* February 15.

Contact: Scholarship Committee
  Phone: 800-793-4636
  E-mail: scholarships@swe.org

DOROTHY LEMKE HOWARTH MEMORIAL SCHOLARSHIP

Six scholarships of $3000 awarded to sophomore women pursuing ABET-accredited Baccalaureate programs in preparation for careers in engineering, engineering technology, and computer science in the United States and Mexico. Must be a U.S. citizen and have a minimum 3.0 GPA.

Academic Fields/Career Goals: Chemical Engineering; Civil Engineering; Electrical Engineering/Electronics; Energy and Power Engineering; Engineering/Technology; Marine/Ocean Engineering; Materials Science, Engineering, and Metallurgy; Mechanical Engineering; Paper and Pulp Engineering.

Award: Scholarship for use in sophomore year; not renewable. *Number:* 6. *Amount:* $3000.

Eligibility Requirements: Applicant must be enrolled or expecting to enroll full-time at a four-year institution or university and female. Applicant or parent of applicant must be member of Society of Women Engineers. Applicant must have 3.0 GPA or higher. Available to U.S. citizens.

Application Requirements: Application form. *Deadline:* February 15.

Contact: Scholarship Committee
  Phone: 800-793-4636
  E-mail: scholarships@swe.org

DOROTHY P. MORRIS SCHOLARSHIP

One $1500 scholarship for a woman pursuing an ABET-accredited Baccalaureate program in preparation for a career in engineering, engineering technology, or computer science in the United States and Mexico. Must be a U.S. citizen and have a minimum 3.0 GPA.

Academic Fields/Career Goals: Chemical Engineering; Civil Engineering; Construction Engineering/Management; Electrical Engineering/Electronics; Energy and Power Engineering; Engineering/Technology; Marine/Ocean Engineering; Materials Science, Engineering, and Metallurgy; Mechanical Engineering; Paper and Pulp Engineering.

Award: Scholarship for use in sophomore, junior, or senior years; not renewable. *Number:* 1. *Amount:* $1500.

Eligibility Requirements: Applicant must be enrolled or expecting to enroll full-time at a four-year institution or university and female. Applicant or parent of applicant must be member of Society of Women Engineers. Applicant must have 3.0 GPA or higher. Available to U.S. citizens.

Application Requirements: Application form, financial need analysis. *Deadline:* February 15.

Contact: Scholarship Committee
  Phone: 800-793-4636
  E-mail: scholarships@swe.org

DUPONT COMPANY SCHOLARSHIP

Two $1000 awards for women pursuing ABET-accredited Baccalaureate programs in preparation for careers in engineering, engineering technology, and computer science in the United States and Mexico.

Minimum 3.0 GPA required. Limited to schools in the following states: AL, AR, CT, DC, DE, FL, GA, IA, IL, IN, KY, LA, MA, MD, ME, MI, MN, MO, MS, NC, NH, NJ, NY,OH, OK, PA, PR, RI, SC, TN, TX, VA, VT, WI and WV.

Academic Fields/Career Goals: Chemical Engineering; Engineering/Technology; Mechanical Engineering.

Award: Scholarship for use in sophomore, junior, or senior years; not renewable. *Number:* 2. *Amount:* $1000.

Eligibility Requirements: Applicant must be enrolled or expecting to enroll full-time at a four-year institution or university and female. Applicant or parent of applicant must be member of Society of Women Engineers. Applicant must have 3.0 GPA or higher. Available to U.S. citizens.

Application Requirements: Application form. *Deadline:* February 15.

Contact: Scholarship Committee
  Phone: 800-793-4636
  E-mail: scholarships@swe.org

EXELON CORPORATION SCHOLARSHIP

Five awards of $1000 for freshmen, sophomore, and junior women pursuing ABET-accredited Baccalaureate programs in preparation for careers in electrical and mechanical engineering in the United States and Mexico. U.S. citizenship, under-represented groups, disabled, and veteran candidates preferred. Inquire for preferred list of schools.

Academic Fields/Career Goals: Chemical Engineering; Civil Engineering; Construction Engineering/Management; Electrical Engineering/Electronics; Energy and Power Engineering; Engineering/Technology; Marine/Ocean Engineering; Materials Science, Engineering, and Metallurgy; Mechanical Engineering; Paper and Pulp Engineering.

Award: Scholarship for use in freshman, sophomore, or junior years; not renewable. *Number:* 5. *Amount:* $1000.

Eligibility Requirements: Applicant must be enrolled or expecting to enroll full-time at a four-year institution or university and female. Applicant or parent of applicant must be member of Society of Women Engineers. Available to U.S. citizens.

Application Requirements: Application form, essay. *Deadline:* February 15.

Contact: Scholarship Committee
  Phone: 800-793-4636
  E-mail: scholarships@swe.org

FCA WOMEN IN ENGINEERING SCHOLARSHIP

$2500 renewable scholarships for women pursuing ABET-accredited Baccalaureate or graduate programs in preparation for careers in engineering, engineering technology, and computer science in the United States and Mexico. Must be a U.S. citizen. Minimum 3.0 GPA required.

Academic Fields/Career Goals: Chemical Engineering; Construction Engineering/Management; Electrical Engineering/Electronics; Energy and Power Engineering; Engineering/Technology; Marine/Ocean Engineering; Materials Science, Engineering, and Metallurgy; Mechanical Engineering; Paper and Pulp Engineering.

Award: Scholarship for use in freshman, sophomore, junior, senior, or graduate years; not renewable. *Number:* 20. *Amount:* $2500.

Eligibility Requirements: Applicant must be enrolled or expecting to enroll full-time at a four-year institution or university and female. Applicant or parent of applicant must be member of Society of Women Engineers. Applicant must have 3.0 GPA or higher. Available to U.S. citizens.

Application Requirements: Application form. *Deadline:* February 15.

Contact: Scholarship Committee
  Phone: 800-793-4636
  E-mail: scholarships@swe.org

HONEYWELL SCHOLARSHIP

Three $5000 scholarships for women pursuing ABET-accredited Baccalaureate programs in preparation for careers in engineering, engineering technology, and computer science in the United States and Mexico. College or home residence must be located in AZ, CA, FL, IN, KS, MN, NM, PR, TX, or WA. U.S. citizenship, 3.5 GPA, and SWE membership required. Financial need and underrepresented students preferred.

Academic Fields/Career Goals: Chemical Engineering; Computer Science/Data Processing; Electrical Engineering/Electronics;

Engineering/Technology; Materials Science, Engineering, and Metallurgy; Mechanical Engineering.

Award: Scholarship for use in sophomore, junior, or senior years; not renewable. *Number:* 3. *Amount:* $5000.

Eligibility Requirements: Applicant must be enrolled or expecting to enroll full-time at a four-year institution or university and female. Applicant or parent of applicant must be member of Society of Women Engineers. Applicant must have 3.5 GPA or higher. Available to U.S. citizens.

Application Requirements: Application form, financial need analysis. *Deadline:* February 15.

Contact: Scholarship Committee
Phone: 800-793-4636
E-mail: scholarships@swe.org

IBM LINDA SANFORD WOMEN'S TECHNICAL ADVANCEMENT SCHOLARSHIP

$1000 renewable scholarship for women pursuing ABET-accredited Baccalaureate or graduate programs in preparation for careers in engineering, engineering technology, and computer science in the United States and Mexico. Must be a U.S. citizen and have a minimum 3.5 GPA.

Academic Fields/Career Goals: Chemical Engineering; Civil Engineering; Construction Engineering/Management; Electrical Engineering/Electronics; Energy and Power Engineering; Engineering/Technology; Marine/Ocean Engineering; Materials Science, Engineering, and Metallurgy; Mechanical Engineering; Paper and Pulp Engineering.

Award: Scholarship for use in freshman, sophomore, junior, senior, or graduate years; not renewable. *Number:* 1. *Amount:* $1000.

Eligibility Requirements: Applicant must be enrolled or expecting to enroll full-time at a four-year institution or university and female. Applicant must have 3.5 GPA or higher. Available to U.S. citizens.

Application Requirements: Application form. *Deadline:* February 15.

Contact: Scholarship Committee
Phone: 800-793-4636
E-mail: scholarships@swe.org

JILL S. TIETJEN P.E. SCHOLARSHIP

$1750 award for a woman pursuing an ABET-accredited Baccalaureate program in preparation for a career in engineering, engineering technology, and computer science in the United States and Mexico. Must be a U.S. citizen and have minimum 3.0 GPA.

Academic Fields/Career Goals: Chemical Engineering; Civil Engineering; Computer Science/Data Processing; Electrical Engineering/Electronics; Energy and Power Engineering; Engineering/Technology; Marine/Ocean Engineering; Materials Science, Engineering, and Metallurgy; Mechanical Engineering; Paper and Pulp Engineering.

Award: Scholarship for use in sophomore, junior, or senior years; not renewable. *Number:* 1. *Amount:* $1750.

Eligibility Requirements: Applicant must be enrolled or expecting to enroll full-time at a four-year institution or university and female. Applicant must have 3.0 GPA or higher. Available to U.S. citizens.

Application Requirements: Application form. *Deadline:* February 15.

Contact: Scholarship Committee
Phone: 800-793-4636
E-mail: scholarships@swe.org

KELLOGG SCHOLARSHIP

Three scholarships for women pursuing ABET-accredited Baccalaureate programs in preparation for careers in engineering, engineering technology, or computer science in the United States and Mexico. Minimum 3.2 GPA and SWE membership required. Two $1000 scholarships (student at Michigan University and Western Michigan University preferred) and one $3000 scholarship (financial need preferred).

Academic Fields/Career Goals: Chemical Engineering; Mechanical Engineering.

Award: Scholarship for use in sophomore or junior years; not renewable. *Number:* 3. *Amount:* $1000–$3000.

Eligibility Requirements: Applicant must be enrolled or expecting to enroll full-time at a four-year institution or university and female. Applicant or parent of applicant must be member of Society of Women Engineers. Available to U.S. citizens.

Application Requirements: Application form. *Deadline:* February 15.

Contact: Scholarship Committee
Phone: 800-793-4636
E-mail: scholarships@swe.org

KOCH DISCOVERY SCHOLARSHIP

Five $2500 awards for women pursuing ABET-accredited Baccalaureate programs in preparation for careers in engineering, engineering technology, and computer science in the United States and Mexico. U.S. citizenship required. Preferred states for school location: AL, AR, FL, GA, IL, IN, IA, KS, MI, MN, MS, MO, NE, NC, ND, OK, OR, SC, SD, TN, TX, UT, VA, WI.

Academic Fields/Career Goals: Chemical Engineering; Civil Engineering; Computer Science/Data Processing; Construction Engineering/Management; Electrical Engineering/Electronics; Energy and Power Engineering; Engineering-Related Technologies; Engineering/Technology; Marine/Ocean Engineering; Mechanical Engineering; Paper and Pulp Engineering.

Award: Scholarship for use in sophomore or junior years; not renewable. *Number:* 5. *Amount:* $2500.

Eligibility Requirements: Applicant must be enrolled or expecting to enroll full-time at a four-year institution or university and female. Applicant must have 3.0 GPA or higher. Available to U.S. citizens.

Application Requirements: Application form, essay. *Deadline:* February 15.

Contact: Scholarship Committee
Phone: 800-793-4636
E-mail: scholarships@swe.org

LILLIAN MOLLER GILBRETH MEMORIAL SCHOLARSHIP

One award of $14,500 for a woman pursuing an ABET-accredited Baccalaureate program in preparation for a career in engineering, engineering technology, and computer science in the United States and Mexico. Renewable for continuing undergraduate study only. Availability dependent upon renewal. Minimum 3.0 GPA required.

Academic Fields/Career Goals: Chemical Engineering; Civil Engineering; Computer Science/Data Processing; Construction Engineering/Management; Electrical Engineering/Electronics; Energy and Power Engineering; Engineering/Technology; Marine/Ocean Engineering; Materials Science, Engineering, and Metallurgy; Mechanical Engineering; Paper and Pulp Engineering.

Award: Scholarship for use in junior or senior years; not renewable. *Number:* 1. *Amount:* $14,500.

Eligibility Requirements: Applicant must be enrolled or expecting to enroll full-time at a four-year institution or university and female. Applicant must have 3.0 GPA or higher. Available to U.S. citizens.

Application Requirements: Application form. *Deadline:* February 15.

Contact: Scholarship Committee
Phone: 800-793-4636
E-mail: scholarships@swe.org

MARY V. MUNGER SCHOLARSHIP

Two $2750 award for women pursuing an ABET-accredited Baccalaureate or graduate program in preparation for a career in engineering, engineering technology, or computer science in the United States and Mexico. Must be a U.S. citizen and a member of SWE. For use by college junior or senior or a re-entry/nontraditional student. Re-entry/nontraditional students must have been out of school and the engineering or technology workforce for a minimum of two years prior to beginning the current course of study. Minimum 3.0 GPA required.

Academic Fields/Career Goals: Chemical Engineering; Civil Engineering; Construction Engineering/Management; Electrical Engineering/Electronics; Energy and Power Engineering; Engineering/Technology; Marine/Ocean Engineering; Materials Science, Engineering, and Metallurgy; Mechanical Engineering; Paper and Pulp Engineering.

Award: Scholarship for use in junior or senior years; not renewable. *Number:* 2. *Amount:* $2750.

Eligibility Requirements: Applicant must be enrolled or expecting to enroll full-time at a four-year institution or university and female. Applicant or parent of applicant must be member of Society of Women Engineers. Applicant must have 3.0 GPA or higher. Available to U.S. citizens.

Application Requirements: Application form. *Deadline:* February 15.

Contact: Scholarship Committee
Phone: 800-793-4636
E-mail: scholarships@swe.org

MASWE SCHOLARSHIP

Four $1500 awards for women pursuing ABET-accredited Baccalaureate programs in preparation for careers in engineering, engineering technology, and computer science in the United States and Mexico. Financial need is taken into consideration. Minimum 3.0 GPA required.

Academic Fields/Career Goals: Chemical Engineering; Civil Engineering; Construction Engineering/Management; Electrical Engineering/Electronics; Energy and Power Engineering; Engineering/Technology; Marine/Ocean Engineering; Materials Science, Engineering, and Metallurgy; Mechanical Engineering; Paper and Pulp Engineering.

Award: Scholarship for use in sophomore, junior, or senior years; not renewable. *Number:* 4. *Amount:* $1500.

Eligibility Requirements: Applicant must be enrolled or expecting to enroll full-time at a four-year institution or university and female. Applicant must have 3.0 GPA or higher. Available to U.S. citizens.

Application Requirements: Application form, financial need analysis. *Deadline:* February 15.

Contact: Scholarship Committee
Phone: 800-793-4636
E-mail: scholarships@swe.org

OLIVE LYNN SALEMBIER MEMORIAL REENTRY SCHOLARSHIP

One $1500 scholarship for a women pursuing an ABET-accredited Baccalaureate or graduate program in preparation for a career in engineering and engineering technology in the United States and Mexico. Must have been out of the engineering work force and out of school for a minimum of two years prior to re-entry. Minimum 3.0 GPA except for first year of reentry.

Academic Fields/Career Goals: Chemical Engineering; Civil Engineering; Construction Engineering/Management; Electrical Engineering/Electronics; Energy and Power Engineering; Engineering/Technology; Marine/Ocean Engineering; Materials Science, Engineering, and Metallurgy; Mechanical Engineering; Paper and Pulp Engineering.

Award: Scholarship for use in freshman, sophomore, junior, senior, or graduate years; not renewable. *Number:* 1. *Amount:* $1500.

Eligibility Requirements: Applicant must be enrolled or expecting to enroll full-time at a four-year institution or university and female. Available to U.S. citizens.

Application Requirements: Application form. *Deadline:* February 15.

Contact: Scholarship Committee
Phone: 800-793-4636
E-mail: scholarships@swe.org

PAULA LORING SIMON SCHOLARSHIP

One $1000 scholarship for a woman pursuing an ABET-accredited Baccalaureate program in preparation for a career in engineering, engineering technology, and computer science in the United States and Mexico. Must have a minimum 3.0 GPA.

Academic Fields/Career Goals: Chemical Engineering; Civil Engineering; Electrical Engineering/Electronics; Engineering/Technology.

Award: Scholarship for use in freshman year; not renewable. *Number:* 1. *Amount:* $1000.

Eligibility Requirements: Applicant must be enrolled or expecting to enroll full-time at a four-year institution or university and female. Applicant must have 3.0 GPA or higher. Available to U.S. citizens.

Application Requirements: Application form. *Deadline:* May 1.

Contact: Scholarship Committee
Phone: 800-793-4636
E-mail: scholarships@swe.org

ROBERTA BANASZAK GLEITER ENGINEERING ENDEAVOR SCHOLARSHIP

One $1250 award for women pursuing ABET-accredited Baccalaureate programs in preparation for careers in engineering, engineering technology, and computer science in the United States and Mexico. Must be U.S. citizen, have a minimum 3.0 GPA, and have SWE membership.

Under-represented groups, reentry candidates, and financial need preferred. Renewal dependent on continued eligibility.

Academic Fields/Career Goals: Chemical Engineering; Computer Science/Data Processing; Construction Engineering/Management; Electrical Engineering/Electronics; Energy and Power Engineering; Engineering-Related Technologies; Engineering/Technology; Marine/Ocean Engineering; Materials Science, Engineering, and Metallurgy; Mechanical Engineering; Paper and Pulp Engineering.

Award: Scholarship for use in sophomore or junior years; not renewable. *Number:* 1. *Amount:* $1250.

Eligibility Requirements: Applicant must be enrolled or expecting to enroll full-time at a four-year institution or university and female. Applicant or parent of applicant must be member of Society of Women Engineers. Applicant must have 3.0 GPA or higher. Available to U.S. citizens.

Application Requirements: Application form, essay, financial need analysis. *Deadline:* February 15.

Contact: Scholarship Committee
Phone: 800-793-4636
E-mail: scholarships@swe.org

ROCHELLE PERRY MEMORIAL SCHOLARSHIP

One $1000 award for women pursuing ABET-accredited Baccalaureate or graduate programs in preparation for careers in engineering, engineering technology, and computer science in the United States and Mexico. Schools in Region E or H preferred. SWE membership and minimum 3.0 GPA required. Community involvement with planning and participating in events or other organizations preferred. High level of dedication and passion for community, organizations, and engineering in general preferred.

Academic Fields/Career Goals: Chemical Engineering; Computer Science/Data Processing; Construction Engineering/Management; Electrical Engineering/Electronics; Energy and Power Engineering; Engineering-Related Technologies; Engineering/Technology; Marine/Ocean Engineering; Materials Science, Engineering, and Metallurgy; Mechanical Engineering; Paper and Pulp Engineering.

Award: Scholarship for use in sophomore, junior, senior, or graduate years; not renewable. *Number:* 1. *Amount:* $1000.

Eligibility Requirements: Applicant must be enrolled or expecting to enroll full-time at a four-year institution or university and female. Applicant or parent of applicant must be member of Society of Women Engineers. Applicant must have 3.0 GPA or higher. Available to U.S. citizens.

Application Requirements: Application form, essay. *Deadline:* February 15.

Contact: Scholarship Committee
Phone: 800-793-4636
E-mail: scholarships@swe.org

SUSAN MISZKOWICZ MEMORIAL SCHOLARSHIP

$1500 award for a woman pursuing an ABET-accredited Baccalaureate program in preparation for a career in engineering, engineering technology, or computer science in the United States and Mexico. Minimum 3.0 GPA required.

Academic Fields/Career Goals: Chemical Engineering; Civil Engineering; Construction Engineering/Management; Electrical Engineering/Electronics; Energy and Power Engineering; Engineering/Technology; Marine/Ocean Engineering; Materials Science, Engineering, and Metallurgy; Mechanical Engineering; Paper and Pulp Engineering.

Award: Scholarship for use in sophomore, junior, or senior years; not renewable. *Number:* 1. *Amount:* $1500.

Eligibility Requirements: Applicant must be enrolled or expecting to enroll full-time at a four-year institution or university and female. Applicant must have 3.0 GPA or higher. Available to U.S. citizens.

Application Requirements: Application form. *Deadline:* February 15.

Contact: Scholarship Committee
Phone: 800-793-4636
E-mail: scholarships@swe.org

SWE BALTIMORE-WASHINGTON SECTION SCHOLARSHIP

One $2000 award for a woman pursuing an ABET-accredited Baccalaureate or graduate program in preparation for a career in engineering, engineering technology, or computer science in the United

States and Mexico. For use at a school in DC, MD, or VA. U.S. citizenship and SWE membership required.

Academic Fields/Career Goals: Chemical Engineering; Civil Engineering; Construction Engineering/Management; Electrical Engineering/Electronics; Energy and Power Engineering; Engineering/Technology; Marine/Ocean Engineering; Materials Science, Engineering, and Metallurgy; Mechanical Engineering; Paper and Pulp Engineering.

Award: Scholarship for use in sophomore, junior, senior, or graduate years; not renewable. *Number:* 1. *Amount:* $2000.

Eligibility Requirements: Applicant must be enrolled or expecting to enroll full-time at a four-year institution or university; female and studying in District of Columbia, Maryland, Virginia. Applicant or parent of applicant must be member of Society of Women Engineers. Applicant must have 3.0 GPA or higher. Available to U.S. citizens.

Application Requirements: Application form. *Deadline:* February 15.

Contact: Scholarship Committee
Phone: 800-793-4636
E-mail: scholarships@swe.org

SWE CENTRAL NEW MEXICO PIONEERS SCHOLARSHIP

Renewable $1500 scholarship for a woman pursuing an ABET-accredited Baccalaureate program in preparation for a career in engineering, engineering technology, or computer science in the United States and Mexico. Must attend a NM university or 4-year engineering/technology school. U.S. citizenship, SWE membership, and minimum 3.0 GPA required. Renewable up to three years. Availability dependent upon renewal.

Academic Fields/Career Goals: Chemical Engineering; Civil Engineering; Construction Engineering/Management; Electrical Engineering/Electronics; Energy and Power Engineering; Engineering/Technology; Marine/Ocean Engineering; Materials Science, Engineering, and Metallurgy; Mechanical Engineering; Paper and Pulp Engineering.

Award: Scholarship for use in sophomore, junior, senior, or graduate years; renewable. *Number:* 1. *Amount:* $1500.

Eligibility Requirements: Applicant must be enrolled or expecting to enroll full-time at a four-year institution or university; female and studying in New Mexico. Applicant or parent of applicant must be member of Society of Women Engineers. Applicant must have 3.0 GPA or higher. Available to U.S. citizens.

Application Requirements: Application form. *Deadline:* February 15.

Contact: Scholarship Committee
Phone: 800-793-4636
E-mail: scholarships@swe.org

SWE CENTRAL NEW MEXICO REENTRY SCHOLARSHIP

$1500 scholarship for a woman pursuing an ABET-accredited Baccalaureate or graduate program in preparation for a career in engineering, engineering technology, or computer science in the United States and Mexico. Must be a U.S. citizen, have SWE membership, and have a minimum 3.0 GPA. Must attend a university located in New Mexico. Reentry for undergraduate sophomore, junior, senior, or graduate student. If there is no qualified candidate, the Scholarship Committee can award a second CNM-Pioneers Scholarship. Renewable up to 6 years.

Academic Fields/Career Goals: Chemical Engineering; Civil Engineering; Construction Engineering/Management; Electrical Engineering/Electronics; Energy and Power Engineering; Engineering/Technology; Marine/Ocean Engineering; Materials Science, Engineering, and Metallurgy; Mechanical Engineering; Paper and Pulp Engineering.

Award: Scholarship for use in sophomore, junior, senior, or graduate years; renewable. *Number:* 1. *Amount:* $1500.

Eligibility Requirements: Applicant must be enrolled or expecting to enroll full-time at a four-year institution or university; female and studying in New Mexico. Applicant or parent of applicant must be member of Society of Women Engineers. Applicant must have 3.0 GPA or higher. Available to U.S. citizens.

Application Requirements: Application form. *Deadline:* February 15.

Contact: Scholarship Committee
Phone: 800-793-4636
E-mail: scholarships@swe.org

SWE MID-HUDSON SECTION SCHOLARSHIP

$1250 scholarship for a woman pursuing an ABET-accredited Baccalaureate or graduate program in preparation for a career in engineering, engineering technology, or computer science in the United States and Mexico. New York is the preferred state for home residence and study. Minimum 3.0 GPA required.

Academic Fields/Career Goals: Chemical Engineering; Civil Engineering; Construction Engineering/Management; Electrical Engineering/Electronics; Energy and Power Engineering; Engineering/Technology; Marine/Ocean Engineering; Materials Science, Engineering, and Metallurgy; Mechanical Engineering; Paper and Pulp Engineering.

Award: Scholarship for use in sophomore, junior, senior, or graduate years; not renewable. *Number:* 1. *Amount:* $1250.

Eligibility Requirements: Applicant must be enrolled or expecting to enroll full-time at a four-year institution or university; female; resident of New York and studying in New York. Applicant must have 3.0 GPA or higher. Available to U.S. citizens.

Application Requirements: Application form. *Deadline:* February 15.

Contact: Scholarship Committee
Phone: 800-793-4636
E-mail: scholarships@swe.org

SWE PHOENIX SECTION SCHOLARSHIP

$3000 scholarship for a woman pursuing an ABET-accredited Baccalaureate program in preparation for a career in engineering, engineering technology, or computer science in the United States and Mexico. Must attend a school in Arizona. SWE membership and minimum 3.0 GPA required.

Academic Fields/Career Goals: Chemical Engineering; Civil Engineering; Construction Engineering/Management; Electrical Engineering/Electronics; Energy and Power Engineering; Engineering/Technology; Marine/Ocean Engineering; Materials Science, Engineering, and Metallurgy; Mechanical Engineering; Paper and Pulp Engineering.

Award: Scholarship for use in sophomore, junior, or senior years; not renewable. *Number:* 1. *Amount:* $3000.

Eligibility Requirements: Applicant must be enrolled or expecting to enroll full-time at a four-year institution or university; female and studying in Arizona. Applicant or parent of applicant must be member of Society of Women Engineers. Applicant must have 3.0 GPA or higher. Available to U.S. citizens.

Application Requirements: Application form. *Deadline:* February 15.

Contact: Scholarship Committee
Phone: 800-793-4636
E-mail: scholarships@swe.org

SWE REGION E SCHOLARSHIP

One $1500 award for women pursuing ABET-accredited Baccalaureate or graduate programs in preparation for careers in engineering, engineering technology, and computer science in the United States and Mexico. SWE membership and minimum 3.0 GPA required. Must be attending school within the Region E boundaries: Delaware, District of Columbia, Eastern Pennsylvania, Maryland, New Jersey, New York, and Virginia.

Academic Fields/Career Goals: Chemical Engineering; Civil Engineering; Computer Science/Data Processing; Construction Engineering/Management; Electrical Engineering/Electronics; Energy and Power Engineering; Engineering-Related Technologies; Engineering/Technology; Marine/Ocean Engineering; Mechanical Engineering; Paper and Pulp Engineering.

Award: Scholarship for use in sophomore, junior, senior, or graduate years; not renewable. *Number:* 1. *Amount:* $1500.

Eligibility Requirements: Applicant must be enrolled or expecting to enroll full-time at a four-year institution or university; female and studying in Delaware, District of Columbia, Maryland, New Jersey, New York, Pennsylvania, Virginia. Applicant or parent of applicant must be member of Society of Women Engineers. Applicant must have 3.0 GPA or higher. Available to U.S. citizens.

Application Requirements: Application form, essay. *Deadline:* February 15.

Contact: Scholarship Committee
Phone: 800-793-4636
E-mail: scholarships@swe.org

SWE REGION G JUDY SIMMONS MEMORIAL SCHOLARSHIP

One $1250 award for women pursuing ABET-accredited Baccalaureate or graduate programs in preparation for careers in engineering, engineering technology, and computer science in the United States and Mexico. May attend any colleges and universities with an active SWE section within Region G, which includes all of Kentucky, Ohio, West Virginia, and the western half of Pennsylvania. SWE membership and minimum 3.0 GPA required.

Academic Fields/Career Goals: Chemical Engineering; Civil Engineering; Computer Science/Data Processing; Construction Engineering/Management; Electrical Engineering/Electronics; Energy and Power Engineering; Engineering-Related Technologies; Engineering/Technology; Marine/Ocean Engineering; Materials Science, Engineering, and Metallurgy; Paper and Pulp Engineering.

Award: Scholarship for use in sophomore, junior, senior, or graduate years; not renewable. *Number:* 1. *Amount:* $1250.

Eligibility Requirements: Applicant must be enrolled or expecting to enroll full-time at a four-year institution or university; female and studying in Kentucky, Ohio, Pennsylvania, West Virginia. Applicant or parent of applicant must be member of Society of Women Engineers. Applicant must have 3.0 GPA or higher. Available to U.S. citizens.

Application Requirements: Application form, essay. *Deadline:* February 15.

Contact: Scholarship Committee
Phone: 800-793-4636
E-mail: scholarships@swe.org

SWE REGION H SCHOLARSHIPS

Two awards ranging from $1250 to $1500 for women pursuing ABET-accredited Baccalaureate or graduate programs in preparation for careers in engineering, engineering technology, and computer science in the United States and Mexico. SWE membership and minimum 3.0 GPA required. Must attend a school within Region H boundaries, which includes ND, SD, MN, IA, WI, IL, MI, and IN. Level of involvement in SWE should be high, as well as the amount of time spent volunteering, level of commitment, and years of service.

Academic Fields/Career Goals: Chemical Engineering; Civil Engineering; Construction Engineering/Management; Electrical Engineering/Electronics; Energy and Power Engineering; Engineering/Technology; Marine/Ocean Engineering; Materials Science, Engineering, and Metallurgy; Mechanical Engineering; Paper and Pulp Engineering.

Award: Scholarship for use in sophomore, junior, senior, or graduate years; not renewable. *Number:* 2. *Amount:* $1250–$1500.

Eligibility Requirements: Applicant must be enrolled or expecting to enroll full-time at a four-year institution or university; female and studying in Illinois, Indiana, Iowa, Michigan, Minnesota, North Dakota, South Dakota, Wisconsin. Applicant or parent of applicant must be member of Society of Women Engineers. Applicant must have 3.0 GPA or higher. Available to U.S. citizens.

Application Requirements: Application form. *Deadline:* February 15.

Contact: Scholarship Committee
Phone: 800-793-4636
E-mail: scholarships@swe.org

SWE REGION J SCHOLARSHIP

$1000 scholarship available to women pursuing ABET-accredited Baccalaureate or graduate programs in preparation for careers in engineering, engineering technology, and computer science in the United States and Mexico. SWE membership required. Must be attending school in the Region J boundaries: Alaska, Washington, Oregon, Montana, and Idaho. Renewable for 5 years. Availability dependent upon renewals.

Academic Fields/Career Goals: Chemical Engineering; Civil Engineering; Construction Engineering/Management; Electrical Engineering/Electronics; Energy and Power Engineering; Engineering/Technology; Marine/Ocean Engineering; Materials Science, Engineering, and Metallurgy; Mechanical Engineering; Paper and Pulp Engineering.

Award: Scholarship for use in sophomore, junior, senior, or graduate years; renewable. *Number:* 1. *Amount:* $1000.

Eligibility Requirements: Applicant must be enrolled or expecting to enroll full-time at a four-year institution or university; female and studying in Alaska, Idaho, Montana, Oregon, Washington. Applicant or parent of applicant must be member of Society of Women Engineers. Applicant must have 3.0 GPA or higher. Available to U.S. citizens.

Application Requirements: Application form, essay. *Deadline:* February 15.

Contact: Scholarship Committee
Phone: 800-793-4636
E-mail: scholarships@swe.org

TURNER CONSTRUCTION SCHOLARSHIP

Two $2500 scholarships available to sophomore women pursuing ABET-accredited Baccalaureate programs in preparation for careers in engineering, engineering technology, and computer science in the United States and Mexico. U.S. citizenship, 3.0 GPA, and SWE membership required.

Academic Fields/Career Goals: Chemical Engineering; Construction Engineering/Management; Engineering/Technology; Mechanical Engineering.

Award: Scholarship for use in sophomore year; not renewable. *Number:* 2. *Amount:* $2500.

Eligibility Requirements: Applicant must be enrolled or expecting to enroll full-time at a four-year institution or university and female. Applicant or parent of applicant must be member of Society of Women Engineers. Applicant must have 3.0 GPA or higher. Available to U.S. citizens.

Application Requirements: Application form, essay. *Deadline:* February 15.

Contact: Scholarship Committee
Phone: 800-793-4636
E-mail: scholarships@swe.org

WANDA MUNN SCHOLARSHIP

One $1500 award for a woman pursuing an ABET-accredited Baccalaureate or graduate program in preparation for a career in engineering, engineering technology, or computer science in the United States and Mexico. Must have satisfactorily completed of a minimum of two years full-time equivalent credits at an ABET-accredited school. Home or school must be in Alaska, Idaho, Montana, Oregon, or Washington.

Academic Fields/Career Goals: Chemical Engineering; Civil Engineering; Construction Engineering/Management; Electrical Engineering/Electronics; Energy and Power Engineering; Engineering/Technology; Marine/Ocean Engineering; Materials Science, Engineering, and Metallurgy; Mechanical Engineering; Paper and Pulp Engineering.

Award: Scholarship for use in sophomore, junior, senior, or graduate years; not renewable. *Number:* 1. *Amount:* $1500.

Eligibility Requirements: Applicant must be enrolled or expecting to enroll full-time at a four-year institution or university and female. Available to U.S. citizens.

Application Requirements: Application form. *Deadline:* February 15.

Contact: Scholarship Committee
Phone: 800-793-4636
E-mail: scholarships@swe.org

SOCIETY OF WOMEN ENGINEERS-ROCKY MOUNTAIN SECTION

http://www.swe-rms.org/

SOCIETY OF WOMEN ENGINEERS-ROCKY MOUNTAIN SECTION SCHOLARSHIP PROGRAM

One-time award for graduating female high school seniors and female college students in Colorado and Wyoming (except zip codes 80800 and 81599). Eligibility: 1. Applicant must be a woman enrolled or planning to enroll as an undergraduate or graduate student in an ABET accredited engineering, computing, or engineering technology program (see http://www.abet.org/ for a list of eligible schools and majors) or other approved program. 2. Applicant must meet minimum GPA requirements. 3. Applicant must be able to accept the scholarship for the academic year starting in the Fall and must not already be receiving full funding from another source. For more information visit the website: http://www.swe-rms.org/scholarships.html.

Academic Fields/Career Goals: Chemical Engineering; Civil Engineering; Computer Science/Data Processing; Construction Engineering/Management; Electrical Engineering/Electronics; Energy and Power Engineering; Engineering-Related Technologies;

Engineering/Technology; Marine/Ocean Engineering; Materials Science, Engineering, and Metallurgy; Mechanical Engineering.

Award: Scholarship for use in freshman, sophomore, junior, senior, or graduate years; not renewable. *Number:* 3–8. *Amount:* $500–$2000.

Eligibility Requirements: Applicant must be enrolled or expecting to enroll full-time at a four-year institution or university; female and resident of Colorado, Wyoming. Applicant must have 3.5 GPA or higher. Available to U.S. citizens.

Application Requirements: Application form, community service, essay. *Deadline:* February 1.

Contact: Christi Wisleder, Scholarship Chair
Society of Women Engineers-Rocky Mountain Section
PO Box 260692
Lakewood, CO 80226-0692
E-mail: christi.wisleder@gmail.com

SONS OF NORWAY FOUNDATION
http://www.sonsofnorway.com/foundation

NANCY LORRAINE JENSEN MEMORIAL SCHOLARSHIP

Scholarship available for full-time undergraduate study in chemistry, physics, or in chemical, electrical, or mechanical engineering by a female student who is a U.S. citizen, and a current member, daughter, or granddaughter of a current member of Sons of Norway. The annual award will be at least 50 percent of the tuition for one semester and no more than 100 percent of the tuition for one year. Must have attained a SAT score of at least 1800, a math score of 600 or better, or an ACT score of at least 26. Applicant must have completed at least one term of studies in the above fields. The award will be made jointly payable to the student and her institution. The award is renewable two times during undergraduate study.

Academic Fields/Career Goals: Chemical Engineering; Electrical Engineering/Electronics; Mechanical Engineering.

Award: Scholarship for use in sophomore, junior, or senior years; not renewable. *Number:* 1–6. *Amount:* $2500–$10,000.

Eligibility Requirements: Applicant must be of Norwegian heritage; age 17-35; enrolled or expecting to enroll full-time at a four-year institution or university; female and must have an interest in science. Applicant must have 3.5 GPA or higher. Available to U.S. citizens.

Application Requirements: Application form, essay, personal photograph, recommendations or references, test scores, transcript. *Deadline:* April 1.

Contact: Scholarship Coordinator
Sons of Norway Foundation
1455 West Lake Street
Minneapolis, MN 55408-2666
Phone: 612-827-3611
Fax: 612-827-0658
E-mail: foundation@sofn.com

STRAIGHTFORWARD MEDIA
http://www.straightforwardmedia.com/

STRAIGHTFORWARD MEDIA ENGINEERING SCHOLARSHIP

Scholarship of $500 to students attending or planning to enroll in a postsecondary engineering program in the United States or abroad. Scholarship is awarded four times per year. Deadlines: March 31, June 30, September 30, and December 31. For more information, see web http://www.straightforwardmedia.com/engineering/form.php.

Academic Fields/Career Goals: Chemical Engineering; Civil Engineering; Electrical Engineering/Electronics; Energy and Power Engineering; Engineering-Related Technologies; Engineering/Technology; Materials Science, Engineering, and Metallurgy; Mechanical Engineering; Paper and Pulp Engineering.

Award: Scholarship for use in freshman, sophomore, junior, or senior years; not renewable. *Number:* 4. *Amount:* $500.

Eligibility Requirements: Applicant must be enrolled or expecting to enroll full- or part-time at a two-year or four-year or technical institution or university. Available to U.S. and non-U.S. citizens.

Application Requirements: Essay. *Deadline:* varies.
Contact: Scholarship Committee
Phone: 605-348-3042

TAU BETA PI ASSOCIATION
http://www.tbp.org/

TAU BETA PI SCHOLARSHIP PROGRAM

One-time award for initiated members of Tau Beta Pi for their senior year of full-time undergraduate engineering study.

Academic Fields/Career Goals: Chemical Engineering; Civil Engineering; Electrical Engineering/Electronics; Engineering-Related Technologies; Engineering/Technology; Materials Science, Engineering, and Metallurgy; Mechanical Engineering.

Award: Scholarship for use in senior year; not renewable. *Number:* 200–245. *Amount:* $1000–$2000.

Eligibility Requirements: Applicant must be enrolled or expecting to enroll full- or part-time at a four-year institution or university. Applicant or parent of applicant must be member of Tau Beta Pi Association. Available to U.S. citizens.

Application Requirements: Application form, essay, personal photograph. *Deadline:* April 1.

Contact: Dylan Lane, Communications Specialist
Phone: 865-546-4578
E-mail: dylan@tbp.org

TRANSTUTORS
http://www.transtutors.com/scholarship

TRANSTUTORS SCHOLARSHIP 2015-16
• See page 85

UNITED NEGRO COLLEGE FUND
http://www.uncf.org/

ANHEUSER-BUSCH LEGENDS OF THE CROWN SCHOLARSHIP PROGRAM
• See page 86

BLUE CROSS BLUE SHIELD OF ILLINOIS AND BLUE CROSS BLUE SHIELD OF TEXAS SCHOLARSHIP
• See page 115

COLGATE–PALMOLIVE CORPORATE SCHOLARS PROGRAM
• See page 86

DAVIS SCHOLARSHIP FOR WOMEN IN STEM

One-time award of up to $5000 for minority female students to pursue a future career in the STEM fields. Must be at least sophomore standing. Preference will be given to students from Massachusetts, although all eligible students are encouraged to apply. Must be a U.S. citizen or permanent resident and have a minimum 3.0 GPA.

Academic Fields/Career Goals: Chemical Engineering; Computer Science/Data Processing; Electrical Engineering/Electronics; Energy and Power Engineering; Engineering/Technology; Mathematics; Mechanical Engineering.

Award: Scholarship for use in sophomore, junior, or senior years; not renewable. *Number:* 2.

Eligibility Requirements: Applicant must be Black (non-Hispanic); enrolled or expecting to enroll full-time at a four-year institution or university and female. Applicant must have 3.0 GPA or higher. Available to U.S. citizens.

Application Requirements: Application form, essay, financial need analysis. *Deadline:* June 3.

Contact: Mary Williams, Director of Outreach and Recruitment
Phone: 800-331-2244

GALACTIC UNITE BYTHEWAY SCHOLARSHIP

Scholarship of up to $7500 for a first-year female college student pursuing STEM degrees at any accredited four-year college or university in the United States. Minimum 2.5 GPA required.

Academic Fields/Career Goals: Chemical Engineering; Computer Science/Data Processing; Energy and Power Engineering; Engineering/Technology; Materials Science, Engineering, and Metallurgy; Mathematics; Mechanical Engineering.

Award: Scholarship for use in freshman year; renewable.

Eligibility Requirements: Applicant must be Black (non-Hispanic); high school student; planning to enroll or expecting to enroll full-time at a four-year institution or university and female. Applicant must have 2.5 GPA or higher. Available to U.S. citizens.

Application Requirements: Application form. *Deadline:* July 29.

Contact: Mary Williams, Director of Outreach and Recruitment
  Phone: 800-331-2244

INTEL SCHOLARSHIP PROGRAM

Up to $8500 to assist college sophomores, juniors, and seniors majoring in computer engineering, computer information Systems, computer science, electrical engineering, information technology or mechanical engineering; attending UNCF institutions and selected universities. Must complete FAFSA, be Pell Grant eligible, and have a demonstrated financial need. Minimum 3.2 GPA required.

Academic Fields/Career Goals: Chemical Engineering; Computer Science/Data Processing; Electrical Engineering/Electronics; Mechanical Engineering.

Award: Scholarship for use in sophomore, junior, or senior years; not renewable. *Amount:* $8500.

Eligibility Requirements: Applicant must be Black (non-Hispanic) and enrolled or expecting to enroll full-time at a four-year institution or university. Applicant must have 3.0 GPA or higher. Available to U.S. citizens.

Application Requirements: Application form, essay, financial need analysis. *Deadline:* January 31.

Contact: Mary Williams, Director of Outreach and Recruitment
  Phone: 800-331-2244

PROCTER & GAMBLE STEM SCHOLARSHIP
• *See page 116*

UNIVERSITIES SPACE RESEARCH ASSOCIATION
http://www.usra.edu/

UNIVERSITIES SPACE RESEARCH ASSOCIATION SCHOLARSHIP AWARD PROGRAM
• *See page 116*

XEROX
http://www.xerox.com//

TECHNICAL MINORITY SCHOLARSHIP

Scholarships are made available to minority students enrolled in technical degree programs at the Bachelor's degree level or above. Eligible students must have a GPA of 3.0 or higher and show financial need. Refer to website http://www.studentcareers-xerox-com.tmpqa.com/ for details.

Academic Fields/Career Goals: Chemical Engineering; Computer Science/Data Processing; Electrical Engineering/Electronics; Engineering-Related Technologies; Engineering/Technology; Materials Science, Engineering, and Metallurgy; Mechanical Engineering; Physical Sciences.

Award: Scholarship for use in freshman, sophomore, junior, senior, graduate, or postgraduate years; not renewable. *Number:* up to 128. *Amount:* $1000–$10,000.

Eligibility Requirements: Applicant must be American Indian/Alaska Native, Asian/Pacific Islander, Black (non-Hispanic), Hispanic and enrolled or expecting to enroll full-time at a four-year institution or university. Applicant must have 3.0 GPA or higher. Available to U.S. citizens.

Application Requirements: Application form, financial need analysis, resume. *Deadline:* September 30.

Contact: Stephanie Michalowski
  Xerox
  150 State Street
  Rochester, NY 14614
  Fax: 585-482-3095
  E-mail: xtmsp@rballiance.com

CHILD AND FAMILY STUDIES

CALIFORNIA STUDENT AID COMMISSION
http://www.csac.ca.gov/

CHILD DEVELOPMENT TEACHER AND SUPERVISOR GRANT PROGRAM

Award is for those students pursuing an approved course of study leading to a Child Development Permit issued by the California Commission on Teacher Credentialing. In exchange for each year funding is received, recipients agree to provide one year of service in a licensed childcare center.

Academic Fields/Career Goals: Child and Family Studies; Education.

Award: Grant for use in freshman, sophomore, junior, senior, or graduate years; renewable. *Number:* up to 300. *Amount:* $1000–$2000.

Eligibility Requirements: Applicant must be enrolled or expecting to enroll full- or part-time at a two-year or four-year institution or university; resident of California and studying in California. Applicant or parent of applicant must have employment or volunteer experience in teaching/education. Available to U.S. citizens.

Application Requirements: Application form, financial need analysis, GPA verification, recommendations or references. *Deadline:* April 16.

Contact: Catalina Mistler, Chief, Program Administration and Services
  Division
  California Student Aid Commission
  PO Box 419026
  Rancho Cordova, CA 95741-9026
  Phone: 916-464-7268
  Fax: 916-526-8004
  E-mail: studentsupport@csac.ca.gov

COMPHEALTH
http://www.comphealth.com

COMPHEALTH MEDICAL SCHOLARSHIP
• *See page 151*

SOCIETY OF PEDIATRIC NURSES
http://www.pedsnurses.org/

SOCIETY OF PEDIATRIC NURSES EDUCATIONAL SCHOLARSHIP

Award to a member engaged in a BSN completion program or a graduate program that will advance the health of children. Nominee must be a current Society of Pediatric Nurses member.

Academic Fields/Career Goals: Child and Family Studies; Health and Medical Sciences; Nursing.

Award: Scholarship for use in freshman, sophomore, junior, senior, or graduate years; not renewable. *Number:* 1. *Amount:* $500.

Eligibility Requirements: Applicant must be enrolled or expecting to enroll full-time at a four-year institution or university. Applicant or parent of applicant must be member of Society of Pediatric Nurses. Applicant or parent of applicant must have employment or volunteer experience in nursing. Available to U.S. citizens.

Application Requirements: Application form, essay, recommendations or references, resume. *Deadline:* November 14.

Contact: Scholarship Committee
Phone: 800-723-2902
Fax: 850-484-8762
E-mail: spn@puetzamc.com

Y'S MEN INTERNATIONAL

http://www.ysmen.org/

ALEXANDER SCHOLARSHIP LOAN FUND
• *See page 171*

CIVIL ENGINEERING

AACE INTERNATIONAL

http://www.aacei.org/

AACE INTERNATIONAL COMPETITIVE SCHOLARSHIP
• *See page 118*

AIST FOUNDATION

http://www.aistfoundation.org/

ASSOCIATION FOR IRON AND STEEL TECHNOLOGY DAVID H. SAMSON CANADIAN SCHOLARSHIP
• *See page 172*

AMERICAN COUNCIL OF ENGINEERING COMPANIES OF PENNSYLVANIA (ACEC/PA)

http://www.acecpa.org/

ERIC J. GENNUSO AND LEROY D. (BUD) LOY, JR. SCHOLARSHIP PROGRAM
• *See page 173*

AMERICAN INDIAN SCIENCE AND ENGINEERING SOCIETY

http://www.aises.org/

A.T. ANDERSON MEMORIAL SCHOLARSHIP PROGRAM
• *See page 109*

AMERICAN PUBLIC POWER ASSOCIATION

http://publicpower.org/DEED

DEED EDUCATIONAL SCHOLARSHIP
• *See page 176*

DEED STUDENT INTERNSHIP
• *See page 176*

DEED STUDENT RESEARCH GRANTS
Student Research Grants are awarded to students who are majoring in a field that could lead to a career in the public power industry. Applicants must be sponsored by a DEED member utility and attend an accredited university/college full-time in the U.S. Email DEED@publicpower.org for access to the application.

Academic Fields/Career Goals: Civil Engineering; Construction Engineering/Management; Electrical Engineering/Electronics; Energy and Power Engineering; Engineering-Related Technologies; Engineering/Technology; Environmental Science; Mechanical Engineering; Natural Resources.

Award: Scholarship for use in freshman, sophomore, junior, senior, graduate, or postgraduate years; not renewable. *Number:* 10. *Amount:* $5000.

Eligibility Requirements: Applicant must be Hispanic and enrolled or expecting to enroll full-time at a two-year or four-year or technical institution or university. Available to U.S. and non-U.S. citizens.

Application Requirements: Application form.

Contact: Richelle Dodds, DEED and Engineering Services Coordinator
E-mail: DEED@publicpower.org

DEED TECHNICAL DESIGN PROJECT
• *See page 176*

AMERICAN PUBLIC TRANSPORTATION FOUNDATION

http://www.apta.com/

TRANSIT HALL OF FAME SCHOLARSHIP AWARD PROGRAM
Renewable award for sophomores, juniors, seniors or graduate students studying transportation or rail transit engineering. Must be sponsored by APTA member organization and complete an internship program with a member organization. Must have a minimum 3.0 GPA and be a U.S. or Canadian citizen.

Academic Fields/Career Goals: Civil Engineering; Electrical Engineering/Electronics; Engineering-Related Technologies; Engineering/Technology; Mechanical Engineering; Transportation.

Award: Scholarship for use in sophomore, junior, senior, or graduate years; renewable. *Number:* 1. *Amount:* $2500.

Eligibility Requirements: Applicant must be enrolled or expecting to enroll full-time at a two-year or four-year institution or university. Applicant must have 3.0 GPA or higher. Available to U.S. and Canadian citizens.

Application Requirements: Application form, essay, financial need analysis, nomination by APTA member, verification of enrollment, copy of fee schedule from the college/university for the academic year, recommendations or references, transcript. *Deadline:* June 16.

Contact: Pamela Boswell, Vice President of Program Management
American Public Transportation Foundation
1666 K Street, NW
Washington, DC 20006-1215
Phone: 202-496-4803
Fax: 202-496-4323

AMERICAN RAILWAY ENGINEERING AND MAINTENANCE OF WAY ASSOCIATION

http://www.aremafoundation.org/

AREMA GRADUATE AND UNDERGRADUATE SCHOLARSHIPS
Railroad interest - Applicants must be enrolled as a student in a Graduate or Undergraduate program leading to a degree in Engineering or Engineering Technology in a curriculum which has been accredited by the Accreditation Board of Engineering and Technology (or comparable accreditation in Canada and Mexico). The applicant must have at least a 2.00 GPA (out of 4.00).

Academic Fields/Career Goals: Civil Engineering; Computer Science/Data Processing; Construction Engineering/Management; Electrical Engineering/Electronics; Engineering-Related Technologies; Engineering/Technology; Mechanical Engineering.

Award: Scholarship for use in freshman, sophomore, junior, senior, or graduate years; not renewable. *Number:* 30–40. *Amount:* $1000–$10,000.

Eligibility Requirements: Applicant must be enrolled or expecting to enroll full- or part-time at a four-year institution or university. Available to U.S. and Canadian citizens.

Application Requirements: Application form. *Deadline:* December 9.

Contact: Alayne Bell, Manager, Committees & Technical Services
Phone: 301-459-3200 Ext. 708
E-mail: abell@arema.org

AMERICAN SOCIETY OF CERTIFIED ENGINEERING TECHNICIANS

http://www.ascet.org/

KURT H. AND DONNA M. SCHULER SMALL GRANT
• See page 176

AMERICAN SOCIETY OF CIVIL ENGINEERS

http://www.asce.org/

EUGENE C. FIGG JR. CIVIL ENGINEERING SCHOLARSHIP

Applicant must be a member of the Society in good standing and be enrolled in an ABET-accredited program who will be registered as an undergraduate in the fall term of the year of award, is a U.S. citizen, and have a passion for bridges.

Academic Fields/Career Goals: Civil Engineering.

Award: Scholarship for use in sophomore, junior, or senior years; not renewable. *Number:* 1. *Amount:* $2500.

Eligibility Requirements: Applicant must be enrolled or expecting to enroll full-time at a four-year institution or university. Applicant or parent of applicant must be member of American Society of Civil Engineers. Available to U.S. citizens.

Application Requirements: Application form, essay, financial need analysis. *Deadline:* February 10.

Contact: Ms. Jane Alspach, Senior Manager, Honors and Awards
American Society of Civil Engineers
1801 Alexander Bell Drive
Reston, VA 20191
Phone: 703-295-6300 Ext. 6382
E-mail: awards@asce.org

JOHN LENARD CIVIL ENGINEERING SCHOLARSHIP

For students engaged in the study of civil engineering with a focus on water supply or environmental engineering. Applicant must be a Society member in good standing, enrolled in an ABET-accredited program.

Academic Fields/Career Goals: Civil Engineering.

Award: Scholarship for use in sophomore, junior, or senior years; not renewable. *Number:* 1–2.

Eligibility Requirements: Applicant must be enrolled or expecting to enroll full-time at a four-year institution or university. Applicant or parent of applicant must be member of American Society of Civil Engineers. Available to U.S. and non-U.S. citizens.

Application Requirements: Application form, essay, financial need analysis. *Deadline:* February 10.

Contact: Ms. Jane Alspach, Senior Manager, Honors and Awards
American Society of Civil Engineers
1801 Alexander Bell Drive
Reston, VA 20191
Phone: 703-295-6300 Ext. 6382
E-mail: awards@asce.org

LAWRENCE W. AND FRANCIS W. COX SCHOLARSHIP

Applicants must be Society members in good standing, enrolled in an ABET-accredited program in civil engineering.

Academic Fields/Career Goals: Civil Engineering.

Award: Scholarship for use in sophomore, junior, or senior years; not renewable. *Number:* 1.

Eligibility Requirements: Applicant must be enrolled or expecting to enroll full-time at a four-year institution or university. Applicant or parent of applicant must be member of American Society of Civil Engineers. Available to U.S. and non-U.S. citizens.

Application Requirements: Application form, essay, financial need analysis. *Deadline:* February 10.

Contact: Ms. Jane Alspach, Senior Manager, Honors and Awards
American Society of Civil Engineers
1801 Alexander Bell Drive
Reston, VA 20191
Phone: 703-295-6300 Ext. 6382
E-mail: awards@asce.org

ROBERT B.B. AND JOSEPHINE N. MOORMAN SCHOLARSHIP

Applicant must be Society member in good standing, enrolled in an ABET-accredited program in civil engineering.

Academic Fields/Career Goals: Civil Engineering.

Award: Scholarship for use in sophomore, junior, or senior years; not renewable. *Number:* 1.

Eligibility Requirements: Applicant must be enrolled or expecting to enroll full-time at a four-year institution or university. Applicant or parent of applicant must be member of American Society of Civil Engineers. Available to U.S. and non-U.S. citizens.

Application Requirements: Application form, essay. *Deadline:* February 10.

Contact: Ms. Jane Alspach, Senior Manager, Honors and Awards
American Society of Civil Engineers
1801 Alexander Bell Drive
Reston, VA 20191
Phone: 703-295-6300 Ext. 6382
E-mail: awards@asce.org

SAMUEL FLETCHER TAPMAN ASCE STUDENT CHAPTER SCHOLARSHIP

Not more than one application may be submitted from the membership of any one ASCE Student Chapter. Awards available to currently enrolled undergraduates. Must be a member of local ASCE Student Chapter and an ASCE Student Member in good standing. Selection is based on the applicant's justification of award, educational plan, academic performance and standing, potential for development, leadership capacity, ASCE activities, and financial need.

Academic Fields/Career Goals: Civil Engineering.

Award: Scholarship for use in sophomore, junior, or senior years; not renewable. *Number:* 1–12. *Amount:* $2000–$2500.

Eligibility Requirements: Applicant must be enrolled or expecting to enroll full-time at a four-year institution or university. Applicant or parent of applicant must be member of American Society of Civil Engineers. Available to U.S. and non-U.S. citizens.

Application Requirements: Application form, essay, financial need analysis. *Deadline:* February 10.

Contact: Ms. Jane Alspach, Senior Manager, Honors and Awards
American Society of Civil Engineers
1801 Alexander Bell Drive
Reston, VA 20191
Phone: 703-295-6300 Ext. 6382
E-mail: awards@asce.org

Y.C. YANG CIVIL ENGINEERING SCHOLARSHIP

Applicants must be student members in good standing of the Society. Currently enrolled civil engineering students at an institution with an ABET-accredited program and an interest in structural engineering may apply.

Academic Fields/Career Goals: Civil Engineering.

Award: Scholarship for use in sophomore, junior, or senior years; not renewable. *Number:* 1–2. *Amount:* $2000.

Eligibility Requirements: Applicant must be enrolled or expecting to enroll full-time at a four-year institution or university. Applicant or parent of applicant must be member of American Society of Civil Engineers. Available to U.S. and non-U.S. citizens.

Application Requirements: Application form, essay, financial need analysis. *Deadline:* February 10.

Contact: Ms. Jane Alspach, Senior Manager, Honors and Awards
American Society of Civil Engineers
1801 Alexander Bell Drive
Reston, VA 20191
Phone: 703-295-6300 Ext. 6382
E-mail: awards@asce.org

AMERICAN SOCIETY OF CIVIL ENGINEERS-MAINE SECTION

http://www.maineasce.org/

AMERICAN SOCIETY OF CIVIL ENGINEERS-MAINE HIGH SCHOOL SCHOLARSHIP

One-time award available to a high school student in senior year, pursuing a course of study in civil engineering. Must be enrolled in a four year ABET accredited Civil Engineering program at the time of award. Must be a resident of Maine. Essay, references and transcript required with application.

Academic Fields/Career Goals: Civil Engineering.

Award: Scholarship for use in freshman year; not renewable. *Number:* 1–4. *Amount:* $1000–$4000.

Eligibility Requirements: Applicant must be high school student; planning to enroll or expecting to enroll full-time at a four-year institution or university and resident of Maine. Available to U.S. citizens.

Application Requirements: Application form, essay. *Deadline:* January 31.

Contact: Ms. Leslie Corrow, Senior Engineer P.E.
American Society of Civil Engineers-Maine Section
141 Main Street, PO Box 650
Pittsfield, ME 04967
Phone: 207-487-3328 Ext. 243
E-mail: leslie.corrow@kleinschmidtgroup.com

AMERICAN SOCIETY OF NAVAL ENGINEERS

http://www.navalengineers.org/

AMERICAN SOCIETY OF NAVAL ENGINEERS SCHOLARSHIP

• *See page 110*

AMERICAN WELDING SOCIETY

http://www.aws.org/

ARSHAM AMIRIKIAN ENGINEERING SCHOLARSHIP

Awarded to an undergraduate pursuing a minimum four-year degree in civil engineering or welding-related program at an accredited university. Applicant must be a minimum of 18 years of age, have a minimum 3.0 GPA and be a citizen of the United States.

Academic Fields/Career Goals: Civil Engineering; Materials Science, Engineering, and Metallurgy; Trade/Technical Specialties.

Award: Scholarship for use in freshman, sophomore, junior, or senior years; not renewable. *Number:* 1.

Eligibility Requirements: Applicant must be enrolled or expecting to enroll full- or part-time at a four-year institution or university. Applicant must have 3.0 GPA or higher. Available to U.S. citizens.

Application Requirements: Application form, financial need analysis. *Deadline:* February 15.

Contact: Vicki Pinsky, Associate Director, Scholarships, Foundation
American Welding Society
8669 NW 36 Street, Suite 130
Miami, FL 33166
Phone: 800-443-9353 Ext. 212
E-mail: vpinsky@aws.org

MATSUO BRIDGE COMPANY LTD. OF JAPAN SCHOLARSHIP

Awarded to a college junior or senior, or graduate student pursuing a minimum four-year degree in civil engineering, welding engineering, welding engineering technology, or related discipline. Applicant must have a minimum 3.0 overall GPA. Financial need is not required to apply. Must be U.S. citizen.

Academic Fields/Career Goals: Civil Engineering; Engineering-Related Technologies; Engineering/Technology; Materials Science, Engineering, and Metallurgy.

Award: Scholarship for use in junior or senior years; not renewable.

Eligibility Requirements: Applicant must be enrolled or expecting to enroll full- or part-time at a two-year or four-year institution or university. Applicant must have 3.0 GPA or higher. Available to U.S. citizens.

Application Requirements: Application form, financial need analysis. *Deadline:* February 15.

Contact: Vicki Pinsky, Associate Director, Scholarships, AWS Foundation
American Welding Society
8669 NW 36 Street, Suite 130
Miami, FL 33166
Phone: 800-443-9353 Ext. 212
E-mail: vpinsky@aws.org

ARRL FOUNDATION INC.

http://www.arrl.org/

ALFRED E. FRIEND JR., W4CF, MEMORIAL SCHOLARSHIP

• *See page 177*

GARY WAGNER, K3OMI, SCHOLARSHIP

• *See page 177*

LOIS MANLEY, K7LMZ, AND RANDALL PITCHFORD, WW7ZZ, SCHOLARSHIP

One $1000 scholarship for a student with active Technical Class amateur radio license who is studying science, technology, engineering, or mathematics at any accredited 2- or 4-year college or university. Must reside in ARRL Northwestern Division (Washington, Oregon, Idaho, Montana, Alaska), with preference given to residents of Oregon.

Academic Fields/Career Goals: Civil Engineering; Electrical Engineering/Electronics; Energy and Power Engineering; Engineering-Related Technologies; Engineering/Technology; Marine/Ocean Engineering; Materials Science, Engineering, and Metallurgy; Mathematics; Natural Sciences; Nuclear Science; Physical Sciences.

Award: Scholarship for use in freshman, sophomore, junior, or senior years; not renewable. *Number:* 1. *Amount:* $1000.

Eligibility Requirements: Applicant must be enrolled or expecting to enroll at a two-year or four-year institution or university; resident of Alaska, Idaho, Montana, Oregon, Washington and must have an interest in amateur radio. Available to U.S. citizens.

Application Requirements: Application form. *Deadline:* January 31.

Contact: Ms. Mary Hobart, Secretary
Phone: 860-594-0397
E-mail: k1mmh@arrl.org

W1FDR SCHOLARSHIP

• *See page 112*

ASSOCIATED GENERAL CONTRACTORS EDUCATION AND RESEARCH FOUNDATION

http://www.agcfoundation.org/

AGC EDUCATION AND RESEARCH FOUNDATION UNDERGRADUATE SCHOLARSHIPS

College sophomores and juniors enrolled or planning to enroll in a full-time, four or five-year ABET or ACCE-accredited construction management or construction-related engineering program are eligible to apply. High school seniors and college freshmen are not eligible.

Academic Fields/Career Goals: Civil Engineering; Construction Engineering/Management.

Award: Scholarship for use in sophomore, junior, or senior years; renewable. *Number:* 100–150. *Amount:* $2500–$7500.

Eligibility Requirements: Applicant must be enrolled or expecting to enroll full-time at a four-year institution or university. Available to U.S. citizens.

Application Requirements: Application form, essay, interview. *Deadline:* November 1.

Contact: Melinda Patrician, Director
Associated General Contractors Education and Research
Foundation
2300 Wilson Boulevard, Suite 300
Arlington, VA 22201
Phone: 703-837-5342
E-mail: patricianm@agc.org

JAMES L. ALLHANDS ESSAY COMPETITION

The competition is open to any senior–level student in a four or five–year ABET or ACCE–accredited university construction management or construction–related engineering program. The first place essay author receives $1,000; faculty sponsor receives $500. Second place wins $500 and third place, $300. Both the recipient and sponsor are invited as guests of the Foundation to the AGC Annual Convention in March.

Academic Fields/Career Goals: Civil Engineering; Construction Engineering/Management.

Award: Prize for use in senior year; not renewable. *Number:* 3. *Amount:* $300–$1000.

Eligibility Requirements: Applicant must be enrolled or expecting to enroll full-time at a four-year institution or university. Available to U.S. citizens.

Application Requirements: Application form, essay. *Deadline:* November 15.

Contact: Melinda Patrician, Director
Associated General Contractors Education and Research
Foundation
2300 Wilson Boulevard, Suite 300
Arlington, VA 22201
Phone: 703-837-5342
E-mail: patricianm@agc.org

ASSOCIATED GENERAL CONTRACTORS OF NEW YORK STATE, LLC

http://www.agcnys.org/

ASSOCIATED GENERAL CONTRACTORS NYS SCHOLARSHIP PROGRAM

Scholarship for students enrolled full-time study in civil engineering, construction management and construction technology and diesel technology. Must have minimum GPA of 2.5. Scholarship value is from $1500 to $5000. Must be resident of New York.

Academic Fields/Career Goals: Civil Engineering; Construction Engineering/Management; Surveying, Surveying Technology, Cartography, or Geographic Information Science; Transportation.

Award: Scholarship for use in sophomore, junior, senior, or graduate years; not renewable. *Number:* 15–25. *Amount:* $1500–$5000.

Eligibility Requirements: Applicant must be enrolled or expecting to enroll full-time at a two-year or four-year institution or university and resident of New York. Applicant must have 2.5 GPA or higher. Available to U.S. citizens.

Application Requirements: Application form, financial need analysis. *Deadline:* May 15.

Contact: Mr. Brendan Manning, Vice President, Education and
Environment
Associated General Contractors of New York State, LLC
10 Airline Drive
Suite 203
Albany, NY 12205
Phone: 518-456-1134
E-mail: bmanning@agcnys.org

ASSOCIATION OF CALIFORNIA WATER AGENCIES

http://www.acwa.com/

ASSOCIATION OF CALIFORNIA WATER AGENCIES SCHOLARSHIPS
• *See page 112*

CLAIR A. HILL SCHOLARSHIP
• *See page 112*

BHW GROUP

https://thebhwgroup.com/

BHW WOMEN IN STEM SCHOLARSHIP
• *See page 74*

BRASKEM ODEBRECHT

http://www.odebrechtaward.com

ODEBRECHT AWARD FOR SUSTAINABLE DEVELOPMENT
• *See page 119*

BROWN AND CALDWELL

http://www.brownandcaldwell.com

ECKENFELDER SCHOLARSHIP
• *See page 155*

MINORITY SCHOLARSHIP PROGRAM
• *See page 155*

CENTER FOR ARCHITECTURE

http://www.cfafoundation.org/scholarships

CENTER FOR ARCHITECTURE DESIGN SCHOLARSHIP
• *See page 119*

THE DALLAS FOUNDATION

http://www.dallasfoundation.org/

JERE W. THOMPSON, JR, SCHOLARSHIP FUND

Renewable scholarships awarded to full-time undergraduate juniors or seniors with disadvantaged backgrounds, who are pursuing a degree in civil engineering and closely related disciplines at Texas colleges and universities. Up to $2000 awarded each semester, beginning with junior year. Must maintain 2.5 GPA. Special consideration given to students from Collin, Dallas, Denton, and Tarrant Counties, Texas.

Academic Fields/Career Goals: Civil Engineering.

Award: Scholarship for use in junior or senior years; renewable. *Number:* 1–2. *Amount:* up to $4000.

Eligibility Requirements: Applicant must be enrolled or expecting to enroll full-time at a four-year institution or university; resident of Texas and studying in Texas. Available to U.S. citizens.

Application Requirements: Application form, essay, financial need analysis, recommendations or references, test scores, transcript. *Deadline:* April 1.

Contact: Rachel Lasseter, Program Associate
The Dallas Foundation
900 Jackson Street, Suite 705
Dallas, TX 75202
Phone: 214-741-9898
Fax: 214-741-9848
E-mail: scholarships@dallasfoundation.org

WHITLEY PLACE SCHOLARSHIP
• *See page 120*

FABRICATORS AND MANUFACTURERS ASSOCIATION FOUNDATION

http://www.nutsandboltsfoundation.org/scholarships/

COLLEGE AND TRADE/TECHNICAL SCHOOL SCHOLARSHIPS
• *See page 178*

FLORIDA ENGINEERING SOCIETY

http://www.fleng.org/scholarships.cfm

DAVID F. LUDOVICI SCHOLARSHIP
• *See page 178*

FECON SCHOLARSHIP
One-time scholarship of $1000 given to Florida citizens in their junior or senior year, who are enrolled or accepted into a Florida university engineering program. Minimum 3.0 GPA required. Applicant must be interested in pursuing a career in the field of construction.

Academic Fields/Career Goals: Civil Engineering; Construction Engineering/Management.

Award: Scholarship for use in junior or senior years; not renewable. *Number:* 1. *Amount:* $1000.

Eligibility Requirements: Applicant must be enrolled or expecting to enroll full-time at an institution or university; resident of Florida and studying in Florida. Applicant must have 3.0 GPA or higher. Available to U.S. citizens.

Application Requirements: Application form, essay. *Deadline:* February 1.

Contact: Amanda Hudson, Director of Information Technology
Florida Engineering Society
125 South Gadsden Street
Tallahassee, FL 32301
Phone: 850-224-7121
E-mail: ahudson@fleng.org

FOUNDATION FOR SCIENCE AND DISABILITY

http://stemd.org/

GRANTS FOR DISABLED GRADUATE STUDENTS IN THE SCIENCES
• *See page 113*

GREAT MINDS IN STEM

www.greatmindsinstem.org

HISPANIC ENGINEER NATIONAL ACHIEVEMENT AWARDS CORPORATION SCHOLARSHIP PROGRAM
• *See page 106*

INDEPENDENT LABORATORIES INSTITUTE SCHOLARSHIP ALLIANCE

http://www.acil.org/

INDEPENDENT LABORATORIES INSTITUTE SCHOLARSHIP ALLIANCE
• *See page 156*

JORGE MAS CANOSA FREEDOM FOUNDATION

http://masscholarships.org/

MAS FAMILY SCHOLARSHIP AWARD
• *See page 165*

KENTUCKY ENERGY AND ENVIRONMENT CABINET

http://dep.ky.gov

ENVIRONMENTAL PROTECTION SCHOLARSHIP
• *See page 157*

KENTUCKY TRANSPORTATION CABINET

http://transportation.ky.gov/Education/Pages/Scholarships.aspx

KENTUCKY TRANSPORTATION CABINET CIVIL ENGINEERING SCHOLARSHIP PROGRAM
Scholarships awarded to qualified Kentucky residents who wish to study civil engineering at University of Kentucky, Western Kentucky University, University of Louisville or Kentucky State University. Applicant should be a graduate of an accredited Kentucky high school or a Kentucky resident. Scholarship recipients are given opportunities to work for the Cabinet during summers and job opportunities upon graduation within the state of KY.

Academic Fields/Career Goals: Civil Engineering.

Award: Scholarship for use in freshman, sophomore, junior, or senior years; renewable. *Number:* 15–25. *Amount:* $12,400–$51,200.

Eligibility Requirements: Applicant must be enrolled or expecting to enroll full-time at a four-year institution or university; resident of Kentucky and studying in Kentucky. Applicant must have 3.0 GPA or higher. Available to U.S. and non-U.S. citizens.

Application Requirements: Application form, essay, interview. *Deadline:* February 1.

Contact: Cherie Mertz, Scholarship Program Coordinator
Kentucky Transportation Cabinet
200 Mero Street, 6th Floor West
Frankfort, KY 40622
Phone: 502-564-4610
E-mail: Cherie.Mertz@ky.gov

LOS ANGELES COUNCIL OF BLACK PROFESSIONAL ENGINEERS

http://www.lablackengineers.org/

AL-BEN SCHOLARSHIP FOR ACADEMIC INCENTIVE
• *See page 179*

AL-BEN SCHOLARSHIP FOR PROFESSIONAL MERIT
• *See page 179*

AL-BEN SCHOLARSHIP FOR SCHOLASTIC ACHIEVEMENT
• *See page 179*

MIDWEST ROOFING CONTRACTORS ASSOCIATION

http://www.mrca.org/

MRCA FOUNDATION SCHOLARSHIP PROGRAM
• *See page 122*

NASA IDAHO SPACE GRANT CONSORTIUM

http://www.id.spacegrant.org/

NASA IDAHO SPACE GRANT CONSORTIUM SCHOLARSHIP PROGRAM
• *See page 157*

NASA MONTANA SPACE GRANT CONSORTIUM

http://www.spacegrant.montana.edu/

MONTANA SPACE GRANT SCHOLARSHIP PROGRAM
• *See page 142*

NATIONAL ASPHALT PAVEMENT ASSOCIATION RESEARCH AND EDUCATION FOUNDATION

http://www.asphaltpavement.org

NATIONAL ASPHALT PAVEMENT ASSOCIATION RESEARCH AND EDUCATION FOUNDATION SCHOLARSHIP PROGRAM

Our scholarship program provides funding for undergraduate and graduate students who are U.S. citizens enrolled in a full-time civil engineering, construction management, or construction engineering curriculum at an accredited four year college/university or two-year technical institution. The student must take at least one course on Hot Mix Asphalt (HMA) Technology. Refer to website for more details at http://www.hotmix.org/index.php?option=com_content&task=view&id=97&Itemid=410.

Academic Fields/Career Goals: Civil Engineering; Construction Engineering/Management.

Award: Scholarship for use in freshman, sophomore, junior, senior, graduate, or postgraduate years; not renewable. *Number:* 50–150. *Amount:* $500–$3000.

Eligibility Requirements: Applicant must be enrolled or expecting to enroll full-time at a two-year or four-year or technical institution or university. Available to U.S. citizens.

Application Requirements: Application form, essay, recommendations or references, transcript. *Deadline:* varies.

Contact: Mrs. Carolyn Wilson, Vice President, Finance and Operations
National Asphalt Pavement Association Research and
Education Foundation
5100 Forbes Boulevard
Lanham, MD 20706
Phone: 301-731-4748 Ext. 127
Fax: 301-731-4621
E-mail: cwilson@asphaltpavement.org

NATIONAL ASSOCIATION OF WATER COMPANIES-NEW JERSEY CHAPTER

http://www.nawc.org

NATIONAL ASSOCIATION OF WATER COMPANIES-NEW JERSEY CHAPTER SCHOLARSHIP
• *See page 80*

NATIONAL ASSOCIATION OF WOMEN IN CONSTRUCTION

http://www.nawic.org/

NAWIC UNDERGRADUATE SCHOLARSHIPS
• *See page 122*

NATIONAL SOCIETY OF PROFESSIONAL ENGINEERS

http://www.nspe.org/

MAUREEN L. AND HOWARD N. BLITMAN, PE SCHOLARSHIP TO PROMOTE DIVERSITY IN ENGINEERING
• *See page 180*

PAUL H. ROBBINS HONORARY SCHOLARSHIP
• *See page 180*

PROFESSIONAL ENGINEERS IN INDUSTRY SCHOLARSHIP
• *See page 180*

NEVADA NASA SPACE GRANT CONSORTIUM

http://www.nvspacegrant.org/

NATIONAL SPACE GRANT COLLEGE AND FELLOWSHIP PROGRAM
• *See page 114*

NEW ENGLAND WATER WORKS ASSOCIATION

http://www.newwa.org/

ELSON T. KILLAM MEMORIAL SCHOLARSHIP

Scholarships are awarded to eligible civil and environmental engineering students on the basis of merit, character, and need. Preference given to those students whose programs are considered by a committee as beneficial to water works practice in New England. NEWWA student membership is required to receive a scholarship award. Applicants for scholarships should be residents or attend school in New England. (Maine, New Hampshire, Vermont, Massachusetts, Rhode Island and Connecticut).

Academic Fields/Career Goals: Civil Engineering; Environmental Science.

Award: Scholarship for use in freshman, sophomore, junior, senior, or graduate years; not renewable. *Number:* 1. *Amount:* up to $1500.

Eligibility Requirements: Applicant must be enrolled or expecting to enroll full-time at a four-year institution or university. Applicant or parent of applicant must be member of New England Water Works Association. Available to U.S. citizens.

Application Requirements: Application form, essay, recommendations or references, transcript. *Fee:* $25. *Deadline:* July 1.

Contact: Thomas MacElhaney, Chair, Scholarship Committee
Phone: 631-231-8100
Fax: 978-418-9156
E-mail: tmacelhaney@preloadinc.com

FRANCIS X. CROWLEY SCHOLARSHIP
• *See page 166*

JOSEPH MURPHY SCHOLARSHIP

Scholarships are awarded to eligible civil or environmental engineering students on the basis of merit, character, and need. Preference given to those students whose programs are considered by a committee as beneficial to water works practice in New England. NEWWA student membership is required to receive a scholarship award.

Academic Fields/Career Goals: Civil Engineering; Environmental Science.

Award: Scholarship for use in freshman, sophomore, junior, senior, or graduate years; not renewable. *Number:* 1. *Amount:* up to $1500.

Eligibility Requirements: Applicant must be enrolled or expecting to enroll full-time at a four-year institution or university. Applicant or parent of applicant must be member of New England Water Works Association. Available to U.S. citizens.

Application Requirements: Application form, essay, recommendations or references, transcript. *Fee:* $25. *Deadline:* July 1.

Contact: Thomas MacElhaney, Chair, Scholarship Committee
Phone: 631-231-8100
Fax: 978-418-9156
E-mail: tmacelhaney@preloadinc.com

WORKS GEORGE E. WATTERS MEMORIAL SCHOLARSHIP.

Scholarships are awarded to eligible Civil Engineering students on the basis of merit, character, and need. Preference given to those students whose programs are considered by a committee as beneficial to water works practice in New England. NEWWA student membership is required to receive a scholarship award. Applicants for scholarships should be residents or attend school in New England. (Maine, New Hampshire, Vermont, Massachusetts, Rhode Island and Connecticut).

Academic Fields/Career Goals: Civil Engineering.

Award: Scholarship for use in freshman, sophomore, junior, senior, or graduate years; not renewable. *Number:* 1. *Amount:* up to $5000.

Eligibility Requirements: Applicant must be enrolled or expecting to enroll full-time at a four-year institution or university. Available to U.S. citizens.

Application Requirements: Application form, essay, recommendations or references, transcript. *Fee:* $25. *Deadline:* July 1.

Contact: Thomas MacElhaney, Chair, Scholarship Committee
    Phone: 631-231-8100
    Fax: 978-418-9156
    E-mail: tmacelhaney@preloadinc.com

NEXTSTEPU

http://www.nextstepu.com/

$1,500 STEM SCHOLARSHIP
• *See page 106*

OREGON STUDENT ASSISTANCE COMMISSION

http://www.GetCollegeFunds.org/

HOME BUILDERS FOUNDATION JIM IRVINE STATEWIDE SCHOLARSHIP
• *See page 123*

SOCIETY OF AMERICAN MILITARY ENGINEERS PORTLAND POST SCHOLARSHIP
• *See page 181*

PLAN NEW HAMPSHIRE

www.plannh.org

PLAN NEW HAMPSHIRE SCHOLARSHIP AND PROGRAM
• *See page 123*

PROFESSIONAL CONSTRUCTION ESTIMATORS ASSOCIATION

http://www.pcea.org/

TED G. WILSON MEMORIAL SCHOLARSHIP FOUNDATION

Amount up to $1000 to a deserving student (high school senior, college freshman, sophomore, or junior) based on their academic ability, need, and desire to enter the construction industry.

Academic Fields/Career Goals: Civil Engineering; Construction Engineering/Management; Drafting; Electrical Engineering/Electronics; Engineering/Technology; Heating, Air-Conditioning, and Refrigeration Mechanics; Landscape Architecture; Mechanical Engineering; Surveying, Surveying Technology, Cartography, or Geographic Information Science; Trade/Technical Specialties.

Award: Scholarship for use in freshman, sophomore, junior, or senior years; not renewable. *Number:* 5. *Amount:* up to $1000.

Eligibility Requirements: Applicant must be enrolled or expecting to enroll full-time at a two-year or four-year or technical institution or university; resident of Florida, Georgia, North Carolina, South Carolina, Virginia and studying in Florida, Georgia, North Carolina, South Carolina, Virginia. Available to U.S. and non-U.S. citizens.

Application Requirements: Application form, financial need analysis, interview, recommendations or references, transcript. *Deadline:* March 15.

Contact: Kim Lybrand, National Office Manager
    Professional Construction Estimators Association
    PO Box 680336
    Charlotte, NC 28216-0336
    Phone: 704-987-9978
    Fax: 704-987-9979
    E-mail: pcea@pcea.org

ROCKY MOUNTAIN COAL MINING INSTITUTE

http://www.rmcmi.org/

ROCKY MOUNTAIN COAL MINING INSTITUTE SCHOLARSHIP

Must be full-time college sophomore or junior at time of application, pursuing a degree in mining-related fields or engineering disciplines such as mining, geology, mineral processing, or metallurgy. For residents of Arizona, Colorado, Montana, New Mexico, North Dakota, Texas, Utah, and Wyoming. Scholarship value is $2500 per year for two-years sent directly to school for tuition.

Academic Fields/Career Goals: Civil Engineering; Earth Science; Engineering-Related Technologies; Engineering/Technology; Materials Science, Engineering, and Metallurgy.

Award: Scholarship for use in junior or senior years; renewable. *Number:* 8. *Amount:* $2500.

Eligibility Requirements: Applicant must be enrolled or expecting to enroll full-time at a four-year institution or university and resident of Arizona, Colorado, Montana, New Mexico, North Dakota, Texas, Utah, Wyoming. Available to U.S. citizens.

Application Requirements: Application form, interview, recommendations or references. *Deadline:* February 1.

Contact: Karen Inzano, Executive Director
    Phone: 303-948-3300
    E-mail: mail@rmcmi.org

SCARLETT FAMILY FOUNDATION SCHOLARSHIP PROGRAM

http://www.scarlettfoundation.org/

SCHOLARSHIP FOR STUDENTS PURSUING A BUSINESS OR STEM DEGREE
• *See page 84*

SIGMA XI, THE SCIENTIFIC RESEARCH SOCIETY

http://www.sigmaxi.org/

SIGMA XI GRANTS-IN-AID OF RESEARCH
• *See page 101*

SOCIETY OF WOMEN ENGINEERS

http://societyofwomenengineers.swe.org/

AMERICAN TRANSMISSION CO. SCHOLARSHIP
• *See page 182*

ANNE SHEN SMITH ENDOWED SCHOLARSHIP
• *See page 182*

BAYER SCHOLARSHIP
• *See page 183*

BETTY LOU BAILEY SWE REGION F SCHOLARSHIP
• *See page 183*

B.J. HARROD SCHOLARSHIP
• *See page 183*

CAROL STEPHENS SWE REGION F SCHOLARSHIP
• *See page 183*

DR. IVY M. PARKER MEMORIAL SCHOLARSHIP
• *See page 184*

DOROTHY LEMKE HOWARTH MEMORIAL SCHOLARSHIP
• See page 184

DOROTHY P. MORRIS SCHOLARSHIP
• See page 184

ELIZABETH MCLEAN MEMORIAL SCHOLARSHIP
$1500 scholarship for a woman pursuing an ABET-accredited Baccalaureate program in preparation for a career in civil engineering in the United States and Mexico. Minimum 3.0 GPA required.

Academic Fields/Career Goals: Civil Engineering; Engineering/Technology.

Award: Scholarship for use in sophomore, junior, or senior years; not renewable. *Number:* 1. *Amount:* $1500.

Eligibility Requirements: Applicant must be enrolled or expecting to enroll full-time at a four-year institution or university and female. Applicant or parent of applicant must be member of Society of Women Engineers. Applicant must have 3.0 GPA or higher. Available to U.S. citizens.

Application Requirements: Application form. *Deadline:* February 15.

Contact: Scholarship Committee
Phone: 800-793-4636
E-mail: scholarships@swe.org

EXELON CORPORATION SCHOLARSHIP
• See page 184

GENERAL ELECTRIC WOMEN'S NETWORK SCHOLARSHIP
Scholarships for women pursuing ABET-accredited Baccalaureate programs in preparation for a careers in engineering, engineering technology, or computer science in the United States and Mexico. U.S. citizenship, minimum 3.0 GPA, and SWE membership required. Applicant should have leadership roles outside of academics and involvement in engineering professional organizations, discipline related internships, and presentation skills. Recipients should be willing to intern at GE. Inquire for list of preferred schools.

Academic Fields/Career Goals: Civil Engineering; Electrical Engineering/Electronics; Engineering/Technology; Mechanical Engineering.

Award: Scholarship for use in sophomore or junior years; not renewable. *Number:* 43. *Amount:* $5000.

Eligibility Requirements: Applicant must be enrolled or expecting to enroll full-time at a four-year institution or university; female and must have an interest in leadership. Applicant or parent of applicant must be member of Society of Women Engineers. Applicant must have 3.0 GPA or higher. Available to U.S. citizens.

Application Requirements: Application form. *Deadline:* February 15.

Contact: Scholarship Committee
Phone: 800-793-4636
E-mail: scholarships@swe.org

IBM LINDA SANFORD WOMEN'S TECHNICAL ADVANCEMENT SCHOLARSHIP
• See page 185

JILL S. TIETJEN P.E. SCHOLARSHIP
• See page 185

KOCH DISCOVERY SCHOLARSHIP
• See page 185

LILLIAN MOLLER GILBRETH MEMORIAL SCHOLARSHIP
• See page 185

MARY V. MUNGER SCHOLARSHIP
• See page 185

MASWE SCHOLARSHIP
• See page 186

OLIVE LYNN SALEMBIER MEMORIAL REENTRY SCHOLARSHIP
• See page 186

PAULA LORING SIMON SCHOLARSHIP
• See page 186

SUSAN MISZKOWICZ MEMORIAL SCHOLARSHIP
• See page 186

SWE BALTIMORE-WASHINGTON SECTION SCHOLARSHIP
• See page 186

SWE CENTRAL NEW MEXICO PIONEERS SCHOLARSHIP
• See page 187

SWE CENTRAL NEW MEXICO REENTRY SCHOLARSHIP
• See page 187

SWE MID-HUDSON SECTION SCHOLARSHIP
• See page 187

SWE PHOENIX SECTION SCHOLARSHIP
• See page 187

SWE REGION E SCHOLARSHIP
• See page 187

SWE REGION G JUDY SIMMONS MEMORIAL SCHOLARSHIP
• See page 188

SWE REGION H SCHOLARSHIPS
• See page 188

SWE REGION J SCHOLARSHIP
• See page 188

WANDA MUNN SCHOLARSHIP
• See page 188

SOCIETY OF WOMEN ENGINEERS-ROCKY MOUNTAIN SECTION
http://www.swe-rms.org/

SOCIETY OF WOMEN ENGINEERS-ROCKY MOUNTAIN SECTION SCHOLARSHIP PROGRAM
• See page 188

STRAIGHTFORWARD MEDIA
http://www.straightforwardmedia.com/

STRAIGHTFORWARD MEDIA ENGINEERING SCHOLARSHIP
• See page 189

TAU BETA PI ASSOCIATION
http://www.tbp.org/

TAU BETA PI SCHOLARSHIP PROGRAM
• See page 189

TEXAS DEPARTMENT OF TRANSPORTATION
http://www.txdot.gov/

CONDITIONAL GRANT PROGRAM
Renewable award to students who are considered economically disadvantaged based on federal guidelines. The maximum amount awarded per semester is $3000 not to exceed $6000 per academic year. Students already enrolled in an undergraduate program should have minimum GPA 2.5 and students newly enrolling should have minimum GPA 3.0.

Academic Fields/Career Goals: Civil Engineering; Computer Science/Data Processing; Occupational Safety and Health.

Award: Grant for use in freshman, sophomore, junior, or senior years; renewable. *Amount:* up to $6000.

Eligibility Requirements: Applicant must be enrolled or expecting to enroll full-time at a four-year institution or university; resident of Texas and studying in Texas. Available to U.S. citizens.

Application Requirements: Application form, essay, interview, recommendations or references, test scores, transcript. *Deadline:* March 1.

Contact: Minnie Brown, Program Coordinator
Texas Department of Transportation
125 East 11th Street
Austin, TX 78701-2483
Phone: 512-416-4979
Fax: 512-416-4980
E-mail: mbrown2@dot.state.tx.us

TIMOTION
http://www.timotion.com/

TIMOTION ENGINEERING AND EXCELLENCE SCHOLARSHIP
In 2005, TiMOTION entered the world of electric linear actuators, quickly becoming the premier global designer and manufacturer of complete motion system solutions. Since its inception, the company has earned a reputation for reliable, high quality, competitively priced products that satisfy the needs of worldwide medical, furniture, ergonomic, and industrial markets. TiMOTION established this annual scholarship opportunity for aspiring engineers, ergonomists, or technology students to continue their education in hopes of powering the worlds towards a better future. Must be a full-time student enrolled in an engineering, ergonomics, or technology-focused program at an accredited undergraduate university or college. Must provide transcripts indicating strong academic performance with a GPA of 3.0 or higher. Must provide information regarding extracurricular activities, volunteering opportunities, or other community-involvement experience. We advise reading all information listed on our website prior to submitting your application, so that you can be better prepared. You will need to submit: 1. a transcript. You will need this as a record of proof to the course level and grades that you received since your freshman year in high school; 2. contact information. You must be prepared to provide us with your name, email address, and phone number so that we may contact you if your application is selected; 3. a school profile. We have an area of the application that asks you to give us the details of the university or college you will attend; 4.the essay. In 500-700 words, you will need to provide us with a comprehensive look into what inspired you to pursue your field of study. Check out sample applications for ideas. Want to be sure that you have gathered all the information you need? Do your research and see what a sample application looks like, but note that we will not accept the sample application in place of the actual application listed below. We wish all students the best as they move forward in continuing their education! See website for full details, http://www.timotion.com/Scholarship%20Program%202017/TiMOTION%20Scholarship%20Program%202017.pdf

Academic Fields/Career Goals: Civil Engineering; Electrical Engineering/Electronics; Energy and Power Engineering; Engineering-Related Technologies; Engineering/Technology; Industrial Design; Mechanical Engineering.

Award: Scholarship for use in freshman, sophomore, junior, senior, or postgraduate years; renewable. *Number:* 5. *Amount:* $2000.

Eligibility Requirements: Applicant must be enrolled or expecting to enroll full-time at a four-year institution or university. Applicant must have 3.0 GPA or higher. Available to U.S. and non-U.S. citizens.

Application Requirements: Application form, essay. *Deadline:* December 1.

Contact: Samantha Rosenfeld, Senior Marketing Associate
TiMOTION
1535 Center Park Drive
Charlotte, NC 28217
Phone: 704-708-6924 Ext. 914
E-mail: scholarships@timotion.com

TRANSTUTORS
http://www.transtutors.com/scholarship

TRANSTUTORS SCHOLARSHIP 2015-16
• *See page 85*

TURNER CONSTRUCTION COMPANY
http://www.turnerconstruction.com/

YOUTHFORCE 2020 SCHOLARSHIP PROGRAM
• *See page 124*

UNITED NEGRO COLLEGE FUND
http://www.uncf.org/

PROCTER & GAMBLE STEM SCHOLARSHIP
• *See page 116*

SUEZ CORPORATE SCHOLARS PROGRAM
• *See page 87*

UNCF STEM SCHOLARS PROGRAM
• *See page 159*

UNITED STATES SOCIETY ON DAMS
http://www.ussdams.org/

UNITED STATES SOCIETY ON DAMS SCHOLARSHIP AWARD
USSD annually awards scholarships to USSD Student Members whose academic program has a potential for developing practical solutions to dam-related issues. Applicants must be U.S. citizens enrolled full-time in U.S. academic institutions

Academic Fields/Career Goals: Civil Engineering; Engineering/Technology; Environmental Science; Hydrology.

Award: Prize for use in senior or graduate years; not renewable. *Number:* 1–4. *Amount:* $1000–$10,000.

Eligibility Requirements: Applicant must be enrolled or expecting to enroll full-time at a four-year institution or university. Applicant or parent of applicant must be member of United States Society on Dams. Available to U.S. citizens.

Application Requirements: Application form. *Deadline:* February 28.

Contact: Tina Stanard, Awards Committee Chair
United States Society on Dams
10431 Morado Circle
Suite 300
Austin, TX 78759
Phone: 512-617-3120
E-mail: ces@freese.com

UNIVERSITIES SPACE RESEARCH ASSOCIATION

http://www.usra.edu/

UNIVERSITIES SPACE RESEARCH ASSOCIATION SCHOLARSHIP AWARD PROGRAM

• See page 116

VECTORWORKS, INC.

http://www.vectorworks.net

VECTORWORKS DESIGN SCHOLARSHIP

• See page 124

VERMONT SPACE GRANT CONSORTIUM

http://www.cems.uvm.edu/vsgc

VERMONT SPACE GRANT CONSORTIUM

• See page 96

WIRE REINFORCEMENT INSTITUTE EDUCATION FOUNDATION

http://www.wirereinforcementinstitute.org/

WRI FOUNDATION COLLEGE SCHOLARSHIP PROGRAM

Academic scholarships for qualified current undergraduate and graduate level students officially declared as or presently pursuing four-year or graduate-level degrees in structural and/or civil engineering at accredited four-year universities or colleges in the U.S. or Canada. Scholarship recipients will also participate in the WRI Mentor Program for the year in which the scholarship is awarded.

Academic Fields/Career Goals: Civil Engineering; Construction Engineering/Management.

Award: Scholarship for use in sophomore, junior, senior, or graduate years; not renewable. *Number:* 2–5. *Amount:* $2000–$4000.

Eligibility Requirements: Applicant must be enrolled or expecting to enroll full-time at a four-year institution or university. Available to U.S. and non-U.S. citizens.

Application Requirements: Application form, essay. *Deadline:* April 15.

Contact: Scholarship Selection Committee
Wire Reinforcement Institute Education Foundation
942 Main Street
Hartford, CT 06103
Phone: 860-240-9545
E-mail: wrischolar@wirereinforcementinstitute.org

CLASSICS

ACL/NJCL NATIONAL LATIN EXAM

http://www.nle.org/

NATIONAL LATIN EXAM SCHOLARSHIP

Scholarships to high school seniors who are gold medal winners in Latin III, III-IV Prose, III-IV Poetry, or Latin V-VI their senior year. Applicants must agree to take at least one year of Latin or classical Greek language in college.

Academic Fields/Career Goals: Classics; Foreign Language.

Award: Scholarship for use in freshman, sophomore, junior, or senior years; renewable. *Number:* 21. *Amount:* $2000.

Eligibility Requirements: Applicant must be high school student; planning to enroll or expecting to enroll full-time at a four-year institution or university and must have an interest in Greek language or Latin language. Available to U.S. and non-U.S. citizens.

Application Requirements: Application form, essay. *Deadline:* May 16.

Contact: Mrs. Ephy Howard, Scholarship Chairperson
Phone: 888-378-7721

AMERICAN CLASSICAL LEAGUE/NATIONAL JUNIOR CLASSICAL LEAGUE

http://www.aclclassics.org/

NATIONAL JUNIOR CLASSICAL LEAGUE SCHOLARSHIP

A one-time award available to graduating high school seniors, who are members of the Junior Classical League. Preference is given to students who plan to major in the classics.

Academic Fields/Career Goals: Classics; Foreign Language; Humanities.

Award: Scholarship for use in freshman year; not renewable. *Number:* 7. *Amount:* $1000–$2000.

Eligibility Requirements: Applicant must be high school student; planning to enroll or expecting to enroll full-time at a two-year or four-year institution or university and must have an interest in foreign language. Applicant or parent of applicant must be member of Junior Classical League. Available to U.S. and non-U.S. citizens.

Application Requirements: Application form, essay. *Deadline:* April 1.

Contact: Sherwin Little, Administrator
American Classical League/National Junior Classical League
860 NW Washington Boulevard
Suite A
Hamilton, OH 45013
Phone: 513-529-7741
E-mail: info@aclclassics.org

AMERICAN SCHOOL OF CLASSICAL STUDIES AT ATHENS

http://www.ascsa.edu.gr/

ASCSA SUMMER SESSIONS SCHOLARSHIPS

• See page 108

SOCIETY FOR CLASSICAL STUDIES

http://www.classicalstudies.org/

MINORITY STUDENT SUMMER SCHOLARSHIP

• See page 118

STRAIGHTFORWARD MEDIA

http://www.straightforwardmedia.com/

STRAIGHTFORWARD MEDIA LIBERAL ARTS SCHOLARSHIP

• See page 126

COMMUNICATIONS

ADC RESEARCH INSTITUTE

http://www.adc.org/

JACK SHAHEEN MASS COMMUNICATIONS SCHOLARSHIP AWARD

Awarded to Arab-American students who excel in the mass communications field (journalism, radio, television or film). Must be a junior or senior undergraduate or graduate student. Must be U.S. citizen. Minimum 3.0 GPA required.

Academic Fields/Career Goals: Communications; Filmmaking/Video; Journalism; TV/Radio Broadcasting.

Award: Scholarship for use in junior, senior, or graduate years; not renewable. *Number:* 4. *Amount:* $2500.

Eligibility Requirements: Applicant must be of Arab heritage and enrolled or expecting to enroll full- or part-time at a four-year institution or university. Applicant must have 3.0 GPA or higher. Available to U.S. citizens.

Application Requirements: Application form, essay. *Deadline:* April 15.

Contact: Mr. Nabil Mohamad, Vice President
ADC Research Institute
1705 Desales street NW, 5th Floor
Washington, DC 20036
Phone: 202-244-2990
E-mail: nmohamad@adc.org

ALPHA OMEGA COUNCIL OF NEW ENGLAND

http://www.alphaomegacouncil.org/

ALPHA OMEGA SCHOLARSHIP IN MEMORY OF PETER AGRIS

Prerequisites for the scholarship include: Greek American heritage; U.S. citizenship; current full-time enrollment as a journalism or communications major at the graduate or undergraduate level in an accredited college or university in the United States; active participation in school, community, church organizations; a minimum of a 3.0 GPA and demonstrated financial need. Interested candidates should visit www.alphaomegacouncil.com or write to The Peter Agris Memorial Scholarships Committee, c/o Nancy Agris Savage, 9 Nonesuch Drive, Natick, MA 01760. Any questions may be directed to: nancyasavage@gmail.com. Applications, transcripts, the required essay and any published work that might enhance the application must be returned by email to nancyasavage@gmail.com, or by mail to the above address, no later than March 1, 2017.

Academic Fields/Career Goals: Communications; Journalism.

Award: Scholarship for use in freshman, sophomore, junior, senior, graduate, or postgraduate years; not renewable. *Number:* 6. *Amount:* $5000.

Eligibility Requirements: Applicant must be Eastern Orthodox; of Greek heritage and enrolled or expecting to enroll full-time at a four-year institution or university. Applicant or parent of applicant must have employment or volunteer experience in journalism/broadcasting. Applicant must have 3.0 GPA or higher. Available to U.S. citizens.

Application Requirements: Application form, essay. *Deadline:* March 1.

Contact: Mrs. Nancy Savage, Executive Director
Alpha Omega Council of New England
Peter Agris Memorial Journalism Scholarships
9 Nonesuch Drive
Natick, MA 01760
Phone: 508-733-6883
E-mail: nancyasavage@gmail.com

AMERICAN INSTITUTE OF POLISH CULTURE INC.

http://www.ampolinstitute.org/

HARRIET IRSAY SCHOLARSHIP GRANT
• *See page 127*

AMERICAN QUARTER HORSE FOUNDATION (AQHF)

http://www.aqha.com/foundation

AQHF JOURNALISM OR COMMUNICATIONS SCHOLARSHIP

Ideal candidate is an AQHA or AQHYA member pursuing a college degree in journalism or communications. Recipient must pursue a career in news, editorial or print journalism, photojournalism or a related field.

Academic Fields/Career Goals: Communications; Journalism; Photojournalism/Photography.

Award: Scholarship for use in freshman, sophomore, junior, senior, or graduate years; renewable. *Number:* 1. *Amount:* $8000.

Eligibility Requirements: Applicant must be enrolled or expecting to enroll full-time at a two-year or four-year institution or university and must have an interest in animal/agricultural competition or writing. Applicant or parent of applicant must be member of American Quarter Horse Association. Applicant must have 2.5 GPA or higher. Available to U.S. and non-U.S. citizens.

Application Requirements: Application form, financial need analysis. *Deadline:* December 1.

Contact: Scholarship Office
American Quarter Horse Foundation (AQHF)
2601 East Interstate 40
Amarillo, TX 79104
Phone: 806-378-5040
E-mail: foundation@aqha.org

ARAB AMERICAN SCHOLARSHIP FOUNDATION

http://www.lahc.org/

LEBANESE AMERICAN HERITAGE CLUB'S SCHOLARSHIP FUND

Scholarship for high school, undergraduate, or graduate students who are of Arab descent. Minimum 3.0 GPA required for high school and undergraduate applicants, 3.5 GPA for graduate student applicants. Must be U.S. citizens.

Academic Fields/Career Goals: Communications; Political Science.

Award: Scholarship for use in freshman, sophomore, junior, senior, or graduate years; not renewable. *Number:* 1. *Amount:* $1000.

Eligibility Requirements: Applicant must be of Arab heritage; enrolled or expecting to enroll full-time at a four-year institution or university and resident of Michigan. Applicant must have 3.0 GPA or higher. Available to U.S. citizens.

Application Requirements: Application form, essay, financial need analysis, recommendations or references, Student Aid Report (SAR), transcript. *Deadline:* April 6.

Contact: Suehalia Amen, Communications Chair
Phone: 313-846-8480
Fax: 313-846-2710
E-mail: sueamen@lahc.org

ARRL FOUNDATION INC.

http://www.arrl.org/

CHARLES CLARKE CORDLE MEMORIAL SCHOLARSHIP

One-time award for licensed amateur radio operators. Must have minimum GPA of 2.5. Preference to students studying electronics, communications, or related fields. Preference given to residents of Georgia or Alabama attending institutions in those states.

Academic Fields/Career Goals: Communications; Electrical Engineering/Electronics.

Award: Scholarship for use in freshman, sophomore, junior, or senior years; not renewable. *Number:* 1. *Amount:* $1000.

Eligibility Requirements: Applicant must be enrolled or expecting to enroll full-time at a four-year institution or university; resident of Alabama, Georgia; studying in Alabama, Georgia and must have an interest in amateur radio. Applicant must have 2.5 GPA or higher. Available to U.S. citizens.

Application Requirements: Application form. *Deadline:* January 31.

Contact: Ms. Mary Hobart, Secretary
   Phone: 860-594-0397
   E-mail: k1mmh@arrl.org

CHARLES N. FISHER MEMORIAL SCHOLARSHIP
• *See page 111*

DR. JAMES L. LAWSON MEMORIAL SCHOLARSHIP

One-time award of $500 available to general amateur radio operators. For Baccalaureate or higher course of study in electronics, communications, or a related field. Preference given to residents of New England states (ME, NH, VT, CT, RI, MA) and New York state and attending college in any of those states.

Academic Fields/Career Goals: Communications; Electrical Engineering/Electronics.

Award: Scholarship for use in freshman, sophomore, junior, senior, or graduate years; not renewable. *Number:* 1. *Amount:* $500.

Eligibility Requirements: Applicant must be enrolled or expecting to enroll full-time at a four-year institution or university; resident of Connecticut, Maine, Massachusetts, New Hampshire, New York, Rhode Island, Vermont; studying in Connecticut, Maine, Massachusetts, New Hampshire, New York, Rhode Island, Vermont and must have an interest in amateur radio. Available to U.S. citizens.

Application Requirements: Application form. *Deadline:* January 31.

Contact: Ms. Mary Hobart, Secretary
   Phone: 860-594-0397
   E-mail: k1mmh@arrl.org

FRED R. MCDANIEL MEMORIAL SCHOLARSHIP

One $500 award is available to students who possess a general class or higher amateur radio license. Must be studying electronics, communications, or related fields at a Bachelor's level. Preference will be given to applicants with a 3.0 GPA or higher who are residents of FCC 5th call district (TX, OK, AR, LA, MS, NM).

Academic Fields/Career Goals: Communications; Electrical Engineering/Electronics.

Award: Scholarship for use in freshman, sophomore, junior, or senior years; not renewable. *Number:* 1. *Amount:* $500.

Eligibility Requirements: Applicant must be enrolled or expecting to enroll full- or part-time at a four-year institution or university; resident of Arkansas, Louisiana, Mississippi, New Mexico, Oklahoma, Texas and must have an interest in amateur radio. Applicant must have 3.0 GPA or higher. Available to U.S. citizens.

Application Requirements: Application form. *Deadline:* January 31.

Contact: Ms. Mary Hobart, Secretary
   Phone: 860-594-0397
   E-mail: k1mmh@arrl.org

IRVING W. COOK, WA0CGS, SCHOLARSHIP

One-time award of $1000 to students pursuing a Baccalaureate or higher degree in communications, electronics, or related fields. Must be a amateur radio operator. Preference to Kansas resident but may attend school in any state.

Academic Fields/Career Goals: Communications; Electrical Engineering/Electronics.

Award: Scholarship for use in freshman, sophomore, junior, senior, or graduate years; not renewable. *Number:* 1. *Amount:* $1000.

Eligibility Requirements: Applicant must be enrolled or expecting to enroll full-time at a four-year institution or university; resident of Kansas and must have an interest in amateur radio. Available to U.S. citizens.

Application Requirements: Application form. *Deadline:* January 31.

Contact: Ms. Mary Hobart, Secretary
   Phone: 860-594-0397
   E-mail: k1mmh@arrl.org

L. PHIL AND ALICE J. WICKER SCHOLARSHIP

One-time award available to a licensed general amateur radio operator. Preference given to residents in the ARRL Roanoke Division (North Carolina, South Carolina, Virginia, West Virginia) and attending school in that division. Preference to Baccalaureate or higher degree studies in electronics, communications, or related fields.

Academic Fields/Career Goals: Communications; Electrical Engineering/Electronics.

Award: Scholarship for use in freshman, sophomore, junior, senior, or graduate years; not renewable. *Number:* 1. *Amount:* $500.

Eligibility Requirements: Applicant must be enrolled or expecting to enroll full-time at a four-year institution or university; resident of North Carolina, South Dakota, Virginia, West Virginia; studying in North Carolina, South Carolina, Virginia, West Virginia and must have an interest in amateur radio. Available to U.S. citizens.

Application Requirements: Application form. *Deadline:* January 31.

Contact: Ms. Mary Hobart, Secretary
   Phone: 860-594-0397
   E-mail: k1mmh@arrl.org

MAGNOLIA DX ASSOCIATION SCHOLARSHIP

One $500 award is available to a student majoring in electronics, communications, computer science, engineering, or a related field. Preference is given to graduating high school seniors who are residents of Mississippi or Delta division planning to study in Mississippi. Must have obtained a technical class or higher amateur radio license.

Academic Fields/Career Goals: Communications; Computer Science/Data Processing; Electrical Engineering/Electronics; Engineering/Technology.

Award: Scholarship for use in freshman, sophomore, junior, or senior years; not renewable. *Number:* 1. *Amount:* $500.

Eligibility Requirements: Applicant must be enrolled or expecting to enroll full- or part-time at a two-year or four-year or technical institution or university; resident of Mississippi; studying in Mississippi and must have an interest in amateur radio. Available to U.S. citizens.

Application Requirements: Application form. *Deadline:* January 31.

Contact: Ms. Mary Hobart, Secretary
   Phone: 860-594-0397
   E-mail: k1mmh@arrl.org

MISSISSIPPI SCHOLARSHIP
• *See page 111*

ORLANDO HAMCATION SCHOLARSHIP

One $1000 scholarship for U.S. citizen studying a technical field that supports the radio art at an accredited four-year college or university. Applicant may have any class of active Amateur Radio license. Must be a resident of Florida, with preference given to residents of Central Florida (Orange, Seminole, Osceola, Lake, Volusia, Brevard and Polk Counties).

Academic Fields/Career Goals: Communications; Electrical Engineering/Electronics.

Award: Scholarship for use in freshman, sophomore, junior, or senior years; not renewable. *Number:* 1. *Amount:* $1000.

Eligibility Requirements: Applicant must be enrolled or expecting to enroll full-time at a four-year institution or university; resident of Florida and must have an interest in amateur radio. Available to U.S. citizens.

Application Requirements: Application form. *Deadline:* January 31.

Contact: Ms. Mary Hobart, Secretary
   Phone: 860-594-0397
   E-mail: k1mmh@arrl.org

PAUL AND HELEN L. GRAUER SCHOLARSHIP
• *See page 111*

ASIAN AMERICAN JOURNALISTS ASSOCIATION

http://www.aaja.org/

CIC/ANNA CHENNAULT SCHOLARSHIP

$5,000 is available to current high school seniors or college students committed to and/or interested in the field of journalism as a career or area of study. The selected student will receive travel, lodging and registration to attend the 2017 AAJA national annual convention July 26 - 29, 2017 in Philadelphia. Depending on the winner's area of study, the student will also be paired with a professional print, online or broadcast mentor at the convention to help them network.

Academic Fields/Career Goals: Communications; Journalism.

Award: Scholarship for use in freshman, sophomore, junior, senior, or graduate years; not renewable. *Number:* 1. *Amount:* $5000.

Eligibility Requirements: Applicant must be enrolled or expecting to enroll full-time at a two-year or four-year institution or university. Available to U.S. citizens.

Application Requirements: Application form, essay, financial need analysis. *Deadline:* April 16.

Contact: Justin Seiter, Program Coordinator
Asian American Journalists Association
5 Third Street
Suite 1108
San Francisco, CA 94103
Phone: 415-346-2051 Ext. 107
E-mail: justins@aaja.org

ASIAN AMERICAN JOURNALISTS ASSOCIATION, SEATTLE CHAPTER

http://www.aajaseattle.org/

NORTHWEST JOURNALISTS OF COLOR SCHOLARSHIP

• See page 88

AUTOMOTIVE WOMEN'S ALLIANCE FOUNDATION

http://www.awafoundation.org/index.php

AUTOMOTIVE WOMEN'S ALLIANCE FOUNDATION SCHOLARSHIPS

• See page 74

BMI FOUNDATION, INC.

http://www.bmifoundation.org/

BMI FOUNDERS AWARD FOR RADIO BROADCASTING

The BMI Founders Award competition is open to radio broadcasting students age 17 - 24 nationwide. A $5,000 scholarship will be awarded for the best original essay response. The program was established in 2015 to recognize future innovators in broadcast radio, and commemorates the group of radio industry leaders who founded Broadcast Music, Inc. in 1939.

Academic Fields/Career Goals: Communications; Journalism.

Award: Scholarship for use in freshman, sophomore, junior, senior, graduate, or postgraduate years; not renewable. *Number:* 1. *Amount:* $5000.

Eligibility Requirements: Applicant must be age 17-24 and enrolled or expecting to enroll full- or part-time at a two-year or four-year or technical institution or university. Available to U.S. and non-U.S. citizens.

Application Requirements: Application form, essay. *Deadline:* February 1.

Contact: Dan Spears, Director
BMI Foundation, Inc.
7 World Trade Center
250 Greenwich Street
New York, NY 10007
Phone: 212-2203103
E-mail: info@bmifoundation.org

CCNMA: LATINO JOURNALISTS OF CALIFORNIA

http://www.ccnma.org/

CCNMA SCHOLARSHIPS

Scholarships for Latinos interested in pursuing a career in journalism. Awards based on scholastic achievement, financial need, and cultural awareness. Submit sample of work. Award limited to California residents or those attending school in California.

Academic Fields/Career Goals: Communications; Graphics/Graphic Arts/Printing; Journalism; Photojournalism/Photography; TV/Radio Broadcasting.

Award: Scholarship for use in freshman, sophomore, junior, senior, or graduate years; not renewable. *Number:* 5–10. *Amount:* $500–$1000.

Eligibility Requirements: Applicant must be of Latin American/Caribbean heritage; Hispanic; enrolled or expecting to enroll full-time at a two-year or four-year institution or university and resident of California. Applicant must have 2.5 GPA or higher. Available to U.S. and non-U.S. citizens.

Application Requirements: Application form, application form may be submitted online (http://www.ccnma.org), essay, financial need analysis, interview, portfolio, recommendations or references, resume, transcript. *Deadline:* April 1.

Contact: Mr. Julio Moran, Executive Director
CCNMA: Latino Journalists of California
ASU Walter Cronkite School of Journalism and Mass Communication
725 Arizona Avenue, Suite 406
Santa Monica, CA 90401-1723
Phone: 424-229-9482
Fax: 424-238-0271
E-mail: ccnmainfo@ccnma.org

CHARLES AND LUCILLE KING FAMILY FOUNDATION, INC.

http://www.kingfoundation.org/

CHARLES AND LUCILLE KING FAMILY FOUNDATION SCHOLARSHIPS

Renewable award for college undergraduates at junior or senior level pursuing television, film, or communication studies to further their education. Must attend a four-year undergraduate institution. Minimum 3.0 GPA required to renew scholarship. Must have completed at least two years of study and be currently enrolled in a U.S. college or university. Application may be downloaded on website.

Academic Fields/Career Goals: Communications; Filmmaking/Video; TV/Radio Broadcasting.

Award: Scholarship for use in junior or senior years; renewable. *Number:* 10–20. *Amount:* $3500–$7000.

Eligibility Requirements: Applicant must be enrolled or expecting to enroll full-time at a four-year institution or university. Applicant must have 3.0 GPA or higher. Available to U.S. and non-U.S. citizens.

Application Requirements: Application form, essay, financial need analysis, recommendations or references, transcript. *Deadline:* March 15.

Contact: Michael Donovan, Educational Director, The Charles and Lucille King Family Foundation
Charles and Lucille King Family Foundation, Inc.
1212 Avenue of the Americas
7th Floor
New York, NY 10036
Phone: 212-682-2913
E-mail: info@kingfoundation.org

CONNECTICUT CHAPTER OF SOCIETY OF PROFESSIONAL JOURNALISTS

http://www.ctspj.org/

CONNECTICUT SPJ BOB EDDY SCHOLARSHIP PROGRAM

One-time awards of $250 to $2000 for college juniors or seniors planning a career in journalism. Must be a Connecticut resident attending a four year college or any student attending a four year college in Connecticut.

Academic Fields/Career Goals: Communications; Journalism; Photojournalism/Photography.

Award: Scholarship for use in junior or senior years; not renewable. *Number:* 5. *Amount:* $250–$2000.

Eligibility Requirements: Applicant must be enrolled or expecting to enroll full-time at a four-year institution or university; resident of Connecticut; studying in Connecticut and must have an interest in writing. Available to U.S. and non-U.S. citizens.

Application Requirements: Application form, entry in a contest, essay, financial need analysis, transcript. *Deadline:* April 4.

Contact: Debra Estock, Scholarship Committee Chairman
Connecticut Chapter of Society of Professional Journalists
71 Kenwood Avenue
Fairfield, CT 06824
Phone: 203-255-2127
E-mail: debae@optonline.net

INSTITUTE FOR HUMANE STUDIES

http://www.theihs.org/

HUMANE STUDIES FELLOWSHIPS

Renewable award for undergraduate and graduate students in selected disciplines. Applicants should have demonstrated interest in classical liberal or libertarian ideas and must intend to pursue a scholarly career. Minimum 3.5 GPA required. Application fee: $25.

Academic Fields/Career Goals: Communications; Economics; History; Humanities; Law/Legal Services; Literature/English/Writing; Political Science; Social Sciences.

Award: Scholarship for use in junior or senior years; not renewable. *Number:* 140–180. *Amount:* $2000–$12,000.

Eligibility Requirements: Applicant must be enrolled or expecting to enroll full-time at a two-year or four-year institution or university. Applicant must have 3.5 GPA or higher. Available to U.S. and Canadian citizens.

Application Requirements: Application form, essay, recommendations or references, resume, test scores, transcript. *Fee:* $25. *Deadline:* December 31.

Contact: Director, Humane Studies Fellowship
E-mail: HSF@TheIHS.org

INTERNATIONAL COMMUNICATIONS INDUSTRIES FOUNDATION

http://www.infocomm.org/scholarships

ICIF SCHOLARSHIP FOR EMPLOYEES AND DEPENDENTS OF MEMBER ORGANIZATIONS

Scholarship for a spouse, child, stepchild or grandchild of an employee of an InfoComm International member organization or for an employee of an InfoComm International member organization. Must be majoring in audiovisual related fields, such as audio, video, audiovisual, electronics, telecommunications, technical theatre, data networking, software development, and information technology. Minimum of 2.75 GPA required. Must show evidence of AV experience (completed course, job, internship, etc.).

Academic Fields/Career Goals: Communications; Computer Science/Data Processing; Electrical Engineering/Electronics; Filmmaking/Video.

Award: Scholarship for use in freshman, sophomore, junior, senior, or graduate years; not renewable. *Number:* 1–50. *Amount:* $1500.

Eligibility Requirements: Applicant must be enrolled or expecting to enroll full-time at a two-year or four-year or technical institution or university. Applicant must have 3.0 GPA or higher. Available to U.S. and non-U.S. citizens.

Application Requirements: Application form, essay, recommendations or references, transcript. *Deadline:* May 10.

Contact: Ms. Shana Rieger, Membership and Social Media Program Manager
International Communications Industries Foundation
11242 Waples Mill Road, Suite 200
Fairfax, VA 22030
Phone: 703-273-7200 Ext. 3690
Fax: 703-278-8082
E-mail: srieger@infocomm.org

INTERNATIONAL COMMUNICATIONS INDUSTRIES FOUNDATION AV SCHOLARSHIP

Scholarship for students majoring in audiovisual related fields such as audio, video, audiovisual, electronics, telecommunications, technical theatre, data networking, software development, information and technology. Minimum 2.75 GPA required. Must provide evidence of audiovisual knowledge (completed course, job, internship, etc.).

Academic Fields/Career Goals: Communications; Computer Science/Data Processing; Electrical Engineering/Electronics; Filmmaking/Video.

Award: Scholarship for use in freshman, sophomore, junior, senior, or graduate years; not renewable. *Number:* 1–50. *Amount:* $1200.

Eligibility Requirements: Applicant must be enrolled or expecting to enroll full-time at a two-year or four-year or technical institution or university. Applicant must have 3.0 GPA or higher. Available to U.S. and Canadian citizens.

Application Requirements: Application form, essay, recommendations or references, transcript. *Deadline:* May 10.

Contact: Ms. Shana Rieger, Membership and Social Media Program Manager
International Communications Industries Foundation
11242 Waples Mill Road, Suite 200
Fairfax, VA 22030
Phone: 703-273-7200 Ext. 3690
Fax: 703-278-8082
E-mail: srieger@infocomm.org

INTERNATIONAL FOODSERVICE EDITORIAL COUNCIL

http://www.ifeconline.com/

INTERNATIONAL FOODSERVICE EDITORIAL COUNCIL COMMUNICATIONS SCHOLARSHIP

• *See page 88*

JOHN BAYLISS BROADCAST FOUNDATION

http://www.beaweb.org/bayliss/radio.html

JOHN BAYLISS BROADCAST RADIO SCHOLARSHIP

One-time award for college juniors or seniors majoring in broadcast communications with a concentration in radio broadcasting. Must have history of radio-related activities and a GPA of at least 3.0.

Academic Fields/Career Goals: Communications; Journalism; TV/Radio Broadcasting.

Award: Scholarship for use in junior or senior years; not renewable. *Number:* 2–6. *Amount:* $5000.

Eligibility Requirements: Applicant must be enrolled or expecting to enroll full-time at a four-year institution or university. Applicant must have 3.0 GPA or higher. Available to U.S. citizens.

Application Requirements: Application form, essay, recommendations or references, resume, self-addressed stamped envelope with application, transcript. *Deadline:* April 30.

Contact: Chairperson
John Bayliss Broadcast Foundation
171 17th Street
Pacific Grove, CA 93950
E-mail: info@baylissfoundation.org

JORGE MAS CANOSA FREEDOM FOUNDATION

http://masscholarships.org/

MAS FAMILY SCHOLARSHIP AWARD

• *See page 165*

LAGRANT FOUNDATION

http://www.lagrantfoundation.org/

LAGRANT FOUNDATION SCHOLARSHIP FOR UNDERGRADUATES

• *See page 88*

NATIONAL ACADEMY OF TELEVISION ARTS & SCIENCES—OHIO VALLEY CHAPTER

http://ohiovalleyemmy.org/

DAVID J. CLARKE MEMORIAL SCHOLARSHIP

One $3000 scholarship offered to a full-time graduate or undergraduate student, majoring in broadcasting (or other designated television major) at an accredited college or university in the designated market area of stations serving the Ohio Valley Chapter of the National Academy of Television Arts and Sciences. The award will be given to a student who has achieved academic excellence; who is involved in co-curricular television activities (through student media, internships, or related employment); who possesses a desire to engage in television as a career; and who has high integrity and personal character. Financial need may also be considered. Must apply online at http://ohiovalleyemmy.org/students/scholarship-application/.

Academic Fields/Career Goals: Communications; Filmmaking/Video; Journalism; TV/Radio Broadcasting.

Award: Scholarship for use in freshman, sophomore, junior, senior, or graduate years; not renewable. *Number:* 1. *Amount:* $3000.

Eligibility Requirements: Applicant must be enrolled or expecting to enroll full-time at a four-year institution or university. Available to U.S. citizens.

Application Requirements: Application form, portfolio. *Deadline:* April 30.

NATIONAL ACADEMY OF TELEVISION ARTS AND SCIENCES

http://www.emmyonline.tv/

DOUGLAS W. MUMMERT SCHOLARSHIP
• *See page 129*

JIM MCKAY MEMORIAL SCHOLARSHIP

The Jim McKay Memorial Scholarship honors sports journalist Jim McKay (1921-2008) and was established in 2009 by the HBO, CBS, NBC, ABC and FOX networks. It is presented at the Sports Emmys each May. It is awarded to a college-bound applicant who demonstrates exceptional talent as a creator of video programming as well as outstanding academic achievement and potential for success in a highly competitive profession.

Academic Fields/Career Goals: Communications; Filmmaking/Video; Journalism; Music; Performing Arts; Photojournalism/Photography; TV/Radio Broadcasting.

Award: Scholarship for use in freshman year; not renewable. *Number:* 1. *Amount:* $10,000.

Eligibility Requirements: Applicant must be high school student and planning to enroll or expecting to enroll full-time at a two-year or four-year or technical institution or university. Available to U.S. citizens.

Application Requirements: Application form, essay. *Deadline:* February 28.

Contact: Mr. Adam Sharp, Chair, Scholarship Committee
Phone: 212-586-8424
Fax: 212-246-8129
E-mail: scholarship@emmyonline.tv

MIKE WALLACE MEMORIAL SCHOLARSHIP

The Mike Wallace Memorial Scholarship is funded by a five-year grant from CBS News in honor of longtime correspondent Mike Wallace (1918-2012) and presented each year at the News & Documentary Emmys. It is awarded to a college-bound applicant who demonstrates exceptional talent as a creator of video programming as well as outstanding academic achievement and potential for success in a highly competitive profession.

Academic Fields/Career Goals: Communications; Filmmaking/Video; Journalism; Music; Performing Arts; Photojournalism/Photography; TV/Radio Broadcasting.

Award: Scholarship for use in freshman year; not renewable. *Number:* 1. *Amount:* $10,000.

Eligibility Requirements: Applicant must be high school student and planning to enroll or expecting to enroll full-time at a two-year or four-year or technical institution or university. Available to U.S. citizens.

Application Requirements: Application form, essay. *Deadline:* February 28.

Contact: Mr. Adam Sharp, Chair, Scholarship Committee
Phone: 212-586-8424
Fax: 212-246-8129
E-mail: scholarship@emmyonline.tv

NATIONAL ACADEMY OF TELEVISION ARTS AND SCIENCES TRUSTEES SCHOLARSHIP

The Trustees Scholarship was established by the NATAS Board of Trustees to recognize standout graduating high school seniors who intend to pursue degrees in pursuit of a career in any aspect of the television industry.

Academic Fields/Career Goals: Communications; Filmmaking/Video; Journalism; Music; Performing Arts; Photojournalism/Photography; TV/Radio Broadcasting.

Award: Scholarship for use in freshman year; not renewable. *Number:* 1. *Amount:* $10,000.

Eligibility Requirements: Applicant must be high school student and planning to enroll or expecting to enroll full-time at a two-year or four-year or technical institution or university. Available to U.S. citizens.

Application Requirements: Application form, essay. *Deadline:* February 28.

Contact: Mr. Adam Sharp, Chair, Scholarship Committee
Phone: 212-586-8424
Fax: 212-246-8129
E-mail: scholarship@emmyonline.tv

RANDY FALCO SCHOLARSHIP

The Falco Scholarship is awarded to a college-bound Hispanic or Latino student who demonstrates exceptional talent as a creator of video programming as well as outstanding academic achievement and potential for success in a highly competitive profession. The $10,000 annual scholarship honors the industry contributions of renowned media executive Randy Falco, currently the President and Chief Executive Officer of Univision Communications Inc. (UCI).

Academic Fields/Career Goals: Communications; Filmmaking/Video; Journalism; Music; Performing Arts; Photojournalism/Photography; TV/Radio Broadcasting.

Award: Scholarship for use in freshman year; not renewable. *Number:* 1. *Amount:* $10,000.

Eligibility Requirements: Applicant must be Hispanic; high school student and planning to enroll or expecting to enroll full-time at a two-year or four-year or technical institution or university. Available to U.S. citizens.

Application Requirements: Application form, essay. *Deadline:* February 28.

Contact: Mr. Adam Sharp, Chair, Scholarship Committee
Phone: 212-586-8424
Fax: 212-246-8129
E-mail: scholarship@emmyonline.tv

NATIONAL ACADEMY OF TELEVISION ARTS AND SCIENCES, MICHIGAN CHAPTER

http://natasmichigan.org

DR. LYNNE BOYLE/JOHN SCHIMPF UNDERGRADUATE SCHOLARSHIP
• *See page 89*

NATIONAL ASSOCIATION OF BLACK JOURNALISTS

http://www.nabj.org/

NABJ SCHOLARSHIP

Scholarship for a student who is currently attending an accredited four-year college or university. Must be enrolled as an undergraduate or graduate student majoring in journalism (print, radio, online, or television). Minimum 2.5 GPA. Must be a member of NABJ. Scholarship value and the number of awards granted varies annually.

Academic Fields/Career Goals: Communications; Journalism; TV/Radio Broadcasting.

Award: Scholarship for use in freshman, sophomore, junior, senior, or graduate years; not renewable.

Eligibility Requirements: Applicant must be enrolled or expecting to enroll full-time at a four-year institution or university. Applicant must have 2.5 GPA or higher. Available to U.S. and non-U.S. citizens.

Application Requirements: Application form, driver's license, essay, interview, recommendations or references, transcript. *Deadline:* March 17.

Contact: Irving Washington, Manager
    Phone: 301-445-7100
    Fax: 301-445-7101
    E-mail: iwashington@nabj.org

NATIONAL ASSOCIATION OF BROADCASTERS

http://www.nab.org/

NATIONAL ASSOCIATION OF BROADCASTERS GRANTS FOR RESEARCH IN BROADCASTING

Award program is intended to fund research on economic, business, social, and policy issues important to station managers and other decision-makers in the United States commercial broadcast industry. Competition is open to all academic personnel. Graduate students and senior undergraduates are invited to submit proposals. For details refer to website http://www.nab.org.

Academic Fields/Career Goals: Communications; Journalism; TV/Radio Broadcasting.

Award: Grant for use in senior, graduate, or postgraduate years; not renewable. *Number:* 2. *Amount:* $5000.

Eligibility Requirements: Applicant must be enrolled or expecting to enroll full-time at a four-year institution or university. Available to U.S. and non-U.S. citizens.

Application Requirements: Application form, recommendations or references, research proposal, budget. *Deadline:* February 1.

Contact: Debbie Milman, Research Director
    National Association of Broadcasters
    1771 N Street, NW
    Washington, DC 20036
    Phone: 202-429-5383
    Fax: 202-429-4199
    E-mail: dmilman@nab.org

NATIONAL ASSOCIATION OF HISPANIC JOURNALISTS (NAHJ)

http://www.nahj.org/

NATIONAL ASSOCIATION OF HISPANIC JOURNALISTS SCHOLARSHIP

One-time award for high school seniors, college undergraduates, and first-year graduate students who are pursuing careers in English- or Spanish-language print, photo, broadcast, or online journalism. Students may major or plan to major in any subject, but must demonstrate a sincere desire to pursue a career in journalism. Must submit resume and work samples. Applications available only on website http://www.nahj.org.

Academic Fields/Career Goals: Communications; Journalism; Photojournalism/Photography; TV/Radio Broadcasting.

Award: Scholarship for use in freshman, sophomore, junior, senior, or graduate years; not renewable. *Amount:* $1000–$2000.

Eligibility Requirements: Applicant must be enrolled or expecting to enroll full-time at a four-year institution or university and must have an interest in photography/photogrammetry/filmmaking or writing. Available to U.S. citizens.

Application Requirements: Application form, essay, financial need analysis, recommendations or references, resume, transcript, work samples. *Deadline:* March 31.

Contact: Virginia Galindo, Program Assistant
    Phone: 202-662-7145
    E-mail: vgalindo@nahj.org

NATIONAL ASSOCIATION OF WATER COMPANIES-NEW JERSEY CHAPTER

http://www.nawc.org

NATIONAL ASSOCIATION OF WATER COMPANIES-NEW JERSEY CHAPTER SCHOLARSHIP
• *See page 80*

NATIONAL CATTLEMEN'S FOUNDATION

http://www.nationalcattlemensfoundation.org/

CME BEEF INDUSTRY SCHOLARSHIP
• *See page 93*

NATIONAL DAIRY SHRINE

http://www.dairyshrine.org/

MARSHALL E. MCCULLOUGH-NATIONAL DAIRY SHRINE SCHOLARSHIPS
• *See page 100*

NATIONAL INSTITUTE FOR LABOR RELATIONS RESEARCH

http://www.nilrr.org/

NATIONAL INSTITUTE FOR LABOR RELATIONS RESEARCH WILLIAM B. RUGGLES JOURNALISM SCHOLARSHIP

One-time award for undergraduate or graduate study in journalism, mass communications or related major. Submit 500-word essay demonstrating an understanding of the right-to-work principle. High school seniors accepted into certified journalism school may apply. Specify "Journalism" or "Ruggles" scholarship on any correspondence.

Academic Fields/Career Goals: Communications; Journalism.

Award: Scholarship for use in freshman, sophomore, junior, senior, graduate, or postgraduate years; not renewable. *Number:* 1. *Amount:* $2000.

Eligibility Requirements: Applicant must be enrolled or expecting to enroll full-time at a four-year institution or university and must have an interest in writing. Available to U.S. citizens.

Application Requirements: Application form, application form may be submitted online (http://www.nilrr.org/resources/online-scholarship-application-401/), essay, transcript. *Deadline:* December 31.

Contact: Cathy Jones, Scholarship Coordinator
    National Institute for Labor Relations Research
    5211 Port Royal Road, Suite 510
    Springfield, VA 22151
    Phone: 703-321-9606 Ext. 2247
    Fax: 703-321-7143
    E-mail: clj@nrtw.org

NEW JERSEY BROADCASTERS ASSOCIATION

http://www.njba.com/

MICHAEL S. LIBRETTI SCHOLARSHIP

Scholarships for undergraduate students in broadcasting, communication and journalism. Must be a New Jersey resident.

Academic Fields/Career Goals: Communications; Journalism; TV/Radio Broadcasting.

Award: Scholarship for use in freshman, sophomore, junior, or senior years; not renewable. *Number:* 1. *Amount:* up to $5000.

Eligibility Requirements: Applicant must be enrolled or expecting to enroll full-time at a four-year institution or university and resident of New Jersey. Available to U.S. citizens.

Application Requirements: Application form. *Deadline:* varies.

Contact: Phil Roberts, Scholarships Coordinator
Phone: 888-652-2366
Fax: 609-860-0110
E-mail: njba@njba.com

OHIO NEWSPAPERS FOUNDATION
http://www.ohionews.org

HAROLD K. DOUTHIT SCHOLARSHIP
• *See page 89*

OHIO NEWSPAPERS FOUNDATION MINORITY SCHOLARSHIP
• *See page 89*

OHIO NEWSPAPERS FOUNDATION UNIVERSITY JOURNALISM SCHOLARSHIP
• *See page 90*

ONWA ANNUAL SCHOLARSHIP
• *See page 90*

OREGON ASSOCIATION OF BROADCASTERS
http://www.theoab.org/

OAB FOUNDATION SCHOLARSHIP
Award for students to begin or continue their education in broadcast and related studies. Must have a minimum GPA of 3.25. Must be a resident of Oregon studying in Oregon. For more details, refer to website at http//www.TheOAB.org.

Academic Fields/Career Goals: Communications; Journalism; TV/Radio Broadcasting.

Award: Scholarship for use in freshman, sophomore, junior, senior, graduate, or postgraduate years; renewable. *Number:* 4. *Amount:* $2500–$3500.

Eligibility Requirements: Applicant must be enrolled or expecting to enroll full-time at a two-year or four-year institution or university and resident of Oregon. Available to U.S. citizens.

Application Requirements: Application form, essay, financial need analysis, recommendations or references, resume, transcript. *Deadline:* May 3.

Contact: Mr. Bill Johnstone, President and Chief Executive Officer
Oregon Association of Broadcasters
9020 SW Washington Square Road
Suite 140
Portland, OR 97223-4433
Phone: 503-443-2299
Fax: 503-443-2488
E-mail: theoab@theoab.org

OUTDOOR WRITERS ASSOCIATION OF AMERICA
http://www.owaa.org/

OUTDOOR WRITERS ASSOCIATION OF AMERICA - BODIE MCDOWELL SCHOLARSHIP AWARD
One-time award for undergraduate and graduate students who demonstrate outdoor communications talent and intend to make a career in this field. Applicants must include a letter of recommendation from their institution and samples of their outdoor communications work.

Academic Fields/Career Goals: Communications; Environmental Science; Filmmaking/Video; Journalism; Literature/English/Writing; Natural Resources; Photojournalism/Photography; TV/Radio Broadcasting.

Award: Scholarship for use in freshman, sophomore, junior, senior, graduate, or postgraduate years; not renewable. *Number:* 2–6. *Amount:* $1000–$5000.

Eligibility Requirements: Applicant must be enrolled or expecting to enroll full-time at a two-year or four-year or technical institution or university and must have an interest in amateur radio, art, athletics/sports, photography/photogrammetry/filmmaking, or writing. Available to U.S. and non-U.S. citizens.

Application Requirements: Application form, essay. *Deadline:* March 15.

Contact: Ms. Jessica Seitz, Membership and Conference Director
Phone: 406-728-7434
Fax: 406-728-7445
E-mail: info@owaa.org

POLISH ARTS CLUB OF BUFFALO SCHOLARSHIP FOUNDATION
http://www.pacb.bfn.org/

POLISH ARTS CLUB OF BUFFALO SCHOLARSHIP FOUNDATION TRUST
• *See page 130*

PRINT AND GRAPHIC SCHOLARSHIP FOUNDATION
http://www.printing.org/

PRINT AND GRAPHICS SCHOLARSHIPS FOUNDATION
Applicant must be interested in a career in graphic communications, printing technology or management, or publishing. Selection is based on academic record, class rank, recommendations, biographical information, and extracurricular activities. All applications and letters of recommendation must be submitted online at www.pgsf.org. All applications high school and college applicants must be submitted by March 1. Awards are available to applicants outside United States, as long as they are attending a U.S. institution and meet the basic criteria of the Print and Graphics Scholarship Foundation.

Academic Fields/Career Goals: Communications; Graphics/Graphic Arts/Printing.

Award: Scholarship for use in freshman, sophomore, junior, senior, or graduate years; renewable. *Number:* 150–200. *Amount:* $1500–$5000.

Eligibility Requirements: Applicant must be enrolled or expecting to enroll full-time at a two-year or four-year or technical institution or university. Applicant must have 3.0 GPA or higher. Available to U.S. and non-U.S. citizens.

Application Requirements: Application form, essay. *Deadline:* March 1.

Contact: Bernie Eckert, Administrator
Print and Graphic Scholarship Foundation
301 Brush Creek Road
Warrendale, PA 15086
Phone: 412-259-1740
E-mail: pgsf@printing.org

PRINTING INDUSTRY MIDWEST EDUCATION FOUDNATION
http://www.pimw.org/scholarships

PRINTING INDUSTRY MIDWEST EDUCATION FOUNDATION SCHOLARSHIP FUND
The fund offers $1000 renewable scholarships to full-time students enrolled in two- or four-year institutions and technical colleges offering degrees in the print communications discipline. Applicant must be a Minnesota resident and be committed to a career in the print communications industry. Minimum 3.0 GPA required. Priority given to children of PIM member company employees.

Academic Fields/Career Goals: Communications; Flexography; Graphics/Graphic Arts/Printing; Journalism; Marketing; Photojournalism/Photography.

Award: Scholarship for use in freshman, sophomore, junior, or senior years; renewable. *Number:* 5–10. *Amount:* $1000.

Eligibility Requirements: Applicant must be enrolled or expecting to enroll full-time at a two-year or four-year or technical institution or university and resident of Iowa, Minnesota, Nebraska, North Dakota, South Dakota. Applicant must have 3.0 GPA or higher. Available to U.S. citizens.

Application Requirements: Application form, essay. *Deadline:* April 1.

Contact: Kristin Pilling-Davis, Education Director
Printing Industry Midwest Education Foudnation
PIM
1300 Godward St. NE Ste. 2650
Minneapolis, MN 55413
Phone: 612-400-6200
E-mail: kdavis@pimw.org

PUBLIC RELATIONS STUDENT SOCIETY OF AMERICA

http://www.prssa.org/

PUBLIC RELATIONS SOCIETY OF AMERICA MULTICULTURAL AFFAIRS SCHOLARSHIP
• *See page 90*

RADIO TELEVISION DIGITAL NEWS ASSOCIATION

www.rtdna.org

CAROLE SIMPSON SCHOLARSHIP

Carole Simpson is a former member of the RTDNF Board of Trustees. In a career of notable firsts, in 1992 Simpson became the first woman and first African American to moderate a presidential debate. She established the scholarship to encourage and help minority students overcome hurdles along their career path.

Academic Fields/Career Goals: Communications; Journalism; Photojournalism/Photography; TV/Radio Broadcasting.

Award: Scholarship for use in junior or senior years; not renewable. *Number:* 1. *Amount:* $2000.

Eligibility Requirements: Applicant must be American Indian/Alaska Native, Asian/Pacific Islander, Black (non-Hispanic), Hispanic and enrolled or expecting to enroll full-time at a four-year institution or university. Available to U.S. and non-U.S. citizens.

Application Requirements: Application form, essay, portfolio. *Deadline:* May 31.

Contact: Ms. Karen Hansen, Membership and Program Manager
Radio Television Digital News Association
529 14th Street, NW
Suite 1240
Washington, DC 20045
Phone: 202-662-7257
E-mail: karenh@rtdna.org

ED BRADLEY SCHOLARSHIP

Ed Bradley was the first black White House television correspondent and enjoyed a long career on CBS 60 Minutes. Bradley was recognized by RTDNA in 2000 for his lifetime commitment to excellence in journalism. He created the award in 1994 to recognize top-tier students, particularly minority students, pursuing journalism careers.

Academic Fields/Career Goals: Communications; Journalism; Photojournalism/Photography; TV/Radio Broadcasting.

Award: Scholarship for use in junior or senior years; not renewable. *Number:* 1. *Amount:* $10,000.

Eligibility Requirements: Applicant must be American Indian/Alaska Native, Asian/Pacific Islander, Black (non-Hispanic), Hispanic and enrolled or expecting to enroll full-time at a four-year institution or university. Available to U.S. and non-U.S. citizens.

Application Requirements: Application form, essay, portfolio. *Deadline:* May 31.

Contact: Ms. Karen Hansen, Membership and Program Manager
Radio Television Digital News Association
529 14th Street, NW
Suite 1240
Washington, DC 20045
Phone: 202-662-7257
E-mail: karenh@rtdna.org

GEORGE FOREMAN TRIBUTE TO LYNDON B. JOHNSON SCHOLARSHIP

George Foreman is a boxing champion, Olympic gold medal winner and celebrated pitchman. As a young man, he was inspired by President Lyndon Johnson and by RTDNF founder Barney Oldfield. The scholarship is a $6,000 award given to a journalism student from the University of Texas at Austin.

Academic Fields/Career Goals: Communications; Journalism; Photojournalism/Photography; TV/Radio Broadcasting.

Award: Scholarship for use in sophomore, junior, or senior years; not renewable. *Number:* 1. *Amount:* $6000.

Eligibility Requirements: Applicant must be enrolled or expecting to enroll full-time at a four-year institution or university and studying in Texas. Available to U.S. and non-U.S. citizens.

Application Requirements: Application form, portfolio. *Deadline:* May 31.

Contact: Ms. Karen Hansen, Membership and Program Manager
Radio Television Digital News Association
529 14th Street, NW
Suite 1240
Washington, DC 20045
Phone: 202-662-7257
E-mail: karenh@rtdna.org

LEE THORNTON SCHOLARSHIP

Lee Thornton was the first African-American woman to cover the White House for a major news network (CBS) and the first African-American host of All Things Considered on National Public Radio. She served as a faculty member at the Howard University School of Communications, earning a tenured position. Later in her career, she taught at the University of Maryland's Philip Merrill College of Journalism and served a term as the school's interim dean. She held a Master's degree from Michigan State University and a doctorate in mass communications from Northwestern University. Ms. Thornton passed away in 2013 at age 71, and endowed in her estate this scholarship in her name. Students from the University of Maryland and Howard University will be given preference. The recipient of the Lee Thornton Scholarship will receive $2,000 and an invitation to the Excellence in Journalism conference.

Academic Fields/Career Goals: Communications; Journalism.

Award: Scholarship for use in sophomore, junior, or senior years; not renewable. *Number:* 1. *Amount:* $2000.

Eligibility Requirements: Applicant must be enrolled or expecting to enroll full-time at a four-year institution or university and studying in District of Columbia, Maryland. Available to U.S. and non-U.S. citizens.

Application Requirements: Application form, essay, portfolio. *Deadline:* May 31.

Contact: Ms. Karen Hansen, Membership and Program Manager
Radio Television Digital News Association
529 14th Street, NW
Suite 1240
Washington, DC 20045
Phone: 202-662-7257
E-mail: karenh@rtdna.org

LOU AND CAROLE PRATO SPORTS REPORTING SCHOLARSHIP

In recognition of his service to RTDNA, and his commitment to excellence in journalism, the Lou and Carole Prato Sports Reporting Scholarship was established in 2001. It is awarded to a journalism student who brings Lou's journalism values to covering sports.

Academic Fields/Career Goals: Communications; Journalism; Photojournalism/Photography; Sports-Related/Exercise Science; TV/Radio Broadcasting.

Award: Scholarship for use in sophomore, junior, or senior years; not renewable. *Number:* 1. *Amount:* $1000.

Eligibility Requirements: Applicant must be enrolled or expecting to enroll full-time at a four-year institution or university. Available to U.S. and non-U.S. citizens.

Application Requirements: Application form, essay, portfolio. *Deadline:* May 31.

Contact: Ms. Karen Hansen, Membership and Program Manager
Radio Television Digital News Association
529 14th Street, NW
Suite 1240
Washington, DC 20045
Phone: 202-662-7257
E-mail: karenh@rtdna.org

MIKE REYNOLDS JOURNALISM SCHOLARSHIP

Mike Reynolds, who died in 1988 at age 45, was managing editor at KCCI-TV in Des Moines, IA. Applicants must have good writing ability, excellent grades, a dedication to the news business, strong interest in pursuing a career in electronic journalism and a demonstrated need for financial assistance.

Academic Fields/Career Goals: Communications; Journalism; Photojournalism/Photography; TV/Radio Broadcasting.

Award: Scholarship for use in sophomore, junior, or senior years; not renewable. *Number:* 1. *Amount:* $1000.

Eligibility Requirements: Applicant must be enrolled or expecting to enroll full-time at a four-year institution or university. Available to U.S. and non-U.S. citizens.

Application Requirements: Application form, essay, portfolio. *Deadline:* May 31.

Contact: Ms. Karen Hansen, Membership and Program Manager
Radio Television Digital News Association
529 14th Street, NW
Suite 1240
Washington, DC 20045
Phone: 202-662-7257
E-mail: karenh@rtdna.org

PETE WILSON SCHOLARSHIP

The Pete Wilson Journalism Scholarship was established in 2007 by Wilson's friends and colleagues. It is granted to a journalism student from the Bay area who shares Wilson's commitment to ethical, responsible journalism. The 2017 Pete Wilson Scholarship is open to undergraduate students, and alternates annually between undergraduates and graduates.

Academic Fields/Career Goals: Communications; Journalism; Photojournalism/Photography; TV/Radio Broadcasting.

Award: Scholarship for use in sophomore, junior, or senior years; not renewable. *Number:* 1. *Amount:* $2000.

Eligibility Requirements: Applicant must be enrolled or expecting to enroll full-time at a four-year institution or university; resident of California and studying in California. Available to U.S. and non-U.S. citizens.

Application Requirements: Application form, essay, portfolio. *Deadline:* May 31.

Contact: Ms. Karen Hansen, Membership and Program Manager
Radio Television Digital News Association
529 14th Street, NW
Suite 1240
Washington, DC 20045
Phone: 202-662-7257
E-mail: karenh@rtdna.org

RHODE ISLAND FOUNDATION

http://www.rifoundation.org/

J. D. EDSAL SCHOLARSHIP

• *See page 90*

RDW GROUP INC. MINORITY SCHOLARSHIP FOR COMMUNICATIONS

Award to provide support for minority students who wish to pursue a course of study in communications at the undergraduate or graduate level. Must be a Rhode Island resident and must demonstrate financial need.

Academic Fields/Career Goals: Communications.

Award: Scholarship for use in freshman, sophomore, junior, senior, or graduate years; not renewable. *Amount:* $2000.

Eligibility Requirements: Applicant must be American Indian/Alaska Native, Asian/Pacific Islander, Black (non-Hispanic), Hispanic; enrolled or expecting to enroll full-time at a four-year institution or university and resident of Rhode Island. Available to U.S. citizens.

Application Requirements: Application form, essay, self-addressed stamped envelope with application, transcript. *Deadline:* April 26.

Contact: Libby Monahan, Funds Administrator
Phone: 401-274-4564 Ext. 3117
E-mail: libbym@rifoundation.org

ROBERT H. MOLLOHAN FAMILY CHARITABLE FOUNDATION, INC.

http://www.mollohanfoundation.org/

HARRY C. HAMM FAMILY SCHOLARSHIP

The Harry C. Hamm Family Scholarship is awarded to a sophomore, junior, or senior college student who is in serious pursuit of a B.A. in Journalism or Communications at a West Virginia four-year institution. Mr. Hamm was a 50 year veteran reporter/editor with Ogden Newspapers. The applicant must be a graduate of a high school in West Virginia and must have at least a 3.0 GPA.

Academic Fields/Career Goals: Communications; Journalism.

Award: Scholarship for use in sophomore, junior, or senior years; not renewable. *Amount:* $1000.

Eligibility Requirements: Applicant must be high school student; planning to enroll or expecting to enroll full-time at a four-year institution or university; resident of West Virginia and studying in West Virginia. Applicant must have 3.0 GPA or higher. Available to U.S. citizens.

Application Requirements: Application form, essay, recommendations or references, resume, test scores, transcript.

Contact: Aime Shaffer, Program Manager
Phone: 304-333-6783
E-mail: ashaffer@wvhtf.org

SOCIETY FOR TECHNICAL COMMUNICATION

http://www.stc.org/

SOCIETY FOR TECHNICAL COMMUNICATION SCHOLARSHIP PROGRAM

Award for study relating to communication of information about technical subjects. Applicants must be full-time graduate students working toward a Master's or Doctoral degree, or undergraduate students working toward a Bachelor's degree. Must have completed at least one year of postsecondary education and have at least one full year of academic work remaining. Two awards available for undergraduate students, two available for graduate students.

Academic Fields/Career Goals: Communications; Science, Technology, and Society.

Award: Scholarship for use in sophomore, junior, senior, or graduate years; not renewable. *Number:* up to 4. *Amount:* up to $1500.

Eligibility Requirements: Applicant must be enrolled or expecting to enroll full-time at a four-year institution or university. Available to U.S. and non-U.S. citizens.

Application Requirements: Application form, essay, recommendations or references, transcript. *Deadline:* February 15.

Contact: Scott DeLoach, Manager, Scholarship Selection Committee
Society for Technical Communication
834 C Dekalb Avenue, NE
Atlanta, GA 30307

SOCIETY FOR TECHNICAL COMMUNICATION–LONE STAR CHAPTER

http://www.stc-dfw.org/

LONE STAR COMMUNITY SCHOLARSHIPS

Scholarship for graduate or undergraduate student working toward a degree or certificate in the technical communication field. We also provide a scholarship for those returning to school to either further their studies in technical communication through approved training courses or career advancement classes. For further information see website http://www.stc-dfw.org.

Academic Fields/Career Goals: Communications.

Award: Scholarship for use in freshman, sophomore, junior, senior, or graduate years; not renewable. *Number:* 1–4.

Eligibility Requirements: Applicant must be Hispanic; enrolled or expecting to enroll full- or part-time at a four-year institution or university and resident of Oklahoma, Texas. Available to U.S. and non-U.S. citizens.

Application Requirements: Application form, recommendations or references, transcript. *Deadline:* March 28.

Contact: Rob Harris, Scholarship Committee Manager
　　　　Phone: 940-391-0167
　　　　E-mail: scholarship@stc-dfw.org

SOCIETY OF MOTION PICTURE AND TELEVISION ENGINEERS

https://www.smpte.org/

LOUIS F. WOLF JR. MEMORIAL SCHOLARSHIP

This scholarship was established to help students further their undergraduate or graduate studies in motion pictures and television, with an emphasis on technology. Open To Currently Enrolled, Full-Time Undergraduate Student Members;, Extra Credit May Be Awarded For Volunteer Work/Leadership.

Academic Fields/Career Goals: Communications; Electrical Engineering/Electronics; Engineering-Related Technologies; Engineering/Technology; Filmmaking/Video; Science, Technology, and Society; TV/Radio Broadcasting.

Award: Scholarship for use in freshman, sophomore, junior, senior, graduate, or postgraduate years; not renewable. *Number:* up to 1. *Amount:* $1000–$5000.

Eligibility Requirements: Applicant must be enrolled or expecting to enroll full-time at a two-year or four-year or technical institution or university. Applicant or parent of applicant must be member of Society of Motion Picture and Television Engineers. Available to U.S. and non-U.S. citizens.

Application Requirements: Application form, essay, financial need analysis, recommendations or references, transcript. *Deadline:* June 1.

Contact: Sally-Ann DAmato, Director of Operations
　　　　Society of Motion Picture and Television Engineers
　　　　SMPTE, 3 Barker Avenue
　　　　White Plains, NY 10601
　　　　Phone: 914-761-1100 Ext. 2375
　　　　E-mail: sdamato@smpte.org

STUDENT PAPER AWARD

Contest for best paper by a current Student Member of SMPTE. Paper must deal with some technical phase of motion pictures, television, photographic instrumentation, or their closely allied arts and sciences. For more information see website http://www.smpte.org.

Academic Fields/Career Goals: Communications; Electrical Engineering/Electronics; Engineering-Related Technologies; Engineering/Technology; Filmmaking/Video; Science, Technology, and Society; TV/Radio Broadcasting.

Award: Prize for use in freshman, sophomore, junior, senior, graduate, or postgraduate years; not renewable. *Number:* 1–2. *Amount:* $1–$1500.

Eligibility Requirements: Applicant must be enrolled or expecting to enroll full- or part-time at a two-year or four-year or technical institution or university. Applicant or parent of applicant must be member of Society of Motion Picture and Television Engineers. Available to U.S. and non-U.S. citizens.

Application Requirements: Application form, entry in a contest, essay, student ID card, transcript. *Deadline:* May 1.

Contact: Sally-Ann DAmato, Director of Operations
　　　　Society of Motion Picture and Television Engineers
　　　　SMPTE, 3 Barker Avenue
　　　　White Plains, NY 10601
　　　　Phone: 914-761-1100 Ext. 2375
　　　　E-mail: sdamato@smpte.org

SOCIETY OF SATELLITE PROFESSIONALS INTERNATIONAL

http://www.sspi.org/

SSPI INTERNATIONAL SCHOLARSHIPS

• *See page 147*

SPECIALTY EQUIPMENT MARKET ASSOCIATION

http://www.sema.org/

SEMA MEMORIAL SCHOLARSHIP FUND

• *See page 85*

STRAIGHTFORWARD MEDIA

http://www.straightforwardmedia.com/

STRAIGHTFORWARD MEDIA MEDIA & COMMUNICATIONS SCHOLARSHIP

• *See page 91*

SUPPORT CREATIVITY

http://wesupportcreativity.org

SUPPORT CREATIVITY SCHOLARSHIP

• *See page 124*

TAMPA BAY TIMES FUND, INC.

http://www.tampabay.com/fund

CAREER JOURNALISM SCHOLARSHIP

These scholarships target high school seniors in the Times' audience area who have a demonstrated interest in pursuing journalism as a major in college and as a career. The scholarship is worth $2,500 per year and may be renewed annually. Up to 4 winners are selected each year. Students from these Florida counties are eligible to apply: Pinellas, Hillsborough, Pasco, Hernando. Application deadline: January 20. Winners are notified by the end of February. On-line applications only.

Academic Fields/Career Goals: Communications; Journalism; Photojournalism/Photography; TV/Radio Broadcasting.

Award: Scholarship for use in freshman, sophomore, junior, or senior years; not renewable. *Number:* 1–10. *Amount:* $1000–$2500.

Eligibility Requirements: Applicant must be age 17-23; enrolled or expecting to enroll full-time at a four-year institution or university; single and resident of Florida. Applicant must have 3.0 GPA or higher. Available to U.S. citizens.

Application Requirements: Application form, essay, portfolio. *Deadline:* January 20.

Contact: Ms. Nancy Waclawek, Scholarship administrator
　　　　Tampa Bay Times Fund, Inc.
　　　　PO Box 1121
　　　　St. Petersburg, FL 33731-1121
　　　　E-mail: tbtschls@gmail.com

TAMPA BAY TIMES FUND CAREER JOURNALISM SCHOLARSHIPS

• *See page 91*

TEXAS ASSOCIATION OF BROADCASTERS

https://www.tab.org/scholarships/available-scholarships

ANN ARNOLD SCHOLARSHIP

Junior, senior or graduate student enrolled in a broadcast curriculum at a four-year college or university in Texas, demonstrating financial need.

Academic Fields/Career Goals: Communications.

Award: Scholarship for use in junior, senior, graduate, or postgraduate years; not renewable. *Number:* 1. *Amount:* $5000.

Eligibility Requirements: Applicant must be enrolled or expecting to enroll full-time at a four-year institution or university; resident of Texas and studying in Texas. Applicant must have 3.5 GPA or higher. Available to U.S. citizens.

Application Requirements: Application form, essay, financial need analysis. *Deadline:* April 15.

Contact: Mr. Craig Bean, Director, Public Service & EEO
Texas Association of Broadcasters
502 East 11th Street, Suite 200
Austin, TX 78701
Phone: 512-322-9944
Fax: 512-322-0522
E-mail: craig@tab.org

BELO TEXAS BROADCAST EDUCATION FOUNDATION SCHOLARSHIP

Scholarship of $2000 to undergraduate and graduate students enrolled in a fully accredited program of instruction that emphasizes radio or television broadcasting or communications at a four-year college or university in Texas. Student must be a member of the Texas Association of Broadcasters. Must have a GPA of 3.0 minimum.

Academic Fields/Career Goals: Communications; TV/Radio Broadcasting.

Award: Scholarship for use in freshman, sophomore, junior, senior, or graduate years; not renewable. *Number:* 1. *Amount:* $2000.

Eligibility Requirements: Applicant must be enrolled or expecting to enroll full-time at a four-year institution or university and studying in Texas. Applicant or parent of applicant must be member of Texas Association of Broadcasters. Applicant must have 3.0 GPA or higher. Available to U.S. and non-U.S. citizens.

Application Requirements: Application form, essay, financial need analysis, recommendations or references. *Deadline:* May 3.

Contact: Craig Bean, Public Service Manager
Texas Association of Broadcasters
502 East 11th Street, Suite 200
Austin, TX 78701
Phone: 512-322-9944
Fax: 512-322-0522
E-mail: craig@tab.org

BONNER MCLANE TEXAS BROADCAST EDUCATION FOUNDATION SCHOLARSHIP

Scholarship of $2000 to a undergraduate and students enrolled in a fully accredited program of instruction that emphasizes radio or television broadcasting or communications at a four-year college or university in Texas. Student must be a member of the Texas Association of Broadcasters. Must have a GPA of 3.0 minimum.

Academic Fields/Career Goals: Communications; TV/Radio Broadcasting.

Award: Scholarship for use in freshman, sophomore, junior, senior, or graduate years; not renewable. *Number:* 1. *Amount:* $2000.

Eligibility Requirements: Applicant must be enrolled or expecting to enroll full-time at a four-year institution or university and studying in Texas. Applicant or parent of applicant must be member of Texas Association of Broadcasters. Applicant must have 3.0 GPA or higher. Available to U.S. and non-U.S. citizens.

Application Requirements: Application form, essay, financial need analysis, recommendations or references. *Deadline:* May 3.

Contact: Craig Bean, Public Service Manager
Texas Association of Broadcasters
502 East 11th Street, Suite 200
Austin, TX 78701
Phone: 512-322-9944
Fax: 512-322-0522
E-mail: craig@tab.org

STUDENT TEXAS BROADCAST EDUCATION FOUNDATION SCHOLARSHIP

Scholarship of $2000 to a undergraduate or a graduate student enrolled in a program of instruction that emphasizes radio or television broadcasting or communications at a two-year or technical school in Texas. Student must be a member of the Texas Association of Broadcasters. Must have a GPA of 3.0 minimum.

Academic Fields/Career Goals: Communications; TV/Radio Broadcasting.

Award: Scholarship for use in freshman, sophomore, junior, or senior years; not renewable. *Number:* 1. *Amount:* $2000.

Eligibility Requirements: Applicant must be enrolled or expecting to enroll full-time at a two-year or technical institution and studying in Texas. Applicant or parent of applicant must be member of Texas Association of Broadcasters. Applicant must have 3.0 GPA or higher. Available to U.S. and non-U.S. citizens.

Application Requirements: Application form, essay, financial need analysis, recommendations or references. *Deadline:* May 3.

Contact: Craig Bean, Public Service Manager
Texas Association of Broadcasters
502 East 11th Street, Suite 200
Austin, TX 78701
Phone: 512-322-9944
Fax: 512-322-0522
E-mail: craig@tab.org

TOM REIFF TEXAS BROADCAST EDUCATION FOUNDATION SCHOLARSHIP

Scholarship of $2000 to undergraduate and graduate students enrolled in a fully accredited program of instruction that emphasizes radio or television broadcasting or communications at a four-year college or university in Texas. Student must be a member of the Texas Association of Broadcasters. Must have a GPA of 3.0 minimum.

Academic Fields/Career Goals: Communications; TV/Radio Broadcasting.

Award: Scholarship for use in freshman, sophomore, junior, senior, or graduate years; not renewable. *Number:* 1. *Amount:* $2000.

Eligibility Requirements: Applicant must be enrolled or expecting to enroll full-time at a four-year institution or university and studying in Texas. Applicant or parent of applicant must be member of Texas Association of Broadcasters. Applicant must have 3.0 GPA or higher. Available to U.S. and non-U.S. citizens.

Application Requirements: Application form, essay, financial need analysis, recommendations or references. *Deadline:* May 3.

Contact: Craig Bean, Public Service Manager
Texas Association of Broadcasters
502 East 11th Street, Suite 200
Austin, TX 78701
Phone: 512-322-9944
Fax: 512-322-0522
E-mail: craig@tab.org

UNDERGRADUATE TEXAS BROADCAST EDUCATION FOUNDATION SCHOLARSHIP

Scholarship of $2000 to a undergraduate student enrolled in a fully accredited program of instruction that emphasizes radio or television broadcasting or communications at a four-year college or university in Texas. Student must be a member of the Texas Association of Broadcasters. Must have a GPA of 3.0 minimum.

Academic Fields/Career Goals: Communications; TV/Radio Broadcasting.

Award: Scholarship for use in freshman, sophomore, junior, or senior years; not renewable. *Number:* 1. *Amount:* $2000.

Eligibility Requirements: Applicant must be enrolled or expecting to enroll full-time at a four-year institution or university and studying in Texas. Applicant or parent of applicant must be member of Texas Association of Broadcasters. Applicant must have 3.0 GPA or higher. Available to U.S. and non-U.S. citizens.

Application Requirements: Application form, essay, financial need analysis, recommendations or references. *Deadline:* May 3.

Contact: Craig Bean, Public Service Manager
Texas Association of Broadcasters
502 East 11th Street, Suite 200
Austin, TX 78701
Phone: 512-322-9944
Fax: 512-322-0522
E-mail: craig@tab.org

VANN KENNEDY TEXAS BROADCAST EDUCATION FOUNDATION SCHOLARSHIP

Scholarship of $2000 to a undergraduate or graduate student enrolled in a fully accredited program of instruction that emphasizes radio or television broadcasting or communications at college or university in

Texas. Student must be a member of the Texas Association of Broadcasters. Must have a GPA of 3.0 minimum.

Academic Fields/Career Goals: Communications; TV/Radio Broadcasting.

Award: Scholarship for use in freshman, sophomore, junior, or senior years; not renewable. *Number:* 1. *Amount:* $2000.

Eligibility Requirements: Applicant must be enrolled or expecting to enroll full-time at a two-year or four-year institution or university and studying in Texas. Applicant or parent of applicant must be member of Texas Association of Broadcasters. Applicant must have 3.0 GPA or higher. Available to U.S. and non-U.S. citizens.

Application Requirements: Application form, essay, financial need analysis, recommendations or references. *Deadline:* May 3.

Contact: Craig Bean, Public Service Manager
Texas Association of Broadcasters
502 East 11th Street, Suite 200
Austin, TX 78701
Phone: 512-322-9944
Fax: 512-322-0522
E-mail: craig@tab.org

TEXAS GRIDIRON CLUB INC.

http://www.spjfw.org/

TEXAS GRIDIRON CLUB SCHOLARSHIPS

$500 to $4000 scholarships for full-time or part-time college juniors, seniors, or graduate students majoring in newspaper, photojournalism, or broadcast fields. Must be Texas resident or going to school in Texas.

Academic Fields/Career Goals: Communications; Journalism; Photojournalism/Photography; TV/Radio Broadcasting.

Award: Scholarship for use in sophomore, junior, senior, or graduate years; not renewable. *Number:* 10–15. *Amount:* $500–$4000.

Eligibility Requirements: Applicant must be enrolled or expecting to enroll full- or part-time at a four-year institution or university. Applicant must have 2.5 GPA or higher. Available to U.S. citizens.

Application Requirements: Application form, essay, financial need analysis. *Deadline:* March 3.

Contact: Angie Summers, Scholarships Coordinator
Texas Gridiron Club Inc.
709 Houston Street
Arlington, TX 76012
E-mail: asummers@star-telegram.com

TKE EDUCATIONAL FOUNDATION

http://www.tke.org/

GEORGE W. WOOLERY MEMORIAL SCHOLARSHIP

$300 scholarship available to initiated undergraduate members of Tau Kappa Epsilon who are full-time students in good standing with a cumulative GPA of 3.0 or higher. Preference will first be given to a graduate of the TKE Leadership Academy but, if there is no qualified applicant, the scholarship will be open to any other qualified Teke.

Academic Fields/Career Goals: Communications.

Award: Scholarship for use in sophomore, junior, or senior years; not renewable. *Number:* 1. *Amount:* $300.

Eligibility Requirements: Applicant must be enrolled or expecting to enroll full-time at a four-year institution or university; male and must have an interest in leadership. Applicant or parent of applicant must be member of Tau Kappa Epsilon. Applicant must have 3.0 GPA or higher. Available to U.S. and non-U.S. citizens.

Application Requirements: Application form, application form may be submitted online (http://www.tke.org/member_resources/scholarships/apply_online), essay, narrative summary of how TKE membership has benefited applicant, personal photograph, transcript. *Deadline:* March 15.

Contact: Offices of the Grand Chapter
TKE Educational Foundation
7439 Woodland Drive, Suite 100
Indianapolis, IN 46278
E-mail: tkeogc@tke.org

TURF AND ORNAMENTAL COMMUNICATORS ASSOCIATION

http://www.toca.org/

TURF AND ORNAMENTAL COMMUNICATORS ASSOCIATION SCHOLARSHIP PROGRAM

• *See page 102*

UNITED METHODIST COMMUNICATIONS

http://www.umcom.org/

LEONARD M. PERRYMAN COMMUNICATIONS SCHOLARSHIP FOR ETHNIC MINORITY STUDENTS

One-time award to assist United Methodist ethnic minority students who are college students intending to pursue careers in religious communications.

Academic Fields/Career Goals: Communications; Journalism; Photojournalism/Photography; Religion/Theology; TV/Radio Broadcasting.

Award: Scholarship for use in junior or senior years; not renewable. *Number:* 1. *Amount:* $2500.

Eligibility Requirements: Applicant must be Methodist; American Indian/Alaska Native, Asian/Pacific Islander, Black (non-Hispanic), Hispanic and enrolled or expecting to enroll full-time at a two-year or four-year institution or university. Available to U.S. citizens.

Application Requirements: Application form, essay, personal photograph, recommendations or references, transcript. *Deadline:* March 15.

Contact: Michael Neff, Executive Director
Phone: 703-836-4606 Ext. 325
Fax: 703-836-2024
E-mail: mwneff@ashs.org

UNITED NEGRO COLLEGE FUND

http://www.uncf.org/

ASHLEY STEWART SCHOLARSHIP

• *See page 169*

JOHN LENNON ENDOWED SCHOLARSHIP PROGRAM

Scholarship up to $5000 based on need, to support deserving students. Must attend one of the 37 UNCF member institutions. Applicants must be majoring in communications, mass communications, mass media arts, music and performing arts.

Academic Fields/Career Goals: Communications; Music; Performing Arts.

Award: Scholarship for use in freshman, sophomore, junior, or senior years.

Eligibility Requirements: Applicant must be Black (non-Hispanic) and enrolled or expecting to enroll at a four-year institution or university. Applicant must have 3.0 GPA or higher. Available to U.S. citizens.

Application Requirements: Application form, financial need analysis. *Deadline:* February 19.

Contact: Mary Williams, Director of Outreach and Recruitment
Phone: 800-331-2244

MICHAEL JACKSON SCHOLARSHIP

One-time scholarships up to $5000 for students majoring in communication arts and social science who are attending UNCF member colleges and universities. Funds may be used for tuition, room and board, books, or to repay federal student loans. Minimum 2.5 GPA required.

Academic Fields/Career Goals: Communications; Social Sciences.

Award: Scholarship for use in freshman, sophomore, junior, senior, or graduate years; not renewable.

Eligibility Requirements: Applicant must be Black (non-Hispanic) and enrolled or expecting to enroll full-time at a four-year institution or university. Applicant must have 2.5 GPA or higher. Available to U.S. citizens.

Application Requirements: Application form, essay. *Deadline:* October 1.

Contact: Mary Williams, Director of Outreach and Recruitment
Phone: 800-331-2244

NASCAR BLACK HISTORY MONTH AWARDS
• *See page 86*

OSSIE DAVIS ENDOWMENT SCHOLARSHIP PROGRAM
• *See page 132*

RHYTHM NATION/JANET JACKSON SCHOLARSHIP
• *See page 132*

SUEZ CORPORATE SCHOLARS PROGRAM
• *See page 87*

UNCF/ALLIANCE DATA SCHOLARSHIP AND INTERNSHIP PROGRAM
• *See page 91*

UNCF/ANTHEM CORPORATE SCHOLARS PROGRAM
• *See page 170*

UNCF/CARNIVAL CORPORATE SCHOLARS PROGRAM
• *See page 170*

VALLEY PRESS CLUB
http://www.valleypressclub.com/

VALLEY PRESS CLUB SCHOLARSHIPS, THE REPUBLICAN SCHOLARSHIP, CHANNEL 22 SCHOLARSHIP
Nonrenewable award for graduating high school seniors from Connecticut and Massachusetts, who are interested in television journalism, photojournalism, broadcast journalism, or print journalism.

Academic Fields/Career Goals: Communications; Journalism; Photojournalism/Photography; TV/Radio Broadcasting.

Award: Scholarship for use in freshman year; not renewable. *Number:* 4–6. *Amount:* $1000.

Eligibility Requirements: Applicant must be high school student; planning to enroll or expecting to enroll full-time at a four-year institution or university; resident of Connecticut, Massachusetts and must have an interest in writing. Available to U.S. citizens.

Application Requirements: Application form, community service, financial need analysis, interview. *Deadline:* April 1.

Contact: Noreen Tassinari, Scholarship Committee Chair
Valley Press Club
PO Box 5475
Springfield, MA 01101
Phone: 413-205-5037
E-mail: ntassinari@thebige.com

VIRGINIA ASSOCIATION OF BROADCASTERS
http://www.vabonline.com/

VIRGINIA ASSOCIATION OF BROADCASTERS SCHOLARSHIP AWARD
Scholarships are available to entering juniors and seniors majoring in mass communications-related courses. Must either be a resident of Virginia or be enrolled at a Virginia college or university. Must be U.S. citizen and enrolled full-time.

Academic Fields/Career Goals: Communications.

Award: Scholarship for use in junior or senior years; renewable. *Number:* 4. *Amount:* $500–$1000.

Eligibility Requirements: Applicant must be enrolled or expecting to enroll full-time at a four-year institution or university; resident of Virginia and studying in Virginia. Available to U.S. and non-U.S. citizens.

Application Requirements: Application form, essay, financial need analysis, transcript. *Deadline:* February 15.

Contact: Ruby Seal, Director of Administration
Phone: 434-977-3716
Fax: 434-979-2439
E-mail: ruby.seal@easterassociates.com

WHOMENTORS.COM, INC.
http://www.WHOmentors.com/

1B USD WORLDWIDE VENTURE CAPITAL
• *See page 116*

WISCONSIN BROADCASTERS ASSOCIATION FOUNDATION
http://www.wi-broadcasters.org/

WISCONSIN BROADCASTERS ASSOCIATION FOUNDATION SCHOLARSHIP
Four $2000 scholarships offered to assist students enrolled in broadcasting-related educational programs at four-year public or private institutions. Applicants must either have graduated from a Wisconsin high school, or be attending a Wisconsin college or university, must have completed at least 60 credits, and must be planning a career in radio or television broadcasting.

Academic Fields/Career Goals: Communications; TV/Radio Broadcasting.

Award: Scholarship for use in freshman, sophomore, junior, or senior years; not renewable. *Number:* 4. *Amount:* $2000.

Eligibility Requirements: Applicant must be enrolled or expecting to enroll full-time at a four-year institution or university and studying in Wisconsin. Available to U.S. citizens.

Application Requirements: Application form, essay, recommendations or references, transcript. *Deadline:* October 20.

Contact: John Laabs, President
Phone: 608-255-2600
Fax: 608-256-3986
E-mail: jlaabs@aol.com

WOMEN'S BASKETBALL COACHES ASSOCIATION
http://www.wbca.org/

ROBIN ROBERTS/WBCA SPORTS COMMUNICATIONS SCHOLARSHIP AWARD
One-time award for female student athletes who have completed their eligibility and plan to go to graduate school. Must major in communications. Must be nominated by the head coach of women's basketball who is a member of the WBCA.

Academic Fields/Career Goals: Communications; Journalism.

Award: Scholarship for use in senior, graduate, or postgraduate years; not renewable. *Number:* 1. *Amount:* $4000.

Eligibility Requirements: Applicant must be enrolled or expecting to enroll full- or part-time at a four-year institution or university; female and must have an interest in athletics/sports. Available to U.S. and non-U.S. citizens.

Application Requirements: Application form, recommendations or references, statistics. *Deadline:* February 15.

Contact: Betty Jaynes, Consultant
Phone: 770-279-8027 Ext. 102
Fax: 770-279-6290
E-mail: bettyj@wbca.org

WYOMING TRUCKING ASSOCIATION SCHOLARSHIP FUND TRUST
http://www.wytruck.org/

WYOMING TRUCKING ASSOCIATION SCHOLARSHIP TRUST FUND
• *See page 87*

COMPUTER SCIENCE/ DATA PROCESSING

AIST FOUNDATION

http://www.aistfoundation.org/

ASSOCIATION FOR IRON AND STEEL TECHNOLOGY OHIO VALLEY CHAPTER SCHOLARSHIP
• See page 153

ASSOCIATION FOR IRON AND STEEL TECHNOLOGY WILLY KORF MEMORIAL SCHOLARSHIP
• See page 172

ALICE L. HALTOM EDUCATIONAL FUND

http://www.alhef.org/

ALICE L. HALTOM EDUCATIONAL FUND
• See page 160

AMERICAN FOUNDATION FOR THE BLIND

http://www.afb.org/

PAUL W. RUCKES SCHOLARSHIP
Scholarship of $1000 to an undergraduate or graduate student studying in the field of engineering or in computer, physical, or life sciences. For more information and application requirements, please visit http://www.afb.org/scholarships.asp.

Academic Fields/Career Goals: Computer Science/Data Processing; Electrical Engineering/Electronics; Engineering/Technology; Natural Sciences; Physical Sciences.

Award: Scholarship for use in freshman, sophomore, junior, or senior years; not renewable. *Number:* 1. *Amount:* $1000.

Eligibility Requirements: Applicant must be visually impaired and enrolled or expecting to enroll full-time at a two-year or four-year institution or university. Applicant must be visually impaired. Available to U.S. citizens.

Application Requirements: Application form, essay, proof of post-secondary acceptance and legal blindness, proof of citizenship, FAFSA, recommendations or references, transcript. *Deadline:* April 30.

Contact: Dawn Bodrogi, Information Center
American Foundation for the Blind
11 Penn Plaza, Suite 300
New York, NY 10001
Phone: 212-502-7661
Fax: 212-502-7771
E-mail: afbinfo@afb.net

AMERICAN INDIAN SCIENCE AND ENGINEERING SOCIETY

http://www.aises.org/

A.T. ANDERSON MEMORIAL SCHOLARSHIP PROGRAM
• See page 109

AMERICAN RAILWAY ENGINEERING AND MAINTENANCE OF WAY ASSOCIATION

http://www.aremafoundation.org/

AREMA GRADUATE AND UNDERGRADUATE SCHOLARSHIPS
• See page 191

AMERICAN SOCIETY FOR INFORMATION SCIENCE AND TECHNOLOGY

http://www.asis.org/

JOHN WILEY & SONS BEST JASIST PAPER AWARD
Award of $1500 to recognize the best refereed paper published in the volume year of the JASIT preceding the ASIST annual meeting. John Wiley & Sons Inc., shall contribute $500 towards travel expenses to attend the ASIST annual meeting. No nomination procedure is used for this award. All eligible papers are considered.

Academic Fields/Career Goals: Computer Science/Data Processing; Library and Information Sciences.

Award: Prize for use in freshman, sophomore, junior, senior, graduate, or postgraduate years; not renewable. *Number:* 1. *Amount:* $2000.

Eligibility Requirements: Applicant must be enrolled or expecting to enroll full-time at a four-year institution or university. Available to U.S. and non-U.S. citizens.

Application Requirements: Application form, essay. *Deadline:* varies.

Contact: Awards Coordinator
Phone: 301-495-0900
Fax: 301-495-0810
E-mail: asis@asis.org

ARMED FORCES COMMUNICATIONS AND ELECTRONICS ASSOCIATION, EDUCATIONAL FOUNDATION

http://www.afcea.org/site/?q=foundation/scholarships

ARMED FORCES COMMUNICATIONS AND ELECTRONICS ASSOCIATION ROTC SCHOLARSHIP PROGRAM
• See page 137

STEM MAJORS SCHOLARSHIPS FOR UNDERGRADUATE STUDENTS
• See page 110

VADM SAMUEL L. GRAVELY, JR, USN(RET.) MEMORIAL SCHOLARSHIP
• See page 111

VETERANS OF ENDURING FREEDOM (AFGHANISTAN) AND IRAQI FREEDOM SCHOLARSHIP
Scholarships for active-duty and honorably discharged U.S. military veterans (to include Reservists and National Guard personnel) of the Enduring Freedom (Afghanistan) or Iraqi Freedom operations who are actively pursuing an undergraduate degree in an eligible major at accredited two- or four-year institutions in the United States. Distance-learning or online programs affiliated with a major U.S. institution are eligible. Candidates must be majoring in the following or related fields: electrical, aerospace, systems or computer engineering; computer engineering technology; computer information systems; information systems management; computer science; physics; mathematics; or science or mathematics education. Majors directly related to the support of U.S. intelligence or homeland security enterprises with relevance to the mission of AFCEA will also be eligible.

Academic Fields/Career Goals: Computer Science/Data Processing; Electrical Engineering/Electronics; Mathematics; Physical Sciences.

Award: Scholarship for use in sophomore or junior years; not renewable. *Number:* 5–10. *Amount:* $2500.

Eligibility Requirements: Applicant must be enrolled or expecting to enroll full- or part-time at a four-year institution or university. Applicant must have 3.0 GPA or higher. Available to U.S. citizens. Applicant must have general military experience.

Application Requirements: Application form, essay, financial need analysis. *Deadline:* April 15.

Contact: Mrs. Casmere Kistner, Director, Scholarships and Awards
Armed Forces Communications and Electronics Association,
Educational Foundation
4400 Fair Lakes Court
Fairfax, VA 22033
Phone: 703-631-6147
E-mail: edfoundation@afcea.org

ARRL FOUNDATION INC.

http://www.arrl.org/

ANDROSCOGGIN AMATEUR RADIO CLUB SCHOLARSHIP

Up to 2 awards to students in the ARRL Maine or New England Division (Maine, New Hampshire, Vermont, Rhode Island, Massachusetts or Connecticut) who have an active technician class amateur radio license or higher. Preference given to students studying computer science, TV/radio electronics, or electrical engineering at a two- or four-year college.

Academic Fields/Career Goals: Computer Science/Data Processing; Electrical Engineering/Electronics; TV/Radio Broadcasting.

Award: Scholarship for use in freshman, sophomore, junior, or senior years; not renewable. *Number:* 1–2. *Amount:* $500–$1000.

Eligibility Requirements: Applicant must be enrolled or expecting to enroll full- or part-time at a two-year or four-year or technical institution; resident of Connecticut, Maine, Massachusetts, New Hampshire, Rhode Island, Vermont and must have an interest in amateur radio. Available to U.S. citizens.

Application Requirements: Application form. *Deadline:* January 31.

Contact: Ms. Mary Hobart, Secretary
Phone: 860-594-0397
E-mail: k1mmh@arrl.org

INDIANAPOLIS AMATEUR RADIO ASSOCIATION SCHOLARSHIP

$1000 award for a student who is a resident of Indiana or the ARRL Central Division (Illinois, Indiana, and Wisconsin). Must be studying electrical or electronics engineering, computer science, or related fields and have an amateur radio license.

Academic Fields/Career Goals: Computer Science/Data Processing; Electrical Engineering/Electronics.

Award: Scholarship for use in freshman, sophomore, junior, or senior years; not renewable. *Number:* 1. *Amount:* $1000.

Eligibility Requirements: Applicant must be enrolled or expecting to enroll full- or part-time at a two-year or four-year or technical institution or university; resident of Illinois, Indiana, Wisconsin and must have an interest in amateur radio. Available to U.S. citizens.

Application Requirements: Application form. *Deadline:* January 31.

Contact: Ms. Mary Hobart, Secretary
Phone: 860-594-0397
E-mail: k1mmh@arrl.org

JAKE MCCLAIN DRIVER, KC5WXA, SCHOLARSHIP

$1000 scholarship for a resident of Tennessee or the ARRL Delta Division (Arkansas, Louisiana, Mississippi, Tennessee). Must have a Technical Class or higher license and provide at least one QLSL card received within the past 12 months. Must be studying electronics, computers, or journalism.

Academic Fields/Career Goals: Computer Science/Data Processing; Electrical Engineering/Electronics; Journalism.

Award: Scholarship for use in freshman, sophomore, junior, or senior years; not renewable. *Number:* 1. *Amount:* $1000.

Eligibility Requirements: Applicant must be enrolled or expecting to enroll full- or part-time at a two-year or four-year or technical institution or university; resident of Arkansas, Louisiana, Mississippi, Tennessee and must have an interest in amateur radio. Available to U.S. citizens.

Application Requirements: Application form. *Deadline:* January 31.

Contact: Ms. Mary Hobart, Secretary
Phone: 860-594-0397
E-mail: k1mmh@arrl.org

MAGNOLIA DX ASSOCIATION SCHOLARSHIP

• See page 202

NORTH FULTON AMATEUR RADIO LEAGUE SCHOLARSHIP

$900 scholarship for an ARRL member who is studying engineering or computer science. Must be a resident in GA and a member of ARRL. If no qualified applicant, preference will be awarded to an applicant from the ARRL Southeastern Division (Alabama, Florida, Georgia, Puerto Rico, and the U.S. Virgin Islands).

Academic Fields/Career Goals: Computer Science/Data Processing; Engineering/Technology.

Award: Scholarship for use in freshman, sophomore, junior, or senior years; not renewable. *Number:* 1. *Amount:* $900.

Eligibility Requirements: Applicant must be enrolled or expecting to enroll full- or part-time at a two-year or four-year or technical institution or university; resident of Alabama, Florida, Georgia, Puerto Rico and must have an interest in amateur radio. Applicant or parent of applicant must be member of American Radio Relay League. Available to U.S. citizens.

Application Requirements: Application form. *Deadline:* January 31.

Contact: Ms. Mary Hobart, Secretary
Phone: 860-594-0397
E-mail: k1mmh@arrl.org

PHD SCHOLARSHIP

One $1000 award for journalism, computer science, or electronic engineering students who are amateur radio operators. Preference given to residents of ARRL Midwest Division (IA, KS, MO, NE). Applicant may be a student who is a child of a deceased amateur radio operator.

Academic Fields/Career Goals: Computer Science/Data Processing; Electrical Engineering/Electronics; Journalism.

Award: Scholarship for use in freshman, sophomore, junior, or senior years; not renewable. *Number:* 1. *Amount:* $1000.

Eligibility Requirements: Applicant must be enrolled or expecting to enroll full-time at a four-year institution or university; resident of Iowa, Kansas, Missouri, Nebraska and must have an interest in amateur radio. Applicant or parent of applicant must be member of American Radio Relay League. Available to U.S. citizens.

Application Requirements: Application form. *Deadline:* January 31.

Contact: Ms. Mary Hobart, Secretary
Phone: 860-594-0397
E-mail: k1mmh@arrl.org

RAY, N0RP, & KATIE, W0KTE, PAUTZ SCHOLARSHIP

One award of up to $1000 is available to a resident of the ARRL Midwest Division (IA, KS, NE, MO) studying electronics or computer science at an accredited four-year college or university. Applicant should possess a general class or higher amateur radio license and be a member of the ARRL.

Academic Fields/Career Goals: Computer Science/Data Processing; Electrical Engineering/Electronics.

Award: Scholarship for use in freshman, sophomore, junior, or senior years; not renewable. *Number:* 1. *Amount:* $500–$1000.

Eligibility Requirements: Applicant must be enrolled or expecting to enroll full- or part-time at a four-year institution or university; resident of Iowa, Kansas, Missouri, Nebraska and must have an interest in amateur radio. Applicant or parent of applicant must be member of American Radio Relay League. Available to U.S. citizens.

Application Requirements: Application form. *Deadline:* January 31.

Contact: Ms. Mary Hobart, Secretary
Phone: 860-594-0397
E-mail: k1mmh@arrl.org

SOUTHEASTERN DX CLUB SCHOLARSHIP

$500 scholarship for an active member of an amateur radio club affiliated with the ARRL. Preference given to students pursuing engineering or computer science. Must be a resident of Georgia. If no qualified applicant, preference will be awarded to an applicant from the ARRL Southeastern Division (Alabama, Florida, Georgia, Puerto Rico and the U.S. Virgin Islands).

Academic Fields/Career Goals: Computer Science/Data Processing; Engineering/Technology.

Award: Scholarship for use in freshman, sophomore, junior, or senior years; not renewable. *Number:* 1. *Amount:* $500.

Eligibility Requirements: Applicant must be enrolled or expecting to enroll full- or part-time at a two-year or four-year or technical institution or university; resident of Alabama, Florida, Georgia, Puerto Rico and must have an interest in amateur radio. Available to U.S. citizens.

Application Requirements: Application form. *Deadline:* January 31.

Contact: Ms. Mary Hobart, Secretary
Phone: 860-594-0397
E-mail: k1mmh@arrl.org

ASSOCIATION OF FORMER INTELLIGENCE OFFICERS

http://www.afio.com

AFIO UNDERGRADUATE AND GRADUATE SCHOLARSHIPS
• *See page 103*

ASTRONAUT SCHOLARSHIP FOUNDATION

http://www.astronautscholarship.org/

ASTRONAUT SCHOLARSHIP FOUNDATION
• *See page 112*

AUTOMOTIVE WOMEN'S ALLIANCE FOUNDATION

http://www.awafoundation.org/index.php

AUTOMOTIVE WOMEN'S ALLIANCE FOUNDATION SCHOLARSHIPS
• *See page 74*

BARRY GOLDWATER SCHOLARSHIP AND EXCELLENCE IN EDUCATION FOUNDATION

https://goldwater.scholarsapply.org

BARRY M. GOLDWATER SCHOLARSHIP AND EXCELLENCE IN EDUCATION PROGRAM
• *See page 112*

BHW GROUP

https://thebhwgroup.com/

BHW WOMEN IN STEM SCHOLARSHIP
• *See page 74*

CATCHING THE DREAM

http://www.catchingthedream.org/

MATH, ENGINEERING, SCIENCE, BUSINESS, EDUCATION, COMPUTERS SCHOLARSHIPS
• *See page 162*

TRIBAL BUSINESS MANAGEMENT PROGRAM (TBM)
• *See page 74*

ELECTRONIC DOCUMENT SYSTEMS FOUNDATION

http://www.edsf.org/

LYNDA BABOYIAN MEMORIAL SCHOLARSHIP
• *See page 163*

FOUNDATION FOR SCIENCE AND DISABILITY

http://stemd.org/

GRANTS FOR DISABLED GRADUATE STUDENTS IN THE SCIENCES
• *See page 113*

GREAT MINDS IN STEM

www.greatmindsinstem.org

HISPANIC ENGINEER NATIONAL ACHIEVEMENT AWARDS CORPORATION SCHOLARSHIP PROGRAM
• *See page 106*

INSTITUTE OF MANAGEMENT ACCOUNTANTS

https://www.imanet.org/students/scholarships-and-awards/scholarships?ssopc=1

ROLF S. JAEHNIGEN FAMILY SCHOLARSHIP
• *See page 79*

INTERNATIONAL COMMUNICATIONS INDUSTRIES FOUNDATION

http://www.infocomm.org/scholarships

ICIF SCHOLARSHIP FOR EMPLOYEES AND DEPENDENTS OF MEMBER ORGANIZATIONS
• *See page 204*

INTERNATIONAL COMMUNICATIONS INDUSTRIES FOUNDATION AV SCHOLARSHIP
• *See page 204*

LOS ANGELES COUNCIL OF BLACK PROFESSIONAL ENGINEERS

http://www.lablackengineers.org/

AL-BEN SCHOLARSHIP FOR ACADEMIC INCENTIVE
• *See page 179*

AL-BEN SCHOLARSHIP FOR PROFESSIONAL MERIT
• *See page 179*

AL-BEN SCHOLARSHIP FOR SCHOLASTIC ACHIEVEMENT
• *See page 179*

MICROSOFT CORPORATION

http://www.microsoft.com/

YOU CAN MAKE A DIFFERENCE SCHOLARSHIP
Scholarship for high school students who want make an impact with technology. All students who submit proposals will receive a free copy of Microsoft Visual Studio NET Academic Edition.

Academic Fields/Career Goals: Computer Science/Data Processing.

Award: Scholarship for use in freshman year; not renewable. *Number:* 10. *Amount:* $5000.

Eligibility Requirements: Applicant must be high school student and planning to enroll or expecting to enroll full- or part-time at a four-year institution or university. Available to U.S. citizens.

Application Requirements: Application form, transcript. *Deadline:* April 30.

Contact: Scholarship Committee
E-mail: scholars@microsoft.com

NASA IDAHO SPACE GRANT CONSORTIUM

http://www.id.spacegrant.org/

NASA IDAHO SPACE GRANT CONSORTIUM SCHOLARSHIP PROGRAM
• See page 157

NASA/MARYLAND SPACE GRANT CONSORTIUM

http://md.spacegrant.org/

NASA MARYLAND SPACE GRANT CONSORTIUM UNDERGRADUATE SCHOLARSHIPS
• See page 142

NASA MINNESOTA SPACE GRANT CONSORTIUM

http://www.aem.umn.edu/mnsgc

MINNESOTA SPACE GRANT CONSORTIUM SCHOLARSHIP PROGRAM
• See page 142

NASA MONTANA SPACE GRANT CONSORTIUM

http://www.spacegrant.montana.edu/

MONTANA SPACE GRANT SCHOLARSHIP PROGRAM
• See page 142

NASA'S VIRGINIA SPACE GRANT CONSORTIUM

http://www.vsgc.odu.edu/

COMMUNITY COLLEGE STEM SCHOLARSHIPS
• See page 114

UNDERGRADUATE STEM RESEARCH SCHOLARSHIPS
• See page 114

NATIONAL ASSOCIATION OF WATER COMPANIES-NEW JERSEY CHAPTER

http://www.nawc.org

NATIONAL ASSOCIATION OF WATER COMPANIES-NEW JERSEY CHAPTER SCHOLARSHIP
• See page 80

NATIONAL SECURITY AGENCY

http://www.nsa.gov/Careers

NATIONAL SECURITY AGENCY STOKES EDUCATIONAL SCHOLARSHIP PROGRAM

Renewable awards for high school students planning to attend a four-year undergraduate institution to study computer science, electrical engineering, or computer engineering. Must be at least 16 to apply. Must be a U.S. citizen. Minimum 3.0 GPA required, and minimum SAT score of 1600. For application visit website http://www.nsa.gov/careers

Academic Fields/Career Goals: Computer Science/Data Processing; Electrical Engineering/Electronics.

Award: Scholarship for use in freshman, sophomore, junior, or senior years; renewable. *Number:* 15–20. *Amount:* $1000–$30,000.

Eligibility Requirements: Applicant must be high school student and planning to enroll or expecting to enroll full-time at a four-year institution or university. Applicant must have 3.0 GPA or higher. Available to U.S. citizens.

Application Requirements: Application form, application form may be submitted online (http://www.nsa.gov/careers), essay, interview, recommendations or references, resume, test scores, transcript. *Deadline:* October 31.

Contact: Anne Clark, Program Manager
National Security Agency
9800 Savage Road, Suite 6779
Fort Meade, MD 20755-6779
Phone: 866-672-4473
Fax: 410-854-3002
E-mail: amclark@nsa.gov

NEVADA NASA SPACE GRANT CONSORTIUM

http://www.nvspacegrant.org/

NATIONAL SPACE GRANT COLLEGE AND FELLOWSHIP PROGRAM
• See page 114

NEXTSTEPU

http://www.nextstepu.com/

$1,500 STEM SCHOLARSHIP
• See page 106

NORTH AMERICAN NETWORK OPERATORS GROUP (NANOG)

http://www.scholarshipamerica.org

NANOG SCHOLARSHIP PROGRAM

The North American Network Operator' Group (NANOG), is the professional association for Internet engineering, architecture and operations. Our core focus is on continuous improvement of the data transmission technologies, practices, and facilities that make the Internet function. In an effort to support the next generation of network operators, NANOG has established a scholarship program to assist current undergraduate and graduate level students pursuing a degree in computer engineering, computer science, electrical engineering, network engineering or telecommunications (at the graduate-level only) with $10,000 scholarships. To apply, students must plan to enroll part-time (at least six credits) or full-time in undergraduate or graduate study at an accredited two- or four-year college or university for the entire 2017–2018 academic year. Applicants must have a minimum 3.0 grade point average on a 4.0 scale or its equivalent. Qualified students are encouraged to apply early!

Academic Fields/Career Goals: Computer Science/Data Processing.

Award: Scholarship for use in freshman, sophomore, junior, senior, or graduate years; not renewable. *Number:* 4. *Amount:* $10,000.

Eligibility Requirements: Applicant must be enrolled or expecting to enroll full- or part-time at a two-year or four-year institution. Applicant must have 3.0 GPA or higher. Available to U.S. citizens.

Application Requirements: Application form, essay. *Deadline:* June 2.

Contact: Program Manager
North American Network Operators Group (NANOG)
One Scholarship Way
Saint Peter, MN 56082
Phone: 800-537-4180
E-mail: nanog@scholarshipamerica.org

ROBERT H. MOLLOHAN FAMILY CHARITABLE FOUNDATION, INC.

http://www.mollohanfoundation.org/

HIGH TECHNOLOGY SCHOLARS PROGRAM
• See page 158

COMPUTER SCIENCE/DATA PROCESSING

RURAL TECHNOLOGY FUND

http://ruraltechfund.org/

SOCIAL ENTREPRENEURSHIP SCHOLARSHIP

This scholarship is open to students from schools in Kentucky who have a passion for using technology skills to make a positive social change in the world or at home in their communities. Applicants must be an active member of the Student Technology Leadership Program at his or her respective high school.

Academic Fields/Career Goals: Computer Science/Data Processing.

Award: Scholarship for use in freshman year; not renewable. *Number:* 1. *Amount:* $500.

Eligibility Requirements: Applicant must be high school student; planning to enroll or expecting to enroll full- or part-time at a four-year institution and studying in Kentucky. Available to U.S. citizens.

Application Requirements: Application form, essay. *Deadline:* April 15.

SCARLETT FAMILY FOUNDATION SCHOLARSHIP PROGRAM

http://www.scarlettfoundation.org/

SCHOLARSHIP FOR STUDENTS PURSUING A BUSINESS OR STEM DEGREE
• *See page 84*

SEMICONDUCTOR RESEARCH CORPORATION (SRC)

http://www.src.org/

MASTER'S SCHOLARSHIP PROGRAM
• *See page 181*

SIGMA XI, THE SCIENTIFIC RESEARCH SOCIETY

http://www.sigmaxi.org/

SIGMA XI GRANTS-IN-AID OF RESEARCH
• *See page 101*

SOCIETY OF WOMEN ENGINEERS

http://societyofwomenengineers.swe.org/

ADMIRAL GRACE MURRAY HOPPER SCHOLARSHIP

Three $1500 scholarships for freshman women pursuing ABET-accredited baccalaureate program in preparation for careers in engineering, engineering technology, and computer science in the United States and Mexico. Preference is given to student in computer-related engineering majors. Minimum 3.5 GPA required.

Academic Fields/Career Goals: Computer Science/Data Processing; Engineering-Related Technologies.

Award: Scholarship for use in freshman year; not renewable. *Number:* 3. *Amount:* $1500.

Eligibility Requirements: Applicant must be enrolled or expecting to enroll full-time at a four-year institution or university and female. Applicant must have 3.5 GPA or higher. Available to U.S. citizens.

Application Requirements: Application form, essay. *Deadline:* May 1.

Contact: Scholarship Committee
    Phone: 800-793-4636
    E-mail: scholarships@swe.org

CUMMINS SCHOLARSHIP
• *See page 183*

HONEYWELL SCHOLARSHIP
• *See page 184*

JILL S. TIETJEN P.E. SCHOLARSHIP
• *See page 185*

KOCH DISCOVERY SCHOLARSHIP
• *See page 185*

LILLIAN MOLLER GILBRETH MEMORIAL SCHOLARSHIP
• *See page 185*

LOCKHEED MARTIN CORPORATION SCHOLARSHIP

Eight $2000 scholarships for women pursuing ABET-accredited Baccalaureate programs in preparation for careers in engineering, engineering technology, or computer science in the United States and Mexico. Must have authorization to work in the U.S. without sponsorship. Includes travel grant for the SWE Annual Conference. 3.2 minimum GPA required.

Academic Fields/Career Goals: Computer Science/Data Processing; Electrical Engineering/Electronics; Engineering/Technology.

Award: Scholarship for use in junior or senior years; not renewable. *Number:* 8. *Amount:* $2000.

Eligibility Requirements: Applicant must be enrolled or expecting to enroll full-time at a four-year institution or university and female. Available to U.S. citizens.

Application Requirements: Application form. *Deadline:* February 15.

Contact: Scholarship Committee
    Phone: 800-793-4636
    E-mail: scholarships@swe.org

ROBERTA BANASZAK GLEITER ENGINEERING ENDEAVOR SCHOLARSHIP
• *See page 186*

ROCHELLE PERRY MEMORIAL SCHOLARSHIP
• *See page 186*

ROCKWELL COLLINS SCHOLARSHIP

Three $2500 scholarships for women pursuing ABET-accredited Baccalaureate programs in preparation for careers in engineering, engineering technology, and computer science in the United States and Mexico. SWE membership and minimum 3.0 GPA required.

Academic Fields/Career Goals: Computer Science/Data Processing; Electrical Engineering/Electronics; Engineering/Technology; Mechanical Engineering.

Award: Scholarship for use in sophomore, junior, or senior years; not renewable. *Number:* 3. *Amount:* $2500.

Eligibility Requirements: Applicant must be enrolled or expecting to enroll full-time at a four-year institution or university and female. Applicant or parent of applicant must be member of Society of Women Engineers. Applicant must have 3.0 GPA or higher. Available to U.S. citizens.

Application Requirements: Application form. *Deadline:* February 15.

Contact: Scholarship Committee
    Phone: 800-793-4636
    E-mail: scholarships@swe.org

SWE REGION E SCHOLARSHIP
• *See page 187*

SWE REGION G JUDY SIMMONS MEMORIAL SCHOLARSHIP
• *See page 188*

SOCIETY OF WOMEN ENGINEERS-DALLAS SECTION

http://www.dallaswe.org/

DALLAS SWE ANNIE COLAÇO COLLEGIATE LEADER SCHOLARSHIP

Four maximum scholarships named in honor of Annie Colaço(1899-1991), the grandmother to SWE lifetime member Nandika D'Souza. Annie Colaço epitomized selfless service and lifelong learning, which is reflected in the SWE mission. Award: $100 to a student leader and $150

COMPUTER SCIENCE/ DATA PROCESSING

to the SWE student section where the student serves. A maximum of 2 (two) award recipients may be from the same SWE section.

Academic Fields/Career Goals: Computer Science/Data Processing; Engineering/Technology.

Award: Scholarship for use in sophomore, junior, senior, graduate, or postgraduate years; not renewable. *Number:* 1–4. *Amount:* $100–$150.

Eligibility Requirements: Applicant must be enrolled or expecting to enroll full-time at a four-year institution or university; female; resident of Texas and studying in Texas. Applicant must have 3.0 GPA or higher. Available to U.S. citizens.

Application Requirements: Application form, essay, personal photograph. *Deadline:* April 30.

Contact: Shelley Stracener, FY17 President
E-mail: dallas.swe@gmail.com

SOCIETY OF WOMEN ENGINEERS-ROCKY MOUNTAIN SECTION
http://www.swe-rms.org/

SOCIETY OF WOMEN ENGINEERS-ROCKY MOUNTAIN SECTION SCHOLARSHIP PROGRAM
• See page 188

SOCIETY OF WOMEN ENGINEERS-TWIN TIERS SECTION
http://www.swetwintiers.org/

SOCIETY OF WOMEN ENGINEERS-TWIN TIERS SECTION SCHOLARSHIP

Scholarship available to female students who reside or attend school in the Twin Tiers SWE section of New York. This is limited to zip codes that begin with 148, 149, 169 and residents of Bradford County, Pennsylvania. Applicant must be accepted or enrolled in an undergraduate degree program in engineering or computer science at an ABET-, CSAB- or SWE-accredited school.

Academic Fields/Career Goals: Computer Science/Data Processing; Engineering/Technology.

Award: Scholarship for use in freshman year; not renewable. *Number:* 5. *Amount:* $2000.

Eligibility Requirements: Applicant must be high school student; planning to enroll or expecting to enroll full-time at a four-year institution or university; female and resident of New York, Pennsylvania. Applicant must have 3.0 GPA or higher. Available to U.S. citizens.

Application Requirements: Application form, essay. *Deadline:* March 24.

Contact: Jessica Ortiz
E-mail: scholarship@swetwintiers.org

SPECIALTY EQUIPMENT MARKET ASSOCIATION
http://www.sema.org/

SEMA MEMORIAL SCHOLARSHIP FUND
• See page 85

TECHNOLOGY FIRST
https://technologyfirst.org/

ROBERT V. MCKENNA SCHOLARSHIPS

Must have at least sophomore standing (30 semester hours) at his/her respective university or college and currently be enrolled as an undergraduate student as defined by the applicant's institution. Must be able to prove that his/her major relates to the information technology field. Approved majors include but are not limited to the following: computer systems, computer science, computer information systems, management information systems, and industrial/computer engineering. Must have a minimum cumulative GPA of 3.0 and a minimum major GPA of 3.25 on a 4.0 scale at the date of submission. Must have a strong

interest in pursuing an IT career in Southwest Ohio. Must be a permanent resident of or attend a North Central accredited degree-granting college within the Southwest Ohio region including Adams, Brown, Butler, Champaign, Clark, Clermont, Clinton, Darke, Greene, Hamilton, Logan, Miami, Montgomery, Preble, Shelby and Warren counties. Financial need, character, and personal work ethic will be important selection criteria.

Academic Fields/Career Goals: Computer Science/Data Processing; Engineering-Related Technologies; Engineering/Technology; Health Information Management/Technology; Science, Technology, and Society.

Award: Scholarship for use in sophomore or junior years; not renewable. *Number:* 2–4. *Amount:* $750–$1500.

Eligibility Requirements: Applicant must be enrolled or expecting to enroll full-time at a four-year institution; resident of Ohio and studying in Ohio. Applicant must have 3.0 GPA or higher. Available to U.S. citizens.

Application Requirements: Application form. *Deadline:* March 15.

TEXAS DEPARTMENT OF TRANSPORTATION
http://www.txdot.gov/

CONDITIONAL GRANT PROGRAM
• See page 199

TKE EDUCATIONAL FOUNDATION
http://www.tke.org/

ERIC D. DUNNING SCHOLARSHIP

One-time award of $300 given to an undergraduate member of Tau Kappa Epsilon who has demonstrated leadership ability within his chapter, campus, or community. Must be a full-time student in good standing with a GPA of 2.75 or higher. Must be at least a sophomore or higher and be pursuing a degree in engineering, computer science, or any of the pure sciences (chemistry, mathematics, physics, geology, etc.). Preference will be given to Tekes at Missouri University of Science and Technology. If there are no qualified candidates from Beta-Eta Chapter, this scholarship will be open to any Frater who meets the criteria.

Academic Fields/Career Goals: Computer Science/Data Processing; Earth Science; Engineering/Technology; Mathematics; Physical Sciences.

Award: Scholarship for use in sophomore, junior, or senior years; not renewable. *Number:* 1. *Amount:* $300.

Eligibility Requirements: Applicant must be enrolled or expecting to enroll full-time at a four-year institution or university; male and must have an interest in leadership. Applicant or parent of applicant must be member of Tau Kappa Epsilon. Available to U.S. and non-U.S. citizens.

Application Requirements: Application form, application form may be submitted online (http://www.tke.org/member_resources/scholarships/apply_online), essay, personal photograph, transcript. *Deadline:* March 15.

Contact: Offices of the Grand Chapter
TKE Educational Foundation
7439 Woodland Drive, Suite 100
Indianapolis, IN 46278
E-mail: tkeogc@tke.org

TRANSTUTORS
http://www.transtutors.com/scholarship

TRANSTUTORS SCHOLARSHIP 2015-16
• See page 85

UNITED DAUGHTERS OF THE CONFEDERACY
http://www.hqudc.org/

WALTER REED SMITH SCHOLARSHIP
• See page 168

www.petersons.com 219

UNITED NEGRO COLLEGE FUND

http://www.uncf.org/

ANHEUSER-BUSCH LEGENDS OF THE CROWN SCHOLARSHIP PROGRAM
• *See page 86*

BASF/ALFRED CHISHOLM ENDOWED MEMORIAL SCHOLARSHIP
• *See page 86*

BLUE CROSS BLUE SHIELD OF ILLINOIS AND BLUE CROSS BLUE SHIELD OF TEXAS SCHOLARSHIP
• *See page 115*

COLGATE–PALMOLIVE CORPORATE SCHOLARS PROGRAM
• *See page 86*

DAVIS SCHOLARSHIP FOR WOMEN IN STEM
• *See page 189*

DELL CORPORATE SCHOLARS PROGRAM
• *See page 169*

DELL CORPORATE SCHOLARS PROGRAM
• *See page 169*

GALACTIC UNITE BYTHEWAY SCHOLARSHIP
• *See page 190*

INTEL SCHOLARSHIP PROGRAM
• *See page 190*

NASCAR BLACK HISTORY MONTH AWARDS
• *See page 86*

ORACLE CORPORATE SCHOLARS PROGRAM
• *See page 169*

PROCTER & GAMBLE GENERAL SCHOLARSHIP
• *See page 91*

SUEZ CORPORATE SCHOLARS PROGRAM
• *See page 87*

UNCF/ALLIANCE DATA SCHOLARSHIP AND INTERNSHIP PROGRAM
• *See page 91*

UNCF/ANTHEM CORPORATE SCHOLARS PROGRAM
• *See page 170*

UNCF NORTHROP GRUMMAN SCHOLARSHIP

Scholarship available for a freshman, sophomore, or junior in college who is a U.S. citizen, an African- American, and enrolled full-time as a college undergraduate. Minimum 3.0 GPA required. Must be pursuing a major in computer science, computer engineering, electrical engineering, software engineering, or systems engineering. Must have an unmet financial need.

Academic Fields/Career Goals: Computer Science/Data Processing; Electrical Engineering/Electronics; Engineering/Technology.

Award: Scholarship for use in freshman, sophomore, or junior years; not renewable.

Eligibility Requirements: Applicant must be Black (non-Hispanic) and enrolled or expecting to enroll full-time at a four-year institution or university. Applicant must have 3.0 GPA or higher. Available to U.S. citizens.

Application Requirements: Application form, financial need analysis. *Deadline:* March 16.

Contact: Mary Williams, Director of Outreach and Recruitment
Phone: 800-331-2244

UNCF STEM SCHOLARS PROGRAM
• *See page 159*

UNIVERSITIES SPACE RESEARCH ASSOCIATION

http://www.usra.edu/

UNIVERSITIES SPACE RESEARCH ASSOCIATION SCHOLARSHIP AWARD PROGRAM
• *See page 116*

VERMONT SPACE GRANT CONSORTIUM

http://www.cems.uvm.edu/vsgc

VERMONT SPACE GRANT CONSORTIUM
• *See page 96*

VISIONARY INTEGRATION PROFESSIONALS (VIP)

http://www.trustvip.com/

WOMEN IN TECHNOLOGY SCHOLARSHIP (WITS)

Scholarship for women who are enrolled at, or accepted into, either a two or four-year college or university within the United States. Must be planning a career in computer science, information technology, management information systems, or other related fields. 3.0 GPA or higher required. Selection based upon academic performance, essay, and level of participation in community services and/or extracurricular activities.

Academic Fields/Career Goals: Computer Science/Data Processing; Earth Science; Engineering/Technology.

Award: Scholarship for use in freshman, sophomore, junior, senior, graduate, or postgraduate years; not renewable. *Number:* 1–20. *Amount:* $500–$2500.

Eligibility Requirements: Applicant must be enrolled or expecting to enroll full-time at a two-year or four-year institution or university and female. Applicant must have 3.0 GPA or higher. Available to U.S. citizens.

Application Requirements: Application form, application form may be submitted online (http://www.vipconsulting.com/vip/index.cfm/about-vip/community-support/women-in-technology-scholarship-wits/), community service, essay, explanation of major, transcript. *Deadline:* March 10.

Contact: Dawn Johnson, Marketing Associate
Visionary Integration Professionals (VIP)
80 Iron Point Circle #100
Folsom, CA 95630
Phone: 916-985-9625
E-mail: WITS@vipconsulting.com

WHOMENTORS.COM, INC.

http://www.WHOmentors.com/

IB USD WORLDWIDE VENTURE CAPITAL
• *See page 116*

WYOMING TRUCKING ASSOCIATION SCHOLARSHIP FUND TRUST

http://www.wytruck.org/

WYOMING TRUCKING ASSOCIATION SCHOLARSHIP TRUST FUND
• *See page 87*

XEROX
http://www.xerox.com//

TECHNICAL MINORITY SCHOLARSHIP
• *See page 190*

CONSTRUCTION ENGINEERING/ MANAGEMENT

AACE INTERNATIONAL
http://www.aacei.org/

AACE INTERNATIONAL COMPETITIVE SCHOLARSHIP
• *See page 118*

AMERICAN COUNCIL OF ENGINEERING COMPANIES OF PENNSYLVANIA (ACEC/PA)
http://www.acecpa.org/

ERIC J. GENNUSO AND LEROY D. (BUD) LOY, JR. SCHOLARSHIP PROGRAM
• *See page 173*

AMERICAN INDIAN SCIENCE AND ENGINEERING SOCIETY
http://www.aises.org/

A.T. ANDERSON MEMORIAL SCHOLARSHIP PROGRAM
• *See page 109*

AMERICAN PUBLIC POWER ASSOCIATION
http://publicpower.org/DEED

DEED EDUCATIONAL SCHOLARSHIP
• *See page 176*

DEED STUDENT INTERNSHIP
• *See page 176*

DEED STUDENT RESEARCH GRANTS
• *See page 191*

DEED TECHNICAL DESIGN PROJECT
• *See page 176*

AMERICAN RAILWAY ENGINEERING AND MAINTENANCE OF WAY ASSOCIATION
http://www.aremafoundation.org/

AREMA GRADUATE AND UNDERGRADUATE SCHOLARSHIPS
• *See page 191*

AMERICAN SOCIETY OF CERTIFIED ENGINEERING TECHNICIANS
http://www.ascet.org/

KURT H. AND DONNA M. SCHULER SMALL GRANT
• *See page 176*

AMERICAN SOCIETY OF HEATING, REFRIGERATING, AND AIR CONDITIONING ENGINEERS, INC.
http://www.ashrae.org/

ASHRAE REGION III BOGGARM SETTY SCHOLARSHIP
• *See page 176*

ARRL FOUNDATION INC.
http://www.arrl.org/

ALFRED E. FRIEND JR., W4CF, MEMORIAL SCHOLARSHIP
• *See page 177*

GARY WAGNER, K3OMI, SCHOLARSHIP
• *See page 177*

ASSOCIATED GENERAL CONTRACTORS EDUCATION AND RESEARCH FOUNDATION
http://www.agcfoundation.org/

AGC EDUCATION AND RESEARCH FOUNDATION UNDERGRADUATE SCHOLARSHIPS
• *See page 193*

JAMES L. ALLHANDS ESSAY COMPETITION
• *See page 194*

WORKFORCE DEVELOPMENT SCHOLARSHIP
Applicant can be anyone who is planning to attend a technical school or approved craft training program in any discipline of construction, including a high school senior, military member, or postsecondary student. Find application here: https://app.wizehive.com/appform/login/AGCTrade

Academic Fields/Career Goals: Construction Engineering/Management; Engineering-Related Technologies; Engineering/Technology; Trade/Technical Specialties.

Award: Scholarship for use in freshman or sophomore years; renewable. *Number:* 5–10. *Amount:* $1000.

Eligibility Requirements: Applicant must be enrolled or expecting to enroll full- or part-time at a two-year or technical institution. Available to U.S. citizens.

Application Requirements: Application form, essay. *Deadline:* June 1.

Contact: Melinda Patrician, Director
Associated General Contractors Education and Research Foundation
2300 Wilson Boulevard, Suite 300
Arlington, VA 22201
Phone: 703-837-5342
E-mail: patricianm@agc.org

ASSOCIATED GENERAL CONTRACTORS OF NEW YORK STATE, LLC

http://www.agcnys.org/

ASSOCIATED GENERAL CONTRACTORS NYS SCHOLARSHIP PROGRAM
• *See page 194*

BHW GROUP

https://thebhwgroup.com/

BHW WOMEN IN STEM SCHOLARSHIP
• *See page 74*

BRASKEM ODEBRECHT

http://www.odebrechtaward.com

ODEBRECHT AWARD FOR SUSTAINABLE DEVELOPMENT
• *See page 119*

BROWN AND CALDWELL

http://www.brownandcaldwell.com

ECKENFELDER SCHOLARSHIP
• *See page 155*

MINORITY SCHOLARSHIP PROGRAM
• *See page 155*

COLORADO CONTRACTORS ASSOCIATION INC.

http://www.coloradocontractors.org/

COLORADO CONTRACTORS ASSOCIATION SCHOLARSHIP PROGRAM
Scholarships of $2500 for junior and senior students who are interested in pursuing a career in heavy-highway-municipal-utility construction. Scholarships are only awarded to students who attend the following institutions: Colorado School of Mines, Colorado State University-Fort Collins, Colorado State University-Pueblo.

Academic Fields/Career Goals: Construction Engineering/Management.

Award: Scholarship for use in junior or senior years; not renewable. *Amount:* $2500.

Eligibility Requirements: Applicant must be enrolled or expecting to enroll full- or part-time at a four-year institution or university. Available to U.S. citizens.

Application Requirements: Application form. *Deadline:* varies.

Contact: Scholarship Program Coordinator
Phone: 290-290-6611
Fax: 290-290-9141
E-mail: info@coloradocontractors.org

FLORIDA EDUCATIONAL FACILITIES PLANNERS' ASSOCIATION

http://www.fefpa.org/

FEFPA ASSISTANTSHIP
• *See page 121*

FLORIDA ENGINEERING SOCIETY

http://www.fleng.org/scholarships.cfm

DAVID F. LUDOVICI SCHOLARSHIP
• *See page 178*

FECON SCHOLARSHIP
• *See page 195*

GRAND RAPIDS COMMUNITY FOUNDATION

http://www.grfoundation.org/

DAROOGE FAMILY SCHOLARSHIP FOR CONSTRUCTION TRADES
Student is a high school senior residing in Kent County Michigan pursuing an undergrad degree in a construction-related field at an accredited 2 or 4 year college/university/trade school in Michigan. Must have financial need.

Academic Fields/Career Goals: Construction Engineering/Management.

Award: Scholarship for use in freshman year; not renewable. *Number:* 1–5. *Amount:* $1000–$5000.

Eligibility Requirements: Applicant must be high school student; planning to enroll or expecting to enroll full-time at a two-year or four-year or technical institution and resident of Michigan. Available to U.S. citizens.

Application Requirements: Application form, essay, financial need analysis, transcript. *Deadline:* April 1.

Contact: Ms. Ruth Bishop, Education Program Officer
Grand Rapids Community Foundation
185 Oakes SW
Grand Rapids, MI 49503
Phone: 616-454-1751 Ext. 103
E-mail: rbishop@grfoundation.org

GREATER KANAWHA VALLEY FOUNDATION

http://www.tgkvf.org/

STEVEN ENGINEERING SCHOLARSHIP
• *See page 178*

GREAT MINDS IN STEM

www.greatmindsinstem.org

HISPANIC ENGINEER NATIONAL ACHIEVEMENT AWARDS CORPORATION SCHOLARSHIP PROGRAM
• *See page 106*

INTERNATIONAL FACILITY MANAGEMENT ASSOCIATION FOUNDATION

http://www.ifmafoundation.org/

IFMA FOUNDATION SCHOLARSHIPS
• See page 122

MIDWEST ROOFING CONTRACTORS ASSOCIATION

http://www.mrca.org/

MRCA FOUNDATION SCHOLARSHIP PROGRAM
• *See page 122*

NASA'S VIRGINIA SPACE GRANT CONSORTIUM

http://www.vsgc.odu.edu/

COMMUNITY COLLEGE STEM SCHOLARSHIPS
• *See page 114*

NATIONAL ASPHALT PAVEMENT ASSOCIATION RESEARCH AND EDUCATION FOUNDATION

http://www.asphaltpavement.org

NATIONAL ASPHALT PAVEMENT ASSOCIATION RESEARCH AND EDUCATION FOUNDATION SCHOLARSHIP PROGRAM
• See page 196

NATIONAL ASSOCIATION OF WATER COMPANIES-NEW JERSEY CHAPTER

http://www.nawc.org

NATIONAL ASSOCIATION OF WATER COMPANIES-NEW JERSEY CHAPTER SCHOLARSHIP
• See page 80

NATIONAL CONSTRUCTION EDUCATION FOUNDATION

http://www.abc.org/

TRIMMER EDUCATION FOUNDATION SCHOLARSHIPS FOR CONSTRUCTION MANAGEMENT

Scholarships are available to students in a major related to the construction industry. Applicants must be enrolled at an educational institution with an ABC student chapter, and be current, active members or employed by an ABC member firm. Architecture and most engineering programs are excluded. Applicants must have a minimum overall GPA of 2.85 and 3.0 in the major. If no courses have been taken in the major, a minimum overall GPA of 3.0 is required. Visit website http://www.abc.org.

Academic Fields/Career Goals: Construction Engineering/Management.

Award: Scholarship for use in sophomore, junior, or senior years; not renewable. *Number:* 10–15. *Amount:* up to $5000.

Eligibility Requirements: Applicant must be enrolled or expecting to enroll full-time at a two-year or four-year institution or university. Available to U.S. citizens.

Application Requirements: Application form, essay, financial need analysis, recommendations or references, Student Aid Report (SAR), transcript. *Deadline:* May 22.

Contact: John Strock, Director, Career and Constructions
Phone: 703-812-2008
E-mail: strock@abc.org

NEXTSTEPU

http://www.nextstepu.com/

$1,500 STEM SCHOLARSHIP
• See page 106

PROFESSIONAL CONSTRUCTION ESTIMATORS ASSOCIATION

http://www.pcea.org/

TED G. WILSON MEMORIAL SCHOLARSHIP FOUNDATION
• See page 197

SOCIETY OF WOMEN ENGINEERS

http://societyofwomenengineers.swe.org/

ADA I. PRESSMAN MEMORIAL SCHOLARSHIP
• See page 182

AMERICAN TRANSMISSION CO. SCHOLARSHIP
• See page 182

ANNE MAUREEN WHITNEY BARROW MEMORIAL SCHOLARSHIP
• See page 182

ANNE SHEN SMITH ENDOWED SCHOLARSHIP
• See page 182

BAYER SCHOLARSHIP
• See page 183

BETTY LOU BAILEY SWE REGION F SCHOLARSHIP
• See page 183

B.J. HARROD SCHOLARSHIP
• See page 183

BK KRENZER MEMORIAL REENTRY SCHOLARSHIP
• See page 183

CAROL STEPHENS SWE REGION F SCHOLARSHIP
• See page 183

DR. IVY M. PARKER MEMORIAL SCHOLARSHIP
• See page 184

DOROTHY P. MORRIS SCHOLARSHIP
• See page 184

EXELON CORPORATION SCHOLARSHIP
• See page 184

FCA WOMEN IN ENGINEERING SCHOLARSHIP
• See page 184

IBM LINDA SANFORD WOMEN'S TECHNICAL ADVANCEMENT SCHOLARSHIP
• See page 185

KOCH DISCOVERY SCHOLARSHIP
• See page 185

LILLIAN MOLLER GILBRETH MEMORIAL SCHOLARSHIP
• See page 185

MARY V. MUNGER SCHOLARSHIP
• See page 185

MASWE SCHOLARSHIP
• See page 186

OLIVE LYNN SALEMBIER MEMORIAL REENTRY SCHOLARSHIP
• See page 186

ROBERTA BANASZAK GLEITER ENGINEERING ENDEAVOR SCHOLARSHIP
• See page 186

ROCHELLE PERRY MEMORIAL SCHOLARSHIP
• See page 186

SUSAN MISZKOWICZ MEMORIAL SCHOLARSHIP
• See page 186

SWE BALTIMORE-WASHINGTON SECTION SCHOLARSHIP
• See page 186

SWE CENTRAL NEW MEXICO PIONEERS SCHOLARSHIP
• See page 187

SWE CENTRAL NEW MEXICO REENTRY SCHOLARSHIP
• See page 187

SWE MID-HUDSON SECTION SCHOLARSHIP
• See page 187

SWE PHOENIX SECTION SCHOLARSHIP
• See page 187

SWE REGION E SCHOLARSHIP
• See page 187

SWE REGION G JUDY SIMMONS MEMORIAL SCHOLARSHIP
• See page 188

SWE REGION H SCHOLARSHIPS
• See page 188

SWE REGION J SCHOLARSHIP
• See page 188

TURNER CONSTRUCTION SCHOLARSHIP
• See page 188

WANDA MUNN SCHOLARSHIP
• See page 188

SOCIETY OF WOMEN ENGINEERS-ROCKY MOUNTAIN SECTION

http://www.swe-rms.org/

SOCIETY OF WOMEN ENGINEERS-ROCKY MOUNTAIN SECTION SCHOLARSHIP PROGRAM
• See page 188

TURNER CONSTRUCTION COMPANY

http://www.turnerconstruction.com/

YOUTHFORCE 2020 SCHOLARSHIP PROGRAM
• See page 124

UNITED NEGRO COLLEGE FUND

http://www.uncf.org/

UNCF STEM SCHOLARS PROGRAM
• See page 159

VECTORWORKS, INC.

http://www.vectorworks.net

VECTORWORKS DESIGN SCHOLARSHIP
• See page 124

WIRE REINFORCEMENT INSTITUTE EDUCATION FOUNDATION

http://www.wirereinforcementinstitute.org/

WRI FOUNDATION COLLEGE SCHOLARSHIP PROGRAM
• See page 200

COSMETOLOGY

AVACARE MEDICAL

https://avacaremedical.com

AVACARE MEDICAL SCHOLARSHIP
• See page 105

JOE FRANCIS HAIRCARE SCHOLARSHIP FOUNDATION

http://www.joefrancis.com

JOE FRANCIS HAIRCARE SCHOLARSHIP PROGRAM
Cosmetology or Barber School scholarships are awarded for $1200 each, with 20 to 28 scholarships awarded annually. Applicants are evaluated for their potential to successfully complete school, their financial need, and their commitment to a long-term career in cosmetology. Deadline to apply is June 1st. Students who graduate before September of the award year are not eligible to apply. Applications are found on our website (apply online) www.joefrancis.com.

Academic Fields/Career Goals: Cosmetology.

Award: Scholarship for use in freshman, sophomore, junior, or senior years; not renewable. *Number:* 20–28. *Amount:* $1200.

Eligibility Requirements: Applicant must be enrolled or expecting to enroll full- or part-time at a technical institution. Available to U.S. citizens.

Application Requirements: Application form, application form may be submitted online (http://www.joefrancis.com), essay, financial need analysis, recommendations or references. *Deadline:* June 1.

Contact: Kim Larson, Administrator
Joe Francis Haircare Scholarship Foundation
PO Box 50625
Minneapolis, MN 55405
Phone: 651-769-1757
Fax: 651-459-8371
E-mail: kimlarsonmn@gmail.com

MEDICAL SCRUBS COLLECTION

http://medicalscrubscollection.com

MEDICAL SCRUBS COLLECTION SCHOLARSHIP
• See page 106

STRAIGHTFORWARD MEDIA

http://www.straightforwardmedia.com/

STRAIGHTFORWARD MEDIA VOCATIONAL-TECHNICAL SCHOOL SCHOLARSHIP
• See page 107

CRIMINAL JUSTICE/ CRIMINOLOGY

AMERICAN CRIMINAL JUSTICE ASSOCIATION-LAMBDA ALPHA EPSILON

http://www.acjalae.org/

AMERICAN CRIMINAL JUSTICE ASSOCIATION-LAMBDA ALPHA EPSILON NATIONAL SCHOLARSHIP
Awarded only to members of the American Criminal Justice Association. One-time award of $100 to $400. Members may reapply each year. Must

have minimum 3.0 GPA. Must pursue studies in law/legal services, criminal justice/law, or the social sciences.

Academic Fields/Career Goals: Criminal Justice/Criminology; Law/Legal Services; Social Sciences.

Award: Scholarship for use in freshman, sophomore, junior, senior, or graduate years; not renewable. *Number:* 9. *Amount:* $100–$400.

Eligibility Requirements: Applicant must be enrolled or expecting to enroll full- or part-time at a two-year or four-year institution or university. Applicant or parent of applicant must be member of American Criminal Justice Association. Applicant must have 3.0 GPA or higher. Available to U.S. citizens.

Application Requirements: Application form. *Deadline:* December 31.

Contact: Karen Campbell, Executive Secretary
American Criminal Justice Association-Lambda Alpha Epsilon
PO Box 601047
Sacramento, CA 95860-1047
Phone: 916-484-6553
E-mail: acjalae@aol.com

AMERICAN SOCIETY OF CRIMINOLOGY

http://www.asc41.com/

AMERICAN SOCIETY OF CRIMINOLOGY GENE CARTE STUDENT PAPER COMPETITION

Award for full-time undergraduate or graduate students. Must submit a conceptual or empirical paper on a subject directly relating to criminology. Papers must be 7500 words or less.

Academic Fields/Career Goals: Criminal Justice/Criminology; Law Enforcement/Police Administration; Law/Legal Services; Social Sciences.

Award: Prize for use in freshman, sophomore, junior, senior, or graduate years; not renewable. *Number:* 3. *Amount:* $200–$500.

Eligibility Requirements: Applicant must be enrolled or expecting to enroll full-time at a four-year institution or university and must have an interest in writing. Available to U.S. and non-U.S. citizens.

Application Requirements: Conceptual or empirical paper on a subject directly relating to criminology, entry in a contest. *Deadline:* April 15.

Contact: Andrew Hochstetlet, Scholarship Committee
American Society of Criminology
Iowa State University, 203D East Hall
Ames, IA 50011-4504
Phone: 515-294-2841
E-mail: hochstet@iastate.edu

ASSOCIATION OF CERTIFIED FRAUD EXAMINERS

http://www.acfe.com/

RITCHIE-JENNINGS MEMORIAL SCHOLARSHIP
• *See page 74*

ASSOCIATION OF FORMER INTELLIGENCE OFFICERS

http://www.afio.com

AFIO UNDERGRADUATE AND GRADUATE SCHOLARSHIPS
• *See page 103*

CANTOR CRANE INJURY LAW

http://cantorcrane.com

CANTOR CRANE PERSONAL INJURY LAWYER $1,000 SCHOLARSHIP

At the Law Firm of Cantor Crane Personal Injury Lawyers, we believe in achieving a higher education just as much as we take pride in representing people who have been injured in an accident. We understand and appreciate the importance that a solid education can factor in the future of successful law school students. We also understand the potential

difficulties of obtaining a law degree because of increasing costs of tuition, text books, and the everyday necessities of life. In order to help make a college education more affordable opportunity and to help spread awareness about Driving Under the Influence and Distracted Driving, the Arizona law firm of Cantor Crane is offering a $1,000 law student scholarship to help current, or soon-to-be, law students ease the burden of higher education costs. The scholarship funds may be used for law school tuition at a college or university. It is not required that the applicant be enrolled in an educational program at the time of his or her application. The winner will have one year from the date of the award to provide a tuition invoice from the school of their choice. A check for $1,000 will then be sent to the educational institution. Submitting the application is easy. Simply take the pledge to not drive under the influence and to not drive while distracted by things such as texting and fill out the contact information.

Academic Fields/Career Goals: Criminal Justice/Criminology; Law/Legal Services.

Award: Scholarship for use in freshman, sophomore, junior, senior, graduate, or postgraduate years; renewable. *Number:* 1. *Amount:* $1000.

Eligibility Requirements: Applicant must be enrolled or expecting to enroll full- or part-time at a two-year or four-year institution or university. Available to U.S. and non-U.S. citizens.

Application Requirements: Application form. *Deadline:* July 31.

Contact: Bryan Young, Media Director
Cantor Crane Injury Law
1 East Washington Street
Suite 1800
Phoenix, AZ 85004
Phone: 602-254-2701
E-mail: b.young@cantorcrane.com

CONNECTICUT ASSOCIATION OF WOMEN POLICE

http://www.cawp.net/

CONNECTICUT ASSOCIATION OF WOMEN POLICE SCHOLARSHIP

Available to Connecticut residents graduating from an accredited high school, and entering a college or university in Connecticut as a criminal justice major.

Academic Fields/Career Goals: Criminal Justice/Criminology; Law Enforcement/Police Administration.

Award: Scholarship for use in freshman year; not renewable. *Number:* 1–3. *Amount:* $200–$500.

Eligibility Requirements: Applicant must be high school student; planning to enroll or expecting to enroll full-time at a two-year or four-year institution or university; resident of Connecticut and studying in Connecticut. Available to U.S. citizens.

Application Requirements: Application form, essay, financial need analysis, recommendations or references, transcript. *Deadline:* April 30.

Contact: Gail McDonnell, Scholarship Committee
Connecticut Association of Women Police
PO Box 1653
Hartford, CT 06144
Phone: 860-527-7300

INDIANA SHERIFFS' ASSOCIATION

http://www.indianasheriffs.org/

INDIANA SHERIFFS' ASSOCIATION SCHOLARSHIP PROGRAM

Applicant must be an Indiana resident majoring in a criminal justice/law enforcement field at an Indiana college or university. Must be a member or dependent child or grandchild of a member of the association. Must be a full-time student with at least 12 credit hours.

Academic Fields/Career Goals: Criminal Justice/Criminology; Law Enforcement/Police Administration.

Award: Scholarship for use in freshman, sophomore, junior, or senior years; not renewable. *Number:* 40. *Amount:* $500.

Eligibility Requirements: Applicant must be enrolled or expecting to enroll full-time at a two-year or four-year institution or university; resident of Indiana and studying in Indiana. Applicant or parent of applicant must be member of Indiana Sheriffs' Association. Available to U.S. citizens.

Application Requirements: Application form, essay. *Deadline:* April 1.

Contact: Laura Vest, Administrative Director
Indiana Sheriffs' Association
147 East Maryland Street
Indianapolis, IN 46204
Phone: 317-356-3633
E-mail: lvest@indianasheriffs.org

LIVSECURE

https://www.livsecure.com

LIVSECURE STUDENT SCHOLARSHIP

At LivSecure, we are proud to support those who are studying to make our neighborhoods a safer place. If you are currently studying law enforcement, law, criminal justice, or a related field, then you are eligible to submit a security-focused essay for a chance to win a $1,000 scholarship to put toward your college tuition.

Academic Fields/Career Goals: Criminal Justice/Criminology; Law Enforcement/Police Administration; Law/Legal Services.

Award: Scholarship for use in freshman or sophomore years; not renewable. *Number:* 1–3. *Amount:* $500–$1000.

Eligibility Requirements: Applicant must be enrolled or expecting to enroll full- or part-time at a two-year or four-year or technical institution or university.

Application Requirements: Essay. *Deadline:* July 1.

Contact: Megan Nonemacher, Marketing Manager
LivSecure
3803 West Chester Pike
Suite 100
Newtown Square, PA 19073
Phone: 484-420-0314
E-mail: megan.nonemacher@myalarmcenter.com

MISSOURI SHERIFFS' ASSOCIATION

http://www.mosheriffs.com/

JOHN DENNIS SCHOLARSHIP

Awards for Missouri high school seniors planning to attend a Missouri college or university and pursuing a career in criminal justice. Students must be in upper one-third of their graduating class and participate in extracurricular activities. Minimum 2.0 GPA required.

Academic Fields/Career Goals: Criminal Justice/Criminology.

Award: Scholarship for use in freshman year; not renewable. *Number:* 16. *Amount:* $1000.

Eligibility Requirements: Applicant must be high school student; planning to enroll or expecting to enroll full-time at a two-year or four-year institution or university; resident of Missouri and studying in Missouri. Available to U.S. citizens.

Application Requirements: Application form, community service, essay, financial need analysis, test scores. *Deadline:* January 31.

Contact: Ms. Karen Logan, Administrative Assistant
Phone: 573-635-5925 Ext. 100
E-mail: karen@mosheriffs.com

NAQVI INJURY LAW

http://www.naqvilaw.com/

NAQVI LAW SCHOLARSHIP

This is a primarily needs-based scholarship offered to Nevada high school students and graduates seeking a law-oriented college degree. The application is submitted online, and the successful applicant will receive $2000.

Academic Fields/Career Goals: Criminal Justice/Criminology; Law/Legal Services; Political Science.

Award: Scholarship for use in freshman year; not renewable. *Number:* 1. *Amount:* $2000.

Eligibility Requirements: Applicant must be enrolled or expecting to enroll full-time at a four-year institution or university and resident of

Nevada. Applicant must have 3.0 GPA or higher. Available to U.S. citizens.

Application Requirements: Application form, application form may be submitted online (http://naqvilaw.com/scholarship-application/), financial need analysis, transcript. *Deadline:* December 31.

NATIONAL BLACK POLICE ASSOCIATION

http://www.blackpolice.org/

ALPHONSO DEAL SCHOLARSHIP AWARD

$500 scholarship for high school senior and U.S. citizen to attend a two-year college or university. Must study law enforcement or other related criminal justice field. Minimum 2.5 GPA required.

Academic Fields/Career Goals: Criminal Justice/Criminology; Law Enforcement/Police Administration; Law/Legal Services; Social Sciences; Social Services.

Award: Scholarship for use in freshman year; not renewable. *Number:* 4. *Amount:* $500.

Eligibility Requirements: Applicant must be high school student and planning to enroll or expecting to enroll full-time at a two-year or four-year institution or university. Available to U.S. citizens.

Application Requirements: Application form, letter of acceptance, personal photograph, recommendations or references, transcript. *Deadline:* June 1.

Contact: Ronald Hampton, Executive Director
National Black Police Association
30 Kennedy Street, NW, Suite 101
Washington, DC 20011
Phone: 202-986-2070
Fax: 202-986-0410
E-mail: nbpanatofc@worldnet.att.net

NORTH CAROLINA STATE EDUCATION ASSISTANCE AUTHORITY

http://www.ncseaa.edu/

NORTH CAROLINA SHERIFFS' ASSOCIATION UNDERGRADUATE CRIMINAL JUSTICE SCHOLARSHIPS

One-time award for full-time North Carolina resident undergraduate students majoring in criminal justice at a University of North Carolina school. Priority given to child of any North Carolina law enforcement officer. Letter of recommendation from county sheriff required.

Academic Fields/Career Goals: Criminal Justice/Criminology; Law Enforcement/Police Administration.

Award: Scholarship for use in freshman, sophomore, junior, or senior years; not renewable. *Number:* 10. *Amount:* $1000–$2000.

Eligibility Requirements: Applicant must be enrolled or expecting to enroll full-time at a four-year institution or university; resident of North Carolina and studying in North Carolina. Applicant or parent of applicant must have employment or volunteer experience in police/firefighting. Available to U.S. citizens.

Application Requirements: Application form, financial need analysis.

Contact: Michele Goldston, Assistant, Scholarship and Grant Division
North Carolina State Education Assistance Authority
PO Box 13663
Research Triangle Park, NC 27709
Phone: 919-549-8614
E-mail: mgoldston@ncseaa.edu

OREGON ASSOCIATION CHIEFS OF POLICE

http://www.policechief.org/

LAW ENFORCEMENT AND CRIMINAL JUSTICE COLLEGE SCHOLARSHIP PROGRAM

Each year, the Oregon Association Chiefs of Police (OACP) provides $1000 college scholarships to students who plan to enter a law enforcement or other criminal justice career. The OACP is committed to promoting professionalism and we value the presence and contributions of educated men and women in Law Enforcement and Criminal Justice.

To further our commitment, the OACP provides competitive college scholarships for qualifying students. The following information will help you determine if you qualify for scholarship consideration and will help you understand the application process. Each year, the Oregon Association Chiefs of Police (OACP) provides $1000 college scholarships to students who plan to enter a law enforcement or other criminal justice career. The OACP is committed to promoting professionalism and we value the presence and contributions of educated men and women in Law Enforcement and Criminal Justice. To further our commitment, the OACP provides competitive college scholarships for qualifying students. The following information will help you determine if you qualify for scholarship consideration and will help you understand the application process. 1. Have you completed at least 36 college credit hours or 30 semester hours? In lieu of 36 college credit hours, have you logged at least 240-hours of service over the last year as a cadet, explorer, or reserve police officer? 2. Have you maintained a grade point average (GPA) of at least 2.5? 3. Do you plan to enter a law enforcement or other criminal justice career? Preference will be given to immediate family members of an Oregon Police Officer killed or disabled in the line of duty, as well as dependents of OACP members.

Academic Fields/Career Goals: Criminal Justice/Criminology.

Award: Scholarship for use in freshman, sophomore, junior, senior, graduate, or postgraduate years; not renewable. *Number:* 5. *Amount:* $1000.

Eligibility Requirements: Applicant must be enrolled or expecting to enroll full- or part-time at a two-year or four-year institution or university and resident of Oregon. Applicant must have 2.5 GPA or higher. Available to U.S. citizens.

Application Requirements: Application form, personal photograph. *Deadline:* December 31.

Contact: Mrs. Marie Campbell, Association Executive
Oregon Association Chiefs of Police
1191 Capitol St NE
Salem, OR 97301
Phone: 503-315-1411
Fax: 503-315-1416
E-mail: marie@victorygrp.com

WASHINGTON STATE ASSOCIATION FOR JUSTICE

http://www.washingtonjustice.org/

WASHINGTON STATE ASSOCIATION FOR JUSTICE AMERICAN JUSTICE ESSAY & VIDEO SCHOLARSHIP

As part of the Washington State Association for Justice's (WSAJ) commitment to foster an awareness and understanding of the important role that the civil justice system plays in our society, WSAJ sponsors an annual statewide student essay and video scholarship program. For 2017, WSAJ will award two, $3,750 scholarships, one to an essayist and one to a videographer. The video scholarship winner's piece will be posted on WSAJ's Facebook and Twitter accounts, and may be aired on TV. This scholarship is available to high school seniors who are residents attending high school in Washington state. Students need not attend a Washington college, but must start college within the next two years to receive the funds. If you have questions about the prompt or the practice of law, please contact anita@washingtonjustice.org and we will connect you with an attorney to answer your questions. The prompt for both scholarships is—Forced arbitration clauses in consumer contracts: How do they affect us? Essay option: Write a 700-800 word essay on this subject. Video option: Create a video of no more than 60 seconds in length on this subject in the format of a Public Service Announcement, as well as writing a 300-400 word summary on this subject and the inspiration for the video. The video must be uploaded on YouTube or Vimeo and the link shared with the scholarship committee. WSAJ reserves the right to make the winning video available to the general public. By submitting a video, you grant WSAJ a royalty-free license to copy, distribute, modify, display and perform publicly and otherwise use and authorize others to use your video for any purpose. You also guarantee that no other person, corporation or organization has a copyright interest in your video. Applications must be postmarked on or before March 17, 2017.

Academic Fields/Career Goals: Criminal Justice/Criminology; Law/Legal Services; Peace and Conflict Studies; Political Science; Public Policy and Administration; Social Sciences.

Award: Scholarship for use in freshman year; not renewable. *Number:* 2. *Amount:* $3750.

Eligibility Requirements: Applicant must be high school student; planning to enroll or expecting to enroll full-time at a four-year institution or university; resident of Washington and studying in Washington. Available to U.S. and non-U.S. citizens.

Application Requirements: Application form, essay. *Deadline:* March 17.

Contact: Anita Yandle, Scholarship Coordinator
Washington State Association for Justice
1809 7th Ave
Suite 1500
Seattle, WA 98101
Phone: 206-464-1011
E-mail: anita@washingtonjustice.org

WIFLE FOUNDATION, INC.

http://www.wifle.org/

WIFLE SCHOLARSHIP

Scholarship to encourage women to pursue a career in federal law enforcement. Applicant must be enrolled in, or be transferring to, a four-year program in criminal justice, social sciences, public administration, chemistry, physics, computer science, or related studies and have a minimum GPA of 3.0. May also be in a graduate program. Must demonstrate commitment to the community through volunteer community service or an internship in a law enforcement agency. Must be a United States citizen.

Academic Fields/Career Goals: Criminal Justice/Criminology; Law Enforcement/Police Administration; Law/Legal Services; Social Sciences.

Award: Scholarship for use in sophomore, junior, senior, graduate, or postgraduate years; not renewable. *Number:* 1–6. *Amount:* $1000–$2500.

Eligibility Requirements: Applicant must be enrolled or expecting to enroll full-time at a four-year institution or university and female. Applicant must have 3.0 GPA or higher. Available to U.S. citizens.

Application Requirements: Application form, community service, essay. *Deadline:* May 1.

Contact: Ms. Catherine Sanz, President
WIFLE Foundation, Inc.
2200 Wilson Boulevard
Suite 102, PMB 204
Arlington, VA 22201
Phone: 301-805-2180
E-mail: wifle@comcast.net

CULINARY ARTS

AMERICAN HOTEL AND LODGING EDUCATIONAL FOUNDATION

http://www.ahlef.org/

AH&LEF ANNUAL SCHOLARSHIP GRANT PROGRAM

Students are selected for this award by their school which must be an AH&LEF affiliated program. Available to full-time students who have completed at least one or two years of a hospitality-related degree, are U.S. citizens or have permanent U.S. resident status. Minimum GPA of 3.0. A list of affiliated schools and designated contacts at the schools is available on http://www.ahlef.org.

Academic Fields/Career Goals: Culinary Arts; Food Service/Hospitality; Hospitality Management; Recreation, Parks, Leisure Studies; Travel/Tourism.

Award: Scholarship for use in sophomore, junior, or senior years; not renewable. *Amount:* $500–$3000.

Eligibility Requirements: Applicant must be enrolled or expecting to enroll full-time at a two-year or four-year institution or university. Applicant must have 3.0 GPA or higher. Available to U.S. citizens.

Application Requirements: Application form, essay, financial need analysis, nomination from school, recommendations or references, transcript. *Deadline:* May 1.

Contact: Ms. Kelsey Allagood, Foundation Manager
American Hotel and Lodging Educational Foundation
1201 New York Avenue, NW, Suite 600
Washington, DC 20005-3931
Phone: 202-289-3139
Fax: 202-289-3199
E-mail: kallagood@ahlef.org

AMERICAN HOTEL & LODGING EDUCATIONAL FOUNDATION PEPSI SCHOLARSHIP

Scholarships of $500 to $3000 awarded to graduates of Hospitality High School in Washington, DC. The scholarship recipients are selected by Hospitality High based upon a set of minimum eligibility criteria which includes graduate of Hospitality High, a minimum 2.5 GPA, and at least 250 hours in the hotel/hospitality industry.

Academic Fields/Career Goals: Culinary Arts; Food Service/Hospitality; Hospitality Management; Recreation, Parks, Leisure Studies; Travel/Tourism.

Award: Scholarship for use in freshman, sophomore, junior, or senior years; not renewable. *Amount:* $500–$3000.

Eligibility Requirements: Applicant must be enrolled or expecting to enroll full-time at a two-year or four-year institution or university and resident of District of Columbia. Applicant must have 2.5 GPA or higher. Available to U.S. and non-U.S. citizens.

Application Requirements: Application form, essay, financial need analysis, nomination from Hospitality High School, resume, transcript. *Deadline:* May 1.

Contact: Ms. Kelsey Allagood, Foundation Manager
American Hotel and Lodging Educational Foundation
1201 New York Avenue, NW, Suite 600
Washington, DC 20005
Phone: 202-289-3139
Fax: 202-289-3199
E-mail: scholarships@ahlef.org

ECOLAB SCHOLARSHIP PROGRAM

Award for students enrolled full-time in United States Baccalaureate or associate program leading to degree in hospitality management.

Academic Fields/Career Goals: Culinary Arts; Food Service/Hospitality; Hospitality Management; Recreation, Parks, Leisure Studies; Travel/Tourism.

Award: Scholarship for use in freshman, sophomore, junior, or senior years; not renewable. *Number:* 10–15. *Amount:* $1000–$2000.

Eligibility Requirements: Applicant must be enrolled or expecting to enroll full-time at a two-year or four-year institution or university. Available to U.S. and non-U.S. citizens.

Application Requirements: Application form, essay, financial need analysis, resume, transcript. *Deadline:* May 1.

Contact: Ms. Kelsey Allagood, Foundation Manager
American Hotel and Lodging Educational Foundation
1201 New York Avenue, SW, Suite 600
Washington, DC 20005-3931
Phone: 202-289-3139
Fax: 202-289-3199
E-mail: kallagood@ahlef.org

HYATT HOTELS FUND FOR MINORITY LODGING MANAGEMENT

Scholarship available for African-American, Hispanic, American Indian, Alaskan Native, Asian, or Pacific Islander in a Baccalaureate hospitality management program. Must be at least a junior in a four-year program to receive the scholarship monies.

Academic Fields/Career Goals: Culinary Arts; Food Service/Hospitality; Hospitality Management; Recreation, Parks, Leisure Studies; Travel/Tourism.

Award: Scholarship for use in sophomore, junior, or senior years; not renewable. *Number:* 10–15. *Amount:* $2000.

Eligibility Requirements: Applicant must be American Indian/Alaska Native, Asian/Pacific Islander, Black (non-Hispanic), Hispanic and

enrolled or expecting to enroll full-time at a four-year institution or university. Available to U.S. citizens.

Application Requirements: Application form, essay, financial need analysis, recommendations or references, resume, transcript. *Deadline:* May 1.

Contact: Ms. Kelsey Allagood, Foundation Manager
American Hotel and Lodging Educational Foundation
1201 New York Avenue, Suite 600
Washington, DC 20005
Phone: 202-289-3139
Fax: 202-289-3199
E-mail: scholarships@ahlef.org

INCOMING FRESHMAN SCHOLARSHIPS

This program is exclusively for incoming freshman interested in pursuing hospitality-related undergraduate programs. Preference will be given to any applicant who is a graduate of the Educational Institute's Lodging Management Program (LMP, which is a two-year high school program.) Must have a minimum 2.0 GPA.

Academic Fields/Career Goals: Culinary Arts; Food Service/Hospitality; Hospitality Management; Recreation, Parks, Leisure Studies; Travel/Tourism.

Award: Scholarship for use in freshman year; not renewable. *Number:* 5–10. *Amount:* $1000–$2000.

Eligibility Requirements: Applicant must be high school student and planning to enroll or expecting to enroll full-time at a two-year or four-year institution or university. Available to U.S. citizens.

Application Requirements: Application form, essay, financial need analysis, resume, transcript. *Deadline:* May 1.

Contact: Ms. Kelsey Allagood, Foundation Manager
American Hotel and Lodging Educational Foundation
1201 New York Avenue, NW, Suite 600
Washington, DC 20005-3197
Phone: 202-289-3139
Fax: 202-289-3199
E-mail: scholarships@ahlef.org

RAMA SCHOLARSHIP FOR THE AMERICAN DREAM

Schools participating in this program include Bethune-Cookman College, California State Polytechnic University, Cornell University, Florida International University, Georgia State university, Greenville Technical College, Howard University, Johnson & Wales University, New York University, University of Central Florida, University of Houston, University of South Carolina, and Virginia Tech. The participating schools select the student nominees based upon a set of minimum eligibility criteria which include: enrolled in at least 9 credit hours for the fall and spring semesters, majoring in an undergraduate or graduate hospitality management program, minimum GPA of 2.5, U.S. citizenship or permanent resident, and schools must give preference to students of Asian-Indian descent or other minority groups, as well as JHM employees and their dependents.

Academic Fields/Career Goals: Culinary Arts; Food Service/Hospitality; Hospitality Management; Recreation, Parks, Leisure Studies; Travel/Tourism.

Award: Scholarship for use in sophomore, junior, senior, or graduate years; not renewable. *Amount:* $1000–$3000.

Eligibility Requirements: Applicant must be American Indian/Alaska Native, Asian/Pacific Islander, Black (non-Hispanic), Hispanic and enrolled or expecting to enroll full- or part-time at a two-year or four-year institution or university. Applicant must have 2.5 GPA or higher. Available to U.S. citizens.

Application Requirements: Application form, essay, financial need analysis, nomination from school, recommendations or references, transcript. *Deadline:* May 1.

Contact: Ms. Kelsey Allagood, Foundation Manager
American Hotel and Lodging Educational Foundation
1201 New York Avenue, NW, Suite 600
Washington, DC 20005
Phone: 202-289-3139
Fax: 202-289-3199
E-mail: kallagood@ahlef.org

CANFIT

http://www.canfit.org/

CANFIT NUTRITION, PHYSICAL EDUCATION AND CULINARY ARTS SCHOLARSHIP

Awards undergraduate and graduate African-American, American-Indian/Alaska Native, Asian-American, Pacific Islander or Latino/Hispanic students who express financial need and are studying nutrition, physical education, or culinary arts in California. GPA of minimum 2.5 for undergraduates and 3.0 for graduates. See website for essay topic http://www.canfit.org.

Academic Fields/Career Goals: Culinary Arts; Food Science/Nutrition; Food Service/Hospitality; Health and Medical Sciences; Sports-Related/Exercise Science.

Award: Scholarship for use in junior, senior, or graduate years; not renewable. *Number:* 5–10. *Amount:* $500–$1500.

Eligibility Requirements: Applicant must be of African, Chinese, Hispanic, Indian, Japanese heritage; American Indian/Alaska Native, Asian/Pacific Islander, Black (non-Hispanic); enrolled or expecting to enroll full-time at a four-year or technical institution or university; resident of California and studying in California. Applicant must have 2.5 GPA or higher. Available to U.S. citizens.

Application Requirements: Application form, essay, financial need analysis, personal photograph, recommendations or references, transcript. *Deadline:* March 31.

Contact: Ms. Arnell Hinkle, Executive Director
Phone: 510-644-1533 Ext. 12
Fax: 510-644-1535
E-mail: info@canfit.org

CAREERS THROUGH CULINARY ARTS PROGRAM INC.

http://www.ccapinc.org/

CAREERS THROUGH CULINARY ARTS PROGRAM COOKING COMPETITION FOR SCHOLARSHIPS

Applicants must be a senior in a C-CAP designated partner high school in Arizona; Prince George's County, Maryland; Tidewater, Virginia; or the cities of Boston, Chicago, Los Angeles, New York, Philadelphia or Washington, DC. Applicants must be accepted into the cooking competition for scholarships.

Academic Fields/Career Goals: Culinary Arts; Hospitality Management.

Award: Scholarship for use in freshman, sophomore, junior, or senior years; not renewable. *Number:* 50–70. *Amount:* $1000–$90,000.

Eligibility Requirements: Applicant must be high school student; planning to enroll or expecting to enroll full- or part-time at a two-year or four-year or technical institution and resident of Arizona, California, Illinois, Maryland, New York, Pennsylvania, Virginia. Available to U.S. and non-U.S. citizens.

Application Requirements: Application form, entry in a contest, essay, financial need analysis, interview, recommendations or references, test scores, transcript. *Deadline:* varies.

Contact: Check website for local coordinator's contact information.

THE CULINARY TRUST

http://www.theculinarytrust.org/

CULINARY TRUST SCHOLARSHIP PROGRAM FOR CULINARY STUDY AND RESEARCH

Scholarships provides funds to qualified applicants for beginning, continuing, and specialty education courses at accredited culinary schools worldwide, as well as, independent study for research projects. Applicants must have at least, a minimum 3.0 GPA, must write an essay, submit two letters of recommendation. Application fee: $35.

Academic Fields/Career Goals: Culinary Arts; Food Science/Nutrition; Food Service/Hospitality.

Award: Scholarship for use in freshman, sophomore, junior, senior, graduate, or postgraduate years; not renewable. *Number:* 21. *Amount:* $1000–$5000.

Eligibility Requirements: Applicant must be enrolled or expecting to enroll full- or part-time at a two-year or four-year or technical institution or university. Applicant must have 3.0 GPA or higher. Available to U.S. and non-U.S. citizens.

Application Requirements: Application form, application form may be submitted online (http://www.theculinarytrust.org), essay, interview, recommendations or references, resume, transcript. *Fee:* $35. *Deadline:* March 1.

Contact: Heather Johnston, Administrator
The Culinary Trust
PO Box 273
New York, NY 10013
Phone: 888-345-4666
Fax: 888-345-4666
E-mail: heather@theculinarytrust.org

GOLDEN GATE RESTAURANT ASSOCIATION

http://www.ggra.org/

GOLDEN GATE RESTAURANT ASSOCIATION SCHOLARSHIP FOUNDATION

One-time award for any student pursuing a food service degree at a 501(c)(3) institution, or institutions approved by the Board of Trustees. California residency and personal interview in San Francisco is required. Minimum GPA of 2.75 required. For further information email donnalyn@ggra.org, or visit http://ggra.org/scholarships/.

Academic Fields/Career Goals: Culinary Arts; Food Service/Hospitality; Hospitality Management.

Award: Scholarship for use in freshman, sophomore, junior, or senior years; renewable. *Number:* 9–15. *Amount:* $1000–$6000.

Eligibility Requirements: Applicant must be enrolled or expecting to enroll full- or part-time at a two-year or four-year or technical institution or university and resident of California. Applicant must have 2.5 GPA or higher. Available to U.S. citizens.

Application Requirements: Application form, essay, financial need analysis, interview. *Deadline:* April 30.

Contact: Donnalyn Murphy, Trustee and Secretary
Golden Gate Restaurant Association
220 Montgomery Street
Suite 990
San Francisco, CA 94104
Phone: 415-781-5350
E-mail: donnalyn@ggra.org

ILLINOIS RESTAURANT ASSOCIATION EDUCATIONAL FOUNDATION

http://www.illinoisrestaurants.org/

ILLINOIS RESTAURANT ASSOCIATION EDUCATIONAL FOUNDATION SCHOLARSHIPS

Scholarship available to Illinois residents enrolled in a food service management, culinary arts, or hospitality management concentration in an accredited program of a two- or four-year college or university. Must be a U.S. citizen.

Academic Fields/Career Goals: Culinary Arts; Food Science/Nutrition; Food Service/Hospitality; Hospitality Management.

Award: Scholarship for use in freshman, sophomore, junior, senior, graduate, or postgraduate years; not renewable. *Number:* 50–70. *Amount:* $1000–$10,000.

Eligibility Requirements: Applicant must be age 17-25; enrolled or expecting to enroll full- or part-time at a two-year or four-year institution or university and resident of Illinois. Applicant or parent of applicant must have employment or volunteer experience in food service, hospitality/hotel administration/operations. Applicant must have 2.5 GPA or higher. Available to U.S. citizens.

Application Requirements: Application form, essay, personal photograph, recommendations or references, transcript. *Deadline:* April 27.

Contact: Jenna Zera, IRA Educational Foundation Scholarship
Committee
Illinois Restaurant Association Educational Foundation
33 West Monroe, Suite 250
Chicago, IL 60603
Phone: 312-380-4117
Fax: 312-787-4792

INTERNATIONAL FOODSERVICE EDITORIAL COUNCIL

http://www.ifeconline.com/

INTERNATIONAL FOODSERVICE EDITORIAL COUNCIL COMMUNICATIONS SCHOLARSHIP
• *See page 88*

JAMES BEARD FOUNDATION INC.

http://www.jamesbeard.org/

ANDREW ZIMMERN "SECOND CHANCES" SCHOLARSHIP

Up to one $10,000 scholarship available to students planning to enroll or currently enrolled at a licensed or accredited culinary school. Student must submit an essay (of 250 words) describing extreme challenges (health, family, military, employment, etc.) they have faced, and explain how this scholarship in culinary studies will give them the second chance they deserve in overcoming these hardships.

Academic Fields/Career Goals: Culinary Arts.

Award: Scholarship for use in freshman, sophomore, junior, senior, or graduate years; not renewable. *Number:* 1. *Amount:* $10,000.

Eligibility Requirements: Applicant must be enrolled or expecting to enroll full- or part-time at a four-year institution or university. Available to U.S. and non-U.S. citizens.

Application Requirements: Application form, essay. *Deadline:* May 15.

Contact: Scholarship Management Services
James Beard Foundation Inc.
One Scholarship Way
Saint Peter, MN 56082
Phone: 507-931-1682
E-mail: jamesbeard@scholarshipamerica.org

BERN LAXER MEMORIAL SCHOLARSHIP

Scholarship for students seeking careers in food service and hospitality management. Up to one scholarship will be given in one of three programs: culinary, hospitality management, and viticulture/oenology. Program and school must be accredited in accordance with the James Beard Foundation scholarship criteria. Must be resident of Florida and substantiate residency, have a high school diploma or the equivalent, and have a minimum of one-year culinary experience either as a student or employee.

Academic Fields/Career Goals: Culinary Arts; Food Science/Nutrition; Hospitality Management.

Award: Scholarship for use in freshman, sophomore, junior, or senior years; not renewable. *Number:* 1. *Amount:* $10,250.

Eligibility Requirements: Applicant must be enrolled or expecting to enroll full- or part-time at a four-year institution or university and resident of Florida. Available to U.S. and non-U.S. citizens.

Application Requirements: Application form, essay, financial need analysis. *Deadline:* May 15.

Contact: Scholarship Management Services
James Beard Foundation Inc.
One Scholarship Way
Saint Peter, MN 56082
Phone: 507-931-1682
E-mail: jamesbeard@scholarshipamerica.org

CHARLIE TROTTER SCHOLARSHIP

Up to four scholarships of $15,000 for high school seniors or graduates who plan to enroll or students who are already enrolled at least part-time in a course of study at a licensed or accredited culinary school.

Academic Fields/Career Goals: Culinary Arts.

Award: Scholarship for use in freshman, sophomore, junior, or senior years; not renewable. *Number:* 4. *Amount:* $15,000.

Eligibility Requirements: Applicant must be enrolled or expecting to enroll full- or part-time at a four-year institution or university. Available to U.S. citizens.

Application Requirements: Application form, essay, financial need analysis. *Deadline:* May 15.

Contact: Scholarship Management Services
James Beard Foundation Inc.
One Scholarship Way
Saint Peter, MN 56082
E-mail: jamesbeard@scholarshipamerica.org

CHICAGO JBF EATS WEEK SCHOLARSHIP

$11,600 scholarship for residents of Illinois who are enrolled in an accredited program of hospitality, culinary, baking, or beverage studies. Must be able to verify residency.

Academic Fields/Career Goals: Culinary Arts.

Award: Scholarship for use in freshman, sophomore, junior, or senior years; not renewable. *Number:* 1. *Amount:* $11,600.

Eligibility Requirements: Applicant must be enrolled or expecting to enroll full- or part-time at a four-year institution or university and resident of Illinois. Available to U.S. citizens.

Application Requirements: Application form. *Deadline:* May 15.

Contact: Scholarship Manager
James Beard Foundation Inc.
One Scholarship Way
Saint Peter, MN 56082
Phone: 507-931-1682
E-mail: jamesbeard@scholarshipamerica.org

CHRISTIAN WOLFFER SCHOLARSHIP

Up to one $2000 award is available to New York residents planning to enroll or currently enrolled at a licensed or accredited culinary school or wine studies program. Minimum GPA of 3.0 required.

Academic Fields/Career Goals: Culinary Arts.

Award: Scholarship for use in freshman, sophomore, junior, or senior years; not renewable. *Number:* 1. *Amount:* $2000.

Eligibility Requirements: Applicant must be enrolled or expecting to enroll full- or part-time at a two-year or four-year institution or university and resident of New York. Applicant must have 3.0 GPA or higher. Available to U.S. citizens.

Application Requirements: Application form. *Deadline:* May 15.

Contact: Scholarship Management Services
James Beard Foundation Inc.
One Scholarship Way
Saint Peter, MN 56082
Phone: 507-931-1682
E-mail: jamesbeard@scholarshipamerica.org

CONNECTONE BANK SCHOLARSHIP

Up to one scholarship of $4,250 for high school seniors or graduates who are already enrolled at least part-time in a course of study at a licensed or accredited culinary school. Must reside and/or attend school in New Jersey.

Academic Fields/Career Goals: Culinary Arts.

Award: Scholarship for use in freshman, sophomore, junior, or senior years; not renewable. *Number:* 1. *Amount:* $4250.

Eligibility Requirements: Applicant must be enrolled or expecting to enroll full- or part-time at a two-year or four-year or technical institution or university. Available to U.S. citizens.

Application Requirements: Application form. *Deadline:* May 15.

Contact: Scholarship Management Services
James Beard Foundation Inc.
One Scholarship Way
Saint Peter, MN 56082
Phone: 507-931-1682
E-mail: jamesbeard@scholarshipamerica.org

HIGH SOUTH BENTONVILLE CULINARY SCHOLARSHIP

Up to one scholarship of $3,750 for high school seniors or graduates who plan to enroll or students who are already enrolled at least part-time in a course of study at a licensed or accredited culinary school. Preference will be given to applicants residing in, or attending school in the state of Arkansas.

Academic Fields/Career Goals: Culinary Arts.

Award: Scholarship for use in freshman, sophomore, junior, or senior years; not renewable. *Number:* 1. *Amount:* $3750.

Eligibility Requirements: Applicant must be enrolled or expecting to enroll full- or part-time at a two-year or four-year or technical institution or university. Available to U.S. citizens.

Application Requirements: Application form. *Deadline:* May 15.

Contact: Scholarship Management Services
James Beard Foundation Inc.
One Scholarship Way
Saint Peter, MN 56082
Phone: 507-931-1682
E-mail: jamesbeard@scholarshipamerica.org

JAMES BEARD FOUNDATION NATIONAL SCHOLARSHIP

Up to ten awards of $20,000 each based on academic merit, worthiness, and personal and professional recommendations. To ensure regional diversity of this national program, one awardee will be selected from each of the ten geographic regions defined by the historic James Beard Foundation Awards. Must demonstrate leadership, community involvement, and academic excellence, and aspire to leadership roles in the culinary arts, food studies, agriculture, hospitality management, and more.

Academic Fields/Career Goals: Culinary Arts.

Award: Scholarship for use in freshman, sophomore, junior, or senior years; not renewable. *Number:* 10. *Amount:* $20,000.

Eligibility Requirements: Applicant must be enrolled or expecting to enroll full- or part-time at a four-year institution or university. Available to U.S. citizens.

Application Requirements: Application form, essay. *Deadline:* May 15.

Contact: Scholarship Manager
James Beard Foundation Inc.
One Scholarship Way
Saint Peter, MN 56082
Phone: 507-931-1682
E-mail: jamesbeard@scholarshipamerica.org

MILJENKO "MIKE"GRGICH'S AMERICAN DREAM SCHOLARSHIP

Up to one $5000 award is available to students planning to enroll or currently enrolled at an accredited wine studies program.

Academic Fields/Career Goals: Culinary Arts.

Award: Scholarship for use in freshman, sophomore, junior, senior, or graduate years; not renewable. *Number:* 1. *Amount:* $5000.

Eligibility Requirements: Applicant must be enrolled or expecting to enroll full- or part-time at a four-year institution or university. Available to U.S. and non-U.S. citizens.

Application Requirements: Application form. *Deadline:* May 15.

Contact: Scholarship Management Services
James Beard Foundation Inc.
One Scholarship Way
Saint Peter, MN 56082
Phone: 507-931-1682
E-mail: jamesbeard@scholarshipamerica.org

PETER CAMERON/HOUSEWARES CHARITY FOUNDATION SCHOLARSHIP

Up to four scholarships of $6000 for high school seniors planning to enroll at a licensed or accredited culinary school. Must have a minimum 3.0 GPA.

Academic Fields/Career Goals: Culinary Arts.

Award: Scholarship for use in freshman year; not renewable. *Number:* 1–4. *Amount:* $6000.

Eligibility Requirements: Applicant must be high school student and planning to enroll or expecting to enroll full-time at a four-year institution or university. Applicant must have 3.0 GPA or higher. Available to U.S. and non-U.S. citizens.

Application Requirements: Application form, essay, financial need analysis. *Deadline:* May 15.

Contact: Scholarship Management Services
James Beard Foundation Inc.
One Scholarship Way
Saint Peter, MN 56082
Phone: 507-931-1682
E-mail: jamesbeard@scholarshipamerica.org

PETER KUMP MEMORIAL SCHOLARSHIP

Up to 5 scholarships of $10,000 towards tuition at an accredited or licensed culinary school of student's choice. Candidates must have a minimum of one year of experience in the culinary field, demonstrate financial need, and have at least a 3.0 GPA.

Academic Fields/Career Goals: Culinary Arts.

Award: Scholarship for use in freshman year; not renewable. *Number:* 1–5. *Amount:* $10,000.

Eligibility Requirements: Applicant must be high school student and planning to enroll or expecting to enroll full- or part-time at a four-year institution or university. Applicant must have 3.0 GPA or higher. Available to U.S. and non-U.S. citizens.

Application Requirements: Application form, essay, financial need analysis. *Deadline:* May 15.

Contact: Scholarship Management Services
James Beard Foundation Inc.
One Scholarship Way
Saint Peter, MN 56082
Phone: 507-931-1682
E-mail: jamesbeard@scholarshipamerica.org

STEVEN SCHER MEMORIAL SCHOLARSHIP FOR ASPIRING RESTAURANTEURS

Up to two awards of $5,000 available to students enrolled or accepted in a culinary or hospitality management program at an accredited institution. Must detail work experience, submit essay, and include a list of top three favorite restaurants and explain why they have earned that ranking. Special consideration will be given to career changers.

Academic Fields/Career Goals: Culinary Arts.

Award: Scholarship for use in freshman, sophomore, junior, or senior years; not renewable. *Number:* 1–2. *Amount:* $5000.

Eligibility Requirements: Applicant must be enrolled or expecting to enroll full- or part-time at a two-year or four-year institution or university. Available to U.S. citizens.

Application Requirements: Application form, essay. *Deadline:* May 15.

Contact: Scholarship Management Services
James Beard Foundation Inc.
One Scholarship Way
Saint Peter, MN 56082
Phone: 507-931-1682
E-mail: jamesbeard@scholarshipamerica.org

TASTE AMERICA SCHOLARSHIPS

Up to 10 scholarships of $2,500 each for students residing or attending school in the states that hosted the JBF nationwide celebration of American Taste: Arizona, California (2), Florida, Illinois, Louisiana, Massachusetts, Minnesota, South Carolina, and Washington.

Academic Fields/Career Goals: Culinary Arts.

Award: Scholarship for use in freshman, sophomore, junior, or senior years; not renewable. *Number:* 1–10. *Amount:* $2500.

Eligibility Requirements: Applicant must be enrolled or expecting to enroll full- or part-time at a two-year or four-year or technical institution or university. Available to U.S. citizens.

Application Requirements: Application form. *Deadline:* May 15.

Contact: Scholarship Management Services
James Beard Foundation Inc.
One Scholarship Way
Saint Peter, MN 56082
Phone: 507-931-1682
E-mail: jamesbeard@scholarshipamerica.org

LES DAMES D'ESCOFFIER INTERNATIONAL, COLORADO CHAPTER

www.lesdamescolorado.org

LES DAMES D'ESCOFFIER INTERNATIONAL, COLORADO CHAPTER SCHOLARSHIP
• *See page 93*

MAINE RESTAURANT ASSOCIATION

http://www.mainerestaurant.com/

MAINE RESTAURANT ASSOCIATION EDUCATION FOUNDATION SCHOLARSHIP FUND

Scholarship available to students (Maine Residents Only) who wish to pursue higher education in culinary arts, restaurant, and hotel or hospitality management. Preference will be given to ProStart students.

Academic Fields/Career Goals: Culinary Arts; Hospitality Management.

Award: Scholarship for use in freshman, sophomore, junior, or senior years; not renewable. *Number:* 1–8. *Amount:* $500–$2000.

Eligibility Requirements: Applicant must be enrolled or expecting to enroll full- or part-time at a two-year or four-year or technical institution or university and resident of Maine. Available to U.S. citizens.

Application Requirements: Application form, essay. *Deadline:* April 28.

Contact: Becky Jacobson, Operations Manager
Maine Restaurant Association
45 Melville St.
Augusta, ME 04330
Phone: 207-623-2178
E-mail: becky@mainerestaurant.com

OREGON STUDENT ASSISTANCE COMMISSION

http://www.GetCollegeFunds.org/

OREGON WINE BROTHERHOOD SCHOLARSHIP

Award for residents of Oregon or Washington majoring in enology, viticulture, or culinary arts (preference for wine emphasis). Must attend Chemeketa, Central Oregon, Lane, Linn-Benton, Mt. Hood, Southwestern Oregon, Umpqua, Walla Walla Community College, Oregon State University, University of California at Davis, or Washington State University. Apply/compete annually.

Academic Fields/Career Goals: Culinary Arts; Food Science/Nutrition; Hospitality Management.

Award: Scholarship for use in freshman, sophomore, junior, senior, or graduate years; not renewable.

Eligibility Requirements: Applicant must be enrolled or expecting to enroll full-time at a two-year or four-year institution or university; resident of Oregon, Washington and studying in Oregon, Washington. Available to U.S. citizens.

Application Requirements: Application form, financial need analysis. *Deadline:* March 1.

Contact: Melissa Adams, Scholarship Processing Coordinator
Phone: 541-687-7409
E-mail: melissa.adams@hecc.oregon.gov

TECHNICAL TRAINING FUND SCHOLARSHIP
• *See page 130*

PROFESSIONAL REPS

http://www.professionalreps.com/

HUNGRY TO LEAD SCHOLARSHIP

Those eligible to apply are high school seniors, or college students registered/pre-registered to attend an accredited school in the United States. Applicant must be pursuing a degree in a foodservice/hospitality program, or directly related. The scholarship is merit based on high school records, ACT and/or SAT scores, college transcripts if applicable, and extracurricular activities. Minimum requirements as follows: high

school or college cumulative GPA of 2.5, SAT of 1300, or ACT of 18. Applicants will also be judged on their ability to demonstrate leadership capabilities. Top four finalists will be awarded scholarships in the following order: first place, The Amana Leadership Scholarship ($2,500); second place, The Hungry To Lead Scholarship ($1,500); third place, Leadership Recognition Award ($500); fourth place, Leadership Recognition Award ($500)

Academic Fields/Career Goals: Culinary Arts; Food Science/Nutrition; Food Service/Hospitality.

Award: Scholarship for use in freshman, sophomore, junior, or senior years; not renewable. *Number:* 4. *Amount:* $500–$2500.

Eligibility Requirements: Applicant must be enrolled or expecting to enroll full-time at a two-year or four-year or technical institution or university. Applicant must have 2.5 GPA or higher. Available to U.S. and non-U.S. citizens.

Application Requirements: Application form, essay. *Deadline:* July 1.

Contact: Tessa Bucklin
Professional Reps
750 E. Covey Lane #110
Phoenix, AZ 85024
Phone: 877-995-8922
E-mail: scholarships@professionalreps.com

SOUTH CAROLINA RESTAURANT AND LODGING ASSOCIATION

http://www.scrla.org/

SOUTH CAROLINA TOURISM AND HOSPITALITY EDUCATIONAL FOUNDATION SCHOLARSHIPS

The South Carolina Restaurant and Lodging Educational Foundation (SCRLEF) manages scholarships on behalf of a variety of organizations that support hospitality education. These scholarships are designed to assist students who demonstrate an interest in and commitment to the hospitality (restaurant, foodservice, lodging, tourism) industry.

Academic Fields/Career Goals: Culinary Arts; Food Service/Hospitality; Hospitality Management.

Award: Scholarship for use in freshman, sophomore, junior, or senior years; not renewable. *Number:* 5–16. *Amount:* $750–$2500.

Eligibility Requirements: Applicant must be enrolled or expecting to enroll full-time at a two-year or four-year or technical institution or university; resident of South Carolina and studying in South Carolina. Available to U.S. citizens.

Application Requirements: Application form, essay. *Deadline:* May 1.

Contact: Douglas OFlaherty, Vice President
South Carolina Restaurant and Lodging Association
PO Box 7577
Columbia, SC 29202
Phone: 803-765-9000

STRAIGHTFORWARD MEDIA

http://www.straightforwardmedia.com/

STRAIGHTFORWARD MEDIA VOCATIONAL-TECHNICAL SCHOOL SCHOLARSHIP
• *See page 107*

SUPPORT CREATIVITY

http://wesupportcreativity.org

SUPPORT CREATIVITY SCHOLARSHIP
• *See page 124*

TEXAS RESTAURANT ASSOCIATION

http://www.restaurantville.com/

W. PRICE, JR. MEMORIAL SCHOLARSHIP

Each year the Texas Restaurant Association awards the W. Price Jr. Memorial Scholarship to students with a growing passion for the foodservice industry. The scholarship is named for W. Price Jr., the first executive director of the Texas Restaurant Association who served from

1953 until 1974. Seven scholarships of $1,000 are awarded to students graduating high school or those currently enrolled in a postsecondary culinary programs.

Academic Fields/Career Goals: Culinary Arts; Food Service/Hospitality.

Award: Scholarship for use in freshman, sophomore, junior, senior, or graduate years; not renewable. *Number:* 5–7. *Amount:* $1000.

Eligibility Requirements: Applicant must be enrolled or expecting to enroll full-time at a two-year or four-year institution or university and resident of Texas. Applicant or parent of applicant must have employment or volunteer experience in food service, hospitality/hotel administration/operations. Available to U.S. citizens.

Application Requirements: Application form, essay. *Deadline:* February 15.

Contact: Jerrica Deloney, Program Manager
Texas Restaurant Association
PO Box 1429
Austin, TX 78767
Phone: 800-395.2872
E-mail: foundation@tramail.org

UNITED NEGRO COLLEGE FUND

http://www.uncf.org/

UNCF/CARNIVAL CORPORATE SCHOLARS PROGRAM
• *See page 170*

WISCONSIN BAKERS ASSOCIATION (WBA)

http://www.wibakers.com/

ROBERT W. HILLER SCHOLARSHIP FUND
Scholarship of $1000 awarded for students at all levels in a baking/pastry arts-related program that prepares candidates for a retail baking profession. Minimum 2.85 GPA required.

Academic Fields/Career Goals: Culinary Arts; Food Science/Nutrition; Food Service/Hospitality.

Award: Scholarship for use in freshman, sophomore, junior, senior, graduate, or postgraduate years; not renewable. *Amount:* $1000.

Eligibility Requirements: Applicant must be enrolled or expecting to enroll full-time at a two-year or four-year institution or university. Available to U.S. citizens.

Application Requirements: Application form, essay. *Deadline:* December 1.

Contact: Jessica Hoover
Phone: 414-258-5552
Fax: 414-258-5582
E-mail: jessica@wibakers.com

WBA SCHOLARSHIP
The Wisconsin Bakers Association's education committee submitted recommendations to the Board of Governors on Oct. 24, 1983, to implement the WBA Scholarship Program. The first scholarship awards were later presented in 1984. Since then, the WBA has awarded more than $25,000 in WBA Scholarships! Wisconsin residents only can apply for the WBA Scholarship.

Academic Fields/Career Goals: Culinary Arts; Food Science/Nutrition; Food Service/Hospitality.

Award: Scholarship for use in freshman, sophomore, junior, senior, graduate, or postgraduate years; not renewable.

Eligibility Requirements: Applicant must be enrolled or expecting to enroll full- or part-time at a two-year or four-year or technical institution or university and resident of Wisconsin. Available to U.S. citizens.

Application Requirements: Application form, essay, interview. *Deadline:* continuous.

Contact: Jessica Hoover
Phone: 414-258-5552
Fax: 414-258-5582
E-mail: jessica@wibakers.com

WOMEN CHEFS AND RESTAURATEURS

http://www.womenchefs.org/

FRENCH CULINARY INSTITUTE/ITALIAN CULINARY EXPERIENCE SCHOLARSHIP
Scholarship intended for a culinary student wishing to specialize in Italian cuisine. Recipient must be a new enrollment and satisfy all entrance requirements of the FCI. Scholarship award is applied to total program fee.

Academic Fields/Career Goals: Culinary Arts; Food Service/Hospitality.

Award: Scholarship for use in freshman, sophomore, junior, senior, graduate, or postgraduate years; not renewable. *Number:* 1. *Amount:* $5000.

Eligibility Requirements: Applicant must be enrolled or expecting to enroll full-time at a four-year institution or university. Available to U.S. and non-U.S. citizens.

Application Requirements: Application form, essay. *Fee:* $25. *Deadline:* March 31.

Contact: Dori Sacksteder, Director of Programs
Phone: 502-581-0300 Ext. 219
Fax: 502-589-3602
E-mail: dsacksteder@hqtrs.com

DENTAL HEALTH/ SERVICES

101ST AIRBORNE DIVISION ASSOCIATION

http://www.screamingeaglefoundation.org/

AL & WILLIAMARY VISTE SCHOLARSHIP
Scholarship to provide financial assistance to students who have the potential to become assets to our nation. The major factors to be considered in the evaluation and rating of applicants are eligibility, career objectives, academic record, and insight gained from the letter requesting consideration and letters of recommendation. Preference will be given, but is not limited, to obtaining a degree in one of the physical sciences, medical, or scientific research fields. Must be an upperclassman and have a minimum 3.75 GPA. Applicants parents, grandparent, husband or wife is (or if deceased was) a regular or life (not Associate) member of the 101st Airborne Division Association.

Academic Fields/Career Goals: Dental Health/Services; Health and Medical Sciences; Physical Sciences; Radiology; Therapy/Rehabilitation.

Award: Scholarship for use in junior, senior, or graduate years; not renewable. *Number:* 1–2.

Eligibility Requirements: Applicant must be enrolled or expecting to enroll full-time at a four-year institution or university. Available to U.S. citizens.

Application Requirements: Application form, essay, personal photograph. *Deadline:* April 11.

Contact: Mr. Randal Underhill, Executive Director
101st Airborne Division Association
P.O. Box 929
Fort Campbell, KY 42223
Phone: 931-431-0199
E-mail: 101exec@comcast.net

ALBERTA HERITAGE SCHOLARSHIP FUND

http://www.alis.alberta.ca/

ABORIGINAL HEALTH CAREERS BURSARY
• *See page 153*

JASON LANG SCHOLARSHIP
Award of CAN$1000 to reward the outstanding academic achievement of Alberta postsecondary students who are studying full-time in Alberta.

Must be a Canadian citizen or permanent resident and Alberta resident. Must be enrolled full-time in an undergraduate or professional program, such as law, medicine, pharmacy, or dentistry at an eligible Alberta postsecondary institution. Nominated by Awards Office at institution on the basis of achieving a minimum GPA of 3.2 in the previous academic year. May be awarded up to three times to one student. Contact the Student Awards Office for application deadline. For additional information, see website http://alis.alberta.ca.

Academic Fields/Career Goals: Dental Health/Services; Health and Medical Sciences; Law/Legal Services; Pharmacy.

Award: Scholarship for use in sophomore, junior, or senior years; not renewable.

Eligibility Requirements: Applicant must be Canadian citizen; enrolled or expecting to enroll full-time at a two-year or four-year or technical institution or university; resident of Alberta and studying in Alberta.

Application Requirements: Application form, test scores, transcript. *Deadline:* varies.

Contact: Scholarship Committee
Phone: 780-427-8640
E-mail: scholarships@gov.ab.ca

NORTHERN ALBERTA DEVELOPMENT COUNCIL BURSARY

Return service bursary awards CAN$6000 per year for up to two years to increase the number of trained professionals in Northern Alberta and to encourage students from Northern Alberta to obtain a postsecondary education. Must be residents of Alberta, and planning to enroll in a full-time postsecondary program in a field in demand in Northern Alberta. Fields in demand include education, health and medical, engineering, technical fields, and social work. Applicants must also be within two years of completion of their postsecondary program. Students must live and work for one year in Northern Alberta for each year of assistance awarded. For additional information, go to website http://alis.alberta.ca.

Academic Fields/Career Goals: Dental Health/Services; Education; Engineering/Technology; Health and Medical Sciences; Social Services.

Award: Scholarship for use in junior or senior years; not renewable.

Eligibility Requirements: Applicant must be Canadian citizen; enrolled or expecting to enroll full-time at a four-year or technical institution or university; resident of Alberta and studying in Alberta.

Application Requirements: Application form, essay, financial need analysis, transcript. *Deadline:* April 30.

Contact: Scholarship Committee
Phone: 780-427-8640
E-mail: scholarships@gov.ab.ca

AMERICAN ACADEMY OF ORAL AND MAXILLOFACIAL RADIOLOGY

http://www.aaomr.org/

CHARLES R. MORRIS STUDENT RESEARCH AWARD

Award to applicants from accredited programs performing research in oral and maxillofacial radiology. Applicant must be a full-time undergraduate or predoctoral student at the time of research, be nominated by the institution where research was carried out, and submit a manuscript detailing the research project.

Academic Fields/Career Goals: Dental Health/Services.

Award: Grant for use in junior, senior, or graduate years; not renewable. *Number:* 1. *Amount:* $1000.

Eligibility Requirements: Applicant must be enrolled or expecting to enroll full-time at a four-year institution or university. Available to U.S. and non-U.S. citizens.

Application Requirements: Application form, manuscript, recommendations or references. *Deadline:* June 16.

Contact: Dr. Michael Shrout, Executive Director
American Academy of Oral and Maxillofacial Radiology
Box 1010
Evans, GA 30809-1010
Phone: 706-271-2881
E-mail: mshrout@mcg.edu

AMERICAN DENTAL ASSISTANTS ASSOCIATION

http://www.adaausa.org

JULIETTE A. SOUTHARD SCHOLARSHIP

Leadership-based award available to students enrolled in an ADAA dental assistant's program. Proof of acceptance into ADAA program and two letters of reference are required.

Academic Fields/Career Goals: Dental Health/Services.

Award: Scholarship for use in freshman, sophomore, junior, senior, graduate, or postgraduate years; not renewable. *Number:* 1–10. *Amount:* $1–$900.

Eligibility Requirements: Applicant must be enrolled or expecting to enroll full- or part-time at a two-year or four-year institution or university and must have an interest in leadership. Applicant or parent of applicant must be member of American Dental Assistants Association. Available to U.S. citizens.

Application Requirements: Application form, essay, financial need analysis. *Deadline:* March 15.

Contact: Jay Kasper, Associate Executive Director
Phone: 630-9944247
Fax: 630-3518490
E-mail: jaykasper@adaausa.org

AMERICAN DENTAL ASSOCIATION (ADA) FOUNDATION

http://www.adafoundation.org/

AMERICAN DENTAL ASSOCIATION FOUNDATION DENTAL HYGIENE SCHOLARSHIP PROGRAM

Applicant must be enrolled full-time with a minimum of 12 Credit hours as a student in an accredited dental hygiene program accredited by the Commission of Dental Accreditation of the American Dental Association. Must be U.S. citizen, permanent resident is ineligible to apply. Must have a minimum 3.5 GPA on a 4.0 scale. Applicants must be recommended by the dental hygiene program director and may request application materials from that same individual at the school where they are currently enrolled as an entering final year student in a dental hygiene program. Applicants must demonstrate a minimum financial need of $1000.

Academic Fields/Career Goals: Dental Health/Services.

Award: Scholarship for use in senior year; not renewable. *Number:* up to 15. *Amount:* up to $1000.

Eligibility Requirements: Applicant must be enrolled or expecting to enroll full-time at a four-year institution or university. Applicant must have 3.5 GPA or higher. Available to U.S. citizens.

Application Requirements: Application form, essay, financial need analysis, recommendations or references. *Deadline:* April 23.

Contact: Rose Famularo, Coordinator
Phone: 312-440-2763
E-mail: famularor@ada.org

AMERICAN DENTAL ASSOCIATION FOUNDATION DENTAL STUDENT SCHOLARSHIP PROGRAM

One-time award for entering second-year students at a dental school accredited by the American Dental Association Commission on Dental Accreditation. Must have 3.0 GPA, and be enrolled full-time (minimum of 12 hours). Must show financial need and be a U.S. citizen, a permanent resident is ineligible to apply. Applicants may request application materials from associate dean for student affairs at the dental school where they are currently enrolled. An applicant must be recommended to the ADA Foundation by the school official.

Academic Fields/Career Goals: Dental Health/Services.

Award: Scholarship for use in sophomore year; not renewable. *Number:* up to 25. *Amount:* up to $2500.

Eligibility Requirements: Applicant must be enrolled or expecting to enroll full-time at a four-year institution or university. Applicant must have 3.0 GPA or higher. Available to U.S. citizens.

Application Requirements: Application form, essay, financial need analysis, recommendations or references. *Deadline:* October 4.

Contact: Rose Famularo, Coordinator
Phone: 312-440-2763
E-mail: famularor@ada.org

AMERICAN DENTAL HYGIENISTS' ASSOCIATION (ADHA) INSTITUTE FOR ORAL HEALTH

http://www.adha.org/ioh

CAROL BAUHS BENSON SCHOLARSHIP

Established in the memory of Carol Bauhs Benson, this scholarship is awarded to students at the Certificate/Associate educational level who have completed (or who will complete by the time of the award) a minimum of one year in a dental hygiene curriculum. This scholarship is restricted to students who reside in the following states: Minnesota, North Dakota, South Dakota or Wisconsin.

Academic Fields/Career Goals: Dental Health/Services.

Award: Scholarship for use in sophomore year; not renewable. *Number:* 1. *Amount:* $1000.

Eligibility Requirements: Applicant must be enrolled or expecting to enroll full-time at a two-year institution or university and resident of Minnesota, North Dakota, South Dakota, Wisconsin. Applicant must have 3.5 GPA or higher. Available to U.S. citizens.

Application Requirements: Application form, essay, recommendations or references. *Deadline:* February 1.

Contact: Jessica Mitton, Development Manager
American Dental Hygienists' Association (ADHA) Institute
For Oral Health
444 North Michigan Avenue
Suite 3400
Chicago, IL 60611
Phone: 312-440-8944
Fax: 312-440-6764
E-mail: institute@adha.net

COLGATE "BRIGHT SMILES, BRIGHT FUTURES" MINORITY SCHOLARSHIP

One time award for members of minority groups currently underrepresented in dental hygiene programs at the certificate educational level. Must be an active student member of ADHA. Applicant must have completed one year of dental hygiene curricula at an accredited dental hygiene program in United States. Applicant must demonstrate GPA of at least 3.0, and financial need of $1500 or more.

Academic Fields/Career Goals: Dental Health/Services.

Award: Scholarship for use in sophomore year; not renewable. *Number:* 1–2. *Amount:* $1250.

Eligibility Requirements: Applicant must be American Indian/Alaska Native, Asian/Pacific Islander, Black (non-Hispanic), Hispanic and enrolled or expecting to enroll full-time at a two-year or technical institution. Applicant or parent of applicant must be member of American Dental Hygienist's Association. Applicant must have 3.0 GPA or higher. Available to U.S. citizens.

Application Requirements: Application form, essay, recommendations or references. *Deadline:* February 1.

Contact: Jessica Mitton, Development Manager
American Dental Hygienists' Association (ADHA) Institute
For Oral Health
444 North Michigan Avenue
Suite 3400
Chicago, IL 60611
Phone: 312-440-8944
Fax: 312-440-6764
E-mail: institute@adha.net

CREST ORAL-B LABORATORIES DENTAL HYGIENE SCHOLARSHIP

Scholarships to Baccalaureate degree students who demonstrate intent to encourage professional excellence, promote quality research, and support dental hygiene through public and private education. Must be an active SADHA or ADHA member. Must have completed one year of dental hygiene curricula at an accredited dental hygiene program in United States. Must demonstrate GPA of at least 3.5.

Academic Fields/Career Goals: Dental Health/Services.

Award: Scholarship for use in sophomore, junior, or senior years; not renewable. *Number:* 1–2. *Amount:* $1000.

Eligibility Requirements: Applicant must be enrolled or expecting to enroll full-time at a four-year institution or university. Applicant or parent of applicant must be member of American Dental Hygienist's Association. Applicant must have 3.5 GPA or higher. Available to U.S. citizens.

Application Requirements: Application form, essay, recommendations or references. *Deadline:* May 1.

Contact: Jessica Mitton, Development Manager
American Dental Hygienists' Association (ADHA) Institute
For Oral Health
444 North Michigan Avenue
Suite 3400
Chicago, IL 60611
Phone: 312-440-8944
Fax: 312-440-6764
E-mail: institute@adha.net

HU-FRIEDY/ESTHER WILKINS INSTRUMENT SCHOLARSHIP

These scholarships are awarded to applicants at the certificate/associate or Baccalaureate degree level who have completed a minimum of one year in a dental hygiene curriculum. The program awards recipients with the Hu-Friedy dental hygiene instruments of their choice, equivalent to a retail value of $1,000.

Academic Fields/Career Goals: Dental Health/Services.

Award: Scholarship for use in sophomore, junior, or senior years; not renewable. *Amount:* $1000.

Eligibility Requirements: Applicant must be enrolled or expecting to enroll full-time at a two-year or four-year institution or university. Applicant must have 3.0 GPA or higher. Available to U.S. citizens.

Application Requirements: Application form, essay, recommendations or references. *Deadline:* February 1.

Contact: Jessica Mitton, Development Manager
American Dental Hygienists' Association (ADHA) Institute
For Oral Health
444 North Michigan Avenue
Suite 3400
Chicago, IL 60611
Phone: 312-440-8944
Fax: 312-440-6764
E-mail: institute@adha.net

JOHNSON & JOHNSON SCHOLARSHIP

These scholarships are awarded to applicants pursuing a certificate/associate or Baccalaureate degree in dental hygiene and have completed a minimum of one year in a dental hygiene curriculum.

Academic Fields/Career Goals: Dental Health/Services.

Award: Scholarship for use in sophomore, junior, or senior years; not renewable. *Number:* 5. *Amount:* $1000.

Eligibility Requirements: Applicant must be enrolled or expecting to enroll full-time at a two-year or four-year institution or university. Applicant must have 3.5 GPA or higher. Available to U.S. citizens.

Application Requirements: Application form, essay, recommendations or references. *Deadline:* February 1.

Contact: Jessica Mitton, Development Manager
American Dental Hygienists' Association (ADHA) Institute
For Oral Health
444 North Michigan Avenue
Suite 3400
Chicago, IL 60611
Phone: 312-440-8944
Fax: 312-440-6764
E-mail: institute@adha.net

KARLA GIRTS MEMORIAL COMMUNITY OUTREACH SCHOLARSHIP

These scholarships are awarded to students enrolled in an associate, Baccalaureate or degree completion program and completed a minimum of one year in a dental hygiene curriculum. Applicants will display a commitment to improving oral health within the geriatric population.

Academic Fields/Career Goals: Dental Health/Services.

Award: Scholarship for use in sophomore, junior, or senior years; not renewable. *Number:* 2. *Amount:* $2000.

Eligibility Requirements: Applicant must be enrolled or expecting to enroll full-time at a two-year or four-year institution. Applicant must have 3.0 GPA or higher. Available to U.S. citizens.

Application Requirements: Additional essay as part of the application, application form, essay, recommendations or references. *Deadline:* February 1.

Contact: Jessica Mitton, Development Manager
American Dental Hygienists' Association (ADHA) Institute
For Oral Health
444 North Michigan Avenue
Suite 3400
Chicago, IL 60611
Phone: 312-440-8944
Fax: 312-440-6764
E-mail: institute@adha.net

SIGMA PHI ALPHA UNDERGRADUATE SCHOLARSHIP

Awarded to an outstanding Sigma Phi Alpha member pursuing a certificate/associate or Baccalaureate degree at a school with an active chapter of the Sigma Phi Alpha Dental Hygiene Honor Society. Applicant must demonstrate GPA of at least 3.5. Must have completed one year of dental hygiene curricula at an accredited dental hygiene program in United States. Must demonstrate a financial need of $1500 or more. Must be an active SADHA or ADHA member.

Academic Fields/Career Goals: Dental Health/Services.

Award: Scholarship for use in sophomore, junior, or senior years; not renewable. *Number:* 1. *Amount:* $1000.

Eligibility Requirements: Applicant must be enrolled or expecting to enroll full-time at a two-year or four-year or technical institution or university. Applicant or parent of applicant must be member of American Dental Hygienist's Association. Applicant must have 3.5 GPA or higher. Available to U.S. citizens.

Application Requirements: Application form, essay, recommendations or references. *Deadline:* February 1.

Contact: Jessica Mitton, Development Manager
American Dental Hygienists' Association (ADHA) Institute
For Oral Health
444 North Michigan Avenue
Suite 3400
Chicago, IL 60611
Phone: 312-440-8944
Fax: 312-440-6764
E-mail: institute@adha.net

WILMA E. MOTLEY SCHOLARSHIP

This scholarship is awarded to applicant(s) pursuing a Baccalaureate degree at an accredited dental hygiene program and will have completed a minimum of one year in a dental hygiene curriculum.

Academic Fields/Career Goals: Dental Health/Services.

Award: Scholarship for use in sophomore, junior, or senior years; not renewable. *Number:* 1. *Amount:* $1000.

Eligibility Requirements: Applicant must be enrolled or expecting to enroll full-time at an institution or university. Applicant must have 3.5 GPA or higher. Available to U.S. citizens.

Application Requirements: Application form, essay, recommendations or references. *Deadline:* February 1.

Contact: Jessica Mitton, Development Manager
American Dental Hygienists' Association (ADHA) Institute
For Oral Health
444 North Michigan Avenue
Suite 3400
Chicago, IL 60611
Phone: 312-440-8944
Fax: 312-440-6764
E-mail: institute@adha.net

AMERICAN INDIAN SCIENCE AND ENGINEERING SOCIETY

http://www.aises.org/

A.T. ANDERSON MEMORIAL SCHOLARSHIP PROGRAM
• See page 109

AMERICAN LEGION AUXILIARY DEPARTMENT OF COLORADO

http://www.alacolorado.com

AMERICAN LEGION AUXILIARY DEPARTMENT OF COLORADO PAST PRESIDENTS' PARLEY HEALTH CARE PROFESSIONAL SCHOLARSHIPNURSES SCHOLARSHIP
• See page 133

AMERICAN LEGION DEPARTMENT OF NORTH DAKOTA

http://www.ndlegion.org/

O. NESHEIM MEMORIAL SCHOLARSHIP
• See page 96

ARRL FOUNDATION INC.

http://www.arrl.org/

CAROLE J. STREETER, KB9JBR, SCHOLARSHIP

One $1000 award is available to a student with any class of active Amateur Radio license with preference for basic Morse code capability. Preference for students studying in the health and medical fields. Must demonstrate basic Morse Code proficiency, be a U.S. citizen, and attend an accredited college or university.

Academic Fields/Career Goals: Dental Health/Services; Health and Medical Sciences; Nursing; Oncology; Optometry; Osteopathy; Therapy/Rehabilitation.

Award: Scholarship for use in freshman, sophomore, junior, senior, or graduate years; not renewable. *Number:* 1. *Amount:* $1000.

Eligibility Requirements: Applicant must be enrolled or expecting to enroll full- or part-time at a two-year or four-year institution or university and must have an interest in amateur radio. Available to U.S. citizens.

Application Requirements: Application form. *Deadline:* January 31.

Contact: Ms. Mary Hobart, Secretary
Phone: 860-594-0397
E-mail: k1mmh@arrl.org

ASSOCIATION ON AMERICAN INDIAN AFFAIRS, INC.

http://www.indian-affairs.org/

ELIZABETH AND SHERMAN ASCHE MEMORIAL SCHOLARSHIP FUND
• See page 98

AVACARE MEDICAL

https://avacaremedical.com

AVACARE MEDICAL SCHOLARSHIP
• See page 105

BETHESDA LUTHERAN COMMUNITIES

http://www.bethesdalutherancommunities.org/scholarships

DEVELOPMENTAL DISABILITIES SCHOLASTIC ACHIEVEMENT SCHOLARSHIP FOR COLLEGE STUDENTS WHO ARE LUTHERAN

One-time award for Lutheran students who are currently enrolled in studies related to developmental disabilities. Awards of up to $3000. 3.0 GPA required.

Academic Fields/Career Goals: Dental Health/Services; Education; Health Administration; Health and Medical Sciences; Health Information Management/Technology; Humanities; Religion/Theology; Social Services; Special Education; Therapy/Rehabilitation.

Award: Scholarship for use in freshman, sophomore, junior, or senior years; not renewable. *Number:* 2–3. *Amount:* $500–$3000.

Eligibility Requirements: Applicant must be Lutheran and enrolled or expecting to enroll full-time at a four-year institution or university. Applicant must have 3.0 GPA or higher. Available to U.S. citizens.

Application Requirements: Application form, community service, essay. *Deadline:* May 1.

Contact: Barb Schultz, Program Coordinator
Bethesda Lutheran Communities
600 Hoffmann Drive
Watertown, WI 53094-6294
Phone: 920-206-4427
E-mail: barb.schultz@mailblc.org

BHW GROUP

https://thebhwgroup.com/

BHW WOMEN IN STEM SCHOLARSHIP
• *See page 74*

COMPHEALTH

http://www.comphealth.com

COMPHEALTH MEDICAL SCHOLARSHIP
• *See page 151*

DDSRANK

https://www.ddsrank.com

DDSRANK DENTAL SCHOLARSHIP

The DDSRank Dental Scholarship is awarded to one aspiring dental student to help them pay for the cost of tuition or books.

Academic Fields/Career Goals: Dental Health/Services.

Award: Scholarship for use in freshman, sophomore, junior, senior, or graduate years; not renewable. *Number:* 1. *Amount:* $500.

Eligibility Requirements: Applicant must be enrolled or expecting to enroll full-time at a four-year institution or university. Available to U.S. citizens.

Application Requirements: Essay. *Deadline:* August 30.

Contact: Scholarship Administrator
E-mail: scholarships@ddsrank.com

THE EXPERT INSTITUTE

https://www.theexpertinstitute.com

ANNUAL HEALTHCARE AND LIFE SCIENCES SCHOLARSHIP
• *See page 156*

HEALTH PROFESSIONS EDUCATION FOUNDATION

http://www.healthprofessions.ca.gov/

ALLIED HEALTHCARE SCHOLARSHIP PROGRAM
• *See page 151*

HELLENIC UNIVERSITY CLUB OF PHILADELPHIA

http://www.hucphiladelphia.org/

NICHOLAS S. HETOS, DDS MEMORIAL GRADUATE SCHOLARSHIP

$2000 scholarships for a senior undergraduate or graduate student with financial need pursuing studies leading to a Doctor of Dental Medicine or Doctor of Dental Surgery degree. Must be a U.S. citizen of Greek descent and a resident of particular counties in NJ or PA.

Academic Fields/Career Goals: Dental Health/Services.

Award: Scholarship for use in senior or graduate years; not renewable. *Number:* up to 1. *Amount:* $2000.

Eligibility Requirements: Applicant must be of Greek heritage; enrolled or expecting to enroll full-time at a four-year institution or university and resident of New Jersey, Pennsylvania. Available to U.S. citizens.

Application Requirements: Application form, financial need analysis, transcript. *Deadline:* April 21.

Contact: Anna Hadgis, Scholarship Chairman
Phone: 610-613-4310
E-mail: www.hucphiladelphia.org

HISPANIC DENTAL ASSOCIATION FOUNDATION

http://www.hdassoc.org/

DR. JUAN D. VILLARREAL/HISPANIC DENTAL ASSOCIATION FOUNDATION

Scholarship offered to Hispanic U.S. students who have been accepted into or are currently enrolled in an accredited dental or dental hygiene program in the state of Texas. Scholarship will obligate the grantees to complete the current year of their dental or dental hygiene program. Scholastic achievement, leadership skills, community service and commitment to improving the health of the Hispanic community will all be considered. Must be a current member of the Hispanic Dental Association.

Academic Fields/Career Goals: Dental Health/Services.

Award: Scholarship for use in freshman, sophomore, junior, or senior years; not renewable. *Number:* up to 3. *Amount:* $500–$1000.

Eligibility Requirements: Applicant must be of Hispanic heritage; enrolled or expecting to enroll full-time at a two-year or four-year institution or university; resident of Texas and studying in Texas. Available to U.S. citizens.

Application Requirements: Application form, essay, recommendations or references, transcript. *Deadline:* June 1.

Contact: David Pena, Executive Director
Hispanic Dental Association Foundation
1111 14th Street
Suite 1100
Washington, DC 20005
Phone: 202-629-3726
E-mail: dpena@hdassoc.org

PROCTOR AND GAMBLE ORAL CARE AND HDA FOUNDATION SCHOLARSHIP

Scholarships available to Hispanic students entering into their first year of an accredited dental, dental hygiene, dental assisting, or dental technician program. Scholastic achievement, community service, leadership, and commitment to improving health of the Hispanic community will all be considered. Must be member of the Hispanic Dental Association.

Academic Fields/Career Goals: Dental Health/Services.

Award: Scholarship for use in freshman year; not renewable. *Number:* up to 15. *Amount:* up to $1000.

Eligibility Requirements: Applicant must be high school student and planning to enroll or expecting to enroll full-time at a two-year or four-year or technical institution or university. Available to U.S. citizens.

Application Requirements: Application form, community service, essay, recommendations or references, transcript. *Deadline:* June 1.

Contact: David Pena, Executive Director
Hispanic Dental Association Foundation
1111 14th Street
Suite 1100
Washington, DC 20005
Phone: 202-629-6108
E-mail: dpena@hdassoc.org

INTERNATIONAL ORDER OF THE KING'S DAUGHTERS AND SONS

http://www.iokds.org/

HEALTH CAREERS SCHOLARSHIP

Award for students preparing for careers in medicine, dentistry, pharmacy, physical or occupational therapy, and medical technologies. Must be a U.S. or Canadian citizen, enrolled full-time in a school accredited in the field involved and located in the U.S. or Canada. For all students, except those preparing for an RN degree, application must be for at least the third year of college. RN students must have completed the first year of schooling. Premedicine students are not eligible to apply. For those students seeking degrees of MD or DDS application must be for at least the second year of medical or dental school. Each applicant must supply proof of acceptance in the school involved.

Academic Fields/Career Goals: Dental Health/Services; Health and Medical Sciences; Nursing; Therapy/Rehabilitation.

Award: Scholarship for use in junior, senior, or graduate years; not renewable. *Number:* 20–30. *Amount:* $500–$1000.

Eligibility Requirements: Applicant must be enrolled or expecting to enroll full-time at a four-year institution or university. Available to U.S. and Canadian citizens.

Application Requirements: Application form, essay, itemized budget, recommendations or references, resume, self-addressed stamped envelope with application, transcript. *Deadline:* April 1.

Contact: Director, Health Careers Department
International Order of The King's Daughters and Sons
PO Box 1017
Chautauqua, NY 14722-1017
Phone: 716-357-4951

MARYLAND STATE HIGHER EDUCATION COMMISSION

http://www.mhec.state.md.us/

GRADUATE AND PROFESSIONAL SCHOLARSHIP PROGRAM-MARYLAND

Graduate and professional scholarships provide need-based financial assistance to students attending a Maryland school of medicine, dentistry, law, pharmacy, social work, or nursing. Funds are provided to specific Maryland colleges and universities. Students must demonstrate financial need and be Maryland residents. Contact institution financial aid office for more information.

Academic Fields/Career Goals: Dental Health/Services; Health and Medical Sciences; Law/Legal Services; Nursing; Social Services.

Award: Scholarship for use in freshman, sophomore, junior, or senior years; renewable. *Number:* up to 584. *Amount:* $1000–$5000.

Eligibility Requirements: Applicant must be enrolled or expecting to enroll full- or part-time at a four-year institution or university; resident of Maryland and studying in Maryland. Available to U.S. citizens.

Application Requirements: Application form, contact institution financial aid office, financial need analysis. *Deadline:* March 1.

Contact: Monica Wheatley, Program Manager
Maryland State Higher Education Commission
839 Bestgate Road, Suite 400
Annapolis, MD 21401
Phone: 410-260-4560
Fax: 410-260-3202
E-mail: mwheatle@mhec.state.md.us

MEDICAL SCRUBS COLLECTION

http://medicalscrubscollection.com

MEDICAL SCRUBS COLLECTION SCHOLARSHIP

• See page 106

NATIONAL DENTAL ASSOCIATION FOUNDATION

http://www.ndaonline.org/

NATIONAL DENTAL ASSOCIATION FOUNDATION COLGATE-PALMOLIVE SCHOLARSHIP PROGRAM (UNDERGRADUATES)

A scholarship of up to $1000 is given to sophomores through juniors in a dental school who are under-represented minority students. Applicants should be a member of NDA. Number of scholarships granted varies.

Academic Fields/Career Goals: Dental Health/Services.

Award: Scholarship for use in sophomore, junior, or senior years; not renewable. *Number:* up to 100. *Amount:* $700–$1000.

Eligibility Requirements: Applicant must be American Indian/Alaska Native, Asian/Pacific Islander, Black (non-Hispanic), Hispanic and enrolled or expecting to enroll full-time at a four-year institution or university. Available to U.S. citizens.

Application Requirements: Application form, financial need analysis, letter of request, recommendations or references, resume, transcript. *Deadline:* May 15.

Contact: Roosevelt Brown, President
Phone: 501-681-6110
Fax: 541-376-4008
E-mail: rbndaf1@comcast.net

OREGON STUDENT ASSISTANCE COMMISSION

http://www.GetCollegeFunds.org/

CLARK-PHELPS SCHOLARSHIP

Award for high school graduates who are residents of Oregon or Alaska and are studying nursing (undergraduate or graduate), dentistry, or medicine. Must be enrolled in a public institution in Oregon, with preference for Oregon Health & Science University, and working toward a 4-year degree or graduate degree. Must reapply annually for award renewal. FAFSA is required.

Academic Fields/Career Goals: Dental Health/Services; Health and Medical Sciences; Nursing.

Award: Scholarship for use in freshman, sophomore, junior, senior, or graduate years; not renewable.

Eligibility Requirements: Applicant must be enrolled or expecting to enroll full-time at a four-year institution or university; resident of Alaska, Oregon and studying in Oregon. Available to U.S. citizens.

Application Requirements: Application form, essay, financial need analysis. *Deadline:* March 1.

Contact: Melissa Adams, Scholarship Processing Coordinator
Phone: 541-687-7409
E-mail: melissa.adams@hecc.oregon.gov

PLATINUM EDUCATIONAL GROUP

www.platinumed.com

PLATINUM EDUCATIONAL GROUP SCHOLARSHIPS PROGRAM FOR EMS, NURSING, AND ALLIED HEALTH

• See page 107

THE RECOVERY VILLAGE

https://www.therecoveryvillage.com/

RECOVERY VILLAGE HEALTHCARE SCHOLARSHIP

A $500 award will be given to a student pursuing a health-related degree program. Areas of study that will be considered include, but are not limited to, counseling, social work, emergency medicine, pre-med, nursing, psychology (with a focus on addiction counseling or a substance-abuse related field). In order to be eligible, students must meet the following criteria: U.S. citizen or permanent U.S. resident; enrolled or accepted in an accredited college or university and plan to continue enrollment; graduating high school seniors who meet the above criteria are encouraged to apply; consent to a talent release, and will provide a digital photograph and quote for display on ARS websites if notified as the winner. Selection will be based upon: 1) Completed of application; 2) Originality (20%); 3) Creativity (20%); 4) Writing Skills (20%); 5) Inspiration (20%); 6) Demonstrated interest in addiction treatment and recovery (20%). The winner will be notified following the deadline and the award will be credited to the student's school. Certain information must be provided by the student to The Recovery Village in order for the school to receive the funds.

Academic Fields/Career Goals: Dental Health/Services; Nursing; Occupational Safety and Health; Psychology; Public Health; Public Policy and Administration; Therapy/Rehabilitation.

Award: Scholarship for use in freshman, sophomore, junior, senior, graduate, or postgraduate years; not renewable. *Number:* 1–2. *Amount:* $1–$500.

Eligibility Requirements: Applicant must be enrolled or expecting to enroll full- or part-time at a two-year or four-year institution or university. Applicant or parent of applicant must have employment or volunteer experience in occupational health and safety. Available to U.S. citizens.

Application Requirements: Application form, essay. *Deadline:* July 31.

Contact: Amy Campbell
E-mail: amy.campbell@laneterralever.com

SCARLETT FAMILY FOUNDATION SCHOLARSHIP PROGRAM

http://www.scarlettfoundation.org/

SCHOLARSHIP FOR STUDENTS PURSUING A BUSINESS OR STEM DEGREE
• *See page 84*

STRAIGHTFORWARD MEDIA

http://www.straightforwardmedia.com/

STRAIGHTFORWARD MEDIA MEDICAL PROFESSIONS SCHOLARSHIP

Scholarship of $500 available to full-time students in any health-related field. Awarded four times per year. Deadlines: March 31, June 30, September 30, and December 31.

Academic Fields/Career Goals: Dental Health/Services; Environmental Health; Health Administration; Health and Medical Sciences; Health Information Management/Technology; Nursing; Occupational Safety and Health; Oncology; Optometry; Osteopathy; Pharmacy; Therapy/Rehabilitation.

Award: Scholarship for use in freshman, sophomore, junior, or senior years; not renewable. *Number:* 4. *Amount:* $500.

Eligibility Requirements: Applicant must be enrolled or expecting to enroll full- or part-time at a two-year or four-year or technical institution or university. Available to U.S. and non-U.S. citizens.

Application Requirements: Essay. *Deadline:* varies.

Contact: Scholarship Committee
Phone: 605-348-3042

STRAIGHTFORWARD MEDIA VOCATIONAL-TECHNICAL SCHOOL SCHOLARSHIP
• *See page 107*

SUPREME GUARDIAN COUNCIL, INTERNATIONAL ORDER OF JOB'S DAUGHTERS

http://www.iojd.org/

GROTTO SCHOLARSHIP

Scholarships of $1500 to aid Job's Daughters students of outstanding ability whom have a sincerity of purpose. High school seniors, or graduates, junior college, technical school, or college students who are in early graduation programs, and pursuing an education in dentistry, preferably with some training in the handicapped field are eligible to apply.

Academic Fields/Career Goals: Dental Health/Services.

Award: Scholarship for use in freshman, sophomore, junior, senior, graduate, or postgraduate years; not renewable. *Number:* 1. *Amount:* $1500.

Eligibility Requirements: Applicant must be age 18-30; enrolled or expecting to enroll full- or part-time at a two-year or four-year or technical institution or university and single female. Applicant or parent of applicant must be member of Jobs Daughters. Available to U.S. and non-U.S. citizens.

Application Requirements: Application form, community service, essay, recommendations or references, transcript. *Deadline:* April 30.

Contact: Christal Bindrich, Scholarship Committee Chairman
Supreme Guardian Council, International Order of Job's Daughters
5351 South Butterfield Way
Greenfield, WI 53221
Phone: 414-423-0016
E-mail: christalbindrich@wi.rr.com

U.S. DEPARTMENT OF HEALTH AND HUMAN SERVICES

http://www.hhs.gov/

U. S. PUBLIC HEALTH SERVICE-HEALTH RESOURCES AND SERVICES ADMINISTRATION, BUREAU OF HEALTH PROFESSIONS SCHOLARSHIPS FOR DISADVANTAGED STUDENTS

One-time award for full-time students from disadvantaged backgrounds enrolled in health professions and nursing programs. Institution must apply for funding and must be eligible to receive SDS funds. Students must contact financial aid office to apply.

Academic Fields/Career Goals: Dental Health/Services; Health and Medical Sciences; Nursing; Therapy/Rehabilitation.

Award: Scholarship for use in freshman, sophomore, junior, senior, or graduate years; not renewable.

Eligibility Requirements: Applicant must be enrolled or expecting to enroll full-time at a two-year or four-year institution or university. Available to U.S. citizens.

Application Requirements: Application form, financial need analysis. *Deadline:* varies.

Contact: Andrea Stampone, Public Health Analyst
U.S. Department of Health and Human Services
Division of Student Loans and Scholarships
Parklawn Building, Suite 9-105
Rockville, MD 20857
Phone: 301-443-4776
Fax: 301-446-0846
E-mail: callcenter@hrsa.gov

DRAFTING

AMERICAN SOCIETY OF CERTIFIED ENGINEERING TECHNICIANS

http://www.ascet.org/

KURT H. AND DONNA M. SCHULER SMALL GRANT
• *See page 176*

MIDWEST ROOFING CONTRACTORS ASSOCIATION

http://www.mrca.org/

MRCA FOUNDATION SCHOLARSHIP PROGRAM
• *See page 122*

NASA'S VIRGINIA SPACE GRANT CONSORTIUM

http://www.vsgc.odu.edu/

COMMUNITY COLLEGE STEM SCHOLARSHIPS
• *See page 114*

NATIONAL ASSOCIATION OF WOMEN IN CONSTRUCTION

http://www.nawic.org/

NAWIC UNDERGRADUATE SCHOLARSHIPS
• *See page 122*

ONLINE LOGO MAKER

http://onlinelogomaker.com

OLM MALALA YOUSAFZAI SCHOLARSHIP 2017-2018
• *See page 129*

PROFESSIONAL CONSTRUCTION ESTIMATORS ASSOCIATION

http://www.pcea.org/

TED G. WILSON MEMORIAL SCHOLARSHIP FOUNDATION
• *See page 197*

SUPPORT CREATIVITY

http://wesupportcreativity.org

SUPPORT CREATIVITY SCHOLARSHIP
• *See page 124*

VECTORWORKS, INC.

http://www.vectorworks.net

VECTORWORKS DESIGN SCHOLARSHIP
• *See page 124*

EARTH SCIENCE

AEG FOUNDATION

http://www.aegfoundation.org/

AEG FOUNDATION MARLIAVE FUND

One-time award to support undergraduate and graduate students studying engineering geology and geological engineering.

Academic Fields/Career Goals: Earth Science; Engineering/Technology; Science, Technology, and Society.

Award: Scholarship for use in senior or graduate years; not renewable. *Number:* 1. *Amount:* $4000.

Eligibility Requirements: Applicant must be enrolled or expecting to enroll full-time at a four-year institution or university. Available to U.S. and Canadian citizens.

Application Requirements: Application form, application form may be submitted online (http://www.aegfoundation.org), essay, recommendations or references, resume, transcript. *Deadline:* February 1.

Contact: Becky Roland, Executive Director
AEG Foundation
PO Box 460518
Denver, CO 80246
Phone: 303-757-2926
Fax: 720-230-4846
E-mail: staff@aegfoundation.org

TILFORD FIELD STUDIES SCHOLARSHIP

Scholarship of $1000 for student members of AEG. Three to four awards are granted annually. For undergraduate students, the scholarship goes toward the cost of a geology field camp course or senior thesis field research. For graduate students, the scholarship would apply to field research.

Academic Fields/Career Goals: Earth Science.

Award: Scholarship for use in freshman, sophomore, junior, senior, graduate, or postgraduate years; not renewable. *Number:* 4–5. *Amount:* $500–$2500.

Eligibility Requirements: Applicant must be enrolled or expecting to enroll full-time at a four-year institution or university. Applicant or parent of applicant must be member of Association of Engineering Geologists. Available to U.S. and non-U.S. citizens.

Application Requirements: Application form, application form may be submitted online (http://www.aegfoundation.org), essay, recommendations or references, resume, transcript. *Deadline:* February 1.

Contact: Becky Roland, AEG Foundation
AEG Foundation
PO Box 460518
Denver, CO 80246
Phone: 303-757-2926
Fax: 720-230-4846
E-mail: staff@aegfoundation.org

ALASKA GEOLOGICAL SOCIETY INC.

http://www.alaskageology.org/

ALASKA GEOLOGICAL SOCIETY SCHOLARSHIP

Scholarship available for a full-time junior or senior undergraduate or graduate student enrolled at any college or university with academic emphasis in earth sciences. Student must have a project based in Alaska or on a topic directly related to Alaskan geology.

Academic Fields/Career Goals: Earth Science.

Award: Scholarship for use in junior, senior, or graduate years; not renewable. *Number:* 3–8. *Amount:* $500–$2500.

Eligibility Requirements: Applicant must be enrolled or expecting to enroll full-time at a four-year institution or university and studying in Alaska. Available to U.S. and non-U.S. citizens.

Application Requirements: Application form, essay, financial need analysis. *Deadline:* February 1.

Contact: Susan Karl, Chair of Scholarship Committee
Alaska Geological Society Inc.
Alaska Geological Society
PO Box 101288
Anchorage, AK 99510
Phone: 907-786-7428
E-mail: skarl@usgs.gov

AMERICAN ALPINE CLUB

https://americanalpineclub.org/

AAC RESEARCH GRANTS
• *See page 153*

AMERICAN GROUND WATER TRUST

http://www.agwt.org/

AMERICAN GROUND WATER TRUST-AMTROL INC. SCHOLARSHIP

Award for college/university entry-level students intending to pursue a career in ground water-related field. Must either have completed a science/environmental project involving ground water resources or have had vacation work experience related to the environment and natural resources. Must be U.S. citizen or legal resident with minimum 3.0 GPA. Submit two letters of recommendation and transcript.

Academic Fields/Career Goals: Earth Science; Hydrology; Natural Resources.

Award: Scholarship for use in freshman year; not renewable. *Number:* 2. *Amount:* up to $1500.

Eligibility Requirements: Applicant must be enrolled or expecting to enroll full-time at a four-year institution or university. Applicant must have 3.0 GPA or higher. Available to U.S. citizens.

Application Requirements: Application form, essay, recommendations or references, transcript. *Deadline:* June 1.

Contact: Andrew Stone, Executive Director
American Ground Water Trust
50 Pleasant Street, Suite 2
Concord, NH 03301-4073
Phone: 603-228-5444
Fax: 603-228-6557
E-mail: trustinfo@agwt.org

AMERICAN GROUND WATER TRUST-BAROID SCHOLARSHIP

Award for entry-level students intending to pursue a career in ground water-related field. Must either have completed a science/environmental project involving ground water resources or have had vacation work experience related to the environment and natural resources. Must be a U.S. citizen or legal resident with minimum 3.0 GPA. Submit two letters of recommendation and transcript.

Academic Fields/Career Goals: Earth Science; Hydrology; Natural Resources.

Award: Scholarship for use in freshman year; not renewable. *Number:* 1. *Amount:* up to $2000.

Eligibility Requirements: Applicant must be enrolled or expecting to enroll full-time at a four-year institution or university. Applicant must have 3.0 GPA or higher. Available to U.S. citizens.

Application Requirements: Application form, essay, recommendations or references, transcript. *Deadline:* June 1.

Contact: Andrew Stone, Executive Director
American Ground Water Trust
50 Pleasant Street, Suite 2
Concord, NH 03301-4073
Phone: 603-228-5444
Fax: 603-228-6557
E-mail: trustinfo@agwt.org

AMERICAN GROUND WATER TRUST-THOMAS STETSON SCHOLARSHIP

For students entering their freshman year in a full-time program of study at a four-year accredited university or college located west of the Mississippi River and intending to pursue a career in ground water-related field. Must be U.S. citizen or legal resident with 3.0 GPA or higher. For more information see website http://www.agwt.org.

Academic Fields/Career Goals: Earth Science; Hydrology; Natural Resources.

Award: Scholarship for use in freshman year; not renewable. *Number:* 1. *Amount:* up to $2000.

Eligibility Requirements: Applicant must be enrolled or expecting to enroll full-time at a four-year institution or university. Applicant must have 3.0 GPA or higher. Available to U.S. citizens.

Application Requirements: Application form, essay, recommendations or references, transcript. *Deadline:* June 1.

Contact: Andrew Stone, Executive Director
American Ground Water Trust
50 Pleasant Street, Suite 2
Concord, NH 03301-4073
Phone: 603-228-5444
Fax: 603-228-6557
E-mail: trustinfo@agwt.org

AMERICAN INDIAN SCIENCE AND ENGINEERING SOCIETY

http://www.aises.org/

A.T. ANDERSON MEMORIAL SCHOLARSHIP PROGRAM
• *See page 109*

AMERICAN SOCIETY OF AGRONOMY, CROP SCIENCE SOCIETY OF AMERICA, SOIL SCIENCE SOCIETY OF AMERICA

http://www.agronomy.org

J. FIELDING REED SCHOLARSHIP
• *See page 97*

ARIZONA HYDROLOGICAL SOCIETY

http://www.azhydrosoc.org/

ARIZONA HYDROLOGICAL SOCIETY SCHOLARSHIP

One-time award to outstanding upper-level undergraduate or graduate students who have demonstrated academic excellence in water resources related fields as a means of encouraging them to continue to develop as water resources professionals. Must be a resident of Arizona and be enrolled in a postsecondary Arizona institution.

Academic Fields/Career Goals: Earth Science; Hydrology; Natural Resources; Nuclear Science; Science, Technology, and Society.

Award: Scholarship for use in junior, senior, or graduate years; not renewable. *Number:* 3. *Amount:* $2000.

Eligibility Requirements: Applicant must be enrolled or expecting to enroll full-time at a two-year or four-year or technical institution or university; resident of Arizona and studying in Arizona. Available to U.S. citizens.

Application Requirements: Application form, essay, financial need analysis, recommendations or references, transcript. *Deadline:* April 30.

Contact: Aregai Tecle, Professor
Phone: 928-523-6642
Fax: 928-556-7112
E-mail: aregai.tecle@nau.edu

ARMED FORCES COMMUNICATIONS AND ELECTRONICS ASSOCIATION, EDUCATIONAL FOUNDATION

http://www.afcea.org/site/?q=foundation/scholarships

STEM TEACHERS SCHOLARSHIP
• *See page 111*

ASSOCIATION FOR WOMEN GEOSCIENTISTS (AWG)

http://www.awg.org/

AWG ETHNIC MINORITY SCHOLARSHIP

The Minority Scholarship encourages young women of a minority background, or heritage, to pursue a major and career in the geosciences. The scholarship provides financial support for college expenses and matches the student with a mentor who has a career similar to that desired by the awardee.

Academic Fields/Career Goals: Earth Science; Education; Environmental Science; Gemology; Geography; Hydrology; Meteorology/Atmospheric Science; Museum Studies; Natural Resources; Natural Sciences; Oceanography; Physical Sciences.

Award: Scholarship for use in freshman, sophomore, junior, or senior years; not renewable. *Number:* 1–5. *Amount:* $500–$3000.

Eligibility Requirements: Applicant must be American Indian/Alaska Native, Black (non-Hispanic), Hispanic; enrolled or expecting to enroll full- or part-time at a four-year institution or university and female. Available to U.S. citizens.

Application Requirements: Application form, community service, recommendations or references, statement of academic or career goals, test scores, transcript. *Deadline:* June 30.

Contact: Christina Tapia, Ethnic Minority Scholarship Coordinator

AWG MARIA LUISA CRAWFORD FIELD CAMP SCHOLARSHIP
• *See page 117*

AWG SALT LAKE CHAPTER (SLC) RESEARCH SCHOLARSHIP
• *See page 117*

AWG UNDERGRADUATE EXCELLENCE IN PALEONTOLOGY AWARD
• *See page 112*

JANET CULLEN TANAKA GEOSCIENCES UNDERGRADUATE SCHOLARSHIP
• *See page 117*

LONE STAR RISING CAREER SCHOLARSHIP
The Lone Star Rising Career Scholarship provides professional development funding for women geoscience professionals seeking to resume their geoscience careers after having been out of the work force, or women geoscience students seeking to enter the workforce in a geoscience-related field within the next two years.

Academic Fields/Career Goals: Earth Science; Education; Environmental Science; Gemology; Hydrology; Meteorology/Atmospheric Science; Museum Studies; Natural Resources; Natural Sciences; Oceanography; Physical Sciences; Science, Technology, and Society.

Award: Scholarship for use in freshman, sophomore, junior, senior, graduate, or postgraduate years; not renewable. *Number:* 1–2. *Amount:* $1–$3000.

Eligibility Requirements: Applicant must be enrolled or expecting to enroll full- or part-time at a two-year or four-year institution or university and single female. Applicant or parent of applicant must have employment or volunteer experience in physical or natural sciences. Available to U.S. citizens.

Application Requirements: Application form, financial need analysis, recommendations or references. *Deadline:* October 31.

Contact: AWG Lone Star Rising Career Scholarship Coordinator
Association for Women Geoscientists (AWG)
AWG Lone Star Chapter
PO Box 542042
Houston, TX 77254
E-mail: awglonestar@gmail.com

OSAGE CHAPTER UNDERGRADUATE SERVICE SCHOLARSHIP
• *See page 117*

SUSAN EKDALE MEMORIAL FIELD CAMP SCHOLARSHIP
The scholarship will be awarded to a female student in the geosciences to help defray field camp expenses. Applicant must be attending a Utah institution of higher learning, or be a Utah resident attending college elsewhere.

Academic Fields/Career Goals: Earth Science; Environmental Science; Hydrology; Meteorology/Atmospheric Science; Museum Studies; Natural Resources; Natural Sciences; Oceanography; Physical Sciences.

Award: Scholarship for use in freshman, sophomore, junior, senior, or graduate years; not renewable. *Amount:* $1000–$2000.

Eligibility Requirements: Applicant must be enrolled or expecting to enroll full- or part-time at a four-year institution or university; female; resident of Utah and studying in Utah. Available to U.S. citizens.

Application Requirements: Application form, essay, letter of eligibility from the department verifying field of study, recommendations or references. *Deadline:* March 12.

Contact: Janae Wallace, Ekdale Scholarship Committee Chair
Association for Women Geoscientists (AWG)
AWG Salt Lake Chapter
PO Box 58691
Salt Lake City, UT 84158-0691
Phone: 801-537-3387
E-mail: janaewallace@utah.gov

ASSOCIATION ON AMERICAN INDIAN AFFAIRS, INC.
http://www.indian-affairs.org/

ELIZABETH AND SHERMAN ASCHE MEMORIAL SCHOLARSHIP FUND
• *See page 98*

ASTRONAUT SCHOLARSHIP FOUNDATION
http://www.astronautscholarship.org/

ASTRONAUT SCHOLARSHIP FOUNDATION
• *See page 112*

BARRY GOLDWATER SCHOLARSHIP AND EXCELLENCE IN EDUCATION FOUNDATION
https://goldwater.scholarsapply.org

BARRY M. GOLDWATER SCHOLARSHIP AND EXCELLENCE IN EDUCATION PROGRAM
• *See page 112*

BHW GROUP
https://thebhwgroup.com/

BHW WOMEN IN STEM SCHOLARSHIP
• *See page 74*

B.O.G. PEST CONTROL
http://www.bogpestcontrol.com/

B.O.G. PEST CONTROL SCHOLARSHIP FUND
• *See page 155*

BROWN AND CALDWELL
http://www.brownandcaldwell.com

ECKENFELDER SCHOLARSHIP
• *See page 155*

MINORITY SCHOLARSHIP PROGRAM
• *See page 155*

GARDEN CLUB OF AMERICA
http://www.gcamerica.org/

ELIZABETH GARDNER NORWEB SUMMER ENVIRONMENTAL STUDIES SCHOLARSHIP
• *See page 98*

GREAT MINDS IN STEM
www.greatmindsinstem.org

HISPANIC ENGINEER NATIONAL ACHIEVEMENT AWARDS CORPORATION SCHOLARSHIP PROGRAM
• *See page 106*

INDEPENDENT LABORATORIES INSTITUTE SCHOLARSHIP ALLIANCE

http://www.acil.org/

INDEPENDENT LABORATORIES INSTITUTE SCHOLARSHIP ALLIANCE
• *See page 156*

KENTUCKY ENERGY AND ENVIRONMENT CABINET

http://dep.ky.gov

ENVIRONMENTAL PROTECTION SCHOLARSHIP
• *See page 157*

THE LAND CONSERVANCY OF NEW JERSEY

http://tlc-nj.org/

ROGERS FAMILY SCHOLARSHIP

The scholarship program is administered by the Board of Trustees of The Land Conservancy of New Jersey and is awarded annually to deserving individuals who plan careers in environmental science, natural resource management, conservation, horticulture, park administration, or a related field. An applicant must be a student in good standing with at least 15 credits completed, have an academic average equivalent to a 3.0 or higher, be a resident of New Jersey and considering a career in New Jersey that is consistent with the goals of the Conservancy. Selected finalist will have to attend an interview in early June.

Academic Fields/Career Goals: Earth Science; Environmental Science; Horticulture/Floriculture; Landscape Architecture; Natural Resources; Recreation, Parks, Leisure Studies; Urban and Regional Planning.

Award: Scholarship for use in freshman, sophomore, junior, senior, or graduate years; not renewable. *Amount:* up to $7500.

Eligibility Requirements: Applicant must be enrolled or expecting to enroll full-time at a four-year institution or university and resident of New Jersey. Applicant must have 3.0 GPA or higher. Available to U.S. citizens.

Application Requirements: Application form, essay, recommendations or references, resume, transcript. *Deadline:* April 1.

Contact: Scholarship Program
The Land Conservancy of New Jersey
19 Boonton Avenue
Boonton, NJ 07005
Phone: 973-541-1010 Ext. 10
E-mail: info@tlc-nj.org

MEDICAL SCRUBS COLLECTION

http://medicalscrubscollection.com

MEDICAL SCRUBS COLLECTION SCHOLARSHIP
• *See page 106*

MONTANA FEDERATION OF GARDEN CLUBS

http://www.mtfgc.org/

LIFE MEMBER MONTANA FEDERATION OF GARDEN CLUBS SCHOLARSHIP

Applicant must be at least a sophomore, majoring in conservation, horticulture, park or forestry, floriculture, greenhouse management, land management, or related subjects. Must be in need of assistance. Must have a potential for a successful future. Must be ranked in upper half of class or have a minimum 2.7 GPA. Must be a Montana resident and all study must be done in Montana.

Academic Fields/Career Goals: Earth Science; Horticulture/Floriculture; Landscape Architecture; Natural Resources.

Award: Scholarship for use in sophomore, junior, or senior years; not renewable. *Number:* 1. *Amount:* $1000.

Eligibility Requirements: Applicant must be enrolled or expecting to enroll full-time at a four-year institution or university; resident of Montana and studying in Montana. Applicant must have 2.5 GPA or higher. Available to U.S. citizens.

Application Requirements: Driver's license, recommendations or references, transcript. *Deadline:* May 1.

Contact: Joyce Backa, Life Members Scholarship Chairman
Montana Federation of Garden Clubs
513 Skyline Drive
Craig, MT 59404-8712
Phone: 406-235-4229
E-mail: rjback@bresnan.net

NASA FLORIDA SPACE GRANT CONSORTIUM

http://www.floridaspacegrant.org/

FLORIDA SPACE RESEARCH PROGRAM
• *See page 142*

NASA IDAHO SPACE GRANT CONSORTIUM

http://www.id.spacegrant.org/

NASA IDAHO SPACE GRANT CONSORTIUM SCHOLARSHIP PROGRAM
• *See page 157*

NASA/MARYLAND SPACE GRANT CONSORTIUM

http://md.spacegrant.org/

NASA MARYLAND SPACE GRANT CONSORTIUM UNDERGRADUATE SCHOLARSHIPS
• *See page 142*

NASA MINNESOTA SPACE GRANT CONSORTIUM

http://www.aem.umn.edu/mnsgc

MINNESOTA SPACE GRANT CONSORTIUM SCHOLARSHIP PROGRAM
• *See page 142*

NASA SOUTH CAROLINA SPACE GRANT CONSORTIUM

http://www.cofc.edu/~scsgrant

UNDERGRADUATE RESEARCH AWARD PROGRAM
• *See page 143*

NATIONAL ASSOCIATION OF GEOSCIENCE TEACHERS & FAR WESTERN SECTION

http://www.nagt-fws.org

NATIONAL ASSOCIATION OF GEOSCIENCE TEACHERS-FAR WESTERN SECTION SCHOLARSHIP

Academically superior students currently enrolled in school in Hawaii, Nevada, or California are eligible to apply for one of three $500 scholarships to the school of their choice. Must be a high school senior or community college student enrolling full-time (12 quarter units) in a Bachelor's degree program in geology at a four-year institution or an undergraduate geology major enrolling in an upper division field geology course of approximately 30 field mapping days.

Academic Fields/Career Goals: Earth Science.

Award: Scholarship for use in sophomore, junior, or senior years; not renewable. *Number:* 3. *Amount:* $500.

Eligibility Requirements: Applicant must be enrolled or expecting to enroll full- or part-time at a four-year institution or university and studying in California, Hawaii, Nevada. Available to U.S. citizens.

Application Requirements: Application form, endorsement signature of a regular member of NAGT-FWS in the reference letter, recommendations or references, transcript. *Deadline:* April 1.

Contact: Mike Martin, Geology Scholarship Coordinator
Phone: 951-789-5690
E-mail: mmartin@rusd.k12.ca.us

NATIONAL ASSOCIATION OF WATER COMPANIES-NEW JERSEY CHAPTER

http://www.nawc.org

NATIONAL ASSOCIATION OF WATER COMPANIES-NEW JERSEY CHAPTER SCHOLARSHIP
• *See page 80*

NATIONAL GARDEN CLUBS INC.

http://www.gardenclub.org/

NATIONAL GARDEN CLUBS INC. SCHOLARSHIP PROGRAM
• *See page 100*

NEVADA NASA SPACE GRANT CONSORTIUM

http://www.nvspacegrant.org/

NATIONAL SPACE GRANT COLLEGE AND FELLOWSHIP PROGRAM
• *See page 114*

NEXTSTEPU

http://www.nextstepu.com/

$1,500 STEM SCHOLARSHIP
• *See page 106*

NGWA FOUNDATION

http://www.ngwa.org/Foundation/Pages/default.aspx

NGWA FOUNDATION'S LEN ASSANTE SCHOLARSHIP

Applicant must be in a field of study that serves, supports, or promotes the groundwater industry. Qualifying majors: geology, hydrology, hydrogeology, environmental sciences, microbiology, and well-drilling two-year associate degree programs. Minimum 2.5 GPA required.

Academic Fields/Career Goals: Earth Science; Environmental Science; Hydrology.

Award: Scholarship for use in freshman, sophomore, junior, senior, graduate, or postgraduate years; not renewable. *Number:* 1–15. *Amount:* $1000–$5000.

Eligibility Requirements: Applicant must be enrolled or expecting to enroll full-time at a two-year or four-year or technical institution or university. Applicant must have 2.5 GPA or higher. Available to U.S. and non-U.S. citizens.

Application Requirements: Application form, essay, personal photograph. *Deadline:* January 15.

Contact: Foundation Administrator
NGWA Foundation
601 Dempsey Road
Westerville, OH 43081
Phone: 614-898-7791 Ext. 1504
E-mail: foundation@ngwa.org

OREGON STUDENT ASSISTANCE COMMISSION

http://www.GetCollegeFunds.org/

ANDY AITKENHEAD SCHOLARSHIP
• *See page 115*

SEHAR SALEHA AHMAD AND ABRAHIM EKRAMULLAH ZAFAR FOUNDATION SCHOLARSHIP
• *See page 115*

ROCKY MOUNTAIN COAL MINING INSTITUTE

http://www.rmcmi.org/

ROCKY MOUNTAIN COAL MINING INSTITUTE SCHOLARSHIP
• *See page 197*

SCARLETT FAMILY FOUNDATION SCHOLARSHIP PROGRAM

http://www.scarlettfoundation.org/

SCHOLARSHIP FOR STUDENTS PURSUING A BUSINESS OR STEM DEGREE
• *See page 84*

SIGMA XI, THE SCIENTIFIC RESEARCH SOCIETY

http://www.sigmaxi.org/

SIGMA XI GRANTS-IN-AID OF RESEARCH
• *See page 101*

SOIL AND WATER CONSERVATION SOCIETY

http://www.swcs.org

DONALD A. WILLIAMS SCHOLARSHIP SOIL CONSERVATION SCHOLARSHIP
• *See page 95*

SOIL AND WATER CONSERVATION SOCIETY-MISSOURI SHOW-ME CHAPTER

http://www.moswcs.org/

MO SHOW-ME CHAPTER SWCS SCHOLARSHIP
• *See page 95*

SOIL AND WATER CONSERVATION SOCIETY-NEW JERSEY CHAPTER

http://www.geocities.com/njswcs

EDWARD R. HALL SCHOLARSHIP
• *See page 95*

TKE EDUCATIONAL FOUNDATION

http://www.tke.org/

CARROL C. HALL MEMORIAL SCHOLARSHIP
• *See page 115*

ERIC D. DUNNING SCHOLARSHIP
• See page 219

UNIVERSITIES SPACE RESEARCH ASSOCIATION
http://www.usra.edu/

UNIVERSITIES SPACE RESEARCH ASSOCIATION SCHOLARSHIP AWARD PROGRAM
• See page 116

VERMONT SPACE GRANT CONSORTIUM
http://www.cems.uvm.edu/vsgc

VERMONT SPACE GRANT CONSORTIUM
• See page 96

VISIONARY INTEGRATION PROFESSIONALS (VIP)
http://www.trustvip.com/

WOMEN IN TECHNOLOGY SCHOLARSHIP (WITS)
• See page 220

ECONOMICS

280 GROUP
https://280group.com/contact/280-group-product-management-scholarship/

280 GROUP PRODUCT MANAGEMENT SCHOLARSHIP
• See page 160

THE ACTUARIAL FOUNDATION
http://www.actuarialfoundation.org

ACTUARY OF TOMORROW—STUART A. ROBERTSON MEMORIAL SCHOLARSHIP
• See page 160

CURTIS E. HUNTINGTON MEMORIAL SCHOLARSHIP (FORMERLY THE JOHN CULVER WOODDY SCHOLARSHIP)

The Curtis E. Huntington Memorial Scholarship (formerly the John Culver Wooddy Scholarship) is awarded annually to college seniors who have successfully completed at least one actuarial examination, rank in the top quartile of their class and are nominated by a professor at their school.

Academic Fields/Career Goals: Economics; Finance; Insurance and Actuarial Science; Mathematics; Statistics.

Award: Scholarship for use in senior year; not renewable. *Amount:* $2000.

Eligibility Requirements: Applicant must be enrolled or expecting to enroll full-time at a four-year institution or university. Applicant must have 2.5 GPA or higher. Available to U.S. and non-U.S. citizens.

Application Requirements: Application form, essay. *Deadline:* June 16.

Contact: Curtis E. Huntington Memorial Scholarship
The Actuarial Foundation
475 North Martingale Road, Suite 600
Schaumburg, IL 60173
Phone: 847-706-3535
E-mail: scholarships@actfnd.org

AUTOMOTIVE WOMEN'S ALLIANCE FOUNDATION
http://www.awafoundation.org/index.php

AUTOMOTIVE WOMEN'S ALLIANCE FOUNDATION SCHOLARSHIPS
• See page 74

CATCHING THE DREAM
http://www.catchingthedream.org/

TRIBAL BUSINESS MANAGEMENT PROGRAM (TBM)
• See page 74

FUKUNAGA SCHOLARSHIP FOUNDATION
http://fukunagascholarship.com

FUKUNAGA SCHOLARSHIP FOUNDATION
• See page 77

GOVERNMENT FINANCE OFFICERS ASSOCIATION
http://www.gfoa.org/

MINORITIES IN GOVERNMENT FINANCE SCHOLARSHIP
• See page 78

INSTITUTE FOR HUMANE STUDIES
http://www.theihs.org/

HUMANE STUDIES FELLOWSHIPS
• See page 204

JORGE MAS CANOSA FREEDOM FOUNDATION
http://masscholarships.org/

MAS FAMILY SCHOLARSHIP AWARD
• See page 165

NATIONAL ASSOCIATION OF NEGRO BUSINESS AND PROFESSIONAL WOMEN'S CLUBS INC.
http://www.nanbpwc.org/

JULIANNE MALVEAUX SCHOLARSHIP

Scholarship for African-American women who are college sophomores or juniors enrolled in an accredited college or university. Applicants must be majoring in journalism, economics, or a related field. Minimum 3.0 GPA required. Must be a U.S. citizen.

Academic Fields/Career Goals: Economics; Journalism.

Award: Scholarship for use in sophomore or junior years; not renewable. *Number:* 1. *Amount:* $1000.

Eligibility Requirements: Applicant must be Black (non-Hispanic); enrolled or expecting to enroll full-time at a four-year institution or university and female. Applicant must have 3.0 GPA or higher. Available to U.S. citizens.

Application Requirements: Application form, essay, recommendations or references, transcript. *Deadline:* April 30.

Contact: Scholarship Program Director
National Association of Negro Business and Professional
Women's Clubs Inc.
1806 New Hampshire Avenue, NW
Washington, DC 20009-3298
Phone: 202-483-4206
E-mail: info@nanbpwc.org

NATIONAL ASSOCIATION OF WATER COMPANIES-NEW JERSEY CHAPTER

http://www.nawc.org

NATIONAL ASSOCIATION OF WATER COMPANIES-NEW JERSEY CHAPTER SCHOLARSHIP
• *See page 80*

NATIONAL SECURITY EDUCATION PROGRAM

http://www.iie.org/

NATIONAL SECURITY EDUCATION PROGRAM (NSEP) DAVID L. BOREN UNDERGRADUATE SCHOLARSHIPS
• *See page 126*

NATIONAL SOCIETY DAUGHTERS OF THE AMERICAN REVOLUTION

http://www.dar.org/

NATIONAL SOCIETY DAUGHTERS OF THE AMERICAN REVOLUTION ENID HALL GRISWOLD MEMORIAL SCHOLARSHIP

Scholarship of $1000 awarded to a deserving junior or senior enrolled in an accredited college or university in the United States who is majoring in political science, history, government, or economics.

Academic Fields/Career Goals: Economics; History; Political Science.

Award: Scholarship for use in junior or senior years; not renewable. *Number:* 2. *Amount:* $5000.

Eligibility Requirements: Applicant must be enrolled or expecting to enroll full-time at a four-year institution or university. Available to U.S. citizens.

Application Requirements: Application form, essay, financial need analysis. *Deadline:* February 10.

Contact: Lakeisha Graham, Manager, Office of the Reporter General
Phone: 202-628-1776
Fax: 202-879-3348
E-mail: nsdarscholarships@dar.org

NEW ENGLAND EMPLOYEE BENEFITS COUNCIL

http://www.neebc.org/

NEW ENGLAND EMPLOYEE BENEFITS COUNCIL SCHOLARSHIP PROGRAM
• *See page 81*

OFFICE AND PROFESSIONAL EMPLOYEES INTERNATIONAL UNION

http://www.opeiu.org/

JOHN KELLY LABOR STUDIES SCHOLARSHIP FUND

Scholarship of up to $3000 given to graduate or undergraduate students who have labor studies, social sciences, industrial relation as their major. Ten scholarships are granted. Applicants should be a member or associate member of the union.

Academic Fields/Career Goals: Economics; Social Sciences.

Award: Scholarship for use in freshman, sophomore, junior, senior, or graduate years; not renewable. *Number:* 10. *Amount:* up to $3000.

Eligibility Requirements: Applicant must be enrolled or expecting to enroll full-time at a four-year institution or university. Available to U.S. citizens.

Application Requirements: Application form, essay, transcript. *Deadline:* March 31.

Contact: Mary Mahoney, Secretary-Treasurer
Phone: 202-393-4464
Fax: 202-887-0910
E-mail: mmahoney@opeiudc.org

OREGON STUDENT ASSISTANCE COMMISSION

http://www.GetCollegeFunds.org/

OREGON STATE FISCAL ASSOCIATION SCHOLARSHIP

One-time award for OSFA members or their dependents. Members must enroll in an Oregon public or nonprofit institution at least half-time and must study public administration, finance, economics, or related fields. Children of members must enroll full-time in an Oregon institution and may enter any program of study. Must reapply annually.

Academic Fields/Career Goals: Economics; Finance; Public Policy and Administration.

Award: Scholarship for use in freshman, sophomore, junior, senior, or graduate years; not renewable.

Eligibility Requirements: Applicant must be enrolled or expecting to enroll full- or part-time at a two-year or four-year institution; resident of Oregon and studying in Oregon. Applicant or parent of applicant must be member of Oregon State Fiscal Association. Available to U.S. citizens.

Application Requirements: Application form, financial need analysis. *Deadline:* March 1.

Contact: Melissa Adams, Scholarship Processing Coordinator
Phone: 541-687-7409
E-mail: melissa.adams@hecc.oregon.gov

RISK MANAGEMENT ASSOCIATION FOUNDATION

www.scholarshipamerica.org

RISK MANAGEMENT ASSOCIATION FOUNDATION SCHOLARSHIP PROGRAM
• *See page 83*

SCARLETT FAMILY FOUNDATION SCHOLARSHIP PROGRAM

http://www.scarlettfoundation.org/

SCHOLARSHIP FOR STUDENTS PURSUING A BUSINESS OR STEM DEGREE
• *See page 84*

SOCIETY OF AUTOMOTIVE ANALYSTS

http://saaauto.com/

SOCIETY OF AUTOMOTIVE ANALYSTS SCHOLARSHIP
• *See page 84*

STRAIGHTFORWARD MEDIA

http://www.straightforwardmedia.com/

STRAIGHTFORWARD MEDIA BUSINESS SCHOOL SCHOLARSHIP
• *See page 90*

STRAIGHTFORWARD MEDIA LIBERAL ARTS SCHOLARSHIP
• *See page 126*

TRANSTUTORS

http://www.transtutors.com/scholarship

TRANSTUTORS SCHOLARSHIP 2015-16
• *See page 85*

UNITED NEGRO COLLEGE FUND

http://www.uncf.org/

COLGATE–PALMOLIVE CORPORATE SCHOLARS PROGRAM
• *See page 86*

UNCF/KOCH SCHOLARS PROGRAM FOR UNDERGRADUATES
• *See page 87*

EDUCATION

ALBERTA HERITAGE SCHOLARSHIP FUND

http://www.alis.alberta.ca/

ANNA AND JOHN KOLESAR MEMORIAL SCHOLARSHIPS

Award of CAN$1500 to recognize and reward the academic excellence of a high school student entering a Faculty of Education. Must be resident of Alberta and plan to enroll full-time in the first year of an education program. Must be from a family where neither parent obtained a university degree. Selection based on the highest average obtained on three grade 12 subjects. Must be a Canadian citizen or permanent resident. For additional information and application, visit website http://alis.alberta.ca.

Academic Fields/Career Goals: Education; Special Education.

Award: Scholarship for use in freshman year; not renewable. *Number:* 1.

Eligibility Requirements: Applicant must be Canadian citizen; high school student; planning to enroll or expecting to enroll full-time at a two-year or four-year institution or university and resident of Alberta. Applicant must have 3.0 GPA or higher.

Application Requirements: Application form, test scores, transcript. *Deadline:* July 1.

Contact: Scholarship Committee
Phone: 780-427-8640
E-mail: scholarships@gov.ab.ca

LANGUAGES IN TEACHER EDUCATION SCHOLARSHIPS

One-time awards of CAN$2500 to Alberta students enrolled full-time in the final two years of a recognized teacher preparation program in Alberta, taking courses that will allow them to teach languages other than English in Alberta schools. Must be Canadian citizen or permanent resident and a resident of Alberta. Must intend to teach in Alberta after graduation. Nominations by faculty of education. For additional information, visit website http://alis.alberta.ca.

Academic Fields/Career Goals: Education; Foreign Language.

Award: Scholarship for use in junior or senior years; not renewable. *Number:* 16.

Eligibility Requirements: Applicant must be enrolled or expecting to enroll full-time at a four-year institution or university; resident of Alberta and studying in Alberta. Available to Canadian citizens.

Application Requirements: Nomination by institution. *Deadline:* varies.

Contact: Scholarship Committee
Phone: 780-427-8640
E-mail: scholarships@gov.ab.ca

NORTHERN ALBERTA DEVELOPMENT COUNCIL BURSARY
• *See page 234*

AMERICAN ASSOCIATION OF PHYSICS TEACHERS

http://aapt.org

BARBARA LOTZE SCHOLARSHIPS FOR FUTURE TEACHERS

Undergraduate students enrolled, or planning to enroll, in physics teacher preparation curricula and high school seniors entering such programs are eligible. Successful applicants receive a stipend of up to $2,000 and a complimentary AAPT Student Membership for one year. The scholarship may be granted to an individual for each of four years. Students who meet the following criteria are eligible to apply for the Barbara Lotze Scholarship for Future Teachers. Applicants must declare their intent to prepare for, and engage in, a career in physics teaching at the high school level and must, at the time the scholarship funds are received by the student; be an undergraduate student enrolled in an accredited two-year college, four-year college or a university, or a high school senior accepted for such enrollment; be pursuing, or planning to pursue, a course of study leading toward a career in physics teaching in the high schools; showing promise of success in their studies; and be a citizen of the United States of America. Applications will be accepted at any time and will be considered for recommendation to the Executive Board at each AAPT Winter Meeting. All applications in which all materials, including letters of recommendation, are received by December 1 will be considered for recommendation at the winter meeting of the AAPT Executive Board.

Academic Fields/Career Goals: Education; Physical Sciences.

Award: Scholarship for use in freshman, sophomore, junior, or senior years; not renewable. *Number:* 5–7. *Amount:* $2000.

Eligibility Requirements: Applicant must be enrolled or expecting to enroll full- or part-time at a two-year or four-year institution. Available to U.S. citizens.

Application Requirements: Application form, portfolio. *Deadline:* December 1.

Contact: Mrs. Rachel Sweeney, Executive Assistant
E-mail: rsweeney@aapt.org

AMERICAN FEDERATION OF TEACHERS

http://www.aft.org/

ROBERT G. PORTER SCHOLARS PROGRAM-AFT MEMBERS

Nonrenewable grant provides continuing education for school teachers, paraprofessionals and school-related personnel, higher education faculty and professionals, employees of state and local governments, nurses and other health professionals. Must be member of the American Federation of Teachers for at least one year.

Academic Fields/Career Goals: Education.

Award: Grant for use in freshman, sophomore, junior, or senior years; not renewable. *Number:* up to 10. *Amount:* $1000.

Eligibility Requirements: Applicant must be enrolled or expecting to enroll full- or part-time at a four-year institution or university. Applicant or parent of applicant must have employment or volunteer experience in nursing, teaching/education. Available to U.S. citizens.

Application Requirements: Application form, essay, recommendations or references, statement of need. *Deadline:* March 31.

Contact: Bernadette Bailey, Scholarship Coordinator
American Federation of Teachers
555 New Jersey Avenue, NW
Washington, DC 20001
Phone: 202-879-4481
Fax: 202-879-4406
E-mail: bbailey@aft.org

AMERICAN FOUNDATION FOR THE BLIND

http://www.afb.org/

DELTA GAMMA FOUNDATION FLORENCE MARGARET HARVEY MEMORIAL SCHOLARSHIP

One scholarship of $1000 to an undergraduate or graduate student who has exhibited academic excellence, and is studying in the field of rehabilitation and/or education of persons who are blind or visually impaired. Must submit proof of legal blindness. For additional information and application requirements, refer to website http://www.afb.org/scholarships.asp.

Academic Fields/Career Goals: Education; Therapy/Rehabilitation.

Award: Scholarship for use in freshman, sophomore, junior, or senior years; not renewable. *Number:* 1. *Amount:* $1000.

Eligibility Requirements: Applicant must be visually impaired and enrolled or expecting to enroll full- or part-time at a two-year or four-year institution or university. Applicant must be visually impaired. Available to U.S. citizens.

Application Requirements: Application form, essay, proof of post-secondary acceptance and legal blindness, recommendations or references, transcript. *Deadline:* April 30.

Contact: Dawn Bodrogi, Information Center and Library Coordinator
American Foundation for the Blind
11 Penn Plaza, Suite 300
New York, NY 10001
Phone: 212-502-7661
Fax: 212-502-7771
E-mail: afbinfo@afb.net

RUDOLPH DILLMAN MEMORIAL SCHOLARSHIP

One-time award not open to previous recipients. Four scholarships of $2500 each to undergraduate or graduate students who are studying in the field of rehabilitation and/or education of persons who are blind or visually impaired. One of these grants is specifically for a student who meets all requirements and submits evidence of economic need. Must submit proof of legal blindness. For additional information and application requirements, visit website http://www.afb.org/scholarships.asp.

Academic Fields/Career Goals: Education; Therapy/Rehabilitation.

Award: Scholarship for use in freshman, sophomore, junior, or senior years; not renewable. *Number:* up to 4. *Amount:* $2500.

Eligibility Requirements: Applicant must be visually impaired and enrolled or expecting to enroll full- or part-time at a two-year or four-year institution or university. Applicant must be visually impaired. Available to U.S. citizens.

Application Requirements: Application form, essay, financial need analysis, proof of legal blindness, acceptance letter, recommendations or references, transcript. *Deadline:* April 30.

Contact: Dawn Bodrogi, Information Center and Library Coordinator
American Foundation for the Blind
11 Penn Plaza, Suite 300
New York, NY 10001
Phone: 212-502-7661
Fax: 212-502-7771
E-mail: afbinfo@afb.net

AMERICAN INSTITUTE OF POLISH CULTURE INC.

http://www.ampolinstitute.org/

HARRIET IRSAY SCHOLARSHIP GRANT
• *See page 127*

AMERICAN LEGION AUXILIARY DEPARTMENT OF IOWA

http://www.ialegion.org/ala

AMERICAN LEGION AUXILIARY DEPARTMENT OF IOWA HARRIET HOFFMAN MEMORIAL MERIT AWARD FOR TEACHER TRAINING

One-time award for Iowa residents attending Iowa institutions who are the children, grandchildren, or great-grandchildren of veterans. Preference given to descendants of deceased veterans.

Academic Fields/Career Goals: Education.

Award: Scholarship for use in freshman, sophomore, junior, or senior years; not renewable. *Number:* 1. *Amount:* $400.

Eligibility Requirements: Applicant must be enrolled or expecting to enroll full-time at a four-year institution or university; resident of Iowa

and studying in Iowa. Available to U.S. citizens. Applicant or parent must meet one or more of the following requirements: general military experience; retired from active duty; disabled or killed as a result of military service; prisoner of war; or missing in action.

Application Requirements: Application form, essay, financial need analysis, personal photograph, recommendations or references, self-addressed stamped envelope with application, test scores, transcript. *Deadline:* June 1.

Contact: Marlene Valentine, Secretary and Treasurer
American Legion Auxiliary Department of Iowa
720 Lyon Street
Des Moines, IA 50309
Phone: 515-282-7987
Fax: 515-282-7583
E-mail: alasectreas@ialegion.org

AMERICAN LEGION DEPARTMENT OF MISSOURI

http://www.missourilegion.org/

ERMAN W. TAYLOR MEMORIAL SCHOLARSHIP

Two $500 awards are given annually to a student planning on obtaining a degree in education. Applicants must be unmarried Missouri resident below age 21, and must use the scholarship as a full-time student in an accredited college or university. Must be an unmarried descendant of a veteran having served 90 days on active duty in the Army, Air Force, Navy, Marine Corps, or Coast Guard of the United States, and having an honorable discharge.

Academic Fields/Career Goals: Education.

Award: Scholarship for use in freshman year; not renewable. *Number:* 2. *Amount:* $500.

Eligibility Requirements: Applicant must be high school student; planning to enroll or expecting to enroll full-time at a two-year or four-year institution or university; single and resident of Missouri. Available to U.S. citizens. Applicant or parent must meet one or more of the following requirements: general military experience; retired from active duty; disabled or killed as a result of military service; prisoner of war; or missing in action.

Application Requirements: Application form, discharge certificate, essay, test scores. *Deadline:* April 20.

Contact: John Doane, Chairman
Phone: 417-924-8596
Fax: 573-225-1406
E-mail: info@missourilegion.org

AMERICAN MONTESSORI SOCIETY

http://www.amshq.org/

AMERICAN MONTESSORI SOCIETY TEACHER EDUCATION SCHOLARSHIP FUND

One-time award for aspiring Montessori teacher candidates. Requires verification that applicant has been accepted into an AMS Montessori Teacher Education program. Awards are considered on the basis of financial need, a compelling personal statement, and 3 letters of recommendation.

Academic Fields/Career Goals: Education.

Award: Scholarship for use in freshman, sophomore, junior, senior, or graduate years; not renewable. *Number:* 10–20. *Amount:* $1000–$3000.

Eligibility Requirements: Applicant must be enrolled or expecting to enroll full-time at a two-year or four-year or technical institution or university. Available to U.S. and non-U.S. citizens.

Application Requirements: Application form, essay, financial need analysis. *Deadline:* May 1.

Contact: Abbie Kelly, Director of Teacher Education
American Montessori Society
116 East 16th Street, 6th Floor
New York, NY 10003
Phone: 212-358-1250 Ext. 315
E-mail: abbie@amshq.org

AMERICAN PHYSICAL THERAPY ASSOCIATION

http://www.apta.org/honorsawards

MARY MCMILLAN SCHOLARSHIP AWARD

Students may be nominated from physical therapist assistant education programs and physical therapist professional education programs accredited by the Commission on Accreditation in Physical Therapy Education (CAPTE) of the association. Physical therapist assistant education program students must be enrolled in the final year of study. For physical therapist assistant education programs that have a part-time curriculum, all nominees must be in the final year of the curriculum of that institution. Minimum 3.0 GPA required.

Academic Fields/Career Goals: Education; Health and Medical Sciences; Therapy/Rehabilitation.

Award: Scholarship for use in senior, graduate, or postgraduate years; not renewable. *Number:* 1–6. *Amount:* $3000–$5000.

Eligibility Requirements: Applicant must be enrolled or expecting to enroll full-time at a two-year or four-year institution or university. Applicant or parent of applicant must have employment or volunteer experience in physical therapy/rehabilitation. Applicant must have 3.0 GPA or higher. Available to U.S. citizens.

Application Requirements: Application form, application form may be submitted online, community service, essay, recommendations or references, resume, transcript. *Deadline:* December 1.

Contact: Stephanie Sadowski, Honors and Awards Program Specialist
American Physical Therapy Association
1111 North Fairfax Street
Alexandria, VA 22314
Phone: 800-999-2782 Ext. 3127
Fax: 703-706-8536
E-mail: stephaniesadowski@apta.org

AMERICAN WELDING SOCIETY

http://www.aws.org/

JOHN M. STROPKI STEM SCHOLARSHIP

Awarded to a college undergraduate student. Priority will be given to the sons and daughters of current Lincoln Electric employees in the United States and Canada. Students must have a 3.0 overall GPA, and be attending school full time. One $2,500 scholarship award will be made to any student pursuing a degree as an educator of a STEM subject.

Academic Fields/Career Goals: Education.

Award: Scholarship for use in freshman, sophomore, junior, or senior years; not renewable.

Eligibility Requirements: Applicant must be high school student and planning to enroll or expecting to enroll full-time at a four-year institution. Applicant must have 3.0 GPA or higher. Available to U.S. and Canadian citizens.

Application Requirements: Application form, financial need analysis. *Deadline:* February 15.

Contact: Ms. Vicki Pinsky, Associate Director, Scholarships
American Welding Society
8669 NW 36 Street, #130
Miami, FL 33166
Phone: 305-443-9353 Ext. 212
E-mail: vpinsky@aws.org

ARCTIC INSTITUTE OF NORTH AMERICA

http://www.arctic.ucalgary.ca/

JIM BOURQUE SCHOLARSHIP

One-time award of CAN$1000 to Canadian aboriginal student enrolled in postsecondary training in education, environmental studies, traditional knowledge or telecommunications. Must submit, in 500 words or less, a description of their intended program of study and reasons for their choice of program. Must include most recent high school or college/university transcript; a signed letter of recommendation from a community leader, a statement of financial need which indicates funding already received or expected; and proof of enrollment in, or application to, a post secondary institution. Applicants must also provide proof of

Canadian Aboriginal descent. Applicants are evaluated based on need, relevance of study, achievements, return of investment and overall presentation of the application.

Academic Fields/Career Goals: Education; Environmental Science; Natural Resources; Natural Sciences.

Award: Scholarship for use in freshman, sophomore, junior, or senior years; not renewable. *Number:* 1.

Eligibility Requirements: Applicant must be of Canadian heritage and Canadian citizen; American Indian/Alaska Native; enrolled or expecting to enroll full-time at a four-year institution or university and resident of Alberta, British Columbia, Manitoba, New Brunswick, Newfoundland, Northwest Territories, Nova Scotia, Ontario, Prince Edward Island, Quebec, Saskatchewan, Yukon.

Application Requirements: Essay, financial need analysis. *Deadline:* July 15.

Contact: Melanie Paulson, Administrative Assistant
Phone: 403-220-7515
E-mail: arctic@ucalgary.ca

ARIZONA BUSINESS EDUCATION ASSOCIATION

http://www.azbea.org/

ABEA STUDENT TEACHER SCHOLARSHIPS

Scholarships awarded to future business education teachers. Must be member of ABEA. Must be a student in last semester or two of an undergraduate Arizona business education teacher program at an accredited university or four-year college or in a post-Baccalaureate Arizona business education teacher certification program at an accredited university or four-year college.

Academic Fields/Career Goals: Education.

Award: Scholarship for use in junior or senior years; not renewable. *Number:* up to 3. *Amount:* $500.

Eligibility Requirements: Applicant must be enrolled or expecting to enroll full-time at a four-year institution or university and resident of Arizona. Applicant or parent of applicant must be member of Arizona Business Education Association. Available to U.S. citizens.

Application Requirements: Application form, recommendations or references, resume, transcript. *Deadline:* April 1.

Contact: Shirley Eittreim, Scholarships Committee Chair
Arizona Business Education Association
Northland Pioneer College
PO Box 610
Holbrook, AZ 86025
Phone: 928-532-6151
E-mail: sjeittreim@cybertrails.com

ARMED FORCES COMMUNICATIONS AND ELECTRONICS ASSOCIATION, EDUCATIONAL FOUNDATION

http://www.afcea.org/site/?q=foundation/scholarships

STEM TEACHERS SCHOLARSHIP

• *See page 111*

ARRL FOUNDATION INC.

http://www.arrl.org/

CTRI/CHRIS SEEBER, KA1GEU, MEMORIAL SCHOLARSHIP

One $500 scholarship for a student with active Amateur Radio license who is studying science, science education, math, math education, engineering, or technology at any accredited 2- or 4-year college or university. Student must reside in ARRL New England Division (Connecticut, Rhode Island, Vermont, Maine, New Hampshire).

Academic Fields/Career Goals: Education; Engineering/Technology; Materials Science, Engineering, and Metallurgy; Mathematics; Natural Sciences; Nuclear Science; Physical Sciences.

Award: Scholarship for use in freshman, sophomore, junior, or senior years; not renewable. *Number:* 1. *Amount:* $500.

Eligibility Requirements: Applicant must be enrolled or expecting to enroll full-time at a two-year or four-year institution or university; resident of Connecticut, Maine, New Hampshire, Rhode Island, Vermont and must have an interest in amateur radio. Available to U.S. citizens.

Application Requirements: Application form. *Deadline:* January 31.

Contact: Ms. Mary Hobart, Secretary
Phone: 860-594-0397
E-mail: k1mmh@arrl.org

ASSOCIATION FOR EDUCATION AND REHABILITATION OF THE BLIND AND VISUALLY IMPAIRED

http://www.aerbvi.org/

WILLIAM AND DOROTHY FERRELL SCHOLARSHIP

Nonrenewable scholarship given in even years for postsecondary education leading to career in services for blind or visually impaired. Applicant must submit proof of legal blindness or visual field impairment of 20 percent or less.

Academic Fields/Career Goals: Education; Health and Medical Sciences; Occupational Safety and Health; Therapy/Rehabilitation.

Award: Scholarship for use in freshman, sophomore, junior, senior, or graduate years; not renewable. *Number:* 1–2. *Amount:* $500–$1000.

Eligibility Requirements: Applicant must be visually impaired and enrolled or expecting to enroll full-time at a two-year or four-year institution or university. Applicant must be visually impaired. Available to U.S. and non-U.S. citizens.

Application Requirements: Application form. *Deadline:* March 25.

Contact: Scholarship Coordinator
Association for Education and Rehabilitation of the Blind and Visually Impaired
1703 North Beauregard Street, Suite 440
Alexandria, VA 22311-1744
Phone: 703-671-4500
E-mail: scholarships@aerbvi.org

ASSOCIATION FOR WOMEN GEOSCIENTISTS (AWG)

http://www.awg.org/

AWG ETHNIC MINORITY SCHOLARSHIP
• *See page 241*

AWG MARIA LUISA CRAWFORD FIELD CAMP SCHOLARSHIP
• *See page 117*

AWG SALT LAKE CHAPTER (SLC) RESEARCH SCHOLARSHIP
• *See page 117*

LONE STAR RISING CAREER SCHOLARSHIP
• *See page 242*

ASSOCIATION OF RETIRED TEACHERS OF CONNECTICUT

http://www.artct.org/

ARTC GLEN MOON SCHOLARSHIP

Renewable scholarship to Connecticut high school seniors, who intend to pursue a career in teaching. Must demonstrate a positive financial need.

Academic Fields/Career Goals: Education.

Award: Scholarship for use in freshman year; renewable. *Number:* 2–3. *Amount:* $1500–$2000.

Eligibility Requirements: Applicant must be high school student; planning to enroll or expecting to enroll full- or part-time at a four-year institution or university and resident of Connecticut. Available to U.S. citizens.

Application Requirements: Application form, community service, driver's license, financial need analysis, recommendations or references, test scores, transcript. *Deadline:* March 31.

Contact: Teresa Barton, Scholarship Committee
Phone: 866-343-2782
E-mail: info@ctretiredteachers.org

BETHESDA LUTHERAN COMMUNITIES

http://www.bethesdalutherancommunities.org/scholarships

DEVELOPMENTAL DISABILITIES SCHOLASTIC ACHIEVEMENT SCHOLARSHIP FOR COLLEGE STUDENTS WHO ARE LUTHERAN
• *See page 236*

BULKOFFICESUPPLY.COM

http://www.bulkofficesupply.com

OFFICE SUPPLY SCHOLARSHIP
• *See page 128*

CALIFORNIA STUDENT AID COMMISSION

http://www.csac.ca.gov/

CHILD DEVELOPMENT TEACHER AND SUPERVISOR GRANT PROGRAM
• *See page 190*

CALIFORNIA TEACHERS ASSOCIATION (CTA)

http://www.cta.org/

L. GORDON BITTLE MEMORIAL SCHOLARSHIP

Awards scholarships annually to active SCTA members for study in a teacher preparatory program. Students may reapply each year. Not available to those who are currently working in public schools as members of CTA. Minimum 3.5 GPA.

Academic Fields/Career Goals: Education.

Award: Scholarship for use in freshman, sophomore, junior, senior, or graduate years; not renewable. *Number:* up to 3. *Amount:* $2500.

Eligibility Requirements: Applicant must be enrolled or expecting to enroll full-time at a two-year or four-year institution or university and resident of California. Applicant or parent of applicant must be member of California Teachers Association. Applicant must have 3.5 GPA or higher. Available to U.S. citizens.

Application Requirements: Application form, essay, recommendations or references, transcript. *Deadline:* February 8.

Contact: Janeya Collins, Scholarship Coordinator
California Teachers Association (CTA)
PO Box 921
Burlingame, CA 94011-0921
Phone: 650-552-5468
Fax: 650-552-5001
E-mail: scholarships@cta.org

MARTIN LUTHER KING, JR. MEMORIAL SCHOLARSHIP

Awards for ethnic minority members of the California Teachers Association, their dependent children, and ethnic minority members of Student California Teachers Association who want to pursue degrees or credentials in public education. Minimum 3.5 GPA.

Academic Fields/Career Goals: Education.

Award: Scholarship for use in freshman, sophomore, junior, senior, or graduate years; not renewable. *Amount:* $1000–$2000.

Eligibility Requirements: Applicant must be American Indian/Alaska Native, Asian/Pacific Islander, Black (non-Hispanic), Hispanic; enrolled or expecting to enroll full-time at a two-year or four-year institution or university and resident of California. Applicant or parent of applicant must be member of California Teachers Association. Applicant must have 3.5 GPA or higher. Available to U.S. citizens.

Application Requirements: Application form, essay, financial need analysis, recommendations or references. *Deadline:* March 14.

Contact: Janeya Collins, Scholarship Coordinator
California Teachers Association (CTA)
PO Box 921
Burlingame, CA 94011-0921
Phone: 650-552-5468
Fax: 650-552-5001
E-mail: scholarships@cta.org

CANADIAN INSTITUTE OF UKRAINIAN STUDIES

http://www.cius.ca/

LEO J. KRYSA UNDERGRADUATE SCHOLARSHIP
• *See page 125*

CATCHING THE DREAM

http://www.catchingthedream.org/

MATH, ENGINEERING, SCIENCE, BUSINESS, EDUCATION, COMPUTERS SCHOLARSHIPS
• *See page 162*

NATIVE AMERICAN LEADERSHIP IN EDUCATION (NALE)
• *See page 163*

CONNECTICUT EDUCATION FOUNDATION INC.

http://www.cea.org/cef/

SCHOLARSHIP FOR ETHNIC MINORITY COLLEGE STUDENTS
An award for qualified minority candidates who have been accepted into a teacher preparation program at an accredited Connecticut college or university. Must have a 3.0 GPA.

Academic Fields/Career Goals: Education.

Award: Scholarship for use in freshman, sophomore, junior, or senior years; renewable. *Number:* 1–2. *Amount:* $1000–$2000.

Eligibility Requirements: Applicant must be American Indian/Alaska Native, Asian/Pacific Islander, Black (non-Hispanic), Hispanic; enrolled or expecting to enroll full-time at a two-year or four-year institution or university; resident of Connecticut and studying in Connecticut. Applicant must have 3.0 GPA or higher. Available to U.S. citizens.

Application Requirements: Application form, essay. *Deadline:* May 1.

Contact: Mr. Jeffrey Leake, President
Connecticut Education Foundation Inc.
21 Oak Street, Suite 500
Hartford, CT 06106
Phone: 860-525-5641 Ext. 6308
E-mail: jeffl@cea.org

SCHOLARSHIP FOR MINORITY HIGH SCHOOL STUDENTS
Award for qualified minority candidates who have been accepted into an accredited four-year Connecticut college or university and intend to enter the teaching profession. Must have 3.0 GPA.

Academic Fields/Career Goals: Education.

Award: Scholarship for use in freshman, sophomore, junior, or senior years; renewable. *Number:* 1–2. *Amount:* $1000–$2000.

Eligibility Requirements: Applicant must be American Indian/Alaska Native, Asian/Pacific Islander, Black (non-Hispanic), Hispanic; high school student; planning to enroll or expecting to enroll full-time at a four-year institution or university; resident of Connecticut and studying in Connecticut. Applicant must have 3.0 GPA or higher. Available to U.S. citizens.

Application Requirements: Application form, essay. *Deadline:* May 1.

Contact: Mr. Jeffrey Leake, President
Connecticut Education Foundation Inc.
21 Oak Street, Suite 500
Hartford, CT 06106
Phone: 860-525-5641 Ext. 6308
E-mail: jeffl@cea.org

CONNECTICUT OFFICE OF HIGHER EDUCATION

http://www.ctohe.org

MINORITY TEACHER INCENTIVE GRANT PROGRAM
Program provides up to $5,000 a year for two years of full-time study in a teacher preparation program for the junior or senior year at a Connecticut college or university. Applicant must be African-American, Hispanic/Latino, Asian American or Native American heritage and be nominated by the Education Dean. Program graduates who teach in Connecticut public schools may be eligible for loan reimbursement stipends up to $2,500 per year for up to four years.

Academic Fields/Career Goals: Education.

Award: Grant for use in junior or senior years; renewable. *Number:* 72. *Amount:* $2500–$5000.

Eligibility Requirements: Applicant must be American Indian/Alaska Native, Asian/Pacific Islander, Black (non-Hispanic), Hispanic; enrolled or expecting to enroll full-time at a four-year institution or university and studying in Connecticut. Available to U.S. citizens.

Application Requirements: Application form. *Deadline:* October 15.

Contact: Ms. Lynne Goodwin, Executive Assistant
Connecticut Office of Higher Education
39 Woodland Street
Hartford, CT 06105
Phone: 860-947-1855
E-mail: mtip@ctohe.org

CONTINENTAL SOCIETY, DAUGHTERS OF INDIAN WARS

http://www.csdiw.org/

CONTINENTAL SOCIETY, DAUGHTERS OF INDIAN WARS SCHOLARSHIP
Award for a certified Indian tribal member enrolled in an undergraduate degree program in education or social service. Must maintain minimum 3.0 GPA and work with Native Americans in a social service or educational role after graduation. Preference given to those in or entering junior year.

Academic Fields/Career Goals: Education; Social Services.

Award: Scholarship for use in freshman, sophomore, junior, or senior years; not renewable. *Amount:* $5000.

Eligibility Requirements: Applicant must be American Indian/Alaska Native and enrolled or expecting to enroll full-time at a two-year or four-year institution or university. Applicant must have 3.0 GPA or higher. Available to U.S. citizens.

Application Requirements: Application form, essay, financial need analysis. *Deadline:* June 15.

Contact: Mrs. J.B. Richards, II, National Scholarship Chairman
Continental Society, Daughters of Indian Wars
PO Box 6695
Chesterfield, MO 63006-6695
Phone: 636-220-2442
E-mail: leslie@khs65.com

CULTURAL SERVICES OF THE FRENCH EMBASSY

http://www.frenchculture.org/

TEACHING ASSISTANT PROGRAM IN FRANCE
• *See page 104*

DECA (DISTRIBUTIVE EDUCATION CLUBS OF AMERICA)

http://www.deca.org/

HARRY A. APPLEGATE SCHOLARSHIP
• *See page 75*

EASTERN STAR-GRAND CHAPTER OF CALIFORNIA

http://www.oescal.org/

SCHOLARSHIPS FOR EDUCATION, BUSINESS AND RELIGION
• *See page 163*

GENERAL BOARD OF HIGHER EDUCATION AND MINISTRY

http://www.gbhem.org

EDITH M. ALLEN SCHOLARSHIP
Scholarship for outstanding African-American graduate or undergraduate students pursuing a degree in education, social work, medicine, and/or other health professions. Must be enrolled at a United Methodist college or university and be an active, full member of the United Methodist Church for at least three years.

Academic Fields/Career Goals: Education; Health and Medical Sciences; Social Services.

Award: Scholarship for use in freshman, sophomore, junior, or senior years; not renewable. *Number:* 2. *Amount:* $1200.

Eligibility Requirements: Applicant must be Methodist; Black (non-Hispanic) and enrolled or expecting to enroll full-time at a four-year institution or university. Available to U.S. citizens.

Application Requirements: Application form, essay, recommendations or references, transcript. *Deadline:* March 1.

Contact: Ms. Marcie Bigord, Assistant Director of Loans & Scholarships
General Board of Higher Education and Ministry
PO Box 340007
Nashville, TN 37203-0007
Phone: 615-340-7388
Fax: 615-340-7529
E-mail: mbigord@gbhem.org

GENERAL FEDERATION OF WOMEN'S CLUBS OF MASSACHUSETTS

http://www.gfwcma.org/

NEWTONVILLE WOMAN'S CLUB SCHOLARSHIP
Applicant must be a senior in a Massachusetts high school in who will enroll in a four-year accredited college or university in a teacher-training program that leads to certification to teach.

Academic Fields/Career Goals: Education.

Award: Scholarship for use in freshman year; not renewable. *Number:* 1. *Amount:* $600.

Eligibility Requirements: Applicant must be high school student; planning to enroll or expecting to enroll full-time at a four-year institution or university and resident of Massachusetts. Available to U.S. citizens.

Application Requirements: Application form, driver's license, essay. *Deadline:* March 1.

Contact: Scholarship Chairman
General Federation of Women's Clubs of Massachusetts
245 Dutton Road
Sudbury, MA 01776
Phone: 978-443-4569
E-mail: gfwcma@aol.com

GEORGIA ASSOCIATION OF EDUCATORS

http://www.gae.org/

GAE GFIE SCHOLARSHIP FOR ASPIRING TEACHERS
Scholarships will be awarded to graduating seniors who currently attend a fully accredited public Georgia high school and will attend a fully accredited Georgia college or university within the next twelve months. Must have a 3.0 GPA. Must submit three letters of recommendation. Must have plans to enter the teaching profession.

Academic Fields/Career Goals: Education.

Award: Scholarship for use in freshman year; not renewable. *Number:* up to 20. *Amount:* $1000.

Eligibility Requirements: Applicant must be enrolled or expecting to enroll full-time at a two-year or four-year institution or university; resident of Georgia and studying in Georgia. Applicant must have 3.0 GPA or higher. Available to U.S. citizens.

Application Requirements: Application form, recommendations or references, transcript. *Deadline:* February 1.

Contact: Sharon Henderson, Staff Associate
Phone: 678-837-1114
Fax: 678-837-1150
E-mail: sharon.henderson@gae.org

GOLDEN APPLE FOUNDATION

http://www.goldenapple.org/

GOLDEN APPLE SCHOLARS OF ILLINOIS
Applicants must be between the ages of 16 and 21 and maintain a GPA of 2.5. Eligible applicants must be residents of Illinois studying education in Illinois. Recipients must agree to teach in an Illinois school school-of-need for 5 years.

Academic Fields/Career Goals: Education.

Award: Scholarship for use in freshman, sophomore, junior, or senior years; renewable. *Number:* 200. *Amount:* $23,000.

Eligibility Requirements: Applicant must be age 16-21; enrolled or expecting to enroll full-time at a two-year or four-year institution or university; resident of Illinois and studying in Illinois. Applicant must have 2.5 GPA or higher. Available to U.S. citizens.

Application Requirements: Application form, essay, interview, personal photograph. *Deadline:* February 15.

Contact: Ms. Patricia Kilduff, Director of Recruitment and Placement
Phone: 312-477-7515
E-mail: kilduff@goldenapple.org

GOLDEN KEY INTERNATIONAL HONOUR SOCIETY

http://www.goldenkey.org/

EDUCATION ACHIEVEMENT AWARDS
Awards members who excel in the study of education. Eligible applicants are undergraduate, graduate and postgraduate members who are currently enrolled in classes at a degree-granting program. One winner will receive a $1000 award. The second place winner will receive $750 and the third place winner will receive $500.

Academic Fields/Career Goals: Education.

Award: Prize for use in freshman, sophomore, junior, senior, graduate, or postgraduate years; not renewable. *Number:* 3. *Amount:* $500–$1000.

Eligibility Requirements: Applicant must be enrolled or expecting to enroll full- or part-time at a four-year institution or university. Available to U.S. and non-U.S. citizens.

Application Requirements: Application form, education related paper or report, entry in a contest, essay, recommendations or references, transcript. *Deadline:* March 3.

Contact: Scholarship Program Administrators
Golden Key International Honour Society
PO Box 23737
Nashville, TN 37202-3737
Phone: 800-377-2401
E-mail: scholarships@goldenkey.org

GREATER KANAWHA VALLEY FOUNDATION

http://www.tgkvf.org/

JOSEPH C. BASILE, II MEMORIAL SCHOLARSHIP FUND

Award for residents of West Virginia who are majoring in education. Must be an undergraduate at a college or university in West Virginia. Award based on financial need.

Academic Fields/Career Goals: Education.

Award: Scholarship for use in freshman, sophomore, junior, or senior years; not renewable. *Number:* 1. *Amount:* $1500.

Eligibility Requirements: Applicant must be enrolled or expecting to enroll full-time at a four-year institution or university; resident of West Virginia and studying in West Virginia. Available to U.S. citizens.

Application Requirements: Application form, essay, financial need analysis, recommendations or references, self-addressed stamped envelope with application, test scores, transcript. *Deadline:* January 15.

Contact: Susan Hoover, Scholarship Coordinator
Greater Kanawha Valley Foundation
900 Lee Street East, 16th Floor
Charleston, WV 25301
E-mail: shoover@tgkvf.org

HAWAII EDUCATION ASSOCIATION

http://www.heaed.com/

HAWAII EDUCATION ASSOCIATION STUDENT TEACHER SCHOLARSHIP

Scholarship available to HEA members, children of HEA members, or grandchildren or legally adopted grandchildren of HEA members. Members must be in good standing and shall have been members for at least one year. Intent is to minimize the need for employment during student teaching semester. Must be enrolled full-time in an undergraduate or post-baccalaureate program in accredited institution of higher learning.

Academic Fields/Career Goals: Education.

Award: Scholarship for use in senior, graduate, or postgraduate years; not renewable. *Number:* up to 2. *Amount:* up to $3000.

Eligibility Requirements: Applicant must be enrolled or expecting to enroll full-time at a four-year institution or university. Applicant or parent of applicant must be member of Hawaii Education Association. Available to U.S. citizens.

Application Requirements: Application, application form, essay, financial need analysis, personal photograph, recommendations or references, transcript. *Deadline:* April 1.

Contact: Laurie Togami, Scholarship Committee
Hawaii Education Association
1953 South Beretania Street, Suite 5C
Honolulu, HI 96826-1304
Phone: 808-949-6657
Fax: 808-944-2032
E-mail: hea.office@heaed.com

HIROSHI BARBARA KIM YAMASHITA HEA SCHOLARSHIP

One $2000 scholarship awarded to full-time undergraduate education majors currently attending an accredited institution of higher learning and intending to teach in a Hawaii public school. Minimum 3.2 GPA required.

Academic Fields/Career Goals: Education.

Award: Scholarship for use in freshman, sophomore, junior, or senior years; not renewable. *Number:* 1. *Amount:* $2000.

Eligibility Requirements: Applicant must be enrolled or expecting to enroll full-time at a four-year institution or university. Available to U.S. citizens.

Application Requirements: Application form, essay, financial need analysis, personal photograph, recommendations or references, test scores, transcript. *Deadline:* April 1.

Contact: Laurie Togami, Staff Specialist
Hawaii Education Association
1953 South Beretania Street, Suite 5C
Honolulu, HI 96826
Phone: 808-949-6657
Fax: 808-944-2032
E-mail: hea.office@heaed.com

ILLINOIS PTA

http://www.illinoispta.org

ILLINOIS PTA SCHOLARSHIP

Scholarship has evolved to encourage Illinois college-bound high school seniors entering the field of education or an education-related field at the college/university of their choice. Minimum 3.0 GPA required.

Academic Fields/Career Goals: Education.

Award: Scholarship for use in freshman year; not renewable. *Number:* 2. *Amount:* $2000–$3000.

Eligibility Requirements: Applicant must be high school student; planning to enroll or expecting to enroll full-time at a four-year institution or university and resident of Illinois. Applicant must have 3.0 GPA or higher. Available to U.S. citizens.

Application Requirements: Application form, application form may be submitted online (http://www.illinoispta.org), community service, essay, personal photograph, resume, test scores, transcript. *Deadline:* February 15.

Contact: Barb Miller, Scholarship Director
Illinois PTA
PO Box 907
Springfield, IL 62705-0907
Phone: 217-528-9617
Fax: 217-528-9490
E-mail: Bmiller@illinoispta.org

ILLINOIS STUDENT ASSISTANCE COMMISSION (ISAC)

http://www.isac.org/

MINORITY TEACHERS OF ILLINOIS SCHOLARSHIP PROGRAM

Award for minority students intending to become school teachers; teaching commitment attached to receipt. Number of scholarships and the individual dollar amounts vary.

Academic Fields/Career Goals: Education.

Award: Scholarship for use in freshman, sophomore, junior, senior, graduate, or postgraduate years; not renewable.

Eligibility Requirements: Applicant must be American Indian/Alaska Native, Asian/Pacific Islander, Black (non-Hispanic), Hispanic; enrolled or expecting to enroll full- or part-time at a two-year or four-year institution or university; resident of Illinois and studying in Illinois. Available to U.S. citizens.

Application Requirements: Application form. *Deadline:* March 1.

Contact: ISAC Call Center Representative
Illinois Student Assistance Commission (ISAC)
1755 Lake Cook Road
Deerfield, IL 60015-5209
Phone: 800-899-4722
E-mail: isac.studentservices@isac.illinois.gov

INDIANA RETIRED TEACHER'S ASSOCIATION (IRTA)

http://www.retiredteachers.org/

INDIANA RETIRED TEACHERS FOUNDATION SCHOLARSHIP

Scholarship available to college sophomores or juniors who are enrolled full-time in an education program at an Indiana college or university for a baccalaureate degree. The applicant must be the child, grandchild, legal dependent or spouse of an active, retired or deceased member of the Indiana State Teachers Retirement Fund and Indiana Retired Teachers Association.

Academic Fields/Career Goals: Education.

Award: Scholarship for use in sophomore or junior years; not renewable. *Number:* 10. *Amount:* $2000.

Eligibility Requirements: Applicant must be physically disabled; enrolled or expecting to enroll full-time at a four-year institution or university; resident of Indiana and studying in Indiana. Applicant or parent of applicant must have employment or volunteer experience in teaching/education. Applicant must be physically disabled. Available to U.S. citizens.

Application Requirements: Application form, community service, essay, financial need analysis. *Deadline:* April 28.

Contact: Executive Director
Indiana Retired Teacher's Association (IRTA)
150 West Market Street, Suite 610
Indianapolis, IN 46204-2812
Phone: 888-454-9333

INTERNATIONAL LITERACY ASSOCIATION

https://literacyworldwide.org/home

JEANNE S. CHALL RESEARCH FELLOWSHIP

This fellowship is a US$5,000 grant established to encourage and support reading research by promising scholars. Its special emphasis is to support research efforts in the following areas: beginning reading (theory, research, and practice that improves the effectiveness of learning to read); readability (methods of predicting the difficulty of texts); reading difficulty (diagnosis, treatment, and prevention); stages of reading development; the relation of vocabulary to reading; and diagnosing and teaching adults with limited reading ability. Applicants must be ILA members.

Academic Fields/Career Goals: Education; Literature/English/Writing; Special Education.

Award: Grant for use in senior, graduate, or postgraduate years; not renewable. *Number:* 1. *Amount:* $5000.

Eligibility Requirements: Applicant must be enrolled or expecting to enroll full- or part-time at a four-year institution or university. Applicant or parent of applicant must have employment or volunteer experience in teaching/education. Available to U.S. and non-U.S. citizens.

Application Requirements: Application form. *Deadline:* January 15.

Contact: Wendy Logan, Special Projects Associate
E-mail: ILAAwards@reading.org

INTERNATIONAL TECHNOLOGY EDUCATION ASSOCIATION

http://www.iteaconnect.org/

INTERNATIONAL TECHNOLOGY EDUCATION ASSOCIATION UNDERGRADUATE SCHOLARSHIP IN TECHNOLOGY EDUCATION

A scholarship for undergraduate students pursuing a degree in technology education and technological studies. Applicants must be members of the association.

Academic Fields/Career Goals: Education; Engineering/Technology; Science, Technology, and Society.

Award: Scholarship for use in freshman, sophomore, junior, or senior years; not renewable. *Number:* 3. *Amount:* $1000.

Eligibility Requirements: Applicant must be enrolled or expecting to enroll full-time at a four-year institution or university. Applicant or parent of applicant must be member of International Technology Education Association. Applicant must have 2.5 GPA or higher. Available to U.S. and non-U.S. citizens.

Application Requirements: Application form, recommendations or references, resume, transcript. *Deadline:* December 1.

Contact: Scholarship Committee
International Technology Education Association
1914 Association Drive, Suite 201
Reston, VA 20191
Phone: 703-860-2100
Fax: 703-860-0353
E-mail: iteaordr@iris.org

JACK J. ISGUR FOUNDATION

www.isgur.org

JACK J. ISGUR FOUNDATION SCHOLARSHIP

• See page 129

KANSAS BOARD OF REGENTS

http://www.kansasregents.org/

KANSAS TEACHER SERVICE SCHOLARSHIP

Scholarship to encourage talented students to enter the teaching profession and teach in Kansas in specific curriculum areas or in underserved areas of Kansas. Students must be Kansas residents attending a postsecondary institution in Kansas. For more details, refer to website http://www.kansasregents.org.

Academic Fields/Career Goals: Education.

Award: Scholarship for use in junior, senior, or graduate years; renewable. *Amount:* $2206–$5514.

Eligibility Requirements: Applicant must be enrolled or expecting to enroll full- or part-time at a four-year institution or university; resident of Kansas and studying in Kansas. Applicant must have 3.0 GPA or higher. Available to U.S. citizens.

Application Requirements: Application form, essay, financial need analysis. *Fee:* $12. *Deadline:* May 1.

Contact: Diane Lindeman, Director of Student Financial Assistance
Kansas Board of Regents
1000 SW Jackson, Suite 520
Topeka, KS 66612
Phone: 785-430-4255
Fax: 785-430-4233
E-mail: dlindeman@ksbor.org

MARYLAND STATE HIGHER EDUCATION COMMISSION

http://www.mhec.state.md.us/

JANET L. HOFFMANN LOAN ASSISTANCE REPAYMENT PROGRAM

Provides assistance for repayment of loan debt to Maryland residents working full-time in nonprofit organizations and state or local governments. Must submit Employment Verification Form and Lender Verification Form.

Academic Fields/Career Goals: Education; Law/Legal Services; Nursing; Social Services; Therapy/Rehabilitation.

Award: Grant for use in freshman, sophomore, junior, or senior years; not renewable. *Number:* up to 700. *Amount:* $1500–$10,000.

Eligibility Requirements: Applicant must be enrolled or expecting to enroll full-time at a four-year institution or university; resident of Maryland and studying in Maryland. Applicant or parent of applicant must have employment or volunteer experience in government/politics. Available to U.S. citizens.

Application Requirements: Application form, IRS 1040 form, transcript. *Deadline:* September 30.

Contact: Tamika McKelvin, Office of Student Financial Assistance
Maryland State Higher Education Commission
839 Bestgate Road, Suite 400
Annapolis, MD 21401
Phone: 410-260-4546
Fax: 410-260-3203
E-mail: tmckelvil@mhec.state.md.us

MASSACHUSETTS OFFICE OF STUDENT FINANCIAL ASSISTANCE

http://www.osfa.mass.edu/

EARLY CHILDHOOD EDUCATORS SCHOLARSHIP PROGRAM

Scholarship to provide financial assistance for currently employed early childhood educators and providers who enroll in an associate or bachelor degree program in Early Childhood Education or related programs.

Awards are not based on financial need. Individuals taking their first college-level ECE course are eligible for 100 percent tuition, while subsequent ECE courses are awarded at 50 percent tuition. Can be used for one class each semester.

Academic Fields/Career Goals: Education.

Award: Scholarship for use in freshman, sophomore, junior, or senior years; not renewable. *Amount:* $150–$3600.

Eligibility Requirements: Applicant must be enrolled or expecting to enroll full- or part-time at a four-year institution or university. Available to U.S. citizens.

Application Requirements: Application form. *Deadline:* July 1.

Contact: Robert Brun, Director of Scholarships and Grants
Phone: 617-727-9420
Fax: 617-727-0667
E-mail: osfa@osfa.mass.edu

PARAPROFESSIONAL TEACHER PREPARATION GRANT

Grant providing financial aid assistance to Massachusetts residents, who are currently employed as paraprofessionals in Massachusetts public schools and wish to obtain higher education and become certified as full-time teachers.

Academic Fields/Career Goals: Education.

Award: Grant for use in freshman, sophomore, junior, or senior years; not renewable. *Amount:* $250–$7500.

Eligibility Requirements: Applicant must be enrolled or expecting to enroll full- or part-time at a two-year or four-year institution or university and resident of Massachusetts. Available to U.S. citizens.

Application Requirements: Application form, FAFSA. *Deadline:* August 1.

Contact: Robert Brun, Director of Scholarships and Grants
Phone: 617-727-9420
Fax: 617-727-0667
E-mail: osfa@osfa.mass.edu

MICHAEL MOODY FITNESS

http://www.michaelmoodyfitness.com/

MICHAEL MOODY FITNESS SCHOLARSHIP

The Michael Moody Fitness Scholarship offers a college scholarship of $1,500 to a high school senior, undergraduate, or graduate student who has demonstrated outstanding achievement, participation and leadership in school activities and work experience, and interest in pursuing a career in the health and fitness related fields. She or he may apply and use the money for education-related expenses, including tuition, fees, books, supplies, room, and board. The scholarship is sponsored by Michael Moody Fitness. The 2017 program will be accepting scholarship applications from October 1st, 2016 until 1,000 scholarship applications are submitted or April 15th, 2017, whichever comes first. Your scholarship application MUST be one of the first 1,000 submitted by the deadline date. Please visit http://www.michaelmoodyfitness.com/student-scholarship-chicago/ for more details.

Academic Fields/Career Goals: Education; Food Science/Nutrition; Health and Medical Sciences; Health Information Management/Technology; Public Health; Sports-Related/Exercise Science; Therapy/Rehabilitation.

Award: Scholarship for use in freshman, sophomore, junior, senior, or graduate years; not renewable. *Number:* 1. *Amount:* $1500.

Eligibility Requirements: Applicant must be enrolled or expecting to enroll full-time at a two-year or four-year institution or university. Available to U.S. and non-U.S. citizens.

Application Requirements: Application form. *Deadline:* July 15.

Contact: Michael Moody
Michael Moody Fitness
900 N. North Branch St.
Chicago, IL 60642
Phone: 773-4848094
E-mail: michael@michaelmoodyfitness.com

NASA RHODE ISLAND SPACE GRANT CONSORTIUM

http://brown/initiatives/ri-space-grant

NASA RISGC SUMMER SCHOLARSHIP FOR UNDERGRADUATE STUDENTS
• See page 143

NATIONAL ASSOCIATION FOR CAMPUS ACTIVITIES

http://www.naca.org/

NATIONAL ASSOCIATION FOR CAMPUS ACTIVITIES MID ATLANTIC HIGHER EDUCATION RESEARCH SCHOLARSHIP
• See page 171

NATIONAL COUNCIL OF TEACHERS OF MATHEMATICS

http://www.nctm.org/

PROSPECTIVE SECONDARY TEACHER COURSE WORK SCHOLARSHIPS

Grant provides financial support to college students preparing for teaching secondary school mathematics. Award of $10,000 will be granted in two phases, with $5000 for the recipient's third year of full-time study, and $5000 for fourth year. Must be student members of NCTM and cannot reapply. Must submit proposal, essay, letters of recommendation, and transcripts.

Academic Fields/Career Goals: Education; Mathematics.

Award: Scholarship for use in junior or senior years; not renewable. *Number:* 2. *Amount:* up to $5000.

Eligibility Requirements: Applicant must be enrolled or expecting to enroll full-time at a four-year institution or university. Available to U.S. and non-U.S. citizens.

Application Requirements: Application form, essay, recommendations or references, transcript, written proposal. *Deadline:* May 9.

Contact: Mathematics Education Trust
Phone: 703-620-9840 Ext. 2112
Fax: 703-476-2970
E-mail: exec@nctm.org

NATIONAL INSTITUTE FOR LABOR RELATIONS RESEARCH

http://www.nilrr.org/

APPLEGATE/JACKSON/PARKS FUTURE TEACHER SCHOLARSHIP

Scholarship available to all education majors currently attending institution of higher learning in the United States. High school seniors accepted into a teacher education program may also apply under certain conditions. Award is based on an essay demonstrating knowledge of and interest in the issue of compulsory unionism in education. Specify "Education" or "Future Teacher Scholarship" on any correspondence.

Academic Fields/Career Goals: Education; Special Education.

Award: Scholarship for use in freshman, sophomore, junior, senior, graduate, or postgraduate years; not renewable. *Number:* 1. *Amount:* $1000.

Eligibility Requirements: Applicant must be enrolled or expecting to enroll full- or part-time at a four-year institution or university. Available to U.S. citizens.

Application Requirements: Application form, essay. *Deadline:* December 31.

Contact: Cathy Jones, Scholarship Coordinator
National Institute for Labor Relations Research
5211 Port Royal Road
Springfield, VA 22151
Phone: 703-321-9606 Ext. 2247
E-mail: clj@nrtw.org

NORTH CAROLINA ASSOCIATION OF EDUCATORS

http://www.ncae.org/

MARY MORROW-EDNA RICHARDS SCHOLARSHIP

One-time award for junior year of study in four-year education degree program. Preference given to members of the student branch of the North Carolina Association of Educators. Must be North Carolina resident attending a North Carolina institution. Must agree to teach in North Carolina for two years after graduation. Must be a junior in college when application is filed.

Academic Fields/Career Goals: Education.

Award: Scholarship for use in senior year; not renewable. *Number:* 3–8. *Amount:* up to $1000.

Eligibility Requirements: Applicant must be enrolled or expecting to enroll full-time at a four-year institution or university; resident of North Carolina and studying in North Carolina. Applicant or parent of applicant must be member of Other Student Academic Clubs. Available to U.S. citizens.

Application Requirements: Application form, essay, financial need analysis, recommendations or references, transcript. *Deadline:* January 13.

Contact: Annette Montgomery, Communications Secretary
Phone: 800-662-7924
Fax: 919-839-8229
E-mail: annette.montgomery@ncae.org

OKLAHOMA STATE REGENTS FOR HIGHER EDUCATION

http://www.okhighered.org/

FUTURE TEACHER SCHOLARSHIP-OKLAHOMA

Open to outstanding Oklahoma high school graduates who agree to teach in shortage areas. Must rank in top 15 percent of graduating class or score above 85th percentile on ACT or similar test, or be accepted in an educational program. Students nominated by institution. Reapply to renew. Must attend college/university in Oklahoma.

Academic Fields/Career Goals: Education.

Award: Scholarship for use in freshman, sophomore, junior, senior, or graduate years; not renewable. *Amount:* $500–$1500.

Eligibility Requirements: Applicant must be enrolled or expecting to enroll full- or part-time at a two-year or four-year institution or university; resident of Oklahoma and studying in Oklahoma. Available to U.S. citizens.

Application Requirements: Application form, essay.

Contact: Scholarship Programs Coordinator
Oklahoma State Regents for Higher Education
PO Box 108850
Oklahoma City, OK 73101-8850
Phone: 800-858-1840
E-mail: studentinfo@osrhe.edu

OREGON PTA

http://www.oregonpta.org/

TEACHER EDUCATION SCHOLARSHIP

Nonrenewable scholarships to high school seniors or college students who are Oregon residents who want to teach in Oregon at an elementary or secondary school. The scholarship may be used at any Oregon public college or university that trains teachers or that transfers credits in education.

Academic Fields/Career Goals: Education.

Award: Scholarship for use in freshman, sophomore, junior, or senior years; not renewable. *Amount:* $500.

Eligibility Requirements: Applicant must be enrolled or expecting to enroll full-time at a two-year or four-year institution or university; resident of Oregon and studying in Oregon. Available to U.S. citizens.

Application Requirements: Application form, essay, recommendations or references, self-addressed stamped envelope with application, test scores, transcript. *Deadline:* March 21.

Contact: Scholarship Committee
Oregon PTA
4506 Southeast Belmont Street, Suite 108-B
Portland, OR 97215
Fax: 503-234-6024
E-mail: or_office@pta.org

OREGON STUDENT ASSISTANCE COMMISSION

http://www.GetCollegeFunds.org/

HARRIET A. SIMMONS SCHOLARSHIP

One-time award available to Oregon residents who are enrolled in an elementary or secondary education program in an Oregon college or university, entering senior or fifth-year, or graduate students in a fifth year for elementary or secondary teaching certificate.

Academic Fields/Career Goals: Education.

Award: Scholarship for use in senior or graduate years; not renewable.

Eligibility Requirements: Applicant must be enrolled or expecting to enroll full-time at a four-year institution or university; resident of Oregon and studying in Oregon. Available to U.S. citizens.

Application Requirements: Application form, financial need analysis. *Deadline:* March 1.

Contact: Melissa Adams, Scholarship Processing Coordinator
Phone: 541-687-7409
E-mail: melissa.adams@hecc.oregon.gov

JAMES CARLSON MEMORIAL SCHOLARSHIP

One-time award for elementary or secondary education majors entering the final year of their program, or graduate students in fifth year for elementary or secondary certificate. Applicants may qualify according to one of the following: (1) Diverse environments (essay required); (2) dependents of Oregon Education Association members (essay recommended); or (3) students committed to teaching autistic children (essay recommended).

Academic Fields/Career Goals: Education; Special Education.

Award: Scholarship for use in senior or graduate years; not renewable.

Eligibility Requirements: Applicant must be enrolled or expecting to enroll full-time at a four-year institution or university and resident of Oregon. Available to U.S. citizens.

Application Requirements: Application form, essay, financial need analysis. *Deadline:* March 1.

Contact: Melissa Adams, Scholarship Processing Coordinator
Phone: 541-687-7409
E-mail: melissa.adams@hecc.oregon.gov

OREGON COLLEGE SAVINGS PLAN EDUCATION CELEBRATION SCHOLARSHIP

One-time award for education majors studying at least half-time at Oregon public or nonprofit schools. Preference given to college seniors or 5th-year seniors seeking MAT or 2nd-year community college students pursuing AAOT or equivalent. High school seniors must have at least a 3.0 GPA (3.4 preferred) and college students must have a minimum GPA of 3.25. Awardees must be willing to participate in publicity with Oregon 529 College Savings Network. Apply/compete annually.

Academic Fields/Career Goals: Education.

Award: Scholarship for use in freshman, sophomore, junior, senior, or graduate years; not renewable.

Eligibility Requirements: Applicant must be enrolled or expecting to enroll full- or part-time at a two-year or four-year institution or university and studying in Oregon. Available to U.S. citizens.

Application Requirements: Application form, financial need analysis. *Deadline:* March 1.

Contact: Melissa Adams, Scholarship Processing Coordinator
Phone: 541-687-7409
E-mail: melissa.adams@hecc.oregon.gov

PADDLE CANADA

https://www.paddlecanada.com/

BILL MASON SCHOLARSHIP FUND

The Bill Mason Memorial Scholarship Fund is a tribute to the late Bill Mason, a Canadian recognized both nationally and internationally as an avid canoeist, environmentalist, filmmaker, photographer, artist and public speaker. The scholarship is intended to incorporate some of the characteristics that made Bill Mason unique and to help ensure that the memory, spirit and ideals that he represented are kept fresh in the minds of Canadians. Applicants must demonstrate experience and competency in any or all of the following: canoeing and kayaking skills, wilderness travel experience, wilderness leadership and guiding, environmental issues, communication skills.

Academic Fields/Career Goals: Education; Environmental Science; Natural Resources; Natural Sciences; Recreation, Parks, Leisure Studies; Sports-Related/Exercise Science.

Award: Scholarship for use in sophomore, junior, or senior years; not renewable. *Number:* up to 1. *Amount:* $943.

Eligibility Requirements: Applicant must be Canadian citizen; enrolled or expecting to enroll full-time at a two-year or four-year institution or university; resident of Alberta, British Columbia, Manitoba, New Brunswick, Newfoundland, Northwest Territories, Nova Scotia, Ontario, Prince Edward Island, Quebec, Saskatchewan, Yukon and studying in Alberta, British Columbia, Manitoba, New Brunswick, Newfoundland, Northwest Territories, Nova Scotia, Ontario, Prince Edward Island, Quebec, Saskatchewan, Yukon. Applicant must have 3.0 GPA or higher.

Application Requirements: Application form, community service, driver's license, entry in a contest, financial need analysis, resume, transcript. *Deadline:* August 30.

Contact: Mr. Graham Ketcheson, Executive Director
Paddle Canada
PO Box 126 Station Main
Kingston, ON K7L 4V6
CAN
Phone: 888-252 6292
E-mail: info@paddlingcanada.com

PI LAMBDA THETA INC.

http://www.pilambda.org/

DISTINGUISHED STUDENT SCHOLAR AWARD

The award is presented in recognition of an education major who has displayed leadership potential and a strong dedication to education. Award given out in odd years. Minimum 3.5 GPA required.

Academic Fields/Career Goals: Education.

Award: Prize for use in freshman, sophomore, junior, or senior years; not renewable. *Number:* 1. *Amount:* $500.

Eligibility Requirements: Applicant must be enrolled or expecting to enroll full- or part-time at a four-year institution or university and must have an interest in leadership. Applicant or parent of applicant must have employment or volunteer experience in community service. Applicant must have 3.5 GPA or higher. Available to U.S. and non-U.S. citizens.

Application Requirements: 2 letters of support from faculty members other than the nominator, letter of endorsement from the nominee's chapter, application form, recommendations or references, resume, transcript. *Deadline:* April 16.

Contact: Scholarships
Pi Lambda Theta Inc.
PO Box 7888
Bloomington, IN 47407-7888
Phone: 812-339-1156
Fax: 812-339-0018
E-mail: scholarships@pdkintl.org

GRADUATE STUDENT SCHOLAR AWARD

The award is presented in recognition of an outstanding graduate student who is an education major. Award given out in odd years. Minimum 3.5 GPA required.

Academic Fields/Career Goals: Education.

Award: Prize for use in senior or graduate years; not renewable. *Number:* 1. *Amount:* $1000.

Eligibility Requirements: Applicant must be enrolled or expecting to enroll full- or part-time at a four-year institution or university and must have an interest in leadership. Applicant or parent of applicant must have employment or volunteer experience in community service. Applicant must have 3.5 GPA or higher. Available to U.S. and non-U.S. citizens.

Application Requirements: Application form, essay, letter of endorsement from nominee's chapter, recommendations or references, resume, transcript. *Deadline:* April 16.

Contact: Scholarships
Pi Lambda Theta Inc.
PO Box 7888
Bloomington, IN 47407-7888
Phone: 812-339-1156
Fax: 812-339-0018
E-mail: scholarships@pdkintl.org

NADEEN BURKEHOLDER WILLIAMS MUSIC SCHOLARSHIP

The scholarship provides $1000 to an outstanding K-12 teacher who is pursuing a graduate degree at an accredited college or university and who is either a music education teacher or applies music systematically in teaching another subject. Minimum 3.5 GPA required.

Academic Fields/Career Goals: Education; Music.

Award: Scholarship for use in freshman, sophomore, junior, senior, or graduate years; not renewable. *Number:* up to 1. *Amount:* $1000.

Eligibility Requirements: Applicant must be enrolled or expecting to enroll full- or part-time at a four-year institution or university and must have an interest in music. Applicant or parent of applicant must have employment or volunteer experience in teaching/education. Applicant must have 3.5 GPA or higher. Available to U.S. and non-U.S. citizens.

Application Requirements: Application form, essay, portfolio, recommendations or references, resume. *Deadline:* April 16.

Contact: Scholarships
Pi Lambda Theta Inc.
PO Box 7888
Bloomington, IN 47407-7888
Phone: 812-339-1156
Fax: 812-339-0018
E-mail: scholarships@pdkintl.org

STUDENT SUPPORT SCHOLARSHIP

The scholarship is available to current members of Pi Lambda Theta who will be a full-time or part-time student enrolled in a minimum of three semester hours at a regionally accredited institution during the year following the award. Minimum 3.5 GPA required.

Academic Fields/Career Goals: Education.

Award: Scholarship for use in sophomore, junior, senior, graduate, or postgraduate years; not renewable. *Number:* 1–30. *Amount:* $1500.

Eligibility Requirements: Applicant must be enrolled or expecting to enroll full- or part-time at a two-year or four-year or technical institution or university. Applicant or parent of applicant must be member of Greek Organization. Applicant must have 3.5 GPA or higher. Available to U.S. and non-U.S. citizens.

Application Requirements: Application form, essay, transcript. *Deadline:* April 16.

Contact: Scholarships
Pi Lambda Theta Inc.
PO Box 7888
Bloomington, IN 47407-7888
Phone: 812-339-1156
Fax: 812-339-0018
E-mail: scholarships@pdkintl.org

TOBIN SORENSON PHYSICAL EDUCATION SCHOLARSHIP

The scholarship provides $1000 for tuition to an outstanding student who intends to pursue a career at the K-12 level as a physical education teacher, adaptive physical education teacher, coach, recreational therapist, dance therapist, or similar professional focusing on teaching the knowledge and use of the human body. Awarded in odd years only. Minimum 3.5 GPA required.

Academic Fields/Career Goals: Education; Sports-Related/Exercise Science; Therapy/Rehabilitation.

Award: Scholarship for use in sophomore, junior, senior, or graduate years; not renewable. *Number:* 1. *Amount:* $1000.

Eligibility Requirements: Applicant must be enrolled or expecting to enroll full- or part-time at a two-year or four-year institution or university. Applicant must have 3.5 GPA or higher. Available to U.S. and non-U.S. citizens.

Application Requirements: Application form, recommendations or references, resume, transcript. *Deadline:* April 16.

Contact: Scholarships
Pi Lambda Theta Inc.
PO Box 7888
Bloomington, IN 47407-7888
Phone: 812-339-1156
Fax: 812-339-0018
E-mail: scholarships@pdkintl.org

PRESBYTERIAN CHURCH (USA)

http://www.pcusa.org/financialaid

STUDENT OPPORTUNITY SCHOLARSHIP

Designed to assist undergraduate students with their sophomore, junior and senior year of college. Restricted to members of the Presbyterian Church (USA).

Academic Fields/Career Goals: Education; Health and Medical Sciences; Religion/Theology; Social Sciences; Social Services.

Award: Scholarship for use in sophomore, junior, or senior years; renewable. *Number:* 68. *Amount:* up to $3000.

Eligibility Requirements: Applicant must be Presbyterian and enrolled or expecting to enroll full-time at a four-year institution or university. Applicant must have 2.5 GPA or higher. Available to U.S. citizens.

Application Requirements: Application form, essay, financial need analysis, recommendations or references, resume, transcript. *Deadline:* June 1.

Contact: Ms. Laura Bryan, Associate, Financial Aid for Studies
Presbyterian Church (USA)
100 Witherspoon Street
Louisville, KY 40202
Phone: 800-728-7228 Ext. 5735
Fax: 502-569-8766
E-mail: finaid@pcusa.org

SARAH KLENKE MEMORIAL TEACHING SCHOLARSHIP

http://www.sarahklenkescholarship.org/

SARAH ELIZABETH KLENKE MEMORIAL TEACHING SCHOLARSHIP

Scholarship for deserving young adults to achieve the goal of becoming teachers. Must have a 2.0 GPA or higher, participate in JROTC or a team sport, and a desire to major in education.

Academic Fields/Career Goals: Education.

Award: Scholarship for use in freshman or senior years; not renewable. *Number:* 1. *Amount:* $1000.

Eligibility Requirements: Applicant must be enrolled or expecting to enroll full-time at a two-year or four-year institution or university. Available to U.S. and non-U.S. citizens.

Application Requirements: Application form, essay, letter from coach or teacher confirming participation in ROTC or team sport, recommendations or references. *Deadline:* April 15.

Contact: William Klenke, Scholarship Committee
Sarah Klenke Memorial Teaching Scholarship
9108 Charred Oak Drive
Bethesda, MD 20817
Phone: 202-412-2812
E-mail: wjk40@yahoo.com

THE SOCIETY FOR THE SCIENTIFIC STUDY OF SEXUALITY

http://www.sexscience.org/

THE SOCIETY FOR THE SCIENTIFIC STUDY OF SEXUALITY STUDENT RESEARCH GRANT

• See page 109

SOUTH DAKOTA BOARD OF REGENTS

http://www.sdbor.edu/

HAINES MEMORIAL SCHOLARSHIP

One-time scholarship for South Dakota public university students who are sophomores, juniors, or seniors having at least a 2.5 GPA and majoring in a teacher education program. Must include resume with application. Must be South Dakota resident.

Academic Fields/Career Goals: Education.

Award: Scholarship for use in sophomore, junior, or senior years; not renewable. *Number:* 1. *Amount:* $2150.

Eligibility Requirements: Applicant must be enrolled or expecting to enroll full-time at an institution or university; resident of South Dakota and studying in South Dakota. Applicant must have 3.5 GPA or higher. Available to U.S. citizens.

Application Requirements: Application form, essay, resume, typed statement describing personal philosophy and philosophy of education. *Deadline:* February 8.

Contact: Dr. Paul Turman, System Vice President for Research and Economic Development
South Dakota Board of Regents
301 East Capital Avenue, Suite 200
Pierre, SD 57501
Phone: 605-773-3455
Fax: 605-773-2422
E-mail: paul.turman@sdbor.edu

SOUTH DAKOTA BOARD OF REGENTS ANNIS I. FOWLER/KADEN SCHOLARSHIP

Scholarship for graduating South Dakota high school seniors to pursue a career in elementary education at a South Dakota public university. Must attend BHSU, BSU, NSU or USD. Applicants must have a cumulative GPA of 3.0 after three years of high school. One-time award.

Academic Fields/Career Goals: Education.

Award: Scholarship for use in freshman year; not renewable. *Number:* 2. *Amount:* $1000.

Eligibility Requirements: Applicant must be high school student; planning to enroll or expecting to enroll full-time at a four-year institution or university; resident of South Dakota and studying in South Dakota. Applicant must have 3.0 GPA or higher. Available to U.S. citizens.

Application Requirements: ACT scores, application form, essay, recommendations or references, test scores, transcript. *Deadline:* February 15.

Contact: Dr. Paul Turman, System Vice President for Research and Economic Development
South Dakota Board of Regents
301 East Capital Avenue, Suite 200
Pierre, SD 57501
Phone: 605-773-3455
Fax: 605-773-2422
E-mail: paul.turman@sdbor.edu

STRAIGHTFORWARD MEDIA

http://www.straightforwardmedia.com/

STRAIGHTFORWARD MEDIA TEACHER SCHOLARSHIP

Scholarship of $500 for students planning to be teachers of any kind and at any level. Must be U.S. citizen. Awarded four times per year. Deadlines are January 14, April 14, July 14, and October 14. For more information, see website at http://www.straightforwardmedia.com/education/form.php.

Academic Fields/Career Goals: Education; Special Education.

Award: Scholarship for use in freshman, sophomore, junior, or senior years; not renewable. *Number:* 4. *Amount:* $500.

Eligibility Requirements: Applicant must be enrolled or expecting to enroll full- or part-time at a two-year or four-year or technical institution or university. Available to U.S. citizens.

Application Requirements: Essay. *Deadline:* varies.

Contact: Scholarship Committee
Phone: 605-348-3042

TEACHER.ORG

http://www.teacher.org

"INSPIRE OUR FUTURE" $2,500 SCHOLARSHIP

Teacher.org offers a $2500 scholarship for college students studying to become teachers or work in the field of education.

Academic Fields/Career Goals: Education.

Award: Scholarship for use in sophomore, junior, senior, graduate, or postgraduate years; not renewable. *Number:* 1. *Amount:* $2500.

Eligibility Requirements: Applicant must be enrolled or expecting to enroll full- or part-time at a two-year or four-year or technical institution or university. Applicant must have 3.5 GPA or higher. Available to U.S. citizens.

Application Requirements: Application form, application form may be submitted online (http://www.teacher.org), essay, transcript. *Deadline:* April 1.

Contact: Salpy Baharian, Co-founder
Teacher.org
7120 Hayvenhurst Avenue
Van Nuys, CA 91406
Phone: 818-860-8620
E-mail: scholarships@teacher.org

TENNESSEE EDUCATION ASSOCIATION

http://www.teateachers.org/

TEA DON SAHLI-KATHY WOODALL FUTURE TEACHERS OF AMERICA SCHOLARSHIP

Scholarship is available to a high school senior planning to major in education, attending a high school which has an FTA Chapter affiliated with TEA, and planning to enroll in a Tennessee college.

Academic Fields/Career Goals: Education.

Award: Scholarship for use in freshman year; not renewable. *Number:* 1. *Amount:* $1000.

Eligibility Requirements: Applicant must be high school student; planning to enroll or expecting to enroll full-time at a four-year institution or university; resident of Tennessee and studying in Tennessee. Available to U.S. citizens.

Application Requirements: Application form, essay. *Deadline:* March 1.

Contact: Jeanette DeMain
Tennessee Education Association
801 Second Avenue North
Nashville, TN 37201
Phone: 615-242-8392 Ext. 210
E-mail: jdemain@tnea.org

TEA DON SAHLI-KATHY WOODALL MINORITY SCHOLARSHIP

Scholarship is available to a minority high school senior planning to major in education and planning to enroll in a Tennessee college. Application must be made by an FTA Chapter, or by the student with the recommendation of an active TEA member.

Academic Fields/Career Goals: Education.

Award: Scholarship for use in freshman year; not renewable. *Number:* 1. *Amount:* $1000.

Eligibility Requirements: Applicant must be American Indian/Alaska Native, Asian/Pacific Islander, Black (non-Hispanic), Hispanic; high school student; planning to enroll or expecting to enroll full-time at a four-year institution or university; resident of Tennessee and studying in Tennessee. Available to U.S. citizens.

Application Requirements: Application form, essay. *Deadline:* March 1.

Contact: Jeanette DeMain
Tennessee Education Association
801 Second Avenue North
Nashville, TN 37201
Phone: 615-242-8392 Ext. 210
E-mail: jdemain@tnea.org

TEA DON SAHLI-KATHY WOODALL SONS AND DAUGHTERS SCHOLARSHIP

Scholarship is available to a TEA member's child who is a high school senior, undergraduate or graduate student, and is planning to enroll, or is already enrolled, in a Tennessee college, majoring in education.

Academic Fields/Career Goals: Education.

Award: Scholarship for use in freshman, sophomore, junior, senior, or graduate years; not renewable. *Number:* 1. *Amount:* $1000.

Eligibility Requirements: Applicant must be enrolled or expecting to enroll full-time at a four-year institution or university; resident of Tennessee and studying in Tennessee. Applicant or parent of applicant must be member of Tennessee Education Association. Applicant or parent of applicant must have employment or volunteer experience in teaching/education. Available to U.S. citizens.

Application Requirements: Application form, essay. *Deadline:* March 1.

Contact: Jeanette DeMain
Tennessee Education Association
801 Second North
Nashville, TN 37201
Phone: 615-242-8392 Ext. 210
E-mail: jdemain@tnea.org

TEA DON SAHLI-KATHY WOODALL STEA SCHOLARSHIP

Scholarship is available to undergraduate students who are student TEA members. Application must be made through the local STEA Chapter. Amount varies from $500 to $1000.

Academic Fields/Career Goals: Education.

Award: Scholarship for use in freshman, sophomore, junior, or senior years; not renewable. *Number:* 4. *Amount:* $500–$1000.

Eligibility Requirements: Applicant must be enrolled or expecting to enroll full- or part-time at a four-year institution or university; resident of Tennessee and studying in Tennessee. Available to U.S. citizens.

Application Requirements: Application form, essay. *Deadline:* March 1.

Contact: Jeanette DeMain
Tennessee Education Association
801 Second Avenue North
Nashville, TN 37201
Phone: 615-242-8392 Ext. 210
E-mail: jdemain@tnea.org

TENNESSEE STUDENT ASSISTANCE CORPORATION

http://www.tn.gov/collegepays

CHRISTA MCAULIFFE SCHOLARSHIP PROGRAM

Scholarship to assist and support Tennessee students who have demonstrated a commitment to a career in educating the youth of Tennessee. Offered to college seniors for a period of one academic year. Must have a minimum college GPA of 3.5. Must have attained scores on either the ACT or SAT which meet or exceed the national norms. Must be enrolled full time and not be in default or owe repayment on a federal or state student loan. Award is made on a periodic basis as funding becomes available.

Academic Fields/Career Goals: Education.

Award: Scholarship for use in senior year; not renewable.

Eligibility Requirements: Applicant must be enrolled or expecting to enroll full-time at a four-year institution or university; resident of Tennessee and studying in Tennessee. Applicant must have 3.5 GPA or higher. Available to U.S. citizens.

Application Requirements: Application form, essay. *Deadline:* April 1.

Contact: Ms. Kathy Stripling, Grant and Scholarship Analyst
Tennessee Student Assistance Corporation
Parkway Towers
404 James Robertson Parkway, Suite 1510
Nashville, TN 37243-0820
Phone: 615-253-7480
E-mail: kathy.stripling@tn.gov

TKE EDUCATIONAL FOUNDATION

http://www.tke.org/

CARROL C. HALL MEMORIAL SCHOLARSHIP

• See page 115

FRANCIS J. FLYNN MEMORIAL SCHOLARSHIP

Award of $800 for an undergraduate member of TKE who is a full-time student pursuing a degree in mathematics or education. Minimum 2.75 GPA required. Leadership within chapter or campus organizations recognized. Preference will first be given to a member of Theta-Sigma Chapter, but if there is no qualified applicant, the scholarship will be open to any other qualified Teke.

Academic Fields/Career Goals: Education; Mathematics.

Award: Scholarship for use in sophomore, junior, or senior years; not renewable. *Number:* 1. *Amount:* $800.

Eligibility Requirements: Applicant must be enrolled or expecting to enroll full-time at a four-year institution or university; male and must have an interest in leadership. Applicant or parent of applicant must be member of Tau Kappa Epsilon. Available to U.S. and non-U.S. citizens.

Application Requirements: Application form, application form may be submitted online (http://www.tke.org/member_resources/scholarships/apply_online), essay, narrative summary of how TKE membership has benefited applicant, personal photograph, transcript. *Deadline:* March 15.

Contact: Offices of the Grand Chapter
TKE Educational Foundation
7439 Woodland Drive, Suite 100
Indianapolis, IN 46278
E-mail: tkeogc@tke.org

TRANSTUTORS

http://www.transtutors.com/scholarship

TRANSTUTORS SCHOLARSHIP 2015-16

• See page 85

ULMAN CANCER FUND FOR YOUNG ADULTS

http://www.ulmanfund.org/scholarships

JAMES AND PATRICIA SOOD SCHOLARSHIP

The Ulman Cancer Fund for Young Adults is committed to helping young adults continue their education after being affected by cancer through their own diagnosis or the diagnosis of a loved one. Many scholarships offered by UCF share similar applicant criteria. Applicants need only submit one application, which will be considered for any and all scholarships for which the student applies and is eligible.

Academic Fields/Career Goals: Education.

Award: Scholarship for use in freshman, sophomore, junior, senior, or graduate years; not renewable. *Number:* 1. *Amount:* $2500.

Eligibility Requirements: Applicant must be age 15-39 and enrolled or expecting to enroll full- or part-time at a four-year institution or university. Available to U.S. citizens.

Application Requirements: Application form, essay. *Deadline:* March 1.

Contact: Lauriann Parker, Scholarship Coordinator
Ulman Cancer Fund for Young Adults
1215 E. Fort Ave.
Ste. 104
Baltimore, MD 21230
Phone: 410-964-0202 Ext. 105
E-mail: scholarship@ulmanfund.org

UNITED NEGRO COLLEGE FUND

http://www.uncf.org/

GATES MILLENNIUM SCHOLARS (GMS) PROGRAM

Award is aimed at increasing minority enrollment in undergraduate degree programs. This program is available to entering freshman with at least a 3.3 GPA attending any college or university. Award is for students intending to study computer science, education, engineering, library science, mathematics, public health, or science. Must have demonstrated leadership abilities through participation in community service, extracurricular, or other activities. Must meet Federal Pell Grant eligibility criteria.

Academic Fields/Career Goals: Education; Engineering/Technology; Library and Information Sciences; Mathematics; Physical Sciences; Public Health; Science, Technology, and Society.

Award: Scholarship for use in freshman year; renewable.

Eligibility Requirements: Applicant must be American Indian/Alaska Native, Asian/Pacific Islander, Black (non-Hispanic), Hispanic; enrolled or expecting to enroll full-time at a four-year institution or university and must have an interest in leadership. Applicant must have 3.0 GPA or higher. Available to U.S. citizens.

Application Requirements: Application form, financial need analysis. *Deadline:* January 13.

Contact: Mary Williams, Director of Outreach and Recruitment
Phone: 800-331-2244

MARGIE H. VERBAL EMERGENCY SCHOLARSHIP FUND

Scholarship of up to $2500 for a college senior majoring in engineering or education, experiencing an emergency financial need that prevents them from paying the outstanding balance on the bill from their institution for educational costs in order to graduate. Minimum 2.8 GPA and FAFSA are required. Must attend a UNCF school located in North Carolina with preference give to students attending Shaw University.

Academic Fields/Career Goals: Education; Engineering/Technology.

Award: Scholarship for use in senior year; not renewable.

Eligibility Requirements: Applicant must be Black (non-Hispanic); enrolled or expecting to enroll full-time at a four-year institution or university and studying in North Carolina. Applicant must have 2.5 GPA or higher. Available to U.S. citizens.

Application Requirements: Application form, essay, financial need analysis. *Deadline:* April 16.

Contact: Mary Williams, Director of Outreach and Recruitment
Phone: 800-331-2244

UNIVERSITY OF WYOMING

http://www.uwyo.edu/scholarships

SUPERIOR STUDENT IN EDUCATION SCHOLARSHIP-WYOMING

Scholarship available each year to sixteen Wyoming high school graduates who plan to teach in Wyoming. The award covers costs of undergraduate tuition at the University of Wyoming or any Wyoming community college.

Academic Fields/Career Goals: Education.

Award: Scholarship for use in freshman, sophomore, junior, or senior years; renewable. *Number:* 16–16. *Amount:* $1000.

Eligibility Requirements: Applicant must be enrolled or expecting to enroll full-time at a two-year or four-year institution or university; resident of Wyoming and studying in Wyoming. Applicant must have 3.0 GPA or higher. Available to U.S. citizens.

Application Requirements: Application form, recommendations or references, test scores, transcript. *Deadline:* October 31.

Contact: Tammy Mack, Assistant Director, Scholarships
University of Wyoming
Department 3335
1000 East University Avenue
Laramie, WY 82071
Phone: 307-766-2412
Fax: 307-766-3800
E-mail: FinAid@uwyo.edu

VERMONT-NEA

http://www.vtnea.org/

VERMONT-NEA/MAIDA F. TOWNSEND SCHOLARSHIP

Scholarship of $1000 to sons and daughters of Vermont-NEA members in their last year of high school, undergraduates, and graduate students.

Students majoring in any discipline are eligible to apply, but preference may be given to those majoring in education, or having that intention.

Academic Fields/Career Goals: Education.

Award: Scholarship for use in freshman, sophomore, junior, senior, or graduate years; not renewable. *Number:* 5. *Amount:* $1000.

Eligibility Requirements: Applicant must be enrolled or expecting to enroll full- or part-time at a two-year or four-year or technical institution or university. Applicant or parent of applicant must be member of Vermont-NEA. Applicant or parent of applicant must have employment or volunteer experience in teaching/education. Available to U.S. and non-U.S. citizens.

Application Requirements: Application form, community service, cover letter, essay, recommendations or references, test scores, transcript. *Deadline:* February 1.

Contact: Sandy Perkins, Administrative Assistant
Vermont-NEA
10 Wheelock Street
Montpelier, VT 05602-3737
Phone: 802-223-6375
E-mail: sperkins@vtnea.org

VIRGINIA CONGRESS OF PARENTS AND TEACHERS

http://www.vapta.org/

FRIEDA L. KOONTZ SCHOLARSHIP

Scholarship of $1200 to graduating high school students planning to enter teaching or other youth-serving professions in Virginia. Must be Virginia residents graduating from a Virginia public high school with a Parent-Teacher-Student Association (PTSA) and attending a Virginia college or university. Minimum 2.5 GPA required.

Academic Fields/Career Goals: Education.

Award: Scholarship for use in freshman year; not renewable. *Number:* 1. *Amount:* $1200.

Eligibility Requirements: Applicant must be high school student; planning to enroll or expecting to enroll full-time at a four-year institution or university; resident of Virginia and studying in Virginia. Applicant or parent of applicant must be member of Parent-Teacher Association/Organization. Applicant must have 2.5 GPA or higher. Available to U.S. citizens.

Application Requirements: Application form, essay, recommendations or references, test scores, transcript. *Deadline:* March 1.

Contact: Daniel Phillips, Scholarship Chair
Phone: 804-264-1234
E-mail: info@vapta.org

GENERAL SCHOLARSHIPS

General scholarships in addition to the Frieda L. Koontz and John S. Davis Scholarships. Only graduating students enrolled in a Virginia school that is a PTA or PTSA school may apply. See website for application details.

Academic Fields/Career Goals: Education.

Award: Scholarship for use in freshman year; not renewable. *Number:* 10–20. *Amount:* $1000.

Eligibility Requirements: Applicant must be high school student; planning to enroll or expecting to enroll full-time at a four-year institution or university and resident of Virginia. Applicant or parent of applicant must be member of Parent-Teacher Association/Organization. Applicant must have 2.5 GPA or higher. Available to U.S. citizens.

Application Requirements: Application form, essay, recommendations or references, test scores, transcript. *Deadline:* March 1.

Contact: Daniel Phillips, Scholarship Chair
Phone: 804-264-1234
E-mail: info@vapta.org

S. JOHN DAVIS SCHOLARSHIP

Scholarship of $1200 to Virginia residents graduating from a Virginia public school that has a Parent-Teacher-Student Association (PTSA) or PTA. Must be planning to attend a Virginia college or university and pursuing a career in teaching or qualifying for service with a youth-serving agency in Virginia. Minimum 2.5 GPA required.

Academic Fields/Career Goals: Education.

Award: Scholarship for use in freshman year; not renewable. *Number:* 1. *Amount:* $1200.

Eligibility Requirements: Applicant must be high school student; planning to enroll or expecting to enroll full-time at a four-year institution or university; resident of Virginia and studying in Virginia. Applicant or parent of applicant must be member of Parent-Teacher Association/Organization. Applicant must have 2.5 GPA or higher. Available to U.S. citizens.

Application Requirements: Application form, essay. *Deadline:* March 1.

Contact: Daniel Phillips, Scholarship Chair
Phone: 804-264-1234
E-mail: info@vapta.org

WISCONSIN CONGRESS OF PARENTS AND TEACHERS INC.

http://www.wisconsinpta.org/

BROOKMIRE-HASTINGS SCHOLARSHIPS

One-time award to graduating high school seniors from Wisconsin public schools. Must pursue a degree in education. High school must have an active PTA in good standing of the Wisconsin PTA.

Academic Fields/Career Goals: Education; Special Education.

Award: Scholarship for use in freshman year; not renewable. *Number:* up to 2. *Amount:* $1000.

Eligibility Requirements: Applicant must be high school student; planning to enroll or expecting to enroll full-time at a four-year institution or university and resident of Wisconsin. Available to U.S. citizens.

Application Requirements: Application form, essay, interview, recommendations or references, transcript. *Deadline:* March 1.

Contact: Kim Schwantes, Executive Administrator
Wisconsin Congress of Parents and Teachers Inc.
4797 Hayes Road, Suite 2
Madison, WI 53704-3256
Phone: 608-244-1455

WISCONSIN MATHEMATICS EDUCATION FOUNDATION

http://wmefonline.org/

ARNE ENGEBRETSEN WISCONSIN MATHEMATICS COUNCIL SCHOLARSHIP

Scholarship for Wisconsin high school senior who is planning to study mathematics education and teach mathematics at K-12 level.

Academic Fields/Career Goals: Education; Mathematics.

Award: Scholarship for use in freshman year; not renewable. *Number:* 1. *Amount:* $2000.

Eligibility Requirements: Applicant must be high school student; planning to enroll or expecting to enroll full-time at a four-year institution or university and resident of Wisconsin. Available to U.S. citizens.

Application Requirements: Application form, essay, recommendations or references, resume, transcript. *Deadline:* March 1.

ETHEL A. NEIJAHR WISCONSIN MATHEMATICS COUNCIL SCHOLARSHIP

Scholarship for a Wisconsin resident who is currently enrolled in teacher education programs in a Wisconsin institution studying mathematics education. Minimum GPA of 3.0 required.

Academic Fields/Career Goals: Education; Mathematics.

Award: Scholarship for use in junior or senior years; not renewable. *Number:* 1. *Amount:* $2000.

Eligibility Requirements: Applicant must be enrolled or expecting to enroll full-time at a four-year institution or university; resident of Wisconsin and studying in Wisconsin. Applicant must have 3.0 GPA or higher. Available to U.S. citizens.

Application Requirements: Application form, essay, recommendations or references, resume, transcript. *Deadline:* March 1.

SISTER MARY PETRONIA VAN STRATEN WISCONSIN MATHEMATICS COUNCIL SCHOLARSHIP

Scholarship for a Wisconsin resident who is currently enrolled in teacher education programs in Wisconsin institution studying mathematics education. Minimum GPA of 3.0 required.

Academic Fields/Career Goals: Education; Mathematics.

Award: Scholarship for use in junior or senior years; not renewable. *Number:* 1. *Amount:* $2000.

Eligibility Requirements: Applicant must be enrolled or expecting to enroll full-time at a four-year institution or university; resident of Wisconsin and studying in Wisconsin. Applicant must have 3.0 GPA or higher. Available to U.S. citizens.

Application Requirements: Application form, essay, recommendations or references, resume, transcript. *Deadline:* March 1.

WOMEN BAND DIRECTORS INTERNATIONAL

http://www.womenbanddirectors.org/

CHARLOTTE PLUMMER OWEN MEMORIAL SCHOLARSHIP

One-time award for women instrumental music majors enrolled in a four-year institution. Applicants must be working toward a degree in music education with the intention of becoming a band director. See website for application http://www.womenbanddirectors.org/.

Academic Fields/Career Goals: Education; Music; Performing Arts.

Award: Scholarship for use in freshman, sophomore, junior, or senior years; not renewable. *Number:* 4. *Amount:* $300.

Eligibility Requirements: Applicant must be enrolled or expecting to enroll full-time at a four-year institution or university; female and must have an interest in music/singing. Available to U.S. and non-U.S. citizens.

Application Requirements: Application form, essay, personal photograph, recommendations or references, transcript. *Deadline:* December 1.

Contact: Nicole Aakre-Rubis, Scholarship Chair
Women Band Directors International
16085 Excel Way
Rosemount, MN 55068

MARTHA ANN STARK MEMORIAL SCHOLARSHIP

One-time award for women instrumental music majors enrolled in a four-year institution. Applicants must be working toward a degree in music education with the intention of becoming a band director. Three of the scholarships are designated for college upperclassmen, and one is open to all levels. See website for application http://www.womenbanddirectors.org/.

Academic Fields/Career Goals: Education; Music; Performing Arts.

Award: Scholarship for use in freshman, sophomore, junior, or senior years; not renewable. *Number:* 1. *Amount:* $300.

Eligibility Requirements: Applicant must be enrolled or expecting to enroll full-time at a four-year institution or university; female and must have an interest in music/singing. Available to U.S. and non-U.S. citizens.

Application Requirements: Application form, essay, personal photograph, recommendations or references, transcript. *Deadline:* December 1.

Contact: Nicole Aakre-Rubis, Scholarship Chair
Women Band Directors International
16085 Excel Way
Rosemount, MN 55068

VOLKWEIN MEMORIAL SCHOLARSHIP

One-time award for female instrumental music majors enrolled in a four-year institution. Applicants must be working toward a degree in music education with the intention of becoming a band director. Three of the scholarships are designated for college upperclassmen, and one is open to all levels. See website for application http://www.womenbanddirectors.org/.

Academic Fields/Career Goals: Education; Music; Performing Arts.

Award: Scholarship for use in freshman, sophomore, junior, senior, or graduate years; not renewable. *Number:* 4. *Amount:* $300–$500.

Eligibility Requirements: Applicant must be enrolled or expecting to enroll full-time at a four-year institution or university; female and must have an interest in music/singing. Available to U.S. and non-U.S. citizens.

Application Requirements: Application form, essay, personal photograph, recommendations or references, self-addressed stamped envelope with application, transcript. *Deadline:* December 1.

Contact: Nicole Aakre-Rubis, Scholarship Chair
Women Band Directors International
16085 Excel Way
Rosemount, MN 55068

WOMEN'S SPORTS FOUNDATION

http://www.womenssportsfoundation.org/

DOROTHEA DEITZ ENDOWED MEMORIAL SCHOLARSHIP

The Dorothea Deitz Endowed Memorial Scholarship was established in 2005 by the Dorothea Deitz Memorial Scholarship Fund Board of Trustees to encourage young women in New York to pursue careers in the physical education teaching profession.

Academic Fields/Career Goals: Education.

Award: Scholarship for use in freshman year; not renewable. *Number:* 3–9. *Amount:* $1000.

Eligibility Requirements: Applicant must be high school student; planning to enroll or expecting to enroll full-time at a four-year institution; female and resident of New York. Applicant must have 3.0 GPA or higher. Available to U.S. citizens.

Application Requirements: Application form. *Deadline:* March 31.

Contact: Elizabeth Flores
Phone: 516-307-3915
E-mail: lflores@womenssportsfoundation.org

Y'S MEN INTERNATIONAL

http://www.ysmen.org/

ALEXANDER SCHOLARSHIP LOAN FUND

• See page 171

ELECTRICAL ENGINEERING/ ELECTRONICS

AACE INTERNATIONAL

http://www.aacei.org/

AACE INTERNATIONAL COMPETITIVE SCHOLARSHIP

• See page 118

AHS INTERNATIONAL—THE VERTICAL FLIGHT TECHNICAL SOCIETY

http://www.vtol.org/

VERTICAL FLIGHT FOUNDATION SCHOLARSHIP

• See page 134

AIST FOUNDATION

http://www.aistfoundation.org/

AISI/AIST FOUNDATION PREMIER SCHOLARSHIP

This award is granted to the highest scoring FeMET at StEEL scholarship applicants. $10,000 scholarships are for full-time students of metallurgy, materials science, chemical, electrical, mechanical, environmental, computer science, and industrial engineering. Students must have an interest in a career in the steel industry as demonstrated by an internship or related experience, or who have plans to pursue such experiences during college. Students must commit to a summer internship at a steel producing company (placement assistance is provided) prior to receiving this scholarship. Student may apply during their sophomore and junior years. Applications are accepted from September 1 through December 31 each year.

Academic Fields/Career Goals: Electrical Engineering/Electronics; Materials Science, Engineering, and Metallurgy; Mechanical Engineering.

Award: Scholarship for use in sophomore or junior years; not renewable. *Number:* 1. *Amount:* $10,000.

Eligibility Requirements: Applicant must be enrolled or expecting to enroll full-time at a four-year institution or university. Applicant must have 2.5 GPA or higher. Available to U.S. and non-U.S. citizens.

Application Requirements: Application form, essay, recommendations or references, resume, transcript. *Deadline:* December 31.

Contact: Lori Wharrey, AIST Manager, Board Services
AIST Foundation
186 Thorn Hill Road
Warrendale, PA 15086
Phone: 724-814-3044
E-mail: lwharrey@aist.org

AIST WILLIAM E. SCHWABE MEMORIAL SCHOLARSHIP

Scholarship for full-time students of metallurgy, materials science, chemical, mechanical, electrical, environmental, computer science, and industrial engineering. Students must have an interest in a career in the steel industry as demonstrated by an internship or related experience, or who have plans to pursue such experiences during college. Student may apply after first term of freshman year of college. Applications are accepted from 1 Sep through 31 Dec each year. Note: High school students do not qualify but are encouraged to learn about the steel industry and the career opportunities available therein, during their freshman year.

Academic Fields/Career Goals: Electrical Engineering/Electronics; Engineering/Technology; Materials Science, Engineering, and Metallurgy; Mechanical Engineering.

Award: Scholarship for use in sophomore, junior, or senior years; not renewable. *Number:* 1. *Amount:* $3000.

Eligibility Requirements: Applicant must be enrolled or expecting to enroll full-time at a four-year institution or university. Applicant must have 2.5 GPA or higher. Available to U.S. and non-U.S. citizens.

Application Requirements: Application form, essay, recommendations or references, resume, transcript. *Deadline:* December 31.

Contact: Lori Wharrey, AIST Manager, Board Services
Phone: 724-814-3044
E-mail: lwharrey@aist.org

ASSOCIATION FOR IRON AND STEEL TECHNOLOGY BENJAMIN F. FAIRLESS SCHOLARSHIP (AIME)
• See page 172

ASSOCIATION FOR IRON AND STEEL TECHNOLOGY DAVID H. SAMSON CANADIAN SCHOLARSHIP
• See page 172

ASSOCIATION FOR IRON AND STEEL TECHNOLOGY OHIO VALLEY CHAPTER SCHOLARSHIP
• See page 153

ASSOCIATION FOR IRON AND STEEL TECHNOLOGY RONALD E. LINCOLN SCHOLARSHIP

Scholarship for full-time students of metallurgy, materials science, chemical, mechanical, electrical, environmental, computer science, and industrial engineering. Students must have an interest in a career in the steel industry as demonstrated by an internship or related experience, or who have plans to pursue such experiences during college. Student may apply after first term of freshman year of college. Applications are accepted from 1 Sep through 31 Dec each year. Note: High school students do not qualify but are encouraged to learn about the steel industry and the career opportunities available therein, during their freshman year.

Academic Fields/Career Goals: Electrical Engineering/Electronics; Materials Science, Engineering, and Metallurgy; Mechanical Engineering.

Award: Scholarship for use in sophomore, junior, or senior years; not renewable. *Number:* 2. *Amount:* $3000.

Eligibility Requirements: Applicant must be enrolled or expecting to enroll full-time at a four-year institution or university. Applicant must have 2.5 GPA or higher. Available to U.S. and non-U.S. citizens.

Application Requirements: Application form, essay, recommendations or references, resume, transcript. *Deadline:* December 31.

Contact: Lori Wharrey, AIST Manager, Board Services
AIST Foundation
186 Thorn Hill Road
Warrendale, PA 15086
Phone: 724-814-3044
E-mail: lwharrey@aist.org

ASSOCIATION FOR IRON AND STEEL TECHNOLOGY WILLY KORF MEMORIAL SCHOLARSHIP
• See page 172

STEEL ENGINEERING EDUCATION LINK (STEEL) SCHOLARSHIPS

Scholarships are for full-time students of chemical, electrical, mechanical, computer science, environment, and industrial engineering. Students must have an interest in a career in the steel industry as demonstrated by an internship or related experience, or who have plans to pursue such experiences during college. Students must commit to a paid summer internship at a steel producing company (placement assistance is provided) prior to receiving this scholarship. Student may apply during their sophomore and junior years. Applications are accepted from 1 Sep through 31 Dec each year.

Academic Fields/Career Goals: Electrical Engineering/Electronics; Mechanical Engineering.

Award: Scholarship for use in sophomore or junior years; not renewable. *Number:* 1–10. *Amount:* $5000.

Eligibility Requirements: Applicant must be enrolled or expecting to enroll full-time at a four-year institution or university. Applicant must have 2.5 GPA or higher. Available to U.S. and non-U.S. citizens.

Application Requirements: Application form, essay, recommendations or references, resume, transcript. *Deadline:* December 31.

Contact: Lori Wharrey, AIST Manager, Board Services
AIST Foundation
186 Thorn Hill Road
Warrendale, PA 15086
Phone: 724-814-3044
E-mail: lwharrey@aist.org

AMERICAN CHEMICAL SOCIETY, RUBBER DIVISION

http://www.rubber.org/

AMERICAN CHEMICAL SOCIETY, RUBBER DIVISION UNDERGRADUATE SCHOLARSHIP
• See page 109

AMERICAN COUNCIL OF ENGINEERING COMPANIES OF PENNSYLVANIA (ACEC/PA)

http://www.acecpa.org/

ERIC J. GENNUSO AND LEROY D. (BUD) LOY, JR. SCHOLARSHIP PROGRAM
• See page 173

AMERICAN FOUNDATION FOR THE BLIND

http://www.afb.org/

PAUL W. RUCKES SCHOLARSHIP
• See page 214

AMERICAN INDIAN SCIENCE AND ENGINEERING SOCIETY

http://www.aises.org/

A.T. ANDERSON MEMORIAL SCHOLARSHIP PROGRAM
• *See page 109*

AMERICAN INSTITUTE OF AERONAUTICS AND ASTRONAUTICS

http://www.aiaafoundation.org/

AIAA FOUNDATION UNDERGRADUATE SCHOLARSHIPS
• *See page 110*

LEATRICE GREGORY PENDRAY SCHOLARSHIP
• *See page 110*

AMERICAN PUBLIC POWER ASSOCIATION

http://publicpower.org/DEED

DEED EDUCATIONAL SCHOLARSHIP
• *See page 176*

DEED STUDENT INTERNSHIP
• *See page 176*

DEED STUDENT RESEARCH GRANTS
• *See page 191*

DEED TECHNICAL DESIGN PROJECT
• *See page 176*

AMERICAN PUBLIC TRANSPORTATION FOUNDATION

http://www.apta.com/

LOUIS T. KLAUDER SCHOLARSHIP

Scholarships for study towards a career in the rail transit industry as an electrical or mechanical engineer. Must be sponsored by APTA member organization and complete internship with APTA member organization. Minimum GPA of 3.0 required.

Academic Fields/Career Goals: Electrical Engineering/Electronics; Mechanical Engineering.

Award: Scholarship for use in sophomore, junior, senior, or graduate years; renewable. *Number:* 1. *Amount:* $2500.

Eligibility Requirements: Applicant must be enrolled or expecting to enroll full-time at a two-year or four-year institution or university. Applicant must have 3.0 GPA or higher. Available to U.S. and Canadian citizens.

Application Requirements: Application form, essay, financial need analysis, recommendations or references, transcript, verification of enrollment for the current semester, copy of fee schedule from the college/university. *Deadline:* June 16.

Contact: Pamela Boswell, Vice President of Program Management
American Public Transportation Foundation
1666 K Street, NW
Washington, DC 20006-1215
Phone: 202-496-4803
Fax: 202-496-2323
E-mail: pboswell@apta.com

TRANSIT HALL OF FAME SCHOLARSHIP AWARD PROGRAM
• *See page 191*

AMERICAN RAILWAY ENGINEERING AND MAINTENANCE OF WAY ASSOCIATION

http://www.aremafoundation.org/

AREMA GRADUATE AND UNDERGRADUATE SCHOLARSHIPS
• *See page 191*

AMERICAN SOCIETY OF CERTIFIED ENGINEERING TECHNICIANS

http://www.ascet.org/

KURT H. AND DONNA M. SCHULER SMALL GRANT
• *See page 176*

AMERICAN SOCIETY OF HEATING, REFRIGERATING, AND AIR CONDITIONING ENGINEERS, INC.

http://www.ashrae.org/

ALWIN B. NEWTON SCHOLARSHIP

Scholarship available to undergraduate students pursuing a bachelor of science or engineering degree, who are enrolled full-time in a program accredited by the Accreditation Board for Engineering and Technology. Application and additional information on Website http://www.ashrae.org.

Academic Fields/Career Goals: Electrical Engineering/Electronics; Engineering-Related Technologies; Engineering/Technology; Heating, Air-Conditioning, and Refrigeration Mechanics; Mechanical Engineering; Trade/Technical Specialties.

Award: Scholarship for use in sophomore, junior, or senior years; not renewable. *Number:* 1. *Amount:* $5000.

Eligibility Requirements: Applicant must be enrolled or expecting to enroll full-time at a four-year institution or university. Applicant must have 3.0 GPA or higher. Available to U.S. and non-U.S. citizens.

Application Requirements: Application form, financial need analysis. *Deadline:* December 1.

Contact: Lois Benedict, Scholarship Administrator
Phone: 404-636-8400 Ext. 1120
E-mail: lbenedict@ashrae.org

ASHRAE REGION III BOGGARM SETTY SCHOLARSHIP
• *See page 176*

DUANE HANSON SCHOLARSHIP

One-time, $5000 scholarship available to undergraduate students pursuing a bachelor of science or engineering degree, who are enrolled full-time in a program. For study in heating, ventilating, refrigeration, and air conditioning in an ABET-accredited program at an accredited school. See Website for application and additional information, http://www.ashrae.org.

Academic Fields/Career Goals: Electrical Engineering/Electronics; Engineering-Related Technologies; Engineering/Technology; Heating, Air-Conditioning, and Refrigeration Mechanics; Trade/Technical Specialties.

Award: Scholarship for use in freshman, sophomore, junior, or senior years; not renewable. *Number:* 1. *Amount:* $5000.

Eligibility Requirements: Applicant must be enrolled or expecting to enroll full-time at a four-year institution or university. Applicant must have 3.0 GPA or higher. Available to U.S. and non-U.S. citizens.

Application Requirements: Application form, financial need analysis. *Deadline:* December 1.

Contact: Lois Benedict, Scholarship Administrator
Phone: 404-636-8400 Ext. 1120
E-mail: lbenedict@ashrae.org

FRANK M. CODA SCHOLARSHIP

$5000 award to undergraduate students enrolled full-time in an ABET-accredited program leading to bachelor of science or engineering degree in a course of study that traditionally has been a preparatory curriculum for the HVAC&R profession. Future service to the HVAC&R profession, character and leadership ability are taken into consideration. For application and additional information see Website, http://www.ashrae.org.

Academic Fields/Career Goals: Electrical Engineering/Electronics; Engineering-Related Technologies; Engineering/Technology; Heating, Air-Conditioning, and Refrigeration Mechanics; Mechanical Engineering; Trade/Technical Specialties.

Award: Scholarship for use in sophomore, junior, or senior years; not renewable. *Number:* 1. *Amount:* $5000.

Eligibility Requirements: Applicant must be enrolled or expecting to enroll full-time at a four-year institution or university and must have an interest in leadership. Applicant must have 3.0 GPA or higher. Available to U.S. and non-U.S. citizens.

Application Requirements: Application form, financial need analysis. *Deadline:* December 1.

Contact: Lois Benedict, Scholarship Administrator
Phone: 404-636-8400 Ext. 1120
E-mail: lbenedict@ashrae.org

HENRY ADAMS SCHOLARSHIP

One-time $3000 award for full-time study in heating, ventilating, refrigeration, and air conditioning in an ABET-accredited program at an accredited school. Must be pursuing a bachelor of science or engineering degree. See Website for application and additional information, http://www.ashrae.org.

Academic Fields/Career Goals: Electrical Engineering/Electronics; Engineering-Related Technologies; Engineering/Technology; Heating, Air-Conditioning, and Refrigeration Mechanics; Trade/Technical Specialties.

Award: Scholarship for use in freshman, sophomore, junior, or senior years; not renewable. *Number:* 1. *Amount:* $3000.

Eligibility Requirements: Applicant must be enrolled or expecting to enroll full-time at a four-year institution or university and must have an interest in leadership. Applicant must have 3.0 GPA or higher. Available to U.S. and non-U.S. citizens.

Application Requirements: Application form, financial need analysis. *Deadline:* December 1.

Contact: Lois Benedict, Scholarship Administrator
Phone: 404-636-8400 Ext. 1120
E-mail: lbenedict@ashrae.org

LYNN G. BELLENGER SCHOLARSHIP

One-year $5,000 scholarship available to a female undergraduate engineering technology student enrolled full-time in a post-secondary educational institution and pursuing a bachelor or an associate degree in a course of study which has traditionally been a preparatory curriculum for the HVAC&R profession.

Academic Fields/Career Goals: Electrical Engineering/Electronics; Engineering-Related Technologies; Engineering/Technology; Heating, Air-Conditioning, and Refrigeration Mechanics; Mechanical Engineering; Trade/Technical Specialties.

Award: Scholarship for use in sophomore, junior, or senior years; not renewable. *Number:* 1. *Amount:* $5000.

Eligibility Requirements: Applicant must be enrolled or expecting to enroll full-time at a two-year or four-year institution or university; female and must have an interest in leadership. Applicant must have 3.0 GPA or higher. Available to U.S. citizens.

Application Requirements: Application form, financial need analysis. *Deadline:* December 1.

Contact: Lois Benedict, Scholarship Administrator
Phone: 404-636-8400 Ext. 1120
E-mail: lbenedict@ashrae.org

REUBEN TRANE SCHOLARSHIP

Undergraduate engineering scholarships awarded in two disbursements of $5000 each at the beginning of the student's junior and senior year. Must be a full-time student enrolled in a bachelor of science or engineering degree accredited by the Accreditation Board for Engineering and Technology. See Website for application package and additional information, http://www.ashrae.org.

Academic Fields/Career Goals: Electrical Engineering/Electronics; Energy and Power Engineering; Engineering/Technology; Heating, Air-

Conditioning, and Refrigeration Mechanics; Mechanical Engineering; Trade/Technical Specialties.

Award: Scholarship for use in junior or senior years; renewable. *Number:* 4. *Amount:* $10,000.

Eligibility Requirements: Applicant must be enrolled or expecting to enroll full-time at a four-year institution or university and must have an interest in leadership. Applicant must have 3.0 GPA or higher. Available to U.S. and non-U.S. citizens.

Application Requirements: Application form, financial need analysis. *Deadline:* December 1.

Contact: Lois Benedict, Scholarship Administrator
Phone: 404-636-8400 Ext. 1120
E-mail: lbenedict@ashrae.org

WILLIS H. CARRIER SCHOLARSHIPS

Two, one-year scholarships of $10,000 available to undergraduate students enrolled full time in an ABET-accredited program leading to a bachelor of science or engineering degree. Minimum 3.0 GPA required. See Website for application and further details, http://www.ashrae.org.

Academic Fields/Career Goals: Electrical Engineering/Electronics; Engineering-Related Technologies; Engineering/Technology; Heating, Air-Conditioning, and Refrigeration Mechanics.

Award: Scholarship for use in sophomore, junior, or senior years; not renewable. *Number:* 2. *Amount:* $10,000.

Eligibility Requirements: Applicant must be enrolled or expecting to enroll full-time at a four-year institution or university. Applicant must have 3.0 GPA or higher. Available to U.S. citizens.

Application Requirements: Application form, financial need analysis. *Deadline:* December 1.

Contact: Lois Benedict, Scholarship Administrator
Phone: 404-636-8400 Ext. 1120
E-mail: lbenedict@ashrae.org

AMERICAN SOCIETY OF NAVAL ENGINEERS

http://www.navalengineers.org/

AMERICAN SOCIETY OF NAVAL ENGINEERS SCHOLARSHIP

• *See page 110*

ARMED FORCES COMMUNICATIONS AND ELECTRONICS ASSOCIATION, EDUCATIONAL FOUNDATION

http://www.afcea.org/site/?q=foundation/scholarships

ARMED FORCES COMMUNICATIONS AND ELECTRONICS ASSOCIATION ROTC SCHOLARSHIP PROGRAM

• *See page 137*

STEM MAJORS SCHOLARSHIPS FOR UNDERGRADUATE STUDENTS

• *See page 110*

VADM SAMUEL L. GRAVELY, JR, USN(RET.) MEMORIAL SCHOLARSHIP

• *See page 111*

VETERANS OF ENDURING FREEDOM (AFGHANISTAN) AND IRAQI FREEDOM SCHOLARSHIP

• *See page 214*

ARRL FOUNDATION INC.

http://www.arrl.org/

ALFRED E. FRIEND JR, W4CF, MEMORIAL SCHOLARSHIP

• *See page 177*

ANDROSCOGGIN AMATEUR RADIO CLUB SCHOLARSHIP
• See page 215

BETTY WEATHERFORD, KQ6RE, MEMORIAL SCHOLARSHIP

$1000 award for a student with an Amateur Radio license in any class. Must be studying electrical or communications engineering.

Academic Fields/Career Goals: Electrical Engineering/Electronics; Engineering/Technology.

Award: Scholarship for use in freshman, sophomore, junior, or senior years; not renewable. *Number:* 1. *Amount:* $1000.

Eligibility Requirements: Applicant must be enrolled or expecting to enroll full- or part-time at a two-year or four-year or technical institution or university and must have an interest in amateur radio. Available to U.S. citizens.

Application Requirements: Application form. *Deadline:* January 31.

Contact: Ms. Mary Hobart, Secretary
　　　Phone: 860-594-0397
　　　E-mail: k1mmh@arrl.org

CHARLES CLARKE CORDLE MEMORIAL SCHOLARSHIP
• See page 201

CHARLES N. FISHER MEMORIAL SCHOLARSHIP
• See page 111

DR. JAMES L. LAWSON MEMORIAL SCHOLARSHIP
• See page 202

EDMOND A. METZGER SCHOLARSHIP

Scholarship for licensed amateur radio operators, at the novice class or above. Applicants must be undergraduate or graduate electrical engineering students and members of the Amateur Radio Relay League. Preference given to residents of ARRL Central Division (IL, IN, WI) and to students attending school in the Central Division states.

Academic Fields/Career Goals: Electrical Engineering/Electronics.

Award: Scholarship for use in freshman, sophomore, junior, senior, or graduate years; not renewable. *Number:* 1. *Amount:* $500.

Eligibility Requirements: Applicant must be enrolled or expecting to enroll full-time at a four-year institution or university; resident of Illinois, Indiana, Wisconsin; studying in Illinois, Indiana, Wisconsin and must have an interest in amateur radio. Applicant or parent of applicant must be member of American Radio Relay League. Available to U.S. citizens.

Application Requirements: Application form. *Deadline:* January 31.

Contact: Ms. Mary Hobart, Secretary
　　　Phone: 860-594-0397
　　　E-mail: k1mmh@arrl.org

FRED R. MCDANIEL MEMORIAL SCHOLARSHIP
• See page 202

GARY WAGNER, K3OMI, SCHOLARSHIP
• See page 177

INDIANAPOLIS AMATEUR RADIO ASSOCIATION SCHOLARSHIP
• See page 215

IRARC MEMORIAL, JOSEPH P. RUBINO, WA4MMD, SCHOLARSHIP

Need-based award available to licensed amateur radio operators. Preference is given to Brevard County, FL residents or to all Florida residents. Must maintain 2.5 GPA and pursue an undergraduate degree or electronic technician certification at an accredited institution.

Academic Fields/Career Goals: Electrical Engineering/Electronics.

Award: Scholarship for use in freshman, sophomore, junior, or senior years; not renewable. *Amount:* $750.

Eligibility Requirements: Applicant must be enrolled or expecting to enroll full-time at a two-year or four-year or technical institution or university; resident of Florida and must have an interest in amateur radio. Applicant or parent of applicant must be member of American Radio Relay League. Applicant must have 2.5 GPA or higher. Available to U.S. citizens.

Application Requirements: Application form, financial need analysis. *Deadline:* January 31.

Contact: Ms. Mary Hobart, Secretary
　　　Phone: 860-594-0397
　　　E-mail: k1mmh@arrl.org

IRVING W. COOK, WA0CGS, SCHOLARSHIP
• See page 202

JAKE MCCLAIN DRIVER, KC5WXA, SCHOLARSHIP
• See page 215

LOIS MANLEY, K7LMZ, AND RANDALL PITCHFORD, WW7ZZ, SCHOLARSHIP
• See page 193

L. PHIL AND ALICE J. WICKER SCHOLARSHIP
• See page 202

MAGNOLIA DX ASSOCIATION SCHOLARSHIP
• See page 202

MISSISSIPPI SCHOLARSHIP
• See page 111

ORLANDO HAMCATION SCHOLARSHIP
• See page 202

PAUL AND HELEN L. GRAUER SCHOLARSHIP
• See page 111

PHD SCHOLARSHIP
• See page 215

RAY, N0RP, & KATIE, W0KTE, PAUTZ SCHOLARSHIP
• See page 215

VICTOR POOR, W5SMM, MEMORIAL SCHOLARSHIP

$2500 scholarship for a student of electrical engineering, with a preference for concentration in digital communications. Must have an active radio license.

Academic Fields/Career Goals: Electrical Engineering/Electronics.

Award: Scholarship for use in freshman, sophomore, junior, or senior years; not renewable. *Number:* 1. *Amount:* $2500.

Eligibility Requirements: Applicant must be enrolled or expecting to enroll full- or part-time at a two-year or four-year or technical institution or university and must have an interest in amateur radio. Available to U.S. citizens.

Application Requirements: Application form. *Deadline:* January 31.

Contact: Ms. Mary Hobart, Secretary
　　　Phone: 860-594-0397
　　　E-mail: k1mmh@arrl.org

W1FDR SCHOLARSHIP
• See page 112

ASSOCIATION OF FEDERAL COMMUNICATIONS CONSULTING ENGINEERS

http://www.afcce.org

JULES COHEN SCHOLARSHIP

AFCCE/IEEE-BTS Scholarships provide financial assistance to students who are undertaking a full-time undergraduate or graduate program in engineering or science and demonstrate an interest in careers in telecommunications consulting or broadcast engineering. AFCCE Scholarships generally range between $500 to $2,500 per semester and the IEEE-BTS Jules Cohen Scholarships, administered by the AFCCE, are either $5,000 or $10,000. A single application to the AFCCE will automatically enter the student for consideration for all scholarships for which you are eligible during each semester.

Academic Fields/Career Goals: Electrical Engineering/Electronics; Engineering-Related Technologies; Science, Technology, and Society.

Award: Scholarship for use in junior, senior, or graduate years; not renewable. *Number:* 1–13. *Amount:* $5000–$10,000.

Eligibility Requirements: Applicant must be enrolled or expecting to enroll full-time at a four-year institution or university and studying in Alabama, Alaska, Arizona, Arkansas, California, Colorado, Connecticut, Delaware, District of Columbia, Florida, Georgia, Guam, Hawaii, Idaho, Illinois, Indiana, Iowa, Kansas, Kentucky, Louisiana, Maine, Maryland, Massachusetts, Michigan, Minnesota, Mississippi, Missouri, Montana, Nebraska, Nevada, New Hampshire, New Jersey, New Mexico, New York, North Carolina, North Dakota, Ohio, Oklahoma, Oregon, Pennsylvania, Puerto Rico, Rhode Island, South Carolina, South Dakota, Tennessee, Texas, Utah, Vermont, Virginia, Washington, West Virginia, Wisconsin, Wyoming. Available to U.S. and non-U.S. citizens.

Application Requirements: Application form, essay. *Deadline:* April 30.

Contact: Mr. Marshall Cross, Chair, AFCCE Scholarship Committee
Association of Federal Communications Consulting Engineers
MegaWave Corporation
100 Jackson Road
Devens, MA 01434
Phone: 978-615-7200 Ext. 14
Fax: 978-615-7241
E-mail: mcross@megawave.com

ASTRONAUT SCHOLARSHIP FOUNDATION

http://www.astronautscholarship.org/

ASTRONAUT SCHOLARSHIP FOUNDATION
• *See page 112*

AUTOMOTIVE WOMEN'S ALLIANCE FOUNDATION

http://www.awafoundation.org/index.php

AUTOMOTIVE WOMEN'S ALLIANCE FOUNDATION SCHOLARSHIPS
• *See page 74*

BARRY GOLDWATER SCHOLARSHIP AND EXCELLENCE IN EDUCATION FOUNDATION

https://goldwater.scholarsapply.org

BARRY M. GOLDWATER SCHOLARSHIP AND EXCELLENCE IN EDUCATION PROGRAM
• *See page 112*

BHW GROUP

https://thebhwgroup.com/

BHW WOMEN IN STEM SCHOLARSHIP
• *See page 74*

BRASKEM ODEBRECHT

http://www.odebrechtaward.com

ODEBRECHT AWARD FOR SUSTAINABLE DEVELOPMENT
• *See page 119*

BROWN AND CALDWELL

http://www.brownandcaldwell.com

ECKENFELDER SCHOLARSHIP
• *See page 155*

MINORITY SCHOLARSHIP PROGRAM
• *See page 155*

CATCHING THE DREAM

http://www.catchingthedream.org/

TRIBAL BUSINESS MANAGEMENT PROGRAM (TBM)
• *See page 74*

CENTER FOR ARCHITECTURE

http://www.cfafoundation.org/scholarships

CENTER FOR ARCHITECTURE DESIGN SCHOLARSHIP
• *See page 119*

THE ELECTROCHEMICAL SOCIETY

http://www.electrochem.org/

H.H. DOW MEMORIAL STUDENT ACHIEVEMENT AWARD OF THE INDUSTRIAL ELECTROLYSIS AND ELECTROCHEMICAL ENGINEERING DIVISION OF THE ELECTROCHEMICAL SOCIETY INC.
• *See page 113*

STUDENT RESEARCH AWARDS OF THE BATTERY DIVISION OF THE ELECTROCHEMICAL SOCIETY INC.
• *See page 113*

FABRICATORS AND MANUFACTURERS ASSOCIATION FOUNDATION

http://www.nutsandboltsfoundation.org/scholarships/

COLLEGE AND TRADE/TECHNICAL SCHOOL SCHOLARSHIPS
• *See page 178*

FLORIDA ENGINEERING SOCIETY

http://www.fleng.org/scholarships.cfm

DAVID F. LUDOVICI SCHOLARSHIP
• *See page 178*

FOUNDATION FOR SCIENCE AND DISABILITY

http://stemd.org/

GRANTS FOR DISABLED GRADUATE STUDENTS IN THE SCIENCES
• *See page 113*

GREATER KANAWHA VALLEY FOUNDATION

http://www.tgkvf.org/

STEVEN ENGINEERING SCHOLARSHIP
• *See page 178*

GREAT MINDS IN STEM

www.greatmindsinstem.org

HISPANIC ENGINEER NATIONAL ACHIEVEMENT AWARDS CORPORATION SCHOLARSHIP PROGRAM
• See page 106

ILLUMINATING ENGINEERING SOCIETY OF NORTH AMERICA–GOLDEN GATE SECTION

http://www.iesgg.org/

ALAN LUCAS MEMORIAL EDUCATIONAL SCHOLARSHIP
• See page 122

INDEPENDENT LABORATORIES INSTITUTE SCHOLARSHIP ALLIANCE

http://www.acil.org/

INDEPENDENT LABORATORIES INSTITUTE SCHOLARSHIP ALLIANCE
• See page 156

INTERNATIONAL COMMUNICATIONS INDUSTRIES FOUNDATION

http://www.infocomm.org/scholarships

ICIF SCHOLARSHIP FOR EMPLOYEES AND DEPENDENTS OF MEMBER ORGANIZATIONS
• See page 204

INTERNATIONAL COMMUNICATIONS INDUSTRIES FOUNDATION AV SCHOLARSHIP
• See page 204

INTERNATIONAL SOCIETY FOR OPTICAL ENGINEERING-SPIE

http://www.spie.org/scholarships

SPIE EDUCATIONAL SCHOLARSHIPS IN OPTICAL SCIENCE AND ENGINEERING
• See page 114

JORGE MAS CANOSA FREEDOM FOUNDATION

http://masscholarships.org/

MAS FAMILY SCHOLARSHIP AWARD
• See page 165

LOS ANGELES COUNCIL OF BLACK PROFESSIONAL ENGINEERS

http://www.lablackengineers.org/

AL-BEN SCHOLARSHIP FOR ACADEMIC INCENTIVE
• See page 179

AL-BEN SCHOLARSHIP FOR PROFESSIONAL MERIT
• See page 179

AL-BEN SCHOLARSHIP FOR SCHOLASTIC ACHIEVEMENT
• See page 179

MINERALS, METALS, AND MATERIALS SOCIETY (TMS)

http://www.tms.org/

KAUFMAN CALPHAD SCHOLARSHIP
The applicant must be a student member of Material Advantage. Applicants must be undergraduate sophomores or junior unless otherwise noted. Applicants must be enrolled full time in a metallurgical/materials science engineering program at a qualified college or university. Relatives of members of the funding committee/division are not eligible. Submitted coursework must be relevant to the scholarship for which the student is applying.

Academic Fields/Career Goals: Electrical Engineering/Electronics; Engineering-Related Technologies; Engineering/Technology; Mechanical Engineering.

Award: Scholarship for use in junior or senior years; not renewable. *Number:* 1. *Amount:* $1000.

Eligibility Requirements: Applicant must be enrolled or expecting to enroll full-time at a four-year institution or university. Applicant or parent of applicant must have employment or volunteer experience in engineering/technology. Available to U.S. and non-U.S. citizens.

Application Requirements: Application form, essay. *Deadline:* March 15.

Contact: Ms. Bryn Simpson
E-mail: bsimpson@tms.org

NASA IDAHO SPACE GRANT CONSORTIUM

http://www.id.spacegrant.org/

NASA IDAHO SPACE GRANT CONSORTIUM SCHOLARSHIP PROGRAM
• See page 157

NASA MINNESOTA SPACE GRANT CONSORTIUM

http://www.aem.umn.edu/mnsgc

MINNESOTA SPACE GRANT CONSORTIUM SCHOLARSHIP PROGRAM
• See page 142

NASA MONTANA SPACE GRANT CONSORTIUM

http://www.spacegrant.montana.edu/

MONTANA SPACE GRANT SCHOLARSHIP PROGRAM
• See page 142

NASA'S VIRGINIA SPACE GRANT CONSORTIUM

http://www.vsgc.odu.edu/

COMMUNITY COLLEGE STEM SCHOLARSHIPS
• See page 114

UNDERGRADUATE STEM RESEARCH SCHOLARSHIPS
• See page 114

NATIONAL ASSOCIATION OF WOMEN IN CONSTRUCTION

http://www.nawic.org/

NAWIC UNDERGRADUATE SCHOLARSHIPS
• See page 122

NATIONAL BOARD OF BOILER AND PRESSURE VESSEL INSPECTORS

http://www.nationalboard.org/

NATIONAL BOARD TECHNICAL SCHOLARSHIP
• *See page 180*

NATIONAL SECURITY AGENCY

http://www.nsa.gov/Careers

NATIONAL SECURITY AGENCY STOKES EDUCATIONAL SCHOLARSHIP PROGRAM
• *See page 217*

NATIONAL SOCIETY OF PROFESSIONAL ENGINEERS

http://www.nspe.org/

MAUREEN L. AND HOWARD N. BLITMAN, PE SCHOLARSHIP TO PROMOTE DIVERSITY IN ENGINEERING
• *See page 180*

PAUL H. ROBBINS HONORARY SCHOLARSHIP
• *See page 180*

PROFESSIONAL ENGINEERS IN INDUSTRY SCHOLARSHIP
• *See page 180*

NEXTSTEPU

http://www.nextstepu.com/

$1,500 STEM SCHOLARSHIP
• *See page 106*

OREGON STUDENT ASSISTANCE COMMISSION

http://www.GetCollegeFunds.org/

HOME BUILDERS FOUNDATION JIM IRVINE STATEWIDE SCHOLARSHIP
• *See page 123*

SOCIETY OF AMERICAN MILITARY ENGINEERS PORTLAND POST SCHOLARSHIP
• *See page 181*

PROFESSIONAL CONSTRUCTION ESTIMATORS ASSOCIATION

http://www.pcea.org/

TED G. WILSON MEMORIAL SCHOLARSHIP FOUNDATION
• *See page 197*

ROBERT H. MOLLOHAN FAMILY CHARITABLE FOUNDATION, INC.

http://www.mollohanfoundation.org/

HIGH TECHNOLOGY SCHOLARS PROGRAM
• *See page 158*

SCARLETT FAMILY FOUNDATION SCHOLARSHIP PROGRAM

http://www.scarlettfoundation.org/

SCHOLARSHIP FOR STUDENTS PURSUING A BUSINESS OR STEM DEGREE
• *See page 84*

SEMICONDUCTOR RESEARCH CORPORATION (SRC)

http://www.src.org/

MASTER'S SCHOLARSHIP PROGRAM
• *See page 181*

SIGMA XI, THE SCIENTIFIC RESEARCH SOCIETY

http://www.sigmaxi.org/

SIGMA XI GRANTS-IN-AID OF RESEARCH
• *See page 101*

SOCIETY OF AUTOMOTIVE ENGINEERS

http://www.sae.org/

BMW/SAE ENGINEERING SCHOLARSHIP
• *See page 146*

EDWARD D. HENDRICKSON/SAE ENGINEERING SCHOLARSHIP
• *See page 146*

TMC/SAE DONALD D. DAWSON TECHNICAL SCHOLARSHIP
• *See page 147*

SOCIETY OF MANUFACTURING ENGINEERS EDUCATION FOUNDATION

http://www.smeef.org/

WILLIAM E. WEISEL SCHOLARSHIP FUND
Scholarship will be given to a full-time undergraduate student enrolled in an engineering or technology degree program in the U.S. or Canada, seeking a career in manufacturing. Consideration will be given to students who intend to apply their knowledge in the sub-specialty of medical robotics. Minimum of 3.0 GPA is required. Scholarships will be limited to United States and Canadian citizens.

Academic Fields/Career Goals: Electrical Engineering/Electronics; Engineering/Technology; Mechanical Engineering; Trade/Technical Specialties.

Award: Scholarship for use in sophomore, junior, or senior years; not renewable. *Number:* 1–10. *Amount:* $1000–$5000.

Eligibility Requirements: Applicant must be enrolled or expecting to enroll full-time at a four-year institution or university. Applicant must have 3.0 GPA or higher. Available to U.S. and Canadian citizens.

Application Requirements: Application form, essay, recommendations or references, resume, transcript. *Deadline:* February 1.

SOCIETY OF MOTION PICTURE AND TELEVISION ENGINEERS

https://www.smpte.org/

LOUIS F. WOLF JR. MEMORIAL SCHOLARSHIP
• *See page 210*

STUDENT PAPER AWARD
• See page 210

SOCIETY OF PLASTICS ENGINEERS FOUNDATION (SPE)
http://www.4spe.org/

FLEMING/BASZCAK SCHOLARSHIP
• See page 181

SOCIETY OF PLASTICS ENGINEERS SCHOLARSHIP PROGRAM
• See page 182

SOCIETY OF WOMEN ENGINEERS
http://societyofwomenengineers.swe.org/

ADA I. PRESSMAN MEMORIAL SCHOLARSHIP
• See page 182

AMERICAN TRANSMISSION CO. SCHOLARSHIP
• See page 182

ANNE MAUREEN WHITNEY BARROW MEMORIAL SCHOLARSHIP
• See page 182

ANNE SHEN SMITH ENDOWED SCHOLARSHIP
• See page 182

BAYER SCHOLARSHIP
• See page 183

BETTY LOU BAILEY SWE REGION F SCHOLARSHIP
• See page 183

B.J. HARROD SCHOLARSHIP
• See page 183

BK KRENZER MEMORIAL REENTRY SCHOLARSHIP
• See page 183

CAROL STEPHENS SWE REGION F SCHOLARSHIP
• See page 183

CUMMINS SCHOLARSHIP
• See page 183

DR. IVY M. PARKER MEMORIAL SCHOLARSHIP
• See page 184

DOROTHY LEMKE HOWARTH MEMORIAL SCHOLARSHIP
• See page 184

DOROTHY P. MORRIS SCHOLARSHIP
• See page 184

EXELON CORPORATION SCHOLARSHIP
• See page 184

FCA WOMEN IN ENGINEERING SCHOLARSHIP
• See page 184

FORD MOTOR COMPANY SCHOLARSHIP
$1250 scholarship for women pursuing ABET-accredited Baccalaureate programs in preparation for careers in engineering and engineering technology in the United States and Mexico. Scholarship for one college sophomore and two juniors. Must have leadership potential and minimum 3.5 GPA.

Academic Fields/Career Goals: Electrical Engineering/Electronics; Engineering/Technology; Mechanical Engineering.

Award: Scholarship for use in sophomore or junior years; not renewable. *Number:* 3. *Amount:* $1250.

Eligibility Requirements: Applicant must be enrolled or expecting to enroll full-time at a four-year institution or university; female and must have an interest in leadership. Applicant or parent of applicant must be member of Society of Women Engineers. Applicant must have 3.5 GPA or higher. Available to U.S. citizens.

Application Requirements: Application form. *Deadline:* February 15.
Contact: Scholarship Committee
Phone: 800-793-4636
E-mail: scholarships@swe.org

GENERAL ELECTRIC WOMEN'S NETWORK SCHOLARSHIP
• See page 198

HONEYWELL SCHOLARSHIP
• See page 184

IBM LINDA SANFORD WOMEN'S TECHNICAL ADVANCEMENT SCHOLARSHIP
• See page 185

JILL S. TIETJEN P.E. SCHOLARSHIP
• See page 185

KOCH DISCOVERY SCHOLARSHIP
• See page 185

LILLIAN MOLLER GILBRETH MEMORIAL SCHOLARSHIP
• See page 185

LOCKHEED MARTIN CORPORATION SCHOLARSHIP
• See page 218

MARY V. MUNGER SCHOLARSHIP
• See page 185

MASWE SCHOLARSHIP
• See page 186

OLIVE LYNN SALEMBIER MEMORIAL REENTRY SCHOLARSHIP
• See page 186

PAULA LORING SIMON SCHOLARSHIP
• See page 186

ROBERTA BANASZAK GLEITER ENGINEERING ENDEAVOR SCHOLARSHIP
• See page 186

ROCHELLE PERRY MEMORIAL SCHOLARSHIP
• See page 186

ROCKWELL COLLINS SCHOLARSHIP
• See page 218

SUSAN MISZKOWICZ MEMORIAL SCHOLARSHIP
• See page 186

SWE BALTIMORE-WASHINGTON SECTION SCHOLARSHIP
• See page 186

SWE CENTRAL NEW MEXICO PIONEERS SCHOLARSHIP
• See page 187

SWE CENTRAL NEW MEXICO REENTRY SCHOLARSHIP
• See page 187

SWE MID-HUDSON SECTION SCHOLARSHIP
• See page 187

SWE PHOENIX SECTION SCHOLARSHIP
• See page 187

SWE REGION E SCHOLARSHIP
• See page 187

SWE REGION G JUDY SIMMONS MEMORIAL SCHOLARSHIP
• See page 188

SWE REGION H SCHOLARSHIPS
• See page 188

SWE REGION J SCHOLARSHIP
• See page 188

WANDA MUNN SCHOLARSHIP
• See page 188

SOCIETY OF WOMEN ENGINEERS-ROCKY MOUNTAIN SECTION

http://www.swe-rms.org/

SOCIETY OF WOMEN ENGINEERS-ROCKY MOUNTAIN SECTION SCHOLARSHIP PROGRAM
• See page 188

SONS OF NORWAY FOUNDATION

http://www.sonsofnorway.com/foundation

NANCY LORRAINE JENSEN MEMORIAL SCHOLARSHIP
• See page 189

SPECIALTY EQUIPMENT MARKET ASSOCIATION

http://www.sema.org/

SEMA MEMORIAL SCHOLARSHIP FUND
• See page 85

STRAIGHTFORWARD MEDIA

http://www.straightforwardmedia.com/

STRAIGHTFORWARD MEDIA ENGINEERING SCHOLARSHIP
• See page 189

TAU BETA PI ASSOCIATION

http://www.tbp.org/

TAU BETA PI SCHOLARSHIP PROGRAM
• See page 189

TIMOTION

http://www.timotion.com/

TIMOTION ENGINEERING AND EXCELLENCE SCHOLARSHIP
• See page 199

TRANSTUTORS

http://www.transtutors.com/scholarship

TRANSTUTORS SCHOLARSHIP 2015-16
• See page 85

TURNER CONSTRUCTION COMPANY

http://www.turnerconstruction.com/

YOUTHFORCE 2020 SCHOLARSHIP PROGRAM
• See page 124

UNITED NEGRO COLLEGE FUND

http://www.uncf.org/

ANHEUSER-BUSCH LEGENDS OF THE CROWN SCHOLARSHIP PROGRAM
• See page 86

BASF/ALFRED CHISHOLM ENDOWED MEMORIAL SCHOLARSHIP
• See page 86

BLUE CROSS BLUE SHIELD OF ILLINOIS AND BLUE CROSS BLUE SHIELD OF TEXAS SCHOLARSHIP
• See page 115

COLGATE–PALMOLIVE CORPORATE SCHOLARS PROGRAM
• See page 86

DAVIS SCHOLARSHIP FOR WOMEN IN STEM
• See page 189

DELL CORPORATE SCHOLARS PROGRAM
• See page 169

INTEL SCHOLARSHIP PROGRAM
• See page 190

PROCTER & GAMBLE STEM SCHOLARSHIP
• See page 116

SUEZ CORPORATE SCHOLARS PROGRAM
• See page 87

UNCF NORTHROP GRUMMAN SCHOLARSHIP
• See page 220

UNCF STEM SCHOLARS PROGRAM
• See page 159

UNIVERSITIES SPACE RESEARCH ASSOCIATION

http://www.usra.edu/

UNIVERSITIES SPACE RESEARCH ASSOCIATION SCHOLARSHIP AWARD PROGRAM
• See page 116

VERMONT SPACE GRANT CONSORTIUM

http://www.cems.uvm.edu/vsgc

VERMONT SPACE GRANT CONSORTIUM
• See page 96

WOMEN IN AVIATION, INTERNATIONAL

http://www.wai.org/

DELTA AIR LINES ENGINEERING SCHOLARSHIP
• *See page 149*

XEROX

http://www.xerox.com//

TECHNICAL MINORITY SCHOLARSHIP
• *See page 190*

ENERGY AND POWER ENGINEERING

AMERICAN CHEMICAL SOCIETY, RUBBER DIVISION

http://www.rubber.org/

AMERICAN CHEMICAL SOCIETY, RUBBER DIVISION UNDERGRADUATE SCHOLARSHIP
• *See page 109*

AMERICAN COUNCIL OF ENGINEERING COMPANIES OF PENNSYLVANIA (ACEC/PA)

http://www.acecpa.org/

ERIC J. GENNUSO AND LEROY D. (BUD) LOY, JR. SCHOLARSHIP PROGRAM
• *See page 173*

AMERICAN INDIAN SCIENCE AND ENGINEERING SOCIETY

http://www.aises.org/

A.T. ANDERSON MEMORIAL SCHOLARSHIP PROGRAM
• *See page 109*

AMERICAN NUCLEAR SOCIETY

http://www.ans.org/

DECOMMISSIONING, DECONTAMINATION, AND REUTILIZATION UNDERGRADUATE SCHOLARSHIP
Undergraduate scholarship for students who have completed two or more years in a course of study leading to a degree in nuclear science, nuclear engineering, or a nuclear-related field.
Academic Fields/Career Goals: Energy and Power Engineering; Nuclear Science.
Award: Scholarship for use in junior or senior years; not renewable. *Number:* 1. *Amount:* $2000.
Eligibility Requirements: Applicant must be enrolled or expecting to enroll full-time at a four-year institution or university. Available to U.S. citizens.
Application Requirements: Application form, essay, recommendations or references, transcript. *Deadline:* February 1.

Contact: Scholarship Coordinator
American Nuclear Society
555 North Kensington Avenue
La Grange Park, IL 60526
Phone: 708-352-6611
Fax: 708-352-0499
E-mail: outreach@ans.org

AMERICAN PUBLIC POWER ASSOCIATION

http://publicpower.org/DEED

DEED EDUCATIONAL SCHOLARSHIP
• *See page 176*

DEED STUDENT INTERNSHIP
• *See page 176*

DEED STUDENT RESEARCH GRANTS
• *See page 191*

DEED TECHNICAL DESIGN PROJECT
• *See page 176*

AMERICAN SOCIETY OF CERTIFIED ENGINEERING TECHNICIANS

http://www.ascet.org/

KURT H. AND DONNA M. SCHULER SMALL GRANT
• *See page 176*

AMERICAN SOCIETY OF HEATING, REFRIGERATING, AND AIR CONDITIONING ENGINEERS, INC.

http://www.ashrae.org/

ASHRAE REGION III BOGGARM SETTY SCHOLARSHIP
• *See page 176*

REUBEN TRANE SCHOLARSHIP
• *See page 265*

AMERICAN SOCIETY OF NAVAL ENGINEERS

http://www.navalengineers.org/

AMERICAN SOCIETY OF NAVAL ENGINEERS SCHOLARSHIP
• *See page 110*

ARRL FOUNDATION INC.

http://www.arrl.org/

ALFRED E. FRIEND JR., W4CF, MEMORIAL SCHOLARSHIP
• *See page 177*

GARY WAGNER, K3OMI, SCHOLARSHIP
• *See page 177*

LOIS MANLEY, K7LMZ, AND RANDALL PITCHFORD, WW7ZZ, SCHOLARSHIP
• *See page 193*

W1FDR SCHOLARSHIP
• *See page 112*

ASSOCIATION FOR WOMEN GEOSCIENTISTS (AWG)

http://www.awg.org/

AWG MARIA LUISA CRAWFORD FIELD CAMP SCHOLARSHIP
• *See page 117*

AUTOMOTIVE WOMEN'S ALLIANCE FOUNDATION

http://www.awafoundation.org/index.php

AUTOMOTIVE WOMEN'S ALLIANCE FOUNDATION SCHOLARSHIPS
• *See page 74*

BARRY GOLDWATER SCHOLARSHIP AND EXCELLENCE IN EDUCATION FOUNDATION

https://goldwater.scholarsapply.org

BARRY M. GOLDWATER SCHOLARSHIP AND EXCELLENCE IN EDUCATION PROGRAM
• *See page 112*

BHW GROUP

https://thebhwgroup.com/

BHW WOMEN IN STEM SCHOLARSHIP
• *See page 74*

BRASKEM ODEBRECHT

http://www.odebrechtaward.com

ODEBRECHT AWARD FOR SUSTAINABLE DEVELOPMENT
• *See page 119*

BROWN AND CALDWELL

http://www.brownandcaldwell.com

ECKENFELDER SCHOLARSHIP
• *See page 155*

MINORITY SCHOLARSHIP PROGRAM
• *See page 155*

THE ELECTROCHEMICAL SOCIETY

http://www.electrochem.org/

H.H. DOW MEMORIAL STUDENT ACHIEVEMENT AWARD OF THE INDUSTRIAL ELECTROLYSIS AND ELECTROCHEMICAL ENGINEERING DIVISION OF THE ELECTROCHEMICAL SOCIETY INC.
• *See page 113*

STUDENT RESEARCH AWARDS OF THE BATTERY DIVISION OF THE ELECTROCHEMICAL SOCIETY INC.
• *See page 113*

FLORIDA ENGINEERING SOCIETY

http://www.fleng.org/scholarships.cfm

DAVID F. LUDOVICI SCHOLARSHIP
• *See page 178*

GREATER KANAWHA VALLEY FOUNDATION

http://www.tgkvf.org/

LEOPOLD & ELIZABETH MARMET SCHOLARSHIP
Renewable award to West Virginia residents pursuing full-time postsecondary studies in science, production or conservation of energy, or natural resources. Award may not be used for medical studies. Minimum 2.5 GPA required. Preference given to graduate students.

Academic Fields/Career Goals: Energy and Power Engineering; Natural Resources.

Award: Scholarship for use in freshman, sophomore, junior, senior, or graduate years; renewable. *Amount:* $3000.

Eligibility Requirements: Applicant must be enrolled or expecting to enroll full-time at a four-year institution or university and resident of West Virginia. Applicant must have 2.5 GPA or higher. Available to U.S. citizens.

Application Requirements: Application form, recommendations or references, test scores, transcript. *Deadline:* January 15.

Contact: Susan Hoover, Scholarship Program Officer
Phone: 304-346-3620
E-mail: shoover@tgkvf.org

STEVEN ENGINEERING SCHOLARSHIP
• *See page 178*

GREAT MINDS IN STEM

www.greatmindsinstem.org

HISPANIC ENGINEER NATIONAL ACHIEVEMENT AWARDS CORPORATION SCHOLARSHIP PROGRAM
• *See page 106*

NEXTSTEPU

http://www.nextstepu.com/

$1,500 STEM SCHOLARSHIP
• *See page 106*

PLAN NEW HAMPSHIRE

www.plannh.org

PLAN NEW HAMPSHIRE SCHOLARSHIP AND PROGRAM
• *See page 123*

ROBERT H. MOLLOHAN FAMILY CHARITABLE FOUNDATION, INC.

http://www.mollohanfoundation.org/

HIGH TECHNOLOGY SCHOLARS PROGRAM
• *See page 158*

SCARLETT FAMILY FOUNDATION SCHOLARSHIP PROGRAM

http://www.scarlettfoundation.org/

SCHOLARSHIP FOR STUDENTS PURSUING A BUSINESS OR STEM DEGREE
• *See page 84*

SIGMA XI, THE SCIENTIFIC RESEARCH SOCIETY

http://www.sigmaxi.org/

SIGMA XI GRANTS-IN-AID OF RESEARCH
• *See page 101*

SOCIETY OF WOMEN ENGINEERS

http://societyofwomenengineers.swe.org/

ADA I. PRESSMAN MEMORIAL SCHOLARSHIP
• *See page 182*

AMERICAN TRANSMISSION CO. SCHOLARSHIP
• *See page 182*

ANNE MAUREEN WHITNEY BARROW MEMORIAL SCHOLARSHIP
• *See page 182*

ANNE SHEN SMITH ENDOWED SCHOLARSHIP
• *See page 182*

BAYER SCHOLARSHIP
• *See page 183*

BETTY LOU BAILEY SWE REGION F SCHOLARSHIP
• *See page 183*

B.J. HARROD SCHOLARSHIP
• *See page 183*

BK KRENZER MEMORIAL REENTRY SCHOLARSHIP
• *See page 183*

CAROL STEPHENS SWE REGION F SCHOLARSHIP
• *See page 183*

DR. IVY M. PARKER MEMORIAL SCHOLARSHIP
• *See page 184*

DOROTHY LEMKE HOWARTH MEMORIAL SCHOLARSHIP
• *See page 184*

DOROTHY P. MORRIS SCHOLARSHIP
• *See page 184*

EXELON CORPORATION SCHOLARSHIP
• *See page 184*

FCA WOMEN IN ENGINEERING SCHOLARSHIP
• *See page 184*

IBM LINDA SANFORD WOMEN'S TECHNICAL ADVANCEMENT SCHOLARSHIP
• *See page 185*

JILL S. TIETJEN P.E. SCHOLARSHIP
• *See page 185*

KOCH DISCOVERY SCHOLARSHIP
• *See page 185*

LILLIAN MOLLER GILBRETH MEMORIAL SCHOLARSHIP
• *See page 185*

MARY V. MUNGER SCHOLARSHIP
• *See page 185*

MASWE SCHOLARSHIP
• *See page 186*

OLIVE LYNN SALEMBIER MEMORIAL REENTRY SCHOLARSHIP
• *See page 186*

ROBERTA BANASZAK GLEITER ENGINEERING ENDEAVOR SCHOLARSHIP
• *See page 186*

ROCHELLE PERRY MEMORIAL SCHOLARSHIP
• *See page 186*

SUSAN MISZKOWICZ MEMORIAL SCHOLARSHIP
• *See page 186*

SWE BALTIMORE-WASHINGTON SECTION SCHOLARSHIP
• *See page 186*

SWE CENTRAL NEW MEXICO PIONEERS SCHOLARSHIP
• *See page 187*

SWE CENTRAL NEW MEXICO REENTRY SCHOLARSHIP
• *See page 187*

SWE MID-HUDSON SECTION SCHOLARSHIP
• *See page 187*

SWE PHOENIX SECTION SCHOLARSHIP
• *See page 187*

SWE REGION E SCHOLARSHIP
• *See page 187*

SWE REGION G JUDY SIMMONS MEMORIAL SCHOLARSHIP
• *See page 188*

SWE REGION H SCHOLARSHIPS
• *See page 188*

SWE REGION J SCHOLARSHIP
• *See page 188*

WANDA MUNN SCHOLARSHIP
• *See page 188*

SOCIETY OF WOMEN ENGINEERS-ROCKY MOUNTAIN SECTION

http://www.swe-rms.org/

SOCIETY OF WOMEN ENGINEERS-ROCKY MOUNTAIN SECTION SCHOLARSHIP PROGRAM
• *See page 188*

STRAIGHTFORWARD MEDIA

http://www.straightforwardmedia.com/

STRAIGHTFORWARD MEDIA ENGINEERING SCHOLARSHIP
• *See page 189*

TIMOTION

http://www.timotion.com/

TIMOTION ENGINEERING AND EXCELLENCE SCHOLARSHIP
• *See page 199*

TRANSTUTORS

http://www.transtutors.com/scholarship

TRANSTUTORS SCHOLARSHIP 2015-16
• *See page 85*

UNITED NEGRO COLLEGE FUND

http://www.uncf.org/

DAVIS SCHOLARSHIP FOR WOMEN IN STEM
• *See page 189*

GALACTIC UNITE BYTHEWAY SCHOLARSHIP
• *See page 190*

UNCF STEM SCHOLARS PROGRAM
• *See page 159*

VERMONT SPACE GRANT CONSORTIUM

http://www.cems.uvm.edu/vsgc

VERMONT SPACE GRANT CONSORTIUM
• *See page 96*

ENGINEERING-RELATED TECHNOLOGIES

AACE INTERNATIONAL

http://www.aacei.org/

AACE INTERNATIONAL COMPETITIVE SCHOLARSHIP
• *See page 118*

AHS INTERNATIONAL—THE VERTICAL FLIGHT TECHNICAL SOCIETY

http://www.vtol.org/

VERTICAL FLIGHT FOUNDATION SCHOLARSHIP
• *See page 134*

AIST FOUNDATION

http://www.aistfoundation.org/

ASSOCIATION FOR IRON AND STEEL TECHNOLOGY BALTIMORE CHAPTER SCHOLARSHIP

Scholarship for child, grandchild, or spouse of a member of the Baltimore Chapter of AIST. Must be high school seniors who are currently enrolled undergraduate students pursuing a career in engineering or metallurgy. Student may reapply each year for the term of their college education.

Academic Fields/Career Goals: Engineering-Related Technologies; Engineering/Technology; Materials Science, Engineering, and Metallurgy.

Award: Scholarship for use in freshman, sophomore, junior, or senior years; not renewable. *Number:* 1. *Amount:* $1500.

Eligibility Requirements: Applicant must be enrolled or expecting to enroll full-time at a four-year institution or university. Applicant or parent of applicant must be member of Association for Iron and Steel Technology. Available to U.S. citizens.

Application Requirements: Application form, essay, test scores, transcript. *Deadline:* April 30.

Contact: Thomas Russo, Program Coordinator
AIST Foundation
1430 Sparrows Point Boulevard
Sparrows Point, MD 21219-1014

ASSOCIATION FOR IRON AND STEEL TECHNOLOGY BENJAMIN F. FAIRLESS SCHOLARSHIP (AIME)
• *See page 172*

ASSOCIATION FOR IRON AND STEEL TECHNOLOGY OHIO VALLEY CHAPTER SCHOLARSHIP
• *See page 153*

AMERICAN CHEMICAL SOCIETY, RUBBER DIVISION

http://www.rubber.org/

AMERICAN CHEMICAL SOCIETY, RUBBER DIVISION UNDERGRADUATE SCHOLARSHIP
• *See page 109*

AMERICAN COUNCIL OF ENGINEERING COMPANIES OF PENNSYLVANIA (ACEC/PA)

http://www.acecpa.org/

ERIC J. GENNUSO AND LEROY D. (BUD) LOY, JR. SCHOLARSHIP PROGRAM
• *See page 173*

AMERICAN INDIAN SCIENCE AND ENGINEERING SOCIETY

http://www.aises.org/

A.T. ANDERSON MEMORIAL SCHOLARSHIP PROGRAM
• *See page 109*

AMERICAN INSTITUTE OF AERONAUTICS AND ASTRONAUTICS

http://www.aiaafoundation.org/

AIAA FOUNDATION UNDERGRADUATE SCHOLARSHIPS
• *See page 110*

LEATRICE GREGORY PENDRAY SCHOLARSHIP
• *See page 110*

AMERICAN PUBLIC POWER ASSOCIATION

http://publicpower.org/DEED

DEED EDUCATIONAL SCHOLARSHIP
• *See page 176*

DEED STUDENT INTERNSHIP
• *See page 176*

DEED STUDENT RESEARCH GRANTS
• *See page 191*

DEED TECHNICAL DESIGN PROJECT
• *See page 176*

AMERICAN PUBLIC TRANSPORTATION FOUNDATION

http://www.apta.com/

TRANSIT HALL OF FAME SCHOLARSHIP AWARD PROGRAM
• *See page 191*

AMERICAN RAILWAY ENGINEERING AND MAINTENANCE OF WAY ASSOCIATION

http://www.aremafoundation.org/

AREMA GRADUATE AND UNDERGRADUATE SCHOLARSHIPS
• *See page 191*

AMERICAN SOCIETY FOR ENGINEERING EDUCATION

http://www.asee.org/

SCIENCE, MATHEMATICS, AND RESEARCH FOR TRANSFORMATION DEFENSE SCHOLARSHIP FOR SERVICE PROGRAM
• *See page 110*

AMERICAN SOCIETY FOR NONDESTRUCTIVE TESTING

http://www.asnt.org

ASNT ENGINEERING UNDERGRADUATE SCHOLARSHIP

The Engineering Undergraduate Scholarship provides incentive to engineering undergraduate students enrolled in colleges and universities in the U.S. to choose nondestructive testing and evaluation as their field of specialization.

Academic Fields/Career Goals: Engineering-Related Technologies.

Award: Scholarship for use in freshman, sophomore, junior, or senior years; not renewable. *Number:* 3. *Amount:* $3000.

Eligibility Requirements: Applicant must be enrolled or expecting to enroll full-time at a two-year or four-year institution or university. Applicant or parent of applicant must have employment or volunteer experience in engineering/technology. Available to U.S. citizens.

Application Requirements: Application form. *Deadline:* December 15.

Contact: Jessica VanDervort, Program Coordinator
    E-mail: jvandervort@asnt.org

AMERICAN SOCIETY OF CERTIFIED ENGINEERING TECHNICIANS

http://www.ascet.org/

KURT H. AND DONNA M. SCHULER SMALL GRANT
• *See page 176*

AMERICAN SOCIETY OF HEATING, REFRIGERATING, AND AIR CONDITIONING ENGINEERS, INC.

http://www.ashrae.org/

ALWIN B. NEWTON SCHOLARSHIP
• *See page 264*

ASHRAE GENERAL SCHOLARSHIPS

One-time award of $5000 for full-time study in heating, ventilating, refrigeration, and air conditioning in an ABET-accredited program at an accredited school. Must be pursuing a bachelor of science or engineering degree and have a minimum GPA of 3.0. See Website for application and additional information, http://www.ashrae.org.

Academic Fields/Career Goals: Engineering-Related Technologies; Engineering/Technology; Heating, Air-Conditioning, and Refrigeration Mechanics; Trade/Technical Specialties.

Award: Scholarship for use in freshman, sophomore, junior, or senior years; not renewable. *Number:* 2. *Amount:* $5000.

Eligibility Requirements: Applicant must be enrolled or expecting to enroll full-time at a four-year institution or university and must have an interest in leadership. Applicant must have 3.0 GPA or higher. Available to U.S. and non-U.S. citizens.

Application Requirements: Application form, financial need analysis. *Deadline:* December 1.

Contact: Lois Benedict, Scholarship Administrator
    Phone: 404-636-8400 Ext. 1120
    E-mail: lbenedict@ashrae.org

ASHRAE REGION III BOGGARM SETTY SCHOLARSHIP
• *See page 176*

ASHRAE REGION VIII SCHOLARSHIP

One-year scholarship available to undergraduate engineering student enrolled full time in an ABET-accredited program at a school located within the geographic boundaries of ASHRAE'S Region VIII or accredited by the Consejo de Acreditacion de la Ensenanza de la Ingenieria in Mexico. This region includes Arkansas, Louisiana, Texas, and Oklahoma as well as Mexico. See Website for application and additional information, http://www.ashrae.org.

Academic Fields/Career Goals: Engineering-Related Technologies; Engineering/Technology.

Award: Scholarship for use in freshman, sophomore, junior, or senior years; not renewable. *Number:* 1. *Amount:* $3000.

Eligibility Requirements: Applicant must be enrolled or expecting to enroll full-time at a four-year institution or university and studying in Arkansas, Louisiana, Oklahoma, Texas. Applicant must have 3.0 GPA or higher. Available to U.S. and non-U.S. citizens.

Application Requirements: Application form, financial need analysis. *Deadline:* December 1.

Contact: Lois Benedict, Scholarship Administrator
    Phone: 404-636-8400 Ext. 1120
    E-mail: lbenedict@ashrae.org

DUANE HANSON SCHOLARSHIP
• *See page 264*

FRANK M. CODA SCHOLARSHIP
• *See page 264*

HENRY ADAMS SCHOLARSHIP
• *See page 265*

LYNN G. BELLENGER SCHOLARSHIP
• *See page 265*

WILLIS H. CARRIER SCHOLARSHIPS
• *See page 265*

AMERICAN WELDING SOCIETY

http://www.aws.org/

AIRGAS-JERRY BAKER SCHOLARSHIP

Awarded to full-time undergraduate pursuing a minimum four-year degree in welding engineering or welding engineering technology. Applicant must be a minimum of 18 years of age and have a 3.0 GPA. Priority will be given to those individuals residing or attending school in the states of Alabama, Georgia or Florida.

Academic Fields/Career Goals: Engineering-Related Technologies; Materials Science, Engineering, and Metallurgy.

Award: Scholarship for use in freshman, sophomore, junior, or senior years; not renewable. *Number:* 1. *Amount:* $2500.

Eligibility Requirements: Applicant must be enrolled or expecting to enroll full-time at a four-year institution or university. Applicant must have 3.0 GPA or higher. Available to U.S. and Canadian citizens.

Application Requirements: Application form, essay, financial need analysis. *Deadline:* February 15.

Contact: Vicki Pinsky, Associate Director, Scholarships, Foundation
American Welding Society
8669 NW 36 Street, Suite 130
Miami, FL 33166
Phone: 800-443-9353 Ext. 212
E-mail: vpinsky@aws.org

AIRGAS-TERRY JARVIS MEMORIAL SCHOLARSHIP

Award for a full-time undergraduate pursuing a minimum four-year degree in welding engineering or welding engineering technology. Must have a minimum 2.8 overall GPA with a 3.0 GPA in engineering courses. Priority given to applicants residing or attending school in Florida, Georgia, or Alabama.

Academic Fields/Career Goals: Engineering-Related Technologies; Engineering/Technology; Materials Science, Engineering, and Metallurgy.

Award: Scholarship for use in freshman, sophomore, junior, or senior years; not renewable. *Number:* 1. *Amount:* $2500.

Eligibility Requirements: Applicant must be enrolled or expecting to enroll full-time at a four-year institution or university. Applicant must have 3.0 GPA or higher. Available to U.S. and Canadian citizens.

Application Requirements: Application form, essay, financial need analysis. *Deadline:* February 15.

Contact: Vicki Pinsky, Associate Director Scholarships, Foundation
American Welding Society
8669 NW 36 Street, Suite 130
Miami, FL 33166
Phone: 800-443-9353 Ext. 212
E-mail: vpinsky@aws.org

AIR PRODUCTS WOMEN IN GASES AND WELDING SCHOLARSHIP

Awarded to a female pursing higher education in a welding or engineering discipline, who has proven to be an exceptional student and is eager to start her career in the industry. The student must be a US citizen, a full time student with a 2.5 overall GPA, and pursuing a two-year or four-year degree at a US school.

Academic Fields/Career Goals: Engineering-Related Technologies; Engineering/Technology; Materials Science, Engineering, and Metallurgy.

Award: Scholarship for use in freshman, sophomore, junior, or senior years; not renewable. *Number:* 1. *Amount:* $2500.

Eligibility Requirements: Applicant must be enrolled or expecting to enroll full-time at a two-year or four-year institution and female. Applicant must have 3.5 GPA or higher. Available to U.S. citizens.

Application Requirements: Application form, financial need analysis. *Deadline:* February 15.

Contact: Ms. Vicki Pinsky, Associate Director, Scholarships
American Welding Society
8669 NW 36 Street, Suite 130
Miami, FL 33166
Phone: 305-443-9353 Ext. 212
E-mail: vpinsky@aws.org

AMERICAN WELDING SOCIETY DISTRICT SCHOLARSHIP PROGRAM

Award for students in vocational training, community college, or a degree program in welding or a related field of study. Applicants must be high school graduates or equivalent. Must reside in the United States and attend a U.S. institution. Recipients may reapply. Must include personal statement of career goals.

Academic Fields/Career Goals: Engineering-Related Technologies; Trade/Technical Specialties.

Award: Scholarship for use in freshman, sophomore, junior, or senior years; not renewable. *Number:* 150–200. *Amount:* $100–$2500.

Eligibility Requirements: Applicant must be enrolled or expecting to enroll full- or part-time at a two-year or four-year or technical institution or university. Available to U.S. citizens.

Application Requirements: Application form, financial need analysis. *Deadline:* March 1.

Contact: Nazdhia Prado-Pulido, Assistant, Foundation
American Welding Society
8669 NW 36 Street, Suite 130
Miami, FL 33166
Phone: 800-443-9353 Ext. 250
E-mail: nprado-pulido@aws.org

AMERICAN WELDING SOCIETY INTERNATIONAL SCHOLARSHIP

Award for full-time international students pursuing a bachelor's or graduate degree in joining technologies. Scholarship not available to students residing in North America. Applicants must have completed at least one year of welding or related field of study at a baccalaureate degree-granting institution and be in the top 20 percent of that institution's grading system. For more information see website http://www.aws.org/foundation/intl_scholarships.html.

Academic Fields/Career Goals: Engineering-Related Technologies; Engineering/Technology; Materials Science, Engineering, and Metallurgy; Trade/Technical Specialties.

Award: Scholarship for use in freshman, sophomore, junior, senior, or graduate years; not renewable. *Number:* 1. *Amount:* $2500.

Eligibility Requirements: Applicant must be enrolled or expecting to enroll full-time at a four-year institution or university. Available to citizens of countries other than the U.S. or Canada.

Application Requirements: Application form, essay, financial need analysis. *Deadline:* April 1.

Contact: Vicki Pinsky, Manager, Foundation
American Welding Society
8669 Doral Boulevard, Suite 130
Doral, FL 33166
Phone: 800-443-9353 Ext. 212
E-mail: vpinsky@aws.org

DONALD F. HASTINGS SCHOLARSHIP

Award for undergraduate pursuing a four-year degree either full-time or part-time in welding engineering or welding engineering technology. Preference given to students residing or attending school in California or Ohio. Submit copy of proposed curriculum. Must rank in upper half of class or have a minimum GPA of 2.5. Must also include acceptance letter.

Academic Fields/Career Goals: Engineering-Related Technologies; Engineering/Technology; Trade/Technical Specialties.

Award: Scholarship for use in freshman, sophomore, junior, or senior years; renewable. *Number:* 1.

Eligibility Requirements: Applicant must be enrolled or expecting to enroll full- or part-time at a four-year institution or university. Applicant must have 3.5 GPA or higher. Available to U.S. citizens.

Application Requirements: Application form, financial need analysis. *Deadline:* February 15.

Contact: Vicki Pinsky, Associate Director, Scholarships, Foundation
American Welding Society
8669 NW 36 Street, Suite 130
Miami, FL 33166
Phone: 800-443-9353 Ext. 212
E-mail: vpinsky@aws.org

EDWARD J. BRADY MEMORIAL SCHOLARSHIP

Award for an undergraduate student pursuing a four-year degree either full- or part-time in welding engineering or welding engineering technology.

Academic Fields/Career Goals: Engineering-Related Technologies; Engineering/Technology; Trade/Technical Specialties.

Award: Scholarship for use in freshman, sophomore, junior, or senior years; not renewable.

Eligibility Requirements: Applicant must be enrolled or expecting to enroll full- or part-time at a four-year institution or university. Available to U.S. citizens.

Application Requirements: Application form, essay, financial need analysis. *Deadline:* February 15.

Contact: Ms. Vicki Pinsky, Associate Director, Scholarships, AWS Foundation
American Welding Society
8669 NW 36 Street, Suite 130
Miami, FL 33166
Phone: 305-443-9353 Ext. 212

HOWARD E. AND WILMA J. ADKINS MEMORIAL SCHOLARSHIP

Award for a full-time junior or senior in welding engineering or welding engineering technology. Preference to welding engineering students and those residing or attending school in Wisconsin or Kentucky. Must have at least 3.2 GPA in engineering, scientific, and technical subjects and a 2.8 GPA overall. No financial need is required to apply. Award may be granted a maximum of two years. Reapply each year. Submit copy of proposed curriculum and an acceptance letter.

Academic Fields/Career Goals: Engineering-Related Technologies; Engineering/Technology; Trade/Technical Specialties.

Award: Scholarship for use in junior or senior years; not renewable.

Eligibility Requirements: Applicant must be enrolled or expecting to enroll full-time at a four-year institution. Available to U.S. citizens.

Application Requirements: Application form, essay, financial need analysis. *Deadline:* February 15.

Contact: Vicki Pinsky, Associate Director, Scholarships, Foundation
American Welding Society
8669 NW 36 Street, Suite 130
Miami, FL 33166
Phone: 800-443-9353 Ext. 212
E-mail: vpinsky@aws.org

JOHN C. LINCOLN MEMORIAL SCHOLARSHIP

Award for an undergraduate pursuing a four-year degree either full time or part time in engineering or welding engineering technology. Priority given to welding engineering students residing or attending school in the states of Ohio or Arizona. Applicant must have a minimum 2.5 overall GPA. Proof of financial need is required to qualify.

Academic Fields/Career Goals: Engineering-Related Technologies; Engineering/Technology; Materials Science, Engineering, and Metallurgy.

Award: Scholarship for use in freshman, sophomore, junior, or senior years; not renewable. *Number:* 1. *Amount:* $3500.

Eligibility Requirements: Applicant must be enrolled or expecting to enroll full- or part-time at a four-year institution. Applicant must have 3.5 GPA or higher. Available to U.S. citizens.

Application Requirements: Application form, financial need analysis. *Deadline:* February 15.

Contact: Vicki Pinsky, Associate Director, Foundation
American Welding Society
8669 NW 36 Street, Suite 130
Miami, FL 33166
Phone: 800-443-9353 Ext. 212
E-mail: vpinsky@aws.org

JOHN M. STROPKI SCHOLARSHIP

Awarded to a college undergraduate student pursuing a minimum four-year Bachelor's degree in welding engineering or a related engineering or science major. Priority will be given to the sons and daughters of current Lincoln Electric employees in the United States and Canada. Students must have a 3.0 overall GPA, and be attending school full time. Three $5,000 scholarship awards will be made to children of current Lincoln Electric employees in the U.S. or Canada pursuing a welding engineering, or related engineering or science bachelors degree. One $5,000 scholarship award will be made to any student pursuing a welding engineering, or related engineering or science bachelors degree.

Academic Fields/Career Goals: Engineering-Related Technologies; Engineering/Technology.

Award: Scholarship for use in freshman, sophomore, junior, or senior years; not renewable.

Eligibility Requirements: Applicant must be enrolled or expecting to enroll full-time at a four-year institution. Available to U.S. and Canadian citizens.

Application Requirements: Application form, financial need analysis. *Deadline:* February 15.

Contact: Ms. Vicki Pinsky, Associate Director, Scholarships
American Welding Society
8669 NW 36 Street, #130
Miami, FL 33166
Phone: 305-443-9353 Ext. 212
E-mail: vpinsky@aws.org

MATSUO BRIDGE COMPANY LTD. OF JAPAN SCHOLARSHIP

• *See page 193*

MILLER ELECTRIC INTERNATIONAL WORLD SKILLS COMPETITION SCHOLARSHIP

Applicant must compete in the National Skills USA-VICA Competition for Welding, and advance to the AWS Weld Trials at the AWS International Welding and Fabricating Exposition and Convention, which is held on a bi-annual basis. The winner of the U.S. Weld Trial Competition will receive the scholarship for $10,000 and runner up will receive $1000. For additional information, see website http://www.aws.org.

Academic Fields/Career Goals: Engineering-Related Technologies; Engineering/Technology; Materials Science, Engineering, and Metallurgy; Trade/Technical Specialties.

Award: Grant for use in freshman, sophomore, junior, or senior years; renewable.

Eligibility Requirements: Applicant must be enrolled or expecting to enroll full- or part-time at a four-year institution or university. Available to U.S. citizens.

Application Requirements: Interview.

Contact: Vicki Pinsky, Associate Director, Scholarships, AWS Foundation
American Welding Society
8669 NW 36 Street, Suite 130
Miami, FL 33166
Phone: 800-443-9353 Ext. 212
E-mail: vpinsky@aws.org

MILLER ELECTRIC MFG. CO. SCHOLARSHIP

Two awards of $3000 each are available for undergraduate students who will be seniors in a four-year bachelor's degree in welding engineering technology or welding engineering. Applicant must be U.S. citizen planning to attend a U.S. institution and have a minimum 3.0 GPA. Priority given to students attending Ferris State University. Must exhibit a strong interest in welding equipment and have prior work experience in the welding equipment field.

Academic Fields/Career Goals: Engineering-Related Technologies; Engineering/Technology; Materials Science, Engineering, and Metallurgy; Trade/Technical Specialties.

Award: Scholarship for use in senior year; not renewable.

Eligibility Requirements: Applicant must be enrolled or expecting to enroll full- or part-time at a four-year institution or university. Applicant must have 3.0 GPA or higher. Available to U.S. citizens.

Application Requirements: Application form, financial need analysis. *Deadline:* February 15.

Contact: Vicki Pinsky, Associate Director, Scholarships, AWS
Foundation
American Welding Society
8669 NW 36 Street, Suite 130
Miami, FL 33166
Phone: 800-443-9353 Ext. 212
E-mail: vpinsky@aws.org

PRAXAIR INTERNATIONAL SCHOLARSHIP

Award for a full-time student demonstrating leadership and pursuing a
four-year degree in welding engineering or welding engineering
technology. Priority given to welding engineering students. Must be a
U.S. or Canadian citizen. Financial need is not required. Must have
minimum 2.5 GPA.

Academic Fields/Career Goals: Engineering-Related Technologies;
Engineering/Technology; Materials Science, Engineering, and
Metallurgy.

Award: Scholarship for use in freshman, sophomore, junior, or senior
years; not renewable.

Eligibility Requirements: Applicant must be enrolled or expecting to
enroll full-time at a four-year institution or university. Applicant must
have 3.5 GPA or higher. Available to U.S. and Canadian citizens.

Application Requirements: Application form, financial need analysis.
Deadline: February 15.

Contact: Vicki Pinsky, Associate Director, Scholarships, AWS
Foundation
American Welding Society
8669 NW 36 Street, Suite 130
Miami, FL 33166
Phone: 800-443-9353 Ext. 212
E-mail: vpinsky@aws.org

RICHARD J. SEIF TECHNICAL SALES AND MARKETING SCHOLARSHIP

• *See page 161*

ROBERT G. AND ANNETTE H. PALI SCHOLARSHIP

This scholarship is sponsored by Robert Pali, Past AWS Treasurer, and
his wife, Annette. The student must be a US citizen, with a 3.0 overall
GPA, and be pursuing a bachelors degree in engineering, or science
related to math, physics, or chemistry. Preference will be given to
students attending Lafayette College. Preference will be given to women.
Annual award is $3,000. The application deadline is February 15th.

Academic Fields/Career Goals: Engineering-Related Technologies.

Award: Scholarship for use in junior or senior years; renewable.

Eligibility Requirements: Applicant must be enrolled or expecting to
enroll full- or part-time at a four-year institution. Applicant must have 3.0
GPA or higher. Available to U.S. citizens.

Application Requirements: Application form, financial need analysis.
Deadline: February 15.

Contact: Ms. Vicki Pinsky, Associate Director, Scholarships, AWS
Foundation
American Welding Society
8669 NW 36 Street, #130
Miami, FL 33166
Phone: 305-443-9353 Ext. 212
E-mail: vpinsky@aws.org

VICTOR TECHNOLOGIES AWARD FOR EXCELLENCE IN CUTTING AND WELDING

Awarded to a student who is a senior or in their final year of a 4-year
degree in WET or WE. Minimum 3.0 overall GPA, US citizen.

Academic Fields/Career Goals: Engineering-Related Technologies;
Engineering/Technology.

Award: Scholarship for use in senior year; not renewable.

Eligibility Requirements: Applicant must be enrolled or expecting to
enroll full- or part-time at a four-year institution. Applicant must have 3.0
GPA or higher. Available to U.S. citizens.

Application Requirements: Application form, financial need analysis.
Deadline: February 15.

Contact: Ms. Vicki Pinsky, Associate Director, Scholarships, AWS
Foundation
American Welding Society
8669 NW 36 Street, Suite 130
Miami, FL 33166
Phone: 305-443-9353 Ext. 212
E-mail: vpinsky@aws.org

VICTOR TECHNOLOGIES CUTTING AND WELDING SCHOLARSHIP

Awarded to an undergraduate pursuing a four-year degree in Welding
Engineering Technology or Welding Engineering.

Academic Fields/Career Goals: Engineering-Related Technologies;
Engineering/Technology; Materials Science, Engineering, and
Metallurgy.

Award: Scholarship for use in freshman, sophomore, or junior years; not
renewable.

Eligibility Requirements: Applicant must be enrolled or expecting to
enroll full- or part-time at a four-year institution. Applicant must have 3.5
GPA or higher. Available to U.S. citizens.

Application Requirements: Application form, financial need analysis.
Deadline: February 15.

Contact: Ms. Vicki Pinsky, Associate Director, Scholarships, AWS
Foundation
American Welding Society
8669 NW 36 Street, Suite 130
Miami, FL 33166
Phone: 305-443-9353 Ext. 212
E-mail: vpinsky@aws.org

WILLIAM A. AND ANN M. BROTHERS SCHOLARSHIP

Awarded to a full-time undergraduate pursuing a bachelor's degree in
welding or welding-related program at an accredited university.
Applicant must have a minimum 2.5 overall GPA. Proof of financial need
is required.

Academic Fields/Career Goals: Engineering-Related Technologies;
Materials Science, Engineering, and Metallurgy.

Award: Scholarship for use in freshman, sophomore, junior, or senior
years; not renewable.

Eligibility Requirements: Applicant must be enrolled or expecting to
enroll full-time at a four-year institution or university. Applicant must
have 3.5 GPA or higher. Available to U.S. citizens.

Application Requirements: Application form, financial need analysis.
Deadline: February 15.

Contact: Vicki Pinsky, Associate Director, Scholarships, AWS
Foundation
American Welding Society
8669 NW 36 Street, Suite 130
Miami, FL 33166
Phone: 800-443-9353 Ext. 212
E-mail: vpinsky@aws.org

WILLIAM A. RICE FAMILY, WOMEN IN WELDING SCHOLARSHIP

Awarded to a female candidate attending one of the following
universities: Ferris State University, The Ohio State University,
LeTourneau University, Pennsylvania College of Technology, or
Montana Tech of the University of Montana. The candidate must be
pursuing a bachelors degree in welding engineering, welding engineering
technology, materials joining engineering, materials joining technology.
Applicant must be a citizen of the United States.

Academic Fields/Career Goals: Engineering-Related Technologies;
Engineering/Technology; Materials Science, Engineering, and
Metallurgy.

Award: Scholarship for use in freshman, sophomore, junior, or senior
years; not renewable.

Eligibility Requirements: Applicant must be enrolled or expecting to
enroll full- or part-time at a four-year institution and female. Available to
U.S. citizens.

Application Requirements: Application form, financial need analysis.
Deadline: February 15.

Contact: Ms. Vicki Pinsky, Associate Director, Scholarships, AWS
Foundation
American Welding Society
8669 NW 36 Street, Suite 130
Miami, FL 33166
Phone: 305-443-9353 Ext. 212
E-mail: vpinsky@aws.org

WILLIAM B. HOWELL MEMORIAL SCHOLARSHIP

Awarded to a full-time undergraduate student pursuing a minimum four-year degree in a welding program at an accredited university. Priority will be given to those individuals residing or attending schools in the state of Florida, Michigan, and Ohio. Minimum 2.5 GPA required.

Academic Fields/Career Goals: Engineering-Related Technologies; Engineering/Technology; Materials Science, Engineering, and Metallurgy.

Award: Scholarship for use in freshman, sophomore, junior, or senior years; not renewable.

Eligibility Requirements: Applicant must be enrolled or expecting to enroll full-time at a four-year institution; resident of Florida, Michigan, Ohio and studying in Florida, Michigan, Ohio. Applicant must have 3.5 GPA or higher. Available to U.S. citizens.

Application Requirements: Application form, essay, financial need analysis. *Deadline:* February 15.

Contact: Vicki Pinsky, Associate Director, Scholarships, AWS
Foundation
American Welding Society
8669 NW 36 Street, Suite 130
Miami, FL 33166
Phone: 305-443-9353 Ext. 212
E-mail: vpinsky@aws.org

ARMED FORCES COMMUNICATIONS AND ELECTRONICS ASSOCIATION, EDUCATIONAL FOUNDATION

http://www.afcea.org/site/?q=foundation/scholarships

ARMED FORCES COMMUNICATIONS AND ELECTRONICS ASSOCIATION ROTC SCHOLARSHIP PROGRAM
• *See page 137*

STEM MAJORS SCHOLARSHIPS FOR UNDERGRADUATE STUDENTS
• *See page 110*

VADM SAMUEL L. GRAVELY, JR., USN(RET.) MEMORIAL SCHOLARSHIP
• *See page 111*

ARRL FOUNDATION INC.

http://www.arrl.org/

DAN HUETTL, WZ7U, MEMORIAL SCHOLARSHIP

$1000 scholarship for a student with active Amateur Radio license who is studying science, technology, engineering, or mathematics at any accredited college or university. Preference will be given to previous recipients if eligibility requirements continue to be met. If no such applicant is identified, preference is given to applicants attending Arizona State University. Minimum 3.0 GPA required. Applicants may receive this scholarship multiple times provided they reapply each year and continue to meet eligibility requirements, up to four years for undergraduate study and up to two years for graduate study.

Academic Fields/Career Goals: Engineering-Related Technologies; Engineering/Technology; Mathematics; Natural Sciences; Nuclear Science; Physical Sciences.

Award: Scholarship for use in freshman, sophomore, junior, senior, or graduate years; not renewable. *Amount:* $1000.

Eligibility Requirements: Applicant must be enrolled or expecting to enroll full-time at a four-year institution or university and must have an interest in amateur radio. Applicant must have 3.0 GPA or higher. Available to U.S. citizens.

Application Requirements: Application form. *Deadline:* January 31.
Contact: Ms. Mary Hobart, Secretary
Phone: 860-594-0397
E-mail: k1mmh@arrl.org

GARY WAGNER, K3OMI, SCHOLARSHIP
• *See page 177*

HENRY BROUGHTON, K2AE, MEMORIAL SCHOLARSHIP

At least one $1000 award is available to students located within 70 miles of Schenectady, NY. Must possess a general class amateur radio license and pursue a Baccalaureate or higher course of study in engineering, sciences, or similar field at an accredited four-year college or university.

Academic Fields/Career Goals: Engineering-Related Technologies; Engineering/Technology.

Award: Scholarship for use in freshman, sophomore, junior, senior, or graduate years; not renewable. *Number:* 1. *Amount:* $1000.

Eligibility Requirements: Applicant must be enrolled or expecting to enroll full- or part-time at a four-year institution or university; resident of New York and must have an interest in amateur radio. Available to U.S. citizens.

Application Requirements: Application form. *Deadline:* January 31.
Contact: Ms. Mary Hobart, Secretary
Phone: 860-594-0397
E-mail: k1mmh@arrl.org

LOIS MANLEY, K7LMZ, AND RANDALL PITCHFORD, WW7ZZ, SCHOLARSHIP
• *See page 193*

WILSE MORGAN, WX7P, MEMORIAL ARRL NORTHWESTERN DIVISION SCHOLARSHIP
• *See page 162*

YASME FOUNDATION SCHOLARSHIP
• *See page 154*

ASSOCIATED GENERAL CONTRACTORS EDUCATION AND RESEARCH FOUNDATION

http://www.agcfoundation.org/

WORKFORCE DEVELOPMENT SCHOLARSHIP
• *See page 221*

ASSOCIATION OF FEDERAL COMMUNICATIONS CONSULTING ENGINEERS

http://www.afcce.org

JULES COHEN SCHOLARSHIP
• *See page 266*

ASTRONAUT SCHOLARSHIP FOUNDATION

http://www.astronautscholarship.org/

ASTRONAUT SCHOLARSHIP FOUNDATION
• *See page 112*

AUTOMOTIVE WOMEN'S ALLIANCE FOUNDATION

http://www.awafoundation.org/index.php

AUTOMOTIVE WOMEN'S ALLIANCE FOUNDATION SCHOLARSHIPS
• *See page 74*

BARRY GOLDWATER SCHOLARSHIP AND EXCELLENCE IN EDUCATION FOUNDATION
https://goldwater.scholarsapply.org

BARRY M. GOLDWATER SCHOLARSHIP AND EXCELLENCE IN EDUCATION PROGRAM
• See page 112

BHW GROUP
https://thebhwgroup.com/

BHW WOMEN IN STEM SCHOLARSHIP
• See page 74

BROWN AND CALDWELL
http://www.brownandcaldwell.com

ECKENFELDER SCHOLARSHIP
• See page 155

MINORITY SCHOLARSHIP PROGRAM
• See page 155

CATCHING THE DREAM
http://www.catchingthedream.org/

TRIBAL BUSINESS MANAGEMENT PROGRAM (TBM)
• See page 74

DELAWARE HIGHER EDUCATION OFFICE
http://www.doe.k12.de.us

DELAWARE SOLID WASTE AUTHORITY JOHN P. "PAT" HEALY SCHOLARSHIP
Award for legal residents of Delaware who are U.S. citizens or eligible non-citizens. Must be high school seniors or full-time college students in their freshman or sophomore years. Must major in either environmental engineering or environmental sciences at a Delaware college. Selection based on financial need, academic performance, community and school involvement, and leadership ability.

Academic Fields/Career Goals: Engineering-Related Technologies; Environmental Science.

Award: Scholarship for use in freshman or sophomore years; renewable. *Number:* 1. *Amount:* $2000.

Eligibility Requirements: Applicant must be enrolled or expecting to enroll full-time at a two-year or four-year institution or university; resident of Delaware; studying in Delaware and must have an interest in leadership. Applicant or parent of applicant must have employment or volunteer experience in community service. Applicant must have 3.0 GPA or higher. Available to U.S. citizens.

Application Requirements: Application form, FAFSA, Student Aid Report (SAR), financial need analysis. *Deadline:* March 14.

Contact: Ms. Carylin Brinkley, Program Administrator
Delaware Higher Education Office
401 Federal Street
Suite 2
Dover, DE 19901
Phone: 302-735-4120
Fax: 302-739-5894
E-mail: cbrinkley@doe.k12.de.us

THE ELECTROCHEMICAL SOCIETY
http://www.electrochem.org/

H.H. DOW MEMORIAL STUDENT ACHIEVEMENT AWARD OF THE INDUSTRIAL ELECTROLYSIS AND

ELECTROCHEMICAL ENGINEERING DIVISION OF THE ELECTROCHEMICAL SOCIETY INC.
• See page 113

STUDENT RESEARCH AWARDS OF THE BATTERY DIVISION OF THE ELECTROCHEMICAL SOCIETY INC.
• See page 113

ENGINEERS FOUNDATION OF OHIO
http://www.ohioengineer.com/

ENGINEERS FOUNDATION OF OHIO GENERAL FUND SCHOLARSHIP
Applicant must be a college junior or senior at the end of the academic year in which the application is submitted. Must be enrolled full-time at an Ohio college or university in a curriculum leading to a BS degree in engineering or its equivalent. Minimum GPA of 3.0 required. Must be a U.S. citizen and permanent resident of Ohio.

Academic Fields/Career Goals: Engineering-Related Technologies.

Award: Scholarship for use in junior or senior years; not renewable. *Number:* 1. *Amount:* $1000.

Eligibility Requirements: Applicant must be enrolled or expecting to enroll full-time at a four-year institution or university; resident of Ohio and studying in Ohio. Applicant must have 3.0 GPA or higher. Available to U.S. citizens.

Application Requirements: Application form, essay, financial need analysis, recommendations or references, test scores, transcript. *Deadline:* December 15.

Contact: Pam McClure, Manager of Administration
Phone: 614-223-1177
E-mail: efo@ohioengineer.com

LLOYD A. CHACEY, PE-OHIO SOCIETY OF PROFESSIONAL ENGINEERS MEMORIAL SCHOLARSHIP
Scholarship available for a son, daughter, brother, sister, niece, nephew, spouse or grandchild of a current member of the Ohio Society of Professional Engineers, or of a deceased member who was in good standing at the time of his or her death. Must be enrolled full-time at an Ohio college or university in a curriculum leading to a degree in engineering or its equivalent. Must have a minimum of 3.0 GPA. Must be a U.S. citizen and permanent resident of Ohio.

Academic Fields/Career Goals: Engineering-Related Technologies.

Award: Scholarship for use in junior or senior years; renewable. *Number:* up to 2. *Amount:* $2000.

Eligibility Requirements: Applicant must be enrolled or expecting to enroll full-time at a four-year institution or university; resident of Ohio and studying in Ohio. Applicant must have 3.0 GPA or higher. Available to U.S. citizens.

Application Requirements: Application form, essay, financial need analysis, recommendations or references, test scores, transcript. *Deadline:* December 15.

Contact: Pam McClure, Manager of Administration
Phone: 614-223-1177
E-mail: efo@ohioengineer.com

RAYMOND H. FULLER, PE MEMORIAL SCHOLARSHIP
Scholarship of $1000 to graduating high school seniors who will enter their freshman year in college the next fall. Recipients must be accepted for enrollment in an engineering program at an Ohio college or university. Must have a minimum of 3.0 GPA. Must be a U.S. citizen and permanent resident of Ohio. Consideration will be given to the prospective recipient's academic achievement, interest in a career in engineering and financial need as determined by interviews and from references.

Academic Fields/Career Goals: Engineering-Related Technologies.

Award: Scholarship for use in freshman year; not renewable. *Number:* 1. *Amount:* $1000.

Eligibility Requirements: Applicant must be high school student; planning to enroll or expecting to enroll full-time at a four-year institution or university; resident of Ohio and studying in Ohio. Applicant must have 3.0 GPA or higher. Available to U.S. citizens.

Application Requirements: Application form, essay, financial need analysis, interview, recommendations or references, test scores, transcript. *Deadline:* December 15.

Contact: Pam McClure, Manager of Administration
Phone: 614-223-1177
E-mail: efo@ohioengineer.com

FLORIDA ENGINEERING SOCIETY

http://www.fleng.org/scholarships.cfm

DAVID F. LUDOVICI SCHOLARSHIP
• *See page 178*

GLOBAL AUTOMOTIVE AFTERMARKET SYMPOSIUM

http://www.automotivescholarships.com/

AUTOMOTIVE AFTERMARKET SCHOLARSHIP CENTRAL
• *See page 164*

GREAT MINDS IN STEM

www.greatmindsinstem.org

HISPANIC ENGINEER NATIONAL ACHIEVEMENT AWARDS CORPORATION SCHOLARSHIP PROGRAM
• *See page 106*

ILLUMINATING ENGINEERING SOCIETY OF NORTH AMERICA

http://www.ies.org/

ROBERT W. THUNEN MEMORIAL SCHOLARSHIPS
• *See page 122*

INDEPENDENT LABORATORIES INSTITUTE SCHOLARSHIP ALLIANCE

http://www.acil.org/

INDEPENDENT LABORATORIES INSTITUTE SCHOLARSHIP ALLIANCE
• *See page 156*

INTERNATIONAL FACILITY MANAGEMENT ASSOCIATION FOUNDATION

http://www.ifmafoundation.org/

IFMA FOUNDATION SCHOLARSHIPS
• *See page 122*

INTERNATIONAL SOCIETY FOR OPTICAL ENGINEERING-SPIE

http://www.spie.org/scholarships

SPIE EDUCATIONAL SCHOLARSHIPS IN OPTICAL SCIENCE AND ENGINEERING
• *See page 114*

INTERNATIONAL SOCIETY OF AUTOMATION

http://www.isa.org/

ISA EDUCATIONAL FOUNDATION SCHOLARSHIPS

Scholarships to graduate and undergraduate students who demonstrate outstanding potential for long-range contribution to the fields of automation, systems, and control.

Academic Fields/Career Goals: Engineering-Related Technologies.

Award: Scholarship for use in sophomore, junior, or graduate years; not renewable. *Number:* up to 15. *Amount:* $500–$5000.

Eligibility Requirements: Applicant must be enrolled or expecting to enroll full-time at a two-year or four-year institution or university. Applicant must have 2.5 GPA or higher. Available to U.S. and non-U.S. citizens.

Application Requirements: Application form, essay, recommendations or references, transcript. *Deadline:* February 15.

Contact: Scholarship Committee
International Society of Automation
67 Alexander Drive
Research Triangle Park, NC 27709

INTERNATIONAL SOCIETY OF EXPLOSIVES ENGINEERS

http://www.isee.org/

JERRY MCDOWELL FUND

Scholarship of $1500 to $5000 to students whose field of education is related to the commercial explosives industry.

Academic Fields/Career Goals: Engineering-Related Technologies; Engineering/Technology.

Award: Scholarship for use in freshman, sophomore, junior, senior, or graduate years; not renewable. *Number:* 1–3. *Amount:* $1500–$5000.

Eligibility Requirements: Applicant must be enrolled or expecting to enroll full-time at a two-year or four-year institution or university. Available to U.S. and non-U.S. citizens.

Application Requirements: Application form, financial need analysis. *Deadline:* May 1.

Contact: Patrick Lang, Manager - Education Foundation
Phone: 440-349-4400
Fax: 440-349-3788
E-mail: isee@isee.org

JORGE MAS CANOSA FREEDOM FOUNDATION

http://masscholarships.org/

MAS FAMILY SCHOLARSHIP AWARD
• *See page 165*

LOGISTICS & TRANSPORTATION ASSOCIATION OF NORTH AMERICA

http://www.ltna.org

TRANSPORTATION CLUBS INTERNATIONAL FRED A. HOOPER MEMORIAL SCHOLARSHIP

Merit-based award available to currently enrolled college students majoring in traffic management, transportation, physical distribution, logistics, or a related field. Must have completed at least one year of post-high school education. One-time award of $1500. Must submit three references. Available to citizens of the United States, Canada, and Mexico.

Academic Fields/Career Goals: Engineering-Related Technologies; Transportation.

Award: Scholarship for use in freshman, sophomore, junior, or senior years; not renewable. *Number:* 1. *Amount:* $1500.

Eligibility Requirements: Applicant must be enrolled or expecting to enroll full- or part-time at a two-year or four-year or technical institution or university. Available to U.S. and non-U.S. citizens.

Application Requirements: Application form, essay, personal photograph, recommendations or references, transcript. *Deadline:* April 30.

Contact: Katie deJonge, Executive Director
Phone: 360-898-3344
E-mail: executive.director@ltna.org

LOS ANGELES COUNCIL OF BLACK PROFESSIONAL ENGINEERS

http://www.lablackengineers.org/

AL-BEN SCHOLARSHIP FOR ACADEMIC INCENTIVE
• *See page 179*

AL-BEN SCHOLARSHIP FOR PROFESSIONAL MERIT
• *See page 179*

AL-BEN SCHOLARSHIP FOR SCHOLASTIC ACHIEVEMENT
• *See page 179*

MAINE SOCIETY OF PROFESSIONAL ENGINEERS

http://www.mespe.org/

MAINE SOCIETY OF PROFESSIONAL ENGINEERS VERNON T. SWAINE-ROBERT E. CHUTE SCHOLARSHIP

Nonrenewable scholarship for full-time study for freshmen only. Must be a Maine resident. Application can also be obtained by sending e-mail to rgmglads@twi.net.

Academic Fields/Career Goals: Engineering-Related Technologies; Engineering/Technology.

Award: Scholarship for use in freshman year; not renewable. *Number:* 1–2. *Amount:* $1500.

Eligibility Requirements: Applicant must be high school student; planning to enroll or expecting to enroll full-time at a four-year institution or university; resident of Maine and studying in Maine. Applicant must have 2.5 GPA or higher. Available to U.S. citizens.

Application Requirements: Application form, essay, interview, recommendations or references, self-addressed stamped envelope with application, test scores, transcript. *Deadline:* March 1.

Contact: Robert Martin, Scholarship Committee Chairman
Maine Society of Professional Engineers
1387 Augusta Road
Belgrade, ME 04917
Phone: 207-495-2244
E-mail: rgmglads@twi.net

MANUFACTURERS ASSOCIATION OF MAINE

http://www.mainemfg.com/

MAINE MANUFACTURING CAREER AND TRAINING FOUNDATION SCHOLARSHIP
• *See page 142*

MINERALS, METALS, AND MATERIALS SOCIETY (TMS)

http://www.tms.org/

KAUFMAN CALPHAD SCHOLARSHIP
• *See page 268*

MATERIALS PROCESSING & MANUFACTURING DIVISION SCHOLARSHIP

The applicant must be a student member of Material Advantage. Applicants must be undergraduate sophomores or junior unless otherwise noted. Applicants must be enrolled full time in a metallurgical/materials science engineering program at a qualified college or university. Relatives of members of the funding committee/division are not eligible. Submitted coursework must be relevant to the scholarship for which the student is applying.

Academic Fields/Career Goals: Engineering-Related Technologies; Engineering/Technology; Materials Science, Engineering, and Metallurgy.

Award: Scholarship for use in sophomore or junior years; not renewable. *Number:* 1–2. *Amount:* $2500.

Eligibility Requirements: Applicant must be enrolled or expecting to enroll full-time at a four-year institution or university. Applicant or parent of applicant must have employment or volunteer experience in engineering/technology. Available to U.S. and non-U.S. citizens.

Application Requirements: Application form, essay. *Deadline:* March 15.

Contact: Ms. Bryn Simpson
E-mail: bsimpson@tms.org

TMS/EPD SCHOLARSHIP

The applicant must be a student member of Material Advantage. Applicants must be undergraduate sophomores or junior unless otherwise noted. Applicants must be enrolled full time in a metallurgical/materials science engineering program at a qualified college or university. Relatives of members of the funding committee/division are not eligible. Submitted coursework must be relevant to the scholarship for which the student is applying.

Academic Fields/Career Goals: Engineering-Related Technologies; Engineering/Technology; Materials Science, Engineering, and Metallurgy.

Award: Scholarship for use in sophomore or junior years; not renewable. *Number:* 3. *Amount:* $3000.

Eligibility Requirements: Applicant must be enrolled or expecting to enroll full-time at a four-year institution or university. Applicant or parent of applicant must have employment or volunteer experience in engineering/technology. Available to U.S. and non-U.S. citizens.

Application Requirements: Application form, essay. *Deadline:* March 15.

Contact: Ms. Bryn Simpson, TMS Student Awards Program
E-mail: bsimpson@tms.org

TMS/FMD GILBERT CHIN SCHOLARSHIP

The applicant must be a student member of Material Advantage. Applicants must be undergraduate sophomores or junior unless otherwise noted. Applicants must be enrolled full time in a metallurgical/materials science engineering program at a qualified college or university. Relatives of members of the funding committee/division are not eligible. Submitted coursework must be relevant to the scholarship for which the student is applying.

Academic Fields/Career Goals: Engineering-Related Technologies; Engineering/Technology; Materials Science, Engineering, and Metallurgy.

Award: Scholarship for use in sophomore or junior years; not renewable. *Number:* 1. *Amount:* $2000.

Eligibility Requirements: Applicant must be enrolled or expecting to enroll full-time at a four-year institution or university. Available to U.S. and non-U.S. citizens.

Application Requirements: Application form, essay. *Deadline:* March 15.

Contact: Ms. Bryn Simpson, TMS Student Awards Program
Phone: 724-776-9000
E-mail: bsimpson@tms.org

TMS/INTERNATIONAL SYMPOSIUM ON SUPERALLOYS SCHOLARSHIP PROGRAM

The applicant must be a student member of Material Advantage. Applicants must be undergraduate sophomores or junior unless otherwise noted. Applicants must be enrolled full time in a metallurgical/materials science engineering program at a qualified college or university. Relatives of members of the funding committee/division are not eligible. Submitted coursework must be relevant to the scholarship for which the student is applying.

Academic Fields/Career Goals: Engineering-Related Technologies; Engineering/Technology; Materials Science, Engineering, and Metallurgy.

Award: Scholarship for use in sophomore, junior, senior, or graduate years; not renewable. *Number:* 2. *Amount:* $2500.

Eligibility Requirements: Applicant must be enrolled or expecting to enroll full-time at a four-year institution or university. Applicant or parent of applicant must have employment or volunteer experience in engineering/technology. Available to U.S. and non-U.S. citizens.

Application Requirements: Application form, essay. *Deadline:* March 15.

Contact: Ms. Bryn Simpson
  E-mail: bsimpson@tms.org

TMS/LIGHT METALS DIVISION SCHOLARSHIP PROGRAM

The applicant must be a student member of Material Advantage. Applicants must be undergraduate sophomores or junior unless otherwise noted. Applicants must be enrolled full time in a metallurgical/materials science engineering program at a qualified college or university. Relatives of members of the funding committee/division are not eligible. Submitted coursework must be relevant to the scholarship for which the student is applying.

Academic Fields/Career Goals: Engineering-Related Technologies; Engineering/Technology; Materials Science, Engineering, and Metallurgy.

Award: Scholarship for use in sophomore or junior years; not renewable. *Number:* 1. *Amount:* $4000.

Eligibility Requirements: Applicant must be enrolled or expecting to enroll full-time at a four-year institution or university. Applicant or parent of applicant must have employment or volunteer experience in engineering/technology. Available to U.S. and non-U.S. citizens.

Application Requirements: Application form, essay. *Deadline:* March 15.

Contact: Ms. Bryn Simpson
  E-mail: bsimpson@tms.org

TMS OUTSTANDING STUDENT PAPER CONTEST-UNDERGRADUATE

The paper should be prepared by one author. It should be the original work of that author as far as possible. If a faculty member is listed as co-author, include a letter from the faculty member confirming that you are the primary author. Papers must be written in English, utilizing good communication skills and quality photocopying. Poor copies of figures and texts are unacceptable. The paper should be neither less than 2,000 nor more than 4,000 words. A cover letter from a faculty member should be included with each entry, verifying your graduate or undergraduate status and original contribution. The front page of the entry should specify whether you are entering the undergraduate or graduate division as well as the subject discipline. The front page should also include your complete address, telephone, fax, and e-mail information. To submit your paper, or for additional information, please contact the TMS Student Awards program.

Academic Fields/Career Goals: Engineering-Related Technologies; Engineering/Technology; Materials Science, Engineering, and Metallurgy.

Award: Prize for use in freshman, sophomore, junior, or senior years; not renewable. *Number:* 2. *Amount:* $250.

Eligibility Requirements: Applicant must be enrolled or expecting to enroll full-time at a four-year institution or university. Applicant or parent of applicant must have employment or volunteer experience in engineering/technology. Available to U.S. and non-U.S. citizens.

Application Requirements: Application form, essay. *Deadline:* May 1.

Contact: Ms. Bryn Simpson
  E-mail: bsimpson@tms.org

TMS/STRUCTURAL MATERIALS DIVISION SCHOLARSHIP

The applicant must be a student member of Material Advantage. Applicants must be undergraduate sophomores or junior unless otherwise noted. Applicants must be enrolled full time in a metallurgical/materials science engineering program at a qualified college or university. Relatives of members of the funding committee/division are not eligible. Submitted coursework must be relevant to the scholarship for which the student is applying.

Academic Fields/Career Goals: Engineering-Related Technologies; Engineering/Technology; Materials Science, Engineering, and Metallurgy.

Award: Scholarship for use in sophomore or junior years; not renewable. *Number:* 2. *Amount:* $2500.

Eligibility Requirements: Applicant must be enrolled or expecting to enroll full-time at a four-year institution or university. Available to U.S. and non-U.S. citizens.

Application Requirements: Application form, essay. *Deadline:* March 15.

Contact: Ms. Bryn Simpson
  E-mail: bsimpson@tms.org

NASA RHODE ISLAND SPACE GRANT CONSORTIUM

http://brown/initiatives/ri-space-grant

NASA RHODE ISLAND SPACE GRANT CONSORTIUM OUTREACH SCHOLARSHIP FOR UNDERGRADUATE STUDENTS

Scholarship for undergraduate students attending a Rhode Island Space Grant Consortium participating institution and studying in any space-related field of science, math, engineering, or other field with applications in space study. Recipients are expected to devote a maximum of 8 hours per week to outreach activities in science education for K-12 children and teachers.

Academic Fields/Career Goals: Engineering-Related Technologies; Mathematics; Science, Technology, and Society.

Award: Scholarship for use in sophomore, junior, or senior years; not renewable. *Number:* up to 2. *Amount:* up to $4000.

Eligibility Requirements: Applicant must be enrolled or expecting to enroll full-time at a four-year institution or university and studying in Rhode Island. Applicant must have 3.0 GPA or higher. Available to U.S. citizens.

Application Requirements: Application form, essay, letter of interest, recommendations or references, resume, transcript. *Deadline:* varies.

Contact: Nancy Ciminelli, Program Manager
  NASA Rhode Island Space Grant Consortium
  Brown University
  Box 1846, Lincoln Field
  Providence, RI 02912
  Phone: 401-863-1151
  Fax: 401-863-3978
  E-mail: nancy_ciminelli@brown.edu

NASA SOUTH CAROLINA SPACE GRANT CONSORTIUM

http://www.cofc.edu/~scsgrant

UNDERGRADUATE RESEARCH AWARD PROGRAM
• See page 143

NASA'S VIRGINIA SPACE GRANT CONSORTIUM

http://www.vsgc.odu.edu/

UNDERGRADUATE STEM RESEARCH SCHOLARSHIPS
• See page 114

NATIONAL ASSOCIATION FOR THE ADVANCEMENT OF COLORED PEOPLE

http://www.naacp.org/

HUBERTUS W.V. WELLEMS SCHOLARSHIP FOR MALE STUDENTS
• See page 180

NATIONAL ASSOCIATION OF WATER COMPANIES-NEW JERSEY CHAPTER

http://www.nawc.org

NATIONAL ASSOCIATION OF WATER COMPANIES-NEW JERSEY CHAPTER SCHOLARSHIP
• See page 80

NATIONAL ASSOCIATION OF WOMEN IN CONSTRUCTION

http://www.nawic.org/

NAWIC UNDERGRADUATE SCHOLARSHIPS
• See page 122

NATIONAL SECURITY EDUCATION PROGRAM

http://www.iie.org/

NATIONAL SECURITY EDUCATION PROGRAM (NSEP) DAVID L. BOREN UNDERGRADUATE SCHOLARSHIPS
• See page 126

NATIONAL SOCIETY OF BLACK ENGINEERS

http://www.nsbe.org/

NSBE O-I CORPORATE SCHOLARSHIP PROGRAM

The goals of this scholarship are to encourage and reward academic excellence for African-American students and to promote O-I's Wellness Culture that values each person, encourages him/her to be great and appreciates individual unique talents and strengths. Applicants should major in: chemical, mechanical, material science, ceramic, glass, manufacturing, or industrial Engineering; and have demonstrated leadership and community service.

Academic Fields/Career Goals: Engineering-Related Technologies; Engineering/Technology.

Award: Scholarship for use in junior or senior years. *Number:* 2. *Amount:* $2500.

Eligibility Requirements: Applicant must be Black (non-Hispanic) and enrolled or expecting to enroll full- or part-time at a four-year institution or university. Applicant must have 3.0 GPA or higher. Available to U.S. citizens.

Application Requirements: *Deadline:* June 30.

NATIONAL SOCIETY OF PROFESSIONAL ENGINEERS

http://www.nspe.org/

MAUREEN L. AND HOWARD N. BLITMAN, PE SCHOLARSHIP TO PROMOTE DIVERSITY IN ENGINEERING
• See page 180

PAUL H. ROBBINS HONORARY SCHOLARSHIP
• See page 180

PROFESSIONAL ENGINEERS IN INDUSTRY SCHOLARSHIP
• See page 180

NATIONAL STONE, SAND AND GRAVEL ASSOCIATION (NSSGA)

http://www.nssga.org/

BARRY K. WENDT MEMORIAL SCHOLARSHIP

Scholarship is restricted to a student in an engineering school who plans to pursue a career in the aggregates industry. Eligible students will be enrolled in a mining-related degree program and will have completed at least one year of college coursework.

Academic Fields/Career Goals: Engineering-Related Technologies; Materials Science, Engineering, and Metallurgy.

Award: Scholarship for use in sophomore, junior, or senior years; not renewable. *Number:* 1. *Amount:* up to $2500.

Eligibility Requirements: Applicant must be enrolled or expecting to enroll full-time at a four-year institution or university. Available to U.S. and non-U.S. citizens.

Application Requirements: 300- to 500-word statement of plans for career in the aggregates industry, application form, application form may be submitted online (http://www.nssga.org/education/scholarships/), essay, recommendations or references. *Deadline:* May 29.

Contact: Catherine Whalen, Barry K. Wendt Memorial Scholarship Committee, c/o NSSGA
National Stone, Sand and Gravel Association (NSSGA)
1605 King Street
Alexandria, VA 22314
Phone: 703-525-8788
Fax: 703-525-7782
E-mail: info@nssga.org

NEXTSTEPU

http://www.nextstepu.com/

$1,500 STEM SCHOLARSHIP
• See page 106

OREGON STUDENT ASSISTANCE COMMISSION

http://www.GetCollegeFunds.org/

FRED FIELDS SCHOLARSHIP
• See page 167

PLUMBING-HEATING-COOLING CONTRACTORS EDUCATION FOUNDATION

http://www.phccfoundation.org/scholarships

DELTA FAUCET COMPANY SCHOLARSHIP PROGRAM
• See page 167

PHCC EDUCATIONAL FOUNDATION NEED-BASED SCHOLARSHIP
• See page 167

PHCC EDUCATIONAL FOUNDATION SCHOLARSHIP PROGRAM
• See page 167

ROBERT H. MOLLOHAN FAMILY CHARITABLE FOUNDATION, INC.

http://www.mollohanfoundation.org/

HIGH TECHNOLOGY SCHOLARS PROGRAM
• See page 158

ROCKY MOUNTAIN COAL MINING INSTITUTE

http://www.rmcmi.org/

ROCKY MOUNTAIN COAL MINING INSTITUTE SCHOLARSHIP

• *See page 197*

SCARLETT FAMILY FOUNDATION SCHOLARSHIP PROGRAM

http://www.scarlettfoundation.org/

SCHOLARSHIP FOR STUDENTS PURSUING A BUSINESS OR STEM DEGREE

• *See page 84*

SIMPLEHUMAN

http://www.simplehuman.com/

SIMPLE SOLUTIONS DESIGN COMPETITION

IDSA-endorsed competition to promote creative problem-solving through product design and increase public awareness of industrial design. Applicants must be enrolled in an Industrial Design program or a closely related program at a design school or university and must design a new, innovative product/technology/concept for making household chores easier. Entries evaluated on utility, efficiency, innovation, research, and aesthetics. See website for details http://www.simplehuman.com/design.

Academic Fields/Career Goals: Engineering-Related Technologies; Engineering/Technology; Industrial Design.

Award: Prize for use in freshman, sophomore, junior, or senior years; not renewable. *Number:* 1. *Amount:* $5000.

Eligibility Requirements: Applicant must be enrolled or expecting to enroll full- or part-time at a two-year or four-year or technical institution or university. Available to U.S. and non-U.S. citizens.

Application Requirements: Application form, entry in a contest, one PDF or JPEG of design, specs, materials, explanation. *Deadline:* February 27.

Contact: Sarah Beachler, Marketing and Communications Associate
Phone: 310-436-2278
Fax: 310-538-9196
E-mail: sbeachler@simplehuman.com

SOCIETY FOR IMAGING SCIENCE AND TECHNOLOGY

http://www.imaging.org/

RAYMOND DAVIS SCHOLARSHIP

Award available to an undergraduate junior or senior or graduate student enrolled full-time in an accredited program of photographic, imaging science or engineering. Minimum award is $1000. Applications processed between October 1 and December 15 only.

Academic Fields/Career Goals: Engineering-Related Technologies; Engineering/Technology; Photojournalism/Photography; Science, Technology, and Society.

Award: Scholarship for use in junior, senior, graduate, or postgraduate years; not renewable. *Number:* 1–2. *Amount:* $1000.

Eligibility Requirements: Applicant must be enrolled or expecting to enroll full-time at a four-year institution or university. Available to U.S. and non-U.S. citizens.

Application Requirements: Application form. *Deadline:* October 1.

Contact: ms. Donna Smith, Executive Assistant
Society for Imaging Science and Technology
7003 Kilworth Lane
Springfield, VA 22151
Phone: 703-642-9090 Ext. 107
E-mail: info@imaging.org

SOCIETY OF AUTOMOTIVE ENGINEERS

http://www.sae.org/

BMW/SAE ENGINEERING SCHOLARSHIP

• *See page 146*

DETROIT SECTION SAE TECHNICAL SCHOLARSHIP

$2500 renewable scholarships for graduating high school seniors. Applicant must be US resident, a child or grandchild of a current SAE Detroit Section member and have demonstrated financial need. Must enroll full time in a two- or four-year engineering or science program at an ABET accredited college or university.

Academic Fields/Career Goals: Engineering-Related Technologies; Engineering/Technology; Mechanical Engineering.

Award: Scholarship for use in freshman year; renewable. *Number:* 2. *Amount:* $2500.

Eligibility Requirements: Applicant must be enrolled or expecting to enroll full-time at a two-year or four-year institution or university. Applicant or parent of applicant must be member of Society of Automotive Engineers. Applicant must have 3.0 GPA or higher. Available to U.S. citizens.

Application Requirements: Application form, financial need analysis. *Deadline:* February 27.

Contact: SAE Detroit Section
Society of Automotive Engineers
28535 Orchard Lake Rd., Ste. 200
Farmington Hills, MI 48334
Phone: 248-324-4445 Ext. 3
E-mail: scholarships@sae-detroit.org

EDWARD D. HENDRICKSON/SAE ENGINEERING SCHOLARSHIP

• *See page 146*

RALPH K. HILLQUIST HONORARY SAE SCHOLARSHIP

A $1000 nonrenewable scholarship awarded every other year at the SAE Noise and Vibration Conference. Applicants must be U.S. citizens enrolled full-time as a junior in a U.S. university. A minimum 3.0 GPA with significant academic and leadership achievements is required. The student must also have a declared major in mechanical engineering or an automotive-related engineering discipline, with preference given to those with studies in the areas of expertise related to noise and vibration.

Academic Fields/Career Goals: Engineering-Related Technologies; Engineering/Technology; Mechanical Engineering.

Award: Scholarship for use in junior year; not renewable. *Number:* 1. *Amount:* $1000.

Eligibility Requirements: Applicant must be enrolled or expecting to enroll full-time at a four-year institution or university. Applicant or parent of applicant must be member of Society of Automotive Engineers. Applicant must have 3.0 GPA or higher. Available to U.S. citizens.

Application Requirements: Application form, essay, transcript. *Deadline:* February 1.

Contact: Connie Harnish, SAE Educational Relations
Society of Automotive Engineers
400 Commonwealth Drive
Warrendale, PA 15096-0001
Phone: 724-772-4047
E-mail: connie@sae.org

TMC/SAE DONALD D. DAWSON TECHNICAL SCHOLARSHIP

• *See page 147*

YANMAR/SAE SCHOLARSHIP

Eligible applicants will be citizens of North America (U.S., Canada, Mexico) and will be entering their junior year of undergraduate engineering or enrolled in a postgraduate engineering or related science program. Applicants must be pursuing a course of study or research related to the conservation of energy in transportation, agriculture, construction, and power generation. Emphasis will be placed on research or study related to the internal combustion engine.

Academic Fields/Career Goals: Engineering-Related Technologies; Engineering/Technology; Materials Science, Engineering, and Metallurgy; Mechanical Engineering.

Award: Scholarship for use in junior, senior, or graduate years; renewable. *Number:* 1. *Amount:* $1000.

Eligibility Requirements: Applicant must be enrolled or expecting to enroll full-time at a four-year institution or university. Available to U.S. and non-U.S. citizens.

Application Requirements: Application form, essay, self-addressed stamped envelope with application, test scores, transcript. *Deadline:* April 1.

Contact: Connie Harnish, SAE Educational Relations
Society of Automotive Engineers
400 Commonwealth Drive
Warrendale, PA 15096
Phone: 724-772-4047
E-mail: connie@sae.org

SOCIETY OF MANUFACTURING ENGINEERS EDUCATION FOUNDATION

http://www.smeef.org/

MYRTLE AND EARL WALKER SCHOLARSHIP FUND

Scholarship available to full-time undergraduate students enrolled in a degree program in manufacturing engineering or technology in the United States or Canada. Minimum GPA of 3.0. Scholarship value and number of awards granted varies.

Academic Fields/Career Goals: Engineering-Related Technologies; Engineering/Technology; Mechanical Engineering.

Award: Scholarship for use in freshman, sophomore, junior, or senior years; not renewable. *Number:* 1–25. *Amount:* $1000–$7000.

Eligibility Requirements: Applicant must be enrolled or expecting to enroll full-time at a two-year or four-year or technical institution or university. Applicant must have 3.0 GPA or higher. Available to U.S. and Canadian citizens.

Application Requirements: Application form, essay, recommendations or references, resume, test scores, transcript. *Deadline:* February 1.

Contact: SME Education Foundation
Society of Manufacturing Engineers Education Foundation
One SME Drive, PO Box 930
Dearborn, MI 48121
Phone: 313-425-3300
Fax: 313-425-3411
E-mail: foundation@sme.org

SOCIETY OF MOTION PICTURE AND TELEVISION ENGINEERS

https://www.smpte.org/

LOUIS F. WOLF JR. MEMORIAL SCHOLARSHIP
• See page 210

STUDENT PAPER AWARD
• See page 210

SOCIETY OF PLASTICS ENGINEERS FOUNDATION (SPE)

http://www.4spe.org/

GULF COAST HURRICANE SCHOLARSHIP
• See page 181

SOCIETY OF WOMEN ENGINEERS

http://societyofwomenengineers.swe.org/

ADMIRAL GRACE MURRAY HOPPER SCHOLARSHIP
• See page 218

KOCH DISCOVERY SCHOLARSHIP
• See page 185

MEREDITH THOMS MEMORIAL SCHOLARSHIPS

Five $2700 scholarships for women pursuing ABET-accredited Baccalaureate programs in preparation for careers in engineering and engineering technology in the United States and Mexico. Minimum 3.0 GPA required.

Academic Fields/Career Goals: Engineering-Related Technologies; Engineering/Technology.

Award: Scholarship for use in sophomore, junior, or senior years; not renewable. *Number:* 5. *Amount:* $2700.

Eligibility Requirements: Applicant must be enrolled or expecting to enroll full-time at a four-year institution or university and female. Applicant must have 3.0 GPA or higher. Available to U.S. citizens.

Application Requirements: Application form. *Deadline:* February 15.

Contact: Scholarship Committee
Phone: 800-793-4636
E-mail: scholarships@swe.org

PAST PRESIDENTS SCHOLARSHIP

Two $2000 scholarships for women pursuing ABET-accredited Baccalaureate or graduate programs in preparation for careers in engineering and engineering technology in the United States and Mexico. Must be a U.S. citizen and have a minimum 3.0 GPA.

Academic Fields/Career Goals: Engineering-Related Technologies; Engineering/Technology.

Award: Scholarship for use in sophomore, junior, senior, or graduate years; not renewable. *Number:* 2. *Amount:* $2000.

Eligibility Requirements: Applicant must be enrolled or expecting to enroll full-time at a four-year institution or university and female. Applicant must have 3.0 GPA or higher. Available to U.S. citizens.

Application Requirements: Application form. *Deadline:* February 15.

Contact: Scholarship Committee
Phone: 800-793-4636
E-mail: scholarships@swe.org

ROBERTA BANASZAK GLEITER ENGINEERING ENDEAVOR SCHOLARSHIP
• See page 186

ROCHELLE PERRY MEMORIAL SCHOLARSHIP
• See page 186

SWE CENTRAL INDIANA SECTION SCHOLARSHIP

$2000 scholarship for women pursuing ABET-accredited Baccalaureate or graduate programs in preparation for careers in engineering, engineering technology, and computer science in the United States and Mexico. Must be a U.S. citizen, go to school in Indiana, and have a minimum 3.0 GPA. Financial need preferred.

Academic Fields/Career Goals: Engineering-Related Technologies; Engineering/Technology.

Award: Scholarship for use in sophomore, junior, senior, or graduate years; not renewable. *Number:* 1. *Amount:* $2000.

Eligibility Requirements: Applicant must be enrolled or expecting to enroll full-time at a four-year institution or university; female and studying in Indiana. Applicant must have 3.0 GPA or higher. Available to U.S. citizens.

Application Requirements: Application form, financial need analysis. *Deadline:* February 15.

Contact: Scholarship Committee
Phone: 800-793-4636
E-mail: scholarships@swe.org

SWE REGION E SCHOLARSHIP
• See page 187

SWE REGION G JUDY SIMMONS MEMORIAL SCHOLARSHIP
• See page 188

SOCIETY OF WOMEN ENGINEERS-ROCKY MOUNTAIN SECTION

http://www.swe-rms.org/

SOCIETY OF WOMEN ENGINEERS-ROCKY MOUNTAIN SECTION SCHOLARSHIP PROGRAM
• *See page 188*

STRAIGHTFORWARD MEDIA

http://www.straightforwardmedia.com/

STRAIGHTFORWARD MEDIA ENGINEERING SCHOLARSHIP
• *See page 189*

TAG AND LABEL MANUFACTURERS INSTITUTE, INC.

http://www.tlmi.com/

TLMI 4 YEAR COLLEGE DEGREE SCHOLARSHIP PROGRAM
A $5000 scholarship awarded to a sophomore or junior attending a four-year accredited college or university on a full-time basis for their junior or senior year studies. Applicants must demonstrate interest in pursuing a career in the tag and label industry.

Academic Fields/Career Goals: Engineering-Related Technologies; Flexography; Graphics/Graphic Arts/Printing.

Award: Scholarship for use in junior or senior years; not renewable. *Number:* 1–6. *Amount:* $2500–$5000.

Eligibility Requirements: Applicant must be enrolled or expecting to enroll full-time at a four-year institution or university. Applicant must have 3.0 GPA or higher. Available to U.S. and Canadian citizens.

Application Requirements: Application form, interview, portfolio. *Deadline:* March 31.

Contact: Scholarship Committee
Tag and Label Manufacturers Institute, Inc.
One Blackburn Center
Gloucester, MA 01930
Phone: 978-282-1400
E-mail: office@tlmi.com

TAU BETA PI ASSOCIATION

http://www.tbp.org/

TAU BETA PI SCHOLARSHIP PROGRAM
• *See page 189*

TECHNICAL ASSOCIATION OF THE PULP & PAPER INDUSTRY (TAPPI)

http://www.tappi.org/

CORRUGATED PACKAGING DIVISION SCHOLARSHIPS
Award to applicants working full time or part time in the box business and attending day/night school for a graduate or undergraduate degree or to a full-time student in a two- or four-year college, university or technical school. Information can be found at http://www.tappi.org/Education/College-and-University-Programs/Scholarship-Overview/.

Academic Fields/Career Goals: Engineering-Related Technologies; Paper and Pulp Engineering.

Award: Scholarship for use in freshman, sophomore, junior, senior, or graduate years; not renewable. *Number:* 1–4. *Amount:* $1000–$2000.

Eligibility Requirements: Applicant must be enrolled or expecting to enroll full- or part-time at a four-year or technical institution or university. Applicant must have 3.0 GPA or higher. Available to U.S. and non-U.S. citizens.

Application Requirements: Application form. *Deadline:* March 15.

Contact: Mr. Laurence Womack, Director of Standards and Awards
Technical Association of the Pulp & Paper Industry (TAPPI)
15 Technology Parkway South
Peachtree Corners, GA 30092
Phone: 770-209-7276
E-mail: standards@tappi.org

TECHNOLOGY FIRST

https://technologyfirst.org/

ROBERT V. MCKENNA SCHOLARSHIPS
• *See page 219*

TIMOTION

http://www.timotion.com/

TIMOTION ENGINEERING AND EXCELLENCE SCHOLARSHIP
• *See page 199*

TRANSTUTORS

http://www.transtutors.com/scholarship

TRANSTUTORS SCHOLARSHIP 2015-16
• *See page 85*

TURNER CONSTRUCTION COMPANY

http://www.turnerconstruction.com/

YOUTHFORCE 2020 SCHOLARSHIP PROGRAM
• *See page 124*

UNITED NEGRO COLLEGE FUND

http://www.uncf.org/

PROCTER & GAMBLE STEM SCHOLARSHIP
• *See page 116*

UNCF STEM SCHOLARS PROGRAM
• *See page 159*

VECTORWORKS, INC.

http://www.vectorworks.net

VECTORWORKS DESIGN SCHOLARSHIP
• *See page 124*

VERMONT SPACE GRANT CONSORTIUM

http://www.cems.uvm.edu/vsgc

VERMONT SPACE GRANT CONSORTIUM
• *See page 96*

WOMEN IN AEROSPACE FOUNDATION

http://www.womeninaerospace.org/index.html

WIA FOUNDATION SCHOLARSHIP
• *See page 149*

XEROX

http://www.xerox.com//

TECHNICAL MINORITY SCHOLARSHIP
• *See page 190*

ENGINEERING/ TECHNOLOGY

AACE INTERNATIONAL
http://www.aacei.org/

AACE INTERNATIONAL COMPETITIVE SCHOLARSHIP
• See page 118

AEG FOUNDATION
http://www.aegfoundation.org/

AEG FOUNDATION MARLIAVE FUND
• See page 240

AHS INTERNATIONAL—THE VERTICAL FLIGHT TECHNICAL SOCIETY
http://www.vtol.org/

VERTICAL FLIGHT FOUNDATION SCHOLARSHIP
• See page 134

AIST FOUNDATION
http://www.aistfoundation.org/

AIST ALFRED B. GLOSSBRENNER AND JOHN KLUSCH SCHOLARSHIPS
Scholarship intended to award high school senior who plans on pursuing a degree in metallurgy or engineering. Student must have previous academic excellence in science courses. Applicant must be a dependent of a AIST Northeastern Ohio chapter member.

Academic Fields/Career Goals: Engineering/Technology; Materials Science, Engineering, and Metallurgy.

Award: Scholarship for use in freshman year; not renewable. *Number:* 2. *Amount:* $1000.

Eligibility Requirements: Applicant must be high school student and planning to enroll or expecting to enroll full-time at a four-year institution or university. Applicant or parent of applicant must be member of Association for Iron and Steel Technology. Available to U.S. and non-U.S. citizens.

Application Requirements: Application form, essay, recommendations or references, resume, test scores, transcript. *Deadline:* April 30.

Contact: Richard Kurz, Chapter Secretary
AIST Foundation
22831 East State Street, Route 62
Alliance, OH 44601

AIST WILLIAM E. SCHWABE MEMORIAL SCHOLARSHIP
• See page 263

ASSOCIATION FOR IRON AND STEEL TECHNOLOGY BALTIMORE CHAPTER SCHOLARSHIP
• See page 275

ASSOCIATION FOR IRON AND STEEL TECHNOLOGY DAVID H. SAMSON CANADIAN SCHOLARSHIP
• See page 172

ASSOCIATION FOR IRON AND STEEL TECHNOLOGY MIDWEST CHAPTER BETTY MCKERN SCHOLARSHIP
Scholarship awarded to a graduating female high school senior, or to an undergraduate freshman, sophomore, or junior enrolled in a fully AIST-accredited college or university. Applicant must be in good academic standing. Must be a dependent of an AIST Midwest chapter member.

Academic Fields/Career Goals: Engineering/Technology.

Award: Scholarship for use in freshman, sophomore, junior, or senior years; not renewable. *Number:* 1. *Amount:* $3000.

Eligibility Requirements: Applicant must be enrolled or expecting to enroll full-time at a four-year institution or university and female. Applicant or parent of applicant must be member of Association for Iron and Steel Technology. Available to U.S. and non-U.S. citizens.

Application Requirements: Application form, essay, recommendations or references, resume, test scores, transcript. *Deadline:* March 15.

Contact: AIST Midwest Member Chapter Scholarships Chair
AIST Foundation
c/o Barry Felton
250 West U.S. Highway 12
Burns Harbor, IN 46304

ASSOCIATION FOR IRON AND STEEL TECHNOLOGY MIDWEST CHAPTER DON NELSON SCHOLARSHIP
One scholarship for a graduating high school senior, or undergraduate freshman, sophomore or junior enrolled in a fully AIST-accredited college or university. Applicant must be in good academic standing. Must be a dependent of an AIST Midwest chapter member. May reapply each year for the duration of college education.

Academic Fields/Career Goals: Engineering/Technology.

Award: Scholarship for use in freshman, sophomore, junior, or senior years; not renewable. *Number:* 1. *Amount:* up to $1000.

Eligibility Requirements: Applicant must be enrolled or expecting to enroll full-time at a four-year institution or university. Applicant or parent of applicant must be member of Association for Iron and Steel Technology. Available to U.S. and non-U.S. citizens.

Application Requirements: Application form, essay, recommendations or references, resume, test scores, transcript. *Deadline:* March 15.

Contact: AIST Midwest Member Chapter Scholarships Chair
AIST Foundation
c/o Barry Felton
250 West U.S. Highway 12
Burns Harbor, IN 46304

ASSOCIATION FOR IRON AND STEEL TECHNOLOGY MIDWEST CHAPTER ENGINEERING SCHOLARSHIP
Two four-year scholarships awarded to graduating high school senior or undergraduate freshman, sophomore or junior enrolled in a fully AIST-accredited college or university majoring engineering. Applicant must be in good academic standing. Must be a dependent of an AIST Midwest chapter member. May reapply each year for the duration of college education.

Academic Fields/Career Goals: Engineering/Technology.

Award: Scholarship for use in freshman, sophomore, or junior years; renewable. *Number:* 2. *Amount:* $1500.

Eligibility Requirements: Applicant must be enrolled or expecting to enroll full-time at a four-year institution or university. Applicant or parent of applicant must be member of Association for Iron and Steel Technology. Available to U.S. and non-U.S. citizens.

Application Requirements: Application form, essay, recommendations or references, resume, test scores, transcript. *Deadline:* March 15.

Contact: AIST Midwest Member Chapter Scholarships Chair
AIST Foundation
c/o Barry Felton
250 West U.S. Highway 12
Burns Harbor, IN 46304

ASSOCIATION FOR IRON AND STEEL TECHNOLOGY MIDWEST CHAPTER JACK GILL SCHOLARSHIP
Scholarship for a graduating high school senior, or undergraduate freshman, sophomore, or junior enrolled in a fully AIST-accredited college or university majoring engineering. Applicant must be in good academic standing. Must be a dependent of an AIST Midwest chapter member. May reapply each year for the duration of college education.

Academic Fields/Career Goals: Engineering/Technology.

Award: Scholarship for use in freshman, sophomore, junior, or senior years; not renewable. *Number:* 1. *Amount:* $3000.

Eligibility Requirements: Applicant must be enrolled or expecting to enroll full-time at a four-year institution or university. Applicant or parent of applicant must be member of Association for Iron and Steel Technology. Available to U.S. and non-U.S. citizens.

Application Requirements: Application form, essay, recommendations or references, resume, test scores, transcript. *Deadline:* March 15.

Contact: AIST Midwest Member Chapter Scholarships Chair
AIST Foundation
c/o Barry Felton
250 West U.S. Highway 12
Burns Harbor, IN 46304

ASSOCIATION FOR IRON AND STEEL TECHNOLOGY MIDWEST CHAPTER MEL NICKEL SCHOLARSHIP

Scholarship awarded to a graduating high school senior, or undergraduate freshman, sophomore or junior enrolled in a fully AIST-accredited college or university majoring engineering. Applicant must be in good academic standing. Must be a dependent of an AIST Midwest chapter member. May reapply each year for the term of their college education.

Academic Fields/Career Goals: Engineering/Technology.

Award: Scholarship for use in freshman, sophomore, junior, or senior years; not renewable. *Number:* 1. *Amount:* $3000.

Eligibility Requirements: Applicant must be enrolled or expecting to enroll full-time at a four-year institution or university. Applicant or parent of applicant must be member of Association for Iron and Steel Technology. Available to U.S. and non-U.S. citizens.

Application Requirements: Application form, essay, recommendations or references, resume, test scores, transcript. *Deadline:* March 15.

Contact: AIST Midwest Member Chapter Scholarships Chair
AIST Foundation
c/o Barry Felton
250 West U.S. Highway 12
Burns Harbor, IN 46304

ASSOCIATION FOR IRON AND STEEL TECHNOLOGY MIDWEST CHAPTER NON-ENGINEERING SCHOLARSHIP

Scholarship for graduating high school senior, or undergraduate freshman, sophomore, or junior enrolled in a fully AIST-accredited college or university. Applicant must be in good academic standing and dependent of an AIST Midwest chapter member. Recipients may reapply each year for the term of their college education.

Academic Fields/Career Goals: Engineering/Technology.

Award: Scholarship for use in freshman, sophomore, junior, or senior years; not renewable. *Number:* 3. *Amount:* $1500.

Eligibility Requirements: Applicant must be enrolled or expecting to enroll full-time at a four-year institution or university. Applicant or parent of applicant must be member of Association for Iron and Steel Technology. Available to U.S. and non-U.S. citizens.

Application Requirements: Application form, essay, recommendations or references, resume, test scores, transcript. *Deadline:* March 15.

Contact: AIST Midwest Member Chapter Scholarships Chair
AIST Foundation
c/o Barry Felton
250 West U.S. Highway 12
Burns Harbor, IN 46304

ASSOCIATION FOR IRON AND STEEL TECHNOLOGY MIDWEST CHAPTER WESTERN STATES SCHOLARSHIP

Scholarship of $3000 awarded to a graduating high school senior, or undergraduate freshman, sophomore, junior, or senior enrolled in a fully AIST-accredited college or university. Applicant must be in good academic standing and a dependent of an AIST Midwest chapter member. Recipients may reapply each year for the term of their college education.

Academic Fields/Career Goals: Engineering/Technology.

Award: Scholarship for use in freshman, sophomore, junior, or senior years; not renewable. *Number:* 1. *Amount:* $3000.

Eligibility Requirements: Applicant must be enrolled or expecting to enroll full-time at a four-year institution or university. Applicant or parent of applicant must be member of Association for Iron and Steel Technology. Available to U.S. and non-U.S. citizens.

Application Requirements: Application form, essay, recommendations or references, resume, test scores, transcript. *Deadline:* March 15.

Contact: AIST Midwest Member Chapter Scholarships Chair
AIST Foundation
c/o Barry Felton
250 West U.S. Highway 12
Burns Harbor, IN 46304

ASSOCIATION FOR IRON AND STEEL TECHNOLOGY NORTHWEST MEMBER CHAPTER SCHOLARSHIP

Scholarships of $1000 available to encourage a Pacific Northwest area student to prepare for a career in engineering. Must be the child, grandchild, spouse, or niece/nephew of a member in good standing of the AIST Northwest Chapter. Award based on academic achievements in chemistry, mathematics, and physics.

Academic Fields/Career Goals: Engineering/Technology; Materials Science, Engineering, and Metallurgy.

Award: Scholarship for use in freshman, sophomore, junior, or senior years; not renewable. *Number:* 2. *Amount:* $1000.

Eligibility Requirements: Applicant must be enrolled or expecting to enroll full- or part-time at a four-year institution or university. Applicant or parent of applicant must be member of Association for Iron and Steel Technology. Available to U.S. citizens.

Application Requirements: Application form, essay, recommendations or references, resume, test scores, transcript. *Deadline:* April 30.

Contact: Gerardo Giraldo, AIST Northwest Chapter Secretary
AIST Foundation
2434 Eyres Place West
Seattle, WA 98199
Phone: 206-285-7897
E-mail: acero9938@comcast.net

ASSOCIATION FOR IRON AND STEEL TECHNOLOGY OHIO VALLEY CHAPTER SCHOLARSHIP

• *See page 153*

ASSOCIATION FOR IRON AND STEEL TECHNOLOGY PITTSBURGH CHAPTER SCHOLARSHIP

Scholarships of $2500 for children, stepchildren, grandchildren, or spouse of a member in good standing of the Pittsburgh Chapter. Applicant must be a high school senior or currently enrolled undergraduate preparing for a career in engineering or metallurgy.

Academic Fields/Career Goals: Engineering/Technology; Materials Science, Engineering, and Metallurgy.

Award: Scholarship for use in freshman, sophomore, junior, or senior years; not renewable. *Number:* 2–3. *Amount:* $2500.

Eligibility Requirements: Applicant must be enrolled or expecting to enroll full-time at a four-year institution or university. Applicant or parent of applicant must be member of Association for Iron and Steel Technology. Available to U.S. citizens.

Application Requirements: Application form, essay, recommendations or references, resume, test scores, transcript. *Deadline:* April 30.

Contact: Daniel Kos, Program Coordinator
AIST Foundation
375 Saxonburg Boulevard
Saxonburg, PA 16056
E-mail: dkos@ii-vi.com

ASSOCIATION FOR IRON AND STEEL TECHNOLOGY SOUTHEAST MEMBER CHAPTER SCHOLARSHIP

Scholarship of $3000 for children, stepchildren, grandchildren, or spouse of active Southeast Chapter members who are pursuing a career in engineering, the sciences, or other majors relating to iron and steel production. Students may reapply for the scholarship each year for their term of college.

Academic Fields/Career Goals: Engineering/Technology; Materials Science, Engineering, and Metallurgy.

Award: Scholarship for use in freshman, sophomore, junior, or senior years; renewable. *Number:* 1. *Amount:* $3000.

Eligibility Requirements: Applicant must be enrolled or expecting to enroll full- or part-time at a four-year institution or university. Applicant or parent of applicant must be member of Association for Iron and Steel Technology. Available to U.S. citizens.

Application Requirements: Application form, essay, recommendations or references, resume, test scores, transcript. *Deadline:* April 30.

Contact: Mike Hutson, AIST Southeast Chapter Secretary
AIST Foundation
803 Floyd Street
Kings Mountain, NC 29086
Phone: 704-730-8320
Fax: 704-730-8321
E-mail: mike@johnhutsoncompany.com

ALBERTA HERITAGE SCHOLARSHIP FUND

http://www.alis.alberta.ca/

NORTHERN ALBERTA DEVELOPMENT COUNCIL BURSARY
• See page 234

AMERICAN CHEMICAL SOCIETY, RUBBER DIVISION

http://www.rubber.org/

AMERICAN CHEMICAL SOCIETY, RUBBER DIVISION UNDERGRADUATE SCHOLARSHIP
• See page 109

AMERICAN COUNCIL OF ENGINEERING COMPANIES OF PENNSYLVANIA (ACEC/PA)

http://www.acecpa.org/

ERIC J. GENNUSO AND LEROY D. (BUD) LOY, JR. SCHOLARSHIP PROGRAM
• See page 173

AMERICAN FOUNDATION FOR THE BLIND

http://www.afb.org/

PAUL W. RUCKES SCHOLARSHIP
• See page 214

AMERICAN INDIAN SCIENCE AND ENGINEERING SOCIETY

http://www.aises.org/

A.T. ANDERSON MEMORIAL SCHOLARSHIP PROGRAM
• See page 109

AMERICAN INSTITUTE OF AERONAUTICS AND ASTRONAUTICS

http://www.aiaafoundation.org/

AIAA FOUNDATION UNDERGRADUATE SCHOLARSHIPS
• See page 110

LEATRICE GREGORY PENDRAY SCHOLARSHIP
• See page 110

AMERICAN PUBLIC POWER ASSOCIATION

http://publicpower.org/DEED

DEED EDUCATIONAL SCHOLARSHIP
• See page 176

DEED STUDENT INTERNSHIP
• See page 176

DEED STUDENT RESEARCH GRANTS
• See page 191

DEED TECHNICAL DESIGN PROJECT
• See page 176

AMERICAN PUBLIC TRANSPORTATION FOUNDATION

http://www.apta.com/

JACK GILSTRAP SCHOLARSHIP
Awarded the APTF scholarship to the applicant with the highest score. Must be in public transportation industry-related fields of study. Must be sponsored by AFTA member organization and complete an internship program with a member organization. Minimum 3.0 GPA required.

Academic Fields/Career Goals: Engineering/Technology; Transportation.

Award: Scholarship for use in sophomore, junior, senior, or graduate years; renewable. *Number:* 1. *Amount:* $2500.

Eligibility Requirements: Applicant must be enrolled or expecting to enroll full-time at a two-year or four-year institution or university. Applicant must have 3.0 GPA or higher. Available to U.S. and Canadian citizens.

Application Requirements: Application form, essay, financial need analysis, recommendations or references, transcript, verification of enrollment for the current semester and copy of fee schedule from the college/university. *Deadline:* June 16.

Contact: Pamela Boswell, Vice President of Program Management
American Public Transportation Foundation
1666 K Street, NW
Washington, DC 20006-1215
Phone: 202-496-4803
Fax: 202-496-2323
E-mail: pboswell@apta.com

TRANSIT HALL OF FAME SCHOLARSHIP AWARD PROGRAM
• See page 191

AMERICAN RAILWAY ENGINEERING AND MAINTENANCE OF WAY ASSOCIATION

http://www.aremafoundation.org/

AREMA GRADUATE AND UNDERGRADUATE SCHOLARSHIPS
• See page 191

AMERICAN SOCIETY FOR ENGINEERING EDUCATION

http://www.asee.org/

SCIENCE, MATHEMATICS, AND RESEARCH FOR TRANSFORMATION DEFENSE SCHOLARSHIP FOR SERVICE PROGRAM
• See page 110

AMERICAN SOCIETY OF AGRICULTURAL AND BIOLOGICAL ENGINEERS

http://www.asabe.org/

ASABE FOUNDATION SCHOLARSHIP
Award for full-time engineering undergraduate student in the U.S. or Canada. Must be active student member of the American Society of Agricultural Engineers. Must have a minimum of 3.0 GPA. Write for more information and special application procedures. One-time award of $1000. Must have completed one year of school, and must submit paper titled "My Goals in the Engineering Profession".

Academic Fields/Career Goals: Engineering/Technology.

Award: Scholarship for use in sophomore, junior, or senior years; not renewable. *Number:* 1. *Amount:* $1200.

Eligibility Requirements: Applicant must be enrolled or expecting to enroll full-time at a four-year institution or university. Applicant or parent of applicant must be member of Other Student Academic Clubs. Applicant must have 3.0 GPA or higher. Available to U.S. and Canadian citizens.

Application Requirements: Application form, essay, financial need analysis, recommendations or references, resume. *Deadline:* March 15.

Contact: Carol Flautt, Scholarship Program
American Society of Agricultural and Biological Engineers
2950 Niles Road
St. Joseph, MI 49085
Phone: 269-932-7036
Fax: 269-429-3852
E-mail: flautt@asabe.org

AMERICAN SOCIETY OF CERTIFIED ENGINEERING TECHNICIANS

http://www.ascet.org/

JOSEPH C. JOHNSON MEMORIAL GRANT

Grant for $750 given to qualified applicants in order to offset the cost of tuition, books and lab fees. Applicant must be a U.S. citizen or a legal resident of the country in which the applicant is currently living, as well as be either a student, certified, regular, registered or associate member of ASCET. Student must be enrolled in an engineering technology program. For further information, visit http://www.ascet.org.

Academic Fields/Career Goals: Engineering/Technology.

Award: Grant for use in freshman, sophomore, junior, or senior years; not renewable. *Number:* 1. *Amount:* $750.

Eligibility Requirements: Applicant must be enrolled or expecting to enroll full- or part-time at a two-year or four-year or technical institution or university. Applicant must have 3.0 GPA or higher. Available to U.S. citizens.

Application Requirements: Application form, financial need analysis, personal photograph, recommendations or references, transcript. *Deadline:* April 1.

Contact: Mr. Tim Latham, General Manager
American Society of Certified Engineering Technicians
PO Box 1536
Brandon, MS 39043
Phone: 601-824-8991
E-mail: tim-latham@ascet.org

JOSEPH M. PARISH MEMORIAL GRANT

Grant of $500 will be awarded to a student to be used to offset the cost of tuition, books and lab fees. Applicant must be a student member of ASCET and be a U.S. citizen or a legal resident of the country in which the applicant is currently living. The award will be given to full-time students enrolled in an engineering technology program; students pursuing a BS degree in engineering are not eligible for this grant. For more information, visit http://www.ascet.org.

Academic Fields/Career Goals: Engineering/Technology.

Award: Grant for use in freshman, sophomore, junior, or senior years; not renewable. *Number:* 1. *Amount:* $500.

Eligibility Requirements: Applicant must be enrolled or expecting to enroll full- or part-time at a two-year or four-year or technical institution or university. Applicant must have 3.0 GPA or higher. Available to U.S. citizens.

Application Requirements: Application form, financial need analysis, personal photograph, recommendations or references, transcript. *Deadline:* April 1.

Contact: Mr. Tim Latham, General Manager
American Society of Certified Engineering Technicians
PO Box 1536
Brandon, MS 39043
Phone: 601-824-8991
E-mail: tim-latham@ascet.org

KURT H. AND DONNA M. SCHULER SMALL GRANT
• See page 176

AMERICAN SOCIETY OF HEATING, REFRIGERATING, AND AIR CONDITIONING ENGINEERS, INC.

http://www.ashrae.org/

ALWIN B. NEWTON SCHOLARSHIP
• See page 264

ASHRAE GENERAL SCHOLARSHIPS
• See page 276

ASHRAE REGION III BOGGARM SETTY SCHOLARSHIP
• See page 176

ASHRAE REGION IV BENNY BOOTLE SCHOLARSHIP
• See page 119

ASHRAE REGION VIII SCHOLARSHIP
• See page 276

DUANE HANSON SCHOLARSHIP
• See page 264

FRANK M. CODA SCHOLARSHIP
• See page 264

HENRY ADAMS SCHOLARSHIP
• See page 265

LYNN G. BELLENGER SCHOLARSHIP
• See page 265

REUBEN TRANE SCHOLARSHIP
• See page 265

WILLIS H. CARRIER SCHOLARSHIPS
• See page 265

AMERICAN SOCIETY OF MECHANICAL ENGINEERS AUXILIARY INC.

http://www.asme.org/

ASME AUXILIARY UNDERGRADUATE SCHOLARSHIP CHARLES B. SHARP

Award of $3000 available only to ASME student members to be used in final year of undergraduate study in mechanical engineering. Must be a U.S. citizen.

Academic Fields/Career Goals: Engineering/Technology.

Award: Scholarship for use in junior year; not renewable. *Number:* 1–2. *Amount:* $3000.

Eligibility Requirements: Applicant must be enrolled or expecting to enroll full-time at a four-year institution or university. Applicant or parent of applicant must be member of American Society of Mechanical Engineers. Available to U.S. citizens.

Application Requirements: Application form, financial need analysis. *Deadline:* March 1.

Contact: RuthAnn Bigley, ASME Auxiliary Staff Coordinator
American Society of Mechanical Engineers Auxiliary Inc.
Two Park Avenue
Mailstop RB
New York, NY 10016
Phone: 212-591-7650
E-mail: bigleyr@asme.org

AMERICAN SOCIETY OF NAVAL ENGINEERS

http://www.navalengineers.org/

AMERICAN SOCIETY OF NAVAL ENGINEERS SCHOLARSHIP
• See page 110

AMERICAN SOCIETY OF PLUMBING ENGINEERS

http://www.aspe.org/

ALFRED STEELE ENGINEERING SCHOLARSHIP

Scholarships of $1000 are awarded for the members of American society of plumbing engineers towards education and professional development on plumbing engineering and designing.

Academic Fields/Career Goals: Engineering/Technology; Industrial Design.

Award: Scholarship for use in freshman, sophomore, junior, or senior years; not renewable. *Number:* 5. *Amount:* $1000.

Eligibility Requirements: Applicant must be enrolled or expecting to enroll full-time at a two-year or four-year or technical institution or university. Applicant must have 3.0 GPA or higher. Available to U.S. and non-U.S. citizens.

Application Requirements: Application form, community service, essay, recommendations or references, statement of personal achievement, transcript. *Deadline:* September 1.

Contact: Stacey Kidd, Membership Director
Phone: 773-693-2773
Fax: 773-695-9007
E-mail: skidd@aspe.org

AMERICAN WELDING SOCIETY

http://www.aws.org/

AIRGAS-TERRY JARVIS MEMORIAL SCHOLARSHIP
• See page 277

AIR PRODUCTS WOMEN IN GASES AND WELDING SCHOLARSHIP
• See page 277

AMERICAN WELDING SOCIETY INTERNATIONAL SCHOLARSHIP
• See page 277

D. FRED AND MARIAN L. BOVIE NATIONAL SCHOLARSHIP

Scholarship for welding engineering at The Ohio State University.

Academic Fields/Career Goals: Engineering/Technology.

Award: Scholarship for use in freshman, sophomore, junior, or senior years; not renewable.

Eligibility Requirements: Applicant must be enrolled or expecting to enroll full-time at an institution or university and studying in Ohio. Applicant must have 3.0 GPA or higher. Available to U.S. citizens.

Application Requirements: Application form, financial need analysis. *Deadline:* February 15.

Contact: Vicki Pinsky, Associate Director, Scholarships, AWS Foundation
American Welding Society
8669 NW 36 Street, Suite 130
Miami, FL 33166
Phone: 305-443-9353 Ext. 212
E-mail: vpinsky@aws.org

DONALD AND SHIRLEY HASTINGS SCHOLARSHIP

Award for U.S. citizen at least 18 years of age pursuing a four-year undergraduate degree in welding engineering or welding engineering technology. Priority given to welding engineering students. Preference is given to students residing or attending school in California or Ohio. Submit copy of proposed curriculum. Minimum GPA of 2.5 required.

Academic Fields/Career Goals: Engineering/Technology; Materials Science, Engineering, and Metallurgy.

Award: Scholarship for use in freshman, sophomore, junior, or senior years; not renewable. *Number:* 1.

Eligibility Requirements: Applicant must be enrolled or expecting to enroll full- or part-time at a four-year institution or university. Available to U.S. citizens.

Application Requirements: Application form, financial need analysis. *Deadline:* February 15.

Contact: Vicki Pinsky, Associate Director, Scholarships, Foundation
American Welding Society
8669 NW 36 Street, Suite 130
Miami, FL 33166
Phone: 800-443-9353 Ext. 212
E-mail: vpinsky@aws.org

DONALD F. HASTINGS SCHOLARSHIP
• See page 277

EDWARD J. BRADY MEMORIAL SCHOLARSHIP
• See page 278

HOWARD E. AND WILMA J. ADKINS MEMORIAL SCHOLARSHIP
• See page 278

JACK R. BARCKHOFF WELDING MANAGEMENT SCHOLARSHIP

Scholarship for a college junior at The Ohio State University. Essay required on improving the world of welding and the welding industry in the US.

Academic Fields/Career Goals: Engineering/Technology.

Award: Scholarship for use in junior year; not renewable.

Eligibility Requirements: Applicant must be enrolled or expecting to enroll full- or part-time at an institution or university and studying in Ohio. Available to U.S. citizens.

Application Requirements: Application form, essay, financial need analysis. *Deadline:* February 15.

Contact: Vicki Pinsky, Associate Director, AWS Foundation
American Welding Society
8669 NW 36 Street, Suite 130
Miami, FL 33166
Phone: 305-443-9353 Ext. 212
E-mail: vpinsky@aws.org

JOHN C. LINCOLN MEMORIAL SCHOLARSHIP
• See page 278

JOHN M. STROPKI SCHOLARSHIP
• See page 278

MATSUO BRIDGE COMPANY LTD. OF JAPAN SCHOLARSHIP
• See page 193

MILLER ELECTRIC INTERNATIONAL WORLD SKILLS COMPETITION SCHOLARSHIP
• See page 278

MILLER ELECTRIC MFG. CO. SCHOLARSHIP
• See page 278

PAST PRESIDENTS' SCHOLARSHIP

Scholarship available to students pursuing a bachelor's degree in welding engineering, welding engineering technology, or an engineering program with emphasis on welding. Also open to graduate students pursuing a master's or doctorate in engineering or management.

Academic Fields/Career Goals: Engineering/Technology; Mechanical Engineering.

Award: Scholarship for use in junior or senior years; not renewable.

Eligibility Requirements: Applicant must be enrolled or expecting to enroll full- or part-time at a four-year institution. Available to U.S. citizens.

Application Requirements: Application form, financial need analysis. *Deadline:* February 15.

Contact: Ms. Vicki Pinsky, Associate Director, Scholarships, AWS Foundation
American Welding Society
8669 NW 36 Street, Suite 130
Miami, FL 33166
E-mail: vpinsky@aws.org

PRAXAIR INTERNATIONAL SCHOLARSHIP
• *See page 279*

RICHARD J. SEIF TECHNICAL SALES AND MARKETING SCHOLARSHIP
• *See page 161*

ROBERT L. PEASLEE BRAZING SCHOLARSHIP

Award for students pursuing a minimum four-year bachelor's degree in welding engineering or welding engineering technology with an emphasis on brazing applications. Must show brazing coursework. Must be minimum 18 years of age and at least a college junior. 3.0 GPA required.

Academic Fields/Career Goals: Engineering/Technology; Materials Science, Engineering, and Metallurgy.

Award: Scholarship for use in junior or senior years; not renewable.

Eligibility Requirements: Applicant must be enrolled or expecting to enroll full- or part-time at a four-year institution or university. Applicant must have 3.0 GPA or higher. Available to U.S. and Canadian citizens.

Application Requirements: Application form, financial need analysis. *Deadline:* February 15.

Contact: Vicki Pinsky, Associate Director, Scholarships, AWS Foundation
American Welding Society
8669 NW 36 Street, Suite 130
Miami, FL 33166
Phone: 800-443-9353 Ext. 212
E-mail: vpinsky@aws.org

VICTOR TECHNOLOGIES AWARD FOR EXCELLENCE IN CUTTING AND WELDING
• *See page 279*

VICTOR TECHNOLOGIES CUTTING AND WELDING SCHOLARSHIP
• *See page 279*

WILLIAM A. RICE FAMILY, WOMEN IN WELDING SCHOLARSHIP
• *See page 279*

WILLIAM B. HOWELL MEMORIAL SCHOLARSHIP
• *See page 280*

ARIZONA PROFESSIONAL CHAPTER OF AISES

http://www.aises.org/scholarships

ARIZONA PROFESSIONAL CHAPTER OF AISES SCHOLARSHIP

Scholarship awarded to American Indian/Alaska Natives attending Arizona schools of higher education pursuing degrees in the sciences, engineering, medicine, natural resources, math, and technology. Student must be a full-time undergraduate student (at least 12 hours per semester) at an accredited two-year or four-year college or university.

Academic Fields/Career Goals: Engineering/Technology; Health and Medical Sciences; Natural Resources; Physical Sciences.

Award: Scholarship for use in freshman, sophomore, junior, or senior years; not renewable.

Eligibility Requirements: Applicant must be American Indian/Alaska Native; enrolled or expecting to enroll full-time at a two-year or four-year institution or university and studying in Arizona. Applicant must have 2.5 GPA or higher. Available to U.S. citizens.

Application Requirements: Application form, essay, portfolio, proof of tribal enrollment, copy of AISES membership card, recommendations or references, resume, transcript. *Deadline:* August 17.

Contact: Jaime Ashike, Scholarship Committee
Arizona Professional Chapter of AISES
PO Box 2528
Phoenix, AZ 85002
Phone: 480-326-0958
E-mail: amazing_butterfly@hotmail.com

ARMED FORCES COMMUNICATIONS AND ELECTRONICS ASSOCIATION, EDUCATIONAL FOUNDATION

http://www.afcea.org/site/?q=foundation/scholarships

ARMED FORCES COMMUNICATIONS AND ELECTRONICS ASSOCIATION ROTC SCHOLARSHIP PROGRAM
• *See page 137*

STEM MAJORS SCHOLARSHIPS FOR UNDERGRADUATE STUDENTS
• *See page 110*

STEM TEACHERS SCHOLARSHIP
• *See page 111*

VADM SAMUEL L. GRAVELY, JR, USN(RET.) MEMORIAL SCHOLARSHIP
• *See page 111*

ARRL FOUNDATION INC.

http://www.arrl.org/

ALFRED E. FRIEND JR, W4CF, MEMORIAL SCHOLARSHIP
• *See page 177*

ALLEN AND BERTHA WATSON MEMORIAL SCHOLARSHIP

$500 award for the study of science, technology, or engineering. Must be a resident of Oklahoma or attend a 4-year university or college in Oklahoma. If no qualified applicant is identified, an applicant from the ARRL West Gulf Division (Texas and Oklahoma) will be chosen.

Academic Fields/Career Goals: Engineering/Technology; Science, Technology, and Society.

Award: Scholarship for use in freshman, sophomore, junior, or senior years; not renewable. *Number:* 1. *Amount:* $500.

Eligibility Requirements: Applicant must be enrolled or expecting to enroll full- or part-time at a four-year institution or university; resident of Oklahoma and must have an interest in amateur radio. Available to U.S. citizens.

Application Requirements: Application form. *Deadline:* January 31.

Contact: Ms. Mary Hobart, Secretary
Phone: 860-594-0397
E-mail: k1mmh@arrl.org

BETTY WEATHERFORD, KQ6RE, MEMORIAL SCHOLARSHIP
• *See page 266*

CHARLES N. FISHER MEMORIAL SCHOLARSHIP
• *See page 111*

CTRI/CHRIS SEEBER, KA1GEU, MEMORIAL SCHOLARSHIP
• *See page 249*

DAN HUETTL, WZ7U, MEMORIAL SCHOLARSHIP
• *See page 280*

GARY WAGNER, K3OMI, SCHOLARSHIP
• *See page 177*

HENRY BROUGHTON, K2AE, MEMORIAL SCHOLARSHIP
• *See page 280*

LOIS MANLEY, K7LMZ, AND RANDALL PITCHFORD, WW7ZZ, SCHOLARSHIP
• *See page 193*

MAGNOLIA DX ASSOCIATION SCHOLARSHIP
• *See page 202*

MISSISSIPPI SCHOLARSHIP
• *See page 111*

NORTH FULTON AMATEUR RADIO LEAGUE SCHOLARSHIP
• *See page 215*

PAUL AND HELEN L. GRAUER SCHOLARSHIP
• *See page 111*

SOUTHEASTERN DX CLUB SCHOLARSHIP
• *See page 215*

W1FDR SCHOLARSHIP
• *See page 112*

WILSE MORGAN, WX7P, MEMORIAL ARRL NORTHWESTERN DIVISION SCHOLARSHIP
• *See page 162*

YASME FOUNDATION SCHOLARSHIP
• *See page 154*

ASM MATERIALS EDUCATION FOUNDATION

http://www.asmfoundation.org/

ASM OUTSTANDING SCHOLARS AWARDS

Awards for student members of ASM International studying metallurgy or materials science and engineering. Must have completed at least one year of college to apply. Awards are merit-based; financial need is not considered.

Academic Fields/Career Goals: Engineering/Technology; Materials Science, Engineering, and Metallurgy.

Award: Scholarship for use in sophomore, junior, or senior years; not renewable. *Number:* 3. *Amount:* $2000.

Eligibility Requirements: Applicant must be enrolled or expecting to enroll full-time at a four-year institution or university. Applicant or parent of applicant must be member of ASM International. Available to U.S. and non-U.S. citizens.

Application Requirements: Application form, essay, personal photograph. *Deadline:* May 1.

Contact: Pergentina Deatherage, Administrator, Foundation Programs
ASM Materials Education Foundation
9639 Kinsman Road
Materials Park, OH 44073-0002
Phone: 440-338-5151

EDWARD J. DULIS SCHOLARSHIP

Award of $1500 for student members of ASM International studying metallurgy or materials science and engineering. Award is merit based; financial need is not considered.

Academic Fields/Career Goals: Engineering/Technology; Materials Science, Engineering, and Metallurgy.

Award: Scholarship for use in freshman, sophomore, junior, or senior years; not renewable. *Number:* 1. *Amount:* $1500.

Eligibility Requirements: Applicant must be enrolled or expecting to enroll full-time at a four-year institution or university. Applicant or parent of applicant must be member of ASM International. Available to U.S. and Canadian citizens.

Application Requirements: Application form, personal photograph. *Deadline:* May 1.

Contact: Pergentina Deatherage, Administrator, Foundation Programs
ASM Materials Education Foundation
9639 Kinsman Road
Materials Park, OH 44073-0002
Phone: 440-338-5151
E-mail: jeane.deatherage@asminternational.org

GEORGE A. ROBERTS SCHOLARSHIP

Awards for college juniors or seniors studying metallurgy or materials engineering in North America. Applicants must be student members of ASM International. Awards based on need, interest in field, academics, and character.

Academic Fields/Career Goals: Engineering/Technology; Materials Science, Engineering, and Metallurgy.

Award: Scholarship for use in junior or senior years; not renewable. *Number:* 7. *Amount:* $6000.

Eligibility Requirements: Applicant must be enrolled or expecting to enroll full-time at an institution or university. Applicant or parent of applicant must be member of ASM International. Available to U.S. and Canadian citizens.

Application Requirements: Application form, essay, financial need analysis, personal photograph. *Deadline:* May 1.

Contact: Pergentina Deatherage, Administrator, Foundation Programs
ASM Materials Education Foundation
9639 Kinsman Road
Materials Park, OH 44073-0002
Phone: 440-338-5151
E-mail: jeane.deatherage@asminternational.org

JOHN M. HANIAK SCHOLARSHIP

Award for student members of ASM International studying metallurgy or materials science and engineering. Must have completed at least one year of college to apply. Award is merit based; financial need is not considered.

Academic Fields/Career Goals: Engineering/Technology; Materials Science, Engineering, and Metallurgy.

Award: Scholarship for use in freshman, sophomore, junior, or senior years; not renewable. *Number:* 1. *Amount:* $1500.

Eligibility Requirements: Applicant must be enrolled or expecting to enroll full-time at a four-year institution or university. Applicant or parent of applicant must be member of ASM International. Available to U.S. and Canadian citizens.

Application Requirements: Application form, essay. *Deadline:* May 1.

Contact: Pergentina Deatherage, Administrator, Foundation Programs
ASM Materials Education Foundation
9639 Kinsman Road
Materials Park, OH 44073-0002
Phone: 440-338-5151 Ext. 5533
E-mail: scholarshipsUG@asminternational.org

WILLIAM P. WOODSIDE FOUNDER'S SCHOLARSHIP

$10,000 scholarship for college junior or senior studying metallurgy or materials engineering in North America. Must be a student member of ASM International. Award based on need, interest in field, academics, and character.

Academic Fields/Career Goals: Engineering/Technology; Materials Science, Engineering, and Metallurgy.

Award: Scholarship for use in junior or senior years; not renewable. *Number:* 1. *Amount:* $10,000.

Eligibility Requirements: Applicant must be enrolled or expecting to enroll full-time at an institution or university. Applicant or parent of applicant must be member of ASM International. Available to U.S. and Canadian citizens.

Application Requirements: Application form, essay, financial need analysis, personal photograph. *Deadline:* May 1.

Contact: Pergentina Deatherage, Administrator, Foundation Programs
ASM Materials Education Foundation
9639 Kinsman Road
Materials Park, OH 44073-0002
Phone: 440-338-5151 Ext. 5533
E-mail: scholarshipsUG@asminternational.org

ASPRS, THE IMAGING AND GEOSPATIAL INFORMATION SOCIETY

http://www.asprs.org/

ABRAHAM ANSON MEMORIAL SCHOLARSHIP

Award to encourage students to pursue education in geospatial science or technology related to photogrammetry, remote sensing, surveying and mapping. Must be enrolled or intending to enroll in a U.S. college or university in geospatial science, surveying and mapping and related fields. Must submit with application a list of all applicable courses taken, a statement of work experience including internships, special projects, technical papers, and courses taught that may support the student's capabilities in this field. For additional information and online application, see website http://www.asprs.org/membership/scholar.html.

Academic Fields/Career Goals: Engineering/Technology; Surveying, Surveying Technology, Cartography, or Geographic Information Science.

Award: Scholarship for use in freshman, sophomore, junior, or senior years; not renewable. *Number:* 1. *Amount:* $2000.

Eligibility Requirements: Applicant must be enrolled or expecting to enroll full-time at a four-year institution or university. Available to U.S. citizens.

Application Requirements: Application form, essay, recommendations or references, resume, transcript. *Deadline:* October 17.

Contact: Scholarship Administrator
Phone: 301-493-0290
E-mail: scholarships@asprs.org

FRANCIS H. MOFFITT MEMORIAL SCHOLARSHIP

Award to encourage upper-division undergraduate and graduate-level students to pursue a course of study in surveying and photogrammetry leading to a career in the mapping profession. Must be enrolled or intending to enroll in a college or university in the U.S. in the field of surveying or photogrammetry. Application must include listing of all courses taken in the field, internships, special projects, courses taught, technical papers that demonstrate applicant's capabilities in the field, two letters of recommendation, and a short statement detailing contributions to the field and future career plans. For additional information, see website http://www.asprs.org.

Academic Fields/Career Goals: Engineering/Technology; Surveying, Surveying Technology, Cartography, or Geographic Information Science.

Award: Scholarship for use in junior or senior years; not renewable. *Number:* 1. *Amount:* $6500.

Eligibility Requirements: Applicant must be enrolled or expecting to enroll full-time at a four-year institution or university. Available to U.S. citizens.

Application Requirements: Application form, essay, recommendations or references, transcript. *Deadline:* October 17.

Contact: Jesse Winch, Scholarship Administrator
Phone: 301-493-0290
E-mail: scholarships@asprs.org

JOHN O. BEHRENS INSTITUTE FOR LAND INFORMATION MEMORIAL SCHOLARSHIP

Award to encourage study in geospatial science or technology or land information systems/records. Must be an undergraduate student enrolled or intending to enroll in a U.S. college or university in the designated field. Application must be submitted electronically and must include a list of completed courses in the field, papers, research reports, or other items produced by the applicant that demonstrate capability in the field, and internships, work experience, special projects or courses taught that support potential excellence in the field. Additional information and application on website http://www.asprs.org/membership/scholar.html.

Academic Fields/Career Goals: Engineering/Technology; Surveying, Surveying Technology, Cartography, or Geographic Information Science.

Award: Scholarship for use in freshman, sophomore, junior, or senior years; not renewable. *Number:* 1. *Amount:* $2000.

Eligibility Requirements: Applicant must be enrolled or expecting to enroll full-time at a four-year institution or university. Available to U.S. citizens.

Application Requirements: Application form, essay, recommendations or references, resume, transcript. *Deadline:* October 17.

Contact: Scholarship Administrator
Phone: 301-493-0290
E-mail: scholarships@asprs.org

KENNETH J. OSBORN MEMORIAL SCHOLARSHIP

Award to encourage students who display the interest and aptitude to enter the profession of surveying, mapping, geospatial information and technology, and photogrammetry. Student must be enrolled or intending to enroll in a college or university in the U.S. in a program of study to prepare for the profession. Application must be submitted electronically. For additional requirements that must accompany electronic application, visit website http://www.asprs.org/membership/scholar.html.

Academic Fields/Career Goals: Engineering/Technology; Surveying, Surveying Technology, Cartography, or Geographic Information Science.

Award: Scholarship for use in freshman, sophomore, junior, or senior years; not renewable. *Number:* 1. *Amount:* $2000.

Eligibility Requirements: Applicant must be enrolled or expecting to enroll full-time at a four-year institution or university. Available to U.S. citizens.

Application Requirements: Application form, essay, recommendations or references, resume, transcript. *Deadline:* October 17.

Contact: Scholarship Administrator
Phone: 301-493-0290
E-mail: scholarships@asprs.org

ROBERT E. ALTENHOFEN MEMORIAL SCHOLARSHIP

One-time award of $2000 available for undergraduate or graduate study in theoretical photogrammetry. Applicant must supply a sample of work in photogrammetry and a statement of plans for future study in the field. Must be a member of ASPRS.

Academic Fields/Career Goals: Engineering/Technology; Surveying, Surveying Technology, Cartography, or Geographic Information Science.

Award: Scholarship for use in junior, senior, or graduate years; not renewable. *Number:* 1. *Amount:* $2000.

Eligibility Requirements: Applicant must be enrolled or expecting to enroll full-time at a four-year institution or university and must have an interest in photography/photogrammetry/filmmaking. Applicant or parent of applicant must be member of American Society for Photogrammetry and Remote Sensing. Available to U.S. and non-U.S. citizens.

Application Requirements: Application form, essay, recommendations or references, transcript, work sample. *Deadline:* October 17.

Contact: Program Manager
ASPRS, The Imaging and Geospatial Information Society
5410 Grosvenor Lane, Suite 210
Bethesda, MD 20814-2160
Phone: 301-493-0290
Fax: 301-493-0208
E-mail: scholarships@asprs.org

ASSOCIATED GENERAL CONTRACTORS EDUCATION AND RESEARCH FOUNDATION

http://www.agcfoundation.org/

WORKFORCE DEVELOPMENT SCHOLARSHIP

• *See page 221*

AUTOMOTIVE WOMEN'S ALLIANCE FOUNDATION

http://www.awafoundation.org/index.php

AUTOMOTIVE WOMEN'S ALLIANCE FOUNDATION SCHOLARSHIPS

• *See page 74*

BARRY GOLDWATER SCHOLARSHIP AND EXCELLENCE IN EDUCATION FOUNDATION

https://goldwater.scholarsapply.org

BARRY M. GOLDWATER SCHOLARSHIP AND EXCELLENCE IN EDUCATION PROGRAM
• See page 112

BHW GROUP

https://thebhwgroup.com/

BHW WOMEN IN STEM SCHOLARSHIP
• See page 74

BOYS AND GIRLS CLUBS OF GREATER SAN DIEGO

http://www.sdyouth.org/

SPENCE REESE SCHOLARSHIP
Renewable scholarship for graduating male high school seniors in the United States for study of law, medicine, engineering, and political science. Awarded based on academic standing, academic ability, financial need, and character.

Academic Fields/Career Goals: Engineering/Technology; Health and Medical Sciences; Law/Legal Services; Political Science.

Award: Scholarship for use in freshman, sophomore, junior, or senior years; renewable. *Number:* up to 8. *Amount:* $2000.

Eligibility Requirements: Applicant must be high school student; planning to enroll or expecting to enroll full-time at a four-year institution or university and male. Applicant must have 3.5 GPA or higher. Available to U.S. citizens.

Application Requirements: Application form, application form may be submitted online (http://www.sdyouth.org/about/college-scholarships), essay, financial need analysis, interview, recommendations or references, self-addressed stamped envelope with application, test scores, transcript. *Deadline:* April 1.

Contact: Spence Reese Scholarship Administrator
Boys and Girls Clubs of Greater San Diego
4635 Clairemont Mesa Boulevard
San Diego, CA 92117
E-mail: mahazzard@sdyouth.org

BROWN AND CALDWELL

http://www.brownandcaldwell.com

ECKENFELDER SCHOLARSHIP
• See page 155

MINORITY SCHOLARSHIP PROGRAM
• See page 155

CATCHING THE DREAM

http://www.catchingthedream.org/

MATH, ENGINEERING, SCIENCE, BUSINESS, EDUCATION, COMPUTERS SCHOLARSHIPS
• See page 162

CENTER FOR ARCHITECTURE

http://www.cfafoundation.org/scholarships

CENTER FOR ARCHITECTURE, DOUGLAS HASKELL AWARD FOR STUDENT JOURNALS
• See page 119

COMMUNITY FOUNDATION FOR GREATER ATLANTA, INC.

http://cfgreateratlanta.org/

TECH HIGH SCHOOL ALUMNI ASSOCIATION/W.O. CHENEY MERIT SCHOLARSHIP FUND
Scholarship for students pursuing degrees in mathematics, engineering, or one of the physical sciences. Cumulative high school GPA of 3.0 or higher or in upper 15 percent of graduating class. SAT (math and critical reading) of at least 1300. For complete eligibility requirements and application, visit http://www.cfgreateratlanta.org.

Academic Fields/Career Goals: Engineering/Technology; Mathematics; Physical Sciences.

Award: Scholarship for use in freshman, sophomore, junior, or senior years; renewable. *Number:* 1–4. *Amount:* $5000.

Eligibility Requirements: Applicant must be high school student; planning to enroll or expecting to enroll full-time at a four-year institution or university and resident of Georgia. Applicant must have 3.0 GPA or higher. Available to U.S. citizens.

Application Requirements: Application form, community service, essay, financial need analysis. *Deadline:* February 15.

THE DALLAS FOUNDATION

http://www.dallasfoundation.org/

WHITLEY PLACE SCHOLARSHIP
• See page 120

DAVIDSON INSTITUTE FOR TALENT DEVELOPMENT

http://www.davidsongifted.org/

DAVIDSON FELLOWS SCHOLARSHIP PROGRAM
• See page 113

EAA AVIATION FOUNDATION, INC.

http://www.eaa.org/

PAYZER SCHOLARSHIP
• See page 140

THE ELECTROCHEMICAL SOCIETY

http://www.electrochem.org/

H.H. DOW MEMORIAL STUDENT ACHIEVEMENT AWARD OF THE INDUSTRIAL ELECTROLYSIS AND ELECTROCHEMICAL ENGINEERING DIVISION OF THE ELECTROCHEMICAL SOCIETY INC.
• See page 113

STUDENT RESEARCH AWARDS OF THE BATTERY DIVISION OF THE ELECTROCHEMICAL SOCIETY INC.
• See page 113

FABRICATORS AND MANUFACTURERS ASSOCIATION FOUNDATION

http://www.nutsandboltsfoundation.org/scholarships/

COLLEGE AND TRADE/TECHNICAL SCHOOL SCHOLARSHIPS
• See page 178

FLORIDA ENGINEERING SOCIETY

http://www.fleng.org/scholarships.cfm

ACEC/FLORIDA SCHOLARSHIP

One-time scholarship of $5000 given to Florida citizen pursuing a bachelor's, master's or doctoral degree in an ABET-approved engineering program or in an accredited land surveying program. Students must be entering their junior, senior, or fifth year of college.

Academic Fields/Career Goals: Engineering/Technology; Surveying, Surveying Technology, Cartography, or Geographic Information Science.

Award: Scholarship for use in junior or senior years; not renewable. *Number:* 1. *Amount:* $5000.

Eligibility Requirements: Applicant must be enrolled or expecting to enroll full-time at a four-year institution or university; resident of Florida and studying in Florida. Available to U.S. citizens.

Application Requirements: Application form, essay. *Deadline:* March 6.

Contact: Chad Faison, Director of Marketing & Communications
Florida Engineering Society
125 South Gadsden Street
Tallahassee, FL 32301
Phone: 850-224-7121
E-mail: cfaison@fleng.org

DAVID F. LUDOVICI SCHOLARSHIP

• *See page 178*

ERIC PRIMAVERA MEMORIAL SCHOLARSHIP

One-time scholarship of $1000 given to students in their junior or senior year in a Florida university engineering program. Minimum 3.0 GPA required.

Academic Fields/Career Goals: Engineering/Technology.

Award: Scholarship for use in junior or senior years; not renewable. *Number:* 1. *Amount:* $1000.

Eligibility Requirements: Applicant must be enrolled or expecting to enroll full-time at an institution or university; resident of Florida and studying in Florida. Applicant must have 3.0 GPA or higher. Available to U.S. citizens.

Application Requirements: Application form. *Deadline:* February 1.

Contact: Amanda Hudson, Director of Information Technology
Florida Engineering Society
125 S Gadsden Street
Tallahassee, FL 32301
Phone: 850-224-7121
E-mail: ahudson@fleng.org

HIGH SCHOOL SCHOLARSHIP

One-time scholarship given to high school seniors who are residents of Florida. Minimum 3.5 GPA required. Applicant must have genuine interest in engineering.

Academic Fields/Career Goals: Engineering/Technology.

Award: Scholarship for use in freshman year; not renewable. *Number:* 6. *Amount:* $1500–$2500.

Eligibility Requirements: Applicant must be high school student; planning to enroll or expecting to enroll full-time at a four-year institution or university and resident of Florida. Applicant or parent of applicant must have employment or volunteer experience in engineering/technology. Applicant must have 3.5 GPA or higher. Available to U.S. citizens.

Application Requirements: Application form, interview. *Deadline:* February 1.

Contact: Amanda Hudson, Director of Information Technology
Florida Engineering Society
125 S Gadsden Street
Tallahassee, FL 32301
Phone: 850-224-7121
E-mail: ahudson@fleng.org

RAYMOND W. MILLER, PE SCHOLARSHIP

One-time scholarship given to students in their junior or senior year in a Florida university engineering program. Minimum 3.0 GPA required.

Academic Fields/Career Goals: Engineering/Technology.

Award: Scholarship for use in junior or senior years; not renewable. *Number:* 1. *Amount:* $1500–$2500.

Eligibility Requirements: Applicant must be enrolled or expecting to enroll full-time at an institution or university; resident of Florida and studying in Florida. Applicant must have 3.0 GPA or higher. Available to U.S. citizens.

Application Requirements: Application form. *Deadline:* February 1.

Contact: Amanda Hudson, Director of Information Technology
Florida Engineering Society
125 S Gadsden Street
Tallahassee, FL 32301
Phone: 850-224-7121
E-mail: ahudson@fleng.org

RICHARD B. GASSETT, PE SCHOLARSHIP

One-time scholarship given to students in their junior or senior year in a Florida university engineering program. Minimum 3.0 GPA required.

Academic Fields/Career Goals: Engineering/Technology.

Award: Scholarship for use in junior or senior years; not renewable. *Number:* 1. *Amount:* $1500–$2500.

Eligibility Requirements: Applicant must be enrolled or expecting to enroll full-time at an institution or university; resident of Florida and studying in Florida. Applicant must have 3.0 GPA or higher. Available to U.S. citizens.

Application Requirements: Application form. *Deadline:* February 1.

Contact: Amanda Hudson, Director of Information Technology
Florida Engineering Society
125 S Gadsden Street
Tallahassee, FL 32301
Phone: 850-224-7121
E-mail: ahudson@fleng.org

FOUNDATION FOR SCIENCE AND DISABILITY

http://stemd.org/

GRANTS FOR DISABLED GRADUATE STUDENTS IN THE SCIENCES

• *See page 113*

GEORGIA SOCIETY OF PROFESSIONAL ENGINEERS/GEORGIA ENGINEERING FOUNDATION

http://www.gefinc.org/

GEORGIA ENGINEERING FOUNDATION SCHOLARSHIP PROGRAM

Awards scholarships to students who are preparing for a career in engineering or engineering technology. Must be U.S. citizens and legal residents of Georgia. Must be attending or accepted in an ABET-accredited program. Separate applications are available: one for use by high school seniors and new college freshmen and one for use by college upperclassmen.

Academic Fields/Career Goals: Engineering/Technology.

Award: Scholarship for use in freshman, sophomore, junior, or senior years; not renewable. *Number:* 45. *Amount:* $1000–$5000.

Eligibility Requirements: Applicant must be enrolled or expecting to enroll full-time at a four-year institution or university and resident of Georgia. Applicant or parent of applicant must have employment or volunteer experience in community service. Available to U.S. citizens.

Application Requirements: Application form, personal photograph, recommendations or references, test scores, transcript. *Deadline:* August 31.

Contact: Roseana Richards, Scholarship Committee Chairman
Georgia Society of Professional Engineers/Georgia
Engineering Foundation
233 Peachtree Street, Suite 700, Harris Tower
Atlanta, GA 30303
Phone: 404-521-2324
E-mail: richardsr@pondco.com

GOLDEN KEY INTERNATIONAL HONOUR SOCIETY

http://www.goldenkey.org/

ENGINEERING/TECHNOLOGY ACHIEVEMENT AWARD

Award to members who excel in the study of engineering or technology. Applicants will be asked to respond to a problem posed by an honorary member within the discipline. One winner will receive a $1000 award. The second place winner will receive $750 and the third place winner will receive $500.

Academic Fields/Career Goals: Engineering/Technology.

Award: Prize for use in freshman, sophomore, junior, senior, graduate, or postgraduate years; not renewable. *Number:* 3. *Amount:* $500–$1000.

Eligibility Requirements: Applicant must be enrolled or expecting to enroll full- or part-time at a four-year institution or university. Available to U.S. and non-U.S. citizens.

Application Requirements: Application form, engineering-related report, cover page from the online registration, entry in a contest, essay, recommendations or references, transcript. *Deadline:* March 3.

Contact: Scholarship Program Administrators
Golden Key International Honour Society
PO Box 23737
Nashville, TN 37202-3737
Phone: 800-377-2401
E-mail: scholarships@goldenkey.org

GREATER KANAWHA VALLEY FOUNDATION

http://www.tgkvf.org/

MATH AND SCIENCE SCHOLARSHIP
• *See page 156*

STEVEN ENGINEERING SCHOLARSHIP
• *See page 178*

GREAT MINDS IN STEM

www.greatmindsinstem.org

HISPANIC ENGINEER NATIONAL ACHIEVEMENT AWARDS CORPORATION SCHOLARSHIP PROGRAM
• *See page 106*

HELLENIC UNIVERSITY CLUB OF PHILADELPHIA

http://www.hucphiladelphia.org/

DIMITRI J. VERVERELLI MEMORIAL SCHOLARSHIP FOR ARCHITECTURE AND/OR ENGINEERING
• *See page 121*

IDAHO STATE BROADCASTERS ASSOCIATION

http://www.idahobroadcasters.org/

WAYNE C. CORNILS MEMORIAL SCHOLARSHIP
• *See page 165*

ILLINOIS SOCIETY OF PROFESSIONAL ENGINEERS

http://www.illinoisengineer.com/

ILLINOIS SOCIETY OF PROFESSIONAL ENGINEERS/MELVIN E. AMSTUTZ MEMORIAL AWARD

Applicant must attend an Illinois university approved by the Accreditation Board of Engineering. Applicant must be at least a junior in university he or she attends, and must prove financial need. Essay must address why applicant wishes to become a professional engineer. Must have a B average.

Academic Fields/Career Goals: Engineering/Technology.

Award: Scholarship for use in junior or senior years; not renewable. *Number:* 1. *Amount:* $1500.

Eligibility Requirements: Applicant must be enrolled or expecting to enroll full-time at a four-year institution and studying in Illinois. Applicant must have 3.0 GPA or higher. Available to U.S. and non-U.S. citizens.

Application Requirements: Application form, application form may be submitted online (http://illinoisengineer.com/scholarships.shtml), essay, financial need analysis, recommendations or references, resume, transcript. *Deadline:* March 31.

Contact: Mrs. Nicole Palmisano, Scholarship Coordinator
Phone: 217-544-7424 Ext. 238
Fax: 217-528-6545
E-mail: NicolePalmisano@illinoisengineer.com

ILLUMINATING ENGINEERING SOCIETY OF NORTH AMERICA

http://www.ies.org/

ROBERT W. THUNEN MEMORIAL SCHOLARSHIPS
• *See page 122*

INDEPENDENT LABORATORIES INSTITUTE SCHOLARSHIP ALLIANCE

http://www.acil.org/

INDEPENDENT LABORATORIES INSTITUTE SCHOLARSHIP ALLIANCE
• *See page 156*

INDIANA SOCIETY OF PROFESSIONAL ENGINEERS

http://www.indspe.org/

INDIANA ENGINEERING SCHOLARSHIP

Award for Indiana resident who attends an Indiana educational institution, or commutes daily to a school outside Indiana. Applicant must have accrued the minimum of one-half the credits required for an undergraduate ABET-accredited engineering degree. For details and an application visit website http://indspe.org.

Academic Fields/Career Goals: Engineering/Technology.

Award: Scholarship for use in junior or senior years; not renewable. *Number:* 3. *Amount:* $750.

Eligibility Requirements: Applicant must be enrolled or expecting to enroll full- or part-time at a four-year institution or university and resident of Indiana. Available to U.S. citizens.

Application Requirements: Application form, community service, recommendations or references, resume, transcript. *Deadline:* May 1.

Contact: Mr. Harold Dungan, Scholarship Coordinator
Indiana Society of Professional Engineers
HNTB, 111 Monument Circle, Suite 1200
Indianapolis, IN 46204
Phone: 317-636-4682 Ext. 75245
Fax: 317-917-5211
E-mail: hdungan@hntb.com

INSTITUTE OF INDUSTRIAL ENGINEERS

http://www.iienet.org/

A.O. PUTNAM MEMORIAL SCHOLARSHIP

$700 award for undergraduate students enrolled in any school in the United States and its territories, Canada, and Mexico pursuing a course of study in industrial engineering. The school's industrial engineering program or equivalent must be accredited by an agency or organization recognized by IIE. Priority is given to students who have demonstrated an interest in management consulting. Minimum 3.4 GPA required.

Academic Fields/Career Goals: Engineering/Technology.

Award: Scholarship for use in freshman, sophomore, junior, or senior years; not renewable. *Number:* 1. *Amount:* up to $4000.

Eligibility Requirements: Applicant must be enrolled or expecting to enroll full-time at a four-year institution or university. Applicant or parent of applicant must be member of Institute of Industrial Engineers. Available to U.S. and non-U.S. citizens.

Application Requirements: Application form, nomination, recommendations or references, transcript. *Deadline:* November 15.

Contact: Bonnie Cameron, Operations Administrator
Phone: 770-449-0461 Ext. 105
E-mail: bcameron@iienet.org

C.B. GAMBRELL UNDERGRADUATE SCHOLARSHIP

One-time award for undergraduate industrial engineering students who are U.S. citizens, have graduated from a U.S. high school, and have a class standing above freshman level in an ABET-accredited IE program. Must be a member of Industrial Engineers, have a minimum GPA of 3.4, and be nominated by a department head.

Academic Fields/Career Goals: Engineering/Technology.

Award: Scholarship for use in sophomore, junior, or senior years; not renewable. *Number:* 1. *Amount:* up to $4000.

Eligibility Requirements: Applicant must be enrolled or expecting to enroll full-time at a four-year institution or university. Applicant or parent of applicant must be member of Institute of Industrial Engineers. Available to U.S. citizens.

Application Requirements: Application form, nomination, recommendations or references, transcript. *Deadline:* November 15.

Contact: Bonnie Cameron, Operations Administrator
Phone: 770-449-0461 Ext. 105
E-mail: bcameron@iienet.org

CIE UNDERGRADUATE SCHOLARSHIP

$2000 scholarship will be awarded to an undergraduate industrial engineering student for the best application of corporate social responsibility, resilience, or sustainability principals aligned with classic industrial engineering techniques to a project for an enterprise. Interested candidates must complete an application form, as well as submit a complete description of the project, including provision of a financial analysis using the triple-bottom line definitions of sustainability, showing a positive cash flow or return on investment to the enterprise over the project life. Applicants should have at least a 3.4 GPA.

Academic Fields/Career Goals: Engineering/Technology.

Award: Scholarship for use in freshman, sophomore, junior, or senior years; not renewable. *Number:* 1. *Amount:* $2000.

Eligibility Requirements: Applicant must be enrolled or expecting to enroll full-time at a four-year institution or university. Available to U.S. citizens.

Application Requirements: Application form, project description, recommendations or references, transcript. *Deadline:* February 1.

Contact: Bonnie Cameron, Operations Administrator
Phone: 770-449-0461 Ext. 105
E-mail: bcameron@iienet.org

DWIGHT D. GARDNER SCHOLARSHIP

$3000 scholarship available to undergraduate students enrolled in an industrial engineering program in any school in the United States and its territories, Canada, and Mexico, provided the school's engineering program or equivalent is accredited by an agency recognized by IIE. Must be an IIE member. Minimum 3.4 GPA required. Must be nominated by department head.

Academic Fields/Career Goals: Engineering/Technology.

Award: Scholarship for use in freshman, sophomore, junior, or senior years; not renewable. *Number:* 3. *Amount:* up to $4000.

Eligibility Requirements: Applicant must be enrolled or expecting to enroll full-time at a four-year institution or university. Applicant or parent of applicant must be member of Institute of Industrial Engineers. Available to U.S. and non-U.S. citizens.

Application Requirements: Application form, essay, financial need analysis, nomination, recommendations or references, transcript. *Deadline:* November 15.

Contact: Bonnie Cameron, Operations Administrator
Phone: 770-449-0461 Ext. 105
E-mail: bcameron@iienet.org

HAROLD AND INGE MARCUS SCHOLARSHIP

Available to undergraduate students enrolled in any school in the United States provided the school's engineering program is accredited by an agency recognized by IIE and the student is pursuing a course of study in industrial engineering. This award is intended to recognize academic excellence and noteworthy contribution to the development of the industrial engineering profession. Must have at least a 3.4 GPA.

Academic Fields/Career Goals: Engineering/Technology.

Award: Scholarship for use in freshman, sophomore, junior, or senior years; not renewable. *Amount:* up to $4000.

Eligibility Requirements: Applicant must be enrolled or expecting to enroll full-time at a two-year or four-year institution or university. Available to U.S. citizens.

Application Requirements: Application form, nominations, recommendations or references, transcript. *Deadline:* November 15.

Contact: Bonnie Cameron, Operations Administrator
Phone: 770-449-0461 Ext. 105
E-mail: bcameron@iienet.org

IIE COUNCIL OF FELLOWS UNDERGRADUATE SCHOLARSHIP

Awards to undergraduate students enrolled in any school in the United States and its territories, Canada and Mexico, provided the school's engineering program or equivalent is accredited by an agency recognized by IIE and the student is pursuing a course of study in industrial engineering. Must be IIE member and have minimum 3.4 GPA.

Academic Fields/Career Goals: Engineering/Technology.

Award: Scholarship for use in freshman, sophomore, junior, or senior years; not renewable. *Amount:* up to $4000.

Eligibility Requirements: Applicant must be enrolled or expecting to enroll full-time at a four-year institution or university. Applicant or parent of applicant must be member of Institute of Industrial Engineers. Available to U.S. and non-U.S. citizens.

Application Requirements: Application form, nomination form, recommendations or references, transcript. *Deadline:* November 15.

Contact: Bonnie Cameron, Operations Administrator
Phone: 770-449-0461 Ext. 105
E-mail: bcameron@iienet.org

JOHN L. IMHOFF SCHOLARSHIP

At least one award for a student pursuing an industrial engineering degree who, by academic, employment and/or professional achievements, has made noteworthy contributions to the development of the industrial engineering profession through international understanding. IIE membership is not required. Must have at least a 3.4 GPA.

Academic Fields/Career Goals: Engineering/Technology.

Award: Scholarship for use in freshman, sophomore, junior, or senior years; not renewable. *Number:* 1. *Amount:* $1000.

Eligibility Requirements: Applicant must be enrolled or expecting to enroll full-time at a four-year institution or university. Available to U.S. citizens.

Application Requirements: Application form, essay, nomination, recommendations or references, transcript. *Deadline:* November 15.

Contact: Bonnie Cameron, Operations Administrator
Phone: 770-449-0461 Ext. 105
E-mail: bcameron@iienet.org

LISA ZAKEN AWARD FOR EXCELLENCE

Award for undergraduate and graduate students enrolled in any school, and pursuing a course of study in industrial engineering. Award is intended to recognize excellence in scholarly activities and leadership related to the industrial engineering profession on campus. Must maintain at least a 3.0 GPA.

Academic Fields/Career Goals: Engineering/Technology.

Award: Prize for use in freshman, sophomore, junior, senior, or graduate years; not renewable. *Number:* up to 1. *Amount:* up to $4000.

Eligibility Requirements: Applicant must be enrolled or expecting to enroll full-time at a four-year institution or university. Applicant or parent of applicant must be member of Institute of Industrial Engineers.

Applicant must have 3.0 GPA or higher. Available to U.S. and non-U.S. citizens.

Application Requirements: Application form, essay, nomination form, recommendations or references, transcript. *Deadline:* November 15.

Contact: Bonnie Cameron, Operations Administrator
Phone: 770-449-0461 Ext. 105
E-mail: bcameron@iienet.org

MARVIN MUNDEL MEMORIAL SCHOLARSHIP

Scholarship awarded to undergraduate students enrolled in any school in the United States, Canada, or Mexico with an accredited industrial engineering program. Priority given to students who have demonstrated an interest in work measurement and methods engineering. Must be active Institute members with 3.4 GPA or above. Must be nominated by department head or faculty adviser.

Academic Fields/Career Goals: Engineering/Technology.

Award: Scholarship for use in freshman, sophomore, junior, or senior years; not renewable. *Amount:* up to $4000.

Eligibility Requirements: Applicant must be enrolled or expecting to enroll full-time at a four-year institution or university. Applicant or parent of applicant must be member of Institute of Industrial Engineers. Available to U.S. and non-U.S. citizens.

Application Requirements: Application form, nomination, recommendations or references, transcript. *Deadline:* November 15.

Contact: Bonnie Cameron, Operations Administrator
Phone: 770-449-0461 Ext. 105
E-mail: bcameron@iienet.org

PRESIDENTS SCHOLARSHIP

$1000 scholarship available to undergraduate student pursuing a course of study in industrial engineering. This award is intended to recognize excellence in scholarly activities and leadership of the industrial engineering profession. Must be active in a student chapter and must have demonstrated leadership and promoted IIE involvement on campus. Must have at least a 3.4 GPA.

Academic Fields/Career Goals: Engineering/Technology.

Award: Scholarship for use in freshman, sophomore, junior, or senior years; not renewable. *Number:* 1. *Amount:* $1000.

Eligibility Requirements: Applicant must be enrolled or expecting to enroll full-time at a four-year institution or university. Applicant or parent of applicant must be member of Institute of Industrial Engineers. Available to U.S. citizens.

Application Requirements: Application form, nomination, recommendations or references, transcript. *Deadline:* November 15.

Contact: Bonnie Cameron, Operations Administrator
Phone: 770-449-0461 Ext. 105
E-mail: bcameron@iienet.org

SOCIETY FOR HEALTH SYSTEMS SCHOLARSHIP

$1000 award for undergraduate students enrolled full-time in an industrial engineering program in any accredited school in the United States and its territories, Canada and Mexico. Must be pursuing a course of study in industrial engineering and operations research with a definite interest in the area of health care. Must be an active Society for Health Systems student member with a minimum 3.4 GPA. Nomination required.

Academic Fields/Career Goals: Engineering/Technology.

Award: Scholarship for use in freshman, sophomore, junior, or senior years; not renewable. *Amount:* $1000.

Eligibility Requirements: Applicant must be enrolled or expecting to enroll full-time at a four-year institution or university. Available to U.S. citizens.

Application Requirements: Application form, essay, nomination, recommendations or references, resume, transcript. *Deadline:* December 1.

Contact: Bonnie Cameron, Operations Administrator
Phone: 770-449-0461 Ext. 105
E-mail: bcameron@iienet.org

UPS SCHOLARSHIP FOR FEMALE STUDENTS

One-time award for female undergraduate students enrolled at any school in the United States, Canada, or Mexico in an industrial engineering program. Must be a member of Institute of Industrial Engineers, have a minimum GPA of 3.4, and be nominated by a department head.

Academic Fields/Career Goals: Engineering/Technology.

Award: Scholarship for use in freshman, sophomore, junior, or senior years; not renewable. *Number:* 1. *Amount:* up to $4000.

Eligibility Requirements: Applicant must be enrolled or expecting to enroll full-time at a four-year or technical institution or university and female. Applicant or parent of applicant must be member of Institute of Industrial Engineers. Available to U.S. and non-U.S. citizens.

Application Requirements: Application form, nomination, recommendations or references, transcript. *Deadline:* November 15.

Contact: Bonnie Cameron, Operations Administrator
Phone: 770-449-0461 Ext. 105
E-mail: bcameron@iienet.org

UPS SCHOLARSHIP FOR MINORITY STUDENTS

One-time award for minority undergraduate students enrolled at any school in the United States, Canada, or Mexico in an industrial engineering program. Must be a member of Institute of Industrial Engineers. Nominated students by IE department heads will be sent an application package to complete and return before November 15. Minimum GPA of 3.4 required.

Academic Fields/Career Goals: Engineering/Technology.

Award: Scholarship for use in freshman, sophomore, junior, or senior years; not renewable. *Number:* 1. *Amount:* up to $4000.

Eligibility Requirements: Applicant must be American Indian/Alaska Native, Asian/Pacific Islander, Black (non-Hispanic), Hispanic and enrolled or expecting to enroll full-time at a four-year institution or university. Applicant or parent of applicant must be member of Institute of Industrial Engineers. Available to U.S. and non-U.S. citizens.

Application Requirements: Application form, nomination, recommendations or references, transcript. *Deadline:* November 15.

Contact: Bonnie Cameron, Operations Administrator
Phone: 770-449-0461 Ext. 105
E-mail: bcameron@iienet.org

INTERNATIONAL FACILITY MANAGEMENT ASSOCIATION FOUNDATION

http://www.ifmafoundation.org/

IFMA FOUNDATION SCHOLARSHIPS
• *See page 122*

INTERNATIONAL SOCIETY FOR OPTICAL ENGINEERING-SPIE

http://www.spie.org/scholarships

SPIE EDUCATIONAL SCHOLARSHIPS IN OPTICAL SCIENCE AND ENGINEERING
• *See page 114*

INTERNATIONAL SOCIETY OF EXPLOSIVES ENGINEERS

http://www.isee.org/

JERRY MCDOWELL FUND
• *See page 282*

INTERNATIONAL TECHNOLOGY EDUCATION ASSOCIATION

http://www.iteaconnect.org/

INTERNATIONAL TECHNOLOGY EDUCATION ASSOCIATION UNDERGRADUATE SCHOLARSHIP IN TECHNOLOGY EDUCATION
• *See page 254*

LEAGUE OF UNITED LATIN AMERICAN CITIZENS NATIONAL EDUCATIONAL SERVICE CENTERS INC.

http://www.lnesc.org/

GE/LULAC SCHOLARSHIP
• *See page 166*

GM/LULAC SCHOLARSHIP

Renewable award for minority students who are pursuing an undergraduate degree in engineering at an accredited college or university. Must maintain a minimum 3.0 GPA. Selection is based in part on the likelihood of pursuing a successful career in engineering.

Academic Fields/Career Goals: Engineering/Technology.

Award: Scholarship for use in freshman, sophomore, junior, or senior years; renewable. *Number:* up to 20. *Amount:* up to $2000.

Eligibility Requirements: Applicant must be American Indian/Alaska Native, Asian/Pacific Islander, Black (non-Hispanic), Hispanic and enrolled or expecting to enroll full-time at a four-year institution or university. Applicant must have 3.0 GPA or higher. Available to U.S. citizens.

Application Requirements: Application form, essay, recommendations or references, transcript. *Deadline:* July 15.

Contact: Scholarship Administrator
League of United Latin American Citizens National
Educational Service Centers Inc.
2000 L Street, NW, Suite 610
Washington, DC 20036
Phone: 202-835-9646 Ext. 10
Fax: 202-835-9685

LOS ANGELES COUNCIL OF BLACK PROFESSIONAL ENGINEERS

http://www.lablackengineers.org/

AL-BEN SCHOLARSHIP FOR ACADEMIC INCENTIVE
• *See page 179*

AL-BEN SCHOLARSHIP FOR PROFESSIONAL MERIT
• *See page 179*

AL-BEN SCHOLARSHIP FOR SCHOLASTIC ACHIEVEMENT
• *See page 179*

MAINE SOCIETY OF PROFESSIONAL ENGINEERS

http://www.mespe.org/

MAINE SOCIETY OF PROFESSIONAL ENGINEERS VERNON T. SWAINE-ROBERT E. CHUTE SCHOLARSHIP
• *See page 283*

MANUFACTURERS ASSOCIATION OF MAINE

http://www.mainemfg.com/

MAINE MANUFACTURING CAREER AND TRAINING FOUNDATION SCHOLARSHIP
• *See page 142*

MARINE TECHNOLOGY SOCIETY

http://www.mtsociety.org/

MTS STUDENT SCHOLARSHIP FOR GRADUATING HIGH SCHOOL SENIORS

Scholarship of $2000 available to high school seniors who have been accepted into a full-time undergraduate program and have an interest in marine technology.

Academic Fields/Career Goals: Engineering/Technology; Marine/Ocean Engineering.

Award: Scholarship for use in freshman year; not renewable. *Amount:* $2000.

Eligibility Requirements: Applicant must be high school student and planning to enroll or expecting to enroll full-time at a four-year institution or university. Available to U.S. and non-U.S. citizens.

Application Requirements: Application form, college acceptance letter, essay, recommendations or references, transcript. *Deadline:* April 15.

Contact: Suzanne Voelker, Operations Administrator
Marine Technology Society
5565 Sterrett Place, Suite 108
Columbia, MD 21044
Phone: 410-884-5330
E-mail: suzanne.voelker@mtsociety.org

MASSACHUSETTS ASSOCIATION OF LAND SURVEYORS AND CIVIL ENGINEERS

http://www.malsce.org/

MALSE SCHOLARSHIPS

A scholarship awarded to a student presently enrolled full time (days) as an undergraduate in an accredited College, University, Junior College, Technical Institute or Community College and majoring in Land Surveying, Civil Engineering or Environmental Engineering. The MALSCE Education Trust may select one or more applicants to receive scholarships per year and currently plans to award one or two scholarships. Typically 2-3 scholarships are awarded each year with varying denominations of $500, $1000 or $2000 each. The MALSCE Education Trust Chair will contact winning applicants. Applicant must be presently enrolled full-time (days) in an accredited College, University, Junior College, Technical Institute, or Community College and majoring in Land Surveying, Civil Engineering or Environmental Engineering; be a Massachusetts resident (based upon parents' full time residence, if still a dependent); however, he/she may attend an out-of-state school. Complete and sign the application and give it to a qualified Sponsor. A Sponsor must be a department head, dean, professor, or instructor who has personal knowledge of the applicant. An applicant's employer may also be a sponsor, if that employer is a MALSCE member in good standing. Friends and relatives of the applicant may not be sponsors. The Trustees will not accept a letter of recommendation from a sponsor other than the types listed above.

Academic Fields/Career Goals: Engineering/Technology; Environmental Science; Surveying, Surveying Technology, Cartography, or Geographic Information Science.

Award: Scholarship for use in sophomore, junior, senior, or postgraduate years; not renewable. *Number:* 1–2. *Amount:* $500–$2000.

Eligibility Requirements: Applicant must be enrolled or expecting to enroll full- or part-time at a two-year or four-year or technical institution or university and resident of Massachusetts. Available to U.S. citizens.

Application Requirements: Application form, essay. *Deadline:* February 15.

Contact: Mrs. Mary Ann Corcoran, MALSCE Education Trust Chair
Massachusetts Association of Land Surveyors and Civil
Engineers
MALSCE
One Walnut Street
Boston, MA 02108
Phone: 413-841-0355
E-mail: mcorcoran@hillengineers.com

MIDWEST ROOFING CONTRACTORS ASSOCIATION

http://www.mrca.org/

MRCA FOUNDATION SCHOLARSHIP PROGRAM
• *See page 122*

MINERALS, METALS, AND MATERIALS SOCIETY (TMS)

http://www.tms.org/

KAUFMAN CALPHAD SCHOLARSHIP
• *See page 268*

MATERIALS PROCESSING & MANUFACTURING DIVISION SCHOLARSHIP
• *See page 283*

TMS/EPD SCHOLARSHIP
• *See page 283*

TMS/FMD GILBERT CHIN SCHOLARSHIP
• *See page 283*

TMS/INTERNATIONAL SYMPOSIUM ON SUPERALLOYS SCHOLARSHIP PROGRAM
• *See page 283*

TMS/LIGHT METALS DIVISION SCHOLARSHIP PROGRAM
• *See page 284*

TMS OUTSTANDING STUDENT PAPER CONTEST-UNDERGRADUATE
• *See page 284*

TMS/STRUCTURAL MATERIALS DIVISION SCHOLARSHIP
• *See page 284*

NASA/MARYLAND SPACE GRANT CONSORTIUM

http://md.spacegrant.org/

NASA MARYLAND SPACE GRANT CONSORTIUM UNDERGRADUATE SCHOLARSHIPS
• *See page 142*

NASA MINNESOTA SPACE GRANT CONSORTIUM

http://www.aem.umn.edu/mnsgc

MINNESOTA SPACE GRANT CONSORTIUM SCHOLARSHIP PROGRAM
• *See page 142*

NASA MONTANA SPACE GRANT CONSORTIUM

http://www.spacegrant.montana.edu/

MONTANA SPACE GRANT SCHOLARSHIP PROGRAM
• *See page 142*

NASA RHODE ISLAND SPACE GRANT CONSORTIUM

http://brown/initiatives/ri-space-grant

NASA RHODE ISLAND SPACE GRANT CONSORTIUM UNDERGRADUATE RESEARCH SCHOLARSHIP
• *See page 143*

NASA RISGC SCIENCE EN ESPANOL SCHOLARSHIP FOR UNDERGRADUATE STUDENTS
• *See page 143*

NASA SOUTH CAROLINA SPACE GRANT CONSORTIUM

http://www.cofc.edu/~scsgrant

UNDERGRADUATE RESEARCH AWARD PROGRAM
• *See page 143*

NASA'S VIRGINIA SPACE GRANT CONSORTIUM

http://www.vsgc.odu.edu/

COMMUNITY COLLEGE STEM SCHOLARSHIPS
• *See page 114*

NATIONAL ACTION COUNCIL FOR MINORITIES IN ENGINEERING-NACME INC.

http://www.nacme.org/

NACME PRE-ENGINEERING SCHOLARSHIP PROGRAM

$2500 award recognizing the nation's highest achieving African American, American Indian, and Latino high school seniors who have demonstrated academic excellence, leadership skills, and a commitment to science and engineering as a career goal. Must be admitted into an engineering program as a full-time student. Priority will be given to applicants who have been admitted to a NACME Partner Institution. Applicant should be a participant in an Academy of Engineering (a National Academy Foundation national network of career-themed academies) or a pre-college or high school program focused on math, science, and engineering. Minimum 3.0 GPA and U.S. citizenship or permanent residence required. Must have a preferred combined SAT score of 1650 for critical reading, writing, and math, and a preferred math score of 550; or preferred composite ACT score of 24 and a preferred score from the math section of 24.

Academic Fields/Career Goals: Engineering/Technology.

Award: Scholarship for use in freshman year; not renewable. *Amount:* $2500.

Eligibility Requirements: Applicant must be American Indian/Alaska Native, Black (non-Hispanic), Hispanic; high school student and planning to enroll or expecting to enroll full-time at a four-year institution or university. Applicant must have 3.0 GPA or higher. Available to U.S. citizens.

Application Requirements: Application form, financial need analysis, recommendations or references. *Deadline:* March 15.

Contact: Aileen Walter, Vice President
　　　　Phone: 914-539-4010
　　　　Fax: 914-539-4032
　　　　E-mail: scholarships@nacme.org

NACME SCHOLARS PROGRAM

Renewable award for African-American, American-Indian, or Latino student enrolled in a Baccalaureate engineering program. Award money is given to participating institutions who select applicants and disperse funds. High school seniors must be accepted by a College of Engineering (at the end of the freshman year, NACME assumes a minimum GPA of 2.5 on a scale of 4.0). Two-year community college transfers, i.e., those accepted for their third year of engineering study, must enter with at least a 2.7 cumulative GPA on a scale of a 4.0 and an Associate's degree in engineering science (or the equivalent program of study). Check website for details, http://www.nacme.org.

Academic Fields/Career Goals: Engineering/Technology.

Award: Scholarship for use in freshman, sophomore, junior, or senior years; renewable. *Amount:* up to $5000.

Eligibility Requirements: Applicant must be American Indian/Alaska Native, Black (non-Hispanic), Hispanic and enrolled or expecting to enroll full-time at a four-year institution or university. Available to U.S. citizens.

Application Requirements: Application form, financial need analysis, recommendations or references. *Deadline:* March 15.

Contact: Aileen Walter, Vice President
> Phone: 914-539-4010
> Fax: 914-539-4032
> E-mail: scholarships@nacme.org

NATIONAL ASSOCIATION FOR THE ADVANCEMENT OF COLORED PEOPLE

http://www.naacp.org/

HUBERTUS W.V. WELLEMS SCHOLARSHIP FOR MALE STUDENTS
• *See page 180*

NATIONAL ASSOCIATION OF WATER COMPANIES-NEW JERSEY CHAPTER

http://www.nawc.org

NATIONAL ASSOCIATION OF WATER COMPANIES-NEW JERSEY CHAPTER SCHOLARSHIP
• *See page 80*

NATIONAL ASSOCIATION OF WOMEN IN CONSTRUCTION

http://www.nawic.org/

NAWIC UNDERGRADUATE SCHOLARSHIPS
• *See page 122*

NATIONAL SOCIETY OF BLACK ENGINEERS

http://www.nsbe.org/

NSBE O-I CORPORATE SCHOLARSHIP PROGRAM
• *See page 285*

S. D. BECHTEL JR. FOUNDATION ENGINEERING SCHOLARSHIP

The purpose of this scholarship is to provide financial scholarships for students pursuing undergraduate degrees in Engineering and collegiate members of the National Society of Black Engineers (NSBE). Applicants must be NSBE members, majoring in civil engineering or mechanical engineering.

Academic Fields/Career Goals: Engineering/Technology.

Award: Scholarship for use in freshman, sophomore, junior, or senior years; renewable. *Number:* 3. *Amount:* $15,000.

Eligibility Requirements: Applicant must be Black (non-Hispanic) and enrolled or expecting to enroll full- or part-time at a four-year institution or university. Applicant must have 3.0 GPA or higher. Available to U.S. citizens.

Application Requirements: *Deadline:* June 30.

NATIONAL SOCIETY OF PROFESSIONAL ENGINEERS

http://www.nspe.org/

MAUREEN L. AND HOWARD N. BLITMAN, PE SCHOLARSHIP TO PROMOTE DIVERSITY IN ENGINEERING
• *See page 180*

PAUL H. ROBBINS HONORARY SCHOLARSHIP
• *See page 180*

PROFESSIONAL ENGINEERS IN INDUSTRY SCHOLARSHIP
• *See page 180*

NEVADA NASA SPACE GRANT CONSORTIUM

http://www.nvspacegrant.org/

NATIONAL SPACE GRANT COLLEGE AND FELLOWSHIP PROGRAM
• *See page 114*

NEXTSTEPU

http://www.nextstepu.com/

$1,500 STEM SCHOLARSHIP
• *See page 106*

OREGON STUDENT ASSISTANCE COMMISSION

http://www.GetCollegeFunds.org/

ANDY AITKENHEAD SCHOLARSHIP
• *See page 115*

HOME BUILDERS FOUNDATION JIM IRVINE STATEWIDE SCHOLARSHIP
• *See page 123*

JEFFREY ALAN SCOGGINS MEMORIAL SCHOLARSHIP

Award for college junior or above for fall term/semester in undergraduate study in engineering at an Oregon four-year nonprofit college or university. Oregon State University is preferred. Membership in the Sigma Chi fraternity is preferred. May reapply for additional year of funding, which may be used towards graduate study. Minimum 3.0 GPA is preferred.

Academic Fields/Career Goals: Engineering/Technology.

Award: Scholarship for use in junior, senior, or graduate years; not renewable.

Eligibility Requirements: Applicant must be enrolled or expecting to enroll full-time at a four-year institution or university; resident of Oregon and studying in Oregon. Applicant must have 3.0 GPA or higher. Available to U.S. citizens.

Application Requirements: Application form, financial need analysis. *Deadline:* March 1.

Contact: Melissa Adams, Scholarship Processing Coordinator
> Phone: 541-687-7409
> E-mail: melissa.adams@hecc.oregon.gov

SOCIETY OF AMERICAN MILITARY ENGINEERS PORTLAND POST SCHOLARSHIP
• *See page 181*

PLAN NEW HAMPSHIRE

www.plannh.org

PLAN NEW HAMPSHIRE SCHOLARSHIP AND PROGRAM
• *See page 123*

PLUMBING-HEATING-COOLING CONTRACTORS EDUCATION FOUNDATION

http://www.phccfoundation.org/scholarships

DELTA FAUCET COMPANY SCHOLARSHIP PROGRAM
• *See page 167*

PHCC EDUCATIONAL FOUNDATION NEED-BASED SCHOLARSHIP
• *See page 167*

PHCC EDUCATIONAL FOUNDATION SCHOLARSHIP PROGRAM
• *See page 167*

PROFESSIONAL CONSTRUCTION ESTIMATORS ASSOCIATION

http://www.pcea.org/

TED G. WILSON MEMORIAL SCHOLARSHIP FOUNDATION
• *See page 197*

ROBERT H. MOLLOHAN FAMILY CHARITABLE FOUNDATION, INC.

http://www.mollohanfoundation.org/

HIGH TECHNOLOGY SCHOLARS PROGRAM
• *See page 158*

ROCKY MOUNTAIN COAL MINING INSTITUTE

http://www.rmcmi.org/

ROCKY MOUNTAIN COAL MINING INSTITUTE SCHOLARSHIP
• *See page 197*

SALT RIVER PROJECT (SRP)

http://www.srpnet.com/

NAVAJO GENERATING STATION NAVAJO SCHOLARSHIP

Applicants must be enrolled members of the Navajo Nation who will be full-time students at an accredited college or university. Priority will be given to the math, engineering and environmental studies. Awards are made based on the field of study, and academic excellence and achievement. Award amounts are determined by the NGS Scholarship Committee following an evaluation of the Financial Needs Analysis of each applicant.

Academic Fields/Career Goals: Engineering/Technology; Environmental Science; Mathematics.

Award: Scholarship for use in junior year; renewable.

Eligibility Requirements: Applicant must be American Indian/Alaska Native and enrolled or expecting to enroll full-time at a four-year institution or university. Applicant must have 3.0 GPA or higher.

Application Requirements: *Deadline:* April 25.

SCARLETT FAMILY FOUNDATION SCHOLARSHIP PROGRAM

http://www.scarlettfoundation.org/

SCHOLARSHIP FOR STUDENTS PURSUING A BUSINESS OR STEM DEGREE
• *See page 84*

SEMICONDUCTOR RESEARCH CORPORATION (SRC)

http://www.src.org/

MASTER'S SCHOLARSHIP PROGRAM
• *See page 181*

SIGMA XI, THE SCIENTIFIC RESEARCH SOCIETY

http://www.sigmaxi.org/

SIGMA XI GRANTS-IN-AID OF RESEARCH
• *See page 101*

SILICON VALLEY COMMUNITY FOUNDATION

www.siliconvalleycf.org

SAMSUNG@FIRST SCHOLARS

Samsung Semiconductor Inc.'s theme of Collaborate. Innovate. Grow. has served as the company's mantra to drive technology innovation today and for the next 30 years in Silicon Valley. To help support the valley's continued legacy as the epicenter of innovation and growth in high-tech, the company has made a commitment to the next-generation of innovators by establishing its Samsung@First Scholars program. The scholarship program's goal is to support those outstanding scientists, technologists, engineers, and mathematicians who will lead the world for the next 30 years and beyond. Current undergraduate student entering their sophomore, junior, or senior year in the upcoming academic school year or Master's student planning to enroll on a full-time basis (as defined by the program of study) in a public four-year college/university in the greater Bay Area (includes Santa Clara, San Mateo, San Francisco, Marin, Alameda, Contra Costa, Napa, Solano, Sonoma) may apply. Must have declared a major in science, technology, engineering, or math (STEM). Preference given to computer science and engineering (CISE) and engineering majors. Minimum grade point average of 3.0 on a 4.0 scale. Must be United States citizen or legal resident.

Academic Fields/Career Goals: Engineering/Technology; Science, Technology, and Society.

Award: Scholarship for use in sophomore, junior, senior, or graduate years; not renewable. *Number:* 3. *Amount:* $15,000.

Eligibility Requirements: Applicant must be enrolled or expecting to enroll full-time at a four-year institution or university and studying in California. Applicant must have 3.0 GPA or higher. Available to U.S. citizens.

Application Requirements: Application form, community service, essay, financial need analysis. *Deadline:* March 27.

SIMPLEHUMAN

http://www.simplehuman.com/

SIMPLE SOLUTIONS DESIGN COMPETITION
• *See page 286*

SOCIETY FOR IMAGING SCIENCE AND TECHNOLOGY

http://www.imaging.org/

RAYMOND DAVIS SCHOLARSHIP
• *See page 286*

SOCIETY OF AUTOMOTIVE ENGINEERS

http://www.sae.org/

BMW/SAE ENGINEERING SCHOLARSHIP
• *See page 146*

DETROIT SECTION SAE TECHNICAL SCHOLARSHIP
• *See page 286*

EDWARD D. HENDRICKSON/SAE ENGINEERING SCHOLARSHIP
• *See page 146*

FRED M. YOUNG SR./SAE ENGINEERING SCHOLARSHIP
Scholarship of $4000 awarded at $1000 per year for four years. Applicants must have a 3.75 GPA, rank in the 90th percentile in both math and critical reading on SAT or composite ACT scores, and pursue an engineering degree accredited by ABET. A 3.0 GPA and continued engineering enrollment must be maintained to renew the scholarship.

Academic Fields/Career Goals: Engineering/Technology.

Award: Scholarship for use in freshman year; renewable. *Number:* 1. *Amount:* $1000.

Eligibility Requirements: Applicant must be high school student and planning to enroll or expecting to enroll full-time at a four-year institution or university. Available to U.S. citizens.

Application Requirements: Application form, essay, test scores, transcript. *Deadline:* December 15.

Contact: Connie Harnish, SAE Educational Relations
Society of Automotive Engineers
400 Commonwealth Drive
Warrendale, PA 15096
Phone: 724-772-4047
E-mail: connie@sae.org

RALPH K. HILLQUIST HONORARY SAE SCHOLARSHIP
• *See page 286*

SAE LONG TERM MEMBER SPONSORED SCHOLARSHIP
The scholarship recognizes outstanding SAE student members who actively support SAE and its activities. Applications may be submitted by the student or by the SAE faculty advisor, an SAE Section officer or a community leader. The student must be a junior who will be entering the senior year of undergraduate engineering studies. Number of award varies.

Academic Fields/Career Goals: Engineering/Technology.

Award: Scholarship for use in senior year; not renewable. *Amount:* $1000.

Eligibility Requirements: Applicant must be enrolled or expecting to enroll full-time at a four-year institution or university. Applicant or parent of applicant must be member of Society of Automotive Engineers. Available to U.S. citizens.

Application Requirements: Application form, recommendations or references. *Deadline:* April 1.

Contact: Connie Harnish, SAE Educational Relations
Society of Automotive Engineers
400 Commonwealth Drive
Warrendale, PA 15096
Phone: 724-772-4047
E-mail: connie@sae.org

TAU BETA PI/SAE ENGINEERING SCHOLARSHIP
Six scholarships valued at $1000 each will be awarded for the freshman year only. Applicants must have a 3.75 GPA, rank in the 90th percentile in both math and critical reading for SAT scores or for composite ACT scores, and pursue an engineering program accredited by the engineering accreditation commission of the Accreditation Board for Engineering and Technology.

Academic Fields/Career Goals: Engineering/Technology.

Award: Scholarship for use in freshman year; not renewable. *Number:* 6. *Amount:* $1000.

Eligibility Requirements: Applicant must be high school student and planning to enroll or expecting to enroll full- or part-time at a four-year institution or university. Available to U.S. citizens.

Application Requirements: Application form, essay, test scores, transcript. *Deadline:* December 15.

Contact: Connie Harnish, SAE Educational Relations
Society of Automotive Engineers
400 Commonwealth Drive
Warrendale, PA 15096
Phone: 724-772-4047
E-mail: connie@sae.org

TMC/SAE DONALD D. DAWSON TECHNICAL SCHOLARSHIP
• *See page 147*

YANMAR/SAE SCHOLARSHIP
• *See page 286*

SOCIETY OF MANUFACTURING ENGINEERS EDUCATION FOUNDATION

http://www.smeef.org/

ALBERT E. WISCHMEYER MEMORIAL SCHOLARSHIP AWARD
Applicants must be residents of Western New York State, graduating high school seniors or current undergraduate students enrolled in an accredited degree program in manufacturing engineering, manufacturing engineering technology or mechanical technology in New York. Must have an GPA of 3.0.

Academic Fields/Career Goals: Engineering/Technology.

Award: Scholarship for use in freshman, sophomore, junior, or senior years; not renewable. *Number:* 1–10. *Amount:* $1000–$5000.

Eligibility Requirements: Applicant must be enrolled or expecting to enroll full-time at a four-year institution or university; resident of New York and studying in New York. Applicant must have 3.0 GPA or higher. Available to U.S. citizens.

Application Requirements: Application form, essay, recommendations or references, resume, transcript. *Deadline:* February 1.

ARTHUR AND GLADYS CERVENKA SCHOLARSHIP AWARD
One-time award to full-time students enrolled in a degree program in manufacturing engineering or technology. Preference given to students attending a Florida institution. Minimum 3.0 GPA required.

Academic Fields/Career Goals: Engineering/Technology.

Award: Scholarship for use in freshman, sophomore, junior, or senior years; not renewable. *Number:* 1–10. *Amount:* $1000–$5000.

Eligibility Requirements: Applicant must be enrolled or expecting to enroll full-time at a four-year institution or university. Applicant must have 3.0 GPA or higher. Available to U.S. citizens.

Application Requirements: Application form, essay, recommendations or references, resume, transcript. *Deadline:* February 1.

CATERPILLAR SCHOLARS AWARD FUND
Supports five one-time scholarships for full-time students enrolled in a manufacturing engineering program. Minority applicants may apply as incoming freshmen. Applicants must have an overall minimum GPA of 3.0.

Academic Fields/Career Goals: Engineering/Technology.

Award: Scholarship for use in freshman, sophomore, junior, or senior years; not renewable. *Number:* 1–15. *Amount:* $1000–$5000.

Eligibility Requirements: Applicant must be enrolled or expecting to enroll full-time at a four-year institution or university. Applicant must have 3.0 GPA or higher. Available to U.S. and Canadian citizens.

Application Requirements: Application form, essay, recommendations or references, resume, transcript. *Deadline:* February 1.

CHAPTER 17-ST. LOUIS SCHOLARSHIP

Scholarship will be given to full-time or part-time students enrolled in a manufacturing engineering, industrial technology, or other related program. Must study in Missouri or Illinois. Minimum 2.5 GPA is required.

Academic Fields/Career Goals: Engineering/Technology.

Award: Scholarship for use in freshman, sophomore, junior, or senior years; not renewable.

Eligibility Requirements: Applicant must be enrolled or expecting to enroll full-time at a four-year institution or university and studying in Illinois, Missouri. Applicant must have 2.5 GPA or higher. Available to U.S. and Canadian citizens.

Application Requirements: Application form, essay, recommendations or references, resume, transcript. *Deadline:* February 1.

CHAPTER 198-DOWNRIVER DETROIT SCHOLARSHIP

One-time award for an individual seeking an Associate's degree, Bachelor's degree, or graduate degree in manufacturing, mechanical or industrial engineering, engineering technology, or industrial technology at an accredited public or private college or university in Michigan. Must have a minimum GPA of 2.5. Preference is given to applicants who are a child or grandchild of a current SME Downriver Chapter No. 198 member, a member of its student chapter, or a Michigan resident.

Academic Fields/Career Goals: Engineering/Technology; Industrial Design; Mechanical Engineering; Trade/Technical Specialties.

Award: Scholarship for use in freshman, sophomore, junior, senior, or graduate years; not renewable. *Number:* 1–5. *Amount:* $1000–$5000.

Eligibility Requirements: Applicant must be enrolled or expecting to enroll full-time at a two-year or four-year institution or university and studying in Michigan. Applicant must have 2.5 GPA or higher. Available to U.S. citizens.

Application Requirements: Application form, essay, recommendations or references, resume, student statement letter, test scores, transcript. *Deadline:* February 1.

CHAPTER 23-QUAD CITIES IOWA/ILLINOIS SCHOLARSHIP

Scholarship applicant must be entering freshman or current undergraduate student pursuing a Bachelor's degree in manufacturing engineering or a related field at an accredited college or university in Iowa or Illinois.

Academic Fields/Career Goals: Engineering/Technology.

Award: Scholarship for use in freshman, sophomore, or junior years; not renewable. *Number:* up to 5. *Amount:* $1000–$5000.

Eligibility Requirements: Applicant must be enrolled or expecting to enroll full-time at a four-year institution or university and studying in Illinois, Iowa. Available to U.S. and Canadian citizens.

Application Requirements: Application form, essay, recommendations or references, resume, test scores, transcript. *Deadline:* February 1.

CHAPTER 31-TRI CITY SCHOLARSHIP

Applicants must be seeking a Bachelor's degree in manufacturing, mechanical, or industrial engineering, engineering technology, industrial technology or closely related field of study. Must be enrolled in or plan to attend an accredited college or university in the state of Michigan.

Academic Fields/Career Goals: Engineering/Technology.

Award: Scholarship for use in freshman, sophomore, junior, or senior years; not renewable. *Number:* up to 5. *Amount:* $1000–$5000.

Eligibility Requirements: Applicant must be enrolled or expecting to enroll full-time at a two-year or four-year or technical institution or university and studying in Michigan. Applicant must have 3.0 GPA or higher. Available to U.S. and Canadian citizens.

Application Requirements: Application form, essay, resume, test scores, transcript. *Deadline:* February 1.

CHAPTER 3-PEORIA ENDOWED SCHOLARSHIP

Applicants must be seeking a Bachelor's degree in manufacturing engineering, industrial engineering, manufacturing technology, or a manufacturing-related degree program at either Bradley University (Peoria, Illinois) or Illinois State University (Normal, Illinois).

Academic Fields/Career Goals: Engineering/Technology.

Award: Scholarship for use in freshman, sophomore, or junior years; not renewable. *Number:* up to 5. *Amount:* $1000–$5000.

Eligibility Requirements: Applicant must be enrolled or expecting to enroll full-time at a two-year or four-year or technical institution or university; resident of Illinois and studying in Illinois. Applicant must have 3.0 GPA or higher. Available to U.S. and Canadian citizens.

Application Requirements: Application form, essay, recommendations or references, resume, test scores, transcript. *Deadline:* February 1.

CHAPTER 4-LAWRENCE A. WACKER MEMORIAL SCHOLARSHIP

Awards available to full-time students enrolled in or accepted to a degree program in manufacturing, mechanical or industrial engineering at a college or university in the state of Wisconsin. One scholarship will be granted to a graduating high school senior and the other will be granted to a current undergraduate student. Minimum GPA of 3.0 required.

Academic Fields/Career Goals: Engineering/Technology; Mechanical Engineering.

Award: Scholarship for use in freshman, sophomore, junior, or senior years; not renewable. *Number:* 1–10. *Amount:* $1000–$5000.

Eligibility Requirements: Applicant must be enrolled or expecting to enroll full-time at a four-year institution or university and studying in Wisconsin. Applicant must have 3.0 GPA or higher. Available to U.S. citizens.

Application Requirements: Application form, essay, recommendations or references, resume, transcript. *Deadline:* February 1.

CHAPTER 63-PORTLAND JAMES E. MORROW SCHOLARSHIP

Applicants must be pursuing a career in manufacturing or a related field. Preference will be given to students planning to attend Oregon or southwest Washington schools. Preference will also be given to applicants who reside within the states of Oregon or southwest Washington.

Academic Fields/Career Goals: Engineering/Technology.

Award: Scholarship for use in freshman, sophomore, or junior years; not renewable. *Number:* up to 5. *Amount:* $1000–$5000.

Eligibility Requirements: Applicant must be enrolled or expecting to enroll full-time at a two-year or four-year or technical institution or university; resident of Oregon, Washington and studying in Oregon, Washington. Available to U.S. and Canadian citizens.

Application Requirements: Application form, essay, recommendations or references, resume, test scores, transcript. *Deadline:* February 1.

CHAPTER 63-PORTLAND UNCLE BUD SMITH SCHOLARSHIP

Applicants must be pursuing a career in manufacturing or a related field. Preference will be given to students planning to attend Oregon or southwest Washington schools. Preference will also be given to applicants who reside within the states of Oregon or southwest Washington.

Academic Fields/Career Goals: Engineering/Technology.

Award: Scholarship for use in freshman, sophomore, or junior years; not renewable. *Number:* up to 5. *Amount:* $1000–$5000.

Eligibility Requirements: Applicant must be enrolled or expecting to enroll full-time at a two-year or four-year or technical institution or university; resident of Oregon, Washington and studying in Oregon, Washington. Available to U.S. and Canadian citizens.

Application Requirements: Application form, essay, recommendations or references, resume, test scores, transcript. *Deadline:* February 1.

CHAPTER 67-PHOENIX SCHOLARSHIP

Award for a high school senior who plans on enrolling in a manufacturing program technology or manufacturing technology program or an undergraduate student enrolled in a manufacturing engineering technology, manufacturing technology, industrial technology, or closely related program at an accredited college or university in Arizona. Applicants must have an overall GPA of 2.5. Scholarship ranges from $1000 to $5000.

Academic Fields/Career Goals: Engineering/Technology; Industrial Design; Mechanical Engineering; Trade/Technical Specialties.

Award: Scholarship for use in freshman, sophomore, junior, or senior years; not renewable. *Number:* 1–5. *Amount:* $1000–$5000.

Eligibility Requirements: Applicant must be enrolled or expecting to enroll full-time at a two-year or four-year institution or university and studying in Arizona. Applicant must have 2.5 GPA or higher. Available to U.S. citizens.

Application Requirements: Application form, essay, recommendations or references, resume, test scores, transcript. *Deadline:* February 1.

CHAPTER 6-FAIRFIELD COUNTY SCHOLARSHIP

Scholarship applicants must be full-time undergraduate students enrolled in a degree program in manufacturing engineering, technology, or a closely related field in the United States or Canada. Preference is given to residents of, or students studying in, the eastern part of the United States.

Academic Fields/Career Goals: Engineering/Technology.

Award: Scholarship for use in freshman, sophomore, or junior years; not renewable. *Number:* up to 4. *Amount:* $1000–$5000.

Eligibility Requirements: Applicant must be enrolled or expecting to enroll full-time at a two-year or four-year or technical institution. Applicant must have 3.0 GPA or higher. Available to U.S. and Canadian citizens.

Application Requirements: Application form, essay, recommendations or references, resume, test scores, transcript. *Deadline:* February 1.

CHAPTER 93-ALBUQUERQUE SCHOLARSHIP

Scholarship to students entering freshmen or current undergraduate students pursuing a Bachelor's degree in manufacturing engineering or a related field who plan to or are attending an accredited college or university in New Mexico.

Academic Fields/Career Goals: Engineering/Technology.

Award: Scholarship for use in freshman, sophomore, junior, or senior years; not renewable. *Number:* 1–5. *Amount:* $1000–$5000.

Eligibility Requirements: Applicant must be enrolled or expecting to enroll full-time at a four-year institution or university and studying in New Mexico. Available to U.S. citizens.

Application Requirements: Application form, essay, recommendations or references, resume, test scores, transcript. *Deadline:* February 1.

CLARENCE AND JOSEPHINE MYERS SCHOLARSHIP

Applicants must be an undergraduate or graduate student pursuing a degree in engineering or a manufacturing-related field at a college within the state of Indiana.

Academic Fields/Career Goals: Engineering/Technology.

Award: Scholarship for use in freshman, sophomore, junior, or senior years; not renewable. *Number:* up to 5. *Amount:* $1000–$5000.

Eligibility Requirements: Applicant must be enrolled or expecting to enroll full-time at a two-year or four-year or technical institution or university and studying in Indiana. Available to U.S. and Canadian citizens.

Application Requirements: Application form, essay, recommendations or references, test scores, transcript. *Deadline:* February 1.

CLINTON J. HELTON MANUFACTURING SCHOLARSHIP AWARD FUND

One-time award to full-time students enrolled in a degree program in manufacturing engineering or technology at Colorado State University or University of Colorado. Applicants must possess an overall minimum GPA of 3.3.

Academic Fields/Career Goals: Engineering/Technology; Trade/Technical Specialties.

Award: Scholarship for use in freshman, sophomore, junior, or senior years; not renewable. *Number:* 1–5. *Amount:* $1000–$5000.

Eligibility Requirements: Applicant must be enrolled or expecting to enroll full-time at a four-year institution or university and studying in Colorado. Available to U.S. citizens.

Application Requirements: Application form, essay, recommendations or references, test scores, transcript. *Deadline:* February 1.

CONNIE AND ROBERT T. GUNTER SCHOLARSHIP

One-time award will be given for full-time undergraduate students enrolled in a degree program in manufacturing engineering or technology. Minimum 3.5 GPA is required. Must study in Georgia.

Academic Fields/Career Goals: Engineering/Technology.

Award: Scholarship for use in freshman, sophomore, junior, or senior years; not renewable. *Number:* 1–5. *Amount:* $1000–$5000.

Eligibility Requirements: Applicant must be enrolled or expecting to enroll full-time at a four-year institution or university and studying in

Georgia. Applicant must have 3.5 GPA or higher. Available to U.S. citizens.

Application Requirements: Application form, essay, recommendations or references, resume, transcript. *Deadline:* February 1.

DETROIT CHAPTER ONE-FOUNDING CHAPTER SCHOLARSHIP

Several awards will be available in each of the following: Associate's degree and equivalent, Baccalaureate degree, and graduate degree programs. Minimum GPA of 3.5 is required. Preference given to undergraduate or graduate student enrolled in a manufacturing engineering or technology program at one of the sponsored institutions.

Academic Fields/Career Goals: Engineering/Technology.

Award: Scholarship for use in freshman, sophomore, junior, senior, or graduate years; not renewable. *Number:* 3. *Amount:* $1000.

Eligibility Requirements: Applicant must be enrolled or expecting to enroll full- or part-time at a two-year or four-year institution or university and studying in Michigan. Applicant must have 3.5 GPA or higher. Available to U.S. citizens.

Application Requirements: Application form, recommendations or references. *Deadline:* February 1.

DIRECTOR'S SCHOLARSHIP AWARD

Scholarship award for full-time undergraduate students enrolled in a manufacturing or related degree program in the United States or Canada. Preference will be given to students who demonstrate leadership skills in a community, academic, or professional environment. Average GPA of 3.5 required.

Academic Fields/Career Goals: Engineering/Technology.

Award: Scholarship for use in freshman, sophomore, junior, or senior years; not renewable. *Number:* 1–5. *Amount:* $1000–$10,000.

Eligibility Requirements: Applicant must be enrolled or expecting to enroll full-time at a four-year institution or university and must have an interest in leadership. Applicant must have 3.5 GPA or higher. Available to U.S. and Canadian citizens.

Application Requirements: Application form, essay, recommendations or references, resume, transcript. *Deadline:* February 1.

EDWARD S. ROTH MANUFACTURING ENGINEERING SCHOLARSHIP

Award to a graduating high school senior, a current full-time undergraduate or graduate student enrolled in an accredited four-year degree program in manufacturing engineering at a sponsored ABET-accredited school. Minimum GPA of 3.0 and be a U.S. citizen.

Academic Fields/Career Goals: Engineering/Technology.

Award: Scholarship for use in freshman, sophomore, junior, senior, or graduate years; not renewable. *Number:* 1–10. *Amount:* $1000–$5000.

Eligibility Requirements: Applicant must be enrolled or expecting to enroll full-time at a four-year institution or university and studying in California, Florida, Illinois, Massachusetts, Minnesota, Ohio, Texas, Utah. Applicant must have 3.0 GPA or higher. Available to U.S. citizens.

Application Requirements: Application form, interview, recommendations or references, resume, transcript. *Deadline:* February 1.

E. WAYNE KAY COMMUNITY COLLEGE SCHOLARSHIP AWARD

One-time award to full-time students enrolled at an accredited community college or trade school which offers programs in manufacturing or closely related field in the United States or Canada. Minimum GPA of 3.0 required. Scholarship applicants may be entering freshmen or sophomore students with less than 60 college credit hours completed and be seeking a career in manufacturing engineering or technology.

Academic Fields/Career Goals: Engineering/Technology; Trade/Technical Specialties.

Award: Scholarship for use in freshman or sophomore years; not renewable. *Number:* 1–20. *Amount:* $1000–$10,000.

Eligibility Requirements: Applicant must be enrolled or expecting to enroll full-time at a two-year or four-year or technical institution or university. Applicant must have 3.0 GPA or higher. Available to U.S. and Canadian citizens.

Application Requirements: Application form, essay, recommendations or references, resume, transcript. *Deadline:* February 1.

E. WAYNE KAY CO-OP SCHOLARSHIP

Scholarship will be awarded for graduating high school senior or full-time undergraduate student enrolled in a degree program in manufacturing or a closely related field at a two-year community college or trade school in the United States or Canada. Average of 3.0 GPA is required.

Academic Fields/Career Goals: Engineering/Technology.

Award: Scholarship for use in freshman, sophomore, junior, or senior years; not renewable. *Number:* 1–10. *Amount:* $1000–$5000.

Eligibility Requirements: Applicant must be enrolled or expecting to enroll full-time at a two-year or four-year or technical institution or university. Applicant must have 3.0 GPA or higher. Available to U.S. and non-U.S. citizens.

Application Requirements: Application form, essay, recommendations or references, resume, transcript. *Deadline:* February 1.

E. WAYNE KAY HIGH SCHOOL SCHOLARSHIP

Scholarship available for student enrolled full-time in manufacturing engineering or technology program at an accredited college or university. Minimum 3.0 GPA required.

Academic Fields/Career Goals: Engineering/Technology.

Award: Scholarship for use in freshman, sophomore, junior, or senior years; renewable. *Number:* 1–20. *Amount:* $1000–$2500.

Eligibility Requirements: Applicant must be enrolled or expecting to enroll full-time at a four-year institution or university. Applicant must have 3.0 GPA or higher. Available to U.S. and Canadian citizens.

Application Requirements: Application form, essay, recommendations or references, test scores, transcript. *Deadline:* February 1.

E. WAYNE KAY SCHOLARSHIP

Scholarship for full-time undergraduate students enrolled in a degree program in manufacturing engineering, technology, or a closely related field in the United States or Canada. Minimum of 3.0 GPA is required.

Academic Fields/Career Goals: Engineering/Technology; Trade/Technical Specialties.

Award: Scholarship for use in freshman, sophomore, junior, or senior years; not renewable. *Number:* 10–30. *Amount:* $2500–$7500.

Eligibility Requirements: Applicant must be enrolled or expecting to enroll full-time at a four-year institution or university. Applicant must have 3.0 GPA or higher. Available to U.S. and Canadian citizens.

Application Requirements: Application form, essay, recommendations or references, resume, test scores, transcript. *Deadline:* February 1.

FORT WAYNE CHAPTER 56 SCHOLARSHIP

One-time award for an individual seeking an Associate's degree, Bachelor's degree, or graduate degree in manufacturing, mechanical or industrial engineering, engineering technology, or industrial technology at an accredited public or private college or university in Indiana. Must have a minimum GPA of 2.5. Preference given to applicants who are a child or grandchild of a current SME Fort Wayne Chapter No. 56 member, a member of its student chapter, or an Indiana resident.

Academic Fields/Career Goals: Engineering/Technology; Industrial Design; Mechanical Engineering; Trade/Technical Specialties.

Award: Scholarship for use in freshman, sophomore, junior, senior, or graduate years; not renewable. *Number:* 1–10. *Amount:* $1000–$5000.

Eligibility Requirements: Applicant must be enrolled or expecting to enroll full-time at a two-year or four-year institution or university and studying in Indiana. Applicant must have 2.5 GPA or higher. Available to U.S. citizens.

Application Requirements: Application form, essay, recommendations or references, resume, transcript. *Deadline:* February 1.

GUILIANO MAZZETTI SCHOLARSHIP AWARD

One-time award available to full-time students enrolled in a degree program in manufacturing engineering or technology in the United States or Canada. Minimum GPA of 3.0 required.

Academic Fields/Career Goals: Engineering/Technology.

Award: Scholarship for use in freshman, sophomore, junior, or senior years; not renewable. *Number:* 1–10. *Amount:* $1000–$5000.

Eligibility Requirements: Applicant must be enrolled or expecting to enroll full-time at a four-year institution or university. Applicant must have 3.0 GPA or higher. Available to U.S. and Canadian citizens.

Application Requirements: Application form, essay, recommendations or references, resume, transcript. *Deadline:* February 1.

LUCILE B. KAUFMAN WOMEN'S SCHOLARSHIP

Scholarships available for female full-time undergraduate students enrolled in a degree program in manufacturing engineering, technology or a closely related field in the United States or Canada. Minimum of 3.0 GPA is required. Scholarship value and the number of awards granted varies.

Academic Fields/Career Goals: Engineering/Technology.

Award: Scholarship for use in freshman, sophomore, junior, or senior years; not renewable. *Number:* 1–5. *Amount:* $1000–$5000.

Eligibility Requirements: Applicant must be enrolled or expecting to enroll full-time at a four-year institution or university and female. Applicant must have 3.0 GPA or higher. Available to U.S. and Canadian citizens.

Application Requirements: Application form, essay, recommendations or references, resume, transcript. *Deadline:* February 1.

MYRTLE AND EARL WALKER SCHOLARSHIP FUND

• See page 287

NORTH CENTRAL REGION 9 SCHOLARSHIP

Award to a full-time student enrolled in a manufacturing, mechanical, or industrial engineering degree program in North Central Region 9 (Iowa, Minnesota, Nebraska, North Dakota, South Dakota, Wisconsin, and the upper peninsula of Michigan). Applicants must have a 3.0 GPA.

Academic Fields/Career Goals: Engineering/Technology; Industrial Design; Mechanical Engineering; Trade/Technical Specialties.

Award: Scholarship for use in freshman, sophomore, junior, or senior years; not renewable. *Number:* 1–10. *Amount:* $1000–$5000.

Eligibility Requirements: Applicant must be enrolled or expecting to enroll full-time at a four-year institution or university and studying in Iowa, Michigan, Minnesota, Nebraska, North Dakota, South Dakota, Wisconsin. Applicant must have 3.0 GPA or higher. Available to U.S. citizens.

Application Requirements: Application form, essay, recommendations or references, resume, transcript. *Deadline:* February 1.

SME FAMILY SCHOLARSHIP

Scholarships awarded to children or grandchildren of Society of Manufacturing Engineers members. Must be graduating high school senior planning to pursue full-time studies for an undergraduate degree in manufacturing engineering, manufacturing engineering technology, or a closely related engineering study at an accredited college or university. Minimum GPA of 3.0 required. Scholarship value and the number of awards granted varies annually.

Academic Fields/Career Goals: Engineering/Technology.

Award: Scholarship for use in freshman, sophomore, junior, or senior years; renewable. *Number:* 1–10. *Amount:* $5000–$80,000.

Eligibility Requirements: Applicant must be enrolled or expecting to enroll full-time at a four-year institution or university. Applicant must have 3.0 GPA or higher. Available to U.S. and non-U.S. citizens.

Application Requirements: Application form, essay, interview, personal photograph, recommendations or references, resume, test scores, transcript. *Deadline:* February 1.

WALT BARTRAM MEMORIAL EDUCATION AWARD

Scholarship available for graduating high school seniors who commit to enroll in, or full-time college or university students pursuing a degree in, manufacturing engineering or a closely related field within the areas of New Mexico, Arizona or Southern California.

Academic Fields/Career Goals: Engineering/Technology.

Award: Scholarship for use in freshman, sophomore, junior, or senior years; not renewable. *Number:* 1. *Amount:* $1500.

Eligibility Requirements: Applicant must be enrolled or expecting to enroll full-time at a four-year institution or university; resident of Arizona, California, New Mexico and studying in Arizona, California, New Mexico. Applicant or parent of applicant must be member of Soil and Water Conservation Society. Available to U.S. and Canadian citizens.

Application Requirements: 2 copies of student statement letter, application form, recommendations or references, resume, transcript. *Deadline:* February 1.

WICHITA CHAPTER 52 SCHOLARSHIP

Award for an individual seeking an Associate's degree, Bachelor's degree, or graduate degree in manufacturing, mechanical or industrial engineering, engineering technology, or industrial technology at an accredited public or private college or university in Kansas, Oklahoma or Missouri. Applicants must have a minimum GPA of 2.5. Preference given to applicants who are a relative of a current SME Wichita Chapter No. 52 member or a Kansas resident.

Academic Fields/Career Goals: Engineering/Technology; Industrial Design; Mechanical Engineering; Trade/Technical Specialties.

Award: Scholarship for use in freshman, sophomore, junior, senior, or graduate years; not renewable. *Number:* 1. *Amount:* up to $1500.

Eligibility Requirements: Applicant must be enrolled or expecting to enroll full-time at a two-year or four-year institution or university and studying in Kansas, Missouri, Oklahoma. Applicant must have 2.5 GPA or higher. Available to U.S. citizens.

Application Requirements: Application form, recommendations or references, resume, student statement letter, transcript. *Deadline:* February 1.

WILLIAM E. WEISEL SCHOLARSHIP FUND
• *See page 269*

SOCIETY OF MOTION PICTURE AND TELEVISION ENGINEERS

https://www.smpte.org/

LOUIS F. WOLF JR. MEMORIAL SCHOLARSHIP
• *See page 210*

STUDENT PAPER AWARD
• *See page 210*

SOCIETY OF PETROLEUM ENGINEERS

http://www.spe.org/

GUS ARCHIE MEMORIAL SCHOLARSHIPS

Renewable award for students who have not attended college or university before and are planning to enroll in a petroleum engineering degree program at a four-year institution. Must have minimum 3.0 GPA.

Academic Fields/Career Goals: Engineering/Technology.

Award: Scholarship for use in freshman, sophomore, junior, or senior years; renewable. *Number:* 1–2. *Amount:* $6000.

Eligibility Requirements: Applicant must be enrolled or expecting to enroll full-time at a four-year institution or university. Applicant must have 3.0 GPA or higher. Available to U.S. and non-U.S. citizens.

Application Requirements: Application form, financial need analysis, personal photograph, recommendations or references, test scores, transcript. *Deadline:* April 30.

Contact: Young Member Program
Society of Petroleum Engineers
PO Box 833836
Richardson, TX 75083
Phone: 972-952-9448
Fax: 972-952-9435
E-mail: studentactivities@spe.org

SOCIETY OF PLASTICS ENGINEERS FOUNDATION (SPE)

http://www.4spe.org/

FLEMING/BASZCAK SCHOLARSHIP
• *See page 181*

GULF COAST HURRICANE SCHOLARSHIP
• *See page 181*

PLASTICS PIONEERS ASSOCIATION SCHOLARSHIPS
• *See page 182*

SOCIETY OF PLASTICS ENGINEERS SCHOLARSHIP PROGRAM
• *See page 182*

SOCIETY OF WOMEN ENGINEERS

http://societyofwomenengineers.swe.org/

ADA I. PRESSMAN MEMORIAL SCHOLARSHIP
• *See page 182*

AMERICAN TRANSMISSION CO. SCHOLARSHIP
• *See page 182*

ANNE MAUREEN WHITNEY BARROW MEMORIAL SCHOLARSHIP
• *See page 182*

ANNE SHEN SMITH ENDOWED SCHOLARSHIP
• *See page 182*

BAYER SCHOLARSHIP
• *See page 183*

BECHTEL CORPORATION SCHOLARSHIP

Two $1400 scholarships for women pursuing ABET-accredited Baccalaureate or graduate programs in preparation for careers in engineering, engineering technology, and computer science in the United States and Mexico. SWE membership and minimum 3.0 GPA required.

Academic Fields/Career Goals: Engineering/Technology.

Award: Scholarship for use in sophomore, junior, senior, or graduate years; not renewable. *Number:* 2. *Amount:* $1400.

Eligibility Requirements: Applicant must be enrolled or expecting to enroll full-time at a four-year institution or university and female. Applicant or parent of applicant must be member of Society of Women Engineers. Applicant must have 3.0 GPA or higher. Available to U.S. citizens.

Application Requirements: Application form. *Deadline:* February 15.

Contact: Scholarship Committee
Phone: 800-793-4636
E-mail: scholarships@swe.org

BETTY LOU BAILEY SWE REGION F SCHOLARSHIP
• *See page 183*

B.J. HARROD SCHOLARSHIP
• *See page 183*

BK KRENZER MEMORIAL REENTRY SCHOLARSHIP
• *See page 183*

BRILL FAMILY SCHOLARSHIP

$1500 award for a woman pursuing an ABET-accredited Baccalaureate or graduate program in preparation for a career in engineering, engineering technology, and computer science in the United States and Mexico. Preference given to a student pursuing study in aeronautical/aerospace engineering or biomedical engineering. Minimum 3.0 GPA required.

Academic Fields/Career Goals: Engineering/Technology.

Award: Scholarship for use in sophomore, junior, or senior years; not renewable. *Number:* 1. *Amount:* $1500.

Eligibility Requirements: Applicant must be enrolled or expecting to enroll full-time at a four-year institution or university and female. Applicant must have 3.0 GPA or higher. Available to U.S. citizens.

Application Requirements: Application form. *Deadline:* February 15.

Contact: Scholarship Committee
Phone: 800-793-4636
E-mail: scholarships@swe.org

CAROL STEPHENS SWE REGION F SCHOLARSHIP
• *See page 183*

CUMMINS SCHOLARSHIP
• *See page 183*

DR. IVY M. PARKER MEMORIAL SCHOLARSHIP
• *See page 184*

DOROTHY LEMKE HOWARTH MEMORIAL SCHOLARSHIP
• *See page 184*

DOROTHY P. MORRIS SCHOLARSHIP
• *See page 184*

DUPONT COMPANY SCHOLARSHIP
• *See page 184*

ELIZABETH MCLEAN MEMORIAL SCHOLARSHIP
• *See page 198*

ELLEN HIPPELI MEMORIAL SCHOLARSHIP
$1000 scholarship for women pursuing ABET-accredited Baccalaureate programs in preparation for careers in engineering, engineering technology, and computer science in the United States and Mexico. U.S. citizenship required. Nuclear engineering major preferred. Minimum 3.5 GPA required.

Academic Fields/Career Goals: Engineering/Technology.

Award: Scholarship for use in freshman year; not renewable. *Number:* 1. *Amount:* $1000.

Eligibility Requirements: Applicant must be high school student; planning to enroll or expecting to enroll full-time at a four-year institution or university and female. Applicant or parent of applicant must be member of Society of Women Engineers. Applicant must have 3.5 GPA or higher. Available to U.S. citizens.

Application Requirements: Application form, essay. *Deadline:* May 1.

Contact: Scholarship Committee
Phone: 800-793-4636
E-mail: scholarships@swe.org

EXELON CORPORATION SCHOLARSHIP
• *See page 184*

FCA WOMEN IN ENGINEERING SCHOLARSHIP
• *See page 184*

FORD MOTOR COMPANY SCHOLARSHIP
• *See page 270*

GENERAL ELECTRIC WOMEN'S NETWORK SCHOLARSHIP
• *See page 198*

HONDA SCHOLARSHIP
$1000 renewable scholarships for 5 junior and senior women pursuing ABET-accredited Baccalaureate programs in preparation for careers in engineering, engineering technology, and computer science in the United States and Mexico. Must be a U.S. citizen and have a minimum 3.0 GPA. Under-represented groups and financial need candidates preferred. College or home location: Illinois, Indiana, Michigan, Ohio, Pennsylvania, or Wisconsin. Renewable for 2 years; availability dependent upon renewals.

Academic Fields/Career Goals: Engineering/Technology.

Award: Scholarship for use in junior or senior years; not renewable. *Number:* 5. *Amount:* $1000.

Eligibility Requirements: Applicant must be enrolled or expecting to enroll full-time at a four-year institution or university; female; resident of Illinois, Indiana, Michigan, Ohio, Pennsylvania, Wisconsin and studying in Illinois, Indiana, Michigan, Ohio, Pennsylvania, Wisconsin. Applicant or parent of applicant must be member of Society of Women Engineers. Applicant must have 3.0 GPA or higher. Available to U.S. citizens.

Application Requirements: Application form, financial need analysis. *Deadline:* February 15.

Contact: Scholarship Committee
Phone: 800-793-4636
E-mail: scholarships@swe.org

HONEYWELL SCHOLARSHIP
• *See page 184*

IBM LINDA SANFORD WOMEN'S TECHNICAL ADVANCEMENT SCHOLARSHIP
• *See page 185*

JILL S. TIETJEN P.E. SCHOLARSHIP
• *See page 185*

JOHN DEERE SWE SCHOLARSHIP
$2000 renewable scholarships for women pursuing ABET-accredited Baccalaureate or graduate programs in preparation for careers in engineering, engineering technology, and computer science in the United States and Mexico. Must be a U.S. citizen and have a minimum 3.0 GPA. Preferred geographic region by state: GA, IL, IN, IA, KS, LA, MI, MN, MO, MT, NE, NC, ND, OH, OK, SD, TN.

Academic Fields/Career Goals: Engineering/Technology.

Award: Scholarship for use in sophomore, junior, senior, or graduate years; not renewable. *Number:* 2. *Amount:* $2000.

Eligibility Requirements: Applicant must be enrolled or expecting to enroll full-time at a four-year institution or university and female. Applicant must have 3.0 GPA or higher. Available to U.S. citizens.

Application Requirements: Application form. *Deadline:* February 15.

Contact: Scholarship Committee
Phone: 800-793-4636
E-mail: scholarships@swe.org

JUDITH RESNICK MEMORIAL SCHOLARSHIP
$3500 scholarship for a women pursuing an ABET-accredited Baccalaureate program in preparation for a career in engineering, engineering technology, and computer science in the United States and Mexico. Must have a minimum 3.0 GPA, be a member of SWE, and pursue a space-related engineering major.

Academic Fields/Career Goals: Engineering/Technology.

Award: Scholarship for use in sophomore, junior, or senior years; not renewable. *Number:* 1. *Amount:* $3500.

Eligibility Requirements: Applicant must be enrolled or expecting to enroll full-time at a four-year institution or university and female. Applicant or parent of applicant must be member of Society of Women Engineers. Applicant must have 3.0 GPA or higher. Available to U.S. citizens.

Application Requirements: Application form. *Deadline:* February 15.

Contact: Scholarship Committee
Phone: 800-793-4636
E-mail: scholarships@swe.org

KOCH DISCOVERY SCHOLARSHIP
• *See page 185*

LILLIAN MOLLER GILBRETH MEMORIAL SCHOLARSHIP
• *See page 185*

LOCKHEED MARTIN CORPORATION SCHOLARSHIP
• *See page 218*

MARY GUNTHER MEMORIAL SCHOLARSHIP
Four $3000 scholarships for women pursuing ABET-accredited Baccalaureate programs in preparation for careers in engineering, engineering technology, and computer science in the United States and Mexico. Preference given to students pursuing studies in architectural and environmental engineering. 3.5 GPA required for freshmen, 3.0 GPA required for all other grade levels.

Academic Fields/Career Goals: Engineering/Technology.

Award: Scholarship for use in freshman, sophomore, junior, or senior years; not renewable. *Number:* 4. *Amount:* $3000.

Eligibility Requirements: Applicant must be enrolled or expecting to enroll full-time at a four-year institution or university and female. Available to U.S. citizens.

Application Requirements: Application form. *Deadline:* February 15.

Contact: Scholarship Committee
Phone: 800-793-4636
E-mail: scholarships@swe.org

MARY V. MUNGER SCHOLARSHIP
• *See page 185*

MASWE SCHOLARSHIP
• *See page 186*

MEREDITH THOMS MEMORIAL SCHOLARSHIPS
• *See page 287*

OLIVE LYNN SALEMBIER MEMORIAL REENTRY SCHOLARSHIP
• *See page 186*

PAST PRESIDENTS SCHOLARSHIP
• *See page 287*

PAULA LORING SIMON SCHOLARSHIP
• *See page 186*

ROBERTA BANASZAK GLEITER ENGINEERING ENDEAVOR SCHOLARSHIP
• *See page 186*

ROCHELLE PERRY MEMORIAL SCHOLARSHIP
• *See page 186*

ROCKWELL COLLINS SCHOLARSHIP
• *See page 218*

SUSAN MISZKOWICZ MEMORIAL SCHOLARSHIP
• *See page 186*

SWE BALTIMORE-WASHINGTON SECTION SCHOLARSHIP
• *See page 186*

SWE CENTRAL INDIANA SECTION SCHOLARSHIP
• *See page 287*

SWE CENTRAL NEW MEXICO PIONEERS SCHOLARSHIP
• *See page 187*

SWE CENTRAL NEW MEXICO REENTRY SCHOLARSHIP
• *See page 187*

SWE MID-HUDSON SECTION SCHOLARSHIP
• *See page 187*

SWE NEW JERSEY SECTION SCHOLARSHIP

Scholarship available for a female New Jersey resident majoring in engineering. Available to incoming freshman. Minimum 3.5 GPA required. Must have attended high school in New Jersey.

Academic Fields/Career Goals: Engineering/Technology.

Award: Scholarship for use in freshman year; not renewable. *Number:* 1. *Amount:* $2000.

Eligibility Requirements: Applicant must be enrolled or expecting to enroll full-time at a four-year institution or university; female and resident of New Jersey. Applicant must have 3.5 GPA or higher. Available to U.S. citizens.

Application Requirements: Application form, essay. *Deadline:* May 1.

Contact: Scholarship Committee
Phone: 800-793-4636
E-mail: scholarships@swe.org

SWE PHOENIX SECTION SCHOLARSHIP
• *See page 187*

SWE REGION E SCHOLARSHIP
• *See page 187*

SWE REGION G JUDY SIMMONS MEMORIAL SCHOLARSHIP
• *See page 188*

SWE REGION H SCHOLARSHIPS
• *See page 188*

SWE REGION J SCHOLARSHIP
• *See page 188*

TURNER CONSTRUCTION SCHOLARSHIP
• *See page 188*

WANDA MUNN SCHOLARSHIP
• *See page 188*

SOCIETY OF WOMEN ENGINEERS-DALLAS SECTION

http://www.dallaswe.org/

DALLAS SWE ANNIE COLA·COLLEGIATE LEADER SCHOLARSHIP
• *See page 218*

DALLAS SWE HIGH SCHOOL SENIOR SCHOLARSHIP

Scholarship for graduating high school senior women who wish to pursue a degree in engineering. Applicant must be a Texas resident and attend a Texas Region 10 high school. Please refer to website for further details http://www.dallaswe.org/scholarships.

Academic Fields/Career Goals: Engineering/Technology.

Award: Scholarship for use in freshman year; not renewable. *Number:* 2–4. *Amount:* $500–$1000.

Eligibility Requirements: Applicant must be high school student; planning to enroll or expecting to enroll full-time at a four-year institution or university; female and resident of Texas. Applicant must have 3.0 GPA or higher. Available to U.S. citizens.

Application Requirements: Application form, essay, personal photograph. *Deadline:* April 15.

Contact: Shelley Stracener, FY17 President
E-mail: dallas.swe@gmail.com

SOCIETY OF WOMEN ENGINEERS-ROCKY MOUNTAIN SECTION

http://www.swe-rms.org/

SOCIETY OF WOMEN ENGINEERS-ROCKY MOUNTAIN SECTION SCHOLARSHIP PROGRAM
• *See page 188*

SOCIETY OF WOMEN ENGINEERS-TWIN TIERS SECTION

http://www.swetwintiers.org/

SOCIETY OF WOMEN ENGINEERS-TWIN TIERS SECTION SCHOLARSHIP
• *See page 219*

SPECIALTY EQUIPMENT MARKET ASSOCIATION

http://www.sema.org/

SEMA MEMORIAL SCHOLARSHIP FUND
• *See page 85*

STRAIGHTFORWARD MEDIA

http://www.straightforwardmedia.com/

STRAIGHTFORWARD MEDIA ENGINEERING SCHOLARSHIP
• *See page 189*

TAU BETA PI ASSOCIATION

http://www.tbp.org/

TAU BETA PI SCHOLARSHIP PROGRAM
• *See page 189*

TECHNICAL ASSOCIATION OF THE PULP & PAPER INDUSTRY (TAPPI)

http://www.tappi.org/

PAPER AND BOARD DIVISION SCHOLARSHIPS

Award to TAPPI student member or an undergraduate member of a TAPPI Student Chapter enrolled as a college or university undergraduate in an engineering or science program. Must be sophomore, junior, or senior and able to show a significant interest in the paper industry. Information can be found at http://www.tappi.org/Education/ College-and-University-Programs/Scholarship-Overview/.

Academic Fields/Career Goals: Engineering/Technology; Paper and Pulp Engineering.

Award: Scholarship for use in sophomore, junior, or senior years; not renewable. *Number:* 1–4. *Amount:* $1000–$1500.

Eligibility Requirements: Applicant must be enrolled or expecting to enroll full-time at a four-year institution or university. Available to U.S. and non-U.S. citizens.

Application Requirements: Application form. *Deadline:* February 15.

Contact: Mr. Laurence Womack, Director of Standards and Awards
Technical Association of the Pulp & Paper Industry (TAPPI)
15 Technology Parkway South
Peachtree Corners, GA 30092
Phone: 770-209-7276
E-mail: standards@tappi.org

TAPPI PROCESS AND PRODUCT QUALITY DIVISION SCHOLARSHIP

The TAPPI Process and Product Quality Scholarship is awarded to TAPPI student members or student chapter members to encourage them to pursue careers in the pulp and paper industry and to develop awareness of quality management.

Academic Fields/Career Goals: Engineering/Technology.

Award: Scholarship for use in sophomore, junior, or senior years; not renewable. *Number:* 1. *Amount:* $1000.

Eligibility Requirements: Applicant must be enrolled or expecting to enroll full-time at a four-year institution or university. Available to U.S. and non-U.S. citizens.

Application Requirements: Application form. *Deadline:* February 15.

Contact: Mr. Charles Bohanan, Director of Standards and Awards
Technical Association of the Pulp & Paper Industry (TAPPI)
15 Technology Parkway South
Peachtree Corners, GA 30092
Phone: 770-209-7276
E-mail: standards@tappi.org

TECHNOLOGY FIRST

https://technologyfirst.org/

ROBERT V. MCKENNA SCHOLARSHIPS
• *See page 219*

TIMOTION

http://www.timotion.com/

TIMOTION ENGINEERING AND EXCELLENCE SCHOLARSHIP
• *See page 199*

TKE EDUCATIONAL FOUNDATION

http://www.tke.org/

ERIC D. DUNNING SCHOLARSHIP
• *See page 219*

TRANSTUTORS

http://www.transtutors.com/scholarship

TRANSTUTORS SCHOLARSHIP 2015-16
• *See page 85*

TURNER CONSTRUCTION COMPANY

http://www.turnerconstruction.com/

YOUTHFORCE 2020 SCHOLARSHIP PROGRAM
• *See page 124*

UNITED NEGRO COLLEGE FUND

http://www.uncf.org/

ANHEUSER-BUSCH LEGENDS OF THE CROWN SCHOLARSHIP PROGRAM
• *See page 86*

BASF/ALFRED CHISHOLM ENDOWED MEMORIAL SCHOLARSHIP
• *See page 86*

BLUE CROSS BLUE SHIELD OF ILLINOIS AND BLUE CROSS BLUE SHIELD OF TEXAS SCHOLARSHIP
• *See page 115*

COLGATE–PALMOLIVE CORPORATE SCHOLARS PROGRAM
• *See page 86*

COOPER INDUSTRIES
• *See page 169*

DAVIS SCHOLARSHIP FOR WOMEN IN STEM
• *See page 189*

DELL CORPORATE SCHOLARS PROGRAM
• *See page 169*

GALACTIC UNITE BYTHEWAY SCHOLARSHIP
• *See page 190*

GATES MILLENNIUM SCHOLARS (GMS) PROGRAM
• *See page 260*

MARGIE H. VERBAL EMERGENCY SCHOLARSHIP FUND
• *See page 260*

NASCAR BLACK HISTORY MONTH AWARDS
• *See page 86*

PROCTER & GAMBLE STEM SCHOLARSHIP
• *See page 116*

RICOH SCHOLARSHIP PROGRAM
• *See page 86*

UNCF/KOCH SCHOLARS PROGRAM FOR UNDERGRADUATES
• *See page 87*

UNCF/NISSAN SCHOLARSHIP
• *See page 170*

UNCF NORTHROP GRUMMAN SCHOLARSHIP
• *See page 220*

UNCF STEM SCHOLARS PROGRAM
• *See page 159*

UNITED STATES SOCIETY ON DAMS

http://www.ussdams.org/

UNITED STATES SOCIETY ON DAMS SCHOLARSHIP AWARD
• *See page 199*

UNIVERSITIES SPACE RESEARCH ASSOCIATION

http://www.usra.edu/

UNIVERSITIES SPACE RESEARCH ASSOCIATION SCHOLARSHIP AWARD PROGRAM
• *See page 116*

VECTORWORKS, INC.

http://www.vectorworks.net

VECTORWORKS DESIGN SCHOLARSHIP
• *See page 124*

VERMONT SPACE GRANT CONSORTIUM

http://www.cems.uvm.edu/vsgc

VERMONT SPACE GRANT CONSORTIUM
• *See page 96*

VISIONARY INTEGRATION PROFESSIONALS (VIP)

http://www.trustvip.com/

WOMEN IN TECHNOLOGY SCHOLARSHIP (WITS)
• *See page 220*

WISCONSIN SOCIETY OF PROFESSIONAL ENGINEERS

http://www.wspe.org/

WISCONSIN SOCIETY OF PROFESSIONAL ENGINEERS SCHOLARSHIPS
Scholarships are awarded each year to high school seniors having qualifications for success in engineering education. Must be a U.S. citizen and Wisconsin resident, ACT composite score and have a minimum GPA of 3.0.
Academic Fields/Career Goals: Engineering/Technology.
Award: Scholarship for use in freshman year; not renewable. *Number:* 7. *Amount:* $1000–$2000.
Eligibility Requirements: Applicant must be high school student; planning to enroll or expecting to enroll full-time at a four-year institution or university and resident of Wisconsin. Applicant must have 3.0 GPA or higher. Available to U.S. citizens.
Application Requirements: Application form, essay, interview, recommendations or references, self-addressed stamped envelope with application, test scores, transcript. *Deadline:* December 19.
Contact: Al Linder
       E-mail: Al.lindner@graef-usa.com

WOMEN IN AEROSPACE FOUNDATION

http://www.womeninaerospace.org/index.html

WIA FOUNDATION SCHOLARSHIP
• *See page 149*

XEROX

http://www.xerox.com//

TECHNICAL MINORITY SCHOLARSHIP
• *See page 190*

ENTOMOLOGY

AMERICAN INDIAN SCIENCE AND ENGINEERING SOCIETY

http://www.aises.org/

A.T. ANDERSON MEMORIAL SCHOLARSHIP PROGRAM
• *See page 109*

AMERICAN SOCIETY OF AGRONOMY, CROP SCIENCE SOCIETY OF AMERICA, SOIL SCIENCE SOCIETY OF AMERICA

http://www.agronomy.org

J. FIELDING REED SCHOLARSHIP
• *See page 97*

BARRY GOLDWATER SCHOLARSHIP AND EXCELLENCE IN EDUCATION FOUNDATION

https://goldwater.scholarsapply.org

BARRY M. GOLDWATER SCHOLARSHIP AND EXCELLENCE IN EDUCATION PROGRAM
• *See page 112*

BHW GROUP

https://thebhwgroup.com/

BHW WOMEN IN STEM SCHOLARSHIP
• *See page 74*

COLEOPTERISTS SOCIETY

http://coleopsoc.org/default.asp

YOUTH INCENTIVE AWARD
Each of the two awards (Junior, grades 7-9 and Senior, grades 10-12) will receive a monetary grant of $200 and $400, respectively, and a matching equipment credit from the BioQuip Products new window catalog. In addition to monetary and BioQuip grants, award recipients will receive a one year subscription to the society journal, The Coleopterists Bulletin.

This is for students of grades 7-12 only. The selection committee invites proposals for topics such as field collecting trips to conduct beetle species inventories or diversity studies, attending workshops or visiting entomology or natural history museums for special training and projects on beetles, studying aspects of beetle biology, etc. The proposed activities or projects will be evaluated on their degree of creativity, educational benefit to the applicant, scientific merit, feasibility and budgetary planning.

Academic Fields/Career Goals: Entomology.

Award: Prize for use in freshman year; not renewable. *Number:* 2. *Amount:* $200–$400.

Eligibility Requirements: Applicant must be high school student and planning to enroll or expecting to enroll full- or part-time at a two-year or four-year institution or university. Available to U.S. citizens.

Application Requirements: Application form. *Deadline:* November 1.

Contact: Dr. David Furth, Award Program Coordinator
Coleopterists Society
Entomology, NHB, MRC 165
P.O. Box 37012; Smithsonian Institution
Washington, DC 20013-7012
Phone: 202-633-0990
Fax: 202-786-2894
E-mail: furthd@si.edu

GREAT MINDS IN STEM

www.greatmindsinstem.org

HISPANIC ENGINEER NATIONAL ACHIEVEMENT AWARDS CORPORATION SCHOLARSHIP PROGRAM
• *See page 106*

HORTICULTURAL RESEARCH INSTITUTE

http://www.hriresearch.org/

BRYAN A. CHAMPION MEMORIAL SCHOLARSHIP
• *See page 92*

CARVILLE M. AKEHURST MEMORIAL SCHOLARSHIP

Scholarship is available to resident of Maryland, Virginia, or West Virginia. Applicant must be enrolled in an accredited undergraduate or graduate landscape/ horticulture program or related discipline at a two- or four-year institution and must have minimum 3.0 GPA. Online application only. http//www.HRIresearch.org for complete information.

Academic Fields/Career Goals: Entomology; Horticulture/Floriculture; Landscape Architecture.

Award: Scholarship for use in junior or senior years; not renewable. *Number:* 2. *Amount:* $2000.

Eligibility Requirements: Applicant must be enrolled or expecting to enroll full-time at a two-year or four-year or technical institution or university and resident of Maryland, Virginia, West Virginia. Applicant must have 3.0 GPA or higher. Available to U.S. citizens.

Application Requirements: Application form, essay, financial need analysis, recommendations or references, resume, transcript. *Deadline:* May 31.

Contact: Ms. Teresa Jodon, Executive Director
Horticultural Research Institute
1200 G Street, NW, Suite 800
Washington, DC 20005
Phone: 202-695-2474
Fax: 888-761-7883
E-mail: scholarships@hriresearch.org

TIMOTHY AND PALMER W. BIGELOW JR, SCHOLARSHIP
• *See page 92*

USREY FAMILY SCHOLARSHIP

Award for students accredited in undergraduate or graduate landscape horticulture program or related discipline at a two- or four-year institution. Preference given to applicants who plan to work within the industry. Must have a minimum 2.5 GPA. For more information, visit website http://www.hriresearch.org.

Academic Fields/Career Goals: Entomology; Horticulture/Floriculture; Landscape Architecture.

Award: Scholarship for use in sophomore, junior, senior, or graduate years; not renewable. *Amount:* $500.

Eligibility Requirements: Applicant must be enrolled or expecting to enroll full-time at a two-year or four-year or technical institution or university and studying in California. Applicant must have 2.5 GPA or higher. Available to U.S. and non-U.S. citizens.

Application Requirements: Application form, application form may be submitted online (http://hriresearch.org/HRI/Scholarship/HRI/ Scholarship/Scholarships.aspx?hkey=eef3ef34-c1e1-44b4-9964-8dbd26745f2c), essay, financial need analysis, recommendations or references, resume, transcript. *Deadline:* May 31.

Contact: Teresa Jodon
Horticultural Research Institute
1200 G Street, NW, Suite 800
Washington, DC 20005
Phone: 202-695-2474
Fax: 888-761-7883
E-mail: scholarships@hriresearch.org

MEDICAL SCRUBS COLLECTION

http://medicalscrubscollection.com

MEDICAL SCRUBS COLLECTION SCHOLARSHIP
• *See page 106*

ENVIRONMENTAL HEALTH

AMERICAN INDIAN SCIENCE AND ENGINEERING SOCIETY

http://www.aises.org/

A.T. ANDERSON MEMORIAL SCHOLARSHIP PROGRAM
• *See page 109*

ASSOCIATION OF ENVIRONMENTAL HEALTH ACADEMIC PROGRAMS (AEHAP)

http://www.aehap.org/

NSF INTERNATIONAL SCHOLAR PROGRAM

Award available for college junior or senior in an AEHAP Environmental Health Academic Program. Student will spend summer on an independent research project in conjunction with their home university and NSF International and the AEHAP Office. Must have consent and commitment from advisor to help develop and oversee research project. Stipend will be paid in two sums, and advisor will receive $500 stipend.

Academic Fields/Career Goals: Environmental Health.

Award: Scholarship for use in junior or senior years; not renewable. *Number:* 1. *Amount:* $3500.

Eligibility Requirements: Applicant must be enrolled or expecting to enroll full-time at a four-year institution or university. Available to U.S. citizens.

Application Requirements: Application form, essay. *Deadline:* December 31.

Contact: Leslie Mitchell, AEHAP Scholarship Committee
Association of Environmental Health Academic Programs (AEHAP)
P.O. Box 66057
Burien, WA 98166
Phone: 206-522-5272
E-mail: info@aehap.org

BHW GROUP

https://thebhwgroup.com/

BHW WOMEN IN STEM SCHOLARSHIP
• See page 74

BROWN AND CALDWELL

http://www.brownandcaldwell.com

ECKENFELDER SCHOLARSHIP
• See page 155

MINORITY SCHOLARSHIP PROGRAM
• See page 155

CYNTHIA E. MORGAN SCHOLARSHIP FUND (CEMS)

http://www.cemsfund.com/

CYNTHIA E. MORGAN MEMORIAL SCHOLARSHIP FUND, INC.

Award for a high school junior or senior, or a current college student, who is a Maryland resident and first generation college student. No previous generation (parents or grandparents) may have attended any college/university. Scholarship for use only at a Maryland post-secondary school or medical school. Must be majoring in, or plan to enter, a medical-related field (for example: doctor, nurse, radiologist).

Academic Fields/Career Goals: Environmental Health; Health and Medical Sciences; Health Information Management/Technology; Neurobiology; Nursing; Occupational Safety and Health; Oncology; Osteopathy; Pharmacy; Psychology; Radiology; Therapy/Rehabilitation.

Award: Scholarship for use in freshman, sophomore, junior, senior, graduate, or postgraduate years; not renewable. *Number:* up to 1. *Amount:* $1000.

Eligibility Requirements: Applicant must be enrolled or expecting to enroll full- or part-time at a two-year or four-year or technical institution or university; resident of Maryland and studying in Maryland. Available to U.S. citizens.

Application Requirements: Application form, essay. *Deadline:* February 25.

Contact: Mr. John Kantorski, Founder and President
Cynthia E. Morgan Scholarship Fund (CEMS)
5516 Maudes Way
White Marsh, MD 21162-3417
Phone: 410-458-6312
Fax: 443-927-7321
E-mail: administrator@cemsfund.com

FLORIDA ENVIRONMENTAL HEALTH ASSOCIATION

http://www.feha.org/

FLORIDA ENVIRONMENTAL HEALTH ASSOCIATION EDUCATIONAL SCHOLARSHIP AWARDS

Scholarships offered to students interested in pursuing a career in the field of environmental health, or to enhance an existing career in environmental health. Applicant must be a member of FEHA in good standing.

Academic Fields/Career Goals: Environmental Health; Public Health.

Award: Scholarship for use in junior, senior, graduate, or postgraduate years; not renewable. *Number:* 1–4. *Amount:* $500–$1000.

Eligibility Requirements: Applicant must be enrolled or expecting to enroll full- or part-time at a four-year institution or university. Applicant or parent of applicant must be member of Florida Environmental Health Association. Applicant must have 2.5 GPA or higher. Available to U.S. and non-U.S. citizens.

Application Requirements: Application form, recommendations or references, transcript. *Deadline:* varies.

Contact: Kim Duffek, Scholarship Committee Chair
Florida Environmental Health Association
400 West Robinson Street, Suite S-529
Orlando, FL 32801
Phone: 407-317-7325
E-mail: duffekkj@gmail.com

GREAT MINDS IN STEM

www.greatmindsinstem.org

HISPANIC ENGINEER NATIONAL ACHIEVEMENT AWARDS CORPORATION SCHOLARSHIP PROGRAM
• See page 106

NATIONAL ENVIRONMENTAL HEALTH ASSOCIATION/AMERICAN ACADEMY OF SANITARIANS

http://www.neha.org/

NATIONAL ENVIRONMENTAL HEALTH ASSOCIATION/AMERICAN ACADEMY OF SANITARIANS SCHOLARSHIP

One-time award for college juniors, seniors, and graduate students pursuing studies in environmental health sciences or public health. Undergraduates must be enrolled full-time in an approved program that is accredited by the Environmental Health Accreditation Council (EHAC) or a NEHA institutional/educational or sustaining member school.

Academic Fields/Career Goals: Environmental Health; Public Health.

Award: Scholarship for use in junior or senior years; renewable. *Number:* 3–4. *Amount:* $1000–$2000.

Eligibility Requirements: Applicant must be enrolled or expecting to enroll full- or part-time at a four-year institution or university. Available to U.S. citizens.

Application Requirements: Application form, recommendations or references, transcript. *Deadline:* February 1.

Contact: Cindy Dimmitt, Scholarship Coordinator
National Environmental Health Association/American
Academy of Sanitarians
720 South Colorado Boulevard, Suite 1000-N
Denver, CO 80246-1926
Phone: 303-756-9090
Fax: 303-691-9490
E-mail: cdimmitt@neha.org

NEXTSTEPU

http://www.nextstepu.com/

$1,500 STEM SCHOLARSHIP
• See page 106

OREGON STUDENT ASSISTANCE COMMISSION

http://www.GetCollegeFunds.org/

WILLIAM E. KEENE MEMORIAL SCHOLARSHIP

Award for residents of Oregon or Washington whose career plans include public health, with strong interest in epidemiology. Preference given to those majoring in public health, epidemiology, environmental health science, health care management, and health education behavioral science. Must be enrolled at least half-time at four-year public and nonprofit colleges or universities. 3.0 GPA preferred. Apply/compete annually.

Academic Fields/Career Goals: Environmental Health; Environmental Science; Health Information Management/Technology; Public Health.

Award: Scholarship for use in freshman, sophomore, junior, or senior years; not renewable.

Eligibility Requirements: Applicant must be enrolled or expecting to enroll full- or part-time at a four-year institution or university and resident of Oregon, Washington. Available to U.S. and non-U.S. citizens.

Application Requirements: Application form. *Deadline:* March 1.

Contact: Melissa Adams, Scholarship Processing Coordinator
Phone: 541-687-7409
E-mail: melissa.adams@hecc.oregon.gov

SOCIETY OF TOXICOLOGY

http://www.toxicology.org/

UNDERGRADUATE DIVERSITY STUDENT AWARDS
• *See page 159*

SOIL AND WATER CONSERVATION SOCIETY-MISSOURI SHOW-ME CHAPTER

http://www.moswcs.org/

MO SHOW-ME CHAPTER SWCS SCHOLARSHIP
• *See page 95*

STRAIGHTFORWARD MEDIA

http://www.straightforwardmedia.com/

STRAIGHTFORWARD MEDIA MEDICAL PROFESSIONS SCHOLARSHIP
• *See page 239*

TED ROLLINS AND TXG CAPITAL

http://www.txgcapital.com/

TED ROLLINS ECO SCHOLARSHIP
• *See page 168*

TRANSTUTORS

http://www.transtutors.com/scholarship

TRANSTUTORS SCHOLARSHIP 2015-16
• *See page 85*

WASHINGTON STATE ENVIRONMENTAL HEALTH ASSOCIATION

http://www.wseha.org/

CIND M. TRESER MEMORIAL SCHOLARSHIP PROGRAM

Scholarships are available for undergraduate students pursuing a major in environmental health or related science and intending to practice environmental health. Must be a resident of Washington. For more details see website http://www.wseha.org.

Academic Fields/Career Goals: Environmental Health.

Award: Scholarship for use in junior or senior years; not renewable. *Number:* 1–2. *Amount:* $500–$2000.

Eligibility Requirements: Applicant must be enrolled or expecting to enroll full-time at a four-year institution or university; resident of Washington and studying in Washington. Applicant must have 3.0 GPA or higher. Available to U.S. citizens.

Application Requirements: Application form. *Deadline:* March 15.

Contact: Mr. Charles Treser, Principle Lecturer Emeritus
Washington State Environmental Health Association
Univ. of Washington, SPH, DEOHS
1959 NE Pacific Street, F-226D
Seattle, WA 98195-7234
Phone: 206-616-2097
E-mail: ctreser@uw.edu

WISCONSIN ASSOCIATION FOR FOOD PROTECTION

http://www.wifoodprotection.org

E.H. MARTH FOOD PROTECTION AND FOOD SCIENCES SCHOLARSHIP

Scholarship awarded to promote and sustain interest in the fields of study that may lead to a career in dairy, food, or environmental sanitation. One scholarship is awarded per year and previous applicants and recipients may reapply.

Academic Fields/Career Goals: Environmental Health; Food Science/Nutrition.

Award: Scholarship for use in sophomore, junior, senior, or graduate years; not renewable. *Number:* 1. *Amount:* $1500.

Eligibility Requirements: Applicant must be enrolled or expecting to enroll full-time at a four-year institution or university; resident of Wisconsin and studying in Wisconsin. Available to U.S. citizens.

Application Requirements: Application form, recommendations or references, transcript. *Deadline:* July 1.

Contact: Mr. Jim Wickert, Chairman, Scholarship Committee
Wisconsin Association for Food Protection
3834 Ridgeway Avenue
Madison, WI 53704
Phone: 608-241-2438
E-mail: jwick16060@tds.net

ENVIRONMENTAL SCIENCE

ABBIE SARGENT MEMORIAL SCHOLARSHIP INC.

http://www.nhfarmbureau.org/

ABBIE SARGENT MEMORIAL SCHOLARSHIP
• *See page 91*

AIR & WASTE MANAGEMENT ASSOCIATION, ALLEGHENY MOUNTAIN SECTION

http://www.ams-awma.org/

ALLEGHENY MOUNTAIN SECTION AIR & WASTE MANAGEMENT ASSOCIATION SCHOLARSHIP

Scholarships for qualified students enrolled in an undergraduate program leading to a career in a field related directly to the environment. Open to current undergraduate students or high school students accepted full-time in a four-year college or university program in Western Pennsylvania or West Virginia. Applicants must have a minimum B average or a 3.0 GPA.

Academic Fields/Career Goals: Environmental Science; Meteorology/Atmospheric Science.

Award: Scholarship for use in freshman, sophomore, junior, or senior years; not renewable. *Number:* 1–5. *Amount:* $500–$2000.

Eligibility Requirements: Applicant must be enrolled or expecting to enroll full-time at a four-year institution or university; resident of Pennsylvania, West Virginia and studying in Pennsylvania, West Virginia. Applicant must have 3.0 GPA or higher. Available to U.S. citizens.

Application Requirements: Application form, community service, essay. *Deadline:* March 31.

Contact: David Testa, Scholarship Chair
Air & Waste Management Association, Allegheny Mountain Section
c/o AECOM
681 Andersen Drive, Foster Plaza 6
Pittsburgh, PA 15220
Phone: 412-503-4560
E-mail: david.testa@aecom.com

AIR & WASTE MANAGEMENT ASSOCIATION–COASTAL PLAINS CHAPTER

http://www.awmacoastalplains.org/

COASTAL PLAINS CHAPTER OF THE AIR AND WASTE MANAGEMENT ASSOCIATION ENVIRONMENTAL STEWARD SCHOLARSHIP

Scholarships awarded to first- or second-year students pursuing a career in environmental science or physical science. Minimum high school and college GPA of 2.5 required. A 500-word paper on personal and professional goals must be submitted.

Academic Fields/Career Goals: Environmental Science; Physical Sciences.

Award: Scholarship for use in freshman or sophomore years; not renewable. *Number:* 5. *Amount:* $800.

Eligibility Requirements: Applicant must be enrolled or expecting to enroll full-time at a two-year or four-year institution or university. Applicant must have 2.5 GPA or higher. Available to U.S. citizens.

Application Requirements: 500-word paper on personal and professional goals, application form, recommendations or references, test scores. *Deadline:* varies.

Contact: Dwain Waters, Treasurer
Air & Waste Management Association–Coastal Plains Chapter
One Energy Place
Pensacola, FL 32520-0328
Phone: 850-444-6527
Fax: 850-444-6217
E-mail: gdwaters@southernco.com

AIST FOUNDATION

http://www.aistfoundation.org/

ASSOCIATION FOR IRON AND STEEL TECHNOLOGY WILLY KORF MEMORIAL SCHOLARSHIP
• *See page 172*

AMERICAN ALPINE CLUB

https://americanalpineclub.org/

AAC RESEARCH GRANTS
• *See page 153*

AMERICAN CHEMICAL SOCIETY

http://www.acs.org/

AMERICAN CHEMICAL SOCIETY SCHOLARS PROGRAM
• *See page 172*

AMERICAN COUNCIL OF ENGINEERING COMPANIES OF PENNSYLVANIA (ACEC/PA)

http://www.acecpa.org/

ERIC J. GENNUSO AND LEROY D. (BUD) LOY, JR. SCHOLARSHIP PROGRAM
• *See page 173*

AMERICAN INDIAN SCIENCE AND ENGINEERING SOCIETY

http://www.aises.org/

A.T. ANDERSON MEMORIAL SCHOLARSHIP PROGRAM
• *See page 109*

AMERICAN INSTITUTE OF CHEMICAL ENGINEERS

http://www.aiche.org/

ENVIRONMENTAL DIVISION UNDERGRADUATE STUDENT PAPER AWARD
• *See page 173*

AMERICAN PHYSIOLOGICAL SOCIETY

http://www.the-aps.org

DAVID S. BRUCE AWARDS FOR EXCELLENCE IN UNDERGRADUATE RESEARCH
• *See page 105*

AMERICAN PUBLIC POWER ASSOCIATION

http://publicpower.org/DEED

DEED EDUCATIONAL SCHOLARSHIP
• *See page 176*

DEED STUDENT INTERNSHIP
• *See page 176*

DEED STUDENT RESEARCH GRANTS
• *See page 191*

DEED TECHNICAL DESIGN PROJECT
• *See page 176*

AMERICAN SOCIETY OF AGRONOMY, CROP SCIENCE SOCIETY OF AMERICA, SOIL SCIENCE SOCIETY OF AMERICA

http://www.agronomy.org

J. FIELDING REED SCHOLARSHIP
• *See page 97*

ARCTIC INSTITUTE OF NORTH AMERICA

http://www.arctic.ucalgary.ca/

JIM BOURQUE SCHOLARSHIP
• *See page 249*

ARRL FOUNDATION INC.

http://www.arrl.org/

ROBERT D., W8ST, AND DONNA J., W9DJS, STREETER SCHOLARSHIP

$1000 scholarship for a student with any active Amateur Radio License Class attending college or university. Student should be studying horticulture and/or environmental sciences.

Academic Fields/Career Goals: Environmental Science; Horticulture/Floriculture.

Award: Scholarship for use in freshman, sophomore, junior, or senior years; not renewable. *Number:* 1. *Amount:* $1000.

Eligibility Requirements: Applicant must be enrolled or expecting to enroll full-time at a two-year or four-year or technical institution or university and must have an interest in amateur radio. Available to U.S. citizens.

Application Requirements: Application form. *Deadline:* January 31.

Contact: Ms. Mary Hobart, Secretary
Phone: 860-594-0397
E-mail: k1mmh@arrl.org

W1FDR SCHOLARSHIP
• *See page 112*

ASSOCIATION FOR WOMEN GEOSCIENTISTS (AWG)

http://www.awg.org/

AWG ETHNIC MINORITY SCHOLARSHIP
• *See page 241*

AWG MARIA LUISA CRAWFORD FIELD CAMP SCHOLARSHIP
• *See page 117*

AWG SALT LAKE CHAPTER (SLC) RESEARCH SCHOLARSHIP
• *See page 117*

JANET CULLEN TANAKA GEOSCIENCES UNDERGRADUATE SCHOLARSHIP
• *See page 117*

LONE STAR RISING CAREER SCHOLARSHIP
• *See page 242*

OSAGE CHAPTER UNDERGRADUATE SERVICE SCHOLARSHIP
• *See page 117*

SUSAN EKDALE MEMORIAL FIELD CAMP SCHOLARSHIP
• *See page 242*

ASSOCIATION OF CALIFORNIA WATER AGENCIES

http://www.acwa.com/

ASSOCIATION OF CALIFORNIA WATER AGENCIES SCHOLARSHIPS
• *See page 112*

CLAIR A. HILL SCHOLARSHIP
• *See page 112*

ASSOCIATION OF NEW JERSEY ENVIRONMENTAL COMMISSIONS

http://www.anjec.org/

LECHNER SCHOLARSHIP

Award of $1000 scholarship for a student entering his/her junior or senior year at an accredited New Jersey college or university. Must be a New Jersey resident and have a minimum GPA of 3.0.

Academic Fields/Career Goals: Environmental Science.

Award: Scholarship for use in junior or senior years; not renewable. *Number:* 1. *Amount:* $1000.

Eligibility Requirements: Applicant must be enrolled or expecting to enroll full-time at a four-year institution or university; resident of New Jersey and studying in New Jersey. Applicant must have 3.0 GPA or higher. Available to U.S. citizens.

Application Requirements: Application form, essay, recommendations or references, transcript.

Contact: Jennifer Coffey, Executive Director
Phone: 973-539-7547
Fax: 973-539-7713
E-mail: jcoffey@anjec.org

AUDUBON SOCIETY OF WESTERN PENNSYLVANIA

http://www.aswp.org/

BEULAH FREY ENVIRONMENTAL SCHOLARSHIP

Scholarship available to high school seniors pursuing studies in the environmental and natural sciences. Students who are applying to a two- or four-year college to further their studies in an environmentally-related field are eligible to apply. Scholarship is restricted to the residents of the seven counties around Pittsburgh.

Academic Fields/Career Goals: Environmental Science; Natural Sciences.

Award: Scholarship for use in freshman year; not renewable. *Number:* 1–2. *Amount:* $1000.

Eligibility Requirements: Applicant must be high school student; planning to enroll or expecting to enroll full-time at a two-year or four-year institution or university and resident of Pennsylvania. Available to U.S. citizens.

Application Requirements: Application form, essay, recommendations or references, test scores, transcript. *Deadline:* March 31.

Contact: Patricia O'Neill, Director of Education
Audubon Society of Western Pennsylvania
614 Dorseyville Road
Pittsburgh, PA 15238
Phone: 412-963-6100
Fax: 412-963-6761
E-mail: toneill@aswp.org

AUTOMOTIVE WOMEN'S ALLIANCE FOUNDATION

http://www.awafoundation.org/index.php

AUTOMOTIVE WOMEN'S ALLIANCE FOUNDATION SCHOLARSHIPS
• *See page 74*

BARRY GOLDWATER SCHOLARSHIP AND EXCELLENCE IN EDUCATION FOUNDATION

https://goldwater.scholarsapply.org

BARRY M. GOLDWATER SCHOLARSHIP AND EXCELLENCE IN EDUCATION PROGRAM
• *See page 112*

BHW GROUP

https://thebhwgroup.com/

BHW WOMEN IN STEM SCHOLARSHIP
• *See page 74*

B.O.G. PEST CONTROL

http://www.bogpestcontrol.com/

B.O.G. PEST CONTROL SCHOLARSHIP FUND
• *See page 155*

BROWN AND CALDWELL

http://www.brownandcaldwell.com

ECKENFELDER SCHOLARSHIP
• See page 155

MINORITY SCHOLARSHIP PROGRAM
• See page 155

CONSERVATION FEDERATION OF MISSOURI

http://www.confedmo.org/

CHARLES P. BELL CONSERVATION SCHOLARSHIP

Eight scholarships of $250 to $600 for Missouri students and/or teachers whose studies or projects are related to natural science, resource conservation, earth resources, or environmental protection. Must be used for study in Missouri. See application for eligibility details.

Academic Fields/Career Goals: Environmental Science; Natural Resources; Natural Sciences.

Award: Scholarship for use in freshman, sophomore, junior, senior, or graduate years; not renewable. *Number:* 8. *Amount:* $250–$600.

Eligibility Requirements: Applicant must be enrolled or expecting to enroll full- or part-time at a four-year institution or university; resident of Missouri and studying in Missouri. Available to U.S. citizens.

Application Requirements: Application form, community service, financial need analysis. *Deadline:* January 31.

Contact: Laurie Coleman, Membership Director
Conservation Federation of Missouri
728 W Main Street
Jefferson City, MO 65101
Phone: 573-634-2322
Fax: 573-634-8205
E-mail: lcoleman@confedmo.org

COSTA RICAN VACATIONS

http://www.vacationscostarica.com/

COSTA RICAN VACATIONS SCHOLARSHIP

The Costa Rican Vacations scholarship program recognizes and rewards innovation and ideas within the areas of tourism studies and sustainable tourism. Every year Costa Rican Vacations will award two scholarships of $1,000 each to students who are interested in pursuing their studies and their career in tourism, hospitality or sustainable development. Scholarships are not renewable; however, a recipient may re-apply. Additional information can be found on the Costa Rican Vacations website: http://www.vacationscostarica.com/about-us/scholarships/

Academic Fields/Career Goals: Environmental Science; Hospitality Management; Natural Resources; Travel/Tourism.

Award: Scholarship for use in freshman, sophomore, junior, or senior years; not renewable. *Number:* 2. *Amount:* $1000.

Eligibility Requirements: Applicant must be enrolled or expecting to enroll full- or part-time at a four-year institution or university and studying in Alabama, Alaska, Arizona, Arkansas, California, Colorado, Connecticut, Delaware, District of Columbia, Florida, Georgia, Hawaii, Idaho, Illinois, Indiana, Iowa, Kansas, Kentucky, Louisiana, Maine, Maryland, Massachusetts, Michigan, Minnesota, Mississippi, Missouri, Montana, Nebraska, Nevada, New Hampshire, New Jersey, New Mexico, New York, North Carolina, North Dakota, Ohio, Oklahoma, Oregon, Pennsylvania, Puerto Rico, Rhode Island, South Carolina, South Dakota, Tennessee, Texas, Utah, Vermont, Virginia, Washington, West Virginia, Wisconsin, Wyoming. Applicant must have 3.0 GPA or higher. Available to U.S. and non-U.S. citizens.

Application Requirements: Essay. *Deadline:* February 15.

Contact: Current Editor, Senior Online Content Editor
Phone: 800-606-1860 Ext. 1304
E-mail: scholarships@namutravel.com

DELAWARE HIGHER EDUCATION OFFICE

http://www.doe.k12.de.us

DELAWARE SOLID WASTE AUTHORITY JOHN P. "PAT" HEALY SCHOLARSHIP
• See page 281

ENVIRONMENTAL PROFESSIONALS' ORGANIZATION OF CONNECTICUT

http://www.epoc.org/

EPOC ENVIRONMENTAL SCHOLARSHIP FUND

Scholarships awarded annually to junior, senior, and graduate level students (full- or part-time) enrolled in accepted programs of study leading the student to become an environmental professional in Connecticut.

Academic Fields/Career Goals: Environmental Science.

Award: Scholarship for use in junior, senior, or graduate years; not renewable. *Number:* 2–3.

Eligibility Requirements: Applicant must be enrolled or expecting to enroll full- or part-time at a four-year institution or university. Available to U.S. citizens.

Application Requirements: Application form, essay, financial need analysis, recommendations or references, transcript. *Deadline:* May 7.

Contact: John Figurelli, Scholarship Fund Coordinator
Environmental Professionals' Organization of Connecticut
PO Box 176
Amston, CT 06231-0176
Phone: 860-513-1473
Fax: 860-228-4902
E-mail: figurelj@wseinc.com

GARDEN CLUB OF AMERICA

http://www.gcamerica.org/

CAROLINE THORN KISSEL SUMMER ENVIRONMENTAL STUDIES SCHOLARSHIP

Scholarship for students to promote environmental studies by students who are either residents of the state of New Jersey or non-residents pursuing study in New Jersey or its surrounding waters. Open to college students, graduate students, Ph.D. candidates, or non-degree-seeking applicants above the high school level. Must be a U.S. citizen.

Academic Fields/Career Goals: Environmental Science.

Award: Scholarship for use in freshman, sophomore, junior, senior, or graduate years; not renewable. *Number:* 1. *Amount:* $3000.

Eligibility Requirements: Applicant must be enrolled or expecting to enroll full- or part-time at a two-year or four-year or technical institution or university; resident of New Jersey and studying in New Jersey. Available to U.S. citizens.

Application Requirements: Application form, essay. *Deadline:* February 10.

Contact: Garden Club of America
14 East 60th Street
New York, NY 10022-1006
Phone: 212-753-8287
E-mail: scholarshipapplications@gcamerica.org

CLARA CARTER HIGGINS SUMMER ENVIRONMENTAL STUDIES SCHOLARSHIP

Scholarship to encourage studies and careers in the environmental field, with the opportunity to gain knowledge and experience beyond the regular course of study. Annually funds one Clara Carter Higgins scholar and one or more GCA Summer Environmental Studies scholars at $3,000 per recipient in financial assistance for summer coursework in environmental studies.

Academic Fields/Career Goals: Environmental Science.

Award: Scholarship for use in sophomore, junior, or senior years; not renewable. *Number:* 1. *Amount:* $3000.

Eligibility Requirements: Applicant must be enrolled or expecting to enroll full- or part-time at a four-year institution or university. Available to U.S. citizens.

Application Requirements: Application form, essay. *Deadline:* February 10.

Contact: Scholarship Committee Administrator
Phone: 212-753-8287
E-mail: scholarshipapplications@gcamerica.org

ELIZABETH GARDNER NORWEB SUMMER ENVIRONMENTAL STUDIES SCHOLARSHIP
• *See page 98*

GCA AWARD IN DESERT STUDIES
• *See page 121*

GCA AWARDS FOR SUMMER ENVIRONMENTAL STUDIES

$3,000 award to encourage studies and careers in the environmental field, with the opportunity to gain knowledge and experience beyond the regular course of study. Open to college students following their freshman, sophomore, or junior year. Eligibility is open to U.S. citizens and permanent residents who are enrolled in a U.S.–based institution.

Academic Fields/Career Goals: Environmental Science.

Award: Scholarship for use in sophomore, junior, or senior years; not renewable. *Amount:* $3000.

Eligibility Requirements: Applicant must be enrolled or expecting to enroll full-time at a four-year institution or university. Available to U.S. citizens.

Application Requirements: Application form, essay. *Deadline:* February 10.

Contact: Garden Club of America
Scholarship Applications
14 East 60th Street
New York, NY 10022-1006
Phone: 212-753-8287
E-mail: scholarshipapplications@gcamerica.org

MARY T. CAROTHERS SUMMER ENVIRONMENTAL STUDIES SCHOLARSHIP

Scholarship to encourage studies and careers in the environmental field, with the opportunity to gain knowledge and experience beyond the regular course of study. Provides financial assistance of $3,000 to one student annually for field work, research, or classroom work. Open to college undergraduates for summer study following the freshman, sophomore, or junior year.

Academic Fields/Career Goals: Environmental Science.

Award: Scholarship for use in sophomore, junior, or senior years; not renewable. *Number:* 1. *Amount:* $3000.

Eligibility Requirements: Applicant must be enrolled or expecting to enroll full-time at a four-year institution or university. Available to U.S. citizens.

Application Requirements: Application form, essay. *Deadline:* February 10.

Contact: Scholarship Committee Administrator
Phone: 212-753-8287
E-mail: scholarshipapplications@gcamerica.org

GREAT MINDS IN STEM

www.greatmindsinstem.org

HISPANIC ENGINEER NATIONAL ACHIEVEMENT AWARDS CORPORATION SCHOLARSHIP PROGRAM
• *See page 106*

GREEN CHEMISTRY INSTITUTE-AMERICAN CHEMICAL SOCIETY

http://www.acs.org/greenchemistry

CIBA TRAVEL AWARDS IN GREEN CHEMISTRY

The award sponsors the participation of students (high school, undergraduate, and graduate students) in an American Chemical Society (ACS) technical meeting, conference or training program, having a significant green chemistry or sustainability component, to expand the students' education in green chemistry. The applicant must demonstrate research or educational interest in green chemistry. The award amount is based on estimated travel expenses.

Academic Fields/Career Goals: Environmental Science.

Award: Grant for use in freshman, sophomore, junior, senior, graduate, or postgraduate years; not renewable. *Number:* 3–4. *Amount:* up to $2000.

Eligibility Requirements: Applicant must be enrolled or expecting to enroll full-time at a four-year institution or university. Available to U.S. citizens.

Application Requirements: Application form, application form may be submitted online, essay, recommendations or references, resume, transcript. *Deadline:* October 12.

Contact: Ms. Joyce Kilgore, Program Manager
Green Chemistry Institute-American Chemical Society
1155 16th Street, NW
Washington, DC 20036
Phone: 202-872-6109
E-mail: gci@acs.org

KENNETH G. HANCOCK MEMORIAL AWARD IN GREEN CHEMISTRY

Award of $1000 for the students who have completed their education or research in green chemistry. The scholarship provides national recognition for outstanding student contributions to furthering the goals of green chemistry through research or education.

Academic Fields/Career Goals: Environmental Science.

Award: Prize for use in freshman, sophomore, junior, senior, or graduate years; not renewable. *Number:* 1–2. *Amount:* $1000.

Eligibility Requirements: Applicant must be enrolled or expecting to enroll full-time at a four-year institution or university. Available to U.S. and non-U.S. citizens.

Application Requirements: Application form, application form may be submitted online, essay. *Deadline:* March 1.

Contact: Mrs. Jennifer MacKellar, Program Manager
Green Chemistry Institute-American Chemical Society
1155 16th Street, NW
Washington, DC 20036
Phone: 202-872-6173
E-mail: gci@acs.org

INDEPENDENT LABORATORIES INSTITUTE SCHOLARSHIP ALLIANCE

http://www.acil.org/

INDEPENDENT LABORATORIES INSTITUTE SCHOLARSHIP ALLIANCE
• *See page 156*

INDIANA WILDLIFE FEDERATION ENDOWMENT

http://www.indianawildlife.org/

CHARLES A. HOLT INDIANA WILDLIFE FEDERATION ENDOWMENT SCHOLARSHIP

A $1000.00 scholarship will be award to one Indiana resident enrolled in a course of study related to resource conservation or environmental education at a sophomore level or above in an accredited college or university. The scholarship recipient will receive priority consideration for an Indiana Wildlife Federation internship position.

Academic Fields/Career Goals: Environmental Science; Natural Resources.

Award: Scholarship for use in sophomore, junior, or senior years; not renewable. *Number:* 1. *Amount:* $1000.

Eligibility Requirements: Applicant must be enrolled or expecting to enroll full-time at a four-year institution or university; resident of Indiana and studying in Indiana. Available to U.S. citizens.

Application Requirements: Application form, essay. *Deadline:* June 1.

Contact: Barbara Simpson, Executive Director
Indiana Wildlife Federation Endowment
708 East Michigan Street
Indianapolis, IN 46202
Phone: 317-875-9453
E-mail: info@indianawildlife.org

INTERTRIBAL TIMBER COUNCIL

http://www.itcnet.org/

TRUMAN D. PICARD SCHOLARSHIP
• *See page 93*

KENTUCKY ENERGY AND ENVIRONMENT CABINET

http://dep.ky.gov

ENVIRONMENTAL PROTECTION SCHOLARSHIP
• *See page 157*

THE LAND CONSERVANCY OF NEW JERSEY

http://tlc-nj.org/

ROGERS FAMILY SCHOLARSHIP
• *See page 243*

RUSSELL W. MYERS SCHOLARSHIP
• *See page 99*

MASSACHUSETTS ASSOCIATION OF LAND SURVEYORS AND CIVIL ENGINEERS

http://www.malsce.org/

MALSE SCHOLARSHIPS
• *See page 302*

NASA/MARYLAND SPACE GRANT CONSORTIUM

http://md.spacegrant.org/

NASA MARYLAND SPACE GRANT CONSORTIUM UNDERGRADUATE SCHOLARSHIPS
• *See page 142*

NASA MINNESOTA SPACE GRANT CONSORTIUM

http://www.aem.umn.edu/mnsgc

MINNESOTA SPACE GRANT CONSORTIUM SCHOLARSHIP PROGRAM
• *See page 142*

NASA'S VIRGINIA SPACE GRANT CONSORTIUM

http://www.vsgc.odu.edu/

COMMUNITY COLLEGE STEM SCHOLARSHIPS
• *See page 114*

NATIONAL ASSOCIATION OF WATER COMPANIES-NEW JERSEY CHAPTER

http://www.nawc.org

NATIONAL ASSOCIATION OF WATER COMPANIES-NEW JERSEY CHAPTER SCHOLARSHIP
• *See page 80*

NATIONAL COUNCIL OF STATE GARDEN CLUBS INC. SCHOLARSHIP

http://www.gardenclub.org/

NATIONAL COUNCIL OF STATE GARDEN CLUBS INC. SCHOLARSHIP
• *See page 99*

NATIONAL GARDEN CLUBS INC.

http://www.gardenclub.org/

NATIONAL GARDEN CLUBS INC. SCHOLARSHIP PROGRAM
• *See page 100*

NATIONAL SAFETY COUNCIL

http://www.cshema.org/

CAMPUS SAFETY, HEALTH AND ENVIRONMENTAL MANAGEMENT ASSOCIATION SCHOLARSHIP AWARD PROGRAM

One $2000 scholarship available to full-time undergraduate or graduate students in all majors to encourage the study of safety and environmental management. The program is open to all college undergraduate and graduate students in all majors/disciplines enrolled in 12 credit hours per semester, trimester, or quarter.

Academic Fields/Career Goals: Environmental Science; Occupational Safety and Health.

Award: Scholarship for use in freshman, sophomore, junior, senior, or graduate years; not renewable. *Number:* 1. *Amount:* $2000.

Eligibility Requirements: Applicant must be enrolled or expecting to enroll full-time at a four-year institution or university. Available to U.S. and Canadian citizens.

Application Requirements: Application form, essay, transcript. *Deadline:* March 31.

Contact: Scholarship Committee
National Safety Council
120 West 7th Street, Suite 204
Bloomington, IN 47404
Phone: 812-245-8084
Fax: 812-245-0590

NATIONAL SECURITY EDUCATION PROGRAM

http://www.iie.org/

NATIONAL SECURITY EDUCATION PROGRAM (NSEP) DAVID L. BOREN UNDERGRADUATE SCHOLARSHIPS
• *See page 126*

NEW ENGLAND WATER WORKS ASSOCIATION

http://www.newwa.org/

ELSON T. KILLAM MEMORIAL SCHOLARSHIP
• *See page 196*

FRANCIS X. CROWLEY SCHOLARSHIP
• *See page 166*

JOSEPH MURPHY SCHOLARSHIP
• *See page 196*

NEXTSTEPU

http://www.nextstepu.com/

$1,500 STEM SCHOLARSHIP
• *See page 106*

NGWA FOUNDATION

http://www.ngwa.org/Foundation/Pages/default.aspx

NGWA FOUNDATION'S LEN ASSANTE SCHOLARSHIP
• *See page 244*

OHIO ACADEMY OF SCIENCE/OHIO ENVIRONMENTAL EDUCATION FUND

http://www.ohiosci.org/

OHIO ENVIRONMENTAL SCIENCE & ENGINEERING SCHOLARSHIPS

Merit-based, non-renewable, tuition-only scholarships awarded to undergraduate students admitted to Ohio state or private colleges and universities. Must be able to demonstrate knowledge of, and commitment to, careers in environmental sciences or environmental engineering.

Academic Fields/Career Goals: Environmental Science.

Award: Scholarship for use in senior year; not renewable. *Number:* 18. *Amount:* $1250–$2500.

Eligibility Requirements: Applicant must be enrolled or expecting to enroll full- or part-time at a two-year or four-year institution or university and studying in Ohio. Applicant must have 3.0 GPA or higher. Available to U.S. citizens.

Application Requirements: Application form, application form may be submitted online (https://mc04.manuscriptcentral.com/oas), community service, essay, recommendations or references, resume, self-addressed stamped envelope with application, transcript. *Deadline:* April 15.

Contact: Dr. Stephen McConoughey, Chief Executive Officer
Ohio Academy of Science/Ohio Environmental
Education Fund
1500 West Third Avenue, Suite 228
Columbus, OH 43212-2817
Phone: 614-488-2228
Fax: 614-488-7629
E-mail: smcconoughey@ohiosci.org

OREGON STUDENT ASSISTANCE COMMISSION

http://www.GetCollegeFunds.org/

ANDY AITKENHEAD SCHOLARSHIP
• *See page 115*

ROBERTS SCHOLARSHIP
• *See page 158*

ROYDEN M. BODLEY SCHOLARSHIP

Award open to Oregon high school graduates who earned their Eagle rank in Boy Scouts of America Cascade Pacific Council. Must be enrolled, or planning to enroll, in an Oregon college or university in an undergraduate program in forestry, wildlife conservation, environmental studies, or related fields that continue interest in the outdoors. Must reapply annually to renew award. Must specify the date you were awarded the rank of Eagle Scout and the name of the Council.

Academic Fields/Career Goals: Environmental Science; Natural Resources; Natural Sciences.

Award: Scholarship for use in freshman year; not renewable.

Eligibility Requirements: Applicant must be enrolled or expecting to enroll full-time at a four-year institution or university; male; resident of Oregon and studying in Oregon. Applicant or parent of applicant must be member of Boy Scouts. Available to U.S. citizens.

Application Requirements: Application form, financial need analysis. *Deadline:* March 1.

Contact: Melissa Adams, Scholarship Processing Coordinator
Phone: 541-687-7409
E-mail: melissa.adams@hecc.oregon.gov

WILLIAM E. KEENE MEMORIAL SCHOLARSHIP
• *See page 316*

OUTDOOR WRITERS ASSOCIATION OF AMERICA

http://www.owaa.org/

OUTDOOR WRITERS ASSOCIATION OF AMERICA - BODIE MCDOWELL SCHOLARSHIP AWARD
• *See page 207*

PADDLE CANADA

https://www.paddlecanada.com/

BILL MASON SCHOLARSHIP FUND
• *See page 257*

PLAN NEW HAMPSHIRE

www.plannh.org

PLAN NEW HAMPSHIRE SCHOLARSHIP AND PROGRAM
• *See page 123*

PRICE BENOWITZ LLP

http://pricebenowitz.com/

STEVE DUCKETT CONSERVATION SCHOLARSHIP

As a dedicated local attorney and an active member of Ducks Unlimited, Steve Duckett is an outspoken proponent of conservation initiatives throughout the country. He believes that it is our responsibility as American citizens to be active stewards of the land that we inherited from our forefathers. To learn more, visit https://www.virginiacriminallaws.com/#scholarship

Academic Fields/Career Goals: Environmental Science.

Award: Scholarship for use in freshman, sophomore, junior, senior, or graduate years; not renewable. *Number:* 1. *Amount:* $500.

Eligibility Requirements: Applicant must be enrolled or expecting to enroll full- or part-time at a two-year or four-year or technical institution or university. Applicant or parent of applicant must have employment or volunteer experience in environmental-related field. Applicant must have 3.0 GPA or higher. Available to U.S. citizens.

Application Requirements: Essay. *Deadline:* January 31.

Contact: Steve Duckett
E-mail: info@virginiacriminallaws.com

SALT RIVER PROJECT (SRP)

http://www.srpnet.com/

NAVAJO GENERATING STATION NAVAJO SCHOLARSHIP
• *See page 305*

SCARLETT FAMILY FOUNDATION SCHOLARSHIP PROGRAM

http://www.scarlettfoundation.org/

SCHOLARSHIP FOR STUDENTS PURSUING A BUSINESS OR STEM DEGREE
• See page 84

SIGMA XI, THE SCIENTIFIC RESEARCH SOCIETY

http://www.sigmaxi.org/

SIGMA XI GRANTS-IN-AID OF RESEARCH
• See page 101

SOCIETY FOR RANGE MANAGEMENT

http://www.rangelands.org/

MASONIC RANGE SCIENCE SCHOLARSHIP
• See page 94

SOCIETY OF TOXICOLOGY

http://www.toxicology.org/

UNDERGRADUATE DIVERSITY STUDENT AWARDS
• See page 159

SOIL AND WATER CONSERVATION SOCIETY

http://www.swcs.org

DONALD A. WILLIAMS SCHOLARSHIP SOIL CONSERVATION SCHOLARSHIP
• See page 95

SOIL AND WATER CONSERVATION SOCIETY-MISSOURI SHOW-ME CHAPTER

http://www.moswcs.org/

MO SHOW-ME CHAPTER SWCS SCHOLARSHIP
• See page 95

SOIL AND WATER CONSERVATION SOCIETY-NEW JERSEY CHAPTER

http://www.geocities.com/njswcs

EDWARD R. HALL SCHOLARSHIP
• See page 95

TAILOR MADE LAWNS

http://www.tailormadelawns.com

2017 TAILOR MADE LAWNS SCHOLARSHIP FUND
• See page 102

TECHNICAL ASSOCIATION OF THE PULP & PAPER INDUSTRY (TAPPI)

http://www.tappi.org/

ENVIRONMENTAL WORKING GROUP SCHOLARSHIP

Scholarship for full-time students in a college program or applicants working full-time or part-time in the corrugated industry. Must demonstrate an interest in the corrugated packaging industry.

Academic Fields/Career Goals: Environmental Science; Paper and Pulp Engineering.

Award: Scholarship for use in sophomore, junior, or senior years; not renewable. *Number:* 1. *Amount:* $2500.

Eligibility Requirements: Applicant must be enrolled or expecting to enroll full-time at a four-year institution or university. Applicant must have 3.0 GPA or higher. Available to U.S. and non-U.S. citizens.

Application Requirements: Application form, interview. *Deadline:* February 15.

Contact: Mr. Laurence Womack, Director of Standards and Awards
Technical Association of the Pulp & Paper Industry (TAPPI)
15 Technology Parkway South
Peachtree Corners, GA 30092
Phone: 770-209-7276
E-mail: standards@tappi.org

TED ROLLINS AND TXG CAPITAL

http://www.txgcapital.com/

TED ROLLINS ECO SCHOLARSHIP
• See page 168

TRANSTUTORS

http://www.transtutors.com/scholarship

TRANSTUTORS SCHOLARSHIP 2015-16
• See page 85

UNITED NEGRO COLLEGE FUND

http://www.uncf.org/

SUEZ CORPORATE SCHOLARS PROGRAM
• See page 87

UNITED STATES ENVIRONMENTAL PROTECTION AGENCY

http://www.epa.gov/enviroed

NATIONAL NETWORK FOR ENVIRONMENTAL MANAGEMENT STUDIES FELLOWSHIP

Fellowship program designed to provide undergraduate and graduate students with research opportunities at one of EPA's facilities nationwide. EPA awards approximately 40 NNEMS fellowships per year. Selected students receive a stipend for performing their research project. EPA develops an annual catalog of research projects available for student application. Submit a complete application package as described in the annual catalog. Minimum 3.0 GPA required.

Academic Fields/Career Goals: Environmental Science; Natural Resources.

Award: Grant for use in freshman, sophomore, junior, senior, graduate, or postgraduate years; not renewable. *Number:* 20–25.

Eligibility Requirements: Applicant must be enrolled or expecting to enroll full- or part-time at a two-year or four-year institution or university. Applicant must have 3.0 GPA or higher. Available to U.S. citizens.

Application Requirements: Application form, recommendations or references, resume, transcript. *Deadline:* January 22.

Contact: Michael Baker, Acting Director
United States Environmental Protection Agency
Environmental Education Division
1200 Pennsylvania Avenue, NW, MC 1704A
Washington, DC 20460
Phone: 202-564-0446
Fax: 202-564-2754
E-mail: baker.michael@epa.gov

UNITED STATES SOCIETY ON DAMS

http://www.ussdams.org/

UNITED STATES SOCIETY ON DAMS SCHOLARSHIP AWARD
• *See page 199*

EUROPEAN STUDIES

CANADIAN INSTITUTE OF UKRAINIAN STUDIES

http://www.cius.ca/

CANADIAN INSTITUTE OF UKRAINIAN STUDIES RESEARCH GRANTS
• *See page 124*

CULTURAL SERVICES OF THE FRENCH EMBASSY

http://www.frenchculture.org/

TEACHING ASSISTANT PROGRAM IN FRANCE
• *See page 104*

FASHION DESIGN

AMERICAN SHEEP INDUSTRY ASSOCIATION

http://www.sheepusa.org/

NATIONAL MAKE IT WITH WOOL COMPETITION
Awards available for entrants ages 13 years & older. Must enter at district and/or state level with home-constructed garment of at least 60 percent wool. Applicant must model garment. National entry fee is $12 for regular contest and $20 for Fashion/Apparel Design students. District and state entry fees may also apply. Complete rules available from State Director, National Coordinator, and online. www.NationalMakeItWithWool.com

Academic Fields/Career Goals: Fashion Design.

Award: Prize for use in freshman, sophomore, junior, senior, or graduate years; not renewable. *Number:* 2–26. *Amount:* $25–$1500.

Eligibility Requirements: Applicant must be enrolled or expecting to enroll full- or part-time at a two-year or four-year or technical institution or university; resident of Alberta, California, Colorado, Connecticut, Delaware, Florida, Georgia, Idaho, Illinois, Indiana, Kansas, Kentucky, Maine, Maryland, Massachusetts, Michigan, Minnesota, Missouri, Montana, Nebraska, New Hampshire, New Jersey, New York, North Carolina, North Dakota, Ohio, Oklahoma, Oregon, Pennsylvania, Rhode Island, South Dakota, Tennessee, Texas, Utah, Vermont, Washington, Wisconsin, Wyoming; studying in Alabama, Alaska, Arizona, Arkansas, California, Colorado, Connecticut, Delaware, District of Columbia, Florida, Georgia, Idaho, Illinois, Indiana, Iowa, Kansas, Kentucky, Louisiana, Maine, Maryland, Massachusetts, Michigan, Minnesota, Mississippi, Missouri, Montana, Nebraska, Nevada, New Hampshire, New Jersey, New Mexico, New York, North Carolina, North Dakota, Ohio, Oklahoma, Oregon, Pennsylvania, Rhode Island, South Carolina, South Dakota, Tennessee, Texas, Utah, Vermont, Virginia, Washington, West Virginia, Wisconsin, Wyoming and must have an interest in sewing. Available to U.S. citizens.

Application Requirements: Application form. *Fee:* $12.

Contact: Mary Roediger, National Coordinator
American Sheep Industry Association
PO Box 123
Albany, OH 45710
Phone: 740-591-5149
E-mail: wool@sewtruedesigns.com

CONGRESSIONAL BLACK CAUCUS FOUNDATION, INC.

http://www.cbcfinc.org/

CBC SPOUSES VISUAL ARTS SCHOLARSHIP
• *See page 120*

DECA (DISTRIBUTIVE EDUCATION CLUBS OF AMERICA)

http://www.deca.org/

HARRY A. APPLEGATE SCHOLARSHIP
• *See page 75*

QUALITY BATH

www.qualitybath.com

QUALITYBATH.COM SCHOLARSHIP PROGRAM
• *See page 123*

SUPPORT CREATIVITY

http://wesupportcreativity.org

SUPPORT CREATIVITY SCHOLARSHIP
• *See page 124*

WHOMENTORS.COM, INC.

http://www.WHOmentors.com/

IB USD WORLDWIDE VENTURE CAPITAL
• *See page 116*

FILMMAKING/VIDEO

ACADEMY FOUNDATION OF THE ACADEMY OF MOTION PICTURE ARTS AND SCIENCES

http://www.oscars.org/saa

ACADEMY OF MOTION PICTURE ARTS AND SCIENCES STUDENT ACADEMY AWARDS
Award available to students who have made a narrative, documentary, alternative, foreign or animated film of up to 60 minutes within the curricular structure of an accredited college or university. Initial entry must be on DVD-R. 16mm or larger format print, digital beta-cam tape, HD-Cam or DCP required for further rounds. Prizes awarded in four categories. Each category awards gold ($5000), silver ($3000), and bronze ($2000). Visit website for details and application http://www.oscars.org/saa.

Academic Fields/Career Goals: Filmmaking/Video.

Award: Prize for use in freshman, sophomore, junior, senior, or graduate years; not renewable. *Number:* 3–15. *Amount:* $2000–$5000.

Eligibility Requirements: Applicant must be enrolled or expecting to enroll full-time at a two-year or four-year institution or university. Available to U.S. and non-U.S. citizens.

Application Requirements: 16mm or larger format film print or NTSC digital betacam version of the entry (BetaSP format is not acceptable), DVD, application form, entry in a contest. *Deadline:* April 1.

Contact: Shawn Guthrie, Program Administrator
Academy Foundation of the Academy of Motion Picture Arts and Sciences
8949 Wilshire Boulevard
Beverly Hills, CA 90211-1972
Phone: 310-247-3000 Ext. 3306
Fax: 310-859-9619
E-mail: sguthrie@oscars.org

ADC RESEARCH INSTITUTE
http://www.adc.org/

JACK SHAHEEN MASS COMMUNICATIONS SCHOLARSHIP AWARD
• *See page 200*

ASIAN AMERICAN JOURNALISTS ASSOCIATION, SEATTLE CHAPTER
http://www.aajaseattle.org/

NORTHWEST JOURNALISTS OF COLOR SCHOLARSHIP
• *See page 88*

CHARLES AND LUCILLE KING FAMILY FOUNDATION, INC.
http://www.kingfoundation.org/

CHARLES AND LUCILLE KING FAMILY FOUNDATION SCHOLARSHIPS
• *See page 203*

CONGRESSIONAL BLACK CAUCUS FOUNDATION, INC.
http://www.cbcfinc.org/

CBC SPOUSES VISUAL ARTS SCHOLARSHIP
• *See page 120*

ILLUMINATING ENGINEERING SOCIETY OF NORTH AMERICA–GOLDEN GATE SECTION
http://www.iesgg.org/

ALAN LUCAS MEMORIAL EDUCATIONAL SCHOLARSHIP
• *See page 122*

INTERNATIONAL COMMUNICATIONS INDUSTRIES FOUNDATION
http://www.infocomm.org/scholarships

ICIF SCHOLARSHIP FOR EMPLOYEES AND DEPENDENTS OF MEMBER ORGANIZATIONS
• *See page 204*

INTERNATIONAL COMMUNICATIONS INDUSTRIES FOUNDATION AV SCHOLARSHIP
• *See page 204*

ISLAMIC SCHOLARSHIP FUND
http://islamicscholarshipfund.org/

ISF NATIONAL SCHOLARSHIP
• *See page 108*

NATIONAL ACADEMY OF TELEVISION ARTS & SCIENCES—OHIO VALLEY CHAPTER
http://ohiovalleyemmy.org/

DAVID J. CLARKE MEMORIAL SCHOLARSHIP
• *See page 205*

NATIONAL ACADEMY OF TELEVISION ARTS AND SCIENCES
http://www.emmyonline.tv/

DOUGLAS W. MUMMERT SCHOLARSHIP
• *See page 129*

JIM MCKAY MEMORIAL SCHOLARSHIP
• *See page 205*

MIKE WALLACE MEMORIAL SCHOLARSHIP
• *See page 205*

NATIONAL ACADEMY OF TELEVISION ARTS AND SCIENCES TRUSTEES SCHOLARSHIP
• *See page 205*

RANDY FALCO SCHOLARSHIP
• *See page 205*

NATIONAL ACADEMY OF TELEVISION ARTS AND SCIENCES, MICHIGAN CHAPTER
http://natasmichigan.org

DR. LYNNE BOYLE/JOHN SCHIMPF UNDERGRADUATE SCHOLARSHIP
• *See page 89*

OUTDOOR WRITERS ASSOCIATION OF AMERICA
http://www.owaa.org/

OUTDOOR WRITERS ASSOCIATION OF AMERICA - BODIE MCDOWELL SCHOLARSHIP AWARD
• *See page 207*

POLISH ARTS CLUB OF BUFFALO SCHOLARSHIP FOUNDATION
http://www.pacb.bfn.org/

POLISH ARTS CLUB OF BUFFALO SCHOLARSHIP FOUNDATION TRUST
• *See page 130*

PRINCESS GRACE FOUNDATION-USA

http://www.pgfusa.org/

PRINCESS GRACE AWARDS IN DANCE, THEATER, AND FILM

One-time scholarship for students enrolled full-time in film or video, dance, or theater program. For dance, applicant must have completed at least one year of undergraduate study; for theater, final year of study in either undergraduate or graduate level; and for film, must be in thesis program. The number of scholarships varies from ten to twelve annually.

Academic Fields/Career Goals: Filmmaking/Video; Performing Arts.

Award: Grant for use in sophomore, junior, senior, or graduate years; not renewable. *Number:* 15–25. *Amount:* $5000–$25,000.

Eligibility Requirements: Applicant must be enrolled or expecting to enroll full-time at a four-year institution or university. Available to U.S. citizens.

Application Requirements: Application form, essay, personal photograph, portfolio.

Contact: Ms. Diana Kemppainen, Program Director
Phone: 212-317-1470
E-mail: grants@pgfusa.org

QUALITY BATH

www.qualitybath.com

QUALITYBATH.COM SCHOLARSHIP PROGRAM
• *See page 123*

RHODE ISLAND FOUNDATION

http://www.rifoundation.org/

J. D. EDSAL SCHOLARSHIP
• *See page 90*

SOCIETY OF MOTION PICTURE AND TELEVISION ENGINEERS

https://www.smpte.org/

LOUIS F. WOLF JR. MEMORIAL SCHOLARSHIP
• *See page 210*

STUDENT PAPER AWARD
• *See page 210*

SUPPORT CREATIVITY

http://wesupportcreativity.org

SUPPORT CREATIVITY SCHOLARSHIP
• *See page 124*

TELETOON

http://www.teletoon.com/

TELETOON ANIMATION SCHOLARSHIP
• *See page 131*

UNIVERSITY FILM AND VIDEO ASSOCIATION

http://www.ufva.org/

UNIVERSITY FILM AND VIDEO ASSOCIATION CAROLE FIELDING STUDENT GRANTS

Up to $4000 is available for production grants in narrative, documentary, experimental, new-media/installation, or animation. Up to $1000 is available for grants in research. Applicant must be sponsored by a faculty person who is an active member of the University Film and Video Association. Fifty percent of award distributed upon completion of project.

Academic Fields/Career Goals: Filmmaking/Video.

Award: Grant for use in freshman, sophomore, junior, senior, or graduate years; not renewable. *Number:* up to 5. *Amount:* $1000–$4000.

Eligibility Requirements: Applicant must be enrolled or expecting to enroll full- or part-time at a two-year or four-year institution or university. Available to U.S. and non-U.S. citizens.

Application Requirements: Application form, essay, project description, budget, recommendations or references, resume. *Deadline:* December 15.

Contact: Prof. Robert Johnson, Chair
University Film and Video Association
Framingham State College, 100 State Street
Framingham, MA 01701-9101
Phone: 508-626-4684
Fax: 508-626-4847
E-mail: rjohnso@frc.mass.edu

WHOMENTORS.COM, INC.

http://www.WHOmentors.com/

1 B USD WORLDWIDE VENTURE CAPITAL
• *See page 116*

FINANCE

THE ACTUARIAL FOUNDATION

http://www.actuarialfoundation.org

ACTUARY OF TOMORROW—STUART A. ROBERTSON MEMORIAL SCHOLARSHIP
• *See page 160*

CURTIS E. HUNTINGTON MEMORIAL SCHOLARSHIP (FORMERLY THE JOHN CULVER WOODDY SCHOLARSHIP)
• *See page 245*

AUTOMOTIVE WOMEN'S ALLIANCE FOUNDATION

http://www.awafoundation.org/index.php

AUTOMOTIVE WOMEN'S ALLIANCE FOUNDATION SCHOLARSHIPS
• *See page 74*

CHECKS SUPERSTORE

http://www.checks-superstore.com/

CHECKS SUPERSTORE SCHOLARSHIP

Checks SuperStore is offering an annual $1,000 scholarship to one college/university student in the United States. The scholarship will be awarded to the student who submits the best overall essay. Essay must be between 500 and 1,000 words long and must fully answer one of the questions. Entry deadline is on August 15th.

Academic Fields/Career Goals: Finance.

Award: Scholarship for use in freshman, sophomore, junior, or senior years; renewable. *Number:* 1. *Amount:* $1000.

Eligibility Requirements: Applicant must be enrolled or expecting to enroll full-time at a four-year institution. Applicant must have 3.0 GPA or higher. Available to U.S. citizens.

Application Requirements: Application form may be submitted online(www.checks-superstore.com/scholarship.aspx), essay. *Deadline:* August 15.

Contact: Ryan Skidmore, Scholarship Manager
     E-mail: scholarship@checks-superstore.com

DECA (DISTRIBUTIVE EDUCATION CLUBS OF AMERICA)

http://www.deca.org/

HARRY A. APPLEGATE SCHOLARSHIP
• *See page 75*

FUKUNAGA SCHOLARSHIP FOUNDATION

http://fukunagascholarship.com

FUKUNAGA SCHOLARSHIP FOUNDATION
• *See page 77*

GEORGIA GOVERNMENT FINANCE OFFICERS ASSOCIATION

http://www.ggfoa.org/

GGFOA ANNUAL COLLEGE SCHOLARSHIP
• *See page 77*

INSTITUTE OF MANAGEMENT ACCOUNTANTS

https://www.imanet.org/students/scholarships-and-awards/scholarships?ssopc=1

ROLF S. JAEHNIGEN FAMILY SCHOLARSHIP
• *See page 79*

OREGON STUDENT ASSISTANCE COMMISSION

http://www.GetCollegeFunds.org/

OREGON STATE FISCAL ASSOCIATION SCHOLARSHIP
• *See page 246*

RISK MANAGEMENT ASSOCIATION FOUNDATION

www.scholarshipamerica.org

RISK MANAGEMENT ASSOCIATION FOUNDATION SCHOLARSHIP PROGRAM
• *See page 83*

SCARLETT FAMILY FOUNDATION SCHOLARSHIP PROGRAM

http://www.scarlettfoundation.org/

SCHOLARSHIP FOR STUDENTS PURSUING A BUSINESS OR STEM DEGREE
• *See page 84*

SPECIALTY EQUIPMENT MARKET ASSOCIATION

http://www.sema.org/

SEMA MEMORIAL SCHOLARSHIP FUND
• *See page 85*

STRAIGHTFORWARD MEDIA

http://www.straightforwardmedia.com/

STRAIGHTFORWARD MEDIA BUSINESS SCHOOL SCHOLARSHIP
• *See page 90*

TRANSTUTORS

http://www.transtutors.com/scholarship

TRANSTUTORS SCHOLARSHIP 2015-16
• *See page 85*

UNITED NEGRO COLLEGE FUND

http://www.uncf.org/

ANHEUSER-BUSCH LEGENDS OF THE CROWN SCHOLARSHIP PROGRAM
• *See page 86*

ASHLEY STEWART SCHOLARSHIP
• *See page 169*

BASF/ALFRED CHISHOLM ENDOWED MEMORIAL SCHOLARSHIP
• *See page 86*

CVS PHARMACY, INC. BUSINESS SCHOLARSHIPS
• *See page 86*

RICOH SCHOLARSHIP PROGRAM
• *See page 86*

SUEZ CORPORATE SCHOLARS PROGRAM
• *See page 87*

UNCF/ANTHEM CORPORATE SCHOLARS PROGRAM
• *See page 170*

UNCF/CARNIVAL CORPORATE SCHOLARS PROGRAM
• *See page 170*

UNCF/NISSAN SCHOLARSHIP
• *See page 170*

FIRE SCIENCES

AMERICAN SOCIETY OF CERTIFIED ENGINEERING TECHNICIANS

http://www.ascet.org/

KURT H. AND DONNA M. SCHULER SMALL GRANT
• *See page 176*

INDEPENDENT LABORATORIES INSTITUTE SCHOLARSHIP ALLIANCE

http://www.acil.org/

INDEPENDENT LABORATORIES INSTITUTE SCHOLARSHIP ALLIANCE
• *See page 156*

INTERNATIONAL ASSOCIATION OF FIRE CHIEFS FOUNDATION

http://www.iafcf.org/

INTERNATIONAL ASSOCIATION OF FIRE CHIEFS FOUNDATION SCHOLARSHIP AWARD

One-time award, open to any person who is an active member (volunteer or paid) of an emergency or fire department. Must use the scholarship funds for an accredited, recognized institution of higher education.

Academic Fields/Career Goals: Fire Sciences.

Award: Scholarship for use in freshman, sophomore, junior, senior, or graduate years; not renewable. *Number:* 20–30. *Amount:* $500–$2500.

Eligibility Requirements: Applicant must be enrolled or expecting to enroll full- or part-time at a two-year or four-year or technical institution or university. Applicant must have 2.5 GPA or higher. Available to U.S. and Canadian citizens.

Application Requirements: Application form, essay, letters of endorsement, recommendations or references, resume, transcript. *Deadline:* June 1.

Contact: Sharon Baroncelli, Association and Services Manager
Phone: 703-896-4822
Fax: 703-273-9363
E-mail: sbaroncelli@iafc.org

LEARNING FOR LIFE

http://www.learning-for-life.org/

INTERNATIONAL ASSOCIATIONS OF FIRE CHIEFS FOUNDATION SCHOLARSHIP

Applicant must be a graduating high school senior in May or June of the year the application is issued and a Fire Service Explorer. The school selected by the applicant must be an accredited public or proprietary institution.

Academic Fields/Career Goals: Fire Sciences.

Award: Scholarship for use in freshman year; not renewable. *Number:* 2. *Amount:* $500.

Eligibility Requirements: Applicant must be high school student and planning to enroll or expecting to enroll full- or part-time at a two-year or four-year institution or university. Applicant or parent of applicant must be member of Explorer Program/Learning for Life. Available to U.S. citizens.

Application Requirements: Application form, essay, personal photograph, recommendations or references, transcript. *Deadline:* July 1.

Contact: William Taylor, Scholarships and Awards Coordinator
E-mail: btaylor@lflmail.org

LEARNING FOR LIFE/EXPLORING

http://www.learning-for-life.org/

INTERNATIONAL ASSOCIATION OF FIRE CHIEFS FOUNDATION SCHOLARSHIP

Two $500 scholarships for Explorers who are pursuing a full-time career in the fire sciences. Must be high school senior and participant of the Learning for Life Exploring program.

Academic Fields/Career Goals: Fire Sciences.

Award: Scholarship for use in freshman year; not renewable. *Number:* 2. *Amount:* $500.

Eligibility Requirements: Applicant must be high school student and planning to enroll or expecting to enroll full-time at a four-year institution or university. Available to U.S. and non-U.S. citizens.

Application Requirements: Application form, essay, personal photograph, recommendations or references, test scores, transcript. *Deadline:* July 1.

Contact: Scholarship Committee
Learning for Life/Exploring
S210, PO Box 152079
Irving, TX 75015

MARYLAND STATE HIGHER EDUCATION COMMISSION

http://www.mhec.state.md.us/

CHARLES W. RILEY FIRE AND EMERGENCY MEDICAL SERVICES TUITION REIMBURSEMENT PROGRAM

Award intended to reimburse members of rescue organizations serving Maryland communities for tuition costs of course work towards a degree or certificate in fire service or medical technology. Must attend a two- or four-year school in Maryland. Minimum 2.0 GPA. The scholarship is worth up to $6500.

Academic Fields/Career Goals: Fire Sciences; Health and Medical Sciences; Trade/Technical Specialties.

Award: Scholarship for use in freshman, sophomore, junior, or senior years; not renewable. *Number:* 1–150. *Amount:* $1–$6500.

Eligibility Requirements: Applicant must be enrolled or expecting to enroll full- or part-time at a two-year or four-year institution or university; resident of Maryland and studying in Maryland. Applicant or parent of applicant must have employment or volunteer experience in police/firefighting. Available to U.S. citizens.

Application Requirements: Application form. *Deadline:* June 1.

Contact: Donna Thomas, Office of Student Financial Assistance
Maryland State Higher Education Commission
6 North Liberty Street
Baltimore, MD 21202
Phone: 410-767-3109
E-mail: donnae.thomas@maryland.gov

OREGON STUDENT ASSISTANCE COMMISSION

http://www.GetCollegeFunds.org/

NWFEDA—NORTHWEST FIRE EQUIPMENT DEALERS ASSOCIATION SCHOLARSHIP

Award for Oregon or Washington residents enrolled at least half-time and studying fire protection/suppression, fire science, fire investigation, or emergency medical services/technology and intending on careers in emergency services. Minimum 3.0 GPA preferred.

Academic Fields/Career Goals: Fire Sciences.

Award: Scholarship for use in freshman, sophomore, junior, senior, or graduate years; not renewable.

Eligibility Requirements: Applicant must be enrolled or expecting to enroll full- or part-time at a two-year or four-year or technical institution or university; resident of Oregon, Washington and studying in Oregon, Washington. Available to U.S. citizens.

Application Requirements: Application form. *Deadline:* March 1.

Contact: Melissa Adams, Scholarship Processing Coordinator
Phone: 541-687-7409
E-mail: melissa.adams@hecc.oregon.gov

STRAIGHTFORWARD MEDIA

http://www.straightforwardmedia.com/

STRAIGHTFORWARD MEDIA VOCATIONAL-TECHNICAL SCHOOL SCHOLARSHIP

• *See page 107*

FLEXOGRAPHY

FOUNDATION OF FLEXOGRAPHIC TECHNICAL ASSOCIATION

http://www.flexography.org/

FOUNDATION OF FLEXOGRAPHIC TECHNICAL ASSOCIATION SCHOLARSHIP COMPETITION

Awards students enrolled in a FFTA Flexo in Education Program with plans to attend a postsecondary institution, or be currently enrolled in a postsecondary institution offering a course of study in flexography. Must demonstrate an interest in a career in flexography, and maintain an overall GPA of at least 3.0. Must reapply.

Academic Fields/Career Goals: Flexography.

Award: Scholarship for use in freshman, sophomore, junior, or senior years; not renewable. *Number:* 6–8. *Amount:* up to $3000.

Eligibility Requirements: Applicant must be enrolled or expecting to enroll full-time at a two-year or four-year or technical institution or university. Applicant must have 3.0 GPA or higher. Available to U.S. and Canadian citizens.

Application Requirements: Application form, application form may be submitted online (http://www.flexography.org), essay, recommendations or references, transcript. *Deadline:* March 15.

Contact: Shelley Rubin, Manager of Educational Programs
Foundation of Flexographic Technical Association
3920 Veterans Memorial Highway, Suite 9
Bohemia, NY 11716
Phone: 631-737-6020 Ext. 36
Fax: 631-737-6813

PRINTING INDUSTRY MIDWEST EDUCATION FOUDNATION

http://www.pimw.org/scholarships

PRINTING INDUSTRY MIDWEST EDUCATION FOUNDATION SCHOLARSHIP FUND

• See page 207

TAG AND LABEL MANUFACTURERS INSTITUTE, INC.

http://www.tlmi.com/

TLMI 2 YEAR COLLEGE DEGREE SCHOLARSHIP PROGRAM

Scholarship program for students enrolled at a two-year college or in a degree technical program whose major course work includes courses appropriate for future work in the tag and label manufacturing industry. Must submit statements including personal information, financial circumstances, career and/or educational goals, employment experience, and reasons applicant should be selected for this award.

Academic Fields/Career Goals: Flexography.

Award: Scholarship for use in sophomore year; not renewable. *Number:* 1–4. *Amount:* $500–$1000.

Eligibility Requirements: Applicant must be enrolled or expecting to enroll full-time at a two-year or technical institution. Applicant must have 3.0 GPA or higher. Available to U.S. and Canadian citizens.

Application Requirements: Application form, essay, portfolio. *Deadline:* March 31.

Contact: Scholarship Committee
Tag and Label Manufacturers Institute, Inc.
510 King Street
Suite 410
Alexandria, VA 22314
Phone: 703-645-5086
E-mail: office@tlmi.com

TLMI 4 YEAR COLLEGE DEGREE SCHOLARSHIP PROGRAM

• See page 288

FOOD SCIENCE/ NUTRITION

AACC INTERNATIONAL

http://www.aaccnet.org/

UNDERGRADUATE SCHOLARSHIP AWARD

The purposes of the undergraduate scholarship program are to encourage scholastically outstanding advanced undergraduate students in academic preparation for a career in grain-based food science and technology, and to attract and encourage outstanding students to enter the field of grain-based food science and technology.

Academic Fields/Career Goals: Food Science/Nutrition.

Award: Scholarship for use in freshman, sophomore, junior, or senior years; not renewable. *Number:* 1. *Amount:* $825.

Eligibility Requirements: Applicant must be enrolled or expecting to enroll full-time at an institution or university. Applicant must have 3.0 GPA or higher. Available to U.S. and non-U.S. citizens.

Application Requirements: Application form, essay. *Deadline:* March 3.

Contact: Lauren McGinty, Membership Experience Manager
AACC International
3340 Pilot Knob Road
St. Paul, MN 55121
Phone: 651-4547250
E-mail: lmcginty@scisoc.org

ACADEMY OF NUTRITION AND DIETETICS

http://www.eatright.org/

ACADEMY OF NUTRITION AND DIETETICS FOUNDATION SCHOLARSHIP PROGRAM

Academy of Nutrition and Dietetics Foundation scholarships are available for undergraduate and graduate students enrolled in programs, including dietetic internships, preparing for entry to dietetics practice as well as dietetics professionals engaged in continuing education at the graduate level. Scholarship funds are provided by many state dietetic associations, dietetic practice groups, past ADA leaders and corporate donors. Scholarships require Academy of Nutrition and Dietetics membership. Details available on website: http://eatrightfoundation.org/scholarships-funding/#Scholarships

Academic Fields/Career Goals: Food Science/Nutrition.

Award: Scholarship for use in sophomore, junior, senior, or graduate years; not renewable. *Number:* 200–250. *Amount:* $500–$10,000.

Eligibility Requirements: Applicant must be enrolled or expecting to enroll full- or part-time at a two-year or four-year institution or university. Applicant or parent of applicant must be member of American Dietetic Association. Available to U.S. citizens.

Application Requirements: Application form, essay, financial need analysis. *Deadline:* April 17.

Contact: Beth Labrador, Development Director
E-mail: scholarship@eatright.org

AMERICAN INDIAN SCIENCE AND ENGINEERING SOCIETY

http://www.aises.org/

A.T. ANDERSON MEMORIAL SCHOLARSHIP PROGRAM

• See page 109

AMERICAN INSTITUTE OF WINE AND FOOD-PACIFIC NORTHWEST CHAPTER

http://www.aiwf.org/

CULINARY, VINIFERA, AND HOSPITALITY SCHOLARSHIP

One-time award available to residents of Washington State. Must be enrolled full-time in an accredited culinary, vinifera, or hospitality program in Washington State. Must have completed two years. Minimum 3.0 GPA required.

Academic Fields/Career Goals: Food Science/Nutrition; Food Service/Hospitality; Hospitality Management.

Award: Scholarship for use in junior or senior years; not renewable. *Number:* 4. *Amount:* $1500.

Eligibility Requirements: Applicant must be enrolled or expecting to enroll full-time at a two-year or four-year or technical institution or university; resident of Washington and studying in Washington. Applicant must have 3.0 GPA or higher. Available to U.S. and non-U.S. citizens.

Application Requirements: Application form, recommendations or references, resume. *Deadline:* continuous.

Contact: Brad Sturman, Scholarship Coordinator
American Institute of Wine and Food-Pacific Northwest
   Chapter
224 18th Avenue
Kirkland, WA 98033
Phone: 206-679-6228

AMERICAN LEGION DEPARTMENT OF NORTH DAKOTA

http://www.ndlegion.org/

O. NESHEIM MEMORIAL SCHOLARSHIP
• *See page 96*

AMERICAN OIL CHEMISTS' SOCIETY

http://www.aocs.org/

AOCS ANALYTICAL DIVISION STUDENT AWARD
• *See page 175*

AOCS BIOTECHNOLOGY STUDENT EXCELLENCE AWARD
• *See page 97*

AOCS HEALTH AND NUTRITION DIVISION STUDENT EXCELLENCE AWARD

$500 award and certificate to recognize the outstanding merit and performance of a student in the health and nutrition field. Student will present a paper at the Annual Meeting of the Society.

Academic Fields/Career Goals: Food Science/Nutrition.

Award: Prize for use in senior or graduate years; not renewable. *Number:* 1. *Amount:* $500.

Eligibility Requirements: Applicant must be enrolled or expecting to enroll full-time at a four-year institution or university. Available to U.S. and non-U.S. citizens.

Application Requirements: Abstract, application form, essay, recommendations or references. *Deadline:* October 15.

Contact: Barbara Semeraro, Area Manager, Membership
American Oil Chemists' Society
AOCS
PO Box 17190
Urbana, IL 61803
Phone: 217-693-4804
Fax: 217-693-4849
E-mail: awards@aocs.org

AOCS PROCESSING DIVISION AWARDS
• *See page 175*

AMERICAN SOCIETY FOR ENOLOGY AND VITICULTURE

http://www.asev.org/

AMERICAN SOCIETY FOR ENOLOGY AND VITICULTURE SCHOLARSHIPS
• *See page 97*

ASSOCIATION FOR FOOD AND DRUG OFFICIALS

http://www.afdo.org/

ASSOCIATION FOR FOOD AND DRUG OFFICIALS SCHOLARSHIP FUND
• *See page 162*

AVACARE MEDICAL

https://avacaremedical.com

AVACARE MEDICAL SCHOLARSHIP
• *See page 105*

BHW GROUP

https://thebhwgroup.com/

BHW WOMEN IN STEM SCHOLARSHIP
• *See page 74*

CANFIT

http://www.canfit.org/

CANFIT NUTRITION, PHYSICAL EDUCATION AND CULINARY ARTS SCHOLARSHIP
• *See page 229*

THE CULINARY TRUST

http://www.theculinarytrust.org/

CULINARY TRUST SCHOLARSHIP PROGRAM FOR CULINARY STUDY AND RESEARCH
• *See page 229*

GREAT MINDS IN STEM

www.greatmindsinstem.org

HISPANIC ENGINEER NATIONAL ACHIEVEMENT AWARDS CORPORATION SCHOLARSHIP PROGRAM
• *See page 106*

HOMEKITCHENARY

http://homekitchenary.com

SHARE YOUR STORY WITH HOMEKITCHENARY

Homekitchenary is starting a breast cancer awareness campaign named Share your story with Homekitchenary. Sharing your personal story can provide solace to yourself and offer hope for others. In this campaign, we will award a scholarship of up to $1,000 to a college-bound high school senior who is living with a parent who has a life-threatening illness, breast cancer patients, and survivors.

Academic Fields/Career Goals: Food Science/Nutrition; Food Service/Hospitality; Social Sciences; Travel/Tourism; Women's Studies.

Award: Scholarship for use in freshman or sophomore years; renewable. *Number:* 2. *Amount:* $1000.

Eligibility Requirements: Applicant must be enrolled or expecting to enroll full- or part-time at a technical institution or university and female. Applicant must have 3.5 GPA or higher. Available to U.S. citizens.

Application Requirements: Essay, personal photograph, portfolio. *Deadline:* June 30.

Contact: Edna Francis
  E-mail: scholarships@homekitchenary.com

ILLINOIS RESTAURANT ASSOCIATION EDUCATIONAL FOUNDATION

http://www.illinoisrestaurants.org/

ILLINOIS RESTAURANT ASSOCIATION EDUCATIONAL FOUNDATION SCHOLARSHIPS
• See page 229

INSTITUTE OF FOOD TECHNOLOGISTS

http://www.ift.org/

EDLONG DAIRY TECHNOLOGIES SCHOLARSHIP

One $2,000 scholarship to a graduate student and one $1,000 scholarship to a junior/senior undergraduate student. The student must be enrolled in a Master's or Ph.D. food science program with a focus in dairy science and/or dairy flavors or pursuing an undergraduate degree in food science with a focus in dairy flavors and/or dairy science at an IFT approved university. Minimum 3.0 GPA required.

Academic Fields/Career Goals: Food Science/Nutrition.

Award: Scholarship for use in junior, senior, graduate, or postgraduate years; not renewable. *Number:* 1. *Amount:* $1000.

Eligibility Requirements: Applicant must be enrolled or expecting to enroll full-time at a four-year institution or university. Applicant must have 3.0 GPA or higher. Available to U.S. and non-U.S. citizens.

Application Requirements: Application form. *Deadline:* February 15.

Contact: IFT Foundation Coordinator
  Institute of Food Technologists
  525 West Van Buren, Suite 1000
  Chicago, IL 60607
  Phone: 312-782-8424
  E-mail: info@ift.org

EVAN TUREK MEMORIAL SCHOLARSHIP
• See page 98

EVAN TUREK MEMORIAL SCHOLARSHIP AND INTERNSHIP
• See page 98

FEEDING TOMORROW FRESHMAN SCHOLARSHIP

$1000 scholarship for high school seniors who demonstrate exceptional scholastic achievements, leadership experience, and a keen interest in the food science and technology profession. Must be pursuing an undergraduate degree in food science within an IFT-approved food science program.

Academic Fields/Career Goals: Food Science/Nutrition.

Award: Scholarship for use in freshman year; not renewable. *Amount:* $1000.

Eligibility Requirements: Applicant must be high school student and planning to enroll or expecting to enroll full-time at a four-year institution or university. Applicant must have 3.0 GPA or higher. Available to U.S. citizens.

Application Requirements: Application form. *Deadline:* April 15.

Contact: IFT Foundation Coordinator
  Institute of Food Technologists
  525 West Van Buren, Suite 1000
  Chicago, IL 60607
  Phone: 312-782-8424
  E-mail: info@ift.org

FEEDING TOMORROW UNDERGRADUATE GENERAL EDUCATION SCHOLARSHIPS

Multiple scholarships for college sophomores, juniors, and seniors demonstrating exceptional scholastic achievements, leadership

experience and a devotion to the food science and technology profession. Minimum 3.0 GPA required.

Academic Fields/Career Goals: Food Science/Nutrition.

Award: Scholarship for use in freshman, sophomore, junior, or senior years; not renewable. *Amount:* $1000–$2500.

Eligibility Requirements: Applicant must be enrolled or expecting to enroll full-time at a four-year institution or university. Applicant must have 3.0 GPA or higher. Available to U.S. and non-U.S. citizens.

Application Requirements: Application form. *Deadline:* February 15.

Contact: IFT Foundation Coordinator
  Institute of Food Technologists
  525 West Van Buren, Suite 1000
  Chicago, IL 60607
  Phone: 312-782-8424
  E-mail: info@ift.org

IFT FOOD ENGINEERING DIVISION SCHOLARSHIP

Available to an undergraduate student who will pursue a research project focusing on any aspect of food process engineering. The research will occur during the academic year or summer. Applicant must be a student member of IFT at the time of application. Will submit a recommendation letter from a research mentor who is a member of the Food Engineering Division of IFT stating that the mentor will supervise the student to do research in their lab.

Academic Fields/Career Goals: Food Science/Nutrition.

Award: Scholarship for use in sophomore, junior, or senior years; not renewable. *Number:* 1. *Amount:* $1000.

Eligibility Requirements: Applicant must be enrolled or expecting to enroll full-time at a four-year institution or university. Applicant must have 3.0 GPA or higher. Available to U.S. and non-U.S. citizens.

Application Requirements: Application form. *Deadline:* February 15.

Contact: IFT Foundation Coordinator
  Institute of Food Technologists
  525 West Van Buren, Suite 1000
  Chicago, IL 60607
  Phone: 312-782-8424
  E-mail: info@ift.org

IFT FOOD MICROBIOLOGY DIVISION UNDERGRADUATE SCHOLARSHIP

$1000 scholarship available to an undergraduate student studying food microbiology. Minimum 3.0 GPA required. Applicant must be a student member of IFT at the time of application.

Academic Fields/Career Goals: Food Science/Nutrition.

Award: Scholarship for use in sophomore, junior, or senior years; not renewable. *Number:* 1. *Amount:* $1000.

Eligibility Requirements: Applicant must be enrolled or expecting to enroll full-time at a four-year institution or university. Applicant must have 3.0 GPA or higher. Available to U.S. and non-U.S. citizens.

Application Requirements: Application form. *Deadline:* February 15.

Contact: IFT Foundation Coordinator
  Institute of Food Technologists
  525 West Van Buren, Suite 1000
  Chicago, IL 60607
  Phone: 312-782-8424
  E-mail: info@ift.org

INSTITUTE FOR THERMAL PROCESSING SPECIALISTS IRVING PFLUG MEMORIAL SCHOLARSHIP

One $1500 scholarship for an undergraduate student studying food science, food engineering, or food microbiology as it relates to food preservation. Minimum 3.0 GPA required. Must reapply each year. Applicant must be a student member of IFT at the time of application.

Academic Fields/Career Goals: Food Science/Nutrition.

Award: Scholarship for use in junior or senior years; not renewable. *Number:* 1. *Amount:* $1500.

Eligibility Requirements: Applicant must be enrolled or expecting to enroll full-time at a four-year institution or university. Applicant must have 3.0 GPA or higher. Available to U.S. and non-U.S. citizens.

Application Requirements: Application form. *Deadline:* February 15.

Contact: IFT Foundation Coordinator
Institute of Food Technologists
525 West Van Buren, Suite 1000
Chicago, IL 60607
Phone: 312-782-8424
E-mail: info@ift.org

KRAFT HEINZ RESEARCH SCHOLARSHIP
• *See page 99*

PEPSICO SCHOLARSHIP AND INTERNSHIP

One scholarship and internship at PepsiCo in New York. Applicant must be enrolled in an IFT approved undergraduate or graduate program at the standing of junior or above, majoring in biochemistry, dairy science, food chemistry, food packaging, non-thermal processing or related discipline. Applicant must demonstrate exceptional leadership experience and be an IFT member at the time of application. Must have 3.0 cumulative GPA in food science.

Academic Fields/Career Goals: Food Science/Nutrition; Physical Sciences.

Award: Scholarship for use in junior, senior, or graduate years; not renewable. *Number:* 1. *Amount:* $1000.

Eligibility Requirements: Applicant must be enrolled or expecting to enroll full-time at a four-year institution or university. Applicant must have 3.0 GPA or higher. Available to U.S. citizens.

Application Requirements: Application form, interview. *Deadline:* October 15.

Contact: IFT Foundation Coordinator
Institute of Food Technologists
525 West Van Buren, Suite 1000
Chicago, IL 60607
Phone: 312-782-8424
E-mail: info@ift.org

INTERNATIONAL FOODSERVICE EDITORIAL COUNCIL
http://www.ifeconline.com/

INTERNATIONAL FOODSERVICE EDITORIAL COUNCIL COMMUNICATIONS SCHOLARSHIP
• *See page 88*

JAMES BEARD FOUNDATION INC.
http://www.jamesbeard.org/

BERN LAXER MEMORIAL SCHOLARSHIP
• *See page 230*

LES DAMES D'ESCOFFIER INTERNATIONAL, COLORADO CHAPTER
www.lesdamescolorado.org

LES DAMES D'ESCOFFIER INTERNATIONAL, COLORADO CHAPTER SCHOLARSHIP
• *See page 93*

MEDICAL SCRUBS COLLECTION
http://medicalscrubscollection.com

MEDICAL SCRUBS COLLECTION SCHOLARSHIP
• *See page 106*

MICHAEL MOODY FITNESS
http://www.michaelmoodyfitness.com/

MICHAEL MOODY FITNESS SCHOLARSHIP
• *See page 255*

NATIONAL DAIRY SHRINE
http://www.dairyshrine.org/

NATIONAL DAIRY SHRINE/DAIRY MARKETING INC. MILK MARKETING SCHOLARSHIPS
• *See page 100*

NDS STUDENT RECOGNITION AWARD
• *See page 94*

NATIONAL POULTRY AND FOOD DISTRIBUTORS ASSOCIATION
http://www.npfda.org/

NATIONAL POULTRY AND FOOD DISTRIBUTORS ASSOCIATION SCHOLARSHIP FOUNDATION
• *See page 94*

NEXTSTEPU
http://www.nextstepu.com/

$1,500 STEM SCHOLARSHIP
• *See page 106*

OREGON STUDENT ASSISTANCE COMMISSION
http://www.GetCollegeFunds.org/

OREGON WINE BROTHERHOOD SCHOLARSHIP
• *See page 232*

PROFESSIONAL REPS
http://www.professionalreps.com/

HUNGRY TO LEAD SCHOLARSHIP
• *See page 232*

SCARLETT FAMILY FOUNDATION SCHOLARSHIP PROGRAM
http://www.scarlettfoundation.org/

SCHOLARSHIP FOR STUDENTS PURSUING A BUSINESS OR STEM DEGREE
• *See page 84*

SCHOOL NUTRITION FOUNDATION
https://schoolnutrition.org/snf/

NANCY CURRY SCHOLARSHIP

Scholarship assists members of the American School Food Service Association and their dependents to pursue educational and career advancement in school food-service or child nutrition.

Academic Fields/Career Goals: Food Science/Nutrition; Food Service/Hospitality.

Award: Scholarship for use in freshman, sophomore, junior, senior, graduate, or postgraduate years; not renewable.

Eligibility Requirements: Applicant must be enrolled or expecting to enroll full- or part-time at a two- or four-year or technical institution or university. Applicant or parent of applicant must have employment or volunteer experience in food service. Applicant must have 3.0 GPA or higher. Available to U.S. citizens.

Application Requirements: Application form, essay, proof of enrollment, recommendations or references, resume, test scores, transcript. *Deadline:* April 15.

Contact: Ruth O'Brien, Scholarship Manager
School Nutrition Foundation
700 South Washington Street, Suite 300
Alexandria, VA 22314
Phone: 703-739-3900 Ext. 150
E-mail: robrien@asfsa.org

PROFESSIONAL GROWTH SCHOLARSHIP

Scholarships for child nutrition professionals who are pursuing graduate education in a food science management or nutrition-related field of study.

Academic Fields/Career Goals: Food Science/Nutrition; Food Service/Hospitality.

Award: Scholarship for use in freshman, sophomore, junior, senior, graduate, or postgraduate years; not renewable.

Eligibility Requirements: Applicant must be enrolled or expecting to enroll full- or part-time at a two-year or four-year or technical institution or university. Applicant or parent of applicant must have employment or volunteer experience in food service. Applicant must have 3.5 GPA or higher. Available to U.S. citizens.

Application Requirements: Application form, essay, proof of enrollment, official program requirement, recommendations or references, resume, transcript. *Deadline:* April 15.

Contact: Scholarship Manager
School Nutrition Foundation
700 South Washington Street, Suite 300
Alexandria, VA 22314
Phone: 703-739-3900 Ext. 150
Fax: 703-739-3915
E-mail: robrien@asfsa.org

SCHWAN'S FOOD SERVICE SCHOLARSHIP

Program is designed to assist members of the American School Food Service Association and their dependents as they pursue educational advancement in the field of child nutrition.

Academic Fields/Career Goals: Food Science/Nutrition; Food Service/Hospitality.

Award: Scholarship for use in freshman, sophomore, junior, senior, graduate, or postgraduate years; not renewable.

Eligibility Requirements: Applicant must be enrolled or expecting to enroll full- or part-time at a two-year or four-year or technical institution or university. Applicant or parent of applicant must have employment or volunteer experience in food service. Applicant must have 2.5 GPA or higher. Available to U.S. citizens.

Application Requirements: Application form, essay, proof of enrollment, official program requirements, recommendations or references, resume, transcript. *Deadline:* April 15.

Contact: Ruth O'Brien, Scholarship Manager
School Nutrition Foundation
700 South Washington Street, Suite 300
Alexandria, VA 22314
Phone: 703-739-3900 Ext. 150
E-mail: robrien@asfsa.org

SOIL AND WATER CONSERVATION SOCIETY

http://www.swcs.org

DONALD A. WILLIAMS SCHOLARSHIP SOIL CONSERVATION SCHOLARSHIP
• *See page 95*

UNITED DAUGHTERS OF THE CONFEDERACY

http://www.hqudc.org/

WALTER REED SMITH SCHOLARSHIP
• *See page 168*

UNITED STATES DEPARTMENT OF AGRICULTURE

http://www.usda.gov/

USDA/1994 TRIBAL SCHOLARS PROGRAM
• *See page 102*

WASHINGTON ASSOCIATION OF WINE GRAPE GROWERS

http://www.wawgg.org/

WALTER J. CLORE SCHOLARSHIP
• *See page 103*

WISCONSIN ASSOCIATION FOR FOOD PROTECTION

http://www.wifoodprotection.org

E.H. MARTH FOOD PROTECTION AND FOOD SCIENCES SCHOLARSHIP
• *See page 317*

WISCONSIN BAKERS ASSOCIATION (WBA)

http://www.wibakers.com/

ROBERT W. HILLER SCHOLARSHIP FUND
• *See page 233*

WBA SCHOLARSHIP
• *See page 233*

FOOD SERVICE/ HOSPITALITY

AMERICAN HOTEL AND LODGING EDUCATIONAL FOUNDATION

http://www.ahlef.org/

AH&LEF ANNUAL SCHOLARSHIP GRANT PROGRAM
• *See page 227*

AMERICAN HOTEL & LODGING EDUCATIONAL FOUNDATION PEPSI SCHOLARSHIP
• *See page 228*

ECOLAB SCHOLARSHIP PROGRAM
• *See page 228*

HYATT HOTELS FUND FOR MINORITY LODGING MANAGEMENT
• *See page 228*

INCOMING FRESHMAN SCHOLARSHIPS
• *See page 228*

RAMA SCHOLARSHIP FOR THE AMERICAN DREAM
• *See page 228*

AMERICAN INSTITUTE OF WINE AND FOOD-PACIFIC NORTHWEST CHAPTER

http://www.aiwf.org/

CULINARY, VINIFERA, AND HOSPITALITY SCHOLARSHIP
• *See page 331*

CALIFORNIA RESTAURANT ASSOCIATION EDUCATIONAL FOUNDATION

http://www.calrest.org/

ACADEMIC SCHOLARSHIP FOR HIGH SCHOOL SENIORS

One-time scholarship awarded to high school seniors to support their education in the restaurant and/or food service industry. Applicants must be citizens of the United States or its territories (American Samoa, Guam, Puerto Rico, and U.S. Virgin Islands).

Academic Fields/Career Goals: Food Service/Hospitality.

Award: Scholarship for use in freshman year; not renewable. *Amount:* up to $2000.

Eligibility Requirements: Applicant must be high school student; planning to enroll or expecting to enroll full-time at a two-year or four-year or technical institution or university and resident of California. Applicant must have 2.5 GPA or higher. Available to U.S. and non-U.S. citizens.

Application Requirements: Application form, essay, interview, recommendations or references, resume, transcript. *Deadline:* April 15.

Contact: Mrs. Kathie Griley, Director, Industry Education
Phone: 800-765-4842 Ext. 2756
E-mail: kgriley@calrest.org

ACADEMIC SCHOLARSHIP FOR UNDERGRADUATE STUDENTS

Scholarships awarded to college students to support their education in the restaurant and food service industry. Minimum 2.75 GPA required. Individuals must be citizens of the United States or its territories (American Samoa, Guam, Puerto Rico, and U.S. Virgin Islands).

Academic Fields/Career Goals: Food Service/Hospitality.

Award: Scholarship for use in freshman, sophomore, junior, or senior years; not renewable.

Eligibility Requirements: Applicant must be enrolled or expecting to enroll full-time at a four-year institution or university and resident of California. Applicant must have 2.5 GPA or higher. Available to U.S. and non-U.S. citizens.

Application Requirements: Application form, essay, interview, recommendations or references, transcript. *Deadline:* March 31.

Contact: Mrs. Kathie Griley, Director, Industry Education
Phone: 800-765-4842 Ext. 2756
E-mail: kgriley@calrest.org

CANFIT

http://www.canfit.org/

CANFIT NUTRITION, PHYSICAL EDUCATION AND CULINARY ARTS SCHOLARSHIP
• *See page 229*

COLORADO RESTAURANT ASSOCIATION

http://www.coloradorestaurant.com/

CRA UNDERGRADUATE SCHOLARSHIPS

Scholarship of $1000 to $2000 for applicants intending to pursue education in the undergraduate level in the field of food service or hospitality and have a GPA of at least 2.75.

Academic Fields/Career Goals: Food Service/Hospitality.

Award: Scholarship for use in freshman, sophomore, junior, or senior years; not renewable. *Number:* 15. *Amount:* $1000–$2000.

Eligibility Requirements: Applicant must be enrolled or expecting to enroll full- or part-time at a four-year institution or university. Available to U.S. and non-U.S. citizens.

Application Requirements: Application form, recommendations or references, resume, transcript. *Deadline:* April 6.

Contact: Mary Mino, President
Phone: 800-522-2972
Fax: 303-830-2973
E-mail: info@coloradorestaurant.com

PROSTART SCHOLARSHIPS

Scholarship of $500 to $1000 for applicants currently in high school and intending to pursue education in the field of food service or hospitality and have a GPA of at least 3.0.

Academic Fields/Career Goals: Food Service/Hospitality.

Award: Scholarship for use in freshman year; not renewable. *Number:* 15. *Amount:* $500–$1000.

Eligibility Requirements: Applicant must be high school student and planning to enroll or expecting to enroll full- or part-time at a four-year institution or university. Applicant must have 3.0 GPA or higher. Available to U.S. and non-U.S. citizens.

Application Requirements: Application form, recommendations or references, resume, transcript. *Deadline:* April 6.

Contact: Mary Mino, President
Phone: 800-522-2972
Fax: 303-830-2973
E-mail: info@coloradorestaurant.com

THE CULINARY TRUST

http://www.theculinarytrust.org/

CULINARY TRUST SCHOLARSHIP PROGRAM FOR CULINARY STUDY AND RESEARCH
• *See page 229*

DECA (DISTRIBUTIVE EDUCATION CLUBS OF AMERICA)

http://www.deca.org/

HARRY A. APPLEGATE SCHOLARSHIP
• *See page 75*

GOLDEN GATE RESTAURANT ASSOCIATION

http://www.ggra.org/

GOLDEN GATE RESTAURANT ASSOCIATION SCHOLARSHIP FOUNDATION
• *See page 229*

HOMEKITCHENARY

http://homekitchenary.com

SHARE YOUR STORY WITH HOMEKITCHENARY
• *See page 331*

ILLINOIS RESTAURANT ASSOCIATION EDUCATIONAL FOUNDATION

http://www.illinoisrestaurants.org/

ILLINOIS RESTAURANT ASSOCIATION EDUCATIONAL FOUNDATION SCHOLARSHIPS
• *See page 229*

INTERNATIONAL EXECUTIVE HOUSEKEEPERS ASSOCIATION

http://www.ieha.org/

INTERNATIONAL EXECUTIVE HOUSEKEEPERS EDUCATIONAL FOUNDATION

One-time award of up to $1000 for students planning careers in the area of facilities management. Awards are for enrollment in IEHA-approved self-study courses. Must be a member of IEHA.

Academic Fields/Career Goals: Food Service/Hospitality; Home Economics; Trade/Technical Specialties.

Award: Scholarship for use in freshman, sophomore, junior, or senior years; not renewable. *Number:* 1–2. *Amount:* $500–$1000.

Eligibility Requirements: Applicant must be enrolled or expecting to enroll full- or part-time at a two-year or four-year or technical institution or university. Applicant or parent of applicant must be member of International Executive Housekeepers Association. Available to U.S. and non-U.S. citizens.

Application Requirements: Application form, essay. *Deadline:* January 10.

Contact: Mary Remson, Executive Director
International Executive Housekeepers Association
Education Department, 1001 Eastwind Drive, Suite 301
Westerville, OH 43081-3361
Phone: 800-200-6342
Fax: 614-895-7166
E-mail: excel@ieha.org

INTERNATIONAL FOODSERVICE EDITORIAL COUNCIL

http://www.ifeconline.com/

INTERNATIONAL FOODSERVICE EDITORIAL COUNCIL COMMUNICATIONS SCHOLARSHIP
• *See page 88*

INTERNATIONAL FOOD SERVICE EXECUTIVES ASSOCIATION

http://www.ifsea.com/

INTERNATIONAL FOOD SERVICE EXECUTIVES ASSOCIATION / WORTHY GOAL SCHOLARSHIP FUND

Scholarships to assist individuals in receiving food service, vocational or hospitality training beyond high school. Applicant must be enrolled or accepted as full-time student in an accredited program at an institution of higher education.

Academic Fields/Career Goals: Food Service/Hospitality.

Award: Scholarship for use in freshman, sophomore, junior, senior, graduate, or postgraduate years; not renewable. *Number:* 1–23,000. *Amount:* $1000–$2000.

Eligibility Requirements: Applicant must be enrolled or expecting to enroll full-time at a two-year or four-year or technical institution or university. Available to U.S. and non-U.S. citizens.

Application Requirements: Application form, essay, financial need analysis, financial statement summary, work experience documentation, recommendations or references, transcript. *Deadline:* March 1.

Contact: David Orosz, Chairman, Board of Trustees, Worthy Goal Foundation
International Food Service Executives Association
4435 Colchester Creek Drive
Cumming, GA 30040
Phone: 952-402-9686
Fax: 317-863-0586
E-mail: dave@orosz.us

LES DAMES D'ESCOFFIER INTERNATIONAL, COLORADO CHAPTER

www.lesdamescolorado.org

LES DAMES D'ESCOFFIER INTERNATIONAL, COLORADO CHAPTER SCHOLARSHIP
• *See page 93*

MISSOURI TRAVEL COUNCIL

http://www.missouritravel.com/

BOB SMITH TOURISM SCHOLARSHIP

One-time award for Missouri resident pursuing hospitality-related major such as hotel/restaurant management or tourism. Applicant must be currently enrolled in an accredited four-year college or university in the state of Missouri. Selection is based on responses to set-forth scholarship criteria.

Academic Fields/Career Goals: Food Service/Hospitality; Hospitality Management; Travel/Tourism.

Award: Scholarship for use in sophomore, junior, or senior years; not renewable. *Number:* 2. *Amount:* $1000.

Eligibility Requirements: Applicant must be enrolled or expecting to enroll full-time at a four-year institution or university; resident of Missouri and studying in Missouri. Applicant must have 3.0 GPA or higher. Available to U.S. citizens.

Application Requirements: Application form, essay. *Deadline:* March 1.

Contact: Mr. Chuck Martin, Executive Director
Missouri Travel Council
1505 East Riverside Drive
Cape Girardeau, MO 63701-2219
Phone: 573-803-3777
E-mail: CMartin@MissouriTravel.com

NATIONAL POULTRY AND FOOD DISTRIBUTORS ASSOCIATION

http://www.npfda.org/

NATIONAL POULTRY AND FOOD DISTRIBUTORS ASSOCIATION SCHOLARSHIP FOUNDATION
• *See page 94*

NATIONAL RESTAURANT ASSOCIATION EDUCATIONAL FOUNDATION

http://www.nraef.org/

NATIONAL RESTAURANT ASSOCIATION EDUCATIONAL FOUNDATION UNDERGRADUATE SCHOLARSHIPS FOR COLLEGE STUDENTS

Awarded to college students who have demonstrated a commitment to both postsecondary hospitality education and to a career in the industry with 750 hours of industry work experience. Minimum 2.75 GPA required. Application deadlines: March 31, July 31 and October 31.

Academic Fields/Career Goals: Food Service/Hospitality; Hospitality Management.

Award: Scholarship for use in sophomore, junior, or senior years; not renewable. *Amount:* $2000.

Eligibility Requirements: Applicant must be enrolled or expecting to enroll full- or part-time at a four-year institution or university. Applicant or parent of applicant must have employment or volunteer experience in food service. Available to U.S. citizens.

Application Requirements: Application form, copies of paycheck stubs or a letter from employers verifying total work hours, essay, recommendations or references, resume, transcript. *Deadline:* varies.

Contact: Shanna Young, Manager
Phone: 800-765-2122 Ext. 744
Fax: 312-566-9733
E-mail: syoung@nraef.org

NATIONAL RESTAURANT ASSOCIATION EDUCATIONAL FOUNDATION UNDERGRADUATE SCHOLARSHIPS FOR HIGH SCHOOL SENIORS AND GENERAL EDUCATION DIPLOMA (GED) GRADUATE S

Scholarship awarded to high school students who have demonstrated a commitment to both postsecondary hospitality education and to a career in the industry. Must have 250 hours of industry experience, be between ages of 17 and 19, and have minimum 2.75 GPA.

Academic Fields/Career Goals: Food Service/Hospitality; Hospitality Management.

Award: Scholarship for use in freshman year; not renewable. *Amount:* $2000.

Eligibility Requirements: Applicant must be age 17-19 and enrolled or expecting to enroll full-time at a four-year institution or university. Applicant or parent of applicant must have employment or volunteer experience in food service. Available to U.S. citizens.

Application Requirements: Application form, essay, letter of acceptance, industrial experience letter, recommendations or references, transcript. *Deadline:* May 16.

Contact: Shanna Young, Manager
 Phone: 800-765-2122 Ext. 744
 Fax: 312-566-9733
 E-mail: syoung@nraef.org

PROSTART® NATIONAL CERTIFICATE OF ACHIEVEMENT SCHOLARSHIP

For high school junior and senior students who have earned Pro Start National Certificate of Achievement and are continuing their education in a restaurant or foodservice program. For application and details visit website http://nraef.org.

Academic Fields/Career Goals: Food Service/Hospitality.

Award: Scholarship for use in freshman year; not renewable. *Amount:* $2000.

Eligibility Requirements: Applicant must be high school student and planning to enroll or expecting to enroll full- or part-time at a four-year institution or university. Available to U.S. citizens.

Application Requirements: Application form. *Deadline:* August 15.

Contact: Shanna Young, Manager
 Phone: 800-765-2122 Ext. 744
 Fax: 312-566-9733
 E-mail: syoung@nraef.org

PROFESSIONAL REPS

http://www.professionalreps.com/

HUNGRY TO LEAD SCHOLARSHIP
• See page 232

SCHOOL NUTRITION FOUNDATION

https://schoolnutrition.org/snf/

NANCY CURRY SCHOLARSHIP
• See page 333

PROFESSIONAL GROWTH SCHOLARSHIP
• See page 334

SCHWAN'S FOOD SERVICE SCHOLARSHIP
• See page 334

SOUTH CAROLINA RESTAURANT AND LODGING ASSOCIATION

http://www.scrla.org/

SOUTH CAROLINA TOURISM AND HOSPITALITY EDUCATIONAL FOUNDATION SCHOLARSHIPS
• See page 232

TEXAS RESTAURANT ASSOCIATION

http://www.restaurantville.com/

W. PRICE, JR. MEMORIAL SCHOLARSHIP
• See page 232

TOURISM CARES

http://www.tourismcares.org.

NEW HORIZONS KATHY LETARTE SCHOLARSHIP

One $1000 scholarship awarded to an undergraduate student entering his or her junior year of study. Applicant must be enrolled in a tourism-related program at an accredited four-year college or university. Must have minimum 3.0 GPA. Applicant must be Michigan resident. Refer to website for further details http://www.ntfonline.com/scholarships/index.php.

Academic Fields/Career Goals: Food Service/Hospitality; Hospitality Management; Travel/Tourism.

Award: Scholarship for use in freshman, sophomore, junior, or senior years; not renewable. *Number:* 1. *Amount:* $1000.

Eligibility Requirements: Applicant must be enrolled or expecting to enroll full-time at a two-year or four-year institution or university and resident of Michigan. Applicant must have 3.0 GPA or higher. Available to U.S. citizens.

Application Requirements: Application form, essay, recommendations or references, resume, transcript. *Deadline:* May 10.

Contact: Amanda D'Aiuto, Student Programs Manager
 Phone: 781-821-5990
 Fax: 781-821-8949
 E-mail: info@tourismcares.org

UNITED NEGRO COLLEGE FUND

http://www.uncf.org/

NATIONAL BLACK MCDONALD'S OWNERS ASSOCIATION HOSPITALITY SCHOLARS PROGRAM
• See page 86

WISCONSIN BAKERS ASSOCIATION (WBA)

http://www.wibakers.com/

ROBERT W. HILLER SCHOLARSHIP FUND
• See page 233

WBA SCHOLARSHIP
• See page 233

WOMEN CHEFS AND RESTAURATEURS

http://www.womenchefs.org/

FRENCH CULINARY INSTITUTE/ITALIAN CULINARY EXPERIENCE SCHOLARSHIP
• See page 233

WOMEN GROCERS OF AMERICA

http://www.nationalgrocers.org/

MARY MACEY SCHOLARSHIP
• See page 103

FOREIGN LANGUAGE

ACL/NJCL NATIONAL LATIN EXAM

http://www.nle.org/

NATIONAL LATIN EXAM SCHOLARSHIP
• *See page 200*

ALBERTA HERITAGE SCHOLARSHIP FUND

http://www.alis.alberta.ca/

FELLOWSHIPS FOR FULL-TIME STUDIES IN FRENCH

Awards of between CAN$500 and CAN$1000 per semester to assist Albertans in pursuing postsecondary studies taught in French. Must be Alberta resident, Canadian citizen, or landed immigrant, and plan to register full-time in a postsecondary program in Alberta of at least one semester in length. Must be enrolled in a minimum of three courses per semester which have French as the language of instruction. For additional information and application, see website http://alis.alberta.ca.

Academic Fields/Career Goals: Foreign Language.

Award: Scholarship for use in freshman, sophomore, junior, or senior years; not renewable.

Eligibility Requirements: Applicant must be Canadian citizen; enrolled or expecting to enroll full-time at a two-year or four-year or technical institution or university; resident of Alberta and must have an interest in French language.

Application Requirements: Application form, transcript. *Deadline:* November 15.

Contact: Scholarship Committee
    Phone: 780-427-8640
    E-mail: scholarships@gov.ab.ca

LANGUAGE BURSARY PROGRAM FOR TEACHING FNMI LANGUAGES

Award of CAN$2500 to assist Alberta teachers, Elders, or instructors who currently provide instruction of an FNMI language and intend to take a summer post-secondary program. Applicants must hold a valid Alberta professional teaching certificate or be working towards Alberta certification, have been teaching in Alberta for a minimum of one year by the end of the current school year, demonstrate a background in FNMI language learning and culture, or have recently initiated the study of an FNMI language. For additional information, see website http://alis.alberta.ca.

Academic Fields/Career Goals: Foreign Language.

Award: Scholarship for use in freshman, sophomore, junior, senior, or graduate years; not renewable. *Number:* up to 2.

Eligibility Requirements: Applicant must be Canadian citizen; enrolled or expecting to enroll full- or part-time at a two-year or four-year institution or university and resident of Alberta. Applicant or parent of applicant must have employment or volunteer experience in teaching/education.

Application Requirements: Application form, recommendations or references. *Deadline:* February 10.

Contact: Scholarship Committee
    Phone: 780-427-8640
    E-mail: scholarships@gov.ab.ca

LANGUAGES IN TEACHER EDUCATION SCHOLARSHIPS
• *See page 247*

ALPHA MU GAMMA, THE NATIONAL COLLEGIATE FOREIGN LANGUAGE SOCIETY

http://www.amgnational.org/

NATIONAL ALPHA MU GAMMA SCHOLARSHIPS

One-time award to student members of Alpha Mu Gamma with a minimum 3.5 GPA, who plan to continue study of a foreign language. Must participate in a national scholarship competition. Apply through local chapter advisers. Freshmen are not eligible. Must submit a copy of Alpha Mu Gamma membership certificate. Can study overseas if part of his/her school program.

Academic Fields/Career Goals: Foreign Language.

Award: Scholarship for use in sophomore, junior, or senior years; not renewable. *Number:* 2–3. *Amount:* $500–$1000.

Eligibility Requirements: Applicant must be enrolled or expecting to enroll full- or part-time at a two-year or four-year institution or university. Applicant or parent of applicant must be member of Alpha Mu Gamma. Applicant must have 3.5 GPA or higher. Available to U.S. and non-U.S. citizens.

Application Requirements: Application form, essay. *Deadline:* February 1.

Contact: Ms. Leslie Brazier, Administrative Assistant
    Alpha Mu Gamma, The National Collegiate Foreign Language Society
    1073 North Benson Rd.
    Department of Modern Languages and Literatures-- Fairfield University
    Fairfield, CT 06824
    Phone: 203-254-4000 Ext. 2676
    E-mail: AMGNational@fairfield.edu

AMERICAN CLASSICAL LEAGUE/NATIONAL JUNIOR CLASSICAL LEAGUE

http://www.aclclassics.org/

NATIONAL JUNIOR CLASSICAL LEAGUE SCHOLARSHIP
• *See page 200*

AMERICAN FOUNDATION FOR TRANSLATION AND INTERPRETATION

http://www.afti.org/

AFTI SCHOLARSHIPS IN SCIENTIFIC AND TECHNICAL TRANSLATION, LITERARY TRANSLATION, AND INTERPRETATION

AFTI offers various awards and scholarships for translators and interpreters. Please see www.afti.org.

Academic Fields/Career Goals: Foreign Language.

Award: Scholarship for use in sophomore, junior, or senior years; not renewable. *Number:* 1–3. *Amount:* $500–$1000.

Eligibility Requirements: Applicant must be enrolled or expecting to enroll full-time at a four-year institution or university.

Application Requirements: Application form. *Deadline:* June 1.

Contact: Walter Bacak, Executive Directorary
    American Foundation for Translation and Interpretation
    225 Reinekers Lane, Suite 590
    Alexandria, VA 22314
    Phone: 703-683-6100
    E-mail: walter@atanet.org

AMERICAN INSTITUTE OF POLISH CULTURE INC.

http://www.ampolinstitute.org/

HARRIET IRSAY SCHOLARSHIP GRANT
• *See page 127*

ASSOCIATION OF FORMER INTELLIGENCE OFFICERS

http://www.afio.com

AFIO UNDERGRADUATE AND GRADUATE SCHOLARSHIPS
• *See page 103*

CULTURAL SERVICES OF THE FRENCH EMBASSY

http://www.frenchculture.org/

TEACHING ASSISTANT PROGRAM IN FRANCE
• *See page 104*

GERMAN ACADEMIC EXCHANGE SERVICE (DAAD)

http://www.daad.org/

DAAD UNIVERSITY SUMMER COURSE GRANT

Scholarships are awarded to full-time degree students of Canadian or US colleges, sophomore/2nd year and higher, for the pursuit of summer courses at universities in Germany. It is open to applicants of any major but there is a prerequisite of at least two years of college level German or the equivalent German language fluency. Courses are three to four weeks in duration, take place at many locations in Germany (universities), are taught in German, and topics include German language, literature, current affairs, political science, history, culture, arts, film and media, economics, linguistics, law, translation and interpretation, and test prep for German language proficiency examinations. Accommodations are arranged by the host institution.

Academic Fields/Career Goals: Foreign Language.

Award: Grant for use in sophomore, junior, senior, or graduate years; not renewable.

Eligibility Requirements: Applicant must be enrolled or expecting to enroll full-time at a four-year institution or university and must have an interest in German language/culture. Available to U.S. and non-U.S. citizens.

Application Requirements: Application form, essay. *Deadline:* December 15.

Contact: DAAD New York
German Academic Exchange Service (DAAD)
871 UN Plaza
New York, NY 10017
Phone: 212-758-3223
E-mail: daadny@daad.org

KOSCIUSZKO FOUNDATION

http://www.thekf.org

YEAR ABROAD PROGRAM IN POLAND
• *See page 125*

NATIONAL ASSOCIATION OF HISPANIC JOURNALISTS (NAHJ)

http://www.nahj.org/

MARIA ELENA SALINAS SCHOLARSHIP

One-time scholarship for high school seniors, college undergraduates, and first-year graduate students who are pursuing careers in Spanish-language broadcast (radio or TV) journalism. Students may major or plan to major in any subject, but must demonstrate a sincere desire to pursue a career in this field. Must submit essays and demo tapes (audio or video) in Spanish. Scholarship includes the opportunity to serve an internship with Univision Spanish-language television news network.

Academic Fields/Career Goals: Foreign Language; Journalism; TV/Radio Broadcasting.

Award: Scholarship for use in freshman, sophomore, junior, senior, or graduate years; not renewable. *Number:* 2. *Amount:* $5000.

Eligibility Requirements: Applicant must be enrolled or expecting to enroll full-time at a four-year institution or university and must have an interest in Spanish language. Available to U.S. citizens.

Application Requirements: Application form, driver's license, essay, financial need analysis, recommendations or references, resume, transcript. *Deadline:* March 31.

Contact: Virginia Galindo, Program Assistant
Phone: 202-662-7145
E-mail: vgalindo@nahj.org

NATIONAL SECURITY EDUCATION PROGRAM

http://www.iie.org/

NATIONAL SECURITY EDUCATION PROGRAM (NSEP) DAVID L. BOREN UNDERGRADUATE SCHOLARSHIPS
• *See page 126*

NORWICH JUBILEE ESPERANTO FOUNDATION

http://www.esperanto-gb.org/

NOJEF TRAVEL GRANTS

Grants to help young Esperanto-speakers to use and improve their knowledge of the language, by traveling to congresses, and summer courses. Applicant must already speak Esperanto sufficiently well enough to take part in planned activity, and should be under 26 years old. For more information, refer to website http://www.esperanto-gb.org/nojef/nojef-en.htm.

Academic Fields/Career Goals: Foreign Language.

Award: Grant for use in freshman, sophomore, junior, senior, or graduate years; not renewable. *Number:* 1–20. *Amount:* $64–$1600.

Eligibility Requirements: Applicant must be enrolled or expecting to enroll full- or part-time at a two-year or four-year or technical institution or university and must have an interest in Spanish language. Available to U.S. and non-U.S. citizens.

Application Requirements: Application form, essay, recommendations or references. *Deadline:* continuous.

Contact: Dr. Kathleen Hall, Scholarship Committee
Norwich Jubilee Esperanto Foundation
37 Granville Court, Cheney Lane
Oxford OX3 0HS
GBR
Phone: 44-1865-245-509

SOCIETY FOR CLASSICAL STUDIES

http://www.classicalstudies.org/

MINORITY STUDENT SUMMER SCHOLARSHIP
• *See page 118*

SONS OF ITALY FOUNDATION

http://www.osia.org/

SONS OF ITALY NATIONAL LEADERSHIP GRANTS COMPETITION LANGUAGE SCHOLARSHIP

Scholarships for undergraduate students in their junior or senior year of study who are majoring in Italian language studies. Must be a U.S. citizen of Italian descent. For more details see website http://www.osia.org.

Academic Fields/Career Goals: Foreign Language.

Award: Scholarship for use in junior or senior years; not renewable. *Number:* up to 1. *Amount:* $4000–$10,000.

Eligibility Requirements: Applicant must be of Italian heritage and enrolled or expecting to enroll full-time at a four-year institution or university. Available to U.S. citizens.

Application Requirements: Application form, essay, recommendations or references, resume, test scores, transcript. *Fee:* $30. *Deadline:* February 28.

Contact: Ms. Laura Kelly, Scholarship Coordinator
Phone: 202-547-2900
E-mail: scholarships@osia.org

STRAIGHTFORWARD MEDIA

http://www.straightforwardmedia.com/

STRAIGHTFORWARD MEDIA LIBERAL ARTS SCHOLARSHIP

• *See page 126*

UNITED NATIONS ASSOCIATION OF CONNECTICUT

http://www.unausa.org

UNITED NATIONS ASSOCIATION OF CONNECTICUT SCHOLARSHIP

• *See page 133*

FUNERAL SERVICES/ MORTUARY SCIENCE

ALABAMA FUNERAL DIRECTORS ASSOCIATION INC.

http://www.alabamafda.org/

ALABAMA FUNERAL DIRECTORS ASSOCIATION SCHOLARSHIP

Two $1000 scholarships available to Alabama residents. Applicant must have been accepted by an accredited mortuary science school and be sponsored by a member of the AFDA. Must maintain a minimum 2.5 GPA. Deadline: no later than 30 days prior to the AFDA mid winter meeting and annual convention.

Academic Fields/Career Goals: Funeral Services/Mortuary Science.

Award: Scholarship for use in freshman, sophomore, junior, or senior years; not renewable. *Number:* 2. *Amount:* $1000.

Eligibility Requirements: Applicant must be enrolled or expecting to enroll full- or part-time at a four-year institution or university and resident of Alabama. Applicant must have 2.5 GPA or higher. Available to U.S. citizens.

Application Requirements: Application form, essay, personal photograph, recommendations or references, transcript, two proofs of residency (such as voter registration, drivers license, or tax returns). *Deadline:* varies.

Contact: Denise Edmisten, Executive Director
Alabama Funeral Directors Association Inc.
7956 Vaughn Road, PO Box 380
Montgomery, AL 36116
Phone: 334-956-8000
Fax: 334-956-8001

AMERICAN BOARD OF FUNERAL SERVICE EDUCATION

http://www.abfse.org/

AMERICAN BOARD OF FUNERAL SERVICE EDUCATION SCHOLARSHIPS

One-time award for students who are enrolled in an accredited funeral science education program and have completed at least one term/semester. Deadlines: March 1 and September 1. For more details see website, http//www.abfse.org.

Academic Fields/Career Goals: Funeral Services/Mortuary Science.

Award: Scholarship for use in freshman, sophomore, junior, or senior years; not renewable. *Number:* 5–15. *Amount:* $500–$2500.

Eligibility Requirements: Applicant must be enrolled or expecting to enroll full-time at a two-year or four-year institution or university. Available to U.S. and non-U.S. citizens.

Application Requirements: Application form, essay, financial need analysis, recommendations or references, transcript. *Deadline:* varies.

Contact: Dr. Michael Smith, Executive Director
American Board of Funeral Service Education
3414 Ashland Avenue Suite G
St. Joseph, MO 64506
Phone: 816-233-3747
Fax: 816-233-3793
E-mail: exdir@abfse.org

MISSOURI FUNERAL DIRECTORS & EMBALMERS ASSOCIATION

http://www.mofuneral.org/

MISSOURI FUNERAL DIRECTORS ASSOCIATION SCHOLARSHIPS

Scholarship to Missouri residents pursuing a career in funeral services or mortuary science.

Academic Fields/Career Goals: Funeral Services/Mortuary Science.

Award: Scholarship for use in freshman, sophomore, junior, or senior years; not renewable. *Number:* up to 5. *Amount:* $300–$600.

Eligibility Requirements: Applicant must be enrolled or expecting to enroll full- or part-time at a technical institution and resident of Missouri. Available to U.S. citizens.

Application Requirements: Application form, recommendations or references, resume. *Deadline:* April 15.

Contact: Don Otto, Executive Director
Missouri Funeral Directors & Embalmers Association
1105 Southwest Boulevard, Suite A
Jefferson City, MO 65109
Phone: 573-635-1661
Fax: 573-635-9494
E-mail: info@mofuneral.org

NATIONAL FUNERAL DIRECTORS AND MORTICIANS ASSOCIATION

http://www.nfdma.com/

NATIONAL FUNERAL DIRECTORS AND MORTICIANS ASSOCIATION SCHOLARSHIP

Awards for high school graduates who have preferably worked in or had one year of apprenticeship in the funeral home business.

Academic Fields/Career Goals: Funeral Services/Mortuary Science.

Award: Scholarship for use in freshman year; not renewable. *Number:* 1. *Amount:* $1500.

Eligibility Requirements: Applicant must be high school student and planning to enroll or expecting to enroll full- or part-time at a four-year institution or university. Available to U.S. citizens.

Application Requirements: Application form, recommendations or references, resume, test scores. *Deadline:* April 15.

Contact: Eva Cranford, Scholarship Coordinator
Phone: 718-625-4656
E-mail: lladyc23@aol.com

THE ORDER OF THE GOLDEN RULE FOUNDATION

http://www.ogr.org/charitable-foundation

ORDER OF THE GOLDEN RULE FOUNDATION AWARDS OF EXCELLENCE SCHOLARSHIP PROGRAM

One-time scholarship for mortuary science students to prepare for a career in funeral service. Must be enrolled in a mortuary science degree program at an accredited mortuary school, have a minimum 3.0 GPA, commit to working at an independently owned funeral home, and be scheduled to graduate within this calendar year.

Academic Fields/Career Goals: Funeral Services/Mortuary Science.

Award: Scholarship for use in freshman, sophomore, junior, or senior years; not renewable. *Number:* 2. *Amount:* $2000–$3500.

Eligibility Requirements: Applicant must be enrolled or expecting to enroll full- or part-time at a two-year or four-year or technical institution or university. Applicant must have 3.0 GPA or higher. Available to U.S. and non-U.S. citizens.

Application Requirements: Application form, community service, essay. *Deadline:* February 28.

Contact: Jessica Smith, Assistant Executive Director
The Order of the Golden Rule Foundation
9101 Burnet Road
Suite 120
Austin, TX 78758
Phone: 800-637-8030
Fax: 512-334-5514
E-mail: jsmith@ogr.org

WALLACE S. AND WILMA K. LAUGHLIN FOUNDATION TRUST

http://www.nefda.org/

SWANSON SCHOLARSHIP

Scholarship for a Nebraska student entering the mortuary science program at a Kansas City community college. Must be a US citizen, a high school graduate and have completed Nebraska pre-mortuary science hours. Scholarship value and number of awards varies annually.

Academic Fields/Career Goals: Funeral Services/Mortuary Science.

Award: Scholarship for use in junior or senior years; not renewable. *Number:* 1–10. *Amount:* $1000–$10,000.

Eligibility Requirements: Applicant must be enrolled or expecting to enroll full-time at a two-year institution and resident of Nebraska. Available to U.S. citizens.

Application Requirements: Application form, financial need analysis, interview. *Deadline:* June 30.

Contact: Craig Draucker, Chairman
Wallace S. and Wilma K. Laughlin Foundation Trust
PO Box 10
521 First Street
Milford, NE 68405
Phone: 402-761-2217
E-mail: Staff@nefda.org

GEMOLOGY

AMERICAN INDIAN SCIENCE AND ENGINEERING SOCIETY

http://www.aises.org/

A.T. ANDERSON MEMORIAL SCHOLARSHIP PROGRAM
• See page 109

ASSOCIATION FOR WOMEN GEOSCIENTISTS (AWG)

http://www.awg.org/

AWG ETHNIC MINORITY SCHOLARSHIP
• See page 241

AWG MARIA LUISA CRAWFORD FIELD CAMP SCHOLARSHIP
• See page 117

LONE STAR RISING CAREER SCHOLARSHIP
• See page 242

OSAGE CHAPTER UNDERGRADUATE SERVICE SCHOLARSHIP
• See page 117

BHW GROUP

https://thebhwgroup.com/

BHW WOMEN IN STEM SCHOLARSHIP
• See page 74

GEOGRAPHY

AMERICAN ALPINE CLUB

https://americanalpineclub.org/

AAC RESEARCH GRANTS
• See page 153

AMERICAN ASSOCIATION OF GEOGRAPHERS

http://www.aag.org/

DARREL HESS COMMUNITY COLLEGE GEOGRAPHY SCHOLARSHIPS

Two $1,000 scholarships will be awarded to students from community colleges, junior colleges, city colleges, or similar two-year educational institutions who will be transferring as geography majors to four year colleges and universities.

Academic Fields/Career Goals: Geography.

Award: Grant for use in junior year; not renewable. *Number:* 2–4. *Amount:* $1000.

Eligibility Requirements: Applicant must be enrolled or expecting to enroll full-time at a two-year institution. Applicant must have 3.5 GPA or higher. Available to U.S. and non-U.S. citizens.

Application Requirements: *Deadline:* November 1.

Contact: Ms. Candida Mannozzi, Deputy Direcetor for Operations
American Association of Geographers
1710 16th Street, NW
Washington, DC 20009
Phone: 202-234-1450
E-mail: grantsawards@aag.org

AMERICAN INDIAN SCIENCE AND ENGINEERING SOCIETY

http://www.aises.org/

A.T. ANDERSON MEMORIAL SCHOLARSHIP PROGRAM
• See page 109

ASSOCIATION FOR WOMEN GEOSCIENTISTS (AWG)

http://www.awg.org/

AWG ETHNIC MINORITY SCHOLARSHIP
• See page 241

AWG SALT LAKE CHAPTER (SLC) RESEARCH SCHOLARSHIP
• See page 117

OSAGE CHAPTER UNDERGRADUATE SERVICE SCHOLARSHIP
• See page 117

BHW GROUP

https://thebhwgroup.com/

BHW WOMEN IN STEM SCHOLARSHIP
• *See page 74*

BROWN AND CALDWELL

http://www.brownandcaldwell.com

ECKENFELDER SCHOLARSHIP
• *See page 155*

MINORITY SCHOLARSHIP PROGRAM
• *See page 155*

GAMMA THETA UPSILON-INTERNATIONAL GEOGRAPHIC HONOR SOCIETY

http://www.gtuhonors.org/

BUZZARD-MAXFIELD-RICHASON AND RECHLIN SCHOLARSHIP
Award is granted to a student who is a Gamma Theta Upsilon member, majoring in geography, will be a senior undergraduate and who has been accepted into a graduate program in geography.

Academic Fields/Career Goals: Geography.

Award: Scholarship for use in senior or graduate years; not renewable. *Number:* 5. *Amount:* $1000.

Eligibility Requirements: Applicant must be enrolled or expecting to enroll full-time at a four-year institution or university. Applicant or parent of applicant must be member of Gamma Theta Upsilon. Applicant must have 3.0 GPA or higher. Available to U.S. and non-U.S. citizens.

Application Requirements: Application form, recommendations or references, transcript. *Deadline:* May 31.

Contact: Dr. Donald Zeigler, Scholarship Committee
Gamma Theta Upsilon-International Geographic Honor Society
Old Dominion University
1881 University Drive
Virginia Beach, VA 23453
E-mail: dzeigler@odu.edu

NASA IDAHO SPACE GRANT CONSORTIUM

http://www.id.spacegrant.org/

NASA IDAHO SPACE GRANT CONSORTIUM SCHOLARSHIP PROGRAM
• *See page 157*

SCARLETT FAMILY FOUNDATION SCHOLARSHIP PROGRAM

http://www.scarlettfoundation.org/

SCHOLARSHIP FOR STUDENTS PURSUING A BUSINESS OR STEM DEGREE
• *See page 84*

SIGMA XI, THE SCIENTIFIC RESEARCH SOCIETY

http://www.sigmaxi.org/

SIGMA XI GRANTS-IN-AID OF RESEARCH
• *See page 101*

GRAPHICS/GRAPHIC ARTS/PRINTING

AUTOMOTIVE WOMEN'S ALLIANCE FOUNDATION

http://www.awafoundation.org/index.php

AUTOMOTIVE WOMEN'S ALLIANCE FOUNDATION SCHOLARSHIPS
• *See page 74*

CCNMA: LATINO JOURNALISTS OF CALIFORNIA

http://www.ccnma.org/

CCNMA SCHOLARSHIPS
• *See page 203*

CONGRESSIONAL BLACK CAUCUS FOUNDATION, INC.

http://www.cbcfinc.org/

CBC SPOUSES VISUAL ARTS SCHOLARSHIP
• *See page 120*

ELECTRONIC DOCUMENT SYSTEMS FOUNDATION

http://www.edsf.org/

ANDY AND JULIE PLATA HONORARY SCHOLARSHIP
This scholarship is provided to a student in a graphic arts related program who displays an entrepreneurial spirit and is pursuing a career in the graphic communications / printing industry.

Academic Fields/Career Goals: Graphics/Graphic Arts/Printing.

Award: Scholarship for use in freshman, sophomore, junior, senior, or graduate years; not renewable. *Number:* 1. *Amount:* $2000.

Eligibility Requirements: Applicant must be enrolled or expecting to enroll full-time at a two-year or four-year or technical institution or university. Applicant must have 3.0 GPA or higher. Available to U.S. and non-U.S. citizens.

Application Requirements: Application form, community service, essay. *Deadline:* May 1.

Contact: Ms. Brenda Kai, Executive Director
Phone: 817-849-1145
E-mail: brenda.kai@edsf.org

EDSF BOARD OF DIRECTORS SCHOLARSHIPS
Scholarships awarded to full-time students who are committed to pursuing a career in the document management and graphic communications marketplace. The career choices are very broad and include, but are not limited to, computer science and engineering, graphic design, graphic communications, media communications, and business. Preference is given to college-level juniors, seniors and advanced degree students. Minimum 3.0 GPA required.

Academic Fields/Career Goals: Graphics/Graphic Arts/Printing.

Award: Scholarship for use in freshman, sophomore, junior, senior, or graduate years; not renewable. *Number:* 1–40. *Amount:* $1000–$5000.

Eligibility Requirements: Applicant must be enrolled or expecting to enroll full-time at a two-year or four-year institution or university. Applicant must have 3.0 GPA or higher. Available to U.S. and non-U.S. citizens.

Application Requirements: Application form, community service, essay. *Deadline:* May 1.

Contact: Ms. Brenda Kai, Executive Director
Phone: 817-849-1145
E-mail: brenda.kai@edsf.org

HOODS MEMORIAL SCHOLARSHIP

$2000 award for students whose academic focus includes all document management and graphic communications careers with special consideration given to students interested in marketing and public relations. Minimum 3.0 GPA required.

Academic Fields/Career Goals: Graphics/Graphic Arts/Printing.

Award: Scholarship for use in freshman, sophomore, junior, senior, or graduate years; not renewable. *Number:* 1. *Amount:* $2000.

Eligibility Requirements: Applicant must be enrolled or expecting to enroll full-time at a two-year or four-year institution or university. Applicant must have 3.0 GPA or higher. Available to U.S. and non-U.S. citizens.

Application Requirements: Application form, community service, essay. *Deadline:* May 1.

Contact: Ms. Brenda Kai, Executive Director
Phone: 817-849-1145
E-mail: brenda.kai@edsf.org

LYNDA BABOYIAN MEMORIAL SCHOLARSHIP

• *See page 163*

GOLDEN KEY INTERNATIONAL HONOUR SOCIETY

http://www.goldenkey.org/

VISUAL AND PERFORMING ARTS ACHIEVEMENT AWARDS

• *See page 128*

INTERNATIONAL FOODSERVICE EDITORIAL COUNCIL

http://www.ifeconline.com/

INTERNATIONAL FOODSERVICE EDITORIAL COUNCIL COMMUNICATIONS SCHOLARSHIP

• *See page 88*

NATIONAL ASSOCIATION OF HISPANIC JOURNALISTS (NAHJ)

http://www.nahj.org/

NEWHOUSE SCHOLARSHIP PROGRAM

Two-year $5000 annually award for students who are pursuing careers in the newspaper industry as reporters, editors, graphic artists, or photojournalists. Recipient is expected to participate in summer internship at a Newhouse newspaper following their junior year. Students must submit resume and writing samples.

Academic Fields/Career Goals: Graphics/Graphic Arts/Printing; Journalism; Photojournalism/Photography.

Award: Scholarship for use in junior or senior years; not renewable. *Amount:* $5000.

Eligibility Requirements: Applicant must be enrolled or expecting to enroll full-time at a four-year institution or university. Available to U.S. citizens.

Application Requirements: Application form, essay, financial need analysis, recommendations or references, resume, transcript, work samples. *Deadline:* March 31.

Contact: Virginia Galindo, Program Assistant
Phone: 202-662-7145
E-mail: vgalindo@nahj.org

NEBRASKA PRESS ASSOCIATION

http://www.nebpress.com/

NEBRASKA PRESS ASSOCIATION FOUNDATION SCHOLARSHIP

• *See page 89*

NEW ENGLAND PRINTING AND PUBLISHING COUNCIL

http://www.gcsfne.org/

GRAPHIC COMMUNICATIONS SCHOLARSHIP FUND OF NEW ENGLAND

Applicants must be residents of New England who have been admitted to, or are currently attending, an accredited two-year vocational or technical college or a four-year college or university that offers a degree program related to printing or graphic communications. Renewable for up to four years if student maintains 2.5 GPA.

Academic Fields/Career Goals: Graphics/Graphic Arts/Printing.

Award: Scholarship for use in freshman, sophomore, junior, or senior years; renewable. *Number:* 16–35. *Amount:* $1350–$2500.

Eligibility Requirements: Applicant must be enrolled or expecting to enroll full-time at a two-year or four-year or technical institution or university and resident of Connecticut, Maine, Massachusetts, New Hampshire, Rhode Island, Vermont. Applicant must have 2.5 GPA or higher. Available to U.S. citizens.

Application Requirements: Application form, financial need analysis. *Deadline:* June 15.

Contact: Tad Parker, Scholarship Administrator
New England Printing and Publishing Council
5 Crystal Pond Road
Southboro, MA 01772
E-mail: chair@gcsfne.org

OREGON STUDENT ASSISTANCE COMMISSION

http://www.GetCollegeFunds.org/

HB DESIGN SCHOLARSHIP

Award for college junior or above studying graphic design or interactive/web design at any U.S. college or university. Semifinalists will be required to e-mail a design sample along with a 200-word description about the concept. Apply/compete annually.

Academic Fields/Career Goals: Graphics/Graphic Arts/Printing.

Award: Scholarship for use in junior, senior, or graduate years; not renewable.

Eligibility Requirements: Applicant must be enrolled or expecting to enroll full-time at a four-year institution or university and resident of Oregon. Applicant must have 3.0 GPA or higher. Available to U.S. citizens.

Application Requirements: Application form, essay, financial need analysis. *Deadline:* March 1.

Contact: Melissa Adams, Scholarship Processing Coordinator
Phone: 541-687-7409
E-mail: melissa.adams@hecc.oregon.gov

KERDRAGON SCHOLARSHIP

• *See page 130*

KIRCHHOFF FAMILY FINE ARTS SCHOLARSHIP

• *See page 130*

PRINT AND GRAPHIC SCHOLARSHIP FOUNDATION

http://www.printing.org/

PRINT AND GRAPHICS SCHOLARSHIPS FOUNDATION

• *See page 207*

PRINTING INDUSTRY MIDWEST EDUCATION FOUDNATION

http://www.pimw.org/scholarships

PRINTING INDUSTRY MIDWEST EDUCATION FOUNDATION SCHOLARSHIP FUND
• *See page 207*

QUALITY BATH

www.qualitybath.com

QUALITYBATH.COM SCHOLARSHIP PROGRAM
• *See page 123*

RHODE ISLAND FOUNDATION

http://www.rifoundation.org/

J. D. EDSAL SCHOLARSHIP
• *See page 90*

ROBERT H. MOLLOHAN FAMILY CHARITABLE FOUNDATION, INC.

http://www.mollohanfoundation.org/

MARY OLIVE EDDY JONES ART SCHOLARSHIP
• *See page 126*

SUPPORT CREATIVITY

http://wesupportcreativity.org

SUPPORT CREATIVITY SCHOLARSHIP
• *See page 124*

TAG AND LABEL MANUFACTURERS INSTITUTE, INC.

http://www.tlmi.com/

TLMI 4 YEAR COLLEGE DEGREE SCHOLARSHIP PROGRAM
• *See page 288*

TECHNICAL ASSOCIATION OF THE PULP & PAPER INDUSTRY (TAPPI)

http://www.tappi.org/

COATING AND GRAPHIC ARTS DIVISION SCHOLARSHIP
Scholarship to encourage talented science and engineering students to pursue careers in the paper industry and to utilize their capabilities in advancing the science and technology of coated paper and paperboard manufacturing and the graphic arts industry. The division may award up to four $1000 awards annually. Information can be found at http://www.tappi.org/s_tappi/sec.asp?CID=6101&DID=546695.
Academic Fields/Career Goals: Graphics/Graphic Arts/Printing; Paper and Pulp Engineering.
Award: Scholarship for use in freshman, sophomore, junior, or senior years; not renewable. *Number:* 1–4. *Amount:* $1000.
Eligibility Requirements: Applicant must be enrolled or expecting to enroll full-time at a four-year institution or university. Applicant must have 3.0 GPA or higher. Available to U.S. and non-U.S. citizens.
Application Requirements: Application form. *Deadline:* March 15.

Contact: Mr. Laurence Womack, Director of Standards and Awards
Technical Association of the Pulp & Paper Industry (TAPPI)
15 Technology Parkway South
Peachtree Corners, GA 30092
Phone: 770-209-7276
E-mail: standards@tappi.org

VECTORWORKS, INC.

http://www.vectorworks.net

VECTORWORKS DESIGN SCHOLARSHIP
• *See page 124*

WORLDSTUDIO FOUNDATION

http://www.aiga.org/

WORLDSTUDIO AIGA SCHOLARSHIPS
• *See page 133*

HEALTH ADMINISTRATION

ALBERTA HERITAGE SCHOLARSHIP FUND

http://www.alis.alberta.ca/

ABORIGINAL HEALTH CAREERS BURSARY
• *See page 153*

ALICE L. HALTOM EDUCATIONAL FUND

http://www.alhef.org/

ALICE L. HALTOM EDUCATIONAL FUND
• *See page 160*

AMERICAN LEGION AUXILIARY DEPARTMENT OF COLORADO

http://www.alacolorado.com

AMERICAN LEGION AUXILIARY DEPARTMENT OF COLORADO PAST PRESIDENTS' PARLEY HEALTH CARE PROFESSIONAL SCHOLARSHIPNURSES SCHOLARSHIP
• *See page 133*

AMERICAN LEGION DEPARTMENT OF NORTH DAKOTA

http://www.ndlegion.org/

O. NESHEIM MEMORIAL SCHOLARSHIP
• *See page 96*

ASRT FOUNDATION

http://foundation.asrt.org

PROFESSIONAL ADVANCEMENT SCHOLARSHIP
Open to ASRT members only who are certificate, undergraduate or graduate students pursuing any degree or certificate intended to further a career in the radiologic sciences profession. One of the following must also be true: applicant holds an unrestricted state license, is registered by the American Registry of Radiologic Technologists, or registered with an equivalent certifying body.

Academic Fields/Career Goals: Health Administration; Health and Medical Sciences; Oncology; Radiology.

Award: Scholarship for use in freshman, sophomore, junior, senior, graduate, or postgraduate years; not renewable. *Number:* 10–20. *Amount:* up to $2000.

Eligibility Requirements: Applicant must be enrolled or expecting to enroll full- or part-time at a two-year or four-year or technical institution or university. Applicant or parent of applicant must be member of American Society of Radiologic Technologists. Applicant must have 3.0 GPA or higher. Available to U.S. citizens.

Application Requirements: Application form, application form may be submitted online (http://aim.applyists.net), essay, financial need analysis, recommendations or references, resume. *Deadline:* February 1.

AVACARE MEDICAL

https://avacaremedical.com

AVACARE MEDICAL SCHOLARSHIP
• *See page 105*

BETHESDA LUTHERAN COMMUNITIES

http://www.bethesdalutherancommunities.org/scholarships

DEVELOPMENTAL DISABILITIES SCHOLASTIC ACHIEVEMENT SCHOLARSHIP FOR COLLEGE STUDENTS WHO ARE LUTHERAN
• *See page 236*

BHW GROUP

https://thebhwgroup.com/

BHW WOMEN IN STEM SCHOLARSHIP
• *See page 74*

CANADIAN SOCIETY FOR MEDICAL LABORATORY SCIENCE

http://www.csmls.org/

E.V. BOOTH SCHOLARSHIP AWARD
The fund was established to assist CSMLS members in fulfilling their vision of achieving university level education in the medical laboratory sciences. One-time award of up to CAN$1000. Must be a Canadian citizen.

Academic Fields/Career Goals: Health Administration; Health and Medical Sciences; Health Information Management/Technology.

Award: Scholarship for use in freshman, sophomore, junior, or senior years; not renewable. *Number:* 1.

Eligibility Requirements: Applicant must be Canadian citizen and enrolled or expecting to enroll full- or part-time at a four-year institution or university. Applicant or parent of applicant must be member of Canadian Society for Medical Laboratory Science.

Application Requirements: Application form, essay. *Deadline:* May 1.

Contact: Katherine Coles, HR & Operations Coordinator
Phone: 905-528-8642 Ext. 8602
E-mail: awards@csmls.org

COMPHEALTH

http://www.comphealth.com

COMPHEALTH MEDICAL SCHOLARSHIP
• *See page 151*

GREATER KANAWHA VALLEY FOUNDATION

http://www.tgkvf.org/

WILLARD H. ERWIN JR. MEMORIAL SCHOLARSHIP FUND
• *See page 165*

HEALTHCARE INFORMATION AND MANAGEMENT SYSTEMS SOCIETY FOUNDATION

http://www.himss.org/

HIMSS FOUNDATION SCHOLARSHIP PROGRAM
The Foundation Scholarships can be awarded to undergraduate, Master's or Ph.D. students enrolled in a program related to the healthcare information and management systems field. In addition to the $5000 scholarship award, the winner also receives an all-expense paid trip to the Annual HIMSS Conference and Exhibition. Applicants must be member in good standing of HIMS. Primary occupation must be that of student in an accredited program related to the healthcare information or management systems field. The specific degree program is not a critical factor, although it is expected that programs similar to those in industrial engineering, operations research, healthcare informatics, computer science and information systems, mathematics, and quantitative programs in business administration and hospital administration will predominate. Undergraduate applicants must be at least a first-term junior when the scholarship is awarded. Previous Foundation Scholarship winners are ineligible.

Academic Fields/Career Goals: Health Administration; Health and Medical Sciences; Health Information Management/Technology; Science, Technology, and Society.

Award: Scholarship for use in junior, senior, graduate, or postgraduate years; not renewable. *Number:* 4–12. *Amount:* $5000.

Eligibility Requirements: Applicant must be enrolled or expecting to enroll full-time at a four-year institution or university. Applicant or parent of applicant must be member of Healthcare Information and Management Systems Society. Available to U.S. and non-U.S. citizens.

Application Requirements: Application form, community service, essay, recommendations or references, resume, transcript. *Deadline:* October 15.

Contact: Helen Figge, Senior Director, Professional Development, Career Services
Healthcare Information and Management Systems Society Foundation
33 West Monroe Street, Suite 1700
Chicago, IL 60603
Phone: 312-915-9548
E-mail: hfigge@himss.org

HEALTH RESEARCH COUNCIL OF NEW ZEALAND

http://www.hrc.govt.nz/

PACIFIC HEALTH WORKFORCE AWARD
Intended to support students studying towards a health or health-related qualification. The eligible courses of study are: health, health administration, or a recognized qualification aligned with the Pacific Island. Priority given to management training, medical, and nursing students. Applicants should be New Zealand citizens or hold residency in New Zealand at the time of application and be of Pacific Island descent. The value of the awards and dollar value will vary and for one year of study.

Academic Fields/Career Goals: Health Administration; Health and Medical Sciences; Health Information Management/Technology; Nursing.

Award: Scholarship for use in freshman, sophomore, junior, senior, graduate, or postgraduate years; not renewable.

Eligibility Requirements: Applicant must be New Zealander citizen; Asian/Pacific Islander and enrolled or expecting to enroll full-time at a two-year or four-year institution or university. Available to citizens of countries other than the U.S. or Canada.

Application Requirements: Application form, driver's license, essay, financial need analysis, recommendations or references, transcript. *Deadline:* October 10.

Contact: Ngamau Wichman Tou, Manager, Pacific Health Research
    Phone: 64 9 3035255
    Fax: 64 9 377 9988
    E-mail: nwichmantou@hrc.govt.nz

PACIFIC MENTAL HEALTH WORK FORCE AWARD

Intended to provide one year of support for students studying towards a mental health or mental health-related qualification. Eligible courses of study include: nursing, psychology, health, health administration or a recognized qualification aligned with the Pacific Island mental health priority areas. Applicants should be New Zealand citizens or hold residency in New Zealand at the time of application and be of Pacific Island descent.

Academic Fields/Career Goals: Health Administration; Health and Medical Sciences; Health Information Management/Technology; Nursing; Psychology.

Award: Scholarship for use in freshman, sophomore, junior, senior, graduate, or postgraduate years; not renewable.

Eligibility Requirements: Applicant must be New Zealander citizen; Asian/Pacific Islander and enrolled or expecting to enroll full-time at a two-year or four-year institution or university. Available to citizens of countries other than the U.S. or Canada.

Application Requirements: Application form, essay, financial need analysis, recommendations or references, resume, transcript. *Deadline:* October 10.

Contact: Ngamau Wichman Tou, Manager, Pacific Health Research
    Phone: 64 9 3035255
    Fax: 64 9 377 9988
    E-mail: nwichmantou@hrc.govt.nz

MEDICAL SCRUBS COLLECTION

http://medicalscrubscollection.com

MEDICAL SCRUBS COLLECTION SCHOLARSHIP
• *See page 106*

THE NATIONAL SOCIETY OF THE COLONIAL DAMES OF AMERICA

http://www.nscda.org/

AMERICAN INDIAN NURSE SCHOLARSHIP PROGRAM

The current goal is to grant a $1,500 scholarship each semester, as long as the student remains in academic good standing. The scholarship money is restricted to tuition and specific academic expenses.

Academic Fields/Career Goals: Health Administration; Nursing.

Award: Scholarship for use in freshman, sophomore, junior, senior, graduate, or postgraduate years; renewable. *Number:* 5–10. *Amount:* $500–$1500.

Eligibility Requirements: Applicant must be American Indian/Alaska Native and enrolled or expecting to enroll full-time at a two-year or four-year or technical institution or university. Applicant must have 2.5 GPA or higher. Available to U.S. citizens.

Application Requirements: Application form, driver's license, financial need analysis, personal photograph, recommendations or references, transcript. *Deadline:* continuous.

Contact: NSCDA Membership Coordinator
    Phone: 202-337-2288 Ext. 227
    E-mail: dames@dumbartonhouse.org

NEW ENGLAND EMPLOYEE BENEFITS COUNCIL

http://www.neebc.org/

NEW ENGLAND EMPLOYEE BENEFITS COUNCIL SCHOLARSHIP PROGRAM
• *See page 81*

SCARLETT FAMILY FOUNDATION SCHOLARSHIP PROGRAM

http://www.scarlettfoundation.org/

SCHOLARSHIP FOR STUDENTS PURSUING A BUSINESS OR STEM DEGREE
• *See page 84*

STRAIGHTFORWARD MEDIA

http://www.straightforwardmedia.com/

STRAIGHTFORWARD MEDIA MEDICAL PROFESSIONS SCHOLARSHIP
• *See page 239*

UNITED NEGRO COLLEGE FUND

http://www.uncf.org/

UNCF/ANTHEM CORPORATE SCHOLARS PROGRAM
• *See page 170*

HEALTH AND MEDICAL SCIENCES

101ST AIRBORNE DIVISION ASSOCIATION

http://www.screamingeaglefoundation.org/

AL & WILLIAMARY VISTE SCHOLARSHIP
• *See page 233*

ALBERTA HERITAGE SCHOLARSHIP FUND

http://www.alis.alberta.ca/

ABORIGINAL HEALTH CAREERS BURSARY
• *See page 153*

JASON LANG SCHOLARSHIP
• *See page 233*

NORTHERN ALBERTA DEVELOPMENT COUNCIL BURSARY
• *See page 234*

ALPENA REGIONAL MEDICAL CENTER

http://www.alpenaregionalmedicalcenter.org/

THELMA ORR MEMORIAL SCHOLARSHIP

Two $1500 scholarships for students pursuing a course of study related to human medicine at any state accredited Michigan college or university.

Academic Fields/Career Goals: Health and Medical Sciences.

Award: Scholarship for use in freshman, sophomore, junior, or senior years; not renewable. *Number:* 2. *Amount:* $1500.

Eligibility Requirements: Applicant must be enrolled or expecting to enroll full-time at a four-year institution or university; resident of Michigan and studying in Michigan. Available to U.S. citizens.

Application Requirements: Application form. *Deadline:* April 15.

Contact: Marlene Pear, Director, Voluntary Services
    Phone: 989-356-7351
    E-mail: info@agh.org

AMERICAN INDIAN SCIENCE AND ENGINEERING SOCIETY

http://www.aises.org/

A.T. ANDERSON MEMORIAL SCHOLARSHIP PROGRAM
• See page 109

AMERICAN LEGION AUXILIARY DEPARTMENT OF ARIZONA

http:/wwwaladeptaz.org

AMERICAN LEGION AUXILIARY DEPARTMENT OF ARIZONA HEALTH CARE OCCUPATION SCHOLARSHIPS

Award for Arizona residents enrolled at an institution in Arizona that awards degrees or certificates in health occupations. Preference given to an immediate family member of a veteran. Must be a U.S. citizen and Arizona resident for at least one year.

Academic Fields/Career Goals: Health and Medical Sciences.

Award: Scholarship for use in freshman, sophomore, junior, or senior years; not renewable. *Amount:* $500.

Eligibility Requirements: Applicant must be enrolled or expecting to enroll full- or part-time at a two-year or four-year or technical institution or university; resident of Arizona and studying in Arizona. Available to U.S. citizens.

Application Requirements: Application form, essay, financial need analysis, personal photograph. *Deadline:* May 15.

Contact: Mrs. Barbara Matteson, Department Secretary and Treasurer
American Legion Auxiliary Department of Arizona
4701 North 19th Avenue, Suite 100
Phoenix, AZ 85015-3727
Phone: 602-241-1080
E-mail: secretary@aladeptaz.org

AMERICAN LEGION AUXILIARY DEPARTMENT OF COLORADO

http://www.alacolorado.com

AMERICAN LEGION AUXILIARY DEPARTMENT OF COLORADO PAST PRESIDENTS' PARLEY HEALTH CARE PROFESSIONAL SCHOLARSHIPNURSES SCHOLARSHIP
• See page 133

AMERICAN LEGION AUXILIARY DEPARTMENT OF MAINE

http://www.mainelegion.org/

AMERICAN LEGION AUXILIARY DEPARTMENT OF MAINE PAST PRESIDENTS' PARLEY NURSES SCHOLARSHIP

One-time award for child, grandchild, sister, or brother of veteran. Must be resident of Maine and wishing to continue education at accredited school in medical field. Must submit photo, doctor's statement, and evidence of civic activity. Minimum 3.5 GPA required.

Academic Fields/Career Goals: Health and Medical Sciences; Nursing.

Award: Scholarship for use in freshman, sophomore, junior, or senior years; not renewable. *Number:* 1. *Amount:* $300.

Eligibility Requirements: Applicant must be enrolled or expecting to enroll full-time at a two-year or four-year or technical institution or university and resident of Maine. Applicant or parent of applicant must have employment or volunteer experience in community service. Applicant must have 2.5 GPA or higher. Available to U.S. citizens. Applicant or parent must meet one or more of the following requirements: general military experience; retired from active duty; disabled or killed as a result of military service; prisoner of war; or missing in action.

Application Requirements: Application form, doctor's statement, personal photograph, recommendations or references, transcript. *Deadline:* March 31.

Contact: Mary Wells, Education Chairman
Phone: 207-532-6007
E-mail: aladeptsecme@verizon.net

AMERICAN LEGION AUXILIARY DEPARTMENT OF MICHIGAN

http://www.michalaux.org/

AMERICAN LEGION AUXILIARY DEPARTMENT OF MICHIGAN MEDICAL CAREER SCHOLARSHIP

Award for training in Michigan as registered nurse, licensed practical nurse, physical therapist, respiratory therapist, or in any medical career. Must be child, grandchild, great-grandchild, wife, or widow of honorably discharged or deceased veteran who has served during the eligibility dates for American Legion membership. Must be Michigan resident attending a Michigan school.

Academic Fields/Career Goals: Health and Medical Sciences; Nursing; Therapy/Rehabilitation.

Award: Scholarship for use in freshman year; not renewable. *Number:* 10–20. *Amount:* $500.

Eligibility Requirements: Applicant must be enrolled or expecting to enroll full-time at a two-year or four-year or technical institution or university; resident of Michigan and studying in Michigan. Applicant must have 3.5 GPA or higher. Available to U.S. citizens. Applicant must have general military experience.

Application Requirements: Application form, financial need analysis. *Deadline:* March 15.

Contact: Scholarship Coordinator
American Legion Auxiliary Department of Michigan
212 North Verlinden Avenue, Suite B
Lansing, MI 48915
Phone: 517-267-8809 Ext. 21
E-mail: info@michalaux.org

AMERICAN LEGION AUXILIARY DEPARTMENT OF MINNESOTA

http://www.mnlegion.org/

AMERICAN LEGION AUXILIARY DEPARTMENT OF MINNESOTA PAST PRESIDENTS' PARLEY HEALTH CARE SCHOLARSHIP

One-time $1000 award for American Legion Auxiliary Department of Minnesota member for at least three years who is needy and deserving, to begin or continue education in any phase of the health care field. Must be a Minnesota resident, attend a vocational or postsecondary institution and maintain at least a C average in school.

Academic Fields/Career Goals: Health and Medical Sciences.

Award: Scholarship for use in freshman, sophomore, junior, or senior years; not renewable. *Number:* 1–10. *Amount:* $1000.

Eligibility Requirements: Applicant must be enrolled or expecting to enroll full-time at a two-year or four-year or technical institution or university; resident of Minnesota and studying in Minnesota. Applicant or parent of applicant must be member of American Legion or Auxiliary. Available to U.S. citizens.

Application Requirements: Application form, financial need analysis. *Deadline:* March 15.

Contact: Eleanor Johnson, Executive Secretary
American Legion Auxiliary Department of Minnesota
State Veterans Service Building
20 West 12th Street, Room 314
St. Paul, MN 55155
Phone: 651-224-7634
Fax: 651-224-5243

AMERICAN LEGION AUXILIARY DEPARTMENT OF TEXAS

http://www.alatexas.org/

AMERICAN LEGION AUXILIARY DEPARTMENT OF TEXAS PAST PRESIDENTS' PARLEY MEDICAL SCHOLARSHIP

Scholarships available for full-time students pursuing studies in human health care. Must be a resident of Texas. Must be a veteran or child, grandchild, great grandchild of a veteran who served in the Armed Forces during period of eligibility.

Academic Fields/Career Goals: Health and Medical Sciences.

Award: Scholarship for use in freshman, sophomore, junior, or senior years; not renewable. *Number:* 1–10. *Amount:* $1000.

Eligibility Requirements: Applicant must be enrolled or expecting to enroll full-time at a two-year or four-year or technical institution or university and resident of Texas. Available to U.S. citizens. Applicant must have general military experience.

Application Requirements: Application form, community service, financial need analysis, letter stating qualifications and intentions, recommendations or references, transcript. *Deadline:* June 1.

Contact: Paula Raney, State Secretary
     Phone: 512-476-7278
     Fax: 512-482-8391
     E-mail: alatexas@txlegion.org

AMERICAN LEGION DEPARTMENT OF NORTH DAKOTA

http://www.ndlegion.org/

O. NESHEIM MEMORIAL SCHOLARSHIP
• *See page 96*

AMERICAN OCCUPATIONAL THERAPY FOUNDATION INC.

http://www.aotf.org/

CARLOTTA WELLES SCHOLARSHIP

Award for study leading to an occupational therapy Associate degree at an accredited institution.

Academic Fields/Career Goals: Health and Medical Sciences; Therapy/Rehabilitation.

Award: Scholarship for use in sophomore year; not renewable. *Number:* up to 1. *Amount:* $500–$500.

Eligibility Requirements: Applicant must be enrolled or expecting to enroll full-time at a two-year institution. Applicant or parent of applicant must be member of American Occupational Therapy Association. Available to U.S. citizens.

Application Requirements: Application form, application form may be submitted online (http://www.aotf.org), Curriculum Director's Statement, essay, recommendations or references. *Deadline:* varies.

Contact: Ms. Jeanne Cooper, Scholarship Program Manager
     Phone: 240-292-1034
     Fax: 240-396-6188
     E-mail: JCooper@aotf.org

AMERICAN PHYSICAL THERAPY ASSOCIATION

http://www.apta.org/honorsawards

MARY MCMILLAN SCHOLARSHIP AWARD
• *See page 249*

AMERICAN PHYSIOLOGICAL SOCIETY

http://www.the-aps.org

DAVID S. BRUCE AWARDS FOR EXCELLENCE IN UNDERGRADUATE RESEARCH
• *See page 105*

AMERICAN RESPIRATORY CARE FOUNDATION

http://www.arcfoundation.org/

JIMMY A. YOUNG MEMORIAL EDUCATION RECOGNITION AWARD

Award available to students studying respiratory care at an American Medical Association-approved institution. Preference given to minority students. Must submit letters of recommendation and a paper on a respiratory care topic. Must have a minimum 3.0 GPA.

Academic Fields/Career Goals: Health and Medical Sciences; Therapy/Rehabilitation.

Award: Prize for use in freshman, sophomore, junior, or senior years; not renewable. *Number:* 1. *Amount:* up to $1000.

Eligibility Requirements: Applicant must be enrolled or expecting to enroll full- or part-time at a two-year or four-year institution or university. Applicant must have 3.0 GPA or higher. Available to U.S. citizens.

Application Requirements: Application form, paper on respiratory care topic, recommendations or references, transcript. *Deadline:* June 16.

Contact: Jill Nelson, Administrative Coordinator
     American Respiratory Care Foundation
     9425 North MacArthur Boulevard, Suite 100
     Irving, TX 75063-4706
     Phone: 972-243-2272
     Fax: 972-484-2720
     E-mail: info@arcfoundation.org

MORTON B. DUGGAN, JR. MEMORIAL EDUCATION RECOGNITION AWARD

Awards students with a minimum 3.0 GPA, enrolled in an American Medical Association-approved respiratory care program. Must be U.S. citizen or permanent resident. Need proof of college enrollment. Must submit an original referenced paper on respiratory care. Preference given to Georgia and South Carolina residents. One-time merit-based award of up to $1000, and includes airfare, registration to AARC Congress, and one night's lodging.

Academic Fields/Career Goals: Health and Medical Sciences; Therapy/Rehabilitation.

Award: Scholarship for use in freshman, sophomore, junior, or senior years; not renewable. *Number:* 1. *Amount:* up to $1000.

Eligibility Requirements: Applicant must be enrolled or expecting to enroll full- or part-time at a two-year or four-year institution or university. Applicant must have 3.0 GPA or higher. Available to U.S. citizens.

Application Requirements: Application form, paper on respiratory care, recommendations or references, transcript. *Deadline:* June 16.

Contact: Jill Nelson, Administrative Coordinator
     American Respiratory Care Foundation
     9425 North MacArthur Boulevard, Suite 100
     Irving, TX 75063-4706
     Phone: 972-243-2272
     Fax: 972-484-2720
     E-mail: info@arcfoundation.org

SEPRACOR ACHIEVEMENT AWARD FOR EXCELLENCE IN PULMONARY DISEASE STATE MANAGEMENT

Nominations may be made by anyone by submitting a paper of not more than 1000 words describing why a nominee should be considered for the award. Must be a member of the American Association for Respiratory Care. Must be a respiratory therapist or other healthcare professional, including physician. Nominees must have demonstrated the attainment of positive healthcare outcomes as a direct result of their disease-oriented practice of respiratory care, regardless of care setting.

Academic Fields/Career Goals: Health and Medical Sciences; Therapy/Rehabilitation.

Award: Prize for use in freshman, sophomore, junior, senior, graduate, or postgraduate years; not renewable. *Number:* 1. *Amount:* up to $2500.

Eligibility Requirements: Applicant must be enrolled or expecting to enroll full- or part-time at a four-year institution or university. Applicant or parent of applicant must have employment or volunteer experience in physical therapy/rehabilitation. Available to U.S. and non-U.S. citizens.

Application Requirements: Paper describing why a nominee should be considered for the award, recommendations or references, resume. *Deadline:* June 1.

Contact: Jill Nelson, Administrative Coordinator
American Respiratory Care Foundation
9425 North MacArthur Boulevard, Suite 100
Irving, TX 75063-4706
Phone: 972-243-2272
Fax: 972-484-2720
E-mail: info@arcfoundation.org

ARIZONA PROFESSIONAL CHAPTER OF AISES

http://www.aises.org/scholarships

ARIZONA PROFESSIONAL CHAPTER OF AISES SCHOLARSHIP
• *See page 294*

ARRL FOUNDATION INC.

http://www.arrl.org/

CAROLE J. STREETER, KB9JBR, SCHOLARSHIP
• *See page 236*

WIFDR SCHOLARSHIP
• *See page 112*

ASRT FOUNDATION

http://foundation.asrt.org

ELEKTA RADIATION THERAPY SCHOLARSHIP

Open to students in the 2nd or 3rd year of an entry-level radiation therapy program. Is a merit-based scholarship awarded on financial need, academic performance, recommendation, and essays.

Academic Fields/Career Goals: Health and Medical Sciences.

Award: Scholarship for use in sophomore, junior, or senior years; not renewable. *Number:* 4. *Amount:* $5000.

Eligibility Requirements: Applicant must be enrolled or expecting to enroll full- or part-time at a two-year or four-year or technical institution or university. Applicant or parent of applicant must be member of American Society of Radiologic Technologists. Applicant must have 3.0 GPA or higher. Available to U.S. citizens.

Application Requirements: Application form, essay, financial need analysis. *Deadline:* February 1.

JERMAN-CAHOON STUDENT SCHOLARSHIP

Merit scholarship for certificate or undergraduate students. Must have completed at least one semester in the radiological sciences to apply (does not include prerequisites). Financial need is a factor. Requirements include 3.0 GPA, recommendation and several short answer essays.

Academic Fields/Career Goals: Health and Medical Sciences; Oncology; Radiology.

Award: Scholarship for use in sophomore or junior years; not renewable. *Number:* 6. *Amount:* up to $2500.

Eligibility Requirements: Applicant must be enrolled or expecting to enroll full- or part-time at a two-year or four-year or technical institution or university. Applicant must have 3.0 GPA or higher. Available to U.S. citizens.

Application Requirements: Application form, application form may be submitted online (http://aim.applyists.net), essay, financial need analysis, recommendations or references, transcript. *Deadline:* February 1.

PROFESSIONAL ADVANCEMENT SCHOLARSHIP
• *See page 344*

ROYCE OSBORN MINORITY STUDENT SCHOLARSHIP

Minority scholarship for certificate or undergraduate students. Must have completed at least one semester in the radiological sciences to apply (does not include prerequisites). Financial need is a factor. Requirements include 3.0 GPA, recommendation and several short answer essays.

Academic Fields/Career Goals: Health and Medical Sciences; Radiology.

Award: Scholarship for use in sophomore or junior years; not renewable. *Number:* 5. *Amount:* up to $4000.

Eligibility Requirements: Applicant must be American Indian/Alaska Native, Asian/Pacific Islander, Black (non-Hispanic), Hispanic and enrolled or expecting to enroll full- or part-time at a two-year or four-year or technical institution or university. Applicant must have 3.0 GPA or higher. Available to U.S. citizens.

Application Requirements: Application form, application form may be submitted online (http://aim.applyists.net), essay, financial need analysis, recommendations or references, transcript. *Deadline:* February 1.

SIEMENS CLINICAL ADVANCEMENT SCHOLARSHIP

Open to ASRT members only who are medical imaging professionals pursuing a Bachelor's or Master's degree in the radiologic sciences to advance patient care skills or pursuing a certificate in a specialty discipline and seek to enhance their clinical practice skills and provide excellent patient care should apply. One of the following must also be true: applicant holds an unrestricted state license, is registered by the American Registry of Radiologic Technologists, or registered with an equivalent certifying body.

Academic Fields/Career Goals: Health and Medical Sciences; Oncology; Radiology.

Award: Scholarship for use in sophomore, junior, senior, graduate, or postgraduate years; not renewable. *Number:* 4. *Amount:* $5000.

Eligibility Requirements: Applicant must be enrolled or expecting to enroll full- or part-time at a two-year or four-year or technical institution or university. Applicant or parent of applicant must be member of American Society of Radiologic Technologists. Applicant must have 3.0 GPA or higher. Available to U.S. citizens.

Application Requirements: Application form, application form may be submitted online (http://aim.applyists.net), essay, financial need analysis, recommendations or references, resume. *Deadline:* February 1.

VARIAN RADIATION THERAPY ADVANCEMENT SCHOLARSHIP

Merit scholarship for radiation therapists and medical dosimetrists or for current radiologic technologists in an entry-level radiation therapy program. Financial need is a factor. Requirements include recommendation and several short answer essays.

Academic Fields/Career Goals: Health and Medical Sciences; Oncology.

Award: Scholarship for use in sophomore, junior, senior, graduate, or postgraduate years; not renewable. *Number:* 19. *Amount:* $5000.

Eligibility Requirements: Applicant must be enrolled or expecting to enroll full- or part-time at a two-year or four-year or technical institution or university. Applicant must have 3.0 GPA or higher. Available to U.S. citizens.

Application Requirements: Application form, application form may be submitted online (http://aim.applyists.net), essay, financial need analysis, recommendations or references, transcript. *Deadline:* February 1.

ASSOCIATION FOR EDUCATION AND REHABILITATION OF THE BLIND AND VISUALLY IMPAIRED

http://www.aerbvi.org/

WILLIAM AND DOROTHY FERRELL SCHOLARSHIP
• *See page 250*

ASSOCIATION OF SURGICAL TECHNOLOGISTS

http://www.ast.org/

FOUNDATION STUDENT SCHOLARSHIP

Scholarship to encourage and reward educational excellence as well as to respond to the financial need demonstrated by the surgical technology student and offer assistance to those who seek a career in surgical technology. High school students also eligible to apply. Minimum GPA 3.2 is required.

Academic Fields/Career Goals: Health and Medical Sciences.

Award: Scholarship for use in freshman, sophomore, junior, or senior years; not renewable. *Number:* up to 12. *Amount:* $500–$2000.

Eligibility Requirements: Applicant must be enrolled or expecting to enroll full-time at a two-year or four-year institution or university. Available to U.S. citizens.

Application Requirements: Application form, essay, financial need analysis, recommendations or references, self-addressed stamped envelope with application, transcript. *Deadline:* April 1.

Contact: Karen Ludwig, Director of Publishing
    Phone: 800-637-7433
    Fax: 303-694-9169
    E-mail: kludwig@ast.org

ASSOCIATION ON AMERICAN INDIAN AFFAIRS, INC.

http://www.indian-affairs.org/

ELIZABETH AND SHERMAN ASCHE MEMORIAL SCHOLARSHIP FUND

• *See page 98*

AVACARE MEDICAL

https://avacaremedical.com

AVACARE MEDICAL SCHOLARSHIP

• *See page 105*

BETHESDA LUTHERAN COMMUNITIES

http://www.bethesdalutherancommunities.org/scholarships

DEVELOPMENTAL DISABILITIES SCHOLASTIC ACHIEVEMENT SCHOLARSHIP FOR COLLEGE STUDENTS WHO ARE LUTHERAN

• *See page 236*

BHW GROUP

https://thebhwgroup.com/

BHW WOMEN IN STEM SCHOLARSHIP

• *See page 74*

BOYS AND GIRLS CLUBS OF GREATER SAN DIEGO

http://www.sdyouth.org/

SPENCE REESE SCHOLARSHIP

• *See page 297*

CANADIAN SOCIETY FOR MEDICAL LABORATORY SCIENCE

http://www.csmls.org/

CANADIAN SOCIETY FOR MEDICAL LABORATORY SCIENCE FOUNDERS FUND AWARDS

Award available for members of the Canadian Society for Medical Laboratory Science to pursue professional development education. Must be a Canadian resident. One-time award of up to CAN$500.

Academic Fields/Career Goals: Health and Medical Sciences.

Award: Grant for use in freshman, sophomore, junior, senior, or graduate years; not renewable. *Number:* 1–10. *Amount:* $200–$500.

Eligibility Requirements: Applicant must be Canadian citizen and enrolled or expecting to enroll full- or part-time at a two-year or four-year or technical institution or university. Applicant or parent of applicant must be member of Canadian Society for Medical Laboratory Science.

Application Requirements: Application form. *Deadline:* May 1.

Contact: Katherine Coles
    Canadian Society for Medical Laboratory Science
    33 Wellington St. N
    Hamilton, ON
    Phone: 800-2638277 Ext. 8602
    E-mail: awards@csmls.org

CANADIAN SOCIETY OF LABORATORY TECHNOLOGISTS STUDENT SCHOLARSHIP PROGRAM

A Scholarship of up to CAD$1000 will be awarded to one student enrolled in either full time or part-time studies. Must be member of Canadian Society for Medical Laboratory Science, and Canadian citizen or permanent resident of Canada.

Academic Fields/Career Goals: Health and Medical Sciences.

Award: Scholarship for use in freshman, sophomore, junior, senior, or graduate years; not renewable. *Number:* 1. *Amount:* $1–$1000.

Eligibility Requirements: Applicant must be Canadian citizen and enrolled or expecting to enroll full- or part-time at an institution or university. Applicant or parent of applicant must be member of Canadian Society for Medical Laboratory Science.

Application Requirements: Application form. *Deadline:* May 1.

Contact: Katherine Coles, HR & Operations Coordinator
    Phone: 905-528-8642 Ext. 8602
    E-mail: awards@csmls.org

E.V. BOOTH SCHOLARSHIP AWARD

• *See page 345*

CANFIT

http://www.canfit.org/

CANFIT NUTRITION, PHYSICAL EDUCATION AND CULINARY ARTS SCHOLARSHIP

• *See page 229*

CHRISTIANA CARE HEALTH SYSTEMS

http://www.christianacare.org/

RUTH SHAW JUNIOR BOARD SCHOLARSHIP

Offers financial assistance to students currently enrolled in nursing and selected allied health programs. Applicants are selected based on academic achievement and a proven commitment to quality patient care. Students receiving assistance are required to commit to a minimum of one year of employment with Christiana Care.

Academic Fields/Career Goals: Health and Medical Sciences; Nursing.

Award: Scholarship for use in freshman, sophomore, junior, or senior years; not renewable.

Eligibility Requirements: Applicant must be enrolled or expecting to enroll full- or part-time at a four-year institution or university. Applicant or parent of applicant must have employment or volunteer experience in nursing. Available to U.S. citizens.

Application Requirements: Application form, driver's license, recommendations or references, resume, transcript. *Deadline:* April 30.

Contact: Wendy Gable, Scholarship Committee
Christiana Care Health Systems
200 Hygeia Drive, PO Box 6001
Newark, DE 19713
Phone: 302-428-5710
E-mail: wgable@christianacare.org

COMMUNITY FOUNDATION FOR GREATER ATLANTA, INC.

http://cfgreateratlanta.org/

STEVE DEARDUFF SCHOLARSHIP

Scholarship for undergraduate and graduate students pursuing degrees in medicine or social work. Legal resident of Georgia. Minimum 2.0 GPA. Previous recipients are encouraged to reapply, but are not guaranteed additional awards. For complete eligibility requirements or to submit an application, visit http://www.cfgreateratlanta.org.

Academic Fields/Career Goals: Health and Medical Sciences; Social Services.

Award: Scholarship for use in freshman, sophomore, junior, senior, or graduate years; not renewable. *Number:* 1–3. *Amount:* $1000–$2500.

Eligibility Requirements: Applicant must be enrolled or expecting to enroll full- or part-time at a four-year institution or university and resident of Georgia. Applicant must have 2.5 GPA or higher. Available to U.S. citizens.

Application Requirements: Application form, essay, financial need analysis. *Deadline:* February 15.

COMPHEALTH

http://www.comphealth.com

COMPHEALTH MEDICAL SCHOLARSHIP
• *See page 151*

CROHN'S & COLITIS FOUNDATION OF AMERICA INC.

http://www.ccfa.org/

CROHN'S & COLITIS FOUNDATION OF AMERICA STUDENT RESEARCH FELLOWSHIP AWARDS

Student Research Fellowship Awards will be available for full-time research with a mentor investigating a subject relevant to IBD. Mentors may not be a relative of the applicant and may not work in their lab. The mentor must be a faculty member who directs a research project highly relevant to the study of IBD at an accredited institution. Awards will be payable to the institution, not the individual. A complete financial statement and scientific report are due September 1 of the year of the award. All publications arising from work funded by this project must acknowledge support of CCFA. Candidates may be undergraduate, medical or graduate students (not yet engaged in thesis research) in accredited United States institutions. Candidates may not hold similar salary support from other agencies.

Academic Fields/Career Goals: Health and Medical Sciences.

Award: Scholarship for use in freshman, sophomore, junior, senior, or graduate years; not renewable. *Amount:* $2500–$2500.

Eligibility Requirements: Applicant must be enrolled or expecting to enroll full-time at a four-year institution or university. Available to U.S. and non-U.S. citizens.

Application Requirements: Abstract, research plan description, application form, resume. *Deadline:* March 15.

Contact: Mr. Moustafa Ibrahim, National Manager of Grants and Contracts
Crohn's & Colitis Foundation of America Inc.
733 Third Avenue
Suite 510
New York, NY 10017
Phone: 646-943-7505
Fax: 212-779-4098
E-mail: grants@ccfa.org

CYNTHIA E. MORGAN SCHOLARSHIP FUND (CEMS)

http://www.cemsfund.com/

CYNTHIA E. MORGAN MEMORIAL SCHOLARSHIP FUND, INC.
• *See page 316*

DIAGNOSIS DELAYED

www.myinjuryattorney.com

DIAGNOSIS DELAYED SCHOLARSHIP

The Diagnosis Delayed scholarship is open to all students pursuing a medical or legal degree. Students must be enrolled in a program at the date of application. Student must be enrolled in a medical or legal program at the date of application; a U.S. citizen; no minimum GPA. Please include all of the following materials in an email to info@diagnosisdelayed.com: proof of enrollment--acceptance letter, current class schedule, etc.; unofficial transcript; a word document containing the following information: name, address, birthdate, program/school attending, GPA, short essay of 500 word maximum describing why you deserve to win the scholarship.

Academic Fields/Career Goals: Health and Medical Sciences; Law/Legal Services.

Award: Scholarship for use in freshman, sophomore, junior, senior, graduate, or postgraduate years; not renewable. *Number:* 1. *Amount:* $500.

Eligibility Requirements: Applicant must be enrolled or expecting to enroll full-time at a two-year or four-year institution or university. Available to U.S. citizens.

Application Requirements: Application form, essay. *Deadline:* August 1.

Contact: Melissa Taggart
E-mail: marketing@consoleandhollawell.com

THE EXPERT INSTITUTE

https://www.theexpertinstitute.com

ANNUAL HEALTHCARE AND LIFE SCIENCES SCHOLARSHIP
• *See page 156*

FOUNDATION FOR SCIENCE AND DISABILITY

http://stemd.org/

GRANTS FOR DISABLED GRADUATE STUDENTS IN THE SCIENCES
• *See page 113*

FOUNDATION FOR SEACOAST HEALTH

www.ffsh.org

FOUNDATION FOR SEACOAST HEALTH SCHOLARSHIPS

In keeping with the mission of the organization to invest its resources to improve the health and well being of Seacoast residents, candidates must be pursuing an undergraduate or graduate degree in a health-related field of study. The awards are based primarily on scholastic aptitude and performance, personal achievements, leadership, and community involvement. The applicant's primary residence must be in one of the following towns: Portsmouth, Rye, Newcastle, Greenland, Newington, and North Hampton, New Hampshire; Kittery, Elliot and York, Maine.

Academic Fields/Career Goals: Health and Medical Sciences.

Award: Scholarship for use in freshman, sophomore, junior, senior, graduate, or postgraduate years; renewable. *Number:* 2–6. *Amount:* $1000–$5000.

Eligibility Requirements: Applicant must be enrolled or expecting to enroll full- or part-time at a two-year or four-year or technical institution or university and resident of Maine, New Hampshire. Available to U.S. citizens.

Application Requirements: Application form, essay. *Deadline:* April 1.

Contact: Noreen Hodgdon
Foundation for Seacoast Health
100 Campus Drive Suite 1
Portsmouth, NH 03801
Phone: 603-422-8204
Fax: 603-422-8207
E-mail: nhodgdon@communitycampus.org

GARDEN CLUB OF AMERICA

http://www.gcamerica.org/

ZELLER SUMMER SCHOLARSHIP IN MEDICINAL BOTANY

One $2,000 award open to undergraduate students enrolled in an accredited U.S. college or university for study or work during the summer following the freshman, sophomore, junior, or senior year. Program aims to encourage students to expand their knowledge of medicinal botany by pursuing summer study in various projects, courses, and/or internship with supervision and structure.

Academic Fields/Career Goals: Health and Medical Sciences; Horticulture/Floriculture; Natural Sciences.

Award: Scholarship for use in sophomore, junior, or senior years; not renewable. *Number:* 1. *Amount:* $2000.

Eligibility Requirements: Applicant must be enrolled or expecting to enroll full-time at a four-year institution or university. Available to U.S. citizens.

Application Requirements: Application form, essay. *Deadline:* February 1.

Contact: Garden Club of America
14 East 60th Street
New York, NY 10022-1006
Phone: 212-753-8287
E-mail: scholarshipapplications@gcamerica.org

GENERAL BOARD OF HIGHER EDUCATION AND MINISTRY

http://www.gbhem.org

EDITH M. ALLEN SCHOLARSHIP
• *See page 252*

GEORGIA BOARD FOR PHYSICIAN WORKFORCE (GBPW)

www.gbpw.georgia.gov

PHYSICIANS FOR RURAL AREAS ASSISTANCE PROGRAM

Service repayable medical school scholarship for a maximum of $20,000 per year for four years available to Georgia residents enrolled in U.S. accredited medical school. Repay by practicing medicine for one year in rural Georgia for each year that the scholarship is received. Service payment begins upon completion of residency training.

Academic Fields/Career Goals: Health and Medical Sciences.

Award: Scholarship for use in freshman, sophomore, junior, or senior years; renewable. *Number:* 20–25. *Amount:* up to $20,000.

Eligibility Requirements: Applicant must be enrolled or expecting to enroll full-time at an institution or university and resident of Georgia. Available to U.S. citizens.

Application Requirements: Application form, essay, financial need analysis, interview, personal photograph, proof of GA residency, test scores, transcript. *Deadline:* June 1.

Contact: Ms. Pamela Smith, Administration Manager
Georgia Board for Physician Workforce (GBPW)
2 Peachtree Street, NW
36th Floor
Atlanta, GA 30303
Phone: 404-232-7972
E-mail: psmith@dch.ga.gov

GRAND RAPIDS COMMUNITY FOUNDATION

http://www.grfoundation.org/

HARRY J. MORRIS, JR. EMERGENCY SERVICES SCHOLARSHIP

Scholarship is for students who are residents of Kent, Allegan, Barry, Ionia, Ottawa, Montcalm, Muskegon or Newaygo Counties pursuing an undergraduate certificate or degree at an accredited education program in Michigan in the field of emergency medical technician, paramedic, or firefighter training. Must have a 2.5 cumulative GPA or verified GED Certificate and demonstrate financial need.

Academic Fields/Career Goals: Health and Medical Sciences.

Award: Scholarship for use in freshman, sophomore, junior, or senior years; not renewable. *Number:* 1. *Amount:* $1000.

Eligibility Requirements: Applicant must be enrolled or expecting to enroll full- or part-time at a two-year or four-year or technical institution; resident of Michigan and studying in Michigan. Applicant must have 2.5 GPA or higher. Available to U.S. citizens.

Application Requirements: Application form, application form may be submitted online (http://grfoundation.org), essay, financial need analysis, transcript. *Deadline:* April 1.

Contact: Ms. Ruth Bishop, Education Program Officer
Grand Rapids Community Foundation
185 Oakes SW
Grand Rapids, MI 49503
Phone: 616-454-1751 Ext. 103
E-mail: rbishop@grfoundation.org

GREATER KANAWHA VALLEY FOUNDATION

http://www.tgkvf.org/

NICHOLAS AND MARY AGNES TRIVILLIAN MEMORIAL SCHOLARSHIP FUND

Renewable award for West Virginia residents pursuing medical or pharmacy programs. Must show financial need and academic merit.

Academic Fields/Career Goals: Health and Medical Sciences; Pharmacy.

Award: Scholarship for use in freshman, sophomore, junior, or senior years; renewable. *Amount:* $1000.

Eligibility Requirements: Applicant must be enrolled or expecting to enroll full-time at a four-year institution or university and resident of West Virginia. Available to U.S. citizens.

Application Requirements: Application form, essay, financial need analysis, recommendations or references, self-addressed stamped envelope with application, test scores, transcript. *Deadline:* January 15.

Contact: Susan Hoover, Scholarship Program Officer
Greater Kanawha Valley Foundation
900 Lee Street East, 16th Floor
Charleston, WV 25301
Phone: 304-346-3620
E-mail: shoover@tgkvf.org

HEALTHCARE INFORMATION AND MANAGEMENT SYSTEMS SOCIETY FOUNDATION

http://www.himss.org/

HIMSS FOUNDATION SCHOLARSHIP PROGRAM
• *See page 345*

HEALTH PROFESSIONS EDUCATION FOUNDATION

http://www.healthprofessions.ca.gov/

ALLIED HEALTHCARE SCHOLARSHIP PROGRAM
• *See page 151*

HEALTH RESEARCH COUNCIL OF NEW ZEALAND

http://www.hrc.govt.nz/

PACIFIC HEALTH WORKFORCE AWARD
• *See page 345*

PACIFIC MENTAL HEALTH WORK FORCE AWARD
• *See page 346*

HELLENIC UNIVERSITY CLUB OF PHILADELPHIA

http://www.hucphiladelphia.org/

DR. PETER A. THEODOS MEMORIAL GRADUATE SCHOLARSHIP
$2500 scholarship awarded to a senior undergraduate or graduate student with financial need pursuing studies leading to a Doctor of Medicine degree. Must be a U.S. citizen of Greek descent and a resident of particular counties in NJ or PA.

Academic Fields/Career Goals: Health and Medical Sciences.

Award: Scholarship for use in senior or graduate years; not renewable. *Number:* up to 1. *Amount:* up to $1500.

Eligibility Requirements: Applicant must be of Greek heritage; enrolled or expecting to enroll full-time at a four-year institution or university and resident of New Jersey, Pennsylvania. Available to U.S. citizens.

Application Requirements: Application form, financial need analysis, transcript. *Deadline:* April 21.

Contact: Anna Hadgis, Scholarship Chairman
Phone: 610-613-4310
E-mail: www.hucphiladelphia.org

INDIAN HEALTH SERVICES, UNITED STATES DEPARTMENT OF HEALTH AND HUMAN SERVICES

http://www.ihs.gov/scholarship

HEALTH PROFESSIONS PREPARATORY SCHOLARSHIP PROGRAM
• *See page 152*

INDIAN HEALTH SERVICE HEALTH PROFESSIONS PRE-GRADUATE SCHOLARSHIPS
• *See page 114*

INTERNATIONAL ORDER OF THE KING'S DAUGHTERS AND SONS

http://www.iokds.org/

HEALTH CAREERS SCHOLARSHIP
• *See page 238*

KETAMINE CLINICS OF LOS ANGELES

http://www.ketamineclinics.com/

KETAMINE CLINICS OF LOS ANGELES SCHOLARSHIP PROGRAM
• *See page 152*

LADIES AUXILIARY TO THE VETERANS OF FOREIGN WARS, DEPARTMENT OF MAINE

http://mainevfw.org/

FRANCES L. BOOTH MEDICAL SCHOLARSHIP SPONSORED BY LAVFW DEPARTMENT OF MAINE
Award for an undergraduate student majoring in the field of medicine who has a parent or grandparent who is a member of the Maine VFW or VFW auxiliary. Applicant must have sponsor from the VFW/Ladies Auxiliary to the Veterans of Foreign Wars.

Academic Fields/Career Goals: Health and Medical Sciences; Humanities; Nursing; Therapy/Rehabilitation.

Award: Scholarship for use in freshman, sophomore, junior, or senior years; renewable. *Number:* 1. *Amount:* $1000.

Eligibility Requirements: Applicant must be enrolled or expecting to enroll full-time at a two-year or four-year institution or university and resident of Maine. Applicant or parent of applicant must be member of Veterans of Foreign Wars or Auxiliary. Applicant must have 3.0 GPA or higher. Available to U.S. citizens.

Application Requirements: Application form, community service, essay, financial need analysis, personal letter, recommendations or references, resume, transcript. *Deadline:* March 31.

Contact: Sheila Webber, Chairman, FBMS
Ladies Auxiliary to the Veterans of Foreign Wars, Department of Maine
PO Box 493
Old Orchard Beach, ME 04064
Phone: 207-934-2405
E-mail: swebber2@maine.rr.com

MAINE OSTEOPATHIC ASSOCIATION

http://www.mainedo.org/

MAINE OSTEOPATHIC ASSOCIATION SCHOLARSHIP
One award of $1000 to a student who is a resident of Maine and able to present proof of enrollment at an approved osteopathic college.

Academic Fields/Career Goals: Health and Medical Sciences; Osteopathy.

Award: Scholarship for use in freshman year; not renewable. *Number:* 1. *Amount:* $1000.

Eligibility Requirements: Applicant must be enrolled or expecting to enroll full-time at a four-year institution or university and resident of Maine. Available to U.S. citizens.

Application Requirements: Application form, proof of Maine residence, recommendations or references. *Deadline:* June 1.

Contact: Dianne Dubord, Office Manager
Phone: 207-623-1101
E-mail: ddubord@mainedo.org

MARYLAND STATE HIGHER EDUCATION COMMISSION

http://www.mhec.state.md.us/

CHARLES W. RILEY FIRE AND EMERGENCY MEDICAL SERVICES TUITION REIMBURSEMENT PROGRAM
• *See page 329*

GRADUATE AND PROFESSIONAL SCHOLARSHIP PROGRAM-MARYLAND
• *See page 238*

MEDICAL SCRUBS COLLECTION

http://medicalscrubscollection.com

MEDICAL SCRUBS COLLECTION SCHOLARSHIP
• *See page 106*

MICHAEL MOODY FITNESS

http://www.michaelmoodyfitness.com/

MICHAEL MOODY FITNESS SCHOLARSHIP
• See page 255

NATIONAL ATHLETIC TRAINERS' ASSOCIATION RESEARCH AND EDUCATION FOUNDATION

http://www.natafoundation.org/

NATIONAL ATHLETIC TRAINERS' ASSOCIATION RESEARCH AND EDUCATION FOUNDATION SCHOLARSHIP PROGRAM

One-time award available to full-time students who are members of NATA. Minimum 3.2 GPA required. Open to undergraduate upperclassmen and graduate/postgraduate students.

Academic Fields/Career Goals: Health and Medical Sciences; Health Information Management/Technology; Sports-Related/Exercise Science; Therapy/Rehabilitation.

Award: Scholarship for use in junior, senior, graduate, or postgraduate years; not renewable. *Number:* 70. *Amount:* $2000.

Eligibility Requirements: Applicant must be enrolled or expecting to enroll full-time at a four-year institution or university. Applicant or parent of applicant must be member of National Athletic Trainers Association. Available to U.S. and non-U.S. citizens.

Application Requirements: Application form, essay, recommendations or references, transcript. *Deadline:* February 10.

Contact: Patsy Brown, Scholarship Coordinator
National Athletic Trainers' Association Research and Education Foundation
2952 Stemmons Freeway, Suite 200
Dallas, TX 75247
Phone: 214-637-6282 Ext. 151
Fax: 214-637-2206
E-mail: patsyb@nata.org

NATIONAL INSTITUTES OF HEALTH

http://www.nih.gov/

NIH UNDERGRADUATE SCHOLARSHIP PROGRAM FOR STUDENTS FROM DISADVANTAGED BACKGROUNDS
• See page 152

NATIONAL SOCIETY FOR HISTOTECHNOLOGY

http://nsh.org/

IRWIN S. LERNER STUDENT SCHOLARSHIPS

Student scholarships support the educational endeavors of aspiring histotechnologists.

Academic Fields/Career Goals: Health and Medical Sciences.

Award: Scholarship for use in freshman, sophomore, junior, or senior years; not renewable. *Number:* 5. *Amount:* $500.

Eligibility Requirements: Applicant must be enrolled or expecting to enroll full- or part-time at a two-year or four-year institution or university. Available to U.S. and non-U.S. citizens.

Application Requirements: Application form. *Deadline:* March 1.

Contact: Natalie Paskoski
Phone: 4435354060
E-mail: natalie@nsh.org

NEXTSTEPU

http://www.nextstepu.com/

$1,500 STEM SCHOLARSHIP
• See page 106

OREGON COMMUNITY FOUNDATION

http://www.oregoncf.org/

FRANZ STENZEL M.D. AND KATHRYN STENZEL SCHOLARSHIP FUND

Scholarships for Oregon residents, with a focus on three types of students: (a) those pursuing any type of undergraduate degree, (b) those pursuing a nursing education through a two-year, four-year, or graduate program, and (c) medical students.

Academic Fields/Career Goals: Health and Medical Sciences; Nursing.

Award: Scholarship for use in freshman, sophomore, junior, or senior years; renewable. *Number:* up to 70. *Amount:* $2000–$5000.

Eligibility Requirements: Applicant must be enrolled or expecting to enroll full-time at a two-year or four-year institution or university and resident of Oregon. Available to U.S. citizens.

Application Requirements: Application form, recommendations or references. *Deadline:* March 1.

Contact: Dianne Causey, Program Associate for Scholarships and Grants
Phone: 503-227-6846 Ext. 1418
E-mail: dcausey@oregoncf.org

OREGON STUDENT ASSISTANCE COMMISSION

http://www.GetCollegeFunds.org/

ANDY AITKENHEAD SCHOLARSHIP
• See page 115

CHESTER AND HELEN LUTHER SCHOLARSHIP

Award available to graduates of any high school in Oregon or Clark County, Washington. Applicants must also be residents of either Oregon or Clark County, Washington. Preference is given to first-generation college attendees. Must attend a college or university in Oregon or Clark County, Washington, enroll at least half-time, and be at least 25 years old as of the March scholarship deadline. Minimum 3.0 GPA and FAFSA are required.

Academic Fields/Career Goals: Health and Medical Sciences; Nursing.

Award: Scholarship for use in freshman, sophomore, junior, senior, or graduate years; not renewable.

Eligibility Requirements: Applicant must be enrolled or expecting to enroll full- or part-time at a two-year or four-year institution or university; resident of Oregon, Washington and studying in Oregon, Washington. Applicant must have 3.0 GPA or higher. Available to U.S. citizens.

Application Requirements: Application form, financial need analysis. *Deadline:* March 1.

Contact: Melissa Adams, Scholarship Processing Coordinator
Phone: 541-687-7409
E-mail: melissa.adams@hecc.oregon.gov

CLARK-PHELPS SCHOLARSHIP
• See page 238

MARION A. LINDEMAN SCHOLARSHIP

Award for Willamette View Health Center or Willamette View Terrace employees who have completed one or more years of service. Must be pursuing a degree or certificate in nursing, speech, physical or occupational therapy, or other health-related fields at a public or nonprofit college. Must enroll at least half time in a public or non-profit college and reapply annually for award renewal.

Academic Fields/Career Goals: Health and Medical Sciences; Nursing; Therapy/Rehabilitation.

Award: Scholarship for use in freshman, sophomore, junior, or senior years; not renewable.

Eligibility Requirements: Applicant must be enrolled or expecting to enroll full- or part-time at a two-year or four-year institution. Applicant or parent of applicant must be affiliated with Willamette View. Available to U.S. citizens.

Application Requirements: Application form, financial need analysis. *Deadline:* March 1.

Contact: Melissa Adams, Scholarship Processing Coordinator
    Phone: 541-687-7409
    E-mail: melissa.adams@hecc.oregon.gov

PEARL SCHOLARSHIP

Award for students in Oregon public colleges and universities who are or have been in foster care. College students must have a minimum 3.0 GPA. Must be enrolled at least part-time and studying health sciences.

Academic Fields/Career Goals: Health and Medical Sciences.

Award: Scholarship for use in freshman, sophomore, junior, or senior years; not renewable.

Eligibility Requirements: Applicant must be enrolled or expecting to enroll full- or part-time at a four-year institution or university and studying in Oregon. Available to U.S. citizens.

Application Requirements: Application form, financial need analysis. *Deadline:* March 1.

Contact: Melissa Adams, Scholarship Processing Coordinator
    Phone: 541-687-7409
    E-mail: melissa.adams@hecc.oregon.gov

PACERS FOUNDATION INC.

http://www.pacersfoundation.org/

LINDA CRAIG MEMORIAL SCHOLARSHIP PRESENTED BY ST. VINCENT SPORTS MEDICINE

Scholarship presented by St. Vincent Sports Medicine is for currently-enrolled juniors and seniors with declared majors of medicine, sports medicine, and/or physical therapy. Students must have completed at least 4 semesters and attend a school in Indiana. Minimum 3.0 GPA required.

Academic Fields/Career Goals: Health and Medical Sciences; Sports-Related/Exercise Science; Therapy/Rehabilitation.

Award: Scholarship for use in junior, senior, graduate, or postgraduate years; renewable. *Number:* 1–2. *Amount:* $2000.

Eligibility Requirements: Applicant must be enrolled or expecting to enroll full-time at a two-year or four-year institution or university and studying in Indiana. Applicant must have 3.0 GPA or higher. Available to U.S. citizens.

Application Requirements: Application form, essay, recommendations or references, transcript. *Deadline:* March 1.

Contact: Jami Marsh, Executive Director
    Pacers Foundation Inc.
    125 South Pennsylvania Street
    Indianapolis, IN 46204
    Phone: 317-917-2856
    E-mail: foundation@pacers.com

PILOT INTERNATIONAL FOUNDATION

http://www.pilotinternational.org/

PILOT INTERNATIONAL SCHOLARSHIP

The Pilot International Scholarship was established in 1988 to provide financial Assistance to undergraduate students preparing for a career working with youth leadership and development, helping people with brain safety or fitness, or caring for families during times of need. Scholarships are based on financial need, academic success, and application contents. Scholarships are awarded for one academic year. A student may re-apply and be granted the Pilot International Scholarship for no more than 3 additional years.

Academic Fields/Career Goals: Health and Medical Sciences; Nursing; Psychology; Special Education; Therapy/Rehabilitation.

Award: Scholarship for use in freshman, sophomore, or junior years; not renewable. *Number:* 5–10. *Amount:* $500–$1500.

Eligibility Requirements: Applicant must be enrolled or expecting to enroll full- or part-time at a two-year or four-year or technical institution. Applicant must have 3.0 GPA or higher. Available to U.S. citizens.

Application Requirements: Application form, community service, financial need analysis. *Deadline:* March 15.

Contact: Sierra Martin, Founders Fund Specialist
    Pilot International Foundation
    102 Preston Court
    Macon, GA 31210
    Phone: 478-4771208 Ext. 304
    Fax: 478-4776978
    E-mail: sierra@pilothq.org

RUBY NEWHALL MEMORIAL SCHOLARSHIP

Ruby Newhall Memorial Scholarship are for students from outside the United States pursuing a degree in either the US or Canada. The field of study must be of a nature that it improves the quality of life for the community in the student's home country. An applicant for the Ruby Newhall Memorial Scholarship must be from a foreign country, pursuing a degree in the United States or Canada. The field of study must be of a nature that it improves the quality of life for the community in their home country. The applicant must have spent at least one semester in a college in the United States or Canada by the application submission date and have a cumulative grade point average of 3.0 on a 4.0 scale. The applicant must be a full time student and remain a full time student for the duration of the scholarship. The student must have a documented Visa at the time the application is completed, submitted, graded and the scholarship is awarded. Failure to have a valid Visa at any time during this process could disqualify the student.

Academic Fields/Career Goals: Health and Medical Sciences; Nursing; Psychology; Public Health; Social Services; Special Education; Therapy/Rehabilitation.

Award: Scholarship for use in freshman, sophomore, junior, senior, or graduate years; not renewable. *Number:* 5–10. *Amount:* $1500.

Eligibility Requirements: Applicant must be enrolled or expecting to enroll full- or part-time at a two-year or four-year or technical institution or university. Applicant must have 3.0 GPA or higher. Available to Canadian and non-U.S. citizens.

Application Requirements: Application form, financial need analysis. *Deadline:* March 15.

Contact: Sierra Martin
    Phone: 478-477-1208 Ext. 304
    E-mail: sierra@pilothq.org

PLATINUM EDUCATIONAL GROUP

www.platinumed.com

PLATINUM EDUCATIONAL GROUP SCHOLARSHIPS PROGRAM FOR EMS, NURSING, AND ALLIED HEALTH
• *See page 107*

PRESBYTERIAN CHURCH (USA)

http://www.pcusa.org/financialaid

STUDENT OPPORTUNITY SCHOLARSHIP
• *See page 258*

SCARLETT FAMILY FOUNDATION SCHOLARSHIP PROGRAM

http://www.scarlettfoundation.org/

SCHOLARSHIP FOR STUDENTS PURSUING A BUSINESS OR STEM DEGREE
• *See page 84*

SIGMA XI, THE SCIENTIFIC RESEARCH SOCIETY

http://www.sigmaxi.org/

SIGMA XI GRANTS-IN-AID OF RESEARCH
• *See page 101*

THE SOCIETY FOR THE SCIENTIFIC STUDY OF SEXUALITY
http://www.sexscience.org/

THE SOCIETY FOR THE SCIENTIFIC STUDY OF SEXUALITY STUDENT RESEARCH GRANT
• *See page 109*

SOCIETY OF PEDIATRIC NURSES
http://www.pedsnurses.org/

SOCIETY OF PEDIATRIC NURSES EDUCATIONAL SCHOLARSHIP
• *See page 190*

STRAIGHTFORWARD MEDIA
http://www.straightforwardmedia.com/

STRAIGHTFORWARD MEDIA MEDICAL PROFESSIONS SCHOLARSHIP
• *See page 239*

ULTRASOUNDTECHNICIANSCHOOLS.COM
http://www.ultrasoundtechnicianschools.com

ULTRASOUNDTECHNICIANSCHOOLS.COM SCHOLARSHIP
We are offering you the chance to win a $1,000 ultrasound technician scholarship. A winner will be selected from the list of all eligible candidates. We will be awarding two different scholarships each year. When one deadline ends, the next scholarship will begin.

Academic Fields/Career Goals: Health and Medical Sciences; Health Information Management/Technology; Radiology.

Award: Scholarship for use in freshman, sophomore, junior, or senior years; not renewable. *Number:* 2. *Amount:* $1000.

Eligibility Requirements: Applicant must be enrolled or expecting to enroll full-time at a two-year or four-year or technical institution or university. Available to U.S. citizens.

Application Requirements: Application form. *Deadline:* July 15.

Contact: Jennifer Moody, Website Marketing Strategist
UltrasoundTechnicianSchools.com
15500 W 113th St
#200
Lenexa, KS 66219
Phone: 913-254-6000 Ext. 6063
E-mail: jennifer.moody@marketing.keypathedu.com

UNITED NATIONS ASSOCIATION OF CONNECTICUT
http://www.unausa.org

UNITED NATIONS ASSOCIATION OF CONNECTICUT SCHOLARSHIP
• *See page 133*

UNITED NEGRO COLLEGE FUND
http://www.uncf.org/

UNCF STEM SCHOLARS PROGRAM
• *See page 159*

UNITED HEALTH FOUNDATION DIVERSE SCHOLARS INITIATIVE
• *See page 152*

U.S. DEPARTMENT OF HEALTH AND HUMAN SERVICES
http://www.hhs.gov/

U. S. PUBLIC HEALTH SERVICE-HEALTH RESOURCES AND SERVICES ADMINISTRATION, BUREAU OF HEALTH PROFESSIONS SCHOLARSHIPS FOR DISADVANTAGED STUDENTS
• *See page 239*

VESALIUS TRUST FOR VISUAL COMMUNICATION IN THE HEALTH SCIENCES
http://www.vesaliustrust.org/

STUDENT RESEARCH SCHOLARSHIP
Scholarships available to students currently enrolled in an undergraduate or graduate school program of bio-communications (medical illustration) who have completed one full year of the curriculum.

Academic Fields/Career Goals: Health and Medical Sciences.

Award: Scholarship for use in junior, senior, or graduate years; not renewable. *Number:* 10–15. *Amount:* $500.

Eligibility Requirements: Applicant must be enrolled or expecting to enroll full- or part-time at a four-year institution or university and must have an interest in art. Available to U.S. and non-U.S. citizens.

Application Requirements: Application form, portfolio, recommendations or references, resume, transcript. *Deadline:* November 7.

Contact: Wendy Gee, Student Grants and Scholarships
Vesalius Trust for Visual Communication in the Health Sciences
1100 Grundy Lane
San Bruno, CA 94066
Phone: 650-244-4320
E-mail: wendy.hillergee@krames.com

WISCONSIN MEDICAL SOCIETY FOUNDATION
http://www.wisconsinmedicalsocietyfoundation.org

AMY HUNTER-WILSON, MD SCHOLARSHIP
Scholarship assists American Indians with proof of tribal membership who pursue training or advanced education as doctors of medicine, nurses, or in related health careers. Award amounts are determined based on the students field of study and financial need and will vary depending on the number of eligible applicants and funds available.

Academic Fields/Career Goals: Health and Medical Sciences.

Award: Scholarship for use in freshman, sophomore, junior, senior, or graduate years; not renewable.

Eligibility Requirements: Applicant must be American Indian/Alaska Native; enrolled or expecting to enroll full-time at a two-year or four-year or technical institution or university; resident of Wisconsin and studying in Wisconsin. Available to U.S. citizens.

Application Requirements: Application form, essay, financial need analysis. *Deadline:* February 1.

Contact: Ms. Elizabeth Ringle, Scholarship Coordinator
Phone: 866-442-3800
Fax: 608-442-3851

HEALTH INFORMATION MANAGEMENT/ TECHNOLOGY

AHIMA FOUNDATION

http://ahimafoundation.org/

AHIMA FOUNDATION STUDENT MERIT SCHOLARSHIP

Merit scholarships for undergraduate, Master's, and Doctoral health information management students. Must be a member of AHIMA. One standard application for all available scholarships. Applicant must have a minimum cumulative GPA of 3.5 (out of 4.0) or 4.5 (out of 5.0). Applications information is available at: http://ahimafoundation.org/education/MeritScholarships.aspx

Academic Fields/Career Goals: Health Information Management/Technology.

Award: Scholarship for use in sophomore, junior, senior, graduate, or postgraduate years; not renewable. *Number:* 1. *Amount:* $1000–$2500.

Eligibility Requirements: Applicant must be enrolled or expecting to enroll full- or part-time at a two-year or four-year institution or university. Applicant or parent of applicant must be member of American Health Information Management Association. Applicant must have 3.5 GPA or higher. Available to U.S. and non-U.S. citizens.

Application Requirements: Application form, application form may be submitted online (http://ahimafoundation.org/education/MeritScholarships.aspx), community service, essay, program director verification, recommendations or references, transcript. *Deadline:* September 30.

Contact: AHIMA Foundation
233 North Michigan Avenue, 21st Floor
Chicago, IL 60601-5800
Phone: 312-233-1131
E-mail: fore@ahima.org

ALICE L. HALTOM EDUCATIONAL FUND

http://www.alhef.org/

ALICE L. HALTOM EDUCATIONAL FUND
• *See page 160*

AMERICAN LEGION AUXILIARY DEPARTMENT OF COLORADO

http://www.alacolorado.com

AMERICAN LEGION AUXILIARY DEPARTMENT OF COLORADO PAST PRESIDENTS' PARLEY HEALTH CARE PROFESSIONAL SCHOLARSHIPNURSES SCHOLARSHIP
• *See page 133*

AVACARE MEDICAL

https://avacaremedical.com

AVACARE MEDICAL SCHOLARSHIP
• *See page 105*

BETHESDA LUTHERAN COMMUNITIES

http://www.bethesdalutherancommunities.org/scholarships

DEVELOPMENTAL DISABILITIES SCHOLASTIC ACHIEVEMENT SCHOLARSHIP FOR COLLEGE STUDENTS WHO ARE LUTHERAN
• *See page 236*

BHW GROUP

https://thebhwgroup.com/

BHW WOMEN IN STEM SCHOLARSHIP
• *See page 74*

CANADIAN SOCIETY FOR MEDICAL LABORATORY SCIENCE

http://www.csmls.org/

E.V. BOOTH SCHOLARSHIP AWARD
• *See page 345*

CYNTHIA E. MORGAN SCHOLARSHIP FUND (CEMS)

http://www.cemsfund.com/

CYNTHIA E. MORGAN MEMORIAL SCHOLARSHIP FUND, INC.
• *See page 316*

HEALTHCARE INFORMATION AND MANAGEMENT SYSTEMS SOCIETY FOUNDATION

http://www.himss.org/

HIMSS FOUNDATION SCHOLARSHIP PROGRAM
• *See page 345*

HEALTH RESEARCH COUNCIL OF NEW ZEALAND

http://www.hrc.govt.nz/

PACIFIC HEALTH WORKFORCE AWARD
• *See page 345*

PACIFIC MENTAL HEALTH WORK FORCE AWARD
• *See page 346*

MEDICAL SCRUBS COLLECTION

http://medicalscrubscollection.com

MEDICAL SCRUBS COLLECTION SCHOLARSHIP
• *See page 106*

MICHAEL MOODY FITNESS

http://www.michaelmoodyfitness.com/

MICHAEL MOODY FITNESS SCHOLARSHIP
• *See page 255*

NATIONAL ATHLETIC TRAINERS' ASSOCIATION RESEARCH AND EDUCATION FOUNDATION

http://www.natafoundation.org/

NATIONAL ATHLETIC TRAINERS' ASSOCIATION RESEARCH AND EDUCATION FOUNDATION SCHOLARSHIP PROGRAM
• *See page 354*

NEXTSTEPU

http://www.nextstepu.com/

$1,500 STEM SCHOLARSHIP
• *See page 106*

OREGON STUDENT ASSISTANCE COMMISSION

http://www.GetCollegeFunds.org/

WILLIAM E. KEENE MEMORIAL SCHOLARSHIP
• *See page 316*

SCARLETT FAMILY FOUNDATION SCHOLARSHIP PROGRAM

http://www.scarlettfoundation.org/

SCHOLARSHIP FOR STUDENTS PURSUING A BUSINESS OR STEM DEGREE
• *See page 84*

STRAIGHTFORWARD MEDIA

http://www.straightforwardmedia.com/

STRAIGHTFORWARD MEDIA MEDICAL PROFESSIONS SCHOLARSHIP
• *See page 239*

TECHNOLOGY FIRST

https://technologyfirst.org/

ROBERT V. MCKENNA SCHOLARSHIPS
• *See page 219*

ULTRASOUNDTECHNICIANSCHOOLS.COM

http://www.ultrasoundtechnicianschools.com

ULTRASOUNDTECHNICIANSCHOOLS.COM SCHOLARSHIP
• *See page 356*

HEATING, AIR-CONDITIONING, AND REFRIGERATION MECHANICS

AMERICAN INDIAN SCIENCE AND ENGINEERING SOCIETY

http://www.aises.org/

A.T. ANDERSON MEMORIAL SCHOLARSHIP PROGRAM
• *See page 109*

AMERICAN SOCIETY OF HEATING, REFRIGERATING, AND AIR CONDITIONING ENGINEERS, INC.

http://www.ashrae.org/

ALWIN B. NEWTON SCHOLARSHIP
• *See page 264*

ASHRAE GENERAL SCHOLARSHIPS
• *See page 276*

DUANE HANSON SCHOLARSHIP
• *See page 264*

FRANK M. CODA SCHOLARSHIP
• *See page 264*

HENRY ADAMS SCHOLARSHIP
• *See page 265*

LYNN G. BELLENGER SCHOLARSHIP
• *See page 265*

REUBEN TRANE SCHOLARSHIP
• *See page 265*

WILLIS H. CARRIER SCHOLARSHIPS
• *See page 265*

BHW GROUP

https://thebhwgroup.com/

BHW WOMEN IN STEM SCHOLARSHIP
• *See page 74*

FABRICATORS AND MANUFACTURERS ASSOCIATION FOUNDATION

http://www.nutsandboltsfoundation.org/scholarships/

COLLEGE AND TRADE/TECHNICAL SCHOOL SCHOLARSHIPS
• *See page 178*

PLUMBING-HEATING-COOLING CONTRACTORS EDUCATION FOUNDATION

http://www.phccfoundation.org/scholarships

BRADFORD WHITE CORPORATION SCHOLARSHIP
Scholarship for students enrolled in either an approved four-year PHCC apprenticeship program or at an accredited two-year community college, technical college, or trade school.

Academic Fields/Career Goals: Heating, Air-Conditioning, and Refrigeration Mechanics; Trade/Technical Specialties.

Award: Scholarship for use in freshman, sophomore, junior, or senior years; not renewable. *Number:* 3. *Amount:* $2500.

Eligibility Requirements: Applicant must be enrolled or expecting to enroll full-time at a two-year or technical institution. Applicant must have 2.5 GPA or higher. Available to U.S. and Canadian citizens.

Application Requirements: Application form, essay. *Deadline:* May 1.
Contact: John Zink, Scholarship Coordinator
　　　Phone: 800-533-7694
　　　E-mail: scholarships@naphcc.org

DELTA FAUCET COMPANY SCHOLARSHIP PROGRAM
• *See page 167*

PHCC EDUCATIONAL FOUNDATION NEED-BASED SCHOLARSHIP
• See page 167

PHCC EDUCATIONAL FOUNDATION SCHOLARSHIP PROGRAM
• See page 167

PROFESSIONAL CONSTRUCTION ESTIMATORS ASSOCIATION

http://www.pcea.org/

TED G. WILSON MEMORIAL SCHOLARSHIP FOUNDATION
• See page 197

SOUTH CAROLINA ASSOCIATION OF HEATING AND AIR CONDITIONING CONTRACTORS

http://www.schvac.org/

SOUTH CAROLINA ASSOCIATION OF HEATING AND AIR CONDITIONING CONTRACTORS SCHOLARSHIP

Scholarship of $500 to pursue a career in the heating and air conditioning industry. Participating students must maintain an overall GPA of 2.5 and a GPA of 3.0 in all major topics. Deadline varies.

Academic Fields/Career Goals: Heating, Air-Conditioning, and Refrigeration Mechanics.

Award: Scholarship for use in freshman year; renewable. *Amount:* $500.

Eligibility Requirements: Applicant must be high school student and planning to enroll or expecting to enroll full- or part-time at a technical institution. Applicant must have 2.5 GPA or higher. Available to U.S. and non-U.S. citizens.

Application Requirements: Application form, recommendations or references. *Deadline:* varies.

Contact: Leigh Faircloth, Scholarship Committee
Phone: 800-395-9276
Fax: 803-252-7799
E-mail: staff@schvac.org

STRAIGHTFORWARD MEDIA

http://www.straightforwardmedia.com/

STRAIGHTFORWARD MEDIA VOCATIONAL-TECHNICAL SCHOOL SCHOLARSHIP
• See page 107

HISTORIC PRESERVATION AND CONSERVATION

AMERICAN SCHOOL OF CLASSICAL STUDIES AT ATHENS

http://www.ascsa.edu.gr/

ASCSA SUMMER SESSIONS SCHOLARSHIPS
• See page 108

COSTUME SOCIETY OF AMERICA

http://www.costumesocietyamerica.com/

ADELE FILENE STUDENT PRESENTER GRANT
• See page 125

STELLA BLUM STUDENT RESEARCH GRANT
• See page 125

THE GEORGIA TRUST FOR HISTORIC PRESERVATION

http://www.georgiatrust.org/

B. PHINIZY SPALDING, HUBERT B. OWENS, AND THE NATIONAL SOCIETY OF THE COLONIAL DAMES OF AMERICA IN THE STATE OF GEORGIA ACADEMIC SCHOLARSHIPS
• See page 104

J. NEEL REID PRIZE
• See page 121

PLAN NEW HAMPSHIRE

www.plannh.org

PLAN NEW HAMPSHIRE SCHOLARSHIP AND PROGRAM
• See page 123

HISTORY

AMERICAN FEDERATION OF STATE, COUNTY, AND MUNICIPAL EMPLOYEES

http://www.afscme.org/

AFSCME/UNCF UNION SCHOLARS PROGRAM
• See page 103

AMERICAN SCHOOL OF CLASSICAL STUDIES AT ATHENS

http://www.ascsa.edu.gr/

ASCSA SUMMER SESSIONS SCHOLARSHIPS
• See page 108

ASSOCIATION OF FORMER INTELLIGENCE OFFICERS

http://www.afio.com

AFIO UNDERGRADUATE AND GRADUATE SCHOLARSHIPS
• See page 103

CANADIAN INSTITUTE OF UKRAINIAN STUDIES

http://www.cius.ca/

LEO J. KRYSA UNDERGRADUATE SCHOLARSHIP
• See page 125

COSTUME SOCIETY OF AMERICA

http://www.costumesocietyamerica.com/

ADELE FILENE STUDENT PRESENTER GRANT
• See page 125

STELLA BLUM STUDENT RESEARCH GRANT
• *See page 125*

CULTURAL SERVICES OF THE FRENCH EMBASSY
http://www.frenchculture.org/

TEACHING ASSISTANT PROGRAM IN FRANCE
• *See page 104*

THE GEORGIA TRUST FOR HISTORIC PRESERVATION
http://www.georgiatrust.org/

B. PHINIZY SPALDING, HUBERT B. OWENS, AND THE NATIONAL SOCIETY OF THE COLONIAL DAMES OF AMERICA IN THE STATE OF GEORGIA ACADEMIC SCHOLARSHIPS
• *See page 104*

GREATER SALINA COMMUNITY FOUNDATION
http://www.gscf.org/

KANSAS FEDERATION OF REPUBLICAN WOMEN SCHOLARSHIP

Awards female students currently attending a Kansas college or university with declared major of political science, history, or public administration. Must be entering junior or senior year of undergraduate study, or attending graduate school. Must be Kansas residents and maintain cumulative GPA of 3.0 or better. Applicants must be registered members of the Republican Party. Must be involved in extracurricular activities.

Academic Fields/Career Goals: History; Political Science; Public Policy and Administration.

Award: Scholarship for use in junior, senior, or graduate years; renewable. *Number:* 1. *Amount:* up to $1000.

Eligibility Requirements: Applicant must be enrolled or expecting to enroll full-time at a two-year or four-year institution or university; female; resident of Kansas and studying in Kansas. Applicant must have 3.0 GPA or higher. Available to U.S. citizens.

Application Requirements: Application form, essay. *Deadline:* March 31.

Contact: Michelle Griffin, Scholarship and Affiliate Coordinator
Greater Salina Community Foundation
PO Box 2876
Salina, KS 67402-2876
Phone: 785-823-1800
E-mail: michellegriffin@gscf.org

INSTITUTE FOR HUMANE STUDIES
http://www.theihs.org/

HUMANE STUDIES FELLOWSHIPS
• *See page 204*

ISLAMIC SCHOLARSHIP FUND
http://islamicscholarshipfund.org/

ISF NATIONAL SCHOLARSHIP
• *See page 108*

THE LYNDON BAINES JOHNSON FOUNDATION
http://www.lbjlibrary.org/page/foundation/

MOODY RESEARCH GRANTS
• *See page 104*

NATIONAL SOCIETY DAUGHTERS OF THE AMERICAN REVOLUTION
http://www.dar.org/

NATIONAL SOCIETY DAUGHTERS OF THE AMERICAN REVOLUTION DR. AURA-LEE A. PITTENGER AND JAMES HOBBS PITTENGER AMERICAN HISTORY SCHOLARSHIP

Scholarship of $2000 each year for up to four consecutive years to a graduating high school senior who will have a concentrated study of a minimum of 24 credit hours in American history or American government while in college. United States citizens residing abroad may apply through a Units Overseas chapter.

Academic Fields/Career Goals: History; Political Science.

Award: Scholarship for use in freshman year; renewable. *Number:* 1. *Amount:* $2000.

Eligibility Requirements: Applicant must be high school student and planning to enroll or expecting to enroll full-time at a four-year institution or university. Available to U.S. citizens.

Application Requirements: Application form, essay. *Deadline:* February 10.

Contact: Lakeisha Graham, Manager, Office of the Reporter General
Phone: 202-628-1776
Fax: 202-879-3348
E-mail: nsdarscholarships@dar.org

NATIONAL SOCIETY DAUGHTERS OF THE AMERICAN REVOLUTION ENID HALL GRISWOLD MEMORIAL SCHOLARSHIP
• *See page 246*

PHI ALPHA THETA HISTORY HONOR SOCIETY, INC.
http://www.phialphatheta.org/

PHI ALPHA THETA PAPER PRIZES

Award for best graduate and undergraduate student papers. Grants $500 prize for best graduate student paper, $500 prize for best undergraduate paper, and four $350 prizes for either graduate or undergraduate papers. All applicants must be members of the association.

Academic Fields/Career Goals: History.

Award: Prize for use in freshman, sophomore, junior, senior, or graduate years; not renewable. *Number:* 6. *Amount:* $350–$500.

Eligibility Requirements: Applicant must be enrolled or expecting to enroll full-time at a four-year institution or university. Applicant or parent of applicant must be member of Phi Alpha Theta. Applicant must have 3.0 GPA or higher. Available to U.S. and non-U.S. citizens.

Application Requirements: Essay, recommendations or references. *Deadline:* June 30.

Contact: Dr. Clayton Drees, Department of History
Phi Alpha Theta History Honor Society, Inc.
Virginia Wesleyan College
1584 Wesleyan Drive
Norfolk, VA 23502-5599
E-mail: cdrees@vwc.edu

PHI ALPHA THETA UNDERGRADUATE STUDENT SCHOLARSHIP

Awards of $1000 available to exceptional juniors entering the senior year and majoring in modern European history (1815 to present). Must be Phi Alpha Theta members. Based on both financial need and merit.

Academic Fields/Career Goals: History.

Award: Scholarship for use in senior year; not renewable. *Number:* 1. *Amount:* $1000.

Eligibility Requirements: Applicant must be enrolled or expecting to enroll full-time at a four-year institution or university. Applicant or parent of applicant must be member of Phi Alpha Theta. Available to U.S. and non-U.S. citizens.

Application Requirements: Application form, recommendations or references, resume, transcript. *Deadline:* March 1.

Contact: Dr. Graydon Tunstall, Executive Director
Phi Alpha Theta History Honor Society, Inc.
University of South Florida
4202 East Fowler Avenue, SOC 107
Tampa, FL 33620-8100
Phone: 800-394-8195
Fax: 813-974-8215
E-mail: info@phialphatheta.org

PHI ALPHA THETA/WESTERN FRONT ASSOCIATION PAPER PRIZE

Essay competition open to full-time undergraduate members of the association. The paper must be from 12 to 15 typed pages and must address the American experience in World War I, must be dealing with virtually any aspect of American involvement during the period from 1912 (second Moroccan crisis) to 1924 (Dawes plan). Primary source material must be used. For further details visit http://www.phialphatheta.org.

Academic Fields/Career Goals: History.

Award: Prize for use in freshman, sophomore, junior, or senior years; not renewable. *Number:* 1. *Amount:* $1000.

Eligibility Requirements: Applicant must be enrolled or expecting to enroll full-time at a four-year institution or university and must have an interest in writing. Applicant or parent of applicant must be member of Phi Alpha Theta. Applicant must have 3.0 GPA or higher. Available to U.S. and non-U.S. citizens.

Application Requirements: 5 copies of the paper, CD-ROM containing a file of the paper and cover letter, application form, essay. *Deadline:* December 1.

Contact: Dr. Graydon Tunstall, Executive Director
Phi Alpha Theta History Honor Society, Inc.
University of South Florida
4202 East Fowler Avenue, SOC 107
Tampa, FL 33620-8100
Phone: 800-394-8195
Fax: 813-974-8215
E-mail: info@phialphatheta.org

PHI ALPHA THETA WORLD HISTORY ASSOCIATION PAPER PRIZE

Awards one undergraduate and one graduate-level prize for papers examining any historical issue with global implications such as: exchange or interchange of cultures, comparison of civilizations or cultures. This is a joint award with the World History Association. Must be a member of the World History Association or Phi Alpha Theta. Paper must have been composed while enrolled at an accredited college or university. Must send in four copies of paper along with professor's letter.

Academic Fields/Career Goals: History; Humanities; International Studies; Social Sciences.

Award: Prize for use in freshman, sophomore, junior, senior, or graduate years; not renewable. *Number:* 2. *Amount:* $500.

Eligibility Requirements: Applicant must be enrolled or expecting to enroll full-time at a four-year institution or university. Applicant or parent of applicant must be member of Other Student Academic Clubs, Phi Alpha Theta. Applicant must have 3.0 GPA or higher. Available to U.S. and non-U.S. citizens.

Application Requirements: 4 copies of paper, abstract, letter from faculty member or professor, recommendations or references. *Deadline:* June 30.

Contact: Prof. Merry Wiesner-Hanks
Phi Alpha Theta History Honor Society, Inc.
Department of History
University of Wisconsin-Madison
Madison, WI 53201
E-mail: merrywh@uwm.edu

SOCIETY FOR CLASSICAL STUDIES

http://www.classicalstudies.org/

MINORITY STUDENT SUMMER SCHOLARSHIP
• *See page 118*

SOUTHERN BAPTIST HISTORICAL LIBRARY AND ARCHIVES

http://www.sbhla.org/

LYNN E. MAY JR. STUDY GRANT
• *See page 104*

STRAIGHTFORWARD MEDIA

http://www.straightforwardmedia.com/

STRAIGHTFORWARD MEDIA LIBERAL ARTS SCHOLARSHIP
• *See page 126*

TOPSFIELD HISTORICAL SOCIETY

http://www.topsfieldhistory.org/

JOHN KIMBALL MEMORIAL TRUST SCHOLARSHIP PROGRAM FOR THE STUDY OF HISTORY

Scholarship grants funds for tuition, books, and other educational and research expenses to undergraduate and graduate students; as well as college, university, and graduate school instructors and professors who have excelled in, and/or have a passion for the study of history and related disciplines; and who reside in, or have a substantial connection to Topsfield, Massachusetts.

Academic Fields/Career Goals: History.

Award: Grant for use in freshman, sophomore, junior, senior, graduate, or postgraduate years; not renewable. *Number:* 3–10. *Amount:* $300–$5000.

Eligibility Requirements: Applicant must be enrolled or expecting to enroll full- or part-time at a two-year or four-year or technical institution or university; resident of Massachusetts and studying in Massachusetts. Available to U.S. citizens.

Application Requirements: Application form. *Deadline:* April 15.

Contact: Mr. Norman Isler, Trustee, John Kimball Scholarship Program
Topsfield Historical Society
PO Box 323
Topsfield, MA 01983
Phone: 978-887-9724
E-mail: normisler@comcast.net

UNITED DAUGHTERS OF THE CONFEDERACY

http://www.hqudc.org/

HELEN JAMES BREWER SCHOLARSHIP

Award for full-time undergraduate student who is a descendant of a Confederate soldier, sailor or marine. Must be from Alabama, Florida, Georgia, South Carolina, Tennessee or Virginia. Recipient must be enrolled in an accredited college or university and studying history and literature. Must be a member or former member of the Children of the Confederacy. Minimum 3.0 GPA required.

Academic Fields/Career Goals: History; Literature/English/Writing.

Award: Scholarship for use in freshman, sophomore, junior, or senior years; renewable. *Number:* 1–2. *Amount:* $800–$1000.

Eligibility Requirements: Applicant must be enrolled or expecting to enroll full-time at a four-year institution or university and resident of Alabama, Florida, Georgia, South Carolina, Tennessee, Virginia. Applicant or parent of applicant must be member of Children of the Confederacy, United Daughters of the Confederacy. Applicant must have 3.0 GPA or higher. Available to U.S. citizens.

Application Requirements: Application form, copy of applicant's birth certificate, copy of confederate ancestor's proof of service, essay, financial need analysis, personal photograph, recommendations or references, self-addressed stamped envelope with application, test scores, transcript. *Deadline:* March 15.

Contact: Ms. Jamie Davis, Second Vice President General
Phone: 804-355-1636
E-mail: hqudc@rcn.com

UNITED NEGRO COLLEGE FUND
http://www.uncf.org/

CATHERINE W. PIERCE SCHOLARSHIP
• See page 127

UNCF/KOCH SCHOLARS PROGRAM FOR UNDERGRADUATES
• See page 87

WILLA CATHER FOUNDATION
http://www.willacather.org/

ANTONETTE WILLA SKUPA TURNER SCHOLARSHIP
The purpose of the Antonette Willa Skupa Turner Scholarship is to provide financial assistance to graduates of Nebraska high schools who plan to enroll as English or history majors in accredited colleges or universities.

Academic Fields/Career Goals: History; Literature/English/Writing.

Award: Scholarship for use in freshman year; not renewable. *Number:* 1. *Amount:* $500.

Eligibility Requirements: Applicant must be high school student; planning to enroll or expecting to enroll full-time at a four-year institution or university and resident of Nebraska. Applicant must have 3.0 GPA or higher. Available to U.S. citizens.

Application Requirements: Application form, essay. *Deadline:* February 28.

Contact: Ashley Olson, Executive Director
Willa Cather Foundation
413 North Webster Street
Red Cloud, NE 68970
Phone: 402-746-2653
E-mail: info@willacather.org

HOME ECONOMICS

ABBIE SARGENT MEMORIAL SCHOLARSHIP INC.
http://www.nhfarmbureau.org/

ABBIE SARGENT MEMORIAL SCHOLARSHIP
• See page 91

AMERICAN ASSOCIATION OF FAMILY & CONSUMER SERVICES
http://www.aafcs.org/

AMERICAN ASSOCIATION OF FAMILY & CONSUMER SCIENCES NATIONAL UNDERGRADUATE SCHOLARSHIP
The association awards scholarships to individuals who have exhibited the potential to make contributions to the family and consumer sciences profession.

Academic Fields/Career Goals: Home Economics.

Award: Scholarship for use in sophomore, junior, or senior years; not renewable. *Number:* up to 1. *Amount:* up to $5000.

Eligibility Requirements: Applicant must be enrolled or expecting to enroll full-time at a four-year institution or university. Available to U.S. citizens.

Application Requirements: Application form, application form may be submitted online (http://www.aafcs.org), recommendations or references, resume, transcript. *Deadline:* January 15.

COSTUME SOCIETY OF AMERICA
http://www.costumesocietyamerica.com/

ADELE FILENE STUDENT PRESENTER GRANT
• See page 125

STELLA BLUM STUDENT RESEARCH GRANT
• See page 125

FAMILY, CAREER AND COMMUNITY LEADERS OF AMERICA-TEXAS ASSOCIATION
http://www.texasfccla.org/

C.J. DAVIDSON SCHOLARSHIP FOR FCCLA
Renewable award for graduating high school seniors enrolled in full-time program in family and consumer sciences. Must be Texas resident and should study in Texas. Must have minimum GPA of 2.5.

Academic Fields/Career Goals: Home Economics.

Award: Scholarship for use in freshman year; renewable. *Number:* 1–10. *Amount:* up to $18,000.

Eligibility Requirements: Applicant must be high school student; planning to enroll or expecting to enroll full-time at a four-year institution or university; single; resident of Texas and studying in Texas. Applicant or parent of applicant must be member of Family, Career and Community Leaders of America. Applicant must have 2.5 GPA or higher. Available to U.S. citizens.

Application Requirements: Application form, essay, recommendations or references, test scores, transcript. *Deadline:* March 1.

Contact: Staff
Family, Career and Community Leaders of America-Texas Association
1107 West 45th
Austin, TX 78756
Phone: 512-306-0099
Fax: 512-442-7100
E-mail: fccla@texasfccla.org

FCCLA REGIONAL SCHOLARSHIPS
• See page 164

FCCLA TEXAS FARM BUREAU SCHOLARSHIP
• See page 164

INTERNATIONAL EXECUTIVE HOUSEKEEPERS ASSOCIATION
http://www.ieha.org/

INTERNATIONAL EXECUTIVE HOUSEKEEPERS EDUCATIONAL FOUNDATION
• See page 336

INTERNATIONAL FOODSERVICE EDITORIAL COUNCIL
http://www.ifeconline.com/

INTERNATIONAL FOODSERVICE EDITORIAL COUNCIL COMMUNICATIONS SCHOLARSHIP
• See page 88

LES DAMES D'ESCOFFIER INTERNATIONAL, COLORADO CHAPTER

www.lesdamescolorado.org

LES DAMES D'ESCOFFIER INTERNATIONAL, COLORADO CHAPTER SCHOLARSHIP
• *See page 93*

UNITED DAUGHTERS OF THE CONFEDERACY

http://www.hqudc.org/

WALTER REED SMITH SCHOLARSHIP
• *See page 168*

HORTICULTURE/ FLORICULTURE

ABBIE SARGENT MEMORIAL SCHOLARSHIP INC.

http://www.nhfarmbureau.org/

ABBIE SARGENT MEMORIAL SCHOLARSHIP
• *See page 91*

ALABAMA GOLF COURSE SUPERINTENDENTS ASSOCIATION

http://www.agcsa.org/

ALABAMA GOLF COURSE SUPERINTENDENT'S ASSOCIATION'S DONNIE ARTHUR MEMORIAL SCHOLARSHIP
• *See page 96*

AMERICAN INDIAN SCIENCE AND ENGINEERING SOCIETY

http://www.aises.org/

A.T. ANDERSON MEMORIAL SCHOLARSHIP PROGRAM
• *See page 109*

AMERICAN SOCIETY FOR ENOLOGY AND VITICULTURE

http://www.asev.org/

AMERICAN SOCIETY FOR ENOLOGY AND VITICULTURE SCHOLARSHIPS
• *See page 97*

ARIZONA NURSERY ASSOCIATION

http://www.azna.org/

ARIZONA NURSERY ASSOCIATION FOUNDATION SCHOLARSHIP
Provides research grants and scholarships for the Green Industry. Applicant must be an Arizona resident currently or planning to be enrolled in a horticultural related curriculum at an Arizona university, community college, or continuing education program. See website for further details http://www.azna.org.

Academic Fields/Career Goals: Horticulture/Floriculture.
Award: Scholarship for use in freshman, sophomore, junior, or senior years; renewable. *Number:* 12–16. *Amount:* $500–$3000.
Eligibility Requirements: Applicant must be enrolled or expecting to enroll full- or part-time at a two-year or four-year or technical institution or university. Available to U.S. citizens.
Application Requirements: Application form, recommendations or references, transcript. *Deadline:* April 15.
Contact: Cheryl Goar, Executive Director
Phone: 480-966-1610
E-mail: cgoar@azna.org

ARRL FOUNDATION INC.

http://www.arrl.org/

ROBERT D., W8ST, AND DONNA J., W9DJS, STREETER SCHOLARSHIP
• *See page 318*

BHW GROUP

https://thebhwgroup.com/

BHW WOMEN IN STEM SCHOLARSHIP
• *See page 74*

CALIFORNIA ASSOCIATION OF NURSERYMEN ENDOWMENT FOR RESEARCH AND SCHOLARSHIPS

http://www.cangc.org/

CANERS FOUNDATION ENDOWMENT SCHOLARSHIP
Applicants must be college students who are currently enrolled in no fewer than six units within a program related to the nursery industry and who are entering or returning to college in a horticulture-related field in the fall.
Academic Fields/Career Goals: Horticulture/Floriculture.
Award: Scholarship for use in freshman, sophomore, junior, or senior years; not renewable.
Eligibility Requirements: Applicant must be enrolled or expecting to enroll full-time at a four-year institution or university. Available to U.S. citizens.
Application Requirements: Application form, transcript. *Deadline:* varies.
Contact: Darrelyn Adams, Membership Director
Phone: 916-928-3900 Ext. 13
Fax: 916-567-0505
E-mail: dadams@cangc.org

CHS FOUNDATION

http://www.chsfoundation.org/

CHS FOUNDATION HIGH SCHOOL SCHOLARSHIPS
• *See page 91*

CHS FOUNDATION TWO-YEAR COLLEGE SCHOLARSHIPS
• *See page 92*

ENVIRONMENTAL CARE ASSOCIATION OF IDAHO

http://www.eacofidaho.org

ECA SCHOLARSHIP
The scholarship will be given directly to the recipient. Applicants must be a son or daughter of ECA member, OR be employed in the Lawn Care, Pest Control or Grounds Management Industries, OR Applicant must be enrolled as a full-time student in an accredited college level in Pest

Control, Lawn Care or related industry. A reference letter and two letters of recommendation are required along with a one-page typed essay stating the benefits of the Lawn Care or Pest Control Industries.

Academic Fields/Career Goals: Horticulture/Floriculture; Trade/Technical Specialties.

Award: Scholarship for use in freshman, sophomore, junior, or senior years; not renewable. *Number:* 1–2. *Amount:* $500.

Eligibility Requirements: Applicant must be enrolled or expecting to enroll full- or part-time at a two-year or four-year or technical institution or university and resident of Idaho.

Application Requirements: Application form, essay. *Deadline:* November 10.

Contact: Ann Bates, Executive Coordinator
    Phone: 208-681-4769
    E-mail: abates@ecaofidaho.org

FEDERATED GARDEN CLUBS OF CONNECTICUT

http://www.ctgardenclubs.org/

FEDERATED GARDEN CLUBS OF CONNECTICUT INC. SCHOLARSHIPS
• *See page 156*

FEDERATED GARDEN CLUBS OF MARYLAND

http://www.fgcofmd.org/

ROBERT LEWIS BAKER SCHOLARSHIP

Scholarship awards of up to $5000 to encourage the study of ornamental horticulture, and landscape design. Applicants must be high school graduates, current college and/or graduate students, and Maryland residents. Can attend any accredited college/university in the United States.

Academic Fields/Career Goals: Horticulture/Floriculture; Landscape Architecture.

Award: Scholarship for use in freshman, sophomore, junior, senior, or graduate years; not renewable. *Number:* 1. *Amount:* $5000.

Eligibility Requirements: Applicant must be enrolled or expecting to enroll full-time at a four-year institution or university and resident of Maryland. Available to U.S. citizens.

Application Requirements: Application form. *Deadline:* June 30.

Contact: Marjorie Schiebel, Scholarship Chair
    Phone: 410-296-6961
    E-mail: fgcofmd@aol.com

GARDEN CLUB OF AMERICA

http://www.gcamerica.org/

CORLISS KNAPP ENGLE SCHOLARSHIP IN HORTICULTURE

$3,000 award to support horticultural study at an accredited college, university, or major botanic garden or arboretum. Open to college undergraduates and graduate students, advanced degree candidates, or non-degree-seeking applicants above the high school level.

Academic Fields/Career Goals: Horticulture/Floriculture.

Award: Scholarship for use in freshman, sophomore, junior, senior, or graduate years; not renewable. *Number:* 1. *Amount:* $3000.

Eligibility Requirements: Applicant must be enrolled or expecting to enroll full- or part-time at a four-year institution or university. Available to U.S. citizens.

Application Requirements: Application form, essay. *Deadline:* February 1.

Contact: Garden Club of America
    14 East 60th Street
    New York, NY 10022
    Phone: 212-753-8287
    E-mail: scholarshipapplications@gcamerica.org

GCA AWARD IN DESERT STUDIES
• *See page 121*

GCA SUMMER SCHOLARSHIP IN FIELD BOTANY

Scholarship of $2,500 to undergraduate or graduate students up to Master's level wishing to pursue summer field work in botany. All candidates must be enrolled in a U.S. college or university. Research must be conducted in the Western Hemisphere.

Academic Fields/Career Goals: Horticulture/Floriculture; Natural Sciences.

Award: Scholarship for use in freshman, sophomore, junior, senior, or graduate years; not renewable. *Number:* 1. *Amount:* $2500.

Eligibility Requirements: Applicant must be enrolled or expecting to enroll full-time at a four-year institution or university. Available to U.S. citizens.

Application Requirements: Application form, essay. *Deadline:* February 1.

Contact: Garden Club of America
    14 East 60th Street
    New York, NY 10022-1006
    Phone: 212-753-8287
    E-mail: scholarshipapplications@gcamerica.org

JOAN K. HUNT AND RACHEL M. HUNT SUMMER SCHOLARSHIP IN FIELD BOTANY

One scholarship of $2,500 towards summer study in field botany to promote the awareness of the importance of botany to horticulture. Open to undergraduates and graduate students up to the Master's degree level with preference given to undergraduate students. Must be enrolled in an accredited United States institution.

Academic Fields/Career Goals: Horticulture/Floriculture; Natural Sciences.

Award: Scholarship for use in freshman, sophomore, junior, senior, or graduate years; not renewable. *Number:* 1. *Amount:* $2500.

Eligibility Requirements: Applicant must be enrolled or expecting to enroll full-time at a four-year institution or university. Available to U.S. citizens.

Application Requirements: Application form, essay. *Deadline:* February 1.

Contact: Garden Club of America
    14 East 60th Street
    New York, NY 10022-1006
    Phone: 212-753-8287
    E-mail: scholarshipapplications@gcamerica.org

KATHARINE M. GROSSCUP SCHOLARSHIPS IN HORTICULTURE

Scholarships of up to $3,500 to encourage the study of horticulture and related fields by providing financial assistance to college sophomores, juniors, seniors, or graduate students who wish to pursue these academic endeavors. Preference is given to students from Ohio, Pennsylvania, West Virginia, Michigan, Indiana, and Kentucky.

Academic Fields/Career Goals: Horticulture/Floriculture; Landscape Architecture.

Award: Scholarship for use in sophomore, junior, senior, or graduate years; not renewable.

Eligibility Requirements: Applicant must be enrolled or expecting to enroll full-time at a four-year institution or university and resident of Indiana, Kentucky, Michigan, Ohio, Pennsylvania, West Virginia. Available to U.S. citizens.

Application Requirements: Application form, interview. *Deadline:* January 15.

Contact: Grosscup Scholarship Committee
    Garden Club of America
    14 East 60th Street, 3rd Floor
    New York, NY 10022-1006
    E-mail: grosscupscholarship@gmail.com

LOY MCCANDLESS MARKS SCHOLARSHIP IN TROPICAL HORTICULTURE

Award of $5,000 to graduate or advanced undergraduate student specializing in tropical horticulture, botany, or landscape architecture. Provides an opportunity to study at a leading foreign institution that specializes in the field of tropical plants. Travel must commence within 12 months of the award. Awarded only in even numbered years.

Academic Fields/Career Goals: Horticulture/Floriculture.

Award: Scholarship for use in junior, senior, or graduate years; not renewable. *Number:* 1. *Amount:* $5000.

Eligibility Requirements: Applicant must be enrolled or expecting to enroll full-time at a four-year institution or university. Available to U.S. citizens.

Application Requirements: Application form, interview. *Deadline:* February 1.

Contact: Garden Club of America
14 East 60th Street
New York, NY 10022-1006
Phone: 212-753-8287
E-mail: scholarshipapplications@gcamerica.org

SARA SHALLENBERGER BROWN GCA NATIONAL PARKS CONSERVATION SCHOLARSHIP

Scholarship provides training, transportation, and a $250/week stipend for each student as an SCA apprentice crew leader working directly under two experienced leaders on a 3 or 4 week summer trail crew in one of America's national parks. Open to college undergraduates aged 19 to 20, with preference given to those with prior SCA experience.

Academic Fields/Career Goals: Horticulture/Floriculture; Natural Resources.

Award: Scholarship for use in freshman or sophomore years; not renewable.

Eligibility Requirements: Applicant must be age 19-20 and enrolled or expecting to enroll full-time at a four-year institution or university. Available to U.S. citizens.

Application Requirements: Application form. *Deadline:* February 17.

Contact: Marlee Leveille
Garden Club of America
Student Conservation Association
Phone: 603-504-3202
E-mail: mleveille@thesca.org

ZELLER SUMMER SCHOLARSHIP IN MEDICINAL BOTANY
• *See page 352*

GOLDEN STATE BONSAI FEDERATION

http://www.gsbf-bonsai.org/

HORTICULTURE SCHOLARSHIPS

Scholarship for study towards a certificate in ornamental horticulture from an accredited school. Applicant must be a current member of a GSBF member club and have a letter of recommendation from club president, or a responsible spokesperson from GSBF. Deadline varies.

Academic Fields/Career Goals: Horticulture/Floriculture.

Award: Scholarship for use in freshman, sophomore, junior, senior, graduate, or postgraduate years; not renewable. *Number:* 1–5. *Amount:* up to $400.

Eligibility Requirements: Applicant must be enrolled or expecting to enroll full-time at a two-year or four-year or technical institution or university. Applicant or parent of applicant must be member of Golden State Bonsai Federation. Available to U.S. citizens.

Application Requirements: Application form, recommendations or references. *Deadline:* varies.

Contact: Abe Far, Grants and Scholarship Committee
Golden State Bonsai Federation
2451 Galahad Road
San Diego, CA 92123
Phone: 619-234-3434
E-mail: abefar@cox.net

GOLF COURSE SUPERINTENDENTS ASSOCIATION OF AMERICA

http://www.eifg.org/

GCSAA SCHOLARS COMPETITION

Competition for outstanding students planning careers in golf course management. Must be full-time college undergraduates currently enrolled

in a two-year or more accredited program related to golf course management and have completed one year of program. Must be member of GCSAA.

Academic Fields/Career Goals: Horticulture/Floriculture.

Award: Scholarship for use in sophomore, junior, or senior years; not renewable. *Amount:* $500–$6000.

Eligibility Requirements: Applicant must be enrolled or expecting to enroll full-time at a two-year or four-year institution or university. Applicant or parent of applicant must be member of Golf Course Superintendents Association of America. Available to U.S. and non-U.S. citizens.

Application Requirements: Application form, essay. *Deadline:* June 1.

Contact: Mischia Wright, Associate Director
Golf Course Superintendents Association of America
1421 Research Park Drive
Lawrence, KS 66049
Phone: 800-472-7878 Ext. 4445
Fax: 785-832-4448
E-mail: mwright@gcsaa.org

HERB SOCIETY OF AMERICA, WESTERN RESERVE UNIT

http://www.herbsociety.org/units/western-reserve.html

FRANCIS SYLVIA ZVERINA SCHOLARSHIP

Awards are given to needy Ohio students who plan a career in horticulture or related field. Preference will be given to applicants whose horticultural career goals involve teaching, research, or work in the public or nonprofit sector, such as public gardens, botanical gardens, parks, arboreta, city planning, public education, and awareness. Students must be America citizens. Applications are only accepted online.

Academic Fields/Career Goals: Horticulture/Floriculture.

Award: Scholarship for use in sophomore, junior, or senior years; not renewable. *Number:* 1. *Amount:* $12,500.

Eligibility Requirements: Applicant must be enrolled or expecting to enroll full-time at a four-year institution or university and studying in Ohio. Available to U.S. citizens.

Application Requirements: Application form, essay. *Deadline:* April 1.

Contact: WRHS Scholarship Committee
Herb Society of America, Western Reserve Unit
Cleveland Botanical Garden
11030 East Boulevard
Cleveland, OH 44106
E-mail: scholarship@westernreserveherbsociety.org

WESTERN RESERVE HERB SOCIETY SCHOLARSHIP

Awards are given to needy students who plan a career in horticulture or related field. Preference will be given to applicants whose horticultural career goals involve teaching, research, or work in the public or nonprofit sector, such as public gardens, botanical gardens, parks, arboreta, city planning, public education and awareness.

Academic Fields/Career Goals: Horticulture/Floriculture.

Award: Scholarship for use in junior, senior, or graduate years; not renewable. *Number:* 1. *Amount:* $9500.

Eligibility Requirements: Applicant must be enrolled or expecting to enroll full-time at a four-year institution or university and resident of Ohio. Available to U.S. citizens.

Application Requirements: Application form, essay. *Deadline:* April 1.

Contact: WRHS Scholarship Committee
Herb Society of America, Western Reserve Unit
c/o Cleveland Botanical Garden
11030 East Blvd.
Cleveland, OH 44106
E-mail: scholarship@westernreserveherbsociety.org

HORTICULTURAL RESEARCH INSTITUTE

http://www.hriresearch.org/

BRYAN A. CHAMPION MEMORIAL SCHOLARSHIP
• *See page 92*

CARVILLE M. AKEHURST MEMORIAL SCHOLARSHIP
• *See page 315*

MUGGETS SCHOLARSHIP

Annual scholarship available to students enrolled in an accredited undergraduate or graduate horticulture, landscape, or related discipline at a two- or four-year institution. Students in vocational agriculture programs will also be considered. High school seniors may apply for this scholarship. Minimum 2.5 GPA required. Online application submission. Visit http//www.HRIresearch.org for details.

Academic Fields/Career Goals: Horticulture/Floriculture; Landscape Architecture.

Award: Scholarship for use in sophomore, junior, senior, or graduate years; not renewable. *Number:* 1. *Amount:* $1500.

Eligibility Requirements: Applicant must be enrolled or expecting to enroll full-time at a two-year or four-year or technical institution or university. Applicant must have 2.5 GPA or higher. Available to U.S. and non-U.S. citizens.

Application Requirements: Application form, essay, financial need analysis, recommendations or references, resume, transcript. *Deadline:* May 31.

Contact: Ms. Teresa Jodon, Executive Director
Horticultural Research Institute
1200 G Street, NW, Suite 800
Washington, DC 20005
Phone: 202-695-2474
Fax: 888-761-7883
E-mail: scholarships@hriresearch.org

SPRING MEADOW NURSERY SCHOLARSHIP

Scholarship for the full-time study of horticulture or landscape architecture students in undergraduate or graduate horticulture program or related discipline at a two- or four-year institution. Applicant must have minimum 2.5 GPA. Spring Meadow Nursery's goal is to grant scholarships to students with an interest in woody plant production, woody plant propagation, woody plant breeding, horticultural sales and marketing. Undergraduate: Applicant must have at least a Sophomore standing in a four-year curriculum or Senior standing in a two-year curriculum as of the Fall semester of scholarship application year. Graduate: All applicants in graduate school regardless of year in school may apply. Online application only.

Academic Fields/Career Goals: Horticulture/Floriculture; Landscape Architecture.

Award: Scholarship for use in junior, senior, or graduate years; not renewable. *Number:* 3. *Amount:* $3000.

Eligibility Requirements: Applicant must be enrolled or expecting to enroll full-time at a two-year or four-year or technical institution or university. Applicant must have 2.5 GPA or higher. Available to U.S. and Canadian citizens.

Application Requirements: Application form, essay, financial need analysis, recommendations or references, resume, transcript. *Deadline:* May 31.

Contact: Ms. Teresa Jodon, Executive Director
Horticultural Research Institute
1200 G Street, NW, Suite 800
Washington, DC 20005
Phone: 202-695-2474
Fax: 888-761-7883
E-mail: scholarships@hriresearch.org

TIMOTHY AND PALMER W. BIGELOW JR. SCHOLARSHIP
• *See page 92*

USREY FAMILY SCHOLARSHIP
• *See page 315*

IDAHO NURSERY AND LANDSCAPE ASSOCIATION

http://www.inlagrow.org/

IDAHO NURSERY AND LANDSCAPE ASSOCIATION SCHOLARSHIPS

To encourage study of Horticulture, Floriculture, Plant Pathology, Landscape Design, Turfgrass Management, Botany and other allied subjects that pertain to the green industry. Applicant must be an Idaho resident.

Academic Fields/Career Goals: Horticulture/Floriculture.

Award: Scholarship for use in freshman, sophomore, junior, or senior years; not renewable. *Number:* 1–4. *Amount:* $750.

Eligibility Requirements: Applicant must be enrolled or expecting to enroll full- or part-time at a two-year or four-year or technical institution or university; resident of Idaho and studying in Idaho. Available to U.S. citizens.

Application Requirements: Application form, community service, essay. *Deadline:* December 1.

Contact: Ann Bates, Executive Director
Phone: 208-681-4769
Fax: 208-529-0832
E-mail: abates@inlagrow.org

JOSEPH SHINODA MEMORIAL SCHOLARSHIP FOUNDATION

http://www.shinodascholarship.org/

JOSEPH SHINODA MEMORIAL SCHOLARSHIP

One-time award for undergraduates in accredited colleges and universities. Must be furthering their education in the field of floriculture (production, distribution, research, or retail).

Academic Fields/Career Goals: Horticulture/Floriculture.

Award: Scholarship for use in sophomore, junior, or senior years; not renewable. *Number:* 8–15. *Amount:* $1000–$5000.

Eligibility Requirements: Applicant must be enrolled or expecting to enroll full-time at a four-year institution or university. Available to U.S. citizens.

Application Requirements: Application form, essay, financial need analysis, recommendations or references, transcript. *Deadline:* March 30.

Contact: Barbara McCaleb, Executive Secretary
Joseph Shinoda Memorial Scholarship Foundation
234 Via La Paz
San Luis Obispo, CA 93401
Phone: 805-544-0717

THE LAND CONSERVANCY OF NEW JERSEY

http://tlc-nj.org/

ROGERS FAMILY SCHOLARSHIP
• *See page 243*

RUSSELL W. MYERS SCHOLARSHIP
• *See page 99*

LANDSCAPE ARCHITECTURE FOUNDATION

www.lafoundation.org

RAIN BIRD INTELLIGENT USE OF WATER SCHOLARSHIP

This award recognizes an outstanding landscape architecture, horticulture or irrigation science student. Eligible applicants are in the final two years of undergraduate study with demonstrated commitment to these professions through participation in extracurricular activities and exemplary scholastic achievements.

Academic Fields/Career Goals: Horticulture/Floriculture; Landscape Architecture.

Award: Scholarship for use in junior or senior years; not renewable. *Number:* 1. *Amount:* $2500.

Eligibility Requirements: Applicant must be enrolled or expecting to enroll full- or part-time at a four-year institution or university. Available to U.S. and non-U.S. citizens.

Application Requirements: Application form, essay, personal photograph. *Fee:* $5. *Deadline:* February 15.

Contact: Scholarships Coordinator
Phone: 202-331-7070 Ext. 14
E-mail: scholarships@lafoundation.org

MONTANA FEDERATION OF GARDEN CLUBS

http://www.mtfgc.org/

LIFE MEMBER MONTANA FEDERATION OF GARDEN CLUBS SCHOLARSHIP
• *See page 243*

NATIONAL GARDEN CLUBS SCHOLARSHIP

Scholarship for a college student majoring in some branch of horticulture. Applicants must have sophomore or higher standing and be a legal resident of Montana.

Academic Fields/Career Goals: Horticulture/Floriculture.

Award: Scholarship for use in sophomore, junior, or senior years; not renewable. *Number:* 1. *Amount:* up to $3500.

Eligibility Requirements: Applicant must be enrolled or expecting to enroll full-time at a four-year institution or university and resident of Montana. Available to U.S. citizens.

Application Requirements: Application form, financial need analysis. *Deadline:* February 28.

Contact: Margaret Yaw, Scholarship Committee, State Chairman
Montana Federation of Garden Clubs
2603 Spring Creek Drive
Bozeman, MT 59715-3621
Phone: 406-587-3621

NATIONAL COUNCIL OF STATE GARDEN CLUBS INC. SCHOLARSHIP

http://www.gardenclub.org/

NATIONAL COUNCIL OF STATE GARDEN CLUBS INC. SCHOLARSHIP
• *See page 99*

NATIONAL GARDEN CLUBS INC.

http://www.gardenclub.org/

NATIONAL GARDEN CLUBS INC. SCHOLARSHIP PROGRAM
• *See page 100*

SOIL AND WATER CONSERVATION SOCIETY-NEW JERSEY CHAPTER

http://www.geocities.com/njswcs

EDWARD R. HALL SCHOLARSHIP
• *See page 95*

SOUTHERN NURSERY ASSOCIATION

http://www.sna.org/

SIDNEY B. MEADOWS SCHOLARSHIP ENDOWMENT FUND

Scholarship of at least $1500 to students enrolled in an accredited undergraduate or graduate ornamental horticulture program or related

discipline at a four-year institution. Student must be in a junior or senior or graduate standing at time of application. For undergraduate students minimum grade point average of 2.25 on a scale of 4.0, or 3.0 for graduate students. Students must be a US Citizen and a resident of the following states in the United States: Alabama, Arkansas, Florida, Georgia, Kentucky, Louisiana, Maryland, Mississippi, Missouri, North Carolina, Oklahoma, South Carolina, Tennessee, Texas, Virginia and West Virginia.

Academic Fields/Career Goals: Horticulture/Floriculture.

Award: Scholarship for use in junior, senior, or graduate years; not renewable. *Number:* 10–12. *Amount:* $1500.

Eligibility Requirements: Applicant must be enrolled or expecting to enroll full-time at a four-year institution or university and resident of Alabama, Arkansas, Florida, Georgia, Kentucky, Louisiana, Maryland, Mississippi, Missouri, North Carolina, Oklahoma, South Carolina, Tennessee, Texas, Virginia, West Virginia. Applicant must have 3.0 GPA or higher. Available to U.S. citizens.

Application Requirements: Application form. *Deadline:* May 30.

Contact: Mr. Danny Summers, Executive Vice President
Southern Nursery Association
PO Box 801513
Acworth, GA 30101
Phone: 678-813-1880
E-mail: danny@sbmsef.org

TURF AND ORNAMENTAL COMMUNICATORS ASSOCIATION

http://www.toca.org/

TURF AND ORNAMENTAL COMMUNICATORS ASSOCIATION SCHOLARSHIP PROGRAM
• *See page 102*

HOSPITALITY MANAGEMENT

AMERICAN HOTEL AND LODGING EDUCATIONAL FOUNDATION

http://www.ahlef.org/

AH&LEF ANNUAL SCHOLARSHIP GRANT PROGRAM
• *See page 227*

AMERICAN EXPRESS SCHOLARSHIP PROGRAM

Award for full- and part-time students in undergraduate program leading to degree in hospitality management. Must be employed at hotel which is a member of AH&LA, and must work a minimum of 20 hours per week. Dependents of hotel employees may also apply.

Academic Fields/Career Goals: Hospitality Management.

Award: Scholarship for use in freshman, sophomore, junior, or senior years; not renewable. *Number:* 5–8. *Amount:* $500–$2000.

Eligibility Requirements: Applicant must be enrolled or expecting to enroll full- or part-time at a two-year or four-year institution or university. Applicant or parent of applicant must have employment or volunteer experience in hospitality/hotel administration/operations. Available to U.S. and non-U.S. citizens.

Application Requirements: Application form, essay, financial need analysis, resume, transcript. *Deadline:* May 1.

Contact: Kelsey Allagood, Foundation Manager
American Hotel and Lodging Educational Foundation
1201 New York Avenue, NW, Suite 600
Washington, DC 20005-3931
Phone: 202-289-3139
Fax: 202-289-3199
E-mail: kallagood@ahlef.org

AMERICAN HOTEL & LODGING EDUCATIONAL FOUNDATION PEPSI SCHOLARSHIP
• *See page 228*

ECOLAB SCHOLARSHIP PROGRAM
• *See page 228*

HYATT HOTELS FUND FOR MINORITY LODGING MANAGEMENT
• *See page 228*

INCOMING FRESHMAN SCHOLARSHIPS
• *See page 228*

RAMA SCHOLARSHIP FOR THE AMERICAN DREAM
• *See page 228*

AMERICAN INSTITUTE OF WINE AND FOOD-PACIFIC NORTHWEST CHAPTER
http://www.aiwf.org/

CULINARY, VINIFERA, AND HOSPITALITY SCHOLARSHIP
• *See page 331*

CAREERS THROUGH CULINARY ARTS PROGRAM INC.
http://www.ccapinc.org/

CAREERS THROUGH CULINARY ARTS PROGRAM COOKING COMPETITION FOR SCHOLARSHIPS
• *See page 229*

CLUB FOUNDATION
http://www.clubfoundation.org/

JOE PERDUE SCHOLARSHIP PROGRAM
Awards for candidates seeking a managerial career in the private club industry and currently attending an accredited four year college or university. Must have completed freshman year and be enrolled full-time. Must have achieved and continue to maintain a GPA of at least 2.5. Minimum two awards of $2500 granted annually.

Academic Fields/Career Goals: Hospitality Management.

Award: Scholarship for use in sophomore, junior, or senior years; not renewable. *Number:* 2. *Amount:* $2500.

Eligibility Requirements: Applicant must be enrolled or expecting to enroll full-time at a four-year institution or university. Applicant must have 2.5 GPA or higher. Available to U.S. citizens.

Application Requirements: Application form, essay, recommendations or references, resume, self-addressed stamped envelope with application, transcript. *Deadline:* May 1.

Contact: Ashleigh Hill, Program Specialist
 Phone: 703-299-4268 Ext. 268
 Fax: 703-739-0124
 E-mail: ashleigh.hill@cmaa.org

COSTA RICAN VACATIONS
http://www.vacationscostarica.com/

COSTA RICAN VACATIONS SCHOLARSHIP
• *See page 320*

DECA (DISTRIBUTIVE EDUCATION CLUBS OF AMERICA)
http://www.deca.org/

HARRY A. APPLEGATE SCHOLARSHIP
• *See page 75*

FUKUNAGA SCHOLARSHIP FOUNDATION
http://fukunagascholarship.com

FUKUNAGA SCHOLARSHIP FOUNDATION
• *See page 77*

GOLDEN GATE RESTAURANT ASSOCIATION
http://www.ggra.org/

GOLDEN GATE RESTAURANT ASSOCIATION SCHOLARSHIP FOUNDATION
• *See page 229*

HAWAII LODGING & TOURISM ASSOCIATION
www.hawaiilodging.org

CLEM JUDD, JR. MEMORIAL SCHOLARSHIP
Scholarship for a Hawaii resident who must be able to prove Hawaiian ancestry. Applicant must be enrolled full-time at a U.S. accredited university/college majoring in hotel management. Must have a minimum 3.0 GPA.

Academic Fields/Career Goals: Hospitality Management.

Award: Scholarship for use in junior or senior years; not renewable. *Number:* 2. *Amount:* $1000–$2500.

Eligibility Requirements: Applicant must be Asian/Pacific Islander; enrolled or expecting to enroll full-time at a four-year institution and resident of Hawaii. Applicant must have 3.0 GPA or higher. Available to U.S. citizens.

Application Requirements: Application form, essay, personal photograph, recommendations or references, resume. *Deadline:* July 1.

Contact: Scholarship Committee
 Hawaii Lodging & Tourism Association
 2270 Kalakaua Avenue, Suite 1506
 Honolulu, HI 96815
 Phone: 808-923-0407
 Fax: 808-924-3843
 E-mail: info@hawaiilodging.org

R.W. "BOB" HOLDEN SCHOLARSHIP
One $1000 award for a student attending an accredited university or college in Hawaii, majoring in hotel management. Must be a Hawaii resident and a U.S. citizen. Must have a minimum 3.0 GPA.

Academic Fields/Career Goals: Hospitality Management; Travel/Tourism.

Award: Scholarship for use in junior or senior years; not renewable. *Number:* 1–5. *Amount:* $1000.

Eligibility Requirements: Applicant must be enrolled or expecting to enroll full-time at a four-year institution or university. Applicant must have 3.0 GPA or higher. Available to U.S. citizens.

Application Requirements: Application form, essay, personal photograph, recommendations or references, resume, self-addressed stamped envelope with application, transcript. *Deadline:* July 1.

Contact: Dean Nakasone, Vice President
 Hawaii Lodging & Tourism Association
 2270 Kalakaua Avenue, Suite 1702
 Honolulu, HI 96815
 Phone: 808-923-0407
 E-mail: info@hawaiilodging.org

HOMETEAM CARE

http://www.hometeamcare.com

HOMETEAM HOMECARE SCHOLARSHIP

The new Hometeam homecare and nursing scholarship program provides $2,000 in support to outstanding students. Eligible applicants must be admitted or enrolled in a nursing school or home care certification program. We also accept students, who are currently enrolled in a high-school program, but have been accepted in a nursing or home health aide program. Deadline: February 1st, 2016

Academic Fields/Career Goals: Hospitality Management; Nursing.

Award: Scholarship for use in freshman, sophomore, junior, or senior years; not renewable. *Number:* 1. *Amount:* $2000.

Eligibility Requirements: Applicant must be enrolled or expecting to enroll full- or part-time at a two-year or four-year or technical institution or university. Available to U.S. citizens.

Application Requirements: Application form, application form may be submitted online (https://www.hometeamcare.com/scholarship). *Deadline:* February 1.

Contact: Hometeam Care
    E-mail: scholarships@homteamcare.com

ILLINOIS RESTAURANT ASSOCIATION EDUCATIONAL FOUNDATION

http://www.illinoisrestaurants.org/

ILLINOIS RESTAURANT ASSOCIATION EDUCATIONAL FOUNDATION SCHOLARSHIPS
• *See page 229*

INTERNATIONAL AIRLINES TRAVEL AGENT NETWORK

http://www.iatan.org/

IATAN RONALD A SANTANA SCHOLARSHIP

Scholarships available annually to individuals who are pursuing or enhancing their careers in travel. Must be U.S. citizens or permanent legal residents of the United States or it's territories. Applicants must be a junior or senior at a 2 or 4 year college or university located in the United States or Canada OR be pursuing a travel certificate professional development course.

Academic Fields/Career Goals: Hospitality Management; Travel/Tourism.

Award: Scholarship for use in junior or senior years; not renewable. *Number:* 10–20. *Amount:* $1000–$1000.

Eligibility Requirements: Applicant must be enrolled or expecting to enroll full- or part-time at a two-year or four-year or technical institution or university. Applicant or parent of applicant must have employment or volunteer experience in travel and tourism industry. Applicant must have 3.0 GPA or higher. Available to U.S. and Canadian citizens.

Application Requirements: Application form, essay, recommendations or references, resume, transcript. *Deadline:* April 25.

Contact: Amanda DAiuto, Student Program Manager
    International Airlines Travel Agent Network
    275 Turnpike Street, Suite 307
    Canton, MA 02021
    Phone: 781-821-5990
    E-mail: scholarships@tourismcares.org

INTERNATIONAL FOODSERVICE EDITORIAL COUNCIL

http://www.ifeconline.com/

INTERNATIONAL FOODSERVICE EDITORIAL COUNCIL COMMUNICATIONS SCHOLARSHIP
• *See page 88*

JAMES BEARD FOUNDATION INC.

http://www.jamesbeard.org/

BERN LAXER MEMORIAL SCHOLARSHIP
• *See page 230*

MAINE RESTAURANT ASSOCIATION

http://www.mainerestaurant.com/

MAINE RESTAURANT ASSOCIATION EDUCATION FOUNDATION SCHOLARSHIP FUND
• *See page 232*

MISSOURI TRAVEL COUNCIL

http://www.missouritravel.com/

BOB SMITH TOURISM SCHOLARSHIP
• *See page 336*

NATIONAL RESTAURANT ASSOCIATION EDUCATIONAL FOUNDATION

http://www.nraef.org/

NATIONAL RESTAURANT ASSOCIATION EDUCATIONAL FOUNDATION UNDERGRADUATE SCHOLARSHIPS FOR COLLEGE STUDENTS
• *See page 336*

NATIONAL RESTAURANT ASSOCIATION EDUCATIONAL FOUNDATION UNDERGRADUATE SCHOLARSHIPS FOR HIGH SCHOOL SENIORS AND GENERAL EDUCATION DIPLOMA (GED) GRADUATE S
• *See page 337*

OHIO TRAVEL ASSOCIATION

http://www.ohiotravel.org/

BILL SCHWARTZ MEMORIAL SCHOLARSHIP

Scholarship will be granted to a qualified full-time, Ohio student after the completion of their freshman year. Must be studying hospitality management or travel/tourism with a minimum 2.5 GPA. As part of the scholarship program, the recipient will be invited to various OTA events throughout the year.

Academic Fields/Career Goals: Hospitality Management; Travel/Tourism.

Award: Scholarship for use in sophomore, junior, or senior years; not renewable. *Number:* 1. *Amount:* $1000.

Eligibility Requirements: Applicant must be enrolled or expecting to enroll full-time at a two-year or four-year or technical institution or university; resident of Ohio and studying in Ohio. Applicant or parent of applicant must have employment or volunteer experience in travel and tourism industry. Applicant must have 2.5 GPA or higher. Available to U.S. citizens.

Application Requirements: Application form, financial need analysis, recommendations or references, transcript. *Deadline:* June 15.

Contact: Ms. Betsy Decillis, Membership and Community Manager
    Phone: 800-896-4682 Ext. 0#
    E-mail: betsy@ohiotravel.org

OREGON STUDENT ASSISTANCE COMMISSION

http://www.GetCollegeFunds.org/

OREGON WINE BROTHERHOOD SCHOLARSHIP
• *See page 232*

SCARLETT FAMILY FOUNDATION SCHOLARSHIP PROGRAM

http://www.scarlettfoundation.org/

SCHOLARSHIP FOR STUDENTS PURSUING A BUSINESS OR STEM DEGREE
• *See page 84*

SOUTH CAROLINA RESTAURANT AND LODGING ASSOCIATION

http://www.scrla.org/

SOUTH CAROLINA TOURISM AND HOSPITALITY EDUCATIONAL FOUNDATION SCHOLARSHIPS
• *See page 232*

TOURISM CARES

http://www.tourismcares.org.

NEW HORIZONS KATHY LETARTE SCHOLARSHIP
• *See page 337*

PAT AND JIM HOST SCHOLARSHIP
Award for students who have a degree emphasis in a travel and tourism related field. Must maintain a 3.0 GPA for renewal.
Academic Fields/Career Goals: Hospitality Management; Travel/Tourism.
Award: Scholarship for use in freshman, sophomore, junior, or senior years; renewable. *Number:* 1. *Amount:* $2000–$8000.
Eligibility Requirements: Applicant must be enrolled or expecting to enroll full-time at a four-year institution or university. Applicant must have 3.0 GPA or higher. Available to U.S. citizens.
Application Requirements: Application form, essay, recommendations or references, resume, transcript. *Deadline:* May 10.
Contact: Amanda D'Aiuto, Student Programs Manager
    Phone: 781-821-5990
    Fax: 781-821-8949
    E-mail: info@tourismcares.org

UNITED NEGRO COLLEGE FUND

http://www.uncf.org/

NATIONAL BLACK MCDONALD'S OWNERS ASSOCIATION HOSPITALITY SCHOLARS PROGRAM
• *See page 86*

UNCF/CARNIVAL CORPORATE SCHOLARS PROGRAM
• *See page 170*

HUMANITIES

AMERICAN CLASSICAL LEAGUE/NATIONAL JUNIOR CLASSICAL LEAGUE

http://www.aclclassics.org/

NATIONAL JUNIOR CLASSICAL LEAGUE SCHOLARSHIP
• *See page 200*

AMERICAN SCHOOL OF CLASSICAL STUDIES AT ATHENS

http://www.ascsa.edu.gr/

ASCSA SUMMER SESSIONS SCHOLARSHIPS
• *See page 108*

BETHESDA LUTHERAN COMMUNITIES

http://www.bethesdalutherancommunities.org/scholarships

DEVELOPMENTAL DISABILITIES SCHOLASTIC ACHIEVEMENT SCHOLARSHIP FOR COLLEGE STUDENTS WHO ARE LUTHERAN
• *See page 236*

CANADIAN INSTITUTE OF UKRAINIAN STUDIES

http://www.cius.ca/

LEO J. KRYSA UNDERGRADUATE SCHOLARSHIP
• *See page 125*

CATCHING THE DREAM

http://www.catchingthedream.org/

MATH, ENGINEERING, SCIENCE, BUSINESS, EDUCATION, COMPUTERS SCHOLARSHIPS
• *See page 162*

NATIVE AMERICAN LEADERSHIP IN EDUCATION (NALE)
• *See page 163*

COMMUNITY FOUNDATION FOR GREATER ATLANTA, INC.

http://cfgreateratlanta.org/

JAMES M. AND VIRGINIA M. SMYTH SCHOLARSHIP
• *See page 128*

CULTURAL SERVICES OF THE FRENCH EMBASSY

http://www.frenchculture.org/

TEACHING ASSISTANT PROGRAM IN FRANCE
• *See page 104*

INSTITUTE FOR HUMANE STUDIES

http://www.theihs.org/

HUMANE STUDIES FELLOWSHIPS
• *See page 204*

JACK J. ISGUR FOUNDATION

www.isgur.org

JACK J. ISGUR FOUNDATION SCHOLARSHIP
• *See page 129*

LADIES AUXILIARY TO THE VETERANS OF FOREIGN WARS, DEPARTMENT OF MAINE

http://mainevfw.org/

FRANCES L. BOOTH MEDICAL SCHOLARSHIP SPONSORED BY LAVFW DEPARTMENT OF MAINE
• *See page 353*

NOET SCHOLARLY TOOLS

http://www.noet.com

NOET HUMANITIES SCHOLARSHIP
The Noet Humanities Scholarship seeks to award students enrolled in a humanities program at the undergraduate or graduate level. There is one scholarship available at $500. To enter, students must be currently enrolled (or enrolling in the upcoming quarter) in an undergraduate or graduate program in the humanities.

Academic Fields/Career Goals: Humanities.

Award: Scholarship for use in freshman, sophomore, junior, senior, graduate, or postgraduate years; not renewable. *Number:* up to 1. *Amount:* $500–$500.

Eligibility Requirements: Applicant must be enrolled or expecting to enroll full- or part-time at a two-year or four-year institution or university. Available to U.S. and non-U.S. citizens.

Application Requirements: Application form may be submitted online (http://noet.com/scholarships), email address, transcript. *Deadline:* varies.

Contact: Mr. Benjamin Amundgaard, Noet Brand/Product Manager
Noet Scholarly Tools
1313 Commercial Street
Bellingham, WA 98226
Phone: 360-398-5145
E-mail: ben.amundgaard@noet.com

PHI ALPHA THETA HISTORY HONOR SOCIETY, INC.

http://www.phialphatheta.org/

PHI ALPHA THETA WORLD HISTORY ASSOCIATION PAPER PRIZE
• *See page 361*

POLISH ARTS CLUB OF BUFFALO SCHOLARSHIP FOUNDATION

http://www.pacb.bfn.org/

POLISH ARTS CLUB OF BUFFALO SCHOLARSHIP FOUNDATION TRUST
• *See page 130*

STRAIGHTFORWARD MEDIA

http://www.straightforwardmedia.com/

STRAIGHTFORWARD MEDIA LIBERAL ARTS SCHOLARSHIP
• *See page 126*

UNITED NEGRO COLLEGE FUND

http://www.uncf.org/

OSSIE DAVIS ENDOWMENT SCHOLARSHIP PROGRAM
• *See page 132*

HUMAN RESOURCES

AUTOMOTIVE WOMEN'S ALLIANCE FOUNDATION

http://www.awafoundation.org/index.php

AUTOMOTIVE WOMEN'S ALLIANCE FOUNDATION SCHOLARSHIPS
• *See page 74*

FUKUNAGA SCHOLARSHIP FOUNDATION

http://fukunagascholarship.com

FUKUNAGA SCHOLARSHIP FOUNDATION
• *See page 77*

NEW ENGLAND EMPLOYEE BENEFITS COUNCIL

http://www.neebc.org/

NEW ENGLAND EMPLOYEE BENEFITS COUNCIL SCHOLARSHIP PROGRAM
• *See page 81*

SCARLETT FAMILY FOUNDATION SCHOLARSHIP PROGRAM

http://www.scarlettfoundation.org/

SCHOLARSHIP FOR STUDENTS PURSUING A BUSINESS OR STEM DEGREE
• *See page 84*

SHRM FOUNDATION-SOCIETY FOR HUMAN RESOURCE MANAGEMENT

www.shrmfoundation.org

SHRM FOUNDATION STUDENT SCHOLARSHIPS
Applicants must be SHRM members and must be pursuing a college degree in HR or a related field. Undergraduates must have a cumulative GPA of at least 3.0 on a 4.0 point scale, and graduate applicants must have at least a 3.5 GPA on a 4.0 scale. Course work in HR management is required. Awards are primarily merit-based.

Academic Fields/Career Goals: Human Resources.

Award: Scholarship for use in junior, senior, or graduate years; not renewable. *Number:* 44. *Amount:* $2500–$10,000.

Eligibility Requirements: Applicant must be enrolled or expecting to enroll full- or part-time at a four-year institution or university. Applicant or parent of applicant must be member of Society for Human Resource Management. Applicant must have 3.0 GPA or higher. Available to U.S. and non-U.S. citizens.

Application Requirements: Application form, community service, essay. *Deadline:* October 10.

Contact: Dorothy Mebane, Manager, Foundation Programs
SHRM Foundation-Society for Human Resource Management
1800 Duke Street
Alexandria, VA 22314
Phone: 703-535-6219
E-mail: dorothy.mebane@shrm.org

UNITED NEGRO COLLEGE FUND

http://www.uncf.org/

CVS PHARMACY, INC. BUSINESS SCHOLARSHIPS
• *See page 86*

ORACLE CORPORATE SCHOLARS PROGRAM
• *See page 169*

SUEZ CORPORATE SCHOLARS PROGRAM
• *See page 87*

Y'S MEN INTERNATIONAL

http://www.ysmen.org/

ALEXANDER SCHOLARSHIP LOAN FUND
• *See page 171*

HYDROLOGY

AMERICAN ALPINE CLUB

https://americanalpineclub.org/

AAC RESEARCH GRANTS
• *See page 153*

AMERICAN GROUND WATER TRUST

http://www.agwt.org/

AMERICAN GROUND WATER TRUST-AMTROL INC. SCHOLARSHIP
• *See page 240*

AMERICAN GROUND WATER TRUST-BAROID SCHOLARSHIP
• *See page 241*

AMERICAN GROUND WATER TRUST-THOMAS STETSON SCHOLARSHIP
• *See page 241*

AMERICAN INDIAN SCIENCE AND ENGINEERING SOCIETY

http://www.aises.org/

A.T. ANDERSON MEMORIAL SCHOLARSHIP PROGRAM
• *See page 109*

ARIZONA HYDROLOGICAL SOCIETY

http://www.azhydrosoc.org/

ARIZONA HYDROLOGICAL SOCIETY SCHOLARSHIP
• *See page 241*

ASSOCIATION FOR WOMEN GEOSCIENTISTS (AWG)

http://www.awg.org/

AWG ETHNIC MINORITY SCHOLARSHIP
• *See page 241*

AWG MARIA LUISA CRAWFORD FIELD CAMP SCHOLARSHIP
• *See page 117*

AWG SALT LAKE CHAPTER (SLC) RESEARCH SCHOLARSHIP
• *See page 117*

JANET CULLEN TANAKA GEOSCIENCES UNDERGRADUATE SCHOLARSHIP
• *See page 117*

LONE STAR RISING CAREER SCHOLARSHIP
• *See page 242*

OSAGE CHAPTER UNDERGRADUATE SERVICE SCHOLARSHIP
• *See page 117*

SUSAN EKDALE MEMORIAL FIELD CAMP SCHOLARSHIP
• *See page 242*

ASSOCIATION OF CALIFORNIA WATER AGENCIES

http://www.acwa.com/

ASSOCIATION OF CALIFORNIA WATER AGENCIES SCHOLARSHIPS
• *See page 112*

CLAIR A. HILL SCHOLARSHIP
• *See page 112*

BARRY GOLDWATER SCHOLARSHIP AND EXCELLENCE IN EDUCATION FOUNDATION

https://goldwater.scholarsapply.org

BARRY M. GOLDWATER SCHOLARSHIP AND EXCELLENCE IN EDUCATION PROGRAM
• *See page 112*

BHW GROUP

https://thebhwgroup.com/

BHW WOMEN IN STEM SCHOLARSHIP
• *See page 74*

BROWN AND CALDWELL

http://www.brownandcaldwell.com

ECKENFELDER SCHOLARSHIP
• *See page 155*

MINORITY SCHOLARSHIP PROGRAM
• *See page 155*

CALIFORNIA GROUNDWATER ASSOCIATION

http://www.groundh2o.org/

CALIFORNIA GROUNDWATER ASSOCIATION SCHOLARSHIP

Award for California residents who demonstrate an interest in some facet of groundwater technology. One to two $1000 awards. Must use for study in California. Submit letter of recommendation.

Academic Fields/Career Goals: Hydrology; Natural Resources.

Award: Scholarship for use in freshman, sophomore, junior, or senior years; not renewable. *Number:* 1–2. *Amount:* $1000.

Eligibility Requirements: Applicant must be enrolled or expecting to enroll full-time at a two-year or four-year or technical institution or university; resident of California and studying in California. Available to U.S. citizens.

Application Requirements: Application form, essay, recommendations or references, transcript. *Deadline:* April 1.

Contact: Mike Mortensson, Executive Director
California Groundwater Association
PO Box 14369
Santa Rosa, CA 95402
Phone: 707-578-4408
Fax: 707-546-4906
E-mail: wellguy@groundh2o.org

GREAT MINDS IN STEM

www.greatmindsinstem.org

HISPANIC ENGINEER NATIONAL ACHIEVEMENT AWARDS CORPORATION SCHOLARSHIP PROGRAM
• *See page 106*

KENTUCKY ENERGY AND ENVIRONMENT CABINET

http://dep.ky.gov

ENVIRONMENTAL PROTECTION SCHOLARSHIP
• *See page 157*

NGWA FOUNDATION

http://www.ngwa.org/Foundation/Pages/default.aspx

NGWA FOUNDATION'S LEN ASSANTE SCHOLARSHIP
• *See page 244*

SIGMA XI, THE SCIENTIFIC RESEARCH SOCIETY

http://www.sigmaxi.org/

SIGMA XI GRANTS-IN-AID OF RESEARCH
• *See page 101*

SOIL AND WATER CONSERVATION SOCIETY

http://www.swcs.org

DONALD A. WILLIAMS SCHOLARSHIP SOIL CONSERVATION SCHOLARSHIP
• *See page 95*

SOIL AND WATER CONSERVATION SOCIETY-MISSOURI SHOW-ME CHAPTER

http://www.moswcs.org/

MO SHOW-ME CHAPTER SWCS SCHOLARSHIP
• *See page 95*

UNITED STATES SOCIETY ON DAMS

http://www.ussdams.org/

UNITED STATES SOCIETY ON DAMS SCHOLARSHIP AWARD
• *See page 199*

INDUSTRIAL DESIGN

AIST FOUNDATION

http://www.aistfoundation.org/

ASSOCIATION FOR IRON AND STEEL TECHNOLOGY WILLY KORF MEMORIAL SCHOLARSHIP
• *See page 172*

AMERICAN INSTITUTE OF CHEMICAL ENGINEERS

http://www.aiche.org/

SAFETY AND HEALTH NATIONAL STUDENT DESIGN COMPETITION AWARD FOR SAFETY
• *See page 175*

AMERICAN SOCIETY OF PLUMBING ENGINEERS

http://www.aspe.org/

ALFRED STEELE ENGINEERING SCHOLARSHIP
• *See page 293*

AUTOMOTIVE WOMEN'S ALLIANCE FOUNDATION

http://www.awafoundation.org/index.php

AUTOMOTIVE WOMEN'S ALLIANCE FOUNDATION SCHOLARSHIPS
• *See page 74*

BHW GROUP

https://thebhwgroup.com/

BHW WOMEN IN STEM SCHOLARSHIP
• *See page 74*

CENTER FOR ARCHITECTURE

http://www.cfafoundation.org/scholarships

CENTER FOR ARCHITECTURE DESIGN SCHOLARSHIP
• *See page 119*

GREAT MINDS IN STEM

www.greatmindsinstem.org

HISPANIC ENGINEER NATIONAL ACHIEVEMENT AWARDS CORPORATION SCHOLARSHIP PROGRAM
• *See page 106*

IFDA EDUCATIONAL FOUNDATION

http://www.ifdaef.org/

RUTH CLARK FURNITURE DESIGN SCHOLARSHIP
• *See page 129*

INDUSTRIAL DESIGNERS SOCIETY OF AMERICA

http://www.idsa.org/

INDUSTRIAL DESIGNERS SOCIETY OF AMERICA UNDERGRADUATE SCHOLARSHIP

One-time award to a U.S. citizen or permanent U.S. resident currently enrolled in an industrial design program. Must submit twenty visual examples of work and study full-time.

Academic Fields/Career Goals: Industrial Design.

Award: Scholarship for use in junior year; not renewable. *Number:* 2. *Amount:* $2500.

Eligibility Requirements: Applicant must be enrolled or expecting to enroll full-time at an institution or university. Applicant must have 3.0 GPA or higher. Available to U.S. citizens.

Application Requirements: Application form, recommendations or references, transcript, twenty visual examples of work. *Deadline:* May 18.

Contact: Max Taylor, Executive Assistant
Industrial Designers Society of America
45195 Business Court, Suite 250
Dulles, VA 20166
Phone: 703-707-6000
Fax: 703-787-8501
E-mail: maxt@idsa.org

MANUFACTURERS ASSOCIATION OF MAINE

http://www.mainemfg.com/

MAINE MANUFACTURING CAREER AND TRAINING FOUNDATION SCHOLARSHIP
• *See page 142*

MIDWEST ROOFING CONTRACTORS ASSOCIATION

http://www.mrca.org/

MRCA FOUNDATION SCHOLARSHIP PROGRAM
• *See page 122*

NASA'S VIRGINIA SPACE GRANT CONSORTIUM

http://www.vsgc.odu.edu/

COMMUNITY COLLEGE STEM SCHOLARSHIPS
• *See page 114*

ONLINE LOGO MAKER

http://onlinelogomaker.com

OLM MALALA YOUSAFZAI SCHOLARSHIP 2017-2018
• *See page 129*

RHODE ISLAND FOUNDATION

http://www.rifoundation.org/

JAMES J. BURNS AND C. A. HAYNES SCHOLARSHIP

Award of $1000 for students enrolled in a textile program at an educational institution offering this type of program. Preference given to children of members of National Association of Textile Supervisors. Must demonstrate financial need.

Academic Fields/Career Goals: Industrial Design.

Award: Scholarship for use in freshman, sophomore, junior, or senior years; not renewable. *Amount:* $1000.

Eligibility Requirements: Applicant must be enrolled or expecting to enroll full-time at a two-year or four-year institution or university. Available to U.S. citizens.

Application Requirements: Application form, essay, financial need analysis, recommendations or references, transcript. *Deadline:* June 3.

Contact: Libby Monahan, Funds Administrator
Phone: 401-274-4564 Ext. 3117
E-mail: libbym@rifoundation.org

SIMPLEHUMAN

http://www.simplehuman.com/

SIMPLE SOLUTIONS DESIGN COMPETITION
• *See page 286*

SOCIETY OF MANUFACTURING ENGINEERS EDUCATION FOUNDATION

http://www.smeef.org/

CHAPTER 198-DOWNRIVER DETROIT SCHOLARSHIP
• *See page 307*

CHAPTER 67-PHOENIX SCHOLARSHIP
• *See page 307*

FORT WAYNE CHAPTER 56 SCHOLARSHIP
• *See page 309*

NORTH CENTRAL REGION 9 SCHOLARSHIP
• *See page 309*

WICHITA CHAPTER 52 SCHOLARSHIP
• *See page 310*

SOCIETY OF PLASTICS ENGINEERS FOUNDATION (SPE)

http://www.4spe.org/

FLEMING/BASZCAK SCHOLARSHIP
• *See page 181*

GULF COAST HURRICANE SCHOLARSHIP
• *See page 181*

SOCIETY OF PLASTICS ENGINEERS SCHOLARSHIP PROGRAM
• *See page 182*

SUPPORT CREATIVITY

http://wesupportcreativity.org

SUPPORT CREATIVITY SCHOLARSHIP
• *See page 124*

TIMOTION

http://www.timotion.com/

TIMOTION ENGINEERING AND EXCELLENCE SCHOLARSHIP
• *See page 199*

TRANSTUTORS

http://www.transtutors.com/scholarship

TRANSTUTORS SCHOLARSHIP 2015-16
• *See page 85*

VECTORWORKS, INC.

http://www.vectorworks.net

VECTORWORKS DESIGN SCHOLARSHIP
• See page 124

WHOMENTORS.COM, INC.

http://www.WHOmentors.com/

IB USD WORLDWIDE VENTURE CAPITAL
• See page 116

INSURANCE AND ACTUARIAL SCIENCE

THE ACTUARIAL FOUNDATION

http://www.actuarialfoundation.org

ACTUARIAL DIVERSITY SCHOLARSHIP

The Actuarial Diversity Scholarship promotes diversity through an annual scholarship program for Black/African American, Hispanic, Native North American and Pacific Islander students. The scholarship award recognizes and encourages the academic achievements of full-time undergraduate students pursuing a degree that may lead to a career in the actuarial profession.

Academic Fields/Career Goals: Insurance and Actuarial Science; Mathematics.

Award: Scholarship for use in freshman, sophomore, junior, or senior years; not renewable. *Amount:* $1000–$4000.

Eligibility Requirements: Applicant must be American Indian/Alaska Native, Asian/Pacific Islander, Black (non-Hispanic), Hispanic and enrolled or expecting to enroll full-time at a two-year or four-year institution or university. Applicant must have 3.0 GPA or higher. Available to U.S. and non-U.S. citizens.

Application Requirements: Application form, essay, personal photograph. *Deadline:* May 1.

Contact: The Actuarial Foundation
    Attention: Actuarial Diversity Scholarship
    475 North Martingale Road, Suite 600
    Schaumburg, IL 60173-2226
    Phone: 847-706-3535
    E-mail: scholarships@actfnd.org

ACTUARY OF TOMORROW—STUART A. ROBERTSON MEMORIAL SCHOLARSHIP
• See page 160

CURTIS E. HUNTINGTON MEMORIAL SCHOLARSHIP (FORMERLY THE JOHN CULVER WOODDY SCHOLARSHIP)
• See page 245

BHW GROUP

https://thebhwgroup.com/

BHW WOMEN IN STEM SCHOLARSHIP
• See page 74

D.W. SIMPSON & COMPANY

http://www.dwsimpson.com/

D.W. SIMPSON ACTUARIAL SCIENCE SCHOLARSHIP

One-time award for full-time actuarial science students. Must be entering senior year of undergraduate study in actuarial science. GPA of 3.2 or better in actuarial science and an overall GPA of 3.0 or better required. Must have passed at least one actuarial exam and be eligible to work in the U.S. Deadlines: April 30 for fall and October 31 for spring.

Academic Fields/Career Goals: Insurance and Actuarial Science.

Award: Scholarship for use in senior year; not renewable. *Number:* up to 2. *Amount:* up to $1000.

Eligibility Requirements: Applicant must be enrolled or expecting to enroll full-time at a four-year institution or university. Applicant must have 3.0 GPA or higher. Available to U.S. citizens.

Application Requirements: Application form, essay, resume, test scores. *Deadline:* varies.

Contact: Bethany Rave, Partner-Operations
    Phone: 312-867-2300
    Fax: 312-951-8386
    E-mail: scholarship@dwsimpson.com

MISSOURI INSURANCE EDUCATION FOUNDATION

http://www.mief.org

MISSOURI INSURANCE EDUCATION FOUNDATION SCHOLARSHIP

One $2500 scholarship and five $2000 scholarships available to college and university students in their junior or senior year. Must be Missouri resident and attending school in Missouri.

Academic Fields/Career Goals: Insurance and Actuarial Science.

Award: Scholarship for use in junior or senior years; not renewable. *Number:* 6. *Amount:* $2000–$2500.

Eligibility Requirements: Applicant must be enrolled or expecting to enroll full-time at a four-year institution or university; resident of Missouri and studying in Missouri. Applicant must have 2.5 GPA or higher. Available to U.S. citizens.

Application Requirements: Application form, financial need analysis, recommendations or references, transcript. *Deadline:* March 31.

Contact: Amy Hamacher, Assistant
    Missouri Insurance Education Foundation
    PO Box 1654
    Jefferson City, MO 65102
    Phone: 573-893-4234
    Fax: 573-893-4996
    E-mail: miis@midamerica.net

NEW ENGLAND EMPLOYEE BENEFITS COUNCIL

http://www.neebc.org/

NEW ENGLAND EMPLOYEE BENEFITS COUNCIL SCHOLARSHIP PROGRAM
• See page 81

SCARLETT FAMILY FOUNDATION SCHOLARSHIP PROGRAM

http://www.scarlettfoundation.org/

SCHOLARSHIP FOR STUDENTS PURSUING A BUSINESS OR STEM DEGREE
• See page 84

SPENCER EDUCATIONAL FOUNDATION INC.

http://www.spencered.org/

SPENCER EDUCATIONAL FOUNDATION SCHOLARSHIP

Scholarship is available to outstanding applicants who are focused on a career in risk management, insurance, and related disciplines. If student is attending a two year college, he/she must have intentions of transferring to a four year college.

Academic Fields/Career Goals: Insurance and Actuarial Science.

Award: Scholarship for use in junior, senior, graduate, or postgraduate years; renewable. *Number:* 30–40. *Amount:* $5000–$10,000.

Eligibility Requirements: Applicant must be enrolled or expecting to enroll full- or part-time at a two-year or four-year institution or university. Applicant must have 3.0 GPA or higher. Available to U.S. and non-U.S. citizens.

Application Requirements: Application form, application form may be submitted online (http://www.spencered.org), essay, resume, transcript. *Deadline:* January 31.

Contact: Ms. Angela Sabatino, Programs Director
Spencer Educational Foundation Inc.
1065 Avenue of the Americas, 13th Floor
New York, NY 10018
Phone: 212-655-6223
E-mail: asabatino@spencered.org

UNITED NEGRO COLLEGE FUND

http://www.uncf.org/

LIBERTY MUTUAL SCHOLARSHIP
• *See page 169*

UNCF/TRAVELERS INSURANCE SCHOLARSHIP
• *See page 170*

INTERIOR DESIGN

AMERICAN SOCIETY OF INTERIOR DESIGNERS (ASID) EDUCATION FOUNDATION INC.

http://www.asidfoundation.org

ASID FOUNDATION LEGACY SCHOLARSHIP FOR UNDERGRADUATES

Open to all students in their junior or senior year of undergraduate study enrolled in at least a three-year program of interior design. The award will be given to a creatively outstanding student as demonstrated through their portfolio.

Academic Fields/Career Goals: Interior Design.

Award: Scholarship for use in junior or senior years; not renewable. *Number:* 1. *Amount:* $4000.

Eligibility Requirements: Applicant must be enrolled or expecting to enroll full- or part-time at a four-year institution or university. Available to U.S. citizens.

Application Requirements: Application form, application form may be submitted online (http://www.asidfoundation.org), portfolio, recommendations or references, transcript. *Deadline:* March 12.

Contact: Valerie O'Keefe, Executive Assistant and Foundation Manager
Phone: 202-546-3480
Fax: 202-546-3240
E-mail: foundation@asid.org

CENTER FOR ARCHITECTURE

http://www.cfafoundation.org/scholarships

CENTER FOR ARCHITECTURE DESIGN SCHOLARSHIP
• *See page 119*

IFDA EDUCATIONAL FOUNDATION

http://www.ifdaef.org/

GREEN/SUSTAINABLE SCHOLARSHIP
• *See page 121*

IFDA LEADERS COMMEMORATIVE SCHOLARSHIP

Scholarship available to students who have completed four courses related to the field of interior design. Award is made to a to full-time student. Applicant does not have to be IFDA student member. Applicant must submit 300 to 500 word essay explaining future plans and goals, indicating why they believe that they are deserving of this award. Decision based upon student's academic achievement, awards and accomplishments, future plans and goals, and letter of recommendation. Documents sent along with the application should be sent via email

Academic Fields/Career Goals: Interior Design.

Award: Scholarship for use in sophomore, junior, or senior years; not renewable. *Number:* 1. *Amount:* $1500.

Eligibility Requirements: Applicant must be enrolled or expecting to enroll full-time at a four-year institution or university. Available to U.S. and non-U.S. citizens.

Application Requirements: Application form, essay. *Deadline:* March 31.

Contact: Earline Feldman, Director of Scholarships and Grants
IFDA Educational Foundation
112 Hidden Lake
Canton, GA 30114
Phone: 770-378-7221
E-mail: ef.ifda@tapestries.org

IFDA STUDENT MEMBER SCHOLARSHIP

Scholarship available to students who have completed four courses related to the field of interior design. Award of $2000 to full-time student. Applicant must be IFDA student member. Applicant must submit 300 to 500 word essay explaining why they joined IFDA, discuss future plans and goals, and indicate why they are deserving of this award. Decision based upon student's academic achievement, awards and accomplishments, future plans and goals, and letter of recommendation. Documents sent along with the application should be sent individually to the four judges (4 copies).

Academic Fields/Career Goals: Interior Design; Trade/Technical Specialties.

Award: Scholarship for use in sophomore, junior, or senior years; not renewable. *Number:* 1. *Amount:* $2000.

Eligibility Requirements: Applicant must be enrolled or expecting to enroll full-time at a four-year institution or university. Available to U.S. and non-U.S. citizens.

Application Requirements: Application form, essay. *Deadline:* March 31.

Contact: Earline Feldman, Director of Scholarships and Grants
IFDA Educational Foundation
112 Hidden Lake Circle
Canton, GA 30114
Phone: 770-378-7221
E-mail: ef.ifda@tapestries.org

PART TIME STUDENT SCHOLARSHIP

$1500 scholarship supported by IFDA Educational Foundation. Applicant must be a part-time student currently enrolled in at least 2 interior design or related field courses in a nationally accredited school in the United States.

Academic Fields/Career Goals: Interior Design.

Award: Scholarship for use in sophomore, junior, or senior years; not renewable. *Number:* 1. *Amount:* $1500.

Eligibility Requirements: Applicant must be enrolled or expecting to enroll part-time at a four-year institution or university. Available to U.S. and non-U.S. citizens.

Application Requirements: Application form, essay. *Deadline:* March 31.

Contact: Earline Feldman, IFDA Director of Scholarships and Grants
IFDA Educational Foundation
112 Hidden Lake Circle
Canton, GA 30114
Phone: 770-378-7221
E-mail: ef.ifta@tapestries.org

RUTH CLARK FURNITURE DESIGN SCHOLARSHIP
• *See page 129*

ILLUMINATING ENGINEERING SOCIETY OF NORTH AMERICA

http://www.ies.org/

ROBERT W. THUNEN MEMORIAL SCHOLARSHIPS
• See page 122

ILLUMINATING ENGINEERING SOCIETY OF NORTH AMERICA–GOLDEN GATE SECTION

http://www.iesgg.org/

ALAN LUCAS MEMORIAL EDUCATIONAL SCHOLARSHIP
• See page 122

INTERNATIONAL FACILITY MANAGEMENT ASSOCIATION FOUNDATION

http://www.ifmafoundation.org/

IFMA FOUNDATION SCHOLARSHIPS
• See page 122

NATIONAL ASSOCIATION OF WOMEN IN CONSTRUCTION

http://www.nawic.org/

NAWIC UNDERGRADUATE SCHOLARSHIPS
• See page 122

ONLINE LOGO MAKER

http://onlinelogomaker.com

OLM MALALA YOUSAFZAI SCHOLARSHIP 2017-2018
• See page 129

OREGON STUDENT ASSISTANCE COMMISSION

http://www.GetCollegeFunds.org/

HOME BUILDERS FOUNDATION JIM IRVINE STATEWIDE SCHOLARSHIP
• See page 123

PLAN NEW HAMPSHIRE

www.plannh.org

PLAN NEW HAMPSHIRE SCHOLARSHIP AND PROGRAM
• See page 123

QUALITY BATH

www.qualitybath.com

QUALITYBATH.COM SCHOLARSHIP PROGRAM
• See page 123

RUG & HOME

http://www.rugandhome.com/

RUG & HOME SCHOLARS PROGRAM

The Rug & Home Scholars Program offers two $1,000 annual scholarships to two eligible candidates decided upon by committee. Our first scholarship is designed specifically for a student interested in pursuing a college degree in interior design. Rug & Home is an interior design destination, known regionally and nationally for its great sense of color and design, with specific interest and expertise in the age-old tradition of handmade rugs. Therefore, supporting students pursuing a career in home fashions and interior design is an extension of who we are as a company, and we are happy to be able to support future design professionals in this way. The second scholarship will be awarded to a humanitarian student who gives back to their community and has demonstrated exceptional character. Our founders are big believers in giving back to the communities who have supported Rug & Home, whether it be locally in the areas where our stores operate or abroad in the places where our products are made. It has always been a deep passion of our founders to inspire this same love of helping others in young people, and that's what this scholarship is intended to celebrate. A demonstrated interest-based scholarship awarded to a currently enrolled university student each year. The awarded student is recognized for his or her interest and aptitude. Applications are being accepted now until October 31, 2016. Applicants should currently be a freshman, sophomore, or junior student at an accredited university.

Academic Fields/Career Goals: Interior Design.

Award: Scholarship for use in freshman, sophomore, junior, or senior years; renewable. *Number:* 2. *Amount:* $1000.

Eligibility Requirements: Applicant must be enrolled or expecting to enroll full-time at a two-year or four-year or technical institution or university. Applicant must have 3.0 GPA or higher. Available to U.S. citizens.

Application Requirements: Application form, essay. *Deadline:* October 31.

Contact: Aanchal Gupta, Principal
E-mail: scholarships@rugandhome.com

SUPPORT CREATIVITY

http://wesupportcreativity.org

SUPPORT CREATIVITY SCHOLARSHIP
• See page 124

TURNER CONSTRUCTION COMPANY

http://www.turnerconstruction.com/

YOUTHFORCE 2020 SCHOLARSHIP PROGRAM
• See page 124

VECTORWORKS, INC.

http://www.vectorworks.net

VECTORWORKS DESIGN SCHOLARSHIP
• See page 124

INTERNATIONAL MIGRATION

UNITED NATIONS ASSOCIATION OF CONNECTICUT

http://www.unausa.org

UNITED NATIONS ASSOCIATION OF CONNECTICUT SCHOLARSHIP
• See page 133

INTERNATIONAL STUDIES

ARRL FOUNDATION INC.

http://www.arrl.org/

DON RIEBHOFF MEMORIAL SCHOLARSHIP
One $1000 award available to students with a technician or higher class license for radio operation. Must be pursuing a Baccalaureate or higher degree in international studies at any accredited institution above the high school level. Preference given to ARRL members. Must demonstrate academic merit, financial need, and interest in promoting amateur radio.
Academic Fields/Career Goals: International Studies.
Award: Scholarship for use in freshman, sophomore, junior, senior, or graduate years; not renewable. *Number:* 1. *Amount:* $1000.
Eligibility Requirements: Applicant must be enrolled or expecting to enroll full-time at a four-year institution or university and must have an interest in amateur radio. Applicant or parent of applicant must be member of American Radio Relay League. Available to U.S. citizens.
Application Requirements: Application form, financial need analysis. *Deadline:* January 31.
Contact: Ms. Mary Hobart, Secretary
Phone: 860-594-0397
E-mail: k1mmh@arrl.org

ASSOCIATION OF FORMER INTELLIGENCE OFFICERS

http://www.afio.com

AFIO UNDERGRADUATE AND GRADUATE SCHOLARSHIPS
• See page 103

AUTOMOTIVE WOMEN'S ALLIANCE FOUNDATION

http://www.awafoundation.org/index.php

AUTOMOTIVE WOMEN'S ALLIANCE FOUNDATION SCHOLARSHIPS
• See page 74

CULTURAL SERVICES OF THE FRENCH EMBASSY

http://www.frenchculture.org/

TEACHING ASSISTANT PROGRAM IN FRANCE
• See page 104

ISLAMIC SCHOLARSHIP FUND

http://islamicscholarshipfund.org/

ISF NATIONAL SCHOLARSHIP
• See page 108

JORGE MAS CANOSA FREEDOM FOUNDATION

http://masscholarships.org/

MAS FAMILY SCHOLARSHIP AWARD
• See page 165

THE LYNDON BAINES JOHNSON FOUNDATION

http://www.lbjlibrary.org/page/foundation/

MOODY RESEARCH GRANTS
• See page 104

NATIONAL SECURITY EDUCATION PROGRAM

http://www.iie.org/

NATIONAL SECURITY EDUCATION PROGRAM (NSEP) DAVID L. BOREN UNDERGRADUATE SCHOLARSHIPS
• See page 126

PHI ALPHA THETA HISTORY HONOR SOCIETY, INC.

http://www.phialphatheta.org/

PHI ALPHA THETA WORLD HISTORY ASSOCIATION PAPER PRIZE
• See page 361

UNITED NATIONS ASSOCIATION OF CONNECTICUT

http://www.unausa.org

UNITED NATIONS ASSOCIATION OF CONNECTICUT SCHOLARSHIP
• See page 133

WOMEN IN INTERNATIONAL TRADE (WIIT)

http://www.wiit.org/

WIIT CHARITABLE TRUST SCHOLARSHIP PROGRAM
2 scholarships of $1500 each (one for an undergraduate female student and one for a graduate female student) may be awarded for the Summer or Fall Semester and the Spring Semester of each year. Applicants must: (1) be currently enrolled or accepted at an undergraduate or graduate program at an accredited U.S. university or college, either full-time or part- time; and (2) demonstrate interest in international development, international relations, international trade, international economics, or international business. A completed application includes a 3-5 page essay, applicant information, and proof of acceptance or current enrollment in an accredited U.S. college or university. All materials should be submitted by email ONLY to info@wiittrust.org using the following subject line - "Submission for WIIT TRUST Essay Writing Contest". Only one submission entry will be accepted from each entrant. Awards are based on the quality of the applicants' essays in response to the assigned topic for that year. Application information is available at https://www.wiit.org/wiit-charitable-trust/; click on "new scholarship program" to download the information for the current year.

Academic Fields/Career Goals: International Studies.

Award: Scholarship for use in freshman, sophomore, junior, senior, graduate, or postgraduate years; not renewable. *Number:* 1–4. *Amount:* $1500.

Eligibility Requirements: Applicant must be enrolled or expecting to enroll full- or part-time at a two-year or four-year institution or university and female. Available to U.S. citizens.

Application Requirements: Application form, essay. *Deadline:* June 15.

Contact: Ms. Nicole Bivens Collinson, Chair, WIIT Charitable Trust
   E-mail: info@wiittrust.org

JOURNALISM

ADC RESEARCH INSTITUTE

http://www.adc.org/

JACK SHAHEEN MASS COMMUNICATIONS SCHOLARSHIP AWARD
• *See page 200*

ALPHA OMEGA COUNCIL OF NEW ENGLAND

http://www.alphaomegacouncil.org/

ALPHA OMEGA SCHOLARSHIP IN MEMORY OF PETER AGRIS
• *See page 201*

AMERICAN INSTITUTE OF POLISH CULTURE INC.

http://www.ampolinstitute.org/

HARRIET IRSAY SCHOLARSHIP GRANT
• *See page 127*

AMERICAN QUARTER HORSE FOUNDATION (AQHF)

http://www.aqha.com/foundation

AQHF JOURNALISM OR COMMUNICATIONS SCHOLARSHIP
• *See page 201*

ARRL FOUNDATION INC.

http://www.arrl.org/

JAKE MCCLAIN DRIVER, KC5WXA, SCHOLARSHIP
• *See page 215*

PHD SCHOLARSHIP
• *See page 215*

ASIAN AMERICAN JOURNALISTS ASSOCIATION

http://www.aaja.org/

CIC/ANNA CHENNAULT SCHOLARSHIP
• *See page 202*

MARY QUON MOY ING MEMORIAL SCHOLARSHIP AWARD

One-time award of up to $2000 for a deserving high school senior or current undergraduate or graduate student. Must intend to pursue a journalism career and must show a commitment to the Asian-American community. Visit website http://www.aaja.org for application and details.

Academic Fields/Career Goals: Journalism.

Award: Scholarship for use in freshman, sophomore, junior, senior, or graduate years; not renewable. *Number:* 1. *Amount:* $2000.

Eligibility Requirements: Applicant must be Asian/Pacific Islander and enrolled or expecting to enroll full-time at a two-year or four-year institution or university. Available to U.S. and non-U.S. citizens.

Application Requirements: Application form, essay, financial need analysis. *Deadline:* April 16.

Contact: Justin Seiter, Program Coordinator
   Asian American Journalists Association
   5 Third Street
   Suite 1108
   San Francisco, CA 94103
   Phone: 415-346-2051 Ext. 107
   E-mail: justins@aaja.org

VINCENT CHIN MEMORIAL SCHOLARSHIP

$500 award to a journalism student committed to keeping Vincent Chin's memory alive. Minimum GPA of 2.5.

Academic Fields/Career Goals: Journalism.

Award: Scholarship for use in freshman, sophomore, junior, senior, or graduate years; not renewable. *Number:* 1. *Amount:* $500.

Eligibility Requirements: Applicant must be Asian/Pacific Islander and enrolled or expecting to enroll full-time at a two-year or four-year technical institution or university. Applicant must have 2.5 GPA or higher. Available to U.S. and non-U.S. citizens.

Application Requirements: Application form, essay, financial need analysis. *Deadline:* April 16.

Contact: Justin Seiter, Program Coordinator
   Asian American Journalists Association
   5 Third Street
   Suite 1108
   San Francisco, CA 94103
   Phone: 415-346-2051 Ext. 107
   E-mail: justins@aaja.org

ASIAN AMERICAN JOURNALISTS ASSOCIATION, SEATTLE CHAPTER

http://www.aajaseattle.org/

NORTHWEST JOURNALISTS OF COLOR SCHOLARSHIP
• *See page 88*

ASSOCIATED PRESS

http://www.aptra.org/

ASSOCIATED PRESS TELEVISION/RADIO ASSOCIATION-CLETE ROBERTS JOURNALISM SCHOLARSHIP AWARDS

Award for college undergraduates and graduate students studying in California, Nevada or Hawaii and pursuing careers in broadcast journalism. Submit application, references, and examples of broadcast-related work.

Academic Fields/Career Goals: Journalism; TV/Radio Broadcasting.

Award: Scholarship for use in freshman, sophomore, junior, or senior years; not renewable. *Number:* 3. *Amount:* $1500.

Eligibility Requirements: Applicant must be enrolled or expecting to enroll full-time at a two-year or four-year institution or university and studying in California, Hawaii, Nevada. Available to U.S. citizens.

Application Requirements: Application form, recommendations or references. *Deadline:* December 14.

Contact: Roberta Gonzales, Scholarship Committee
Associated Press
CBS 5 TV, 855 Battery Street
San Francisco, CA 94111

KATHRYN DETTMAN MEMORIAL JOURNALISM SCHOLARSHIP

One-time award of $1500 for broadcast journalism students, enrolled at a California, Hawaii, or Nevada college or university. Must submit entry form and examples of broadcast-related work.

Academic Fields/Career Goals: Journalism; TV/Radio Broadcasting.

Award: Scholarship for use in freshman, sophomore, junior, or senior years; renewable. *Number:* 1–4. *Amount:* $1500.

Eligibility Requirements: Applicant must be enrolled or expecting to enroll full-time at a two-year or four-year institution or university and studying in California, Hawaii, Nevada. Available to U.S. citizens.

Application Requirements: Application form, examples of broadcast-related work. *Deadline:* December 14.

Contact: Roberta Gonzales, Scholarship Committee
Associated Press
CBS 5 TV, 855 Battery Street
San Francisco, CA 94111

ASSOCIATION FOR WOMEN IN COMMUNICATIONS-SEATTLE PROFESSIONAL CHAPTER

http://www.seattleawc.org/

SEATTLE PROFESSIONAL CHAPTER OF THE ASSOCIATION FOR WOMEN IN COMMUNICATIONS

Scholarship of $3000 for women pursuing journalism in the state of Washington. For more details on eligibility criteria or selection procedure, refer to website at http://www.seattleawc.org/scholarships.html.

Academic Fields/Career Goals: Journalism.

Award: Scholarship for use in sophomore, junior, or senior years; not renewable. *Number:* 2. *Amount:* $3000.

Eligibility Requirements: Applicant must be enrolled or expecting to enroll full-time at a two-year or four-year or technical institution or university; female; resident of Washington and studying in Washington. Available to U.S. citizens.

Application Requirements: Application form, resume, sample of work, cover letter, transcript. *Deadline:* March 16.

Contact: Jaron Snow, Office Administrator
Phone: 425-771-4189
E-mail: awcseattle@verizon.net

BMI FOUNDATION, INC.

http://www.bmifoundation.org/

BMI FOUNDERS AWARD FOR RADIO BROADCASTING
• *See page 203*

CCNMA: LATINO JOURNALISTS OF CALIFORNIA

http://www.ccnma.org/

CCNMA SCHOLARSHIPS
• *See page 203*

COMMUNITY FOUNDATION OF WESTERN MASSACHUSETTS

http://www.communityfoundation.org/

WILLIAM J. (BILL) AND LORETTA M. O'NEIL SCHOLARSHIP

Scholarship available to residents from western MA pursuing English, journalism, or a related field. For details, please see website http://communityfoundation.org/.

Academic Fields/Career Goals: Journalism.

Award: Scholarship for use in freshman, sophomore, junior, senior, or graduate years; not renewable.

Eligibility Requirements: Applicant must be enrolled or expecting to enroll full- or part-time at a two-year or four-year institution or university and resident of Massachusetts. Available to U.S. citizens.

Application Requirements: Application form, essay, financial need analysis, transcript. *Deadline:* March 31.

Contact: Dotty Theriaque, Program Assistant for Scholarships
Community Foundation of Western Massachusetts
1500 Main Street
PO Box 15769
Springfield, MA 01115
Phone: 413-732-2858
Fax: 413-733-8565
E-mail: scholar@communityfoundation.org

CONNECTICUT CHAPTER OF SOCIETY OF PROFESSIONAL JOURNALISTS

http://www.ctspj.org/

CONNECTICUT SPJ BOB EDDY SCHOLARSHIP PROGRAM
• *See page 203*

DOW JONES NEWS FUND, INC.

https://www.newsfund.org/

DOW JONES NEWS FUND HIGH SCHOOL JOURNALISM WORKSHOPS WRITING, PHOTOGRAPHY AND MULTIMEDIA COMPETITION

Participants in DJNF summer workshops are nominated for writing, multimedia and photography awards based on their published work. Scholarships are presented to the best writers, digital producers and photographers to pursue media careers.

Academic Fields/Career Goals: Journalism.

Award: Scholarship for use in freshman year; not renewable. *Number:* 8. *Amount:* up to $1000.

Eligibility Requirements: Applicant must be high school student and planning to enroll or expecting to enroll full-time at a four-year institution or university. Available to U.S. and non-U.S. citizens.

Application Requirements: Application form, entry in a contest, essay, portfolio, recommendations or references. *Deadline:* October 1.

Contact: Mrs. Linda Shockley, Managing Director
Dow Jones News Fund, Inc.
PO Box 300
Princeton, NJ 08543-0300
Phone: 609-452-2820
Fax: 609-520-5804
E-mail: djnf@dowjones.com

FREEDOM FORUM

http://www.newseuminstitute.org

AL NEUHARTH FREE SPIRIT AND JOURNALISM CONFERENCE PROGRAM

One-time award for high school juniors interested in pursuing a career in journalism. Must be actively involved in high school journalism and demonstrate qualities such as being a visionary, an innovative leader, an entrepreneur or a courageous achiever. One student selected from each state and the District of Columbia. Scholars come to Washington D.C. to receive their awards and participate in an all-expense paid journalism conference. See website at http://www.freespirit.org for further information.

Academic Fields/Career Goals: Journalism.

Award: Scholarship for use in freshman year; not renewable. *Number:* 51. *Amount:* $1000.

Eligibility Requirements: Applicant must be high school student; planning to enroll or expecting to enroll full-time at a two-year or four-year institution or university and must have an interest in entrepreneurship, leadership, photography/photogrammetry/filmmaking, or writing. Available to U.S. citizens.

Application Requirements: Application form, essay, personal photograph. *Deadline:* February 1.

Contact: Karen Catone, Director, Al Neuharth Free Spirit Program
Freedom Forum
555 Pennsylvania Avenue, NW
Washington, DC 20001
Phone: 202-292-6271
E-mail: kcatone@freedomforum.org

GEORGIA PRESS EDUCATIONAL FOUNDATION INC.

http://gapress.org/scholarships-internships/

DURWOOD MCALISTER SCHOLARSHIP

Scholarship awarded annually to an outstanding student majoring in print journalism at a Georgia college or university.

Academic Fields/Career Goals: Journalism.

Award: Scholarship for use in freshman, sophomore, junior, senior, graduate, or postgraduate years; not renewable. *Number:* 1. *Amount:* $500–$2000.

Eligibility Requirements: Applicant must be enrolled or expecting to enroll full-time at a two-year or four-year or technical institution or university; resident of Georgia and studying in Georgia. Available to U.S. citizens.

Application Requirements: Application form, essay, personal photograph. *Deadline:* March 1.

Contact: Sean Ireland, Manager
Phone: 770-454-6776
Fax: 770-454-6778
E-mail: sireland@gapress.org

GEORGIA PRESS EDUCATIONAL FOUNDATION SCHOLARSHIPS

One-time awards to Georgia high school seniors and college undergraduates. Based on prior interest in newspaper journalism. Must be recommended by high school counselor, professor, and/or Georgia Press Educational Foundation member. Must reside and attend school in Georgia.

Academic Fields/Career Goals: Journalism.

Award: Scholarship for use in freshman, sophomore, junior, or senior years; not renewable. *Number:* 1–5. *Amount:* $500–$2000.

Eligibility Requirements: Applicant must be enrolled or expecting to enroll full-time at a two-year or four-year institution or university; resident of Georgia and studying in Georgia. Available to U.S. citizens.

Application Requirements: Application form, financial need analysis, interview, personal photograph. *Deadline:* March 1.

Contact: Jenifer Farmer, Manager
Georgia Press Educational Foundation Inc.
3066 Mercer University Drive, Suite 200
Atlanta, GA 30341-4137
Phone: 770-454-6776

KIRK SUTLIVE SCHOLARSHIP

Scholarship awarded annually to a junior or senior majoring in either the news-editorial or public relations sequence.

Academic Fields/Career Goals: Journalism.

Award: Scholarship for use in junior or senior years; not renewable. *Number:* 1. *Amount:* $500–$2000.

Eligibility Requirements: Applicant must be enrolled or expecting to enroll full-time at a four-year institution or university. Available to U.S. citizens.

Application Requirements: Application form, essay, financial need analysis, personal photograph, transcript. *Deadline:* March 1.

Contact: Sean Ireland, Manager
Phone: 770-454-6776
Fax: 770-454-6778
E-mail: sireland@gapress.org

MORRIS NEWSPAPER CORPORATION SCHOLARSHIP

Scholarship awarded annually to an outstanding print journalism student. Applications are submitted through newspapers in the Morris Newspaper Corporation chain and recipients are named by the Foundation.

Academic Fields/Career Goals: Journalism.

Award: Scholarship for use in freshman, sophomore, junior, or senior years; not renewable. *Number:* 1. *Amount:* $500–$2000.

Eligibility Requirements: Applicant must be enrolled or expecting to enroll full-time at a four-year or technical institution or university; resident of Georgia and studying in Georgia. Available to U.S. citizens.

Application Requirements: Application form, essay, personal photograph. *Deadline:* March 1.

Contact: Sean Ireland, Manager
Phone: 770-454-6776
Fax: 770-454-6778
E-mail: sireland@gapress.org

WILLIAM C. ROGERS SCHOLARSHIP

Scholarship awarded to a junior or senior majoring in the news-editorial sequence. For full-time study only. Must be a resident of Georgia.

Academic Fields/Career Goals: Journalism.

Award: Scholarship for use in junior or senior years; not renewable. *Number:* 1. *Amount:* $500–$2000.

Eligibility Requirements: Applicant must be enrolled or expecting to enroll full-time at a four-year institution or university; resident of Georgia and must have an interest in writing. Available to U.S. citizens.

Application Requirements: Application form, essay, personal photograph, recommendations or references, transcript. *Deadline:* March 1.

Contact: Sean Ireland, Manager
Phone: 770-454-6776
Fax: 770-454-6778
E-mail: sireland@gapress.org

IDAHO STATE BROADCASTERS ASSOCIATION

http://www.idahobroadcasters.org/

WAYNE C. CORNILS MEMORIAL SCHOLARSHIP
• *See page 165*

INDIANA BROADCASTERS ASSOCIATION

http://www.indianabroadcasters.org/

INDIANA BROADCASTERS FOUNDATION SCHOLARSHIP

Awards a student majoring in broadcasting, electronic media, or journalism. Must maintain a 3.0 GPA and be a resident of Indiana. One-time award for full-time undergraduate study in Indiana.

Academic Fields/Career Goals: Journalism; TV/Radio Broadcasting.

Award: Scholarship for use in freshman, sophomore, junior, or senior years; not renewable. *Number:* up to 10. *Amount:* $500–$2000.

Eligibility Requirements: Applicant must be enrolled or expecting to enroll full-time at a two-year or four-year or technical institution or university; resident of Indiana and studying in Indiana. Applicant must have 3.0 GPA or higher. Available to U.S. citizens.

Application Requirements: Application form, application form may be submitted online (http://www.indianabroadcasters.org), essay, recommendations or references, transcript. *Deadline:* March 4.

Contact: Gwen Piening, Scholarship Administrator
Indiana Broadcasters Association
3003 East 98th Street, Suite 161
Indianapolis, IN 46280
Phone: 317-573-0119
Fax: 317-573-0895
E-mail: indba@aol.com

INTERNATIONAL FOODSERVICE EDITORIAL COUNCIL

http://www.ifeconline.com/

INTERNATIONAL FOODSERVICE EDITORIAL COUNCIL COMMUNICATIONS SCHOLARSHIP
• See page 88

ISLAMIC SCHOLARSHIP FUND

http://islamicscholarshipfund.org/

ISF NATIONAL SCHOLARSHIP
• See page 108

JAPANESE AMERICAN CITIZENS LEAGUE (JACL)

http://www.jacl.org/

NATIONAL JACL HEADQUARTERS SCHOLARSHIP
• See page 99

JOHN BAYLISS BROADCAST FOUNDATION

http://www.beaweb.org/bayliss/radio.html

JOHN BAYLISS BROADCAST RADIO SCHOLARSHIP
• See page 204

JORGE MAS CANOSA FREEDOM FOUNDATION

http://masscholarships.org/

MAS FAMILY SCHOLARSHIP AWARD
• See page 165

MAINE COMMUNITY FOUNDATION, INC.

http://www.mainecf.org/

GUY P. GANNETT SCHOLARSHIP FUND

Scholarship for students majoring in journalism or a field reasonably related, including all forms of print, broadcast, or electronic media. Recipients must be graduates of Maine high schools or home-schooled in a Maine community during their last year of secondary education. Students will be chosen based on demonstrated interest in journalism, financial need, and academic achievement.

Academic Fields/Career Goals: Journalism.

Award: Scholarship for use in freshman year; not renewable.

Eligibility Requirements: Applicant must be high school student and planning to enroll or expecting to enroll full-time at a four-year institution or university. Available to U.S. citizens.

Application Requirements: Application form, financial need analysis, transcript. *Deadline:* May 1.

Contact: Ms. Amy Pollien, Grants Administration
Phone: 207-667-9735 Ext. 1109
E-mail: apollien@mainecf.org

MARYLAND/DELAWARE/DISTRICT OF COLUMBIA PRESS FOUNDATION

http://www.mddcpress.com/

MICHAEL J. POWELL HIGH SCHOOL JOURNALIST OF THE YEAR

Scholarship of $1500 to an outstanding high school student. Applicant must submit five samples of work, mounted on unlined paper, a letter of recommendation from the nominee's advisor, an autobiography geared to the publication activities in which the nominee participated, and the nominee should write a paragraph or two on the most important aspect of scholastic journalism.

Academic Fields/Career Goals: Journalism.

Award: Scholarship for use in freshman year; not renewable. *Number:* 1. *Amount:* $1500.

Eligibility Requirements: Applicant must be high school student; planning to enroll or expecting to enroll full-time at a four-year institution or university; resident of Delaware, District of Columbia, Maryland and must have an interest in writing. Available to U.S. citizens.

Application Requirements: Application form, driver's license, entry in a contest, five sample articles, recommendations or references. *Deadline:* January 31.

Contact: Jennifer Thornberry, Membership Services Coordinator
Maryland/Delaware/District of Columbia Press Foundation
60 West Street
Suite 107
Annapolis, MD 21401-2479
Phone: 855-721-6332 Ext. 2
Fax: 855-721-6332
E-mail: service@mddcpress.com

MISSISSIPPI ASSOCIATION OF BROADCASTERS

http://www.msbroadcasters.org/

MISSISSIPPI ASSOCIATION OF BROADCASTERS SCHOLARSHIP

Scholarship available to a student enrolled in a fully accredited broadcast curriculum at a Mississippi two- or four-year college.

Academic Fields/Career Goals: Journalism; TV/Radio Broadcasting.

Award: Scholarship for use in freshman, sophomore, junior, or senior years; not renewable. *Number:* up to 8. *Amount:* $2000.

Eligibility Requirements: Applicant must be enrolled or expecting to enroll full-time at a two-year or four-year institution or university; resident of Mississippi and studying in Mississippi. Available to U.S. citizens.

Application Requirements: Application form, extracurricular activities and community involvement also considered, financial need analysis, recommendations or references. *Deadline:* May 1.

Contact: Jackie Lett, Scholarship Coordinator
Phone: 601-957-9121
Fax: 601-957-9175
E-mail: jackie@msbroadcasters.org

MISSISSIPPI PRESS ASSOCIATION EDUCATION FOUNDATION

http://www.mspress.org/

MISSISSIPPI PRESS ASSOCIATION EDUCATION FOUNDATION SCHOLARSHIP

The foundation annually offers $1000 ($500 per semester) scholarships to qualified students enrolled in print journalism, and who are residents of Mississippi. The recipient who maintains a 3.0 GPA. Total value of the scholarship can be as much as $4000 when awarded to an incoming freshman who remains qualified throughout their four years of print journalism education.

Academic Fields/Career Goals: Journalism.

Award: Scholarship for use in freshman, sophomore, junior, or senior years; renewable. *Number:* 1. *Amount:* $1000–$4000.

Eligibility Requirements: Applicant must be enrolled or expecting to enroll full-time at a two-year or four-year institution or university and resident of Mississippi. Applicant must have 3.0 GPA or higher. Available to U.S. citizens.

Application Requirements: Application form, recommendations or references, resume, sample of work. *Deadline:* April 1.

Contact: Beth Boone, Scholarship Coordinator
Phone: 601-981-3060
Fax: 601-981-3676
E-mail: bboone@mspress.org

NATIONAL ACADEMY OF TELEVISION ARTS & SCIENCES—OHIO VALLEY CHAPTER

http://ohiovalleyemmy.org/

DAVID J. CLARKE MEMORIAL SCHOLARSHIP
• See page 205

NATIONAL ACADEMY OF TELEVISION ARTS AND SCIENCES

http://www.emmyonline.tv/

DOUGLAS W. MUMMERT SCHOLARSHIP
• See page 129

JIM MCKAY MEMORIAL SCHOLARSHIP
• See page 205

MIKE WALLACE MEMORIAL SCHOLARSHIP
• See page 205

NATIONAL ACADEMY OF TELEVISION ARTS AND SCIENCES TRUSTEES SCHOLARSHIP
• See page 205

RANDY FALCO SCHOLARSHIP
• See page 205

NATIONAL ACADEMY OF TELEVISION ARTS AND SCIENCES, MICHIGAN CHAPTER

http://natasmichigan.org

DR. LYNNE BOYLE/JOHN SCHIMPF UNDERGRADUATE SCHOLARSHIP
• See page 89

NATIONAL ACADEMY OF TELEVISION ARTS AND SCIENCES-NATIONAL CAPITAL/CHESAPEAKE BAY CHAPTER

http://www.natasdc.org/

BETTY ENDICOTT/NTA-NCCB STUDENT SCHOLARSHIP

Scholarship for a full-time sophomore, junior or non-graduating senior student pursuing a career in communication, television or broadcast journalism. Must be enrolled in an accredited four-year college or university in Maryland, Virginia or Washington, D.C. Minimum GPA of 3.0 required. Must demonstrate an aptitude or interest in communication, television or broadcast journalism. Application URL http://capitalemmys.tv/betty_endicott.htm.

Academic Fields/Career Goals: Journalism; TV/Radio Broadcasting.

Award: Scholarship for use in sophomore, junior, or senior years; not renewable. *Number:* 1. *Amount:* $5000.

Eligibility Requirements: Applicant must be enrolled or expecting to enroll full-time at a four-year institution or university and studying in District of Columbia, Maryland, Virginia. Applicant must have 3.0 GPA or higher. Available to U.S. citizens.

Application Requirements: Application form, essay, recommendations or references, resume, transcript, work samples (resume tape in VHS format and radio or television broadcast scripts). *Deadline:* April 22.

Contact: Diane Bruno, Student Affairs Committee
National Academy of Television Arts and Sciences-National Capital/Chesapeake Bay Chapter
9405 Russell Road
Silver Spring, MD 20910
Phone: 301-587-3993
E-mail: capitalemmys@aol.com

NATIONAL ASSOCIATION OF BLACK JOURNALISTS

http://www.nabj.org/

ALLISON FISHER SCHOLARSHIP

Scholarship for students currently attending an accredited college or university. Must be majoring in print journalism and maintain a 3.0 GPA. Recipient will attend NABJ convention and participate in the mentor program. Scholarship value and the number of awards granted varies.

Academic Fields/Career Goals: Journalism.

Award: Scholarship for use in freshman, sophomore, junior, senior, or graduate years; not renewable.

Eligibility Requirements: Applicant must be enrolled or expecting to enroll full-time at a four-year institution or university. Applicant must have 3.0 GPA or higher. Available to U.S. and non-U.S. citizens.

Application Requirements: Driver's license, proof of enrollment, recommendations or references. *Deadline:* March 17.

Contact: Irving Washington, Manager
Phone: 301-445-7100
Fax: 301-445-7101
E-mail: iwashington@nabj.org

GERALD BOYD/ROBIN STONE NON-SUSTAINING SCHOLARSHIP

One-time scholarship for students enrolled in an accredited four-year institution. Must be enrolled as an undergraduate or graduate student and maintain a 3.0 GPA. Must major in print journalism. Must be a member of NABJ. Scholarship value and the number of awards granted annually varies.

Academic Fields/Career Goals: Journalism.

Award: Scholarship for use in freshman, sophomore, junior, senior, or graduate years; not renewable.

Eligibility Requirements: Applicant must be enrolled or expecting to enroll full-time at a four-year institution or university. Applicant must have 3.0 GPA or higher. Available to U.S. and non-U.S. citizens.

Application Requirements: 6 samples of work, application form, essay, personal photograph, recommendations or references, transcript. *Deadline:* March 17.

Contact: Irving Washington, Manager
Phone: 301-445-7100
Fax: 301-445-7101
E-mail: iwashington@nabj.org

NABJ SCHOLARSHIP
• See page 205

NATIONAL ASSOCIATION OF BLACK JOURNALISTS AND NEWHOUSE FOUNDATION SCHOLARSHIP

Award for high school seniors planning to attend an accredited four-year college or university and major in journalism. Minimum 3.0 GPA required. Must be a member of NABJ. The scholarship value and the number of awards granted varies.

Academic Fields/Career Goals: Journalism.

Award: Scholarship for use in freshman, sophomore, junior, or senior years; not renewable.

Eligibility Requirements: Applicant must be enrolled or expecting to enroll full-time at a four-year institution or university and must have an interest in writing. Applicant must have 3.0 GPA or higher. Available to U.S. and non-U.S. citizens.

Application Requirements: Application form, driver's license, essay, interview, recommendations or references, transcript. *Deadline:* March 17.

Contact: Irving Washington, Manager
Phone: 301-445-7100
Fax: 301-445-7101
E-mail: iwashington@nabj.org

NATIONAL ASSOCIATION OF BLACK JOURNALISTS NON-SUSTAINING SCHOLARSHIP AWARDS

One-time award for college students attending a four-year institution and majoring in journalism. Minimum 2.5 GPA required. Must be a member of NABJ. Scholarship value and the number of awards varies annually.

Academic Fields/Career Goals: Journalism; Photojournalism/Photography; TV/Radio Broadcasting.

Award: Scholarship for use in freshman, sophomore, junior, or senior years; not renewable.

Eligibility Requirements: Applicant must be enrolled or expecting to enroll full-time at a four-year institution or university and must have an interest in writing. Applicant must have 2.5 GPA or higher. Available to U.S. and non-U.S. citizens.

Application Requirements: Application form, driver's license, personal photograph, proof of enrollment, recommendations or references, transcript. *Deadline:* March 17.

Contact: Irving Washington, Manager
Phone: 301-445-7100
Fax: 301-445-7101
E-mail: iwashington@nabj.org

NATIONAL ASSOCIATION OF BROADCASTERS

http://www.nab.org/

NATIONAL ASSOCIATION OF BROADCASTERS GRANTS FOR RESEARCH IN BROADCASTING
• *See page 206*

NATIONAL ASSOCIATION OF HISPANIC JOURNALISTS (NAHJ)

http://www.nahj.org/

GERALDO RIVERA SCHOLARSHIP

Awards available to college undergraduates and graduate students pursuing careers in English- or Spanish-language TV broadcast journalism. Applications available on website, http://www.nahj.org.

Academic Fields/Career Goals: Journalism; TV/Radio Broadcasting.

Award: Scholarship for use in senior or graduate years; not renewable. *Amount:* $1000–$5000.

Eligibility Requirements: Applicant must be enrolled or expecting to enroll full-time at a four-year institution or university. Available to U.S. citizens.

Application Requirements: Application form, financial need analysis, recommendations or references, resume, transcript. *Deadline:* March 31.

Contact: Virginia Galindo, Program Assistant
Phone: 202-662-7145
E-mail: vgalindo@nahj.org

MARIA ELENA SALINAS SCHOLARSHIP
• *See page 339*

NATIONAL ASSOCIATION OF HISPANIC JOURNALISTS SCHOLARSHIP
• *See page 206*

NEWHOUSE SCHOLARSHIP PROGRAM
• *See page 343*

WASHINGTON POST YOUNG JOURNALISTS SCHOLARSHIP

Four-year award of $10,000 for high school seniors in D.C. metropolitan area. Contact educational programs manager for application and information.

Academic Fields/Career Goals: Journalism.

Award: Scholarship for use in freshman year; not renewable. *Amount:* $10,000.

Eligibility Requirements: Applicant must be high school student; planning to enroll or expecting to enroll full-time at a four-year institution or university and resident of District of Columbia, Maryland, Virginia. Available to U.S. citizens.

Application Requirements: Application form, recommendations or references, transcript. *Deadline:* March 31.

Contact: Virginia Galindo, Program Assistant
Phone: 202-662-7145
E-mail: vgalindo@nahj.org

NATIONAL ASSOCIATION OF NEGRO BUSINESS AND PROFESSIONAL WOMEN'S CLUBS INC.

http://www.nanbpwc.org/

JULIANNE MALVEAUX SCHOLARSHIP
• *See page 245*

NATIONAL DAIRY SHRINE

http://www.dairyshrine.org/

MARSHALL E. MCCULLOUGH-NATIONAL DAIRY SHRINE SCHOLARSHIPS
• *See page 100*

NATIONAL INSTITUTE FOR LABOR RELATIONS RESEARCH

http://www.nilrr.org/

NATIONAL INSTITUTE FOR LABOR RELATIONS RESEARCH WILLIAM B. RUGGLES JOURNALISM SCHOLARSHIP
• *See page 206*

NATIONAL PRESS CLUB

http://www.press.org/

NATIONAL PRESS CLUB SCHOLARSHIP FOR JOURNALISM DIVERSITY

Scholarship of $2500 per year awarded to a talented minority student planning to pursue a career in journalism. Applicant must be a high school senior. Must have applied to or been accepted by a college or university for the upcoming year.

Academic Fields/Career Goals: Journalism.

Award: Scholarship for use in freshman year; not renewable. *Number:* 1. *Amount:* $2500.

Eligibility Requirements: Applicant must be American Indian/Alaska Native, Asian/Pacific Islander, Black (non-Hispanic), Hispanic; high school student and planning to enroll or expecting to enroll full-time at a four-year institution or university. Applicant must have 3.0 GPA or higher. Available to U.S. and non-U.S. citizens.

Application Requirements: Application form, essay, financial need analysis, recommendations or references, transcript, work samples demonstrating an ongoing interest in journalism. *Deadline:* March 1.

Contact: Joann Booze, Scholarship Coordinator
Phone: 202-662-7532
Fax: 202-662-7512
E-mail: jbooze@press.org

NATIONAL SCHOLASTIC PRESS ASSOCIATION

http://www.studentpress.org/

NSPA JOURNALISM HONOR ROLL SCHOLARSHIP

Scholarship to student journalists who have achieved a 3.75 or higher GPA and have worked in student media for two or more years.

Academic Fields/Career Goals: Journalism.

Award: Scholarship for use in freshman year; not renewable. *Number:* 1–3. *Amount:* $1000.

Eligibility Requirements: Applicant must be high school student and planning to enroll or expecting to enroll full-time at a four-year institution or university. Applicant or parent of applicant must have employment or volunteer experience in journalism/broadcasting. Available to U.S. and non-U.S. citizens.

Application Requirements: Application form, essay, proof of NSPA membership required, recommendations or references, resume, transcript. *Deadline:* February 15.

Contact: Marisa Dobson, Sponsorship Contest Coordinator
Phone: 612-625-6519
Fax: 612-626-0720
E-mail: marisa@studentpress.org

NATIONAL WRITERS ASSOCIATION FOUNDATION

http://www.nationalwriters.com/

NATIONAL WRITERS ASSOCIATION FOUNDATION SCHOLARSHIPS

Scholarships available to talented young writers with serious interest in any writing field.

Academic Fields/Career Goals: Journalism; Literature/English/Writing.

Award: Scholarship for use in freshman, sophomore, junior, senior, graduate, or postgraduate years; not renewable. *Number:* 1–4. *Amount:* $1000.

Eligibility Requirements: Applicant must be enrolled or expecting to enroll full- or part-time at a two-year or four-year or technical institution or university and must have an interest in writing. Available to U.S. and non-U.S. citizens.

Application Requirements: Application form. *Deadline:* December 31.

Contact: Sandy Whelchel, Executive Director
National Writers Association Foundation
10940 South Parker Road, Suite 508
Parker, CO 80134
Phone: 303-841-0246
Fax: 303-841-2607
E-mail: natlwritersassn@hotmail.com

NATIVE AMERICAN JOURNALISTS ASSOCIATION

http://www.naja.com/

NATIVE AMERICAN JOURNALISTS ASSOCIATION SCHOLARSHIPS

• *See page 89*

NEBRASKA PRESS ASSOCIATION

http://www.nebpress.com/

NEBRASKA PRESS ASSOCIATION FOUNDATION SCHOLARSHIP

• *See page 89*

NEW JERSEY BROADCASTERS ASSOCIATION

http://www.njba.com/

MICHAEL S. LIBRETTI SCHOLARSHIP

• *See page 206*

NEW JERSEY PRESS FOUNDATION

http://www.njpressfoundation.org/

BERNARD KILGORE MEMORIAL SCHOLARSHIP FOR THE NJ HIGH SCHOOL JOURNALIST OF THE YEAR

Program co-sponsored with the Garden State Scholastic Press Association. Winning student is nominated to the Journalism Education Association for the National High School Journalist of the Year Competition. Must be in high school with plans of entering a four-year college or university on a full-time basis. Minimum 3.0 GPA required.

Academic Fields/Career Goals: Journalism.

Award: Scholarship for use in freshman year; not renewable. *Number:* 1. *Amount:* $5000.

Eligibility Requirements: Applicant must be high school student; planning to enroll or expecting to enroll full-time at a four-year institution or university; resident of New Jersey and must have an interest in writing. Applicant must have 3.0 GPA or higher. Available to U.S. citizens.

Application Requirements: Application form, entry in a contest, essay, portfolio, recommendations or references, resume, transcript. *Deadline:* February 15.

Contact: Thomas Engleman, Program Director
Phone: 609-406-0600 Ext. 19
E-mail: programs@njpressfoundation.org

OHIO NEWSPAPERS FOUNDATION

http://www.ohionews.org

HAROLD K. DOUTHIT SCHOLARSHIP

• *See page 89*

OHIO NEWSPAPERS FOUNDATION MINORITY SCHOLARSHIP

• *See page 89*

OHIO NEWSPAPERS FOUNDATION UNIVERSITY JOURNALISM SCHOLARSHIP

• *See page 90*

ONWA ANNUAL SCHOLARSHIP

• *See page 90*

OREGON ASSOCIATION OF BROADCASTERS

http://www.theoab.org/

OAB FOUNDATION SCHOLARSHIP

• *See page 207*

OREGON COMMUNITY FOUNDATION

http://www.oregoncf.org/

JACKSON FOUNDATION JOURNALISM SCHOLARSHIP FUND

Scholarship for students attending an Oregon college or university and majoring in, or with emphasis on, journalism. For both full-time and part-time. Must be a resident of Oregon.

Academic Fields/Career Goals: Journalism.

Award: Scholarship for use in freshman, sophomore, junior, or senior years; renewable. *Number:* 5. *Amount:* $1500–$2000.

Eligibility Requirements: Applicant must be enrolled or expecting to enroll full-time at a four-year institution or university; resident of Oregon and studying in Oregon. Available to U.S. citizens.

Application Requirements: Application form. *Deadline:* March 1.

Contact: Dianne Causey, Program Associate for Scholarships and Grants
Phone: 503-227-6846 Ext. 1418
E-mail: dcausey@oregoncf.org

OREGON STUDENT ASSISTANCE COMMISSION

http://www.GetCollegeFunds.org/

JACKSON FOUNDATION JOURNALISM SCHOLARSHIP

Renewable award for students at Oregon public and nonprofit colleges who are journalism majors or whose course of study emphasizes journalism. Preference given to students who have taken the SAT and have received good essay scores.

Academic Fields/Career Goals: Journalism.

Award: Scholarship for use in freshman, sophomore, junior, or senior years; not renewable.

Eligibility Requirements: Applicant must be enrolled or expecting to enroll full-time at a two-year or four-year institution; resident of Oregon and studying in Oregon. Available to U.S. citizens.

Application Requirements: Application form, financial need analysis. *Deadline:* March 1.

Contact: Melissa Adams, Scholarship Processing Coordinator
Phone: 541-687-7409
E-mail: melissa.adams@hecc.oregon.gov

OUTDOOR WRITERS ASSOCIATION OF AMERICA

http://www.owaa.org/

OUTDOOR WRITERS ASSOCIATION OF AMERICA - BODIE MCDOWELL SCHOLARSHIP AWARD

• *See page 207*

OVERSEAS PRESS CLUB FOUNDATION

www.overseaspressclubfoundation.org/

OVERSEAS PRESS CLUB FOUNDATION SCHOLAR AWARDS

Students aspiring to become foreign correspondents can apply. Must write an essay of no more than 500 words concentrating on an area of the world or an international issue that is in keeping with the applicant's interest. Must be studying at an American college or university or be an American student studying abroad. Winners receive either a $2,000 scholarship or a $3,000 fellowship to be used to fund an experience at an overseas media organization.

Academic Fields/Career Goals: Journalism.

Award: Scholarship for use in freshman, sophomore, junior, senior, or graduate years; not renewable. *Number:* 15. *Amount:* $2000–$3000.

Eligibility Requirements: Applicant must be enrolled or expecting to enroll full-time at a two-year or four-year institution or university and must have an interest in writing. Available to U.S. and non-U.S. citizens.

Application Requirements: Essay. *Deadline:* December 1.

Contact: Jane Reilly, Executive Director
Overseas Press Club Foundation
40 West 45th Street
New York, NY 10036
Phone: 201-493-9087
E-mail: foundation@opcofamerica.org

PALM BEACH ASSOCIATION OF BLACK JOURNALISTS

PALM BEACH ASSOCIATION OF BLACK JOURNALISTS SCHOLARSHIP

Scholarship of $1000 are awarded to African-American graduating high school seniors plan to pursue a degree in journalism-print, television, radio broadcasting or photography industries. Have a GPA of 2.7 or better.

Academic Fields/Career Goals: Journalism; Photojournalism/Photography; TV/Radio Broadcasting.

Award: Scholarship for use in freshman year; not renewable. *Number:* 1. *Amount:* $1000.

Eligibility Requirements: Applicant must be Black (non-Hispanic); high school student and planning to enroll or expecting to enroll full- or part-time at a four-year institution or university. Available to U.S. and non-U.S. citizens.

Application Requirements: Application form, college acceptance proof, driver's license, transcript. *Deadline:* March 30.

Contact: Christopher Smith, Scholarship Chair
Palm Beach Association of Black Journalists
PO Box 19533
West Palm Beach, FL 33416

PHILADELPHIA ASSOCIATION OF BLACK JOURNALISTS

http://www.pabj.org/

PHILADELPHIA ASSOCIATION OF BLACK JOURNALISTS SCHOLARSHIP

One-time award available to deserving high school students in the Delaware Valley who are interested in becoming journalists. Must have a 2.5 GPA. All applicants must state their intention to pursue journalism careers.

Academic Fields/Career Goals: Journalism.

Award: Scholarship for use in freshman, sophomore, junior, or senior years; not renewable. *Number:* 2. *Amount:* up to $1000.

Eligibility Requirements: Applicant must be Black (non-Hispanic); enrolled or expecting to enroll full-time at a four-year institution or university; resident of Pennsylvania and must have an interest in writing. Applicant must have 2.5 GPA or higher. Available to U.S. citizens.

Application Requirements: Application form, driver's license, essay, recommendations or references, transcript. *Deadline:* May 1.

Contact: Manny Smith, Scholarship Committee
Philadelphia Association of Black Journalists
PO Box 8232
Philadelphia, PA 19101
E-mail: manuelsmith@gmail.com

PRINTING INDUSTRY MIDWEST EDUCATION FOUDNATION

http://www.pimw.org/scholarships

PRINTING INDUSTRY MIDWEST EDUCATION FOUNDATION SCHOLARSHIP FUND

• *See page 207*

QUILL AND SCROLL FOUNDATION

http://www.quillandscroll.org

EDWARD J. NELL MEMORIAL SCHOLARSHIP IN JOURNALISM

Merit-based award for high school seniors planning to major in journalism. Must have won a National Quill and Scroll Writing Award or a Photography or Yearbook Excellence contest. Entry forms available from journalism adviser or Quill and Scroll. Must rank in upper third of class or have a minimum 3.0 GPA.

Academic Fields/Career Goals: Journalism.

Award: Scholarship for use in freshman year; not renewable. *Number:* 1–6. *Amount:* $500–$1500.

Eligibility Requirements: Applicant must be high school student; planning to enroll or expecting to enroll full-time at a four-year institution or university and must have an interest in photography/photogrammetry/filmmaking or writing. Applicant must have 3.0 GPA or higher. Available to U.S. citizens.

Application Requirements: Application form, entry in a contest, essay, personal photograph, recommendations or references, test scores, transcript. *Deadline:* May 10.

Contact: Vanessa Shelton, Executive Director
Quill and Scroll Foundation
School of Journalism, E346 AJB
Iowa City, IA 52242-1528
Phone: 319-335-3457
Fax: 319-335-3989
E-mail: quill-scroll@uiowa.edu

RADIO TELEVISION DIGITAL NEWS ASSOCIATION

www.rtdna.org

CAROLE SIMPSON SCHOLARSHIP
• *See page 208*

ED BRADLEY SCHOLARSHIP
• *See page 208*

GEORGE FOREMAN TRIBUTE TO LYNDON B. JOHNSON SCHOLARSHIP
• *See page 208*

LEE THORNTON SCHOLARSHIP
• *See page 208*

LOU AND CAROLE PRATO SPORTS REPORTING SCHOLARSHIP
• *See page 208*

MIKE REYNOLDS JOURNALISM SCHOLARSHIP
• *See page 209*

PETE WILSON SCHOLARSHIP
• *See page 209*

ROBERT H. MOLLOHAN FAMILY CHARITABLE FOUNDATION, INC.

http://www.mollohanfoundation.org/

HARRY C. HAMM FAMILY SCHOLARSHIP
• *See page 209*

SIGMA DELTA CHI FOUNDATION OF WASHINGTON D.C.

http://www.sdxdc.org

SIGMA DELTA CHI SCHOLARSHIPS

One-time award to help pay tuition for full-time students in their junior or senior year demonstrating a clear intention to become journalists. Must demonstrate financial need. Grades and skills are also considered. Must be enrolled in a college or university in the Washington, D.C., metropolitan area. Sponsored by the Society of Professional Journalists.

Academic Fields/Career Goals: Journalism.

Award: Scholarship for use in junior or senior years; not renewable. *Number:* 4–7. *Amount:* $3000–$5000.

Eligibility Requirements: Applicant must be enrolled or expecting to enroll full-time at a four-year institution or university and studying in District of Columbia, Maryland, Virginia. Applicant must have 3.0 GPA or higher. Available to U.S. and non-U.S. citizens.

Application Requirements: Application form, essay, financial need analysis, interview, portfolio. *Deadline:* February 28.

Contact: Maura Judkis
E-mail: scholarship@sdxdc.org

SOCIETY OF PROFESSIONAL JOURNALISTS, LOS ANGELES CHAPTER

http://www.spj.org/losangeles

BILL FARR SCHOLARSHIP

Award available to a student who is either a resident of Los Angeles, Ventura or Orange counties or is enrolled at a university in one of those counties. Must have completed sophomore year and be enrolled in or accepted to a journalism program.

Academic Fields/Career Goals: Journalism.

Award: Scholarship for use in junior, senior, or graduate years; not renewable. *Number:* 1. *Amount:* $500–$1000.

Eligibility Requirements: Applicant must be enrolled or expecting to enroll full-time at a four-year institution or university; resident of California and studying in California. Available to U.S. citizens.

Application Requirements: Application form, essay, financial need analysis, recommendations or references, resume, work samples. *Deadline:* April 15.

Contact: Daniel Garvey, Scholarship Chairman
Society of Professional Journalists, Los Angeles Chapter
1250 Bellflower
Long Beach, CA 90840
Phone: 562-985-5779

CARL GREENBERG SCHOLARSHIP

Award for a student who is either a resident of Los Angeles, Ventura or Orange counties or is enrolled at a university in one of those three California counties. Must have completed sophomore year and be enrolled in or accepted to an investigative or political journalism program.

Academic Fields/Career Goals: Journalism.

Award: Scholarship for use in junior, senior, or graduate years; not renewable. *Number:* 1. *Amount:* $1000.

Eligibility Requirements: Applicant must be enrolled or expecting to enroll full-time at a four-year institution or university; resident of California and studying in California. Available to U.S. citizens.

Application Requirements: Application form, essay, financial need analysis, recommendations or references, resume, work samples. *Deadline:* April 15.

Contact: Daniel Garvey, Scholarship Chairman
Society of Professional Journalists, Los Angeles Chapter
1250 Bellflower
Long Beach, CA 90840
Phone: 562-985-5779

HELEN JOHNSON SCHOLARSHIP

Awards are available to a student who is a resident of Los Angeles, Ventura or Orange counties or is enrolled at a university in one of those three California counties. Must have completed sophomore year and be enrolled in or accepted to a broadcast journalism program.

Academic Fields/Career Goals: Journalism; TV/Radio Broadcasting.

Award: Scholarship for use in junior, senior, or graduate years; not renewable. *Number:* 1. *Amount:* $500–$1000.

Eligibility Requirements: Applicant must be enrolled or expecting to enroll full-time at a four-year institution or university; resident of California and studying in California. Available to U.S. citizens.

Application Requirements: Application form, essay, financial need analysis, recommendations or references, resume, work samples. *Deadline:* April 15.

Contact: Daniel Garvey, Scholarship Chairman
Society of Professional Journalists, Los Angeles Chapter
1250 Bellflower
Long Beach, CA 90840
Phone: 562-985-5779

KEN INOUYE SCHOLARSHIP

Awards are available to a minority student who is either a resident of Los Angeles, Ventura, or Orange counties or is enrolled at a university in one of those three California counties. Must have completed sophomore year and be enrolled in or accepted to a journalism program.

Academic Fields/Career Goals: Journalism.

Award: Scholarship for use in junior, senior, or graduate years; renewable. *Number:* 1. *Amount:* $500–$1000.

Eligibility Requirements: Applicant must be American Indian/Alaska Native, Asian/Pacific Islander, Black (non-Hispanic), Hispanic; enrolled or expecting to enroll full-time at a four-year institution or university; resident of California and studying in California. Available to U.S. citizens.

Application Requirements: Application form, essay, financial need analysis, recommendations or references, resume, work samples. *Deadline:* April 15.

Contact: Daniel Garvey, Scholarship Chairman
Society of Professional Journalists, Los Angeles Chapter
1250 Bellflower
Long Beach, CA 90840
Phone: 562-985-5779

SOCIETY OF PROFESSIONAL JOURNALISTS MARYLAND PRO CHAPTER

http://www.spj.org/mdpro

MARYLAND SPJ PRO CHAPTER COLLEGE SCHOLARSHIP

Scholarships for journalism students whose regular home residence is in Maryland. May attend colleges or universities in Virginia, Washington D.C., or Pennsylvania.

Academic Fields/Career Goals: Journalism.

Award: Scholarship for use in freshman, sophomore, junior, or senior years; not renewable.

Eligibility Requirements: Applicant must be enrolled or expecting to enroll full- or part-time at a four-year institution or university; resident of Maryland and studying in District of Columbia, Maryland, Pennsylvania, Virginia. Available to U.S. citizens.

Application Requirements: Application form, awards or honors received, essay, financial need analysis, recommendations or references, transcript. *Deadline:* May 9.

Contact: Sue Katcef, Scholarship Chair
Society of Professional Journalists Maryland Pro Chapter
402 Fox Hollow Lane
Annapolis, MD 21403
Phone: 301-405-7526
E-mail: susiekk@aol.com

SOUTH ASIAN JOURNALISTS ASSOCIATION (SAJA)

http://www.saja.org/

SAJA JOURNALISM SCHOLARSHIP

Scholarships for students in North America who are of South Asian descent (includes Bangladesh, Bhutan, India, Maldives, Nepal, Pakistan and Sri Lanka, Indo-Caribbean) or those with a demonstrated interest in South Asia or South Asian issues. Must be interested in pursuing journalism. Applicant must be a high school senior, undergraduate student or graduate-level student.

Academic Fields/Career Goals: Journalism.

Award: Scholarship for use in freshman, sophomore, junior, senior, graduate, or postgraduate years; not renewable. *Number:* 1–4. *Amount:* $1000–$2000.

Eligibility Requirements: Applicant must be Asian/Pacific Islander and enrolled or expecting to enroll full-time at a two-year or four-year institution or university. Available to U.S. and non-U.S. citizens.

Application Requirements: Application form, essay, financial need analysis, journalism clips or work samples, portfolio, recommendations or references, resume. *Deadline:* February 15.

Contact: Amita Parashar, Student Committee and Scholarships
Phone: 202-513-2845
E-mail: students@saja.org

STRAIGHTFORWARD MEDIA

http://www.straightforwardmedia.com/

STRAIGHTFORWARD MEDIA MEDIA & COMMUNICATIONS SCHOLARSHIP

• *See page 91*

TAMPA BAY TIMES FUND, INC.

http://www.tampabay.com/fund

CAREER JOURNALISM SCHOLARSHIP

• *See page 210*

TAMPA BAY TIMES FUND CAREER JOURNALISM SCHOLARSHIPS

• *See page 91*

TEXAS GRIDIRON CLUB INC.

http://www.spjfw.org/

TEXAS GRIDIRON CLUB SCHOLARSHIPS

• *See page 212*

UNITED METHODIST COMMUNICATIONS

http://www.umcom.org/

LEONARD M. PERRYMAN COMMUNICATIONS SCHOLARSHIP FOR ETHNIC MINORITY STUDENTS

• *See page 212*

UNITED NEGRO COLLEGE FUND

http://www.uncf.org/

RHYTHM NATION/JANET JACKSON SCHOLARSHIP

• *See page 132*

VALLEY PRESS CLUB

http://www.valleypressclub.com/

VALLEY PRESS CLUB SCHOLARSHIPS, THE REPUBLICAN SCHOLARSHIP, CHANNEL 22 SCHOLARSHIP

• *See page 213*

THE WALTER J. TRAVIS SOCIETY

http://www.travissociety.com

THE WALTER J. TRAVIS MEMORIAL SCHOLARSHIP

This scholarship is awarded to students who are pursuing a career in one of the following golf-related professions: golf course architecture, golf course superintendent/turfgrass manager, sports journalism, or professional golf management. Also, any college student who is an outstanding amateur golfer is eligible. Awards based on academic record, extracurricular activities including volunteer service, work experience, and golf-related interests and accomplishments. Award may be used for any educational expenses.

Academic Fields/Career Goals: Journalism; Landscape Architecture; Recreation, Parks, Leisure Studies; Sports-Related/Exercise Science.

Award: Scholarship for use in freshman, sophomore, junior, senior, or graduate years; not renewable. *Number:* 1–5. *Amount:* $1000.

Eligibility Requirements: Applicant must be enrolled or expecting to enroll full-time at a four-year or technical institution or university and must have an interest in golf. Applicant must have 3.0 GPA or higher. Available to U.S. and non-U.S. citizens.

Application Requirements: Application form, community service, essay. *Deadline:* June 1.

Contact: Mr. Edward Homsey, Scholarship Chairman
The Walter J. Travis Society
24 Sandstone Drive
Rochester, NY 14616
Phone: 585-663-6120
E-mail: TravisSociety@yahoo.com

WOMEN'S BASKETBALL COACHES ASSOCIATION

http://www.wbca.org/

ROBIN ROBERTS/WBCA SPORTS COMMUNICATIONS SCHOLARSHIP AWARD
• *See page 213*

LANDSCAPE ARCHITECTURE

AMERICAN SOCIETY OF CERTIFIED ENGINEERING TECHNICIANS

http://www.ascet.org/

KURT H. AND DONNA M. SCHULER SMALL GRANT
• *See page 176*

BHW GROUP

https://thebhwgroup.com/

BHW WOMEN IN STEM SCHOLARSHIP
• *See page 74*

CENTER FOR ARCHITECTURE

http://www.cfafoundation.org/scholarships

CENTER FOR ARCHITECTURE DESIGN SCHOLARSHIP
• *See page 119*

CENTER FOR ARCHITECTURE, DOUGLAS HASKELL AWARD FOR STUDENT JOURNALS
• *See page 119*

THE DALLAS FOUNDATION

http://www.dallasfoundation.org/

WHITLEY PLACE SCHOLARSHIP
• *See page 120*

FEDERATED GARDEN CLUBS OF CONNECTICUT

http://www.ctgardenclubs.org/

FEDERATED GARDEN CLUBS OF CONNECTICUT INC. SCHOLARSHIPS
• *See page 156*

FEDERATED GARDEN CLUBS OF MARYLAND

http://www.fgcofmd.org/

ROBERT LEWIS BAKER SCHOLARSHIP
• *See page 364*

GARDEN CLUB OF AMERICA

http://www.gcamerica.org/

GCA AWARD IN DESERT STUDIES
• *See page 121*

KATHARINE M. GROSSCUP SCHOLARSHIPS IN HORTICULTURE
• *See page 364*

THE GEORGIA TRUST FOR HISTORIC PRESERVATION

http://www.georgiatrust.org/

B. PHINIZY SPALDING, HUBERT B. OWENS, AND THE NATIONAL SOCIETY OF THE COLONIAL DAMES OF AMERICA IN THE STATE OF GEORGIA ACADEMIC SCHOLARSHIPS
• *See page 104*

J. NEEL REID PRIZE
• *See page 121*

HORTICULTURAL RESEARCH INSTITUTE

http://www.hriresearch.org/

BRYAN A. CHAMPION MEMORIAL SCHOLARSHIP
• *See page 92*

CARVILLE M. AKEHURST MEMORIAL SCHOLARSHIP
• *See page 315*

MUGGETS SCHOLARSHIP
• *See page 366*

SPRING MEADOW NURSERY SCHOLARSHIP
• *See page 366*

TIMOTHY AND PALMER W. BIGELOW JR., SCHOLARSHIP
• *See page 92*

USREY FAMILY SCHOLARSHIP
• *See page 315*

THE LAND CONSERVANCY OF NEW JERSEY

http://tlc-nj.org/

ROGERS FAMILY SCHOLARSHIP
• *See page 243*

RUSSELL W. MYERS SCHOLARSHIP
• *See page 99*

LANDSCAPE ARCHITECTURE FOUNDATION

www.lafoundation.org

ASLA COUNCIL OF FELLOWS SCHOLARSHIP

This scholarship was established to: 1) aid outstanding students with unmet financial need; 2) increase participation of economically disadvantaged and under-represented populations; and 3) enrich the profession of landscape architecture through a more diverse population. Eligible applicants must be Student ASLA members and third, fourth, or fifth-year undergraduates in Landscape Architecture Accreditation Board (LAAB) accredited programs.

Academic Fields/Career Goals: Landscape Architecture.

Award: Scholarship for use in junior or senior years; not renewable. *Number:* 1–3. *Amount:* $5000.

Eligibility Requirements: Applicant must be enrolled or expecting to enroll full- or part-time at a four-year institution or university. Available to U.S. citizens.

Application Requirements: Application form, essay, financial need analysis, personal photograph. *Fee:* $5. *Deadline:* February 15.

Contact: Scholarships Coordinator
Phone: 202-331-7070 Ext. 14
E-mail: scholarships@lafoundation.org

COURTLAND PAUL SCHOLARSHIP

This scholarship honors the memory of Courtland P. Paul, FASLA (1927-2003) and his lifelong commitment to the landscape architecture profession. A native Californian, he became one of the state's first licensed landscape architects in 1954. Mr. Paul and Peridian International, the landscape architecture firm he founded over fifty years ago, were well known for community design and master planning, and for the golf courses, hotels, and theme parks they created in Southern California and throughout the world.

Academic Fields/Career Goals: Landscape Architecture.

Award: Scholarship for use in junior or senior years; not renewable. *Number:* 1. *Amount:* $5000.

Eligibility Requirements: Applicant must be enrolled or expecting to enroll full- or part-time at a four-year institution or university. Available to U.S. citizens.

Application Requirements: Application form, essay, financial need analysis, personal photograph. *Fee:* $5. *Deadline:* February 15.

Contact: Scholarships Coordinator
Phone: 202-331-7070 Ext. 14
E-mail: scholarships@lafoundation.org

EDSA MINORITY SCHOLARSHIP

Scholarship established to help African American, Hispanic, Native American and minority students of other cultural and ethnic backgrounds to continue their landscape architecture education as they pursue a graduate degree or enter into their final two years of undergraduate study.

Academic Fields/Career Goals: Landscape Architecture.

Award: Scholarship for use in junior, senior, or graduate years; not renewable. *Number:* 1. *Amount:* $5000.

Eligibility Requirements: Applicant must be American Indian/Alaska Native, Asian/Pacific Islander, Black (non-Hispanic), Hispanic and enrolled or expecting to enroll full- or part-time at a four-year institution or university. Available to U.S. and non-U.S. citizens.

Application Requirements: Application form, essay, personal photograph. *Fee:* $5. *Deadline:* February 15.

Contact: Scholarships Coordinator
Phone: 202-331-7070 Ext. 14
E-mail: scholarships@lafoundation.org

HAWAII CHAPTER/DAVID T. WOOLSEY SCHOLARSHIP

The award provides funds for educational or professional development purposes for a third-, fourth-, or fifth-year undergraduate or graduate student of landscape architecture in a Landscape Architecture Accreditation Board (LAAB) accredited program. Student must be a permanent resident of Hawaii.

Academic Fields/Career Goals: Landscape Architecture.

Award: Scholarship for use in junior, senior, or graduate years; not renewable. *Number:* 1–2000.

Eligibility Requirements: Applicant must be enrolled or expecting to enroll full- or part-time at a four-year institution or university and resident of Hawaii. Available to U.S. and non-U.S. citizens.

Application Requirements: Application form, essay, personal photograph. *Fee:* $5. *Deadline:* February 15.

Contact: Scholarships Coordinator
Phone: 202-331-7070 Ext. 14
E-mail: scholarships@lafoundation.org

LANDSCAPE FORMS DESIGN FOR PEOPLE SCHOLARSHIP

This $3,000 scholarship honors landscape architecture students with a proven contribution to the design of public spaces that integrate landscape design and the use of amenities to promote social interaction.

Academic Fields/Career Goals: Landscape Architecture.

Award: Scholarship for use in senior year; not renewable. *Number:* 1. *Amount:* $3000.

Eligibility Requirements: Applicant must be enrolled or expecting to enroll full-time at a four-year institution or university. Available to U.S. and non-U.S. citizens.

Application Requirements: Application form, essay, personal photograph. *Fee:* $5. *Deadline:* February 15.

Contact: Scholarships Coordinator
Phone: 202-331-7070 Ext. 14
E-mail: scholarships@lafoundation.org

RAIN BIRD INTELLIGENT USE OF WATER SCHOLARSHIP

• See page 366

STEVEN G. KING PLAY ENVIRONMENTS SCHOLARSHIP

This $5,000 scholarship, created by Steven G. King, FASLA, founder and Chairman of Landscape Structures Inc., recognizes a student who has high potential in the design of play environments. This student must show an interest in the value of integrating playgrounds into parks, schools and other play environments and understand the significant social and educational value of play. Key qualities in the student receiving the Scholarship are creativity, openness to innovation, and a demonstrated interest in park and playground planning.

Academic Fields/Career Goals: Landscape Architecture.

Award: Scholarship for use in junior, senior, or graduate years; not renewable. *Number:* 1. *Amount:* $5000.

Eligibility Requirements: Applicant must be enrolled or expecting to enroll full- or part-time at a four-year institution or university. Available to U.S. and non-U.S. citizens.

Application Requirements: Application form, essay, personal photograph. *Fee:* $5. *Deadline:* February 15.

Contact: Scholarships Coordinator
Phone: 202-331-7070 Ext. 14
E-mail: scholarships@lafoundation.org

MONTANA FEDERATION OF GARDEN CLUBS

http://www.mtfgc.org/

LIFE MEMBER MONTANA FEDERATION OF GARDEN CLUBS SCHOLARSHIP

• See page 243

NATIONAL ASSOCIATION OF WOMEN IN CONSTRUCTION

http://www.nawic.org/

NAWIC UNDERGRADUATE SCHOLARSHIPS

• See page 122

NATIONAL GARDEN CLUBS INC.

http://www.gardenclub.org/

NATIONAL GARDEN CLUBS INC. SCHOLARSHIP PROGRAM
• See page 100

OREGON STUDENT ASSISTANCE COMMISSION

http://www.GetCollegeFunds.org/

HOME BUILDERS FOUNDATION JIM IRVINE STATEWIDE SCHOLARSHIP
• See page 123

PLAN NEW HAMPSHIRE

www.plannh.org

PLAN NEW HAMPSHIRE SCHOLARSHIP AND PROGRAM
• See page 123

PROFESSIONAL CONSTRUCTION ESTIMATORS ASSOCIATION

http://www.pcea.org/

TED G. WILSON MEMORIAL SCHOLARSHIP FOUNDATION
• See page 197

QUALITY BATH

www.qualitybath.com

QUALITYBATH.COM SCHOLARSHIP PROGRAM
• See page 123

SUPPORT CREATIVITY

http://wesupportcreativity.org

SUPPORT CREATIVITY SCHOLARSHIP
• See page 124

TURNER CONSTRUCTION COMPANY

http://www.turnerconstruction.com/

YOUTHFORCE 2020 SCHOLARSHIP PROGRAM
• See page 124

VECTORWORKS, INC.

http://www.vectorworks.net

VECTORWORKS DESIGN SCHOLARSHIP
• See page 124

THE WALTER J. TRAVIS SOCIETY

http://www.travissociety.com

THE WALTER J. TRAVIS MEMORIAL SCHOLARSHIP
• See page 388

LAW ENFORCEMENT/ POLICE ADMINISTRATION

AMERICAN SOCIETY OF CRIMINOLOGY

http://www.asc41.com/

AMERICAN SOCIETY OF CRIMINOLOGY GENE CARTE STUDENT PAPER COMPETITION
• See page 225

ASSOCIATION OF FORMER INTELLIGENCE OFFICERS

http://www.afio.com

AFIO UNDERGRADUATE AND GRADUATE SCHOLARSHIPS
• See page 103

CONNECTICUT ASSOCIATION OF WOMEN POLICE

http://www.cawp.net/

CONNECTICUT ASSOCIATION OF WOMEN POLICE SCHOLARSHIP
• See page 225

FALES & FALES, P.A.

https://www.faleslaw.com/

LAW ENFORCEMENT FAMILY MEMBER SCHOLARSHIP
This scholarship will be awarded to a student (undergraduate or graduate) enrolled at either an accredited law school or an accredited university. The student must have a family member (such as a parent, spouse or sibling) who is or was an active duty member of law enforcement, including reserve officers and retired, deceased or disabled officers. To be eligible, a candidate must submit a 1-3 page typed essay describing the impact of the law enforcement member on the candidate's life. Candidates must be full-time students with a current GPA of at least a 3.0. To apply, candidates must submit the following by 5:00 pm (CST) on August 31st, 2017 to the included address—a completed application (which can be found on our website), personal essay (described above), and a certified copy of the applicant's current transcript confirming satisfaction of the eligibility requirements listed above.

Academic Fields/Career Goals: Law Enforcement/Police Administration; Law/Legal Services.

Award: Scholarship for use in freshman, sophomore, junior, senior, graduate, or postgraduate years; not renewable. *Number:* 1. *Amount:* $1000.

Eligibility Requirements: Applicant must be enrolled or expecting to enroll full-time at a four-year institution or university. Applicant must have 3.0 GPA or higher. Available to U.S. citizens.

Application Requirements: Application form, essay. *Deadline:* August 31.

Contact: Anthony Ferguson
Fales & Fales, P.A.
192 Lisbon Street
Lewiston, ME 04240
E-mail: aferguson@faleslaw.com

INDIANA SHERIFFS' ASSOCIATION

http://www.indianasheriffs.org/

INDIANA SHERIFFS' ASSOCIATION SCHOLARSHIP PROGRAM
• See page 225

ISLAMIC SCHOLARSHIP FUND

http://islamicscholarshipfund.org/

ISF NATIONAL SCHOLARSHIP
• *See page 108*

LEARNING FOR LIFE

http://www.learning-for-life.org/

CAPTAIN JAMES J. REGAN SCHOLARSHIP

Two one-time $500 scholarships are presented annually to Law Enforcement Explorers graduating from high school or from an accredited college program. Evaluation will be based on academic record.

Academic Fields/Career Goals: Law Enforcement/Police Administration.

Award: Scholarship for use in freshman, sophomore, junior, or senior years; not renewable. *Number:* 2. *Amount:* $500.

Eligibility Requirements: Applicant must be enrolled or expecting to enroll full-time at a two-year or four-year or technical institution or university. Applicant or parent of applicant must be member of Explorer Program/Learning for Life. Available to U.S. citizens.

Application Requirements: Application form, essay, personal photograph, recommendations or references, transcript. *Deadline:* March 31.

Contact: William Taylor, Scholarships and Awards Coordinator
Learning for Life
1329 West Walnut Hill Lane, PO Box 152225
Irving, TX 75015-2225
Phone: 972-580-2241
E-mail: btaylor@lflmail.org

SHERYL A. HORAK MEMORIAL SCHOLARSHIP

Award for graduating high school students who are Law Enforcement Explorers joining a program in law enforcement in accredited college or university. Provides a one-time scholarship of $1000.

Academic Fields/Career Goals: Law Enforcement/Police Administration.

Award: Scholarship for use in freshman year; not renewable. *Number:* 1. *Amount:* $1000.

Eligibility Requirements: Applicant must be enrolled or expecting to enroll full-time at a two-year or four-year institution or university. Applicant or parent of applicant must be member of Explorer Program/Learning for Life. Available to U.S. citizens.

Application Requirements: Application form, essay, personal photograph, recommendations or references, transcript. *Deadline:* March 31.

Contact: William Taylor, Scholarships and Awards Coordinator
E-mail: btaylor@lflmail.org

LEARNING FOR LIFE/EXPLORING

http://www.learning-for-life.org/

SHERYL A. HORAK MEMORIAL SCHOLARSHIP

$1000 one-time scholarship for students enrolled either for full- or part-time study in a law enforcement field. Must be participant of the Learning for Life Exploring program.

Academic Fields/Career Goals: Law Enforcement/Police Administration.

Award: Scholarship for use in freshman, sophomore, junior, or senior years; not renewable. *Number:* 1. *Amount:* $1000.

Eligibility Requirements: Applicant must be enrolled or expecting to enroll full- or part-time at a two-year or four-year or technical institution or university. Available to U.S. and non-U.S. citizens.

Application Requirements: Application form, essay, personal photograph, recommendations or references, transcript. *Deadline:* March 31.

Contact: Scholarship Committee
Learning for Life/Exploring
1325 West Walnut Hill Lane, PO Box 152079
Irving, TX 75015-2079

LIVSECURE

https://www.livsecure.com

LIVSECURE STUDENT SCHOLARSHIP
• *See page 226*

NATIONAL BLACK POLICE ASSOCIATION

http://www.blackpolice.org/

ALPHONSO DEAL SCHOLARSHIP AWARD
• *See page 226*

NORTH CAROLINA STATE EDUCATION ASSISTANCE AUTHORITY

http://www.ncseaa.edu/

NORTH CAROLINA SHERIFFS' ASSOCIATION UNDERGRADUATE CRIMINAL JUSTICE SCHOLARSHIPS
• *See page 226*

WIFLE FOUNDATION, INC.

http://www.wifle.org/

WIFLE SCHOLARSHIP
• *See page 227*

LAW/LEGAL SERVICES

ALBERTA HERITAGE SCHOLARSHIP FUND

http://www.alis.alberta.ca/

JASON LANG SCHOLARSHIP
• *See page 233*

AMERICAN CRIMINAL JUSTICE ASSOCIATION-LAMBDA ALPHA EPSILON

http://www.acjalae.org/

AMERICAN CRIMINAL JUSTICE ASSOCIATION-LAMBDA ALPHA EPSILON NATIONAL SCHOLARSHIP
• *See page 224*

AMERICAN SOCIETY OF CRIMINOLOGY

http://www.asc41.com/

AMERICAN SOCIETY OF CRIMINOLOGY GENE CARTE STUDENT PAPER COMPETITION
• *See page 225*

BAURKOT & BAURKOT: THE IMMIGRATION LAW GROUP

http://nationalimmigrationlawyers.com/

ATTORNEY RAYMOND LAHOUD SCHOLAR PROGRAM

All scholarship candidates must be enrolled in a 4-year college or university program and about to embark on their sophomore, junior, or senior year; or be accepted, or already enrolled in an ABA-accredited law school and about to embark on their first, second, or third year of law school; wish to pursue, or already be pursuing a career in the legal profession; have maintained a minimum GPA of 3.0 at their current college, university, or law school; and submit an application, resume, unofficial transcripts, and an essay discussing why the candidate wishes to pursue a career in the legal profession. The essay must be no less than 3,000 words. The application deadline is March 1 of each year. Selected candidates will be notified no later than April 1 of the same year. The scholarship may be used by the selected recipient for any education related expense. To learn more, please visit: http://nationalimmigrationlawyers.com/legalscholars/ or e-mail legalscholars@baurkotlaw.com. No phone calls or faxes, please.

Academic Fields/Career Goals: Law/Legal Services.

Award: Scholarship for use in sophomore, junior, senior, graduate, or postgraduate years; not renewable. *Number:* 5. *Amount:* $10,000.

Eligibility Requirements: Applicant must be enrolled or expecting to enroll full-time at a four-year institution or university. Applicant must have 3.0 GPA or higher. Available to U.S. and non-U.S. citizens.

Application Requirements: Application form, essay. *Deadline:* March 1.

Contact: Yenny Bautista, Office Director
Baurkot & Baurkot: The Immigration Law Group
205 South 7th Street
Easton, PA 18042
Phone: 484-5440022
E-mail: legalscholars@baurkotlaw.com

BENSON & BINGHAM

https://www.bensonbingham.com/

BENSON & BINGHAM FIRST ANNUAL SCHOLARSHIP

In 2017, Benson & Bingham decided to once again give back to the community with the inception of its first annual Law Scholarship. Benson & Bingham understand the rigors of law school accompanied with the expense to become an attorney, and felt obliged to help alleviate the financial strain with their annual scholarship offer. In order to be eligible for the scholarship award, applicants must adhere to the following scholarship criteria. Must be currently enrolled in or recently accepted to an accredited law school; be a United States citizen or permanent resident; have a cumulative GPA of 3.0 or higher; provide a copy of your college transcript (unofficial); and submit proof of law school acceptance or attendance. Applications must be received electronically by August 31, 2017 to the following email address: scholarship@bensonbingham.com. In the subject line, please reference: Benson & Bingham First Annual Scholarship Application. Questions regarding the application or process may be submitted to the above email address. Please, no phone calls. One grand prize winner will receive a one-time payment of $2,000 to be applied to the law school of their admission/attendance. Essays may be published by Benson & Bingham, so please refrain from submitting anything personal, vulgar or inappropriate for the web. The winner of the award will be announced by October 31st, 2017. Entrants for our scholarship must submit a minimum of a 600-word typed essay on one of the below topics to be judged by partners Joe Benson and Ben Bingham at the conclusion of the deadline--The future of driver-less cars and how this will affect the field of personal injury. Investigate and report on the past five years of historical motor vehicle accident data in any state, and analyze what state level laws or programs have been instituted during this time to decrease the rate of such accidents.

Academic Fields/Career Goals: Law/Legal Services.

Award: Scholarship for use in senior or postgraduate years; not renewable. *Number:* 1. *Amount:* $2000.

Eligibility Requirements: Applicant must be enrolled or expecting to enroll full-time at an institution or university; resident of Alabama, Alaska, Alberta, Arizona, Arkansas, British Columbia, California, Colorado, Connecticut, Delaware, District of Columbia, Florida, Georgia, Guam, Hawaii, Idaho, Illinois, Indiana, Iowa, Kansas, Kentucky, Louisiana, Maine, Manitoba, Maryland, Massachusetts, Michigan, Minnesota, Mississippi, Missouri, Montana, Nebraska, Nevada, New Brunswick, Newfoundland, New Hampshire, New Jersey, New Mexico, New York, North Carolina, North Dakota, Northwest Territories, Nova Scotia, Ohio, Oklahoma, Ontario, Oregon, Pennsylvania, Prince Edward Island, Puerto Rico, Quebec, Rhode Island, Saskatchewan, South Carolina, South Dakota, Tennessee, Texas, Utah, Vermont, Virginia, Washington, West Virginia, Wisconsin, Wyoming, Yukon and studying in Alabama, Alaska, Alberta, Arizona, Arkansas, British Columbia, California, Colorado, Connecticut, Delaware, District of Columbia, Florida, Georgia, Guam, Hawaii, Idaho, Illinois, Indiana,

Iowa, Kansas, Kentucky, Louisiana, Maine, Manitoba, Maryland, Massachusetts, Michigan, Minnesota, Mississippi, Missouri, Montana, Nebraska, Nevada, New Brunswick, Newfoundland, New Hampshire, New Jersey, New Mexico, New York, North Carolina, North Dakota, Northwest Territories, Nova Scotia, Ohio, Oklahoma, Ontario, Oregon, Pennsylvania, Prince Edward Island, Puerto Rico, Quebec, Rhode Island, Saskatchewan, South Carolina, South Dakota, Tennessee, Texas, Utah, Vermont, Virginia, Washington, West Virginia, Wisconsin, Wyoming, Yukon. Applicant or parent of applicant must have employment or volunteer experience in agriculture. Applicant must have 3.0 GPA or higher. Available to U.S. citizens.

Application Requirements: Application form, essay. *Deadline:* August 31.

Contact: Justin Simpson, Scholarship Adminstrator
Benson & Bingham
11441 Allerton Park Dr. Ste. # 100
Las Vegas, NV 89135
Phone: 702-684-6900
Fax: 702-382-9798
E-mail: scholarship@bensonbingham.com

BLACK ENTERTAINMENT AND SPORTS LAWYERS ASSOCIATION INC.

http://www.besla.org/

BESLA SCHOLARSHIP LEGAL WRITING COMPETITION

$1500 award for the best 1000-word, or two-page essay on a compelling legal issue facing the entertainment or sports industry. Essay must be written by law school student who has completed at least one full year at an accredited law school. Minimum GPA of 2.8 required.

Academic Fields/Career Goals: Law/Legal Services.

Award: Scholarship for use in frfreshman, sophomore, junior, senior, or graduate years; not renewable. *Number:* 2. *Amount:* $1500.

Eligibility Requirements: Applicant must be enrolled or expecting to enroll full-time at a four-year institution or university. Available to U.S. and non-U.S. citizens.

Application Requirements: Application form, essay, resume, transcript. *Deadline:* varies.

Contact: Rev. Phyllicia Hatton, Executive Administrator
Phone: 301-248-1818
Fax: 301-248-0700
E-mail: beslamailbox@aol.com

BOYS AND GIRLS CLUBS OF GREATER SAN DIEGO

http://www.sdyouth.org/

SPENCE REESE SCHOLARSHIP

• *See page 297*

CANTOR CRANE INJURY LAW

http://cantorcrane.com

CANTOR CRANE PERSONAL INJURY LAWYER $1,000 SCHOLARSHIP

• *See page 225*

CRUSH THE CPA EXAM

http://crushthecpaexam.com

CRUSH THE LSAT SCHOLARSHIP

One Grand Prize Winner will receive a $175 reimbursement of LSAT fees plus free access to a Magoosh review course that is valued at $399! This is an annual scholarship for potential law school students. Applicants must enter prior to May 31st, 2017, when the winner will be chosen and announced.

Academic Fields/Career Goals: Law/Legal Services.

Award: Scholarship for use in junior, senior, or graduate years; not renewable. *Number:* 1. *Amount:* $500–$574.

Eligibility Requirements: Applicant must be enrolled or expecting to enroll full-time at a four-year institution or university. Applicant must have 3.0 GPA or higher. Available to U.S. and non-U.S. citizens.

Application Requirements: Application form, essay. *Deadline:* May 31.

Contact: Stephanie Murguia
    E-mail: stephanie@crushempire.com

DIAGNOSIS DELAYED

www.myinjuryattorney.com

DIAGNOSIS DELAYED SCHOLARSHIP

• See page 351

DUDLEY DEBOSIER INJURY LAWYERS

http://www.dudleydebosier.com/home

DUDLEY DEBOSIER LAW SCHOOL SCHOLARSHIP

The Dudley DeBosier Injury Lawyers Law School Scholarship program was organized to enhance the legal educational opportunities available to law students within our community. Dudley DeBosier Injury Lawyers believes a solid legal education foundation is instrumental in a rewarding and fulfilling career. Dudley DeBosier will award two (2) $2,500 scholarships to eligible law school students. To apply and further information, please visit our website.

Academic Fields/Career Goals: Law/Legal Services.

Award: Scholarship for use in senior or graduate years; not renewable. *Number:* 2. *Amount:* $2500.

Eligibility Requirements: Applicant must be enrolled or expecting to enroll full-time at an institution or university. Available to U.S. citizens.

Application Requirements: Application form, essay, personal photograph. *Deadline:* June 2.

Contact: Elizabeth Demopulos, Director of Marketing
    Dudley DeBosier Injury Lawyers
    1075 Government St
    Baton Rouge, LA 70808
    Phone: 225-379-3333
    Fax: 225-379-4952
    E-mail: EDemopulos@dudleydebosier.com

FALES & FALES, P.A.

https://www.faleslaw.com/

LAW ENFORCEMENT FAMILY MEMBER SCHOLARSHIP

• See page 391

GRAND RAPIDS COMMUNITY FOUNDATION

http://www.grfoundation.org/

WARNER NORCROSS AND JUDD LLP SCHOLARSHIP FOR STUDENTS OF COLOR

Financial assistance to students of color who are residents of Michigan, or attend a college/university/vocational school in Michigan, pursuing a career in law, paralegal, or a legal secretarial program. Law school scholarship ($5000), paralegal scholarship ($2000), legal secretary scholarship ($1000).

Academic Fields/Career Goals: Law/Legal Services.

Award: Scholarship for use in freshman, sophomore, junior, senior, or graduate years; not renewable. *Number:* up to 3. *Amount:* $1000–$5000.

Eligibility Requirements: Applicant must be American Indian/Alaska Native, Asian/Pacific Islander, Black (non-Hispanic), Hispanic; enrolled or expecting to enroll full-time at a two-year or four-year institution or university; resident of Michigan and studying in Michigan. Applicant must have 2.5 GPA or higher. Available to U.S. citizens.

Application Requirements: Application form, application form may be submitted online (http://grfoundation.org), essay, financial need analysis, recommendations or references, transcript. *Deadline:* April 1.

Contact: Ms. Ruth Bishop, Education Program Officer
    Grand Rapids Community Foundation
    185 Oakes SW
    Grand Rapids, MI 49503
    Phone: 616-454-1751 Ext. 103
    E-mail: rbishop@grfoundation.org

GREATER KANAWHA VALLEY FOUNDATION

http://www.tgkvf.org/

BERNICE PICKINS PARSONS FUND

Renewable award of $1000 open to students pursuing education or training in the fields of library science, nursing, and paraprofessional training in the legal field. Grant based on financial need. Must be a resident of West Virginia; preference given to Jackson county residents.

Academic Fields/Career Goals: Law/Legal Services; Library and Information Sciences; Nursing.

Award: Grant for use in freshman, sophomore, junior, or senior years; renewable. *Amount:* $1000.

Eligibility Requirements: Applicant must be enrolled or expecting to enroll full-time at a two-year or four-year institution or university and resident of West Virginia. Available to U.S. citizens.

Application Requirements: Application form, essay, financial need analysis, recommendations or references, self-addressed stamped envelope with application, test scores, transcript. *Deadline:* January 15.

Contact: Susan Hoover, Scholarship Program Officer
    Greater Kanawha Valley Foundation
    900 Lee Street East, 16th Floor
    Charleston, WV 25301
    Phone: 304-346-3620
    E-mail: shoover@tgkvf.org

INSTITUTE FOR HUMANE STUDIES

http://www.theihs.org/

HUMANE STUDIES FELLOWSHIPS

• See page 204

ISLAMIC SCHOLARSHIP FUND

http://islamicscholarshipfund.org/

ISF NATIONAL SCHOLARSHIP

• See page 108

JAPANESE AMERICAN CITIZENS LEAGUE (JACL)

http://www.jacl.org/

NATIONAL JACL HEADQUARTERS SCHOLARSHIP

• See page 99

LAW OFFICES OF GOODWIN & SCIESZKA

http://www.1888goodwin.com/

GOODWIN & SCIESZKA INNOVATION SCHOLARSHIP

The Innovation Scholarship will be awarded to three high-achieving students intending to pursue a career in law. Applicants will be judged on their academic performance and their essay addressing one of two law-related questions provided on the application. Applicant must be either a current law student at an accredited law school within the U.S. or at an accredited undergraduate university planning to attend law school.

Academic Fields/Career Goals: Law/Legal Services.

Award: Scholarship for use in freshman, sophomore, junior, senior, or graduate years; not renewable. *Number:* 3. *Amount:* $500–$1000.

Eligibility Requirements: Applicant must be enrolled or expecting to enroll full- or part-time at a two-year or four-year institution or university. Applicant must have 3.0 GPA or higher. Available to U.S. citizens.

Application Requirements: Application form, essay. *Deadline:* June 1.
Contact: Michael Cianfarani
E-mail: mcianfarani@trafficdigitalagency.com

LIVSECURE
https://www.livsecure.com

LIVSECURE STUDENT SCHOLARSHIP
• *See page 226*

MARYLAND STATE HIGHER EDUCATION COMMISSION
http://www.mhec.state.md.us/

GRADUATE AND PROFESSIONAL SCHOLARSHIP PROGRAM-MARYLAND
• *See page 238*

JANET L. HOFFMANN LOAN ASSISTANCE REPAYMENT PROGRAM
• *See page 254*

MORROW & SHEPPARD LLP
https://www.morrowsheppard.com

MORROW & SHEPPARD COLLEGE SCHOLARSHIP
Morrow & Sheppard LLP is a law firm founded by Nick Morrow and John Sheppard. Both partners are Houston lawyers representing clients with cases relating to maritime injuries, truck accidents, oil field accidents, and other types of civil and commercial litigation. It can be very difficult to pay for college, and the expense can be a heavy financial burden. Morrow & Sheppard LLP offers this legal scholarship to students starting their journey into college and to those intending to explore a legal career, as a way to provide financial assistance. The winner of this scholarship will receive $500 towards their education. Any high school senior or current college student who is interested in pursuing law within the U.S. is allowed to apply. For full details see our website: https://www.morrowsheppard.com/college-scholarship/
Academic Fields/Career Goals: Law/Legal Services.
Award: Scholarship for use in freshman, sophomore, junior, or senior years; not renewable. *Number:* 1. *Amount:* $500.
Eligibility Requirements: Applicant must be high school student; planning to enroll or expecting to enroll full- or part-time at a two-year or four-year institution or university and studying in Alabama, Alaska, Arizona, Arkansas, California, Colorado, Connecticut, Delaware, District of Columbia, Florida, Georgia, Hawaii, Idaho, Illinois, Indiana, Iowa, Kansas, Kentucky, Louisiana, Maine, Maryland, Massachusetts, Michigan, Minnesota, Mississippi, Missouri, Montana, Nebraska, Nevada, New Hampshire, New Jersey, New Mexico, New York, North Carolina, North Dakota, Ohio, Oklahoma, Oregon, Pennsylvania, Rhode Island, South Carolina, South Dakota, Tennessee, Texas, Utah, Vermont, Virginia, Washington, West Virginia, Wisconsin, Wyoming. Available to U.S. citizens.
Application Requirements: Application form, essay. *Deadline:* July 10.
Contact: Nick Morrow
Morrow & Sheppard LLP
3701 Kirby Drive, Suite 840
Houston, TX 77098
Phone: 713-489-1206
E-mail: scholarship@morrowsheppard.com

NAQVI INJURY LAW
http://www.naqvilaw.com/

NAQVI LAW SCHOLARSHIP
• *See page 226*

NATIONAL ASSOCIATION OF WATER COMPANIES-NEW JERSEY CHAPTER
http://www.nawc.org

NATIONAL ASSOCIATION OF WATER COMPANIES-NEW JERSEY CHAPTER SCHOLARSHIP
• *See page 80*

NATIONAL BLACK POLICE ASSOCIATION
http://www.blackpolice.org/

ALPHONSO DEAL SCHOLARSHIP AWARD
• *See page 226*

NATIONAL COURT REPORTERS ASSOCIATION
http://ncra.org

COUNCIL ON APPROVED STUDENT EDUCATION'S SCHOLARSHIP FUND
Applicant must have a writing speed of 140 to 180 words/min; must be in an NCRA certified court reporting program; write a two-page essay on topic chosen for the year; and submit a letter of recommendation.
Academic Fields/Career Goals: Law/Legal Services.
Award: Scholarship for use in sophomore year; not renewable. *Number:* 3. *Amount:* $500–$1500.
Eligibility Requirements: Applicant must be enrolled or expecting to enroll full- or part-time at a two-year or four-year or technical institution. Applicant must have 3.0 GPA or higher. Available to U.S. and Canadian citizens.
Application Requirements: Application form, entry in a contest, essay, recommendations or references, transcript. *Deadline:* April 1.
Contact: Cynthia Andrews, Director, Professional Development Programs
National Court Reporters Association
8224 Old Courthouse Road
Vienna, VA 22182
Phone: 703-584-9058
E-mail: candrews@ncra.org

FRANK SARLI MEMORIAL SCHOLARSHIP
One-time award to a student who is nearing graduation from a trade/technical school or four-year college. Must be enrolled in a court reporting program. Minimum 3.5 GPA required.
Academic Fields/Career Goals: Law/Legal Services.
Award: Scholarship for use in senior year; not renewable. *Number:* 1. *Amount:* $2000.
Eligibility Requirements: Applicant must be enrolled or expecting to enroll full- or part-time at a four-year or technical institution or university. Applicant or parent of applicant must be member of National Federation of Press Women. Applicant must have 3.5 GPA or higher. Available to U.S. and non-U.S. citizens.
Application Requirements: Application form. *Deadline:* February 28.
Contact: B.J. Shorak, Deputy Executive Director
National Court Reporters Association
8224 Old Courthouse Road
Vienna, VA 22182-3808
Phone: 703-556-6272 Ext. 126
Fax: 703-556-6291
E-mail: BJSHORAK@ncra.org

STUDENT MEMBER TUITION GRANT
Four $500 awards for students in good academic standing in a court reporting program. Students are required to write 120 to 200 words/min.
Academic Fields/Career Goals: Law/Legal Services.
Award: Grant for use in freshman, sophomore, junior, or senior years; not renewable. *Number:* 4. *Amount:* $500.
Eligibility Requirements: Applicant must be enrolled or expecting to enroll full- or part-time at a four-year or technical institution or university. Available to U.S. and non-U.S. citizens.

Application Requirements: Application form. *Deadline:* May 31.

Contact: Amy Davidson, Assistant Director of Membership
National Court Reporters Association
8224 Old Courthouse Road
Vienna, VA 22182
Phone: 703-556-6272 Ext. 123
E-mail: adavidson@ncrahq.org

NATIONAL FEDERATION OF PARALEGAL ASSOCIATIONS INC. (NFPA)

http://www.paralegals.org/

NATIONAL FEDERATION OF PARALEGAL ASSOCIATES INC. THOMSON REUTERS SCHOLARSHIP

Applicants must be full- or part-time students enrolled in an accredited paralegal education program or college-level program with emphasis in paralegal studies. Minimum GPA of 3.0 required. NFPA membership is not required. Travel stipend to annual convention, where recipients will receive awards, also provided.

Academic Fields/Career Goals: Law/Legal Services.

Award: Scholarship for use in freshman, sophomore, junior, senior, graduate, or postgraduate years; not renewable. *Number:* 2. *Amount:* $2000–$3000.

Eligibility Requirements: Applicant must be enrolled or expecting to enroll full- or part-time at a two-year or four-year or technical institution or university. Applicant must have 3.0 GPA or higher. Available to U.S. and non-U.S. citizens.

Application Requirements: Application form, essay, recommendations or references, transcript. *Deadline:* July 1.

Contact: Michelle Bushnell, Assistant Director
Phone: 425-967-0045
E-mail: info@paralegals.org

NEW ENGLAND EMPLOYEE BENEFITS COUNCIL

http://www.neebc.org/

NEW ENGLAND EMPLOYEE BENEFITS COUNCIL SCHOLARSHIP PROGRAM

• *See page 81*

ROBINSON & HENRY, P.C.

https://www.robinsonandhenry.com/

ROBINSON & HENRY FAMILY LAW SCHOLARSHIP

This scholarship is available to high school seniors and current college students nationwide who plan on attending, or are attending, an accredited 4-year college/university or 2-year accredited community college in the Fall of 2017. The Family Law Scholarship is open only to applicants whose parents have gone through a divorce or are planning on pursuing a career in family law.

Academic Fields/Career Goals: Law/Legal Services.

Award: Scholarship for use in freshman, sophomore, junior, or senior years; not renewable. *Number:* 1. *Amount:* $1000.

Eligibility Requirements: Applicant must be enrolled or expecting to enroll full-time at a two-year or four-year institution or university. Applicant must have 3.0 GPA or higher. Available to U.S. citizens.

Application Requirements: Application form, essay. *Deadline:* May 31.

Contact: Amador Cahvez
E-mail: amador@niftymarketing.com

ROBINSON & HENRY INJURY SCHOLARSHIP

This scholarship is available to high school seniors and current college students nationwide who plan on attending, or are attending, an accredited 4-year college/university or 2-year accredited community college in the Fall of 2017. The applicant or the applicant's family must have been involved in a personal injury accident. Special preferences will be given to members of a family that has recently been injured in a car accident.

Academic Fields/Career Goals: Law/Legal Services.

Award: Scholarship for use in freshman, sophomore, junior, or senior years; not renewable. *Number:* 1. *Amount:* $1500.

Eligibility Requirements: Applicant must be enrolled or expecting to enroll full-time at a two-year or four-year institution or university. Applicant must have 3.0 GPA or higher. Available to U.S. citizens.

Application Requirements: Application form, essay. *Deadline:* May 31.

Contact: Amador Cahvez
E-mail: amador@niftymarketing.com

SOCIETY OF SATELLITE PROFESSIONALS INTERNATIONAL

http://www.sspi.org/

SSPI INTERNATIONAL SCHOLARSHIPS

• *See page 147*

TKE EDUCATIONAL FOUNDATION

http://www.tke.org/

HARRY J. DONNELLY MEMORIAL SCHOLARSHIP

• *See page 85*

UNITARIAN UNIVERSALIST ASSOCIATION

http://www.uua.org/

STANFIELD AND D'ORLANDO ART SCHOLARSHIP

• *See page 132*

UNITED NEGRO COLLEGE FUND

http://www.uncf.org/

SUEZ CORPORATE SCHOLARS PROGRAM

• *See page 87*

VIRGINIA STATE BAR

http://www.vsb.org/

LAW IN SOCIETY AWARD COMPETITION

Participants write an essay in response to a hypothetical situation dealing with legal issues. Awards are based on superior understanding of the value of law in everyday life. The top thirty essays are awarded prizes of a plaque and dictionary/thesaurus set. First place receives $2000 U.S. Savings Bond or $1000 cash; second place, $1,500 bond or $750 cash; third place, $1000 bond or $500 cash; honorable mentions, $200 bond or $100 cash.

Academic Fields/Career Goals: Law/Legal Services.

Award: Prize for use in freshman year; not renewable. *Number:* up to 10. *Amount:* $100–$1000.

Eligibility Requirements: Applicant must be high school student; planning to enroll or expecting to enroll full- or part-time at a four-year institution or university; resident of Virginia and must have an interest in writing. Available to U.S. citizens.

Application Requirements: Application form, entry in a contest, essay. *Deadline:* February 1.

Contact: Sandy Adkins, Public Relations Assistant
Virginia State Bar
707 East Main Street, Suite 1500
Richmond, VA 23219-2800
Phone: 804-775-0594
Fax: 804-775-0582
E-mail: adkins@vsb.org

WASHINGTON STATE ASSOCIATION FOR JUSTICE

http://www.washingtonjustice.org/

WASHINGTON STATE ASSOCIATION FOR JUSTICE AMERICAN JUSTICE ESSAY & VIDEO SCHOLARSHIP

• *See page 227*

WASHINGTON STATE ASSOCIATION FOR JUSTICE PAST PRESIDENTS' SCHOLARSHIP

The Washington State Association for Justice (WSAJ) created the WSAJ Past President's Scholarship Fund in 1991. One $7,500 scholarship will be awarded in 2017. Winners must have 1. Demonstrated academic achievement and planned advancement toward a degree in an institution of higher learning. 2. A documented need for financial assistance. 3. A history of achievement despite having been a victim of injury or overcoming a disability, handicap, or similar challenge. 4. A record of commitment to helping people in need or protecting the rights of injured persons. 5. A plan or commitment to apply your education toward helping people. 6. Residency in Washington State. 7. High school seniors only. Application for this scholarship must be made as follows. Incomplete applications will not be reviewed or considered. 1. Send a letter (written by the student/applicant) to the scholarship committee describing the qualifications of the applicant and explaining the reasons why s/he feels they deserve the scholarship. 2. Include all high school and community college academic transcripts; name, address, and telephone number of two (2) references, at least one of which must be outside of the school environment (please do not submit more than two); brief written financial statement indicating what resources are available to the applicant and why this scholarship is necessary to fund the applicant's college education (copies of FAFSA are acceptable); name, address, telephone number and email (if they have one) of the applicant; any other documentation the applicant wishes to attach in support of their qualifications and; completed Application Checklist form. Applications must be postmarked on or before March 17, 2017.

Academic Fields/Career Goals: Law/Legal Services.

Award: Scholarship for use in freshman year; not renewable. *Number:* 1. *Amount:* $7500.

Eligibility Requirements: Applicant must be high school student; planning to enroll or expecting to enroll full-time at a four-year institution or university and resident of Washington. Applicant or parent of applicant must have employment or volunteer experience in community service. Available to U.S. citizens.

Application Requirements: Application form, driver's license, essay, financial need analysis. *Deadline:* March 17.

Contact: Anita Yandle, Scholarship Coordinator
Washington State Association for Justice
1809 7th Ave
Suite 1500
Seattle, WA 98101
Phone: 206-464-1011
E-mail: anita@washingtonjustice.org

WIFLE FOUNDATION, INC.

http://www.wifle.org/

WIFLE SCHOLARSHIP

• *See page 227*

LIBRARY AND INFORMATION SCIENCES

ALICE L. HALTOM EDUCATIONAL FUND

http://www.alhef.org/

ALICE L. HALTOM EDUCATIONAL FUND

• *See page 160*

AMERICAN SOCIETY FOR INFORMATION SCIENCE AND TECHNOLOGY

http://www.asis.org/

JOHN WILEY & SONS BEST JASIST PAPER AWARD

• *See page 214*

BIBLIOGRAPHICAL SOCIETY OF AMERICA

http://www.bibsocamer.org/

JUSTIN G. SCHILLER PRIZE FOR BIBLIOGRAPHICAL WORK IN PRE-20TH-CENTURY CHILDREN'S BOOKS

Award for bibliographic work in the field of pre-20th century children's books. Winner will receive a cash award of $2000 and a year's membership in the Society.

Academic Fields/Career Goals: Library and Information Sciences; Literature/English/Writing.

Award: Prize for use in freshman, sophomore, junior, or senior years; not renewable. *Number:* 1. *Amount:* $2000.

Eligibility Requirements: Applicant must be enrolled or expecting to enroll full- or part-time at a four-year institution or university. Available to U.S. and non-U.S. citizens.

Application Requirements: Application form, documentation regarding the approval of a thesis or dissertation or confirming the date of publication, entry in a contest, resume. *Deadline:* September 1.

Contact: Michele Randall, Executive Secretary
Bibliographical Society of America
PO Box 1537, Lenox Hill Station
New York, NY 10021
Phone: 212-452-2710
Fax: 212-452-2710
E-mail: bsa@bibsocamer.org

FLORIDA ASSOCIATION FOR MEDIA IN EDUCATION

http://www.floridamediaed.org/ssyra.html

FAME/SANDY ULM SCHOLARSHIP

Scholarship for students studying to be school library media specialists. The scholarship awards at least $1000 to one or more students each year. Deadlines are September 15 and February 15.

Academic Fields/Career Goals: Library and Information Sciences.

Award: Scholarship for use in freshman year; not renewable. *Amount:* $1000.

Eligibility Requirements: Applicant must be high school student; planning to enroll or expecting to enroll full-time at a two-year or four-year or technical institution or university and studying in Florida. Available to U.S. citizens.

Application Requirements: Application form. *Deadline:* varies.

Contact: Larry Bodkin, Executive Director
Phone: 850-531-8350
Fax: 850-531-8344
E-mail: lbodkin@floridamedia.org

FLORIDA LIBRARY ASSOCIATION

http://www.flalib.org/

FLORIDA LIBRARY ASSOCIATION-ASSOCIATE'S DEGREE SCHOLARSHIP

Scholarship will be awarded to a Florida resident with library experience who is pursuing an Associate degree. Applicants must be members of the Florida Library Association. For further details, visit website http://www.flalib.org.

Academic Fields/Career Goals: Library and Information Sciences.

Award: Scholarship for use in freshman or sophomore years; not renewable. *Number:* 1. *Amount:* $1–$350.

Eligibility Requirements: Applicant must be enrolled or expecting to enroll full- or part-time at a two-year or four-year institution or university; resident of Florida and studying in Florida. Applicant or parent of applicant must have employment or volunteer experience in library work. Available to U.S. and non-U.S. citizens.

Application Requirements: Application form, application form may be submitted online (http://www.flalib.org/scholarships.php), essay, recommendations or references, resume. *Deadline:* February 1.

Contact: Dawn Pollock, Interim Executive Director
Florida Library Association
541 East Tennessee Street, Suite 103
Tallahassee, FL 32308
Phone: 850-270-9205
E-mail: dawn@flalib.org

FLORIDA LIBRARY ASSOCIATION-BACHELOR'S DEGREE SCHOLARSHIP

Scholarship will be awarded to a Florida resident with library experience who is pursuing a Bachelor's degree. Applicants must be members of Florida Library Association. For further details, visit website http://www.flalib.org.

Academic Fields/Career Goals: Library and Information Sciences.

Award: Scholarship for use in freshman, sophomore, junior, or senior years; not renewable. *Number:* 1. *Amount:* $1–$750.

Eligibility Requirements: Applicant must be enrolled or expecting to enroll full- or part-time at a two-year or four-year institution or university; resident of Florida and studying in Florida. Applicant or parent of applicant must have employment or volunteer experience in library work. Available to U.S. and non-U.S. citizens.

Application Requirements: Application form, application form may be submitted online (http://www.flalib.org/scholarships.php), essay, recommendations or references, resume. *Deadline:* February 1.

Contact: Dawn Pollock, Interim Executive Director
Florida Library Association
541 East Tennessee Street, Suite 103
Tallahassee, FL 32308
Phone: 850-270-9205
E-mail: dawn@flalib.org

GREATER KANAWHA VALLEY FOUNDATION

http://www.tgkvf.org/

BERNICE PICKINS PARSONS FUND
• *See page 394*

IDAHO LIBRARY ASSOCIATION

http://www.idaholibraries.org/

IDAHO LIBRARY ASSOCIATION GARDNER HANKS SCHOLARSHIP

Scholarship for students who are beginning or continuing formal library education, pursuing a Master's of Library Science degree or Media Generalist certification. Must be an Idaho Library Association member.

Academic Fields/Career Goals: Library and Information Sciences.

Award: Scholarship for use in freshman, sophomore, junior, senior, graduate, or postgraduate years; not renewable. *Number:* 1. *Amount:* $600.

Eligibility Requirements: Applicant must be enrolled or expecting to enroll full-time at a four-year institution or university and resident of Idaho. Applicant or parent of applicant must be member of Idaho Library Association. Available to U.S. citizens.

Application Requirements: Application form, financial need analysis. *Deadline:* May 31.

Contact: Jennifer Hills, Scholarships and Awards Committee Chair
Phone: 208-733-2964 Ext. 206
E-mail: jhills@twinfallspubliclibrary.org

INDIANA LIBRARY FEDERATION

http://www.ilfonline.org/

SUE MARSH WELLER SCHOLARSHIP FUND

Scholarships are provided for undergraduate or graduate students entering or currently enrolled in a program to receive educational certification in the field of school library media services. For more details, visit http//www.ilfonline.org.

Academic Fields/Career Goals: Library and Information Sciences.

Award: Scholarship for use in freshman, sophomore, junior, senior, or graduate years; not renewable.

Eligibility Requirements: Applicant must be enrolled or expecting to enroll full-time at a four-year institution or university; resident of Indiana and studying in Indiana. Available to U.S. citizens.

Application Requirements: Application form, essay. *Deadline:* June 30.

Contact: Tisa Davis, Communications
Phone: 317-257-2040
Fax: 317-257-1389
E-mail: tdavis@ilfonline.org

UNITED NEGRO COLLEGE FUND

http://www.uncf.org/

GATES MILLENNIUM SCHOLARS (GMS) PROGRAM
• *See page 260*

WISCONSIN LIBRARY ASSOCIATION

http://www.wla.wisconsinlibraries.org/

SCHOLARSHIP FOR THE EDUCATION OF RURAL LIBRARIANS GLORIA HOEGH MEMORIAL FUND

Scholarship awarded to librarians planning to attend a workshop, conference, and/or a continuing education program within or outside Wisconsin. Applicant must be a library employee working in a Wisconsin community with a current population of 5000 or less or who works with library employees in those communities.

Academic Fields/Career Goals: Library and Information Sciences.

Award: Scholarship for use in freshman, sophomore, junior, senior, or graduate years; not renewable. *Number:* 1. *Amount:* $900.

Eligibility Requirements: Applicant must be enrolled or expecting to enroll full- or part-time at a four-year institution or university and resident of Wisconsin. Available to U.S. citizens.

Application Requirements: Application form, essay, financial need analysis. *Deadline:* July 17.

Contact: Brigitte Rupp Vacha, WLA Conference Liaison
Wisconsin Library Association
4610 S Biltmore Lane
Suite 100
Madison, WI 53718
Phone: 608-245-3640
Fax: 608-245-3646
E-mail: ruppvacha@wisconsinlibraries.org

WLA CONTINUING EDUCATION SCHOLARSHIP

Scholarship awarded to employee who is planning to attend a continuing education program within or outside of Wisconsin. Applicant must be able to communicate the knowledge gained from the continuing education program to fellow librarians and information professionals in Wisconsin, employed in a library and information agency in Wisconsin.

Academic Fields/Career Goals: Library and Information Sciences.

Award: Scholarship for use in freshman, sophomore, junior, senior, graduate, or postgraduate years; not renewable. *Number:* 1.

Eligibility Requirements: Applicant must be enrolled or expecting to enroll full- or part-time at a four-year institution or university and resident of Wisconsin. Available to U.S. citizens.

Application Requirements: Application form. *Deadline:* July 17.

Contact: Brigitte Rupp Vacha, WLA Conference Liaison
Wisconsin Library Association
4610 S Biltmore Lane
Suite 100
Madison, WI 53718
Phone: 608-245-3640
Fax: 608-245-3646
E-mail: ruppvacha@wisconsinlibraries.org

LITERATURE/ENGLISH/ WRITING

ALLIANCE FOR YOUNG ARTISTS AND WRITERS INC.

http://www.artandwriting.org/

SCHOLASTIC ART AND WRITING AWARDS-WRITING SECTION SCHOLARSHIP
• *See page 127*

AMERICAN FOUNDATION FOR THE BLIND

http://www.afb.org/

R.L. GILLETTE SCHOLARSHIP

Two scholarships of $1000 each to women who are enrolled in a four-year undergraduate degree program in literature or music. In addition to the general requirements, applicants must submit a performance tape not to exceed 30 minutes, or a creative writing sample. Must submit proof of legal blindness. For additional information and application requirements, refer to website http://www.afb.org/scholarships.asp.

Academic Fields/Career Goals: Literature/English/Writing; Music.

Award: Scholarship for use in freshman, sophomore, junior, or senior years; not renewable. *Number:* up to 2. *Amount:* $1000.

Eligibility Requirements: Applicant must be visually impaired; enrolled or expecting to enroll full-time at a four-year institution or university and female. Applicant must be visually impaired. Available to U.S. citizens.

Application Requirements: Application form, essay, financial need analysis, performance tape (not to exceed 30 minutes) or creative writing sample, proof of legal blindness, acceptance letter, recommendations or references, transcript. *Deadline:* April 30.

Contact: Dawn Bodrogi, Information Center and Library Coordinator
American Foundation for the Blind
11 Penn Plaza, Suite 300
New York, NY 10001
Phone: 212-502-7661
Fax: 212-502-7771
E-mail: afbinfo@afb.net

AMERICAN-SCANDINAVIAN FOUNDATION

http://www.amscan.org/

AMERICAN-SCANDINAVIAN FOUNDATION TRANSLATION PRIZE

Two prizes are awarded for outstanding English translations of poetry, fiction, drama or literary prose originally written in Danish, Finnish, Icelandic, Norwegian or Swedish. The Nadia Christensen Prize includes a $2,500 award, publication of an excerpt in Scandinavian Review, and a commemorative bronze medallion. The Leif and Inger Sj?g Award, given to an individual whose literature translations have not previously been published, includes a $2,000 award, publication of an excerpt in Scandinavian Review, and a commemorative bronze medallion.

Academic Fields/Career Goals: Literature/English/Writing.

Award: Prize for use in freshman, sophomore, junior, senior, graduate, or postgraduate years; not renewable. *Number:* 2. *Amount:* $2000–$2500.

Eligibility Requirements: Applicant must be enrolled or expecting to enroll full- or part-time at a two-year or four-year or technical institution or university and must have an interest in Scandinavian language. Available to U.S. and non-U.S. citizens.

Application Requirements: Application form. *Deadline:* June 15.

Contact: Director of Fellowships and Grants
American-Scandinavian Foundation
58 Park Avenue
New York, NY 10016
Phone: 212-779-3587
E-mail: grants@amscan.org

BIBLIOGRAPHICAL SOCIETY OF AMERICA

http://www.bibsocamer.org/

JUSTIN G. SCHILLER PRIZE FOR BIBLIOGRAPHICAL WORK IN PRE-20TH-CENTURY CHILDREN'S BOOKS
• *See page 397*

CULTURAL SERVICES OF THE FRENCH EMBASSY

http://www.frenchculture.org/

TEACHING ASSISTANT PROGRAM IN FRANCE
• *See page 104*

DAVIDSON INSTITUTE FOR TALENT DEVELOPMENT

http://www.davidsongifted.org/

DAVIDSON FELLOWS SCHOLARSHIP PROGRAM
• *See page 113*

GOLDEN KEY INTERNATIONAL HONOUR SOCIETY

http://www.goldenkey.org/

LITERARY ACHIEVEMENT AWARDS

Award of $1000 will be given to winners in each of the following four categories: fiction, non-fiction, poetry, and feature writing. Eligible applicants are undergraduate, graduate and postgraduate members who are currently enrolled in classes at a degree-granting program.

Academic Fields/Career Goals: Literature/English/Writing.

Award: Prize for use in freshman, sophomore, junior, senior, graduate, or postgraduate years; not renewable. *Number:* 4. *Amount:* $1000.

Eligibility Requirements: Applicant must be enrolled or expecting to enroll full- or part-time at a four-year institution or university and must have an interest in writing. Available to U.S. and non-U.S. citizens.

Application Requirements: Application form, entry in a contest, essay, original composition. *Deadline:* April 1.

Contact: Scholarship Program Administrators
Golden Key International Honour Society
PO Box 23737
Nashville, TN 37202-3737
Phone: 800-377-2401
E-mail: scholarships@goldenkey.org

INSTITUTE FOR HUMANE STUDIES

http://www.theihs.org/

HUMANE STUDIES FELLOWSHIPS
• *See page 204*

INTERNATIONAL FOODSERVICE EDITORIAL COUNCIL

http://www.ifeconline.com/

INTERNATIONAL FOODSERVICE EDITORIAL COUNCIL COMMUNICATIONS SCHOLARSHIP
• *See page 88*

INTERNATIONAL LITERACY ASSOCIATION

https://literacyworldwide.org/home

JEANNE S. CHALL RESEARCH FELLOWSHIP
• *See page 254*

JAPANESE AMERICAN CITIZENS LEAGUE (JACL)

http://www.jacl.org/

NATIONAL JACL HEADQUARTERS SCHOLARSHIP
• *See page 99*

NATIONAL WRITERS ASSOCIATION FOUNDATION

http://www.nationalwriters.com/

NATIONAL WRITERS ASSOCIATION FOUNDATION SCHOLARSHIPS
• *See page 385*

OUTDOOR WRITERS ASSOCIATION OF AMERICA

http://www.owaa.org/

OUTDOOR WRITERS ASSOCIATION OF AMERICA - BODIE MCDOWELL SCHOLARSHIP AWARD
• *See page 207*

STRAIGHTFORWARD MEDIA

http://www.straightforwardmedia.com/

STRAIGHTFORWARD MEDIA LIBERAL ARTS SCHOLARSHIP
• *See page 126*

UNITED DAUGHTERS OF THE CONFEDERACY

http://www.hqudc.org/

HELEN JAMES BREWER SCHOLARSHIP
• *See page 361*

UNITED NEGRO COLLEGE FUND

http://www.uncf.org/

RETHA M. FORD SCHOLARSHIP FOR ENGLISH MAJORS
Up to $5000 scholarship for a student pursuing a degree in English at a four-year college or university affiliated with UNCF. Minimum 2.5 GPA required.

Academic Fields/Career Goals: Literature/English/Writing.

Award: Scholarship for use in freshman, sophomore, junior, senior, or graduate years; not renewable.

Eligibility Requirements: Applicant must be Black (non-Hispanic) and enrolled or expecting to enroll full-time at a four-year institution or university. Applicant must have 2.5 GPA or higher. Available to U.S. citizens.

Application Requirements: Application form, essay, financial need analysis. *Deadline:* October 21.

Contact: Mary Williams, Director of Outreach and Recruitment
    Phone: 800-331-2244

WILLA CATHER FOUNDATION

http://www.willacather.org/

ANTONETTE WILLA SKUPA TURNER SCHOLARSHIP
• *See page 362*

NORMA ROSS WALTER SCHOLARSHIP
Applicants must be female high school seniors who are prospective first year college students and plan to continue their education as English majors in accredited colleges or universities. Selection is based on intellectual promise, creativity, and character of the applicant.

Academic Fields/Career Goals: Literature/English/Writing.

Award: Scholarship for use in freshman year; not renewable. *Number:* 1–3. *Amount:* $1250–$2500.

Eligibility Requirements: Applicant must be high school student; planning to enroll or expecting to enroll full-time at a four-year institution or university; female and resident of Nebraska. Applicant must have 3.0 GPA or higher. Available to U.S. citizens.

Application Requirements: Application form, essay. *Deadline:* January 31.

Contact: Ashley Olson, Executive Director
    Willa Cather Foundation
    413 North Webster Street
    Red Cloud, NE 68970
    Phone: 402-746-2653
    E-mail: info@willacather.org

MARINE BIOLOGY

AMERICAN INDIAN SCIENCE AND ENGINEERING SOCIETY

http://www.aises.org/

A.T. ANDERSON MEMORIAL SCHOLARSHIP PROGRAM
• *See page 109*

AMERICAN PHYSIOLOGICAL SOCIETY

http://www.the-aps.org

DAVID S. BRUCE AWARDS FOR EXCELLENCE IN UNDERGRADUATE RESEARCH
• *See page 105*

ASSOCIATION FOR WOMEN GEOSCIENTISTS (AWG)

http://www.awg.org/

AWG UNDERGRADUATE EXCELLENCE IN PALEONTOLOGY AWARD
• *See page 112*

ASSOCIATION ON AMERICAN INDIAN AFFAIRS, INC.

http://www.indian-affairs.org/

ELIZABETH AND SHERMAN ASCHE MEMORIAL SCHOLARSHIP FUND
• See page 98

BARRY GOLDWATER SCHOLARSHIP AND EXCELLENCE IN EDUCATION FOUNDATION

https://goldwater.scholarsapply.org

BARRY M. GOLDWATER SCHOLARSHIP AND EXCELLENCE IN EDUCATION PROGRAM
• See page 112

CUSHMAN FOUNDATION FOR FORAMINIFERAL RESEARCH

http://www.cushmanfoundation.org/index.php

LOEBLICH AND TAPPAN STUDENT RESEARCH AWARD
• See page 156

THE EXPERT INSTITUTE

https://www.theexpertinstitute.com

ANNUAL HEALTHCARE AND LIFE SCIENCES SCHOLARSHIP
• See page 156

GREAT MINDS IN STEM

www.greatmindsinstem.org

HISPANIC ENGINEER NATIONAL ACHIEVEMENT AWARDS CORPORATION SCHOLARSHIP PROGRAM
• See page 106

THE LAND CONSERVANCY OF NEW JERSEY

http://tlc-nj.org/

RUSSELL W. MYERS SCHOLARSHIP
• See page 99

LOUISIANA OFFICE OF STUDENT FINANCIAL ASSISTANCE

http://www.osfa.la.gov/

ROCKEFELLER STATE WILDLIFE SCHOLARSHIP
• See page 157

MARINE TECHNOLOGY SOCIETY

http://www.mtsociety.org/

CHARLES H. BUSSMAN UNDERGRADUATE SCHOLARSHIP
Scholarship for undergraduate students enrolled full-time in a marine-related field. Must be a member of Marine Technology Society.

Academic Fields/Career Goals: Marine Biology; Marine/Ocean Engineering; Oceanography.

Award: Scholarship for use in freshman, sophomore, junior, or senior years; not renewable. *Amount:* up to $2500.

Eligibility Requirements: Applicant must be enrolled or expecting to enroll full-time at a four-year institution or university. Applicant or parent of applicant must be member of Marine Technology Society. Available to U.S. and non-U.S. citizens.

Application Requirements: Application form, driver's license, proof of acceptance for an undergraduate course, recommendations or references, transcript. *Deadline:* April 15.

Contact: Suzanne Voelker, Operations Administrator
  Phone: 410-884-5330
  Fax: 410-884-9060
  E-mail: suzanne.voelker@mtsociety.org

JOHN C. BAJUS SCHOLARSHIP
Scholarship available to undergraduate and graduate students enrolled full-time in a marine-related field. Must be a MTS student member with demonstrated commitment to community service/volunteer activities.

Academic Fields/Career Goals: Marine Biology; Marine/Ocean Engineering; Oceanography.

Award: Scholarship for use in freshman, sophomore, junior, senior, or graduate years; not renewable. *Amount:* up to $1000.

Eligibility Requirements: Applicant must be enrolled or expecting to enroll full-time at a four-year institution or university. Applicant or parent of applicant must be member of Marine Technology Society. Available to U.S. and non-U.S. citizens.

Application Requirements: Application form, driver's license, recommendations or references, transcript. *Deadline:* April 15.

Contact: Suzanne Voelker, Operations Administrator
  Phone: 410-884-5330
  Fax: 410-884-9060
  E-mail: suzanne.voelker@mtsociety.org

MTS STUDENT SCHOLARSHIP
Scholarships available to both Marine Technology Society members and non-members, undergraduates and graduate students, enrolled full-time in a marine-related field.

Academic Fields/Career Goals: Marine Biology; Marine/Ocean Engineering; Oceanography.

Award: Scholarship for use in freshman, sophomore, junior, senior, or graduate years; not renewable. *Amount:* up to $2000.

Eligibility Requirements: Applicant must be enrolled or expecting to enroll full-time at a four-year institution or university. Available to U.S. and non-U.S. citizens.

Application Requirements: Application form, driver's license, recommendations or references, transcript. *Deadline:* April 15.

Contact: Suzanne Voelker, Operations Administrator
  Phone: 410-884-5330
  Fax: 410-884-9060
  E-mail: suzanne.voelker@mtsociety.org

MTS STUDENT SCHOLARSHIP FOR GRADUATE AND UNDERGRADUATE STUDENTS
Scholarship of $2000 available to undergraduate students who are enrolled full-time in a marine-related field.

Academic Fields/Career Goals: Marine Biology; Marine/Ocean Engineering.

Award: Scholarship for use in freshman, sophomore, junior, senior, or graduate years; not renewable. *Amount:* $2000.

Eligibility Requirements: Applicant must be enrolled or expecting to enroll full-time at a four-year institution or university. Available to U.S. and non-U.S. citizens.

Application Requirements: Application form, essay, recommendations or references, transcript. *Deadline:* April 15.

Contact: Suzanne Voelker, Operations Administrator
  Marine Technology Society
  5565 Sterrett Place, Suite 108
  Columbia, MD 21044
  Phone: 410-884-5330
  E-mail: suzanne.voelker@mtsociety.org

MTS STUDENT SCHOLARSHIP FOR TWO-YEAR TECHNICAL, ENGINEERING AND COMMUNITY COLLEGE STUDENTS

Scholarship of $2000 available to students enrolled in a two-year technical, engineering, or community college in a marine-related field.

Academic Fields/Career Goals: Marine Biology; Marine/Ocean Engineering.

Award: Scholarship for use in freshman or sophomore years; not renewable. *Amount:* $2000.

Eligibility Requirements: Applicant must be enrolled or expecting to enroll full-time at a two-year institution. Available to U.S. and non-U.S. citizens.

Application Requirements: Application form, essay, recommendations or references, transcript. *Deadline:* April 15.

Contact: Suzanne Voelker, Operations Administrator
Marine Technology Society
5565 Sterrett Place, Suite 108
Columbia, MD 21044
Phone: 410-884-5330
E-mail: suzanne.voelker@mtsociety.org

PAROS-DIGIQUARTZ SCHOLARSHIP

Scholarships available to both MTS members and non-members, undergraduates and graduate students, enrolled full-time in a marine-related field with an interest in marine instrumentation. High school seniors who have been accepted into a full-time undergraduate program in a marine-related field are also eligible to apply.

Academic Fields/Career Goals: Marine Biology; Marine/Ocean Engineering; Oceanography.

Award: Scholarship for use in freshman, sophomore, junior, senior, or graduate years; not renewable. *Amount:* up to $2000.

Eligibility Requirements: Applicant must be enrolled or expecting to enroll full-time at a four-year institution or university. Available to U.S. and non-U.S. citizens.

Application Requirements: Application form, driver's license, recommendations or references, transcript. *Deadline:* April 15.

Contact: Suzanne Voelker, Operations Administrator
Phone: 410-884-5330
Fax: 410-884-9060
E-mail: suzanne.voelker@mtsociety.org

ROV SCHOLARSHIP

Scholarships for undergraduate and graduate students interested in remotely operated vehicles or underwater work that furthers the use of ROVs. Open to MTS student members and non-MTS members.

Academic Fields/Career Goals: Marine Biology; Marine/Ocean Engineering; Oceanography.

Award: Scholarship for use in freshman, sophomore, junior, senior, or graduate years; not renewable. *Amount:* up to $10,000.

Eligibility Requirements: Applicant must be enrolled or expecting to enroll full-time at a four-year institution or university. Available to U.S. and non-U.S. citizens.

Application Requirements: Application form, driver's license, essay, recommendations or references, transcript. *Deadline:* April 15.

Contact: Chuck Richards, Chair, Scholarship Committee
Marine Technology Society
c/o C.A. Richards and Associates Inc.
777 North Eldridge Parkway, Suite 280
Houston, TX 77079

MEDICAL SCRUBS COLLECTION

http://medicalscrubscollection.com

MEDICAL SCRUBS COLLECTION SCHOLARSHIP
• *See page 106*

NEXTSTEPU

http://www.nextstepu.com/

$1,500 STEM SCHOLARSHIP
• *See page 106*

SCARLETT FAMILY FOUNDATION SCHOLARSHIP PROGRAM

http://www.scarlettfoundation.org/

SCHOLARSHIP FOR STUDENTS PURSUING A BUSINESS OR STEM DEGREE
• *See page 84*

SIGMA XI, THE SCIENTIFIC RESEARCH SOCIETY

http://www.sigmaxi.org/

SIGMA XI GRANTS-IN-AID OF RESEARCH
• *See page 101*

SOCIETY FOR INTEGRATIVE AND COMPARATIVE BIOLOGY

http://www.sicb.org/

LIBBIE H. HYMAN MEMORIAL SCHOLARSHIP
• *See page 159*

WOMAN'S SEAMEN'S FRIEND SOCIETY OF CONNECTICUT INC.

FINANCIAL SUPPORT FOR MARINE OR MARITIME STUDIES

Applicant must be full-time student. High school students not considered. Award available to U.S. citizens. Must be majoring in marine sciences at any college or university.

Academic Fields/Career Goals: Marine Biology; Oceanography.

Award: Scholarship for use in freshman, sophomore, junior, or senior years; not renewable.

Eligibility Requirements: Applicant must be enrolled or expecting to enroll full-time at a four-year institution or university. Available to U.S. citizens.

Application Requirements: Application form, financial need analysis, recommendations or references, resume, test scores, transcript. *Deadline:* varies.

Contact: Marshall Davidson, Executive Director
Phone: 203-777-2165
Fax: 203-777-5774
E-mail: wsfsofct@earthlink.net

YOUTH MARITIME TRAINING ASSOCIATION

http://ymta.net/

NORM MANLY—YMTA MARITIME EDUCATIONAL SCHOLARSHIPS

The scholarships may be used by students pursuing marine-related and maritime training and education in community colleges, technical and vocational programs, colleges, universities, maritime academies or other educational institutions. Scholarships will be awarded in the amounts of one $5,000, one $3,000, two $2,500, and two $1,000. In addition, Pacific Maritime Magazine will award a $500 scholarship to one of the finalists planning to pursue a seagoing maritime career. Requires 2.5 GPA or submit an additional letter of recommendation from a second teacher.

Academic Fields/Career Goals: Marine Biology; Marine/Ocean Engineering; Oceanography; Trade/Technical Specialties.

Award: Scholarship for use in freshman year; not renewable. *Number:* 6–7. *Amount:* $1000–$5000.

Eligibility Requirements: Applicant must be high school student; planning to enroll or expecting to enroll full- or part-time at a two-year or four-year or technical institution or university and resident of Washington. Applicant must have 2.5 GPA or higher. Available to U.S. citizens.

Application Requirements: Application form, essay. *Deadline:* March 22.

Contact: Alicia Barnes, Director
Youth Maritime Training Association
PO Box 81142
Seattle, WA 98108
Phone: 206-812-5464
E-mail: ymta@pugetmaritime.org

MARINE/OCEAN ENGINEERING

AMERICAN COUNCIL OF ENGINEERING COMPANIES OF PENNSYLVANIA (ACEC/PA)

http://www.acecpa.org/

ERIC J. GENNUSO AND LEROY D. (BUD) LOY, JR. SCHOLARSHIP PROGRAM
• *See page 173*

AMERICAN INDIAN SCIENCE AND ENGINEERING SOCIETY

http://www.aises.org/

A.T. ANDERSON MEMORIAL SCHOLARSHIP PROGRAM
• *See page 109*

AMERICAN SOCIETY OF CERTIFIED ENGINEERING TECHNICIANS

http://www.ascet.org/

KURT H. AND DONNA M. SCHULER SMALL GRANT
• *See page 176*

AMERICAN SOCIETY OF NAVAL ENGINEERS

http://www.navalengineers.org/

AMERICAN SOCIETY OF NAVAL ENGINEERS SCHOLARSHIP
• *See page 110*

ARRL FOUNDATION INC.

http://www.arrl.org/

ALFRED E. FRIEND JR, W4CF, MEMORIAL SCHOLARSHIP
• *See page 177*

LOIS MANLEY, K7LMZ, AND RANDALL PITCHFORD, WW7ZZ, SCHOLARSHIP
• *See page 193*

W1FDR SCHOLARSHIP
• *See page 112*

BARRY GOLDWATER SCHOLARSHIP AND EXCELLENCE IN EDUCATION FOUNDATION

https://goldwater.scholarsapply.org

BARRY M. GOLDWATER SCHOLARSHIP AND EXCELLENCE IN EDUCATION PROGRAM
• *See page 112*

BHW GROUP

https://thebhwgroup.com/

BHW WOMEN IN STEM SCHOLARSHIP
• *See page 74*

BROWN AND CALDWELL

http://www.brownandcaldwell.com

ECKENFELDER SCHOLARSHIP
• *See page 155*

MINORITY SCHOLARSHIP PROGRAM
• *See page 155*

FABRICATORS AND MANUFACTURERS ASSOCIATION FOUNDATION

http://www.nutsandboltsfoundation.org/scholarships/

COLLEGE AND TRADE/TECHNICAL SCHOOL SCHOLARSHIPS
• *See page 178*

GREATER KANAWHA VALLEY FOUNDATION

http://www.tgkvf.org/

STEVEN ENGINEERING SCHOLARSHIP
• *See page 178*

GREAT MINDS IN STEM

www.greatmindsinstem.org

HISPANIC ENGINEER NATIONAL ACHIEVEMENT AWARDS CORPORATION SCHOLARSHIP PROGRAM
• *See page 106*

LOUISIANA OFFICE OF STUDENT FINANCIAL ASSISTANCE

http://www.osfa.la.gov/

ROCKEFELLER STATE WILDLIFE SCHOLARSHIP
• *See page 157*

MANUFACTURERS ASSOCIATION OF MAINE

http://www.mainemfg.com/

MAINE MANUFACTURING CAREER AND TRAINING FOUNDATION SCHOLARSHIP
• *See page 142*

MARINE TECHNOLOGY SOCIETY
http://www.mtsociety.org/

CHARLES H. BUSSMAN UNDERGRADUATE SCHOLARSHIP
• See page 401

JOHN C. BAJUS SCHOLARSHIP
• See page 401

MTS STUDENT SCHOLARSHIP
• See page 401

MTS STUDENT SCHOLARSHIP FOR GRADUATE AND UNDERGRADUATE STUDENTS
• See page 401

MTS STUDENT SCHOLARSHIP FOR GRADUATING HIGH SCHOOL SENIORS
• See page 302

MTS STUDENT SCHOLARSHIP FOR TWO-YEAR TECHNICAL, ENGINEERING AND COMMUNITY COLLEGE STUDENTS
• See page 402

PAROS-DIGIQUARTZ SCHOLARSHIP
• See page 402

ROV SCHOLARSHIP
• See page 402

NEXTSTEPU
http://www.nextstepu.com/

$1,500 STEM SCHOLARSHIP
• See page 106

SCARLETT FAMILY FOUNDATION SCHOLARSHIP PROGRAM
http://www.scarlettfoundation.org/

SCHOLARSHIP FOR STUDENTS PURSUING A BUSINESS OR STEM DEGREE
• See page 84

SIGMA XI, THE SCIENTIFIC RESEARCH SOCIETY
http://www.sigmaxi.org/

SIGMA XI GRANTS-IN-AID OF RESEARCH
• See page 101

SNAME
http://www.sname.org

GENERAL UNDERGRADUATE SCHOLARSHIPS
General Undergraduate Scholarships are part of the SNAME Undergraduate Scholarships Program. It is open to U.S., Canadian and international applicants. SNAME membership required four months prior to the application submission deadline (i.e. February 1). Applicants must study in approved universities with SNAME student sections. Awards are made for one year of study leading to a Bachelor of Science degree in naval architecture, marine engineering, ocean engineering, ship hydrodynamics and wave theory, ship and offshore structures, or in other fields directly related to the marine industry. Applicants must not receive their Bachelor's degree prior to April 15 of the academic year they are applying for their scholarship. Undergraduate scholarships may be awarded to an individual more than once and applicants remain eligible

for a graduate scholarship. Applications must be received prior to June 1, with all supporting data by June 15 for Scholarships Committee review. Selection in July based upon Scholarships Committee recommendations and Executive Committee approval. Scholarship funds may be used for student tuition, textbooks, academic fees or other academic related expenses for study and research. Application forms downloaded from the SNAME website are to be submitted electronically to Sofia Iliogrammenou at scholarships@sname.org.

Academic Fields/Career Goals: Marine/Ocean Engineering.

Award: Scholarship for use in freshman, sophomore, junior, or senior years; not renewable. *Amount:* up to $5000.

Eligibility Requirements: Applicant must be enrolled or expecting to enroll full-time at an institution or university. Available to U.S. and non-U.S. citizens.

Application Requirements: Application form, essay. *Deadline:* June 1.

Contact: Sofia Iliogrammenou, Director of Regional Member Services
    E-mail: scholarships@sname.org

MANDELL AND LESTER ROSENBLATT UNDERGRADUATE SCHOLARSHIP
First awarded in 2007, the Mandell and Lester Rosenblatt Scholarship provides a maximum of $6,000 to an undergraduate scholar having a passion for naval architecture, marine or ocean engineering, and displaying evidence of professionalism and involvement in SNAME. The Mandell and Lester Rosenblatt Scholarship is part of the SNAME Undergraduate Scholarships Program. It is open to U.S., Canadian and international applicants. SNAME membership required four months prior to the application submission deadline (i.e. February 1). Currently be an actively involved member of a SNAME student section and be committed to future membership. Awards are made for one year of study leading to a Bachelor of Science degree in naval architecture, marine engineering, ocean engineering, ship hydrodynamics and wave theory, ship and offshore structures, or in other fields directly related to the marine industry. Applicants must not receive their Bachelor's degree prior to April 15th of the academic year they are applying for their scholarship. Undergraduate scholarships may be awarded to an individual more than once and applicants remain eligible for a graduate scholarship. Applications must be received prior to June 1, with all supporting data by June 15 for Scholarships Committee review. Selection in July based upon Scholarships Committee recommendations and Executive Committee approval. Scholarship funds may be used for student tuition, textbooks, academic fees or other academic related expenses for study and research. Application forms downloaded from the SNAME website are to be submitted electronically to Sofia Iliogrammenou at scholarships@sname.org.

Academic Fields/Career Goals: Marine/Ocean Engineering.

Award: Scholarship for use in freshman, sophomore, junior, or senior years; not renewable. *Amount:* up to $6000.

Eligibility Requirements: Applicant must be enrolled or expecting to enroll full-time at an institution or university. Available to U.S. and non-U.S. citizens.

Application Requirements: Application form, essay. *Deadline:* June 1.

Contact: Sofia Iliogrammenou, Director of Regional Member Services
    E-mail: scholarships@sname.org

ROBERT N. HERBERT UNDERGRADUATE SCHOLARSHIP
First awarded in 2008, the Robert N. Herbert Undergraduate Scholarship provides a maximum award of $6,000 to an undergraduate scholar having a passion for naval architecture, marine or ocean engineering, and displaying evidence of professionalism and involvement in SNAME. The Robert N. Herbert Undergraduate Scholarship is part of the SNAME Undergraduate Scholarships Program. It is open to U.S., Canadian and International applicants. SNAME membership required four months prior to the application submission deadline (i.e. February 1). Currently be an actively involved member of a SNAME student section and be committed to future membership. Awards are made for one year of study leading to a Bachelor of Science degree in naval architecture, marine engineering, ocean engineering, ship hydrodynamics and wave theory, ship and offshore structures, or in other fields directly related to the marine industry. Applicants must not receive their Bachelor's degree prior to April 15th of the academic year they are applying for their scholarship. Undergraduate scholarships may be awarded to an individual more than once and applicants remain eligible for a graduate scholarship. Applications must be received prior to June 1, with all supporting data by June 15 for Scholarships Committee review. Selection in July based upon Scholarships Committee recommendations and Executive Committee

approval. Scholarship funds may be used for student tuition, textbooks, academic fees or other academic related expenses for study and research. Application forms downloaded from the SNAME website are to be submitted electronically to Sofia Iliogrammenou at scholarships@ sname.org.

Academic Fields/Career Goals: Marine/Ocean Engineering.

Award: Scholarship for use in freshman, sophomore, junior, or senior years; not renewable. *Amount:* up to $6000.

Eligibility Requirements: Applicant must be enrolled or expecting to enroll full-time at an institution or university. Available to U.S. and non-U.S. citizens.

Application Requirements: Application form, essay. *Deadline:* June 1.

Contact: Sofia Iliogrammenou, Director of Regional Member Serivces
E-mail: scholarships@sname.org

SOCIETY OF WOMEN ENGINEERS

http://societyofwomenengineers.swe.org/

ADA I. PRESSMAN MEMORIAL SCHOLARSHIP
• *See page 182*

AMERICAN TRANSMISSION CO. SCHOLARSHIP
• *See page 182*

ANNE MAUREEN WHITNEY BARROW MEMORIAL SCHOLARSHIP
• *See page 182*

ANNE SHEN SMITH ENDOWED SCHOLARSHIP
• *See page 182*

BAYER SCHOLARSHIP
• *See page 183*

BETTY LOU BAILEY SWE REGION F SCHOLARSHIP
• *See page 183*

B.J. HARROD SCHOLARSHIP
• *See page 183*

BK KRENZER MEMORIAL REENTRY SCHOLARSHIP
• *See page 183*

CAROL STEPHENS SWE REGION F SCHOLARSHIP
• *See page 183*

DR. IVY M. PARKER MEMORIAL SCHOLARSHIP
• *See page 184*

DOROTHY LEMKE HOWARTH MEMORIAL SCHOLARSHIP
• *See page 184*

DOROTHY P. MORRIS SCHOLARSHIP
• *See page 184*

EXELON CORPORATION SCHOLARSHIP
• *See page 184*

FCA WOMEN IN ENGINEERING SCHOLARSHIP
• *See page 184*

IBM LINDA SANFORD WOMEN'S TECHNICAL ADVANCEMENT SCHOLARSHIP
• *See page 185*

JILL S. TIETJEN P.E. SCHOLARSHIP
• *See page 185*

KOCH DISCOVERY SCHOLARSHIP
• *See page 185*

LILLIAN MOLLER GILBRETH MEMORIAL SCHOLARSHIP
• *See page 185*

MARY V. MUNGER SCHOLARSHIP
• *See page 185*

MASWE SCHOLARSHIP
• *See page 186*

OLIVE LYNN SALEMBIER MEMORIAL REENTRY SCHOLARSHIP
• *See page 186*

ROBERTA BANASZAK GLEITER ENGINEERING ENDEAVOR SCHOLARSHIP
• *See page 186*

ROCHELLE PERRY MEMORIAL SCHOLARSHIP
• *See page 186*

SUSAN MISZKOWICZ MEMORIAL SCHOLARSHIP
• *See page 186*

SWE BALTIMORE-WASHINGTON SECTION SCHOLARSHIP
• *See page 186*

SWE CENTRAL NEW MEXICO PIONEERS SCHOLARSHIP
• *See page 187*

SWE CENTRAL NEW MEXICO REENTRY SCHOLARSHIP
• *See page 187*

SWE MID-HUDSON SECTION SCHOLARSHIP
• *See page 187*

SWE PHOENIX SECTION SCHOLARSHIP
• *See page 187*

SWE REGION E SCHOLARSHIP
• *See page 187*

SWE REGION G JUDY SIMMONS MEMORIAL SCHOLARSHIP
• *See page 188*

SWE REGION H SCHOLARSHIPS
• *See page 188*

SWE REGION J SCHOLARSHIP
• *See page 188*

WANDA MUNN SCHOLARSHIP
• *See page 188*

SOCIETY OF WOMEN ENGINEERS-ROCKY MOUNTAIN SECTION

http://www.swe-rms.org/

SOCIETY OF WOMEN ENGINEERS-ROCKY MOUNTAIN SECTION SCHOLARSHIP PROGRAM
• *See page 188*

YOUTH MARITIME TRAINING ASSOCIATION

http://ymta.net/

NORM MANLY—YMTA MARITIME EDUCATIONAL SCHOLARSHIPS
• *See page 402*

MARKETING

280 GROUP

https://280group.com/contact/280-group-product-management-scholarship/

280 GROUP PRODUCT MANAGEMENT SCHOLARSHIP
• *See page 160*

AMERICAN NATIONAL CATTLE WOMEN INC.

https://ancw.org

COLLEGIATE BEEF ADVOCACY PROGRAM

Award's purpose is to train young spokespersons in the beef industry. Applicant must be fully prepared to answer questions and debate focusing on topic related to beef consumption and distribution, as well as social factors related to the industry. The prize value is $2,000. Details and tools for preparation are available on the website https://ancw.org

Academic Fields/Career Goals: Marketing.

Award: Scholarship for use in freshman, sophomore, junior, or senior years; not renewable. *Number:* 5. *Amount:* $2000.

Eligibility Requirements: Applicant must be age 18-24; enrolled or expecting to enroll full-time at a two-year or four-year institution or university and single. Applicant or parent of applicant must have employment or volunteer experience in agriculture, farming, food service. Applicant must have 2.5 GPA or higher. Available to U.S. citizens.

Application Requirements: Application form, community service, driver's license, personal photograph, portfolio. *Deadline:* December 31.

Contact: Evelyn Brown, Manager
American National Cattle Women Inc.
5802 Lee Rd 27
Auburn, AL 36803
Phone: 256-708-4833
E-mail: ancw.cbap@gmail.com

AUTOMOTIVE WOMEN'S ALLIANCE FOUNDATION

http://www.awafoundation.org/index.php

AUTOMOTIVE WOMEN'S ALLIANCE FOUNDATION SCHOLARSHIPS
• *See page 74*

BALTIMORE CHAPTER OF THE AMERICAN MARKETING ASSOCIATION

http://www.amabaltimore.org/

UNDERGRADUATE MARKETING EDUCATION MERIT SCHOLARSHIPS
• *See page 162*

DECA (DISTRIBUTIVE EDUCATION CLUBS OF AMERICA)

http://www.deca.org/

HARRY A. APPLEGATE SCHOLARSHIP
• *See page 75*

DIGITAL THIRD COAST INTERNET MARKETING

http://www.digitalthirdcoast.net/

DIGITAL MARKETING SCHOLARSHIP
• *See page 88*

FUKUNAGA SCHOLARSHIP FOUNDATION

http://fukunagascholarship.com

FUKUNAGA SCHOLARSHIP FOUNDATION
• *See page 77*

GLOBAL AUTOMOTIVE AFTERMARKET SYMPOSIUM

http://www.automotivescholarships.com/

AUTOMOTIVE AFTERMARKET SCHOLARSHIP CENTRAL
• *See page 164*

INTERNATIONAL FOODSERVICE EDITORIAL COUNCIL

http://www.ifeconline.com/

INTERNATIONAL FOODSERVICE EDITORIAL COUNCIL COMMUNICATIONS SCHOLARSHIP
• *See page 88*

NATIONAL DAIRY SHRINE

http://www.dairyshrine.org/

NATIONAL DAIRY SHRINE/DAIRY MARKETING INC. MILK MARKETING SCHOLARSHIPS
• *See page 100*

NEXT STEPS DIGITAL

https://www.nextstepsdigital.com/

NEXT STEPS DIGITAL SCHOLARSHIP

The recipient will receive a one-time $5,000 scholarship to be applied to qualified expenses, including graduate and undergraduate tuition, fees, books, and on-campus room and board for the 2017 Spring Semester. Funds are provided by Next Steps Digital. Payments are issued by Next Steps Digital and made payable to the student's approved college or university and mailed after Dec. 31, 2016 directly to the accredited college or university last designated by the student.

Academic Fields/Career Goals: Marketing.

Award: Scholarship for use in freshman, sophomore, junior, senior, or graduate years; not renewable. *Number:* 1. *Amount:* $5000.

Eligibility Requirements: Applicant must be enrolled or expecting to enroll full-time at a four-year institution or university. Applicant must have 3.5 GPA or higher. Available to U.S. citizens.

Application Requirements: Application form, essay. *Deadline:* December 15.

Contact: Josh Blanton, CMO
E-mail: josh@nextstepsdigital.com

OHIO NEWSPAPERS FOUNDATION

http://www.ohionews.org

HAROLD K. DOUTHIT SCHOLARSHIP
• *See page 89*

OHIO NEWSPAPERS FOUNDATION MINORITY SCHOLARSHIP
• *See page 89*

OHIO NEWSPAPERS FOUNDATION UNIVERSITY JOURNALISM SCHOLARSHIP
• *See page 90*

ONWA ANNUAL SCHOLARSHIP
• *See page 90*

PRINTING INDUSTRY MIDWEST EDUCATION FOUDNATION

http://www.pimw.org/scholarships

PRINTING INDUSTRY MIDWEST EDUCATION FOUNDATION SCHOLARSHIP FUND
• *See page 207*

RHODE ISLAND FOUNDATION

http://www.rifoundation.org/

J. D. EDSAL SCHOLARSHIP
• *See page 90*

SCARLETT FAMILY FOUNDATION SCHOLARSHIP PROGRAM

http://www.scarlettfoundation.org/

SCHOLARSHIP FOR STUDENTS PURSUING A BUSINESS OR STEM DEGREE
• *See page 84*

SPECIALTY EQUIPMENT MARKET ASSOCIATION

http://www.sema.org/

SEMA MEMORIAL SCHOLARSHIP FUND
• *See page 85*

STRAIGHTFORWARD MEDIA

http://www.straightforwardmedia.com/

STRAIGHTFORWARD MEDIA BUSINESS SCHOOL SCHOLARSHIP
• *See page 90*

STRAIGHTFORWARD MEDIA MEDIA & COMMUNICATIONS SCHOLARSHIP
• *See page 91*

SUPPORT CREATIVITY

http://wesupportcreativity.org

SUPPORT CREATIVITY SCHOLARSHIP
• *See page 124*

TAMPA BAY TIMES FUND, INC.

http://www.tampabay.com/fund

TAMPA BAY TIMES FUND CAREER JOURNALISM SCHOLARSHIPS
• *See page 91*

TRANSTUTORS

http://www.transtutors.com/scholarship

TRANSTUTORS SCHOLARSHIP 2015-16
• *See page 85*

UNITED NEGRO COLLEGE FUND

http://www.uncf.org/

ANHEUSER-BUSCH LEGENDS OF THE CROWN SCHOLARSHIP PROGRAM
• *See page 86*

ASHLEY STEWART SCHOLARSHIP
• *See page 169*

NASCAR BLACK HISTORY MONTH AWARDS
• *See page 86*

NATIONAL BLACK MCDONALD'S OWNERS ASSOCIATION HOSPITALITY SCHOLARS PROGRAM
• *See page 86*

ORACLE CORPORATE SCHOLARS PROGRAM
• *See page 169*

PROCTER & GAMBLE GENERAL SCHOLARSHIP
• *See page 91*

RICOH SCHOLARSHIP PROGRAM
• *See page 86*

SUEZ CORPORATE SCHOLARS PROGRAM
• *See page 87*

UNCF/ALLIANCE DATA SCHOLARSHIP AND INTERNSHIP PROGRAM
• *See page 91*

UNCF/ANTHEM CORPORATE SCHOLARS PROGRAM
• *See page 170*

UNCF/CARNIVAL CORPORATE SCHOLARS PROGRAM
• *See page 170*

UNCF/NISSAN SCHOLARSHIP
• *See page 170*

WHOMENTORS.COM, INC.

http://www.WHOmentors.com/

1 B USD WORLDWIDE VENTURE CAPITAL
• *See page 116*

WYOMING TRUCKING ASSOCIATION SCHOLARSHIP FUND TRUST

http://www.wytruck.org/

WYOMING TRUCKING ASSOCIATION SCHOLARSHIP TRUST FUND
• See page 87

MATERIALS SCIENCE, ENGINEERING, AND METALLURGY

AIST FOUNDATION

http://www.aistfoundation.org/

AISI/AIST FOUNDATION PREMIER SCHOLARSHIP
• See page 262

AIST ALFRED B. GLOSSBRENNER AND JOHN KLUSCH SCHOLARSHIPS
• See page 289

AIST WILLIAM E. SCHWABE MEMORIAL SCHOLARSHIP
• See page 263

ASSOCIATION FOR IRON AND STEEL TECHNOLOGY BALTIMORE CHAPTER SCHOLARSHIP
• See page 275

ASSOCIATION FOR IRON AND STEEL TECHNOLOGY BENJAMIN F. FAIRLESS SCHOLARSHIP (AIME)
• See page 172

ASSOCIATION FOR IRON AND STEEL TECHNOLOGY DAVID H. SAMSON CANADIAN SCHOLARSHIP
• See page 172

ASSOCIATION FOR IRON AND STEEL TECHNOLOGY NORTHWEST MEMBER CHAPTER SCHOLARSHIP
• See page 290

ASSOCIATION FOR IRON AND STEEL TECHNOLOGY OHIO VALLEY CHAPTER SCHOLARSHIP
• See page 153

ASSOCIATION FOR IRON AND STEEL TECHNOLOGY PITTSBURGH CHAPTER SCHOLARSHIP
• See page 290

ASSOCIATION FOR IRON AND STEEL TECHNOLOGY RONALD E. LINCOLN SCHOLARSHIP
• See page 263

ASSOCIATION FOR IRON AND STEEL TECHNOLOGY SOUTHEAST MEMBER CHAPTER SCHOLARSHIP
• See page 290

ASSOCIATION FOR IRON AND STEEL TECHNOLOGY WILLY KORF MEMORIAL SCHOLARSHIP
• See page 172

FERROUS METALLURGY EDUCATION TODAY (FEMET)
Scholarships are for full-time students of metallurgy or materials science engineering. Students must have an interest in a career in the steel industry as demonstrated by an internship or related experience, or who have plans to pursue such experiences during college. Students must commit to a summer internship at a steel producing company (placement assistance is provided) prior to receiving this scholarship. Student may apply during their sophomore and junior years. Applications are accepted from 1 Sep through 31 Dec each year.

Academic Fields/Career Goals: Materials Science, Engineering, and Metallurgy.

Award: Scholarship for use in sophomore or junior years; not renewable. *Number:* 1–10. *Amount:* $5000.

Eligibility Requirements: Applicant must be enrolled or expecting to enroll full-time at a four-year institution or university. Applicant must have 2.5 GPA or higher. Available to U.S. and non-U.S. citizens.

Application Requirements: Application form, essay, recommendations or references, resume, transcript. *Deadline:* December 31.

Contact: Lori Wharrey, AIST Manager, Board Services
AIST Foundation
186 Thorn HIll Road
Warrendale, PA 15086
Phone: 724-814-3044
E-mail: lwharrey@aist.org

AMERICAN ALPINE CLUB

https://americanalpineclub.org/

AAC RESEARCH GRANTS
• See page 153

AMERICAN CHEMICAL SOCIETY

http://www.acs.org/

AMERICAN CHEMICAL SOCIETY SCHOLARS PROGRAM
• See page 172

AMERICAN CHEMICAL SOCIETY, RUBBER DIVISION

http://www.rubber.org/

AMERICAN CHEMICAL SOCIETY, RUBBER DIVISION UNDERGRADUATE SCHOLARSHIP
• See page 109

AMERICAN COUNCIL OF ENGINEERING COMPANIES OF PENNSYLVANIA (ACEC/PA)

http://www.acecpa.org/

ERIC J. GENNUSO AND LEROY D. (BUD) LOY, JR. SCHOLARSHIP PROGRAM
• See page 173

AMERICAN INDIAN SCIENCE AND ENGINEERING SOCIETY

http://www.aises.org/

A.T. ANDERSON MEMORIAL SCHOLARSHIP PROGRAM
• See page 109

AMERICAN INSTITUTE OF AERONAUTICS AND ASTRONAUTICS

http://www.aiaafoundation.org/

AIAA FOUNDATION UNDERGRADUATE SCHOLARSHIPS
• See page 110

LEATRICE GREGORY PENDRAY SCHOLARSHIP
• See page 110

AMERICAN SOCIETY OF CERTIFIED ENGINEERING TECHNICIANS
http://www.ascet.org/

KURT H. AND DONNA M. SCHULER SMALL GRANT
• See page 176

AMERICAN SOCIETY OF NAVAL ENGINEERS
http://www.navalengineers.org/

AMERICAN SOCIETY OF NAVAL ENGINEERS SCHOLARSHIP
• See page 110

AMERICAN WELDING SOCIETY
http://www.aws.org/

AIRGAS-JERRY BAKER SCHOLARSHIP
• See page 277

AIRGAS-TERRY JARVIS MEMORIAL SCHOLARSHIP
• See page 277

AIR PRODUCTS WOMEN IN GASES AND WELDING SCHOLARSHIP
• See page 277

AMERICAN WELDING SOCIETY INTERNATIONAL SCHOLARSHIP
• See page 277

ARSHAM AMIRIKIAN ENGINEERING SCHOLARSHIP
• See page 193

DONALD AND SHIRLEY HASTINGS SCHOLARSHIP
• See page 293

DONALD J. BENETEAU SCHOLARSHIP
Awarded to an undergraduate student pursuing a full time or part time education in welding or a related program. The applicant must have a minimum overall GPA of 3.0, have proof of financial need, and be a student member of the American Welding Society. The applicant must be a U.S. or Canadian citizen, and plan to attend an academic institution in the U. S. or Canada.

Academic Fields/Career Goals: Materials Science, Engineering, and Metallurgy.

Award: Scholarship for use in freshman, sophomore, junior, or senior years; not renewable.

Eligibility Requirements: Applicant must be enrolled or expecting to enroll full- or part-time at a four-year institution. Applicant must have 3.0 GPA or higher. Available to U.S. and Canadian citizens.

Application Requirements: Application form, financial need analysis. *Deadline:* February 15.

Contact: Ms. Vicki Pinsky, Associate Director, Scholarships
American Welding Society
8669 NW 36 Street, #130
Miami, FL 33166
Phone: 305-443-9353 Ext. 212
E-mail: vpinsky@aws.org

JOHN C. LINCOLN MEMORIAL SCHOLARSHIP
• See page 278

MATSUO BRIDGE COMPANY LTD. OF JAPAN SCHOLARSHIP
• See page 193

MILLER ELECTRIC INTERNATIONAL WORLD SKILLS COMPETITION SCHOLARSHIP
• See page 278

MILLER ELECTRIC MFG. CO. SCHOLARSHIP
• See page 278

PRAXAIR INTERNATIONAL SCHOLARSHIP
• See page 279

ROBERT L. PEASLEE BRAZING SCHOLARSHIP
• See page 294

ROBERT W. WHITE, SR. SCHOLARSHIP
For a junior or senior college student in a welding program. Preference to students in resistance welding program. Full time, US citizen. Minimum overall GPA 3.2

Academic Fields/Career Goals: Materials Science, Engineering, and Metallurgy.

Award: Scholarship for use in junior or senior years; not renewable.

Eligibility Requirements: Applicant must be enrolled or expecting to enroll full-time at an institution or university. Applicant must have 3.0 GPA or higher. Available to U.S. citizens.

Application Requirements: Application form, financial need analysis. *Deadline:* February 15.

Contact: Ms. Vicki Pinsky, Associate Director, Scholarships, AWS Foundation
American Welding Society
8669 NW 36 Street, #130
Miami, FL 33166
Phone: 305-443-9353 Ext. 212
E-mail: vpinsky@aws.org

VICTOR TECHNOLOGIES CUTTING AND WELDING SCHOLARSHIP
• See page 279

WILLIAM A. AND ANN M. BROTHERS SCHOLARSHIP
• See page 279

WILLIAM A. RICE FAMILY, WOMEN IN WELDING SCHOLARSHIP
• See page 279

WILLIAM B. HOWELL MEMORIAL SCHOLARSHIP
• See page 280

ARMED FORCES COMMUNICATIONS AND ELECTRONICS ASSOCIATION, EDUCATIONAL FOUNDATION
http://www.afcea.org/site/?q=foundation/scholarships

ARMED FORCES COMMUNICATIONS AND ELECTRONICS ASSOCIATION ROTC SCHOLARSHIP PROGRAM
• See page 137

STEM MAJORS SCHOLARSHIPS FOR UNDERGRADUATE STUDENTS
• See page 110

VADM SAMUEL L. GRAVELY, JR, USN(RET.) MEMORIAL SCHOLARSHIP
• See page 111

ARRL FOUNDATION INC.

http://www.arrl.org/

ALFRED E. FRIEND JR., W4CF, MEMORIAL SCHOLARSHIP

CTRI/CHRIS SEEBER, KA1GEU, MEMORIAL SCHOLARSHIP

GARY WAGNER, K3OMI, SCHOLARSHIP

LOIS MANLEY, K7LMZ, AND RANDALL PITCHFORD, WW7ZZ, SCHOLARSHIP

W1FDR SCHOLARSHIP

ASM MATERIALS EDUCATION FOUNDATION

http://www.asmfoundation.org/

ASM OUTSTANDING SCHOLARS AWARDS

EDWARD J. DULIS SCHOLARSHIP

GEORGE A. ROBERTS SCHOLARSHIP

JOHN M. HANIAK SCHOLARSHIP

WILLIAM P. WOODSIDE FOUNDER'S SCHOLARSHIP

ASTRONAUT SCHOLARSHIP FOUNDATION

http://www.astronautscholarship.org/

ASTRONAUT SCHOLARSHIP FOUNDATION

AUTOMOTIVE WOMEN'S ALLIANCE FOUNDATION

http://www.awafoundation.org/index.php

AUTOMOTIVE WOMEN'S ALLIANCE FOUNDATION SCHOLARSHIPS

BARRY GOLDWATER SCHOLARSHIP AND EXCELLENCE IN EDUCATION FOUNDATION

https://goldwater.scholarsapply.org

BARRY M. GOLDWATER SCHOLARSHIP AND EXCELLENCE IN EDUCATION PROGRAM

BHW GROUP

https://thebhwgroup.com/

BHW WOMEN IN STEM SCHOLARSHIP

BROWN AND CALDWELL

http://www.brownandcaldwell.com

MINORITY SCHOLARSHIP PROGRAM

THE ELECTROCHEMICAL SOCIETY

http://www.electrochem.org/

STUDENT RESEARCH AWARDS OF THE BATTERY DIVISION OF THE ELECTROCHEMICAL SOCIETY INC.

FABRICATORS AND MANUFACTURERS ASSOCIATION FOUNDATION

http://www.nutsandboltsfoundation.org/scholarships/

COLLEGE AND TRADE/TECHNICAL SCHOOL SCHOLARSHIPS

GREATER KANAWHA VALLEY FOUNDATION

http://www.tgkvf.org/

STEVEN ENGINEERING SCHOLARSHIP

GREAT MINDS IN STEM

www.greatmindsinstem.org

HISPANIC ENGINEER NATIONAL ACHIEVEMENT AWARDS CORPORATION SCHOLARSHIP PROGRAM

INDEPENDENT LABORATORIES INSTITUTE SCHOLARSHIP ALLIANCE

http://www.acil.org/

INDEPENDENT LABORATORIES INSTITUTE SCHOLARSHIP ALLIANCE

INTERNATIONAL SOCIETY FOR OPTICAL ENGINEERING-SPIE

http://www.spie.org/scholarships

SPIE EDUCATIONAL SCHOLARSHIPS IN OPTICAL SCIENCE AND ENGINEERING

JORGE MAS CANOSA FREEDOM FOUNDATION

http://masscholarships.org/

MAS FAMILY SCHOLARSHIP AWARD

LOS ANGELES COUNCIL OF BLACK PROFESSIONAL ENGINEERS

http://www.lablackengineers.org/

AL-BEN SCHOLARSHIP FOR ACADEMIC INCENTIVE
• *See page 179*

AL-BEN SCHOLARSHIP FOR PROFESSIONAL MERIT
• *See page 179*

AL-BEN SCHOLARSHIP FOR SCHOLASTIC ACHIEVEMENT
• *See page 179*

MANUFACTURERS ASSOCIATION OF MAINE

http://www.mainemfg.com/

MAINE MANUFACTURING CAREER AND TRAINING FOUNDATION SCHOLARSHIP
• *See page 142*

MEDICAL SCRUBS COLLECTION

http://medicalscrubscollection.com

MEDICAL SCRUBS COLLECTION SCHOLARSHIP
• *See page 106*

MIDWEST ROOFING CONTRACTORS ASSOCIATION

http://www.mrca.org/

MRCA FOUNDATION SCHOLARSHIP PROGRAM
• *See page 122*

MINERALS, METALS, AND MATERIALS SOCIETY (TMS)

http://www.tms.org/

MATERIALS PROCESSING & MANUFACTURING DIVISION SCHOLARSHIP
• *See page 283*

TMS/EPD SCHOLARSHIP
• *See page 283*

TMS/FMD GILBERT CHIN SCHOLARSHIP
• *See page 283*

TMS/INTERNATIONAL SYMPOSIUM ON SUPERALLOYS SCHOLARSHIP PROGRAM
• *See page 283*

TMS/LIGHT METALS DIVISION SCHOLARSHIP PROGRAM
• *See page 284*

TMS OUTSTANDING STUDENT PAPER CONTEST-UNDERGRADUATE
• *See page 284*

TMS/STRUCTURAL MATERIALS DIVISION SCHOLARSHIP
• *See page 284*

NASA FLORIDA SPACE GRANT CONSORTIUM

http://www.floridaspacegrant.org/

FLORIDA SPACE RESEARCH PROGRAM
• *See page 142*

NASA IDAHO SPACE GRANT CONSORTIUM

http://www.id.spacegrant.org/

NASA IDAHO SPACE GRANT CONSORTIUM SCHOLARSHIP PROGRAM
• *See page 157*

NASA/MARYLAND SPACE GRANT CONSORTIUM

http://md.spacegrant.org/

NASA MARYLAND SPACE GRANT CONSORTIUM UNDERGRADUATE SCHOLARSHIPS
• *See page 142*

NASA'S VIRGINIA SPACE GRANT CONSORTIUM

http://www.vsgc.odu.edu/

COMMUNITY COLLEGE STEM SCHOLARSHIPS
• *See page 114*

UNDERGRADUATE STEM RESEARCH SCHOLARSHIPS
• *See page 114*

NATIONAL SOCIETY OF PROFESSIONAL ENGINEERS

http://www.nspe.org/

MAUREEN L. AND HOWARD N. BLITMAN, PE SCHOLARSHIP TO PROMOTE DIVERSITY IN ENGINEERING
• *See page 180*

PAUL H. ROBBINS HONORARY SCHOLARSHIP
• *See page 180*

PROFESSIONAL ENGINEERS IN INDUSTRY SCHOLARSHIP
• *See page 180*

NATIONAL STONE, SAND AND GRAVEL ASSOCIATION (NSSGA)

http://www.nssga.org/

BARRY K. WENDT MEMORIAL SCHOLARSHIP
• *See page 285*

NEXTSTEPU

http://www.nextstepu.com/

$1,500 STEM SCHOLARSHIP
• *See page 106*

ROCKY MOUNTAIN COAL MINING INSTITUTE

http://www.rmcmi.org/

ROCKY MOUNTAIN COAL MINING INSTITUTE SCHOLARSHIP
• *See page 197*

SCARLETT FAMILY FOUNDATION SCHOLARSHIP PROGRAM

http://www.scarlettfoundation.org/

SCHOLARSHIP FOR STUDENTS PURSUING A BUSINESS OR STEM DEGREE
• *See page 84*

SEMICONDUCTOR RESEARCH CORPORATION (SRC)

http://www.src.org/

MASTER'S SCHOLARSHIP PROGRAM
• *See page 181*

SIGMA XI, THE SCIENTIFIC RESEARCH SOCIETY

http://www.sigmaxi.org/

SIGMA XI GRANTS-IN-AID OF RESEARCH
• *See page 101*

SOCIETY OF AUTOMOTIVE ENGINEERS

http://www.sae.org/

TMC/SAE DONALD D. DAWSON TECHNICAL SCHOLARSHIP
• *See page 147*

YANMAR/SAE SCHOLARSHIP
• *See page 286*

SOCIETY OF PLASTICS ENGINEERS FOUNDATION (SPE)

http://www.4spe.org/

FLEMING/BASZCAK SCHOLARSHIP
• *See page 181*

GULF COAST HURRICANE SCHOLARSHIP
• *See page 181*

SOCIETY OF PLASTICS ENGINEERS SCHOLARSHIP PROGRAM
• *See page 182*

SOCIETY OF WOMEN ENGINEERS

http://societyofwomenengineers.swe.org/

AMERICAN TRANSMISSION CO. SCHOLARSHIP
• *See page 182*

ANNE SHEN SMITH ENDOWED SCHOLARSHIP
• *See page 182*

BAYER SCHOLARSHIP
• *See page 183*

BETTY LOU BAILEY SWE REGION F SCHOLARSHIP
• *See page 183*

B.J. HARROD SCHOLARSHIP
• *See page 183*

BK KRENZER MEMORIAL REENTRY SCHOLARSHIP
• *See page 183*

CAROL STEPHENS SWE REGION F SCHOLARSHIP
• *See page 183*

CUMMINS SCHOLARSHIP
• *See page 183*

DR. IVY M. PARKER MEMORIAL SCHOLARSHIP
• *See page 184*

DOROTHY LEMKE HOWARTH MEMORIAL SCHOLARSHIP
• *See page 184*

DOROTHY P. MORRIS SCHOLARSHIP
• *See page 184*

EXELON CORPORATION SCHOLARSHIP
• *See page 184*

FCA WOMEN IN ENGINEERING SCHOLARSHIP
• *See page 184*

HONEYWELL SCHOLARSHIP
• *See page 184*

IBM LINDA SANFORD WOMEN'S TECHNICAL ADVANCEMENT SCHOLARSHIP
• *See page 185*

JILL S. TIETJEN P.E. SCHOLARSHIP
• *See page 185*

LILLIAN MOLLER GILBRETH MEMORIAL SCHOLARSHIP
• *See page 185*

MARY V. MUNGER SCHOLARSHIP
• *See page 185*

MASWE SCHOLARSHIP
• *See page 186*

OLIVE LYNN SALEMBIER MEMORIAL REENTRY SCHOLARSHIP
• *See page 186*

ROBERTA BANASZAK GLEITER ENGINEERING ENDEAVOR SCHOLARSHIP
• *See page 186*

ROCHELLE PERRY MEMORIAL SCHOLARSHIP
• *See page 186*

SUSAN MISZKOWICZ MEMORIAL SCHOLARSHIP
• *See page 186*

SWE BALTIMORE-WASHINGTON SECTION SCHOLARSHIP
• *See page 186*

SWE CENTRAL NEW MEXICO PIONEERS SCHOLARSHIP
• *See page 187*

SWE CENTRAL NEW MEXICO REENTRY SCHOLARSHIP
• *See page 187*

SWE MID-HUDSON SECTION SCHOLARSHIP
• *See page 187*

SWE PHOENIX SECTION SCHOLARSHIP
• *See page 187*

SWE REGION G JUDY SIMMONS MEMORIAL SCHOLARSHIP
• *See page 188*

SWE REGION H SCHOLARSHIPS
• *See page 188*

SWE REGION J SCHOLARSHIP
• *See page 188*

WANDA MUNN SCHOLARSHIP
• *See page 188*

SOCIETY OF WOMEN ENGINEERS-ROCKY MOUNTAIN SECTION

http://www.swe-rms.org/

SOCIETY OF WOMEN ENGINEERS-ROCKY MOUNTAIN SECTION SCHOLARSHIP PROGRAM
• *See page 188*

STRAIGHTFORWARD MEDIA

http://www.straightforwardmedia.com/

STRAIGHTFORWARD MEDIA ENGINEERING SCHOLARSHIP
• *See page 189*

TAU BETA PI ASSOCIATION

http://www.tbp.org/

TAU BETA PI SCHOLARSHIP PROGRAM
• *See page 189*

TURNER CONSTRUCTION COMPANY

http://www.turnerconstruction.com/

YOUTHFORCE 2020 SCHOLARSHIP PROGRAM
• *See page 124*

UNITED NEGRO COLLEGE FUND

http://www.uncf.org/

BLUE CROSS BLUE SHIELD OF ILLINOIS AND BLUE CROSS BLUE SHIELD OF TEXAS SCHOLARSHIP
• *See page 115*

GALACTIC UNITE BYTHEWAY SCHOLARSHIP
• *See page 190*

PROCTER & GAMBLE STEM SCHOLARSHIP
• *See page 116*

UNCF STEM SCHOLARS PROGRAM
• *See page 159*

UNIVERSITIES SPACE RESEARCH ASSOCIATION

http://www.usra.edu/

UNIVERSITIES SPACE RESEARCH ASSOCIATION SCHOLARSHIP AWARD PROGRAM
• *See page 116*

VERMONT SPACE GRANT CONSORTIUM

http://www.cems.uvm.edu/vsgc

VERMONT SPACE GRANT CONSORTIUM
• *See page 96*

WHOMENTORS.COM, INC.

http://www.WHOmentors.com/

1 B USD WORLDWIDE VENTURE CAPITAL
• *See page 116*

XEROX

http://www.xerox.com//

TECHNICAL MINORITY SCHOLARSHIP
• *See page 190*

MATHEMATICS

THE ACTUARIAL FOUNDATION

http://www.actuarialfoundation.org

ACTUARIAL DIVERSITY SCHOLARSHIP
• *See page 375*

ACTUARY OF TOMORROW—STUART A. ROBERTSON MEMORIAL SCHOLARSHIP
• *See page 160*

CURTIS E. HUNTINGTON MEMORIAL SCHOLARSHIP (FORMERLY THE JOHN CULVER WOODDY SCHOLARSHIP)
• *See page 245*

AMERICAN INDIAN SCIENCE AND ENGINEERING SOCIETY

http://www.aises.org/

A.T. ANDERSON MEMORIAL SCHOLARSHIP PROGRAM
• *See page 109*

AMERICAN LEGION DEPARTMENT OF MARYLAND

http://www.mdlegion.org/

AMERICAN LEGION DEPARTMENT OF MARYLAND MATH-SCIENCE SCHOLARSHIP
Scholarship for study in math or the sciences. Must be a Maryland resident and the dependent child of a veteran. Must submit essay, financial need analysis, and transcript with application. Nonrenewable award for freshman. Application available on website http://mdlegion.org.

Academic Fields/Career Goals: Mathematics; Physical Sciences.

Award: Scholarship for use in freshman, sophomore, junior, or senior years; not renewable. *Number:* 1–3. *Amount:* $500–$1500.

Eligibility Requirements: Applicant must be high school student; planning to enroll or expecting to enroll full-time at a two-year or four-year institution or university and resident of Maryland. Available to U.S. citizens. Applicant must have general military experience.

Application Requirements: Application form, essay, financial need analysis, transcript. *Deadline:* April 1.

Contact: Russell Myers, Department Adjutant
American Legion Department of Maryland
101 North Gay, Room E
Baltimore, MD 21202
Phone: 410-752-1405
Fax: 410-752-3822
E-mail: russell@mdlegion.org

AMERICAN MATHEMATICAL ASSOCIATION OF TWO YEAR COLLEGES

http://www.amatyc.org/

CHARLES MILLER SCHOLARSHIP

A grand prize of $3000 for the qualified individual with the highest total score of the student mathematics league exam. Funds to continue education at an accredited four-year institution. In the case of a tie for the grand prize, the scholarship will be evenly divided.

Academic Fields/Career Goals: Mathematics.

Award: Scholarship for use in freshman or sophomore years; not renewable. *Number:* 1. *Amount:* $3000.

Eligibility Requirements: Applicant must be enrolled or expecting to enroll full-time at a two-year institution. Available to U.S. citizens.

Application Requirements: Entry in a contest, test scores. *Deadline:* September 30.

Contact: Cheryl Cleaves, Executive Director of Office Operations
Phone: 901-333-4643
Fax: 901-333-4651
E-mail: amatyc@amatyc.org

AMERICAN SOCIETY FOR ENGINEERING EDUCATION

http://www.asee.org/

SCIENCE, MATHEMATICS, AND RESEARCH FOR TRANSFORMATION DEFENSE SCHOLARSHIP FOR SERVICE PROGRAM
• See page 110

ARMED FORCES COMMUNICATIONS AND ELECTRONICS ASSOCIATION, EDUCATIONAL FOUNDATION

http://www.afcea.org/site/?q=foundation/scholarships

ARMED FORCES COMMUNICATIONS AND ELECTRONICS ASSOCIATION ROTC SCHOLARSHIP PROGRAM
• See page 137

STEM MAJORS SCHOLARSHIPS FOR UNDERGRADUATE STUDENTS
• See page 110

STEM TEACHERS SCHOLARSHIP
• See page 111

VADM SAMUEL L. GRAVELY, JR., USN(RET.) MEMORIAL SCHOLARSHIP
• See page 111

VETERANS OF ENDURING FREEDOM (AFGHANISTAN) AND IRAQI FREEDOM SCHOLARSHIP
• See page 214

ARRL FOUNDATION INC.

http://www.arrl.org/

CTRI/CHRIS SEEBER, KA1GEU, MEMORIAL SCHOLARSHIP
• See page 249

DAN HUETTL, WZ7U, MEMORIAL SCHOLARSHIP
• See page 280

LOIS MANLEY, K7LMZ, AND RANDALL PITCHFORD, WW7ZZ, SCHOLARSHIP
• See page 193

W1FDR SCHOLARSHIP
• See page 112

ASSOCIATION FOR WOMEN IN MATHEMATICS

http://www.awm-math.org/

ALICE T. SCHAFER MATHEMATICS PRIZE FOR EXCELLENCE IN MATHEMATICS BY AN UNDERGRADUATE WOMAN

One-time merit award for women undergraduates in the math field. Based on quality of performance in math courses and special programs, ability to work independently, interest in math, and performance in competitions. Must be nominated by a professor or an adviser.

Academic Fields/Career Goals: Mathematics.

Award: Prize for use in freshman, sophomore, junior, or senior years; not renewable. *Number:* 1. *Amount:* $250–$1000.

Eligibility Requirements: Applicant must be enrolled or expecting to enroll full-time at a four-year institution or university and female. Available to U.S. citizens.

Application Requirements: Application form. *Deadline:* September 15.

Contact: Jennifer Lewis, Managing Director
Phone: 703-934-0163 Ext. 213
Fax: 703-359-7562
E-mail: jennifer@awm-math.org

AUTOMOTIVE WOMEN'S ALLIANCE FOUNDATION

http://www.awafoundation.org/index.php

AUTOMOTIVE WOMEN'S ALLIANCE FOUNDATION SCHOLARSHIPS
• See page 74

BARRY GOLDWATER SCHOLARSHIP AND EXCELLENCE IN EDUCATION FOUNDATION

https://goldwater.scholarsapply.org

BARRY M. GOLDWATER SCHOLARSHIP AND EXCELLENCE IN EDUCATION PROGRAM
• See page 112

BHW GROUP

https://thebhwgroup.com/

BHW WOMEN IN STEM SCHOLARSHIP
• See page 74

CALIFORNIA MATHEMATICS COUNCIL-SOUTH

http://www.cmc-math.org/

CALIFORNIA MATHEMATICS COUNCIL-SOUTH SECONDARY EDUCATION SCHOLARSHIPS

Scholarships for students enrolled in accredited Southern California secondary education credential programs with math as a major. Applicants must be members of the California Math Council-South.

Academic Fields/Career Goals: Mathematics.

Award: Scholarship for use in freshman, sophomore, junior, or senior years; renewable. *Number:* 2–5. *Amount:* $100–$2000.

Eligibility Requirements: Applicant must be enrolled or expecting to enroll full- or part-time at a four-year institution or university; resident of California and studying in California. Available to U.S. and non-U.S. citizens.

Application Requirements: Application form, essay, recommendations or references, transcript. *Deadline:* January 31.

Contact: Dr. Sid Kolpas, Professor of Mathematics
    Phone: 818-240-1000 Ext. 5378
    E-mail: sjkolpas@sprintmail.com

COMMUNITY FOUNDATION FOR GREATER ATLANTA, INC.

http://cfgreateratlanta.org/

TECH HIGH SCHOOL ALUMNI ASSOCIATION/W.O. CHENEY MERIT SCHOLARSHIP FUND

• *See page 297*

THE DALLAS FOUNDATION

http://www.dallasfoundation.org/

WHITLEY PLACE SCHOLARSHIP

• *See page 120*

DAVIDSON INSTITUTE FOR TALENT DEVELOPMENT

http://www.davidsongifted.org/

DAVIDSON FELLOWS SCHOLARSHIP PROGRAM

• *See page 113*

GREATER KANAWHA VALLEY FOUNDATION

http://www.tgkvf.org/

MATH AND SCIENCE SCHOLARSHIP

• *See page 156*

GREAT MINDS IN STEM

www.greatmindsinstem.org

HISPANIC ENGINEER NATIONAL ACHIEVEMENT AWARDS CORPORATION SCHOLARSHIP PROGRAM

• *See page 106*

MICHIGAN COUNCIL OF TEACHERS OF MATHEMATICS

http://www.mictm.org/

MIRIAM SCHAEFER SCHOLARSHIP

A scholarship of $2500 is given to a senior or a junior enrolled full-time in undergraduate degree with mathematics specialty. Applicants should be a resident of Michigan but citizenship does not matter.

Academic Fields/Career Goals: Mathematics.

Award: Scholarship for use in junior or senior years; not renewable. *Number:* 3–5. *Amount:* $2500.

Eligibility Requirements: Applicant must be enrolled or expecting to enroll full-time at a four-year institution or university and resident of Michigan. Applicant must have 3.0 GPA or higher. Available to U.S. and non-U.S. citizens.

Application Requirements: Application form, essay. *Deadline:* May 1.

Contact: Mr. Chris Berry, Executive Director
    Michigan Council of Teachers of Mathematics
    4767 Stadler Road
    Monroe, MI 48162
    Phone: 734-477-0421
    Fax: 734-241-4128
    E-mail: info@mictm.org

NASA FLORIDA SPACE GRANT CONSORTIUM

http://www.floridaspacegrant.org/

FLORIDA SPACE RESEARCH PROGRAM

• *See page 142*

NASA IDAHO SPACE GRANT CONSORTIUM

http://www.id.spacegrant.org/

NASA IDAHO SPACE GRANT CONSORTIUM SCHOLARSHIP PROGRAM

• *See page 157*

NASA/MARYLAND SPACE GRANT CONSORTIUM

http://md.spacegrant.org/

NASA MARYLAND SPACE GRANT CONSORTIUM UNDERGRADUATE SCHOLARSHIPS

• *See page 142*

NASA MINNESOTA SPACE GRANT CONSORTIUM

http://www.aem.umn.edu/mnsgc

MINNESOTA SPACE GRANT CONSORTIUM SCHOLARSHIP PROGRAM

• *See page 142*

NASA MONTANA SPACE GRANT CONSORTIUM

http://www.spacegrant.montana.edu/

MONTANA SPACE GRANT SCHOLARSHIP PROGRAM

• *See page 142*

NASA RHODE ISLAND SPACE GRANT CONSORTIUM

http://brown/initiatives/ri-space-grant

NASA RHODE ISLAND SPACE GRANT CONSORTIUM OUTREACH SCHOLARSHIP FOR UNDERGRADUATE STUDENTS
• See page 284

NASA RISGC SCIENCE EN ESPANOL SCHOLARSHIP FOR UNDERGRADUATE STUDENTS
• See page 143

NASA'S VIRGINIA SPACE GRANT CONSORTIUM

http://www.vsgc.odu.edu/

COMMUNITY COLLEGE STEM SCHOLARSHIPS
• See page 114

UNDERGRADUATE STEM RESEARCH SCHOLARSHIPS
• See page 114

NATIONAL COUNCIL OF TEACHERS OF MATHEMATICS

http://www.nctm.org/

PROSPECTIVE SECONDARY TEACHER COURSE WORK SCHOLARSHIPS
• See page 255

NEVADA NASA SPACE GRANT CONSORTIUM

http://www.nvspacegrant.org/

NATIONAL SPACE GRANT COLLEGE AND FELLOWSHIP PROGRAM
• See page 114

NEXTSTEPU

http://www.nextstepu.com/

$1,500 STEM SCHOLARSHIP
• See page 106

OREGON STUDENT ASSISTANCE COMMISSION

http://www.GetCollegeFunds.org/

ANDY AITKENHEAD SCHOLARSHIP
• See page 115

SEHAR SALEHA AHMAD AND ABRAHIM EKRAMULLAH ZAFAR FOUNDATION SCHOLARSHIP
• See page 115

PIRATE'S ALLEY FAULKNER SOCIETY

http://www.wordsandmusic.org/

WILLIAM FAULKNER-WILLIAM WISDOM CREATIVE WRITING COMPETITION

Prizes for unpublished manuscripts written in English. One prize awarded in each category: $7500, novel; $2500, novella; $2000, book-length narrative non-fiction; $1,500, novel-in-progress; $1500, short story; $750, essay; $750, poem; $750 high school short story-student author, $250 sponsoring teacher. Manuscripts must be submitted by e-mail; entry forms and accompanying entry fee ranging from $10 for high school category to $40 for novel must be submitted hard copy by snail mail.

Academic Fields/Career Goals: Mathematics.

Award: Prize for use in freshman, sophomore, junior, senior, graduate, or postgraduate years; not renewable. *Number:* 8. *Amount:* $250–$7500.

Eligibility Requirements: Applicant must be age 15-80; enrolled or expecting to enroll full- or part-time at a two-year or four-year institution or university and must have an interest in English language or writing. Applicant or parent of applicant must have employment or volunteer experience in human services. Available to U.S. and non-U.S. citizens.

Application Requirements: Application form. *Fee:* $25. *Deadline:* May 1.

Contact: Ms. Rosemary James, Director
Pirate's Alley Faulkner Society
624 Pirate's Alley
New Orleans, LA 70116
Phone: 504-586-1609
E-mail: faulkhouse@aol.com

SALT RIVER PROJECT (SRP)

http://www.srpnet.com/

NAVAJO GENERATING STATION NAVAJO SCHOLARSHIP
• See page 305

SCARLETT FAMILY FOUNDATION SCHOLARSHIP PROGRAM

http://www.scarlettfoundation.org/

SCHOLARSHIP FOR STUDENTS PURSUING A BUSINESS OR STEM DEGREE
• See page 84

SIGMA XI, THE SCIENTIFIC RESEARCH SOCIETY

http://www.sigmaxi.org/

SIGMA XI GRANTS-IN-AID OF RESEARCH
• See page 101

TKE EDUCATIONAL FOUNDATION

http://www.tke.org/

ERIC D. DUNNING SCHOLARSHIP
• See page 219

FRANCIS J. FLYNN MEMORIAL SCHOLARSHIP
• See page 260

TRANSTUTORS

http://www.transtutors.com/scholarship

TRANSTUTORS SCHOLARSHIP 2015-16
• See page 85

UNITED NEGRO COLLEGE FUND

http://www.uncf.org/

BASF/ALFRED CHISHOLM ENDOWED MEMORIAL SCHOLARSHIP
• See page 86

MECHANICAL ENGINEERING

AMERICAN INDIAN SCIENCE AND ENGINEERING SOCIETY

http://www.aises.org/

A.T. ANDERSON MEMORIAL SCHOLARSHIP PROGRAM
• *See page 109*

AMERICAN INSTITUTE OF AERONAUTICS AND ASTRONAUTICS

http://www.aiaafoundation.org/

AIAA FOUNDATION UNDERGRADUATE SCHOLARSHIPS
• *See page 110*

LEATRICE GREGORY PENDRAY SCHOLARSHIP
• *See page 110*

AMERICAN PUBLIC POWER ASSOCIATION

http://publicpower.org/DEED

DEED EDUCATIONAL SCHOLARSHIP
• *See page 176*

DEED STUDENT INTERNSHIP
• *See page 176*

DEED STUDENT RESEARCH GRANTS
• *See page 191*

DEED TECHNICAL DESIGN PROJECT
• *See page 176*

AMERICAN PUBLIC TRANSPORTATION FOUNDATION

http://www.apta.com/

LOUIS T. KLAUDER SCHOLARSHIP
• *See page 264*

TRANSIT HALL OF FAME SCHOLARSHIP AWARD PROGRAM
• *See page 191*

AMERICAN RAILWAY ENGINEERING AND MAINTENANCE OF WAY ASSOCIATION

http://www.aremafoundation.org/

AREMA GRADUATE AND UNDERGRADUATE SCHOLARSHIPS
• *See page 191*

AMERICAN SOCIETY OF CERTIFIED ENGINEERING TECHNICIANS

http://www.ascet.org/

KURT H. AND DONNA M. SCHULER SMALL GRANT
• *See page 176*

AMERICAN SOCIETY OF HEATING, REFRIGERATING, AND AIR CONDITIONING ENGINEERS, INC.

http://www.ashrae.org/

ALWIN B. NEWTON SCHOLARSHIP
• *See page 264*

ASHRAE REGION III BOGGARM SETTY SCHOLARSHIP
• *See page 176*

FRANK M. CODA SCHOLARSHIP
• *See page 264*

LYNN G. BELLENGER SCHOLARSHIP
• *See page 265*

REUBEN TRANE SCHOLARSHIP
• *See page 265*

AMERICAN SOCIETY OF MECHANICAL ENGINEERS AUXILIARY INC.

http://www.asme.org/

AGNES MALAKATE KEZIOS SCHOLARSHIP

Scholarship to college juniors for use in final year at a four year college. Must be majoring in mechanical engineering, be member of ASME (if available), and exhibit leadership values. Must be U.S. citizen enrolled in a college/university in the United States that has ABET accreditation. Scholarship value is $3000 and the number of awards granted varies.

Academic Fields/Career Goals: Mechanical Engineering.

Award: Scholarship for use in junior or senior years; not renewable. *Number:* 1–2. *Amount:* $3000.

Eligibility Requirements: Applicant must be enrolled or expecting to enroll full-time at a four-year institution or university. Available to U.S. citizens.

Application Requirements: Application form, essay, financial need analysis. *Deadline:* March 1.

Contact: Saraswati Sahay, Undergraduate Scholarships
American Society of Mechanical Engineers Auxiliary Inc.
170 East Opal Drive
Glastonbury, CT 06033
Phone: 860-659-3828
E-mail: uma.sahay@gmail.com

ALLEN J. BALDWIN SCHOLARSHIP

Scholarship available to college juniors for use in final year at a four year college. Must be majoring in mechanical engineering, be member of ASME (if available), and exhibit leadership values. Must be U.S. citizen enrolled in a college/university in the United States that has ABET accreditation. Scholarship value is $2000 and the number of awards granted varies.

Academic Fields/Career Goals: Mechanical Engineering.

Award: Scholarship for use in junior year; not renewable. *Number:* 1–2. *Amount:* $3000.

Eligibility Requirements: Applicant must be enrolled or expecting to enroll full-time at a four-year institution or university. Available to U.S. citizens.

Application Requirements: Application form, driver's license, financial need analysis, recommendations or references, self-addressed stamped envelope with application, transcript. *Deadline:* March 15.

Contact: Saraswati Sahay, Undergraduate Scholarships
American Society of Mechanical Engineers Auxiliary Inc.
170 East Opal Drive
Glastonbury, CT 06033
Phone: 860-659-3828
E-mail: uma.sahay@gmail.com

BERNA LOU CARTWRIGHT SCHOLARSHIP

Scholarship for college juniors for use in final year at a four year college. Must be majoring in mechanical engineering. Must be a U.S. citizen, enrolled in a college/university in the United States that has ABET accreditation. Number of awards varies.

Academic Fields/Career Goals: Mechanical Engineering.

Award: Scholarship for use in junior year; not renewable. *Number:* 1–2. *Amount:* $3000.

Eligibility Requirements: Applicant must be enrolled or expecting to enroll full-time at a four-year institution or university and must have an interest in leadership. Applicant or parent of applicant must be member of Other Student Academic Clubs. Available to U.S. citizens.

Application Requirements: Application form, financial need analysis, recommendations or references, resume, transcript. *Deadline:* March 15.

Contact: Saraswati Sahay, Undergraduate Scholarships
American Society of Mechanical Engineers Auxiliary Inc.
170 East Opal Drive
Glastonbury, CT 06033
Phone: 860-659-3828
E-mail: uma.sahay@gmail.com

SYLVIA W. FARNY SCHOLARSHIP

One-time awards of $2000 to ASME student members for the final year of undergraduate study in mechanical engineering. Must be a U.S. citizen, enrolled in a college/university in the United States that has ABET accreditation. Number of scholarships granted varies.

Academic Fields/Career Goals: Mechanical Engineering.

Award: Scholarship for use in junior year; not renewable. *Number:* 1–2. *Amount:* $3000.

Eligibility Requirements: Applicant must be enrolled or expecting to enroll full-time at a four-year institution or university. Applicant or parent of applicant must be member of Other Student Academic Clubs. Available to U.S. citizens.

Application Requirements: Application form, recommendations or references, transcript. *Deadline:* March 15.

Contact: Saraswati Sahay, Undergraduate Scholarships
American Society of Mechanical Engineers Auxiliary Inc.
170 East Opal Drive
Glastonbury, CT 06033
Phone: 860-659-3828
E-mail: uma.sahay@gmail.com

AMERICAN SOCIETY OF NAVAL ENGINEERS

http://www.navalengineers.org/

AMERICAN SOCIETY OF NAVAL ENGINEERS SCHOLARSHIP
• *See page 110*

AMERICAN WELDING SOCIETY

http://www.aws.org/

PAST PRESIDENTS' SCHOLARSHIP
• *See page 293*

ARRL FOUNDATION INC.

http://www.arrl.org/

ALFRED E. FRIEND JR., W4CF, MEMORIAL SCHOLARSHIP
• *See page 177*

GARY WAGNER, K3OMI, SCHOLARSHIP
• *See page 177*

W I FDR SCHOLARSHIP
• *See page 112*

ASTRONAUT SCHOLARSHIP FOUNDATION

http://www.astronautscholarship.org/

ASTRONAUT SCHOLARSHIP FOUNDATION
• *See page 112*

AUTOMOTIVE WOMEN'S ALLIANCE FOUNDATION

http://www.awafoundation.org/index.php

AUTOMOTIVE WOMEN'S ALLIANCE FOUNDATION SCHOLARSHIPS
• *See page 74*

BARRY GOLDWATER SCHOLARSHIP AND EXCELLENCE IN EDUCATION FOUNDATION

https://goldwater.scholarsapply.org

BARRY M. GOLDWATER SCHOLARSHIP AND EXCELLENCE IN EDUCATION PROGRAM
• *See page 112*

BHW GROUP

https://thebhwgroup.com/

BHW WOMEN IN STEM SCHOLARSHIP
• *See page 74*

BRASKEM ODEBRECHT

http://www.odebrechtaward.com

ODEBRECHT AWARD FOR SUSTAINABLE DEVELOPMENT
• *See page 119*

BROWN AND CALDWELL

http://www.brownandcaldwell.com

ECKENFELDER SCHOLARSHIP
• *See page 155*

MINORITY SCHOLARSHIP PROGRAM
• *See page 155*

CENTER FOR ARCHITECTURE

http://www.cfafoundation.org/scholarships

CENTER FOR ARCHITECTURE DESIGN SCHOLARSHIP
• *See page 119*

THE DALLAS FOUNDATION

http://www.dallasfoundation.org/

WHITLEY PLACE SCHOLARSHIP
• *See page 120*

THE ELECTROCHEMICAL SOCIETY

http://www.electrochem.org/

STUDENT RESEARCH AWARDS OF THE BATTERY DIVISION OF THE ELECTROCHEMICAL SOCIETY INC.
• *See page 113*

ENGINEERS' SOCIETY OF WESTERN PENNSYLVANIA

http://www.eswp.com/

JOSEPH A. LEVENDUSKY MEMORIAL SCHOLARSHIP
• *See page 178*

FABRICATORS AND MANUFACTURERS ASSOCIATION FOUNDATION

http://www.nutsandboltsfoundation.org/scholarships/

COLLEGE AND TRADE/TECHNICAL SCHOOL SCHOLARSHIPS
• *See page 178*

FOUNDATION FOR SCIENCE AND DISABILITY

http://stemd.org/

GRANTS FOR DISABLED GRADUATE STUDENTS IN THE SCIENCES
• *See page 113*

GLOBAL AUTOMOTIVE AFTERMARKET SYMPOSIUM

http://www.automotivescholarships.com/

AUTOMOTIVE AFTERMARKET SCHOLARSHIP CENTRAL
• *See page 164*

GREATER KANAWHA VALLEY FOUNDATION

http://www.tgkvf.org/

STEVEN ENGINEERING SCHOLARSHIP
• *See page 178*

GREAT MINDS IN STEM

www.greatmindsinstem.org

HISPANIC ENGINEER NATIONAL ACHIEVEMENT AWARDS CORPORATION SCHOLARSHIP PROGRAM
• *See page 106*

INDEPENDENT LABORATORIES INSTITUTE SCHOLARSHIP ALLIANCE

http://www.acil.org/

INDEPENDENT LABORATORIES INSTITUTE SCHOLARSHIP ALLIANCE
• *See page 156*

INTERNATIONAL SOCIETY FOR OPTICAL ENGINEERING-SPIE

http://www.spie.org/scholarships

SPIE EDUCATIONAL SCHOLARSHIPS IN OPTICAL SCIENCE AND ENGINEERING
• *See page 114*

JORGE MAS CANOSA FREEDOM FOUNDATION

http://masscholarships.org/

MAS FAMILY SCHOLARSHIP AWARD
• *See page 165*

KENTUCKY ENERGY AND ENVIRONMENT CABINET

http://dep.ky.gov

ENVIRONMENTAL PROTECTION SCHOLARSHIP
• *See page 157*

LOS ANGELES COUNCIL OF BLACK PROFESSIONAL ENGINEERS

http://www.lablackengineers.org/

AL-BEN SCHOLARSHIP FOR ACADEMIC INCENTIVE
• *See page 179*

AL-BEN SCHOLARSHIP FOR PROFESSIONAL MERIT
• *See page 179*

AL-BEN SCHOLARSHIP FOR SCHOLASTIC ACHIEVEMENT
• *See page 179*

MANUFACTURERS ASSOCIATION OF MAINE

http://www.mainemfg.com/

MAINE MANUFACTURING CAREER AND TRAINING FOUNDATION SCHOLARSHIP
• *See page 142*

MINERALS, METALS, AND MATERIALS SOCIETY (TMS)

http://www.tms.org/

KAUFMAN CALPHAD SCHOLARSHIP
• *See page 268*

NASA FLORIDA SPACE GRANT CONSORTIUM

http://www.floridaspacegrant.org/

FLORIDA SPACE RESEARCH PROGRAM
• *See page 142*

NASA IDAHO SPACE GRANT CONSORTIUM

http://www.id.spacegrant.org/

NASA IDAHO SPACE GRANT CONSORTIUM SCHOLARSHIP PROGRAM
• *See page 157*

NASA MINNESOTA SPACE GRANT CONSORTIUM

http://www.aem.umn.edu/mnsgc

MINNESOTA SPACE GRANT CONSORTIUM SCHOLARSHIP PROGRAM
• *See page 142*

NASA MONTANA SPACE GRANT CONSORTIUM

http://www.spacegrant.montana.edu/

MONTANA SPACE GRANT SCHOLARSHIP PROGRAM
• *See page 142*

NASA'S VIRGINIA SPACE GRANT CONSORTIUM

http://www.vsgc.odu.edu/

COMMUNITY COLLEGE STEM SCHOLARSHIPS
• *See page 114*

UNDERGRADUATE STEM RESEARCH SCHOLARSHIPS
• *See page 114*

NATIONAL ASSOCIATION OF WOMEN IN CONSTRUCTION

http://www.nawic.org/

NAWIC UNDERGRADUATE SCHOLARSHIPS
• *See page 122*

NATIONAL BOARD OF BOILER AND PRESSURE VESSEL INSPECTORS

http://www.nationalboard.org/

NATIONAL BOARD TECHNICAL SCHOLARSHIP
• *See page 180*

NATIONAL SOCIETY OF PROFESSIONAL ENGINEERS

http://www.nspe.org/

MAUREEN L. AND HOWARD N. BLITMAN, PE SCHOLARSHIP TO PROMOTE DIVERSITY IN ENGINEERING
• *See page 180*

PAUL H. ROBBINS HONORARY SCHOLARSHIP
• *See page 180*

PROFESSIONAL ENGINEERS IN INDUSTRY SCHOLARSHIP
• *See page 180*

NEVADA NASA SPACE GRANT CONSORTIUM

http://www.nvspacegrant.org/

NATIONAL SPACE GRANT COLLEGE AND FELLOWSHIP PROGRAM
• *See page 114*

NEXTSTEPU

http://www.nextstepu.com/

$1,500 STEM SCHOLARSHIP
• *See page 106*

OREGON STUDENT ASSISTANCE COMMISSION

http://www.GetCollegeFunds.org/

FRED FIELDS SCHOLARSHIP
• *See page 167*

SOCIETY OF AMERICAN MILITARY ENGINEERS PORTLAND POST SCHOLARSHIP
• *See page 181*

PLAN NEW HAMPSHIRE

www.plannh.org

PLAN NEW HAMPSHIRE SCHOLARSHIP AND PROGRAM
• *See page 123*

PLUMBING-HEATING-COOLING CONTRACTORS EDUCATION FOUNDATION

http://www.phccfoundation.org/scholarships

DELTA FAUCET COMPANY SCHOLARSHIP PROGRAM
• *See page 167*

PHCC EDUCATIONAL FOUNDATION NEED-BASED SCHOLARSHIP
• *See page 167*

PHCC EDUCATIONAL FOUNDATION SCHOLARSHIP PROGRAM
• *See page 167*

PROFESSIONAL CONSTRUCTION ESTIMATORS ASSOCIATION

http://www.pcea.org/

TED G. WILSON MEMORIAL SCHOLARSHIP FOUNDATION
• *See page 197*

ROBERT H. MOLLOHAN FAMILY CHARITABLE FOUNDATION, INC.

http://www.mollohanfoundation.org/

HIGH TECHNOLOGY SCHOLARS PROGRAM
• *See page 158*

SCARLETT FAMILY FOUNDATION SCHOLARSHIP PROGRAM

http://www.scarlettfoundation.org/

SCHOLARSHIP FOR STUDENTS PURSUING A BUSINESS OR STEM DEGREE
• *See page 84*

SIGMA XI, THE SCIENTIFIC RESEARCH SOCIETY

http://www.sigmaxi.org/

SIGMA XI GRANTS-IN-AID OF RESEARCH
• *See page 101*

SOCIETY OF AUTOMOTIVE ENGINEERS

http://www.sae.org/

BMW/SAE ENGINEERING SCHOLARSHIP
• *See page 146*

DETROIT SECTION SAE TECHNICAL SCHOLARSHIP
• *See page 286*

EDWARD D. HENDRICKSON/SAE ENGINEERING SCHOLARSHIP
• *See page 146*

RALPH K. HILLQUIST HONORARY SAE SCHOLARSHIP
• *See page 286*

TMC/SAE DONALD D. DAWSON TECHNICAL SCHOLARSHIP
• *See page 147*

YANMAR/SAE SCHOLARSHIP
• *See page 286*

SOCIETY OF MANUFACTURING ENGINEERS EDUCATION FOUNDATION

http://www.smeef.org/

CHAPTER 198-DOWNRIVER DETROIT SCHOLARSHIP
• *See page 307*

CHAPTER 4-LAWRENCE A. WACKER MEMORIAL SCHOLARSHIP
• *See page 307*

CHAPTER 67-PHOENIX SCHOLARSHIP
• *See page 307*

FORT WAYNE CHAPTER 56 SCHOLARSHIP
• *See page 309*

MYRTLE AND EARL WALKER SCHOLARSHIP FUND
• *See page 287*

NORTH CENTRAL REGION 9 SCHOLARSHIP
• *See page 309*

WICHITA CHAPTER 52 SCHOLARSHIP
• *See page 310*

WILLIAM E. WEISEL SCHOLARSHIP FUND
• *See page 269*

SOCIETY OF PLASTICS ENGINEERS FOUNDATION (SPE)

http://www.4spe.org/

GULF COAST HURRICANE SCHOLARSHIP
• *See page 181*

SOCIETY OF WOMEN ENGINEERS

http://societyofwomenengineers.swe.org/

ADA I. PRESSMAN MEMORIAL SCHOLARSHIP
• *See page 182*

AMERICAN TRANSMISSION CO. SCHOLARSHIP
• *See page 182*

ANNE MAUREEN WHITNEY BARROW MEMORIAL SCHOLARSHIP
• *See page 182*

ANNE SHEN SMITH ENDOWED SCHOLARSHIP
• *See page 182*

BAYER SCHOLARSHIP
• *See page 183*

BETTY LOU BAILEY SWE REGION F SCHOLARSHIP
• *See page 183*

B.J. HARROD SCHOLARSHIP
• *See page 183*

BK KRENZER MEMORIAL REENTRY SCHOLARSHIP
• *See page 183*

CAROL STEPHENS SWE REGION F SCHOLARSHIP
• *See page 183*

CUMMINS SCHOLARSHIP
• *See page 183*

DR. IVY M. PARKER MEMORIAL SCHOLARSHIP
• *See page 184*

DOROTHY LEMKE HOWARTH MEMORIAL SCHOLARSHIP
• *See page 184*

DOROTHY P. MORRIS SCHOLARSHIP
• *See page 184*

DUPONT COMPANY SCHOLARSHIP
• *See page 184*

EXELON CORPORATION SCHOLARSHIP
• *See page 184*

FCA WOMEN IN ENGINEERING SCHOLARSHIP
• *See page 184*

FORD MOTOR COMPANY SCHOLARSHIP
• *See page 270*

GENERAL ELECTRIC WOMEN'S NETWORK SCHOLARSHIP
• *See page 198*

HONEYWELL SCHOLARSHIP
• *See page 184*

IBM LINDA SANFORD WOMEN'S TECHNICAL ADVANCEMENT SCHOLARSHIP
• *See page 185*

JILL S. TIETJEN P.E. SCHOLARSHIP
• *See page 185*

KELLOGG SCHOLARSHIP
• *See page 185*

KOCH DISCOVERY SCHOLARSHIP
• *See page 185*

LILLIAN MOLLER GILBRETH MEMORIAL SCHOLARSHIP
• *See page 185*

MARY V. MUNGER SCHOLARSHIP
• *See page 185*

MASWE SCHOLARSHIP
• *See page 186*

OLIVE LYNN SALEMBIER MEMORIAL REENTRY SCHOLARSHIP
• *See page 186*

ROBERTA BANASZAK GLEITER ENGINEERING ENDEAVOR SCHOLARSHIP
• *See page 186*

ROCHELLE PERRY MEMORIAL SCHOLARSHIP
• *See page 186*

ROCKWELL COLLINS SCHOLARSHIP
• *See page 218*

SUSAN MISZKOWICZ MEMORIAL SCHOLARSHIP
• *See page 186*

SWE BALTIMORE-WASHINGTON SECTION SCHOLARSHIP
• *See page 186*

SWE CENTRAL NEW MEXICO PIONEERS SCHOLARSHIP
• *See page 187*

SWE CENTRAL NEW MEXICO REENTRY SCHOLARSHIP
• *See page 187*

SWE MID-HUDSON SECTION SCHOLARSHIP
• *See page 187*

SWE PHOENIX SECTION SCHOLARSHIP
• *See page 187*

SWE REGION E SCHOLARSHIP
• *See page 187*

SWE REGION H SCHOLARSHIPS
• *See page 188*

SWE REGION J SCHOLARSHIP
• *See page 188*

TURNER CONSTRUCTION SCHOLARSHIP
• *See page 188*

WANDA MUNN SCHOLARSHIP
• *See page 188*

SOCIETY OF WOMEN ENGINEERS-ROCKY MOUNTAIN SECTION
http://www.swe-rms.org/

SOCIETY OF WOMEN ENGINEERS-ROCKY MOUNTAIN SECTION SCHOLARSHIP PROGRAM
• *See page 188*

SONS OF NORWAY FOUNDATION
http://www.sonsofnorway.com/foundation

NANCY LORRAINE JENSEN MEMORIAL SCHOLARSHIP
• *See page 189*

SPECIALTY EQUIPMENT MARKET ASSOCIATION
http://www.sema.org/

SEMA MEMORIAL SCHOLARSHIP FUND
• *See page 85*

STRAIGHTFORWARD MEDIA
http://www.straightforwardmedia.com/

STRAIGHTFORWARD MEDIA ENGINEERING SCHOLARSHIP
• *See page 189*

TAU BETA PI ASSOCIATION
http://www.tbp.org/

TAU BETA PI SCHOLARSHIP PROGRAM
• *See page 189*

TIMOTION
http://www.timotion.com/

TIMOTION ENGINEERING AND EXCELLENCE SCHOLARSHIP
• *See page 199*

TRANSTUTORS
http://www.transtutors.com/scholarship

TRANSTUTORS SCHOLARSHIP 2015-16
• *See page 85*

TURNER CONSTRUCTION COMPANY
http://www.turnerconstruction.com/

YOUTHFORCE 2020 SCHOLARSHIP PROGRAM
• *See page 124*

UNITED NEGRO COLLEGE FUND
http://www.uncf.org/

ANHEUSER-BUSCH LEGENDS OF THE CROWN SCHOLARSHIP PROGRAM
• *See page 86*

BLUE CROSS BLUE SHIELD OF ILLINOIS AND BLUE CROSS BLUE SHIELD OF TEXAS SCHOLARSHIP
• *See page 115*

COLGATE–PALMOLIVE CORPORATE SCHOLARS PROGRAM
• *See page 86*

DAVIS SCHOLARSHIP FOR WOMEN IN STEM
• *See page 189*

GALACTIC UNITE BYTHEWAY SCHOLARSHIP
• *See page 190*

INTEL SCHOLARSHIP PROGRAM
• *See page 190*

PROCTER & GAMBLE STEM SCHOLARSHIP
• *See page 116*

SUEZ CORPORATE SCHOLARS PROGRAM
• *See page 87*

UNCF STEM SCHOLARS PROGRAM
• *See page 159*

UNIVERSITIES SPACE RESEARCH ASSOCIATION

http://www.usra.edu/

UNIVERSITIES SPACE RESEARCH ASSOCIATION SCHOLARSHIP AWARD PROGRAM
• *See page 116*

VERMONT SPACE GRANT CONSORTIUM

http://www.cems.uvm.edu/vsgc

VERMONT SPACE GRANT CONSORTIUM
• *See page 96*

WOMEN IN AVIATION, INTERNATIONAL

http://www.wai.org/

DELTA AIR LINES ENGINEERING SCHOLARSHIP
• *See page 149*

XEROX

http://www.xerox.com//

TECHNICAL MINORITY SCHOLARSHIP
• *See page 190*

METEOROLOGY/ ATMOSPHERIC SCIENCE

AIR & WASTE MANAGEMENT ASSOCIATION, ALLEGHENY MOUNTAIN SECTION

http://www.ams-awma.org/

ALLEGHENY MOUNTAIN SECTION AIR & WASTE MANAGEMENT ASSOCIATION SCHOLARSHIP
• *See page 317*

AMERICAN INDIAN SCIENCE AND ENGINEERING SOCIETY

http://www.aises.org/

A.T. ANDERSON MEMORIAL SCHOLARSHIP PROGRAM
• *See page 109*

AMERICAN METEOROLOGICAL SOCIETY

http://www.ametsoc.org/

AMERICAN METEOROLOGICAL SOCIETY MINORITY SCHOLARSHIPS

Two-year scholarship of $3,000 per year for minority students entering their freshman year of college. Must plan to pursue careers in the atmospheric and related oceanic and hydrologic sciences. Must be U.S. citizen or permanent resident to apply.

Academic Fields/Career Goals: Meteorology/Atmospheric Science.

Award: Scholarship for use in freshman year; renewable. *Number:* 3. *Amount:* $3000–$6000.

Eligibility Requirements: Applicant must be of African, Chinese, Hispanic, Indian, Latin American/Caribbean, Spanish heritage; American Indian/Alaska Native, Asian/Pacific Islander, Black (non-Hispanic); high school student and planning to enroll or expecting to enroll full-time at a two-year or four-year institution or university. Applicant must have 3.0 GPA or higher. Available to U.S. and Canadian citizens.

Application Requirements: Application form. *Deadline:* February 10.

Contact: Donna Fernandez, Development and Student Program Manager
American Meteorological Society
45 Beacon Street
Boston, MA 02108-3693
Phone: 617-227-2426 Ext. 307
E-mail: dfernand@ametsoc.org

AMS FRESHMAN UNDERGRADUATE SCHOLARSHIP

Scholarships will be awarded, based on academic excellence, to high school seniors entering their freshman year of study in the atmospheric, oceanic, or hydrologic sciences. For use in freshman and sophomore years, with second-year funding dependent on successful completion of first year.

Academic Fields/Career Goals: Meteorology/Atmospheric Science.

Award: Scholarship for use in freshman year; renewable. *Number:* 14. *Amount:* $2500–$5000.

Eligibility Requirements: Applicant must be high school student and planning to enroll or expecting to enroll full-time at a two-year or four-year or technical institution or university. Applicant must have 3.0 GPA or higher. Available to U.S. and Canadian citizens.

Application Requirements: Application form, essay. *Deadline:* February 10.

Contact: Ms. Donna Fernandez, Development and Student Program Manager
American Meteorological Society
45 Beacon Street
Boston, MA 02108
Phone: 617-227-2426 Ext. 246
E-mail: dfernand@ametsoc.org

FATHER JAMES B. MACELWANE ANNUAL AWARDS

Available to enrolled undergraduates who submit a paper on a phase of atmospheric sciences with a statement from a supervisor on the student's original contribution to the work. Minimum 3.0 GPA required. No more than two students from any one institution may enter papers in one contest. Must submit letter from department head or faculty member confirming applicant's undergraduate status and paper's originality. Must be a U.S. citizen.

Academic Fields/Career Goals: Meteorology/Atmospheric Science.

Award: Prize for use in sophomore, junior, or senior years; not renewable. *Number:* 1. *Amount:* $1000.

Eligibility Requirements: Applicant must be enrolled or expecting to enroll full-time at a two-year or four-year institution or university. Applicant must have 3.0 GPA or higher. Available to U.S. and Canadian citizens.

Application Requirements: *Deadline:* June 10.

Contact: Donna Fernandez, Development and Student Program Manager
E-mail: dfernandez@ametsoc.org

ASSOCIATION FOR WOMEN GEOSCIENTISTS (AWG)

http://www.awg.org/

AWG ETHNIC MINORITY SCHOLARSHIP
• See page 241

AWG MARIA LUISA CRAWFORD FIELD CAMP SCHOLARSHIP
• See page 117

AWG SALT LAKE CHAPTER (SLC) RESEARCH SCHOLARSHIP
• See page 117

JANET CULLEN TANAKA GEOSCIENCES UNDERGRADUATE SCHOLARSHIP
• See page 117

LONE STAR RISING CAREER SCHOLARSHIP
• See page 242

OSAGE CHAPTER UNDERGRADUATE SERVICE SCHOLARSHIP
• See page 117

SUSAN EKDALE MEMORIAL FIELD CAMP SCHOLARSHIP
• See page 242

ASTRONAUT SCHOLARSHIP FOUNDATION

http://www.astronautscholarship.org/

ASTRONAUT SCHOLARSHIP FOUNDATION
• See page 112

BARRY GOLDWATER SCHOLARSHIP AND EXCELLENCE IN EDUCATION FOUNDATION

https://goldwater.scholarsapply.org

BARRY M. GOLDWATER SCHOLARSHIP AND EXCELLENCE IN EDUCATION PROGRAM
• See page 112

BHW GROUP

https://thebhwgroup.com/

BHW WOMEN IN STEM SCHOLARSHIP
• See page 74

BROWN AND CALDWELL

http://www.brownandcaldwell.com

ECKENFELDER SCHOLARSHIP
• See page 155

MINORITY SCHOLARSHIP PROGRAM
• See page 155

GREAT MINDS IN STEM

www.greatmindsinstem.org

HISPANIC ENGINEER NATIONAL ACHIEVEMENT AWARDS CORPORATION SCHOLARSHIP PROGRAM
• See page 106

NASA MINNESOTA SPACE GRANT CONSORTIUM

http://www.aem.umn.edu/mnsgc

MINNESOTA SPACE GRANT CONSORTIUM SCHOLARSHIP PROGRAM
• See page 142

NASA RHODE ISLAND SPACE GRANT CONSORTIUM

http://brown/initiatives/ri-space-grant

NASA RHODE ISLAND SPACE GRANT CONSORTIUM UNDERGRADUATE RESEARCH SCHOLARSHIP
• See page 143

NEXTSTEPU

http://www.nextstepu.com/

$1,500 STEM SCHOLARSHIP
• See page 106

SCARLETT FAMILY FOUNDATION SCHOLARSHIP PROGRAM

http://www.scarlettfoundation.org/

SCHOLARSHIP FOR STUDENTS PURSUING A BUSINESS OR STEM DEGREE
• See page 84

SIGMA XI, THE SCIENTIFIC RESEARCH SOCIETY

http://www.sigmaxi.org/

SIGMA XI GRANTS-IN-AID OF RESEARCH
• See page 101

SOCIETY OF SATELLITE PROFESSIONALS INTERNATIONAL

http://www.sspi.org/

SSPI INTERNATIONAL SCHOLARSHIPS
• See page 147

TKE EDUCATIONAL FOUNDATION

http://www.tke.org/

CARROL C. HALL MEMORIAL SCHOLARSHIP
• See page 115

MILITARY AND DEFENSE STUDIES

ARMED FORCES COMMUNICATIONS AND ELECTRONICS ASSOCIATION, EDUCATIONAL FOUNDATION

http://www.afcea.org/site/?q=foundation/scholarships

STEM MAJORS SCHOLARSHIPS FOR UNDERGRADUATE STUDENTS
• See page 110

VADM SAMUEL L. GRAVELY, JR, USN(RET.) MEMORIAL SCHOLARSHIP
• See page 111

ASSOCIATION OF FORMER INTELLIGENCE OFFICERS

http://www.afio.com

AFIO UNDERGRADUATE AND GRADUATE SCHOLARSHIPS
• See page 103

BHW GROUP

https://thebhwgroup.com/

BHW WOMEN IN STEM SCHOLARSHIP
• See page 74

THE LYNDON BAINES JOHNSON FOUNDATION

http://www.lbjlibrary.org/page/foundation/

MOODY RESEARCH GRANTS
• See page 104

NATIONAL MILITARY INTELLIGENCE FOUNDATION

http://www.nmia.org/

NATIONAL MILITARY INTELLIGENCE ASSOCIATION SCHOLARSHIP

Scholarships to support the growth of professional studies in the field of military intelligence and to recognize and reward excellence in the development and transfer of knowledge about military and associated intelligence disciplines.

Academic Fields/Career Goals: Military and Defense Studies.

Award: Scholarship for use in freshman, sophomore, junior, or senior years; not renewable. *Number:* 3. *Amount:* $1000.

Eligibility Requirements: Applicant must be enrolled or expecting to enroll full-time at a four-year institution or university. Applicant or parent of applicant must be member of National Military Intelligence Association. Applicant must have 3.0 GPA or higher. Available to U.S. citizens.

Application Requirements: Application form, test scores. *Deadline:* August 1.

Contact: Dr. Forrest Frank, Secretary-Treasurer
National Military Intelligence Foundation
PO Box 6844
Arlington, VA 22311
Phone: 434-542-5929
E-mail: ffrank54@comcast.net

SOCIETY OF SATELLITE PROFESSIONALS INTERNATIONAL

http://www.sspi.org/

SSPI INTERNATIONAL SCHOLARSHIPS
• See page 147

WOMEN IN DEFENSE (WID), A NATIONAL SECURITY ORGANIZATION

http://wid.ndia.org

HORIZONS SCHOLARSHIP

Scholarships awarded to provide financial assistance to further educational objectives of women either currently employed in, or planning careers in, defense or national security arenas (not law enforcement or criminal justice). Must be U.S. citizen. Minimum 3.5 GPA required.

Academic Fields/Career Goals: Military and Defense Studies.

Award: Scholarship for use in junior, senior, graduate, or postgraduate years; renewable. *Number:* 5–6. *Amount:* $500–$10,000.

Eligibility Requirements: Applicant must be enrolled or expecting to enroll full- or part-time at a four-year institution or university and female. Applicant must have 3.5 GPA or higher. Available to U.S. citizens.

Application Requirements: Application form, essay, financial need analysis, proof of citizenship, recommendations or references, transcript. *Deadline:* July 1.

Contact: Trina Dickey
Women In Defense (WID), A National Security Organization
2111 Wilson Boulevard, Suite 400
Arlington, VA 22201-3061
Phone: 703-247-2589
Fax: 703-522-1885
E-mail: tdickey@ndia.org

MUSEUM STUDIES

AMERICAN SCHOOL OF CLASSICAL STUDIES AT ATHENS

http://www.ascsa.edu.gr/

ASCSA SUMMER SESSIONS SCHOLARSHIPS
• See page 108

ASSOCIATION FOR WOMEN GEOSCIENTISTS (AWG)

http://www.awg.org/

AWG ETHNIC MINORITY SCHOLARSHIP
• See page 241

AWG SALT LAKE CHAPTER (SLC) RESEARCH SCHOLARSHIP
• See page 117

LONE STAR RISING CAREER SCHOLARSHIP
• See page 242

OSAGE CHAPTER UNDERGRADUATE SERVICE SCHOLARSHIP
• See page 117

SUSAN EKDALE MEMORIAL FIELD CAMP SCHOLARSHIP
• See page 242

COSTUME SOCIETY OF AMERICA

http://www.costumesocietyamerica.com/

ADELE FILENE STUDENT PRESENTER GRANT
• *See page 125*

STELLA BLUM STUDENT RESEARCH GRANT
• *See page 125*

THE LYNDON BAINES JOHNSON FOUNDATION

http://www.lbjlibrary.org/page/foundation/

MOODY RESEARCH GRANTS
• *See page 104*

MUSIC

AMERICAN COLLEGE OF MUSICIANS/NATIONAL GUILD OF PIANO TEACHERS

http://www.pianoguild.com/

AMERICAN COLLEGE OF MUSICIANS/NATIONAL GUILD OF PIANO TEACHERS $200 SCHOLARSHIPS

Award available only to student affiliate members who have participated in National Guild of Piano Teachers auditions over a ten-year period. Must be Paderewski Medal winner and be sponsored by Guild member. Contact American College of Musicians for more information.

Academic Fields/Career Goals: Music.

Award: Scholarship for use in freshman, sophomore, junior, or senior years; not renewable. *Number:* up to 150. *Amount:* $200.

Eligibility Requirements: Applicant must be enrolled or expecting to enroll full-time at a two-year or four-year or technical institution or university and must have an interest in music. Applicant or parent of applicant must be member of American College of Musicians. Available to U.S. and non-U.S. citizens.

Application Requirements: Application form, test scores. *Deadline:* September 15.

Contact: Scholarship Committee
American College of Musicians/National Guild of Piano
Teachers
PO Box 1807
Austin, TX 78767-1807

AMERICAN FOUNDATION FOR THE BLIND

http://www.afb.org/

GLADYS C. ANDERSON MEMORIAL SCHOLARSHIP

Non-renewable award available to a legally-blind female undergraduate or graduate student studying religious or classical music. Must submit a letter from a post-secondary institution as proof of enrollment in a program in music. For online application and more information, visit website http://www.afb.org.

Academic Fields/Career Goals: Music.

Award: Scholarship for use in freshman, sophomore, junior, or senior years; not renewable. *Number:* 1. *Amount:* $1000.

Eligibility Requirements: Applicant must be visually impaired; enrolled or expecting to enroll full-time at a four-year institution or university and female. Applicant must be visually impaired. Available to U.S. citizens.

Application Requirements: Application form, essay, proof of enrollment letter from post secondary institution, proof of blindness letter from

agency or medical doctor, recommendations or references, transcript. *Deadline:* April 30.

Contact: Dawn Bodrogi, Information Center and Library Coordinator
Phone: 212-502-7661
E-mail: dbodrogi@afb.net

R.L. GILLETTE SCHOLARSHIP
• *See page 399*

AMERICAN LEGION DEPARTMENT OF KANSAS

http://www.ksamlegion.org/

MUSIC COMMITTEE SCHOLARSHIP

One-time award open to a high school senior or college freshman or sophomore. Must be a Kansas resident. Must have distinguished background in the field of music at an approved Kansas junior college, college or university. Award of $1000, with the disbursement as $500 award for each of the two semesters.

Academic Fields/Career Goals: Music; Performing Arts.

Award: Scholarship for use in freshman or sophomore years; not renewable. *Number:* 1. *Amount:* $1000.

Eligibility Requirements: Applicant must be enrolled or expecting to enroll full-time at a two-year or four-year or technical institution or university; resident of Kansas; studying in Kansas and must have an interest in music/singing. Available to U.S. citizens.

Application Requirements: Application form, financial need analysis, personal photograph. *Deadline:* February 15.

Contact: Mike Oppy, Chairman, Scholarship Committee
American Legion Department of Kansas
1314 SW Topeka Boulevard
Topeka, KS 66612
Phone: 785-232-9315

BMI FOUNDATION, INC.

http://www.bmifoundation.org/

BMI STUDENT COMPOSER AWARDS
• *See page 127*

THE CHOPIN FOUNDATION OF THE UNITED STATES

http://www.chopin.org/

SCHOLARSHIP PROGRAM FOR YOUNG AMERICAN PIANISTS

Program is open to qualified American pianists not younger than 14 and not older than 17 years of age on their first year of application. Renewable for up to four years, if eligible. Students will be assisted in preparing music repertoire required for the National Chopin Piano Competition. Must be U.S. citizens or legal residents. For more information, see website http://www.chopin.org.

Academic Fields/Career Goals: Music; Performing Arts.

Award: Grant for use in freshman, sophomore, or junior years; renewable. *Number:* 1–10. *Amount:* $1000.

Eligibility Requirements: Applicant must be age 14-17; enrolled or expecting to enroll full- or part-time at a two-year or four-year institution and must have an interest in music. Available to U.S. citizens.

Application Requirements: Application form. *Fee:* $25. *Deadline:* May 15.

Contact: Jadwiga Gewert, Executive Director
The Chopin Foundation of the United States
1440 79th Street Causeway, Suite 117
Miami, FL 33141
Phone: 305-868-0624
E-mail: info@chopin.org

COMMUNITY FOUNDATION FOR GREATER ATLANTA, INC.

http://cfgreateratlanta.org/

JAMES M. AND VIRGINIA M. SMYTH SCHOLARSHIP
• *See page 128*

CONGRESSIONAL BLACK CAUCUS FOUNDATION, INC.

http://www.cbcfinc.org/

CBC SPOUSES HEINEKEN USA PERFORMING ARTS SCHOLARSHIP

This program was established in 2000 in honor of the late Curtis Mayfield to ensure that students pursuing a degree in the performing arts receive financial assistance. Performing arts includes theater, drama, comedy, music, dance, opera, marching bands, etc.

Academic Fields/Career Goals: Music; Performing Arts.

Award: Scholarship for use in freshman, sophomore, junior, or senior years; not renewable. *Number:* 10. *Amount:* $3000.

Eligibility Requirements: Applicant must be Black (non-Hispanic); enrolled or expecting to enroll full-time at a two-year or four-year institution or university; studying in Alabama, Alaska, Arizona, Arkansas, California, Colorado, Connecticut, Delaware, District of Columbia, Florida, Georgia, Guam, Hawaii, Idaho, Illinois, Indiana, Iowa, Kansas, Kentucky, Louisiana, Maine, Maryland, Massachusetts, Michigan, Minnesota, Mississippi, Missouri, Montana, Nebraska, Nevada, New Hampshire, New Jersey, New Mexico, New York, North Carolina, North Dakota, Ohio, Oklahoma, Oregon, Pennsylvania, Puerto Rico, Rhode Island, South Carolina, South Dakota, Tennessee, Texas, Utah, Vermont, Virginia, Washington, West Virginia, Wisconsin, Wyoming and must have an interest in music, music/singing, or theater. Applicant must have 2.5 GPA or higher. Available to U.S. citizens.

Application Requirements: Application form, essay, financial need analysis, personal photograph. *Deadline:* April 21.

Contact: Ms. Katrina Finch, Program Administrator, Scholarships
Phone: 202-263-2800
E-mail: scholarships@cbcfinc.org

DAVIDSON INSTITUTE FOR TALENT DEVELOPMENT

http://www.davidsongifted.org/

DAVIDSON FELLOWS SCHOLARSHIP PROGRAM
• *See page 113*

DELTA OMICRON FOUNDATION, INC.

http://www.delta-omicron.org

DELTA OMICRON FOUNDATION EDUCATIONAL GRANTS IN MUSIC

Grants available toward tuition awarded to undergraduate and graduate music students at a four-year college or university. Grants primarily available for Delta Omicron Fraternity members.

Academic Fields/Career Goals: Music.

Award: Grant for use in freshman, sophomore, junior, senior, graduate, or postgraduate years; not renewable. *Number:* 8. *Amount:* $500.

Eligibility Requirements: Applicant must be enrolled or expecting to enroll full- or part-time at a four-year institution or university and must have an interest in music. Applicant must have 3.5 GPA or higher. Available to U.S. and non-U.S. citizens.

Application Requirements: Application form, personal photograph. *Deadline:* April 30.

Contact: Dr. Jonny Ramsey, President
Delta Omicron Foundation, Inc.
2500 Potomac Parkway
Denton, TX 76210
Phone: 940-566-3170
E-mail: jramsey18@verizon.net

DELTA OMICRON SUMMER SCHOLARSHIPS

Scholarships awarded to assist with summer study in the area of music for summer workshops, seminars and study abroad. Award cannot be used for college tuition. Recipients must be members of Delta Omicron International Music Fraternity.

Academic Fields/Career Goals: Music.

Award: Scholarship for use in freshman, sophomore, junior, or senior years; not renewable. *Number:* 8. *Amount:* $400–$500.

Eligibility Requirements: Applicant must be enrolled or expecting to enroll part-time at a four-year institution or university and must have an interest in music. Available to U.S. and non-U.S. citizens.

Application Requirements: Application form. *Deadline:* April 2.

Contact: Ms. Michelle May, Chair, Summer Scholarships
Delta Omicron Foundation, Inc.
1635 West Boston Boulevard
Detroit, MI 48206
Phone: 313-865-1149
E-mail: maybiz@aol.com

GENERAL FEDERATION OF WOMEN'S CLUBS OF MASSACHUSETTS

http://www.gfwcma.org/

DORCHESTER WOMEN'S CLUB MUSIC SCHOLARSHIP

Scholarship for undergraduate major in voice. Applicant must be a Massachusetts resident and an undergraduate currently enrolled in a four-year accredited college, university or school of music, majoring in voice.

Academic Fields/Career Goals: Music; Performing Arts.

Award: Scholarship for use in sophomore, junior, or senior years; not renewable. *Number:* 1. *Amount:* $500.

Eligibility Requirements: Applicant must be enrolled or expecting to enroll full-time at a four-year institution or university and resident of Massachusetts. Available to U.S. citizens.

Application Requirements: Application form, driver's license, interview. *Deadline:* March 1.

Contact: Scholarship Chairman
General Federation of Women's Clubs of Massachusetts
245 Dutton Road
Sudbury, MA 01776
Phone: 978-443-4569
E-mail: gfwcma@aol.com

GLENN MILLER BIRTHPLACE SOCIETY

http://www.glennmiller.org/

GMBS-3RD PLACE INSTRUMENTAL SCHOLARSHIP

One scholarship for a male or female instrumentalist will be awarded as a competition prize to be used for any education-related expenses. Must submit 10-minute, high-quality audio tape of pieces selected for competition or those of similar style. Applicant is responsible for travel to and lodging during the competition. One-time award for high school seniors and college freshmen.

Academic Fields/Career Goals: Music.

Award: Scholarship for use in freshman year; not renewable. *Number:* 1. *Amount:* up to $1000.

Eligibility Requirements: Applicant must be enrolled or expecting to enroll full-time at a four-year institution or university. Available to U.S. and non-U.S. citizens.

Application Requirements: Application form, essay, performance tape or CD. *Deadline:* March 10.

Contact: Arlene Leonard, Secretary
Glenn Miller Birthplace Society
PO Box 61
Clarinda, IA 51632
Phone: 712-542-2461
Fax: 712-542-2461
E-mail: gmbs@heartland.net

GMBS-BILL BAKER/HANS STARREVELD SCHOLARSHIP

One scholarship for a male or female instrumentalist will be awarded as a competition prize to be used for any education-related expenses. Must submit 10-minute, high-quality audio tape of pieces selected for competition or those of similar style. Applicant is responsible for travel to and lodging during the competition. One-time award for high school seniors and college freshmen.

Academic Fields/Career Goals: Music.

Award: Scholarship for use in freshman year; not renewable. *Number:* 1. *Amount:* up to $2000.

Eligibility Requirements: Applicant must be enrolled or expecting to enroll full-time at a four-year institution or university. Available to U.S. and non-U.S. citizens.

Application Requirements: Application form, essay, performance tape or CD. *Deadline:* March 10.

Contact: Arlene Leonard, Secretary
Glenn Miller Birthplace Society
PO Box 61
Clarinda, IA 51632
Phone: 712-542-2461
Fax: 712-542-2461
E-mail: gmbs@heartland.net

GMBS-RAY EBERLE VOCAL SCHOLARSHIP

One scholarship for a male or female vocalist will be awarded as a competition prize to be used for any education-related expenses. Must submit 10-minute, high-quality audio tape of pieces selected for competition or those of similar style. Applicant is responsible for travel to and lodging during the competition. One-time award for high school seniors and college freshmen.

Academic Fields/Career Goals: Music.

Award: Scholarship for use in freshman year; not renewable. *Number:* 1. *Amount:* up to $4000.

Eligibility Requirements: Applicant must be enrolled or expecting to enroll full-time at a four-year institution. Available to U.S. and non-U.S. citizens.

Application Requirements: Application form, essay, performance tape or CD. *Deadline:* March 10.

Contact: Arlene Leonard, Secretary
Glenn Miller Birthplace Society
PO Box 61
Clarinda, IA 51632
Phone: 712-542-2461
Fax: 712-542-2461
E-mail: gmbs@heartland.net

GRAND RAPIDS COMMUNITY FOUNDATION

http://www.grfoundation.org/

LLEWELLYN L. CAYVAN STRING INSTRUMENT SCHOLARSHIP

Scholarship for undergraduate students studying the violin, the viola, the violoncello, and/or the bass viol. High school students not considered. To apply, submit required application form, transcript, essay, reference.

Academic Fields/Career Goals: Music.

Award: Scholarship for use in freshman, sophomore, junior, senior, or graduate years; not renewable. *Number:* 1–6. *Amount:* $1000–$2000.

Eligibility Requirements: Applicant must be enrolled or expecting to enroll full-time at a four-year institution or university and must have an interest in music. Available to U.S. citizens.

Application Requirements: Application form, application form may be submitted online (http://grfoundation.org), essay, transcript. *Deadline:* April 1.

Contact: Ms. Ruth Bishop, Education Program Officer
Grand Rapids Community Foundation
185 Oakes SW
Grand Rapids, MI 49503
Phone: 616-454-1751 Ext. 103
E-mail: rbishop@grfoundation.org

GREATER KANAWHA VALLEY FOUNDATION

http://www.tgkvf.org/

HERB SMITH/EUNICE FLEMING SCHOLARSHIP

Renewable award for a West Virginia resident pursuing full-time postsecondary studies in music, theater, musical theatre, and/or dance. Preference given to Fayette, Kanawha, or Wood County residents. Minimum 3.5 GPA required.

Academic Fields/Career Goals: Music; Performing Arts.

Award: Scholarship for use in freshman, sophomore, junior, or senior years; renewable. *Amount:* $500.

Eligibility Requirements: Applicant must be enrolled or expecting to enroll full-time at a four-year institution or university and resident of West Virginia. Applicant must have 3.5 GPA or higher. Available to U.S. citizens.

Application Requirements: Application form, financial need analysis, recommendations or references, test scores, transcript. *Deadline:* January 15.

Contact: Susan Hoover, Scholarship Program Officer
Greater Kanawha Valley Foundation
900 Lee Street East, 16th Floor
Charleston, WV 25301
Phone: 304-346-3620
E-mail: shoover@tgkvf.org

HAPCO MUSIC FOUNDATION INC.

http://www.hapcopromo.org/

TRADITIONAL MARCHING BAND EXTRAVAGANZA SCHOLARSHIP AWARD

Scholarship is offered to deserving students who will continue their participation in any college music program. Minimum 3.0 GPA required. Applicant should have best composite score of 970 SAT or 20 ACT.

Academic Fields/Career Goals: Music.

Award: Scholarship for use in freshman year; not renewable. *Amount:* $250–$1000.

Eligibility Requirements: Applicant must be enrolled or expecting to enroll full-time at a two-year or four-year institution or university and must have an interest in music. Applicant must have 3.0 GPA or higher. Available to U.S. citizens.

Application Requirements: Application form, essay, personal photograph, recommendations or references, test scores, transcript. *Deadline:* varies.

Contact: Joseph McMullen, President
Phone: 407-877-2262
Fax: 407-654-0308
E-mail: hapcopromo@aol.com

HARTFORD JAZZ SOCIETY INC.

http://www.hartfordjazzsociety.com/

HARTFORD JAZZ SOCIETY SCHOLARSHIPS

Scholarship of up to $3000 is awarded to graduating high school senior attending a four-year college or university. Must be a Connecticut resident. Music major with interest in jazz required.

Academic Fields/Career Goals: Music.

Award: Scholarship for use in freshman year; not renewable. *Number:* 2–3. *Amount:* up to $3000.

Eligibility Requirements: Applicant must be high school student; planning to enroll or expecting to enroll full- or part-time at a four-year institution or university; resident of Connecticut and must have an interest in music. Available to U.S. and Canadian citizens.

Application Requirements: Application form, cassette tape or CD, recommendations or references. *Deadline:* May 1.

Contact: Scholarship Committee Chairperson
Hartford Jazz Society Inc.
116 Cottage Grove Road
Bloomfield, CT 06002
Phone: 860-242-6688
Fax: 860-243-8871
E-mail: hartjazzsocinc@aol.com

HOUSTON SYMPHONY

http://www.houstonsymphony.org/

HOUSTON SYMPHONY IMA HOGG COMPETITION

Competition for musicians ages 16 to 29 who play standard instruments of the symphony orchestra. Goal is to offer a review by panel of music professionals and further career of an advanced student or a professional musician. Participants must be U.S. citizens or studying in the United States. Application fee is $30.

Academic Fields/Career Goals: Music.

Award: Prize for use in freshman, sophomore, junior, senior, graduate, or postgraduate years; not renewable. *Number:* 5. *Amount:* $300–$5000.

Eligibility Requirements: Applicant must be age 16-29; enrolled or expecting to enroll full- or part-time at a two-year or four-year or technical institution or university and must have an interest in music. Available to U.S. and non-U.S. citizens.

Application Requirements: Application form, CD with required repertoire, entry in a contest. *Fee:* $30. *Deadline:* February 13.

Contact: Carol Wilson, Manager, Music Matters!
Houston Symphony
615 Louisiana Street, Suite 102
Houston, TX 77002
Phone: 713-238-1447
Fax: 713-224-0453
E-mail: e&o@houstonsymphony.org

HOUSTON SYMPHONY LEAGUE CONCERTO COMPETITION

Competition is open to student musicians 18 years of age or younger who have not yet graduated from high school and who play any standard orchestral instrument or piano. Must live within a 200-mile radius of Houston and submit a screening CD of one movement of their concerto.

Academic Fields/Career Goals: Music.

Award: Prize for use in freshman year; not renewable. *Number:* up to 3. *Amount:* $250–$1000.

Eligibility Requirements: Applicant must be high school student; planning to enroll or expecting to enroll full-time at a two-year or four-year institution; resident of Texas and must have an interest in music. Available to U.S. citizens.

Application Requirements: Application form, CD, entry in a contest. *Fee:* $25. *Deadline:* November 18.

Contact: Carol Wilson, Manager, Music Matters!
Houston Symphony
615 Louisiana Street, Suite 102
Houston, TX 77002
Phone: 713-238-1449
Fax: 713-224-0453
E-mail: e&o@houstonsymphony.org

JACK J. ISGUR FOUNDATION

www.isgur.org

JACK J. ISGUR FOUNDATION SCHOLARSHIP

• *See page 129*

NATIONAL ACADEMY OF TELEVISION ARTS AND SCIENCES

http://www.emmyonline.tv/

DOUGLAS W. MUMMERT SCHOLARSHIP

• *See page 129*

JIM MCKAY MEMORIAL SCHOLARSHIP

• *See page 205*

MIKE WALLACE MEMORIAL SCHOLARSHIP

• *See page 205*

NATIONAL ACADEMY OF TELEVISION ARTS AND SCIENCES TRUSTEES SCHOLARSHIP

• *See page 205*

RANDY FALCO SCHOLARSHIP

• *See page 205*

NATIONAL ASSOCIATION OF PASTORAL MUSICIANS

http://www.npm.org/

DAN SCHUTTE SCHOLARSHIP

Scholarship for NPM members enrolled full-or part-time in an undergraduate or graduate pastoral music program. Applicant must intend to work at least two years in the field of pastoral music following graduation/program completion.

Academic Fields/Career Goals: Music.

Award: Scholarship for use in freshman, sophomore, junior, senior, or graduate years; not renewable. *Number:* 1. *Amount:* $1000.

Eligibility Requirements: Applicant must be enrolled or expecting to enroll full- or part-time at a two-year or four-year institution or university and must have an interest in music/singing. Applicant or parent of applicant must be member of National Association of Pastoral Musicians. Available to U.S. and non-U.S. citizens.

Application Requirements: Application form, CD of performance, essay, financial need analysis, recommendations or references, resume. *Deadline:* March 5.

Contact: Ms. Kathleen Haley, Director of Membership Services
Phone: 240-247-3000
E-mail: haley@npm.org

ELAINE RENDLER-RENE DOSOGNE-GEORGETOWN CHORALE SCHOLARSHIP

Awards NPM members enrolled full-time or part-time in a graduate or undergraduate degree program of studies related to the field of pastoral music. Applicant must intend to work at least two years in the field of pastoral music following graduation or program completion.

Academic Fields/Career Goals: Music; Religion/Theology.

Award: Scholarship for use in freshman, sophomore, junior, senior, or graduate years; not renewable. *Number:* 1. *Amount:* $1000.

Eligibility Requirements: Applicant must be enrolled or expecting to enroll full- or part-time at a two-year or four-year institution or university and must have an interest in music/singing. Applicant or parent of applicant must be member of National Association of Pastoral Musicians. Available to U.S. and non-U.S. citizens.

Application Requirements: Application form, CD of performance, essay, financial need analysis, recommendations or references, resume. *Deadline:* March 5.

Contact: Ms. Kathleen Haley, Director of Membership Services
Phone: 240-247-3000
E-mail: haley@npm.org

FUNK FAMILY MEMORIAL SCHOLARSHIP

Awards NPM members enrolled full-time or part-time in a graduate or undergraduate degree program of studies related to the field of pastoral music. Applicant must intend to work at least two years in the field of pastoral music following graduation or program completion.

Academic Fields/Career Goals: Music; Religion/Theology.

Award: Scholarship for use in freshman, sophomore, junior, senior, or graduate years; not renewable. *Number:* 1. *Amount:* $1000.

Eligibility Requirements: Applicant must be enrolled or expecting to enroll full- or part-time at a two-year or four-year or technical institution or university and must have an interest in music/singing. Applicant or parent of applicant must be member of National Association of Pastoral Musicians. Available to U.S. and non-U.S. citizens.

Application Requirements: Application form, CD of performance, essay, financial need analysis, recommendations or references, resume. *Deadline:* March 5.

Contact: Ms. Kathleen Haley, Director of Membership Services
Phone: 240-247-3000
E-mail: haley@npm.org

GIA PUBLICATION PASTORAL MUSICIAN SCHOLARSHIP

Awards NPM members enrolled full-time or part-time in a graduate or undergraduate degree program of studies related to the field of pastoral music. Applicant must intend to work at least two years in the field of pastoral music following graduation or program completion.

Academic Fields/Career Goals: Music; Religion/Theology.

Award: Scholarship for use in freshman, sophomore, junior, senior, or graduate years; not renewable. *Number:* 1. *Amount:* $2000.

Eligibility Requirements: Applicant must be enrolled or expecting to enroll full- or part-time at a two-year or four-year institution or university and must have an interest in music/singing. Applicant or parent of applicant must be member of National Association of Pastoral Musicians. Available to U.S. and non-U.S. citizens.

Application Requirements: Application form, CD of performance, essay, financial need analysis, recommendations or references, resume. *Deadline:* March 5.

Contact: Ms. Kathleen Haley, Director of Membership Services
Phone: 240-247-3000
E-mail: haley@npm.org

MUSONICS SCHOLARSHIP

Awards NPM members enrolled full-time or part-time in a graduate or undergraduate degree program of studies related to the field of pastoral music. Applicant must intend to work at least two years in the field of pastoral music following graduation or program completion. One award available for graduate study and one award available for undergraduate study.

Academic Fields/Career Goals: Music; Religion/Theology.

Award: Scholarship for use in freshman, sophomore, junior, senior, or graduate years; not renewable. *Number:* 2. *Amount:* $2000.

Eligibility Requirements: Applicant must be enrolled or expecting to enroll full- or part-time at a two-year or four-year institution or university and must have an interest in music/singing. Applicant or parent of applicant must be member of National Association of Pastoral Musicians. Available to U.S. and non-U.S. citizens.

Application Requirements: Application form, CD of performance, essay, financial need analysis, recommendations or references, resume. *Deadline:* March 5.

Contact: Ms. Kathleen Haley, Director of Membership Services
Phone: 240-247-3000
E-mail: haley@npm.org

NATIONAL ASSOCIATION OF PASTORAL MUSICIANS MEMBERS' SCHOLARSHIP

Awards NPM members enrolled full-time or part-time in a graduate or undergraduate degree program of studies related to the field of pastoral music. Applicant must intend to work at least two years in the field of pastoral music following graduation or program completion.

Academic Fields/Career Goals: Music; Religion/Theology.

Award: Scholarship for use in freshman, sophomore, junior, senior, or graduate years; not renewable. *Number:* 1. *Amount:* $3000.

Eligibility Requirements: Applicant must be enrolled or expecting to enroll full- or part-time at a two-year or four-year or technical institution or university and must have an interest in music/singing. Applicant or parent of applicant must be member of National Association of Pastoral Musicians. Available to U.S. and non-U.S. citizens.

Application Requirements: Application form, CD of performance, essay, financial need analysis, recommendations or references, resume. *Deadline:* March 5.

Contact: Ms. Kathleen Haley, Director of Membership Services
Phone: 240-247-3000
E-mail: haley@npm.org

NPM BOARD OF DIRECTORS SCHOLARSHIP

Scholarship for NPM members enrolled full- or part-time in an undergraduate or graduate pastoral music program. Must intend to work at least two years in the field of pastoral music following graduation/program completion.

Academic Fields/Career Goals: Music.

Award: Scholarship for use in freshman, sophomore, junior, senior, or graduate years; not renewable. *Number:* 1. *Amount:* $2000.

Eligibility Requirements: Applicant must be enrolled or expecting to enroll full- or part-time at a two-year or four-year institution or university and must have an interest in music/singing. Applicant or parent of applicant must be member of National Association of Pastoral Musicians. Available to U.S. and non-U.S. citizens.

Application Requirements: Application form, CD of performance, essay, financial need analysis, recommendations or references, resume. *Deadline:* March 5.

Contact: Ms. Kathleen Haley, Director of Membership Services
Phone: 240-247-3000
E-mail: haley@npm.org

NPM KOINONIA/BOARD OF DIRECTORS SCHOLARSHIP

Awards NPM members enrolled full-time or part-time in a graduate or undergraduate degree program of studies related to the field of pastoral music. Applicant must intend to work at least two years in the field of pastoral music following graduation or program completion.

Academic Fields/Career Goals: Music; Religion/Theology.

Award: Scholarship for use in freshman, sophomore, junior, senior, or graduate years; not renewable. *Number:* 1. *Amount:* $2000.

Eligibility Requirements: Applicant must be enrolled or expecting to enroll full- or part-time at a two-year or four-year institution or university and must have an interest in music/singing. Applicant or parent of applicant must be member of National Association of Pastoral Musicians. Available to U.S. and non-U.S. citizens.

Application Requirements: Application form, CD of performance, essay, financial need analysis, recommendations or references, resume. *Deadline:* March 5.

Contact: Ms. Kathleen Haley, Director of Membership Services
Phone: 240-247-3000
E-mail: haley@npm.org

NPM PERROT SCHOLARSHIP

Awards NPM members enrolled full-time or part-time in a graduate or undergraduate degree program of studies related to the field of pastoral music. Applicant must intend to work at least two years in the field of pastoral music following graduation or program completion.

Academic Fields/Career Goals: Music.

Award: Scholarship for use in freshman, sophomore, junior, senior, or graduate years; not renewable. *Number:* 1. *Amount:* $3000.

Eligibility Requirements: Applicant must be enrolled or expecting to enroll full- or part-time at a two-year or four-year institution or university. Applicant or parent of applicant must be member of National Association of Pastoral Musicians. Available to U.S. and non-U.S. citizens.

Application Requirements: Application form, CD of performance, essay, financial need analysis, recommendations or references, resume. *Deadline:* March 5.

Contact: Ms. Kathleen Haley, Director of Membership Services
Phone: 240-247-3000
E-mail: haley@npm.org

OREGON CATHOLIC PRESS SCHOLARSHIP

Awards NPM members enrolled full-time or part-time in a graduate or undergraduate degree program of studies related to the field of pastoral music. Applicant must intend to work at least two years in the field of pastoral music following graduation or program completion.

Academic Fields/Career Goals: Music; Religion/Theology.

Award: Scholarship for use in freshman, sophomore, junior, senior, or graduate years; not renewable. *Number:* 1. *Amount:* up to $2500.

Eligibility Requirements: Applicant must be enrolled or expecting to enroll full- or part-time at a two-year or four-year institution or university and must have an interest in music/singing. Available to U.S. and non-U.S. citizens.

Application Requirements: Application form, CD of performance, essay, financial need analysis, recommendations or references, resume. *Deadline:* March 5.

Contact: Ms. Kathleen Haley, Director of Membership Services
Phone: 240-247-3000
E-mail: haley@npm.org

PALUCH FAMILY FOUNDATION/WORLD LIBRARY PUBLICATIONS SCHOLARSHIP

Awards NPM members enrolled full-time or part-time in a graduate or undergraduate degree program of studies related to the field of pastoral music. Applicant must intend to work at least two years in the field of pastoral music following graduation or program completion.

Academic Fields/Career Goals: Music; Religion/Theology.

Award: Scholarship for use in freshman, sophomore, junior, senior, or graduate years; not renewable. *Number:* 1. *Amount:* up to $2500.

Eligibility Requirements: Applicant must be enrolled or expecting to enroll full- or part-time at a two-year or four-year institution or university and must have an interest in music/singing. Available to U.S. and non-U.S. citizens.

Application Requirements: Application form, CD of performance, essay, financial need analysis, recommendations or references, resume. *Deadline:* March 5.

Contact: Ms. Kathleen Haley, Director of Membership Services
Phone: 240-247-3000
E-mail: haley@npm.org

STEVEN C. WARNER SCHOLARSHIP

Scholarship for NPM members enrolled full-or part-time in an undergraduate or graduate pastoral music program. Applicant must intend to work at least two years in the field of pastoral music following graduation/program completion.

Academic Fields/Career Goals: Music.

Award: Scholarship for use in freshman, sophomore, junior, senior, or graduate years; not renewable. *Number:* 1. *Amount:* $1000.

Eligibility Requirements: Applicant must be enrolled or expecting to enroll full- or part-time at a two-year or four-year institution or university and must have an interest in music/singing. Applicant or parent of applicant must be member of National Association of Pastoral Musicians. Available to U.S. and non-U.S. citizens.

Application Requirements: Application form, CD of performance, essay, financial need analysis, recommendations or references, resume. *Deadline:* March 5.

Contact: Ms. Kathleen Haley, Director of Membership Services
Phone: 240-247-3000
E-mail: haley@npm.org

OREGON STUDENT ASSISTANCE COMMISSION

http://www.GetCollegeFunds.org/

FARROLD STEPHENS SCHOLARSHIP

Awards for students that have experience in vocal performance or music education. Must enroll at least half time as college junior or above for fall term working towards a degree as a vocal performer or music educator. Oregon residency is not required. Semifinalists will be invited to submit a non-returnable CD of a musical performance. FAFSA is required.

Academic Fields/Career Goals: Music.

Award: Scholarship for use in junior, senior, or graduate years; not renewable.

Eligibility Requirements: Applicant must be enrolled or expecting to enroll full- or part-time at a four-year institution or university. Available to U.S. citizens.

Application Requirements: Application form, financial need analysis. *Deadline:* March 1.

Contact: Melissa Adams, Scholarship Processing Coordinator
Phone: 541-687-7409
E-mail: melissa.adams@hecc.oregon.gov

LIMING AND ULMER MUSIC SCHOLARSHIP

Award for undergraduate students who are enrolled at least half-time at any public or non-profit college and majoring in music. Not open to high school seniors. Apply/compete annually.

Academic Fields/Career Goals: Music.

Award: Scholarship for use in sophomore, junior, or senior years; not renewable.

Eligibility Requirements: Applicant must be enrolled or expecting to enroll full- or part-time at a two-year or four-year institution or university. Available to U.S. citizens.

Application Requirements: Application form, financial need analysis. *Deadline:* March 1.

Contact: Melissa Adams, Scholarship Processing Coordinator
Phone: 541-687-7409
E-mail: melissa.adams@hecc.oregon.gov

TECHNICAL TRAINING FUND SCHOLARSHIP
• *See page 130*

PI LAMBDA THETA INC.

http://www.pilambda.org/

NADEEN BURKEHOLDER WILLIAMS MUSIC SCHOLARSHIP
• *See page 257*

POLISH ARTS CLUB OF BUFFALO SCHOLARSHIP FOUNDATION

http://www.pacb.bfn.org/

POLISH ARTS CLUB OF BUFFALO SCHOLARSHIP FOUNDATION TRUST
• *See page 130*

QUALITY BATH

www.qualitybath.com

QUALITYBATH.COM SCHOLARSHIP PROGRAM
• *See page 123*

QUEEN ELISABETH INTERNATIONAL MUSIC COMPETITION OF BELGIUM

http://www.qeimc.be

QUEEN ELISABETH COMPETITION

Competition is open to musicians who have already completed their training and who are ready to launch their international careers. The competition covers the following musical disciplines: piano, voice and violin.

Academic Fields/Career Goals: Music.

Award: Prize for use in freshman, sophomore, junior, senior, or graduate years; not renewable.

Eligibility Requirements: Applicant must be age 18-30; enrolled or expecting to enroll full- or part-time at a two-year or four-year or technical institution or university and must have an interest in music or music/singing. Available to U.S. and non-U.S. citizens.

Application Requirements: Application form, application form may be submitted online (http://www.qeimc.be), CD/DVD recording, personal photograph. *Fee:* $130. *Deadline:* January 15.

Contact: Michel-Etienne Van Neste, Secretary General
Phone: 32 2 213 40 50
Fax: 32 2 514 32 97
E-mail: info@qeimc.be

RHODE ISLAND FOUNDATION

http://www.rifoundation.org/

BACH ORGAN AND KEYBOARD MUSIC SCHOLARSHIP

Scholarship for college music majors who are Rhode Island residents or attending college in Rhode Island. Must demonstrate good grades, financial need, and be an ABO member. Must include music sample.

Academic Fields/Career Goals: Music.

Award: Scholarship for use in freshman, sophomore, junior, or senior years; not renewable. *Amount:* $800–$1000.

Eligibility Requirements: Applicant must be enrolled or expecting to enroll full-time at a two-year or four-year institution or university; resident of Rhode Island and must have an interest in music/singing. Available to U.S. citizens.

Application Requirements: Application form, financial need analysis, recommendations or references, self-addressed stamped envelope with application, transcript. *Deadline:* June 14.

Contact: Libby Monahan, Funds Administrator
Phone: 401-274-4564 Ext. 3117
E-mail: libbym@rifoundation.org

UNITED NEGRO COLLEGE FUND

http://www.uncf.org/

JOHN LENNON ENDOWED SCHOLARSHIP PROGRAM
• *See page 212*

RHYTHM NATION/JANET JACKSON SCHOLARSHIP
• *See page 132*

VSA

http://www.kennedy-center.org/education/vsa/

VSA INTERNATIONAL YOUNG SOLOISTS AWARD

Each year outstanding young musicians with disabilities from around the world receive the VSA International Young Soloists Award, $2,000, and the opportunity to perform at the John F. Kennedy Center for the Performing Arts in Washington, D.C., which is live-streamed and archived on the Kennedy Center website. This program is open to soloists and ensembles of any instrument or genre including classical, jazz, hip-hop, rock, and more!

Academic Fields/Career Goals: Music; Performing Arts.

Award: Prize for use in freshman, sophomore, junior, or senior years; not renewable. *Number:* 4. *Amount:* $2000.

Eligibility Requirements: Applicant must be hearing impaired, learning disabled, physically disabled, or visually impaired; age 14-25; enrolled or expecting to enroll full- or part-time at a four-year institution or university and must have an interest in music or music/singing. Applicant must be hearing impaired, learning disabled, physically disabled, or visually impaired. Available to U.S. and non-U.S. citizens.

Application Requirements: Application form. *Deadline:* February 8.

Contact: Megan Bailey, Administrative Assistant
VSA
2700 F St NW
Washington, DC 20566
Phone: 202-416-8822
E-mail: vsainfo@kennedy-center.org

WOMEN BAND DIRECTORS INTERNATIONAL

http://www.womenbanddirectors.org/

CHARLOTTE PLUMMER OWEN MEMORIAL SCHOLARSHIP
• *See page 262*

MARTHA ANN STARK MEMORIAL SCHOLARSHIP
• *See page 262*

VOLKWEIN MEMORIAL SCHOLARSHIP
• *See page 262*

NATURAL RESOURCES

AMERICAN ALPINE CLUB

https://americanalpineclub.org/

AAC RESEARCH GRANTS
• *See page 153*

AMERICAN GROUND WATER TRUST

http://www.agwt.org/

AMERICAN GROUND WATER TRUST-AMTROL INC. SCHOLARSHIP
• *See page 240*

AMERICAN GROUND WATER TRUST-BAROID SCHOLARSHIP
• *See page 241*

AMERICAN GROUND WATER TRUST-THOMAS STETSON SCHOLARSHIP
• *See page 241*

AMERICAN INDIAN SCIENCE AND ENGINEERING SOCIETY

http://www.aises.org/

A.T. ANDERSON MEMORIAL SCHOLARSHIP PROGRAM
• *See page 109*

AMERICAN PUBLIC POWER ASSOCIATION

http://publicpower.org/DEED

DEED EDUCATIONAL SCHOLARSHIP
• *See page 176*

DEED STUDENT INTERNSHIP
• *See page 176*

DEED STUDENT RESEARCH GRANTS
• *See page 191*

DEED TECHNICAL DESIGN PROJECT
• *See page 176*

AMERICAN SOCIETY OF AGRONOMY, CROP SCIENCE SOCIETY OF AMERICA, SOIL SCIENCE SOCIETY OF AMERICA

http://www.agronomy.org

J. FIELDING REED SCHOLARSHIP
• *See page 97*

AMERICAN WATER RESOURCES ASSOCIATION

http://www.awra.org/

AWRA RICHARD A. HERBERT MEMORIAL SCHOLARSHIP

At least two scholarships are available: one for full-time undergraduate student and one for a full-time graduate student, each working toward a degree in water resources. All applicants must be national AWRA members.

Academic Fields/Career Goals: Natural Resources.

Award: Scholarship for use in freshman, sophomore, junior, senior, or graduate years; not renewable. *Number:* 2–4. *Amount:* $1000–$2000.

Eligibility Requirements: Applicant must be enrolled or expecting to enroll full-time at a four-year institution or university. Available to U.S. and non-U.S. citizens.

Application Requirements: Application form, application form may be submitted online (http://www.awra.org), essay, recommendations or references, resume, transcript. *Deadline:* April 22.

Contact: Jacque Towner, Office Manager
American Water Resources Association
4 West Federal Street, PO Box 1626
Middleburg, VA 20118-1626
Phone: 540-687-8390
Fax: 540-687-8395
E-mail: info@awra.org

ARCTIC INSTITUTE OF NORTH AMERICA

http://www.arctic.ucalgary.ca/

JIM BOURQUE SCHOLARSHIP
• *See page 249*

ARIZONA HYDROLOGICAL SOCIETY

http://www.azhydrosoc.org/

ARIZONA HYDROLOGICAL SOCIETY SCHOLARSHIP
• *See page 241*

ARIZONA PROFESSIONAL CHAPTER OF AISES

http://www.aises.org/scholarships

ARIZONA PROFESSIONAL CHAPTER OF AISES SCHOLARSHIP
• *See page 294*

ASSOCIATION FOR WOMEN GEOSCIENTISTS (AWG)

http://www.awg.org/

AWG ETHNIC MINORITY SCHOLARSHIP
• *See page 241*

AWG MARIA LUISA CRAWFORD FIELD CAMP SCHOLARSHIP
• *See page 117*

AWG SALT LAKE CHAPTER (SLC) RESEARCH SCHOLARSHIP
• *See page 117*

JANET CULLEN TANAKA GEOSCIENCES UNDERGRADUATE SCHOLARSHIP
• *See page 117*

LONE STAR RISING CAREER SCHOLARSHIP
• *See page 242*

OSAGE CHAPTER UNDERGRADUATE SERVICE SCHOLARSHIP
• *See page 117*

SUSAN EKDALE MEMORIAL FIELD CAMP SCHOLARSHIP
• *See page 242*

ASSOCIATION OF CALIFORNIA WATER AGENCIES

http://www.acwa.com/

ASSOCIATION OF CALIFORNIA WATER AGENCIES SCHOLARSHIPS
• *See page 112*

CLAIR A. HILL SCHOLARSHIP
• *See page 112*

BHW GROUP

https://thebhwgroup.com/

BHW WOMEN IN STEM SCHOLARSHIP
• *See page 74*

B.O.G. PEST CONTROL

http://www.bogpestcontrol.com/

B.O.G. PEST CONTROL SCHOLARSHIP FUND
• *See page 155*

BROWN AND CALDWELL

http://www.brownandcaldwell.com

ECKENFELDER SCHOLARSHIP
• *See page 155*

MINORITY SCHOLARSHIP PROGRAM
• *See page 155*

CALIFORNIA GROUNDWATER ASSOCIATION

http://www.groundh2o.org/

CALIFORNIA GROUNDWATER ASSOCIATION SCHOLARSHIP
• *See page 372*

CONSERVATION FEDERATION OF MISSOURI

http://www.confedmo.org/

CHARLES P. BELL CONSERVATION SCHOLARSHIP
• *See page 320*

COSTA RICAN VACATIONS

http://www.vacationscostarica.com/

COSTA RICAN VACATIONS SCHOLARSHIP
• *See page 320*

GARDEN CLUB OF AMERICA

http://www.gcamerica.org/

ELIZABETH GARDNER NORWEB SUMMER ENVIRONMENTAL STUDIES SCHOLARSHIP
• *See page 98*

SARA SHALLENBERGER BROWN GCA NATIONAL PARKS CONSERVATION SCHOLARSHIP
• *See page 365*

GREATER KANAWHA VALLEY FOUNDATION

http://www.tgkvf.org/

LEOPOLD & ELIZABETH MARMET SCHOLARSHIP
• *See page 273*

GREAT MINDS IN STEM

www.greatmindsinstem.org

HISPANIC ENGINEER NATIONAL ACHIEVEMENT AWARDS CORPORATION SCHOLARSHIP PROGRAM
• *See page 106*

INDIANA WILDLIFE FEDERATION ENDOWMENT

http://www.indianawildlife.org/

CHARLES A. HOLT INDIANA WILDLIFE FEDERATION ENDOWMENT SCHOLARSHIP
• *See page 321*

INTERTRIBAL TIMBER COUNCIL

http://www.itcnet.org/

NATIVE AMERICAN NATURAL RESOURCE RESEARCH SCHOLARSHIP

The Intertribal Timber Council (ITC), in partnership with the USDA Forest Service Southern and Pacific Northwest Research Stations is pleased to announce scholarship opportunities for Native American students who are planning or currently conducting tribally relevant research in a natural resource issue. Application deadline is January 20, 2017, 5:00 p.m. PST Award: Up to $4,000. The ITC Research Scholarship is designed to support tribally relevant, natural resource based, research being conducted by Native American scholars (graduate or undergraduate).The ITC Research Sub-Committee will review and rank only those applications that completely address the following criteria: 1. letter of application. The letter must include your name, permanent mailing address, email address and phone number. Discuss your current educational program and how the proposed research fits into both your degree in natural resources and your future plans; 2. Resume; 3. evidence of validated enrollment in a federally recognized tribe or Alaska Native Corporation, as established by the U.S. Government. A photocopy of your enrollment card, front and back, or Certificate of Indian Blood (CIB) is sufficient; 4. mini research proposal. Please keep this concise (4 page maximum not counting budget and justification). Required elements include a) abstract stating research merit and explaining how this research is relevant to tribal natural resource interests b) timeline and methodology c) dissemination plan, including a tribal component d) budget and budget justification; 5. letters of reference/support from an academic advisor or committee member is required. Additionally, a second letter of support from a tribal resource manager or a tribal representative with tribal approval of the project or the relevancy of the project to the tribe is required. All requested material must be received by close of business (5:00 p.m. PST) January 20, 2017. Incomplete applications will not be considered. Applicatins should be submitted electronically by email (itc1@teleport.com), or (fax 503-282-1274).

Academic Fields/Career Goals: Natural Resources; Natural Sciences.

Award: Scholarship for use in senior or graduate years; not renewable. *Amount:* $4000.

Eligibility Requirements: Applicant must be American Indian/Alaska Native and enrolled or expecting to enroll full-time at a four-year institution or university. Available to U.S. citizens.

Application Requirements: Application form. *Deadline:* January 20.

Contact: Education Committee
Intertribal Timber Council
1112 NE 21st Avenue, Suite 4
Portland, OR 97232
Phone: 503-282-4296
Fax: 503-282-1274
E-mail: itc1@teleport.com

TRUMAN D. PICARD SCHOLARSHIP
• *See page 93*

THE LAND CONSERVANCY OF NEW JERSEY

http://tlc-nj.org/

ROGERS FAMILY SCHOLARSHIP
• *See page 243*

RUSSELL W. MYERS SCHOLARSHIP
• *See page 99*

LOUISIANA OFFICE OF STUDENT FINANCIAL ASSISTANCE

http://www.osfa.la.gov/

ROCKEFELLER STATE WILDLIFE SCHOLARSHIP
• *See page 157*

MONTANA FEDERATION OF GARDEN CLUBS

http://www.mtfgc.org/

LIFE MEMBER MONTANA FEDERATION OF GARDEN CLUBS SCHOLARSHIP
• *See page 243*

NATIONAL ASSOCIATION OF WATER COMPANIES-NEW JERSEY CHAPTER

http://www.nawc.org

NATIONAL ASSOCIATION OF WATER COMPANIES-NEW JERSEY CHAPTER SCHOLARSHIP
• *See page 80*

OHIO FORESTRY ASSOCIATION

http://www.ohioforest.org/

E. B MILLER MEMORIAL SCHOLARSHIP

Minimum of one scholarship will be awarded to provide assistance toward forest resource education to quality college students. Preference given to students attending Ohio colleges and universities.

Academic Fields/Career Goals: Natural Resources.

Award: Scholarship for use in freshman, sophomore, junior, or senior years; not renewable. *Number:* 1–2. *Amount:* $1000–$2000.

Eligibility Requirements: Applicant must be enrolled or expecting to enroll full-time at a two-year or four-year or technical institution or university and resident of Ohio. Available to U.S. citizens.

Application Requirements: Application form, essay. *Deadline:* April 15.

Contact: Gayla Fleming, Association Services
Ohio Forestry Association
1100-H Brandywine Boulevard
Zanesville, OH 43701
Phone: 888-388-7337 Ext. 5
E-mail: gayla@ohioforest.org

OREGON STUDENT ASSISTANCE COMMISSION

http://www.GetCollegeFunds.org/

ROYDEN M. BODLEY SCHOLARSHIP

• *See page 323*

OUTDOOR WRITERS ASSOCIATION OF AMERICA

http://www.owaa.org/

OUTDOOR WRITERS ASSOCIATION OF AMERICA - BODIE MCDOWELL SCHOLARSHIP AWARD

• *See page 207*

PADDLE CANADA

https://www.paddlecanada.com/

BILL MASON SCHOLARSHIP FUND

• *See page 257*

PLAN NEW HAMPSHIRE

www.plannh.org

PLAN NEW HAMPSHIRE SCHOLARSHIP AND PROGRAM

• *See page 123*

RAILWAY TIE ASSOCIATION

http://www.rta.org/

JOHN MABRY FORESTRY SCHOLARSHIP

One-time award to potential forestry industry leaders. Open to junior and senior undergraduates who will be enrolled in accredited forestry schools. One scholarship is also available to second-year students in a two-year college. Applications reviewed with emphasis on leadership qualities, career objectives, scholastic achievement, and financial need.

Academic Fields/Career Goals: Natural Resources.

Award: Scholarship for use in junior or senior years; not renewable. *Number:* 2. *Amount:* $2000.

Eligibility Requirements: Applicant must be enrolled or expecting to enroll full-time at a two-year or four-year or technical institution or university. Available to U.S. and Canadian citizens.

Application Requirements: Application form, essay, financial need analysis, personal photograph. *Deadline:* June 30.

Contact: Mrs. Barbara Stacey, Website and Committee Coordinator
Railway Tie Association
115 Commerce Drive, Suite C
Fayetteville, GA 30214
Phone: 770-460-5553
E-mail: ties@rta.org

ROCKY MOUNTAIN ELK FOUNDATION

http://www.rmef.org

WILDLIFE LEADERSHIP AWARDS

Program established to recognize, encourage and promote leadership among future wildlife management professionals. Candidates must be an undergraduate in a recognized wildlife program, have at least a junior standing (completed a minimum of 56 semester hours or 108 quarter hours), and have at least one semester or two quarters remaining in their degree program.

Academic Fields/Career Goals: Natural Resources; Natural Sciences.

Award: Scholarship for use in junior or senior years; not renewable. *Number:* 1–5. *Amount:* $3000.

Eligibility Requirements: Applicant must be enrolled or expecting to enroll full-time at a four-year institution or university and must have an interest in wildlife conservation/animal rescue. Available to U.S. and Canadian citizens.

Application Requirements: Application form. *Deadline:* March 1.

Contact: Toni O'Hara, Lands & Conservation Office Administrator
E-mail: tohara@rmef.org

SOCIETY FOR RANGE MANAGEMENT

http://www.rangelands.org/

MASONIC RANGE SCIENCE SCHOLARSHIP

• *See page 94*

SOIL AND WATER CONSERVATION SOCIETY

http://www.swcs.org

DONALD A. WILLIAMS SCHOLARSHIP SOIL CONSERVATION SCHOLARSHIP

• *See page 95*

SOIL AND WATER CONSERVATION SOCIETY-MISSOURI SHOW-ME CHAPTER

http://www.moswcs.org/

MO SHOW-ME CHAPTER SWCS SCHOLARSHIP

• *See page 95*

SOIL AND WATER CONSERVATION SOCIETY-NEW JERSEY CHAPTER

http://www.geocities.com/njswcs

EDWARD R. HALL SCHOLARSHIP

• *See page 95*

SOUTH DAKOTA BOARD OF REGENTS

http://www.sdbor.edu/

SOUTH DAKOTA BOARD OF REGENTS BJUGSTAD SCHOLARSHIP

• *See page 95*

TECHNICAL ASSOCIATION OF THE PULP & PAPER INDUSTRY (TAPPI)

http://www.tappi.org/

WILLIAM L. CULLISON SCHOLARSHIP

Scholarship provides incentive for students to pursue an academic path related to the pulp and paper industry. Eligible students must meet all criteria and will have completed two years of undergraduate school with two years (or three years in a five-year program) remaining. For details, refer to website http://www.tappi.org/s_tappi/doc.asp?CID=6101&DID=561682.

Academic Fields/Career Goals: Natural Resources; Paper and Pulp Engineering.

Award: Scholarship for use in junior or senior years; renewable. *Number:* 1–2. *Amount:* $2000–$4000.

Eligibility Requirements: Applicant must be enrolled or expecting to enroll full-time at a four-year institution or university. Available to U.S. and non-U.S. citizens.

Application Requirements: Application form. *Deadline:* May 1.

Contact: Mr. Laurence Womack, Director of Standards and Awards
Technical Association of the Pulp & Paper Industry (TAPPI)
15 Technology Parkway South
Peachtree Corners, GA 30092
Phone: 770-209-7276
E-mail: standards@tappi.org

UNITED STATES DEPARTMENT OF AGRICULTURE

http://www.usda.gov/

USDA/1994 TRIBAL SCHOLARS PROGRAM
• See page 102

UNITED STATES ENVIRONMENTAL PROTECTION AGENCY

http://www.epa.gov/enviroed

NATIONAL NETWORK FOR ENVIRONMENTAL MANAGEMENT STUDIES FELLOWSHIP
• See page 324

VIRGINIA ASSOCIATION OF SOIL AND WATER CONSERVATION DISTRICTS EDUCATIONAL FOUNDATION INC.

http://www.vaswcd.org/

VASWCD EDUCATIONAL FOUNDATION INC. SCHOLARSHIP AWARDS PROGRAM

Scholarship to provide financial support to Virginia residents majoring in, or showing a strong desire to major in, a course curriculum related to natural resource conservation and/or environmental studies. Applicants must be full-time students who have applied to an undergraduate freshman-level curriculum. Must rank in the top 20 percent of graduating class or have a 3.0 or greater GPA, and demonstrate an active interest in conservation. Recipients may reapply to their individual SWCD for scholarship consideration in ensuing years.

Academic Fields/Career Goals: Natural Resources.

Award: Scholarship for use in freshman year; not renewable. *Number:* 4. *Amount:* $1000.

Eligibility Requirements: Applicant must be high school student; planning to enroll or expecting to enroll full-time at a four-year institution or university and resident of Virginia. Applicant must have 3.0 GPA or higher. Available to U.S. citizens.

Application Requirements: Application form, essay, financial need analysis. *Deadline:* March 1.

Contact: Jennifer Hoysa, District Manager
  Phone: 540-316-6984 Ext. 6984
  E-mail: jennifer.hoysa@fauquiercounty.gov

WILSON ORNITHOLOGICAL SOCIETY

http://www.wilsonsociety.org/

GEORGE A. HALL/HAROLD F. MAYFIELD AWARD
• See page 108

PAUL A. STEWART AWARDS
• See page 108

NATURAL SCIENCES

AMERICAN ALPINE CLUB

https://americanalpineclub.org/

AAC RESEARCH GRANTS
• See page 153

AMERICAN CHEMICAL SOCIETY

http://www.acs.org/

AMERICAN CHEMICAL SOCIETY SCHOLARS PROGRAM
• See page 172

AMERICAN FOUNDATION FOR THE BLIND

http://www.afb.org/

PAUL W. RUCKES SCHOLARSHIP
• See page 214

AMERICAN INDIAN SCIENCE AND ENGINEERING SOCIETY

http://www.aises.org/

A.T. ANDERSON MEMORIAL SCHOLARSHIP PROGRAM
• See page 109

AMERICAN PHYSIOLOGICAL SOCIETY

http://www.the-aps.org

DAVID S. BRUCE AWARDS FOR EXCELLENCE IN UNDERGRADUATE RESEARCH
• See page 105

AMERICAN SOCIETY OF AGRONOMY, CROP SCIENCE SOCIETY OF AMERICA, SOIL SCIENCE SOCIETY OF AMERICA

http://www.agronomy.org

J. FIELDING REED SCHOLARSHIP
• See page 97

ARCTIC INSTITUTE OF NORTH AMERICA

http://www.arctic.ucalgary.ca/

JIM BOURQUE SCHOLARSHIP
• See page 249

ARMED FORCES COMMUNICATIONS AND ELECTRONICS ASSOCIATION, EDUCATIONAL FOUNDATION

http://www.afcea.org/site/?q=foundation/scholarships

STEM TEACHERS SCHOLARSHIP
• See page 111

ARRL FOUNDATION INC.

http://www.arrl.org/

CTRI/CHRIS SEEBER, KA1GEU, MEMORIAL SCHOLARSHIP
• See page 249

DAN HUETTL, WZ7U, MEMORIAL SCHOLARSHIP
• See page 280

LOIS MANLEY, K7LMZ, AND RANDALL PITCHFORD, WW7ZZ, SCHOLARSHIP
• See page 193

WIFDR SCHOLARSHIP
• *See page 112*

YASME FOUNDATION SCHOLARSHIP
• *See page 154*

ASSOCIATION FOR WOMEN GEOSCIENTISTS (AWG)

http://www.awg.org/

AWG ETHNIC MINORITY SCHOLARSHIP
• *See page 241*

AWG MARIA LUISA CRAWFORD FIELD CAMP SCHOLARSHIP
• *See page 117*

AWG SALT LAKE CHAPTER (SLC) RESEARCH SCHOLARSHIP
• *See page 117*

AWG UNDERGRADUATE EXCELLENCE IN PALEONTOLOGY AWARD
• *See page 112*

JANET CULLEN TANAKA GEOSCIENCES UNDERGRADUATE SCHOLARSHIP
• *See page 117*

LONE STAR RISING CAREER SCHOLARSHIP
• *See page 242*

SUSAN EKDALE MEMORIAL FIELD CAMP SCHOLARSHIP
• *See page 242*

ASSOCIATION OF CALIFORNIA WATER AGENCIES

http://www.acwa.com/

ASSOCIATION OF CALIFORNIA WATER AGENCIES SCHOLARSHIPS
• *See page 112*

CLAIR A. HILL SCHOLARSHIP
• *See page 112*

ASSOCIATION OF FORMER INTELLIGENCE OFFICERS

http://www.afio.com

AFIO UNDERGRADUATE AND GRADUATE SCHOLARSHIPS
• *See page 103*

ASSOCIATION ON AMERICAN INDIAN AFFAIRS, INC.

http://www.indian-affairs.org/

ELIZABETH AND SHERMAN ASCHE MEMORIAL SCHOLARSHIP FUND
• *See page 98*

AUDUBON SOCIETY OF WESTERN PENNSYLVANIA

http://www.aswp.org/

BEULAH FREY ENVIRONMENTAL SCHOLARSHIP
• *See page 319*

BARRY GOLDWATER SCHOLARSHIP AND EXCELLENCE IN EDUCATION FOUNDATION

https://goldwater.scholarsapply.org

BARRY M. GOLDWATER SCHOLARSHIP AND EXCELLENCE IN EDUCATION PROGRAM
• *See page 112*

BHW GROUP

https://thebhwgroup.com/

BHW WOMEN IN STEM SCHOLARSHIP
• *See page 74*

B.O.G. PEST CONTROL

http://www.bogpestcontrol.com/

B.O.G. PEST CONTROL SCHOLARSHIP FUND
• *See page 155*

BROWN AND CALDWELL

http://www.brownandcaldwell.com

ECKENFELDER SCHOLARSHIP
• *See page 155*

MINORITY SCHOLARSHIP PROGRAM
• *See page 155*

COMMUNITY FOUNDATION FOR GREATER ATLANTA, INC.

http://cfgreateratlanta.org/

JAMES M. AND VIRGINIA M. SMYTH SCHOLARSHIP
• *See page 128*

COMPHEALTH

http://www.comphealth.com

COMPHEALTH MEDICAL SCHOLARSHIP
• *See page 151*

CONSERVATION FEDERATION OF MISSOURI

http://www.confedmo.org/

CHARLES P. BELL CONSERVATION SCHOLARSHIP
• *See page 320*

THE ELECTROCHEMICAL SOCIETY

http://www.electrochem.org/

STUDENT RESEARCH AWARDS OF THE BATTERY DIVISION OF THE ELECTROCHEMICAL SOCIETY INC.
• *See page 113*

EXPLORERS CLUB

http://www.explorers.org/

YOUTH ACTIVITY FUND

Award given to college students or high school students pursuing a research project in the field of science. Applicants must have two letter of recommendation, one-page description of project, a budget or plan, and proof of student enrollment with dates.

Academic Fields/Career Goals: Natural Sciences; Science, Technology, and Society.

Award: Grant for use in freshman, sophomore, junior, or senior years; not renewable. *Number:* 10–30. *Amount:* $500–$5000.

Eligibility Requirements: Applicant must be enrolled or expecting to enroll full-time at a four-year institution or university. Available to U.S. and non-U.S. citizens.

Application Requirements: Application form, essay, financial need analysis, recommendations or references. *Deadline:* varies.

Contact: Annie Lee, Member Services
Explorers Club
46 East 70th Street
New York, NY 10021
Fax: 212-288-4449
E-mail: alee@explorers.org

GARDEN CLUB OF AMERICA

http://www.gcamerica.org/

FRANCES M. PEACOCK SCHOLARSHIP FOR NATIVE BIRD HABITAT

Up to $4500 award provides financial aid to study areas in the United States that provide seasonal habitat for threatened or endangered native birds and to tend useful information for land-management decisions. Open to college seniors and graduate students only (second-semester juniors may apply for their senior year).

Academic Fields/Career Goals: Natural Sciences.

Award: Scholarship for use in senior or graduate years; not renewable. *Amount:* $4500.

Eligibility Requirements: Applicant must be enrolled or expecting to enroll full- or part-time at a four-year institution or university. Available to U.S. citizens.

Application Requirements: Application form, essay. *Deadline:* January 15.

Contact: Prof. Irby Lovette, Scholarship Committee
Garden Club of America
Cornell Lab of Ornithology
159 Sapsucker Woods Road
Ithaca, NY 14850-1999
E-mail: ijl2@cornell.edu

GCA AWARD IN DESERT STUDIES
• *See page 121*

GCA SUMMER SCHOLARSHIP IN FIELD BOTANY
• *See page 364*

JOAN K. HUNT AND RACHEL M. HUNT SUMMER SCHOLARSHIP IN FIELD BOTANY
• *See page 364*

ZELLER SUMMER SCHOLARSHIP IN MEDICINAL BOTANY
• *See page 352*

GREAT MINDS IN STEM

www.greatmindsinstem.org

HISPANIC ENGINEER NATIONAL ACHIEVEMENT AWARDS CORPORATION SCHOLARSHIP PROGRAM
• *See page 106*

INTERTRIBAL TIMBER COUNCIL

http://www.itcnet.org/

NATIVE AMERICAN NATURAL RESOURCE RESEARCH SCHOLARSHIP
• *See page 435*

KENTUCKY ENERGY AND ENVIRONMENT CABINET

http://dep.ky.gov

ENVIRONMENTAL PROTECTION SCHOLARSHIP
• *See page 157*

MEDICAL SCRUBS COLLECTION

http://medicalscrubscollection.com

MEDICAL SCRUBS COLLECTION SCHOLARSHIP
• *See page 106*

NASA IDAHO SPACE GRANT CONSORTIUM

http://www.id.spacegrant.org/

NASA IDAHO SPACE GRANT CONSORTIUM SCHOLARSHIP PROGRAM
• *See page 157*

NASA MINNESOTA SPACE GRANT CONSORTIUM

http://www.aem.umn.edu/mnsgc

MINNESOTA SPACE GRANT CONSORTIUM SCHOLARSHIP PROGRAM
• *See page 142*

NATIONAL ASSOCIATION OF WATER COMPANIES-NEW JERSEY CHAPTER

http://www.nawc.org

NATIONAL ASSOCIATION OF WATER COMPANIES-NEW JERSEY CHAPTER SCHOLARSHIP
• *See page 80*

NEVADA NASA SPACE GRANT CONSORTIUM

http://www.nvspacegrant.org/

NATIONAL SPACE GRANT COLLEGE AND FELLOWSHIP PROGRAM
• *See page 114*

NEXTSTEPU

http://www.nextstepu.com/

$1,500 STEM SCHOLARSHIP
• *See page 106*

OREGON STUDENT ASSISTANCE COMMISSION

http://www.GetCollegeFunds.org/

ANDY AITKENHEAD SCHOLARSHIP
• *See page 115*

ROBERTS SCHOLARSHIP
• *See page 158*

ROYDEN M. BODLEY SCHOLARSHIP
• *See page 323*

SEHAR SALEHA AHMAD AND ABRAHIM EKRAMULLAH ZAFAR FOUNDATION SCHOLARSHIP
• *See page 115*

PADDLE CANADA

https://www.paddlecanada.com/

BILL MASON SCHOLARSHIP FUND
• *See page 257*

ROBERT H. MOLLOHAN FAMILY CHARITABLE FOUNDATION, INC.

http://www.mollohanfoundation.org/

JOHN M. MURPHY SCHOLARSHIP
The John M. Murphy Scholarship is a $500 scholarship that will be awarded to a Pendleton County High School senior who is planning to major in any natural science related field at a West Virginia college or university. Furthermore, the recipient will be eligible for summer internship opportunities within his or her field of study.

Academic Fields/Career Goals: Natural Sciences.

Award: Scholarship for use in senior year; not renewable. *Amount:* $500.

Eligibility Requirements: Applicant must be high school student; planning to enroll or expecting to enroll full- or part-time at a four-year institution or university; resident of West Virginia and studying in West Virginia. Available to U.S. citizens.

Application Requirements: Application form, essay, recommendations or references, resume, test scores, transcript.

Contact: Aime Shaffer, Program Manager
    Phone: 304-333-6783
    E-mail: ashaffer@wvhtf.org

ROCKY MOUNTAIN ELK FOUNDATION

http://www.rmef.org

WILDLIFE LEADERSHIP AWARDS
• *See page 436*

SCARLETT FAMILY FOUNDATION SCHOLARSHIP PROGRAM

http://www.scarlettfoundation.org/

SCHOLARSHIP FOR STUDENTS PURSUING A BUSINESS OR STEM DEGREE
• *See page 84*

SIGMA XI, THE SCIENTIFIC RESEARCH SOCIETY

http://www.sigmaxi.org/

SIGMA XI GRANTS-IN-AID OF RESEARCH
• *See page 101*

SOIL AND WATER CONSERVATION SOCIETY

http://www.swcs.org

DONALD A. WILLIAMS SCHOLARSHIP SOIL CONSERVATION SCHOLARSHIP
• *See page 95*

SOIL AND WATER CONSERVATION SOCIETY-MISSOURI SHOW-ME CHAPTER

http://www.moswcs.org/

MO SHOW-ME CHAPTER SWCS SCHOLARSHIP
• *See page 95*

SOIL AND WATER CONSERVATION SOCIETY-NEW JERSEY CHAPTER

http://www.geocities.com/njswcs

EDWARD R. HALL SCHOLARSHIP
• *See page 95*

TED ROLLINS AND TXG CAPITAL

http://www.txgcapital.com/

TED ROLLINS ECO SCHOLARSHIP
• *See page 168*

UNITED NATIONS ASSOCIATION OF CONNECTICUT

http://www.unausa.org

UNITED NATIONS ASSOCIATION OF CONNECTICUT SCHOLARSHIP
• *See page 133*

UNITED NEGRO COLLEGE FUND

http://www.uncf.org/

PROCTER & GAMBLE STEM SCHOLARSHIP
• *See page 116*

NEAR AND MIDDLE EAST STUDIES

ASSOCIATION OF FORMER INTELLIGENCE OFFICERS

http://www.afio.com

AFIO UNDERGRADUATE AND GRADUATE SCHOLARSHIPS
• *See page 103*

BHW GROUP

https://thebhwgroup.com/

BHW WOMEN IN STEM SCHOLARSHIP
• *See page 74*

ISLAMIC SCHOLARSHIP FUND

http://islamicscholarshipfund.org/

ISF NATIONAL SCHOLARSHIP
• *See page 108*

UNITED NATIONS ASSOCIATION OF CONNECTICUT

http://www.unausa.org

UNITED NATIONS ASSOCIATION OF CONNECTICUT SCHOLARSHIP
• *See page 133*

NEUROBIOLOGY

AMERICAN INDIAN SCIENCE AND ENGINEERING SOCIETY

http://www.aises.org/

A.T. ANDERSON MEMORIAL SCHOLARSHIP PROGRAM
• *See page 109*

AMERICAN PHYSIOLOGICAL SOCIETY

http://www.the-aps.org

DAVID S. BRUCE AWARDS FOR EXCELLENCE IN UNDERGRADUATE RESEARCH
• *See page 105*

AVACARE MEDICAL

https://avacaremedical.com

AVACARE MEDICAL SCHOLARSHIP
• *See page 105*

BARRY GOLDWATER SCHOLARSHIP AND EXCELLENCE IN EDUCATION FOUNDATION

https://goldwater.scholarsapply.org

BARRY M. GOLDWATER SCHOLARSHIP AND EXCELLENCE IN EDUCATION PROGRAM
• *See page 112*

BHW GROUP

https://thebhwgroup.com/

BHW WOMEN IN STEM SCHOLARSHIP
• *See page 74*

COMPHEALTH

http://www.comphealth.com

COMPHEALTH MEDICAL SCHOLARSHIP
• *See page 151*

CYNTHIA E. MORGAN SCHOLARSHIP FUND (CEMS)

http://www.cemsfund.com/

CYNTHIA E. MORGAN MEMORIAL SCHOLARSHIP FUND, INC.
• *See page 316*

THE EXPERT INSTITUTE

https://www.theexpertinstitute.com

ANNUAL HEALTHCARE AND LIFE SCIENCES SCHOLARSHIP
• *See page 156*

GREAT MINDS IN STEM

www.greatmindsinstem.org

HISPANIC ENGINEER NATIONAL ACHIEVEMENT AWARDS CORPORATION SCHOLARSHIP PROGRAM
• *See page 106*

KETAMINE CLINICS OF LOS ANGELES

http://www.ketamineclinics.com/

KETAMINE CLINICS OF LOS ANGELES SCHOLARSHIP PROGRAM
• *See page 152*

MEDICAL SCRUBS COLLECTION

http://medicalscrubscollection.com

MEDICAL SCRUBS COLLECTION SCHOLARSHIP
• *See page 106*

NEXTSTEPU

http://www.nextstepu.com/

$1,500 STEM SCHOLARSHIP
• *See page 106*

SCARLETT FAMILY FOUNDATION SCHOLARSHIP PROGRAM

http://www.scarlettfoundation.org/

SCHOLARSHIP FOR STUDENTS PURSUING A BUSINESS OR STEM DEGREE
• *See page 84*

NUCLEAR SCIENCE

AMERICAN CHEMICAL SOCIETY, RUBBER DIVISION

http://www.rubber.org/

AMERICAN CHEMICAL SOCIETY, RUBBER DIVISION UNDERGRADUATE SCHOLARSHIP
• *See page 109*

AMERICAN INDIAN SCIENCE AND ENGINEERING SOCIETY

http://www.aises.org/

A.T. ANDERSON MEMORIAL SCHOLARSHIP PROGRAM
• See page 109

AMERICAN NUCLEAR SOCIETY

http://www.ans.org/

AMERICAN NUCLEAR SOCIETY OPERATIONS AND POWER SCHOLARSHIP

Undergraduate scholarship for students who have completed two or more years in a course of study leading to a degree in nuclear science, nuclear engineering, or a nuclear-related field.

Academic Fields/Career Goals: Nuclear Science.

Award: Scholarship for use in junior or senior years; not renewable. *Number:* 1. *Amount:* $2500.

Eligibility Requirements: Applicant must be enrolled or expecting to enroll full- or part-time at a four-year institution or university. Available to U.S. citizens.

Application Requirements: Application form, recommendations or references, transcript. *Deadline:* February 1.

Contact: Scholarship Coordinator
American Nuclear Society
555 North Kensington Avenue
La Grange Park, IL 60526
Phone: 708-352-6611
Fax: 708-352-0499
E-mail: outreach@ans.org

AMERICAN NUCLEAR SOCIETY UNDERGRADUATE SCHOLARSHIPS

Maximum of four scholarships for students who have completed one year in a course of study leading to a degree in nuclear science, nuclear engineering, or a nuclear-related field and who will be sophomores in the upcoming academic year; and a maximum of twenty one scholarships for students who have completed two or more years and will be entering as juniors or seniors. Must be sponsored by ANS member or branch. Must be U.S. citizen or permanent resident.

Academic Fields/Career Goals: Nuclear Science.

Award: Scholarship for use in junior or senior years; not renewable. *Number:* 4–21. *Amount:* $2000.

Eligibility Requirements: Applicant must be enrolled or expecting to enroll full-time at a four-year institution or university. Available to U.S. citizens.

Application Requirements: Application form, recommendations or references, transcript. *Deadline:* February 1.

Contact: Scholarship Coordinator
American Nuclear Society
555 North Kensington Avenue
La Grange Park, IL 60526
Phone: 708-352-6611
Fax: 708-352-0499
E-mail: outreach@ans.org

ANS INCOMING FRESHMAN SCHOLARSHIP

Scholarship for graduating high school seniors who have enrolled or plan to enroll full-time in a nuclear engineering degree program. Scholarships will be awarded based on an applicant's high school academic achievement and course of undergraduate study.

Academic Fields/Career Goals: Nuclear Science.

Award: Scholarship for use in freshman year; not renewable. *Number:* 1–4. *Amount:* $1000.

Eligibility Requirements: Applicant must be high school student and planning to enroll or expecting to enroll full-time at a four-year institution or university. Available to U.S. and non-U.S. citizens.

Application Requirements: Application form, essay, recommendations or references, transcript. *Deadline:* April 1.

Contact: Scholarship Committee
American Nuclear Society
555 North Kensington Avenue
La Grange Park, IL 60526
Phone: 708-352-6611
Fax: 708-352-0499

CHARLES (TOMMY) THOMAS MEMORIAL SCHOLARSHIP DIVISION SCHOLARSHIP

Undergraduate scholarship for students who have completed two or more years in a course of study leading to a degree in nuclear science, nuclear engineering, or a nuclear-related field.

Academic Fields/Career Goals: Nuclear Science.

Award: Scholarship for use in junior or senior years; not renewable. *Number:* 1. *Amount:* $3000.

Eligibility Requirements: Applicant must be enrolled or expecting to enroll full-time at a four-year institution or university. Available to U.S. citizens.

Application Requirements: Application form, recommendations or references, transcript. *Deadline:* February 1.

Contact: Scholarship Coordinator
American Nuclear Society
555 North Kensington Avenue
La Grange Park, IL 60526
Phone: 708-352-6611
Fax: 708-352-0499
E-mail: outreach@ans.org

DECOMMISSIONING, DECONTAMINATION, AND REUTILIZATION UNDERGRADUATE SCHOLARSHIP
• See page 272

DELAYED EDUCATION FOR WOMEN SCHOLARSHIPS

One-time award given to enable mature women whose formal studies in nuclear science, nuclear engineering, or related fields have been delayed or interrupted at least one year. Must be U.S. citizen or permanent resident. Minimum GPA of 2.5 required.

Academic Fields/Career Goals: Nuclear Science.

Award: Scholarship for use in freshman, sophomore, junior, or senior years; not renewable. *Number:* 1. *Amount:* $5000.

Eligibility Requirements: Applicant must be enrolled or expecting to enroll full-time at a four-year institution or university and female. Applicant must have 2.5 GPA or higher. Available to U.S. citizens.

Application Requirements: Application form, financial need analysis, recommendations or references, transcript. *Deadline:* February 1.

Contact: Scholarship Coordinator
American Nuclear Society
555 North Kensington Avenue
La Grange Park, IL 60526
Phone: 708-352-6611
Fax: 708-352-0499
E-mail: outreach@ans.org

JOHN AND MURIEL LANDIS SCHOLARSHIP AWARDS

Maximum of eight scholarships are awarded to undergraduate and graduate students who have greater than average financial need. Applicants should be planning a career in nuclear science, nuclear engineering, or a nuclear related field and be enrolled or planning to enroll in a college or university located in the United States, but need not be U.S. citizens.

Academic Fields/Career Goals: Nuclear Science.

Award: Scholarship for use in freshman, sophomore, junior, senior, or graduate years; not renewable. *Number:* 1–8. *Amount:* $5000.

Eligibility Requirements: Applicant must be enrolled or expecting to enroll full-time at a four-year institution or university. Available to U.S. and non-U.S. citizens.

Application Requirements: Application form, financial need analysis, recommendations or references, transcript. *Deadline:* February 1.

Contact: Scholarship Coordinator
American Nuclear Society
555 North Kensington Avenue
La Grange Park, IL 60526
Phone: 708-352-6611
Fax: 708-352-0469
E-mail: outreach@ans.org

JOHN R. LAMARSH SCHOLARSHIP

Undergraduate scholarship for students who have completed two or more years in a course of study leading to a degree in nuclear science, nuclear engineering, or a nuclear-related field.

Academic Fields/Career Goals: Nuclear Science.

Award: Scholarship for use in junior or senior years; not renewable. *Number:* 1. *Amount:* $2000.

Eligibility Requirements: Applicant must be enrolled or expecting to enroll full- or part-time at a four-year institution or university. Available to U.S. citizens.

Application Requirements: Application form, recommendations or references, transcript. *Deadline:* February 1.

Contact: Scholarship Coordinator
American Nuclear Society
555 North Kensington Avenue
La Grange Park, IL 60526
Phone: 708-352-6611
Fax: 708-352-0499
E-mail: outreach@ans.org

JOSEPH R. DIETRICH SCHOLARSHIP

Undergraduate scholarship for students who have completed two or more years in a course of study leading to a degree in nuclear science, nuclear engineering, or a nuclear-related field.

Academic Fields/Career Goals: Nuclear Science.

Award: Scholarship for use in junior or senior years; not renewable. *Number:* 1. *Amount:* $2000.

Eligibility Requirements: Applicant must be enrolled or expecting to enroll full- or part-time at a four-year institution or university. Available to U.S. citizens.

Application Requirements: Application form, recommendations or references, transcript. *Deadline:* February 1.

Contact: Scholarship Coordinator
American Nuclear Society
555 North Kensington Avenue
La Grange Park, IL 60526
Phone: 708-352-6611
Fax: 708-352-0499
E-mail: outreach@ans.org

RAYMOND DISALVO SCHOLARSHIP

Undergraduate scholarship for students who have completed two or more years in a course of study leading to a degree in nuclear science, nuclear engineering, or a nuclear-related field.

Academic Fields/Career Goals: Nuclear Science.

Award: Scholarship for use in junior or senior years; not renewable. *Number:* 1–21. *Amount:* $2000.

Eligibility Requirements: Applicant must be enrolled or expecting to enroll full-time at a four-year institution or university. Available to U.S. and non-U.S. citizens.

Application Requirements: Application form, recommendations or references, sponsorship letter from ANS organization, transcript. *Deadline:* February 1.

Contact: Scholarship Coordinator
Phone: 708-352-6611
Fax: 708-352-0499
E-mail: outreach@ans.org

ROBERT G. LACY SCHOLARSHIP

Undergraduate scholarship for students who have completed two or more years in a course of study leading to a degree in nuclear science, nuclear engineering, or a nuclear-related field.

Academic Fields/Career Goals: Nuclear Science.

Award: Scholarship for use in junior or senior years; not renewable. *Number:* 1. *Amount:* $2000.

Eligibility Requirements: Applicant must be enrolled or expecting to enroll full-time at a four-year institution or university. Available to U.S. and non-U.S. citizens.

Application Requirements: Application form, recommendations or references, sponsorship letter from ANS organization, transcript. *Deadline:* February 1.

Contact: Scholarship Coordinator
Phone: 708-352-6611
Fax: 708-352-0499
E-mail: outreach@ans.org

ROBERT T. "BOB" LINER SCHOLARSHIP

Undergraduate scholarship for students who have completed two or more years in a course of study leading to a degree in nuclear science, nuclear engineering, or a nuclear-related field.

Academic Fields/Career Goals: Nuclear Science.

Award: Scholarship for use in junior or senior years; not renewable. *Number:* 1. *Amount:* $2000.

Eligibility Requirements: Applicant must be enrolled or expecting to enroll full-time at a four-year institution or university. Available to U.S. and non-U.S. citizens.

Application Requirements: Application form, recommendations or references, sponsorship letter from ANS organization, transcript. *Deadline:* February 1.

Contact: Scholarship Coordinator
Phone: 708-352-6611
Fax: 708-352-0499
E-mail: outreach@ans.org

AMERICAN SOCIETY OF NAVAL ENGINEERS

http://www.navalengineers.org/

AMERICAN SOCIETY OF NAVAL ENGINEERS SCHOLARSHIP
• See page 110

ARIZONA HYDROLOGICAL SOCIETY

http://www.azhydrosoc.org/

ARIZONA HYDROLOGICAL SOCIETY SCHOLARSHIP
• See page 241

ARRL FOUNDATION INC.

http://www.arrl.org/

CTRI/CHRIS SEEBER, KA1GEU, MEMORIAL SCHOLARSHIP
• See page 249

DAN HUETTL, WZ7U, MEMORIAL SCHOLARSHIP
• See page 280

LOIS MANLEY, K7LMZ, AND RANDALL PITCHFORD, WW7ZZ, SCHOLARSHIP
• See page 193

W1FDR SCHOLARSHIP
• See page 112

BARRY GOLDWATER SCHOLARSHIP AND EXCELLENCE IN EDUCATION FOUNDATION

https://goldwater.scholarsapply.org

BARRY M. GOLDWATER SCHOLARSHIP AND EXCELLENCE IN EDUCATION PROGRAM
• See page 112

BHW GROUP

https://thebhwgroup.com/

BHW WOMEN IN STEM SCHOLARSHIP
• *See page 74*

COMPHEALTH

http://www.comphealth.com

COMPHEALTH MEDICAL SCHOLARSHIP
• *See page 151*

GREAT MINDS IN STEM

www.greatmindsinstem.org

HISPANIC ENGINEER NATIONAL ACHIEVEMENT AWARDS CORPORATION SCHOLARSHIP PROGRAM
• *See page 106*

NASA MINNESOTA SPACE GRANT CONSORTIUM

http://www.aem.umn.edu/mnsgc

MINNESOTA SPACE GRANT CONSORTIUM SCHOLARSHIP PROGRAM
• *See page 142*

NEXTSTEPU

http://www.nextstepu.com/

$1,500 STEM SCHOLARSHIP
• *See page 106*

OREGON STUDENT ASSISTANCE COMMISSION

http://www.GetCollegeFunds.org/

ANDY AITKENHEAD SCHOLARSHIP
• *See page 115*

SCARLETT FAMILY FOUNDATION SCHOLARSHIP PROGRAM

http://www.scarlettfoundation.org/

SCHOLARSHIP FOR STUDENTS PURSUING A BUSINESS OR STEM DEGREE
• *See page 84*

SIGMA XI, THE SCIENTIFIC RESEARCH SOCIETY

http://www.sigmaxi.org/

SIGMA XI GRANTS-IN-AID OF RESEARCH
• *See page 101*

TAILOR MADE LAWNS

http://www.tailormadelawns.com

2017 TAILOR MADE LAWNS SCHOLARSHIP FUND
• *See page 102*

UNITED NATIONS ASSOCIATION OF CONNECTICUT

http://www.unausa.org

UNITED NATIONS ASSOCIATION OF CONNECTICUT SCHOLARSHIP
• *See page 133*

UNITED NEGRO COLLEGE FUND

http://www.uncf.org/

PROCTER & GAMBLE STEM SCHOLARSHIP
• *See page 116*

UNIVERSITIES SPACE RESEARCH ASSOCIATION

http://www.usra.edu/

UNIVERSITIES SPACE RESEARCH ASSOCIATION SCHOLARSHIP AWARD PROGRAM
• *See page 116*

NURSING

AIR FORCE RESERVE OFFICER TRAINING CORPS

http://www.afrotc.com/

AIR FORCE ROTC FOUR-YEAR NURSING SCHOLARSHIP
Scholarship offers qualified individuals the chance to compete for scholarships of up to $15,000 per academic year. Nursing students can compete for scholarships through the In-College Scholarship Program, or may qualify for a nursing scholarship.

Academic Fields/Career Goals: Nursing.

Award: Scholarship for use in sophomore, junior, or senior years; not renewable. *Amount:* up to $15,000.

Eligibility Requirements: Applicant must be enrolled or expecting to enroll full-time at a four-year institution or university. Available to U.S. citizens.

Application Requirements: Application form. *Deadline:* varies.

Contact: Capt. Elmarko Magee, Chief of Advertising
Air Force Reserve Officer Training Corps
551 East Maxwell Boulevard
Maxwell AFB, AL 36112-6106
Phone: 866-423-7682

ALBERTA HERITAGE SCHOLARSHIP FUND

http://www.alis.alberta.ca/

ABORIGINAL HEALTH CAREERS BURSARY
• *See page 153*

AMARILLO AREA FOUNDATION

http://www.amarilloareafoundation.org/

E. EUGENE WAIDE, MD MEMORIAL SCHOLARSHIP
Scholarship for graduating senior from Ochiltree, Hansford, Lipscomb, Hutchinson, Roberts or Hemphill counties. Applicant must pursue a career as LVN, BSN (junior or senior), or MSN.

Academic Fields/Career Goals: Nursing.

Award: Scholarship for use in freshman, sophomore, junior, senior, or graduate years; not renewable.

Eligibility Requirements: Applicant must be enrolled or expecting to enroll full- or part-time at a two-year or four-year or technical institution or university and resident of Texas. Available to U.S. citizens.

Application Requirements: Application form, personal photograph. *Deadline:* February 1.

Contact: Scholarship Screening Committee
Phone: 806-376-4521
Fax: 806-373-3656

NANCY GERALD MEMORIAL NURSING SCHOLARSHIP

Scholarship of $500 for graduating senior from one of the 26 counties in Texas. Applicant must be majoring in the field of nursing at Amarillo College or West Texas A & M University pursuing AAS, BSN, or MSN degree.

Academic Fields/Career Goals: Nursing.

Award: Scholarship for use in freshman, sophomore, junior, senior, or graduate years; not renewable. *Amount:* $500.

Eligibility Requirements: Applicant must be enrolled or expecting to enroll full- or part-time at a two-year or four-year institution or university; resident of Texas and studying in Texas. Applicant must have 2.5 GPA or higher. Available to U.S. citizens.

Application Requirements: Application form, personal photograph. *Deadline:* February 1.

Contact: Scholarship Screening Committee
Phone: 806-376-4521
Fax: 806-373-3656

AMERICAN INDIAN SCIENCE AND ENGINEERING SOCIETY

http://www.aises.org/

A.T. ANDERSON MEMORIAL SCHOLARSHIP PROGRAM
• See page 109

AMERICAN LEGION AUXILIARY DEPARTMENT OF ARIZONA

http://wwwaladeptaz.org

AMERICAN LEGION AUXILIARY DEPARTMENT OF ARIZONA NURSES' SCHOLARSHIPS

Award for Arizona residents enrolled in their second year at an institution in Arizona awarding degrees as a registered nurse. Preference given to immediate family member of a veteran. Must be a U.S. citizen and resident of Arizona for one year.

Academic Fields/Career Goals: Nursing.

Award: Scholarship for use in freshman, sophomore, junior, senior, or graduate years; not renewable. *Number:* 4. *Amount:* $600.

Eligibility Requirements: Applicant must be enrolled or expecting to enroll full- or part-time at a two-year or four-year or technical institution or university; resident of Arizona and studying in Arizona. Available to U.S. citizens.

Application Requirements: Application form, essay, financial need analysis, personal photograph. *Deadline:* May 15.

Contact: Mrs. Barbara Matteson, Department Secretary and Treasurer
American Legion Auxiliary Department of Arizona
4701 North 19th Avenue, Suite 100
Phoenix, AZ 85015-3727
Phone: 602-241-1080
E-mail: secretary@aladeptaz.org

AMERICAN LEGION AUXILIARY DEPARTMENT OF CALIFORNIA

http://www.calegionaux.org/

AMERICAN LEGION AUXILIARY DEPARTMENT OF CALIFORNIA PAST PRESIDENTS' PARLEY NURSING SCHOLARSHIPS

Award for student entering into or continuing studies in a nursing program.

Academic Fields/Career Goals: Nursing.

Award: Scholarship for use in freshman, sophomore, junior, or senior years; not renewable. *Number:* 1–2. *Amount:* $4000–$4000.

Eligibility Requirements: Applicant must be enrolled or expecting to enroll full- or part-time at a four-year institution or university and resident of California. Available to U.S. citizens. Applicant must have general military experience.

Application Requirements: Application form, recommendations or references, transcript. *Deadline:* April 4.

Contact: Ruby Kapsalis, Secretary/Treasurer
Phone: 415-862-5092
Fax: 415-861-8365
E-mail: calegionaux@calegionaux.org

AMERICAN LEGION AUXILIARY DEPARTMENT OF COLORADO

http://www.alacolorado.com

AMERICAN LEGION AUXILIARY DEPARTMENT OF COLORADO PAST PRESIDENTS' PARLEY HEALTH CARE PROFESSIONAL SCHOLARSHIPNURSES SCHOLARSHIP
• See page 133

AMERICAN LEGION AUXILIARY DEPARTMENT OF IDAHO

http://www.idahoala.org/

AMERICAN LEGION AUXILIARY DEPARTMENT OF IDAHO NURSING SCHOLARSHIP

Scholarship available to veterans or the children of veterans who are majoring in nursing. Applicants must be 17 to 35 years of age and residents of Idaho for five years prior to applying. One-time award of $1000.

Academic Fields/Career Goals: Nursing.

Award: Scholarship for use in freshman, sophomore, junior, or senior years; not renewable. *Number:* 1. *Amount:* $1000.

Eligibility Requirements: Applicant must be age 17-35; enrolled or expecting to enroll full- or part-time at a four-year institution or university and resident of Idaho. Available to U.S. citizens. Applicant or parent must meet one or more of the following requirements: general military experience; retired from active duty; disabled or killed as a result of military service; prisoner of war; or missing in action.

Application Requirements: Application form, financial need analysis, personal photograph, recommendations or references, self-addressed stamped envelope with application, transcript. *Deadline:* May 15.

Contact: Mary Sue Chase, Secretary
American Legion Auxiliary Department of Idaho
905 Warren Street
Boise, ID 83706-3825
Phone: 208-342-7066
Fax: 208-342-7066
E-mail: idalegionaux@msn.com

AMERICAN LEGION AUXILIARY DEPARTMENT OF IOWA

http://www.ialegion.org/ala

AMERICAN LEGION AUXILIARY DEPARTMENT OF IOWA M.V. MCCRAE MEMORIAL NURSES MERIT AWARD

One-time award available to the child of an Iowa American Legion Post member or Iowa American Legion Auxiliary Unit member. Award is for full-time study in an accredited nursing program. Must be U.S. citizen and Iowa resident. Must attend an Iowa institution.

Academic Fields/Career Goals: Nursing.

Award: Scholarship for use in freshman, sophomore, junior, or senior years; not renewable. *Number:* 1. *Amount:* $400.

Eligibility Requirements: Applicant must be enrolled or expecting to enroll full-time at a two-year or four-year or technical institution or university; resident of Iowa and studying in Iowa. Applicant or parent of applicant must be member of American Legion or Auxiliary. Available to U.S. citizens. Applicant or parent must meet one or more of the following requirements: general military experience; retired from active duty; disabled or killed as a result of military service; prisoner of war; or missing in action.

Application Requirements: Application form, essay, financial need analysis, personal photograph, recommendations or references, self-addressed stamped envelope with application, test scores, transcript. *Deadline:* June 1.

Contact: Marlene Valentine, Secretary and Treasurer
American Legion Auxiliary Department of Iowa
720 Lyon Street
Des Moines, IA 50309
Phone: 515-282-7987
Fax: 515-282-7583
E-mail: alasectreas@ialegion.org

AMERICAN LEGION AUXILIARY DEPARTMENT OF MAINE

http://www.mainelegion.org/

AMERICAN LEGION AUXILIARY DEPARTMENT OF MAINE PAST PRESIDENTS' PARLEY NURSES SCHOLARSHIP
• See page 347

AMERICAN LEGION AUXILIARY DEPARTMENT OF MICHIGAN

http://www.michalaux.org/

AMERICAN LEGION AUXILIARY DEPARTMENT OF MICHIGAN MEDICAL CAREER SCHOLARSHIP
• See page 347

AMERICAN LEGION AUXILIARY DEPARTMENT OF MISSOURI

http://www.missourilegion.org/

AMERICAN LEGION AUXILIARY DEPARTMENT OF MISSOURI PAST PRESIDENTS' PARLEY SCHOLARSHIP

Scholarship of $500 is awarded to high school graduate who has chosen to study nursing. $500 will be awarded upon receipt of verification from the college that student is enrolled. The applicant must be a resident of Missouri and a member of a veteran's family. The applicant must be validated by the sponsoring unit. Check with sponsoring unit for details on required recommendation letters.

Academic Fields/Career Goals: Nursing.

Award: Scholarship for use in freshman year; not renewable. *Number:* 2. *Amount:* $500.

Eligibility Requirements: Applicant must be high school student; planning to enroll or expecting to enroll full-time at a two-year or four-year or technical institution or university and resident of Missouri. Applicant or parent of applicant must be member of American Legion or Auxiliary. Available to U.S. citizens. Applicant or parent must meet one or more of the following requirements: general military experience; retired from active duty; disabled or killed as a result of military service; prisoner of war; or missing in action.

Application Requirements: Application form, personal photograph, resume. *Deadline:* March 1.

Contact: Karen Larson, Department Secretary/Treasurer
American Legion Auxiliary Department of Missouri
600 Ellis Boulevard
Jefferson City, MO 65101
Phone: 573-636-9133
Fax: 573-635-3467
E-mail: dptmoala@embarqmail.com

AMERICAN LEGION AUXILIARY DEPARTMENT OF NORTH DAKOTA

http://www.ndlegion.org/

AMERICAN LEGION AUXILIARY DEPARTMENT OF NORTH DAKOTA PAST PRESIDENTS' PARLEY NURSES SCHOLARSHIP

One-time award for North Dakota resident who is the child, grandchild, or great-grandchild of a member of the American Legion or Auxiliary. Must be a graduate of a North Dakota high school and attending a nursing program in North Dakota. A minimum 2.5 GPA is required.

Academic Fields/Career Goals: Nursing.

Award: Scholarship for use in freshman year; not renewable. *Number:* 5. *Amount:* $500.

Eligibility Requirements: Applicant must be enrolled or expecting to enroll full- or part-time at a four-year institution or university; resident of North Dakota and studying in North Dakota. Applicant or parent of applicant must be member of American Legion or Auxiliary. Applicant must have 2.5 GPA or higher. Available to U.S. citizens. Applicant or parent must meet one or more of the following requirements: general military experience; retired from active duty; disabled or killed as a result of military service; prisoner of war; or missing in action.

Application Requirements: Application form, driver's license, essay, financial need analysis, self-addressed stamped envelope with application, test scores, transcript. *Deadline:* May 15.

Contact: Myrna Ronholm, Department Secretary
American Legion Auxiliary Department of North Dakota
PO Box 1060
Jamestown, ND 58402-1060
Phone: 701-253-5992
E-mail: ala-hq@ndlegion.org

AMERICAN LEGION AUXILIARY DEPARTMENT OF OHIO

http://www.alaohio.org/

AMERICAN LEGION AUXILIARY DEPARTMENT OF OHIO PAST PRESIDENTS' PARLEY NURSES SCHOLARSHIP

One-time award worth $300 to $500 for Ohio residents who are the children or grandchildren of a veteran, living or deceased. Must enroll or be enrolled in a nursing program. Application requests must be received by May 1.

Academic Fields/Career Goals: Nursing.

Award: Scholarship for use in freshman, sophomore, junior, or senior years; not renewable. *Number:* 15–20. *Amount:* $300–$500.

Eligibility Requirements: Applicant must be enrolled or expecting to enroll full-time at a two-year or four-year institution or university and resident of Ohio. Available to U.S. citizens. Applicant or parent must meet one or more of the following requirements: general military experience; retired from active duty; disabled or killed as a result of military service; prisoner of war; or missing in action.

Application Requirements: Application form, recommendations or references. *Deadline:* May 1.

Contact: Katie Tucker, Scholarship Coordinator
Phone: 740-452-8245
Fax: 740-452-2620
E-mail: ala_katie@rrohio.com

AMERICAN LEGION AUXILIARY DEPARTMENT OF OREGON

http://www.alaoregon.org/

AMERICAN LEGION AUXILIARY DEPARTMENT OF OREGON NURSES SCHOLARSHIP

One-time award for Oregon residents who are in their senior year of high school, who are the children of veterans who served during eligibility dates for American Legion membership. Must enroll in a nursing program. Contact local units for application.

Academic Fields/Career Goals: Nursing.

Award: Scholarship for use in freshman year; not renewable. *Number:* 1. *Amount:* $1500.

Eligibility Requirements: Applicant must be high school student; planning to enroll or expecting to enroll full- or part-time at a four-year institution or university and resident of Oregon. Available to U.S. citizens.

Application Requirements: Application form, essay, financial need analysis, interview. *Deadline:* March 20.

Contact: Virginia Biddle, Secretary/Treasurer
American Legion Auxiliary Department of Oregon
PO Box 1730
Wilsonville, OR 97070
Phone: 503-682-3162
E-mail: alaor@pcez.com

AMERICAN LEGION AUXILIARY DEPARTMENT OF PENNSYLVANIA

http://pa-legion.com

AMERICAN LEGION AUXILIARY DEPARTMENT OF PENNSYLVANIA PAST DEPARTMENT PRESIDENTS' MEMORIAL SCHOLARSHIP

Renewable award of $400 given each year to high school seniors. Must be residents of Pennsylvania. Total award $1200

Academic Fields/Career Goals: Nursing.

Award: Scholarship for use in freshman, sophomore, or junior years; renewable. *Number:* 1. *Amount:* $1200.

Eligibility Requirements: Applicant must be high school student; planning to enroll or expecting to enroll full-time at a four-year institution or university; single; resident of Pennsylvania and studying in Pennsylvania. Available to U.S. citizens.

Application Requirements: Application form. *Deadline:* March 15.

Contact: Colleen Watson, Executive Secretary and Treasurer
Phone: 717-763-7545
Fax: 717-763-0617
E-mail: paalad@hotmail.com

AMERICAN LEGION AUXILIARY DEPARTMENT OF WISCONSIN

http://www.amlegionauxwi.org/

AMERICAN LEGION AUXILIARY DEPARTMENT OF WISCONSIN PAST PRESIDENTS' PARLEY REGISTERED NURSE SCHOLARSHIP

One-time award of $1000. Applicant must be in nursing school or have positive acceptance to an accredited hospital or university registered nursing program. Applicant must be a direct descendant, wife, or widow of a veteran. Must submit certification of an American Legion Auxiliary unit president, copy of proof that veteran was in service (i.e. discharge papers), letters of recommendation, transcripts, and essay. Must have minimum 3.5 GPA, show financial need, and be a resident of Wisconsin or member of the Wisconsin American Legion Family. Applications available on website http://www.amlegionauxwi.org.

Academic Fields/Career Goals: Nursing.

Award: Scholarship for use in freshman, sophomore, junior, or senior years; not renewable. *Number:* 1–2. *Amount:* $1000.

Eligibility Requirements: Applicant must be enrolled or expecting to enroll full- or part-time at an institution or university and resident of Wisconsin. Applicant or parent of applicant must be member of American Legion or Auxiliary. Applicant must have 3.5 GPA or higher. Available to U.S. citizens. Applicant or parent must meet one or more of the following requirements: general military experience; retired from active duty; disabled or killed as a result of military service; prisoner of war; or missing in action.

Application Requirements: Application form, essay, financial need analysis. *Deadline:* March 15.

Contact: Bonnie Dorniak, Department Secretary
American Legion Auxiliary Department of Wisconsin
PO Box 140
Portage, WI 53901
Phone: 608-745-0124
Fax: 608-745-1947
E-mail: deptsec@amlegionauxwi.org

AMERICAN LEGION DEPARTMENT OF KANSAS

http://www.ksamlegion.org/

HOBBLE (LPN) NURSING SCHOLARSHIP

Award of $300, payable one-time at the start of the first semester. Awarded only upon acceptance and verification of enrollment by the scholarship winner in an accredited Kansas school which awards a diploma for Licensed Practical Nursing (LPN). Must pursue this profession in a health related institution such as a nursing home or hospital in Kansas. Must have attained the age of 18 prior to taking the Kansas state board examination. Must be a Kansas resident.

Academic Fields/Career Goals: Nursing.

Award: Scholarship for use in freshman year; not renewable. *Number:* 1. *Amount:* $300.

Eligibility Requirements: Applicant must be enrolled or expecting to enroll full-time at a two-year or technical institution; resident of Kansas and studying in Kansas. Available to U.S. citizens.

Application Requirements: Application form, essay, financial need analysis, personal photograph. *Deadline:* February 15.

Contact: Mike Oppy, Chairman, Scholarship Committee
American Legion Department of Kansas
1314 SW Topeka Boulevard
Topeka, KS 66612
Phone: 785-232-9315

AMERICAN LEGION DEPARTMENT OF MISSOURI

http://www.missourilegion.org/

M.D. "JACK" MURPHY MEMORIAL SCHOLARSHIP

One $750 award for two successive semesters will be given to a Missouri resident who is a RN and under the age of 21. Applicant must be unmarried and a descendant of a veteran with at least ninety days active service in the U.S. Army, Navy, Air Force, Marines, or Coast Guard receiving a Honorable Discharge for service. Applicant must have graduated in the top forty percent of their high school class or have a "C" average or equivalent.

Academic Fields/Career Goals: Nursing.

Award: Scholarship for use in freshman year; not renewable. *Number:* 1. *Amount:* $750.

Eligibility Requirements: Applicant must be high school student; planning to enroll or expecting to enroll full-time at a two-year or four-year institution or university; single female and resident of Missouri. Available to U.S. citizens. Applicant or parent must meet one or more of the following requirements: general military experience; retired from active duty; disabled or killed as a result of military service; prisoner of war; or missing in action.

Application Requirements: Application form, copy of the veteran's discharge or separation notice, financial need analysis, test scores. *Deadline:* April 20.

Contact: John Doane, Chairman
American Legion Department of Missouri
PO Box 179
Jefferson City, MO 65102-0179
Phone: 417-924-8186
Fax: 573-893-2980

ARRL FOUNDATION INC.

http://www.arrl.org/

CAROLE J. STREETER, KB9JBR, SCHOLARSHIP
• *See page 236*

ASSOCIATION ON AMERICAN INDIAN AFFAIRS, INC.

http://www.indian-affairs.org/

ELIZABETH AND SHERMAN ASCHE MEMORIAL SCHOLARSHIP FUND
• *See page 98*

AVACARE MEDICAL

https://avacaremedical.com

AVACARE MEDICAL SCHOLARSHIP
• *See page 105*

BESTNURSINGDEGREE.COM

http://www.bestnursingdegree.com

2017 BACK TO SCHOOL NURSING SCHOLARSHIP PROGRAM

Are you ready to chase your dream of becoming a nurse, but aren't sure how you'll pay for your education? We want to help you realize your dream of becoming a nurse by offering you the chance to win a $2,500 nursing scholarship. A winner will be randomly selected from the list of all eligible candidates. We award four different scholarships each year. When one deadline ends, the next scholarship will begin. Deadlines are as follows: January 31, April 30, July 30, and October 31. Apply for the scholarship at http://www.bestnursingdegree.com/scholarship/

Academic Fields/Career Goals: Nursing.

Award: Scholarship for use in freshman, sophomore, junior, senior, or graduate years; not renewable. *Number:* 1. *Amount:* $2500.

Eligibility Requirements: Applicant must be enrolled or expecting to enroll full- or part-time at a two-year or four-year or technical institution or university. Available to U.S. and non-U.S. citizens.

Application Requirements: Application form. *Deadline:* continuous.

Contact: Joann Do, Website Specialist
BestNursingDegree.com
15500 West 113th Street, #200
Lenexa, KS 66219
Phone: 913-254-6742
E-mail: joann.do@keypathedu.com

BHW GROUP

https://thebhwgroup.com/

BHW WOMEN IN STEM SCHOLARSHIP
• *See page 74*

CANADIAN NURSES FOUNDATION

http://www.cnf-fiic.ca/

CANADIAN NURSES FOUNDATION SCHOLARSHIPS

Study awards are granted annually to Canadian nurses wishing to pursue education and research. Must be a Canadian citizen or permanent resident and provide proof of citizenship. Must be studying in Canada at a Canadian institution. Baccalaureate students must be full-time, masters and doctoral students may be full- or part-time. Additional restrictions vary by specific scholarship.

Academic Fields/Career Goals: Nursing.

Award: Scholarship for use in sophomore, junior, senior, graduate, or postgraduate years; not renewable. *Number:* 50–60. *Amount:* $1500–$9000.

Eligibility Requirements: Applicant must be Canadian citizen and enrolled or expecting to enroll full- or part-time at a four-year institution or university. Applicant or parent of applicant must have employment or volunteer experience in nursing.

Application Requirements: Application form, community service. *Fee:* $30. *Deadline:* March 31.

Contact: Foundation Coordinator
Canadian Nurses Foundation
50 Driveway
Ottawa, ON
CAN
Phone: 613-680-0879 Ext. 221
E-mail: info@cnf-fiic.ca

CHRISTIANA CARE HEALTH SYSTEMS

http://www.christianacare.org/

RUTH SHAW JUNIOR BOARD SCHOLARSHIP
• *See page 350*

COMPHEALTH

http://www.comphealth.com

COMPHEALTH MEDICAL SCHOLARSHIP
• *See page 151*

CRUSH THE CPA EXAM

http://crushthecpaexam.com

CRUSH THE NCLEX SCHOLARSHIP PROGRAM

One Grand Prize Winner will receive $300 toward cost of licensure for the NCLEX plus free access to a Graduate review course that is valued at $289! This is an annual scholarship for nursing candidates who need to get certified. Applicants must enter prior to May 31st, 2017, when the winner will be chosen and announced by our staff.

Academic Fields/Career Goals: Nursing.

Award: Scholarship for use in junior, senior, or graduate years; not renewable. *Number:* 1. *Amount:* $500–$589.

Eligibility Requirements: Applicant must be enrolled or expecting to enroll full-time at a four-year institution or university. Applicant must have 3.0 GPA or higher. Available to U.S. and non-U.S. citizens.

Application Requirements: Application form, essay. *Deadline:* May 31.

Contact: Stephanie Murguia
E-mail: stephanie@crushempire.com

CYNTHIA E. MORGAN SCHOLARSHIP FUND (CEMS)

http://www.cemsfund.com/

CYNTHIA E. MORGAN MEMORIAL SCHOLARSHIP FUND, INC.
• *See page 316*

DELAWARE COMMUNITY FOUNDATION

https://delcf.org/

MARGARET A. STAFFORD NURSING SCHOLARSHIP

Must be a resident of Delaware to apply.

Academic Fields/Career Goals: Nursing.

Award: Scholarship for use in freshman, sophomore, or junior years; not renewable. *Number:* 1–2. *Amount:* $1000–$2000.

Eligibility Requirements: Applicant must be enrolled or expecting to enroll full- or part-time at a two-year or four-year institution or university and resident of Delaware. Available to U.S. citizens.

Application Requirements: Application form, essay, financial need analysis. *Deadline:* March 15.

Contact: Kelly Sheridan, Scholarship Administrator
Delaware Community Foundation
36 The circle
Georgetown, DE 19947
Phone: 302-856-4393
E-mail: ksheridan@delcf.org

DEPARTMENT OF THE ARMY

http://www.goarmy.com/rotc

U.S. ARMY ROTC FOUR-YEAR NURSING SCHOLARSHIP

One-time award for freshman interested in nursing and accepted into an accredited nursing program. Must join ROTC program at the institution, pass physical evaluation, and have minimum GPA of 2.5. Applicant must be a U.S. citizen, have a qualifying SAT or ACT score, and be at least 17 years of age by college enrollment and under 31 years of age at time of graduation. Online application available.

Academic Fields/Career Goals: Nursing.

Award: Scholarship for use in freshman, sophomore, junior, or senior years; renewable. *Number:* 100. *Amount:* $5000–$50,000.

Eligibility Requirements: Applicant must be age 17-26 and enrolled or expecting to enroll full-time at a four-year institution or university. Applicant must have 2.5 GPA or higher. Available to U.S. citizens. Applicant must have national guard experience.

Application Requirements: Application form, essay, interview. *Deadline:* January 10.

Contact: Mr. Timothy Borgerding, Chief of Scholarship Management Branch
Department of the Army
U.S. Army Cadet Command
Building 1002, 204 1st Cavalry Regiment Road
Fort Knox, KY 40121-5123
Phone: 502-624-2309
E-mail: timothy.b.borgerding.civ@mail.mil

DERMATOLOGY NURSES' ASSOCIATION

http://www.dnanurse.org/

CAREER MOBILITY SCHOLARSHIP

Provides financial assistance to members of the Dermatology Nurses' Association (DNA) who are pursuing an undergraduate or graduate degree. The candidate must be a DNA member for two years, and be employed in the specialty of dermatology.

Academic Fields/Career Goals: Nursing.

Award: Scholarship for use in freshman, sophomore, junior, senior, or graduate years; not renewable. *Number:* 2. *Amount:* $2500.

Eligibility Requirements: Applicant must be enrolled or expecting to enroll full- or part-time at a four-year or technical institution or university. Applicant or parent of applicant must be member of Dermatology Nurses' Association. Applicant or parent of applicant must have employment or volunteer experience in nursing. Available to U.S. and non-U.S. citizens.

Application Requirements: Application form, essay, financial need analysis, recommendations or references, transcript. *Deadline:* August 31.

Contact: DNA Recognition Program
Dermatology Nurses' Association
15000 Commerce Parkway
Suite C
Mount Laurel, NJ 08054
Phone: 800-454-4362
Fax: 856-439-0525
E-mail: dna@dnanurse.org

EQUALITY SCHOLARSHIP COLLABORATIVE

http://www.equalityscholarship.org

NURSING SCHOLARSHIP

Applicants must be enrolled or accepted for enrollment by the interview date in an accredited ADN or BSN RN program in California. Master's prepared programs with a BA/BS in a field other than nursing will be considered eligible. Current Kaiser Permanente employees or their dependents, RN reentry programs, or current RN to BSN or MSN programs are not eligible for these scholarships. Diploma programs are not eligible.

Academic Fields/Career Goals: Nursing.

Award: Scholarship for use in freshman, sophomore, junior, senior, or graduate years; not renewable. *Number:* 1–2. *Amount:* $6000.

Eligibility Requirements: Applicant must be enrolled or expecting to enroll full- or part-time at a two-year or four-year institution or university; studying in California and must have an interest in LGBT issues. Applicant or parent of applicant must have employment or volunteer experience in community service. Applicant must have 3.0 GPA or higher. Available to U.S. and non-U.S. citizens.

Application Requirements: Application form, essay, interview. *Deadline:* February 1.

EXCEPTIONALNURSE.COM

http://www.exceptionalnurse.com/

ANNA MAY ROLANDO SCHOLARSHIP AWARD

Scholarship of $500 awarded to a nursing student with a disability. Preference will be given to a graduate student who has demonstrated a commitment to working with people with disabilities.

Academic Fields/Career Goals: Nursing.

Award: Scholarship for use in freshman, sophomore, junior, senior, graduate, or postgraduate years; not renewable. *Number:* 1. *Amount:* $500.

Eligibility Requirements: Applicant must be hearing impaired, learning disabled, physically disabled, or visually impaired and enrolled or expecting to enroll full-time at a four-year institution or university. Applicant must be hearing impaired, learning disabled, physically disabled, or visually impaired. Available to U.S. citizens.

Application Requirements: Application form, essay, medical verification of disability form, recommendations or references, transcript. *Deadline:* June 1.

Contact: Donna Maheady, Founder
E-mail: exceptionalnurse@aol.com

BRUNO ROLANDO SCHOLARSHIP AWARD

Scholarship of $250 awarded to a nursing student with a disability. Preference will be given to a nursing student who is employed at a Veteran's Hospital.

Academic Fields/Career Goals: Nursing.

Award: Scholarship for use in freshman, sophomore, junior, senior, graduate, or postgraduate years; not renewable. *Number:* 1. *Amount:* $250.

Eligibility Requirements: Applicant must be hearing impaired, learning disabled, physically disabled, or visually impaired and enrolled or expecting to enroll full-time at a four-year institution or university. Applicant or parent of applicant must have employment or volunteer experience in nursing. Applicant must be hearing impaired, learning disabled, physically disabled, or visually impaired. Available to U.S. citizens.

Application Requirements: Application form, essay, medical verification of disability form, recommendations or references, transcript. *Deadline:* June 1.

Contact: Donna Maheady, Founder
E-mail: exceptionalnurse@aol.com

CAROLINE SIMPSON MAHEADY SCHOLARSHIP AWARD

Scholarship of $250 awarded to a nursing student with a disability. Preference will be given to an undergraduate student, of Scottish descent, who has demonstrated a commitment to working with people with disabilities.

Academic Fields/Career Goals: Nursing.

Award: Scholarship for use in freshman, sophomore, junior, senior, graduate, or postgraduate years; not renewable. *Number:* 1. *Amount:* $250.

Eligibility Requirements: Applicant must be hearing impaired, learning disabled, physically disabled, or visually impaired and enrolled or expecting to enroll full-time at a four-year institution or university. Applicant must be hearing impaired, learning disabled, physically disabled, or visually impaired. Available to U.S. citizens.

Application Requirements: Application form, essay, medical verification of disability form, recommendations or references, transcript. *Deadline:* June 1.

Contact: Donna Maheady, Founder
E-mail: exceptionalnurse@aol.com

GENEVIEVE SARAN RICHMOND AWARD

Scholarship of $500 awarded to a nursing student with a disability.

Academic Fields/Career Goals: Nursing.

Award: Scholarship for use in freshman, sophomore, junior, senior, graduate, or postgraduate years; not renewable. *Number:* 1. *Amount:* $500.

Eligibility Requirements: Applicant must be hearing impaired, learning disabled, physically disabled, or visually impaired and enrolled or expecting to enroll full-time at a four-year institution or university. Applicant must be hearing impaired, learning disabled, physically disabled, or visually impaired. Available to U.S. citizens.

Application Requirements: Application form, essay, medical verification of disability form, recommendations or references, transcript. *Deadline:* June 1.

Contact: Donna Maheady, Founder
E-mail: exceptionalnurse@aol.com

JILL LAURA CREEDON SCHOLARSHIP AWARD

Scholarship of $500 awarded to a nursing student with a disability or medical challenge.

Academic Fields/Career Goals: Nursing.

Award: Scholarship for use in freshman, sophomore, junior, senior, graduate, or postgraduate years; not renewable. *Number:* 1. *Amount:* $500.

Eligibility Requirements: Applicant must be hearing impaired, learning disabled, physically disabled, or visually impaired and enrolled or expecting to enroll full-time at a four-year institution or university. Applicant must be hearing impaired, learning disabled, physically disabled, or visually impaired. Available to U.S. citizens.

Application Requirements: Application form, essay, medical verification of disability form, recommendations or references, transcript. *Deadline:* June 1.

Contact: Donna Maheady, Founder
E-mail: exceptionalnurse@aol.com

MARY SERRA GILI SCHOLARSHIP AWARD

Scholarship of $250 awarded to a nursing student with a disability.

Academic Fields/Career Goals: Nursing.

Award: Scholarship for use in freshman, sophomore, junior, senior, graduate, or postgraduate years; not renewable. *Number:* 1. *Amount:* $250.

Eligibility Requirements: Applicant must be hearing impaired, learning disabled, physically disabled, or visually impaired and enrolled or expecting to enroll full-time at a four-year institution or university. Applicant must be hearing impaired, learning disabled, physically disabled, or visually impaired. Available to U.S. citizens.

Application Requirements: Application form, essay, medical verification of disability form, recommendations or references, transcript. *Deadline:* June 1.

Contact: Donna Maheady, Founder
E-mail: exceptionalnurse@aol.com

PETER GILI SCHOLARSHIP AWARD

Scholarship of $500 awarded to a nursing student with a disability.

Academic Fields/Career Goals: Nursing.

Award: Scholarship for use in freshman, sophomore, junior, senior, graduate, or postgraduate years; not renewable. *Number:* 1. *Amount:* $500.

Eligibility Requirements: Applicant must be hearing impaired, learning disabled, physically disabled, or visually impaired and enrolled or expecting to enroll full-time at a four-year institution or university. Applicant must be hearing impaired, learning disabled, physically disabled, or visually impaired. Available to U.S. citizens.

Application Requirements: Application form, essay, medical verification of disability form, recommendations or references, transcript. *Deadline:* June 1.

Contact: Donna Maheady, Founder
E-mail: exceptionalnurse@aol.com

THE EXPERT INSTITUTE

https://www.theexpertinstitute.com

ANNUAL HEALTHCARE AND LIFE SCIENCES SCHOLARSHIP

• *See page 156*

FLORIDA NURSES ASSOCIATION

http://www.floridanurse.org/

AGNES NAUGHTON RN-BSN FUND

This fund is established to honor Agnes Naughton who was a lifelong FNA member and the mother of FNA Executive Director Paula Massey. She valued education and this scholarship will assist a RN who is continuing his or her education.

Academic Fields/Career Goals: Nursing.

Award: Scholarship for use in freshman, sophomore, junior, or senior years; not renewable. *Number:* 1. *Amount:* $500.

Eligibility Requirements: Applicant must be enrolled or expecting to enroll full- or part-time at a four-year institution or university; resident of Florida and studying in Florida. Applicant must have 2.5 GPA or higher. Available to U.S. citizens.

Application Requirements: Application form, application form may be submitted online (http://www.floridanurse.org), essay, recommendations or references, transcript, validation of Florida residency.

Contact: Willa Fuller, Executive Director
E-mail: foundation@floridanurse.org

EDNA HICKS FUND SCHOLARSHIP

Applicant should be enrolled in a nationally accredited nursing program. Must be in Associate, Baccalaureate, or Master's degree nursing programs or doctoral programs. Preference given to nurse researchers from South Florida.

Academic Fields/Career Goals: Nursing.

Award: Scholarship for use in freshman, sophomore, junior, senior, graduate, or postgraduate years; not renewable. *Number:* 1. *Amount:* $500.

Eligibility Requirements: Applicant must be enrolled or expecting to enroll full- or part-time at a two-year or four-year institution or university; resident of Florida and studying in Florida. Applicant must have 2.5 GPA or higher. Available to U.S. citizens.

Application Requirements: Application form, driver's license, recommendations or references, transcript. *Deadline:* June 1.

Contact: Willa Fuller, Executive Director
Florida Nurses Association
PO Box 536985
Orlando, FL 32803
E-mail: foundation@floridanurse.org

MARY YORK SCHOLARSHIP FUND

Need criteria for the Mary York Scholarship Fund is not restricted at this time.

Academic Fields/Career Goals: Nursing.

Award: Scholarship for use in freshman, sophomore, junior, senior, graduate, or postgraduate years; not renewable. *Number:* 1. *Amount:* $500.

Eligibility Requirements: Applicant must be enrolled or expecting to enroll full- or part-time at a two-year or four-year or technical institution or university; resident of Florida and studying in Florida. Applicant must have 2.5 GPA or higher. Available to U.S. citizens.

Application Requirements: Application form, essay, financial need analysis, proof of Florida residency, recommendations or references, transcript. *Deadline:* June 1.

Contact: Willa Fuller, Executive Director
Florida Nurses Association
PO Box 536985
Orlando, FL 32803
Phone: 407-896-3261
E-mail: foundation@floridanurse.org

RUTH FINAMORE SCHOLARSHIP FUND

The Ruth Finamore Scholarship Fund is available to all levels of Florida nursing students.

Academic Fields/Career Goals: Nursing.

Award: Scholarship for use in freshman, sophomore, junior, senior, graduate, or postgraduate years; not renewable. *Number:* 1. *Amount:* $500.

Eligibility Requirements: Applicant must be enrolled or expecting to enroll full- or part-time at a two-year or four-year or technical institution or university; resident of Florida and studying in Florida. Applicant must have 2.5 GPA or higher. Available to U.S. citizens.

Application Requirements: Application form, driver's license, essay, financial need analysis, recommendations or references, transcript, validation of Florida residency. *Deadline:* June 1.

Contact: Willa Fuller, Executive Director
Florida Nurses Association
PO Box 536985
Orlando, FL 32803
E-mail: foundation@floridanurse.org

UNDINE SAMS AND FRIENDS SCHOLARSHIP FUND

The Undine Sams and Friends Scholarship Fund is available statewide to all levels of Nursing students.

Academic Fields/Career Goals: Nursing.

Award: Scholarship for use in freshman, sophomore, junior, senior, or graduate years; not renewable. *Number:* 1. *Amount:* $500.

Eligibility Requirements: Applicant must be enrolled or expecting to enroll full- or part-time at a two-year or four-year or technical institution or university; resident of Florida and studying in Florida. Applicant must have 2.5 GPA or higher. Available to U.S. citizens.

Application Requirements: Application form, application form may be submitted online (http://www.floridanurse.org), financial need analysis, proof of Florida residency, recommendations or references, transcript. *Deadline:* June 1.

Contact: Willa Fuller, Executive Director
Florida Nurses Association
PO Box 536985
Orlando, FL 32803
Phone: 407-896-3261
E-mail: foundation@floridanurse.org

FOUNDATION OF THE NATIONAL STUDENT NURSES' ASSOCIATION

http://www.nsna.org/

BREAKTHROUGH TO NURSING SCHOLARSHIPS FOR RACIAL/ETHNIC MINORITIES

Available to minority students enrolled in nursing or pre-nursing programs. Awards based on need, scholarship, and health-related activities. Application fee of $10. Send self-addressed stamped envelope with two stamps along with application request. Number of awards varies based on donors.

Academic Fields/Career Goals: Nursing.

Award: Scholarship for use in freshman, sophomore, junior, or senior years; not renewable. *Amount:* $1000–$2500.

Eligibility Requirements: Applicant must be American Indian/Alaska Native, Asian/Pacific Islander, Black (non-Hispanic), Hispanic and enrolled or expecting to enroll full- or part-time at a two-year or four-year institution or university. Available to U.S. citizens.

Application Requirements: Application form, financial need analysis, self-addressed stamped envelope with application, transcript. *Fee:* $10. *Deadline:* January 11.

Contact: Lauren Sperle, Scholarship Chairperson
Phone: 718-210-0705
Fax: 718-210-0710
E-mail: lauren@nsna.org

FOUNDATION OF THE NATIONAL STUDENT NURSES' ASSOCIATION CAREER MOBILITY SCHOLARSHIP

One-time award open to registered nurses enrolled in nursing or licensed practical or vocational nurses enrolled in a program leading to licensure as a registered nurse. The award value is $1000 to $2500 and the number of awards varies. Submit copy of license. Application fee: $10. Send self-addressed stamped envelope.

Academic Fields/Career Goals: Nursing.

Award: Scholarship for use in freshman, sophomore, junior, or senior years; not renewable. *Amount:* $1000–$2500.

Eligibility Requirements: Applicant must be enrolled or expecting to enroll full- or part-time at a two-year or four-year institution or university. Available to U.S. citizens.

Application Requirements: Application form, financial need analysis, self-addressed stamped envelope with application, transcript. *Fee:* $10. *Deadline:* January 11.

Contact: Lauren Sperle, Scholarship Chairperson
Phone: 718-210-0705
Fax: 718-210-0710
E-mail: lauren@nsna.org

FOUNDATION OF THE NATIONAL STUDENT NURSES' ASSOCIATION GENERAL SCHOLARSHIPS

One-time award for National Student Nurses' Association members and nonmembers enrolled in nursing programs. Graduating high school seniors are not eligible. Send self-addressed stamped envelope with two stamps for application.

Academic Fields/Career Goals: Nursing.

Award: Scholarship for use in freshman, sophomore, junior, or senior years; not renewable. *Amount:* $1000–$2500.

Eligibility Requirements: Applicant must be enrolled or expecting to enroll full- or part-time at a two-year or four-year institution or university. Available to U.S. citizens.

Application Requirements: Application form, financial need analysis, self-addressed stamped envelope with application, transcript. *Fee:* $10. *Deadline:* January 11.

Contact: Lauren Sperle, Scholarship Chairperson
Phone: 718-210-0705
Fax: 718-210-0710
E-mail: lauren@nsna.org

FOUNDATION OF THE NATIONAL STUDENT NURSES' ASSOCIATION SPECIALTY SCHOLARSHIP

One-time award available to students currently enrolled in a state-approved school of nursing or prenursing. Must have interest in a specialty area of nursing. The award value is $1000 to $2500 and the number of awards granted varies.

Academic Fields/Career Goals: Nursing.

Award: Scholarship for use in freshman, sophomore, junior, or senior years; not renewable. *Amount:* $1000–$2500.

Eligibility Requirements: Applicant must be enrolled or expecting to enroll full- or part-time at a two-year or four-year institution or university. Available to U.S. citizens.

Application Requirements: Application form, financial need analysis, self-addressed stamped envelope with application, transcript. *Fee:* $10. *Deadline:* January 11.

Contact: Lauren Sperle, Scholarship Chairperson
Phone: 718-210-0705
Fax: 718-210-0710
E-mail: lauren@nsna.org

PROMISE OF NURSING SCHOLARSHIP

Applicants attending nursing school in California, South Florida, Georgia, Illinois, Massachusetts, Michigan, New Jersey, Tennessee, or Dallas/Fort Worth, Texas are eligible. Number of awards granted varies.

Academic Fields/Career Goals: Nursing.

Award: Scholarship for use in freshman, sophomore, junior, or senior years; renewable. *Amount:* $1000–$5000.

Eligibility Requirements: Applicant must be enrolled or expecting to enroll full- or part-time at a two-year or four-year institution or university and studying in California, Florida, Georgia, Illinois, Massachusetts, Michigan, New Jersey, Tennessee, Texas. Available to U.S. citizens.

Application Requirements: Application form, financial need analysis, self-addressed stamped envelope with application, transcript. *Fee:* $10. *Deadline:* January 11.

Contact: Lauren Sperle, Scholarship Chairperson
      Phone: 718-210-0705
      Fax: 718-210-0710
      E-mail: lauren@nsna.org

GENESIS HEALTH SERVICES FOUNDATION
http://www.genesishealth.com/

GALA NURSING SCHOLARSHIPS
Scholarships of $6000 for up to five recipients who are seeking admission to, or have been accepted into, an undergraduate Baccalaureate program in nursing.

Academic Fields/Career Goals: Nursing.

Award: Scholarship for use in freshman, sophomore, junior, or senior years; not renewable. *Number:* up to 5. *Amount:* $6000.

Eligibility Requirements: Applicant must be enrolled or expecting to enroll full-time at a four-year institution or university; resident of Illinois, Iowa and studying in Illinois, Iowa. Available to U.S. citizens.

Application Requirements: Application form, transcript. *Deadline:* March 8.

Contact: Melinda Gowey, Executive Director
      Phone: 563-421-6865
      Fax: 563-421-6869
      E-mail: goweym@genesishealth.com

GOOD SAMARITAN FOUNDATION
http://www.gsftx.org/

GOOD SAMARITAN FOUNDATION SCHOLARSHIP
Scholarship for nursing students in their clinical level of education. Must be a resident of Texas and plan to work in a U.S. health-care system.

Academic Fields/Career Goals: Nursing.

Award: Scholarship for use in freshman, sophomore, junior, senior, graduate, or postgraduate years; renewable. *Amount:* $1000.

Eligibility Requirements: Applicant must be enrolled or expecting to enroll full-time at a four-year institution or university and resident of Texas. Available to U.S. and non-U.S. citizens.

Application Requirements: Application form. *Deadline:* varies.

Contact: Kay Crawford, Scholarship Director
      Phone: 713-529-4646
      Fax: 713-521-1169
      E-mail: kcrawford@gsftx.org

GREATER KANAWHA VALLEY FOUNDATION
http://www.tgkvf.org/

BERNICE PICKINS PARSONS FUND
• *See page 394*

ELEANORA G. WYLIE SCHOLARSHIP
Renewable award for West Virginia residents pursuing postsecondary studies in nursing or gerontology. Minimum 2.5 GPA required. Must show financial need.

Academic Fields/Career Goals: Nursing.

Award: Scholarship for use in freshman, sophomore, junior, senior, or graduate years; renewable. *Amount:* $300.

Eligibility Requirements: Applicant must be enrolled or expecting to enroll full-time at a four-year institution or university and resident of West Virginia. Applicant must have 2.5 GPA or higher. Available to U.S. citizens.

Application Requirements: Application form, financial need analysis, recommendations or references, test scores, transcript. *Deadline:* January 15.

Contact: Susan Hoover, Scholarship Program Officer
      Greater Kanawha Valley Foundation
      900 Lee Street East, 16th Floor
      Charleston, WV 25301
      Phone: 304-346-3620
      E-mail: shoover@tgkvf.org

GUSTAVUS B. CAPITO FUND
Scholarships awarded to students who show financial need and are seeking education in nursing at any accredited college or university with a nursing program in West Virginia. Scholarships are awarded for one or more years. Must be a resident of West Virginia.

Academic Fields/Career Goals: Nursing.

Award: Scholarship for use in freshman, sophomore, junior, or senior years; renewable. *Amount:* $2000.

Eligibility Requirements: Applicant must be enrolled or expecting to enroll full-time at a four-year institution or university; resident of West Virginia and studying in West Virginia. Available to U.S. citizens.

Application Requirements: Application form, essay, financial need analysis, recommendations or references, transcript. *Deadline:* January 15.

Contact: Susan Hoover, Scholarship Program Officer
      Greater Kanawha Valley Foundation
      900 Lee Street East, 16th Floor
      Charleston, WV 25301
      Phone: 304-346-3620
      E-mail: shoover@tgkvf.org

REBECCA GOLDMAN SCHOLARSHIP
Renewable award for a West Virginia resident pursuing full-time postsecondary studies. Must be studying nursing and have a minimum 3.0 GPA.

Academic Fields/Career Goals: Nursing.

Award: Scholarship for use in freshman, sophomore, junior, or senior years; renewable. *Number:* 1.

Eligibility Requirements: Applicant must be enrolled or expecting to enroll full-time at a four-year institution or university and resident of West Virginia. Applicant must have 3.0 GPA or higher. Available to U.S. citizens.

Application Requirements: Application form, financial need analysis, recommendations or references, test scores, transcript. *Deadline:* January 15.

Contact: Susan Hoover, Scholarship Program Officer
      Greater Kanawha Valley Foundation
      900 Lee Street East, 16th Floor
      Charleston, WV 25301
      Phone: 304-346-3620
      E-mail: shoover@tgkvf.org

HEALTH PROFESSIONS EDUCATION FOUNDATION
http://www.healthprofessions.ca.gov/

ASSOCIATE DEGREE NURSING SCHOLARSHIP PROGRAM
One-time award to nursing students accepted to or enrolled in associate degree nursing programs. Eligible applicants may receive up to $10,000 per year in financial assistance. Deadlines: Check website http://oshpd.ca.gov/HPEF/. Must be a resident of California. Minimum 2.0 GPA.

Academic Fields/Career Goals: Nursing.

Award: Scholarship for use in freshman, sophomore, junior, or senior years; not renewable. *Number:* 20–40. *Amount:* up to $10,000.

Eligibility Requirements: Applicant must be enrolled or expecting to enroll full- or part-time at a two-year or four-year institution or university; resident of California and studying in California. Available to U.S. citizens.

Application Requirements: Application form, application form may be submitted online (http://calreach.oshpd.ca.gov), community service, essay, financial need analysis, graduation date verification form, verification of language fluency, recommendations or references, transcript. *Deadline:* varies.

Contact: Charlene Almazan, Senior Program Officer
Health Professions Education Foundation
400 R Street
Sacramento, CA 95811
Phone: 800-773-1669
Fax: 916-324-6585
E-mail: HPEF-EMail@oshpd.ca.gov

BACHELOR OF SCIENCE NURSING LOAN REPAYMENT PROGRAM

Repays governmental and commercial loans that were obtained for tuition expenses, books, equipment, and reasonable living expenses associated with attending college. In return for the repayment of educational debt, loan repayment recipients are required to practice full-time in direct patient care in a medically underserved area or county health facility. Deadlines: check website http://oshpd.ca.gov/HPEF. Must be resident of California.

Academic Fields/Career Goals: Nursing.

Award: Grant for use in senior, graduate, or postgraduate years; not renewable. *Number:* 50–70. *Amount:* up to $11,000.

Eligibility Requirements: Applicant must be enrolled or expecting to enroll full- or part-time at a four-year institution or university; resident of California and studying in California. Available to U.S. citizens.

Application Requirements: Application form, application form may be submitted online (http://calreach.oshpd.ca.gov), community service, Employment Verification Form, financial need analysis, recommendations or references, transcript. *Deadline:* varies.

Contact: Charlene Almazan, Senior Program Officer
Health Professions Education Foundation
400 R Street
Sacramento, CA 95811
Phone: 800-773-1669
Fax: 916-324-6585
E-mail: HPEF-EMail@oshpd.ca.gov

BACHELOR OF SCIENCE NURSING SCHOLARSHIP PROGRAM

One-time award to nursing students accepted to or enrolled in baccalaureate degree nursing programs in California. Eligible applicants may receive up to $13,000 per year in financial assistance. Deadlines: check website. Must be resident of California and a U.S. citizen. Minimum 2.0 GPA.

Academic Fields/Career Goals: Nursing.

Award: Scholarship for use in freshman, sophomore, junior, or senior years; not renewable. *Number:* 50–70. *Amount:* up to $13,000.

Eligibility Requirements: Applicant must be age 18-99; enrolled or expecting to enroll full- or part-time at a two-year or four-year institution or university; resident of California and studying in California. Applicant must have 2.5 GPA or higher. Available to U.S. citizens.

Application Requirements: Application form, application form may be submitted online (http://calreach.oshpd.ca.gov/), employment verification form, proof of RN license, verification of language fluency, essay, financial need analysis, recommendations or references, transcript. *Deadline:* varies.

Contact: Charlene Almazan, Senior Program Officer
Health Professions Education Foundation
400 R Street
Sacramento, CA 95811
Phone: 800-773-1669
Fax: 916-324-6585
E-mail: HPEF-EMail@oshpd.ca.gov

VOCATIONAL NURSE & LICENSED VOCATIONAL NURSE TO ASSOCIATE DEGREE NURSING SCHOLARSHIP PROGRAM

Scholarships are available to students who are enrolled or accepted in an accredited Vocational Nurse program. Eligible applicants may receive up to $8,000 per year in financial assistance. Deadlines: Check website http://oshpd.ca.gov/HPEF/. Must be a resident of California. Minimum 2.0 GPA.

Academic Fields/Career Goals: Nursing.

Award: Scholarship for use in freshman or sophomore years; not renewable. *Amount:* $4000–$8000.

Eligibility Requirements: Applicant must be enrolled or expecting to enroll full- or part-time at a two-year or technical institution and resident of California. Available to U.S. citizens.

Application Requirements: Application form, application form may be submitted online (http://calreach.oshpd.ca.gov), community service, essay, financial need analysis, recommendations or references, Student Aid Report (SAR), personal statement, educational debt reporting form, transcript. *Deadline:* varies.

Contact: Meaghan HArrington, Program Officer
Health Professions Education Foundation
400 R Street
Sacramento, CA 95811
Phone: 800-773-1669
Fax: 916-324-6585
E-mail: HPEF-EMail@oshpd.ca.gov

HEALTH RESEARCH COUNCIL OF NEW ZEALAND

http://www.hrc.govt.nz/

PACIFIC HEALTH WORKFORCE AWARD

• *See page 345*

PACIFIC MENTAL HEALTH WORK FORCE AWARD

• *See page 346*

HOMETEAM CARE

http://www.hometeamcare.com

HOMETEAM HOMECARE SCHOLARSHIP

• *See page 369*

ILLINOIS NURSES ASSOCIATION

http://www.illinoisnurses.com/

SONNE SCHOLARSHIP

One-time award of up to $3000 available to nursing students. Funds may be used to cover tuition, fees, or any other cost encountered by students enrolled in Illinois state-approved nursing program. Award limited to U.S. citizens who are residents of Illinois. Recipients will receive a year's free membership in INA upon graduation.

Academic Fields/Career Goals: Nursing.

Award: Scholarship for use in freshman, sophomore, junior, or senior years; not renewable. *Number:* 2–4. *Amount:* $1000–$3000.

Eligibility Requirements: Applicant must be enrolled or expecting to enroll full-time at a four-year institution or university; resident of Illinois and studying in Illinois. Applicant must have 3.5 GPA or higher. Available to U.S. citizens.

Application Requirements: Application form, essay, financial need analysis, recommendations or references, transcript. *Deadline:* March 15.

Contact: Melinda Sweeney, Sonne Scholarship Committee
Illinois Nurses Association
105 West Adams Street, Suite 2101
Chicago, IL 60603
Phone: 312-419-2900 Ext. 222
Fax: 312-419-2920
E-mail: msweeney@illinoisnurses.com

INDEPENDENT COLLEGE FUND OF NEW JERSEY

http://www.njcolleges.org/

C.R. BARD FOUNDATION, INC. NURSING SCHOLARSHIP

Applicant must be entering at least the second semester of their sophomore year or the second semester of the second year of their nursing program and be enrolled full-time at an ICFNJ member college or university. Must maintain a minimum GPA of 3.0.

Academic Fields/Career Goals: Nursing.

Award: Scholarship for use in junior or senior years; not renewable. *Number:* 10. *Amount:* $2500.

Eligibility Requirements: Applicant must be enrolled or expecting to enroll full-time at a four-year institution or university and studying in New Jersey. Applicant must have 3.0 GPA or higher. Available to U.S. citizens.

Application Requirements: Application form, community service, essay, financial need analysis, recommendations or references, resume, transcript. *Deadline:* April 30.

Contact: Ms. Yvette Panella, Scholarship Coordinator
Independent College Fund of New Jersey
797 Springfield Avenue
Summit, NJ 07901
Phone: 908-277-3424
Fax: 908-277-0851
E-mail: scholarships@njcolleges.org

INDIANA HEALTH CARE POLICY INSTITUTE

http://www.ihca.org/

INDIANA HEALTH CARE POLICY INSTITUTE NURSING SCHOLARSHIP

Scholarship is for students pursuing a career in long-term care. One-time award of up to $5000 for Indiana residents studying nursing at an institution in Indiana, Ohio, Kentucky, Illinois or Michigan. Minimum 2.5 GPA required. Total number of awards varies.

Academic Fields/Career Goals: Nursing.

Award: Scholarship for use in freshman, sophomore, junior, or senior years; not renewable. *Number:* 1–5. *Amount:* $750–$5000.

Eligibility Requirements: Applicant must be enrolled or expecting to enroll full- or part-time at a two-year or four-year or technical institution or university; resident of Indiana and studying in Illinois, Indiana, Kentucky, Michigan, Ohio. Applicant must have 2.5 GPA or higher. Available to U.S. citizens.

Application Requirements: Application form, essay, interview, recommendations or references, transcript. *Deadline:* May 13.

Contact: Dorothy Henry, Executive Director
Indiana Health Care Policy Institute
One North Capitol Avenue, Suite 100
Indianapolis, IN 46204
Phone: 317-616-9028
Fax: 877-298-3749
E-mail: dhenry@ihca.org

INDIAN HEALTH SERVICES, UNITED STATES DEPARTMENT OF HEALTH AND HUMAN SERVICES

http://www.ihs.gov/scholarship

HEALTH PROFESSIONS PREPARATORY SCHOLARSHIP PROGRAM
• *See page 152*

INTERNATIONAL ORDER OF THE KING'S DAUGHTERS AND SONS

http://www.iokds.org/

HEALTH CAREERS SCHOLARSHIP
• *See page 238*

KETAMINE CLINICS OF LOS ANGELES

http://www.ketamineclinics.com/

KETAMINE CLINICS OF LOS ANGELES SCHOLARSHIP PROGRAM
• *See page 152*

KEVIN'S REVIEW

http://www.kevinsreview.com

KEVIN'S REVIEW NCLEX ASSISTANCE SCHOLARSHIP

In order to stay true to our student-centered intent and mission, KevinsReview.com is introducing a new and very unique scholarship. Platinum Tests has also joined us in this mission and has graciously contributed for each award recipient! The scholarship is awarded on a quarterly basis, meaning there will be 4 award recipients each year. Each recipient of the scholarship will receive an award of $250, enough to cover half or more of the cost of an NCLEX Review Course or an NCLEX Application. Lifetime access to Platinum Tests, a Computerized Adaptive Testing simulator that can predict your NCLEX readiness ($80 Value).Drawings will take place February 1st, May 1st, August 1st, and November 1st of each year. August 1st, 2017 will be the first award of this scholarship program. This money is meant to help pay for remedial classes, if necessary, or to help allay the costs of re-registration and re-application. Students must upload proof that they have unsuccessfully attempted the NCLEX. This can be in the form of NCLEX "Quick Results" (a screenshot from the Pearson Vue website), or a photo or photocopy of your NCLEX notification letter in the mail. Students must upload proof that they are either attempting the NCLEX again or are undergoing a paid NCLEX Review or remedial course. This can be in the form of a receipt or confirmation email from Pearson Vue, your State Board of Nursing, or an NCLEX Review company. Apply and upload your documents now! http://www.kevinsreview.com/nclex/nclex-assistance.php

Academic Fields/Career Goals: Nursing.

Award: Prize for use in sophomore or senior years; renewable. *Number:* 4. *Amount:* $330.

Eligibility Requirements: Applicant must be enrolled or expecting to enroll full- or part-time at a two-year or four-year or technical institution or university. Available to U.S. and non-U.S. citizens.

Application Requirements: Application form. *Deadline:* continuous.

Contact: Kevin Pan
Phone: 630-776-5801
E-mail: kevin@kevinsreview.com

LADIES AUXILIARY TO THE VETERANS OF FOREIGN WARS, DEPARTMENT OF MAINE

http://mainevfw.org/

FRANCES L. BOOTH MEDICAL SCHOLARSHIP SPONSORED BY LAVFW DEPARTMENT OF MAINE
• *See page 353*

LAW FIRM OF JACK TOLLIVER, MD & ASSOCIATES, PLLC

www.kymedicalmalpractice.com

TOLLIVER ANNUAL NURSING SCHOLARSHIP

Open to current high school seniors living in Kentucky, currently attending a Kentucky high school, and interested in pursuing a nursing degree. Applicants must be applying to a Kentucky college or university offering an accredited program of study in nursing. Apply through online application only.

Academic Fields/Career Goals: Nursing.

Award: Scholarship for use in freshman year; not renewable. *Number:* 5. *Amount:* $1000.

Eligibility Requirements: Applicant must be high school student; planning to enroll or expecting to enroll full- or part-time at a two-year or four-year institution or university; resident of Kentucky and studying in Kentucky. Available to U.S. citizens.

Application Requirements: Application form, essay. *Deadline:* March 15.

Contact: Nick Gowen
Phone: 502-827-1588
E-mail: nick@kymedicalmalpractice.com

MARION D. AND EVA S. PEEPLES FOUNDATION TRUST SCHOLARSHIP PROGRAM

http://www.jccf.org/apply-for-a-scholarship/

MARION A. AND EVA S. PEEPLES SCHOLARSHIPS

The Peeples Foundation Trust Fund provides for the awarding of annual scholarships in three fields of study to graduates of Indiana high schools who will attend an Indiana college or university. Eligible students must be pursuing or planning to pursue a major in: Nursing, Dietetics, or Technology Education.

Academic Fields/Career Goals: Nursing.

Award: Scholarship for use in freshman, sophomore, junior, or senior years; renewable. *Number:* 5–20. *Amount:* $1000–$5500.

Eligibility Requirements: Applicant must be enrolled or expecting to enroll full-time at a two-year or four-year or technical institution or university; resident of Indiana and studying in Indiana. Applicant must have 2.5 GPA or higher. Available to U.S. citizens.

Application Requirements: Application form, essay, financial need analysis. *Deadline:* February 21.

Contact: Stephanie Fox, Program Officer: Grants and Scholarships
    Marion D. and Eva S. Peeples Foundation Trust Scholarship Program
    PO Box 217
    Franklin, IN 46131
    Phone: 317-738-2213
    Fax: 317-738-9113
    E-mail: stephanief@jccf.org

MARYLAND STATE HIGHER EDUCATION COMMISSION

http://www.mhec.state.md.us/

GRADUATE AND PROFESSIONAL SCHOLARSHIP PROGRAM-MARYLAND

• *See page 238*

JANET L. HOFFMANN LOAN ASSISTANCE REPAYMENT PROGRAM

• *See page 254*

TUITION REDUCTION FOR NON-RESIDENT NURSING STUDENTS

Available to nonresidents of Maryland who attend a two-year or four-year public institution in Maryland. It is renewable provided student maintains academic requirements designated by institution attended. Recipient must agree to serve as a full-time nurse in a hospital or related institution for two to four years.

Academic Fields/Career Goals: Nursing.

Award: Scholarship for use in freshman, sophomore, junior, or senior years; renewable.

Eligibility Requirements: Applicant must be enrolled or expecting to enroll full- or part-time at a two-year or four-year institution and studying in Maryland. Available to U.S. citizens.

Application Requirements: Application form. *Deadline:* varies.

Contact: Robert Parker, Director
    Phone: 410-260-4558
    E-mail: rparker@mhec.state.md.us

MEDICAL SCRUBS COLLECTION

http://medicalscrubscollection.com

MEDICAL SCRUBS COLLECTION SCHOLARSHIP

• *See page 106*

MICHIGAN LEAGUE FOR NURSING

http://www.michleaguenursing.org

NURSING STUDENT SCHOLARSHIP

Four $500 scholarships will be awarded to students currently enrolled in a licensed practical nurse, Associate degree, or Bachelor's degree nursing education program. Must have successfully completed at least one nursing course with a clinical component. For Michigan residents to use at colleges and universities within the state of Michigan.

Academic Fields/Career Goals: Nursing.

Award: Scholarship for use in sophomore, junior, or senior years; not renewable. *Number:* 4. *Amount:* $500.

Eligibility Requirements: Applicant must be enrolled or expecting to enroll full-time at a two-year or four-year institution; resident of Michigan and studying in Michigan. Available to U.S. and non-U.S. citizens.

Application Requirements: Application form, community service, essay, letters of endorsement, recommendations or references, transcript. *Deadline:* January 1.

Contact: Carole Stacy, Director
    Michigan League for Nursing
    2410 Woodlake Drive
    Okemos, MI 48864
    Phone: 517-347-8091
    Fax: 517-347-4096
    E-mail: cstacy@mhc.org

MISSISSIPPI NURSES' ASSOCIATION (MNA)

http://www.msnurses.org/

MISSISSIPPI NURSES' ASSOCIATION FOUNDATION SCHOLARSHIP

Scholarship of $1000 to a Mississippi resident. Applicant should major in nursing and be a member of MASN.

Academic Fields/Career Goals: Nursing.

Award: Scholarship for use in freshman, sophomore, junior, or senior years; not renewable. *Number:* 1. *Amount:* $1000.

Eligibility Requirements: Applicant must be enrolled or expecting to enroll full- or part-time at a four-year institution or university and resident of Mississippi. Available to U.S. citizens.

Application Requirements: Application form, essay, recommendations or references, transcript. *Deadline:* October 1.

Contact: Scholarship Committee
    Mississippi Nurses' Association (MNA)
    31 Woodgreen Place
    Madison, MS 39110
    Phone: 601-898-0850
    E-mail: foundation@msnurses.org

MOUNT SINAI HOSPITAL DEPARTMENT OF NURSING

http://www.mountsinai.org/

BSN STUDENT SCHOLARSHIP/WORK REPAYMENT PROGRAM

$3000 award for senior nursing student or in the last semester/year of the program. Minimum GPA is 3.25.

Academic Fields/Career Goals: Nursing.

Award: Scholarship for use in senior year; not renewable. *Amount:* $3000.

Eligibility Requirements: Applicant must be enrolled or expecting to enroll full-time at a four-year institution or university. Available to U.S. citizens.

Application Requirements: Application form, recommendations or references, resume, transcript. *Deadline:* October 1.

Contact: Maria Vezina, Director, Nursing Education and Recruitment
    Mount Sinai Hospital Department of Nursing
    One Gustave Levy Place, PO Box 1144
    New York, NY 10029

NATIONAL ASSOCIATION DIRECTORS OF NURSING ADMINISTRATION

http://www.nadona.org/

NADONA STEPHANIE CARROLL MEMORIAL SCHOLARSHIP

Scholarship is for nursing student enrolled in an accredited nursing program or nursing student in an undergraduate or graduate program. Also for employees in the long term care continuum achieving an LPN/LVN.

Academic Fields/Career Goals: Nursing.

Award: Scholarship for use in freshman, sophomore, junior, senior, graduate, or postgraduate years; not renewable. *Number:* 1–13. *Amount:* $1000–$5000.

Eligibility Requirements: Applicant must be enrolled or expecting to enroll full- or part-time at a two-year or four-year or technical institution or university. Applicant or parent of applicant must have employment or volunteer experience in nursing. Available to U.S. citizens.

Application Requirements: Application form, essay, financial need analysis, personal photograph. *Deadline:* May 20.

Contact: Sherrie Dornberger, Executive Director
National Association Directors of Nursing Administration
1349 E. Kemper Road
Suite 4100A
Springdale, OH 45246
Phone: 800-222-0539
E-mail: sherrie@nadona.org

NATIONAL ASSOCIATION OF HISPANIC NURSES

http://www.nahnnet.org

NAHN SCHOLARSHIPS

Awards are presented to NAHN members only (must be a member for at least 6 months) enrolled in Associate, diploma, Baccalaureate, graduate or practical/vocational nursing programs. Selection based on current academic standing. Scholarship award recipients are a select group of Hispanic students who demonstrate promise of future professional contributions to the nursing profession and who have the potential to act as role models for other aspiring nursing students.

Academic Fields/Career Goals: Nursing.

Award: Scholarship for use in freshman, sophomore, junior, senior, or graduate years; not renewable.

Eligibility Requirements: Applicant must be of Hispanic heritage and enrolled or expecting to enroll full-time at a four-year or technical institution or university. Available to U.S. citizens.

Application Requirements: Application form, essay, recommendations or references, transcript. *Deadline:* varies.

Contact: Celia Besore, Executive Director and CEO
Phone: 202-387-2477
Fax: 202-483-7183
E-mail: info@thehispanicnurses.org

NATIONAL BLACK NURSES ASSOCIATION INC.

http://www.nbna.org/

DR. HILDA RICHARDS SCHOLARSHIP

Scholarship for nurses currently enrolled in a nursing program who are members of NBNA. Applicant must have at least one full year of school remaining.

Academic Fields/Career Goals: Nursing.

Award: Scholarship for use in freshman, sophomore, junior, senior, graduate, or postgraduate years; not renewable. *Number:* 1. *Amount:* $1000–$2000.

Eligibility Requirements: Applicant must be enrolled or expecting to enroll full-time at a two-year or four-year institution or university. Applicant or parent of applicant must be member of National Black Nurses' Association. Applicant or parent of applicant must have

employment or volunteer experience in community service. Available to U.S. and non-U.S. citizens.

Application Requirements: Application form, essay, personal photograph, recommendations or references, self-addressed stamped envelope with application, transcript. *Deadline:* April 15.

Contact: Scholarship Committee
Phone: 301-589-3200
Fax: 301-589-3223
E-mail: nbna@erols.com

DR. LAURANNE SAMS SCHOLARSHIP

Award available for NBNA member who is currently enrolled full-time in a nursing program. Applicant must have at least one full year of school remaining. Scholarships will range from $1000 to $2000.

Academic Fields/Career Goals: Nursing.

Award: Scholarship for use in freshman, sophomore, junior, senior, graduate, or postgraduate years; not renewable. *Number:* up to 5. *Amount:* $1000–$2000.

Eligibility Requirements: Applicant must be enrolled or expecting to enroll full-time at a two-year or four-year institution or university. Applicant or parent of applicant must be member of National Black Nurses' Association. Available to U.S. and non-U.S. citizens.

Application Requirements: Application form, essay, recommendations or references, self-addressed stamped envelope with application, transcript. *Deadline:* April 15.

Contact: Scholarship Committee
Phone: 301-589-3200
Fax: 301-589-3223
E-mail: nbna@erols.com

KAISER PERMANENTE SCHOOL OF ANESTHESIA SCHOLARSHIP

Scholarship for nurses currently enrolled in a nursing program who are active members of NBNA. Must have at least one full year of school remaining.

Academic Fields/Career Goals: Nursing.

Award: Scholarship for use in freshman, sophomore, junior, senior, graduate, or postgraduate years; not renewable. *Number:* 1. *Amount:* $1000–$2000.

Eligibility Requirements: Applicant must be enrolled or expecting to enroll full-time at a two-year or four-year institution or university. Applicant or parent of applicant must be member of National Black Nurses' Association. Available to U.S. and non-U.S. citizens.

Application Requirements: Application form, essay, recommendations or references, self-addressed stamped envelope with application, transcript. *Deadline:* April 15.

Contact: Scholarship Committee
Phone: 301-589-3200
Fax: 301-589-3223
E-mail: nbna@erols.com

MARTHA R. DUDLEY LVN/LPN SCHOLARSHIP

Scholarship available for nurses currently enrolled full-time in a nursing program and must be a member of NBNA. Applicant must have at least one full year of school remaining. Scholarships will range from $1000 to $2000.

Academic Fields/Career Goals: Nursing.

Award: Scholarship for use in freshman, sophomore, junior, senior, graduate, or postgraduate years; not renewable. *Number:* 1. *Amount:* $1000–$2000.

Eligibility Requirements: Applicant must be Black (non-Hispanic) and enrolled or expecting to enroll full-time at a two-year or four-year institution or university. Applicant or parent of applicant must be member of National Black Nurses' Association. Applicant or parent of applicant must have employment or volunteer experience in community service. Available to U.S. and non-U.S. citizens.

Application Requirements: Application form, essay, personal photograph, recommendations or references, self-addressed stamped envelope with application, transcript. *Deadline:* April 15.

Contact: Scholarship Committee
Phone: 301-589-3200
Fax: 301-589-3223
E-mail: nbna@erols.com

MAYO FOUNDATIONS SCHOLARSHIP

Scholarship for nurses currently enrolled full-time in a nursing program who are members of NBNA. Applicant must have at least one full year of school remaining.

Academic Fields/Career Goals: Nursing.

Award: Scholarship for use in freshman, sophomore, junior, senior, graduate, or postgraduate years; not renewable. *Number:* 1. *Amount:* $1000–$2000.

Eligibility Requirements: Applicant must be enrolled or expecting to enroll full-time at a two-year or four-year institution or university. Applicant or parent of applicant must be member of National Black Nurses' Association. Available to U.S. and non-U.S. citizens.

Application Requirements: Application form, essay, personal photograph, recommendations or references, self-addressed stamped envelope with application, transcript. *Deadline:* April 15.

Contact: Scholarship Committee
Phone: 301-589-3200
Fax: 301-589-3223
E-mail: nbna@erols.com

NBNA BOARD OF DIRECTORS SCHOLARSHIP

The scholarship enables nurses to grow and better contribute their talents to the health and healthcare of communities. Candidate must be currently enrolled in a nursing program with at least one full year of school remaining and must be a member of NBNA.

Academic Fields/Career Goals: Nursing.

Award: Scholarship for use in freshman, sophomore, junior, senior, graduate, or postgraduate years; not renewable. *Number:* up to 2. *Amount:* $1000–$2000.

Eligibility Requirements: Applicant must be enrolled or expecting to enroll full-time at a two-year or four-year institution or university. Applicant or parent of applicant must be member of National Black Nurses' Association. Applicant or parent of applicant must have employment or volunteer experience in community service. Available to U.S. and non-U.S. citizens.

Application Requirements: Application form, essay, personal photograph, recommendations or references, self-addressed stamped envelope with application, transcript. *Deadline:* April 15.

Contact: Scholarship Committee
Phone: 301-589-3200
Fax: 301-589-3223
E-mail: nbna@erols.com

NURSING SPECTRUM SCHOLARSHIP

Scholarship enables nurses to grow and better contribute their talents to the health and healthcare of communities. Candidate must be currently enrolled in a nursing program and be a member of NBNA. Applicant must have at least one full year of school remaining.

Academic Fields/Career Goals: Nursing.

Award: Scholarship for use in freshman, sophomore, junior, senior, graduate, or postgraduate years; not renewable. *Number:* 1. *Amount:* $1000–$2000.

Eligibility Requirements: Applicant must be enrolled or expecting to enroll full-time at a two-year or four-year institution or university. Applicant or parent of applicant must be member of National Black Nurses' Association. Available to U.S. and non-U.S. citizens.

Application Requirements: Application form, essay, recommendations or references, self-addressed stamped envelope with application, transcript. *Deadline:* April 15.

Contact: Scholarship Committee
Phone: 301-589-3200
Fax: 301-589-3223
E-mail: nbna@erols.com

NATIONAL COUNCIL OF JEWISH WOMEN LOS ANGELES (NCJW L LA)

http://ncjwla.org/

INGER LAWRENCE-M.R. BAUER FOUNDATION NURSING STUDIES SCHOLARSHIP

This award is given to woman or man enrolled in or accepted to a degree program in nursing. Some units toward the degree are preferred, but not

required. Applicants to the Inger Lawrence-M.R. Bauer award are also eligible for the June Miller Nursing Education Scholarship. The National Council of Jewish Women l Los Angeles (NCJW l LA) provides scholarships, regardless of race, ethnicity, religion, age, gender identity, sexuality or national origin to those who live and attend school in the Greater Los Angeles area, including Los Angeles, Orange, Riverside, and Ventura Counties.

Academic Fields/Career Goals: Nursing.

Award: Scholarship for use in freshman, sophomore, junior, senior, or graduate years; not renewable. *Number:* 2. *Amount:* $2000.

Eligibility Requirements: Applicant must be enrolled or expecting to enroll full- or part-time at a two-year or four-year or technical institution or university; resident of California and studying in California. Available to U.S. citizens.

Application Requirements: Application form, essay, financial need analysis. *Deadline:* continuous.

Contact: Stephanie Flax, Program and Scholarship Coordinator
National Council of Jewish Women Los Angeles (NCJW l LA)
543 North Fairfax Avenue
Los Angeles, CA 90036
Phone: 323-852-8515
E-mail: scholarship@ncjwla.org

JUNE MILLER NURSING EDUCATION SCHOLARSHIP

This award is given to woman or man enrolled in or accepted to a degree program in nursing. Some units toward the degree are preferred, but not required. Applicants to the June Miller Nursing Education Scholarship are also eligible for the Inger Lawrence-M.R. Bauer award. The National Council of Jewish Women l Los Angeles (NCJW l LA) provides scholarships, regardless of race, ethnicity, religion, age, gender identity, sexuality or national origin to those who live and attend school in the Greater Los Angeles area, including Los Angeles, Orange, Riverside, and Ventura Counties.

Academic Fields/Career Goals: Nursing.

Award: Scholarship for use in freshman, sophomore, junior, senior, or graduate years; not renewable. *Number:* 4. *Amount:* $2000.

Eligibility Requirements: Applicant must be enrolled or expecting to enroll full- or part-time at a two-year or four-year or technical institution or university; resident of California and studying in California. Available to U.S. and non-U.S. citizens.

Application Requirements: Application form, essay, financial need analysis. *Deadline:* May 1.

Contact: Ms. Stephanie Flax, Scholarship and Program Coordinator
National Council of Jewish Women Los Angeles (NCJW l LA)
543 North Fairfax Avenue
Los Angeles, CA 90036
Phone: 323-852-8515
E-mail: scholarship@ncjwla.org

NATIONAL SOCIETY DAUGHTERS OF THE AMERICAN REVOLUTION

http://www.dar.org/

NATIONAL SOCIETY DAUGHTERS OF THE AMERICAN REVOLUTION CAROLINE E. HOLT NURSING SCHOLARSHIPS

One-time award for students who are in financial need and have been accepted or are enrolled in an accredited school of nursing. A letter of acceptance into the nursing program or the transcript stating that the applicant is enrolled in the nursing program must be included with the application.

Academic Fields/Career Goals: Nursing.

Award: Scholarship for use in freshman, sophomore, junior, or senior years; not renewable.

Eligibility Requirements: Applicant must be enrolled or expecting to enroll full-time at a two-year or four-year institution or university. Available to U.S. citizens.

Application Requirements: Application form, essay, financial need analysis. *Deadline:* February 10.

Contact: Lakeisha Graham, Manager, Office of the Reporter General
Phone: 202-628-1776
Fax: 202-879-3348
E-mail: nsdarscholarships@dar.org

NATIONAL SOCIETY DAUGHTERS OF THE AMERICAN REVOLUTION MADELINE PICKETT (HALBERT) COGSWELL NURSING SCHOLARSHIP

Scholarship available to students who have been accepted or are currently enrolled in an accredited school of nursing, who are members of NSDAR, descendants of members of NSDAR, or are eligible to be members of NSDAR. A letter of acceptance into the nursing program or transcript showing enrollment in nursing program must be included with the application. DAR member number must be on the application.

Academic Fields/Career Goals: Nursing.

Award: Scholarship for use in freshman, sophomore, junior, or senior years; not renewable. *Amount:* $2500.

Eligibility Requirements: Applicant must be enrolled or expecting to enroll full-time at a two-year or four-year institution or university. Applicant or parent of applicant must be member of Daughters of the American Revolution. Available to U.S. and non-U.S. citizens.

Application Requirements: Application form. *Deadline:* February 15.

Contact: Lakeisha Graham, Manager, Office of the Reporter General
Phone: 202-628-1776
Fax: 202-879-3348
E-mail: nsdarscholarships@dar.org

NATIONAL SOCIETY DAUGHTERS OF THE AMERICAN REVOLUTION MILDRED NUTTING NURSING SCHOLARSHIP

A one-time $1000 scholarship for students who are in financial need and who have been accepted or are currently enrolled in an accredited school of nursing. A letter of acceptance into the nursing program or the transcript stating that the applicant is in the nursing program must be enclosed with the application. Preference will be given to candidates from the Lowell, Massachusetts area.

Academic Fields/Career Goals: Nursing.

Award: Scholarship for use in freshman, sophomore, junior, or senior years; not renewable. *Amount:* $1000.

Eligibility Requirements: Applicant must be enrolled or expecting to enroll full-time at a two-year or four-year institution or university. Available to U.S. citizens.

Application Requirements: Application form, essay, financial need analysis. *Deadline:* February 15.

Contact: Lakeisha Graham, Manager, Office of the Reporter General
Phone: 202-628-1776
Fax: 202-879-3348
E-mail: nsdarscholarships@dar.org

THE NATIONAL SOCIETY OF THE COLONIAL DAMES OF AMERICA

http://www.nscda.org/

AMERICAN INDIAN NURSE SCHOLARSHIP PROGRAM
• See page 346

NEW JERSEY STATE NURSES ASSOCIATION

http://www.njsna.org/

INSTITUTE FOR NURSING SCHOLARSHIP

Applicants must be New Jersey residents currently enrolled in a diploma, associate, baccalaureate, master's, or doctoral program in nursing or a related field. The amount awarded in each scholarship will be $1000 per recipient.

Academic Fields/Career Goals: Nursing.

Award: Scholarship for use in freshman, sophomore, junior, senior, or graduate years; not renewable. *Number:* 14. *Amount:* $1000.

Eligibility Requirements: Applicant must be enrolled or expecting to enroll full-time at a two-year or four-year institution or university and resident of New Jersey. Available to U.S. citizens.

Application Requirements: Application form.

Contact: Sandy Kerr, Executive Assistant
Phone: 609-883-5335
Fax: 609-883-5343
E-mail: sandy@njsna.org

NEW YORK STATE EMERGENCY NURSES ASSOCIATION (ENA)

http://www.ena.org/

NEW YORK STATE ENA SEPTEMBER 11 SCHOLARSHIP FUND

Scholarships to rescue workers who are going to school to obtain their undergraduate nursing degree. Eligible rescue workers include prehospital care providers, fire fighters, and police officers. The scholarship is not limited geographically. The scholarship winner will also be awarded a complimentary one year ENA membership.

Academic Fields/Career Goals: Nursing.

Award: Scholarship for use in freshman, sophomore, junior, senior, graduate, or postgraduate years; not renewable. *Number:* 1. *Amount:* $2000.

Eligibility Requirements: Applicant must be enrolled or expecting to enroll full- or part-time at a four-year institution or university. Available to U.S. citizens.

Application Requirements: Application form. *Deadline:* varies.

Contact: Educational Services
Phone: 847-460-4123
Fax: 847-460-4005
E-mail: education@ena.org

NEW YORK STATE GRANGE

http://www.nysgrange.org/

JUNE GILL NURSING SCHOLARSHIP

One annual scholarship award to verified NYS Grange member pursuing a career in nursing. Selection based on verification of NYS Grange membership and enrollment in a nursing program, as well as applicant's career statement, academic records, and financial need. Payment made after successful completion of one term.

Academic Fields/Career Goals: Nursing.

Award: Scholarship for use in freshman, sophomore, junior, or senior years; not renewable. *Number:* 1. *Amount:* $1000.

Eligibility Requirements: Applicant must be enrolled or expecting to enroll full-time at a two-year or four-year institution and resident of New York. Applicant or parent of applicant must be member of Grange Association. Available to U.S. citizens.

Application Requirements: Application form, financial need analysis. *Deadline:* April 15.

Contact: Scholarship Committee
New York State Grange
100 Grange Place
Cortland, NY 13045
Phone: 607-756-7553
E-mail: nysgrange@nysgrange.org

NEXTSTEPU

http://www.nextstepu.com/

$1,500 STEM SCHOLARSHIP
• See page 106

ODD FELLOWS AND REBEKAHS

http://www.ioofme.org/

ODD FELLOWS AND REBEKAHS ELLEN F. WASHBURN NURSES TRAINING AWARD

Award for high school seniors and college undergraduates to attend an accredited Maine institution and pursue a registered nursing degree. Must have a minimum 2.5 GPA. Can reapply for award for up to four years.

Academic Fields/Career Goals: Nursing.

Award: Scholarship for use in freshman, sophomore, junior, or senior years; renewable. *Number:* up to 30. *Amount:* $150–$400.

Eligibility Requirements: Applicant must be enrolled or expecting to enroll full- or part-time at a two-year or four-year institution or university and studying in Maine. Applicant must have 2.5 GPA or higher. Available to U.S. citizens.

Application Requirements: Application form, financial need analysis, personal photograph, recommendations or references. *Deadline:* April 15.

Contact: Joyce Young, Chairman
　　　　Phone: 207-839-4723

ONS FOUNDATION

http://www.onsfoundation.org

ONS FOUNDATION JOSH GOTTHEIL MEMORIAL BONE MARROW TRANSPLANT CAREER DEVELOPMENT AWARDS

Awards available to any professional registered nurse in field of bone marrow transplant nursing for further study in a Bachelor's or Master's program. Submit examples of contributions to BMT nursing.

Academic Fields/Career Goals: Nursing.

Award: Scholarship for use in junior, senior, or graduate years; not renewable. *Number:* 4. *Amount:* $2000.

Eligibility Requirements: Applicant must be enrolled or expecting to enroll full- or part-time at a four-year institution or university. Available to U.S. and non-U.S. citizens.

Application Requirements: Application form, essay, recommendations or references, resume. *Deadline:* December 1.

Contact: Bonny Revo, Executive Assistant
　　　　Phone: 412-859-6278
　　　　E-mail: brevo@onsfoundation.org

ONS FOUNDATION/ONCOLOGY NURSING CERTIFICATION CORPORATION BACHELOR'S SCHOLARSHIPS

One-time awards to improve oncology nursing by assisting registered nurses in furthering their education. Applicants must hold a current license to practice and be enrolled in an undergraduate nursing degree program at an NLN-accredited school.

Academic Fields/Career Goals: Nursing; Oncology.

Award: Scholarship for use in freshman, sophomore, junior, or senior years; not renewable. *Amount:* $2000.

Eligibility Requirements: Applicant must be enrolled or expecting to enroll full- or part-time at a four-year institution or university. Available to U.S. and non-U.S. citizens.

Application Requirements: Application form, transcript. *Fee:* $5. *Deadline:* February 1.

Contact: Bonny Revo, Executive Assistant
　　　　Phone: 412-859-6278
　　　　E-mail: brevo@onsfoundation.org

ONS FOUNDATION/PEARL MOORE CAREER DEVELOPMENT AWARDS

Awards to practicing staff nurses who possess or are pursuing a BSN and have two years oncology practice experience.

Academic Fields/Career Goals: Nursing; Oncology.

Award: Prize for use in junior, senior, or graduate years; not renewable. *Number:* 3. *Amount:* $3000.

Eligibility Requirements: Applicant must be enrolled or expecting to enroll full- or part-time at a four-year institution or university. Available to U.S. citizens.

Application Requirements: Application form, recommendations or references. *Deadline:* December 1.

Contact: Bonny Revo, Executive Assistant
　　　　Phone: 412-859-6278
　　　　E-mail: brevo@onsfoundation.org

OREGON COMMUNITY FOUNDATION

http://www.oregoncf.org/

FRANZ STENZEL M.D. AND KATHRYN STENZEL SCHOLARSHIP FUND

• *See page 354*

NLN ELLA MCKINNEY SCHOLARSHIP FUND

Award for Oregon high school graduates (or the equivalent) for use in the pursuit of an undergraduate or graduate nursing education. Must attend a nonprofit college or university in Oregon accredited by the NLN Accrediting Commission. For more information, see web http://www.getcollegefunds.org.

Academic Fields/Career Goals: Nursing.

Award: Scholarship for use in freshman, sophomore, junior, or senior years; renewable. *Number:* up to 2. *Amount:* $1000–$2000.

Eligibility Requirements: Applicant must be enrolled or expecting to enroll full-time at a two-year or four-year institution or university; resident of Oregon and studying in Oregon. Available to U.S. citizens.

Application Requirements: Application form, recommendations or references. *Deadline:* March 1.

Contact: Dianne Causey, Program Associate for Scholarships and Grants
　　　　Phone: 503-227-6846 Ext. 1418
　　　　E-mail: dcausey@oregoncf.org

OREGON STUDENT ASSISTANCE COMMISSION

http://www.GetCollegeFunds.org/

BERTHA P. SINGER NURSES SCHOLARSHIP

Renewable award for Oregon residents pursuing a nursing career. Must attend a college or university in Oregon. Minimum GPA of 3.0 required. Proof of enrollment in second year of nursing degree program is required. U.S. Bank employees, their children, or close relatives are not eligible.

Academic Fields/Career Goals: Nursing.

Award: Scholarship for use in sophomore, junior, senior, or graduate years; renewable.

Eligibility Requirements: Applicant must be enrolled or expecting to enroll full-time at a four-year institution or university and studying in Oregon. Applicant must have 3.0 GPA or higher. Available to U.S. citizens.

Application Requirements: Application form, financial need analysis. *Deadline:* March 1.

Contact: Melissa Adams, Scholarship Processing Coordinator
　　　　Phone: 541-687-7409
　　　　E-mail: melissa.adams@hecc.oregon.gov

CHESTER AND HELEN LUTHER SCHOLARSHIP

• *See page 354*

CLARK-PHELPS SCHOLARSHIP

• *See page 238*

FRANKS FOUNDATION SCHOLARSHIP

Awards to students who are nursing or theology majors and residents of Crook, Deschutes, or Jefferson County (first preference) or residents of Grant, Harney, Klamath, or Lake County (second preference). High school seniors must have a minimum GPA of 2.5, college students must have a minimum GPA of 2.0. Must reapply annually for renewal. U.S. Bank employees, their children, and near relatives are not eligible. FAFSA is required.

Academic Fields/Career Goals: Nursing; Religion/Theology.

Award: Scholarship for use in freshman, sophomore, junior, senior, or graduate years; not renewable.

Eligibility Requirements: Applicant must be enrolled or expecting to enroll full- or part-time at a four-year institution or university and resident of Oregon. Available to U.S. citizens.

Application Requirements: Application form, financial need analysis. *Deadline:* March 1.

Contact: Melissa Adams, Scholarship Processing Coordinator
　　　　Phone: 541-687-7409
　　　　E-mail: melissa.adams@hecc.oregon.gov

MARION A. LINDEMAN SCHOLARSHIP

• *See page 354*

WALTER C. AND MARIE C. SCHMIDT SCHOLARSHIP

Scholarship available to Oregon students enrolling in programs to become registered nurses and intending to pursue careers in geriatric health care. Preference given to (1) students attending Lane County Community College, (2) students enrolled in any other two-year college nursing program, (3) students enrolled in a four-year college nursing program. U.S. Bank employees, their children, or near relatives are not eligible.

Academic Fields/Career Goals: Nursing.

Award: Scholarship for use in freshman year; not renewable.

Eligibility Requirements: Applicant must be enrolled or expecting to enroll full- or part-time at a two-year or four-year institution or university and resident of Oregon. Available to U.S. citizens.

Application Requirements: Application form, essay, financial need analysis. *Deadline:* March 1.

Contact: Melissa Adams, Scholarship Processing Coordinator
    Phone: 541-687-7409
    E-mail: melissa.adams@hecc.oregon.gov

PILOT INTERNATIONAL FOUNDATION

http://www.pilotinternational.org/

PILOT INTERNATIONAL SCHOLARSHIP
• See page 355

RUBY NEWHALL MEMORIAL SCHOLARSHIP
• See page 355

PLATINUM EDUCATIONAL GROUP

www.platinumed.com

PLATINUM EDUCATIONAL GROUP SCHOLARSHIPS PROGRAM FOR EMS, NURSING, AND ALLIED HEALTH
• See page 107

THE RECOVERY VILLAGE

https://www.therecoveryvillage.com/

RECOVERY VILLAGE HEALTHCARE SCHOLARSHIP
• See page 238

RHODE ISLAND FOUNDATION

http://www.rifoundation.org/

ALBERT E. AND FLORENCE W. NEWTON NURSE SCHOLARSHIP

Scholarship for student studying nursing on a full- or part-time basis. Preference will be given to Rhode Island residents committed to practicing in Rhode Island. Must be able to demonstrate financial need. Must be either a licensed RN enrolled in a nursing Baccalaureate degree program; a student enrolled in a Baccalaureate nursing program; a student in a diploma nursing program; or a student in a two-year Associate degree nursing program.

Academic Fields/Career Goals: Nursing.

Award: Scholarship for use in freshman, sophomore, junior, or senior years; renewable. *Amount:* $500–$2000.

Eligibility Requirements: Applicant must be enrolled or expecting to enroll full- or part-time at a two-year or four-year institution or university. Available to U.S. citizens.

Application Requirements: Application form, copy of college acceptance letter, copy of most recent income tax return, essay, financial need analysis, self-addressed stamped envelope with application, transcript. *Deadline:* April 19.

Contact: Libby Monahan, Funds Administrator
    Phone: 401-274-4564 Ext. 3117
    E-mail: libbym@rifoundation.org

EDWARD J. AND VIRGINIA M. ROUTHIER NURSING SCHOLARSHIP

Renewable scholarship for licensed RNs seeking Baccalaureate or graduate nursing degrees in Rhode Island. Must demonstrate financial need.

Academic Fields/Career Goals: Nursing.

Award: Scholarship for use in freshman, sophomore, junior, senior, or graduate years; renewable. *Amount:* $500–$3000.

Eligibility Requirements: Applicant must be enrolled or expecting to enroll full- or part-time at a four-year institution or university and studying in Rhode Island. Available to U.S. citizens.

Application Requirements: Application form. *Deadline:* April 19.

Contact: Libby Monahan, Funds Administrator
    Phone: 401-274-4564 Ext. 3117
    E-mail: libbym@rifoundation.org

WILLARD & MARJORIE SCHEIBE NURSING SCHOLARSHIP

Renewable scholarship for Rhode Island residents pursuing LPN, RN, or advanced nursing degrees. Must demonstrate financial need.

Academic Fields/Career Goals: Nursing.

Award: Scholarship for use in freshman, sophomore, junior, senior, or graduate years; renewable.

Eligibility Requirements: Applicant must be enrolled or expecting to enroll full-time at a four-year institution or university and resident of Rhode Island. Available to U.S. citizens.

Application Requirements: Application form, financial need analysis. *Deadline:* April 19.

Contact: Libby Monahan, Funds Administrator
    Phone: 401-274-4564 Ext. 3117
    E-mail: libbym@rifoundation.org

SCARLETT FAMILY FOUNDATION SCHOLARSHIP PROGRAM

http://www.scarlettfoundation.org/

SCHOLARSHIP FOR STUDENTS PURSUING A BUSINESS OR STEM DEGREE
• See page 84

THE SOCIETY FOR THE SCIENTIFIC STUDY OF SEXUALITY

http://www.sexscience.org/

THE SOCIETY FOR THE SCIENTIFIC STUDY OF SEXUALITY STUDENT RESEARCH GRANT
• See page 109

SOCIETY OF PEDIATRIC NURSES

http://www.pedsnurses.org/

SOCIETY OF PEDIATRIC NURSES EDUCATIONAL SCHOLARSHIP
• See page 190

STATE STUDENT ASSISTANCE COMMISSION OF INDIANA (SSACI)

http://www.in.gov/ssaci

INDIANA NURSING SCHOLARSHIP FUND

Need-based tuition funding for nursing students enrolled full- or part-time at an eligible Indiana institution. Must be a U.S. citizen and an Indiana resident and have a minimum 2.0 GPA or meet the minimum requirements for the nursing program. Upon graduation, recipients must practice as a nurse in an Indiana health care setting for two years.

Academic Fields/Career Goals: Nursing.

Award: Scholarship for use in freshman, sophomore, junior, or senior years; not renewable. *Number:* 490–690. *Amount:* $200–$5000.

Eligibility Requirements: Applicant must be enrolled or expecting to enroll full- or part-time at a two-year or four-year institution or university; resident of Indiana and studying in Indiana. Available to U.S. citizens.

Application Requirements: Application form, FAFSA, financial need analysis. *Deadline:* continuous.

Contact: Yvonne Heflin, Director, Special Programs
State Student Assistance Commission of Indiana (SSACI)
150 West Market Street, Suite 500
Indianapolis, IN 46204-2805
Phone: 317-232-2350
Fax: 317-232-3260

STRAIGHTFORWARD MEDIA
http://www.straightforwardmedia.com/

STRAIGHTFORWARD MEDIA MEDICAL PROFESSIONS SCHOLARSHIP
• *See page 239*

STRAIGHTFORWARD MEDIA NURSING SCHOOL SCHOLARSHIP
Scholarship of $500 available to students majoring in nursing. Awarded four times per year. Deadlines are April 14, July 14, October 14, and January 14. To apply, go to http://www.straightforwardmedia.com/nursing/form.php.

Academic Fields/Career Goals: Nursing.

Award: Scholarship for use in freshman, sophomore, junior, or senior years; not renewable. *Number:* 4. *Amount:* $500.

Eligibility Requirements: Applicant must be enrolled or expecting to enroll full- or part-time at a two-year or four-year or technical institution or university. Available to U.S. and non-U.S. citizens.

Application Requirements: Essay. *Deadline:* varies.

Contact: Scholarship Committee
Phone: 605-348-3042

TAFFORD UNIFORMS
http://www.tafford.com/

TAFFORD UNIFORMS NURSING SCHOLARSHIP PROGRAM
Two scholarships of $1000 each awarded to nursing students enrolled in undergraduate and graduate study. Minimum 2.5 GPA required.

Academic Fields/Career Goals: Nursing.

Award: Scholarship for use in freshman, sophomore, junior, or senior years; not renewable. *Number:* 2. *Amount:* $1000.

Eligibility Requirements: Applicant must be enrolled or expecting to enroll full-time at a two-year or four-year institution or university. Applicant must have 2.5 GPA or higher. Available to U.S. citizens.

Application Requirements: Application form. *Deadline:* continuous.

Contact: Scholarship Coordinator
Phone: 215-643-9666

TOUCHMARK FOUNDATION
http://www.touchmarkfoundation.org/

TOUCHMARK FOUNDATION NURSING SCHOLARSHIP
Students pursuing nursing degrees at any level are encouraged to apply, including nurses interested pursuing advanced degrees in order to teach. Applications reviewed throughout the year. Scholarships are offered to students attending schools in the following states: WI, WA, ID, OR, ND, SD, MN, OK, MT, and AZ.

Academic Fields/Career Goals: Nursing.

Award: Scholarship for use in freshman, sophomore, junior, senior, graduate, or postgraduate years; not renewable. *Number:* 8–16. *Amount:* $1000–$2000.

Eligibility Requirements: Applicant must be enrolled or expecting to enroll full-time at a four-year institution or university and studying in Alberta, Idaho, Minnesota, Montana, North Dakota, Oklahoma, Oregon, South Dakota, Washington, Wisconsin. Available to U.S. citizens.

Application Requirements: Application form, essay, FAFSA, copy of acceptance letter, recommendations or references, transcript. *Deadline:* continuous.

Contact: Bret Cope, Chairman
Touchmark Foundation
5150 SW Griffith Drive
Beaverton, OR 97005
Phone: 503-646-5186
E-mail: bjc@touchmark.com

UNICO FOUNDATION INC.
http://www.unico.org/

BERNARD AND CAROLYN TORRACO MEMORIAL NURSING SCHOLARSHIP PROGRAM
$2,500 award for students currently enrolled in an accredited nursing degree program in the United States, completing core nursing courses at either an associate degree School of Nursing, a collegiate School of Nursing, or a diploma School of Nursing. Proof of enrollment must be provided. Preference will be given to applicants demonstrating financial need. A current FAFSA Student Aid Report (SAR) or previous year tax return is required. Must hold U.S. citizenship. A candidate must reside in the home state of an active UNICO chapter. Applications maybe acquired from and submitted through a UNICO chapter, a District Governor or the UNICO National Office. To locate contact information for the nearest chapter, access the UNICO National web-site, unico.org, and click on Find a Chapter.

Academic Fields/Career Goals: Nursing.

Award: Scholarship for use in freshman, sophomore, junior, or senior years; not renewable. *Number:* 10. *Amount:* $2500.

Eligibility Requirements: Applicant must be enrolled or expecting to enroll full- or part-time at a two-year or four-year institution or university. Applicant must have 3.0 GPA or higher. Available to U.S. citizens.

Application Requirements: Application form, financial need analysis. *Deadline:* April 15.

Contact: Joan Tidona, Scholarship Director
Phone: 973-808-0035
Fax: 973-808-0043
E-mail: uniconational@unico.org

UNITED DAUGHTERS OF THE CONFEDERACY
http://www.hqudc.org/

PHOEBE PEMBER MEMORIAL SCHOLARSHIP
Award for full-time undergraduate students who are descendants of a Confederate soldier, enrolled in a school of nursing. Must be enrolled in an accredited college or university and have a minimum 3.0 GPA. Submit letter of endorsement from sponsoring Chapter of the United Daughters of the Confederacy.

Academic Fields/Career Goals: Nursing.

Award: Scholarship for use in freshman, sophomore, junior, or senior years; renewable. *Number:* 1–2. *Amount:* $800–$1000.

Eligibility Requirements: Applicant must be enrolled or expecting to enroll full-time at a four-year institution or university. Applicant or parent of applicant must be member of United Daughters of the Confederacy. Applicant must have 3.0 GPA or higher. Available to U.S. citizens.

Application Requirements: Application form, copy of applicant's birth certificate, copy of confederate ancestor's proof of service, essay, financial need analysis, personal photograph, recommendations or references, self-addressed stamped envelope with application, test scores, transcript. *Deadline:* March 15.

Contact: Ms. Jamie Davis, Second Vice President General
Phone: 804-355-1636
E-mail: hqudc@rcn.com

WALTER REED SMITH SCHOLARSHIP
• *See page 168*

UNITED NEGRO COLLEGE FUND

http://www.uncf.org/

UNITED HEALTH FOUNDATION DIVERSE SCHOLARS INITIATIVE
• *See page 152*

U.S. DEPARTMENT OF HEALTH AND HUMAN SERVICES

http://www.hhs.gov/

U. S. PUBLIC HEALTH SERVICE-HEALTH RESOURCES AND SERVICES ADMINISTRATION, BUREAU OF HEALTH PROFESSIONS SCHOLARSHIPS FOR DISADVANTAGED STUDENTS
• *See page 239*

VIRGINIA DEPARTMENT OF HEALTH, OFFICE OF MINORITY HEALTH AND HEALTH EQUITY

http://www.vdh.virginia.gov/

MARY MARSHALL PRACTICAL NURSING SCHOLARSHIP (LPN)

Awards for students who are accepted or enrolled as a full-time or part-time student in a practical school of nursing in the state of Virginia. Must be a Virginia resident for at least one year and have submitted a completed application form and a recommendation from the Director regarding scholastic attainment and financial need prior to June 30. Students pursuing a nursing degree not available in Virginia, are not eligible for the scholarship. Scholarship amount varies.

Academic Fields/Career Goals: Nursing.

Award: Scholarship for use in freshman, sophomore, junior, or senior years; not renewable. *Number:* 26–88. *Amount:* $600–$1200.

Eligibility Requirements: Applicant must be enrolled or expecting to enroll full- or part-time at a two-year or four-year or technical institution or university; resident of Virginia and studying in Virginia. Applicant must have 2.5 GPA or higher. Available to U.S. citizens.

Application Requirements: Application form, driver's license, essay, financial need analysis, recommendations or references, transcript. *Deadline:* June 30.

Contact: Miss. Sarahbeth Jones, Communications Specialist
Virginia Department of Health, Office of Minority Health and Health Equity
PO Box 2448, 109 Governor Street, Suite 1016-E
Richmond, VA 23218-2448
Phone: 804-864-7422
Fax: 804-864-7440
E-mail: IncentivePrograms@vdh.virginia.gov

MARY MARSHALL REGISTERED NURSING SCHOLARSHIPS

Scholarship for Virginia residents who have been accepted or is enrollment as a full-time or part-time student in a school of nursing in the state of Virginia. Must demonstrate financial need, verified by the Financial Aid Office/authorized person at the applicant's nursing school. Must also be a resident of Virginia for at least one year and have a minimum 3.0 GPA in required courses. Must have submitted a completed application form and an official grade transcript to The Office of Minority Health and Public Health Policy prior to June 30. If no college courses attempted an official high school transcript or equivalent must be submitted.

Academic Fields/Career Goals: Nursing.

Award: Scholarship for use in freshman, sophomore, junior, or senior years; not renewable. *Number:* 28–95. *Amount:* $600–$2000.

Eligibility Requirements: Applicant must be enrolled or expecting to enroll full- or part-time at a two-year or four-year institution or university; resident of Virginia and studying in Virginia. Applicant must have 2.5 GPA or higher. Available to U.S. citizens.

Application Requirements: Application form, driver's license, essay, financial need analysis, recommendations or references, transcript. *Deadline:* June 30.

Contact: Miss. Sarahbeth Jones, Communications Specialist
Virginia Department of Health, Office of Minority Health and Health Equity
PO Box 2448, 109 Governor Street, Suite 1016-E
Richmond, VA 23218-2448
Phone: 804-864-7422
Fax: 804-864-7440
E-mail: IncentivePrograms@vdh.virginia.gov

WISCONSIN LEAGUE FOR NURSING, INC.

http://www.wisconsinwln.org/

NURSING SCHOLARSHIP FOR HIGH SCHOOL SENIORS

One scholarship for a Wisconsin high school senior who will be pursuing a professional nursing career. The senior must have been accepted by a Wisconsin NLN accredited school of nursing, have financial need, demonstrate scholastic excellence and leadership potential. Contact the WLN office by mail to request an application.

Academic Fields/Career Goals: Nursing.

Award: Scholarship for use in freshman year; not renewable. *Number:* 1. *Amount:* $500.

Eligibility Requirements: Applicant must be high school student; planning to enroll or expecting to enroll full-time at a two-year or four-year institution or university; resident of Wisconsin and studying in Wisconsin. Available to U.S. citizens.

Application Requirements: Application form, financial need analysis. *Deadline:* March 1.

Contact: Mary Ann Tanner, Administrative Secretary
Phone: 888-755-3329
E-mail: wln@wisconsinwln.org

WISCONSIN LEAGUE FOR NURSING, INC. SCHOLARSHIP

One-time award for Wisconsin residents who have completed half of an accredited Wisconsin school of nursing program. Financial need of student must be demonstrated. Scholarship applications are mailed by WLN office ONLY to Wisconsin nursing schools in January for distribution to students. Students interested in obtaining an application must contact their nursing school and submit completed applications to their school. Applications sent directly to WLN office will be returned to applicant. For further information visit website http://www.wisconsinwln.org/Scholarships.htm.

Academic Fields/Career Goals: Nursing.

Award: Scholarship for use in junior or senior years; not renewable. *Number:* 11–35. *Amount:* $500–$1000.

Eligibility Requirements: Applicant must be enrolled or expecting to enroll full-time at a two-year or four-year or technical institution or university; resident of Wisconsin and studying in Wisconsin. Available to U.S. citizens.

Application Requirements: Application form, essay, financial need analysis. *Deadline:* March 1.

Contact: Mary Ann Tanner, Administrative Secretary
Phone: 888-755-3329
E-mail: wln@wisconsinwln.org

WOUND, OSTOMY AND CONTINENCE NURSES SOCIETY

http://www.wocn.org

WOCN ACCREDITED NURSING EDUCATION PROGRAM SCHOLARSHIP

Scholarships are awarded to deserving individuals committed to working within the wound, ostomy and continence nursing specialty. Applicants must agree to support the WOCN Society philosophy and scope of practice. Number of scholarships and the dollar value varies annually. Deadlines: May 1 or November 1.

Academic Fields/Career Goals: Nursing.

Award: Scholarship for use in freshman, sophomore, junior, or senior years; not renewable. *Number:* 20. *Amount:* $2000.

Eligibility Requirements: Applicant must be enrolled or expecting to enroll full-time at a two-year or four-year or technical institution or university. Applicant or parent of applicant must have employment or volunteer experience in nursing. Available to U.S. and non-U.S. citizens.

Application Requirements: Application form. *Deadline:* May 1.

Contact: Heather Martinek, Assistant Executive Director
Wound, Ostomy and Continence Nurses Society
1120 Route 73
Suite 200
Mount Laurel, NJ 08054
Phone: 888-224-9626
Fax: 856-439-0525
E-mail: info@wocn.org

OCCUPATIONAL SAFETY AND HEALTH

AMERICAN INDIAN SCIENCE AND ENGINEERING SOCIETY

http://www.aises.org/

A.T. ANDERSON MEMORIAL SCHOLARSHIP PROGRAM
• *See page 109*

AMERICAN SOCIETY OF SAFETY ENGINEERS (ASSE) FOUNDATION

http://www.asse.org/

ALASKA CHAPTER SCHOLARSHIP

$1000 award for full-time students pursing Associate or Bachelor's degrees in occupational safety. Priority given to Alaska chapter members attending UAA or other school, Alaska residents attending school elsewhere, or students residing in Region I. Minimum 3.0 GPA required.

Academic Fields/Career Goals: Occupational Safety and Health.

Award: Scholarship for use in freshman, sophomore, junior, or senior years; not renewable. *Number:* 1. *Amount:* $1000.

Eligibility Requirements: Applicant must be enrolled or expecting to enroll full-time at a two-year or four-year institution or university. Applicant or parent of applicant must be member of American Society of Safety Engineers. Applicant must have 3.0 GPA or higher. Available to U.S. and non-U.S. citizens.

Application Requirements: Application form. *Deadline:* December 1.

Contact: Matthew Sells, Scholarship Coordinator
American Society of Safety Engineers (ASSE) Foundation
1800 East Oakton Street
Des Plaines, IL 60018
E-mail: msells@asse.org

AMERICA RESPONDS MEMORIAL SCHOLARSHIP

Scholarship of $1000 will be awarded to a student pursuing a degree in occupational safety and health or a closely related field. Must have completed 60 semester hours and maintain at least a 3.0 GPA. Must be a member of ASSE and be a U.S. citizen. Priority given to students who have experience working as an emergency responders.

Academic Fields/Career Goals: Occupational Safety and Health.

Award: Scholarship for use in freshman, sophomore, junior, senior, graduate, or postgraduate years; not renewable. *Number:* 1. *Amount:* $1000.

Eligibility Requirements: Applicant must be enrolled or expecting to enroll full-time at a four-year institution or university. Applicant or parent of applicant must be member of American Society of Safety Engineers. Applicant must have 3.0 GPA or higher. Available to U.S. citizens.

Application Requirements: Application form, essay, financial need analysis. *Deadline:* December 1.

Contact: Matthew Sells, Scholarship Coordinator
American Society of Safety Engineers (ASSE) Foundation
1800 East Oakton Street
Des Plaines, IL 60018
E-mail: msells@asse.org

APPLICATIONS INTERNATIONAL CORPORATION IMPACT SCHOLARSHIP

Scholarship awarded to a student pursuing an undergraduate, graduate, or postgraduate degree in occupational safety and health or a closely related field. Priority will be given to students that have served in the military and are attending an ABET-accredited school. GPA of 3.0 required for undergraduates, 3.5 for all other students. ASSE membership is preferred but not required.

Academic Fields/Career Goals: Occupational Safety and Health.

Award: Scholarship for use in sophomore, junior, senior, graduate, or postgraduate years; not renewable. *Number:* 4. *Amount:* $10,000–$15,000.

Eligibility Requirements: Applicant must be enrolled or expecting to enroll full-time at a four-year institution or university. Available to U.S. citizens.

Application Requirements: Application form, essay, financial need analysis. *Deadline:* December 1.

Contact: Matthew Sells, Scholarship Coordinator
American Society of Safety Engineers (ASSE) Foundation
1800 East Oakton Street
Des Plaines, IL 60018
E-mail: msells@asse.org

ASSE CONSTRUCTION SAFETY SCHOLARSHIP

One $2000 scholarship for a student pursuing an undergraduate degree in occupational safety and health or a closely related field. Must have completed 60 semester hours and maintain at least a 3.0 GPA. Priority will be given to students with an emphasis in construction safety, and enrolled in an ABET-accredited OSH program.

Academic Fields/Career Goals: Occupational Safety and Health.

Award: Scholarship for use in sophomore, junior, or senior years; not renewable. *Number:* 1. *Amount:* $2000.

Eligibility Requirements: Applicant must be enrolled or expecting to enroll full-time at a four-year institution or university. Applicant must have 3.0 GPA or higher. Available to U.S. citizens.

Application Requirements: Application form, essay, financial need analysis. *Deadline:* December 1.

Contact: Matthew Sells, Scholarship Coordinator
American Society of Safety Engineers (ASSE) Foundation
1800 East Oakton Street
Des Plaines, IL 60018
E-mail: msells@asse.org

ASSE DIVERSITY COMMITTEE SCHOLARSHIP

Scholarship of $1000 will be awarded to a student pursuing an undergraduate or graduate degree in occupational safety and health or a closely related field. Award is open to any individual regardless of race, ethnicity, gender, religion, personal beliefs, age, sexual orientation, physical challenges, geographic location, university or specific area of study. Minimum 3.0 GPA required for undergraduates, 3.5 for graduates.

Academic Fields/Career Goals: Occupational Safety and Health.

Award: Scholarship for use in sophomore, junior, senior, or graduate years; not renewable. *Number:* 1. *Amount:* $1000.

Eligibility Requirements: Applicant must be enrolled or expecting to enroll full-time at a four-year institution or university. Available to U.S. citizens.

Application Requirements: Application form, essay, financial need analysis. *Deadline:* December 1.

Contact: Matthew Sells, Scholarship Coordinator
American Society of Safety Engineers (ASSE) Foundation
1800 East Oakton Street
Des Plaines, IL 60018
E-mail: msells@asse.org

ASSE-GULF COAST PAST PRESIDENTS SCHOLARSHIP

Scholarship of $1500 will be awarded to a part- or full-time student pursuing an associate or undergraduate degree in occupational safety and health or a closely related field. Must have completed 60 semester hours and maintain at least a 3.0 GPA. ASSE general or professional membership preferred if applicant is a part-time student.

Academic Fields/Career Goals: Occupational Safety and Health.

Award: Scholarship for use in freshman, sophomore, junior, or senior years; not renewable. *Number:* 2. *Amount:* $1500.

Eligibility Requirements: Applicant must be enrolled or expecting to enroll full- or part-time at a four-year institution or university. Applicant or parent of applicant must be member of American Society of Safety Engineers. Applicant must have 3.0 GPA or higher. Available to U.S. citizens.

Application Requirements: Application form, essay, financial need analysis. *Deadline:* December 1.

Contact: Matthew Sells, Scholarship Coordinator
American Society of Safety Engineers (ASSE) Foundation
1800 East Oakton Street
Des Plaines, IL 60018
E-mail: msells@asse.org

ASSE MEMBER GET A MEMBER SCHOLARSHIP

$2500 scholarship for full-time students pursing undergraduate degrees in occupational safety. Minimum 3.0 GPA required.

Academic Fields/Career Goals: Occupational Safety and Health.

Award: Scholarship for use in freshman, sophomore, junior, or senior years; not renewable. *Number:* 1. *Amount:* $2500.

Eligibility Requirements: Applicant must be enrolled or expecting to enroll full-time at a four-year institution or university. Applicant or parent of applicant must be member of American Society of Safety Engineers. Applicant must have 3.0 GPA or higher. Available to U.S. and non-U.S. citizens.

Application Requirements: Application form. *Deadline:* December 1.

Contact: Matthew Sells, Scholarship Coordinator
American Society of Safety Engineers (ASSE) Foundation
1800 East Oakton Street
Des Plaines, IL 60018
E-mail: msells@asse.org

ASSE-UNITED PARCEL SERVICE SCHOLARSHIP

Scholarships for students pursuing a four-year BS or BA degree in occupational safety and health or related area. Completion of at least 60 current semester hours and a minimum 3.0 GPA is required. Must be a student member of ASSE.

Academic Fields/Career Goals: Occupational Safety and Health.

Award: Scholarship for use in sophomore, junior, or senior years; not renewable. *Number:* 3. *Amount:* $5250.

Eligibility Requirements: Applicant must be enrolled or expecting to enroll full-time at a four-year institution or university. Applicant or parent of applicant must be member of American Society of Safety Engineers. Applicant must have 3.0 GPA or higher. Available to U.S. and non-U.S. citizens.

Application Requirements: Application form, essay. *Deadline:* December 1.

Contact: Matthew Sells, Scholarship Coordinator
American Society of Safety Engineers (ASSE) Foundation
1800 East Oakton Street
Des Plaines, IL 60018
E-mail: msells@asse.org

BCSP MARGARET M. CARROLL PROFESSIONAL SCHOLARSHIP

$5000 scholarship for students pursuing undergraduate or graduate degrees in occupational safety. Priority given to students attending a school with an ASAC/ABET program. Minimum 3.0 GPA required for undergraduates, 3.5 for graduate students.

Academic Fields/Career Goals: Occupational Safety and Health.

Award: Scholarship for use in freshman, sophomore, junior, senior, or graduate years; not renewable. *Number:* 1. *Amount:* $5000.

Eligibility Requirements: Applicant must be enrolled or expecting to enroll full-time at a four-year institution or university. Available to U.S. citizens.

Application Requirements: Application form. *Deadline:* December 1.

Contact: Matthew Sells, Scholarship Coordinator
American Society of Safety Engineers (ASSE) Foundation
1800 East Oakton Street
Des Plaines, IL 60018
E-mail: msells@asse.org

BCSP MARK COSTELLO TECHNICIAN/TECHNOLOGIST SUPERVISORY SCHOLARSHIP

$5000 scholarship for students pursuing undergraduate or graduate degrees in occupational safety. Priority given to students attending a school with an ASAC/ABET program. Minimum 3.0 GPA for undergraduates, 3.5 for graduate students.

Academic Fields/Career Goals: Occupational Safety and Health.

Award: Scholarship for use in freshman, sophomore, junior, senior, or graduate years; not renewable. *Number:* 1. *Amount:* $5000.

Eligibility Requirements: Applicant must be enrolled or expecting to enroll full-time at a four-year institution or university. Available to U.S. citizens.

Application Requirements: Application form. *Deadline:* December 1.

Contact: Matthew Sells, Scholarship Coordinator
American Society of Safety Engineers (ASSE) Foundation
1800 East Oakton Street
Des Plaines, IL 60018
E-mail: msells@asse.org

BERVIN HALL MEMORIAL SCHOLARSHIP

Scholarship of $1000 will be awarded to a student pursuing an Associate or Bachelor's degree in occupational safety and health or a closely related field. Must have completed 60 semester hours and maintain at least a 3.0 GPA. Priority will be given to Colorado Chapter members or to students attending school within Region II.

Academic Fields/Career Goals: Occupational Safety and Health.

Award: Scholarship for use in freshman, sophomore, junior, or senior years; not renewable. *Number:* 1. *Amount:* $1000.

Eligibility Requirements: Applicant must be enrolled or expecting to enroll full-time at a two-year or four-year institution or university. Applicant must have 3.0 GPA or higher. Available to U.S. citizens.

Application Requirements: Application form, essay, financial need analysis. *Deadline:* December 1.

Contact: Matthew Sells, Scholarship Coordinator
American Society of Safety Engineers (ASSE) Foundation
1800 East Oakton Street
Des Plaines, IL 60018
E-mail: msells@asse.org

BLACKS IN SAFETY ENGINEERING SCHOLARSHIP

Scholarship of $1000 will be awarded to a black student pursuing an undergraduate degree in occupational safety and health or a closely related field. Must have completed 60 semester hours and maintain at least a 3.0 GPA.

Academic Fields/Career Goals: Occupational Safety and Health.

Award: Scholarship for use in sophomore, junior, or senior years; not renewable. *Number:* 1. *Amount:* $1000.

Eligibility Requirements: Applicant must be Black (non-Hispanic) and enrolled or expecting to enroll full-time at a four-year institution or university. Applicant must have 3.0 GPA or higher. Available to U.S. citizens.

Application Requirements: Application form, essay, financial need analysis. *Deadline:* December 1.

Contact: Matthew Sells, Scholarship Coordinator
American Society of Safety Engineers (ASSE) Foundation
1800 East Oakton Street
Des Plaines, IL 60018
E-mail: msells@asse.org

CENTRAL FLORIDA CHAPTER SCHOLARSHIP

$1000 scholarship for students pursing degrees in occupational safety. Priority will be given to Central Florida Chapter members or students residing in Region IV. Minimum 3.0 GPA required for undergraduates and 3.5 for graduate students.

Academic Fields/Career Goals: Occupational Safety and Health.

Award: Scholarship for use in freshman, sophomore, junior, senior, or graduate years; not renewable. *Number:* 1. *Amount:* $1000.

Eligibility Requirements: Applicant must be enrolled or expecting to enroll full- or part-time at a two-year or four-year institution or university. Applicant or parent of applicant must be member of American Society of Safety Engineers. Available to U.S. and non-U.S. citizens.

Application Requirements: Application form. *Deadline:* December 1.

Contact: Matthew Sells, Scholarship Coordinator
American Society of Safety Engineers (ASSE) Foundation
1800 East Oakton Street
Des Plaines, IL 60018
E-mail: msells@asse.org

CENTRAL INDIANA ASSE JIM KRINER MEMORIAL SCHOLARSHIP

Scholarship awarded to a student pursuing an undergraduate or graduate degree in occupational safety and health or a closely related field. Priority will be given to Indiana residents attending school in Indiana or anywhere in the U.S. or to non-residents attending an Indiana university. Minimum 3.0 GPA for undergraduate students, 3.5 GPA for graduate students.

Academic Fields/Career Goals: Occupational Safety and Health.

Award: Scholarship for use in sophomore, junior, senior, or graduate years; not renewable. *Number:* 1. *Amount:* $3000.

Eligibility Requirements: Applicant must be enrolled or expecting to enroll full-time at a four-year institution or university. Available to U.S. citizens.

Application Requirements: Application form, essay, financial need analysis. *Deadline:* December 1.

Contact: Matthew Sells, Scholarship Coordinator
American Society of Safety Engineers (ASSE) Foundation
1800 East Oakton Street
Des Plaines, IL 60018
E-mail: msells@asse.org

COLUMBIA-WILLAMETTE CHAPTER PRESIDENT SCHOLARSHIP

One $1000 scholarship will be awarded to a student pursuing an undergraduate or graduate degree in occupational safety and health or a closely related field. Minimum 3.0 GPA for undergraduate students, 3.5 for graduate students. Priority will be given to Columbia-Willamette chapter members, students attending school in Oregon or Washington state, or to residents of Oregon or Washington state attending school elsewhere.

Academic Fields/Career Goals: Occupational Safety and Health.

Award: Scholarship for use in sophomore, junior, senior, or graduate years; not renewable. *Number:* 1. *Amount:* $1000.

Eligibility Requirements: Applicant must be enrolled or expecting to enroll full-time at a four-year institution or university. Available to U.S. citizens.

Application Requirements: Application form, essay, financial need analysis. *Deadline:* December 1.

Contact: Matthew Sells, Scholarship Coordinator
American Society of Safety Engineers (ASSE) Foundation
1800 East Oakton Street
Des Plaines, IL 60018
E-mail: msells@asse.org

FABENCO-LACOOK INVESTMENT FOR EXCELLENCE IN OCCUPATIONAL SAFETY & HEALTH SCHOLARSHIP

$4000 scholarship for students pursuing degrees in occupational safety. Priority will be given to a student from the Gulf Coast Chapter or a student from Region III. Minimum 3.0 GPA required for undergraduates, 3.5 for graduate students.

Academic Fields/Career Goals: Occupational Safety and Health.

Award: Scholarship for use in freshman, sophomore, junior, senior, or graduate years; not renewable. *Number:* 1. *Amount:* $4000.

Eligibility Requirements: Applicant must be enrolled or expecting to enroll full- or part-time at a two-year or four-year institution or university. Applicant or parent of applicant must be member of American Society of Safety Engineers. Available to U.S. and non-U.S. citizens.

Application Requirements: Application form. *Deadline:* December 1.

Contact: Matthew Sells, Scholarship Coordinator
American Society of Safety Engineers (ASSE) Foundation
1800 East Oakton Street
Des Plaines, IL 60018
E-mail: msells@asse.org

FLATIRON CONSTRUCTION CHRISTOPHER GONZALEZ MEMORIAL SCHOLARSHIP

One scholarship of $4700 will be awarded to a student pursuing an undergraduate degree in occupational safety and health or a closely related field. Must have completed 60 semester hours and maintain at least a 3.0 GPA. Priority will be given to students with an emphasis in construction safety.

Academic Fields/Career Goals: Occupational Safety and Health.

Award: Scholarship for use in sophomore, junior, or senior years; not renewable. *Number:* 1. *Amount:* $4700.

Eligibility Requirements: Applicant must be enrolled or expecting to enroll full-time at a four-year institution or university. Applicant must have 3.0 GPA or higher. Available to U.S. citizens.

Application Requirements: Application form, essay, financial need analysis. *Deadline:* December 1.

Contact: Matthew Sells, Scholarship Coordinator
American Society of Safety Engineers (ASSE) Foundation
1800 East Oakton Street
Des Plaines, IL 60018
E-mail: msells@asse.org

FOUR CORNERS CHAPTER SCHOLARSHIP

Scholarship of $1000 will be awarded to a student pursuing an undergraduate degree in occupational safety and health or a closely related field. Must have completed 60 semester hours and maintain at least a 3.0 GPA. Priority will be given to students from the Four Corner's Chapter, a New Mexico or Colorado Chapter member, or from a student that resides in Region II (in that order).

Academic Fields/Career Goals: Occupational Safety and Health.

Award: Scholarship for use in sophomore, junior, or senior years; not renewable. *Number:* 1. *Amount:* $1000.

Eligibility Requirements: Applicant must be enrolled or expecting to enroll full-time at a four-year institution or university. Applicant must have 3.0 GPA or higher. Available to U.S. citizens.

Application Requirements: Application form, essay, financial need analysis. *Deadline:* December 1.

Contact: Matthew Sells, Scholarship Coordinator
American Society of Safety Engineers (ASSE) Foundation
1800 East Oakton Street
Des Plaines, IL 60018
E-mail: msells@asse.org

GEORGE GUSTAFSON HSE MEMORIAL SCHOLARSHIP

Scholarship of $2000 will be awarded to a student pursuing an undergraduate or a graduate degree in occupational safety and health or a closely related field. Minimum GPA of 3.0 for undergraduates, 3.5 for graduate students. Priority will be given to students residing in Texas or attending a Texas university.

Academic Fields/Career Goals: Occupational Safety and Health.

Award: Scholarship for use in sophomore, junior, senior, or graduate years; not renewable. *Number:* 1. *Amount:* $2000.

Eligibility Requirements: Applicant must be enrolled or expecting to enroll full-time at a four-year institution or university. Available to U.S. citizens.

Application Requirements: Application form, essay, financial need analysis. *Deadline:* December 1.

Contact: Matthew Sells, Scholarship Coordinator
American Society of Safety Engineers (ASSE) Foundation
1800 East Oakton Street
Des Plaines, IL 60018
E-mail: msells@asse.org

GEORGIA CHAPTER SCHOLARSHIP

$1000 scholarship for students pursuing degrees in occupational safety. Priority will be given to students residing or attending school in Georgia. Minimum 3.0 GPA required.

Academic Fields/Career Goals: Occupational Safety and Health.

Award: Scholarship for use in freshman, sophomore, junior, or senior years; not renewable. *Number:* 1. *Amount:* $1000.

Eligibility Requirements: Applicant must be enrolled or expecting to enroll full- or part-time at a two-year institution. Applicant or parent of applicant must be member of American Society of Safety Engineers. Applicant must have 3.0 GPA or higher. Available to U.S. and non-U.S. citizens.

Application Requirements: Application form. *Deadline:* December 1.

Contact: Matthew Sells, Scholarship Coordinator
American Society of Safety Engineers (ASSE) Foundation
1800 East Oakton Street
Des Plaines, IL 60018
E-mail: msells@asse.org

GRANBERRY, FLEMING & ROSS SCHOLARSHIP

Scholarship of $1500 will be awarded to a student pursuing an undergraduate degree in occupational safety and health or a closely related field. Must have completed 60 semester hours and maintain at least a 3.0 GPA. Priority will be given to students that attend school within the Region IV area.

Academic Fields/Career Goals: Occupational Safety and Health.

Award: Scholarship for use in sophomore, junior, or senior years; not renewable. *Number:* 1. *Amount:* $1500.

Eligibility Requirements: Applicant must be enrolled or expecting to enroll full-time at a four-year institution or university. Applicant must have 3.0 GPA or higher. Available to U.S. citizens.

Application Requirements: Application form, essay, financial need analysis. *Deadline:* December 1.

Contact: Matthew Sells, Scholarship Coordinator
American Society of Safety Engineers (ASSE) Foundation
1800 Oakton Street
Des Plaines, IL 60018
E-mail: msells@asse.org

GREATER BATON ROUGE CHAPTER DON JONES EXCELLENCE IN SAFETY SCHOLARSHIP

$1500 scholarship to students pursuing degrees in occupational safety. Priority will be given to a student that attends a school associated with a student section from the Greater Baton Rouge chapter, a student from Louisiana, or a student from Region IV (in that order). Minimum 3.0 GPA required for undergraduate students, 3.5 for graduate students.

Academic Fields/Career Goals: Occupational Safety and Health.

Award: Scholarship for use in freshman, sophomore, junior, senior, or graduate years; not renewable. *Number:* 1. *Amount:* $1500.

Eligibility Requirements: Applicant must be enrolled or expecting to enroll full- or part-time at a two-year or four-year or technical institution or university. Applicant or parent of applicant must be member of American Society of Safety Engineers. Available to U.S. and non-U.S. citizens.

Application Requirements: Application form. *Deadline:* December 1.

Contact: Matthew Sells, Scholarship Coordinator
American Society of Safety Engineers (ASSE) Foundation
1800 East Oakton Street
Des Plaines, IL 60018
E-mail: msells@asse.org

GREATER BOSTON CHAPTER LEADERSHIP AWARD

$1000-$2000 scholarships for students pursuing undergraduate or graduate degrees in occupational safety. Priority given to Greater Boston, Connecticut Valley, Granite State, Maine, Nutmeg, or Worcester County chapter members; the spouse or child of any New England chapter member; or New England Student Section member (in that order). Minimum 3.0 GPA for undergraduates, 3.5 for graduate students.

Academic Fields/Career Goals: Occupational Safety and Health.

Award: Scholarship for use in freshman, sophomore, junior, senior, or graduate years; not renewable. *Number:* 2. *Amount:* $1000–$2000.

Eligibility Requirements: Applicant must be enrolled or expecting to enroll full-time at a four-year institution or university. Available to U.S. citizens.

Application Requirements: Application form. *Deadline:* December 1.

Contact: Matthew Sells, Scholarship Coordinator
American Society of Safety Engineers (ASSE) Foundation
1800 East Oakton Street
Des Plaines, IL 60018
E-mail: msells@asse.org

GREAT PLAINES CHAPTER SCHOLARSHIP

$1000 scholarship for students pursuing degrees in occupational safety. Priority will be given to Great Plains Chapter members, non-chapter members attending school in NE, IA, SD, or MN, or residents of NE, IA, SD or MN attending school elsewhere (Nebraska takes priority). Minimum 3.0 GPA required for undergraduates, 3.5 for graduate students.

Academic Fields/Career Goals: Occupational Safety and Health.

Award: Scholarship for use in freshman, sophomore, junior, senior, or graduate years; not renewable. *Number:* 1. *Amount:* $1000.

Eligibility Requirements: Applicant must be enrolled or expecting to enroll full- or part-time at a four-year institution or university. Applicant or parent of applicant must be member of American Society of Safety Engineers. Available to U.S. and non-U.S. citizens.

Application Requirements: Application form. *Deadline:* December 1.

Contact: Matthew Sells, Scholarship Coordinator
American Society of Safety Engineers (ASSE) Foundation
1800 East Oakton Street
Des Plaines, IL 60018
E-mail: msells@asse.org

HAROLD F. POLSTON SCHOLARSHIP

Scholarship of $1500 for students pursuing undergraduate or graduate degree in occupational safety and health or a closely related field. Priority will be given to students that belong to the Middle Tennessee Chapter, attending Middle Tennessee State University in Murfreesboro, TN, Murray State University in Murray, KY, and those that live in Region VII. Must have a minimum GPA of 3.0 for undergraduate study and 3.5 for graduate study. Must be a student member of ASSE.

Academic Fields/Career Goals: Occupational Safety and Health.

Award: Scholarship for use in sophomore, junior, senior, or graduate years; not renewable. *Number:* 1. *Amount:* $1500.

Eligibility Requirements: Applicant must be enrolled or expecting to enroll full-time at a four-year institution or university. Applicant or parent of applicant must be member of American Society of Safety Engineers. Available to U.S. and non-U.S. citizens.

Application Requirements: Application form, essay, financial need analysis. *Deadline:* December 1.

Contact: Matthew Sells, Scholarship Coordinator
American Society of Safety Engineers (ASSE) Foundation
1800 East Oakton Street
Des Plaines, IL 60018
E-mail: msells@asse.org

HARRY TABACK 9/11 MEMORIAL SCHOLARSHIP

Scholarship for students pursuing an undergraduate or graduate degree in occupational safety and health or a closely related field. Preference given to student who is a natural born United States citizen. Minimum GPA is 3.0 for undergraduates and 3.5 for graduates. Must be a student member of ASSE.

Academic Fields/Career Goals: Occupational Safety and Health.

Award: Scholarship for use in sophomore, junior, senior, or graduate years; not renewable. *Number:* 1. *Amount:* $1000.

Eligibility Requirements: Applicant must be enrolled or expecting to enroll full-time at a four-year institution or university. Applicant or parent of applicant must be member of American Society of Safety Engineers. Available to U.S. citizens.

Application Requirements: Application form, financial need analysis. *Deadline:* December 1.

Contact: Matthew Sells, Scholarship Coordinator
American Society of Safety Engineers (ASSE) Foundation
1800 East Oakton Street
Des Plaines, IL 60018
E-mail: msells@asse.org

HEART OF AMERICA SCHOLARSHIP

Scholarships of $1000 will be awarded to students pursuing an undergraduate or graduate degree in occupational safety and health or a closely related field. Minimum GPA of 3.0 for undergraduate students, 3.5 for graduate students. Priority will be given to students attending University of Central Missouri in Warrensburg, MO or Pittsburg State University in Pittsburg, KS or to those attending a university in KS or MO, or to those attending a university within Region V (in that order).

Academic Fields/Career Goals: Occupational Safety and Health.

Award: Scholarship for use in sophomore, junior, senior, or graduate years; not renewable. *Number:* 2. *Amount:* $1000.

Eligibility Requirements: Applicant must be enrolled or expecting to enroll full-time at a four-year institution or university. Available to U.S. citizens.

Application Requirements: Application form, essay, financial need analysis. *Deadline:* December 1.

Contact: Matthew Sells, Scholarship Coordinator
American Society of Safety Engineers (ASSE) Foundation
1800 East Oakton Street
Des Plaines, IL 60018
E-mail: msells@asse.org

ISNETWORLD SCHOLARSHIP

Scholarship of $1000 will be awarded to students pursuing an undergraduate degree in occupational safety and health or a closely related field. Must have completed 60 semester hours and maintain at least a 3.0 GPA. Priority will be given to students living in OK, TX, NM, LA, or AK.

Academic Fields/Career Goals: Occupational Safety and Health.

Award: Scholarship for use in sophomore, junior, or senior years; not renewable. *Number:* 3. *Amount:* $1000.

Eligibility Requirements: Applicant must be enrolled or expecting to enroll full-time at a four-year institution or university and resident of Arkansas, Louisiana, New Mexico, Oklahoma, Texas. Applicant must have 3.0 GPA or higher. Available to U.S. citizens.

Application Requirements: Application form, essay, financial need analysis. *Deadline:* December 1.

Contact: Matthew Sells, Scholarship Coordinator
American Society of Safety Engineers (ASSE) Foundation
1800 East Oakton Street
Des Plaines, IL 60018
E-mail: msells@asse.org

JAMES JOSEPH DAVIS SCHOLARSHIP

$10,000 scholarship for full-time students pursuing undergraduate or graduate degrees in occupational safety. Priority will be given to students that have served in the military and are attending an ABET-accredited school. Minimum 3.0 GPA required for undergraduates, 3.5 for graduate students.

Academic Fields/Career Goals: Occupational Safety and Health.

Award: Scholarship for use in freshman, sophomore, junior, senior, or graduate years; not renewable. *Number:* 1. *Amount:* $10,000.

Eligibility Requirements: Applicant must be enrolled or expecting to enroll full-time at a four-year institution or university. Applicant or parent of applicant must be member of American Society of Safety Engineers. Available to U.S. and non-U.S. citizens.

Application Requirements: Application form. *Deadline:* December 1.

Contact: Matthew Sells, Scholarship Coordinator
American Society of Safety Engineers (ASSE) Foundation
1800 East Oakton Street
Des Plaines, IL 60018
E-mail: msells@asse.org

JANET SPRICKMAN AWARD

$1000 scholarship awarded to a student pursuing an undergraduate or graduate degree in occupational safety and health or a closely related field. Minimum GPA of 3.0 for undergraduates, 3.5 for graduate students. Students from Region VI, IV, VII, and VIII will have priority (in that order).

Academic Fields/Career Goals: Occupational Safety and Health.

Award: Scholarship for use in sophomore, junior, senior, or graduate years; not renewable. *Number:* 1. *Amount:* $1000.

Eligibility Requirements: Applicant must be enrolled or expecting to enroll full-time at a four-year institution or university. Available to U.S. citizens.

Application Requirements: Application form, essay, financial need analysis. *Deadline:* December 1.

Contact: Matthew Sells, Scholarship Coordinator
American Society of Safety Engineers (ASSE) Foundation
1800 East Oakton Street
Des Plaines, IL 60018
E-mail: msells@asse.org

KEITH BAIN SCHOLARSHIP

$1500 scholarship for students pursuing an undergraduate or graduate degree in occupational safety and health or a closely related field. Minimum 3.0 GPA required for undergraduates and 3.5 for graduate students. Priority will be given to students that belong to the Middle Tennessee Chapter, attending Middle Tennessee State University in Murfreesboro, TN, Murray State University in Murray, KY and those that live in the Region VII area (in that order).

Academic Fields/Career Goals: Occupational Safety and Health.

Award: Scholarship for use in sophomore, junior, senior, or graduate years; not renewable. *Number:* 1. *Amount:* $1500.

Eligibility Requirements: Applicant must be enrolled or expecting to enroll full-time at a four-year institution or university. Available to U.S. citizens.

Application Requirements: Application form, essay, financial need analysis. *Deadline:* December 1.

Contact: Matthew Sells, Scholarship Coordinator
American Society of Safety Engineers (ASSE) Foundation
1800 East Oakton Street
Des Plaines, IL 60018
E-mail: msells@asse.org

LANCASTER COUNTY INDUSTRIAL SAFETY COUNCIL SCHOLARSHIP IN HONOR OF CRAIG SCHROLL & JAN GETZ

$1000 scholarship for students pursuing undergraduate degrees in occupational safety. Priority will be given to LCISC members, students residing in PA, or students attending Millersville University. Minimum 3.0 GPA required.

Academic Fields/Career Goals: Occupational Safety and Health.

Award: Scholarship for use in freshman, sophomore, junior, or senior years; not renewable. *Number:* 1. *Amount:* $1000.

Eligibility Requirements: Applicant must be enrolled or expecting to enroll full- or part-time at a four-year institution or university. Applicant or parent of applicant must be member of American Society of Safety Engineers. Applicant must have 3.0 GPA or higher. Available to U.S. and non-U.S. citizens.

Application Requirements: Application form. *Deadline:* December 1.

Contact: Matthew Sells, Scholarship Coordinator
American Society of Safety Engineers (ASSE) Foundation
1800 East Oakton Street
Des Plaines, IL 60018
E-mail: msells@asse.org

LIBERTY MUTUAL SCHOLARSHIP

Scholarship of $4000 for students pursuing an undergraduate degree in occupational safety and health or a closely related field. ASSE student membership required. Minimum 3.0 GPA required. Must have completed 60 semester hours in the study program. Students may also be provided with the opportunity to attend a professional development conference related to safety.

Academic Fields/Career Goals: Occupational Safety and Health.

Award: Scholarship for use in sophomore, junior, or senior years; not renewable. *Number:* 2. *Amount:* $4000.

Eligibility Requirements: Applicant must be enrolled or expecting to enroll full-time at a four-year institution or university. Applicant or parent of applicant must be member of American Society of Safety Engineers. Applicant must have 3.0 GPA or higher. Available to U.S. and non-U.S. citizens.

Application Requirements: Application form, financial need analysis. *Deadline:* December 1.

Contact: Matthew Sells, Scholarship Coordinator
American Society of Safety Engineers (ASSE) Foundation
1800 East Oakton Street
Des Plaines, IL 60018
E-mail: msells@asse.org

LINDA & BRAD GILES SCHOLARSHIP

One $2500 scholarship will be awarded to a student pursuing an undergraduate degree in occupational safety and health or a closely related field. Must have completed 60 semester hours and maintain at least a 3.0 GPA. Priority will be given to students with a military background attending Murray State University, Oakland, or Central

Missouri University. Priority will also be given to students attending a school with an ASAC/ABET accredited safety program.

Academic Fields/Career Goals: Occupational Safety and Health.

Award: Scholarship for use in sophomore, junior, or senior years; not renewable. *Number:* 1. *Amount:* $2500.

Eligibility Requirements: Applicant must be enrolled or expecting to enroll full-time at a four-year institution or university. Applicant must have 3.0 GPA or higher. Available to U.S. citizens.

Application Requirements: Application form, essay, financial need analysis. *Deadline:* December 1.

Contact: Matthew Sells, Scholarship Coordinator
American Society of Safety Engineers (ASSE) Foundation
1800 East Oakton Street
Des Plaines, IL 60018
E-mail: msells@asse.org

NEW ENGLAND AREA FUTURE LEADERSHIP AWARD

One $1500 award will be given to a student pursuing an undergraduate or graduate degree in occupational safety and health or a closely related field. Minimum GPA of 3.0 for undergraduates, 3.5 for graduate students. Priority will be given to students residing in the New England area, or the Region VIII area (in that order).

Academic Fields/Career Goals: Occupational Safety and Health.

Award: Scholarship for use in sophomore, junior, senior, or graduate years; not renewable. *Number:* 1. *Amount:* $1500.

Eligibility Requirements: Applicant must be enrolled or expecting to enroll full-time at a four-year institution or university. Available to U.S. citizens.

Application Requirements: Application form, essay, financial need analysis. *Deadline:* December 1.

Contact: Matthew Sells, Scholarship Coordinator
American Society of Safety Engineers (ASSE) Foundation
1800 East Oakton Street
Des Plaines, IL 60018
E-mail: msells@asse.org

NICK D. YIN SCHOLARSHIP

One $1200 award will be given to a student pursuing an undergraduate or graduate degree in occupational safety and health or a closely related field. Minimum GPA of 3.0 for undergraduates, 3.5 for graduate students. Must be a foreign student from Greater China Region (China, Taiwan, Hong Kong, Macau) studying in the U.S.

Academic Fields/Career Goals: Occupational Safety and Health.

Award: Scholarship for use in sophomore, junior, senior, graduate, or postgraduate years; not renewable. *Number:* 1. *Amount:* $2000.

Eligibility Requirements: Applicant must be enrolled or expecting to enroll full-time at a four-year institution or university. Available to citizens of countries other than the U.S. or Canada.

Application Requirements: Application form, essay, financial need analysis. *Deadline:* December 1.

Contact: Matthew Sells, Scholarship Coordinator
American Society of Safety Engineers (ASSE) Foundation
1800 East Oakton Street
Des Plaines, IL 60018
E-mail: msells@asse.org

NORTHEASTERN ILLINOIS CHAPTER SCHOLARSHIP

Scholarship of $2000 for students pursuing an undergraduate or graduate degree in occupational safety and health or a closely related field. Priority will be given to students that attend Northern Illinois University in DeKalb, IL; members of the NE IL chapter, regardless of school location; offspring of NE IL chapter members, regardless of school location; or to students attending school in the northeastern Illinois region. ASSE student membership required. Undergraduate students must have completed at least 60 semester hours. Minimum GPA is 3.0 for undergraduates and 3.5 for graduates.

Academic Fields/Career Goals: Occupational Safety and Health.

Award: Scholarship for use in sophomore, junior, senior, graduate, or postgraduate years; not renewable. *Number:* 1. *Amount:* $2000.

Eligibility Requirements: Applicant must be enrolled or expecting to enroll full-time at a four-year institution or university and resident of Illinois. Applicant or parent of applicant must be member of American Society of Safety Engineers. Available to U.S. citizens.

Application Requirements: Application form, financial need analysis. *Deadline:* December 1.

Contact: Matthew Sells, Scholarship Coordinator
American Society of Safety Engineers (ASSE) Foundation
1800 East Oakton Street
Des Plaines, IL 60018
E-mail: msells@asse.org

NORTHERN OHIO CHAPTER SCHOLARSHIP

$1000 scholarship for full-time students pursuing undergraduate degrees in occupational safety. Minimum 3.0 GPA required.

Academic Fields/Career Goals: Occupational Safety and Health.

Award: Scholarship for use in freshman, sophomore, junior, or senior years; not renewable. *Number:* 1. *Amount:* $1000.

Eligibility Requirements: Applicant must be enrolled or expecting to enroll full-time at a four-year institution or university. Applicant or parent of applicant must be member of American Society of Safety Engineers. Applicant must have 3.0 GPA or higher. Available to U.S. and non-U.S. citizens.

Application Requirements: Application form. *Deadline:* December 1.

Contact: Matthew Sells, Scholarship Coordinator
American Society of Safety Engineers (ASSE) Foundation
1800 East Oakton Street
Des Plaines, IL 60018
E-mail: msells@asse.org

NORTH FLORIDA CHAPTER SAFETY EDUCATION SCHOLARSHIP

One $1000 scholarship for a student pursuing an undergraduate or graduate degree in occupational safety and health or a closely related field. Minimum GPA of 3.0 for undergraduates, 3.5 for graduate students. Priority will be given to North Florida Chapter members, full-time students that attend any Florida college or university, or to full-time students that attend an ASAC/ABET accredited program nationwide (in that order). ASSE general or professional membership is preferred if applicant is a part-time student.

Academic Fields/Career Goals: Occupational Safety and Health.

Award: Scholarship for use in sophomore, junior, senior, or graduate years; not renewable. *Number:* 1. *Amount:* $1000.

Eligibility Requirements: Applicant must be enrolled or expecting to enroll full- or part-time at a four-year institution or university. Available to U.S. citizens.

Application Requirements: Application form, essay, financial need analysis. *Deadline:* December 1.

Contact: Matthew Sells, Scholarship Coordinator
American Society of Safety Engineers (ASSE) Foundation
1800 East Oakton Street
Des Plaines, IL 60018
E-mail: msells@asse.org

PERMIAN BASIN CHAPTER ENDOWMENT SCHOLARSHIP

Scholarship of $1000 will be awarded to a student pursuing an undergraduate or graduate degree in occupational safety and health or a closely related field. Minimum GPA of 3.0 for undergraduates, 3.5 for graduate students. Priority will be given to students that attend a school within the Region III area.

Academic Fields/Career Goals: Occupational Safety and Health.

Award: Scholarship for use in sophomore, junior, senior, or graduate years; not renewable. *Number:* 1. *Amount:* $1000.

Eligibility Requirements: Applicant must be enrolled or expecting to enroll full-time at a four-year institution or university. Available to U.S. citizens.

Application Requirements: Application form, essay, financial need analysis. *Deadline:* December 1.

Contact: Matthew Sells, Scholarship Coordinator
American Society of Safety Engineers (ASSE) Foundation
1800 East Oakton Street
Des Plaines, IL 60018
E-mail: msells@asse.org

PUGENT SOUND CHAPTER MARTIN BROWN MEMORIAL SCHOLARSHIP

One $1000 award will be given to a student pursuing an undergraduate degree in occupational safety and health or a closely related field.

Minimum GPA of 3.0 required. First priority given to full-time student who is a Puget Sound Chapter member. Second priority given to part-time student who is a Puget Sound Chapter member.

Academic Fields/Career Goals: Occupational Safety and Health.

Award: Scholarship for use in sophomore, junior, or senior years; not renewable. *Number:* 1. *Amount:* $1000.

Eligibility Requirements: Applicant must be enrolled or expecting to enroll full- or part-time at a four-year institution or university. Applicant must have 3.0 GPA or higher. Available to U.S. citizens.

Application Requirements: Application form, essay, financial need analysis. *Deadline:* December 1.

Contact: Matthew Sells, Scholarship Coordinator
American Society of Safety Engineers (ASSE) Foundation
1800 East Oakton Street
Des Plaines, IL 60018
E-mail: msells@asse.org

REGION II SCHOLARSHIP

$1000 scholarship for full-time students pursuing Bachelor's or Master's degrees in occupational safety. Priority will be given to students from Region II. Minimum 3.0 GPA required for undergraduates, 3.5 for graduate students.

Academic Fields/Career Goals: Occupational Safety and Health.

Award: Scholarship for use in freshman, sophomore, junior, senior, or graduate years; not renewable. *Number:* 1. *Amount:* $1000.

Eligibility Requirements: Applicant must be enrolled or expecting to enroll full-time at a four-year institution or university. Applicant or parent of applicant must be member of American Society of Safety Engineers. Available to U.S. and non-U.S. citizens.

Application Requirements: Application form. *Deadline:* December 1.

Contact: Matthew Sells, Scholarship Coordinator
American Society of Safety Engineers (ASSE) Foundation
1800 East Oakton Street
Des Plaines, IL 60018
E-mail: msells@asse.org

RIXIO MEDINA & ASSOCIATES HISPANICS IN SAFETY SCHOLARSHIP

$4000 award for a student pursuing an undergraduate or graduate degree in occupational safety and health or a closely related field. Minimum GPA of 3.0 for undergraduates, 3.5 for graduate students. Must be bilingual (Spanish-English); Hispanic ethnicity preferred. Student attending an ASAC/ABET accredited safety program is also preferred.

Academic Fields/Career Goals: Occupational Safety and Health.

Award: Scholarship for use in sophomore, junior, senior, or graduate years; not renewable. *Number:* 1. *Amount:* $4000.

Eligibility Requirements: Applicant must be enrolled or expecting to enroll full-time at a four-year institution or university. Available to U.S. citizens.

Application Requirements: Application form, essay, financial need analysis. *Deadline:* December 1.

Contact: Matthew Sells, Scholarship Coordinator
American Society of Safety Engineers (ASSE) Foundation
1800 East Oakton Street
Des Plaines, IL 60018
E-mail: msells@asse.org

SAFESTART SCHOLARSHIP

$5000 scholarship for students pursuing undergraduate degrees in occupational safety. Minimum 3.0 GPA required.

Academic Fields/Career Goals: Occupational Safety and Health.

Award: Scholarship for use in freshman, sophomore, junior, or senior years; not renewable. *Number:* 1. *Amount:* $5000.

Eligibility Requirements: Applicant must be enrolled or expecting to enroll full-time at a four-year institution or university. Applicant must have 3.0 GPA or higher. Available to U.S. citizens.

Application Requirements: Application form. *Deadline:* December 1.

Contact: Matthew Sells, Scholarship Coordinator
American Society of Safety Engineers (ASSE) Foundation
1800 East Oakton Street
Des Plaines, IL 60018
E-mail: msells@asse.org

SCOTT DOMINGUEZ-CRATERS OF THE MOON CHAPTER SCHOLARSHIP

Scholarship for part-or full-time students pursuing an undergraduate or graduate degree in occupational safety and health or a closely related field. Students residing within the Craters of the Moon Chapter, Idaho, and Region II (MT, ID, WY, CO, UT, NV, AZ, NM) will have priority. Students that are employees or dependents of a sponsoring organization, serve the country through active duty in the armed forces or honorably discharged, members of the Boy Scouts, Girl Scouts, FFA, 4H, etc. in previous years, recipients of awards from service organizations, or have provided volunteer service to an ASSE chapter in a leadership role will also receive priority on this award. ASSE student membership required for full-time student. ASSE general or professional membership required for part-time students. Minimum GPA is 3.0 for undergraduates and 3.5 for graduates.

Academic Fields/Career Goals: Occupational Safety and Health.

Award: Scholarship for use in sophomore, junior, senior, or graduate years; not renewable. *Number:* 1. *Amount:* $1000.

Eligibility Requirements: Applicant must be enrolled or expecting to enroll full- or part-time at a four-year institution or university and resident of Arizona, Colorado, Idaho, Montana, Nevada, New Mexico, Utah, Wyoming. Applicant or parent of applicant must be member of American Society of Safety Engineers. Available to U.S. citizens.

Application Requirements: Application form, financial need analysis. *Deadline:* December 1.

Contact: Matthew Sells, Scholarship Coordinator
American Society of Safety Engineers (ASSE) Foundation
1800 East Oakton Street
Des Plaines, IL 60018
E-mail: msells@asse.org

SITEHAWK SAFETY SCHOLARSHIP

Scholarship of $1000 will be awarded to a full-time student pursuing an undergraduate degree in occupational safety and health or a closely related field. Must have completed 60 semester hours and maintain at least a 3.0 GPA.

Academic Fields/Career Goals: Occupational Safety and Health.

Award: Scholarship for use in sophomore, junior, or senior years; not renewable. *Number:* 1. *Amount:* $1000.

Eligibility Requirements: Applicant must be enrolled or expecting to enroll full-time at a four-year institution or university. Applicant must have 3.0 GPA or higher. Available to U.S. citizens.

Application Requirements: Application form, essay, financial need analysis. *Deadline:* December 1.

Contact: Matthew Sells, Scholarship Coordinator
American Society of Safety Engineers (ASSE) Foundation
1800 East Oakton Street
Des Plaines, IL 60018
E-mail: msells@asse.org

STEVEN F. KANE MEMORIAL SCHOLARSHIP

$2000 scholarship for students pursuing an undergraduate or graduate degree in occupational safety and health or a closely related field. Minimum 3.0 GPA required for undergraduates and 3.5 for graduate students. Preference for Master's students with an undergraduate degree in core engineering or mathematics.

Academic Fields/Career Goals: Occupational Safety and Health.

Award: Scholarship for use in sophomore, junior, senior, or graduate years; not renewable. *Number:* 1. *Amount:* $2000.

Eligibility Requirements: Applicant must be enrolled or expecting to enroll full-time at a four-year institution or university. Available to U.S. citizens.

Application Requirements: Application form, essay, financial need analysis. *Deadline:* December 1.

Contact: Matthew Sells, Scholarship Coordinator
American Society of Safety Engineers (ASSE) Foundation
1800 East Oakton Street
Des Plaines, IL 60018
E-mail: msells@asse.org

UL SCHOLARSHIP

Two $5000 scholarships for students pursuing undergraduate or graduate degrees in occupational safety. Minimum 3.0 GPA required for undergraduates, 3.5 for graduate students.

Academic Fields/Career Goals: Occupational Safety and Health.

Award: Scholarship for use in freshman, sophomore, junior, senior, or graduate years; not renewable. *Number:* 2. *Amount:* $5000.

Eligibility Requirements: Applicant must be enrolled or expecting to enroll full-time at a four-year institution or university. Available to U.S. citizens.

Application Requirements: Application form. *Deadline:* December 1.

Contact: Matthew Sells, Scholarship Coordinator
American Society of Safety Engineers (ASSE) Foundation
1800 East Oakton Street
Des Plaines, IL 60018
E-mail: msells@asse.org

UNITED PARCEL SERVICE DIVERSITY SCHOLARSHIP PROGRAM

Scholarship for students pursuing an undergraduate degree in occupational safety and health or a closely related field. Must be of a minority ethnic or racial group. U.S. citizenship preferred but not required. Must be an ASSE member and have a minimum 3.0 GPA. Students may also be provided with the opportunity to attend a professional development conference related to safety.

Academic Fields/Career Goals: Occupational Safety and Health.

Award: Scholarship for use in sophomore, junior, or senior years; not renewable. *Number:* 3. *Amount:* $5250.

Eligibility Requirements: Applicant must be American Indian/Alaska Native, Asian/Pacific Islander, Black (non-Hispanic), Hispanic and enrolled or expecting to enroll full-time at a four-year institution or university. Applicant or parent of applicant must be member of American Society of Safety Engineers. Applicant must have 3.0 GPA or higher. Available to U.S. citizens.

Application Requirements: Application form, essay, financial need analysis. *Deadline:* December 1.

Contact: Matthew Sells, Scholarship Coordinator
American Society of Safety Engineers (ASSE) Foundation
1800 East Oakton Street
Des Plaines, IL 60018
E-mail: msells@asse.org

URS SAFETY SCHOLARSHIP

$6000 scholarship awarded to a student pursuing an undergraduate degree in occupational safety and health or a closely related field. Must have completed 60 semester hours and maintain at least a 3.0 GPA. Applicant must be attending a school with an ASAC/ABET-accredited safety program. Student may also be provided with the opportunity to attend a professional development conference as it relates to safety and an internship that includes salary and living expenses.

Academic Fields/Career Goals: Occupational Safety and Health.

Award: Scholarship for use in sophomore, junior, or senior years; not renewable. *Number:* 1. *Amount:* $6000.

Eligibility Requirements: Applicant must be enrolled or expecting to enroll full-time at a four-year institution or university. Applicant must have 3.0 GPA or higher. Available to U.S. citizens.

Application Requirements: Application form, essay, financial need analysis. *Deadline:* December 1.

Contact: Matthew Sells, Scholarship Coordinator
American Society of Safety Engineers (ASSE) Foundation
1800 East Oakton Street
Des Plaines, IL 60018
E-mail: msells@asse.org

UTAH CHAPTER ASSE SCHOLARSHIP

Two awards of $1000 will be awarded to students pursuing an undergraduate or graduate degree in occupational safety and health or a closely related field. Minimum GPA of 3.0 for undergraduates, 3.5 for graduate students. Priority will be given to students residing in Utah or Wyoming.

Academic Fields/Career Goals: Occupational Safety and Health.

Award: Scholarship for use in sophomore, junior, senior, or graduate years; not renewable. *Number:* 2. *Amount:* $1000.

Eligibility Requirements: Applicant must be enrolled or expecting to enroll full-time at a four-year institution or university and resident of Utah, Washington. Available to U.S. citizens.

Application Requirements: Application form, essay, financial need analysis. *Deadline:* December 1.

Contact: Matthew Sells, Scholarship Coordinator
American Society of Safety Engineers (ASSE) Foundation
1800 East Oakton Street
Des Plaines, IL 60018
E-mail: msells@asse.org

WILLIAM C. RAY, CIH, CSP ARIZONA SCHOLARSHIP

Two scholarships of $2500 will be awarded to students pursuing undergraduate or graduate degrees in occupational safety and health or a closely related field. Minimum GPA of 3.0 for undergraduates, 3.5 for graduate students. Priority will be given to students residing in Arizona or within the Region II area.

Academic Fields/Career Goals: Occupational Safety and Health.

Award: Scholarship for use in sophomore, junior, senior, or graduate years; not renewable. *Number:* 2. *Amount:* $2500.

Eligibility Requirements: Applicant must be enrolled or expecting to enroll full-time at a four-year institution or university. Available to U.S. citizens.

Application Requirements: Application form, essay, financial need analysis. *Deadline:* December 1.

Contact: Matthew Sells, Scholarship Coordinator
American Society of Safety Engineers (ASSE) Foundation
1800 East Oakton Street
Des Plaines, IL 60018
E-mail: msells@asse.org

ASSOCIATION FOR EDUCATION AND REHABILITATION OF THE BLIND AND VISUALLY IMPAIRED

http://www.aerbvi.org/

WILLIAM AND DOROTHY FERRELL SCHOLARSHIP
• *See page 250*

BHW GROUP

https://thebhwgroup.com/

BHW WOMEN IN STEM SCHOLARSHIP
• *See page 74*

COMPHEALTH

http://www.comphealth.com

COMPHEALTH MEDICAL SCHOLARSHIP
• *See page 151*

CYNTHIA E. MORGAN SCHOLARSHIP FUND (CEMS)

http://www.cemsfund.com/

CYNTHIA E. MORGAN MEMORIAL SCHOLARSHIP FUND, INC.
• *See page 316*

NATIONAL SAFETY COUNCIL

http://www.cshema.org/

CAMPUS SAFETY, HEALTH AND ENVIRONMENTAL MANAGEMENT ASSOCIATION SCHOLARSHIP AWARD PROGRAM
• *See page 322*

THE RECOVERY VILLAGE

https://www.therecoveryvillage.com/

RECOVERY VILLAGE HEALTHCARE SCHOLARSHIP
• *See page 238*

STRAIGHTFORWARD MEDIA

http://www.straightforwardmedia.com/

STRAIGHTFORWARD MEDIA MEDICAL PROFESSIONS SCHOLARSHIP
- *See page 239*

TEXAS DEPARTMENT OF TRANSPORTATION

http://www.txdot.gov/

CONDITIONAL GRANT PROGRAM
- *See page 199*

OCEANOGRAPHY

AMERICAN INDIAN SCIENCE AND ENGINEERING SOCIETY

http://www.aises.org/

A.T. ANDERSON MEMORIAL SCHOLARSHIP PROGRAM
- *See page 109*

ASSOCIATION FOR WOMEN GEOSCIENTISTS (AWG)

http://www.awg.org/

AWG ETHNIC MINORITY SCHOLARSHIP
- *See page 241*

AWG MARIA LUISA CRAWFORD FIELD CAMP SCHOLARSHIP
- *See page 117*

AWG SALT LAKE CHAPTER (SLC) RESEARCH SCHOLARSHIP
- *See page 117*

JANET CULLEN TANAKA GEOSCIENCES UNDERGRADUATE SCHOLARSHIP
- *See page 117*

LONE STAR RISING CAREER SCHOLARSHIP
- *See page 242*

OSAGE CHAPTER UNDERGRADUATE SERVICE SCHOLARSHIP
- *See page 117*

SUSAN EKDALE MEMORIAL FIELD CAMP SCHOLARSHIP
- *See page 242*

BARRY GOLDWATER SCHOLARSHIP AND EXCELLENCE IN EDUCATION FOUNDATION

https://goldwater.scholarsapply.org

BARRY M. GOLDWATER SCHOLARSHIP AND EXCELLENCE IN EDUCATION PROGRAM
- *See page 112*

BHW GROUP

https://thebhwgroup.com/

BHW WOMEN IN STEM SCHOLARSHIP
- *See page 74*

BROWN AND CALDWELL

http://www.brownandcaldwell.com

ECKENFELDER SCHOLARSHIP
- *See page 155*

MINORITY SCHOLARSHIP PROGRAM
- *See page 155*

GREAT MINDS IN STEM

www.greatmindsinstem.org

HISPANIC ENGINEER NATIONAL ACHIEVEMENT AWARDS CORPORATION SCHOLARSHIP PROGRAM
- *See page 106*

LOUISIANA OFFICE OF STUDENT FINANCIAL ASSISTANCE

http://www.osfa.la.gov/

ROCKEFELLER STATE WILDLIFE SCHOLARSHIP
- *See page 157*

MARINE TECHNOLOGY SOCIETY

http://www.mtsociety.org/

CHARLES H. BUSSMAN UNDERGRADUATE SCHOLARSHIP
- *See page 401*

JOHN C. BAJUS SCHOLARSHIP
- *See page 401*

MTS STUDENT SCHOLARSHIP
- *See page 401*

PAROS-DIGIQUARTZ SCHOLARSHIP
- *See page 402*

ROV SCHOLARSHIP
- *See page 402*

NASA MINNESOTA SPACE GRANT CONSORTIUM

http://www.aem.umn.edu/mnsgc

MINNESOTA SPACE GRANT CONSORTIUM SCHOLARSHIP PROGRAM
- *See page 142*

NEXTSTEPU

http://www.nextstepu.com/

$1,500 STEM SCHOLARSHIP
- *See page 106*

SCARLETT FAMILY FOUNDATION SCHOLARSHIP PROGRAM

http://www.scarlettfoundation.org/

SCHOLARSHIP FOR STUDENTS PURSUING A BUSINESS OR STEM DEGREE
• *See page 84*

WOMAN'S SEAMEN'S FRIEND SOCIETY OF CONNECTICUT INC.

FINANCIAL SUPPORT FOR MARINE OR MARITIME STUDIES
• *See page 402*

YOUTH MARITIME TRAINING ASSOCIATION

http://ymta.net/

NORM MANLY—YMTA MARITIME EDUCATIONAL SCHOLARSHIPS
• *See page 402*

ONCOLOGY

AMERICAN INDIAN SCIENCE AND ENGINEERING SOCIETY

http://www.aises.org/

A.T. ANDERSON MEMORIAL SCHOLARSHIP PROGRAM
• *See page 109*

AMERICAN LEGION AUXILIARY DEPARTMENT OF COLORADO

http://www.alacolorado.com

AMERICAN LEGION AUXILIARY DEPARTMENT OF COLORADO PAST PRESIDENTS' PARLEY HEALTH CARE PROFESSIONAL SCHOLARSHIPNURSES SCHOLARSHIP
• *See page 133*

ARRL FOUNDATION INC.

http://www.arrl.org/

CAROLE J. STREETER, KB9JBR, SCHOLARSHIP
• *See page 236*

ASRT FOUNDATION

http://foundation.asrt.org

JERMAN-CAHOON STUDENT SCHOLARSHIP
• *See page 349*

PROFESSIONAL ADVANCEMENT SCHOLARSHIP
• *See page 344*

SIEMENS CLINICAL ADVANCEMENT SCHOLARSHIP
• *See page 349*

VARIAN RADIATION THERAPY ADVANCEMENT SCHOLARSHIP
• *See page 349*

AVACARE MEDICAL

https://avacaremedical.com

AVACARE MEDICAL SCHOLARSHIP
• *See page 105*

BHW GROUP

https://thebhwgroup.com/

BHW WOMEN IN STEM SCHOLARSHIP
• *See page 74*

COMPHEALTH

http://www.comphealth.com

COMPHEALTH MEDICAL SCHOLARSHIP
• *See page 151*

CYNTHIA E. MORGAN SCHOLARSHIP FUND (CEMS)

http://www.cemsfund.com/

CYNTHIA E. MORGAN MEMORIAL SCHOLARSHIP FUND, INC.
• *See page 316*

THE EXPERT INSTITUTE

https://www.theexpertinstitute.com

ANNUAL HEALTHCARE AND LIFE SCIENCES SCHOLARSHIP
• *See page 156*

GREAT MINDS IN STEM

www.greatmindsinstem.org

HISPANIC ENGINEER NATIONAL ACHIEVEMENT AWARDS CORPORATION SCHOLARSHIP PROGRAM
• *See page 106*

MEDICAL SCRUBS COLLECTION

http://medicalscrubscollection.com

MEDICAL SCRUBS COLLECTION SCHOLARSHIP
• *See page 106*

NEXTSTEPU

http://www.nextstepu.com/

$1,500 STEM SCHOLARSHIP
• *See page 106*

ONS FOUNDATION

http://www.onsfoundation.org

ONS FOUNDATION/ONCOLOGY NURSING CERTIFICATION CORPORATION BACHELOR'S SCHOLARSHIPS
• *See page 459*

ONS FOUNDATION/PEARL MOORE CAREER DEVELOPMENT AWARDS
• See page 459

SCARLETT FAMILY FOUNDATION SCHOLARSHIP PROGRAM

http://www.scarlettfoundation.org/

SCHOLARSHIP FOR STUDENTS PURSUING A BUSINESS OR STEM DEGREE
• See page 84

STRAIGHTFORWARD MEDIA

http://www.straightforwardmedia.com/

STRAIGHTFORWARD MEDIA MEDICAL PROFESSIONS SCHOLARSHIP
• See page 239

OPTOMETRY

AMERICAN INDIAN SCIENCE AND ENGINEERING SOCIETY

http://www.aises.org/

A.T. ANDERSON MEMORIAL SCHOLARSHIP PROGRAM
• See page 109

AMERICAN LEGION AUXILIARY DEPARTMENT OF COLORADO

http://www.alacolorado.com

AMERICAN LEGION AUXILIARY DEPARTMENT OF COLORADO PAST PRESIDENTS' PARLEY HEALTH CARE PROFESSIONAL SCHOLARSHIPNURSES SCHOLARSHIP
• See page 133

AMERICAN OPTOMETRIC FOUNDATION

http://www.aaopt.org/

VISTAKON AWARD OF EXCELLENCE IN CONTACT LENS PATIENT CARE

Open to any fourth-year student attending any school or college of optometry. Must have 3.0 GPA. Student's knowledge of subject matter and skillful, professional clinical contact lens patient care are considered. School makes selection and sends application to AOF.

Academic Fields/Career Goals: Optometry.

Award: Scholarship for use in senior or graduate years; not renewable. *Number:* 19. *Amount:* $1000.

Eligibility Requirements: Applicant must be enrolled or expecting to enroll full-time at a four-year institution or university. Applicant must have 3.0 GPA or higher. Available to U.S. and non-U.S. citizens.

Application Requirements: Application form, recommendations or references. *Deadline:* September 1.

Contact: Alisa Moore, Program Administrator
　　　　Phone: 240-880-3084
　　　　Fax: 301-984-4737
　　　　E-mail: alisam@aaopt.org

ARRL FOUNDATION INC.

http://www.arrl.org/

CAROLE J. STREETER, KB9JBR, SCHOLARSHIP
• See page 236

AVACARE MEDICAL

https://avacaremedical.com

AVACARE MEDICAL SCHOLARSHIP
• See page 105

BHW GROUP

https://thebhwgroup.com/

BHW WOMEN IN STEM SCHOLARSHIP
• See page 74

COMPHEALTH

http://www.comphealth.com

COMPHEALTH MEDICAL SCHOLARSHIP
• See page 151

THE EXPERT INSTITUTE

https://www.theexpertinstitute.com

ANNUAL HEALTHCARE AND LIFE SCIENCES SCHOLARSHIP
• See page 156

GREAT MINDS IN STEM

www.greatmindsinstem.org

HISPANIC ENGINEER NATIONAL ACHIEVEMENT AWARDS CORPORATION SCHOLARSHIP PROGRAM
• See page 106

KETAMINE CLINICS OF LOS ANGELES

http://www.ketamineclinics.com/

KETAMINE CLINICS OF LOS ANGELES SCHOLARSHIP PROGRAM
• See page 152

MEDICAL SCRUBS COLLECTION

http://medicalscrubscollection.com

MEDICAL SCRUBS COLLECTION SCHOLARSHIP
• See page 106

NEXTSTEPU

http://www.nextstepu.com/

$1,500 STEM SCHOLARSHIP
• See page 106

SCARLETT FAMILY FOUNDATION SCHOLARSHIP PROGRAM

http://www.scarlettfoundation.org/

SCHOLARSHIP FOR STUDENTS PURSUING A BUSINESS OR STEM DEGREE
• *See page 84*

STRAIGHTFORWARD MEDIA

http://www.straightforwardmedia.com/

STRAIGHTFORWARD MEDIA MEDICAL PROFESSIONS SCHOLARSHIP
• *See page 239*

OSTEOPATHY

AMERICAN INDIAN SCIENCE AND ENGINEERING SOCIETY

http://www.aises.org/

A.T. ANDERSON MEMORIAL SCHOLARSHIP PROGRAM
• *See page 109*

AMERICAN LEGION AUXILIARY DEPARTMENT OF COLORADO

http://www.alacolorado.com

AMERICAN LEGION AUXILIARY DEPARTMENT OF COLORADO PAST PRESIDENTS' PARLEY HEALTH CARE PROFESSIONAL SCHOLARSHIPNURSES SCHOLARSHIP
• *See page 133*

ARRL FOUNDATION INC.

http://www.arrl.org/

CAROLE J. STREETER, KB9JBR, SCHOLARSHIP
• *See page 236*

AVACARE MEDICAL

https://avacaremedical.com

AVACARE MEDICAL SCHOLARSHIP
• *See page 105*

BHW GROUP

https://thebhwgroup.com/

BHW WOMEN IN STEM SCHOLARSHIP
• *See page 74*

COMPHEALTH

http://www.comphealth.com

COMPHEALTH MEDICAL SCHOLARSHIP
• *See page 151*

CYNTHIA E. MORGAN SCHOLARSHIP FUND (CEMS)

http://www.cemsfund.com/

CYNTHIA E. MORGAN MEMORIAL SCHOLARSHIP FUND, INC.
• *See page 316*

GREAT MINDS IN STEM

www.greatmindsinstem.org

HISPANIC ENGINEER NATIONAL ACHIEVEMENT AWARDS CORPORATION SCHOLARSHIP PROGRAM
• *See page 106*

MAINE OSTEOPATHIC ASSOCIATION

http://www.mainedo.org/

MAINE OSTEOPATHIC ASSOCIATION SCHOLARSHIP
• *See page 353*

MEDICAL SCRUBS COLLECTION

http://medicalscrubscollection.com

MEDICAL SCRUBS COLLECTION SCHOLARSHIP
• *See page 106*

NEXTSTEPU

http://www.nextstepu.com/

$1,500 STEM SCHOLARSHIP
• *See page 106*

SCARLETT FAMILY FOUNDATION SCHOLARSHIP PROGRAM

http://www.scarlettfoundation.org/

SCHOLARSHIP FOR STUDENTS PURSUING A BUSINESS OR STEM DEGREE
• *See page 84*

STRAIGHTFORWARD MEDIA

http://www.straightforwardmedia.com/

STRAIGHTFORWARD MEDIA MEDICAL PROFESSIONS SCHOLARSHIP
• *See page 239*

PAPER AND PULP ENGINEERING

AMERICAN CHEMICAL SOCIETY

http://www.acs.org/

AMERICAN CHEMICAL SOCIETY SCHOLARS PROGRAM
• *See page 172*

AMERICAN INDIAN SCIENCE AND ENGINEERING SOCIETY

http://www.aises.org/

A.T. ANDERSON MEMORIAL SCHOLARSHIP PROGRAM
• *See page 109*

AMERICAN SOCIETY OF HEATING, REFRIGERATING, AND AIR CONDITIONING ENGINEERS, INC.

http://www.ashrae.org/

ASHRAE REGION III BOGGARM SETTY SCHOLARSHIP
• *See page 176*

ARRL FOUNDATION INC.

http://www.arrl.org/

ALFRED E. FRIEND JR., W4CF, MEMORIAL SCHOLARSHIP
• *See page 177*

W1FDR SCHOLARSHIP
• *See page 112*

BHW GROUP

https://thebhwgroup.com/

BHW WOMEN IN STEM SCHOLARSHIP
• *See page 74*

BROWN AND CALDWELL

http://www.brownandcaldwell.com

ECKENFELDER SCHOLARSHIP
• *See page 155*

MINORITY SCHOLARSHIP PROGRAM
• *See page 155*

GREATER KANAWHA VALLEY FOUNDATION

http://www.tgkvf.org/

STEVEN ENGINEERING SCHOLARSHIP
• *See page 178*

GREAT MINDS IN STEM

www.greatmindsinstem.org

HISPANIC ENGINEER NATIONAL ACHIEVEMENT AWARDS CORPORATION SCHOLARSHIP PROGRAM
• *See page 106*

NEXTSTEPU

http://www.nextstepu.com/

$1,500 STEM SCHOLARSHIP
• *See page 106*

SOCIETY OF WOMEN ENGINEERS

http://societyofwomenengineers.swe.org/

ADA I. PRESSMAN MEMORIAL SCHOLARSHIP
• *See page 182*

AMERICAN TRANSMISSION CO. SCHOLARSHIP
• *See page 182*

ANNE MAUREEN WHITNEY BARROW MEMORIAL SCHOLARSHIP
• *See page 182*

ANNE SHEN SMITH ENDOWED SCHOLARSHIP
• *See page 182*

BAYER SCHOLARSHIP
• *See page 183*

BETTY LOU BAILEY SWE REGION F SCHOLARSHIP
• *See page 183*

B.J. HARROD SCHOLARSHIP
• *See page 183*

BK KRENZER MEMORIAL REENTRY SCHOLARSHIP
• *See page 183*

CAROL STEPHENS SWE REGION F SCHOLARSHIP
• *See page 183*

DR. IVY M. PARKER MEMORIAL SCHOLARSHIP
• *See page 184*

DOROTHY LEMKE HOWARTH MEMORIAL SCHOLARSHIP
• *See page 184*

DOROTHY P. MORRIS SCHOLARSHIP
• *See page 184*

EXELON CORPORATION SCHOLARSHIP
• *See page 184*

FCA WOMEN IN ENGINEERING SCHOLARSHIP
• *See page 184*

IBM LINDA SANFORD WOMEN'S TECHNICAL ADVANCEMENT SCHOLARSHIP
• *See page 185*

JILL S. TIETJEN P.E. SCHOLARSHIP
• *See page 185*

KOCH DISCOVERY SCHOLARSHIP
• *See page 185*

LILLIAN MOLLER GILBRETH MEMORIAL SCHOLARSHIP
• *See page 185*

MARY V. MUNGER SCHOLARSHIP
• *See page 185*

MASWE SCHOLARSHIP
• *See page 186*

OLIVE LYNN SALEMBIER MEMORIAL REENTRY SCHOLARSHIP
• *See page 186*

ROBERTA BANASZAK GLEITER ENGINEERING ENDEAVOR SCHOLARSHIP
• See page 186

ROCHELLE PERRY MEMORIAL SCHOLARSHIP
• See page 186

SUSAN MISZKOWICZ MEMORIAL SCHOLARSHIP
• See page 186

SWE BALTIMORE-WASHINGTON SECTION SCHOLARSHIP
• See page 186

SWE CENTRAL NEW MEXICO PIONEERS SCHOLARSHIP
• See page 187

SWE CENTRAL NEW MEXICO REENTRY SCHOLARSHIP
• See page 187

SWE MID-HUDSON SECTION SCHOLARSHIP
• See page 187

SWE PHOENIX SECTION SCHOLARSHIP
• See page 187

SWE REGION E SCHOLARSHIP
• See page 187

SWE REGION G JUDY SIMMONS MEMORIAL SCHOLARSHIP
• See page 188

SWE REGION H SCHOLARSHIPS
• See page 188

SWE REGION J SCHOLARSHIP
• See page 188

WANDA MUNN SCHOLARSHIP
• See page 188

STRAIGHTFORWARD MEDIA
http://www.straightforwardmedia.com/

STRAIGHTFORWARD MEDIA ENGINEERING SCHOLARSHIP
• See page 189

TECHNICAL ASSOCIATION OF THE PULP & PAPER INDUSTRY (TAPPI)
http://www.tappi.org/

COATING AND GRAPHIC ARTS DIVISION SCHOLARSHIP
• See page 344

CORRUGATED PACKAGING DIVISION SCHOLARSHIPS
• See page 288

ENGINEERING DIVISION SCHOLARSHIP
Up to two $1500 scholarships offered. One may be awarded to a student who will be in his or her junior year, and the other will be offered to a student who will be in his or her senior year at the beginning of the next academic year. Information can be found at http://www.tappi.org/Education/College-and-University-Programs/Scholarship-Overview.

Academic Fields/Career Goals: Paper and Pulp Engineering.
Award: Scholarship for use in junior or senior years; not renewable. *Number:* 1–2. *Amount:* $2000.
Eligibility Requirements: Applicant must be enrolled or expecting to enroll full-time at a four-year institution or university. Applicant must have 3.0 GPA or higher. Available to U.S. and non-U.S. citizens.
Application Requirements: Application form. *Deadline:* February 15.
Contact: Mr. Laurence Womack, Director of Standards and Awards
Technical Association of the Pulp & Paper Industry (TAPPI)
15 Technology Parkway South
Peachtree Corners, GA 30092
Phone: 770-209-7276
E-mail: standards@tappi.org

ENVIRONMENTAL WORKING GROUP SCHOLARSHIP
• See page 324

PAPER AND BOARD DIVISION SCHOLARSHIPS
• See page 313

TAPPI PROCESS CONTROL SCHOLARSHIP
The TAPPI Process Control Scholarship is designed to encourage talented engineering students to pursue careers in the pulp and paper industry and to develop professional skills in process control fields.
Academic Fields/Career Goals: Paper and Pulp Engineering.
Award: Scholarship for use in sophomore, junior, or senior years; not renewable. *Number:* 1. *Amount:* $1000.
Eligibility Requirements: Applicant must be high school student and planning to enroll or expecting to enroll full-time at a two-year or four-year institution or university. Applicant must have 3.0 GPA or higher. Available to U.S. and non-U.S. citizens.
Application Requirements: Application form. *Deadline:* February 15.
Contact: Mr. Laurence Womack, Director of Standards and Awards
Technical Association of the Pulp & Paper Industry (TAPPI)
15 Technology Parkway South
Suite 115
Peachtree Corners, GA 30092
Phone: 770-209-7276
E-mail: standards@tappi.org

WILLIAM L. CULLISON SCHOLARSHIP
• See page 436

PEACE AND CONFLICT STUDIES

ASSOCIATION OF FORMER INTELLIGENCE OFFICERS
http://www.afio.com

AFIO UNDERGRADUATE AND GRADUATE SCHOLARSHIPS
• See page 103

NATIONAL SECURITY EDUCATION PROGRAM
http://www.iie.org/

NATIONAL SECURITY EDUCATION PROGRAM (NSEP) DAVID L. BOREN UNDERGRADUATE SCHOLARSHIPS
• See page 126

UNITED NATIONS ASSOCIATION OF CONNECTICUT

http://www.unausa.org

UNITED NATIONS ASSOCIATION OF CONNECTICUT SCHOLARSHIP
• See page 133

WASHINGTON STATE ASSOCIATION FOR JUSTICE

http://www.washingtonjustice.org/

WASHINGTON STATE ASSOCIATION FOR JUSTICE AMERICAN JUSTICE ESSAY & VIDEO SCHOLARSHIP
• See page 227

PERFORMING ARTS

AMERICAN LEGION DEPARTMENT OF KANSAS

http://www.ksamlegion.org/

MUSIC COMMITTEE SCHOLARSHIP
• See page 427

THE CHOPIN FOUNDATION OF THE UNITED STATES

http://www.chopin.org/

SCHOLARSHIP PROGRAM FOR YOUNG AMERICAN PIANISTS
• See page 427

CONGRESSIONAL BLACK CAUCUS FOUNDATION, INC.

http://www.cbcfinc.org/

CBC SPOUSES HEINEKEN USA PERFORMING ARTS SCHOLARSHIP
• See page 428

COSTUME SOCIETY OF AMERICA

http://www.costumesocietyamerica.com/

ADELE FILENE STUDENT PRESENTER GRANT
• See page 125

STELLA BLUM STUDENT RESEARCH GRANT
• See page 125

GENERAL FEDERATION OF WOMEN'S CLUBS OF MASSACHUSETTS

http://www.gfwcma.org/

DORCHESTER WOMEN'S CLUB MUSIC SCHOLARSHIP
• See page 428

GREATER KANAWHA VALLEY FOUNDATION

http://www.tgkvf.org/

HERB SMITH/EUNICE FLEMING SCHOLARSHIP
• See page 429

HOSTESS COMMITTEE SCHOLARSHIPS/MISS AMERICA PAGEANT

http://www.missamerica.org/

EUGENIA VELLNER FISCHER AWARD FOR PERFORMING ARTS
Scholarship for Miss America contestants pursuing degree in performing arts. Award available to women who have competed within the Miss America system on the local, state, or national level from 1998 to the present, regardless of whether title was won. One or more scholarships are awarded annually, depending on qualifications of applicants. Late or incomplete applications are not accepted.

Academic Fields/Career Goals: Performing Arts.

Award: Scholarship for use in freshman, sophomore, junior, senior, or graduate years; not renewable.

Eligibility Requirements: Applicant must be enrolled or expecting to enroll full- or part-time at a four-year institution or university; female and must have an interest in beauty pageant. Available to U.S. citizens.

Application Requirements: Application form, essay, financial need analysis, recommendations or references, transcript. *Deadline:* June 30.

Contact: Doreen Lindell Gordon, Controller and Scholarship
          Administrator
          Phone: 609-345-7571 Ext. 27
          Fax: 609-347-6079
          E-mail: doreen@missamerica.org

ILLUMINATING ENGINEERING SOCIETY OF NORTH AMERICA

http://www.ies.org/

ROBERT W. THUNEN MEMORIAL SCHOLARSHIPS
• See page 122

NATIONAL ACADEMY OF TELEVISION ARTS AND SCIENCES

http://www.emmyonline.tv/

DOUGLAS W. MUMMERT SCHOLARSHIP
• See page 129

JIM MCKAY MEMORIAL SCHOLARSHIP
• See page 205

MIKE WALLACE MEMORIAL SCHOLARSHIP
• See page 205

NATIONAL ACADEMY OF TELEVISION ARTS AND SCIENCES TRUSTEES SCHOLARSHIP
• See page 205

RANDY FALCO SCHOLARSHIP
• See page 205

NATIONAL ACADEMY OF TELEVISION ARTS AND SCIENCES, MICHIGAN CHAPTER

http://natasmichigan.org

DR. LYNNE BOYLE/JOHN SCHIMPF UNDERGRADUATE SCHOLARSHIP
• See page 89

NATIONAL OPERA ASSOCIATION

http://www.noa.org/

NOA VOCAL COMPETITION/LEGACY AWARD PROGRAM
• See page 129

ONLINE LOGO MAKER

http://onlinelogomaker.com

OLM MALALA YOUSAFZAI SCHOLARSHIP 2017-2018
• See page 129

POLISH ARTS CLUB OF BUFFALO SCHOLARSHIP FOUNDATION

http://www.pacb.bfn.org/

POLISH ARTS CLUB OF BUFFALO SCHOLARSHIP FOUNDATION TRUST
• See page 130

PRINCESS GRACE FOUNDATION-USA

http://www.pgfusa.org/

PRINCESS GRACE AWARDS IN DANCE, THEATER, AND FILM
• See page 327

QUALITY BATH

www.qualitybath.com

QUALITYBATH.COM SCHOLARSHIP PROGRAM
• See page 123

SERVICE EMPLOYEES INTERNATIONAL UNION (SEIU)

http://www.seiu.org/

SEIU MOE FONER SCHOLARSHIP PROGRAM FOR VISUAL AND PERFORMING ARTS
• See page 131

UNITED NEGRO COLLEGE FUND

http://www.uncf.org/

JOHN LENNON ENDOWED SCHOLARSHIP PROGRAM
• See page 212

OSSIE DAVIS ENDOWMENT SCHOLARSHIP PROGRAM
• See page 132

VSA

http://www.kennedy-center.org/education/vsa/

VSA INTERNATIONAL YOUNG SOLOISTS AWARD
• See page 433

WAMSO-MINNESOTA ORCHESTRA VOLUNTEER ASSOCIATION

http://www.wamso.org/

YOUNG ARTIST COMPETITION
Scholarship of $500 to $5000 for graduates and undergraduates. Applicant should be Canadian/ U.S citizens.

Academic Fields/Career Goals: Performing Arts.

Award: Prize for use in freshman, sophomore, junior, senior, graduate, or postgraduate years; not renewable. *Number:* 8. *Amount:* $500–$5000.

Eligibility Requirements: Applicant must be age 15-26; enrolled or expecting to enroll full- or part-time at a two-year or four-year or technical institution or university; resident of Illinois, Indiana, Iowa, Kansas, Manitoba, Michigan, Minnesota, Missouri, Nebraska, North Dakota, Ontario, South Dakota, Wisconsin and must have an interest in music. Available to U.S. and Canadian citizens.

Application Requirements: Application form, entry in a contest, taped performance of specific repertoire. *Fee:* $75. *Deadline:* varies.

Contact: Eloise Breikjern, Executive Director
    Phone: 612-371-5654
    E-mail: wamso@mnorch.org

WOMEN BAND DIRECTORS INTERNATIONAL

http://www.womenbanddirectors.org/

CHARLOTTE PLUMMER OWEN MEMORIAL SCHOLARSHIP
• See page 262

MARTHA ANN STARK MEMORIAL SCHOLARSHIP
• See page 262

VOLKWEIN MEMORIAL SCHOLARSHIP
• See page 262

PHARMACY

ALBERTA HERITAGE SCHOLARSHIP FUND

http://www.alis.alberta.ca/

JASON LANG SCHOLARSHIP
• See page 233

AMERICAN INDIAN SCIENCE AND ENGINEERING SOCIETY

http://www.aises.org/

A.T. ANDERSON MEMORIAL SCHOLARSHIP PROGRAM
• See page 109

AMERICAN LEGION AUXILIARY DEPARTMENT OF COLORADO

http://www.alacolorado.com

AMERICAN LEGION AUXILIARY DEPARTMENT OF COLORADO PAST PRESIDENTS' PARLEY HEALTH

CARE PROFESSIONAL SCHOLARSHIPNURSES SCHOLARSHIP
• *See page 133*

AMERICAN LEGION DEPARTMENT OF NORTH DAKOTA

http://www.ndlegion.org/

O. NESHEIM MEMORIAL SCHOLARSHIP
• *See page 96*

AVACARE MEDICAL

https://avacaremedical.com

AVACARE MEDICAL SCHOLARSHIP
• *See page 105*

BARRY GOLDWATER SCHOLARSHIP AND EXCELLENCE IN EDUCATION FOUNDATION

https://goldwater.scholarsapply.org

BARRY M. GOLDWATER SCHOLARSHIP AND EXCELLENCE IN EDUCATION PROGRAM
• *See page 112*

BHW GROUP

https://thebhwgroup.com/

BHW WOMEN IN STEM SCHOLARSHIP
• *See page 74*

COMPHEALTH

http://www.comphealth.com

COMPHEALTH MEDICAL SCHOLARSHIP
• *See page 151*

CYNTHIA E. MORGAN SCHOLARSHIP FUND (CEMS)

http://www.cemsfund.com/

CYNTHIA E. MORGAN MEMORIAL SCHOLARSHIP FUND, INC.
• *See page 316*

GREATER KANAWHA VALLEY FOUNDATION

http://www.tgkvf.org/

NICHOLAS AND MARY AGNES TRIVILLIAN MEMORIAL SCHOLARSHIP FUND
• *See page 352*

GREAT MINDS IN STEM

www.greatmindsinstem.org

HISPANIC ENGINEER NATIONAL ACHIEVEMENT AWARDS CORPORATION SCHOLARSHIP PROGRAM
• *See page 106*

HEALTH PROFESSIONS EDUCATION FOUNDATION

http://www.healthprofessions.ca.gov/

ALLIED HEALTHCARE SCHOLARSHIP PROGRAM
• *See page 151*

INDIAN HEALTH SERVICES, UNITED STATES DEPARTMENT OF HEALTH AND HUMAN SERVICES

http://www.ihs.gov/scholarship

HEALTH PROFESSIONS PREPARATORY SCHOLARSHIP PROGRAM
• *See page 152*

MEDICAL SCRUBS COLLECTION

http://medicalscrubscollection.com

MEDICAL SCRUBS COLLECTION SCHOLARSHIP
• *See page 106*

NATIONAL COMMUNITY PHARMACIST ASSOCIATION (NCPA) FOUNDATION

http://www.ncpanet.org/

NATIONAL COMMUNITY PHARMACIST ASSOCIATION FOUNDATION PRESIDENTIAL SCHOLARSHIP

One-time award to student members of NCPA. Must be enrolled in an accredited U.S. school or college of pharmacy on a full-time basis. Award based on leadership qualities and accomplishments with a demonstrated interest in independent pharmacy, as well as involvement in extracurricular activities.

Academic Fields/Career Goals: Pharmacy.

Award: Scholarship for use in freshman, sophomore, junior, or senior years; not renewable. *Number:* up to 15. *Amount:* up to $2000.

Eligibility Requirements: Applicant must be enrolled or expecting to enroll full-time at a four-year institution or university and must have an interest in leadership. Applicant must have 2.5 GPA or higher. Available to U.S. citizens.

Application Requirements: Application form, essay, recommendations or references, resume, transcript. *Deadline:* March 15.

Contact: Jackie Lopez, Administrative Assistant
National Community Pharmacist Association (NCPA)
    Foundation
100 Daingerfield Road
Alexandria, VA 22314
Phone: 703-683-8200
Fax: 703-683-3619
E-mail: jackie.lopez@ncpanet.org

NEXTSTEPU

http://www.nextstepu.com/

$1,500 STEM SCHOLARSHIP
• *See page 106*

PLATINUM EDUCATIONAL GROUP

www.platinumed.com

PLATINUM EDUCATIONAL GROUP SCHOLARSHIPS PROGRAM FOR EMS, NURSING, AND ALLIED HEALTH
• *See page 107*

SCARLETT FAMILY FOUNDATION SCHOLARSHIP PROGRAM

http://www.scarlettfoundation.org/

SCHOLARSHIP FOR STUDENTS PURSUING A BUSINESS OR STEM DEGREE
• *See page 84*

STRAIGHTFORWARD MEDIA

http://www.straightforwardmedia.com/

STRAIGHTFORWARD MEDIA MEDICAL PROFESSIONS SCHOLARSHIP
• *See page 239*

STRAIGHTFORWARD MEDIA VOCATIONAL-TECHNICAL SCHOOL SCHOLARSHIP
• *See page 107*

UNITED NEGRO COLLEGE FUND

http://www.uncf.org/

CVS PHARMACY, INC. PHARMACY SCHOLARSHIP
$5000 scholarship for college undergraduate or graduate student pursuing pharmacy studies on a full-time basis. Minimum 3.0 GPA required. Must have demonstrated unmet financial need (as verified by college or university). Open to US citizens, nationals and permanent residents.

Academic Fields/Career Goals: Pharmacy.

Award: Scholarship for use in sophomore, junior, senior, or graduate years; not renewable. *Amount:* $5000.

Eligibility Requirements: Applicant must be Black (non-Hispanic) and enrolled or expecting to enroll full-time at a four-year institution or university. Applicant must have 3.0 GPA or higher. Available to U.S. and non-U.S. citizens.

Application Requirements: Application form, essay, financial need analysis. *Deadline:* March 31.

Contact: Mary Williams, Director of Outreach and Recruitment
Phone: 800-331-2244

UNITED HEALTH FOUNDATION DIVERSE SCHOLARS INITIATIVE
• *See page 152*

PHILOSOPHY

AMERICAN SCHOOL OF CLASSICAL STUDIES AT ATHENS

http://www.ascsa.edu.gr/

ASCSA SUMMER SESSIONS SCHOLARSHIPS
• *See page 108*

DAVIDSON INSTITUTE FOR TALENT DEVELOPMENT

http://www.davidsongifted.org/

DAVIDSON FELLOWS SCHOLARSHIP PROGRAM
• *See page 113*

STRAIGHTFORWARD MEDIA

http://www.straightforwardmedia.com/

STRAIGHTFORWARD MEDIA LIBERAL ARTS SCHOLARSHIP
• *See page 126*

UNITED NEGRO COLLEGE FUND

http://www.uncf.org/

UNCF/KOCH SCHOLARS PROGRAM FOR UNDERGRADUATES
• *See page 87*

PHOTOJOURNALISM/ PHOTOGRAPHY

AMERICAN QUARTER HORSE FOUNDATION (AQHF)

http://www.aqha.com/foundation

AQHF JOURNALISM OR COMMUNICATIONS SCHOLARSHIP
• *See page 201*

ASIAN AMERICAN JOURNALISTS ASSOCIATION, SEATTLE CHAPTER

http://www.aajaseattle.org/

NORTHWEST JOURNALISTS OF COLOR SCHOLARSHIP
• *See page 88*

CCNMA: LATINO JOURNALISTS OF CALIFORNIA

http://www.ccnma.org/

CCNMA SCHOLARSHIPS
• *See page 203*

COLLEGE PHOTOGRAPHER OF THE YEAR

http://www.cpoy.org/

COLLEGE PHOTOGRAPHER OF THE YEAR COMPETITION
Awards undergraduate and graduate students for juried contest of individual photographs, picture stories and photographic essay and multimedia presentations. Two awards in the dollar value of $500 and $1000 are granted. Deadline varies.

Academic Fields/Career Goals: Photojournalism/Photography.

Award: Prize for use in freshman, sophomore, junior, senior, or graduate years; not renewable. *Number:* up to 2. *Amount:* $500–$1000.

Eligibility Requirements: Applicant must be enrolled or expecting to enroll full- or part-time at a four-year institution or university. Available to U.S. and non-U.S. citizens.

Application Requirements: Application form, entry in a contest, essay, personal photograph, portfolio. *Deadline:* varies.

Contact: Rita Ann Reed, Program Director
College Photographer of the Year
University of Missouri, School of Journalism
107 Lee Hills Hall
Columbia, MO 65211
Phone: 573-882-2198
Fax: 573-884-4999
E-mail: info@cpoy.org

CONNECTICUT CHAPTER OF SOCIETY OF PROFESSIONAL JOURNALISTS

http://www.ctspj.org/

CONNECTICUT SPJ BOB EDDY SCHOLARSHIP PROGRAM

• *See page 203*

INTERNATIONAL FOODSERVICE EDITORIAL COUNCIL

http://www.ifeconline.com/

INTERNATIONAL FOODSERVICE EDITORIAL COUNCIL COMMUNICATIONS SCHOLARSHIP

• *See page 88*

NATIONAL ACADEMY OF TELEVISION ARTS AND SCIENCES

http://www.emmyonline.tv/

DOUGLAS W. MUMMERT SCHOLARSHIP

• *See page 129*

JIM MCKAY MEMORIAL SCHOLARSHIP

• *See page 205*

MIKE WALLACE MEMORIAL SCHOLARSHIP

• *See page 205*

NATIONAL ACADEMY OF TELEVISION ARTS AND SCIENCES TRUSTEES SCHOLARSHIP

• *See page 205*

RANDY FALCO SCHOLARSHIP

• *See page 205*

NATIONAL ASSOCIATION OF BLACK JOURNALISTS

http://www.nabj.org/

NATIONAL ASSOCIATION OF BLACK JOURNALISTS NON-SUSTAINING SCHOLARSHIP AWARDS

• *See page 384*

VISUAL TASK FORCE SCHOLARSHIP

Scholarship for students attending an accredited four-year college or university and majoring in visual journalism. Minimum 3.0 GPA required. Must be a member of NABJ. Scholarship value and the number of scholarships granted varies annually.

Academic Fields/Career Goals: Photojournalism/Photography.

Award: Scholarship for use in freshman, sophomore, junior, senior, or graduate years; not renewable.

Eligibility Requirements: Applicant must be enrolled or expecting to enroll full-time at a four-year institution or university. Applicant must have 3.0 GPA or higher. Available to U.S. and non-U.S. citizens.

Application Requirements: Application form, driver's license, essay, interview, recommendations or references, transcript. *Deadline:* March 17.

Contact: Irving Washington, Manager
Phone: 301-445-7100
Fax: 301-445-7101
E-mail: iwashington@nabj.org

NATIONAL ASSOCIATION OF HISPANIC JOURNALISTS (NAHJ)

http://www.nahj.org/

NATIONAL ASSOCIATION OF HISPANIC JOURNALISTS SCHOLARSHIP

• *See page 206*

NEWHOUSE SCHOLARSHIP PROGRAM

• *See page 343*

NATIVE AMERICAN JOURNALISTS ASSOCIATION

http://www.naja.com/

NATIVE AMERICAN JOURNALISTS ASSOCIATION SCHOLARSHIPS

• *See page 89*

NEBRASKA PRESS ASSOCIATION

http://www.nebpress.com/

NEBRASKA PRESS ASSOCIATION FOUNDATION SCHOLARSHIP

• *See page 89*

OREGON STUDENT ASSISTANCE COMMISSION

http://www.GetCollegeFunds.org/

KERDRAGON SCHOLARSHIP

• *See page 130*

OUTDOOR WRITERS ASSOCIATION OF AMERICA

http://www.owaa.org/

OUTDOOR WRITERS ASSOCIATION OF AMERICA - BODIE MCDOWELL SCHOLARSHIP AWARD

• *See page 207*

PALM BEACH ASSOCIATION OF BLACK JOURNALISTS

PALM BEACH ASSOCIATION OF BLACK JOURNALISTS SCHOLARSHIP

• *See page 386*

PRINTING INDUSTRY MIDWEST EDUCATION FOUDNATION

http://www.pimw.org/scholarships

PRINTING INDUSTRY MIDWEST EDUCATION FOUNDATION SCHOLARSHIP FUND

• *See page 207*

QUALITY BATH

www.qualitybath.com

QUALITYBATH.COM SCHOLARSHIP PROGRAM
• See page 123

RADIO TELEVISION DIGITAL NEWS ASSOCIATION

www.rtdna.org

CAROLE SIMPSON SCHOLARSHIP
• See page 208

ED BRADLEY SCHOLARSHIP
• See page 208

GEORGE FOREMAN TRIBUTE TO LYNDON B. JOHNSON SCHOLARSHIP
• See page 208

LOU AND CAROLE PRATO SPORTS REPORTING SCHOLARSHIP
• See page 208

MIKE REYNOLDS JOURNALISM SCHOLARSHIP
• See page 209

PETE WILSON SCHOLARSHIP
• See page 209

SOCIETY FOR IMAGING SCIENCE AND TECHNOLOGY

http://www.imaging.org/

RAYMOND DAVIS SCHOLARSHIP
• See page 286

STRAIGHTFORWARD MEDIA

http://www.straightforwardmedia.com/

STRAIGHTFORWARD MEDIA MEDIA & COMMUNICATIONS SCHOLARSHIP
• See page 91

SUPPORT CREATIVITY

http://wesupportcreativity.org

SUPPORT CREATIVITY SCHOLARSHIP
• See page 124

TAMPA BAY TIMES FUND, INC.

http://www.tampabay.com/fund

CAREER JOURNALISM SCHOLARSHIP
• See page 210

TAMPA BAY TIMES FUND CAREER JOURNALISM SCHOLARSHIPS
• See page 91

TEXAS GRIDIRON CLUB INC.

http://www.spjfw.org/

TEXAS GRIDIRON CLUB SCHOLARSHIPS
• See page 212

UNITARIAN UNIVERSALIST ASSOCIATION

http://www.uua.org/

PAULY D'ORLANDO MEMORIAL ART SCHOLARSHIP
• See page 132

UNITED METHODIST COMMUNICATIONS

http://www.umcom.org/

LEONARD M. PERRYMAN COMMUNICATIONS SCHOLARSHIP FOR ETHNIC MINORITY STUDENTS
• See page 212

UNITED NEGRO COLLEGE FUND

http://www.uncf.org/

RHYTHM NATION/JANET JACKSON SCHOLARSHIP
• See page 132

VALLEY PRESS CLUB

http://www.valleypressclub.com/

VALLEY PRESS CLUB SCHOLARSHIPS, THE REPUBLICAN SCHOLARSHIP, CHANNEL 22 SCHOLARSHIP
• See page 213

PHYSICAL SCIENCES

101ST AIRBORNE DIVISION ASSOCIATION

http://www.screamingeaglefoundation.org/

AL & WILLIAMARY VISTE SCHOLARSHIP
• See page 233

AIR & WASTE MANAGEMENT ASSOCIATION–COASTAL PLAINS CHAPTER

http://www.awmacoastalplains.org/

COASTAL PLAINS CHAPTER OF THE AIR AND WASTE MANAGEMENT ASSOCIATION ENVIRONMENTAL STEWARD SCHOLARSHIP
• See page 318

AIST FOUNDATION

http://www.aistfoundation.org/

ASSOCIATION FOR IRON AND STEEL TECHNOLOGY OHIO VALLEY CHAPTER SCHOLARSHIP
• See page 153

AMERICAN ALPINE CLUB

https://americanalpineclub.org/

AAC RESEARCH GRANTS
• See page 153

AMERICAN ASSOCIATION OF PHYSICS TEACHERS

http://aapt.org

BARBARA LOTZE SCHOLARSHIPS FOR FUTURE TEACHERS
• *See page 247*

AMERICAN FOUNDATION FOR THE BLIND

http://www.afb.org/

PAUL W. RUCKES SCHOLARSHIP
• *See page 214*

AMERICAN INDIAN SCIENCE AND ENGINEERING SOCIETY

http://www.aises.org/

A.T. ANDERSON MEMORIAL SCHOLARSHIP PROGRAM
• *See page 109*

AMERICAN INSTITUTE OF AERONAUTICS AND ASTRONAUTICS

http://www.aiaafoundation.org/

AIAA FOUNDATION UNDERGRADUATE SCHOLARSHIPS
• *See page 110*

LEATRICE GREGORY PENDRAY SCHOLARSHIP
• *See page 110*

AMERICAN LEGION DEPARTMENT OF MARYLAND

http://www.mdlegion.org/

AMERICAN LEGION DEPARTMENT OF MARYLAND MATH-SCIENCE SCHOLARSHIP
• *See page 413*

AMERICAN SOCIETY FOR ENGINEERING EDUCATION

http://www.asee.org/

SCIENCE, MATHEMATICS, AND RESEARCH FOR TRANSFORMATION DEFENSE SCHOLARSHIP FOR SERVICE PROGRAM
• *See page 110*

AMERICAN SOCIETY OF NAVAL ENGINEERS

http://www.navalengineers.org/

AMERICAN SOCIETY OF NAVAL ENGINEERS SCHOLARSHIP
• *See page 110*

ARIZONA PROFESSIONAL CHAPTER OF AISES

http://www.aises.org/scholarships

ARIZONA PROFESSIONAL CHAPTER OF AISES SCHOLARSHIP
• *See page 294*

ARMED FORCES COMMUNICATIONS AND ELECTRONICS ASSOCIATION, EDUCATIONAL FOUNDATION

http://www.afcea.org/site/?q=foundation/scholarships

ARMED FORCES COMMUNICATIONS AND ELECTRONICS ASSOCIATION ROTC SCHOLARSHIP PROGRAM
• *See page 137*

STEM MAJORS SCHOLARSHIPS FOR UNDERGRADUATE STUDENTS
• *See page 110*

STEM TEACHERS SCHOLARSHIP
• *See page 111*

VADM SAMUEL L. GRAVELY, JR., USN(RET.) MEMORIAL SCHOLARSHIP
• *See page 111*

VETERANS OF ENDURING FREEDOM (AFGHANISTAN) AND IRAQI FREEDOM SCHOLARSHIP
• *See page 214*

ARRL FOUNDATION INC.

http://www.arrl.org/

CTRI/CHRIS SEEBER, KA1GEU, MEMORIAL SCHOLARSHIP
• *See page 249*

DAN HUETTL, WZ7U, MEMORIAL SCHOLARSHIP
• *See page 280*

LOIS MANLEY, K7LMZ, AND RANDALL PITCHFORD, WW7ZZ, SCHOLARSHIP
• *See page 193*

W1FDR SCHOLARSHIP
• *See page 112*

ASSOCIATION FOR WOMEN GEOSCIENTISTS (AWG)

http://www.awg.org/

AWG ETHNIC MINORITY SCHOLARSHIP
• *See page 241*

AWG MARIA LUISA CRAWFORD FIELD CAMP SCHOLARSHIP
• *See page 117*

AWG SALT LAKE CHAPTER (SLC) RESEARCH SCHOLARSHIP
• *See page 117*

JANET CULLEN TANAKA GEOSCIENCES UNDERGRADUATE SCHOLARSHIP
• *See page 117*

LONE STAR RISING CAREER SCHOLARSHIP
• See page 242

OSAGE CHAPTER UNDERGRADUATE SERVICE SCHOLARSHIP
• See page 117

SUSAN EKDALE MEMORIAL FIELD CAMP SCHOLARSHIP
• See page 242

ASSOCIATION ON AMERICAN INDIAN AFFAIRS, INC.
http://www.indian-affairs.org/

ELIZABETH AND SHERMAN ASCHE MEMORIAL SCHOLARSHIP FUND
• See page 98

BARRY GOLDWATER SCHOLARSHIP AND EXCELLENCE IN EDUCATION FOUNDATION
https://goldwater.scholarsapply.org

BARRY M. GOLDWATER SCHOLARSHIP AND EXCELLENCE IN EDUCATION PROGRAM
• See page 112

BHW GROUP
https://thebhwgroup.com/

BHW WOMEN IN STEM SCHOLARSHIP
• See page 74

CATCHING THE DREAM
http://www.catchingthedream.org/

MATH, ENGINEERING, SCIENCE, BUSINESS, EDUCATION, COMPUTERS SCHOLARSHIPS
• See page 162

NATIVE AMERICAN LEADERSHIP IN EDUCATION (NALE)
• See page 163

COMMUNITY FOUNDATION FOR GREATER ATLANTA, INC.
http://cfgreateratlanta.org/

JAMES M. AND VIRGINIA M. SMYTH SCHOLARSHIP
• See page 128

TECH HIGH SCHOOL ALUMNI ASSOCIATION/W.O. CHENEY MERIT SCHOLARSHIP FUND
• See page 297

COMPHEALTH
http://www.comphealth.com

COMPHEALTH MEDICAL SCHOLARSHIP
• See page 151

THE DALLAS FOUNDATION
http://www.dallasfoundation.org/

WHITLEY PLACE SCHOLARSHIP
• See page 120

EAA AVIATION FOUNDATION, INC.
http://www.eaa.org/

PAYZER SCHOLARSHIP
• See page 140

THE ELECTROCHEMICAL SOCIETY
http://www.electrochem.org/

H.H. DOW MEMORIAL STUDENT ACHIEVEMENT AWARD OF THE INDUSTRIAL ELECTROLYSIS AND ELECTROCHEMICAL ENGINEERING DIVISION OF THE ELECTROCHEMICAL SOCIETY INC.
• See page 113

STUDENT RESEARCH AWARDS OF THE BATTERY DIVISION OF THE ELECTROCHEMICAL SOCIETY INC.
• See page 113

FOUNDATION FOR SCIENCE AND DISABILITY
http://stemd.org/

GRANTS FOR DISABLED GRADUATE STUDENTS IN THE SCIENCES
• See page 113

GREATER KANAWHA VALLEY FOUNDATION
http://www.tgkvf.org/

MATH AND SCIENCE SCHOLARSHIP
• See page 156

GREAT MINDS IN STEM
www.greatmindsinstem.org

HISPANIC ENGINEER NATIONAL ACHIEVEMENT AWARDS CORPORATION SCHOLARSHIP PROGRAM
• See page 106

INDEPENDENT LABORATORIES INSTITUTE SCHOLARSHIP ALLIANCE
http://www.acil.org/

INDEPENDENT LABORATORIES INSTITUTE SCHOLARSHIP ALLIANCE
• See page 156

INSTITUTE OF FOOD TECHNOLOGISTS
http://www.ift.org/

PEPSICO SCHOLARSHIP AND INTERNSHIP
• See page 333

LOS ANGELES COUNCIL OF BLACK PROFESSIONAL ENGINEERS

http://www.lablackengineers.org/

AL-BEN SCHOLARSHIP FOR ACADEMIC INCENTIVE
• *See page 179*

AL-BEN SCHOLARSHIP FOR PROFESSIONAL MERIT
• *See page 179*

AL-BEN SCHOLARSHIP FOR SCHOLASTIC ACHIEVEMENT
• *See page 179*

MEDICAL SCRUBS COLLECTION

http://medicalscrubscollection.com

MEDICAL SCRUBS COLLECTION SCHOLARSHIP
• *See page 106*

NASA IDAHO SPACE GRANT CONSORTIUM

http://www.id.spacegrant.org/

NASA IDAHO SPACE GRANT CONSORTIUM SCHOLARSHIP PROGRAM
• *See page 157*

NASA/MARYLAND SPACE GRANT CONSORTIUM

http://md.spacegrant.org/

NASA MARYLAND SPACE GRANT CONSORTIUM UNDERGRADUATE SCHOLARSHIPS
• *See page 142*

NASA MINNESOTA SPACE GRANT CONSORTIUM

http://www.aem.umn.edu/mnsgc

MINNESOTA SPACE GRANT CONSORTIUM SCHOLARSHIP PROGRAM
• *See page 142*

NASA'S VIRGINIA SPACE GRANT CONSORTIUM

http://www.vsgc.odu.edu/

UNDERGRADUATE STEM RESEARCH SCHOLARSHIPS
• *See page 114*

NATIONAL ASSOCIATION FOR THE ADVANCEMENT OF COLORED PEOPLE

http://www.naacp.org/

HUBERTUS W.V. WELLEMS SCHOLARSHIP FOR MALE STUDENTS
• *See page 180*

NATIONAL ASSOCIATION OF WATER COMPANIES-NEW JERSEY CHAPTER

http://www.nawc.org

NATIONAL ASSOCIATION OF WATER COMPANIES-NEW JERSEY CHAPTER SCHOLARSHIP
• *See page 80*

NATIONAL SOCIETY OF BLACK PHYSICISTS

http://www.nsbp.org/

AMERICAN PHYSICAL SOCIETY CORPORATE-SPONSORED SCHOLARSHIP FOR MINORITY UNDERGRADUATE STUDENTS WHO MAJOR IN PHYSICS

Scholarship available for minority undergraduate students majoring in physics. Award of $2000 per year for new corporate scholars, and $3000 per year for renewal students. In addition, each physics department that hosts one or more APS minority undergraduate scholars and assigns a mentor for their students will receive a $500 award for programs to encourage minority students.

Academic Fields/Career Goals: Physical Sciences.

Award: Scholarship for use in freshman, sophomore, junior, or senior years; not renewable. *Amount:* $2000–$3000.

Eligibility Requirements: Applicant must be American Indian/Alaska Native, Asian/Pacific Islander, Black (non-Hispanic), Hispanic and enrolled or expecting to enroll full- or part-time at a two-year or four-year institution or university. Available to U.S. citizens.

Application Requirements: Application form, recommendations or references, transcript. *Deadline:* December 1.

Contact: Dr. Stephen Roberson, Scholarship Chairman
Phone: 703-536-4207
Fax: 703-536-4203
E-mail: adminofficer@nsbp.org

CHARLES S. BROWN SCHOLARSHIP IN PHYSICS

Scholarship providing and African-American student with financial assistance while enrolled in a physics degree program. Number of awards and dollar value varies.

Academic Fields/Career Goals: Physical Sciences.

Award: Scholarship for use in freshman, sophomore, junior, senior, or graduate years; not renewable.

Eligibility Requirements: Applicant must be Black (non-Hispanic) and enrolled or expecting to enroll full- or part-time at a four-year institution or university. Available to U.S. and non-U.S. citizens.

Application Requirements: Application form, financial need analysis, self-addressed stamped envelope with application. *Deadline:* January 12.

Contact: Scholarship Committee Chair
National Society of Black Physicists
6704G Lee Highway
Arlington, VA 22205
Phone: 703-536-4207
Fax: 703-536-4203
E-mail: scholarship@nsbp.org

ELMER S. IMES SCHOLARSHIP IN PHYSICS

Graduating high school seniors and undergraduate students already enrolled in college as physics majors may apply for the scholarship. U.S citizenship is required.

Academic Fields/Career Goals: Physical Sciences.

Award: Scholarship for use in freshman, sophomore, junior, or senior years; not renewable. *Number:* 1. *Amount:* $1000.

Eligibility Requirements: Applicant must be enrolled or expecting to enroll full-time at a two-year or four-year institution or university. Available to U.S. citizens.

Application Requirements: Application form, driver's license, essay, recommendations or references, resume, transcript. *Deadline:* January 12.

Contact: Scholarship Committee Chair
National Society of Black Physicists
6704G Lee Highway
Arlington, VA 22205
Phone: 703-536-4207
Fax: 703-536-4203
E-mail: scholarship@nsbp.org

HARVEY WASHINGTON BANKS SCHOLARSHIP IN ASTRONOMY

One-time award for an African American student pursuing an undergraduate degree in astronomy/physics.

Academic Fields/Career Goals: Physical Sciences.

Award: Scholarship for use in freshman, sophomore, junior, or senior years; not renewable. *Number:* 1. *Amount:* $1000.

Eligibility Requirements: Applicant must be Black (non-Hispanic) and enrolled or expecting to enroll full-time at a two-year or four-year institution or university. Available to U.S. citizens.

Application Requirements: Application form, essay, recommendations or references, transcript. *Deadline:* January 12.

Contact: Dr. Stephen Roberson, Scholarship Chairman
Phone: 703-536-4207
Fax: 703-536-4203
E-mail: adminofficer@nsbp.org

MICHAEL P. ANDERSON SCHOLARSHIP IN SPACE SCIENCE

One-time award for an African American undergraduate student majoring in space science/physics.

Academic Fields/Career Goals: Physical Sciences.

Award: Scholarship for use in freshman, sophomore, junior, or senior years; not renewable. *Number:* 1. *Amount:* $1000.

Eligibility Requirements: Applicant must be Black (non-Hispanic) and enrolled or expecting to enroll full-time at a two-year or four-year institution or university. Available to U.S. citizens.

Application Requirements: Application form, essay, recommendations or references, transcript. *Deadline:* January 12.

Contact: Dr. Stephen Roberson, Scholarship Chairman
Phone: 703-536-4207
Fax: 703-536-4203
E-mail: adminofficer@nsbp.org

NATIONAL SOCIETY OF BLACK PHYSICISTS AND LAWRENCE LIVERMORE NATIONAL LIBRARY UNDERGRADUATE SCHOLARSHIP

Scholarship for a graduating high school senior or undergraduate student enrolled in a physics major. Scholarship renewable up to four years if student maintains a 3.0 GPA and remains a physics major.

Academic Fields/Career Goals: Physical Sciences.

Award: Scholarship for use in freshman, sophomore, junior, or senior years; renewable. *Number:* 1. *Amount:* $5000.

Eligibility Requirements: Applicant must be Black (non-Hispanic) and enrolled or expecting to enroll full-time at a two-year or four-year institution or university. Applicant must have 3.0 GPA or higher. Available to U.S. citizens.

Application Requirements: Application form, essay, recommendations or references, transcript. *Deadline:* December 1.

Contact: Dr. Stephen Roberson, Scholarship Chairman
Phone: 703-536-4207
Fax: 703-536-4203
E-mail: adminofficer@nsbp.org

RONALD E. MCNAIR SCHOLARSHIP IN SPACE AND OPTICAL PHYSICS

One-time award for African American undergraduate student majoring in physics. Must be U.S. citizen.

Academic Fields/Career Goals: Physical Sciences.

Award: Scholarship for use in freshman, sophomore, junior, or senior years; not renewable. *Number:* 1. *Amount:* $1000.

Eligibility Requirements: Applicant must be Black (non-Hispanic) and enrolled or expecting to enroll full-time at a two-year or four-year institution or university. Available to U.S. citizens.

Application Requirements: Application form, essay, recommendations or references, transcript. *Deadline:* January 12.

Contact: Dr. Stephen Roberson, Scholarship Chairman
Phone: 703-536-4207
Fax: 703-536-4203
E-mail: adminofficer@nsbp.org

WALTER SAMUEL MCAFEE SCHOLARSHIP IN SPACE PHYSICS

One-time scholarship for African American full-time undergraduate student majoring in physics. Must be U.S. citizen.

Academic Fields/Career Goals: Physical Sciences.

Award: Scholarship for use in freshman, sophomore, junior, or senior years; not renewable. *Number:* 1. *Amount:* $1000.

Eligibility Requirements: Applicant must be Black (non-Hispanic) and enrolled or expecting to enroll full-time at a two-year or four-year institution or university. Available to U.S. citizens.

Application Requirements: Application form, essay, recommendations or references, transcript. *Deadline:* January 12.

Contact: Dr. Stephen Roberson, Scholarship Chairman
Phone: 703-536-4207
Fax: 703-536-4203
E-mail: adminofficer@nsbp.org

WILLIE HOBBS MOORE, HARRY L. MORRISON, AND ARTHUR B.C. WALKER PHYSICS SCHOLARSHIPS

Scholarships are intended for African American undergraduate physics majors. Applicants should be either sophomores or juniors. Award for use in junior or senior year of study.

Academic Fields/Career Goals: Physical Sciences.

Award: Scholarship for use in sophomore, junior, or senior years; not renewable. *Number:* 3. *Amount:* $1000.

Eligibility Requirements: Applicant must be Black (non-Hispanic) and enrolled or expecting to enroll full-time at a two-year or four-year institution or university. Available to U.S. citizens.

Application Requirements: Application form, essay, recommendations or references, transcript. *Deadline:* January 12.

Contact: Dr. Stephen Roberson, Scholarship Chairman
Phone: 703-536-4207
Fax: 703-536-4203
E-mail: adminofficer@nsbp.org

NEVADA NASA SPACE GRANT CONSORTIUM

http://www.nvspacegrant.org/

NATIONAL SPACE GRANT COLLEGE AND FELLOWSHIP PROGRAM

• See page 114

NEXTSTEPU

http://www.nextstepu.com/

$1,500 STEM SCHOLARSHIP

• See page 106

OREGON STUDENT ASSISTANCE COMMISSION

http://www.GetCollegeFunds.org/

ANDY AITKENHEAD SCHOLARSHIP

• See page 115

SEHAR SALEHA AHMAD AND ABRAHIM EKRAMULLAH ZAFAR FOUNDATION SCHOLARSHIP

• See page 115

ROBERT H. MOLLOHAN FAMILY CHARITABLE FOUNDATION, INC.

http://www.mollohanfoundation.org/

HIGH TECHNOLOGY SCHOLARS PROGRAM
• *See page 158*

SCARLETT FAMILY FOUNDATION SCHOLARSHIP PROGRAM

http://www.scarlettfoundation.org/

SCHOLARSHIP FOR STUDENTS PURSUING A BUSINESS OR STEM DEGREE
• *See page 84*

SIGMA XI, THE SCIENTIFIC RESEARCH SOCIETY

http://www.sigmaxi.org/

SIGMA XI GRANTS-IN-AID OF RESEARCH
• *See page 101*

SOCIETY OF PHYSICS STUDENTS

http://www.spsnational.org/

SOCIETY OF PHYSICS STUDENTS LEADERSHIP SCHOLARSHIPS

Scholarships of $2000 to $5000 are awarded to members of Society of Physics Students (SPS) for undergraduate study. The number of awards granted ranges from 17 to 22.

Academic Fields/Career Goals: Physical Sciences.

Award: Scholarship for use in sophomore, junior, or senior years; not renewable. *Number:* 17–22. *Amount:* $2000–$5000.

Eligibility Requirements: Applicant must be enrolled or expecting to enroll full-time at a two-year or four-year institution or university. Applicant or parent of applicant must be member of Society of Physics Students. Available to U.S. and non-U.S. citizens.

Application Requirements: Application form, recommendations or references, transcript. *Deadline:* February 15.

Contact: Scholarship Committee
Society of Physics Students
One Physics Ellipse
College Park, MD 20740
Phone: 301-209-3007
Fax: 301-209-0839
E-mail: sps@aip.org

SOCIETY OF PHYSICS STUDENTS OUTSTANDING STUDENT IN RESEARCH

Available to members of the Society of Physics Students. Winners will receive a $500 honorarium and a $500 award for their SPS Chapter. In addition, expenses for transportation, room, board, and registration for the ICPS will by paid by SPS.

Academic Fields/Career Goals: Physical Sciences.

Award: Prize for use in freshman, sophomore, junior, or senior years; not renewable. *Number:* 1–2. *Amount:* $500–$2500.

Eligibility Requirements: Applicant must be enrolled or expecting to enroll full-time at a two-year or four-year institution or university. Applicant or parent of applicant must be member of Society of Physics Students. Available to U.S. and non-U.S. citizens.

Application Requirements: Abstract, application form, recommendations or references. *Deadline:* April 15.

Contact: Secretary
Society of Physics Students
One Physics Ellipse
College Park, MD 20740
Phone: 301-209-3007
Fax: 301-209-0839
E-mail: sps@aip.org

SOCIETY OF PHYSICS STUDENTS PEGGY DIXON TWO-YEAR COLLEGE SCHOLARSHIP

Scholarship available to Society of Physics Students (SPS) members. Award based on performance both in physics and overall studies, and SPS participation. Must have completed at least one semester or quarter of the introductory physics sequence, and be currently registered in the appropriate subsequent physics courses.

Academic Fields/Career Goals: Physical Sciences.

Award: Scholarship for use in freshman or sophomore years; not renewable. *Number:* 1. *Amount:* $2000.

Eligibility Requirements: Applicant must be enrolled or expecting to enroll full-time at a two-year or four-year institution or university. Applicant or parent of applicant must be member of Society of Physics Students. Available to U.S. and non-U.S. citizens.

Application Requirements: Application form, financial need analysis, letters from at least two faculty members, transcript. *Deadline:* February 15.

Contact: Sacha Purnell, Administrative Assistant
Phone: 301-209-3007
E-mail: sps@aip.org

TAILOR MADE LAWNS

http://www.tailormadelawns.com

2017 TAILOR MADE LAWNS SCHOLARSHIP FUND
• *See page 102*

TKE EDUCATIONAL FOUNDATION

http://www.tke.org/

CARROL C. HALL MEMORIAL SCHOLARSHIP
• *See page 115*

ERIC D. DUNNING SCHOLARSHIP
• *See page 219*

UNITED NEGRO COLLEGE FUND

http://www.uncf.org/

ANHEUSER-BUSCH LEGENDS OF THE CROWN SCHOLARSHIP PROGRAM
• *See page 86*

BASF/ALFRED CHISHOLM ENDOWED MEMORIAL SCHOLARSHIP
• *See page 86*

BLUE CROSS BLUE SHIELD OF ILLINOIS AND BLUE CROSS BLUE SHIELD OF TEXAS SCHOLARSHIP
• *See page 115*

GATES MILLENNIUM SCHOLARS (GMS) PROGRAM
• *See page 260*

UNCF STEM SCHOLARS PROGRAM
• *See page 159*

UNIVERSITIES SPACE RESEARCH ASSOCIATION

http://www.usra.edu/

UNIVERSITIES SPACE RESEARCH ASSOCIATION SCHOLARSHIP AWARD PROGRAM
• *See page 116*

VERMONT SPACE GRANT CONSORTIUM

http://www.cems.uvm.edu/vsgc

VERMONT SPACE GRANT CONSORTIUM
• See page 96

XEROX

http://www.xerox.com//

TECHNICAL MINORITY SCHOLARSHIP
• See page 190

POLITICAL SCIENCE

AMERICAN FEDERATION OF STATE, COUNTY, AND MUNICIPAL EMPLOYEES

http://www.afscme.org/

AFSCME/UNCF UNION SCHOLARS PROGRAM
• See page 103

JERRY CLARK MEMORIAL SCHOLARSHIP
Renewable award for a student majoring in political science for his or her junior and senior years of study. Must be a child of an AFSCME member. Minimum 2.5 GPA required. Once awarded, the scholarship will be renewed for the senior year provided the student remains enrolled full-time as a political science major.

Academic Fields/Career Goals: Political Science.

Award: Scholarship for use in junior or senior years; renewable. *Number:* 2. *Amount:* $5000.

Eligibility Requirements: Applicant must be enrolled or expecting to enroll full-time at a four-year institution or university. Applicant or parent of applicant must be member of American Federation of State, County, and Municipal Employees. Applicant must have 2.5 GPA or higher. Available to U.S. citizens.

Application Requirements: Application form, proof of parent, transcript. *Deadline:* July 1.

Contact: Philip Allen, Scholarship Coordinator
Phone: 202-429-1250
Fax: 202-429-1293
E-mail: pallen@asscme.org

AMERICAN LEGION AUXILIARY DEPARTMENT OF ARIZONA

http:/wwwaladeptaz.org

AMERICAN LEGION AUXILIARY DEPARTMENT OF ARIZONA WILMA HOYAL-MAXINE CHILTON MEMORIAL SCHOLARSHIP
Annual scholarship to a student in second year or higher in one of the three state universities in Arizona. Must be enrolled in a program of study in political science, public programs, or special education. Must be a citizen of United States and of Arizona for at least one year. Honorably discharged veterans or immediate family members are given preference.

Academic Fields/Career Goals: Political Science; Public Policy and Administration; Social Services; Special Education.

Award: Scholarship for use in freshman, sophomore, junior, senior, graduate, or postgraduate years; not renewable. *Number:* 3. *Amount:* $1000.

Eligibility Requirements: Applicant must be enrolled or expecting to enroll full- or part-time at a four-year institution or university; resident of Arizona and studying in Arizona. Available to U.S. citizens.

Application Requirements: Application form, essay, financial need analysis, personal photograph. *Deadline:* May 15.

Contact: Barbara Matteson, Department Secretary/Treasurer
American Legion Auxiliary Department of Arizona
4701 North 19th Avenue, Suite 100
Phoenix, AZ 85015
Phone: 602-241-1080
E-mail: secretary@aladeptaz.org

ARAB AMERICAN SCHOLARSHIP FOUNDATION

http://www.lahc.org/

LEBANESE AMERICAN HERITAGE CLUB'S SCHOLARSHIP FUND
• See page 201

ASSOCIATION OF FORMER INTELLIGENCE OFFICERS

http://www.afio.com

AFIO UNDERGRADUATE AND GRADUATE SCHOLARSHIPS
• See page 103

BOYS AND GIRLS CLUBS OF GREATER SAN DIEGO

http://www.sdyouth.org/

SPENCE REESE SCHOLARSHIP
• See page 297

CULTURAL SERVICES OF THE FRENCH EMBASSY

http://www.frenchculture.org/

TEACHING ASSISTANT PROGRAM IN FRANCE
• See page 104

GOVERNMENT FINANCE OFFICERS ASSOCIATION

http://www.gfoa.org/

MINORITIES IN GOVERNMENT FINANCE SCHOLARSHIP
• See page 78

GREATER SALINA COMMUNITY FOUNDATION

http://www.gscf.org/

KANSAS FEDERATION OF REPUBLICAN WOMEN SCHOLARSHIP
• See page 360

HARRY S. TRUMAN SCHOLARSHIP FOUNDATION

http://www.truman.gov/

HARRY S. TRUMAN SCHOLARSHIP
Scholarships for U.S. citizens or U.S. nationals who are college or university students with junior-level academic standing and who wish to attend professional or graduate school to prepare for careers in government or the nonprofit and advocacy sectors. Candidates must be nominated by their institution. Public service and leadership record considered. Visit website http://www.truman.gov for further information and application.

Academic Fields/Career Goals: Political Science; Public Policy and Administration.

Award: Scholarship for use in junior year; renewable. *Number:* 65. *Amount:* $30,000.

Eligibility Requirements: Applicant must be enrolled or expecting to enroll full-time at a four-year institution or university and must have an interest in leadership. Available to U.S. citizens.

Application Requirements: Application form, interview, policy proposal, recommendations or references. *Deadline:* February 5.

Contact: Tonji Wade, Program Officer
Harry S. Truman Scholarship Foundation
712 Jackson Place, NW
Washington, DC 20006
Phone: 202-395-4831
Fax: 202-395-6995
E-mail: office@truman.gov

INSTITUTE FOR HUMANE STUDIES
http://www.theihs.org/

HUMANE STUDIES FELLOWSHIPS
• *See page 204*

THE LYNDON BAINES JOHNSON FOUNDATION
http://www.lbjlibrary.org/page/foundation/

MOODY RESEARCH GRANTS
• *See page 104*

NAQVI INJURY LAW
http://www.naqvilaw.com/

NAQVI LAW SCHOLARSHIP
• *See page 226*

NATIONAL SOCIETY DAUGHTERS OF THE AMERICAN REVOLUTION
http://www.dar.org/

NATIONAL SOCIETY DAUGHTERS OF THE AMERICAN REVOLUTION DR. AURA-LEE A. PITTENGER AND JAMES HOBBS PITTENGER AMERICAN HISTORY SCHOLARSHIP
• *See page 360*

NATIONAL SOCIETY DAUGHTERS OF THE AMERICAN REVOLUTION ENID HALL GRISWOLD MEMORIAL SCHOLARSHIP
• *See page 246*

STRAIGHTFORWARD MEDIA
http://www.straightforwardmedia.com/

STRAIGHTFORWARD MEDIA LIBERAL ARTS SCHOLARSHIP
• *See page 126*

TKE EDUCATIONAL FOUNDATION
http://www.tke.org/

BRUCE B. MELCHERT SCHOLARSHIP
One-time award of $300 given to an undergraduate member of Tau Kappa Epsilon with sophomore, junior, or senior standing. Must be pursuing a degree in political science or government and have a record of leadership within his fraternity and other campus organizations. Should have as a goal to serve in a political or government position. Recent head and shoulders photograph must be submitted with application. Minimum 3.0 GPA required. Preference will first be given to a member of Beta-Theta Chapter but, if there is no qualified applicant, the scholarship will be open to any other qualified Teke.

Academic Fields/Career Goals: Political Science.

Award: Scholarship for use in sophomore, junior, or senior years; not renewable. *Number:* 1. *Amount:* $300.

Eligibility Requirements: Applicant must be enrolled or expecting to enroll full-time at a four-year institution or university; male and must have an interest in leadership. Applicant or parent of applicant must be member of Tau Kappa Epsilon. Applicant must have 3.0 GPA or higher. Available to U.S. and non-U.S. citizens.

Application Requirements: Application form, application form may be submitted online (http://www.tke.org/member_resources/scholarships/apply_online), essay, narrative summary of how TKE membership has benefited applicant, personal photograph, transcript. *Deadline:* March 15.

Contact: Offices of the Grand Chapter
TKE Educational Foundation
7439 Woodland Drive, Suite 100
Indianapolis, IN 46278
E-mail: tkeogc@tke.org

UNITED NATIONS ASSOCIATION OF CONNECTICUT
http://www.unausa.org

UNITED NATIONS ASSOCIATION OF CONNECTICUT SCHOLARSHIP
• *See page 133*

UNITED NEGRO COLLEGE FUND
http://www.uncf.org/

OSSIE DAVIS ENDOWMENT SCHOLARSHIP PROGRAM
• *See page 132*

SUEZ CORPORATE SCHOLARS PROGRAM
• *See page 87*

UNCF/KOCH SCHOLARS PROGRAM FOR UNDERGRADUATES
• *See page 87*

WASHINGTON CROSSING FOUNDATION
http://www.gwcf.org/

WASHINGTON CROSSING FOUNDATION SCHOLARSHIP
Merit-based awards available to high school seniors who are planning a career in government service. Must write an essay stating reason for deciding on a career in public service. Minimum 3.0 GPA required.

Academic Fields/Career Goals: Political Science; Public Policy and Administration.

Award: Scholarship for use in freshman year; not renewable. *Amount:* $500–$5000.

Eligibility Requirements: Applicant must be high school student and planning to enroll or expecting to enroll full-time at a four-year institution or university. Applicant must have 3.0 GPA or higher. Available to U.S. citizens.

Application Requirements: Application form, essay, interview, personal photograph. *Deadline:* January 15.

Contact: Washington Crossing Foundation
Washington Crossing Foundation
PO Box 503
Levittown, PA 19058-0503
Phone: 215-949-8841
E-mail: info@gwcf.org

WASHINGTON STATE ASSOCIATION FOR JUSTICE

http://www.washingtonjustice.org/

WASHINGTON STATE ASSOCIATION FOR JUSTICE AMERICAN JUSTICE ESSAY & VIDEO SCHOLARSHIP
• *See page 227*

PSYCHOLOGY

AMERICAN FEDERATION OF STATE, COUNTY, AND MUNICIPAL EMPLOYEES

http://www.afscme.org/

AFSCME/UNCF UNION SCHOLARS PROGRAM
• *See page 103*

AVACARE MEDICAL

https://avacaremedical.com

AVACARE MEDICAL SCHOLARSHIP
• *See page 105*

BHW GROUP

https://thebhwgroup.com/

BHW WOMEN IN STEM SCHOLARSHIP
• *See page 74*

COMPHEALTH

http://www.comphealth.com

COMPHEALTH MEDICAL SCHOLARSHIP
• *See page 151*

CYNTHIA E. MORGAN SCHOLARSHIP FUND (CEMS)

http://www.cemsfund.com/

CYNTHIA E. MORGAN MEMORIAL SCHOLARSHIP FUND, INC.
• *See page 316*

HEALTH PROFESSIONS EDUCATION FOUNDATION

http://www.healthprofessions.ca.gov/

ALLIED HEALTHCARE SCHOLARSHIP PROGRAM
• *See page 151*

HEALTH RESEARCH COUNCIL OF NEW ZEALAND

http://www.hrc.govt.nz/

PACIFIC MENTAL HEALTH WORK FORCE AWARD
• *See page 346*

INDIAN HEALTH SERVICES, UNITED STATES DEPARTMENT OF HEALTH AND HUMAN SERVICES

http://www.ihs.gov/scholarship

HEALTH PROFESSIONS PREPARATORY SCHOLARSHIP PROGRAM
• *See page 152*

KETAMINE CLINICS OF LOS ANGELES

http://www.ketamineclinics.com/

KETAMINE CLINICS OF LOS ANGELES SCHOLARSHIP PROGRAM
• *See page 152*

MEDICAL SCRUBS COLLECTION

http://medicalscrubscollection.com

MEDICAL SCRUBS COLLECTION SCHOLARSHIP
• *See page 106*

ONLINEPSYCHOLOGYDEGREES.COM

http://www.onlinepsychologydegrees.com/

ONLINEPSYCHOLOGYDEGREES.COM EDUCATION SCHOLARSHIPS
If you're ready to begin your career of helping change lives, get started by applying for the OnlinePsychologyDegrees.com $1,000 scholarship. Apply now, and then find the psychology programs that fit your career path.

Academic Fields/Career Goals: Psychology.

Award: Scholarship for use in freshman, sophomore, junior, senior, graduate, or postgraduate years; renewable. *Number:* 2. *Amount:* $1000.

Eligibility Requirements: Applicant must be enrolled or expecting to enroll full- or part-time at a two-year or four-year or technical institution or university and resident of Alabama, Alaska, Arizona, Arkansas, California, Colorado, Connecticut, Delaware, District of Columbia, Georgia, Hawaii, Idaho, Illinois, Indiana, Iowa, Kansas, Kentucky, Louisiana, Maine, Manitoba, Maryland, Massachusetts, Michigan, Minnesota, Mississippi, Missouri, Montana, Nebraska, Nevada, New Hampshire, New Jersey, New Mexico, North Carolina, North Dakota, Northwest Territories, Ohio, Oklahoma, Ontario, Oregon, Pennsylvania, South Carolina, South Dakota, Tennessee, Texas, Utah, Vermont, Virginia, Washington, West Virginia, Wisconsin, Wyoming. Available to U.S. citizens.

Application Requirements: Application form, essay. *Deadline:* January 15.

PILOT INTERNATIONAL FOUNDATION

http://www.pilotinternational.org/

PILOT INTERNATIONAL SCHOLARSHIP
• *See page 355*

RUBY NEWHALL MEMORIAL SCHOLARSHIP
• *See page 355*

THE RECOVERY VILLAGE

https://www.therecoveryvillage.com/

RECOVERY VILLAGE HEALTHCARE SCHOLARSHIP
• *See page 238*

SIGMA XI, THE SCIENTIFIC RESEARCH SOCIETY

http://www.sigmaxi.org/

SIGMA XI GRANTS-IN-AID OF RESEARCH
• *See page 101*

THE SOCIETY FOR THE SCIENTIFIC STUDY OF SEXUALITY

http://www.sexscience.org/

THE SOCIETY FOR THE SCIENTIFIC STUDY OF SEXUALITY STUDENT RESEARCH GRANT
• *See page 109*

STRAIGHTFORWARD MEDIA

http://www.straightforwardmedia.com/

STRAIGHTFORWARD MEDIA LIBERAL ARTS SCHOLARSHIP
• *See page 126*

VIRTUOUS PROM

http://www.virtuousprom.com

VIRTUOUS PROM PEACE SCHOLARSHIP
This scholarship is for women studying in the areas of psychology, anthropology, sociology and theology at both the undergraduate and graduate level.

Academic Fields/Career Goals: Psychology.

Award: Scholarship for use in freshman, sophomore, junior, senior, graduate, or postgraduate years; not renewable. *Number:* 1. *Amount:* $250.

Eligibility Requirements: Applicant must be enrolled or expecting to enroll full- or part-time at a four-year institution or university and female. Available to U.S. and non-U.S. citizens.

Application Requirements: Essay. *Deadline:* January 31.

Contact: Ms. Megan MacNeal, Creative Director

PUBLIC HEALTH

AMERICAN ALPINE CLUB

https://americanalpineclub.org/

AAC RESEARCH GRANTS
• *See page 153*

ASSOCIATION ON AMERICAN INDIAN AFFAIRS, INC.

http://www.indian-affairs.org/

ELIZABETH AND SHERMAN ASCHE MEMORIAL SCHOLARSHIP FUND
• *See page 98*

AVACARE MEDICAL

https://avacaremedical.com

AVACARE MEDICAL SCHOLARSHIP
• *See page 105*

COMPHEALTH

http://www.comphealth.com

COMPHEALTH MEDICAL SCHOLARSHIP
• *See page 151*

THE EXPERT INSTITUTE

https://www.theexpertinstitute.com

ANNUAL HEALTHCARE AND LIFE SCIENCES SCHOLARSHIP
• *See page 156*

FLORIDA ENVIRONMENTAL HEALTH ASSOCIATION

http://www.feha.org/

FLORIDA ENVIRONMENTAL HEALTH ASSOCIATION EDUCATIONAL SCHOLARSHIP AWARDS
• *See page 316*

GENERAL FEDERATION OF WOMEN'S CLUBS OF MASSACHUSETTS

http://www.gfwcma.org/

CATHERINE E. PHILBIN SCHOLARSHIP
One scholarship of up to $500 will be awarded to a graduate or undergraduate student studying public health. Eligible applicants will be residents of Massachusetts. Along with the application, students must send a personal statement of no more than 500 words addressing professional goals and financial need.

Academic Fields/Career Goals: Public Health.

Award: Scholarship for use in freshman, sophomore, junior, senior, or graduate years; not renewable. *Number:* 1. *Amount:* $500.

Eligibility Requirements: Applicant must be enrolled or expecting to enroll full-time at a four-year institution or university and resident of Massachusetts. Available to U.S. citizens.

Application Requirements: Application form, essay. *Deadline:* March 1.

Contact: Scholarship Chairman
General Federation of Women's Clubs of Massachusetts
PO Box 679
Sudbury, MA 01776-0679
E-mail: gfwcma@aol.com

MEDICAL SCRUBS COLLECTION

http://medicalscrubscollection.com

MEDICAL SCRUBS COLLECTION SCHOLARSHIP
• *See page 106*

MICHAEL MOODY FITNESS

http://www.michaelmoodyfitness.com/

MICHAEL MOODY FITNESS SCHOLARSHIP
• *See page 255*

NATIONAL ENVIRONMENTAL HEALTH ASSOCIATION/AMERICAN ACADEMY OF SANITARIANS

http://www.neha.org/

NATIONAL ENVIRONMENTAL HEALTH ASSOCIATION/AMERICAN ACADEMY OF SANITARIANS SCHOLARSHIP

• *See page 316*

NEW ENGLAND EMPLOYEE BENEFITS COUNCIL

http://www.neebc.org/

NEW ENGLAND EMPLOYEE BENEFITS COUNCIL SCHOLARSHIP PROGRAM

• *See page 81*

OREGON STUDENT ASSISTANCE COMMISSION

http://www.GetCollegeFunds.org/

LAURENCE R. FOSTER MEMORIAL SCHOLARSHIP

One-time award to students enrolled or planning to enroll in a public health degree program. First preference given to those working in the public health field and those pursuing a graduate degree in public health. Undergraduates entering junior or senior year health programs may apply if seeking a public health career, and not private practice. Applicants from diverse environments preferred.

Academic Fields/Career Goals: Public Health.

Award: Scholarship for use in junior, senior, or graduate years; not renewable.

Eligibility Requirements: Applicant must be enrolled or expecting to enroll full- or part-time at a four-year institution or university. Available to U.S. citizens.

Application Requirements: Application form, essay, financial need analysis. *Deadline:* March 1.

Contact: Melissa Adams, Scholarship Processing Coordinator
    Phone: 541-687-7409
    E-mail: melissa.adams@hecc.oregon.gov

WILLIAM E. KEENE MEMORIAL SCHOLARSHIP

• *See page 316*

PILOT INTERNATIONAL FOUNDATION

http://www.pilotinternational.org/

RUBY NEWHALL MEMORIAL SCHOLARSHIP

• *See page 355*

PLATINUM EDUCATIONAL GROUP

www.platinumed.com

PLATINUM EDUCATIONAL GROUP SCHOLARSHIPS PROGRAM FOR EMS, NURSING, AND ALLIED HEALTH

• *See page 107*

THE RECOVERY VILLAGE

https://www.therecoveryvillage.com/

RECOVERY VILLAGE HEALTHCARE SCHOLARSHIP

• *See page 238*

THE SOCIETY FOR THE SCIENTIFIC STUDY OF SEXUALITY

http://www.sexscience.org/

THE SOCIETY FOR THE SCIENTIFIC STUDY OF SEXUALITY STUDENT RESEARCH GRANT

• *See page 109*

SOUTH CAROLINA PUBLIC HEALTH ASSOCIATION

http://www.scpha.com/

SOUTH CAROLINA PUBLIC HEALTH ASSOCIATION PUBLIC HEALTH SCHOLARSHIPS

Current member of the SCPHA with more than 6 hours remaining and enrolled in a accredited higher education program for public health or related field. Dantzler- exhibit significant commitment to the public health profession through volunteer and/or professional activity as indicated on the application. Public Health Scholarship- exhibit significant commitment to the public health profession through volunteer and/or professional activity as indicated on the application.

Academic Fields/Career Goals: Public Health.

Award: Scholarship for use in freshman, sophomore, junior, senior, graduate, or postgraduate years; not renewable. *Number:* 2. *Amount:* $500–$750.

Eligibility Requirements: Applicant must be enrolled or expecting to enroll full- or part-time at a four-year institution or university. Applicant must have 3.5 GPA or higher. Available to U.S. citizens.

Application Requirements: Application form, proof of number of hours remaining, transcript. *Deadline:* March 31.

Contact: Mr. Larry White, Scholarship Committee Chair
    South Carolina Public Health Association
    PO Box 3051
    Conway, SC 29528
    Phone: 843-488-1329 Ext. 225
    Fax: 843-488-1330
    E-mail: larry@smokefreehorry.org

UNITED NEGRO COLLEGE FUND

http://www.uncf.org/

GATES MILLENNIUM SCHOLARS (GMS) PROGRAM

• *See page 260*

UNITED HEALTH FOUNDATION DIVERSE SCHOLARS INITIATIVE

• *See page 152*

PUBLIC POLICY AND ADMINISTRATION

AMERICAN INSTITUTE OF POLISH CULTURE INC.

http://www.ampolinstitute.org/

HARRIET IRSAY SCHOLARSHIP GRANT

• *See page 127*

AMERICAN LEGION AUXILIARY DEPARTMENT OF ARIZONA

http:/wwwaladeptaz.org

AMERICAN LEGION AUXILIARY DEPARTMENT OF ARIZONA WILMA HOYAL-MAXINE CHILTON MEMORIAL SCHOLARSHIP
• *See page 488*

ASSOCIATION OF FORMER INTELLIGENCE OFFICERS

http://www.afio.com

AFIO UNDERGRADUATE AND GRADUATE SCHOLARSHIPS
• *See page 103*

THE DALLAS FOUNDATION

http://www.dallasfoundation.org/

WHITLEY PLACE SCHOLARSHIP
• *See page 120*

GEORGIA GOVERNMENT FINANCE OFFICERS ASSOCIATION

http://www.ggfoa.org/

GGFOA ANNUAL COLLEGE SCHOLARSHIP
• *See page 77*

GOVERNMENT FINANCE OFFICERS ASSOCIATION

http://www.gfoa.org/

MINORITIES IN GOVERNMENT FINANCE SCHOLARSHIP
• *See page 78*

GREATER SALINA COMMUNITY FOUNDATION

http://www.gscf.org/

KANSAS FEDERATION OF REPUBLICAN WOMEN SCHOLARSHIP
• *See page 360*

HARRY S. TRUMAN SCHOLARSHIP FOUNDATION

http://www.truman.gov/

HARRY S. TRUMAN SCHOLARSHIP
• *See page 488*

JAPANESE AMERICAN CITIZENS LEAGUE (JACL)

http://www.jacl.org/

NATIONAL JACL HEADQUARTERS SCHOLARSHIP
• *See page 99*

NATIONAL ACADEMY OF TELEVISION ARTS AND SCIENCES

http://www.emmyonline.tv/

DOUGLAS W. MUMMERT SCHOLARSHIP
• *See page 129*

NEW ENGLAND EMPLOYEE BENEFITS COUNCIL

http://www.neebc.org/

NEW ENGLAND EMPLOYEE BENEFITS COUNCIL SCHOLARSHIP PROGRAM
• *See page 81*

OREGON STUDENT ASSISTANCE COMMISSION

http://www.GetCollegeFunds.org/

OREGON STATE FISCAL ASSOCIATION SCHOLARSHIP
• *See page 246*

THE RECOVERY VILLAGE

https://www.therecoveryvillage.com/

RECOVERY VILLAGE HEALTHCARE SCHOLARSHIP
• *See page 238*

WASHINGTON CROSSING FOUNDATION

http://www.gwcf.org/

WASHINGTON CROSSING FOUNDATION SCHOLARSHIP
• *See page 489*

WASHINGTON STATE ASSOCIATION FOR JUSTICE

http://www.washingtonjustice.org/

WASHINGTON STATE ASSOCIATION FOR JUSTICE AMERICAN JUSTICE ESSAY & VIDEO SCHOLARSHIP
• *See page 227*

RADIOLOGY

101ST AIRBORNE DIVISION ASSOCIATION

http://www.screamingeaglefoundation.org/

AL & WILLIAMARY VISTE SCHOLARSHIP
• *See page 233*

AMERICAN INDIAN SCIENCE AND ENGINEERING SOCIETY

http://www.aises.org/

A.T. ANDERSON MEMORIAL SCHOLARSHIP PROGRAM
• *See page 109*

ASRT FOUNDATION

http://foundation.asrt.org

JERMAN-CAHOON STUDENT SCHOLARSHIP
• *See page 349*

PROFESSIONAL ADVANCEMENT SCHOLARSHIP
• *See page 344*

ROYCE OSBORN MINORITY STUDENT SCHOLARSHIP
• *See page 349*

SIEMENS CLINICAL ADVANCEMENT SCHOLARSHIP
• *See page 349*

COMPHEALTH

http://www.comphealth.com

COMPHEALTH MEDICAL SCHOLARSHIP
• *See page 151*

CYNTHIA E. MORGAN SCHOLARSHIP FUND (CEMS)

http://www.cemsfund.com/

CYNTHIA E. MORGAN MEMORIAL SCHOLARSHIP FUND, INC.
• *See page 316*

HEALTH PROFESSIONS EDUCATION FOUNDATION

http://www.healthprofessions.ca.gov/

ALLIED HEALTHCARE SCHOLARSHIP PROGRAM
• *See page 151*

MEDICAL SCRUBS COLLECTION

http://medicalscrubscollection.com

MEDICAL SCRUBS COLLECTION SCHOLARSHIP
• *See page 106*

NEXTSTEPU

http://www.nextstepu.com/

$1,500 STEM SCHOLARSHIP
• *See page 106*

PLATINUM EDUCATIONAL GROUP

www.platinumed.com

PLATINUM EDUCATIONAL GROUP SCHOLARSHIPS PROGRAM FOR EMS, NURSING, AND ALLIED HEALTH
• *See page 107*

ULTRASOUNDTECHNICIANSCHOOLS.COM

http://www.ultrasoundtechnicianschools.com

ULTRASOUNDTECHNICIANSCHOOLS.COM SCHOLARSHIP
• *See page 356*

UNITED NEGRO COLLEGE FUND

http://www.uncf.org/

UNITED HEALTH FOUNDATION DIVERSE SCHOLARS INITIATIVE
• *See page 152*

REAL ESTATE

APPRAISAL INSTITUTE EDUCATION TRUST

http://www.aiedtrust.org/

AIET MINORITIES AND WOMEN EDUCATIONAL SCHOLARSHIP

Awarded to minorities and women undergraduate students pursuing academic degrees in real estate appraisal or related fields.

Academic Fields/Career Goals: Real Estate.

Award: Scholarship for use in freshman, sophomore, junior, senior, graduate, or postgraduate years; not renewable. *Amount:* $1000.

Eligibility Requirements: Applicant must be hearing impaired, learning disabled, physically disabled, or visually impaired; American Indian/Alaska Native, Asian/Pacific Islander, Black (non-Hispanic), Hispanic; enrolled or expecting to enroll full- or part-time at a four-year institution or university and female. Applicant must be hearing impaired, learning disabled, physically disabled, or visually impaired. Applicant must have 2.5 GPA or higher. Available to U.S. citizens.

Application Requirements: Application form, essay, financial need analysis, personal photograph, recommendations or references, resume, transcript. *Deadline:* April 15.

Contact: Sarah Walsh
Appraisal Institute Education Trust
200 West Madison
Suite 1500
Chicago, IL 60607
Phone: 312-335-4133
Fax: 312-335-4134
E-mail: educationtrust@appraisalinstitute.org

APPRAISAL INSTITUTE EDUCATION TRUST EDUCATION SCHOLARSHIPS

Awarded on the basis of academic excellence, this scholarship helps finance the educational endeavors of undergraduate and graduate students concentrating in real estate appraisal, land economics, real estate or allied fields.

Academic Fields/Career Goals: Real Estate.

Award: Scholarship for use in sophomore, junior, senior, or graduate years; not renewable. *Amount:* $1000–$2000.

Eligibility Requirements: Applicant must be enrolled or expecting to enroll full-time at a four-year institution or university. Available to U.S. citizens.

Application Requirements: Application form, essay, recommendations or references, resume, transcript. *Deadline:* February 15.

Contact: Sarah Walsh, Coordinator
Appraisal Institute Education Trust
200 West Madison
Suite 1500
Chicago, IL 60606
Phone: 312-335-4133
Fax: 312-335-4134
E-mail: educationtrust@appraisalinstitute.org

ARMED FORCES COMMUNICATIONS AND ELECTRONICS ASSOCIATION, EDUCATIONAL FOUNDATION

http://www.afcea.org/site/?q=foundation/scholarships

AFGHANISTAN AND IRAQ WAR VETERANS SCHOLARSHIP

Applications are requested from U.S. Armed forces and national guard personnel either currently on active-duty or honorably discharged veterans or reservists who have served in either Enduring Freedo, Afghanistan, or Iraqi Freedom. Candidates must be majoring in the following or c4i-related fields related to the mission of AFCEA—biometry/biometrics, computer engineering, computer forensics science, computer programming, computer science, computer systems, cybersecurity, electrical engineering, electronics engineering, geospatial science, information science, information technology, information resource, management, intelligence, mathematics, network engineering, network security, operations, research, physics, robotics engineering, robotics technology, statistics, strategic intelligence, and telecommunications engineering. Must be studying at an accredited community college, 4-year college, or university.

Academic Fields/Career Goals: Real Estate.

Award: Scholarship for use in sophomore or junior years; not renewable. *Number:* 6–9. *Amount:* $2500.

Eligibility Requirements: Applicant must be of Yemeni heritage and enrolled or expecting to enroll full- or part-time at a four-year institution or university. Applicant must have 3.0 GPA or higher. Available to U.S. citizens.

Application Requirements: Application form, community service, essay, financial need analysis. *Deadline:* April 15.

Contact: Mrs. Casmere Kistner, Scholarships, Awards and Grants
Armed Forces Communications and Electronics Association, Educational Foundation
4400 Fair Lakes Court
Fairfax, VA 22033
Phone: 703-631-6147
E-mail: edfoundation@afcea.org

C.A.R. SCHOLARSHIP FOUNDATION

http://www.car.org/

C.A.R. SCHOLARSHIP FOUNDATION AWARD

Scholarships to students enrolled at a California College or University for professions which are centered on, or support a career in real estate transactional activity. Must have maintained a cumulative GPA of 2.6 or higher.

Academic Fields/Career Goals: Real Estate.

Award: Scholarship for use in sophomore, junior, senior, or graduate years; not renewable. *Number:* 10–25. *Amount:* $2000–$4000.

Eligibility Requirements: Applicant must be enrolled or expecting to enroll full- or part-time at a two-year or four-year institution or university; resident of California and studying in California. Available to U.S. citizens.

Application Requirements: Application form, driver's license, essay, interview. *Deadline:* continuous.

Contact: Lindsey Moss, Scholarship Coordinator
C.A.R. Scholarship Foundation
525 South Virgil Avenue
Los Angeles, CA 90020
Phone: 213-739-8200
Fax: 213-480-7724
E-mail: scholarship@car.org

ILLINOIS REAL ESTATE EDUCATIONAL FOUNDATION

http://www.ilreef.org/

ILLINOIS REAL ESTATE EDUCATIONAL FOUNDATION ACADEMIC SCHOLARSHIPS

Awards for Illinois residents attending an accredited two-or four-year junior college, college or university in Illinois. Must have completed 30 college credit hours and be pursuing a degree with an emphasis in real estate. Must be a U.S. citizen.

Academic Fields/Career Goals: Real Estate.

Award: Scholarship for use in freshman, sophomore, junior, or senior years; not renewable. *Amount:* $1000.

Eligibility Requirements: Applicant must be enrolled or expecting to enroll full-time at a two-year or four-year institution or university; resident of Illinois and studying in Illinois. Available to U.S. citizens.

Application Requirements: Application form, essay, recommendations or references, resume, transcript. *Deadline:* April 1.

Contact: Laurie Clayton, Foundation Manager
Illinois Real Estate Educational Foundation
522 South 5th Street, PO Box 2607
Springfield, IL 62708
Phone: 866-854-7333
Fax: 217-529-5893
E-mail: lclayton@iar.org

THOMAS F. SEAY SCHOLARSHIP

Award of $2000 to students pursuing a degree with an emphasis in real estate. Must be a U.S. citizen and attending any accredited U.S. college or university full-time. Must have completed at least 30 college credit hours. Minimum 3.5 GPA required.

Academic Fields/Career Goals: Real Estate.

Award: Scholarship for use in junior or senior years; not renewable. *Amount:* $2000.

Eligibility Requirements: Applicant must be enrolled or expecting to enroll full-time at a four-year institution or university; resident of Illinois and studying in Illinois. Applicant must have 3.5 GPA or higher. Available to U.S. citizens.

Application Requirements: Application form, community service, essay, recommendations or references, resume, transcript. *Deadline:* April 1.

Contact: Laurie Clayton, Foundation Manager
Illinois Real Estate Educational Foundation
522 South 5th Street, PO Box 2607
Springfield, IL 62708
Phone: 866-854-7333
Fax: 217-529-5893
E-mail: lclayton@iar.org

INTERNATIONAL COUNCIL OF SHOPPING CENTERS FOUNDATION

http://www.icsc.org/foundation/

JOHN T. RIORDAN SCHOOL FOR PROFESSIONAL DEVELOPMENT

Award for higher education for shopping center professionals. Must be a official ICSC member in good standing, actively employed in the shopping center industry for a minimum of one year, or recent graduate of college/university with coursework emphasis in real estate; or a graduate of REAP or Inroads programs within the past eighteen months prior to year end when the application is submitted.

Academic Fields/Career Goals: Real Estate.

Award: Scholarship for use in freshman, sophomore, junior, senior, graduate, or postgraduate years; not renewable. *Number:* 10–15. *Amount:* $2999–$3000.

Eligibility Requirements: Applicant must be enrolled or expecting to enroll full- or part-time at a technical institution. Available to U.S. and non-U.S. citizens.

Application Requirements: Application form, essay. *Deadline:* March 29.

Contact: Amy Reinharz, Development and Program Director
Phone: 646-728-3618
E-mail: areinharz@icsc.org

NEW JERSEY ASSOCIATION OF REALTORS

http://www.njar.com/

NEW JERSEY ASSOCIATION OF REALTORS EDUCATIONAL FOUNDATION SCHOLARSHIP PROGRAM

One-time awards for New Jersey residents who are high school seniors pursuing studies in real estate or allied fields. Preference to students considering a career in real estate. Must be member of NJAR or relative of a member. Selected candidates are interviewed in June. Must be a U.S. citizen.

Academic Fields/Career Goals: Real Estate.

Award: Scholarship for use in freshman year; not renewable. *Number:* 20–32. *Amount:* $1000–$2500.

Eligibility Requirements: Applicant must be high school student; planning to enroll or expecting to enroll full-time at a four-year institution or university and resident of New Jersey. Applicant or parent of applicant must be member of New Jersey Association of Realtors. Available to U.S. citizens.

Application Requirements: Application form, essay, financial need analysis, interview, letter of verification of realtor/realtor associate/association staff, transcript. *Deadline:* April 9.

Contact: Diane Hatley, Educational Foundation
New Jersey Association of Realtors
PO Box 2098
Edison, NJ 08818
Phone: 732-494-5616
Fax: 732-494-4723

STRAIGHTFORWARD MEDIA

http://www.straightforwardmedia.com/

STRAIGHTFORWARD MEDIA VOCATIONAL-TECHNICAL SCHOOL SCHOLARSHIP
• *See page 107*

RECREATION, PARKS, LEISURE STUDIES

AMERICAN ALLIANCE FOR HEALTH, PHYSICAL EDUCATION, RECREATION AND DANCE

http://www.shapeamerica.org/

RUTH ABERNATHY PRESIDENTIAL SCHOLARSHIP

Three award for undergraduate students and two for graduate students in January of each year. Must be majoring in the field of health, physical education, recreation or dance. Undergraduate awards are in the amount of $1,250 each and graduate awards are in the amount of $1,750 each. Recipients also receive a complimentary three-year AAHPERD membership. Applicant must be current member of AAHPERD.

Academic Fields/Career Goals: Recreation, Parks, Leisure Studies; Sports-Related/Exercise Science.

Award: Scholarship for use in junior, senior, or graduate years; not renewable. *Number:* 5. *Amount:* $1250–$1750.

Eligibility Requirements: Applicant must be enrolled or expecting to enroll full-time at a four-year institution or university and must have an interest in leadership. Applicant must have 3.5 GPA or higher. Available to U.S. and non-U.S. citizens.

Application Requirements: Application form, letter from the school's dean/registrar indicating full-time status, recommendations or references, transcript. *Deadline:* October 15.

Contact: Deb Callis, Secretary to Chief Executive Officer
American Alliance for Health, Physical Education, Recreation and Dance
1900 Association Drive
Reston, VA 20191
Phone: 703-476-3405
Fax: 703-476-9537
E-mail: dcallis@aahperd.org

AMERICAN ALPINE CLUB

https://americanalpineclub.org/

AAC RESEARCH GRANTS
• *See page 153*

AMERICAN HOTEL AND LODGING EDUCATIONAL FOUNDATION

http://www.ahlef.org/

AH&LEF ANNUAL SCHOLARSHIP GRANT PROGRAM
• *See page 227*

AMERICAN HOTEL & LODGING EDUCATIONAL FOUNDATION PEPSI SCHOLARSHIP
• *See page 228*

ECOLAB SCHOLARSHIP PROGRAM
• *See page 228*

HYATT HOTELS FUND FOR MINORITY LODGING MANAGEMENT
• *See page 228*

INCOMING FRESHMAN SCHOLARSHIPS
• *See page 228*

RAMA SCHOLARSHIP FOR THE AMERICAN DREAM
• *See page 228*

THE LAND CONSERVANCY OF NEW JERSEY

http://tlc-nj.org/

ROGERS FAMILY SCHOLARSHIP
• *See page 243*

RUSSELL W. MYERS SCHOLARSHIP
• *See page 99*

NATIONAL RECREATION AND PARK ASSOCIATION

http://www.nrpa.org/

AFRS STUDENT SCHOLARSHIP

Applicant must be currently enrolled in a NRPA accredited recreation/parks curriculum or related field. Number of awards varies.

Academic Fields/Career Goals: Recreation, Parks, Leisure Studies.

Award: Scholarship for use in freshman or sophomore years; not renewable. *Amount:* $500.

Eligibility Requirements: Applicant must be enrolled or expecting to enroll full- or part-time at a four-year institution or university. Applicant must have 3.0 GPA or higher. Available to U.S. citizens.

Application Requirements: Application form, essay, recommendations or references, test scores, transcript. *Deadline:* June 1.

Contact: Jessica Lytle, Senior Manager
Phone: 703-858-2150
Fax: 703-858-0974
E-mail: jlytle@nrpa.org

PADDLE CANADA

https://www.paddlecanada.com/

BILL MASON SCHOLARSHIP FUND
• *See page 257*

SOIL AND WATER CONSERVATION SOCIETY-MISSOURI SHOW-ME CHAPTER

http://www.moswcs.org/

MO SHOW-ME CHAPTER SWCS SCHOLARSHIP
• *See page 95*

THE WALTER J. TRAVIS SOCIETY

http://www.travissociety.com

THE WALTER J. TRAVIS MEMORIAL SCHOLARSHIP
• *See page 388*

RELIGION/THEOLOGY

AMERICAN SCHOOL OF CLASSICAL STUDIES AT ATHENS

http://www.ascsa.edu.gr/

ASCSA SUMMER SESSIONS SCHOLARSHIPS
• *See page 108*

BETHESDA LUTHERAN COMMUNITIES

http://www.bethesdalutherancommunities.org/scholarships

DEVELOPMENTAL DISABILITIES SCHOLASTIC ACHIEVEMENT SCHOLARSHIP FOR COLLEGE STUDENTS WHO ARE LUTHERAN
• *See page 236*

COMMUNITY FOUNDATION FOR GREATER ATLANTA, INC.

http://cfgreateratlanta.org/

JAMES M. AND VIRGINIA M. SMYTH SCHOLARSHIP
• *See page 128*

EASTERN STAR-GRAND CHAPTER OF CALIFORNIA

http://www.oescal.org/

SCHOLARSHIPS FOR EDUCATION, BUSINESS AND RELIGION
• *See page 163*

ED E. AND GLADYS HURLEY FOUNDATION

ED E. AND GLADYS HURLEY FOUNDATION SCHOLARSHIP
Provides scholarships up to $1000 per year per student. Applicant must be Protestant enrolled or expecting to enroll full or part-time at a two-year or four-year institution or university and studying in Texas. Available to U.S. citizens.

Academic Fields/Career Goals: Religion/Theology.

Award: Scholarship for use in freshman, sophomore, junior, senior, graduate, or postgraduate years; not renewable. *Number:* 100–150. *Amount:* up to $1000.

Eligibility Requirements: Applicant must be Protestant; enrolled or expecting to enroll full- or part-time at a two-year or four-year institution or university; resident of Arkansas, Louisiana, Texas and studying in Texas. Available to U.S. citizens.

Application Requirements: Application form, financial need analysis, recommendations or references. *Deadline:* April 30.

Contact: Rose Davis, Financial Aid Coordinator
Ed E. and Gladys Hurley Foundation
Houston Graduate School-Theology
2501 Central Parkway, Suite A19
Houston, TX 77092
Phone: 713-942-9505
E-mail: rdavis@hgst.edu

NATIONAL ASSOCIATION OF PASTORAL MUSICIANS

http://www.npm.org/

ELAINE RENDLER-RENE DOSOGNE-GEORGETOWN CHORALE SCHOLARSHIP
• *See page 430*

FUNK FAMILY MEMORIAL SCHOLARSHIP
• *See page 430*

GIA PUBLICATION PASTORAL MUSICIAN SCHOLARSHIP
• *See page 431*

MUSONICS SCHOLARSHIP
• *See page 431*

NATIONAL ASSOCIATION OF PASTORAL MUSICIANS MEMBERS' SCHOLARSHIP
• *See page 431*

NPM KOINONIA/BOARD OF DIRECTORS SCHOLARSHIP
• *See page 431*

OREGON CATHOLIC PRESS SCHOLARSHIP
• *See page 431*

PALUCH FAMILY FOUNDATION/WORLD LIBRARY PUBLICATIONS SCHOLARSHIP
• *See page 432*

OREGON STUDENT ASSISTANCE COMMISSION

http://www.GetCollegeFunds.org/

FRANKS FOUNDATION SCHOLARSHIP
• *See page 459*

PRESBYTERIAN CHURCH (USA)

http://www.pcusa.org/financialaid

STUDENT OPPORTUNITY SCHOLARSHIP
• *See page 258*

THE SOCIETY FOR THE SCIENTIFIC STUDY OF SEXUALITY

http://www.sexscience.org/

THE SOCIETY FOR THE SCIENTIFIC STUDY OF SEXUALITY STUDENT RESEARCH GRANT
• See page 109

SOUTHERN BAPTIST HISTORICAL LIBRARY AND ARCHIVES

http://www.sbhla.org/

LYNN E. MAY JR. STUDY GRANT
• See page 104

UNITARIAN UNIVERSALIST ASSOCIATION

http://www.uua.org/

ROY H. POLLACK SCHOLARSHIP
Scholarship given to a junior or senior student with academic excellence and good character, studying for ordained ministry who actively participates in extracurricular activities at their theological school. Applicant must be pursuing in Divinity degree.

Academic Fields/Career Goals: Religion/Theology.

Award: Scholarship for use in junior or senior years; not renewable.

Eligibility Requirements: Applicant must be Unitarian Universalist and enrolled or expecting to enroll full- or part-time at a four-year institution or university. Available to U.S. citizens.

Application Requirements: Application form, financial need analysis. *Deadline:* April 15.

Contact: Ms. Hillary Goodridge, Program Director
Phone: 617-971-9600
Fax: 617-971-0029
E-mail: uufp@aol.com

UNITED METHODIST COMMUNICATIONS

http://www.umcom.org/

LEONARD M. PERRYMAN COMMUNICATIONS SCHOLARSHIP FOR ETHNIC MINORITY STUDENTS
• See page 212

SCIENCE, TECHNOLOGY, AND SOCIETY

ADELANTE! U.S. EDUCATION LEADERSHIP FUND

http://www.adelantefund.org/

ADELANTE FUND SCHOLARSHIPS
• See page 160

AEG FOUNDATION

http://www.aegfoundation.org/

AEG FOUNDATION MARLIAVE FUND
• See page 240

AMERICAN INDIAN SCIENCE AND ENGINEERING SOCIETY

http://www.aises.org/

A.T. ANDERSON MEMORIAL SCHOLARSHIP PROGRAM
• See page 109

AMERICAN INSTITUTE OF AERONAUTICS AND ASTRONAUTICS

http://www.aiaafoundation.org/

AIAA FOUNDATION UNDERGRADUATE SCHOLARSHIPS
• See page 110

LEATRICE GREGORY PENDRAY SCHOLARSHIP
• See page 110

AMERICAN LEGION DEPARTMENT OF TENNESSEE

http://www.tennesseelegion.org/

JROTC SCHOLARSHIP
One scholarship of $3000 available to a Tennessee JROTC cadet who has been awarded either The American Legion General Military Excellence, or The American Legion Scholastic Award Medal and The American Legion Certificate. JROTC Senior Instructor must provide the recommendation for the award. Information and recommendation forms are provided each JROTC Unit in Tennessee. Must be U.S. citizen.

Academic Fields/Career Goals: Science, Technology, and Society.

Award: Scholarship for use in freshman, sophomore, junior, or senior years; not renewable. *Number:* 1. *Amount:* $3000.

Eligibility Requirements: Applicant must be high school student; planning to enroll or expecting to enroll full- or part-time at a four-year institution or university; resident of Tennessee and studying in Tennessee. Applicant or parent of applicant must have employment or volunteer experience in journalism/broadcasting. Available to U.S. citizens.

Application Requirements: Application form. *Deadline:* April 15.

Contact: Sherri Mayberry, Program Secretary
Phone: 615-391-5088
E-mail: Sherri@TNLegion.org

ARIZONA HYDROLOGICAL SOCIETY

http://www.azhydrosoc.org/

ARIZONA HYDROLOGICAL SOCIETY SCHOLARSHIP
• See page 241

ARRL FOUNDATION INC.

http://www.arrl.org/

ALLEN AND BERTHA WATSON MEMORIAL SCHOLARSHIP
• See page 294

WILSE MORGAN, WX7P, MEMORIAL ARRL NORTHWESTERN DIVISION SCHOLARSHIP
• See page 162

YASME FOUNDATION SCHOLARSHIP
• See page 154

ASSOCIATION FOR WOMEN GEOSCIENTISTS (AWG)

http://www.awg.org/

LONE STAR RISING CAREER SCHOLARSHIP
• *See page 242*

ASSOCIATION OF FEDERAL COMMUNICATIONS CONSULTING ENGINEERS

http://www.afcce.org

JULES COHEN SCHOLARSHIP
• *See page 266*

AUTOMOTIVE WOMEN'S ALLIANCE FOUNDATION

http://www.awafoundation.org/index.php

AUTOMOTIVE WOMEN'S ALLIANCE FOUNDATION SCHOLARSHIPS
• *See page 74*

BHW GROUP

https://thebhwgroup.com/

BHW WOMEN IN STEM SCHOLARSHIP
• *See page 74*

BROWN AND CALDWELL

http://www.brownandcaldwell.com

ECKENFELDER SCHOLARSHIP
• *See page 155*

CATCHING THE DREAM

http://www.catchingthedream.org/

MATH, ENGINEERING, SCIENCE, BUSINESS, EDUCATION, COMPUTERS SCHOLARSHIPS
• *See page 162*

NATIVE AMERICAN LEADERSHIP IN EDUCATION (NALE)
• *See page 163*

COMPHEALTH

http://www.comphealth.com

COMPHEALTH MEDICAL SCHOLARSHIP
• *See page 151*

DAVIDSON INSTITUTE FOR TALENT DEVELOPMENT

http://www.davidsongifted.org/

DAVIDSON FELLOWS SCHOLARSHIP PROGRAM
• *See page 113*

EXPLORERS CLUB

http://www.explorers.org/

YOUTH ACTIVITY FUND
• *See page 439*

HEALTHCARE INFORMATION AND MANAGEMENT SYSTEMS SOCIETY FOUNDATION

http://www.himss.org/

HIMSS FOUNDATION SCHOLARSHIP PROGRAM
• *See page 345*

INTERNATIONAL TECHNOLOGY EDUCATION ASSOCIATION

http://www.iteaconnect.org/

INTERNATIONAL TECHNOLOGY EDUCATION ASSOCIATION UNDERGRADUATE SCHOLARSHIP IN TECHNOLOGY EDUCATION
• *See page 254*

NASA RHODE ISLAND SPACE GRANT CONSORTIUM

http://brown/initiatives/ri-space-grant

NASA RHODE ISLAND SPACE GRANT CONSORTIUM OUTREACH SCHOLARSHIP FOR UNDERGRADUATE STUDENTS
• *See page 284*

NASA'S VIRGINIA SPACE GRANT CONSORTIUM

http://www.vsgc.odu.edu/

UNDERGRADUATE STEM RESEARCH SCHOLARSHIPS
• *See page 114*

NATIONAL ASSOCIATION OF WATER COMPANIES-NEW JERSEY CHAPTER

http://www.nawc.org

NATIONAL ASSOCIATION OF WATER COMPANIES-NEW JERSEY CHAPTER SCHOLARSHIP
• *See page 80*

NEXTSTEPU

http://www.nextstepu.com/

$1,500 STEM SCHOLARSHIP
• *See page 106*

NOVUS BIOLOGICALS, LLC

https://www.novusbio.com/

NOVUS BIOLOGICALS SCHOLARSHIP PROGRAM

Applicants must have a major declared in a science related field. Enrolled or accepted for enrollment (baccalaureate, graduate, associate degree, or diploma) with a declared major in a science related field. Fill out the scholarship application form. Submit a transcript of all college/post-secondary coursework (if high school student, submit high school transcript). This may be an official or unofficial copy. Submit a written statement addressing the following topics: Submit a 140 character statement/tweet on your favorite scientist. Write a personal statement of 500 words or less on how you plan to use your degree to further advance science in your field of interest.

Academic Fields/Career Goals: Science, Technology, and Society.

Award: Scholarship for use in freshman, sophomore, junior, senior, graduate, or postgraduate years; not renewable. *Number:* 1. *Amount:* $1500.

Eligibility Requirements: Applicant must be enrolled or expecting to enroll full- or part-time at a two-year or four-year institution or university. Available to U.S. and non-U.S. citizens.

Application Requirements: Application form, essay. *Deadline:* July 17.

Contact: Lisa Ikariyama
Novus Biologicals, LLC
8100 Southpark Way
Unit A-8
Littleton, CO 80120
Phone: 303-7301950
E-mail: lisa@novusbio.com

R & D SYSTEMS INC.
https://www.rndsystems.com/

R&D SYSTEMS SCHOLARSHIP PROGRAM

Scholarship available to students with majors in a science-related field as well as high school students planning on majoring in a science field. High school students must submit a written statement addressing the following topics: Make a top ten list of your favorite emerging technologies.

Academic Fields/Career Goals: Science, Technology, and Society.

Award: Scholarship for use in freshman, sophomore, junior, senior, graduate, or postgraduate years; not renewable. *Number:* 1. *Amount:* $1500.

Eligibility Requirements: Applicant must be enrolled or expecting to enroll full- or part-time at a two-year or four-year institution or university. Available to U.S. and non-U.S. citizens.

Application Requirements: Application form, essay. *Deadline:* July 8.

Contact: Lisa Ikariyama
E-mail: Lisa.Ikariyama@bio-techne.com

SIGMA XI, THE SCIENTIFIC RESEARCH SOCIETY
http://www.sigmaxi.org/

SIGMA XI GRANTS-IN-AID OF RESEARCH
• *See page 101*

SILICON VALLEY COMMUNITY FOUNDATION
www.siliconvalleycf.org

SAMSUNG@FIRST SCHOLARS
• *See page 305*

SOCIETY FOR IMAGING SCIENCE AND TECHNOLOGY
http://www.imaging.org/

RAYMOND DAVIS SCHOLARSHIP
• *See page 286*

SOCIETY FOR TECHNICAL COMMUNICATION
http://www.stc.org/

SOCIETY FOR TECHNICAL COMMUNICATION SCHOLARSHIP PROGRAM
• *See page 209*

SOCIETY OF MOTION PICTURE AND TELEVISION ENGINEERS
https://www.smpte.org/

LOUIS F. WOLF JR. MEMORIAL SCHOLARSHIP
• *See page 210*

STUDENT PAPER AWARD
• *See page 210*

SOCIETY OF PLASTICS ENGINEERS FOUNDATION (SPE)
http://www.4spe.org/

GULF COAST HURRICANE SCHOLARSHIP
• *See page 181*

SOIL AND WATER CONSERVATION SOCIETY
http://www.swcs.org

DONALD A. WILLIAMS SCHOLARSHIP SOIL CONSERVATION SCHOLARSHIP
• *See page 95*

TECHNOLOGY FIRST
https://technologyfirst.org/

ROBERT V. MCKENNA SCHOLARSHIPS
• *See page 219*

THERMO FISHER SCIENTIFIC
https://www.thermofisher.com/antibodyscholarship

ANTIBODY SCHOLARSHIP PROGRAM

The Thermo Fisher Scientific Antibody Scholarship program, awarded annually, is open to graduate and undergraduate students studying biology, chemistry, biochemistry or a related life science field. Applicants are required to demonstrate a strong academic background along with a true passion for science. A total of six scholarships are available for the 2017-2018 academic year; two $10,000 awards and four $5,000 awards will be awarded on August 4, 2017. Complete rules and the application form can be found on our website at http://www.thermofisher.com/antibodyscholarship

Academic Fields/Career Goals: Science, Technology, and Society.

Award: Scholarship for use in freshman, sophomore, junior, senior, graduate, or postgraduate years; not renewable. *Number:* 6. *Amount:* $5000–$10,000.

Eligibility Requirements: Applicant must be enrolled or expecting to enroll full- or part-time at a two-year or four-year institution or university. Applicant must have 3.0 GPA or higher. Available to U.S. and non-U.S. citizens.

Application Requirements: Application form, essay. *Deadline:* June 15.

Contact: Mrs. Sue Boggs
Thermo Fisher Scientific
3747 N Meridian Rd
Rockford, IL 61101
Phone: 815-6684973
E-mail: antibodyscholarship@thermofisher.com

UNITED NEGRO COLLEGE FUND
http://www.uncf.org/

GATES MILLENNIUM SCHOLARS (GMS) PROGRAM
• *See page 260*

PROCTER & GAMBLE STEM SCHOLARSHIP
• *See page 116*

UNIVERSITIES SPACE RESEARCH ASSOCIATION

http://www.usra.edu/

UNIVERSITIES SPACE RESEARCH ASSOCIATION SCHOLARSHIP AWARD PROGRAM
• *See page 116*

VERMONT SPACE GRANT CONSORTIUM

http://www.cems.uvm.edu/vsgc

VERMONT SPACE GRANT CONSORTIUM
• *See page 96*

WHOMENTORS.COM, INC.

http://www.WHOmentors.com/

IB USD WORLDWIDE VENTURE CAPITAL
• *See page 116*

WOMEN IN AEROSPACE FOUNDATION

http://www.womeninaerospace.org/index.html

WIA FOUNDATION SCHOLARSHIP
• *See page 149*

SOCIAL SCIENCES

AMERICAN CRIMINAL JUSTICE ASSOCIATION-LAMBDA ALPHA EPSILON

http://www.acjalae.org/

AMERICAN CRIMINAL JUSTICE ASSOCIATION-LAMBDA ALPHA EPSILON NATIONAL SCHOLARSHIP
• *See page 224*

AMERICAN FEDERATION OF STATE, COUNTY, AND MUNICIPAL EMPLOYEES

http://www.afscme.org/

AFSCME/UNCF UNION SCHOLARS PROGRAM
• *See page 103*

AMERICAN INDIAN SCIENCE AND ENGINEERING SOCIETY

http://www.aises.org/

A.T. ANDERSON MEMORIAL SCHOLARSHIP PROGRAM
• *See page 109*

AMERICAN SOCIETY OF CRIMINOLOGY

http://www.asc41.com/

AMERICAN SOCIETY OF CRIMINOLOGY GENE CARTE STUDENT PAPER COMPETITION
• *See page 225*

BHW GROUP

https://thebhwgroup.com/

BHW WOMEN IN STEM SCHOLARSHIP
• *See page 74*

CANADIAN INSTITUTE OF UKRAINIAN STUDIES

http://www.cius.ca/

LEO J. KRYSA UNDERGRADUATE SCHOLARSHIP
• *See page 125*

CATCHING THE DREAM

http://www.catchingthedream.org/

MATH, ENGINEERING, SCIENCE, BUSINESS, EDUCATION, COMPUTERS SCHOLARSHIPS
• *See page 162*

CULTURAL SERVICES OF THE FRENCH EMBASSY

http://www.frenchculture.org/

TEACHING ASSISTANT PROGRAM IN FRANCE
• *See page 104*

HOMEKITCHENARY

http://homekitchenary.com

SHARE YOUR STORY WITH HOMEKITCHENARY
• *See page 331*

INDIAN HEALTH SERVICES, UNITED STATES DEPARTMENT OF HEALTH AND HUMAN SERVICES

http://www.ihs.gov/scholarship

HEALTH PROFESSIONS PREPARATORY SCHOLARSHIP PROGRAM
• *See page 152*

INSTITUTE FOR HUMANE STUDIES

http://www.theihs.org/

HUMANE STUDIES FELLOWSHIPS
• *See page 204*

NATIONAL BLACK POLICE ASSOCIATION

http://www.blackpolice.org/

ALPHONSO DEAL SCHOLARSHIP AWARD
• *See page 226*

NATIONAL INSTITUTES OF HEALTH

http://www.nih.gov/

NIH UNDERGRADUATE SCHOLARSHIP PROGRAM FOR STUDENTS FROM DISADVANTAGED BACKGROUNDS
• *See page 152*

NATIONAL SECURITY EDUCATION PROGRAM

http://www.iie.org/

NATIONAL SECURITY EDUCATION PROGRAM (NSEP) DAVID L. BOREN UNDERGRADUATE SCHOLARSHIPS
• *See page 126*

OFFICE AND PROFESSIONAL EMPLOYEES INTERNATIONAL UNION

http://www.opeiu.org/

JOHN KELLY LABOR STUDIES SCHOLARSHIP FUND
• *See page 246*

PARAPSYCHOLOGY FOUNDATION

http://www.parapsychology.org/

CHARLES T. AND JUDITH A. TART STUDENT INCENTIVE

An annual incentive is awarded to promote the research of an undergraduate or graduate student, who shows dedication to work within parapsychology. For more details see website http://www.parapsychology.org.

Academic Fields/Career Goals: Social Sciences.

Award: Scholarship for use in freshman, sophomore, junior, senior, graduate, or postgraduate years; not renewable. *Number:* 1. *Amount:* $500.

Eligibility Requirements: Applicant must be enrolled or expecting to enroll full-time at a two-year or four-year institution or university. Available to U.S. citizens.

Application Requirements: Application form, essay, recommendations or references, transcript. *Deadline:* October 15.

Contact: Lisette Coly, Vice President
Phone: 212-628-1550
Fax: 212-628-1559
E-mail: office@parapsychology.org

EILEEN J. GARRETT SCHOLARSHIP FOR PARAPSYCHOLOGICAL RESEARCH

Scholarship requires applicants to demonstrate academic interest in the science of parapsychology through completed research, term papers, and courses for which credit was received. Those with only a general interest will not be considered. Visit website for additional information.

Academic Fields/Career Goals: Social Sciences.

Award: Scholarship for use in freshman, sophomore, junior, senior, graduate, or postgraduate years; not renewable. *Number:* 1. *Amount:* $3000.

Eligibility Requirements: Applicant must be enrolled or expecting to enroll full-time at a two-year or four-year institution or university. Available to U.S. citizens.

Application Requirements: Application form, essay, recommendations or references, transcript. *Deadline:* July 15.

Contact: Lisette Coly, Vice President
Parapsychology Foundation
PO Box 1562
New York, NY 10021-0043
Phone: 212-628-1550
Fax: 212-628-1559
E-mail: office@parapsychology.org

PHI ALPHA THETA HISTORY HONOR SOCIETY, INC.

http://www.phialphatheta.org/

PHI ALPHA THETA WORLD HISTORY ASSOCIATION PAPER PRIZE
• *See page 361*

PRESBYTERIAN CHURCH (USA)

http://www.pcusa.org/financialaid

STUDENT OPPORTUNITY SCHOLARSHIP
• *See page 258*

SIGMA XI, THE SCIENTIFIC RESEARCH SOCIETY

http://www.sigmaxi.org/

SIGMA XI GRANTS-IN-AID OF RESEARCH
• *See page 101*

THE SOCIETY FOR THE SCIENTIFIC STUDY OF SEXUALITY

http://www.sexscience.org/

THE SOCIETY FOR THE SCIENTIFIC STUDY OF SEXUALITY STUDENT RESEARCH GRANT
• *See page 109*

STRAIGHTFORWARD MEDIA

http://www.straightforwardmedia.com/

STRAIGHTFORWARD MEDIA LIBERAL ARTS SCHOLARSHIP
• *See page 126*

UNITED NEGRO COLLEGE FUND

http://www.uncf.org/

MICHAEL JACKSON SCHOLARSHIP
• *See page 212*

OSSIE DAVIS ENDOWMENT SCHOLARSHIP PROGRAM
• *See page 132*

SUEZ CORPORATE SCHOLARS PROGRAM
• *See page 87*

WASHINGTON STATE ASSOCIATION FOR JUSTICE

http://www.washingtonjustice.org/

WASHINGTON STATE ASSOCIATION FOR JUSTICE AMERICAN JUSTICE ESSAY & VIDEO SCHOLARSHIP
• *See page 227*

WIFLE FOUNDATION, INC.

http://www.wifle.org/

WIFLE SCHOLARSHIP
• *See page 227*

Y'S MEN INTERNATIONAL

http://www.ysmen.org/

ALEXANDER SCHOLARSHIP LOAN FUND
• *See page 171*

SOCIAL SERVICES

ALBERTA HERITAGE SCHOLARSHIP FUND

http://www.alis.alberta.ca/

NORTHERN ALBERTA DEVELOPMENT COUNCIL BURSARY
• *See page 234*

AMERICAN FEDERATION OF STATE, COUNTY, AND MUNICIPAL EMPLOYEES

http://www.afscme.org/

AFSCME/UNCF UNION SCHOLARS PROGRAM
• *See page 103*

AMERICAN LEGION AUXILIARY DEPARTMENT OF ARIZONA

http:/wwwaladeptaz.org

AMERICAN LEGION AUXILIARY DEPARTMENT OF ARIZONA WILMA HOYAL-MAXINE CHILTON MEMORIAL SCHOLARSHIP
• *See page 488*

BETHESDA LUTHERAN COMMUNITIES

http://www.bethesdalutherancommunities.org/scholarships

DEVELOPMENTAL DISABILITIES SCHOLASTIC ACHIEVEMENT SCHOLARSHIP FOR COLLEGE STUDENTS WHO ARE LUTHERAN
• *See page 236*

COMMUNITY FOUNDATION FOR GREATER ATLANTA, INC.

http://cfgreateratlanta.org/

STEVE DEARDUFF SCHOLARSHIP
• *See page 351*

COMMUNITY FOUNDATION OF WESTERN MASSACHUSETTS

http://www.communityfoundation.org/

HELEN HAMILTON SCHOLARSHIP FUND
Scholarship for students pursuing degrees in social services, housing studies, urban design, and other related fields with a preference for students who have demonstrated a commitment to community service. For more information, please see website http://communityfoundation.org/.
Academic Fields/Career Goals: Social Services; Urban and Regional Planning.
Award: Scholarship for use in freshman, sophomore, junior, senior, or graduate years; not renewable.
Eligibility Requirements: Applicant must be enrolled or expecting to enroll full- or part-time at a two-year or four-year institution or university and resident of Massachusetts. Applicant or parent of applicant must have employment or volunteer experience in community service. Available to U.S. citizens.
Application Requirements: Application form, essay, financial need analysis, transcript. *Deadline:* March 31.

Contact: Dotty Theriaque, Program Assistant for Scholarships
Community Foundation of Western Massachusetts
1500 Main Street
PO Box 15769
Springfield, MA 01115
Phone: 413-732-2858
Fax: 413-733-8565
E-mail: scholar@communityfoundation.org

COMPHEALTH

http://www.comphealth.com

COMPHEALTH MEDICAL SCHOLARSHIP
• *See page 151*

CONTINENTAL SOCIETY, DAUGHTERS OF INDIAN WARS

http://www.csdiw.org/

CONTINENTAL SOCIETY, DAUGHTERS OF INDIAN WARS SCHOLARSHIP
• *See page 251*

GENERAL BOARD OF HIGHER EDUCATION AND MINISTRY

http://www.gbhem.org

EDITH M. ALLEN SCHOLARSHIP
• *See page 252*

HEALTH PROFESSIONS EDUCATION FOUNDATION

http://www.healthprofessions.ca.gov/

ALLIED HEALTHCARE SCHOLARSHIP PROGRAM
• *See page 151*

MARYLAND STATE HIGHER EDUCATION COMMISSION

http://www.mhec.state.md.us/

GRADUATE AND PROFESSIONAL SCHOLARSHIP PROGRAM-MARYLAND
• *See page 238*

JANET L. HOFFMANN LOAN ASSISTANCE REPAYMENT PROGRAM
• *See page 254*

NATIONAL BLACK POLICE ASSOCIATION

http://www.blackpolice.org/

ALPHONSO DEAL SCHOLARSHIP AWARD
• *See page 226*

PILOT INTERNATIONAL FOUNDATION

http://www.pilotinternational.org/

RUBY NEWHALL MEMORIAL SCHOLARSHIP
• *See page 355*

PRESBYTERIAN CHURCH (USA)

http://www.pcusa.org/financialaid

STUDENT OPPORTUNITY SCHOLARSHIP
• *See page 258*

UNITED COMMUNITY SERVICES FOR WORKING FAMILIES

http://www.ucswf.org

TED BRICKER SCHOLARSHIP

One-time award available to child of a union member who is a parent or guardian. Must be a member of a union affiliated with the Berks County United Labor Council, AFL-CIO. Must submit essay that is clear, concise, persuasive, and shows a commitment to the community.

Academic Fields/Career Goals: Social Services.

Award: Scholarship for use in freshman year; not renewable. *Number:* 1. *Amount:* up to $250.

Eligibility Requirements: Applicant must be high school student; planning to enroll or expecting to enroll full-time at a four-year institution or university and resident of Pennsylvania. Applicant or parent of applicant must be member of AFL-CIO. Available to U.S. citizens.

Application Requirements: Application form, essay, financial need analysis, transcript. *Deadline:* July 31.

Contact: Victoria Henshaw, Executive Director
United Community Services for Working Families
1251 North Front Street
Reading, PA 19601
Phone: 610-374-3319 Ext. 104
E-mail: vhenshaw@ucswf.org

Y'S MEN INTERNATIONAL

http://www.ysmen.org/

ALEXANDER SCHOLARSHIP LOAN FUND
• *See page 171*

SPECIAL EDUCATION

ALBERTA HERITAGE SCHOLARSHIP FUND

http://www.alis.alberta.ca/

ANNA AND JOHN KOLESAR MEMORIAL SCHOLARSHIPS
• *See page 247*

AMERICAN LEGION AUXILIARY DEPARTMENT OF ARIZONA

http:/wwwaladeptaz.org

AMERICAN LEGION AUXILIARY DEPARTMENT OF ARIZONA WILMA HOYAL-MAXINE CHILTON MEMORIAL SCHOLARSHIP
• *See page 488*

ARC OF WASHINGTON TRUST FUND

http://www.arctrustfund.org/

ARC OF WASHINGTON TRUST FUND STIPEND PROGRAM

Stipends of up to $5000 will be awarded to upper division or graduate students in schools in the states of Washington, Alaska, Oregon or Idaho.

Applicants must have a demonstrated interest in the field of intellectual and developmental disabilities. The application can be downloaded from the website http://www.arctrustfund.org/Student-Stipends

Academic Fields/Career Goals: Special Education.

Award: Scholarship for use in junior, senior, graduate, or postgraduate years; not renewable. *Number:* 4–5. *Amount:* $4000–$5000.

Eligibility Requirements: Applicant must be enrolled or expecting to enroll full-time at a four-year institution or university and resident of Alaska, Idaho, Oregon, Washington. Applicant or parent of applicant must have employment or volunteer experience in community service, helping handicapped, human services, physical therapy/rehabilitation, teaching/education. Available to U.S. citizens.

Application Requirements: Application form, essay. *Deadline:* February 29.

Contact: Diana Stadden, Administrative Assistant
ARC of Washington Trust Fund
2638 State Ave NE
Olympia, WA 98506
Phone: 360-357-5596 Ext. 6
E-mail: Diana@arcwa.org

BETHESDA LUTHERAN COMMUNITIES

http://www.bethesdalutherancommunities.org/scholarships

DEVELOPMENTAL DISABILITIES SCHOLASTIC ACHIEVEMENT SCHOLARSHIP FOR COLLEGE STUDENTS WHO ARE LUTHERAN
• *See page 236*

ILLINOIS STUDENT ASSISTANCE COMMISSION (ISAC)

http://www.isac.org/

ILLINOIS SPECIAL EDUCATION TEACHER TUITION WAIVER

Teachers or students who are pursuing a career in special education as public, private or parochial preschool, elementary or secondary school teachers in Illinois may be eligible for this program. This program will exempt such individuals from paying tuition and mandatory fees at an eligible institution, for up to four years. The individual dollar amount awarded are subject to sufficient annual appropriations by the Illinois General Assembly.

Academic Fields/Career Goals: Special Education.

Award: Scholarship for use in freshman, sophomore, junior, senior, or graduate years; renewable.

Eligibility Requirements: Applicant must be enrolled or expecting to enroll full- or part-time at a four-year institution or university; resident of Illinois and studying in Illinois. Applicant must have 2.5 GPA or higher. Available to U.S. citizens.

Application Requirements: Application form. *Deadline:* March 1.

Contact: ISAC Call Center Representative
Illinois Student Assistance Commission (ISAC)
1755 Lake Cook Road
Deerfield, IL 60015-5209
Phone: 800-899-4722
E-mail: isac.studentservices@isac.illinois.gov

INTERNATIONAL LITERACY ASSOCIATION

https://literacyworldwide.org/home

JEANNE S. CHALL RESEARCH FELLOWSHIP
• *See page 254*

NATIONAL INSTITUTE FOR LABOR RELATIONS RESEARCH

http://www.nilrr.org/

APPLEGATE/JACKSON/PARKS FUTURE TEACHER SCHOLARSHIP
• *See page 255*

OREGON STUDENT ASSISTANCE COMMISSION

http://www.GetCollegeFunds.org/

JAMES CARLSON MEMORIAL SCHOLARSHIP
• *See page 256*

MARY ELIZABETH GUEST SCHOLARSHIP
Renewable award for graduates of Oregon high schools (not open to graduating high school seniors) who are attending 4-year private or nonprofit colleges and universities. For those studying special education, with a preference for teaching students with severe behavioral disorders.
Academic Fields/Career Goals: Special Education.
Award: Scholarship for use in sophomore, junior, or senior years; renewable.
Eligibility Requirements: Applicant must be enrolled or expecting to enroll full-time at a four-year institution or university and resident of Oregon. Available to U.S. citizens.
Application Requirements: Application form. *Deadline:* March 1.
Contact: Melissa Adams, Scholarship Processing Coordinator
    Phone: 541-687-7409
    E-mail: melissa.adams@hecc.oregon.gov

P. BUCKLEY MOSS FOUNDATION FOR CHILDREN'S EDUCATION

www.mossfoundation.org

JUDITH CARY MEMORIAL SCHOLARSHIP
The Judith Cary Scholarship is an up-to-$1,000 award given annually to one student who is pursuing either a Bachelor's or Master's Degree in teaching Special Education. Students applying need Proof of Acceptance into a specific program to teach special needs; Completion of two years of undergraduate work; two letters of recommendation (one academic and one personal (not a relative); Nomination by a Moss Society member; Short essay detailing school/community/work activities & achievements.
Academic Fields/Career Goals: Special Education.
Award: Scholarship for use in junior, senior, or graduate years; not renewable. *Number:* 1. *Amount:* $1000.
Eligibility Requirements: Applicant must be enrolled or expecting to enroll full- or part-time at an institution or university. Applicant must have 3.0 GPA or higher. Available to U.S. citizens.
Application Requirements: Application form, essay. *Deadline:* March 31.

PILOT INTERNATIONAL FOUNDATION

http://www.pilotinternational.org/

PILOT INTERNATIONAL SCHOLARSHIP
• *See page 355*

RUBY NEWHALL MEMORIAL SCHOLARSHIP
• *See page 355*

STRAIGHTFORWARD MEDIA

http://www.straightforwardmedia.com/

STRAIGHTFORWARD MEDIA TEACHER SCHOLARSHIP
• *See page 258*

WISCONSIN CONGRESS OF PARENTS AND TEACHERS INC.

http://www.wisconsinpta.org/

BROOKMIRE-HASTINGS SCHOLARSHIPS
• *See page 261*

SPORTS-RELATED/ EXERCISE SCIENCE

AMERICAN ALLIANCE FOR HEALTH, PHYSICAL EDUCATION, RECREATION AND DANCE

http://www.shapeamerica.org/

RUTH ABERNATHY PRESIDENTIAL SCHOLARSHIP
• *See page 496*

AMERICAN INDIAN SCIENCE AND ENGINEERING SOCIETY

http://www.aises.org/

A.T. ANDERSON MEMORIAL SCHOLARSHIP PROGRAM
• *See page 109*

AMERICAN PHYSIOLOGICAL SOCIETY

http://www.the-aps.org

DAVID S. BRUCE AWARDS FOR EXCELLENCE IN UNDERGRADUATE RESEARCH
• *See page 105*

CANFIT

http://www.canfit.org/

CANFIT NUTRITION, PHYSICAL EDUCATION AND CULINARY ARTS SCHOLARSHIP
• *See page 229*

COMPHEALTH

http://www.comphealth.com

COMPHEALTH MEDICAL SCHOLARSHIP
• *See page 151*

MICHAEL MOODY FITNESS

http://www.michaelmoodyfitness.com/

MICHAEL MOODY FITNESS SCHOLARSHIP
• *See page 255*

NATIONAL ATHLETIC TRAINERS' ASSOCIATION RESEARCH AND EDUCATION FOUNDATION

http://www.natafoundation.org/

NATIONAL ATHLETIC TRAINERS' ASSOCIATION RESEARCH AND EDUCATION FOUNDATION SCHOLARSHIP PROGRAM
• *See page 354*

NEXTSTEPU

http://www.nextstepu.com/

$1,500 STEM SCHOLARSHIP
• *See page 106*

PACERS FOUNDATION INC.

http://www.pacersfoundation.org/

LINDA CRAIG MEMORIAL SCHOLARSHIP PRESENTED BY ST. VINCENT SPORTS MEDICINE
• *See page 355*

PADDLE CANADA

https://www.paddlecanada.com/

BILL MASON SCHOLARSHIP FUND
• *See page 257*

PI LAMBDA THETA INC.

http://www.pilambda.org/

TOBIN SORENSON PHYSICAL EDUCATION SCHOLARSHIP
• *See page 257*

RADIO TELEVISION DIGITAL NEWS ASSOCIATION

www.rtdna.org

LOU AND CAROLE PRATO SPORTS REPORTING SCHOLARSHIP
• *See page 208*

SCARLETT FAMILY FOUNDATION SCHOLARSHIP PROGRAM

http://www.scarlettfoundation.org/

SCHOLARSHIP FOR STUDENTS PURSUING A BUSINESS OR STEM DEGREE
• *See page 84*

STRAIGHTFORWARD MEDIA

http://www.straightforwardmedia.com/

STRAIGHTFORWARD MEDIA VOCATIONAL-TECHNICAL SCHOOL SCHOLARSHIP
• *See page 107*

THE WALTER J. TRAVIS SOCIETY

http://www.travissociety.com

THE WALTER J. TRAVIS MEMORIAL SCHOLARSHIP
• *See page 388*

Y'S MEN INTERNATIONAL

http://www.ysmen.org/

ALEXANDER SCHOLARSHIP LOAN FUND
• *See page 171*

STATISTICS

THE ACTUARIAL FOUNDATION

http://www.actuarialfoundation.org

ACTUARY OF TOMORROW—STUART A. ROBERTSON MEMORIAL SCHOLARSHIP
• *See page 160*

CURTIS E. HUNTINGTON MEMORIAL SCHOLARSHIP (FORMERLY THE JOHN CULVER WOODDY SCHOLARSHIP)
• *See page 245*

AMERICAN INDIAN SCIENCE AND ENGINEERING SOCIETY

http://www.aises.org/

A.T. ANDERSON MEMORIAL SCHOLARSHIP PROGRAM
• *See page 109*

ARMED FORCES COMMUNICATIONS AND ELECTRONICS ASSOCIATION, EDUCATIONAL FOUNDATION

http://www.afcea.org/site/?q=foundation/scholarships

STEM MAJORS SCHOLARSHIPS FOR UNDERGRADUATE STUDENTS
• *See page 110*

STEM TEACHERS SCHOLARSHIP
• *See page 111*

VADM SAMUEL L. GRAVELY, JR., USN(RET.) MEMORIAL SCHOLARSHIP
• *See page 111*

AUTOMOTIVE WOMEN'S ALLIANCE FOUNDATION

http://www.awafoundation.org/index.php

AUTOMOTIVE WOMEN'S ALLIANCE FOUNDATION SCHOLARSHIPS
• *See page 74*

GREAT MINDS IN STEM

www.greatmindsinstem.org

HISPANIC ENGINEER NATIONAL ACHIEVEMENT AWARDS CORPORATION SCHOLARSHIP PROGRAM
• *See page 106*

NEXTSTEPU

http://www.nextstepu.com/

$1,500 STEM SCHOLARSHIP
• *See page 106*

TRANSTUTORS

http://www.transtutors.com/scholarship

TRANSTUTORS SCHOLARSHIP 2015-16
• *See page 85*

UNITED NEGRO COLLEGE FUND

http://www.uncf.org/

COLGATE–PALMOLIVE CORPORATE SCHOLARS PROGRAM
• *See page 86*

SURVEYING, SURVEYING TECHNOLOGY, CARTOGRAPHY, OR GEOGRAPHIC INFORMATION SCIENCE

AMERICAN CONGRESS ON SURVEYING AND MAPPING

http://landsurveyorsunited.com/acsm

ACSM FELLOWS SCHOLARSHIP

One-time award available to a student with a junior or higher standing in any ACSM discipline (surveying, mapping, geographic information systems, and geodetic science). Must be ACSM member.

Academic Fields/Career Goals: Surveying, Surveying Technology, Cartography, or Geographic Information Science.

Award: Scholarship for use in freshman, sophomore, junior, or senior years; not renewable. *Number:* 1. *Amount:* $2000.

Eligibility Requirements: Applicant must be enrolled or expecting to enroll full- or part-time at a four-year institution or university. Applicant or parent of applicant must be member of American Congress on Surveying and Mapping. Available to U.S. citizens.

Application Requirements: Application form, essay, membership proof, recommendations or references, transcript. *Deadline:* October 1.

Contact: Ilse Genovese, Communications Director
American Congress on Surveying and Mapping
6 Montgomery Village Avenue, Suite 403
Gaithersburg, MD 20879
Phone: 240-632-9716 Ext. 113
Fax: 240-632-1321
E-mail: ilse.genovese@acsm.net

ACSM LOWELL H. AND DOROTHY LOVING UNDERGRADUATE SCHOLARSHIP

Scholarship available for a junior or senior in a college or university in the U.S. studying surveying. Program of study must include courses in two of the following areas: land surveying, geometric geodesy, photogrammetry/remote sensing, or analysis and design of spatial measurement systems.

Academic Fields/Career Goals: Surveying, Surveying Technology, Cartography, or Geographic Information Science.

Award: Scholarship for use in freshman, sophomore, junior, or senior years; not renewable. *Number:* 1. *Amount:* $2500.

Eligibility Requirements: Applicant must be enrolled or expecting to enroll full- or part-time at a four-year institution or university. Applicant or parent of applicant must be member of American Congress on Surveying and Mapping. Available to U.S. citizens.

Application Requirements: Application form, essay, membership proof, recommendations or references, transcript. *Deadline:* October 1.

Contact: Ilse Genovese, Communications Director
American Congress on Surveying and Mapping
6 Montgomery Village Avenue, Suite 403
Gaithersbutg, MD 20879
Phone: 240-632-9716
Fax: 240-632-1321
E-mail: ilse.genovese@acsm.net

AMERICAN ASSOCIATION FOR GEODETIC SURVEYING JOSEPH F. DRACUP SCHOLARSHIP AWARD

Award for students enrolled in a four-year degree program in surveying (or in closely-related degree programs such as geomatics or surveying engineering). Preference given to applicants from programs with significant focus on geodetic surveying. Must be ACSM member.

Academic Fields/Career Goals: Surveying, Surveying Technology, Cartography, or Geographic Information Science.

Award: Scholarship for use in freshman, sophomore, junior, or senior years; not renewable. *Number:* 1. *Amount:* $2000.

Eligibility Requirements: Applicant must be enrolled or expecting to enroll full- or part-time at a four-year institution or university. Applicant or parent of applicant must be member of American Congress on Surveying and Mapping. Available to U.S. and non-Canadian citizens.

Application Requirements: Application form, essay, recommendations or references, transcript. *Deadline:* October 1.

Contact: Ilse Genovese, ACSM Communications Director
American Congress on Surveying and Mapping
6 Montgomery Village Avenue, Suite 403
Gaithersburg, MD 20879
Phone: 240-632-9716 Ext. 113
Fax: 240-632-1321
E-mail: ilse.genovese@acsm.net

BERNTSEN INTERNATIONAL SCHOLARSHIP IN SURVEYING

Award of $1500 for full-time students enrolled in a four-year degree program in surveying or in a closely-related degree program, such as geomatics or surveying engineering. Must be ACSM member.

Academic Fields/Career Goals: Surveying, Surveying Technology, Cartography, or Geographic Information Science.

Award: Scholarship for use in freshman, sophomore, junior, or senior years; not renewable. *Number:* 1. *Amount:* $1500.

Eligibility Requirements: Applicant must be enrolled or expecting to enroll full-time at a four-year institution or university. Applicant or parent of applicant must be member of American Congress on Surveying and Mapping. Available to U.S. citizens.

Application Requirements: Application form, essay, recommendations or references, transcript. *Deadline:* October 1.

Contact: Ilse Genovese, ACSM Communications Director
American Congress on Surveying and Mapping
6 Montgomery Village Avenue, Suite 403
Gaithersburg, MD 20879
Phone: 240-632-9716 Ext. 113
Fax: 240-632-1321
E-mail: ilse.genovese@acsm.net

BERNTSEN INTERNATIONAL SCHOLARSHIP IN SURVEYING TECHNOLOGY

Award for full-time undergraduate students enrolled in a two-year degree program in surveying technology. For U.S. study only. Must be a member of the American Congress on Surveying and Mapping. See website for application and more details http://www.acsm.net/scholar.html.

Academic Fields/Career Goals: Surveying, Surveying Technology, Cartography, or Geographic Information Science.

Award: Scholarship for use in freshman or sophomore years; not renewable. *Number:* 1. *Amount:* $500.

Eligibility Requirements: Applicant must be enrolled or expecting to enroll full-time at a two-year or four-year institution. Applicant or parent of applicant must be member of American Congress on Surveying and Mapping. Available to U.S. and non-Canadian citizens.

Application Requirements: Application form, essay, proof of membership in ACSM, recommendations or references, transcript. *Deadline:* varies.

Contact: Ilse Genovese, ACSM Communications Director
American Congress on Surveying and Mapping
6 Montgomery Village Avenue, Suite 403
Gaithersburg, MD 20879
Phone: 240-632-9716 Ext. 113
Fax: 240-632-1321
E-mail: ilse.genovese@acsm.net

CADY MCDONNELL MEMORIAL SCHOLARSHIP

Award of $1000 for female surveying student. Must be a resident of one of the following western states: Alaska, Arizona, California, Colorado, Hawaii, Idaho, Montana, Nevada, New Mexico, Oregon, Utah, Washington, and Wyoming. Must provide proof of legal home residence and be a member of the American Congress on Surveying and Mapping.

Academic Fields/Career Goals: Surveying, Surveying Technology, Cartography, or Geographic Information Science.

Award: Scholarship for use in freshman, sophomore, junior, or senior years; not renewable. *Number:* 1. *Amount:* $1000.

Eligibility Requirements: Applicant must be enrolled or expecting to enroll full- or part-time at a two-year or four-year institution or university; female and resident of Alaska, Arizona, California, Colorado, Hawaii, Idaho, Montana, Nevada, New Mexico, Oregon, Utah, Washington, Wyoming. Applicant or parent of applicant must be member of American Congress on Surveying and Mapping. Available to U.S. citizens.

Application Requirements: Application form, essay, financial need analysis, proof of residence, membership proof, personal statement, recommendations or references, transcript. *Deadline:* October 1.

Contact: Ilse Genovese, ACSM Communications Director
American Congress on Surveying and Mapping
6 Montgomery Village Avenue, Suite 403
Gaithersburg, MD 20879
Phone: 240-632-9716 Ext. 113
Fax: 240-632-1321
E-mail: ilse.genovese@acsm.net

NETTIE DRACUP MEMORIAL SCHOLARSHIP

Award for undergraduate student enrolled in a four-year geodetic surveying program at an accredited college or university. Must be U.S. citizen. Must be ACSM member.

Academic Fields/Career Goals: Surveying, Surveying Technology, Cartography, or Geographic Information Science.

Award: Scholarship for use in freshman, sophomore, junior, or senior years; not renewable. *Number:* 2. *Amount:* $2000.

Eligibility Requirements: Applicant must be enrolled or expecting to enroll full-time at a four-year institution or university. Applicant or parent of applicant must be member of American Congress on Surveying and Mapping. Available to U.S. citizens.

Application Requirements: ACSM membership proof, application form, essay, financial need analysis, recommendations or references, transcript. *Deadline:* October 1.

Contact: Ilse Genovese, Communications Director
American Congress on Surveying and Mapping
6 Montgomery Village Avenue, Suite 403
Gaithersburg, MD 20879
Phone: 240-632-9716 Ext. 113
Fax: 240-632-1321
E-mail: ilse.genovese@acsm.net

SCHONSTEDT SCHOLARSHIP IN SURVEYING

Award preference given to applicants with junior or senior standing in a four-year program in surveying. Schonstedt donates magnetic locator to surveying program at each recipient's school. Must be ACSM member.

Academic Fields/Career Goals: Surveying, Surveying Technology, Cartography, or Geographic Information Science.

Award: Scholarship for use in junior or senior years; not renewable. *Number:* 2. *Amount:* $1500.

Eligibility Requirements: Applicant must be enrolled or expecting to enroll full-time at a four-year institution or university. Applicant or parent of applicant must be member of American Congress on Surveying and Mapping. Available to U.S. citizens.

Application Requirements: ACSM membership proof, application form, essay, recommendations or references, transcript. *Deadline:* October 1.

Contact: Ilse Genovese, Communications Director
American Congress on Surveying and Mapping
6 Montgomery Village Avenue, Suite 403
Gaithersburg, MD 20879
Phone: 240-632-9716 Ext. 113
Fax: 240-632-1321
E-mail: ilse.genovese@acsm.net

TRI-STATE SURVEYING AND PHOTOGRAMMETRY KRIS M. KUNZE MEMORIAL SCHOLARSHIP
• *See page 161*

AMERICAN COUNCIL OF ENGINEERING COMPANIES OF PENNSYLVANIA (ACEC/PA)

http://www.acecpa.org/

ERIC J. GENNUSO AND LEROY D. (BUD) LOY, JR. SCHOLARSHIP PROGRAM
• *See page 173*

AMERICAN INDIAN SCIENCE AND ENGINEERING SOCIETY

http://www.aises.org/

A.T. ANDERSON MEMORIAL SCHOLARSHIP PROGRAM
• *See page 109*

AMERICAN SOCIETY OF CERTIFIED ENGINEERING TECHNICIANS

http://www.ascet.org/

KURT H. AND DONNA M. SCHULER SMALL GRANT
• *See page 176*

ASPRS, THE IMAGING AND GEOSPATIAL INFORMATION SOCIETY

http://www.asprs.org/

ABRAHAM ANSON MEMORIAL SCHOLARSHIP
• *See page 296*

FRANCIS H. MOFFITT MEMORIAL SCHOLARSHIP
• *See page 296*

JOHN O. BEHRENS INSTITUTE FOR LAND INFORMATION MEMORIAL SCHOLARSHIP
• *See page 296*

KENNETH J. OSBORN MEMORIAL SCHOLARSHIP
• *See page 296*

ROBERT E. ALTENHOFEN MEMORIAL SCHOLARSHIP
• *See page 296*

ASSOCIATED GENERAL CONTRACTORS OF NEW YORK STATE, LLC

http://www.agcnys.org/

ASSOCIATED GENERAL CONTRACTORS NYS SCHOLARSHIP PROGRAM
• *See page 194*

ASSOCIATION OF CALIFORNIA WATER AGENCIES

http://www.acwa.com/

ASSOCIATION OF CALIFORNIA WATER AGENCIES SCHOLARSHIPS
• *See page 112*

CLAIR A. HILL SCHOLARSHIP
• *See page 112*

BROWN AND CALDWELL

http://www.brownandcaldwell.com

ECKENFELDER SCHOLARSHIP
• *See page 155*

MINORITY SCHOLARSHIP PROGRAM
• *See page 155*

FLORIDA ENGINEERING SOCIETY

http://www.fleng.org/scholarships.cfm

ACEC/FLORIDA SCHOLARSHIP
• *See page 298*

MASSACHUSETTS ASSOCIATION OF LAND SURVEYORS AND CIVIL ENGINEERS

http://www.malsce.org/

MALSE SCHOLARSHIPS
• *See page 302*

NEXTSTEPU

http://www.nextstepu.com/

$1,500 STEM SCHOLARSHIP
• *See page 106*

OREGON STUDENT ASSISTANCE COMMISSION

http://www.GetCollegeFunds.org/

PROFESSIONAL LAND SURVEYORS OF OREGON SCHOLARSHIP

Award for students enrolled in Oregon public and nonprofit colleges and engaged in a course of study leading to land-surveying career. Must intend to take Fundamentals of Land Surveying exam. Additional essay stating education/career goals and their relation to land surveying is required.

Academic Fields/Career Goals: Surveying, Surveying Technology, Cartography, or Geographic Information Science.

Award: Scholarship for use in freshman year; not renewable.

Eligibility Requirements: Applicant must be enrolled or expecting to enroll full-time at a two-year or four-year institution or university and studying in Oregon. Available to U.S. citizens.

Application Requirements: Application form, essay, financial need analysis. *Deadline:* March 1.

Contact: Melissa Adams, Scholarship Processing Coordinator
  Phone: 541-687-7409
  E-mail: melissa.adams@hecc.oregon.gov

PROFESSIONAL CONSTRUCTION ESTIMATORS ASSOCIATION

http://www.pcea.org/

TED G. WILSON MEMORIAL SCHOLARSHIP FOUNDATION
• *See page 197*

RHODE ISLAND SOCIETY OF PROFESSIONAL LAND SURVEYORS

http://www.rispls.org/

PIERRE H. GUILLEMETTE SCHOLARSHIP

Scholarship available to any Rhode Island resident enrolled in a certificate or degree program in land surveying at a qualified institution of higher learning.

Academic Fields/Career Goals: Surveying, Surveying Technology, Cartography, or Geographic Information Science.

Award: Scholarship for use in freshman, sophomore, junior, or senior years; not renewable.

Eligibility Requirements: Applicant must be enrolled or expecting to enroll full- or part-time at a four-year institution or university and resident of Rhode Island. Available to U.S. citizens.

Application Requirements: Application form, resume, transcript. *Deadline:* October 30.

Contact: Scholarship Coordinator
  Rhode Island Society of Professional Land Surveyors
  PO Box 544
  East Greenwich, RI 02818
  Phone: 401-294-1262
  E-mail: info@rispls.org

SOIL AND WATER CONSERVATION SOCIETY-MISSOURI SHOW-ME CHAPTER

http://www.moswcs.org/

MO SHOW-ME CHAPTER SWCS SCHOLARSHIP
• *See page 95*

THERAPY/ REHABILITATION

101ST AIRBORNE DIVISION ASSOCIATION

http://www.screamingeaglefoundation.org/

AL & WILLIAMARY VISTE SCHOLARSHIP
• *See page 233*

ALBERTA HERITAGE SCHOLARSHIP FUND

http://www.alis.alberta.ca/

ABORIGINAL HEALTH CAREERS BURSARY
• *See page 153*

AMERICAN FOUNDATION FOR THE BLIND

http://www.afb.org/

DELTA GAMMA FOUNDATION FLORENCE MARGARET HARVEY MEMORIAL SCHOLARSHIP
• *See page 247*

RUDOLPH DILLMAN MEMORIAL SCHOLARSHIP
• *See page 248*

AMERICAN INDIAN SCIENCE AND ENGINEERING SOCIETY

http://www.aises.org/

A.T. ANDERSON MEMORIAL SCHOLARSHIP PROGRAM
• *See page 109*

AMERICAN LEGION AUXILIARY DEPARTMENT OF COLORADO

http://www.alacolorado.com

AMERICAN LEGION AUXILIARY DEPARTMENT OF COLORADO PAST PRESIDENTS' PARLEY HEALTH CARE PROFESSIONAL SCHOLARSHIPNURSES SCHOLARSHIP
• *See page 133*

AMERICAN LEGION AUXILIARY DEPARTMENT OF MICHIGAN

http://www.michalaux.org/

AMERICAN LEGION AUXILIARY DEPARTMENT OF MICHIGAN MEDICAL CAREER SCHOLARSHIP
• *See page 347*

AMERICAN OCCUPATIONAL THERAPY FOUNDATION INC.

http://www.aotf.org/

CARLOTTA WELLES SCHOLARSHIP
• *See page 348*

AMERICAN PHYSICAL THERAPY ASSOCIATION

http://www.apta.org/honorsawards

MARY MCMILLAN SCHOLARSHIP AWARD
• *See page 249*

AMERICAN QUARTER HORSE FOUNDATION (AQHF)

http://www.aqha.com/foundation

EAAT HIPPOTHERAPY SCHOLARSHIP
Ideal candidate is an AQHA member pursuing a career in the field of hippotherapy through physical therapy, occupational therapy and or speech language pathology. Related majors may include, but are not limited to, communication disorders, sports and exercise science or kinesiology.
Academic Fields/Career Goals: Therapy/Rehabilitation.
Award: Scholarship for use in junior, senior, graduate, or postgraduate years; renewable. *Number:* 1. *Amount:* $10,000.

Eligibility Requirements: Applicant must be enrolled or expecting to enroll full-time at a four-year institution or university. Applicant or parent of applicant must be member of American Quarter Horse Association. Applicant or parent of applicant must have employment or volunteer experience in designated career field, helping handicapped, physical therapy/rehabilitation. Applicant must have 2.5 GPA or higher. Available to U.S. and non-U.S. citizens.
Application Requirements: Application form, financial need analysis. *Deadline:* December 1.
Contact: Scholarship Office
American Quarter Horse Foundation (AQHF)
2601 East Interstate 40
Amarillo, TX 79104
Phone: 806-378-5040
E-mail: foundation@aqha.org

AMERICAN RESPIRATORY CARE FOUNDATION

http://www.arcfoundation.org/

JIMMY A. YOUNG MEMORIAL EDUCATION RECOGNITION AWARD
• *See page 348*

MORTON B. DUGGAN, JR. MEMORIAL EDUCATION RECOGNITION AWARD
• *See page 348*

SEPRACOR ACHIEVEMENT AWARD FOR EXCELLENCE IN PULMONARY DISEASE STATE MANAGEMENT
• *See page 348*

ARRL FOUNDATION INC.

http://www.arrl.org/

CAROLE J. STREETER, KB9JBR, SCHOLARSHIP
• *See page 236*

ASSOCIATION FOR EDUCATION AND REHABILITATION OF THE BLIND AND VISUALLY IMPAIRED

http://www.aerbvi.org/

WILLIAM AND DOROTHY FERRELL SCHOLARSHIP
• *See page 250*

AVACARE MEDICAL

https://avacaremedical.com

AVACARE MEDICAL SCHOLARSHIP
• *See page 105*

BETHESDA LUTHERAN COMMUNITIES

http://www.bethesdalutherancommunities.org/scholarships

DEVELOPMENTAL DISABILITIES SCHOLASTIC ACHIEVEMENT SCHOLARSHIP FOR COLLEGE STUDENTS WHO ARE LUTHERAN
• *See page 236*

COMPHEALTH

http://www.comphealth.com

COMPHEALTH MEDICAL SCHOLARSHIP
• *See page 151*

CYNTHIA E. MORGAN SCHOLARSHIP FUND (CEMS)

http://www.cemsfund.com/

CYNTHIA E. MORGAN MEMORIAL SCHOLARSHIP FUND, INC.
• See page 316

THE EXPERT INSTITUTE

https://www.theexpertinstitute.com

ANNUAL HEALTHCARE AND LIFE SCIENCES SCHOLARSHIP
• See page 156

HEALTH PROFESSIONS EDUCATION FOUNDATION

http://www.healthprofessions.ca.gov/

ALLIED HEALTHCARE SCHOLARSHIP PROGRAM
• See page 151

INTERNATIONAL ORDER OF THE KING'S DAUGHTERS AND SONS

http://www.iokds.org/

HEALTH CAREERS SCHOLARSHIP
• See page 238

KETAMINE CLINICS OF LOS ANGELES

http://www.ketamineclinics.com/

KETAMINE CLINICS OF LOS ANGELES SCHOLARSHIP PROGRAM
• See page 152

LADIES AUXILIARY TO THE VETERANS OF FOREIGN WARS, DEPARTMENT OF MAINE

http://mainevfw.org/

FRANCES L. BOOTH MEDICAL SCHOLARSHIP SPONSORED BY LAVFW DEPARTMENT OF MAINE
• See page 353

MARYLAND STATE HIGHER EDUCATION COMMISSION

http://www.mhec.state.md.us/

JANET L. HOFFMANN LOAN ASSISTANCE REPAYMENT PROGRAM
• See page 254

MEDICAL SCRUBS COLLECTION

http://medicalscrubscollection.com

MEDICAL SCRUBS COLLECTION SCHOLARSHIP
• See page 106

MICHAEL MOODY FITNESS

http://www.michaelmoodyfitness.com/

MICHAEL MOODY FITNESS SCHOLARSHIP
• See page 255

NATIONAL AMBUCS INC.

http://www.ambucs.org/

AMBUCS SCHOLARS-SCHOLARSHIPS FOR THERAPISTS
• See page 134

NATIONAL ATHLETIC TRAINERS' ASSOCIATION RESEARCH AND EDUCATION FOUNDATION

http://www.natafoundation.org/

NATIONAL ATHLETIC TRAINERS' ASSOCIATION RESEARCH AND EDUCATION FOUNDATION SCHOLARSHIP PROGRAM
• See page 354

NATIONAL SOCIETY DAUGHTERS OF THE AMERICAN REVOLUTION

http://www.dar.org/

NATIONAL SOCIETY DAUGHTERS OF THE AMERICAN REVOLUTION OCCUPATIONAL THERAPY SCHOLARSHIP

Scholarship of $1000 for students who are in financial need and have been accepted or are attending an accredited school of occupational therapy including art, music or physical therapy. A letter of acceptance into the occupational therapy program or the transcript stating the applicant is in the occupational therapy program must be included with the application.

Academic Fields/Career Goals: Therapy/Rehabilitation.

Award: Scholarship for use in freshman, sophomore, junior, senior, or graduate years; not renewable. *Amount:* $1000.

Eligibility Requirements: Applicant must be enrolled or expecting to enroll full- or part-time at a two-year or four-year institution or university. Available to U.S. citizens.

Application Requirements: Application form, essay, financial need analysis. *Deadline:* February 15.

Contact: Lakeisha Graham, Manager, Office of the Reporter General
Phone: 202-628-1776
Fax: 202-879-3348
E-mail: nsdarscholarships@dar.org

OREGON STUDENT ASSISTANCE COMMISSION

http://www.GetCollegeFunds.org/

MARION A. LINDEMAN SCHOLARSHIP
• See page 354

PACERS FOUNDATION INC.

http://www.pacersfoundation.org/

LINDA CRAIG MEMORIAL SCHOLARSHIP PRESENTED BY ST. VINCENT SPORTS MEDICINE
• See page 355

PI LAMBDA THETA INC.

http://www.pilambda.org/

TOBIN SORENSON PHYSICAL EDUCATION SCHOLARSHIP
• See page 257

PILOT INTERNATIONAL FOUNDATION

http://www.pilotinternational.org/

PILOT INTERNATIONAL SCHOLARSHIP
• See page 355

RUBY NEWHALL MEMORIAL SCHOLARSHIP
• See page 355

THE RECOVERY VILLAGE

https://www.therecoveryvillage.com/

RECOVERY VILLAGE HEALTHCARE SCHOLARSHIP
• See page 238

SCARLETT FAMILY FOUNDATION SCHOLARSHIP PROGRAM

http://www.scarlettfoundation.org/

SCHOLARSHIP FOR STUDENTS PURSUING A BUSINESS OR STEM DEGREE
• See page 84

STRAIGHTFORWARD MEDIA

http://www.straightforwardmedia.com/

STRAIGHTFORWARD MEDIA MEDICAL PROFESSIONS SCHOLARSHIP
• See page 239

U.S. DEPARTMENT OF HEALTH AND HUMAN SERVICES

http://www.hhs.gov/

U. S. PUBLIC HEALTH SERVICE-HEALTH RESOURCES AND SERVICES ADMINISTRATION, BUREAU OF HEALTH PROFESSIONS SCHOLARSHIPS FOR DISADVANTAGED STUDENTS
• See page 239

TRADE/TECHNICAL SPECIALTIES

AIRCRAFT ELECTRONICS ASSOCIATION EDUCATIONAL FOUNDATION

http://www.aea.net/

DUTCH AND GINGER ARVER SCHOLARSHIP
• See page 135

GARMIN-JERRY SMITH MEMORIAL SCHOLARSHIP
• See page 135

GARMIN SCHOLARSHIP
• See page 135

LEE TARBOX MEMORIAL SCHOLARSHIP
• See page 135

LOWELL GAYLOR MEMORIAL SCHOLARSHIP
• See page 135

MID-CONTINENT INSTRUMENT SCHOLARSHIP
• See page 136

ALBERTA HERITAGE SCHOLARSHIP FUND

http://www.alis.alberta.ca/

REGISTERED APPRENTICESHIP PROGRAM/CAREER AND TECHNOLOGIES STUDIES (RAPS/CTS) SCHOLARSHIPS

Scholarships of CAN$1000 available for high school graduates who are registered as apprentices in a trade while in high school to encourage recipients to continue their apprenticeship or occupational training programs after graduation. Must be a Canadian citizen or landed immigrant and Alberta resident. For more details see website http://alis.alberta.ca.

Academic Fields/Career Goals: Trade/Technical Specialties.

Award: Scholarship for use in freshman year; not renewable. *Number:* 500.

Eligibility Requirements: Applicant must be enrolled or expecting to enroll full-time at a technical institution and resident of Alberta. Available to Canadian citizens.

Application Requirements: Application form, essay, recommendations or references. *Deadline:* June 30.

Contact: Scholarship Committee
Phone: 780-427-8640
E-mail: scholarships@gov.ab.ca

AMERICAN CHEMICAL SOCIETY

http://www.acs.org/

AMERICAN CHEMICAL SOCIETY SCHOLARS PROGRAM
• See page 172

AMERICAN LEGION DEPARTMENT OF PENNSYLVANIA

http://www.pa-legion.com/

ROBERT W. VALIMONT ENDOWMENT FUND SCHOLARSHIP (PART II)

Scholarships for any Pennsylvania high school senior seeking admission to a two-year college, post-high school trade/technical school, or training program. Must attend school in Pennsylvania. Continuation of award is based on grades. Renewable award of $600. Number of awards varies from year to year. Membership in an American Legion post in Pennsylvania is not required, but it must be documented if it does apply.

Academic Fields/Career Goals: Trade/Technical Specialties.

Award: Scholarship for use in freshman year; renewable. *Amount:* $600.

Eligibility Requirements: Applicant must be high school student; planning to enroll or expecting to enroll full-time at a two-year or technical institution; resident of Pennsylvania and studying in Pennsylvania. Applicant must have 2.5 GPA or higher. Available to U.S. citizens.

Application Requirements: Application form, financial need analysis, test scores, transcript. *Deadline:* May 30.

Contact: Debbie Watson, Emblem Sales Supervisor
American Legion Department of Pennsylvania
PO Box 2324
Harrisburg, PA 17105-2324
Phone: 717-730-9100
Fax: 717-975-2836
E-mail: hq@pa-legion.com

AMERICAN SOCIETY OF CERTIFIED ENGINEERING TECHNICIANS

http://www.ascet.org/

KURT H. AND DONNA M. SCHULER SMALL GRANT
• *See page 176*

AMERICAN SOCIETY OF HEATING, REFRIGERATING, AND AIR CONDITIONING ENGINEERS, INC.

http://www.ashrae.org/

ALWIN B. NEWTON SCHOLARSHIP
• *See page 264*

ASHRAE GENERAL SCHOLARSHIPS
• *See page 276*

DUANE HANSON SCHOLARSHIP
• *See page 264*

FRANK M. CODA SCHOLARSHIP
• *See page 264*

HENRY ADAMS SCHOLARSHIP
• *See page 265*

LYNN G. BELLENGER SCHOLARSHIP
• *See page 265*

REUBEN TRANE SCHOLARSHIP
• *See page 265*

AMERICAN WELDING SOCIETY

http://www.aws.org/

AMERICAN WELDING SOCIETY DISTRICT SCHOLARSHIP PROGRAM
• *See page 277*

AMERICAN WELDING SOCIETY INTERNATIONAL SCHOLARSHIP
• *See page 277*

ARSHAM AMIRIKIAN ENGINEERING SCHOLARSHIP
• *See page 193*

DONALD F. HASTINGS SCHOLARSHIP
• *See page 277*

EDWARD J. BRADY MEMORIAL SCHOLARSHIP
• *See page 278*

HOWARD E. AND WILMA J. ADKINS MEMORIAL SCHOLARSHIP
• *See page 278*

MILLER ELECTRIC INTERNATIONAL WORLD SKILLS COMPETITION SCHOLARSHIP
• *See page 278*

MILLER ELECTRIC MFG. CO. SCHOLARSHIP
• *See page 278*

ASSOCIATED GENERAL CONTRACTORS EDUCATION AND RESEARCH FOUNDATION

http://www.agcfoundation.org/

WORKFORCE DEVELOPMENT SCHOLARSHIP
• *See page 221*

ENVIRONMENTAL CARE ASSOCIATION OF IDAHO

http://www.eacofidaho.org

ECA SCHOLARSHIP
• *See page 363*

FABRICATORS AND MANUFACTURERS ASSOCIATION FOUNDATION

http://www.nutsandboltsfoundation.org/scholarships/

COLLEGE AND TRADE/TECHNICAL SCHOOL SCHOLARSHIPS
• *See page 178*

GLOBAL AUTOMOTIVE AFTERMARKET SYMPOSIUM

http://www.automotivescholarships.com/

AUTOMOTIVE AFTERMARKET SCHOLARSHIP CENTRAL
• *See page 164*

IFDA EDUCATIONAL FOUNDATION

http://www.ifdaef.org/

IFDA STUDENT MEMBER SCHOLARSHIP
• *See page 376*

INTERNATIONAL EXECUTIVE HOUSEKEEPERS ASSOCIATION

http://www.ieha.org/

INTERNATIONAL EXECUTIVE HOUSEKEEPERS EDUCATIONAL FOUNDATION
• *See page 336*

MANUFACTURERS ASSOCIATION OF MAINE

http://www.mainemfg.com/

MAINE MANUFACTURING CAREER AND TRAINING FOUNDATION SCHOLARSHIP
• *See page 142*

MARYLAND STATE HIGHER EDUCATION COMMISSION

http://www.mhec.state.md.us/

CHARLES W. RILEY FIRE AND EMERGENCY MEDICAL SERVICES TUITION REIMBURSEMENT PROGRAM
• *See page 329*

MIDWEST ROOFING CONTRACTORS ASSOCIATION

http://www.mrca.org/

MRCA FOUNDATION SCHOLARSHIP PROGRAM
• See page 122

NATIONAL ASSOCIATION OF WATER COMPANIES-NEW JERSEY CHAPTER

http://www.nawc.org

NATIONAL ASSOCIATION OF WATER COMPANIES-NEW JERSEY CHAPTER SCHOLARSHIP
• See page 80

NATIONAL ASSOCIATION OF WOMEN IN CONSTRUCTION

http://www.nawic.org/

NAWIC CONSTRUCTION TRADES SCHOLARSHIP

Scholarship for women pursuing a trade apprenticeship program. Only for students attending school in the United States or Canada.

Academic Fields/Career Goals: Trade/Technical Specialties.

Award: Scholarship for use in sophomore or junior years; not renewable. *Number:* 1. *Amount:* $1000–$2000.

Eligibility Requirements: Applicant must be enrolled or expecting to enroll full-time at a technical institution. Available to U.S. and Canadian citizens.

Application Requirements: Application form, essay, transcript. *Deadline:* March 15.

Contact: Scholarship Committee
National Association of Women in Construction
327 South Adams Street
Fort Worth, TX 76104
Phone: 817-877-5551
Fax: 817-877-0324

NAWIC UNDERGRADUATE SCHOLARSHIPS
• See page 122

NATIONAL COUNCIL OF JEWISH WOMEN LOS ANGELES (NCJW L LA)

http://ncjwla.org/

SINGERMAN/NOSSECK MEMORIAL SCHOLARSHIP

To qualify a candidate must be enrolling or enrolled in a trade school (online course ok) that leads to certification (i.e. massage therapy, dental assistant, CNA), in order to learn a marketable skill which will lead to economic self-sufficiency. The scholarship is intended to ease the burden of the applicant starting or continuing their education, and is not limited to a particular field of study. The National Council of Jewish Women l Los Angeles (NCJW l LA) provides scholarships, regardless of race, ethnicity, religion, age, gender identity, sexuality or national origin to those who live and attend school in the Greater Los Angeles area, including Los Angeles, Orange, Riverside, and Ventura Counties.

Academic Fields/Career Goals: Trade/Technical Specialties.

Award: Scholarship for use in freshman, sophomore, junior, or senior years; not renewable. *Number:* 1. *Amount:* $1000.

Eligibility Requirements: Applicant must be enrolled or expecting to enroll full- or part-time at a technical institution; resident of California and studying in California. Available to U.S. citizens.

Application Requirements: Application form, essay, financial need analysis. *Deadline:* May 1.

Contact: Stephanie Flax, Scholarship and Program Coordinator
National Council of Jewish Women Los Angeles (NCJW l LA)
543 North Fairfax Avenue
Los Angeles, CA 90036
Phone: 323-852-8515
E-mail: scholarship@ncjwla.org

NEXTSTEPU

http://www.nextstepu.com/

$1,500 STEM SCHOLARSHIP
• See page 106

NORTH CAROLINA COMMUNITY COLLEGE SYSTEM-STUDENT DEVELOPMENT SERVICES

http://www.nccommunitycolleges.edu/student-services

WACHOVIA TECHNICAL SCHOLARSHIP PROGRAM

One scholarship per college valued at $500 each. These scholarships are distributed among the 58 colleges in the community college system, which may be distributed in two payments: fall semester, $250; and spring semester, $250. To qualify as a candidate for these scholarships, a person must meet the following criteria: 1. Is a full-time student enrolled in the second year of a two-year educational/technical program. 2. Demonstrate financial need. 3. Demonstrate scholastic promise. 4. Use the scholarship to pay for tuition, books, and transportation. The recipients of the scholarships will be selected each year from applicants meeting the above criteria at local colleges.

Academic Fields/Career Goals: Trade/Technical Specialties.

Award: Scholarship for use in freshman or sophomore years; not renewable. *Amount:* $500.

Eligibility Requirements: Applicant must be enrolled or expecting to enroll full-time at a two-year or technical institution; resident of North Carolina and studying in North Carolina. Available to U.S. citizens.

Application Requirements: Application form, essay. *Deadline:* continuous.

Contact: Charletta Sims Evans, Associate Director of Student Development Services
Phone: 919-807-7106
E-mail: simsc@nccommunitycolleges.edu

OREGON STUDENT ASSISTANCE COMMISSION

http://www.GetCollegeFunds.org/

DAVID L. MASSEE EDUCATION SCHOLARSHIP

Award for first-time freshmen and undergraduate students who are enrolled at least half time in trade or vocational programs in private or two-year public colleges in the U.S. Automatically renewable if renewal criteria is met.

Academic Fields/Career Goals: Trade/Technical Specialties.

Award: Scholarship for use in freshman, sophomore, junior, or senior years; not renewable.

Eligibility Requirements: Applicant must be enrolled or expecting to enroll full- or part-time at a two-year institution. Available to U.S. citizens.

Application Requirements: Application form. *Deadline:* March 1.

Contact: Melissa Adams, Scholarship Processing Coordinator
Phone: 541-687-7409
E-mail: melissa.adams@hecc.oregon.gov

JIM AND DIANNA MURPHY SCHOLARSHIP

Scholarship for graduates of Oregon high schools who are majoring in programs to become diesel mechanic/technician, driver/operator of commercial vehicle/bus/truck, and related areas leading to a career in the commercial trucking industry or in diesel technologies. Must enroll at least half-time at a Oregon two-year community college or for-profit school. Financial need may or may not be considered.

Academic Fields/Career Goals: Trade/Technical Specialties.

Award: Scholarship for use in freshman or sophomore years; not renewable.

Eligibility Requirements: Applicant must be enrolled or expecting to enroll full- or part-time at a two-year or technical institution and studying in Oregon. Available to U.S. citizens.

Application Requirements: Application form. *Deadline:* March 1.

Contact: Melissa Adams, Scholarship Processing Coordinator
Phone: 541-687-7409
E-mail: melissa.adams@hecc.oregon.gov

TECHNICAL TRAINING FUND SCHOLARSHIP
• *See page 130*

PLUMBING-HEATING-COOLING CONTRACTORS EDUCATION FOUNDATION

http://www.phccfoundation.org/scholarships

BRADFORD WHITE CORPORATION SCHOLARSHIP
• *See page 358*

DELTA FAUCET COMPANY SCHOLARSHIP PROGRAM
• *See page 167*

PHCC EDUCATIONAL FOUNDATION NEED-BASED SCHOLARSHIP
• *See page 167*

PHCC EDUCATIONAL FOUNDATION SCHOLARSHIP PROGRAM
• *See page 167*

PROFESSIONAL CONSTRUCTION ESTIMATORS ASSOCIATION

http://www.pcea.org/

TED G. WILSON MEMORIAL SCHOLARSHIP FOUNDATION
• *See page 197*

ROCKY MOUNTAIN COAL MINING INSTITUTE

http://www.rmcmi.org/

ROCKY MOUNTAIN COAL MINING INSTITUTE TECHNICAL SCHOLARSHIP

Scholarship for a first or second year student at a two-year technical/trade school in good standing at the time of selection. The student must be in a discipline related to potential use in the coal mining industry. Must be U.S. citizen and a legal resident of one of the Rocky Mountain Coal Mining Institute member states.

Academic Fields/Career Goals: Trade/Technical Specialties.

Award: Scholarship for use in freshman or sophomore years; not renewable. *Number:* 8. *Amount:* $1000.

Eligibility Requirements: Applicant must be enrolled or expecting to enroll full-time at a technical institution and resident of Arizona, Colorado, Montana, New Mexico, North Dakota, Texas, Utah, Wyoming. Available to U.S. citizens.

Application Requirements: Application form, essay, interview. *Deadline:* February 1.

Contact: Shahreen Salam, Executive Assistant
Rocky Mountain Coal Mining Institute
8057 South Yukon Way
Littleton, CO 80128-5510
Phone: 303-948-3300
Fax: 303-948-1132
E-mail: mail@rmcmi.org

SOCIETY OF MANUFACTURING ENGINEERS EDUCATION FOUNDATION

http://www.smeef.org/

CHAPTER 198-DOWNRIVER DETROIT SCHOLARSHIP
• *See page 307*

CHAPTER 67-PHOENIX SCHOLARSHIP
• *See page 307*

CLINTON J. HELTON MANUFACTURING SCHOLARSHIP AWARD FUND
• *See page 308*

E. WAYNE KAY COMMUNITY COLLEGE SCHOLARSHIP AWARD
• *See page 308*

E. WAYNE KAY SCHOLARSHIP
• *See page 309*

FORT WAYNE CHAPTER 56 SCHOLARSHIP
• *See page 309*

NORTH CENTRAL REGION 9 SCHOLARSHIP
• *See page 309*

WICHITA CHAPTER 52 SCHOLARSHIP
• *See page 310*

WILLIAM E. WEISEL SCHOLARSHIP FUND
• *See page 269*

SOCIETY OF PLASTICS ENGINEERS FOUNDATION (SPE)

http://www.4spe.org/

FLEMING/BASZCAK SCHOLARSHIP
• *See page 181*

GULF COAST HURRICANE SCHOLARSHIP
• *See page 181*

SOCIETY OF PLASTICS ENGINEERS SCHOLARSHIP PROGRAM
• *See page 182*

SPECIALTY EQUIPMENT MARKET ASSOCIATION

http://www.sema.org/

SEMA MEMORIAL SCHOLARSHIP FUND
• *See page 85*

STRAIGHTFORWARD MEDIA

http://www.straightforwardmedia.com/

STRAIGHTFORWARD MEDIA VOCATIONAL-TECHNICAL SCHOOL SCHOLARSHIP
• *See page 107*

TRUCKER TO TRUCKER, LLC

http://www.truckertotrucker.com/

TRUCKER TO TRUCKER SCHOLARSHIP

$500 Scholarship to attend a commercial driver's training program in the US. Applicants will need to fill out a short online application and upload a 300-500 word essay.

Academic Fields/Career Goals: Trade/Technical Specialties.

Award: Scholarship for use in freshman, sophomore, junior, or senior years; not renewable. *Number:* 2. *Amount:* $500.

Eligibility Requirements: Applicant must be age 18-99 and enrolled or expecting to enroll full-time at a technical institution. Available to U.S. citizens.

Application Requirements: Application form, essay. *Deadline:* November 15.

Contact: Scholarship Coordinator
E-mail: scholarship@truckertotrucker.com

UNITED COMMUNITY SERVICES FOR WORKING FAMILIES

http://www.ucswf.org

RONALD LORAH MEMORIAL SCHOLARSHIP

One-time award available to a union member, spouse of a union member, or child of a union member. Must be a resident of Pennsylvania. Must submit essay that is clear, concise, persuasive and show an understanding of unions.

Academic Fields/Career Goals: Trade/Technical Specialties.

Award: Scholarship for use in freshman, sophomore, junior, or senior years; not renewable. *Number:* 2. *Amount:* $500–$750.

Eligibility Requirements: Applicant must be enrolled or expecting to enroll full-time at a two-year or four-year or technical institution or university and resident of Pennsylvania. Applicant or parent of applicant must be member of AFL-CIO. Available to U.S. citizens.

Application Requirements: Application form, essay, financial need analysis, transcript. *Deadline:* July 31.

Contact: Victoria Henshaw, Executive Director
United Community Services for Working Families
1251 North Front Street
Reading, PA 19601
E-mail: vhenshaw@ucswf.org

VERMONT SPACE GRANT CONSORTIUM

http://www.cems.uvm.edu/vsgc

VERMONT SPACE GRANT CONSORTIUM
• See page 96

WOMEN IN LOGISTICS, NORTHERN CALIFORNIA

http://www.womeninlogistics.org/

WOMEN IN LOGISTICS SCHOLARSHIP
• See page 170

WOMEN'S JEWELRY ASSOCIATION

http://www.womensjewelryassociation.com

WOMEN'S JEWELRY ASSOCIATION STUDENT SCHOLARSHIP
• See page 132

WYOMING TRUCKING ASSOCIATION SCHOLARSHIP FUND TRUST

http://www.wytruck.org/

WYOMING TRUCKING ASSOCIATION SCHOLARSHIP TRUST FUND
• See page 87

YOUTH MARITIME TRAINING ASSOCIATION

http://ymta.net/

NORM MANLY—YMTA MARITIME EDUCATIONAL SCHOLARSHIPS
• See page 402

TRANSPORTATION

AMERICAN BUS ASSOCIATION

https://www.buses.org/

ABA ACADEMIC MERIT SCHOLARSHIPS

Academic Merit Scholarships are open to both ABA and non-ABA Members. The applicant must be a freshman, sophomore; junior, senior, or graduate student at an accredited University (4-year university/college or junior college) and must have a declared major or course of study relevant to the transportation, travel and tourism industry and must possess a cumulative GPA of 3.4 or higher. Two scholarships are awarded, in the amount $5,000 each. Apply online between December 7th and April 6th. Create an account to submit applications, as well as check the status of your applications and make any necessary changes before the program deadline.

Academic Fields/Career Goals: Transportation; Travel/Tourism.

Award: Scholarship for use in freshman, sophomore, junior, senior, graduate, or postgraduate years; not renewable. *Number:* 2. *Amount:* $5000.

Eligibility Requirements: Applicant must be enrolled or expecting to enroll full-time at a four-year institution. Applicant must have 3.5 GPA or higher. Available to U.S. and Canadian citizens.

Application Requirements: Application form, essay. *Deadline:* April 6.

Contact: Zoe Deloglos, Special Projects Coordinator
American Bus Association
111 K Street NE
9th Floor
Washington, DC 20002
Phone: 202-202-218-7222
Fax: 202-202-842-0850
E-mail: zdeloglos@buses.org

ABA DIVERSITY SCHOLARSHIPS

The Diversity Scholarship focuses on broadening the number of traditionally underrepresented groups in the management and operation ranks of the transportation, travel, and tourism industry. Eligible candidates must have completed, at a minimum, their first year of college at an accredited university; must have a declared major or course of study relevant to the transportation, travel, and tourism industry; and must have a cumulative 3.0 GPA. Applicants are required to submit a 500-word essay discussing the role they hope to play in advancing the future of the transportation, motorcoach, travel, and tourism/hospitality industry.

Academic Fields/Career Goals: Transportation; Travel/Tourism.

Award: Scholarship for use in sophomore, junior, or senior years; not renewable. *Number:* 1. *Amount:* $5000.

Eligibility Requirements: Applicant must be enrolled or expecting to enroll full-time at an institution or university. Applicant must have 3.0 GPA or higher. Available to U.S. and Canadian citizens.

Application Requirements: Application form, essay. *Deadline:* April 6.

Contact: Zoe Deloglos, Special Projects Coordinator
American Bus Association
111 K Street NE
9th Floor
Washington, DC 20002
Phone: 202-202-218-7222
Fax: 202-202-842-0850
E-mail: zdeloglos@buses.org

AMERICAN COUNCIL OF ENGINEERING COMPANIES OF PENNSYLVANIA (ACEC/PA)

http://www.acecpa.org/

ERIC J. GENNUSO AND LEROY D. (BUD) LOY, JR. SCHOLARSHIP PROGRAM
• See page 173

AMERICAN INDIAN SCIENCE AND ENGINEERING SOCIETY

http://www.aises.org/

A.T. ANDERSON MEMORIAL SCHOLARSHIP PROGRAM
• See page 109

AMERICAN PUBLIC TRANSPORTATION FOUNDATION

http://www.apta.com/

DAN REICHARD JR. SCHOLARSHIP
• See page 161

DR. GEORGE M. SMERK SCHOLARSHIP

Scholarship for study towards a career in career in public transit management. Must be sponsored by APTA member organization. Minimum GPA of 3.0 required. College sophomores (30 hours or more satisfactorily completed), juniors, seniors, or those seeking advanced degrees may apply.

Academic Fields/Career Goals: Transportation.

Award: Scholarship for use in sophomore, junior, senior, or graduate years; not renewable. *Number:* 1. *Amount:* $2500.

Eligibility Requirements: Applicant must be enrolled or expecting to enroll full-time at a two-year or four-year institution or university. Applicant must have 3.0 GPA or higher. Available to U.S. citizens.

Application Requirements: Application form, essay, financial need analysis, recommendations or references, test scores, transcript, verification of enrollment for the fall semester, copy of fee schedule from the college/university. *Deadline:* June 16.

Contact: Pamela Boswell, Vice President of Program Management
American Public Transportation Foundation
1666 K Street, NW
Washington, DC 20006-1215
Phone: 202-496-4803
Fax: 202-496-2323
E-mail: pboswell@apta.com

DONALD C. HYDE ESSAY PROGRAM

Award of $500 for the best response to the required essay component of the program.

Academic Fields/Career Goals: Transportation.

Award: Prize for use in sophomore, junior, senior, or graduate years; not renewable. *Number:* 1. *Amount:* $500.

Eligibility Requirements: Applicant must be enrolled or expecting to enroll full-time at a two-year or four-year institution or university. Applicant must have 3.0 GPA or higher. Available to U.S. and Canadian citizens.

Application Requirements: Application form, entry in a contest, essay, financial need analysis, recommendations or references, transcript. *Deadline:* June 16.

Contact: Pamela Boswell, Vice President of Program Management
American Public Transportation Foundation
1666 K Street, NW
Washington, DC 20006-1215
Phone: 202-496-4803
Fax: 202-496-2323
E-mail: pboswell@apta.com

JACK GILSTRAP SCHOLARSHIP
• See page 291

PARSONS BRINCKERHOFF-JIM LAMMIE SCHOLARSHIP

Scholarship for study in public transportation engineering field. Must be sponsored by APTA member organization and complete internship with APTA member organization. Minimum GPA of 3.0 required.

Academic Fields/Career Goals: Transportation.

Award: Scholarship for use in sophomore, junior, senior, or graduate years; renewable. *Number:* 1. *Amount:* $2500.

Eligibility Requirements: Applicant must be enrolled or expecting to enroll full-time at a two-year or four-year institution or university. Applicant must have 3.0 GPA or higher. Available to U.S. and Canadian citizens.

Application Requirements: Application form, essay, financial need analysis, recommendations or references, transcript, verification of enrollment for the current year and copy of fee schedule from the college/university. *Deadline:* June 16.

Contact: Pamela Boswell, Vice President of Program Management
American Public Transportation Foundation
1666 K Street, NW
Washington, DC 20006-1215
Phone: 202-496-4803
Fax: 202-496-2323
E-mail: pboswell@apta.com

TRANSIT HALL OF FAME SCHOLARSHIP AWARD PROGRAM
• See page 191

AMERICAN SOCIETY OF CERTIFIED ENGINEERING TECHNICIANS

http://www.ascet.org/

KURT H. AND DONNA M. SCHULER SMALL GRANT
• See page 176

ASSOCIATED GENERAL CONTRACTORS OF NEW YORK STATE, LLC

http://www.agcnys.org/

ASSOCIATED GENERAL CONTRACTORS NYS SCHOLARSHIP PROGRAM
• See page 194

AUTOMOTIVE WOMEN'S ALLIANCE FOUNDATION

http://www.awafoundation.org/index.php

AUTOMOTIVE WOMEN'S ALLIANCE FOUNDATION SCHOLARSHIPS
• See page 74

LOGISTICS & TRANSPORTATION ASSOCIATION OF NORTH AMERICA

http://www.ltna.org

ALICE GLAISYER WARFIELD MEMORIAL SCHOLARSHIP

Award is available to currently enrolled students majoring in transportation, logistics, traffic management, or related fields. Available to citizens of the United States, Canada, and Mexico. See website for application, http://www.transportationclubinternational.com/.

Academic Fields/Career Goals: Transportation.

Award: Scholarship for use in freshman, sophomore, junior, or senior years; not renewable. *Number:* 1. *Amount:* $1500.

Eligibility Requirements: Applicant must be enrolled or expecting to enroll full- or part-time at a two-year or four-year or technical institution or university. Applicant or parent of applicant must be member of Transportation Club International. Available to U.S. and non-U.S. citizens.

Application Requirements: Application form, essay, personal photograph, recommendations or references, transcript. *Deadline:* April 30.

Contact: Katie deJonge, Executive Director
Phone: 360-898-3344
E-mail: executive.director@ltna.org

DENNY LYDIC SCHOLARSHIP

Award is available to currently enrolled college students majoring in transportation, logistics, traffic management, or related fields. Available to citizens of the United States, Canada, and Mexico. See website for application, http://www.transportationclubsinternational.com/.

Academic Fields/Career Goals: Transportation.

Award: Scholarship for use in freshman, sophomore, junior, or senior years; not renewable. *Number:* 1. *Amount:* $1000.

Eligibility Requirements: Applicant must be enrolled or expecting to enroll full- or part-time at a two-year or four-year or technical institution or university. Applicant or parent of applicant must be member of Transportation Club International. Available to U.S. and non-U.S. citizens.

Application Requirements: Application form, essay, personal photograph, recommendations or references, transcript. *Deadline:* April 30.

Contact: Katie deJonge, Executive Director
  Phone: 360-898-3344
  E-mail: executive.director@ltna.org

TEXAS TRANSPORTATION SCHOLARSHIP

Merit-based award for a student who is at least a sophomore studying transportation, traffic management, and related fields. Must have been enrolled in a school in Texas during some phase of education (elementary, secondary, high school). Must include photo and submit three references. One-time scholarship of $1000. See website for application http://www.transportationclubsinternational.com/.

Academic Fields/Career Goals: Transportation.

Award: Scholarship for use in sophomore, junior, or senior years; not renewable. *Number:* 1. *Amount:* $1000.

Eligibility Requirements: Applicant must be enrolled or expecting to enroll full- or part-time at a two-year or four-year or technical institution or university. Applicant or parent of applicant must be member of Transportation Club International. Available to U.S. citizens.

Application Requirements: Application form, essay, personal photograph, recommendations or references, transcript. *Deadline:* April 30.

Contact: Katie deJonge, Executive Director
  Phone: 360-898-3344
  E-mail: executive.director@ltna.org

TRANSPORTATION CLUBS INTERNATIONAL CHARLOTTE WOODS SCHOLARSHIP

Award available to an enrolled college student majoring in transportation or traffic management. Must be a member or a dependent of a member of Transportation Clubs International. Must have completed at least one year of post-high school education. One-time award of $1000. See website for application http://www.transportationclubsinternational.com/.

Academic Fields/Career Goals: Transportation.

Award: Scholarship for use in freshman, sophomore, junior, or senior years; not renewable. *Number:* 1. *Amount:* $1000.

Eligibility Requirements: Applicant must be enrolled or expecting to enroll full- or part-time at a two-year or four-year or technical institution or university. Applicant or parent of applicant must be member of Transportation Club International. Available to U.S. and non-U.S. citizens.

Application Requirements: Application form, essay, personal photograph, recommendations or references, transcript. *Deadline:* April 30.

Contact: Crystal Hunter, Program Manager
  Phone: 800-377-2401
  E-mail: awards@goldenkey.org

TRANSPORTATION CLUBS INTERNATIONAL FRED A. HOOPER MEMORIAL SCHOLARSHIP

• *See page 282*

TRANSPORTATION CLUBS INTERNATIONAL GINGER AND FRED DEINES CANADA SCHOLARSHIP

One-time award for a student of Canadian heritage, who is attending college or university in Canada or the United States and majoring in transportation, traffic management, logistics, or a related field. Academic merit is considered. See website for application http://www.transportationclubsinternational.com/.

Academic Fields/Career Goals: Transportation.

Award: Scholarship for use in freshman, sophomore, junior, or senior years; not renewable. *Number:* 1. *Amount:* $1500.

Eligibility Requirements: Applicant must be of Canadian heritage and Canadian citizen and enrolled or expecting to enroll full- or part-time at a two-year or four-year or technical institution or university. Applicant or parent of applicant must be member of Transportation Club International.

Application Requirements: Application form, essay, personal photograph, recommendations or references, transcript. *Deadline:* April 30.

Contact: Katie deJonge, Executive Director
  Phone: 360-898-3344
  E-mail: executive.director@ltna.org

TRANSPORTATION CLUBS INTERNATIONAL GINGER AND FRED DEINES MEXICO SCHOLARSHIP

Scholarship of $2000 for a Mexican student who is enrolled in an accredited institution of higher learning in a vocational or degree program in the fields of transportation, logistics or traffic management, or related fields. May be enrolled in a U.S. or Canadian institution. See website for application http://www.transportationclubsinternational.com/.

Academic Fields/Career Goals: Transportation.

Award: Scholarship for use in freshman, sophomore, junior, or senior years; not renewable. *Number:* 1. *Amount:* $2000.

Eligibility Requirements: Applicant must be Mexican citizen and enrolled or expecting to enroll full- or part-time at a two-year or four-year or technical institution or university. Applicant or parent of applicant must be member of Transportation Club International. Available to Canadian and non-U.S. citizens.

Application Requirements: Application form, essay, personal photograph, recommendations or references, transcript. *Deadline:* April 30.

Contact: Katie deJonge, Executive Director
  Phone: 360-898-3344
  E-mail: executive.director@ltna.org

NATIONAL CUSTOMS BROKERS AND FORWARDERS ASSOCIATION OF AMERICA

http://www.ncbfaa.org/

NATIONAL CUSTOMS BROKERS AND FORWARDERS ASSOCIATION OF AMERICA SCHOLARSHIP AWARD

One-time award for employees of National Customs Broker & Forwarders Association of America, Inc. (NCBFAA) regular member organizations and their children. Must be studying transportation logistics or international trade full time. Require minimum 2.0 GPA.

Academic Fields/Career Goals: Transportation.

Award: Scholarship for use in freshman, sophomore, junior, or senior years; not renewable. *Number:* 1. *Amount:* $5000.

Eligibility Requirements: Applicant must be enrolled or expecting to enroll full-time at a four-year institution or university. Available to U.S. citizens.

Application Requirements: Essay. *Deadline:* January 8.

Contact: Mr. Tom Mathers, Director, Communications
  National Customs Brokers and Forwarders Association of
    America
  1200 18th Street, NW, Suite 901
  Washington, DC 20036
  Phone: 202-466-0222
  E-mail: tom@ncbfaa.org

OREGON STUDENT ASSISTANCE COMMISSION

http://www.GetCollegeFunds.org/

WESTERN ASSOCIATION OF STATE HIGHWAY AND TRANSPORTATION OFFICIALS SCHOLARSHIP

Award for students planning to enroll at least part-time as college juniors or above for fall term/semester at any four-year college or university.

Career interest preference for transportation or a transportation-related field. Apply/compete annually.

Academic Fields/Career Goals: Transportation.

Award: Scholarship for use in junior or senior years; not renewable.

Eligibility Requirements: Applicant must be enrolled or expecting to enroll full- or part-time at a four-year institution or university and resident of Oregon. Applicant must have 3.0 GPA or higher. Available to U.S. citizens.

Application Requirements: Application form, essay, financial need analysis. *Deadline:* March 1.

Contact: Melissa Adams, Scholarship Processing Coordinator
Phone: 541-687-7409
E-mail: melissa.adams@hecc.oregon.gov

PLAN NEW HAMPSHIRE

www.plannh.org

PLAN NEW HAMPSHIRE SCHOLARSHIP AND PROGRAM
• *See page 123*

SPECIALTY EQUIPMENT MARKET ASSOCIATION

http://www.sema.org/

SEMA MEMORIAL SCHOLARSHIP FUND
• *See page 85*

TRANSPORTATION ASSOCIATION OF CANADA FOUNDATION

http://www.tac-foundation.ca

TAC FOUNDATION SCHOLARSHIPS

Candidates must be Canadian citizens or permanent residents; be enrolled at a post-secondary institution (university or college) in an academic program related to the planning, design, construction, operations, maintenance and program management of transportation infrastructure, including urban transit. Students are limited to one TAC Foundation scholarship at each stage of their education (community college, university undergraduate, graduate). TAC Foundation entrance scholarships are not included in this restriction. Must have achieved an overall B average or equivalent average mark in their previous academic year and may apply for and receive scholarships from other sources.

Academic Fields/Career Goals: Transportation; Urban and Regional Planning.

Award: Scholarship for use in senior or graduate years; not renewable. *Number:* 30–45. *Amount:* $2500–$5000.

Eligibility Requirements: Applicant must be Canadian citizen; enrolled or expecting to enroll full-time at a two-year or four-year institution or university and resident of Alberta, British Columbia, Manitoba, New Brunswick, Newfoundland, Northwest Territories, Nova Scotia, Ontario, Prince Edward Island, Quebec, Saskatchewan, Yukon. Applicant must have 3.0 GPA or higher.

Application Requirements: Application form. *Deadline:* February 29.

Contact: Ms. Erica Andersen, Secretary-Treasurer
Phone: 613-736-1350 Ext. 235
Fax: 613-736-1395
E-mail: foundation@tac-atc.ca

TRUCKLOAD CARRIERS ASSOCIATION

http://www.truckload.org/

TRUCKLOAD CARRIERS ASSOCIATION SCHOLARSHIP FUND
• *See page 168*

WOMEN IN LOGISTICS, NORTHERN CALIFORNIA

http://www.womeninlogistics.org/

WOMEN IN LOGISTICS SCHOLARSHIP
• *See page 170*

WYOMING TRUCKING ASSOCIATION SCHOLARSHIP FUND TRUST

http://www.wytruck.org/

WYOMING TRUCKING ASSOCIATION SCHOLARSHIP TRUST FUND
• *See page 87*

TRAVEL/TOURISM

AMERICAN BUS ASSOCIATION

https://www.buses.org/

ABA ACADEMIC MERIT SCHOLARSHIPS
• *See page 516*

ABA DIVERSITY SCHOLARSHIPS
• *See page 516*

AMERICAN HOTEL AND LODGING EDUCATIONAL FOUNDATION

http://www.ahlef.org/

AH&LEF ANNUAL SCHOLARSHIP GRANT PROGRAM
• *See page 227*

AMERICAN HOTEL & LODGING EDUCATIONAL FOUNDATION PEPSI SCHOLARSHIP
• *See page 228*

ECOLAB SCHOLARSHIP PROGRAM
• *See page 228*

HYATT HOTELS FUND FOR MINORITY LODGING MANAGEMENT
• *See page 228*

INCOMING FRESHMAN SCHOLARSHIPS
• *See page 228*

RAMA SCHOLARSHIP FOR THE AMERICAN DREAM
• *See page 228*

AMERICAN SOCIETY OF TRAVEL AGENTS (ASTA) FOUNDATION

http://asta.org/scholarships/

AMERICAN EXPRESS TRAVEL SCHOLARSHIP

Candidate must be enrolled in a travel or tourism program as an incoming freshman in either a two- or four-year college or university located in the United States or Canada. Student must have graduated from an Academic of Hospitality and tourism program through their high school. Minimum 3.0 GPA required

Academic Fields/Career Goals: Travel/Tourism.

Award: Scholarship for use in freshman year; not renewable. *Number:* up to 1. *Amount:* $2000–$2000.

www.petersons.com 519

Eligibility Requirements: Applicant must be high school student and planning to enroll or expecting to enroll full-time at a two-year or four-year institution or university. Applicant must have 3.0 GPA or higher. Available to U.S. and Canadian citizens.

Application Requirements: 500-word paper detailing the student's plans in travel, application form, recommendations or references, resume, transcript. *Deadline:* July 31.

Contact: Amanda DAiuto, Student Program Manager
American Society of Travel Agents (ASTA) Foundation
275 Turnpike Street, Suite 307
Canton, MA 02021
Phone: 781-821-5990
E-mail: scholarships@tourismcares.org

ARIZONA CHAPTER GOLD SCHOLARSHIP

One-time award for college undergraduates who are Arizona residents pursuing a travel or tourism degree at a four-year Arizona institution. Freshmen are not eligible. Must submit essay on career plans and interests. Minimum 2.5 GPA required. Must be a U.S. citizen or Canadian citizen.

Academic Fields/Career Goals: Travel/Tourism.

Award: Scholarship for use in sophomore, junior, or senior years; not renewable. *Number:* 1. *Amount:* $3000.

Eligibility Requirements: Applicant must be enrolled or expecting to enroll full- or part-time at a four-year institution or university; resident of Arizona and studying in Arizona. Applicant must have 2.5 GPA or higher. Available to U.S. and Canadian citizens.

Application Requirements: Application form, recommendations or references, transcript. *Deadline:* July 31.

Contact: Verlette Mitchell, Manager
American Society of Travel Agents (ASTA) Foundation
1101 King Street
Alexandria, VA 22314-2187
Phone: 703-739-8721
Fax: 703-684-8319
E-mail: scholarship@astahq.com

AVIS SCHOLARSHIP

Scholarship of $2000 for individuals who have already gained experience and/or training in the travel industry. Candidate must have a minimum of two years of full-time travel industry experience or an undergraduate degree in travel/tourism and must currently be employed in the travel industry. Must be enrolled in a minimum of two courses per semester in an accredited undergraduate or graduate level degree program in business, or equivalent degree program. Minimum GPA of 3.0 required.

Academic Fields/Career Goals: Travel/Tourism.

Award: Scholarship for use in freshman, sophomore, junior, senior, or graduate years; renewable. *Number:* 1. *Amount:* $2000.

Eligibility Requirements: Applicant must be enrolled or expecting to enroll full- or part-time at a four-year institution or university. Applicant must have 3.0 GPA or higher. Available to U.S. and Canadian citizens.

Application Requirements: Application form, proof of current employment in the travel industry, recommendations or references, transcript. *Deadline:* July 31.

Contact: Verlette Mitchell, Manager
American Society of Travel Agents (ASTA) Foundation
1101 King Street
Alexandria, VA 22314-2187
Phone: 703-739-8721
Fax: 703-684-8319
E-mail: scholarship@astahq.com

GEORGE REINKE SCHOLARSHIPS

Applicant must write a 500-word essay on career goals in the travel or tourism industry. Must be a U.S. citizen living and studying in the United States and enrolled in a travel agent studies program in a junior college or travel school. Must have a minimum GPA of 2.5.

Academic Fields/Career Goals: Travel/Tourism.

Award: Scholarship for use in freshman or sophomore years; not renewable. *Number:* up to 6. *Amount:* $2000.

Eligibility Requirements: Applicant must be enrolled or expecting to enroll full- or part-time at a two-year institution. Applicant must have 2.5 GPA or higher. Available to U.S. citizens.

Application Requirements: 500-word paper entitled "My Objectives in the Travel Agency Industry", application form, recommendations or references, transcript. *Deadline:* July 31.

Contact: Verlette Mitchell, Manager
American Society of Travel Agents (ASTA) Foundation
1101 King Street
Alexandria, VA 22314-2187
Phone: 703-739-8721
Fax: 703-684-8319
E-mail: scholarship@astahq.com

HOLLAND-AMERICA LINE WESTOURS SCHOLARSHIPS

Students must write 500-word essay on the future of the cruise industry and must be enrolled in travel or tourism program at a two- or four-year college or proprietary travel school. Minimum 2.5 GPA required. Must be a U.S. or Canadian citizen.

Academic Fields/Career Goals: Travel/Tourism.

Award: Scholarship for use in freshman, sophomore, junior, or senior years; not renewable. *Number:* 2. *Amount:* $3000.

Eligibility Requirements: Applicant must be enrolled or expecting to enroll full- or part-time at a two-year or four-year institution or university. Applicant must have 2.5 GPA or higher. Available to U.S. and Canadian citizens.

Application Requirements: 500-word paper on the future of the cruise industry, application form, financial need analysis, recommendations or references, resume, transcript. *Deadline:* July 31.

Contact: Verlette Mitchell, Manager
American Society of Travel Agents (ASTA) Foundation
1101 King Street
Alexandria, VA 22314-2187
Phone: 703-739-8721
Fax: 703-684-8319
E-mail: scholarship@astahq.com

JOSEPH R. STONE SCHOLARSHIPS

One-time award for high school senior or college undergraduate pursuing a travel or tourism degree. Must have a parent in the industry and proof of employment. Must submit a 500-word essay explaining career goals. Minimum 2.5 GPA required. Must be a citizen of United States or Canada.

Academic Fields/Career Goals: Travel/Tourism.

Award: Scholarship for use in freshman, sophomore, junior, or senior years; not renewable. *Number:* 3. *Amount:* $2400.

Eligibility Requirements: Applicant must be enrolled or expecting to enroll full- or part-time at a four-year institution or university. Applicant must have 2.5 GPA or higher. Available to U.S. and Canadian citizens.

Application Requirements: 500-word paper on applicant's goals, application form, recommendations or references, transcript. *Deadline:* July 31.

Contact: Verlette Mitchell, Manager
American Society of Travel Agents (ASTA) Foundation
1101 King Street
Alexandria, VA 22314-2187
Phone: 703-739-8721
Fax: 703-684-8319
E-mail: scholarship@astahq.com

NORTHERN CALIFORNIA CHAPTER RICHARD EPPING SCHOLARSHIP

Scholarship of $2000. Applicant must be currently enrolled in a travel and tourism curriculum at a college, university, or proprietary travel and tourism school in Northern California or Northern Nevada. Minimum 2.5 GPA required. Must be a U.S. or Canadian citizen.

Academic Fields/Career Goals: Travel/Tourism.

Award: Scholarship for use in freshman, sophomore, junior, or senior years; not renewable. *Number:* 1. *Amount:* $2000.

Eligibility Requirements: Applicant must be enrolled or expecting to enroll full- or part-time at a two-year or four-year institution or university and studying in California, Nevada. Applicant must have 2.5 GPA or higher. Available to U.S. and Canadian citizens.

Application Requirements: Application form, essay, recommendations or references, transcript. *Deadline:* July 31.

Contact: Verlette Mitchell, Manager
American Society of Travel Agents (ASTA) Foundation
1101 King Street
Alexandria, VA 22314-2187
Phone: 703-739-8721
Fax: 703-684-8319
E-mail: scholarship@astahq.com

PACIFIC NORTHWEST CHAPTER-WILLIAM HUNT SCHOLARSHIP FUND

One-time award for travel professionals. Applicant must be employed in the travel industry in an ASTA office or enrolled in a travel and tourism program in either a two- or four-year college, university or proprietary travel school. Must be a resident of and studying in one of the following states: Alaska, Idaho, Montana, Oregon, or Washington. Must be a U.S. or Canadian citizen. Must have a minimum of 2.5 GPA.

Academic Fields/Career Goals: Travel/Tourism.

Award: Scholarship for use in freshman, sophomore, junior, or senior years; not renewable. *Number:* up to 3. *Amount:* up to $1000.

Eligibility Requirements: Applicant must be enrolled or expecting to enroll full- or part-time at a two-year or four-year or technical institution or university; resident of Alaska, Idaho, Montana, Oregon, Washington and studying in Alaska, Idaho, Montana, Oregon, Washington. Applicant or parent of applicant must be member of American Society of Travel Agents. Applicant must have 2.5 GPA or higher. Available to U.S. and Canadian citizens.

Application Requirements: 300-word letter explaining reasons for interest in further training in travel, application form, essay, recommendations or references, transcript. *Deadline:* July 31.

Contact: Verlette Mitchell, Manager
American Society of Travel Agents (ASTA) Foundation
1101 King Street
Alexandria, VA 22314-2187
Phone: 703-739-8721
Fax: 703-684-8319
E-mail: scholarship@astahq.com

PRINCESS CRUISES AND PRINCESS TOURS SCHOLARSHIP

Merit-based award for student accepted or enrolled as an undergraduate in a travel or tourism program. Submit 300-word essay on two features cruise ships will need to offer passengers in the next ten years. Minimum 2.5 GPA required. Must be a U.S. citizen or Canadian citizen.

Academic Fields/Career Goals: Travel/Tourism.

Award: Scholarship for use in freshman, sophomore, junior, or senior years; not renewable. *Number:* 2. *Amount:* $2000.

Eligibility Requirements: Applicant must be enrolled or expecting to enroll full- or part-time at a two-year or four-year institution or university. Applicant must have 2.5 GPA or higher. Available to U.S. and Canadian citizens.

Application Requirements: 300-word paper on the two features cruise ships will need to offer passengers in the next ten years, application form, recommendations or references, transcript. *Deadline:* July 31.

Contact: Verlette Mitchell, Manager
American Society of Travel Agents (ASTA) Foundation
1101 King Street
Alexandria, VA 22314-2187
Phone: 703-739-8721
Fax: 703-684-8319
E-mail: scholarship@astahq.com

SOUTHERN CALIFORNIA CHAPTER/PLEASANT HAWAIIAN HOLIDAYS SCHOLARSHIP

Two awards for students pursuing travel or tourism degrees. One award given to student attending college in southern California, and one award given to a student attending school anywhere in the United States. Applicant must be U.S. citizens. Minimum 2.5 GPA required.

Academic Fields/Career Goals: Travel/Tourism.

Award: Scholarship for use in freshman, sophomore, junior, or senior years; not renewable. *Number:* 2. *Amount:* $2500.

Eligibility Requirements: Applicant must be enrolled or expecting to enroll full- or part-time at a four-year institution or university. Applicant must have 2.5 GPA or higher. Available to U.S. citizens.

Application Requirements: 500-word paper entitled "My Goals in the Travel Industry", application form, recommendations or references, transcript. *Deadline:* July 31.

Contact: Verlette Mitchell, Manager
American Society of Travel Agents (ASTA) Foundation
1101 King Street
Alexandria, VA 22314-2187
Phone: 703-739-8721
Fax: 703-684-8319
E-mail: scholarship@astahq.com

STAN AND LEONE POLLARD SCHOLARSHIPS

Candidate must be re-entering the job market by being enrolled in a travel and tourism curriculum in either a recognized proprietary travel school or a two-year junior college. Two awards of $2000 each will be given. Must have a minimum GPA of 2.5 and be a U.S. or Canadian citizen.

Academic Fields/Career Goals: Travel/Tourism.

Award: Scholarship for use in freshman or sophomore years; not renewable. *Number:* 2. *Amount:* $2000.

Eligibility Requirements: Applicant must be enrolled or expecting to enroll full- or part-time at a two-year or technical institution. Applicant must have 2.5 GPA or higher. Available to U.S. and Canadian citizens.

Application Requirements: 500-word paper on the student's objectives in the travel and tourism industry, application form, recommendations or references, transcript. *Deadline:* July 31.

Contact: Verlette Mitchell, Manager
American Society of Travel Agents (ASTA) Foundation
1101 King Street
Alexandria, VA 22314-2187
Phone: 703-739-8721
Fax: 703-684-8319
E-mail: scholarship@astahq.com

COSTA RICAN VACATIONS

http://www.vacationscostarica.com/

COSTA RICAN VACATIONS SCHOLARSHIP
• *See page 320*

HAWAII LODGING & TOURISM ASSOCIATION

www.hawaiilodging.org

R.W. "BOB" HOLDEN SCHOLARSHIP
• *See page 368*

HOMEKITCHENARY

http://homekitchenary.com

SHARE YOUR STORY WITH HOMEKITCHENARY
• *See page 331*

INTERNATIONAL AIRLINES TRAVEL AGENT NETWORK

http://www.iatan.org/

IATAN RONALD A SANTANA SCHOLARSHIP
• *See page 369*

MISSOURI TRAVEL COUNCIL

http://www.missouritravel.com/

BOB SMITH TOURISM SCHOLARSHIP
• *See page 336*

OHIO TRAVEL ASSOCIATION

http://www.ohiotravel.org/

BILL SCHWARTZ MEMORIAL SCHOLARSHIP
• *See page 369*

TOURISM CARES

http://www.tourismcares.org.

NEW HORIZONS KATHY LETARTE SCHOLARSHIP
• *See page 337*

PAT AND JIM HOST SCHOLARSHIP
• *See page 370*

UNITED NEGRO COLLEGE FUND

http://www.uncf.org/

UNCF/CARNIVAL CORPORATE SCHOLARS PROGRAM
• *See page 170*

TV/RADIO BROADCASTING

ADC RESEARCH INSTITUTE

http://www.adc.org/

JACK SHAHEEN MASS COMMUNICATIONS SCHOLARSHIP AWARD
• *See page 200*

ALABAMA BROADCASTERS ASSOCIATION

http://www.al-ba.com/

ALABAMA BROADCASTERS ASSOCIATION SCHOLARSHIP

Scholarship available to Alabama residents studying broadcasting at any accredited Alabama technical school, 2- or 4-year college, or university.

Academic Fields/Career Goals: TV/Radio Broadcasting.

Award: Scholarship for use in junior or senior years; not renewable. *Number:* up to 4. *Amount:* up to $2500.

Eligibility Requirements: Applicant must be enrolled or expecting to enroll full-time at a two-year or four-year or technical institution or university; resident of Alabama and studying in Alabama. Available to U.S. citizens.

Application Requirements: Application form, recommendations or references. *Deadline:* April 30.

Contact: Sharon Tinsley, President
   Phone: 205-982-5001
   Fax: 205-982-0015
   E-mail: stinsley@al-ba.com

ALBERTA HERITAGE SCHOLARSHIP FUND

http://www.alis.alberta.ca/

TIESSEN FOUNDATION BROADCAST SCHOLARSHIP

CAN$750 to recognize an outstanding Alberta high school student and to encourage and assist them with their post-secondary studies at any recognized post-secondary institution in Canada that offers degree or diploma programs in broadcasting. For additional information, see website http://alis.alberta.ca.

Academic Fields/Career Goals: TV/Radio Broadcasting.

Award: Scholarship for use in freshman year; not renewable.

Eligibility Requirements: Applicant must be Canadian citizen; high school student; planning to enroll or expecting to enroll full-time at a two-year or four-year or technical institution or university and resident of Alberta.

Application Requirements: Application form, essay, recommendations or references. *Deadline:* June 1.

Contact: Scholarship Committee
   Phone: 780-427-8640
   E-mail: scholarships@gov.ab.ca

ARRL FOUNDATION INC.

http://www.arrl.org/

ANDROSCOGGIN AMATEUR RADIO CLUB SCHOLARSHIP
• *See page 215*

ASIAN AMERICAN JOURNALISTS ASSOCIATION, SEATTLE CHAPTER

http://www.aajaseattle.org/

NORTHWEST JOURNALISTS OF COLOR SCHOLARSHIP
• *See page 88*

ASSOCIATED PRESS

http://www.aptra.org/

ASSOCIATED PRESS TELEVISION/RADIO ASSOCIATION-CLETE ROBERTS JOURNALISM SCHOLARSHIP AWARDS
• *See page 379*

KATHRYN DETTMAN MEMORIAL JOURNALISM SCHOLARSHIP
• *See page 380*

CALIFORNIA BROADCASTERS FOUNDATION

http://www.cabroadcasters.org/

CALIFORNIA BROADCASTERS FOUNDATION INTERN SCHOLARSHIP

Two $500 scholarships awarded to radio interns and two $500 scholarships awarded to television interns each semester. Any enrolled college student working as an intern at any California Broadcasters Foundation or Association member radio or television station is eligible. No minimum number of hours per week required. Immediate family of current Foundation Board Members are not eligible. Deadlines: June 18 for fall and December 10 for spring.

Academic Fields/Career Goals: TV/Radio Broadcasting.

Award: Scholarship for use in freshman, sophomore, junior, senior, graduate, or postgraduate years; not renewable. *Number:* up to 4. *Amount:* $500.

Eligibility Requirements: Applicant must be enrolled or expecting to enroll full- or part-time at a two-year or four-year or technical institution or university and resident of California. Available to U.S. citizens.

Application Requirements: Application form, essay, recommendations or references. *Deadline:* varies.

Contact: Mark Powers, Government Affairs
   California Broadcasters Foundation
   915 L Street, Suite 1150
   Sacramento, CA 95814
   Phone: 916-444-2237
   E-mail: cbapowers@cabroadcasters.org

CCNMA: LATINO JOURNALISTS OF CALIFORNIA

http://www.ccnma.org/

CCNMA SCHOLARSHIPS
• *See page 203*

CHARLES AND LUCILLE KING FAMILY FOUNDATION, INC.

http://www.kingfoundation.org/

CHARLES AND LUCILLE KING FAMILY FOUNDATION SCHOLARSHIPS
• *See page 203*

HAWAII ASSOCIATION OF BROADCASTERS INC.

http://www.hawaiibroadcasters.com/

HAWAII ASSOCIATION OF BROADCASTERS SCHOLARSHIP
Renewable scholarship for full-time college students with the career goal of working in the broadcast industry in Hawaii upon graduation. Minimum GPA of 2.75 required. Number of awards granted ranges between twenty and thirty. For more information, visit website http://www.hawaiibroadcasters.com.

Academic Fields/Career Goals: TV/Radio Broadcasting.

Award: Scholarship for use in freshman, sophomore, junior, or senior years; renewable. *Number:* 20–30. *Amount:* $500–$4500.

Eligibility Requirements: Applicant must be enrolled or expecting to enroll full-time at a two-year or four-year institution or university. Applicant must have 2.5 GPA or higher. Available to U.S. and non-U.S. citizens.

Application Requirements: Application form, recommendations or references, transcript. *Deadline:* April 30.

Contact: Scholarship Committee
Hawaii Association of Broadcasters Inc.
PO Box 61562
Honolulu, HI 96839
Phone: 808-599-1455
Fax: 808-599-7784

IDAHO STATE BROADCASTERS ASSOCIATION

http://www.idahobroadcasters.org/

WAYNE C. CORNILS MEMORIAL SCHOLARSHIP
• *See page 165*

ILLUMINATING ENGINEERING SOCIETY OF NORTH AMERICA

http://www.ies.org/

ROBERT W. THUNEN MEMORIAL SCHOLARSHIPS
• *See page 122*

INDIANA BROADCASTERS ASSOCIATION

http://www.indianabroadcasters.org/

INDIANA BROADCASTERS FOUNDATION SCHOLARSHIP
• *See page 381*

ISLAMIC SCHOLARSHIP FUND

http://islamicscholarshipfund.org/

ISF NATIONAL SCHOLARSHIP
• *See page 108*

JOHN BAYLISS BROADCAST FOUNDATION

http://www.beaweb.org/bayliss/radio.html

JOHN BAYLISS BROADCAST RADIO SCHOLARSHIP
• *See page 204*

LOUISIANA ASSOCIATION OF BROADCASTERS

http://www.broadcasters.org/

BROADCAST SCHOLARSHIP PROGRAM
Scholarship to students enrolled and attending classes, full-time, in a fully accredited broadcast curriculum at a Louisiana four-year college. Must be a Louisiana resident and maintain a minimum 2.5 GPA. Previous LAB Scholarship Award winners are eligible.

Academic Fields/Career Goals: TV/Radio Broadcasting.

Award: Scholarship for use in junior or senior years; not renewable. *Number:* 2. *Amount:* $2000.

Eligibility Requirements: Applicant must be enrolled or expecting to enroll full-time at a four-year institution or university; resident of Louisiana and studying in Louisiana. Applicant must have 2.5 GPA or higher. Available to U.S. citizens.

Application Requirements: Application form, essay, recommendations or references, transcript. *Deadline:* February 1.

Contact: Louise Munson, Scholarship Coordinator
Louisiana Association of Broadcasters
660 Florida Boulevard
Baton Rouge, LA 70801
Phone: 225-267-4522
Fax: 225-267-4329
E-mail: lmunson@broadcasters.org

MICHIGAN ASSOCIATION OF BROADCASTERS FOUNDATION

http://www.michmab.com/

WXYZ-TV BROADCASTING SCHOLARSHIP
One-time $1000 scholarship to assist students who are actively pursuing a career in a broadcast-related field. No limit on the number of awards within the program. Interested applicants should send a cover letter, resume, letters of recommendation, and an essay (200 to 300 words). The scholarship is open to Michigan residents currently attending college in Michigan.

Academic Fields/Career Goals: TV/Radio Broadcasting.

Award: Scholarship for use in freshman year; not renewable. *Number:* 1. *Amount:* $1000.

Eligibility Requirements: Applicant must be high school student; planning to enroll or expecting to enroll full-time at a two-year or four-year institution or university; resident of Michigan and studying in Michigan. Available to U.S. citizens.

Application Requirements: Application form, driver's license, essay, recommendations or references. *Deadline:* January 15.

Contact: Julie Sochay, Executive Vice President
Michigan Association of Broadcasters Foundation
819 North Washington Avenue
Lansing, MI 48906
Phone: 517-484-7444
Fax: 517-484-5810
E-mail: mabf@michmab.com

MISSISSIPPI ASSOCIATION OF BROADCASTERS

http://www.msbroadcasters.org/

MISSISSIPPI ASSOCIATION OF BROADCASTERS SCHOLARSHIP

• *See page 382*

MISSOURI BROADCASTERS ASSOCIATION SCHOLARSHIP PROGRAM

http://www.mbaweb.org/

MISSOURI BROADCASTERS ASSOCIATION SCHOLARSHIP

Scholarship for a Missouri resident enrolled or planning to enroll in a broadcast or related curriculum which provides training and expertise applicable to a broadcast operation. Must maintain a GPA of at least 3.0 or equivalent. Multiple awards may be assigned each year and the amount of the scholarship will vary.

Academic Fields/Career Goals: TV/Radio Broadcasting.

Award: Scholarship for use in freshman, sophomore, junior, or senior years; not renewable. *Number:* 3–5. *Amount:* $1000–$2500.

Eligibility Requirements: Applicant must be enrolled or expecting to enroll full-time at a two-year or four-year institution or university; resident of Missouri and studying in Missouri. Applicant must have 3.0 GPA or higher. Available to U.S. citizens.

Application Requirements: Application form, essay, financial need analysis. *Deadline:* March 31.

Contact: Ms. Terry Harper, Director of Member Services
Phone: 573-636-6692
Fax: 573-634-8258
E-mail: tharper@mbaweb.org

MONTANA BROADCASTERS ASSOCIATION

http://www.mtbroadcasters.org/

GREAT FALLS BROADCASTERS ASSOCIATION SCHOLARSHIP

Scholarship available to a student who has graduated from a north-central Montana high school (Cascade, Meagher, Judith Basin, Fergus, Choteau, Teton, Pondera, Glacier, Toole, Liberty, Hill, Blaine, Phillips, and Valley counties) and is enrolled as at least a second year student in radio-TV at any public or private Montana college or university.

Academic Fields/Career Goals: TV/Radio Broadcasting.

Award: Scholarship for use in sophomore year; not renewable. *Number:* 1. *Amount:* $2000–$5000.

Eligibility Requirements: Applicant must be enrolled or expecting to enroll full-time at a two-year or four-year institution or university; resident of Montana and studying in Montana. Available to U.S. citizens.

Application Requirements: Application form, essay, recommendations or references, transcript. *Deadline:* March 15.

Contact: Gregory McDonald, Scholarship Coordinator
Montana Broadcasters Association
HC 70 PO Box 98
Bonner, MT 59823
Phone: 406-244-4622
Fax: 406-244-5518
E-mail: mba@mtbroadcasters.org

NATIONAL ACADEMY OF TELEVISION ARTS & SCIENCES—OHIO VALLEY CHAPTER

http://ohiovalleyemmy.org/

DAVID J. CLARKE MEMORIAL SCHOLARSHIP

• *See page 205*

NATIONAL ACADEMY OF TELEVISION ARTS AND SCIENCES

http://www.emmyonline.tv/

DOUGLAS W. MUMMERT SCHOLARSHIP

• *See page 129*

JIM MCKAY MEMORIAL SCHOLARSHIP

• *See page 205*

MIKE WALLACE MEMORIAL SCHOLARSHIP

• *See page 205*

NATIONAL ACADEMY OF TELEVISION ARTS AND SCIENCES TRUSTEES SCHOLARSHIP

• *See page 205*

RANDY FALCO SCHOLARSHIP

• *See page 205*

NATIONAL ACADEMY OF TELEVISION ARTS AND SCIENCES, MICHIGAN CHAPTER

http://natasmichigan.org

DR. LYNNE BOYLE/JOHN SCHIMPF UNDERGRADUATE SCHOLARSHIP

• *See page 89*

NATIONAL ACADEMY OF TELEVISION ARTS AND SCIENCES-NATIONAL CAPITAL/CHESAPEAKE BAY CHAPTER

http://www.natasdc.org/

BETTY ENDICOTT/NTA-NCCB STUDENT SCHOLARSHIP

• *See page 383*

NATIONAL ASSOCIATION OF BLACK JOURNALISTS

http://www.nabj.org/

NABJ SCHOLARSHIP

• *See page 205*

NATIONAL ASSOCIATION OF BLACK JOURNALISTS NON-SUSTAINING SCHOLARSHIP AWARDS

• *See page 384*

NATIONAL ASSOCIATION OF BROADCASTERS

http://www.nab.org/

NATIONAL ASSOCIATION OF BROADCASTERS GRANTS FOR RESEARCH IN BROADCASTING

• *See page 206*

NATIONAL ASSOCIATION OF HISPANIC JOURNALISTS (NAHJ)

http://www.nahj.org/

GERALDO RIVERA SCHOLARSHIP

• *See page 384*

MARIA ELENA SALINAS SCHOLARSHIP
• See page 339

NATIONAL ASSOCIATION OF HISPANIC JOURNALISTS SCHOLARSHIP
• See page 206

NATIONAL DAIRY SHRINE
http://www.dairyshrine.org/

MARSHALL E. MCCULLOUGH-NATIONAL DAIRY SHRINE SCHOLARSHIPS
• See page 100

NEW JERSEY BROADCASTERS ASSOCIATION
http://www.njba.com/

MICHAEL S. LIBRETTI SCHOLARSHIP
• See page 206

NORTH CAROLINA ASSOCIATION OF BROADCASTERS
http://www.ncbroadcast.com/

NCAB SCHOLARSHIP
One-time scholarship for high school seniors enrolled as full-time students in a North Carolina college or university with an interest in broadcasting. Must be between ages 17 and 20.
Academic Fields/Career Goals: TV/Radio Broadcasting.
Award: Scholarship for use in freshman year; not renewable. *Number:* 2. *Amount:* $10,000.
Eligibility Requirements: Applicant must be high school student; age 17-20; planning to enroll or expecting to enroll full-time at a two-year or four-year institution or university and studying in North Carolina. Available to U.S. citizens.
Application Requirements: Application form, essay, recommendations or references, transcript. *Deadline:* April 15.
Contact: Lisa Reynolds, Executive Manager
North Carolina Association of Broadcasters
PO Box 627
Raleigh, NC 27602
Phone: 919-821-7300
Fax: 919-839-0304

OREGON ASSOCIATION OF BROADCASTERS
http://www.theoab.org/

OAB FOUNDATION SCHOLARSHIP
• See page 207

OUTDOOR WRITERS ASSOCIATION OF AMERICA
http://www.owaa.org/

OUTDOOR WRITERS ASSOCIATION OF AMERICA - BODIE MCDOWELL SCHOLARSHIP AWARD
• See page 207

PALM BEACH ASSOCIATION OF BLACK JOURNALISTS
PALM BEACH ASSOCIATION OF BLACK JOURNALISTS SCHOLARSHIP
• See page 386

POLISH ARTS CLUB OF BUFFALO SCHOLARSHIP FOUNDATION
http://www.pacb.bfn.org/

POLISH ARTS CLUB OF BUFFALO SCHOLARSHIP FOUNDATION TRUST
• See page 130

RADIO TELEVISION DIGITAL NEWS ASSOCIATION
www.rtdna.org

CAROLE SIMPSON SCHOLARSHIP
• See page 208

ED BRADLEY SCHOLARSHIP
• See page 208

GEORGE FOREMAN TRIBUTE TO LYNDON B. JOHNSON SCHOLARSHIP
• See page 208

LOU AND CAROLE PRATO SPORTS REPORTING SCHOLARSHIP
• See page 208

MIKE REYNOLDS JOURNALISM SCHOLARSHIP
• See page 209

PETE WILSON SCHOLARSHIP
• See page 209

RHODE ISLAND FOUNDATION
http://www.rifoundation.org/

J. D. EDSAL SCHOLARSHIP
• See page 90

SOCIETY OF MOTION PICTURE AND TELEVISION ENGINEERS
https://www.smpte.org/

LOUIS F. WOLF JR. MEMORIAL SCHOLARSHIP
• See page 210

STUDENT PAPER AWARD
• See page 210

SOCIETY OF PROFESSIONAL JOURNALISTS, LOS ANGELES CHAPTER
http://www.spj.org/losangeles

HELEN JOHNSON SCHOLARSHIP
• See page 387

STRAIGHTFORWARD MEDIA

http://www.straightforwardmedia.com/

STRAIGHTFORWARD MEDIA MEDIA & COMMUNICATIONS SCHOLARSHIP
• *See page 91*

TAMPA BAY TIMES FUND, INC.

http://www.tampabay.com/fund

CAREER JOURNALISM SCHOLARSHIP
• *See page 210*

TAMPA BAY TIMES FUND CAREER JOURNALISM SCHOLARSHIPS
• *See page 91*

TEXAS ASSOCIATION OF BROADCASTERS

https://www.tab.org/scholarships/available-scholarships

BELO TEXAS BROADCAST EDUCATION FOUNDATION SCHOLARSHIP
• *See page 211*

BONNER MCLANE TEXAS BROADCAST EDUCATION FOUNDATION SCHOLARSHIP
• *See page 211*

STUDENT TEXAS BROADCAST EDUCATION FOUNDATION SCHOLARSHIP
• *See page 211*

TOM REIFF TEXAS BROADCAST EDUCATION FOUNDATION SCHOLARSHIP
• *See page 211*

UNDERGRADUATE TEXAS BROADCAST EDUCATION FOUNDATION SCHOLARSHIP
• *See page 211*

VANN KENNEDY TEXAS BROADCAST EDUCATION FOUNDATION SCHOLARSHIP
• *See page 211*

TEXAS GRIDIRON CLUB INC.

http://www.spjfw.org/

TEXAS GRIDIRON CLUB SCHOLARSHIPS
• *See page 212*

UNITED METHODIST COMMUNICATIONS

http://www.umcom.org/

LEONARD M. PERRYMAN COMMUNICATIONS SCHOLARSHIP FOR ETHNIC MINORITY STUDENTS
• *See page 212*

UNITED NEGRO COLLEGE FUND

http://www.uncf.org/

RHYTHM NATION/JANET JACKSON SCHOLARSHIP
• *See page 132*

VALLEY PRESS CLUB

http://www.valleypressclub.com/

VALLEY PRESS CLUB SCHOLARSHIPS, THE REPUBLICAN SCHOLARSHIP, CHANNEL 22 SCHOLARSHIP
• *See page 213*

WISCONSIN BROADCASTERS ASSOCIATION FOUNDATION

http://www.wi-broadcasters.org/

WISCONSIN BROADCASTERS ASSOCIATION FOUNDATION SCHOLARSHIP
• *See page 213*

WOWT-TV OMAHA, NEBRASKA

http://www.wowt.com/

WOWT-TV BROADCASTING SCHOLARSHIP PROGRAM
Two annual scholarships of $1000 for high school graduates in the Channel 6 viewing area of Nebraska. Must be pursuing a full-time career in broadcasting and have a minimum GPA of 3.0.
Academic Fields/Career Goals: TV/Radio Broadcasting.
Award: Scholarship for use in freshman year; not renewable. *Number:* 2. *Amount:* $1000.
Eligibility Requirements: Applicant must be high school student; planning to enroll or expecting to enroll full-time at a two-year or four-year institution or university and resident of Nebraska. Applicant must have 3.0 GPA or higher. Available to U.S. citizens.
Application Requirements: Application form, community service, essay, interview. *Deadline:* March 15.
Contact: Brandy Gerry, Programming and Community Affairs Manager
WOWT-TV Omaha, Nebraska
3501 Farnam Street
Omaha, NE 68131
Phone: 402-346-6666
E-mail: scholarship@wowt.com

URBAN AND REGIONAL PLANNING

AMERICAN PLANNING ASSOCIATION

http://www.planning.org/

JUDITH MCMANUS PRICE SCHOLARSHIP
Women and minority (African American, Hispanic American, or Native American) students enrolled in an approved Planning Accreditation Board (PAB) planning program who are citizens of the United States, intend to pursue careers as practicing planners in the public sector, and are able to demonstrate a genuine financial need are eligible to apply for this scholarship. For further information visit https://www.planning.org/scholarships/apa/
Academic Fields/Career Goals: Urban and Regional Planning.
Award: Scholarship for use in freshman, sophomore, junior, senior, or graduate years; not renewable. *Amount:* $2000–$5000.
Eligibility Requirements: Applicant must be American Indian/Alaska Native, Black (non-Hispanic), Hispanic and enrolled or expecting to enroll full-time at a four-year institution or university. Available to U.S. citizens.
Application Requirements: Application form, essay, financial need analysis. *Deadline:* April 30.
Contact: Monica Groh, Director of Emerging Professionals
Phone: 312-786-6363
E-mail: mgroh@planning.org

CENTER FOR ARCHITECTURE

http://www.cfafoundation.org/scholarships

CENTER FOR ARCHITECTURE, DOUGLAS HASKELL AWARD FOR STUDENT JOURNALS
• See page 119

COMMUNITY FOUNDATION OF WESTERN MASSACHUSETTS

http://www.communityfoundation.org/

HELEN HAMILTON SCHOLARSHIP FUND
• See page 503

CONNECTICUT CHAPTER OF THE AMERICAN PLANNING ASSOCIATION

http://www.ccapa.org/

DIANA DONALD SCHOLARSHIP
One-time award of $2500 for full-time students enrolled in a graduate or undergraduate program in city planning or a closely related field. Must be resident of Connecticut and study in Connecticut. Deadline varies.

Academic Fields/Career Goals: Urban and Regional Planning.

Award: Scholarship for use in freshman, sophomore, junior, senior, or graduate years; not renewable. *Number:* up to 1. *Amount:* up to $2500.

Eligibility Requirements: Applicant must be enrolled or expecting to enroll full-time at a four-year institution or university; resident of Connecticut and studying in Connecticut. Available to U.S. and non-U.S. citizens.

Application Requirements: Application form, essay, financial need analysis, recommendations or references, transcript. *Deadline:* varies.

Contact: Mary Savage-Dunham, Town Planner
Connecticut Chapter of the American Planning Association
75 Main Street
Southington, CT 06489
Phone: 860-276-6248
E-mail: savagem@southington.org

INTERNATIONAL FACILITY MANAGEMENT ASSOCIATION FOUNDATION

http://www.ifmafoundation.org/

IFMA FOUNDATION SCHOLARSHIPS
• See page 122

THE LAND CONSERVANCY OF NEW JERSEY

http://tlc-nj.org/

ROGERS FAMILY SCHOLARSHIP
• See page 243

PLAN NEW HAMPSHIRE

www.plannh.org

PLAN NEW HAMPSHIRE SCHOLARSHIP AND PROGRAM
• See page 123

TRANSPORTATION ASSOCIATION OF CANADA FOUNDATION

http://www.tac-foundation.ca

TAC FOUNDATION SCHOLARSHIPS
• See page 519

VECTORWORKS, INC.

http://www.vectorworks.net

VECTORWORKS DESIGN SCHOLARSHIP
• See page 124

WOMEN'S STUDIES

AMERICAN FEDERATION OF STATE, COUNTY, AND MUNICIPAL EMPLOYEES

http://www.afscme.org/

AFSCME/UNCF UNION SCHOLARS PROGRAM
• See page 103

HOMEKITCHENARY

http://homekitchenary.com

SHARE YOUR STORY WITH HOMEKITCHENARY
• See page 331

THE SOCIETY FOR THE SCIENTIFIC STUDY OF SEXUALITY

http://www.sexscience.org/

THE SOCIETY FOR THE SCIENTIFIC STUDY OF SEXUALITY STUDENT RESEARCH GRANT
• See page 109

SOUTHERN BAPTIST HISTORICAL LIBRARY AND ARCHIVES

http://www.sbhla.org/

LYNN E. MAY JR. STUDY GRANT
• See page 104

UNITED NATIONS ASSOCIATION OF CONNECTICUT

http://www.unausa.org

UNITED NATIONS ASSOCIATION OF CONNECTICUT SCHOLARSHIP
• See page 133

Nonacademic/Noncareer Criteria

CIVIC, PROFESSIONAL, SOCIAL, OR UNION AFFILIATION

AIR LINE PILOTS ASSOCIATION, INTERNATIONAL
http://www.alpa.org/

AIRLINE PILOTS ASSOCIATION SCHOLARSHIP PROGRAM
Scholarship for children of medically retired, long-term disabled, or deceased pilot members of the Air Line Pilots Association. The total monetary value is $12,000 with $3000 disbursed annually to the recipient for four consecutive years, provided that a GPA of 3.0 is maintained. An additional $2000 per year is available which may be awarded to one or two additional applicants as a one-year special award, which is not renewable.

Award: Scholarship for use in freshman, sophomore, junior, or senior years; renewable. *Number:* 1–3. *Amount:* $1000–$12,000.

Eligibility Requirements: Applicant must be enrolled or expecting to enroll full-time at a four-year institution or university. Applicant or parent of applicant must be member of Airline Pilots Association. Applicant must have 3.0 GPA or higher. Available to U.S. and Canadian citizens.

Application Requirements: Application form, financial need analysis, recommendations or references, test scores, transcript. *Deadline:* April 1.

Contact: Yvonne Willits, Coordinator
Phone: 703-689-4107
Fax: 703-481-5575
E-mail: Yvonne.Willits@alpa.org

ALBERTA AGRICULTURE FOOD AND RURAL DEVELOPMENT 4-H BRANCH
http://www.4h.ab.ca/

ALBERTA AGRICULTURE FOOD AND RURAL DEVELOPMENT 4-H SCHOLARSHIP PROGRAM
Awards will be given to current and incoming students attending any institute of higher learning. Must have been a member of the Alberta 4-H Program and be a Canadian citizen. Must be a resident of Alberta.

Award: Scholarship for use in freshman, sophomore, junior, senior, or graduate years; not renewable. *Number:* 115–120. *Amount:* $200–$1500.

Eligibility Requirements: Applicant must be enrolled or expecting to enroll full-time at a two-year or four-year or technical institution or university and resident of Alberta. Applicant or parent of applicant must be member of National 4-H. Available to Canadian citizens.

Application Requirements: Application form, essay, recommendations or references, transcript. *Deadline:* May 5.

Contact: Susann Stone, Scholarship Coordinator
Phone: 780-682-2153
Fax: 780-682-3784
E-mail: foundation@4hab.com

AMERICAN FEDERATION OF STATE, COUNTY, AND MUNICIPAL EMPLOYEES
http://www.afscme.org/

AMERICAN FEDERATION OF STATE, COUNTY, AND MUNICIPAL EMPLOYEES SCHOLARSHIP PROGRAM
Scholarship for family dependents of American Federation of State, County, and Municipal Employees members. Must be a graduating high school senior planning to pursue postsecondary education at a four-year institution. Submit proof of parent's membership. Renewable award of $2000.

Award: Scholarship for use in freshman, sophomore, junior, or senior years; renewable. *Number:* 13. *Amount:* $2000.

Eligibility Requirements: Applicant must be high school student and planning to enroll or expecting to enroll full-time at a four-year institution or university. Applicant or parent of applicant must be member of American Federation of State, County, and Municipal Employees. Available to U.S. citizens.

Application Requirements: Application form, essay, recommendations or references, test scores, transcript. *Deadline:* December 31.

Contact: Philip Allen, Scholarship Coordinator
Phone: 202-429-1250
Fax: 202-429-1293
E-mail: pallen@asscme.org

UNION PLUS CREDIT CARD SCHOLARSHIP PROGRAM
One-time award for AFSCME members, their spouses and dependent children. Graduate students and grandchildren are not eligible.

Award: Scholarship for use in freshman, sophomore, junior, or senior years; not renewable. *Amount:* $500–$4000.

Eligibility Requirements: Applicant must be enrolled or expecting to enroll full-time at a two-year or four-year or technical institution or university. Applicant or parent of applicant must be member of American Federation of State, County, and Municipal Employees. Available to U.S. citizens.

Application Requirements: Application form, driver's license, essay, recommendations or references, transcript. *Deadline:* January 31.

Contact: Philip Allen, Scholarship Coordinator
Phone: 202-429-1250
Fax: 202-429-1293
E-mail: pallen@asscme.org

AMERICAN FEDERATION OF TEACHERS

http://www.aft.org/

ROBERT G. PORTER SCHOLARS PROGRAM-AMERICAN FEDERATION OF TEACHERS DEPENDENTS

Scholarship of up to $8000 for high school seniors who are dependents of AFT members. Must submit transcript, test scores, essay, and recommendations with application. Must be U.S. citizen.

Award: Scholarship for use in freshman year; renewable. *Number:* 4. *Amount:* $8000.

Eligibility Requirements: Applicant must be high school student and planning to enroll or expecting to enroll full-time at a four-year institution or university. Applicant or parent of applicant must be member of American Federation of Teachers. Applicant or parent of applicant must have employment or volunteer experience in nursing, teaching/education. Available to U.S. citizens.

Application Requirements: Application form, community service, essay, recommendations or references, test scores, transcript. *Deadline:* March 31.

Contact: Ms. Nina Newkirk, Scholarship Coordinator
Phone: 202-393-5696
E-mail: nnewkirk@aft.org

AMERICAN LEGION AUXILIARY DEPARTMENT OF CONNECTICUT

http://www.ct.legion.org/

AMERICAN LEGION AUXILIARY DEPARTMENT OF CONNECTICUT MEMORIAL EDUCATIONAL GRANT

Half the number of available grants are awarded to children of veterans who are also residents of CT. Remaining grants awarded to child or grandchild of a member (or member at time of death) of the CT Departments of the American Legion/American Legion Auxiliary, regardless of residency; or are members of the CT Departments of the American Legion Auxiliary/Sons of the American Legion, regardless of residency. Contact local unit President. Must include list of community service activities.

Award: Grant for use in freshman, sophomore, junior, or senior years; not renewable. *Number:* 4. *Amount:* $500.

Eligibility Requirements: Applicant must be age 16-23 and enrolled or expecting to enroll full-time at a two-year or four-year or technical institution or university. Applicant or parent of applicant must be member of American Legion or Auxiliary. Available to U.S. citizens. Applicant must have general military experience.

Application Requirements: Application form, community service, essay, financial need analysis, recommendations or references, self-addressed stamped envelope with application, transcript. *Deadline:* March 10.

Contact: Nancy Hansen, State Secretary
American Legion Auxiliary Department of Connecticut
PO Box 266
Rocky Hill, CT 06067-0266
Phone: 860-616-2343
E-mail: ctaladept@gmail.com

AMERICAN LEGION AUXILIARY DEPARTMENT OF CONNECTICUT PAST PRESIDENTS' PARLEY MEMORIAL EDUCATION GRANT

The program gives preference a child or grandchild of an ex-service woman, who was or is a member of the CT departments of the American Legion/American Legion Auxiliary. In the event of a deficiency of preferred applicants, award may be granted to child or grandchild of a member of the CT Departments of the American Legion/American Legion Auxiliary or Sons of the American Legion. Minimum three-year membership required, or three years prior to death. Contact local unit President. Must include list of community service activities.

Award: Grant for use in freshman, sophomore, junior, or senior years; not renewable. *Number:* 4. *Amount:* up to $500.

Eligibility Requirements: Applicant must be age 16-23; enrolled or expecting to enroll full-time at a two-year or four-year or technical institution or university and resident of Connecticut. Applicant or parent of applicant must be member of American Legion or Auxiliary. Available to U.S. citizens. Applicant must have general military experience.

Application Requirements: Application form, community service, financial need analysis, list of school and community activities, recommendations or references, test scores, transcript. *Deadline:* March 10.

Contact: Nancy Hansen, State Secretary
American Legion Auxiliary Department of Connecticut
PO Box 266
Rocky Hill, CT 06067-0266
Phone: 860-616-2343
E-mail: ctaladept@gmail.com

AMERICAN LEGION AUXILIARY DEPARTMENT OF MISSOURI

http://www.missourilegion.org/

AMERICAN LEGION AUXILIARY DEPARTMENT OF MISSOURI LELA MURPHY SCHOLARSHIP

Scholarship of $500 for high school graduate. $250 will be awarded each semester. Applicant must be Missouri resident and the granddaughter or great-granddaughter of a living or deceased Auxiliary member. Sponsoring unit and department must validate application.

Award: Scholarship for use in freshman year; not renewable. *Number:* 1. *Amount:* $500.

Eligibility Requirements: Applicant must be high school student; planning to enroll or expecting to enroll full-time at a two-year or four-year or technical institution or university; female and resident of Missouri. Applicant or parent of applicant must be member of American Legion or Auxiliary. Available to U.S. citizens. Applicant or parent must meet one or more of the following requirements: general military experience; retired from active duty; disabled or killed as a result of military service; prisoner of war; or missing in action.

Application Requirements: Application form. *Deadline:* March 1.

Contact: Karen Larson, Department Secretary/Treasurer
American Legion Auxiliary Department of Missouri
600 Ellis Boulevard
Jefferson City, MO 65101
Phone: 573-636-9133
Fax: 573-635-3467
E-mail: dptmoala@embarqmail.com

AMERICAN LEGION AUXILIARY DEPARTMENT OF MISSOURI NATIONAL PRESIDENT'S SCHOLARSHIP

State-level award. Offers one $500 scholarship. Applicant must complete 50 hours of community service during their high school years. Sponsoring unit and department must validate application. Applicant must be a Missouri resident.

Award: Scholarship for use in freshman year; not renewable. *Number:* 1. *Amount:* $500.

Eligibility Requirements: Applicant must be high school student; planning to enroll or expecting to enroll full-time at a two-year or four-year or technical institution or university and resident of Missouri. Applicant or parent of applicant must be member of American Legion or Auxiliary. Available to U.S. citizens. Applicant or parent must meet one or more of the following requirements: general military experience; retired from active duty; disabled or killed as a result of military service; prisoner of war; or missing in action.

Application Requirements: Application form, community service, resume. *Deadline:* March 1.

Contact: Karen Larson, Department Secretary/Treasurer
American Legion Auxiliary Department of Missouri
600 Ellis Boulevard
Jefferson City, MO 65101
Phone: 573-636-9133
Fax: 573-635-3467
E-mail: dptmoala@embarqmail.com

AMERICAN LEGION AUXILIARY DEPARTMENT OF NEBRASKA

http://www.nebraskalegionaux.net/

AMERICAN LEGION AUXILIARY DEPARTMENT OF NEBRASKA RUBY PAUL CAMPAIGN FUND SCHOLARSHIP

One-time award for Nebraska residents who are children, grandchildren, or great-grandchildren of an American Legion Auxiliary member, or who have been members of the American Legion, American Legion Auxiliary, or Sons of the American Legion or Auxiliary for two years prior to issuing the application. Must rank in upper third of class or have minimum 3.0 GPA.

Award: Scholarship for use in freshman year; not renewable. *Number:* 1–3. *Amount:* $100–$300.

Eligibility Requirements: Applicant must be high school student; planning to enroll or expecting to enroll full-time at a four-year institution or university and resident of Nebraska. Applicant or parent of applicant must be member of American Legion or Auxiliary. Applicant must have 3.0 GPA or higher. Available to U.S. citizens. Applicant or parent must meet one or more of the following requirements: general military experience; retired from active duty; disabled or killed as a result of military service; prisoner of war; or missing in action.

Application Requirements: Application form, essay, financial need analysis, letter of acceptance, proof of enrollment, recommendations or references, test scores, transcript. *Deadline:* March 15.

Contact: Jacki O'Neill, Department Secretary
Phone: 402-466-1808
E-mail: neaux@alltel.net

AMERICAN LEGION AUXILIARY DEPARTMENT OF OREGON

http://www.alaoregon.org/

AMERICAN LEGION AUXILIARY DEPARTMENT OF OREGON SPIRIT OF YOUTH SCHOLARSHIP

One-time award available to Oregon high school seniors. Must be a current female junior member of the American Legion Auxiliary with a three-year membership history. Apply through local units.

Award: Scholarship for use in freshman year; not renewable. *Number:* 1. *Amount:* $1000.

Eligibility Requirements: Applicant must be high school student; planning to enroll or expecting to enroll full- or part-time at a four-year institution or university; female and resident of Oregon. Applicant or parent of applicant must be member of American Legion or Auxiliary. Available to U.S. citizens.

Application Requirements: Application form, essay, financial need analysis, interview. *Deadline:* February 1.

Contact: Virginia Biddle, Secretary/Treasurer
American Legion Auxiliary Department of Oregon
PO Box 1730
Wilsonville, OR 97070
Phone: 503-682-3162
E-mail: alaor@pcez.com

AMERICAN LEGION AUXILIARY DEPARTMENT OF SOUTH DAKOTA

http://www.sdlegion-aux.org/

AMERICAN LEGION AUXILIARY DEPARTMENT OF SOUTH DAKOTA COLLEGE SCHOLARSHIPS

One-time award of $500 to assist veterans children or auxiliary members' children from South Dakota ages 16 to 22 to secure an education at a four-year school. Write for more information.

Award: Scholarship for use in freshman, sophomore, junior, or senior years; not renewable. *Number:* 2. *Amount:* $500.

Eligibility Requirements: Applicant must be age 16-22; enrolled or expecting to enroll full-time at a four-year institution or university and resident of South Dakota. Applicant or parent of applicant must be member of American Legion or Auxiliary. Available to U.S. and non-U.S. citizens. Applicant or parent must meet one or more of the following

requirements: general military experience; retired from active duty; disabled or killed as a result of military service; prisoner of war; or missing in action.

Application Requirements: Application form, entry in a contest, essay, financial need analysis, recommendations or references. *Deadline:* March 1.

Contact: Dianne Hudson, Executive Secretary
American Legion Auxiliary Department of South Dakota
PO Box 1819
Sioux Falls, SD 57101
Phone: 605-338-9774
Fax: 605-332-3032
E-mail: legionauxiliary.sd@gmail.com

AMERICAN LEGION AUXILIARY DEPARTMENT OF SOUTH DAKOTA SENIOR SCHOLARSHIP

Award of $400 for current senior member of South Dakota American Legion Auxiliary who has been a member for three years. Based on financial need.

Award: Scholarship for use in freshman year; not renewable. *Number:* 1. *Amount:* $400.

Eligibility Requirements: Applicant must be high school student; planning to enroll or expecting to enroll full-time at a two-year or four-year or technical institution; female and resident of South Dakota. Applicant or parent of applicant must be member of American Legion or Auxiliary. Available to U.S. and non-U.S. citizens. Applicant or parent must meet one or more of the following requirements: general military experience; retired from active duty; disabled or killed as a result of military service; prisoner of war; or missing in action.

Application Requirements: Application form, essay, financial need analysis, recommendations or references, transcript. *Deadline:* March 1.

Contact: Dianne Hudson, Executive Secretary
American Legion Auxiliary Department of South Dakota
PO Box 1819
Sioux Falls, SD 57101
Phone: 605-338-9774
Fax: 605-332-3032
E-mail: legionauxiliary.sd@gmail.com

AMERICAN LEGION AUXILIARY DEPARTMENT OF SOUTH DAKOTA THELMA FOSTER SCHOLARSHIP FOR SENIOR AUXILIARY MEMBERS

One-time award of $300 must be used within twelve months for a current senior member of the South Dakota American Legion Auxiliary who has been a member for three years. Applicant may be a high school senior or older and must be female.

Award: Scholarship for use in freshman year; not renewable. *Number:* 1. *Amount:* $300.

Eligibility Requirements: Applicant must be enrolled or expecting to enroll full-time at a four-year institution or university and female. Applicant or parent of applicant must be member of American Legion or Auxiliary. Available to U.S. and non-U.S. citizens. Applicant or parent must meet one or more of the following requirements: general military experience; retired from active duty; disabled or killed as a result of military service; prisoner of war; or missing in action.

Application Requirements: Application form, essay, financial need analysis, recommendations or references. *Deadline:* March 1.

Contact: Dianne Hudson, Executive Secretary
American Legion Auxiliary Department of South Dakota
PO Box 1819
Sioux Falls, SD 57101
Phone: 605-338-9774
Fax: 605-332-3032
E-mail: legionauxiliary.sd@gmail.com

AMERICAN LEGION AUXILIARY DEPARTMENT OF UTAH

http://www.legion-aux.org/

AMERICAN LEGION AUXILIARY DEPARTMENT OF UTAH NATIONAL PRESIDENT'S SCHOLARSHIP

Scholarships available for graduating high school seniors. Must be a resident of Utah, a U.S. citizen, and the direct descendant of a veteran.

Award: Scholarship for use in freshman year; not renewable. *Number:* 15. *Amount:* $1000–$2500.

Eligibility Requirements: Applicant must be high school student; planning to enroll or expecting to enroll full-time at a two-year or four-year or technical institution or university; single and resident of Utah. Applicant or parent of applicant must be member of American Legion or Auxiliary. Available to U.S. citizens. Applicant or parent must meet one or more of the following requirements: general military experience; retired from active duty; disabled or killed as a result of military service; prisoner of war; or missing in action.

Application Requirements: Application form, essay, recommendations or references, statement of parent's military service, test scores, transcript. *Deadline:* March 1.

Contact: Lucia Anderson, Public Relations Manager and Associate Editor
Phone: 801-539-1015
Fax: 801-521-9191
E-mail: landerson@legion-aux.org

AMERICAN LEGION AUXILIARY DEPARTMENT OF WISCONSIN

http://www.amlegionauxwi.org/

AMERICAN LEGION AUXILIARY DEPARTMENT OF WISCONSIN DELLA VAN DEUREN MEMORIAL SCHOLARSHIP

One-time award of $1000 for Wisconsin residents. Applicant or mother of applicant must be a member of an American Legion Auxiliary unit. Must submit certification of an American Legion Auxiliary unit president, copy of proof that veteran was in service (i.e. discharge papers), letters of recommendation, transcripts, and essay. Minimum 3.5 GPA required. Must demonstrate financial need. Applications available on website http://www.amlegionauxwi.org.

Award: Scholarship for use in freshman, sophomore, junior, or senior years; not renewable. *Number:* 2. *Amount:* $1000.

Eligibility Requirements: Applicant must be enrolled or expecting to enroll full- or part-time at a two-year or four-year or technical institution or university and resident of Wisconsin. Applicant or parent of applicant must be member of American Legion or Auxiliary. Applicant must have 3.5 GPA or higher. Available to U.S. citizens. Applicant or parent must meet one or more of the following requirements: general military experience; retired from active duty; disabled or killed as a result of military service; prisoner of war; or missing in action.

Application Requirements: Application form, essay, financial need analysis. *Deadline:* March 15.

Contact: Bonnie Dorniak, Department Secretary
American Legion Auxiliary Department of Wisconsin
PO Box 140
Portage, WI 53901
Phone: 608-745-0124
Fax: 608-745-1947
E-mail: deptsec@amlegionauxwi.org

AMERICAN LEGION AUXILIARY DEPARTMENT OF WISCONSIN H.S. AND ANGELINE LEWIS SCHOLARSHIPS

One-time award of $1000. Applicant must be a direct descendant, wife, or widow of a veteran. Must submit certification of an American Legion Auxiliary unit president, copy of proof that veteran was in service (i.e. discharge papers), letters of recommendation, transcripts, and essay. Must have minimum 3.5 GPA, show financial need, and be a resident of Wisconsin or member of the Wisconsin American Legion Family. Applications available on website http://www.amlegionauxwi.org.

Award: Scholarship for use in freshman, sophomore, junior, senior, or graduate years; not renewable. *Number:* 5–6. *Amount:* $1000.

Eligibility Requirements: Applicant must be enrolled or expecting to enroll full- or part-time at a two-year or four-year or technical institution or university and resident of Wisconsin. Applicant or parent of applicant must be member of American Legion or Auxiliary. Applicant must have 3.5 GPA or higher. Available to U.S. citizens. Applicant or parent must meet one or more of the following requirements: general military experience; retired from active duty; disabled or killed as a result of military service; prisoner of war; or missing in action.

Application Requirements: Application form, essay, financial need analysis. *Deadline:* March 15.

Contact: Bonnie Dorniak, Department Secretary
American Legion Auxiliary Department of Wisconsin
PO Box 140
Portage, WI 53901
Phone: 608-745-0124
Fax: 608-745-1947
E-mail: deptsec@amlegionauxwi.org

AMERICAN LEGION AUXILIARY DEPARTMENT OF WISCONSIN MERIT AND MEMORIAL SCHOLARSHIPS

One-time award of $1000. Applicant must be a direct descendant, wife, or widow of a veteran. Must submit certification of an American Legion Auxiliary unit president, copy of proof that veteran was in service (i.e. discharge papers), letters of recommendation, transcripts, and essay. Must have minimum 3.5 GPA, show financial need, and be a resident of Wisconsin or member of the Wisconsin American Legion Family. Applications available on website http://www.amlegionauxwi.org.

Award: Scholarship for use in freshman, sophomore, junior, or senior years; not renewable. *Number:* 7. *Amount:* $1000.

Eligibility Requirements: Applicant must be enrolled or expecting to enroll full- or part-time at a two-year or four-year or technical institution or university and resident of Wisconsin. Applicant or parent of applicant must be member of American Legion or Auxiliary. Applicant must have 3.5 GPA or higher. Available to U.S. citizens. Applicant or parent must meet one or more of the following requirements: general military experience; retired from active duty; disabled or killed as a result of military service; prisoner of war; or missing in action.

Application Requirements: Application form, essay, financial need analysis. *Deadline:* March 15.

Contact: Bonnie Dorniak, Department Secretary
American Legion Auxiliary Department of Wisconsin
PO Box 140
Portage, WI 53901
Phone: 608-745-0124
Fax: 608-745-1947
E-mail: deptsec@amlegionauxwi.org

AMERICAN LEGION AUXILIARY DEPARTMENT OF WISCONSIN PAST PRESIDENTS' PARLEY HEALTH CAREER SCHOLARSHIPS

One-time award of $1000. Course of study need not be a four-year program. A hospital, university, or technical school program is also acceptable. Applicant must be a direct descendant, wife, or widow of a veteran. Must submit certification of an American Legion Auxiliary unit president, copy of proof that veteran was in service (i.e. discharge papers), letters of recommendation, transcripts, and essay. Must have minimum 3.5 GPA, show financial need, and be a resident of Wisconsin or member of the Wisconsin American Legion Family. Applications available on website http://www.amlegionauxwi.org.

Award: Scholarship for use in freshman, sophomore, junior, or senior years; not renewable. *Number:* 1–2. *Amount:* $1000.

Eligibility Requirements: Applicant must be enrolled or expecting to enroll full- or part-time at a two-year or four-year or technical institution or university and resident of Wisconsin. Applicant or parent of applicant must be member of American Legion or Auxiliary. Applicant must have 3.5 GPA or higher. Available to U.S. citizens. Applicant or parent must meet one or more of the following requirements: general military experience; retired from active duty; disabled or killed as a result of military service; prisoner of war; or missing in action.

Application Requirements: Application form, essay, financial need analysis. *Deadline:* March 15.

Contact: Bonnie Dorniak, Department Secretary
American Legion Auxiliary Department of Wisconsin
PO Box 140
Portage, WI 53901
Phone: 608-745-0124
Fax: 608-745-1947
E-mail: deptsec@amlegionauxwi.org

AMERICAN LEGION AUXILIARY DEPARTMENT OF WISCONSIN PRESIDENT'S SCHOLARSHIPS

One-time award of $1000. The mother of the applicant or the applicant must be a member of the Wisconsin American Legion Auxiliary. Must submit certification of an American Legion Auxiliary unit president, copy of proof that veteran was in service (i.e. discharge papers), letters of recommendation, transcripts, and essay. Must have minimum 3.5 GPA, show financial need, and be a resident of Wisconsin. Applications available on website http://www.legion-aux.org.

Award: Scholarship for use in freshman, sophomore, junior, or senior years; not renewable. *Number:* 3. *Amount:* $1000.

Eligibility Requirements: Applicant must be enrolled or expecting to enroll full- or part-time at a four-year institution or university and resident of Wisconsin. Applicant or parent of applicant must be member of American Legion or Auxiliary. Applicant must have 3.5 GPA or higher. Available to U.S. citizens. Applicant or parent must meet one or more of the following requirements: general military experience; retired from active duty; disabled or killed as a result of military service; prisoner of war; or missing in action.

Application Requirements: Application form, essay, financial need analysis. *Deadline:* March 15.

Contact: Bonnie Dorniak, Department Secretary
American Legion Auxiliary Department of Wisconsin
PO Box 140
Portage, WI 53901
Phone: 608-745-0124
Fax: 608-745-1947
E-mail: deptsec@amlegionauxwi.org

AMERICAN LEGION AUXILIARY NATIONAL HEADQUARTERS

http://www.ALAforVeterans.org

AMERICAN LEGION AUXILIARY NON-TRADITIONAL STUDENTS SCHOLARSHIPS

One-time award for students returning to the classroom after some period of time in which his/her formal schooling was interrupted or a student who has had at least one year of college and is in need of financial assistance to pursue an undergraduate degree. Must be a member of the American Legion, American Legion Auxiliary or Sons of the American Legion.

Award: Scholarship for use in freshman, sophomore, junior, senior, graduate, or postgraduate years; not renewable. *Number:* 5. *Amount:* $2000.

Eligibility Requirements: Applicant must be enrolled or expecting to enroll full-time at a two-year or four-year or technical institution or university. Applicant or parent of applicant must be member of American Legion or Auxiliary. Available to U.S. citizens.

Application Requirements: Application form, essay, financial need analysis. *Deadline:* March 1.

Contact: Kristin Hinshaw, Program Coordinator
American Legion Auxiliary National Headquarters
8945 North Meridian Street
Indianapolis, IN 46260
Phone: 317-569-4556
E-mail: khinshaw@ALAforVeterans.org

AMERICAN LEGION AUXILIARY SPIRIT OF YOUTH SCHOLARSHIPS FOR JUNIOR MEMBERS

Renewable scholarship for graduating high school seniors. Must be a woman and a current junior member of the American Legion Auxiliary, with a three-year membership history.

Award: Scholarship for use in freshman, sophomore, junior, or senior years; not renewable. *Number:* 5. *Amount:* $5000.

Eligibility Requirements: Applicant must be high school student; planning to enroll or expecting to enroll full-time at a four-year institution or university and female. Applicant or parent of applicant must be member of American Legion or Auxiliary. Applicant must have 3.0 GPA or higher. Available to U.S. citizens.

Application Requirements: Application form, essay. *Deadline:* March 1.

Contact: Kristin Hinshaw, Program Coordinator
American Legion Auxiliary National Headquarters
8945 North Meridian Street
Indianapolis, IN 46260
Phone: 317-569-4556
E-mail: khinshaw@ALAforVeterans.org

AMERICAN LEGION DEPARTMENT OF IDAHO

http://www.idaholegion.com/

AMERICAN LEGION DEPARTMENT OF IDAHO SCHOLARSHIP

One-time award of $500 to $750 for residents of Idaho studying at an Idaho institution. Must be related to a Idaho American Member.

Award: Scholarship for use in freshman year; not renewable. *Number:* 1–3. *Amount:* $500–$750.

Eligibility Requirements: Applicant must be high school student; planning to enroll or expecting to enroll full-time at a two-year or four-year institution or university; resident of Idaho and studying in Idaho. Applicant or parent of applicant must be member of American Legion or Auxiliary. Available to U.S. citizens. Applicant or parent must meet one or more of the following requirements: general military experience; retired from active duty; disabled or killed as a result of military service; prisoner of war; or missing in action.

Application Requirements: Application form, community service, essay, financial need analysis. *Deadline:* June 1.

Contact: Abe Abrahamson, Adjutant
American Legion Department of Idaho
901 West Warren Street
Boise, ID 83706-3825
Phone: 208-342-7061
E-mail: idlegion@mindspring.com

AMERICAN LEGION DEPARTMENT OF ILLINOIS

http://www.illegion.org/

AMERICAN ESSAY CONTEST SCHOLARSHIP

Scholarship for students in 7th to 12th grades of any accredited Illinois high school. Must write a 500-word essay on selected topic.

Award: Prize for use in freshman year; not renewable. *Number:* up to 60. *Amount:* $100–$1200.

Eligibility Requirements: Applicant must be high school student; planning to enroll or expecting to enroll full- or part-time at a two-year or four-year institution or university; resident of Illinois and must have an interest in writing. Applicant or parent of applicant must be member of American Legion or Auxiliary. Available to U.S. citizens.

Application Requirements: Application form, entry in a contest, essay. *Deadline:* February 1.

Contact: Mr. Gary Jenson, American Legion Department Assistant Adjutant
American Legion Department of Illinois
2720 East Lincoln Street
Bloomington, IL 61704
Phone: 309-663-0361
Fax: 309-663-5783
E-mail: gjenson@illegion.org

AMERICAN LEGION DEPARTMENT OF ILLINOIS BOY SCOUT/EXPLORER SCHOLARSHIP

Scholarship for a graduating high school senior who is a qualified Boy Scout or Explorer and a resident of Illinois. Must write a 500-word essay on Legion's Americanism and Boy Scout programs.

Award: Scholarship for use in freshman year; not renewable. *Number:* up to 5. *Amount:* $200–$1000.

Eligibility Requirements: Applicant must be high school student; planning to enroll or expecting to enroll full- or part-time at a four-year institution or university; male and resident of Illinois. Applicant or parent of applicant must be member of Boy Scouts. Available to U.S. citizens.

Application Requirements: Application form, entry in a contest, essay. *Deadline:* April 30.

Contact: Mr. Gary Jenson, American Legion Assistant Adjutant
American Legion Department of Illinois
2720 East Lincoln Street
Bloomington, IL 61704
Phone: 309-663-0361
Fax: 309-663-5783
E-mail: gjenson@illegion.org

AMERICAN LEGION DEPARTMENT OF INDIANA

http://www.indianalegion.org

AMERICAN LEGION FAMILY SCHOLARSHIP

Scholarship open to children and grandchildren of current members of The American Legion, American Legion Auxiliary, and The Sons of the American Legion. Also open to the children and grandchildren of deceased members who were current paid members of the above organizations at the time of their death. Applicants must be attending or planning to attend an Indiana institution of higher education.

Award: Scholarship for use in freshman, sophomore, junior, or senior years; not renewable. *Number:* 5. *Amount:* $1500–$1500.

Eligibility Requirements: Applicant must be enrolled or expecting to enroll full- or part-time at a two-year or four-year or technical institution or university; resident of Indiana and studying in Indiana. Applicant or parent of applicant must be member of American Legion or Auxiliary. Applicant must have 3.5 GPA or higher. Available to U.S. citizens.

Application Requirements: Application form, essay, transcript. *Deadline:* April 1.

Contact: Butch Miller, Program Coordinator
Phone: 317-630-1391
Fax: 317-237-9891
E-mail: bmiller@indlegion.org

AMERICAN LEGION DEPARTMENT OF IOWA

http://www.ialegion.org/

AMERICAN LEGION DEPARTMENT OF IOWA EAGLE SCOUT OF THE YEAR SCHOLARSHIP

Three one-time award for Eagle Scouts who are residents of Iowa. For full-time study only.

Award: Scholarship for use in freshman year; not renewable. *Number:* up to 3. *Amount:* $250–$1000.

Eligibility Requirements: Applicant must be high school student; planning to enroll or expecting to enroll full-time at a two-year or four-year institution or university; male and resident of Iowa. Applicant or parent of applicant must be member of Boy Scouts. Available to U.S. citizens.

Application Requirements: Application form, entry in a contest, recommendations or references. *Deadline:* March 1.

Contact: Program Director
American Legion Department of Iowa
720 Lyon Street
Des Moines, IA 50309
Phone: 515-282-5068

AMERICAN LEGION DEPARTMENT OF KANSAS

http://www.ksamlegion.org/

ALBERT M. LAPPIN SCHOLARSHIP

Scholarship for children of the members of Kansas American Legion or its auxiliary. Membership must have been active for the past three years. The children of deceased members are also eligible if parents' dues were paid at the time of death. Applicant must be a son/daughter of a veteran. Must be high school senior or college freshman or sophomore. Must use award at a Kansas college, university, or trade school.

Award: Scholarship for use in freshman or sophomore years; not renewable. *Number:* 1. *Amount:* $1000.

Eligibility Requirements: Applicant must be enrolled or expecting to enroll full-time at a two-year or four-year or technical institution or university; resident of Kansas and studying in Kansas. Applicant or parent of applicant must be member of American Legion or Auxiliary. Available to U.S. citizens.

Application Requirements: Application form, essay, financial need analysis, personal photograph. *Deadline:* February 15.

Contact: Mike Oppy, Chairman, Scholarship Committee
American Legion Department of Kansas
1314 SW Topeka Boulevard
Topeka, KS 66612
Phone: 785-232-9513

CHARLES W. AND ANNETTE HILL SCHOLARSHIP

Scholarship of $1000 to the descendants of veterans who are American Legion members or American Legion Auxiliary members holding membership for the past three consecutive years. Descendants of deceased members can also apply. Must be high school seniors or college freshmen or sophomores in a Kansas institution. Scholarship for use at an approved college, university, or trade school in Kansas. Must maintain a 3.0 GPA. Disbursement: $500 at beginning each semester for one year.

Award: Scholarship for use in freshman or sophomore years; not renewable. *Number:* 1. *Amount:* $1000.

Eligibility Requirements: Applicant must be enrolled or expecting to enroll full-time at a two-year or four-year or technical institution or university; resident of Kansas and studying in Kansas. Applicant or parent of applicant must be member of American Legion or Auxiliary. Applicant must have 3.0 GPA or higher. Available to U.S. citizens.

Application Requirements: Application form, essay, financial need analysis, personal photograph. *Deadline:* February 15.

Contact: Mike Oppy, Chairman, Scholarship Committee
American Legion Department of Kansas
1314 SW Topeka Boulevard
Topeka, KS 66612
Phone: 785-232-9315

HUGH A. SMITH SCHOLARSHIP FUND

One-year scholarship of $500 to the children of American Legion/Auxiliary members holding membership for the past three consecutive years. Children of a deceased member can also apply. Parent of the applicant must be a veteran. Must be high school seniors or college freshmen or sophomores in a Kansas institution. Scholarship for use at an approved college, university, or trade school in Kansas. Must maintain a C average in college.

Award: Scholarship for use in freshman or sophomore years; not renewable. *Number:* 1. *Amount:* $500.

Eligibility Requirements: Applicant must be enrolled or expecting to enroll full-time at a two-year or four-year or technical institution or university; resident of Kansas and studying in Kansas. Applicant or parent of applicant must be member of American Legion or Auxiliary. Available to U.S. citizens.

Application Requirements: Application form, essay, financial need analysis, personal photograph. *Deadline:* February 15.

Contact: Mike Oppy, Chairman, Scholarship Committee
American Legion Department of Kansas
1314 SW Topeka Boulevard
Topeka, KS 66612
Phone: 785-232-9315

ROSEDALE POST 346 SCHOLARSHIP

Two scholarships of $1500 each awarded to the children of American Legion members or of American Legion Auxiliary members holding membership for the past three consecutive years. Children of a deceased member can also apply. Parent of the applicant must be a veteran. Must be high school seniors or college freshmen or sophomores in a Kansas institution. Scholarship for use at an approved college, university, or trade school in Kansas. Must maintain a C average in college.

Award: Scholarship for use in freshman or sophomore years; not renewable. *Number:* 2. *Amount:* $1500.

Eligibility Requirements: Applicant must be enrolled or expecting to enroll full-time at a two-year or four-year or technical institution or university; resident of Kansas and studying in Kansas. Applicant or parent of applicant must be member of American Legion or Auxiliary. Available to U.S. citizens.

Application Requirements: Application form, essay, financial need analysis, personal photograph. *Deadline:* February 15.

Contact: Mike Oppy, Chairman, Scholarship Committee
American Legion Department of Kansas
1314 SW Topeka Boulevard
Topeka, KS 66612
Phone: 785-232-9315

TED AND NORA ANDERSON SCHOLARSHIPS

Scholarship of $1000 for each semester (one year only) given to the descendant of American Legion members who are holding membership for the past three consecutive years. Children of a deceased member can also apply. Must be high school seniors or college freshmen or sophomores in a Kansas institution. Scholarship for use at an approved college, university, or trade school in Kansas. Must maintain a C average in college.

Award: Scholarship for use in freshman or sophomore years; not renewable. *Number:* 1. *Amount:* $1000.

Eligibility Requirements: Applicant must be enrolled or expecting to enroll full-time at a two-year or four-year or technical institution or university; resident of Kansas and studying in Kansas. Applicant or parent of applicant must be member of American Legion or Auxiliary. Available to U.S. citizens.

Application Requirements: Application form, essay, financial need analysis, personal photograph. *Deadline:* February 15.

Contact: Mike Oppy, Chairman, Scholarship Committee
American Legion Department of Kansas
1314 SW Topeka Boulevard
Topeka, KS 66612
Phone: 785-232-9315

AMERICAN LEGION DEPARTMENT OF MAINE

http://www.mainelegion.org/

JAMES V. DAY SCHOLARSHIP

One-time $500 award for a Maine resident whose parent is a member of the American Legion or Auxiliary in Maine, or is a member of Sons of the American Legion in Maine. Must be a U.S. citizen. Based on character and financial need.

Award: Scholarship for use in freshman, sophomore, junior, or senior years; not renewable. *Number:* 1–2. *Amount:* up to $500.

Eligibility Requirements: Applicant must be enrolled or expecting to enroll full-time at a two-year or four-year or technical institution or university and resident of Maine. Applicant or parent of applicant must be member of American Legion or Auxiliary. Available to U.S. citizens. Applicant or parent must meet one or more of the following requirements: general military experience; retired from active duty; disabled or killed as a result of military service; prisoner of war; or missing in action.

Application Requirements: Application form, recommendations or references, transcript. *Deadline:* May 1.

Contact: Mr. Paul L'Heureux, Department Adjutant
American Legion Department of Maine
PO Box 900
Waterville, ME 04903
Phone: 207-873-3229
Fax: 207-872-0501
E-mail: legionme@mainelegion.org

THE AMERICAN LEGION, DEPARTMENT OF MINNESOTA

http://www.mnlegion.org/

AMERICAN LEGION DEPARTMENT OF MINNESOTA MEMORIAL SCHOLARSHIP

Scholarship available to Minnesota residents who are dependents of members of the Minnesota American Legion or Auxiliary. One-time award of $500 for study at a Minnesota institution or neighboring state with reciprocating agreement. See website for application information http://www.mnlegion.org.

Award: Scholarship for use in freshman, sophomore, junior, or senior years; not renewable. *Number:* 6. *Amount:* $500.

Eligibility Requirements: Applicant must be enrolled or expecting to enroll full- or part-time at a two-year or four-year or technical institution or university; resident of Minnesota and studying in Iowa, Minnesota, North Dakota, South Dakota, Wisconsin. Applicant or parent of applicant must be member of American Legion or Auxiliary. Available to U.S. citizens. Applicant or parent must meet one or more of the following requirements: general military experience; retired from active duty; disabled or killed as a result of military service; prisoner of war; or missing in action.

Application Requirements: Application form, essay, financial need analysis. *Deadline:* April 1.

Contact: Jennifer Kelley, Program Coordinator
The American Legion, Department of Minnesota
20 West 12th Street, Room 300-A
St. Paul, MN 55155
Phone: 651-291-1800
E-mail: department@mnlegion.org

MINNESOTA LEGIONNAIRES INSURANCE TRUST SCHOLARSHIP

Scholarship for Minnesota residents who are veterans or dependents of veterans. One-time award of $500 for study at a Minnesota institution or neighboring state with reciprocating agreement. All applications must be approved and recommended by a post of the American Legion. See website for application information http://www.mnlegion.org.

Award: Scholarship for use in freshman, sophomore, junior, or senior years; not renewable. *Number:* 3. *Amount:* $500.

Eligibility Requirements: Applicant must be enrolled or expecting to enroll full- or part-time at a two-year or four-year or technical institution or university; resident of Minnesota and studying in Iowa, Minnesota, North Dakota, South Dakota, Wisconsin. Applicant or parent of applicant must be member of American Legion or Auxiliary. Available to U.S. citizens. Applicant or parent must meet one or more of the following requirements: general military experience; retired from active duty; disabled or killed as a result of military service; prisoner of war; or missing in action.

Application Requirements: Application form, essay, financial need analysis. *Deadline:* April 1.

Contact: Jennifer Kelley, Program Coordinator
The American Legion, Department of Minnesota
20 West 12th Street, Room 300-A
St. Paul, MN 55155
Phone: 651-291-1800
E-mail: department@mnlegion.org

AMERICAN LEGION DEPARTMENT OF MISSOURI

http://www.missourilegion.org/

CHARLES L. BACON MEMORIAL SCHOLARSHIP

Two awards of $500 are given to members of The American Legion, the American Legion Auxiliary, or the Sons of The American Legion, or a descendant of a member of any thereof. Applicants must be unmarried Missouri resident below age 21, and must use the scholarship as a full-time student in an accredited college or university in Missouri. Must submit proof of American Legion membership.

Award: Scholarship for use in freshman year; not renewable. *Number:* 2. *Amount:* $500.

Eligibility Requirements: Applicant must be high school student; planning to enroll or expecting to enroll full-time at a two-year or four-year institution or university; single and resident of Missouri. Applicant or parent of applicant must be member of American Legion or Auxiliary. Available to U.S. citizens. Applicant or parent must meet one or more of the following requirements: general military experience; retired from active duty; disabled or killed as a result of military service; prisoner of war; or missing in action.

Application Requirements: Application form, discharge certificate, financial need analysis, test scores. *Deadline:* April 20.

Contact: John Doane, Chairman
Phone: 417-924-8596
Fax: 573-225-1406
E-mail: info@missourilegion.org

AMERICAN LEGION DEPARTMENT OF NEBRASKA

http://www.nebraskalegion.net/

MAYNARD JENSEN AMERICAN LEGION MEMORIAL SCHOLARSHIP

Scholarship for dependents or grandchildren of members, prisoner-of-war, missing-in-action veterans, killed-in-action veterans, or any deceased veterans of the American Legion. One-time award is based on academic achievement and financial need for Nebraska residents attending Nebraska institutions. Several scholarships of $500 each. Must have minimum 2.5 GPA and must submit school certification of GPA.

Award: Scholarship for use in freshman, sophomore, junior, or senior years; not renewable. *Number:* 1–10. *Amount:* $500.

Eligibility Requirements: Applicant must be enrolled or expecting to enroll full-time at a two-year or four-year or technical institution or university; resident of Nebraska and studying in Nebraska. Applicant or parent of applicant must be member of American Legion or Auxiliary. Applicant must have 3.5 GPA or higher. Available to U.S. citizens.

Application Requirements: Application form, financial need analysis. *Deadline:* March 1.

Contact: Brent Hagel-Pitt, Activities Director
Phone: 402-464-6338
Fax: 402-464-6330
E-mail: actdirlegion@windstream.net

AMERICAN LEGION DEPARTMENT OF OHIO

http://www.ohiolegion.com/

OHIO AMERICAN LEGION SCHOLARSHIPS

One-time award for full-time students attending an accredited institution. Open to students of any postsecondary academic year. Must have minimum 3.0 GPA. Must be a member of the American Legion, a direct descendent of a Legionnaire (living or deceased), or surviving spouse or child of a deceased U.S. military person who died on active duty or of injuries received on active duty.

Award: Scholarship for use in freshman, sophomore, junior, or senior years; not renewable. *Number:* 15–18. *Amount:* $2000–$3000.

Eligibility Requirements: Applicant must be enrolled or expecting to enroll full-time at a two-year or four-year or technical institution or university. Applicant or parent of applicant must be member of American Legion or Auxiliary. Applicant must have 3.0 GPA or higher. Available to U.S. and non-U.S. citizens. Applicant or parent must meet one or more of the following requirements: general military experience; retired from active duty; disabled or killed as a result of military service; prisoner of war; or missing in action.

Application Requirements: Application form, resume, transcript. *Deadline:* April 15.

Contact: Donald Lanthorn, Service Director
American Legion Department of Ohio
60 Big Run Road, PO Box 8007
Delaware, OH 43015
Phone: 740-362-7478
Fax: 740-362-1429
E-mail: dlanthorn@iwaynet.net

AMERICAN LEGION DEPARTMENT OF PENNSYLVANIA

http://www.pa-legion.com/

JOSEPH P. GAVENONIS COLLEGE SCHOLARSHIP (PLAN I)

Scholarships for Pennsylvania residents seeking a four-year degree from a Pennsylvania college or university. Must be the child of a member of a Pennsylvania American Legion post. Must be a graduating high school senior. Award amount and number of awards determined annually.

Renewable award. Must maintain 2.5 GPA in college. Total number of awards varies.

Award: Scholarship for use in freshman year; renewable. *Amount:* $500–$1000.

Eligibility Requirements: Applicant must be high school student; planning to enroll or expecting to enroll full-time at a four-year institution or university; resident of Pennsylvania and studying in Pennsylvania. Applicant or parent of applicant must be member of American Legion or Auxiliary. Applicant must have 2.5 GPA or higher. Available to U.S. citizens.

Application Requirements: Application form, financial need analysis, test scores, transcript. *Deadline:* May 30.

Contact: Debbie Watson, Emblem Sales Supervisor
American Legion Department of Pennsylvania
PO Box 2324
Harrisburg, PA 17105-2324
Phone: 717-730-9100
Fax: 717-975-2836
E-mail: hq@pa-legion.com

AMERICAN LEGION DEPARTMENT OF TENNESSEE

http://www.tennesseelegion.org/

AMERICAN LEGION DEPARTMENT OF TENNESSEE EAGLE SCOUT OF THE YEAR

$3000.00 scholarship for graduating high school seniors who are Eagle Scouts, enrolled either part-time or full-time for study in accredited colleges or universities. Deadline varies.

Award: Scholarship for use in freshman, sophomore, junior, or senior years; not renewable. *Number:* 1. *Amount:* $3000.

Eligibility Requirements: Applicant must be high school student; age 15-18; planning to enroll or expecting to enroll full- or part-time at a four-year institution or university; male; resident of Tennessee and studying in Tennessee. Applicant or parent of applicant must be member of Boy Scouts. Available to U.S. citizens.

Application Requirements: Application form, community service, personal photograph, portfolio. *Deadline:* March 1.

Contact: Sherri Mayberry, Program Secretary
Phone: 615-391-5088
E-mail: Sherri@TNLegion.org

AMERICAN LEGION DEPARTMENT OF VERMONT

http://www.vtlegion.org

AMERICAN LEGION EAGLE SCOUT OF THE YEAR

Awarded to the Boy Scout chosen for outstanding service to his religious institution, school, and community. Must receive the award and reside in Vermont.

Award: Scholarship for use in freshman year; not renewable. *Number:* 1. *Amount:* $1000.

Eligibility Requirements: Applicant must be high school student; planning to enroll or expecting to enroll full-time at a two-year or four-year or technical institution or university and resident of Vermont. Applicant or parent of applicant must be member of Boy Scouts. Applicant or parent of applicant must have employment or volunteer experience in community service. Available to U.S. citizens.

Application Requirements: Application form, community service, essay, personal photograph. *Deadline:* March 1.

Contact: Ronald LaRose, Chairman
American Legion Department of Vermont
PO Box 396
Montpelier, VT 05601-0396
Phone: 802-223-7131
E-mail: alvthq@myfairpoint.net

AMERICAN LEGION DEPARTMENT OF WASHINGTON

http://www.walegion.org/

AMERICAN LEGION DEPARTMENT OF WASHINGTON CHILDREN AND YOUTH SCHOLARSHIPS

One-time award for the son or daughter of a Washington American Legion or Auxiliary member, living or deceased. Must be high school senior and Washington resident planning to attend an accredited institution of higher education in Washington. Award based on need.

Award: Scholarship for use in freshman year; not renewable. *Number:* 2. *Amount:* $1500–$2500.

Eligibility Requirements: Applicant must be high school student; planning to enroll or expecting to enroll full- or part-time at a four-year institution or university and resident of Washington. Applicant or parent of applicant must be member of American Legion or Auxiliary. Available to U.S. citizens.

Application Requirements: Application form, financial need analysis. *Deadline:* April 1.

Contact: Department Adjutant
American Legion Department of Washington
PO Box 3917
Lacey, WA 98509
Phone: 360-491-4373
E-mail: americanlegion@walegion.org

AMERICAN LEGION DEPARTMENT OF WEST VIRGINIA

http://www.wvlegion.org/

SONS OF THE AMERICAN LEGION WILLIAM F. "BILL" JOHNSON MEMORIAL SCHOLARSHIP

Applicant is required to write an essay based on a different question each year. Award is given during the second semester of college provided the winner has passing grades in the first semester. Must submit a copy of passing GPA of their first semester of college. Must be a resident of West Virginia and the child or grandchild of a member of The American Legion. Deadline each year is May 15th.

Award: Scholarship for use in freshman year; not renewable.

Eligibility Requirements: Applicant must be high school student; planning to enroll or expecting to enroll full-time at a two-year or four-year institution or university; resident of West Virginia and studying in West Virginia. Applicant or parent of applicant must be member of American Legion or Auxiliary. Available to U.S. citizens. Applicant or parent must meet one or more of the following requirements: general military experience; retired from active duty; disabled or killed as a result of military service; prisoner of war; or missing in action.

Application Requirements: Application form, essay. *Deadline:* May 15.

Contact: Mr. Miles Epling, Department Adjutant
American Legion Department of West Virginia
2016 Kanawha Boulevard East, P.O. Box 3191
Charleston, WV 25332-3191
Phone: 304-343-7591
E-mail: wvlegion@suddenlinkmail.com

AMERICAN POSTAL WORKERS UNION

http://www.apwu.org/

E.C. HALLBECK SCHOLARSHIP FUND

Scholarship for children of American Postal Workers Union members. Applicant must be a child, grandchild, stepchild, or legally adopted child of an active member, Retirees Department member, or deceased member of American Postal Workers Union. Must be a senior attending high school or other corresponding secondary school. Must be 18 years or older. Recipient must attend accredited community college or university as a full-time student. Scholarship will be $1000 for each year of four consecutive years of college. Scholarship will provide five area winners. For additional information and to download applications go to website http://www.apwu.org.

Award: Scholarship for use in freshman year; renewable. *Number:* 5. *Amount:* $1000.

Eligibility Requirements: Applicant must be high school student and planning to enroll or expecting to enroll full-time at a two-year or four-year or technical institution or university. Applicant or parent of applicant must be member of American Postal Workers Union. Applicant or parent of applicant must have employment or volunteer experience in federal/postal service. Available to U.S. citizens.

Application Requirements: Application form, essay, recommendations or references, test scores, transcript. *Deadline:* March 15.

Contact: Terry Stapleton, Secretary and Treasurer
American Postal Workers Union
1300 L Street, NW
Washington, DC 20005
Phone: 202-842-4215
Fax: 202-842-8530

VOCATIONAL SCHOLARSHIP PROGRAM

A scholarship for a child, grandchild, stepchild, or legally adopted child of an active member, Retiree's Department member, or deceased member of the American Postal Workers Union. Applicant must be a senior attending high school who plans on attending an accredited vocational school or community college vocational program as a full-time student. The award is $1000 per year consecutively or until completion of the course. For additional information see website http://www.apwu.org.

Award: Scholarship for use in freshman year; renewable. *Number:* 5. *Amount:* $1000.

Eligibility Requirements: Applicant must be high school student and planning to enroll or expecting to enroll full-time at a four-year institution or university. Applicant or parent of applicant must be member of American Postal Workers Union. Applicant or parent of applicant must have employment or volunteer experience in federal/postal service. Available to U.S. citizens.

Application Requirements: Application form, essay, recommendations or references, test scores, transcript. *Deadline:* March 15.

Contact: Terry Stapleton, Secretary and Treasurer
American Postal Workers Union
1300 L Street, NW
Washington, DC 20005
Phone: 202-842-4215
Fax: 202-842-8530

AMERICAN QUARTER HORSE FOUNDATION (AQHF)

http://www.aqha.com/foundation

AQHF GENERAL SCHOLARSHIP

Ideal candidates are current AQHA or AQHYA members.

Award: Scholarship for use in sophomore, junior, senior, graduate, or postgraduate years; renewable. *Number:* 1–15. *Amount:* $4000.

Eligibility Requirements: Applicant must be enrolled or expecting to enroll full-time at a two-year or four-year or technical institution or university. Applicant or parent of applicant must be member of American Quarter Horse Association. Applicant must have 2.5 GPA or higher. Available to U.S. and non-U.S. citizens.

Application Requirements: Application form, financial need analysis. *Deadline:* December 1.

Contact: Scholarship Office
American Quarter Horse Foundation (AQHF)
2601 East Interstate 40
Amarillo, TX 79104
Phone: 806-378-5040
E-mail: foundation@aqha.org

AQHF RACING SCHOLARSHIPS

Scholarships for applicants who have experience within the racing industry or are seeking a career in the industry. Applicants seeking a career in the racing industry may specialize in veterinary medicine, racetrack management or other related fields.

Award: Scholarship for use in freshman, sophomore, junior, senior, graduate, or postgraduate years; renewable. *Number:* 1–5. *Amount:* $4000–$8000.

Eligibility Requirements: Applicant must be enrolled or expecting to enroll full-time at a two-year or four-year or technical institution or university. Applicant or parent of applicant must be member of American Quarter Horse Association. Applicant or parent of applicant must have employment or volunteer experience in designated career field, harness racing. Applicant must have 2.5 GPA or higher. Available to U.S. and non-U.S. citizens.

Application Requirements: Application form, financial need analysis. *Deadline:* December 1.

Contact: Scholarship Office
American Quarter Horse Foundation (AQHF)
2601 East Interstate 40
Amarillo, TX 79104
Phone: 806-378-5040
E-mail: foundation@aqha.org

AQHF YOUTH SCHOLARSHIPS

Ideal candidates are members of AQHA or AQHYA who have completed a minimum of three years cumulative membership; exhibit an affinity for the American Quarter Horse, and demonstrate leadership potential.

Award: Scholarship for use in freshman, sophomore, junior, senior, or graduate years; renewable. *Number:* 1–15. *Amount:* $8000.

Eligibility Requirements: Applicant must be high school student and planning to enroll or expecting to enroll full-time at a two-year or four-year or technical institution or university. Applicant or parent of applicant must be member of American Quarter Horse Association. Applicant must have 3.5 GPA or higher. Available to U.S. and non-U.S. citizens.

Application Requirements: Application form, financial need analysis. *Deadline:* December 1.

Contact: Scholarship Office
American Quarter Horse Foundation (AQHF)
2601 East Interstate 40
Amarillo, TX 79104
Phone: 806-378-5040
E-mail: foundation@aqha.org

ARIZONA QUARTER HORSE YOUTH SCHOLARSHIP

Ideal candidate is an AQHA or AQHYA member from Arizona who is a current or previous member of the Arizona Quarter Horse Youth Association, and must be actively involved with AzQHA.

Award: Scholarship for use in freshman, sophomore, junior, senior, or graduate years; renewable. *Number:* 1. *Amount:* $5000.

Eligibility Requirements: Applicant must be enrolled or expecting to enroll full-time at a two-year or four-year or technical institution or university and resident of Arizona. Applicant or parent of applicant must be member of American Quarter Horse Association. Applicant must have 2.5 GPA or higher. Available to U.S. citizens.

Application Requirements: Application form, financial need analysis. *Deadline:* December 1.

Contact: Scholarship Office
American Quarter Horse Foundation (AQHF)
2601 East Interstate 40
Amarillo, TX 79104
Phone: 806-378-5040
E-mail: foundation@aqha.org

ARIZONA QUARTER RACING SCHOLARSHIP

Ideal candidate is an AQHA or AQHYA member from Arizona who has experience within, or is seeking a career in the racing industry. Recipient may specialize in veterinary medicine, racetrack management or other related field.

Award: Scholarship for use in freshman, sophomore, junior, senior, graduate, or postgraduate years; not renewable. *Number:* 1. *Amount:* $500.

Eligibility Requirements: Applicant must be enrolled or expecting to enroll full-time at a two-year or four-year or technical institution or university; resident of Arizona and must have an interest in animal/agricultural competition. Applicant or parent of applicant must be member of American Quarter Horse Association. Applicant or parent of applicant must have employment or volunteer experience in designated career field, harness racing. Applicant must have 2.5 GPA or higher. Available to U.S. citizens.

Application Requirements: Application form, financial need analysis. *Deadline:* December 1.

Contact: Scholarship Office
American Quarter Horse Foundation (AQHF)
2601 East Interstate 40
Amarillo, TX 79104
Phone: 806-378-5040
E-mail: foundation@aqha.org

BOON SAN KITTY SCHOLARSHIP

Ideal candidate is a current AQHA or AQHYA member.

Award: Scholarship for use in freshman, sophomore, junior, or senior years; renewable. *Number:* 1. *Amount:* $7500.

Eligibility Requirements: Applicant must be high school student and planning to enroll or expecting to enroll full-time at a two-year or four-year institution or university. Applicant or parent of applicant must be member of American Quarter Horse Association. Applicant must have 3.0 GPA or higher. Available to U.S. and non-U.S. citizens.

Application Requirements: Application form, financial need analysis. *Deadline:* December 1.

Contact: Scholarship Office
American Quarter Horse Foundation (AQHF)
2601 East Interstate 40
Amarillo, TX 79104
Phone: 806-378-5040
E-mail: foundation@aqha.org

CHRISTOPHER LAWRENCE JUNKER NEBRASKA SCHOLARSHIP

Ideal candidate is an AQHA or AQHYA member from Nebraska.

Award: Scholarship for use in freshman, sophomore, junior, or senior years; not renewable. *Number:* 1. *Amount:* $500.

Eligibility Requirements: Applicant must be enrolled or expecting to enroll full-time at a two-year or four-year or technical institution or university and resident of Nebraska. Applicant or parent of applicant must be member of American Quarter Horse Association. Applicant must have 2.5 GPA or higher. Available to U.S. citizens.

Application Requirements: Application form, financial need analysis. *Deadline:* December 1.

Contact: Scholarship Office
American Quarter Horse Foundation (AQHF)
2601 East Interstate 40
Amarillo, TX 79104
Phone: 806-378-5040
E-mail: foundation@aqha.org

DR. GERALD O'CONNOR MICHIGAN QHY SCHOLARSHIP

Ideal candidate is an AQHA or AQHYA member from Michigan. Scholarship is available once every four years.

Award: Scholarship for use in freshman, sophomore, junior, senior, or graduate years; renewable. *Number:* 1. *Amount:* $2000.

Eligibility Requirements: Applicant must be enrolled or expecting to enroll full-time at a two-year or four-year or technical institution or university; resident of Michigan and must have an interest in animal/agricultural competition. Applicant or parent of applicant must be member of American Quarter Horse Association. Applicant must have 2.5 GPA or higher. Available to U.S. citizens.

Application Requirements: Application form, financial need analysis. *Deadline:* December 1.

Contact: Scholarship Office
American Quarter Horse Foundation (AQHF)
2601 East Interstate 40
Amarillo, TX 79104
Phone: 806-378-5040
E-mail: foundation@aqha.org

DOGWOOD SCHOLARSHIP

Ideal candidate is a current AQHA or AQHYA member.

Award: Scholarship for use in freshman, sophomore, junior, or senior years; renewable. *Number:* 1. *Amount:* $4000.

Eligibility Requirements: Applicant must be enrolled or expecting to enroll full-time at a two-year or four-year or technical institution or university. Applicant or parent of applicant must be member of American Quarter Horse Association. Applicant must have 3.0 GPA or higher. Available to U.S. and non-U.S. citizens.

Application Requirements: Application form, financial need analysis. *Deadline:* December 1.

Contact: Scholarship Office
American Quarter Horse Foundation (AQHF)
2601 East Interstate 40
Amarillo, TX 79104
Phone: 806-378-5040
E-mail: foundation@aqha.org

EXCELLENCE IN EQUINE & AGRICULTURAL INVOLVEMENT SCHOLARSHIP

Ideal candidate is an AQHA or AQHYA member who exemplifies the characteristics of leadership and excellence acquired through participation in equine and or agriculture activities. Applicant should not compete in AQHA-approved shows.

Award: Scholarship for use in freshman, sophomore, junior, senior, or graduate years; renewable. *Number:* 1. *Amount:* $25,000.

Eligibility Requirements: Applicant must be enrolled or expecting to enroll full-time at a two-year or four-year institution or university. Applicant or parent of applicant must be member of American Quarter Horse Association. Applicant or parent of applicant must have employment or volunteer experience in agriculture. Applicant must have 3.5 GPA or higher. Available to U.S. and non-U.S. citizens.

Application Requirements: Application form, financial need analysis. *Deadline:* December 1.

Contact: Scholarship Office
American Quarter Horse Foundation (AQHF)
2601 East Interstate 40
Amarillo, TX 79104
Phone: 806-378-5040
E-mail: foundation@aqha.org

FARM AND RANCH HERITAGE SCHOLARSHIP

Ideal candidates are AQHA or AQHYA members from farming and or ranching backgrounds who represent the outstanding education, expertise and life skills gained through participation in agricultural activities. Applicants may not compete in AQHA-approved shows.

Award: Scholarship for use in freshman, sophomore, junior, senior, or graduate years; renewable. *Number:* 1–4. *Amount:* $12,500.

Eligibility Requirements: Applicant must be enrolled or expecting to enroll full-time at a two-year or four-year institution or university. Applicant or parent of applicant must be member of American Quarter Horse Association. Applicant or parent of applicant must have employment or volunteer experience in agriculture, farming. Applicant must have 3.0 GPA or higher. Available to U.S. and non-U.S. citizens.

Application Requirements: Application form, financial need analysis. *Deadline:* December 1.

Contact: Scholarship Office
American Quarter Horse Foundation (AQHF)
2601 East Interstate 40
Amarillo, TX 79104
Phone: 806-378-5040
E-mail: foundation@aqha.org

GUY STOOPS PROFESSIONAL HORSEMEN'S FAMILY SCHOLARSHIP

Ideal candidates are AQHA or AQHYA members whose parent(s) are a current member of the AQHA Professional Horsemen's Association, with membership in good standing for three or more years.

Award: Scholarship for use in freshman, sophomore, junior, or senior years; renewable. *Number:* 1. *Amount:* $3000.

Eligibility Requirements: Applicant must be enrolled or expecting to enroll full-time at a two-year or four-year or technical institution or university. Applicant or parent of applicant must be member of American Quarter Horse Association, Professional Horsemen Association. Applicant must have 2.5 GPA or higher. Available to U.S. and non-U.S. citizens.

Application Requirements: Application form, financial need analysis. *Deadline:* December 1.

Contact: Scholarship Office
American Quarter Horse Foundation (AQHF)
2601 East Interstate 40
Amarillo, TX 79104
Phone: 806-378-5040
E-mail: foundation@aqha.org

INDIANA QUARTER HORSE YOUTH SCHOLARSHIP

Ideal candidate is an AQHA or AQHYA member from Indiana who is a current member of the Indiana Quarter Horse Association, and has maintained two or more years membership with that association.

Award: Scholarship for use in freshman, sophomore, junior, or senior years; not renewable. *Number:* 1. *Amount:* $1000.

Eligibility Requirements: Applicant must be enrolled or expecting to enroll full-time at a two-year or four-year or technical institution or university and resident of Indiana. Applicant or parent of applicant must be member of American Quarter Horse Association. Applicant must have 2.5 GPA or higher. Available to U.S. citizens.

Application Requirements: Application form, financial need analysis. *Deadline:* December 1.

Contact: Scholarship Office
American Quarter Horse Foundation (AQHF)
2601 East Interstate 40
Amarillo, TX 79104
Phone: 806-378-5040
E-mail: foundation@aqha.org

JAMES F. AND DORIS M. BARTON SCHOLARSHIP

Ideal candidate is an AQHA or AQHYA member from New York who is a current member of the Empire State Youth Quarter Horse Association.

Award: Scholarship for use in freshman, sophomore, junior, or senior years; renewable. *Number:* 1. *Amount:* $5000.

Eligibility Requirements: Applicant must be enrolled or expecting to enroll full-time at a two-year or four-year institution or university and resident of New York. Applicant or parent of applicant must be member of American Quarter Horse Association. Applicant must have 3.0 GPA or higher. Available to U.S. citizens.

Application Requirements: Application form, financial need analysis. *Deadline:* December 1.

Contact: Scholarship Office
American Quarter Horse Foundation (AQHF)
2601 East Interstate 40
Amarillo, TX 79104
Phone: 806-378-5040
E-mail: foundation@aqha.org

JOAN CAIN FLORIDA QUARTER HORSE YOUTH SCHOLARSHIP

Ideal candidate is an AQHA or AQHYA member from Florida who is a current member of the Florida Quarter Horse Youth Association, and has maintained two or more years of membership.

Award: Scholarship for use in freshman, sophomore, junior, or senior years; not renewable. *Number:* 1. *Amount:* $1000.

Eligibility Requirements: Applicant must be enrolled or expecting to enroll full-time at a two-year or four-year or technical institution or university and resident of Florida. Applicant or parent of applicant must be member of American Quarter Horse Association. Applicant must have 2.5 GPA or higher. Available to U.S. citizens.

Application Requirements: Application form, financial need analysis. *Deadline:* December 1.

Contact: Scholarship Office
American Quarter Horse Foundation (AQHF)
2601 East Interstate 40
Amarillo, TX 79104
Phone: 806-378-5040
E-mail: foundation@aqha.org

JOYCE WYATT PENNSYLVANIA QUARTER HORSE YOUTH SCHOLARSHIP

Ideal candidate is an AQHA or AQHYA member from Pennsylvania. Scholarship is available once every four years.

Award: Scholarship for use in freshman, sophomore, junior, senior, or graduate years; renewable. *Number:* 1. *Amount:* $2000.

Eligibility Requirements: Applicant must be enrolled or expecting to enroll full-time at a two-year or four-year or technical institution or university and resident of Pennsylvania. Applicant or parent of applicant must be member of American Quarter Horse Association. Applicant must have 3.0 GPA or higher. Available to U.S. citizens.

Application Requirements: Application form, financial need analysis. *Deadline:* December 1.

Contact: Scholarship Office
American Quarter Horse Foundation (AQHF)
2601 East Interstate 40
Amarillo, TX 79104
Phone: 806-378-5040
E-mail: foundation@aqha.org

NEBRASKA QUARTER HORSE YOUTH SCHOLARSHIP

Ideal candidate is an AQHA or AQHYA member from Nebraska.

Award: Scholarship for use in freshman, sophomore, junior, or senior years; renewable. *Number:* 1. *Amount:* $2000.

Eligibility Requirements: Applicant must be enrolled or expecting to enroll full-time at a two-year or four-year or technical institution or university and resident of Nebraska. Applicant or parent of applicant must be member of American Quarter Horse Association. Applicant must have 2.5 GPA or higher. Available to U.S. citizens.

Application Requirements: Application form, financial need analysis. *Deadline:* December 1.

Contact: Scholarship Office
American Quarter Horse Foundation (AQHF)
2601 East Interstate 40
Amarillo, TX 79104
Phone: 806-378-5040
E-mail: foundation@aqha.org

SCOOP VESSELS SCHOLARSHIP

Ideal candidate is a member of AQHA who demonstrates a strong work ethic and financial need.

Award: Scholarship for use in junior or senior years; renewable. *Number:* 1. *Amount:* $5000.

Eligibility Requirements: Applicant must be enrolled or expecting to enroll full-time at a four-year institution or university. Applicant or parent of applicant must be member of American Quarter Horse Association. Applicant must have 2.5 GPA or higher. Available to U.S. and non-U.S. citizens.

Application Requirements: Application form, financial need analysis. *Deadline:* December 1.

Contact: Scholarship Office
American Quarter Horse Foundation (AQHF)
2601 East Interstate 40
Amarillo, TX 79104
Phone: 806-378-5040
E-mail: foundation@aqha.org

SWAYZE WOODRUFF MEMORIAL MID-SOUTH SCHOLARSHIP

Ideal candidate is an AQHA or AQHYA member from Alabama, Arkansas, Louisiana, Mississippi or Tennessee who competes in AQHA-approved shows.

Award: Scholarship for use in freshman, sophomore, junior, or senior years; renewable. *Number:* 1. *Amount:* $9000.

Eligibility Requirements: Applicant must be enrolled or expecting to enroll full-time at a two-year or four-year institution or university; resident of Alabama, Arkansas, Louisiana, Mississippi, Tennessee and must have an interest in animal/agricultural competition. Applicant or parent of applicant must be member of American Quarter Horse Association. Applicant must have 2.5 GPA or higher. Available to U.S. citizens.

Application Requirements: Application form, financial need analysis. *Deadline:* December 1.

Contact: Scholarship Office
American Quarter Horse Foundation (AQHF)
2601 East Interstate 40
Amarillo, TX 79104
Phone: 806-378-5040
E-mail: foundation@aqha.org

AMERICAN WATER SKI EDUCATIONAL FOUNDATION

http://www.waterskihalloffame.com/

AMERICAN WATER SKI EDUCATIONAL FOUNDATION SCHOLARSHIP

Awards for incoming college sophomores through incoming seniors who are members of USA Water Ski. Awards are based upon academics, leadership, extracurricular activities, recommendations, essay and financial need.

Award: Scholarship for use in sophomore, junior, or senior years; renewable. *Number:* 5. *Amount:* $1500–$3000.

Eligibility Requirements: Applicant must be enrolled or expecting to enroll full-time at a two-year or four-year institution or university. Applicant or parent of applicant must be member of USA Water Ski. Available to U.S. citizens.

Application Requirements: Application form, essay, financial need analysis, recommendations or references, self-addressed stamped envelope with application, transcript. *Deadline:* March 1.

Contact: Carole Lowe, Scholarship Director
Phone: 863-324-2472 Ext. 127
Fax: 863-324-3996
E-mail: awsefhalloffame@cs.com

AMVETS AUXILIARY

http://amvetsaux.org/

AMVETS NATIONAL LADIES AUXILIARY SCHOLARSHIP

One-time award of up to $1000 for a member of AMVETS or the Auxiliary. Applicant may also be the family member of a member. Award for full-time study at any accredited U.S. institution. Minimum 2.5 GPA required.

Award: Scholarship for use in sophomore, junior, or senior years; not renewable. *Number:* up to 7. *Amount:* $750–$1000.

Eligibility Requirements: Applicant must be enrolled or expecting to enroll full-time at a two-year or four-year or technical institution. Applicant or parent of applicant must be member of AMVETS Auxiliary. Applicant must have 2.5 GPA or higher. Available to U.S. citizens. Applicant or parent must meet one or more of the following requirements: general military experience; retired from active duty; disabled or killed as a result of military service; prisoner of war; or missing in action.

Application Requirements: Application form, essay, recommendations or references, transcript. *Deadline:* June 1.

Contact: Kellie Haggerty, Executive Administrator
AMVETS Auxiliary
4647 Forbes Boulevard
Lanham, MD 20706-4380
Phone: 301-459-6255
Fax: 301-459-5403
E-mail: auxhdqs@amvets.org

APPALOOSA HORSE CLUB-APPALOOSA YOUTH PROGRAM

http://www.appaloosayouth.com/

APPALOOSA YOUTH EDUCATIONAL SCHOLARSHIPS

Scholarship of up to $1000 available for members or dependents of members of the Appaloosa Youth Association or Appaloosa Horse Club. Based on academics, leadership, sportsmanship, and horsemanship. Printable application is available at website, http://www.appaloosayouth.com.

Award: Scholarship for use in freshman, sophomore, junior, or senior years; not renewable. *Number:* 6–8. *Amount:* $100–$1000.

Eligibility Requirements: Applicant must be enrolled or expecting to enroll full-time at a two-year or four-year institution or university and must have an interest in animal/agricultural competition or leadership. Applicant or parent of applicant must be member of Appaloosa Horse Club/Appaloosa Youth Association. Applicant must have 3.5 GPA or higher. Available to U.S. citizens.

Application Requirements: Application form, entry in a contest, essay, personal photograph, recommendations or references, test scores, transcript. *Deadline:* June 1.

Contact: Anna Brown, AYF Coordinator
Appaloosa Horse Club-Appaloosa Youth Program
2720 West Pullman Road
Moscow, ID 83843
Phone: 208-882-5578 Ext. 264
Fax: 208-882-8150
E-mail: youth@appaloosa.com

ARRL FOUNDATION INC.

http://www.arrl.org/

YOU'VE GOT A FRIEND IN PENNSYLVANIA SCHOLARSHIP

One-time award available to licensed general class or extra class amateur radio operators. Must be a member of American Radio Relay League and have an A or equivalent grade point average including graded courses in mathematics, science, and languages and excluding grades in sports or physical education. Must also be a resident of the Commonwealth of Pennsylvania.

Award: Scholarship for use in freshman, sophomore, junior, senior, graduate, or postgraduate years; not renewable. *Number:* 2. *Amount:* $2000.

Eligibility Requirements: Applicant must be enrolled or expecting to enroll full-time at a two-year or four-year or technical institution or university; resident of Pennsylvania and must have an interest in amateur radio. Applicant or parent of applicant must be member of American Radio Relay League. Applicant must have 3.5 GPA or higher. Available to U.S. citizens.

Application Requirements: Application form. *Deadline:* January 31.

Contact: Ms. Mary Hobart, Secretary
Phone: 860-594-0397
E-mail: k1mmh@arrl.org

ASSURED LIFE ASSOCIATION

http://assuredlife.org

ASSURED LIFE ASSOCIATION ENDOWMENT SCHOLARSHIP PROGRAM

Award for full-time study at a trade/technical school, two-year college, four-year college or university. Applicant must be a benefit member, or a child or grandchild of a benefit member, of Assured Life Association of Colorado. Applicant may reapply each year he/she is a full-time student.

Award: Scholarship for use in freshman, sophomore, junior, senior, or graduate years; not renewable. *Number:* 65–75. *Amount:* $500–$2500.

Eligibility Requirements: Applicant must be enrolled or expecting to enroll full-time at a two-year or four-year or technical institution or university. Applicant or parent of applicant must be member of Woodmen of the World. Applicant must have 2.5 GPA or higher. Available to U.S. and Canadian citizens.

Application Requirements: Application form, community service, essay, personal photograph. *Deadline:* March 15.

Contact: Mr. Jerome Christensen, Vice President
Assured Life Association
PO Box 3169
Englewood, CO 80155
Phone: 303-468-3773
E-mail: jlc@assuredlife.org

AUTOMOTIVE RECYCLERS ASSOCIATION SCHOLARSHIP FOUNDATION

http://www.a-r-a.org/

AUTOMOTIVE RECYCLERS ASSOCIATION SCHOLARSHIP FOUNDATION SCHOLARSHIP

Scholarships are available for the post-high school educational pursuits of the children of employees of direct ARA member companies.

Award: Scholarship for use in freshman, sophomore, junior, or senior years; not renewable.

Eligibility Requirements: Applicant must be enrolled or expecting to enroll full-time at a two-year or four-year institution or university. Applicant or parent of applicant must be member of Automotive Recyclers Association. Applicant must have 3.0 GPA or higher. Available to U.S. and non-U.S. citizens.

Application Requirements: Application form, letter verifying parents' employment, personal photograph, transcript. *Deadline:* March 15.

Contact: Kelly Badillo, Director, Member Services
Automotive Recyclers Association Scholarship Foundation
3975 Fair Ridge Drive, Suite 20-North
Fairfax, VA 22033
Phone: 703-385-1001 Ext. 26
Fax: 703-385-1494
E-mail: kelly@a-r-a.org

CALIFORNIA GRANGE FOUNDATION

http://www.csgfoundation.org/

CALIFORNIA GRANGE FOUNDATION SCHOLARSHIP

Scholarship program available for Grange members residing in California who wish to attend a higher institution of learning of their choice.

Award: Scholarship for use in freshman, sophomore, junior, or senior years; renewable. *Number:* 5–8. *Amount:* $250–$1000.

Eligibility Requirements: Applicant must be enrolled or expecting to enroll full- or part-time at a two-year or four-year or technical institution or university and resident of California. Applicant or parent of applicant must be member of Grange Association. Available to U.S. citizens.

Application Requirements: Application form, community service, essay, financial need analysis, recommendations or references, transcript. *Deadline:* April 1.

Contact: Mrs. Leslie Parker, Executive Assistant
California Grange Foundation
3830 U Street
Sacramento, CA 95817
Phone: 916-454-5805 Ext. 21
Fax: 916-739-8189
E-mail: info@californiagrange.org

CALIFORNIA STATE PARENT-TEACHER ASSOCIATION

http://www.capta.org/

CONTINUING EDUCATION-PTA VOLUNTEERS SCHOLARSHIP

Scholarships are available annually from the California State PTA to be used for continuing education at accredited colleges, universities, trade or technical schools. These scholarships recognize volunteer service in PTA and enable PTA volunteers to continue their education.

Award: Scholarship for use in freshman, sophomore, junior, or senior graduate years; not renewable. *Amount:* $500.

Eligibility Requirements: Applicant must be enrolled or expecting to enroll full- or part-time at a two-year or four-year or technical institution or university and resident of California. Applicant or parent of applicant must be member of Parent-Teacher Association/Organization. Applicant or parent of applicant must have employment or volunteer experience in community service. Available to U.S. citizens.

Application Requirements: Application form, copy of membership card, essay, recommendations or references, transcript. *Deadline:* November 15.

Contact: Becky Reece, Scholarship and Award Chairman
California State Parent-Teacher Association
930 Georgia Street
Los Angeles, CA 90015-1322
Phone: 213-620-1100
Fax: 213-620-1141

CALIFORNIA TEACHERS ASSOCIATION (CTA)

http://www.cta.org/

CALIFORNIA TEACHERS ASSOCIATION SCHOLARSHIP FOR DEPENDENT CHILDREN

Awards scholarships annually for dependent children of active, retired, or deceased members of California Teachers Association. Minimum 3.5 GPA required.

Award: Scholarship for use in freshman, sophomore, junior, senior, or graduate years; not renewable. *Number:* up to 25. *Amount:* $2500.

Eligibility Requirements: Applicant must be enrolled or expecting to enroll full-time at a two-year or four-year or technical institution or university. Applicant or parent of applicant must be member of California Teachers Association. Applicant must have 3.5 GPA or higher. Available to U.S. citizens.

Application Requirements: Application form, essay, recommendations or references, transcript. *Deadline:* February 8.

Contact: Janeya Collins, Scholarship Coordinator
California Teachers Association (CTA)
PO Box 921
Burlingame, CA 94011-0921
Phone: 650-552-5468
Fax: 650-552-5001
E-mail: scholarships@cta.org

CALIFORNIA TEACHERS ASSOCIATION SCHOLARSHIP FOR MEMBERS

Must be an active member of California Teachers Association (including members working on an emergency credential). Available for study in a degree, credential, or graduate program.

Award: Scholarship for use in freshman, sophomore, junior, senior, or graduate years; not renewable. *Number:* 5. *Amount:* $2500.

Eligibility Requirements: Applicant must be enrolled or expecting to enroll full-time at a two-year or four-year institution or university and resident of California. Applicant or parent of applicant must be member of California Teachers Association. Applicant or parent of applicant must have employment or volunteer experience in teaching/education. Applicant must have 3.0 GPA or higher. Available to U.S. citizens.

Application Requirements: Application form, essay, recommendations or references, transcript. *Deadline:* February 8.

Contact: Janeya Collins, Scholarship Coordinator
California Teachers Association (CTA)
PO Box 921
Burlingame, CA 94011-0921
Phone: 650-552-5468
E-mail: scholarships@cta.org

CIVIL AIR PATROL, USAF AUXILIARY

http://www.gocivilairpatrol.com/

CIVIL AIR PATROL ACADEMIC SCHOLARSHIPS

One-time award for active members of the Civil Air Patrol to pursue undergraduate, graduate, or trade or technical education. Must be a current CAP member. Significant restrictions apply. Not open to the general public.

Award: Scholarship for use in freshman, sophomore, junior, senior, or graduate years; not renewable. *Number:* up to 40. *Amount:* $1000–$7500.

Eligibility Requirements: Applicant must be enrolled or expecting to enroll full-time at a two-year or four-year or technical institution or university. Applicant or parent of applicant must be member of Civil Air Patrol. Available to U.S. citizens.

Application Requirements: Application form, essay, personal photograph, recommendations or references, resume, test scores, transcript. *Deadline:* January 31.

Contact: Kelly Easterly, Assistant Program Manager
Civil Air Patrol, USAF Auxiliary
105 South Hansell Street, Building 714
Maxwell Air Force Base, AL 36112-6332
Phone: 334-953-8640
Fax: 334-953-6699
E-mail: cpr@capnhq.gov

COMMUNITY BANKERS ASSOCIATION OF ILLINOIS

http://www.cbai.com/

COMMUNITY BANKERS ASSOC OF IL CHILD OF A BANKER SCHOLARSHIP

Must be a child or grandchild of an eligible CBAI member banker or be a part-time employee of an eligible CBAI member bank.

Award: Prize for use in freshman year; renewable. *Number:* 3. *Amount:* $4000.

Eligibility Requirements: Applicant must be high school student; planning to enroll or expecting to enroll full-time at a two-year or four-year or technical institution or university and resident of Illinois. Applicant or parent of applicant must be member of Community Banker Association of Illinois. Applicant or parent of applicant must have employment or volunteer experience in banking. Available to U.S. citizens.

Application Requirements: Application form. *Deadline:* August 15.

Contact: Ms. Bobbi Watson, Administrative Assistant
Community Bankers Association of Illinois
CBAI
901 Community Drive
Springfield, IL 62715
Phone: 800-736-2224
E-mail: bobbiw@cbai.com

COMMUNITY FOUNDATION OF WESTERN MASSACHUSETTS

http://www.communityfoundation.org/

HORACE HILL SCHOLARSHIP

Scholarships are given to children or grandchildren of a member of the Springfield Newspapers 25-Year Club. For more information or application, visit http://www.communityfoundation.org.

Award: Scholarship for use in freshman, sophomore, junior, senior, or graduate years; not renewable. *Amount:* up to $1000.

Eligibility Requirements: Applicant must be enrolled or expecting to enroll full- or part-time at a two-year or four-year institution or university and resident of Massachusetts. Applicant or parent of applicant must be member of Springfield Newspaper 25-Year Club. Available to U.S. citizens.

Application Requirements: Application form, Student Aid Report (SAR), transcript. *Deadline:* March 31.

Contact: Dotty Theriaque, Program Assistant for Scholarships
Community Foundation of Western Massachusetts
1500 Main Street
PO Box 15769
Springfield, MA 01115
Phone: 413-732-2858
Fax: 413-733-8565
E-mail: scholar@communityfoundation.org

EASTERN ORTHODOX COMMITTEE ON SCOUTING

http://www.eocs.org/

EASTERN ORTHODOX COMMITTEE ON SCOUTING SCHOLARSHIPS

One-time award for high school seniors planning to attend a four-year institution. Must be a registered member of a Boy or Girl Scout unit, an Eagle Scout or Gold Award recipient, active member of an Eastern Orthodox Church, and recipient of the Alpha Omega religious award.

Award: Scholarship for use in freshman year; not renewable. *Number:* 2. *Amount:* $500–$1000.

Eligibility Requirements: Applicant must be Eastern Orthodox; high school student; planning to enroll or expecting to enroll full-time at a four-year institution or university and single. Applicant or parent of applicant must be member of Boy Scouts, Girl Scouts. Available to U.S. citizens.

Application Requirements: Application form, community service, recommendations or references, self-addressed stamped envelope with application, test scores, transcript. *Deadline:* May 1.

Contact: George Boulukos, Scholarship Chairman
Eastern Orthodox Committee on Scouting
862 Guy Lombardo Avenue
Freeport, NY 11520
Phone: 516-868-4050
E-mail: geobou03@aol.com

EASTERN SURFING ASSOCIATION (ESA)

http://www.surfesa.org/

ESA MARSH SCHOLARSHIP PROGRAM

Grants are awarded to ESA current members in good standing on the basis of academics and U.S. citizenship rather than athletic ability.

Award: Scholarship for use in freshman, sophomore, junior, or senior years; not renewable. *Number:* 2. *Amount:* up to $8000.

Eligibility Requirements: Applicant must be enrolled or expecting to enroll full-time at a four-year institution or university. Applicant or parent of applicant must be member of Eastern Surfing Association. Available to U.S. citizens.

Application Requirements: Application form, essay, recommendations or references, transcript. *Deadline:* May 15.

Contact: Debbie Hodges, Scholarship Committee
Phone: 757-233-1790
E-mail: centralhq@surfesa.org

ELKS NATIONAL FOUNDATION

http://www.elks.org/enf

ELKS EMERGENCY EDUCATIONAL GRANTS

Grant available to children of Elks members who are deceased or totally disabled. Disability must be proven by recent doctors note. Parent must have been a member for at least a year before the date of death or onset of disability. Applicants for the one-year renewable awards must be unmarried, under the age of 23, be a full-time undergraduate student, and demonstrate financial need. They must also maintain a minimum 2.0 GPA.

Award: Scholarship for use in freshman, sophomore, junior, or senior years; not renewable. *Amount:* $1000–$4000.

Eligibility Requirements: Applicant must be enrolled or expecting to enroll full-time at a two-year or four-year institution or university and single. Applicant or parent of applicant must be member of Elks Club. Available to U.S. citizens.

Application Requirements: Application form, community service, essay, financial need analysis. *Deadline:* October 31.

Contact: Elks National Foundation Scholarship Office
Elks National Foundation
2750 North Lakeview Avenue
Chicago, IL 60614-2256
Phone: 773-755-4732
E-mail: scholarship@elks.org

ELKS NATIONAL FOUNDATION LEGACY AWARDS

$4,000 four-year scholarships available for children and grandchildren of Elks in good standing. Parent or grandparent must have been an Elk for two years and continue to be a member in good standing. Must be high school senior and apply through the related member's Elks Lodge. Applications available after September 1 online only, enf.elks.org/leg. Must be submitted online through the website.

Award: Scholarship for use in freshman, sophomore, junior, or senior years; renewable. *Number:* 250. *Amount:* $4000.

Eligibility Requirements: Applicant must be high school student and planning to enroll or expecting to enroll full-time at a four-year institution or university. Applicant or parent of applicant must be member of Elks Club. Available to U.S. citizens.

Application Requirements: Application form, community service, essay. *Deadline:* January 26.

Contact: Elks National Foundation Scholarship Office
Elks National Foundation
2750 North Lakeview Avenue
Chicago, IL 60614-2256
Phone: 773-755-4732
E-mail: scholarship@elks.org

FEDERATION OF AMERICAN CONSUMERS AND TRAVELERS

http://www.usafact.org

FEDERATION OF AMERICAN CONSUMERS AND TRAVELERS EDUCATIONAL GRANT PROGRAM

Approximately $75,000 will be awarded this year to members and their immediate families, with the hope of increasing accessibility to advanced education. Some of the highlights of this new program include a single application can be submitted for all types of education, from trade schools to graduate programs, no deadlines! Applications will be accepted year round and will be reviewed quarterly, awards will occur four times annually, and for the first time, graduate students may apply. The program will begin accepting applications on January 1, 2017.

Award: Grant for use in freshman, sophomore, junior, senior, graduate, or postgraduate years; not renewable. *Number:* 4–10. *Amount:* $250–$10,000.

Eligibility Requirements: Applicant must be enrolled or expecting to enroll full-time at a two-year or four-year or technical institution or university. Applicant or parent of applicant must be member of Federation of American Consumers and Travelers. Available to U.S. citizens.

Application Requirements: Application form, community service, essay. *Deadline:* continuous.

Contact: Vicki Rolens, Managing Director
Federation of American Consumers and Travelers
PO Box 104
Edwardsville, IL 62025
Phone: 800-872-3228 Ext. 10
E-mail: vrolens@usafact.org

FEDERATION OF AMERICAN CONSUMERS AND TRAVELERS TRADE/TECHNICAL SCHOOL SCHOLARSHIP

The FACT Trade/Technical School Scholarship is designed for students who wish to, or are currently attending a trade or technical school. Members of FACT, their children and grandchildren are eligible to apply.

Award: Scholarship for use in freshman, sophomore, junior, or senior years; not renewable. *Number:* 1–3. *Amount:* $1000–$5000.

Eligibility Requirements: Applicant must be enrolled or expecting to enroll full- or part-time at a technical institution. Applicant or parent of applicant must be member of Federation of American Consumers and Travelers. Available to U.S. citizens.

Application Requirements: Application form, community service, entry in a contest, essay, recommendations or references, test scores, transcript. *Deadline:* January 15.

Contact: Vicki Rolens, Managing Director
Federation of American Consumers and Travelers
PO Box 104
318 Hillsboro Avenue
Edwardsville, IL 62025
Phone: 800-872-3228
Fax: 618-656-5369
E-mail: vrolens@usafact.org

FIRST CATHOLIC SLOVAK LADIES ASSOCIATION

http://www.fcsla.org/

FIRST CATHOLIC SLOVAK LADIES ASSOCIATION HIGH SCHOOL SCHOLARSHIPS

Scholarship for high school students. A written report of approximately 250 words on "What This High School Scholarship Will Do for Me" must be submitted with application. Candidate must have been a beneficial member of the Association for at least three years prior to date of application.

Award: Scholarship for use in freshman year; renewable. *Number:* up to 32. *Amount:* $1000.

Eligibility Requirements: Applicant must be high school student and planning to enroll or expecting to enroll full-time at a four-year institution or university. Applicant or parent of applicant must be member of First Catholic Slovak Ladies Association. Available to U.S. and Canadian citizens.

Application Requirements: Application form, community service, essay, personal photograph, transcript. *Deadline:* March 1.

Contact: Director of Fraternal Scholarships
First Catholic Slovak Ladies Association
24950 Chagrin Boulevard
Beachwood, OH 44122
Phone: 800-464-4642
E-mail: info@fcsla.com

FLEET RESERVE ASSOCIATION EDUCATION FOUNDATION

http://www.fra.org/foundation

COLONEL HAZEL ELIZABETH BENN U.S.M.C. SCHOLARSHIP

Scholarship only for U.S. citizens who are unmarried, dependent children of a member in good standing of the FRA, currently or at time of death, who served or is now serving in the U.S. Navy as an enlisted medical rating assigned to and serving with the U.S. Marine Corps. Must be enrolled as a freshman or sophomore undergraduate at a state or regionally accredited institution of post-secondary education located in the United States.

Award: Scholarship for use in freshman or sophomore years; not renewable. *Number:* 1–5. *Amount:* $1000–$2000.

Eligibility Requirements: Applicant must be enrolled or expecting to enroll full-time at a two-year or four-year institution and single. Applicant or parent of applicant must be member of Fleet Reserve Association/Auxiliary. Available to U.S. citizens.

Application Requirements: Application form, community service, essay, financial need analysis. *Deadline:* April 15.

Contact: Mrs. Alicia Landis, Program Administrator
Phone: 703-683-1400 Ext. 107
E-mail: scholars@fra.org

DORAN/BLAIR SCHOLARSHIPS

Applicant or sponsor has to be a member in good standing of the FRA, currently or at time of death. Applicant must be an FRA member; spouse; dependent biological, step, or adoptive child; or biological, step, or adoptive grandchild; or biological, step, or adoptive great grandchild of the FRA member. Applicant must be a U.S. citizen, registered as a full time student in an accredited college located in the United States of America.

Award: Scholarship for use in freshman, sophomore, junior, senior, graduate, or postgraduate years; not renewable. *Number:* 1–20. *Amount:* $1000–$5000.

Eligibility Requirements: Applicant must be enrolled or expecting to enroll full-time at a two-year or four-year institution or university. Applicant or parent of applicant must be member of Fleet Reserve Association/Auxiliary. Available to U.S. citizens. Applicant must have served in the Coast Guard.

Application Requirements: Application form, community service, essay, financial need analysis. *Deadline:* April 15.

Contact: Mrs. Alicia Landis, Program Administrator
Phone: 703-683-1400 Ext. 107
E-mail: scholars@fra.org

GIRL SCOUTS OF CONNECTICUT

http://www.gsofct.org/

EMILY CHAISON GOLD AWARD SCHOLARSHIP

An annual scholarship of $750 is awarded each year to one Gold Award recipient from the state of Connecticut during her senior year.

Award: Scholarship for use in freshman year; not renewable. *Number:* 1. *Amount:* $750.

Eligibility Requirements: Applicant must be high school student; planning to enroll or expecting to enroll full-time at a four-year institution or university; female and resident of Connecticut. Applicant or parent of applicant must be member of Girl Scouts. Available to U.S. citizens.

Application Requirements: Application form, community service, essay, recommendations or references. *Deadline:* April 1.

Contact: Nancy Bussman, Scholarship Committee
Girl Scouts of Connecticut
340 Washington Street
Hartford, CT 06106
Phone: 203-239-2922
E-mail: nbussman@gsofct.org

GLASS, MOLDERS, POTTERY, PLASTICS AND ALLIED WORKERS INTERNATIONAL UNION

http://www.gmpiu.org/

GMP MEMORIAL SCHOLARSHIP PROGRAM

Six college scholarships of $4000 per year available to the sons and daughters of members of the union. Renewable each year for a full four-year college program if adequate academic standards are maintained. Four vocational/technical/two-year Associate degree scholarships of $2000 also available (not to exceed the cost of the program).

Award: Scholarship for use in freshman year; renewable. *Number:* 10. *Amount:* $2000–$4000.

Eligibility Requirements: Applicant must be high school student and planning to enroll or expecting to enroll full-time at a two-year or four-year or technical institution or university. Applicant or parent of applicant must be member of Glass, Molders, Pottery, Plastics and Allied Workers International Union. Available to U.S. and Canadian citizens.

Application Requirements: Application form, test scores. *Deadline:* November 1.

Contact: Bruce Smith, International Secretary and Treasurer
Glass, Molders, Pottery, Plastics and Allied Workers
International Union
608 East Baltimore Pike, PO Box 607
Media, PA 19063
Phone: 610-565-5051 Ext. 220
Fax: 610-565-0983

GOLDEN KEY INTERNATIONAL HONOUR SOCIETY

http://www.goldenkey.org/

GEICO LIFE SCHOLARSHIP

Ten $1000 awards will be given to outstanding students while balancing additional responsibilities. Must have completed at least 12 undergraduate credit hours in the previous year. Must be enrolled at the time of application and must be working toward a Baccalaureate degree.

Award: Scholarship for use in freshman, sophomore, junior, or senior years; not renewable. *Number:* 10. *Amount:* $1000.

Eligibility Requirements: Applicant must be enrolled or expecting to enroll full- or part-time at a four-year institution or university. Applicant or parent of applicant must be member of Golden Key National Honor Society. Available to U.S. and non-U.S. citizens.

Application Requirements: Application form, essay, recommendations or references, transcript. *Deadline:* April 1.

Contact: Scholarship Program Administrators
Golden Key International Honour Society
PO Box 23737
Nashville, TN 37202
Phone: 800-377-2401

GOLDEN KEY STUDY ABROAD SCHOLARSHIPS

Ten $1000 scholarships will be awarded each year to assist students in the pursuit of a study abroad program. Eligible members are undergraduate members who are currently enrolled in a study abroad program or will be enrolled in the academic year immediately following the granting of the award. Deadlines: April 15 and October 20.

Award: Scholarship for use in freshman, sophomore, junior, or senior years; not renewable. *Number:* 10. *Amount:* $1000.

Eligibility Requirements: Applicant must be enrolled or expecting to enroll full-time at a four-year institution or university. Applicant or parent of applicant must be member of Golden Key National Honor Society. Available to U.S. and non-U.S. citizens.

Application Requirements: Application form, description of the planned academic program, essay, transcript. *Deadline:* varies.

Contact: Scholarship Program Administrators
Golden Key International Honour Society
PO Box 23737
Nashville, TN 37202-3737
Phone: 800-377-2401
E-mail: scholarships@goldenkey.org

GOLF COURSE SUPERINTENDENTS ASSOCIATION OF AMERICA

http://www.eifg.org/

GOLF COURSE SUPERINTENDENTS ASSOCIATION OF AMERICA LEGACY AWARD

Awards of $1500 for the children or grandchildren of Golf Course Superintendents Association of America members. Applicants must be enrolled full-time at an accredited institution of higher learning, or for high school seniors, they must have been accepted at such an institution for the next academic year.

Award: Scholarship for use in freshman, sophomore, junior, or senior years; not renewable. *Number:* 20. *Amount:* $1500.

Eligibility Requirements: Applicant must be enrolled or expecting to enroll full-time at a two-year or four-year or technical institution or university. Applicant or parent of applicant must be member of Golf Course Superintendents Association of America. Available to U.S. and non-U.S. citizens.

Application Requirements: Application form, essay. *Deadline:* April 15.

Contact: Mischia Wright, Associate Director
Golf Course Superintendents Association of America
1421 Research Park Drive
Lawrence, KS 66049
Phone: 800-472-7878 Ext. 4445
Fax: 785-832-4448
E-mail: mwright@gcsaa.org

JOSEPH S. GARSKE COLLEGIATE GRANT PROGRAM

Award available to children/step children of GCSAA members who have been active members for five or more consecutive years for use at an accredited college or trade school. Applicant must be a graduating high school senior and be accepted at an institution of higher learning for the upcoming year.

Award: Scholarship for use in freshman year; not renewable. *Number:* 1–5. *Amount:* $500–$2500.

Eligibility Requirements: Applicant must be high school student and planning to enroll or expecting to enroll full-time at a two-year or four-year or technical institution or university. Applicant or parent of applicant must be member of Golf Course Superintendents Association of America. Available to U.S. and non-U.S. citizens.

Application Requirements: Application form, essay. *Deadline:* March 15.

Contact: Mischia Wright, Associate Director
Golf Course Superintendents Association of America
1421 Research Park Drive
Lawrence, KS 66049
Phone: 800-472-7878 Ext. 4445
Fax: 785-832-4448
E-mail: mwright@gcsaa.org

HAWAII EDUCATION ASSOCIATION

http://www.heaed.com/

HAWAII EDUCATION ASSOCIATION HIGH SCHOOL STUDENT SCHOLARSHIP

Scholarship available to high school seniors planning on attending four-year college/university. Must be HEA members, children of HEA members, or grandchildren or legally adopted grandchildren of HEA members. Members must be in good standing and shall have been members for at least one year.

Award: Scholarship for use in freshman year; not renewable. *Number:* up to 2. *Amount:* up to $2000.

Eligibility Requirements: Applicant must be high school student; planning to enroll or expecting to enroll full-time at a four-year institution or university and resident of Hawaii. Applicant or parent of applicant must be member of Hawaii Education Association. Available to U.S. citizens.

Application Requirements: Application, application form, essay, financial need analysis, personal photograph, recommendations or references, transcript. *Deadline:* April 1.

Contact: Laurie Togami, Scholarship Committee
Hawaii Education Association
1953 South Beretania Street, Suite 5C
Honolulu, HI 96826-1304
Phone: 808-949-6657
Fax: 808-944-2032
E-mail: hea.office@heaed.com

HAWAII EDUCATION ASSOCIATION UNDERGRADUATE COLLEGE STUDENT SCHOLARSHIP

Two scholarships of $2000 each are offered to deserving continuing, full-time undergraduate college students in any two- or four-year accredited institution of higher learning. HEA offers scholarships to HEA members, children of HEA members, or grandchildren or legally adopted grandchildren of HEA members. Members must be in good standing and shall have been members for at least one year.

Award: Scholarship for use in freshman, sophomore, junior, or senior years; not renewable. *Number:* up to 2. *Amount:* up to $2000.

Eligibility Requirements: Applicant must be enrolled or expecting to enroll full-time at a two-year or four-year institution or university. Applicant or parent of applicant must be member of Hawaii Education Association. Available to U.S. citizens.

Application Requirements: Application, application form, essay, financial need analysis, personal photograph, recommendations or references, transcript. *Deadline:* April 1.

Contact: Laurie Togami, Staff Specialist
Hawaii Education Association
1953 South Beretania Street, Suite 5C
Honolulu, HI 96826-1304
Phone: 808-949-6657
Fax: 808-944-2032

HELLENIC UNIVERSITY CLUB OF PHILADELPHIA

http://www.hucphiladelphia.org/

PAIDEIA SCHOLARSHIP

$3000 merit scholarship awarded to the child of a Hellenic University Club of Philadelphia member. Must be a U.S. citizen of Greek descent and a resident of particular counties in NJ or PA.

Award: Scholarship for use in freshman, sophomore, junior, or senior years; not renewable. *Number:* 1. *Amount:* up to $3000.

Eligibility Requirements: Applicant must be of Greek heritage; enrolled or expecting to enroll full-time at a four-year institution or university and resident of New Jersey, Pennsylvania. Applicant or parent of applicant must be member of Hellenic University Club of Pennsylvania. Available to U.S. citizens.

Application Requirements: Application form, financial need analysis, transcript. *Deadline:* April 3.

Contact: Anna Hadgis, Scholarship Chairman
Phone: 610-613-4310
E-mail: www.hucphiladelphia.org

HONOR SOCIETY OF PHI KAPPA PHI

http://www.PhiKappaPhi.org/

LITERACY GRANT COMPETITION

Grants up to $2500 are awarded to Phi Kappa Phi members for projects relating to a broad definition of literacy (math, science, music, art, reading, health, etc.). These projects should fulfill the spirit of volunteerism and community. Eligible applicants must be Active members of Phi Kappa Phi.

Award: Grant for use in freshman, sophomore, junior, senior, graduate, or postgraduate years; not renewable. *Number:* up to 18. *Amount:* $300–$2500.

Eligibility Requirements: Applicant must be enrolled or expecting to enroll full- or part-time at a two-year or four-year or technical institution or university. Applicant or parent of applicant must be member of Phi Kappa Phi. Available to U.S. and non-U.S. citizens.

Application Requirements: Application form, itemized budget. *Deadline:* April 1.

Contact: Mrs. Kelli Partin, Programs Coordinator
Honor Society of Phi Kappa Phi
7576 Goodwood Boulevard
Baton Rouge, LA 70806
Phone: 225-388-4917 Ext. 35
Fax: 225-388-4900
E-mail: kpartin@phikappaphi.org

INDEPENDENT OFFICE PRODUCTS AND FURNITURE DEALERS ASSOCIATION

http://www.iopfda.org/

NOPA AND OFDA SCHOLARSHIP AWARD

Candidates must have graduated from high school or its equivalent before July 1 of the year in which they would use the scholarship. Must have an academic record sufficient to be accepted by an accredited college, junior college, or technical institute. Must be a relative of a member of NOPA or OFDA.

Award: Scholarship for use in freshman, sophomore, junior, or senior years; not renewable. *Number:* up to 25. *Amount:* $2000.

Eligibility Requirements: Applicant must be enrolled or expecting to enroll full- or part-time at a two-year or four-year or technical institution or university. Applicant or parent of applicant must be member of Independent Office Products and Furniture Dealers Association. Available to U.S. and non-U.S. citizens.

Application Requirements: Application form, recommendations or references, transcript. *Deadline:* March 16.

Contact: Billie Zidek, Scholarship Administrator
Phone: 703-549-9040 Ext. 121
E-mail: bzidek@iopfda.org

INTERNATIONAL BOWLING CAMPUS YOUTH DEVELOPMENT

http://www.bowl.com/

GIFT FOR LIFE SCHOLARSHIP

The Gift for Life Scholarships are available to any USBC Youth member currently in high school and holding a GPA of 2.0 or better who can demonstrate financial need.

Award: Scholarship for use in freshman year; not renewable. *Number:* 12. *Amount:* $1000.

Eligibility Requirements: Applicant must be high school student; planning to enroll or expecting to enroll full- or part-time at a four-year institution or university and must have an interest in bowling. Applicant or parent of applicant must be member of Young American Bowling Alliance. Available to U.S. citizens.

Application Requirements: Application form, recommendations or references, transcript. *Deadline:* April 1.

Contact: Youth Marketing Project Manager
International Bowling Campus Youth Development
621 Six Flags Drive
Arlington, TX 76011
Phone: 800-514-2695 Ext. 8425
E-mail: esienicki@ibcyouth.com

USBC EARL ANTHONY MEMORIAL SCHOLARSHIP

Annually recognizes five USBC Youth bowlers for their community involvement and academic achievements.

Award: Scholarship for use in freshman, sophomore, junior, or senior years; not renewable. *Number:* 5. *Amount:* $5000.

Eligibility Requirements: Applicant must be high school student; planning to enroll or expecting to enroll full- or part-time at a two-year or four-year institution or university and must have an interest in bowling. Applicant or parent of applicant must be member of Young American Bowling Alliance. Applicant must have 3.0 GPA or higher. Available to U.S. citizens.

Application Requirements: Application form, community service, entry in a contest, essay, recommendations or references, transcript. *Deadline:* December 1.

Contact: Roger Noordhoek, Senior Director Youth Marketing
International Bowling Campus Youth Development
621 Six Flags Dr.
Arlington, TX 76011
Phone: 800-514-2695 Ext. 8308
E-mail: contactus@ibcyouth.com

INTERNATIONAL BROTHERHOOD OF TEAMSTERS SCHOLARSHIP FUND

http://www.teamster.org/

JAMES R. HOFFA MEMORIAL SCHOLARSHIP FUND

Scholarships available to children of members of the International Brotherhood of Teamsters (in good standing). The $10,000 awards are renewed on an annual basis. Also awarded are a one-time $1000 awards (non-renewable). The recipient must plan to attend a four-year institution and must maintain 3.0 GPA.

Award: Scholarship for use in freshman, sophomore, junior, or senior years; renewable. *Number:* 1–100. *Amount:* $1000–$10,000.

Eligibility Requirements: Applicant must be high school student and planning to enroll or expecting to enroll full-time at a four-year institution or university. Applicant or parent of applicant must be member of International Brotherhood of Teamsters. Applicant must have 3.0 GPA or higher. Available to U.S. and Canadian citizens.

Application Requirements: Application form, entry in a contest, list of activities, recommendations or references, test scores, transcript. *Deadline:* March 31.

Contact: Mrs. Traci Jacobs, Administrative Manager
International Brotherhood of Teamsters Scholarship Fund
25 Louisiana Avenue, NW
Washington, DC 20001
Phone: 202-624-8735
Fax: 202-624-7457
E-mail: tjacobs@teamster.org

INTERNATIONAL CHEMICAL WORKERS UNION

http://www.icwuc.org/

WALTER L. MITCHELL MEMORIAL AWARDS

Award available to children of International Chemical Workers Union members. Applicants must be starting their freshman year of college.

Award: Scholarship for use in freshman year; not renewable. *Number:* 12. *Amount:* $1500.

Eligibility Requirements: Applicant must be high school student and planning to enroll or expecting to enroll full-time at a two-year or four-year or technical institution or university. Applicant or parent of applicant must be member of International Chemical Workers Union. Available to U.S. citizens.

Application Requirements: Application form, biographical questionnaire, test scores, transcript. *Deadline:* April 23.

Contact: Sue Everhart, Secretary for Research and Education
International Chemical Workers Union
1799 Akron-Peninsula Road
Akron, OH 44313
Phone: 330-926-1444 Ext. 134
Fax: 330-926-0816
E-mail: severhart@icwuc.org

INTERNATIONAL EXECUTIVE HOUSEKEEPERS ASSOCIATION

http://www.ieha.org/

INTERNATIONAL EXECUTIVE HOUSEKEEPERS ASSOCIATION EDUCATIONAL FOUNDATION SPARTAN SCHOLARSHIP

Award available to IEHA members and their immediate families. Scholarship will be awarded to the best qualified candidate as determined by IEHA's education committee.

Award: Scholarship for use in freshman, sophomore, junior, or senior years; not renewable. *Number:* 1. *Amount:* $1500.

Eligibility Requirements: Applicant must be enrolled or expecting to enroll full- or part-time at a four-year institution or university. Applicant or parent of applicant must be member of International Executive Housekeepers Association. Available to U.S. and non-U.S. citizens.

Application Requirements: Application form, financial need analysis. *Deadline:* September 10.

Contact: Scholarship Selection Committee
International Executive Housekeepers Association
1001 Eastwind Drive, Suite 301
Westerville, OH 43081-3361
Phone: 800-200-6342
Fax: 614-895-1248

INTERNATIONAL UNION OF BRICKLAYERS AND ALLIED CRAFTWORKERS

http://www.bacweb.org/

CANADIAN BATES SCHOLARSHIP PROGRAM

The Canadian Bates Scholarship is a renewable scholarship for high school seniors for their undergraduate study. Three scholarships are granted annually and the award value is $1500 CND or $1200 CND. A student must be the son or daughter of a Canadian BAC member in good standing of a Canadian BAC local, and a graduating high school senior planning to attend college in the fall.

Award: Scholarship for use in freshman, sophomore, junior, or senior years; renewable. *Number:* 3. *Amount:* $1200–$1500.

Eligibility Requirements: Applicant must be Canadian citizen; high school student and planning to enroll or expecting to enroll full-time at a four-year institution or university. Applicant or parent of applicant must be member of International Union of Bricklayers and Allied Craftworkers.

Application Requirements: Application form, application form may be submitted online. *Deadline:* May 1.

Contact: Mrs. Constance Lambert, Communications and Education
Director
International Union of Bricklayers and Allied Craftworkers
620 F Street, NW
Washington, DC 20004
Phone: 202-383-3110
E-mail: kward@bacweb.org

U.S. BATES SCHOLARSHIP PROGRAM

The U.S. Bates Scholarship awards a stipend of $2500 per year for up to four years to three students annually. The program is open to sons and daughters of U.S. BAC members (in good standing) of U.S. BAC Locals who are in their junior year of high school, and who either have taken or plan to take the standardized PSAT exam.

Award: Scholarship for use in freshman, sophomore, junior, or senior years; renewable. *Number:* 3. *Amount:* $2500.

Eligibility Requirements: Applicant must be high school student and planning to enroll or expecting to enroll full-time at a four-year institution or university. Applicant or parent of applicant must be member of International Union of Bricklayers and Allied Craftworkers. Available to U.S. citizens.

Application Requirements: Application form. *Deadline:* February 28.

Contact: Mrs. Constance Lambert, Communications and Education
Director
International Union of Bricklayers and Allied Craftworkers
620 F Street, NW
Washington, DC 20004
Phone: 202-383-3110
E-mail: kward@bacweb.org

ITALIAN CATHOLIC FEDERATION

http://www.icf.org/

ITALIAN CATHOLIC FEDERATION FIRST YEAR SCHOLARSHIP

Scholarship for undergraduate students of the Catholic faith and of Italian heritage (or children or grand children of non-Italian ICF members). Must have minimum 3.2 GPA. Must live in AZ, CA, IL and NV.

Award: Scholarship for use in freshman year; not renewable. *Number:* 180–200. *Amount:* $400.

Eligibility Requirements: Applicant must be Roman Catholic; high school student; planning to enroll or expecting to enroll full-time at a two-year or four-year or technical institution or university and resident of Arizona, California, Illinois, Nevada. Applicant or parent of applicant must be member of Italian Catholic Federation. Available to U.S. citizens.

Application Requirements: Application form, essay, financial need analysis, recommendations or references, test scores, transcript. *Deadline:* March 15.

Contact: Scholarship Committee
Italian Catholic Federation
ICF Central Council Office
8393 Capwell Drive, Suite 110
Oakland, CA 94621
Phone: 510-633-9058
Fax: 510-633-9758

JUNIOR ACHIEVEMENT

http://www.ja.org/

JOE FRANCOMANO SCHOLARSHIP

Renewable award to high school seniors who have demonstrated academic achievement, leadership skills, and financial need. May be used at any accredited post secondary educational institution for any field of study resulting in a Baccalaureate degree. Must have completed JA Company Program or JA Economics.

Award: Scholarship for use in freshman year; renewable. *Number:* 1. *Amount:* $5000.

Eligibility Requirements: Applicant must be high school student; planning to enroll or expecting to enroll full-time at a four-year institution or university and must have an interest in leadership. Applicant or parent of applicant must be member of Junior Achievement. Applicant must have 3.0 GPA or higher. Available to U.S. citizens.

Application Requirements: Application form, essay, financial need analysis, recommendations or references, transcript. *Deadline:* February 1.

Contact: Gwen Rose, Scholarship Coordinator
Phone: 719-540-6134
E-mail: dterry@ja.org

KAPPA ALPHA THETA FOUNDATION

http://www.kappaalphathetafoundation.org/

KAPPA ALPHA THETA FOUNDATION NON-DEGREE EDUCATIONAL GRANT PROGRAM

Kappa Alpha Theta Foundation grants provide funds for collegian and alumnae members of Kappa Alpha Theta Fraternity for leadership training and non-degree educational and service-learning opportunities. Individual collegian and alumnae members of the Fraternity and college and alumnae chapters are eligible to apply.

Award: Grant for use in freshman, sophomore, junior, senior, graduate, or postgraduate years; not renewable. *Number:* 1. *Amount:* $100–$5000.

Eligibility Requirements: Applicant must be enrolled or expecting to enroll full- or part-time at an institution or university and female.

Applicant or parent of applicant must be member of Greek Organization. Available to U.S. and non-U.S. citizens.

Application Requirements: Application form. *Deadline:* continuous.

Contact: Ms. Gaylena Merritt, Director of Programs
Phone: 317-876-1870 Ext. 148
E-mail: gmerritt@kappaalphatheta.org

KAPPA ALPHA THETA FOUNDATION SCHOLARSHIP PROGRAM

Kappa Alpha Theta Foundation awards scholarships to graduate and undergraduate members of Kappa Alpha Theta Fraternity. Scholarships are awarded based upon academic performance, fraternity activities, campus and/or community activities, financial need (for need-based awards), and references.

Award: Scholarship for use in sophomore, junior, senior, graduate, or postgraduate years; not renewable. *Amount:* $1000–$12,000.

Eligibility Requirements: Applicant must be enrolled or expecting to enroll full- or part-time at a two-year or four-year institution or university and female. Applicant or parent of applicant must be member of Greek Organization. Available to U.S. and non-U.S. citizens.

Application Requirements: Application form, community service, essay, financial need analysis. *Deadline:* March 8.

Contact: Ms. Gaylena Merritt, Director of Programs
Phone: 317-876-1870 Ext. 148
E-mail: gmerritt@kappaalphatheta.org

KNIGHTS OF COLUMBUS

http://www.kofc.org/

FOURTH DEGREE PRO DEO AND PRO PATRIA (CANADA)

Renewable scholarships for members of Canadian Knights of Columbus councils and their children who are entering first year of study for Baccalaureate degree. Based on academic excellence. Award not limited to Fourth Degree members.

Award: Scholarship for use in freshman year; renewable. *Amount:* $1500.

Eligibility Requirements: Applicant must be Roman Catholic; Canadian citizen and enrolled or expecting to enroll full-time at a four-year institution or university. Applicant or parent of applicant must be member of Knights of Columbus. Applicant must have 3.0 GPA or higher.

Application Requirements: Application form, recommendations or references, test scores, transcript. *Deadline:* May 1.

FOURTH DEGREE PRO DEO AND PRO PATRIA SCHOLARSHIPS

Award available to students entering freshman year at a Catholic university or college in United States. Applicant must be a member or child of a member of Knights of Columbus or Columbian Squires. Scholarships are awarded on the basis of academic excellence. Minimum 3.0 GPA required. See website for additional information http://www.kofc.org.

Award: Scholarship for use in freshman, sophomore, junior, or senior years; renewable. *Amount:* $1500.

Eligibility Requirements: Applicant must be Roman Catholic and enrolled or expecting to enroll full-time at a four-year institution or university. Applicant or parent of applicant must be member of Columbian Squires, Knights of Columbus. Applicant must have 3.0 GPA or higher. Available to U.S. citizens.

Application Requirements: Application form, essay, recommendations or references, test scores, transcript. *Deadline:* March 1.

Contact: Rev. Donald Barry, Scholarship Coordinator
Knights of Columbus
Department of Scholarships, PO Box 1670
New Haven, CT 06507-0901
Phone: 202-336-6800
Fax: 202-408-8102
E-mail: info@kofc.org

FRANCIS P. MATTHEWS AND JOHN E. SWIFT EDUCATIONAL TRUST SCHOLARSHIPS

Available to dependent children of Knights of Columbus who died or became permanently disabled while in military service during a time of conflict, from a cause connected with military service, or who died as the result of criminal violence while in the performance of their duties as full-time law enforcement officers or firemen. The scholarship is awarded at a Catholic college in the amount not covered by other financial aid for tuition up to $25,000 annually.

Award: Scholarship for use in freshman, sophomore, junior, or senior years; renewable. *Amount:* up to $25,000.

Eligibility Requirements: Applicant must be Roman Catholic and enrolled or expecting to enroll full-time at a four-year institution or university. Applicant or parent of applicant must be member of Knights of Columbus. Available to U.S. citizens. Applicant or parent must meet one or more of the following requirements: general military experience; retired from active duty; disabled or killed as a result of military service; prisoner of war; or missing in action.

Application Requirements: Application form, proof of parent's military service or employment in law enforcement services. *Deadline:* March 1.

JOHN W. McDEVITT (FOURTH DEGREE) SCHOLARSHIPS

Scholarship for students entering freshman year at a Catholic college or university in United States. Applicant must submit Pro Deo and Pro Patria Scholarship application. Must be a member or wife, son, or daughter of a member of the Knights of Columbus. Minimum 3.0 GPA required. See website for additional information http://www.fofc.org.

Award: Scholarship for use in freshman year; renewable. *Amount:* $1500.

Eligibility Requirements: Applicant must be Roman Catholic and enrolled or expecting to enroll full-time at a four-year institution or university. Applicant or parent of applicant must be member of Knights of Columbus. Applicant must have 3.0 GPA or higher. Available to U.S. citizens.

Application Requirements: Application form, recommendations or references, test scores, transcript. *Deadline:* March 1.

PERCY J. JOHNSON ENDOWED SCHOLARSHIPS

Renewable scholarship for young men entering freshman year at a Catholic college or university. Applicants must submit Pro Deo and Pro Patria Scholarship application and a copy of Student Aid Report (SAR). Must be a member or a son of a member of the Knights of Columbus. Must also rank in upper third of class or have 3.0 GPA. See website for additional information http://www.kofc.org.

Award: Scholarship for use in freshman year; renewable. *Amount:* $1500.

Eligibility Requirements: Applicant must be Roman Catholic; enrolled or expecting to enroll full-time at a four-year institution or university and male. Applicant or parent of applicant must be member of Knights of Columbus. Applicant must have 3.0 GPA or higher. Available to U.S. citizens.

Application Requirements: Application form, financial need analysis, recommendations or references, test scores, transcript. *Deadline:* March 1.

LADIES AUXILIARY OF THE FLEET RESERVE ASSOCIATION

http://www.fra.org/

LADIES AUXILIARY OF THE FLEET RESERVE ASSOCIATION SCHOLARSHIP

Scholarship for members; spouses; dependent biological, step or adoptive child; or biological, step or adoptive grandchild of LA FRA or FRA member in good standing, currently or at time of death. Applicant must be a U.S. citizen, registered as a full-time student in an accredited college located in the United States.

Award: Scholarship for use in freshman, sophomore, junior, or senior years; not renewable. *Amount:* $1500.

Eligibility Requirements: Applicant must be enrolled or expecting to enroll full-time at a four-year institution or university and female. Applicant or parent of applicant must be member of Fleet Reserve Association/Auxiliary. Available to U.S. citizens. Applicant or parent must meet one or more of the following requirements: Coast Guard, Marine Corps, or Navy experience; retired from active duty; disabled or killed as a result of military service; prisoner of war; or missing in action.

Application Requirements: Application form, essay, recommendations or references, transcript. *Deadline:* April 15.

Contact: National Scholarship Chair
Ladies Auxiliary of the Fleet Reserve Association
PO Box 3459
Pahrump, NV 89041-3459
Phone: 775-751-3309

SAM ROSE MEMORIAL SCHOLARSHIP

Scholarship for members; spouses; dependent biological, step or adoptive child; or biological, step or adoptive grandchild of LA FRA or FRA member in good standing, currently or at time of death. Applicant must be a U.S. citizen, registered as a full-time student in an accredited college located in the United States.

Award: Scholarship for use in freshman, sophomore, junior, or senior years; not renewable. *Amount:* $1500.

Eligibility Requirements: Applicant must be enrolled or expecting to enroll full-time at a four-year institution or university. Applicant or parent of applicant must be member of Fleet Reserve Association/Auxiliary. Available to U.S. citizens. Applicant or parent must meet one or more of the following requirements: Coast Guard, Marine Corps, or Navy experience; retired from active duty; disabled or killed as a result of military service; prisoner of war; or missing in action.

Application Requirements: Application form, essay, recommendations or references, transcript. *Deadline:* April 15.

Contact: National Scholarship Chair
Ladies Auxiliary of the Fleet Reserve Association
PO Box 3459
Pahrump, NV 89041-3459
Phone: 775-751-3309

LEARNING ALLY

http://www.learningally.org

MARION HUBER LEARNING THROUGH LISTENING AWARDS

Awards presented to Learning Ally members who are high school seniors with learning disabilities, in recognition of extraordinary leadership, scholarship, enterprise and service to others. Must have minimum 3.0 GPA.

Award: Prize for use in freshman year; not renewable. *Number:* 6. *Amount:* $2000–$6000.

Eligibility Requirements: Applicant must be learning disabled; high school student and planning to enroll or expecting to enroll full-time at a two-year or four-year institution. Applicant or parent of applicant must be member of Learning Ally. Applicant must be learning disabled. Applicant must have 3.0 GPA or higher. Available to U.S. citizens.

Application Requirements: Application form, community service, essay. *Deadline:* May 31.

Contact: Jessica Kooper, Director of Engagement Marketing
Learning Ally
20 Roszel Road
Princeton, NJ 08540
Phone: 609-243-3089
E-mail: naa@learningally.org

MARY P. OENSLAGER SCHOLASTIC ACHIEVEMENT AWARDS

Award presented to Learning Ally members who are college seniors and blind or visually impaired, in recognition of extraordinary leadership, scholarship, enterprise, and service to others.

Award: Prize for use in senior or graduate years; not renewable. *Number:* 3–9. *Amount:* $1000–$6000.

Eligibility Requirements: Applicant must be visually impaired and enrolled or expecting to enroll full-time at a four-year institution or university. Applicant or parent of applicant must be member of Learning Ally. Applicant must be visually impaired. Applicant must have 3.0 GPA or higher. Available to U.S. citizens.

Application Requirements: Application form, community service, essay. *Deadline:* May 31.

Contact: Jessica Kooper, Director of Engagement Marketing
Learning Ally
20 Roszel Road
Princeton, NJ 08540
Phone: 609-243-7082
E-mail: naa@learningally.org

MINNESOTA AFL-CIO

http://www.mnaflcio.org/

MARTIN DUFFY ADULT LEARNER SCHOLARSHIP AWARD

Scholarship available for union members affiliated with the Minnesota AFL-CIO or the Minnesota Joint Council 32. May be used at any postsecondary institution in Minnesota. Information available on website at http://www.mnaflcio.org.

Award: Scholarship for use in freshman, sophomore, junior, or senior years; not renewable. *Number:* 4. *Amount:* $500.

Eligibility Requirements: Applicant must be enrolled or expecting to enroll full-time at a four-year institution or university; resident of Minnesota and studying in Minnesota. Applicant or parent of applicant must be member of AFL-CIO. Available to U.S. citizens.

Application Requirements: Application form. *Deadline:* April 30.

Contact: Computer Information Specialist
Minnesota AFL-CIO
175 Aurora Avenue
St. Paul, MN 55103
Phone: 651-227-7647
Fax: 651-227-3801

MINNESOTA AFL-CIO SCHOLARSHIPS

Applicant must be attending a college or university located in Minnesota. Must have a parent or legal guardian, who has held a one year membership in a local union which is an affiliate of the Minnesota AFL-CIO. Winners are selected by lot. Academic eligibility based on a straight "B" average or better. See website http://www.mnaflcio.org for information and application.

Award: Scholarship for use in freshman year; not renewable. *Number:* up to 5. *Amount:* $1000.

Eligibility Requirements: Applicant must be high school student; planning to enroll or expecting to enroll full-time at a two-year or four-year or technical institution or university and studying in Minnesota. Applicant or parent of applicant must be member of AFL-CIO. Applicant must have 3.0 GPA or higher. Available to U.S. citizens.

Application Requirements: Application form, transcript. *Deadline:* April 30.

Contact: Computer Information Specialist
Minnesota AFL-CIO
175 Aurora Avenue
St. Paul, MN 55103
Phone: 651-227-7647
Fax: 651-227-3801

NATIONAL ALLIANCE OF POSTAL AND FEDERAL EMPLOYEES (NAPFE)

http://www.napfe.com/

ASHBY B. CARTER MEMORIAL SCHOLARSHIP FUND FOUNDERS AWARD

Scholarships available to high school seniors. Must be a U.S. citizen. Applicant must be a dependent of NAPFE Labor Union member with a minimum three year membership. Applicant must take the SAT on or before March 1 of the year they apply for award.

Award: Scholarship for use in freshman year; not renewable. *Number:* 3. *Amount:* $2000–$5000.

Eligibility Requirements: Applicant must be high school student and planning to enroll or expecting to enroll full-time at a four-year institution or university. Applicant or parent of applicant must be member of National Alliance of Postal and Federal Employees. Available to U.S. citizens.

Application Requirements: Application form, community service, personal photograph, recommendations or references, self-addressed stamped envelope with application, test scores, transcript. *Deadline:* April 1.

Contact: Melissa Jeffries-Stewart, Director
Phone: 202-939-6325 Ext. 239
Fax: 202-939-6389
E-mail: headquarters@napfe.org

NATIONAL ASSOCIATION FOR THE ADVANCEMENT OF COLORED PEOPLE

http://www.naacp.org/

AGNES JONES JACKSON SCHOLARSHIP

Scholarship for undergraduate and graduate students who have been members of the NAACP for at least one year, or fully paid life members. Undergraduates must have 2.5 GPA and graduate students must have 3.0 GPA.

Award: Scholarship for use in freshman, sophomore, junior, senior, or graduate years; not renewable. *Number:* 1. *Amount:* $1500–$2500.

Eligibility Requirements: Applicant must be American Indian/Alaska Native, Asian/Pacific Islander, Black (non-Hispanic), Hispanic and enrolled or expecting to enroll full- or part-time at a two-year or four-year institution or university. Applicant or parent of applicant must be member of National Association for the Advancement of Colored People. Available to U.S. citizens.

Application Requirements: Application form, evidence of NAACP membership, financial need analysis, recommendations or references, transcript. *Deadline:* March 7.

Contact: Victor Goode, Attorney
Phone: 410-580-5760
E-mail: info@naacp.org

NATIONAL ASSOCIATION FOR THE SELF-EMPLOYED

http://www.NASE.org/

NASE SCHOLARSHIPS

Scholarship of $4000 for high school students or college undergraduates enrolled in full-time program of study. Total number of available awards varies. Applicants must be children or dependents of NASE Members and between the ages of 16 and 24.

Award: Scholarship for use in freshman, sophomore, junior, or senior years; not renewable. *Amount:* $4000.

Eligibility Requirements: Applicant must be age 16-24; enrolled or expecting to enroll full-time at a four-year institution or university and must have an interest in leadership. Applicant or parent of applicant must be member of National Association for the Self-Employed. Available to U.S. citizens.

Application Requirements: Application form, application form may be submitted online (http://www.nase.org/Membership/MembersBenefits/BenefitDetails.aspx?BenefitId=71), essay, financial need analysis, recommendations or references, resume, transcript. *Deadline:* April 1.

Contact: Molly Nelson, Member Communications Manager
Phone: 202-466-2100
Fax: 202-466-2123
E-mail: mnelson@NASEadmin.org

NATIONAL ASSOCIATION OF ENERGY SERVICE COMPANIES

http://www.aesc.net/

ASSOCIATION OF ENERGY SERVICE COMPANIES SCHOLARSHIP PROGRAM

Applicant must be the legal dependent of an employee of an AESC member company, or an employee. Dependents of company officers are not eligible. Must submit application to local AESC chapter chairman. Application must include ACT or SAT test scores.

Award: Scholarship for use in freshman, sophomore, junior, senior, or graduate years; renewable. *Number:* 150–200. *Amount:* $1000.

Eligibility Requirements: Applicant must be enrolled or expecting to enroll full-time at a two-year or four-year or technical institution or university. Applicant or parent of applicant must be member of Association of Energy Service Companies. Available to U.S. and non-U.S. citizens.

Application Requirements: Application form, essay. *Deadline:* March 14.

Contact: Susan Dudley, Administrative Assistant
Phone: 800-692-0771
Fax: 713-781-7542
E-mail: sdudley@aesc.net

NATIONAL ASSOCIATION OF LETTER CARRIERS

http://www.nalc.org/

COSTAS G. LEMONOPOULOS SCHOLARSHIP

Scholarships to children of NALC members attending public, four-year colleges or universities supported by the state of Florida or St. Petersburg Junior College. Scholarships are renewable one time.

Award: Scholarship for use in freshman, sophomore, junior, or senior years; renewable. *Number:* 1–20.

Eligibility Requirements: Applicant must be enrolled or expecting to enroll full-time at a two-year or four-year institution or university and studying in Florida. Applicant or parent of applicant must be member of National Association of Letter Carriers. Available to U.S. citizens.

Application Requirements: Application form, recommendations or references, transcript. *Deadline:* June 1.

Contact: Ann Porch, Membership Committee
Phone: 202-393-4695
E-mail: nalcinf@nalc.org

JOHN T. DONELON SCHOLARSHIP

Scholarship for sons and daughters of NALC members who are high school seniors when making application. The $1000 scholarship will be renewable for four years.

Award: Scholarship for use in freshman year; renewable. *Number:* 5. *Amount:* $1000.

Eligibility Requirements: Applicant must be high school student and planning to enroll or expecting to enroll full-time at a four-year institution or university. Applicant or parent of applicant must be member of National Association of Letter Carriers. Available to U.S. citizens.

Application Requirements: Application form, recommendations or references, transcript. *Deadline:* December 31.

Contact: Ann Porch, Membership Committee
Phone: 202-393-4695
E-mail: nalcinf@nalc.org

UNION PLUS SCHOLARSHIP PROGRAM

One-time cash award available for undergraduate and graduate study programs. Scholarship ranges from $500 to $4000. Three awards are granted. Must be children of members of NALC.

Award: Scholarship for use in freshman year; not renewable. *Number:* 3. *Amount:* $500–$4000.

Eligibility Requirements: Applicant must be high school student and planning to enroll or expecting to enroll full-time at a four-year institution or university. Applicant or parent of applicant must be member of National Association of Letter Carriers. Available to U.S. citizens.

Application Requirements: Application form, recommendations or references, transcript. *Deadline:* January 31.

Contact: Ann Porch, Membership Committee
Phone: 202-393-4695
E-mail: nalcinf@nalc.org

WILLIAM C. DOHERTY SCHOLARSHIP FUND

Five scholarships of $4000 each are awarded to children of members in NALC. Renewable for three consecutive years thereafter providing the winner maintains satisfactory grades. Applicant must be a high school senior when making application.

Award: Scholarship for use in freshman year; renewable. *Number:* 5. *Amount:* $4000.

Eligibility Requirements: Applicant must be high school student and planning to enroll or expecting to enroll full-time at a four-year institution or university. Applicant or parent of applicant must be member of National Association of Letter Carriers. Available to U.S. citizens.

Application Requirements: Application form, test scores, transcript. *Deadline:* December 31.

Contact: Ann Porch, Membership Committee
Phone: 202-393-4695
E-mail: nalcinf@nalc.org

NATIONAL ASSOCIATION OF SECONDARY SCHOOL PRINCIPALS

http://www.nhs.us/

NATIONAL HONOR SOCIETY SCHOLARSHIPS

One-time award to high school seniors who are National Honor Society members for use at an accredited two- or four-year college or university in the U.S. Application fee is $6. Contact school counselor or NHS chapter adviser as they must nominate seniors in good standing for the award. Minimum 3.0 GPA.

Award: Scholarship for use in freshman year; not renewable. *Number:* 200. *Amount:* $1000–$13,000.

Eligibility Requirements: Applicant must be high school student and planning to enroll or expecting to enroll full-time at a two-year or four-year institution or university. Applicant or parent of applicant must be member of National Honor Society. Applicant must have 3.0 GPA or higher. Available to U.S. and non-U.S. citizens.

Application Requirements: Application form, essay, nomination by NHS adviser, recommendations or references, test scores, transcript. *Fee:* $6. *Deadline:* January 23.

Contact: Wanda Carroll, Program Manager
Phone: 703-860-0200
E-mail: carrollw@principals.org

NATIONAL BETA CLUB

http://www.betaclub.org/

NATIONAL BETA CLUB SCHOLARSHIP

Applicant must be in twelfth grade and a member of the National Beta Club. Must be nominated by school chapter of the National Beta Club, therefore, applications will not be sent to the individual students. Renewable and nonrenewable awards available. Contact school Beta Club sponsor for more information.

Award: Scholarship for use in freshman year; renewable. *Number:* 221. *Amount:* $1000–$15,000.

Eligibility Requirements: Applicant must be high school student and planning to enroll or expecting to enroll full-time at a two-year or four-year institution or university. Applicant or parent of applicant must be member of National Beta Club. Available to U.S. citizens.

Application Requirements: Application form, application form may be submitted online, essay, recommendations or references, test scores, transcript. *Fee:* $10. *Deadline:* December 10.

Contact: Mrs. Joan Burnett, Scholarship Coordinator
Phone: 864-583-4553
Fax: 864-542-9300
E-mail: jburnett@betaclub.org

NATIONAL FFA ORGANIZATION

http://www.ffa.org

NATIONAL FFA COLLEGIATE SCHOLARSHIP PROGRAM

Scholarships to high school seniors planning to enroll in a full-time course of study at an accredited vocational/technical school, college or university. A smaller number of awards are available to currently enrolled undergraduates. Most awards require the applicant be an FFA member. Some awards are available to non-members.

Award: Scholarship for use in freshman, sophomore, junior, or senior years; not renewable. *Number:* 1700–1800. *Amount:* $300–$28,000.

Eligibility Requirements: Applicant must be age 17-23 and enrolled or expecting to enroll full-time at a two-year or four-year or technical institution or university. Applicant or parent of applicant must be member of Future Farmers of America. Available to U.S. citizens.

Application Requirements: Application form, application form may be submitted online (http://www.ffa.org/scholarships), signature page mailed by deadline. *Deadline:* February 1.

Contact: Scholarship Program Manager
National FFA Organization
PO Box 68960
Indianapolis, IN 46268
Phone: 317-802-6099
E-mail: scholarships@ffa.org

NATIONAL FOSTER PARENT ASSOCIATION

http://www.nfpaonline.org/

NATIONAL FOSTER PARENT ASSOCIATION YOUTH SCHOLARSHIP

Award for high school senior who will be entering first year of college, comparable education, or training program. Six $1000 awards, three for foster children currently in foster care with an NFPA member family, and one each for birth and adopted children of foster parents. NFPA family membership required ($35 membership fee).

Award: Scholarship for use in freshman year; not renewable. *Number:* 6. *Amount:* $1000.

Eligibility Requirements: Applicant must be high school student and planning to enroll or expecting to enroll full- or part-time at a two-year or four-year or technical institution or university. Applicant or parent of applicant must be member of National Foster Parent Association. Available to U.S. citizens.

Application Requirements: Application form, driver's license, essay, recommendations or references, test scores, transcript. *Deadline:* March 31.

Contact: Karen Jorgenson, Executive Director
National Foster Parent Association
7512 Stanich Avenue, Suite 6
Gig Harbor, WA 98335
Phone: 253-853-4000
Fax: 253-853-4001
E-mail: info@nfpaonline.org

NATIONAL JUNIOR ANGUS ASSOCIATION

http://www.angus.org/njaa/

ANGUS FOUNDATION SCHOLARSHIPS

Applicants must have at one time been a National Junior Angus Association member and currently be a junior, regular or life member of the association. Must have applied to undergraduate studies in any field. Applicants must have a minimum 2.0 GPA. See website for further information and to download application.

Award: Scholarship for use in freshman, sophomore, junior, senior, or graduate years; not renewable. *Number:* 75–90. *Amount:* $250–$5000.

Eligibility Requirements: Applicant must be enrolled or expecting to enroll full-time at a two-year or four-year or technical institution or university. Applicant or parent of applicant must be member of American Angus Association. Available to U.S. and Canadian citizens.

Application Requirements: Application form, recommendations or references, transcript. *Deadline:* May 1.

Contact: Mr. Milford Jenkins, Angus Foundation President
National Junior Angus Association
3201 Frederick Avenue
St. Joseph, MO 64506
Phone: 816-383-5100 Ext. 163
Fax: 816-383-5146
E-mail: mjenkins@angusfoundation.org

NATIONAL ORDER OF OMEGA

http://www.orderofomega.org/

FOUNDERS SCHOLARSHIP

Scholarship of $1000 available to juniors or seniors displaying leadership and service to their Order of Omega chapter.

Award: Scholarship for use in junior or senior years; not renewable. *Number:* 1. *Amount:* $1000.

Eligibility Requirements: Applicant must be enrolled or expecting to enroll full-time at a four-year institution or university and must have an interest in leadership. Applicant or parent of applicant must be member of Order of Omega. Available to U.S. and Canadian citizens.

Application Requirements: Application form, essay, personal photograph, recommendations or references, transcript. *Deadline:* November 16.

Contact: Scholarship Committee
National Order of Omega
300 East Border Street
Arlington, TX 76010-1656

NATIONAL SOCIETY DAUGHTERS OF THE AMERICAN REVOLUTION

http://www.dar.org/

NATIONAL SOCIETY DAUGHTERS OF THE AMERICAN REVOLUTION LILLIAN AND ARTHUR DUNN SCHOLARSHIP

A $2500 scholarship awarded for up to four years to well-qualified, deserving sons and daughters of members of the NSDAR. Outstanding recipients will be considered for an additional period of up to four years of study. Must include DAR member number.

Award: Scholarship for use in freshman, sophomore, junior, or senior years; renewable. *Amount:* $2500.

Eligibility Requirements: Applicant must be enrolled or expecting to enroll full-time at a four-year institution or university. Applicant or parent of applicant must be member of Daughters of the American Revolution. Available to U.S. citizens.

Application Requirements: Application form, financial need analysis. *Deadline:* February 15.

Contact: Lakeisha Graham, Manager, Office of the Reporter General
Phone: 202-628-1776
Fax: 202-879-3348
E-mail: nsdarscholarships@dar.org

NATIONAL SOCIETY OF COLLEGIATE SCHOLARS (NSCS)

http://www.nscs.org/

NSCS EXEMPLARY SCHOLAR AWARD

Scholarship of $1000 available to outstanding undergraduates among the NSCS members for their high academic achievement as well as additional scholarly pursuits outside of the classroom. They should exemplify the NSCS mission: "Honoring and inspiring academic excellence and engaged citizenship for a lifetime" and show integrity in everything they do. Must have a completed profile and resume in NSCS database. Apply on website http://www.nscs.org/exemplary_scholar_award.

Award: Scholarship for use in freshman, sophomore, junior, or senior years; not renewable. *Number:* 3. *Amount:* $1000.

Eligibility Requirements: Applicant must be enrolled or expecting to enroll full- or part-time at a four-year institution or university and must have an interest in leadership. Applicant or parent of applicant must be member of National Society of Collegiate Scholars. Available to U.S. and non-U.S. citizens.

Application Requirements: Application form. *Deadline:* April 30.

Contact: Stephen Loflin, Executive Director
Phone: 202-965-9000
E-mail: nscs@nscs.org

NSCS MERIT AWARD

Fifty merit awards to outstanding new NSCS members around the country. Student is chosen based upon how they exemplify the mission of NSCS. Must have a resume in the NSCS database and be a member who has joined between August of the previous year and July of the present year. Must have a minimum GPA of 3.4 and be enrolled in an accredited institution. For additional information, see website http://www.nscs.org.

Award: Scholarship for use in freshman, sophomore, junior, or senior years; not renewable. *Number:* 50. *Amount:* $1000.

Eligibility Requirements: Applicant must be enrolled or expecting to enroll full- or part-time at a two-year or four-year or technical institution or university. Applicant or parent of applicant must be member of

National Society of Collegiate Scholars. Available to U.S. and non-U.S. citizens.

Application Requirements: Application form, recommendations or references, resume, transcript. *Deadline:* July 31.

Contact: Stephen Loflin, Executive Director
Phone: 202-965-9000
E-mail: nscs@nscs.org

NSCS SCHOLAR ABROAD SCHOLARSHIP

Scholarship for an active NSCS member who has been accepted to and enrolled in an accredited study abroad program. One $5000 scholarship is awarded each fall and spring semester and one $2500 scholarship is awarded for the summer term. Must have profile and resume in NSCS database and have a minimum 3.4 GPA. Apply at website http://www.nscs.org/scholar-abroad-scholarship.

Award: Scholarship for use in freshman, sophomore, junior, or senior years; not renewable. *Number:* 3. *Amount:* $2500–$5000.

Eligibility Requirements: Applicant must be enrolled or expecting to enroll full-time at a two-year or four-year institution or university. Applicant or parent of applicant must be member of National Society of Collegiate Scholars. Available to U.S. and non-U.S. citizens.

Application Requirements: Application form, resume. *Deadline:* April 15.

Contact: Stephen Loflin, Executive Director
Phone: 202-965-9000
E-mail: nscs@nscs.org

NATIONAL SOCIETY OF HIGH SCHOOL SCHOLARS

www.nshss.org

ABERCROMBIE & FITCH SCHOLAR AWARDS

Ten scholarships of $1000 to high school seniors who are members of NSHSS. Must submit written response to the question posed by A&F regarding diversity and inclusion.

Award: Scholarship for use in freshman, sophomore, or junior years; not renewable. *Number:* 20. *Amount:* $1000.

Eligibility Requirements: Applicant must be high school student and planning to enroll or expecting to enroll full-time at a four-year institution or university. Applicant or parent of applicant must be member of National Society of High School Scholars. Applicant must have 3.5 GPA or higher. Available to U.S. and non-U.S. citizens.

Application Requirements: Application form, essay, personal photograph. *Deadline:* April 30.

Contact: Dr. Susan Thurman, Scholarship Director
National Society of High School Scholars
1936 North Druid Hills Road
Atlanta, GA 30319
Phone: 866-343-1800
E-mail: susan.thurman@nshss.org

CLAES NOBEL ACADEMIC SCHOLARSHIPS

Scholarships for high school students planning to attend four-year colleges or universities who are members of NSHSS. Minimum 3.5 GPA required.

Award: Scholarship for use in freshman year; not renewable. *Number:* 10. *Amount:* $5000.

Eligibility Requirements: Applicant must be high school student; planning to enroll or expecting to enroll full-time at a four-year institution or university and must have an interest in leadership. Applicant or parent of applicant must be member of National Society of High School Scholars. Applicant must have 3.5 GPA or higher. Available to U.S. and non-U.S. citizens.

Application Requirements: Application form, essay, personal photograph. *Deadline:* March 1.

Contact: Dr. Susan Thurman, Scholarship Director
National Society of High School Scholars
1936 North Druid Hills Road
Atlanta, GA 30319
Phone: 404-235-5500
E-mail: scholarships@nshss.org

NATIONAL SCHOLAR AWARDS FOR NSHSS MEMBERS

Scholarship of $1000 for undergraduate study. Applicant must be a member of NSHSS.

Award: Scholarship for use in freshman year; not renewable. *Number:* 75. *Amount:* $1000.

Eligibility Requirements: Applicant must be high school student; planning to enroll or expecting to enroll full-time at a two-year or four-year or technical institution or university and must have an interest in leadership. Applicant or parent of applicant must be member of National Society of High School Scholars. Applicant must have 3.5 GPA or higher. Available to U.S. and non-U.S. citizens.

Application Requirements: Application form, essay, personal photograph. *Deadline:* March 1.

Contact: Dr. Susan Thurman, Scholarship Director
National Society of High School Scholars
1936 North Druid Hills road
Atlanta, GA 30319
Phone: 404-235-5500
E-mail: scholarships@nshss.org

ROBERT P. SHEPPARD LEADERSHIP AWARD FOR NSHSS MEMBERS

Scholarship of $1000 awarded to an NSHSS member demonstrating outstanding dedication to community service and initiative in volunteer activities.

Award: Scholarship for use in freshman year; not renewable. *Number:* 5. *Amount:* $1000–$2500.

Eligibility Requirements: Applicant must be high school student; planning to enroll or expecting to enroll full-time at a four-year institution or university and must have an interest in leadership. Applicant or parent of applicant must be member of National Society of High School Scholars. Applicant must have 3.5 GPA or higher. Available to U.S. and non-U.S. citizens.

Application Requirements: Application form, essay, personal photograph. *Deadline:* March 10.

Contact: Dr. Susan Thurman, Scholarship Director
National Society of High School Scholars
1936 North Druid Hills Road
Atlanta, GA 30319
Phone: 404-235-5500
E-mail: scholarships@nshss.org

NEW YORK STATE GRANGE

http://www.nysgrange.org/

SUSAN W. FREESTONE EDUCATION AWARD

Grants for members of Junior Grange and Subordinate Grange in New York State. Students must enroll in an approved two or four-year college in New York State. Second grants available with reapplication.

Award: Scholarship for use in freshman or sophomore years; not renewable. *Number:* 1–4. *Amount:* $1000.

Eligibility Requirements: Applicant must be high school student; planning to enroll or expecting to enroll full-time at a two-year or four-year institution; resident of New York and studying in New York. Applicant or parent of applicant must be member of Grange Association. Applicant must have 2.5 GPA or higher. Available to U.S. citizens.

Application Requirements: Application form, financial need analysis. *Deadline:* April 15.

Contact: Scholarship Committee
New York State Grange
100 Grange Place
Cortland, NY 13045
Phone: 607-756-7553
E-mail: nysgrange@nysgrange.com

NORTHEASTERN LOGGERS' ASSOCIATION INC.

http://www.northernlogger.com/

NORTHEASTERN LOGGERS' ASSOCIATION SCHOLARSHIPS

Scholarships available to those whose family is a member of the Northeastern Loggers' Association or whose family member is an employee of an Industrial or Associate Members of the Northeastern Loggers' Association. Must submit paper on topic of "What it means to grow up in the forest industry";

Award: Scholarship for use in freshman, sophomore, junior, or senior years; not renewable. *Number:* 6–10. *Amount:* $500–$1000.

Eligibility Requirements: Applicant must be enrolled or expecting to enroll full-time at a two-year or four-year or technical institution or university. Applicant or parent of applicant must be member of Northeastern Loggers Association. Available to U.S. and Canadian citizens.

Application Requirements: Application form, application form may be submitted online (http://northernlogger.com/content/nela-scholarships), entry in a contest, essay, transcript. *Deadline:* March 31.

Contact: Mona Lincoln, Director, Training and Safety
Northeastern Loggers' Association Inc.
PO Box 69
Old Forge, NY 13420-0069
Phone: 315-369-3078
Fax: 315-369-3736
E-mail: mona@northernlogger.com

NORTH EAST ROOFING EDUCATIONAL FOUNDATION

http://www.nerca.org/

NORTH EAST ROOFING EDUCATIONAL FOUNDATION SCHOLARSHIP

Applicants must be a member of NERCA, their employees, or their respective immediate family. Immediate family is defined as self, spouse, or child. The child may be natural, legally adopted, or a stepchild. Also must be a high school senior or graduate who plans to enroll in a full-time undergraduate course of study at an accredited two-year or four-year college, university, or vocational-technical school.

Award: Scholarship for use in freshman, sophomore, junior, or senior years; not renewable. *Number:* 11. *Amount:* up to $2000.

Eligibility Requirements: Applicant must be enrolled or expecting to enroll full-time at a two-year or four-year or technical institution or university. Applicant or parent of applicant must be member of North East Roofing Contractors Association. Available to U.S. and Canadian citizens.

Application Requirements: Application form, recommendations or references, self-addressed stamped envelope with application, transcript. *Deadline:* May 1.

Contact: Patsy Sweeney, Clerk
North East Roofing Educational Foundation
150 Grossman Drive Street, Suite 313
Braintree, MA 02184
Phone: 781-849-0555
Fax: 781-849-3223
E-mail: info@nerca.org

OFFICE AND PROFESSIONAL EMPLOYEES INTERNATIONAL UNION

http://www.opeiu.org/

OFFICE AND PROFESSIONAL EMPLOYEES INTERNATIONAL UNION HOWARD COUGHLIN MEMORIAL SCHOLARSHIP FUND

Scholarship of twelve full-time awards of $6000 and six part-time awards of $2400 is given to undergraduate students. Applicants should be a member or associate member of the Union.

Award: Scholarship for use in freshman, sophomore, junior, or senior years; not renewable. *Number:* 18. *Amount:* $2400–$6000.

Eligibility Requirements: Applicant must be enrolled or expecting to enroll full- or part-time at a two-year or four-year or technical institution or university. Applicant or parent of applicant must be member of Office and Professional Employees International Union. Available to U.S. citizens.

Application Requirements: Application form, SAT/CAT scores, transcript. *Deadline:* March 31.

Contact: Mary Mahoney, Secretary-Treasurer
    Phone: 202-393-4464
    Fax: 202-887-0910
    E-mail: mmahoney@opeiudc.org

OKLAHOMA ALUMNI & ASSOCIATES OF FHA, HERO AND FCCLA INC.

http://www.okfccla.net/

OKLAHOMA ALUMNI & ASSOCIATES OF FHA, HERO, AND FCCLA INC. SCHOLARSHIP

One-time award for FCCLA members who will be pursuing a postsecondary education. Must be a resident of Oklahoma. Scholarship value is $1000. Two scholarships are granted.

Award: Scholarship for use in freshman year; not renewable. *Number:* 2. *Amount:* $1000.

Eligibility Requirements: Applicant must be high school student; planning to enroll or expecting to enroll full-time at a two-year or four-year or technical institution or university and resident of Oklahoma. Applicant or parent of applicant must be member of Family, Career and Community Leaders of America. Applicant must have 3.0 GPA or higher. Available to U.S. citizens.

Application Requirements: Application form, essay, recommendations or references, transcript. *Deadline:* March 1.

Contact: Denise Morris, State FCCLA Adviser
    Oklahoma Alumni & Associates of FHA, HERO and FCCLA Inc.
    1500 West Seventh Avenue
    Stillwater, OK 74074
    Phone: 405-743-5467
    Fax: 405-743-6809
    E-mail: dmorr@okcareertech.org

OREGON STUDENT ASSISTANCE COMMISSION

http://www.GetCollegeFunds.org/

AFSCME: AMERICAN FEDERATION OF STATE, COUNTY, AND MUNICIPAL EMPLOYEES LOCAL 2067 SCHOLARSHIP

Award for active members in good standing or spouses, children, or grandchildren of active members in good standing of Oregon AFSCME Local 2067. Qualifying members must have been active in AFSCME Local 2067 one+ year as of the March scholarship deadline. Oregon residency is not required. Minimum 2.5 GPA.

Award: Scholarship for use in freshman, sophomore, junior, or senior years; not renewable.

Eligibility Requirements: Applicant must be enrolled or expecting to enroll full- or part-time at a four-year institution or university. Applicant or parent of applicant must be member of American Federation of State, County, and Municipal Employees. Applicant must have 2.5 GPA or higher. Available to U.S. citizens.

Application Requirements: Application form, essay, financial need analysis. *Deadline:* March 1.

Contact: Melissa Adams, Scholarship Processing Coordinator
    Phone: 541-687-7409
    E-mail: melissa.adams@hecc.oregon.gov

AMERICAN FEDERATION OF STATE, COUNTY, AND MUNICIPAL EMPLOYEES OREGON COUNCIL # 75 SCHOLARSHIP

Renewable award for active, laid-off, retired, or disabled members in good standing or spouses (including life partners and their children), natural children, or grandchildren of active, laid-off, retired, disabled, or deceased members of AFSCME #75 in good standing. Qualifying members must have been active in AFSCME Council # 75 one year or more as of the March 1 scholarship deadline or have been a member one year or more preceding the date of layoff, death, disability, or retirement. Enrollment of at least half-time is required. Financial need may or may not be considered.

Award: Scholarship for use in freshman, sophomore, junior, senior, or graduate years; renewable.

Eligibility Requirements: Applicant must be enrolled or expecting to enroll full- or part-time at a two-year or four-year institution or university. Applicant or parent of applicant must be member of American Federation of State, County, and Municipal Employees. Available to U.S. citizens.

Application Requirements: Application form, essay, financial need analysis. *Deadline:* March 1.

Contact: Melissa Adams, Scholarship Processing Coordinator
    Phone: 541-687-7409
    E-mail: melissa.adams@hecc.oregon.gov

CLYDE C. CROSBY/JOSEPH M. EDGAR AND THOMAS J. MALLOY MEMORIAL SCHOLARSHIP

Renewable scholarship available for a graduating high school senior with a minimum 3.0 cumulative GPA who is a child, or dependent stepchild of an active, retired, disabled, or deceased member of local union affiliated with Teamsters 37. Member must have been active for at least one year. FAFSA is required. Scholarship is automatically renewable if renewal criteria met.

Award: Scholarship for use in freshman, sophomore, junior, or senior years; renewable.

Eligibility Requirements: Applicant must be high school student and planning to enroll or expecting to enroll full-time at a four-year institution. Applicant or parent of applicant must be member of Teamsters. Applicant must have 3.0 GPA or higher. Available to U.S. citizens.

Application Requirements: Application form, financial need analysis. *Deadline:* March 1.

Contact: Melissa Adams, Scholarship Processing Coordinator
    Phone: 541-687-7409
    E-mail: melissa.adams@hecc.oregon.gov

INTERNATIONAL BROTHERHOOD OF ELECTRICAL WORKERS LOCAL 280 SCHOLARSHIP

One-time award available for children or grandchildren of active or retired members of IBEW Local 280. Must be graduating high school seniors enrolling as first-time freshman in any college or university in the U.S.

Award: Scholarship for use in freshman year; not renewable.

Eligibility Requirements: Applicant must be enrolled or expecting to enroll full-time at a four-year institution or university. Applicant or parent of applicant must be member of International Brotherhood of Electrical Workers. Available to U.S. citizens.

Application Requirements: Application form, essay. *Deadline:* March 1.

Contact: Melissa Adams, Scholarship Processing Coordinator
    Phone: 541-687-7409
    E-mail: melissa.adams@hecc.oregon.gov

INTERNATIONAL UNION OF OPERATING ENGINEERS LOCAL 701 SCHOLARSHIP

One-time award available for graduating high school seniors who are children of International Union of Operating Engineers Local 701 members.

Award: Scholarship for use in freshman year; not renewable.

Eligibility Requirements: Applicant must be high school student and planning to enroll or expecting to enroll full-time at a four-year institution or university. Applicant or parent of applicant must be member of International Union of Operating Engineers. Available to U.S. citizens.

Application Requirements: Application form. *Deadline:* March 1.

Contact: Melissa Adams, Scholarship Processing Coordinator
    Phone: 541-687-7409
    E-mail: melissa.adams@hecc.oregon.gov

JOSH HIETER MEMORIAL/TEAMSTERS LOCAL 223 SCHOLARSHIP

One-time award for active members or dependent children or stepchildren of active, retired, disabled, or deceased members of Local 223 of the Joint Council of Teamsters #37. Member must have been active 1+ year as of the March scholarship deadline or have been a member 1+ year preceding the date of retirement, disability, or death. For use at an Oregon public or non-profit college. Minimum 3.0 GPA is preferred.

Award: Scholarship for use in freshman, sophomore, junior, or senior years; not renewable.

Eligibility Requirements: Applicant must be enrolled or expecting to enroll full-time at a two-year or four-year or technical institution or university and studying in Oregon. Applicant or parent of applicant must be member of Teamsters. Available to U.S. citizens.

Application Requirements: Application form, essay. *Deadline:* March 1.

Contact: Melissa Adams, Scholarship Processing Coordinator
Phone: 541-687-7409
E-mail: melissa.adams@hecc.oregon.gov

NORTHWEST AUTOMATIC VENDING ASSOCIATION SCHOLARSHIP

One-time award to recent high school graduates who are first-time freshmen and are dependents or grandchildren of members or employees of Northwest Automatic Vending Association. Oregon residency not required. For use at public or nonprofit universities only.

Award: Scholarship for use in freshman year; not renewable.

Eligibility Requirements: Applicant must be high school student and planning to enroll or expecting to enroll full-time at a four-year institution or university. Applicant or parent of applicant must be member of Northwest Automatic Vending Association. Available to U.S. citizens.

Application Requirements: Application form. *Deadline:* March 1.

Contact: Melissa Adams, Scholarship Processing Coordinator
Phone: 541-687-7409
E-mail: melissa.adams@hecc.oregon.gov

TEAMSTERS COUNCIL 37 FEDERAL CREDIT UNION SCHOLARSHIP

One-time award for members (or dependents of members) of Council 37 Federal Credit Union who are active for one year as of the March 1 deadline, in a local that is affiliated with the Joint Council of Teamsters 37. GPA preference between 2.0 and 3.0. Must enroll at least half-time.

Award: Scholarship for use in freshman, sophomore, junior, or senior years; not renewable.

Eligibility Requirements: Applicant must be enrolled or expecting to enroll full- or part-time at a two-year or four-year institution or university. Applicant or parent of applicant must be member of Teamsters. Available to U.S. citizens.

Application Requirements: Application form. *Deadline:* March 1.

Contact: Melissa Adams, Scholarship Processing Coordinator
Phone: 541-687-7409
E-mail: melissa.adams@hecc.oregon.gov

TEAMSTERS LOCAL 305 SCHOLARSHIP

Renewable award for graduating Oregon high school seniors who are dependents of eligible members of Local 305 of the Joint Council of Teamsters #37. Members must have been active at least one year as of the March deadline. Scholarship is automatically renewable if renewal criteria is met.

Award: Scholarship for use in freshman year; renewable.

Eligibility Requirements: Applicant must be high school student and planning to enroll or expecting to enroll full-time at a four-year institution or university. Applicant or parent of applicant must be member of Teamsters. Available to U.S. citizens.

Application Requirements: Application form. *Deadline:* March 1.

Contact: Melissa Adams, Scholarship Processing Coordinator
Phone: 541-687-7409
E-mail: melissa.adams@hecc.oregon.gov

PENNSYLVANIA FEDERATION OF DEMOCRATIC WOMEN INC.

www.pafedofdemwomen.org

PENNSYLVANIA FEDERATION OF DEMOCRATIC WOMEN INC. ANNUAL SCHOLARSHIP AWARDS

Award of up to $1000 for any female resident of Pennsylvania who is a sophomore or junior at an accredited college or university and is a registered Democrat. Award is for their Junior or senior year. Applicants must possess a Democratic Party family background and be an active participant in activities of the Democratic Party.

Award: Scholarship for use in junior or senior years; not renewable. *Number:* 1–5. *Amount:* $250–$1000.

Eligibility Requirements: Applicant must be enrolled or expecting to enroll full-time at a four-year institution or university; female and resident of Pennsylvania. Applicant or parent of applicant must be member of Democratic Party. Available to U.S. citizens.

Application Requirements: Application form, essay. *Deadline:* April 1.

Contact: Michelle Price, Scholarship Chair
Pennsylvania Federation of Democratic Women Inc.
462 W Grant Street
Easton, PA 18042
Phone: 610-235-9599
E-mail: mbernsonprice@gmail.com

PENNSYLVANIA MASONIC YOUTH FOUNDATION

http://www.pmyf.org/

PENNSYLVANIA MASONIC YOUTH FOUNDATION EDUCATIONAL ENDOWMENT FUND SCHOLARSHIPS

Grants for children, stepchildren, grandchildren, siblings, or dependents of members in good standing of a Pennsylvania Masonic Lodge, or members in good standing of a PA Masonic-sponsored youth group. Applicants must be high school graduates or high school seniors pursuing a college education. Minimum GPA 3.0. Proof of relationship to a member of a Lodge under the jurisdiction of the Right Worshipful Grand Lodge of Free and Accepted Masons of PA is required, or proof of membership in one of the youth groups it sponsors.

Award: Grant for use in freshman, sophomore, junior, or senior years; not renewable. *Number:* 25–75. *Amount:* $1000–$3000.

Eligibility Requirements: Applicant must be enrolled or expecting to enroll full-time at a two-year or four-year or technical institution or university. Applicant or parent of applicant must be member of Freemasons. Applicant must have 3.0 GPA or higher. Available to U.S. and non-U.S. citizens.

Application Requirements: Application form, essay, financial need analysis. *Deadline:* March 15.

Contact: Amy Nace, Executive Assistant
Pennsylvania Masonic Youth Foundation
1244 Bainbridge Road
Elizabethtown, PA 17022
Phone: 717-367-1536 Ext. 2
Fax: 717-367-0616
E-mail: pmyf@pagrandlodge.org

PHILIPINO-AMERICAN ASSOCIATION OF NEW ENGLAND

http://www.pamas.org/

PAMAS RESTRICTED SCHOLARSHIP AWARD

Award of $500 for any sons or daughters of PAMAS members who are currently active in PAMAS projects and activities. Must be of Filipino descent, a resident of New England, a high school senior at the time of award, and have college acceptance letter from accredited institution. Minimum of 3.3 GPA required. For application details visit http://www.pamas.org.

Award: Scholarship for use in freshman year; not renewable. *Number:* 1. *Amount:* $500.

Eligibility Requirements: Applicant must be Asian/Pacific Islander; high school student; planning to enroll or expecting to enroll full-time at a four-year institution or university and resident of Connecticut, Maine, Massachusetts, New Hampshire, Rhode Island, Vermont. Applicant or parent of applicant must be member of Philipino-American Association. Available to U.S. citizens.

Application Requirements: Application form, college acceptance letter, essay, recommendations or references, transcript. *Deadline:* May 31.

Contact: Amanda Kalb, First Vice President
Phone: 617-471-3513
E-mail: balic2ss@comcast.net

PHI SIGMA KAPPA INTERNATIONAL HEADQUARTERS

http://www.phisigmakappa.org/

WENDEROTH UNDERGRADUATE SCHOLARSHIP

Available to sophomores and juniors on the basis of academic criteria. Must submit an essay and letter of recommendation along with the application.

Award: Scholarship for use in sophomore or junior years; not renewable. *Number:* 1–4. *Amount:* $1750–$4000.

Eligibility Requirements: Applicant must be enrolled or expecting to enroll full-time at a four-year institution or university. Applicant or parent of applicant must be member of Phi Sigma Kappa. Available to U.S. and non-U.S. citizens.

Application Requirements: Application form, essay, personal photograph, recommendations or references, resume, transcript. *Deadline:* January 31.

Contact: Michael Carey, Executive Director
Phone: 317-573-5420
Fax: 317-573-5430
E-mail: michael@phisigmakappa.org

ZETA SCHOLARSHIP

Scholarships are available following a generous gift to the Phi Sigma Kappa Foundation from the Zeta Alumni Association. Phi Sig or a child of a Phi Sig having minimum 3.0 GPA are eligible to apply.

Award: Scholarship for use in freshman, sophomore, junior, senior, or graduate years; not renewable. *Number:* 2. *Amount:* $2500.

Eligibility Requirements: Applicant must be enrolled or expecting to enroll full-time at a four-year institution or university. Applicant or parent of applicant must be member of Phi Sigma Kappa. Applicant must have 3.0 GPA or higher. Available to U.S. citizens.

Application Requirements: Application form, community service, personal photograph, recommendations or references, resume, test scores, transcript. *Deadline:* January 31.

Contact: Scholarship Program Coordinator
Phi Sigma Kappa International Headquarters
2925 East 96th Street
Indianapolis, IN 46240
Phone: 317-573-5420
Fax: 317-573-5430

PHI SIGMA PI NATIONAL HONOR FRATERNITY

http://www.phisigmapi.org/

RICHARD CECIL TODD AND CLAUDA PENNOCK TODD TRIPOD SCHOLARSHIP

Scholarship to promote the future academic opportunity of brothers (members) of the fraternity, who have excelled in embodying the ideals of scholarship, leadership, and fellowship. One-time award for full-time student, sophomore level or higher, with minimum 3.0 GPA.

Award: Scholarship for use in sophomore, junior, or senior years; not renewable. *Number:* 1. *Amount:* up to $1500.

Eligibility Requirements: Applicant must be enrolled or expecting to enroll full-time at a two-year or four-year or technical institution or university and must have an interest in leadership. Applicant or parent of applicant must be member of Greek Organization. Applicant must have 3.0 GPA or higher. Available to U.S. and non-U.S. citizens.

Application Requirements: Application form, driver's license, essay, recommendations or references, transcript. *Deadline:* April 15.

Contact: Suzanne Schaffer, Executive Director
Phone: 717-299-4710
Fax: 717-390-3054
E-mail: schaffer@phisigmapi.org

PONY OF THE AMERICAS CLUB INC.

http://www.poac.org/

POAC NATIONAL SCHOLARSHIP

Two to four renewable awards that may be used for any year or any institution but must be for full-time undergraduate study. Application and transcript required. Award restricted to those who have interest in animal or agricultural competition and active involvement in Pony Of the Americas organization.

Award: Scholarship for use in freshman, sophomore, junior, or senior years; not renewable. *Number:* 2–4. *Amount:* $500–$1000.

Eligibility Requirements: Applicant must be enrolled or expecting to enroll full- or part-time at a two-year or four-year or technical institution or university and must have an interest in animal/agricultural competition. Applicant or parent of applicant must be member of Pony of the Americas Club. Available to U.S. and non-U.S. citizens.

Application Requirements: Application form, driver's license, entry in a contest, essay, recommendations or references, transcript. *Deadline:* March 1.

Contact: Joyse Banister, Scholarship Administrator/CEO
Pony Of the Americas Club Inc.
3828 South Emerson Avenue
Indianapolis, IN 46203
Phone: 317-788-0107
Fax: 317-788-8974
E-mail: officemanager@poac.org

PROFESSIONAL HORSEMEN'S SCHOLARSHIP FUND INC.

http://www.nationalpha.com/

PROFESSIONAL HORSEMEN'S SCHOLARSHIP FUND

Scholarship provides financial assistance from a fund established for children of professional members of the Professional Horseman's Association who have been professional members for more than two years and who are enrolled in an approved school for the advancement of their education beyond the secondary level.

Award: Scholarship for use in freshman, sophomore, junior, senior, graduate, or postgraduate years; not renewable. *Number:* 10–20. *Amount:* $500–$1000.

Eligibility Requirements: Applicant must be enrolled or expecting to enroll full-time at a two-year or four-year or technical institution or university. Applicant or parent of applicant must be member of Professional Horsemen Association. Available to U.S. and non-U.S. citizens.

Application Requirements: Application form, autobiography, essay, financial need analysis, interview. *Deadline:* May 1.

Contact: Mrs. Ann Grenci, Chairman, Scholarship Committee
Phone: 561-707-9094
E-mail: foxhill33@aol.com

PROJECT BEST SCHOLARSHIP FUND

http://www.projectbest.com/

PROJECT BEST SCHOLARSHIP

One-time award of $1000 to $2000 for employees or children or spouses of employees working for a company or labor union in the construction industry that is affiliated with Project BEST. Must be residents of West Virginia, Pennsylvania, or Ohio and attend a West Virginia or Ohio postsecondary institution. Must be U.S. citizens.

Award: Scholarship for use in freshman, sophomore, junior, senior, or graduate years; renewable. *Number:* 11–22. *Amount:* $1000–$2000.

Eligibility Requirements: Applicant must be enrolled or expecting to enroll full-time at a two-year or four-year institution or university; resident of Ohio, Pennsylvania, West Virginia and studying in Ohio, West Virginia. Applicant or parent of applicant must be member of AFL-CIO.

Applicant or parent of applicant must have employment or volunteer experience in construction. Available to U.S. citizens.

Application Requirements: Application form. *Deadline:* continuous.

Contact: Mary Jo Klempa, Director
Project BEST Scholarship Fund
21 Armory Drive
Wheeling, WV 26003
Phone: 304-242-0520
Fax: 304-242-7261
E-mail: best2003@swave.net

PUEBLO OF ISLETA, DEPARTMENT OF EDUCATION
http://www.isletapueblo.com/

HIGHER EDUCATION SUPPLEMENTAL SCHOLARSHIP
ISLETA PUEBLO HIGHER EDUCATION DEPARTMENT

Applicants must be students seeking a postsecondary degree. The degree granting institution must be a nationally accredited vocational or postsecondary institution offering a certificate, Associate, Bachelor's, Master's, or Doctoral degree. Enrolled tribal members of the Isleta Pueblo may apply for this scholarship if they also apply for additional scholarships from different sources. Deadlines: April 1 for summer, November 1 for spring and July 1 for fall.

Award: Scholarship for use in freshman, sophomore, junior, senior, graduate, or postgraduate years; renewable.

Eligibility Requirements: Applicant must be American Indian/Alaska Native and enrolled or expecting to enroll full- or part-time at a two-year or four-year or technical institution or university. Applicant or parent of applicant must be member of Ice Skating Institute. Available to U.S. citizens.

Application Requirements: Application form, certificate of Indian blood, class schedule, financial need analysis, transcript. *Deadline:* varies.

Contact: Higher Education Director
Pueblo of Isleta, Department of Education
PO Box 1270
Isleta, NM 87022
Phone: 505-869-2680
Fax: 505-869-7690
E-mail: isletahighered@yahoo.com

RAILWAY SUPPLY INSTITUTE
http://www.rsiweb.org/

RSI UNDERGRADUATE SCHOLARSHIP PROGRAM

Scholarships available for the child/in legal custody of a current employee whose employer is a current member of the Railway Supply Institute (RSI) or one of the Coordinated Mechanical Associations (CMA). Must be currently enrolled as a full-time student at an accredited post-secondary institution and studying for an Associate or Bachelor's degree, with at least a sophomore status (30+ credit hours). Refer to website for more information and eligibility requirements, http://rsiweb.org/rsi-scholarship/.

Award: Scholarship for use in sophomore, junior, or senior years; not renewable. *Number:* 5. *Amount:* $5000.

Eligibility Requirements: Applicant must be enrolled or expecting to enroll full-time at a four-year institution or university. Applicant or parent of applicant must be member of Mutual Benefit Society. Available to U.S. and Canadian citizens.

Application Requirements: Application form, essay, recommendations or references, resume, transcript. *Deadline:* May 31.

Contact: Thomas Simpson, Executive Director
Phone: 202-347-4664
E-mail: rsi@railwaysupply.org

RED ANGUS ASSOCIATION OF AMERICA
http://www.redangus.org/

4 RAAA/JUNIOR RED ANGUS SCHOLARSHIP

Scholarship of $500 given to active members of the National Junior Red Angus Association. Must be high school seniors or college underclassmen.

Award: Scholarship for use in freshman or sophomore years; not renewable. *Number:* 2. *Amount:* $500.

Eligibility Requirements: Applicant must be enrolled or expecting to enroll full-time at a two-year or four-year institution or university. Applicant or parent of applicant must be member of National Junior Red Angus Association. Available to U.S. citizens.

Application Requirements: Application form, personal photograph, recommendations or references, transcript. *Deadline:* March 31.

Contact: Betty Grimshaw, Association Administrative Director
Phone: 940-387-3502
Fax: 940-383-4036
E-mail: betty@redangus.org

DEE SONSTEGARD MEMORIAL SCHOLARSHIP

Scholarship of $500 given to active members of the National Junior Red Angus Association. Must be high school seniors or college underclassmen.

Award: Scholarship for use in freshman or sophomore years; not renewable. *Number:* 2. *Amount:* $500.

Eligibility Requirements: Applicant must be enrolled or expecting to enroll full-time at a two-year or four-year institution or university. Applicant or parent of applicant must be member of National Junior Red Angus Association. Available to U.S. citizens.

Application Requirements: Application form, personal photograph, recommendations or references, transcript. *Deadline:* March 31.

Contact: Betty Grimshaw, Association Administrative Director
Phone: 940-387-3502
Fax: 940-383-4036
E-mail: betty@redangus.org

FARM AND RANCH CONNECTION SCHOLARSHIP

Scholarship of $500 given to active members of the National Junior Red Angus Association. Must be high school seniors or college underclassmen.

Award: Scholarship for use in freshman or sophomore years; not renewable. *Number:* 1. *Amount:* $500.

Eligibility Requirements: Applicant must be enrolled or expecting to enroll full-time at a two-year or four-year institution or university. Applicant or parent of applicant must be member of National Junior Red Angus Association. Available to U.S. citizens.

Application Requirements: Application form, personal photograph, recommendations or references, transcript. *Deadline:* March 31.

Contact: Betty Grimshaw, Association Administrative Director
Phone: 940-387-3502
Fax: 940-383-4036
E-mail: betty@redangus.org

LEONARD A. LORENZEN MEMORIAL SCHOLARSHIP

Scholarship of $500 given to active members of the National Junior Red Angus Association. Must be high school seniors or college underclassmen.

Award: Scholarship for use in freshman or sophomore years; not renewable. *Number:* 2. *Amount:* $500.

Eligibility Requirements: Applicant must be enrolled or expecting to enroll full-time at a two-year or four-year institution or university. Applicant or parent of applicant must be member of National Junior Red Angus Association. Available to U.S. citizens.

Application Requirements: Application form, personal photograph, recommendations or references, transcript. *Deadline:* March 31.

Contact: Betty Grimshaw, Association Administrative Director
Phone: 940-387-3502
Fax: 940-383-4036
E-mail: betty@redangus.org

THE RESERVE OFFICERS ASSOCIATION

http://www.roa.org/

HENRY J. REILLY MEMORIAL SCHOLARSHIP-HIGH SCHOOL SENIORS AND FIRST YEAR FRESHMEN

One-time award for high school seniors or college freshmen who are U.S. citizens and children or grandchildren of active members of the Reserve Officers Association. Must demonstrate leadership, have minimum 3.0 GPA and 1250 on the SAT. Must submit sponsor verification. College freshmen must submit college transcript.

Award: Scholarship for use in freshman year; not renewable. *Number:* 25–30. *Amount:* $1000.

Eligibility Requirements: Applicant must be enrolled or expecting to enroll full-time at a four-year institution or university and must have an interest in leadership. Applicant or parent of applicant must be member of Reserve Officers Association. Applicant must have 3.0 GPA or higher. Available to U.S. citizens. Applicant or parent must meet one or more of the following requirements: general military experience; retired from active duty; disabled or killed as a result of military service; prisoner of war; or missing in action.

Application Requirements: Application form, essay, test scores, transcript. *Deadline:* May 15.

Contact: Rebecca Riedler, Executive Administrator
  Phone: 202-646-7706
  E-mail: scholarship@roa.org

HENRY J. REILLY MEMORIAL UNDERGRADUATE SCHOLARSHIP PROGRAM FOR COLLEGE ATTENDEES

One-time award of $1000 for members and children or grandchildren of members of the Reserve Officers Association or its Auxiliary. Must be a U.S. citizen, 26 years old or younger, and enrolled at an accredited four-year institution. Must submit sponsor verification. Minimum 3.0 GPA required. Submit SAT or ACT scores; contact for score requirements.

Award: Scholarship for use in freshman, sophomore, junior, or senior years; not renewable. *Number:* 25–30. *Amount:* $1000.

Eligibility Requirements: Applicant must be enrolled or expecting to enroll full-time at a two-year or four-year institution or university. Applicant or parent of applicant must be member of Reserve Officers Association. Applicant must have 3.0 GPA or higher. Available to U.S. citizens. Applicant or parent must meet one or more of the following requirements: general military experience; retired from active duty; disabled or killed as a result of military service; prisoner of war; or missing in action.

Application Requirements: Application form, essay, sponsor verification, test scores, transcript. *Deadline:* May 15.

Contact: Rebecca Riedler, Executive Administrator
  Phone: 202-646-7706
  E-mail: scholarship@roa.org

RETAIL, WHOLESALE AND DEPARTMENT STORE UNION

http://www.rwdsu.org/

ALVIN E. HEAPS MEMORIAL SCHOLARSHIP

Scholarship for RWDSU members or members of an RWDSU family. Applicant must submit 500-word essay on the benefits of union membership. See website for application, http://www.rwdsu.info/heapsscholar.htm.

Award: Scholarship for use in freshman, sophomore, junior, or senior years; not renewable.

Eligibility Requirements: Applicant must be enrolled or expecting to enroll full- or part-time at a two-year or four-year institution or university. Applicant or parent of applicant must be member of Retail, Wholesale and Department Store Union. Available to U.S. citizens.

Application Requirements: Application form, essay, transcript. *Deadline:* varies.

Contact: Scholarship Committee
  Phone: 212-684-5300
  Fax: 212-779-2809

RHODE ISLAND FOUNDATION

http://www.rifoundation.org/

EDWARD LEON DUHAMEL FREEMASONS SCHOLARSHIP

Renewable scholarship for descendants of members of Franklin Lodge in Westerly Rhode Island. Must be accepted into an accredited postsecondary institution. Must demonstrate scholastic achievement, financial need, and good citizenship.

Award: Scholarship for use in freshman, sophomore, junior, or senior years; renewable. *Amount:* $500–$1000.

Eligibility Requirements: Applicant must be enrolled or expecting to enroll full-time at a four-year institution or university. Applicant or parent of applicant must be member of Freemasons. Available to U.S. citizens.

Application Requirements: Application form, essay, financial need analysis, self-addressed stamped envelope with application, transcript. *Deadline:* varies.

Contact: Libby Monahan, Funds Administrator
  Phone: 401-274-4564 Ext. 3117
  E-mail: libbym@rifoundation.org

SERVICE EMPLOYEES INTERNATIONAL UNION (SEIU)

http://www.seiu.org/

SEIU JESSE JACKSON SCHOLARSHIP PROGRAM

Renewable scholarship of $5000 given to a student whose work and aspirations for economic and social justice reflect the values and accomplishments of the Rev. Jackson.

Award: Scholarship for use in freshman, sophomore, junior, or senior years; renewable. *Number:* 1. *Amount:* $5000.

Eligibility Requirements: Applicant must be enrolled or expecting to enroll full-time at a four-year institution or university. Applicant or parent of applicant must be member of Service Employees International Union. Available to U.S. citizens.

Application Requirements: Application form, essay. *Deadline:* March 1.

Contact: c/o Scholarship Program Administrators, Inc.
  Phone: 615-320-3149
  Fax: 615-320-3151
  E-mail: info@spaprog.com

SEIU JOHN GEAGAN SCHOLARSHIP

Scholarship to SEIU members or their children or SEIU local union staff. Priority will be given to those applicants who are not served by traditional education institutions-typically adults who have been in the workforce and have decided to go, or return to, college.

Award: Scholarship for use in freshman, sophomore, junior, or senior years; not renewable. *Number:* 1. *Amount:* $2500.

Eligibility Requirements: Applicant must be enrolled or expecting to enroll full-time at a two-year or four-year or technical institution or university. Applicant or parent of applicant must be member of Service Employees International Union. Available to U.S. citizens.

Application Requirements: Application form, essay. *Deadline:* March 1.

Contact: c/o Scholarship Program Administrators, Inc.
  Phone: 615-320-3149
  Fax: 615-320-3151
  E-mail: info@spaprog.com

SEIU NORA PIORE SCHOLARSHIP PROGRAM

Renewable award of $4375 to SEIU members enrolled full-time in an undergraduate study. Applicant's financial need will be considered during the selection process.

Award: Scholarship for use in freshman, sophomore, junior, or senior years; renewable. *Number:* 1. *Amount:* $4375.

Eligibility Requirements: Applicant must be enrolled or expecting to enroll full-time at a four-year institution or university. Applicant or parent of applicant must be member of Service Employees International Union. Available to U.S. citizens.

Application Requirements: Application form. *Deadline:* March 1.

Contact: c/o Scholarship Program Administrators, Inc.
Phone: 615-320-3149
Fax: 615-320-3151
E-mail: info@spaprog.com

SEIU SCHOLARSHIP PROGRAM

Fifteen $1000 scholarships available in annual installments for up to four years. Applicants must graduate from a high school or GED program by August. Must be enrolled as a full-time college freshman by the fall semester at an accredited, four-year college or university.

Award: Scholarship for use in freshman year; renewable. *Number:* 15. *Amount:* $1000.

Eligibility Requirements: Applicant must be high school student and planning to enroll or expecting to enroll full-time at a four-year institution or university. Applicant or parent of applicant must be member of Service Employees International Union. Available to U.S. citizens.

Application Requirements: Application form. *Deadline:* March 1.

Contact: c/o Scholarship Program Administrators, Inc.
Phone: 615-320-3149
Fax: 615-320-3151
E-mail: info@spaprog.com

SIGMA ALPHA MU

http://www.sam-fdn.org

UNDERGRADUATE ACHIEVEMENT AWARDS

Scholarship for seniors or juniors of undergraduate students enrolled full-time study. Must be member of Sigma Alpha Mu Foundation. Scholarship value varies.

Award: Scholarship for use in junior or senior years; not renewable. *Number:* 2.

Eligibility Requirements: Applicant must be enrolled or expecting to enroll full-time at a four-year institution or university. Applicant or parent of applicant must be member of Sigma Alpha Mu Foundation. Available to U.S. citizens.

Application Requirements: Application form. *Deadline:* February 1.

Contact: Maria Mandel, Director of Scholarships and Donor Relations
Phone: 317-789-8339
Fax: 317-824-1505
E-mail: mariam@sam-fdn.org

YOUNG SCHOLARS PROGRAM

Scholarship for candidates achieving a 3.75 GPA (or equivalent) for courses taken in the academic term of the undergraduate study. Must be member of Sigma Alpha Mu Foundation. Deadline varies.

Award: Scholarship for use in freshman, sophomore, junior, or senior years; not renewable. *Amount:* $500.

Eligibility Requirements: Applicant must be enrolled or expecting to enroll full-time at a four-year institution or university. Applicant or parent of applicant must be member of Sigma Alpha Mu Foundation. Applicant must have 2.5 GPA or higher. Available to U.S. citizens.

Application Requirements: Application form.

Contact: Maria Mandel, Director of Scholarships and Donor Relations
Phone: 317-789-8339
Fax: 317-824-1505
E-mail: mariam@sam-fdn.org

SIGMA CHI FOUNDATION

http://foundation.sigmachi.org

GENERAL SCHOLARSHIP GRANTS

Applicants must have completed three semesters (or four quarters) of undergraduate study to be considered for current year awards. Funds are available for tuition/fees payments only.

Award: Scholarship for use in sophomore, junior, or senior years; not renewable.

Eligibility Requirements: Applicant must be enrolled or expecting to enroll full-time at a four-year institution or university and male. Applicant or parent of applicant must be member of Sigma Chi Fraternity. Available to U.S. and non-U.S. citizens.

Application Requirements: Application form, financial need analysis, recommendations or references, transcript. *Deadline:* April 13.

Contact: Heidi Holley, Scholarship Administrator
Phone: 847-869-3655 Ext. 270
Fax: 847-869-4906
E-mail: heidi.holley@sigmachi.org

SLOVAK GYMNASTIC UNION SOKOL, USA

http://www.sokolusa.org/

SLOVAK GYMNASTIC UNION SOKOL, USA/MILAN GETTING SCHOLARSHIP

Available to members of SOKOL, U.S.A who have been in good standing for at least three years. Must have plans to attend college. Renewable for a maximum of four years, based upon academic achievement. Minimum GPA 2.5 required.

Award: Grant for use in freshman, sophomore, junior, or senior years; renewable. *Number:* 4–8. *Amount:* $500.

Eligibility Requirements: Applicant must be enrolled or expecting to enroll full-time at a four-year institution or university. Applicant or parent of applicant must be member of SOKOL, USA. Applicant must have 2.5 GPA or higher. Available to U.S. citizens.

Application Requirements: Application form. *Deadline:* April 1.

Contact: Milan Kovac, Fraternal Secretary
Slovak Gymnastic Union SOKOL, USA
276 Prospect Street, PO Box 189
East Orange, NJ 07019
Phone: 973-676-0281
E-mail: sokolusahqs@aol.com

SLOVENIAN WOMEN'S UNION SCHOLARSHIP FOUNDATION

http://www.swusf.org

SLOVENIAN WOMEN'S UNION OF AMERICA SCHOLARSHIP FOUNDATION

one time award for full-time study only. Essay, transcripts, letters of recommendation from principal/teacher, financial need form, photo, civic and church activities information required. Open to high school seniors. One graduate school scholarship of $2,000 available to student majoring in education. Membership in Slovenian Women's Union not required. Applicant must be of Slovenian ancestry. One Graduate school scholarship of $2,000 available to student majoring in science, mathematics, or engineering. Membership in Slovenian Women's Union not required. Applicant must be of Slovenian ancestry.

Award: Scholarship for use in freshman, sophomore, junior, senior, or graduate years; not renewable. *Number:* 6–12. *Amount:* $1000–$2000.

Eligibility Requirements: Applicant must be enrolled or expecting to enroll full- or part-time at a two-year or four-year or technical institution or university. Applicant or parent of applicant must be member of Slovenian Women's Union of America. Available to U.S. citizens.

Application Requirements: Application form, autobiography, community service, essay, financial need analysis, personal photograph. *Deadline:* March 1.

Contact: Mary Turvey, Director
Slovenian Women's Union Scholarship Foundation
4 Lawrence Drive
Marquette, MI 49855
Phone: 906-249-4288
E-mail: mturvey@aol.com

SOIL AND WATER CONSERVATION SOCIETY

http://www.swcs.org

MELVILLE H. COHEE STUDENT LEADER CONSERVATION SCHOLARSHIP

The scholarship honors SWCS members who succeed as leaders in their studies, volunteerism, and work. Members who are in their junior or senior year of full-time undergraduate study or pursuing graduate level studies with a natural resource conservation orientation at a properly accredited college or university are eligible.

Award: Scholarship for use in junior, senior, graduate, or postgraduate years; not renewable. *Number:* 1. *Amount:* up to $500.

Eligibility Requirements: Applicant must be enrolled or expecting to enroll full-time at a four-year institution or university. Applicant or parent of applicant must be member of Soil and Water Conservation Society. Available to U.S. and non-U.S. citizens.

Application Requirements: Application form, essay, recommendations or references, transcript. *Deadline:* February 13.

Contact: SWCS Scholarships Program Coordinator
Soil and Water Conservation Society
945 SW Ankeny Road
Ankeny, IA 50023-9723
Phone: 515-289-2331 Ext. 114
E-mail: scholarships@swcs.org

SONS OF NORWAY FOUNDATION

http://www.sonsofnorway.com/foundation

ASTRID G. CATES AND MYRTLE BEINHAUER SCHOLARSHIP FUNDS

Merit award available to students ages 17 to 22 who are current members, children, or grandchildren of members of the Sons of Norway. School transcript required. Academic potential and clarity of study plan is key criterion for award. Minimum 3.0 GPA required.

Award: Scholarship for use in freshman, sophomore, junior, or senior years; not renewable. *Number:* 2–7. *Amount:* $1000–$3000.

Eligibility Requirements: Applicant must be age 17-22 and enrolled or expecting to enroll full-time at a two-year or four-year or technical institution or university. Applicant or parent of applicant must be member of Mutual Benefit Society. Applicant must have 3.0 GPA or higher. Available to U.S. citizens.

Application Requirements: Application form, application form may be submitted online (http://www.sonsofnorway.com/foundation), community service, essay, personal photograph, recommendations or references, test scores, transcript. *Deadline:* March 1.

Contact: Scholarship Coordinator
Sons of Norway Foundation
1455 West Lake Street
Minneapolis, MN 55408-2666
Phone: 612-827-3611
E-mail: foundation@sofn.com

SOUTH CAROLINA STATE EMPLOYEES ASSOCIATION

http://www.scsea.com/

ANNE A. AGNEW SCHOLARSHIP

Nonrenewable scholarship for full-time study only. Must be a sophomore, junior, senior, graduate or postgraduate student. Application forms are available after January 1 of each year.

Award: Scholarship for use in sophomore, junior, senior, graduate, or postgraduate years; not renewable. *Number:* 3. *Amount:* $1000.

Eligibility Requirements: Applicant must be enrolled or expecting to enroll full-time at a four-year institution or university and resident of South Carolina. Applicant or parent of applicant must be member of South Carolina State Employees Association. Available to U.S. and non-U.S. citizens.

Application Requirements: Application form, essay, financial need analysis, transcript. *Deadline:* March 12.

Contact: Broadus Jamerson, Executive Director
South Carolina State Employees Association
PO Box 8447
Columbia, SC 29202
Phone: 803-765-0680
Fax: 803-779-6558
E-mail: scsea@scsea.com

RICHLAND/LEXINGTON SCSEA SCHOLARSHIP

Scholarships available to SCSEA members or their relatives, with priority given to Richland-Lexington Chapter members, spouses and/or children of Chapter members. The awardees must be currently enrolled at a recognized and accredited college, university, trade school or other institution of higher learning and must have completed at least one academic semester/quarter.

Award: Scholarship for use in sophomore, junior, senior, graduate, or postgraduate years; not renewable. *Number:* 3. *Amount:* $750.

Eligibility Requirements: Applicant must be enrolled or expecting to enroll full-time at a two-year or four-year institution or university and resident of South Carolina. Applicant or parent of applicant must be member of Society of Architectural Historians. Available to U.S. citizens.

Application Requirements: Application form, essay, transcript. *Deadline:* March 12.

Contact: Broadus Jamerson, Executive Director
Phone: 803-765-0680
Fax: 803-779-6558
E-mail: scsea@scsea.com

SUPREME GUARDIAN COUNCIL, INTERNATIONAL ORDER OF JOB'S DAUGHTERS

http://www.iojd.org/

SUPREME GUARDIAN COUNCIL SCHOLARSHIP

Scholarships of $750 to aid Job's Daughters students of outstanding ability whom have a sincerity of purpose. High school seniors, or graduates, junior college, technical school, or college students who are in early graduation programs, are eligible to apply.

Award: Scholarship for use in freshman, sophomore, junior, senior, graduate, or postgraduate years; not renewable. *Number:* 5–10. *Amount:* $750.

Eligibility Requirements: Applicant must be age 18-30; enrolled or expecting to enroll full- or part-time at a two-year or four-year or technical institution or university and single female. Applicant or parent of applicant must be member of Jobs Daughters. Available to U.S. and non-U.S. citizens.

Application Requirements: Application form, community service, essay, financial need analysis, recommendation from Executive Bethel Guardian Council, achievements outside of Job's Daughters, recommendations or references. *Deadline:* April 30.

Contact: Christal Bindrich, Scholarship Committee Chairman
Supreme Guardian Council, International Order of Job's Daughters
5351 South Butterfield Way
Greenfield, WI 53221
Phone: 414-423-0016
E-mail: christalbindrich@wi.rr.com

SUSIE HOLMES MEMORIAL SCHOLARSHIP

Scholarships of $1000 awarded to Job's Daughters high school students with a minimum of 2.5 GPA.

Award: Scholarship for use in freshman, sophomore, junior, senior, graduate, or postgraduate years; not renewable. *Number:* 1. *Amount:* $1000.

Eligibility Requirements: Applicant must be age 18-30; enrolled or expecting to enroll full-time at a two-year or four-year or technical institution or university and single female. Applicant or parent of applicant must be member of Jobs Daughters. Applicant must have 2.5 GPA or higher. Available to U.S. and non-U.S. citizens.

Application Requirements: Application form, community service, essay, recommendations or references, test scores, transcript. *Deadline:* April 30.

Contact: Christal Bindrich, Scholarship Committee Chairman
Supreme Guardian Council, International Order of Job's Daughters
5351 South Butterfield Way
Greenfield, WI 53221
Phone: 414-423-0016
E-mail: christalbindrich@wi.rr.com

TEXAS AFL-CIO

http://www.texasaflcio.org/

TEXAS AFL-CIO SCHOLARSHIP PROGRAM

Award for sons or daughters of members of unions affiliated with the Texas AFL-CIO and the appropriate Central Labor Council. Selection by interview/testing process. One-time awards of $1000. Applicant must be a graduating high school senior and Texas resident. Previous winners may apply for a limited number of continuing scholarships.

Award: Scholarship for use in freshman, sophomore, junior, or senior years; not renewable. *Number:* 20–35. *Amount:* $1000.

Eligibility Requirements: Applicant must be high school student; planning to enroll or expecting to enroll full-time at a two-year or four-year or technical institution or university and resident of Texas. Applicant or parent of applicant must be member of AFL-CIO. Available to U.S. citizens.

Application Requirements: Application form, essay, financial need analysis, interview, personal photograph. *Deadline:* January 31.

Contact: Mr. Edward Sills, Director of Communications
Texas AFL-CIO
PO Box 12727
Austin, TX 78701
Phone: 512-477-6195
Fax: 512-477-2962
E-mail: ed@texasaflcio.org

TKE EDUCATIONAL FOUNDATION

http://www.tke.org/

CHARLES J. TRABOLD SCHOLARSHIP

One-time award of $1200 given to an undergraduate member of Tau Kappa Epsilon who has demonstrated leadership ability within his chapter, campus, or community. Must be a full-time student in good standing with a GPA of 3.0 or higher. Preference will first be given to a member of Kappa-Kappa Chapter (Monmouth) but, if there is no qualified applicant, the scholarship will be open to any other qualified Teke.

Award: Scholarship for use in sophomore, junior, or senior years; not renewable. *Number:* 1. *Amount:* $1200.

Eligibility Requirements: Applicant must be enrolled or expecting to enroll full-time at a four-year institution or university; male and must have an interest in leadership. Applicant or parent of applicant must be member of Tau Kappa Epsilon. Applicant must have 3.0 GPA or higher. Available to U.S. and non-U.S. citizens.

Application Requirements: Application form, application form may be submitted online (http://www.tke.org/member_resources/scholarships/apply_online), essay, personal photograph, transcript. *Deadline:* March 15.

Contact: Offices of the Grand Chapter
TKE Educational Foundation
7439 Woodland Drive, Suite 100
Indianapolis, IN 46278
E-mail: tkeogc@tke.org

CHARLES R. WALGREEN, JR. LEADERSHIP AWARD

This $1400 leadership award is given in recognition of academic achievement with a GPA of at least 3.0 or higher and recognizes outstanding leadership, as demonstrated by activities and accomplishments within the chapter, on campus and in the community.

Award: Scholarship for use in sophomore, junior, or senior years; not renewable. *Number:* 1. *Amount:* $1400.

Eligibility Requirements: Applicant must be enrolled or expecting to enroll full-time at a four-year institution or university; male and must have an interest in leadership. Applicant or parent of applicant must be member of Tau Kappa Epsilon. Applicant must have 3.0 GPA or higher. Available to U.S. and non-U.S. citizens.

Application Requirements: Application form, application form may be submitted online (http://www.tke.org/member_resources/scholarships/apply_online), essay, personal photograph, transcript. *Deadline:* March 15.

Contact: Offices of the Grand Chapter
TKE Educational Foundation
7439 Woodland Drive, Suite 100
Indianapolis, IN 46278
E-mail: tkeogc@tke.org

CHARLES R. WALGREEN, JR. SCHOLARSHIP AWARD

Award given in recognition of outstanding leadership, as demonstrated by the activities and accomplishments of an individual within the chapter, on campus and in the community, while maintaining a good academic record. All initiated undergraduate members of TKE, in good standing with a cumulative GPA of 2.5 or higher, are eligible to apply.

Award: Scholarship for use in sophomore, junior, or senior years; not renewable. *Number:* 1. *Amount:* $1400.

Eligibility Requirements: Applicant must be enrolled or expecting to enroll full-time at a four-year institution or university; male and must have an interest in leadership. Applicant or parent of applicant must be member of Tau Kappa Epsilon. Applicant must have 2.5 GPA or higher. Available to U.S. and non-U.S. citizens.

Application Requirements: Application form, application form may be submitted online (http://www.tke.org/member_resources/scholarships/apply_online), essay, narrative summary of how TKE membership has benefited applicant, personal photograph, transcript. *Deadline:* March 15.

Contact: Offices of the Grand Chapter
TKE Educational Foundation
7439 Woodland Drive, Suite 100
Indianapolis, IN 46278
E-mail: tkeogc@tke.org

CHRISTOPHER GRASSO SCHOLARSHIP

One-time award of $200 given to an undergraduate member of Tau Kappa Epsilon who has demonstrated leadership ability within his chapter, campus, or community. Must be a full-time student in good standing with a GPA of 2.5 or higher. Preference should be given to any member of Alpha-Tau Chapter who applies but is not restricted to members of Alpha-Tau.

Award: Scholarship for use in sophomore, junior, or senior years; not renewable. *Number:* 1. *Amount:* $200.

Eligibility Requirements: Applicant must be enrolled or expecting to enroll full-time at a four-year institution or university; male and must have an interest in leadership. Applicant or parent of applicant must be member of Tau Kappa Epsilon. Applicant must have 2.5 GPA or higher. Available to U.S. and non-U.S. citizens.

Application Requirements: Application form, application form may be submitted online (http://www.tke.org/member_resources/scholarships/apply_online), essay, personal photograph, transcript. *Deadline:* March 15.

Contact: Offices of the Grand Chapter
TKE Educational Foundation
7439 Woodland Drive, Suite 100
Indianapolis, IN 46278
E-mail: tkeogc@tke.org

DONALD A. AND JOHN R. FISHER MEMORIAL SCHOLARSHIP

One-time award of $800 given to an undergraduate member of Tau Kappa Epsilon, who has demonstrated leadership ability within his chapter, campus, or community. Must be a full-time student in good standing with a GPA of 3.0 or higher.

Award: Scholarship for use in sophomore, junior, or senior years; not renewable. *Number:* 1. *Amount:* $800.

Eligibility Requirements: Applicant must be enrolled or expecting to enroll full-time at a four-year institution or university; male and must have an interest in leadership. Applicant or parent of applicant must be member of Tau Kappa Epsilon. Applicant must have 3.0 GPA or higher. Available to U.S. and non-U.S. citizens.

Application Requirements: Application form, application form may be submitted online (http://www.tke.org/member_resources/scholarships/apply_online), essay, personal photograph, transcript. *Deadline:* March 15.

Contact: Offices of the Grand Chapter
TKE Educational Foundation
7439 Woodland Drive, Suite 100
Indianapolis, IN 46278
E-mail: tkeogc@tke.org

DORIS AND ELMER H. SCHMITZ, SR. MEMORIAL SCHOLARSHIP

One-time award of $300 given to an undergraduate member of Tau Kappa Epsilon from Wisconsin who has demonstrated leadership ability within his chapter, campus, or community. Must be a full-time student in good standing with a GPA of 2.5 or higher. Preference will first be given to a member from the state of Wisconsin but, if there is no qualified applicant, the scholarship will be open to any other qualified Teke.

Award: Scholarship for use in sophomore, junior, or senior years; not renewable. *Number:* 1. *Amount:* $300.

Eligibility Requirements: Applicant must be enrolled or expecting to enroll full-time at a four-year institution or university; male; resident of Wisconsin and must have an interest in leadership. Applicant or parent of applicant must be member of Tau Kappa Epsilon. Applicant must have 2.5 GPA or higher. Available to U.S. and non-U.S. citizens.

Application Requirements: Application form, application form may be submitted online (http://www.tke.org/member_resources/scholarships/apply_online), essay, narrative summary of how TKE membership has benefited applicant, personal photograph, transcript. *Deadline:* March 15.

Contact: Offices of the Grand Chapter
TKE Educational Foundation
7439 Woodland Drive, Suite 100
Indianapolis, IN 46278
E-mail: tkeogc@tke.org

DWAYNE R. WOERPEL MEMORIAL LEADERSHIP SCHOLARSHIP

$500 award available to an undergraduate Tau Kappa Epsilon member who is a full-time student and graduate of the TKE Leadership Academy. Applicants should have demonstrated leadership qualities in service to the Fraternity and to the civic and religious community while maintaining a 3.0 GPA or higher. Preference will first be given to a graduate of the TKE Leadership Academy but, if there is no qualified applicant, the scholarship will be open to any other qualified Teke.

Award: Scholarship for use in sophomore, junior, or senior years; not renewable. *Number:* 1. *Amount:* $500.

Eligibility Requirements: Applicant must be enrolled or expecting to enroll full-time at a four-year institution or university; male and must have an interest in leadership. Applicant or parent of applicant must be member of Tau Kappa Epsilon. Applicant must have 3.0 GPA or higher. Available to U.S. and non-U.S. citizens.

Application Requirements: Application form, application form may be submitted online (http://www.tke.org/member_resources/scholarships/apply_online), essay, personal photograph, transcript. *Deadline:* March 15.

Contact: Offices of the Grand Chapter
TKE Educational Foundation
7439 Woodland Drive, Suite 100
Indianapolis, IN 46278
E-mail: tkeogc@tke.org

EUGENE C. BEACH MEMORIAL SCHOLARSHIP

One-time award of $300 given to an undergraduate member of Tau Kappa Epsilon who has demonstrated leadership ability within chapter, campus, or community. Must be a full-time student in good standing with a GPA of 3.0 or higher.

Award: Scholarship for use in freshman, sophomore, junior, or senior years; not renewable. *Number:* 1. *Amount:* $300.

Eligibility Requirements: Applicant must be enrolled or expecting to enroll full-time at a four-year institution or university; male and must have an interest in leadership. Applicant or parent of applicant must be member of Tau Kappa Epsilon. Applicant must have 3.0 GPA or higher. Available to U.S. and non-U.S. citizens.

Application Requirements: Application form, application form may be submitted online (http://www.tke.org/member_resources/scholarships/apply_online), essay, narrative summary of how TKE membership has benefited applicant, personal photograph, transcript. *Deadline:* March 15.

Contact: Offices of the Grand Chapter
TKE Educational Foundation
7439 Woodland Drive, Suite 100
Indianapolis, IN 46278
E-mail: tkeogc@tke.org

FATHER TIMOTHY VAKOC MEMORIAL SCHOLARSHIP

This scholarship is available to any undergraduate member of Tau Kappa Epsilon who is a full-time student. Preference will first be given to members of Theta-Rho Chapter but if no qualified individual applies, the award will be open to any member of TKE.

Award: Scholarship for use in sophomore, junior, or senior years; not renewable. *Number:* 1. *Amount:* $400.

Eligibility Requirements: Applicant must be enrolled or expecting to enroll full-time at a four-year institution or university; male and must

have an interest in leadership. Applicant or parent of applicant must be member of Tau Kappa Epsilon. Available to U.S. and non-U.S. citizens.

Application Requirements: Application form, application form may be submitted online (http://www.tke.org/member_resources/scholarships/apply_online), essay, personal photograph, transcript. *Deadline:* March 15.

Contact: Offices of the Grand Chapter
TKE Educational Foundation
7439 Woodland Drive, Suite 100
Indianapolis, IN 46278
E-mail: tkeogc@tke.org

GABE ANAYA SCHOLARSHIP

One-time award of $300 given to an undergraduate member of Tau Kappa Epsilon who has demonstrated leadership ability within his chapter, campus, or community. Must be a full-time student in good standing with a GPA of 2.75 or higher. Preference will be given to members from Alpha-Omicron chapter.

Award: Scholarship for use in sophomore, junior, or senior years; not renewable. *Number:* 1. *Amount:* $300.

Eligibility Requirements: Applicant must be enrolled or expecting to enroll full-time at a four-year institution or university; male and must have an interest in leadership. Applicant or parent of applicant must be member of Tau Kappa Epsilon. Available to U.S. and non-U.S. citizens.

Application Requirements: Application form, application form may be submitted online (http://www.tke.org/member_resources/scholarships/apply_online), essay, personal photograph, transcript. *Deadline:* March 15.

Contact: Offices of the Grand Chapter
TKE Educational Foundation
7439 Woodland Drive, Suite 100
Indianapolis, IN 46278
E-mail: tkeogc@tke.org

J.D. WILLIAMS SCHOLARSHIP

One-time award of $500 given to an undergraduate member of Tau Kappa Epsilon who has demonstrated leadership ability within his chapter, campus, or community. Must be a full-time student in good standing.

Award: Scholarship for use in sophomore, junior, or senior years; not renewable. *Number:* 1. *Amount:* $500.

Eligibility Requirements: Applicant must be enrolled or expecting to enroll full-time at a four-year institution or university; male and must have an interest in leadership. Applicant or parent of applicant must be member of Tau Kappa Epsilon. Available to U.S. and non-U.S. citizens.

Application Requirements: Application form, application form may be submitted online (http://www.tke.org/member_resources/scholarships/apply_online), essay, personal photograph, transcript. *Deadline:* March 15.

Contact: Offices of the Grand Chapter
TKE Educational Foundation
7439 Woodland Drive, Suite 100
Indianapolis, IN 46278
E-mail: tkeogc@tke.org

JOHN A. COURSON SCHOLARSHIP

This $2200 distinguished scholastic award is the highest academic honor awarded to a member of Tau Kappa Epsilon. Award is given in recognition of academic achievement with a GPA of at least 3.0 or higher and recognizes outstanding leadership, as demonstrated by activities and accomplishments within the chapter, on campus and in the community.

Award: Scholarship for use in sophomore, junior, or senior years; not renewable. *Number:* 1. *Amount:* $2200.

Eligibility Requirements: Applicant must be enrolled or expecting to enroll full-time at a four-year institution or university; male and must have an interest in leadership. Applicant or parent of applicant must be member of Tau Kappa Epsilon. Applicant must have 3.0 GPA or higher. Available to U.S. and non-U.S. citizens.

Application Requirements: Application form, application form may be submitted online (http://www.tke.org/member_resources/scholarships/apply_online), essay, personal photograph, transcript. *Deadline:* March 15.

Contact: Offices of the Grand Chapter
TKE Educational Foundation
7439 Woodland Drive, Suite 100
Indianapolis, IN 46278
E-mail: tkeogc@tke.org

J. RUSSEL SALSBURY MEMORIAL SCHOLARSHIP

One-time award of $200 given to an undergraduate member of Tau Kappa Epsilon who has demonstrated leadership ability within his chapter, campus, or community. Must be a full-time student in good standing with a GPA of 3.0 or higher.

Award: Scholarship for use in sophomore, junior, or senior years; not renewable. *Number:* 1. *Amount:* $200.

Eligibility Requirements: Applicant must be enrolled or expecting to enroll full-time at a four-year institution or university; male and must have an interest in leadership. Applicant or parent of applicant must be member of Tau Kappa Epsilon. Applicant must have 3.0 GPA or higher. Available to U.S. and non-U.S. citizens.

Application Requirements: Application form, application form may be submitted online (http://www.tke.org/member_resources/scholarships/apply_online), essay, personal photograph, transcript. *Deadline:* March 15.

Contact: Offices of the Grand Chapter
TKE Educational Foundation
7439 Woodland Drive, Suite 100
Indianapolis, IN 46278
E-mail: tkeogc@tke.org

KENNETH L. DUKE, SR. MEMORIAL SCHOLARSHIP

One-time award of $200 given to an undergraduate member of Tau Kappa Epsilon who has demonstrated leadership ability within his chapter, campus, or community. Must be a full-time student in good standing with a GPA of 2.5 or higher.

Award: Scholarship for use in sophomore, junior, or senior years; not renewable. *Number:* 1. *Amount:* $200.

Eligibility Requirements: Applicant must be enrolled or expecting to enroll full-time at a four-year institution or university; male and must have an interest in leadership. Applicant or parent of applicant must be member of Tau Kappa Epsilon. Applicant must have 2.5 GPA or higher. Available to U.S. and non-U.S. citizens.

Application Requirements: Application form, application form may be submitted online (http://www.tke.org/member_resources/scholarships/apply_online), essay, personal photograph, transcript. *Deadline:* March 15.

Contact: Offices of the Grand Chapter
TKE Educational Foundation
7439 Woodland Drive, Suite 100
Indianapolis, IN 46278
E-mail: tkeogc@tke.org

LENWOOD S. COCHRAN SCHOLARSHIP

One-time award of $1000 given to an undergraduate member of Tau Kappa Epsilon who has demonstrated leadership ability within his chapter, campus, or community. Must be a full-time student in good standing with a GPA of 3.0 or higher. Preference will first be given to a member of Sigma-Psi and Gamma-Mu, but if there is no qualified applicant, the scholarship will be open to any other qualified Teke.

Award: Scholarship for use in sophomore, junior, or senior years; not renewable. *Number:* 1. *Amount:* $1000.

Eligibility Requirements: Applicant must be enrolled or expecting to enroll full-time at a four-year institution or university; male and must have an interest in leadership. Applicant or parent of applicant must be member of Tau Kappa Epsilon. Applicant must have 3.0 GPA or higher. Available to U.S. and non-U.S. citizens.

Application Requirements: Application form, application form may be submitted online (http://www.tke.org/member_resources/scholarships/apply_online), essay, personal photograph, transcript. *Deadline:* March 15.

Contact: Offices of the Grand Chapter
TKE Educational Foundation
7439 Woodland Drive, Suite 100
Indianapolis, IN 46278
E-mail: tkeogc@tke.org

LON G. JUSTICE SCHOLARSHIP

One-time award of $1000 given to an undergraduate member of Tau Kappa Epsilon. Must be a full-time student in good standing with a GPA of 3.0 or higher and with exceptional academic achievement. Must demonstrate exceptional leadership abilities in campus, community, and Fraternity activities and have a demonstrated record of personal achievement (e.g. awards, citations, Fraternity, campus or community recognitions).

Award: Scholarship for use in sophomore, junior, or senior years; not renewable. *Number:* 1. *Amount:* $1000.

Eligibility Requirements: Applicant must be enrolled or expecting to enroll full-time at a four-year institution or university; male and must have an interest in leadership. Applicant or parent of applicant must be member of Tau Kappa Epsilon. Applicant must have 3.0 GPA or higher. Available to U.S. and non-U.S. citizens.

Application Requirements: Application form, application form may be submitted online (http://www.tke.org/member_resources/scholarships/apply_online), essay, personal photograph, transcript. *Deadline:* March 15.

Contact: Offices of the Grand Chapter
TKE Educational Foundation
7439 Woodland Drive, Suite 100
Indianapolis, IN 46278
E-mail: tkeogc@tke.org

MICHAEL CERUSSI LEADERSHIP SCHOLARSHIP

One-time award of $200 given to an undergraduate member of Tau Kappa Epsilon who has demonstrated leadership ability within his chapter, campus, or community. Awarded to a past or present jeweled officer with a minimum 3.0 GPA. Members from Nu Chapter are preferred, but if there is no qualified applicant, the scholarship will be open to any other eligible Teke.

Award: Scholarship for use in sophomore, junior, or senior years; not renewable. *Number:* 1. *Amount:* $200.

Eligibility Requirements: Applicant must be enrolled or expecting to enroll full-time at a four-year institution or university; male and must have an interest in leadership. Applicant or parent of applicant must be member of Tau Kappa Epsilon. Applicant must have 3.0 GPA or higher. Available to U.S. and non-U.S. citizens.

Application Requirements: Application form, application form may be submitted online (http://www.tke.org/member_resources/scholarships/apply_online), essay, personal photograph, transcript. *Deadline:* March 15.

Contact: Offices of the Grand Chapter
TKE Educational Foundation
7439 Woodland Drive, Suite 100
Indianapolis, IN 46278
E-mail: tkeogc@tke.org

MICHAEL J. MORIN MEMORIAL SCHOLARSHIP

One-time award of $300 for any undergraduate member of Tau Kappa Epsilon who has demonstrated leadership capacity within his chapter, on campus or the community. Must have a cumulative GPA of 3.0 or higher and be a full-time student in good standing.

Award: Scholarship for use in sophomore, junior, or senior years; not renewable. *Number:* 1. *Amount:* $300.

Eligibility Requirements: Applicant must be enrolled or expecting to enroll full-time at a four-year institution or university; male and must have an interest in leadership. Applicant or parent of applicant must be member of Tau Kappa Epsilon. Applicant must have 3.0 GPA or higher. Available to U.S. and non-U.S. citizens.

Application Requirements: Application form, application form may be submitted online (http://www.tke.org/member_resources/scholarships/apply_online), essay, narrative summary of how TKE membership has benefited applicant, personal photograph, transcript. *Deadline:* March 15.

Contact: Offices of the Grand Chapter
TKE Educational Foundation
7439 Woodland Drive, Suite 100
Indianapolis, IN 46278
E-mail: tkeogc@tke.org

MILES GRAY MEMORIAL SCHOLARSHIP

One-time award of $300 given to an undergraduate member of Tau Kappa Epsilon who has demonstrated leadership ability within his chapter, campus, or community. Must be a full-time student in good standing with a GPA of 3.0 or higher.

Award: Scholarship for use in sophomore, junior, or senior years; not renewable. *Number:* 1. *Amount:* $300.

Eligibility Requirements: Applicant must be enrolled or expecting to enroll full-time at a four-year institution or university; male and must have an interest in leadership. Applicant or parent of applicant must be member of Tau Kappa Epsilon. Applicant must have 3.0 GPA or higher. Available to U.S. and non-U.S. citizens.

Application Requirements: Application form, application form may be submitted online (http://www.tke.org/member_resources/scholarships/apply_online), essay, personal photograph, transcript. *Deadline:* March 15.

Contact: Offices of the Grand Chapter
TKE Educational Foundation
7439 Woodland Drive, Suite 100
Indianapolis, IN 46278
E-mail: tkeogc@tke.org

ROBERT D. PLANCK SCHOLARSHIP

One-time award of $300 given to an undergraduate member of Tau Kappa Epsilon. Must be a full-time student in good standing and demonstrate financial need. Preference will first be given to a member in the state of Texas but, if there is no qualified applicant, the scholarship will be open to any other qualified Teke.

Award: Scholarship for use in sophomore, junior, or senior years; not renewable. *Number:* 1. *Amount:* $300.

Eligibility Requirements: Applicant must be enrolled or expecting to enroll full-time at a four-year institution or university and male. Applicant or parent of applicant must be member of Tau Kappa Epsilon. Available to U.S. and non-U.S. citizens.

Application Requirements: Application form, application form may be submitted online (http://www.tke.org/member_resources/scholarships/apply_online), essay, financial need analysis, personal photograph, transcript. *Deadline:* March 15.

Contact: Offices of the Grand Chapter
TKE Educational Foundation
7439 Woodland Drive, Suite 100
Indianapolis, IN 46278
E-mail: tkeogc@tke.org

RONALD REAGAN LEADERSHIP AWARD

One-time award of $1100 for initiated undergraduate member of Tau Kappa Epsilon, given in recognition of outstanding leadership, as demonstrated by activities and accomplishments within chapter, on campus, and in community. Minimum 3.0 GPA required.

Award: Scholarship for use in sophomore, junior, or senior years; not renewable. *Number:* 1. *Amount:* $1100.

Eligibility Requirements: Applicant must be enrolled or expecting to enroll full-time at a four-year institution or university; male and must have an interest in leadership. Applicant or parent of applicant must be member of Tau Kappa Epsilon. Applicant must have 3.0 GPA or higher. Available to U.S. and non-U.S. citizens.

Application Requirements: Application form, application form may be submitted online (http://www.tke.org/member_resources/scholarships/apply_online), essay, narrative summary of how TKE membership has benefited applicant, personal photograph, transcript. *Deadline:* March 15.

Contact: Offices of the Grand Chapter
TKE Educational Foundation
7439 Woodland Drive, Suite 100
Indianapolis, IN 46278
E-mail: tkeogc@tke.org

T.J. SCHMITZ SCHOLARSHIP

$500 award for an initiated undergraduate member of TKE. Must be a full-time student in good standing with a minimum cumulative GPA of 3.0. Must have demonstrated leadership capability within chapter, campus, or community.

Award: Scholarship for use in sophomore, junior, or senior years; not renewable. *Number:* 1. *Amount:* $500.

Eligibility Requirements: Applicant must be enrolled or expecting to enroll full-time at a four-year institution or university; male and must have an interest in leadership. Applicant or parent of applicant must be

member of Tau Kappa Epsilon. Applicant must have 3.0 GPA or higher. Available to U.S. and non-U.S. citizens.

Application Requirements: Application form, application form may be submitted online (http://www.tke.org/member_resources/scholarships/apply_online), essay, narrative summary of how TKE membership has benefited applicant, personal photograph, transcript. *Deadline:* March 15.

Contact: Offices of the Grand Chapter
TKE Educational Foundation
7439 Woodland Drive, Suite 100
Indianapolis, IN 46278
E-mail: tkeogc@tke.org

TKE SERVANT LEADERSHIP SCHOLARSHIP

$800 award open to all initiated undergraduate and graduate studies members of Tau Kappa Epsilon who are currently enrolled students in good standing with a cumulative GPA of 3.0 or higher. Applicants must have a demonstrated record of leadership in service to others. Applicants may apply themselves or may be nominated by any alumnus, his chapter, the chapter's alumni association, school administration official, or faculty member. Awards will be made annually, with the recipients for each biennium prior to the International Conclave of TKE acknowledged and recognized as servant leaders before the Grand Chapter at Conclave.

Award: Scholarship for use in freshman, sophomore, junior, senior, or graduate years; not renewable. *Number:* 1. *Amount:* $800.

Eligibility Requirements: Applicant must be enrolled or expecting to enroll full-time at a four-year institution or university; male and must have an interest in leadership. Applicant or parent of applicant must be member of Tau Kappa Epsilon. Applicant must have 3.0 GPA or higher. Available to U.S. and non-U.S. citizens.

Application Requirements: Application form, application form may be submitted online (http://www.tke.org/member_resources/scholarships/apply_online), essay, personal photograph, transcript. *Deadline:* March 15.

Contact: Offices of the Grand Chapter
TKE Educational Foundation
7439 Woodland Drive, Suite 100
Indianapolis, IN 46278
E-mail: tkeogc@tke.org

WALLACE MCCAULEY MEMORIAL SCHOLARSHIP

One-time $300 award to undergraduate member of Tau Kappa Epsilon with junior or senior standing. Must have demonstrated understanding of the importance of good alumni relations. Must have excelled in the development, promotion, and execution of programs which increase alumni contact, awareness, and participation in fraternity activities. Minimum 3.0 GPA required.

Award: Scholarship for use in junior or senior years; not renewable. *Number:* 1. *Amount:* $300.

Eligibility Requirements: Applicant must be enrolled or expecting to enroll full-time at a four-year institution or university; male and must have an interest in leadership. Applicant or parent of applicant must be member of Tau Kappa Epsilon. Applicant must have 3.0 GPA or higher. Available to U.S. and non-U.S. citizens.

Application Requirements: Application form, application form may be submitted online (http://www.tke.org/member_resources/scholarships/apply_online), essay, narrative summary of how TKE membership has benefited applicant, personal photograph, transcript. *Deadline:* March 15.

Contact: Offices of the Grand Chapter
TKE Educational Foundation
7439 Woodland Drive, Suite 100
Indianapolis, IN 46278
E-mail: tkeogc@tke.org

WILLIAM V. MUSE SCHOLARSHIP

Award of $400 given to an undergraduate member of Tau Kappa Epsilon who has completed at least 30 semester hours of course work. Applicant should demonstrate leadership within chapter and maintain 3.0 GPA. Preference will first be given to a member of Epsilon-Upsilon Chapter but, if there is no qualified applicant, the scholarship will be open to any other qualified Teke.

Award: Scholarship for use in sophomore, junior, or senior years; not renewable. *Number:* 1. *Amount:* $400.

Eligibility Requirements: Applicant must be enrolled or expecting to enroll full-time at a four-year institution or university; male and must have an interest in leadership. Applicant or parent of applicant must be member of Tau Kappa Epsilon. Applicant must have 3.0 GPA or higher. Available to U.S. and non-U.S. citizens.

Application Requirements: Application form, application form may be submitted online (http://www.tke.org/member_resources/scholarships/apply_online), essay, narrative summary of how TKE membership has benefited applicant, personal photograph, transcript. *Deadline:* March 15.

Contact: Offices of the Grand Chapter
TKE Educational Foundation
7439 Woodland Drive, Suite 100
Indianapolis, IN 46278
E-mail: tkeogc@tke.org

WILLIAM WILSON MEMORIAL SCHOLARSHIP

One-time award given to undergraduate member of Tau Kappa Epsilon with junior or senior standing. Must have demonstrated understanding of the importance of good alumni relations. Must have excelled in the development, promotion, and execution of programs which increase alumni contact, awareness, and participation in fraternity activities. If there are no applicants who meet the alumni relations criteria, the scholarship will be open to any other qualified Teke, in recognition of academic achievement with a Grade Point Average of at least 2.5 or higher and recognized outstanding leadership within the chapter and on campus.

Award: Scholarship for use in junior or senior years; not renewable. *Number:* 1. *Amount:* $300.

Eligibility Requirements: Applicant must be enrolled or expecting to enroll full-time at a four-year institution or university; male and must have an interest in leadership. Applicant or parent of applicant must be member of Tau Kappa Epsilon. Applicant must have 3.0 GPA or higher. Available to U.S. and non-U.S. citizens.

Application Requirements: Application form, application form may be submitted online (http://www.tke.org/member_resources/scholarships/apply_online), essay, narrative summary of how TKE membership has benefited applicant, personal photograph, transcript. *Deadline:* March 15.

Contact: Offices of the Grand Chapter
TKE Educational Foundation
7439 Woodland Drive, Suite 100
Indianapolis, IN 46278
E-mail: tkeogc@tke.org

UNION PLUS SCHOLARSHIP PROGRAM

http://www.unionplus.org/

UNION PLUS EDUCATION FOUNDATION SCHOLARSHIP PROGRAM

One-time cash award for current or retired union members in good standing, in unions affiliated with the AFL-CIO, their spouses, and dependent children. Based upon academic achievement, character, leadership, career goals, social awareness of the labor movement and financial need. Must be from Canada or U.S., including Puerto Rico and the Virgin Islands. Members must apply online at our website: http://www.unionplus.org/scholarships.

Award: Scholarship for use in freshman, sophomore, junior, senior, or graduate years; not renewable. *Number:* 100–120. *Amount:* $500–$4000.

Eligibility Requirements: Applicant must be enrolled or expecting to enroll full- or part-time at a two-year or four-year or technical institution or university. Applicant or parent of applicant must be member of AFL-CIO. Applicant must have 2.5 GPA or higher. Available to U.S. and non-U.S. citizens.

Application Requirements: Application form, essay. *Deadline:* January 31.

Contact: Shana Higgins, Program Assistant
Union Plus Scholarship Program
Union Privilege
1100 First Street, NE
Suite 850
Washington, DC 20002
Phone: 202-778-9836
E-mail: shiggins@unionprivilege.org

UNITED DAUGHTERS OF THE CONFEDERACY

http://www.hqudc.org/

BARBARA JACKSON SICHEL MEMORIAL SCHOLARSHIP

Renewable award for undergraduate students who are descendant of a Confederate soldier, sailor or marine. Must be enrolled in an accredited college or university. Minimum of 3.0 GPA required. Submit a letter of endorsement from sponsoring Chapter of the United Daughters of the Confederacy.

Award: Scholarship for use in freshman, sophomore, junior, or senior years; renewable. *Number:* 1–2. *Amount:* $800–$1000.

Eligibility Requirements: Applicant must be enrolled or expecting to enroll full-time at a four-year institution or university. Applicant or parent of applicant must be member of United Daughters of the Confederacy. Applicant must have 3.0 GPA or higher. Available to U.S. citizens.

Application Requirements: Application form, essay, financial need analysis, personal photograph, proof of confederate ancestor's service, copy of applicant's birth certificate, recommendations or references, self-addressed stamped envelope with application, test scores, transcript. *Deadline:* March 15.

Contact: Ms. Jamie Davis, Second Vice President General
Phone: 804-355-1636
E-mail: hqudc@rcn.com

CHARLOTTE M. F. BENTLEY/NEW YORK CHAPTER 103 SCHOLARSHIP

Renewable award for undergraduate students who are descendant of a Confederate soldier, sailor or marine. Must be enrolled in an accredited college or university. Minimum of 3.0 GPA required. Must be members of United Daughters of the Confederacy and Children of the Confederacy from New York.

Award: Scholarship for use in freshman, sophomore, junior, or senior years; renewable. *Number:* 1–2. *Amount:* $800–$1000.

Eligibility Requirements: Applicant must be enrolled or expecting to enroll full-time at a four-year institution or university and resident of New York. Applicant or parent of applicant must be member of Children of the Confederacy, United Daughters of the Confederacy. Applicant must have 3.0 GPA or higher. Available to U.S. citizens.

Application Requirements: Application form, essay, financial need analysis, personal photograph, proof of confederate ancestor's service, copy of applicant's birth certificate, recommendations or references, self-addressed stamped envelope with application, test scores, transcript. *Deadline:* March 15.

Contact: Ms. Jamie Davis, Second Vice President General
Phone: 804-355-1636
E-mail: hqudc@rcn.com

ELIZABETH AND WALLACE KINGSBURY SCHOLARSHIP

Award for full-time undergraduate students who are descendants of a Confederate soldier, studying at an accredited college or university. Must have been a member of the Children of the Confederacy for a minimum of three years. Minimum 3.0 GPA required.

Award: Scholarship for use in freshman, sophomore, junior, or senior years; renewable. *Number:* 1–2. *Amount:* $800–$1000.

Eligibility Requirements: Applicant must be enrolled or expecting to enroll full-time at a four-year institution or university. Applicant or parent of applicant must be member of Children of the Confederacy. Applicant must have 3.0 GPA or higher. Available to U.S. citizens.

Application Requirements: Application form, copy of applicant's birth certificate, copy of confederate ancestor's proof of service, essay, financial need analysis, personal photograph, recommendations or references, self-addressed stamped envelope with application, test scores, transcript. *Deadline:* March 15.

Contact: Ms. Jamie Davis, Second Vice President General
Phone: 804-355-1636
E-mail: hqudc@rcn.com

GERTRUDE BOTTS-SAUCIER SCHOLARSHIP

Award for full-time undergraduate students who are descendants of a Confederate soldier, sailor or marine. Must be from Texas, Mississippi or Louisiana. Must be enrolled in an accredited college or university and have a minimum 3.0 GPA. Submit application and letter of endorsement from sponsoring chapter of the United Daughters of the Confederacy.

Award: Scholarship for use in freshman, sophomore, junior, or senior years; renewable. *Number:* 1–2. *Amount:* $800–$1000.

Eligibility Requirements: Applicant must be enrolled or expecting to enroll full-time at a four-year institution or university and resident of Louisiana, Mississippi, Texas. Applicant or parent of applicant must be member of United Daughters of the Confederacy. Applicant must have 3.0 GPA or higher. Available to U.S. citizens.

Application Requirements: Application form, copy of applicant's birth certificate, copy of confederate ancestor's proof of service, essay, financial need analysis, personal photograph, recommendations or references, self-addressed stamped envelope with application, test scores, transcript. *Deadline:* March 15.

Contact: Ms. Jamie Davis, Second Vice President General
Phone: 804-355-1636
E-mail: hqudc@rcn.com

LOLA B. CURRY SCHOLARSHIP

Award for full-time undergraduate students from Alabama who are descendants of a Confederate soldier. Must be enrolled in an accredited college or university in Alabama. Minimum 3.0 GPA required. Submit letter of endorsement from sponsoring chapter of the United Daughters of the Confederacy.

Award: Scholarship for use in freshman, sophomore, junior, or senior years; renewable. *Number:* 1–2. *Amount:* $800–$1000.

Eligibility Requirements: Applicant must be enrolled or expecting to enroll full-time at a four-year institution or university; resident of Alabama and studying in Alabama. Applicant or parent of applicant must be member of United Daughters of the Confederacy. Applicant must have 3.0 GPA or higher. Available to U.S. citizens.

Application Requirements: Application form, copy of applicant's birth certificate, copy of confederate ancestor's proof of service, essay, financial need analysis, personal photograph, recommendations or references, self-addressed stamped envelope with application, test scores, transcript. *Deadline:* March 15.

Contact: Ms. Jamie Davis, Second Vice President General
Phone: 804-355-1636
E-mail: hqudc@rcn.com

UNITED DAUGHTERS OF THE CONFEDERACY UNDERGRADUATE SCHOLARSHIPS

Renewable award for undergraduate students who are descendants of an eligible Confederate soldier. Must be enrolled in an accredited college or university. Minimum 3.0 GPA required. Applicants must be endorsed by the President and the Second Vice President/Education Chairman of Chapter and Division, and by the Second Vice President General. Applications are submitted through local chapters.

Award: Scholarship for use in freshman, sophomore, junior, or senior years; renewable. *Number:* 18–30. *Amount:* $800–$1000.

Eligibility Requirements: Applicant must be enrolled or expecting to enroll full-time at a two-year or four-year institution or university. Applicant or parent of applicant must be member of United Daughters of the Confederacy. Applicant must have 3.0 GPA or higher. Available to U.S. citizens.

Application Requirements: Application form, copy of applicant's birth certificate, copy of confederate ancestor's proof of service, essay, financial need analysis, personal photograph, recommendations or references, self-addressed stamped envelope with application, test scores, transcript. *Deadline:* March 15.

Contact: Ms. Jamie Davis, Second Vice President General
Phone: 804-355-1636
E-mail: hqudc@rcn.com

WINNIE DAVIS-CHILDREN OF THE CONFEDERACY SCHOLARSHIP

Award for full-time undergraduate students who are descendants of a Confederate soldier, enrolled in an accredited college or university. Recipient must be, or have been until age of 18, a participating member of the Children of the Confederacy and approved by the Third Vice President General. Minimum 3.0 GPA required.

Award: Scholarship for use in freshman, sophomore, junior, or senior years; renewable. *Number:* 1–2. *Amount:* $800–$1000.

Eligibility Requirements: Applicant must be enrolled or expecting to enroll full-time at a four-year institution or university. Applicant or parent

of applicant must be member of Children of the Confederacy. Applicant must have 3.0 GPA or higher. Available to U.S. citizens.

Application Requirements: Application form, copy of applicant's birth certificate, copy of confederate ancestor's proof of service, essay, financial need analysis, personal photograph, recommendations or references, self-addressed stamped envelope with application, test scores, transcript. *Deadline:* March 15.

Contact: Ms. Jamie Davis, Second Vice President General
Phone: 804-355-1636
E-mail: hqudc@rcn.com

UNITED FOOD AND COMMERCIAL WORKERS INTERNATIONAL UNION

http://www.ufcw.org/

JAMES A. SUFFRIDGE UNITED FOOD AND COMMERCIAL WORKERS SCHOLARSHIP PROGRAM

Scholarships available to graduating high school seniors and college students during the specific program year. Must be an active member of UFCW or unmarried dependent under age 20 of a UFCW member. Scholarship is disbursed over a four-year period.

Award: Scholarship for use in freshman, sophomore, junior, or senior years; renewable. *Number:* 14–20. *Amount:* up to $8000.

Eligibility Requirements: Applicant must be enrolled or expecting to enroll full- or part-time at a two-year or four-year or technical institution or university. Applicant or parent of applicant must be member of United Food and Commercial Workers. Available to U.S. and Canadian citizens.

Application Requirements: Application form, community service, essay, transcript. *Deadline:* April 15.

Contact: Field Assistant
United Food and Commercial Workers International Union
1775 K Street, NW
Washington, DC 20006
Phone: 202-223-3111
Fax: 202-721-8008
E-mail: scholarship@ufcw.org

UNITED STATES JUNIOR CHAMBER OF COMMERCE

http://www.usjaycees.org/

CHARLES R. FORD SCHOLARSHIP

One-time award of $3000 available to active members of Jaycee wishing to return to college to complete his/her formal education. Must be U.S. citizen, possess academic potential and leadership qualities and show financial need. To receive an application, send $10 application fee and self-addressed stamped envelope by February 1.

Award: Scholarship for use in freshman, sophomore, junior, senior, graduate, or postgraduate years; not renewable. *Number:* 1. *Amount:* $3000.

Eligibility Requirements: Applicant must be age 18-40 and enrolled or expecting to enroll full- or part-time at a two-year or four-year institution or university. Applicant or parent of applicant must be member of Jaycees. Available to U.S. citizens.

Application Requirements: Application form, financial need analysis, self-addressed stamped envelope with application, transcript. *Fee:* $10. *Deadline:* February 1.

Contact: Karen Fitzgerald, Customer Service and Data Processing
Phone: 918-584-2481
E-mail: customerservice@usjaycees.org

THOMAS WOOD BALDRIDGE SCHOLARSHIP

One-time award of $3000 available to a Jaycee immediate family member or a descendant of a Jaycee member. Must be U.S. citizen, possess academic potential and leadership qualities and show financial need. To receive an application, send $10 application fee and self-addressed stamped envelope by February 1.

Award: Scholarship for use in freshman, sophomore, junior, senior, graduate, or postgraduate years; not renewable. *Number:* 1. *Amount:* $3000.

Eligibility Requirements: Applicant must be age 18-40 and enrolled or expecting to enroll full- or part-time at a two-year or four-year or technical institution or university. Applicant or parent of applicant must be member of Jaycees. Available to U.S. citizens.

Application Requirements: Application form, financial need analysis, self-addressed stamped envelope with application, transcript. *Fee:* $10. *Deadline:* February 1.

Contact: Karen Fitzgerald, Customer Service and Data Processing
Phone: 918-584-2481
E-mail: customerservice@usjaycees.org

UNITED STATES MARINE CORPS SCHOLARSHIP FOUNDATION, INC.

http://www.mcsf.org/

MARINE CORPS SCHOLARSHIP FOUNDATION

Available to the sons and daughters of active duty, veteran, and deceased Marines, and to the children of qualifying Navy Corpsmen, whose family income does not exceed $96,000. Must submit proof of parent's service. Apply online at mcsf.org and or email Scholarship@mcsf.org for further information.

Award: Scholarship for use in freshman, sophomore, junior, or senior years; not renewable. *Number:* 2000–2300. *Amount:* $1500–$10,000.

Eligibility Requirements: Applicant must be enrolled or expecting to enroll full- or part-time at a two-year or four-year or technical institution or university. Applicant or parent of applicant must be member of American Legion or Auxiliary. Available to U.S. citizens.

Application Requirements: Application form, essay, financial need analysis. *Deadline:* March 1.

Contact: Jeanna Adams, Assistant Director, Scholarship Programs
Phone: 866-496-5462
E-mail: scholarship@mcsf.org

UNITED STATES SUBMARINE VETERANS

https://www.ussvi.org/home.asp

UNITED STATES SUBMARINE VETERANS INC. NATIONAL SCHOLARSHIP PROGRAM

Program requires the sponsor to be a qualified Base Member or Member-at-Large in good standing. Must demonstrate financial need, have a minimum 2.5 GPA, and submit an essay. Open to children, stepchildren, and grandchildren of qualified members. Applicants must be between the ages of 17 to 23 and must be unmarried.

Award: Scholarship for use in freshman, sophomore, junior, or senior years; not renewable. *Number:* 2–18. *Amount:* $950–$1500.

Eligibility Requirements: Applicant must be age 17-23; enrolled or expecting to enroll full-time at a two-year or four-year or technical institution or university and single. Applicant or parent of applicant must be member of Veterans of Foreign Wars or Auxiliary. Applicant or parent of applicant must have employment or volunteer experience in seafaring/fishing industry. Applicant must have 3.0 GPA or higher. Available to U.S. citizens. Applicant or parent must meet one or more of the following requirements: Navy experience; retired from active duty; disabled or killed as a result of military service; prisoner of war; or missing in action.

Application Requirements: Application form, essay, financial need analysis, recommendations or references, transcript. *Deadline:* April 15.

Contact: Paul Orstad, National Scholarship Chairman
United States Submarine Veterans
30 Surrey Lane
Norwich, CT 06369-6541
Phone: 860-334-6457
E-mail: hogan343@aol.com

USA BMX

http://usabmx.com

BOB WARNICKE MEMORIAL SCHOLARSHIP PROGRAM

Scholarship assists students and their families in meeting the costs of undergraduate or trade school education. Applicant must be a high school senior, graduate or attending a postsecondary school at the time of application, or accepted and plan to attend an accredited postsecondary school as a full-time or part-time student for the complete award year. Must be an active member or official of USA BMX.

Award: Scholarship for use in freshman, sophomore, junior, senior, graduate, or postgraduate years; not renewable.

Eligibility Requirements: Applicant must be enrolled or expecting to enroll full- or part-time at a two-year or four-year or technical institution or university. Applicant or parent of applicant must be member of National Bicycle League. Available to U.S. and non-U.S. citizens.

Application Requirements: Application form, essay, personal photograph. *Deadline:* March 6.

Contact: Scholarship Committee
Phone: 480-961-1903

UTILITY WORKERS UNION OF AMERICA

http://www.uwua.net/

UTILITY WORKERS UNION OF AMERICA SCHOLARSHIP AWARDS PROGRAM

Renewable award for high school juniors who are children of active members of the Utility Workers Union of America. Must take the PSAT National Merit Scholarship Qualifying Test in junior year and plan to enter college in the fall after high school graduation.

Award: Scholarship for use in freshman, sophomore, junior, or senior years; renewable. *Number:* 2. *Amount:* $500–$2000.

Eligibility Requirements: Applicant must be high school student and planning to enroll or expecting to enroll full-time at a four-year institution or university. Applicant or parent of applicant must be member of Utility Workers Union of America. Available to U.S. citizens.

Application Requirements: Application form. *Deadline:* May 31.

Contact: Ms. Stacy Paulo, Executive Assistant to the National Secretary-Treasurer
Utility Workers Union of America
1300 L St. NW
Suite 1200
Washington, DC 20002
Phone: 202-899-2851
Fax: 202-899-2852
E-mail: spaulo@uwua.net

VIETNOW NATIONAL HEADQUARTERS

http://www.vietnow.com/

VIETNOW NATIONAL SCHOLARSHIP

One-time award available to dependents of members of VietNow only. Applicants' academic achievements, abilities and extracurricular activities will be reviewed. Must be U.S. citizen and under the age of 35.

Award: Scholarship for use in freshman, sophomore, junior, senior, or graduate years; not renewable. *Amount:* $500–$1000.

Eligibility Requirements: Applicant must be enrolled or expecting to enroll full-time at a four-year institution or university. Applicant or parent of applicant must be member of VietNow. Available to U.S. citizens.

Application Requirements: Application form, driver's license, essay, test scores, transcript. *Deadline:* April 1.

Contact: Eileen Shoemaker, Executive Assistant
VietNow National Headquarters
1835 Broadway
Rockford, IL 61104
Phone: 815-227-5100
Fax: 815-227-5127
E-mail: vnnatl@inwave.com

WESTERN FRATERNAL LIFE ASSOCIATION

http://www.wflains.org/

WESTERN FRATERNAL LIFE ASSOCIATION NATIONAL SCHOLARSHIP

Western Fraternal Life Association is pleased to announce 25 national scholarships for its eligible members. They include the following: one four-year academic scholarship, $1,000 per year for a total of $4,000; two $1,000 scholarships to either community college or vocational/trade school; one community involvement scholarship, $1,000; one non-traditional student scholarship, $1,000. Traditional and non-traditional students are eligible. Must be a Western Fraternal Life Association member in good standing for two years prior to the application deadline. A member is an individual who has life insurance or an annuity with Western. High school seniors may apply. Members who are qualified for the National Scholarship may also qualify for state and local lodge scholarships.

Award: Scholarship for use in freshman, sophomore, junior, senior, graduate, or postgraduate years; renewable. *Number:* 25. *Amount:* $1000.

Eligibility Requirements: Applicant must be enrolled or expecting to enroll full-time at a two-year or four-year or technical institution or university and resident of Illinois, Iowa, Kansas, Louisiana, Michigan, Minnesota, Missouri, Nebraska, North Dakota, Oklahoma, Oregon, Pennsylvania, South Dakota, Texas, Washington, Wisconsin. Applicant or parent of applicant must be member of Western Fraternal Life Association. Available to U.S. citizens.

Application Requirements: Application form, essay. *Deadline:* March 1.

Contact: Darcy Hilton, Member Program Coordinator
Phone: 877-935-2467 Ext. 131
Fax: 319-363-8806
E-mail: dhilton@wflains.org

WESTERN FRATERNAL LIFE NATIONAL SCHOLARSHIP

Western Fraternal Life Association is pleased to announce 25 national scholarships for its eligible members. The 25 national scholarships include the following: one four-year academic scholarship, $1,000 per year for a total of $4,000; two $1,000 scholarships to either community college or vocational/trade school; one community involvement scholarship, $1,000; one non-traditional student scholarship, $1,000. Traditional and non-traditional students are eligible. Must be a Western Fraternal Life Association member in good standing for two years prior to the application deadline. A member is an individual who has life insurance or an annuity with Western. High school seniors may apply. Members who are qualified for the national scholarship may also qualify for state and local lodge scholarships.

Award: Scholarship for use in freshman, sophomore, junior, senior, graduate, or postgraduate years; renewable. *Number:* 25. *Amount:* $1000.

Eligibility Requirements: Applicant must be enrolled or expecting to enroll full-time at a two-year or four-year or technical institution or university and resident of Colorado, Illinois, Iowa, Kansas, Louisiana, Michigan, Minnesota, Missouri, Nebraska, North Dakota, Oklahoma, Oregon, Pennsylvania, South Dakota, Texas, Washington, Wisconsin. Applicant or parent of applicant must be member of Western Fraternal Life Association. Available to U.S. citizens.

Application Requirements: Application form, community service, essay, financial need analysis. *Deadline:* March 1.

Contact: Darcy Hilton, Member Program Coordinator
Phone: 877-935-2467 Ext. 131
Fax: 319-363-8806
E-mail: dhilton@wflains.org

WISCONSIN ASSOCIATION FOR FOOD PROTECTION

http://www.wifoodprotection.org

WAFP MEMORIAL SCHOLARSHIP

Scholarship for a child or dependent of a current or deceased WAFP member, or the applicant may be a WAFP student member. Must have been accepted into an accredited degree program in a university, college, or technical institute.

Award: Scholarship for use in sophomore, junior, senior, or graduate years; not renewable. *Number:* 1. *Amount:* $1000.

Eligibility Requirements: Applicant must be enrolled or expecting to enroll full-time at a two-year or four-year or technical institution or university. Applicant or parent of applicant must be member of Wisconsin Association for Food Protection. Available to U.S. and non-U.S. citizens.

Application Requirements: Application form. *Deadline:* July 1.

Contact: Mr. Jim Wickert, Scholarship Committee Chairman
Wisconsin Association for Food Protection
3834 Ridgeway Avenue
Madison, WI 53704
Phone: 608-241-2438
E-mail: jwick16060@tds.net

WYOMING FARM BUREAU FEDERATION

http://www.wyfb.org/

LIVINGSTON FAMILY - H.J. KING MEMORIAL SCHOLARSHIP

One-time award given to graduates of Wyoming high schools. Must attend a Wyoming junior college or the University of Wyoming. Minimum 2.5 GPA required. If Applicant is under 18 years of age, the applicant must have an immediate family member or guardian that is a current member of the Wyoming Farm Bureau Federation at the time of applying.

Award: Scholarship for use in freshman, sophomore, junior, senior, or graduate years; not renewable. *Number:* 1. *Amount:* $1500.

Eligibility Requirements: Applicant must be enrolled or expecting to enroll full-time at a two-year or four-year institution or university; resident of Wyoming and studying in Wyoming. Applicant or parent of applicant must be member of Wyoming Farm Bureau. Applicant must have 2.5 GPA or higher. Available to U.S. and non-U.S. citizens.

Application Requirements: Application form, financial need analysis, personal photograph. *Deadline:* March 1.

Contact: McKenzi Digby, Administrative Assistant
Phone: 307-721-7719
E-mail: mdigby@wyfb.org

WYOMING FARM BUREAU CONTINUING EDUCATION SCHOLARSHIPS

Award to students attending a two-year college in Wyoming or the University of Wyoming. Must be a resident of Wyoming and if 18 years or older, must be a current member of the Wyoming Farm Bureau Federation. If under 18, applicant must have an immediate family member or guardian that is a current member of the Wyoming Farm Bureau Federation at the time of applying. Must submit at least two semesters of college grade transcripts. Freshmen must submit first semester grades and proof of enrollment in second semester. Minimum 2.5 GPA.

Award: Scholarship for use in freshman, sophomore, junior, senior, or graduate years; not renewable. *Number:* 3. *Amount:* $500.

Eligibility Requirements: Applicant must be enrolled or expecting to enroll full-time at a two-year or four-year institution or university; resident of Wyoming and studying in Wyoming. Applicant or parent of applicant must be member of Wyoming Farm Bureau. Applicant must have 2.5 GPA or higher. Available to U.S. and non-U.S. citizens.

Application Requirements: Application form, financial need analysis, personal photograph. *Deadline:* March 1.

Contact: McKenzi Digby, Administrative Assistant
Phone: 307-721-7719
E-mail: mdigby@wyfb.org

WYOMING FARM BUREAU FEDERATION SCHOLARSHIPS

Five $500 scholarships will be given to graduates of Wyoming high schools. Eligible candidates must be enrolled in a two-year college in Wyoming or the University of Wyoming and must have a minimum 2.5 GPA. If 18 years or older, applicant must be a current paid member of the Wyoming Farm Bureau Federation at the time of applying. If under 18, applicant must have an immediate family member or guardian that is a current member of the Wyoming Farm Bureau Federation.

Award: Scholarship for use in freshman, sophomore, junior, senior, or graduate years; not renewable. *Number:* 5. *Amount:* $500.

Eligibility Requirements: Applicant must be enrolled or expecting to enroll full-time at a two-year or four-year institution or university; resident of Wyoming and studying in Wyoming. Applicant or parent of applicant must be member of Wyoming Farm Bureau. Applicant must have 2.5 GPA or higher. Available to U.S. and non-U.S. citizens.

Application Requirements: Application form, financial need analysis, personal photograph. *Deadline:* March 1.

Contact: McKenzi Digby, Administrative Assistant
Phone: 307-721-7719
E-mail: mdigby@wyfb.org

CORPORATE AFFILIATION

DEMOLAY FOUNDATION INCORPORATED

http://www.demolay.org/

FRANK S. LAND SCHOLARSHIP

Scholarship awarded to members of DeMolay International only, who have not yet reached the age of 21, to assist in financing their education. Must be U.S. resident.

Award: Scholarship for use in freshman, sophomore, junior, or senior years; not renewable. *Number:* 10–15. *Amount:* $1000.

Eligibility Requirements: Applicant must be enrolled or expecting to enroll full-time at a two-year or four-year institution or university and male. Applicant or parent of applicant must be affiliated with DeMolay. Available to U.S. citizens.

Application Requirements: Application form, financial need analysis. *Deadline:* April 1.

Contact: Mr. Frank Kell, Scholarship Chairman
DeMolay Foundation Incorporated
10200 Northwest Ambassador Drive
Kansas City, MO 64153
Phone: 800-336-6529
E-mail: admin@demolay.org

DONALDSON COMPANY

http://www.donaldson.com/

THE DONALDSON COMPANY, INC. SCHOLARSHIP PROGRAM

Scholarships for children of U.S. employees of Donaldson Company Inc. Any form of accredited postsecondary education is eligible. The amount of the award can range from $1000 to $3000 for each year of full-time study and may be renewed for up to a total of four years. The number of scholarships awarded is limited to a maximum of 25 percent of the number of applicants.

Award: Scholarship for use in freshman, sophomore, junior, or senior years; renewable. *Amount:* $1000–$3000.

Eligibility Requirements: Applicant must be enrolled or expecting to enroll full-time at a two-year or four-year institution or university. Applicant or parent of applicant must be affiliated with Donaldson Company. Available to U.S. citizens.

Application Requirements: Application form, essay, financial need analysis, recommendations or references, transcript. *Deadline:* March 15.

Contact: Norm Linnell, Vice President, General Counsel and Secretary
Phone: 952-887-3631
Fax: 952-887-3005
E-mail: norm.linnell@donaldson.com

DUKE ENERGY CORPORATION

http://www.duke-energy.com/

DUKE ENERGY SCHOLARS PROGRAM

The scholarship is for undergraduate study at accredited, two-year technical schools or community colleges and/or four-year colleges or universities in the United States and Canada who are children of eligible employees and retirees of Duke Energy and its subsidiaries. Recipients selected by five-member outside committee. The scholarships are merit-based with consideration given to academic record, leadership and participation in school and community activities, honors and awards, adult appraisal, work experience, a statement of educational and career goals, and unusual circumstances.

Award: Scholarship for use in freshman, sophomore, junior, or senior years; renewable. *Number:* 50. *Amount:* $1000–$5000.

Eligibility Requirements: Applicant must be high school student and planning to enroll or expecting to enroll full-time at a two-year or four-year or technical institution or university. Applicant or parent of applicant must be affiliated with Duke Energy Corporation. Available to U.S. citizens.

Application Requirements: Application form, community service, essay. *Deadline:* January 31.

Contact: Celia Beam, Scholarship Administrator
Phone: 704-382-5544
Fax: 704-382-3553
E-mail: chbeam@duke-energy.com

THE FORD FAMILY FOUNDATION

http://www.tfff.org

SCHOLARSHIP PROGRAM FOR SONS & DAUGHTERS OF EMPLOYEES OF ROSEBURG FOREST PRODUCTS CO.

Kenneth W. Ford and The Ford Family Foundation established the Ford Sons & Daughters Program to provide scholarships to sons and daughters of Roseburg Forest Products Co. employees as they pursue education beyond high school. Each year, up to 10% of all eligible applicants are selected to receive the Ford Sons & Daughters Scholarship. An applicant must be a dependent child or stepchild (age 21 or younger) of an employee of Roseburg Forest Products Co. The employee must be full-time and have been employed by Roseburg Forest Products Co. for a minimum of 18 months as of March 1 of the application year.

Award: Scholarship for use in freshman, sophomore, junior, or senior years; renewable. *Number:* 30–47. *Amount:* $3000–$5000.

Eligibility Requirements: Applicant must be enrolled or expecting to enroll full-time at a two-year or four-year or technical institution or university. Applicant or parent of applicant must be affiliated with Roseburg Forest Products.

Application Requirements: Application form, essay, interview. *Deadline:* March 1.

Contact: Tricia Tate, Scholarship Programs Manager
The Ford Family Foundation
440 East Broadway, Suite 200
Eugene, OR 97401
Phone: 541-485-6211
Fax: 541-485-6223
E-mail: fordscholarships@tfff.org

GANNETT FOUNDATION

http://www.gannettfoundation.org/

GANNETT FOUNDATION/MADELYN P. JENNINGS SCHOLARSHIP AWARD

One-time awards for high school students whose parents are current full-time Gannett Company employees. Must be planning to attend a 4-year college or university for full-time study in the fall after graduation. Students must meet all requirements for participation in the National Merit Scholarship Program and take the PSAT/NMSQT in their junior year of high school. For more information, call Tiffany Sanford at Gannett Co., Inc., 703.854.6446.

Award: Scholarship for use in freshman year; not renewable. *Number:* 6. *Amount:* $3000.

Eligibility Requirements: Applicant must be high school student and planning to enroll or expecting to enroll full-time at a four-year institution or university. Applicant or parent of applicant must be affiliated with Gannett Company, Inc. Available to U.S. citizens.

Application Requirements: Application form. *Deadline:* March 1.

Contact: Tiffany Sanford, Senior Benefits Analyst
Gannett Foundation
7950 Jones Branch Drive
McLean, VA 22107
Phone: 703-854-6446
E-mail: tsanford@gannett.com

GATEWAY PRESS INC. OF LOUISVILLE

http://www.gatewaypressinc.com/

GATEWAY PRESS SCHOLARSHIP

Scholarship for graduating high school seniors whose parents have been employees of Gateway Press Inc. for a minimum of 5 years. Applicant must be accepted at a college or university and maintain a minimum GPA of 2.25.

Award: Scholarship for use in freshman year; renewable. *Amount:* up to $3000.

Eligibility Requirements: Applicant must be high school student and planning to enroll or expecting to enroll full-time at a four-year institution or university. Applicant or parent of applicant must be affiliated with Gateway Press Inc. Available to U.S. citizens.

Application Requirements: Application form, recommendations or references, transcript. *Deadline:* January 1.

Contact: Chris Georgehead, Human Resources Manager
Phone: 502-454-0431
Fax: 502-459-7930
E-mail: kit@gatewaypressinc.com

GRACO INC.

http://www.graco.com/

GRACO EXCELLENCE SCHOLARSHIP

Three awards of $7500 (one for athletic achievement) for children of Graco employees with at least one year of company service. Award based on academics, financial need, and tuition costs. Must be under 25 years of age.

Award: Scholarship for use in freshman, sophomore, junior, senior, or graduate years; renewable. *Number:* 3. *Amount:* $7500.

Eligibility Requirements: Applicant must be enrolled or expecting to enroll full-time at a two-year or four-year or technical institution or university and must have an interest in athletics/sports. Applicant or parent of applicant must be affiliated with Graco, Inc. Available to U.S. and non-U.S. citizens.

Application Requirements: Application form, financial need analysis, test scores, transcript. *Deadline:* March 15.

Contact: Kristin Ridley, Grants Administration Manager
Graco Inc.
PO Box 1441
Minneapolis, MN 55440-1441
Phone: 612-623-6684
Fax: 612-623-6944

GRACO INC. SCHOLARSHIP PROGRAM

Renewable award for children of Graco employees under 26 years of age pursuing undergraduate or graduate education. Awards are based upon academics, financial need, and tuition costs. Submit transcripts, test scores, and financial need analysis with application.

Award: Scholarship for use in freshman, sophomore, junior, senior, or graduate years; renewable. *Amount:* $3500–$5000.

Eligibility Requirements: Applicant must be enrolled or expecting to enroll full-time at a two-year or four-year or technical institution or university. Applicant or parent of applicant must be affiliated with Graco, Inc. Available to U.S. and non-U.S. citizens.

Application Requirements: Application form, financial need analysis, test scores, transcript. *Deadline:* March 15.

Contact: Kristin Ridley, Grants Administration Manager
Graco Inc.
PO Box 1441
Minneapolis, MN 55440-1441
Phone: 612-623-6684
Fax: 612-623-6944

HERMAN O. WEST FOUNDATION

http://www.westpharma.com/

HERMAN O. WEST FOUNDATION SCHOLARSHIP PROGRAM

Awards up to fourteen scholarships per year to high school seniors who will be attending college in the fall after graduation. The scholarship may only be applied toward tuition cost up to $3000 per year for up to four years. Available only to children of active employees of West Pharmaceutical Services, Inc.

Award: Scholarship for use in freshman, sophomore, junior, or senior years; renewable. *Number:* 1–14. *Amount:* $3000–$12,000.

Eligibility Requirements: Applicant must be high school student and planning to enroll or expecting to enroll full-time at a two-year or four-year institution or university. Applicant or parent of applicant must be affiliated with West Pharmaceuticals. Available to U.S. citizens.

Application Requirements: Application form, essay. *Deadline:* January 31.

Contact: Laura Pit, Manager, Community Affairs
Herman O. West Foundation
530 Herman O West Drive
Exton, PA 19341
Phone: 610-594-3046
E-mail: laura.pitt@westpharma.com

JOHNSON CONTROLS INC.

http://www.johnsoncontrols.com/

JOHNSON CONTROLS FOUNDATION SCHOLARSHIP PROGRAM

Available to high school seniors who are children of Johnson Controls, Inc. U.S. employees only. 20 one-time awards of $2000 and 40 renewable scholarships of $2000 a year for up to four years.

Award: Scholarship for use in freshman year; renewable. *Number:* up to 60. *Amount:* $2000.

Eligibility Requirements: Applicant must be high school student and planning to enroll or expecting to enroll full-time at a four-year institution or university. Applicant or parent of applicant must be affiliated with Johnson Controls, Inc. Applicant must have 3.5 GPA or higher. Available to U.S. citizens.

Application Requirements: Application form, application form may be submitted online, community service, essay, recommendations or references, test scores, transcript. *Deadline:* March 13.

Contact: Marlene Griffith, Human Resources Administration Coordinator
Phone: 414-524-2425
Fax: 414-524-2299
E-mail: marlene.f.griffith@jci.com

OREGON STUDENT ASSISTANCE COMMISSION

http://www.GetCollegeFunds.org/

ALBINA FUEL COMPANY SCHOLARSHIP

Scholarship available to a dependent child of a current Albina Fuel Company employee. The employee must have been employed for at least one full year as of October 1 prior to the scholarship deadline. Must reapply annually. Oregon residency not required.

Award: Scholarship for use in freshman, sophomore, junior, or senior years; not renewable.

Eligibility Requirements: Applicant must be enrolled or expecting to enroll full-time at a four-year institution. Applicant or parent of applicant must be affiliated with Albina Fuel Company. Available to U.S. citizens.

Application Requirements: Application form, essay. *Deadline:* March 1.

Contact: Director of Grant Programs
Oregon Student Assistance Commission
1500 Valley River Drive, Suite 100
Eugene, OR 97401-7020
Phone: 800-452-8807

A. VICTOR ROSENFELD SCHOLARSHIP

Award for dependents of employees of Calbag Metals who have worked for that company for three or more years prior to the March 1 scholarship deadline. Applicants must be enrolled at any public or nonprofit U.S. college or university. Must reapply annually for award renewal. FAFSA required.

Award: Scholarship for use in freshman, sophomore, junior, or senior years; not renewable.

Eligibility Requirements: Applicant must be enrolled or expecting to enroll full-time at a four-year institution or university and resident of Oregon, Washington. Applicant or parent of applicant must be affiliated with Calbag Metals. Available to U.S. citizens.

Application Requirements: Application form, essay, financial need analysis. *Deadline:* March 1.

Contact: Director of Grant Programs
Oregon Student Assistance Commission
1500 Valley River Drive, Suite 100
Eugene, OR 97401-7020
Phone: 800-452-8807

ESSEX GENERAL CONSTRUCTION SCHOLARSHIP

Award for an employee, or dependent of a current employee of Essex General Construction. Employee must have been continuously employed at Essex for one year or more at no fewer than 20 hours per week as of the March 1 application deadline. Oregon residency is not required. Must be a high school graduate enrolling as an undergraduate in a college or university in the U.S. Must reapply each year to renew award for up to four years.

Award: Scholarship for use in freshman, sophomore, junior, or senior years; not renewable.

Eligibility Requirements: Applicant must be enrolled or expecting to enroll full- or part-time at a four-year institution or university. Applicant or parent of applicant must be affiliated with Essex General Construction. Available to U.S. citizens.

Application Requirements: Application form. *Deadline:* March 1.

Contact: Melissa Adams, Scholarship Processing Coordinator
Phone: 541-687-7409
E-mail: melissa.adams@hecc.oregon.gov

GLENN JACKSON SCHOLARS SCHOLARSHIPS

Renewable award for Oregon graduating high school seniors who are dependents of employees or retirees of Oregon Department of Transportation or Parks and Recreation Department. Employees must have worked in their department at least three years as of the March 1 scholarship deadline. Scholarship is automatically renewable if renewal criteria met.

Award: Scholarship for use in freshman, sophomore, junior, or senior years; renewable.

Eligibility Requirements: Applicant must be high school student; planning to enroll or expecting to enroll full- or part-time at a two-year or four-year institution or university and resident of Oregon. Applicant or parent of applicant must be affiliated with Oregon Department of Transportation Parks and Recreation. Available to U.S. citizens.

Application Requirements: Application form, financial need analysis. *Deadline:* March 1.

Contact: Melissa Adams, Scholarship Processing Coordinator
Phone: 541-687-7409
E-mail: melissa.adams@hecc.oregon.gov

OREGON TRUCKING ASSOCIATION SAFETY MANAGEMENT COUNCIL SCHOLARSHIP

One-time award available to a child of an Oregon Trucking Association member, or child of an employee of OTA member. Applicants must be graduating high school seniors planning to attend a public or nonprofit college or university. Oregon residency is not required.

Award: Scholarship for use in freshman year; not renewable.

Eligibility Requirements: Applicant must be high school student and planning to enroll or expecting to enroll full-time at a four-year institution. Applicant or parent of applicant must be affiliated with Oregon Trucking Association. Available to U.S. citizens.

Application Requirements: Application form. *Deadline:* March 1.

Contact: Melissa Adams, Scholarship Processing Coordinator
Phone: 541-687-7409
E-mail: melissa.adams@hecc.oregon.gov

RICHARD F. BRENTANO MEMORIAL SCHOLARSHIP

Award for legal dependents of eligible employees of Waste Control Systems Inc., and subsidiaries. Employees must be employed at least one year as of the March 1 scholarship deadline. Must reapply annually to renew award.

Award: Scholarship for use in freshman, sophomore, junior, or senior years; not renewable.

Eligibility Requirements: Applicant must be enrolled or expecting to enroll full-time at a four-year institution. Applicant or parent of applicant must be affiliated with Waste Control Systems, Inc. Applicant must have 3.0 GPA or higher. Available to U.S. citizens.

Application Requirements: Application form. *Deadline:* March 1.

Contact: Melissa Adams, Scholarship Processing Coordinator
Phone: 541-687-7409
E-mail: melissa.adams@hecc.oregon.gov

ROBERT D. FORSTER SCHOLARSHIP

Dependents of eligible employees of Walsh Construction Co. Eligible employees must have been employed by Walsh Construction 3+ years (1000+ hours each year) as of the March scholarship deadline. Automatically renewable if renewal criteria are met, and may be used at any four-year college or university in the U.S.

Award: Scholarship for use in freshman, sophomore, junior, or senior years; renewable.

Eligibility Requirements: Applicant must be enrolled or expecting to enroll full-time at a four-year institution or university. Applicant or parent of applicant must be affiliated with Walsh Construction Company. Available to U.S. citizens.

Application Requirements: Application form, financial need analysis. *Deadline:* March 1.

Contact: Melissa Adams, Scholarship Processing Coordinator
Phone: 541-687-7409
E-mail: melissa.adams@hecc.oregon.gov

ROGER W. EMMONS MEMORIAL SCHOLARSHIP

Scholarship available to children and grandchildren of owners or employees (for at least three years) of regular members of the Oregon Refuse and Recycling Association. Award may be used at any accredited U.S. public or nonprofit college or university. Scholarship is automatically renewable if renewal criteria met.

Award: Scholarship for use in freshman year; renewable.

Eligibility Requirements: Applicant must be high school student and planning to enroll or expecting to enroll full-time at a four-year institution. Applicant or parent of applicant must be affiliated with Oregon Refuse and Recycling Association. Available to U.S. citizens.

Application Requirements: Application form. *Deadline:* March 1.

Contact: Melissa Adams, Scholarship Processing Coordinator
Phone: 541-687-7409
E-mail: melissa.adams@hecc.oregon.gov

STIMSON LUMBER COMPANY SCHOLARSHIP

Renewable award for dependents of Stimson Lumber Company employees who are graduating seniors.

Award: Scholarship for use in freshman year; renewable.

Eligibility Requirements: Applicant must be high school student and planning to enroll or expecting to enroll full-time at a two-year or four-year institution. Applicant or parent of applicant must be affiliated with Stimson Lumber Company. Applicant must have 3.0 GPA or higher. Available to U.S. citizens.

Application Requirements: Application form. *Deadline:* March 1.

Contact: Melissa Adams, Scholarship Processing Coordinator
Phone: 541-687-7409
E-mail: melissa.adams@hecc.oregon.gov

TAYLOR MADE LABELS SCHOLARSHIP

Award available to dependents of eligible employees of Taylor Made Label Company. Employee must have been employed by Taylor Made for a minimum of one year as of the March 1 scholarship deadline. Applicant must reapply annually for award renewal.

Award: Scholarship for use in freshman, sophomore, junior, or senior years; not renewable.

Eligibility Requirements: Applicant must be enrolled or expecting to enroll full- or part-time at a four-year institution or university. Applicant or parent of applicant must be affiliated with Taylor Made Label Company. Available to U.S. citizens.

Application Requirements: Application form. *Deadline:* March 1.

Contact: Melissa Adams, Scholarship Processing Coordinator
Phone: 541-687-7409
E-mail: melissa.adams@hecc.oregon.gov

WALTER DAVIES SCHOLARSHIP

Award for eligible employees or dependents of eligible employees of U.S. Bank. Must be an Oregon high school graduate. Oregon residency is not required; must re-apply annually.

Award: Scholarship for use in freshman, sophomore, junior, or senior years; not renewable.

Eligibility Requirements: Applicant must be enrolled or expecting to enroll full- or part-time at a four-year institution. Applicant or parent of applicant must be affiliated with U.S. Bancorp. Available to U.S. citizens.

Application Requirements: Application form, financial need analysis. *Deadline:* March 1.

Contact: Melissa Adams, Scholarship Processing Coordinator
Phone: 541-687-7409
E-mail: melissa.adams@hecc.oregon.gov

WILLETT AND MARGUERITE LAKE SCHOLARSHIP

Scholarships for dependents and grandchildren of eligible employees of Bonita Pioneer Packaging Company who have been employed by the company for two years. May be used at public and non-profit colleges only. Reapply annually.

Award: Scholarship for use in freshman, sophomore, junior, or senior years; not renewable.

Eligibility Requirements: Applicant must be enrolled or expecting to enroll full-time at a four-year institution or university. Applicant or parent of applicant must be affiliated with Bonita Pioneer Packaging Company. Available to U.S. citizens.

Application Requirements: Application form. *Deadline:* March 1.

Contact: Melissa Adams, Scholarship Processing Coordinator
Phone: 541-687-7409
E-mail: melissa.adams@hecc.oregon.gov

WOODARD FAMILY SCHOLARSHIP

Scholarships are available to employees and dependents of eligible employees of Kimwood Corporation. Awards may be used at Oregon public and nonprofit colleges only. May reapply annually for award.

Award: Scholarship for use in freshman, sophomore, junior, or senior years; not renewable.

Eligibility Requirements: Applicant must be enrolled or expecting to enroll full-time at a two-year or four-year institution and studying in Oregon. Applicant or parent of applicant must be affiliated with Kimwood Corporation or Middlefield Village. Available to U.S. citizens.

Application Requirements: Application form. *Deadline:* March 1.

Contact: Melissa Adams, Scholarship Processing Coordinator
Phone: 541-687-7409
E-mail: melissa.adams@hecc.oregon.gov

RHODE ISLAND FOUNDATION

http://www.rifoundation.org/

A.T. CROSS SCHOLARSHIP

Renewable scholarships ranging from $1000 to $3000 for new applicants and from $300 to $2000 for renewals are available to children of full-time employees of A.T. Cross Company. Must be Rhode Island residents.

Award: Scholarship for use in freshman, sophomore, junior, or senior years; renewable. *Amount:* $1000–$3000.

Eligibility Requirements: Applicant must be enrolled or expecting to enroll full-time at a four-year institution or university and resident of Rhode Island. Applicant or parent of applicant must be affiliated with A.T. Cross. Available to U.S. citizens.

Application Requirements: Application form, essay, financial need analysis, recommendations or references, self-addressed stamped envelope with application, transcript. *Deadline:* May 15.

Contact: Libby Monahan, Funds Administrator
Phone: 401-274-4564 Ext. 3117
E-mail: libbym@rifoundation.org

THEODORE R. AND VIVIAN M. JOHNSON SCHOLARSHIP FOUNDATION INC.

http://www.jsf.bz/

THEODORE R. AND VIVIAN M. JOHNSON SCHOLARSHIP PROGRAM FOR CHILDREN OF UPS EMPLOYEES OR UPS RETIREES

The children of United Parcel Service employees or retirees who live in Florida are eligible for scholarship funds to attend college or vocational school in Florida. Awards are for undergraduate study only and ranges

from $1000 to $10,000. Community college students and vocational school students may receive a maximum of $10,000 per year.

Award: Scholarship for use in freshman, sophomore, junior, or senior years; renewable. *Number:* 1–205. *Amount:* $1000–$10,000.

Eligibility Requirements: Applicant must be enrolled or expecting to enroll full- or part-time at a two-year or four-year or technical institution or university; resident of Florida and studying in Florida. Applicant or parent of applicant must be affiliated with Universal American Financial Corporation. Available to U.S. citizens.

Application Requirements: Application form, financial need analysis. *Deadline:* April 15.

Contact: Alexa Thelen, Program Manager
Theodore R. and Vivian M. Johnson Scholarship Foundation Inc.
Scholarship Management Services
One Scholarship Way
Saint Peter, MN 56082
Phone: 507-931-1682
E-mail: athelen@scholarshipamerica.org

TRIANGLE COMMUNITY FOUNDATION

http://www.trianglecf.org

GEORGE AND MARY NEWTON SCHOLARSHIP

Anyone between 16-25, who has received or is expecting a high school degree or equivalent and whose parent or legal guardian is an employee of Newton Instrument Company, Inc., may apply. Applicant must have applied to the institution he or she plans to attend, and must intend to enroll within one year of the application deadline. Recipients will be selected on the basis of academic achievement, financial need, school and community activities, and work experience and educational goals.

Award: Scholarship for use in freshman, sophomore, junior, or senior years; renewable. *Number:* 1. *Amount:* $1000.

Eligibility Requirements: Applicant must be age 16-25; enrolled or expecting to enroll full-time at a two-year or four-year or technical institution or university and resident of North Carolina. Applicant or parent of applicant must be affiliated with Newton Instrument Company. Available to U.S. citizens.

Application Requirements: Application form. *Deadline:* March 15.

Contact: Mrs. Sarah Battersby, Scholarships and Donor Services Officer
Phone: 919-474-8370 Ext. 4015
E-mail: Scholarships@trianglecf.org

WALMART FOUNDATION

http://foundation.walmart.com/

WALMART ASSOCIATE SCHOLARSHIP

The Walmart Foundation offers scholarship programs that benefit qualified Walmart associates. Applicants must be employed with any division of Walmart for at least six consecutive months prior to the application due date for the award period in which the associate is applying. Applicants must have graduated high school/home school or obtained a GED or be a graduating high school senior who intends to enroll in a college or university upon graduation. http://foundation.walmart.com/our-focus/associate-scholarships

Award: Scholarship for use in freshman, sophomore, junior, senior, or graduate years; renewable. *Amount:* up to $16,000.

Eligibility Requirements: Applicant must be enrolled or expecting to enroll full- or part-time at a two-year or four-year or technical institution or university. Applicant or parent of applicant must be affiliated with Wal-Mart Foundation. Available to U.S. citizens.

Application Requirements: Application form, application form may be submitted online (http://foundation.walmart.com/our-focus/associate-scholarships), community service, entry in a contest, financial need analysis. *Deadline:* varies.

Contact: Walmart Foundation Scholarship Administrator
Walmart Foundation
702 SW 8th Street
Bentonville, AR 72716-0150
Fax: 479-273-6850
E-mail: W.Mschol@wal-mart.com

WALMART DEPENDENT SCHOLARSHIP

The Walmart Foundation offers scholarship programs that benefit qualified Walmart associates and their high school senior dependents. Applicants must be the dependent of an actively employed Walmart associate (employee) within any division of Walmart for at least six consecutive months as of April 1 and must be a high school or home school senior graduating or earning a GED between August 1 and July 31. Applicants must have a cumulative high school grade point average (GPA) of at least 2.0 on a 4-point scale. See website for details, https://walmart.scholarsapply.org/dependent/

Award: Scholarship for use in freshman, sophomore, junior, or senior years; renewable. *Amount:* up to $13,000.

Eligibility Requirements: Applicant must be high school student and planning to enroll or expecting to enroll full-time at a two-year or four-year or technical institution or university. Applicant or parent of applicant must be affiliated with Wal-Mart Foundation. Available to U.S. citizens.

Application Requirements: Application form, application form may be submitted online (http://foundation.walmart.com/our-focus/associate-scholarships), entry in a contest, financial need analysis, transcript. *Deadline:* April 1.

Contact: Walmart Foundation Scholarship Administrator
Walmart Foundation
702 SW 8th Street
Bentonville, AR 72716-0150
Fax: 479-273-6850
E-mail: W.Mschol@wal-mart.com

WILLITS FOUNDATION

WILLITS FOUNDATION SCHOLARSHIP PROGRAM

Renewable awards for children of full-time employees of C. R. Bard Inc. Children of Bard officers are not eligible. Must be pursuing, or planning to pursue, full-time postsecondary studies in the year in which the application is made.

Award: Scholarship for use in freshman, sophomore, junior, or senior years; renewable. *Number:* 15–20. *Amount:* $5000.

Eligibility Requirements: Applicant must be enrolled or expecting to enroll full-time at a four-year institution or university. Applicant or parent of applicant must be affiliated with C.R. Bard, Inc. Available to U.S. and Canadian citizens.

Application Requirements: Application form, community service, essay, recommendations or references, test scores, transcript. *Deadline:* March 1.

Contact: Ms. Linda Hrevnack, Program Manager
Willits Foundation
730 Central Avenue
Murray Hill, NJ 07974
Phone: 908-277-8182
Fax: 908-277-8098

EMPLOYMENT/ VOLUNTEER EXPERIENCE

1-800-HANSONS

www.hansons.com

1-800-HANSONS SCHOLARSHIP PROGRAM

To be eligible, applicant must have a minimum of a 3.3 cumulative GPA and submit a 1000–1500-word essay. There are no other requirements for this scholarship, just the desire and drive to be successful in life. Please answer one of the following essay questions: What do you consider to be the single most important societal problem? Why? What do you think your chosen industry will be like in the next 10 years? What is the purpose of life? If you won the lottery for a million dollars, what would you do with it? Mail your official transcript and essay to 1-800-HANSONS, Attention: Hansons Scholarship Program, c/o Brian Elias, 977 E 14 Mile Road, Troy, MI 48083. Be sure to include your name, address, phone number, and email address so we can contact you if you win!

Award: Scholarship for use in freshman, sophomore, junior, senior, graduate, or postgraduate years; not renewable. *Number:* 8. *Amount:* $500–$5000.

Eligibility Requirements: Applicant must be enrolled or expecting to enroll full- or part-time at a two-year or four-year institution or university. Available to U.S. and non-U.S. citizens.

Application Requirements: Essay. *Deadline:* October 15.

Contact: Theresa Baughman
1-800-HANSONS
977 E 14 Mile Rd
Troy, MI 48083
Phone: 248-5813030 Ext. 1011
E-mail: tbaughman@hansons.com

4MYCASH.COM, LLC

https://www.4mycash.com

4MYCASH ST. LOUIS HARD MONEY SCHOLARSHIP

The 4MyCash St. Louis Hard Money Scholarship was created to help students interested in higher education reach their goal of attending college or university. Each year students who have lived in St. Louis, MO, at some point in their lives, will have the chance to provide a short essay. Applicants are asked to explain how their experience living in St. Louis has shaped them as individuals. St. Louis is a dynamic and historic city faced with many challenges, but it is also one of opportunity and growth. We encourage applicants to consider some of those challenges and opportunities in their essay. A committee will select a winner by the end of November. One winner will be selected and receive $1000 towards higher education.

Award: Scholarship for use in freshman, sophomore, junior, senior, graduate, or postgraduate years; renewable. *Number:* 1. *Amount:* $1000.

Eligibility Requirements: Applicant must be enrolled or expecting to enroll full- or part-time at a two-year or four-year or technical institution or university. Available to U.S. citizens.

Application Requirements: Application form, essay. *Deadline:* November 30.

Contact: Mr. Andrew Polsky, Manager
4MyCash.com, LLC
7750 Maryland Avenue
#50004
St. Louis, MO 63105
Phone: 310-764-7656
E-mail: andrew@4mycash.com

A-1 AUTO TRANSPORT, INC.

https://www.a1autotransport.com/a-1-auto-transport-scholarship/

A-1 AUTO TRANSPORT SCHOLARSHIP

The scholarship will be sent directly to the school/university/college's financial aid office. One award available, totaling $1000.

Award: Scholarship for use in freshman, sophomore, junior, senior, graduate, or postgraduate years; renewable. *Number:* 1–2. *Amount:* $1–$1000.

Eligibility Requirements: Applicant must be enrolled or expecting to enroll full- or part-time at a two-year or four-year or technical institution or university. Applicant must have 3.0 GPA or higher. Available to U.S. and non-U.S. citizens.

Application Requirements: Essay. *Deadline:* March 10.

Contact: Joe Webster
Phone: 831-778-4529
E-mail: scholarships@a1autotransport.com

ABBVIE INC.

https://www.abbvie.com/

ABBVIE IMMUNOLOGY SCHOLARSHIP

The AbbVie Immunology Scholarship is available to students living with inflammatory diseases, including ankylosing spondylitis (AS), Crohn's disease (CD), hidradenitis suppurativa (HS), juvenile idiopathic arthritis (JIA), psoriasis (Ps), psoriatic arthritis (PsA), rheumatoid arthritis (RA), ulcerative colitis (UC) or uveitis (UV), who are seeking an undergraduate degree (associate's/two-year college, bachelor's/four-year college, trade/vocational school) or graduate degree (Master's, MD, JD, doctorate) from an accredited United States (US) university/college. Students applying for this scholarship must have completed high school or obtained a General Educational Development (GED) certificate before the end of June 2017. Students applying for the scholarship must enroll in an accredited U.S.-based higher education institution for the 2017–2018 school year. Students in their final year of undergraduate study may only apply if they will be pursuing a graduate program in the 2017–2018 school year.

Award: Scholarship for use in freshman, sophomore, junior, senior, or graduate years; not renewable. *Number:* 45. *Amount:* $15,000.

Eligibility Requirements: Applicant must be enrolled or expecting to enroll full- or part-time at a two-year or four-year or technical institution or university; resident of Alabama, Alaska, Arizona, Arkansas, California, Colorado, Connecticut, Delaware, District of Columbia, Florida, Georgia, Hawaii, Idaho, Illinois, Indiana, Iowa, Kansas, Kentucky, Louisiana, Maine, Maryland, Massachusetts, Michigan, Minnesota, Mississippi, Missouri, Montana, Nebraska, Nevada, New Hampshire, New Jersey, New Mexico, New York, North Carolina, North Dakota, Ohio, Oklahoma, Oregon, Pennsylvania, Rhode Island, South Carolina, South Dakota, Tennessee, Texas, Utah, Vermont, Virginia, Washington, West Virginia, Wisconsin, Wyoming and studying in Alabama, Alaska, Arizona, Arkansas, California, Colorado, Connecticut, Delaware, District of Columbia, Florida, Georgia, Hawaii, Idaho, Illinois, Indiana, Iowa, Kansas, Kentucky, Louisiana, Maine, Maryland, Massachusetts, Michigan, Minnesota, Mississippi, Missouri, Montana, Nebraska, Nevada, New Hampshire, New Jersey, New Mexico, New York, North Carolina, North Dakota, Ohio, Oklahoma, Oregon, Pennsylvania, Rhode Island, South Carolina, South Dakota, Tennessee, Texas, Utah, Vermont, Virginia, Washington, West Virginia, Wisconsin, Wyoming. Available to U.S. citizens.

Application Requirements: Application form, essay. *Deadline:* March 31.

AIR TRAFFIC CONTROL ASSOCIATION INC.

http://www.atca.org/

AIR TRAFFIC CONTROL ASSOCIATION SCHOLARSHIP

Scholarships for students in programs leading to a bachelor's degree or higher in aviation-related courses of study, and for full-time employees engaged in advanced study to improve their skills in air traffic control or aviation. Visit website for additional information http://www.atca.org.

Award: Scholarship for use in freshman, sophomore, junior, senior, graduate, or postgraduate years; not renewable. *Number:* 7–12. *Amount:* $2000–$10,000.

Eligibility Requirements: Applicant must be enrolled or expecting to enroll full- or part-time at a two-year or four-year institution or university and must have an interest in aviation. Applicant or parent of applicant must have employment or volunteer experience in air traffic control. Available to U.S. and non-U.S. citizens.

Application Requirements: Application form, essay, financial need analysis. *Deadline:* May 1.

Contact: Tim Wagner, Membership Manager
Air Traffic Control Association Inc.
1101 King Street, Suite 300
Alexandria, VA 22314
Phone: 703-299-2430
E-mail: info@atca.org

BUCKINGHAM MEMORIAL SCHOLARSHIP

Scholarships granted to children of air traffic control specialists pursuing a bachelor's degree or higher in any course of study. Must be the child, natural or by adoption, of a person serving, or having served as an air traffic control specialist, be it with the U.S. government, U.S. military, or in a private facility in the United States.

Award: Scholarship for use in freshman, sophomore, junior, senior, or graduate years; not renewable. *Number:* 1–4. *Amount:* $2000–$10,000.

Eligibility Requirements: Applicant must be enrolled or expecting to enroll full-time at a four-year institution or university. Applicant or parent of applicant must have employment or volunteer experience in air traffic control. Available to U.S. citizens.

Application Requirements: Application form, community service, essay, financial need analysis. *Deadline:* May 1.

Contact: Tim Wagner, Membership Manager
Air Traffic Control Association Inc.
1101 King Street
Suite 300
Alexandria, VA 22314
Phone: 703-299-2430 Ext. 314
Fax: 703-299-2437
E-mail: tim.wagner@atca.org

LAWRENCE C. FORTIER MEMORIAL SCHOLARSHIP

Awarded to students enrolled in an aviation-related program of study leading to a Bachelor's degree or greater.

Award: Scholarship for use in freshman, sophomore, junior, senior, graduate, or postgraduate years; not renewable. *Number:* 1–5. *Amount:* $2000–$10,000.

Eligibility Requirements: Applicant must be enrolled or expecting to enroll full-time at a two-year or four-year institution or university and must have an interest in aviation. Available to U.S. and non-U.S. citizens.

Application Requirements: Application form, community service, essay, financial need analysis. *Deadline:* May 1.

Contact: Tim Wagner, Membership Manager
Air Traffic Control Association Inc.
1101 King Street
Suite 300
Alexandria, VA 22314
Phone: 703-299-2430 Ext. 314
Fax: 703-299-2437
E-mail: tim.wagner@atca.org

ALERTONE SERVICES LLC

https://www.alert-1.com/

ALERT1 STUDENT FOR SENIORS SCHOLARSHIP

Plan to help seniors in the future? You could be grandma's caregiver or the next great innovator for seniors. Whether you're pursuing technology or the arts, you're committed to improve senior care. To reward your hard work, Alert1 wants to give you a helping hand. As America's #1 medical alert, we are all about helping future leaders in senior care. Alert1 is offering a $3500 scholarship to a student attending an accredited U.S. college or university who wants to help seniors. To apply for this scholarship, follow the instructions below. Submit the online application form and answer the following three questions (under 300 words each): What is your experience with seniors? What is the most important lesson you've learned from seniors? How will you help seniors in your chosen career?

Award: Scholarship for use in freshman, sophomore, junior, senior, or graduate years; not renewable. *Number:* 1. *Amount:* $3500.

Eligibility Requirements: Applicant must be enrolled or expecting to enroll full-time at a two-year or four-year institution or university. Available to U.S. citizens.

Application Requirements: Application form, essay, personal photograph. *Deadline:* May 25.

Contact: Kathy Vo, Marketing Associate
AlertOne Services LLC
60 South Market Street
San Jose, CA 95113
Phone: 866-8023676 Ext. 7415
E-mail: kathy.vo@alert1.com

ALGAECAL INC.

https://www.algaecal.com/

ALGAECAL SCHOLARSHIP

The 2017 AlgaeCal Scholarship originated from the desire to financially assist students in pursuit of higher education as they face the challenge of significantly rising costs of obtaining a college degree. Also, it stemmed from the need for greater focus on the critical issue of health and well-being. With two-thirds of the U.S. reported to be overweight, and one-third obese, more dialogue and solutions are obviously still in need to manage and correct this huge rising health crisis. Applicants will download and fill out an AlgaeCal Health Scholarships Application Form and write an essay up to 750 words, describing "If you could, what, if any, changes to programs, policies, and education etc. would you implement for the general health/ well being of the average modern person?"

Award: Scholarship for use in freshman, sophomore, junior, senior, graduate, or postgraduate years; not renewable. *Number:* 1. *Amount:* $1000.

Eligibility Requirements: Applicant must be age 18-99 and enrolled or expecting to enroll full- or part-time at a two-year or four-year or technical institution or university. Applicant must have 3.0 GPA or higher. Available to U.S. and non-U.S. citizens.

Application Requirements: Essay. *Deadline:* June 30.

Contact: Mr. Philip Wong
Phone: 877-9165901
E-mail: philip@algaecal.com

ALLIANCE FOR YOUNG ARTISTS AND WRITERS INC.

http://www.artandwriting.org/

SCHOLASTIC ART AND WRITING AWARDS

Public, private, or home-school students in the U.S., Canada, or American schools abroad enrolled in grades 7–12 are eligible to participate in the Scholastic Awards in 29 categories of art and wiring. The Scholastic Awards are adjudicated without knowledge of the artists/writers identity using three criteria: originality, technical skill, and emergence of personal voice or vision.

Award: Scholarship for use in freshman year; not renewable. *Number:* 89. *Amount:* $500–$10,000.

Eligibility Requirements: Applicant must be high school student and planning to enroll or expecting to enroll full- or part-time at a two-year or four-year or technical institution or university. Available to U.S. and non-U.S. citizens.

Application Requirements: Application form, essay, personal photograph, portfolio. *Fee:* $5. *Deadline:* continuous.

Contact: General Information
Alliance for Young Artists and Writers Inc.
557 Broadway
New York, NY 10012
Phone: 212-343-7700
E-mail: info@artandwriting.org

ALLTHEROOMS

http://alltherooms.com

ROOM TO TRAVEL - STUDY ABROAD SCHOLARSHIP

University students enrolled in or enrolling in a study abroad program with their university must submit a 600-800 worded essay on what inspires them to travel and the benefits they stand to gain from their study abroad experience. Winning submission receives $1,000 to be used on study abroad costs. Submissions must be received no later than August 1st, 2017 and winner will be announced prior to the 2017 Fall semester. Eligible students have U.S. citizenship or residency and is enrolled in or enrolling in a study abroad program at an accredited university.

Award: Prize for use in freshman, sophomore, junior or senior years; renewable. *Number:* 1. *Amount:* $1000.

Eligibility Requirements: Applicant must be enrolled or expecting to enroll full-time at a four-year institution or university. Available to U.S. citizens.

Application Requirements: Essay. *Deadline:* August 1.

Contact: Victor Bosselaar
AllTheRooms
712 5th Avenue, 14th FL
New York, NY 10019
Phone: 203-561-9767
E-mail: victor.bosselaar@gmail.com

AMERICAN ASSOCIATION OF TEACHERS OF JAPANESE BRIDGING CLEARINGHOUSE FOR STUDY ABROAD IN JAPAN

http://www.aatj.org

BRIDGING SCHOLARSHIP FOR STUDY ABROAD IN JAPAN

Scholarships for U.S. students studying in Japan on semester or year-long programs. Deadlines: April 11 and October 11.

Award: Scholarship for use in sophomore, junior, or senior years; not renewable. *Number:* 70–100. *Amount:* $2500–$4000.

Eligibility Requirements: Applicant must be enrolled or expecting to enroll full-time at a two-year or four-year institution or university. Available to U.S. citizens.

Application Requirements: Application form, essay, financial need analysis. *Deadline:* April 11.

Contact: Susan Schmidt
E-mail: susan.schmidt@colorado.edu

AMERICAN COUNCIL OF THE BLIND

http://www.acb.org/

AMERICAN COUNCIL OF THE BLIND SCHOLARSHIPS

Merit-based award available to undergraduate students who are legally blind in both eyes. Submit certificate of legal blindness and proof of acceptance at an accredited postsecondary institution, as well as scholarship application, high school or college transcripts and other supporting documents (see directions on www.acb.org). Deadline: February 15.

Award: Scholarship for use in freshman, sophomore, junior, senior, graduate, or postgraduate years; not renewable. *Number:* 16–20. *Amount:* $1000–$3500.

Eligibility Requirements: Applicant must be visually impaired and enrolled or expecting to enroll full- or part-time at a two-year or four-year or technical institution or university. Applicant must be visually impaired. Applicant must have 3.5 GPA or higher. Available to U.S. citizens.

Application Requirements: Application form, autobiography, driver's license, essay, interview. *Deadline:* February 15.

Contact: Scholarship Coordinator
American Council of the Blind
6300 Shingle Creek Pkwy
Suite 195
Brooklyn Center, MN 55430
Phone: 612-332-3242
E-mail: info@acb.org

AMERICAN FEDERATION OF TEACHERS

http://www.aft.org/

ROBERT G. PORTER SCHOLARS PROGRAM-AMERICAN FEDERATION OF TEACHERS DEPENDENTS

• *See page 529*

AMERICAN LEGION AUXILIARY DEPARTMENT OF MASSACHUSETTS

http://www.masslegion-aux.org/

AMERICAN LEGION AUXILIARY DEPARTMENT OF MASSACHUSETTS DEPARTMENT PRESIDENT'S SCHOLARSHIP

Awarded to children of veterans who served in the armed forces during the eligibility dates specified by the legion. The applicant must complete 50 hours of community service during high school years to be eligible for this scholarship.

Award: Scholarship for use in freshman, sophomore, junior, or senior years; not renewable. *Number:* 12. *Amount:* $200–$750.

Eligibility Requirements: Applicant must be age 16-22; enrolled or expecting to enroll full-time at a two-year or four-year institution or university; resident of Massachusetts and studying in Massachusetts. Applicant or parent of applicant must have employment or volunteer experience in community service. Available to U.S. citizens. Applicant or parent must meet one or more of the following requirements: general military experience; retired from active duty; disabled or killed as a result of military service; prisoner of war; or missing in action.

Application Requirements: Application form. *Deadline:* March 1.

Contact: Ann Fournier, Secretary and Treasurer
American Legion Auxiliary Department of Massachusetts
State House Room 546-2
Boston, MA 02133
Phone: 617-727-2958
Fax: 617-727-0741
E-mail: masslegion-aux@verizon.net

AMERICAN LEGION AUXILIARY DEPARTMENT OF NORTH DAKOTA

http://www.ndlegion.org/

AMERICAN LEGION AUXILIARY DEPARTMENT OF NORTH DAKOTA NATIONAL PRESIDENT'S SCHOLARSHIP

Three division scholarships for children of veterans who served in the Armed Forces during eligible dates for American Legion membership. Must be U.S. citizen and a high school senior with a minimum 2.5 GPA. Must be entered by local American Legion Auxiliary Unit.

Award: Scholarship for use in freshman year; not renewable. *Number:* 3. *Amount:* $1000–$2500.

Eligibility Requirements: Applicant must be high school student; planning to enroll or expecting to enroll full-time at a four-year institution or university; resident of North Dakota and studying in North Dakota. Applicant or parent of applicant must have employment or volunteer experience in community service. Applicant must have 2.5 GPA or higher. Available to U.S. citizens. Applicant or parent must meet one or more of the following requirements: general military experience; retired from active duty; disabled or killed as a result of military service; prisoner of war; or missing in action.

Application Requirements: Application form, essay, financial need analysis, proof of 50 hours voluntary service, recommendations or references, test scores, transcript. *Deadline:* March 1.

Contact: Myrna Runholm, Department Secretary
Phone: 701-253-5992
Fax: 701-952-5993
E-mail: ala-hq@ndlegion.org

AMERICAN LEGION AUXILIARY DEPARTMENT OF PENNSYLVANIA

http://pa-legion.com

AMERICAN LEGION AUXILIARY DEPARTMENT OF PENNSYLVANIA SCHOLARSHIP FOR DEPENDENTS OF LIVING VETERANS

Renewable award of $600 for high school seniors who are residents of Pennsylvania. Applicants must enroll in a program of full-time study. Total $2,400 award.

Award: Scholarship for use in freshman, sophomore, junior, or senior years; renewable. *Number:* 1. *Amount:* $600.

Eligibility Requirements: Applicant must be high school student; planning to enroll or expecting to enroll full-time at a four-year institution or university; single; resident of Pennsylvania and studying in Pennsylvania. Available to U.S. citizens.

Application Requirements: Application form. *Deadline:* March 15.

Contact: Colleen Watson, Executive Secretary and Treasurer
Phone: 717-763-7545
Fax: 717-763-0617
E-mail: paalad@hotmail.com

AMERICAN LEGION AUXILIARY DEPARTMENT OF WISCONSIN

http://www.amlegionauxwi.org/

AMERICAN LEGION AUXILIARY DEPARTMENT OF WISCONSIN DELLA VAN DEUREN MEMORIAL SCHOLARSHIP
• *See page 531*

AMERICAN LEGION AUXILIARY DEPARTMENT OF WISCONSIN H.S. AND ANGELINE LEWIS SCHOLARSHIPS
• *See page 531*

AMERICAN LEGION AUXILIARY DEPARTMENT OF WISCONSIN MERIT AND MEMORIAL SCHOLARSHIPS
• *See page 531*

AMERICAN LEGION AUXILIARY DEPARTMENT OF WISCONSIN PAST PRESIDENTS' PARLEY HEALTH CAREER SCHOLARSHIPS
• *See page 531*

AMERICAN LEGION AUXILIARY DEPARTMENT OF WISCONSIN PRESIDENT'S SCHOLARSHIPS
• *See page 531*

AMERICAN LEGION AUXILIARY NATIONAL HEADQUARTERS

http://www.ALAforVeterans.org

AMERICAN LEGION AUXILIARY CHILDREN OF WARRIORS NATIONAL PRESIDENTS' SCHOLARSHIP

One-time scholarship for high school children of veterans who served in the Armed Forces during the eligibility dates for The American Legion. The applicant must complete 50 hours of community service during his/her high school years to be eligible for one of these scholarships.

Award: Scholarship for use in freshman year; not renewable. *Number:* 15. *Amount:* $5000.

Eligibility Requirements: Applicant must be high school student and planning to enroll or expecting to enroll full-time at a four-year institution or university. Available to U.S. citizens. Applicant or parent must meet one or more of the following requirements: general military experience; retired from active duty; disabled or killed as a result of military service; prisoner of war; or missing in action.

Application Requirements: Application form, community service, essay. *Deadline:* March 1.

Contact: Kristin Hinshaw, Program Coordinator
American Legion Auxiliary National Headquarters
8945 North Meridian Street
Indianapolis, IN 46260
Phone: 317-569-4556
E-mail: khinshaw@ALAforVeterans.org

AMERICAN LEGION DEPARTMENT OF VERMONT

http://www.vtlegion.org

AMERICAN LEGION EAGLE SCOUT OF THE YEAR
• *See page 535*

AMERICAN POSTAL WORKERS UNION

http://www.apwu.org/

E.C. HALLBECK SCHOLARSHIP FUND
• *See page 536*

VOCATIONAL SCHOLARSHIP PROGRAM
• *See page 536*

AMERICAN QUARTER HORSE FOUNDATION (AQHF)

http://www.aqha.com/foundation

AQHF RACING SCHOLARSHIPS
• *See page 536*

ARIZONA QUARTER RACING SCHOLARSHIP
• *See page 537*

EXCELLENCE IN EQUINE & AGRICULTURAL INVOLVEMENT SCHOLARSHIP
• *See page 538*

FARM AND RANCH HERITAGE SCHOLARSHIP
• *See page 538*

AMERICAN ROAD & TRANSPORTATION BUILDERS ASSOCIATION-TRANSPORTATION DEVELOPMENT FOUNDATION (ARTBA-TDF)

http://www.artba.org/

ARTBA-TDF LANFORD FAMILY HIGHWAY WORKERS MEMORIAL SCHOLARSHIP PROGRAM

The ARTBA-TDF Highway Worker Memorial Scholarship Program provides financial assistance to help the sons, daughters or legally adopted children of highway workers killed or permanently disabled in the line of duty pursue post-high school education. Minimum 2.5 GPA required.

Award: Scholarship for use in freshman, sophomore, junior, senior, or graduate years; not renewable. *Amount:* $1000–$5000.

Eligibility Requirements: Applicant must be enrolled or expecting to enroll full-time at a two-year or four-year or technical institution or university. Applicant or parent of applicant must have employment or volunteer experience in construction, roadway work. Applicant must have 2.5 GPA or higher. Available to U.S. citizens.

Application Requirements: Application form, copy of current year federal tax return, copy of parent's current year federal tax return, essay, financial need analysis, personal photograph, recommendations or references, transcript. *Deadline:* April 4.

Contact: Kashae Williams, Program Manager
American Road & Transportation Builders Association-Transportation Development Foundation (ARTBA-TDF)
1219 28th Street, NW
Washington, DC 20007
Phone: 202-289-4434 Ext. 109
E-mail: kwilliams@artba.org

AMERICAN SAVINGS FOUNDATION

http://www.asfdn.org/

ROBERT T. KENNEY SCHOLARSHIP PROGRAM AT THE AMERICAN SAVINGS FOUNDATION

Scholarship awards range from $1,000 to $3,000 for students entering any year of a two- or four-year undergraduate program or technical/vocational program at an accredited institution. Applicant must be a resident of one of the 64 Connecticut towns within our service area. Minimum 2.5 GPA required.

Award: Scholarship for use in freshman, sophomore, junior, or senior years; renewable. *Number:* 400. *Amount:* $1000–$2500.

Eligibility Requirements: Applicant must be enrolled or expecting to enroll full-time at a two-year or four-year or technical institution or university and resident of Connecticut. Applicant must have 2.5 GPA or higher.

Application Requirements: Application form, essay, financial need analysis. *Deadline:* March 31.

Contact: Heather Hokunson, Associate Program Officer - Scholarships
Phone: 860-827-2572
Fax: 860-832-4582
E-mail: hhokunson@asfdn.org

AMERICAN TRAFFIC SAFETY SERVICES FOUNDATION

http://www.atssa.com/TheFoundation

ROADWAY WORKER MEMORIAL SCHOLARSHIP PROGRAM

Scholarship will provide financial assistance for post-high school education to the dependents (children and spouses) of roadway workers killed or permanently disabled in work zone accidents, including mobile operations and the installation of roadway safety features are eligible for the Foundation's annual scholarships in support of higher education (college or vocational).

Award: Scholarship for use in freshman, sophomore, junior, senior, graduate, or postgraduate years; not renewable. *Number:* 2–5. *Amount:* $5000–$6000.

Eligibility Requirements: Applicant must be enrolled or expecting to enroll full- or part-time at a two-year or four-year or technical institution or university. Applicant or parent of applicant must have employment or volunteer experience in construction, roadway work, transportation industry. Available to U.S. citizens.

Application Requirements: Application form, community service, essay, financial need analysis, interview. *Deadline:* February 15.

Contact: Neil Mullanaphy, Foundation Director
American Traffic Safety Services Foundation
15 Riverside Parkway, Suite 100
Fredericksburg, VA 22406-1077
Phone: 540-368-1701 Ext. 3885
E-mail: neil.mullanaphy@atssa.com

ANKIN LAW

http://ankinlaw.com

ANKIN LAW OFFICE COLLEGE SCHOLARSHIP

Ankin Law understands the financial challenges college students face. As such, we are pleased to announce a $5,000 scholarship to an undergraduate or law school student of need who submits the best essay addressing the topic below. The submission deadline is June 1st, 2017. Qualified applicants should submit a fully completed application no later than June 1, 2017. Must be enrolled as a full-time student in an accredited community college, college or university, or an accredited law school starting in the fall of 2017; write an essay (maximum of 400 words) on the topic below; submit their own original work; submit FAFSA results to verify need and provide proof of enrollment should his/her submission be selected. 2017 Essay Prompt: The Biggest Threat to Social Safety. Submit an essay (maximum 400 words) on the following topic: What effect will driverless-car technology have on personal injury automobile cases? Citations, logical proofs, and sound reasoning are welcome. The winner of the scholarship will be chosen based on the quality of the applicant's essay submission and the accuracy with which they followed the instructions. Submit a completed application no later than June 1st, 2017. Applications received after June 1st, 2017 will not be considered. Applications may only be submitted through the website, http://ankinlaw.com/aaaa_scholarship/. A submission via any other channel will not be considered. Ankin Law, in its sole discretion will pick the scholarship winner. The winner will be selected from all eligible applications and will be announced on AnkinLaw.com by September 1, 2017. The winning applicant will be notified by email. The funds will be distributed after the winner has been announced and proof of post-high school enrollment has been verified.

Award: Scholarship for use in freshman, sophomore, junior, senior, or graduate years; not renewable. *Number:* 1. *Amount:* $5000.

Eligibility Requirements: Applicant must be enrolled or expecting to enroll full-time at a two-year or four-year institution or university. Available to U.S. and non-U.S. citizens.

Application Requirements: Application form, essay, financial need analysis. *Deadline:* June 1.

Contact: Mr. Howard Ankin, Partner
Ankin Law
162 West Grand Avenue
Chicago, IL 60654
Phone: 844-600-0000
E-mail: ankinlaw123@gmail.com

ANTHONY MUNOZ FOUNDATION

www.munozfoundation.org

ANTHONY MUNOZ SCHOLARSHIPS

The Anthony Mu?Scholarship Fund was created by Anthony Mu?and his family to support greater Cincinnati high school youth in achieving their dreams of attending a local college or university. Applications for the scholarship fund will be accepted starting January 1st, 2017 through May 1st, 2017. Recipients of The Anthony Mu?Scholarship Fund must meet several requirements to apply for this scholarship. This includes, but is not limited to attending a high school in our greater Cincinnati impact area; being enrolled in or entering an eligible greater Cincinnati/tri-state college or university; and displaying a desire to overcome adversity and demonstrate a financial need. The Scholarship Fund application and eligibility requirements can be found at www.munozfoundation.org.

Award: Scholarship for use in freshman, sophomore, junior, or senior years; renewable. *Number:* 7. *Amount:* $20,000.

Eligibility Requirements: Applicant must be high school student; planning to enroll or expecting to enroll full-time at a four-year institution; resident of Indiana, Kentucky, Ohio and studying in Indiana, Kentucky, Ohio. Applicant must have 2.5 GPA or higher. Available to U.S. citizens.

Application Requirements: Application form, essay, financial need analysis. *Deadline:* May 1.

Contact: Mrs. Victoria Knepp, Director of Marketing and Events
Anthony Munoz Foundation
8919 Rossash Road
Cincinnati, OH 45236
Phone: 513-772-4900
E-mail: vknepp@munozfoundation.org

ANY INTERN

http://www.anyintern.com

$1,000 5 MINUTE SCHOLARSHIP

All over the world people want Unpaid Internships to be made completely illegal. Anyintern.com is awarding a $1000 scholarship for the best solution to this public debate (in 60 words or less). Do you have a solution to fix Unpaid Internships? It can be anything from Government Legislation to University Rules to Student Union involvement. Write in 60 words or less we suggest trying to find a solution to please both sides of the argument. This is open to all countries. Deadline: 10th Dec 2016. Winner announced 30th Dec 2016 The winner will be chosen from the Top 5 Voted entries. Check it out and submit your entry here www.anyintern.com

Award: Scholarship for use in freshman, sophomore, junior, senior, graduate, or postgraduate years; not renewable. *Number:* 1. *Amount:* $1000.

Eligibility Requirements: Applicant must be enrolled or expecting to enroll full- or part-time at a two-year or four-year or technical institution or university. Available to U.S. and non-U.S. citizens.

Application Requirements: Application form, essay. *Deadline:* December 10.

Contact: Mr. Ross O'Donovan
E-mail: scholarships@anyintern.com

ARKANSAS SINGLE PARENT SCHOLARSHIP FUND

http://www.aspsf.org/

ARKANSAS SINGLE PARENT SCHOLARSHIP FUND

Scholarships are awarded to economically disadvantaged single parents who live anywhere in Arkansas or in Bowie County, Texas. Applicants must have custodial care of at least one minor child. Generally, applicants who have not yet received a 4-year degree are preferred. In some cases, applications from students pursuing a Masters degree will be considered. Application forms, award values, deadlines, and other requirements will vary by county. Visit http://www.aspsf.org for more information.

Award: Scholarship for use in freshman, sophomore, junior, or senior years; not renewable. *Number:* 1–2000. *Amount:* $200–$1800.

Eligibility Requirements: Applicant must be enrolled or expecting to enroll full- or part-time at a two-year or four-year or technical institution or university; single and resident of Arkansas, Texas. Available to U.S. and non-U.S. citizens.

Application Requirements: Application form, essay, financial need analysis, interview. *Deadline:* continuous.

ARRL FOUNDATION INC.

http://www.arrl.org/

TED, W4VHF, AND ITICE, K4LVV, GOLDTHORPE SCHOLARSHIP

One $500 scholarship to a student attending a four-year college or university and possessing an active amateur radio license. Financial need and active volunteer service in the community will be taken into consideration.

Award: Scholarship for use in freshman, sophomore, junior, or senior years; not renewable. *Number:* 1. *Amount:* $500.

Eligibility Requirements: Applicant must be enrolled or expecting to enroll full- or part-time at a four-year institution or university and must have an interest in amateur radio. Applicant or parent of applicant must have employment or volunteer experience in community service. Available to U.S. citizens.

Application Requirements: Application form, community service, financial need analysis. *Deadline:* January 31.

Contact: Ms. Mary Hobart, Secretary
Phone: 860-594-0397
E-mail: k1mmh@arrl.org

ASIAN PACIFIC COMMUNITY FUND

http://www.apcf.org/

ROYAL BUSINESS BANK SCHOLARSHIP PROGRAM

Royal Business Bank is committed to supporting economically-challenged youth residing in its business service territories to fulfill their dreams of obtaining a higher education.

Award: Scholarship for use in freshman year; not renewable. *Number:* 20. *Amount:* $1000.

Eligibility Requirements: Applicant must be high school student; planning to enroll or expecting to enroll full-time at a two-year or four-year institution or university and resident of California, Nevada. Applicant must have 3.0 GPA or higher. Available to U.S. citizens.

Application Requirements: Application form, community service. *Deadline:* March 29.

Contact: Ms. Sandy Southivilay, Communications Manager
Asian Pacific Community Fund
1145 Wilshire Boulevard
Suite 105
Los Angeles, CA 90017
Phone: 213-624-6400 Ext. 6
Fax: 213-624-6406
E-mail: scholarships@apcf.org

ASIAN REPORTER

http://www.arfoundation.net/

ASIAN REPORTER SCHOLARSHIP

Scholarship available to graduating high school student or currently enrolled college student of Asian descent. Must be a resident of Washington or Oregon and attend school full-time in either state. Minimum 3.25 GPA required. Must demonstrate financial need, and involvement in community or school-related activities.

Award: Scholarship for use in freshman, sophomore, junior, senior, graduate, or postgraduate years; not renewable. *Number:* 2–9. *Amount:* $1000–$2000.

Eligibility Requirements: Applicant must be Asian/Pacific Islander; age 17–40; enrolled or expecting to enroll full- or part-time at a two-year or four-year or technical institution or university; resident of Oregon, Washington and studying in Oregon, Washington. Applicant must have 3.0 GPA or higher. Available to U.S. citizens.

Application Requirements: Application form, community service, essay, financial need analysis, personal photograph. *Deadline:* March 1.

Contact: Jason Lim, Program Director
Phone: 503-283-0595
Fax: 503-283-4445
E-mail: arfoundation@asianreporter.com

ASSURED LIFE ASSOCIATION

http://assuredlife.org

ASSURED LIFE ASSOCIATION ENDOWMENT SCHOLARSHIP PROGRAM
• *See page 540*

BARONE DEFENSE FIRM

http://baronedefensefirm.com/

BARONE DEFENSE FIRM WIN BACK YOUR LIFE SCHOLARSHIP
The Win Back Your Life scholarship is open to apply to for any student who is currently enrolled in an accredited community college, undergraduate, or graduate program in the United States. Students who are currently incoming first-year college students and have graduated high school or possesses a GED may also apply. For complete information, please visit http://baronedefensefirm.com/#scholarship

Award: Scholarship for use in freshman, sophomore, junior, senior, graduate, or postgraduate years; not renewable. *Number:* 1. *Amount:* $500.

Eligibility Requirements: Applicant must be enrolled or expecting to enroll full- or part-time at a two-year or four-year or technical institution or university. Applicant must have 3.0 GPA or higher. Available to U.S. and non-U.S. citizens.

Application Requirements: Application form, essay. *Deadline:* May 31.

Contact: Patrick Barone
E-mail: info@baronedefensefirm.com

BOUNCE ENERGY

http://www.bounceenergy.com

BE MORE SCHOLARSHIP
Bounce Energy is excited to announce its fourth annual "BE More" Scholarship! The scholarship is open to all high school senior and college students who live or attend school in the state of Texas. The $2,500 scholarship will be awarded to three qualifying students. In order to be eligible for the scholarship, students must meet the requirements below, submit an online application, and write a short essay of no more than 500 words.

Award: Scholarship for use in freshman, sophomore, junior, senior, graduate, or postgraduate years; not renewable. *Number:* 3. *Amount:* $2500.

Eligibility Requirements: Applicant must be age 13-24; enrolled or expecting to enroll full- or part-time at a two-year or four-year or technical institution or university; resident of Texas and studying in Texas. Applicant must have 3.0 GPA or higher. Available to U.S. and non-U.S. citizens.

Application Requirements: Application form, essay. *Deadline:* June 30.

Contact: Scholarship Coordinator
Bounce Energy
12 Greenway Plaza
Suite 250
Houston, TX 77046
Phone: 855-4526862
E-mail: BEscholarship@directenergy.com

BRAINLY, INC.

http://www.brainly.com

BRAINLY EVERYONE KNOWS SOMETHING SCHOLARSHIP
No one knows everything, but everyone knows something. Tell us how you help teach others and you could win a $1,000 scholarship. Deadline: May 31, 2017. Scholarship amount: $1,000. U.S. high school graduating seniors ages 16+ are eligible. Entrants must have a free Brainly account. Read the Terms & Conditions for full details. Answer our short essay question in 250 words or less: "How have you helped teach another student and how has that impacted you?" Where to apply: https://brainly.com/app/scholarship

Award: Scholarship for use in freshman year; not renewable. *Number:* 1. *Amount:* $1000.

Eligibility Requirements: Applicant must be high school student; age 16-19; planning to enroll or expecting to enroll full-time at a four-year institution or university; resident of Alabama, Alaska, Arizona, Arkansas, California, Colorado, Connecticut, Delaware, District of Columbia, Florida, Georgia, Hawaii, Idaho, Illinois, Indiana, Iowa, Kansas, Kentucky, Louisiana, Maine, Maryland, Massachusetts, Michigan, Minnesota, Mississippi, Missouri, Montana, Nebraska, Nevada, New Hampshire, New Jersey, New Mexico, New York, North Carolina, North Dakota, Ohio, Oklahoma, Oregon, Pennsylvania, Rhode Island, South Carolina, South Dakota, Tennessee, Texas, Utah, Vermont, Virginia, Washington, West Virginia, Wisconsin, Wyoming and studying in Alabama, Alaska, Arizona, Arkansas, California, Colorado, Connecticut, Delaware, District of Columbia, Florida, Georgia, Hawaii, Idaho, Illinois, Indiana, Iowa, Kansas, Kentucky, Louisiana, Maine, Maryland, Massachusetts, Michigan, Minnesota, Mississippi, Missouri, Montana, Nebraska, Nevada, New Hampshire, New Jersey, New Mexico, New York, North Carolina, North Dakota, Ohio, Oklahoma, Oregon, Pennsylvania, Rhode Island, South Carolina, South Dakota, Tennessee, Texas, Utah, Vermont, Virginia, Washington, West Virginia, Wisconsin, Wyoming. Available to U.S. citizens.

Application Requirements: Application form, essay. *Deadline:* May 31.

Contact: US Growth Manager
Brainly, Inc.
161 Bowery
2nd Floor
New York, NY 10002
E-mail: contact@brainly.com

BRANDES INVESTMENT PARTNERS L.P.

https://www.brandes.com

BRANDES SCHOLARSHIP PROGRAM
The Brandes Scholarship Program (BSP) is designed to educate young people between 18 and 22 years of age about the world of investing and to introduce the personality traits that are outlined in the Know-Your-Client (KYC) form, an information form you need to fill out to open an investment account. The program gives students the opportunity to win one of five $4,000 scholarships and includes a multiple-choice investing personality quiz with an essay-based question. Brandes Investment Partners, L.P. (Brandes) is passionate about educating future investors. The Brandes Scholarship Program's aim is to promote fiscal knowledge and responsibility with students and provide financial assistance for students pursuing college education. This marks the third year that Brandes has offered the scholarship program in the U.S. Following the most recent BSP in 2014, quiz results showed that a majority of participants were described as risk tolerant. Winning essays featuring details from the 2014 contest can be found at www.brandesscholarship.com/winners/.

Award: Scholarship for use in freshman, sophomore, junior, senior, graduate, or postgraduate years; not renewable. *Number:* 5. *Amount:* $4000.

Eligibility Requirements: Applicant must be age 18-22 and enrolled or expecting to enroll full- or part-time at a two-year or four-year or technical institution or university. Available to U.S. citizens.

Application Requirements: Essay. *Deadline:* June 15.

Contact: Nancy Allen
Phone: 858.523.3383
E-mail: nancy.allen@brandes.com

BREYER LAW OFFICES PC

http://www.breyerlaw.com/

2017 HUSBAND AND WIFE LAW TEAM ARIZONA SCHOLARSHIP
Breyer Law Offices, P.C. has represented residents of the Phoenix area and throughout the state of Arizona for twenty years. Our firm has very

strong ties to our community, which is why we are thrilled to be able to offer a $1,000 scholarship to a deserving high school senior or current college student who has not only demonstrated excellence in their scholastic endeavors, but has also taken the time to give back to their Arizona community.

Award: Scholarship for use in freshman, sophomore, junior, or senior years; not renewable. *Number:* 1. *Amount:* $1000.

Eligibility Requirements: Applicant must be enrolled or expecting to enroll full- or part-time at a two-year or four-year institution or university and resident of Arizona. Applicant must have 2.5 GPA or higher. Available to U.S. citizens.

Application Requirements: Application form, essay. *Deadline:* April 17.

Contact: Jenn Peterson
Breyer Law Offices PC
3840 E. Ray Road
Phoenix, AZ 85044
Phone: 602-267-1280
E-mail: jenn@breyerlaw.com

BY KIDS FOR KIDS, CO.

http://bkfkeducation.com

CTIA WIRELESS FOUNDATION DRIVE SMART DIGITAL SHORT CONTEST

Create a digital short to help combat distracted driving. This contest is for legal residents of the United States who are between the ages of 13 and 18. Distracted driving is a serious problem, but you can help. Create a 30-60 second digital short to persuade your peers to not drive distracted, and earn a chance to win $5,000! Scholarships and grants will be awarded to students and teachers. See website for details, http://drivesmartnow.com

Award: Prize for use in freshman, sophomore, junior, or senior years; not renewable. *Number:* 6. *Amount:* $1000–$10,000.

Eligibility Requirements: Applicant must be age 13-18 and enrolled or expecting to enroll full- or part-time at a two-year or four-year or technical institution or university. Available to U.S. citizens.

Application Requirements: Application form. *Deadline:* December 19.

Contact: Operations & Events Manager
Phone: 203-321-1226
E-mail: info@bkfk.com

SALLIE MAE® MAKE COLLEGE HAPPEN CHALLENGE

Students are challenged to creatively answer the question, "How do you plan to pay for college?" Entries can be in the form of a video, photo, essay, song, or poem (be creative!).To enter, answer a few questions then either share a link to your creative entry or upload it. Registration is currently open. The contest launches November 1, 2016 at noon (12:00 p.m.) ET and ends December 31 at 5:00 p.m. (ET). See website for details, http://www.makecollegehappenchallenge.com

Award: Prize for use in freshman, sophomore, junior, or senior years; not renewable. *Number:* 10. *Amount:* $1000–$15,000.

Eligibility Requirements: Applicant must be age 14-18 and enrolled or expecting to enroll full- or part-time at a two-year or four-year or technical institution or university. Available to U.S. citizens.

Application Requirements: Application form. *Deadline:* December 31.

Contact: Operations & Events Manager
Phone: 203-321-1226
E-mail: info@bkfk.com

CALIFORNIA COMMUNITY COLLEGES

http://www.cccco.edu/

EOPS (EXTENDED OPPORTUNITY PROGRAMS AND SERVICES)/CARE (COOPERATIVE AGENCIES RESOURCES FOR EDUCATION)

Renewable award available to California residents and individuals who are exempt from paying nonresident tuition. Individuals must be enrolled as a full-time student at a two-year publicly-funded California community college. EOPS students must fulfill program-specific income and educational disadvantage eligibility requirements. CARE students must be in EOPS, currently receive CalWORKs/TANF, have at least one child under fourteen years of age at time of acceptance into CARE

program, be a single head of household, and age 18 or older. EOPS students may also qualify for CARE if their dependent child(ren) receive CalWORKs/TANF cash aid even if the student (i.e., parent) is not a cash aid recipient. Contact local college EOPS/CARE office for an application and more information about supportive services and grants. To locate nearest community college campus, see http://www.cccco.edu/

Award: Grant for use in freshman or sophomore years; renewable. *Number:* 10,000–85,000. *Amount:* $100–$1000.

Eligibility Requirements: Applicant must be enrolled or expecting to enroll full-time at a two-year institution; single; resident of California and studying in California. Available to U.S. citizens.

Application Requirements: Application form, financial need analysis. *Deadline:* continuous.

Contact: Contact local community college EOPS/CARE program.

CALIFORNIA STATE PARENT-TEACHER ASSOCIATION

http://www.capta.org/

CONTINUING EDUCATION-PTA VOLUNTEERS SCHOLARSHIP

• *See page 540*

GRADUATING HIGH SCHOOL SENIOR SCHOLARSHIP

Available to high school seniors graduating between January 1 and June 30 of the current academic year from high schools in California with a PTA/PTSA unit in good standing. Must be a California resident. Must have volunteered in the school and community volunteer service.

Award: Scholarship for use in freshman year; renewable. *Amount:* $500.

Eligibility Requirements: Applicant must be high school student; planning to enroll or expecting to enroll full-time at a two-year or four-year or technical institution or university and resident of California. Applicant or parent of applicant must have employment or volunteer experience in community service. Available to U.S. citizens.

Application Requirements: Application form, community service, copy of current PTA/PTSA membership card, essay, recommendations or references, transcript. *Deadline:* February 1.

Contact: Becky Reece, Scholarship and Award Chairman
California State Parent-Teacher Association
930 Georgia Street
Los Angeles, CA 90015-1322
Phone: 213-620-1100
Fax: 213-620-1411
E-mail: info@capta.org

CALIFORNIA STUDENT AID COMMISSION

http://www.csac.ca.gov/

LAW ENFORCEMENT PERSONNEL DEPENDENTS SCHOLARSHIP

Provides college grants to needy dependents of California law enforcement officers, officers and employees of the Department of Corrections and Department of Youth Authority, and firefighters killed or disabled in the line of duty.

Award: Grant for use in freshman, sophomore, junior, or senior years; renewable. *Amount:* $100–$13,665.

Eligibility Requirements: Applicant must be enrolled or expecting to enroll full- or part-time at a two-year or four-year institution or university; resident of California and studying in California. Applicant or parent of applicant must have employment or volunteer experience in police/firefighting. Available to U.S. citizens.

Application Requirements: Application form, birth certificate, death certificate of parents or spouse, police report, financial need analysis, transcript. *Deadline:* continuous.

Contact: Catalina Mistler, Chief, Program Administration and Services Division
California Student Aid Commission
PO Box 419026
Rancho Cordova, CA 95741-9026
Phone: 916-464-7268
Fax: 916-526-8004
E-mail: studentsupport@csac.ca.gov

CALIFORNIA TABLE GRAPE COMMISSION

http://www.freshcaliforniagrapes.com/

CALIFORNIA TABLE GRAPE FARM WORKERS SCHOLARSHIP PROGRAM

Applicants must be high school graduates who plan to attend any college or university in California. The applicant, a parent, or a legal guardian must have worked in the California table grape harvest during the last season. School activities, personal references, and financial need are considered. Must be a U.S. citizen.

Award: Scholarship for use in freshman year; not renewable. *Number:* 3. *Amount:* $16,000.

Eligibility Requirements: Applicant must be enrolled or expecting to enroll full-time at a four-year institution or university and studying in California. Applicant or parent of applicant must have employment or volunteer experience in agriculture. Available to U.S. citizens.

Application Requirements: Application form, essay, recommendations or references, test scores, transcript. *Deadline:* March 19.

Contact: Scholarship Coordinator
California Table Grape Commission
392 West Fallbrook, Suite 101
Fresno, CA 93711-6150
Phone: 559-447-8350
Fax: 559-447-9184

CALIFORNIA TEACHERS ASSOCIATION (CTA)

http://www.cta.org/

CALIFORNIA TEACHERS ASSOCIATION SCHOLARSHIP FOR MEMBERS

• *See page 541*

CAMP NETWORK

https://www.campnetwork.com/

CAMP COUNSELOR APPRECIATION SCHOLARSHIP

All applicants must be U.S. citizens and current high school seniors attending school in the United States; anticipating completion of high school diploma at time of application; carrying a minimum 3.0 GPA currently. Please create a short, exciting video (3-5 minutes max) that explains your experience as a camp counselor, how you exhibit the 5 qualities above, and how you intend to use your college degree. Upload your video to DropBox.com, YouTube, Vimeo, or another reputable file sharing service (make sure the visibility is set to public). To submit your application send an email to scholarships@campnetwork.com. Please include your full name, school year, name of the college you plan to or are already attending, and a link to your video. By submitting this form you agree to allow Camp Network to use your video for promotional purposes.

Award: Scholarship for use in freshman year; not renewable. *Number:* 1–2. *Amount:* $1000.

Eligibility Requirements: Applicant must be high school student and planning to enroll or expecting to enroll full-time at an institution or university. Applicant must have 3.0 GPA or higher. Available to U.S. citizens.

Application Requirements: Application form. *Deadline:* November 1.

Contact: Andrew Downing
Camp Network
1033 Demonbreun St
Suite 300
Nashville, TN 37203
E-mail: scholarships@campnetwork.com

CARING.COM

http://caring.com

CARING.COM STUDENT-CAREGIVER BI-ANNUAL SCHOLARSHIP

There are two deadlines for this scholarship every calendar year, one in December and one over the summer. The application can always be found at caring.com/scholarship. Additionally, previous winners' submissions can be found at caring.com/scholars. We encourage applicants to view previous winners' submissions when completing their own applications.

Award: Scholarship for use in freshman, sophomore, junior, senior, graduate, or postgraduate years; not renewable. *Number:* 3. *Amount:* $1500.

Eligibility Requirements: Applicant must be enrolled or expecting to enroll full- or part-time at a two-year or four-year or technical institution or university. Available to U.S. and non-U.S. citizens.

Application Requirements: Application form. *Deadline:* continuous.

Contact: Daniel Tachna-Fram, Product Management Intern
E-mail: tfram@caring.com

CENTER FOR REINTEGRATION

www.reintegration.com

BAER REINTEGRATION SCHOLARSHIP

The goal of the Baer Reintegration Scholarship is to help people with schizophrenia, schizoaffective disorder or bipolar disorder acquire the educational and vocational skills necessary to reintegrate into society, secure jobs, and regain their lives

Award: Scholarship for use in freshman, sophomore, junior, senior, graduate, or postgraduate years; renewable. *Number:* 20–30. *Amount:* $1000–$30,000.

Eligibility Requirements: Applicant must be enrolled or expecting to enroll full- or part-time at a two-year or four-year or technical institution or university. Available to U.S. citizens.

Application Requirements: Application form, essay, financial need analysis. *Deadline:* January 31.

Contact: Baer Reintegration Scholarship
Center for Reintegration
PO Box 35218
Phildelphia, PA 19128
E-mail: baerscholarships@reintegration.com

CGTRADER

https://www.cgtrader.com/

ANNUAL CGTRADER SCHOLARSHIP

Each semester CGTrader challenges students to dig into the field of technology writing an essay on how innovative technologies are transforming our lives. Enter the CGTrader Scholarship 2017 challenge to win $3,000 for your education bills. The best submission will be awarded $2,000 while the two runners-up will receive $500 each. How to enter? Write and submit an original essay on the topic "The future of technology in education." Visit our scholarship website at https://www.cgtrader.com/scholarships

Award: Scholarship for use in freshman, sophomore, junior, senior, graduate, or postgraduate years; renewable. *Number:* 3. *Amount:* $500–$2000.

Eligibility Requirements: Applicant must be high school student; age 18-99; planning to enroll or expecting to enroll full- or part-time at a two-year or four-year or technical institution or university; resident of Alabama, Alaska, Alberta, Arizona, Arkansas, British Columbia, California, Colorado, Connecticut, Delaware, District of Columbia, Florida, Georgia, Guam, Hawaii, Idaho, Illinois, Indiana, Iowa, Kansas, Kentucky, Louisiana, Maine, Manitoba, Maryland, Massachusetts, Michigan, Minnesota, Mississippi, Missouri, Montana, Nebraska, Nevada, New Brunswick, Newfoundland, New Hampshire, New Jersey, New Mexico, New York, North Carolina, North Dakota, Northwest Territories, Nova Scotia, Ohio, Oklahoma, Ontario, Oregon, Pennsylvania, Prince Edward Island, Puerto Rico, Quebec, Rhode Island, Saskatchewan, South Carolina, South Dakota, Tennessee, Texas, Utah, Vermont, Virginia, Washington, West Virginia, Wisconsin, Wyoming, Yukon and studying in Alabama, Alaska, Alberta, Arizona, Arkansas, British Columbia, California, Colorado, Connecticut, Delaware, District of Columbia, Florida, Georgia, Guam, Hawaii, Idaho, Illinois, Indiana, Iowa, Kansas, Kentucky, Louisiana, Maine, Manitoba, Maryland, Massachusetts, Michigan, Minnesota, Mississippi, Missouri, Montana, Nebraska, Nevada, New Brunswick, Newfoundland, New Hampshire, New Jersey, New Mexico, New York, North Carolina, North Dakota, Northwest Territories, Nova Scotia, Ohio, Oklahoma, Ontario, Oregon, Pennsylvania, Prince Edward Island, Puerto Rico, Quebec, Rhode Island,

Saskatchewan, South Carolina, South Dakota, Tennessee, Texas, Utah, Vermont, Virginia, Washington, West Virginia, Wisconsin, Wyoming, Yukon. Applicant must have 2.5 GPA or higher. Available to U.S. and non-U.S. citizens.

Application Requirements: Essay. *Deadline:* June 1.

Contact: Laura Paskauskaite, Scholarship Adminsitrator
CGTrader
Antakalnio st. 17
Vilnius 10312
E-mail: laura@cgtrader.com

CHRISTINE GERTSCH ATTORNEY AT LAW

https://www.ctdomesticviolencehelp.com/

CONNECTICUT DOMESTIC VIOLENCE 2017 LEGISLATION REFORM SCHOLARSHIP

This scholarship is offered to any student currently enrolled in an accredited community college, undergraduate, or graduate program in the United States. Students who are incoming first-year college students who are high school graduates or possess a GED can also apply. Please visit this site for complete information about this scholarship: https://www.ctdomesticviolencehelp.com/#scholarship

Award: Scholarship for use in freshman, sophomore, junior, senior, graduate, or postgraduate years; not renewable. *Number:* 1. *Amount:* $500.

Eligibility Requirements: Applicant must be enrolled or expecting to enroll full- or part-time at a two-year or four-year or technical institution or university. Applicant must have 3.0 GPA or higher. Available to U.S. and non-U.S. citizens.

Application Requirements: Application form, essay. *Deadline:* September 1.

Contact: Christine Gertsch
E-mail: info@ctdomesticviolencehelp.com

CHURCH HILL CLASSICS

http://www.diplomaframe.com/

FRAME MY FUTURE SCHOLARSHIP CONTEST

Submit an original creation that communicates: This is how I want to Frame My Future. Some examples of creative entry pieces are: photos, collages, drawings, poem, painting, graphic design piece, short typed essay, or anything you can create in an image.

Award: Scholarship for use in freshman, sophomore, junior, senior, graduate, or postgraduate years; not renewable. *Number:* 1–5. *Amount:* $1000.

Eligibility Requirements: Applicant must be enrolled or expecting to enroll full-time at a two-year or four-year or technical institution or university. Available to U.S. citizens.

Application Requirements: Application form. *Deadline:* March 1.

Contact: Chris Angelone, Digital Marketing Associate
Church Hill Classics
594 Pepper Street
Monroe, CT 06468
Phone: 203-268-1598 Ext. 186
E-mail: christopher@diplomaframe.com

CODA INTERNATIONAL

http://www.coda-international.org

MILLIE BROTHER SCHOLARSHIP FOR CHILDREN OF DEAF ADULTS

Scholarship awarded to any higher education student who is the hearing child of deaf parents. One-time award based on transcripts, letters of reference, and an essay.

Award: Scholarship for use in freshman, sophomore, junior, senior, or graduate years; not renewable. *Number:* 2–5. *Amount:* $1000–$3000.

Eligibility Requirements: Applicant must be enrolled or expecting to enroll full- or part-time at a two-year or four-year or technical institution or university. Available to U.S. and non-U.S. citizens.

Application Requirements: Application form, essay. *Deadline:* April 1.

Contact: Dr. Jennie Pyers, Chair, CODA Scholarship Committee
CODA International
Wellesley College, 106 Central Street
Wellesley, MA 02481
Phone: 413-650-2632
E-mail: scholarships@coda-international.org

COGBURN LAW OFFICES

http://cogburnlaw.com/

$5,000 ADVERSITY SCHOLARSHIP

Cogburn Law Offices offers a broad range of services, with an emphasis on personal injury and consumer law. We understand the increasing costs of college tuition is making it more difficult to obtain a college degree for many outstanding students across the nation. Therefore, we are offering one $5,000 need-based scholarship to the student who submits the winning essay or video demonstrating how he or she has overcome great personal adversity.

Award: Scholarship for use in freshman, sophomore, junior, or senior years; not renewable. *Number:* 1. *Amount:* $5000.

Eligibility Requirements: Applicant must be enrolled or expecting to enroll full-time at a two-year or four-year institution or university. Available to U.S. citizens.

Application Requirements: Application form, essay, financial need analysis. *Deadline:* June 1.

Contact: Pat McCune, Scholarship Coordinator
Cogburn Law Offices
PO Box 1596
620B Academy Drive
Northbrook, IL 60065
Phone: 847-940-4000
E-mail: pat@marketjd.com

COLLEGE ASSISTANCE MIGRANT PROGRAM

https://www.stedwards.edu

COLLEGE ASSISTANCE MIGRANT PROG.

The College Assistance Migrant Program (CAMP) is dedicated to serving the higher education needs of migrant students at St. Edward's University. Through CAMP, you have the opportunity to achieve your dream of a college education. Because CAMP is funded by both the U.S. Department of Education and St. Edward's, we follow federal definitions for migrant and seasonal farmwork. To qualify for CAMP you must meet the admission requirements for St. Edward's, be a U.S. citizen or a legal resident.

Award: Scholarship for use in freshman year; not renewable. *Number:* 35. *Amount:* $25,000.

Eligibility Requirements: Applicant must be enrolled or expecting to enroll full-time at an institution or university. Applicant or parent of applicant must have employment or volunteer experience in farming. Applicant must have 2.5 GPA or higher. Available to U.S. citizens.

Application Requirements: Application form, essay, financial need analysis. *Deadline:* May 1.

Contact: Ms. Rocio Rangel, Assistant Director
College Assistance Migrant Program
3001 S. Congress Ave.
Austin, TX 78704
Phone: 512-448-8502
Fax: 512-464-8877
E-mail: rocior@stedwards.edu

COLORADO MASONS BENEVOLENT FUND ASSOCIATION

http://www.cmbfa.org/scholarship

COLORADO MASONS BENEVOLENT FUND SCHOLARSHIPS

Applicants must be graduating seniors from a Colorado public high school accepted at a Colorado postsecondary institution. The maximum grant is $7000 renewable over four years. Obtain scholarship materials and specific requirements from high school counselor, or our website (www.cmbfa.org/scholarships).

Award: Scholarship for use in freshman, sophomore, junior, or senior years; renewable. *Number:* 6–10. *Amount:* $1000–$7000.

Eligibility Requirements: Applicant must be high school student; planning to enroll or expecting to enroll full-time at a two-year or four-year or technical institution or university; resident of Colorado and studying in Colorado. Available to U.S. citizens.

Application Requirements: Application form, essay, financial need analysis, interview. *Deadline:* March 31.

Contact: Grover Sardeson, Scholarship Administrator
Colorado Masons Benevolent Fund Association
P.O. Box 703
Westminster, CO 80036-0703
Phone: 719-623-5349
E-mail: education@cmbfa.org

COLUMBUS CITIZENS FOUNDATION

http://www.columbuscitizensfd.org/scholarships/scholarships.html

COLUMBUS CITIZENS FOUNDATION COLLEGE SCHOLARSHIP PROGRAM

CCF recipients receive a four-year scholarship that helps underwrite the cost of their college tuition. CCF scholarships, while generous, provide assistance towards tuition but will not cover payment for all school costs. Applications and all support documents must be submitted to FACTS Grant and Aid Assessment by Friday, February 17, 2017 for entering the freshman year of college in fall 2017. Visit the CCF website (columbuscitizensfd.org) for all eligibility information and application instructions.

Award: Scholarship for use in freshman, sophomore, junior, or senior years; renewable.

Eligibility Requirements: Applicant must be of Italian heritage; high school student and planning to enroll or expecting to enroll full-time at a four-year institution or university. Applicant must have 3.0 GPA or higher. Available to U.S. citizens.

Application Requirements: Application form, essay, financial need analysis, interview. *Deadline:* February 17.

Contact: Antonella Recchia, Director, Scholarships/Opportunities Office
Columbus Citizens Foundation
8 E. 69th Street
New York, NY 10021
Phone: 212-249-9923
Fax: 212-517-7619
E-mail: arecchia@columbuscitizens.org

COMCAST LEADERS AND ACHIEVERS SCHOLARSHIP PROGRAM

http://corporate.comcast.com/our-values/community-investment/youth-education-leadership#accordion-2

COMCAST LEADERS AND ACHIEVERS SCHOLARSHIP

Nominees must be full-time high school seniors, must demonstrate a strong commitment to community service and display leadership abilities. Minimum 2.8 GPA required. Must be nominated by their high school principal. Employees of Comcast, its subsidiaries and affiliates, and their families, are not eligible. E-mail for nomination form: comcast@spaprog.com.

Award: Scholarship for use in freshman year; not renewable. *Amount:* $1000.

Eligibility Requirements: Applicant must be high school student and planning to enroll or expecting to enroll full-time at a two-year or four-year institution or university. Applicant or parent of applicant must have employment or volunteer experience in community service. Applicant must have 3.0 GPA or higher. Available to U.S. and non-U.S. citizens.

Application Requirements: Community service. *Deadline:* January 29.

Contact: Executive Director
Comcast Leaders and Achievers Scholarship Program
1500 Market Street, East Tower, 33rd Floor
Philadelphia, PA 19102
Phone: 866-851-4274
E-mail: comcast@spaprog.com

COMMUNITY BANKERS ASSOCIATION OF ILLINOIS

http://www.cbai.com/

COMMUNITY BANKERS ASSOC OF IL CHILD OF A BANKER SCHOLARSHIP

• *See page 541*

COMMUNITY BANKERS ASSOC. OF IL ESSAY CONTEST

Open to Illinois high school seniors who are sponsored by a CBAI member bank. Student bank employees, immediate families of bank employees, board members, stockholders, CBAI employees, and judges are ineligible. Thirteen awards are available at $1,000/year for up to four years of higher education; 13 additional one-time $500 awards are also available. For more details see website http://www.cbai.com.

Award: Prize for use in freshman year; renewable. *Number:* 13–26. *Amount:* $500–$4000.

Eligibility Requirements: Applicant must be high school student; planning to enroll or expecting to enroll full-time at a two-year or four-year or technical institution or university and resident of Illinois. Available to U.S. citizens.

Application Requirements: Application form, essay. *Deadline:* February 3.

Contact: Ms. Bobbi Watson, Administrative Asst.
Community Bankers Association of Illinois
CBAI
901 Community Drive
Springfield, IL 62703-5184
Phone: 217-529-2265
E-mail: bobbiw@cbai.com

COMMUNITY FOUNDATION FOR GREATER ATLANTA, INC.

http://cfgreateratlanta.org/

DREAMS SQUARED SCHOLARSHIP

Scholarship designed to provide scholarship opportunities for deserving students who want to pursue their education. Minimum 2.0 GPA, maximum 3.0 GPA required. For complete eligibility requirements or to submit an application, please visit www.cfgreateratlanta.org.

Award: Scholarship for use in freshman, sophomore, junior, or senior years; not renewable. *Number:* 6. *Amount:* $2000.

Eligibility Requirements: Applicant must be enrolled or expecting to enroll full-time at a two-year or four-year or technical institution or university and studying in Alabama. Available to U.S. citizens.

Application Requirements: Application form, community service, essay, financial need analysis. *Deadline:* February 15.

COUNCIL OF CITIZENS WITH LOW VISION INTERNATIONAL C/O AMERICAN COUNCIL OF THE BLIND

http://www.cclvi.org/

FRED SCHEIGERT SCHOLARSHIP

The Council of Citizens with Low Vision International (CCLVI) annually awards three scholarships in the amount of $3,000 each to one full-time entering freshman, undergraduate and graduate college student who are low vision, maintain a strong GPA and are involved in their school and local community. The application process annually opens January 1 at 12:01am eastern and the materials must annually be received by March 1 at 11:59pm eastern. Scholarship funds will be awarded for the upcoming academic year. To read the scholarship guidelines and complete an online application, please visit https://www.cclvi.org. The link directing you to the online application annually goes live January 1 at 12:01am eastern and annually closes March 1 at 11:59 pm eastern. Questions may be directed to CCLVI at 844-460-0253 or scholarship@cclvi.org.

Award: Scholarship for use in freshman, graduate, or postgraduate years; not renewable. *Number:* 3. *Amount:* $3000.

Eligibility Requirements: Applicant must be visually impaired and enrolled or expecting to enroll full-time at a four-year or technical institution or university. Applicant must be visually impaired. Applicant must have 3.5 GPA or higher. Available to U.S. and non-U.S. citizens.

Application Requirements: Application form, interview. *Deadline:* March 1.

Contact: Lindsey Tilden, Chair
Phone: 844-460-0625
E-mail: scholarship@cclvi.org

CSA MEDICAL SUPPLY

https://csamedicalsupply.com

CSA MEDICAL SUPPLY COLLEGE SCHOLARSHIP

CSA Medical Supply.com is excited to offer our inaugural college scholarship designed to aid college students with mobility disabilities in their academic endeavors. One student will be awarded a $500 scholarship. In order to qualify for this scholarship you must submit an essay, poem, or short story about the chosen topic "Personnel Challenge". This scholarship is open to all students with mobility disabilities enrolled at an accredited 4-year institution.

Award: Scholarship for use in freshman, sophomore, junior, or senior years; renewable. *Number:* 1. *Amount:* $500.

Eligibility Requirements: Applicant must be physically disabled and enrolled or expecting to enroll full-time at a four-year institution or university. Applicant must be physically disabled. Applicant must have 3.0 GPA or higher. Available to U.S. citizens.

Application Requirements: Essay. *Deadline:* May 30.

Contact: Aaron Kish, Director Of Marking
CSA Medical Supply
725 N HWY A1A
STE A106
Jupiter, FL 33477
Phone: 561-203-2191 Ext. 7018
Fax: 561-203-7932
E-mail: scholarships@csamedicalsupply.com

DELAWARE HIGHER EDUCATION OFFICE

http://www.doe.k12.de.us

EDUCATIONAL BENEFITS FOR CHILDREN OF DECEASED VETERANS

Award for children between the ages of 16 and 24 of deceased/MIA/POW veterans or state police officers. Must have been a resident of Delaware for 3 or more years prior to the date of application. If the applicant's parent is a member of the armed forces, the parent must have been a resident of Delaware at the time of death or declaration of missing in action or prisoner of war status. Award will not exceed tuition and fees at a Delaware public college.

Award: Grant for use in freshman, sophomore, junior, or senior years; renewable. *Amount:* $7479–$14,421.

Eligibility Requirements: Applicant must be age 16-24; enrolled or expecting to enroll full-time at a two-year or four-year institution or university and resident of Delaware. Applicant or parent of applicant must have employment or volunteer experience in police/firefighting. Available to U.S. citizens. Applicant or parent must meet one or more of the following requirements: general military experience; retired from active duty; disabled or killed as a result of military service; prisoner of war; or missing in action.

Application Requirements: Application form, verification of service-related death. *Deadline:* continuous.

Contact: Ms. Carylin Brinkley, Program Administrator
Delaware Higher Education Office
401 Federal Street
Suite 2
Dover, DE 19901
Phone: 302-735-4120
Fax: 302-739-5894
E-mail: cbrinkley@doe.k12.de.us

DEMAS LAW GROUP, P.C.

http://www.injury-attorneys.com/

DEMAS LAW GROUP SCHOLARSHIP

Demas Law Group will be awarding $1000 to a qualifying student who has demonstrated a meaningful commitment to improving their local community. The legal team at Demas Law Group values education, and we're thrilled to offer this scholarship to a deserving student who's not only helping build a better community today, but positively shaping the future of that community for a better tomorrow.

Award: Scholarship for use in freshman, sophomore, junior, or senior years; not renewable. *Number:* 1. *Amount:* $1000.

Eligibility Requirements: Applicant must be enrolled or expecting to enroll full-time at a four-year institution or university. Applicant must have 3.0 GPA or higher. Available to U.S. citizens.

Application Requirements: Application form, driver's license, essay. *Deadline:* May 2.

Contact: Sylvia Zawadzka
E-mail: sylvia@injury-attorneys.com

DIAMANTE, INC.

http://www.diamanteinc.org/

LATINO DIAMANTE SCHOLARSHIP FUND

Awards for Hispanic high school seniors recognizing their contributions to the community and their leadership qualities. Graduating high school seniors in North Carolina who plan to enroll at North Carolina institutions of higher education, and first-year undergraduates can apply for this scholarship. Must maintain a GPA of at least 2.5.

Award: Scholarship for use in freshman year; not renewable. *Number:* 2. *Amount:* $500.

Eligibility Requirements: Applicant must be Hispanic; enrolled or expecting to enroll full- or part-time at a two-year or four-year institution or university; resident of North Carolina; studying in North Carolina and must have an interest in leadership. Applicant or parent of applicant must have employment or volunteer experience in community service. Applicant must have 2.5 GPA or higher. Available to U.S. citizens.

Application Requirements: Application form, community service, essay, recommendations or references, transcript.

DIBELLA LAW OFFICES, P.C.

http://www.dibellalawoffice.com

2017 DIBELLA LAW OFFICES, P.C. SCHOLARSHIP

The 2017 DiBella Law Offices, P.C. Scholarship is our way of thanking those students who have committed themselves to bettering the community while still working to pursue their education. We understand the high cost associated with post-secondary education, which is why we are thrilled to be able to help one deserving student with minimizing that cost. Graduating high school seniors and current college students who have earned a 3.0 or higher GPA are welcome to apply for this scholarship. Applicants must be United States Citizens or Permanent Residents.

Award: Scholarship for use in freshman, sophomore, junior, or senior years; not renewable. *Number:* 1. *Amount:* $500.

Eligibility Requirements: Applicant must be enrolled or expecting to enroll full- or part-time at a two-year or four-year institution or university. Applicant must have 3.0 GPA or higher. Available to U.S. citizens.

Application Requirements: Application form, essay. *Deadline:* May 4.

Contact: Mr. Chris DiBella, Attorney
DiBella Law Offices, P.C.
45 Osgood Street, Suite 302
Methuen, MA 01844
Phone: 978-327-5140
Fax: 978-849-5140
E-mail: chris.dibella@dibellalawoffice.com

DIRECT ENERGY
https://www.directenergy.com/

DIRECT ENERGY LIVE BRIGHTER SCHOLARSHIP
Applicant must be a registered college/university student 18 years of age or older; be a resident of any of the states where Direct Energy offers energy services: Connecticut, Delaware, Illinois, Indiana, Maryland, Massachusetts, Michigan, New Hampshire, New Jersey, New York, Ohio, Pennsylvania, Rhode Island, Texas, D.C.; have a minimum of 3.0 GPA on a 4.0 scale; and provide an electronic copy of official or unofficial transcripts. Transcript does not need to bear a University seal or school seal, but must contain all of the relevant academic information of a student, including student name, cumulative grade point average, and school year. Transcript must be in one of the following formats:.doc,.pdf,.txt,.jpg,.png. Other file types will not be accepted and applications with other file types will not be considered. Must submit complete entry online including application form and accept terms and conditions. Submit complete application online between July 1st and September 30th, 2016. Either create a 60 to 120 second video (not including the 10 second title screen) or write a 500 word essay that responds to the following question: Direct Energy offers the tools and technology to use energy wisely and efficiently. We help our customers take advantage of energy choice to live a brighter life with accessible energy plans, innovative product offerings, engaging customer service, and high-end home services. How do you live your life brighter?

Award: Scholarship for use in freshman, sophomore, junior, senior, graduate, or postgraduate years; not renewable. *Number:* 3. *Amount:* $2500–$5000.

Eligibility Requirements: Applicant must be enrolled or expecting to enroll full- or part-time at a two-year or four-year or technical institution or university; resident of Connecticut, Delaware, District of Columbia, Illinois, Indiana, Maryland, Massachusetts, Michigan, New Hampshire, New Jersey, New York, Ohio, Pennsylvania, Rhode Island, Texas and studying in Connecticut, Delaware, District of Columbia, Illinois, Indiana, Maryland, Massachusetts, Michigan, New Hampshire, New Jersey, New York, Ohio, Pennsylvania, Rhode Island, Texas. Applicant must have 3.0 GPA or higher. Available to U.S. citizens.

Application Requirements: Application form, essay. *Deadline:* September 30.

Contact: Scholarship Committee
Direct Energy
12 Greenway Plaza
Houston, TX 77046
E-mail: DEscholarship@directenergy.com

DIRECTTEXTBOOK.COM
http://www.DirectTextbook.com

DIRECTTEXTBOOK.COM 2016 HAIKU SCHOLARSHIP CONTEST
Two $500 scholarships for Haiku entries selected at random from all qualifying entries. Scholarship deadline date: September 15th, 2016. 6 Awards available. Submit your original haiku poem that captures the essence of what the word "Manifest" means to you. Applications will no longer be accepted after September 15th, 2016. Once the contest is closed, all poems will be reviewed. The winners of each award will be notified by email on or before September 30th, 2016. Applicable majors: Must be a high school graduate with a most recent GPA of 2.0 or above, enrolled in an accredited 2 or 4 year college or university for fall of 2016, a legal resident of the United States and not currently incarcerated. See website for more details and to apply, http://www.directtextbook.com/haiku

Award: Scholarship for use in freshman, sophomore, junior, or senior years; not renewable. *Number:* 1–6. *Amount:* $1–$500.

Eligibility Requirements: Applicant must be enrolled or expecting to enroll full- or part-time at a two-year or four-year institution or university. Available to U.S. citizens.

Application Requirements: Application form. *Deadline:* September 15.

Contact: Hanna Wharton, Digital Marketing and Communications Manager
E-mail: hanna@directtextbook.com

DIRECTTEXTBOOK.COM "SHINE" PHOTO ESSAY CONTEST
Two $500 scholarships; photo entries selected at random from all qualifying entries. Scholarship deadline date: January 16th, 2017. Awards available: 6. Submit your original photo that captures the essence of what the theme "Shine" means to you. Applications will no longer be accepted after January 16th, 2017. Once the contest is closed, all entries will be reviewed. The winners of each award will be notified by email on or before January 30th, 2017.Applicable majors: All. Applicant must be a high school graduate with a most recent GPA of 2.0 or above, enrolled in an accredited 2 or 4 year college or university for winter or spring term of 2017, a legal resident of the United States and not currently incarcerated. See website for more details and to apply, http://www.directtextbook.com/photocontest

Award: Scholarship for use in freshman, sophomore, junior, or senior years; not renewable. *Number:* 6. *Amount:* $500.

Eligibility Requirements: Applicant must be enrolled or expecting to enroll full- or part-time at a two-year or four-year institution or university. Available to U.S. citizens.

Application Requirements: Personal photograph. *Deadline:* January 16.

Contact: Hanna Wharton, Digital Marketing and Communications Manager
Phone: 503-791-2414
E-mail: hanna@directtextbook.com

DISABLED AMERICAN VETERANS
http://www.dav.org/

JESSE BROWN MEMORIAL YOUTH SCHOLARSHIP PROGRAM
The Jesse Brown Memorial Youth Scholarship Program honors former National Service Officer and Secretary of Veterans Affairs Jesse Brown. It is given in memory of a DAV leader dedicated to veterans, through the recognition of those who carry on his legacy of service. This scholarship is awarded to youth volunteers who are committed to serving veterans. Each year, one outstanding applicant receives the top scholarship in the amount of $20,000 to help fund their higher education. In addition, the top winner and parent/guardian receive round-trip airfare (lowest non-refundable fare), hotel accommodations, and per diem for three days to attend the DAV National Convention. The winner will be presented the award and be recognized for their dedication and commitment to veterans. Additional scholarships are awarded annually in the following amounts: second prize of $15,000, third prize of $10,000, fourth prize of $7,500 (two awarded annually), fifth prize of $5,000 (three awarded annually).

Award: Scholarship for use in freshman, sophomore, junior, senior, graduate, or postgraduate years; renewable. *Number:* 8. *Amount:* $5000–$20,000.

Eligibility Requirements: Applicant must be enrolled or expecting to enroll full- or part-time at a two-year or four-year or technical institution or university. Applicant or parent of applicant must have employment or volunteer experience in community service, helping handicapped. Available to U.S. citizens.

Application Requirements: Application form, community service, essay. *Deadline:* February 10.

Contact: Ms. Kati Geoppinger, Supervisor of Voluntary Services
Disabled American Veterans
3725 Alexandria Pike
Cold Spring, KY 41076
Phone: 859-442-1012
E-mail: kgeoppinger@dav.org

DISABLEDPERSON INC. COLLEGE SCHOLARSHIP
http://www.disabledperson.com/

DISABLEDPERSON INC. NATIONAL COLLEGE SCHOLARSHIP AWARD FOR COLLEGE STUDENTS WITH DISABILITIES
Essay contest for college students with disabilities who are enrolled as full-time students in a two- or four-year accredited college or university. Length of the essay must not exceed 1000 words. We offer two scholarships per school year.

Award: Scholarship for use in freshman, sophomore, junior, senior, graduate, or postgraduate years; not renewable. *Number:* 1. *Amount:* $2000.

Eligibility Requirements: Applicant must be hearing impaired, learning disabled, physically disabled, or visually impaired and enrolled or expecting to enroll full- or part-time at a two-year or four-year or technical institution or university. Applicant must be hearing impaired, learning disabled, physically disabled, or visually impaired. Available to U.S. citizens.

Application Requirements: Application form, essay. *Deadline:* March 31.

Contact: Michael Corso, Programs Manager
disABLEDperson Inc. College Scholarship
PO Box 230636
Encinitas, CA 92023
E-mail: scholarships@disabledperson.com

DOLLARS 4 TIC SCHOLARS

http://www.dollars4ticscholars.org/

DOLLARS 4 TIC SCHOLARS TOURETTE SYNDROME SCHOLARSHIP

A minimum GPA of 2.5 and a letter of diagnosis of Tourette Syndrome are required. No fee is required to apply. Required components include application, essay, video, FAFSA SAR and financial information, transcripts, letter of acceptance, letter of diagnosis, and three letters of recommendation. Students have the option to apply online and mail in supporting documents (transcript, FAFSA and diagnosis) or complete the entire application process via mailing. Students can find the complete scholarship information by going to our website at http://www.dollars4ticscholars.org/

Award: Scholarship for use in freshman, sophomore, junior, or senior years; not renewable. *Number:* 4–5. *Amount:* $1000.

Eligibility Requirements: Applicant must be enrolled or expecting to enroll full-time at a two-year or four-year institution or university. Applicant must have 2.5 GPA or higher. Available to U.S. citizens.

Application Requirements: Application form, essay. *Deadline:* April 15.

Contact: Diane Diamantis
Dollars 4 Tic Scholars
21801 Little Bear Lane
Boca Raton, FL 33428
Phone: 561-4879526
Fax: 561-4879526
E-mail: info@dollars4ticscholars.org

DOLPHIN SCHOLARSHIP FOUNDATION

http://www.dolphinscholarship.org/

DOLPHIN SCHOLARSHIPS

Renewable award for undergraduate students. Applicant's parent/stepparent must meet one of the following requirements: be current/former member of the U.S. Navy who qualified in submarines and served in the Submarine Force for at least eight years; current or former member of the Navy who served in submarine support activities for at least ten years; Medically discharged or; died while on active duty in the Submarine Force. Must be single, under age 24.

Award: Scholarship for use in freshman, sophomore, junior, or senior years; renewable. *Number:* 25–30. *Amount:* $2000–$3400.

Eligibility Requirements: Applicant must be enrolled or expecting to enroll full-time at a two-year or four-year or technical institution or university and married. Available to U.S. citizens.

Application Requirements: Application form, community service, essay, financial need analysis. *Deadline:* March 15.

Contact: Mr. Andrew Clark, Executive Director
Dolphin Scholarship Foundation
4966 Euclid Road
Suite 109
Virginia Beach, VA 23462
Phone: 757-671-3200 Ext. 4
E-mail: scholars@dolphinscholarship.org

DUDLEY DEBOSIER INJURY LAWYERS

http://www.dudleydebosier.com/home

DUDLEY DEBOSIER SCHOLARSHIP PROGRAM

The Dudley DeBosier Scholarship Program is designed to help students in our community who are interested in attending college upon graduation from high school. That is because our law firm is committed to giving back to our community and the education system. At Dudley DeBosier, we believe education is an important foundation for creating gratifying and advantageous careers. We are proud to support the youth in our community by providing this opportunity, and we look forward to helping students achieve their goals to attend college!

Award: Scholarship for use in freshman year; not renewable. *Number:* 9. *Amount:* $1000–$2000.

Eligibility Requirements: Applicant must be high school student and planning to enroll or expecting to enroll full-time at a two-year or four-year or technical institution or university. Available to U.S. citizens.

Application Requirements: Application form, essay, personal photograph. *Deadline:* March 17.

Contact: Elizabeth Demopulos, Director of Marketing
Dudley DeBosier Injury Lawyers
1075 Government St
Baton Rouge, LA 70808
Phone: 225-379-3333
Fax: 225-379-4952
E-mail: EDemopulos@dudleydebosier.com

DUKE ENERGY CORPORATION

http://www.duke-energy.com/

DUKE ENERGY SCHOLARS PROGRAM
• *See page 568*

ELEARNERS.COM

http://www.elearners.com

ELEARNERS ONLINE STUDENT SCHOLARSHIP

Entering to win our free scholarship for college is fast and easy. All you have to do is complete a short form to tell us a little about yourself and answer one essay question in 250 words or less. What is the essay question you ask? We want you to tell us: How has choosing an online college enabled you to finish your education?

Award: Scholarship for use in freshman, sophomore, junior, senior, graduate, or postgraduate years; not renewable. *Number:* 1–2. *Amount:* $1000.

Eligibility Requirements: Applicant must be enrolled or expecting to enroll full- or part-time at a two-year or four-year or technical institution or university. Available to U.S. citizens.

Application Requirements: Application form, driver's license, essay. *Deadline:* February 28.

Contact: Scholarship Organizer
E-mail: militaryscholarships@elearners.com

ELECTRONIC SECURITY ASSOCIATION (ESA)

http://www.esaweb.org

ESA YOUTH SCHOLARSHIP PROGRAM

One-time award for high school seniors entering postsecondary education, who are deserving sons or daughters of police and fire officials. The number of awards granted varies annually.

Award: Scholarship for use in freshman year; not renewable. *Amount:* $500–$10,000.

Eligibility Requirements: Applicant must be high school student; age 15-20 and planning to enroll or expecting to enroll full-time at a four-year institution or university. Applicant or parent of applicant must have employment or volunteer experience in police/firefighting. Available to U.S. citizens.

Application Requirements: Application form, essay, proof of acceptance to college or university, proof of parent/guardian occupation, recommendations or references, resume, test scores, transcript. *Deadline:* March 28.

Contact: Laurie Knox, Vice President of Communications and Public Relations
Electronic Security Association (ESA)
6333 North State Highway 161
Suite 350
Irving, TX 75038
Phone: 888-447-1689 Ext. 6825
E-mail: laurie.knox@esaweb.org

ELIZABETH GREENSHIELDS FOUNDATION

http://www.elizabethgreenshieldsfoundation.org

THE ELIZABETH GREENSHIELDS FOUNDATION GRANT

The Elizabeth Greenshields Foundation provides financial grants to art students and artists in the early or developmental stage of their career. The Foundation focuses solely on those who work in a representational style of painting, drawing, sculpture or printmaking and who are committed to making the practice of their art a lifetime career. Candidates must be at least 18 years of age at the time of submitting their application. Grants are made directly to the beneficiaries, not through other organizations. First grants are in the amount of CDN$15,000; second and third grants, in the amount of CDN$18,000 Important: The Foundation does not accept applications from commercial artists, graphic designers and illustrators; photographers; cartoonists; animation artists; video artists, filmmakers and digital artists; craft-makers; or any artist whose work falls primarily into these categories. The Foundation does not provide funding for the pursuit of abstract or non-objective art. Applications may only be accessed through the Foundation's website. The Foundation does not mail or provide application forms to applicants. Applications must be completed online, then printed, dated, and signed by the applicant, and submitted by mail. Applicants may not submit applications by fax, email, internet or other electronic means.

Award: Grant for use in freshman, sophomore, junior, senior, graduate, or postgraduate years; not renewable. *Number:* 40–70. *Amount:* $10,500–$13,000.

Eligibility Requirements: Applicant must be enrolled or expecting to enroll full- or part-time at a two-year or four-year institution or university and must have an interest in art. Available to U.S. and non-U.S. citizens.

Application Requirements: Application form, personal photograph, portfolio. *Deadline:* continuous.

Contact: Ms. Diane Pitcher, Applications Coordinator
Phone: 514-937-9225
E-mail: info@greenshieldsfoundation.ca

ENVIRONMENTAL LITIGATION GROUP P.C.

https://www.elglaw.com/

ENVIRONMENTAL LITIGATION GROUP, P.C. ASBESTOS SCHOLARSHIP

Must be 18 years old and a U.S. citizen; be enrolled full-time in a U.S. based accredited two-year or four-year university, community college or junior college, or a graduate degree program; must have a minimum GPA of 3.0 or higher; and must be a student who witnessed a parent, sibling, immediate family member or close friend fighting cancer. Must apply to the contest via online form available on our website at https://www.elglaw.com/scholarship/. Must provide the written essay by the deadline of July 31, 2017. The three winners will be chosen by the end of August 2017 and notified by email.

Award: Scholarship for use in freshman, sophomore, junior, senior, or graduate years; not renewable. *Number:* 3. *Amount:* $2000–$5000.

Eligibility Requirements: Applicant must be enrolled or expecting to enroll full-time at a two-year or four-year institution or university. Applicant must have 3.0 GPA or higher. Available to U.S. citizens.

Application Requirements: Essay, personal photograph. *Deadline:* July 31.

Contact: Ciprian Oltean
Environmental Litigation Group P.C.
2160 Highland Avenue, Suite 200
Birmingham, AL 35205
E-mail: ciprian@elglaw.com

EOD WARRIOR FOUNDATION

http://www.eodwarriorfoundation.org

EXPLOSIVE ORDNANCE DISPOSAL MEMORIAL SCHOLARSHIP

Award based on academic merit, community involvement, and financial need for the children, grandchildren, and spouses of military Explosive Ordnance Disposal technicians. This scholarship is for students enrolled or planning to enroll full-time as an undergraduate in a U.S. accredited two year, four year college. Applications are only available on the website at http://www.eodwarriorfoundation.org.

Award: Scholarship for use in freshman, sophomore, junior, or senior years; not renewable. *Number:* 25–75. *Amount:* $1000–$5000.

Eligibility Requirements: Applicant must be enrolled or expecting to enroll full-time at a two-year or four-year institution or university. Applicant or parent of applicant must have employment or volunteer experience in explosive ordnance disposal. Available to U.S. citizens. Applicant or parent must meet one or more of the following requirements: general military experience; retired from active duty; disabled or killed as a result of military service; prisoner of war; or missing in action.

Application Requirements: Application form, application form may be submitted online (http://www.eodmemorial.org/scholarship), community service, essay, recommendations or references, transcript. *Deadline:* March 15.

Contact: Nicole Motsek, Executive Director
EOD Warrior Foundation
33735 Snickersville Turnpike
PO Box 309
Bluemont, VA 20135
Phone: 540-554-4550
E-mail: nicole.motsek@eodmemorial.org

EQUALITY SCHOLARSHIP COLLABORATIVE

http://www.equalityscholarship.org

EQUALITY SCHOLARSHIPS FOR COMMUNITY COLLEGE TRANSFER STUDENTS

eQuality scholarships for community college transfer students recognize northern and central California community college students for their service to the lesbian/gay/bisexual/transgender community. Applicants must plan to attend or have begun attending an accredited 4-year college or university for the first time in the award year.

Award: Scholarship for use in junior or senior years; not renewable. *Number:* 1–2. *Amount:* $6000.

Eligibility Requirements: Applicant must be enrolled or expecting to enroll full- or part-time at a four-year institution or university; resident of California and must have an interest in LGBT issues. Applicant or parent of applicant must have employment or volunteer experience in community service. Available to U.S. and non-U.S. citizens.

Application Requirements: Application form, essay, interview. *Deadline:* February 1.

SCHOLARSHIPS FOR HIGH SCHOOL GRADUATES

eQuality Scholarships for high school graduates recognize graduating high school seniors and recent graduates in northern and central California students for their service to the lesbian/gay/bisexual/transgender community. Applicants must plan to attend or have begun attending an accredited post-secondary institution for the first time in the award year.

Award: Scholarship for use in freshman, sophomore, junior, or senior years; not renewable. *Number:* 11–12. *Amount:* $6000.

Eligibility Requirements: Applicant must be enrolled or expecting to enroll full- or part-time at a two-year or four-year or technical institution or university; resident of California and must have an interest in LGBT issues. Applicant or parent of applicant must have employment or volunteer experience in community service. Available to U.S. and non-U.S. citizens.

Application Requirements: Application form, community service, essay, interview. *Deadline:* February 1.

ESSAYHUB

https://essayhub.com/

ESSAY WRITING CONTEST BY ESSAYHUB

Any individual choosing to participate in this contest must be undergoing high school or higher level education (university, college). Every submission must meet the minimum word count requirement of 500 words to 1000 words max. All work for this essay contest must be written in English. We understand that the world is multilingual and we would enjoy reading such interesting works in their original language, however it would make conducting such an event nearly impossible. Fill our application form located on this page to take part in the contest. Or send your works in Word or Doc type files as to allow easy access to them to the email address support@essayhub.com with subject line Essay Writing Contest. The email submission requirements need you to place your name in the work itself and in the text of the email letter itself. Example: Essay Writing Contest—Joseph Smith. Avoid continuously looking to debate whether you should be the winner or trying to convince the judges why you think you deserved to win. All judging is done anonymously and based solely on the quality of the essay writer's work. This allows for only the best essays to win. We do not accept the submission of any kind of scholarship essay. Plagiarism is a no go. All those found guilty will be disqualified without being notified. No excuses, no exceptions. There are many referencing guides available on our website for you to use in case you get stuck. In the case of a resubmission from a previous contest it will not be taken into account and regarded as plagiarism. All submissions must be given in by the 30th of April 2017 11:59 PST at the latest. Make sure to include your correct contact information so we may get a hold of you if you have won. The event begins on the 17th of February 2017 at 12:00 PST.

Award: Scholarship for use in freshman, sophomore, junior, senior, graduate, or postgraduate years; not renewable. *Number:* 3. *Amount:* $500.

Eligibility Requirements: Applicant must be hearing impaired, learning disabled, physically disabled, or visually impaired; American Indian/Alaska Native, Asian/Pacific Islander, Black (non-Hispanic), Hispanic; enrolled or expecting to enroll full- or part-time at a two-year or four-year institution or university and must have an interest in writing. Applicant must be hearing impaired, learning disabled, physically disabled, or visually impaired. Available to U.S. and non-U.S. citizens.

Application Requirements: Essay. *Deadline:* April 30.

Contact: Miss. Tia Moreen
Gardena
E-mail: tia.moreen@gmail.com

FARAH & FARAH

http://www.farahandfarah.com/

FARAH & FARAH SCHOLARSHIP

We will be awarding $500 to a student who has not only demonstrated excellence in academics, but also a deep and meaningful commitment to bettering the local community. The 2016 Farah & Farah Scholarship is open to both high school seniors and current college students across the U.S. Farah & Farah truly values education and the drive to do good work, and we want to help students in need. To make things a little easier financially, we are glad to offer this scholarship to students shaping America's present and its bright future.

Award: Scholarship for use in freshman, sophomore, junior, or senior years; not renewable. *Number:* 1. *Amount:* $500.

Eligibility Requirements: Applicant must be enrolled or expecting to enroll full- or part-time at a two-year or four-year institution or university. Applicant must have 3.0 GPA or higher. Available to U.S. citizens.

Application Requirements: Application form, essay. *Deadline:* September 15.

Contact: Eric Baskauskas, Scholarship Manager
Farah & Farah
10 West Adams Street
Jacksonville, FL 32202
Phone: 904-396-5555
E-mail: eric@farahandfarah.com

FELDMAN & ROYLE, ATTORNEYS AT LAW

http://www.feldmanroyle.com/

AUTISM SCHOLARSHIPS

Feldman & Royle, Attorneys at Law is pleased to announce two annual scholarships for individuals diagnosed with Autism Spectrum Disorder (ASD or Autism). The scholarships are designed to assist applicants in furthering their education. Each of the $1,000 scholarships will be for tuition at an educational institution chosen by the applicant. All those who have ASD (DSM-5) are eligible for the scholarships, which will be used to assist you in furthering your educational goals. We may request proof of your ASD diagnosis. Feldman & Royle is offering two annual scholarships. Both of them are for $1,000, and will be used to defray the cost of tuition for a secondary school, community college, trade school or college. You are eligible for a scholarship whether or not you currently attend school. After being awarded the scholarship, you will have one year within which to provide us with a tuition invoice from the educational institution you have chosen to attend. A check for $1,000 will then be issued to the institution.

Award: Scholarship for use in freshman, sophomore, junior, senior, graduate, or postgraduate years; not renewable. *Number:* 2. *Amount:* $1000.

Eligibility Requirements: Applicant must be learning disabled and enrolled or expecting to enroll full- or part-time at a two-year or four-year or technical institution or university. Applicant must be learning disabled. Available to U.S. citizens.

Application Requirements: Application form, essay. *Deadline:* November 7.

Contact: Adam Feldman
E-mail: michael@feldmanroyle.com

FELDMAN LAW FIRM PLLC

http://www.afphoenixcriminalattorney.com/

DISABLED VETERANS SCHOLARSHIP

The Feldman Law Firm, PLLC has announced that it will be offering two annual scholarships for disabled veterans. The scholarships focus on providing tuition assistance to disabled veterans who wish to continue their education. These are two separate $1,000 scholarships offered annually to disabled veterans. The scholarship funds may be used for tuition at a college or university (including a community college), a trade school, or a secondary school. It is not required that the applicant be enrolled in an educational program at the time of his or her application. The winners will have one year from the date of the award to provide a tuition invoice from the school of their choice. A check for $1,000 will then be sent to the educational institution. n order to be eligible for a scholarship, you must be a disabled veteran of the United States Armed Forces with a disability rating of at least 30 percent. You may be asked to provide proof of your disability and your status as a veteran.

Award: Scholarship for use in freshman, sophomore, junior, senior, graduate, or postgraduate years; not renewable. *Number:* 2. *Amount:* $1000.

Eligibility Requirements: Applicant must be physically disabled and enrolled or expecting to enroll full- or part-time at a two-year or four-year or technical institution or university. Applicant must be physically disabled. Available to U.S. citizens. Applicant or parent must meet one or more of the following requirements: general military experience; retired from active duty; disabled or killed as a result of military service; prisoner of war; or missing in action.

Application Requirements: Application form, essay. *Deadline:* November 10.

Contact: Adam Feldman
Phone: 602-540-7887
E-mail: Mike@afphoenixcriminalattorney.com

FINANCE AUTHORITY OF MAINE

http://www.famemaine.com/

TUITION WAIVER PROGRAMS

Provides tuition waivers for children and spouses of EMS personnel, firefighters, and law enforcement officers who have been killed in the line of duty and for students who were foster children under the custody of the Department of Human Services when they graduated from high school. Waivers valid at the University of Maine System, the Maine Technical College System, and Maine Maritime Academy. Applicant must reside and study in Maine.

Award: Grant for use in freshman, sophomore, junior, or senior years; renewable. *Number:* 30.

Eligibility Requirements: Applicant must be enrolled or expecting to enroll full- or part-time at a two-year or four-year institution or university; resident of Maine and studying in Maine. Applicant or parent of applicant must have employment or volunteer experience in police/firefighting. Available to U.S. citizens.

Application Requirements: Application form. *Deadline:* continuous.

Contact: Claude Roy, Education Services Officer
Finance Authority of Maine
5 Community Drive
Augusta, ME 04332
Phone: 207-620-3507
E-mail: education@famemaine.com

FLORIDA PTA/PTSA

http://www.floridapta.org/

FLORIDA PTA/PTSA ANNUAL SCHOLARSHIP

Non-Renewable scholarship of $2000 awarded to students enrolled full-time in their undergraduate study.

Award: Scholarship for use in freshman year; not renewable. *Number:* 2. *Amount:* $2000.

Eligibility Requirements: Applicant must be high school student; planning to enroll or expecting to enroll full-time at a two-year or four-year or technical institution or university and resident of Florida. Applicant must have 2.5 GPA or higher.

Application Requirements: Application form, community service, essay, financial need analysis. *Deadline:* February 1.

Contact: Scholarship Chair, Scholarship Chair
Florida PTA/PTSA
1747 Orlando Central Parkway
Orlando, FL 32809
Phone: 407-855-7604
Fax: 407-240-9577
E-mail: scholarship@floridapta.org

FRATERNAL ORDER OF POLICE ASSOCIATES OF OHIO INC.

http://www.fopaohio.org/

FRATERNAL ORDER OF POLICE ASSOCIATES, STATE LODGE OF OHIO INC., SCHOLARSHIP FUND

Scholarship available to a graduating high school senior whose parent or guardian is a member in good standing of the Fraternal Order of Police, State Lodge of Ohio Inc. The amount of each scholarship will be up to $4000 payable over a four-year period. A one-time award of $500 will be given to the first runner-up. Scholarships will be awarded on the basis of scholastic merit, economic need and goals in life.

Award: Scholarship for use in freshman year; renewable. *Number:* 1–4. *Amount:* $500–$1000.

Eligibility Requirements: Applicant must be high school student; planning to enroll or expecting to enroll full-time at a four-year institution or university and resident of Ohio. Applicant or parent of applicant must have employment or volunteer experience in police/firefighting. Available to U.S. citizens.

Application Requirements: Application form, community service, essay, financial need analysis, personal photograph, proof of guardianship, recommendations or references, test scores, transcript. *Deadline:* May 1.

Contact: Mr. Michael Esposito, FOPA Scholarship Assistance Program
Fraternal Order of Police Associates of Ohio Inc.
PO Box 14564
Cincinnati, OH 45250-0564
Phone: 513-684-4755
E-mail: mje@fopaohio.org

FREEDOM ALLIANCE

https://freedomalliance.org

FREEDOM ALLIANCE SCHOLARSHIP FUND

The mission of the Freedom Alliance Scholarship Fund is two-fold. First, it helps offset the high cost of a college education for the sons and daughters of American heroes. Second, it is a reminder to the recipient that their parent's sacrifice will never be forgotten by a grateful nation. Freedom Alliance Scholarship Fund applicants must be one of the following: the dependent son or daughter of a U.S. Soldier, Sailor, Airman, Guardsman or Marine who has become 100% permanently disabled as a result of an combat mission or training accident; the dependent son or daughter of a U.S. Soldier, Sailor, Airman, Guardsman or Marine who has been killed in action; the dependent son or daughter of a U.S. Soldier, Sailor, Airman, Guardsman or Marine who has been classified as a Prisoner of War (POW) or Missing in Action (MIA). All applicants must also meet the following eligibility requirements in order to qualify for a Freedom Alliance scholarship: currently in their senior year of high school, a high school graduate or a currently enrolled full time undergraduate student; under the age of 26 at the time of application; have a GPA of 2.0 or higher. Eligible students can visit our website, http://www.fascholarship.com, and complete the application to start the process. Should you have any additional questions about eligibility, please feel free to contact us at (800) 475-6620 or (703) 444-7940.

Award: Scholarship for use in freshman, sophomore, junior, or senior years; renewable. *Number:* 250–325. *Amount:* $500–$3500.

Eligibility Requirements: Applicant must be age 17-25 and enrolled or expecting to enroll full-time at a two-year or four-year or technical institution or university. Applicant must have 2.5 GPA or higher. Available to U.S. citizens.

Application Requirements: Application form, essay, personal photograph. *Deadline:* continuous.

Contact: Wanda Cruz, Programs Assistant
Freedom Alliance
22570 Markey Court
Suite 240
Dulles, VA 20166
Phone: 800-475-6620
E-mail: info@fascholarship.com

FUNNEWJERSEY.COM INC.

www.funnewjersey.com

FUNNEWJERSEY.COM SCHOLARSHIP

FunNewJersey.com is awarding scholarships to New Jersey residents who plan on attending an institution of higher learning at one of the many distinguished colleges and/or universities in state. Applicants must submit an essay about New Jersey. Themes may include the following: What is so special about New Jersey? What should tourists, visitors and non-residents know about NJ that they might not know? Do you have any memories of New Jersey that are special? What is your favorite local attraction or place? What makes your town, city, neighborhood or community unique? These are merely suggestions: please feel free to come up with your own creative responses. Applicants must also submit a resume.

Award: Scholarship for use in freshman year; not renewable. *Number:* 1–3. *Amount:* $100–$1000.

Eligibility Requirements: Applicant must be high school student; planning to enroll or expecting to enroll full-time at a two-year or four-year or technical institution or university; resident of New Jersey and studying in New Jersey. Available to U.S. citizens.

Application Requirements: Essay. *Deadline:* April 15.

Contact: Ms. Ray Gallagher, Managing Content Editor
FunNewJersey.com Inc.
241 Forsgate Drive
Suite 113
Jamesburg, NJ 08831
Phone: 732-298-0615 Ext. 551
E-mail: ray@funnewjersey.com

GENERAL FEDERATION OF WOMEN'S CLUBS OF MASSACHUSETTS

http://www.gfwcma.org/

GENERAL FEDERATION OF WOMEN'S CLUBS OF MASSACHUSETTS NICKEL FOR NOTES MUSIC SCHOLARSHIP

Scholarship for high school seniors majoring in piano, instrument, music education, music therapy or voice. Applicant must be a senior in a Massachusetts High School.

Award: Scholarship for use in freshman year; not renewable. *Number:* 1. *Amount:* $500.

Eligibility Requirements: Applicant must be high school student; planning to enroll or expecting to enroll full-time at a four-year institution or university; resident of Massachusetts and must have an interest in music/singing. Available to U.S. citizens.

Application Requirements: Application form, essay, interview. *Deadline:* March 1.

Contact: Scholarship Chairman
General Federation of Women's Clubs of Massachusetts
245 Dutton Road
Sudbury, MA 01776
Phone: 978-443-4569
E-mail: gfwcma@aol.com

GENERAL FEDERATION OF WOMEN'S CLUBS OF MASSACHUSETTS PENNIES FOR ART SCHOLARSHIP

Scholarship for graduating high school senior who is resident of Massachusetts majoring in art. Must submit three (3) pieces of original artwork in three (3) different mediums (no sculpture). Matting is required except for oil on stretched canvas.

Award: Scholarship for use in freshman year; not renewable. *Number:* 1. *Amount:* $500.

Eligibility Requirements: Applicant must be high school student; planning to enroll or expecting to enroll full-time at a four-year institution or university; resident of Massachusetts and must have an interest in art. Available to U.S. citizens.

Application Requirements: Application form, driver's license, essay, portfolio. *Deadline:* March 1.

Contact: Scholarship Chairman
General Federation of Women's Clubs of Massachusetts
245 Dutton Road
Sudbury, MA 01776
Phone: 978-443-4569
E-mail: gfwcma@aol.com

GIFT BASKETS PLUS

www.giftbasketsplus.com

2017 HIGH SCHOOL GRADUATE SCHOLARSHIP CONTEST

We are announcing the Gift Baskets Plus 2017 college scholarship contest for $500. The rules are simple. Seniors in high school will submit an essay of at least 600 words, entitled "The perfect high school graduation gift." Each essay must be submitted by email to 2017scholarship@giftbasketsplus.com. To qualify, each submission must contain a PDF of the essay; student's full name; destination college (or colleges if not yet selected); email address; mailing address; date of birth. Qualifying essays will be published on GiftBasketsPlus.com. Essays must be submitted by May 1st, 2017 to be considered. The winner will be announced on June 1, 2017. Once qualified, one essay will be selected for a $500 scholarship based on the number of social shares that essay gets.

Winners will be notified by email and scholarships will be mailed by check. Good luck, students!

Award: Prize for use in freshman, sophomore, junior, senior, or graduate years; not renewable. *Number:* 1. *Amount:* $500.

Eligibility Requirements: Applicant must be enrolled or expecting to enroll full-time at a two-year or four-year or technical institution or university. Available to U.S. citizens.

Application Requirements: Essay. *Deadline:* May 1.

Contact: Tamara Watson, Marketing Manager
Phone: 800-520-6657 Ext. 0

GOENNOUNCE, LLC

http://GoEnnounce.com/about

GOENNOUNCE YOURSELF $500 MONTHLY SCHOLARSHIP

Our $500 monthly scholarship is a monthly scholarship open to all high school students and college freshmen, sophomores, and juniors. Once you apply, you're considered every month based on the updates you're posting. Not essay or GPA–based. Who are you as a student? An athlete, a history ace, a star on the drums, class treasurer, a student volunteer, or something completely different? We want to reward you for being you and for e–nnouncing your school progress and accomplishments each month.

Award: Prize for use in freshman, sophomore, or junior years; renewable. *Number:* 12. *Amount:* $500.

Eligibility Requirements: Applicant must be enrolled or expecting to enroll full-time at a two-year or four-year institution or university. Available to U.S. citizens.

Application Requirements: *Deadline:* continuous.

GOLF COURSE SUPERINTENDENTS ASSOCIATION OF AMERICA

http://www.eifg.org/

GOLF COURSE SUPERINTENDENTS ASSOCIATION OF AMERICA LEGACY AWARD
• *See page 544*

JOSEPH S. GARSKE COLLEGIATE GRANT PROGRAM
• *See page 544*

GORDON LAW GROUP

https://www.gordonlawltd.com

GORDON LAW GROUP NEED-BASED SCHOLARSHIP

This scholarship is open to any US citizen or permanent US resident who will be enrolled full--time in an accredited community college, college or university, or accredited law school in the fall of 2017. The scholarship will be awarded to an undergraduate or law school student of need who submits the best essay addressing the following topic: "Should the federal income tax code be changed to a flat tax of 18% with no deductions so that every person pays the same tax rate?"

Award: Scholarship for use in freshman, sophomore, junior, or senior years; not renewable. *Number:* 1. *Amount:* $1500.

Eligibility Requirements: Applicant must be enrolled or expecting to enroll full-time at a two-year or four-year institution or university. Available to U.S. citizens.

Application Requirements: Financial need analysis. *Deadline:* June 1.

Contact: Andrew Gordon, Partner
Gordon Law Group
400 Central Ave, Suite 340
Northfield, IL 60093
Phone: 847-580-1279
Fax: 847-305-1202
E-mail: abg@gordonlawltd.com

GREATER WASHINGTON URBAN LEAGUE

http://www.gwul.org/

SAFEWAY/GREATER WASHINGTON URBAN LEAGUE SCHOLARSHIP

Award to graduating high school students who reside in the service area of the League. Applicants must complete an essay on a subject selected by the sponsors and must have completed 90 percent of their school district's community service requirement. Minimum GPA of 2.7 required.

Award: Scholarship for use in freshman year; not renewable. *Number:* 6. *Amount:* $3000.

Eligibility Requirements: Applicant must be high school student; planning to enroll or expecting to enroll full-time at a four-year institution or university and resident of District of Columbia. Applicant or parent of applicant must have employment or volunteer experience in community service. Available to U.S. citizens.

Application Requirements: Application form, community service, entry in a contest, essay, test scores. *Deadline:* February 12.

Contact: Audrey Epperson, Director of Education
Phone: 202-265-8200
Fax: 202-387-7019
E-mail: aepperson@gwul.org

GREENHOUSE SCHOLARS

http://greenhousescholars.org/our-scholars/become-a-scholar/

GREENHOUSE SCHOLARS

Our 4 core values are relentlessness, leadership, community, and accountability. Applicants should be able to demonstrate a strong commitment to the community, an ability to persevere through difficult circumstances, excellent leadership skills, and financial need. Applicants must be/have: i) a graduating high school senior who is planning to attend a 4-year, accredited institution, ii) a resident of selected states, iii) a minimum un-weighted, cumulative GPA of 3.5, and iv) an annual household income no greater than $70,000 for a family of 4.

Award: Scholarship for use in freshman, sophomore, junior, or senior years; renewable. *Number:* 15–25. *Amount:* $1000–$5000.

Eligibility Requirements: Applicant must be high school student; planning to enroll or expecting to enroll full-time at a four-year institution or university; resident of Colorado, Georgia, Illinois, North Carolina; studying in Alabama, Alaska, Arizona, Arkansas, California, Colorado, Connecticut, Delaware, District of Columbia, Florida, Georgia, Hawaii, Idaho, Illinois, Indiana, Iowa, Kansas, Kentucky, Louisiana, Maine, Maryland, Michigan, Mississippi, Missouri, Montana, Nebraska, Nevada, New Hampshire, New Jersey, New Mexico, New York, North Carolina, North Dakota, Ohio, Oklahoma, Oregon, Pennsylvania, Rhode Island, South Carolina, South Dakota, Tennessee, Texas, Utah, Vermont, Virginia, Washington, West Virginia, Wisconsin, Wyoming and must have an interest in leadership. Applicant or parent of applicant must have employment or volunteer experience in community service. Applicant must have 3.5 GPA or higher. Available to U.S. citizens.

Application Requirements: Application form, community service, essay, financial need analysis, interview, personal photograph. *Deadline:* December 1.

Contact: Lindsey Price, Program Director
Greenhouse Scholars
1881 9th Street, Suite 200
Boulder, CO 80302
Phone: 303-459-5470
E-mail: scholars@greenhousescholars.org

GRUNGO COLARULO

https://gcinjurylaw.com/

GRUNGO COLARULO GIVING BACK TO THE COMMUNITY SCHOLARSHIP

The Giving Back to the Community scholarship is open to apply to for any student who is currently enrolled in an accredited community college, undergraduate, or graduate program in the United States. Students who are currently incoming first-year college students and have graduated high school or possesses a GED may also apply. For complete information on this scholarship, please visit https://gcinjurylaw.com/#scholarship

Award: Scholarship for use in freshman, sophomore, junior, senior, graduate, or postgraduate years; not renewable. *Number:* 1. *Amount:* $500.

Eligibility Requirements: Applicant must be enrolled or expecting to enroll full- or part-time at a two-year or four-year or technical institution or university. Applicant must have 3.0 GPA or higher. Available to U.S. and non-U.S. citizens.

Application Requirements: Application form, essay. *Deadline:* October 31.

Contact: Richard Grungo
E-mail: rgrungo@gcinjurylaw.com

HARNESS HORSE YOUTH FOUNDATION

http://www.hhyf.org/

CURT GREENE MEMORIAL SCHOLARSHIP

One-time award with preference given to those under age 24 who have a passion for harness racing. Based on need, merit, need, and passion for harness racing. Available for study in any field. May reapply.

Award: Scholarship for use in freshman, sophomore, junior, or senior years; not renewable. *Number:* 1–2. *Amount:* $2500.

Eligibility Requirements: Applicant must be age 18-24; enrolled or expecting to enroll full-time at a two-year or four-year or technical institution or university and must have an interest in animal/agricultural competition. Applicant or parent of applicant must have employment or volunteer experience in harness racing. Applicant must have 2.5 GPA or higher. Available to U.S. and Canadian citizens.

Application Requirements: Application form, community service, essay, financial need analysis, page 1 of parent's IRS form, test scores, transcript. *Deadline:* April 30.

Contact: Ellen Taylor, Executive Director
Harness Horse Youth Foundation
16575 Carey Road
Westfield, IN 46074
Phone: 317-867-5877
Fax: 317-867-1886
E-mail: ellen@hhyf.org

HARNESS TRACKS OF AMERICA

http://www.harnesstracks.com/

HTA/HAROLD SNYDER MEMORIAL SCHOLARSHIPS

One-time, merit-based award of $5000 for students actively involved in harness racing or the children of licensed drivers, trainers, breeders, or caretakers, living or deceased. Based on financial need, academic merit, and active harness racing involvement by applicant or family member. High school seniors may apply for the following school year award.

Award: Scholarship for use in freshman, sophomore, junior, senior, or graduate years; not renewable. *Number:* 3. *Amount:* $5000.

Eligibility Requirements: Applicant must be enrolled or expecting to enroll full-time at a two-year or four-year or technical institution or university. Applicant or parent of applicant must have employment or volunteer experience in harness racing. Available to U.S. and Canadian citizens.

Application Requirements: Application form, essay, financial need analysis. *Deadline:* June 26.

Contact: Ms. Heather McColloch, Executive Assistant
Harness Tracks of America
10705 Northfield Rd.
Northfield, OH 44067
Phone: 330-467-4101 Ext. 2204
E-mail: hmccolloch@northfieldpark.com

HARRINGTON FAMILY FOUNDATION

http://harringtonfamilyfoundation.org

OREGON COMMUNITY QUARTERBACK SCHOLARSHIP

The Oregon Community Quarterback Scholarship is a renewable four-year collegiate scholarship program for Oregon high school seniors who are emerging leaders, and plan to attend an Oregon trade school, college or university. The program is designed to find and encourage students in the state of Oregon who have shown a take-charge ability in their community, but may need financial help reaching their potential. In addition to the scholarship, each recipient will have a board of mentors available to them throughout and following their schooling to help guide their path to a successful career and future. By helping to open doors in the business sector, these emerging leaders will remain planted and invested in the state of Oregon. This is a need-based scholarship with criteria focusing on an individual's involvement in his or her community, rather than academic or athletic performance. Four scholarships will be issued for the 2017/18 academic year. Each scholarship is worth $2,500 per year for a total commitment of $10,000 per student. Scholarship valid only at an accredited Oregon trade school, college or university. Application deadline is March 31, 2017. Apply online at harringtonfamilyfoundation.slideroom.comBackground

Award: Scholarship for use in freshman, sophomore, junior, or senior years; renewable. *Number:* 4. *Amount:* $10,000.

Eligibility Requirements: Applicant must be enrolled or expecting to enroll full-time at a two-year or four-year or technical institution or university; resident of Oregon and studying in Oregon. Available to U.S. and non-U.S. citizens.

Application Requirements: *Deadline:* March 31.

Contact: Mrs. Madeline Guzzo, Scholarship Manager
Harrington Family Foundation
1355 NW 13th Avenue
Portland, OR 97209
Phone: 855-868-3549
E-mail: madeline@harringtonfamilyfoundation.org

HELEN DILLER FAMILY FOUNDATION

http://www.dillerteenawards.org

DILLER TEEN TIKKUN OLAM AWARDS

The Diller Teen Tikkun Olam Awards celebrate tikkun olam, or repairing the world. The Diller Family Foundation knows that supporting Jewish teen leadership today means creating and inspiring future generations of strong Jewish leaders in the global community. The Awards provide $36,000 for each recipient so that they may use it to further their project or education. If the funds will be used towards education, they will be sent directly to the college or university. Some recipients choose to divide the award between their education and philanthropic work. Applicants must demonstrate leadership via a specific community service project that is already underway. Applications presenting a project that has not yet been initiated will not be considered. Examples of past recipient's work can be found on our website, http://www.dillerteenawards.org.

Award: Prize for use in freshman or sophomore years; not renewable. *Number:* 15. *Amount:* $36,000.

Eligibility Requirements: Applicant must be Jewish; of Jewish heritage and Jewish citizen; age 13-19 and enrolled or expecting to enroll full- or part-time at a two-year or four-year or technical institution or university. Available to U.S. citizens.

Application Requirements: Application form, community service. *Deadline:* January 5.

Contact: Ms. Lindsay Merbaum, Director of Marketing and Outreach
Helen Diller Family Foundation
121 Steuart Street
San Francisco, CA 94105
Phone: 415-512-6438
E-mail: lindsaym@sfjcf.org

HENKEL CONSUMER ADHESIVES INC.

http://www.ducktapeclub.com/

DUCK BRAND DUCT TAPE "STUCK AT PROM" SCHOLARSHIP CONTEST

Contest is open to residents of the United States and Canada. Must be 14 years or older. The Grand Prize winners will each receive a $10000 scholarship, the second place students will each receive $5000, and third place winners will each receive $3000. The remaining seven "runner-up" couples will each receive a $1000 prize. Additionally, the Singles Category winner will receive a $1000 prize.

Award: Prize for use in freshman, sophomore, junior, or senior years; not renewable. *Number:* 1–11. *Amount:* $1000–$10,000.

Eligibility Requirements: Applicant must be high school student; planning to enroll or expecting to enroll full- or part-time at a two-year or four-year or technical institution or university and resident of Alabama, Alaska, Alberta, Arizona, Arkansas, British Columbia, California, Connecticut, Delaware, District of Columbia, Florida, Georgia, Guam, Hawaii, Idaho, Illinois, Indiana, Iowa, Kansas, Kentucky, Louisiana, Maine, Manitoba, Massachusetts, Michigan, Minnesota, Mississippi, Missouri, Montana, Nebraska, Nevada, New Brunswick, Newfoundland, New Hampshire, New Jersey, New Mexico, New York, North Carolina, North Dakota, Northwest Territories, Nova Scotia, Ohio, Oklahoma, Ontario, Oregon, Pennsylvania, Prince Edward Island, Puerto Rico, Rhode Island, Saskatchewan, South Carolina, South Dakota, Tennessee, Texas, Utah, Virginia, Washington, West Virginia, Wisconsin, Wyoming, Yukon. Available to U.S. and Canadian citizens.

Application Requirements: Application form, personal photograph. *Deadline:* May 31.

Contact: Consumer Relations, ShurTech Brands Consumer Relations Department
Henkel Consumer Adhesives Inc.
32150 Just Imagine Drive
Avon, OH 44011-1355
Phone: 800-321-1733

HERB KOHL EDUCATIONAL FOUNDATION INC.

http://www.kohleducation.org/

HERB KOHL EXCELLENCE SCHOLARSHIP PROGRAM

Scholarships of $5000 to Wisconsin high school graduates awarded annually in a competitive selection process. Applicants must be Wisconsin residents. Recipients are chosen for their demonstrated academic potential, outstanding leadership, citizenship, community service, integrity and other special talents.

Award: Scholarship for use in freshman, sophomore, junior, or senior years; not renewable. *Number:* 100. *Amount:* $5000.

Eligibility Requirements: Applicant must be high school student; planning to enroll or expecting to enroll full- or part-time at a two-year or four-year or technical institution or university and resident of Wisconsin. Available to U.S. and non-U.S. citizens.

Application Requirements: Application form, community service, essay. *Deadline:* November 4.

Contact: Ms. Kim Marggraf, Director
Phone: 920-457-1727
E-mail: marggraf@excel.net

HISPANIC ANNUAL SALUTE

http://www.hispanicannualsalute.org/

HISPANIC ANNUAL SALUTE SCHOLARSHIP

Scholarships of $2000 are awarded to graduating high school seniors. Program is intended to help foster a strong Hispanic presence within colleges and universities that will ultimately lead to active community leadership and volunteerism. Applicant must maintain a minimum GPA of 2.5.

Award: Scholarship for use in freshman year; not renewable. *Number:* 10. *Amount:* $2000.

Eligibility Requirements: Applicant must be Hispanic; high school student and planning to enroll or expecting to enroll full-time at a four-year institution or university. Applicant or parent of applicant must have employment or volunteer experience in community service. Applicant must have 2.5 GPA or higher. Available to U.S. citizens.

Application Requirements: Application form, essay, recommendations or references, test scores. *Deadline:* December 4.

Contact: Dan Sandos, President
Phone: 303-699-0715
Fax: 303-627-4205
E-mail: dcsandos@aol.com

HISPANIC METROPOLITAN CHAMBER SCHOLARSHIPS

http://www.hmccoregon.com/

HISPANIC METROPOLITAN CHAMBER SCHOLARSHIPS

Scholarships to encourage Hispanics to pursue higher education. Applicant must have a minimum 3.00 GPA. The award is available only to Hispanic students from Oregon and Southwest Washington.

Award: Scholarship for use in freshman, sophomore, junior, senior, graduate, or postgraduate years; not renewable. *Number:* 45–50. *Amount:* $2000–$8000.

Eligibility Requirements: Applicant must be of Hispanic heritage; enrolled or expecting to enroll full- or part-time at a two-year or four-year institution or university and resident of Oregon. Applicant must have 3.0 GPA or higher. Available to U.S. and non-Canadian citizens.

Application Requirements: Application form, community service, essay. *Deadline:* January 29.

Contact: MaryAnn Potter, Scholarship Director
Hispanic Metropolitan Chamber Scholarships
P.O. Box 1837
Portland, OR 97207
Phone: 503-222-0280
E-mail: scholarship@hmccoregon.com

HOSPITAL CENTRAL SERVICES INC.

http://www.giveapint.org/

HOSPITAL CENTRAL SERVICES STUDENT VOLUNTEER SCHOLARSHIP

Award to a graduating high school senior. Must have completed a minimum of 135 hours of volunteer service to the Blood Center in no less than a two calendar year period. Minimum 2.5 GPA required. Children of employees of Hospital Central Services or its affiliates are not eligible.

Award: Scholarship for use in freshman year; not renewable. *Number:* up to 2. *Amount:* $1000.

Eligibility Requirements: Applicant must be high school student and planning to enroll or expecting to enroll full- or part-time at a two-year or four-year institution or university. Applicant or parent of applicant must have employment or volunteer experience in community service. Applicant must have 2.5 GPA or higher. Available to U.S. citizens.

Application Requirements: Application form, recommendations or references, test scores, transcript. *Deadline:* March 31.

Contact: Sandra Thomas, Director of Development and Customer Service
Hospital Central Services Inc.
1465 Valley Center Parkway
Bethlehem, PA 18017
Phone: 610-691-5850 Ext. 292

HOSTESS COMMITTEE SCHOLARSHIPS/MISS AMERICA PAGEANT

http://www.missamerica.org/

MISS AMERICA COMMUNITY SERVICE SCHOLARSHIPS

Award to assist in the expansion of scholarship provision throughout the state and local programs. Each eligible state will receive a $1000 scholarship for a contestant demonstrating exemplary community service initiatives. Only opened to those contestants competing at the state level.

Award: Scholarship for use in freshman, sophomore, junior, senior, or graduate years; not renewable. *Amount:* $1000.

Eligibility Requirements: Applicant must be enrolled or expecting to enroll full- or part-time at a four-year institution or university; female and must have an interest in beauty pageant. Applicant or parent of applicant must have employment or volunteer experience in community service. Available to U.S. citizens.

Application Requirements: Application form. *Deadline:* varies.

Contact: Doreen Lindell Gordon, Controller and Scholarship Administrator
Phone: 609-345-7571 Ext. 27
Fax: 609-347-6079
E-mail: doreen@missamerica.org

HOUSTON COMMUNITY SERVICES

AZTECA SCHOLARSHIP

Scholarships are awarded annually to a male and a female high school senior planning to attend a university or a college as first-time, first-year students. Must be a Houston Area resident.

Award: Scholarship for use in freshman year; not renewable. *Number:* 2. *Amount:* $500.

Eligibility Requirements: Applicant must be of Hispanic heritage; high school student; planning to enroll or expecting to enroll full-time at a two-year or four-year institution or university and resident of Texas. Available to U.S. citizens.

Application Requirements: Application form, essay, personal photograph. *Deadline:* April 28.

Contact: Edward Castillo, Coordinator
Houston Community Services
5115 Harrisburg Boulevard
Houston, TX 77011
Phone: 713-926-8771
Fax: 713-926-8771
E-mail: hcsaztlan@sbcglobal.net

HOW TO WIN COLLEGE SCHOLARSHIPS

https://how2winscholarships.com

SAVOR SUMMER COLLEGE SCHOLARSHIP

This is a $500 scholarship award open to high school sophomores, juniors, and seniors in the 2016-2017 school year. There is no income limit for this scholarship opportunity. To read the full list of requirements and to download the application, please visit https://how2winscholarships.com.

Award: Scholarship for use in freshman year; not renewable. *Number:* 1. *Amount:* $500.

Eligibility Requirements: Applicant must be high school student and planning to enroll or expecting to enroll full-time at a two-year or four-year institution or university. Applicant must have 3.0 GPA or higher. Available to U.S. citizens.

Application Requirements: Application form, essay. *Deadline:* July 1.

Contact: Monica Matthews, Author, Site/Business Owner
How to Win College Scholarships
PO Box 94
Jeddo, MI 48032
Phone: 810-434-4390
E-mail: info@how2winscholarships.com

HUBSHOUT

http://hubshout.com/

HUBSHOUT INTERNET MARKETING SCHOLARSHIP

The HubShout Internet Marketing Scholarship is designed to help students who are on the path to any type of technical, business, or marketing career that will involve online marketing. Students who have completed at least one year of post-secondary education and have at least a 3.0 GPA are encouraged to apply. Graduate students are also welcome to apply. This is an ongoing scholarship and applications are reviewed twice per year.

Award: Scholarship for use in sophomore, junior, senior, graduate, or postgraduate years; not renewable. *Number:* 1. *Amount:* $1000.

Eligibility Requirements: Applicant must be enrolled or expecting to enroll full-time at a two-year or four-year or technical institution or university. Applicant must have 3.0 GPA or higher. Available to U.S. citizens.

Application Requirements: Application form. *Deadline:* continuous.

Contact: Nick Wiese, Marketing Analyst
HubShout
200 Little Falls Street
Suite 207
Falls Church, VA 22046
Phone: 571-766-0450
E-mail: nickw@hubshout.com

HUMANA FOUNDATION

http://www.humanafoundation.org/

HUMANA FOUNDATION SCHOLARSHIP PROGRAM

Applicants must be under 25 years of age and a United States citizen. Must be a dependent of a Humana Inc. employee. For more information, visit website http://www.humanafoundation.org.

Award: Scholarship for use in freshman, sophomore, junior, or senior years; renewable. *Number:* 74–75. *Amount:* $1500–$3000.

Eligibility Requirements: Applicant must be enrolled or expecting to enroll full-time at a two-year or four-year institution or university. Available to U.S. citizens.

Application Requirements: Application form, financial need analysis. *Deadline:* April 17.

Contact: Charles Jackson, Consultant
Humana Foundation
500 West Main Street, Room 208
Louisville, KY 40202
Phone: 502-580-1245
E-mail: cjackson@humana.com

IDAHO STATE BOARD OF EDUCATION

http://www.boardofed.idaho.gov/

IDAHO GOVERNOR'S CUP SCHOLARSHIP

Idaho Governor's Cup is a renewable scholarship available to Idaho residents enrolled full-time in an undergraduate academic or vocational-technical program at an eligible Idaho public or private college or university. A minimum GPA of 2.8 is required. Applicants must demonstrate commitment to public service and be able to document service. Applicants must be a high school seniors and U.S. citizens.

Award: Scholarship for use in freshman year; renewable. *Number:* 20–40. *Amount:* $3000.

Eligibility Requirements: Applicant must be high school student; planning to enroll or expecting to enroll full-time at a two-year or four-year institution or university; resident of Idaho and studying in Idaho. Applicant or parent of applicant must have employment or volunteer experience in community service. Available to U.S. citizens.

Application Requirements: Application form, community service, essay, portfolio. *Deadline:* February 15.

Contact: Sarah Fuhriman
E-mail: sarah@idahogovernorscup.org

INSTITUTE FOR JUSTICE

http://www.ij.org

LIBERTY IN ACTION ESSAY CONTEST: REMOVING BARRIERS TO ENTREPRENEURSHIP

The Institute for Justice, a nonprofit, civil liberties law firm is are offering high school students in Florida a chance to win a $500 scholarship and the opportunity to help pass a law and increase economic opportunity in their state. The winning student will receive an all-expense-paid trip to the Florida state Capitol in Tallahassee to meet with lawmakers. Interested students should submit an 800-word persuasive essay naming an occupational license in their state that should be repealed. The deadline is May 1, 2016. All details, resources, information on occupational licensing and economic liberty, and submission options can be found on our website at http://ij.org/activism/activism-projects/florida-essay-contest/

Award: Prize for use in freshman year; not renewable. *Number:* 1. *Amount:* $500.

Eligibility Requirements: Applicant must be high school student; age 13-19; planning to enroll or expecting to enroll full- or part-time at a two-year or four-year or technical institution or university and resident of Florida. Available to U.S. and non-U.S. citizens.

Application Requirements: Application form, essay. *Deadline:* May 1.

Contact: Mr. Garrett Atherton, Outreach Coordinator
Institute for Justice
999 Brickell Avenue
Suite # 720
Miami, FL 33131
Phone: 305-721-1600
E-mail: gatherton@ij.org

INTERNATIONAL ASSOCIATION OF FIRE FIGHTERS

http://www.iaff.org/

W. H. "HOWIE" MCCLENNAN SCHOLARSHIP

Sons, daughters, or legally adopted children of IAFF members killed in the line of duty who are planning to attend an institution of higher learning can apply. Award of $2500 for each year. Renewable up to four years. Applicant must have a GPA of 2.0.

Award: Scholarship for use in freshman year; renewable. *Number:* 20–25. *Amount:* $2500.

Eligibility Requirements: Applicant must be enrolled or expecting to enroll full- or part-time at a two-year or four-year or technical institution. Applicant or parent of applicant must have employment or volunteer experience in police/firefighting. Available to U.S. citizens.

Application Requirements: Application form, essay, financial need analysis, recommendations or references, transcript. *Deadline:* February 1.

Contact: L. Harrington, International Association of Fire Fighters
International Association of Fire Fighters
1750 New York Avenue, NW
Education Department, 3rd Floor
Washington, DC 20006-5395
Phone: 202-737-8484
Fax: 202-737-8418

INTERNATIONAL BOWLING CAMPUS YOUTH DEVELOPMENT

http://www.bowl.com/

USBC ANNUAL ZEB SCHOLARSHIP

Scholarship is awarded to a USBC Youth member who achieves academic success and gives back to his/her community through service. Candidates must have a current GPA of 3.0 or better.

Award: Scholarship for use in junior or senior years; not renewable. *Number:* 1. *Amount:* $2500.

Eligibility Requirements: Applicant must be high school student; planning to enroll or expecting to enroll full- or part-time at a four-year institution or university and must have an interest in bowling. Applicant or parent of applicant must have employment or volunteer experience in community service. Applicant must have 3.0 GPA or higher. Available to U.S. citizens.

Application Requirements: Application form, recommendations or references, transcript. *Deadline:* December 1.

Contact: Roger Noordhoek, Senior Director Youth Marketing
International Bowling Campus Youth Development
621 Six Flags Dr.
Arlington, TX 76011
Phone: 800-514-2695 Ext. 8308
E-mail: contactus@ibcyouth.com

INTERNATIONAL COLLEGE COUNSELORS

www.internationalcollegecounselors.com

INTERNATIONAL COLLEGE COUNSELORS SCHOLARSHIP

International College Counselors is giving away two (2) $250 scholarships. High school freshmen, sophomores or juniors must write an essay that addresses the following topic: You have been invited to talk to the future U.S. Secretary of Education. What would you say? Essays must not exceed 500 words. Two winning essays will be selected: one (1) from a student in Miami Dade County, Broward County, or Palm Beach County; and one (1) at large winner from anywhere in the world, domestic or international, including home schooled students. Each winner will receive a $250 check. The goal of the International College Counselors Scholarship is to increase awareness of the value of higher education among students.

Award: Scholarship for use in freshman year; not renewable. *Number:* 2. *Amount:* $250.

Eligibility Requirements: Applicant must be high school student and planning to enroll or expecting to enroll full-time at a two-year or four-year or technical institution or university. Available to U.S. and non-U.S. citizens.

Application Requirements: Application form, essay. *Deadline:* March 1.

Contact: Cheree Liebowitz, Director of Marketing
International College Counselors
3107 Stirling Road
Suite 208
Ft. Lauderdale, FL 33312
E-mail: info@internationalcollegecounselors.com

INTERNATIONAL DAIRY DELI BAKERY ASSOCIATION

http://www.iddba.org

INTERNATIONAL DAIRY DELI BAKERY ASSOCIATION'S SCHOLARSHIP FOR GROWING THE FUTURE

Applicants must work for a member of IDDBA at least 13 hours per week while attending classes. Applicants are eligible for two awards per year.

Award: Scholarship for use in freshman, sophomore, junior, senior, or graduate years; not renewable. *Number:* 100–200. *Amount:* $500–$2000.

Eligibility Requirements: Applicant must be enrolled or expecting to enroll full- or part-time at a two-year or four-year or technical institution or university. Applicant or parent of applicant must have employment or volunteer experience in agriculture, food service. Applicant must have 2.5 GPA or higher. Available to U.S. and non-U.S. citizens.

Application Requirements: Application form. *Deadline:* continuous.

Contact: Mr. Jonathan Whalley, Education Coordinator
International Dairy Deli Bakery Association
636 Science Dr.
Madison, WI 53711
Phone: 608-310-5000
E-mail: scholarships@iddba.org

INTERNATIONAL FLIGHT SERVICES ASSOCIATION

http://www.ifsanet.com

AMI SCHOLARSHIP AWARD

Individuals are selected based on scholastic merit and dedication to an advanced education. Priority is given to those with an onboard hospitality focus, or relationship with member company.

Award: Scholarship for use in freshman, sophomore, junior, senior, graduate, or postgraduate years; not renewable. *Number:* 1. *Amount:* $4500.

Eligibility Requirements: Applicant must be enrolled or expecting to enroll full- or part-time at an institution or university. Applicant must have 3.0 GPA or higher. Available to U.S. and non-U.S. citizens.

Application Requirements: Application form, essay, financial need analysis. *Deadline:* April 30.

Contact: Ms. Kelly McLendon, Programs Manager
International Flight Services Association
1100 Johnson Ferry Road
Suite 300
Atlanta, GA 30342
Phone: 678-303-3042
E-mail: kmclendon@kellencompany.com

DHL AIRLINE BUSINESS SOLUTIONS SCHOLARSHIP AWARD

Individuals are selected to receive the award based on scholastic merit and dedication to an advanced education. Must be an employee of a current IFSA member company in good standing, or a relative of an

employee of a current IFSA member company. Please address financial need within essay.

Award: Scholarship for use in freshman, sophomore, junior, or senior years; not renewable. *Number:* 1. *Amount:* $2250.

Eligibility Requirements: Applicant must be enrolled or expecting to enroll full- or part-time at an institution or university. Applicant or parent of applicant must have employment or volunteer experience in hospitality/hotel administration/operations. Applicant must have 3.0 GPA or higher. Available to U.S. and non-U.S. citizens.

Application Requirements: Application form, essay, recommendations or references, transcript. *Deadline:* May 14.

Contact: Ms. Kelly McLendon, Programs Manager
International Flight Services Association
1100 Johnson Ferry Road, NE
Suite 300
Atlanta, GA 30342
Phone: 678-303-3042
E-mail: kmclendon@kellencompany.com

FLYING FOOD GROUP SCHOLARSHIP AWARD

Individuals are selected to receive the award based on scholastic merit and dedication to an advanced education. Must be an employee of a current IFSA member company in good standing, or a relative of an employee of a current IFSA member company.

Award: Scholarship for use in freshman, sophomore, junior, or senior years; not renewable. *Number:* 1. *Amount:* $2250.

Eligibility Requirements: Applicant must be enrolled or expecting to enroll full- or part-time at an institution or university. Applicant or parent of applicant must have employment or volunteer experience in hospitality/hotel administration/operations. Applicant must have 3.0 GPA or higher. Available to U.S. and non-U.S. citizens.

Application Requirements: Application form, essay, recommendations or references, transcript. *Deadline:* May 14.

Contact: Ms. Kelly McLendon, Programs Manager
International Flight Services Association
1100 Johnson Ferry Road, NE
Suite 300
Atlanta, GA 30342
Phone: 678-303-3042
E-mail: kmclendon@kellencompany.com

IFSA MEMBER FAMILY SCHOLARSHIP AWARD

Individuals are selected based upon scholastic merit and dedication to pursuing an advanced degree. Must be an employee of a current IFSA member company in good standing, or a relative of an employee of a current IFSA member company.

Award: Scholarship for use in freshman, sophomore, junior, or senior years; not renewable. *Number:* 2. *Amount:* $2250.

Eligibility Requirements: Applicant must be enrolled or expecting to enroll full- or part-time at an institution or university. Applicant or parent of applicant must have employment or volunteer experience in hospitality/hotel administration/operations. Applicant must have 3.0 GPA or higher. Available to U.S. and non-U.S. citizens.

Application Requirements: Application form, essay, recommendations or references, transcript. *Deadline:* May 14.

Contact: Ms. Kelly McLendon, Programs Manager
International Flight Services Association
1100 Johnson Ferry Road, NE
Suite 300
Atlanta, GA 30342
Phone: 678-303-3042
E-mail: kmclendon@kellencompany.com

JOHN & GINNIE LONG SCHOLARSHIP AWARD

Individuals are selected to receive the award based on scholastic merit and dedication to an advanced education. Must be an employee of a current IFSA member company in good standing, or a relative of an employee of a current IFSA member company.

Award: Scholarship for use in freshman, sophomore, junior, or senior years; not renewable. *Number:* 1. *Amount:* $2250.

Eligibility Requirements: Applicant must be enrolled or expecting to enroll full- or part-time at an institution or university. Applicant or parent of applicant must have employment or volunteer experience in hospitality/hotel administration/operations. Applicant must have 3.0 GPA or higher. Available to U.S. and non-U.S. citizens.

Application Requirements: Application form, essay, recommendations or references, transcript. *Deadline:* May 14.

Contact: Ms. Kelly McLendon, Programs Manager
International Flight Services Association
1100 Johnson Ferry Road, NE
Suite 300
Atlanta, GA 30342
Phone: 678-303-3042
E-mail: kmclendon@kellencompany.com

JOHN LOUIS FOUNDATION SCHOLARSHIP AWARD

Individuals are selected to receive the award based on scholastic merit and dedication to an advanced education. Must be an employee of a current IFSA member company in good standing, or a relative of an employee of a current IFSA member company. Please address financial need within essay.

Award: Scholarship for use in freshman, sophomore, junior, or senior years; not renewable. *Number:* 1. *Amount:* $5000.

Eligibility Requirements: Applicant must be enrolled or expecting to enroll full- or part-time at an institution or university. Applicant or parent of applicant must have employment or volunteer experience in hospitality/hotel administration/operations. Applicant must have 3.0 GPA or higher. Available to U.S. and non-U.S. citizens.

Application Requirements: Application form, essay, recommendations or references, transcript. *Deadline:* May 14.

Contact: Ms. Kelly McLendon, Programs Manager
International Flight Services Association
1100 Johnson Ferry Road, NE
Suite 300
Atlanta, GA 30342
Phone: 678-303-3042
E-mail: kmclendon@kellencompany.com

KING NUT COMPANIES SCHOLARSHIP AWARD

Individuals are selected to receive the award based on scholastic merit and dedication to an advanced education. Must be an employee of a current IFSA member company in good standing, or a relative of an employee of a current IFSA member company. Please address financial need within essay.

Award: Scholarship for use in freshman, sophomore, junior, or senior years; not renewable. *Number:* 1. *Amount:* $2250.

Eligibility Requirements: Applicant must be enrolled or expecting to enroll full- or part-time at an institution or university. Applicant or parent of applicant must have employment or volunteer experience in hospitality/hotel administration/operations. Applicant must have 3.0 GPA or higher. Available to U.S. and non-U.S. citizens.

Application Requirements: Application form, essay, recommendations or references, transcript. *Deadline:* May 14.

Contact: Ms. Kelly McLendon, Programs Manager
International Flight Services Association
1100 Johnson Ferry Road, NE
Suite 300
Atlanta, GA 30342
Phone: 678-303-3042
E-mail: kmclendon@kellencompany.com

OAKFIELD FARMS SOLUTIONS SCHOLARSHIP AWARD

Individuals are selected to receive the award based on scholastic merit and dedication to pursuing a career in onboard services operations. Must be an employee of a current IFSA member company in good standing, or a relative of an employee of a current IFSA member company.

Award: Scholarship for use in freshman, sophomore, junior, or senior years; not renewable. *Number:* 1. *Amount:* $5000.

Eligibility Requirements: Applicant must be enrolled or expecting to enroll full- or part-time at an institution or university. Applicant or parent of applicant must have employment or volunteer experience in hospitality/hotel administration/operations. Applicant must have 3.0 GPA or higher. Available to U.S. and non-U.S. citizens.

Application Requirements: Application form, essay, recommendations or references, transcript. *Deadline:* May 14.

Contact: Ms. Kelly McLendon, Programs Manager
International Flight Services Association
1100 Johnson Ferry Road, NE
Suite 300
Atlanta, GA 30342
Phone: 678-303-3042
E-mail: kmclendon@kellencompany.com

WESSCO INTERNATIONAL SCHOLARSHIP AWARD

Individuals are selected to receive the award based on scholastic merit and dedication to an advanced education. Must be an employee of a current IFSA member company in good standing, or a relative of an employee of a current IFSA member company. Please address financial need within essay.

Award: Scholarship for use in freshman, sophomore, junior, or senior years; not renewable. *Number:* 1. *Amount:* $5000.

Eligibility Requirements: Applicant must be enrolled or expecting to enroll full- or part-time at an institution or university. Applicant or parent of applicant must have employment or volunteer experience in hospitality/hotel administration/operations. Applicant must have 3.0 GPA or higher. Available to U.S. and non-U.S. citizens.

Application Requirements: Application form, essay, recommendations or references, transcript. *Deadline:* May 14.

Contact: Ms. Kelly McLendon, Programs Manager
International Flight Services Association
1100 Johnson Ferry Road, NE
Suite 300
Atlanta, GA 30342
Phone: 678-303-3042
E-mail: kmclendon@kellencompany.com

INTERNATIONAL VOLUNTEER HQ

https://www.volunteerhq.org/

VOLUNTEER OF THE YEAR SCHOLARSHIP

We make safe, quality and responsible international volunteer travel genuinely affordable. Our volunteers provide assistance to the achievement of long term community goals in countries all over the world. Our programs grow cross-cultural awareness and understanding, and foster global citizenship. We provide cultural immersion experiences, achieved by living and working with local people, communities, organizations and families. International Volunteer HQ provides affordable volunteer programs by partnering with organizations based in each of our program countries. We believe this is the best approach to international volunteering because local organizations are in the best position to see where volunteers are genuinely needed. The staff in these organizations are locals, they have been raised in the area and know it inside and out. They can speak the local language, they know the local people and are in the best position to provide guidance, advice, supervision and support to volunteers. Partnering with local organizations reduces the costs associated with hosting volunteers, making programs more affordable. This means more people are enabled to volunteer and that enables greater social outcomes to be achieved. One of the major strengths of IVHQ is our careful selection process in choosing our partner organizations and the high quality volunteer programs that we offer through these partners. Every program that IVHQ offers has been personally inspected by IVHQ. We have experienced the programs first-hand, we have assessed the local teams and we have provided comprehensive IVHQ training to all of our local teams.

Award: Scholarship for use in freshman, sophomore, junior, senior, graduate, or postgraduate years; not renewable. *Number:* 1. *Amount:* $2500.

Eligibility Requirements: Applicant must be age 18-80 and enrolled or expecting to enroll full- or part-time at a two-year or four-year or technical institution or university. Available to U.S. and non-U.S. citizens.

Application Requirements: Application form, personal photograph. *Deadline:* November 27.

Contact: Taylor Haskell
E-mail: taylor@volunteerhq.org

IOWA STUDENT LOAN

http://www.IowaStudentLoan.org/

IOWA FINANCIAL KNOW-HOW CHALLENGE: SENIOR SCHOLARSHIP

Thirty $2,000 scholarships for Iowa high school seniors who plan to attend college in fall 2017. To qualify, students must register by February 17, 2017, complete two online financial literacy tutorials and complete a related financial literacy assessment test. Go to www.IowaStudentLoan.org/SeniorScholarship to register and see details.

Award: Scholarship for use in freshman year; not renewable. *Number:* 30. *Amount:* $2000.

Eligibility Requirements: Applicant must be high school student; planning to enroll or expecting to enroll full- or part-time at a two-year or four-year or technical institution or university and resident of Iowa. Available to U.S. citizens.

Application Requirements: Application form. *Deadline:* February 17.

Contact: Julie Cahalan, Communications Specialist
Iowa Student Loan
6775 Vista Drive
West Des Moines, IA 50266
Phone: 800-243-7552 Ext. 7226
E-mail: scholarship@studentloan.org

JACKIE ROBINSON FOUNDATION

http://www.jackierobinson.org/

JACKIE ROBINSON SCHOLARSHIP

Scholarship for graduating high school seniors accepted to accredited four-year colleges or universities. Must be a minority student, United States citizen, involved in community service and demonstrate leadership potential and financial need. See website for additional details.

Award: Scholarship for use in freshman, sophomore, junior, or senior years; renewable. *Number:* 40–60. *Amount:* $6000–$6000.

Eligibility Requirements: Applicant must be American Indian/Alaska Native, Asian/Pacific Islander, Black (non-Hispanic), Hispanic; high school student; age 18-22; planning to enroll or expecting to enroll full-time at a four-year institution or university and must have an interest in leadership. Applicant or parent of applicant must have employment or volunteer experience in community service. Applicant must have 3.0 GPA or higher. Available to U.S. citizens.

Application Requirements: Application form, application form may be submitted online (http://jackierobinson.org), community service, essay, financial need analysis, recommendations or references, test scores, transcript. *Deadline:* February 15.

Contact: Mr. John Shaw, Scholarship Application
Jackie Robinson Foundation
75 Varick Street, 2nd Floor
New York, NY 10013
Phone: 212-290-8600
Fax: 212-290-8081
E-mail: scholarships@jackierobinson.org

JASON KALAFAT ATTORNEY AT LAW

https://criminallawyerwashingtondc.com/

JASON KALAFAT MAKE A DIFFERENCE SCHOLARSHIP

Applicants must submit an approximate 750-word essay responding to the following prompt: 1) How will your dreams make a meaningful impact on the world? 2) How will you take the practical steps to achieve these dreams? This scholarship is offered to any student currently enrolled in an accredited community college, undergraduate, or graduate program. This includes incoming first-year college students who are high school graduates or possess a GED. Candidates must have an interest in social justice, as demonstrated by past and present volunteer, professional, and educational experiences. Eligible candidates must be in good academic standing with a minimum cumulative GPA of 3.0 or higher. For more information please visit our scholarship page at http://criminallawyerwashingtondc.com/#scholarship

Award: Scholarship for use in freshman, sophomore, junior, senior, graduate, or postgraduate years; not renewable. *Number:* 1. *Amount:* $500.

Eligibility Requirements: Applicant must be enrolled or expecting to enroll full- or part-time at a two-year or four-year or technical institution or university. Applicant must have 3.0 GPA or higher. Available to U.S. and non-U.S. citizens.

Application Requirements: Application form, essay. *Deadline:* March 31.

Contact: Jason Kalafat
E-mail: scholarship@criminallawyerwashingtondc.com

JOHN B. FABRIELE, III, LLC

https://www.fabrielelaw.com/

FABRIELE DISABILITY AWARENESS SCHOLARSHIP

Applicants must have a minimum cumulative GPA of 3.3 or higher. Applicants must be enrolled in an institution of higher education in the Fall Semester of 2017. If the applicant is still awaiting admission or deciding on a school when submitting the application, that is fine. However, before granting the scholarship we will need to ensure that the applicant is enrolled for the fall of 2017. Applicants must submit a 500-word statement in response to the following the prompt. Mail your application to 214 Route 18, #2A, East Brunswick, NJ 08816. Address your letter to The Fabriele Disability Awareness Scholarship. Please visit the site for complete information.

Award: Scholarship for use in freshman, sophomore, junior, senior, graduate, or postgraduate years; not renewable. *Number:* 1. *Amount:* $1000.

Eligibility Requirements: Applicant must be enrolled or expecting to enroll full- or part-time at a two-year or four-year or technical institution or university. Applicant must have 3.0 GPA or higher. Available to U.S. and non-U.S. citizens.

Application Requirements: Application form, essay. *Deadline:* May 31.

Contact: John Fabriele
John B. Fabriele, III, LLC
214 Route 18 Ste. 2A
East Brunswick, NJ 08816

JUREWITZ LAW GROUP

http://www.jurewitz.com/

JUREWITZ LAW GROUP SCHOLARSHIP

The 2016 Jurewitz Law Group Scholarship is our small way of thanking an exceptional high school senior for the great work they have done in improving their local community and in their education. We at Jurewitz Law Group are aware of the high costs associated with post-secondary education, which is why we are very proud to offer this scholarship to a deserving student. This scholarship opportunity is open to graduating, or recently graduated, high school seniors across the United States who will be entering college this coming academic year. Applicants must have graduated, or be on track to graduate, from high school in the 2015-2016 school year, have at least a 3.0 GPA, and all applicants must be current U.S. Citizens or Permanent Residents.

Award: Scholarship for use in freshman year; not renewable. *Number:* 1. *Amount:* $500.

Eligibility Requirements: Applicant must be high school student and planning to enroll or expecting to enroll full- or part-time at a two-year or four-year institution or university. Applicant must have 3.0 GPA or higher. Available to U.S. citizens.

Application Requirements: Application form, essay. *Deadline:* August 24.

Contact: Ms. Ruthie Sanchez, Marketing Coordinator
Jurewitz Law Group
600 B Street
Suite 1550
San Diego, CA 92101
Phone: 619-452-0716
Fax: 888-233-3180
E-mail: info@jurewitz.com

KAUFMAN & STIGGER, PLLC

http://www.getthetiger.com/

THE ALBERTA C. KAUFMAN SCHOLARSHIP

In order to honor his late mother, Attorney Marshall Kaufman of Kentucky's Kaufman & Stigger, PLLC wished to offer a scholarship to graduating high school seniors and current college students. Alberta C. Kaufman encouraged her son to further his education and to eventually attend law school. It is in that spirit of support that we are sponsoring The Alberta C. Kaufman Scholarship.

Award: Scholarship for use in freshman, sophomore, junior, or senior years; not renewable. *Number:* 1. *Amount:* $500.

Eligibility Requirements: Applicant must be enrolled or expecting to enroll full- or part-time at a two-year or four-year institution or university and resident of Kentucky. Applicant must have 3.0 GPA or higher. Available to U.S. citizens.

Application Requirements: Application form, essay. *Deadline:* May 9.

Contact: Linda Brumleve
Kaufman & Stigger, PLLC
7513 New La Grange Road
Louisville, KY 40222
Phone: 502-458-5555
Fax: 502-458-9101
E-mail: lbrumleve@kstrial.com

KELLER LAW OFFICES

http://www.kellerlawoffices.com/

KELLER LAW OFFICES SCHOLARSHIP FOR HIGHER EDUCATION

The goal of this scholarship is to provide financial assistance to a worthy student. We understand that there are a lot of outstanding young people who, without financial assistance would not be able to go to college. Medical, social or financial obstacles can make higher education a mere dream to some students. To help open the door to the world of higher education Keller Law Offices will be providing an annual $2000 scholarship to an exceptional student enrolled for the fall of 2017. The scholarship committee will base the judging criteria on financial need along with the quality of a written essay. To win this scholarship, all applicants must submit an essay between 500 and 1000 words in length on the following topic—A 19-year-old is convicted of statutory rape with a 15-year-old. Should the 19-year-old be required to register as a sex offender? The quality of the applicants essay and the accuracy with which they followed the instructions included here will be a significant part of the committee's decision-making process. The winners essay submission may be published on KellerLawOffices.com. All applications must be filled out and materials received by June 1st, 2017. Applications submitted via any other channel will not be considered. Applications submitted after this date will not be considered. The decision of the committee is final. The winner will be notified by email or phone by August of 2017. Scholarship funds will be disbursed to the college or university in September of 2017. Our scholarship recipient will also be asked to submit a current photo to be published in an announcement to recognize this year's winner on our website.

Award: Scholarship for use in freshman, sophomore, junior, senior, or graduate years; not renewable. *Number:* 1. *Amount:* $2000.

Eligibility Requirements: Applicant must be enrolled or expecting to enroll full-time at a two-year or four-year institution or university. Available to U.S. citizens.

Application Requirements: Application form, essay, financial need analysis. *Deadline:* June 1.

Contact: Mr. Max Keller, Founding Attorney
Keller Law Offices
310 S 4th Ave #1130
Minneapolis, MN 55415
Phone: 952-913-1421
E-mail: max@kellerlawoffices.com

KELLY & SOTO LAW

http://www.1800lawguys.com

KELLY & SOTO LAW SCHOLARSHIP PROGRAM

The Kelly & Soto Law Scholarship Program is designed to help high school seniors and college students who are attending an institution of higher learning. With combined scholarship grants worth $1,500, we are enthusiastic to provide students a chance to further their education as we recognize its value as a vital foundation for the creation and fulfillment of advantageous careers. All applications will be reviewed by the firm internally and we look forward to reviewing your application, and wish you success in all your future endeavors.

Award: Scholarship for use in freshman, sophomore, junior, or senior years; not renewable. *Number:* 3. *Amount:* $200–$1000.

Eligibility Requirements: Applicant must be enrolled or expecting to enroll full-time at a two-year or four-year institution. Available to U.S. and non-U.S. citizens.

Application Requirements: Essay, personal photograph. *Deadline:* April 15.

Contact: Scholarship Coordinator
Kelly & Soto Law
220 Commercial Street
Boston, MA 02109
Phone: 617-807-0855
E-mail: essay@1800lawguys.com

KELLY LAW TEAM

http://www.jkphoenixpersonalinjuryattorney.com/

DOWN SYNDROME SCHOLARSHIP

The Kelly Law Team takes pleasure in announcing two annual $1,000 scholarships for individuals with Down syndrome. The scholarships are to pursue secondary or post-secondary educational opportunities. The scholarships are open to United States citizens with Down syndrome. Two scholarships, $1,000 each, are being offered annually. They will consist of tuition payment for attendance at a college, trade school, community college, or secondary school. You do not have to be a student at the time you apply in order to qualify for the award. The scholarship money must be used within a year after the award date, and an invoice for tuition must be furnished to the Kelly Law Team within that time period. Upon receipt of the invoice, the Kelly Law Team will issue its check for $1,000 to the educational institution.

Award: Scholarship for use in freshman, sophomore, junior, senior, graduate, or postgraduate years; not renewable. *Number:* 2. *Amount:* $1000.

Eligibility Requirements: Applicant must be learning disabled and enrolled or expecting to enroll full- or part-time at a two-year or four-year or technical institution or university. Applicant must be learning disabled. Available to U.S. citizens.

Application Requirements: Application form, essay. *Deadline:* November 7.

Contact: John Kelly
Phone: 602-283-4122
E-mail: michael@jkphoenixpersonalinjuryattorney.com

KIDGUARD

http://www.kidguard.com/

KIDGUARD FOR EDUCATION ESSAY SCHOLARSHIP

Do you think parents should monitor their children's phones and online activities? We want to hear your honest opinion. The personal opinion expressed in your essay will in no way affect whether or not you are awarded the scholarship. We respect that everyone has their own opinions on the topic and want to hear what you have to say. We want to stress that word count is not a deciding factor in this contest. However, this is a writing contest and you are expected to express your well-thought-out ideas clearly, supported with research and evidence.

Award: Scholarship for use in freshman, sophomore, junior, senior, graduate, or postgraduate years; not renewable. *Number:* 1–2. *Amount:* $500–$1500.

Eligibility Requirements: Applicant must be enrolled or expecting to enroll full-time at a two-year or four-year or technical institution or university. Available to U.S. and non-U.S. citizens.

Application Requirements: Essay. *Deadline:* March 31.

Contact: Jessica Chang
KidGuard
117 W. 9th Street, Suite 1009
Los Angeles, CA 90015
E-mail: jessica@kidguard.com

KIDGUARD FOR EDUCATION ESSAY SCHOLARSHIP FOR HIGH SCHOOL

Statistics show that 42% of teenagers with tech access have been cyberbullied over the past year and that 1 in 4 have been bullied more than once. We believe that you as high school students can give us invaluable feedback. We want to hear your honest opinion. The personal opinion expressed in your essay will in no way affect whether or not you are awarded the scholarship. We respect that everyone has their own opinions on the topic and want to hear what you have to say. There are two parts in the application: essay contest and survey questions (optional.) Please visit our site for more information.

Award: Scholarship for use in freshman, sophomore, junior, or senior years; not renewable. *Number:* 1–3. *Amount:* $500–$1000.

Eligibility Requirements: Applicant must be high school student and planning to enroll or expecting to enroll full-time at a two-year or four-year institution or university. Available to U.S. and non-U.S. citizens.

Application Requirements: Essay. *Deadline:* March 31.

Contact: Jessica Chang
KidGuard
117 West 9th Street, Suite 1009
Los Angeles, CA 90015
E-mail: jessica@kidguard.com

KITCHEN GUIDES
http://www.kitchensguides.com/

SMART KITCHEN IMPROVEMENT SCHOLARSHIP BY KITCHEN GUIDES

Under this scholarship, applicants have to write 1000 words article on the cooking related niche. Topics will provide by us, so you just need to pick one from them and start writing on it and submit it on our website

Award: Scholarship for use in freshman, sophomore, junior, senior, graduate, or postgraduate years; not renewable. *Number:* 1. *Amount:* $500.

Eligibility Requirements: Applicant must be hearing impaired, learning disabled, physically disabled, or visually impaired; American Indian/Alaska Native, Asian/Pacific Islander, Black (non-Hispanic), Hispanic; high school student; age 15-40 and planning to enroll or expecting to enroll full- or part-time at a two-year or four-year or technical institution or university. Applicant must be hearing impaired, learning disabled, physically disabled, or visually impaired. Available to U.S. and non-U.S. citizens. Applicant must have general military experience.

Application Requirements: Application form. *Deadline:* October 15.

Contact: Kitchen Guides. Steven Burton, Kitchen Guides
Kitchen Guides
3548 Wyatt Street
Boca Raton, FL 33432
Phone: 651-3938087
E-mail: info@kitchensguides.com

LARSON JEWELERS
www.larsonjewelers.com

BAND WITH SUCCESS SCHOLARSHIP

Larson Jewelers created the Band With Success Scholarship to band together with both men and women who want to further their education and strive for a successful future. We are proud to offer scholarships to any students, age 16 and older, attending high school or enrolled in undergraduate, graduate and vocational programs in the US. Larson

Jewelers understands the financial difficulties of higher education and would like to help. The application consists of three short essay questions involving career goals and extra-curricular activities and the winner will be announced on our website. The deadline to apply for Fall 2016 is October 25th, 2016. The deadline to apply for Spring 2017 is April 15th, 2017.

Award: Scholarship for use in freshman, sophomore, junior, senior, or graduate years; not renewable. *Number:* 1–2. *Amount:* $1000.

Eligibility Requirements: Applicant must be enrolled or expecting to enroll full-time at a two-year or four-year or technical institution or university. Available to U.S. citizens.

Application Requirements: Application form, essay. *Deadline:* April 15.

Contact: Scholarship Coordinator
E-mail: service@larsonjewelers.com

LATIN AMERICAN EDUCATIONAL FOUNDATION
http://www.laef.org/

LATIN AMERICAN EDUCATIONAL FOUNDATION SCHOLARSHIPS

Scholarship for Colorado residents of Hispanic heritage. Applicant should be accepted in an accredited college, university or vocational school. Must maintain a minimum GPA of 3.0.

Award: Scholarship for use in freshman, sophomore, junior, senior, or graduate years; renewable. *Number:* 100–120. *Amount:* $500–$2000.

Eligibility Requirements: Applicant must be of Hispanic heritage; enrolled or expecting to enroll full- or part-time at a two-year or four-year institution or university and resident of Colorado. Applicant must have 3.0 GPA or higher. Available to U.S. citizens.

Application Requirements: Application form, community service, essay, financial need analysis, interview, personal photograph. *Deadline:* February 15.

Contact: Karley Arguello, Scholarship Selection Committee
Latin American Educational Foundation
561 Santa Fe Drive
Denver, CO 80204
Phone: 303-446-0541 Ext. 10
E-mail: karguello@laef.org

LAW OFFICE OF DAVID D. WHITE, PLLC
http://www.wm-attorneys.com/

ANNUAL TRAUMATIC BRAIN INJURY SCHOLARSHIPS

The Law Office of David D. White takes pleasure in announcing the establishment of an annual scholarship program for the benefit of persons who have suffered traumatic brain injury (TBI). The scholarship program consists of two scholarships, offered annually,* both in the amount of $1,000. The scholarships will take the form of tuition payments for attendance at a school of the applicant's choosing. This may be a university, a college (or a community college), a secondary school, or a trade school. And you do not have to be enrolled as a student currently in order to apply. In order to be eligible to apply for a scholarship, you must have been diagnosed with TBI. We may ask you to provide us with proof of the diagnosis. The winners will have a year in which to provide an invoice for tuition from their school, and we will then pay $1,000 to the school toward the cost reflected in the invoice.

Award: Scholarship for use in freshman, sophomore, junior, senior, graduate, or postgraduate years; not renewable. *Number:* 2. *Amount:* $1000.

Eligibility Requirements: Applicant must be learning disabled and enrolled or expecting to enroll full- or part-time at a two-year or four-year or technical institution or university. Applicant must be learning disabled. Available to U.S. citizens.

Application Requirements: Application form, essay. *Deadline:* November 3.

Contact: David White
E-mail: michael@wm-attorneys.com

LAW OFFICE OF MATTHEW L. SHARP

https://mattsharplaw.com/

LAW OFFICE OF MATTHEW L. SHARP NEED-BASED SCHOLARSHIP

This scholarship is open to any US citizen or permanent US resident who will be enrolled full--time in an accredited community college, college or university, or accredited law school in the fall of 2017. This scholarship will be awarded to the student who demonstrates financial need and who submits the strongest PSA video focusing on the following topic: "Do you think an injured party should be entitled to a trial by jury?"

Award: Scholarship for use in freshman, sophomore, junior, or senior years; not renewable. *Number:* 1. *Amount:* $2000.

Eligibility Requirements: Applicant must be enrolled or expecting to enroll full-time at a two-year or four-year institution or university. Available to U.S. citizens.

Application Requirements: Financial need analysis. *Deadline:* June 1.

Contact: Matthew Sharp, Partner
Law Office of Matthew L. Sharp
432 Ridge St
Reno, NV 89501
Phone: 775-324-1500

LAW OFFICE OF MATTHEW SHRUM

http://www.shrumlawoffice.com/

ANNUAL SINGLE MOTHERS SCHOLARSHIP

The Law Office of Matthew Shrum is delighted to announce the offering of two annual scholarships of $1,000 each for the benefit of single mothers who wish to continue their education. The scholarship is open to single mothers who wish to continue their education on the secondary or post-secondary level. The scholarships will be paid to defray tuition costs at their chosen school. There are two scholarships being offered annually by the Law Office of Matthew Shrum. Each is in the amount of $1,000. The winners will receive the award for payment of tuition in connection with their enrollment/attendance at a college (including community college), trade school or secondary school. Each winner will have a period of one year from the award date in order to provide to us a tuition invoice from the school of her choice. We will then issue a check payable to the order of the school in the sum of $1,000.

Award: Scholarship for use in freshman, sophomore, junior, senior, graduate, or postgraduate years; not renewable. *Number:* 2. *Amount:* $1000.

Eligibility Requirements: Applicant must be enrolled or expecting to enroll full- or part-time at a two-year or four-year or technical institution or university and single female. Available to U.S. citizens.

Application Requirements: Application form, essay. *Deadline:* November 9.

Contact: Matthew Shrum
E-mail: michael@shrumlawoffice.com

LAW OFFICES OF DAVID A. BLACK

http://www.dbphoenixcriminallawyer.com

ANNUAL HEARING IMPAIRED SCHOLARSHIP

The Law Offices of David A. Black is pleased to announce that it is offering two $1,000 educational scholarships annually for hearing impaired and deaf students. Hearing loss can have a negative effect on academic performance, and that effect can be profound. Typically, students with a hearing impairment may experience difficulties with certain school subjects (for example grammar, spelling and vocabulary). They may also have problems taking notes, participating in class discussions, and making oral presentations, among other difficulties. These scholarships are intended to provide assistance that will allow hearing impaired students to continue their education. Applicants must have a 40dB (or greater) bilateral hearing loss, and must be citizens of the United States. The scholarships, each in the amount of $1,000, will be awarded annually for secondary or post-secondary educational classes (secondary school, college, trade school, community college, etc.). You need not be currently enrolled in order to qualify. The winners will have one year from the date of their award to provide a tuition invoice from the educational institution, and the Law Offices of David A. Black will then issue a check payable to the institution in the sum of $1,000.

Award: Scholarship for use in freshman, sophomore, junior, senior, graduate, or postgraduate years; not renewable. *Number:* 2. *Amount:* $1000.

Eligibility Requirements: Applicant must be hearing impaired and enrolled or expecting to enroll full- or part-time at a two-year or four-year or technical institution or university. Applicant must be hearing impaired. Available to U.S. citizens.

Application Requirements: Application form, essay. *Deadline:* November 8.

Contact: David Black
Law Offices of David A. Black
40 North Central Avenue, Suite 1400
Phoenix, AZ 85004
Phone: 480-280-8028
E-mail: michael@dbphoenixcriminallawyer.com

LAW OFFICES OF JUDD S. NEMIRO, PLLC

http://www.jnphoenixfamilylawyer.com/

ANNUAL DYSLEXIA SCHOLARSHIP

The Law Offices of Judd S. Nemiro, PLLC takes pleasure in announcing its annual dyslexia scholarship program. The program consists of two awards annually, each for $1,000, for tuition assistance at an educational institution. We offer these scholarships in order to help those with Dyslexia in continuing their education. You must be diagnosed with Dyslexia. We may ask for proof of the diagnosis. Two scholarships are being offered annually, and each is in the sum of $1,000. Each scholarship will take the form of a tuition payment for enrollment at a university, college, community college, trade school, or secondary school. You need not be currently enrolled at an educational institution at the time you submit your application. The winners, within a year from the award date, will provide us with a tuition invoice from the school they will be attending. A $1,000 check will then be forwarded to the school.

Award: Scholarship for use in freshman, sophomore, junior, senior, graduate, or postgraduate years; not renewable. *Number:* 2. *Amount:* $1000.

Eligibility Requirements: Applicant must be learning disabled and enrolled or expecting to enroll full- or part-time at a two-year or four-year or technical institution or university. Applicant must be learning disabled. Available to U.S. citizens.

Application Requirements: Application form, essay. *Deadline:* November 4.

Contact: Judd Nemiro
E-mail: michael@jnphoenixfamilylawyer.com

LAW OFFICES OF RYAN J. TEGNELIA

http://www.sandiegocriminallawyerrt.com/

ANNUAL VETERANS WITH POST-TRAUMATIC STRESS SCHOLARSHIP

RJT Criminal Defense is pleased to announce that it will be offering two scholarships annually for veterans who suffer from post-traumatic stress disorder (PTSD). Each of the scholarships will provide $1,000 toward tuition to attend an educational program chosen by the recipient. The program is open to veterans of the United States Armed Forces who have been diagnosed with PTSD. RJT Criminal Defense is offering two educational scholarships annually to United States veterans with PTSD. Each of the scholarships is in the amount of $1,000, the funds to be paid for tuition for secondary education, college (or community college), or trade school. Applicants need not currently be students in order to qualify for an award. Within one year from the date of their award, the winners must provide RJT Criminal Defense with a tuition invoice from the educational institution, and a $1,000 check for will be issued to the institution at that time.

Award: Scholarship for use in freshman, sophomore, junior, senior, graduate, or postgraduate years; not renewable. *Number:* 2. *Amount:* $1000.

Eligibility Requirements: Applicant must be enrolled or expecting to enroll full- or part-time at a two-year or four-year or technical institution or university. Available to U.S. citizens. Applicant must have general military experience.

Application Requirements: Application form, essay. *Deadline:* November 14.

Contact: Ryan Tegnelia
    E-mail: mike@sandiegocriminallawyerrt.com

LAW OFFICES OF SHERYL R. RENTZ, P.C.

http://www.srrentzlaw.com/

2017 LAW OFFICES OF SHERYL R. RENTZ SCHOLARSHIP

The 2017 Law Offices of Sheryl R. Rentz Scholarship is our way of thanking those students who have gone above and beyond in order to give back to their local communities. Students who have earned at least a 3.0 GPA in the classroom while pursuing the betterment of the world outside of the classroom are welcome to apply to this scholarship. Applicants should be graduating high school seniors or current undergraduate students. U.S. Citizenship or Permanent Residency is required. Please visit our website for additional information and to submit an application today: http://www.srrentzlaw.com/scholarship/

Award: Scholarship for use in freshman, sophomore, junior, or senior years; not renewable. *Number:* 1. *Amount:* $500.

Eligibility Requirements: Applicant must be enrolled or expecting to enroll full- or part-time at a two-year or four-year institution or university. Applicant must have 3.0 GPA or higher. Available to U.S. citizens.

Application Requirements: Application form, essay. *Deadline:* March 30.

Contact: Ms. Sheryl Rentz, Lead Attorney
    Law Offices of Sheryl R. Rentz, P.C.
    326 W. Lancaster Ave., #100
    Ardmore, PA 19003
    Phone: 610-645-0100
    Fax: 610-645-0111
    E-mail: sheryl@srrentz.com

LAW OFFICES OF THOMAS J. LAVIN

http://www.lawlavinflorida.com/

THOMAS J. LAVIN SCHOLARSHIP

The Law Lavin Scholarship was established to promote and encourage the pursuit of higher education throughout Florida and the rest of the nation. Thomas J. Lavin, founder of the scholarship believes in a bright future for our nation and has committed by offering the annual Law Lavin Scholarship beginning on April 25, 2016 and occurring annually. Our financial award can act as a scholarship for students, a scholarship for graduate students, a scholarship for transfer students, a need based scholarship for moms, scholarship for minorities, and more!

Award: Scholarship for use in freshman, sophomore, junior, senior, graduate, or postgraduate years; not renewable. *Number:* 1–2. *Amount:* $1–$1000.

Eligibility Requirements: Applicant must be age 14-40 and enrolled or expecting to enroll full- or part-time at a two-year or four-year or technical institution or university. Available to U.S. citizens.

Application Requirements: Personal photograph. *Deadline:* November 25.

Contact: Grant Webb, Director
    Law Offices of Thomas J. Lavin
    4731 w. hillsborough ave
    tampa 33611
    Phone: 813-345-4750
    E-mail: contactglw@yahoo.com

LAW OFFICES OF TRAGOS, SARTES & TRAGOS

https://tragoslaw.com/

TRAGOS WRITE YOUR OWN LAW SCHOLARSHIP

This scholarship is offered to any student currently enrolled in an accredited community college, undergraduate, or graduate program in the United States. This includes incoming first-year college students who are high school graduates or possess a GED. All eligible candidates must be in good academic standing, with a minimum cumulative GPA of 3.0 or

above. For more complete information, visit https://tragoslaw.com/#scholarship

Award: Scholarship for use in freshman, sophomore, junior, senior, graduate, or postgraduate years; not renewable. *Number:* 1. *Amount:* $500.

Eligibility Requirements: Applicant must be enrolled or expecting to enroll full- or part-time at a two-year or four-year or technical institution or university. Applicant must have 3.0 GPA or higher. Available to U.S. and non-U.S. citizens.

Application Requirements: Application form, essay. *Deadline:* March 31.

Contact: George Tragos
    E-mail: info@tragoslaw.com

LEPENDORF & SILVERSTEIN, P.C.

http://www.lependorf.com/

LEPENDORF & SILVERSTEIN, P.C. 2017 NEW JERSEY SCHOLARSHIP

With the Lependorf & Silverstein, P.C. 2017 New Jersey Scholarship we have found a new way to support those students who have dedicated themselves not only to their education, but to improving their local communities. We are thrilled to be able to support those high school seniors and current college students who are working to make New Jersey and the world a better place. This $500 scholarship will be awarded to one deserving New Jersey resident student with a minimum 3.0 GPA.

Award: Scholarship for use in freshman, sophomore, junior, or senior years; not renewable. *Number:* 1. *Amount:* $500.

Eligibility Requirements: Applicant must be enrolled or expecting to enroll full- or part-time at a two-year or four-year institution or university and resident of New Jersey. Applicant must have 3.0 GPA or higher. Available to U.S. citizens.

Application Requirements: Application form, essay. *Deadline:* May 29.

Contact: Mr. David Silverstein, Attorney
    Lependorf & Silverstein, P.C.
    4365 US Highway 1
    Suite 104
    Princeton, NJ 08540
    Phone: 609-240-0040
    E-mail: dsilverstein@lependorf.com

LEP FOUNDATION FOR YOUTH EDUCATION

http://www.lepfoundation.org/applications

CURE—CANCER SUPPORT SCHOLARSHIP

The Lep Foundation for Youth Education was formed in 2009 with the specific mission of providing financial assistance to support disabled students who demonstrate academic success and the motivation to move forward despite their disabilities. In addition, the Foundation was proud to have introduced the Cure Cancer Support Scholarship in 2016 to assist students diagnosed with childhood and adolescent cancers. The Lep Foundation is a non-profit charity with 501c3 tax exempt status (E.I.N. #27-0817346).

Award: Scholarship for use in freshman, sophomore, junior, senior, graduate, or postgraduate years; not renewable. *Number:* 1. *Amount:* $5000.

Eligibility Requirements: Applicant must be enrolled or expecting to enroll full- or part-time at a two-year or four-year or technical institution or university. Available to U.S. citizens.

Application Requirements: Application form, essay, financial need analysis. *Deadline:* June 1.

Contact: Scholarship Committee
    Lep Foundation for Youth Education
    9 Whispering Spring Dr.
    Millstone Twp., NJ 08510
    E-mail: lepfoundation@aol.com

JOHN LEPPING MEMORIAL SCHOLARSHIP

The Lep Foundation for Youth Education was formed in 2009 with the specific mission of providing financial assistance to support disabled students who demonstrate academic success and the motivation to move forward despite their disabilities. In addition, the Foundation was proud to have introduced the Cure Cancer Support Scholarship in 2016 to assist students diagnosed with childhood and adolescent cancers. The Lep Foundation is a non-profit charity with 501c3 tax exempt status (E.I.N. #27-0817346).

Award: Scholarship for use in freshman, sophomore, junior, senior, graduate, or postgraduate years; not renewable. *Number:* 1–5. *Amount:* $5000.

Eligibility Requirements: Applicant must be enrolled or expecting to enroll full- or part-time at a two-year or four-year or technical institution or university and resident of New Jersey, New York, Pennsylvania. Available to U.S. citizens.

Application Requirements: Application form, essay, financial need analysis. *Deadline:* May 1.

Contact: Scholarship Committee
Lep Foundation for Youth Education
9 Whispering Spring Dr.
Millstone Twp., NJ 08510
E-mail: lepfoundation@aol.com

LIVE POETS SOCIETY AND JUST POETRY!!! MAGAZINE

http://www.highschoolpoetrycontest.com/

NATIONAL HIGH SCHOOL POETRY CONTEST

Award to encourage the youth of America in the pursuit of literary exploration and excellence, and to help provide a venue in which American High School students may share their poetic works. All U.S. high school students are eligible to enter this contest by submitting an original poem of 20 lines or less according to the Official Rules and Entry Procedures on our website, http://www.highschoolpoetrycontest.com, under the 'To Enter' tab.

Award: Scholarship for use in freshman year; not renewable. *Number:* 1–9. *Amount:* $100–$1000.

Eligibility Requirements: Applicant must be high school student and planning to enroll or expecting to enroll full-time at a two-year or four-year institution or university. Available to U.S. citizens.

Application Requirements: *Deadline:* continuous.

Contact: Mr. D Edwards, Editor
Live Poets Society and JUST POETRY!!! magazine
PO Box 8841
Turnersville, NJ 08012
E-mail: info@highschoolpoetrtycontest.com

MAGIC JOHNSON FOUNDATION INC.

http://www.magicjohnson.org/

TAYLOR MICHAELS SCHOLARSHIP FUND

Scholarship to provide support for deserving minority high school students who exemplify a strong potential for academic achievement but face social-economic conditions that hinder them from reaching their full potential. Must have strong community service involvement.

Award: Scholarship for use in freshman year; renewable. *Amount:* $1000–$5000.

Eligibility Requirements: Applicant must be American Indian/Alaska Native, Asian/Pacific Islander, Black (non-Hispanic), Hispanic; high school student and planning to enroll or expecting to enroll full-time at a four-year institution or university. Applicant or parent of applicant must have employment or volunteer experience in community service. Applicant must have 2.5 GPA or higher. Available to U.S. and non-U.S. citizens.

Application Requirements: Application form, community service, essay, recommendations or references, transcript. *Deadline:* February 5.

Contact: Scholarship Coordinator
Magic Johnson Foundation Inc.
9100 Wilshire Boulevard, Suite 700, East Tower
Beverly Hills, CA 90212
Phone: 310-246-4400

MAINE STATE SOCIETY FOUNDATION OF WASHINGTON, DC INC.

http://mainestatesociety.org/foundation/

MAINE STATE SOCIETY FOUNDATION SCHOLARSHIP

Scholarship(s) awarded to full-time students enrolled in undergraduate courses at a four-year degree-granting, nonprofit institution in Maine. Must be Maine resident. All inquiries must be accompanied by a self-addressed stamped envelope. Applicant must be 25 or younger.

Award: Scholarship for use in sophomore or junior years; not renewable. *Number:* 5–10. *Amount:* $1000–$2500.

Eligibility Requirements: Applicant must be enrolled or expecting to enroll full-time at a four-year institution or university; resident of Maine and studying in Maine. Applicant must have 3.0 GPA or higher. Available to U.S. citizens.

Application Requirements: Application form, essay. *Deadline:* March 15.

Contact: Jessica Stewart
E-mail: mssfscholarship@gmail.com

MAINOR WORTH INJURY LAWYERS

https://mainorwirth.com/

MAINOR WIRTH INJURY LAWYERS NEED-BASED SCHOLARSHIP

This scholarship is open to any US citizen or permanent US resident who will be enrolled full-time in an accredited community college, college or university, or accredited law school in the fall of 2017. The judging criteria is based on financial need and the quality of a PSA video focusing on distracted driving (maximum of 2 minutes).

Award: Scholarship for use in freshman, sophomore, junior, or senior years; not renewable. *Number:* 1. *Amount:* $1000.

Eligibility Requirements: Applicant must be enrolled or expecting to enroll full-time at a two-year or four-year institution or university. Available to U.S. citizens.

Application Requirements: Financial need analysis. *Deadline:* June 1.

Contact: Bradly Mainor, Senior Partner
Mainor Worth Injury Lawyers
6018 South Fort Apache Road
Suite 150
Las Vegas, NV 89148
Phone: 702-464-5000

MANA DE SAN DIEGO

http://www.manasd.org/

MANA DE SAN DIEGO SYLVIA CHAVEZ MEMORIAL SCHOLARSHIP

Scholarship for Latinas with permanent residence in San Diego County who are enrolled or about to enroll in a two-year, four-year, or graduate program. Must have a minimum 2.75 GPA and demonstrate financial need. For an application and additional information visit http://www.sdmana.org.

Award: Scholarship for use in freshman, sophomore, junior, or senior years; not renewable. *Amount:* $500–$2000.

Eligibility Requirements: Applicant must be Hispanic; enrolled or expecting to enroll full- or part-time at a two-year or four-year institution or university; female; resident of California and must have an interest in leadership. Applicant or parent of applicant must have employment or volunteer experience in community service. Available to U.S. citizens.

Application Requirements: Application form, essay, recommendations or references, transcript. *Deadline:* February 13.

Contact: Lucy Hernandez, Scholarship Director
MANA de San Diego
PO Box 81364
San Diego, CA 92138-1364
Phone: 619-225-9594
Fax: 619-225-0500
E-mail: scholarships@sdmana.org

MARYLAND ASSOCIATION OF PRIVATE COLLEGES AND CAREER SCHOOLS

http://www.mapccs.org/

MARYLAND ASSOCIATION OF PRIVATE COLLEGES AND CAREER SCHOOLS SCHOLARSHIP

Awards for study at Maryland private colleges and career schools only. Must enroll in private college or career school same year high school is completed.

Award: Scholarship for use in freshman year; not renewable. *Number:* 50–75. *Amount:* $500–$2000.

Eligibility Requirements: Applicant must be high school student; planning to enroll or expecting to enroll full- or part-time at a technical institution and studying in Maryland. Available to U.S. and non-U.S. citizens.

Application Requirements: Application form, essay. *Deadline:* continuous.

Contact: Frank Russell, Administrative Manager
Maryland Association of Private Colleges and Career Schools
5305 Village Center Drive
Suite 295
Columbia, MD 21044
Phone: 410-282-4012
E-mail: info@mapccs.org

MARYLAND STATE HIGHER EDUCATION COMMISSION

http://www.mhec.state.md.us/

EDWARD T. CONROY MEMORIAL SCHOLARSHIP PROGRAM

Scholarship for dependents of deceased or 100 percent disabled U.S. Armed Forces personnel; the son, daughter, or surviving spouse of a victim of the September 11, 2001 terrorist attacks who died as a result of the attacks on the World Trade Center in New York City, the attack on the Pentagon in Virginia, or the crash of United Airlines Flight 93 in Pennsylvania; a POW/MIA of the Vietnam Conflict or his/her son or daughter; the son, daughter or surviving spouse (who has not remarried) of a state or local public safety employee or volunteer who died in the line of duty; or a state or local public safety employee or volunteer who was 100 percent disabled in the line of duty. Must be Maryland resident at time of disability. Submit applicable VA certification. Must be at least 16 years of age and attend Maryland institution.

Award: Scholarship for use in freshman, sophomore, junior, or senior years; renewable. *Number:* up to 121. *Amount:* $7200–$9000.

Eligibility Requirements: Applicant must be age 16-24; enrolled or expecting to enroll full- or part-time at a two-year or four-year institution or university; resident of Maryland and studying in Maryland. Applicant or parent of applicant must have employment or volunteer experience in police/firefighting. Available to U.S. citizens. Applicant or parent must meet one or more of the following requirements: general military experience; retired from active duty; disabled or killed as a result of military service; prisoner of war; or missing in action.

Application Requirements: Application form, birth and death certificate, disability papers. *Deadline:* July 15.

Contact: Linda Asplin, Office of Student Financial Assistance
Maryland State Higher Education Commission
839 Bestgate Road, Suite 400
Annapolis, MD 21401-3013
Phone: 410-260-4563
Fax: 410-260-3203
E-mail: lasplin@mhec.state.md.us

MASSACHUSETTS OFFICE OF STUDENT FINANCIAL ASSISTANCE

http://www.osfa.mass.edu/

MASSACHUSETTS PUBLIC SERVICE GRANT PROGRAM

Scholarships for children and/or spouses of deceased members of fire, police, and corrections departments, who were killed in the line of duty.

Awards Massachusetts residents attending Massachusetts institutions. Applicant should have not received a prior Bachelor's degree or its equivalent.

Award: Grant for use in freshman, sophomore, junior, or senior years; not renewable. *Amount:* $910–$1714.

Eligibility Requirements: Applicant must be enrolled or expecting to enroll full-time at a four-year institution or university; resident of Massachusetts and studying in Massachusetts. Applicant or parent of applicant must have employment or volunteer experience in police/firefighting. Available to U.S. citizens. Applicant must have general military experience.

Application Requirements: Application form, copy of birth certificate, copy of veteran's death certificate, financial need analysis. *Deadline:* May 1.

Contact: Bridget Lynch
Massachusetts Office of Student Financial Assistance
454 Broadway, Suite 200
Revere, MA 02151
Phone: 617-391-6079
Fax: 617-727-0667
E-mail: osfa@osfa.mass.edu

MATRIX HEALTH GROUP

http://www.matrixhealthgroup.com

JOE HOLIBAUGH MEMORIAL SCHOLARSHIP

Two $1000 scholarships for men and women with hemophilia and an inhibitor. Joe Holibaugh (1971- 2006) was one of the founding figures of Matrix Health Group. Living with severe hemophilia and an inhibitor, Joe met many challenges. He faced these difficulties as opportunities to grow, embracing life fully with his entire being. Joe worked hard to impart this approach to others, bringing many together with his unique style of wit and humor. Joe's work lives on in the hearts of his many friends and family who love him dearly. He will always be remembered for his strength, love, and resolve to make a difference for the bleeding disorders community.

Award: Scholarship for use in freshman, sophomore, junior, senior, graduate, or postgraduate years; not renewable. *Number:* 2. *Amount:* $1000.

Eligibility Requirements: Applicant must be physically disabled and enrolled or expecting to enroll full-time at a two-year or four-year or technical institution or university. Applicant must be physically disabled. Applicant must have 2.5 GPA or higher. Available to U.S. citizens.

Application Requirements: Application form, essay, personal photograph. *Deadline:* August 1.

Contact: Maria Vetter
Matrix Health Group
3300 Corporate Avenue, Suite 104
Weston, FL 33331
Phone: 877-337-3002
E-mail: info@matrixhealthgroup.com

MARK COATS MEMORIAL SCHOLARSHIP

Mark Coats (1956-1963) was just a child when he passed from hemophilia-related issues. He was born in an entirely different era of bleeding disorder treatment and was not able to live a near normal life as most people with hemophilia do today. With his smiling eyes and sweet grin, we are reminded that every child deserves a chance to lead a full and happy life. We look to Mark as a reminder of what living with a bleeding disorder was like not that long ago, how blessed we are to have the treatments we have today, and just how important it is that we continue our quest to find a cure for hemophilia

Award: Scholarship for use in freshman, sophomore, junior, senior, graduate, or postgraduate years; not renewable. *Number:* 1. *Amount:* $1000.

Eligibility Requirements: Applicant must be physically disabled and enrolled or expecting to enroll full-time at a two-year or four-year or technical institution or university. Applicant must be physically disabled. Applicant must have 2.5 GPA or higher. Available to U.S. citizens.

Application Requirements: Application form, essay, personal photograph. *Deadline:* August 1.

Contact: Maria Vetter, Dir. of Corporate Communications
Matrix Health Group
3300 Corporate Avenue, Suite 104
Weston, FL 33331
Phone: 877-337-3002
E-mail: info@matrixhealthgroup.com

RON NIEDERMAN MEMORIAL SCHOLARSHIP

Ron Niederman (1950-1999) was born when treatment for persons with bleeding disorders was largely nonexistent. Many of his generation faced a lifetime of pain and a great struggle for better care, while fighting against stigma and prejudice associated with having HIV in the 1980's. Living with severe hemophilia, Ron endured challenges well beyond that of most, and faced each with grace. He exemplified the meaning of compassion towards others, action in his words and deeds, and practiced more than preached what it meant to be an advocate. He was a great friend and a trusted source of advice and wisdom to all that knew him. Ron's commitment towards the bleeding disorder community was surpassed only by his love for his family.

Award: Scholarship for use in freshman, sophomore, junior, senior, graduate, or postgraduate years; not renewable. *Number:* 1. *Amount:* $1000.

Eligibility Requirements: Applicant must be physically disabled; enrolled or expecting to enroll full-time at a two-year or four-year or technical institution or university and male. Applicant must be physically disabled. Applicant must have 2.5 GPA or higher. Available to U.S. citizens.

Application Requirements: Application form, essay, personal photograph. *Deadline:* August 1.

Contact: Maria Vetter, Dir. Of Corporate Communications
Matrix Health Group
3300 Corporate Avenue, Suite 104
Weston, FL 33331
Phone: 877-337-3002
E-mail: info@matrixhealthgroup.com

TIM KENNEDY MEMORIAL SCHOLARSHIP

Tim Kennedy (1962-2011) was a tenured employee at Matrix Health Group and a respected name in the bleeding disorders community. Those who knew Tim remember him for his ability to make most anyone smile and share a hearty laugh. Though life had dealt him a rough hand, Tim kept an air about him that was truly inspiring. As a father and husband, the love he showed his two children and wife knew no bounds. As a friend, he was always ready to listen, share, and comfort, most often with his signature sense of humor. As a member of the bleeding disorders community, Tim was devoted to helping his peers look past their health conditions and enjoy every moment of life for all it's worth.

Award: Scholarship for use in freshman, sophomore, junior, senior, graduate, or postgraduate years; not renewable. *Number:* 2. *Amount:* $1000.

Eligibility Requirements: Applicant must be physically disabled; enrolled or expecting to enroll full-time at a two-year or four-year or technical institution or university and male. Applicant must be physically disabled. Applicant must have 2.5 GPA or higher. Available to U.S. citizens.

Application Requirements: Application form, essay, personal photograph. *Deadline:* August 1.

Contact: Maria Vetter, Dir. Corporate Communications
Matrix Health Group
3300 Corporate Avenue, Suite 104
Weston, FL 33331
Phone: 877-337-3002
E-mail: info@matrixhealthgroup.com

MENSA FOUNDATION

http://mensafoundation.org

U.S. SCHOLARSHIP PROGRAM

The scholarship program is an essay based program open to students of all ages. Mensa membership is not required.

Award: Scholarship for use in freshman, sophomore, junior, senior, graduate, or postgraduate years; not renewable. *Number:* 100–150. *Amount:* $600–$2500.

Eligibility Requirements: Applicant must be enrolled or expecting to enroll full- or part-time at a two-year or four-year institution or university. Available to U.S. citizens.

Application Requirements: Application form, essay. *Deadline:* January 15.

Contact: Jill Beckham, Foundation Director
Mensa Foundation
1229 Corporate Dr W
Arlington, TX 76006
Phone: 817-607-5577
Fax: 817-649-5232
E-mail: director@mensafoundation.org

MES FOUNDATION

http://www.mesfoundation.org

RICHARD H. PIERCE MEMORIAL SCHOLARSHIP

A $5,000 scholarship per student per year will be awarded. Scholarships will be renewable for up to 4 years (depending on the grade level of the student). A total of 10 scholarships will be awarded to eligible students in 2017. Application period runs from January 1st to April 15th. Must be a Maine resident entering first year of post-secondary education; intend to enroll/be enrolled in a 2 or 4 year degree-granting college or university accredited by the Association of Schools and Colleges; and show a strong desire to complete degree program.

Award: Scholarship for use in freshman, sophomore, junior, or senior years; renewable. *Number:* 10. *Amount:* $5000.

Eligibility Requirements: Applicant must be enrolled or expecting to enroll full-time at a two-year or four-year institution or university and resident of Maine. Available to U.S. citizens.

Application Requirements: Application form, community service, essay, financial need analysis. *Deadline:* April 15.

Contact: Kristie Hurlburt, Program Director
MES Foundation
PO Box 1296
Alfred, ME 04002
Phone: 207-791-3600
E-mail: info@mesfoundation.org

MICHIGAN STATE HORTICULTURAL SOCIETY

www.mihortsociety.org

FRUITS INDUSTRIES SCHOLARSHIPS

This scholarship is only for students who intend to pursue careers in or connected to the Midwest fruit industry.

Award: Scholarship for use in sophomore, junior, senior, or graduate years; not renewable. *Number:* 4–7. *Amount:* $1500.

Eligibility Requirements: Applicant must be enrolled or expecting to enroll full-time at a two-year or four-year institution or university. Applicant or parent of applicant must have employment or volunteer experience in agriculture. Available to U.S. citizens.

Application Requirements: Application form. *Deadline:* September 30.

Contact: Allyn Anthony

MINDSUMO

http://www.mindsumo.com

MINDSUMO 15-MINUTE SCHOLARSHIP

This is the first year we are launching this scholarship program to run in conjunction with our standard MindSumo platform. In terms of total payouts we have provided to college students for merit-based performance on solving business and engineering challenges, we have paid out $600,000 over the last 4 years. Now we want to convert a portion of our prize pool to be dedicated to scholarships. Our reward structure is unique in that the number of winners and the award amount depends on the number of submissions. Our objective is to reward a larger proportion of applicants to encourage them through the tough scholarship application process rather than limit winners to a small select few. Please see website for details, http://www.mindsumo.com/scholarships.

Award: Scholarship for use in freshman, sophomore, junior, senior, graduate, or postgraduate years; not renewable. *Number:* 250–500. *Amount:* $40–$200.

Eligibility Requirements: Applicant must be enrolled or expecting to enroll full- or part-time at a two-year or four-year or technical institution or university. Available to U.S. and non-U.S. citizens.

Application Requirements: *Deadline:* continuous.

Contact: Mr. John Huang, Manager
MindSumo
33 New Montgomery
Suite 220
San Francisco, CA 94105
Phone: 843-453-5176
E-mail: john@mindsumo.com

MINNESOTA MASONIC CHARITIES

http://www.mnmasoniccharities.org

MINNESOTA MASONIC CHARITIES SIGNATURE SCHOLARSHIP

Signature Scholarships are provided each year to students attending a Minnesota high school with a GPA of 3.9 or higher. Applicants must plan to enroll in a four-year college program.

Award: Scholarship for use in freshman, sophomore, junior, or senior years; renewable. *Number:* 5. *Amount:* $5000.

Eligibility Requirements: Applicant must be high school student; planning to enroll or expecting to enroll full-time at a four-year institution or university and resident of Minnesota. Applicant must have 3.5 GPA or higher. Available to U.S. citizens.

Application Requirements: Application form, essay. *Deadline:* March 1.

Contact: Ms. Kim Ramaker, Scholarships Manager
Minnesota Masonic Charities
11501 Masonic Home Drive
Bloomington, MN 55437
Phone: 952-948-6227
E-mail: kim.ramaker@mnmasonic.org

MINNESOTA MASONIC CHARITIES UNDERGRADUATE SCHOLARSHIP

Undergraduate Scholarships are provided each year to current college freshman, sophomores or juniors who graduated from a Minnesota high school and have a GPA of 2.75 or above. Applicants must be enrolled in a four-year college program.

Award: Scholarship for use in sophomore, junior, or senior years; renewable. *Number:* 20. *Amount:* $2000.

Eligibility Requirements: Applicant must be enrolled or expecting to enroll full-time at a four-year institution and resident of Minnesota. Applicant must have 2.5 GPA or higher. Available to U.S. citizens.

Application Requirements: Application form, essay. *Deadline:* March 1.

Contact: Ms. Kim Ramaker, Scholarships Manager
Minnesota Masonic Charities
11501 Masonic Home Drive
Bloomington, MN 55437
Phone: 952-948-6227
E-mail: kim.ramaker@mnmasonic.org

MINNESOTA OFFICE OF HIGHER EDUCATION

http://www.ohe.state.mn.us

SAFETY OFFICERS' SURVIVOR GRANT PROGRAM

Grant for eligible survivors of Minnesota public safety officers killed in the line of duty. Safety officers who have been permanently or totally disabled in the line of duty are also eligible. Must be used at a Minnesota institution participating in State Grant Program. Write for details. Must submit proof of death or disability and Public Safety Officers Benefit Fund Certificate. Must apply for renewal each year. Five-year limit on awards.

Award: Grant for use in freshman, sophomore, junior, senior, or graduate years; not renewable. *Number:* 1–10. *Amount:* $1–$13,840.

Eligibility Requirements: Applicant must be enrolled or expecting to enroll full- or part-time at a two-year or four-year or technical institution or university; resident of Minnesota and studying in Minnesota. Applicant or parent of applicant must have employment or volunteer experience in police/firefighting. Available to U.S. citizens.

Application Requirements: Application form. *Deadline:* continuous.

Contact: Brenda Larter, Program Administrator
Phone: 651-355-0612
E-mail: brenda.larter@state.mn.us

MISSISSIPPI OFFICE OF STUDENT FINANCIAL AID

http://www.mississippi.edu/financialaid

LAW ENFORCEMENT OFFICERS/FIREMEN SCHOLARSHIP

Financial assistance to dependent children and spouses of any Mississippi law enforcement officer, full-time fire fighter or volunteer fire fighter who has suffered fatal injuries or wounds or become permanently and totally disabled as a result of injuries or wounds which occurred in the performance of the official and appointed duties of his or her office. This financial assistance is offered as an eight semester tuition and room scholarship at any state-supported college or university in Mississippi.

Award: Scholarship for use in freshman, sophomore, junior, or senior years; renewable. *Number:* 1–30. *Amount:* $2010–$12,854.

Eligibility Requirements: Applicant must be enrolled or expecting to enroll full-time at a two-year or four-year institution or university; resident of Mississippi and studying in Mississippi. Applicant or parent of applicant must have employment or volunteer experience in police/firefighting. Applicant must have 2.5 GPA or higher. Available to U.S. citizens.

Application Requirements: Application form. *Deadline:* continuous.

Contact: Program Administrator
Mississippi Office of Student Financial Aid
3825 Ridgewood Road
Jackson, MS 39211
Phone: 601-432-6997
Fax: 601-432 Ext. 6527
E-mail: sfa@mississippi.edu

MITCHELL INSTITUTE

http://www.mitchellinstitute.org/

THE SENATOR GEORGE J. MITCHELL SCHOLARSHIP RESEARCH INSTITUTE

The Mitchell Institute awards scholarships to graduating seniors from every public high school in Maine each year. The scholarship award is in the amount of $9000, and Mitchell Scholars have up to six years to use the funds. An award check in the amount of $2250 is disbursed to each Scholar annually for up to four years.

Award: Scholarship for use in freshman, sophomore, junior, or senior years; renewable. *Number:* 133. *Amount:* $9000.

Eligibility Requirements: Applicant must be high school student; planning to enroll or expecting to enroll full- or part-time at a two-year or four-year or technical institution or university and resident of Maine. Available to U.S. citizens.

Application Requirements: Application form, community service, essay, financial need analysis. *Deadline:* April 1.

Contact: Kim Gustafson, Scholarship Director
Mitchell Institute
75 Washington Avenue
Suite 2E
Portland, ME 04101
Phone: 207-773-7700
E-mail: kgustafson@mitchellinstitute.org

MLD WEALTH MANAGEMENT GROUP

http://mywealthmanagement.ca/

ANNUAL MLD SCHOLASTIC SCHOLARSHIP

MLD Wealth Management is offering an annual scholarship to all the students from that meet our qualifications. This scholarship is based on merit, financial need, and community participation. The winning applicant will receive $3000 towards their education costs. The application deadline is May 10, 2017. Scholarship details: http://mywealthmanagement.ca/scholarsip2017/

Award: Scholarship for use in freshman, sophomore, junior, senior, graduate, or postgraduate years; not renewable. *Number:* 1. *Amount:* $3000.

Eligibility Requirements: Applicant must be enrolled or expecting to enroll full-time at a two-year or four-year institution or university. Applicant must have 3.0 GPA or higher. Available to U.S. and Canadian citizens.

Application Requirements: Application form, essay, interview, personal photograph. *Deadline:* May 10.

Contact: Mr. Chris Hilliard, PR Manager
MLD Wealth Management Group
239 - 8th Avenue SW
Suite 200
Calgary T2P 1B9
Phone: 604-3605161
Fax: 403-4109668
E-mail: pr@mywealthmanagement.ca

NATIONAL AIDS MEMORIAL GROVE

http://www.aidsmemorial.org

PEDRO ZAMORA YOUNG LEADERS SCHOLARSHIP

The Pedro Zamora Young Leaders Scholarship is open to all current high school seniors, and college freshman, sophomores and juniors (ages 27 and younger) who demonstrate an active commitment to fighting HIV/AIDS and taking on roles of public service and leadership. Examples include (but are not limited to): serving in peer-education and prevention programs; working in the reproductive-health and sexual health field; pursuing a medical degree to work with HIV-positive individuals; international service providing AIDS-related care and/or HIV-prevention education; research in established and emerging technologies designed to mitigate the epidemic; or activism and social change efforts that address issues contributing to the epidemic, like education and drug sentencing reform, employment and economic justice issues, housing and homelessness. All applicants must describe their current leadership efforts/experience, its significance to the HIV/AIDS epidemic, as well as their how their future career plans or public service will be an extension of their current efforts. Applicants must provide at least one letter of recommendation from a teacher, program coordinator, supervisor/ally/community leader who is directly involved in their HIV/AIDS-related service, leadership, or field of study. A panel of community leaders will judge the applications. Submissions must include the following five items: 1. a complete Application; 2. a brief personal statement (not to exceed 500 words) describing some of the ways that you provide service and/or leadership in the fight against HIV/AIDS and how your studies, career plans, or public service will contribute to the fight against HIV/AIDS; 3. a written essay, not to exceed 1,500 words, in which you reflect on the ways in which your life has been impacted by HIV/AIDS, explore and describe the ways in which you are providing public service or leadership that makes a difference in the lives of people with HIV/AIDS, or people at risk, and det il how the scholarship will help you in your career path and how that career will allow you to continue to fight HIV/AIDS in a way that makes a difference; 4. at least one written letter of recommendation from a teacher, program coordinator, supervisor/ally/community leader or other adult who is directly involved in your HIV/AIDS-related service, leadership, or field of study; 5. a transcript from current high school or college that demonstrates a minimum 2.5 GPA overall, or in the immediate past two semesters or three trimesters. Deadlines: application/personal statement–5:00 PM, PST, Monday, May 1st, 2017; essay/letter(s) of recommendation/transcript–5:00 PM, PST, Friday, May 26th, 2017.

Award: Scholarship for use in freshman, sophomore, junior, or senior years; not renewable. *Number:* 8–10. *Amount:* $5000.

Eligibility Requirements: Applicant must be enrolled or expecting to enroll full- or part-time at a two-year or four-year institution or university and studying in Alabama, Alaska, Arizona, Arkansas, California, Colorado, Connecticut, Delaware, District of Columbia, Florida, Georgia, Hawaii, Idaho, Illinois, Indiana, Iowa, Kansas, Kentucky, Louisiana, Maine, Maryland, Massachusetts, Michigan, Minnesota, Mississippi, Missouri, Montana, Nebraska, Nevada, New Hampshire, New Jersey, New Mexico, New York, North Carolina, North Dakota, Ohio, Oklahoma, Oregon, Pennsylvania, Puerto Rico, Rhode Island,

South Carolina, South Dakota, Tennessee, Texas, Utah, Vermont, Virginia, Washington, West Virginia, Wisconsin, Wyoming. Applicant must have 2.5 GPA or higher. Available to U.S. citizens.

Application Requirements: Application form, essay. *Deadline:* May 1.

Contact: Steve Sagaser, Development Manager
National AIDS Memorial Grove
870 Market Street, Suite 965
San Francisco, CA 94102
Phone: 415-765-0497
Fax: 415-707-6150
E-mail: ssagaser@aidsmemorial.org

NATIONAL ASSOCIATION FOR CAMPUS ACTIVITIES

http://www.naca.org/

LORI RHETT MEMORIAL SCHOLARSHIP

Scholarships will be given to undergraduate or graduate students with a cumulative GPA of 2.5 or better at the time of the application and during the academic term in which the scholarship is awarded. Must demonstrate significant leadership skill and ability while holding a significant leadership position on campus. Applicants must have made contributions via volunteer involvement, either on or off campus.

Award: Scholarship for use in freshman, sophomore, junior, senior, or graduate years; not renewable. *Number:* 1. *Amount:* $300.

Eligibility Requirements: Applicant must be enrolled or expecting to enroll full-time at a two-year or four-year institution or university; studying in Alaska, Arizona, California, Colorado, Idaho, Nevada, New Mexico, Oregon, Utah, Washington and must have an interest in leadership. Applicant or parent of applicant must have employment or volunteer experience in community service. Applicant must have 2.5 GPA or higher. Available to U.S. citizens.

Application Requirements: Application form, autobiography, essay. *Deadline:* June 30.

Contact: Kayla Brennan, Education and Development Coordinator
Phone: 803-217-3471
Fax: 803-749-1047
E-mail: kaylab@naca.org

NATIONAL ASSOCIATION FOR CAMPUS ACTIVITIES MID ATLANTIC UNDERGRADUATE SCHOLARSHIP FOR STUDENT LEADERS

Scholarship for undergraduate students who are in good standing at the time of the application and during the academic term in which the scholarship is awarded. Applicants must maintain a 2.5 GPA, demonstrate leadership skills and abilities while holding a significant leadership position on campus or in community, and have made significant contributions via volunteer involvement. Eligible students must be attending a college or university within the NACA Mid Atlantic Region.

Award: Scholarship for use in freshman, sophomore, junior, or senior years; not renewable. *Number:* 1–2. *Amount:* $300.

Eligibility Requirements: Applicant must be enrolled or expecting to enroll full- or part-time at a two-year or four-year institution or university; studying in Delaware, District of Columbia, Maryland, New Jersey, New York, Pennsylvania and must have an interest in leadership. Applicant or parent of applicant must have employment or volunteer experience in community service. Applicant must have 2.5 GPA or higher. Available to U.S. citizens.

Application Requirements: Application form, autobiography, essay. *Deadline:* March 31.

Contact: Kayla Brennan, Education and Development Coordinator
Phone: 803-217-3471
Fax: 803-749-1047
E-mail: kaylab@naca.org

NATIONAL ASSOCIATION FOR CAMPUS ACTIVITIES NORTHERN PLAINS REGION STUDENT LEADERSHIP SCHOLARSHIP

Scholarships will be awarded to undergraduate or graduate students in good standing and enrolled in the equivalent of at least six academic credits at the time of the application and during the academic term in which the scholarship is awarded. Must be currently enrolled in or received a degree from a college or university within Wisconsin or the upper peninsula of Michigan (area code 906) and have demonstrated leadership skill and significant service to their campus community.

Award: Scholarship for use in freshman, sophomore, junior, senior, or graduate years; not renewable. *Number:* 1. *Amount:* $300.

Eligibility Requirements: Applicant must be enrolled or expecting to enroll full- or part-time at a two-year or four-year institution or university; studying in Michigan, Wisconsin and must have an interest in leadership. Applicant or parent of applicant must have employment or volunteer experience in community service. Available to U.S. citizens.

Application Requirements: Application form, autobiography, essay. *Deadline:* January 15.

Contact: Kayla Brennan, Education and Development Coordinator
    Phone: 803-217-3471
    Fax: 803-749-1047
    E-mail: kaylab@naca.org

NATIONAL ASSOCIATION FOR CAMPUS ACTIVITIES SOUTH REGION STUDENT LEADER SCHOLARSHIP

Scholarships will be given to full-time undergraduate students in good standing at the time of the application and during the academic term in which the scholarship is awarded. Must demonstrate significant leadership skill and ability while holding a significant leadership position on campus. Applicants must have made contributions via volunteer involvement, either on or off campus. Must be enrolled in a college/university in the NACA South Region.

Award: Scholarship for use in freshman, sophomore, junior, or senior years; not renewable. *Number:* 1–4. *Amount:* $300.

Eligibility Requirements: Applicant must be enrolled or expecting to enroll full-time at a two-year or four-year institution or university; studying in Alabama, Florida, Georgia, Mississippi, North Carolina, South Carolina, Tennessee, Virginia and must have an interest in leadership. Applicant or parent of applicant must have employment or volunteer experience in community service. Available to U.S. citizens.

Application Requirements: Application form, autobiography, essay. *Deadline:* March 31.

Contact: Kayla Brennan, Education and Development Coordinator
    Phone: 803-217-3471
    Fax: 803-749-1047
    E-mail: kaylab@naca.org

SCHOLARSHIPS FOR STUDENT LEADERS

Scholarships will be awarded to undergraduate students in good standing at the time of the application and who, during the academic term in which the scholarship is awarded, hold a significant leadership position on their campus. Must make significant contributions to their campus communities and demonstrate leadership skills and abilities.

Award: Scholarship for use in freshman, sophomore, junior, or senior years; not renewable. *Number:* 1–7. *Amount:* $300.

Eligibility Requirements: Applicant must be enrolled or expecting to enroll full- or part-time at a two-year or four-year institution or university and must have an interest in leadership. Applicant or parent of applicant must have employment or volunteer experience in community service. Available to U.S. citizens.

Application Requirements: Application form, essay. *Deadline:* November 1.

Contact: Kayla Brennan, Education and Development Coordinator
    Phone: 803-217-3471
    Fax: 803-749-1047
    E-mail: kaylab@naca.org

NATIONAL COUNCIL OF JEWISH WOMEN LOS ANGELES (NCJW L LA)

http://ncjwla.org/

DODELL WOMEN'S EMPOWERMENT SCHOLARSHIP

To qualify, an applicant must be re-entering or continuing school in order to learn a marketable skill which will lead to economic self-sufficiency. The applicant must be a woman 25 years of age or older for whom the opportunity to return to school will lead to economic independence. The applicant can be either married or single, with or without children. The National Council of Jewish Women l Los Angeles (NCJW l LA) provides scholarships, regardless of race, ethnicity, religion, age, gender identity, sexuality or national origin to those who live and attend school in the Greater Los Angeles area, including Los Angeles, Orange, Riverside, and Ventura Counties.

Award: Scholarship for use in freshman, sophomore, junior, senior, or graduate years; not renewable. *Number:* 2. *Amount:* $1000.

Eligibility Requirements: Applicant must be enrolled or expecting to enroll full- or part-time at a two-year or four-year or technical institution or university; female; resident of California and studying in California. Available to U.S. and non-U.S. citizens.

Application Requirements: Application form, essay, financial need analysis. *Deadline:* May 1.

Contact: Ms. Stephanie Flax, Scholarship and Program Coordinator
    National Council of Jewish Women Los Angeles (NCJW l LA)
    543 North Fairfax Avenue
    Los Angeles, CA 90036
    Phone: 323-852-8515
    E-mail: Scholarship@ncjwla.org

SOPHIE GREENSTADT SCHOLARSHIP FOR MID-LIFE WOMEN

To qualify, an applicant must be re-entering or continuing school in order to learn a marketable skill which will lead to economic self-sufficiency. The applicant must be a woman 35 years of age or older for whom the opportunity to return to school will lead to economic independence. The applicant can be either married or single, with or without children. The National Council of Jewish Women l Los Angeles (NCJW l LA) provides scholarships, regardless of race, ethnicity, religion, age, gender identity, sexuality or national origin to those who live and attend school in the Greater Los Angeles area, including Los Angeles, Orange, Riverside, and Ventura Counties.

Award: Scholarship for use in freshman, sophomore, junior, senior, or graduate years; not renewable. *Number:* 1. *Amount:* $1000.

Eligibility Requirements: Applicant must be enrolled or expecting to enroll full- or part-time at a two-year or four-year or technical institution or university; female; resident of California and studying in California. Available to U.S. and non-U.S. citizens.

Application Requirements: Application form, essay, financial need analysis. *Deadline:* May 1.

Contact: Stephanie Flax, Scholarship and Program Coordinator
    National Council of Jewish Women Los Angeles (NCJW l LA)
    543 North Fairfax Avenue
    Los Angeles, CA 90036
    Phone: 323-852-8515
    E-mail: scholarship@ncjala.org

STEPHEN L. TELLER & RICHARD HOTSON TV, CINEMA, AND THEATER SCHOLARSHIP

To qualify, an applicant must be a full-time student enrolled in a community college Film/ Television/ Cinema/Theater program, and preparing for a career in film, television, or theater production (not acting). Applicant must have completed 12 units of classes in their school's Film/TV/Cinema/Theater program. The National Council of Jewish Women l Los Angeles (NCJW l LA) provides scholarships, regardless of race, ethnicity, religion, age, gender identity, sexuality or national origin to those who live and attend school in the Greater Los Angeles area, including Los Angeles, Orange, Riverside, and Ventura Counties.

Award: Scholarship for use in freshman, sophomore, junior, senior, graduate, or postgraduate years; not renewable. *Number:* 2. *Amount:* $1000.

Eligibility Requirements: Applicant must be enrolled or expecting to enroll full- or part-time at a two-year institution; resident of California and studying in California. Available to U.S. and non-U.S. citizens.

Application Requirements: Application form, essay, financial need analysis. *Deadline:* May 1.

Contact: Stephanie Flax, Scholarship and Program Coordinator
    National Council of Jewish Women Los Angeles (NCJW l LA)
    543 North Fairfax Avenue
    Los Angeles, CA 90036
    Phone: 323-852-8515
    E-mail: scholarship@ncjwla.org

SUSAN SCHULMAN BEGLEY MEMORIAL SCHOLARSHIP

This award is given to a woman who is establishing herself as a head of household and a single parent, and due to extreme circumstances following the dissolution of an abusive or emotionally traumatic relationship has no other adequate financial means, and requires funds to meet immediate needs for herself and her children, including rent & food. The National Council of Jewish Women l Los Angeles (NCJW l LA) provides scholarships, regardless of race, ethnicity, religion, age, gender identity, sexuality or national origin to those who live and attend school in the Greater Los Angeles area, including Los Angeles, Orange, Riverside, and Ventura Counties.

Award: Scholarship for use in freshman, sophomore, junior, senior, graduate, or postgraduate years; not renewable. *Number:* 1. *Amount:* $1000.

Eligibility Requirements: Applicant must be enrolled or expecting to enroll full- or part-time at a two-year or four-year or technical institution or university; single female; resident of California and studying in California. Available to U.S. and non-U.S. citizens.

Application Requirements: Application form, essay, financial need analysis. *Deadline:* May 1.

Contact: Stephanie Flax, Scholarship and Program Coordinator
National Council of Jewish Women Los Angeles (NCJW l LA)
543 North Fairfax Avenue
Los Angeles, CA 90036
Phone: 323-852-8515
E-mail: scholarship@ncjwla.org

NATIONAL FEDERATION OF THE BLIND (NFB)

http://www.nfb.org/scholarships

AAF KENNETH JERNIGAN SCHOLARSHIP FOR $12,000

The American Action Fund for Blind Children & Adults $12,000 award to honor the top blind college student residing in and attending an accredited institution in the US or Puerto Rico. Winner receives financial assistance to attend NFB convention to receive scholarship.

Award: Scholarship for use in freshman, sophomore, junior, senior, graduate, or postgraduate years; not renewable. *Number:* 1. *Amount:* $12,000.

Eligibility Requirements: Applicant must be visually impaired and enrolled or expecting to enroll full- or part-time at a two-year or four-year institution or university. Applicant must be visually impaired. Available to U.S. citizens.

Application Requirements: Application form, essay, interview. *Deadline:* March 31.

Contact: Patti Chang, Chairperson
National Federation of the Blind (NFB)
NFB Scholarship Committee
200 East Wells Street
Baltimore, MD 21230
Phone: 410-659-9314 Ext. 2415
E-mail: scholarships@nfb.org

CHARLES AND MELVA T. OWEN SCHOLARSHIP FOR $10,000

Merit-based scholarship requires academic excellence and leadership, permanently resides in United States/Puerto Rico, and accredited institution's degree program (in US/PR) directed toward financial independence (excludes degrees in religious studies or solely for cultural education). Winner assisted to attend NFB annual convention to receive this award. Membership not required. USA Citizenship is not a requirement, but if the student's home is not in the US/PR, then the student is not eligible.

Award: Scholarship for use in freshman, sophomore, junior, senior, graduate, or postgraduate years; not renewable. *Number:* 1. *Amount:* $10,000.

Eligibility Requirements: Applicant must be visually impaired and enrolled or expecting to enroll full- or part-time at a two-year or four-year institution or university. Applicant must be visually impaired. Available to U.S. and non-U.S. citizens.

Application Requirements: Application form, essay, interview. *Deadline:* March 31.

Contact: Ms. Patti Chang, Chairperson, NFB Scholarship Committee
National Federation of the Blind (NFB)
200 East Wells Street
Baltimore, MD 21230
Phone: 410-659-9314 Ext. 2415
E-mail: scholarships@nfb.org

NATIONAL MULTIPLE SCLEROSIS SOCIETY

http://www.nmss.org/

NATIONAL MULTIPLE SCLEROSIS SOCIETY SCHOLARSHIP PROGRAM

Scholarships available to high school seniors and graduates (or GED) with MS, or who are children of people with MS. Must be attending a postsecondary school for the first time. All applicants must meet the basic eligibility criteria, fully complete the online application and mail supporting documents by deadline. The program is competitive in nature, and not all applicants will be selected for an award. Scholarship finalists will be selected on the basis of demonstrated financial need, academic record, leadership and participation in school or community activities, work experience, an outside appraisal, goals and aspirations, special circumstances, and an essay (written by the applicant) regarding the impact of MS on their life. More information can be found at www.nationalmssociety.org

Award: Scholarship for use in freshman year; not renewable. *Number:* 400. *Amount:* $1500.

Eligibility Requirements: Applicant must be physically disabled and enrolled or expecting to enroll full- or part-time at a two-year or four-year institution or university. Applicant must be physically disabled. Available to U.S. citizens.

Application Requirements: Application form, driver's license, essay, financial need analysis, personal photograph. *Deadline:* January 15.

Contact: Scholarship Management Services
Phone: 507-931-1682
E-mail: mssociety@scholarshipamerica.org

NATIONAL PRESS FOUNDATION

http://www.nationalpress.org/

EVERT CLARK/SETH PAYNE AWARD

Award to recognize outstanding reporting and writing in any field of science. Limited to non-technical, print journalism only. Articles published in newspapers (including college newspapers), magazines, and newsletters are eligible. Both freelancers and staff writers are eligible.

Award: Prize for use in freshman, sophomore, junior, senior, graduate, or postgraduate years; not renewable. *Number:* 1000.

Eligibility Requirements: Applicant must be enrolled or expecting to enroll full- or part-time at a two-year or four-year or technical institution or university. Available to U.S. citizens.

Application Requirements: Application form, portfolio. *Deadline:* June 30.

Contact: Dianeq McGurgan, Administrator
National Press Foundation
P.O. Box 910
Hedgesville, WV 25427
Phone: 304-754-6786
E-mail: diane@casw.org

NATSO FOUNDATION

http://www.natso.com/

BILL MOON SCHOLARSHIP

Available to employees or dependents of NATSO-affiliated truck stops/travel plazas. Visit website at http://www.natsofoundation.org for additional information.

Award: Scholarship for use in freshman, sophomore, junior, senior, or graduate years; not renewable. *Number:* 13. *Amount:* $2500.

Eligibility Requirements: Applicant must be enrolled or expecting to enroll full- or part-time at a two-year or four-year institution or university. Applicant or parent of applicant must have employment or volunteer experience in transportation industry. Available to U.S. and non-U.S. citizens.

Application Requirements: Application form, essay, financial need analysis, recommendations or references, signature from employer, transcript. *Deadline:* April 14.

Contact: Sharon Corigliano, Executive Director
Phone: 703-549-2100 Ext. 8561
Fax: 703-684-9667
E-mail: scorigliano@natso.com

NEBRASKA'S COORDINATING COMMISSION FOR POSTSECONDARY EDUCATION

https://ccpe.nebraska.gov/

NEBRASKA OPPORTUNITY GRANT

Available to undergraduates attending a participating postsecondary institution in Nebraska. Must demonstrate financial need. Nebraska residency required. Awards determined by each participating institution. Student must complete the Free Application for Federal Student Aid (FAFSA) to apply. Contact financial aid office at institution for additional information.

Award: Grant for use in freshman, sophomore, junior, or senior years; not renewable. *Amount:* $100–$4270.

Eligibility Requirements: Applicant must be enrolled or expecting to enroll full- or part-time at a two-year or four-year or technical institution or university; resident of Nebraska and studying in Nebraska. Available to U.S. citizens.

Application Requirements: Application form, financial need analysis. *Deadline:* continuous.

Contact: Mr. J. Ritchie Morrow, Financial Aid Officer
Nebraska's Coordinating Commission for Postsecondary Education
140 North 8th Street, Suite 300
PO Box 95005
Lincoln, NE 68509-5005
Phone: 402-471-2847
E-mail: Ritchie.Morrow@nebraska.gov

NEW JERSEY HIGHER EDUCATION STUDENT ASSISTANCE AUTHORITY

http://www.hesaa.org/

LAW ENFORCEMENT OFFICER MEMORIAL SCHOLARSHIP

Scholarships for full-time undergraduate study at approved New Jersey institutions for the dependent children of New Jersey law enforcement officers killed in the line of duty. Value of scholarship will be established annually. Deadline varies.

Award: Scholarship for use in freshman, sophomore, junior, or senior years; not renewable.

Eligibility Requirements: Applicant must be enrolled or expecting to enroll full-time at a two-year or four-year institution or university; resident of New Jersey and studying in New Jersey. Applicant or parent of applicant must have employment or volunteer experience in police/firefighting. Available to U.S. citizens.

Application Requirements: Application form.

Contact: Jean Hathaway, Assistant Director of Special Grants and Scholarships
New Jersey Higher Education Student Assistance Authority
PO Box 540
Trenton, NJ 08625
Phone: 609-588-3266

SURVIVOR TUITION BENEFITS PROGRAM

The scholarship provides tuition fees for spouses and dependents of law enforcement officers, fire, or emergency services personnel killed in the line of duty. Eligible recipients may attend any independent institution in the state; however, the annual value of the grant cannot exceed the highest tuition charged at a New Jersey public institution.

Award: Scholarship for use in freshman, sophomore, junior, or senior years; renewable.

Eligibility Requirements: Applicant must be enrolled or expecting to enroll full- or part-time at a two-year or four-year institution or university; resident of New Jersey and studying in New Jersey. Applicant or parent of applicant must have employment or volunteer experience in police/firefighting. Available to U.S. citizens.

Application Requirements: Application form.

Contact: Jean Hathaway, Assistant Director of Special Grants and Scholarships
New Jersey Higher Education Student Assistance Authority
PO Box 540
Trenton, NJ 08625
Phone: 609-588-3266
E-mail: jhathaway@hesaa.org

NICODEMUS WILDERNESS PROJECT

http://www.wildernessproject.org/

APPRENTICE ECOLOGIST SCHOLARSHIP

The Apprentice Ecologist Scholarship is open to students interested in protecting wildlife and the environment. This program elevates young people into leadership roles by engaging them in environmental stewardship and conservation projects that benefit native ecosystems and local communities. Applicants should demonstrate personal initiative, leadership, and dedication in their projects.

Award: Scholarship for use in freshman, sophomore, junior, or senior years; not renewable. *Number:* 3. *Amount:* $250–$1000.

Eligibility Requirements: Applicant must be age 13-21 and enrolled or expecting to enroll full- or part-time at a two-year or four-year or technical institution or university. Available to U.S. and non-U.S. citizens.

Application Requirements: Essay. *Deadline:* December 31.

Contact: Dr. Robert Dudley, Director
Nicodemus Wilderness Project
115 Cornell Dr. SE, #40712
Albuquerque, NM 87196-0712
E-mail: mail@wildernessproject.org

NIKKO COSMETIC SURGERY CENTER

http://www.drnikko.com/

BREAST CANCER SURVIVOR SCHOLARSHIPS

Nikko Cosmetic Surgery Center has announced that it will offer two $1,000 scholarships annually for breast cancer survivors. The scholarships are aimed at assisting breast cancer survivors in the pursuit of their educational goals. Nikko Cosmetic Surgery Center is offering two annual scholarships of $1,000 each. The funds will be paid in the form of tuition for attendance at an educational institution. The tuition can be for secondary or for post-secondary education, including college, trade school, and community college. You do not have to be attending school at this time to be eligible for a scholarship. Within a year after the award date, the winner must provide to Nikko Cosmetic Surgery Center a tuition invoice for the chosen school. A check will then be issued to the institution for $1,000. To be eligible, you must be a U.S. citizen who has been diagnosed with breast cancer.

Award: Scholarship for use in freshman, sophomore, junior, senior, graduate, or postgraduate years; not renewable. *Number:* 2. *Amount:* $1000.

Eligibility Requirements: Applicant must be physically disabled and enrolled or expecting to enroll full- or part-time at a two-year or four-year or technical institution or university. Applicant must be physically disabled. Available to U.S. citizens.

Application Requirements: Application form, essay. *Deadline:* September 30.

Contact: Dr. Anthony Nikko
E-mail: michael@drnikko.com

NISEI STUDENT RELOCATION COMMEMORATIVE FUND

http://www.nsrcfund.org/

NISEI STUDENT RELOCATION COMMEMORATIVE FUND

Eligibility: only high school seniors of Southeast Asian (Vietnam, Cambodia, Laos) ancestry living in the U.S. Deadline to apply varies. Scholarships awarded in a different city/region each year. Check the website (www.nsrcfund.org) for current information or email: jeanhibino@aol.com.

Award: Scholarship for use in freshman year; not renewable. *Number:* 30–50. *Amount:* $250–$2000.

Eligibility Requirements: Applicant must be of Lao/Hmong, Vietnamese heritage; Asian/Pacific Islander; high school student and planning to enroll or expecting to enroll full- or part-time at a two-year or four-year or technical institution or university. Available to U.S. citizens.

Application Requirements: Application form, community service, essay, financial need analysis, personal photograph.

Contact: Ms. Jean Hibino, Executive Secretary
Nisei Student Relocation Commemorative Fund
19 Scenic Drive
Portland, CT 06480
E-mail: jeanhibino@aol.com

NO BULL SPORTS

http://nobullsports.org/

NO BULL SPORTS SCHOLARSHIP

No Bull Sports is a non-profit organization dedicated to uniting, educating, and empowering young women. When we set out to build a community of female athletes from all walks of life, a cornerstone of our mission was to offer scholarships to deserving high school students. No Bull Sports provides smart, trailblazing, talented young women the financial resources they need to achieve their academic and athletic goals. No Bull Sports is excited to award our quarterly scholarships of $5,000 in March, June, and December of 2017 to a deserving female high school sophomore, junior or senior to pursue her dreams on and off the field. We will award $15,000 worth of scholarships over the course of a calendar year; awarded 3xs/year, each scholarship is worth $5,000.

Award: Scholarship for use in freshman year; not renewable.

Eligibility Requirements: Applicant must be high school student and planning to enroll or expecting to enroll full- or part-time at a two-year or four-year or technical institution or university. Available to U.S. citizens.

Application Requirements: Application form, essay. *Deadline:* continuous.

Contact: Bridget W.
No Bull Sports
653 W Fallbrook Ave. #101
Fresno, CA 93711
Phone: 877-307-1451
E-mail: hello@nobullsports.org

NOPLAG PLAGIARISM CHECKER

http://noplag.com/

NOPLAG SCHOLARSHIP ESSAY CONTEST

We are happy to announce the start of the Noplag Scholarship Essay contest. In comparison with other writing contests our goal is to help you become successful and nowadays proper education is a key component. We hope that our aid in the amount of $3500 will help the winner in his education in full or partially. Plus, you will have a good chance to test your writing skills and maybe pump them up by participating in this contest.

Award: Scholarship for use in freshman, sophomore, junior, or senior years; not renewable. *Number:* 3. *Amount:* $300–$2500.

Eligibility Requirements: Applicant must be enrolled or expecting to enroll full- or part-time at a two-year or four-year or technical institution or university. Available to U.S. and non-U.S. citizens.

Application Requirements: Application form, essay. *Deadline:* June 25.

Contact: CEO
E-mail: aleks@noplag.com

NORTH CAROLINA DIVISION OF VOCATIONAL REHABILITATION SERVICES

http://www.dhhs.state.nc.us/

TRAINING SUPPORT FOR YOUTH WITH DISABILITIES

Public service program that helps persons with disabilities obtain competitive employment. To qualify: student must have a mental, physical or learning disability that is an impediment to employment. A Rehabilitation Counselor along with the eligible student individually develops a rehabilitation program to achieve an employment outcome which requires post secondary training. Financial assistance is based on NC Division of Vocational Rehabilitation demonstrated financial need and type of program in which the student enrolls.

Award: Grant for use in freshman, sophomore, junior, senior, or graduate years; renewable.

Eligibility Requirements: Applicant must be hearing impaired, learning disabled, physically disabled, or visually impaired; enrolled or expecting to enroll full- or part-time at a two-year or four-year or technical institution or university and resident of North Carolina. Applicant must be hearing impaired, learning disabled, physically disabled, or visually impaired. Available to U.S. citizens.

Application Requirements: Application form, financial need analysis, interview. *Deadline:* continuous.

Contact: Stephanie Hanes, Program Specialist for Transition
Phone: 919-855-3576
E-mail: stephanie.hanes@dhhs.nc.gov

NORTH CAROLINA VIETNAM VETERANS, INC.

http://www.ncvvi.org

NC VIETNAM VETERANS, INC., SCHOLARSHIP PROGRAM

Scholarship is awarded to Vietnam Veterans, their spouses or their offspring including adopted. Students who successfully attend a Lessons of Vietnam class prior to or during the year of submission are eligible. A 600-900 word essay on a different topic each year relating to the Vietnam War era is required.

Award: Scholarship for use in freshman, sophomore, junior, or senior years; not renewable. *Number:* 1–6. *Amount:* $500–$1500.

Eligibility Requirements: Applicant must be enrolled or expecting to enroll full-time at a two-year or four-year or technical institution or university and resident of North Carolina. Available to U.S. and non-U.S. citizens.

Application Requirements: Application form, essay. *Deadline:* February 28.

OHIO DEPARTMENT OF HIGHER EDUCATION

www.ohiohighered.org

OHIO COLLEGE OPPORTUNITY GRANT

OCOG provides grant money to Ohio residents who demonstrate the highest levels of financial need (as determined by the results of the FAFSA) who are enrolled at Ohio public colleges or universities; Ohio private, non-profit colleges or universities; Ohio private, for-profit institutions; or eligible Pennsylvania institutions.

Award: Grant for use in freshman, sophomore, junior, or senior years; not renewable. *Amount:* $888–$2592.

Eligibility Requirements: Applicant must be enrolled or expecting to enroll full- or part-time at a two-year or four-year institution or university; resident of Ohio and studying in Ohio, Pennsylvania. Available to U.S. citizens.

Application Requirements: *Deadline:* October 1.

Contact: Tamika Braswell, Director
Ohio Department of Higher Education
25 South Front Street
Columbus, OH 43215
Phone: 614-728-8862
E-mail: ocog_admin@regents.state.oh.us

OHIO SAFETY OFFICERS COLLEGE MEMORIAL FUND

Renewable award covering up to full tuition is available to children and surviving spouses of peace officers, other safety officers and fire fighters killed in the line of duty in any state. Children must be under 26 years of age. Dollar value of each award varies. Must be an Ohio resident and enroll full-time or part-time at an Ohio college or university. Any spouse/child of a member of the armed services of the U.S., who has been killed in the line duty during Operation Enduring Freedom, Operation

Iraqi Freedom or a combat zone designated by the President of the United States. Dollar value of each award varies.

Award: Scholarship for use in freshman, sophomore, junior, or senior years; renewable.

Eligibility Requirements: Applicant must be enrolled or expecting to enroll full- or part-time at a two-year or four-year institution or university; resident of Ohio and studying in Ohio. Available to U.S. citizens.

Application Requirements: *Deadline:* continuous.

Contact: Ramah Church, Program Manager
Ohio Department of Higher Education
25 South Front Street
Columbus, OH 43215
Phone: 614-752-9528
E-mail: osom_admin@regents.state.oh.us

OHIO WAR ORPHANS SCHOLARSHIP

Aids Ohio residents attending an eligible college in Ohio. Must be between the ages of 16 and 25, the child of a disabled or deceased veteran, and enrolled full-time. Must maintain a minimum GPA of 2.0. Renewable up to five years. Amount of award varies. Must include Form DD214.

Award: Scholarship for use in freshman, sophomore, junior, or senior years; renewable.

Eligibility Requirements: Applicant must be age 16-25; enrolled or expecting to enroll full-time at a two-year or four-year institution or university; resident of Ohio and studying in Ohio. Available to U.S. citizens. Applicant must have general military experience.

Application Requirements: Application form. *Deadline:* May 15.

Contact: Ramah Church, Program Manager
Ohio Department of Higher Education
25 South Front Street
Columbus, OH 43215
Phone: 614-752-9528
E-mail: wo_admin@regents.state.oh.us

ONE LOVE FOUNDATION

www.joinonelove.org

ONE LOVE FOUNDATION PETS VS. PARTNERS SCHOLARSHIP

Pets can and will take advantage of our love. And we forgive them because they're cute and fluffy and don't know any better. But people should know better. Help us highlight the gray areas between love and control by creating your own #OKforpetsnotpartners meme the educates others about unhealthy relationship behaviors. Yep,.. it's that fun and easy! www.petsvspartners.com

Award: Scholarship for use in freshman, sophomore, junior, senior, graduate, or postgraduate years; not renewable. *Number:* 3. *Amount:* $500.

Eligibility Requirements: Applicant must be age 18-26 and enrolled or expecting to enroll full- or part-time at a two-year or four-year or technical institution or university. Available to U.S. and non-U.S. citizens.

Application Requirements: *Deadline:* December 31.

Contact: April Wright
One Love Foundation
119 Pondfield Rd
PO Box 368
Bronxville, NY 10708
E-mail: thatsnotlove@joinonelove.org

OREGON STUDENT ASSISTANCE COMMISSION

http://www.GetCollegeFunds.org/

FRIENDS OF BILL RUTHERFORD EDUCATION SCHOLARSHIP

Award for children of individuals serving in the Oregon State Legislature or holding statewide elected office (Governor, Treasurer, Attorney

General, Secretary of State, Commissioner of Labor, or Superintendent of Public Instruction); this does not include judicial positions. For use at public and nonprofit colleges in the U.S.

Award: Scholarship for use in freshman, sophomore, junior, or senior years; not renewable.

Eligibility Requirements: Applicant must be enrolled or expecting to enroll full-time at a four-year institution or university. Applicant or parent of applicant must have employment or volunteer experience in government/politics. Available to U.S. citizens.

Application Requirements: Application form, financial need analysis. *Deadline:* March 1.

Contact: Melissa Adams, Scholarship Processing Coordinator
Phone: 541-687-7409
E-mail: melissa.adams@hecc.oregon.gov

ORGANIZATION FOR AUTISM RESEARCH

www.researchautism.org

LISA HIGGINS HUSSMAN SCHOLARSHIP

The Lisa Higgins Hussman Scholarship supports students with autism attending two or four year universities, life skills or postsecondary programs, or vocational, technical, or trade schools. Hussman applicants typically make up the pool of talented students who face daily challenges related to autism and attend programs that assist in skill-building, job-readiness, and other transition-related skills.

Award: Scholarship for use in freshman, sophomore, junior, or senior years; not renewable. *Number:* 20. *Amount:* $3000.

Eligibility Requirements: Applicant must be enrolled or expecting to enroll full-time at a two-year or four-year or technical institution or university. Available to U.S. citizens.

Application Requirements: Application form, essay. *Deadline:* May 5.

SCHWALLIE FAMILY SCHOLARSHIP

The Schwallie Family Scholarship supports students with autism attending two or four year universities. Schwallie applicants typically pursue degrees at four year universities and have a diagnosis of Asperger Syndrome.

Award: Scholarship for use in freshman, sophomore, junior, or senior years; not renewable. *Number:* 20. *Amount:* $3000.

Eligibility Requirements: Applicant must be enrolled or expecting to enroll full-time at a two-year or four-year institution or university. Available to U.S. citizens.

Application Requirements: Application form, essay. *Deadline:* May 5.

OSAGE NATION EDUCATION DEPARTMENT

https://www.osagenation-nsn.gov/what-we-do/education-department

OSAGE NATION HIGHER EDUCATION SCHOLARSHIP

The Osage Nation provides scholarships to legally enrolled members of the Osage Nation who are attending colleges and universities throughout the United States and abroad. The annual qualifying application opens on May 15th and closes on June 15th of each year.

Award: Scholarship for use in freshman, sophomore, junior, senior, graduate, or postgraduate years; renewable. *Number:* 1–1200. *Amount:* $150–$4950.

Eligibility Requirements: Applicant must be American Indian/Alaska Native and enrolled or expecting to enroll full- or part-time at a two-year or four-year institution or university. Available to U.S. citizens.

Application Requirements: Application form. *Deadline:* June 15.

Contact: Katie May, Program Manager
Osage Nation Education Department
Scholarship Management Services
One Scholarship Way
Saint Peter, MN 56082
Phone: 855-758-8609
E-mail: OsageNation@scholarshipamerica.org

OUTRIGGER DUKE KAHANAMOKU FOUNDATION

http://www.dukefoundation.org

ODKF GENERAL SCHOLARSHIP AWARD

The Outrigger Duke Kahanamoku Foundation ("ODKF") is an organization created to support the development and growth of individual athletes and teams that compete in local, national and international athletic competitions. As a tribute to Olympic swimmer and gold medal winner Duke Kahanamoku, our scholarships are awarded to competitors in water sports and volleyball. General scholarships are open to student athletes who are Hawaii residents currently competing in water sports or volleyball, who intended to compete in sports in college, have a 3.0 G.P.A. or higher and involved in community service.

Award: Scholarship for use in freshman, sophomore, junior, or senior years; not renewable. *Number:* 30–50. *Amount:* $1450–$15,000.

Eligibility Requirements: Applicant must be enrolled or expecting to enroll full-time at a four-year institution or university; resident of Hawaii and must have an interest in athletics/sports. Applicant must have 3.0 GPA or higher. Available to U.S. citizens.

Application Requirements: Application form, community service, essay, financial need analysis, personal photograph. *Deadline:* March 1.

Contact: Ms. Kathryn Currier, Administrator
Outrigger Duke Kahanamoku Foundation
PO Box 160924
Honolulu, HI 96816
Phone: 808-545-4880
E-mail: info@dukefoundation.org

PACERS FOUNDATION INC.

http://www.pacersfoundation.org/

PACERS TEAMUP SCHOLARSHIP

Scholarship is awarded to Indiana high school seniors for their first year of undergraduate study at any accredited four-year college or university or two-year college or junior college. Primary selection criteria is student involvement in community service.

Award: Scholarship for use in freshman year; not renewable. *Number:* 5. *Amount:* $2000.

Eligibility Requirements: Applicant must be enrolled or expecting to enroll full-time at a two-year or four-year institution or university and resident of Indiana. Applicant or parent of applicant must have employment or volunteer experience in community service. Available to U.S. citizens.

Application Requirements: Application form, community service, essay, recommendations or references, transcript. *Deadline:* March 1.

Contact: Jami Marsh, Executive Director
Pacers Foundation Inc.
125 South Pennsylvania Street
Indianapolis, IN 46204
Phone: 317-917-2856
E-mail: foundation@pacers.com

PANHELLENIC SCHOLARSHIP FOUNDATION

http://www.panhellenicscholarships.org/

PANHELLENIC SCHOLARSHIP AWARDS

The PanHellenic Scholarship Awards are offered to recognize and reward students who have demonstrated exceptional academic performance as well as provide meaningful support to those with the greatest financial need. The application can be downloaded directly from our website, www.panhellenicsf.org. $250,000 in scholarships will be awarded to exceptional undergraduates of Hellenic descent from across the United States. The awards are offered at two levels—twenty (20) awards of $10,000 based on academic achievement and financial need, and twenty (20) awards of $2,500 based solely on academic achievement. To be eligible to apply for a scholarship, applicants must be U.S. Citizens or U.S. permanent residents; be of Hellenic descent; be a full-time undergraduate student at an accredited 4-year university in fall 2016; and have a minimum 3.5 cumulative GPA. Award recipients are selected by

an Academic Committee appointed by the Foundation's Board of Directors. This Committee works independently and makes its decisions based on established criteria set forth in the scholarship application. All award recipients are required to attend the Awards Ceremony & Gala, where they will receive their scholarship. The gala will be held on Saturday, June 17, 2017 at the Hilton Chicago.

Award: Scholarship for use in freshman, sophomore, junior, or senior years; not renewable. *Number:* 40. *Amount:* $2500–$10,000.

Eligibility Requirements: Applicant must be of Greek heritage and enrolled or expecting to enroll full-time at a four-year institution or university. Applicant must have 3.5 GPA or higher. Available to U.S. citizens.

Application Requirements: Application form, autobiography, essay, financial need analysis. *Deadline:* January 31.

Contact: Ms. Allie Clayman, Scholarships Coordinator
PanHellenic Scholarship Foundation
17 N. Wabash Ave.
Ste. 600
Chicago, IL 60602
Phone: 312-357-6432
E-mail: aclayman@panhellenicsf.org

PAPERCHECK

https://www.papercheck.com/

PAPERCHECK, LLC—CHARLES SHAFAE' SCHOLARSHIP FUND

Awards one $1,000 scholarships each year to winners of the Papercheck essay contest. Must be enrolled at an accredited four-year college or university. Must maintain a cumulative GPA of at least 3.2. Scholarship guidelines available at https://www.papercheck.com/papercheck-scholarship/.

Award: Scholarship for use in freshman, sophomore, junior, or senior years; not renewable. *Number:* 1. *Amount:* $1000.

Eligibility Requirements: Applicant must be enrolled or expecting to enroll full-time at a four-year institution or university. Applicant must have 3.0 GPA or higher. Available to U.S. citizens.

Application Requirements: Application form, essay. *Deadline:* January 31.

Contact: Mr. Darren Shafae, Scholarship Coordinator
Papercheck
3905 State Street
Suite 7-516
Santa Barbara, CA 93105
Phone: 866-693-3348
E-mail: scholarships@papercheck.com

PENNSYLVANIA BURGLAR AND FIRE ALARM ASSOCIATION

http://www.pbfaa.com/

PENNSYLVANIA BURGLAR AND FIRE ALARM ASSOCIATION YOUTH SCHOLARSHIP PROGRAM

Non-renewable scholarships available to sons and daughters of active Pennsylvania police and fire personnel, and volunteer fire department personnel for full-time study at a two- or four-year college, or university. Must be a senior attending a Pennsylvania high school. Scholarship amount in the range of $500 to $6500.

Award: Scholarship for use in freshman year; not renewable. *Number:* 6–8. *Amount:* $500–$6500.

Eligibility Requirements: Applicant must be high school student; planning to enroll or expecting to enroll full-time at a two-year or four-year institution or university and resident of Pennsylvania. Applicant or parent of applicant must have employment or volunteer experience in police/firefighting. Available to U.S. citizens.

Application Requirements: Application form, essay, resume, test scores, transcript. *Deadline:* March 1.

Contact: Dale Eller, Executive Director
Phone: 814-838-3093
Fax: 814-838-5127
E-mail: info@pbfaa.com

PENNSYLVANIA FEDERATION OF DEMOCRATIC WOMEN INC.

www.pafedofdemwomen.org

PENNSYLVANIA FEDERATION OF DEMOCRATIC WOMEN INC. ANNUAL SCHOLARSHIP AWARDS
• See page 554

PENNSYLVANIA HIGHER EDUCATION ASSISTANCE AGENCY

http://www.pheaa.org/

BLIND OR DEAF BENEFICIARY GRANT PROGRAM

This state-funded program provides financial aid to blind or deaf students attending a postsecondary institution. This program awards funds on a first-come, first-served basis.

Award: Grant for use in freshman, sophomore, junior, or senior years; not renewable. *Amount:* $500.

Eligibility Requirements: Applicant must be hearing impaired or visually impaired; enrolled or expecting to enroll full- or part-time at a two-year or four-year or technical institution or university and resident of Pennsylvania. Applicant must be hearing impaired or visually impaired.

Application Requirements: Application form. *Deadline:* March 31.

Contact: Keith New, Director of Public Relations
Phone: 717-720-2509
E-mail: knew@pheaa.org

PENNSYLVANIA STATE GRANT PROGRAM

Award for Pennsylvania residents attending an approved postsecondary institution as undergraduates in a program of at least two years duration. Renewable for up to eight semesters if applicants show continued need and academic progress. Must submit FAFSA. Number of awards granted varies annually. Scholarship value is $200 to $4340. Deadlines: May 1 and August 1.

Award: Grant for use in freshman, sophomore, junior, or senior years; renewable. *Amount:* $200–$4340.

Eligibility Requirements: Applicant must be enrolled or expecting to enroll full- or part-time at a two-year or four-year or technical institution or university and resident of Pennsylvania. Available to U.S. citizens.

Application Requirements: Application form, financial need analysis.

Contact: Keith New, Director of Public Relations
Pennsylvania Higher Education Assistance Agency
1200 North Seventh Street
Harrisburg, PA 17102-1444
Phone: 717-720-2509

PILOT INTERNATIONAL FOUNDATION

http://www.pilotinternational.org/

BECKY BURROWS MEMORIAL SCHOLARSHIP

Becky Burrows Memorial Scholarship are for graduate or undergraduate students who are re-entering the job market, beginning "second careers, " or seeking to improve their professional skills for their current occupation by continuing their education in that field. Student must pursue courses of study that further Pilot International's mission to transform communities through education and service in the area of Preparing Youth for Service, Encouraging Brain Safety & Health; Supporting those who care for others.

Award: Scholarship for use in freshman, sophomore, junior, senior, graduate, or postgraduate years; not renewable. *Number:* 1–5. *Amount:* $500–$1000.

Eligibility Requirements: Applicant must be enrolled or expecting to enroll full- or part-time at a four-year or technical institution or university. Applicant must have 3.5 GPA or higher. Available to U.S. citizens.

Application Requirements: Application form, community service, financial need analysis. *Deadline:* March 15.

Contact: Sierra Martin
Phone: 478-477-1208 Ext. 304
E-mail: sierra@pilothq.org

PLAINTIFF RELIEF

http://plaintiffrelief.com/

PLAINTIFF RELIEF SCHOLARSHIP

We are excited to offer one $1,000 scholarship to a high school senior who demonstrates academic achievement, exhibits leadership ability, participates in community service activities, and demonstrates financial need. Applicants must be U.S. citizens or permanent residents and current high school seniors at the time of their application. Current college students are not eligible to apply.

Award: Scholarship for use in senior year; not renewable. *Number:* 1. *Amount:* $1000.

Eligibility Requirements: Applicant must be high school student and planning to enroll or expecting to enroll full-time at a four-year institution or university. Available to U.S. citizens.

Application Requirements: Application form. *Deadline:* November 1.

Contact: Alex Miller
Plaintiff Relief
3379 Peachtree Road NE, Suite 555
Atlanta, GA 30326
Phone: 866-301-0084
E-mail: alex@plaintiffrelief.com

POLSON & POLSON, P.C.

https://www.polsonlawfirm.com/

POLSON & POLSON, P.C. CONQUERING ADVERSITY SCHOLARSHIP

The Polson & Polson, P.C. Conquering Adversity Scholarship is available to individuals currently enrolled in a course of study at any duly accredited community or junior college, undergraduate or graduate degree program anywhere in the United States. Also eligible are high school graduates or GED holders who are about to embark on college-level studies. For full details, please visit https://www.polsonlawfirm.com/#scholarship

Award: Scholarship for use in freshman, sophomore, junior, senior, graduate, or postgraduate years; not renewable. *Number:* 1. *Amount:* $500.

Eligibility Requirements: Applicant must be enrolled or expecting to enroll full- or part-time at a two-year or four-year or technical institution or university. Applicant must have 3.0 GPA or higher. Available to U.S. and non-U.S. citizens.

Application Requirements: Application form, essay. *Deadline:* October 31.

Contact: Mark Polson
E-mail: info@alabamaduidefense.com

PORTUGUESE FOUNDATION INC.

https://www.facebook.com/pfict/

PORTUGUESE FOUNDATION SCHOLARSHIP PROGRAM

Eligibility: Student must be of Portuguese ancestry, resident of Connecticut, U.S. citizen or a permanent resident, applying for, or currently in college, full-time student in an undergraduate degree conferring program or a part-time student in a master's or doctorate program.

Award: Scholarship for use in freshman, sophomore, junior, senior, graduate, or postgraduate years; not renewable. *Number:* 1–4. *Amount:* $4000.

Eligibility Requirements: Applicant must be of Portuguese heritage; high school student; planning to enroll or expecting to enroll full- or part-time at a two-year or four-year or technical institution or university and resident of Connecticut. Applicant must have 2.5 GPA or higher. Available to U.S. citizens.

Application Requirements: Application form, community service, essay, personal photograph. *Deadline:* April 15.

Contact: Gabe Serrano
Portuguese Foundation Inc.
PO Box 331441
West Hartford, CT 06133-1441
Phone: 860-236-9350
E-mail: pfict90@gmail.com

PRICE BENOWITZ LLP

http://pricebenowitz.com/

AMATO SANITA BRIGHTER FUTURE SCHOLARSHIP

For more information please visit
http://criminallawpennsylvania.com/brighter-future-scholarship-2017.html

Award: Scholarship for use in freshman, sophomore, junior, senior, or graduate years; not renewable. *Number:* 1. *Amount:* $500.

Eligibility Requirements: Applicant must be enrolled or expecting to enroll full- or part-time at a two-year or four-year or technical institution or university. Applicant must have 3.0 GPA or higher. Available to U.S. citizens.

Application Requirements: Essay. *Deadline:* March 31.

Contact: Amato Sanita
E-mail: info@criminallawpennsylvania.com

ANGIE DIPIETRO WOMEN IN BUSINESS SCHOLARSHIP

This scholarship is available to any female student who is pursuing post-secondary education (community college, undergraduate college, graduate school, business school, or law school) at an accredited U.S. institution. Please visit http://marylandcriminallaws.com/#scholarship for more information on this opportunity.

Award: Scholarship for use in freshman, sophomore, junior, senior, or graduate years; not renewable. *Number:* 1. *Amount:* $500.

Eligibility Requirements: Applicant must be enrolled or expecting to enroll full- or part-time at a two-year or four-year institution or university and female. Applicant must have 3.0 GPA or higher. Available to U.S. citizens.

Application Requirements: Essay. *Deadline:* March 31.

Contact: Angie DiPietro
E-mail: info@marylandcriminallaws.com

APRIL COCKERHAM DREAM ACT SCHOLARSHIP

The April Cockerham DREAM Act scholarship is designed to support individuals who are interested in making a difference in the lives of immigrants and other non-native individuals living in the United States. For more information, please visit: http://thevisafirm.com/#scholarship

Award: Scholarship for use in freshman, sophomore, junior, senior, or graduate years; not renewable. *Number:* 1. *Amount:* $500.

Eligibility Requirements: Applicant must be enrolled or expecting to enroll full- or part-time at a two-year or four-year or technical institution or university. Applicant must have 3.0 GPA or higher. Available to U.S. citizens.

Application Requirements: Essay. *Deadline:* January 31.

Contact: April Cockerham
E-mail: info@thevisafirm.com

KAREN RILEY PORTER GOOD WORKS SCHOLARSHIP

Karin Riley Porter believes strongly in advancing the cause of the criminal justice system and criminal defense services by ensuring that everyone within the Commonwealth of Virginia receives fair representation and that those who are dedicated to that calling can realize their full academic potential. For more information, please visit: https://www.virginia-criminallawyer.com/#scholarship

Award: Scholarship for use in freshman, sophomore, junior, senior, graduate, or postgraduate years; not renewable. *Number:* 1. *Amount:* $500.

Eligibility Requirements: Applicant must be enrolled or expecting to enroll full-time at a four-year institution or university. Applicant must have 3.0 GPA or higher. Available to U.S. citizens.

Application Requirements: Essay. *Deadline:* November 30.

Contact: Karin Riley Porter
E-mail: info@virginia-criminallawyer.com

KERRI CASTELLINI WOMEN'S LEADERSHIP SCHOLARSHIP

Ms. Castellini feels that educated women have the power to act as strong leaders both in their field and in the community at large. Thus, she is glad to sponsor the Kerri Castellini Women's Leadership Scholarship. The scholarship is open to any female student enrolled full-time in a community college, private or public undergraduate college or university, graduate program, business school, or law school in the United States. All candidates who apply for this scholarship must be in good academic standing and possess a minimum cumulative GPA of 3.0 or higher. For more information, please visit:
https://trustandestateslawyers.com/#scholarship

Award: Scholarship for use in freshman, sophomore, junior, senior, graduate, or postgraduate years; not renewable. *Number:* 1. *Amount:* $500.

Eligibility Requirements: Applicant must be enrolled or expecting to enroll full-time at a two-year or four-year institution or university and female. Applicant must have 3.0 GPA or higher. Available to U.S. and non-U.S. citizens.

Application Requirements: Essay. *Deadline:* November 30.

Contact: Kerri Castellini
E-mail: info@trustandestateslawyers.com

KUSH ARORA FEDERAL CRIMINAL JUSTICE REFORM SCHOLARSHIP

Mr. Arora understands that the success of the criminal justice system depends on the success of the bright young women and men who are pursuing their academic and professional dreams today. To help them achieve their goals, and to further bolster the system that he so proudly serves, Mr. Arora has established the Kush Arora Criminal Justice Reform Scholarship. For more information, please visit:
https://maryland-criminallawyer.com/#scholarship

Award: Scholarship for use in freshman, sophomore, junior, senior, graduate, or postgraduate years; not renewable. *Number:* 1. *Amount:* $500.

Eligibility Requirements: Applicant must be enrolled or expecting to enroll full-time at a two-year or four-year institution or university. Applicant must have 3.0 GPA or higher. Available to U.S. and non-U.S. citizens.

Application Requirements: Essay. *Deadline:* November 30.

Contact: Kush Arora
E-mail: info@maryland-criminallawyer.com

PRICE BENOWITZ SOCIAL JUSTICE SCHOLARSHIP

To further this vision of making the world a better and more equitable place, our firm offers a scholarship to individuals who have demonstrated an outstanding commitment to social justice and community outreach. For more information, please visit:
https://pricebenowitz.com/#scholarship

Award: Scholarship for use in freshman, sophomore, junior, senior, graduate, or postgraduate years; not renewable. *Number:* 1. *Amount:* $500.

Eligibility Requirements: Applicant must be enrolled or expecting to enroll full- or part-time at a two-year or four-year institution or university. Applicant must have 3.0 GPA or higher. Available to U.S. and non-U.S. citizens.

Application Requirements: Essay. *Deadline:* November 30.

Contact: David Benowitz
E-mail: info@pricebenowitz.com

SETH OKIN GOOD DEEDS SCHOLARSHIP

Mr. Okin is proud to contribute to the national discussion on community service and helping to enable those in pursuit of educational goals with the ultimate purpose of creating a meaningful life of service to others. For more information, please visit:
https://criminallawyermaryland.net/#scholarship

Award: Scholarship for use in freshman, sophomore, junior, senior, or graduate years; not renewable. *Number:* 1. *Amount:* $500.

Eligibility Requirements: Applicant must be enrolled or expecting to enroll full- or part-time at a two-year or four-year institution or university. Applicant must have 3.0 GPA or higher. Available to U.S. citizens.

Application Requirements: Essay. *Deadline:* January 31.

Contact: Seth Okin
E-mail: info@criminallawyermaryland.net

THOMAS SOLDAN HEALTHY COMMUNITIES SCHOLARSHIP

To further champion the cause of developing healthy communities, Mr. Soldan is investing in the future and has offered a scholarship of $500 to any student in a post-secondary education seeking means to encourage sustainable and local health-initiatives in his or her own community. For more information, visit http://virginialawfirm.net/#scholarship

Award: Scholarship for use in freshman, sophomore, junior, senior, or graduate years; not renewable. *Number:* 1. *Amount:* $500.

Eligibility Requirements: Applicant must be enrolled or expecting to enroll full- or part-time at a two-year or four-year institution or university. Applicant must have 3.0 GPA or higher. Available to U.S. citizens.

Application Requirements: Essay. *Deadline:* January 31.

Contact: Thomas Soldan
E-mail: info@virginialawfirm.net

PRIVATE AID TEST SURVEY

A TEST PROGRAM NAME

ScholarshipOwl is proudly announcing the new $1,000 "You Deserve it!" Scholarship because we simply believe that students deserve a scholarship for all their hard work! All that is required from students is to be registered with ScholarshipOwl, be at least 16 years of age, and have a complete profile. A winner will be chosen at random. The scholarship winner will have the funds go towards their tuition fees.

Award: Scholarship for use in senior year; not renewable.

Eligibility Requirements: Applicant must be enrolled or expecting to enroll full-time at an institution or university. Applicant must have 2.5 GPA or higher. Available to U.S. citizens.

Application Requirements: Application form. *Deadline:* May 18.

PROJECT BEST SCHOLARSHIP FUND

http://www.projectbest.com/

PROJECT BEST SCHOLARSHIP

• *See page 555*

PROMPT

http://prompt.com

PROMPT'S $20,000 SCHOLARSHIP

Apply for Prompt's $20,000 Scholarship, The Easiest Scholarship Application in History. All you have to do is upload your favorite essay you are using for your college applications. Your GPA, test scores, family income, race, activities, and random adult coloring book you did while bored in class do not matter! The only thing that matters is telling us something compelling about yourself. If you don't have an essay yet, you can start your application now and upload the essay later. If your colleges do not require essays, then submit anything you feel is compelling. Make sure you get started today as we're giving away $2,000 the 15th of every month before our big $10,000 Grand Prize deadline on January 15th. If your essay doesn't win this month, you can always upload a new one for next month. Best of luck!

Award: Scholarship for use in freshman year; not renewable. *Number:* 14. *Amount:* $2000–$10,000.

Eligibility Requirements: Applicant must be high school student and planning to enroll or expecting to enroll full-time at a two-year or four-year institution or university. Available to U.S. and non-U.S. citizens.

Application Requirements: Essay, interview. *Deadline:* continuous.

Contact: Jordan Haines, Co-Founder
Prompt
110 E 25th St.
New York, NY 07070
Phone: 844-5776678
E-mail: scholarship@prompt.com

PUEBLO OF SAN JUAN, DEPARTMENT OF EDUCATION

OHKAY OWINGEH TRIBAL SCHOLARSHIP OF THE PUEBLO OF SAN JUAN

Scholarship for residents of New Mexico enrolled either full-time or part-time in accredited colleges or universities. Minimum GPA of 2.0 required. Must complete required number of hours of community service in the San Juan Pueblo. Up to thirty scholarships are granted and the value of the award ranges from $300 to $600. Deadline varies.

Award: Scholarship for use in freshman, sophomore, junior, or senior years; renewable. *Number:* 1–30. *Amount:* $300–$600.

Eligibility Requirements: Applicant must be American Indian/Alaska Native; enrolled or expecting to enroll full- or part-time at a two-year or four-year or technical institution or university and resident of New Mexico. Applicant or parent of applicant must have employment or volunteer experience in community service. Available to U.S. citizens.

Application Requirements: Application form, letter of acceptance, transcript. *Deadline:* varies.

Contact: Adam Garcia, Education Coordinator
Phone: 505-852-3477
Fax: 505-852-3030
E-mail: wevog68@valornet.com

POP'AY SCHOLARSHIP

Scholarship for members of Pueblo of San Juan tribe pursuing their first Associate or Baccalaureate degree. Must complete a minimum of 20 hours of community service within the San Juan Pueblo. Scholarship value is $2500. Seventeen awards are granted. Deadlines: December 30 for spring, April 30 for summer, and June 30 for fall.

Award: Scholarship for use in freshman, sophomore, junior, or senior years; renewable. *Number:* up to 17. *Amount:* $2500.

Eligibility Requirements: Applicant must be American Indian/Alaska Native; enrolled or expecting to enroll full-time at a two-year or four-year institution or university and resident of New Mexico. Applicant or parent of applicant must have employment or volunteer experience in community service. Available to U.S. citizens.

Application Requirements: Application form, letter of acceptance, transcript. *Deadline:* varies.

Contact: Adam Garcia, Education Coordinator
Phone: 505-852-3477
Fax: 505-852-3030
E-mail: wevog68@valornet.com

REACH HIGHER MONTANA

http://www.ReachHigherMontana.org

REACH HIGHER MONTANA SCHOLARSHIPS

To qualify, applicants must be: Montana high school seniors, Montana residents who graduated from a Montana high school and are currently attending a Montana college or university, planning on attending school at least half time, maintaining a 2.5 grade point average (GPA). To apply: Scholarship applications are available Dec. 1 - Jan. 31. Watch our website for here for more details and the application: www.ReachHigherMontana.org.

Award: Scholarship for use in freshman, sophomore, junior, or senior years; not renewable. *Number:* 75. *Amount:* $1000.

Eligibility Requirements: Applicant must be enrolled or expecting to enroll full- or part-time at a two-year or four-year or technical institution or university; resident of Montana and studying in Montana. Applicant must have 2.5 GPA or higher. Available to U.S. citizens.

Application Requirements: Application form, personal photograph. *Deadline:* January 31.

Contact: Rhonda Safford, Programs Manager
Reach Higher Montana
40 W 6th Ave
Helena, MT 59601
Phone: 406-422-1275 Ext. 800
E-mail: rsafford@reachhighermontana.org

RHINE LAW FIRM, P.C.

http://www.carolinaaccidentattorneys.com/

2017 RHINE LAW FIRM, P.C. SCHOLARSHIP

With the 2017 Rhine Law Firm, P.C. Scholarship we have found a new way to give back to those who have given so much to their local communities. We believe students are the future, which is why we are so excited to be able to support those students who are working to better, not only themselves through education, but the world at large by giving back. This $500 scholarship is open to students who have earned a 3.0 or higher GPA while demonstrating their commitment to improving their communities. Applicants must be graduating high school seniors or currently-enrolled college students.

Award: Scholarship for use in freshman, sophomore, junior, or senior years; not renewable. *Number:* 1. *Amount:* $500.

Eligibility Requirements: Applicant must be enrolled or expecting to enroll full- or part-time at a two-year or four-year institution or university. Applicant must have 3.0 GPA or higher. Available to U.S. citizens.

Application Requirements: Application form, essay. *Deadline:* April 24.

Contact: Mr. Joel Rhine, Attorney
Rhine Law Firm, P.C.
1612 Military Cutoff Road
Suite 300
Wilmington, NC 28403
Phone: 910-772-9960
Fax: 910-772-9062
E-mail: jrr@rhinelawfirm.com

ROSENGREN KOHLMEYER, LAW OFFICE CHTD.

http://rokolaw.com

ROSENGREN KOHLMEYER LAW OFFICE SCHOLARSHIP

This $1,500 scholarship is judged primarily on need basis, but does not exclude achievement standards. The applicant must have a minimum GPA of 3.0. A transcript must be attached with counselor or school representative signature for application to be considered. Although not required, applicants are encouraged to submit recommendation letters and/or resumes to substantiate their application.

Award: Scholarship for use in freshman, sophomore, junior, or senior years; not renewable. *Number:* 1. *Amount:* $1500.

Eligibility Requirements: Applicant must be enrolled or expecting to enroll full-time at a two-year or four-year institution or university. Applicant must have 3.0 GPA or higher. Available to U.S. citizens.

Application Requirements: Application form, financial need analysis. *Deadline:* June 30.

Contact: Jason Kohlmeyer, Partner
Rosengren Kohlmeyer, Law Office Chtd.
150 St. Andrews Court, Suite 110
Mankato, MN 56001
Phone: 507-625-5000
Fax: 507-625-5004
E-mail: Jkohlmeyer@rokolaw.com

ST. CLAIRE REGIONAL MEDICAL CENTER

http://www.st-claire.org/

SR. MARY JEANNETTE WESS, S.N.D. SCHOLARSHIP

Scholarships available for undergraduates in their junior or senior year of study, or graduate students. Must have graduated from an eastern Kentucky high school in one of the following counties: Bath, Carter, Elliott, Fleming, Lewis, Magoffin, Menifee, Montgomery, Morgan, Rowan, or Wolfe. Must demonstrate academic achievement, leadership, service, and financial need.

Award: Scholarship for use in junior, senior, or graduate years; renewable. *Number:* 2. *Amount:* $750.

Eligibility Requirements: Applicant must be enrolled or expecting to enroll full-time at a four-year institution or university; resident of Kentucky and must have an interest in leadership. Applicant or parent of applicant must have employment or volunteer experience in community service. Available to U.S. and non-U.S. citizens.

Application Requirements: Application form, financial need analysis, recommendations or references, self-addressed stamped envelope with application, transcript. *Deadline:* varies.

Contact: Tom Lewis, Director of Development
Phone: 606-783-6511
Fax: 606-783-6795
E-mail: telewis@st-claire.org

SALLIE MAE FUND

http://www.thesalliemaefund.org/

$1,000 PLAN FOR COLLEGE SWEEPSTAKES

Sallie Mae offers a monthly sweepstakes that is free to register for and is available to all high school and college students! Every month we give away $1,000 to a deserving student and registration is simple! At Sallie Mae we encourage students to apply for as many scholarships as they can before turning to alternate ways to pay for school and we believe in this sweepstake's ability to make college happen.

Award: Scholarship for use in freshman, sophomore, junior, senior, graduate, or postgraduate years; renewable. *Number:* 1–12. *Amount:* $1000.

Eligibility Requirements: Applicant must be enrolled or expecting to enroll full- or part-time at a two-year or four-year or technical institution or university. Available to U.S. citizens.

Application Requirements: *Deadline:* continuous.

Contact: Plan for College team
Phone: 703-810-3000
Fax: 703-984-5042

SELECTBLINDS.COM

http://www.selectblinds.com

SELECTBLINDS.COM $1000 COLLEGE SCHOLARSHIP

We love and value innovation, education, and passion, and we have created a scholarship based around that. We want to see your innovative spirit and learn what you are passionate about. It could earn you $1,000 to use toward your college expenses! Here is what you need to know: Applicants must submit an idea on one of these two items (video, photos or images, infographic, etc. Creativity is encouraged.): 1) What is the most creative thing you can do with window coverings? or 2)Come up with new technology for window coverings. Applicants must also submit a 250 to750 word essay that answers one of the following questions: 1) What do you want to do to make the world a better place? 2) What is the importance of your major/area of study in today's society? 3) What are your most meaningful achievements, and how do they relate to your field of study? 4) Why did you choose your field of study, and where do you see yourself in 10 years? 5) Why are you a good candidate to receive this scholarship? Applicants must submit a transcript. An unofficial transcript is acceptable. Applicants may email their submissions or links to their submissions to scholarship@selectshops.com.

Award: Scholarship for use in freshman, sophomore, junior, senior, graduate, or postgraduate years; not renewable. *Number:* 1. *Amount:* $1000.

Eligibility Requirements: Applicant must be enrolled or expecting to enroll full- or part-time at a two-year or four-year or technical institution or university. Applicant must have 2.5 GPA or higher. Available to U.S. citizens.

Application Requirements: Essay, personal photograph. *Deadline:* June 15.

Contact: Nate Kennedy, Vice President, Operations
SelectBlinds.com
1910 S Stapley Dr
Ste 137
Mesa, AZ 85204
Phone: 480-302-5163
E-mail: scholarship@selectshops.com

SEXNER & ASSOCIATES LLC

http://www.sexner.com/personal-injury/

MITCHELL S. SEXNER & ASSOCIATES LLC SCHOLARSHIP

This scholarship opportunity is available to graduating high school students or currently enrolled undergraduate college students who have maintained a 3.0 or higher GPA and are current U.S. Citizens or current U.S. Permanent Residents. Students must complete the application and a short essay demonstrating their commitment to their education and improving their community; both items, as well as additional information are available on our website: http://www.sexner.com/personal-injury/scholarship/

Award: Scholarship for use in freshman, sophomore, junior, or senior years; not renewable. *Number:* 1. *Amount:* $500.

Eligibility Requirements: Applicant must be enrolled or expecting to enroll full-time at a two-year or four-year institution. Applicant must have 3.0 GPA or higher. Available to U.S. citizens.

Application Requirements: Application form, essay. *Deadline:* May 15.

Contact: Mitch Sexner
Sexner & Associates LLC
2126 W Van Buren St.
Chicago, IL 60612
E-mail: mitch@sexner.com

SHAWN SUKUMAR ATTORNEY AT LAW

https://www.washingtondccriminallawyer.net/

SHAWN SUKUMAR CRIMINAL JUSTICE REFORM SCHOLARSHIP

This scholarship is offered to any student currently enrolled in an accredited community college, undergraduate, or graduate program in the United States. This includes incoming first-year college students who are high school graduates or possess a GED. The scholarship candidate must possess an interest in social justice, as demonstrated by past and present volunteer, professional, and educational experiences. For more information, please visit http://www.washingtondccriminallawyer.net/#scholarship

Award: Scholarship for use in freshman, sophomore, junior, senior, graduate, or postgraduate years; not renewable. *Number:* 1. *Amount:* $500.

Eligibility Requirements: Applicant must be enrolled or expecting to enroll full- or part-time at a two-year or four-year or technical institution or university. Applicant must have 3.0 GPA or higher. Available to U.S. and non-U.S. citizens.

Application Requirements: Application form, essay. *Deadline:* March 31.

Contact: Shawn Sukumar
E-mail: scholarships@washingtondccriminallawyer.net

SILICON VALLEY COMMUNITY FOUNDATION

www.siliconvalleycf.org

ABBY SOBRATO SCHOLARSHIP

For graduating high school seniors and graduates of Latino College Preparatory Academy in San Jos?CA who plan to pursue postsecondary education.

Award: Scholarship for use in freshman or sophomore years; renewable. *Number:* 20. *Amount:* $1000–$7500.

Eligibility Requirements: Applicant must be enrolled or expecting to enroll full-time at a two-year or four-year institution or university and resident of California. Applicant must have 2.5 GPA or higher. Available to U.S. and non-Canadian citizens.

Application Requirements: Application form, essay, financial need analysis. *Deadline:* February 22.

BOBETTE BIBO GUGLIOTTA MEMORIAL SCHOLARSHIP FOR CREATIVE WRITING

For students majoring in the creative writing field and who have demonstrated creative writing ability.

Award: Scholarship for use in freshman or sophomore years; not renewable. *Number:* 2. *Amount:* $1000.

Eligibility Requirements: Applicant must be enrolled or expecting to enroll full-time at a four-year institution; resident of California and must have an interest in writing. Available to U.S. and non-Canadian citizens.

Application Requirements: Application form, essay, financial need analysis. *Deadline:* February 22.

CURRY AWARD FOR GIRLS AND YOUNG WOMEN

Scholarship for young woman aged 18 to 26. Maximum cumulative grade point average of 3.3 on a 4.0 scale. Must have the following: demonstrated financial hardship; current resident of San Mateo County, preference given to residents of East Palo Alto, East Menlo Park, Redwood City and San Mateo; current graduating high school senior, graduate or GED certificate holder; preference given to students who attend(ed) East Palo Alto Academy, East Side College Prep, Menlo Atherton, Sequoia, Carlmont and San Mateo high schools; planning to enroll or currently enrolled in a two- or four-year college or university as a full-time student; United States citizen or eligible non-citizen (eligible non-citizens include United States legal residents and A.B. 540 students). See website for details www.siliconvalleycf.org/scholarships

Award: Scholarship for use in freshman year; not renewable. *Number:* 10. *Amount:* $1000.

Eligibility Requirements: Applicant must be age 18-26; enrolled or expecting to enroll full-time at a two-year or four-year institution or university; female and resident of California. Applicant must have 3.0 GPA or higher. Available to U.S. and non-U.S. citizens.

Application Requirements: Application form, community service, essay, financial need analysis. *Deadline:* February 22.

HAROLD JOHNSON LAW ENFORCEMENT SCHOLARSHIP

The Krishnan-Shah Family Scholarship was established by Ajay Shah, Lata Krishnan and their family. This scholarship program seeks to support financially needy students with academic potential and demonstrated community involvement, and provide meaningful and ongoing financial support to ensure that students complete their undergraduate degree. Eligibility Requirements: Graduating high school senior residing in the greater Silicon Valley Region (includes Santa Clara County, San Mateo County, San Francisco County, Alameda County and Santa Cruz County) or current community college student who graduated from a high school within the five listed counties. First generation college student (neither parent earned a four-year college degree), pursuing first undergraduate degree, planning to enroll in a four-year college or university on a full-time basis in the upcoming fall session. Maximum cumulative grade point average of 3.75 on a 4.0 scale. Demonstrated involvement in activities (extracurricular, volunteer, paid, etc.). Demonstrated financial need or hardship.

Award: Scholarship for use in freshman, sophomore, junior, or senior years; not renewable. *Number:* 1–5. *Amount:* $1000–$10,000.

Eligibility Requirements: Applicant must be enrolled or expecting to enroll full-time at a four-year institution or university and resident of California. Applicant must have 3.5 GPA or higher.

Application Requirements: Application form, community service, essay, financial need analysis. *Deadline:* February 22.

HAZEL REED BAUMEISTER SCHOLARSHIP PROGRAM

This program was established in 2001 through the Trust of Mrs. Hazel Reed Baumeister, a longtime resident of Burlingame. Mrs. Baumeister attended business school and worked from 1933 to 1939 as confidential executive secretary to United States Senator Pat McCarran of Nevada. The purpose of the scholarship, established in her memory, is to support high school graduates of high academic achievement who would be unable to pursue higher education without financial assistance. The selection committee looks for academic promise, documented perseverance in activities outside the classroom, the quality of the personal statement and personal characteristics such as honesty, good judgment and commitment to serving the community. Students may apply to both the Crain Educational Grant Program and the Hazel Reed Baumeister Scholarship Program, but may receive only one of these scholarships. Must have demonstrated community involvement over a period of several years; minimum cumulative grade point average of 3.5 on a 4.0 scale; demonstrated financial hardship; be a graduating high school senior or graduate of a public or private high school in San Mateo County or Santa Clara County; planning to enroll or currently enrolled in a four-year college or university as a full-time student; and be a United States citizen.

Award: Scholarship for use in freshman, sophomore, junior, or senior years; not renewable. *Number:* 1–15. *Amount:* $1000–$5000.

Eligibility Requirements: Applicant must be enrolled or expecting to enroll full-time at a four-year institution or university and resident of California. Applicant must have 3.5 GPA or higher. Available to U.S. citizens.

Application Requirements: Application form, community service, essay, financial need analysis. *Deadline:* February 22.

HUANG LEADERSHIP DEVELOPMENT SCHOLARSHIP

Scholarship recipients will be selected based on academic achievement excellence and leadership qualities as evidenced by their personal statement, letters of reference, school and community activities. Must be a current employee or past employee, or a legal dependent or grandchild of a current or past employee of SYNNEX Corporation or its subsidiaries, who left the company in good standing; or a current employee or past employee, or a legal dependent or grandchild of a current or past employee that worked for SYNNEX Corporation or its subsidiaries for a minimum of three years at the time of the application deadline. Must have demonstrated academic excellence and leadership qualities through activities in school, community, or social service activities. Must have been accepted into and confirmed intent to enroll or be enrolled on a full-time basis in an undergraduate program in a four-year college or university ranked as a top college or university according to the current year's U.S. News and World Report college/university rankings or comparable source.

Award: Scholarship for use in freshman, sophomore, junior, or senior years; renewable. *Number:* 1–10. *Amount:* $1000–$8500.

Eligibility Requirements: Applicant must be enrolled or expecting to enroll full-time at a four-year institution or university. Available to U.S. and non-U.S. citizens.

Application Requirements: Application form, essay, financial need analysis. *Deadline:* May 10.

LATINOS IN TECHNOLOGY SCHOLARSHIP

Must be of Latino or Hispanic origin (as defined by U.S. Census Bureau); have a declared major in and been accepted into a STEM program; current college student entering their junior or senior year in the 2017 academic school year and planning to enroll on a full-time or part-time basis. Preference will be given to full-time and rising junior students. Must be a graduate of a high school in the following Northern California counties: Alameda County, Contra Costa County, Marin County, Napa County, San Francisco County, San Mateo County, Santa Clara County, Santa Cruz County and Solano County; OR, enrolled at a college/university within the 10 listed counties. Minimum cumulative college grade point average of 2.5 and demonstrated financial need required. United States citizen or eligible non-citizen (eligible non-citizens include United States legal residents and students who have obtained Deferred Action for Childhood Arrivals). See complete details at www.siliconvalleycf.org/scholarships

Award: Scholarship for use in junior or senior years; renewable. *Number:* 1–100. *Amount:* $1000–$10,000.

Eligibility Requirements: Applicant must be of Hispanic, Mexican heritage; enrolled or expecting to enroll full-time at a four-year institution or university and resident of California. Applicant must have 2.5 GPA or higher. Available to U.S. and non-U.S. citizens.

Application Requirements: Application form, essay, financial need analysis. *Deadline:* December 7.

SOCIETY FOR APPLIED ANTHROPOLOGY

http://www.sfaa.net/

ANNUAL SFAA STUDENT ENDOWED AWARD

The Student Endowed Award consists of a $500 travel stipend to cover costs of attending the annual meeting, plus a one-year SfAA membership, (which includes a one year subscription to the journals Human Organization and Practicing Anthropology).

Award: Prize for use in freshman, sophomore, junior, senior, graduate, or postgraduate years; not renewable. *Number:* 1. *Amount:* $500.

Eligibility Requirements: Applicant must be enrolled or expecting to enroll full- or part-time at a two-year or four-year institution or university. Available to U.S. and non-U.S. citizens.

Application Requirements: Application form, essay. *Deadline:* December 20.

Contact: Student Committee Awards Officer
Society for Applied Anthropology
c/o The Society for Applied Anthropology
PO Box 2436
Oklahoma City, OK 73101-2436
Phone: 405-843-5113
E-mail: student.award@sfaa.net

TOURISM AND HERITAGE STUDENT PAPER COMPETITION

The SfAA seeks to recognize student contributions to the anthropology of tourism and heritage and encourage new and innovative avenues of inquiry. Student papers should entail original research on the themes of "tourism" and/or "heritage" broadly defined, including topics such as heritage, archaeology and tourism, ecotourism, and cultural resource management.

Award: Prize for use in freshman, sophomore, junior, senior, graduate, or postgraduate years; not renewable. *Number:* 1. *Amount:* $500.

Eligibility Requirements: Applicant must be enrolled or expecting to enroll full- or part-time at a two-year or four-year institution or university. Available to U.S. and non-U.S. citizens.

Application Requirements: *Deadline:* September 15.

Contact: Dr. Trish Colvin, Office Manager
Phone: 405-843-5113
Fax: 405-843-8553
E-mail: info@sfaa.net

SOCIETY OF DAUGHTERS OF THE UNITED STATES ARMY

SOCIETY OF DAUGHTERS OF THE UNITED STATES ARMY SCHOLARSHIPS

Scholarship for daughters or granddaughters of career warrant or commissioned officer in the U.S. Army who is on active duty; retired from active duty after 20 years of service; medically retired before 20 years of active service; died while on active duty or died after retiring from active duty. Send the following information to request an application: applicant's name, name of officer, rank, component (active, reserve, retired), dates of active duty service, and relationship to the applicant. Send information only, no documentation at this time. Send to Mary P. Maroney, DUSA Scholarship Chairman, 11804 Grey Birch Place, Reston, VA 20191. Application available November 1 - March 1.

Award: Scholarship for use in freshman, sophomore, junior, or senior years; not renewable. *Number:* 8–12. *Amount:* $1000.

Eligibility Requirements: Applicant must be enrolled or expecting to enroll full-time at a two-year or four-year or technical institution or university and female. Applicant must have 3.0 GPA or higher. Available to U.S. citizens. Applicant or parent must meet one or more of the following requirements: national guard experience; retired from active duty; disabled or killed as a result of military service; prisoner of war; or missing in action.

Application Requirements: Application form, essay. *Deadline:* March 1.

Contact: Mary Maroney, Chairperson, Memorial and Scholarship Funds
Society of Daughters of the United States Army
11804 Grey Birch Place
Reston, VA 20191

SOUTH CAROLINA TUITION GRANTS COMMISSION

http://www.sctuitiongrants.org/

SOUTH CAROLINA TUITION GRANTS PROGRAM

Need-based grant set aside for students attending eligible independent colleges in South Carolina. Student must be a South Carolina resident. Must apply annually by submitting the Free Application for Federal Student Aid (FAFSA). Freshmen must graduate in top 75% of high school class OR score 900 on SAT/19 on ACT OR graduate with at least 2.0 on SC Uniform Grading Scale. Upperclassmen must pass a minimum of 24 credit hours annually.

Award: Grant for use in freshman, sophomore, junior, or senior years; renewable. *Amount:* $100–$3200.

Eligibility Requirements: Applicant must be enrolled or expecting to enroll full-time at a two-year or four-year institution or university; resident of South Carolina and studying in South Carolina. Available to U.S. citizens.

Application Requirements: Financial need analysis. *Deadline:* June 30.

Contact: Zachary Christian, Financial Aid Counselor
South Carolina Tuition Grants Commission
115 Atrium Way, Suite 102
Columbia, SC 29223
Phone: 803-896-1120
E-mail: zachary@sctuitiongrants.org

SPANISHDICT

www.spanishdict.com/traductor

BECA #TRADUCTOR

SpanishDict.com is hosting an inaugural #Traductor scholarship to give students the opportunity to win $1,000. The scholarship competition is open now through Wednesday, August 31, 2016 on www.spanishdict.com/traductor. The application is open to all students from around the world, 13 and older. Students can simply navigate to www.spanishdict.com/traductor, and fill out the form, with a short essay prompt describing a time when they had to translate words from Spanish to English or English to Spanish. The winner will receive $1,000 to help cover education expenses.

Award: Scholarship for use in freshman, sophomore, junior, senior, graduate, or postgraduate years; not renewable. *Number:* 1. *Amount:* $1000.

Eligibility Requirements: Applicant must be enrolled or expecting to enroll full- or part-time at a two-year or four-year or technical institution or university. Available to U.S. and non-U.S. citizens.

Application Requirements: Application form, essay. *Deadline:* August 31.

Contact: Alicia Zelek, Product Growth Lead
SpanishDict
1400 Key Blvd
Suite 1200
Arlington, VA 22209
Phone: 305-505-4667
E-mail: ali@spanishdict.com

SPINE SURGEON DR. VICTOR HAYES

https://tampabaybackpaindoctor.com/

TAMPA BAY SPINE CENTER ROAD TO RECOVERY SCHOLARSHIP

Write a 750-word essay that thoughtfully describes a time in your life in which you suffered a physical or emotional setback, how you recovered, and what that recovery has meant to you. Current official transcript from the applicant's school is required. First-year college students may submit an official transcript from their most recent school, as well as an unofficial transcript from their current post-secondary institution. For more complete information, please visit http://tampabaybackpaindoctor.com/#scholarship

Award: Scholarship for use in freshman, sophomore, junior, senior, graduate, or postgraduate years; not renewable. *Number:* 1. *Amount:* $500.

Eligibility Requirements: Applicant must be enrolled or expecting to enroll full- or part-time at a two-year or four-year or technical institution or university. Applicant must have 3.0 GPA or higher. Available to U.S. and non-U.S. citizens.

Application Requirements: Application form, essay. *Deadline:* July 1.

Contact: Dr. Victor Hayes
E-mail: info@tampabaybackpaindoctor.com

STATE FARM COMPANIES/YOUTH SERVICE AMERICA

http://www.ysa.org/

HARRIS WOFFORD AWARDS

Awards recognize extraordinary achievements in three categories: youth (ages 12 to 25), organization (nonprofit, corporate, foundation), and media (organization or individual) for actively contributing towards, "Making service and service-learning the common expectation and common experience of every young person."

Award: Grant for use in freshman, sophomore, junior, senior, graduate, or postgraduate years; not renewable. *Number:* up to 3. *Amount:* $500–$1000.

Eligibility Requirements: Applicant must be age 12-25 and enrolled or expecting to enroll full- or part-time at a two-year or four-year or technical institution or university. Applicant or parent of applicant must have employment or volunteer experience in community service. Available to U.S. citizens.

Application Requirements: Application form. *Deadline:* October 19.

Contact: Julie Mancuso, Grant Manager
Phone: 202-296-2992 Ext. 111
Fax: 202-296-4030
E-mail: jmancuso@ysa.org

STONEWALL COMMUNITY FOUNDATION

http://www.stonewallfoundation.org/

HARRY BARTEL MEMORIAL SCHOLARSHIP

LGBT students in New York City who are 23 years or younger with a record of community service can apply for this scholarship. Deadline varies. Applications available through Youth Program at The LGBT Center in Manhattan.

Award: Scholarship for use in freshman, sophomore, junior, senior, graduate, or postgraduate years; not renewable. *Number:* 1–2. *Amount:* $500.

Eligibility Requirements: Applicant must be enrolled or expecting to enroll full-time at a two-year or four-year or technical institution or university; male and must have an interest in LGBT issues. Applicant or parent of applicant must have employment or volunteer experience in community service. Available to U.S. citizens.

Application Requirements: Application form.

Contact: Natasha Jones, Director of Youth Leadership and Engagement
Stonewall Community Foundation
c/o The Lesbian, Gay, Bisexual, and Transgender
Community Center
208 West 13th Street
New York, NY 10011
Phone: 212-620-7310
E-mail: youth@gaycenter.org

NEW YORK RAMBLERS SCHOLARSHIP FOR STUDENT ATHLETES

The New York Ramblers Scholarship for Student Athletes was created in 2016 to support student athletes who self-identify as either lesbian, gay, bisexual, queer, or intersex (LGBTQI), or are demonstrated and committed allies. Awardees will receive a one-time scholarship, paid directly to their college, to cover tuition and fees. Up to two scholarships of $2,500 each will be awarded in Summer 2016.

Award: Scholarship for use in freshman, sophomore, or junior years; not renewable. *Number:* 1–2. *Amount:* $1000–$2500.

Eligibility Requirements: Applicant must be enrolled or expecting to enroll full- or part-time at a two-year or four-year institution or university and must have an interest in athletics/sports or LGBT issues. Available to U.S. citizens.

Application Requirements: Application form. *Deadline:* July 12.

Contact: Carlie Steen, Program Manager
Stonewall Community Foundation
446 West 33rd Street
New York, NY 10001-2601
Phone: 212-367.1155
E-mail: grants@stonewallfoundation.org

TRAUB-DICKER RAINBOW SCHOLARSHIP

Non-renewable scholarships available to women-identified students who are involved in LGBTQ activism. Must be graduating high school seniors planning to attend a recognized college, or already matriculated college students in any year of study, including graduate school.

Award: Scholarship for use in freshman, sophomore, junior, senior, graduate, or postgraduate years; not renewable. *Number:* 3–4. *Amount:* $1000–$3000.

Eligibility Requirements: Applicant must be enrolled or expecting to enroll full- or part-time at a four-year institution or university; female and must have an interest in LGBT issues. Available to U.S. citizens.

Application Requirements: Application form, essay. *Deadline:* May 10.

Contact: Carlie Steen, Program Manager
Stonewall Community Foundation
Stonewall Community Foundation
1270 Broadway, Suite 501
New York, NY 10001
Phone: 212-457.1349
E-mail: grants@stonewallfoundation.org

STROM & ASSOCIATES

https://stromlawyers.com

STROM & ASSOCIATES NEED-BASED SCHOLARSHIP

This scholarship is open to any US citizen or permanent US resident who will be enrolled full--time in an accredited community college, college or university, or accredited law school in the fall of 2017. This need--based scholarship will be awarded to the student who demonstrates financial need and who submits the strongest PSA video focusing on the following topic: "What does it take to be a good American?"

Award: Scholarship for use in freshman, sophomore, junior, or senior years; not renewable. *Number:* 1. *Amount:* $1500.

Eligibility Requirements: Applicant must be enrolled or expecting to enroll full-time at a two-year or four-year institution or university. Available to U.S. citizens.

Application Requirements: Financial need analysis. *Deadline:* June 1.

Contact: Neal Strom, Partner
Strom & Associates
180 N. LaSalle Suite #2510
Chicago, IL 60601
Phone: 312-609-0400

TARADASH LAW FIRM

https://taradashlaw.com/

TARADASH LAW FIRM SCHOLARSHIP

This scholarship is open to any US citizen or permanent US resident who will be enrolled full--time in an accredited community college, college or university, or accredited law school in the fall of 2017. The scholarship committee will base the judging criteria on financial need and the quality of a written essay on the topic: Describe what contributions you plan on making to society over the next ten years.

Award: Scholarship for use in freshman, sophomore, junior, or senior years; not renewable. *Number:* 1. *Amount:* $1500.

Eligibility Requirements: Applicant must be enrolled or expecting to enroll full-time at a two-year or four-year institution or university. Available to U.S. citizens.

Application Requirements: Financial need analysis. *Deadline:* June 1.

Contact: Randall Taradash, Partner
Taradash Law Firm
908 S. Illinois Route 31
McHenry, IL 60050
Phone: 815-385-1177
Fax: 815-385-1549

TELEVISION ACADEMY FOUNDATION

http://www.televisionacademy.com/foundation

TELEVISION ACADEMY FOUNDATION

A competition for excellence in college student video, digital, and film productions. Rules and guidelines are updated annually in the fall at televisionacademyfoundation.org. Awards of up to $10,000. Open to those students who have produced their video while enrolled in a community college, college, or university in the United States.

Award: Prize for use in freshman, sophomore, junior, senior, graduate, or postgraduate years; not renewable. *Number:* 20–25. *Amount:* $2000–$10,000.

Eligibility Requirements: Applicant must be enrolled or expecting to enroll full- or part-time at a two-year or four-year or technical institution or university. Available to U.S. citizens.

Application Requirements: Application form, personal photograph. *Deadline:* January 31.

Contact: Jessica Davis, Program Coordinator
Television Academy Foundation
5220 Lankershim Boulevard
North Hollywood, CA 91601
Phone: 818-754-2802
E-mail: ctasupport@televisionacademy.com

TENNESSEE STUDENT ASSISTANCE CORPORATION

http://www.tn.gov/collegepays

DEPENDENT CHILDREN SCHOLARSHIP PROGRAM

Scholarship for Tennessee residents who are dependent children of a Tennessee law enforcement officer, fireman, or an emergency medical service technician who have been killed or totally and permanently disabled while performing duties within the scope of such employment. The scholarship is awarded to full-time undergraduate students for a maximum of four academic years or the period required for the completion of the program of study.

Award: Scholarship for use in freshman, sophomore, junior, or senior years; not renewable. *Amount:* $3000–$30,000.

Eligibility Requirements: Applicant must be enrolled or expecting to enroll full-time at a two-year or four-year institution or university; resident of Tennessee and studying in Tennessee. Available to U.S. citizens.

Application Requirements: Application form. *Deadline:* July 15.

Contact: Ms. Kathy Stripling, Grant and Scholarship Analyst
Tennessee Student Assistance Corporation
Parkway Towers
404 James Robertson Parkway, Suite 1510
Nashville, TN 37243-0820
Phone: 615-253-7480
E-mail: kathy.stripling@tn.gov

HELPING HEROES GRANT

Provides assistance to Tennessee veterans who have been awarded the Iraq Campaign Medal, Afghanistan Campaign Medal, or Global War on Terrorism Expeditionary Medal (on or after 9/11/01) and who meet eligibility requirements for the program. Award is up to $1,000 per semester. For more information, visit http://www.TN.gov/collegepays.

Award: Grant for use in freshman, sophomore, junior, or senior years; renewable. *Amount:* $2000.

Eligibility Requirements: Applicant must be enrolled or expecting to enroll full- or part-time at a two-year or four-year institution or university; resident of Tennessee and studying in Tennessee. Available to U.S. citizens. Applicant must have general military experience.

Application Requirements: Application form. *Deadline:* September 1.

Contact: Mr. Robert Biggers, Assistant Executive Director of Grant & Scholarship Programs
Tennessee Student Assistance Corporation
Parkway Towers
404 James Robertson Parkway, Suite 1510
Nashville, TN 37243
Phone: 615-253-7453
E-mail: robert.biggers@tn.gov

HOPE WITH ASPIRE

HOPE Scholarship of $2,000 per semester (four-year institution) or $1,000 per semester (two-year institution) with $750 supplement per semester. Must meet Tennessee HOPE Scholarship requirements and Adjusted Gross Income (AGI) attributable to the student must be $36,000 or less.

Award: Scholarship for use in freshman, sophomore, junior, or senior years; renewable. *Amount:* $5500.

Eligibility Requirements: Applicant must be enrolled or expecting to enroll full- or part-time at a two-year or four-year institution or university; resident of Tennessee and studying in Tennessee. Applicant must have 3.0 GPA or higher. Available to U.S. citizens.

Application Requirements: *Deadline:* September 1.

Contact: Mr. Robert Biggers, Assistant Executive Director of Grant &
Scholarships Programs
Tennessee Student Assistance Corporation
Parkway Towers
404 James Robertson Parkway, Suite 1510
Nashville, TN 37243-0820
Phone: 615-253-7453
E-mail: robert.biggers@tn.gov

NED MCWHERTER SCHOLARS PROGRAM

Award for Tennessee high school seniors with high academic ability.
Must have minimum high school GPA of 3.5 and a score of 29 on the
ACT or SAT equivalent. Must attend a college or university in Tennessee.
Must be a Tennessee resident and U.S. citizen or permanent resident. For
more information, visit website http://tn.gov/collegepays.

Award: Scholarship for use in freshman, sophomore, junior, or senior
years; renewable. *Amount:* $3000.

Eligibility Requirements: Applicant must be enrolled or expecting to
enroll full-time at a two-year or four-year or technical institution or
university; resident of Tennessee and studying in Tennessee. Applicant
must have 3.5 GPA or higher. Available to U.S. citizens.

Application Requirements: Application form. *Deadline:* February 15.

Contact: Ms. Kathy Stripling, Grants and Scholarship Analyst
Tennessee Student Assistance Corporation
404 James Robertson Parkway, Suite 1510
Parkway Towers
Nashville, TN 37243-0820
Phone: 615-253-7480
E-mail: kathy.stripling@tn.gov

TELS HOPE ACCESS GRANT

Non-renewable award of $2,750 for students at four-year colleges or
$1,750 for students at two-year colleges. Entering freshmen must have a
minimum GPA of 2.75, ACT score of 18-20 (or SAT equivalent), and
adjusted gross income attributable to the student must be $36,000 or less.
Recipients will become eligible for Tennessee HOPE Scholarship by
meeting HOPE Scholarship renewal criteria.

Award: Grant for use in freshman, sophomore, junior, or senior years; not
renewable. *Amount:* $2750.

Eligibility Requirements: Applicant must be enrolled or expecting to
enroll full- or part-time at a two-year or four-year institution or
university; resident of Tennessee and studying in Tennessee. Applicant
must have 3.0 GPA or higher. Available to U.S. citizens.

Application Requirements: *Deadline:* September 1.

Contact: Mr. Robert Biggers, Assistant Executive Director of Grant &
Scholarship Programs
Tennessee Student Assistance Corporation
Parkway Towers
404 James Robertson Parkway, Suite 1510
Nashville, TN 37243-0820
Phone: 615-253-7453
E-mail: robert.biggers@tn.gov

TELS -HOPE WITH GENERAL ASSEMBLY MERIT SCHOLARSHIP (GAMS)

Students who qualify for the HOPE Scholarship can receive GAMS by
earning a minimum 3.75 GPA and a 29 or above on the ACT (or SAT
equivalent). The supplemental award is $500 per semester. Must be a
Tennessee resident. For more information, visit www.tn.gov/collegepays.

Award: Scholarship for use in freshman, sophomore, junior, or senior
years; renewable. *Amount:* $5000.

Eligibility Requirements: Applicant must be enrolled or expecting to
enroll full- or part-time at a two-year or four-year institution or
university; resident of Tennessee and studying in Tennessee. Applicant
must have 3.5 GPA or higher. Available to U.S. citizens.

Application Requirements: *Deadline:* September 1.

Contact: Mr. Robert Biggers, Assistant Executive Director of Grant &
Scholarship Programs
Tennessee Student Assistance Corporation
Parkway Towers
404 James Robertson Parkway, Suite 1510
Nashville, TN 37243-0820
Phone: 615-253-7453
E-mail: robert.biggers@tn.gov

TELS - TENNESSEE HOPE SCHOLARSHIP

Students must achieve a minimum 3.0 GPA or 21 or above on the ACT to
qualify for the scholarship. Award amount is $1,750 for per semester at
four-year institutions and $1,500 per semester at two-year institutions for
entering freshmen who first received HOPE in fall 2015 and thereafter.
Award amount is $2,000 per semester at four-year institutions and $1,000
per semester at two-year institutions for students who first received
HOPE between fall 2009 and summer 2015. Must be a Tennessee
resident attending an eligible postsecondary institution in Tennessee. For
more information, visit http://www.TN.gov/CollegePays.

Award: Scholarship for use in freshman, sophomore, junior, or senior
years; renewable. *Amount:* $2000–$6000.

Eligibility Requirements: Applicant must be enrolled or expecting to
enroll full- or part-time at a two-year or four-year institution or
university; resident of Tennessee and studying in Tennessee. Applicant
must have 3.0 GPA or higher. Available to U.S. citizens.

Application Requirements: *Deadline:* September 1.

Contact: Mr. Robert Biggers, Assistant Executive Director of Grant &
Scholarship Programs
Tennessee Student Assistance Corporation
Parkway Towers
404 James Robertson Parkway, Suite 1510
Nashville, TN 37243-0820
Phone: 615-253-7453
E-mail: robert.biggers@tn.gov

TENNESSEE DUAL ENROLLMENT GRANT

Grant for study at an eligible Tennessee postsecondary institution
awarded to juniors and seniors in a Tennessee high school who have been
admitted to undergraduate study while still pursuing a high school
diploma. For more information, visit website
http://www.tn.gov/collegepays.

Award: Grant for use in freshman year; renewable. *Amount:* $1200.

Eligibility Requirements: Applicant must be high school student;
planning to enroll or expecting to enroll part-time at a two-year or four-
year or technical institution or university; resident of Tennessee and
studying in Tennessee. Available to U.S. citizens.

Application Requirements: Application form. *Deadline:* September 1.

Contact: Mr. Robert Biggers, Assistant Executive Director of Grant &
Scholarship Programs
Tennessee Student Assistance Corporation
Parkway Towers
404 James Robertson Parkway, Suite 1510
Nashville, TN 37243-0820
Phone: 615-253-7453
E-mail: robert.biggers@tn.gov

TENNESSEE EDUCATION LOTTERY SCHOLARSHIP PROGRAM WILDER-NAIFEH TECHNICAL SKILLS GRANT

Award up to $2,000 for students enrolled in a certificate or diploma
program at a Tennessee College of Applied Technology (TCAT). For
more information, visit http://www.TN.gov/CollegePays.

Award: Grant for use in freshman or sophomore years; renewable.
Amount: $2000.

Eligibility Requirements: Applicant must be enrolled or expecting to
enroll full- or part-time at a technical institution; resident of Tennessee
and studying in Tennessee. Available to U.S. citizens.

Application Requirements: *Deadline:* November 1.

Contact: Mr. Robert Biggers, Assistant Executive Director of Grant &
Scholarship Programs
Tennessee Student Assistance Corporation
Parkway Towers
404 James Robertson Parkway, Suite 1510
Nashville, TN 37243-0820
Phone: 615-253-7453
E-mail: robert.biggers@tn.gov

TENNESSEE HOPE FOSTER CHILD TUITION GRANT

Renewable tuition award available for recipients of the HOPE
Scholarship or HOPE Access Grant. Student must have been in
Tennessee state custody as a foster child for at least one year after
reaching age 14. Award amount varies and shall not exceed the tuition
and mandatory fees at an eligible Tennessee public postsecondary
institution. For additional information, visit website
http://www.tn.gov/collegepays.

Award: Scholarship for use in freshman, sophomore, junior, or senior years; renewable.

Eligibility Requirements: Applicant must be enrolled or expecting to enroll full- or part-time at a two-year or four-year institution or university; resident of Tennessee and studying in Tennessee. Applicant must have 3.0 GPA or higher. Available to U.S. citizens.

Application Requirements: *Deadline:* September 1.

Contact: Mr. Robert Biggers, Assistant Executive Director of Grant & Scholarship Programs
Tennessee Student Assistance Corporation
Parkway Towers
404 James Robertson Parkway, Suite 1510
Nashville, TN 37243-0820
Phone: 615-253-7453
E-mail: robert.biggers@tn.gov

TENNESSEE STEP UP SCHOLARSHIP

Scholarship program designed to assist students with intellectual disabilities who have completed high school and enroll in up to a four-year individualized program at an eligible postsecondary institution. For entering students beginning with Fall 2015 and thereafter, students will receive $1,750 per semester. For students who first received the STEP UP Scholarship in Fall 2012 through Summer 2015 students will continue to receive $2,000 per semester.

Award: Scholarship for use in freshman, sophomore, junior, or senior years; not renewable. *Amount:* $2000–$4000.

Eligibility Requirements: Applicant must be enrolled or expecting to enroll full- or part-time at a four-year institution or university; resident of Tennessee and studying in Tennessee. Available to U.S. citizens.

Application Requirements: Application form. *Deadline:* September 1.

Contact: Ms. Tracy Biggers, Grant and Scholarship Analyst
Tennessee Student Assistance Corporation
Parkway Towers
404 James Robertson Parkway, Suite 1510
Nashville, TN 37243
Phone: 615-253-7460
E-mail: Tracy.Biggers@tn.gov

TENNESSEE STUDENT ASSISTANCE AWARD

Award to assist financially-needy Tennessee residents attending an approved college or university within the state. Complete a Free Application for Federal Student Aid form. Students are encourage to complete the FAFSA as soon as possible after October 1 for priority consideration. To apply, go to http://www.fafsa.gov. For more information, go to www.tn.gov/collegepays

Award: Grant for use in freshman, sophomore, junior, or senior years; not renewable. *Amount:* $100–$4000.

Eligibility Requirements: Applicant must be enrolled or expecting to enroll full- or part-time at a two-year or four-year or technical institution or university; resident of Tennessee and studying in Tennessee. Available to U.S. citizens.

Application Requirements: *Deadline:* March 1.

Contact: Mrs. Leah Louallen, Director of Grants and Scholarship Programs
Tennessee Student Assistance Corporation
Parkway Towers
404 James Robertson Parkway, Suite 1510
Nashville, TN 37243-0820
Phone: 615-253-7478
E-mail: leah.louallen@tn.gov

TERRY FOX HUMANITARIAN AWARD

http://terryfoxawards.ca/

TERRY FOX HUMANITARIAN AWARD

The Terry Fox Humanitarian Award is granted to Canadian students working towards their first post-secondary degree or diploma. Criteria includes commitment to voluntary humanitarian work, courage in overcoming obstacles, excellence in academics, fitness and amateur sports. Maximum value of award is CAN$28,000 for a maximum of four years ($7000 annually, subject to renewal).

Award: Scholarship for use in freshman, sophomore, junior, or senior years; renewable. *Number:* 20. *Amount:* $20,744.

Eligibility Requirements: Applicant must be Canadian citizen; enrolled or expecting to enroll full-time at a two-year or four-year institution or university and must have an interest in athletics/sports. Applicant or parent of applicant must have employment or volunteer experience in community service.

Application Requirements: Application form, interview. *Deadline:* February 1.

Contact: Paulina Chow-White, Executive Director
Terry Fox Humanitarian Award
AQ 5003, 8888 University Drive
Burnaby, BC V5A 1S6
CAN
Phone: 778-782-3057
Fax: 778-782-3311
E-mail: info@terryfoxawards.ca

TETHERBOX

http://www.tetherbox.com/

$1,000 CREATIVE VIDEO CHALLENGE COLLEGE SCHOLARSHIP

Make a creative funny, heartwarming, or informational video for the opportunity to win a $1,000 college scholarship. The assignment for the TetherBox Creative Video Challenge College Scholarship is to make a commercial about TetherBox College Care Packages or a video related to care packages, being away from home, etc. Video length should be at least 1 minute but no longer than 4 minutes. You have full creative control on how you storyboard and shoot your video, but here is a few thoughts to help add context: Situation: Think of unique situations, locations, occurrences, etc. or think of common situations, occurrences and locations that you can put a creative, humorous or heartwarming twist on; Dialogue/Narrative: Develop hilarious or touching dialogue and/or narratives; Perspective: Find creative and unique angles and shots; Effects: Try and make use of different video styles and effects to get the video just the way you want it; Think Creatively: Think back on your favorite commercials and the most popular viral commercials on the web and see what unique ideas you can come up with. Go to www.tetherbox.com/scholarship and complete the brief application. When your commercial is ready, upload your video to a file sharing site like Dropbox or Google Drive and send the link to info@tetherbox.com, along with a short bio including your name, year in school, and expected graduation date and a brief overview explaining your video concept. Submission deadline: March 31, 2017. Your personal safety is paramount so please be safe. Entry is subject to the official rules and conditions. By submitting your video to TetherBox for scholarship consideration you agree to assign all rights and ownership of the video to TetherBox and you grant TetherBox full permission to re-publish, edit and otherwise freely use your video in any manner without notice or compensation.

Award: Scholarship for use in freshman, sophomore, junior, or senior years; not renewable. *Number:* 1. *Amount:* $1000.

Eligibility Requirements: Applicant must be enrolled or expecting to enroll full-time at a four-year or technical institution or university. Available to U.S. citizens.

Application Requirements: Application form. *Deadline:* March 31.

Contact: Lynn Holdsworth, Co-Founder
TetherBox
5 Walter E. Foran Blvd.
Suite 2002
Flemington, NJ 08822
Phone: 908-246-3934
Fax: 866-302-2255
E-mail: lynn.holdsworth@tetherbox.com

TEXAS AFL-CIO

http://www.texasaflcio.org/

TEXAS AFL-CIO SCHOLARSHIP PROGRAM
• *See page 559*

TEXAS ASSOCIATION OF DEVELOPING COLLEGES

http://www.txadc.org

THE URBAN SCHOLARSHIPS FUND

Eligibility - United States citizen or eligible non-citizen (permanent resident card I-551 front and back copy) Texas resident, graduate of high school from 29 urban cities: Abilene, Amarillo, Arlington, Austin, Beaumont, Brownsville, Carrollton, Corpus Christi, Dallas, Denton, El Paso, Fort Worth, Frisco, Garland, Grand Prairie, Houston, Irving, Killeen, Laredo, Lubbock, McAllen, McKinney, Mesquite, Midland, Pasadena, Plano, San Antonio, Waco and Wichita Falls

Award: Scholarship for use in freshman, sophomore, junior, or senior years; not renewable. *Number:* 450–500. *Amount:* $700–$1000.

Eligibility Requirements: Applicant must be age 16-65; enrolled or expecting to enroll full-time at a two-year or four-year or technical institution or university and resident of Texas. Available to U.S. citizens.

Application Requirements: Financial need analysis. *Deadline:* July 10.

Contact: Ms. Janice Jackson, Office Programs Administrator
Texas Association of Developing Colleges
1140 Empire Central Drive 550
Dallas, TX 75247
Phone: 214-630-2511
E-mail: janice.jackson@txadc.org

TEXAS MUTUAL INSURANCE COMPANY

http://www.texasmutual.com/

TEXAS MUTUAL INSURANCE COMPANY SCHOLARSHIP PROGRAM

A scholarship program open to qualified family members of policyholder employees who died from on-the-job injuries or accidents, policyholder employees who qualify for lifetime income benefits pursuant to the Texas Workers Compensation Act, and family members of injured employees who qualify for lifetime income benefits.

Award: Scholarship for use in freshman, sophomore, junior, or senior years; not renewable. *Number:* 1–25. *Amount:* $600–$6000.

Eligibility Requirements: Applicant must be enrolled or expecting to enroll full-time at a two-year or four-year or technical institution or university. Applicant must have 2.5 GPA or higher. Available to U.S. and non-U.S. citizens.

Application Requirements: Application form, financial need analysis. *Deadline:* continuous.

Contact: Temetria McVea, Executive Assistant to the President
Texas Mutual Insurance Company
6210 East Highway 290
Austin, TX 78723
Phone: 512-224-3907
E-mail: tmcvea@texasmutual.com

TRUCKER TO TRUCKER, LLC

http://www.truckertotrucker.com/

TRUCKERTOTRUCKER.COM COLLEGE SCHOLARSHIP

$500 college scholarship for individuals and their family members who are part of the transportation industry.

Award: Scholarship for use in freshman, sophomore, junior, senior, graduate, or postgraduate years; not renewable. *Number:* 2. *Amount:* $500.

Eligibility Requirements: Applicant must be age 17-99 and enrolled or expecting to enroll full-time at a two-year or four-year institution or university. Applicant or parent of applicant must have employment or volunteer experience in transportation industry. Available to U.S. citizens.

Application Requirements: Application form, essay. *Deadline:* June 1.

Contact: Scholarship Coordinator
E-mail: scholarship@truckertotrucker.com

TUITION EXCHANGE INC.

http://www.tuitionexchange.org/

TUITION EXCHANGE SCHOLARSHIPS

The Tuition Exchange is an association of over 670 colleges and universities awarding over 7200 full or substantial scholarships each year for children and other family members of faculty and staff employed at participating institutions. Students must maintain satisfactory academic progress and a cumulative GPA as established by each institution. Application procedures and deadlines vary by school. Contact Tuition Exchange Liaison Officer at home institution for details.

Award: Scholarship for use in freshman, sophomore, junior, senior, graduate, or postgraduate years; renewable. *Number:* 7000–9000. *Amount:* $4190–$52,140.

Eligibility Requirements: Applicant must be enrolled or expecting to enroll full- or part-time at a two-year or four-year institution or university. Applicant or parent of applicant must have employment or volunteer experience in teaching/education. Available to U.S. and non-U.S. citizens.

Application Requirements: Application form. *Deadline:* continuous.

Contact: Mr. Robert Shorb, Executive Director/CEO
Tuition Exchange Inc.
3 Bethesda Metro Center
Suite 700
Bethesda, MD 20814
Phone: 301-941-1827
E-mail: info@tuitionexchange.org

TWO TEN FOOTWEAR FOUNDATION

http://www.twoten.org/

CLASSIC SCHOLARSHIPS

Two Ten offers footwear employees and their families higher education scholarships to two or four year undergraduate programs based on financial need, academic ability and personal promise.

Award: Scholarship for use in freshman, sophomore, junior, or senior years; renewable. *Number:* 300–350. *Amount:* $2500–$5000.

Eligibility Requirements: Applicant must be enrolled or expecting to enroll full- or part-time at a two-year or four-year or technical institution or university; resident of Alabama, Alaska, Arizona, Arkansas, California, Colorado, Connecticut, Delaware, Florida, Georgia, Hawaii, Idaho, Illinois, Indiana, Iowa, Kansas, Kentucky, Louisiana, Maine, Maryland, Massachusetts, Michigan, Minnesota, Mississippi, Missouri, Montana, Nebraska, Nevada, New Hampshire, New Jersey, New Mexico, New York, North Carolina, North Dakota, Ohio, Oklahoma, Oregon, Pennsylvania, Puerto Rico, Rhode Island, South Carolina, South Dakota, Tennessee, Texas, Utah, Vermont, Virginia, Washington, West Virginia, Wisconsin, Wyoming and studying in Alabama, Alaska, Arizona, Arkansas, California, Colorado, Connecticut, Delaware, Florida, Georgia, Hawaii, Idaho, Illinois, Indiana, Iowa, Kansas, Kentucky, Louisiana, Maine, Maryland, Massachusetts, Michigan, Minnesota, Mississippi, Missouri, Montana, Nebraska, Nevada, New Hampshire, New Jersey, New Mexico, New York, North Carolina, North Dakota, Ohio, Oklahoma, Oregon, Pennsylvania, Puerto Rico, Rhode Island, South Carolina, South Dakota, Tennessee, Texas, Utah, Vermont, Virginia, Washington, West Virginia, Wisconsin, Wyoming. Applicant must have 2.5 GPA or higher. Available to U.S. citizens.

Application Requirements: Application form, community service, essay, financial need analysis. *Deadline:* April 15.

Contact: Liz Watson, Scholarship Coordinator
Phone: 781-736-1510
E-mail: scholarship@twoten.org

TWO TEN FOOTWEAR FOUNDATION SCHOLARSHIP

Renewable, merit and need-based award available to students who have 500 hours work experience in footwear, leather, or allied industries during year of application, or have a parent employed in one of these fields for at least two years. Must have proof of employment and maintain 2.5 GPA.

Award: Scholarship for use in freshman, sophomore, junior, or senior years; renewable. *Number:* 300–350. *Amount:* $2500–$5000.

Eligibility Requirements: Applicant must be enrolled or expecting to enroll full- or part-time at a two-year or four-year institution or university; resident of Alabama, Alaska, Arizona, Arkansas, California,

Colorado, Connecticut, Delaware, Florida, Georgia, Hawaii, Idaho, Illinois, Indiana, Iowa, Kansas, Kentucky, Louisiana, Maine, Maryland, Massachusetts, Michigan, Minnesota, Mississippi, Missouri, Montana, Nebraska, Nevada, New Hampshire, New Jersey, New Mexico, New York, North Carolina, North Dakota, Ohio, Oklahoma, Ontario, Oregon, Pennsylvania, Puerto Rico, Rhode Island, South Carolina, South Dakota, Tennessee, Texas, Utah, Vermont, Virginia, Washington, West Virginia, Wisconsin, Wyoming and studying in Alabama, Alaska, Arizona, Arkansas, California, Colorado, Connecticut, Delaware, Florida, Georgia, Hawaii, Idaho, Illinois, Indiana, Iowa, Kansas, Kentucky, Louisiana, Maine, Maryland, Massachusetts, Michigan, Minnesota, Mississippi, Missouri, Montana, Nebraska, Nevada, New Hampshire, New Jersey, New Mexico, New York, North Carolina, North Dakota, Ohio, Oklahoma, Oregon, Pennsylvania, Puerto Rico, Rhode Island, South Carolina, South Dakota, Tennessee, Texas, Utah, Vermont, Virginia, Washington, West Virginia, Wisconsin, Wyoming. Applicant or parent of applicant must have employment or volunteer experience in leather/footwear industry. Applicant must have 2.5 GPA or higher. Available to U.S. citizens.

Application Requirements: Application form, essay, financial need analysis. *Deadline:* April 14.

Contact: Liz Watson, Scholarship Coordinator
Phone: 781-736-1510
E-mail: scholarship@twoten.org

ULMAN CANCER FUND FOR YOUNG ADULTS

http://www.ulmanfund.org/scholarships

JACQUELINE SHEARER MEMORIAL SCHOLARSHIP

The Ulman Cancer Fund for Young Adults is committed to helping young adults continue their education after being affected by cancer through their own diagnosis or the diagnosis of a loved one. Many scholarships offered by UCF share similar applicant criteria. Applicants need only submit one application, which will be considered for any and all scholarships for which the student applies and is eligible.

Award: Scholarship for use in freshman, sophomore, junior, or senior years; not renewable. *Number:* 2. *Amount:* $2500.

Eligibility Requirements: Applicant must be age 15-39; enrolled or expecting to enroll full- or part-time at a four-year institution or university and resident of District of Columbia, Maryland, Virginia. Available to U.S. citizens.

Application Requirements: Application form, essay. *Deadline:* March 1.

Contact: Lauriann Parker, Scholarship Coordinator
Ulman Cancer Fund for Young Adults
1215 E. Fort Ave.
Ste. 104
Baltimore, MD 21230
Phone: 410-964-0202 Ext. 105
E-mail: scholarship@ulmanfund.org

JAMIE L. ROBERTS MEMORIAL SCHOLARSHIP AWARD

The Ulman Cancer Fund for Young Adults is committed to helping young adults continue their education after being affected by cancer through their own diagnosis or the diagnosis of a loved one. Many scholarships offered by UCF share similar applicant criteria. Applicants need only submit one application, which will be considered for any and all scholarships for which the student applies and is eligible.

Award: Scholarship for use in freshman, sophomore, junior, senior, or graduate years; not renewable. *Number:* 6. *Amount:* $2500.

Eligibility Requirements: Applicant must be age 15-39 and enrolled or expecting to enroll full- or part-time at a four-year institution or university. Available to U.S. citizens.

Application Requirements: Application form, essay. *Deadline:* March 1.

Contact: Lauriann Parker, Scholarship Coordinator
Ulman Cancer Fund for Young Adults
1215 E. Fort Ave.
Ste. 104
Baltimore, MD 21230
Phone: 410-964-0202 Ext. 105
E-mail: scholarship@ulmanfund.org

JEFFREY P. MEYER MEMORIAL SCHOLARSHIP

The Ulman Cancer Fund for Young Adults is committed to helping young adults continue their education after being affected by cancer through their own diagnosis or the diagnosis of a loved one. Many scholarships offered by UCF share similar applicant criteria. Applicants need only submit one application, which will be considered for any and all scholarships for which the student applies and is eligible.

Award: Scholarship for use in freshman, sophomore, junior, senior, or graduate years; not renewable. *Number:* 1. *Amount:* $2500.

Eligibility Requirements: Applicant must be age 15-39 and enrolled or expecting to enroll full- or part-time at a four-year institution or university. Applicant or parent of applicant must have employment or volunteer experience in community service. Available to U.S. citizens.

Application Requirements: Application form, essay. *Deadline:* March 1.

Contact: Lauriann Parker, Scholarship Coordinator
Ulman Cancer Fund for Young Adults
1215 E. Fort Ave.
Ste. 104
Baltimore, MD 21230
Phone: 410-964-0202 Ext. 105
E-mail: scholarship@ulmanfund.org

JILL WEAVER STARKMAN SCHOLARSHIP

The Ulman Cancer Fund for Young Adults is committed to helping young adults continue their education after being affected by cancer through their own diagnosis or the diagnosis of a loved one. Many scholarships offered by UCF share similar applicant criteria. Applicants need only submit one application, which will be considered for any and all scholarships for which the student applies and is eligible.

Award: Scholarship for use in freshman, sophomore, junior, senior, or graduate years; not renewable. *Number:* 1. *Amount:* $2500.

Eligibility Requirements: Applicant must be age 15-39 and enrolled or expecting to enroll full- or part-time at a four-year institution or university. Applicant or parent of applicant must have employment or volunteer experience in community service. Available to U.S. citizens.

Application Requirements: Application form, community service, essay. *Deadline:* March 1.

Contact: Lauriann Parker, Scholarship Coordinator
Ulman Cancer Fund for Young Adults
1215 E. Fort Ave.
Ste. 104
Baltimore, MD 21230
Phone: 410-964-0202 Ext. 105
E-mail: scholarship@ulmanfund.org

JOHN HANLEY MEMORIAL SCHOLARSHIP

The Ulman Cancer Fund for Young Adults is committed to helping young adults continue their education after being affected by cancer through their own diagnosis or the diagnosis of a loved one. Many scholarships offered by UCF share similar applicant criteria. Applicants need only submit one application, which will be considered for any and all scholarships for which the student applies and is eligible.

Award: Scholarship for use in freshman, sophomore, junior, or senior years; not renewable. *Number:* 6. *Amount:* $2500.

Eligibility Requirements: Applicant must be age 15-25 and enrolled or expecting to enroll full- or part-time at a four-year institution or university. Available to U.S. citizens.

Application Requirements: Application form, essay. *Deadline:* March 1.

Contact: Lauriann Parker, Scholarship Coordinator
Ulman Cancer Fund for Young Adults
1215 E. Fort Ave.
Ste. 104
Baltimore, MD 21230
Phone: 410-964-0202 Ext. 105
E-mail: scholarship@ulmanfund.org

LISA HIGGINS-HUSSMAN FOUNDATION SCHOLARSHIP

The Ulman Cancer Fund for Young Adults is committed to helping young adults continue their education after being affected by cancer through their own diagnosis or the diagnosis of a loved one. Many scholarships offered by UCF share similar applicant criteria. Applicants need only submit one application, which will be considered for any and all scholarships for which the student applies and is eligible.

Award: Scholarship for use in freshman, sophomore, junior, senior, or graduate years; not renewable. *Number:* 1. *Amount:* $2500.

Eligibility Requirements: Applicant must be age 15-39; enrolled or expecting to enroll full- or part-time at a four-year institution or university and resident of District of Columbia, Maryland, Virginia. Available to U.S. citizens.

Application Requirements: Application form, essay. *Deadline:* March 1.

Contact: Lauriann Parker, Scholarship Coordinator
Ulman Cancer Fund for Young Adults
1215 E. Fort Ave.
Ste. 104
Baltimore, MD 21230
Phone: 410-964-0202 Ext. 105
E-mail: scholarship@ulmanfund.org

MARILYN YETSO MEMORIAL SCHOLARSHIP

Provides support for the financial needs of college students who have a parent with cancer or who have lost a parent to cancer. Currently attending, or accepted to, a two- or four-year college, university or vocational program (including graduate and professional schools). Must be a resident of, or attending or planning to attend an educational institution in: Maryland, Virginia, or Washington, D.C.

Award: Scholarship for use in freshman, sophomore, junior, or senior years; not renewable. *Number:* 1–2. *Amount:* $1000.

Eligibility Requirements: Applicant must be age 15-39; enrolled or expecting to enroll full- or part-time at a two-year or four-year or technical institution or university and resident of District of Columbia, Maryland, Virginia. Available to U.S. citizens.

Application Requirements: Application form, essay, financial need analysis. *Deadline:* March 1.

Contact: Lauriann Parker, Scholarship Coordinator
Ulman Cancer Fund for Young Adults
1215 E. Fort Ave.
Ste. 104
Baltimore, MD 21230
Phone: 410-964-0202 Ext. 105
E-mail: scholarship@ulmanfund.org

OLIVIA M. MARQUART SCHOLARSHIP

The Olivia M. Marquart Scholarship was established in honor of a friend, sister, and daughter who continues to demonstrate strength and courage throughout her battle with Synovial Sarcomas in her lungs. The scholarship is awarded annually to a young adult who is either a cancer survivor or currently undergoing treatment. The recipient must demonstrate financial need and be a US citizen attending a college or university in the US. The applicant must reside in Pennsylvania.

Award: Scholarship for use in freshman, sophomore, junior, or senior years; not renewable. *Number:* 1. *Amount:* $2500.

Eligibility Requirements: Applicant must be age 15-39; enrolled or expecting to enroll full- or part-time at a four-year institution or university and resident of Pennsylvania. Available to U.S. citizens.

Application Requirements: Application form, essay. *Deadline:* March 1.

Contact: Lauriann Parker, Scholarship Coordinator
Ulman Cancer Fund for Young Adults
1215 E. Fort Ave.
Ste. 104
Baltimore, MD 21230
Phone: 410-964-0202 Ext. 105
E-mail: scholarship@ulmanfund.org

PERLITA LIWANAG MEMORIAL SCHOLARSHIP

The Perlita Liwanag Memorial Scholarship was established in memory of Perlita Liwanag who lost her life to pancreatic cancer. The purpose of this scholarship is to support the financial needs of a deserving young adult in the Washington, DC metro area (Maryland, Northern Virginia and DC) seeking higher education within the U.S.

Award: Scholarship for use in freshman, sophomore, junior, or senior years; not renewable. *Number:* 1. *Amount:* $2500.

Eligibility Requirements: Applicant must be age 15-39; enrolled or expecting to enroll full- or part-time at a four-year institution or university and resident of District of Columbia, Maryland, Virginia. Available to U.S. citizens.

Application Requirements: Application form, essay. *Deadline:* March 1.

Contact: Lauriann Parker, Scholarship Coordinator
Ulman Cancer Fund for Young Adults
1215 E. Fort Ave.
Ste. 104
Baltimore, MD 21230
Phone: 410-964-0202 Ext. 105
E-mail: scholarship@ulmanfund.org

SATOLA FAMILY SCHOLARSHIP

The Satola Family Scholarship Award was established in 2009 to support the financial needs of young adults who have been affected by cancer, and are seeking higher education. The Satola family wishes to recognize students who have battled cancer or have shown selflessness in supporting a loved one through their cancer experience. This award seeks to honor the applicant who best demonstrates courage, spirit, and determination. The Satola Family Scholarship Award is available to applicants who are young adult cancer survivors diagnosed between the ages of 15-39 OR young adults who have lost a parent/guardian/sibling to cancer OR have a parent/guardian/sibling that has been diagnosed or undergoing treatment for cancer while they were a young adult. Candidates must be degree-seeking and United States citizens.

Award: Scholarship for use in freshman, sophomore, junior, or senior years; not renewable. *Number:* 1. *Amount:* $2500.

Eligibility Requirements: Applicant must be age 15-39 and enrolled or expecting to enroll full- or part-time at a four-year institution or university. Available to U.S. citizens.

Application Requirements: Application form, essay. *Deadline:* March 1.

Contact: Lauriann Parker, Scholarship Coordinator
Ulman Cancer Fund for Young Adults
1215 E. Fort Ave.
Ste. 104
Baltimore, MD 21230
Phone: 410-964-0202 Ext. 105
E-mail: scholarship@ulmanfund.org

SEAN SILVER MEMORIAL SCHOLARSHIP AWARD

Sean Silver was a graduate of Columbia College in Chicago, managing to obtain his degree while in extensive treatment for a rare from of Sarcoma named Chordoma. Sean studies focused on music journalism, combining his passions of music and writing into what he hoped would be a fruitful career as a rock journalist. While undergoing multiple surgeries, radiation and chemotherapy courses, he persevered to obtain his degree from Columbia at the age of 31. Less than a year after graduating from Columbia, Sean lost his battle on May 13, 2007. The Sean Silver Memorial Scholarship Award is available to applicants who are degree seeking United States citizens, age 15-30 at the time of application. Applicants must be currently undergoing active treatment for cancer.

Award: Scholarship for use in freshman, sophomore, junior, or senior years; not renewable. *Number:* 2. *Amount:* $5000.

Eligibility Requirements: Applicant must be age 17-30 and enrolled or expecting to enroll full- or part-time at a four-year institution. Available to U.S. citizens.

Application Requirements: Application form, community service, essay. *Deadline:* March 1.

Contact: Ulman Cancer Fund Scholarship Program Coordinator
Ulman Cancer Fund for Young Adults
1215 East Fort Avenue
Suite 104
Baltimore, MD 21230
Phone: 410-964-0202 Ext. 105
E-mail: scholarship@ulmanfund.org

VERA YIP MEMORIAL SCHOLARSHIP

The Vera Yip Memorial Scholarship Award was established to support the financial needs of young adults who are impacted by cancer and seeking higher education. Vera was committed to promoting a love of learning and helped to inspire and empower others to pursue their personal, educational and professional dreams in the face of adversity. This award seeks to honor the applicant who best demonstrates the courage, determination, motivation and dedication that Vera displayed during her lifetime.

Award: Scholarship for use in freshman, sophomore, junior, or senior years; not renewable. *Number:* 1. *Amount:* $2500.

Eligibility Requirements: Applicant must be age 17-35; enrolled or expecting to enroll full- or part-time at a four-year institution or university; resident of District of Columbia, Maryland, Virginia and studying in District of Columbia, Maryland, Virginia. Available to U.S. citizens.

Application Requirements: Application form, community service, essay. *Deadline:* March 1.

Contact: Lauriann Parker, Scholarship Coordinator
Ulman Cancer Fund for Young Adults
1215 E. Fort Ave.
Ste. 104
Baltimore, MD 21230
Phone: 410-964-0202 Ext. 105
E-mail: scholarship@ulmanfund.org

VITTORIA DIANNA RICARDO MEMORIAL SCHOLARSHIP

The Vittoria Dianna Ricardo Memorial Scholarship is in honor of a worldly woman who preferred to stay out of the limelight and remain quite and reserved. An immigrant from Italy, she worked hard to raise a family and care for her husband who was sick with kidney disease. She lost her battle with lung cancer in 2008. The degree-seeking applicant must be either a cancer survivor or has supported a family member through their cancer experience. Candidates must demonstrate financial need, and be enrolled in any accredited four-year college or university. Applicants must have a 3.0 GPA or better. Freshman may apply but must have a cumulative high school GPA of 3.0 or better.

Award: Scholarship for use in sophomore, junior, senior, or graduate years; not renewable. *Number:* 1. *Amount:* $2500.

Eligibility Requirements: Applicant must be age 17-39 and enrolled or expecting to enroll full- or part-time at a four-year institution or university. Applicant must have 3.0 GPA or higher. Available to U.S. citizens.

Application Requirements: Application form, essay. *Deadline:* March 1.

Contact: Lauriann Parker, Scholarship Coordinator
Ulman Cancer Fund for Young Adults
1215 E. Fort Ave.
Ste. 104
Baltimore, MD 21230
Phone: 410-964-0202 Ext. 105
E-mail: scholarship@ulmanfund.org

UNION PLUS SCHOLARSHIP PROGRAM

http://www.unionplus.org/

UNION PLUS EDUCATION FOUNDATION SCHOLARSHIP PROGRAM

• See page 564

UNITED NEGRO COLLEGE FUND

http://www.uncf.org/

SAR FAMILY EMERGENCY SCHOLARSHIP

Up to $5000 scholarship open to juniors and seniors at HBCUs who are currently expecting a financial crisis that is hindering spring semester matriculation. Students must be actively and heavily involved in community service. Minimum 2.5 GPA required.

Award: Scholarship for use in junior or senior years; not renewable.

Eligibility Requirements: Applicant must be Black (non-Hispanic) and enrolled or expecting to enroll full-time at a four-year institution or university. Applicant or parent of applicant must have employment or volunteer experience in community service. Applicant must have 2.5 GPA or higher. Available to U.S. citizens.

Application Requirements: Application form, essay, financial need analysis. *Deadline:* December 12.

Contact: Mary Williams, Director of Outreach and Recruitment
Phone: 800-331-2244

UNITED STATES SUBMARINE VETERANS

https://www.ussvi.org/home.asp

UNITED STATES SUBMARINE VETERANS INC. NATIONAL SCHOLARSHIP PROGRAM

• See page 566

UNITED TRANSPORTATION UNION INSURANCE ASSOCIATION

http://www.utuia.org/

UTUIA SCHOLARSHIP

Scholarships of $2000 awarded to undergraduate students. Requirements of a UTUIA scholarship applicant are that he or she be a U.S. citizen, at least a high school senior or equivalent, and age 25 or under. Applicants must be associated with the UTUIA by either owning a UTUIA insurance policy, or by being the child or grandchild of a current UTUIA policyholder. Scholarship applicants must also be associated with the SMART Transportation Division by belonging to the union, or by being the child or grandchild of an active or lifetime SMART Transportation Division member. Applicants also must be accepted for admittance, or already enrolled, for at least 12 credit hours per quarter or semester at a recognized institution of higher learning (university, college or junior college, nursing or technical school offering college credit).

Award: Scholarship for use in freshman, sophomore, junior, or senior years; renewable. *Number:* 50. *Amount:* $2000.

Eligibility Requirements: Applicant must be enrolled or expecting to enroll full-time at a two-year or four-year or technical institution or university. Available to U.S. citizens.

Application Requirements: Application form. *Deadline:* March 31.

Contact: Beth Thomas, Compensation Specialist
Phone: 216-227-5254

UNIVERSITY CONSORTIUM FOR LIBERIA

http://ucliberia.com/

JOSEPH N. BOAKAI SR. HIGHER EDUCATION SCHOLARSHIP

The University Consortium for Liberia (UCL) Scholarship Program was established in 2015 by the UCL Board of Directors. A special scholarship was established on behalf of Joseph N. Boakai, Sr., the Vice President of the Republic of Liberia, in dedication of his support to educate our youth. The UCL Scholarship program is open to Liberian students and/or students of Liberian decent pursuing a post-secondary education at a U.S. College or University. Priority will be given to students applying to a UCL college/university noted below who are considered Institutional Partners.

Award: Scholarship for use in freshman, sophomore, junior, senior, graduate, or postgraduate years; not renewable. *Number:* 5–10. *Amount:* $500–$1000.

Eligibility Requirements: Applicant must be of African heritage; Black (non-Hispanic) and enrolled or expecting to enroll full- or part-time at a two-year or four-year or technical institution or university. Applicant must have 3.0 GPA or higher. Available to U.S. and non-U.S. citizens.

Application Requirements: Application form.

Contact: University Consortium for Liberia Scholarship Committee
E-mail: uclscholarship@gmail.com

U.S. COAST GUARD

www.gocoastguard/cspi

COLLEGE STUDENT PRE-COMMISSIONING INITIATIVE (CSPI)

See scholarship information at the following website, http://www.gocoastguard/cspi

Award: Scholarship for use in junior or senior years; renewable. *Number:* 70. *Amount:* $12,850.

Eligibility Requirements: Applicant must be physically disabled or visually impaired; American Indian/Alaska Native, Asian/Pacific Islander, Black (non-Hispanic), Hispanic; age 19-28 and enrolled or expecting to enroll full-time at a four-year institution or university. Applicant must be physically disabled or visually impaired. Applicant must have 2.5 GPA or higher. Available to U.S. citizens. Applicant must have served in the Coast Guard.

Application Requirements: Application form, financial need analysis, interview. *Deadline:* continuous.

Contact: LT. Patrick Bennett
U.S. Coast Guard
2703 Martin Luther King JR Ave SE
Washington, DC 20593
Phone: 202-795-6855
E-mail: patrick.g.bennett@uscg.mil

VALUEPENGUIN

http://www.valuepenguin.com

VALUEPENGUIN SCHOLARSHIP

The cost of education in the U.S. is on the rise. In addition, the National Center for Education Statistics reports that only 12.8% of undergraduate students receive private grants. These facts illustrate how difficult it is for many students across the nation to afford basic necessities, such as textbooks and transportation—let alone tuition. In our coverage of personal finance, we have discovered how these issues have far reaching effects on an individual's financial wellbeing. Oftentimes, they continue to be a burden well after graduation. That's why ValuePenguin is offering a $2,000 scholarship to eligible undergraduate students in the U.S. To be considered for the scholarship, submit a 500 to 750 word response (for a total word count of 1,000 to 1,500) to each of the following two questions:1) Students encounter financial pitfalls of all types while attending colleges and universities. Explain a situation in which you spent too much (or not enough) money on a student expense and explain a creative solution you would share with future students. This could be something you did on your own or as part of a group.2) How did you choose your college and/or major? Submit your responses to scholarships@valuepenguin.com along with the following information—name, school you're attending, expected graduation date, major and career goal, e-mail address, phone number, a picture of you, and whether or not you're a first-generation college student. Your responses can be included in the body of the e-mail or attached as a PDF or Word document (.doc,.docx).

Award: Scholarship for use in freshman, sophomore, junior, or senior years; not renewable. *Number:* 1–3. *Amount:* $2000.

Eligibility Requirements: Applicant must be enrolled or expecting to enroll full- or part-time at a four-year institution or university and studying in Alabama, Alaska, Arizona, Arkansas, California, Colorado, Connecticut, Delaware, District of Columbia, Florida, Georgia, Guam, Hawaii, Idaho, Illinois, Indiana, Iowa, Kansas, Kentucky, Louisiana, Maine, Maryland, Massachusetts, Michigan, Minnesota, Mississippi, Missouri, Montana, Nebraska, Nevada, New Hampshire, New Jersey, New Mexico, New York, North Carolina, North Dakota, Ohio, Oklahoma, Oregon, Pennsylvania, Puerto Rico, Rhode Island, South Carolina, South Dakota, Tennessee, Texas, Utah, Vermont, Virginia, Washington, West Virginia, Wisconsin, Wyoming. Available to U.S. and non-U.S. citizens.

Application Requirements: Application form, essay. *Deadline:* November 10.

Contact: Rebecca Wessell, Scholarship Manager
ValuePenguin
600 Third Avenue
Floor 8
New York, NY 10016
E-mail: scholarships@valuepenguin.com

WARD LAW GROUP, PL

http://thecoveragelawyer.com/

WARD LAW GROUP BETTER FUTURE SCHOLARSHIP

This scholarship is offered to any student currently enrolled in an accredited community college, undergraduate, or graduate program in the United States. This includes incoming first-year college students who are high school graduates or possess a GED. For more information please go to this webpage http://thecoveragelawyer.com/#scholarship

Award: Scholarship for use in freshman, sophomore, junior, senior, graduate, or postgraduate years; not renewable. *Number:* 1. *Amount:* $500.

Eligibility Requirements: Applicant must be enrolled or expecting to enroll full- or part-time at a two-year or four-year or technical institution or university. Applicant must have 3.0 GPA or higher. Available to U.S. and non-U.S. citizens.

Application Requirements: Application form, essay. *Deadline:* November 30.

Contact: Gregory Ward
E-mail: info@thecoveragelawyer.com

WASHINGTON SOCIETY OF CERTIFIED PUBLIC ACCOUNTANTS

http://www.wscpa.org/

WSCPA FOUNDATION SCHOLARSHIPS

The Washington CPA Foundation is a 501(c)(3) not-for-profit foundation committed to ensuring that Washington's diverse communities have awareness of and access to both high quality accounting education and the resources required to make sound financial decisions. In order to make our vision a reality, the Foundation funds education and research in the field of accountancy, scholarships for accounting students, programs designed to improve accounting education and expand knowledge within the profession, and initiatives designed to improve the public's skills in personal financial management.

Award: Scholarship for use in sophomore, junior, senior, graduate, or postgraduate years; not renewable. *Number:* 50–60. *Amount:* $5000.

Eligibility Requirements: Applicant must be enrolled or expecting to enroll full- or part-time at a four-year institution or university. Applicant must have 3.0 GPA or higher. Available to U.S. and non-U.S. citizens.

Application Requirements: Application form, essay. *Deadline:* February 14.

Contact: Ms. Jocelyn Nystrom, Advocacy and Foundation Coordinator
Washington Society of Certified Public Accountants
902 140th Ave NE
Bellevue, WA 98005
Phone: 425-644-4800
E-mail: Jnystrom@wscpa.org

WESTERN GOLF ASSOCIATION EVANS SCHOLARS FOUNDATION

http://www.wgaesf.org

CHICK EVANS CADDIE SCHOLARSHIP

Full tuition and housing scholarship renewable up to four years for high school seniors who have worked at least two years as a caddie at a Western Golf Association member club. Must demonstrate financial need, excellent academics and outstanding character. Visit www.wgaesf.org for more information.

Award: Scholarship for use in freshman, sophomore, junior, or senior years; renewable. *Number:* up to 250. *Amount:* $80,000.

Eligibility Requirements: Applicant must be high school student; planning to enroll or expecting to enroll full-time at a four-year institution or university and studying in Colorado, Illinois, Indiana, Michigan, Minnesota, Missouri, Ohio, Oregon, Washington, Wisconsin. Applicant or parent of applicant must have employment or volunteer experience in private club/caddying. Available to U.S. and non-U.S. citizens.

Application Requirements: Application form, application form may be submitted online (http://www.wgaesf.org/site/c.dwJTKiO0JgI8G/b.7512567/k.47CB/Evans_Scholarship_Application.htm), essay, financial need analysis, interview, personal photograph, recommendations or references, test scores, transcript. *Deadline:* September 30.

Contact: Scholarship Committee
Phone: 847-724-4600
E-mail: applications@wgaesf.org

WILLIAM D. SQUIRES EDUCATIONAL FOUNDATION INC.

http://www.wmdsquiresfoundation.org/

WILLIAM D. SQUIRES SCHOLARSHIP

$3000 Scholarship award. Renewable up to $12,000. For graduating high school seniors from Ohio planning to pursue a four year program. The William D. Squires Scholarship is primarily financial need based but students must also have a clear career goal and be highly motivated. Minimum 3.2 GPA is required. Free to apply: www.wmdsquiresfoundation.org

Award: Scholarship for use in freshman, sophomore, junior, or senior years; renewable. *Number:* 15. *Amount:* $3000.

Eligibility Requirements: Applicant must be high school student; planning to enroll or expecting to enroll full-time at a four-year institution or university and resident of Ohio. Available to U.S. citizens.

Application Requirements: Application form, essay, financial need analysis. *Deadline:* April 5.

Contact: Scholarship Director
William D. Squires Educational Foundation Inc.
PO Box 2940
Jupiter, FL 33468
Phone: 561-741-7751
E-mail: info@wmdsquiresfoundation.org

WOMEN'S JEWELRY ASSOCIATION

http://www.womensjewelryassociation.com

MEMBER GRANTS

This grant is available to WJA Members only and is valid towards any type of professional growth.

Award: Grant for use in freshman, sophomore, junior, senior, graduate, or postgraduate years; renewable. *Number:* 12–25. *Amount:* $500–$1000.

Eligibility Requirements: Applicant must be enrolled or expecting to enroll full- or part-time at a two-year or four-year or technical institution or university and female. Available to U.S. and non-U.S. citizens.

Application Requirements: Application form, essay. *Deadline:* January 31.

Contact: Sue Elliott
E-mail: Selliott@gia.edu

WOMEN'S JEWELRY ASSOCIATIONS VETERANS GRANT

This award is given to a woman veteran of the US armed forces who wants to pursue a Jewelry career. It is a grant and does not have to be used for school, but could be used as a start-up grant for their business. It is essay based and is sponsored by Jewelers Mutual.

Award: Grant for use in freshman, sophomore, junior, senior, graduate, or postgraduate years; renewable. *Number:* 1. *Amount:* $5000.

Eligibility Requirements: Applicant must be enrolled or expecting to enroll full- or part-time at a two-year or four-year or technical institution or university and female. Available to U.S. citizens. Applicant or parent must meet one or more of the following requirements: general military experience; retired from active duty; disabled or killed as a result of military service; prisoner of war; or missing in action.

Application Requirements: Application form, essay. *Deadline:* April 15.

Contact: Isabel Cajulis
E-mail: icajulis@reedexpo.com

WOMEN'S SPORTS FOUNDATION

http://www.womenssportsfoundation.org/

LINDA RIDDLE/SGMA ENDOWED SCHOLARSHIP

One $1,500 scholarship to provide female student-athletes of limited financial means the opportunity to continue to pursue their sport in addition to their college studies. If you plan to participate in intercollegiate sports at a Division I school, consult with your college compliance office to determine whether this scholarship will affect your eligibility. Please check website for application procedures.

Award: Scholarship for use in freshman year; not renewable. *Number:* 1. *Amount:* $1500.

Eligibility Requirements: Applicant must be high school student; planning to enroll or expecting to enroll full-time at a two-year or four-year institution and female. Applicant must have 3.5 GPA or higher. Available to U.S. citizens.

Application Requirements: Application form. *Deadline:* March 31.

Contact: Elizabeth Flores
Phone: 516-307-3915
E-mail: LFlores@WomensSportsFoundation.org

YORKVILLE GOODS LLC

http://yorkvilleblankets.com/

YORKVILLE BLANKETS ASD SCHOLARSHIP

Yorkville Blanket Company's mission to provide comfort to everybody who needs it does not end with making blankets. In order to continue pursuing our mission, we have created the Yorkville Blankets ASD Scholarship for prospective or current college students who are living with ASD as well as students who are parents, siblings, and children of somebody on the autism spectrum to earn an award of $1000 toward continuing their education. The scholarship was created to help provide a means to pursue a post-secondary education for those whose lives have been impacted by Autism Spectrum Disorder (ASD).

Award: Scholarship for use in freshman, sophomore, junior, or senior years; not renewable. *Number:* 1. *Amount:* $1000.

Eligibility Requirements: Applicant must be learning disabled and enrolled or expecting to enroll full- or part-time at a two-year or four-year or technical institution or university. Applicant must be learning disabled. Available to U.S. citizens.

Application Requirements: Essay. *Deadline:* June 1.

Contact: Mr. Thomas Nolan, Owner
Yorkville Goods LLC
65 Linden Dr
Berlin, CT 06037
Phone: 860-335-2447
E-mail: yorkvilleblankets@gmail.com

YOUTH FOUNDATION INC.

http://fdnweb.org/youthfdn

ALEXANDER AND MAUDE HADDEN SCHOLARSHIP

Youth Foundation offers exceptional students with financial need an award of $2500 to $4000 per year which is renewable for four years at the foundation's discretion. Minimum GPA of 3.5 required, community service and extra curricular activities expected. Must write Foundation for information and application request form.

Award: Scholarship for use in freshman, sophomore, junior, or senior years; renewable. *Number:* 96–108. *Amount:* $2500–$4000.

Eligibility Requirements: Applicant must be enrolled or expecting to enroll full-time at a four-year institution or university and resident of Yukon. Applicant or parent of applicant must have employment or volunteer experience in community service. Applicant must have 3.5 GPA or higher. Available to U.S. citizens.

Application Requirements: Application form, community service, essay, financial need analysis, personal photograph. *Deadline:* February 28.

Contact: Ms. Johanna Lee, Executive Administrator
Phone: 212-840-6291
Fax: 212-840-6747
E-mail: YouthFdn@aol.com

IMPAIRMENT

ALEXANDER GRAHAM BELL ASSOCIATION FOR THE DEAF AND HARD OF HEARING

http://www.agbell.org/

AG BELL COLLEGE SCHOLARSHIP PROGRAM

Available to students with pre-lingual bilateral hearing loss in the moderate-severe to profound range who attend a mainstream and accredited college or university on a full-time basis. Specific eligibility criteria, submission guidelines, deadline and application available on AG Bell website at http://www.agbell.org.

Award: Scholarship for use in freshman, sophomore, junior, senior, graduate, or postgraduate years; not renewable. *Number:* 15–25. *Amount:* $2500–$10,000.

Eligibility Requirements: Applicant must be hearing impaired and enrolled or expecting to enroll full-time at a four-year institution or university. Applicant must be hearing impaired. Applicant must have 3.5 GPA or higher. Available to U.S. and non-U.S. citizens.

Application Requirements: Application form, essay. *Deadline:* March 10.

Contact: Ms. Lisa Chutjian, Chief Development Officer
Phone: 202-337-5220
E-mail: scholarships@agbell.org

AMERICAN COUNCIL OF THE BLIND

http://www.acb.org/

AMERICAN COUNCIL OF THE BLIND SCHOLARSHIPS
• See page 574

AMERICAN FOUNDATION FOR THE BLIND

http://www.afb.org/

FERDINAND TORRES SCHOLARSHIP

Awards one scholarship of $2500 to a full-time undergraduate or graduate student who presents evidence of economic need. To be eligible the applicant must reside in the U.S., but need not be a citizen of the U.S. Preference will be given to applicants residing in the New York City metropolitan area and new immigrants to the U.S. Must submit proof of legal blindness. For additional information and application requirements, visit http://www.afb.org/scholarships.asp.

Award: Scholarship for use in freshman, sophomore, junior, senior, or graduate years; not renewable. *Number:* 1. *Amount:* $2500.

Eligibility Requirements: Applicant must be visually impaired and enrolled or expecting to enroll full-time at a two-year or four-year institution or university. Applicant must be visually impaired. Available to U.S. and non-U.S. citizens.

Application Requirements: Application form, essay, financial need analysis, proof of acceptance in an accredited full-time undergraduate or graduate program, proof of legal blindness, recommendations or references, transcript. *Deadline:* April 30.

Contact: Dawn Bodrogi, Information Center and Library Coordinator
American Foundation for the Blind
11 Penn Plaza, Suite 300
New York, NY 10001
Phone: 212-502-7661
Fax: 212-502-7771
E-mail: dbodrogi@afb.net

ARRL FOUNDATION INC.

http://www.arrl.org/

CHALLENGE MET SCHOLARSHIP

Multiple $500 awards are available to students with any active amateur radio license who are studying at an accredited two- or four-year college, university, or technical school. Preference to applicants with documented learning disabilities (by physician or school) and indications that applicant is putting forth substantial effort regardless of resulting academic grades.

Award: Scholarship for use in freshman, sophomore, junior, or senior years; not renewable. *Amount:* $500.

Eligibility Requirements: Applicant must be hearing impaired, learning disabled, physically disabled, or visually impaired; enrolled or expecting to enroll full- or part-time at a two-year or four-year or technical institution or university and must have an interest in amateur radio. Applicant must be hearing impaired, learning disabled, physically disabled, or visually impaired. Available to U.S. citizens.

Application Requirements: Application form. *Deadline:* January 31.

Contact: Ms. Mary Hobart, Secretary
Phone: 860-594-0397
E-mail: k1mmh@arrl.org

BRIDGES FOR THE DEAF AND HARD OF HEARING

http://www.bridgesfordeafandhh.org/

LINDA COWDEN MEMORIAL SCHOLARSHIP

The Linda Cowden Memorial Scholarship is awarded to Deaf or hard of hearing students or hearing students preparing to work in a profession serving the Deaf and/or hard of hearing communities. Applicants must live in the agency's 16 county service area in middle Tennessee.

Award: Scholarship for use in freshman, sophomore, junior, senior, graduate, or postgraduate years; not renewable. *Number:* 1. *Amount:* $1000.

Eligibility Requirements: Applicant must be hearing impaired; enrolled or expecting to enroll full- or part-time at a two-year or four-year or technical institution or university and resident of Tennessee. Applicant must be hearing impaired. Available to U.S. citizens.

Application Requirements: Application form, essay, interview. *Deadline:* April 1.

Contact: Rebecca Nofi
Bridges for the Deaf and Hard of Hearing
935 Edgehill Avenue
Nashville, TN 37203
Phone: 615-248-8828
E-mail: rn@bridgesfordeafandhh.org

CALIFORNIA COUNCIL OF THE BLIND

http://www.ccbnet.org/

CALIFORNIA COUNCIL OF THE BLIND SCHOLARSHIPS

Scholarships available to blind student applicants who are California residents entering or continuing studies at an accredited California college, university, or vocational training school. Must be a full-time student registered for at least twelve units for the entire academic year. Applications must be typed and all blanks must be filled to be considered for scholarship. Applications available at website http://www.ccbnet.org.

Award: Scholarship for use in freshman, sophomore, junior, or senior years; renewable. *Number:* up to 20. *Amount:* $375–$2500.

Eligibility Requirements: Applicant must be visually impaired; enrolled or expecting to enroll full-time at a two-year or four-year or technical institution or university; resident of California and studying in California. Applicant must be visually impaired. Available to U.S. and non-U.S. citizens.

Application Requirements: Application form, interview, proof of blindness, recommendations or references, transcript. *Deadline:* May 15.

Contact: Scholarship Chair, CA Council of the Blind
California Council of the Blind
1303 J Street, Suite 400
Sacramento, CA 95814-2900
Phone: 916-441-2100
Fax: 916-441-2188
E-mail: ccotb@ccbnet.org

RHONDA KING MEMORIAL SCHOLARSHIP

The individual must be either a resident of, or attending an accredited college or university in Sacramento, Yolo, Placer, or El Dorado Counties. It is not required that a resident of Sacramento, Yolo, Placer or El Dorado

Counties be attending an institution in California to submit an application.

Award: Scholarship for use in junior, senior, graduate, or postgraduate years; not renewable. *Number:* 1. *Amount:* $500.

Eligibility Requirements: Applicant must be visually impaired and enrolled or expecting to enroll full-time at a four-year institution or university. Applicant must be visually impaired. Applicant must have 2.5 GPA or higher. Available to U.S. and non-U.S. citizens.

Application Requirements: Application form, application form may be submitted online (http://www.ccbnet.org), essay, interview, recommendations or references, transcript. *Deadline:* July 17.

Contact: Leslie Thom, Scholarship Committee Chair
California Council of the Blind
ACB Capitol Chapter, California Council of the Blind
E-mail: lathom@comcast.net

CHRISTIAN RECORD SERVICES INC.

http://www.christianrecord.org/

CHRISTIAN RECORD SERVICES INC. SCHOLARSHIPS

One-time award for legally blind or blind college undergraduates. Submit application, essay-autobiography, photo, references, and financial information by April 1.

Award: Scholarship for use in freshman, sophomore, junior, or senior years; renewable. *Number:* 7–10. *Amount:* $250–$500.

Eligibility Requirements: Applicant must be visually impaired and enrolled or expecting to enroll full-time at a four-year institution or university. Applicant must be visually impaired. Available to U.S. citizens.

Application Requirements: Application form, driver's license, essay, financial need analysis, personal photograph, recommendations or references. *Deadline:* April 1.

Contact: Shelly Kittleson, Assistant to Treasurer
Phone: 402-488-0981 Ext. 216
Fax: 402-488-7582
E-mail: info@christianrecord.org

COLLEGE WOMEN'S ASSOCIATION OF JAPAN

http://www.cwaj.org/

SCHOLARSHIP FOR THE VISUALLY IMPAIRED TO STUDY ABROAD

Scholarship for visually impaired Japanese nationals or permanent residents of Japan who have been accepted into an undergraduate or graduate degree program at an accredited English-speaking university or research institution. Former recipients of CWAJ awards and members of CWAJ are ineligible. Award value is JPY3 million. Deadline on or between November 1 and November 30.

Award: Scholarship for use in junior or senior years; not renewable. *Number:* 1.

Eligibility Requirements: Applicant must be visually impaired; of Japanese heritage and Japanese citizen and enrolled or expecting to enroll full-time at a four-year institution or university. Applicant must be visually impaired. Available to citizens of countries other than the U.S. or Canada.

Application Requirements: Application form, certificate of disability, essay, recommendations or references, test scores, transcript. *Fee:* $10. *Deadline:* varies.

Contact: Scholarship Committee
E-mail: scholarship@cwaj.org

SCHOLARSHIP FOR THE VISUALLY IMPAIRED TO STUDY IN JAPAN

Scholarship for visually impaired Japanese or permanent resident students for graduate or undergraduate study in Japan. Former recipients of CWAJ awards and members of CWAJ are ineligible. Award Value is JPY2.0 million. Deadline on or between November 1 and November 30.

Award: Scholarship for use in junior or senior years; not renewable. *Number:* 1–2.

Eligibility Requirements: Applicant must be visually impaired; of Japanese heritage and Japanese citizen and enrolled or expecting to enroll full-time at a four-year institution or university. Applicant must be visually impaired. Available to citizens of countries other than the U.S. or Canada.

Application Requirements: Application form, certificate of disability, essay, recommendations or references, self-addressed stamped envelope with application, transcript. *Fee:* $10. *Deadline:* varies.

Contact: Scholarship Committee
E-mail: scholarship@cwaj.org

COUNCIL OF CITIZENS WITH LOW VISION INTERNATIONAL C/O AMERICAN COUNCIL OF THE BLIND

http://www.cclvi.org/

FRED SCHEIGERT SCHOLARSHIP

• See page 582

CSA MEDICAL SUPPLY

https://csamedicalsupply.com

CSA MEDICAL SUPPLY COLLEGE SCHOLARSHIP

• See page 583

CYSTIC FIBROSIS SCHOLARSHIP FOUNDATION

http://www.cfscholarship.org/

CYSTIC FIBROSIS SCHOLARSHIP

One-time $1000 to $10,000 scholarships for young adults with cystic fibrosis to be used to further their education after high school. Awards may be used for tuition, books, and fees. Students may reapply in subsequent years.

Award: Scholarship for use in freshman, sophomore, junior, or senior years; not renewable. *Number:* 40–50. *Amount:* $1000–$10,000.

Eligibility Requirements: Applicant must be physically disabled and enrolled or expecting to enroll full-time at a two-year or four-year or technical institution or university. Applicant must be physically disabled. Available to U.S. citizens.

Application Requirements: Application form, essay, financial need analysis, recommendations or references, test scores, transcript. *Deadline:* March 21.

Contact: Mary Bottorff, President
Cystic Fibrosis Scholarship Foundation
2814 Grant Street
Evanston, IL 60201
Phone: 847-328-0127
Fax: 847-328-0127
E-mail: mkbcfsf@aol.com

DISABLEDPERSON INC. COLLEGE SCHOLARSHIP

http://www.disabledperson.com/

DISABLEDPERSON INC. NATIONAL COLLEGE SCHOLARSHIP AWARD FOR COLLEGE STUDENTS WITH DISABILITIES

• See page 584

EASTERN AMPUTEE GOLF ASSOCIATION

http://www.eagagolf.org/

EASTERN AMPUTEE GOLF ASSOCIATION SCHOLARSHIP FUND

Three (3) new $1000 college scholarships are available in 2017 to any EAGA amputee member and/or a member of his or her family. Amputee is define as one who has had the loss of a limb at a major joint (i.e. Ankle, Wrist etc.) due to trauma or congenital birth defect. Award recipients do not need to be in attendance. Award covers each of the four school years depending on when applications are accepted. Award recipient must maintain a 2.0 GPA.

Award: Scholarship for use in freshman, sophomore, junior, or senior years; renewable. *Number:* 1–6. *Amount:* $1000.

Eligibility Requirements: Applicant must be physically disabled and enrolled or expecting to enroll full-time at a two-year or four-year institution or university. Applicant must be physically disabled. Available to U.S. citizens.

Application Requirements: Application form, community service, essay, financial need analysis, personal photograph. *Fee:* $15. *Deadline:* July 1.

Contact: Mr. Robert Buck, Executive Director
Eastern Amputee Golf Association
20 15 Amherst Drive
Bethlehem, PA 18015-5606
Phone: 610-867-9295
Fax: 610-867-9295
E-mail: rbuck18015@verizon.net

ELAINE CHAPIN MEMORIAL SCHOLARSHIP FUND

https://sites.google.com/site/theelainechapinfund/

ELAINE CHAPIN MEMORIAL SCHOLARSHIP FUND

Scholarship program that benefits students whose lives are impacted by multiple sclerosis.

Award: Scholarship for use in freshman, sophomore, junior, or senior years; not renewable. *Number:* 8. *Amount:* $500–$1000.

Eligibility Requirements: Applicant must be physically disabled; age 17-99 and enrolled or expecting to enroll full-time at a two-year or four-year or technical institution or university. Applicant must be physically disabled. Available to U.S. citizens.

Application Requirements: Application form, essay. *Deadline:* April 30.

Contact: Joseph Chapin
Elaine Chapin Memorial Scholarship Fund
1440 Heritage Landing
Suite 109
St. Charles, MO 63303
E-mail: elainechapinfund@gmail.com

ESSAYHUB

https://essayhub.com/

ESSAY WRITING CONTEST BY ESSAYHUB
• See page 587

FELDMAN & ROYLE, ATTORNEYS AT LAW

http://www.feldmanroyle.com/

AUTISM SCHOLARSHIPS
• See page 587

FELDMAN LAW FIRM PLLC

http://www.afphoenixcriminalattorney.com/

DISABLED VETERANS SCHOLARSHIP
• See page 587

FIT SMALL BUSINESS

http://www.fitsmallbusiness.com

BUSINESS PLAN SCHOLARSHIP FOR STUDENTS WITH DISABILITIES

The Business Plan Scholarship is awarded twice a year, once during the fall semester and once during the spring semester. The winner is judged primarily on the merit of their 500-1000 word response to the essay prompt "What I learned from writing a business plan."

Award: Scholarship for use in freshman, sophomore, junior, senior, graduate, or postgraduate years; not renewable. *Number:* 1–2. *Amount:* $1000–$1000.

Eligibility Requirements: Applicant must be hearing impaired, learning disabled, physically disabled, or visually impaired and enrolled or expecting to enroll full- or part-time at a two-year or four-year or technical institution or university. Applicant must be hearing impaired, learning disabled, physically disabled, or visually impaired. Available to U.S. and non-U.S. citizens.

Application Requirements: Application form may be submitted online(fitsmallbusiness.com/learn-how-to-write-a-business-plan/), essay. *Deadline:* varies.

Contact: Mr. Marc Prosser, Publisher
E-mail: mprosser@fitsmallbusiness.com

GEORGIA STUDENT FINANCE COMMISSION

http://www.GAcollege411.org/

GEORGIA TUITION EQUALIZATION GRANT (GTEG)

Award for Georgia residents pursuing undergraduate study at an accredited two- or four-year Georgia private postsecondary institution.

Award: Grant for use in freshman, sophomore, junior, or senior years; not renewable. *Number:* 1–35,000.

Eligibility Requirements: Applicant must be learning disabled; Hispanic; enrolled or expecting to enroll full-time at a two-year or four-year institution or university; resident of Georgia and studying in Georgia. Applicant must be learning disabled. Available to U.S. citizens.

Application Requirements: Application form, application form may be submitted online (http://www.gacollege411.org), social security number.

Contact: Ms. Caylee French, Director, Student Aid Services
Georgia Student Finance Commission
2082 East Exchange Place, Suite 100
Tucker, GA 30084
Phone: 770-724-9244
Fax: 770-724-9249
E-mail: cayleef@gsfc.org

GOLDIA GOLD & DIAMONDS

http://www.goldia.com

GOLDIA.COM SCHOLARSHIP

Goldia.com is offering one student a $500 paid scholarship towards their academic costs for the 2016 school year. If any alumni wins this scholarship, $500 will be given to the school from which the alumni graduated. Punctuation, grammar, clarity and organization will be considered during the evaluation process, as well as content. Students must currently be residing in the United States, Brazil, India, South Korea, Australia, Japan, United Kingdom or Canada. Please see http://www.goldia.com/scholarship.html for complete information.

Award: Scholarship for use in freshman, sophomore, junior, senior, graduate, or postgraduate years; renewable. *Number:* up to 1. *Amount:* $500–$500.

Eligibility Requirements: Applicant must be hearing impaired, learning disabled, physically disabled, or visually impaired; American Indian/Alaska Native, Asian/Pacific Islander, Black (non-Hispanic), Hispanic; age 17-57 and enrolled or expecting to enroll full- or part-time at a two-year or four-year or technical institution or university. Applicant must be hearing impaired, learning disabled, physically disabled, or visually impaired. Available to U.S. and non-U.S. citizens. Applicant must have general military experience.

Application Requirements: Application form, application form may be submitted online(www.goldia.com/scholarship.html), Please see the details at www.goldia.com/scholarsip.html. *Deadline:* December 31.

Contact: Mr. Mike Ulu, Chief Executive Officer
Goldia Gold & Diamonds
PO Box 5557
New York, NY 10185
Phone: 212-840-6099
E-mail: mike@goldia.com

GREAT LAKES HEMOPHILIA FOUNDATION

http://www.glhf.org/

GLHF INDIVIDUAL CLASS SCHOLARSHIP

Scholarship available to members of the Wisconsin bleeding disorder community, individuals with a bleeding disorder and their immediate families. Provides funding assistance for tuition and enrollment fees relevant to continuing education in a non-traditional or non-degree format.

Award: Scholarship for use in freshman, sophomore, junior, or senior years; not renewable. *Number:* 1. *Amount:* up to $500.

Eligibility Requirements: Applicant must be physically disabled; enrolled or expecting to enroll full- or part-time at a two-year or four-year or technical institution or university and resident of Wisconsin. Applicant must be physically disabled. Available to U.S. citizens.

Application Requirements: Application form, essay, recommendations or references, transcript. *Deadline:* varies.

Contact: Karin Koppen, Program Services Coordinator
Great Lakes Hemophilia Foundation
638 North 18 Street, Suite 108
Milwaukee, WI 53233
Phone: 414-257-0200
Fax: 414-257-1225
E-mail: kkoppen@glhf.org

GREAT LAKES HEMOPHILIA FOUNDATION EDUCATION SCHOLARSHIP

This scholarship not only targets the traditional college and vocational students, but also looks at retraining adults with bleeding disorders who are finding it difficult to function in their chosen field because of health complications. It also targets parents of children with bleeding disorders who through career advancement can better meet the financial needs of caring for their child.

Award: Scholarship for use in freshman, sophomore, junior, senior, graduate, or postgraduate years; not renewable. *Number:* 5–6. *Amount:* $500–$2000.

Eligibility Requirements: Applicant must be physically disabled; enrolled or expecting to enroll full- or part-time at a two-year or four-year or technical institution or university and resident of Wisconsin. Applicant must be physically disabled. Available to U.S. citizens.

Application Requirements: Application form, essay, recommendations or references, transcript. *Deadline:* May 1.

Contact: Karin Koppen, Program Services Coordinator
Great Lakes Hemophilia Foundation
638 North 18 Street, Suite 108
Milwaukee, WI 53233
Phone: 414-257-0200
Fax: 414-257-1225
E-mail: kkoppen@glhf.org

HEMOPHILIA FEDERATION OF AMERICA

http://www.hemophiliafed.org/

HFA EDUCATIONAL SCHOLARSHIPS

This scholarship is for students with a bleeding disorder who are attending/planning to attend a postsecondary school.

Award: Scholarship for use in freshman, sophomore, junior, senior, graduate, or postgraduate years; not renewable. *Number:* 2. *Amount:* $2000.

Eligibility Requirements: Applicant must be physically disabled and enrolled or expecting to enroll full- or part-time at a two-year or four-year or technical institution or university. Applicant must be physically disabled. Applicant must have 3.0 GPA or higher. Available to U.S. citizens.

Application Requirements: Application form, essay, financial need analysis. *Deadline:* May 15.

Contact: Athenna Harrison, Educational Scholarship Committee
Hemophilia Federation of America
820 First Street NE
Suite 720
Washington, DC 20002
Phone: 202-675-6984
Fax: 972-616-6211
E-mail: scholarships@hemophiliafed.org

HFA PARENT/SIBLING/CHILD EDUCATIONAL SCHOLARSHIP

Each year, HFA awards scholarships to promising students in the bleeding disorders community. This scholarship is geared towards those who are immediately related to someone with a bleeding disorder.

Award: Scholarship for use in freshman, sophomore, junior, senior, graduate, or postgraduate years; not renewable. *Number:* 1. *Amount:* $2000.

Eligibility Requirements: Applicant must be physically disabled and enrolled or expecting to enroll full- or part-time at a two-year or four-year or technical institution or university. Applicant must be physically disabled. Applicant must have 3.0 GPA or higher. Available to U.S. citizens.

Application Requirements: Application form, essay, financial need analysis. *Deadline:* May 15.

Contact: Athenna Harrison, Educational Scholarship Committee
Hemophilia Federation of America
820 First Street NE
Suite 720
Washington, DC 20002
Phone: 202-675-6984
Fax: 972-616-6211
E-mail: scholarships@hemophiliafed.org

MEDICAL/HEALTH SERVICES EDUCATION SCHOLARSHIP

One (1) scholarships will be awarded in the amount of $4,000.00 to a student pursuing a degree in the medical/healthcare services field. We have noticed over the years that many of our students in the bleeding disorders community are studying for a career in the medial field. Because we know how costly this can be, we created this scholarship specifically for those students to help further their goals.

Award: Scholarship for use in freshman, sophomore, junior, senior, graduate, or postgraduate years; not renewable. *Number:* 1. *Amount:* $4000.

Eligibility Requirements: Applicant must be physically disabled; high school student and planning to enroll or expecting to enroll full- or part-time at a two-year or four-year or technical institution or university. Applicant must be physically disabled. Available to U.S. citizens.

Application Requirements: Application form, essay, financial need analysis. *Deadline:* April 30.

Contact: Athenna Harrison, Educational Scholarship Committee
Hemophilia Federation of America
820 First Street NE
Suite 720
Washington, DC 20002
Phone: 202-675-6984
Fax: 972-616-6211
E-mail: scholarships@hemophiliafed.org

HEMOPHILIA FOUNDATION OF MICHIGAN

http://www.hfmich.org/

BILL MCADAM SCHOLARSHIP FUND

Scholarship for a person with hemophilia, including their spouse, partner, child or sibling, planning to attend an accredited college, university, trade, or technical school.

Award: Scholarship for use in freshman, sophomore, junior, senior, graduate, or postgraduate years; not renewable. *Number:* 1. *Amount:* $2000.

Eligibility Requirements: Applicant must be physically disabled and enrolled or expecting to enroll full- or part-time at a two-year or four-year or technical institution or university. Applicant must be physically disabled. Available to U.S. citizens.

Application Requirements: Application form. *Deadline:* May 15.

Contact: Academic Scholarship Committee
Phone: 734-544-0015
E-mail: hfm@hfmich.org

HEMOPHILIA FOUNDATION OF MICHIGAN ACADEMIC SCHOLARSHIP

Scholarship for individuals or immediate family members, with hemophilia or other inherited bleeding disorder and residing in Michigan. Must be pursuing education in accredited colleges or universities in the United States.

Award: Scholarship for use in freshman, sophomore, junior, or senior years; not renewable. *Number:* 3. *Amount:* $1500–$2000.

Eligibility Requirements: Applicant must be physically disabled and enrolled or expecting to enroll full- or part-time at a two-year or four-year or technical institution or university. Applicant must be physically disabled. Available to U.S. citizens.

Application Requirements: Application form. *Deadline:* March 14.

Contact: Academic Scholarship Committee
Phone: 734-544-0015
E-mail: hfm@hfmich.org

HEMOPHILIA FOUNDATION OF SOUTHERN CALIFORNIA

http://www.hemosocal.org/

CHRISTOPHER MARK PITKIN MEMORIAL SCHOLARSHIP

Scholarship open to all members of the hemophilia community, including spouses and siblings. Applicants must be pursuing a college or technical/trade school education. Applicants must be part of the HFSC Service Area.

Award: Scholarship for use in freshman, sophomore, junior, senior, graduate, or postgraduate years; not renewable. *Number:* 5–7. *Amount:* $500–$1000.

Eligibility Requirements: Applicant must be physically disabled; enrolled or expecting to enroll full- or part-time at a two-year or four-year or technical institution or university and resident of California. Applicant must be physically disabled. Available to U.S. citizens.

Application Requirements: Application form, autobiography. *Deadline:* June 30.

Contact: Laura Desai, Operations Manager
Hemophilia Foundation of Southern California
959 E Walnut St Suite 114
Pasadena, CA 91106
Phone: 626-765-6656
Fax: 626-765-6657
E-mail: laura@hemosocal.org

ILLINOIS COUNCIL OF THE BLIND

http://www.icbonline.org/

FLOYD R. CARGILL SCHOLARSHIP

Award for a visually impaired Illinois resident attending or planning to attend an Illinois college. One-time award of $1000.

Award: Scholarship for use in freshman, sophomore, junior, or senior years; not renewable. *Number:* 1. *Amount:* $1000.

Eligibility Requirements: Applicant must be visually impaired; enrolled or expecting to enroll full-time at a two-year or four-year or technical institution or university; resident of Illinois and studying in Illinois. Applicant must be visually impaired. Applicant must have 3.5 GPA or higher. Available to U.S. citizens.

Application Requirements: Application form, recommendations or references, test scores, transcript. *Deadline:* July 15.

Contact: Maggie Ulrich, Office Manager
Phone: 217-523-4967
E-mail: icb@icbonline.org

IMMUNE DEFICIENCY FOUNDATION

http://www.primaryimmune.org/

IMMUNE DEFICIENCY FOUNDATION SCHOLARSHIP

One-time award available to individuals diagnosed with a primary immune deficiency disease. Must submit medical verification of diagnosis. Available for study at the undergraduate level at any postsecondary institution. Must be U.S. citizen.

Award: Scholarship for use in freshman, sophomore, junior, or senior years; not renewable. *Number:* 30–40. *Amount:* $750–$2000.

Eligibility Requirements: Applicant must be physically disabled and enrolled or expecting to enroll full- or part-time at a two-year or four-year or technical institution or university. Applicant must be physically disabled. Available to U.S. citizens.

Application Requirements: Application form, driver's license, essay, financial need analysis, medical verification of diagnosis, recommendations or references. *Deadline:* March 31.

Contact: Diana Gill, Director of Patient Programs
Phone: 800-296-4433 Ext. 2545
Fax: 410-321-9165
E-mail: dgill@primaryimmune.org

KELLY LAW TEAM

http://www.jkphoenixpersonalinjuryattorney.com/

DOWN SYNDROME SCHOLARSHIP
• *See page 597*

KITCHEN GUIDES

http://www.kitchensguides.com/

SMART KITCHEN IMPROVEMENT SCHOLARSHIP BY KITCHEN GUIDES
• *See page 598*

LAW OFFICE OF DAVID D. WHITE, PLLC

http://www.wm-attorneys.com/

ANNUAL TRAUMATIC BRAIN INJURY SCHOLARSHIPS
• *See page 598*

LAW OFFICES OF DAVID A. BLACK

http://www.dbphoenixcriminallawyer.com

ANNUAL HEARING IMPAIRED SCHOLARSHIP
• *See page 599*

LAW OFFICES OF JUDD S. NEMIRO, PLLC

http://www.jnphoenixfamilylawyer.com/

ANNUAL DYSLEXIA SCHOLARSHIP
• *See page 599*

LEARNING ALLY

http://www.learningally.org

MARION HUBER LEARNING THROUGH LISTENING AWARDS
• *See page 548*

MARY P. OENSLAGER SCHOLASTIC ACHIEVEMENT AWARDS
• *See page 548*

LIGHTHOUSE GUILD

http://www.lighthouseguild.org

LIGHTHOUSE GUILD SCHOLARSHIP PROGRAM

Annual merit based scholarship program for college-bound high school and graduate school students who are legally blind. The submission deadline is March 31st. Twenty scholarships will be awarded to college bound high school seniors and one for a graduate student.

Award: Scholarship for use in freshman, graduate, or postgraduate years; not renewable. *Number:* 21. *Amount:* $10,000.

Eligibility Requirements: Applicant must be visually impaired and enrolled or expecting to enroll full-time at a four-year institution or university. Applicant must be visually impaired. Applicant must have 3.0 GPA or higher. Available to U.S. citizens.

Application Requirements: Application form, community service, essay. *Deadline:* March 31.

Contact: Mr. Gordon Rovins, Director of Special Programs
Lighthouse Guild
15 West 65th Street
New York, NY 10023
Phone: 212-769-7801
E-mail: scholars@lighthouseguild.org

MATRIX HEALTH GROUP

http://www.matrixhealthgroup.com

JOE HOLIBAUGH MEMORIAL SCHOLARSHIP

• *See page 602*

MARK COATS MEMORIAL SCHOLARSHIP

• *See page 602*

MIKE HYLTON MEMORIAL SCHOLARSHIP

One-time scholarship for men diagnosed with hemophilia or von Willebrand Disease and their immediate family members. Must be attending or entering a college, university, trade or technical school full-time. Minimum GPA 2.5 on a 4.0 scale during senior year of high school or current year of post high school studies. Only U.S. residents are eligible.

Award: Scholarship for use in freshman, sophomore, junior, senior, or graduate years; not renewable. *Number:* 1. *Amount:* $1000.

Eligibility Requirements: Applicant must be physically disabled; enrolled or expecting to enroll full-time at a two-year or four-year or technical institution or university; male and resident of Massachusetts. Applicant must be physically disabled. Applicant must have 2.5 GPA or higher. Available to U.S. citizens.

Application Requirements: Application form, essay, personal photograph. *Deadline:* August 1.

Contact: Maria Vetter, Scholarship Administrator
Matrix Health Group
2202 Brownstone Court
Champaign, IL 61822
Phone: 877-337-3002 Ext. 442
E-mail: maria.vetter@matrixhealthgroup.com

MILLIE GONZALEZ MEMORIAL SCHOLARSHIP

Scholarship for women diagnosed with hemophilia or von Willebrand Disease who are entering or attending a college, university, trade or technical school full-time. Minimum grade point average of 2.5 on a 4.0 scale during entire senior year of high school or current year of college or graduate school. Must be U.S. resident. Must provide medical verification of bleeding disorder.

Award: Scholarship for use in freshman, sophomore, junior, senior, or graduate years; not renewable. *Number:* 2. *Amount:* $1000.

Eligibility Requirements: Applicant must be physically disabled; enrolled or expecting to enroll full-time at a two-year or four-year or technical institution or university and female. Applicant must be physically disabled. Applicant must have 2.5 GPA or higher. Available to U.S. citizens.

Application Requirements: Application form, essay. *Deadline:* August 1.

Contact: Maria Vetter
Matrix Health Group
2202 Brownstone Court
Champaign, IL 61822
Phone: 877-337-3002 Ext. 442
E-mail: maria.vetter@matrixhealthgroup.com

RON NIEDERMAN MEMORIAL SCHOLARSHIP

• *See page 603*

TIM KENNEDY MEMORIAL SCHOLARSHIP

• *See page 603*

NATIONAL CENTER FOR LEARNING DISABILITIES, INC.

http://www.ld.org/

ANNE FORD & ALLEGRA FORD SCHOLARSHIP

Award of $10,000 given to two high school seniors of high merit with an identified learning disability who is pursuing a college degree. The ideal candidate is a person who has faced the challenges of having a learning disability and who, through perseverance and academic endeavor, has created a life of purpose and achievement.

Award: Scholarship for use in freshman, sophomore, junior, or senior years; not renewable. *Number:* 2. *Amount:* $10,000.

Eligibility Requirements: Applicant must be learning disabled; high school student and planning to enroll or expecting to enroll full-time at a four-year institution or university. Applicant must be learning disabled. Applicant must have 3.0 GPA or higher. Available to U.S. citizens.

Application Requirements: Application form, essay, financial need analysis, recommendations or references, test scores, transcript.

Contact: Catherine Boswell, Coordinator
National Center for Learning Disabilities, Inc.
381 Park Avenue South, Suite 1401
New York, NY 10016-8806
Phone: 646-616-1233
Fax: 212-545-9665
E-mail: afscholarship@ncld.org

NATIONAL COUNCIL OF JEWISH WOMEN NEW YORK SECTION

http://www.ncjwny.org/

JACKSON-STRICKS SCHOLARSHIP

Scholarship provides financial aid to a person with significant physical challenges for academic study or vocational training that leads to independent living.

Award: Scholarship for use in sophomore, junior, senior, graduate, or postgraduate years; not renewable. *Number:* 1–2. *Amount:* $1500–$2500.

Eligibility Requirements: Applicant must be physically disabled; enrolled or expecting to enroll full- or part-time at a two-year or four-year institution or university and studying in New York. Applicant must be physically disabled. Available to U.S. and non-U.S. citizens.

Application Requirements: Application form, essay. *Deadline:* March 31.

Contact: Naomi Skop Richter, Jackson-Stricks Scholarship Committee
National Council of Jewish Women New York Section
241 West 72 Street
New York, NY 10023
Phone: 212-687-5030 Ext. 461
E-mail: jss@ncjwny.org

NATIONAL FEDERATION OF THE BLIND (NFB)

http://www.nfb.org/scholarships

AAF KENNETH JERNIGAN SCHOLARSHIP FOR $12,000

• *See page 607*

CHARLES AND MELVA T. OWEN MEMORIAL SCHOLARSHIP FOR $5,000

Merit-based scholarship requires academic excellence and leadership, permanent residency in United States/Puerto Rico, and accredited institution's degree program (in U.S./PR) directed toward financial independence (excludes degrees in religious studies or solely for cultural education). Winner assisted to attend NFB annual convention to receive this award. Membership not required.

Award: Scholarship for use in freshman, sophomore, junior, senior, graduate, or postgraduate years; not renewable. *Number:* 2. *Amount:* $5000.

Eligibility Requirements: Applicant must be visually impaired and enrolled or expecting to enroll full- or part-time at a two-year or four-year institution or university. Applicant must be visually impaired. Available to U.S. and non-U.S. citizens.

Application Requirements: Application form, application form may be submitted online (https://nfb.org//scholarships), essay, interview, proof of legal blindness in both eyes, recommendations or references, test scores, transcript. *Deadline:* March 31.

Contact: Ms. Patti Chang, Chairperson, NFB Scholarship Committee
National Federation of the Blind (NFB)
200 East Wells Street
Baltimore, MD 21230
Phone: 410-659-9314 Ext. 2415
E-mail: scholarships@nfb.org

CHARLES AND MELVA T. OWEN SCHOLARSHIP FOR $10,000

• See page 607

LARRY STREETER MEMORIAL SCHOLARSHIP FOR $3,000

$3000 scholarship for legally blind, permanent residents of the U.S. or Puerto Rico, pursuing a postsecondary degree at an accredited institution in U.S. or PR. Created to assist blind students to elevate their quality of life, equipping them to be active, productive participants in their family, community, and the workplace.

Award: Scholarship for use in freshman, sophomore, junior, or senior years; not renewable. *Number:* 1. *Amount:* $3000.

Eligibility Requirements: Applicant must be visually impaired and enrolled or expecting to enroll full- or part-time at a four-year institution or university. Applicant must be visually impaired. Available to U.S. citizens.

Application Requirements: Application form, essay, financial need analysis, proof of blindness in both eyes, transcript. *Deadline:* March 31.

Contact: Ms. Patti Chang, Chairperson, NFB Scholarship Program
National Federation of the Blind (NFB)
200 East Wells Street
Baltimore, MD 21230
Phone: 410-659-9314 Ext. 2415
E-mail: scholarships@nfb.org

NATIONAL FEDERATION OF THE BLIND SCHOLARSHIP FOR $3,000

$3000 scholarship for legally blind, permanent residents of the U.S. or Puerto Rico, pursuing a postsecondary degree at an accredited institution in U.S. or PR. Selection is merit-based on academic excellence and leadership. With NFB assistance, winner attends NFB annual convention to receive award. Membership in NFB is not required.

Award: Scholarship for use in freshman, sophomore, junior, senior, graduate, or postgraduate years; not renewable. *Number:* 20. *Amount:* $3000.

Eligibility Requirements: Applicant must be visually impaired and enrolled or expecting to enroll full- or part-time at a two-year or four-year institution or university. Applicant must be visually impaired. Available to U.S. and non-U.S. citizens.

Application Requirements: Application form, application form may be submitted online (https://nfb.org//scholarships), essay, interview, proof of legal blindness in both eyes, recommendations or references, test scores, transcript. *Deadline:* March 31.

Contact: Ms. Patti Chang, Chairperson, Scholarship Committee
National Federation of the Blind (NFB)
200 East Wells Street
Baltimore, MD 21230
Phone: 410-659-9314 Ext. 2415
E-mail: scholarships@nfb.org

NATIONAL FEDERATION OF THE BLIND SCHOLARSHIP FOR $7,000

$7000 scholarship for legally blind, permanent residents of the U.S. or Puerto Rico, pursuing a postsecondary degree at an accredited institution in U.S. or PR. Selection is merit-based on academic excellence and leadership. With NFB assistance, winner attends NFB annual convention to receive award. Membership in NFB is not required.

Award: Scholarship for use in freshman, sophomore, junior, senior, graduate, or postgraduate years; not renewable. *Number:* 2. *Amount:* $7000.

Eligibility Requirements: Applicant must be visually impaired and enrolled or expecting to enroll full- or part-time at a two-year or four-year institution or university. Applicant must be visually impaired. Available to U.S. and non-U.S. citizens.

Application Requirements: Application form, application form may be submitted online (http://www.nfb.org//scholarships), entry in a contest, essay, interview, proof of legal blindness in both eyes, recommendations or references, test scores, transcript. *Deadline:* March 31.

Contact: Ms. Patti Chang, Chairperson, NFB Scholarship Committee
National Federation of the Blind (NFB)
200 East Wells Street
Baltimore, MD 21230
Phone: 410-659-9314 Ext. 2415
E-mail: scholarships@nfb.org

NFB SCHOLARSHIP FOR $5,000

$5000 scholarships for legally blind, permanent residents of the U.S. or Puerto Rico, pursuing a postsecondary degree at an accredited institution in U.S. or PR. Selection is merit-based on academic excellence and leadership. With NFB assistance, winner attends NFB annual convention to receive award. Membership in NFB is not required.

Award: Scholarship for use in freshman, sophomore, junior, senior, graduate, or postgraduate years; not renewable. *Number:* 4. *Amount:* $5000.

Eligibility Requirements: Applicant must be visually impaired and enrolled or expecting to enroll full- or part-time at a two-year or four-year institution or university. Applicant must be visually impaired. Available to U.S. and non-U.S. citizens.

Application Requirements: Application form, application form may be submitted online (http://www.nfb.org//scholarships), entry in a contest, essay, interview, proof of legal blindness in both eyes, recommendations or references, test scores, transcript. *Deadline:* March 31.

Contact: Ms. Patti Chang, Chairperson, NFB Scholarship Program
National Federation of the Blind (NFB)
200 East Wells Street
Baltimore, MD 21230
Phone: 410-659-9314 Ext. 2415
E-mail: scholarships@nfb.org

NATIONAL FEDERATION OF THE BLIND OF CALIFORNIA

http://www.nfbcal.org/

GERALD DRAKE MEMORIAL SCHOLARSHIP

One-time award for legally blind students pursuing an undergraduate or graduate degree. Must be a California resident and full-time student.

Award: Scholarship for use in freshman, sophomore, junior, senior, or graduate years; not renewable. *Number:* up to 5. *Amount:* $1500.

Eligibility Requirements: Applicant must be visually impaired; enrolled or expecting to enroll full-time at a four-year institution or university and resident of California. Applicant must be visually impaired. Available to U.S. and non-U.S. citizens.

Application Requirements: Application form. *Deadline:* March 31.

Contact: Robert Stigile, President
Phone: 818-342-6524
Fax: 818-344-7930
E-mail: nfbcal@yahoo.com

JULIE LANDUCCI SCHOLARSHIP

Award for legally blind students pursuing an undergraduate or graduate degree. Must be a California resident and full-time student. Award available to U.S. citizens.

Award: Scholarship for use in freshman, sophomore, junior, senior, or graduate years; renewable. *Number:* 1. *Amount:* up to $2000.

Eligibility Requirements: Applicant must be visually impaired; enrolled or expecting to enroll full-time at a four-year institution or university and resident of California. Applicant must be visually impaired. Available to U.S. citizens.

Application Requirements: Application form. *Deadline:* March 31.

Contact: Robert Stigile, President
 Phone: 818-342-6524
 Fax: 818-344-7930
 E-mail: nfbcal@yahoo.com

LA VYRL "PINKY" JOHNSON MEMORIAL SCHOLARSHIP

One-time award up to $2000 for legally blind students pursuing an undergraduate or graduate degree. Must be a California resident and full-time student.

Award: Scholarship for use in freshman, sophomore, junior, senior, or graduate years; renewable. *Number:* 1. *Amount:* $2000.

Eligibility Requirements: Applicant must be visually impaired; enrolled or expecting to enroll full-time at a four-year institution or university and resident of California. Applicant must be visually impaired. Available to U.S. citizens.

Application Requirements: Application form. *Deadline:* March 31.

Contact: Robert Stigile, President
 Phone: 818-342-6524
 Fax: 818-344-7930
 E-mail: nfbcal@yahoo.com

LAWRENCE "MUZZY" MARCELINO MEMORIAL SCHOLARSHIP

Scholarship provides financial assistance for graduate or undergraduate education to blind students in California. Any legally blind student may apply for a scholarship but must attend the convention of the National Federation of the Blind of California. Selection is based first on academic merit and second on financial need.

Award: Scholarship for use in freshman, sophomore, junior, senior, or graduate years; renewable. *Number:* up to 4. *Amount:* $1500.

Eligibility Requirements: Applicant must be visually impaired; enrolled or expecting to enroll full-time at a four-year institution or university and resident of California. Applicant must be visually impaired. Available to U.S. citizens.

Application Requirements: Application form. *Deadline:* March 15.

Contact: Robert Stigile, President
 Phone: 818-342-6524
 Fax: 818-344-7930
 E-mail: nfbcal@yahoo.com

NATIONAL FEDERATION OF THE BLIND OF CALIFORNIA MERIT SCHOLARSHIPS

Scholarships to qualified blind students pursuing undergraduate or graduate studies in order to achieve an academic degree. This opportunity is also available to high school seniors preparing to enter undergraduate programs.

Award: Scholarship for use in freshman, sophomore, junior, senior, or graduate years; renewable. *Number:* up to 5. *Amount:* $1000.

Eligibility Requirements: Applicant must be visually impaired; enrolled or expecting to enroll full-time at a four-year institution or university and resident of California. Applicant must be visually impaired. Available to U.S. citizens.

Application Requirements: Application form. *Deadline:* March 15.

Contact: Robert Stigile, President
 Phone: 818-342-6524
 Fax: 818-344-7930
 E-mail: nfbcal@yahoo.com

NATIONAL FEDERATION OF THE BLIND OF MISSOURI

http://www.nfbmo.org/

NATIONAL FEDERATION OF THE BLIND OF MISSOURI SCHOLARSHIP PROGRAM FOR LEGALLY BLIND STUDENTS

Awards are based on achievement and commitment to community. Recipients must be legally blind, live in Missouri, and maintain a GPA greater than 2.5.Amount of money each year available for program will vary.

Award: Scholarship for use in freshman, sophomore, or senior years; not renewable. *Number:* 1–3. *Amount:* $500–$2500.

Eligibility Requirements: Applicant must be visually impaired; enrolled or expecting to enroll full- or part-time at a two-year or four-year or technical institution or university; resident of Missouri and studying in Missouri. Applicant must be visually impaired. Applicant must have 3.5 GPA or higher. Available to U.S. citizens.

Application Requirements: Application form, essay, interview. *Deadline:* February 1.

Contact: Shelia Wright
 National Federation of the Blind of Missouri
 7928 NW Milrey Drive
 Kansas City, MO 64152
 Phone: 816-741-6402
 E-mail: sbwright95@att.net

NATIONAL KIDNEY FOUNDATION OF INDIANA INC.

http://www.kidneyindiana.org/

NATIONAL KIDNEY FOUNDATION OF INDIANA SCHOLARSHIP

Scholarship provides financial assistance for kidney dialysis and transplant patients to pursue post-secondary education. Applicant must be resident of Indiana over the age of 18. Must have a high school diploma or its equivalent. Applications are reviewed by committee to choose awardees.

Award: Scholarship for use in freshman, sophomore, junior, or senior years; not renewable. *Number:* 2–8. *Amount:* $250–$1500.

Eligibility Requirements: Applicant must be physically disabled; enrolled or expecting to enroll full- or part-time at a two-year or four-year or technical institution or university and resident of Indiana. Applicant must be physically disabled. Available to U.S. citizens.

Application Requirements: Application form, essay. *Deadline:* March 31.

Contact: Nicki Howard, Public Health Coordinator
 National Kidney Foundation of Indiana Inc.
 911 East 86th Street
 Suite 100
 Indianapolis, IN 46240
 Phone: 317-722-5640
 Fax: 317-722-5650
 E-mail: nhoward@kidneyindiana.org

NATIONAL MULTIPLE SCLEROSIS SOCIETY

http://www.nmss.org/

NATIONAL MULTIPLE SCLEROSIS SOCIETY SCHOLARSHIP PROGRAM

• *See page 607*

NATIONAL PKU NEWS

http://www.pkunews.org/

ROBERT GUTHRIE PKU SCHOLARSHIP AND AWARDS

Scholarship for persons with phenylketonuria (PKU) who are on a special diet for PKU treatment. Award is for full-time or part-time study at any accredited U.S. institution. Up to 8 scholarships of between $500 and $3500 are granted.

Award: Scholarship for use in freshman, sophomore, junior, or senior years; not renewable. *Number:* 4–8. *Amount:* $500–$3500.

Eligibility Requirements: Applicant must be physically disabled and enrolled or expecting to enroll full- or part-time at a two-year or four-year or technical institution or university. Applicant must be physically disabled. Available to U.S. and non-U.S. citizens.

Application Requirements: Application form, essay, personal photograph, recommendations or references, resume, test scores, transcript. *Deadline:* October 15.

Contact: Virginia Schuett, Director
   Phone: 206-525-8140
   E-mail: schuett@pkunews.org

NIKKO COSMETIC SURGERY CENTER

http://www.drnikko.com/

BREAST CANCER SURVIVOR SCHOLARSHIPS
• *See page 608*

NORTH CAROLINA DIVISION OF SERVICES FOR THE BLIND

http://www.ncdhhs.gov/

NORTH CAROLINA DIVISION OF SERVICES FOR THE BLIND REHABILITATION SERVICES

Financial assistance is available for North Carolina residents who are blind or visually impaired and who require vocational rehabilitation to help find employment. Tuition and other assistance provided based on need. Open to U.S. citizens and legal residents of United States. Applicants goal must be to work after receiving vocational services. To apply, contact the local DSB office and apply for vocational rehabilitation services.

Award: Scholarship for use in freshman, sophomore, junior, or senior years; renewable.

Eligibility Requirements: Applicant must be visually impaired; enrolled or expecting to enroll full-time at a two-year or four-year or technical institution or university and resident of North Carolina. Applicant must be visually impaired. Available to U.S. citizens.

Application Requirements: Application form, financial need analysis, interview, proof of eligibility. *Deadline:* continuous.

Contact: JoAnn Strader, Chief of Rehabilitation Field Services
   North Carolina Division of Services for the Blind
   2601 Mail Service Center
   Raleigh, NC 27699-2601
   Phone: 919-733-9700
   Fax: 919-715-8771
   E-mail: joann.strader@ncmail.net

NORTH CAROLINA DIVISION OF VOCATIONAL REHABILITATION SERVICES

http://www.dhhs.state.nc.us/

TRAINING SUPPORT FOR YOUTH WITH DISABILITIES
• *See page 609*

OPTIMIST INTERNATIONAL FOUNDATION

http://www.optimist.org/

COMMUNICATION CONTEST FOR THE DEAF AND HARD OF HEARING

College scholarship (district level) for young people through grade twelve in the U.S. and Canada, to CEGEP in Quebec and grade thirteen in the Caribbean. Students interested in participating must submit the results of an audiogram conducted no longer than twenty four months prior to the date of the contest from a qualified audiologist. Students must be certified to have a hearing loss of forty decibels or more and supported by the audiogram to be eligible to compete. Students attending either

public school or schools providing special services are eligible to enter if criteria are met.

Award: Scholarship for use in freshman, sophomore, junior, or senior years; not renewable. *Number:* 1–30. *Amount:* up to $2500.

Eligibility Requirements: Applicant must be hearing impaired and enrolled or expecting to enroll full- or part-time at a two-year or four-year or technical institution or university. Applicant must be hearing impaired. Available to U.S. and Canadian citizens.

Application Requirements: Application form, entry in a contest, self-addressed stamped envelope with application, speech/presentation, audiogram. *Deadline:* varies.

Contact: Dana Thomas, Director of International Programs
   Optimist International Foundation
   4494 Lindell Boulevard
   St. Louis, MO 63108
   Phone: 800-500-8130
   Fax: 314-371-6006
   E-mail: programs@optimist.org

OREGON COMMUNITY FOUNDATION

http://www.oregoncf.org/

HARRY LUDWIG SCHOLARSHIP FUND

Scholarship for visually impaired students for use in the pursuit of a postsecondary education at a college or university. For full-time students only.

Award: Scholarship for use in freshman, sophomore, junior, or senior years; renewable. *Number:* 1–3. *Amount:* $500–$5000.

Eligibility Requirements: Applicant must be visually impaired and enrolled or expecting to enroll full-time at a four-year institution or university. Applicant must be visually impaired. Available to U.S. citizens.

Application Requirements: Application form, recommendations or references. *Deadline:* March 1.

Contact: Dianne Causey, Program Associate for Scholarships and
   Grants
   Phone: 503-227-6846 Ext. 1418
   E-mail: dcausey@oregoncf.org

OREGON STUDENT ASSISTANCE COMMISSION

http://www.GetCollegeFunds.org/

HARRY LUDWIG MEMORIAL SCHOLARSHIP

Award for visually-impaired Oregon residents planning to enroll full-time in undergraduate or graduate studies at an Oregon college or university. Must document visual impairment with a letter from a physician. Must reapply for award annually.

Award: Scholarship for use in freshman, sophomore, junior, senior, or graduate years; not renewable.

Eligibility Requirements: Applicant must be visually impaired; enrolled or expecting to enroll full-time at a two-year or four-year institution or university; resident of Oregon and studying in Oregon. Applicant must be visually impaired. Available to U.S. citizens.

Application Requirements: Application form, financial need analysis. *Deadline:* March 1.

Contact: Melissa Adams, Scholarship Processing Coordinator
   Phone: 541-687-7409
   E-mail: melissa.adams@hecc.oregon.gov

SALEM FOUNDATION ANSEL & MARIE SOLIE SCHOLARSHIP

Award is available to visually impaired Oregon residents planning to enroll in full-time undergraduate studies. Award may be used only at a four-year public or nonprofit Oregon college or university. Apply/compete annually.

Award: Scholarship for use in freshman, sophomore, junior, or senior years; not renewable.

Eligibility Requirements: Applicant must be visually impaired; enrolled or expecting to enroll full-time at a four-year institution or university; resident of Oregon and studying in Oregon. Applicant must be visually impaired. Available to U.S. citizens.

Application Requirements: Application form. *Deadline:* March 1.

Contact: Melissa Adams, Scholarship Processing Coordinator
Phone: 541-687-7409
E-mail: melissa.adams@hecc.oregon.gov

PENNSYLVANIA HIGHER EDUCATION ASSISTANCE AGENCY

http://www.pheaa.org/

BLIND OR DEAF BENEFICIARY GRANT PROGRAM
• *See page 612*

PETAZI

https://petazi.com/

2017 NURTURE FOR NATURE SCHOLARSHIP

One $1200 scholarship created to help raise everyone's awareness about protecting animals and the environment. All students located and currently studying in the United States or Canada are eligible to apply for this scholarship. Valid statements of current academic status as evidence that candidates are currently attending college. Students can apply by writing an inspirational short story about animals/ pets. Upon sharing it with us, we will then share it online via Petazi websites. The winner of the $1200 prize will be the one whose entry/story receives the most likes after we post all the entries on our Petazi Facebook page. See website for details, https://petazi.com/scholarship

Award: Scholarship for use in freshman, sophomore, junior, senior, graduate, or postgraduate years; renewable. *Number:* 1. *Amount:* $1200.

Eligibility Requirements: Applicant must be hearing impaired, learning disabled, physically disabled, or visually impaired; American Indian/Alaska Native, Asian/Pacific Islander, Black (non-Hispanic), Hispanic and enrolled or expecting to enroll full- or part-time at a two-year or four-year institution or university. Applicant must be hearing impaired, learning disabled, physically disabled, or visually impaired. Available to U.S. and non-U.S. citizens. Applicant or parent must meet one or more of the following requirements: general military experience; retired from active duty; disabled or killed as a result of military service; prisoner of war; or missing in action.

Application Requirements: Application form, personal photograph. *Deadline:* June 30.

Contact: Ms. Rose Larson, $1200 Nurture for Nature Scholarship
Petazi
Scholarship Office
316A Cecil Street
Chicago, IL 60605
Phone: 331-2074154
E-mail: scholarship@petazi.com

RYU FAMILY FOUNDATION, INC.

SEOL BONG SCHOLARSHIP

One-time award to support and advance education and research. Must be Korean residing in DE, PA, NJ, NY, CT, VT, RI, NH, MA, or ME. Minimum 3.5 GPA required.

Award: Scholarship for use in freshman, sophomore, junior, senior, or graduate years; not renewable. *Number:* 21. *Amount:* $2000–$3000.

Eligibility Requirements: Applicant must be learning disabled; of Korean heritage; Asian/Pacific Islander; enrolled or expecting to enroll full-time at a four-year institution or university; resident of Connecticut, Delaware, Maine, Massachusetts, New Hampshire, New Jersey, New York, Pennsylvania, Rhode Island, Vermont and studying in Connecticut, Delaware, Maine, Massachusetts, New Hampshire, New Jersey, New York, Pennsylvania, Rhode Island, Vermont. Applicant must be learning disabled. Applicant must have 3.5 GPA or higher. Available to U.S. and non-Canadian citizens.

Application Requirements: Application form, essay, financial need analysis, personal photograph, portfolio, recommendations or references, resume, test scores, transcript. *Deadline:* November 15.

Contact: Jenny Kang, Scholarship Secretary
Phone: 973-692-9696 Ext. 20
E-mail: jennyk@toplineus.com

SCHOLARSHIP AMERICA

www.scholarshipamerica.org

WELLS FARGO SCHOLARSHIP PROGRAM FOR PEOPLE WITH DISABILITIES

The Wells Fargo Scholarship Program for People with Disabilities is designed to help people with disabilities obtain the education or training necessary to succeed in the career path of their choice. To apply, you must have an identified disability (defined as someone who has, or considers themselves to have, a long-term or recurring issue that impacts one or more major life activity). Applicants must be high school seniors or graduates planning to enroll or who are already enrolled in full- or half-time undergraduate study at an accredited two- or four-year college or university in the United States for the 2017-2018 academic year. The program will award $2,500 renewable scholarships for full-time students and $1,250 renewable scholarships for half-time students. Visit https://scholarsapply.org/pwdscholarship for more information and to apply.

Award: Scholarship for use in freshman, sophomore, junior, or senior years; renewable. *Number:* 25. *Amount:* $2500.

Eligibility Requirements: Applicant must be hearing impaired, learning disabled, physically disabled, or visually impaired and enrolled or expecting to enroll full- or part-time at a two-year or four-year institution or university. Applicant must be hearing impaired, learning disabled, physically disabled, or visually impaired. Applicant must have 2.5 GPA or higher. Available to U.S. citizens.

Application Requirements: Application form. *Deadline:* January 17.

Contact: Program Manager
Scholarship America
Scholarship America
One Scholarship Way
Saint Peter, MN 56082
Phone: 844-402-0357
E-mail: pwdscholarship@scholarshipamerica.org

SERTOMA, INC.

http://www.sertoma.org/

SERTOMA SCHOLARSHIP FOR STUDENTS WHO ARE HARD OF HEARING OR DEAF

Applicants must have a minimum of 40dB bilateral hearing loss, as evidenced on audiogram by an SRT. Must have a minimum cumulative 3.2 GPA on a 4.0 unweighted scale.

Award: Scholarship for use in freshman, sophomore, junior, or senior years; not renewable. *Number:* 45–50. *Amount:* $1000.

Eligibility Requirements: Applicant must be hearing impaired and enrolled or expecting to enroll full-time at a four-year institution or university. Applicant must be hearing impaired. Applicant must have 3.0 GPA or higher. Available to U.S. citizens.

Application Requirements: Application form, Audiogram (Proof of Hearing Loss), recommendations or references, transcript. *Deadline:* May 1.

Contact: Mrs. Bridget Almond, Mission Development Officer, Internal Marketing
Phone: 816-333-8300
E-mail: Balmond@sertomahq.org

SISTER KENNY REHABILITATION INSTITUTE

http://www.allina.com/ahs/ski.nsf

INTERNATIONAL ART SHOW FOR ARTISTS WITH DISABILITIES

One-time award for artwork submitted by artists of any age with visual, hearing, physical, or learning impairment. Contact Sister Kenny Rehabilitation Institute for show information. This is a one-time prize, not an academic scholarship.

Award: Prize for use in freshman, sophomore, junior, senior, or graduate years; not renewable. *Number:* 25–70. *Amount:* $25–$500.

Eligibility Requirements: Applicant must be hearing impaired, learning disabled, physically disabled, or visually impaired; enrolled or expecting to enroll full- or part-time at a four-year institution or university and must have an interest in art. Applicant must be hearing impaired, learning disabled, physically disabled, or visually impaired. Available to U.S. and non-U.S. citizens.

Application Requirements: Application form, entry in a contest. *Deadline:* March 17.

Contact: Laura Swift, Administrative Assistant
Sister Kenny Rehabilitation Institute
800 East 28th Street
Minneapolis, MN 55407-3799
Phone: 612-863-4466
Fax: 612-863-8942
E-mail: laura.swift@allina.com

STICKLER INVOLVED PEOPLE

https://stickler.org/

DR. GUNNAR B. STICKLER SCHOLARSHIPS

Applicant must have a diagnosis of Stickler syndrome and submit letter from physician with application. Scholarship is renewable yearly with 3.0 goals letter provided from school.

Award: Scholarship for use in freshman, sophomore, junior, or senior years; renewable. *Number:* 1. *Amount:* $500.

Eligibility Requirements: Applicant must be hearing impaired, physically disabled, or visually impaired; high school student and planning to enroll or expecting to enroll full-time at a four-year institution. Applicant must be hearing impaired, physically disabled, or visually impaired. Applicant must have 3.0 GPA or higher. Available to U.S. citizens.

Application Requirements: Application form. *Deadline:* June 15.

Contact: James Brown, Scholarship Committee Chair
Stickler Involved People
Gunnar B. Stickler Scholarship Award
PO Box 775
Cologne, NJ 08213

TPA SCHOLARSHIP TRUST FOR THE HEARING IMPAIRED

https://www.tpahq.org/scholarshiptrust/

TPA SCHOLARSHIP TRUST FOR THE HEARING IMPAIRED

Scholarships are awarded to deaf or hearing-impaired persons of any age, race, or religion for specialized education, mechanical devices, or medical or specialized treatment. Based on financial need.

Award: Scholarship for use in freshman, sophomore, junior, senior, graduate, or postgraduate years; not renewable. *Amount:* $100–$1000.

Eligibility Requirements: Applicant must be hearing impaired and enrolled or expecting to enroll full- or part-time at a two-year or four-year or technical institution or university. Applicant must be hearing impaired. Available to U.S. citizens.

Application Requirements: Application form, financial need analysis, personal photograph. *Deadline:* continuous.

Contact: Venita Sedodo, Trust Secretary
TPA Scholarship Trust for the Hearing Impaired
2041 Exchange Drive
Saint Charles, MO 63303
Phone: 636-724-2227
E-mail: vsedodo@tpahq.org

UCB, INC.

http://www.ucb.com/

UCB FAMILY EPILEPSY SCHOLARSHIP

In 2017, UCB, Inc. will award 32 one-time scholarships to people living with epilepsy, their family members and caregivers who are pursuing higher educations. Thirty scholarships of up to $5,000 each will be awarded to outstanding applicants who demonstrate academic and personal achievement. In addition, 2 Epilepsy Leader Scholarships of $10,000 each will be awarded to outstanding applicants who demonstrate academic and personal achievement as well as a passion for advocacy, serving the epilepsy community and a persevering spirit. Students of all ages are welcome to apply and the scholarship can be used for a two-year, four-year, trade or specialty school.

Award: Scholarship for use in freshman, sophomore, junior, senior, or graduate years; not renewable. *Number:* 32. *Amount:* $5000–$10,000.

Eligibility Requirements: Applicant must be physically disabled and enrolled or expecting to enroll full- or part-time at a two-year or four-year or technical institution or university. Applicant must be physically disabled. Available to U.S. citizens.

Application Requirements: Application form, community service, essay, personal photograph. *Deadline:* March 10.

Contact: Mrs. Amy Bryant, UCB Family Epilepsy Scholarship Program
UCB, Inc.
c/o Summit Medical Communications
1421 East Broad Street, Suite 340
Fuquay-Varina, NC 27526
Phone: 866-825-1920
E-mail: ucbepilepsyscholarship@summitmedcomm.com

UNITED NEGRO COLLEGE FUND

http://www.uncf.org/

ROBERT DOLE SCHOLARSHIP FOR DISABLED STUDENTS

Up to $3500 need-base scholarship for physically and mentally challenged students. Must attend one of the 37 UNCF member colleges or universities.

Award: Scholarship for use in freshman, sophomore, junior, or senior years.

Eligibility Requirements: Applicant must be hearing impaired, learning disabled, physically disabled, or visually impaired; American Indian/Alaska Native, Asian/Pacific Islander, Black (non-Hispanic), Hispanic and enrolled or expecting to enroll at a four-year institution or university. Applicant must be hearing impaired, learning disabled, physically disabled, or visually impaired. Applicant must have 2.5 GPA or higher. Available to U.S. citizens.

Application Requirements: Application form, essay, financial need analysis. *Deadline:* October 26.

Contact: Mary Williams, Director of Outreach and Recruitment
Phone: 800-331-2244

UNITED STATES ASSOCIATION FOR BLIND ATHLETES

http://www.usaba.org/

ARTHUR E. AND HELEN COPELAND SCHOLARSHIPS

Scholarship for a full-time college student who is blind or visually impaired. All applicants must be current members of USABA.

Award: Scholarship for use in freshman, sophomore, junior, or senior years; not renewable. *Number:* 1–2. *Amount:* $500.

Eligibility Requirements: Applicant must be visually impaired and enrolled or expecting to enroll full-time at a four-year institution or university. Applicant must be visually impaired. Available to U.S. citizens.

Application Requirements: Application form, driver's license, proof of acceptance, recommendations or references, transcript. *Deadline:* October 1.

Contact: Mark Lucas, Executive Director
United States Association for Blind Athletes
33 North Institute Street
Colorado Springs, CO 80903
Phone: 719-630-0422 Ext. 13
Fax: 719-630-0616
E-mail: mlucas@usaba.org

U.S. COAST GUARD

www.gocoastguard/cspi

COLLEGE STUDENT PRE-COMMISSIONING INITIATIVE (CSPI)
• *See page 625*

WISCONSIN DEPARTMENT OF VETERANS AFFAIRS (WDVA)

http://www.dva.state.wi.us/

VETERANS EDUCATION (VETED) REIMBURSEMENT GRANT

The grant is for eligible Wisconsin veterans enrolled at approved schools who have not yet earned a BS/BA. Reimburses up to 120 credits or eight semesters at the UW Madison rate for the same number of credits taken in one semester or term. The number of credits or semesters is based on length of time serving on active duty in the armed forces (active duty for training does not apply). Application is due no later than 60 days after the course start date. The student must earn a 2.0 or better for the semester. An eligible veteran will have entered active duty as a Wisconsin resident or lived in state for twelve consecutive months since entering active duty.

Award: Grant for use in freshman, sophomore, junior, or senior years; renewable. *Amount:* $1340–$4000.

Eligibility Requirements: Applicant must be hearing impaired, learning disabled, physically disabled, or visually impaired; age 18-75; enrolled or expecting to enroll full- or part-time at a two-year or four-year or technical institution or university; resident of Wisconsin and studying in Minnesota, Wisconsin. Applicant must be hearing impaired, learning disabled, physically disabled, or visually impaired. Applicant must have 3.5 GPA or higher. Available to U.S. citizens. Applicant must have general military experience.

Application Requirements: Application form. *Deadline:* July 15.

Contact: Mrs. Leslie Busby-Amegashie, Analyst
Wisconsin Department of Veterans Affairs (WDVA)
PO Box 7843
Madison, WI 53707-7843
Phone: 800-947-8387
E-mail: leslie.busby-amegashie@dva.wisconsin.gov

WISCONSIN HIGHER EDUCATIONAL AID BOARD

http://www.heab.wi.gov/

HANDICAPPED STUDENT GRANT-WISCONSIN

One-time award available to residents of Wisconsin who have severe or profound hearing or visual impairment. Must be enrolled at least half-time at a nonprofit institution. If the handicap prevents the student from attending a Wisconsin school, the award may be used out-of-state in a specialized college. Refer to website for further details http://www.heab.state.wi.us.

Award: Grant for use in freshman, sophomore, junior, or senior years; not renewable. *Amount:* $250–$1800.

Eligibility Requirements: Applicant must be hearing impaired or visually impaired; enrolled or expecting to enroll full- or part-time at a four-year institution or university and resident of Wisconsin. Applicant must be hearing impaired or visually impaired. Available to U.S. citizens.

Application Requirements: Application form, financial need analysis. *Deadline:* continuous.

Contact: Sandy Thomas, Program Coordinator
Wisconsin Higher Educational Aid Board
PO Box 7885
Madison, WI 53707-7885
Phone: 608-266-0888
Fax: 608-267-2808
E-mail: sandy.thomas@wi.gov

YORKVILLE GOODS LLC

http://yorkvilleblankets.com/

YORKVILLE BLANKETS ASD SCHOLARSHIP

• See page 627

MILITARY SERVICE: AIR FORCE

AIR FORCE AID SOCIETY

http://www.afas.org/

GENERAL HENRY H. ARNOLD EDUCATION GRANT PROGRAM

Need- based grants awarded to dependent sons and daughters of active duty, Title 10 AGR/Reserve, Title 32 AGR performing full-time active duty, retired, retired reserve and deceased Air Force members; spouses of active members and Title 10 AGR/Reservist; and surviving spouses of deceased personnel for their undergraduate studies. Dependent children must be unmarried and under the age of 23. High school seniors may apply. Minimum 2.0 GPA is required. Students must reapply and compete each year. Full-time enrollment status required.

Award: Grant for use in freshman, sophomore, junior, or senior years; not renewable. *Number:* 3000. *Amount:* $500–$4000.

Eligibility Requirements: Applicant must be enrolled or expecting to enroll full-time at a two-year or four-year or technical institution or university. Available to U.S. citizens. Applicant or parent must meet one or more of the following requirements: national guard experience; retired from active duty; disabled or killed as a result of military service; prisoner of war; or missing in action.

Application Requirements: Application form, financial need analysis. *Deadline:* March 11.

Contact: Education Assistance Department
Air Force Aid Society
241 18th Street South, Suite 202
Arlington, VA 22202-3409
Phone: 703-972-2647
E-mail: ED@afas-hq.org

AIR FORCE RESERVE OFFICER TRAINING CORPS

http://www.afrotc.com/

AFROTC HBCU SCHOLARSHIP PROGRAM

Up to $15,000 awarded to student studying at a historically black college or university (HBCU). Please refer to website for more information http://www.afrotc.com/scholarships/incolschol/minority/hbcu.php.

Award: Scholarship for use in freshman, sophomore, junior, or senior years; not renewable. *Number:* up to 15. *Amount:* up to $15,000.

Eligibility Requirements: Applicant must be Black (non-Hispanic) and enrolled or expecting to enroll full-time at a four-year institution or university. Available to U.S. citizens. Applicant must have national guard experience.

Application Requirements: Application form. *Deadline:* varies.

Contact: Elmarko Magee, Chief of Advertising
Air Force Reserve Officer Training Corps
551 East Maxwell Boulevard
Maxwell AFB, AL 36112
Phone: 866-423-7682

AFROTC HSI SCHOLARSHIP PROGRAM

$15,000 scholarships to students at colleges and universities defined as Hispanic Serving Institutions by the United States Department of Education. Student must already be enrolled in school to receive award.

Award: Scholarship for use in freshman, sophomore, junior, or senior years; not renewable. *Number:* up to 15. *Amount:* $15,000.

Eligibility Requirements: Applicant must be enrolled or expecting to enroll full-time at a four-year institution or university. Available to U.S. citizens. Applicant must have national guard experience.

Application Requirements: Application form. *Deadline:* varies.

Contact: Capt. Elmarko Magee, Chief of Advertising
Phone: 334-953-2278
E-mail: elmarko.magee@maxwell.af.mil

AIR FORCE ROTC COLLEGE SCHOLARSHIP

Scholarship program provides three- and four-year scholarships in three different types to high school seniors. All scholarship cadets receive a nontaxable monthly allowance (stipend) during the academic year. For more details refer to website http://www.afrotc.com/scholarships/hsschol/types.php.

Award: Scholarship for use in freshman, sophomore, junior, or senior years; renewable. *Number:* 2000–4000. *Amount:* $9000–$15,000.

Eligibility Requirements: Applicant must be age 17-30 and enrolled or expecting to enroll full-time at a two-year or four-year institution or university. Applicant must have 3.0 GPA or higher. Available to U.S. citizens. Applicant or parent must meet one or more of the following requirements: Air Force experience; retired from active duty; disabled or killed as a result of military service; prisoner of war; or missing in action.

Application Requirements: Application form, interview, test scores, transcript. *Deadline:* December 1.

Contact: Ty Christian, Chief Air Force ROTC Advertising Manager
Air Force Reserve Officer Training Corps
551 East Maxwell Boulevard
Maxwell Air Force Base, AL 36112-6106
Phone: 334-953-2278
Fax: 334-953-4384
E-mail: ty.christian@maxwell.af.mil

AIRMEN MEMORIAL FOUNDATION/AIR FORCE SERGEANTS ASSOCIATION

http://www.hqafsa.org/

AIRMEN MEMORIAL FOUNDATION SCHOLARSHIP

Scholarship for full-time undergraduate studies of dependent children of Air Force, Air Force Reserve Command and Air National Guard members in active duty, retired or veteran status. Must be under age of 23, have minimum combined score of 1650 on SAT or 24 on ACT, and a minimum GPA of 3.5.

Award: Scholarship for use in freshman, sophomore, junior, or senior years; not renewable. *Number:* 20. *Amount:* $500–$2000.

Eligibility Requirements: Applicant must be enrolled or expecting to enroll full-time at a four-year institution or university. Applicant must have 3.5 GPA or higher. Available to U.S. and non-U.S. citizens. Applicant or parent must meet one or more of the following requirements: national guard experience; retired from active duty; disabled or killed as a result of military service; prisoner of war; or missing in action.

Application Requirements: Application form, essay, recommendations or references, transcript. *Deadline:* March 31.

Contact: Melanie Shirley, Scholarship Coordinator
Phone: 301-899-3500
Fax: 301-899-8136
E-mail: staff@afsahq.org

CHIEF MASTER SERGEANTS OF THE AIR FORCE SCHOLARSHIP PROGRAM

Scholarship to financially assist the full-time undergraduate studies of dependent children of Air Force, Air Force Reserve Command and Air National Guard enlisted members in active duty, retired or veteran status. Must be under age twenty-three and participate in the Airmen Memorial Foundation Scholarship Program. Must have minimum combined score of 1650 on SAT or 24 on ACT, and a minimum GPA of 3.5.

Award: Scholarship for use in freshman, sophomore, junior, or senior years; not renewable. *Number:* up to 30. *Amount:* $500–$3000.

Eligibility Requirements: Applicant must be enrolled or expecting to enroll full-time at a four-year institution or university. Applicant must have 3.5 GPA or higher. Available to U.S. and non-U.S. citizens. Applicant or parent must meet one or more of the following requirements: national guard experience; retired from active duty; disabled or killed as a result of military service; prisoner of war; or missing in action.

Application Requirements: Application form, essay, recommendations or references, transcript. *Deadline:* March 31.

Contact: Melanie Shirley, Scholarship Coordinator
Phone: 301-899-3500
Fax: 301-899-8136
E-mail: staff\@afsahq.org

DEPARTMENT OF VETERANS AFFAIRS (VA)

http://www.gibill.va.gov/

MONTGOMERY GI BILL (SELECTED RESERVE)

Educational assistance program for members of the selected reserve of the Army, Navy, Air Force, Marine Corps and Coast Guard, as well as the Army and Air National Guard. Available to all reservists and National Guard personnel who commit to a six-year obligation, and remain in the Reserve or Guard during the six years. Award is renewable. Monthly benefit is $309 for up to thirty-six months for full-time.

Award: Scholarship for use in freshman, sophomore, junior, senior, or postgraduate years; renewable.

Eligibility Requirements: Applicant must be enrolled or expecting to enroll full- or part-time at a two-year or four-year or technical institution or university. Available to U.S. citizens. Applicant or parent must meet one or more of the following requirements: general military experience; retired from active duty; disabled or killed as a result of military service; prisoner of war; or missing in action.

Application Requirements: Application form. *Deadline:* continuous.

Contact: Keith Wilson, Director, Education Service
Phone: 888-442-4551

ELEARNERS.COM

http://www.elearners.com

ELEARNERS MILITARY SCHOLARSHIP

To help ease the burden, eLearners and EducationDynamics is awarding a new $1,000 scholarship to two lucky students who are veterans, active duty service members or spouses of service members or veterans. Winners can use this one-time payment for whatever they choose. The draw will be held on or about September 2nd and recipients will be notified by mail or phone.

Award: Scholarship for use in freshman, sophomore, junior, senior, graduate, or postgraduate years; not renewable. *Number:* 1–2. *Amount:* $1000.

Eligibility Requirements: Applicant must be age 18-99 and enrolled or expecting to enroll full- or part-time at a two-year or four-year or technical institution or university. Available to U.S. citizens. Applicant must have general military experience.

Application Requirements: Driver's license, essay. *Deadline:* February 28.

Contact: Scholarship Organizer
E-mail: militaryscholarships@elearners.com

FOUNDATION OF THE 1ST CAVALRY DIVISION ASSOCIATION

http://www.1cda.org/

FOUNDATION OF THE 1ST CAVALRY DIVISION ASSOCIATION (IA DRANG) SCHOLARSHIP

Award for children and grandchildren of soldiers of 1st Cavalry Division, U.S. Air Force Forward Air Controllers and A1E pilots, and war correspondents who served in designated qualifying units which were involved in battles of the Ia Drang Valley during the period of November 3-19, 1965. Include self-addressed stamped envelope. More information on http://www.1cda.org.

Award: Grant for use in freshman, sophomore, junior, or senior years; not renewable. *Number:* 2–8. *Amount:* $600–$1200.

Eligibility Requirements: Applicant must be enrolled or expecting to enroll full- or part-time at a two-year or four-year or technical institution or university. Available to U.S. citizens. Applicant or parent must meet one or more of the following requirements: Air Force or Army experience; retired from active duty; disabled or killed as a result of military service; prisoner of war; or missing in action.

Application Requirements: Application form. *Deadline:* August 1.

Contact: Dara Wydler, Executive Director
Foundation of the 1st Cavalry Division Association
302 North Main Street
Copperas Cove, TX 76522-1703
Phone: 254-547-6537
E-mail: firstcav@1cda.org

FOUNDATION OF THE 1ST CAVALRY DIVISION ASSOCIATION SCHOLARSHIP

Scholarships for children of soldiers of the 1st Cavalry Division who died or have been declared permanently and totally (100%) disabled from combat with the 1st Cavalry Division. Show proof of service with the division, relationship to parent, death or disability of parent, and acceptance at higher education institution. Include self-addressed stamped envelope.

Award: Grant for use in freshman, sophomore, junior, or senior years; not renewable. *Number:* 1–8. *Amount:* $600–$1200.

Eligibility Requirements: Applicant must be enrolled or expecting to enroll full- or part-time at a two-year or four-year or technical institution or university. Available to U.S. citizens. Applicant or parent must meet one or more of the following requirements: national guard experience; retired from active duty; disabled or killed as a result of military service; prisoner of war; or missing in action.

Application Requirements: Application form. *Deadline:* August 1.

Contact: Dara Wydler, Executive Director
Foundation of the 1st Cavalry Division Association
302 North Main Street
Copperas Cove, TX 76522-1703
Phone: 254-547-6537
E-mail: firstcav@1cda.org

IMAGINE AMERICA FOUNDATION

www.imagine-america.org

MILITARY AWARD PROGRAM (MAP)

The Military Award Program offers scholarships for veterans and other military students who decide to pursue career college training. This $1,000 career education award is available to any qualified active duty, reservist, honorably discharged or retired veteran of a U.S. military service branch for attendance at a participating career college.

Award: Scholarship for use in freshman, sophomore, junior, or senior years; not renewable. *Number:* 1500. *Amount:* $1000.

Eligibility Requirements: Applicant must be enrolled or expecting to enroll full- or part-time at a two-year or four-year or technical institution. Available to U.S. citizens. Applicant must have general military experience.

Application Requirements: Application form. *Deadline:* continuous.

Contact: Lee Doubleday, Student Services Representative
Imagine America Foundation
12001 Sunrise Valley Drive, Suite 203
Reston, VA 20191
Phone: 571-267-3015
E-mail: leroyd@imagine-america.org

INDIANA DEPARTMENT OF VETERANS AFFAIRS

http://www.in.gov/dva

RESIDENT TUITION FOR ACTIVE DUTY MILITARY PERSONNEL

Applicant must be a nonresident of Indiana serving on active duty and stationed in Indiana and attending any state-supported college or university. Dependents remain eligible for the duration of their enrollment, even if the active duty person is no longer in Indiana. Entitlement is to the resident tuition rate.

Award: Grant for use in freshman, sophomore, junior, senior, graduate, or postgraduate years; renewable.

Eligibility Requirements: Applicant must be enrolled or expecting to enroll full- or part-time at a two-year or four-year or technical institution or university and studying in Indiana. Available to U.S. citizens. Applicant or parent must meet one or more of the following requirements: Air Force or Army experience; retired from active duty; disabled or killed as a result of military service; prisoner of war; or missing in action.

Application Requirements: Application form.

Contact: Jon Brinkley, State Service Officer
Phone: 317-232-3910
Fax: 317-232-7721
E-mail: jbrinkley@dva.in.gov

KITCHEN GUIDES

http://www.kitchensguides.com/

SMART KITCHEN IMPROVEMENT SCHOLARSHIP BY KITCHEN GUIDES

• *See page 598*

PETAZI

https://petazi.com/

2017 NURTURE FOR NATURE SCHOLARSHIP

• *See page 637*

WISCONSIN DEPARTMENT OF VETERANS AFFAIRS (WDVA)

http://www.dva.state.wi.us/

VETERANS EDUCATION (VETED) REIMBURSEMENT GRANT

• *See page 639*

MILITARY SERVICE: AIR FORCE NATIONAL GUARD

AIR FORCE AID SOCIETY

http://www.afas.org/

GENERAL HENRY H. ARNOLD EDUCATION GRANT PROGRAM

• *See page 639*

AIR FORCE RESERVE OFFICER TRAINING CORPS

http://www.afrotc.com/

AFROTC HBCU SCHOLARSHIP PROGRAM

• *See page 639*

AFROTC HSI SCHOLARSHIP PROGRAM

• *See page 639*

AIRMEN MEMORIAL FOUNDATION/AIR FORCE SERGEANTS ASSOCIATION

http://www.hqafsa.org/

AIRMEN MEMORIAL FOUNDATION SCHOLARSHIP

• *See page 640*

CHIEF MASTER SERGEANTS OF THE AIR FORCE SCHOLARSHIP PROGRAM

• *See page 640*

ALABAMA COMMISSION ON HIGHER EDUCATION

http://www.ache.alabama.gov/

ALABAMA NATIONAL GUARD EDUCATIONAL ASSISTANCE PROGRAM

Renewable award aids Alabama residents who are members of the Alabama National Guard and are enrolled in a nationally recognized accredited college in Alabama. Forms must be signed by a representative of the Alabama Military Department and financial aid officer. Recipient must be in a degree-seeking program.

Award: Scholarship for use in freshman, sophomore, junior, senior, or graduate years; not renewable. *Number:* 400–800. *Amount:* $100–$2000.

Eligibility Requirements: Applicant must be enrolled or expecting to enroll full- or part-time at a two-year or four-year or technical institution or university; resident of Alabama and studying in Alabama. Available to U.S. citizens. Applicant must have national guard experience.

Application Requirements: Application form, financial need analysis. *Deadline:* continuous.

Contact: Cheryl Newton, Grants Coordinator
Phone: 334-242-2273
Fax: 334-242-2269
E-mail: cheryl.newton@ache.alabama.gov

DELAWARE NATIONAL GUARD

http://www.delawarenationalguard.com/

STATE TUITION ASSISTANCE

You must enlist in the Delaware Air or Army National Guard to be eligible for this scholarship award. Award providing tuition assistance for any member of the Air or Army National Guard attending a Delaware two-year or four-year college. Awards are renewable. Applicant's minimum GPA must be 2.0.

Award: Scholarship for use in freshman, sophomore, junior, or senior years; renewable. *Number:* 1–200. *Amount:* $1–$10,000.

Eligibility Requirements: Applicant must be enrolled or expecting to enroll full- or part-time at a two-year or four-year institution or university and studying in Delaware. Available to U.S. citizens. Applicant or parent must meet one or more of the following requirements: national guard experience; retired from active duty; disabled or killed as a result of military service; prisoner of war; or missing in action.

Application Requirements: Application form, transcript.

Contact: Robert Csizmadia, State Tuition Assistance Manager
Delaware National Guard
1st Regiment Road
Wilmington, DE 19808-2191
Phone: 302-326-7012
Fax: 302-326-7029
E-mail: robert.csizmadia@us.army.mil

DEPARTMENT OF VETERANS AFFAIRS (VA)

http://www.gibill.va.gov/

MONTGOMERY GI BILL (SELECTED RESERVE)

• *See page 640*

RESERVE EDUCATION ASSISTANCE PROGRAM

The program provides educational assistance to members of National Guard and reserve components. Selected Reserve and Individual Ready Reserve (IRR) who are called or ordered to active duty service in response to a war or national emergency as declared by the president or Congress are eligible. For further information see website http://www.GIBILL.va.gov.

Award: Scholarship for use in freshman, sophomore, junior, senior, graduate, or postgraduate years; renewable.

Eligibility Requirements: Applicant must be enrolled or expecting to enroll full- or part-time at a two-year or four-year or technical institution or university. Available to U.S. citizens. Applicant or parent must meet one or more of the following requirements: general military experience; retired from active duty; disabled or killed as a result of military service; prisoner of war; or missing in action.

Application Requirements: Application form. *Deadline:* continuous.

Contact: Keith Wilson, Director, Education Service
Phone: 888-442-4551

ELEARNERS.COM

http://www.elearners.com

ELEARNERS MILITARY SCHOLARSHIP

• *See page 640*

ENLISTED ASSOCIATION OF THE NATIONAL GUARD OF NEW JERSEY

http://www.eang-nj.org/

CSM VINCENT BALDASSARI MEMORIAL SCHOLARSHIP PROGRAM

Scholarships open to the legal children of New Jersey National Guard Members who are also members of the Enlisted Association. Also open to any drilling guardsperson who is a member of the Enlisted Association. Along with application, submit proof of parent's membership and a letter stating the reason for applying and future intents.

Award: Scholarship for use in freshman, sophomore, junior, senior, graduate, or postgraduate years; not renewable. *Number:* 5. *Amount:* $1000.

Eligibility Requirements: Applicant must be enrolled or expecting to enroll full- or part-time at a two-year or four-year or technical institution or university and resident of New Jersey. Available to U.S. and non-U.S. citizens. Applicant or parent must meet one or more of the following requirements: national guard experience; retired from active duty; disabled or killed as a result of military service; prisoner of war; or missing in action.

Application Requirements: Application form, essay, personal photograph, recommendations or references, transcript. *Deadline:* May 15.

Contact: Michael Amoroso, Scholarship Committee Chairman
Phone: 609-562-0754
Fax: 609-562-0731
E-mail: michael.c@us.army.mil

USAA SCHOLARSHIP

Scholarship of $1000 open to any drilling guardsperson (need not be a member of the EANGNJ).

Award: Scholarship for use in freshman, sophomore, junior, senior, graduate, or postgraduate years; not renewable. *Number:* 1. *Amount:* $1000.

Eligibility Requirements: Applicant must be enrolled or expecting to enroll full- or part-time at a two-year or four-year or technical institution or university. Available to U.S. and non-U.S. citizens. Applicant or parent must meet one or more of the following requirements: national guard experience; retired from active duty; disabled or killed as a result of military service; prisoner of war; or missing in action.

Application Requirements: Application form, essay, personal photograph, transcript. *Deadline:* May 15.

Contact: Michael Amoroso, Scholarship Committee Chairman
Phone: 609-562-0754
Fax: 609-562-0731
E-mail: michael.c@us.army.mil

ILLINOIS STUDENT ASSISTANCE COMMISSION (ISAC)

http://www.isac.org/

ILLINOIS NATIONAL GUARD GRANT PROGRAM

Active duty members of the Illinois National Guard, or who are within 12 months of discharge, and who have completed one full year of service are eligible. May be used for study at Illinois two- or four-year public colleges for a maximum of the equivalent of four academic years of full-time enrollment. Deadlines: October 1 of the academic year for full year, March 1 for second/third term, or June 15 for the summer term.

Award: Grant for use in freshman, sophomore, junior, senior, or graduate years; not renewable.

Eligibility Requirements: Applicant must be enrolled or expecting to enroll full- or part-time at a two-year or four-year institution or university; resident of Illinois and studying in Illinois. Available to U.S. citizens. Applicant or parent must meet one or more of the following requirements: national guard experience; retired from active duty; disabled or killed as a result of military service; prisoner of war; or missing in action.

Application Requirements: Application form. *Deadline:* October 1.

Contact: ISAC Call Center Representative
Illinois Student Assistance Commission (ISAC)
1755 Lake Cook Road
Deerfield, IL 60015-5209
Phone: 800-899-4722
E-mail: isac.studentservices@isac.illinois.gov

IMAGINE AMERICA FOUNDATION

www.imagine-america.org

MILITARY AWARD PROGRAM (MAP)

• *See page 641*

INDIANA DEPARTMENT OF VETERANS AFFAIRS

http://www.in.gov/dva

NATIONAL GUARD SCHOLARSHIP EXTENSION PROGRAM

A scholarship extension applicant is eligible for a tuition scholarship under Indiana Code 21-13-5-4 for a period not to exceed the period of scholarship extension the applicant served on active duty as a member of the National Guard (mobilized and deployed). Must apply not later than one (1) year after the applicant ceases to be a member of the Indiana National Guard. Applicant should apply through the education officer of their last unit of assignment.

Award: Grant for use in freshman, sophomore, junior, or senior years; renewable.

Eligibility Requirements: Applicant must be enrolled or expecting to enroll full- or part-time at a two-year or four-year or technical institution or university and studying in Indiana. Available to U.S. citizens. Applicant must have national guard experience.

Application Requirements: Application form.

Contact: Pamela Moody, National Guard Education Officer
Indiana Department of Veterans Affairs
302 West Washington Street, Room E-120
Indianapolis, IN 46204
Phone: 317-964-7017
E-mail: pamela.moody@in.ngb.army.mil

NATIONAL GUARD TUITION SUPPLEMENT PROGRAM

Applicant must be a member of the Indiana National Guard, in active drilling status, who has not been AWOL during the last 12 months, does not possess a bachelor's degree, possesses the requisite academic qualifications, meets the requirements of the state-supported college or university, and meets all National Guard requirements.

Award: Grant for use in freshman, sophomore, junior, or senior years; renewable.

Eligibility Requirements: Applicant must be enrolled or expecting to enroll full- or part-time at a two-year or four-year or technical institution or university and studying in Indiana. Available to U.S. citizens. Applicant must have national guard experience.

Application Requirements: Application form.

Contact: Jon Brinkley, State Service Officer
Phone: 317-232-3910
Fax: 317-232-7721
E-mail: jbrinkley@dva.in.gov

TUITION AND FEE REMISSION FOR CHILDREN AND SPOUSES OF NATIONAL GUARD MEMBERS

Award to an individual whose father, mother or spouse was a member of the Indiana National Guard and suffered a service-connected death while serving on state active duty (which includes mobilized and deployed for federal active duty). The student must be eligible to pay the resident tuition rate at the state-supported college or university and must possess the requisite academic qualifications.

Award: Grant for use in freshman, sophomore, junior, or senior years; renewable.

Eligibility Requirements: Applicant must be enrolled or expecting to enroll full- or part-time at a two-year or four-year or technical institution or university and studying in Indiana. Available to U.S. citizens. Applicant or parent must meet one or more of the following requirements: national guard experience; retired from active duty; disabled or killed as a result of military service; prisoner of war; or missing in action.

Application Requirements: Application form.

Contact: R. Martin Umbarger, Adjutant General
Indiana Department of Veterans Affairs
2002 South Holt Road
Indianapolis, IN 46241
Phone: 317-247-3559
E-mail: r.martin.umbarger@in.ngb.army.mil

IOWA COLLEGE STUDENT AID COMMISSION

http://www.iowacollegeaid.gov/

IOWA NATIONAL GUARD EDUCATION ASSISTANCE PROGRAM

Program provides postsecondary grant assistance to members of Iowa National Guard Units. Must study at a postsecondary institution in Iowa.

Award: Grant for use in freshman, sophomore, junior, or senior years; not renewable.

Eligibility Requirements: Applicant must be enrolled or expecting to enroll full- or part-time at a two-year or four-year or technical institution or university; resident of Iowa and studying in Iowa. Available to U.S. citizens. Applicant must have national guard experience.

Application Requirements: Application form. *Deadline:* July 1.

Contact: Tracy Davis, Executive Officer 1
Iowa College Student Aid Commission
430 E Grand Avenue, FL 3
Des Moines, IA 50309-1920
Phone: 877-272-4456

KENTUCKY HIGHER EDUCATION ASSISTANCE AUTHORITY (KHEAA)

http://www.kheaa.com/

KENTUCKY NATIONAL GUARD TUITION AWARD

Provides tuition assistance for active members of the Kentucky National Guard to attend a Kentucky college or university. Guard members may apply through their unit.

Award: Grant for use in freshman, sophomore, junior, or senior years; not renewable. *Number:* 1000–1500. *Amount:* $100–$11,500.

Eligibility Requirements: Applicant must be enrolled or expecting to enroll full- or part-time at a two-year or four-year or technical institution or university; resident of Kentucky and studying in Kentucky. Available to U.S. citizens. Applicant must have national guard experience.

Application Requirements: Application form. *Deadline:* continuous.

Contact: Michelle Kelley
Kentucky Higher Education Assistance Authority (KHEAA)
Boone National Guard
Frankfort, KY 40601
Phone: 502-607-1039

KITCHEN GUIDES

http://www.kitchensguides.com/

SMART KITCHEN IMPROVEMENT SCHOLARSHIP BY KITCHEN GUIDES

• *See page 598*

LOUISIANA NATIONAL GUARD, JOINT TASK FORCE LA

http://geauxguard.com/organization/joint-force-headquarters-jfhq-la/

LOUISIANA NATIONAL GUARD STATE TUITION EXEMPTION PROGRAM

Renewable award for college undergraduates to receive tuition exemption upon satisfactory performance in the Louisiana National Guard. Applicant must attend a state-funded institution in Louisiana, be a resident and registered voter in Louisiana, meet the academic and residency requirements of the university attended, and provide documentation of Louisiana National Guard enlistment. The exemption can be used for up to 15 semesters. Minimum 2.5 GPA required.

Award: Scholarship for use in freshman, sophomore, junior, or senior years; renewable.

Eligibility Requirements: Applicant must be enrolled or expecting to enroll full- or part-time at a two-year or four-year or technical institution or university; resident of Louisiana and studying in Louisiana. Applicant must have 2.5 GPA or higher. Available to U.S. citizens. Applicant or parent must meet one or more of the following requirements: national guard experience; retired from active duty; disabled or killed as a result of military service; prisoner of war; or missing in action.

Application Requirements: Application form, test scores, transcript. *Deadline:* continuous.

Contact: Jona Hughes, Education Services Officer
Louisiana National Guard, Joint Task Force LA
Building 35, Jackson Barracks, JI-PD
New Orleans, LA 70146-0330
Phone: 504-278-8531 Ext. 8304
Fax: 504-278-8025
E-mail: hughesj@la-arng.ngb.army.mil

NORTH CAROLINA NATIONAL GUARD

http://nc.ng.mil/Pages/default.aspx

NORTH CAROLINA NATIONAL GUARD TUITION ASSISTANCE PROGRAM

Scholarship for members of the North Carolina Air and Army National Guard who will remain in the service for two years following the period for which assistance is provided. Must reapply for each academic period. For use at approved North Carolina institutions.

Award: Grant for use in freshman, sophomore, junior, senior, or graduate years; not renewable. *Amount:* $100–$3440.

Eligibility Requirements: Applicant must be enrolled or expecting to enroll full- or part-time at a two-year or four-year or technical institution or university; resident of North Carolina and studying in North Carolina. Available to U.S. citizens. Applicant or parent must meet one or more of the following requirements: national guard experience; retired from active duty; disabled or killed as a result of military service; prisoner of war; or missing in action.

Application Requirements: Application form. *Deadline:* continuous.

Contact: Ms. Stacy Steinmetz, NCTAP Manager
North Carolina National Guard
1636 Gold Star Drive
Raleigh, NC 27607
Phone: 919-664-6272
E-mail: stacy.m.steinmetz.nfg@mail.mil

OHIO NATIONAL GUARD

http://www.ong.ohio.gov/

OHIO NATIONAL GUARD SCHOLARSHIP PROGRAM

Scholarships are for undergraduate studies at an approved Ohio post-secondary institution. Applicants must enlist for six or three years of Selective Service Reserve Duty in the Ohio National Guard. Scholarship pays 100% instructional and general fees for public institutions and an average of cost of public universities is available for private schools. May reapply up to four years of studies (12 quarters or 8 semesters) for six year enlistment and two years of studies (6 quarters or 4 semesters) for three year enlistment. Deadlines: July 1 (fall), November 1 (winter quarter/spring semester), February 1 (spring quarter), April 1 (summer).

Award: Scholarship for use in freshman, sophomore, junior, or senior years; not renewable. *Number:* up to 3500. *Amount:* up to $4006.

Eligibility Requirements: Applicant must be enrolled or expecting to enroll full- or part-time at a two-year or four-year or technical institution or university; resident of Ohio and studying in Ohio. Available to U.S. citizens. Applicant must have national guard experience.

Application Requirements: Application form. *Deadline:* varies.

Contact: Mrs. Toni Davis, Grants Administrator
Ohio National Guard
2825 West Dublin Granville Road, ONGSP
Columbus, OH 43235-2789
Phone: 614-336-7143
Fax: 614-336-7318
E-mail: toni.davis7@us.army.mil

PENNSYLVANIA HIGHER EDUCATION ASSISTANCE AGENCY

http://www.pheaa.org/

POSTSECONDARY EDUCATION GRATUITY PROGRAM

The program offers waiver of tuition and fees for children of Pennsylvania police officers, firefighters, rescue or ambulance squad members, corrections facility employees, or National Guard members who died in line of duty after January 1, 1976.

Award: Grant for use in freshman, sophomore, junior, or senior years; renewable.

Eligibility Requirements: Applicant must be enrolled or expecting to enroll full-time at a two-year or four-year institution or university; resident of Pennsylvania and studying in Pennsylvania. Available to U.S. citizens. Applicant or parent must meet one or more of the following requirements: national guard experience; retired from active duty; disabled or killed as a result of military service; prisoner of war; or missing in action.

Application Requirements: Application form. *Deadline:* July 1.

Contact: Keith New, Director of Public Relations
Phone: 717-720-2509
E-mail: knew@pheaa.org

PETAZI

https://petazi.com/

2017 NURTURE FOR NATURE SCHOLARSHIP
• *See page 637*

STATE STUDENT ASSISTANCE COMMISSION OF INDIANA (SSACI)

http://www.in.gov/ssaci

INDIANA NATIONAL GUARD SUPPLEMENTAL GRANT

The award is a supplement to the Indiana Higher Education Grant program. Applicants must be members of the Indiana National Guard. All Guard paperwork must be completed prior to the start of each semester. The FAFSA must be received by March 10. Award covers certain tuition and fees at select public colleges.

Award: Grant for use in freshman, sophomore, junior, or senior years; not renewable. *Number:* 503–925. *Amount:* $20–$7110.

Eligibility Requirements: Applicant must be enrolled or expecting to enroll full- or part-time at a two-year or four-year institution or university; resident of Indiana and studying in Indiana. Available to U.S. citizens. Applicant or parent must meet one or more of the following requirements: national guard experience; retired from active duty; disabled or killed as a result of military service; prisoner of war; or missing in action.

Application Requirements: Application form. *Deadline:* March 10.

Contact: Kathryn Moore, Grants Counselor
State Student Assistance Commission of Indiana (SSACI)
150 West Market Street, Suite 500
Indianapolis, IN 46204-2805
Phone: 317-232-2350
Fax: 317-232-2360
E-mail: kmoore@ssaci.in.gov

WISCONSIN DEPARTMENT OF VETERANS AFFAIRS (WDVA)

http://www.dva.state.wi.us/

VETERANS EDUCATION (VETED) REIMBURSEMENT GRANT

• *See page 639*

MILITARY SERVICE: ARMY

AMERICAN LEGION AUXILIARY DEPARTMENT OF KENTUCKY

http://www.kylegion.org/

AMERICAN LEGION AUXILIARY DEPARTMENT OF KENTUCKY LAURA BLACKBURN MEMORIAL SCHOLARSHIP

Scholarship to the child, grandchild, or great grandchild of a veteran who served in the Armed Forces. Applicant must be a Kentucky resident.

Award: Scholarship for use in freshman year; not renewable. *Number:* 1. *Amount:* $1000.

Eligibility Requirements: Applicant must be high school student; planning to enroll or expecting to enroll full-time at a four-year institution or university and resident of Kentucky. Available to U.S. citizens. Applicant or parent must meet one or more of the following requirements: Army experience; retired from active duty; disabled or killed as a result of military service; prisoner of war; or missing in action.

Application Requirements: Application form, financial need analysis, transcript. *Deadline:* March 31.

Contact: Betty Cook, Secretary and Treasurer
Phone: 270-932-7533
Fax: 270-932-7672
E-mail: secretarykyala@aol.com

ARMY OFFICERS' WIVES CLUB OF GREATER WASHINGTON AREA

http://www.aowcgwa.org/

ARMY OFFICERS WIVES CLUB OF THE GREATER WASHINGTON AREA SCHOLARSHIP

Scholarship for high school seniors, college students or children or spouses of U.S. Army personnel. Scholarship awards are based on scholastic merit and community involvement.

Award: Scholarship for use in freshman, sophomore, junior, or senior years; not renewable. *Number:* 1–3. *Amount:* $100–$500.

Eligibility Requirements: Applicant must be enrolled or expecting to enroll full-time at a four-year institution or university. Available to U.S. citizens. Applicant or parent must meet one or more of the following requirements: Army experience; retired from active duty; disabled or killed as a result of military service; prisoner of war; or missing in action.

Application Requirements: Application form, essay, military dependent ID card, recommendations or references, self-addressed stamped envelope with application, transcript. *Deadline:* March 31.

Contact: Janis Waller, Scholarship Committee Chair
Army Officers' Wives Club of Greater Washington Area
12025 William and Mary Circle
Woodbridge, VA 22192-1634

DEPARTMENT OF THE ARMY

http://www.goarmy.com/rotc

ARMY (ROTC) RESERVE OFFICERS TRAINING CORPS TWO-, THREE-, FOUR-YEAR CAMPUS-BASED SCHOLARSHIPS

One-time award for college freshmen, sophomores, or juniors or students with BA who need two years to obtain graduate degree. Must be a member of school's ROTC program. Must pass physical. Minimum 2.5 GPA required. Professor of Military Science must submit application. Applicant must be at least 17 when enrolled in college and under thirty-one years of age in the year of graduation. Must be U.S. citizen/national at time of award. Open year-round.

Award: Scholarship for use in freshman, sophomore, junior, senior, or graduate years; renewable. *Number:* 2000–3500. *Amount:* $10,000–$120,000.

Eligibility Requirements: Applicant must be Asian/Pacific Islander; age 17-30 and enrolled or expecting to enroll full-time at a four-year institution or university. Applicant must have 2.5 GPA or higher. Available to U.S. citizens. Applicant must have served in the Army.

Application Requirements: Application form, interview. *Deadline:* continuous.

Contact: Mr. Timothy Borgerding, Incentives Division Chief
Department of the Army
U.S. Army Cadet Command
Building 1002, 204 1st Cavalry Regiment Road
Fort Knox, KY 40121-5123
Phone: 502-624-2309
E-mail: timothy.b.borgerding.civ@mail.mil

U.S. ARMY ROTC FOUR-YEAR COLLEGE SCHOLARSHIP

One-time award for students entering college for the first time, or freshmen in a documented five-year degree program. Must join school's ROTC program, pass physical, and submit teacher evaluations. Must be a U.S. citizen and have a qualifying SAT or ACT score. Applicant must be at least seventeen years of age by college enrollment and under thirty-one years of age in the year of graduation. Online application available.

Award: Scholarship for use in freshman year; renewable. *Number:* 1000–2500. *Amount:* $9000–$150,000.

Eligibility Requirements: Applicant must be high school student; age 17-26 and planning to enroll or expecting to enroll full-time at a four-year institution or university. Applicant must have 2.5 GPA or higher. Available to U.S. citizens. Applicant must have national guard experience.

Application Requirements: Application form, essay, interview. *Deadline:* January 10.

Contact: Ms. Kathleen Barnes, Supervisor, Human Resources Specialist
Department of the Army
U.S. Army Cadet Command
Building 1002, 204 1st Cavalry Regiment Road
Fort Knox, KY 40121-5123
Phone: 502-624-7371
E-mail: kathleen.m.barnes19.civ@mail.mil

U.S. ARMY ROTC FOUR-YEAR HISTORICALLY BLACK COLLEGE/UNIVERSITY SCHOLARSHIP

One-time award for students attending college for the first time Must attend a historically black college or university and must join school's ROTC program. Must pass physical. Must have a qualifying SAT or ACT score and minimum GPA of 2.5. Applicant must be at least 17 by college enrollment and under thirty-one years of age in the year of graduation. Must be a U.S. citizen/national at time of award. Application available online.

Award: Scholarship for use in freshman, sophomore, junior, senior, or graduate years; renewable. *Number:* 20–200. *Amount:* $9000–$40,000.

Eligibility Requirements: Applicant must be age 17-26 and enrolled or expecting to enroll full-time at a four-year institution or university. Applicant must have 2.5 GPA or higher. Available to U.S. citizens. Applicant must have national guard experience.

Application Requirements: Application form, essay, interview. *Deadline:* January 10.

Contact: Ms. Kathleen Barnes, Supervisor, Human Resources Specialist
Department of the Army
U.S. Army Cadet Command
Building 1002, 204 1st Cavalry Regiment Road
Fort Knox, KY 40121-5123
Phone: 502-624-7371
E-mail: kathleen.m.barnes19.civ@mail.mil

U.S. ARMY ROTC MILITARY JUNIOR COLLEGE (MJC) SCHOLARSHIP

One-time award for high school graduates who wish to attend a two-year military junior college. Must serve simultaneously in the Army National Guard or Reserve and qualify for the ROTC Advanced Course. Must have a minimum GPA of 2.5. Must be a U.S. citizen/national at time of award. Must also be eighteen years of age by October 1 and under twenty-seven years of age on June 30 in the year of graduation. On-line application available. Must be used at one of five military junior colleges. See Professor of Military Science at college for application.

Award: Scholarship for use in freshman or sophomore years; renewable. *Number:* 110–150. *Amount:* $5600–$52,000.

Eligibility Requirements: Applicant must be age 18-26 and enrolled or expecting to enroll full-time at a two-year institution. Applicant must have 2.5 GPA or higher. Available to U.S. citizens. Applicant must have national guard experience.

Application Requirements: Application form, essay, interview. *Deadline:* July 25.

Contact: Mr. Larry Waller, Program Manager
Department of the Army
U.S. Army Cadet Command
Building 1002, 204 1st Cavalry Regiment Road
Fort Knox, KY 40121-5123
Phone: 502-624-7023
E-mail: larry.j.waller.civ@mail.mil

DEPARTMENT OF VETERANS AFFAIRS (VA)

http://www.gibill.va.gov/

MONTGOMERY GI BILL (SELECTED RESERVE)

• *See page 640*

ELEARNERS.COM

http://www.elearners.com

ELEARNERS MILITARY SCHOLARSHIP

• *See page 640*

FOUNDATION OF THE 1ST CAVALRY DIVISION ASSOCIATION

http://www.1cda.org/

FOUNDATION OF THE 1ST CAVALRY DIVISION ASSOCIATION (IA DRANG) SCHOLARSHIP

• *See page 640*

FOUNDATION OF THE 1ST CAVALRY DIVISION ASSOCIATION SCHOLARSHIP

• *See page 641*

IMAGINE AMERICA FOUNDATION

www.imagine-america.org

MILITARY AWARD PROGRAM (MAP)

• *See page 641*

INDIANA DEPARTMENT OF VETERANS AFFAIRS

http://www.in.gov/dva

RESIDENT TUITION FOR ACTIVE DUTY MILITARY PERSONNEL

• *See page 641*

KITCHEN GUIDES

http://www.kitchensguides.com/

SMART KITCHEN IMPROVEMENT SCHOLARSHIP BY KITCHEN GUIDES

• *See page 598*

PETAZI

https://petazi.com/

2017 NURTURE FOR NATURE SCHOLARSHIP

• *See page 637*

SOCIETY OF DAUGHTERS OF THE UNITED STATES ARMY

SOCIETY OF DAUGHTERS OF THE UNITED STATES ARMY SCHOLARSHIPS

• *See page 617*

WISCONSIN DEPARTMENT OF VETERANS AFFAIRS (WDVA)

http://www.dva.state.wi.us/

VETERANS EDUCATION (VETED) REIMBURSEMENT GRANT

• *See page 639*

WOMEN'S ARMY CORPS VETERANS' ASSOCIATION

http://www.armywomen.org/

WOMEN'S ARMY CORPS VETERANS' ASSOCIATION SCHOLARSHIP

Scholarship to graduating high school senior showing academic promise. Must be a child, grandchild, niece or nephew of an Army servicewoman. Minimum cumulative GPA of 3.5 required. Applicants must plan to enroll in a degree program as a full-time student at an accredited college or university in the United States.

Award: Scholarship for use in freshman year; not renewable. *Number:* 1. *Amount:* $1500.

Eligibility Requirements: Applicant must be high school student and planning to enroll or expecting to enroll full-time at a four-year institution or university. Applicant must have 2.5 GPA or higher. Available to U.S. citizens. Applicant or parent must meet one or more of the following requirements: Army experience; retired from active duty; disabled or killed as a result of military service; prisoner of war; or missing in action.

Application Requirements: Application form. *Deadline:* April 1.

Contact: Eldora Engebretson, Scholarship Committee
Phone: 623-566-9299
E-mail: info@armywomen.org

MILITARY SERVICE: ARMY NATIONAL GUARD

ALABAMA COMMISSION ON HIGHER EDUCATION

http://www.ache.alabama.gov/

ALABAMA NATIONAL GUARD EDUCATIONAL ASSISTANCE PROGRAM
• *See page 642*

CONNECTICUT ARMY NATIONAL GUARD

http://ct.ng.mil/Pages/default.aspx

CONNECTICUT ARMY NATIONAL GUARD 100% TUITION WAIVER

Program is for any active member of the Connecticut Army National Guard in good standing. Must be a resident of Connecticut attending any Connecticut state (public) university, community-technical college or regional vocational-technical school. The total number of available awards is unlimited.

Award: Scholarship for use in freshman, sophomore, junior, or senior years; not renewable. *Amount:* $16,000.

Eligibility Requirements: Applicant must be age 17-65; enrolled or expecting to enroll full- or part-time at a two-year or four-year or technical institution or university; resident of Connecticut and studying in Connecticut. Available to U.S. and non-U.S. citizens. Applicant or parent must meet one or more of the following requirements: national guard experience; retired from active duty; disabled or killed as a result of military service; prisoner of war; or missing in action.

Application Requirements: Application form. *Deadline:* July 1.

Contact: Capt. Jeremy Lingenfelser, Education Services Officer
Connecticut Army National Guard
360 Broad Street
Hartford, CT 06105-3795
Phone: 860-524-4816
Fax: 860-524-4904
E-mail: education@ct.ngb.army.mil

DELAWARE NATIONAL GUARD

http://www.delawarenationalguard.com/

STATE TUITION ASSISTANCE
• *See page 642*

DEPARTMENT OF THE ARMY

http://www.goarmy.com/rotc

U.S. ARMY ROTC FOUR-YEAR COLLEGE SCHOLARSHIP
• *See page 645*

U.S. ARMY ROTC FOUR-YEAR HISTORICALLY BLACK COLLEGE/UNIVERSITY SCHOLARSHIP
• *See page 645*

U.S. ARMY ROTC GUARANTEED RESERVE FORCES DUTY (GRFD), (ARNG/USAR) AND DEDICATED ARNG SCHOLARSHIPS

One-time award for college freshmen, sophomores, and juniors, or two-year graduate degree students. Must be a member of school's ROTC program. Must pass physical. Minimum 2.5 GPA required. Applicant must be at least seventeen years of age when enrolled in college and under thirty-one years of age in the year of graduation. Must be a U.S. citizen/national at the time of award.

Award: Scholarship for use in freshman, sophomore, junior, senior, or graduate years; renewable. *Number:* 1000–3000. *Amount:* $10,000–$120,000.

Eligibility Requirements: Applicant must be age 17-30 and enrolled or expecting to enroll full-time at a four-year institution or university. Applicant must have 2.5 GPA or higher. Available to U.S. citizens. Applicant must have national guard experience.

Application Requirements: Application form, interview. *Deadline:* May 15.

Contact: Mr. Kenneth Suratt, Program Manager
Department of the Army
U.S. Army Cadet Command
Building 1002, 204 1st Cavalry Regiment Road
Fort Knox, KY 40121-5123
Phone: 502-624-1257
E-mail: kenneth.s.suratt.ctr@mail.mil

U.S. ARMY ROTC MILITARY JUNIOR COLLEGE (MJC) SCHOLARSHIP
• *See page 646*

DEPARTMENT OF VETERANS AFFAIRS (VA)

http://www.gibill.va.gov/

MONTGOMERY GI BILL (SELECTED RESERVE)
• *See page 640*

RESERVE EDUCATION ASSISTANCE PROGRAM
• *See page 642*

ELEARNERS.COM

http://www.elearners.com

ELEARNERS MILITARY SCHOLARSHIP
• *See page 640*

ENLISTED ASSOCIATION OF THE NATIONAL GUARD OF NEW JERSEY

http://www.eang-nj.org/

CSM VINCENT BALDASSARI MEMORIAL SCHOLARSHIP PROGRAM
• *See page 642*

USAA SCHOLARSHIP
• *See page 642*

FLEET RESERVE ASSOCIATION EDUCATION FOUNDATION

http://www.fra.org/foundation

TREADWELL/PRINGLE SCHOLARSHIPS

Scholarship for members; spouses; dependent biological, step or adoptive children; or biological, step or adoptive grandchildren of a FRA member in good standing, currently or at time of death. Applicant must be a U.S. citizen, registered as a full-time student in an accredited college located in the United States.

Award: Scholarship for use in freshman, sophomore, junior, senior, graduate, or postgraduate years; not renewable.

Eligibility Requirements: Applicant must be enrolled or expecting to enroll full-time at a two-year or four-year institution or university. Available to U.S. citizens. Applicant must have national guard experience.

Application Requirements: Application form, community service, essay, financial need analysis. *Deadline:* April 15.

Contact: Alicia Landis, Program Administrator
Phone: 703-683-1400
E-mail: scholars@fra.org

FOUNDATION OF THE 1ST CAVALRY DIVISION ASSOCIATION

http://www.1cda.org/

FOUNDATION OF THE 1ST CAVALRY DIVISION ASSOCIATION SCHOLARSHIP
• *See page 641*

ILLINOIS STUDENT ASSISTANCE COMMISSION (ISAC)

http://www.isac.org/

ILLINOIS NATIONAL GUARD GRANT PROGRAM
• *See page 642*

IMAGINE AMERICA FOUNDATION

www.imagine-america.org

MILITARY AWARD PROGRAM (MAP)
• *See page 641*

INDIANA DEPARTMENT OF VETERANS AFFAIRS

http://www.in.gov/dva

NATIONAL GUARD SCHOLARSHIP EXTENSION PROGRAM
• *See page 643*

NATIONAL GUARD TUITION SUPPLEMENT PROGRAM
• *See page 643*

TUITION AND FEE REMISSION FOR CHILDREN AND SPOUSES OF NATIONAL GUARD MEMBERS
• *See page 643*

IOWA COLLEGE STUDENT AID COMMISSION

http://www.iowacollegeaid.gov/

IOWA NATIONAL GUARD EDUCATION ASSISTANCE PROGRAM
• *See page 643*

KENTUCKY HIGHER EDUCATION ASSISTANCE AUTHORITY (KHEAA)

http://www.kheaa.com/

KENTUCKY NATIONAL GUARD TUITION AWARD
• *See page 643*

KITCHEN GUIDES

http://www.kitchensguides.com/

SMART KITCHEN IMPROVEMENT SCHOLARSHIP BY KITCHEN GUIDES
• *See page 598*

LOUISIANA NATIONAL GUARD, JOINT TASK FORCE LA

http://geauxguard.com/organization/joint-force-headquarters-jfhq-la/

LOUISIANA NATIONAL GUARD STATE TUITION EXEMPTION PROGRAM
• *See page 644*

NORTH CAROLINA NATIONAL GUARD

http://nc.ng.mil/Pages/default.aspx

NORTH CAROLINA NATIONAL GUARD TUITION ASSISTANCE PROGRAM
• *See page 644*

OHIO NATIONAL GUARD

http://www.ong.ohio.gov/

OHIO NATIONAL GUARD SCHOLARSHIP PROGRAM
• *See page 644*

PENNSYLVANIA HIGHER EDUCATION ASSISTANCE AGENCY

http://www.pheaa.org/

POSTSECONDARY EDUCATION GRATUITY PROGRAM
• *See page 644*

PETAZI

https://petazi.com/

2017 NURTURE FOR NATURE SCHOLARSHIP
• *See page 637*

SOCIETY OF DAUGHTERS OF THE UNITED STATES ARMY

SOCIETY OF DAUGHTERS OF THE UNITED STATES ARMY SCHOLARSHIPS
• *See page 617*

STATE STUDENT ASSISTANCE COMMISSION OF INDIANA (SSACI)

http://www.in.gov/ssaci

INDIANA NATIONAL GUARD SUPPLEMENTAL GRANT
• *See page 644*

WISCONSIN DEPARTMENT OF VETERANS AFFAIRS (WDVA)

http://www.dva.state.wi.us/

VETERANS EDUCATION (VETED) REIMBURSEMENT GRANT
• *See page 639*

MILITARY SERVICE: COAST GUARD

DEPARTMENT OF VETERANS AFFAIRS (VA)

http://www.gibill.va.gov/

MONTGOMERY GI BILL (SELECTED RESERVE)
• *See page 640*

ELEARNERS.COM

http://www.elearners.com

ELEARNERS MILITARY SCHOLARSHIP
• *See page 640*

FLEET RESERVE ASSOCIATION EDUCATION FOUNDATION

http://www.fra.org/foundation

DORAN/BLAIR SCHOLARSHIPS
• *See page 543*

FLEET RESERVE ASSOCIATION EDUCATION FOUNDATION SCHOLARSHIPS

Applicant or sponsor has to be an FRA non-member, living, on active duty, reserve, retired, or honorably discharged veteran of the Navy, Marine Corps or Coast Guard. The applicant must be an FRA non-member; spouse; dependent biological, step, or adoptive child; or biological, step, or adoptive grandchild; or biological, step, or adoptive great grandchild of the FRA non-member. Applicant must be a U.S. citizen, registered as a full-time student in an accredited college located in the United States of America.

Award: Scholarship for use in freshman, sophomore, junior, senior, graduate, or postgraduate years; not renewable. *Number:* 1–10. *Amount:* $1000–$5000.

Eligibility Requirements: Applicant must be enrolled or expecting to enroll full-time at a two-year or four-year institution or university. Available to U.S. citizens. Applicant must have served in the Coast Guard.

Application Requirements: Application form, community service, essay, financial need analysis. *Deadline:* April 15.

Contact: Alicia Landis, Program Administrator
Phone: 703-683-1400 Ext. 107
E-mail: scholars@fra.org

TREADWELL/PRINGLE SCHOLARSHIPS
• *See page 647*

IMAGINE AMERICA FOUNDATION

www.imagine-america.org

MILITARY AWARD PROGRAM (MAP)
• *See page 641*

KITCHEN GUIDES

http://www.kitchensguides.com/

SMART KITCHEN IMPROVEMENT SCHOLARSHIP BY KITCHEN GUIDES
• *See page 598*

LADIES AUXILIARY OF THE FLEET RESERVE ASSOCIATION

http://www.fra.org/

LADIES AUXILIARY OF THE FLEET RESERVE ASSOCIATION SCHOLARSHIP
• *See page 547*

SAM ROSE MEMORIAL SCHOLARSHIP
• *See page 548*

PETAZI

https://petazi.com/

2017 NURTURE FOR NATURE SCHOLARSHIP
• *See page 637*

TAILHOOK EDUCATIONAL FOUNDATION

http://www.tailhook.org/

TAILHOOK EDUCATIONAL FOUNDATION SCHOLARSHIP

Applicant must be a high school graduate and the natural, step or adopted son or daughter of a current or former Naval Aviator, Naval Flight Officer or Naval Air-crewman. Individuals or children of individuals serving or having served on board a U.S. Navy Aircraft Carrier in ship's company or the Air Wing also eligible.

Award: Scholarship for use in freshman, sophomore, junior, or senior years; not renewable. *Number:* 70. *Amount:* $2000–$10,000.

Eligibility Requirements: Applicant must be enrolled or expecting to enroll full-time at a two-year or four-year institution or university. Applicant must have 3.0 GPA or higher. Available to U.S. citizens. Applicant or parent must meet one or more of the following requirements: Coast Guard, Marine Corps, or Navy experience; retired from active duty; disabled or killed as a result of military service; prisoner of war; or missing in action.

Application Requirements: Application form, essay, proof of eligibility, recommendations or references, test scores, transcript. *Deadline:* March 15.

Contact: Marc Ostertag, Executive Director of Education
Tailhook Educational Foundation
9696 Businesspark Avenue
San Diego, CA 92196
Phone: 800-269-8267
Fax: 858-578-8839
E-mail: tag@tailhook.net

U.S. COAST GUARD

www.gocoastguard/cspi

COLLEGE STUDENT PRE-COMMISSIONING INITIATIVE (CSPI)
• *See page 625*

WISCONSIN DEPARTMENT OF VETERANS AFFAIRS (WDVA)

http://www.dva.state.wi.us/

VETERANS EDUCATION (VETED) REIMBURSEMENT GRANT
• *See page 639*

MILITARY SERVICE: GENERAL

AMERICAN LEGION AUXILIARY DEPARTMENT OF ALABAMA

http://www.legional.org/

AMERICAN LEGION AUXILIARY DEPARTMENT OF ALABAMA SCHOLARSHIP PROGRAM

Merit-based scholarships for Alabama residents, preferably ages 17 to 25, who are children or grandchildren of veterans of World War I, World War II, Korea, Vietnam, Operation Desert Storm, Beirut, Grenada, or Panama. Submit proof of relationship and service record. Renewable awards of $850 each. Must send self-addressed stamped envelope for application.

Award: Scholarship for use in freshman, sophomore, junior, or senior years; renewable. *Number:* up to 40. *Amount:* $850.

Eligibility Requirements: Applicant must be age 17-25; enrolled or expecting to enroll full-time at a four-year institution or university and resident of Alabama. Applicant must have 3.5 GPA or higher. Available to U.S. citizens. Applicant or parent must meet one or more of the following requirements: general military experience; retired from active duty; disabled or killed as a result of military service; prisoner of war; or missing in action.

Application Requirements: Application form, birth certificate, service record, financial need analysis, personal photograph, recommendations or references, self-addressed stamped envelope with application, test scores, transcript. *Deadline:* April 1.

Contact: Education and Scholarship Chairperson
American Legion Auxiliary Department of Alabama
120 North Jackson Street
Montgomery, AL 36104-3811
Phone: 334-262-1176
Fax: 334-262-1176
E-mail: americanlegionaux1@juno.com

AMERICAN LEGION AUXILIARY DEPARTMENT OF CALIFORNIA

http://www.calegionaux.org/

AMERICAN LEGION AUXILIARY DEPARTMENT OF CALIFORNIA GENERAL SCHOLARSHIP

Award ranges from $500 to $1000 for high school senior or graduate of an accredited high school who has not been able to begin college due to circumstances of illness or finance. Student must attend a California college or university. Deadline March 16.

Award: Scholarship for use in freshman, sophomore, junior, or senior years; not renewable. *Amount:* $500–$1000.

Eligibility Requirements: Applicant must be high school student; planning to enroll or expecting to enroll full- or part-time at a two-year or four-year institution or university; resident of California and studying in California. Available to U.S. citizens. Applicant must have general military experience.

Application Requirements: Application form. *Deadline:* March 16.

Contact: Ruby Kapsalis, Secretary/Treasurer
Phone: 415-862-5092
Fax: 415-861-8365
E-mail: calegionaux@calegionaux.org

AMERICAN LEGION AUXILIARY DEPARTMENT OF CONNECTICUT

http://www.ct.legion.org/

AMERICAN LEGION AUXILIARY DEPARTMENT OF CONNECTICUT MEMORIAL EDUCATIONAL GRANT

• *See page 529*

AMERICAN LEGION AUXILIARY DEPARTMENT OF CONNECTICUT PAST PRESIDENTS' PARLEY MEMORIAL EDUCATION GRANT

• *See page 529*

AMERICAN LEGION AUXILIARY DEPARTMENT OF IOWA

http://www.ialegion.org/ala

AMERICAN LEGION AUXILIARY DEPARTMENT OF IOWA CHILDREN OF VETERANS MERIT AWARD

One-time award available to a high school senior, child of a veteran who served in the armed forces during eligibility dates for American Legion membership. Must be U.S. citizen and Iowa resident enrolled at an Iowa institution.

Award: Scholarship for use in freshman year; not renewable. *Number:* 10. *Amount:* $400.

Eligibility Requirements: Applicant must be high school student; planning to enroll or expecting to enroll full- or part-time at a two-year or four-year or technical institution or university; resident of Iowa and studying in Iowa. Available to U.S. citizens. Applicant or parent must meet one or more of the following requirements: general military experience; retired from active duty; disabled or killed as a result of military service; prisoner of war; or missing in action.

Application Requirements: Application form, essay, financial need analysis, personal photograph. *Deadline:* June 1.

Contact: Marlene Valentine, Executive SExecutive Director
American Legion Auxiliary Department of Iowa
720 Lyon Street
Des Moines, IA 50309
Phone: 515-282-7987
E-mail: alasectreas@ialegion.org

AMERICAN LEGION AUXILIARY DEPARTMENT OF KENTUCKY

http://www.kylegion.org/

AMERICAN LEGION AUXILIARY DEPARTMENT OF KENTUCKY MARY BARRETT MARSHALL SCHOLARSHIP

Scholarship to the daughter or grand daughter of a veteran in The American Legion. Applicant must attend a Kentucky college, and demonstrate financial need.

Award: Scholarship for use in freshman year; not renewable. *Number:* 1. *Amount:* $1000.

Eligibility Requirements: Applicant must be high school student; planning to enroll or expecting to enroll full-time at a four-year institution or university; female and studying in Kentucky. Available to U.S. citizens. Applicant or parent must meet one or more of the following requirements: general military experience; retired from active duty; disabled or killed as a result of military service; prisoner of war; or missing in action.

Application Requirements: Application form, financial need analysis, transcript. *Deadline:* April 1.

Contact: Betty Cook, Secretary and Treasurer
Phone: 270-932-7533
Fax: 270-932-7672
E-mail: secretarykyala@aol.com

AMERICAN LEGION AUXILIARY DEPARTMENT OF MAINE

http://www.mainelegion.org/

AMERICAN LEGION AUXILIARY DEPARTMENT OF MAINE DANIEL E. LAMBERT MEMORIAL SCHOLARSHIP

Scholarships to assist young men and women in continuing their education beyond high school. Must demonstrate financial need, must be a resident of the State of Maine, U.S. citizen, and parent must be a veteran.

Award: Scholarship for use in freshman year; not renewable. *Number:* up to 2. *Amount:* $1000.

Eligibility Requirements: Applicant must be high school student; planning to enroll or expecting to enroll full-time at a four-year institution or university and resident of Maine. Available to U.S. citizens. Applicant or parent must meet one or more of the following requirements: general military experience; retired from active duty; disabled or killed as a result of military service; prisoner of war; or missing in action.

Application Requirements: Application form, financial need analysis. *Deadline:* May 1.

Contact: Mary Wells, Education Chairman
Phone: 207-532-6007
E-mail: aladeptsecme@verizon.net

AMERICAN LEGION AUXILIARY DEPARTMENT OF MASSACHUSETTS

http://www.masslegion-aux.org/

AMERICAN LEGION AUXILIARY DEPARTMENT OF MASSACHUSETTS DEPARTMENT PRESIDENT'S SCHOLARSHIP

• *See page 574*

AMERICAN LEGION AUXILIARY DEPARTMENT OF MASSACHUSETTS PAST PRESIDENTS' PARLEY SCHOLARSHIP

One-time awards of $200 to $750 for residents of Massachusetts who are children of living or deceased veterans. Must be between the ages of 16 to 22 years and enrolled full-time at a Massachusetts institution.

Award: Scholarship for use in freshman, sophomore, junior, or senior years; not renewable. *Number:* 1. *Amount:* $200–$750.

Eligibility Requirements: Applicant must be age 16-22; enrolled or expecting to enroll full-time at a two-year or four-year institution or university; resident of Massachusetts and studying in Massachusetts. Available to U.S. citizens. Applicant or parent must meet one or more of the following requirements: general military experience; retired from active duty; disabled or killed as a result of military service; prisoner of war; or missing in action.

Application Requirements: Application form. *Deadline:* March 1.

Contact: Ann Fournier, Secretary and Treasurer
American Legion Auxiliary Department of Massachusetts
State House Room 546-2
Boston, MA 02133
Phone: 617-727-2958
Fax: 617-727-0741
E-mail: masslegion-aux@verizon.net

AMERICAN LEGION AUXILIARY DEPARTMENT OF MICHIGAN

http://www.michalaux.org/

AMERICAN LEGION AUXILIARY DEPARTMENT OF MICHIGAN MEMORIAL SCHOLARSHIP

Scholarship for daughter, granddaughter, and great-granddaughter of any honorably discharged or deceased veteran of U.S. wars or conflicts. Must be Michigan resident for minimum of one year, female between 16 and 21 years, and attend college in Michigan. Must include copy of military discharge and copy of parent or guardian's IRS 1040 form.

Award: Scholarship for use in freshman or sophomore years; not renewable. *Number:* 10–20. *Amount:* $500.

Eligibility Requirements: Applicant must be age 16-21; enrolled or expecting to enroll full-time at a two-year or four-year or technical institution or university; female; resident of Michigan and studying in Michigan. Available to U.S. citizens. Applicant must have general military experience.

Application Requirements: Application form, financial need analysis. *Deadline:* March 15.

Contact: Scholarship Coordinator
American Legion Auxiliary Department of Michigan
212 North Verlinden Avenue, Suite B
Lansing, MI 48915
Phone: 517-267-8809 Ext. 21
E-mail: info@michalaux.org

AMERICAN LEGION AUXILIARY DEPARTMENT OF MICHIGAN SCHOLARSHIP FOR NON-TRADITIONAL STUDENT

Applicant must be a dependent of a veteran. Must be one of the following: nontraditional student returning to classroom after some period of time in which their education was interrupted, student over the age of 22 attending college for the first time to pursue a degree, or student over the age of 22 attending a trade or vocational school. Applicants must be Michigan residents only and attend Michigan institution. Judging based on need, character/leadership, scholastic standing, and initiative/goal.

Award: Scholarship for use in freshman, sophomore, junior, or senior years; renewable. *Number:* 1. *Amount:* $500.

Eligibility Requirements: Applicant must be age 22-99; enrolled or expecting to enroll full- or part-time at a two-year or four-year or technical institution or university; resident of Michigan and studying in Michigan. Available to U.S. citizens. Applicant must have general military experience.

Application Requirements: Application form, financial need analysis. *Deadline:* March 15.

Contact: Scholarship Coordinator
American Legion Auxiliary Department of Michigan
212 North Verlinden Avenue, Suite B
Lansing, MI 48915
Phone: 517-267-8809 Ext. 22
E-mail: info@michalaux.org

AMERICAN LEGION AUXILIARY NATIONAL PRESIDENT'S SCHOLARSHIP

One-time scholarship for son or daughter of veterans, who were in armed forces during the eligibility dates for American Legion membership. Must be high school senior. Only one candidate per Auxiliary Unit. Applicant must complete 50 hours of volunteer service in the community. Must submit essay of no more than 1000 words on a specified topic.

Award: Scholarship for use in freshman year; not renewable. *Number:* 15. *Amount:* $2500–$3500.

Eligibility Requirements: Applicant must be high school student and planning to enroll or expecting to enroll full-time at a two-year or four-year institution or university. Available to U.S. citizens. Applicant must have general military experience.

Application Requirements: Application form, community service, essay, financial need analysis. *Deadline:* March 1.

Contact: Scholarship Coordinator
American Legion Auxiliary Department of Michigan
212 North Verlinden Avenue, Suite B
Lansing, MI 48915
Phone: 517-267-8809 Ext. 21
E-mail: info@michalaux.org

AMERICAN LEGION AUXILIARY SPIRIT OF YOUTH SCHOLARSHIP

Scholarship valued at $5000 is available to one Junior American Legion Auxiliary member in each division. The applicant must have held membership in the American Legion Auxiliary for the past three years, must hold a current membership card, and must continue to maintain their membership throughout the four-year scholarship period.

Award: Scholarship for use in freshman, sophomore, junior, or senior years; renewable. *Number:* 5. *Amount:* $5000.

Eligibility Requirements: Applicant must be high school student; planning to enroll or expecting to enroll full-time at a two-year or four-year or technical institution or university and female. Applicant must have 3.0 GPA or higher. Available to U.S. citizens. Applicant must have general military experience.

Application Requirements: Application form, essay, financial need analysis. *Deadline:* March 1.

Contact: Scholarship Coordinator
American Legion Auxiliary Department of Michigan
212 North Verlinden Avenue, Suite B
Lansing, MI 48915
Phone: 517-267-8809 Ext. 21
E-mail: info@michalaux.org

AMERICAN LEGION AUXILIARY DEPARTMENT OF MINNESOTA

http://www.mnlegion.org/

AMERICAN LEGION AUXILIARY DEPARTMENT OF MINNESOTA SCHOLARSHIPS

Seven $1000 awards for the sons, daughters, grandsons, or granddaughters of veterans who served in the Armed Forces during specific eligibility dates. Must be a Minnesota resident, a high school senior or graduate, in need of financial assistance, of good character, having a good scholastic record and at least a C average. Must be planning to attend a Minnesota post secondary institution.

Award: Scholarship for use in freshman, sophomore, junior, or senior years; not renewable. *Number:* up to 7. *Amount:* $1000.

Eligibility Requirements: Applicant must be enrolled or expecting to enroll full-time at a two-year or four-year or technical institution or university; resident of Minnesota and studying in Minnesota. Available to U.S. citizens. Applicant or parent must meet one or more of the following requirements: general military experience; retired from active duty; disabled or killed as a result of military service; prisoner of war; or missing in action.

Application Requirements: Application form, essay, financial need analysis, recommendations or references, transcript. *Deadline:* March 15.

Contact: Eleanor Johnson, Executive Secretary
American Legion Auxiliary Department of Minnesota
State Veterans Service Building
20 West 12th Street, Room 314
St. Paul, MN 55155
Phone: 651-224-7634
Fax: 651-224-5243

AMERICAN LEGION AUXILIARY DEPARTMENT OF MISSOURI

http://www.missourilegion.org/

AMERICAN LEGION AUXILIARY DEPARTMENT OF MISSOURI LELA MURPHY SCHOLARSHIP

• *See page 529*

AMERICAN LEGION AUXILIARY DEPARTMENT OF MISSOURI NATIONAL PRESIDENT'S SCHOLARSHIP

• *See page 529*

AMERICAN LEGION AUXILIARY DEPARTMENT OF NEBRASKA

http://www.nebraskalegionaux.net/

AMERICAN LEGION AUXILIARY DEPARTMENT OF NEBRASKA RUBY PAUL CAMPAIGN FUND SCHOLARSHIP

• *See page 530*

AMERICAN LEGION AUXILIARY DEPARTMENT OF NORTH DAKOTA

http://www.ndlegion.org/

AMERICAN LEGION AUXILIARY DEPARTMENT OF NORTH DAKOTA NATIONAL PRESIDENT'S SCHOLARSHIP

• *See page 575*

AMERICAN LEGION AUXILIARY DEPARTMENT OF OHIO

http://www.alaohio.org/

AMERICAN LEGION AUXILIARY DEPARTMENT OF OHIO CONTINUING EDUCATION FUND

One-time award for Ohio residents who are the children or grandchildren of veterans, living or deceased, honorably discharged during eligibility dates for American Legion membership. Awards are for undergraduate use, based on need. Freshmen not eligible. Application must be signed by a unit representative.

Award: Scholarship for use in sophomore, junior, or senior years; not renewable. *Number:* 15. *Amount:* $200.

Eligibility Requirements: Applicant must be enrolled or expecting to enroll full-time at a two-year or four-year institution or university and resident of Ohio. Available to U.S. citizens. Applicant or parent must meet one or more of the following requirements: general military experience; retired from active duty; disabled or killed as a result of military service; prisoner of war; or missing in action.

Application Requirements: Application form, financial need analysis, transcript. *Deadline:* November 1.

Contact: Katie Tucker, Scholarship Coordinator
Phone: 740-452-8245
Fax: 740-452-2620
E-mail: ala_katie@rrohio.com

AMERICAN LEGION AUXILIARY DEPARTMENT OF OHIO DEPARTMENT PRESIDENT'S SCHOLARSHIP

Scholarship for children or grandchildren of veterans who served in Armed Forces during eligibility dates for American Legion membership. Must be high school senior, ages 16 to 18, Ohio resident, and U.S. citizen. Award for full-time undergraduate study. One-time award of $1000 to $1500.

Award: Scholarship for use in freshman year; not renewable. *Number:* 2. *Amount:* $1000–$1500.

Eligibility Requirements: Applicant must be high school student; age 16-18; planning to enroll or expecting to enroll full-time at a two-year or four-year institution or university and resident of Ohio. Available to U.S. citizens. Applicant or parent must meet one or more of the following requirements: general military experience; retired from active duty; disabled or killed as a result of military service; prisoner of war; or missing in action.

Application Requirements: Application form, essay, financial need analysis, recommendations or references, transcript. *Deadline:* March 1.

Contact: Department Scholarship Coordinator
American Legion Auxiliary Department of Ohio
PO Box 2760
Zanesville, OH 43702-2760
Phone: 740-452-8245
Fax: 740-452-2620

AMERICAN LEGION AUXILIARY DEPARTMENT OF SOUTH DAKOTA

http://www.sdlegion-aux.org/

AMERICAN LEGION AUXILIARY DEPARTMENT OF SOUTH DAKOTA COLLEGE SCHOLARSHIPS

• *See page 530*

AMERICAN LEGION AUXILIARY DEPARTMENT OF SOUTH DAKOTA SENIOR SCHOLARSHIP

• *See page 530*

AMERICAN LEGION AUXILIARY DEPARTMENT OF SOUTH DAKOTA THELMA FOSTER SCHOLARSHIP FOR SENIOR AUXILIARY MEMBERS

• *See page 530*

AMERICAN LEGION AUXILIARY DEPARTMENT OF TEXAS

http://www.alatexas.org/

AMERICAN LEGION AUXILIARY DEPARTMENT OF TEXAS GENERAL EDUCATION SCHOLARSHIP

Scholarships available for Texas residents. Must be a child of a veteran who served in the Armed Forces during eligibility dates. Some additional criteria used for selection are recommendations, academics, and finances.

Award: Scholarship for use in freshman, sophomore, junior, or senior years; not renewable. *Number:* 1–10. *Amount:* $500.

Eligibility Requirements: Applicant must be enrolled or expecting to enroll full-time at a two-year or four-year or technical institution or university and resident of Texas. Available to U.S. citizens. Applicant must have general military experience.

Application Requirements: Application form, community service, financial need analysis, letter stating qualifications and intentions, recommendations or references, resume, transcript. *Deadline:* June 1.

Contact: Paula Raney, State Secretary
American Legion Auxiliary Department of Texas
PO Box 140407
Austin, TX 78714
Phone: 512-476-7278
Fax: 512-482-8391
E-mail: alatexas@txlegion.org

AMERICAN LEGION AUXILIARY DEPARTMENT OF UTAH

http://www.legion-aux.org/

AMERICAN LEGION AUXILIARY DEPARTMENT OF UTAH NATIONAL PRESIDENT'S SCHOLARSHIP
• *See page 530*

AMERICAN LEGION AUXILIARY DEPARTMENT OF WISCONSIN

http://www.amlegionauxwi.org/

AMERICAN LEGION AUXILIARY DEPARTMENT OF WISCONSIN DELLA VAN DEUREN MEMORIAL SCHOLARSHIP
• *See page 531*

AMERICAN LEGION AUXILIARY DEPARTMENT OF WISCONSIN H.S. AND ANGELINE LEWIS SCHOLARSHIPS
• *See page 531*

AMERICAN LEGION AUXILIARY DEPARTMENT OF WISCONSIN MERIT AND MEMORIAL SCHOLARSHIPS
• *See page 531*

AMERICAN LEGION AUXILIARY DEPARTMENT OF WISCONSIN PAST PRESIDENTS' PARLEY HEALTH CAREER SCHOLARSHIPS
• *See page 531*

AMERICAN LEGION AUXILIARY DEPARTMENT OF WISCONSIN PRESIDENT'S SCHOLARSHIPS
• *See page 531*

AMERICAN LEGION AUXILIARY NATIONAL HEADQUARTERS

http://www.ALAforVeterans.org

AMERICAN LEGION AUXILIARY CHILDREN OF WARRIORS NATIONAL PRESIDENTS' SCHOLARSHIP
• *See page 575*

AMERICAN LEGION DEPARTMENT OF IDAHO

http://www.idaholegion.com/

AMERICAN LEGION DEPARTMENT OF IDAHO SCHOLARSHIP
• *See page 532*

AMERICAN LEGION DEPARTMENT OF MAINE

http://www.mainelegion.org/

AMERICAN LEGION DEPARTMENT OF MAINE CHILDREN AND YOUTH SCHOLARSHIP

Scholarships available to high school seniors, college students, and veterans who are residents of Maine. Must be in upper half of high school class. One-time award of $500.

Award: Scholarship for use in freshman, sophomore, junior, or senior years; not renewable. *Number:* 7. *Amount:* $500.

Eligibility Requirements: Applicant must be enrolled or expecting to enroll full-time at a two-year or four-year or technical institution or university and resident of Maine. Available to U.S. citizens. Applicant or parent must meet one or more of the following requirements: general military experience; retired from active duty; disabled or killed as a result of military service; prisoner of war; or missing in action.

Application Requirements: Application form, essay, financial need analysis, recommendations or references, transcript. *Deadline:* May 1.

Contact: Mr. Paul L'Heureux, Department Adjutant
American Legion Department of Maine
PO Box 900
Waterville, ME 04903
Phone: 207-873-3229
Fax: 207-872-0501
E-mail: legionme@mainelegion.org

DANIEL E. LAMBERT MEMORIAL SCHOLARSHIP

One-time award for undergraduate and graduate student whose parents are veterans. Award is based on financial need and good character. Must be U.S. citizen. Applicant must show evidence of being enrolled, or attending accredited college or vocational technical school. Scholarship value is from $500 to $1000.

Award: Scholarship for use in freshman, sophomore, junior, or senior years; not renewable. *Number:* 1–2. *Amount:* $500–$1000.

Eligibility Requirements: Applicant must be enrolled or expecting to enroll full-time at a two-year or four-year or technical institution or university and resident of Maine. Available to U.S. citizens. Applicant or parent must meet one or more of the following requirements: general military experience; retired from active duty; disabled or killed as a result of military service; prisoner of war; or missing in action.

Application Requirements: Application form, recommendations or references. *Deadline:* May 1.

Contact: Mr. Paul L'Heureux, Department Adjutant
American Legion Department of Maine
PO Box 900
Waterville, ME 04903
Phone: 207-873-3229
Fax: 207-872-0501
E-mail: legionme@mainelegion.org

JAMES V. DAY SCHOLARSHIP
• *See page 534*

AMERICAN LEGION DEPARTMENT OF MARYLAND

http://www.mdlegion.org/

AMERICAN LEGION DEPARTMENT OF MARYLAND GENERAL SCHOLARSHIP FUND

Nonrenewable scholarship for veterans or children of veterans who served in the Armed Forces during dates of eligibility for American

Legion membership. Merit-based award. Application available on website http://mdlegion.org.

Award: Scholarship for use in freshman, sophomore, junior, or senior years; not renewable. *Number:* 1–10. *Amount:* up to $500.

Eligibility Requirements: Applicant must be high school student; planning to enroll or expecting to enroll full-time at a four-year institution or university and resident of Maryland. Available to U.S. citizens. Applicant must have general military experience.

Application Requirements: Application form, essay, financial need analysis, transcript. *Deadline:* April 1.

Contact: Russell Myers, Department Adjutant
American Legion Department of Maryland
101 North Gay, Room E
Baltimore, MD 21202
Phone: 410-752-1405
Fax: 410-752-3822
E-mail: russell@mdlegion.org

AMERICAN LEGION DEPARTMENT OF MICHIGAN

http://www.michiganlegion.org/

GUY M. WILSON SCHOLARSHIPS

Scholarship for undergraduate use at a Michigan college. Must be resident of Michigan and the son, daughter, grandchild, or great grandchild of a veteran, living or deceased. Must submit copy of veteran's honorable discharge. Must have minimum 2.5 GPA. Total number of awards given vary each year depending upon the number of applications received. Applicants have to refer the website for the deadline.

Award: Scholarship for use in freshman year; not renewable. *Number:* 9. *Amount:* $500.

Eligibility Requirements: Applicant must be high school student; planning to enroll or expecting to enroll full- or part-time at a two-year or four-year institution or university; resident of Michigan and studying in Michigan. Applicant must have 2.5 GPA or higher. Available to U.S. citizens. Applicant or parent must meet one or more of the following requirements: general military experience; retired from active duty; disabled or killed as a result of military service; prisoner of war; or missing in action.

Application Requirements: Application form, essay, financial need analysis. *Deadline:* January 9.

Contact: Roxanne Osga, Programs Coordinator
American Legion Department of Michigan
212 North Verlinden Avenue, Suite A
Lansing, MI 48915
Phone: 517-371-4720 Ext. 23
E-mail: programs@michiganlegion.org

WILLIAM D. AND JEWELL W. BREWER SCHOLARSHIP TRUSTS

One-time award for residents of Michigan who are the son, daughter, grandchild, or great grandchild of veterans, living or deceased. Must submit copy of veteran's honorable discharge. Several scholarships of $500 each. Must have minimum 2.5 GPA. Scholarship can be applied to any college or university within the United States.

Award: Scholarship for use in freshman, sophomore, junior, or senior years; not renewable. *Number:* 4. *Amount:* $500.

Eligibility Requirements: Applicant must be enrolled or expecting to enroll full- or part-time at a two-year or four-year institution or university and resident of Michigan. Applicant must have 2.5 GPA or higher. Available to U.S. citizens. Applicant or parent must meet one or more of the following requirements: general military experience; retired from active duty; disabled or killed as a result of military service; prisoner of war; or missing in action.

Application Requirements: Application form, essay, financial need analysis. *Deadline:* January 9.

Contact: Roxanne Osga, Programs Coordinator
American Legion Department of Michigan
212 North Verlinden Avenue, Suite A
Lansing, MI 48915
Phone: 517-371-4720 Ext. 23
E-mail: programs@michiganlegion.org

THE AMERICAN LEGION, DEPARTMENT OF MINNESOTA

http://www.mnlegion.org/

AMERICAN LEGION DEPARTMENT OF MINNESOTA MEMORIAL SCHOLARSHIP
• See page 534

MINNESOTA LEGIONNAIRES INSURANCE TRUST SCHOLARSHIP
• See page 534

AMERICAN LEGION DEPARTMENT OF MISSOURI

http://www.missourilegion.org/

CHARLES L. BACON MEMORIAL SCHOLARSHIP
• See page 534

LILLIE LOIS FORD SCHOLARSHIP FUND

Two awards of $1000 each are given each year to one boy and one girl. Applicant must have attended a full session of Missouri Boys/Girls State or Missouri Cadet Patrol Academy. Must be a Missouri resident below age 21, attending an accredited college/university as a full-time student. Must be an unmarried descendant of a veteran having served at least 90 days on active duty in the Army, Air Force, Navy, Marine Corps, or Coast Guard of the United States.

Award: Scholarship for use in freshman year; not renewable. *Number:* 2. *Amount:* $1000.

Eligibility Requirements: Applicant must be high school student; planning to enroll or expecting to enroll full-time at a two-year or four-year institution or university; single and resident of Missouri. Available to U.S. citizens. Applicant or parent must meet one or more of the following requirements: general military experience; retired from active duty; disabled or killed as a result of military service; prisoner of war; or missing in action.

Application Requirements: Application form, copy of the veteran's discharge certificate, financial need analysis, test scores. *Deadline:* April 20.

Contact: John Doane, Chairman, Education and Scholarship Committee
American Legion Department of Missouri
PO Box 179
Jefferson City, MO 65102-0179
Phone: 417-924-8186

AMERICAN LEGION DEPARTMENT OF OHIO

http://www.ohiolegion.com/

OHIO AMERICAN LEGION SCHOLARSHIPS
• See page 535

AMERICAN LEGION DEPARTMENT OF WEST VIRGINIA

http://www.wvlegion.org/

SONS OF THE AMERICAN LEGION WILLIAM F. "BILL" JOHNSON MEMORIAL SCHOLARSHIP
• See page 536

AMVETS AUXILIARY

http://amvetsaux.org/

AMVETS NATIONAL LADIES AUXILIARY SCHOLARSHIP
• See page 539

ARKANSAS DEPARTMENT OF HIGHER EDUCATION

http://www.adhe.edu/

MILITARY DEPENDENT'S SCHOLARSHIP PROGRAM

Renewable waiver of tuition, fees, room and board undergraduate students seeking a Bachelor's degree or certificate of completion at any public college, university or technical school in Arkansas who qualify as a spouse or dependent child of an Arkansas resident who has been declared to be missing in action, killed in action, a POW, or killed on ordnance delivery, or a veteran who has been declared to be 100 percent totally and permanently disabled during, or as a result of, active military service.

Award: Scholarship for use in freshman, sophomore, junior, or senior years; renewable. *Number:* 1–60.

Eligibility Requirements: Applicant must be enrolled or expecting to enroll full-time at a two-year or four-year or technical institution or university; resident of Arkansas and studying in Arkansas. Available to U.S. citizens. Applicant or parent must meet one or more of the following requirements: general military experience; retired from active duty; disabled or killed as a result of military service; prisoner of war; or missing in action.

Application Requirements: Application form, recommendations or references, report of casualty. *Deadline:* June 1.

Contact: Tara Smith, Director of Financial Aid
Arkansas Department of Higher Education
114 East Capitol Avenue
Little Rock, AR 72201-3818
Phone: 501-371-2000
Fax: 501-371-2001
E-mail: taras@adhe.edu

DEFENSE COMMISSARY AGENCY

http://www.militaryscholar.org/

SCHOLARSHIPS FOR MILITARY CHILDREN

One-time award to unmarried dependents of military personnel for full-time undergraduate study at a four-year institution. Minimum 3.0 GPA required. Further information and applications available at website http://www.militaryscholar.org.

Award: Scholarship for use in freshman, sophomore, or junior years; not renewable. *Number:* 700. *Amount:* $2000.

Eligibility Requirements: Applicant must be enrolled or expecting to enroll full-time at a four-year institution or university and single. Applicant must have 3.0 GPA or higher. Available to U.S. citizens. Applicant or parent must meet one or more of the following requirements: general military experience; retired from active duty; disabled or killed as a result of military service; prisoner of war; or missing in action.

Application Requirements: Application form, essay. *Deadline:* February 17.

Contact: Mr. Bernard Cote
Phone: 856-573-9400
E-mail: militaryscholar@scholarshipmanagers.com

DELAWARE HIGHER EDUCATION OFFICE

http://www.doe.k12.de.us

EDUCATIONAL BENEFITS FOR CHILDREN OF DECEASED VETERANS

• *See page 583*

DEPARTMENT OF VETERANS AFFAIRS (VA)

http://www.gibill.va.gov/

MONTGOMERY GI BILL (ACTIVE DUTY) CHAPTER 30

Award provides up to thirty-six months of education benefits to eligible veterans for college, business school, technical courses, vocational courses, correspondence courses, apprenticeships/job training, or flight training. Must be an eligible veteran with an Honorable Discharge and have high school diploma or GED before applying for benefits.

Award: Scholarship for use in freshman, sophomore, junior, senior, or graduate years; renewable.

Eligibility Requirements: Applicant must be enrolled or expecting to enroll full- or part-time at a two-year or four-year or technical institution or university. Available to U.S. citizens. Applicant or parent must meet one or more of the following requirements: general military experience; retired from active duty; disabled or killed as a result of military service; prisoner of war; or missing in action.

Application Requirements: Application form. *Deadline:* continuous.

Contact: Keith Wilson, Director, Education Service
Phone: 888-442-4551

MONTGOMERY GI BILL (SELECTED RESERVE)

• *See page 640*

RESERVE EDUCATION ASSISTANCE PROGRAM

• *See page 642*

SURVIVORS AND DEPENDENTS EDUCATIONAL ASSISTANCE (CHAPTER 35)-VA

Monthly $860 benefits for up to 45 months. Must be spouses or children under age 26 of current veterans missing in action or of deceased or totally and permanently disabled (service-related) service persons. For more information visit the following website http://www.gibill.va.gov.

Award: Scholarship for use in freshman, sophomore, junior, or senior years; renewable.

Eligibility Requirements: Applicant must be enrolled or expecting to enroll full- or part-time at a two-year or four-year or technical institution or university. Available to U.S. and non-U.S. citizens. Applicant or parent must meet one or more of the following requirements: general military experience; retired from active duty; disabled or killed as a result of military service; prisoner of war; or missing in action.

Application Requirements: Application form. *Deadline:* continuous.

Contact: Keith Wilson, Director, Education Service
Phone: 888-442-4551

ELEARNERS.COM

http://www.elearners.com

ELEARNERS MILITARY SCHOLARSHIP

• *See page 640*

EOD WARRIOR FOUNDATION

http://www.eodwarriorfoundation.org

EXPLOSIVE ORDNANCE DISPOSAL MEMORIAL SCHOLARSHIP

• *See page 586*

FELDMAN LAW FIRM PLLC

http://www.afphoenixcriminalattorney.com/

DISABLED VETERANS SCHOLARSHIP

• *See page 587*

FIRST COMMAND EDUCATIONAL FOUNDATION

http://www.fcef.com/

DONALDSON D. FRIZZELL SCHOLARSHIP

Scholarship awarded to students seeking associate, undergraduate, or graduate degrees. Also available to those seeking professional certification or attending vocational school. Details announced in February of each year.

Award: Scholarship for use in freshman, sophomore, junior, senior, or graduate years; not renewable. *Number:* 5–14. *Amount:* $1000–$5000.

Eligibility Requirements: Applicant must be enrolled or expecting to enroll full- or part-time at a two-year or four-year or technical institution or university. Applicant must have 3.0 GPA or higher. Available to U.S. citizens. Applicant or parent must meet one or more of the following requirements: general military experience; retired from active duty; disabled or killed as a result of military service; prisoner of war; or missing in action.

Application Requirements: Application form, community service, essay. *Deadline:* April 7.

Contact: Bill Johnson, Director, Military Affairs
First Command Educational Foundation
1 FirstComm Plaza
Fort Worth, TX 76109
Phone: 817-569-2500
Fax: 817-569-2970
E-mail: Scholarships@fcef.com

FLORIDA STATE DEPARTMENT OF EDUCATION

http://www.floridastudentfinancialaid.org/

SCHOLARSHIPS FOR CHILDREN & SPOUSES OF DECEASED OR DISABLED VETERANS

Renewable scholarships for children and spouses of deceased or disabled veterans. Children must be between the ages of 16 and 22, and attend an eligible Florida postsecondary institution and enrolled at least part-time. Must ensure that the Florida Department of Veterans Affairs certifies the applicant's eligibility. Must maintain GPA of 2.0. For more details, visit the website at http://www.FloridaStudentFinancialAid.org/SSFAD/home/uamain.htm.

Award: Scholarship for use in freshman, sophomore, junior, or senior years; renewable.

Eligibility Requirements: Applicant must be age 16-22; enrolled or expecting to enroll full- or part-time at a two-year or four-year or technical institution or university; resident of Florida and studying in Florida. Available to U.S. citizens. Applicant or parent must meet one or more of the following requirements: general military experience; retired from active duty; disabled or killed as a result of military service; prisoner of war; or missing in action.

Application Requirements: Application form. *Deadline:* April 1.

Contact: Florida Department of Education, Office of Student Financial Assistance, Customer Service
Florida State Department of Education
325 West Gaines Street
Tallahassee, FL 32399
Phone: 888-827-2004
E-mail: osfa@fldoe.org

GOLDIA GOLD & DIAMONDS

http://www.goldia.com

GOLDIA.COM SCHOLARSHIP
• *See page 630*

ILLINOIS AMVETS

http://www.ilamvets.org/

ILLINOIS AMVETS LADIES AUXILIARY MEMORIAL SCHOLARSHIP

Applicant must be an Illinois student and a child of an honorably discharged veteran who served after September 15, 1940. Must submit ACT scores, IRS 1040 form, high school rank and grades.

Award: Scholarship for use in freshman year; not renewable. *Number:* 1–3. *Amount:* $500.

Eligibility Requirements: Applicant must be high school student; planning to enroll or expecting to enroll full-time at a two-year or four-year or technical institution or university and resident of Illinois. Available to U.S. citizens. Applicant or parent must meet one or more of the following requirements: general military experience; retired from

active duty; disabled or killed as a result of military service; prisoner of war; or missing in action.

Application Requirements: Application form, financial need analysis, IRS 1040 form, test scores, transcript. *Deadline:* March 1.

Contact: Scholarship Director
Illinois AMVETS
2200 South Sixth Street
Springfield, IL 62703-3496
Phone: 217-528-4713
Fax: 217-528-9896
E-mail: scholarship@amvetsillinois.com

ILLINOIS AMVETS LADIES AUXILIARY WORCHID SCHOLARSHIPS

Applicant must be an Illinois student and the child of an honorably discharged, deceased veteran who served after September 15, 1940. Must submit ACT score and IRS 1040 form.

Award: Scholarship for use in freshman year; not renewable. *Number:* 1–3. *Amount:* $500.

Eligibility Requirements: Applicant must be high school student; age 17-18; planning to enroll or expecting to enroll full-time at a two-year or four-year or technical institution or university and resident of Illinois. Available to U.S. citizens. Applicant or parent must meet one or more of the following requirements: general military experience; retired from active duty; disabled or killed as a result of military service; prisoner of war; or missing in action.

Application Requirements: Application form, financial need analysis, IRS 1040 form, test scores, transcript. *Deadline:* March 1.

Contact: Scholarship Director
Illinois AMVETS
2200 South Sixth Street
Springfield, IL 62703-3496
Phone: 217-528-4713
Fax: 217-528-9896
E-mail: scholarship@amvetsillinois.com

ILLINOIS AMVETS SERVICE FOUNDATION

Applicant must be a resident of Illinois. Preference given to child or grandchild of veteran or active duty.

Award: Scholarship for use in freshman year; not renewable. *Number:* 10. *Amount:* $1000.

Eligibility Requirements: Applicant must be high school student; planning to enroll or expecting to enroll full-time at a two-year or four-year or technical institution or university; resident of Illinois and studying in Illinois. Available to U.S. citizens. Applicant must have general military experience.

Application Requirements: Application form, community service, financial need analysis. *Deadline:* March 1.

Contact: Scholarship Director
Illinois AMVETS
2200 South Sixth Street
Springfield, IL 62703-3496
Phone: 217-528-4713

ILLINOIS AMVETS TRADE SCHOOL SCHOLARSHIP

Applicant must be an Illinois student who has been accepted in a pre-approved trade school program. Must be a child or grandchild of a veteran or active-duty.

Award: Scholarship for use in freshman year; not renewable. *Number:* 5. *Amount:* $1000.

Eligibility Requirements: Applicant must be high school student; planning to enroll or expecting to enroll full-time at a technical institution and resident of Illinois. Available to U.S. citizens. Applicant or parent must meet one or more of the following requirements: general military experience; retired from active duty; disabled or killed as a result of military service; prisoner of war; or missing in action.

Application Requirements: Application form. *Deadline:* March 1.

Contact: Crystal Blakeman, Programs Director
Illinois AMVETS
2200 S. 6th St.
Springfield, IL 62703
Phone: 217-528-4713 Ext. 207
E-mail: Crystal@ilamvets.org

ILLINOIS DEPARTMENT OF VETERANS' AFFAIRS

https://www.illinois.gov/veterans/Pages/default.aspx

MIA/POW SCHOLARSHIP

Any Spouse, natural child, adopted child, or any step child of a veteran. Child must attend school prior to 26th birthday. No age limit for spouse. Veteran must be MIA, POW, died as the result of service connected disability determined by the U.S. Department of Veterans' Affairs or is 100% service connected disabled permanent and total established by the U.S. Department of Veterans' Affairs. Veteran must have been an Illinois resident at time of entry into service or became an Illinois resident within 6 months after entering service. Scholarship is equivalent to four full years of college, including summer terms. Based on a point system with 120 points as the maximum. Applicant has 12 years to utilize scholarship from the date they begin using it.

Award: Scholarship for use in freshman, sophomore, junior, or senior years; renewable.

Eligibility Requirements: Applicant must be enrolled or expecting to enroll full- or part-time at a two-year or four-year institution or university; married; resident of Illinois and studying in Illinois. Available to U.S. citizens. Applicant must have general military experience.

Application Requirements: Application form. *Deadline:* continuous.

Contact: Ms. Tracy Kimmel, Grants Section
Illinois Department of Veterans' Affairs
833 South Spring Street
Springfield, IL 62794-9432
Phone: 217-782-3564
Fax: 217-782-4161

VETERANS' CHILDREN EDUCATIONAL OPPORTUNITIES

$250 award for each child aged 10 to 18 of a veteran who died or became totally disabled as a result of active duty. Must be Illinois resident studying in Illinois. Death must be service-connected. Disability must be rated 100 percent for two or more years.

Award: Grant for use in freshman year; not renewable. *Amount:* $250.

Eligibility Requirements: Applicant must be age 10-18; enrolled or expecting to enroll full- or part-time at a two-year or four-year institution or university; single; resident of Illinois and studying in Illinois. Available to U.S. citizens. Applicant must have general military experience.

Application Requirements: Application form. *Deadline:* June 30.

Contact: Tracy Kimmel, Grants Section
Illinois Department of Veterans' Affairs
833 South Spring Street
Springfield, IL 62794-9432
Phone: 217-782-3564
Fax: 217-782-4161

ILLINOIS STUDENT ASSISTANCE COMMISSION (ISAC)

http://www.isac.org/

ILLINOIS VETERAN GRANT PROGRAM-IVG

Awards qualified veterans and pays eligible tuition and fees for study in Illinois public universities or community colleges. Program eligibility units are based on the enrolled hours for a particular term, not the dollar amount of the benefits paid. Applications are available at college financial aid office and can be submitted any time during the academic year for which assistance is being requested.

Award: Grant for use in freshman, sophomore, junior, senior, or graduate years; renewable.

Eligibility Requirements: Applicant must be enrolled or expecting to enroll full- or part-time at a two-year or four-year institution or university; resident of Illinois and studying in Illinois. Available to U.S. citizens. Applicant or parent must meet one or more of the following requirements: general military experience; retired from active duty;

disabled or killed as a result of military service; prisoner of war; or missing in action.

Application Requirements: Application form. *Deadline:* continuous.

Contact: ISAC Call Center Representative
Illinois Student Assistance Commission (ISAC)
1755 Lake Cook Road
Deerfield, IL 60015-5209
Phone: 800-899-4722
E-mail: isac.studentservices@isac.illinois.gov

IMAGINE AMERICA FOUNDATION

www.imagine-america.org

MILITARY AWARD PROGRAM (MAP)

• *See page 641*

KANSAS COMMISSION ON VETERANS AFFAIRS

http://www.kcva.org/

KANSAS EDUCATIONAL BENEFITS FOR CHILDREN OF MIA, POW, AND DECEASED VETERANS OF THE VIETNAM WAR

Scholarship awarded to students who are children of veterans. Must show proof of parent's status as missing in action, prisoner-of-war, or killed in action in the Vietnam War. Kansas residence required of veteran at time of entry to service. Must attend a state-supported postsecondary school.

Award: Scholarship for use in freshman, sophomore, junior, or senior years; not renewable. *Number:* 1.

Eligibility Requirements: Applicant must be enrolled or expecting to enroll full-time at a two-year or four-year or technical institution or university and studying in Kansas. Available to U.S. citizens. Applicant or parent must meet one or more of the following requirements: general military experience; retired from active duty; disabled or killed as a result of military service; prisoner of war; or missing in action.

Application Requirements: Application form, birth certificate, school acceptance letter, military discharge of veteran. *Deadline:* varies.

Contact: Wayne Bollig, Program Director
Phone: 785-296-3976
Fax: 785-296-1462
E-mail: wbollig@kcva.org

KITCHEN GUIDES

http://www.kitchensguides.com/

SMART KITCHEN IMPROVEMENT SCHOLARSHIP BY KITCHEN GUIDES

• *See page 598*

KNIGHTS OF COLUMBUS

http://www.kofc.org/

FRANCIS P. MATTHEWS AND JOHN E. SWIFT EDUCATIONAL TRUST SCHOLARSHIPS

• *See page 547*

LAW OFFICES OF RYAN J. TEGNELIA

http://www.sandiegocriminallawyerrt.com/

ANNUAL VETERANS WITH POST-TRAUMATIC STRESS SCHOLARSHIP

• *See page 599*

LOUISIANA DEPARTMENT OF VETERAN AFFAIRS

http://www.vetaffairs.la.gov

LOUISIANA DEPARTMENT OF VETERANS AFFAIRS STATE EDUCATIONAL AID PROGRAM

Waiver of tuition and school-imposed fees at any state supported college, university, or technical institute in Louisiana for dependent children, aged 16-25, of service connected disabled veterans, service connected deceased veterans, or veterans rated 100% service connected due to individual unemployability. Tuition waiver also available for an unremarried surviving spouse of a service connected deceased veteran. Residency restricted to Louisiana.

Award: Scholarship for use in freshman, sophomore, junior, or senior years; not renewable.

Eligibility Requirements: Applicant must be age 16-25; enrolled or expecting to enroll full-time at a two-year or four-year or technical institution or university; resident of Louisiana and studying in Louisiana. Available to U.S. citizens. Applicant or parent must meet one or more of the following requirements: general military experience; retired from active duty; disabled or killed as a result of military service; prisoner of war; or missing in action.

Application Requirements: Application form. *Deadline:* continuous.

Contact: Mr. Barry Robinson, Regional Manager/Training Officer
Louisiana Department of Veteran Affairs
PO Box 94095 Capitol Station
Baton Rouge, LA 70804-9095
Phone: 225-219-5017
Fax: 225-219-5590
E-mail: barry.robinson@vetaffairs.la.gov

MAINE VETERANS SERVICES

http://www.maine.gov/dvem/bvs

VETERANS DEPENDENTS EDUCATIONAL BENEFITS-MAINE

Tuition waiver award for dependent children who have not reached their 22nd birthday or spouses of veterans permanently and totally disabled resulting from service-connected disability; died from a service-connected disability; at time of death was totally and permanently disabled due to service-connected disability, but whose death was not related to the service-connected disability; or member of the Armed Forces on active duty who has been listed for more than 90 days as missing in action, captured or forcibly detained or interned in the line of duty. Benefits apply only to the University of Maine System, Maine community colleges and Maine Maritime Academy. Must be high school graduate. Must submit with application proof of veteran's VA disability along with dependent verification paperwork such as birth, marriage, or adoption certificate and proof of enrollment in degree program.

Award: Scholarship for use in freshman, sophomore, junior, or senior years; not renewable.

Eligibility Requirements: Applicant must be enrolled or expecting to enroll full- or part-time at a two-year or four-year institution or university; resident of Maine and studying in Maine. Available to U.S. citizens. Applicant or parent must meet one or more of the following requirements: general military experience; retired from active duty; disabled or killed as a result of military service; prisoner of war; or missing in action.

Application Requirements: Application form, see application.

Contact: Mrs. Paula Gagnon, Office Associate II
Maine Veterans Services
State House Station 117
Augusta, ME 04333-0117
Phone: 207-430-6035
Fax: 207-626-4471
E-mail: mainebvs@maine.gov

MARYLAND STATE HIGHER EDUCATION COMMISSION

http://www.mhec.state.md.us/

EDWARD T. CONROY MEMORIAL SCHOLARSHIP PROGRAM

• *See page 602*

VETERANS OF THE AFGHANISTAN AND IRAQ CONFLICTS SCHOLARSHIP PROGRAM

Provides financial assistance to Maryland resident U.S. Armed Forces personnel who served in Afghanistan or Iraq conflicts and their children or spouses who are attending Maryland institutions.

Award: Scholarship for use in freshman, sophomore, junior, or senior years; renewable. *Number:* 123. *Amount:* $8850.

Eligibility Requirements: Applicant must be enrolled or expecting to enroll full- or part-time at a two-year or four-year institution or university; resident of Maryland and studying in Maryland. Available to U.S. citizens. Applicant or parent must meet one or more of the following requirements: general military experience; retired from active duty; disabled or killed as a result of military service; prisoner of war; or missing in action.

Application Requirements: Application form, birth certificate/marriage certificate, documentation of military order, financial need analysis. *Deadline:* March 1.

Contact: Linda Asplin, Program Administrator
Maryland State Higher Education Commission
839 Bestgate Road, Suite 400
Annapolis, MD 21401-3013
Phone: 410-260-4563
Fax: 410-260-3203
E-mail: lasplin@mhec.state.md.us

MASSACHUSETTS OFFICE OF STUDENT FINANCIAL ASSISTANCE

http://www.osfa.mass.edu/

MASSACHUSETTS PUBLIC SERVICE GRANT PROGRAM

• *See page 602*

MILITARY ORDER OF THE PURPLE HEART

http://www.purpleheart.org/

MILITARY ORDER OF THE PURPLE HEART SCHOLARSHIP

Scholarship for Military Order of the Purple Heart (MOPH) Members/spouses or children, stepchildren, adopted children or grandchildren, veterans killed-in-action or veterans who died of wounds and did not have the opportunity to join the MOPH. Must submit $10 application fee, essay, high school/college transcript, and letters of recommendation. Must be U.S. citizen and high school graduate with minimum GPA of 2.75 and accepted or enrolled as a full-time student at a U.S. college, university of trade school at the time the scholarship is awarded.

Award: Scholarship for use in freshman, sophomore, junior, or senior years; not renewable. *Number:* up to 83. *Amount:* $3000.

Eligibility Requirements: Applicant must be enrolled or expecting to enroll full-time at a two-year or four-year or technical institution or university. Applicant must have 3.0 GPA or higher. Available to U.S. citizens. Applicant or parent must meet one or more of the following requirements: general military experience; retired from active duty; disabled or killed as a result of military service; prisoner of war; or missing in action.

Application Requirements: Application form, essay, proof of MOPH membership, recommendations or references, transcript. *Fee:* $10. *Deadline:* February 17.

Contact: Mr. Stewart Mckeown, Scholarship Coordinator
Military Order of the Purple Heart
5413-B Backlick Road
Springfield, VA 22151-3960
Phone: 703-642-5360
Fax: 703-642-2054
E-mail: info@purpleheart.org

NATIONAL MILITARY FAMILY ASSOCIATION

http://www.MilitaryFamily.org

NATIONAL MILITARY FAMILY ASSOCIATION'S MILITARY SPOUSE SCHOLARSHIPS

Scholarships ranging from $500 to $2000 are awarded to spouses of
Uniformed Services members (active duty, National Guard and Reserve,
retirees, and survivors) for professional funding such as licensure and
certification or any level of degree. Award number and amount varies.
You must be a military spouse to apply.

Award: Scholarship for use in freshman, sophomore, junior, senior,
graduate, or postgraduate years; not renewable. *Number:* 300–600.
Amount: $500–$2000.

Eligibility Requirements: Applicant must be enrolled or expecting to
enroll full- or part-time at a two-year or four-year or technical institution
or university and married. Available to U.S. and non-U.S. citizens.
Applicant or parent must meet one or more of the following
requirements: general military experience; retired from active duty;
disabled or killed as a result of military service; prisoner of war; or
missing in action.

Application Requirements: Application form, essay. *Deadline:*
continuous.

Contact: Mrs. Allison Jones, Military Spouse Scholarship Program
Manager
National Military Family Association
3601 Eisenhower Avenue
Suite 425
Alexandria, VA 22304
Phone: 703-931-6632
E-mail: scholarships@militaryfamily.org

NEW JERSEY DEPARTMENT OF MILITARY AND VETERANS AFFAIRS

http://www.state.nj.us/military

NEW JERSEY WAR ORPHANS TUITION ASSISTANCE

$500 scholarship to children of those service personnel who died while in
the military or due to service-connected disabilities, or who are officially
listed as missing in action by the U.S. Department of Defense. Must be a
resident of New Jersey for at least one year immediately preceding the
filing of the application and be between the ages of 16 and 21 at the time
of application.

Award: Scholarship for use in freshman, sophomore, junior, or senior
years; renewable. *Amount:* $500.

Eligibility Requirements: Applicant must be age 16-21; enrolled or
expecting to enroll full-time at a four-year institution or university and
resident of New Jersey. Available to U.S. citizens. Applicant or parent
must meet one or more of the following requirements: general military
experience; retired from active duty; disabled or killed as a result of
military service; prisoner of war; or missing in action.

Application Requirements: Application form, transcript. *Deadline:*
varies.

Contact: Patricia Richter, Grants Manager
New Jersey Department of Military and Veterans Affairs
PO Box 340
Trenton, NJ 08625-0340
Phone: 609-530-6854
Fax: 609-530-6970
E-mail: patricia.richter@njdmava.state.nj.us

POW-MIA TUITION BENEFIT PROGRAM

Free undergraduate college tuition provided to any child born or adopted
before or during the period of time his or her parent was officially
declared a prisoner of war or person missing in action after January 1,

1960. The POW-MIA must have been a New Jersey resident at the time
he or she entered the service. Child of veteran must attend either a public
or private institution in New Jersey. A copy of DD 1300 must be
furnished with the application. Minimum 2.5 GPA required.

Award: Scholarship for use in freshman, sophomore, junior, or senior
years; renewable.

Eligibility Requirements: Applicant must be enrolled or expecting to
enroll full-time at a two-year or four-year or technical institution or
university; resident of New Jersey and studying in New Jersey. Applicant
must have 2.5 GPA or higher. Available to U.S. citizens. Applicant or
parent must meet one or more of the following requirements: general
military experience; retired from active duty; disabled or killed as a result
of military service; prisoner of war; or missing in action.

Application Requirements: Application form, copy of DD 1300,
transcript. *Deadline:* varies.

Contact: Patricia Richter, Grants Manager
New Jersey Department of Military and Veterans Affairs
PO Box 340
Trenton, NJ 08625-0340
Phone: 609-530-6854
Fax: 609-530-6970
E-mail: patricia.richter@njdmava.state.nj.us

VETERANS TUITION CREDIT PROGRAM-NEW JERSEY

Award for New Jersey resident veterans who served in the armed forces
between December 31, 1960, and May 7, 1975. Must have been a New
Jersey resident at time of induction or discharge or for two years
immediately prior to application.

Award: Scholarship for use in freshman, sophomore, junior, or senior
years; renewable. *Amount:* $200–$400.

Eligibility Requirements: Applicant must be enrolled or expecting to
enroll full- or part-time at a two-year or four-year or technical institution
or university and resident of New Jersey. Available to U.S. citizens.
Applicant or parent must meet one or more of the following
requirements: general military experience; retired from active duty;
disabled or killed as a result of military service; prisoner of war; or
missing in action.

Application Requirements: Application form. *Deadline:* varies.

Contact: Patricia Richter, Grants Manager
New Jersey Department of Military and Veterans Affairs
PO Box 340
Trenton, NJ 08625-0340
Phone: 609-530-6854
Fax: 609-530-6970
E-mail: patricia.richter@njdmava.state.nj.us

NEW MEXICO COMMISSION ON HIGHER EDUCATION

http://www.hed.state.nm.us/

VIETNAM VETERANS' SCHOLARSHIP PROGRAM

Renewable scholarship program created to provide aid for Vietnam
veterans who are undergraduate and graduate students attending public
postsecondary institutions or select private colleges in New Mexico.
Private colleges include: College of Santa Fe, St. John's College and
College of the Southwest.

Award: Scholarship for use in freshman, sophomore, junior, or senior
years; renewable. *Number:* 1.

Eligibility Requirements: Applicant must be enrolled or expecting to
enroll full-time at a two-year or four-year institution; resident of New
Mexico and studying in New Mexico. Available to U.S. citizens.
Applicant or parent must meet one or more of the following
requirements: general military experience; retired from active duty;
disabled or killed as a result of military service; prisoner of war; or
missing in action.

Application Requirements: Application form, certification by the NM
Veteran's commission. *Deadline:* varies.

Contact: Tashina Moore, Director of Financial Aid
New Mexico Commission on Higher Education
1068 Cerrillos Road
Santa Fe, NM 87505-1650
Phone: 505-476-6549
Fax: 505-476-6511
E-mail: tashina.banks-moore@state.nm.us

NEW MEXICO DEPARTMENT OF VETERANS' SERVICES

http://www.nmdvs.org

NEW MEXICO WARTIME VETERANS SCHOLARSHIP

Award for Wartime Veterans who have been a New Mexico resident for a minimum of ten years and are attending state-funded postsecondary schools. Must have been awarded a campaign medal such as the Southwest Asia Service Medal, Global War on Terrorism Expeditionary Medal, Iraq Campaign Medal, Afghanistan Campaign Medal or any other medal issued for service in the Armed Forces of the United States in support of any US Military Campaign or armed conflict as defined by congress or presidential order or service after August 1, 1990.

Award: Scholarship for use in freshman, sophomore, junior, or senior years; renewable. *Number:* 100. *Amount:* $3500–$4000.

Eligibility Requirements: Applicant must be enrolled or expecting to enroll full- or part-time at a two-year or four-year or technical institution or university; resident of New Mexico and studying in New Mexico. Available to U.S. citizens. Applicant must have general military experience.

Contact: Mr. Dale Movius, Director, State Benefits
New Mexico Department of Veterans' Services
407 Galiesteo St, Room 142
Santa Fe, NM 87501
Phone: 505-827-6374
E-mail: dalej.movius@state.nm.us

NEW YORK STATE HIGHER EDUCATION SERVICES CORPORATION

https://www.hesc.ny.gov/

NEW YORK VIETNAM/PERSIAN GULF/AFGHANISTAN VETERANS TUITION AWARDS

Scholarship for veterans who served in Vietnam, the Persian Gulf, or Afghanistan. Must be a New York resident attending a New York institution. Must establish eligibility by September 1.

Award: Scholarship for use in freshman, sophomore, junior, or senior years; renewable.

Eligibility Requirements: Applicant must be enrolled or expecting to enroll full- or part-time at a two-year or four-year or technical institution or university; resident of New York and studying in New York. Available to U.S. citizens. Applicant or parent must meet one or more of the following requirements: general military experience; retired from active duty; disabled or killed as a result of military service; prisoner of war; or missing in action.

Application Requirements: Application form, financial need analysis. *Deadline:* May 1.

Contact: Associate HESC Information Representative
Phone: 888-NYS-HESC
E-mail: scholarship@hesc.com

REGENTS AWARD FOR CHILD OF VETERAN

Award for students whose parent, as a result of service in U.S. Armed Forces during war or national emergency, died; suffered a 40 percent or more disability; or is classified as missing in action or a prisoner of war. Veteran must be current New York State resident or have been so at time of death. Student must be a New York resident, attending, or planning to attend, college in New York State. Must establish eligibility before applying for payment.

Award: Scholarship for use in freshman, sophomore, junior, or senior years; not renewable. *Amount:* up to $450.

Eligibility Requirements: Applicant must be enrolled or expecting to enroll full-time at a two-year or four-year institution or university; resident of New York and studying in New York. Available to U.S. citizens. Applicant or parent must meet one or more of the following requirements: general military experience; retired from active duty; disabled or killed as a result of military service; prisoner of war; or missing in action.

Application Requirements: Application form, proof of eligibility. *Deadline:* May 1.

Contact: Rita McGivern, Student Information
New York State Higher Education Services Corporation
99 Washington Avenue, Room 1320
Albany, NY 12255
E-mail: rmcgivern@hesc.com

N.H. DEPARTMENT OF EDUCATION, DIVISION OF HIGHER EDUCATION - HIGHER EDUCATION COMMISSION

http://www.education.nh.gov/highered

SCHOLARSHIPS FOR ORPHANS OF VETERANS

Scholarship to provide financial assistance (room, board, books and supplies) to children of parents who served in World War II, Korean Conflict, Vietnam (Southeast Asian Conflict) or the Gulf Wars, or any other operation for which the armed forces expeditionary medal or theater of operations service medal was awarded to the veteran. Must be between the ages of 16 and 25 to qualify and be residents of New Hampshire studying at New Hampshire colleges and universities.

Award: Scholarship for use in freshman, sophomore, junior, or senior years; renewable. *Number:* 1–10. *Amount:* $1500–$2500.

Eligibility Requirements: Applicant must be age 16-25; enrolled or expecting to enroll full-time at a two-year or four-year institution or university; resident of New Hampshire and studying in New Hampshire. Available to U.S. citizens. Applicant or parent must meet one or more of the following requirements: general military experience; retired from active duty; disabled or killed as a result of military service; prisoner of war; or missing in action.

Application Requirements: Application form. *Deadline:* September 1.

Contact: Mrs. Pat Moquin, Program Assistant
N.H. Department of Education, Division of Higher Education -
Higher Education Commission
101 Pleasant Street
Concord, NH 03301
Phone: 603-271-0289
Fax: 603-271-1953
E-mail: patricia.moquin@doe.nh.gov

NORTH CAROLINA DIVISION OF VETERANS AFFAIRS

http://www.milvets.nc.gov/

NORTH CAROLINA VETERANS SCHOLARSHIPS CLASS I-A

Scholarships for children of certain deceased, disabled or POW/MIA veterans. Award value is $4500 per nine-month academic year in private colleges and junior colleges. No limit on number awarded each year.

Award: Scholarship for use in freshman, sophomore, junior, or senior years; renewable. *Amount:* $4500.

Eligibility Requirements: Applicant must be enrolled or expecting to enroll full-time at a two-year or four-year or technical institution or university; resident of North Carolina and studying in North Carolina. Available to U.S. citizens. Applicant or parent must meet one or more of the following requirements: general military experience; retired from active duty; disabled or killed as a result of military service; prisoner of war; or missing in action.

Application Requirements: Application form, financial need analysis, interview, transcript. *Deadline:* continuous.

Contact: Charles Smith, Assistant Secretary
Phone: 919-733-3851
Fax: 919-733-2834
E-mail: charlie.smith@ncmail.net

NORTH CAROLINA VETERANS SCHOLARSHIPS CLASS I-B

Awards for children of veterans rated by USDVA as 100 percent disabled due to wartime service as defined in the law, and currently or at time of death drawing compensation for such disability. Parent must have been a North Carolina resident at time of entry into service. Duration of the scholarship is four academic years (8 semesters) if used within 8 years. No limit on number awarded each year.

Award: Scholarship for use in freshman, sophomore, junior, or senior years; renewable. *Amount:* $1500.

Eligibility Requirements: Applicant must be enrolled or expecting to enroll full- or part-time at a two-year or four-year or technical institution or university; resident of North Carolina and studying in North Carolina. Available to U.S. citizens. Applicant or parent must meet one or more of the following requirements: general military experience; retired from active duty; disabled or killed as a result of military service; prisoner of war; or missing in action.

Application Requirements: Application form, financial need analysis, interview, transcript. *Deadline:* continuous.

Contact: Charles Smith, Assistant Secretary
  Phone: 919-733-3851
  Fax: 919-733-2834
  E-mail: charlie.smith@ncmail.net

NORTH CAROLINA VETERANS SCHOLARSHIPS CLASS II

Awards for children of veterans rated by USDVA as much as 20 percent but less than 100 percent disabled due to wartime service as defined in the law, or awarded Purple Heart Medal for wounds received. Parent must have been a North Carolina resident at time of entry into service. Duration of the scholarship is four academic years (8 semesters) if used within 8 years. Free tuition and exemption from certain mandatory fees as set forth in the law in Public, Community and Technical Colleges.

Award: Scholarship for use in freshman, sophomore, junior, or senior years; renewable. *Number:* up to 100. *Amount:* $4500.

Eligibility Requirements: Applicant must be enrolled or expecting to enroll full- or part-time at a two-year or four-year or technical institution or university; resident of North Carolina and studying in North Carolina. Available to U.S. citizens. Applicant or parent must meet one or more of the following requirements: general military experience; retired from active duty; disabled or killed as a result of military service; prisoner of war; or missing in action.

Application Requirements: Application form, financial need analysis, interview, transcript. *Deadline:* March 1.

Contact: Charles Smith, Assistant Secretary
  Phone: 919-733-3851
  Fax: 919-733-2834
  E-mail: charlie.smith@ncmail.net

NORTH CAROLINA VETERANS SCHOLARSHIPS CLASS III

Awards for children of a deceased war veteran, who was honorably discharged and who does not qualify under any other provision within this synopsis or veteran who served in a combat zone or waters adjacent to a combat zone and received a campaign badge or medal and who does not qualify under any other provision within this synopsis. Duration of the scholarship is four academic years (8 semesters) if used within 8 years.

Award: Scholarship for use in freshman, sophomore, junior, or senior years; renewable. *Number:* up to 100. *Amount:* $4500.

Eligibility Requirements: Applicant must be enrolled or expecting to enroll full- or part-time at a two-year or four-year or technical institution or university; resident of North Carolina and studying in North Carolina. Available to U.S. citizens. Applicant or parent must meet one or more of the following requirements: general military experience; retired from active duty; disabled or killed as a result of military service; prisoner of war; or missing in action.

Application Requirements: Application form, financial need analysis, interview, transcript. *Deadline:* March 1.

Contact: Charles Smith, Assistant Secretary
  Phone: 919-733-3851
  Fax: 919-733-2834
  E-mail: charlie.smith@ncmail.net

NORTH CAROLINA VETERANS SCHOLARSHIPS CLASS IV

Awards for children of veterans, who were prisoner of war or missing in action. Duration of the scholarship is four academic years (8 semesters) if used within 8 years. No limit on number awarded each year. Award value is $4500 per nine-month academic year in private colleges and junior colleges.

Award: Scholarship for use in freshman, sophomore, junior, or senior years; renewable. *Amount:* $4500.

Eligibility Requirements: Applicant must be enrolled or expecting to enroll full- or part-time at a two-year or four-year or technical institution or university; resident of North Carolina and studying in North Carolina. Available to U.S. citizens. Applicant or parent must meet one or more of the following requirements: general military experience; retired from active duty; disabled or killed as a result of military service; prisoner of war; or missing in action.

Application Requirements: Application form, financial need analysis, interview, transcript. *Deadline:* continuous.

Contact: Charles Smith, Assistant Secretary
  Phone: 919-733-3851
  Fax: 919-733-2834
  E-mail: charlie.smith@ncmail.net

OHIO DEPARTMENT OF HIGHER EDUCATION

www.ohiohighered.org

OHIO WAR ORPHANS SCHOLARSHIP

• *See page 610*

OREGON DEPARTMENT OF VETERANS' AFFAIRS

http://www.oregon.gov/odva

OREGON VETERANS' EDUCATION AID

To be eligible, veteran must have actively served in U.S. armed forces 90 days and been discharged under honorable conditions. Must be U.S. citizen and Oregon resident. Korean War veteran or received campaign or expeditionary medal or ribbon awarded by U.S. armed forces for services after June 30, 1958. Full-time students receive up to $150 per month, and part-time students receive up to $100 per month for a maximum of 36 months. Length of benefits depend on length of service. Payments contingent upon available funding.

Award: Grant for use in freshman, sophomore, junior, senior, graduate, or postgraduate years; not renewable. *Number:* 1–200. *Amount:* $3600–$5400.

Eligibility Requirements: Applicant must be enrolled or expecting to enroll full- or part-time at a two-year or four-year or technical institution or university; resident of Oregon and studying in Oregon. Available to U.S. citizens. Applicant must have general military experience.

Application Requirements: Application form, certified copy of DD Form 214. *Deadline:* continuous.

Contact: Loriann Sheridan, Veterans Programs Consultant
  Oregon Department of Veterans' Affairs
  700 Summer Street, NE
  Salem, OR 97301-1289
  Phone: 503-373-2264
  Fax: 503-373-2393
  E-mail: sheridl@odva.state.or.us

PETAZI

https://petazi.com/

2017 NURTURE FOR NATURE SCHOLARSHIP
• *See page 637*

THE RESERVE OFFICERS ASSOCIATION

http://www.roa.org/

HENRY J. REILLY MEMORIAL SCHOLARSHIP-HIGH SCHOOL SENIORS AND FIRST YEAR FRESHMEN
• *See page 557*

HENRY J. REILLY MEMORIAL UNDERGRADUATE SCHOLARSHIP PROGRAM FOR COLLEGE ATTENDEES
• *See page 557*

RETIRED ENLISTED ASSOCIATION

http://www.trea.org/

RETIRED ENLISTED ASSOCIATION SCHOLARSHIP

One-time award for dependent children or grandchildren of a TREA member or TREA auxiliary member in good standing.

Award: Scholarship for use in freshman, sophomore, junior, senior, graduate, or postgraduate years; not renewable. *Amount:* $1000–$1500.

Eligibility Requirements: Applicant must be enrolled or expecting to enroll full-time at a two-year or four-year or technical institution or university. Available to U.S. citizens. Applicant or parent must meet one or more of the following requirements: general military experience; retired from active duty; disabled or killed as a result of military service; prisoner of war; or missing in action.

Application Requirements: Application form, copy of IRS tax forms, essay, financial need analysis, personal photograph, recommendations or references, test scores, transcript. *Deadline:* April 30.

Contact: Donnell Minnis, Executive Assistant
Phone: 303-752-0660
Fax: 303-752-0835
E-mail: execasst@trea.org

SCHOLARSHIP AMERICA

www.scholarshipamerica.org

WELLS FARGO VETERANS SCHOLARSHIP PROGRAM

The Wells Fargo Veterans Scholarship Program is designed to help meet the needs of veterans after military benefits and other grants and scholarships have been utilized. The scholarship program will award renewable scholarships for up to $7,000 per year to honorably-discharged veterans or spouses of disabled veterans who are high school or GED graduates and who have served in the United States military. Qualified applicants must have a minimum grade point average of 2.5 on a 4.0 scale or its equivalent and plan to enroll in full-time undergraduate or graduate (first Masters degree) study at an accredited two- or four-year college, university, or vocational-technical school for the 2017-2018 academic year. Each award renewal will increase by $1,000 over the previous year to encourage program completion. Visit www.scholarsapply.org/wellsfargoveterans for more information and to apply.

Award: Scholarship for use in freshman, sophomore, junior, senior, or graduate years; renewable.

Eligibility Requirements: Applicant must be enrolled or expecting to enroll part-time at a two-year or four-year or technical institution or university. Applicant must have 2.5 GPA or higher. Available to U.S. citizens. Applicant must have general military experience.

Application Requirements: Application form. *Deadline:* February 28.

Contact: Program Manager Scholarship America
Scholarship America
One Scholarship Way
St. Peter, MN 56082
Phone: 800-537-4180
E-mail: wellsfargoveterans@scholarshipamerica.org

SOUTH CAROLINA DIVISION OF VETERANS AFFAIRS

http://www.govoepp.state.sc.us/vetaff.htm

EDUCATIONAL ASSISTANCE FOR CERTAIN WAR VETERANS DEPENDENTS SCHOLARSHIP-SOUTH CAROLINA

Free tuition for South Carolina residents whose parent is a resident, wartime veteran, and meets one of these criteria. Must be awarded Purple Heart or Congressional Medal of Honor; permanently and totally disabled or killed as a result of military service; prisoner of war; or missing in action. Must be age 18 to 26 and enrolled or expecting to enroll full or part-time at a two-year or four-year technical institution or university in South Carolina. Complete information and qualifications for this award are on website http://www.govoepp.state.sc.us.

Award: Scholarship for use in freshman, sophomore, junior, or senior years; not renewable.

Eligibility Requirements: Applicant must be age 18-26; enrolled or expecting to enroll full- or part-time at a two-year or four-year or technical institution or university; resident of South Carolina and studying in South Carolina. Available to U.S. citizens. Applicant or parent must meet one or more of the following requirements: general military experience; retired from active duty; disabled or killed as a result of military service; prisoner of war; or missing in action.

Application Requirements: Application form, proof of qualification of veteran, transcript. *Deadline:* continuous.

Contact: Adm. Dorian Sease-Phillips, Free Tuition Coordinator
Phone: 803-647-2434
E-mail: va@oepp.sc.gov

TENNESSEE STUDENT ASSISTANCE CORPORATION

http://www.tn.gov/collegepays

HELPING HEROES GRANT

• *See page 619*

UNIVERSITY OF WYOMING

http://www.uwyo.edu/scholarships

VIETNAM VETERANS AWARD-WYOMING

Scholarship available to Wyoming residents who served in the armed forces between August 5, 1964 and May 7, 1975, and received a Vietnam service medal.

Award: Scholarship for use in freshman, sophomore, junior, or senior years; renewable.

Eligibility Requirements: Applicant must be enrolled or expecting to enroll full- or part-time at a two-year or four-year institution or university and resident of Wyoming. Available to U.S. citizens. Applicant or parent must meet one or more of the following requirements: general military experience; retired from active duty; disabled or killed as a result of military service; prisoner of war; or missing in action.

Application Requirements: Application form. *Deadline:* continuous.

Contact: Tammy Mack, Assistant Director, Scholarships
University of Wyoming
Department 3335
1000 East University Avenue
Laramie, WY 82071
Phone: 307-766-2412
Fax: 307-766-3800
E-mail: FinAid@uwyo.edu

VETERANS UNITED FOUNDATION

http://www.enhancelives.com

VETERANS UNITED FOUNDATION SCHOLARSHIP

This scholarship is for active military members, veterans, spouses of military members, and children of military members currently pursuing a post-secondary degree. The program's primary goal is to assist military service members and their families by awarding up to twenty $2000 scholarships per semester to help pay for tuition and books. For more information visit http://www.enhancelives.com/scholarships

Award: Scholarship for use in freshman, sophomore, junior, senior, graduate, or postgraduate years; not renewable. *Number:* 5–20. *Amount:* $2000.

Eligibility Requirements: Applicant must be enrolled or expecting to enroll full- or part-time at a two-year or four-year or technical institution or university. Applicant must have 2.5 GPA or higher. Available to U.S. citizens. Applicant or parent must meet one or more of the following requirements: general military experience; retired from active duty; disabled or killed as a result of military service; prisoner of war; or missing in action.

Application Requirements: Application form, application form may be submitted online (http://www.enhancelives.com/scholarships), essay, personal photograph, transcript. *Deadline:* April 30.

Contact: Mrs. Miranda Giger, Foundation Outreach Coordinator
Veterans United Foundation
1400 Veterans United Drive
Columbia, MO 65203
E-mail: miranda.giger@veteransunited.com

VIRGINIA DEPARTMENT OF VETERANS SERVICES

http://www.dvs.virginia.gov/

VIRGINIA MILITARY SURVIVORS AND DEPENDENTS EDUCATION PROGRAM

Scholarships for post-secondary students between ages 16 and 29 to attend Virginia state-supported institutions. Must be child or surviving spouse of veteran who has either been permanently or totally disabled due to war or other armed conflict; died as a result of war or other armed conflict; or been listed as a POW or MIA. Parent must also meet Virginia residency requirements.

Award: Scholarship for use in freshman, sophomore, junior, senior, or graduate years; renewable.

Eligibility Requirements: Applicant must be age 16-29; enrolled or expecting to enroll full-time at a two-year or four-year or technical institution or university; resident of Virginia and studying in Virginia. Available to U.S. citizens. Applicant or parent must meet one or more of the following requirements: general military experience; retired from active duty; disabled or killed as a result of military service; prisoner of war; or missing in action.

Application Requirements: Application form, DD214 of service member, birth certificate of applicant, marriage certificate, acceptance letter from institution. *Deadline:* varies.

Contact: Mrs. Doris Sullivan, Coordinator
Virginia Department of Veterans Services
1351 Hershberger Road, Suite 220
Roanoke, VA 24012
Phone: 540-561-6625
Fax: 540-857-7573

WISCONSIN DEPARTMENT OF VETERANS AFFAIRS (WDVA)

http://www.dva.state.wi.us/

VETERANS EDUCATION (VETED) REIMBURSEMENT GRANT
• *See page 639*

WOMEN'S JEWELRY ASSOCIATION

http://www.womensjewelryassociation.com

WOMEN'S JEWELRY ASSOCIATIONS VETERANS GRANT
• *See page 627*

MILITARY SERVICE: MARINES

ELEARNERS.COM

http://www.elearners.com

ELEARNERS MILITARY SCHOLARSHIP
• *See page 640*

FIRST MARINE DIVISION ASSOCIATION

http://www.1stmarinedivisionassociation.org/

FIRST MARINE DIVISION ASSOCIATION SCHOLARSHIP FUND

Scholarship to assist dependents of deceased or 100 percent permanently disabled veterans of service with the 1st Marine Division in furthering their education towards a Bachelor's degree. Awarded to full-time, undergraduate students who are attending an accredited college, university, or higher technical trade school, up to a maximum of four years.

Award: Scholarship for use in freshman, sophomore, junior, or senior years; not renewable. *Amount:* up to $1750.

Eligibility Requirements: Applicant must be enrolled or expecting to enroll full-time at a four-year or technical institution or university and single. Available to U.S. citizens. Applicant or parent must meet one or more of the following requirements: Marine Corps experience; retired from active duty; disabled or killed as a result of military service; prisoner of war; or missing in action.

Application Requirements: Application form, essay, personal photograph, social security number, birth certificate, proof of parent's death, transcript. *Deadline:* continuous.

Contact: Col. Len Hayes, Executive Director
Phone: 760-967-8561
Fax: 760-967-8567
E-mail: oldbreed@sbcglobal.net

IMAGINE AMERICA FOUNDATION

www.imagine-america.org

MILITARY AWARD PROGRAM (MAP)
• *See page 641*

KITCHEN GUIDES

http://www.kitchensguides.com/

SMART KITCHEN IMPROVEMENT SCHOLARSHIP BY KITCHEN GUIDES
• *See page 598*

LADIES AUXILIARY OF THE FLEET RESERVE ASSOCIATION

http://www.fra.org/

LADIES AUXILIARY OF THE FLEET RESERVE ASSOCIATION SCHOLARSHIP
• *See page 547*

SAM ROSE MEMORIAL SCHOLARSHIP
• *See page 548*

MARINE CORPS TANKERS ASSOCIATION INC.

http://www.USMarinetankers.org/

MARINE CORPS TANKERS ASSOCIATION, JOHN CORNELIUS/MAX ENGLISH SCHOLARSHIP

Award for Marine tankers or former Marine tankers, or dependents of Marines who served in a tank unit and are on active duty, retired, reserve or have been honorably discharged. Applicant must be a high school graduate or planning to graduate in June. May be enrolled in college, undergraduate or graduate or have previously attended college. Must be a member of MCTA or intends to join in the future.

Award: Scholarship for use in freshman, sophomore, junior, senior, or graduate years; not renewable. *Number:* 10. *Amount:* up to $2000.

Eligibility Requirements: Applicant must be enrolled or expecting to enroll full-time at a two-year or four-year or technical institution or university. Available to U.S. citizens. Applicant or parent must meet one or more of the following requirements: Marine Corps experience; retired from active duty; disabled or killed as a result of military service; prisoner of war; or missing in action.

Application Requirements: Application form, essay, personal photograph, recommendations or references, test scores, transcript. *Deadline:* March 15.

Contact: Phil Morell, Scholarship Chair
Marine Corps Tankers Association Inc.
1112 Alpine Heights Road
Alpine, CA 91901-2814
Phone: 619-445-8423
Fax: 619-445-8423
E-mail: mpmorell@cox.net

PETAZI

https://petazi.com/

2017 NURTURE FOR NATURE SCHOLARSHIP
• See page 637

SECOND MARINE DIVISION ASSOCIATION

http://www.2dmardiv.com/

SECOND MARINE DIVISION ASSOCIATION MEMORIAL SCHOLARSHIP FUND

Renewable award for students who are unmarried, dependent sons, daughters or grandchildren of former or current members of Second Marine Division or attached units. Must submit proof of parent's or grandparent's service. Family adjusted gross income must not exceed $75,000. Award is merit-based. Minimum 2.5 GPA required.

Award: Scholarship for use in freshman, sophomore, junior, or senior years; not renewable. *Number:* 35–42. *Amount:* $1200–$1500.

Eligibility Requirements: Applicant must be enrolled or expecting to enroll full-time at a two-year or four-year or technical institution or university and single. Applicant must have 2.5 GPA or higher. Available to U.S. and non-U.S. citizens. Applicant must have served in the Marine Corps or Navy.

Application Requirements: Application form, essay, financial need analysis, personal photograph, recommendations or references, self-addressed stamped envelope with application, transcript. *Deadline:* April 1.

Contact: Mr. Martin McNulty, Chairman, Board of Trustees, SMDA
Memorial Scholarship Fund
Second Marine Division Association
280 Briarwood Road
Tyrone, GA 30290
Phone: 678-364-1328

TAILHOOK EDUCATIONAL FOUNDATION

http://www.tailhook.org/

TAILHOOK EDUCATIONAL FOUNDATION SCHOLARSHIP
• See page 649

WISCONSIN DEPARTMENT OF VETERANS AFFAIRS (WDVA)

http://www.dva.state.wi.us/

VETERANS EDUCATION (VETED) REIMBURSEMENT GRANT
• See page 639

MILITARY SERVICE: NAVY

ANCHOR SCHOLARSHIP FOUNDATION

http://www.anchorscholarship.com/

ANCHOR SCHOLARSHIP FOUNDATION PROGRAM

Must be dependent child or spouse of U.S. Navy service member (active or retired) having served at least six years under administrative control of U.S. Naval Surface Forces, Atlantic or Pacific Fleets. Dependent child must be pursuing full-time their first Bachelor's degree at a four-year college or university. Spouse applicants may attend either full or part-time at either a two- or four-year college or university in pursuit of their first Associate's or Bachelor's degree. Eligibility must first be determined by submitting an eligibility application. This application is available online in the fall. Be prepared to submit sponsor's full name, rank/rate, list of duty stations, home-ports, ship hull numbers, dates served aboard, and supporting documentation. Once eligibility is confirmed, the scholarship application will be sent via e-mail. Selection basis: academics, extracurricular activities, character, and financial need.

Award: Scholarship for use in freshman, sophomore, junior, or senior years; not renewable. *Number:* 35–43. *Amount:* $2000–$5000.

Eligibility Requirements: Applicant must be enrolled or expecting to enroll full- or part-time at a two-year or four-year institution or university. Available to U.S. citizens. Applicant or parent must meet one or more of the following requirements: Navy experience; retired from active duty; disabled or killed as a result of military service; prisoner of war; or missing in action.

Application Requirements: Application form, eligibility application (online), essay, financial need analysis, recommendations or references, self-addressed stamped envelope with application, test scores, transcript. *Deadline:* March 1.

Contact: Mrs. Ingrid Turner, Director of Operations
Anchor Scholarship Foundation
4966 Euclid Road
Suite 109
Virginia Beach, VA 23462
Phone: 757-671-3200 Ext. Opt 3
E-mail: scholarshipadmin@anchorscholarship.com

ELEARNERS.COM

http://www.elearners.com

ELEARNERS MILITARY SCHOLARSHIP
• See page 640

GAMEWARDENS OF VIETNAM ASSOCIATION INC.

http://www.tf116.org/

GAMEWARDENS OF VIETNAM SCHOLARSHIP

Scholarship for entering freshman who is a descendant of a U.S. Navy man or woman who worked with TF-116 in Vietnam. One-time award, but applicant may reapply.

Award: Scholarship for use in freshman year; not renewable. *Number:* 1–3. *Amount:* $500.

Eligibility Requirements: Applicant must be high school student; age 16-21 and planning to enroll or expecting to enroll full-time at a two-year or four-year or technical institution or university. Applicant must have 2.5 GPA or higher. Available to U.S. and non-U.S. citizens. Applicant or parent must meet one or more of the following requirements: Navy experience; retired from active duty; disabled or killed as a result of military service; prisoner of war; or missing in action.

Application Requirements: Application form, recommendations or references, resume, test scores, transcript. *Deadline:* April 1.

Contact: David Ajax, Scholarship Coordinator
Gamewardens of Vietnam Association Inc.
6630 Perry Court
Arvada, CO 80003
Phone: 303-426-6385
Fax: 303-426-6186
E-mail: dpajax@comcast.net

IMAGINE AMERICA FOUNDATION

www.imagine-america.org

MILITARY AWARD PROGRAM (MAP)
• *See page 641*

KITCHEN GUIDES

http://www.kitchensguides.com/

SMART KITCHEN IMPROVEMENT SCHOLARSHIP BY KITCHEN GUIDES
• *See page 598*

LADIES AUXILIARY OF THE FLEET RESERVE ASSOCIATION

http://www.fra.org/

LADIES AUXILIARY OF THE FLEET RESERVE ASSOCIATION SCHOLARSHIP
• *See page 547*

SAM ROSE MEMORIAL SCHOLARSHIP
• *See page 548*

PETAZI

https://petazi.com/

2017 NURTURE FOR NATURE SCHOLARSHIP
• *See page 637*

SECOND MARINE DIVISION ASSOCIATION

http://www.2dmardiv.com/

SECOND MARINE DIVISION ASSOCIATION MEMORIAL SCHOLARSHIP FUND
• *See page 664*

TAILHOOK EDUCATIONAL FOUNDATION

http://www.tailhook.org/

TAILHOOK EDUCATIONAL FOUNDATION SCHOLARSHIP
• *See page 649*

UDT-SEAL ASSOCIATION

http://www.nswfoundation.org/

HAD RICHARDS UDT-SEAL MEMORIAL SCHOLARSHIP

One-time award for dependent children of UDT-SEAL association members. Freshmen given priority. Applicant may not be older than 22 and not married. Must be U.S. citizen.

Award: Scholarship for use in freshman, sophomore, junior, or senior years; not renewable. *Number:* 1–2.

Eligibility Requirements: Applicant must be enrolled or expecting to enroll full-time at a two-year or four-year institution or university and single. Available to U.S. citizens. Applicant or parent must meet one or more of the following requirements: Navy experience; retired from active duty; disabled or killed as a result of military service; prisoner of war; or missing in action.

Application Requirements: Application form, essay, personal photograph, proof of active duty or parent/spouse's active duty, test scores, transcript. *Deadline:* varies.

Contact: Robert Rieve, President and CEO
Phone: 757-363-7490
E-mail: info@nswfoundation.org

NAVAL SPECIAL WARFARE SCHOLARSHIP

Awards given to active duty SEAL's, SWCC's, and other active duty military serving in a Naval Special Warfare command or their spouses and dependents.

Award: Scholarship for use in freshman, sophomore, junior, or senior years; not renewable. *Number:* 80–100.

Eligibility Requirements: Applicant must be enrolled or expecting to enroll full- or part-time at a two-year or four-year institution or university. Available to U.S. citizens. Applicant or parent must meet one or more of the following requirements: Navy experience; retired from active duty; disabled or killed as a result of military service; prisoner of war; or missing in action.

Application Requirements: Application form, essay, personal photograph, proof of active duty or parent/spouse's active duty, transcript.

Contact: Robert Rieve, President and CEO
Phone: 757-363-7490
E-mail: info@nswfoundation.org

UDT-SEAL SCHOLARSHIP

Award for dependent children of UDT-SEAL association members. Freshmen given priority. Applicant may not be older than 22 and not married. Must be U.S. citizen.

Award: Scholarship for use in freshman, sophomore, junior, or senior years; not renewable. *Number:* 10–20.

Eligibility Requirements: Applicant must be enrolled or expecting to enroll full-time at a two-year or four-year or technical institution or university and single. Available to U.S. citizens. Applicant or parent must meet one or more of the following requirements: Navy experience; retired from active duty; disabled or killed as a result of military service; prisoner of war; or missing in action.

Application Requirements: Application form, essay, personal photograph, proof of active duty or parent/spouse's active duty, test scores, transcript. *Deadline:* varies.

Contact: Robert Rieve, President and CEO
Phone: 757-363-7490
E-mail: info@nswfoundation.org

UNITED STATES SUBMARINE VETERANS

https://www.ussvi.org/home.asp

UNITED STATES SUBMARINE VETERANS INC. NATIONAL SCHOLARSHIP PROGRAM
• *See page 566*

WINGS OVER AMERICA SCHOLARSHIP FOUNDATION

http://www.wingsoveramerica.us/

WINGS OVER AMERICA SCHOLARSHIP FOUNDATION

Applicant must be graduates of an accredited high school or the equivalent home school or institution and must plan to attend an accredited academic institution. Scholarship awardees must be enrolled full-time in order to receive their award. Awards may be used for tuition and tuition-related fees only.

Award: Scholarship for use in freshman, sophomore, or junior years; not renewable. *Number:* 50. *Amount:* $3000.

Eligibility Requirements: Applicant must be enrolled or expecting to enroll full-time at a two-year or four-year or technical institution or university. Available to U.S. citizens. Applicant must have served in the Navy.

Application Requirements: Application form, community service, essay. *Deadline:* February 1.

Contact: Melissa Garrison, Scholarship Administrator
Wings Over America Scholarship Foundation
4966 Euclid Drive
Suite 109
Virginia Beach, VA 23452
Phone: 757-671-3200 Ext. 2
E-mail: scholarship@wingsoveramerica.us

WISCONSIN DEPARTMENT OF VETERANS AFFAIRS (WDVA)

http://www.dva.state.wi.us/

VETERANS EDUCATION (VETED) REIMBURSEMENT GRANT
• *See page 639*

NATIONALITY OR ETHNIC HERITAGE

1-800-HANSONS

www.hansons.com

1-800-HANSONS SCHOLARSHIP PROGRAM
• *See page 572*

4MYCASH.COM, LLC

https://www.4mycash.com

4MYCASH ST. LOUIS HARD MONEY SCHOLARSHIP
• *See page 572*

THE 5 STRONG SCHOLARSHIP FOUNDATION, INC.

http://5strongscholars.org

5 STRONG SCHOLARS SCHOLARSHIP

The applicants must reside in the Metropolitan Atlanta area (Cobb, Fulton, Clayton, Fayette, Douglas, Gwinett, DeKalb, etc). If chosen, applicants must be able to attend bi-monthly college prep sessions. Minimum requirements: GPA: 2.5 and ACT: 21, SAT: 1010

Award: Scholarship for use in freshman, sophomore, junior, or senior years; renewable. *Number:* 25. *Amount:* $10,000–$16,000.

Eligibility Requirements: Applicant must be American Indian/Alaska Native, Asian/Pacific Islander, Black (non-Hispanic), Hispanic; high school student; age 17-19; planning to enroll or expecting to enroll full-time at a four-year institution or university; resident of Georgia and studying in Georgia. Applicant must have 3.0 GPA or higher. Available to U.S. citizens.

Application Requirements: Application form, interview. *Deadline:* December 31.

Contact: Drew Ragland
The 5 Strong Scholarship Foundation, Inc.
103 Pinegate Rd
Peachtree City 30269
E-mail: 5strongscholars@gmail.com

A-1 AUTO TRANSPORT, INC.

https://www.a1autotransport.com/a-1-auto-transport-scholarship/

A-1 AUTO TRANSPORT SCHOLARSHIP
• *See page 572*

ABBVIE INC.

https://www.abbvie.com/

ABBVIE IMMUNOLOGY SCHOLARSHIP
• *See page 572*

AIR FORCE RESERVE OFFICER TRAINING CORPS

http://www.afrotc.com/

AFROTC HBCU SCHOLARSHIP PROGRAM
• *See page 639*

AIR TRAFFIC CONTROL ASSOCIATION INC.

http://www.atca.org/

AIR TRAFFIC CONTROL ASSOCIATION SCHOLARSHIP
• *See page 573*

BUCKINGHAM MEMORIAL SCHOLARSHIP
• *See page 573*

LAWRENCE C. FORTIER MEMORIAL SCHOLARSHIP
• *See page 573*

ALBERTA HERITAGE SCHOLARSHIP FUND

http://www.alis.alberta.ca/

ADULT HIGH SCHOOL EQUIVALENCY SCHOLARSHIPS

Awards of CAN$500 to recognize and reward the academic achievement of mature students in the attainment of high school equivalency and provide an incentive for students to continue their education at the postsecondary level. Applicants must be residents of Alberta, have been out of high school for a minimum of three years prior to commencing a high school equivalency program, and be enrolled full-time in a high school equivalency program. Must be nominated by high school. See website for additional information and application http://alis.alberta.ca.

Award: Scholarship for use in freshman year; not renewable. *Number:* up to 200.

Eligibility Requirements: Applicant must be Canadian citizen; enrolled or expecting to enroll full-time at a two-year or four-year or technical institution or university and resident of Alberta. Applicant must have 3.0 GPA or higher.

Application Requirements: Application form, nomination. *Deadline:* September 1.

Contact: Scholarship Committee
Alberta Heritage Scholarship Fund
9940 106th Street, Fourth Floor
PO Box 28000, Station Main
Edmonton, AB T5J 4R4
CAN
Phone: 780-427-8640
Fax: 780-422-4516
E-mail: scholarships@gov.ab.ca

ALBERTA CENTENNIAL SCHOLARSHIPS-ALBERTA

25 awards of CAN$2005 have been established to commemorate the province of Alberta's centennial. Must be Canadian citizens or permanent residents of Canada and Alberta residents. Awards students entering any level of postsecondary study at any university, college, technical institute, or apprenticeship program in Canada. Each high school in Alberta nominates a recipient and all are considered for the 25 awards. For additional information and application form, visit website http://alis.alberta.ca.

Award: Scholarship for use in freshman, sophomore, junior, or senior years; not renewable. *Number:* 25.

Eligibility Requirements: Applicant must be Canadian citizen; high school student; planning to enroll or expecting to enroll full-time at a two-year or four-year or technical institution or university and resident of Alberta.

Application Requirements: Nomination from high school counselors. *Deadline:* June 1.

Contact: Scholarship Committee
Phone: 780-427-8640
E-mail: scholarships@gov.ab.ca

ALEXANDER RUTHERFORD SCHOLARSHIPS FOR HIGH SCHOOL ACHIEVEMENT

Award of up to CAN$2500 available to high school students who are residents of Alberta and plan to enroll in or are enrolled in a full-time postsecondary program of at least one semester. Awarded on the basis of achieving an 75 percent average on five designated subjects in grades 10, 11, and 12. Application deadlines are May 1 for September start date and December 1 for January start date. For additional information, see website http://alis.alberta.ca.

Award: Scholarship for use in freshman year; not renewable.

Eligibility Requirements: Applicant must be Canadian citizen; high school student; planning to enroll or expecting to enroll full-time at a two-year or four-year or technical institution or university and resident of Alberta.

Application Requirements: Application form, transcript. *Deadline:* varies.

Contact: Scholarship Committee
Phone: 780-427-8640
E-mail: scholarships@gov.ab.ca

CHARLES S. NOBLE JUNIOR FOOTBALL SCHOLARSHIPS

Scholarships of up to CAN$1000 available to reward the athletic and academic excellence of junior football players at universities, colleges, and technical institutes in Alberta. Must be Alberta residents and enrolled full-time in an undergraduate, professional, or graduate program at a university, college, or technical institute in Alberta. Must be a playing member on an Alberta junior football team and maintain 2.0 average in the previous semester. Students entering their first semester of post-secondary study do not have to meet this requirement. Interested applicants should contact their team coach or manager as nominations must come from the football team. For additional information, visit website http://alis.alberta.ca.

Award: Scholarship for use in freshman, sophomore, junior, senior, or graduate years; not renewable. *Number:* 30.

Eligibility Requirements: Applicant must be Canadian citizen; enrolled or expecting to enroll full-time at a two-year or four-year or technical institution or university; resident of Alberta; studying in Alberta and must have an interest in athletics/sports.

Application Requirements: Nomination from junior football team. *Deadline:* October 1.

Contact: Scholarship Committee
Phone: 780-427-8640
E-mail: scholarships@gov.ab.ca

CHARLES S. NOBLE JUNIOR HOCKEY SCHOLARSHIPS

Awards of CAN$2000 to reward the athletic and academic excellence of junior hockey league players and to provide an incentive and means for these players to continue their postsecondary education. Must be Alberta residents and enrolled full-time at a postsecondary institution in Alberta. Interested applicants should contact their team coach or manager, as nominations must come from the participant's hockey team. Applicants must have maintained a minimum average of 2.0 on a 4.0 scale in their previous semester. Students entering their first semester of post-secondary study do not have to meet this requirement. For additional information, see website http://alis.alberta.ca.

Award: Scholarship for use in freshman, sophomore, junior, or senior years; not renewable. *Number:* 10.

Eligibility Requirements: Applicant must be Canadian citizen; enrolled or expecting to enroll full-time at a two-year or four-year or technical institution or university; resident of Alberta; studying in Alberta and must have an interest in athletics/sports.

Application Requirements: Application form, essay, transcript. *Deadline:* December 1.

Contact: Scholarship Committee
Phone: 780-427-8640
E-mail: scholarships@gov.ab.ca

INTERNATIONAL EDUCATION AWARDS-UKRAINE

Awards of CAN$5000 to enable Alberta post-secondary students, post-graduates, professionals, and scholars to undertake career-related training, research, or study in Ukraine, and Ukrainian post-secondary students, post-graduates, professionals and scholars to undertake career-related training, research, or study in Alberta. Selection will be based on academic merit, past accomplishments, the purpose or validity of the proposal, reference letter, and institutional support and benefit to the recipient's institution. For additional information and application, see website http://alis.alberta.ca.

Award: Scholarship for use in freshman, sophomore, junior, or senior years; not renewable. *Number:* 5.

Eligibility Requirements: Applicant must be Canadian, Ukrainian citizen; enrolled or expecting to enroll full-time at a two-year or four-year or technical institution or university and studying in Alberta. Available to Canadian and non-U.S. citizens.

Application Requirements: Application form, recommendations or references. *Deadline:* February 1.

Contact: Scholarship Committee
Phone: 780-427-8640
E-mail: scholarships@gov.ab.ca

JIMMIE CONDON ATHLETIC SCHOLARSHIPS

Award of CAN$1800 available to Alberta residents enrolled full-time in an undergraduate, professional, or graduate program at a university, college, or technical institute in Alberta. Must be a member of a designated sports team or a Provincial Disabled Athletic Team recognized by the Alberta Athlete Development Program, and must be nominated by coach. For additional information, go to website http://alis.alberta.ca.

Award: Scholarship for use in freshman, sophomore, junior, or senior years; not renewable.

Eligibility Requirements: Applicant must be Canadian citizen; enrolled or expecting to enroll full-time at a two-year or four-year or technical institution or university; resident of Alberta; studying in Alberta and must have an interest in athletics/sports.

Application Requirements: Application form, nomination by athletic coach. *Deadline:* continuous.

Contact: Scholarship Committee
Phone: 780-427-8640
E-mail: scholarships@gov.ab.ca

JO-ANNE KOCH-ABC SOCIETY SCHOLARSHIP

Up to two scholarships of CAN$500 supporting gifted learners in their post-secondary studies. Applicants must have completed Grade 12 requirements at a publicly funded high school in Alberta and plan to pursue post-secondary studies. Applicants must meet the criteria for Giftedness as determined by their school jurisdiction. Preference will be given to applicants who have received extra support for their learning needs. For additional information, see website http://alis.alberta.ca.

Award: Scholarship for use in freshman year; not renewable. *Number:* up to 2.

Eligibility Requirements: Applicant must be Canadian citizen; high school student; planning to enroll or expecting to enroll full-time at a two-year or four-year institution or university and resident of Alberta.

Application Requirements: Application form, essay, recommendations or references. *Deadline:* April 1.

Contact: Scholarship Committee
Phone: 780-427-8640
E-mail: scholarships@gov.ab.ca

KEYERA ENERGY-PETER J. RENTON MEMORIAL SCHOLARSHIP

The scholarship is intended to assist and encourage Alberta students to pursue full-time studies in a post-secondary program in a field related to the oil and gas industry. CAN$3,000 for first year of study and CAN$3,000 renewable in second year providing recipient remains in good standing and continues into the second year. Family of Keyera Energy employees are eligible to apply. Relatives of the selection committee members are not eligible. For additional information, see website http://alis.alberta.ca.

Award: Scholarship for use in freshman or sophomore years; renewable.

Eligibility Requirements: Applicant must be Canadian citizen; high school student; planning to enroll or expecting to enroll full-time at a two-year or four-year or technical institution or university; resident of Alberta and studying in Alberta.

Application Requirements: Application form, essay, recommendations or references. *Deadline:* May 1.

Contact: Scholarship Committee
Phone: 780-427-8640
E-mail: scholarships@gov.ab.ca

LAURENCE DECORE AWARDS FOR STUDENT LEADERSHIP

Awards of CAN$1,000 for postsecondary students who have demonstrated outstanding dedication and leadership to fellow students and to their community. Must be Alberta residents who are currently enrolled in a minimum of three full courses at a designated Alberta postsecondary institution. Selected on the basis of involvement in either student government or student societies, clubs, or organizations. For additional information, visit website http://alis.alberta.ca.

Award: Scholarship for use in freshman, sophomore, junior, or senior years; not renewable. *Number:* 100.

Eligibility Requirements: Applicant must be Canadian citizen; enrolled or expecting to enroll full- or part-time at a two-year or four-year or technical institution or university; resident of Alberta; studying in Alberta and must have an interest in leadership.

Application Requirements: Application form, nomination from school. *Deadline:* March 1.

Contact: Scholarship Committee
Phone: 780-427-8640
E-mail: scholarships@gov.ab.ca

LOUISE MCKINNEY POST-SECONDARY SCHOLARSHIPS

Student awards of up to CAN$2500 to residents of Alberta who are enrolled at a university, college, or technical institute in the second or subsequent year of full-time study. Alberta students studying out-of-province because their program of study is not offered in Alberta will be considered for a scholarship if their class standing is in the top two percent of their program. Deadlines vary. For additional information, go to website http://alis.alberta.ca.

Award: Scholarship for use in sophomore, junior, or senior years; not renewable.

Eligibility Requirements: Applicant must be Canadian citizen; enrolled or expecting to enroll full-time at a two-year or four-year or technical institution or university and resident of Alberta.

Application Requirements: Application form, test scores, transcript. *Deadline:* varies.

Contact: Scholarship Committee
Phone: 780-427-8640
E-mail: scholarships@gov.ab.ca

PERSONS CASE SCHOLARSHIPS

Awards of up to CAN$5000 to assist female students whose studies will ultimately contribute to the advancement of women, or who are studying in a field that is non-traditional for women. Applicants must be residents of Alberta and enrolled full-time at a postsecondary institution in Alberta. Students studying out-of-province may be considered for this award if their program of study is not available in Alberta. Selection is based on chosen program of study, financial need, and academic achievement. For additional information and application, visit website http://alis.alberta.ca.

Award: Scholarship for use in freshman, sophomore, junior, senior, or graduate years; not renewable.

Eligibility Requirements: Applicant must be Canadian citizen; enrolled or expecting to enroll full-time at a four-year institution or university; female; resident of Alberta and studying in Alberta. Applicant must have 3.0 GPA or higher.

Application Requirements: Application form, essay, financial need analysis, resume, transcript. *Deadline:* September 30.

Contact: Scholarship Committee
Phone: 780-427-8640
E-mail: scholarships@gov.ab.ca

QUEEN ELIZABETH II GOLDEN JUBILEE CITIZENSHIP MEDAL

Award of CAN$5000, a medal and a letter of commendation from the Lieutenant Governor to recognize the eight most outstanding students among the recipients of a Premier's Citizenship Award in recognition of the Queen's Golden Jubilee. Applicant must be a Canadian citizen or permanent resident and be nominated for this award. For additional information, see website http://alis.alberta.ca.

Award: Prize for use in freshman year; not renewable. *Number:* 8.

Eligibility Requirements: Applicant must be Canadian citizen; high school student; planning to enroll or expecting to enroll full-time at a four-year institution or university and resident of Alberta.

Application Requirements: Nomination. *Deadline:* June 1.

Contact: Scholarship Committee
Phone: 780-427-8640
E-mail: scholarships@gov.ab.ca

RUTHERFORD SCHOLARS

Award of CAN $2500 for Alberta residents based of results obtained on Diploma Examinations in English 30, or Francais 30, Social Studies 30, and three other subjects. Averages normally are in the 98.0 to 98.8 percent range. Only the first writing of the diploma exam will be considered. No application is required. Recipients are selected from all Alexander Rutherford Scholarship applications received before August 1.

Award: Scholarship for use in freshman year; not renewable. *Number:* 10.

Eligibility Requirements: Applicant must be Canadian citizen; high school student; planning to enroll or expecting to enroll full-time at a four-year institution or university and resident of Alberta.

Application Requirements: Test scores, transcript. *Deadline:* August 1.

Contact: Scholarship Committee
Phone: 780-427-8640
E-mail: scholarships@gov.ab.ca

ALERTONE SERVICES LLC

https://www.alert-1.com/

ALERT1 STUDENT FOR SENIORS SCHOLARSHIP
• *See page 573*

ALGAECAL INC.

https://www.algaecal.com/

ALGAECAL SCHOLARSHIP
• *See page 573*

ALLIANCE FOR YOUNG ARTISTS AND WRITERS INC.

http://www.artandwriting.org/

SCHOLASTIC ART AND WRITING AWARDS
• *See page 574*

ALLTHEROOMS

http://alltherooms.com

ROOM TO TRAVEL - STUDY ABROAD SCHOLARSHIP
• *See page 574*

AMERICAN ASSOCIATION OF TEACHERS OF JAPANESE BRIDGING CLEARINGHOUSE FOR STUDY ABROAD IN JAPAN

http://www.aatj.org

BRIDGING SCHOLARSHIP FOR STUDY ABROAD IN JAPAN
• *See page 574*

AMERICAN COUNCIL OF THE BLIND

http://www.acb.org/

AMERICAN COUNCIL OF THE BLIND SCHOLARSHIPS
• *See page 574*

AMERICAN INDIAN EDUCATION FOUNDATION

http://www.aiefprograms.org/

AMERICAN INDIAN EDUCATION FOUNDATION SCHOLARSHIP

AIEF provides tuition and books for American Indian students. 200 undergraduate, 25 graduate scholarships.

Award: Scholarship for use in freshman, sophomore, junior, senior, or graduate years; not renewable. *Number:* 200. *Amount:* $2000.

Eligibility Requirements: Applicant must be of Indian heritage; American Indian/Alaska Native and enrolled or expecting to enroll full- or part-time at a two-year or four-year or technical institution or university. Available to U.S. citizens.

Application Requirements: Application form, certificate of Tribal enrollment, community service, essay, personal photograph, transcript. *Deadline:* April 4.

Contact: Murray Lee, Scholarship Specialist
American Indian Education Foundation
2401 Eglin Street
Rapid City, SD 57703
Phone: 605-342-9968
E-mail: mlee@nrc1.org

AMERICAN INDIAN GRADUATE CENTER

http://www.aigcs.org/

ACCENTURE AMERICAN INDIAN SCHOLARSHIP

Scholarships awarded to American Indian and Alaska Natives from U.S. federally recognized tribes. This program is for first year college freshmen (undergraduate) students. Must have a cumulative GPA of a 3.25 on a 4.0 scale and demonstrate financial need. Areas of study: engineering, computer science, operations management, finance, marketing and business.

Award: Scholarship for use in freshman year; renewable.

Eligibility Requirements: Applicant must be American Indian/Alaska Native; high school student and planning to enroll or expecting to enroll full-time at a four-year institution or university. Available to U.S. citizens.

Application Requirements: Application form, community service, essay, financial need analysis, personal photograph, recommendations or references, transcript, tribal eligibility certificate. *Deadline:* January 30.

Contact: Marveline Vallo Gabbard, Program Associate
American Indian Graduate Center
3701 San Mateo Boulevard, NE, Suite 200
Albuquerque, NM 87110
Phone: 505-881-4584
Fax: 505-884-0427
E-mail: fellowships@aigcs.org

GATES MILLENNIUM SCHOLARS PROGRAM

Award enables American-Indian/Alaska native students to complete an undergraduate and graduate education. Must be entering a U.S. accredited college or university as a full-time student. Minimum 3.3 GPA required. Must demonstrate leadership abilities. Must meet federal Pell Grant eligibility criteria. Visit website at http://www.gmsp.org.

Award: Scholarship for use in freshman, sophomore, junior, senior, or graduate years; renewable. *Number:* 150. *Amount:* $500–$20,000.

Eligibility Requirements: Applicant must be American Indian/Alaska Native; enrolled or expecting to enroll full-time at a two-year or four-year institution or university and must have an interest in leadership. Available to U.S. citizens.

Application Requirements: Application form, financial need analysis, nomination packet, recommendations or references. *Deadline:* January 16.

Contact: Christa Moya, GMS Representative
American Indian Graduate Center
4520 Montgomery Boulevard, NE
Suite 1-B
Albuquerque, NM 87109
Phone: 866-884-7007
Fax: 505-884-8683
E-mail: christa@aigcs.org

WELLS FARGO SCHOLARSHIP AMERICAN INDIAN SCHOLARSHIP

Must be an enrolled member of a U.S. federally recognized American Indian or Alaska Native tribe. Be pursuing a degree in the banking, resort management, gaming operations, management and administration, including accounting, finance, information technology and human resources. Must have a cumulative GPA of a 3.0 on a 4.0 scale and demonstrate financial need.

Award: Scholarship for use in junior, senior, or graduate years; renewable.

Eligibility Requirements: Applicant must be American Indian/Alaska Native and enrolled or expecting to enroll full-time at a four-year institution or university. Applicant must have 3.0 GPA or higher. Available to U.S. citizens.

Application Requirements: Application form, community service, essay, financial need analysis, personal photograph, transcript, tribal eligibility certificate. *Deadline:* May 15.

Contact: Marveline Vallo Gabbard, Program Associate
American Indian Graduate Center
3701 San Mateo Boulevard, NE, Suite 200
Albuquerque, NM 87110
Phone: 505-881-4584
Fax: 505-884-0427
E-mail: fellowships@aigcs.org

AMERICAN INSTITUTE FOR FOREIGN STUDY

http://www.aifsabroad.com/

AIFS DIVERSITYABROAD.COM SCHOLARSHIP

Scholarships are available for students studying abroad on any program offered by a DiversityAbroad.com member organization. African-American, Asian-American, Hispanic/Latino and Native-American students are strongly encouraged to apply. Visit http://www.aifsabroad.com/scholarships.asp for more information.

Award: Scholarship for use in freshman, sophomore, junior, or senior years; not renewable. *Number:* up to 20. *Amount:* up to $1000.

Eligibility Requirements: Applicant must be American Indian/Alaska Native, Asian/Pacific Islander, Black (non-Hispanic), Hispanic; enrolled or expecting to enroll full-time at a two-year or four-year institution or university and must have an interest in international exchange. Applicant must have 3.5 GPA or higher. Available to U.S. citizens.

Application Requirements: Application form, essay, personal photograph, recommendations or references, resume, transcript. *Fee:* $95. *Deadline:* varies.

Contact: David Mauro, Admissions Counselor
American Institute for Foreign Study
River Plaza, 9 West Broad Street
Stamford, CT 06902-3788
Phone: 800-727-2437 Ext. 5163
Fax: 203-399-5463
E-mail: dmauro@aifs.com

AIFS-HACU SCHOLARSHIPS

Scholarships to outstanding Hispanic students to study abroad with AIFS. Available to students attending HACU member schools. Students will receive scholarships of up to 50 percent of the full program fee. Students must meet all standard AIFS eligibility requirements. Deadlines: April 15 for fall, October 1 for spring, and March 15 for summer.

Award: Scholarship for use in freshman, sophomore, junior, or senior years; not renewable. *Number:* up to 1. *Amount:* $6000–$8000.

Eligibility Requirements: Applicant must be Hispanic; enrolled or expecting to enroll full-time at a two-year or four-year institution or university and must have an interest in international exchange. Applicant must have 3.0 GPA or higher. Available to U.S. and non-U.S. citizens.

Application Requirements: Application form, essay, personal photograph, recommendations or references, transcript. *Fee:* $95. *Deadline:* varies.

Contact: David Mauro, Admissions Counselor
American Institute for Foreign Study
1 High Ridge Park
Stamford, CT 06905
Phone: 800-727-2437 Ext. 5163
Fax: 203-399-5463
E-mail: dmauro@aifs.com

AMERICAN LEGION AUXILIARY DEPARTMENT OF WISCONSIN

http://www.amlegionauxwi.org/

AMERICAN LEGION AUXILIARY DEPARTMENT OF WISCONSIN DELLA VAN DEUREN MEMORIAL SCHOLARSHIP
• *See page 531*

AMERICAN LEGION AUXILIARY DEPARTMENT OF WISCONSIN H.S. AND ANGELINE LEWIS SCHOLARSHIPS
• *See page 531*

AMERICAN LEGION AUXILIARY DEPARTMENT OF WISCONSIN MERIT AND MEMORIAL SCHOLARSHIPS
• *See page 531*

AMERICAN LEGION AUXILIARY DEPARTMENT OF WISCONSIN PAST PRESIDENTS' PARLEY HEALTH CAREER SCHOLARSHIPS
• *See page 531*

AMERICAN LEGION AUXILIARY DEPARTMENT OF WISCONSIN PRESIDENT'S SCHOLARSHIPS
• *See page 531*

AMERICAN LEGION AUXILIARY NATIONAL HEADQUARTERS

http://www.ALAforVeterans.org

AMERICAN LEGION AUXILIARY CHILDREN OF WARRIORS NATIONAL PRESIDENTS' SCHOLARSHIP
• *See page 575*

AMERICAN LEGION DEPARTMENT OF WASHINGTON

http://www.walegion.org/

AMERICAN LEGION DEPARTMENT OF WASHINGTON CHILDREN AND YOUTH SCHOLARSHIPS
• *See page 536*

AMERICAN SAVINGS FOUNDATION

http://www.asfdn.org/

ROBERT T. KENNEY SCHOLARSHIP PROGRAM AT THE AMERICAN SAVINGS FOUNDATION
• *See page 576*

ANKIN LAW

http://ankinlaw.com

ANKIN LAW OFFICE COLLEGE SCHOLARSHIP
• *See page 576*

ANTHONY MUNOZ FOUNDATION

www.munozfoundation.org

ANTHONY MUNOZ SCHOLARSHIPS
• *See page 577*

ANY INTERN

http://www.anyintern.com

$1,000 5 MINUTE SCHOLARSHIP
• *See page 577*

ARKANSAS SINGLE PARENT SCHOLARSHIP FUND

http://www.aspsf.org/

ARKANSAS SINGLE PARENT SCHOLARSHIP FUND
• *See page 577*

ARMENIAN RELIEF SOCIETY OF EASTERN USA INC.-REGIONAL OFFICE

http://www.arseastusa.org/

ARMENIAN RELIEF SOCIETY UNDERGRADUATE SCHOLARSHIP

Applicant must be an undergraduate student of Armenian heritage attending an accredited four-year college or university in the United States. Award for full-time students only. Must be U.S. or Canadian citizen. High school students may not apply.

Award: Scholarship for use in freshman, sophomore, junior, or senior years; not renewable. *Amount:* $13,000–$15,000.

Eligibility Requirements: Applicant must be of Armenian heritage and Armenian citizen and enrolled or expecting to enroll full-time at a four-year institution or university. Available to U.S. and Canadian citizens.

Application Requirements: Application form, financial need analysis. *Deadline:* April 1.

Contact: Mrs. Vart Chiloyan, Scholarship Committee
Armenian Relief Society of Eastern USA Inc.-Regional Office
80 Bigelow Avenue, Suite 200
Watertown, MA 02472
Phone: 617-926-3801
E-mail: arseastus@gmail.com

ARMENIAN STUDENTS ASSOCIATION OF AMERICA INC.

http://www.asainc.org/

ARMENIAN STUDENTS ASSOCIATION OF AMERICA INC. SCHOLARSHIPS

One-time award for students of Armenian descent. Must be an undergraduate in sophomore, junior, or senior years, or graduate student, attending an accredited U.S. institution. Award based on need, merit, and character. Application fee: $15.

Award: Scholarship for use in sophomore, junior, senior, or graduate years; not renewable. *Number:* 35. *Amount:* $3300–$6700.

Eligibility Requirements: Applicant must be of Armenian heritage and enrolled or expecting to enroll full-time at a four-year institution or university. Available to U.S. citizens.

Application Requirements: Application form, essay, financial need analysis. *Fee:* $15. *Deadline:* March 15.

Contact: Nathalie Yaghoobian, ASA Scholarship Committee
Phone: 401-461-6114
Fax: 401-461-6112
E-mail: asa@asainc.org

ASIAN PACIFIC COMMUNITY FUND

http://www.apcf.org/

ROYAL BUSINESS BANK SCHOLARSHIP PROGRAM
• *See page 577*

TAIWANESE AMERICAN SCHOLARSHIP FUND

The Taiwanese American Scholarship Fund is focused on helping economically-challenged Taiwanese American youth fulfill their dreams of obtaining higher education. Must be a U.S. citizen or U.S. permanent resident (holders of a Permanent Resident Card); a direct blood descendant of a Taiwanese citizen; a high school senior or first year college student residing in the United States; and plan to attend a university or college as a full-time first or second year student in the fall of 2016 in the United States. If selected, high school seniors must submit college acceptance letter for verification. Must have a minimum cumulative unweighted high school/college GPA of 3.0 and a household income at or below the Federal/State/County Low Income Level (must be able to show 2014 or 2015 tax return should applicant be selected for award).The scholarship is open to all majors. Previous award recipients are eligible to apply as long as they meet the eligibility requirements.

Award: Scholarship for use in freshman or sophomore years; not renewable. *Number:* 20. *Amount:* $2500.

Eligibility Requirements: Applicant must be of Chinese heritage; Asian/Pacific Islander and enrolled or expecting to enroll full-time at a four-year institution or university. Applicant must have 3.0 GPA or higher. Available to U.S. citizens.

Application Requirements: Application form. *Deadline:* March 29.

Contact: Ms. Sandy Southivilay, Communications Manager
Asian Pacific Community Fund
1145 Wilshire Boulevard
Suite 105
Los Angeles, CA 90017
Phone: 213-624-6400 Ext. 6
Fax: 213-624-6406
E-mail: scholarships@apcf.org

ASIAN PROFESSIONAL EXTENSION INC.

http://www.apex-ny.org/

APEX SCHOLARSHIP

Scholarship to students based on academic excellence, personal essays, letters of recommendation, extracurricular activities/volunteer service, and financial need. Two winners will receive scholarships of $500 and $1000. Deadline varies.

Award: Scholarship for use in freshman, sophomore, junior, senior, or graduate years; not renewable. *Number:* 2. *Amount:* $500–$1000.

Eligibility Requirements: Applicant must be American Indian/Alaska Native or Asian/Pacific Islander and enrolled or expecting to enroll full- or part-time at a four-year institution or university. Available to U.S. citizens.

Application Requirements: Application form, entry in a contest, essay, financial need analysis, recommendations or references, transcript. *Deadline:* varies.

Contact: Trang Le-Chan, Deputy Director of Programs
Phone: 212-748-1225 Ext. 101
Fax: 212-748-1250
E-mail: trang.le-chan@apex-ny.org

ASIAN REPORTER

http://www.arfoundation.net/

ASIAN REPORTER SCHOLARSHIP
• *See page 577*

ASSOCIATION ON AMERICAN INDIAN AFFAIRS, INC.

http://www.indian-affairs.org/

ADOLPH VAN PELT SPECIAL FUND FOR INDIAN SCHOLARSHIPS

Scholarship is open to undergraduate students pursuing a Bachelor's degree in any curriculum. Must be an American Indian/Alaska Native. See http://www.indian-affairs.org for specific details. Must be seeking an Associate's degree or higher at an accredited school.

Award: Scholarship for use in freshman, sophomore, junior, or senior years; not renewable. *Number:* 5–15. *Amount:* up to $1500.

Eligibility Requirements: Applicant must be American Indian/Alaska Native and enrolled or expecting to enroll full-time at a two-year or four-year or technical institution or university. Available to U.S. citizens.

Application Requirements: Application form, essay, Tribal Enrollment. *Deadline:* June 1.

Contact: Lisa Wyzlic, Director of Scholarship Programs
Association on American Indian Affairs, Inc.
966 Hungerford Drive, Suite 12-B
Rockville, MD 20850
Phone: 240-314-7155
Fax: 240-314-7155
E-mail: lw.aaia@indian-affairs.org

ALLOGAN SLAGLE MEMORIAL SCHOLARSHIP

Scholarship available for American Indian/Alaska Native undergraduate and graduate students who are members of tribes that are not yet recognized by the federal government. Students must apply each year. See http://www.indian-affairs.org for specific details. Must be seeking an Associate's degree or higher at an accredited school.

Award: Scholarship for use in freshman, sophomore, junior, senior, or graduate years; not renewable. *Number:* 4–8. *Amount:* $1500.

Eligibility Requirements: Applicant must be American Indian/Alaska Native and enrolled or expecting to enroll full-time at a two-year or four-year or technical institution or university. Available to U.S. citizens.

Application Requirements: Application form, essay, Tribal Enrollment. *Deadline:* June 1.

Contact: Lisa Wyzlic, Director of Scholarship Programs
Association on American Indian Affairs, Inc.
966 Hungerford Drive, Suite 12-B
Rockville, MD 20850
Phone: 240-314-7155
Fax: 240-314-7159
E-mail: lw.aaia@indian-affairs.org

DAVID RISLING EMERGENCY AID SCHOLARSHIP

This scholarship is very limited in the amount available as well as the situation covered (eviction, utility disconnection, child removed from daycare for non-payment, some very limited car expenses for commuting students). Scholarship is for acute, temporary, unexpected emergencies that would keep students from attending school. Tuition, books, computers and other expected expenses are NOT considered emergencies. Must be Native American/Alaska Native. See our website at http://www.indian-affairs.org for details AND call the Rockville office prior to submission to see if funding is available and if your situation qualifies as an emergency. We do not fund summer session or expenses incurred over the summer.

Award: Scholarship for use in freshman, sophomore, junior, senior, or graduate years; not renewable. *Amount:* $100–$400.

Eligibility Requirements: Applicant must be American Indian/Alaska Native and enrolled or expecting to enroll full-time at a two-year or four-year institution or university. Available to U.S. citizens.

Application Requirements: Application form, essay, financial need analysis, recommendations or references, transcript, Tribal Enrollment, financial aid award letter, full time class schedule, explanation of need, proof of need. *Deadline:* continuous.

Contact: Lisa Wyzlic, Director of Scholarship Programs
Association on American Indian Affairs, Inc.
966 Hungerford Drive, Suite 12-B
Rockville, MD 20850
Phone: 240-314-7155
Fax: 240-314-7159
E-mail: lw.aaia@indian-affairs.org

DISPLACED HOMEMAKER SCHOLARSHIP

This undergraduate scholarship is for men and women 30+ who would not otherwise be able to complete their educational goals due to family responsibilities. Must be an American Indian/Alaska Native. See our website http://www.indian-affairs.org for complete details. Must be an Associate's degree or higher. Must be an accredited institution.

Award: Scholarship for use in freshman, sophomore, junior, or senior years; not renewable. *Number:* 2–10. *Amount:* $1500.

Eligibility Requirements: Applicant must be American Indian/Alaska Native and enrolled or expecting to enroll full-time at a two-year or four-year or technical institution or university. Available to U.S. citizens.

Application Requirements: Application form, essay, Tribal Enrollment. *Deadline:* June 3.

Contact: Lisa Wyzlic, Director of Scholarship Programs
Association on American Indian Affairs, Inc.
966 Hungerford Drive, Suite 12-B
Rockville, MD 20850
Phone: 240-314-7155
Fax: 240-314-7159
E-mail: lw.aaia@indian-affairs.org

OWANAH ANDERSON SCHOLARSHIP

This scholarship is for Native American and Alaska Native undergraduate women who are entering their Junior year of college. Students must be enrolled in a federally recognized tribe. Students must be seeking a Bachelors Degree and may be enrolled in any curriculum. This scholarship renews each semester through the student's Senior year pending satisfactory progress. Each award is $1,500 per school year. $750 is disbursed in late September and $750 is disbursed in late January. This scholarship is for two years only. See our website at www.indian-affairs.org for complete details.

Award: Scholarship for use in junior year; renewable. *Number:* 1–5. *Amount:* $1500.

Eligibility Requirements: Applicant must be American Indian/Alaska Native; enrolled or expecting to enroll full-time at a four-year institution or university and female. Available to U.S. citizens.

Application Requirements: Application form, copy of Tribal Enrollment, essay. *Deadline:* June 1.

Contact: Lisa Wyzlic, Director of Scholarship Program
Association on American Indian Affairs, Inc.
966 Hungerford Drive, Suite 12-B
Rockville, DC 20850
Phone: 240-314-7155
Fax: 240-314-7159
E-mail: lw.aaia@indian-affairs.org

ASSURED LIFE ASSOCIATION

http://assuredlife.org

ASSURED LIFE ASSOCIATION ENDOWMENT SCHOLARSHIP PROGRAM

• *See page 540*

AWEBER COMMUNICATIONS

http://www.aweber.com/

AWEBER DEVELOPING FUTURES SCHOLARSHIP

The AWeber Developing Futures Scholarship, which grants a $2,500 scholarship to one college student each year, is awarded to undergraduate students studying in the Business/Marketing/Communications fields, as they pursue their educational and professional goals. It is AWeber's mission to help entrepreneurs and small business owners be successful as they connect with and grow their communities. As part of that mission, we know that drive is something that is nurtured over time—and it all begins with investing in the young individuals who will be the entrepreneurs, business owners and hard-working professionals of the future. See more at http://www.aweber.com/email-marketing-scholarship.htm#sthash.SVlP9Kh4.dpuf

Award: Scholarship for use in freshman, sophomore, junior, or senior years; not renewable. *Number:* 1. *Amount:* $2500.

Eligibility Requirements: Applicant must be enrolled or expecting to enroll full- or part-time at a four-year institution or university. Available to U.S. and non-U.S. citizens.

Application Requirements: Essay. *Deadline:* May 31.

Contact: Ms. Rebecca Pollard
E-mail: rebeccap@aweber.com

BARONE DEFENSE FIRM

http://baronedefensefirm.com/

BARONE DEFENSE FIRM WIN BACK YOUR LIFE SCHOLARSHIP

• *See page 578*

BLACKFEET NATION HIGHER EDUCATION PROGRAM

http://www.blackfeetnation.com/

BLACKFEET NATION HIGHER EDUCATION GRANT

Grants of $2800-$3000 will be awarded to students who are enrolled members of the Blackfeet Tribe and actively pursuing an undergraduate degree. Must submit a certification of Blackfeet blood.

Award: Grant for use in freshman, sophomore, junior, or senior years; not renewable. *Number:* 180. *Amount:* $2800–$3000.

Eligibility Requirements: Applicant must be American Indian/Alaska Native and enrolled or expecting to enroll full-time at a two-year or four-year or technical institution or university. Available to U.S. citizens.

Application Requirements: Application form, certification of Blackfeet blood, essay, financial need analysis, transcript. *Deadline:* March 1.

Contact: Conrad LaFromboise, Director
Blackfeet Nation Higher Education Program
PO Box 850
Browning, MT 59417
Phone: 406-338-7539
Fax: 406-338-7529
E-mail: bhep@3rivers.net

BOUNCE ENERGY

http://www.bounceenergy.com

BE MORE SCHOLARSHIP

• *See page 578*

BRAINLY, INC.

http://www.brainly.com

BRAINLY EVERYONE KNOWS SOMETHING SCHOLARSHIP

• *See page 578*

BRANDES INVESTMENT PARTNERS L.P.

https://www.brandes.com

BRANDES SCHOLARSHIP PROGRAM

• *See page 578*

BREYER LAW OFFICES PC

http://www.breyerlaw.com/

2017 HUSBAND AND WIFE LAW TEAM ARIZONA SCHOLARSHIP

• *See page 578*

BUREAU OF INDIAN AFFAIRS OFFICE OF INDIAN EDUCATION PROGRAMS

http://www.bie.edu/

BUREAU OF INDIAN EDUCATION GRANT PROGRAM

Grants are provided to supplement financial assistance to eligible American Indian/Alaska Native students entering college seeking a Baccalaureate degree. A student must be a member of, or at least one-quarter degree Indian blood descendent of a member of an American Indian tribe who are eligible for the special programs and services provided by the United States through the Bureau of Indian Affairs to Indians because of their status as Indians.

Award: Grant for use in freshman year; not renewable.

Eligibility Requirements: Applicant must be American Indian/Alaska Native; high school student and planning to enroll or expecting to enroll full-time at a two-year or four-year institution or university. Available to U.S. citizens.

Application Requirements: Application form, recommendations or references, test scores, transcript. *Deadline:* varies.

Contact: Paulina Bell, Office Automation Assistant
Phone: 202-208-6123
Fax: 202-208-3312

BY KIDS FOR KIDS, CO.

http://bkfkeducation.com

CTIA WIRELESS FOUNDATION DRIVE SMART DIGITAL SHORT CONTEST

• *See page 579*

SALLIE MAE® MAKE COLLEGE HAPPEN CHALLENGE

• *See page 579*

CABRILLO CIVIC CLUBS OF CALIFORNIA INC.

http://www.cabrillocivicclubs.org/scholarship.asp

CABRILLO CIVIC CLUBS OF CALIFORNIA SCHOLARSHIP

Applicants must be graduating California high school seniors of Portuguese heritage and American citizenship, with an overall 3.5 GPA.

Award: Scholarship for use in freshman year; not renewable. *Number:* 75–100. *Amount:* $500.

Eligibility Requirements: Applicant must be of Portuguese heritage; high school student; planning to enroll or expecting to enroll full-time at a technical institution and resident of California. Applicant must have 3.5 GPA or higher. Available to U.S. citizens.

Application Requirements: Application form, driver's license, personal photograph, recommendations or references, resume, self-addressed stamped envelope with application, transcript. *Deadline:* March 15.

Contact: Breck Austin, Scholarship Chairperson
Cabrillo Civic Clubs of California Inc.
2174 South Coast Highway
Oceanside, CA 92054
E-mail: shampoobla@sbcglobal.net

CAFÉ BUSTELO

http://cafebustelo.com

CAFÉ BUSTELO EL CAFE DEL FUTURO SCHOLARSHIP ESSAY CONTEST

Café Bustelo and the Hispanic Association of Colleges and Universities (HACU) have teamed up to present El Café Bustelo Futuro Scholarship Essay Contest. Eligible students can enter for a chance to win one of nine $5,000 college scholarships. Permanent legal residents of the 50 United States and D.C., age 18 or older and of Latino decent, that are currently enrolled full-time in a college of university, are eligible to apply for the scholarship. To enter/apply, complete the online application on the HACU website: www.hacu.net; and respond to and upload your original essay on the following topic: Describe how your Latino heritage, family, and the community in which you grew up have impacted your desire and motivation to obtain a college degree. Additionally, describe what you intend to accomplish with your degree and how you will give back to your community. Attach the required supporting documents to the application. Scholarship closes on May 26.

Award: Scholarship for use in freshman, sophomore, junior, or senior years; not renewable. *Number:* 9. *Amount:* $5000.

Eligibility Requirements: Applicant must be of Hispanic heritage and enrolled or expecting to enroll full-time at a four-year institution or university. Available to U.S. citizens.

Application Requirements: Application form, essay. *Deadline:* May 26.

Contact: Hispanic Association of Colleges & Universities
Café Bustelo
8415 Datapoint Drive, Suite 400
San Antonio, TX 78229
Phone: 210-692-3805
Fax: 210-692-0823
E-mail: hacu@hacu.net

CALIFORNIA COMMUNITY COLLEGES

http://www.ccco.edu/

EOPS (EXTENDED OPPORTUNITY PROGRAMS AND SERVICES)/CARE (COOPERATIVE AGENCIES RESOURCES FOR EDUCATION)

• *See page 579*

CAMP NETWORK

https://www.campnetwork.com/

CAMP COUNSELOR APPRECIATION SCHOLARSHIP

• *See page 580*

CARING.COM

http://caring.com

CARING.COM STUDENT-CAREGIVER BI-ANNUAL SCHOLARSHIP

• *See page 580*

CENTER FOR REINTEGRATION

www.reintegration.com

BAER REINTEGRATION SCHOLARSHIP

• *See page 580*

CENTRAL COUNCIL, TLINGIT AND HAIDA INDIAN TRIBES OF ALASKA

http://www.hied.org/

ALUMNI STUDENT ASSISTANCE PROGRAM

The program provides annual scholarship awards to all enrolled Tlingit or Haida tribal members regardless of service area, community affiliation, origination, residence, tribal compact, or signatory status.

Award: Scholarship for use in freshman, sophomore, junior, senior, graduate, or postgraduate years; not renewable. *Number:* 1–100. *Amount:* $300–$500.

Eligibility Requirements: Applicant must be American Indian/Alaska Native and enrolled or expecting to enroll full-time at a two-year or four-year institution or university. Applicant must have 2.5 GPA or higher. Available to U.S. citizens.

Application Requirements: Application form, community service, essay, financial need analysis, recommendations or references, transcript, tribal enrollment certification form, letter of admission. *Deadline:* September 15.

Contact: Miss. Leslie Rae Isturis, Education Specialist
Central Council, Tlingit and Haida Indian Tribes of Alaska
3239 Hospital Drive
Juneau, AK 99801
Phone: 907-463-7375
Fax: 907-463-7173
E-mail: listuris@ccthita.org

COLLEGE STUDENT ASSISTANCE PROGRAM

A federally funded program which authorizes a program of assistance, by educational grants, to Indians seeking higher education. Awards available only to enrolled T&H members. Minimum 2.0 GPA required.

Award: Scholarship for use in freshman, sophomore, junior, senior, graduate, or postgraduate years; renewable. *Number:* 1–200. *Amount:* up to $2000.

Eligibility Requirements: Applicant must be American Indian/Alaska Native and enrolled or expecting to enroll full-time at a two-year or four-year institution or university. Available to U.S. citizens.

Application Requirements: Application form, letter of admission, test scores, transcript. *Deadline:* May 15.

Contact: Miss. Leslie Rae Isturis, Education Specialist
Central Council, Tlingit and Haida Indian Tribes of Alaska
3239 Hospital Drive
Juneau, AK 99801
Phone: 907-463-7375
Fax: 907-463-7173
E-mail: listuris@ccthita.org

CENTRAL SCHOLARSHIP

http://www.central-scholarship.org

LESSANS FAMILY SCHOLARSHIP

Scholarship available for Jewish students from Maryland who attend undergraduate colleges, universities or vocational schools full-time. Students can attend any accredited U.S. college or university. Awards are based on need and merit. The scholarship committee determines award amounts. For more information, visit website http://www.centralsb.org.

Award: Scholarship for use in freshman, sophomore, junior, or senior years; renewable. *Number:* 12–20. *Amount:* $1000–$2500.

Eligibility Requirements: Applicant must be Jewish; of Jewish heritage; enrolled or expecting to enroll full-time at a two-year or four-year institution or university and resident of Maryland. Applicant must have 3.0 GPA or higher. Available to U.S. citizens.

Application Requirements: Application form, essay, financial need analysis, interview, resume, transcript. *Deadline:* May 1.

Contact: Roberta Goldman, Program Director
Phone: 410-415-5558
Fax: 410-415-5501
E-mail: rgoldman@central-scholarship.org

CGTRADER

https://www.cgtrader.com/

ANNUAL CGTRADER SCHOLARSHIP

• *See page 580*

CHEROKEE NATION OF OKLAHOMA

http://www.cherokee.org/

CHEROKEE NATION HIGHER EDUCATION SCHOLARSHIP

A supplementary program that provides financial assistance to Cherokee Nation Members only. It is a need-based program which provides assistance in seeking a Bachelor's degree.

Award: Scholarship for use in freshman, sophomore, junior, or senior years; renewable. *Number:* up to 2800. *Amount:* $100–$1000.

Eligibility Requirements: Applicant must be American Indian/Alaska Native and enrolled or expecting to enroll full-time at a four-year institution or university. Applicant must have 2.5 GPA or higher. Available to U.S. citizens.

Application Requirements: Test scores, transcript, written request for application. *Deadline:* June 13.

Contact: Nita Wilson, Higher Education Specialist
Cherokee Nation of Oklahoma
PO Box 948
Tahlequah, OK 74465
Phone: 918-458-6195
E-mail: nwilson@cherokee.org

CHICANA/LATINA FOUNDATION

http://www.chicanalatina.org/

SCHOLARSHIPS FOR LATINA STUDENTS ENROLLED IN COLLEGES/UNIVERSITIES IN NORTHERN CALIFORNIA

Scholarships are awarded to female Latina students enrolled in two-year, four-year or graduate levels. Applicants must be from and/or attending colleges in the nine counties of Northern California listed on the application.

Award: Scholarship for use in freshman, sophomore, junior, or senior years; not renewable. *Number:* 25–30. *Amount:* $1500.

Eligibility Requirements: Applicant must be of Hispanic heritage; enrolled or expecting to enroll full-time at a two-year or four-year institution or university; female and resident of California. Available to U.S. citizens.

Application Requirements: Application form, essay, interview. *Deadline:* March 31.

Contact: Stephanie Segovia, Program Director
Chicana/Latina Foundation
1419 Burlingame Avenue, Suite W2
Burlingame, CA 94010
Phone: 650-548-1049
E-mail: stephanie@chicanalatina.org

CHINESE AMERICAN ASSOCIATION OF MINNESOTA

http://www.caam.org/

CHINESE AMERICAN ASSOCIATION OF MINNESOTA (CAAM) SCHOLARSHIPS

Merit and need scholarships of $1000 each are available for college and graduate students of Chinese descent and a resident of Minnesota. Applicants will be evaluated on their academic records, leadership qualities, and community service.

Award: Scholarship for use in freshman, sophomore, junior, senior, or graduate years; not renewable. *Amount:* $1000.

Eligibility Requirements: Applicant must be of Chinese heritage; Asian/Pacific Islander; enrolled or expecting to enroll full-time at a two-year or four-year or technical institution or university and resident of Minnesota. Available to U.S. citizens.

Application Requirements: Application form, financial need analysis, recommendations or references, SAT score. *Deadline:* November 15.

Contact: Scholarship Committee
Chinese American Association of Minnesota
PO Box 582584
Minneapolis, MN 55458-2584

CHRISTINE GERTSCH ATTORNEY AT LAW

https://www.ctdomesticviolencehelp.com/

CONNECTICUT DOMESTIC VIOLENCE 2017 LEGISLATION REFORM SCHOLARSHIP

• *See page 581*

CHURCH HILL CLASSICS

http://www.diplomaframe.com/

FRAME MY FUTURE SCHOLARSHIP CONTEST

• *See page 581*

CITIZEN POTAWATOMI NATION

http://www.potawatomi.org/

CITIZEN POTAWATOMI NATION TRIBAL SCHOLARSHIP

Provides financial assistance for payment of tuition for members of the Citizen Potawatomi Nation. Minimum 2.0 GPA required. Deadlines are December 1 for spring, August 1 for fall, and June 1 for summer. Award amount varies from $750 to $1500.

Award: Scholarship for use in freshman, sophomore, junior, senior, or graduate years; renewable. *Amount:* $750–$1500.

Eligibility Requirements: Applicant must be American Indian/Alaska Native and enrolled or expecting to enroll full- or part-time at a two-year or four-year or technical institution or university. Available to U.S. citizens.

Application Requirements: Application form, financial need analysis, test scores, transcript. *Deadline:* varies.

Contact: Charles Clark, Director, Tribal Rolls
Phone: 800-880-9880
Fax: 405-275-0198
E-mail: cclark@potawatomi.org

CODA INTERNATIONAL

http://www.coda-international.org

MILLIE BROTHER SCHOLARSHIP FOR CHILDREN OF DEAF ADULTS

• *See page 581*

COGBURN LAW OFFICES

http://cogburnlaw.com/

$5,000 ADVERSITY SCHOLARSHIP

• *See page 581*

COLLEGE ASSISTANCE MIGRANT PROGRAM

https://www.stedwards.edu

COLLEGE ASSISTANCE MIGRANT PROG.

• *See page 581*

COLLEGEBOUND FOUNDATION

http://www.collegeboundfoundation.org/

LORENZO FELDER SCHOLARSHIP

You must: be an African-American male; be a graduate of a Baltimore City public school; have a cumulative GPA of 3.0 or better; have demonstrated financial need; have verifiable community service or extracurricular activity; write an essay of 500-1,000 words describing the environment you live in and the most meaningful contribution you have made as a volunteer in your community.

Award: Scholarship for use in freshman year; not renewable. *Number:* 1–3. *Amount:* $1000–$1500.

Eligibility Requirements: Applicant must be Black (non-Hispanic); high school student; planning to enroll or expecting to enroll full-time at a two-year or four-year institution; male and resident of Maryland. Applicant must have 3.0 GPA or higher. Available to U.S. citizens.

Application Requirements: Application form, community service, essay. *Deadline:* March 1.

Contact: Jennifer Covahey, Associate Program Director, Scholarship Programs
CollegeBound Foundation
300 Water Street, Suite 300
Baltimore, MD 21202
Phone: 410-783-2905 Ext. 207
E-mail: jcovahey@collegeboundfoundation.org

COLLEGE WOMEN'S ASSOCIATION OF JAPAN

http://www.cwaj.org/

SCHOLARSHIP FOR THE VISUALLY IMPAIRED TO STUDY ABROAD

• *See page 629*

SCHOLARSHIP FOR THE VISUALLY IMPAIRED TO STUDY IN JAPAN

• *See page 629*

COLORADO MASONS BENEVOLENT FUND ASSOCIATION

http://www.cmbfa.org/scholarship

COLORADO MASONS BENEVOLENT FUND SCHOLARSHIPS

• *See page 581*

COLUMBUS CITIZENS FOUNDATION

http://www.columbuscitizensfd.org/scholarships/scholarships.html

COLUMBUS CITIZENS FOUNDATION COLLEGE SCHOLARSHIP PROGRAM

• *See page 582*

COMMUNITY BANKERS ASSOCIATION OF ILLINOIS

http://www.cbai.com/

COMMUNITY BANKERS ASSOC OF IL CHILD OF A BANKER SCHOLARSHIP

• *See page 541*

COMMUNITY BANKERS ASSOC. OF IL ESSAY CONTEST

• *See page 582*

COMMUNITY FOUNDATION FOR GREATER ATLANTA, INC.

http://cfgreateratlanta.org/

DREAMS SQUARED SCHOLARSHIP

• *See page 582*

COMMUNITY FOUNDATION OF WESTERN MASSACHUSETTS

http://www.communityfoundation.org/

HELLESPONT SOCIETY SCHOLARSHIP FUND

Scholarship available to high school graduates who attend a two or four year college, who are persons of Greek descent, with a preference given to descendants of past Hellespont Society Members. For more information, please see website http://communityfoundation.org/.

Award: Scholarship for use in freshman year; not renewable.

Eligibility Requirements: Applicant must be of Greek heritage; high school student; planning to enroll or expecting to enroll full- or part-time at a two-year or four-year institution and resident of Massachusetts. Available to U.S. citizens.

Application Requirements: Application form, essay, financial need analysis, transcript. *Deadline:* March 31.

Contact: Dotty Theriaque, Program Assistant for Scholarships
Community Foundation of Western Massachusetts
1500 Main Street
PO Box 15769
Springfield, MA 01115
Phone: 413-732-2858
Fax: 413-733-8565
E-mail: scholar@communityfoundation.org

CONGRESSIONAL BLACK CAUCUS FOUNDATION, INC.

http://www.cbcfinc.org/

CBC SPOUSES EDUCATION SCHOLARSHIP

The CBC Spouses Education Scholarship was established in 1988 by the spouses of Congressional Black Caucus members in response to federal cuts in spending for education programs and scholarships, which disproportionately affect people of color. This scholarship awards scholarships to academically talented and highly motivated students of all majors who intend to pursue full-time undergraduate, graduate, or doctoral degrees.

Award: Scholarship for use in freshman, sophomore, junior, senior, or graduate years; not renewable. *Number:* 250–350. *Amount:* $500–$8200.

Eligibility Requirements: Applicant must be Black (non-Hispanic); enrolled or expecting to enroll full-time at a two-year or four-year institution or university and studying in Alabama, Alaska, Arizona, Arkansas, California, Colorado, Connecticut, Delaware, District of Columbia, Florida, Georgia, Guam, Hawaii, Idaho, Illinois, Indiana, Iowa, Kansas, Kentucky, Louisiana, Maine, Maryland, Massachusetts, Michigan, Minnesota, Mississippi, Missouri, Montana, Nebraska, Nevada, New Hampshire, New Jersey, New Mexico, New York, North Carolina, North Dakota, Ohio, Oklahoma, Oregon, Pennsylvania, Puerto Rico, Rhode Island, South Carolina, South Dakota, Tennessee, Texas, Utah, Vermont, Virginia, Washington, West Virginia, Wisconsin, Wyoming. Applicant must have 2.5 GPA or higher. Available to U.S. citizens.

Application Requirements: Application form, essay, financial need analysis, personal photograph. *Deadline:* May 19.

Contact: Ms. Katrina Finch, Program Administrator, Scholarships
Phone: 202-263-2800
E-mail: scholarships@cbcfinc.org

CONGRESSIONAL HISPANIC CAUCUS INSTITUTE

http://www.chci.org/

CONGRESSIONAL HISPANIC CAUCUS INSTITUTE SCHOLARSHIP AWARDS

Needs Based Scholarship award for Latino students who have a history of public service-oriented activities. Provides scholarships to students enrolled full-time in school. Scholarship levels are: $1000 for community college, $2500 for four year academic institution, $5000 for graduate level institution. See website at http://www.chci.org for further information.

Award: Scholarship for use in freshman, sophomore, junior, senior, or graduate years; renewable. *Number:* 100–150. *Amount:* $1000–$5000.

Eligibility Requirements: Applicant must be Hispanic and enrolled or expecting to enroll full-time at a two-year or four-year institution or university. Available to U.S. citizens.

Application Requirements: Application form, application form may be submitted online (http://www.chci.org), community service, essay, financial need analysis, recommendations or references, resume, transcript. *Deadline:* April 16.

Contact: Anissa Perez, Scholarship Specialist
Congressional Hispanic Caucus Institute
911 2nd Street, NE
Washington, DC 20002
Phone: 202-543-1771
Fax: 202-546-2143
E-mail: aperez@chci.org

CONNECTICUT ASSOCIATION OF LATINOS IN HIGHER EDUCATION (CALAHE)

http://www.calahe.org/

CONNECTICUT ASSOCIATION OF LATINOS IN HIGHER EDUCATION SCHOLARSHIPS

Must demonstrate involvement with, and commitment to, activities that promote Latinos in pursuit of education. Must have a 2.75 GPA, be a U.S. citizen or permanent resident, be a resident of Connecticut.

Award: Scholarship for use in freshman, sophomore, junior, or senior years; not renewable. *Number:* 20. *Amount:* $1000.

Eligibility Requirements: Applicant must be of Hispanic heritage; enrolled or expecting to enroll full-time at a two-year or four-year institution or university and resident of Connecticut. Applicant must have 2.5 GPA or higher. Available to U.S. citizens.

Application Requirements: Application form, essay, financial need analysis. *Deadline:* May 6.

Contact: Dr. Wilson Luna, Gateway Community-Technical College
Connecticut Association of Latinos in Higher Education (CALAHE)
20 Church Street
New Haven, CT 06510
Phone: 203-285-2210
E-mail: wluna@gatewayct.edu

CONNECTICUT OFFICE OF HIGHER EDUCATION

http://www.ctohe.org

ROBERTA B. WILLIS SCHOLARSHIP PROGRAM—NEED-BASED GRANT

This program provides need-based grants to eligible Connecticut residents attending eligible institutions of higher education in Connecticut. Students must file a Free Application for Federal Student Aid (FAFSA) by their college's deadline, if applicable. Students, as a result of filing the FAFSA must have an Expected Family Contribution (EFC) equal to or less than the allowable annual EFC. There is no application to fill out.

Award: Grant for use in freshman, sophomore, junior, or senior years; renewable. *Amount:* $650–$3000.

Eligibility Requirements: Applicant must be Ukrainian citizen; enrolled or expecting to enroll full- or part-time at a two-year or four-year institution or university; resident of Connecticut and studying in Connecticut. Available to U.S. citizens.

Application Requirements: Financial need analysis.

Contact: Ms. Lynne Goodwin, Financial Aid Consultant
Connecticut Office of Higher Education
39 Woodland Street
Hartford, CT 06105
Phone: 860-947-1855
E-mail: sfa@ctohe.org

COUNCIL OF CITIZENS WITH LOW VISION INTERNATIONAL C/O AMERICAN COUNCIL OF THE BLIND

http://www.cclvi.org/

FRED SCHEIGERT SCHOLARSHIP
• *See page 582*

CROATIAN SCHOLARSHIP FUND

http://www.croatianscholarship.org/

CROATIAN SCHOLARSHIP FUND

Scholarship for students of Croatian heritage. Award based on academic achievement and financial need. Must demonstrate appropriate degree selection. Scholarships are awarded depending on availability of funds and number of applicants.

Award: Scholarship for use in freshman, sophomore, junior, or senior years; renewable. *Amount:* $1500.

Eligibility Requirements: Applicant must be of Croatian/Serbian heritage; age 18-25 and enrolled or expecting to enroll full-time at a four-year institution or university. Applicant must have 2.5 GPA or higher. Available to U.S. and non-U.S. citizens.

Application Requirements: Application form, application form may be submitted online, autobiography, financial need analysis, personal photograph, recommendations or references, test scores, transcript. *Deadline:* May 15.

Contact: Vesna Brekalo, Scholarship Liaison
Croatian Scholarship Fund
31 Mesa Vista Court
PO Box 290
San Ramon, CA 94583
Phone: 925-556-6263
Fax: 925-556-6263
E-mail: vbrekalo@msn.com

CSA MEDICAL SUPPLY

https://csamedicalsupply.com

CSA MEDICAL SUPPLY COLLEGE SCHOLARSHIP
• *See page 583*

THE DALLAS FOUNDATION

http://www.dallasfoundation.org/

DR. DAN J. AND PATRICIA S. PICKARD SCHOLARSHIP

The Dr. Dan J. and Patricia S. Pickard Scholarship Fund was established at the Dallas Foundation in 2004 to assist African-American male students in Dallas County. Dr. Pickard was an optometrist and founder of the Pickard eye clinic. He believed that if you did something nice for someone and they do something nice for someone else, you can affect the lives of many people. The Scholarship Fund is his way of "passing it on".

Award: Scholarship for use in freshman year; renewable. *Number:* 1–2. *Amount:* $1000–$2000.

Eligibility Requirements: Applicant must be Black (non-Hispanic); high school student; planning to enroll or expecting to enroll full-time at a two-year or four-year institution; male; resident of Texas and studying in Texas. Applicant must have 2.5 GPA or higher. Available to U.S. citizens.

Application Requirements: Application form, community service, essay, financial need analysis, recommendations or references, transcript. *Deadline:* April 1.

Contact: Ms. Rachel Lasseter, Program Associate
The Dallas Foundation
900 Jackson Street, Suite 705
Dallas, TX 75202
Phone: 214-741-9898
Fax: 214-741-9848
E-mail: scholarships@dallasfoundation.org

DEMAS LAW GROUP, P.C.

http://www.injury-attorneys.com/

DEMAS LAW GROUP SCHOLARSHIP
• *See page 583*

DEPARTMENT OF THE ARMY

http://www.goarmy.com/rotc

ARMY (ROTC) RESERVE OFFICERS TRAINING CORPS TWO-, THREE-, FOUR-YEAR CAMPUS-BASED SCHOLARSHIPS
• *See page 645*

DIAMANTE, INC.

http://www.diamanteinc.org/

LATINO DIAMANTE SCHOLARSHIP FUND
• *See page 583*

DIBELLA LAW OFFICES, P.C.

http://www.dibellalawoffice.com

2017 DIBELLA LAW OFFICES, P.C. SCHOLARSHIP
• *See page 583*

DIRECT ENERGY

https://www.directenergy.com/

DIRECT ENERGY LIVE BRIGHTER SCHOLARSHIP
• *See page 584*

DIRECTTEXTBOOK.COM

http://www.DirectTextbook.com

DIRECTTEXTBOOK.COM 2016 HAIKU SCHOLARSHIP CONTEST
• *See page 584*

DIRECTTEXTBOOK.COM "SHINE" PHOTO ESSAY CONTEST
• *See page 584*

DISABLED AMERICAN VETERANS

http://www.dav.org/

JESSE BROWN MEMORIAL YOUTH SCHOLARSHIP PROGRAM
• *See page 584*

DISABLEDPERSON INC. COLLEGE SCHOLARSHIP

http://www.disabledperson.com/

DISABLEDPERSON INC. NATIONAL COLLEGE SCHOLARSHIP AWARD FOR COLLEGE STUDENTS WITH DISABILITIES
• *See page 584*

DISCIPLESHIP MINISTRIES

http://umcyoungpeople.org

RICHARD S. SMITH SCHOLARSHIP

Open to racial/ethnic minority youth only. Must be a United Methodist Youth who has been active in local church for at least one year prior to application. Must be a graduating senior in high school (who maintained at least a "C" average) entering the first year of undergraduate study and be pursuing a "church-related" career.

Award: Scholarship for use in freshman year; not renewable. *Number:* 1–5. *Amount:* $100–$1300.

Eligibility Requirements: Applicant must be Methodist; American Indian/Alaska Native, Asian/Pacific Islander, Black (non-Hispanic), Hispanic; high school student and planning to enroll or expecting to enroll full-time at a two-year or four-year or technical institution or university. Applicant must have 2.5 GPA or higher. Available to U.S. citizens.

Application Requirements: Application form, essay, financial need analysis. *Deadline:* March 1.

Contact: Kelsey Tinker Hannum, Grant and Scholarships Administrator
Phone: 615-340-7184
E-mail: youngpeople@umcdiscipleship.org

DOLLARS 4 TIC SCHOLARS

http://www.dollars4ticscholars.org/

DOLLARS 4 TIC SCHOLARS TOURETTE SYNDROME SCHOLARSHIP
• *See page 585*

DOLPHIN SCHOLARSHIP FOUNDATION

http://www.dolphinscholarship.org/

DOLPHIN SCHOLARSHIPS
• *See page 585*

DORMBEDDING.COM

http://www.dormbedding.com

#FORTONFLEEK CHALLENGE SCHOLARSHIP
The award asks students to build a fort out of sheets and blankets (does not have to be from DormBedding.com) and share an image or video of their creation on Instagram or Facebook with the hashtag #FortOnFleek and the tag @dormbedding. Participants may tag their friends who they wish to participate in the challenge. If one of the tagged friends wins, the student that first tagged them will receive $200 for their referral. The DormBedding team will choose the winner based on quality and creativity.

Award: Scholarship for use in freshman, sophomore, junior, senior, graduate, or postgraduate years; not renewable. *Number:* 1. *Amount:* $1000.

Eligibility Requirements: Applicant must be American Indian/Alaska Native, Asian/Pacific Islander, Black (non-Hispanic), Hispanic and enrolled or expecting to enroll full- or part-time at a two-year or four-year institution or university. Applicant must have 2.5 GPA or higher. Available to U.S. and non-U.S. citizens.

Application Requirements: Entry in a contest, personal photograph, transcript. *Deadline:* September 28.

Contact: Mr. Josh Pribyl, CEO
DormBedding.com
1610 93rd Lane NE
Blaine, MN 55449
Phone: 612-213-2833
E-mail: admin@dormbedding.com

DUDLEY DEBOSIER INJURY LAWYERS

http://www.dudleydebosier.com/home

DUDLEY DEBOSIER SCHOLARSHIP PROGRAM
• *See page 585*

DUKE ENERGY CORPORATION

http://www.duke-energy.com/

DUKE ENERGY SCHOLARS PROGRAM
• *See page 568*

EDGAR ALLEN POE LITERARY SOCIETY

http://www.ravens.org/

DISTINGUISHED RAVEN FAC MEMORIAL SCHOLARSHIP
Scholarship provides educational assistance to the descendants of those Lao/Hmong who served alongside the Ravens in defense of their country.

Award: Scholarship for use in freshman, sophomore, junior, or senior years; not renewable. *Number:* 10. *Amount:* $1000–$2500.

Eligibility Requirements: Applicant must be of Lao/Hmong heritage; Asian/Pacific Islander and enrolled or expecting to enroll full-time at a two-year or four-year or technical institution or university. Available to U.S. and non-U.S. citizens.

Application Requirements: Application form, essay. *Deadline:* February 29.

Contact: Col. Jerry Milam, Scholarship Chairman
Edgar Allen Poe Literary Society
4320 Saddle Ridge Trail
Flower Mound, TX 75028
Phone: 972-691-2569
E-mail: spikemilam@verizon.net

ELEARNERS.COM

http://www.elearners.com

ELEARNERS ONLINE STUDENT SCHOLARSHIP
• *See page 585*

ELIZABETH GREENSHIELDS FOUNDATION

http://www.elizabethgreenshieldsfoundation.org

THE ELIZABETH GREENSHIELDS FOUNDATION GRANT
• *See page 586*

ENVIRONMENTAL LITIGATION GROUP P.C.

https://www.elglaw.com/

ENVIRONMENTAL LITIGATION GROUP, P.C. ASBESTOS SCHOLARSHIP
• *See page 586*

EPSILON SIGMA ALPHA

http://www.epsilonsigmaalpha.org/scholarships

EPSILON SIGMA ALPHA FOUNDATION SCHOLARSHIPS
Awards for various fields of study. Required GPA vary with scholarship. Applications must be sent to the Epsilon Sigma Alpha designated state counselor. See website at http://www.esaintl.com/esaf for further information, application forms, and a list of state counselors.

Award: Scholarship for use in freshman, sophomore, junior, senior, graduate, or postgraduate years; not renewable. *Number:* 125–175. *Amount:* $350–$7500.

Eligibility Requirements: Applicant must be American Indian/Alaska Native, Asian/Pacific Islander, Black (non-Hispanic), Hispanic and enrolled or expecting to enroll full- or part-time at a two-year or four-year or technical institution or university. Applicant must have 3.0 GPA or higher. Available to U.S. and non-U.S. citizens.

Application Requirements: Application form, essay, recommendations or references, test scores, transcript. *Fee:* $5. *Deadline:* February 1.

Contact: Kathy Loyd, Scholarship Chairman
Epsilon Sigma Alpha
1222 NW 651
Blairstown, MO 64726
Phone: 660-678-2611
Fax: 660-747-0807
E-mail: kloyd@knoxy.net

EQUALITY SCHOLARSHIP COLLABORATIVE

http://www.equalityscholarship.org

EQUALITY SCHOLARSHIPS FOR COMMUNITY COLLEGE TRANSFER STUDENTS
• *See page 586*

SCHOLARSHIPS FOR HIGH SCHOOL GRADUATES
• *See page 586*

ESSAYHUB

https://essayhub.com/

ESSAY WRITING CONTEST BY ESSAYHUB
• *See page 587*

FARAH & FARAH

http://www.farahandfarah.com/

FARAH & FARAH SCHOLARSHIP
• *See page 587*

FELDMAN & ROYLE, ATTORNEYS AT LAW

http://www.feldmanroyle.com/

AUTISM SCHOLARSHIPS
• *See page 587*

FELDMAN LAW FIRM PLLC

http://www.afphoenixcriminalattorney.com/

DISABLED VETERANS SCHOLARSHIP
• *See page 587*

FIRST CATHOLIC SLOVAK LADIES ASSOCIATION

http://www.fcsla.org/

FIRST CATHOLIC SLOVAK LADIES ASSOCIATION FRATERNAL SCHOLARSHIP AWARD
Must be FCSLA member in good standing for at least three years. Must attend accredited college in the United States or Canada in undergraduate or graduate degree program. Must submit certified copy of college acceptance. Award value is $1250 for undergraduate and $1750 for graduate students.

Award: Scholarship for use in freshman, sophomore, junior, senior, or graduate years; not renewable. *Number:* 133. *Amount:* $1250–$1750.

Eligibility Requirements: Applicant must be of Slavic/Czech heritage and enrolled or expecting to enroll full-time at a two-year or four-year institution or university. Available to U.S. and Canadian citizens.

Application Requirements: Application form, driver's license, essay, personal photograph, recommendations or references, test scores, transcript. *Deadline:* March 1.

Contact: Dorothy Szumski, Director of Fraternal Scholarships
First Catholic Slovak Ladies Association
24950 Chagrin Boulevard
Beachwood, OH 44122
Phone: 216-464-8015 Ext. 134
Fax: 216-464-9260
E-mail: info@fcsla.com

FLORIDA PTA/PTSA

http://www.floridapta.org/

FLORIDA PTA/PTSA ANNUAL SCHOLARSHIP
• *See page 588*

FLORIDA STATE DEPARTMENT OF EDUCATION

http://www.floridastudentfinancialaid.org/

JOSE MARTI SCHOLARSHIP CHALLENGE GRANT FUND
Award available to Hispanic-American students who were born in, or whose parent was born in a Hispanic country. Must be a Florida resident, be enrolled full-time in Florida at an eligible school, and have a GPA of 3.0 or above. Must be U.S. citizen or eligible non-citizen. FAFSA must be processed by May 15. For more details, visit the website at http://www.FloridaStudentFinancialAid.org/SSFAD/home/uamain.htm.

Award: Scholarship for use in freshman, sophomore, junior, or senior years; renewable. *Amount:* $2000.

Eligibility Requirements: Applicant must be of Hispanic heritage; high school student; planning to enroll or expecting to enroll full-time at a two-year or four-year institution or university; resident of Florida and studying in Florida. Applicant must have 3.0 GPA or higher. Available to U.S. citizens.

Application Requirements: Application form, financial need analysis. *Deadline:* April 1.

Contact: Florida Department of Education, Office of Student Financial Assistance, Customer Service
Florida State Department of Education
325 West Gaines Street
Tallahassee, FL 32399
Phone: 888-827-2004
E-mail: osfa@fldoe.org

FREEDOM ALLIANCE

https://freedomalliance.org

FREEDOM ALLIANCE SCHOLARSHIP FUND
• *See page 588*

FUNNEWJERSEY.COM INC.

www.funnewjersey.com

FUNNEWJERSEY.COM SCHOLARSHIP
• *See page 588*

GENERAL BOARD OF HIGHER EDUCATION AND MINISTRY

http://www.gbhem.org

BISHOP JOSEPH B. BETHEA SCHOLARSHIP
Undergraduate scholarship for full-time African American students. Must be a member of the Southeastern Jurisdiction Black Methodists for Church Renewal (SEJBMCR) and an active, full member of a United Methodist Church for at least one year prior to applying. Must be U.S. citizen or permanent resident, maintain a GPA of 2.8, and demonstrate financial need.

Award: Scholarship for use in freshman, sophomore, junior, or senior years; not renewable.

Eligibility Requirements: Applicant must be Methodist; Black (non-Hispanic) and enrolled or expecting to enroll full-time at a four-year institution or university. Available to U.S. citizens.

Application Requirements: Application form, application form may be submitted online (http://www.gbhem.org/loans-scholarships), essay, recommendations or references, transcript. *Deadline:* March 1.

Contact: Ms. Marcie Bigord, Assistant Director of Loans &
Scholarships
General Board of Higher Education and Ministry
PO Box 340007
Nashville, TN 37203-0007
Phone: 615-340-7388
Fax: 615-340-7529
E-mail: mbigord@gbhem.org

GENERAL FEDERATION OF WOMEN'S CLUBS OF MASSACHUSETTS

http://www.gfwcma.org/

GENERAL FEDERATION OF WOMEN'S CLUBS OF MASSACHUSETTS NICKEL FOR NOTES MUSIC SCHOLARSHIP
• *See page 589*

GENERAL FEDERATION OF WOMEN'S CLUBS OF MASSACHUSETTS PENNIES FOR ART SCHOLARSHIP
• *See page 589*

GEORGIA STUDENT FINANCE COMMISSION

http://www.GAcollege411.org/

GEORGIA TUITION EQUALIZATION GRANT (GTEG)
• *See page 630*

GIFT BASKETS PLUS

www.giftbasketsplus.com

2017 HIGH SCHOOL GRADUATE SCHOLARSHIP CONTEST
• *See page 589*

GOENNOUNCE, LLC

http://GoEnnounce.com/about

GOENNOUNCE YOURSELF $500 MONTHLY SCHOLARSHIP
• *See page 589*

GOLDIA GOLD & DIAMONDS

http://www.goldia.com

GOLDIA.COM SCHOLARSHIP
• *See page 630*

GOLF COURSE SUPERINTENDENTS ASSOCIATION OF AMERICA

http://www.eifg.org/

GOLF COURSE SUPERINTENDENTS ASSOCIATION OF AMERICA LEGACY AWARD
• *See page 544*

JOSEPH S. GARSKE COLLEGIATE GRANT PROGRAM
• *See page 544*

GORDON LAW GROUP

https://www.gordonlawltd.com

GORDON LAW GROUP NEED-BASED SCHOLARSHIP
• *See page 589*

GREENHOUSE SCHOLARS

http://greenhousescholars.org/our-scholars/become-a-scholar/

GREENHOUSE SCHOLARS
• *See page 590*

GRUNGO COLARULO

https://gcinjurylaw.com/

GRUNGO COLARULO GIVING BACK TO THE COMMUNITY SCHOLARSHIP
• *See page 590*

HARRINGTON FAMILY FOUNDATION

http://harringtonfamilyfoundation.org

OREGON COMMUNITY QUARTERBACK SCHOLARSHIP
• *See page 590*

HBCUCONNECT.COM

http://www.hbcuconnect.com/

HBCUCONNECT.COM MINORITY SCHOLARSHIP PROGRAM
Scholarship to minorities attending a historically Black college or university. Must attend or be enrolled into an HBCU. Selection based on quality of content in the online registration, and/or an essay, and financial need.

Award: Scholarship for use in freshman, sophomore, junior, senior, graduate, or postgraduate years; not renewable. *Number:* 1. *Amount:* $1000–$2500.

Eligibility Requirements: Applicant must be American Indian/Alaska Native, Asian/Pacific Islander, Black (non-Hispanic), Hispanic and enrolled or expecting to enroll full- or part-time at a two-year or four-year institution or university. Available to U.S. citizens.

Application Requirements: Application form, essay. *Deadline:* May 1.

Contact: Mr. William Moss, CEO
Phone: 614-416-5515
Fax: 614-864-8901
E-mail: wrmoss@hbcuconnect.com

HELEN DILLER FAMILY FOUNDATION

http://www.dillerteenawards.org

DILLER TEEN TIKKUN OLAM AWARDS
• *See page 591*

HELLENIC TIMES SCHOLARSHIP FUND

http://www.htsf.org/

HELLENIC TIMES SCHOLARSHIP FUND
One-time award to students of Greek/Hellenic descent. Must be between the ages of 17 and 25. For use in any year of undergraduate education. Employees of the Hellenic Times and their families are not eligible.

Award: Scholarship for use in freshman, sophomore, junior, or senior years; not renewable. *Number:* 30–40. *Amount:* $500–$10,000.

Eligibility Requirements: Applicant must be of Greek heritage; age 17-25 and enrolled or expecting to enroll full-time at a two-year or four-year or technical institution or university. Available to U.S. and non-U.S. citizens.

Application Requirements: Application form, financial need analysis, recommendations or references, resume, transcript. *Deadline:* February 19.

Contact: Nick Katsoris, President of Scholarship Fund
Hellenic Times Scholarship Fund
823 11th Avenue, Fifth Floor
New York, NY 10019-3535
Phone: 212-986-6881
Fax: 212-977-3662
E-mail: htsfund@aol.com

HELLENIC UNIVERSITY CLUB OF NEW YORK

http://www.hucny.com

HELLENIC UNIVERSITY CLUB UNDERGRADUATE SCHOLARSHIP AWARDS PROGRAM

The Hellenic University Club Undergraduate Scholarship Awards are offered in recognition and honor of Greek American students who have exemplified high scholastic achievement. The Hellenic University Club of New York will offer a total of four (4) awards of $1,500 each based on academic achievement and financial need. All applicants must meet the eligibility requirements and submit a complete Hellenic University Club Undergraduate Scholarship Application to the organization. Must be a high school student that will graduate in spring 2017 from a state certified high school, or equivalent, and will enroll at an accredited university/college in the U.S. in fall 2017 as a full-time student pursuing a Bachelor's degree; must be U.S. citizens or U.S. permanent residents and living in the tri-state New York area (New York, New Jersey and Connecticut); must be of Hellenic descent, at least one great grandparent with Hellenic roots; must have a cumulative average of at least 90% (or 3.5 GPA) or be in the top 10% of their class; must have a minimum SAT score of 1800/2400 (old SAT) or 1300/1600 (new SAT) and/or minimum ACT score of 27/36; must be able to demonstrate financial need. For more information, visit our website: http://www.hucny.com

Award: Grant for use in freshman year; not renewable. *Number:* 4. *Amount:* $1500.

Eligibility Requirements: Applicant must be of Cypriot, Greek heritage; high school student; planning to enroll or expecting to enroll full-time at a four-year institution or university and resident of Connecticut, New Jersey, New York. Applicant must have 3.5 GPA or higher. Available to U.S. citizens.

Application Requirements: Application form, essay. *Deadline:* April 1.

HELLENIC UNIVERSITY CLUB OF PHILADELPHIA

http://www.hucphiladelphia.org/

CHRISTOPHER DEMETRIS SCHOLARSHIP

$1500 scholarship for a full-time student enrolled in a degree program at an accredited four-year college or university. High school seniors accepted for enrollment in such a degree program may also apply. Must be a U.S. citizen of Greek descent and a resident of particular counties in NJ or PA.

Award: Scholarship for use in freshman, sophomore, junior, or senior years; not renewable. *Amount:* up to $1500.

Eligibility Requirements: Applicant must be of Greek heritage; enrolled or expecting to enroll full-time at a four-year institution or university and resident of New Jersey, Pennsylvania. Available to U.S. citizens.

Application Requirements: Application form, financial need analysis, transcript. *Deadline:* April 3.

Contact: Anna Hadgis, Scholarship Chairman
Phone: 610-613-4310
E-mail: www.hucphiladelphia.org

DR. NICHOLAS PADIS MEMORIAL GRADUATE SCHOLARSHIP

$5000 scholarship for a qualifying senior undergraduate or graduate student pursuing a full-time degree at an accredited university or professional school. Must be a U.S. citizen of Greek descent and a resident of particular counties in NJ or PA. Academic excellence is the primary consideration for this scholarship.

Award: Scholarship for use in senior or graduate years; not renewable. *Number:* up to 1. *Amount:* up to $5000.

Eligibility Requirements: Applicant must be of Greek heritage; enrolled or expecting to enroll full-time at a four-year institution or university and resident of New Jersey, Pennsylvania. Available to U.S. citizens.

Application Requirements: Application form, financial need analysis, transcript. *Deadline:* April 3.

Contact: Anna Hadgis, Scholarship Chairman
Phone: 610-613-4310
E-mail: www.hucphiladelphia.org

DORIZAS MEMORIAL SCHOLARSHIP

$3000 award for a full-time student enrolled in a degree program at an accredited four-year college or university. Must be a U.S. citizen of Greek descent and a resident of particular counties in NJ or PA.

Award: Scholarship for use in freshman, sophomore, junior, or senior years; not renewable. *Amount:* up to $3000.

Eligibility Requirements: Applicant must be of Greek heritage; enrolled or expecting to enroll full-time at a four-year institution or university and resident of New Jersey, Pennsylvania. Available to U.S. citizens.

Application Requirements: Application form, financial need analysis, transcript. *Deadline:* April 3.

Contact: Anna Hadgis, Scholarship Chairman
Phone: 610-613-4310
E-mail: www.hucphiladelphia.org

FOUNDERS SCHOLARSHIP

$3000 award for a full-time student enrolled in a degree program at an accredited four-year college or university. Must be a U.S. citizen of Greek descent and a resident of particular counties in NJ or PA.

Award: Scholarship for use in freshman, sophomore, junior, or senior years; not renewable. *Amount:* up to $3000.

Eligibility Requirements: Applicant must be of Greek heritage; enrolled or expecting to enroll full-time at a four-year institution or university and resident of New Jersey, Pennsylvania. Available to U.S. citizens.

Application Requirements: Application form, financial need analysis, transcript. *Deadline:* April 3.

Contact: Anna Hadgis, Scholarship Chairman
Phone: 610-613-4310
E-mail: www.hucphiladelphia.org

PAIDEIA SCHOLARSHIP
• *See page 544*

HENKEL CONSUMER ADHESIVES INC.

http://www.ducktapeclub.com/

DUCK BRAND DUCT TAPE "STUCK AT PROM" SCHOLARSHIP CONTEST
• *See page 591*

HERB KOHL EDUCATIONAL FOUNDATION INC.

http://www.kohleducation.org/

HERB KOHL EXCELLENCE SCHOLARSHIP PROGRAM
• *See page 591*

HISPANIC ANNUAL SALUTE

http://www.hispanicannualsalute.org/

HISPANIC ANNUAL SALUTE SCHOLARSHIP
• *See page 591*

HISPANIC METROPOLITAN CHAMBER SCHOLARSHIPS

http://www.hmccoregon.com/

HISPANIC METROPOLITAN CHAMBER SCHOLARSHIPS
• *See page 592*

HISPANIC SCHOLARSHIP FUND

http://HSF.net

HSF/GENERAL COLLEGE SCHOLARSHIP PROGRAM

Merit-based award for U.S. citizens, permanent residents, eligible non-citizens or DACA of Hispanic heritage with plans to enroll full time in an accredited U.S. 4 year university in the upcoming academic year. Applicants must have a minimum 3.0 GPA. Must complete FAFSA or state based financial aid (if available). Must include official transcript. Award ranges from $500-$5,000 depending on need. For additional information please go to HSF.net

Award: Scholarship for use in freshman, sophomore, junior, senior, graduate, or postgraduate years; not renewable. *Number:* 2200–5000. *Amount:* $500–$5000.

Eligibility Requirements: Applicant must be of Hispanic heritage and enrolled or expecting to enroll full-time at a four-year institution or university. Applicant must have 3.0 GPA or higher. Available to U.S. citizens.

Application Requirements: Application form, community service, essay, financial need analysis, personal photograph. *Deadline:* March 30.

Contact: Ms. Ricardo Deleon, COO
Hispanic Scholarship Fund
1411 West 190th Street
Suite 700
Gardena, CA 90248
Phone: 310-975-3700
E-mail: scholar1@hsf.net

HOPI TRIBE

http://www.hopi-nsn.gov/

BIA HIGHER EDUCATION GRANT

Grant provides financial support for eligible Hopi individuals pursuing postsecondary education. Minimum 2.5 CGPA required. Deadlines are July 1 for fall, and December 1 for spring.

Award: Grant for use in freshman, sophomore, junior, or senior years; not renewable. *Number:* 1–150. *Amount:* $50–$2500.

Eligibility Requirements: Applicant must be American Indian/Alaska Native and enrolled or expecting to enroll full-time at a two-year or four-year institution or university. Applicant must have 2.5 GPA or higher. Available to U.S. citizens.

Application Requirements: Application form, financial need analysis, test scores, transcript, verification of Hopi Indian blood. *Deadline:* varies.

Contact: Theresa Lomakema, Financial Aid Processor/Monitor
Phone: 928-734-3533
E-mail: info@hopi.nsn.us

HOPI EDUCATION AWARD

Grant provides financial support for eligible Hopi individuals pursuing postsecondary education. Minimum 2.5 CGPA required. Deadlines are April 1 for summer, July 1 for fall, and December 1 for spring.

Award: Scholarship for use in freshman, sophomore, junior, or senior years; not renewable. *Number:* 1–400. *Amount:* $50–$2500.

Eligibility Requirements: Applicant must be American Indian/Alaska Native and enrolled or expecting to enroll full- or part-time at a two-year or four-year institution or university. Applicant must have 2.5 GPA or higher. Available to U.S. citizens.

Application Requirements: Application form, financial need analysis, test scores, transcript, verification of Hopi Indian blood. *Deadline:* varies.

Contact: Theresa Lomakema, Financial Aid Processor/Monitor
Phone: 928-734-3533
E-mail: info@hopi.nsn.us

TRIBAL PRIORITY AWARD

Scholarship provides financial support for eligible Hopi individuals pursuing postsecondary education. Minimum 3.0 GPA required.

Award: Scholarship for use in junior or senior years; not renewable. *Number:* 1–5. *Amount:* $2500–$15,000.

Eligibility Requirements: Applicant must be American Indian/Alaska Native and enrolled or expecting to enroll full-time at a two-year or four-year institution or university. Applicant must have 3.0 GPA or higher. Available to U.S. citizens.

Application Requirements: Application form, financial need analysis, interview, recommendations or references, test scores, transcript, verification of Hopi Indian blood. *Deadline:* July 1.

Contact: Theresa Lomakema, Financial Aid Processor/Monitor
Phone: 928-734-3533
E-mail: info@hopi.nsn.us

HOUSTON COMMUNITY SERVICES

AZTECA SCHOLARSHIP

• *See page 592*

HOW TO WIN COLLEGE SCHOLARSHIPS

https://how2winscholarships.com

SAVOR SUMMER COLLEGE SCHOLARSHIP

• *See page 592*

HUBSHOUT

http://hubshout.com/

HUBSHOUT INTERNET MARKETING SCHOLARSHIP

• *See page 592*

HUMANA FOUNDATION

http://www.humanafoundation.org/

HUMANA FOUNDATION SCHOLARSHIP PROGRAM

• *See page 593*

INDIAN AMERICAN CULTURAL ASSOCIATION

http://www.iasf.org/

INDIAN AMERICAN SCHOLARSHIP FUND

Scholarships for descendants of families who are from modern-day India and are graduating from public or private high schools in Georgia. They must be enrolled in four-year colleges or universities. There are both academic and need-based awards available through this program.

Award: Scholarship for use in freshman year; renewable. *Number:* 3. *Amount:* $500–$5000.

Eligibility Requirements: Applicant must be of Indian heritage; Asian/Pacific Islander; high school student; planning to enroll or expecting to enroll full-time at a four-year institution or university and resident of Georgia. Applicant must have 3.0 GPA or higher. Available to U.S. citizens.

Application Requirements: Application form, essay, financial need analysis, IRS 1040 form, resume, test scores, transcript. *Deadline:* varies.

Contact: Rajesh Kurup, Scholarship Coordinator
E-mail: rajnina@mindspring.com

INSTITUTE FOR JUSTICE

http://www.ij.org

LIBERTY IN ACTION ESSAY CONTEST: REMOVING BARRIERS TO ENTREPRENEURSHIP

• *See page 593*

INTERNATIONAL ASSOCIATION OF BLACK ACTUARIES

http://www.blackactuaries.org

IABA SCHOLARSHIP

The International Association of Black Actuaries scholarship program advances its mission by providing scholarships at the undergraduate and graduate level to qualified black students who are interested in pursuing an actuarial career. IABA's mission is to contribute to an increase in the number of black actuaries and to influence the successful career development, civic growth and achievement of black actuaries.

Award: Scholarship for use in freshman, sophomore, junior, senior, or graduate years; renewable. *Number:* 20–30. *Amount:* $3000–$5000.

Eligibility Requirements: Applicant must be Black (non-Hispanic) and enrolled or expecting to enroll full-time at a two-year or four-year institution or university. Applicant must have 3.0 GPA or higher. Available to U.S. and non-U.S. citizens.

Application Requirements: Application form, essay. *Deadline:* May 1.

Contact: Kate Weaver, Executive Director
E-mail: iaba@blackactuaries.org

INTERNATIONAL COLLEGE COUNSELORS

www.internationalcollegecounselors.com

INTERNATIONAL COLLEGE COUNSELORS SCHOLARSHIP

• *See page 593*

INTERNATIONAL DAIRY DELI BAKERY ASSOCIATION

http://www.iddba.org

INTERNATIONAL DAIRY DELI BAKERY ASSOCIATION'S SCHOLARSHIP FOR GROWING THE FUTURE

• *See page 594*

INTERNATIONAL FLIGHT SERVICES ASSOCIATION

http://www.ifsanet.com

AMI SCHOLARSHIP AWARD

• *See page 594*

INTERNATIONAL ORDER OF THE KING'S DAUGHTERS AND SONS

http://www.iokds.org/

INTERNATIONAL ORDER OF THE KING'S DAUGHTERS AND SONS NORTH AMERICAN INDIAN SCHOLARSHIP

Scholarships available for Native American students. Proof of reservation registration, college acceptance letter, and financial aid office address required. Merit-based award. Send self-addressed stamped envelope. Must maintain minimum 2.5 GPA.

Award: Scholarship for use in freshman, sophomore, junior, or senior years; renewable. *Number:* 45–60. *Amount:* $500–$650.

Eligibility Requirements: Applicant must be American Indian/Alaska Native and enrolled or expecting to enroll full-time at a two-year or four-year or technical institution or university. Applicant must have 2.5 GPA or higher. Available to U.S. and Canadian citizens.

Application Requirements: Application form, essay, financial need analysis, recommendations or references, self-addressed stamped envelope with application, transcript, written documentation of reservation registration. *Deadline:* varies.

Contact: Scholarship Committee
Phone: 312-799-8015
E-mail: lillyfellowship@poetryfoundation.org

INTERNATIONAL UNION OF BRICKLAYERS AND ALLIED CRAFTWORKERS

http://www.bacweb.org/

CANADIAN BATES SCHOLARSHIP PROGRAM

• *See page 546*

INTERNATIONAL VOLUNTEER HQ

https://www.volunteerhq.org/

VOLUNTEER OF THE YEAR SCHOLARSHIP

• *See page 595*

IOWA STUDENT LOAN

http://www.IowaStudentLoan.org/

IOWA FINANCIAL KNOW-HOW CHALLENGE: SENIOR SCHOLARSHIP

• *See page 596*

ITALIAN-AMERICAN CHAMBER OF COMMERCE OF CHICAGO

http://www.iacc-chicago.com/

ITALIAN-AMERICAN CHAMBER OF COMMERCE OF CHICAGO SCHOLARSHIP

One-time awards for Illinois residents of Italian descent. Available to high school seniors and college students for use at a four-year institution. Applicants must have a 3.5 GPA. Must reside in Cook, Du Page, Kane, Lake, McHenry, or Will counties of Illinois. Must submit a letter including a biographical account of themselves and two letters of recommendation, one from a teacher and one from their counselor.

Award: Scholarship for use in freshman, sophomore, junior, or senior years; not renewable. *Number:* 1. *Amount:* up to $1000.

Eligibility Requirements: Applicant must be of Italian heritage; enrolled or expecting to enroll full-time at a four-year institution and resident of Illinois. Applicant must have 2.5 GPA or higher. Available to U.S. and non-U.S. citizens.

Application Requirements: Application form, essay, personal photograph, recommendations or references, self-addressed stamped envelope with application, transcript. *Deadline:* May 31.

Contact: Frank Pugno, Scholarship Chairman
Italian-American Chamber of Commerce of Chicago
30 South Michigan Avenue, Suite 504
Chicago, IL 60603
Phone: 312-553-9137 Ext. 13
Fax: 312-553-9142
E-mail: info.chicago@italchambers.net

ITALIAN CATHOLIC FEDERATION

http://www.icf.org/

MARIO CUGIA ITALIAN STUDIES SCHOLARSHIP PROGRAM

Two awards for full-time students who are juniors or seniors in college and residents of Arizona, California, Illinois, or Nevada and of Italian descent. Must also be Roman Catholic.

Award: Scholarship for use in junior or senior years; not renewable. *Number:* 2. *Amount:* $600–$1000.

Eligibility Requirements: Applicant must be Roman Catholic; of Italian heritage; enrolled or expecting to enroll full-time at a four-year institution and resident of Arizona, California, Illinois, Nevada. Available to U.S. citizens.

Application Requirements: Application form, essay, financial need analysis, recommendations or references, test scores, transcript. *Deadline:* August 15.

Contact: Italian Catholic Federation
Italian Catholic Federation
8393 Capwell Drive, Suite 110
Oakland, CA 94621
Phone: 510-633-9058
Fax: 510-633-9758
E-mail: info@icf.org

JACKIE ROBINSON FOUNDATION

http://www.jackierobinson.org/

JACKIE ROBINSON SCHOLARSHIP
• *See page 596*

JA LIVING LEGACY

http://www.jalivinglegacy.org/

TERI AND ART IWASAKI SCHOLARSHIP

The scholarship is to support the rising costs of education. Applicant must be a descendent of a Japanese-American World War II veteran that served in the United States military units. Descendents include grandchild, great grandchild, grand niece/nephew as well as extended family.

Award: Scholarship for use in freshman year; not renewable. *Number:* 1. *Amount:* $2000.

Eligibility Requirements: Applicant must be of Japanese heritage; Asian/Pacific Islander; high school student and planning to enroll or expecting to enroll full- or part-time at an institution or university. Available to U.S. citizens.

Application Requirements: *Deadline:* continuous.

JASON KALAFAT ATTORNEY AT LAW

https://criminallawyerwashingtondc.com/

JASON KALAFAT MAKE A DIFFERENCE SCHOLARSHIP
• *See page 596*

JEWISH VOCATIONAL SERVICE LOS ANGELES

http://www.jvsla.org/

JVS SCHOLARSHIP PROGRAM

Need-based scholarships to support Jewish students from Los Angeles County in their pursuit of college, graduate, and vocational education. Applicants must be Jewish, permanent residents of Los Angeles, maintain a minimum 2.7 GPA, and demonstrate verifiable financial need.

Award: Scholarship for use in freshman, sophomore, junior, senior, or graduate years; not renewable. *Number:* 125–200. *Amount:* $1000–$5000.

Eligibility Requirements: Applicant must be Jewish; of Jewish heritage; enrolled or expecting to enroll full-time at a two-year or four-year or technical institution or university and resident of California. Applicant must have 3.0 GPA or higher. Available to U.S. citizens.

Application Requirements: Application form, essay, FAFSA, Student Aid Report (SAR), financial need analysis, interview, recommendations or references, resume, transcript. *Deadline:* March 15.

Contact: Patricia Sills, Scholarship Program Manager
Jewish Vocational Service Los Angeles
6505 Wilshire Boulevard, Suite 200
Los Angeles, CA 90048
Phone: 323-761-8888 Ext. 8868
Fax: 323-761-8575
E-mail: scholarship@jvsla.org

JEWISH WAR VETERANS OF THE UNITED STATES OF AMERICA

http://www.jwv.org/

BERNARD ROTBERG MEMORIAL SCHOLARSHIPS

This is a grant for high school seniors (at the time of application) to help them pay the costs of their tuition. Applicants must have been accepted by an accredited college, university, community college, or hospital school of nursing as a member of the freshman class entering in the fall of the year the student graduates. Applicants must be a direct descendant (children, grand-children, great-grand-children, etc.) of Jewish War Veterans members in good standing. All members, including posthumous members, must have joined before 2013.

Award: Grant for use in freshman year; not renewable. *Number:* 1. *Amount:* $1000.

Eligibility Requirements: Applicant must be high school student and planning to enroll or expecting to enroll full-time at a two-year or four-year institution or university. Available to U.S. citizens.

Application Requirements: Application form. *Deadline:* May 27.

JOHN B. FABRIELE, III, LLC

https://www.fabrielelaw.com/

FABRIELE DISABILITY AWARENESS SCHOLARSHIP
• *See page 596*

JOHN M. AZARIAN MEMORIAL ARMENIAN YOUTH SCHOLARSHIP FUND

http://azariangroup.com/scholarship.html

JOHN M. AZARIAN MEMORIAL ARMENIAN YOUTH SCHOLARSHIP FUND

Grants awarded to undergraduate students of Armenian descent, attending a full-time four-year college or university within the United States. Compelling financial need is the main criteria. Minimum 2.5 GPA required. Activity / involvement in the Armenian church / community a plus.

Award: Grant for use in freshman, sophomore, junior, or senior years; not renewable. *Number:* 1–5. *Amount:* $500–$5000.

Eligibility Requirements: Applicant must be of Armenian heritage and enrolled or expecting to enroll full-time at a four-year institution or university. Applicant must have 2.5 GPA or higher. Available to U.S. citizens.

Application Requirements: Application form, autobiography, essay, financial need analysis, personal photograph. *Deadline:* May 30.

Contact: Mr. John Azarian, CEO
John M. Azarian Memorial Armenian Youth Scholarship Fund
The Azarian Group, LLC, The Azarian Building
6 Prospect Street, Suite 1B
Midland Park, NJ 07432
Phone: 201-444-7111 Ext. 101
E-mail: jazarian@azariangroup.com

JUREWITZ LAW GROUP

http://www.jurewitz.com/

JUREWITZ LAW GROUP SCHOLARSHIP
• *See page 596*

JVS CHICAGO

http://jvschicago.org/

JEWISH FEDERATION OF METROPOLITAN CHICAGO ACADEMIC SCHOLARSHIP PROGRAM

Educational scholarship funds from grants administered by the Jewish Federation of Metropolitan Chicago are available for Jewish college and graduate students. Approximately $500,000 is available each year for full-time students, predominantly those legally domiciled in the metropolitan Chicago area, with career promise in their chosen fields.

Assistance is available primarily for those with FINANCIAL NEED who are pursuing careers in the helping professions.

Award: Scholarship for use in junior, senior, graduate, or postgraduate years; not renewable. *Number:* 100–125. *Amount:* $1000–$8000.

Eligibility Requirements: Applicant must be Jewish; of Jewish heritage and enrolled or expecting to enroll full-time at a four-year institution or university. Available to U.S. citizens.

Application Requirements: Application form, financial need analysis. *Deadline:* February 1.

Contact: Sally Yarberry, Scholarship Administrator
JVS Chicago
216 W. Jackson Blvd.
Suite 700
Chicago, IL 60606
Phone: 312-673-3444
E-mail: jvsscholarship@jvschicago.org

KANSAS BOARD OF REGENTS

http://www.kansasregents.org/

KANSAS ETHNIC MINORITY SCHOLARSHIP

Scholarship program designed to assist financially needy, academically competitive students who are identified as members of any of the following ethnic/racial groups: African-American, American Indian or Alaskan Native, Asian or Pacific Islander, or Hispanic. Priority is given to applicants who are freshmen. Students must be Kansas residents attending postsecondary institutions in Kansas. For more details refer to website http://www.kansasregents.org/students/student_financial_aid/scholarships_and_grants.

Award: Scholarship for use in freshman, sophomore, junior, or senior years; renewable. *Number:* 100–250. *Amount:* $50–$1850.

Eligibility Requirements: Applicant must be American Indian/Alaska Native, Asian/Pacific Islander, Black (non-Hispanic), Hispanic; enrolled or expecting to enroll full-time at a two-year or four-year institution or university; resident of Kansas and studying in Kansas. Applicant must have 3.0 GPA or higher. Available to U.S. citizens.

Application Requirements: Application form, financial need analysis. *Fee:* $12. *Deadline:* May 1.

Contact: Diane Lindeman, Director of Student Financial Assistance
Kansas Board of Regents
1000 SW Jackson, Suite 520
Topeka, KS 66612
Phone: 785-430-4255
Fax: 785-430-4233
E-mail: dlindeman@ksbor.org

KAUFMAN & STIGGER, PLLC

http://www.getthetiger.com/

THE ALBERTA C. KAUFMAN SCHOLARSHIP
• *See page 597*

KELLER LAW OFFICES

http://www.kellerlawoffices.com/

KELLER LAW OFFICES SCHOLARSHIP FOR HIGHER EDUCATION
• *See page 597*

KELLY & SOTO LAW

http://www.1800lawguys.com

KELLY & SOTO LAW SCHOLARSHIP PROGRAM
• *See page 597*

KELLY LAW TEAM

http://www.jkphoenixpersonalinjuryattorney.com/

DOWN SYNDROME SCHOLARSHIP
• *See page 597*

KIDGUARD

http://www.kidguard.com/

KIDGUARD FOR EDUCATION ESSAY SCHOLARSHIP
• *See page 597*

KIDGUARD FOR EDUCATION ESSAY SCHOLARSHIP FOR HIGH SCHOOL
• *See page 598*

KIMBO FOUNDATION

http://www.kimbofoundation.org/

KIMBO FOUNDATION SCHOLARSHIP

Scholarship available to Korean-American students only. Full time study only. Application deadline varies every year.

Award: Scholarship for use in freshman, sophomore, junior, senior, graduate, or postgraduate years; not renewable. *Number:* 30–50. *Amount:* $1500.

Eligibility Requirements: Applicant must be of Korean heritage; Asian/Pacific Islander and enrolled or expecting to enroll full-time at a two-year or four-year or technical institution or university. Available to citizens of countries other than the U.S. or Canada.

Application Requirements: Application form, copy of household income tax return, essay, recommendations or references, transcript. *Deadline:* varies.

Contact: Jennifer Chung, Program Coordinator
Kimbo Foundation
430 Shotwell Street
San Francisco, CA 94110
Phone: 415-285-4100
Fax: 415-285-4103
E-mail: info@kimbofoundation.org

KITCHEN GUIDES

http://www.kitchensguides.com/

SMART KITCHEN IMPROVEMENT SCHOLARSHIP BY KITCHEN GUIDES
• *See page 598*

KNIGHTS OF COLUMBUS

http://www.kofc.org/

FOURTH DEGREE PRO DEO AND PRO PATRIA (CANADA)
• *See page 547*

KOREAN AMERICAN SCHOLARSHIP FOUNDATION

http://www.kasf.org/

KOREAN-AMERICAN SCHOLARSHIP FOUNDATION EASTERN REGION SCHOLARSHIPS

Scholarships available to Korean-American and Korean students enrolled in a full-time undergraduate or graduate program in the United States. Selection based on financial need, academic achievement, school activities, and community services. Each applicant must submit an application to the respective KASF region. For more details and an application see website http://www.kasf.org.

Award: Scholarship for use in freshman, sophomore, junior, senior, or graduate years; not renewable. *Amount:* $1000.

Eligibility Requirements: Applicant must be of Korean heritage; Asian/Pacific Islander; enrolled or expecting to enroll full-time at a four-year institution or university and studying in Delaware, District of Columbia, Kentucky, Maryland, North Carolina, Pennsylvania, Virginia, West Virginia. Available to U.S. and non-U.S. citizens.

Application Requirements: Application form, essay, financial need analysis, personal photograph, recommendations or references, self-addressed stamped envelope with application, transcript. *Deadline:* May 31.

Contact: Dr. Brandon Yi, Scholarship Committee
Korean American Scholarship Foundation
803 Russell Avenue, Suite 2C
Reston, VA 20879
E-mail: eastern@kasf.org

KOREAN-AMERICAN SCHOLARSHIP FOUNDATION NORTHEASTERN REGION SCHOLARSHIPS

Scholarships available to Korean-American and Korean students enrolled in a full-time undergraduate or graduate program in the United States. Selection based on financial need, academic achievement, school activities, and community services. Each applicant must submit an application to the respective KASF region. For more details and an application see website http://www.kasf.org.

Award: Scholarship for use in freshman, sophomore, junior, senior, graduate, or postgraduate years; not renewable. *Number:* 60. *Amount:* $1000–$2500.

Eligibility Requirements: Applicant must be of Korean heritage; Asian/Pacific Islander; enrolled or expecting to enroll full-time at a four-year institution or university and studying in Connecticut, Maine, Massachusetts, New Hampshire, New Jersey, New York, Rhode Island, Vermont. Available to U.S. citizens.

Application Requirements: Application form, essay, financial need analysis, personal photograph, recommendations or references, transcript. *Deadline:* June 23.

Contact: Mr. William Kim, Scholarship Committee Chairman
Korean American Scholarship Foundation
51 West Overlook
Port Washington, NY 11050
Phone: 516-883-1142
Fax: 516-883-1964
E-mail: kim.william@gmail.com

KOREAN-AMERICAN SCHOLARSHIP FOUNDATION SOUTHERN REGION SCHOLARSHIPS

Scholarships available to Korean-American and Korean students enrolled in a full-time undergraduate or graduate program in the United States. Selection based on financial need, academic achievement, school activities, and community services. Each applicant must submit an application to the respective KASF region. For more details and an application see website http://www.kasf.org.

Award: Scholarship for use in freshman, sophomore, junior, senior, or graduate years; not renewable. *Number:* up to 45. *Amount:* $1000.

Eligibility Requirements: Applicant must be of Korean heritage; Asian/Pacific Islander; enrolled or expecting to enroll full-time at a four-year institution or university and studying in Alabama, Arkansas, Florida, Georgia, Louisiana, Mississippi, North Carolina, Oklahoma, South Carolina, Tennessee, Texas. Available to U.S. citizens.

Application Requirements: Application form, essay, financial need analysis, personal photograph, recommendations or references, transcript. *Deadline:* June 10.

Contact: Dr. Sam Sook Chung, Scholarship Committee
Korean American Scholarship Foundation
2989 Preston Drive
Rex, GA 30273
Phone: 770-968-6768
E-mail: samsookchung@hotmail.com

KOREAN-AMERICAN SCHOLARSHIP FOUNDATION WESTERN REGION SCHOLARSHIPS

Scholarships available to Korean-American and Korean students enrolled in a full-time undergraduate or graduate program in the United States. Selection based on financial need, academic achievement, school activities, and community services. Each applicant must submit an application to the respective KASF region. For more details and an application see website http://www.kasf.org.

Award: Scholarship for use in freshman, sophomore, junior, senior, or graduate years; not renewable. *Amount:* $2000.

Eligibility Requirements: Applicant must be of Korean heritage; Asian/Pacific Islander; enrolled or expecting to enroll full-time at a four-year institution or university and studying in Alaska, Arizona, California, Colorado, Hawaii, Idaho, Montana, Nevada, New Mexico, Oregon, Utah, Washington, Wyoming. Applicant must have 3.0 GPA or higher. Available to U.S. citizens.

Application Requirements: Application form, essay, financial need analysis, personal photograph, recommendations or references, transcript. *Deadline:* May 31.

Contact: KASF Western Regional Chapter
Korean American Scholarship Foundation
3435 Wilshire Boulevard, Suite 2450B
Los Angeles, CA 90010
Phone: 213-380-5273
Fax: 213-380-5273
E-mail: western@kasf.org

KOSCIUSZKO FOUNDATION

http://www.thekf.org

MASSACHUSETTS FEDERATION OF POLISH WOMEN'S CLUBS SCHOLARSHIPS

Nonrenewable award to American students of Polish descent for sophomore, junior, and senior year who are attending an accredited four-year college or university. The scholarship is awarded to residents of Massachusetts. If no residents of Massachusetts apply, the award(s) may be offered to residents of New England. Applicants must submit proof of Polish ancestry. Minimum 3.0 GPA required.

Award: Scholarship for use in sophomore, junior, or senior years; not renewable. *Number:* 1–3. *Amount:* $1250.

Eligibility Requirements: Applicant must be of Polish heritage; enrolled or expecting to enroll full-time at a four-year institution or university and resident of Connecticut, Maine, Massachusetts, New Hampshire, Rhode Island, Vermont. Applicant must have 3.0 GPA or higher. Available to U.S. citizens.

Application Requirements: Application form, application form may be submitted online (http://www.thekf.org/kf/scholarships/tuition/mfpw/), essay, financial need analysis, personal photograph, proof of Polish ancestry, recommendations or references, transcript. *Fee:* $35. *Deadline:* January 16.

Contact: Ms. Addy Tymczyszyn, Scholarship and Grant Officer for Americans
Kosciuszko Foundation
15 East 65th Street
New York, NY 10065
Phone: 212-734-2130 Ext. 210
E-mail: Addy@thekf.org

POLISH AMERICAN CLUB OF NORTH JERSEY SCHOLARSHIPS

Scholarships of $1000 to $1700 awarded to qualified students for full-time undergraduate and graduate studies at accredited colleges and universities in the United States. The scholarship is renewable. U.S. citizens of Polish descent and Polish citizens with permanent residency status in the United States with minimum GPA of 3.0 are eligible. Applicants must be members of the Polish American Club of North Jersey.

Award: Scholarship for use in freshman, sophomore, junior, senior, or graduate years; not renewable. *Number:* 1–5. *Amount:* $1000–$1700.

Eligibility Requirements: Applicant must be of Polish heritage; enrolled or expecting to enroll full-time at a four-year institution or university and resident of New Jersey. Applicant must have 3.0 GPA or higher. Available to U.S. citizens.

Application Requirements: Application form, essay, personal photograph, proof of Polish ancestry, recommendations or references, transcript. *Fee:* $35. *Deadline:* January 15.

Contact: Ms. Addy Tymczyszyn, Scholarship and Grant Officer for
Americans
Kosciuszko Foundation
15 East 65th Street
New York, NY 10065
Phone: 212-734-2130 Ext. 210
E-mail: addy@thekf.org

POLISH NATIONAL ALLIANCE OF BROOKLYN USA INC. SCHOLARSHIPS

Scholarships of $2000 available to qualified undergraduate students for full-time studies at accredited colleges and universities in the United States. U.S. citizens of Polish descent and Polish citizens with permanent residency status in the United States with minimum GPA of 3.0 are eligible. Applicants must be members in good standing of the Polish National Alliance of Brooklyn Lodge#1903.

Award: Scholarship for use in freshman, sophomore, junior, or senior years; not renewable. *Number:* 1–2. *Amount:* $2000.

Eligibility Requirements: Applicant must be of Polish heritage; enrolled or expecting to enroll full-time at a four-year institution or university and resident of New York. Applicant must have 3.0 GPA or higher. Available to U.S. and non-Canadian citizens.

Application Requirements: Application form, essay, personal photograph, proof of Polish ancestry, recommendations or references, transcript. *Fee:* $35. *Deadline:* January 5.

Contact: Ms. Addy Tymczyszyn, Scholarship and Grant Officer for
Americans
Kosciuszko Foundation
15 East 65th Street
New York, NY 10065
Phone: 212-734-2130 Ext. 210
E-mail: Addy@thekf.org

TOMASZKIEWICZ-FLORIO SCHOLARSHIP

The Tomaszkiewicz-Florio Scholarship supports Kosciuszko Foundation's Summer language and culture program at the Jagiellonian University in Krakow, Poland. The scholarship covers program fees (tuition, 3 meals a day, sightseeing on weekends and a shared room) for a 3 week intensive language program. Some funding may be awarded towards airfare. High school seniors who expect to be 18 and have a high school diploma by the first day of the program may apply. Credit is available. Students who receive scholarship funding are responsible for $95 non-refundable registration fees, airfare and spending money. Group flights are available.

Award: Scholarship for use in freshman, sophomore, junior, or senior years; not renewable. *Number:* up to 13. *Amount:* $1985.

Eligibility Requirements: Applicant must be of Polish heritage and enrolled or expecting to enroll full-time at a four-year institution or university. Applicant must have 3.0 GPA or higher. Available to U.S. citizens.

Application Requirements: Application fee, application form, essay, financial need analysis, personal photograph, recommendations or references, transcript. *Fee:* $35. *Deadline:* April 15.

Contact: Addy Tymczyszyn, Summer Study Abroad Coordinator
Kosciuszko Foundation
15 East 65th Street
New York, NY 10065
Phone: 212-734-2130 Ext. 210

LARSON JEWELERS

www.larsonjewelers.com

BAND WITH SUCCESS SCHOLARSHIP
• *See page 598*

LATIN AMERICAN EDUCATIONAL FOUNDATION

http://www.laef.org/

LATIN AMERICAN EDUCATIONAL FOUNDATION SCHOLARSHIPS
• *See page 598*

LAW OFFICE OF DAVID D. WHITE, PLLC

http://www.wm-attorneys.com/

ANNUAL TRAUMATIC BRAIN INJURY SCHOLARSHIPS
• *See page 598*

LAW OFFICE OF MATTHEW L. SHARP

https://mattsharplaw.com/

LAW OFFICE OF MATTHEW L. SHARP NEED-BASED SCHOLARSHIP
• *See page 599*

LAW OFFICE OF MATTHEW SHRUM

http://www.shrumlawoffice.com/

ANNUAL SINGLE MOTHERS SCHOLARSHIP
• *See page 599*

LAW OFFICES OF DAVID A. BLACK

http://www.dbphoenixcriminallawyer.com

ANNUAL HEARING IMPAIRED SCHOLARSHIP
• *See page 599*

LAW OFFICES OF JUDD S. NEMIRO, PLLC

http://www.jnphoenixfamilylawyer.com/

ANNUAL DYSLEXIA SCHOLARSHIP
• *See page 599*

LAW OFFICES OF RYAN J. TEGNELIA

http://www.sandiegocriminallawyerrt.com/

ANNUAL VETERANS WITH POST-TRAUMATIC STRESS SCHOLARSHIP
• *See page 599*

LAW OFFICES OF SHERYL R. RENTZ, P.C.

http://www.srrentzlaw.com/

2017 LAW OFFICES OF SHERYL R. RENTZ SCHOLARSHIP
• *See page 600*

LAW OFFICES OF THOMAS J. LAVIN

http://www.lawlavinflorida.com/

THOMAS J. LAVIN SCHOLARSHIP
• *See page 600*

LAW OFFICES OF TRAGOS, SARTES & TRAGOS

https://tragoslaw.com/

TRAGOS WRITE YOUR OWN LAW SCHOLARSHIP
• *See page 600*

LEAGUE OF UNITED LATIN AMERICAN CITIZENS NATIONAL EDUCATIONAL SERVICE CENTERS INC.

http://www.lnesc.org/

LULAC NATIONAL SCHOLARSHIP FUND

Awards scholarships to Hispanic students who are enrolled or planning to enroll in accredited colleges or universities in the United States. Applicants must be U.S. citizens or legal residents. Scholarships may be used for the payment of tuition, academic fees, room, board and the purchase of required educational materials. For additional information visit website http://www.lnesc.org to see a list of participating councils or send a self-addressed stamped envelope.

Award: Scholarship for use in freshman, sophomore, junior, or senior years; not renewable. *Number:* 1000. *Amount:* $250–$2000.

Eligibility Requirements: Applicant must be Hispanic and enrolled or expecting to enroll full-time at a two-year or four-year institution or university. Available to U.S. citizens.

Application Requirements: Application form, driver's license, essay, financial need analysis, interview, recommendations or references, self-addressed stamped envelope with application, test scores, transcript. *Deadline:* March 31.

Contact: Scholarship Coordinator
League of United Latin American Citizens National
Educational Service Centers Inc.
2000 L Street, NW, Suite 610
Washington, DC 20036
Phone: 202-835-9646
Fax: 202-835-9685

LEPENDORF & SILVERSTEIN, P.C.

http://www.lependorf.com/

LEPENDORF & SILVERSTEIN, P.C. 2017 NEW JERSEY SCHOLARSHIP

• *See page 600*

LEP FOUNDATION FOR YOUTH EDUCATION

http://www.lepfoundation.org/applications

CURE—CANCER SUPPORT SCHOLARSHIP

• *See page 600*

JOHN LEPPING MEMORIAL SCHOLARSHIP

• *See page 600*

LIVE POETS SOCIETY AND JUST POETRY!!! MAGAZINE

http://www.highschoolpoetrycontest.com/

NATIONAL HIGH SCHOOL POETRY CONTEST

• *See page 601*

LOS PADRES FOUNDATION

http://www.lospadresfoundation.com/

COLLEGE TUITION ASSISTANCE PROGRAM

Program for eligible students who are the first family member to attend college. Must be a legal resident or citizen of the U.S. and a resident of New York or New Jersey. Must have a 3.0 GPA. For further information, refer to website at http://www.lospadresfoundation.com.

Award: Scholarship for use in freshman, sophomore, junior, or senior years; not renewable. *Number:* 25–30. *Amount:* $2000–$3000.

Eligibility Requirements: Applicant must be of Hispanic heritage; high school student; planning to enroll or expecting to enroll full-time at a two-year or four-year institution or university and resident of New Jersey, New York. Applicant must have 3.0 GPA or higher. Available to U.S. citizens.

Application Requirements: Application form, application form may be submitted online (http://www.lospadresfoundation.com), essay, financial need analysis, interview, personal photograph, recommendations or references, test scores, transcript. *Deadline:* January 16.

Contact: Mrs. Andrea Betancourt, Office Manager
Phone: 800-528-4105
Fax: 866-810-1361
E-mail: lpfadmin@lospadresfoundation.com

SECOND CHANCE SCHOLARSHIPS

Scholarships granted to Puerto Rican/Latinos students who wish to return to college, trade school or apprenticeship program. Must be a resident of New York or New Jersey. Must demonstrate financial need. For further information, refer to website at http://www.lospadresfoundation.com.

Award: Scholarship for use in freshman year; renewable. *Number:* 1–5. *Amount:* $2000.

Eligibility Requirements: Applicant must be of Hispanic, Latin American/Caribbean heritage; enrolled or expecting to enroll full-time at a two-year or four-year or technical institution or university and resident of New Jersey, New York. Applicant must have 3.0 GPA or higher. Available to U.S. citizens.

Application Requirements: Application form, application form may be submitted online (http://www.lospadresfoundation.com), essay, financial need analysis, interview, personal photograph, recommendations or references, transcript. *Deadline:* June 1.

Contact: Mrs. Andrea Betancourt, Office Manager
Phone: 800-528-4105
Fax: 866-810-1361
E-mail: lpfadmin@lospadresfoundation.com

MAGIC JOHNSON FOUNDATION INC.

http://www.magicjohnson.org/

TAYLOR MICHAELS SCHOLARSHIP FUND

• *See page 601*

MAINE STATE SOCIETY FOUNDATION OF WASHINGTON, DC INC.

http://mainestatesociety.org/foundation/

MAINE STATE SOCIETY FOUNDATION SCHOLARSHIP

• *See page 601*

MAINOR WORTH INJURY LAWYERS

https://mainorwirth.com/

MAINOR WIRTH INJURY LAWYERS NEED-BASED SCHOLARSHIP

• *See page 601*

MANA DE SAN DIEGO

http://www.manasd.org/

MANA DE SAN DIEGO SYLVIA CHAVEZ MEMORIAL SCHOLARSHIP

• *See page 601*

MARKET INSPECTOR

http://www.market-inspector.co.uk/

MARKET INSPECTOR $1,000 SCHOLARSHIP IN SUPPORT OF THOSE UNDER THE REVISED U.S. TRAVEL BAN

We at Market Inspector, are a multicultural team of digital marketing enthusiasts, many of which have left their country of origin to work here. Unity in diversity has allowed us to grow immensely as a company and is something we want to actively promote all over. So, we gladly announce our first scholarship of $1,000 to support students from the 6 travel banned countries by the Trump administration: Iran, Libya, Somalia, Sudan, Syria, and Yemen. Eligibility Criteria: There are two main prerequisites that must be met to be eligible for the scholarship: 1. All the participants should have been born in one of the following countries: Iran, Libya, Somalia, Sudan, Syria and Yemen. 2. All the participants should be either currently enrolled or have been accepted at an accredited UK/US post-secondary educational institution within 2017. The applicant must also be able to provide the following documentation: 1. A copy of a valid passport or birth certificate. 2. Transcripts or similar documentation proving that the applicant is currently enrolled or has been accepted at an accredited UK or US university 3. An essay outlining why they feel that they should be chosen to receive the scholarship. The essay should represent you, where do you plan to spend the money, why do you want to obtain this specific degree, and why you are the most suitable candidate for the scholarship. The essay must be written in English and the number of words should be between 1,000–1,500. All documents must be submitted in MS Word or PDF format and the content of the essay must be written by the applicant and be 100% original. The applicants should submit all the documents via email at scholarship@ market-inspector.co.uk.

Award: Scholarship for use in freshman, sophomore, junior, or senior years; not renewable. *Number:* 1. *Amount:* $1000.

Eligibility Requirements: Applicant must be of African, Arab, Syrian, Yemeni heritage and African, Arab, Syrian, Yemeni citizen and enrolled or expecting to enroll full- or part-time at an institution or university.

Application Requirements: Application form, essay. *Deadline:* October 31.

Contact: Mr. Aris Vourvoulias, SEO and Content Manager
Phone: 44-0330 828 0745
E-mail: info@market-inspector.co.uk

MARYLAND ASSOCIATION OF PRIVATE COLLEGES AND CAREER SCHOOLS

http://www.mapccs.org/

MARYLAND ASSOCIATION OF PRIVATE COLLEGES AND CAREER SCHOOLS SCHOLARSHIP
• *See page 602*

MATRIX HEALTH GROUP

http://www.matrixhealthgroup.com

JOE HOLIBAUGH MEMORIAL SCHOLARSHIP
• *See page 602*

MARK COATS MEMORIAL SCHOLARSHIP
• *See page 602*

RON NIEDERMAN MEMORIAL SCHOLARSHIP
• *See page 603*

TIM KENNEDY MEMORIAL SCHOLARSHIP
• *See page 603*

MENOMINEE INDIAN TRIBE OF WISCONSIN

http://www.menominee-nsn.gov/

MENOMINEE INDIAN TRIBE ADULT VOCATIONAL TRAINING PROGRAM

Renewable award for enrolled Menominee tribal members to use at vocational or technical schools. Must be at least 1/4 Menominee and show proof of Indian blood. Must complete financial aid form.

Award: Grant for use in freshman or sophomore years; renewable. *Number:* 50–70. *Amount:* $100–$2200.

Eligibility Requirements: Applicant must be American Indian/Alaska Native and enrolled or expecting to enroll full- or part-time at a two-year or technical institution. Available to U.S. citizens.

Application Requirements: Application form, financial need analysis, proof of Indian blood. *Deadline:* varies.

Contact: Virginia Nuske, Education Director
Menominee Indian Tribe of Wisconsin
PO Box 910
Keshena, WI 54135
Phone: 715-799-5110
Fax: 715-799-5102
E-mail: vnuske@mitw.org

MENOMINEE INDIAN TRIBE OF WISCONSIN HIGHER EDUCATION GRANTS

Renewable award for only enrolled Menominee tribal members to use at a two- or four-year college or university. Must be at least 1/4 Menominee and show proof of Indian blood. Must complete the Free Application for Federal Student Aid (FAFSA)financial aid form and demonstrate financial need.

Award: Grant for use in freshman, sophomore, junior, or senior years; renewable. *Number:* 136. *Amount:* $100–$2200.

Eligibility Requirements: Applicant must be American Indian/Alaska Native and enrolled or expecting to enroll full- or part-time at a two-year or four-year institution or university. Available to U.S. citizens.

Application Requirements: Application form, financial need analysis, proof of Indian blood. *Deadline:* continuous.

Contact: Virginia Nuske, Education Director
Menominee Indian Tribe of Wisconsin
PO Box 910
Keshena, WI 54135
Phone: 715-799-5110
Fax: 715-799-5102
E-mail: vnuske@mitw.org

MENSA FOUNDATION

http://mensafoundation.org

U.S. SCHOLARSHIP PROGRAM
• *See page 603*

MES FOUNDATION

http://www.mesfoundation.org

RICHARD H. PIERCE MEMORIAL SCHOLARSHIP
• *See page 603*

THE MIAMI FOUNDATION

http://www.miamifoundation.org

RODNEY THAXTON/MARTIN E. SEGAL SCHOLARSHIP

Award available to a graduating high school senior who is African American and a Miami-Dade county area resident. Must demonstrate a commitment to social justice and have financial need. For additional information and application, visit website at http://www.dadecommunityfoundation.org.

Award: Scholarship for use in freshman year; not renewable. *Number:* 11. *Amount:* $1000.

Eligibility Requirements: Applicant must be Black (non-Hispanic); high school student; planning to enroll or expecting to enroll full-time at a four-year institution or university and resident of Florida. Available to U.S. citizens.

Application Requirements: Application form, resume, transcript. *Deadline:* April 17.

Contact: Lauren Mayfield, Programs Assistant
The Miami Foundation
40 NW 3rd Street
Miami, FL 33128
Phone: 305-371-2711
E-mail: lmayfield@miamifoundation.org

SIDNEY M. ARONOVITZ SCHOLARSHIP

Award available for minority students who are seniors at a Miami-Dade county public school or GED recipient from Miami-Dade area. Must be enrolled or planning to enroll in a college or university and plan to live and work in South Florida. Must have a minimum of 3.0 GPA. Additional information and application on website http://www.dadecommunityfoundation.org.

Award: Scholarship for use in freshman year; not renewable. *Number:* 1. *Amount:* $500.

Eligibility Requirements: Applicant must be American Indian/Alaska Native, Black (non-Hispanic), Hispanic; high school student; planning to enroll or expecting to enroll full-time at a four-year institution or university and resident of Florida. Applicant must have 3.0 GPA or higher. Available to U.S. citizens.

Application Requirements: Application form, financial need analysis, transcript. *Deadline:* March 20.

Contact: Lauren Mayfield, Programs Assistant
The Miami Foundation
40 NW 3rd Street
Miami, FL 33128
Phone: 305-371-2711
E-mail: lmayfield@miamifoundation.org

MINDSUMO

http://www.mindsumo.com

MINDSUMO 15-MINUTE SCHOLARSHIP
• *See page 603*

MINNESOTA MASONIC CHARITIES

http://www.mnmasoniccharities.org

MINNESOTA MASONIC CHARITIES SIGNATURE SCHOLARSHIP
• *See page 604*

MINNESOTA MASONIC CHARITIES UNDERGRADUATE SCHOLARSHIP
• *See page 604*

MINNESOTA OFFICE OF HIGHER EDUCATION

http://www.ohe.state.mn.us

MINNESOTA INDIAN SCHOLARSHIP

The Minnesota Indian Scholarship Program provides postsecondary financial assistance to eligible Minnesota resident students who are of one-fourth or more American Indian ancestry and demonstrate financial need for an award. Scholarships are available to eligible American Indian undergraduate students enrolled at least ¾ time and graduate students enrolled at least half time. The award amount is based on need up to $4,000 per year for undergraduate students and up to $6,000 for graduate students.

Award: Scholarship for use in freshman, sophomore, junior, senior, graduate, or postgraduate years; not renewable.

Eligibility Requirements: Applicant must be of Arumanian/Ulacedo-Romanian heritage; American Indian/Alaska Native; high school student; planning to enroll or expecting to enroll full- or part-time at a two-year or four-year or technical institution or university; resident of Minnesota and studying in Minnesota. Available to U.S. and Canadian citizens.

Application Requirements: Application form, financial need analysis. *Deadline:* continuous.

Contact: Meghan Flores, State Grant Manager
Phone: 651-355-0610
E-mail: meghan.flores@state.mn.us

MITCHELL INSTITUTE

http://www.mitchellinstitute.org/

THE SENATOR GEORGE J. MITCHELL SCHOLARSHIP RESEARCH INSTITUTE
• *See page 604*

MLD WEALTH MANAGEMENT GROUP

http://mywealthmanagement.ca/

ANNUAL MLD SCHOLASTIC SCHOLARSHIP
• *See page 604*

NAACP LEGAL DEFENSE AND EDUCATIONAL FUND INC.

http://www.naacpldf.org/

HERBERT LEHMAN SCHOLARSHIP PROGRAM

Renewable award for successful African-American high school seniors and freshmen to attend a four-year college on a full-time basis. Candidates are required to be U.S. citizens and must have outstanding potential as evidenced by their high school academic records, test scores, and personal essays.

Award: Scholarship for use in freshman, sophomore, junior, or senior years; renewable. *Number:* 25–30. *Amount:* $2000.

Eligibility Requirements: Applicant must be Black (non-Hispanic) and enrolled or expecting to enroll full-time at a four-year institution or university. Applicant must have 2.5 GPA or higher. Available to U.S. citizens.

Application Requirements: Application form, community service, essay, personal photograph, recommendations or references, resume, test scores, transcript. *Deadline:* March 31.

Contact: Program Director
NAACP Legal Defense and Educational Fund Inc.
99 Hudson Street
Suite 1600
New York, NY 10013
Phone: 212-965-2225
Fax: 212-219-1595
E-mail: scholarships@naacpldf.org

NANA (NORTHWEST ALASKA NATIVE ASSOCIATION) REGIONAL CORPORATION

http://www.nana.com/

ROBERT AQQALUK NEWLIN SR. MEMORIAL TRUST SCHOLARSHIP

Scholarship for NANA shareholders, descendants of NANA shareholders, or dependents of NANA shareholders or their descendants. Applicant must be enrolled or accepted for admittance at a postsecondary educational institution or vocational school.

Award: Scholarship for use in freshman, sophomore, junior, or senior years; not renewable. *Number:* 250–400. *Amount:* $1000–$2000.

Eligibility Requirements: Applicant must be American Indian/Alaska Native and enrolled or expecting to enroll full- or part-time at a two-year or four-year or technical institution or university. Available to U.S. citizens.

Application Requirements: Application form, college acceptance letter, enrollment proof, financial need analysis, recommendations or references, transcript. *Deadline:* varies.

Contact: Erica Nelson, Education Director
NANA (Northwest Alaska Native Association) Regional
Corporation
PO Box 509
Kotzebue, AK 99752
Phone: 907-442-1607
Fax: 907-442-2289
E-mail: erica.nelson@nana.org

NATIONAL AIDS MEMORIAL GROVE

http://www.aidsmemorial.org

PEDRO ZAMORA YOUNG LEADERS SCHOLARSHIP
• *See page 605*

NATIONAL ASSOCIATION FOR THE ADVANCEMENT OF COLORED PEOPLE

http://www.naacp.org/

AGNES JONES JACKSON SCHOLARSHIP
• *See page 549*

NATIONAL ASSOCIATION OF COLORED WOMEN'S CLUBS

http://www.nacwc.org/

HALLIE Q. BROWN SCHOLARSHIP
One-time $1000-$2000 scholarship for high school graduates who have completed at least one semester in a postsecondary accredited institution with a minimum "C" average.

Award: Scholarship for use in freshman year; not renewable. *Number:* 4–6. *Amount:* $1000–$2000.

Eligibility Requirements: Applicant must be Black (non-Hispanic); high school student and planning to enroll or expecting to enroll full-time at a two-year or four-year institution or university. Available to U.S. citizens.

Application Requirements: Application form, recommendations or references, transcript. *Deadline:* March 30.

Contact: Dr. Gerldine Jenkins, Program Coordinator
National Association of Colored Women's Clubs
Program Coordinator
Washington, DC 20009
Phone: 202-667-4080
Fax: 202-667-2574

NATIONAL ASSOCIATION OF NEGRO BUSINESS AND PROFESSIONAL WOMEN'S CLUBS INC.

http://www.nanbpwc.org/

NATIONAL SCHOLARSHIP
Scholarship for African-American graduating high school seniors with a minimum 3.0 GPA. Must submit 300-word essay on the topic "Why Education is Important to Me."

Award: Scholarship for use in freshman year; not renewable. *Number:* 6–8. *Amount:* $500–$1000.

Eligibility Requirements: Applicant must be Black (non-Hispanic); high school student and planning to enroll or expecting to enroll full-time at a four-year institution or university. Applicant must have 3.0 GPA or higher. Available to U.S. citizens.

Application Requirements: Application form, community service, essay, recommendations or references, test scores, transcript. *Deadline:* March 1.

Contact: Twyla Whitby, National Director of Education Scholarship
Program
National Association of Negro Business and Professional
Women's Clubs Inc.
1806 New Hampshire Avenue, NW
Washington, DC 20009-3298
Phone: 202-483-4206
E-mail: info@nanbpwc.org

NATIONAL COUNCIL OF JEWISH WOMEN LOS ANGELES (NCJW L LA)

http://ncjwla.org/

DODELL WOMEN'S EMPOWERMENT SCHOLARSHIP
• *See page 606*

SOPHIE GREENSTADT SCHOLARSHIP FOR MID-LIFE WOMEN
• *See page 606*

STEPHEN L. TELLER & RICHARD HOTSON TV, CINEMA, AND THEATER SCHOLARSHIP
• *See page 606*

SUSAN SCHULMAN BEGLEY MEMORIAL SCHOLARSHIP
• *See page 606*

NATIONAL FEDERATION OF THE BLIND (NFB)

http://www.nfb.org/scholarships

AAF KENNETH JERNIGAN SCHOLARSHIP FOR $12,000
• *See page 607*

CHARLES AND MELVA T. OWEN SCHOLARSHIP FOR $10,000
• *See page 607*

NATIONAL ITALIAN AMERICAN FOUNDATION

http://www.niaf.org/

NATIONAL ITALIAN AMERICAN FOUNDATION CATEGORY I SCHOLARSHIP
Award available to Italian-American students who have outstanding potential and high academic achievements. Minimum 3.5 GPA required. Must be a U.S. citizen and be enrolled in an accredited institution of higher education. Application can only be submitted online. For further information, deadlines, and online application visit website http://www.niaf.org/scholarships/index.asp.

Award: Scholarship for use in freshman, sophomore, junior, senior, graduate, or postgraduate years; not renewable. *Number:* 40–45. *Amount:* $2500–$10,000.

Eligibility Requirements: Applicant must be of Italian heritage and enrolled or expecting to enroll full-time at a two-year or four-year institution or university. Applicant must have 3.5 GPA or higher. Available to U.S. citizens.

Application Requirements: Application form, application form may be submitted online (http://www.niaf.org/scholarships), essay, recommendations or references, transcript. *Deadline:* March 2.

Contact: NIAF Education and Culture Department
National Italian American Foundation
1860 19th Street, NW
Washington, DC 20009
Phone: 202-387-0600
E-mail: scholarships@niaf.org

NATIONAL MULTIPLE SCLEROSIS SOCIETY

http://www.nmss.org/

NATIONAL MULTIPLE SCLEROSIS SOCIETY SCHOLARSHIP PROGRAM
• *See page 607*

NATIONAL PRESS FOUNDATION

http://www.nationalpress.org/

EVERT CLARK/SETH PAYNE AWARD
• *See page 607*

NATIONAL SOCIETY DAUGHTERS OF THE AMERICAN REVOLUTION

http://www.dar.org/

NATIONAL SOCIETY DAUGHTERS OF THE AMERICAN REVOLUTION AMERICAN INDIAN SCHOLARSHIP

One-time scholarship available to Native Americans. All awards are judged based on financial need and academic achievement. Undergraduate students are given preference. GPA of 2.75 or higher is required. Deadline is February 15th each calendar year

Award: Scholarship for use in freshman, sophomore, junior, senior, or graduate years; not renewable. *Amount:* $4000.

Eligibility Requirements: Applicant must be American Indian/Alaska Native and enrolled or expecting to enroll full-time at a two-year or four-year or technical institution or university. Available to U.S. citizens.

Application Requirements: Application form, essay. *Deadline:* February 15.

Contact: Lakeisha Graham, Manager, Office of the Reporter General
Phone: 202-628-1776
Fax: 202-879-3348
E-mail: nsdarscholarships@dar.org

NATIONAL SOCIETY DAUGHTERS OF THE AMERICAN REVOLUTION FRANCES CRAWFORD MARVIN AMERICAN INDIAN SCHOLARSHIP

Nonrenewable award available for a Native American to attend any two- or four-year college or university. Must demonstrate financial need, academic achievement, and have a 3.0 GPA or higher. Must submit a self-addressed stamped envelope to be considered.

Award: Scholarship for use in freshman, sophomore, junior, or senior years; not renewable. *Number:* 1.

Eligibility Requirements: Applicant must be American Indian/Alaska Native and enrolled or expecting to enroll full-time at a two-year or four-year institution or university. Applicant must have 3.0 GPA or higher. Available to U.S. citizens.

Application Requirements: Application form, financial need analysis. *Deadline:* February 15.

Contact: Lakeisha Graham, Manager, Office of the Reporter General
Phone: 202-628-1776
Fax: 202-879-3348
E-mail: nsdarscholarships@dar.org

NATIVE VISION SCHOLARSHIP

http://www.nativevision.org/

NATIVEVISION

Scholarship available to any Native American high school senior who has been accepted to college.

Award: Scholarship for use in freshman year; not renewable. *Number:* 2. *Amount:* $5000.

Eligibility Requirements: Applicant must be American Indian/Alaska Native; high school student and planning to enroll or expecting to enroll full-time at a four-year institution or university. Applicant must have 3.0 GPA or higher. Available to U.S. and non-U.S. citizens.

Application Requirements: Application form, community service, essay, financial need analysis. *Deadline:* May 12.

Contact: Marlena Hammen, Scholarship Coordinator
Native Vision Scholarship
415 North Washington Street
4th Floor
Baltimore, MD 21231
Phone: 443-287-5167
Fax: 410-955-2010
E-mail: mhammen@jhu.edu

NEBRASKA'S COORDINATING COMMISSION FOR POSTSECONDARY EDUCATION

https://ccpe.nebraska.gov/

NEBRASKA OPPORTUNITY GRANT

• See page 608

NEED

http://www.needld.org/

UNMET NEED GRANT PROGRAM

The program provides "last dollar" funding to lower-income students that still have a need for aid after all federal, state, local and private scholarships and grants have been secured. Must be a U.S. citizen, high school graduate, resident of one of nine participating counties in Southwestern Pennsylvania (Allegheny, Armstrong, Beaver, Butler, Fayette, Greene, Lawrence, Washington or Westmoreland county), and have a minimum 2.0 GPA.

Award: Grant for use in freshman, sophomore, junior, or senior years; not renewable. *Number:* 10–500. *Amount:* $1000–$3500.

Eligibility Requirements: Applicant must be Black (non-Hispanic); enrolled or expecting to enroll full- or part-time at a two-year or four-year or technical institution or university and resident of Pennsylvania. Available to U.S. citizens.

Application Requirements: Application form, essay, financial need analysis, personal photograph, transcript. *Deadline:* May 31.

Contact: Rhonda Brooks, Director of Student Services
Phone: 412-566-2760
E-mail: rbrooks@needld.org

NEW YORK STATE HIGHER EDUCATION SERVICES CORPORATION

https://www.hesc.ny.gov/

NEW YORK STATE AID TO NATIVE AMERICANS

Award for enrolled members of a New York State tribe and their children who are attending or planning to attend a New York State college and who are New York State residents. Deadlines: July 15 for the fall semester, December 31 for the spring semester, and May 20 for summer session.

Award: Scholarship for use in freshman, sophomore, junior, or senior years; renewable. *Amount:* $85–$2000.

Eligibility Requirements: Applicant must be American Indian/Alaska Native; enrolled or expecting to enroll full- or part-time at a two-year or four-year or technical institution or university; resident of New York and studying in New York. Available to U.S. citizens.

Application Requirements: Application form, financial need analysis, recommendations or references, transcript. *Deadline:* varies.

Contact: Native American Education Unit
New York State Higher Education Services Corporation
EBA Room 475
Albany, NY 12234
Phone: 518-474-0537

NICODEMUS WILDERNESS PROJECT

http://www.wildernessproject.org/

APPRENTICE ECOLOGIST SCHOLARSHIP

• See page 608

NIKKO COSMETIC SURGERY CENTER

http://www.drnikko.com/

BREAST CANCER SURVIVOR SCHOLARSHIPS

• See page 608

NISEI STUDENT RELOCATION COMMEMORATIVE FUND

http://www.nsrcfund.org/

NISEI STUDENT RELOCATION COMMEMORATIVE FUND

• See page 608

NO BULL SPORTS

http://nobullsports.org/

NO BULL SPORTS SCHOLARSHIP

• See page 609

NOPLAG PLAGIARISM CHECKER

http://noplag.com/

NOPLAG SCHOLARSHIP ESSAY CONTEST

• See page 609

NORTH CAROLINA DIVISION OF VOCATIONAL REHABILITATION SERVICES

http://www.dhhs.state.nc.us/

TRAINING SUPPORT FOR YOUTH WITH DISABILITIES

• See page 609

NORTH CAROLINA SOCIETY OF HISPANIC PROFESSIONALS

http://www.thencshp.org/

NORTH CAROLINA HISPANIC COLLEGE FUND SCHOLARSHIP

Four-year renewable scholarship for Hispanic students. Must have graduated from a North Carolina high school within the past two years, have a four-year cumulative GPA of 2.5, and be accepted into a two- or four-year college or university. Preference is given to full-time students but part-time students may apply. Preference will be given to foreign-born applicants or native-born children of foreign-born parents. Applications are available online at http://www.thencshp.org/.

Award: Scholarship for use in freshman, sophomore, junior, or senior years; renewable. *Amount:* $500–$2500.

Eligibility Requirements: Applicant must be Hispanic; enrolled or expecting to enroll full- or part-time at a two-year or four-year institution or university and resident of North Carolina. Applicant must have 2.5 GPA or higher. Available to U.S. and non-U.S. citizens.

Application Requirements: Application form, application form may be submitted online (http://www.thencshp.org), transcript. *Deadline:* continuous.

Contact: Marco Zarate, President
North Carolina Society of Hispanic Professionals
8450 Chapel Hill Road, Suite 209
Cary, NC 27513
Phone: 919-467-8424
Fax: 919-469-1785
E-mail: mailbox@thencshp.org

NORTH CAROLINA VIETNAM VETERANS, INC.

http://www.ncvvi.org

NC VIETNAM VETERANS, INC., SCHOLARSHIP PROGRAM

• See page 609

NORTH DAKOTA UNIVERSITY SYSTEM

www.ndus.edu/

NORTH DAKOTA INDIAN SCHOLARSHIP PROGRAM

The North Dakota Indian Scholarship program was established to provide scholarship awards to Native American Students attending qualifying colleges or universities within North Dakota. Students must be ND residents as defined by the college, enrolled full-time (limited exceptions), and maintain a GPA of at least 2.0. Awards are available to both undergraduate and graduate students. Students who maintain a 3.50 GPA qualify for the scholarship based on merit. Students who have a GPA lower than 3.50 must show unmet need. The minimum required GPA is 2.0. The priority application date is July 15. Not all eligible applicants are awarded due to limited appropriations.

Award: Scholarship for use in freshman, sophomore, junior, senior, graduate, or postgraduate years; not renewable. *Number:* 230–270. *Amount:* $1–$2000.

Eligibility Requirements: Applicant must be American Indian/Alaska Native; enrolled or expecting to enroll full-time at a two-year or four-year or technical institution or university; resident of North Dakota and studying in North Dakota. Available to U.S. citizens.

Application Requirements: Application form, financial need analysis. *Deadline:* July 15.

Contact: Brenda Zastoupil, Director of Financial Aid
North Dakota University System
600 E Boulevard Ave, Dept 21
Bismarck, ND 58505-0602
Phone: 701-328-2906
Fax: 701-328-2979
E-mail: ndfinaid@ndus.edu

NORTHERN CHEYENNE TRIBAL EDUCATION DEPARTMENT

http://www.cheyennenation.com/education.html

HIGHER EDUCATION SCHOLARSHIP PROGRAM

Scholarships will be provided for enrolled Northern Cheyenne Tribal members who meet the requirements listed in the higher education guidelines and meet the deadlines December1, Fall Quarter/Semester October 1, Winter quarter/Spring Semester and April 1 for summer. Northern Cheyenne students must be enrolled in an accredited post secondary institution.

Award: Scholarship for use in freshman, sophomore, junior, senior, or graduate years; renewable. *Number:* 60–72. *Amount:* $50–$6000.

Eligibility Requirements: Applicant must be American Indian/Alaska Native and enrolled or expecting to enroll full- or part-time at a two-year or four-year institution or university. Available to U.S. citizens.

Application Requirements: Application form, essay, financial need analysis. *Deadline:* December 1.

Contact: Norma Bixby, Director
Northern Cheyenne Tribal Education Department
Box 307
Lame Deer, MT 59043
Phone: 406-477-6567
E-mail: norma.bixby@cheyennenation.com

NORTHWEST DANISH ASSOCIATION

www.northwestdanish.org

NORTHWEST DANISH ASSOCIATION SCHOLARSHIP

The scholarship program is designated for people with some kind of Danish connection, living in WA or Oregon states, but study may be at any other location in the United States.

Award: Scholarship for use in freshman, sophomore, junior, senior, or graduate years; not renewable. *Number:* 1–5. *Amount:* $500–$1000.

Eligibility Requirements: Applicant must be of Danish heritage; enrolled or expecting to enroll full-time at a two-year or four-year institution or university and resident of Oregon, Washington. Available to U.S. citizens.

Application Requirements: Application form, essay, financial need analysis. *Deadline:* April 30.

Contact: Dr. Edith Christensen, Scholarship Awards
Northwest Danish Association
1833 N. 105th St.
Suite 101
Seattle, WA 98133
Phone: 206-523-3263
E-mail: seattle@nwdanish.org

OCA

http://www.ocanational.org/

OCA-AXA ACHIEVEMENT SCHOLARSHIP

College achievement scholarship for Asian Pacific Americans entering their first year of college. For full-time study only. Must have an minimum GPA of 3.0.

Award: Scholarship for use in freshman year; not renewable. *Number:* 10. *Amount:* $2000.

Eligibility Requirements: Applicant must be Asian/Pacific Islander; high school student and planning to enroll or expecting to enroll full-time at a two-year or four-year institution or university. Applicant must have 3.0 GPA or higher. Available to U.S. citizens.

Application Requirements: Application form, application form may be submitted online (http://www.ocanational.org), essay, financial need analysis, self-addressed stamped envelope with application, transcript. *Deadline:* April 18.

Contact: Jeffrey Moy, Scholarship Coordinator
OCA
1322 18th Street, NW
Washington, DC 20036
Phone: 202-223-5500 Ext. 116
Fax: 202-296-0540
E-mail: jmoy@ocanational.org

OCA/UPS FOUNDATION GOLD MOUNTAIN SCHOLARSHIP

Scholarships for Asian Pacific Americans who are the first person in their immediate family to attend college. Must be entering first year of college in the upcoming fall. Please see website, http//www.ocanational.org for more information.

Award: Scholarship for use in freshman year; not renewable. *Number:* 10–15. *Amount:* $2000.

Eligibility Requirements: Applicant must be Asian/Pacific Islander; high school student and planning to enroll or expecting to enroll full-time at a two-year or four-year institution or university. Applicant must have 3.0 GPA or higher. Available to U.S. citizens.

Application Requirements: Application form, application form may be submitted online (http://www.ocanational.org), essay, financial need analysis, resume, self-addressed stamped envelope with application, transcript. *Deadline:* April 18.

Contact: Jeffrey Moy, Scholarship Coordinator
OCA
1322 18th Street, NW
Washington, DC 20036
Phone: 202-223-5500
Fax: 202-296-0540
E-mail: oca@ocanational.org

OCA-VERIZON COLLEGE SCHOLARSHIP

Up to $3000 award for students who are Asian/Pacific Islanders having a minimum 3.0 GPA. For more information, see the OCA website at http//www.ocanational.org.

Award: Scholarship for use in sophomore, junior, or senior years; not renewable. *Number:* 15. *Amount:* up to $2000.

Eligibility Requirements: Applicant must be Asian/Pacific Islander and enrolled or expecting to enroll full-time at a two-year or four-year institution or university. Applicant must have 3.0 GPA or higher. Available to U.S. citizens.

Application Requirements: Application form, essay, financial need analysis, self-addressed stamped envelope with application, transcript. *Deadline:* April 18.

Contact: Jeffrey Moy, Scholarship Coordinator
OCA
1322 18th Street, NW
Washington, DC 20036
Phone: 202-223-5500 Ext. 116
E-mail: jmoy@ocanational.org

OFFICE OF NAVAJO NATION SCHOLARSHIP AND FINANCIAL ASSISTANCE

http://www.onnsfa.org/

CHIEF MANUELITO SCHOLARSHIP PROGRAM

Award programs established to recognize and award undergraduate students with high test scores and GPA of 3.0. Priorities to Navajo Nation applicants. Must be enrolled as a full-time undergraduate and pursue a degree program leading to a Baccalaureate. For further details visit website http://www.onnsfa.org/docs/polproc.pdf.

Award: Scholarship for use in freshman, sophomore, junior, or senior years; not renewable. *Number:* 1. *Amount:* $7000.

Eligibility Requirements: Applicant must be American Indian/Alaska Native and enrolled or expecting to enroll full-time at a two-year or four-year institution or university. Applicant must have 3.0 GPA or higher. Available to U.S. citizens.

Application Requirements: Application form, financial need analysis, test scores, transcript. *Deadline:* April 1.

Contact: Maxine Damon, Financial Aid Counselor
Phone: 800-243-2956
Fax: 928-871-6561
E-mail: maxinedamon@navajo.org

OHIO DEPARTMENT OF HIGHER EDUCATION

www.ohiohighered.org

OHIO COLLEGE OPPORTUNITY GRANT

• *See page 609*

OHIO SAFETY OFFICERS COLLEGE MEMORIAL FUND

• *See page 609*

OHIO WAR ORPHANS SCHOLARSHIP

• *See page 610*

ONEIDA TRIBE OF INDIANS OF WISCONSIN

http://www.oneida-nsn.gov

ONEIDA HIGHER EDUCATION SCHOLARSHIP PROGRAM

Renewable award available to enrolled members of the Oneida Tribe of Indians of Wisconsin, who are accepted into an accredited postsecondary institution within the United States. Must have a high school diploma, HSED or GED. Maximum funding varies based on the post-secondary costs and level of degree seeking. Please see website for more details.

Award: Grant for use in freshman, sophomore, junior, senior, graduate, or postgraduate years; renewable.

Eligibility Requirements: Applicant must be American Indian/Alaska Native and enrolled or expecting to enroll full- or part-time at a two-year or four-year or technical institution or university. Available to U.S. citizens.

Application Requirements: Application form, financial need analysis. *Deadline:* continuous.

Contact: Higher Education Advisor
Oneida Tribe of Indians of Wisconsin
PO Box 365
Oneida, WI 54155
Phone: 920-869-4033
E-mail: highered@oneidanation.org

ONE LOVE FOUNDATION

www.joinonelove.org

ONE LOVE FOUNDATION PETS VS. PARTNERS SCHOLARSHIP
• *See page 610*

OREGON NATIVE AMERICAN CHAMBER OF COMMERCE SCHOLARSHIP

http://www.onacc.org/

OREGON NATIVE AMERICAN CHAMBER OF COMMERCE SCHOLARSHIP
Scholarships available to Native American students studying in Oregon. Must verify Native American status and be actively involved in the Native American community.

Award: Scholarship for use in freshman, sophomore, junior, or senior years; not renewable. *Number:* 1. *Amount:* $1000.

Eligibility Requirements: Applicant must be American Indian/Alaska Native; enrolled or expecting to enroll full- or part-time at a four-year institution or university and studying in Oregon. Available to U.S. and Canadian citizens.

Application Requirements: Application form, proof of Native American descent, transcript. *Deadline:* varies.

Contact: James Parker, Director of Operations
  Phone: 503-894-4525
  E-mail: support@onacc.org

ORGANIZATION FOR AUTISM RESEARCH

www.researchautism.org

LISA HIGGINS HUSSMAN SCHOLARSHIP
• *See page 610*

SCHWALLIE FAMILY SCHOLARSHIP
• *See page 610*

ORTHODOX UNION

http://ou.org

SARA AND MAX GOLDSAMMLER SCHOLARSHIP FUND
This award is open to any Jewish student. Applicants should write a short essay describing in 500 to 1000 words how they have demonstrated leadership ability both in and outside of school.

Award: Scholarship for use in freshman, sophomore, junior, or senior years; not renewable. *Number:* 3. *Amount:* $300–$1000.

Eligibility Requirements: Applicant must be Jewish; of Jewish heritage and enrolled or expecting to enroll full- or part-time at a two-year or four-year or technical institution or university. Available to U.S. citizens.

Application Requirements: Application form, essay. *Deadline:* August 10.

Contact: Mrs. Rachel Shammah, Alumni Assistant
  Orthodox Union
  11 Broadway
  New York, NY 10004
  Phone: 212-613-8155
  E-mail: shammahr@ncsy.org

OSAGE NATION EDUCATION DEPARTMENT

https://www.osagenation-nsn.gov/what-we-do/education-department

OSAGE NATION HIGHER EDUCATION SCHOLARSHIP
• *See page 610*

OUTRIGGER DUKE KAHANAMOKU FOUNDATION

http://www.dukefoundation.org

ODKF GENERAL SCHOLARSHIP AWARD
• *See page 611*

PANHELLENIC SCHOLARSHIP FOUNDATION

http://www.panhellenicscholarships.org/

PANHELLENIC SCHOLARSHIP AWARDS
• *See page 611*

PAPERCHECK

https://www.papercheck.com/

PAPERCHECK, LLC—CHARLES SHAFAE' SCHOLARSHIP FUND
• *See page 611*

PENNSYLVANIA FEDERATION OF DEMOCRATIC WOMEN INC.

www.pafedofdemwomen.org

PENNSYLVANIA FEDERATION OF DEMOCRATIC WOMEN INC. ANNUAL SCHOLARSHIP AWARDS
• *See page 554*

PENNSYLVANIA HIGHER EDUCATION ASSISTANCE AGENCY

http://www.pheaa.org/

BLIND OR DEAF BENEFICIARY GRANT PROGRAM
• *See page 612*

PENNSYLVANIA STATE GRANT PROGRAM
• *See page 612*

PETAZI

https://petazi.com/

2017 NURTURE FOR NATURE SCHOLARSHIP
• *See page 637*

PETER AND ALICE KOOMRUIAN FUND

PETER AND ALICE KOOMRUIAN ARMENIAN EDUCATION FUND
Award for students of Armenian descent to pursue postsecondary studies in any field at any accredited college or university in the U.S. Submit student identification and letter of enrollment. Must rank in upper third of class or have minimum GPA of 3.0.

Award: Scholarship for use in freshman, sophomore, junior, senior, or graduate years; not renewable. *Number:* 4–10. *Amount:* $1000–$5000.

Eligibility Requirements: Applicant must be of Armenian heritage and Armenian citizen and enrolled or expecting to enroll full-time at a two-year or four-year institution or university. Applicant must have 3.0 GPA or higher. Available to U.S. and non-U.S. citizens.

Application Requirements: Application form, personal photograph. *Deadline:* April 30.

Contact: Mr. Terenik Koujakian, Awards Committee Member
Peter and Alice Koomruian Fund
16654 1/2 Calneva Drive
Encino, CA 91436
Phone: 818-990-7454
E-mail: terenikkoujakian@hotmail.com

PETER DOCTOR MEMORIAL INDIAN SCHOLARSHIP FOUNDATION INC.

PETER DOCTOR MEMORIAL INDIAN SCHOLARSHIP FOUNDATION INC.

One-time award available to enrolled New York State Iroquois Indian students. Must be a full-time student at the Freshman level and above.

Award: Scholarship for use in freshman, sophomore, junior, senior, or graduate years; not renewable. *Number:* 2. *Amount:* $700–$1500.

Eligibility Requirements: Applicant must be American Indian/Alaska Native; enrolled or expecting to enroll full-time at a two-year or four-year or technical institution or university and resident of New York. Available to U.S. citizens.

Application Requirements: Application form, driver's license, financial need analysis, recommendations or references, tribal certification. *Deadline:* May 31.

Contact: Clara Hill, Treasurer
Peter Doctor Memorial Indian Scholarship Foundation Inc.
PO Box 431
Basom, NY 14013
Phone: 716-542-2025
E-mail: ceh3936@hughes.net

PHILIPINO-AMERICAN ASSOCIATION OF NEW ENGLAND

http://www.pamas.org/

BLESSED LEON OF OUR LADY OF THE ROSARY AWARD

Award for any Filipino-American high school student. Must be of Filipino descent, and have a minimum GPA of 3.3. Application details are available at http://www.pamas.org.

Award: Scholarship for use in freshman year; not renewable. *Number:* 1. *Amount:* $250.

Eligibility Requirements: Applicant must be Asian/Pacific Islander; high school student; planning to enroll or expecting to enroll full-time at a two-year or four-year or technical institution or university and resident of Connecticut, Maine, Massachusetts, New Hampshire, Rhode Island, Vermont. Available to U.S. citizens.

Application Requirements: Application form, college acceptance letter, essay, recommendations or references, transcript. *Deadline:* May 31.

Contact: Amanda Kalb, First Vice President
Phone: 617-471-3513
E-mail: balic2ss@comcast.net

PAMAS RESTRICTED SCHOLARSHIP AWARD
• *See page 554*

RAVENSCROFT FAMILY AWARD

Award for any Filipino-American high school student, who is active in the Filipino community. Must be of Filipino descent, a resident of New England, and have a minimum GPA of 3.3. Application details are available at http://www.pamas.org.

Award: Scholarship for use in freshman year; not renewable. *Number:* 1. *Amount:* $250.

Eligibility Requirements: Applicant must be Asian/Pacific Islander; high school student; planning to enroll or expecting to enroll full-time at a four-year institution or university and resident of Connecticut, Maine, Massachusetts, New Hampshire, Rhode Island, Vermont. Available to U.S. citizens.

Application Requirements: Application form, college acceptance letter, essay, recommendations or references, transcript. *Deadline:* May 31.

Contact: Amanda Kalb, First Vice President
Phone: 617-471-3513
E-mail: balic2ss@comcast.net

PILOT INTERNATIONAL FOUNDATION

http://www.pilotinternational.org/

BECKY BURROWS MEMORIAL SCHOLARSHIP
• *See page 612*

PLAINTIFF RELIEF

http://plaintiffrelief.com/

PLAINTIFF RELIEF SCHOLARSHIP
• *See page 612*

POLISH HERITAGE ASSOCIATION OF MARYLAND

http://www.pha-md.org/

POLISH HERITAGE SCHOLARSHIP

$2500 scholarships given to individuals of Polish descent (at least two Polish grandparents) who demonstrates academic excellence, financial need, and promotes their Polish Heritage. Must be a legal Maryland resident.

Award: Scholarship for use in freshman, sophomore, junior, or senior years; not renewable. *Number:* 1–9. *Amount:* $1500–$2500.

Eligibility Requirements: Applicant must be of Polish heritage; enrolled or expecting to enroll full-time at a two-year or four-year institution or university and resident of Maryland. Available to U.S. citizens.

Application Requirements: Application form, essay, financial need analysis, interview, recommendations or references, transcript. *Deadline:* March 15.

Contact: Thomas Hollowak, Scholarship Chair
Phone: 410-837-4268
E-mail: thollowalk@ubmail.ubalt.edu

POLISH WOMEN'S ALLIANCE

http://www.pwaa.org/

POLISH WOMEN'S ALLIANCE ACADEMIC COLLEGE UNDERGRADUATE SCHOLARSHIPS

Scholarships are given to members of the Polish Women's Alliance of America who have been in good standing for five years. Awards are given for the sophomore, junior, and senior year level of undergraduate study. For details visit website http://www.pwaa.org.

Award: Scholarship for use in sophomore, junior, or senior years; renewable. *Number:* 5. *Amount:* $1000.

Eligibility Requirements: Applicant must be of Polish heritage and enrolled or expecting to enroll full-time at a four-year institution or university. Available to U.S. citizens.

Application Requirements: Application form, essay, personal photograph, transcript. *Deadline:* May 15.

Contact: Sharon Zago, Vice President and Scholarship Chairman
Phone: 847-384-1208
E-mail: vpres@pwaa.org

POLSON & POLSON, P.C.

https://www.polsonlawfirm.com/

POLSON & POLSON, P.C. CONQUERING ADVERSITY SCHOLARSHIP
• *See page 612*

PORTUGUESE FOUNDATION INC.

https://www.facebook.com/pfict/

PORTUGUESE FOUNDATION SCHOLARSHIP PROGRAM
• *See page 612*

PRESBYTERIAN CHURCH (USA)

http://www.pcusa.org/financialaid

NATIVE AMERICAN SUPPLEMENTAL GRANT

Award for Undergrad students who are registered Members of a Native American Tribe. Students must be members of a PC(USA) church.

Award: Grant for use in freshman, sophomore, junior, or senior years; not renewable.

Eligibility Requirements: Applicant must be Presbyterian; American Indian/Alaska Native and enrolled or expecting to enroll full-time at a four-year institution or university. Available to U.S. citizens.

Application Requirements: Application form. *Deadline:* June 1.

Contact: Ms. Laura Bryan, Associate, Financial Aid for Studies
Presbyterian Church (USA)
100 Witherspoon Street
Louisville, KY 40202
Phone: 800-728-7228 Ext. 5735
Fax: 502-569-8766
E-mail: finaid@pcusa.org

PRICE BENOWITZ LLP

http://pricebenowitz.com/

AMATO SANITA BRIGHTER FUTURE SCHOLARSHIP
• *See page 613*

ANGIE DIPIETRO WOMEN IN BUSINESS SCHOLARSHIP
• *See page 613*

APRIL COCKERHAM DREAM ACT SCHOLARSHIP
• *See page 613*

KAREN RILEY PORTER GOOD WORKS SCHOLARSHIP
• *See page 613*

KERRI CASTELLINI WOMEN'S LEADERSHIP SCHOLARSHIP
• *See page 613*

KUSH ARORA FEDERAL CRIMINAL JUSTICE REFORM SCHOLARSHIP
• *See page 613*

PRICE BENOWITZ SOCIAL JUSTICE SCHOLARSHIP
• *See page 613*

SETH OKIN GOOD DEEDS SCHOLARSHIP
• *See page 613*

THOMAS SOLDAN HEALTHY COMMUNITIES SCHOLARSHIP
• *See page 614*

PRIVATE AID TEST SURVEY

A TEST PROGRAM NAME
• *See page 614*

PROMPT

http://prompt.com

PROMPT'S $20,000 SCHOLARSHIP
• *See page 614*

PUEBLO OF ISLETA, DEPARTMENT OF EDUCATION

http://www.isletapueblo.com/

HIGHER EDUCATION SUPPLEMENTAL SCHOLARSHIP ISLETA PUEBLO HIGHER EDUCATION DEPARTMENT
• *See page 556*

PUEBLO OF SAN JUAN, DEPARTMENT OF EDUCATION

OHKAY OWINGEH TRIBAL SCHOLARSHIP OF THE PUEBLO OF SAN JUAN
• *See page 614*

POP'AY SCHOLARSHIP
• *See page 614*

REACH HIGHER MONTANA

http://www.ReachHigherMontana.org

REACH HIGHER MONTANA SCHOLARSHIPS
• *See page 614*

RHINE LAW FIRM, P.C.

http://www.carolinaaccidentattorneys.com/

2017 RHINE LAW FIRM, P.C. SCHOLARSHIP
• *See page 615*

ROMAN CATHOLIC DIOCESE OF TULSA

http://www.dioceseoftulsa.org

MAE LASSLEY OSAGE SCHOLARSHIP

This scholarship fund gives the Catholic Church an opportunity to continue it's educational work with the Osage Tribe.

Award: Scholarship for use in freshman, sophomore, junior, senior, or graduate years; renewable. *Amount:* $500–$1000.

Eligibility Requirements: Applicant must be Roman Catholic; American Indian/Alaska Native and enrolled or expecting to enroll full-time at a two-year or four-year institution or university. Applicant must have 2.5 GPA or higher. Available to U.S. citizens.

Application Requirements: Application form, financial need analysis. *Deadline:* April 15.

Contact: Mrs. Sarah Jameson, Assistant Director, Youth,
Young Adult and Campus Ministry
Roman Catholic Diocese of Tulsa
PO Box 690240
Tulsa, OK 74169-0240
Phone: 918-307-4939
E-mail: sarah.jameson@dioceseoftulsa.org

RON BROWN SCHOLAR FUND

http://www.ronbrown.org/

RON BROWN SCHOLAR PROGRAM

The program seeks to identify African-American high school seniors who will make significant contributions to the society. Applicants must excel academically, show exceptional leadership potential, participate in community service activities, and demonstrate financial need. Must be a U.S. citizen or hold permanent resident visa. Must plan to attend a four-year college or university. Deadlines: November 1 and January 9.

Award: Scholarship for use in freshman, sophomore, junior, or senior years; renewable. *Number:* 10–20. *Amount:* $10,000–$40,000.

Eligibility Requirements: Applicant must be Black (non-Hispanic); high school student; planning to enroll or expecting to enroll full-time at a four-year institution or university and must have an interest in leadership. Available to U.S. citizens.

Application Requirements: Application form, community service, essay, financial need analysis, interview, personal photograph, recommendations or references, test scores, transcript.

Contact: Ms. Vanessa Evans, Associate Director
Ron Brown Scholar Fund
1160 Pepsi Place, Suite 206
Charlottesville, VA 22901
Phone: 434-964-1588
Fax: 434-964-1589
E-mail: info@ronbrown.org

ROSENGREN KOHLMEYER, LAW OFFICE CHTD.

http://rokolaw.com

ROSENGREN KOHLMEYER LAW OFFICE SCHOLARSHIP
• *See page 615*

RYU FAMILY FOUNDATION, INC.

SEOL BONG SCHOLARSHIP
• *See page 637*

SACHS FOUNDATION

http://www.sachsfoundation.org/

SACHS FOUNDATION SCHOLARSHIPS
Award to undergraduate students based on performance, financial need, and applicant's area of study and life goals. Must be African-American and a resident of Colorado. Minimum 3.5 GPA required.

Award: Scholarship for use in freshman year; renewable. *Number:* up to 50. *Amount:* up to $4000.

Eligibility Requirements: Applicant must be Black (non-Hispanic); high school student; planning to enroll or expecting to enroll full-time at a four-year institution or university and resident of Colorado. Applicant must have 3.5 GPA or higher. Available to U.S. citizens.

Application Requirements: Application form, financial need analysis, personal photograph. *Deadline:* March 1.

Contact: Lisa Harris, Secretary and Treasurer
Phone: 719-633-2353
E-mail: lisa@sachsfoundation.org

SAINT ANDREW'S SOCIETY OF THE STATE OF NEW YORK

http://www.standrewsny.org/

ST. ANDREWS SCHOLARSHIP
Scholarship for senior undergraduate students who will obtain a Bachelor's degree from an accredited college or university in the spring and can demonstrate the significance of studying in Scotland. Proof of application to their selected school will be required for finalists. Applicant must be of Scottish descent.

Award: Scholarship for use in senior year; not renewable. *Number:* 2. *Amount:* $20,000–$30,000.

Eligibility Requirements: Applicant must be of Scottish heritage and enrolled or expecting to enroll full-time at a four-year institution or university. Applicant must have 2.5 GPA or higher. Available to U.S. citizens.

Application Requirements: Application form. *Deadline:* December 15.

Contact: James Heggie, President
Phone: 212-223-4248
Fax: 212-223-0748
E-mail: office@standrewsny.org

ST. ANDREW'S SOCIETY OF WASHINGTON, DC

http://www.saintandrewsociety.org/

DONALD MALCOLM MACARTHUR SCHOLARSHIP
One-time award is available for U.S. students to study in Scotland or students from Scotland to study in the United States. Special attention will be given to applicants whose work would demonstrably contribute to enhanced knowledge of Scottish history or culture. Must be a college junior, senior, or graduate student to apply. Need for financial assistance and academic record considered. Visit website for details and application http://www.thecapitalscot.com/standrew/scholarships.html.

Award: Scholarship for use in junior, senior, or graduate years; not renewable. *Number:* 1. *Amount:* up to $2500.

Eligibility Requirements: Applicant must be of Scottish heritage; enrolled or expecting to enroll full-time at a four-year institution or university and resident of Delaware, District of Columbia, Maryland, New Jersey, North Carolina, Pennsylvania, Virginia, Wisconsin. Available to U.S. and non-U.S. citizens.

Application Requirements: Application form, essay, financial need analysis, interview, recommendations or references, self-addressed stamped envelope with application. *Deadline:* April 30.

Contact: T.J. Holland, Chairman, Scholarship Committee
St. Andrew's Society of Washington, DC
1443 Laurel Hill Road
Vienna, VA 22182-1711
E-mail: tjholland@wmalumni.com

SALLIE MAE FUND

http://www.thesalliemaefund.org/

$1,000 PLAN FOR COLLEGE SWEEPSTAKES
• *See page 615*

SALVADORAN AMERICAN LEADERSHIP AND EDUCATIONAL FUND

http://www.salef.org/

FULFILLING OUR DREAMS SCHOLARSHIP FUND
Up to 60 scholarships ranging from $500 to $2500 will be awarded to students who come from a Latino heritage. Must have a 2.5 GPA. See website for more details, http://www.salef.org.

Award: Scholarship for use in freshman, sophomore, junior, senior, graduate, or postgraduate years; not renewable. *Number:* 50–60. *Amount:* $500–$2500.

Eligibility Requirements: Applicant must be of Hispanic, Latin American/Caribbean heritage; enrolled or expecting to enroll full- or part-time at a two-year or four-year institution or university; resident of California and studying in California. Applicant must have 2.5 GPA or higher. Available to U.S. and non-U.S. citizens.

Application Requirements: Application form, community service, essay, financial need analysis, interview, personal photograph, recommendations or references, resume, self-addressed stamped envelope with application, test scores, transcript. *Deadline:* June 30.

Contact: Mayra Soriano, Educational and Youth Programs Manager
Salvadoran American Leadership and Educational Fund
1625 West Olympic Boulevard, Suite 718
Los Angeles, CA 90015
Phone: 213-480-1052
Fax: 213-487-2530
E-mail: msoriano@salef.org

SANTO DOMINGO SCHOLARSHIP PROGRAM

SANTO DOMINGO SCHOLARSHIP
An organization instituted for the welfare of the Santo Domingo Pueblo enrolled members. Santo Domingo Tribe—Education Office offers scholarships in Higher Education and Adult Education. To be considered

an applicant, you must fill out an application. Deadlines: Fall semester—March 1 and Spring semester—October 1.

Award: Scholarship for use in freshman, sophomore, junior, or senior years; renewable. *Amount:* $200–$1000.

Eligibility Requirements: Applicant must be American Indian/Alaska Native and enrolled or expecting to enroll full- or part-time at a two-year or four-year or technical institution or university. Applicant must have 2.5 GPA or higher. Available to U.S. citizens.

Application Requirements: Application form, certificate of Indian blood, financial need analysis, recommendations or references, transcript. *Deadline:* varies.

Contact: Rita Lujan, Education Director
Santo Domingo Scholarship Program
PO Box 160
Santo Domingo Pueblo, NM 87052
Phone: 505-465-2214 Ext. 2211
Fax: 505-465-2542
E-mail: rlujan@kewa-nsn.us

SELECTBLINDS.COM

http://www.selectblinds.com

SELECTBLINDS.COM $1000 COLLEGE SCHOLARSHIP
• *See page 615*

SEXNER & ASSOCIATES LLC

http://www.sexner.com/personal-injury/

MITCHELL S. SEXNER & ASSOCIATES LLC SCHOLARSHIP
• *See page 616*

SHAWN SUKUMAR ATTORNEY AT LAW

https://www.washingtondccriminallawyer.net/

SHAWN SUKUMAR CRIMINAL JUSTICE REFORM SCHOLARSHIP
• *See page 616*

SILICON VALLEY COMMUNITY FOUNDATION

www.siliconvalleycf.org

ABBY SOBRATO SCHOLARSHIP
• *See page 616*

BOBETTE BIBO GUGLIOTTA MEMORIAL SCHOLARSHIP FOR CREATIVE WRITING
• *See page 616*

CURRY AWARD FOR GIRLS AND YOUNG WOMEN
• *See page 616*

HAZEL REED BAUMEISTER SCHOLARSHIP PROGRAM
• *See page 616*

HUANG LEADERSHIP DEVELOPMENT SCHOLARSHIP
• *See page 617*

LATINOS IN TECHNOLOGY SCHOLARSHIP
• *See page 617*

SNOW, CARPIO & WEEKLEY, PLC

http://workinjuryaz.com

SCW DREAMERS SCHOLARSHIP
Must be a DREAMer with a GPA of 3.0 or higher. This is a video submission scholarship. For all requirements and more info please visit our website http://workinjuryaz.com/tucson-social-security-disability-attorneys/#dreamers. Only submissions on our website will be considered.

Award: Scholarship for use in freshman or sophomore years; not renewable. *Number:* 2. *Amount:* $2500.

Eligibility Requirements: Applicant must be of Hispanic heritage; age 16-25 and enrolled or expecting to enroll full- or part-time at a two-year or four-year institution or university. Applicant must have 3.0 GPA or higher. Available to U.S. and non-U.S. citizens.

Application Requirements: Application form. *Deadline:* May 31.

Contact: April Snow
E-mail: snowcarpioaz@gmail.com

SOCIETY FOR APPLIED ANTHROPOLOGY

http://www.sfaa.net/

ANNUAL SFAA STUDENT ENDOWED AWARD
• *See page 617*

TOURISM AND HERITAGE STUDENT PAPER COMPETITION
• *See page 617*

SOCIETY OF DAUGHTERS OF THE UNITED STATES ARMY

SOCIETY OF DAUGHTERS OF THE UNITED STATES ARMY SCHOLARSHIPS
• *See page 617*

SONS OF ITALY FOUNDATION

http://www.osia.org/

SONS OF ITALY FOUNDATION'S NATIONAL LEADERSHIP GRANT COMPETITION
Scholarships for undergraduate or graduate students who are U.S. citizens of Italian descent. Must demonstrate academic excellence. For more details see Website, http://www.osia.org.

Award: Scholarship for use in freshman, sophomore, junior, senior, or graduate years; not renewable. *Number:* 9–10. *Amount:* $4000–$10,000.

Eligibility Requirements: Applicant must be of Italian heritage and enrolled or expecting to enroll full-time at a four-year institution or university. Available to U.S. citizens.

Application Requirements: Application form, community service, essay, recommendations or references, resume, test scores, transcript. *Fee:* $30. *Deadline:* February 28.

Contact: Ms. Laura Kelly
Phone: 202-547-2900
Fax: 202-546-8168
E-mail: scholarships@osia.org

SONS OF ITALY NATIONAL LEADERSHIP GRANTS COMPETITION/ HENRY SALVATORI SCHOLARSHIP
Scholarships for college-bound high school seniors who demonstrate exceptional leadership, distinguished scholarship, and a deep understanding and respect for the principles upon which our nation was founded: liberty, freedom, and equality. Must be a U.S. citizen of Italian descent. For more details see website http://www.osia.org.

Award: Scholarship for use in freshman year; not renewable. *Number:* up to 1. *Amount:* up to $5000.

Eligibility Requirements: Applicant must be of Italian heritage; high school student and planning to enroll or expecting to enroll full-time at a four-year institution or university. Available to U.S. citizens.

Application Requirements: Application form, community service, essay, recommendations or references, resume, test scores, transcript. *Fee:* $30. *Deadline:* February 27.

Contact: Ms. Laura Kelly
Phone: 202-547-2900
Fax: 202-546-8168
E-mail: scholarships@osia.org

SOURCE SUPPLY COMPANY

http://sourcesupplycompany.com/

SOURCE SUPPLY SCHOLARSHIP

To apply for the 2014-2015 Source Supply Scholarship, respond to the following essay prompt in 1,000 words: Please discuss the importance of keeping the environment clean. How does recycling make an impact on the environment? And how can the systems we, as a nation, have in place be improved? To be eligible, please email your essay to info@ sourcesupplycompany.com by May 31, 2015. Please be sure to reference Source Supply College Scholarship Essay Content in the subject line of your email.

Award: Scholarship for use in freshman, sophomore, or junior years; not renewable. *Number:* up to 1. *Amount:* $1000–$1000.

Eligibility Requirements: Applicant must be American Indian/Alaska Native, Asian/Pacific Islander, Black (non-Hispanic), Hispanic and enrolled or expecting to enroll full-time at a two-year or four-year or technical institution or university. Available to U.S. citizens.

Application Requirements: Entry in a contest, essay. *Deadline:* May 31.

Contact: Dave Brown, Owner
Source Supply Company
6 Bellecor Drive
Suite 104
New Castle, PA 19720
Phone: 302-328-5110
E-mail: Info@SourceSupplyCompany.com

SOUTH CAROLINA TUITION GRANTS COMMISSION

http://www.sctuitiongrants.org/

SOUTH CAROLINA TUITION GRANTS PROGRAM
• *See page 617*

SPANISHDICT

www.spanishdict.com/traductor

BECA #TRADUCTOR
• *See page 618*

SPINE SURGEON DR. VICTOR HAYES

https://tampabaybackpaindoctor.com/

TAMPA BAY SPINE CENTER ROAD TO RECOVERY SCHOLARSHIP
• *See page 618*

STATE EMPLOYEES ASSOCIATION OF NORTH CAROLINA (SEANC)

http://www.seanc.org/

STATE EMPLOYEES ASSOCIATION OF NORTH CAROLINA (SEANC) SCHOLARSHIPS

Scholarships available to SEANC members, their spouses and dependents seeking postsecondary education. Awarded in three categories: based on academic merit, financial need, and awards for SEANC members only. For application and more information visit http://www.seanc.org/.

Award: Scholarship for use in freshman, sophomore, junior, or senior years; not renewable. *Number:* 47. *Amount:* $500–$1000.

Eligibility Requirements: Applicant must be enrolled or expecting to enroll full-time at a two-year or four-year or technical institution or university and resident of North Carolina. Applicant must have 3.5 GPA or higher. Available to U.S. citizens.

Application Requirements: Application form, financial need analysis. *Deadline:* April 15.

Contact: Renee Vaughan
Phone: 919-833-6436

STONEWALL COMMUNITY FOUNDATION

http://www.stonewallfoundation.org/

NEW YORK RAMBLERS SCHOLARSHIP FOR STUDENT ATHLETES
• *See page 618*

TRAUB-DICKER RAINBOW SCHOLARSHIP
• *See page 618*

STRAIGHTFORWARD MEDIA

http://www.straightforwardmedia.com/

STRAIGHTFORWARD MEDIA MINORITY SCHOLARSHIP

Four scholarships a year offered to students who are members of racial or ethnic minority groups and who are currently enrolled in or planning to enroll in postsecondary education. For more information, see website at http://www.straightforwardmedia.com/minority/form.php.

Award: Scholarship for use in freshman, sophomore, junior, or senior years; not renewable. *Number:* 4. *Amount:* $500.

Eligibility Requirements: Applicant must be American Indian/Alaska Native, Asian/Pacific Islander, Black (non-Hispanic), Hispanic and enrolled or expecting to enroll full- or part-time at a two-year or four-year or technical institution or university. Available to U.S. and non-U.S. citizens.

Application Requirements: Essay. *Deadline:* varies.

Contact: Scholarship Committee
Phone: 605-348-3042

STROM & ASSOCIATES

https://stromlawyers.com

STROM & ASSOCIATES NEED-BASED SCHOLARSHIP
• *See page 619*

SWISS BENEVOLENT SOCIETY

http://www.sbssf.com/

WILLY ISLER SCHOLARSHIPS

The Swiss Benevolent Society helps qualified applicants obtain a higher education in any field of endeavor at any accredited university or college in the United States. The scholarships are limited to students who are residents of Northern California. Students may apply every year while enrolled. Applicants must be of Swiss descent by demonstrating that applicant or at least one parent is a Swiss national, registered with the Swiss Consulate General of San Francisco (or carry a valid Swiss passport). Must have resided in Northern California for a minimum of three years preceding the date of initial application. Must have applied for admission to any accredited institution of higher learning in the United States offering a baccalaureate or graduate degree (in exceptional cases, students attending a community college or an accredited vocational school in California may be considered). Must be a full time student completing 12 undergraduate or 9 graduate units per term. Additional requirements regarding scholastic merit and financial need, as well as the application form and guidelines, are available on the SBSSF website. Only complete applications, including all supporting documents, postmarked no later than April 30th, can be considered.

Award: Scholarship for use in freshman, sophomore, junior, senior, graduate, or postgraduate years; renewable.

Eligibility Requirements: Applicant must be of Swiss heritage; enrolled or expecting to enroll full-time at a four-year institution or university and resident of California. Applicant must have 3.0 GPA or higher.

Application Requirements: Application form, essay, financial need analysis. *Deadline:* April 30.

Contact: John Andrew, Scholarship Committee Chair
Swiss Benevolent Society
Pier 17, Ste 600
San Francisco, CA 94111
E-mail: scholarships@sbssf.com

SWISS BENEVOLENT SOCIETY OF CHICAGO

http://www.sbschicago.org/

SWISS BENEVOLENT SOCIETY OF CHICAGO SCHOLARSHIPS

Scholarship for undergraduate college students of Swiss descent, having permanent residence in Illinois or Southern Wisconsin. Must have 3.3 GPA. High school students need a 26 on ACT or 1050 on SAT.

Award: Scholarship for use in freshman, sophomore, or junior years; not renewable. *Number:* 30. *Amount:* $500–$2500.

Eligibility Requirements: Applicant must be of Swiss heritage; enrolled or expecting to enroll full-time at a four-year institution or university and resident of Illinois, Wisconsin. Available to U.S. citizens.

Application Requirements: Application form, essay. *Deadline:* April 15.

Contact: John Paluch, Chair
Swiss Benevolent Society of Chicago
PO Box 2137
Chicago, IL 60690-2137
Phone: 847-491-8081
E-mail: education@sbschicago.org

SWISS BENEVOLENT SOCIETY OF NEW YORK

http://www.sbsny.org/

MEDICUS STUDENT EXCHANGE

One-time award to students of Swiss nationality or parentage. Open to U.S. residents for study in Switzerland and to Swiss residents for study in the U.S. Must be proficient in foreign language of instruction.

Award: Grant for use in junior, senior, or graduate years; not renewable. *Number:* 1–10. *Amount:* $2000–$10,000.

Eligibility Requirements: Applicant must be of Swiss heritage; enrolled or expecting to enroll full-time at a four-year institution or university and must have an interest in foreign language. Applicant must have 2.5 GPA or higher. Available to U.S. and non-Canadian citizens.

Application Requirements: Application form. *Fee:* $75. *Deadline:* March 31.

Contact: Scholarship Committee
Swiss Benevolent Society of New York
500 Fifth Avenue, Suite 1800
New York, NY 10110
Phone: 212-246-0655

PELLEGRINI SCHOLARSHIP GRANTS

Award to students who have a minimum 3.0 GPA and show financial need. Must submit proof of Swiss nationality or descent. Must be a permanent resident of Connecticut, Delaware, New Jersey, New York, or Pennsylvania.

Award: Scholarship for use in freshman, sophomore, junior, senior, or graduate years; not renewable. *Number:* 50. *Amount:* $500–$5000.

Eligibility Requirements: Applicant must be of Swiss heritage; enrolled or expecting to enroll full-time at a two-year or four-year or technical institution or university and resident of Connecticut, Delaware, New Jersey, New York, Pennsylvania. Applicant must have 3.0 GPA or higher. Available to U.S. citizens.

Application Requirements: Application form, financial need analysis. *Fee:* $75. *Deadline:* March 31.

Contact: Scholarship Committee
Swiss Benevolent Society of New York
500 Fifth Avenue, Room 1800
New York, NY 10110
Phone: 212-246-0655

TARADASH LAW FIRM

https://taradashlaw.com/

TARADASH LAW FIRM SCHOLARSHIP
• See page 619

TELEVISION ACADEMY FOUNDATION

http://www.televisionacademy.com/foundation

TELEVISION ACADEMY FOUNDATION
• See page 619

TENNESSEE STUDENT ASSISTANCE CORPORATION

http://www.tn.gov/collegepays

DEPENDENT CHILDREN SCHOLARSHIP PROGRAM
• See page 619

HELPING HEROES GRANT
• See page 619

HOPE WITH ASPIRE
• See page 619

NED MCWHERTER SCHOLARS PROGRAM
• See page 620

TELS HOPE ACCESS GRANT
• See page 620

TELS -HOPE WITH GENERAL ASSEMBLY MERIT SCHOLARSHIP (GAMS)
• See page 620

TELS - TENNESSEE HOPE SCHOLARSHIP
• See page 620

TENNESSEE DUAL ENROLLMENT GRANT
• See page 620

TENNESSEE EDUCATION LOTTERY SCHOLARSHIP PROGRAM WILDER-NAIFEH TECHNICAL SKILLS GRANT
• See page 620

TENNESSEE HOPE FOSTER CHILD TUITION GRANT
• See page 620

TENNESSEE STEP UP SCHOLARSHIP
• See page 621

TENNESSEE STUDENT ASSISTANCE AWARD
• See page 621

TERRY FOX HUMANITARIAN AWARD

http://terryfoxawards.ca/

TERRY FOX HUMANITARIAN AWARD
• See page 621

TETHERBOX

http://www.tetherbox.com/

$1,000 CREATIVE VIDEO CHALLENGE COLLEGE SCHOLARSHIP
• See page 621

TEXAS ASSOCIATION OF DEVELOPING COLLEGES

http://www.txadc.org

THE URBAN SCHOLARSHIPS FUND
• *See page 622*

TEXAS BLACK BAPTIST SCHOLARSHIP COMMITTEE

http://www.bgct.org/

TEXAS BLACK BAPTIST SCHOLARSHIP

Renewable award for Texas residents attending a Baptist educational institution in Texas. Must be of African-American descent with a minimum 2.0 GPA. Must be a member in good standing of a Baptist church.

Award: Scholarship for use in freshman, sophomore, junior, or senior years; renewable. *Amount:* $1600.

Eligibility Requirements: Applicant must be Baptist; Black (non-Hispanic); enrolled or expecting to enroll full- or part-time at a two-year or four-year institution or university; resident of Texas and studying in Texas. Available to U.S. citizens.

Application Requirements: Application form, driver's license, financial need analysis, interview, personal photograph, portfolio, recommendations or references, resume, test scores, transcript. *Deadline:* continuous.

Contact: Charlie Singleton, Director
          Phone: 214-828-5130
          Fax: 214-828-5284
          E-mail: charlie.singleton@bgct.org

TEXAS MUTUAL INSURANCE COMPANY

http://www.texasmutual.com/

TEXAS MUTUAL INSURANCE COMPANY SCHOLARSHIP PROGRAM
• *See page 622*

TLICHO GOVERNMENT

http://www.tlicho.ca/

BHP BILLITON UNIVERSITY SCHOLARSHIPS

Award for undergraduate, Master's or Ph.D. degree students of Tlicho ancestry. Applicants should be a member of Tlicho Citizens. Must be enrolled full-time in a Canadian university degree program and be interested and active in community affairs. Scholarship value is $5000.

Award: Scholarship for use in junior, senior, graduate, or postgraduate years; not renewable. *Number:* 4. *Amount:* $5000.

Eligibility Requirements: Applicant must be Canadian citizen; American Indian/Alaska Native and enrolled or expecting to enroll full-time at an institution or university. Applicant must have 2.5 GPA or higher.

Application Requirements: Application form, Indian Status Card, acceptance letter, recommendations or references, transcript. *Deadline:* July 15.

Contact: Bertha Black, Career Development Coordinator
          Tlicho Government
          PO Box 412
          Behchoko, NT X0E 0Y0
          CAN
          Phone: 867-392-6381 Ext. 211
          E-mail: berthablack@tlicho.com

DIAVIK DIAMONDS INC. SCHOLARSHIPS FOR COLLEGE STUDENTS

Scholarship for students enrolled full-time in a Canadian college diploma program. Must be of Tlicho ancestry. Must be interested and active in community affairs. Applicants should be a member of Tilcho Citizens. Scholarship value is $3000.

Award: Scholarship for use in freshman, sophomore, junior, or senior years; not renewable. *Number:* 10. *Amount:* $3000.

Eligibility Requirements: Applicant must be Canadian citizen; American Indian/Alaska Native and enrolled or expecting to enroll full-time at a two-year or four-year or technical institution. Applicant must have 2.5 GPA or higher.

Application Requirements: Application form, essay, personal letter, acceptance letter, and Indian Status Card, recommendations or references, transcript. *Deadline:* July 15.

Contact: Bertha Black, Career Development Coordinator
          Tlicho Government
          PO Box 412
          Behchoko, NT X0E 0Y0
          CAN
          Phone: 867-392-6381 Ext. 211
          E-mail: berthablack@tlicho.com

TWO TEN FOOTWEAR FOUNDATION

http://www.twoten.org/

CLASSIC SCHOLARSHIPS
• *See page 622*

ULMAN CANCER FUND FOR YOUNG ADULTS

http://www.ulmanfund.org/scholarships

JACQUELINE SHEARER MEMORIAL SCHOLARSHIP
• *See page 623*

JAMIE L. ROBERTS MEMORIAL SCHOLARSHIP AWARD
• *See page 623*

JEFFREY P. MEYER MEMORIAL SCHOLARSHIP
• *See page 623*

JILL WEAVER STARKMAN SCHOLARSHIP
• *See page 623*

JOHN HANLEY MEMORIAL SCHOLARSHIP
• *See page 623*

LISA HIGGINS-HUSSMAN FOUNDATION SCHOLARSHIP
• *See page 623*

MARILYN YETSO MEMORIAL SCHOLARSHIP
• *See page 624*

OLIVIA M. MARQUART SCHOLARSHIP
• *See page 624*

PERLITA LIWANAG MEMORIAL SCHOLARSHIP
• *See page 624*

SATOLA FAMILY SCHOLARSHIP
• *See page 624*

SEAN SILVER MEMORIAL SCHOLARSHIP AWARD
• *See page 624*

VERA YIP MEMORIAL SCHOLARSHIP
• *See page 624*

VITTORIA DIANNA RICARDO MEMORIAL SCHOLARSHIP
• *See page 625*

UNICO FOUNDATION INC.
http://www.unico.org/

ALPHONSE A. MIELE SCHOLARSHIP
Candidates must be of Italian heritage and reside in the home state of an active UNICO Chapter. Applications may be acquired from and submitted through a State Chapter, the District Governor or the UNICO National Office. Scholarship is available to a graduating high school senior. Application must be signed by student's guidance counselor. This scholarship is valued at $6,000; paid out at $1,500 per year, over four years.

Award: Scholarship for use in freshman, sophomore, junior, or senior years; renewable. *Number:* 1. *Amount:* $1500.

Eligibility Requirements: Applicant must be of Italian heritage; high school student and planning to enroll or expecting to enroll full-time at a four-year institution or university. Applicant must have 3.0 GPA or higher. Available to U.S. citizens.

Application Requirements: Application form, essay, financial need analysis. *Deadline:* April 15.

Contact: Joan Tidona, Scholarship Director
Phone: 973-808-0035
Fax: 973-808-0043
E-mail: uniconational@unico.org

DIMATTIO CELLI FAMILY STUDY ABROAD SCHOLARSHIP
This award is for study in Italy. Candidates must be currently enrolled, full-time, in an accredited college/university in the United States. The study abroad program must be eligible for credit by the student's college/university. Candidates must be of Italian heritage and reside in the home state of an active UNICO Chapter. Applications may be acquired from and submitted through a State Chapter, the District Governor or the UNICO National Office.

Award: Scholarship for use in freshman, sophomore, junior, or senior years; not renewable. *Number:* 2. *Amount:* $1250.

Eligibility Requirements: Applicant must be of Bulgarian heritage and enrolled or expecting to enroll full-time at a four-year institution or university. Applicant must have 3.0 GPA or higher. Available to U.S. citizens.

Application Requirements: Application form. *Deadline:* March 1.

Contact: Joan Tidona, Scholarship Director
Phone: 973-808-0035
Fax: 973-808-0043
E-mail: uniconational@unico.org

ELLA T. GRASSO LITERARY SCHOLARSHIP
Application is open to matriculated college students. The candidate is required to submit a short story or essay celebrating their Italian heritage. Participants must reside in the home state of an active UNICO Chapter. Applications may be acquired from and submitted through a State Chapter, the District Governor or the UNICO National Office. The signature of a School Administrator is required.

Award: Scholarship for use in sophomore, junior, senior, graduate, or postgraduate years; not renewable. *Number:* 2. *Amount:* $1000.

Eligibility Requirements: Applicant must be of Italian heritage and enrolled or expecting to enroll full-time at a four-year institution or university. Applicant must have 3.0 GPA or higher. Available to U.S. citizens.

Application Requirements: Application form, essay. *Deadline:* April 15.

Contact: Joan Tidona, Scholarship Director
Phone: 973-808-0035
Fax: 973-808-0043
E-mail: uniconational@unico.org

MAJOR DON S. GENTILE SCHOLARSHIP
Candidates must be of Italian heritage and reside in the home state of an active UNICO Chapter. Applications may be acquired from and submitted through a State Chapter, the District Governor or the UNICO National Office. Scholarship is available to a graduating high school senior. Application must be signed by student's guidance counselor. This scholarship is valued at $6,000; paid out at $1,500 per year, over four years.

Award: Scholarship for use in freshman, sophomore, junior, or senior years; renewable. *Number:* 1. *Amount:* $1500.

Eligibility Requirements: Applicant must be of Italian heritage; high school student and planning to enroll or expecting to enroll full-time at a four-year institution or university. Applicant must have 3.0 GPA or higher. Available to U.S. citizens.

Application Requirements: Application form, essay, financial need analysis. *Deadline:* April 15.

Contact: Joan Tidona, Scholarship Director
Phone: 973-808-0035
Fax: 973-808-0043
E-mail: uniconational@unico.org

THEODORE MAZZA SCHOLARSHIP
Candidates must be of Italian heritage and reside in the home state of an active UNICO Chapter. Applications may be acquired from and submitted through a State Chapter, the District Governor or the UNICO National Office. Scholarship is available to a graduating high school senior. Application must be signed by student's guidance counselor. This scholarship is valued at $6,000; paid out at $1,500 per year, over four years.

Award: Scholarship for use in freshman, sophomore, junior, or senior years; renewable. *Number:* 1. *Amount:* $1500.

Eligibility Requirements: Applicant must be of Italian heritage; high school student and planning to enroll or expecting to enroll full-time at a four-year institution or university. Applicant must have 3.0 GPA or higher. Available to U.S. citizens.

Application Requirements: Application form, essay, financial need analysis. *Deadline:* April 15.

Contact: Joan Tidona, Scholarship Director
Phone: 973-808-0035
Fax: 973-808-0043
E-mail: uniconational@unico.org

WILLIAM C. DAVINI SCHOLARSHIP
Candidates must be of Italian heritage and reside in the home state of an active UNICO Chapter. Applications may be acquired from and submitted through a State Chapter, the District Governor or the UNICO National Office. Scholarship is available to a graduating high school senior. Application must be signed by student's guidance counselor. This scholarship is valued at $6,000; paid out at $1,500 per year, over four years.

Award: Scholarship for use in freshman, sophomore, junior, or senior years; renewable. *Number:* 1. *Amount:* $1500.

Eligibility Requirements: Applicant must be of Italian heritage; high school student and planning to enroll or expecting to enroll full-time at a four-year institution or university. Applicant must have 3.0 GPA or higher. Available to U.S. citizens.

Application Requirements: Application form, essay, financial need analysis. *Deadline:* April 15.

Contact: Joan Tidona, Scholarship Director
Phone: 973-808-0035
Fax: 973-808-0043
E-mail: uniconational@unico.org

UNION PLUS SCHOLARSHIP PROGRAM
http://www.unionplus.org/

UNION PLUS EDUCATION FOUNDATION SCHOLARSHIP PROGRAM
• See page 564

UNITED NEGRO COLLEGE FUND
http://www.uncf.org/

CITY OF CHICAGO SCHOLARSHIP
Scholarship directed to students who are dependents of current or retired employees (parent, legal guardian, or foster parent) of the City of Chicago and their sister agencies. Applicants must attend HBCU or UNCF-affiliated colleges and have a financial.

Award: Scholarship for use in freshman, sophomore, junior, or senior years.

Eligibility Requirements: Applicant must be Black (non-Hispanic) and enrolled or expecting to enroll at a four-year institution or university. Applicant must have 2.5 GPA or higher. Available to U.S. citizens.

Application Requirements: Application form, financial need analysis. *Deadline:* January 23.

Contact: Mary Williams, Director of Outreach and Recruitment
Phone: 800-331-2244

DEBORAH L. VINCENT FAHRO EDUCATION SCHOLARSHIP AWARD

Up to $1500 award for residents of federally assisted housing or a recipient of assistance through the Community Development Block Grant program in Florida. Must be a high school senior and meet income requirements as defined by HUD for public/assisted housing and Community Development Block Grant targeted area recipients. Must have a sponsor that is an active member of FAHRO as a housing authority/agency or community development agency that is willing to support travel expenses to attend Annual Convention awards banquet to receive scholarship if selected. Minimum 2.5 GPA required.

Award: Scholarship for use in freshman year; renewable.

Eligibility Requirements: Applicant must be Black (non-Hispanic); high school student; planning to enroll or expecting to enroll full-time at a two-year or four-year institution and resident of Florida. Applicant must have 2.5 GPA or higher. Available to U.S. citizens.

Application Requirements: Application form. *Deadline:* June 30.

Contact: Mary Williams, Director of Outreach and Recruitment
Phone: 800-331-2244

FEDEX/UNCF SCHOLARSHIP PROGRAM

Up to $4500 scholarships for high school seniors entering any Historically Black College or University (HBCU). Applicants must have a demonstrated, unmet, financial need.

Award: Scholarship for use in freshman year; renewable. *Number:* 5.

Eligibility Requirements: Applicant must be Black (non-Hispanic) and enrolled or expecting to enroll full-time at a four-year institution or university. Available to U.S. citizens.

Application Requirements: Application form, essay, financial need analysis. *Deadline:* June 3.

Contact: Mary Williams, Director of Outreach and Recruitment
Phone: 800-331-2244

FOOT LOCKER FOUNDATION, INC./UNCF SCHOLARSHIP

Scholarship of up to $5000 for African American high school seniors or students attending or planning to attend a UNCF member college or university. Minimum GPA of 2.5 required. Officers and directors of the Foundation and of Foot Locker, Inc. and its affiliates and family members of these officers and directors are not eligible to apply.

Award: Scholarship for use in freshman, sophomore, junior, or senior years; not renewable.

Eligibility Requirements: Applicant must be Black (non-Hispanic) and enrolled or expecting to enroll full-time at a four-year institution or university. Applicant must have 2.5 GPA or higher. Available to U.S. citizens.

Application Requirements: Application form, essay, financial need analysis. *Deadline:* May 13.

Contact: Mary Williams, Director of Outreach and Recruitment
Phone: 800-331-2244

FOUR PROMISES SCHOLARSHIP

Scholarship of up to $5000 for an African American or Hispanic graduating high school senior from Minnesota who will be attending a UNCF college/university or an HBCU. Scholarship is a renewable pending the student continues to be eligible. Minimum 3.0 GPA required.

Award: Scholarship for use in freshman year; renewable.

Eligibility Requirements: Applicant must be Black (non-Hispanic), Hispanic; high school student; planning to enroll or expecting to enroll full-time at a four-year institution or university and resident of Minnesota. Applicant must have 3.0 GPA or higher. Available to U.S. citizens.

Application Requirements: Application form. *Deadline:* April 4.

Contact: Mary Williams, Director of Outreach and Recruitment
Phone: 800-331-2244

HAUSMAN FAMILY CHARITABLE TRUST SCHOLARSHIP

Scholarship for students from the New England region of the United States (CT, VT, ME, MA, RI). Candidates must be college freshmen at a UNCF-affiliated college at the time of application. Annually renewable at $5,000 per year for a total scholarship of $20,000.

Award: Scholarship for use in freshman year. *Number:* 4. *Amount:* $5000.

Eligibility Requirements: Applicant must be Black (non-Hispanic); enrolled or expecting to enroll full-time at a four-year institution or university and resident of Connecticut, Maine, Massachusetts, Rhode Island, Vermont. Applicant must have 2.5 GPA or higher. Available to U.S. citizens.

Application Requirements: Application form, essay, financial need analysis. *Deadline:* November 14.

Contact: Mary Williams, Director of Outreach and Recruitment
Phone: 800-331-2244

JACK AND JILL OF AMERICA FOUNDATION SCHOLARSHIP

Scholarship available to any African-American high school senior. The applicant must become and maintain full-time status at an accredited, four year post-secondary institution beginning in the fall of the year working toward a Bachelor's degree. Dependents of members of Jack & Jill of America are not eligible to apply. Minimum 3.0 GPA required.

Award: Scholarship for use in freshman year; not renewable. *Amount:* $1500–$2500.

Eligibility Requirements: Applicant must be Black (non-Hispanic); high school student and planning to enroll or expecting to enroll full-time at a four-year institution or university. Applicant must have 3.0 GPA or higher. Available to U.S. citizens.

Application Requirements: Application form, essay. *Deadline:* June 1.

Contact: Mary Williams, Director of Outreach and Recruitment
Phone: 800-331-2244

JOSEPH A. TOWLES AFRICAN STUDY ABROAD SCHOLARSHIP

Scholarship enabling black Americans, conscious of their African descent, to have an opportunity to experience the richness of African cultures. Available to UNCF students who have been accepted into a study abroad program in Africa and have a minimum 3.0 GPA.

Award: Scholarship for use in sophomore, junior, or graduate years; not renewable.

Eligibility Requirements: Applicant must be Black (non-Hispanic) and enrolled or expecting to enroll full-time at a four-year institution or university. Applicant must have 3.0 GPA or higher. Available to U.S. citizens.

Application Requirements: Application form, essay. *Deadline:* November 4.

Contact: Mary Williams, Director of Outreach and Recruitment
Phone: 800-331-2244

KROGER MICHIGAN SCHOLARSHIP

Two, one-time scholarships of up to $5000 each available to graduating high school seniors that reside in the Michigan area. Minimum 2.5 GPA required.

Award: Scholarship for use in freshman year; not renewable. *Number:* 2. *Amount:* $5000.

Eligibility Requirements: Applicant must be Black (non-Hispanic); high school student; planning to enroll or expecting to enroll full-time at a four-year institution or university and resident of Michigan. Applicant must have 2.5 GPA or higher. Available to U.S. citizens.

Application Requirements: Application form. *Deadline:* April 4.

Contact: Mary Williams, Director of Outreach and Recruitment
Phone: 800-331-2244

MINNESOTA STUDENT AID SCHOLARSHIP

Scholarship for residents of Minnesota attending select UNCF colleges/universities. Minimum 2.5 GPA required.

Award: Scholarship for use in freshman, sophomore, junior, or senior years; not renewable.

Eligibility Requirements: Applicant must be Black (non-Hispanic); enrolled or expecting to enroll full-time at a four-year institution or university and resident of Minnesota. Applicant must have 2.5 GPA or higher. Available to U.S. citizens.

Application Requirements: Application form, essay. *Deadline:* September 9.

Contact: Mary Williams, Director of Outreach and Recruitment
Phone: 800-331-2244

MUTUAL SAVINGS LIFE COMPANY SCHOLARSHIP (KEMPER)

Up to $2500 scholarship for qualifying students who attend a Historically Black College or University. The recipient's parent or legal guardian must be a policy holder of Kemper Mutual Savings Life Insurance. Children or dependents of Kemper Home Services Companies' employees are ineligible to apply.

Award: Scholarship for use in freshman, sophomore, junior, or senior years.

Eligibility Requirements: Applicant must be Black (non-Hispanic); enrolled or expecting to enroll at a four-year institution or university and resident of Alabama. Applicant must have 2.5 GPA or higher. Available to U.S. citizens.

Application Requirements: Application form. *Deadline:* June 10.

Contact: Mary Williams, Director of Outreach and Recruitment
Phone: 800-331-2244

NATIONAL BLACK MBA ASSOCIATION UNDERGRADUATE SCHOLARSHIP

Scholarship of up to $5000 for student who is a financially active member of the National Black MBA Association. Must be a student in their first, second, third, or fourth year enrolled full-time at an accredited college or university at the time of award. Must be recommended by faculty advisor, have a minimum 3.0 GPA, and demonstrate exceptional leadership potential.

Award: Scholarship for use in freshman, sophomore, junior, or senior years; not renewable.

Eligibility Requirements: Applicant must be Black (non-Hispanic); enrolled or expecting to enroll full-time at a four-year institution or university and must have an interest in leadership. Applicant must have 3.0 GPA or higher. Available to U.S. and Canadian citizens.

Application Requirements: Application form, essay, personal photograph. *Deadline:* June 29.

Contact: Mary Williams, Director of Outreach and Recruitment
Phone: 800-331-2244

PENNSYLVANIA STATE EMPLOYEES COMBINED CAMPAIGN SCHOLARSHIP (SECA)

Up to $4000 scholarship program for qualified students entering or enrolled in a UNCF member college/university. Applicant must be Pell Grant eligible and have a demonstrated financial need.

Award: Scholarship for use in freshman, sophomore, junior, senior, or graduate years.

Eligibility Requirements: Applicant must be Black (non-Hispanic); enrolled or expecting to enroll full-time at a two-year or four-year institution or university and resident of Pennsylvania. Applicant must have 2.5 GPA or higher. Available to U.S. citizens.

Application Requirements: Application form, financial need analysis. *Deadline:* August 18.

Contact: Mary Williams, Director of Outreach and Recruitment
Phone: 800-331-2244

PEPSICO FOUNDATION-UNCF LAST DOLLAR SCHOLARSHIP

Up to $5000 scholarship open to students at HBCUs who have a demonstrated, unmet financial need that can be verified by their attending college or university. Students should be actively involved in community service. Minimum 2.5 GPA required.

Award: Scholarship for use in freshman, sophomore, junior, or senior years; not renewable.

Eligibility Requirements: Applicant must be Black (non-Hispanic) and enrolled or expecting to enroll full-time at a four-year institution or university. Applicant must have 2.5 GPA or higher. Available to U.S. citizens.

Application Requirements: Application form, essay. *Deadline:* March 18.

Contact: Mary Williams, Director of Outreach and Recruitment
Phone: 800-331-2244

RELIABLE LIFE INSURANCE COMPANY SCHOLARSHIP (KEMPER)

Up to $2500 scholarship for qualifying students who attend a Historically Black College or University (HBCU). The recipient's parent or legal guardian must be a policy holder of Kemper Reliable Life Insurance. Children or dependents of Kemper Home Services Companies' employees are ineligible to apply.

Award: Scholarship for use in freshman, sophomore, junior, or senior years.

Eligibility Requirements: Applicant must be Black (non-Hispanic); enrolled or expecting to enroll at a four-year institution or university and resident of Arkansas, Missouri, Oklahoma, Texas. Applicant must have 2.5 GPA or higher. Available to U.S. citizens.

Application Requirements: Application form. *Deadline:* October 15.

Contact: Mary Williams, Director of Outreach and Recruitment
Phone: 800-331-2244

ROBERT DOLE SCHOLARSHIP FOR DISABLED STUDENTS

• *See page 638*

ROLLIN M. GERSTACKER FOUNDATION SCHOLARSHIP

Scholarship for students from the state of Michigan attending an accredited 4-year college or university in the United States.

Award: Scholarship for use in freshman, sophomore, junior, senior, or graduate years.

Eligibility Requirements: Applicant must be Black (non-Hispanic); enrolled or expecting to enroll at a four-year institution or university and resident of Michigan. Applicant must have 2.5 GPA or higher. Available to U.S. citizens.

Application Requirements: Application form, essay. *Deadline:* June 7.

Contact: Mary Williams, Director of Outreach and Recruitment
Phone: 800-331-2244

RONALD MCDONALD HOUSE OF CHARITIES FOR CENTRAL INDIANA SCHOLARSHIP

Up to $2500 scholarships for students from Indiana currently attending a 4-year U.S. accredited college or university.

Award: Scholarship for use in freshman, sophomore, junior, or senior years. *Number:* 8.

Eligibility Requirements: Applicant must be Black (non-Hispanic); enrolled or expecting to enroll full-time at a four-year institution or university and resident of Indiana. Applicant must have 2.5 GPA or higher. Available to U.S. citizens.

Application Requirements: Application form. *Deadline:* December 5.

Contact: Mary Williams, Director of Outreach and Recruitment
Phone: 800-331-2244

SAR FAMILY EMERGENCY SCHOLARSHIP

• *See page 625*

UNCF GENERAL SCHOLARSHIP PROGRAM

Up to $5000 scholarships for students enrolled full-time and attending UNCF Institutes. Must have a demonstrated financial need. Minimum 2.5 GPA required. This application information will be used to match students to specific programs administered by UNCF. For more information see website, http://www.uncf.org.

Award: Scholarship for use in freshman, sophomore, junior, or senior, or graduate years; not renewable.

Eligibility Requirements: Applicant must be Black (non-Hispanic) and enrolled or expecting to enroll full-time at a four-year institution or university. Applicant must have 2.5 GPA or higher. Available to U.S. citizens.

Application Requirements: Application form, financial need analysis. *Deadline:* March 24.

Contact: Mary Williams, Director of Outreach and Recruitment
Phone: 800-331-2244

UNCF HONDA MANUFACTURING OF INDIANA SCHOLARSHIP

$2500 scholarship for graduating high school seniors enrolled in a Student Development and/or Youth Leadership Program through an organization in Indiana. Eligible students must be residents of Indiana and show certification of enrollment or completion of a Student Development/Youth Leadership Program. Minimum 2.5 GPA required. Priority given to STEM majors.

Award: Scholarship for use in freshman year; not renewable. *Amount:* $2500.

Eligibility Requirements: Applicant must be Black (non-Hispanic); high school student; planning to enroll or expecting to enroll full-time at a four-year institution or university and resident of Indiana. Applicant must have 2.5 GPA or higher. Available to U.S. citizens.

Application Requirements: Application form. *Deadline:* May 31.

Contact: Mary Williams, Director of Outreach and Recruitment
Phone: 800-331-2244

UNION NATIONAL LIFE INSURANCE COMPANY SCHOLARSHIP (KEMPER)

Up to $2500 for students who attend a Historically Black College or University (HBCU). the scholarship recipient's parent or legal guardian must be a policy holder Kemper United National Life Insurance. Children or dependents of Kemper Home Services Companies' employees are ineligible to apply.

Award: Scholarship for use in freshman, sophomore, junior, or senior years.

Eligibility Requirements: Applicant must be Black (non-Hispanic); enrolled or expecting to enroll at a four-year institution or university and resident of Louisiana, Mississippi. Applicant must have 2.5 GPA or higher. Available to U.S. citizens.

Application Requirements: Application form. *Deadline:* June 10.

Contact: Mary Williams, Director of Outreach and Recruitment
Phone: 800-331-2244

UNITED INSURANCE COMPANY SCHOLARSHIP (KEMPER)

Up to $2500 award for students attending a Historically Black College or University (HBCU). Parent or legal guardian must be a policy holder of Kemper United Insurance. Applicant must reside in California, District of Columbia, Florida, Georgia, Illinois, Indiana, Maryland, Michigan, New Jersey, North Carolina, Ohio, Pennsylvania, South Carolina, Tennessee, or Virginia. Children or dependents of Kemper Home Services Companies' employees are ineligible to apply.

Award: Scholarship for use in freshman, sophomore, junior, or senior years.

Eligibility Requirements: Applicant must be Black (non-Hispanic); enrolled or expecting to enroll at a four-year institution or university and resident of California, District of Columbia, Florida, Georgia, Illinois, Indiana, Maryland, Michigan, New Jersey, North Carolina, Ohio, Pennsylvania, South Carolina, Tennessee, Virginia. Applicant must have 2.5 GPA or higher. Available to U.S. citizens.

Application Requirements: Application form. *Deadline:* June 10.

Contact: Mary Williams, Director of Outreach and Recruitment
Phone: 800-331-2244

USA FUNDS SCHOLARSHIP

Scholarships of up to $5,000 to assist students and their families in gaining access to postsecondary education at UNCF or other HBCU colleges/universities in Indiana. Students must be resident of Indiana and be a U.S. citizen or permanent resident. Minimum 2.5 GPA required.

Award: Scholarship for use in freshman, sophomore, junior, or senior years; not renewable.

Eligibility Requirements: Applicant must be Black (non-Hispanic); enrolled or expecting to enroll full-time at a four-year institution or university; resident of Indiana and studying in Indiana. Applicant must have 2.5 GPA or higher. Available to U.S. citizens.

Application Requirements: Application form, essay. *Deadline:* February 10.

Contact: Mary Williams, Director of Outreach and Recruitment
Phone: 800-331-2244

VOYA UNCF MALE INITIATIVE

Scholarship for male, African-American colleges sophomores attending UNCF affiliated colleges or universities on a full-time basis. Must have a demonstrated unmet, financial need as verified by college or university. Minimum 2.5 GPA required.

Award: Scholarship for use in sophomore year; not renewable.

Eligibility Requirements: Applicant must be Black (non-Hispanic); enrolled or expecting to enroll full-time at a four-year institution or university and male. Applicant must have 2.5 GPA or higher. Available to U.S. citizens.

Application Requirements: Application form, essay, financial need analysis. *Deadline:* December 9.

Contact: Mary Williams, Director of Outreach and Recruitment
Phone: 800-331-2244

WELLS FARGO SCHOLARSHIP PROGRAM

Scholarship to support full-time students in good academic standing at a UNCF member college or university. Must have a demonstrated unmet, financial need as verified by college or university. Minimum 2.5 GPA.

Award: Scholarship for use in freshman, sophomore, junior, or senior years; not renewable.

Eligibility Requirements: Applicant must be Black (non-Hispanic) and enrolled or expecting to enroll full-time at a four-year institution or university. Applicant must have 2.5 GPA or higher. Available to U.S. citizens.

Application Requirements: Application form, financial need analysis. *Deadline:* April 6.

Contact: Mary Williams, Director of Outreach and Recruitment
Phone: 800-331-2244

UNITED SOUTH AND EASTERN TRIBES INC.

http://www.usetinc.org/

UNITED SOUTH AND EASTERN TRIBES SCHOLARSHIP FUND

One-time scholarship for Native American students who are members of United South and Eastern Tribes, enrolled or accepted in a postsecondary educational institution.

Award: Scholarship for use in freshman, sophomore, junior, or senior years; not renewable. *Number:* 4–8. *Amount:* $500.

Eligibility Requirements: Applicant must be Indian citizen; American Indian/Alaska Native and enrolled or expecting to enroll full- or part-time at a four-year institution or university.

Application Requirements: Application form, essay, financial need analysis, proof of tribal enrollment, transcript. *Deadline:* April 30.

Contact: Theresa Embry, Executive Assistant to Director
United South and Eastern Tribes Inc.
711 Stewarts Ferry Pike, Suite 100
Nashville, TN 37214-2634
Phone: 615-872-7900
Fax: 615-872-7417

UNITED STATES DEPARTMENT OF AGRICULTURE

http://www.usda.gov/

USDA/PUBLIC SERVICE LEADER SCHOLARS (PSLS)

The Public Service Leaders Scholarship Program provides combined scholarship and internship opportunities to undergraduate and graduate students leading to permanent employment upon completion of their degree. Benefits include: Full-tuition scholarships; paid internship (minimum 640 hours) prior to graduation, leading to permanent employment; employee benefits such as mentoring, career development, leadership training, use of a personal computer.

Award: Scholarship for use in sophomore, junior, senior, or graduate years.

Eligibility Requirements: Applicant must be Hispanic and enrolled or expecting to enroll full- or part-time at a four-year institution or university. Available to U.S. citizens.

Application Requirements: *Deadline:* May 20.

Contact: Sandra Cortez, HSI National Student Program Manager
Phone: 202-720-6506
E-mail: Sandra.Cortez@ars.usda.gov

UNITED STATES HISPANIC LEADERSHIP INSTITUTE

http://www.ushli.org/

DR. JUAN ANDRADE, JR. SCHOLARSHIP

Scholarship for young Hispanic leaders. Applicants must be enrolled or accepted for enrollment as a full-time student in a four-year institution in the United States or U.S. territories, and demonstrate a verifiable need for financial support. At least one parent must be of Hispanic ancestry.

Award: Scholarship for use in freshman, sophomore, junior, or senior years; not renewable. *Number:* 30. *Amount:* $500–$1000.

Eligibility Requirements: Applicant must be Hispanic and enrolled or expecting to enroll full-time at a two-year or four-year institution or university. Available to U.S. citizens.

Application Requirements: Application form, driver's license, essay, personal photograph, recommendations or references, resume, transcript. *Deadline:* January 11.

Contact: Isabel Reyes, Scholarship Coordinator
Phone: 312-427-8683
Fax: 312-427-5183
E-mail: ireyes@ushli.org

UNITED TRANSPORTATION UNION INSURANCE ASSOCIATION

http://www.utuia.org/

UTUIA SCHOLARSHIP

• See page 625

UNIVERSITY CONSORTIUM FOR LIBERIA

http://ucliberia.com/

JOSEPH N. BOAKAI SR. HIGHER EDUCATION SCHOLARSHIP

• See page 625

U.S. COAST GUARD

www.gocoastguard/cspi

COLLEGE STUDENT PRE-COMMISSIONING INITIATIVE (CSPI)

• See page 625

U.S. NEWS & WORLD REPORT

U.S. NEWS PATH TO COLLEGE SCHOLARSHIP PROGRAM

U.S. News & World Report has established the U.S. News Path to College Scholarship program to assist high school students who plan to continue their education at a 4-year U.S. college or university. Applicants of the U.S. News Path to College Scholarship must be a freshman, sophomore, junior or senior attending a U.S. public or private high school. They must plan to enroll in full-time undergraduate study at an accredited four-year college or university in the United States immediately following high school graduation. Applicants must have a minimum grade point average of 3.0 on a 4.0 scale (or the equivalent) and be a United States citizen or lawful permanent resident.

Award: Scholarship for use in freshman, sophomore, junior, or senior years; not renewable. *Number:* 2. *Amount:* $2500.

Eligibility Requirements: Applicant must be high school student and planning to enroll or expecting to enroll full-time at a four-year institution. Applicant must have 3.0 GPA or higher. Available to U.S. citizens.

Application Requirements: Application form. *Deadline:* June 2.

Contact: Program Manager
U.S. News & World Report
One Scholarship Way
St. Peter, MN 56082
Phone: 800-537-4180
E-mail: usnews@scholarshipamerica.org

US PAN ASIAN AMERICAN CHAMBER OF COMMERCE EDUCATION FOUNDATION

http://www.uspaacc.com/

AMPCUS HALLMARK SCHOLARSHIP

The applicant should demonstrate academic achievement of 3.3 GPA or higher, leadership in extracurricular activities, involvement in community service, and financial need. The amount of the scholarship depends on the sponsors' contributions and varies between $2000 and $5000.

Award: Scholarship for use in freshman year; renewable. *Amount:* $2000–$5000.

Eligibility Requirements: Applicant must be Asian/Pacific Islander; high school student and planning to enroll or expecting to enroll full-time at a four-year institution or university. Applicant must have 3.0 GPA or higher. Available to U.S. citizens.

Application Requirements: Application form. *Deadline:* March 17.

Contact: Diana Yee, Program Associate
US Pan Asian American Chamber of Commerce Education
Foundation
1329 18th Street N.W.
Washington D.C. 20036
Phone: 202-378-1121
E-mail: diana@uspaacc.com

INGERSOLL RAND SCHOLARSHIP

The applicant should demonstrate academic achievement of 3.3 GPA or higher, leadership in extracurricular activities, involvement in community service, and financial need. The amount of the scholarship depends on the sponsors' contributions and varies between $2000 and $5000.

Award: Scholarship for use in freshman year; not renewable. *Amount:* $2000–$5000.

Eligibility Requirements: Applicant must be Asian/Pacific Islander; high school student and planning to enroll or expecting to enroll full-time at a four-year institution or university. Available to U.S. citizens.

Application Requirements: Application form. *Deadline:* March 17.

Contact: Diana Yee, Program Associate
US Pan Asian American Chamber of Commerce Education
Foundation
1329 18th Street N.W.
Washington D.C. 20036
Phone: 202-378-1121
E-mail: Diana@uspaacc.com

PEPSICO HALLMARK SCHOLARSHIPS

The applicant should demonstrate academic achievement of 3.3 GPA or higher, leadership in extracurricular activities, involvement in community service, and financial need. The amount of the scholarship depends on the sponsors' contributions and varies between $2000 and $5000.

Award: Scholarship for use in freshman year; not renewable. *Number:* 1. *Amount:* $2000–$5000.

Eligibility Requirements: Applicant must be Asian/Pacific Islander; high school student and planning to enroll or expecting to enroll full-time at an institution or university. Available to U.S. citizens.

Application Requirements: Application form. *Deadline:* March 17.

Contact: Diana Yee
US Pan Asian American Chamber of Commerce Education
Foundation
1329 18th Street N.W.
Washington D.C. 20036
Phone: 202-3781121
E-mail: diana@uspaacc.com

UPS HALLMARK SCHOLARSHIPS

The applicant should demonstrate academic achievement of 3.3 GPA or higher, leadership in extracurricular activities, involvement in community service, and financial need. The amount of the scholarship depends on the sponsors' contributions and varies between $2000 and $5000.

Award: Scholarship for use in freshman year; not renewable. *Amount:* $2000–$5000.

Eligibility Requirements: Applicant must be Asian/Pacific Islander; high school student and planning to enroll or expecting to enroll full-time at an institution or university. Available to U.S. citizens.

Application Requirements: Application form. *Deadline:* March 17.

Contact: Diana Yee
US Pan Asian American Chamber of Commerce Education Foundation
1329 18th Street N.W.
Washington D.C. 20036
Phone: 202-3781121

WINWIN PRODUCTS, INC. SCHOLARSHIP

The applicant should demonstrate academic achievement of 3.3 GPA or higher, leadership in extracurricular activities, involvement in community service, and financial need. The amount of the scholarship depends on the sponsors' contributions and varies between $2000 and $5000.

Award: Scholarship for use in freshman year; not renewable. *Amount:* $2000–$5000.

Eligibility Requirements: Applicant must be Asian/Pacific Islander; high school student and planning to enroll or expecting to enroll full-time at a four-year institution or university. Available to U.S. citizens.

Application Requirements: Application form. *Deadline:* March 13.

Contact: Diana Yee, Program Associate
US Pan Asian American Chamber of Commerce Education Foundation
1329 18th Street N.W.
Washington, D.C. 20036
Phone: 202-378-1121
Fax: 202-296-5221
E-mail: diana@uspaacc.com

VALUEPENGUIN

http://www.valuepenguin.com

VALUEPENGUIN SCHOLARSHIP

• See page 626

WARD LAW GROUP, PL

http://thecoveragelawyer.com/

WARD LAW GROUP BETTER FUTURE SCHOLARSHIP

• See page 626

WASHINGTON SOCIETY OF CERTIFIED PUBLIC ACCOUNTANTS

http://www.wscpa.org/

WSCPA FOUNDATION SCHOLARSHIPS

• See page 626

WHITE EARTH TRIBAL COUNCIL

http://www.whiteearth.com/

WHITE EARTH SCHOLARSHIP PROGRAM

Renewable scholarship for students who are enrolled in postsecondary institutions. Must have a GPA of 2.5. Must be U.S. citizen.

Award: Scholarship for use in freshman, sophomore, junior, senior, graduate, or postgraduate years; renewable. *Number:* 200. *Amount:* $3000.

Eligibility Requirements: Applicant must be American Indian/Alaska Native and enrolled or expecting to enroll full- or part-time at a two-year or four-year or technical institution or university. Applicant must have 2.5 GPA or higher. Available to U.S. citizens.

Application Requirements: Application form, financial need analysis, transcript. *Deadline:* May 31.

Contact: Leslie Nessman, Scholarship Manager
Phone: 218-983-3285
Fax: 218-983-4299

WILLIAM D. SQUIRES EDUCATIONAL FOUNDATION INC.

http://www.wmdsquiresfoundation.org/

WILLIAM D. SQUIRES SCHOLARSHIP

• See page 627

WILLIAM E. DOCTER EDUCATIONAL FUND/ST. MARY ARMENIAN CHURCH

http://www.wedfund.org/

WILLIAM ERVANT DOCTER EDUCATIONAL FUND

Grant up to $2000 available to worthy students regardless of age, gender, or level of education or training. Funds given to American citizens of Armenian ancestry to pursue studies and training in the United States or Canada.

Award: Grant for use in freshman, sophomore, junior, senior, graduate, or postgraduate years; not renewable. *Number:* 20. *Amount:* $1000–$2000.

Eligibility Requirements: Applicant must be of Armenian heritage and enrolled or expecting to enroll full- or part-time at a two-year or four-year or technical institution or university. Available to U.S. citizens.

Application Requirements: Application form, essay, financial need analysis, proof of U.S. citizenship, test scores, transcript. *Deadline:* June 30.

Contact: Edward Alexander, Scholarship Committee Chairman
Fax: 202-364-1441
E-mail: wedfund@aol.com

WISCONSIN HIGHER EDUCATIONAL AID BOARD

http://www.heab.wi.gov/

MINORITY UNDERGRADUATE RETENTION GRANT-WISCONSIN

The grant provides financial assistance to African-American, Native-American, Hispanic, and former citizens of Laos, Vietnam, and Cambodia, for study in Wisconsin. Must be Wisconsin resident, enrolled at least half-time in Wisconsin Technical College System schools, non-profit independent colleges and universities, and tribal colleges. Refer to website for further details http://www.heab.state.wi.us.

Award: Grant for use in sophomore, junior, or senior years; not renewable. *Amount:* $250–$2500.

Eligibility Requirements: Applicant must be American Indian/Alaska Native, Asian/Pacific Islander, Black (non-Hispanic), Hispanic; enrolled or expecting to enroll full- or part-time at a two-year or four-year or technical institution or university; resident of Wisconsin and studying in Wisconsin. Available to U.S. and non-U.S. citizens.

Application Requirements: Application form, financial need analysis. *Deadline:* continuous.

Contact: Mary Lou Kuzdas, Program Coordinator
Wisconsin Higher Educational Aid Board
PO Box 7885
Madison, WI 53707-7885
Phone: 608-267-2212
Fax: 608-267-2808
E-mail: mary.kuzdas@wi.gov

WISCONSIN NATIVE AMERICAN/INDIAN STUDENT ASSISTANCE GRANT

Grants for Wisconsin residents who are at least one-quarter American Indian. Must be attending a college or university within the state. Refer to website for further details, http://www.heab.state.wi.us.

Award: Grant for use in freshman, sophomore, junior, or senior years; not renewable. *Amount:* $250–$1100.

Eligibility Requirements: Applicant must be American Indian/Alaska Native; enrolled or expecting to enroll full- or part-time at a two-year or four-year or technical institution or university; resident of Wisconsin and studying in Wisconsin. Available to U.S. citizens.

Application Requirements: Application form, financial need analysis. *Deadline:* continuous.

Contact: Sandra Thomas, Program Coordinator
Wisconsin Higher Educational Aid Board
PO Box 7885
Madison, WI 53707-7885
Phone: 608-266-0888
Fax: 608-267-2808
E-mail: sandy.thomas@wi.gov

WOMEN OF THE EVANGELICAL LUTHERAN CHURCH IN AMERICA

http://www.womenoftheelca.org/

AMELIA KEMP SCHOLARSHIP

Scholarship for ELCA women who are of an ethnic minority in undergraduate, graduate, professional, or vocational courses of study. Must be at least 21 years old and hold membership in the ELCA. Must have experienced an interruption of two or more years in education since the completion of high school.

Award: Scholarship for use in freshman, sophomore, junior, senior, or graduate years; not renewable. *Number:* 1. *Amount:* up to $1000.

Eligibility Requirements: Applicant must be Lutheran; American Indian/Alaska Native, Asian/Pacific Islander, Black (non-Hispanic), Hispanic; enrolled or expecting to enroll full- or part-time at a two-year or four-year or technical institution or university and female. Available to U.S. citizens.

Application Requirements: Application form, recommendations or references, resume, transcript. *Deadline:* February 15.

Contact: Emily Hansen, Scholarship Committee
Phone: 800-638-3522 Ext. 2736
Fax: 773-380-2419
E-mail: womenelca@elca.org

WOMEN'S JEWELRY ASSOCIATION

http://www.womensjewelryassociation.com

MEMBER GRANTS
• See page 627

WOMEN'S JEWELRY ASSOCIATIONS VETERANS GRANT
• See page 627

WOMEN'S SPORTS FOUNDATION

http://www.womenssportsfoundation.org/

LINDA RIDDLE/SGMA ENDOWED SCHOLARSHIP
• See page 627

YORKVILLE GOODS LLC

http://yorkvilleblankets.com/

YORKVILLE BLANKETS ASD SCHOLARSHIP
• See page 627

RELIGIOUS AFFILIATION

1-800-HANSONS

www.hansons.com

1-800-HANSONS SCHOLARSHIP PROGRAM
• See page 572

4MYCASH.COM, LLC

https://www.4mycash.com

4MYCASH ST. LOUIS HARD MONEY SCHOLARSHIP
• See page 572

A-1 AUTO TRANSPORT, INC.

https://www.a1autotransport.com/a-1-auto-transport-scholarship/

A-1 AUTO TRANSPORT SCHOLARSHIP
• See page 572

ABBVIE INC.

https://www.abbvie.com/

ABBVIE IMMUNOLOGY SCHOLARSHIP
• See page 572

AIR TRAFFIC CONTROL ASSOCIATION INC.

http://www.atca.org/

AIR TRAFFIC CONTROL ASSOCIATION SCHOLARSHIP
• See page 573

BUCKINGHAM MEMORIAL SCHOLARSHIP
• See page 573

LAWRENCE C. FORTIER MEMORIAL SCHOLARSHIP
• See page 573

ALERTONE SERVICES LLC

https://www.alert-1.com/

ALERT1 STUDENT FOR SENIORS SCHOLARSHIP
• See page 573

ALGAECAL INC.

https://www.algaecal.com/

ALGAECAL SCHOLARSHIP
• See page 573

ALLIANCE FOR YOUNG ARTISTS AND WRITERS INC.

http://www.artandwriting.org/

SCHOLASTIC ART AND WRITING AWARDS
• See page 574

ALLTHEROOMS

http://alltherooms.com

ROOM TO TRAVEL - STUDY ABROAD SCHOLARSHIP
• *See page 574*

AMERICAN ASSOCIATION OF TEACHERS OF JAPANESE BRIDGING CLEARINGHOUSE FOR STUDY ABROAD IN JAPAN

http://www.aatj.org

BRIDGING SCHOLARSHIP FOR STUDY ABROAD IN JAPAN
• *See page 574*

AMERICAN BAPTIST FINANCIAL AID PROGRAM

http://www.abhms.org/

AMERICAN BAPTIST FINANCIAL AID PROGRAM
The American Baptist Financial Aid Program supports American Baptist college students, graduate students, and seminarians. Applicants must hold an active membership in an American Baptist church, maintain a GPA of 2.75 or higher, and be enrolled at an accredited institution in the United States or Puerto Rico.

Award: Scholarship for use in freshman, sophomore, junior, senior, or graduate years; not renewable. *Number:* 1–250. *Amount:* $500–$1000.

Eligibility Requirements: Applicant must be Baptist and enrolled or expecting to enroll full-time at a four-year institution or university. Applicant must have 3.0 GPA or higher. Available to U.S. citizens.

Application Requirements: Application form, essay, financial need analysis. *Deadline:* May 31.

Contact: Ms. Sarah Strosahl-Kagi, Director of Emerging Leaders and Scholarships Program
American Baptist Financial Aid Program
PO Box 851
Valley Forge, PA 19482-0851
Phone: 800-222-3872 Ext. 2462
Fax: 610-768-2470
E-mail: sarah.strosahl-kagi@abhms.org

AMERICAN COUNCIL OF THE BLIND

http://www.acb.org/

AMERICAN COUNCIL OF THE BLIND SCHOLARSHIPS
• *See page 574*

AMERICAN LEGION AUXILIARY DEPARTMENT OF WISCONSIN

http://www.amlegionauxwi.org/

AMERICAN LEGION AUXILIARY DEPARTMENT OF WISCONSIN DELLA VAN DEUREN MEMORIAL SCHOLARSHIP
• *See page 531*

AMERICAN LEGION AUXILIARY DEPARTMENT OF WISCONSIN H.S. AND ANGELINE LEWIS SCHOLARSHIPS
• *See page 531*

AMERICAN LEGION AUXILIARY DEPARTMENT OF WISCONSIN MERIT AND MEMORIAL SCHOLARSHIPS
• *See page 531*

AMERICAN LEGION AUXILIARY DEPARTMENT OF WISCONSIN PAST PRESIDENTS' PARLEY HEALTH CAREER SCHOLARSHIPS
• *See page 531*

AMERICAN LEGION AUXILIARY DEPARTMENT OF WISCONSIN PRESIDENT'S SCHOLARSHIPS
• *See page 531*

AMERICAN LEGION AUXILIARY NATIONAL HEADQUARTERS

http://www.ALAforVeterans.org

AMERICAN LEGION AUXILIARY CHILDREN OF WARRIORS NATIONAL PRESIDENTS' SCHOLARSHIP
• *See page 575*

AMERICAN LEGION DEPARTMENT OF WASHINGTON

http://www.walegion.org/

AMERICAN LEGION DEPARTMENT OF WASHINGTON CHILDREN AND YOUTH SCHOLARSHIPS
• *See page 536*

AMERICAN SAVINGS FOUNDATION

http://www.asfdn.org/

ROBERT T. KENNEY SCHOLARSHIP PROGRAM AT THE AMERICAN SAVINGS FOUNDATION
• *See page 576*

AMERICAN SEPHARDI FOUNDATION

http://www.americansephardifederation.org/

BROOME AND ALLEN BOYS CAMP AND SCHOLARSHIP FUND
The Broome and Allen Scholarship is awarded to students of Sephardic origin or those working in Sephardic studies. Both graduate and undergraduate degree candidates as well as those doing research projects will be considered. It is awarded for one year and must be renewed for successive years. Enclose copy of tax returns with application.

Award: Scholarship for use in freshman, sophomore, junior, senior, graduate, or postgraduate years; not renewable. *Number:* 20–60. *Amount:* $500–$2000.

Eligibility Requirements: Applicant must be Jewish and enrolled or expecting to enroll full- or part-time at a two-year or four-year or technical institution or university. Available to U.S. and non-U.S. citizens.

Application Requirements: Application form, copy of tax returns, essay, financial need analysis, recommendations or references, transcript. *Deadline:* May 15.

Contact: Ms. Ellen Cohen, Membership and Outreach Coordinator
American Sephardi Foundation
15 West 16th Street
New York, NY 10011
Phone: 212-294-8350 Ext. 4
Fax: 212-294-8348
E-mail: ecohen@asf.cjh.org

ANKIN LAW

http://ankinlaw.com

ANKIN LAW OFFICE COLLEGE SCHOLARSHIP
• *See page 576*

ANTHONY MUNOZ FOUNDATION

www.munozfoundation.org

ANTHONY MUNOZ SCHOLARSHIPS
• *See page 577*

ANY INTERN

http://www.anyintern.com

$1,000 5 MINUTE SCHOLARSHIP
• *See page 577*

ARKANSAS SINGLE PARENT SCHOLARSHIP FUND

http://www.aspsf.org/

ARKANSAS SINGLE PARENT SCHOLARSHIP FUND
• *See page 577*

ARMENIAN RELIEF SOCIETY OF EASTERN USA INC.-REGIONAL OFFICE

http://www.arseastusa.org/

ARMENIAN RELIEF SOCIETY UNDERGRADUATE SCHOLARSHIP
• *See page 670*

ASIAN PACIFIC COMMUNITY FUND

http://www.apcf.org/

ROYAL BUSINESS BANK SCHOLARSHIP PROGRAM
• *See page 577*

ASIAN REPORTER

http://www.arfoundation.net/

ASIAN REPORTER SCHOLARSHIP
• *See page 577*

ASSURED LIFE ASSOCIATION

http://assuredlife.org

ASSURED LIFE ASSOCIATION ENDOWMENT SCHOLARSHIP PROGRAM
• *See page 540*

AWEBER COMMUNICATIONS

http://www.aweber.com/

AWEBER DEVELOPING FUTURES SCHOLARSHIP
• *See page 672*

BARONE DEFENSE FIRM

http://baronedefensefirm.com/

BARONE DEFENSE FIRM WIN BACK YOUR LIFE SCHOLARSHIP
• *See page 578*

BOUNCE ENERGY

http://www.bounceenergy.com

BE MORE SCHOLARSHIP
• *See page 578*

BRAINLY, INC.

http://www.brainly.com

BRAINLY EVERYONE KNOWS SOMETHING SCHOLARSHIP
• *See page 578*

BRANDES INVESTMENT PARTNERS L.P.

https://www.brandes.com

BRANDES SCHOLARSHIP PROGRAM
• *See page 578*

BREYER LAW OFFICES PC

http://www.breyerlaw.com/

2017 HUSBAND AND WIFE LAW TEAM ARIZONA SCHOLARSHIP
• *See page 578*

BY KIDS FOR KIDS, CO.

http://bkfkeducation.com

CTIA WIRELESS FOUNDATION DRIVE SMART DIGITAL SHORT CONTEST
• *See page 579*

SALLIE MAE® MAKE COLLEGE HAPPEN CHALLENGE
• *See page 579*

CAMP NETWORK

https://www.campnetwork.com/

CAMP COUNSELOR APPRECIATION SCHOLARSHIP
• *See page 580*

CARING.COM

http://caring.com

CARING.COM STUDENT-CAREGIVER BI-ANNUAL SCHOLARSHIP
• *See page 580*

CATHOLIC UNITED FINANCIAL

http://www.catholicunitedfinancial.org

POST HIGH SCHOOL TUITION SCHOLARSHIPS
Catholic United Financial membership requirement of 2 years by application deadline.

Award: Scholarship for use in freshman, sophomore, junior, or senior years; not renewable. *Number:* 461. *Amount:* $300.

Eligibility Requirements: Applicant must be Roman Catholic and enrolled or expecting to enroll full- or part-time at a two-year or four-year or technical institution or university. Available to U.S. citizens.

Application Requirements: Application form, personal photograph. *Deadline:* April 30.

Contact: Member Engagement Department
Phone: 18005686670
E-mail: engage@catholicunited.org

CENTER FOR REINTEGRATION

www.reintegration.com

BAER REINTEGRATION SCHOLARSHIP
• *See page 580*

CENTRAL SCHOLARSHIP

http://www.central-scholarship.org

LESSANS FAMILY SCHOLARSHIP
• *See page 674*

CGTRADER

https://www.cgtrader.com/

ANNUAL CGTRADER SCHOLARSHIP
• *See page 580*

CHRISTINE GERTSCH ATTORNEY AT LAW

https://www.ctdomesticviolencehelp.com/

**CONNECTICUT DOMESTIC VIOLENCE 2017
LEGISLATION REFORM SCHOLARSHIP**
• *See page 581*

CHURCH HILL CLASSICS

http://www.diplomaframe.com/

FRAME MY FUTURE SCHOLARSHIP CONTEST
• *See page 581*

CODA INTERNATIONAL

http://www.coda-international.org

**MILLIE BROTHER SCHOLARSHIP FOR CHILDREN OF
DEAF ADULTS**
• *See page 581*

COGBURN LAW OFFICES

http://cogburnlaw.com/

$5,000 ADVERSITY SCHOLARSHIP
• *See page 581*

COLLEGE ASSISTANCE MIGRANT PROGRAM

https://www.stedwards.edu

COLLEGE ASSISTANCE MIGRANT PROG.
• *See page 581*

COLORADO MASONS BENEVOLENT FUND ASSOCIATION

http://www.cmbfa.org/scholarship

**COLORADO MASONS BENEVOLENT FUND
SCHOLARSHIPS**
• *See page 581*

COLUMBUS CITIZENS FOUNDATION

http://www.columbuscitizensfd.org/scholarships/scholarships.html

**COLUMBUS CITIZENS FOUNDATION COLLEGE
SCHOLARSHIP PROGRAM**
• *See page 582*

COMMUNITY BANKERS ASSOCIATION OF ILLINOIS

http://www.cbai.com/

**COMMUNITY BANKERS ASSOC OF IL CHILD OF A
BANKER SCHOLARSHIP**
• *See page 541*

**COMMUNITY BANKERS ASSOC. OF IL ESSAY
CONTEST**
• *See page 582*

COMMUNITY FOUNDATION FOR GREATER ATLANTA, INC.

http://cfgreateratlanta.org/

DREAMS SQUARED SCHOLARSHIP
• *See page 582*

COUNCIL OF CITIZENS WITH LOW VISION INTERNATIONAL C/O AMERICAN COUNCIL OF THE BLIND

http://www.cclvi.org/

FRED SCHEIGERT SCHOLARSHIP
• *See page 582*

CSA MEDICAL SUPPLY

https://csamedicalsupply.com

CSA MEDICAL SUPPLY COLLEGE SCHOLARSHIP
• *See page 583*

DANIEL P. BUTTAFUOCO & ASSOCIATES

http://www.1800nowhurt.com

YOUNG CHRISTIAN LEADERS SCHOLARSHIP
Two awards of $1000 given each month to students under the age of 24 who are either high school seniors entering college or are currently full-time undergraduates. Must be a full-time resident of either New York, New Jersey, Connecticut, or Pennsylvania. Applications submitted by the 15th of the month will be considered in the following month's selection process. (e.g., apply by April 15th for a May award). Each applicant may receive a maximum total of three awards per 12-month period. Must be an attending, active members of a local church and have a minimum 3.0 GPA.

Award: Scholarship for use in freshman, sophomore, junior, or senior years; not renewable. *Amount:* $1000.

Eligibility Requirements: Applicant must be Christian; age 18-24; enrolled or expecting to enroll full-time at a four-year institution or university and resident of Connecticut, New Jersey, New York, Pennsylvania. Applicant must have 3.0 GPA or higher. Available to U.S. citizens.

Application Requirements: Application form, essay, personal photograph.

Contact: Ms. Maciel Almonte, Scholarship Administrator
Daniel P. Buttafuoco & Associates
9 Broadman Parkway
Jersey City, NJ 07305
Phone: 201-432-7300
E-mail: info@yclscholarship.org

DEMAS LAW GROUP, P.C.

http://www.injury-attorneys.com/

DEMAS LAW GROUP SCHOLARSHIP
• *See page 583*

DIBELLA LAW OFFICES, P.C.

http://www.dibellalawoffice.com

2017 DIBELLA LAW OFFICES, P.C. SCHOLARSHIP
• *See page 583*

DIRECT ENERGY

https://www.directenergy.com/

DIRECT ENERGY LIVE BRIGHTER SCHOLARSHIP
• *See page 584*

DIRECTTEXTBOOK.COM

http://www.DirectTextbook.com

DIRECTTEXTBOOK.COM 2016 HAIKU SCHOLARSHIP CONTEST
• *See page 584*

DIRECTTEXTBOOK.COM "SHINE" PHOTO ESSAY CONTEST
• *See page 584*

DISABLED AMERICAN VETERANS

http://www.dav.org/

JESSE BROWN MEMORIAL YOUTH SCHOLARSHIP PROGRAM
• *See page 584*

DISABLEDPERSON INC. COLLEGE SCHOLARSHIP

http://www.disabledperson.com/

DISABLEDPERSON INC. NATIONAL COLLEGE SCHOLARSHIP AWARD FOR COLLEGE STUDENTS WITH DISABILITIES
• *See page 584*

DISCIPLESHIP MINISTRIES

http://umcyoungpeople.org

DAVID W. SELF SCHOLARSHIP
Must be a United Methodist Youth who has been active in local church for at least one year prior to application. Must be a graduating senior in high school entering the first year of undergraduate study. Must be pursuing a "church-related" career and should have maintained at least a "C" average throughout high school.

Award: Scholarship for use in freshman year; not renewable. *Number:* 1–5. *Amount:* $100–$1000.
Eligibility Requirements: Applicant must be Methodist; high school student and planning to enroll or expecting to enroll full-time at a two-year or four-year institution or university. Applicant must have 2.5 GPA or higher. Available to U.S. citizens.
Application Requirements: Application form, essay, financial need analysis. *Deadline:* March 1.
Contact: Kelsey Tinker Hannum, Grant and Scholarships Administrator
Phone: 615-340-7184
E-mail: youngpeople@umcdiscipleship.org

RICHARD S. SMITH SCHOLARSHIP
• *See page 677*

DOLLARS 4 TIC SCHOLARS

http://www.dollars4ticscholars.org/

DOLLARS 4 TIC SCHOLARS TOURETTE SYNDROME SCHOLARSHIP
• *See page 585*

DOLPHIN SCHOLARSHIP FOUNDATION

http://www.dolphinscholarship.org/

DOLPHIN SCHOLARSHIPS
• *See page 585*

DUDLEY DEBOSIER INJURY LAWYERS

http://www.dudleydebosier.com/home

DUDLEY DEBOSIER SCHOLARSHIP PROGRAM
• *See page 585*

DUKE ENERGY CORPORATION

http://www.duke-energy.com/

DUKE ENERGY SCHOLARS PROGRAM
• *See page 568*

EASTERN ORTHODOX COMMITTEE ON SCOUTING

http://www.eocs.org/

EASTERN ORTHODOX COMMITTEE ON SCOUTING SCHOLARSHIPS
• *See page 541*

ELEARNERS.COM

http://www.elearners.com

ELEARNERS ONLINE STUDENT SCHOLARSHIP
• *See page 585*

ELIZABETH GREENSHIELDS FOUNDATION

http://www.elizabethgreenshieldsfoundation.org

THE ELIZABETH GREENSHIELDS FOUNDATION GRANT
• *See page 586*

ENVIRONMENTAL LITIGATION GROUP P.C.

https://www.elglaw.com/

ENVIRONMENTAL LITIGATION GROUP, P.C. ASBESTOS SCHOLARSHIP

• *See page 586*

EQUALITY SCHOLARSHIP COLLABORATIVE

http://www.equalityscholarship.org

EQUALITY SCHOLARSHIPS FOR COMMUNITY COLLEGE TRANSFER STUDENTS

• *See page 586*

SCHOLARSHIPS FOR HIGH SCHOOL GRADUATES

• *See page 586*

ESSAYHUB

https://essayhub.com/

ESSAY WRITING CONTEST BY ESSAYHUB

• *See page 587*

FADEL EDUCATIONAL FOUNDATION, INC.

http://www.fadelfoundation.org/

ANNUAL AWARD PROGRAM

Grants of $800 to $3500 awarded on the basis of merit and financial need.

Award: Grant for use in freshman, sophomore, junior, senior, or graduate years; renewable. *Number:* 3–5. *Amount:* $800–$3500.

Eligibility Requirements: Applicant must be Muslim faith and enrolled or expecting to enroll full- or part-time at a two-year or four-year or technical institution or university. Available to U.S. citizens.

Application Requirements: Application form, essay, financial need analysis. *Deadline:* May 28.

Contact: Mr. Ayman Fadel, Secretary
E-mail: secretary@fadelfoundation.org

FARAH & FARAH

http://www.farahandfarah.com/

FARAH & FARAH SCHOLARSHIP

• *See page 587*

FELDMAN & ROYLE, ATTORNEYS AT LAW

http://www.feldmanroyle.com/

AUTISM SCHOLARSHIPS

• *See page 587*

FELDMAN LAW FIRM PLLC

http://www.afphoenixcriminalattorney.com/

DISABLED VETERANS SCHOLARSHIP

• *See page 587*

FLORIDA PTA/PTSA

http://www.floridapta.org/

FLORIDA PTA/PTSA ANNUAL SCHOLARSHIP

• *See page 588*

FOUNDATION FOR CHRISTIAN COLLEGE LEADERS

http://www.collegechristianleader.com/

FOUNDATION FOR COLLEGE CHRISTIAN LEADERS SCHOLARSHIP

Applicant must be accepted to or currently enrolled in an undergraduate degree program. Candidate must demonstrate Christian leadership. Combined income of parents and student must be less than $60,000. Minimum 3.0 GPA required.

Award: Scholarship for use in freshman, sophomore, junior, senior, or graduate years; not renewable.

Eligibility Requirements: Applicant must be Christian; enrolled or expecting to enroll full- or part-time at a four-year institution or university and must have an interest in leadership. Applicant must have 3.0 GPA or higher. Available to U.S. citizens.

Application Requirements: Application form, financial need analysis, interview, leadership assessment form, cover sheet, recommendations or references. *Deadline:* May 7.

Contact: Scholarship Committee
Phone: 858-481-0848
Fax: 858-481-0848
E-mail: lmhays@aol.com

FREEDOM ALLIANCE

https://freedomalliance.org

FREEDOM ALLIANCE SCHOLARSHIP FUND

• *See page 588*

FREEDOM FROM RELIGION FOUNDATION

http://www.ffrf.org/

FREEDOM FROM RELIGION FOUNDATION MICHAEL HAKEEM MEMORIAL ONGOING COLLEGE ESSAY COMPETITION

Any currently enrolled college student may submit essay. Any college-bound high school seniors enter our high school contest. "My morals do not come from God, they come from.." is the open-ended topic offered to ongoing college students in the Michael Hakeem Memorial Contest. College students are asked to write essays of 450-650 words due by July 1, with winners announced in August. All the rules and online application are here: https://www.surveymonkey.com/r/B8F3235

Award: Scholarship for use in freshman, sophomore, junior, or senior years; not renewable. *Number:* 6–20. *Amount:* $200–$3000.

Eligibility Requirements: Applicant must be age 16-24; enrolled or expecting to enroll full- or part-time at a two-year or four-year or technical institution or university and must have an interest in writing. Available to U.S. and Canadian citizens.

Application Requirements: Application form, essay. *Deadline:* July 1.

Contact: FFRF College Essay Contest
Freedom From Religion Foundation
PO Box 750
Madison, WI 53701

FREEDOM FROM RELIGION FOUNDATION WILLIAM J. SCHULZ MEMORIAL COLLEGE-BOUND HIGH SCHOOL SENIOR ESSAY COMPETITION

College-bound high school seniors write on the topic: "If there was one thing I could tell my family or a believer about why I'm a nonbeliever, this would be it." June 1 deadline. Word limits of 350 words, with winners announced in July. See all rules at: https://www.surveymonkey.com/r/QBHT9XG

Award: Scholarship for use in freshman year; not renewable. *Number:* 6–20. *Amount:* $200–$3000.

Eligibility Requirements: Applicant must be high school student; age 15-20; planning to enroll or expecting to enroll full- or part-time at a two-year or four-year or technical institution or university and must have an interest in writing. Available to U.S. and Canadian citizens.

Application Requirements: Application form, essay. *Deadline:* June 1.

Contact: High School Essay Competition
Freedom From Religion Foundation
PO Box 750
Madison, WI 53701

FUNNEWJERSEY.COM INC.

www.funnewjersey.com

FUNNEWJERSEY.COM SCHOLARSHIP
• *See page 588*

GENERAL BOARD OF HIGHER EDUCATION AND MINISTRY

http://www.gbhem.org

BISHOP JOSEPH B. BETHEA SCHOLARSHIP
• *See page 679*

E. CRAIG BRANDENBURG GRADUATE AWARD

Scholarship for students 35 years of age or older, desiring to continue their education or to go into a second career. Must be enrolled full-time at an accredited institution, and be active, full-time members of the United Methodist Church for at least one year.

Award: Scholarship for use in freshman, sophomore, junior, senior, or graduate years; not renewable.

Eligibility Requirements: Applicant must be Methodist and enrolled or expecting to enroll full-time at a four-year institution or university. Available to U.S. citizens.

Application Requirements: Application form, application form may be submitted online (http://www.gbhem.org), essay, recommendations or references, resume, transcript. *Deadline:* March 1.

Contact: Ms. Marcie Bigord, Assistant Director of Loans &
Scholarships
General Board of Higher Education and Ministry
PO Box 340007
Nashville, TN 37203-0007
Phone: 615-340-7388
Fax: 615-340-7529
E-mail: mbigord@gbhem.org

HELEN AND ALLEN BROWN SCHOLARSHIP

Scholarship for outstanding high school graduates and undergraduate college students who are members of the Nashville District of the Tennessee Annual Conference of UMC or members of the New Orleans District of the Louisiana Annual Conference of UMC. Must have been full and active members of The United Methodist Church for at least three years and maintain a GPA of 3.0.

Award: Scholarship for use in freshman, sophomore, junior, or senior years; not renewable.

Eligibility Requirements: Applicant must be Methodist and enrolled or expecting to enroll full-time at a four-year institution or university. Applicant must have 3.0 GPA or higher. Available to U.S. citizens.

Application Requirements: Application form, application form may be submitted online (http://www.gbhem.org/loans-scholarships), essay, recommendations or references, transcript. *Deadline:* March 1.

Contact: Ms. Marcie Bigord, Assistant Director of Loans &
Scholarships
General Board of Higher Education and Ministry
PO Box 340007
Nashville, TN 37203-0007
Phone: 615-340-7388
Fax: 615-340-7529
E-mail: mbigord@gbhem.org

THE REV. DR. KAREN LAYMAN GIFT OF HOPE: 21ST CENTURY SCHOLARS PROGRAM

$1000 scholarship to United Methodist undergraduate students who are full-time, active members of UMC for at least three years prior to applying. Must demonstrate leadership in the United Methodist Church

and be enrolled in a full-time degree program at a regionally accredited U.S. institution. Cumulative GPA of 3.0 or higher required.

Award: Scholarship for use in freshman, sophomore, junior, or senior years; not renewable. *Amount:* $1000.

Eligibility Requirements: Applicant must be Methodist; enrolled or expecting to enroll full-time at a two-year or four-year institution or university and must have an interest in leadership. Applicant must have 3.0 GPA or higher. Available to U.S. and non-Canadian citizens.

Application Requirements: Application form, application form may be submitted online (http://www.gbhem.org), essay, recommendations or references, transcript. *Deadline:* March 1.

Contact: Ms. Marcie Bigord, Assistant Director of Loans &
Scholarships
General Board of Higher Education and Ministry
PO Box 340007
Nashville, TN 37203-0007
Phone: 615-340-7388
Fax: 615-340-7529
E-mail: mbigord@gbhem.org

GENERAL FEDERATION OF WOMEN'S CLUBS OF MASSACHUSETTS

http://www.gfwcma.org/

GENERAL FEDERATION OF WOMEN'S CLUBS OF MASSACHUSETTS NICKEL FOR NOTES MUSIC SCHOLARSHIP
• *See page 589*

GENERAL FEDERATION OF WOMEN'S CLUBS OF MASSACHUSETTS PENNIES FOR ART SCHOLARSHIP
• *See page 589*

GIFT BASKETS PLUS

www.giftbasketsplus.com

2017 HIGH SCHOOL GRADUATE SCHOLARSHIP CONTEST
• *See page 589*

GOENNOUNCE, LLC

http://GoEnnounce.com/about

GOENNOUNCE YOURSELF $500 MONTHLY SCHOLARSHIP
• *See page 589*

GOLF COURSE SUPERINTENDENTS ASSOCIATION OF AMERICA

http://www.eifg.org/

GOLF COURSE SUPERINTENDENTS ASSOCIATION OF AMERICA LEGACY AWARD
• *See page 544*

JOSEPH S. GARSKE COLLEGIATE GRANT PROGRAM
• *See page 544*

GORDON LAW GROUP

https://www.gordonlawltd.com

GORDON LAW GROUP NEED-BASED SCHOLARSHIP
• *See page 589*

GREATER KANAWHA VALLEY FOUNDATION

http://www.tgkvf.org/

STUART & LUCILLE ARMSTRONG SCHOLARSHIP

Renewable scholarship for an Episcopalian in the Diocese of West Virginia. Must maintain a 3.0 GPA and continue to pursue the same major or degree program. Seminarians are not eligible. Preference given to applicants from St. Christopher in Charleston.

Award: Scholarship for use in freshman, sophomore, junior, or senior years; renewable. *Amount:* $1000.

Eligibility Requirements: Applicant must be Episcopalian; enrolled or expecting to enroll full-time at a four-year institution or university and resident of West Virginia. Applicant must have 3.0 GPA or higher. Available to U.S. citizens.

Application Requirements: Application form, essay, financial need analysis, name and location of home parish along with Rectors name and contact information, recommendations or references, test scores, transcript. *Deadline:* January 15.

Contact: Susan Hoover, Scholarship Program Officer
Greater Kanawha Valley Foundation
900 Lee Street East, 16th Floor
Charleston, WV 25301
Phone: 304-346-3620
E-mail: shoover@tgkvf.org

GREENHOUSE SCHOLARS

http://greenhousescholars.org/our-scholars/become-a-scholar/

GREENHOUSE SCHOLARS

• *See page 590*

GRUNGO COLARULO

https://gcinjurylaw.com/

GRUNGO COLARULO GIVING BACK TO THE COMMUNITY SCHOLARSHIP

• *See page 590*

HARRINGTON FAMILY FOUNDATION

http://harringtonfamilyfoundation.org

OREGON COMMUNITY QUARTERBACK SCHOLARSHIP

• *See page 590*

HELEN DILLER FAMILY FOUNDATION

http://www.dillerteenawards.org

DILLER TEEN TIKKUN OLAM AWARDS

• *See page 591*

HENKEL CONSUMER ADHESIVES INC.

http://www.ducktapeclub.com/

DUCK BRAND DUCT TAPE "STUCK AT PROM" SCHOLARSHIP CONTEST

• *See page 591*

HISPANIC METROPOLITAN CHAMBER SCHOLARSHIPS

http://www.hmccoregon.com/

HISPANIC METROPOLITAN CHAMBER SCHOLARSHIPS

• *See page 592*

HOUSTON COMMUNITY SERVICES

AZTECA SCHOLARSHIP

• *See page 592*

HOW TO WIN COLLEGE SCHOLARSHIPS

https://how2winscholarships.com

SAVOR SUMMER COLLEGE SCHOLARSHIP

• *See page 592*

HUBSHOUT

http://hubshout.com/

HUBSHOUT INTERNET MARKETING SCHOLARSHIP

• *See page 592*

HUMANA FOUNDATION

http://www.humanafoundation.org/

HUMANA FOUNDATION SCHOLARSHIP PROGRAM

• *See page 593*

INSTITUTE FOR JUSTICE

http://www.ij.org

LIBERTY IN ACTION ESSAY CONTEST: REMOVING BARRIERS TO ENTREPRENEURSHIP

• *See page 593*

INTERNATIONAL COLLEGE COUNSELORS

www.internationalcollegecounselors.com

INTERNATIONAL COLLEGE COUNSELORS SCHOLARSHIP

• *See page 593*

INTERNATIONAL DAIRY DELI BAKERY ASSOCIATION

http://www.iddba.org

INTERNATIONAL DAIRY DELI BAKERY ASSOCIATION'S SCHOLARSHIP FOR GROWING THE FUTURE

• *See page 594*

INTERNATIONAL FLIGHT SERVICES ASSOCIATION

http://www.ifsanet.com

AMI SCHOLARSHIP AWARD

• *See page 594*

INTERNATIONAL VOLUNTEER HQ

https://www.volunteerhq.org/

VOLUNTEER OF THE YEAR SCHOLARSHIP

• *See page 595*

IOWA STUDENT LOAN

http://www.IowaStudentLoan.org/

IOWA FINANCIAL KNOW-HOW CHALLENGE: SENIOR SCHOLARSHIP
• *See page 596*

ITALIAN CATHOLIC FEDERATION

http://www.icf.org/

ITALIAN CATHOLIC FEDERATION FIRST YEAR SCHOLARSHIP
• *See page 546*

MARIO CUGIA ITALIAN STUDIES SCHOLARSHIP PROGRAM
• *See page 683*

JASON KALAFAT ATTORNEY AT LAW

https://criminallawyerwashingtondc.com/

JASON KALAFAT MAKE A DIFFERENCE SCHOLARSHIP
• *See page 596*

JEWISH VOCATIONAL SERVICE LOS ANGELES

http://www.jvsla.org/

JVS SCHOLARSHIP PROGRAM
• *See page 684*

JOHN B. FABRIELE, III, LLC

https://www.fabrielelaw.com/

FABRIELE DISABILITY AWARENESS SCHOLARSHIP
• *See page 596*

JUREWITZ LAW GROUP

http://www.jurewitz.com/

JUREWITZ LAW GROUP SCHOLARSHIP
• *See page 596*

JVS CHICAGO

http://jvschicago.org/

JEWISH FEDERATION OF METROPOLITAN CHICAGO ACADEMIC SCHOLARSHIP PROGRAM
• *See page 684*

KAUFMAN & STIGGER, PLLC

http://www.getthetiger.com/

THE ALBERTA C. KAUFMAN SCHOLARSHIP
• *See page 597*

KELLER LAW OFFICES

http://www.kellerlawoffices.com/

KELLER LAW OFFICES SCHOLARSHIP FOR HIGHER EDUCATION
• *See page 597*

KELLY & SOTO LAW

http://www.1800lawguys.com

KELLY & SOTO LAW SCHOLARSHIP PROGRAM
• *See page 597*

KELLY LAW TEAM

http://www.jkphoenixpersonalinjuryattorney.com/

DOWN SYNDROME SCHOLARSHIP
• *See page 597*

KIDGUARD

http://www.kidguard.com/

KIDGUARD FOR EDUCATION ESSAY SCHOLARSHIP
• *See page 597*

KIDGUARD FOR EDUCATION ESSAY SCHOLARSHIP FOR HIGH SCHOOL
• *See page 598*

KITCHEN GUIDES

http://www.kitchensguides.com/

SMART KITCHEN IMPROVEMENT SCHOLARSHIP BY KITCHEN GUIDES
• *See page 598*

KNIGHTS OF COLUMBUS

http://www.kofc.org/

FOURTH DEGREE PRO DEO AND PRO PATRIA (CANADA)
• *See page 547*

FOURTH DEGREE PRO DEO AND PRO PATRIA SCHOLARSHIPS
• *See page 547*

FRANCIS P. MATTHEWS AND JOHN E. SWIFT EDUCATIONAL TRUST SCHOLARSHIPS
• *See page 547*

JOHN W. MCDEVITT (FOURTH DEGREE) SCHOLARSHIPS
• *See page 547*

PERCY J. JOHNSON ENDOWED SCHOLARSHIPS
• *See page 547*

LARSON JEWELERS

www.larsonjewelers.com

BAND WITH SUCCESS SCHOLARSHIP
• *See page 598*

LATIN AMERICAN EDUCATIONAL FOUNDATION

http://www.laef.org/

LATIN AMERICAN EDUCATIONAL FOUNDATION SCHOLARSHIPS
• *See page 598*

LAW OFFICE OF DAVID D. WHITE, PLLC

http://www.wm-attorneys.com/

ANNUAL TRAUMATIC BRAIN INJURY SCHOLARSHIPS
• *See page 598*

LAW OFFICE OF MATTHEW L. SHARP

https://mattsharplaw.com/

LAW OFFICE OF MATTHEW L. SHARP NEED-BASED SCHOLARSHIP
• *See page 599*

LAW OFFICE OF MATTHEW SHRUM

http://www.shrumlawoffice.com/

ANNUAL SINGLE MOTHERS SCHOLARSHIP
• *See page 599*

LAW OFFICES OF DAVID A. BLACK

http://www.dbphoenixcriminallawyer.com

ANNUAL HEARING IMPAIRED SCHOLARSHIP
• *See page 599*

LAW OFFICES OF JUDD S. NEMIRO, PLLC

http://www.jnphoenixfamilylawyer.com/

ANNUAL DYSLEXIA SCHOLARSHIP
• *See page 599*

LAW OFFICES OF RYAN J. TEGNELIA

http://www.sandiegocriminallawyerrt.com/

ANNUAL VETERANS WITH POST-TRAUMATIC STRESS SCHOLARSHIP
• *See page 599*

LAW OFFICES OF SHERYL R. RENTZ, P.C.

http://www.srrentzlaw.com/

2017 LAW OFFICES OF SHERYL R. RENTZ SCHOLARSHIP
• *See page 600*

LAW OFFICES OF THOMAS J. LAVIN

http://www.lawlavinflorida.com/

THOMAS J. LAVIN SCHOLARSHIP
• *See page 600*

LAW OFFICES OF TRAGOS, SARTES & TRAGOS

https://tragoslaw.com/

TRAGOS WRITE YOUR OWN LAW SCHOLARSHIP
• *See page 600*

LEPENDORF & SILVERSTEIN, P.C.

http://www.lependorf.com/

LEPENDORF & SILVERSTEIN, P.C. 2017 NEW JERSEY SCHOLARSHIP
• *See page 600*

LEP FOUNDATION FOR YOUTH EDUCATION

http://www.lepfoundation.org/applications

CURE—CANCER SUPPORT SCHOLARSHIP
• *See page 600*

JOHN LEPPING MEMORIAL SCHOLARSHIP
• *See page 600*

LIVE POETS SOCIETY AND JUST POETRY!!! MAGAZINE

http://www.highschoolpoetrycontest.com/

NATIONAL HIGH SCHOOL POETRY CONTEST
• *See page 601*

MAINE STATE SOCIETY FOUNDATION OF WASHINGTON, DC INC.

http://mainestatesociety.org/foundation/

MAINE STATE SOCIETY FOUNDATION SCHOLARSHIP
• *See page 601*

MAINOR WORTH INJURY LAWYERS

https://mainorwirth.com/

MAINOR WIRTH INJURY LAWYERS NEED-BASED SCHOLARSHIP
• *See page 601*

MARYLAND ASSOCIATION OF PRIVATE COLLEGES AND CAREER SCHOOLS

http://www.mapccs.org/

MARYLAND ASSOCIATION OF PRIVATE COLLEGES AND CAREER SCHOOLS SCHOLARSHIP
• *See page 602*

MATRIX HEALTH GROUP

http://www.matrixhealthgroup.com

JOE HOLIBAUGH MEMORIAL SCHOLARSHIP
• *See page 602*

MARK COATS MEMORIAL SCHOLARSHIP
• *See page 602*

RON NIEDERMAN MEMORIAL SCHOLARSHIP
• *See page 603*

TIM KENNEDY MEMORIAL SCHOLARSHIP
• *See page 603*

MENSA FOUNDATION

http://mensafoundation.org

U.S. SCHOLARSHIP PROGRAM
• *See page 603*

MES FOUNDATION

http://www.mesfoundation.org

RICHARD H. PIERCE MEMORIAL SCHOLARSHIP
• *See page 603*

MINDSUMO

http://www.mindsumo.com

MINDSUMO 15-MINUTE SCHOLARSHIP
• *See page 603*

MINNESOTA MASONIC CHARITIES

http://www.mnmasoniccharities.org

MINNESOTA MASONIC CHARITIES SIGNATURE SCHOLARSHIP
• *See page 604*

MINNESOTA MASONIC CHARITIES UNDERGRADUATE SCHOLARSHIP
• *See page 604*

MITCHELL INSTITUTE

http://www.mitchellinstitute.org/

THE SENATOR GEORGE J. MITCHELL SCHOLARSHIP RESEARCH INSTITUTE
• *See page 604*

MLD WEALTH MANAGEMENT GROUP

http://mywealthmanagement.ca/

ANNUAL MLD SCHOLASTIC SCHOLARSHIP
• *See page 604*

NATIONAL AIDS MEMORIAL GROVE

http://www.aidsmemorial.org

PEDRO ZAMORA YOUNG LEADERS SCHOLARSHIP
• *See page 605*

NATIONAL COUNCIL OF JEWISH WOMEN LOS ANGELES (NCJW L LA)

http://ncjwla.org/

DODELL WOMEN'S EMPOWERMENT SCHOLARSHIP
• *See page 606*

SOPHIE GREENSTADT SCHOLARSHIP FOR MID-LIFE WOMEN
• *See page 606*

STEPHEN L. TELLER & RICHARD HOTSON TV, CINEMA, AND THEATER SCHOLARSHIP
• *See page 606*

SUSAN SCHULMAN BEGLEY MEMORIAL SCHOLARSHIP
• *See page 606*

NATIONAL FEDERATION OF THE BLIND (NFB)

http://www.nfb.org/scholarships

AAF KENNETH JERNIGAN SCHOLARSHIP FOR $12,000
• *See page 607*

CHARLES AND MELVA T. OWEN SCHOLARSHIP FOR $10,000
• *See page 607*

NATIONAL MULTIPLE SCLEROSIS SOCIETY

http://www.nmss.org/

NATIONAL MULTIPLE SCLEROSIS SOCIETY SCHOLARSHIP PROGRAM
• *See page 607*

NATIONAL PRESS FOUNDATION

http://www.nationalpress.org/

EVERT CLARK/SETH PAYNE AWARD
• *See page 607*

NEBRASKA'S COORDINATING COMMISSION FOR POSTSECONDARY EDUCATION

https://ccpe.nebraska.gov/

NEBRASKA OPPORTUNITY GRANT
• *See page 608*

NICODEMUS WILDERNESS PROJECT

http://www.wildernessproject.org/

APPRENTICE ECOLOGIST SCHOLARSHIP
• *See page 608*

NIKKO COSMETIC SURGERY CENTER

http://www.drnikko.com/

BREAST CANCER SURVIVOR SCHOLARSHIPS
• *See page 608*

NISEI STUDENT RELOCATION COMMEMORATIVE FUND

http://www.nsrcfund.org/

NISEI STUDENT RELOCATION COMMEMORATIVE FUND
• *See page 608*

NO BULL SPORTS

http://nobullsports.org/

NO BULL SPORTS SCHOLARSHIP
• *See page 609*

NOPLAG PLAGIARISM CHECKER

http://noplag.com/

NOPLAG SCHOLARSHIP ESSAY CONTEST

• See page 609

NORTH CAROLINA DIVISION OF VOCATIONAL REHABILITATION SERVICES

http://www.dhhs.state.nc.us/

TRAINING SUPPORT FOR YOUTH WITH DISABILITIES

• See page 609

NORTH CAROLINA VIETNAM VETERANS, INC.

http://www.ncvvi.org

NC VIETNAM VETERANS, INC., SCHOLARSHIP PROGRAM

• See page 609

OHIO DEPARTMENT OF HIGHER EDUCATION

www.ohiohighered.org

OHIO COLLEGE OPPORTUNITY GRANT

• See page 609

OHIO SAFETY OFFICERS COLLEGE MEMORIAL FUND

• See page 609

OHIO WAR ORPHANS SCHOLARSHIP

• See page 610

ONE LOVE FOUNDATION

www.joinonelove.org

ONE LOVE FOUNDATION PETS VS. PARTNERS SCHOLARSHIP

• See page 610

ORGANIZATION FOR AUTISM RESEARCH

www.researchautism.org

LISA HIGGINS HUSSMAN SCHOLARSHIP

• See page 610

SCHWALLIE FAMILY SCHOLARSHIP

• See page 610

ORTHODOX UNION

http://ou.org

SARA AND MAX GOLDSAMMLER SCHOLARSHIP FUND

• See page 695

OUTRIGGER DUKE KAHANAMOKU FOUNDATION

http://www.dukefoundation.org

ODKF GENERAL SCHOLARSHIP AWARD

• See page 611

PANHELLENIC SCHOLARSHIP FOUNDATION

http://www.panhellenicscholarships.org/

PANHELLENIC SCHOLARSHIP AWARDS

• See page 611

PAPERCHECK

https://www.papercheck.com/

PAPERCHECK, LLC—CHARLES SHAFAE' SCHOLARSHIP FUND

• See page 611

PENNSYLVANIA FEDERATION OF DEMOCRATIC WOMEN INC.

www.pafedofdemwomen.org

PENNSYLVANIA FEDERATION OF DEMOCRATIC WOMEN INC. ANNUAL SCHOLARSHIP AWARDS

• See page 554

PENNSYLVANIA HIGHER EDUCATION ASSISTANCE AGENCY

http://www.pheaa.org/

BLIND OR DEAF BENEFICIARY GRANT PROGRAM

• See page 612

PILOT INTERNATIONAL FOUNDATION

http://www.pilotinternational.org/

BECKY BURROWS MEMORIAL SCHOLARSHIP

• See page 612

PLAINTIFF RELIEF

http://plaintiffrelief.com/

PLAINTIFF RELIEF SCHOLARSHIP

• See page 612

POLSON & POLSON, P.C.

https://www.polsonlawfirm.com/

POLSON & POLSON, P.C. CONQUERING ADVERSITY SCHOLARSHIP

• See page 612

PRESBYTERIAN CHURCH (USA)

http://www.pcusa.org/financialaid

NATIONAL PRESBYTERIAN COLLEGE SCHOLARSHIP

Scholarships between $1000 and $1500 available to incoming undergraduate enrolled in full-time programs in colleges associated with the Presbyterian Church (U.S.A.). Applicants must have a minimum GPA of 2.5 and demonstrate financial need. Students are required to participate in campus ministry or a worshiping community proximate to the college they attend and respond to an annual essay question exploring aspects of vocation.

Award: Scholarship for use in freshman, sophomore, junior, or senior years; not renewable. *Number:* 25–100. *Amount:* $1000–$1500.

Eligibility Requirements: Applicant must be Presbyterian and enrolled or expecting to enroll full-time at a four-year institution or university. Applicant must have 2.5 GPA or higher. Available to U.S. and non-U.S. citizens.

Application Requirements: Application form, essay, financial need analysis, recommendations or references, resume, transcript. *Deadline:* March 1.

Contact: Ms. Laura Bryan, Associate, Financial Aid for Studies
Presbyterian Church (USA)
100 Witherspoon Street
Louisville, KY 40202-1396
Phone: 800-728-7228 Ext. 5735
Fax: 502-569-8776
E-mail: finaid@pcusa.org

NATIVE AMERICAN SUPPLEMENTAL GRANT
• *See page 697*

SAMUEL ROBINSON AWARD

Prize granted to full-time junior and senior students attending a Presbyterian related college or university who successfully recite answers to the Westminster Shorter Catechism and write an essay on an assigned topic.

Award: Prize for use in junior or senior years; not renewable. *Number:* 16. *Amount:* $250–$5000.

Eligibility Requirements: Applicant must be Presbyterian and enrolled or expecting to enroll full-time at a four-year institution or university. Available to U.S. citizens.

Application Requirements: Application form, entry in a contest, essay. *Deadline:* April 1.

Contact: Ms. Laura Bryan, Associate, Financial Aid for Studies
Presbyterian Church (USA)
100 Witherspoon Street
Louisville, KY 40202
Phone: 800-728-7228 Ext. 5735
Fax: 502-569-8766
E-mail: finaid@pcusa.org

PRICE BENOWITZ LLP
http://pricebenowitz.com/

AMATO SANITA BRIGHTER FUTURE SCHOLARSHIP
• *See page 613*

ANGIE DIPIETRO WOMEN IN BUSINESS SCHOLARSHIP
• *See page 613*

APRIL COCKERHAM DREAM ACT SCHOLARSHIP
• *See page 613*

KAREN RILEY PORTER GOOD WORKS SCHOLARSHIP
• *See page 613*

KERRI CASTELLINI WOMEN'S LEADERSHIP SCHOLARSHIP
• *See page 613*

KUSH ARORA FEDERAL CRIMINAL JUSTICE REFORM SCHOLARSHIP
• *See page 613*

PRICE BENOWITZ SOCIAL JUSTICE SCHOLARSHIP
• *See page 613*

SETH OKIN GOOD DEEDS SCHOLARSHIP
• *See page 613*

THOMAS SOLDAN HEALTHY COMMUNITIES SCHOLARSHIP
• *See page 614*

PRIVATE AID TEST SURVEY

A TEST PROGRAM NAME
• *See page 614*

PROMPT
http://prompt.com

PROMPT'S $20,000 SCHOLARSHIP
• *See page 614*

REACH HIGHER MONTANA
http://www.ReachHigherMontana.org

REACH HIGHER MONTANA SCHOLARSHIPS
• *See page 614*

RHINE LAW FIRM, P.C.
http://www.carolinaaccidentattorneys.com/

2017 RHINE LAW FIRM, P.C. SCHOLARSHIP
• *See page 615*

ROMAN CATHOLIC DIOCESE OF TULSA
http://www.dioceseoftulsa.org

MAE LASSLEY OSAGE SCHOLARSHIP
• *See page 697*

ROSENGREN KOHLMEYER, LAW OFFICE CHTD.
http://rokolaw.com

ROSENGREN KOHLMEYER LAW OFFICE SCHOLARSHIP
• *See page 615*

SALLIE MAE FUND
http://www.thesalliemaefund.org/

$1,000 PLAN FOR COLLEGE SWEEPSTAKES
• *See page 615*

SELECTBLINDS.COM
http://www.selectblinds.com

SELECTBLINDS.COM $1000 COLLEGE SCHOLARSHIP
• *See page 615*

SEXNER & ASSOCIATES LLC
http://www.sexner.com/personal-injury/

MITCHELL S. SEXNER & ASSOCIATES LLC SCHOLARSHIP
• *See page 616*

SHAWN SUKUMAR ATTORNEY AT LAW
https://www.washingtondccriminallawyer.net/

SHAWN SUKUMAR CRIMINAL JUSTICE REFORM SCHOLARSHIP
• *See page 616*

SILICON VALLEY COMMUNITY FOUNDATION

www.siliconvalleycf.org

ABBY SOBRATO SCHOLARSHIP
• *See page 616*

BOBETTE BIBO GUGLIOTTA MEMORIAL SCHOLARSHIP FOR CREATIVE WRITING
• *See page 616*

CURRY AWARD FOR GIRLS AND YOUNG WOMEN
• *See page 616*

HAZEL REED BAUMEISTER SCHOLARSHIP PROGRAM
• *See page 616*

HUANG LEADERSHIP DEVELOPMENT SCHOLARSHIP
• *See page 617*

LATINOS IN TECHNOLOGY SCHOLARSHIP
• *See page 617*

SOCIETY FOR APPLIED ANTHROPOLOGY

http://www.sfaa.net/

ANNUAL SFAA STUDENT ENDOWED AWARD
• *See page 617*

TOURISM AND HERITAGE STUDENT PAPER COMPETITION
• *See page 617*

SOCIETY OF DAUGHTERS OF THE UNITED STATES ARMY

SOCIETY OF DAUGHTERS OF THE UNITED STATES ARMY SCHOLARSHIPS
• *See page 617*

SOUTH CAROLINA TUITION GRANTS COMMISSION

http://www.sctuitiongrants.org/

SOUTH CAROLINA TUITION GRANTS PROGRAM
• *See page 617*

SPANISHDICT

www.spanishdict.com/traductor

BECA #TRADUCTOR
• *See page 618*

SPINE SURGEON DR. VICTOR HAYES

https://tampabaybackpaindoctor.com/

TAMPA BAY SPINE CENTER ROAD TO RECOVERY SCHOLARSHIP
• *See page 618*

STATE EMPLOYEES ASSOCIATION OF NORTH CAROLINA (SEANC)

http://www.seanc.org/

STATE EMPLOYEES ASSOCIATION OF NORTH CAROLINA (SEANC) SCHOLARSHIPS
• *See page 700*

STONEWALL COMMUNITY FOUNDATION

http://www.stonewallfoundation.org/

NEW YORK RAMBLERS SCHOLARSHIP FOR STUDENT ATHLETES
• *See page 618*

TRAUB-DICKER RAINBOW SCHOLARSHIP
• *See page 618*

STROM & ASSOCIATES

https://stromlawyers.com

STROM & ASSOCIATES NEED-BASED SCHOLARSHIP
• *See page 619*

TARADASH LAW FIRM

https://taradashlaw.com/

TARADASH LAW FIRM SCHOLARSHIP
• *See page 619*

TELEVISION ACADEMY FOUNDATION

http://www.televisionacademy.com/foundation

TELEVISION ACADEMY FOUNDATION
• *See page 619*

TENNESSEE STUDENT ASSISTANCE CORPORATION

http://www.tn.gov/collegepays

HELPING HEROES GRANT
• *See page 619*

HOPE WITH ASPIRE
• *See page 619*

NED MCWHERTER SCHOLARS PROGRAM
• *See page 620*

TELS HOPE ACCESS GRANT
• *See page 620*

TELS -HOPE WITH GENERAL ASSEMBLY MERIT SCHOLARSHIP (GAMS)
• *See page 620*

TELS - TENNESSEE HOPE SCHOLARSHIP
• *See page 620*

TENNESSEE DUAL ENROLLMENT GRANT
• *See page 620*

TENNESSEE EDUCATION LOTTERY SCHOLARSHIP PROGRAM WILDER-NAIFEH TECHNICAL SKILLS GRANT
• *See page 620*

TENNESSEE HOPE FOSTER CHILD TUITION GRANT
• *See page 620*

TENNESSEE STEP UP SCHOLARSHIP
• *See page 621*

TENNESSEE STUDENT ASSISTANCE AWARD
• *See page 621*

TETHERBOX
http://www.tetherbox.com/

$1,000 CREATIVE VIDEO CHALLENGE COLLEGE SCHOLARSHIP
• *See page 621*

TEXAS ASSOCIATION OF DEVELOPING COLLEGES
http://www.txadc.org

THE URBAN SCHOLARSHIPS FUND
• *See page 622*

TEXAS BLACK BAPTIST SCHOLARSHIP COMMITTEE
http://www.bgct.org/

TEXAS BLACK BAPTIST SCHOLARSHIP
• *See page 702*

TEXAS MUTUAL INSURANCE COMPANY
http://www.texasmutual.com/

TEXAS MUTUAL INSURANCE COMPANY SCHOLARSHIP PROGRAM
• *See page 622*

TWO TEN FOOTWEAR FOUNDATION
http://www.twoten.org/

CLASSIC SCHOLARSHIPS
• *See page 622*

ULMAN CANCER FUND FOR YOUNG ADULTS
http://www.ulmanfund.org/scholarships

JACQUELINE SHEARER MEMORIAL SCHOLARSHIP
• *See page 623*

JAMIE L. ROBERTS MEMORIAL SCHOLARSHIP AWARD
• *See page 623*

JEFFREY P. MEYER MEMORIAL SCHOLARSHIP
• *See page 623*

JILL WEAVER STARKMAN SCHOLARSHIP
• *See page 623*

JOHN HANLEY MEMORIAL SCHOLARSHIP
• *See page 623*

LISA HIGGINS-HUSSMAN FOUNDATION SCHOLARSHIP
• *See page 623*

MARILYN YETSO MEMORIAL SCHOLARSHIP
• *See page 624*

OLIVIA M. MARQUART SCHOLARSHIP
• *See page 624*

PERLITA LIWANAG MEMORIAL SCHOLARSHIP
• *See page 624*

SATOLA FAMILY SCHOLARSHIP
• *See page 624*

SEAN SILVER MEMORIAL SCHOLARSHIP AWARD
• *See page 624*

VERA YIP MEMORIAL SCHOLARSHIP
• *See page 624*

VITTORIA DIANNA RICARDO MEMORIAL SCHOLARSHIP
• *See page 625*

UNION PLUS SCHOLARSHIP PROGRAM
http://www.unionplus.org/

UNION PLUS EDUCATION FOUNDATION SCHOLARSHIP PROGRAM
• *See page 564*

UNITARIAN UNIVERSALIST ASSOCIATION
http://www.uua.org/

CHILDREN OF UNITARIAN UNIVERSALIST MINISTERS
Non-renewable scholarship available to children of Unitarian Universalist Ministers to defray undergraduate college expenses. Dollar value and number of awards varies. Priority is given to applicants whose family income does not exceed $50,000.

Award: Scholarship for use in freshman, sophomore, junior, or senior years; not renewable.

Eligibility Requirements: Applicant must be Unitarian Universalist and enrolled or expecting to enroll full- or part-time at a four-year institution or university. Available to U.S. citizens.

Application Requirements: Application form. *Deadline:* July 31.

Contact: Ms. Hillary Goodridge, Program Director
Phone: 617-971-9600
Fax: 617-971-0029
E-mail: uufp@aol.com

JOSEPH SUMNER SMITH SCHOLARSHIP
Funds are available for Unitarian Universalist (UU) students attending Antioch (including satellite and nonresidential campuses) and Harvard. While there is no restriction on the course of studies the student may elect to pursue, nor any restrictions on choice of career, student interested in pursuing the ministry after graduation are especially urged to apply.

Award: Scholarship for use in freshman, sophomore, junior, senior, or graduate years; not renewable. *Amount:* $500–$1000.

Eligibility Requirements: Applicant must be Unitarian Universalist and enrolled or expecting to enroll full- or part-time at a two-year or four-year or technical institution or university. Available to U.S. citizens.

Application Requirements: Application form. *Deadline:* April 30.

Contact: Ms. Hillary Goodridge, Program Director
Phone: 617-971-9600
Fax: 617-971-0029
E-mail: uufp@aol.com

UNITED TRANSPORTATION UNION INSURANCE ASSOCIATION

http://www.utuia.org/

UTUIA SCHOLARSHIP
• *See page 625*

UNIVERSITY CONSORTIUM FOR LIBERIA

http://ucliberia.com/

JOSEPH N. BOAKAI SR. HIGHER EDUCATION SCHOLARSHIP
• *See page 625*

U.S. COAST GUARD

www.gocoastguard/cspi

COLLEGE STUDENT PRE-COMMISSIONING INITIATIVE (CSPI)
• *See page 625*

VALUEPENGUIN

http://www.valuepenguin.com

VALUEPENGUIN SCHOLARSHIP
• *See page 626*

WARD LAW GROUP, PL

http://thecoveragelawyer.com/

WARD LAW GROUP BETTER FUTURE SCHOLARSHIP
• *See page 626*

WASHINGTON SOCIETY OF CERTIFIED PUBLIC ACCOUNTANTS

http://www.wscpa.org/

WSCPA FOUNDATION SCHOLARSHIPS
• *See page 626*

WILLIAM D. SQUIRES EDUCATIONAL FOUNDATION INC.

http://www.wmdsquiresfoundation.org/

WILLIAM D. SQUIRES SCHOLARSHIP
• *See page 627*

WOMEN OF THE EVANGELICAL LUTHERAN CHURCH IN AMERICA

http://www.womenoftheelca.org/

AMELIA KEMP SCHOLARSHIP
• *See page 709*

BELMER/FLORA PRINCE SCHOLARSHIP
Scholarship for women who have experienced an interruption of two or more years in education since the completion of high school. Must be member of ELCA and be at least 21 years old.

Award: Scholarship for use in freshman, sophomore, junior, senior, or graduate years; not renewable. *Number:* 2. *Amount:* up to $1000.

Eligibility Requirements: Applicant must be Lutheran; enrolled or expecting to enroll full- or part-time at a two-year or four-year or technical institution or university and female. Available to U.S. citizens.

Application Requirements: Application form, recommendations or references, resume, transcript. *Deadline:* February 15.

Contact: Emily Hansen, Scholarship Committee
Phone: 800-638-3522 Ext. 2736
Fax: 773-380-2419
E-mail: womenelca@elca.org

WOMEN'S JEWELRY ASSOCIATION

http://www.womensjewelryassociation.com

MEMBER GRANTS
• *See page 627*

WOMEN'S JEWELRY ASSOCIATIONS VETERANS GRANT
• *See page 627*

WOMEN'S SPORTS FOUNDATION

http://www.womenssportsfoundation.org/

LINDA RIDDLE/SGMA ENDOWED SCHOLARSHIP
• *See page 627*

YORKVILLE GOODS LLC

http://yorkvilleblankets.com/

YORKVILLE BLANKETS ASD SCHOLARSHIP
• *See page 627*

RESIDENCE

180 MEDICAL, INC.

http://www.180medical.com

180 MEDICAL COLLEGE SCHOLARSHIP PROGRAM
Seven $1,000 scholarships will be awarded to students attending a two-year, four-year, or graduate school program full time in the fall are eligible to apply. Applicants must be under a physician's care for a spinal cord injury, spina bifida, transverse myelitis, neurogenic bladder, or ostomy (ileostomy, colostomy, or urostomy). Must be a legal resident in the United States. Deadline is June 1st.

Award: Scholarship for use in freshman, sophomore, junior, senior, graduate, or postgraduate years; not renewable. *Number:* 7. *Amount:* $1000.

Eligibility Requirements: Applicant must be enrolled or expecting to enroll full-time at a two-year or four-year or technical institution or university and resident of Alabama, Alaska, Alberta, Arizona, Arkansas, California, Colorado, Connecticut, Delaware, District of Columbia, Florida, Georgia, Guam, Hawaii, Idaho, Illinois, Indiana, Iowa, Kansas, Kentucky, Louisiana, Maine, Manitoba, Maryland, Massachusetts, Michigan, Minnesota, Mississippi, Missouri, Montana, Nebraska, Nevada, New Hampshire, New Jersey, New Mexico, New York, North Carolina, North Dakota, Ohio, Oklahoma, Oregon, Pennsylvania, Puerto Rico, Rhode Island, Saskatchewan, South Carolina, South Dakota, Tennessee, Texas, Utah, Vermont, Virginia, Washington, West Virginia, Wisconsin, Wyoming. Available to U.S. citizens.

Application Requirements: Application form, essay. *Deadline:* June 1.

THE 5 STRONG SCHOLARSHIP FOUNDATION, INC.

http://5strongscholars.org

5 STRONG SCHOLARS SCHOLARSHIP
• *See page 666*

ABBVIE INC.

https://www.abbvie.com/

ABBVIE IMMUNOLOGY SCHOLARSHIP

• *See page 572*

ALABAMA COMMISSION ON HIGHER EDUCATION

http://www.ache.alabama.gov/

ALABAMA NATIONAL GUARD EDUCATIONAL ASSISTANCE PROGRAM

• *See page 642*

ALABAMA STUDENT ASSISTANCE PROGRAM

Scholarship award of $300 to $5000 per academic year given to undergraduate students residing in the state of Alabama and attending a college or university in Alabama.

Award: Grant for use in freshman, sophomore, junior, or senior years; not renewable. *Number:* 3500–4500. *Amount:* $300–$5000.

Eligibility Requirements: Applicant must be enrolled or expecting to enroll full- or part-time at a two-year or four-year or technical institution or university; resident of Alabama and studying in Alabama. Available to U.S. citizens.

Application Requirements: Application form, financial need analysis. *Deadline:* continuous.

Contact: Cheryl Newton, Grants Coordinator
 Phone: 334-242-2273
 Fax: 334-242-2269
 E-mail: cheryl.newton@ache.alabama.gov

ALABAMA STUDENT GRANT PROGRAM

Nonrenewable awards available to Alabama residents for undergraduate study at certain independent colleges within the state. Both full and half-time students are eligible. Deadlines: September 15, January 15, and February 15.

Award: Grant for use in freshman, sophomore, junior, or senior years; not renewable. *Number:* 3500–5200. *Amount:* $200–$1200.

Eligibility Requirements: Applicant must be enrolled or expecting to enroll full- or part-time at a four-year institution or university; resident of Alabama and studying in Alabama. Available to U.S. citizens.

Application Requirements: Application form.

Contact: Cheryl Newton, Grants Coordinator
 Phone: 334-242-2273
 Fax: 334-242-2269
 E-mail: cheryl.newton@ache.alabama.gov

POLICE OFFICERS AND FIREFIGHTERS SURVIVORS EDUCATION ASSISTANCE PROGRAM-ALABAMA

Provides tuition, fees, books, and supplies to dependents of full-time police officers and firefighters killed or totally disabled in the line of duty. Must attend an Alabama public college as an undergraduate. Must be Alabama resident.

Award: Scholarship for use in freshman, sophomore, junior, or senior years; renewable. *Number:* 15–30. *Amount:* $1600–$12,000.

Eligibility Requirements: Applicant must be enrolled or expecting to enroll full- or part-time at a two-year or technical institution or university; resident of Alabama and studying in Alabama. Available to U.S. citizens.

Application Requirements: Application form. *Deadline:* continuous.

Contact: Cheryl Newton, Grants Coordinator
 Phone: 334-242-2273
 Fax: 334-242-2269
 E-mail: cheryl.newton@ache.alabama.gov

ALABAMA DEPARTMENT OF VETERANS AFFAIRS

http://www.va.alabama.gov/

ALABAMA G.I. DEPENDENTS SCHOLARSHIP PROGRAM

Scholarship pays for tuition, textbooks and laboratory fees for eligible dependents of Alabama disabled, prisoner-of-war, or missing-in-action veterans. Child or stepchild must initiate training before 26th birthday; age 30 deadline may apply in certain situations. No age deadline for spouses or widows. The veteran and the step child's parent must have been married prior the child's 19th birthday.

Award: Scholarship for use in freshman, sophomore, junior, or senior years; renewable.

Eligibility Requirements: Applicant must be enrolled or expecting to enroll full- or part-time at a two-year or four-year or technical institution or university; resident of Alabama and studying in Alabama. Available to U.S. citizens.

Application Requirements: Application form.

Contact: Kayla Kyle, Department Operations Manager
 Alabama Department of Veterans Affairs
 PO Box 1509
 Montgomery, AL 36102-1509
 Phone: 334-242-5077

ALASKA COMMISSION ON POSTSECONDARY EDUCATION

http://www.acpe.alaska.gov

ALASKADVANTAGE EDUCATION GRANT

The Alaska legislature created the AlaskAdvantage Education Grant Program (AEG) to provide need-based financial assistance to eligible Alaska students attending qualifying postsecondary educational institutions in Alaska. Students apply by completing the FAFSA annually.

Award: Grant for use in freshman, sophomore, junior, or senior years; not renewable. *Amount:* $500–$3000.

Eligibility Requirements: Applicant must be enrolled or expecting to enroll full- or part-time at a two-year or four-year institution or university; resident of Alaska and studying in Alaska. Available to U.S. and non-U.S. citizens.

Application Requirements: Completed FAFSA.

Contact: Adam Weed, Special Programs Coordinator
 Phone: 907-465-6685
 E-mail: customer_service@acpe.state.ak.us

ALASKA PERFORMANCE SCHOLARSHIP

To qualify, students must take a specific, rigorous high school curriculum; earn a minimum 2.5 GPA; and do well on college or career readiness exam. Students apply by completing the FAFSA by the annual deadline. Awards can be used at any regionally accredited college or university in Alaska, or for approved career and technical education programs in the state. Students must use scholarship within 6 years of high school graduation. Students cannot receive award for more than 8 semesters.

Award: Scholarship for use in freshman, sophomore, junior, senior, graduate, or postgraduate years; not renewable. *Amount:* $500–$4755.

Eligibility Requirements: Applicant must be enrolled or expecting to enroll full- or part-time at a two-year or four-year or technical institution or university; resident of Alaska and studying in Alaska. Applicant must have 2.5 GPA or higher. Available to U.S. and non-U.S. citizens.

Application Requirements: FAFSA.

Contact: Adam Weed, Special Programs Coordinator
 Phone: 907-465-6685
 E-mail: customer_service@acpe.state.ak.us

ALBERTA AGRICULTURE FOOD AND RURAL DEVELOPMENT 4-H BRANCH

http://www.4h.ab.ca/

ALBERTA AGRICULTURE FOOD AND RURAL DEVELOPMENT 4-H SCHOLARSHIP PROGRAM
• *See page 528*

ALBERTA HERITAGE SCHOLARSHIP FUND

http://www.alis.alberta.ca/

ADULT HIGH SCHOOL EQUIVALENCY SCHOLARSHIPS
• *See page 666*

ALBERTA APPRENTICESHIP AND INDUSTRY TRAINING SCHOLARSHIPS

Awards of CAN$1000 to recognize the accomplishments of Alberta high school students taking the registered apprenticeship program and to encourage recipients to continue their apprenticeship training after completing high school. Must be a Canadian citizen or landed immigrant and a resident of Alberta, must have completed the requirements for high school graduation between August 1 and July 31 of the current year and must be registered as an Alberta apprentice in a trade while still attending high school. For additional information, please visit website http://alis.alberta.ca.

Award: Scholarship for use in freshman year; not renewable.

Eligibility Requirements: Applicant must be enrolled or expecting to enroll full-time at a two-year or four-year or technical institution or university and resident of Alberta. Available to Canadian citizens.

Application Requirements: Application form, employer recommendation, essay, recommendations or references. *Deadline:* June 30.

Contact: Scholarship Committee
Phone: 780-427-8640
E-mail: scholarships@gov.ab.ca

ALBERTA CENTENNIAL SCHOLARSHIPS-ALBERTA
• *See page 666*

ALBERTA PRE-APPRENTICESHIP SCHOLARSHIPS

CAN$1000 to encourage those completing pre-apprenticeship programs to continue in the trades and complete their training. Programs must include at least four weeks of trades-related instruction, not including work experience. Applicants must be registered apprentices and demonstrate financial need. For additional information, see website http://alis.alberta.ca.

Award: Scholarship for use in freshman or sophomore years; not renewable. *Number:* 11.

Eligibility Requirements: Applicant must be enrolled or expecting to enroll full-time at a technical institution; resident of Alberta and studying in Alberta. Available to Canadian citizens.

Application Requirements: Application form, essay, recommendations or references, transcript. *Deadline:* June 30.

Contact: Scholarship Committee
Phone: 780-427-8640
E-mail: scholarships@gov.ab.ca

ALEXANDER RUTHERFORD SCHOLARSHIPS FOR HIGH SCHOOL ACHIEVEMENT
• *See page 667*

CHARLES S. NOBLE JUNIOR FOOTBALL SCHOLARSHIPS
• *See page 667*

CHARLES S. NOBLE JUNIOR HOCKEY SCHOLARSHIPS
• *See page 667*

CHINA-ALBERTA AWARD FOR EXCELLENCE IN CHINESE

Award of CAN$500 for Canadian citizens or permanent residents who are Alberta residents currently enrolled in Grade 12. Must have taken high school Chinese Language and Culture Program 10 and 20 and currently be enrolled or have completed level 30; and have obtained an average of 80% in all courses, and a minimum average of 90% in Chinese Language and Culture 10 and 20. Applicant's parents or a parent must reside in Alberta. For more information, see website http://alis.alberta.ca/.

Award: Grant for use in freshman year; not renewable.

Eligibility Requirements: Applicant must be high school student; planning to enroll or expecting to enroll full-time at a four-year institution or university and resident of Alberta.

Application Requirements: Application form, essay, recommendations or references, transcript. *Deadline:* April 30.

Contact: Scholarship Committee
Phone: 780-427-8640
E-mail: scholarships@gov.ab.ca

DUKE AND DUTCHESS OF CAMBRIDGE SCHOLARSHIP

Awards of CAN$2500 available to students who have been in government care and have overcome significant challenges in their lives while pursing their postsecondary studies. Eligible students must be Advancing Futures Bursary recipients and be returning to full-time postsecondary studies. Awarded on the basis of academic achievement; the highest GPA (grade point average) while working toward a degree, diploma, or certificate. Advancing Futures Bursary recipients who are taking postsecondary upgrading courses or attending a specialized high school are also eligible. For more information, see website http://alis.alberta.ca/.

Award: Scholarship for use in freshman, sophomore, junior, or senior years; not renewable. *Number:* 25.

Eligibility Requirements: Applicant must be enrolled or expecting to enroll full-time at a four-year institution or university and resident of Alberta.

Application Requirements: Application form, transcript. *Deadline:* August 1.

Contact: Scholarship Committee
Phone: 780-427-8640
E-mail: scholarships@gov.ab.ca

JIMMIE CONDON ATHLETIC SCHOLARSHIPS
• *See page 667*

JO-ANNE KOCH-ABC SOCIETY SCHOLARSHIP
• *See page 667*

KEYERA ENERGY-PETER J. RENTON MEMORIAL SCHOLARSHIP
• *See page 667*

LAURENCE DECORE AWARDS FOR STUDENT LEADERSHIP
• *See page 668*

LOUISE MCKINNEY POST-SECONDARY SCHOLARSHIPS
• *See page 668*

PERSONS CASE SCHOLARSHIPS
• *See page 668*

PRAIRIE BASEBALL ACADEMY SCHOLARSHIPS

Scholarships of between CAN$500 and CAN$2500 reward athletic and academic excellence of Alberta baseball players, and provides an incentive and means for these players to continue with their postsecondary education. Must be Alberta residents and enrolled full-time at a postsecondary institution in Alberta. Applicants must be a participant in the Prairie Baseball Academy and must have achieved a minimum GPA of 2.0 in their previous semester. For additional information, visit website http://alis.alberta.ca.

Award: Scholarship for use in freshman, sophomore, junior, or senior years; not renewable.

Eligibility Requirements: Applicant must be enrolled or expecting to enroll full-time at a two-year or four-year or technical institution or university; resident of Alberta; studying in Alberta and must have an interest in athletics/sports. Available to Canadian citizens.

Application Requirements: Application form, community service, recommendations or references. *Deadline:* October 15.

Contact: Scholarship Committee
Phone: 780-427-8640
E-mail: scholarships@gov.ab.ca

QUEEN ELIZABETH II GOLDEN JUBILEE CITIZENSHIP MEDAL
• *See page 668*

RUTHERFORD SCHOLARS
• *See page 668*

ALBUQUERQUE COMMUNITY FOUNDATION
http://www.albuquerquefoundation.org/

NEW MEXICO MANUFACTURED HOUSING SCHOLARSHIP PROGRAM

The scholarship is to be used for study in a four-year college or university. The total number of available awards and the dollar value of each award varies. Deadline varies. Refer to website for details and application http://www.albuquerquefoundation.org.

Award: Scholarship for use in freshman year; not renewable. *Number:* 1–2. *Amount:* $740–$1000.

Eligibility Requirements: Applicant must be high school student; planning to enroll or expecting to enroll full-time at a four-year institution or university; resident of New Mexico and studying in New Mexico. Applicant must have 3.0 GPA or higher. Available to U.S. citizens.

Application Requirements: Application form, recommendations or references, resume, test scores, transcript.

Contact: Ms. Nancy Johnson, Grant Director
Albuquerque Community Foundation
PO Box 25266
Albuquerque, NM 87125
Phone: 505-883-6240
E-mail: njohnson@albuquerquefoundation.org

SUSSMAN-MILLER EDUCATIONAL ASSISTANCE FUND

The program provides financial aid to enable students to continue with an undergraduate program. This is a gap program based on financial need. Must be resident of New Mexico. Minimum 3.0 GPA required. Deadline varies. The fund requests not to write or call for information. Please visit website http://www.albuquerquefoundation.org for complete information.

Award: Scholarship for use in freshman, sophomore, junior, or senior years; not renewable. *Number:* 25–30. *Amount:* $500–$2500.

Eligibility Requirements: Applicant must be enrolled or expecting to enroll full-time at a two-year or four-year institution or university and resident of New Mexico. Applicant must have 3.0 GPA or higher. Available to U.S. citizens.

Application Requirements: Application form, essay, financial need analysis, recommendations or references, resume, test scores, transcript.

Contact: Ms. Nancy Johnson, Grant Director
Albuquerque Community Foundation
PO Box 25266
Albuquerque, NM 87125
Phone: 505-883-6240
E-mail: njohnson@albuquerquefoundation.org

YOUTH IN FOSTER CARE SCHOLARSHIP PROGRAM

This award is designed to support youth who have been in the New Mexico foster care system.

Award: Scholarship for use in freshman, sophomore, junior, or senior years; not renewable. *Number:* 1–4. *Amount:* $500–$1000.

Eligibility Requirements: Applicant must be age 17-21; enrolled or expecting to enroll full- or part-time at a two-year or four-year or

technical institution or university and resident of New Mexico. Available to U.S. citizens.

Application Requirements: Application form, essay, resume, transcript. *Deadline:* March 18.

Contact: Ms. Nancy Johnson, Grant Director
Albuquerque Community Foundation
PO Box 25266
Albuquerque, NM 87125
Phone: 505-883-6240
E-mail: njohnson@albuquerquefoundation.org

ALERT SCHOLARSHIP
http://www.alertmagazine.org/

ALERT SCHOLARSHIP

$500 scholarship for the best essay on drug / alcohol abuse from each state. Applicant must be current high school senior in Alaska, Nebraska, Oregon, Washington, Idaho, Montana, Minnesota, Wyoming, Colorado, North Dakota, or South Dakota. Minimum 2.5 GPA required. For more information visit: http://www.alertmagazine.org/scholarship.php.

Award: Scholarship for use in freshman year; not renewable. *Amount:* $500.

Eligibility Requirements: Applicant must be high school student; planning to enroll or expecting to enroll full- or part-time at a four-year institution or university; resident of Alaska, Colorado, Idaho, Minnesota, Montana, Nebraska, North Dakota, Oregon, South Dakota, Washington, Wyoming and must have an interest in writing. Applicant must have 2.5 GPA or higher. Available to U.S. citizens.

Application Requirements: Essay, personal photograph. *Deadline:* continuous.

Contact: Alert Magazine
Phone: 208-375-7911
Fax: 208-376-0770
E-mail: alertmagazine@aol.com

THE ALEXANDER FOUNDATION
http://www.thealexanderfoundation.org/

THE ALEXANDER FOUNDATION SCHOLARSHIP PROGRAM

Alexander scholarships provide financial assistance to undergraduate or graduate students accepted or enrolled in Colorado institutions of higher education. Applicants must be gay, lesbian, bisexual, or transgendered and reside in Colorado, must demonstrate financial need, and should be active/supporting/contributing members of the community.

Award: Scholarship for use in freshman, sophomore, junior, senior, graduate, or postgraduate years; not renewable. *Number:* 6–35. *Amount:* $300–$3000.

Eligibility Requirements: Applicant must be enrolled or expecting to enroll full- or part-time at a two-year or four-year or technical institution or university; resident of Colorado; studying in Colorado and must have an interest in LGBT issues. Available to U.S. citizens.

Application Requirements: Application form, essay, financial need analysis, recommendations or references, transcript. *Deadline:* April 15.

Contact: Scholarship Committee
The Alexander Foundation
PO Box 1995
Denver, CO 80201-1995
Phone: 303-331-7733
Fax: 303-331-1953
E-mail: infoalexander@thealexanderfoundation.org

ALS ASSOCIATION
http://webdc.alsa.org/site/PageServer?pagename=DC_homepage

PAULA KOVARICK SEGALMAN FAMILY SCHOLARSHIP FUND

The Paula Kovarick Segalman Family Scholarship Fund for ALS was established by the Segalman Family to provide educational funding to students affected by ALS, also known as Lou Gehrig's disease. ALS is a

fatal disease affecting families physically, emotionally and financially. The cost of care for someone with ALS can exceed $200,000 a year. The fund looks to alleviate some of the additional financial burdens that families will face when paying for college. Applicant must have a parent or legal guardian currently battling ALS or who has passed away from the disease. Annual household income must be less than $50,000. See the URL link for more about the scholarship, eligibility requirements, and the application process
http://webdc.alsa.org/site/PageNavigator/DC_Chapter/DC_6_Paula_Seg alman_Scholarship.html

Award: Scholarship for use in freshman, sophomore, junior, or senior years; not renewable. *Amount:* up to $25,000.

Eligibility Requirements: Applicant must be age 17-25; enrolled or expecting to enroll full-time at a two-year or four-year or technical institution or university and resident of District of Columbia, Maryland, Virginia. Applicant must have 2.5 GPA or higher. Available to U.S. citizens.

Application Requirements: Essay. *Deadline:* May 1.

Contact: Judy Taylor
ALS Association
7507 Standish Place
Rockville, MD 20855
Phone: 240-240.672.3742 Ext. 213
E-mail: info@ALSinfo.org

AMERICAN LEGION AUXILIARY DEPARTMENT OF ALABAMA

http://www.legional.org/

AMERICAN LEGION AUXILIARY DEPARTMENT OF ALABAMA SCHOLARSHIP PROGRAM
• *See page 650*

AMERICAN LEGION AUXILIARY DEPARTMENT OF CALIFORNIA

http://www.calegionaux.org/

AMERICAN LEGION AUXILIARY DEPARTMENT OF CALIFORNIA GENERAL SCHOLARSHIP
• *See page 650*

AMERICAN LEGION AUXILIARY DEPARTMENT OF CONNECTICUT

http://www.ct.legion.org/

AMERICAN LEGION AUXILIARY DEPARTMENT OF CONNECTICUT PAST PRESIDENTS' PARLEY MEMORIAL EDUCATION GRANT
• *See page 529*

AMERICAN LEGION AUXILIARY DEPARTMENT OF IOWA

http://www.ialegion.org/ala

AMERICAN LEGION AUXILIARY DEPARTMENT OF IOWA CHILDREN OF VETERANS MERIT AWARD
• *See page 650*

AMERICAN LEGION AUXILIARY DEPARTMENT OF KENTUCKY

http://www.kylegion.org/

AMERICAN LEGION AUXILIARY DEPARTMENT OF KENTUCKY LAURA BLACKBURN MEMORIAL SCHOLARSHIP
• *See page 645*

AMERICAN LEGION AUXILIARY DEPARTMENT OF MAINE

http://www.mainelegion.org/

AMERICAN LEGION AUXILIARY DEPARTMENT OF MAINE DANIEL E. LAMBERT MEMORIAL SCHOLARSHIP
• *See page 650*

AMERICAN LEGION AUXILIARY DEPARTMENT OF MASSACHUSETTS

http://www.masslegion-aux.org/

AMERICAN LEGION AUXILIARY DEPARTMENT OF MASSACHUSETTS DEPARTMENT PRESIDENT'S SCHOLARSHIP
• *See page 574*

AMERICAN LEGION AUXILIARY DEPARTMENT OF MASSACHUSETTS PAST PRESIDENTS' PARLEY SCHOLARSHIP
• *See page 651*

AMERICAN LEGION AUXILIARY DEPARTMENT OF MICHIGAN

http://www.michalaux.org/

AMERICAN LEGION AUXILIARY DEPARTMENT OF MICHIGAN MEMORIAL SCHOLARSHIP
• *See page 651*

AMERICAN LEGION AUXILIARY DEPARTMENT OF MICHIGAN SCHOLARSHIP FOR NON-TRADITIONAL STUDENT
• *See page 651*

AMERICAN LEGION AUXILIARY DEPARTMENT OF MINNESOTA

http://www.mnlegion.org/

AMERICAN LEGION AUXILIARY DEPARTMENT OF MINNESOTA SCHOLARSHIPS
• *See page 652*

AMERICAN LEGION AUXILIARY DEPARTMENT OF MISSOURI

http://www.missourilegion.org/

AMERICAN LEGION AUXILIARY DEPARTMENT OF MISSOURI LELA MURPHY SCHOLARSHIP
• *See page 529*

AMERICAN LEGION AUXILIARY DEPARTMENT OF MISSOURI NATIONAL PRESIDENT'S SCHOLARSHIP
• *See page 529*

AMERICAN LEGION AUXILIARY DEPARTMENT OF NEBRASKA

http://www.nebraskalegionaux.net/

AMERICAN LEGION AUXILIARY DEPARTMENT OF NEBRASKA RUBY PAUL CAMPAIGN FUND SCHOLARSHIP
• *See page 530*

AMERICAN LEGION AUXILIARY DEPARTMENT OF NORTH DAKOTA

http://www.ndlegion.org/

AMERICAN LEGION AUXILIARY DEPARTMENT OF NORTH DAKOTA NATIONAL PRESIDENT'S SCHOLARSHIP
• See page 575

AMERICAN LEGION AUXILIARY DEPARTMENT OF NORTH DAKOTA SCHOLARSHIPS

One-time award for North Dakota residents who are already attending a North Dakota institution of higher learning. Contact local or nearest American Legion Auxiliary Unit for more information. Must be a U.S. citizen.

Award: Scholarship for use in sophomore, junior, senior, or graduate years; not renewable. *Number:* 3. *Amount:* $400.

Eligibility Requirements: Applicant must be enrolled or expecting to enroll full-time at a two-year or four-year or technical institution or university; resident of North Dakota and studying in North Dakota. Available to U.S. citizens.

Application Requirements: Application form, driver's license, essay, financial need analysis, recommendations or references, self-addressed stamped envelope with application, test scores, transcript. *Deadline:* January 15.

Contact: Myrna Runholm, Department Secretary
American Legion Auxiliary Department of North Dakota
PO Box 1060
Jamestown, ND 58402-1060
Phone: 701-253-5992
E-mail: ala-hq@ndlegion.org

AMERICAN LEGION AUXILIARY DEPARTMENT OF OHIO

http://www.alaohio.org/

AMERICAN LEGION AUXILIARY DEPARTMENT OF OHIO CONTINUING EDUCATION FUND
• See page 652

AMERICAN LEGION AUXILIARY DEPARTMENT OF OHIO DEPARTMENT PRESIDENT'S SCHOLARSHIP
• See page 652

AMERICAN LEGION AUXILIARY DEPARTMENT OF OREGON

http://www.alaoregon.org/

AMERICAN LEGION AUXILIARY DEPARTMENT OF OREGON DEPARTMENT GRANTS

One-time award for educational use in the state of Oregon. Must be a resident of Oregon who is the child or widow of a veteran or the wife of a disabled veteran.

Award: Scholarship for use in freshman year; not renewable. *Number:* 2. *Amount:* $1000.

Eligibility Requirements: Applicant must be enrolled or expecting to enroll full- or part-time at a two-year or four-year or technical institution or university and resident of Oregon. Available to U.S. citizens.

Application Requirements: Application form, essay, financial need analysis, interview. *Deadline:* February 10.

Contact: Virginia Biddle, Secretary/Treasurer
American Legion Auxiliary Department of Oregon
PO Box 1730
Wilsonville, OR 97070
Phone: 503-682-3162
E-mail: alaor@pcez.com

AMERICAN LEGION AUXILIARY DEPARTMENT OF OREGON NATIONAL PRESIDENT'S SCHOLARSHIP

One-time award for children of veterans who served in the Armed Forces during eligibility dates for American Legion membership. Must be high school senior and Oregon resident. Must be entered by a local American Legion auxiliary unit. Three scholarships of varying amounts.

Award: Scholarship for use in freshman year; not renewable. *Number:* 3. *Amount:* $1000–$2500.

Eligibility Requirements: Applicant must be high school student; planning to enroll or expecting to enroll full-time at a four-year institution or university and resident of Oregon. Available to U.S. citizens.

Application Requirements: Application form, essay, financial need analysis, interview. *Deadline:* February 1.

Contact: Virginia Biddle, Secretary/Treasurer
American Legion Auxiliary Department of Oregon
PO Box 1730
Wilsonville, OR 97070
Phone: 503-682-3162
E-mail: alaor@pcez.com

AMERICAN LEGION AUXILIARY DEPARTMENT OF OREGON SPIRIT OF YOUTH SCHOLARSHIP
• See page 530

AMERICAN LEGION AUXILIARY DEPARTMENT OF PENNSYLVANIA

http://pa-legion.com

AMERICAN LEGION AUXILIARY DEPARTMENT OF PENNSYLVANIA SCHOLARSHIP FOR DEPENDENTS OF DISABLED OR DECEASED VETERANS

Renewable award of $600 to high school seniors who are residents of Pennsylvania. Applicants must enroll in full-time studies.

Award: Scholarship for use in freshman year; renewable. *Number:* 1. *Amount:* $600.

Eligibility Requirements: Applicant must be high school student; planning to enroll or expecting to enroll full-time at a four-year institution or university and resident of Pennsylvania. Available to U.S. citizens.

Application Requirements: Application form. *Deadline:* March 15.

Contact: Colleen Watson, Executive Secretary and Treasurer
Phone: 717-763-7545
Fax: 717-763-0617
E-mail: paalad@hotmail.com

AMERICAN LEGION AUXILIARY DEPARTMENT OF PENNSYLVANIA SCHOLARSHIP FOR DEPENDENTS OF LIVING VETERANS
• See page 575

AMERICAN LEGION AUXILIARY DEPARTMENT OF SOUTH DAKOTA

http://www.sdlegion-aux.org/

AMERICAN LEGION AUXILIARY DEPARTMENT OF SOUTH DAKOTA COLLEGE SCHOLARSHIPS
• See page 530

AMERICAN LEGION AUXILIARY DEPARTMENT OF SOUTH DAKOTA SENIOR SCHOLARSHIP
• See page 530

AMERICAN LEGION AUXILIARY DEPARTMENT OF TEXAS

http://www.alatexas.org/

AMERICAN LEGION AUXILIARY DEPARTMENT OF TEXAS GENERAL EDUCATION SCHOLARSHIP

• *See page 653*

AMERICAN LEGION AUXILIARY DEPARTMENT OF UTAH

http://www.legion-aux.org/

AMERICAN LEGION AUXILIARY DEPARTMENT OF UTAH NATIONAL PRESIDENT'S SCHOLARSHIP

• *See page 530*

AMERICAN LEGION AUXILIARY DEPARTMENT OF WISCONSIN

http://www.amlegionauxwi.org/

AMERICAN LEGION AUXILIARY DEPARTMENT OF WISCONSIN DELLA VAN DEUREN MEMORIAL SCHOLARSHIP

• *See page 531*

AMERICAN LEGION AUXILIARY DEPARTMENT OF WISCONSIN H.S. AND ANGELINE LEWIS SCHOLARSHIPS

• *See page 531*

AMERICAN LEGION AUXILIARY DEPARTMENT OF WISCONSIN MERIT AND MEMORIAL SCHOLARSHIPS

• *See page 531*

AMERICAN LEGION AUXILIARY DEPARTMENT OF WISCONSIN PAST PRESIDENTS' PARLEY HEALTH CAREER SCHOLARSHIPS

• *See page 531*

AMERICAN LEGION AUXILIARY DEPARTMENT OF WISCONSIN PRESIDENT'S SCHOLARSHIPS

• *See page 531*

AMERICAN LEGION DEPARTMENT OF ARIZONA

http://www.azlegion.org/programs

AMERICAN LEGION DEPARTMENT OF ARIZONA HIGH SCHOOL ORATORICAL CONTEST

Each student must present an 8 to 10 minute prepared oration on any part of the U.S. Constitution without any notes, podiums, or coaching. The student will then be asked to do a 3 to 5 minute oration on one of four possible topics. Which one of the four topics will not be known in advance, so students must be prepared to respond to any of the four. Open to students in grades 9 to 12.

Award: Scholarship for use in freshman year; not renewable. *Number:* 10–20. *Amount:* $50–$1500.

Eligibility Requirements: Applicant must be high school student; planning to enroll or expecting to enroll full-time at a two-year or four-year institution or university; resident of Arizona and must have an interest in public speaking. Available to U.S. citizens.

Application Requirements: Application form. *Deadline:* January 1.

Contact: Roger Munchbach, Department Oratorical Chairman
American Legion Department of Arizona
4701 North 19th Avenue, Suite 200
Phoenix, AZ 85015-3799
Phone: 602-264-7706
E-mail: legionoratoricalcontest@msn.com

AMERICAN LEGION DEPARTMENT OF ARKANSAS

http://www.arklegion.homestead.com/

AMERICAN LEGION DEPARTMENT OF ARKANSAS HIGH SCHOOL ORATORICAL CONTEST

Oratorical contest open to students in ninth to twelfth grades of any accredited Arkansas high school. Begins with finalists at the post level and proceeds through area and district levels to national contest.

Award: Prize for use in freshman year; not renewable. *Number:* 4. *Amount:* $1250–$3500.

Eligibility Requirements: Applicant must be high school student; planning to enroll or expecting to enroll full-time at a four-year institution or university; resident of Arkansas and must have an interest in public speaking. Applicant must have 2.5 GPA or higher. Available to U.S. citizens.

Application Requirements: Application form, entry in a contest, personal photograph, recommendations or references. *Deadline:* December 15.

Contact: William Winchell, Department Adjutant
American Legion Department of Arkansas
PO Box 3280
Little Rock, AR 72203-3280
Phone: 501-375-1104
Fax: 501-375-4236
E-mail: alegion@swbell.net

AMERICAN LEGION DEPARTMENT OF HAWAII

http://www.legion.org/

AMERICAN LEGION DEPARTMENT OF HAWAII HIGH SCHOOL ORATORICAL CONTEST

Oratorical contest open to students in ninth to twelfth grades of any accredited Hawaii high school. Must be under 20 years of age. Speech contests begin in January at post level and continue on to the national competition. Contact local American Legion Post or department for deadlines and application details.

Award: Prize for use in freshman year; not renewable. *Number:* 1–3. *Amount:* $50–$1500.

Eligibility Requirements: Applicant must be high school student; age 14–20; planning to enroll or expecting to enroll full-time at a four-year institution or university and resident of Hawaii. Available to U.S. citizens.

Application Requirements: Application form. *Deadline:* January 1.

Contact: Adm. Bernard Lee, Department Adjutant
American Legion Department of Hawaii
612 McCully Street
Honolulu, HI 96826-3935
Phone: 808-946-6383
E-mail: aldepthi@hawaii.rr.com

AMERICAN LEGION DEPARTMENT OF IDAHO

http://www.idaholegion.com/

AMERICAN LEGION DEPARTMENT OF IDAHO SCHOLARSHIP

• *See page 532*

AMERICAN LEGION DEPARTMENT OF ILLINOIS

http://www.illegion.org/

AMERICAN ESSAY CONTEST SCHOLARSHIP

• *See page 532*

AMERICAN LEGION DEPARTMENT OF ILLINOIS BOY SCOUT/EXPLORER SCHOLARSHIP

• *See page 532*

AMERICAN LEGION DEPARTMENT OF ILLINOIS HIGH SCHOOL ORATORICAL CONTEST

Single oratorical contest with winners advancing to the next level. Open to students in 9th to 12th grades of any accredited Illinois high school. Seniors must be in attendance as of January 1. Must contact local American Legion post or department headquarters for complete information and applications, which will be available in the fall.

Award: Scholarship for use in freshman year; not renewable. *Number:* 1–30. *Amount:* $100–$2000.

Eligibility Requirements: Applicant must be high school student; planning to enroll or expecting to enroll full- or part-time at a four-year institution or university; resident of Illinois and must have an interest in English language or public speaking. Available to U.S. citizens.

Application Requirements: Application form, entry in a contest. *Fee:* $125. *Deadline:* varies.

Contact: Mr. Gary Jenson, American Legion Department Assistant Adjutant
American Legion Department of Illinois
2720 East Lincoln Street
Bloomington, IL 61704
Phone: 309-663-0361
Fax: 309-663-5783
E-mail: gjenson@illegion.org

AMERICAN LEGION DEPARTMENT OF INDIANA

http://www.indianalegion.org

AMERICAN LEGION DEPARTMENT OF INDIANA, AMERICANISM AND GOVERNMENT TEST

Study guides are provided to high schools. Students take a test and write an essay. One male and one female student from each grade (10 to 12) are selected as state winners.

Award: Scholarship for use in freshman, sophomore, junior, or senior years; not renewable. *Number:* 6. *Amount:* $1000.

Eligibility Requirements: Applicant must be high school student; planning to enroll or expecting to enroll full- or part-time at a two-year or four-year or technical institution or university and resident of Indiana. Available to U.S. citizens.

Application Requirements: Entry in a contest, essay, test scores. *Deadline:* December 1.

Contact: Butch Miller, Program Coordinator
Phone: 317-630-1391
Fax: 317-237-9891
E-mail: bmiller@indlegion.org

AMERICAN LEGION DEPARTMENT OF INDIANA HIGH SCHOOL ORATORICAL CONTEST

Oratorical contest open to students in grades nine to twelve of any accredited Indiana high school or home schooled students in an equivalent grade. All contestants must be a citizen of or lawful permanent resident of the United States. Students may only enter one district/zone/state competition. The student must compete in the district in which his/her sponsoring post is located. Speech contests begin in November at post level and continue on to national competition. Contact local American Legion post for application details or visit our website at http//www.indianalegion.org.

Award: Scholarship for use in freshman, sophomore, junior, or senior years; not renewable. *Number:* 4–8. *Amount:* $200–$4200.

Eligibility Requirements: Applicant must be high school student; planning to enroll or expecting to enroll full- or part-time at a two-year or four-year or technical institution or university; resident of Indiana and must have an interest in public speaking. Available to U.S. citizens.

Application Requirements: Application form, application form may be submitted online (http://www.indianalegion.org), assigned and prepared speech contest, entry in a contest. *Deadline:* December 15.

Contact: Butch Miller, Program Coordinator
Phone: 317-630-1391
Fax: 317-237-9891
E-mail: bmiller@indlegion.org

AMERICAN LEGION FAMILY SCHOLARSHIP

• *See page 533*

FRANK W. MCHALE MEMORIAL SCHOLARSHIPS

One-time award for Indiana high school junior boys who participated in The American Legion Hoosier Boys State Program. Must be nominated by Boys State official while in attendance at Hoosier Boys State. Write for more information and deadline.

Award: Scholarship for use in freshman, sophomore, junior, or senior years; not renewable. *Number:* 3. *Amount:* $1000–$1500.

Eligibility Requirements: Applicant must be high school student; planning to enroll or expecting to enroll full- or part-time at a two-year or four-year or technical institution or university; male; resident of Indiana and must have an interest in leadership. Available to U.S. citizens.

Application Requirements: Application form, essay, participation in the Boys State Program, nomination from Boys State official. *Deadline:* June 16.

Contact: Susan Long, Program Coordinator
American Legion Department of Indiana
777 North Meridan Street, Room 104
Indianapolis, IN 46204-1189
Phone: 317-630-1264
Fax: 317-237-9891
E-mail: slong@indlegion.org

AMERICAN LEGION DEPARTMENT OF IOWA

http://www.ialegion.org/

AMERICAN LEGION DEPARTMENT OF IOWA EAGLE SCOUT OF THE YEAR SCHOLARSHIP

• *See page 533*

AMERICAN LEGION DEPARTMENT OF IOWA HIGH SCHOOL ORATORICAL CONTEST

All contestants in the department of Iowa American Legion High School Oratorical Contest shall be citizens or lawful permanent residents of the United States. The department of Iowa American Legion High School Oratorical Contest shall consist of one contestant from each of the three area contests. The area contest shall consist of one contestant from each district in the designated Area.

Award: Prize for use in freshman year; not renewable. *Number:* up to 3. *Amount:* $1000–$2000.

Eligibility Requirements: Applicant must be high school student; planning to enroll or expecting to enroll full-time at a two-year or four-year institution or university; resident of Iowa and must have an interest in public speaking. Available to U.S. citizens.

Application Requirements: Application form, entry in a contest. *Deadline:* varies.

Contact: Kathy Nees, Program Director, Youth Programs
Phone: 515-282-5068
Fax: 515-282-7583
E-mail: knees@ialegion.org

AMERICAN LEGION DEPARTMENT OF IOWA OUTSTANDING SENIOR BASEBALL PLAYER

One-time award for Iowa residents who participated in the American Legion Senior Baseball Program and display outstanding sportsmanship, athletic ability, and proven academic achievements. Must be recommended by Baseball Committee.

Award: Scholarship for use in freshman year; not renewable. *Number:* 1. *Amount:* $750–$1500.

Eligibility Requirements: Applicant must be high school student; age 15-18; planning to enroll or expecting to enroll full-time at a two-year or four-year institution or university; resident of Iowa and must have an interest in athletics/sports. Available to U.S. citizens.

Application Requirements: Application form, entry in a contest, recommendations or references. *Deadline:* July 15.

Contact: Kathy Nees, Program Director, Youth Programs
Phone: 515-282-5068
Fax: 515-282-7583
E-mail: knees@ialegion.org

AMERICAN LEGION DEPARTMENT OF KANSAS

http://www.ksamlegion.org/

ALBERT M. LAPPIN SCHOLARSHIP
• *See page 533*

AMERICAN LEGION DEPARTMENT OF KANSAS HIGH SCHOOL ORATORICAL CONTEST
Awards a total of $2400 ($1500, $500, $250, and $150) in scholarships to the top four winners in each state. The state winner's school receives $500. The top three contestants in the nation are awarded scholarships totaling $48,000 ($18,000, $16,000, and $14,000).

Award: Prize for use in freshman year; not renewable. *Number:* 4. *Amount:* $150–$18,000.

Eligibility Requirements: Applicant must be high school student; planning to enroll or expecting to enroll full-time at a four-year institution or university; resident of Kansas and must have an interest in public speaking. Available to U.S. citizens.

Application Requirements: Application form. *Deadline:* January 15.

Contact: Jeff Bond, Oratorical Contest Committee
American Legion Department of Kansas
1314 SW Topeka Boulevard
Topeka, KS 66612
Phone: 785-232-9315

CHARLES W. AND ANNETTE HILL SCHOLARSHIP
• *See page 533*

DR. CLICK COWGER BASEBALL SCHOLARSHIP
Scholarship available to a high school senior or college freshman or sophomore enrolled in a Kansas institution. Applicant may intend to enroll in a junior college, university or trade school in Kansas only. Must be a male and should play or has played Kansas American Legion baseball. Must be an average or a better student scholastically.

Award: Scholarship for use in freshman or sophomore years; not renewable. *Number:* 1. *Amount:* $500.

Eligibility Requirements: Applicant must be enrolled or expecting to enroll full-time at a two-year or four-year or technical institution or university; male; resident of Kansas; studying in Kansas and must have an interest in athletics/sports. Available to U.S. citizens.

Application Requirements: Application form, essay, financial need analysis, personal photograph. *Deadline:* July 15.

Contact: Mike Oppy, Chairman, Scholarship Committee
American Legion Department of Kansas
1314 SW Topeka Boulevard
Topeka, KS 66612
Phone: 785-232-9315

HUGH A. SMITH SCHOLARSHIP FUND
• *See page 533*

PAUL FLAHERTY ATHLETIC SCHOLARSHIP
Scholarship available to high school seniors, college level freshmen or sophomores enrolled or intending to enroll in an approved junior college, college, university, or trade school. Must have participated in any form of high school athletics. Must be an average or a better student scholastically.

Award: Scholarship for use in freshman or sophomore years; not renewable. *Number:* 1. *Amount:* $250.

Eligibility Requirements: Applicant must be enrolled or expecting to enroll full-time at a two-year or four-year or technical institution or university; resident of Kansas; studying in Kansas and must have an interest in athletics/sports. Available to U.S. citizens.

Application Requirements: Application form, essay, financial need analysis, personal photograph. *Deadline:* July 15.

Contact: Mike Oppy, Chairman, Scholarship Committee
American Legion Department of Kansas
1314 SW Topeka Boulevard
Topeka, KS 66612
Phone: 785-232-9513

ROSEDALE POST 346 SCHOLARSHIP
• *See page 533*

TED AND NORA ANDERSON SCHOLARSHIPS
• *See page 534*

AMERICAN LEGION DEPARTMENT OF MAINE

http://www.mainelegion.org/

AMERICAN LEGION DEPARTMENT OF MAINE CHILDREN AND YOUTH SCHOLARSHIP
• *See page 653*

DANIEL E. LAMBERT MEMORIAL SCHOLARSHIP
• *See page 653*

JAMES V. DAY SCHOLARSHIP
• *See page 534*

AMERICAN LEGION DEPARTMENT OF MARYLAND

http://www.mdlegion.org/

AMERICAN LEGION DEPARTMENT OF MARYLAND GENERAL SCHOLARSHIP FUND
• *See page 653*

MARYLAND BOYS STATE SCHOLARSHIP
Scholarship awarded from applicants that have graduated from Maryland Boys State program. Applications must be received by May 1st of the Boys State graduate's senior year in High School. Application available at http://www.mdlegion.org/Forms/bsschol.pdf

Award: Scholarship for use in freshman, sophomore, junior, or senior years; not renewable. *Number:* 1–10. *Amount:* up to $500.

Eligibility Requirements: Applicant must be high school student; planning to enroll or expecting to enroll full-time at a two-year or four-year institution or university; male and resident of Maryland. Available to U.S. citizens.

Application Requirements: Application form, test scores, transcript. *Deadline:* May 1.

Contact: Russell Myers, Department Adjutant
American Legion Department of Maryland
101 North Gay Street
Room E
Baltimore, MD 21202
Phone: 410-752-1405
Fax: 410-752-3822
E-mail: russell@mdlegion.org

AMERICAN LEGION DEPARTMENT OF MICHIGAN

http://www.michiganlegion.org/

AMERICAN LEGION DEPARTMENT OF MICHIGAN ORATORICAL SCHOLARSHIP PROGRAM
Oratorical contest open to students in ninth to twelfth grades of any accredited Michigan high school or state accredited home school. Five one-time awards of varying amounts. State winner advances to National Competition for scholarship money ranging from $14,000 to $18,000. Application Due in November

Award: Scholarship for use in freshman year; not renewable. *Number:* 5. *Amount:* $800–$1500.

Eligibility Requirements: Applicant must be high school student; planning to enroll or expecting to enroll full- or part-time at a two-year or four-year institution or university; resident of Michigan and must have an interest in public speaking. Available to U.S. citizens.

Application Requirements: Application form, essay. *Deadline:* November 19.

Contact: Roxanne Osga, Programs Coordinator
American Legion Department of Michigan
212 North Verlinden Avenue
Lansing, MI 48915
Phone: 517-371-4720 Ext. 23
E-mail: programs@michiganlegion.org

GUY M. WILSON SCHOLARSHIPS
• *See page 654*

WILLIAM D. AND JEWELL W. BREWER SCHOLARSHIP TRUSTS
• *See page 654*

THE AMERICAN LEGION, DEPARTMENT OF MINNESOTA
http://www.mnlegion.org/

AMERICAN LEGION DEPARTMENT OF MINNESOTA HIGH SCHOOL ORATORICAL CONTEST
Oratorical contest open to students in ninth to twelfth grades of any accredited Minnesota high school or home-schooled students. Must be Minnesota resident. Speech must be student's original work on the general subject of the Constitution. Speech contests begin in December at local Legion post level and continue on to the national competition. See website for specific topic and application details http://www.mnlegion.org.

Award: Scholarship for use in freshman year; not renewable. *Number:* 4. *Amount:* $500–$1500.

Eligibility Requirements: Applicant must be high school student; planning to enroll or expecting to enroll full- or part-time at a two-year or four-year or technical institution or university; resident of Minnesota and must have an interest in public speaking. Available to U.S. citizens.

Application Requirements: *Deadline:* November 30.

Contact: Jennifer Kelley, Program Coordinator
The American Legion, Department of Minnesota
20 West 12th Street, Room 300-A
St. Paul, MN 55155
Phone: 651-291-1800
E-mail: department@mnlegion.org

AMERICAN LEGION DEPARTMENT OF MINNESOTA MEMORIAL SCHOLARSHIP
• *See page 534*

MINNESOTA LEGIONNAIRES INSURANCE TRUST SCHOLARSHIP
• *See page 534*

AMERICAN LEGION DEPARTMENT OF MISSOURI
http://www.missourilegion.org/

CHARLES L. BACON MEMORIAL SCHOLARSHIP
• *See page 534*

LILLIE LOIS FORD SCHOLARSHIP FUND
• *See page 654*

AMERICAN LEGION DEPARTMENT OF MONTANA
http://www.mtlegion.org/

AMERICAN LEGION DEPARTMENT OF MONTANA HIGH SCHOOL ORATORICAL CONTEST
Applicants participate in a statewide memorized oratorical contest on the U.S. Constitution. Four places are awarded. Must be a Montana high school student. Contact state adjutant American Legion Department of Montana for further details. Each state winner who competes in the first round of the national contest will receive a $1000 scholarship. Participants in the second round who do not advance to the national final round will receive an additional $1000 scholarship.

Award: Scholarship for use in freshman year; not renewable. *Number:* 1–4. *Amount:* $300–$2000.

Eligibility Requirements: Applicant must be high school student; planning to enroll or expecting to enroll full-time at a two-year or four-year or technical institution or university; resident of Montana and must have an interest in public speaking. Available to U.S. citizens.

Contact: Gary White, State Adjutant
Phone: 406-324-3989
Fax: 406-324-3991
E-mail: amlegmt29@mtlegion.org

AMERICAN LEGION DEPARTMENT OF NEBRASKA
http://www.nebraskalegion.net/

AMERICAN LEGION DEPARTMENT OF NEBRASKA HIGH SCHOOL ORATORICAL CONTEST
Local high school winners advance to District. Fifteen District Winners advance to Area contest. Area contestants awarded $100. Four Area winners advance to State contest. State prizes range from $200 to $1000. State winner advances to National contest. National prizes range from $14,000 to $18,000.

Award: Prize for use in freshman year; not renewable. *Number:* 4–19. *Amount:* $100–$1000.

Eligibility Requirements: Applicant must be high school student; planning to enroll or expecting to enroll full- or part-time at a two-year or four-year or technical institution or university; resident of Nebraska and must have an interest in public speaking. Available to U.S. citizens.

Application Requirements: *Deadline:* October 1.

Contact: Brent Hagel-Pitt, Activities Director
Phone: 402-464-6338
Fax: 402-464-6330
E-mail: actdirlegion@windstream.net

AMERICAN LEGION DEPARTMENT OF NEBRASKA JIM HURLBERT MEMORIAL BASEBALL SCHOLARSHIP
Award to a Nebraska American Legion Baseball player in last year of eligibility and/or graduating senior. One applicant nominated by each Senior American Legion Baseball team. Student must attend a postsecondary educational institution within the state of Nebraska, and must have maintained a GPA in the upper half of his/her graduating class.

Award: Scholarship for use in freshman year; not renewable. *Number:* 1–4. *Amount:* $500.

Eligibility Requirements: Applicant must be high school student; planning to enroll or expecting to enroll full-time at a two-year or four-year or technical institution or university; resident of Nebraska; studying in Nebraska and must have an interest in athletics/sports. Applicant must have 3.5 GPA or higher. Available to U.S. citizens.

Application Requirements: Application form, community service, financial need analysis. *Deadline:* June 15.

Contact: Brent Hagel-Pitt, Activities Director
Phone: 402-464-6338
Fax: 402-464-6330
E-mail: actdirlegion@windstream.net

MAYNARD JENSEN AMERICAN LEGION MEMORIAL SCHOLARSHIP
• *See page 535*

AMERICAN LEGION DEPARTMENT OF NEW YORK

http://www.ny.legion.org/

AMERICAN LEGION DEPARTMENT OF NEW YORK HIGH SCHOOL ORATORICAL CONTEST

Oratorical contest open to students under 20 years in 9th-12th grades of any accredited New York high school. Speech contests begin in November at post levels and continue to national competition. Must be U.S. citizen or permanent resident. Payments are made directly to college and are awarded over a four-year period. Deadline varies.

Award: Scholarship for use in freshman year; not renewable. *Amount:* $2000–$6000.

Eligibility Requirements: Applicant must be high school student; planning to enroll or expecting to enroll full-time at a four-year institution or university; resident of New York and must have an interest in public speaking. Available to U.S. citizens.

Application Requirements: Application form, entry in a contest. *Deadline:* varies.

Contact: Richard Pedro, Department Adjutant
American Legion Department of New York
112 State Street, Suite 400
Albany, NY 12207
Phone: 518-463-2215
Fax: 518-427-8443
E-mail: newyork@legion.org

AMERICAN LEGION DEPARTMENT OF NORTH CAROLINA

http://www.nclegion.org/

AMERICAN LEGION DEPARTMENT OF NORTH CAROLINA HIGH SCHOOL ORATORICAL CONTEST

This is a speaking contest. The objective of the contest is to develop a deeper knowledge and appreciation of the U.S. Constitution, develop leadership qualities, the ability to think and speak clearly and intelligently, and prepare for acceptance of duties, responsibilities, rights, and privileges of American citizenship. Open to North Carolina high school students. Must be U.S. citizen or lawful permanent resident. The contestant must have a prepared eight to ten minute oration on some aspect of the Constitution of the United States, as well as 4 three to five minute discourses on specific assigned topics to test the speaker's knowledge of the subject.

Award: Scholarship for use in freshman year; not renewable. *Number:* 5. *Amount:* $1000–$2500.

Eligibility Requirements: Applicant must be high school student; planning to enroll or expecting to enroll full-time at a two-year or four-year or technical institution; resident of North Carolina and must have an interest in public speaking. Available to U.S. citizens.

Application Requirements: *Deadline:* December 18.

Contact: Deborah Rose, Department Executive Secretary
American Legion Department of North Carolina
4 North Blount Street, PO Box 26657
Raleigh, NC 27611-6657
Phone: 919-832-7506
E-mail: drose-nclegion@nc.rr.com

AMERICAN LEGION DEPARTMENT OF NORTH DAKOTA

http://www.ndlegion.org/

AMERICAN LEGION DEPARTMENT OF NORTH DAKOTA NATIONAL HIGH SCHOOL ORATORICAL CONTEST

Oratorical contest for high school students in grades nine to twelve. Contestants must prepare to speak on the topic of the U.S. Constitution. Must graduate from an accredited North Dakota high school. Contest begins at the local level and continues to the national level. Several one-time awards of $100 to $2000.

Award: Prize for use in freshman, sophomore, junior, or senior years; not renewable. *Number:* 38. *Amount:* $100–$2000.

Eligibility Requirements: Applicant must be high school student; planning to enroll or expecting to enroll full-time at a four-year institution or university; resident of North Dakota; studying in North Dakota and must have an interest in public speaking. Available to U.S. citizens.

Application Requirements: Application form. *Deadline:* October 30.

Contact: Teri Bryant
American Legion Department of North Dakota
405 West Main Avenue, Suite 4A
West Fargo, ND 58078
Phone: 701-293-3120
E-mail: programs@ndlegion.org

HATTIE TEDROW MEMORIAL FUND SCHOLARSHIP

Applicants must be legal residents of North Dakota, high school seniors, and direct descendants of a veteran with honorable service in the U.S. military. The student will have two years from the date of graduation from high school to use his/her award.

Award: Scholarship for use in freshman, sophomore, junior, or senior years; not renewable. *Amount:* $200–$500.

Eligibility Requirements: Applicant must be high school student; age 17-18; planning to enroll or expecting to enroll full-time at a two-year or four-year or technical institution or university; resident of North Dakota and studying in North Dakota. Available to U.S. citizens.

Application Requirements: Application form, essay. *Deadline:* March 15.

Contact: Teri Bryant
American Legion Department of North Dakota
405 West Main Avenue, Suite 4A
West Fargo, ND 58078
Phone: 701-293-3120
E-mail: programs@ndlegion.org

NORTH DAKOTA CARING CITIZEN SCHOLARSHIP

One-time award for North Dakota high school juniors who participated in the Boys State Program. Must be nominated by Boys State official. Must demonstrate care and concern for fellow students.

Award: Scholarship for use in freshman year; not renewable.

Eligibility Requirements: Applicant must be high school student; planning to enroll or expecting to enroll full-time at a two-year or four-year or technical institution or university; male and resident of North Dakota. Available to U.S. citizens.

Application Requirements: Application form.

Contact: Teri Bryant
American Legion Department of North Dakota
405 West Main Avenue, Suite 4A
West Fargo, ND 58078
Phone: 701-293-3120
E-mail: programs@ndlegion.org

AMERICAN LEGION DEPARTMENT OF OREGON

http://www.orlegion.org/

AMERICAN LEGION DEPARTMENT OF OREGON HIGH SCHOOL ORATORICAL CONTEST

Students give two orations, one prepared and one extemporaneous on an assigned topic pertaining to the Constitution of the United States of America. Awards are given at Post, District, and State level with the state winner advancing to the National level contest. Open to students enrolled in high schools within the state of Oregon.

Award: Scholarship for use in freshman year; not renewable. *Number:* up to 4. *Amount:* $200–$500.

Eligibility Requirements: Applicant must be high school student; planning to enroll or expecting to enroll full-time at a four-year institution or university; resident of Oregon and must have an interest in public speaking. Available to U.S. citizens.

Application Requirements: Application form, entry in a contest. *Deadline:* December 1.

Contact: Barry Snyder, Adjutant
Phone: 503-685-5006
Fax: 503-968-5432
E-mail: orlegion@aol.com

AMERICAN LEGION DEPARTMENT OF PENNSYLVANIA

http://www.pa-legion.com/

AMERICAN LEGION DEPARTMENT OF PENNSYLVANIA HIGH SCHOOL ORATORICAL CONTEST

Oratorical contest open to students in 9th-12th grades of any accredited Pennsylvania high school. Speech contests begin in January at post level and continue on to national competition. Contact local American Legion post for deadlines and application details. Three one-time awards ranging from $7500 for first place, second place $5000, and third place $4000.

Award: Prize for use in freshman year; not renewable. *Number:* 3. *Amount:* $4000–$7500.

Eligibility Requirements: Applicant must be high school student; planning to enroll or expecting to enroll full-time at a two-year or four-year or technical institution or university; resident of Pennsylvania and must have an interest in public speaking. Available to U.S. citizens.

Application Requirements: Application form, entry in a contest. *Deadline:* varies.

Contact: Colleen Washinger, Executive Secretary
American Legion Department of Pennsylvania
PO Box 2324
Harrisburg, PA 17105-2324
Phone: 717-730-9100
Fax: 717-975-2836
E-mail: hq@pa-legion.com

JOSEPH P. GAVENONIS COLLEGE SCHOLARSHIP (PLAN I)
• *See page 535*

AMERICAN LEGION DEPARTMENT OF SOUTH DAKOTA

http://www.sdlegion.org/

AMERICAN LEGION DEPARTMENT OF SOUTH DAKOTA HIGH SCHOOL ORATORICAL CONTEST

Provide an 8 to 10 minute oration on some phase of the U.S. Constitution. Be prepared to speak extemporaneously for 3 to 5 minutes on specified articles or amendments. Compete at Local, District, and State levels. State winner goes on to National Contest and opportunity to win $18,000 in scholarships. Contact local American Legion post for contest dates.

Award: Prize for use in freshman, sophomore, junior, or senior years; not renewable. *Number:* 1–4. *Amount:* $200–$1000.

Eligibility Requirements: Applicant must be enrolled or expecting to enroll full-time at a two-year or four-year or technical institution or university; resident of South Dakota and must have an interest in public speaking. Available to U.S. citizens.

Application Requirements: Entry in a contest, oration. *Deadline:* varies.

Contact: Dennis Brendan, Department Adjutant
American Legion Department of South Dakota
PO Box 67
Watertown, SD 57201-0067
Phone: 605-886-3604
Fax: 605-886-2870
E-mail: sdlegion@dailypost.com

AMERICAN LEGION DEPARTMENT OF TENNESSEE

http://www.tennesseelegion.org/

AMERICAN LEGION DEPARTMENT OF TENNESSEE EAGLE SCOUT OF THE YEAR
• *See page 535*

AMERICAN LEGION DEPARTMENT OF TENNESSEE HIGH SCHOOL ORATORICAL CONTEST

Scholarship for graduating Tennessee high school seniors enrolled either part-time or full-time in accredited colleges or universities.

Award: Scholarship for use in freshman, sophomore, junior, or senior years; not renewable. *Number:* 1–3. *Amount:* $1000–$3000.

Eligibility Requirements: Applicant must be high school student; planning to enroll or expecting to enroll full- or part-time at a two-year or four-year institution or university; resident of Tennessee and must have an interest in public speaking. Available to U.S. citizens.

Application Requirements: Application form, essay.

Contact: Sherri Mayberry, Program Secretary
Phone: 615-391-5088
E-mail: Sherri@TNLegion.org

AMERICAN LEGION DEPARTMENT OF TEXAS

http://www.txlegion.org/

AMERICAN LEGION DEPARTMENT OF TEXAS HIGH SCHOOL ORATORICAL CONTEST

Scholarships will be given to the winners of oratorical contests. Contestants must be in high school with plans to further their education in a postsecondary institution. The winner of first place will be certified to national headquarters as the Texas representative in the quarter finals and the department will award a $2000 scholarship to the college of the applicant's choice. The department champion will receive additional scholarships each time he/she advances to the next level.

Award: Prize for use in freshman year; not renewable. *Number:* up to 20. *Amount:* $500–$2000.

Eligibility Requirements: Applicant must be high school student; planning to enroll or expecting to enroll full-time at a two-year or four-year or technical institution or university; resident of Texas and must have an interest in public speaking. Available to U.S. citizens.

Application Requirements: Application form, copy of prepared oration, entry in a contest, essay, interview. *Deadline:* varies.

Contact: Robert Squyres, Director of Internal Affairs
American Legion Department of Texas
3401 Ed Bluestein Boulevard
Austin, TX 78721-2902
Phone: 512-472-4138
Fax: 512-472-0603
E-mail: programs@txlegion.org

AMERICAN LEGION DEPARTMENT OF VERMONT

http://www.vtlegion.org

AMERICAN LEGION DEPARTMENT OF VERMONT DEPARTMENT SCHOLARSHIPS

Awards for high school seniors who attend a Vermont high school or similar school in an adjoining state whose parents are legal residents of Vermont, or reside in an adjoining state and attend a Vermont secondary school.

Award: Scholarship for use in freshman year; not renewable. *Number:* 1–12. *Amount:* $500–$1500.

Eligibility Requirements: Applicant must be high school student; planning to enroll or expecting to enroll full- or part-time at a two-year or four-year or technical institution or university and resident of New Hampshire, New York, Vermont. Available to U.S. citizens.

Application Requirements: Application form, essay, financial need analysis. *Deadline:* April 1.

Contact: Huzon "Jerry" Stewart, Chairman
American Legion Department of Vermont
PO Box 396
Montpelier, VT 05601-0396
Phone: 802-223-7131
E-mail: alvthq@myfairpoint.net

AMERICAN LEGION DEPARTMENT OF VERMONT HIGH SCHOOL ORATORICAL CONTEST

Students in grades 9 to 12 are eligible to compete. Must attend an accredited Vermont high school. Must be a U.S. citizen. Selection based on oration.

Award: Prize for use in freshman year; not renewable. *Number:* 1–2. *Amount:* $200–$1500.

Eligibility Requirements: Applicant must be high school student; planning to enroll or expecting to enroll full- or part-time at a two-year or four-year or technical institution or university; resident of Vermont and must have an interest in public speaking. Available to U.S. citizens.

Application Requirements: Application form. *Deadline:* January 1.

Contact: Karlene DeVine, Chairman
American Legion Department of Vermont
126 State Street
Montpelier, VT 05601
Phone: 802-223-7131
E-mail: alvthq@myfairpoint.net

AMERICAN LEGION EAGLE SCOUT OF THE YEAR
• See page 535

AMERICAN LEGION DEPARTMENT OF VIRGINIA

http://www.valegion.org/

AMERICAN LEGION DEPARTMENT OF VIRGINIA HIGH SCHOOL ORATORICAL CONTEST

Three one-time awards of up to $1100. Oratorical contest open to applicants who are winners of the Virginia department oratorical contest and who attend high school in Virginia. Competitors must demonstrate their knowledge of the U.S. Constitution. Must be students in ninth to twelfth grades at accredited Virginia high schools.

Award: Prize for use in freshman year; not renewable. *Number:* 3. *Amount:* $600–$1100.

Eligibility Requirements: Applicant must be high school student; planning to enroll or expecting to enroll full-time at a four-year institution or university and resident of Virginia. Available to U.S. citizens.

Application Requirements: Application form, entry in a contest. *Deadline:* December 1.

Contact: Dale Chapman, Adjutant
American Legion Department of Virginia
1708 Commonwealth Avenue
Richmond, VA 23230
Phone: 804-353-6606
Fax: 804-358-1940
E-mail: eeccleston@valegion.org

AMERICAN LEGION DEPARTMENT OF WASHINGTON

http://www.walegion.org/

AMERICAN LEGION DEPARTMENT OF WASHINGTON CHILDREN AND YOUTH SCHOLARSHIPS
• See page 536

AMERICAN LEGION DEPARTMENT OF WEST VIRGINIA

http://www.wvlegion.org/

AMERICAN LEGION DEPARTMENT OF WEST VIRGINIA BOARD OF REGENTS SCHOLARSHIP

One-time prize awarded annually to the winner of the West Virginia American Legion State Oratorical Scholarship Program Contest. Must be in ninth to twelfth grade of an accredited West Virginia high school to compete. For use at a West Virginia institution only.

Award: Scholarship for use in freshman year; not renewable. *Number:* 1. *Amount:* up to $2000.

Eligibility Requirements: Applicant must be high school student; planning to enroll or expecting to enroll full-time at a four-year institution or university; resident of West Virginia; studying in West Virginia and must have an interest in public speaking. Available to U.S. citizens.

Application Requirements: Application form. *Deadline:* January 1.

Contact: Mr. Miles Epling, State Adjutant
American Legion Department of West Virginia
2016 Kanawha Boulevard East, PO Box 3191
Charleston, WV 25332-3191
Phone: 304-343-7591
E-mail: wvlegion@suddenlinkmail.com

AMERICAN LEGION DEPARTMENT OF WEST VIRGINIA HIGH SCHOOL ORATORICAL CONTEST

Oratorical Scholarship Program Contest open to students in ninth to twelfth grades of any accredited West Virginia high school. Speech contests begin in January at post level and continue on to national competition. Contact local American Legion Post for deadlines and application details, or American Legion State Headquarters 304-343-7591.

Award: Scholarship for use in freshman year; not renewable. *Number:* 25–39. *Amount:* $200.

Eligibility Requirements: Applicant must be high school student; planning to enroll or expecting to enroll full-time at a four-year institution or university; resident of West Virginia; studying in West Virginia and must have an interest in public speaking. Available to U.S. citizens.

Application Requirements: Application form. *Deadline:* January 1.

Contact: Mr. Miles Epling, Department Adjutant
American Legion Department of West Virginia
2016 Kanawha Boulevard East, PO Box 3191
Charleston, WV 25332-3191
Phone: 304-343-7591
E-mail: wvlegion@suddenlinkmail.com

SONS OF THE AMERICAN LEGION WILLIAM F. "BILL" JOHNSON MEMORIAL SCHOLARSHIP
• See page 536

AMERICAN QUARTER HORSE FOUNDATION (AQHF)

http://www.aqha.com/foundation

ARIZONA QUARTER HORSE YOUTH SCHOLARSHIP
• See page 537

ARIZONA QUARTER RACING SCHOLARSHIP
• See page 537

CHRISTOPHER LAWRENCE JUNKER NEBRASKA SCHOLARSHIP
• See page 537

DR. GERALD O'CONNOR MICHIGAN QHY SCHOLARSHIP
• See page 537

INDIANA QUARTER HORSE YOUTH SCHOLARSHIP
• See page 538

JAMES F. AND DORIS M. BARTON SCHOLARSHIP
• See page 538

JOAN CAIN FLORIDA QUARTER HORSE YOUTH SCHOLARSHIP
• See page 538

JOYCE WYATT PENNSYLVANIA QUARTER HORSE YOUTH SCHOLARSHIP
• See page 538

NEBRASKA QUARTER HORSE YOUTH SCHOLARSHIP
• See page 539

SWAYZE WOODRUFF MEMORIAL MID-SOUTH SCHOLARSHIP
• See page 539

AMERICAN SAVINGS FOUNDATION

http://www.asfdn.org/

ROBERT T. KENNEY SCHOLARSHIP PROGRAM AT THE AMERICAN SAVINGS FOUNDATION
• *See page 576*

ANTHONY MUNOZ FOUNDATION

www.munozfoundation.org

ANTHONY MUNOZ SCHOLARSHIPS
• *See page 577*

ARIZONA COMMISSION FOR POSTSECONDARY EDUCATION

https://highered.az.gov/

LEVERAGING EDUCATIONAL ASSISTANCE PARTNERSHIP

Grants to financially needy students, who enroll in and attend postsecondary education or training in Arizona schools. Program was formerly known as the State Student Incentive Grant or SSIG Program.

Award: Grant for use in freshman, sophomore, junior, senior, or graduate years; not renewable. *Amount:* $100–$2500.

Eligibility Requirements: Applicant must be enrolled or expecting to enroll full- or part-time at a two-year or four-year or technical institution or university; resident of Arizona and studying in Arizona. Available to U.S. citizens.

Application Requirements: Application form, financial need analysis, transcript. *Deadline:* April 30.

Contact: Mila Zaporteza, Business Manager and LEAP Financial Aid Manager
Arizona Commission for Postsecondary Education
2020 North Central Avenue, Suite 650
Phoenix, AZ 85004-4503
Phone: 602-258-2435 Ext. 102
Fax: 602-258-2483
E-mail: mila@azhighered.gov

ARIZONA PRIVATE SCHOOL ASSOCIATION

http://www.arizonapsa.org/

ARIZONA PRIVATE SCHOOL ASSOCIATION SCHOLARSHIP

Scholarships are for graduating students from Arizona and the high school determines the recipients of the awards. Each spring the Arizona Private School Association awards two $1000 scholarships to every private high school in Arizona.

Award: Scholarship for use in freshman year; not renewable. *Number:* 600. *Amount:* $1000.

Eligibility Requirements: Applicant must be high school student; planning to enroll or expecting to enroll full-time at a four-year institution or university and resident of Arizona. Available to U.S. citizens.

Application Requirements: Application form, essay. *Deadline:* April 30.

Contact: Fred Lockhart, Executive Director
Arizona Private School Association
202 East McDowell Road, Suite 273
Phoenix, AZ 85004
Phone: 602-254-5199
Fax: 602-254-5073
E-mail: apsa@eschelon.com

ARKANSAS DEPARTMENT OF HIGHER EDUCATION

http://www.adhe.edu/

ARKANSAS ACADEMIC CHALLENGE SCHOLARSHIP PROGRAM

Awards for Arkansas residents who are graduating high school seniors, currently enrolled college students and nontraditional students to study at an approved Arkansas institution. Must have at least a 2.5 GPA or 19 ACT composite score (or the equivalent). Renewable up to three additional years.

Award: Scholarship for use in freshman, sophomore, junior, or senior years; renewable. *Number:* 30,000–35,000. *Amount:* $1250–$4500.

Eligibility Requirements: Applicant must be enrolled or expecting to enroll full- or part-time at a two-year or four-year institution or university; resident of Arkansas and studying in Arkansas. Applicant must have 2.5 GPA or higher. Available to U.S. citizens.

Application Requirements: Application form, application form may be submitted online (http://www.adhe.edu), financial need analysis, test scores, transcript. *Deadline:* June 1.

Contact: Philip Axelroth, Financial Aid Program Coordinator
Phone: 501-371-2000

ARKANSAS GOVERNOR'S SCHOLARS PROGRAM

Awards for outstanding Arkansas high school seniors. Must be an Arkansas resident and have a high school GPA of at least 3.5 or have scored at least 27 on the ACT. Award is $4000 per year for four years of full-time undergraduate study. Applicants who attain 32 or above on ACT, 1410 or above on SAT and have an academic 3.5 GPA, or are selected as National Merit or National Achievement finalists may receive an award equal to tuition, mandatory fees, room, and board up to $10,000 per year at any Arkansas institution.

Award: Scholarship for use in freshman, sophomore, junior, senior, or graduate years; renewable. *Number:* 75–375. *Amount:* $4000–$10,000.

Eligibility Requirements: Applicant must be high school student; planning to enroll or expecting to enroll full-time at a two-year or four-year institution or university; resident of Arkansas and studying in Arkansas. Applicant must have 3.5 GPA or higher. Available to U.S. citizens.

Application Requirements: Application form, application form may be submitted online (http://www.adhe.edu), community service, test scores, transcript. *Deadline:* February 1.

Contact: Philip Axelroth, Financial Aid Program Coordinator
Phone: 501-371-2000

LAW ENFORCEMENT OFFICERS' DEPENDENTS SCHOLARSHIP–ARKANSAS

Scholarship for dependents, under 23 years old, of Arkansas law-enforcement officers killed or permanently disabled in the line of duty. Renewable award is a waiver of tuition, fees, and room at two- or four-year Arkansas institution. Submit birth certificate, death certificate, and claims commission report of findings of fact. Proof of disability from State Claims Commission may also be submitted.

Award: Scholarship for use in freshman, sophomore, junior, or senior years; renewable. *Number:* 27–32.

Eligibility Requirements: Applicant must be enrolled or expecting to enroll full- or part-time at a two-year or four-year or technical institution or university; resident of Arkansas and studying in Arkansas. Available to U.S. citizens.

Application Requirements: Application form. *Deadline:* continuous.

Contact: Tara Smith, Director of Financial Aid
Arkansas Department of Higher Education
114 East Capitol Avenue
Little Rock, AR 72201-3818
Phone: 501-371-2000
Fax: 501-371-2001
E-mail: taras@adhe.edu

MILITARY DEPENDENT'S SCHOLARSHIP PROGRAM
• *See page 655*

SECOND EFFORT SCHOLARSHIP

Awarded to those scholars who achieved one of the 10 highest scores on the Arkansas High School Diploma Test (GED). Must be at least age 18 and not have graduated from high school. Students do not apply for this award, they are contacted by the Arkansas Department of Higher Education.

Award: Scholarship for use in freshman, sophomore, junior, or senior years; renewable. *Number:* 10. *Amount:* up to $1000.

Eligibility Requirements: Applicant must be enrolled or expecting to enroll full- or part-time at a two-year or four-year institution or university; resident of Arkansas and studying in Arkansas. Available to U.S. citizens.

Application Requirements: Application form, application form may be submitted online (http://www.adhe.edu). *Deadline:* varies.

Contact: Philip Axelroth, Financial Aid Program Coordinator
Phone: 501-371-2000

ARKANSAS SINGLE PARENT SCHOLARSHIP FUND

http://www.aspsf.org/

ARKANSAS SINGLE PARENT SCHOLARSHIP FUND
• *See page 577*

ARKANSAS STUDENT LOAN AUTHORITY

http://www.asla.info/

R. PRESTON WOODRUFF JR. SCHOLARSHIP

Up to twenty $1,000 scholarships awarded annually. Online entries only and only one entry per applicant. Eligible entries will be drawn at random to select the scholarship winners. Winners must submit a 500-word essay in order to receive a $1,000 scholarship. One renewable scholarship (up to 4 years) will be awarded to the student with the most outstanding essay.

Award: Scholarship for use in freshman, sophomore, junior, senior, or graduate years; renewable. *Number:* 20. *Amount:* $1000.

Eligibility Requirements: Applicant must be enrolled or expecting to enroll full- or part-time at a two-year or four-year or technical institution or university and resident of Arkansas. Available to U.S. citizens.

Application Requirements: Application form. *Deadline:* April 1.

Contact: Amy Neathery, Higher Education Programs Manager
Arkansas Student Loan Authority
3801 Woodland Heights
Suite 200
Little Rock, AR 72212
Phone: 800-443-6030 Ext. 4130
E-mail: aneathery@asla.info

ARRL FOUNDATION INC.

http://www.arrl.org/

ALBERT H. HIX, W8AH, MEMORIAL SCHOLARSHIP

One-time $500 award available to general class or higher class amateur radio operators. Preference is given to the residents of the West Virginia section who are attending postsecondary school in the West Virginia section. Minimum GPA of 3.0 or higher required.

Award: Scholarship for use in freshman, sophomore, junior, or senior years; not renewable. *Number:* 1. *Amount:* $500.

Eligibility Requirements: Applicant must be enrolled or expecting to enroll full-time at a two-year or four-year or technical institution or university; resident of West Virginia; studying in West Virginia and must have an interest in amateur radio. Applicant must have 3.0 GPA or higher. Available to U.S. citizens.

Application Requirements: Application form. *Deadline:* January 31.

Contact: Ms. Mary Hobart, Secretary
Phone: 860-594-0397
E-mail: k1mmh@arrl.org

ARRL ROCKY MOUNTAIN DIVISION SCHOLARSHIP

One $500 award to a student with an active amateur radio license attending an accredited two- or four-year college or university.

Preference given to residents of the ARRL Rocky Mountain Division (Colorado, New Mexico, Utah or Wyoming). Must be a U.S. citizen, and a graduating high school senior or undergraduate student. Must submit a letter of recommendation from a sitting officer of an ARRL-affiliated club attesting to regular activity on the amateur radio spectrum and within the Amateur Radio community.

Award: Scholarship for use in freshman, sophomore, junior, or senior years; not renewable. *Number:* 1. *Amount:* $500.

Eligibility Requirements: Applicant must be enrolled or expecting to enroll full- or part-time at a two-year or four-year institution or university; resident of Colorado, New Mexico, Utah, Wyoming and must have an interest in amateur radio. Available to U.S. citizens.

Application Requirements: Application form. *Deadline:* January 31.

Contact: Ms. Mary Hobart, Secretary
Phone: 860-594-0397
E-mail: k1mmh@arrl.org

ATLANTA RADIO CLUB SCHOLARSHIP

One $500 scholarship for a Georgia resident who is a student with an active Amateur Radio license studying at an accredited 4-year college or university. Must be between the ages of 17 and 25 at the time of the award. Preference is given to students performing at a high academic level.

Award: Scholarship for use in freshman, sophomore, junior, senior, or graduate years; not renewable. *Number:* 1. *Amount:* $500.

Eligibility Requirements: Applicant must be age 17-25; enrolled or expecting to enroll full- or part-time at a four-year institution or university; resident of Georgia and must have an interest in amateur radio. Available to U.S. citizens.

Application Requirements: Application form. *Deadline:* January 31.

Contact: Ms. Mary Hobart, Secretary
Phone: 860-594-0397
E-mail: k1mmh@arrl.org

BYRON BLANCHARD, N1EKV, MEMORIAL SCHOLARSHIP

One $500 scholarship for a student in residence in ARRL New England Division (Massachusetts, New Hampshire, Connecticut, Rhode Island, Vermont and Maine). Must have an active Amateur Radio License Class license.

Award: Scholarship for use in freshman, sophomore, junior, or senior years; not renewable. *Number:* 1. *Amount:* $500.

Eligibility Requirements: Applicant must be enrolled or expecting to enroll full- or part-time at a two-year or four-year or technical institution or university; resident of Connecticut, Maine, Massachusetts, New Hampshire, Rhode Island, Vermont and must have an interest in amateur radio. Available to U.S. citizens.

Application Requirements: Application form. *Deadline:* January 31.

Contact: Ms. Mary Hobart, Secretary
Phone: 860-594-0397
E-mail: k1mmh@arrl.org

CENTRAL ARIZONA DX ASSOCIATION SCHOLARSHIP

One $1000 award is a available to a student who is an Arizona resident and who possesses a Technician class or higher radio license. Must have a cumulative GPA of 3.2 or above. Graduating high school students will be considered before current college students.

Award: Scholarship for use in freshman, sophomore, junior, or senior years; not renewable. *Number:* 1. *Amount:* $1000.

Eligibility Requirements: Applicant must be enrolled or expecting to enroll full- or part-time at a two-year or four-year institution or university; resident of Arizona and must have an interest in amateur radio. Available to U.S. citizens.

Application Requirements: Application form. *Deadline:* January 31.

Contact: Ms. Mary Hobart, Secretary
Phone: 860-594-0397
E-mail: k1mmh@arrl.org

CHICAGO FM CLUB SCHOLARSHIP FUND

Multiple awards available to amateur radio operators with technician license who are U.S. citizens or within 3 months of citizenship. Preference given to residents of FCC Ninth Call District (Indiana, Illinois, Wisconsin) pursuing post-secondary course of study at accredited 2- or 4-year college or trade school.

Award: Scholarship for use in freshman, sophomore, junior, or senior years; not renewable. *Amount:* $500.

Eligibility Requirements: Applicant must be enrolled or expecting to enroll full-time at a two-year or four-year or technical institution or university; resident of Illinois, Wisconsin and must have an interest in amateur radio. Available to U.S. citizens.

Application Requirements: Application form. *Deadline:* January 31.

Contact: Ms. Mary Hobart, Secretary
  Phone: 860-594-0397
  E-mail: k1mmh@arrl.org

DAVID KNAUS MEMORIAL SCHOLARSHIP

One $1500 award for a student with an active amateur radio license pursuing a Bachelor's degree or a 2-year Associate's degree. Preference given to a resident of Wisconsin or, if no qualified applicant from Wisconsin, to applicant from the ARRL Central Division (Illinois, Indiana, Wisconsin).

Award: Scholarship for use in freshman, sophomore, junior, or senior years; not renewable. *Number:* 1. *Amount:* $1500.

Eligibility Requirements: Applicant must be enrolled or expecting to enroll full- or part-time at a two-year or four-year institution; resident of Illinois, Indiana, Wisconsin and must have an interest in amateur radio. Available to U.S. citizens.

Application Requirements: Application form. *Deadline:* January 31.

Contact: Ms. Mary Hobart, Secretary
  Phone: 860-594-0397
  E-mail: k1mmh@arrl.org

GWINNETT AMATEUR RADIO SOCIETY SCHOLARSHIP

One $500 award available to a Georgia resident possessing an active amateur radio license. Preference is given to students from Gwinnett County, GA or from the state of Georgia studying at four-year colleges or universities.

Award: Scholarship for use in freshman, sophomore, junior, or senior years; not renewable. *Number:* 1. *Amount:* $1000.

Eligibility Requirements: Applicant must be enrolled or expecting to enroll full- or part-time at a four-year institution or university; resident of Georgia and must have an interest in amateur radio. Available to U.S. citizens.

Application Requirements: Application form. *Deadline:* January 31.

Contact: Ms. Mary Hobart, Secretary
  Phone: 860-594-0397
  E-mail: k1mmh@arrl.org

JACKSON COUNTY ARA SCHOLARSHIP

One $500 award for a student with an active amateur radio license. Preference given to students from Mississippi. If no applicant is identified, preference will be given to a student from the ARRL Delta Division (Arkansas, Louisiana, Mississippi, and Tennessee).

Award: Scholarship for use in freshman, sophomore, junior, or senior years; not renewable. *Number:* 1. *Amount:* $500.

Eligibility Requirements: Applicant must be enrolled or expecting to enroll full- or part-time at a two-year or four-year or technical institution or university; resident of Arkansas, Louisiana, Mississippi, Tennessee and must have an interest in amateur radio. Available to U.S. citizens.

Application Requirements: Application form. *Deadline:* January 31.

Contact: Ms. Mary Hobart, Secretary
  Phone: 860-594-0397
  E-mail: k1mmh@arrl.org

JAMES COTHRAN, KD3NI, SCHOLARSHIP

$2000 scholarship for a student with any active Amateur Radio License Class who is a resident of the Atlantic Division (DE, MD, PA, Southern NJ, Western NY), the Roanoke Division (NC, SC, VA, WV), the Southeastern Division (AL, FL, GA) or Washington, D.C.

Award: Scholarship for use in freshman, sophomore, junior, or senior years; not renewable. *Number:* 1. *Amount:* $2000.

Eligibility Requirements: Applicant must be enrolled or expecting to enroll full-time at a two-year or four-year or technical institution or university; resident of Alabama, Delaware, District of Columbia, Florida, Georgia, Maryland, New Jersey, New York, North Carolina, Pennsylvania, South Carolina, Virginia, West Virginia and must have an interest in amateur radio. Available to U.S. citizens.

Application Requirements: Application form. *Deadline:* January 31.

Contact: Ms. Mary Hobart, Secretary
  Phone: 860-594-0397
  E-mail: k1mmh@arrl.org

MARY LOU BROWN SCHOLARSHIP

Multiple awards available to amateur radio operators with general license. Preference given to residents of Alaska, Idaho, Montana, Oregon, and Washington pursuing Baccalaureate or higher course of study. GPA of 3.0 or higher required. Must demonstrate interest in promoting Amateur Radio Service.

Award: Scholarship for use in freshman, sophomore, junior, senior, or graduate years; not renewable. *Amount:* $2500.

Eligibility Requirements: Applicant must be enrolled or expecting to enroll full-time at a four-year institution or university; resident of Alaska, Idaho, Montana, Oregon, Washington and must have an interest in amateur radio. Applicant must have 3.0 GPA or higher. Available to U.S. citizens.

Application Requirements: Application form. *Deadline:* January 31.

Contact: Ms. Mary Hobart, Secretary
  Phone: 860-594-0397
  E-mail: k1mmh@arrl.org

NEW ENGLAND FEMARA SCHOLARSHIPS

One-time award of $2000 available to students licensed as amateur radio operator technicians. Multiple awards per year. Preference is given to the residents of Vermont, Maine, New Hampshire, Rhode Island, Massachusetts, or Connecticut.

Award: Scholarship for use in freshman, sophomore, junior, or senior years; not renewable. *Amount:* $2000.

Eligibility Requirements: Applicant must be enrolled or expecting to enroll full-time at a four-year institution or university; resident of Connecticut, Maine, Massachusetts, New Hampshire, Rhode Island, Vermont and must have an interest in amateur radio. Available to U.S. citizens.

Application Requirements: Application form. *Deadline:* January 31.

Contact: Ms. Mary Hobart, Secretary
  Phone: 860-594-0397
  E-mail: k1mmh@arrl.org

NORMAN E. STROHMEIER, W2VRS, MEMORIAL SCHOLARSHIP

One $500 award is available to students who are residents of western New York and who possess technician class or higher amateur radio licenses. Preference is given to graduating high school seniors with a 3.2 GPA. Must provide documentation of Amateur Radio activities and achievements and any honor from community service.

Award: Scholarship for use in freshman, sophomore, junior, or senior, or graduate years; not renewable. *Number:* 1. *Amount:* $500.

Eligibility Requirements: Applicant must be enrolled or expecting to enroll full- or part-time at a two-year or four-year or technical institution or university; resident of New York and must have an interest in amateur radio. Applicant must have 3.0 GPA or higher. Available to U.S. citizens.

Application Requirements: Application form, community service. *Deadline:* January 31.

Contact: Ms. Mary Hobart, Secretary
  Phone: 860-594-0397
  E-mail: k1mmh@arrl.org

PEORIA AREA AMATEUR RADIO CLUB SCHOLARSHIP

One $500 award is available to residents of the Central Illinois counties of Peoria, Tazewell, Woodford, Knox, McLean, Fulton, Logan, Marshall, and Stark. Applicants must possess a technician class or higher amateur radio license and attend an accredited two- or four-year college or university.

Award: Scholarship for use in freshman, sophomore, junior, or senior years; not renewable. *Number:* 1. *Amount:* $500.

Eligibility Requirements: Applicant must be enrolled or expecting to enroll full- or part-time at a two-year or four-year institution or university; resident of Illinois and must have an interest in amateur radio. Available to U.S. citizens.

Application Requirements: Application form. *Deadline:* January 31.

Contact: Ms. Mary Hobart, Secretary
Phone: 860-594-0397
E-mail: k1mmh@arrl.org

SIX METER CLUB OF CHICAGO SCHOLARSHIP

One-time $500 award for licensed amateur radio operators. Preference given to students with grade point average of 2.5 or better and in good academic standing. Must be a resident of Illinois, or resident of ARRL Central Division (Indiana, Wisconsin) attending school at a regionally accredited technical school, community college, college, or university and pursuing an undergraduate degree.

Award: Scholarship for use in freshman, sophomore, junior, or senior years; not renewable. *Number:* 1. *Amount:* $500.

Eligibility Requirements: Applicant must be enrolled or expecting to enroll full- or part-time at a two-year or four-year or technical institution or university; resident of Illinois, Indiana, Wisconsin and must have an interest in amateur radio. Applicant must have 2.5 GPA or higher. Available to U.S. citizens.

Application Requirements: Application form. *Deadline:* January 31.

Contact: Ms. Mary Hobart, Secretary
Phone: 860-594-0397
E-mail: k1mmh@arrl.org

THOMAS W. PORTER, W8KYZ, SCHOLARSHIP HONORING MICHAEL DAUGHERTY, W8LSE

One $1000 award available to a student with a technician class or higher amateur radio license. Preference given to students from Ohio or West Virginia at accredited 2- or 4-year colleges/universities or technical schools.

Award: Scholarship for use in freshman, sophomore, junior, or senior years; not renewable. *Number:* 1. *Amount:* $1000.

Eligibility Requirements: Applicant must be enrolled or expecting to enroll full- or part-time at a two-year or four-year or technical institution or university; resident of Ohio, West Virginia and must have an interest in amateur radio. Available to U.S. citizens.

Application Requirements: Application form. *Deadline:* January 31.

Contact: Ms. Mary Hobart, Secretary
Phone: 860-594-0397
E-mail: k1mmh@arrl.org

TOM AND JUDITH COMSTOCK SCHOLARSHIP

One-time award of $2000 for high school seniors. Preference given to residents of Texas and Oklahoma. Must be licensed amateur radio operator and be accepted at a two- or four-year institution.

Award: Scholarship for use in freshman year; not renewable. *Number:* 1. *Amount:* $2000.

Eligibility Requirements: Applicant must be high school student; planning to enroll or expecting to enroll full-time at a two-year or four-year institution or university; resident of Oklahoma, Texas and must have an interest in amateur radio. Available to U.S. citizens.

Application Requirements: Application form. *Deadline:* January 31.

Contact: Ms. Mary Hobart, Secretary
Phone: 860-594-0397
E-mail: k1mmh@arrl.org

WAYNE NELSON, KB4UT, MEMORIAL SCHOLARSHIP

One $1000 award for a U.S. citizen and Florida resident studying in a technical field at any four-year college or university. May have any class of active Amateur Radio license. Preference given to resident of Central FL (Orange, Seminole, Osceola, Lake, Volusia, Brevard and Polk counties). If none identified, residence in FL. Minimum GPA of 3.0 or better on a 4.0 scale in high school or for the previous undergraduate year.

Award: Scholarship for use in freshman, sophomore, junior, or senior years; not renewable. *Number:* 1. *Amount:* $1000.

Eligibility Requirements: Applicant must be enrolled or expecting to enroll full-time at a four-year institution or university; resident of Florida and must have an interest in amateur radio. Applicant must have 3.0 GPA or higher. Available to U.S. citizens.

Application Requirements: Application form. *Deadline:* January 31.

Contact: Ms. Mary Hobart, Secretary
Phone: 860-594-0397
E-mail: k1mmh@arrl.org

WILLIAM BENNETT, W7PHO, MEMORIAL SCHOLARSHIP

One $500 award is available to residents of ARRL's Northwest, Pacific, and Southwest divisions. Must have a general class or higher amateur radio license, attend a four-year college or university, and have a minimum 3.0 GPA.

Award: Scholarship for use in freshman, sophomore, junior, or senior years; not renewable. *Number:* 1. *Amount:* $500.

Eligibility Requirements: Applicant must be enrolled or expecting to enroll full- or part-time at a four-year institution or university; resident of Arizona, California, Colorado, Idaho, Montana, Nevada, New Mexico, Oregon, Utah, Washington, Wyoming and must have an interest in amateur radio. Applicant must have 3.0 GPA or higher. Available to U.S. citizens.

Application Requirements: Application form. *Deadline:* January 31.

Contact: Ms. Mary Hobart, Secretary
Phone: 860-594-0397
E-mail: k1mmh@arrl.org

YANKEE CLIPPER CONTEST CLUB YOUTH SCHOLARSHIP

One-time award available to general class or higher licensed amateur radio operators. Must reside and attend an accredited college or university within a 175-mile radius of YCCC Center in Erving, MA. Recipient must be 22 years or younger as of June 1 of the year of the grant.

Award: Scholarship for use in freshman, sophomore, junior, or senior years; not renewable. *Number:* 1. *Amount:* $1200.

Eligibility Requirements: Applicant must be enrolled or expecting to enroll full-time at a two-year or four-year institution or university; resident of Connecticut, Maine, Massachusetts, New Hampshire, New Jersey, New York, Pennsylvania, Rhode Island, Vermont and must have an interest in amateur radio. Available to U.S. citizens.

Application Requirements: Application form. *Deadline:* January 31.

Contact: Ms. Mary Hobart, Secretary
Phone: 860-594-0397
E-mail: k1mmh@arrl.org

YOU'VE GOT A FRIEND IN PENNSYLVANIA SCHOLARSHIP

• *See page 540*

ZACHARY TAYLOR STEVENS SCHOLARSHIP

One $750 award is available to students who possess a technician class or higher amateur radio license. Preference will be given to residents of Michigan, Ohio, and West Virginia. Must attend an accredited 2-year or 4-year college, university, or technical school.

Award: Scholarship for use in freshman, sophomore, junior, or senior years; not renewable. *Number:* 1. *Amount:* $750.

Eligibility Requirements: Applicant must be enrolled or expecting to enroll full- or part-time at a two-year or four-year or technical institution or university; resident of Michigan, Ohio, West Virginia and must have an interest in amateur radio. Available to U.S. citizens.

Application Requirements: Application form. *Deadline:* January 31.

Contact: Ms. Mary Hobart, Secretary
Phone: 860-594-0397
E-mail: k1mmh@arrl.org

ASIAN PACIFIC COMMUNITY FUND

http://www.apcf.org/

THE CHEN FOUNDATION SCHOLARSHIP PROGRAM

The Chen Foundation is focused on helping economically-challenged youth fulfill their dreams of obtaining higher education. The scholarship is renewable, allowing scholarship recipients to receive an additional $2,000 award for the fall quarter/semester of their second year of college if they maintain a minimum 3.0 GPA and active service in the community. Must be a high school senior who resides in California and planning to attend a California State University or California community college as a first year full-time student in the fall of 2017 (if selected, must submit college acceptance letter for verification). Must have a minimum cumulative unweighted high school GPA of 3.0 and a household income at or below California State Low Income Level (must be able to show 2015 or 2016 tax return should applicant be selected for award).The scholarship is open to all majors and there is no ethnicity requirement.

Award: Scholarship for use in freshman or sophomore years; renewable. *Number:* 10. *Amount:* $2000.

Eligibility Requirements: Applicant must be high school student; planning to enroll or expecting to enroll full-time at a two-year or four-year institution or university; resident of California and studying in California. Applicant must have 3.0 GPA or higher. Available to U.S. and non-U.S. citizens.

Application Requirements: Application form, essay. *Deadline:* March 29.

Contact: Ms. Sandy Southivilay, Communications Manager
Asian Pacific Community Fund
1145 Wilshire Boulevard
Suite 105
Los Angeles, CA 90017
Phone: 213-624-6400 Ext. 6
Fax: 213-624-6406
E-mail: scholarships@apcf.org

ROYAL BUSINESS BANK SCHOLARSHIP PROGRAM
• *See page 577*

ASIAN REPORTER

http://www.arfoundation.net/

ASIAN REPORTER SCHOLARSHIP
• *See page 577*

BLUE GRASS ENERGY

http://www.bgenergy.com/

BLUE GRASS ENERGY ACADEMIC SCHOLARSHIP
Scholarships for Kentucky high school seniors living with parents or guardians who are members of Blue Grass Energy. Must have minimum GPA of 3.0 and have demonstrated academic achievement, extracurricular involvement and financial need. For application and information, visit website http://www.bgenergy.com/forStudents.aspx.

Award: Scholarship for use in freshman year; not renewable. *Number:* 10. *Amount:* $1000.

Eligibility Requirements: Applicant must be high school student; planning to enroll or expecting to enroll full-time at a two-year or four-year or technical institution or university and resident of Kentucky. Applicant must have 3.0 GPA or higher. Available to U.S. citizens.

Application Requirements: Application form, essay, explanation of how scholarship is necessary to further education, financial need analysis, resume, test scores, transcript. *Deadline:* April 1.

Contact: Ms. Magen Howard, Communications Adviser
Phone: 859-885-2104
E-mail: magenh@bgenergy.com

BOETTCHER FOUNDATION

http://www.boettcherfoundation.org/

BOETTCHER FOUNDATION SCHOLARSHIP
Merit-based scholarship available to graduating seniors in the state of Colorado. Selection based on academic achievement, leadership, service and character. Renewable for four years and can be used at any Colorado university or college. Includes full tuition and fees, living stipend of $2800 per year, and a stipend for books.

Award: Scholarship for use in freshman, sophomore, junior, or senior years; renewable. *Number:* 42. *Amount:* $13,000–$40,000.

Eligibility Requirements: Applicant must be high school student; planning to enroll or expecting to enroll full-time at a four-year institution or university; resident of Colorado; studying in Colorado and must have an interest in leadership. Available to U.S. citizens.

Application Requirements: Application form, essay, interview. *Deadline:* November 1.

Contact: Ms. Stephanie Panion, Scholarship Program Coordinator
Boettcher Foundation
600 17th Street, Suite 2210 S
Denver, CO 80202-5422
Phone: 303-285-6207
E-mail: scholarships@boettcherfoundation.org

BOUNCE ENERGY

http://www.bounceenergy.com

BE MORE SCHOLARSHIP
• *See page 578*

BRAINLY, INC.

http://www.brainly.com

BRAINLY EVERYONE KNOWS SOMETHING SCHOLARSHIP
• *See page 578*

BREAD & ROSES COMMUNITY FUND

http://www.breadrosesfund.org

JONATHAN LAX SCHOLARSHIP FOR GAY MEN
The Lax Scholarship Fund was established in 1994 by the late entrepreneur and inventor Jonathan R. Lax for the purpose of encouraging gay men to obtain additional education; aspiring to positions in which they contribute to society; being out about their sexual orientation; and acting as role models for other gay men with similar potential. Tuition scholarships are awarded in amounts $4,000 and $8,000 to men who live in the five-county Philadelphia region (Bucks, Chester, Delaware, Montgomery and Philadelphia counties) and Camden County in NJ, who are attending accredited colleges, graduate or professional schools anywhere, or to men attending such schools within the Philadelphia region. For more questions, please contact lax@breadrosesfund.org.

Award: Scholarship for use in freshman, sophomore, junior, senior, graduate, or postgraduate years; not renewable. *Number:* 4–20. *Amount:* $4000–$8000.

Eligibility Requirements: Applicant must be enrolled or expecting to enroll full-time at a four-year institution or university; male; resident of Pennsylvania and studying in Pennsylvania. Available to U.S. citizens.

Application Requirements: Application form. *Deadline:* February 1.

Contact: Aarati Kasturirangan, Director of Programs
Bread & Roses Community Fund
1315 Walnut Street
Suite 1300
Philadelphia, PA 19107
Phone: 215-731-1107 Ext. 206
Fax: 215-731.0453
E-mail: lax@breadrosesfund.org

BREYER LAW OFFICES PC

http://www.breyerlaw.com/

2017 HUSBAND AND WIFE LAW TEAM ARIZONA SCHOLARSHIP
• *See page 578*

BRIDGES FOR THE DEAF AND HARD OF HEARING

http://www.bridgesfordeafandhh.org/

LINDA COWDEN MEMORIAL SCHOLARSHIP
• *See page 628*

CABRILLO CIVIC CLUBS OF CALIFORNIA INC.

http://www.cabrillocivicclubs.org/scholarship.asp

CABRILLO CIVIC CLUBS OF CALIFORNIA SCHOLARSHIP
• *See page 673*

CALIFORNIA ASSOCIATION OF WINE GRAPE GROWERS FOUNDATION

http://www.cawgfoundation.org/

CALIFORNIA WINE GRAPE GROWERS FOUNDATION SCHOLARSHIP

Scholarship for high school seniors whose parents or legal guardians are vineyard employees of wine grape growers. Recipients may study the subject of their choice at any campus of the University of California system, the California State University system, or the California Community College system.

Award: Scholarship for use in freshman year; renewable. *Number:* 6–7. *Amount:* $2000–$8000.

Eligibility Requirements: Applicant must be high school student; planning to enroll or expecting to enroll full-time at a two-year or four-year institution or university; resident of California and studying in California. Available to U.S. citizens.

Application Requirements: Application form, community service, essay, financial need analysis. *Deadline:* March 24.

Contact: Carolee Williams, Assistant Executive Director
California Association of Wine Grape Growers Foundation
1121 L Street, #304
Sacramento, CA 95814
Phone: 916-379-8995
E-mail: carolee@cawg.org

CALIFORNIA COMMUNITY COLLEGES

http://www.cccco.edu/

EOPS (EXTENDED OPPORTUNITY PROGRAMS AND SERVICES)/CARE (COOPERATIVE AGENCIES RESOURCES FOR EDUCATION)
• *See page 579*

CALIFORNIA COUNCIL OF THE BLIND

http://www.ccbnet.org/

CALIFORNIA COUNCIL OF THE BLIND SCHOLARSHIPS
• *See page 628*

CALIFORNIA GRANGE FOUNDATION

http://www.csgfoundation.org/

CALIFORNIA GRANGE FOUNDATION SCHOLARSHIP
• *See page 540*

CALIFORNIA INTERSCHOLASTIC FEDERATION

http://www.cifstate.org/

CIF SCHOLAR-ATHLETE OF THE YEAR

Honors one male and one female statewide and is based on excellence in athletics, academics and character.

Award: Scholarship for use in freshman year; not renewable. *Number:* 2. *Amount:* $5000.

Eligibility Requirements: Applicant must be high school student; planning to enroll or expecting to enroll full-time at a four-year institution or university; resident of California and must have an interest in athletics/sports. Applicant must have 3.5 GPA or higher. Available to U.S. citizens.

Application Requirements: Application form, community service, essay. *Deadline:* February 11.

Contact: Jade Chin, Assistant to the Executive Director
California Interscholastic Federation
4658 Duckhorn Dr
Sacramento, CA 95624
Phone: 916-239-4477
E-mail: jchin@cifstate.org

CIF SPIRIT OF SPORT AWARD

This award seeks to recognize student-athletes who display good sportsmanship and school leadership, regardless of athletic ability.

Award: Scholarship for use in freshman year; not renewable. *Number:* 6. *Amount:* $500.

Eligibility Requirements: Applicant must be high school student; planning to enroll or expecting to enroll full-time at a four-year institution or university; resident of California and must have an interest in athletics/sports. Available to U.S. citizens.

Application Requirements: Application form, community service, essay. *Deadline:* continuous.

Contact: Jade Chin, Assistant to the Executive Director
California Interscholastic Federation
4658 Duckhorn Dr.
Sacramento, CA 95624
Phone: 916-239-4477
E-mail: jchin@cifstate.org

CALIFORNIA JUNIOR MISS SCHOLARSHIP PROGRAM

http://www.ajm.org/

CALIFORNIA JUNIOR MISS SCHOLARSHIP PROGRAM

Scholarship program to recognize and reward outstanding high school junior females in the areas of academics, leadership, athletics, public speaking, and the performing arts. Must be single, U.S. citizen, and resident of California. Minimum 3.0 GPA required.

Award: Scholarship for use in freshman year; not renewable. *Number:* 25. *Amount:* $500–$10,000.

Eligibility Requirements: Applicant must be high school student; age 15-17; planning to enroll or expecting to enroll full-time at a four-year institution or university; single female; resident of California and must have an interest in beauty pageant, leadership, or public speaking. Applicant must have 3.0 GPA or higher. Available to U.S. citizens.

Application Requirements: Application form, essay, interview, test scores, transcript. *Deadline:* varies.

Contact: Joan McDonald, Chairman
California Junior Miss Scholarship Program
385 Via Montanosa
Encinitas, CA 92024
Phone: 760-420-4177
E-mail: jmcdonald@bellmicro.com

CALIFORNIA SCHOOL LIBRARY ASSOCIATION

http://www.csla.net/

CSLA NORTHERN REGION PARAPROFESSIONAL SCHOLARSHIP

This scholarship is intended to assist a school library paraprofessional who is enrolled in a 2-year paraprofessional program working towards the goal of becoming a school library media technician, or enrolled in a class to support the library program through job-related skills.

Award: Scholarship for use in freshman or sophomore years; not renewable. *Number:* 1–2. *Amount:* $500–$500.

Eligibility Requirements: Applicant must be enrolled or expecting to enroll full- or part-time at a two-year institution and resident of California. Available to U.S. citizens.

Application Requirements: Application form, essay, recommendations or references, transcript. *Deadline:* September 30.

Contact: Jessica Lee, CSLA Northern Region Scholarship Committee
California School Library Association
6444 E. Spring Street #237
Long Beach, CA 90815-1553
Phone: 888-655-8480
E-mail: info@csla.net

CALIFORNIA STATE PARENT-TEACHER ASSOCIATION

http://www.capta.org/

CONTINUING EDUCATION-PTA VOLUNTEERS SCHOLARSHIP
• See page 540

GRADUATING HIGH SCHOOL SENIOR SCHOLARSHIP
• See page 579

CALIFORNIA STUDENT AID COMMISSION

http://www.csac.ca.gov/

CAL GRANT C
Award for California residents who are enrolled in a short-term vocational training program. Program must lead to a recognized degree or certificate. Course length must be a minimum of 4 months and no longer than 24 months. Students must be attending an approved California institution and show financial need.

Award: Grant for use in freshman or sophomore years; renewable. *Number:* up to 7761. *Amount:* $576–$3168.

Eligibility Requirements: Applicant must be enrolled or expecting to enroll full- or part-time at a two-year or technical institution; resident of California and studying in California. Available to U.S. citizens.

Application Requirements: Application form, financial need analysis, GPA verification. *Deadline:* March 2.

Contact: Catalina Mistler, Chief, Program Administration and Services Division
California Student Aid Commission
PO Box 419026
Rancho Cordova, CA 95741-9026
Phone: 916-464-7268
Fax: 916-526-8004
E-mail: studentsupport@csac.ca.gov

COMPETITIVE CAL GRANT A
Award for California residents who are not recent high school graduates attending an approved college or university within the state. Must show financial need and meet minimum 3.00 GPA requirement.

Award: Grant for use in freshman, sophomore, junior, or senior years; renewable. *Number:* 1000–2000. *Amount:* $5472–$12,192.

Eligibility Requirements: Applicant must be enrolled or expecting to enroll full- or part-time at a two-year or four-year institution or university; resident of California and studying in California. Applicant must have 3.0 GPA or higher. Available to U.S. citizens.

Application Requirements: Application form, financial need analysis, GPA verification. *Deadline:* March 2.

Contact: Catalina Mistler, Chief, Program Administration and Services Division
California Student Aid Commission
PO Box 419026
Rancho Cordova, CA 95741-9026
Phone: 916-464-7268
Fax: 916-526-8004
E-mail: studentsupport@csac.ca.gov

ENTITLEMENT CAL GRANT B
Provide grant funds for access costs for low-income students in an amount not to exceed $1648 and tuition/fee expenses of up to $12,192. Must be California residents and enroll in an undergraduate academic program of not less than one academic year at a qualifying postsecondary institution. Must show financial need and meet the minimum 2.00 GPA requirement.

Award: Grant for use in freshman, sophomore, junior, or senior years; renewable. *Number:* 61,340. *Amount:* $700–$13,665.

Eligibility Requirements: Applicant must be enrolled or expecting to enroll full- or part-time at a two-year or four-year or technical institution or university; resident of California and studying in California. Available to U.S. citizens.

Application Requirements: Application form, financial need analysis. *Deadline:* March 2.

Contact: Catalina Mistler, Chief, Program Administration and Services Division
California Student Aid Commission
PO Box 419026
Rancho Cordova, CA 95741-9026
Phone: 916-464-7268
Fax: 916-526-8004
E-mail: studentsupport@csac.ca.gov

LAW ENFORCEMENT PERSONNEL DEPENDENTS SCHOLARSHIP
• See page 579

CALIFORNIA TEACHERS ASSOCIATION (CTA)

http://www.cta.org/

CALIFORNIA TEACHERS ASSOCIATION SCHOLARSHIP FOR MEMBERS
• See page 541

CAREER COLLEGES AND SCHOOLS OF TEXAS

http://www.ccst.org/

CAREER COLLEGES AND SCHOOLS OF TEXAS SCHOLARSHIP PROGRAM
One-time award available to graduating high school seniors who plan to attend a Texas trade or technical institution. Must be a Texas resident. Criteria selection, which is determined independently by each school's guidance counselors, may be based on academic excellence, financial need, or student leadership. Must be U.S. citizen. Deadline: continuous.

Award: Scholarship for use in freshman year; not renewable. *Number:* up to 27,770. *Amount:* $1000.

Eligibility Requirements: Applicant must be high school student; planning to enroll or expecting to enroll full- or part-time at a technical institution; resident of Texas and studying in Texas. Available to U.S. citizens.

Application Requirements: Application form, recommendations or references. *Deadline:* continuous.

Contact: Jennifer George, Association Manager
Career Colleges and Schools of Texas
823 Congress Avenue, Suite 230
Austin, TX 78701
Phone: 512-479-0425 Ext. 17
Fax: 512-495-9031
E-mail: jgeorge@eami.com

CENTRAL SCHOLARSHIP

http://www.central-scholarship.org

LESSANS FAMILY SCHOLARSHIP
• See page 674

SHOE CITY-WB54/WB50 SCHOLARSHIP
Scholarship for high school seniors who are permanent residents of Maryland or Washington D.C. Four $1500 awards are granted annually. For more information, visit website http://www.centralsb.org.

Award: Scholarship for use in freshman year; not renewable. *Number:* 4. *Amount:* up to $1500.

Eligibility Requirements: Applicant must be high school student; planning to enroll or expecting to enroll full-time at a four-year institution or university and resident of District of Columbia, Maryland. Available to U.S. citizens.

Application Requirements: Application form, community service, essay, financial need analysis, interview, recommendations or references, resume, test scores, transcript. *Deadline:* May 1.

Contact: Roberta Goldman, Program Director
    Phone: 410-415-5558
    Fax: 410-415-5501
    E-mail: rgoldman@central-scholarship.org

STRAUS SCHOLARSHIP PROGRAM FOR UNDERGRADUATE EDUCATION

Scholarship provides assistance to Maryland residents who are full-time undergraduate students in their sophomore, junior, or senior years at an accredited college or university. Renewable grants of up to $5000 each per year will be awarded. If the recipient graduates within four years with a cumulative GPA of 3.0 or higher, an additional $5000 grant will be awarded to apply toward student loan debt.

Award: Scholarship for use in sophomore, junior, or senior years; renewable. *Number:* 5–8. *Amount:* up to $5000.

Eligibility Requirements: Applicant must be enrolled or expecting to enroll full-time at a four-year institution or university and resident of Maryland. Applicant must have 3.0 GPA or higher. Available to U.S. citizens.

Application Requirements: Application form, CSB online application, essay, financial need analysis, interview, resume, transcript. *Deadline:* May 1.

Contact: Roberta Goldman, Program Director
    Phone: 410-415-5558
    Fax: 410-415-5501
    E-mail: rgoldman@central-scholarship.org

CGTRADER

https://www.cgtrader.com/

ANNUAL CGTRADER SCHOLARSHIP

• See page 580

CHICANA/LATINA FOUNDATION

http://www.chicanalatina.org/

SCHOLARSHIPS FOR LATINA STUDENTS ENROLLED IN COLLEGES/UNIVERSITIES IN NORTHERN CALIFORNIA

• See page 674

CHINESE AMERICAN ASSOCIATION OF MINNESOTA

http://www.caam.org/

CHINESE AMERICAN ASSOCIATION OF MINNESOTA (CAAM) SCHOLARSHIPS

• See page 674

COLLEGEBOUND FOUNDATION

http://www.collegeboundfoundation.org/

BALTIMORE RAVENS SCHOLARSHIP PROGRAM

The Baltimore Ravens established this scholarship program to enable local youth to continue their education on a collegiate level. The team has a long-standing history of service to local communities, and this fund will support those who do the same. In addition, this renewable scholarship will be based on financial need and academic achievement. You must: have a cumulative 3.0 GPA or better; demonstrate financial need (include a SAR if available); be accepted to and attend a 4-year college or university; have verifiable community service; submit one (1) reference from an individual who can attest to your commitment to helping others; submit one (1) reference from a teacher, school counselor or administrator; and submit a 1-2 page essay describing the environment in which you live, and the most meaningful contribution you have made as a volunteer to the betterment of your community.

Award: Scholarship for use in freshman, sophomore, junior, or senior years; renewable. *Number:* 1–5. *Amount:* $1–$5000.

Eligibility Requirements: Applicant must be high school student; planning to enroll or expecting to enroll full-time at a four-year institution or university and resident of Maryland. Applicant must have 3.0 GPA or higher. Available to U.S. citizens.

Application Requirements: Application form, community service, essay, interview. *Deadline:* March 1.

Contact: Jennifer Covahey, Associate Program Director, Scholarship
    Programs
    CollegeBound Foundation
    300 Water Street, Suite 300
    Baltimore, MD 21202
    E-mail: jcovahey@collegeboundfoundation.org

CARMEN V. D'ANNA MEMORIAL SCHOLARSHIP OF THE MARS SUPERMARKET EDUCATIONAL FUND

Must be a senior in a Baltimore City public high school. You must be accepted to and attend a Maryland four-year public state college or university; demonstrate financial need; exhibit a strong desire to achieve; and submit an essay providing a "personal statement" or an essay which describes the challenges you have overcome and why you want to attend college (500-1000 words; 2-4 pages).

Award: Scholarship for use in freshman, sophomore, junior, or senior years; renewable. *Number:* 1. *Amount:* $1–$10,000.

Eligibility Requirements: Applicant must be high school student; planning to enroll or expecting to enroll full-time at a four-year institution or university; resident of Maryland and studying in Maryland. Available to U.S. citizens.

Application Requirements: Application form, application form may be submitted online (http://www.collegeboundfoundation.org), essay, financial need analysis, recommendations or references, resume, transcript. *Deadline:* March 1.

Contact: Michael Thornton, Associate Program Director, Scholarship
    Programs
    CollegeBound Foundation
    300 Water Street
    Suite 300
    Baltimore, MD 21202
    Phone: 410-783-2905 Ext. 207
    Fax: 410-727-5786
    E-mail: mthornton@collegeboundfoundation.org

COLLEGEBOUND FOUNDATION LAST DOLLAR GRANT

The Last Dollar Grant is a need-based award for Baltimore City public high school graduates whose expected family contribution and financial aid package total less than the cost to attend college. Students who are awarded a CollegeBound Foundation Last Dollar Grant are eligible to receive a grant of up to $3,000 per year, renewable for up to five (5) years of college. Students must be a current academic year graduate of a Baltimore City public high school. Applicants must demonstrate financial need and be eligible to receive a Pell Grant. Family income must not exceed $75,000 annually.

Award: Grant for use in freshman, sophomore, junior, or senior years; renewable. *Number:* 40–70. *Amount:* $500–$3000.

Eligibility Requirements: Applicant must be high school student; planning to enroll or expecting to enroll full-time at a four-year institution or university and resident of Maryland. Available to U.S. citizens.

Application Requirements: Application form, financial need analysis. *Deadline:* June 1.

Contact: Ms. Jennifer Covahey, Associate Program Director,
    Scholarship Programs
    CollegeBound Foundation
    300 Water Street, Suite 300
    Baltimore, MD 21202
    Phone: 410-783-2905 Ext. 207
    E-mail: jcovahey@collegeboundfoundation.org

DUNBAR CLASS OF 1958 SCHOLARSHIP

The Dunbar Class of 1958 established this scholarship with the intention to give back to the community in which they were raised and went to school. The Class of 1958 views Dunbar as the source of their many successes, and hopes to provide financial assistance so that current graduates have the same opportunities to succeed. You must: be a senior at Paul Laurence Dunbar High School; have a cumulative high school GPA between a 2.0 and a 3.0; and demonstrate financial need.

Award: Scholarship for use in freshman, sophomore, junior, or senior years; not renewable. *Number:* 1–3. *Amount:* $1–$1000.

Eligibility Requirements: Applicant must be high school student; planning to enroll or expecting to enroll full-time at a two-year or four-year institution or university and resident of Maryland. Applicant must have 2.5 GPA or higher. Available to U.S. citizens.

Application Requirements: Application form, essay. *Deadline:* March 1.

Contact: Ms. Jennifer Covahey, Associate Program Director of Scholarships
CollegeBound Foundation
300 Water Street
Baltimore, MD 21202
Phone: 410-783-2905 Ext. 207
E-mail: jcovahey@collegeboundfoundation.org

HY ZOLET STUDENT ATHLETE SCHOLARSHIP

You must be a Baltimore City public high school student-athlete; have a cumulative 2.5 GPA or better; submit at least two (2) letters verifying your participation in high school athletics and evidence you possess the qualities Hy Zolet exemplified, including a good work ethic, fairness and courage, in addition to outstanding leadership and athletic skills; and submit an essay describing your academic and professional goals, why you have chosen them and what you have done to prepare yourself thus far (500-1,000 words; 2-4 pages).

Award: Scholarship for use in freshman, sophomore, junior, or senior years; renewable. *Number:* 4. *Amount:* $1000.

Eligibility Requirements: Applicant must be high school student; planning to enroll or expecting to enroll full-time at a four-year institution or university; resident of Maryland and must have an interest in athletics/sports. Applicant must have 2.5 GPA or higher. Available to U.S. citizens.

Application Requirements: Application form, essay. *Deadline:* March 1.

Contact: Jennifer Covahey, Associate Program Director, Scholarship Programs
CollegeBound Foundation
300 Water Street
Suite 300
Baltimore, MD 21202
Phone: 410-783-2905 Ext. 207
E-mail: jcovahey@collegeboundfoundation.org

KHIA "DJ K-SWIFT" MEMORIAL SCHOLARSHIP

You must: have a cumulative 2.5 GPA or better; submit SAT (CR+M) scores; demonstrate financial need; and submit an essay (500 words) describing the importance of a college education and why you should receive this award.

Award: Scholarship for use in freshman year; not renewable. *Number:* 1–2. *Amount:* $1–$1000.

Eligibility Requirements: Applicant must be high school student; planning to enroll or expecting to enroll full-time at a two-year or four-year institution and resident of Maryland. Applicant must have 2.5 GPA or higher. Available to U.S. citizens.

Application Requirements: Application form. *Deadline:* March 1.

Contact: Ms. Jennifer Covahey, Asscoiate Program Director of Scholarships
CollegeBound Foundation
300 Water Street
Suite 300
Baltimore, MD 21202
Phone: 410-783-2905 Ext. 207
E-mail: jcovahey@collegeboundfoundation.org

LESLIE MOORE FOUNDATION SCHOLARSHIP

You must have verifiable community service; have a cumulative 2.0 GPA or better; submit an essay describing the environment you live in, then describe the most meaningful contribution you have made as a volunteer in your community (500-1000 words; 2-4 pages); and be accepted to and attend a 2 or four-year college or technical school. Finalists must be available to interview with the selection committee.

Award: Scholarship for use in freshman, sophomore, junior, or senior years; renewable. *Number:* 5. *Amount:* $2500.

Eligibility Requirements: Applicant must be high school student; planning to enroll or expecting to enroll full-time at a two-year or four-year institution and resident of Maryland. Available to U.S. citizens.

Application Requirements: Application form, community service, essay, financial need analysis, interview. *Deadline:* March 1.

Contact: Jennifer Covahey, Associate Program Director, Scholarship Programs
CollegeBound Foundation
300 Water Street
Suite 300
Baltimore, MD 21202
Phone: 410-783-2905 Ext. 207
E-mail: jcovahey@collegeboundfoundation.org

LORENZO FELDER SCHOLARSHIP

• *See page 675*

MANAGERIAL AND PROFESSIONAL SOCIETY (MAPS) OF BALTIMORE MERIT SCHOLARSHIP

You must have a cumulative 3.0 GPA or better; an SAT (CR+M) score of at least 950; verifiable community service; and submit an essay (500-1000 words) describing the importance of a college education and community service you have been involved in. Only dues-paying MAPS members and their immediate family members are eligible to apply. Winners must attend a MAPS quarterly meeting held in September.

Award: Scholarship for use in freshman year; not renewable. *Number:* up to 3. *Amount:* $1000.

Eligibility Requirements: Applicant must be high school student; planning to enroll or expecting to enroll full-time at a two-year or four-year institution and resident of Maryland. Applicant must have 3.0 GPA or higher. Available to U.S. citizens.

Application Requirements: *Deadline:* March 1.

Contact: Jennifer Covahey, Associate Program Director, Scholarship Programs
CollegeBound Foundation
300 Water Street
Suite 300
Baltimore, MD 21202
Phone: 410-783-2905 Ext. 207
Fax: 410-727-5786
E-mail: jcovahey@collegeboundfoundation.org

MANAGERIAL AND PROFESSIONAL SOCIETY (MAPS) OF BALTIMORE SERVICE AWARD SCHOLARSHIP

You must have verifiable community service; have a cumulative 2.5 GPA or better; and submit an essay (500-1000 words) describing the importance of a college education and community service you have been involved in. Only dues-paying MAPS members and their immediate family members are eligible to apply. Winners must attend a MAPS quarterly meeting held in September.

Award: Scholarship for use in freshman year; not renewable. *Number:* up to 2. *Amount:* $1000.

Eligibility Requirements: Applicant must be high school student; planning to enroll or expecting to enroll full-time at a two-year or four-year institution or university and resident of Maryland. Applicant must have 2.5 GPA or higher. Available to U.S. citizens.

Application Requirements: *Deadline:* March 1.

Contact: Jennifer Covahey, Associate Program Director, Scholarship Programs
CollegeBound Foundation
300 Water Street
Suite 300
Baltimore, MD 21202
Phone: 410-783-2905 Ext. 207
Fax: 410-727-5786
E-mail: jcovahey@collegeboundfoundation.org

COLLEGE NOW GREATER CLEVELAND, INC.

http://www.collegenowgc.org/

COLLEGE NOW GREATER CLEVELAND ADULT LEARNER PROGRAM SCHOLARSHIP

Scholarship for students pursuing first Associate or Bachelor's degree in an eligible two- or four-year program. Individuals already having a Bachelor's degree are not eligible. Students must be 19 years old or older and must have interrupted the education for at least one year. Applicants must be a resident of Ashtabula, Cuyahoga, Geauga, Lake, Lorain, Mahoning, Medina, Portage, Stark, Summit or Trumbull County. Student must meet income guidelines and maintain a 2.5 GPA. Student must be attending a public or private not for profit institution.

Award: Scholarship for use in freshman, sophomore, junior, or senior years; renewable. *Number:* 250–450. *Amount:* $500–$4000.

Eligibility Requirements: Applicant must be enrolled or expecting to enroll full- or part-time at a two-year or four-year or technical institution or university and resident of Ohio. Applicant must have 2.5 GPA or higher. Available to U.S. citizens.

Application Requirements: Application form, essay, financial need analysis, transcript. *Deadline:* April 15.

Contact: Mr. Robert Durham, Director of Scholarship Services and Financial Aid
College Now Greater Cleveland, Inc.
50Public Square, Suite 1800
Cleveland, OH 44113
Phone: 216-635-0450
Fax: 216-241-6184
E-mail: rdurham@collegenowgc.org

COLLEGE SUCCESS FOUNDATION

http://www.collegesuccessfoundation.org/

GOVERNORS' SCHOLARSHIP FOR FOSTER YOUTH PROGRAM

The Washington State Governor's Scholarship for Foster Youth is a scholarship program that helps young men and women from foster care continue their education and earn a college degree from Washington state. Eligible students must meet specific criteria. The program has been supported by the current and former governors in Proceeds from the Governor's Cup, an annual golf tournament, provide funding for approximately 30-50 new scholars each year. Scholarship award amounts range from $2000 to $4000 depending on the college of attendance. The scholarship can be accessed for up to five years to complete an undergraduate study. Students much be enrolled full-time and maintain satisfactory academic progress in order to renew the scholarship each year.

Award: Scholarship for use in freshman, sophomore, junior, or senior years; renewable. *Number:* 30–50. *Amount:* $2000–$4000.

Eligibility Requirements: Applicant must be high school student; planning to enroll or expecting to enroll full- or part-time at a two-year or four-year institution or university; resident of Washington and studying in Washington. Available to U.S. citizens.

Application Requirements: Application form, application form may be submitted online (http://www.collegesuccessfoundation.org/wa/students/governors-eligibility), essay, recommendations or references, transcript. *Deadline:* March 9.

Contact: Erica Meier, Director, Scholarship Services
Phone: 425-416-2000
Fax: 425-416-2001
E-mail: info@collegesuccessfoundation.org

COLORADO COMMISSION ON HIGHER EDUCATION

http://highered.colorado.gov/cche/mission.html

COLORADO STUDENT GRANT

Grants for Colorado residents attending eligible public, private, or vocational institutions within the state. Students must complete a Free Application for Federal Student Aid (FAFSA) and demonstrate need.

Application deadlines vary by institution. Renewable award for undergraduates. Contact the financial aid office at the college/institution for application and more information.

Award: Grant for use in freshman, sophomore, junior, or senior years; not renewable. *Amount:* $300–$5000.

Eligibility Requirements: Applicant must be enrolled or expecting to enroll full- or part-time at a two-year or four-year or technical institution; resident of Colorado and studying in Colorado. Available to U.S. citizens.

Application Requirements: Application form, financial need analysis. *Deadline:* continuous.

Contact: Celina Duran, Financial Aid Administrator
Colorado Commission on Higher Education
1560 Broadway
Suite 1600
Denver, CO 80202
Phone: 303-866-2723
E-mail: celina.duran@dhe.state.co.us

COLORADO EDUCATIONAL SERVICES AND DEVELOPMENT ASSOCIATION

http://www.cesda.org

CESDA DIVERSITY SCHOLARSHIPS

Award for underrepresented, economically, and disadvantaged high school seniors planning to pursue undergraduate studies at a Colorado college or university. Must be Colorado resident. Applicant must be a first generation student, or member of an underrepresented ethnic or racial minority, and/or show financial need. Minimum 2.8 GPA required.

Award: Scholarship for use in freshman year; not renewable. *Number:* 6. *Amount:* $1000.

Eligibility Requirements: Applicant must be high school student; planning to enroll or expecting to enroll full- or part-time at a two-year or four-year or technical institution or university; resident of Colorado and studying in Colorado. Applicant must have 3.0 GPA or higher. Available to U.S. and non-Canadian citizens.

Application Requirements: Application form, essay, financial need analysis. *Deadline:* April 1.

Contact: Maria Castro Barajas, CESDA Chair
Colorado Educational Services and Development Association
Center for Community, Suite 485
108 UCB
Boulder, CO 80309
Phone: 303-492-2178
E-mail: maria.barajas@colorado.edu

COLORADO MASONS BENEVOLENT FUND ASSOCIATION

http://www.cmbfa.org/scholarship

COLORADO MASONS BENEVOLENT FUND SCHOLARSHIPS

• *See page 581*

COMMUNITY BANKERS ASSOCIATION OF GEORGIA

http://www.cbaofga.com/

JULIAN AND JAN HESTER MEMORIAL SCHOLARSHIP

Scholarship available to Georgia high school seniors who will be entering a Georgia two- or four-year college or university, or a program at a technical institution. Recipients will be named on the basis of merit, and family financial need is not considered. Application must be sponsored by a local community bank, and must include an essay on community banking and what it represents.

Award: Scholarship for use in freshman year; not renewable. *Number:* 4. *Amount:* $1000.

Eligibility Requirements: Applicant must be high school student; planning to enroll or expecting to enroll full-time at a two-year or four-year or technical institution or university; resident of Georgia and studying in Georgia. Available to U.S. citizens.

Application Requirements: Application form, community service, recommendations or references, test scores, transcript. *Deadline:* March 30.

Contact: Lauren Dismuke, Public Relations and Marketing Coordinator
Phone: 770-541-4490
Fax: 770-541-4496
E-mail: lauren@cbaofga.com

COMMUNITY BANKERS ASSOCIATION OF ILLINOIS

http://www.cbai.com/

COMMUNITY BANKERS ASSOC OF IL CHILD OF A BANKER SCHOLARSHIP
• *See page 541*

COMMUNITY BANKERS ASSOC. OF IL ESSAY CONTEST
• *See page 582*

COMMUNITY FOUNDATION FOR GREATER ATLANTA, INC.

http://cfgreateratlanta.org/

GEORGE AND PEARL STRICKLAND SCHOLARSHIP

For undergraduate or graduate students with financial need pursuing degrees at Atlanta University Center Colleges. For complete eligibility requirements and for an application, please visit cfgreateratlanta.org.

Award: Scholarship for use in freshman, sophomore, junior, senior, or graduate years; not renewable. *Number:* 1–25. *Amount:* $1000–$3000.

Eligibility Requirements: Applicant must be enrolled or expecting to enroll full- or part-time at a four-year institution or university; resident of Georgia and studying in Georgia. Applicant must have 2.5 GPA or higher. Available to U.S. citizens.

Application Requirements: Application form, community service, essay, financial need analysis. *Deadline:* February 15.

NANCY PENN LYONS SCHOLARSHIP FUND

Award for graduating high school seniors with financial need living in Georgia who have been accepted for enrollment at prestigious or out-of-state universities. (Due to the timing of application, college acceptance will be verified before scholarships are awarded but are not necessary at time of application). Please visit the website (www.cfgreateratlanta.org) for complete eligibility requirements and link to the application.

Award: Scholarship for use in freshman, sophomore, junior, or senior years; renewable. *Number:* 1–5. *Amount:* $5000.

Eligibility Requirements: Applicant must be high school student; planning to enroll or expecting to enroll full-time at a four-year institution or university and resident of Georgia. Applicant must have 3.0 GPA or higher. Available to U.S. citizens.

Application Requirements: Application form, community service, driver's license, essay, financial need analysis, interview. *Deadline:* February 15.

COMMUNITY FOUNDATION OF WESTERN MASSACHUSETTS

http://www.communityfoundation.org/

CALEB L. BUTLER SCHOLARSHIP

Scholarship for graduating high school seniors from western MA who are in the custody of the Department of Children and Families (DCF), formerly the Department of Social Services (DSS). Preference given to former or current residents of Hillcrest Educational Centers. For more information, please see website http://communityfoundation.org/.

Award: Scholarship for use in freshman year; not renewable.

Eligibility Requirements: Applicant must be high school student; planning to enroll or expecting to enroll full- or part-time at a two-year or four-year institution or university and resident of Massachusetts. Available to U.S. citizens.

Application Requirements: Application form, essay, financial need analysis, transcript. *Deadline:* March 31.

Contact: Dotty Theriaque, Program Assistant for Scholarships
Community Foundation of Western Massachusetts
1500 Main Street
PO Box 15769
Springfield, MA 01115
Phone: 413-732-2858
Fax: 413-733-8565
E-mail: scholar@communityfoundation.org

CHRISTINE MITUS ROSE MEMORIAL SCHOLARSHIP

Scholarship for students who have had a parent die; preference to those who have had a parent die from cancer. Must be from western Massachusetts. For more information, see website http://communityfoundation.org/.

Award: Scholarship for use in freshman, sophomore, junior, senior, or graduate years; not renewable.

Eligibility Requirements: Applicant must be enrolled or expecting to enroll full- or part-time at a two-year or four-year institution or university and resident of Massachusetts. Available to U.S. citizens.

Application Requirements: Application form, essay, financial need analysis, transcript. *Deadline:* March 31.

Contact: Dotty Theriaque, Program Assistant for Scholarships
Community Foundation of Western Massachusetts
1500 Main Street
PO Box 15769
Springfield, MA 01115
Phone: 413-732-2858
Fax: 413-733-8565
E-mail: scholar@communityfoundation.org

DIANA & LEON FEFFER SCHOLARSHIP

Scholarship available to residents of western Massachusetts. For more information, please see website http://communityfoundation.org/.

Award: Scholarship for use in freshman, sophomore, junior, senior, or graduate years; not renewable.

Eligibility Requirements: Applicant must be enrolled or expecting to enroll full- or part-time at a two-year or four-year institution or university and resident of Massachusetts. Available to U.S. citizens.

Application Requirements: Application form, essay, financial need analysis, transcript. *Deadline:* March 31.

Contact: Dotty Theriaque, Program Assistant for Scholarships
Community Foundation of Western Massachusetts
1500 Main Street
PO Box 15769
Springfield, MA 01115
Phone: 413-732-2858
Fax: 413-733-8565
E-mail: scholar@communityfoundation.org

FRED K. LANE SCHOLARSHIP

Scholarship for graduating high school seniors who are past or current members (individual or family) or employees of the Orchards Golf Course in South Hadley. For more information, see website http://communityfoundation.org/.

Award: Scholarship for use in freshman year; not renewable.

Eligibility Requirements: Applicant must be high school student; planning to enroll or expecting to enroll full- or part-time at a two-year or four-year institution or university and resident of Massachusetts. Available to U.S. citizens.

Application Requirements: Application form, essay, financial need analysis, transcript. *Deadline:* March 31.

Contact: Dotty Theriaque, Program Assistant for Scholarships
Community Foundation of Western Massachusetts
1500 Main Street
PO Box 15769
Springfield, MA 01115
Phone: 413-732-2858
Fax: 413-733-8565
E-mail: scholar@communityfoundation.org

HELLESPONT SOCIETY SCHOLARSHIP FUND
• *See page 675*

HORACE HILL SCHOLARSHIP
• *See page 541*

JAMES L. SHRIVER SCHOLARSHIP
Scholarships available to students from western MA pursuing technical careers. For additional information, see website communityfoundation.org/.

Award: Scholarship for use in freshman, sophomore, junior, senior, or graduate years; not renewable.

Eligibility Requirements: Applicant must be enrolled or expecting to enroll full- or part-time at a four-year institution or university and resident of Massachusetts. Available to U.S. citizens.

Application Requirements: Application form, essay, financial need analysis. *Deadline:* March 31.

Contact: Dotty Theriaque, Program Assistant for Scholarships
Community Foundation of Western Massachusetts
1500 Main Street
PO Box 15769
Springfield, MA 01115
Phone: 413-732-2858
Fax: 413-733-8565
E-mail: scholar@communityfoundation.org

KIMBER RICHTER FAMILY SCHOLARSHIP
Scholarship available to graduating high school seniors of the Baha'i faith from western Massachusetts. For more information, see website http://communityfoundation.org/.

Award: Scholarship for use in freshman year; not renewable.

Eligibility Requirements: Applicant must be high school student; planning to enroll or expecting to enroll full- or part-time at a two-year or four-year institution or university and resident of Massachusetts. Available to U.S. citizens.

Application Requirements: Application form, essay, financial need analysis, transcript. *Deadline:* March 31.

Contact: Dotty Theriaque, Program Assistant for Scholarships
Community Foundation of Western Massachusetts
1500 Main Street
PO Box 15769
Springfield, MA 01115
Phone: 413-732-2858
Fax: 413-733-8565
E-mail: scholar@communityfoundation.org

VIRGINILLO-FALVO SCHOLARSHIP FUND
Scholarship for needy youth of western Massachusetts to attend college. For more information, please see website http://communityfoundation.org/.

Award: Scholarship for use in freshman, sophomore, junior, senior, or graduate years; not renewable.

Eligibility Requirements: Applicant must be enrolled or expecting to enroll full- or part-time at a two-year or four-year institution or university and resident of Massachusetts. Available to U.S. citizens.

Application Requirements: Application form, essay, financial need analysis, transcript. *Deadline:* March 31.

Contact: Dotty Theriaque, Program Assistant for Scholarships
Community Foundation of Western Massachusetts
1500 Main Street
PO Box 15769
Springfield, MA 01115
Phone: 413-732-2858
Fax: 413-733-8565
E-mail: scholar@communityfoundation.org

WILLIAM A. AND VINNIE E. DEXTER SCHOLARSHIP
Scholarship for graduating high school seniors in western Massachusetts. For more information, please see website http://communityfoundation.org/.

Award: Scholarship for use in freshman year; not renewable.

Eligibility Requirements: Applicant must be high school student; planning to enroll or expecting to enroll full- or part-time at a two-year or four-year institution or university and resident of Massachusetts. Available to U.S. citizens.

Application Requirements: Application form, essay, financial need analysis, transcript. *Deadline:* March 31.

Contact: Dotty Theriaque, Program Assistant for Scholarships
Community Foundation of Western Massachusetts
1500 Main Street
PO Box 15769
Springfield, MA 01115
Phone: 413-732-2858
Fax: 413-733-8565
E-mail: scholar@communityfoundation.org

CONNECTICUT ARMY NATIONAL GUARD
http://ct.ng.mil/Pages/default.aspx

CONNECTICUT ARMY NATIONAL GUARD 100% TUITION WAIVER
• *See page 647*

CONNECTICUT ASSOCIATION OF LATINOS IN HIGHER EDUCATION (CALAHE)
http://www.calahe.org/

CONNECTICUT ASSOCIATION OF LATINOS IN HIGHER EDUCATION SCHOLARSHIPS
• *See page 676*

CONNECTICUT COMMUNITY FOUNDATION
http://www.conncf.org/

REGIONAL AND RESTRICTED SCHOLARSHIP AWARD PROGRAM
Supports accredited college or university study for residents of the Connecticut community twenty-one town service area. In addition, a variety of restricted award programs are based on specific fund criteria (residency, school, course of study, etc.). Scholarships are awarded on a competitive basis with consideration given to academic record, extracurricular activities, work experience, financial need, reference letter, and an essay.

Award: Scholarship for use in freshman, sophomore, junior, or senior years; renewable. *Number:* 200–300. *Amount:* $2000–$5000.

Eligibility Requirements: Applicant must be enrolled or expecting to enroll full-time at a two-year or four-year institution or university and resident of Connecticut. Applicant must have 3.0 GPA or higher. Available to U.S. citizens.

Application Requirements: Application form, community service, essay, financial need analysis. *Deadline:* March 15.

Contact: Ms. Tallitha Richardson, Program and Scholarship Associate
Connecticut Community Foundation
43 Field Street
Waterbury, CT 06702
Phone: 203-753-1315 Ext. 126
E-mail: scholarships@conncf.org

CONNECTICUT OFFICE OF HIGHER EDUCATION
http://www.ctohe.org

GOVERNOR'S SCHOLARSHIP PROGRAM—ACADEMIC INCENTIVE AWARD
The Academic Incentive Award provides additional grant funds to Governor's Scholarship Program need-based aid recipients who are on track to complete their degree in the required time frame, 2 or 4 years. Eligible students must also demonstrate strong academic performance while in college.

Award: Grant for use in sophomore, junior, or senior years; renewable. *Number:* 603. *Amount:* $1000–$1200.

Eligibility Requirements: Applicant must be enrolled or expecting to enroll full-time at a two-year or four-year institution or university; resident of Connecticut and studying in Connecticut. Applicant must have 3.0 GPA or higher. Available to U.S. citizens.

Application Requirements: Financial need analysis. *Deadline:* continuous.

Contact: Ms. Lynne Little, Financial Aid Consultant
Connecticut Office of Higher Education
61 Woodland Street
Hartford, CT 06105
Phone: 860-947-1855
E-mail: gsp@ctohe.org

GOVERNOR'S SCHOLARSHIP PROGRAM—NEED/MERIT SCHOLARSHIP

This program provides scholarships to eligible Connecticut residents attending eligible institutions of higher education in Connecticut. Eligibility is based on a minimum SAT score of 1800, or a minimum ACT score of 27 and/or top 20% ranking in the students junior year high school class. Applications must be filed through the students high school counseling office. In addition, all students must file a Free Application for Federal Student Aid (FAFSA) and, as a result, have an Expected Family Contribution (EFC) equal to or less than the annual allowable maximum EFC. Both the application and FAFSA must be processed by February 15th.

Award: Scholarship for use in freshman, sophomore, junior, or senior years; renewable. *Number:* 2404. *Amount:* $900–$5000.

Eligibility Requirements: Applicant must be enrolled or expecting to enroll full- or part-time at a two-year or four-year institution or university; resident of Connecticut and studying in Connecticut. Applicant must have 3.5 GPA or higher. Available to U.S. citizens.

Application Requirements: Application form, financial need analysis. *Deadline:* February 15.

Contact: Ms. Lynne Goodwin, Student Financial Aid Consultant
Connecticut Office of Higher Education
39 Woodland Street
Hartford, CT 06105
Phone: 860-947-1855
E-mail: sfa@ctohe.org

ROBERTA B. WILLIS SCHOLARSHIP PROGRAM—NEED-BASED GRANT

• *See page 676*

CONNECTICUT WOMEN'S HALL OF FAME

http://www.cwhf.org

EILEEN KRAUS SCHOLARSHIP

The Eileen Kraus Scholarship honors Connecticut Women's Hall of Fame 2002 Inductee Eileen Kraus and recognizes an outstanding young Connecticut woman embarking on her first year of college or university. Applicants should be a female residing in Connecticut in their final year of high school or a recent high school graduate. She must be intending to enroll in her first year of college or university to obtain an Associate or Bachelor degree. Applicants should visit the scholarship website for an application form and instructions. A two-page essay is required answering the question, "Among the 115 Inductees of the Hall, who do you find the most inspiring, and how do you see the legacy of this woman reflected in your own goals?" Deadline for submission is February 15, 2017. Award winner will be announced March 31, 2017. Award recipient is asked to attend the CWHF 24th Annual Induction Ceremony on November 9, 2017, in Hartford, CT.

Award: Scholarship for use in freshman year; not renewable. *Number:* 1. *Amount:* $5000.

Eligibility Requirements: Applicant must be high school student; planning to enroll or expecting to enroll full- or part-time at a two-year or four-year institution or university; female and resident of Connecticut. Available to U.S. citizens.

Application Requirements: Application form, essay. *Deadline:* February 15.

Contact: Ms. Tina Carlson, Programs Coordinator
Connecticut Women's Hall of Fame
Connecticut Women's Hall of Fame
320 Fitch Street
New Haven, CT 06515
Phone: 203-3929008
Fax: 203-3929012
E-mail: scholarships@cwhf.org

CORPORATION FOR OHIO APPALACHIAN DEVELOPMENT (COAD)

http://www.coadinc.org/

DAVID V. STIVISON APPALACHIAN COMMUNITY ACTION SCHOLARSHIP FUND

Provides financial assistance to students who are residents in the Corporation for Ohio Appalachian Development's service area and want to attend college but lack the required resources. Individual income must not exceed 200 percent of Federal Poverty Level. See website for application information - http://www.coadinc.org/scholarships

Award: Scholarship for use in freshman, sophomore, junior, or senior years; not renewable. *Number:* 1–30. *Amount:* $500–$1500.

Eligibility Requirements: Applicant must be enrolled or expecting to enroll full-time at a two-year or four-year institution or university and resident of Ohio. Available to U.S. citizens.

Application Requirements: Application form, financial need analysis, personal photograph. *Deadline:* April 1.

Contact: Allyssa Mefford, Operations Director
Phone: 740-594-8499 Ext. 213
E-mail: amefford@coadinc.org

COURAGE KENNY REHABILITATION INSTITUTE, VOCATIONAL SERVICES DEPARTMENT

http://www.allinahealth.org/couragekenny

SCHOLARSHIP FOR PEOPLE WITH DISABILITIES

Award provides financial assistance to students with sensory or physical disabilities. May reapply each year. Applicant must be pursuing educational goals or technical expertise beyond high school. Must be U.S. citizen and resident of Minnesota, or participate in Courage Kenny Rehabilitation Services. A Statement of Intention essay must be submitted along with application form - http://www.allinahealth.org/Courage-Kenny-Rehabilitation-Institute/Programs-and-services/Scholarship-for-people-with-disabilities/

Award: Scholarship for use in freshman, sophomore, junior, or senior years; not renewable. *Number:* 15–19. *Amount:* $500–$1000.

Eligibility Requirements: Applicant must be enrolled or expecting to enroll full-time at a two-year or four-year or technical institution or university and resident of Minnesota. Available to U.S. citizens.

Application Requirements: Application form, essay, financial need analysis, interview. *Deadline:* May 31.

Contact: Ms. Leanne Jackson, Vocational Evaluator
Courage Kenny Rehabilitation Institute, Vocational Services Department
Courage Kenny Rehabilitation Institute
MR #78404
Minneapolis, MN 55422
Phone: 612-775-2564
E-mail: leanne.jackson-butala@allina.com

CRUMLEY ROBERTS ATTORNEYS AT LAW

http://www.crumleyroberts.com/

CRUMLEY ROBERTS FOUNDER'S SCHOLARSHIP

The Founder's Scholarship is awarded to graduating North Carolina High School Seniors who will be attending a four-year college or university in pursuit of a degree.

Award: Scholarship for use in freshman year; not renewable. *Number:* 3–5. *Amount:* $2500.

Eligibility Requirements: Applicant must be high school student; planning to enroll or expecting to enroll full-time at a four-year institution or university and resident of North Carolina. Available to U.S. citizens.

Application Requirements: Application form, essay. *Deadline:* February 1.

Contact: Mr. Adam Amundson
Crumley Roberts Attorneys at Law
2400 Freeman Mill Road
Suite 200
Greensboro, NC 27406
Phone: 800-288-1529
E-mail: acamundson@crumleyroberts.com

CRUMLEY ROBERTS NEXT STEP SCHOLARSHIP

Each year, Crumley Roberts awards three $2,500 scholarships to North Carolina community college students planning to transfer to accredited four-year colleges or universities.

Award: Scholarship for use in freshman year; not renewable. *Number:* 3–5. *Amount:* $2500.

Eligibility Requirements: Applicant must be enrolled or expecting to enroll full-time at a four-year institution or university and resident of North Carolina. Available to U.S. citizens.

Application Requirements: Application form, essay. *Deadline:* February 1.

Contact: Adam Amundson
Crumley Roberts Attorneys at Law
2400 Freeman Mill Road
Suite 200
Greensboro, NC 27406
Phone: 800-288-1529
E-mail: acamundson@crumleyroberts.com

THE DALLAS FOUNDATION

http://www.dallasfoundation.org/

THE AKIN AYODELE SCHOLARSHIP IN MEMORY OF MICHAEL TILMON

Michael Tilmon was a best friend and teammate of Dallas Cowboy Akin Ayodele while at MacArthur High School. Sadly, he passed away in a car accident in March of 1997. This scholarship program is intended to honor those who demonstrate the type of character and integrity that Michael possessed.

Award: Scholarship for use in freshman year; not renewable. *Amount:* $10,000.

Eligibility Requirements: Applicant must be high school student; planning to enroll or expecting to enroll full-time at a two-year or four-year institution or university and resident of Texas.

Application Requirements: Application form, transcript. *Deadline:* April 15.

Contact: Rachel Lasseter, Program Associate
Phone: 214-741-9898
E-mail: scholarships@dallasfoundation.org

DR. DAN J. AND PATRICIA S. PICKARD SCHOLARSHIP
• *See page 677*

DR. DON AND ROSE MARIE BENTON SCHOLARSHIP

Award is available to students, parents of students and volunteers who have been affiliated with Trinity River Mission in Dallas, Texas. Must be enrolled in a graduate or undergraduate program in a regionally accredited college or university. Scholarship is renewable for two years if the student maintains a specified grade point average and fulfills all reporting requirements as determined by the Scholarship Committee.

Award: Scholarship for use in freshman, sophomore, junior, senior, graduate, or postgraduate years; renewable. *Number:* 1–3. *Amount:* $1500.

Eligibility Requirements: Applicant must be enrolled or expecting to enroll full-time at a two-year or four-year institution or university and resident of Texas.

Application Requirements: Application form, transcript. *Deadline:* April 1.

Contact: Ms. Dolores Sosa Green, Trinity River Mission
The Dallas Foundation
2060 Singleton Boulevard, Suite 104
Dallas, TX 75212
Phone: 214-744-5648

THE LANDON RUSNAK SCHOLARSHIP

The Landon Rusnak Scholarship Fund was established at The Dallas Foundation in 2007. This scholarship is established by the employees of LEAM Drilling Systems, Inc. and Conroe Machine, LLC in memory of Landon Rusnak, son of David and Janet Rusnak and brother of Cady Rusnak. Landon's sister Cady is an active member of the Mexia High School Black Cat Band.

Award: Scholarship for use in freshman year; not renewable. *Number:* 1. *Amount:* $3000.

Eligibility Requirements: Applicant must be high school student; planning to enroll or expecting to enroll full-time at a two-year or four-year institution or university; resident of Texas and must have an interest in music.

Application Requirements: Application form, financial need analysis, transcript. *Deadline:* February 28.

Contact: Rachel Lasseter, Program Associate
Phone: 214-741-9898
E-mail: scholarships@dallasfoundation.org

THE MAYOR'S CHESAPEAKE ENERGY SCHOLARSHIP

The Mayor's Chesapeake Energy Scholarship was established at The Dallas Foundation by Chesapeake Energy Corporation. The goal of the Fund is to make a college degree or vocational certification possible for minority and socially disadvantaged youth. Graduating students in the Dallas ISD are eligible to apply. Applicants should be female or a member of a minority group. Applicants must have participated in the Education is Freedom program.

Award: Scholarship for use in freshman, sophomore, junior, or senior years; renewable. *Amount:* $20,000.

Eligibility Requirements: Applicant must be high school student; planning to enroll or expecting to enroll full-time at a two-year or four-year or technical institution or university and resident of Texas. Applicant must have 3.0 GPA or higher. Available to U.S. citizens.

Application Requirements: Application form, financial need analysis, test scores, transcript. *Deadline:* April 15.

Contact: Rachel Lasseter, Program Associate
Phone: 214-741-9898
E-mail: scholarships@dallasfoundation.org

TOMMY TRANCHIN AWARD

Established at The Dallas Foundation to support students with physical, emotional or intellectual disabilities who have excelled or shown promise in a chosen field of interest. Tommy's family wants to recognize his creativity and his refusal to allow his disability to limit his personal growth by helping others to develop their own talents. Applicants should be residents of North Texas.

Award: Scholarship for use in freshman year; not renewable. *Amount:* $1500.

Eligibility Requirements: Applicant must be high school student; planning to enroll or expecting to enroll full-time at a two-year or four-year or technical institution or university and resident of Texas.

Application Requirements: Application form, physical, proof of physical, emotional or intellectual disability. *Deadline:* March 5.

Contact: Rachel Lasseter, Program Associate
Phone: 214-741-9898
E-mail: scholarships@dallasfoundation.org

DANIEL P. BUTTAFUOCO & ASSOCIATES

http://www.1800nowhurt.com

YOUNG CHRISTIAN LEADERS SCHOLARSHIP
• *See page 712*

DANIELS FUND

http://www.danielsfund.org/Scholarships/Scholars/Index.asp#hide1

DANIELS SCHOLARSHIP PROGRAM

The Daniels Scholarship is an exciting and challenging program that provides the opportunity to obtain a four-year college education at any accredited nonprofit college or university in the United States, complete with financial and personal support throughout the journey. The Daniels Scholarship Program offers resources, encouragement, and inspiration far beyond the financial assistance needed to earn a college degree. Our goal is not only to help Daniels Scholars succeed in college, but to ensure that they thrive beyond their years in college. Every year, Daniels Scholars are selected from our four-state region of Colorado, New Mexico, Utah, and Wyoming. Daniels Scholars currently attend more than 200 colleges and universities in 44 states. To date, the Daniels Scholarship Program has provided more than $108.5 million in undergraduate scholarships to more than 3,000 students.

Award: Scholarship for use in freshman, sophomore, junior, or senior years; renewable. *Number:* 230.

Eligibility Requirements: Applicant must be high school student; planning to enroll or expecting to enroll full-time at a four-year institution or university and resident of Colorado, New Mexico, Utah, Wyoming. Available to U.S. citizens.

Application Requirements: Application form, application form may be submitted online(www.danielsfund.org/Scholarships/Scholars/Index.asp#hide1), community service, driver's license, essay, financial need analysis, interview, personal photograph, recommendations or references, test scores, transcript. *Deadline:* November 13.

Contact: Adm. Laura Steffen, Assistant Vice President
Daniels Fund
101 Monroe Street
Denver, CO 80206
Phone: 720-941-4455
E-mail: lsteffen@danielsfund.org

DELAWARE HIGHER EDUCATION OFFICE

http://www.doe.k12.de.us

DIAMOND STATE SCHOLARSHIP

Award for legal residents of Delaware who are U.S. citizens or eligible non-citizens. Must be enrolled as a full-time student in a degree program at a nonprofit, regionally accredited institution. Minimum 3.0 GPA required. High school seniors should rank in upper quarter of class and have a combined score of at least 1800 on the SAT.

Award: Scholarship for use in freshman year; renewable. *Number:* 50. *Amount:* $1250.

Eligibility Requirements: Applicant must be high school student; planning to enroll or expecting to enroll full-time at a four-year institution or university and resident of Delaware. Applicant must have 3.0 GPA or higher. Available to U.S. citizens.

Application Requirements: Application form, essay, test scores, transcript. *Deadline:* March 22.

Contact: Ms. Carylin Brinkley, Program Administrator
Delaware Higher Education Office
401 Federal Street
Suite 2
Dover, DE 19901
Phone: 302-735-4120
Fax: 302-739-5894
E-mail: cbrinkley@doe.k12.de.us

EDUCATIONAL BENEFITS FOR CHILDREN OF DECEASED VETERANS

• *See page 583*

FIRST STATE MANUFACTURED HOUSING ASSOCIATION SCHOLARSHIP

Award for legal residents of Delaware who are high school seniors or former graduates seeking to further their education. Must have been a resident of a manufactured home for at least one year prior to the application. Evaluated on scholastic record, financial need, essay, and recommendations. Award for any type of accredited two- or four-year degree program, or for any accredited training, licensing, or certification program.

Award: Scholarship for use in freshman, sophomore, junior, or senior years; renewable. *Number:* up to 2. *Amount:* up to $2000.

Eligibility Requirements: Applicant must be enrolled or expecting to enroll full- or part-time at a two-year or four-year or technical institution or university and resident of Delaware. Available to U.S. citizens.

Application Requirements: Application form, essay, FAFSA, financial need analysis, recommendations or references, transcript. *Deadline:* March 7.

Contact: Ms. Carylin Brinkley, Program Administrator
Delaware Higher Education Office
401 Federal Street
Suite 2
Dover, DE 19901
Phone: 302-735-4120
Fax: 302-739-5894
E-mail: cbrinkley@doe.k12.de.us

GOVERNOR'S EDUCATION GRANT FOR WORKING ADULTS

Grants for part-time undergraduate students attending Delaware College of Art and Design, Delaware State University, Delaware Technical and Community College, Goldey-Beacom College, University of Delaware, Wesley College, Widener University (Delaware Campus), PolyTech Adult division, Sussex Tech Adult division, or Wilmington College. Must be at least 18 years old, a resident of Delaware, and employed by a company in Delaware that contributes to the Blue Collar Training Fund Program.

Award: Grant for use in freshman, sophomore, junior, or senior years; not renewable. *Number:* up to 100. *Amount:* $2000.

Eligibility Requirements: Applicant must be enrolled or expecting to enroll full- or part-time at a two-year or four-year or technical institution or university; resident of Delaware and studying in Delaware. Available to U.S. and non-U.S. citizens.

Application Requirements: Application form. *Deadline:* varies.

Contact: Ms. Carylin Brinkley, Program Administrator
Delaware Higher Education Office
401 Federal Street
Suite 2
Dover, DE 19901
Phone: 302-735-4120
Fax: 302-739-5894
E-mail: cbrinkley@doe.k12.de.us

SCHOLARSHIP INCENTIVE PROGRAM (SCIP)

Award for legal residents of Delaware who are U.S. citizens or eligible non-citizens. Must demonstrate substantial financial need and enroll full-time in an undergraduate degree program at a nonprofit, regionally accredited institution in Delaware or Pennsylvania. Minimum 2.5 GPA required.

Award: Grant for use in freshman, sophomore, junior, senior, or graduate years; not renewable. *Number:* 700–2200. *Amount:* $700–$2200.

Eligibility Requirements: Applicant must be enrolled or expecting to enroll full-time at a two-year or four-year institution or university; resident of Delaware and studying in Delaware, Pennsylvania. Applicant must have 2.5 GPA or higher. Available to U.S. citizens.

Application Requirements: Application form, FAFSA, financial need analysis, transcript. *Deadline:* April 15.

Contact: Ms. Carylin Brinkley, Program Administrator
Delaware Higher Education Office
401 Federal Street
Suite 2
Dover, DE 19901
Phone: 302-735-4120
Fax: 302-739-5894
E-mail: cbrinkley@doe.k12.de.us

DENVER FOUNDATION

http://www.denverfoundation.org/

REISHER FAMILY SCHOLARSHIP FUND

Scholarships awarded to Colorado residents who attend Metropolitan State College, the University of Northern Colorado, and the University of Colorado at Denver. Sophomores or transferring juniors who do not have sufficient funding to otherwise complete their degrees are eligible to apply. Must have at least a 3.0 GPA.

Award: Scholarship for use in sophomore or junior years; not renewable.

Eligibility Requirements: Applicant must be enrolled or expecting to enroll full-time at a four-year institution or university; resident of Colorado and studying in Colorado. Applicant must have 3.0 GPA or higher. Available to U.S. citizens.

Application Requirements: Application form. *Deadline:* varies.

Contact: Karla Bieniulis, Scholarship Committee
Phone: 303-300-1790 Ext. 103
Fax: 303-300-6547
E-mail: info@denverfoundation.org

DIAMANTE, INC.

http://www.diamanteinc.org/

LATINO DIAMANTE SCHOLARSHIP FUND

• See page 583

DIRECT ENERGY

https://www.directenergy.com/

DIRECT ENERGY LIVE BRIGHTER SCHOLARSHIP

• See page 584

DISTRICT OF COLUMBIA OFFICE OF THE STATE SUPERINTENDENT OF EDUCATION

http://www.osse.dc.gov/

DC TUITION ASSISTANCE GRANT PROGRAM (DCTAG)

Grant pays the difference between in-state and out-of-state tuition and fees at any public college or university in the United States, Guam, Puerto Rico or U.S. Virgin Islands, up to $10,000 per year. It also pays up to $2500 per year of tuition and fees at private colleges and universities in the Washington metropolitan area and at historically black colleges and universities throughout the United States. Students must be enrolled in a degree-granting program at an eligible institution, and be domiciled in the District of Columbia.

Award: Grant for use in freshman, sophomore, junior, or senior years; not renewable. *Number:* 5999–6000. *Amount:* $2500–$10,000.

Eligibility Requirements: Applicant must be enrolled or expecting to enroll full- or part-time at a two-year or four-year institution or university and resident of District of Columbia. Available to U.S. citizens.

Application Requirements: Application form, financial need analysis. *Deadline:* June 30.

Contact: Dr. Antoinette Mitchell, Assistant Superintendent, Postsecondary and Career Education
District of Columbia Office of the State Superintendent of Education
810 First Street, NE, 3rd Floor
Washington, DC 20002
Phone: 202-727-2824
E-mail: antoinette.mitchell@dc.gov

DIXIE BOYS BASEBALL

http://www.dixie.org/boys

DIXIE BOYS BASEBALL BERNIE VARNADORE SCHOLARSHIP PROGRAM

Eleven scholarships presented annually to deserving high school seniors who have participated in the Dixie Boys Baseball Program. Citizenship, scholarship, residency in a state with Dixie Baseball Programs and financial need are considered in determining the awards.

Award: Scholarship for use in freshman year; not renewable. *Number:* 11. *Amount:* $1250.

Eligibility Requirements: Applicant must be high school student; planning to enroll or expecting to enroll full-time at a two-year or four-year institution or university; resident of Alabama, Arkansas, Florida, Georgia, Louisiana, Mississippi, North Carolina, South Carolina, Tennessee, Texas, Virginia and must have an interest in athletics/sports. Available to U.S. citizens.

Application Requirements: Application form, financial need analysis, personal photograph. *Deadline:* April 1.

Contact: Mr. James Jones, Commissioner/CEO
Dixie Boys Baseball
PO Box 8263
Dothan, AL 36304
Phone: 334-793-3331
E-mail: jjones29@sw.rr.com

DIXIE YOUTH SCHOLARSHIP PROGRAM

Scholarships are presented annually to deserving high school seniors who participated in the Dixie Youth Baseball program while age 12 and under. Financial need is considered. Scholarship value is $2000.

Award: Scholarship for use in freshman year; not renewable. *Number:* up to 70. *Amount:* $2000.

Eligibility Requirements: Applicant must be high school student; planning to enroll or expecting to enroll full-time at a two-year or four-year or technical institution or university; resident of Alabama, Arkansas, Florida, Georgia, Louisiana, Mississippi, North Carolina, South Carolina, Tennessee, Texas, Virginia and must have an interest in athletics/sports. Available to U.S. citizens.

Application Requirements: 1040 form, application form, essay, financial need analysis, personal photograph, recommendations or references, transcript. *Deadline:* March 1.

Contact: Scholarship Chairman
Dixie Boys Baseball
PO Box 877
Marshall, TX 75671-0877
E-mail: dyb@dixie.org

DON'T MESS WITH TEXAS

http://www.dontmesswithtexas.org/

DON'T MESS WITH TEXAS SCHOLARSHIP PROGRAM

Scholarship for Texas graduating high school seniors who plan to attend accredited two- or four-year colleges or public or private universities in Texas.

Award: Scholarship for use in freshman year; not renewable. *Number:* 2–3. *Amount:* $2000–$6000.

Eligibility Requirements: Applicant must be high school student; planning to enroll or expecting to enroll full- or part-time at a two-year or four-year institution or university; resident of Texas and studying in Texas. Available to U.S. and non-U.S. citizens.

Application Requirements: Application form, essay. *Deadline:* March 26.

Contact: Brenda Flores-Dollar, Programs Manager
Don't Mess With Texas
Texas Department of Transportation
Don't mess with Texas, 150 E. Riverside Dr.
Austin, TX 78704
Phone: 512-486-5904
E-mail: scholarship@dontmesswithtexas.org

EAST BAY COLLEGE FUND

http://www.eastbaycollegefund.org/

GREAT EXPECTATIONS AWARD

Program provides renewable scholarships, mentoring, college counseling, and life skills training. Must have at least 3.0 cumulative GPA. Restricted to graduating seniors of Oakland, California public high schools.

Award: Scholarship for use in freshman, sophomore, junior, or senior years; renewable. *Number:* 50. *Amount:* $16,000.

Eligibility Requirements: Applicant must be high school student; planning to enroll or expecting to enroll full-time at a four-year institution or university and resident of California. Applicant must have 3.0 GPA or higher. Available to U.S. citizens.

Application Requirements: Application form, application form may be submitted online (https://www.scholarselect.com/scholarships/13454-2014-east-bay-college-fund-great-expectations-scholarship-program), essay, financial need analysis, interview, recommendations or references, transcript. *Deadline:* February 13.

Contact: Yancie Davis, College Access and Success Manager
East Bay College Fund
2201 Broadway, Suite 208
Oakland, CA 94612
Phone: 510-836-8900
Fax: 510-550-7876
E-mail: yancie@eastbaycollegefund.org

EAST LOS ANGELES COMMUNITY UNION (TELACU) SCHOLARSHIP PROGRAM

http://www.telacu.com/

TELACU EDUCATION FOUNDATION

Applicant must be a first-generation college student from a low-income family and have a minimum GPA of 2.5. Must attend partnering colleges and universities and be enrolled full-time for the entire academic year. California applicants: Must be permanent resident of unincorporated East Los Angeles, Bell Gardens, Commerce, Huntington Park, City of Los Angeles, Montebello, Monterey Park, Pico Rivera, Pomona and the Inland Empire, Santa Ana, South Gate, or other communities selected by foundation. Texas applicants: Must be permanent resident of San Antonio or Austin. Illinois Applicants: Must be permanent resident of Greater Chicagoland Area. New York applicants: Must be permanent resident of the state of New York.

Award: Scholarship for use in freshman, sophomore, junior, or senior years; not renewable. *Number:* 350–600. *Amount:* $500–$7500.

Eligibility Requirements: Applicant must be enrolled or expecting to enroll full-time at a two-year or four-year institution or university and resident of California, Illinois, New York, Texas. Applicant must have 2.5 GPA or higher. Available to U.S. citizens.

Application Requirements: Application form, essay, financial need analysis, interview, recommendations or references, resume, test scores, transcript. *Deadline:* March 14.

  Contact: Mr. Daniel Garcia, Associate Director
      East Los Angeles Community Union (TELACU) Scholarship
        Program
      5400 East Olympic Boulevard
      Los Angeles, CA 90022
      Phone: 323-721-1655 Ext. 486
      E-mail: dgarcia@TELACU.com

EDMUND F. MAXWELL FOUNDATION

http://www.maxwell.org/

EDMUND F. MAXWELL FOUNDATION SCHOLARSHIP

Scholarships awarded to residents of Western Washington to attend accredited independent colleges or universities. Awards up to $5000 per year based on need, merit, citizenship, and activities. Renewable for up to four years if academic progress is suitable and financial need is unchanged.

Award: Scholarship for use in freshman year; renewable. *Number:* 110. *Amount:* up to $5000.

Eligibility Requirements: Applicant must be enrolled or expecting to enroll full-time at a four-year institution or university and resident of Washington. Available to U.S. citizens.

Application Requirements: Application form, employment history, essay, financial need analysis, test scores, transcript. *Deadline:* April 30.

  Contact: Jane Thomas, Administrator
      Edmund F. Maxwell Foundation
      PO Box 22537
      Seattle, WA 98122
      Phone: 206-303-4402
      Fax: 206-303-4419
      E-mail: admin@maxwell.org

EDWARDS SCHOLARSHIP FUND

http://www.edwardsfund.org

EDWARDS SCHOLARSHIP

The Edwards Scholarship is for legal, permanent residents of the City of Boston, MA only. Applicants must be residents of Boston from the beginning of their junior year in high school to the present. Recipients must maintain a 2.0 GPA on a 4-point scale or a comparable GPA on another scale. Students must apply on-line.

Award: Scholarship for use in freshman, sophomore, junior, or senior years; renewable. *Number:* 100–125. *Amount:* $2500.

Eligibility Requirements: Applicant must be enrolled or expecting to enroll full-time at a two-year or four-year institution or university and resident of Alberta. Available to U.S. citizens.

Application Requirements: Application form, essay, financial need analysis. *Deadline:* March 15.

  Contact: Kathryn Osmond, Director
      Edwards Scholarship Fund
      89 South Street
      Suite 603
      Boston, MA 02111
      Phone: 617-737-3400
      E-mail: info@edwardsfund.org

ENLISTED ASSOCIATION OF THE NATIONAL GUARD OF NEW JERSEY

http://www.eang-nj.org/

CSM VINCENT BALDASSARI MEMORIAL SCHOLARSHIP PROGRAM

• See page 642

EQUALITY SCHOLARSHIP COLLABORATIVE

http://www.equalityscholarship.org

EQUALITY SCHOLARSHIPS FOR COMMUNITY COLLEGE TRANSFER STUDENTS

• See page 586

SCHOLARSHIPS FOR HIGH SCHOOL GRADUATES

• See page 586

ESSAYJOLT.COM

http://www.essayjolt.com/

ESSAYJOLT SCHOLARSHIP

Essay contest open to high school juniors and seniors who may be citizens of any country, but must live in New Jersey. Essays are judged on originality, insight, and quality of writing by an independent panel of writers and editors. Only one winner is selected. See website for current essay question and guidelines http://www.essayjolt.com.

Award: Prize for use in freshman year; not renewable. *Number:* 1. *Amount:* $500.

Eligibility Requirements: Applicant must be high school student; planning to enroll or expecting to enroll full- or part-time at a two-year or four-year or technical institution or university; resident of New Jersey and must have an interest in writing. Available to U.S. and non-U.S. citizens.

Application Requirements: Entry in a contest, essay. *Deadline:* varies.

  Contact: Meg Hartmann, Director
      Phone: 917-575-3165
      E-mail: scholarship@essayjolt.com

FINANCE AUTHORITY OF MAINE

http://www.famemaine.com/

STATE OF MAINE GRANT PROGRAM

Scholarship for residents of Maine, attending an eligible school in Maine, Connecticut, Massachusetts, New Hampshire, Rhode Island, or Vermont. Award based on need. Students attending out-of-state institutions must be participating in the New England Regional Tuition Break Program to be eligible. Students must apply annually. Complete free application for Federal Student Aid to apply. One-time award for undergraduate study. For further information see website http://www.famemaine.com.

Award: Grant for use in freshman, sophomore, junior, or senior years; not renewable. *Number:* 15,831. *Amount:* $1500.

Eligibility Requirements: Applicant must be enrolled or expecting to enroll full- or part-time at a two-year or four-year or technical institution or university; resident of Maine and studying in Connecticut, Maine, Massachusetts, New Hampshire, Rhode Island, Vermont. Available to U.S. citizens.

Application Requirements: Application form, financial need analysis. *Deadline:* May 1.

Contact: Claude Roy, Education Services Officer
Finance Authority of Maine
5 Community Drive
Augusta, ME 04332
Phone: 207-620-3507
E-mail: education@famemaine.com

TUITION WAIVER PROGRAMS

• See page 588

FLORIDA ASSOCIATION FOR MEDIA IN EDUCATION

http://www.floridamediaed.org/ssyra.html

INTELLECTUAL FREEDOM STUDENT SCHOLARSHIP

Scholarship in the amount of $1000 is awarded annually to a graduating senior from a high school in Florida. Only students whose library media specialists are members of FAME are eligible. Essays written by senior students will be submitted to the FAME Intellectual Freedom Committee.

Award: Scholarship for use in freshman year; not renewable. *Number:* 1. *Amount:* $1000.

Eligibility Requirements: Applicant must be high school student; planning to enroll or expecting to enroll full-time at a two-year or four-year or technical institution or university and resident of Florida. Available to U.S. citizens.

Application Requirements: Application form, essay. *Deadline:* March 15.

Contact: Larry Bodkin, Executive Director
Phone: 850-531-8350
Fax: 850-531-8344
E-mail: lbodkin@floridamedia.org

FLORIDA PTA/PTSA

http://www.floridapta.org/

FLORIDA PTA/PTSA ANNUAL SCHOLARSHIP

• See page 588

FLORIDA PTA/PTSA COMMUNITY/JUNIOR COLLEGE SCHOLARSHIP

One time award of $1000 to high school students who enrolled in a community or junior college. Must be a resident of Florida for at least 2 years. Must be a U.S. citizen and have at least a two-year attendance in a Florida PTA/PTSA high school. Minimum 2.5 GPA or higher.

Award: Scholarship for use in freshman year; not renewable. *Number:* 1–2. *Amount:* $1000.

Eligibility Requirements: Applicant must be enrolled or expecting to enroll full-time at a two-year institution and resident of Florida. Applicant must have 2.5 GPA or higher. Available to U.S. citizens.

Application Requirements: Application form, essay, proof of enrollment, recommendations or references. *Deadline:* March 1.

Contact: Scholarship Chair, Scholarship Chair
Florida PTA/PTSA
1747 Orlando Central Parkway
Orlando, FL 32809
Phone: 407-855-7604
Fax: 407-240-9577
E-mail: scholarship@floridapta.org

FLORIDA PTA/PTSA VOCATIONAL/TECHNICAL SCHOLARSHIP

Scholarship of $1000 is awarded to graduating senior enrolled full-time in a vocational/technical institution within the state of Florida. Must have at least a two-year attendance in a Florida PTA/PTSA high school. Minimum GPA is 2.0.

Award: Scholarship for use in freshman year; not renewable. *Number:* 3. *Amount:* $1000.

Eligibility Requirements: Applicant must be high school student; planning to enroll or expecting to enroll full-time at a two-year or technical institution; resident of Florida and studying in Florida. Available to U.S. citizens.

Application Requirements: Application form, essay, proof of enrollment, recommendations or references. *Deadline:* March 1.

Contact: Scholarship Chair, Scholarship Chair
Florida PTA/PTSA
1747 Orlando Central Parkway
Orlando, FL 32809
Phone: 407-855-7604
Fax: 407-240-9577
E-mail: scholarship@floridapta.org

FLORIDA STATE DEPARTMENT OF EDUCATION

http://www.floridastudentfinancialaid.org/

ACCESS TO BETTER LEARNING AND EDUCATION GRANT

Grant program provides tuition assistance to Florida undergraduate students enrolled in degree programs at eligible private Florida colleges or universities. Must be a U.S. citizen or eligible non-citizen and must meet Florida residency requirements. The participating institution determines application procedures, deadlines, and student eligibility. An eligible student must complete and submit the FAFSA in order to receive program funding. For more details, visit the website at http://www.FloridaStudentFinancialAid.org/SSFAD/home/uamain.htm.

Award: Grant for use in freshman, sophomore, junior, or senior years; renewable. *Amount:* up to $1500.

Eligibility Requirements: Applicant must be enrolled or expecting to enroll full-time at a four-year institution or university; resident of Florida and studying in Florida. Available to U.S. citizens.

Application Requirements: Application form.

Contact: Florida Department of Education, Office of Student Financial Assistance, Customer Service
Florida State Department of Education
325 West Gaines Street
Tallahassee, FL 32399
Phone: 888-827-2007
E-mail: osfa@fldoe.org

FIRST GENERATION MATCHING GRANT PROGRAM

Need-based grants to Florida resident undergraduate students who are enrolled in state universities and community colleges in Florida and whose parents have not earned baccalaureate degrees. Available state funds are contingent upon matching contributions from private sources on a dollar-for-dollar basis. Institutions determine application procedures, deadlines, and student eligibility. For more details, visit the website at http://www.FloridaStudentFinancialAid.org/SSFAD/home/uamain.htm.

Award: Grant for use in freshman, sophomore, junior, or senior years; renewable.

Eligibility Requirements: Applicant must be enrolled or expecting to enroll full- or part-time at a two-year or four-year institution or university; resident of Florida and studying in Florida. Available to U.S. citizens.

Application Requirements: Application form, financial need analysis.

Contact: Florida Department of Education, Office of Student Financial Assistance, Customer Service
Florida State Department of Education
325 West Gaines Street
Tallahassee, FL 32399
Phone: 888-827-2004
E-mail: osfa@fldoe.org

FLORIDA BRIGHT FUTURES SCHOLARSHIP PROGRAM

Three lottery-funded scholarships reward Florida high school graduates for high academic achievement. Program is comprised of the following three awards: Florida Academic Scholars Award, Florida Medallion Scholars Award and Florida Gold Seal Vocational Scholars Award. An eligible student must complete and submit the FAFSA in order to receive program funding. For more details, visit the website at http://www.FloridaStudentFinancialAid.org/SSFAD/home/uamain.htm.

Award: Scholarship for use in freshman, sophomore, junior, or senior years; renewable.

Eligibility Requirements: Applicant must be high school student; planning to enroll or expecting to enroll full- or part-time at a two-year or four-year or technical institution or university; resident of Florida and studying in Florida. Applicant must have 3.0 GPA or higher. Available to U.S. citizens.

Application Requirements: Application form, application form may be submitted online, community service, test scores, transcript.

Contact: Florida Department of Education, Office of Student Financial Assistance, Customer Service
Florida State Department of Education
325 West Gaines Street
Tallahassee, FL 32399
Phone: 888-827-2004
E-mail: osfa@fldoe.org

FLORIDA POSTSECONDARY STUDENT ASSISTANCE GRANT

Scholarships to degree-seeking, resident, undergraduate students who demonstrate substantial financial need and are enrolled in eligible degree-granting private colleges and universities not eligible under the Florida Private Student Assistance Grant. FSAG is a decentralized program, and each participating institution determines application procedures, deadlines and student eligibility. Number of awards varies. For more details, visit the website at http://www.FloridaStudentFinancialAid.org/SSFAD/home/uamain.htm.

Award: Grant for use in freshman, sophomore, junior, or senior years; renewable. *Amount:* $200–$2610.

Eligibility Requirements: Applicant must be enrolled or expecting to enroll full-time at a two-year or four-year institution or university; resident of Florida and studying in Florida. Available to U.S. citizens.

Application Requirements: Financial need analysis.

Contact: Florida Department of Education, Office of Student Financial Assistance, Customer Service
Florida State Department of Education
325 West Gaines Street
Tallahassee, FL 32399
Phone: 888-827-2004
E-mail: osfa@fldoe.org

FLORIDA PRIVATE STUDENT ASSISTANCE GRANT

Grants for Florida residents who are U.S. citizens or eligible non-citizens attending eligible private, nonprofit, four-year colleges and universities in Florida. Must be a full-time student and demonstrate substantial financial need. For renewal, must have earned a minimum cumulative GPA of 2.0 at the last institution attended. For more details, visit the website at http://www.FloridaStudentFinancialAid.org/SSFAD/home/uamain.htm.

Award: Grant for use in freshman, sophomore, junior, or senior years; renewable. *Amount:* $200–$2610.

Eligibility Requirements: Applicant must be enrolled or expecting to enroll full-time at a four-year institution or university; resident of Florida and studying in Florida. Available to U.S. citizens.

Application Requirements: Application form, financial need analysis.

Contact: Florida Department of Education, Office of Student Financial Assistance, Customer Service
Florida State Department of Education
325 West Gaines Street
Tallahassee, FL 32399
Phone: 888-827-2004
E-mail: osfa@fldoe.org

FLORIDA PUBLIC STUDENT ASSISTANCE GRANT

Grants for Florida residents, U.S. citizens or eligible non-citizens who attend state universities and public community colleges and demonstrate substantial financial need. For renewal, must have earned a minimum cumulative GPA of 2.0 at the last institution attended. For more details, visit the website at http://www.FloridaStudentFinancialAid.org/SSFAD/home/uamain.htm.

Award: Grant for use in freshman, sophomore, junior, or senior years; renewable. *Amount:* $200–$2610.

Eligibility Requirements: Applicant must be enrolled or expecting to enroll full- or part-time at a two-year or four-year institution or university; resident of Florida and studying in Florida. Available to U.S. citizens.

Application Requirements: Application form, financial need analysis.

Contact: Florida Department of Education, Office of Student Financial Assistance, Customer Service
Florida State Department of Education
325 West Gaines Street
Tallahassee, FL 32399
Phone: 888-827-2004
E-mail: osfa@fldoe.org

FLORIDA STUDENT ASSISTANCE GRANT-CAREER EDUCATION

Need-based grant program available to Florida residents enrolled in certificate programs of 450 or more clock hours at participating community colleges or career centers operated by district school boards. FSAG-CE is a decentralized state of Florida program, which means that each participating institution determines application procedures, deadlines, student eligibility, and award amounts. For more details, visit the website at http://www.FloridaStudentFinancialAid.org/SSFAD/home/uamain.htm.

Award: Grant for use in freshman, sophomore, junior, or senior years; renewable. *Amount:* $200–$2610.

Eligibility Requirements: Applicant must be enrolled or expecting to enroll full- or part-time at a two-year or technical institution; resident of Florida and studying in Florida. Available to U.S. citizens.

Application Requirements: Application form may be submitted online, financial need analysis.

Contact: Florida Department of Education, Office of Student Financial Assistance, Customer Service
Florida State Department of Education
325 West Gaines Street
Tallahassee, FL 32399
Phone: 888-827-2004
E-mail: osfa@fldoe.org

FLORIDA WORK EXPERIENCE PROGRAM

Need-based program providing eligible Florida residents work experiences that will complement and reinforce their educational and career goals. Must maintain GPA of 2.0. Postsecondary institution will determine applicant's eligibility, number of hours to be worked per week, and the award amount. For more details, visit the website at http://www.FloridaStudentFinancialAid.org/SSFAD/home/uamain.htm.

Award: Grant for use in freshman, sophomore, junior, or senior years; renewable.

Eligibility Requirements: Applicant must be enrolled or expecting to enroll full- or part-time at a two-year or four-year institution or university; resident of Florida and studying in Florida. Available to U.S. citizens.

Application Requirements: Financial need analysis.

Contact: Florida Department of Education, Office of Student Financial Assistance, Customer Service
Florida State Department of Education
325 West Gaines Street
Tallahassee, FL 32399
Phone: 888-827-2004
E-mail: osfa@fldoe.com

JOSE MARTI SCHOLARSHIP CHALLENGE GRANT FUND

• *See page 679*

MARY MCLEOD BETHUNE SCHOLARSHIP

Renewable award to Florida residents with a GPA of 3.0 or above, who will attend Bethune-Cookman University, Edward Waters College, Florida A&M University, or Florida Memorial University. Must not have previously received a baccalaureate degree. Must demonstrate financial need as specified by the institution. For more details, visit the website at http://www.FloridaStudentFinancialAid.org/SSFAD/home/uamain.htm.

Award: Scholarship for use in freshman, sophomore, junior, or senior years; renewable. *Amount:* $3000.

Eligibility Requirements: Applicant must be enrolled or expecting to enroll full-time at a four-year institution or university; resident of Florida and studying in Florida. Applicant must have 3.0 GPA or higher. Available to U.S. citizens.

Application Requirements: Financial need analysis.

Contact: Florida Department of Education, Office of Student Financial
Assistance, Customer Service
Florida State Department of Education
325 West Gaines Street
Tallahassee, FL 32399
Phone: 888-827-2004
E-mail: osfa@fldoe.org

SCHOLARSHIPS FOR CHILDREN & SPOUSES OF DECEASED OR DISABLED VETERANS

• *See page 656*

WILLIAM L. BOYD IV FLORIDA RESIDENT ACCESS GRANT

Renewable awards to Florida undergraduate residents attending an
eligible private, nonprofit Florida college or university. Postsecondary
institution will determine applicant's eligibility. Renewal applicant must
have earned a minimum institutional GPA of 2.0. An eligible student
must complete and submit the FAFSA in order to receive program
funding. For more details, visit the website at
http://www.FloridaStudentFinancialAid.org/SSFAD/home/uamain.htm.

Award: Grant for use in freshman, sophomore, junior, or senior years;
renewable. *Amount:* up to $3000.

Eligibility Requirements: Applicant must be enrolled or expecting to
enroll full-time at a four-year institution or university; resident of Florida
and studying in Florida. Available to U.S. citizens.

Application Requirements: Application form.

Contact: Florida Department of Education, Office of Student Financial
Assistance, Customer Service
Florida State Department of Education
325 West Gaines Street
Tallahassee, FL 32399
Phone: 888-827-2004
E-mail: osfa@fldoe.org

FLORIDA WOMEN'S STATE GOLF ASSOCIATION

CLUB EMPLOYEES AND DEPENDENTS SCHOLARSHIP

Scholarship was designed to employees, and dependents of employees, of
FSGA Member Clubs that utilize the GHIN Handicap System.

Award: Scholarship for use in freshman, sophomore, junior, or senior
years; renewable. *Number:* 1. *Amount:* $500–$2000.

Eligibility Requirements: Applicant must be enrolled or expecting to
enroll full-time at a two-year or four-year or technical institution or
university; resident of Florida and must have an interest in golf.
Applicant must have 3.0 GPA or higher. Available to U.S. citizens.

Application Requirements: Application form, application form may be
submitted online (http://www.fsga.org/sections/Foundation/College-
Scholarships/38), community service, essay, financial need analysis,
personal photograph, recommendations or references, test scores,
transcript. *Deadline:* June 1.

Contact: Kyle Walkiewicz, Director of Junior Golf
Florida Women's State Golf Association
12630 Telecom Drive
Tampa, FL 33637
Phone: 813-632-3742
Fax: 813-910-2125
E-mail: kyle@fsga.org

FSGA SCHOLARS

FSGA Scholars is a scholarship program made possible by the Florida
State Golf Association and our Future of Golf Foundation. In the Spring
each year, the FSGA selects a minimum of five golfers from the FJT's
graduating class to be awarded a renewable four-year scholarship. A total
of $10,000 in college scholarships will be awarded each year, resulting in
$40,000 granted to each graduating class.

Award: Scholarship for use in freshman, sophomore, junior, or senior
years; renewable. *Number:* 1–8. *Amount:* $500–$2000.

Eligibility Requirements: Applicant must be high school student;
planning to enroll or expecting to enroll full-time at a two-year or four-
year or technical institution or university; resident of Florida and must
have an interest in golf. Applicant must have 3.0 GPA or higher.
Available to U.S. citizens.

Application Requirements: Application form, application form may be
submitted online (http://www.fsga.org/sections/Foundation/College-
Scholarships/38), community service, essay, financial need analysis,
personal photograph, recommendations or references, test scores,
transcript. *Deadline:* July 1.

Contact: Kyle Walkiewica, Director of Junior Golf
Florida Women's State Golf Association
12630 Telecom Drive
Tampa, FL 33637
Phone: 813-632-3742
Fax: 813-910-2125
E-mail: kyle@fsga.org

SARAH E. HUNEYCUTT SCHOLARSHIP

This four-year scholarship of $5000 per academic year ($20,000 total) is
awarded annually to a deserving high school senior woman who is a
Florida resident, will be attending an accredited Florida college or
university, has demonstrated an interest in golf but is not eligible for a
golf athletic scholarship, shows financial need, and maintains a grade
point average of 3.0 or higher.

Award: Scholarship for use in freshman, sophomore, junior, or senior
years; renewable. *Number:* 1–5. *Amount:* $5000.

Eligibility Requirements: Applicant must be high school student;
planning to enroll or expecting to enroll full-time at a two-year or four-
year or technical institution or university; female; resident of Florida;
studying in Florida and must have an interest in golf. Applicant must
have 3.0 GPA or higher. Available to U.S. citizens.

Application Requirements: Application form, application form may be
submitted online (http://www.jggsf.org/), community service, essay,
financial need analysis, personal photograph, test scores, transcript.
Deadline: June 1.

Contact: Jan Demarco, President
E-mail: jan@jggsf.org

THE FORD FAMILY FOUNDATION

http://www.tfff.org

FORD OPPORTUNITY PROGRAM

Hallie E. Ford and The Ford Family Foundation established the Ford
Opportunity Scholarship Program to provide scholarships to college
students who are single parents with custody of dependent children (18
years of age or younger) and be the head of household as defined by IRS
regulations. The intention of this scholarship is to assist single parents
who do not have the support of a live-in partner. Recipients must have at
least one year remaining in their undergraduate program and attend
college in their home start of Oregon or California and plan to pursue a
Bachelor's degree. Minimum 3.0 GPA required.

Award: Scholarship for use in freshman, sophomore, junior, senior,
graduate, or postgraduate years; renewable. *Number:* 30–50. *Amount:*
$1000–$25,000.

Eligibility Requirements: Applicant must be enrolled or expecting to
enroll full-time at a two-year or four-year institution or university; single;
resident of California, Oregon and studying in California, Oregon.
Applicant must have 3.0 GPA or higher. Available to U.S. citizens.

Application Requirements: Application form, essay, financial need
analysis, interview. *Deadline:* March 1.

Contact: Tricia Tate, Scholarship Programs Manager
The Ford Family Foundation
440 East Broadway, Suite 200
Eugene, OR 97401
Phone: 541-485-6211
Fax: 541-485-6223
E-mail: fordscholarships@tfff.org

FORD RESTART PROGRAM

The Ford Family Foundation established the Ford ReStart Scholarship
Program to encourage adults, age 25 or older, to begin or return to full-
time, post-secondary education. Each year, up to 46 applicants are
selected from Oregon and Siskiyou County, California to receive a Ford
ReStart scholarship. An applicant must be at least 25 years old by March
1 of the application year, be no more than halfway through their degree
program, and seek an associate's degree or a Bachelor's degree at an
eligible institution in CA or Oregon (and not previously have earned a
Bachelor's degree).

RESIDENCE

Award: Scholarship for use in freshman, sophomore, junior, senior, graduate, or postgraduate years; renewable. *Number:* 45–46. *Amount:* $1000–$25,000.

Eligibility Requirements: Applicant must be enrolled or expecting to enroll full-time at a two-year or four-year institution or university; resident of California, Oregon and studying in California, Oregon. Applicant must have 3.0 GPA or higher. Available to U.S. citizens.

Application Requirements: Application form, essay, financial need analysis, interview. *Deadline:* March 1.

Contact: Tricia Tate, Scholarship Programs Manager
The Ford Family Foundation
440 East Broadway, Suite 200
Eugene, OR 97401
Phone: 541-485-6211
Fax: 541-485-6223
E-mail: fordscholarships@tfff.org

FORD SCHOLARS PROGRAM

The Ford Scholars Program is need-based and open to 1) graduating high school seniors and, 2) entering college freshmen and (3) continuing community college students ready to transfer to a four-year college, who are seeking a Bachelor's degree in Oregon or California. This program is available to residents of Oregon and Siskiyou County, California. The Ford Scholars Program was created by Kenneth W. Ford (1908-1997), a founder of The Ford Family Foundation, to assist students who otherwise would find it impossible, or at least very difficult, to obtain a college degree without financial assistance.

Award: Scholarship for use in freshman, sophomore, junior, senior, graduate, or postgraduate years; renewable. *Number:* 100–120. *Amount:* $1000–$25,000.

Eligibility Requirements: Applicant must be enrolled or expecting to enroll full-time at a two-year or four-year institution or university; resident of California, Oregon and studying in California, Oregon. Applicant must have 3.0 GPA or higher. Available to U.S. citizens.

Application Requirements: Application form, essay, financial need analysis, interview. *Deadline:* March 1.

Contact: Tricia Tate, Scholarship Programs Manager
The Ford Family Foundation
440 East Broadway, Suite 200
Eugene, OR 97401
Phone: 541-485-6211
Fax: 541-485-6223
E-mail: fordscholarships@tfff.org

FRATERNAL ORDER OF POLICE ASSOCIATES OF OHIO INC.

http://www.fopaohio.org/

FRATERNAL ORDER OF POLICE ASSOCIATES, STATE LODGE OF OHIO INC., SCHOLARSHIP FUND

• *See page 588*

FRESH START SCHOLARSHIP FOUNDATION

www.freshstartscholarship.org

FRESH START SCHOLARSHIP

Must be entering an undergraduate program at a college or university in Delaware. Scholarship offering a fresh start to women who are returning to school after a hiatus of at least two years to better their life and opportunities. Applicants must be Delaware residents or employed in Delaware for at least 12 months. US Citizenship or Permanent Resident status required.

Award: Scholarship for use in freshman, sophomore, junior, or senior years; not renewable. *Number:* 25–30. *Amount:* $1000–$4000.

Eligibility Requirements: Applicant must be enrolled or expecting to enroll full- or part-time at a two-year or four-year institution or university; female; resident of Delaware and studying in Delaware. Applicant must have 2.5 GPA or higher. Available to U.S. citizens.

Application Requirements: Application form, essay, financial need analysis. *Deadline:* May 15.

Contact: Scholarship Chair
Fresh Start Scholarship Foundation
PO Box 7784
Wilmington, DE 19803
Phone: 302-397-3440
E-mail: fsscholar@comcast.net

FRIENDS OF 440 SCHOLARSHIP FUND INC.

http://www.440scholarship.org/

FRIENDS OF 440 SCHOLARSHIP FUND, INC.

Scholarships to students who are dependents of workers who were injured or killed in the course and scope of their employment and who are eligible to receive benefits under the Florida Workers' Compensation system, or are dependents of those primarily engaged in the administration of the Florida Workers' Compensation Law.

Award: Scholarship for use in freshman, sophomore, junior, or senior years; renewable. *Number:* 1–60. *Amount:* $500–$6000.

Eligibility Requirements: Applicant must be enrolled or expecting to enroll full-time at a two-year or four-year or technical institution or university and resident of Florida. Available to U.S. and non-U.S. citizens.

Application Requirements: Application form, copy of tax return, transcript. *Deadline:* February 28.

Contact: Ms. Lori Gerson, Managing Director
Phone: 305-423-8710
Fax: 305-670-0716
E-mail: info@440scholarship.org

FULFILLMENT FUND

http://www.fulfillment.org/

FULFILLMENT FUND SCHOLARSHIPS

Award is for undergraduates. Serving students in seven partner high schools, Fremont, Hamilton, Locke, Los Angeles, Manual Arts, Crenshaw and Wilson. Only students who participated in the Fulfillment Fund High School Program for at least two years are eligible to apply for the scholarship.

Award: Scholarship for use in freshman, sophomore, junior, or senior years; not renewable. *Amount:* $1000–$1500.

Eligibility Requirements: Applicant must be enrolled or expecting to enroll full- or part-time at a four-year institution or university and resident of California. Available to U.S. citizens.

Application Requirements: Application form. *Deadline:* varies.

Contact: Darcine Thomas, Community Outreach Manager
Phone: 323-900-8753
Fax: 525-3095

FUNNEWJERSEY.COM INC.

www.funnewjersey.com

FUNNEWJERSEY.COM SCHOLARSHIP

• *See page 588*

GENERAL FEDERATION OF WOMEN'S CLUBS OF MASSACHUSETTS

http://www.gfwcma.org/

GENERAL FEDERATION OF WOMEN'S CLUBS OF MASSACHUSETTS NICKEL FOR NOTES MUSIC SCHOLARSHIP

• *See page 589*

GENERAL FEDERATION OF WOMEN'S CLUBS OF MASSACHUSETTS PENNIES FOR ART SCHOLARSHIP

• *See page 589*

GENERAL FEDERATION OF WOMEN'S CLUBS OF MASSACHUSETTS STUDY ABROAD SCHOLARSHIP

Scholarship for undergraduate or graduate students to study abroad. Applicant must submit personal statement and letter of endorsement from the president of the sponsoring General Federation of Women's Clubs of Massachusetts. Must be resident of Massachusetts.

Award: Scholarship for use in freshman, sophomore, junior, senior, or graduate years; not renewable. *Number:* 1. *Amount:* $800.

Eligibility Requirements: Applicant must be enrolled or expecting to enroll full-time at a four-year institution or university and resident of Massachusetts. Available to U.S. citizens.

Application Requirements: Application form, essay, interview, recommendations or references, self-addressed stamped envelope with application, transcript. *Deadline:* March 1.

Contact: Marta DiBenedetto, Scholarship Chairperson
General Federation of Women's Clubs of Massachusetts
PO Box 679, 245 Dutton Road
Sudbury, MA 01776-0679
Phone: 978-444-9105
E-mail: marta_dibenedetto@nylim.com

GENERAL FEDERATION OF WOMEN'S CLUBS OF VERMONT

BARBARA JEAN BARKER MEMORIAL SCHOLARSHIP FOR A DISPLACED HOMEMAKER

Applicants must be Vermont residents who have been homemakers (primarily) for at least fifteen years and have lost their main means of support through death, divorce, separation, spouse's long-time illness, or spouse's long-time unemployment. Provides one to three scholarships ranging from $500 to $1500.

Award: Grant for use in freshman, sophomore, junior, senior, or graduate years; not renewable. *Number:* 1–3. *Amount:* $500–$1500.

Eligibility Requirements: Applicant must be enrolled or expecting to enroll full- or part-time at a two-year or four-year or technical institution or university; female and resident of Vermont. Available to U.S. citizens.

Application Requirements: Application form, driver's license, financial need analysis, interview. *Deadline:* March 15.

Contact: Mrs. Joyce Lindamood
General Federation of Women's Clubs of Vermont
P.O. Box 92
Springfield, VT 05156
Phone: 802-885-4690
E-mail: jmood@vermontel.net

GEORGIA STUDENT FINANCE COMMISSION

http://www.GAcollege411.org/

GEORGIA HOPE SCHOLARSHIP PROGRAM

Scholarship and Grant program for Georgia residents who are college undergraduates to attend an accredited two or four-year Georgia institution. Pays a percentage of actual undergraduate tuition charged at public postsecondary institutions. Percentage paid will vary from year to year. At private postsecondary institutions in Georgia, students may receive up to $3600 per year for full-time study or $1800 per year for part-time. Minimum 3.0 GPA required. Renewable if student maintains grades. See http://www.GAcollege411.org for full details.

Award: Scholarship for use in freshman, sophomore, junior, or senior years; renewable. *Number:* 200,000–230,000. *Amount:* up to $6000.

Eligibility Requirements: Applicant must be enrolled or expecting to enroll full- or part-time at a two-year or four-year institution or university; resident of Georgia and studying in Georgia. Applicant must have 3.0 GPA or higher. Available to U.S. citizens.

Application Requirements: Application form, high schools must report transcripts to GSFC. *Deadline:* continuous.

Contact: Tracy Ireland, Vice President
Georgia Student Finance Commission
2082 East Exchange Place, Suite 100
Tucker, GA 30084
Phone: 800-505-4732
E-mail: tracyi@gsfc.org

GEORGIA PUBLIC SAFETY MEMORIAL GRANT

Award for children of Georgia Public Safety Officers, prison guards, fire fighters, law enforcement officers or emergency medical technicians killed or permanently disabled in the line of duty. Must attend an accredited postsecondary Georgia school. Complete the Public Safety Memorial Grant application.

Award: Grant for use in freshman, sophomore, junior, or senior years; not renewable. *Number:* 20–40. *Amount:* $2000.

Eligibility Requirements: Applicant must be enrolled or expecting to enroll full-time at a two-year or four-year or technical institution or university; resident of Georgia and studying in Georgia. Available to U.S. citizens.

Application Requirements: Application form, selective service registration. *Deadline:* continuous.

Contact: Caylee French, Division Director
Georgia Student Finance Commission
2082 East Exchange Place, Suite 100
Tucker, GA 30084
Phone: 770-724-9244
E-mail: cayleef@gsfc.org

GEORGIA TUITION EQUALIZATION GRANT (GTEG)
• *See page 630*

GIRL SCOUTS OF CONNECTICUT

http://www.gsofct.org/

EMILY CHAISON GOLD AWARD SCHOLARSHIP
• *See page 543*

GOLDBERG & OSBORNE

https://1800theeagle.com

ARIZONA DON'T TEXT AND DRIVE SCHOLARSHIP

We invite anyone who lives in the United States and knows someone who lives in Arizona currently attending college or trade school, or getting ready to attend one, to make the pledge not to text and drive. That means you can pledge not to text and drive and enter the scholarship drawing either on your behalf or on behalf of someone else. We award one (1) $1,000 scholarship every month. New scholarships begin on the first day of each month and close on the last day of each month. Applications do not carry forward from month to month so please return and take the don't text and drive pledge again to apply for a new month. Winners are announced on our Facebook and Twitter feeds.

Award: Scholarship for use in freshman, sophomore, junior, senior, graduate, or postgraduate years; not renewable. *Number:* 1. *Amount:* $1000.

Eligibility Requirements: Applicant must be enrolled or expecting to enroll full- or part-time at a two-year or four-year or technical institution or university; resident of Arizona and studying in Arizona. Available to U.S. citizens.

Application Requirements: Application form. *Deadline:* continuous.

Contact: Mr. Dan Bradley, Marketing Director
Goldberg & Osborne
2815 S Alma School Rd
Mesa, AZ 85210
Phone: 602-808-6600
E-mail: scholarships@1800theeagle.com

NATIONAL DON'T TEXT AND DRIVE SCHOLARSHIP

Applicants for the Second Quarter 2017 National Goldberg & Osborne Don't Text and Drive College Scholarship must either be attending college or trade school currently or planning to attend college or trade school this semester or the fall 2017 semester. You can pledge not to text and drive and enter the scholarship drawing either on your behalf or on behalf of someone else. We award one (1) $1,000 scholarship every over month (bimonthly) for a total of six scholarships per year. New scholarships begin on the first day of every other month and close on the last day of every other month. Applications do not carry forward from one bimonthly period to the next so please return and take the don't text and drive pledge again to apply for a new period. Winners are announced on our Facebook and Twitter feeds.

Award: Scholarship for use in freshman, sophomore, junior, senior, graduate, or postgraduate years; not renewable. *Number:* 1. *Amount:* $1000.

Eligibility Requirements: Applicant must be enrolled or expecting to enroll full- or part-time at a two-year or four-year or technical institution or university and resident of Alabama, Alaska, Arizona, Arkansas, California, Colorado, Connecticut, Delaware, District of Columbia, Florida, Georgia, Hawaii, Idaho, Illinois, Indiana, Iowa, Kansas, Kentucky, Louisiana, Maine, Maryland, Massachusetts, Michigan, Minnesota, Mississippi, Missouri, Montana, Nebraska, Nevada, New Hampshire, New Jersey, New Mexico, New York, North Carolina, North Dakota, Ohio, Oklahoma, Oregon, Pennsylvania, Rhode Island, South Carolina, South Dakota, Tennessee, Texas, Utah, Vermont, Virginia, Washington, West Virginia, Wisconsin, Wyoming. Available to U.S. citizens.

Application Requirements: Application form. *Deadline:* continuous.

Contact: Mr. Dan Bradley, Marketing Director
Goldberg & Osborne
2815 S Alma School Rd
Mesa, AZ 85210
Phone: 602-808-6600
E-mail: scholarships@1800theeagle.com

GREATER KANAWHA VALLEY FOUNDATION

http://www.tgkvf.org/

C. RAYMOND & DELSIA R. COLLINS SCHOLARSHIP

Renewable award for a full-time student who is a resident of West Virginia pursing postsecondary studies. Must demonstrate academic excellence.

Award: Scholarship for use in freshman, sophomore, junior, or senior years; renewable. *Amount:* $1000.

Eligibility Requirements: Applicant must be enrolled or expecting to enroll full-time at a four-year institution or university and resident of West Virginia. Available to U.S. citizens.

Application Requirements: Application form, financial need analysis, recommendations or references, test scores, transcript. *Deadline:* January 15.

Contact: Susan Hoover, Scholarship Program Officer
Greater Kanawha Valley Foundation
900 Lee Street East, 16th Floor
Charleston, WV 25301
Phone: 304-346-3620
E-mail: shoover@tgkvf.org

DRS. CHARLENE & CHARLES BYRD SCHOLARSHIP

Renewable award for a West Virginia resident pursuing full-time postsecondary studies. Minimum 2.5 GPA required.

Award: Scholarship for use in freshman, sophomore, junior, or senior years; renewable. *Amount:* $1000.

Eligibility Requirements: Applicant must be enrolled or expecting to enroll full-time at a four-year institution or university and resident of West Virginia. Applicant must have 2.5 GPA or higher. Available to U.S. citizens.

Application Requirements: Application form, recommendations or references, transcript. *Deadline:* January 15.

Contact: Susan Hoover, Scholarship Program Officer
Greater Kanawha Valley Foundation
900 Lee Street East, 16th Floor
Charleston, WV 25301
Phone: 304-346-3620
E-mail: shoover@tgkvf.org

EVANS MEMORIAL SCHOLARSHIP

Renewable award available to West Virginia resident who is enrolling or has enrolled in a two-year or four-year college/university in West Virginia. Must demonstrate financial need.

Award: Scholarship for use in freshman, sophomore, junior, or senior years; renewable. *Amount:* $1000.

Eligibility Requirements: Applicant must be enrolled or expecting to enroll full-time at a two-year or four-year institution or university;

resident of West Virginia and studying in West Virginia. Available to U.S. citizens.

Application Requirements: Application form, financial need analysis, test scores, transcript. *Deadline:* January 15.

Contact: Susan Hoover, Scholarship Program Officer
Greater Kanawha Valley Foundation
900 Lee Street East, 16th Floor
Charleston, WV 25301
Phone: 304-346-3620
E-mail: shoover@tgkvf.org

HENRY E. KING SCHOLARSHIP FUND

Award available for immediate family members of owners, or employees, of companies that are current members of, and have been members of, the Home Builders Association of Greater Charleston, West Virginia. Award to be used for full-time study in a two- or four-year college/university. Must be a resident of West Virginia and demonstrate financial need. Renewable only for current members.

Award: Scholarship for use in freshman, sophomore, junior, or senior years; not renewable. *Amount:* $1000.

Eligibility Requirements: Applicant must be enrolled or expecting to enroll full-time at a two-year or four-year institution or university and resident of West Virginia. Available to U.S. citizens.

Application Requirements: Application form, financial need analysis, transcript. *Deadline:* January 15.

Contact: Susan Hoover, Scholarship Program Officer
Greater Kanawha Valley Foundation
900 Lee Street East, 16th Floor
Charleston, WV 25301
Phone: 304-346-3620
E-mail: shoover@tgkvf.org

JAMES & MARIANNE LANE SCHOLARSHIP

Renewable award for a West Virginia resident pursuing postsecondary studies. Minimum 2.5 GPA required. Preference given to students attending Washington & Jefferson College.

Award: Scholarship for use in freshman, sophomore, junior, or senior years; renewable.

Eligibility Requirements: Applicant must be enrolled or expecting to enroll full-time at a four-year institution or university and resident of West Virginia. Applicant must have 2.5 GPA or higher. Available to U.S. citizens.

Application Requirements: Application form, recommendations or references, test scores, transcript. *Deadline:* January 15.

Contact: Susan Hoover, Scholarship Program Officer
Greater Kanawha Valley Foundation
900 Lee Street East, 16th Floor
Charleston, WV 25301
Phone: 304-346-3620
E-mail: shoover@tgkvf.org

KID'S CHANCE OF WEST VIRGINIA SCHOLARSHIP

Award for children (between the ages of 16 and 25) of a parent injured in a WV work-related accident. Preference shall be given to students with financial need, academic performance, leadership abilities, demonstrated and potential contributions to school and community who are pursuing any field of study in any accredited trade, vocational school, college, or university. Must attach a copy of the order or letter from the worker's compensation carrier granting a permanent total disability award or dependent's benefits.

Award: Scholarship for use in freshman, sophomore, junior, or senior years; renewable. *Amount:* $2000.

Eligibility Requirements: Applicant must be age 16-25; enrolled or expecting to enroll full-time at a two-year or four-year or technical institution or university; resident of West Virginia and must have an interest in leadership. Available to U.S. citizens.

Application Requirements: Application form, essay, financial need analysis, recommendations or references, transcript, worker's compensation order/letter. *Deadline:* January 15.

Contact: Susan Hoover, Scholarship Program Officer
Greater Kanawha Valley Foundation
900 Lee Street East, 16th Floor
Charleston, WV 25301
Phone: 304-346-3620
E-mail: shoover@tgkvf.org

LAWRENCE C. YEARDLEY SCHOLARSHIP

Renewable award for resident of West Virginia pursuing postsecondary studies. Must demonstrate academic excellence, financial need, and have a minimum 2.5 GPA.

Award: Scholarship for use in freshman, sophomore, junior, or senior years; renewable. *Amount:* $1000.

Eligibility Requirements: Applicant must be enrolled or expecting to enroll full-time at a four-year institution or university and resident of West Virginia. Applicant must have 2.5 GPA or higher. Available to U.S. citizens.

Application Requirements: Application form, financial need analysis, recommendations or references, test scores, transcript. *Deadline:* January 15.

Contact: Susan Hoover, Scholarship Program Officer
Greater Kanawha Valley Foundation
900 Lee Street East, 16th Floor
Charleston, WV 25301
Phone: 304-346-3620
E-mail: shoover@tgkvf.org

LEFF MOORE SCHOLARSHIP

Renewable award for a West Virginia resident pursuing full-time postsecondary studies. Must be affiliated with the Democratic Party and demonstrate financial need. Minimum 2.5 GPA required.

Award: Scholarship for use in freshman, sophomore, junior, or senior years; renewable.

Eligibility Requirements: Applicant must be enrolled or expecting to enroll full-time at a four-year institution or university and resident of West Virginia. Applicant must have 2.5 GPA or higher. Available to U.S. citizens.

Application Requirements: Application form, financial need analysis, recommendations or references, transcript. *Deadline:* January 15.

Contact: Susan Hoover, Scholarship Program Officer
Greater Kanawha Valley Foundation
900 Lee Street East, 16th Floor
Charleston, WV 25301
Phone: 304-346-3620
E-mail: shoover@tgkvf.org

MABEL W. WALKER SCHOLARSHIP

Renewable award for West Virginia residents pursuing full-time postsecondary studies. Minimum 2.5 GPA required. Preference given to residents of Campbell Creek and then Upper Kanawha.

Award: Scholarship for use in freshman, sophomore, junior, or senior years; renewable. *Amount:* $1000.

Eligibility Requirements: Applicant must be enrolled or expecting to enroll full-time at a four-year institution or university and resident of West Virginia. Applicant must have 2.5 GPA or higher. Available to U.S. citizens.

Application Requirements: Application form, financial need analysis, recommendations or references, test scores, transcript. *Deadline:* January 15.

Contact: Susan Hoover, Scholarship Program Officer
Greater Kanawha Valley Foundation
900 Lee Street East, 16th Floor
Charleston, WV 25301
Phone: 304-346-3620
E-mail: shoover@tgkvf.org

MILLIE SNYDER SCHOLARSHIP

Renewable award for a West Virginia resident pursuing full-time postsecondary studies. Must be a member of Weight Watchers. Minimum 2.5 GPA required.

Award: Scholarship for use in freshman, sophomore, junior, or senior years; renewable. *Amount:* $1000.

Eligibility Requirements: Applicant must be enrolled or expecting to enroll full-time at a four-year institution or university and resident of West Virginia. Applicant must have 2.5 GPA or higher. Available to U.S. citizens.

Application Requirements: Application form, financial need analysis, recommendations or references, transcript. *Deadline:* January 15.

Contact: Susan Hoover, Scholarship Program Officer
Greater Kanawha Valley Foundation
900 Lee Street East, 16th Floor
Charleston, WV 25301
Phone: 304-346-3620
E-mail: shoover@tgkvf.org

NORMAN S. AND BETTY M. FITZHUGH FUND

Award available to West Virginia residents who demonstrate academic excellence and financial need to attend any accredited college or university. Scholarships are awarded for full-time study for one or more years.

Award: Scholarship for use in freshman, sophomore, junior, or senior years; renewable. *Number:* 1. *Amount:* $750.

Eligibility Requirements: Applicant must be enrolled or expecting to enroll full-time at a two-year or four-year or technical institution or university and resident of West Virginia. Available to U.S. citizens.

Application Requirements: Application form, essay, financial need analysis, recommendations or references, transcript. *Deadline:* January 15.

Contact: Susan Hoover, Scholarship Program Officer
Greater Kanawha Valley Foundation
900 Lee Street East, 16th Floor
Charleston, WV 25301
Phone: 304-346-3620
E-mail: shoover@tgkvf.org

O'HAIR SCHOLARSHIP

Renewable award for West Virginia residents pursuing full-time postsecondary studies. Must demonstrate academic ability. Minimum 2.5 GPA required.

Award: Scholarship for use in freshman, sophomore, junior, or senior years; renewable. *Amount:* $1000.

Eligibility Requirements: Applicant must be enrolled or expecting to enroll full-time at a four-year institution or university and resident of West Virginia. Applicant must have 2.5 GPA or higher. Available to U.S. citizens.

Application Requirements: Application form, financial need analysis, recommendations or references, test scores, transcript. *Deadline:* January 15.

Contact: Susan Hoover, Scholarship Program Officer
Greater Kanawha Valley Foundation
900 Lee Street East, 16th Floor
Charleston, WV 25301
Phone: 304-346-3620
E-mail: shoover@tgkvf.org

RHUDY SCHOLARSHIP

Renewable award for a West Virginia resident pursuing full-time postsecondary studies. Minimum 2.5 GPA required. Must demonstrate academic ability and financial need.

Award: Scholarship for use in freshman, sophomore, junior, or senior years; renewable. *Amount:* $500.

Eligibility Requirements: Applicant must be enrolled or expecting to enroll full-time at a four-year institution or university and resident of West Virginia. Applicant must have 2.5 GPA or higher. Available to U.S. citizens.

Application Requirements: Application form, financial need analysis, recommendations or references, test scores, transcript. *Deadline:* January 15.

Contact: Susan Hoover, Scholarship Program Officer
Greater Kanawha Valley Foundation
900 Lee Street East, 16th Floor
Charleston, WV 25301
Phone: 304-346-3620
E-mail: shoover@tgkvf.org

R. RAY SINGLETON FUND

Renewable award available for undergraduate or graduate study in a West Virginia college/university. Applicant must be resident of Kanawha, Boone, Clay, Putnam, Lincoln, or Fayette counties, and demonstrate financial need and academic excellence.

Award: Scholarship for use in freshman, sophomore, junior, senior, or graduate years; renewable. *Amount:* $1000.

Eligibility Requirements: Applicant must be enrolled or expecting to enroll full-time at a four-year institution or university; resident of West Virginia and studying in West Virginia. Available to U.S. citizens.

Application Requirements: Application form, financial need analysis, transcript. *Deadline:* January 15.

Contact: Susan Hoover, Scholarship Program Officer
Greater Kanawha Valley Foundation
900 Lee Street East, 16th Floor
Charleston, WV 25301
Phone: 304-346-3620
E-mail: shoover@tgkvf.org

RUTH ANN JOHNSON SCHOLARSHIP

Renewable award for a full-time postsecondary student who is a resident of West Virginia. Must demonstrate academic excellence. Minimum 2.5 GPA required.

Award: Scholarship for use in freshman, sophomore, junior, or senior years; renewable. *Amount:* $1000.

Eligibility Requirements: Applicant must be enrolled or expecting to enroll full-time at a four-year institution or university and resident of West Virginia. Applicant must have 2.5 GPA or higher. Available to U.S. citizens.

Application Requirements: Application form, financial need analysis, recommendations or references, test scores, transcript. *Deadline:* January 15.

Contact: Susan Hoover, Scholarship Program Officer
Greater Kanawha Valley Foundation
900 Lee Street East, 16th Floor
Charleston, WV 25301
Phone: 304-346-3620
E-mail: shoover@tgkvf.org

STUART & LUCILLE ARMSTRONG SCHOLARSHIP
• *See page 716*

THALHEIMER FAMILY SUPPLEMENTAL SCHOLARSHIP

Award available to West Virginia students who are current scholarship winners to provide supplemental funds for goods and services necessary for the student to attend college. Must be a resident of Kanawha, Putnam, Boone, Clay, Fayette, or Lincoln counties and submit a written request for additional aid, listing all financial aid that has been awarded and reason for request.

Award: Scholarship for use in freshman, sophomore, junior, or senior years; not renewable. *Amount:* $1000.

Eligibility Requirements: Applicant must be enrolled or expecting to enroll full-time at a two-year or four-year institution or university and resident of West Virginia. Available to U.S. citizens.

Application Requirements: Application form, financial need analysis, letter requesting aid, transcript. *Deadline:* January 15.

Contact: Susan Hoover, Scholarship Program Officer
Greater Kanawha Valley Foundation
900 Lee Street East, 16th Floor
Charleston, WV 25301
Phone: 304-346-3620
E-mail: shoover@tgkvf.org

WEST VIRGINIA GOLF ASSOCIATION FUND

Award of $1000 available to students at any accredited West Virginia college or university. This fund is open to individuals who (1) have played golf in WV as an amateur for recreation or competition, or (2) have been or are presently employed in WV as a caddie, groundskeeper, bag boy, etc. Must also include a reference by a coach, golf professional, or employer and an essay explaining how the game of golf has made an impact in applicant's life.

Award: Scholarship for use in freshman, sophomore, junior, or senior years; not renewable. *Number:* 2. *Amount:* $1000.

Eligibility Requirements: Applicant must be enrolled or expecting to enroll full-time at a two-year or four-year or technical institution or university; resident of West Virginia; studying in West Virginia and must have an interest in golf. Available to U.S. citizens.

Application Requirements: Application form, essay, recommendations or references, transcript. *Deadline:* January 15.

Contact: Susan Hoover, Scholarship Program Officer
Greater Kanawha Valley Foundation
900 Lee Street East, 16th Floor
Charleston, WV 25301
Phone: 304-346-3620
E-mail: shoover@tgkvf.org

W. P. BLACK SCHOLARSHIP FUND

Renewable award for West Virginia residents who demonstrate academic excellence and financial need and who are enrolled in an undergraduate program in any accredited college or university.

Award: Scholarship for use in freshman, sophomore, junior, or senior years; renewable. *Amount:* $1000.

Eligibility Requirements: Applicant must be enrolled or expecting to enroll full-time at a four-year institution or university and resident of West Virginia. Available to U.S. citizens.

Application Requirements: Application form, essay, financial need analysis, recommendations or references, self-addressed stamped envelope with application, test scores, transcript. *Deadline:* January 15.

Contact: Susan Hoover, Scholarship Coordinator
Greater Kanawha Valley Foundation
900 Lee Street East, 16th Floor
Charleston, WV 25301
Phone: 304-346-3620
E-mail: shoover@tgkvf.org

GREATER SEATTLE BUSINESS ASSOCIATION

http://thegsba.org/

GSBA SCHOLARSHIP FUND

GSBA awards educational scholarships to LGBTQ and allied students who are committed to making a difference in the world. Our scholarships range up to $13,000 annually and are meant to provide significant support as you pursue your educational goals.

Award: Scholarship for use in freshman, sophomore, junior, or senior years; renewable. *Number:* 40–45. *Amount:* $2000–$13,000.

Eligibility Requirements: Applicant must be enrolled or expecting to enroll full- or part-time at a two-year or four-year or technical institution or university; resident of Washington and must have an interest in LGBT issues. Available to U.S. and non-U.S. citizens.

Application Requirements: Application form, community service, essay, financial need analysis, interview. *Deadline:* January 13.

Contact: Travis Mears, Director of Development and Scholarship Programs
Greater Seattle Business Association
400 East Pine Street
Suite 322
Seattle, WA 98122
Phone: 206-363-9188
E-mail: travis@thegsba.org

GREATER WASHINGTON URBAN LEAGUE

http://www.gwul.org/

SAFEWAY/GREATER WASHINGTON URBAN LEAGUE SCHOLARSHIP
• *See page 590*

GREAT LAKES HEMOPHILIA FOUNDATION

http://www.glhf.org/

GLHF INDIVIDUAL CLASS SCHOLARSHIP
• *See page 631*

GREAT LAKES HEMOPHILIA FOUNDATION EDUCATION SCHOLARSHIP
• *See page 631*

GREENHOUSE SCHOLARS

http://greenhousescholars.org/our-scholars/become-a-scholar/

GREENHOUSE SCHOLARS
• *See page 590*

HARRINGTON FAMILY FOUNDATION

http://harringtonfamilyfoundation.org

OREGON COMMUNITY QUARTERBACK SCHOLARSHIP
• *See page 590*

HAWAIIAN LODGE, F&AM

www.hawaiianlodgefreemasons.org

HAWAIIAN LODGE SCHOLARSHIPS

The Hawaiian Lodge, Free and Accepted Masons Scholarship Program is dedicated to worthy High School seniors who wish to pursue a degree in the areas of Engineering, the Sciences, Hawaiian studies, or Education - who may otherwise not be able to attend college. First and foremost, we look for a consistently good GPA throughout High School - with an eye towards the difficulty of the classes attended. Applicants will be asked to submit with their application, a written (or typed) essay which will enlighten the committee on the applicant's views and opinions on a selected topic or philosophy. Also requested will be recommendation letters from the applicant's mentors and role models. An applicant's (family) financial need will be judged by the submission of a (sanitized) IRS Form 1040 showing their household income. Hawaiian Lodge encourages awardees to maintain good study habits, and rewards steadfast follow-on applicants with continuing awards throughout their Baccalaureate studies. Hawaiian Lodge reserves the right to choose their awardees based on the above criteria, with GPA being important, the Essay being essential and financial need being a strong driver towards the Scholarship selection. Masonic Membership or Affiliation through family is noted by the committee.

Award: Scholarship for use in freshman, sophomore, junior, or senior years; not renewable. *Number:* 10–16. *Amount:* $1500.

Eligibility Requirements: Applicant must be age 18-25; enrolled or expecting to enroll full-time at a two-year or four-year institution or university and resident of Hawaii. Applicant must have 3.0 GPA or higher. Available to U.S. citizens.

Application Requirements: Application form, essay, financial need analysis, interview. *Deadline:* May 31.

Contact: Mr. Robert Schultz, Chairman, Scholarship Committee
Hawaiian Lodge, F&AM
94-1002 Lauwi Place
Waipahu, HI 96797
Phone: 808-220-3859
E-mail: robert.schultz@icloud.com

HAWAII EDUCATION ASSOCIATION

http://www.heaed.com/

HAWAII EDUCATION ASSOCIATION HIGH SCHOOL STUDENT SCHOLARSHIP
• *See page 544*

HAWAII SCHOOLS FEDERAL CREDIT UNION

http://www.hawaiischoolsfcu.org/

EDWIN KUNIYUKI MEMORIAL SCHOLARSHIP

Annual scholarship for an incoming college freshman in recognition of academic excellence. Applicant must be Hawaii Schools Federal Credit Union member for one year prior to scholarship application.

Award: Scholarship for use in freshman year; not renewable. *Number:* 1. *Amount:* $1000.

Eligibility Requirements: Applicant must be high school student; planning to enroll or expecting to enroll full-time at a two-year or four-year or technical institution or university and resident of Hawaii. Applicant must have 3.0 GPA or higher. Available to U.S. citizens.

Application Requirements: Application form, essay, recommendations or references, transcript. *Deadline:* February 28.

Contact: Kristy Garan, Administrative Assistant
Phone: 808-521-0302
Fax: 808-791-6229
E-mail: kgaran@hawaiischoolsfcu.org

HAWAII STATE POSTSECONDARY EDUCATION COMMISSION

HAWAII STATE STUDENT INCENTIVE GRANT

Grants are given to residents of Hawaii who are enrolled in a participating Hawaiian state school. Funds are for undergraduate tuition only. Applicants must submit a financial need analysis.

Award: Grant for use in freshman, sophomore, junior, or senior years; renewable. *Number:* 470. *Amount:* $200–$2000.

Eligibility Requirements: Applicant must be enrolled or expecting to enroll full- or part-time at a two-year or four-year or technical institution or university; resident of Hawaii and studying in Hawaii. Available to U.S. citizens.

Application Requirements: Application form, financial need analysis. *Deadline:* continuous.

Contact: Janine Oyama, Financial Aid Specialist
Hawaii State Postsecondary Education Commission
University of Hawaii
Honolulu, HI 96822
Phone: 808-956-6066

HELLENIC UNIVERSITY CLUB OF NEW YORK

http://www.hucny.com

HELLENIC UNIVERSITY CLUB UNDERGRADUATE SCHOLARSHIP AWARDS PROGRAM
• *See page 681*

HELLENIC UNIVERSITY CLUB OF PHILADELPHIA

http://www.hucphiladelphia.org/

CHRISTOPHER DEMETRIS SCHOLARSHIP
• *See page 681*

DR. NICHOLAS PADIS MEMORIAL GRADUATE SCHOLARSHIP
• *See page 681*

DORIZAS MEMORIAL SCHOLARSHIP
• *See page 681*

FOUNDERS SCHOLARSHIP
• *See page 681*

PAIDEIA SCHOLARSHIP
• *See page 544*

HEMOPHILIA FOUNDATION OF SOUTHERN CALIFORNIA

http://www.hemosocal.org/

CHRISTOPHER MARK PITKIN MEMORIAL SCHOLARSHIP
• *See page 632*

HENKEL CONSUMER ADHESIVES INC.

http://www.ducktapeclub.com/

DUCK BRAND DUCT TAPE "STUCK AT PROM" SCHOLARSHIP CONTEST

• See page 591

HERB KOHL EDUCATIONAL FOUNDATION INC.

http://www.kohleducation.org/

HERB KOHL EXCELLENCE SCHOLARSHIP PROGRAM

• See page 591

HISPANIC METROPOLITAN CHAMBER SCHOLARSHIPS

http://www.hmccoregon.com/

HISPANIC METROPOLITAN CHAMBER SCHOLARSHIPS

• See page 592

HOOVER PRESIDENTIAL FOUNDATION

http://www.hooverpresidentialfoundation.org/

HERBERT HOOVER UNCOMMON STUDENT AWARD

Award for juniors attending an Iowa high school or home school program only. Grades and test scores are not evaluated. Applicants are chosen on the basis of submitted project proposals. Those chosen will complete their proposed project and make a presentation to receive $1000. Three are chosen for $5000 scholarships.

Award: Scholarship for use in freshman or sophomore years; not renewable. *Number:* 15. *Amount:* $1000–$5000.

Eligibility Requirements: Applicant must be high school student; planning to enroll or expecting to enroll full-time at a two-year or four-year or technical institution or university and resident of Iowa. Available to U.S. citizens.

Application Requirements: Application form. *Deadline:* March 15.

Contact: Ms. Delene McConnaha, Membership and Academic Programs Manager
Hoover Presidential Foundation
PO Box 696
302 Parkside Drive
West Branch, IA 52358-0696
Phone: 319-643-5327
E-mail: DMcConnaha@HooverPF.org

HOUSTON COMMUNITY SERVICES

AZTECA SCHOLARSHIP

• See page 592

HUMANE SOCIETY OF THE UNITED STATES

http://www.hsus.org/

SHAW-WORTH MEMORIAL SCHOLARSHIP

Scholarship for a New England high school senior, who has made a meaningful contribution to animal protection over a significant amount of time. Passive liking of animals or the desire to enter an animal care field does not justify the award.

Award: Scholarship for use in freshman year; not renewable. *Number:* 1. *Amount:* $2000.

Eligibility Requirements: Applicant must be high school student; planning to enroll or expecting to enroll full-time at a four-year institution or university and resident of Connecticut, Maine, Massachusetts, New Hampshire, Rhode Island, Vermont. Available to U.S. citizens.

Application Requirements: Essay, recommendations or references. *Deadline:* March 17.

Contact: Administrator
Humane Society of the United States
PO Box 619
Jacksonville, VT 05342-0619
Phone: 802-368-2790
Fax: 802-368-2756

IDAHO STATE BOARD OF EDUCATION

http://www.boardofed.idaho.gov/

IDAHO GOVERNOR'S CUP SCHOLARSHIP

• See page 593

IDAHO OPPORTUNITY SCHOLARSHIP

The Idaho Opportunity Scholarship is an award open to Idaho citizens who have graduated from Idaho high schools. The application is open to any high school or college students who attended an Idaho high school, are Idaho residents, and are attending or who are planning on attending an eligible Idaho college or university. Students must be earning their first undergraduate degree. The required GPA is a 3.0 and applicants must show need by completing the FAFSA by March 1 each year. The award is renewable for a total of 4 years.

Award: Scholarship for use in freshman, sophomore, junior, or senior years; renewable. *Number:* 700–2000. *Amount:* $1–$3000.

Eligibility Requirements: Applicant must be enrolled or expecting to enroll full-time at a two-year or four-year or technical institution or university; resident of Idaho and studying in Idaho. Applicant must have 3.0 GPA or higher. Available to U.S. citizens.

Application Requirements: Application form, financial need analysis. *Deadline:* March 1.

Contact: Joy Miller, Scholarships Program Manager
Idaho State Board of Education
650 West State Street, #307
Boise, ID 83720-0037
Phone: 208-332-1595
E-mail: joy.miller@osbe.idaho.gov

ILLINOIS AMVETS

http://www.ilamvets.org/

ILLINOIS AMVETS JUNIOR ROTC SCHOLARSHIPS

One year, $1000 scholarship (non-renewal) for high school seniors who have taken the ACT or SAT tests. Preference will be given to children or grandchildren of veterans and active-duty. Student must be enrolled in JROTC program.

Award: Scholarship for use in freshman year; not renewable. *Number:* 5. *Amount:* $1000.

Eligibility Requirements: Applicant must be high school student; planning to enroll or expecting to enroll full-time at a two-year or four-year or technical institution or university and resident of Illinois. Available to U.S. citizens.

Application Requirements: Application form. *Deadline:* March 1.

Contact: Crystal Blakeman, Programs Director
Illinois AMVETS
2200 S. 6th St.
Springfield, IL 62703
Phone: 217-528-4713 Ext. 207
E-mail: Crystal@ilamvets.org

ILLINOIS AMVETS LADIES AUXILIARY MEMORIAL SCHOLARSHIP

• See page 656

ILLINOIS AMVETS LADIES AUXILIARY WORCHID SCHOLARSHIPS

• See page 656

ILLINOIS AMVETS SERVICE FOUNDATION

• See page 656

ILLINOIS AMVETS TRADE SCHOOL SCHOLARSHIP
• *See page 656*

ILLINOIS COUNCIL OF THE BLIND
http://www.icbonline.org/

FLOYD R. CARGILL SCHOLARSHIP
• *See page 632*

ILLINOIS COUNTIES ASSOCIATION
http://www.illinoiscountiesassociation.org/

ILLINOIS COUNTIES ASSOCIATION SCHOLARSHIP
Preferential treatment will be given to: 1) individuals demonstrating a dedicated pursuit toward a career in government, public service or public administration as evidenced by involvement in a course of study, work and volunteer service or internships in public, government, community and/or legislative environments; and, 2) students with immediate family members employed by a county participating in the Nationwide Retirement Solutions 457 program.

Award: Scholarship for use in freshman year; not renewable. *Number:* 15. *Amount:* $3000.

Eligibility Requirements: Applicant must be high school student; planning to enroll or expecting to enroll full-time at a four-year institution or university and resident of Illinois. Applicant must have 3.0 GPA or higher. Available to U.S. citizens.

Application Requirements: Application form, essay, financial need analysis. *Deadline:* April 28.

Contact: Courtney Adams, Scholarship Coordinator
Illinois Counties Association
100 East Washington
Springfield, IL 62701
Phone: 217-528-3434
E-mail: courtneyadams@frontline-online.net

ILLINOIS DEPARTMENT OF VETERANS' AFFAIRS
https://www.illinois.gov/veterans/Pages/default.aspx

MIA/POW SCHOLARSHIP
• *See page 657*

VETERANS' CHILDREN EDUCATIONAL OPPORTUNITIES
• *See page 657*

ILLINOIS STUDENT ASSISTANCE COMMISSION (ISAC)
http://www.isac.org/

GRANT PROGRAM FOR DEPENDENTS OF POLICE, FIRE, OR CORRECTIONAL OFFICERS
Awards available to Illinois residents who are dependents of police, fire, and correctional officers killed or disabled in line of duty. Provides for tuition and fees at approved Illinois institutions. Number of grants and individual dollar amount awarded vary.

Award: Grant for use in freshman, sophomore, junior, senior, graduate, or postgraduate years; renewable.

Eligibility Requirements: Applicant must be enrolled or expecting to enroll full- or part-time at a two-year or four-year or technical institution or university; resident of Illinois and studying in Illinois. Available to U.S. citizens.

Application Requirements: Application form. *Deadline:* October 1.

Contact: ISAC Call Center Representative
Illinois Student Assistance Commission (ISAC)
1755 Lake Cook Road
Deerfield, IL 60015-5209
Phone: 800-899-4722
E-mail: isac.studentservices@isac.illinois.gov

HIGHER EDUCATION LICENSE PLATE PROGRAM-HELP
Grants for students who attend Illinois colleges for which the special collegiate license plates are available. The Illinois Secretary of State issues the license plates, and part of the proceeds are used for grants for undergraduate students attending these colleges, to pay tuition and mandatory fees.

Award: Grant for use in freshman, sophomore, junior, or senior years; not renewable.

Eligibility Requirements: Applicant must be enrolled or expecting to enroll full- or part-time at a two-year or four-year institution or university; resident of Illinois and studying in Illinois. Available to U.S. citizens.

Application Requirements: Application form, financial need analysis. *Deadline:* continuous.

Contact: ISAC Call Center Representative
Illinois Student Assistance Commission (ISAC)
1755 Lake Cook Road
Deerfield, IL 60015-5209
Phone: 800-899-4722
E-mail: isac.studentservices@isac.illinois.gov

ILLINOIS MONETARY AWARD PROGRAM
Awards to Illinois residents enrolled in a minimum of 3 hours per term in a degree program at an approved Illinois institution. See website for complete list of participating schools. Must demonstrate financial need, based on the information provided on the Free Application for Federal Student Aid. Number of grants and the individual dollar amount awarded vary. Deadline: As soon as possible after October 1 of the year before the student will enter college.

Award: Grant for use in freshman, sophomore, junior, or senior years; not renewable. *Amount:* $2987.

Eligibility Requirements: Applicant must be enrolled or expecting to enroll full- or part-time at a two-year or four-year or technical institution or university; resident of Illinois and studying in Illinois. Available to U.S. citizens.

Application Requirements: Financial need analysis. *Deadline:* June 30.

Contact: ISAC Call Center Representative
Illinois Student Assistance Commission (ISAC)
1755 Lake Cook Road
Deerfield, IL 60015-5209
Phone: 800-899-4722
E-mail: isac.studentservices@isac.illinois.gov

ILLINOIS NATIONAL GUARD GRANT PROGRAM
• *See page 642*

ILLINOIS VETERAN GRANT PROGRAM-IVG
• *See page 657*

INDIANA DEPARTMENT OF VETERANS AFFAIRS
http://www.in.gov/dva

CHILD OF DISABLED VETERAN GRANT OR PURPLE HEART RECIPIENT GRANT
Free tuition at Indiana state-supported colleges or universities for children of disabled veterans or Purple Heart recipients. Must submit form DD214 or service record. Covers tuition and mandatory fees.

Award: Grant for use in freshman, sophomore, junior, senior, graduate, or postgraduate years; renewable.

Eligibility Requirements: Applicant must be enrolled or expecting to enroll full- or part-time at a two-year or four-year institution or university; resident of Indiana and studying in Indiana. Available to U.S. citizens.

Application Requirements: Application form.

Contact: Jon Brinkley, State Service Officer
Phone: 317-232-3910
Fax: 317-232-7721
E-mail: jbrinkley@dva.in.gov

DEPARTMENT OF VETERANS AFFAIRS FREE TUITION FOR CHILDREN OF POW/MIA'S IN VIETNAM

Renewable award for residents of Indiana who are the children of veterans declared missing in action or prisoner-of-war after January 1, 1960. Provides tuition at Indiana state-supported institutions for undergraduate study.

Award: Grant for use in freshman, sophomore, junior, senior, graduate, or postgraduate years; renewable.

Eligibility Requirements: Applicant must be enrolled or expecting to enroll full- or part-time at a two-year or four-year institution or university; resident of Indiana and studying in Indiana. Available to U.S. citizens.

Application Requirements: Application form.

Contact: Jon Brinkley, State Service Officer
Phone: 317-232-3910
Fax: 317-232-7721
E-mail: jbrinkley@dva.in.gov

INDIAN AMERICAN CULTURAL ASSOCIATION

http://www.iasf.org/

INDIAN AMERICAN SCHOLARSHIP FUND

• *See page 682*

INSTITUTE FOR JUSTICE

http://www.ij.org

LIBERTY IN ACTION ESSAY CONTEST: REMOVING BARRIERS TO ENTREPRENEURSHIP

• *See page 593*

INTER-COUNTY ENERGY

http://www.intercountyenergy.net/

INTER-COUNTY ENERGY SCHOLARSHIP

One $1,000 scholarship given to a high school senior in each of Inter-County Energy's six directorial districts: Boyle, Lincoln, Mercer, Garrard, Casey and Marion. Applicant's parent or legal guardian must be a member of Inter-County Energy with the primary residence being on the cooperative lines.

Award: Scholarship for use in freshman year; not renewable. *Number:* 6. *Amount:* $1000.

Eligibility Requirements: Applicant must be high school student; planning to enroll or expecting to enroll full-time at a four-year institution or university and resident of Kentucky. Available to U.S. citizens.

Application Requirements: Application form, community service, financial need analysis. *Deadline:* March 17.

Contact: April Burgess, Member Services Advisor
Inter-County Energy
PO Box 87
Danville, KY 40423
Phone: 859-236-4561 Ext. 7822
Fax: 859-236-5012
E-mail: april@intercountyenergy.net

IOWA COLLEGE STUDENT AID COMMISSION

http://www.iowacollegeaid.gov/

IOWA NATIONAL GUARD EDUCATION ASSISTANCE PROGRAM

• *See page 643*

IOWA TUITION GRANT PROGRAM

Program assists students who attend independent postsecondary institutions in Iowa. Iowa residents currently enrolled, or planning to enroll, for at least 3 semester hours at one of the eligible Iowa postsecondary institutions may apply. Awards currently range from $100 to $5650. Grants may not exceed the difference between independent college and university tuition fees and the average tuition fees at the three public Regent universities.

Award: Grant for use in freshman, sophomore, junior, or senior years; not renewable. *Number:* 16,500–19,000. *Amount:* $100–$5650.

Eligibility Requirements: Applicant must be enrolled or expecting to enroll full- or part-time at a two-year or four-year institution or university; resident of Iowa and studying in Iowa. Available to U.S. citizens.

Application Requirements: Financial need analysis. *Deadline:* July 1.

Contact: Tristan Lynn, Executive Officer 1
Iowa College Student Aid Commission
430 E Grand Avenue, FL 3
Des Moines, IA 50309-1920
Phone: 515-725-3409
E-mail: tristan.lynn@iowa.gov

IOWA VOCATIONAL-TECHNICAL TUITION GRANT PROGRAM

Program provides need-based financial assistance to Iowa residents enrolled in career education (vocational-technical), and career option programs at Iowa area community colleges. Grants range from $150 to $1200, depending on the length of the program, financial need, and available funds.

Award: Grant for use in freshman or sophomore years; not renewable. *Number:* 2500–3500. *Amount:* $150–$1200.

Eligibility Requirements: Applicant must be enrolled or expecting to enroll full- or part-time at a two-year or technical institution; resident of Iowa and studying in Iowa. Available to U.S. citizens.

Application Requirements: Financial need analysis. *Deadline:* July 1.

Contact: Tristan Lynn, Executive Officer 1
Iowa College Student Aid Commission
430 E Grand Avenue, FL 3
Des Moines, IA 50309-1920
Phone: 515-725-3409
E-mail: tristan.lynn@iowa.gov

IOWA STUDENT LOAN

http://www.IowaStudentLoan.org/

COME 2 IOWA (C2IA) SENIOR SCHOLARSHIP

To participate in the C2IA Senior Scholarship, eligible students may register at http://www.IowaStudentLoan.org/Come2Iowa and then complete two online financial literacy tutorials plus an assessment. A short essay may be required to break ties among students who achieve a top score on the assessment.

Award: Scholarship for use in freshman year; not renewable. *Number:* 5. *Amount:* $1000.

Eligibility Requirements: Applicant must be high school student; age 13-99; planning to enroll or expecting to enroll full- or part-time at a two-year or four-year or technical institution or university; resident of Illinois, Minnesota, Missouri, Nebraska, South Dakota, Wisconsin and studying in Iowa. Available to U.S. citizens.

Application Requirements: Application form. *Deadline:* May 12.

Contact: Matt Brown, Communications, Program and Research Liaison
Iowa Student Loan
6775 Vista Drive
West Des Moines, IA 50266
Phone: 515-273-7656
E-mail: scholarship@studentloan.org

IOWA FINANCIAL KNOW-HOW CHALLENGE: SENIOR SCHOLARSHIP

• *See page 596*

ITALIAN-AMERICAN CHAMBER OF COMMERCE OF CHICAGO

http://www.iacc-chicago.com/

ITALIAN-AMERICAN CHAMBER OF COMMERCE OF CHICAGO SCHOLARSHIP

• *See page 683*

ITALIAN CATHOLIC FEDERATION

http://www.icf.org/

ITALIAN CATHOLIC FEDERATION FIRST YEAR SCHOLARSHIP

• *See page 546*

MARIO CUGIA ITALIAN STUDIES SCHOLARSHIP PROGRAM

• *See page 683*

JACKSON ENERGY COOPERATIVE

http://www.jacksonenergy.com/

JACKSON ENERGY SCHOLARSHIP ESSAY CONTEST

Applicant must be a high school senior. Scholarships are awarded to winners in an essay contest. Applicants, their parents, or legal guardians must be members of Jackson Energy Cooperative; may not be a spouse or an employee or director of Jackson Energy. Scholarships are paid directly to winner's college, university, or institution of higher education.

Award: Scholarship for use in freshman, sophomore, junior, or senior years; not renewable. *Number:* 8. *Amount:* $2000.

Eligibility Requirements: Applicant must be high school student; planning to enroll or expecting to enroll full-time at a two-year or four-year or technical institution or university and resident of Kentucky. Available to U.S. citizens.

Application Requirements: Application form, essay. *Deadline:* November 25.

Contact: Jamie Gaddis, Director of Community and Economic
  Development
  Jackson Energy Cooperative
  115 Jackson Energy Lane
  McKee, KY 40447
  Phone: 606-364-9233
  E-mail: jamiegaddis@jacksonenergy.com

JAMES F. BYRNES FOUNDATION

http://www.byrnesscholars.org/

JAMES F. BYRNES SCHOLARSHIP

Renewable award for residents of South Carolina ages in their Senior year High School, with one or both parents deceased. Must show financial need; a satisfactory scholastic record; and qualities of character, ability, and enterprise. Award is for undergraduate study. Results of SAT must be provided. Information available on website http://www.byrnesscholars.org.

Award: Scholarship for use in freshman year; renewable. *Number:* 6–10. *Amount:* up to $14,000.

Eligibility Requirements: Applicant must be high school student; age 17-19; planning to enroll or expecting to enroll full-time at a four-year institution and resident of South Carolina. Available to U.S. citizens.

Application Requirements: Application form, essay, financial need analysis, interview, personal photograph. *Deadline:* February 6.

Contact: Kenya White, Executive Secretary
  James F. Byrnes Foundation
  PO Box 6781
  Columbia, SC 29260-6781
  Phone: 803-254-9325
  E-mail: info@byrnesscholars.org

J. CRAIG AND PAGE T. SMITH SCHOLARSHIP FOUNDATION

http://www.jcraigsmithfoundation.org/

FIRST IN FAMILY SCHOLARSHIP

Scholarships are available for graduating Alabama high school seniors. Must be planning to enroll in an Alabama institution in fall and pursue a four-year degree. Students who apply must want to give back to their community by volunteer and civic work. Special consideration will be given to applicants who would be the first in either their mother's or father's family (or both) to attend college.

Award: Scholarship for use in freshman year; renewable. *Number:* 10. *Amount:* $12,500–$15,000.

Eligibility Requirements: Applicant must be high school student; planning to enroll or expecting to enroll full-time at a four-year institution or university; resident of Alabama and studying in Alabama. Applicant must have 2.5 GPA or higher. Available to U.S. citizens.

Application Requirements: Application form, community service, essay, financial need analysis, recommendations or references, test scores, transcript. *Deadline:* January 15.

Contact: Ahrian Tyler, Administrator/Chairman of the Board
  Phone: 205-250-6669
  Fax: 205-328-7234
  E-mail: ahrian@jcraigsmithfoundation.org

JEWISH VOCATIONAL SERVICE LOS ANGELES

http://www.jvsla.org/

JVS SCHOLARSHIP PROGRAM

• *See page 684*

J. WOOD PLATT CADDIE SCHOLARSHIP TRUST

http://www.plattcaddiescholarship.org/

J. WOOD PLATT CADDIE SCHOLARSHIP TRUST

The Platt Caddie Scholarship is available to individuals who caddie at Golf Association of Philadelphia Member Clubs and is solely based on financial need, as a result of submitting the FAFSA application and other financial documents. This is not an athletic or golf scholarship.

Award: Scholarship for use in freshman, sophomore, junior, senior, graduate, or postgraduate years; renewable. *Amount:* $1000–$10,000.

Eligibility Requirements: Applicant must be enrolled or expecting to enroll full-time at a two-year or four-year or technical institution or university and resident of Delaware, New Jersey, Pennsylvania. Available to U.S. and non-U.S. citizens.

Application Requirements: Application form, essay, financial need analysis, interview. *Deadline:* November 30.

Contact: Bradley Kane, Director, Platt Caddie Scholarship
  J. Wood Platt Caddie Scholarship Trust
  1974 Sproul Road
  Suite 400
  Broomall, PA 19008
  Phone: 610-687-2340 Ext. 21
  Fax: 610-687-2082
  E-mail: bkane@gapgolf.org

KANSAS BOARD OF REGENTS

http://www.kansasregents.org/

KANSAS ETHNIC MINORITY SCHOLARSHIP

• *See page 685*

KAUFMAN & STIGGER, PLLC

http://www.getthetiger.com/

THE ALBERTA C. KAUFMAN SCHOLARSHIP

• *See page 597*

KENTUCKY ASSOCIATION OF ELECTRIC COOPERATIVES, INC.

http://www.kaec.com/

WOMEN IN RURAL ELECTRIFICATION (WIRE) SCHOLARSHIPS

Scholarship available to Kentucky students who are juniors or seniors in a Kentucky college or university and have 60 credit hours by the fall semester. Immediate family of student must be served by one of the state's 24 rural electric distribution cooperatives. Awards based on academic achievement, extracurricular activities, career goals, recommendations.

Award: Scholarship for use in junior, senior, graduate, or postgraduate years; not renewable. *Number:* 3. *Amount:* $1000.

Eligibility Requirements: Applicant must be enrolled or expecting to enroll full-time at a two-year or four-year or technical institution or university; resident of Kentucky and studying in Kentucky. Available to U.S. citizens.

Application Requirements: Application form. *Deadline:* April 10.

Contact: Mary Beth Dennis, Meeting Coordinator
Kentucky Association of Electric Cooperatives, Inc.
PO Box 32170
Louisville, KY 40232
Phone: 502-815-6302
E-mail: mbdennis@kaec.org

KENTUCKY DEPARTMENT OF VETERANS AFFAIRS

http://www.veterans.ky.gov/

DEPARTMENT OF VETERANS AFFAIRS TUITION WAIVER-KY KRS 164-507

Scholarship available to college students who are residents of Kentucky under the age of 26.

Award: Scholarship for use in freshman, sophomore, junior, or senior years; not renewable. *Number:* 400.

Eligibility Requirements: Applicant must be enrolled or expecting to enroll full- or part-time at a two-year or four-year institution or university and resident of Kentucky. Available to U.S. citizens.

Application Requirements: Application form. *Deadline:* varies.

Contact: Barbara Sipek, Tuition Waiver Coordinator
Phone: 502-595-4447
E-mail: barbaraa.sipek@ky.gov

KENTUCKY HIGHER EDUCATION ASSISTANCE AUTHORITY (KHEAA)

http://www.kheaa.com/

COLLEGE ACCESS PROGRAM (CAP) GRANT

Award for U.S. citizens and Kentucky residents seeking their first undergraduate degree. Applicants enrolled in sectarian institutions are not eligible. Must submit Free Application for Federal Student Aid to demonstrate financial need. Funding is limited. Awards are made on a first-come, first-serve basis.

Award: Grant for use in freshman, sophomore, junior, or senior years; not renewable. *Number:* 44,900–45,000. *Amount:* $475–$1900.

Eligibility Requirements: Applicant must be enrolled or expecting to enroll full- or part-time at a two-year or four-year or technical institution or university; resident of Kentucky and studying in Kentucky. Available to U.S. citizens.

Application Requirements: Application form. *Deadline:* continuous.

Contact: Sheila Roe, Program Coordinator
Kentucky Higher Education Assistance Authority (KHEAA)
PO Box 798
Frankfort, KY 40602-0798
Phone: 800-928-8926 Ext. 67393
E-mail: sroe@kheaa.com

EARLY CHILDHOOD DEVELOPMENT SCHOLARSHIP

Awards scholarship with conditional service commitment for part-time students currently employed by participating ECD facility or providing training in ECD for an approved organization. For more information, visit website http://www.kheaa.com.

Award: Scholarship for use in freshman, sophomore, junior, or senior years; not renewable. *Number:* 500–800. *Amount:* $100–$1800.

Eligibility Requirements: Applicant must be enrolled or expecting to enroll part-time at a two-year or four-year institution or university; resident of Kentucky and studying in Kentucky. Available to U.S. citizens.

Application Requirements: Application form. *Deadline:* continuous.

Contact: Danny Prather, Program Coordinator
Kentucky Higher Education Assistance Authority (KHEAA)
PO Box 798
Frankfort, KY 40602-0798
Phone: 800-928-8926 Ext. 67399
E-mail: danprather@kheaa.com

GO HIGHER GRANT

Need-based grant for adult students pursuing their first undergraduate degree. Completion of the FAFSA is required.

Award: Grant for use in freshman year; not renewable. *Number:* 100–300. *Amount:* $50–$1000.

Eligibility Requirements: Applicant must be enrolled or expecting to enroll full- or part-time at a two-year or four-year or technical institution or university; resident of Kentucky and studying in Kentucky. Available to U.S. citizens.

Application Requirements: Application form. *Deadline:* continuous.

Contact: Sheila Roe, Grant Program Coordinator
Kentucky Higher Education Assistance Authority (KHEAA)
PO Box 798
Frankfort, KY 40206-0798
Phone: 800-928-8926 Ext. 67393
E-mail: sroe@kheaa.com

KENTUCKY EDUCATIONAL EXCELLENCE SCHOLARSHIP (KEES)

Annual award based on yearly high school GPA and highest ACT or SAT score received by high school graduation. Awards are renewable, if required cumulative GPA is maintained at a Kentucky postsecondary school. Must be a Kentucky resident, and a graduate of a Kentucky high school. Low-income students who qualify for the free/reduced lunch program at least one year of high school may receive supplemental awards for passing scores on Advanced Placement (AP) or International Baccalaureate (IB) exams.

Award: Scholarship for use in freshman, sophomore, junior, or senior years; renewable. *Number:* 65,000–75,000. *Amount:* $125–$2500.

Eligibility Requirements: Applicant must be enrolled or expecting to enroll full- or part-time at a two-year or four-year or technical institution or university; resident of Kentucky and studying in Kentucky. Available to U.S. citizens.

Contact: Becky Gilpatrick, Director of Student Aid Services
Kentucky Higher Education Assistance Authority (KHEAA)
PO Box 798
Frankfort, KY 40602
Phone: 800-928-8926 Ext. 67394
E-mail: rgilpatrick@kheaa.com

KENTUCKY NATIONAL GUARD TUITION AWARD

• See page 643

KENTUCKY TUITION GRANT (KTG)

Grants available to Kentucky residents who are full-time undergraduates at an independent college within the state. Based on financial need. Must submit FAFSA.

Award: Grant for use in freshman, sophomore, junior, or senior years; not renewable. *Number:* 10,000–12,500. *Amount:* $200–$3000.

Eligibility Requirements: Applicant must be enrolled or expecting to enroll full-time at a two-year or four-year institution or university; resident of Kentucky and studying in Kentucky. Available to U.S. citizens.

Application Requirements: Application form. *Deadline:* continuous.

Contact: Sheila Roe, Grant Program Coordinator
Kentucky Higher Education Assistance Authority (KHEAA)
PO Box 798
Frankfort, KY 40602-0798
Phone: 800-928-8926 Ext. 67393
E-mail: sroe@kheaa.com

MARY JO YOUNG SCHOLARSHIP

Provides financial assistance for tuition and textbook expenses incurred by Kentucky high school students taking college/dual credit coursework.

Award: Scholarship for use in freshman year; not renewable. *Number:* 700–1000. *Amount:* $125–$840.

Eligibility Requirements: Applicant must be high school student; planning to enroll or expecting to enroll part-time at a two-year or four-year or technical institution or university; resident of Kentucky and studying in Kentucky. Applicant must have 2.5 GPA or higher. Available to U.S. citizens.

Application Requirements: Application form. *Deadline:* May 1.

Contact: Danny Prather, Program Coordinator
Kentucky Higher Education Assistance Authority (KHEAA)
PO Box 798
Frankfort, KY 40602-0798
Phone: 800-938-8926 Ext. 67399
E-mail: danprather@kheaa.com

KENTUCKY TOUCHSTONE ENERGY COOPERATIVES

http://www.ekpc.coop

TOUCHSTONE ENERGY ALL "A" CLASSIC SCHOLARSHIP

Award of $1000 for senior student in good standing at a Kentucky high school which is a member of the All Classic. Applicant must be a U.S. citizen and must plan to attend a postsecondary institution in Kentucky in the upcoming year as a full-time student and be drug free.

Award: Scholarship for use in freshman year; not renewable. *Number:* 12. *Amount:* $1000.

Eligibility Requirements: Applicant must be high school student; planning to enroll or expecting to enroll full-time at a two-year or four-year or technical institution or university; resident of Kentucky and studying in Kentucky. Available to U.S. citizens.

Application Requirements: Application form, essay, personal photograph, recommendations or references, transcript. *Deadline:* December 3.

Contact: David Cowden, Chairperson, Scholarship Committee
Kentucky Touchstone Energy Cooperatives
1320 Lincoln Road
Lewisport, KY 42351
Phone: 859-744-4812
E-mail: allaclassic@alltel.net

KOSCIUSZKO FOUNDATION

http://www.thekf.org

MASSACHUSETTS FEDERATION OF POLISH WOMEN'S CLUBS SCHOLARSHIPS
• *See page 686*

POLISH AMERICAN CLUB OF NORTH JERSEY SCHOLARSHIPS
• *See page 686*

POLISH NATIONAL ALLIANCE OF BROOKLYN USA INC. SCHOLARSHIPS
• *See page 687*

LATIN AMERICAN EDUCATIONAL FOUNDATION

http://www.laef.org/

LATIN AMERICAN EDUCATIONAL FOUNDATION SCHOLARSHIPS
• *See page 598*

LEE-JACKSON EDUCATIONAL FOUNDATION

http://www.lee-jackson.org/

LEE-JACKSON EDUCATIONAL FOUNDATION SCHOLARSHIP COMPETITION

Essay contest for junior and senior Virginia high school students. Must demonstrate appreciation for the exemplary character and soldierly virtues of Generals Robert E. Lee and Thomas J. "Stonewall" Jackson. Three one-time awards of $1000 in each of Virginia's eight regions. A bonus scholarship of $1000 will be awarded to the author of the best essay in each of the eight regions. An additional award of $8000 will go to the essay judged the best in the state.

Award: Scholarship for use in freshman, sophomore, junior, or senior years; not renewable. *Number:* 27. *Amount:* $1000–$10,000.

Eligibility Requirements: Applicant must be high school student; planning to enroll or expecting to enroll full-time at a four-year institution or university; resident of Virginia and must have an interest in writing. Available to U.S. citizens.

Application Requirements: Application form, entry in a contest, essay, transcript. *Deadline:* December 21.

Contact: Stephanie Leech, Administrator
Lee-Jackson Educational Foundation
PO Box 8121
Charlottesville, VA 22906
Phone: 434-977-1861
E-mail: salp_leech@yahoo.com

LEPENDORF & SILVERSTEIN, P.C.

http://www.lependorf.com/

LEPENDORF & SILVERSTEIN, P.C. 2017 NEW JERSEY SCHOLARSHIP
• *See page 600*

LEP FOUNDATION FOR YOUTH EDUCATION

http://www.lepfoundation.org/applications

JOHN LEPPING MEMORIAL SCHOLARSHIP
• *See page 600*

LIBERTY GRAPHICS INC.

http://www.lgtees.com

ANNUAL LIBERTY GRAPHICS ART CONTEST

One-time scholarship to the successful student who submits the winning artwork depicting appreciation of the natural environment of Maine. Applicants must be residents of Maine and be a high school seniors. Original works in traditional flat media are the required format. Photography, sculpture and computer-generated work will not be considered. Multiple submissions are allowed.

Award: Prize for use in freshman year; not renewable. *Number:* 1. *Amount:* $1000.

Eligibility Requirements: Applicant must be high school student; planning to enroll or expecting to enroll full- or part-time at a two-year or four-year or technical institution or university; resident of Maine and must have an interest in art. Available to U.S. citizens.

Application Requirements: Application form. *Deadline:* March 13.

Contact: Mr. Jay Sproul, Scholarship Coordinator
Liberty Graphics Inc.
PO Box 5
44 Main Street
Liberty, ME 04949
Phone: 207-589-4596
E-mail: jay@lgtees.com

LOS ALAMOS NATIONAL LABORATORY FOUNDATION

http://www.lanlfoundation.org/

LOS ALAMOS EMPLOYEES' SCHOLARSHIP

Scholarship supports students in Northern New Mexico who are pursuing undergraduate degrees in fields that will serve the region. Financial need, diversity, and regional representation are integral components of the selections process. Applicant should be a permanent resident of Northern New Mexico with at least a 3.25 cumulative GPA and 19 ACT or 930 SAT score.

Award: Scholarship for use in freshman, sophomore, junior, or senior years; renewable. *Number:* 50. *Amount:* $1000–$30,000.

Eligibility Requirements: Applicant must be enrolled or expecting to enroll full- or part-time at a two-year or four-year institution or university and resident of New Mexico. Available to U.S. and non-U.S. citizens.

Application Requirements: Application form, essay, personal photograph, recommendations or references, test scores, transcript. *Deadline:* January 22.

Contact: Tony Fox, Program Officer
Phone: 505-753-8890 Ext. 16
Fax: 505-753-8915
E-mail: tfox@lanlfoundation.org

LOS PADRES FOUNDATION

http://www.lospadresfoundation.com/

COLLEGE TUITION ASSISTANCE PROGRAM
• *See page 688*

SECOND CHANCE SCHOLARSHIPS
• *See page 688*

LOUISIANA DEPARTMENT OF VETERAN AFFAIRS

http://www.vetaffairs.la.gov

LOUISIANA DEPARTMENT OF VETERANS AFFAIRS STATE EDUCATIONAL AID PROGRAM
• *See page 658*

LOUISIANA NATIONAL GUARD, JOINT TASK FORCE LA

http://geauxguard.com/organization/joint-force-headquarters-jfhq-la/

LOUISIANA NATIONAL GUARD STATE TUITION EXEMPTION PROGRAM
• *See page 644*

LOUISIANA OFFICE OF STUDENT FINANCIAL ASSISTANCE

http://www.osfa.la.gov/

TAYLOR OPPORTUNITY PROGRAM FOR STUDENTS HONORS LEVEL

Program awards 8 semesters or 12 terms of tuition to any Louisiana State postsecondary institution plus $400 stipend per semester. Program awards 8 semesters or 12 terms of an amount equal to the weighted average public tuition to students attending a LAICU (Louisiana Association of Independent Colleges and Universities) institution plus $400 stipend per semester. Program awards 8 semesters or 12 terms of an amount equal to the weighted average public tuition to two out-of-state Institutions for Hearing Impaired Students: Gallaudet University and Rochester Institute of Technology plus $400 stipend per semester. Program awards $1744 per year to Approved Proprietary and Cosmetology schools plus a stipend of $800 per year. When you submit the FAFSA, you have automatically applied for all four levels of TOPS, for Federal Pell Grants and Go Grants and for Federal Student Loans. Please do not send separate letters of application to the TOPS office.

Award: Scholarship for use in freshman, sophomore, junior, or senior years; renewable. *Number:* 9661. *Amount:* $836–$6736.

Eligibility Requirements: Applicant must be enrolled or expecting to enroll full-time at a two-year or four-year or technical institution or university; resident of Louisiana and studying in Louisiana. Applicant must have 3.0 GPA or higher. Available to U.S. citizens.

Application Requirements: Application form, application form may be submitted online (http://www.osfa.la.gov), FAFSA, test scores, transcript. *Deadline:* July 1.

Contact: Public Information
Louisiana Office of Student Financial Assistance
PO Box 91202
Baton Rouge, LA 70821-9202
Phone: 800-259-5626 Ext. 1012
Fax: 225-208-1496
E-mail: custserv@osfa.la.gov

TAYLOR OPPORTUNITY PROGRAM FOR STUDENTS OPPORTUNITY LEVEL

Program awards 8 semesters or 12 terms of tuition to any Louisiana State postsecondary institution. Program awards 8 semesters or 12 terms of an amount equal to the weighted average public tuition to students attending a LAICU (Louisiana Association of Independent Colleges and Universities) institution. Program awards 8 semesters or 12 terms of an amount equal to the weighted average public tuition to two out-of-state Institutions for Hearing Impaired Students: Gallaudet University and Rochester Institute of Technology. Program awards $1744 per year to Approved Proprietary and Cosmetology schools. When you submit the FAFSA, you have automatically applied for all four levels of TOPS, and for Federal Pell Grants and Go Grants. Please do not send separate letters of application to the TOPS office.

Award: Scholarship for use in freshman, sophomore, junior, or senior years; renewable. *Number:* 24,633. *Amount:* $436–$5936.

Eligibility Requirements: Applicant must be enrolled or expecting to enroll full-time at a two-year or four-year or technical institution or university; resident of Louisiana and studying in Louisiana. Applicant must have 2.5 GPA or higher. Available to U.S. citizens.

Application Requirements: Application form, application form may be submitted online (http://www.osfa.la.gov), FAFSA, test scores, transcript. *Deadline:* July 1.

Contact: Public Information
Louisiana Office of Student Financial Assistance
PO Box 91202
Baton Rouge, LA 70821-9202
Phone: 800-259-5626 Ext. 1012
Fax: 225-208-1496
E-mail: custserv@osfa.la.gov

TAYLOR OPPORTUNITY PROGRAM FOR STUDENTS PERFORMANCE LEVEL

Program awards 8 semesters or 12 terms of tuition to any Louisiana State postsecondary institution plus $200 stipend per semester. Program awards 8 semesters or 12 terms of an amount equal to the weighted average public tuition to students attending a LAICU (Louisiana Association of Independent Colleges and Universities) institution plus $200 stipend per semester. Program awards 8 semesters or 12 terms of an amount equal to the weighted average public tuition to two out-of-state Institutions for Hearing Impaired Students: Gallaudet University and Rochester Institute of Technology plus $200 stipend per semester. Program awards $1744 plus $400 per year to Approved Proprietary and Cosmetology schools. When you submit the FAFSA, you have automatically applied for all four levels of TOPS, for Federal Pell Grants and Go Grants and for Federal Student Loans. Please do not send separate letters of application to the TOPS office.

Award: Scholarship for use in freshman, sophomore, junior, or senior years; renewable. *Number:* 11,928. *Amount:* $636–$6336.

Eligibility Requirements: Applicant must be enrolled or expecting to enroll full-time at a two-year or four-year or technical institution or university; resident of Louisiana and studying in Louisiana. Applicant must have 3.0 GPA or higher. Available to U.S. citizens.

Application Requirements: Application form, application form may be submitted online (http://www.osfa.la.gov), FAFSA, test scores, transcript. *Deadline:* July 1.

Contact: Public Information
Louisiana Office of Student Financial Assistance
PO Box 91202
Baton Rouge, LA 70821-9202
Phone: 800-259-5626 Ext. 1012
Fax: 225-208-1496
E-mail: custserv@osfa.la.gov

TAYLOR OPPORTUNITY PROGRAM FOR STUDENTS TECH LEVEL

Program awards an amount equal to tuition for up to 4 semesters and two summers of technical training at a Louisiana postsecondary institution that offers a vocational or technical education certificate or diploma program, or a non-academic degree program; or up to $1744 to an approved Proprietary or Cosmetology school. Must have completed the TOPS Opportunity core curriculum or the TOPS Tech core curriculum, must have achieved a 2.50 grade point average over the core curriculum only, and must have achieved an ACT score of 17 or an SAT score of 810. Program awards an amount equal to the weighted average public tuition for technical programs to students attending a LAICU private institution for technical training. When you submit the FAFSA, you have automatically applied for all four levels of TOPS, for Federal Pell Grants and Go Grants and Federal Student Loans. Please do not send separate letters of application to the TOPS office.

Award: Scholarship for use in freshman or sophomore years; renewable. *Number:* 1671. *Amount:* $436–$3985.

Eligibility Requirements: Applicant must be enrolled or expecting to enroll full-time at a technical institution; resident of Louisiana and studying in Louisiana. Applicant must have 2.5 GPA or higher. Available to U.S. citizens.

Application Requirements: Application form, application form may be submitted online (http://www.osfa.la.gov), FAFSA, test scores, transcript. *Deadline:* July 1.

Contact: Public Information
Louisiana Office of Student Financial Assistance
PO Box 91202
Baton Rouge, LA 70821-9202
Phone: 800-259-5626 Ext. 1012
Fax: 225-208-1496
E-mail: custserv@osfa.la.gov

MAINE COMMUNITY COLLEGE SYSTEM

http://www.mccs.me.edu/

EARLY COLLEGE FOR ME

Scholarship for high school students who in their junior year have not made plans for college but are academically capable of success in college. Recipients are selected by their school principal or Guidance Director. Students must be entering a Maine Community College. Refer to website http://www.mccs.me.edu/our-programs/programs-for-high-school-students/early-college/

Award: Scholarship for use in freshman or sophomore years; renewable. *Number:* 400–500. *Amount:* $2000.

Eligibility Requirements: Applicant must be high school student; planning to enroll or expecting to enroll full-time at a two-year institution; resident of Maine and studying in Maine. Available to U.S. citizens.

Application Requirements: Application form, financial need analysis. *Deadline:* April 15.

Contact: Mercedes Pour, State Director, Early College for ME
Maine Community College System
6 Fundy Road, Suite 300
Falmouth, ME 04105
Phone: 207-699-4897
E-mail: mpour@mccs.me.edu

MAINE STATE SOCIETY FOUNDATION OF WASHINGTON, DC INC.

http://mainestatesociety.org/foundation/

MAINE STATE SOCIETY FOUNDATION SCHOLARSHIP
• *See page 601*

MAINE VETERANS SERVICES

http://www.maine.gov/dvem/bvs

VETERANS DEPENDENTS EDUCATIONAL BENEFITS-MAINE
• *See page 658*

MAKING THE TURN AGAINST PARKINSON'S

http://www.makingtheturngolf.com/3/scholarship-award.htm

MAKING THE TURN AGAINST PARKINSON'S SCHOLARSHIP

Making the Turn Against Parkinson's will award a $2,500 scholarship to the student demonstrating the most effort and creativity in achieving the Scholarship Committee's objectives of raising awareness and developing a greater understanding of what it means to live with Parkinson's disease. Additional honorable mention scholarships may be awarded at the discretion of the committee.

Award: Scholarship for use in freshman, sophomore, junior, senior, graduate, or postgraduate years; not renewable. *Number:* 1–4. *Amount:* $1000–$2500.

Eligibility Requirements: Applicant must be enrolled or expecting to enroll full-time at a two-year or four-year institution or university and resident of Michigan. Available to U.S. citizens.

Application Requirements: Application form, driver's license, essay. *Deadline:* March 1.

Contact: Mr. Todd Gardner, President
Williamston, MI 48895
E-mail: scholarship@makingtheturngolf.com

MANA DE SAN DIEGO

http://www.manasd.org/

MANA DE SAN DIEGO SYLVIA CHAVEZ MEMORIAL SCHOLARSHIP
• *See page 601*

MARYLAND STATE HIGHER EDUCATION COMMISSION

http://www.mhec.state.md.us/

DELEGATE SCHOLARSHIP PROGRAM-MARYLAND

Delegate scholarships help Maryland residents attending Maryland degree-granting institutions, certain career schools, or nursing diploma schools. May attend out-of-state institution if Maryland Higher Education Commission deems major to be unique and not offered at a Maryland institution. Free Application for Federal Student Aid may be required. Students interested in this program should apply by contacting their legislative district delegate.

Award: Scholarship for use in freshman, sophomore, junior, or senior years; not renewable. *Number:* up to 3500. *Amount:* $200–$8650.

Eligibility Requirements: Applicant must be enrolled or expecting to enroll full- or part-time at a two-year or four-year or technical institution or university; resident of Maryland and studying in Maryland. Available to U.S. citizens.

Application Requirements: Application form, FAFSA. *Deadline:* continuous.

Contact: Monica Wheatley, Office of Student Financial Assistance
Maryland State Higher Education Commission
839 Bestgate Road, Suite 400
Annapolis, MD 21401-3013
Phone: 800-974-1024
Fax: 410-260-3200
E-mail: osfamail@mhec.state.md.us

EDWARD T. CONROY MEMORIAL SCHOLARSHIP PROGRAM

• See page 602

HOWARD P. RAWLINGS EDUCATIONAL EXCELLENCE AWARDS EDUCATIONAL ASSISTANCE GRANT

Award for Maryland residents accepted or enrolled in a full-time undergraduate degree or certificate program at a Maryland institution or hospital nursing school. Must submit financial aid form by March 1. Must earn 2.0 GPA in college to maintain award.

Award: Grant for use in freshman, sophomore, junior, or senior years; renewable. *Number:* 15,000–30,000. *Amount:* $400–$2700.

Eligibility Requirements: Applicant must be enrolled or expecting to enroll full-time at a two-year or four-year institution or university; resident of Maryland and studying in Maryland. Available to U.S. citizens.

Application Requirements: Application form, financial need analysis. *Deadline:* March 1.

Contact: Office of Student Financial Assistance
Maryland State Higher Education Commission
839 Bestgate Road, Suite 400
Annapolis, MD 21401-3013
Phone: 800-974-1024
Fax: 410-260-3200
E-mail: osfamail@mhec.state.md.us

HOWARD P. RAWLINGS EDUCATIONAL EXCELLENCE AWARDS GUARANTEED ACCESS GRANT

Award for Maryland resident enrolling full-time in an undergraduate program at a Maryland institution. Must be under 21 at time of first award and begin college within one year of completing high school in Maryland with a minimum 2.5 GPA. Must have an annual family income less than 130 percent of the federal poverty level guideline.

Award: Grant for use in freshman, sophomore, junior, or senior years; renewable. *Number:* up to 1000. *Amount:* $400–$14,800.

Eligibility Requirements: Applicant must be enrolled or expecting to enroll full-time at a two-year or four-year institution or university; resident of Maryland and studying in Maryland. Applicant must have 3.5 GPA or higher. Available to U.S. citizens.

Application Requirements: Application form, financial need analysis, transcript. *Deadline:* March 1.

Contact: Theresa Lowe, Office of Student Financial Assistance
Maryland State Higher Education Commission
839 Bestgate Road, Suite 400
Annapolis, MD 21401-3013
Phone: 410-260-4555
Fax: 410-260-3200
E-mail: osfamail@mhec.state.md.us

J.F. TOLBERT MEMORIAL STUDENT GRANT PROGRAM

Awards of $500 granted to Maryland residents attending a private career school in Maryland. The scholarship deadline continues.

Award: Grant for use in freshman or sophomore years; not renewable. *Number:* 522. *Amount:* $500.

Eligibility Requirements: Applicant must be enrolled or expecting to enroll full-time at a technical institution; resident of Maryland and studying in Maryland. Available to U.S. citizens.

Application Requirements: Application form, financial need analysis. *Deadline:* continuous.

Contact: Glenda Hamlet, Office of Student Financial Assistance
Maryland State Higher Education Commission
839 Bestgate Road, Suite 400
Annapolis, MD 21401-3013
Phone: 800-974-1024
Fax: 410-260-3200
E-mail: osfamail@mhec.state.md.us

PART-TIME GRANT PROGRAM-MARYLAND

Funds provided to Maryland colleges and universities. Eligible students must be enrolled on a part-time basis (6 to 11 credits) in an undergraduate degree program. Must demonstrate financial need and also be Maryland resident. Contact financial aid office at institution for more information.

Award: Grant for use in freshman, sophomore, junior, or senior years; renewable. *Number:* 1800–9000. *Amount:* $200–$1500.

Eligibility Requirements: Applicant must be enrolled or expecting to enroll part-time at a two-year or four-year institution or university; resident of Maryland and studying in Maryland. Available to U.S. citizens.

Application Requirements: Application form, financial need analysis. *Deadline:* March 1.

Contact: Monica Wheatley, Program Manager
Maryland State Higher Education Commission
839 Bestgate Road, Suite 400
Annapolis, MD 21401
Phone: 410-260-4560
Fax: 410-260-3202
E-mail: mwheatle@mhec.state.md.us

SENATORIAL SCHOLARSHIPS-MARYLAND

Renewable award for Maryland residents attending a Maryland degree-granting institution, nursing diploma school, or certain private career schools. May be used out-of-state only if Maryland Higher Education Commission deems major to be unique and not offered at Maryland institution. The scholarship value is $400 to $7000.

Award: Scholarship for use in freshman, sophomore, junior, or senior years; renewable. *Number:* up to 7000. *Amount:* $400–$7000.

Eligibility Requirements: Applicant must be enrolled or expecting to enroll full- or part-time at a two-year or four-year or technical institution or university; resident of Maryland and studying in Maryland. Available to U.S. citizens.

Application Requirements: Application form, financial need analysis, test scores. *Deadline:* March 1.

Contact: Monica Wheatley, Office of Student Financial Assistance
Maryland State Higher Education Commission
839 Bestgate Road, Suite 400
Annapolis, MD 21401-3013
Phone: 800-974-1024
Fax: 410-260-3200
E-mail: osfamail@mhec.state.md.us

TUITION WAIVER FOR FOSTER CARE RECIPIENTS

Applicant must be a high school graduate or GED recipient and under the age of 21. Must either have resided in a foster care home in Maryland at the time of high school graduation or GED reception, or until 14th birthday, and been adopted after 14th birthday. Applicant, if status approved, will be exempt from paying tuition and mandatory fees at a public college in Maryland.

Award: Grant for use in freshman, sophomore, junior, senior, or graduate years; renewable.

Eligibility Requirements: Applicant must be enrolled or expecting to enroll full- or part-time at a two-year or four-year institution or university; resident of Maryland and studying in Maryland. Available to U.S. citizens.

Application Requirements: Application form, financial need analysis, must inquire at financial aid office of schools. *Deadline:* March 1.

Contact: Robert Parker, Director
Phone: 410-260-4558
E-mail: rparker@mhec.state.md.us

VETERANS OF THE AFGHANISTAN AND IRAQ CONFLICTS SCHOLARSHIP PROGRAM

• See page 658

WORKFORCE SHORTAGE STUDENT ASSISTANCE GRANT PROGRAM

Scholarship of $4000 available to students who will be required to major in specific areas and will be obligated to serve in the state of Maryland after completion of degree.

Award: Scholarship for use in freshman, sophomore, junior, or senior years; renewable. *Number:* 1300. *Amount:* $4000.

Eligibility Requirements: Applicant must be enrolled or expecting to enroll full- or part-time at a two-year or four-year institution or university; resident of Maryland and studying in Maryland. Available to U.S. citizens.

Application Requirements: Application form, certain majors require additional documentation, essay, financial need analysis, recommendations or references, resume, transcript. *Deadline:* July 1.

Contact: Maura Sappington, Program Manager
Maryland State Higher Education Commission
839 Bestgate Road, Suite 400
Annapolis, MD 21401-3013
Phone: 410-260-4569
Fax: 410-260-3203
E-mail: msapping@mhec.state.md.us

MASSACHUSETTS AFL-CIO

http://www.massaflcio.org/

MASSACHUSETTS AFL-CIO SCHOLARSHIP

Scholarships to union members, their children/stepchildren, grandchildren, nieces, nephews, and non-union Massachusetts high school seniors.

Award: Scholarship for use in freshman year; not renewable. *Number:* 100–150. *Amount:* $250–$12,000.

Eligibility Requirements: Applicant must be high school student; planning to enroll or expecting to enroll full-time at a four-year institution or university; resident of Massachusetts and studying in Massachusetts. Available to U.S. citizens.

Application Requirements: Application form. *Deadline:* December 21.

Contact: Jackie Bergantino, Scholarship Administrator
Phone: 781-324-8230
Fax: 781-324-8225
E-mail: jbergantino@massaflcio.org

MASSACHUSETTS OFFICE OF STUDENT FINANCIAL ASSISTANCE

http://www.osfa.mass.edu/

AGNES M. LINDSAY SCHOLARSHIP

Scholarships for students with demonstrated financial need who are from rural areas of Massachusetts and attend public institutions of higher education in Massachusetts. Deadline varies.

Award: Scholarship for use in freshman, sophomore, junior, or senior years; not renewable.

Eligibility Requirements: Applicant must be enrolled or expecting to enroll full-time at a two-year or four-year institution or university; resident of Massachusetts and studying in Massachusetts. Available to U.S. citizens.

Application Requirements: Application form, financial need analysis. *Deadline:* varies.

Contact: Robert Brun, Director of Scholarships and Grants
Phone: 617-727-9420
Fax: 617-727-0667
E-mail: osfa@osfa.mass.edu

CHRISTIAN A. HERTER MEMORIAL SCHOLARSHIP

Renewable award for Massachusetts residents who are in the tenth and eleventh grades, and whose socio-economic backgrounds and environment may inhibit their ability to attain educational goals. Must exhibit severe personal or family-related difficulties, medical problems, or have overcome a personal obstacle. Provides up to 50 percent of the student's calculated need, as determined by federal methodology, at the college of their choice within the continental United States.

Award: Scholarship for use in freshman, sophomore, junior, or senior years; renewable. *Number:* 25. *Amount:* up to $15,000.

Eligibility Requirements: Applicant must be high school student; planning to enroll or expecting to enroll full-time at a two-year or four-year or technical institution or university and resident of Massachusetts. Applicant must have 2.5 GPA or higher. Available to U.S. citizens.

Application Requirements: Application form, community service, financial need analysis, interview, recommendations or references. *Deadline:* February 1.

Contact: Robert Brun, Director of Scholarships and Grants
Phone: 617-727-9420
Fax: 617-727-0667
E-mail: osfa@osfa.mass.edu

DSS ADOPTED CHILDREN TUITION WAIVER

Need-based tuition waiver for Massachusetts residents who are full-time undergraduate students. Must attend a Massachusetts public institution of higher education and be under 24 years of age. File the FAFSA after January 1. Contact school financial aid office for more information.

Award: Scholarship for use in freshman, sophomore, junior, or senior years; renewable.

Eligibility Requirements: Applicant must be enrolled or expecting to enroll full-time at a two-year or four-year institution and resident of Massachusetts. Available to U.S. and non-Canadian citizens.

Application Requirements: Application form, FAFSA, financial need analysis. *Deadline:* varies.

Contact: Robert Brun, Director of Scholarships and Grants
Phone: 617-727-9420
Fax: 617-727-0667
E-mail: osfa@osfa.mass.edu

JOHN AND ABIGAIL ADAMS SCHOLARSHIP

Scholarship to reward and inspire student achievement, attract more high-performing students to Massachusetts public higher education, and provide families of college-bound students with financial assistance. Must be a U.S. citizen or an eligible non-citizen. There is no application process for the scholarship. Students who are eligible will be notified in the fall of their senior year in high school.

Award: Scholarship for use in freshman year; not renewable.

Eligibility Requirements: Applicant must be high school student; planning to enroll or expecting to enroll full-time at a two-year or four-year institution or university; resident of Massachusetts and studying in Massachusetts. Applicant must have 3.0 GPA or higher. Available to U.S. citizens.

Application Requirements: *Deadline:* varies.

Contact: Robert Brun, Director of Scholarships and Grants
Phone: 617-727-9420
Fax: 617-727-0667
E-mail: osfa@osfa.mass.edu

MASSACHUSETTS ASSISTANCE FOR STUDENT SUCCESS PROGRAM

Provides need-based financial assistance to Massachusetts residents to attend undergraduate postsecondary institutions in Connecticut, Maine, Massachusetts, New Hampshire, Pennsylvania, Rhode Island, Vermont, and District of Columbia. High school seniors may apply. Expected Family Contribution (EFC) should be $3850. Timely filing of FAFSA required.

Award: Grant for use in freshman, sophomore, junior, or senior years; not renewable. *Number:* 50,000–57,000. *Amount:* $300–$1600.

Eligibility Requirements: Applicant must be enrolled or expecting to enroll full-time at a two-year or four-year or technical institution or university; resident of Massachusetts and studying in Connecticut, District of Columbia, Maine, Massachusetts, New Hampshire, Pennsylvania, Rhode Island, Vermont. Available to U.S. citizens.

Application Requirements: FAFSA, financial need analysis. *Deadline:* May 1.

Contact: Robert Brun, Director of Scholarships and Grants
Phone: 617-727-9420
Fax: 617-727-0667
E-mail: osfa@osfa.mass.edu

MASSACHUSETTS CASH GRANT PROGRAM

A need-based grant to assist with mandatory fees and non-state supported tuition. This supplemental award is available to Massachusetts residents, who are undergraduates at public two-year, four-year colleges and universities in Massachusetts. Must file FAFSA before May 1. Contact college financial aid office for information.

Award: Grant for use in freshman, sophomore, junior, or senior years; not renewable.

Eligibility Requirements: Applicant must be enrolled or expecting to enroll full-time at a two-year or four-year institution or university and resident of Massachusetts. Available to U.S. citizens.

Application Requirements: Application form, FAFSA, financial need analysis. *Deadline:* continuous.

Contact: Robert Brun, Director of Scholarships and Grants
 Phone: 617-727-9420
 Fax: 617-727-0667
 E-mail: osfa@osfa.mass.edu

MASSACHUSETTS GILBERT MATCHING STUDENT GRANT PROGRAM

Grants for permanent Massachusetts residents attending an independent, regionally accredited Massachusetts school or school of nursing full-time. Must be U.S. citizen and permanent legal resident of Massachusetts. File the Free Application for Federal Student Aid after January 1. Contact college financial aid office for complete details and deadlines.

Award: Grant for use in freshman, sophomore, junior, or senior years; not renewable. *Amount:* $200–$2500.

Eligibility Requirements: Applicant must be enrolled or expecting to enroll full-time at a four-year institution or university; resident of Massachusetts and studying in Massachusetts. Available to U.S. citizens.

Application Requirements: FAFSA, financial need analysis. *Deadline:* varies.

Contact: Robert Brun, Director of Scholarships and Grants
 Massachusetts Office of Student Financial Assistance
 454 Broadway, Suite 200
 Revere, MA 02151
 Phone: 617-727-9420
 Fax: 617-727-0667
 E-mail: rbrun@osfa.mass.edu

MASSACHUSETTS PART-TIME GRANT PROGRAM

Award for permanent Massachusetts residents who have enrolled part-time for at least one year in a state-approved postsecondary school. The recipient must not have a Bachelor's degree. FAFSA must be filed before May 1. Contact college financial aid office for further information.

Award: Grant for use in freshman, sophomore, junior, or senior years; not renewable. *Number:* 200. *Amount:* $200–$1150.

Eligibility Requirements: Applicant must be enrolled or expecting to enroll part-time at a two-year or four-year or technical institution or university and resident of Massachusetts. Available to U.S. citizens.

Application Requirements: Application form, FAFSA, financial need analysis. *Deadline:* varies.

Contact: Robert Brun, Director of Scholarships and Grants
 Phone: 617-727-9420
 Fax: 617-727-0667
 E-mail: osfa@osfa.mass.edu

MASSACHUSETTS PUBLIC SERVICE GRANT PROGRAM
• *See page 602*

PAUL TSONGAS SCHOLARSHIP PROGRAM

Scholarship to recognize achievement and reward Massachusetts students, who have graduated from high school within three years with a GPA of 3.75 and a SAT score of at least 1200, and who also meet the one year residency requirement for tuition classification at the state colleges.

Award: Scholarship for use in freshman, sophomore, junior, or senior years; renewable.

Eligibility Requirements: Applicant must be enrolled or expecting to enroll full-time at a two-year or four-year institution or university; resident of Massachusetts and studying in Massachusetts. Available to U.S. citizens.

Application Requirements: Application form, test scores. *Deadline:* varies.

Contact: Robert Brun, Director of Scholarships and Grants
 Phone: 617-727-9420
 Fax: 617-727-0667
 E-mail: osfa@osfa.mass.edu

MATRIX HEALTH GROUP
http://www.matrixhealthgroup.com

MIKE HYLTON MEMORIAL SCHOLARSHIP
• *See page 633*

MCCURRY FOUNDATION INC.
http://www.mccurryfoundation.org/

MCCURRY FOUNDATION SCHOLARSHIP

Scholarship open to all public high school seniors, with preference given to applicants from Clay, Duval, Nassau, and St. Johns Counties, Florida and from Glynn County, Georgia. Scholarship emphasizes leadership, work ethic, and academic excellence. A minimum GPA of 3.0 is required and family income cannot exceed a maximum of $75,000 (AGI).

Award: Scholarship for use in freshman, sophomore, junior, or senior years; renewable. *Number:* 1–10. *Amount:* $1000–$1500.

Eligibility Requirements: Applicant must be high school student; planning to enroll or expecting to enroll full-time at a two-year or four-year or technical institution or university; single; resident of Florida, Georgia and must have an interest in leadership. Applicant must have 3.0 GPA or higher. Available to U.S. citizens.

Application Requirements: Application form, essay, financial need analysis, interview. *Deadline:* February 15.

Contact: Leslie Fine, Scholarship Selection Committee
 Phone: 904-910-4414
 E-mail: info@mccurryfoundation.org

MES FOUNDATION
http://www.mesfoundation.org

RICHARD H. PIERCE MEMORIAL SCHOLARSHIP
• *See page 603*

THE MIAMI FOUNDATION
http://www.miamifoundation.org

ALAN R. EPSTEIN SCHOLARSHIP

Award available for a high school senior who is a Dade county resident. Must have a 3.0 GPA and attach a copy of acceptance letter to two- or four-year college or university. For additional information and application, visit website at http://www.dadecommunityfoundation.org.

Award: Scholarship for use in freshman year; not renewable.

Eligibility Requirements: Applicant must be high school student; planning to enroll or expecting to enroll full-time at a two-year or four-year institution or university and resident of Florida. Applicant must have 3.0 GPA or higher. Available to U.S. citizens.

Application Requirements: Acceptance letter, personal statement, application form, financial need analysis, recommendations or references, transcript. *Deadline:* April 10.

Contact: Lauren Mayfield, Programs Assistant
 The Miami Foundation
 40 NW 3rd Street
 Miami, FL 33128
 Phone: 305-371-2711
 E-mail: lmayfield@miamifoundation.org

RODNEY THAXTON/MARTIN E. SEGAL SCHOLARSHIP
• *See page 689*

SIDNEY M. ARONOVITZ SCHOLARSHIP
• *See page 689*

MICHIGAN DEPARTMENT OF TREASURY - STUDENT FINANCIAL SERVICES BUREAU
http://www.michigan.gov/mistudentaid

MICHIGAN COMPETITIVE SCHOLARSHIP

Renewable awards for Michigan resident to pursue undergraduate study at a Michigan institution. Awards limited to tuition. Must maintain at least a 2.0 grade point average and meet the college's academic progress requirements. Must file Free Application for Federal Student Aid. http://www.michigan.gov/mistudentaid/0,4636,7-128-60969_61016-274563—,00.html

Award: Scholarship for use in freshman, sophomore, junior, or senior years; renewable.

Eligibility Requirements: Applicant must be enrolled or expecting to enroll full- or part-time at a two-year or four-year institution or university; resident of Michigan and studying in Michigan. Available to U.S. citizens.

Application Requirements: Application form, financial need analysis. *Deadline:* March 1.

Contact: Student Scholarships and Grants Division
Michigan Department of Treasury - Student Financial Services
Bureau
PO Box 30466
Lansing, MI 48909-7962
Phone: 888-447-2687
E-mail: ssg@michigan.gov

MICHIGAN TUITION GRANT

Need-based program. Students must be Michigan residents and attend a Michigan private, nonprofit, degree-granting college. Must file the Free Application for Federal Student Aid and meet the college's academic progress requirements. http://www.michigan.gov/mistudentaid/0,4636,7-128-60969_61016-274564—,00.html

Award: Grant for use in freshman, sophomore, junior, or senior years; renewable.

Eligibility Requirements: Applicant must be enrolled or expecting to enroll full- or part-time at a four-year institution or university; resident of Michigan and studying in Michigan. Available to U.S. citizens.

Application Requirements: Financial need analysis. *Deadline:* June 30.

Contact: Student Scholarships and Grants Division
Michigan Department of Treasury - Student Financial Services
Bureau
PO Box 30462
Lansing, MI 48909-7962
Phone: 888-447-2687
E-mail: ssg@michigan.gov

TUITION INCENTIVE PROGRAM

The Tuition Incentive Program (TIP) was established in 1987 under the Annual Higher Education Appropriations Act as an incentive program that encourages eligible students to complete high school by providing tuition assistance for the first two years of college and beyond. Students must be enrolled in courses leading to an associate degree or certificate. Certificate courses are defined as at least a one-year training program that leads to a certificate (or other recognized educational credential), which prepares students for gainful employment in a recognized occupation. Students must meet a Medicaid eligibility history requirement. Eligible students must apply prior to high school graduation (high school diploma or its recognized equivalent). The program targets students with financial need so students are encouraged to also complete the FAFSA. Funds are appropriated annually in the Higher Education Appropriations Act. This program is administered by the Student Scholarships and Grants Division.

Award: Grant for use in freshman, sophomore, junior, or senior years; renewable.

Eligibility Requirements: Applicant must be enrolled or expecting to enroll full- or part-time at a two-year or four-year institution or university; resident of Michigan and studying in Michigan. Available to U.S. citizens.

Application Requirements: Application form.

Contact: Student Scholarships and Grants Division
Michigan Department of Treasury - Student Financial Services
Bureau
PO Box 30462
Lansing, MI 48909-7962
Phone: 888-447-2687
E-mail: ssg@michigan.gov

MINNESOTA AFL-CIO

http://www.mnaflcio.org/

MARTIN DUFFY ADULT LEARNER SCHOLARSHIP AWARD

• *See page 548*

MINNESOTA MASONIC CHARITIES

http://www.mnmasoniccharities.org

MINNESOTA MASONIC CHARITIES LEGACY SCHOLARSHIP

Legacy Scholarships are provided each year to students attending a Minnesota high school with a GPA of 3.6 to 3.89. Applicants must plan to enroll in a four-year college program.

Award: Scholarship for use in freshman, sophomore, or senior years; renewable. *Number:* 10. *Amount:* $4000.

Eligibility Requirements: Applicant must be high school student; planning to enroll or expecting to enroll full-time at a four-year institution and resident of Minnesota. Applicant must have 3.5 GPA or higher. Available to U.S. citizens.

Application Requirements: Application form, essay. *Deadline:* March 1.

Contact: Ms. Kim Ramaker, Scholarships Manager
Minnesota Masonic Charities
11501 Masonic Home Drive
Bloomington, MN 55437
Phone: 952-948-6227
E-mail: kim.ramaker@mnmasonic.org

MINNESOTA MASONIC CHARITIES SIGNATURE SCHOLARSHIP

• *See page 604*

MINNESOTA MASONIC CHARITIES UNDERGRADUATE SCHOLARSHIP

• *See page 604*

MINNESOTA OFFICE OF HIGHER EDUCATION

http://www.ohe.state.mn.us

MINNESOTA GI BILL PROGRAM

The Minnesota GI Bill program provides postsecondary financial assistance to eligible Minnesota veterans and service members as well as eligible spouses and children of deceased or severely disabled eligible Minnesota veterans. Full-time undergraduate or graduate students may be eligible to receive up to $1,000 per semester or term and part-time students may be eligible to receive up to $500 per semester or term. Eligible students may receive up to $3,000 per award year and up to the lifetime maximum of $10,000.

Award: Grant for use in freshman, sophomore, junior, senior, graduate, or postgraduate years; not renewable. *Amount:* $50–$3000.

Eligibility Requirements: Applicant must be enrolled or expecting to enroll full- or part-time at a two-year or four-year or technical institution or university; resident of Minnesota and studying in Minnesota. Available to U.S. citizens.

Application Requirements: Application form. *Deadline:* continuous.

Contact: Meghan Flores, State Grant Manager
Phone: 651-355-0610
E-mail: meghan.flores@state.mn.us

MINNESOTA INDIAN SCHOLARSHIP

• *See page 690*

MINNESOTA STATE GRANT PROGRAM

Need-based grant program available for Minnesota residents attending Minnesota colleges. Student covers 50% of cost with remainder covered by Pell Grant, parent contribution and state grant. Students apply with FAFSA and colleges administer the program on campus.

Award: Grant for use in freshman, sophomore, junior, or senior years; not renewable. *Number:* 71,000–120,000. *Amount:* $100–$11,334.

Eligibility Requirements: Applicant must be enrolled or expecting to enroll full- or part-time at a two-year or four-year or technical institution or university; resident of Minnesota and studying in Minnesota. Available to U.S. citizens.

Application Requirements: Application form, financial need analysis. *Deadline:* continuous.

Contact: Grant Staff
Minnesota Office of Higher Education
1450 Energy Park Drive, Suite 350
St. Paul, MN 55108
Phone: 651-642-0567 Ext. 2

MINNESOTA STATE VETERANS' DEPENDENTS ASSISTANCE PROGRAM

Tuition assistance to dependents of persons considered to be prisoner-of-war or missing in action after August 1, 1958. Must be Minnesota resident attending Minnesota two- or four-year school.

Award: Scholarship for use in freshman, sophomore, junior, or senior years; renewable. *Number:* 100–200. *Amount:* $249–$250.

Eligibility Requirements: Applicant must be enrolled or expecting to enroll full- or part-time at a two-year or four-year institution; resident of Minnesota and studying in Minnesota. Available to U.S. citizens.

Application Requirements: Application form. *Deadline:* continuous.

Contact: Meghan Flores, State Grant Manager
Phone: 651-355-0610
E-mail: meghan.flores@state.mn.us

POSTSECONDARY CHILD CARE GRANT PROGRAM-MINNESOTA

Grant available for students who are not receiving MFIP (TANF) and have children in day care. Based on financial need. Cannot exceed actual child care costs or maximum award chart (based on income). Must be Minnesota resident. For use at Minnesota two- or four-year school, including public technical colleges. Available until student has attended college for the equivalent of four full-time academic years.

Award: Grant for use in freshman, sophomore, junior, or senior years; not renewable. *Number:* 1–3500. *Amount:* $100–$2800.

Eligibility Requirements: Applicant must be enrolled or expecting to enroll full- or part-time at a two-year or four-year or technical institution or university; resident of Minnesota and studying in Minnesota. Available to U.S. citizens.

Application Requirements: Application form, financial need analysis. *Deadline:* continuous.

Contact: Brenda Larter, Program Administrator
Minnesota Office of Higher Education
1450 Energy Park Drive, Suite 350
St. Paul, MN 55108-5227
Phone: 651-355-0612
E-mail: brenda.larter@state.mn.us

SAFETY OFFICERS' SURVIVOR GRANT PROGRAM

• *See page 604*

MISSISSIPPI OFFICE OF STUDENT FINANCIAL AID

http://www.mississippi.edu/financialaid

HIGHER EDUCATION LEGISLATIVE PLAN (HELP)

Eligible applicant must be resident of Mississippi and apply for the first time as a freshman and/or sophomore student who graduated from high school within the immediate past two years. Must demonstrate need as determined by the results of the FAFSA, documenting an average family adjusted gross income of $36,500 or less over the prior two years. Must be enrolled full-time at a Mississippi college or university, have a GPA of 2.5, have completed a specific high school core curriculum, and have scored 20 on the ACT.

Award: Grant for use in freshman, sophomore, junior, or senior years; renewable. *Number:* 2661. *Amount:* $340–$7344.

Eligibility Requirements: Applicant must be enrolled or expecting to enroll full-time at a two-year or four-year institution or university; resident of Mississippi and studying in Mississippi. Applicant must have 3.0 GPA or higher. Available to U.S. citizens.

Application Requirements: Application form, financial need analysis. *Deadline:* March 31.

Contact: Program Administrator
Mississippi Office of Student Financial Aid
3825 Ridgewood Road
Jackson, MS 39211
Phone: 601-432-6997
Fax: 601-432 Ext. 6527
E-mail: sfa@mississippi.edu

LAW ENFORCEMENT OFFICERS/FIREMEN SCHOLARSHIP

• *See page 604*

MISSISSIPPI EMINENT SCHOLARS GRANT

Award for an entering freshmen or as a renewal for sophomore, junior or senior, who are residents of Mississippi. Applicants must achieve a GPA of 3.5 and must have scored 29 on the ACT. Must enroll full-time at an eligible Mississippi college or university.

Award: Grant for use in freshman, sophomore, junior, or senior years; not renewable. *Amount:* $1157–$2500.

Eligibility Requirements: Applicant must be enrolled or expecting to enroll full-time at a two-year or four-year institution or university; resident of Mississippi and studying in Mississippi. Applicant must have 3.5 GPA or higher. Available to U.S. citizens.

Application Requirements: Application form. *Deadline:* September 15.

Contact: Program Administrator
Mississippi Office of Student Financial Aid
3825 Ridgewood Road
Jackson, MS 39211
Phone: 601-432-6997
Fax: 601-432 Ext. 6527
E-mail: sfa@mississippi.edu

MISSISSIPPI RESIDENT TUITION ASSISTANCE GRANT

Must be a resident of Mississippi enrolled full-time at an eligible Mississippi college or university. Must maintain a minimum 2.5 GPA each semester. MTAG awards may be up to $500 per academic year for freshman and sophomores and $1000 per academic year for juniors and seniors.

Award: Grant for use in freshman, sophomore, junior, or senior years; not renewable. *Amount:* $17–$1000.

Eligibility Requirements: Applicant must be enrolled or expecting to enroll full-time at a two-year or four-year institution or university; resident of Mississippi and studying in Mississippi. Applicant must have 2.5 GPA or higher. Available to U.S. citizens.

Application Requirements: Application form. *Deadline:* September 15.

Contact: Program Administrator
Mississippi Office of Student Financial Aid
3825 Ridgewood Road
Jackson, MS 39211
Phone: 601-432-6997
Fax: 601-432 Ext. 6527
E-mail: sfa@mississippi.edu

NISSAN SCHOLARSHIP

Renewable award for Mississippi residents attending a Mississippi institution. Must be graduating from a Mississippi high school in the current year. The scholarship will pay full tuition and a book allowance. Minimum GPA of 2.5 as well as an ACT composite of at least 20 or combined SAT scores of 940 or better. Must demonstrate financial need and leadership abilities.

Award: Scholarship for use in freshman, sophomore, junior, or senior years; renewable. *Number:* 1. *Amount:* $8002.

Eligibility Requirements: Applicant must be high school student; planning to enroll or expecting to enroll full-time at a two-year or four-year institution or university; resident of Mississippi and studying in Mississippi. Applicant must have 2.5 GPA or higher. Available to U.S. citizens.

Application Requirements: Application form, essay, financial need analysis. *Deadline:* March 1.

Contact: Program Administrator
Mississippi Office of Student Financial Aid
3825 Ridgewood Road
Jackson, MS 39211
Phone: 601-432-6997
Fax: 601-432 Ext. 6527
E-mail: sfa@mississippi.edu

MISSOURI CONSERVATION AGENTS ASSOCIATION SCHOLARSHIP

http://www.moagent.com/

MISSOURI CONSERVATION AGENTS ASSOCIATION SCHOLARSHIP

Scholarship of up to $500 per student per year for full-time undergraduate students who reside in the state of Missouri. The applicant must be a U.S. citizen.

Award: Scholarship for use in freshman, sophomore, junior, or senior years; not renewable. *Amount:* up to $500.

Eligibility Requirements: Applicant must be enrolled or expecting to enroll full-time at a four-year or technical institution or university and resident of Missouri. Applicant must have 2.5 GPA or higher. Available to U.S. citizens.

Application Requirements: Essay, transcript. *Deadline:* February 1.

Contact: Brian Ham, Scholarship Committee
Phone: 573-896-8628

MISSOURI DEPARTMENT OF HIGHER EDUCATION

http://www.dhe.mo.gov/

ACCESS MISSOURI FINANCIAL ASSISTANCE PROGRAM

Need-based program that provides awards to students who are enrolled full-time and have an expected family contribution (EFC) of $12,000 or less based on their Free Application for Federal Student Aid (FAFSA). Awards vary depending on EFC and the type of postsecondary school.

Award: Grant for use in freshman, sophomore, junior, or senior years; not renewable.

Eligibility Requirements: Applicant must be enrolled or expecting to enroll full-time at a two-year or technical institution or university; resident of Missouri and studying in Missouri. Applicant must have 2.5 GPA or higher. Available to U.S. citizens.

Application Requirements: FAFSA on file by April 1.

Contact: Information Center
Phone: 800-473-6757 Ext. 4
Fax: 573-751-6635
E-mail: info@dhe.mo.gov

MARGUERITE ROSS BARNETT MEMORIAL SCHOLARSHIP

Scholarship was established for students who are employed while attending school part-time. Must be enrolled at least half-time but less than full-time at a participating Missouri postsecondary school, be employed and compensated for at least 20 hours per week, be 18 years of age, be a Missouri resident and a U.S. citizen or a permanent resident.

Award: Scholarship for use in freshman, sophomore, junior, or senior years; renewable.

Eligibility Requirements: Applicant must be enrolled or expecting to enroll part-time at a two-year or four-year or technical institution or university; resident of Missouri and studying in Missouri. Applicant must have 2.5 GPA or higher. Available to U.S. citizens.

Application Requirements: FAFSA on file by August 1. *Deadline:* August 1.

Contact: Information Center
Phone: 800-473-6757 Ext. 4
Fax: 573-751-6635
E-mail: info@dhe.mo.gov

MISSOURI HIGHER EDUCATION ACADEMIC SCHOLARSHIP (BRIGHT FLIGHT)

Program encourages top-ranked high school seniors to attend approved Missouri postsecondary schools. Must be a Missouri resident and a U.S. citizen or permanent resident. Must have a composite score on the ACT or SAT in the top 5 percent of all Missouri students taking those tests. Students with scores in the top 3 percent are eligible for an annual award of up to $3000 (up to $1500 each semester). Students with scores in the top 4% and 5% are eligible for an annual award of up to $1000 (up to $500 each semester). Award amounts, and the availability of the award for students in the 4% and 5%, are subject to change based on the amount of funding allocated for the program in the legislative session.

Award: Scholarship for use in freshman, sophomore, junior, or senior years; renewable. *Amount:* $1000–$3000.

Eligibility Requirements: Applicant must be enrolled or expecting to enroll full-time at a two-year or four-year or technical institution or university; resident of Missouri and studying in Missouri. Applicant must have 2.5 GPA or higher. Available to U.S. citizens.

Application Requirements: Test scores.

Contact: Information Center
Phone: 800-473-6757 Ext. 4
Fax: 573-751-6635
E-mail: info@dhe.mo.gov

MITCHELL INSTITUTE

http://www.mitchellinstitute.org/

THE SENATOR GEORGE J. MITCHELL SCHOLARSHIP RESEARCH INSTITUTE

• See page 604

MONTANA UNIVERSITY SYSTEM, OFFICE OF COMMISSIONER OF HIGHER EDUCATION

http://www.mus.edu

MONTANA HIGHER EDUCATION OPPORTUNITY GRANT

This grant is awarded based on need to undergraduate students attending either part-time or full-time who are residents of Montana and attending participating Montana schools. Awards are limited to the most needy students. A specific major or program of study is not required. This grant does not need to be repaid, and students may apply each year. Apply by filing FAFSA by March 1 and contacting the financial aid office at the admitting college.

Award: Grant for use in freshman, sophomore, junior, or senior years; not renewable. *Number:* up to 800. *Amount:* $400–$600.

Eligibility Requirements: Applicant must be enrolled or expecting to enroll full- or part-time at a two-year or four-year institution or university; resident of Montana and studying in Montana. Available to U.S. citizens.

Application Requirements: FAFSA, financial need analysis. *Deadline:* March 1.

Contact: Jamie Dushin, Budget Analyst
Montana University System, Office of Commissioner of Higher Education
PO Box 203101
Helena, MT 59620-3101
Phone: 406-444-0638
Fax: 406-444-1869
E-mail: jdushin@mgslp.state.mt.us

MONTANA TUITION ASSISTANCE PROGRAM-BAKER GRANT

Need-based grant for Montana residents attending participating Montana schools who have earned at least $2575 during the previous calendar year. Must be enrolled full-time. Grant does not need to be repaid. Award covers the first undergraduate degree or certificate. Apply by filing FAFSA by March 1 and contacting the financial aid office at the admitting college.

Award: Grant for use in freshman, sophomore, junior, or senior years; not renewable. *Number:* 1000–3000. *Amount:* $100–$1000.

Eligibility Requirements: Applicant must be enrolled or expecting to enroll full-time at a two-year or four-year institution or university; resident of Montana and studying in Montana. Available to U.S. citizens.

Application Requirements: Application form, FAFSA, financial need analysis, resume. *Deadline:* March 1.

Contact: Jamie Dushin, Budget Analyst
Montana University System, Office of Commissioner of Higher Education
PO Box 203101
Helena, MT 59620-3101
Phone: 406-444-0638
Fax: 406-444-1869
E-mail: jdushin@mgslp.state.mt.us

MONTANA UNIVERSITY SYSTEM HONOR SCHOLARSHIP

Scholarship will be awarded annually to high school seniors graduating from accredited Montana high schools. The MUS Honor Scholarship is a four year renewable scholarship that waives the tuition and registration fee at one of the Montana University System campuses or one of the three community colleges (Flathead Valley in Kalispell, Miles in Miles City or Dawson in Glendive). The scholarship must be used within 9 months after high school graduation. Applicant must have a minimum GPA of 3.4.

Award: Scholarship for use in freshman, sophomore, junior, or senior years; renewable. *Number:* up to 200. *Amount:* $4000–$6000.

Eligibility Requirements: Applicant must be high school student; planning to enroll or expecting to enroll full-time at a two-year or four-year institution or university; resident of Montana and studying in Montana. Applicant must have 3.5 GPA or higher. Available to U.S. citizens.

Application Requirements: Application form, college acceptance letter, test scores, transcript. *Deadline:* March 15.

Contact: Sheila Newlun, Grants and Scholarship Coordinator
Phone: 406-444-0638
Fax: 406-444-1869
E-mail: snewlun@montana.edu

MOUNT VERNON URBAN RENEWAL AGENCY

http://www.ci.mount-vernon.ny.us/

MAYORS EDUCATIONAL ASSISTANCE PROGRAM

Awards offered only to the low and moderate income residents of the city of Mount Vernon for the purpose of pursuing higher education at a vocational/technical school or college.

Award: Grant for use in freshman, sophomore, junior, or senior years; renewable.

Eligibility Requirements: Applicant must be enrolled or expecting to enroll full-time at a two-year or four-year or technical institution or university and resident of New York. Applicant must have 3.5 GPA or higher. Available to U.S. citizens.

Application Requirements: Application form, essay, financial need analysis. *Deadline:* July 1.

Contact: Mary Fleming, Director, Scholarship Programs
Mount Vernon Urban Renewal Agency
Department of Planning, One Roosevelt Square, City Hall
Mount Vernon, NY 10550
Phone: 914-699-7230
E-mail: mfleming@ci.mount-vernon.ny.us

NATIONAL COUNCIL OF JEWISH WOMEN LOS ANGELES (NCJW L LA)

http://ncjwla.org/

DODELL WOMEN'S EMPOWERMENT SCHOLARSHIP

• *See page 606*

SOPHIE GREENSTADT SCHOLARSHIP FOR MID-LIFE WOMEN

• *See page 606*

STEPHEN L. TELLER & RICHARD HOTSON TV, CINEMA, AND THEATER SCHOLARSHIP

• *See page 606*

SUSAN SCHULMAN BEGLEY MEMORIAL SCHOLARSHIP

• *See page 606*

NATIONAL DEFENSE TRANSPORTATION ASSOCIATION-SCOTT ST. LOUIS CHAPTER

http://www.ndtascottstlouis.org/

NATIONAL DEFENSE TRANSPORTATION ASSOCIATION, SCOTT AIR FORCE BASE-ST. LOUIS AREA CHAPTER SCHOLARSHIP

The Scott/St. Louis Chapter of the NDTA intends to award a minimum of two (2) scholarships of $3500 each and four (4) scholarships of $2000 each. Additional awards may be granted pending availability of funds. Scholarships are open to any high school student that meets the eligibility criteria. High school students must be reside and go to school in Illinois or Missouri. College applicants must be a full-time student in the following states: CO, IA, IL, IN, KS, MI, MN, MO, MT, ND, NE, SD, WI, or WY.

Award: Scholarship for use in freshman, sophomore, junior, or senior years; not renewable. *Number:* 6. *Amount:* $2000–$3500.

Eligibility Requirements: Applicant must be enrolled or expecting to enroll full-time at a two-year or four-year institution or university; resident of Illinois, Missouri and studying in Colorado, Illinois, Indiana, Iowa, Kansas, Michigan, Minnesota, Missouri, Montana, Nebraska, North Dakota, South Dakota, Wisconsin, Wyoming. Applicant must have 3.0 GPA or higher. Available to U.S. citizens.

Application Requirements: Application form, community service, essay, recommendations or references, test scores, transcript. *Deadline:* March 1.

Contact: Mr. Michael Carnes, Chairman, Professional Development Committee
National Defense Transportation Association-Scott St. Louis Chapter
PO Box 25486
Scott AFB, IL 62225
Phone: 618-229-4756
E-mail: michael.carnes.ctr@ustranscom.mil

NATIONAL FEDERATION OF THE BLIND OF CALIFORNIA

http://www.nfbcal.org/

GERALD DRAKE MEMORIAL SCHOLARSHIP

• *See page 634*

JULIE LANDUCCI SCHOLARSHIP

• *See page 635*

LA VYRL "PINKY" JOHNSON MEMORIAL SCHOLARSHIP

• *See page 635*

LAWRENCE "MUZZY" MARCELINO MEMORIAL SCHOLARSHIP

• *See page 635*

NATIONAL FEDERATION OF THE BLIND OF CALIFORNIA MERIT SCHOLARSHIPS

• *See page 635*

NATIONAL FEDERATION OF THE BLIND OF MISSOURI

http://www.nfbmo.org/

NATIONAL FEDERATION OF THE BLIND OF MISSOURI SCHOLARSHIP PROGRAM FOR LEGALLY BLIND STUDENTS
• *See page 635*

NATIONAL KIDNEY FOUNDATION OF INDIANA INC.

http://www.kidneyindiana.org/

NATIONAL KIDNEY FOUNDATION OF INDIANA SCHOLARSHIP
• *See page 635*

NEBRASKA'S COORDINATING COMMISSION FOR POSTSECONDARY EDUCATION

https://ccpe.nebraska.gov/

NEBRASKA OPPORTUNITY GRANT
• *See page 608*

NEED

http://www.needld.org/

UNMET NEED GRANT PROGRAM
• *See page 692*

NEVADA OFFICE OF THE STATE TREASURER

http://www.nevadatreasurer.gov/

GOVERNOR GUINN MILLENNIUM SCHOLARSHIP
Scholarship for Nevada residents. Student must graduate from a public or private high school within Nevada with a minimum GPA of 3.25. Must complete core curriculum. Maximum award is $10,000. Student must acknowledge award and use it within 6 years of high school graduation.

Award: Scholarship for use in freshman, sophomore, junior, or senior years; renewable. *Number:* 1. *Amount:* up to $10,000.

Eligibility Requirements: Applicant must be enrolled or expecting to enroll full-time at a two-year or four-year institution or university; resident of Nevada and studying in Nevada. Available to U.S. citizens.

Application Requirements: Application form may be submitted online (http://nevadatreasurer.gov), high schools determine eligibility; student must accept award. *Deadline:* varies.

Contact: Linda English, Executive Director
Phone: 702-486-3889
Fax: 702-486-3246
E-mail: info@nevadatreasurer.gov

NEW ENGLAND BOARD OF HIGHER EDUCATION

http://www.nebhe.org/

NEW ENGLAND REGIONAL STUDENT PROGRAM-TUITION BREAK
Tuition discount for residents of six New England states (Connecticut, Maine, Massachusetts, New Hampshire, Rhode Island, Vermont). Students pay reduced out-of-state tuition at public colleges or universities in other New England states when enrolling in certain majors not offered at public institutions in home state. Details are available at http://www.nebhe.org/tuitionbreak.

Award: Scholarship for use in freshman, sophomore, junior, senior, or graduate years; renewable.

Eligibility Requirements: Applicant must be enrolled or expecting to enroll full- or part-time at a two-year or four-year institution or university; resident of Connecticut, Maine, Massachusetts, New Hampshire, Rhode Island, Vermont and studying in Connecticut, Maine, Massachusetts, New Hampshire, Rhode Island, Vermont. Available to U.S. citizens.

Application Requirements: *Deadline:* continuous.

Contact: Wendy Lindsay, Senior Director of Regional Student Program
New England Board of Higher Education
45 Temple Place
Boston, MA 02111
Phone: 617-533-9511
E-mail: tuitionbreak@nebhe.org

NEW JERSEY DEPARTMENT OF MILITARY AND VETERANS AFFAIRS

http://www.state.nj.us/military

NEW JERSEY WAR ORPHANS TUITION ASSISTANCE
• *See page 659*

POW-MIA TUITION BENEFIT PROGRAM
• *See page 659*

VETERANS TUITION CREDIT PROGRAM-NEW JERSEY
• *See page 659*

NEW JERSEY HALL OF FAME

http://njhalloffame.org/

NJHOF ARTÊ SCHOLARSHIP AWARD
The New Jersey Hall of Fame is proud to announce the renewal of the Arête Scholarship Fund. The Arête Scholarships will be awarded to a deserving male and female student graduating in 2017 from a New Jersey high school. Each recipient will receive a $5,000 scholarship from the New Jersey Hall of Fame (NJHOF). Ar? is a concept that Plato referred to more than 3,000 years ago that refers to the act of actualizing one's highest sense of self. The term Ar? essentially means that the individual should strive to pursue their passions in life, and realize their dreams regardless of their circumstances or the adversities that they are likely to face on the path to greatness. The successful applicants will embody the meaning of Ar?, and will distinguish themselves as New Jerseyans who are on their way to realizing their dreams. The NJHOF Ar? Scholarship Award will be one of the highest honors that the NJHOF and the State of N.J. can bestow upon a student, and each student will be recognized at the NJHOF's annual induction ceremony! The recipients of the Ar? scholarship are young people who demonstrate that sense of Jersey pride and that willingness to go above and beyond the call of duty. The successful applicants must demonstrate the qualities such as academic engagement, moral character, and a commitment to their community. These recipients do not necessarily have to be at the very top of their school class from an academic standpoint, but should demonstrate a focus in school and life, and have a well thought out plan on how they intend to realize their highest sense of self, their Ar?.

Award: Scholarship for use in freshman year; not renewable. *Number:* 2. *Amount:* $5000.

Eligibility Requirements: Applicant must be high school student; planning to enroll or expecting to enroll full- or part-time at a two-year or four-year institution or university and resident of New Jersey. Available to U.S. citizens.

Application Requirements: Application form. *Deadline:* February 28.

Contact: Ms. Emaleigh Kaithern
E-mail: emaleigh@princetonscgroup.com

NEW JERSEY HIGHER EDUCATION STUDENT ASSISTANCE AUTHORITY

http://www.hesaa.org/

LAW ENFORCEMENT OFFICER MEMORIAL SCHOLARSHIP

• *See page 608*

NEW JERSEY STUDENT TUITION ASSISTANCE REWARD SCHOLARSHIP II

Earn an associate degree from the home New Jersey county college as an NJ STARS recipient and graduate with a cumulative GPA of 3.25 or higher. Family income (taxable and untaxed income) must be less than $250,000 as derived from the FAFSA. NJ STARS II students may receive up to $1,250 per semester, paid completely by the State, after all other sources of federal and State grants and scholarships are applied to tuition charges.

Award: Scholarship for use in junior or senior years; renewable.

Eligibility Requirements: Applicant must be enrolled or expecting to enroll full-time at a four-year institution or university; resident of New Jersey and studying in New Jersey. Applicant must have 3.0 GPA or higher. Available to U.S. citizens.

Application Requirements: Application form.

Contact: Jossette Greene, Program Officer
Phone: 609-584-4480
E-mail: jgreene@hesaa.org

NEW JERSEY WORLD TRADE CENTER SCHOLARSHIP

Scholarship was established by the legislature to aid the dependent children and surviving spouses of New Jersey residents who were killed in the terrorist attacks, or who are missing and officially presumed dead as a direct result of the attacks; applies to instate and out-of-state institutions for students seeking undergraduate degrees.

Award: Scholarship for use in freshman, sophomore, junior, or senior years; not renewable. *Amount:* $1–$6500.

Eligibility Requirements: Applicant must be enrolled or expecting to enroll full-time at a two-year or four-year institution or university and resident of New Jersey. Available to U.S. citizens.

Application Requirements: Application form.

Contact: Jean Hathaway, Assistant Director of Special Grants and Scholarships
New Jersey Higher Education Student Assistance Authority
PO Box 540
Trenton, NJ 08625
Phone: 609-588-3266
E-mail: jhathaway@hesaa.org

NJ STUDENT TUITION ASSISTANCE REWARD SCHOLARSHIP

Students must enroll in a full time course of study at their home county colleges. The award covers tuition charges for up to 18 credit hours per term.

Award: Scholarship for use in freshman or sophomore years; renewable. *Amount:* $500–$2600.

Eligibility Requirements: Applicant must be enrolled or expecting to enroll full-time at a two-year institution; resident of New Jersey and studying in New Jersey. Applicant must have 3.0 GPA or higher. Available to U.S. citizens.

Application Requirements: Application form.

Contact: Ms. Jossette Greene, Program Officer
New Jersey Higher Education Student Assistance Authority
PO Box 540
Trenton, NJ 08625
Phone: 609-584-4480
E-mail: jgreene@hessa.org

PART-TIME TUITION AID GRANT FOR COUNTY COLLEGES

Provides financial aid to eligible part-time undergraduate students enrolled for 9 to 11 credits at New Jersey community colleges.

Award: Grant for use in freshman or sophomore years; not renewable. *Amount:* $500–$1900.

Eligibility Requirements: Applicant must be enrolled or expecting to enroll part-time at a two-year institution; resident of New Jersey and studying in New Jersey. Available to U.S. citizens.

Application Requirements: Application form.

Contact: Jean Hathaway, AS of Grants and Scholarships
New Jersey Higher Education Student Assistance Authority
PO Box 540
Trenton, NJ 08625
Phone: 609-584-4480
E-mail: jhathaway@hesaa.org

SURVIVOR TUITION BENEFITS PROGRAM

• *See page 608*

TUITION AID GRANT

The program provides grants to eligible undergraduate students attending participating in-state institutions.

Award: Grant for use in freshman, sophomore, junior, or senior years; not renewable. *Amount:* $1012–$12,190.

Eligibility Requirements: Applicant must be enrolled or expecting to enroll full-time at a two-year or four-year institution or university; resident of New Jersey and studying in New Jersey. Available to U.S. citizens.

Application Requirements: Application form, financial need analysis.

Contact: Kathyrn Safran, Director of Grants and Scholarships
New Jersey Higher Education Student Assistance Authority
PO Box 540
Trenton, NJ 08625
Phone: 609-584-4480
E-mail: ksafran@hesaa.org

NEW JERSEY VIETNAM VETERANS' MEMORIAL FOUNDATION

http://www.njvvmf.org/college-scholarships

NEW JERSEY VIETNAM VETERANS' MEMORIAL FOUNDATION SCHOLARSHIP

Applicant must be a New Jersey resident, be a graduating high school senior, and visited the New Jersey Vietnam Veterans' Memorial (on their own /class trip/ scholarship tour).

Award: Scholarship for use in freshman year; not renewable. *Number:* 2. *Amount:* $2500.

Eligibility Requirements: Applicant must be high school student; planning to enroll or expecting to enroll full-time at a two-year or four-year or technical institution or university and resident of New Jersey. Available to U.S. citizens.

Application Requirements: Application form, essay. *Deadline:* April 14.

NEW MEXICO COMMISSION ON HIGHER EDUCATION

http://www.hed.state.nm.us/

COLLEGE AFFORDABILITY GRANT

Grant available to New Mexico students with financial need who do not qualify for other state grants and scholarships to attend and complete educational programs at a New Mexico public college or university. Student must have unmet need after all other financial aid has been awarded. Student may not be receiving any other state grants or scholarships. Renewable upon satisfactory academic progress.

Award: Grant for use in freshman, sophomore, junior, or senior years; renewable. *Number:* 1. *Amount:* up to $1000.

Eligibility Requirements: Applicant must be enrolled or expecting to enroll full- or part-time at a two-year or four-year institution or university; resident of New Mexico and studying in New Mexico. Available to U.S. citizens.

Application Requirements: Application form, FAFSA, financial need analysis. *Deadline:* continuous.

Contact: Tashina Acker, Director of Financial Aid
New Mexico Commission on Higher Education
1068 Cerrillos Road
Santa Fe, NM 87505-1650
Phone: 505-476-6549
Fax: 505-476-6511
E-mail: tashina.banks-moore@state.nm.us

LEGISLATIVE ENDOWMENT SCHOLARSHIPS

Renewable scholarships to provide aid for undergraduate students with substantial financial need who are attending public postsecondary institutions in New Mexico. Four-year schools may award up to $2500 per academic year, two-year schools may award up to $1000 per academic year. Deadlines varies.

Award: Scholarship for use in freshman, sophomore, junior, or senior years; renewable. *Number:* 1. *Amount:* $1000–$2500.

Eligibility Requirements: Applicant must be enrolled or expecting to enroll full- or part-time at a two-year or four-year institution or university; resident of New Mexico and studying in New Mexico. Available to U.S. citizens.

Application Requirements: Application form, FAFSA, financial need analysis. *Deadline:* varies.

Contact: Tashina Moore, Director of Financial Aid
New Mexico Commission on Higher Education
1068 Cerrillos Road
Santa Fe, NM 87505-1650
Phone: 505-475-6549
Fax: 505-476-6511
E-mail: tashina.banks-moore@state.nm.us

LEGISLATIVE LOTTERY SCHOLARSHIP

Renewable Scholarship for New Mexico high school graduates or GED recipients who plan to attend an eligible New Mexico public college or university. Must be enrolled full-time and maintain 2.5 GPA.

Award: Scholarship for use in freshman year; renewable. *Number:* 1.

Eligibility Requirements: Applicant must be high school student; planning to enroll or expecting to enroll full-time at a four-year institution or university; resident of New Mexico and studying in New Mexico. Applicant must have 3.5 GPA or higher. Available to U.S. citizens.

Application Requirements: Application form, FAFSA. *Deadline:* varies.

Contact: Tashina Moore, Director of Financial Aid
New Mexico Commission on Higher Education
1068 Cerrillos Road
Santa Fe, NM 87505
Phone: 505-476-6549
Fax: 505-476-6511
E-mail: tashina.banks-moore@state.nm.us

NEW MEXICO SCHOLARS' PROGRAM

Renewable award program created to encourage New Mexico high school students to attend public postsecondary institutions or the following private colleges in New Mexico: College of Santa Fe, St. John's College, College of the Southwest. For details visit http://fin.hed.state.nm.us.

Award: Scholarship for use in freshman year; renewable. *Number:* 1.

Eligibility Requirements: Applicant must be high school student; planning to enroll or expecting to enroll full-time at a two-year or four-year institution; resident of New Mexico and studying in New Mexico. Available to U.S. citizens.

Application Requirements: Application form, FAFSA, financial need analysis, test scores. *Deadline:* varies.

Contact: Tashina Moore, Director of Financial Aid
New Mexico Commission on Higher Education
1068 Cerrillos Road
Santa Fe, NM 87505-1650
Phone: 505-476-6549
Fax: 505-476-6511
E-mail: tashina.banks-moore@state.nm.us

NEW MEXICO STUDENT INCENTIVE GRANT

Grant created to provide aid for undergraduate students with substantial financial need who are attending public colleges or universities or the following eligible colleges in New Mexico: College of Santa Fe, St. John's College, College of the Southwest, Institute of American Indian Art, Crownpoint Institute of Technology, Dine College and Southwestern Indian Polytechnic Institute. Part-time students are eligible for pro-rated awards.

Award: Grant for use in freshman, sophomore, junior, or senior years; not renewable. *Number:* 1. *Amount:* $200–$2500.

Eligibility Requirements: Applicant must be enrolled or expecting to enroll full- or part-time at a two-year or four-year or technical institution or university; resident of New Mexico and studying in New Mexico. Available to U.S. citizens.

Application Requirements: Application form, FAFSA, financial need analysis. *Deadline:* varies.

Contact: Tashina Moore, Director of Financial Aid
New Mexico Commission on Higher Education
1068 Cerrillos Road
Santa Fe, NM 87505-1650
Phone: 505-476-6549
Fax: 505-476-6511
E-mail: tashina.banks-moore@state.nm.us

VIETNAM VETERANS' SCHOLARSHIP PROGRAM
• *See page 659*

NEW MEXICO DEPARTMENT OF VETERANS' SERVICES

http://www.nmdvs.org

CHILDREN OF DECEASED VETERANS SCHOLARSHIP-NEW MEXICO

Award for New Mexico residents who are children of veterans killed as a result of service, prisoner of war, or veterans missing in action. Must be between ages 16 and 26. For use at New Mexico schools for undergraduate study. Must submit parent's death certificate and DD form 214.

Award: Scholarship for use in freshman, sophomore, junior, or senior years; not renewable. *Number:* 49–50. *Amount:* $300.

Eligibility Requirements: Applicant must be age 16-26; enrolled or expecting to enroll full- or part-time at a two-year or four-year or technical institution or university; resident of New Mexico and studying in New Mexico. Available to U.S. citizens.

Application Requirements: Application form.

Contact: Mr. Dale Movius, Director, State Benefits
New Mexico Department of Veterans' Services
407 Galisteo St, Room 142
Santa Fe, NM 87501
Phone: 505-827-6300
E-mail: dalej.movius@state.nm.us

NEW MEXICO VIETNAM VETERAN SCHOLARSHIP

Award for Vietnam veterans who have been New Mexico residents for a minimum of ten years and are attending state-funded postsecondary schools. Must have been awarded the Vietnam Campaign medal. Must submit DD 214 and discharge papers.

Award: Scholarship for use in freshman, sophomore, junior, or senior years; renewable. *Number:* 100. *Amount:* $3500–$4000.

Eligibility Requirements: Applicant must be enrolled or expecting to enroll full- or part-time at a two-year or four-year or technical institution or university; resident of New Mexico and studying in New Mexico. Available to U.S. citizens.

Application Requirements: Application form.

Contact: Mr. Dale Movius, Director, State Benefits
New Mexico Department of Veterans' Services
407 Galisteo St, Room 142
Santa Fe, NM 87501
Phone: 505-827-6300
E-mail: Dalej.movius@state.nm.us

NEW MEXICO WARTIME VETERANS SCHOLARSHIP
• *See page 660*

NEW YORK STATE EDUCATION DEPARTMENT

http://www.highered.nysed.gov/

SCHOLARSHIP FOR ACADEMIC EXCELLENCE

Renewable award for New York residents. Scholarship winners must attend a college or university in New York. 2000 scholarships are for $1500 and 6000 are for $500. The selection criteria used are based on Regents test scores or rank in class or local exam. Must be U.S. citizen or permanent resident.

Award: Scholarship for use in freshman year; renewable. *Number:* up to 8000. *Amount:* $500–$1500.

Eligibility Requirements: Applicant must be high school student; planning to enroll or expecting to enroll full-time at a two-year or four-year institution or university; resident of New York and studying in New York. Available to U.S. citizens.

Application Requirements: Application form. *Deadline:* December 19.

Contact: Lewis Hall, Supervisor
    Phone: 518-486-1319
    Fax: 518-486-5346
    E-mail: scholar@mail.nysed.gov

NEW YORK STATE GRANGE

http://www.nysgrange.org/

SUSAN W. FREESTONE EDUCATION AWARD
• *See page 552*

NEW YORK STATE HIGHER EDUCATION SERVICES CORPORATION

https://www.hesc.ny.gov/

NEW YORK AID FOR PART-TIME STUDY (APTS)

Renewable scholarship provides tuition assistance to part-time undergraduate students who are New York residents, meet income eligibility requirements and are attending New York accredited institutions. Deadline varies. Must be U.S. citizen.

Award: Grant for use in freshman, sophomore, junior, or senior years; renewable. *Amount:* up to $2000.

Eligibility Requirements: Applicant must be enrolled or expecting to enroll part-time at a two-year or four-year institution or university; resident of New York and studying in New York. Available to U.S. citizens.

Application Requirements: Application form, financial need analysis. *Deadline:* varies.

Contact: Student Information
    New York State Higher Education Services Corporation
    99 Washington Avenue, Room 1320
    Albany, NY 12255
    Phone: 518-473-3887
    Fax: 518-474-2839

NEW YORK MEMORIAL SCHOLARSHIPS FOR FAMILIES OF DECEASED POLICE OFFICERS, FIRE FIGHTERS, AND PEACE OFFICERS

Renewable scholarship for children, spouses and financial dependents of deceased fire fighters, volunteer firefighters, police officers, peace officers and emergency medical service workers who died in the line of duty. Provides up to the cost of SUNY educational expenses.

Award: Scholarship for use in freshman, sophomore, junior, or senior years; renewable.

Eligibility Requirements: Applicant must be enrolled or expecting to enroll full-time at a four-year institution or university; resident of New York and studying in New York. Available to U.S. citizens.

Application Requirements: Application form, financial need analysis, transcript. *Deadline:* May 1.

Contact: Scholarships
    Phone: 888-697-4372

NEW YORK STATE AID TO NATIVE AMERICANS
• *See page 692*

NEW YORK STATE TUITION ASSISTANCE PROGRAM

Award for New York state residents attending a New York postsecondary institution. Must be full-time student in approved program with tuition over $200 per year. Must show financial need and not be in default in any other state program. Renewable award of $500 to $5000 dependent on family income and tuition charged.

Award: Grant for use in freshman, sophomore, junior, or senior years; renewable. *Number:* 350,000–360,000. *Amount:* $500–$5000.

Eligibility Requirements: Applicant must be enrolled or expecting to enroll full-time at a two-year or four-year institution or university; resident of New York and studying in New York. Available to U.S. citizens.

Application Requirements: Application form, financial need analysis. *Deadline:* May 1.

Contact: Student Information
    New York State Higher Education Services Corporation
    99 Washington Avenue, Room 1400
    Albany, NY 12255
    Phone: 888-697-4372

NEW YORK VIETNAM/PERSIAN GULF/AFGHANISTAN VETERANS TUITION AWARDS
• *See page 660*

REGENTS AWARD FOR CHILD OF VETERAN
• *See page 660*

SCHOLARSHIPS FOR ACADEMIC EXCELLENCE

Renewable awards of up to $1500 for academically outstanding New York State high school graduates planning to attend an approved postsecondary institution in New York State. For full-time study only. Contact high school guidance counselor to apply.

Award: Scholarship for use in freshman, sophomore, junior, or senior years; renewable. *Number:* up to 8000. *Amount:* $500–$1500.

Eligibility Requirements: Applicant must be high school student; planning to enroll or expecting to enroll full-time at a four-year institution or university; resident of New York and studying in New York. Available to U.S. citizens.

Application Requirements: Application form. *Deadline:* varies.

Contact: Rita McGivern, Student Information
    New York State Higher Education Services Corporation
    99 Washington Avenue, Room 1320
    Albany, NY 12255
    E-mail: scholarship@hesc.com

N.H. DEPARTMENT OF EDUCATION, DIVISION OF HIGHER EDUCATION - HIGHER EDUCATION COMMISSION

http://www.education.nh.gov/highered

SCHOLARSHIPS FOR ORPHANS OF VETERANS
• *See page 660*

NORTH CAROLINA ASSOCIATION OF EDUCATORS

http://www.ncae.org/

NORTH CAROLINA ASSOCIATION OF EDUCATORS MARTIN LUTHER KING JR SCHOLARSHIP

One-time award for high school seniors who are North Carolina residents to attend a postsecondary institution. Must be a U.S. citizen. Based upon financial need, GPA, and essay. Must have a GPA of at least 3.5 on a 5.0 scale or a 2.5 on a 4.0 scale.

Award: Scholarship for use in freshman year; not renewable. *Number:* 3–4. *Amount:* $500–$1000.

Eligibility Requirements: Applicant must be high school student; planning to enroll or expecting to enroll full-time at a four-year institution or university and resident of North Carolina. Available to U.S. citizens.

Application Requirements: Application form, community service, essay, financial need analysis. *Deadline:* February 1.

Contact: Derevana Leach, Scholarship Coordinator
North Carolina Association of Educators
700 S Salisbury St
Raleigh, NC 27601
Phone: 800-662-7924 Ext. 203
E-mail: derevana.leach@ncae.org

NORTH CAROLINA BAR ASSOCIATION

http://www.ncbar.org/

NORTH CAROLINA BAR ASSOCIATION YOUNG LAWYERS DIVISION SCHOLARSHIP

Renewable award for children or step-children of North Carolina Law Enforcement Officers killed or permanently disabled in the line of duty, studying full-time in accredited colleges or universities. Must be resident of North Carolina and under 26 years of age for first time application. The number of awards and the dollar value of the award varies annually.

Award: Scholarship for use in freshman, sophomore, junior, senior, graduate, or postgraduate years; renewable.

Eligibility Requirements: Applicant must be enrolled or expecting to enroll full-time at a two-year or four-year or technical institution or university and resident of North Carolina. Available to U.S. citizens.

Application Requirements: Application form, essay, financial need analysis, personal photograph. *Deadline:* April 1.

Contact: Ms. Jacquelyn Terrell, Director of Sections/Divisions
Activities, YLD Staff Liaison
North Carolina Bar Association
PO Box 3688
Cary, NC 27519
Phone: 919-657-0561
E-mail: jterrell@ncbar.org

NORTH CAROLINA DIVISION OF SERVICES FOR THE BLIND

http://www.ncdhhs.gov/

NORTH CAROLINA DIVISION OF SERVICES FOR THE BLIND REHABILITATION SERVICES
• *See page 636*

NORTH CAROLINA DIVISION OF VETERANS AFFAIRS

http://www.milvets.nc.gov/

NORTH CAROLINA VETERANS SCHOLARSHIPS CLASS I-A
• *See page 660*

NORTH CAROLINA VETERANS SCHOLARSHIPS CLASS I-B
• *See page 660*

NORTH CAROLINA VETERANS SCHOLARSHIPS CLASS II
• *See page 661*

NORTH CAROLINA VETERANS SCHOLARSHIPS CLASS III
• *See page 661*

NORTH CAROLINA VETERANS SCHOLARSHIPS CLASS IV
• *See page 661*

NORTH CAROLINA DIVISION OF VOCATIONAL REHABILITATION SERVICES

http://www.dhhs.state.nc.us/

TRAINING SUPPORT FOR YOUTH WITH DISABILITIES
• *See page 609*

NORTH CAROLINA NATIONAL GUARD

http://nc.ng.mil/Pages/default.aspx

NORTH CAROLINA NATIONAL GUARD TUITION ASSISTANCE PROGRAM
• *See page 644*

NORTH CAROLINA SOCIETY OF HISPANIC PROFESSIONALS

http://www.thencshp.org/

NORTH CAROLINA HISPANIC COLLEGE FUND SCHOLARSHIP
• *See page 693*

NORTH CAROLINA STATE EDUCATION ASSISTANCE AUTHORITY

http://www.ncseaa.edu/

AUBREY LEE BROOKS SCHOLARSHIPS

A renewable scholarship for graduating high school seniors who are residents of designated North Carolina counties: Alamance, Bertie, Caswell, Durham. Forsyth, Granville, Guilford, Orange, Person, Rockingham, Stokes, Surry, Swain and Warren counties. The scholarship may be used at North Carolina State University, the University of North Carolina at Chapel Hill or the University of North Carolina at Greensboro. Scholarship is renewable, provided the recipient has continued financial need, remains enrolled full-time at an eligible institution and maintains specified academic standards. Additional details and application at http://www.CFNC.org/Brooks

Award: Scholarship for use in freshman, sophomore, junior, or senior years; renewable. *Number:* 17. *Amount:* $12,000.

Eligibility Requirements: Applicant must be high school student; planning to enroll or expecting to enroll full-time at a four-year institution or university; resident of North Carolina and studying in North Carolina. Available to U.S. citizens.

Application Requirements: Application form, essay, financial need analysis, interview. *Deadline:* continuous.

Contact: Ms. Rashonn Albritton, Scholarship and Grant Manager
North Carolina State Education Assistance Authority
PO Box 13663
Research Triangle Park, NC 27709-3663
Phone: 919-248-4632
E-mail: ewilliams@ncseaa.edu

JAGANNATHAN SCHOLARSHIP

Available to graduating high school seniors who plan to enroll as college freshmen in a full-time degree program at one of the constituent institutions of The University of North Carolina. Applicant must be resident of North Carolina. Applicant must document financial need.

Award: Scholarship for use in freshman year; renewable.

Eligibility Requirements: Applicant must be enrolled or expecting to enroll full-time at a four-year institution or university; resident of North Carolina and studying in North Carolina. Applicant must have 3.0 GPA or higher. Available to U.S. citizens.

Application Requirements: Application form, financial need analysis. *Deadline:* January 15.

Contact: Edna Williams, Manager, Award and Loan Origination
Services
North Carolina State Education Assistance Authority
PO Box 13663
Research Triangle Park, NC 27709
Phone: 919-549-8614
E-mail: ewilliams@ncseaa.edu

NORTH CAROLINA COMMUNITY COLLEGE GRANT PROGRAM

Grants are available to North Carolina residents who demonstrate
financial need and are enrolled at NC community colleges. The applicant
must be a N.C. resident for tuition purposes; enroll for at least six credit
hours per semester in a curriculum program; and meet the Satisfactory
Academic Progress requirements of the institution. Eligibility is
determined based on the same criteria as the Federal Pell Grant; students
not eligible for the Federal Pell Grant may be considered for the grant
based on the expected family contribution (EFC). Student who have
earned a Bachelor's degree already are ineligible. Applicants must
complete the Free Application for Federal Student Aid (FAFSA).
Consideration is automatic once the FAFSA is filed. Please contact the
financial aid office at the local community college for more specific
information regarding institutional processes.

Award: Grant for use in freshman or sophomore years; not renewable.
Number: 25,000. *Amount:* $150–$1150.

Eligibility Requirements: Applicant must be enrolled or expecting to
enroll full- or part-time at a two-year or technical institution; resident of
North Carolina and studying in North Carolina. Available to U.S.
citizens.

Application Requirements: Financial need analysis.

Contact: Edna Williams, Manager, Award and Loan Origination
Services
North Carolina State Education Assistance Authority
PO Box 13663
Research Triangle Park, NC 27709-3663
Phone: 919-248-4632
E-mail: ewilliams@ncseaa.edu

UNIVERSITY OF NORTH CAROLINA NEED-BASED GRANT

Applicants must be enrolled in at least 6 credit hours at one of sixteen
UNC system universities. Eligibility based on need; award varies,
consideration for grant automatic when FAFSA is filed. Late applications
may be denied due to insufficient funds.

Award: Grant for use in freshman, sophomore, junior, or senior years;
renewable.

Eligibility Requirements: Applicant must be enrolled or expecting to
enroll full- or part-time at an institution or university; resident of North
Carolina and studying in North Carolina. Available to U.S. citizens.

Application Requirements: Application form, financial need analysis.

Contact: Edna Williams, Manager, Award and Loan Origination
Services
North Carolina State Education Assistance Authority
PO Box 13663
Research Triangle Park, NC 27709
Phone: 919-549-8614
E-mail: ewilliams@ncseaa.edu

NORTH CAROLINA VIETNAM VETERANS, INC.

http://www.ncvvi.org

NC VIETNAM VETERANS, INC., SCHOLARSHIP PROGRAM

• See page 609

NORTH DAKOTA UNIVERSITY SYSTEM

www.ndus.edu/

NORTH DAKOTA ACADEMIC SCHOLARSHIP

This scholarship rewards high schools students from ND for taking
rigorous coursework in high school. Applicants must earn a cumulative
high school GPA of 3.0 and have a minimum ACT score of 24. Full-time
enrollment is required and is defined as 12 credits in the first two terms
and 15 credits in subsequent terms. A minimum cumulative college GPA
of 2.75 is required to renew the scholarship. This scholarship is based on
merit. Awards are $750/sem. or $500/qtr. up to a total of $6,000. Students
have up to 6 years following high school to utilize the scholarship.

Award: Scholarship for use in freshman, sophomore, junior, senior, or
graduate years; renewable. *Number:* 1–5000. *Amount:* $6000.

Eligibility Requirements: Applicant must be high school student;
planning to enroll or expecting to enroll full-time at a two-year or four-
year institution or university; resident of North Dakota and studying in
North Dakota. Applicant must have 3.0 GPA or higher. Available to U.S.
citizens.

Application Requirements: Application form. *Deadline:* June 2.

Contact: Brenda Zastoupil, Director of Financial Aid
North Dakota University System
600 E Boulevard Ave, Dept 21
Bismarck, ND 58505-0602
Phone: 701-328-2906
Fax: 701-328-2979
E-mail: ndfinaid@ndus.edu

NORTH DAKOTA CAREER AND TECHNICAL EDUCATION SCHOLARSHIP

The ND Career and Technical Education Scholarship's goal is to reward
students taking rigorous courses in high school, to increase awareness of
career and technical programs, and to retain students within ND. The
scholarship has an ACT or WorkKeys exam score requirement, a GPA
requirement, and a specific high school course list that must be
completed to qualify. Full-time enrollment is required and is defined as
12 credits in the first two terms and 15 credits in subsequent terms. A
minimum cumulative college GPA of 2.75 is required to renew the
scholarship. This scholarship is based on merit. Awards are $750/sem. or
$500/qtr. up to a total of $6,000. Students have up to 6 years following
high school to utilize the scholarship.

Award: Scholarship for use in freshman, sophomore, junior, senior, or
graduate years; renewable. *Number:* 1–4000. *Amount:* $6000.

Eligibility Requirements: Applicant must be high school student;
planning to enroll or expecting to enroll full-time at a two-year or four-
year institution or university; resident of North Dakota and studying in
North Dakota. Applicant must have 3.0 GPA or higher. Available to U.S.
citizens.

Application Requirements: Application form. *Deadline:* June 2.

Contact: Brenda Zastoupil, Director of Financial Aid
North Dakota University System
600 E Boulevard Ave, Dept 21
Bismarck, ND 58505-0602
Phone: 701-328-2906
Fax: 701-328-2979
E-mail: ndfinaid@ndus.edu

NORTH DAKOTA INDIAN SCHOLARSHIP PROGRAM

• See page 693

NORTH DAKOTA SCHOLARS PROGRAM

The purpose of the ND Scholars Scholarship is to retain within ND, the
brightest and best students who are pursuing post-secondary education.
The scholarship amount equates to the tuition charged at the Scholar's
eligible institution, not to exceed the highest regular resident
undergraduate tuition rate in the NDUS system. This program provides
merit-based, full-tuition scholarships to ND high school graduates who
attend a qualifying college within ND. High school juniors who score in
the top 95th percentile of all ND ACT test-takers prior to July 1 of the
year preceding their freshman year of college will be considered as a
candidate for this award. Not all eligible students will qualify due to
limited appropriations. Students are ranked based on ACT test scores.
This scholarship is renewable for up to three years. Recipients must be
enrolled at qualifying institutions in ND at full-time status (12 cr.
minimum per semester) and must maintain a cumulative GPA of 3.50.
Only 40-50 new awards are made each year to new students.

Award: Scholarship for use in freshman, sophomore, junior, or senior
years; renewable. *Number:* 40–50. *Amount:* $6652–$13,848.

Eligibility Requirements: Applicant must be high school student;
planning to enroll or expecting to enroll full-time at a two-year or four-
year institution or university; resident of North Dakota and studying in
North Dakota. Available to U.S. citizens.

Application Requirements: *Deadline:* June 30.

Contact: Brenda Zastoupil, Director of Financial Aid
North Dakota University System
600 E Boulevard Ave, Dept 21
Bismarck, ND 58505-0602
Phone: 701-328-2906
Fax: 701-328-2979
E-mail: ndfinaid@ndus.edu

NORTH DAKOTA STATE STUDENT INCENTIVE GRANT PROGRAM

The North Dakota State Grant is the premier need-based state grant in North Dakota. Maximum award of $975 per semester or $650 per quarter. The North Dakota State Grant supports ND residents attending an eligible college or university within North Dakota in a program of study that is at least one year in length. The FAFSA is required annually. Awards are available for up to 8 full-time equivalent semesters or 12 full-time equivalent quarters of undergraduate study. Students must meet the SAP guidelines of their institution and meet all title IV eligibility criteria, including having verification complete, if required.

Award: Grant for use in freshman, sophomore, junior, or senior years; not renewable. *Number:* 7000–8000. *Amount:* $1–$975.

Eligibility Requirements: Applicant must be enrolled or expecting to enroll full- or part-time at a two-year or four-year institution or university; resident of North Dakota and studying in North Dakota. Available to U.S. citizens.

Application Requirements: *Deadline:* continuous.

Contact: Brenda Zastoupil, Director of Financial Aid
North Dakota University System
600 E Boulevard Ave, Dept 21
Bismarck, ND 58505-0602
Phone: 701-328-2906
Fax: 701-328-2979
E-mail: ndfinaid@ndus.edu

NORTHWEST DANISH ASSOCIATION

www.northwestdanish.org

NORTHWEST DANISH ASSOCIATION SCHOLARSHIP
• See page 693

OHIO ASSOCIATION OF CAREER COLLEGES AND SCHOOLS

http://www.ohiocareercolleges.org/

OHIOLEADS! SCHOLARSHIP

One-time scholarship for graduating high school seniors enrolling in a career college or school that is a participating member of OACCS. The applicant must be an Ohio high school student with a 2.0 GPA or better and does not have to demonstrate a financial need. The scholarship amount and the number of scholarships granted varies.

Award: Scholarship for use in freshman, sophomore, junior, or senior years; not renewable. *Number:* 200–250. *Amount:* $1500–$40,000.

Eligibility Requirements: Applicant must be high school student; planning to enroll or expecting to enroll full-time at a two-year or four-year or technical institution; resident of Ohio and studying in Ohio. Available to U.S. and non-U.S. citizens.

Application Requirements: Application form, essay. *Deadline:* April 14.

Contact: Michelle "Mike" Widner, Admin Asst
Ohio Association of Career Colleges and Schools
2109 Stella Ct
Ste 125
Columbus, OH 43215
Phone: 614-487-8180
E-mail: admin@ohiocareercolleges.org

OHIO DEPARTMENT OF HIGHER EDUCATION

www.ohiohighered.org

OHIO COLLEGE OPPORTUNITY GRANT
• See page 609

OHIO SAFETY OFFICERS COLLEGE MEMORIAL FUND
• See page 609

OHIO WAR ORPHANS SCHOLARSHIP
• See page 610

OHIO NATIONAL GUARD

http://www.ong.ohio.gov/

OHIO NATIONAL GUARD SCHOLARSHIP PROGRAM
• See page 644

OKLAHOMA ALUMNI & ASSOCIATES OF FHA, HERO AND FCCLA INC.

http://www.okfccla.net/

OKLAHOMA ALUMNI & ASSOCIATES OF FHA, HERO, AND FCCLA INC. SCHOLARSHIP
• See page 553

OKLAHOMA STATE REGENTS FOR HIGHER EDUCATION

http://www.okhighered.org/

OKLAHOMA TUITION AID GRANT

Award for Oklahoma residents enrolled at an Oklahoma institution at least part time each semester in a degree program. May be enrolled in two- or four-year or approved vocational-technical institution. Award for students attending public institutions or private colleges. Application is made through FAFSA.

Award: Grant for use in freshman, sophomore, junior, or senior years; not renewable. *Amount:* $1000–$1300.

Eligibility Requirements: Applicant must be enrolled or expecting to enroll full- or part-time at a two-year or four-year or technical institution or university; resident of Oklahoma and studying in Oklahoma. Available to U.S. citizens.

Application Requirements: Application form, financial need analysis.

Contact: Mrs. Linette McMurtrey, Scholarship Programs Coordinator
Phone: 405-225-9131
E-mail: lmcmurtrey@osrhe.edu

REGIONAL UNIVERSITY BACCALAUREATE SCHOLARSHIP

Renewable award for Oklahoma residents attending one of 11 participating Oklahoma public universities. Must have an ACT composite score of at least 30 or be a National Merit semifinalist or commended student. In addition to the award amount, each recipient will receive a resident tuition waiver from the institution. Must maintain a 3.25 GPA. Deadlines vary depending upon the institution attended.

Award: Scholarship for use in freshman, sophomore, junior, or senior years; renewable. *Amount:* $3000.

Eligibility Requirements: Applicant must be enrolled or expecting to enroll full-time at an institution or university; resident of Oklahoma and studying in Oklahoma. Available to U.S. citizens.

Application Requirements: Application form.

Contact: Scholarship Programs Coordinator
Oklahoma State Regents for Higher Education
PO Box 108850
Oklahoma City, OK 73101-8850
Phone: 405-858-1840
E-mail: studentinfo@osrhe.edu

WILLIAM P. WILLIS SCHOLARSHIP

Renewable award for low-income Oklahoma residents attending an Oklahoma institution. Must be a full-time undergraduate. Deadline varies.

Award: Scholarship for use in freshman, sophomore, junior, or senior years; renewable. *Amount:* $2000–$3000.

Eligibility Requirements: Applicant must be enrolled or expecting to enroll full-time at a two-year or four-year institution or university; resident of Oklahoma and studying in Oklahoma. Available to U.S. citizens.

Application Requirements: Application form.

Contact: Scholarship Programs Coordinator
Oklahoma State Regents for Higher Education
PO Box 108850
Oklahoma City, OK 73101-8850
Phone: 405-858-1840
E-mail: studentinfo@osrhe.edu

ONE MILLION DEGREES

http://www.onemilliondegrees.org

ONE MILLION DEGREES SIGNATURE FUND SCHOLARSHIP

The One Million Degrees Signature Scholarship Program offers groundbreaking, whole-student programming to low-income, highly motivated community college students.

Award: Scholarship for use in freshman, sophomore, junior, or senior years; renewable. *Number:* 1–80. *Amount:* $500–$3000.

Eligibility Requirements: Applicant must be enrolled or expecting to enroll full-time at a two-year institution; resident of Illinois and studying in Illinois. Available to U.S. citizens.

Application Requirements: Application form, community service, completion of FAFSA, essay, financial need analysis, interview, recommendations or references, test scores, transcript. *Deadline:* June 1.

Contact: Ms. Nina Sanchez, Director, Scholarship and Academics
Phone: 312-920-9605
E-mail: apply@onemilliondegrees.org

OREGON COMMUNITY FOUNDATION

http://www.oregoncf.org/

ERNEST ALAN AND BARBARA PARK MEYER SCHOLARSHIP FUND

Scholarship for Oregon high school graduates for use in the pursuit of a postsecondary education (undergraduate or graduate) at a nonprofit two- or four-year college or university.

Award: Scholarship for use in freshman, sophomore, junior, or senior years; renewable. *Number:* up to 5. *Amount:* $1000–$4500.

Eligibility Requirements: Applicant must be enrolled or expecting to enroll full-time at a two-year or four-year or technical institution or university and resident of Oregon. Available to U.S. citizens.

Application Requirements: Application form, recommendations or references. *Deadline:* March 1.

Contact: Dianne Causey, Program Associate for Scholarships and Grants
Phone: 503-227-6846 Ext. 1418
E-mail: dcausey@oregoncf.org

FRIENDS OF BILL RUTHERFORD EDUCATION FUND

Scholarship for Oregon high school graduates or GED recipients who are dependent children of individuals holding statewide elected office or currently serving in the Oregon State Legislature. Students must be enrolled full-time in a two- or four-year college or university. For more information, see web http://www.getcollegefunds.org.

Award: Scholarship for use in freshman, sophomore, junior, or senior years; renewable. *Number:* 1–2. *Amount:* $1000–$2500.

Eligibility Requirements: Applicant must be enrolled or expecting to enroll full-time at a two-year or four-year institution or university and resident of Oregon. Available to U.S. citizens.

Application Requirements: Application form, recommendations or references. *Deadline:* March 1.

Contact: Dianne Causey, Program Associate for Scholarships and Grants
Phone: 503-227-6846 Ext. 1418
E-mail: dcausey@oregoncf.org

MARY E. HORSTKOTTE SCHOLARSHIP FUND

Award available for academically talented and financially needy students for use in the pursuit of a postsecondary education. Must be an Oregon resident. For full-time study only.

Award: Scholarship for use in freshman, sophomore, junior, or senior years; not renewable. *Number:* 1–10. *Amount:* $2000.

Eligibility Requirements: Applicant must be enrolled or expecting to enroll full-time at a two-year or four-year or technical institution or university and resident of Oregon. Available to U.S. citizens.

Application Requirements: Application form, recommendations or references. *Deadline:* March 1.

Contact: Dianne Causey, Program Associate for Scholarships and Grants
Phone: 503-227-6846 Ext. 1418
E-mail: dcausey@oregoncf.org

RUBE AND MINAH LESLIE EDUCATIONAL FUND

Scholarship for Oregon residents for the pursuit of a postsecondary education. Selection is based on financial need.

Award: Scholarship for use in freshman, sophomore, junior, or senior years; renewable. *Number:* up to 50. *Amount:* $2000.

Eligibility Requirements: Applicant must be enrolled or expecting to enroll full-time at a two-year or four-year institution or university and resident of Oregon. Available to U.S. citizens.

Application Requirements: Application form, financial need analysis. *Deadline:* March 1.

Contact: Dianne Causey, Program Associate for Scholarships and Grants
Phone: 503-227-6846 Ext. 1418
E-mail: dcausey@oregoncf.org

OREGON DEPARTMENT OF VETERANS' AFFAIRS

http://www.oregon.gov/odva

OREGON VETERANS' EDUCATION AID
• *See page 661*

OREGON STUDENT ASSISTANCE COMMISSION

http://www.GetCollegeFunds.org/

ANDEO SCHOLARSHIP

One-time award for graduating seniors (including GED recipients and home-schooled seniors) of Oregon or Washington high schools. Must have hosted an international student through ANDEO International Homestays during the current academic year or the year immediately prior to the current year and taken 3+ years of a foreign language by the end of the current academic year. Minimum 3.5 GPA preferred. FAFSA is required. Must enroll at least half time at any U.S. college or university.

Award: Scholarship for use in freshman year; not renewable.

Eligibility Requirements: Applicant must be high school student; planning to enroll or expecting to enroll full- or part-time at a four-year institution or university and resident of Oregon, Washington. Applicant must have 3.5 GPA or higher. Available to U.S. citizens.

Application Requirements: Application form, financial need analysis. *Deadline:* March 1.

Contact: Melissa Adams, Scholarship Processing Coordinator
Phone: 541-687-7409
E-mail: melissa.adams@hecc.oregon.gov

A. VICTOR ROSENFELD SCHOLARSHIP
• *See page 569*

BANDON SUBMARINE CABLE COUNCIL'S LENNY MONTALBANO MEMORIAL SCHOLARSHIP

Award for members or dependent children of members of the Bandon Submarine Cable Council. Residents of Coos County are preferred. Minimum 2.75 GPA required. Award is automatically renewable if criteria is met.

Award: Scholarship for use in freshman, sophomore, junior, senior, or graduate years; renewable.

Eligibility Requirements: Applicant must be enrolled or expecting to enroll full-time at a four-year institution and resident of Oregon. Available to U.S. citizens.

Application Requirements: Application form, essay. *Deadline:* March 1.

Contact: Melissa Adams, Scholarship Processing Coordinator
Phone: 541-687-7409
E-mail: melissa.adams@hecc.oregon.gov

BANK OF THE CASCADES SCHOLARSHIP

Award for residents of Oregon or Washington who are dependents of eligible employees of Bank of the Cascades. Eligible employee must have been employed by Bank of the Cascades one+ year as of the March scholarship deadline. Must be attending a public or nonprofit college with a preferred GPA of at least 2.5.

Award: Scholarship for use in freshman, sophomore, junior, or senior years; not renewable.

Eligibility Requirements: Applicant must be enrolled or expecting to enroll full-time at a four-year institution or university and resident of Idaho, Oregon, Washington. Applicant must have 2.5 GPA or higher. Available to U.S. citizens.

Application Requirements: Application form, essay. *Deadline:* March 1.

Contact: Melissa Adams, Scholarship Processing Coordinator
Phone: 541-687-7409
E-mail: melissa.adams@hecc.oregon.gov

BEN SELLING SCHOLARSHIP

Award for Oregon residents enrolling as undergraduate sophomores, juniors, or seniors. Minimum college GPA of 3.5 and FAFSA are required. Recipients must attend any Oregon or U.S. Rabbinical public and nonprofit college. Apply/compete annually.

Award: Scholarship for use in sophomore, junior, or senior years; not renewable.

Eligibility Requirements: Applicant must be enrolled or expecting to enroll full-time at a two-year or four-year institution and resident of Oregon. Applicant must have 3.5 GPA or higher. Available to U.S. citizens.

Application Requirements: Application form, financial need analysis. *Deadline:* March 1.

Contact: Melissa Adams, Scholarship Processing Coordinator
Phone: 541-687-7409
E-mail: melissa.adams@hecc.oregon.gov

CONGRESSMAN PETER DEFAZIO SCHOLARSHIP

One-time award available to dislocated workers residing in Oregon's Fourth Congressional District, which includes parts of Benton, Coos, Curry, Douglas, Josephine, Lane, and Linn counties. Recipients must attend one of Lane, Linn-Benton, Rogue, Southwestern Oregon or Umpqua Community Colleges and enroll at least half-time. If selected as a semi-finalist for the scholarship, verification of status as a dislocated worker is required. FAFSA is required.

Award: Scholarship for use in freshman or sophomore years; not renewable.

Eligibility Requirements: Applicant must be enrolled or expecting to enroll full- or part-time at a two-year institution; resident of Oregon and studying in Oregon. Available to U.S. citizens.

Application Requirements: Application form, financial need analysis. *Deadline:* March 1.

Contact: Melissa Adams, Scholarship Processing Coordinator
Phone: 541-687-7409
E-mail: melissa.adams@hecc.oregon.gov

DOROTHY CAMPBELL MEMORIAL SCHOLARSHIP

Renewable award for female Oregon high school graduates with a minimum 2.75 GPA. Must submit essay describing strong, continuing interest in golf and the contribution that sport has made to applicant's development. Preference for participation in high school golf team (including intramural), if available, and planning to enroll at a four-year Oregon public or nonprofit college. FAFSA required.

Award: Scholarship for use in freshman year; renewable.

Eligibility Requirements: Applicant must be enrolled or expecting to enroll full-time at a four-year institution or university; female; resident of Oregon; studying in Oregon and must have an interest in golf. Available to U.S. citizens.

Application Requirements: Application form, essay, financial need analysis. *Deadline:* March 1.

Contact: Melissa Adams, Scholarship Processing Coordinator
Phone: 541-687-7409
E-mail: melissa.adams@hecc.oregon.gov

FORD OPPORTUNITY PROGRAM

Renewable award for Oregon or Siskiyou County residents who are single heads of household with custody of a dependent child or children and without the support of a domestic partner. Must be planning to earn a Bachelor's degree and study full-time at an Oregon or California college or university. Minimum cumulative GPA of 3.0 required. If minimum requirements are not met, special recommendation form required (see high school counselor or contact OSAC). FAFSA required.

Award: Scholarship for use in freshman, sophomore, junior, or senior years; renewable.

Eligibility Requirements: Applicant must be enrolled or expecting to enroll full-time at a four-year institution or university; single; resident of California, Oregon and studying in California, Oregon. Applicant must have 3.0 GPA or higher. Available to U.S. citizens.

Application Requirements: Application form, essay, financial need analysis, interview. *Deadline:* March 1.

Contact: Ford Family Foundation Scholarship Office
Oregon Student Assistance Commission
44 Club Road, Suite 100
Eugene, OR 97401
Phone: 877-864-2872
E-mail: fordscholarships@tfff.org

FORD RESTART PROGRAM

Award to support nontraditional, full-time adult students who wish to begin or continue education at the postsecondary level in Oregon or California. Must be an Oregon or Siskiyou County resident and at least 25 years of age by March 1 of the application year. Must have a high school diploma or GED certificate and must not have previously earned a Bachelor's degree. A Restart Reference Form is required and must be submitted with the application. Strong preference given to applicants with little or no recent college experience. FAFSA is required. Scholarship is automatically renewable if renewal criteria met.

Award: Scholarship for use in freshman, sophomore, junior, or senior years; renewable.

Eligibility Requirements: Applicant must be enrolled or expecting to enroll full-time at a two-year or four-year institution or university; resident of California, Oregon and studying in California, Oregon. Available to U.S. citizens.

Application Requirements: Application form, financial need analysis, interview. *Deadline:* March 1.

Contact: Melissa Adams, Scholarship Processing Coordinator
Phone: 541-687-7409
E-mail: melissa.adams@hecc.oregon.gov

FORD SCHOLARS PROGRAM

Renewable award for Oregon or Siskiyou County residents who are graduating high school seniors, GED recipients or students at the point of transferring from a community college to a four-year college in Oregon or California. Must have minimum cumulative GPA of 3.0, be planning to earn a Bachelor's degree, and be enrolled as a full-time student. If minimum requirements are not met, special recommendation form required (see high school counselor or contact OSAC). FAFSA required. Scholarship is automatically renewable if renewal criteria met.

Award: Scholarship for use in freshman, sophomore, junior, or senior years; renewable.

Eligibility Requirements: Applicant must be enrolled or expecting to enroll full-time at a four-year institution or university; resident of California, Oregon and studying in California, Oregon. Applicant must have 3.0 GPA or higher. Available to U.S. citizens.

Application Requirements: Application form, financial need analysis, interview. *Deadline:* March 1.

Contact: Melissa Adams, Scholarship Processing Coordinator
Phone: 541-687-7409
E-mail: melissa.adams@hecc.oregon.gov

GLENN JACKSON SCHOLARS SCHOLARSHIPS
• *See page 570*

GRAY COMMUNITY COLLEGE SCHOLARSHIP
Scholarship available to students attending Oregon community colleges at least half time. Not open to graduating high school seniors. Minimum GPA of 2.5 to 3.5. Scholarship is automatically renewable if renewal criteria met.

Award: Scholarship for use in freshman or sophomore years; not renewable.

Eligibility Requirements: Applicant must be enrolled or expecting to enroll full- or part-time at a two-year institution; resident of Oregon and studying in Oregon. Applicant must have 2.5 GPA or higher. Available to U.S. citizens.

Application Requirements: Application form, financial need analysis. *Deadline:* March 1.

Contact: Melissa Adams, Scholarship Processing Coordinator
Phone: 541-687-7409
E-mail: melissa.adams@hecc.oregon.gov

HARRY LUDWIG MEMORIAL SCHOLARSHIP
• *See page 636*

IDA M. CRAWFORD SCHOLARSHIP
Scholarship available to graduates of accredited Oregon high schools. Not available to applicants majoring in law, medicine, theology, teaching, or music. U.S. Bank employees, their children or near relatives, are not eligible. Reapply annually for award renewal.

Award: Scholarship for use in freshman year; not renewable.

Eligibility Requirements: Applicant must be enrolled or expecting to enroll full-time at a four-year institution and resident of Oregon. Applicant must have 3.5 GPA or higher. Available to U.S. citizens.

Application Requirements: Application form, essay, financial need analysis. *Deadline:* March 1.

Contact: Melissa Adams, Scholarship Processing Coordinator
Phone: 541-687-7409
E-mail: melissa.adams@hecc.oregon.gov

JEROME B. STEINBACH SCHOLARSHIP
Award for Oregon residents enrolled in Oregon institutions as sophomore or above. Award for undergraduate study only. U.S. Bank employees, their children, or near relatives are not eligible.

Award: Scholarship for use in sophomore, junior, or senior years; not renewable.

Eligibility Requirements: Applicant must be enrolled or expecting to enroll full-time at a four-year institution or university and resident of Oregon. Applicant must have 3.5 GPA or higher. Available to U.S. citizens.

Application Requirements: Application form, financial need analysis. *Deadline:* March 1.

Contact: Melissa Adams, Scholarship Processing Coordinator
Phone: 541-687-7409
E-mail: melissa.adams@hecc.oregon.gov

MARIA C. JACKSON/GENERAL GEORGE A. WHITE SCHOLARSHIP
Available to Oregon residents who served or whose parents serve or have served in the U.S. Armed Forces and resided in Oregon at time of enlistment. Must have at least 3.75 GPA and submit documentation of service. (No GPA requirement for graduate-level students and students attending a technical school). U.S. Bank employees, their children, and near relatives are not eligible.

Award: Scholarship for use in freshman, sophomore, junior, senior, or graduate years; not renewable.

Eligibility Requirements: Applicant must be enrolled or expecting to enroll full-time at a two-year or four-year or technical institution or university; resident of Oregon and studying in Oregon. Available to U.S. citizens.

Application Requirements: Application form, financial need analysis. *Deadline:* March 1.

Contact: Melissa Adams, Scholarship Processing Coordinator
Phone: 541-687-7409
E-mail: melissa.adams@hecc.oregon.gov

OREGON DUNGENESS CRAB COMMISSION SCHOLARSHIP
One-time scholarship available to children, stepchildren, or legal dependents of licensed Oregon Dungeness Crab fishermen or crew. Must be 23 years of age or under as of the March scholarship deadline.

Award: Scholarship for use in freshman, sophomore, junior, or senior years; not renewable.

Eligibility Requirements: Applicant must be enrolled or expecting to enroll full-time at a four-year institution or university and resident of Oregon. Available to U.S. citizens.

Application Requirements: Application form. *Deadline:* March 1.

Contact: Melissa Adams, Scholarship Processing Coordinator
Phone: 541-687-7409
E-mail: melissa.adams@hecc.oregon.gov

OREGON STUDENT ACCESS COMMISSION EMPLOYEE AND DEPENDENTS SCHOLARSHIP
Award for eligible employees of the Office of Student Access and Completion and their dependents. Children and dependents must enroll full-time and be 23 or under as of the March scholarship deadline. Employees must enroll at least half time. Apply/compete annually.

Award: Scholarship for use in freshman, sophomore, junior, or senior years; not renewable.

Eligibility Requirements: Applicant must be enrolled or expecting to enroll full- or part-time at a four-year institution or university and resident of Oregon. Available to U.S. citizens.

Application Requirements: Application form. *Deadline:* March 1.

Contact: Melissa Adams, Scholarship Processing Coordinator
Phone: 541-687-7409
E-mail: melissa.adams@hecc.oregon.gov

OREGON TRAWL COMMISSION JOE EASLEY MEMORIAL SCHOLARSHIP
Award for students in any accredited U.S. college or university who are dependents of licensed Oregon Trawl fishermen or crew. Must reapply annually for renewal.

Award: Scholarship for use in freshman, sophomore, junior, or senior years; not renewable.

Eligibility Requirements: Applicant must be enrolled or expecting to enroll full-time at a four-year institution or university; resident of Oregon and studying in Yukon. Available to U.S. citizens.

Application Requirements: Application form, financial need analysis. *Deadline:* March 1.

Contact: Melissa Adams, Scholarship Processing Coordinator
Phone: 541-687-7409
E-mail: melissa.adams@hecc.oregon.gov

PACIFIC NW FEDERAL CREDIT UNION SCHOLARSHIP
Scholarship available to members of Pacific North West Federal Credit Union. Must submit an essay on 'Why My Credit Union is an Important Consumer Choice.' Immediate family members of Pacific NW Federal Credit Union employees and credit union elected or appointed officials are not eligible.

Award: Scholarship for use in freshman, sophomore, junior, or senior years; not renewable.

Eligibility Requirements: Applicant must be enrolled or expecting to enroll full-time at a four-year institution or university and resident of Oregon, Washington. Available to U.S. citizens.

Application Requirements: Application form, essay. *Deadline:* March 1.

Contact: Melissa Adams, Scholarship Processing Coordinator
Phone: 541-687-7409
E-mail: melissa.adams@hecc.oregon.gov

PETER CROSSLEY MEMORIAL SCHOLARSHIP
Renewable award for graduating seniors of Oregon public alternative high schools. Must be highly motivated to succeed despite overcoming a

severe personal obstacle or challenge during high school career. Must plan to enroll at least half-time in an Oregon college or university. Preferred GPA is between 2.0 and 3.5.

Award: Scholarship for use in freshman year; not renewable.

Eligibility Requirements: Applicant must be high school student; planning to enroll or expecting to enroll full- or part-time at a four-year institution or university; resident of Oregon and studying in Oregon. Available to U.S. citizens.

Application Requirements: Application form, essay, financial need analysis. *Deadline:* March 1.

Contact: Melissa Adams, Scholarship Processing Coordinator
Phone: 541-687-7409
E-mail: melissa.adams@hecc.oregon.gov

SALEM ELECTRIC COOPERATIVE SCHOLARSHIP

Award for high school graduates (including GED recipients and home-schooled graduates) who is or whose parents/legal guardians are receiving service from Salem Electric at their primary residence. Salem Electric staff, board members, and immediate family are not eligible. Apply/compete annually.

Award: Scholarship for use in freshman, sophomore, junior, or senior years; not renewable.

Eligibility Requirements: Applicant must be enrolled or expecting to enroll full-time at a four-year institution or university and resident of Oregon. Available to U.S. citizens.

Application Requirements: Application form. *Deadline:* March 1.

Contact: Melissa Adams, Scholarship Processing Coordinator
Phone: 541-687-7409
E-mail: melissa.adams@hecc.oregon.gov

SALEM FOUNDATION ANSEL & MARIE SOLIE SCHOLARSHIP

• See page 636

SEIU LOCAL 503/OPEU STUDENT FINANCIAL AID SCHOLARSHIP

Award for students who are SEIU Local 503/OPEU active members; laid-off members; children, grandchildren, spouses, or domestic partners of active or retired members in good standing; or dependents of deceased members who were active members at time of death. Qualifying members must have been active (full membership dues payer) 1+ year as of the March scholarship deadline. Children, grandchildren, or dependents of qualifying members must be 24 or younger as of the March scholarship deadline, must enroll full time, and will be considered only for undergraduate programs. Part-time enrollment (minimum six credit hours) or graduate program enrollment will be considered only for active members, spouses, domestic partners, or laid-off members.

Award: Scholarship for use in freshman, sophomore, junior, senior, or graduate years; not renewable.

Eligibility Requirements: Applicant must be enrolled or expecting to enroll full- or part-time at a four-year institution or university and resident of Oregon. Available to U.S. citizens.

Application Requirements: Application form, financial need analysis. *Deadline:* March 1.

Contact: Melissa Adams, Scholarship Processing Coordinator
Phone: 541-687-7409
E-mail: melissa.adams@hecc.oregon.gov

W.C. AND PEARL CAMPBELL SCHOLARSHIP

One-time award for graduating seniors of Oregon high schools. 1220+ combined math and critical reading SAT scores or ACT composite of 27+ required. Minimum GPA of 3.85 required.

Award: Scholarship for use in freshman year; not renewable.

Eligibility Requirements: Applicant must be high school student; planning to enroll or expecting to enroll full-time at a four-year institution or university; resident of Oregon and studying in Oregon. Applicant must have 3.5 GPA or higher. Available to U.S. citizens.

Application Requirements: Application form, financial need analysis. *Deadline:* March 1.

Contact: Melissa Adams, Scholarship Processing Coordinator
Phone: 541-687-7409
E-mail: melissa.adams@hecc.oregon.gov

OUTRIGGER DUKE KAHANAMOKU FOUNDATION

http://www.dukefoundation.org

ODKF GENERAL SCHOLARSHIP AWARD

• See page 611

PACERS FOUNDATION INC.

http://www.pacersfoundation.org/

PACERS TEAMUP SCHOLARSHIP

• See page 611

PACIFIC AND ASIAN AFFAIRS COUNCIL

http://www.paachawaii.org/

PAAC ACADEMIC SCHOLARSHIPS

PAAC's academic scholarships are available to college-bound seniors and underclassmen attending Hawaii public or private high school. Applicants must be active in PAAC's high school program (PAAC clubs or PAAC After-School Classes).

Award: Scholarship for use in freshman year; not renewable. *Number:* 5. *Amount:* $300–$1000.

Eligibility Requirements: Applicant must be high school student; planning to enroll or expecting to enroll full-time at a two-year or four-year or technical institution or university and resident of Hawaii. Available to U.S. and non-U.S. citizens.

Application Requirements: Application form, essay. *Deadline:* April 1.

Contact: Jason Shon, High School Program Director
Pacific and Asian Affairs Council
1601 East-West Road, 4th Floor
Honolulu, HI 96848
Phone: 808-944-7759

PENNSYLVANIA BURGLAR AND FIRE ALARM ASSOCIATION

http://www.pbfaa.com/

PENNSYLVANIA BURGLAR AND FIRE ALARM ASSOCIATION YOUTH SCHOLARSHIP PROGRAM

• See page 611

PENNSYLVANIA FEDERATION OF DEMOCRATIC WOMEN INC.

www.pafedofdemwomen.org

PENNSYLVANIA FEDERATION OF DEMOCRATIC WOMEN INC. ANNUAL SCHOLARSHIP AWARDS

• See page 554

PENNSYLVANIA HIGHER EDUCATION ASSISTANCE AGENCY

http://www.pheaa.org/

BLIND OR DEAF BENEFICIARY GRANT PROGRAM

• See page 612

PENNSYLVANIA STATE GRANT PROGRAM

• See page 612

POSTSECONDARY EDUCATION GRATUITY PROGRAM

• See page 644

READY TO SUCCEED SCHOLARSHIP PROGRAM

RTSS provides scholarships to high academic achievers that, in combination with the Pennsylvania State Grant Program, offer a total award up to $2,000 for full-time and $1,000 for part-time students. The minimum award is $500. Awards can be used to cover tuition, books, fees, supplies, and living expenses. Students must be nominated by their post-secondary institution for participation in the program. Funding is limited for the program and awards are made on a first-come, first-served basis. The program, which is funded by the Pennsylvania General Assembly, provides awards to high-achieving students whose annual family income does not exceed $110,000.

Award: Scholarship for use in sophomore, junior, or senior years; not renewable. *Amount:* $500–$2000.

Eligibility Requirements: Applicant must be enrolled or expecting to enroll full- or part-time at a two-year or four-year or technical institution or university; resident of Pennsylvania and studying in Pennsylvania. Applicant must have 3.5 GPA or higher.

Application Requirements: Application form, financial need analysis.

Contact: Keith New, Director of Public Relations
Phone: 717-720-2509
E-mail: knew@pheaa.org

PETER DOCTOR MEMORIAL INDIAN SCHOLARSHIP FOUNDATION INC.

PETER DOCTOR MEMORIAL INDIAN SCHOLARSHIP FOUNDATION INC.
• *See page 696*

PFUND FOUNDATION

http://www.pfundfoundation.org

PFUND FOUNDATION SCHOLARSHIP PROGRAM

The PFund Foundation Scholarship Program annually awards $60,000 in scholarships to Lesbian, Gay, Bisexual, Transgender, Queer and allied students in recognition of their courageous leadership, community service and academic achievement. Powered by a diverse panel of community leaders who select scholars each year and numerous donors who establish the scholarship awards, the PFund Scholarship Program is developing every generation of LGBTQ leadership. Scholarship awards range from $1,000 to $10,000. To learn more about how to apply, visit www.PFundFoundation.org for the Scholarship Guidelines & Application Form or contact (612) 870-1806 or email: scholarships@pfundfoundation.org

Award: Scholarship for use in freshman, sophomore, junior, senior, graduate, or postgraduate years; not renewable. *Number:* 15–30. *Amount:* $2000–$10,000.

Eligibility Requirements: Applicant must be enrolled or expecting to enroll full- or part-time at a two-year or four-year or technical institution or university; resident of Iowa, Minnesota, North Dakota, South Dakota, Wisconsin and studying in Iowa, Minnesota, North Dakota, South Dakota, Wisconsin. Available to U.S. and non-U.S. citizens.

Application Requirements: Application form, community service, essay. *Deadline:* January 15.

Contact: Trina Olson, Executive Director
PFund Foundation
2801 21st Ave. S
Suite 132B
Minneapolis, MN 55407
Phone: 612-870-1806
E-mail: scholarships@pfundfoundation.org

PHILIPINO-AMERICAN ASSOCIATION OF NEW ENGLAND

http://www.pamas.org/

BLESSED LEON OF OUR LADY OF THE ROSARY AWARD
• *See page 696*

PAMAS RESTRICTED SCHOLARSHIP AWARD
• *See page 554*

RAVENSCROFT FAMILY AWARD
• *See page 696*

PINE TREE STATE 4-H CLUB FOUNDATION/4-H POSTSECONDARY SCHOLARSHIP

http://www.umaine.edu/

PARKER-LOVEJOY SCHOLARSHIP

One-time scholarship of $1000 is available to a graduating high school senior. Applicants must be residents of Maine.

Award: Scholarship for use in freshman year; not renewable. *Number:* 1. *Amount:* $1000.

Eligibility Requirements: Applicant must be high school student; planning to enroll or expecting to enroll full-time at a two-year or four-year institution or university and resident of Maine. Available to U.S. citizens.

Application Requirements: Application form. *Deadline:* March 14.

Contact: Angela Martin, Administrative Assistant
Phone: 207-581-3739
Fax: 207-581-1387
E-mail: angela.martin@maine.edu

WAYNE S. RICH SCHOLARSHIP

Scholarship for an outstanding Maine or New Hampshire 4-H member for postsecondary study. Awarded to a Maine student in odd numbered years and a New Hampshire student in even numbered years.

Award: Scholarship for use in freshman year; not renewable. *Number:* 1. *Amount:* up to $1000.

Eligibility Requirements: Applicant must be high school student; planning to enroll or expecting to enroll full-time at a two-year or four-year institution or university and resident of Maine, New Hampshire. Available to U.S. citizens.

Application Requirements: Application form. *Deadline:* March 14.

Contact: Angela Martin, Administrative Assistant
Phone: 207-581-3739
Fax: 207-581-1387
E-mail: angela.martin@maine.edu

POINTE PEST CONTROL

http://pointepestcontrol.net

GREEN PEST SERVICES SCHOLARSHIP

$750 scholarship available to graduating high school seniors and college freshman who are residents of D.C. and Maryland. Minimum 3.0 GPA required.

Award: Scholarship for use in freshman year; not renewable. *Number:* 4. *Amount:* $750.

Eligibility Requirements: Applicant must be enrolled or expecting to enroll full- or part-time at a two-year or four-year or technical institution or university; resident of Maryland and studying in District of Columbia. Applicant must have 3.0 GPA or higher. Available to U.S. citizens.

Application Requirements: Application form, financial need analysis. *Deadline:* April 14.

Contact: Jodelle Maglaya, Communications Manager
E-mail: pr@pointepestcontrol.net

ILLINOIS SCHOLARSHIP

$750 scholarship available to graduating high school seniors and college freshman who are residents of Illinois. Minimum 3.0 GPA required.

Award: Scholarship for use in freshman year; not renewable. *Number:* 4. *Amount:* $750.

Eligibility Requirements: Applicant must be enrolled or expecting to enroll full- or part-time at a two-year or four-year or technical institution or university and resident of Illinois. Applicant must have 3.0 GPA or higher. Available to U.S. citizens.

Application Requirements: Application form, financial need analysis. *Deadline:* April 14.

Contact: Jodelle Maglaya, Communications Manager
E-mail: pr@pointepestcontrol.net

VIRGINIA GREEN PEST SERVICES

$750 scholarship available to graduating high school seniors and college freshman who are residents of Virginia. Minimum 3.0 GPA required.

Award: Scholarship for use in freshman year; not renewable. *Number:* 4. *Amount:* $750.

Eligibility Requirements: Applicant must be enrolled or expecting to enroll full- or part-time at a two-year or four-year or technical institution or university and resident of Virginia. Applicant must have 3.0 GPA or higher. Available to U.S. citizens.

Application Requirements: Application form, financial need analysis. *Deadline:* April 14.

Contact: Jodelle Maglaya, Communications Manager
E-mail: pr@pointepestcontrol.net

POLISH HERITAGE ASSOCIATION OF MARYLAND

http://www.pha-md.org/

POLISH HERITAGE SCHOLARSHIP
• See page 696

PORTUGUESE FOUNDATION INC.

https://www.facebook.com/pfict/

PORTUGUESE FOUNDATION SCHOLARSHIP PROGRAM
• See page 612

POTENTIAL MAGAZINE

http://potentialmagazine.com/

$1000 COUNTDOWN TO COLLEGE SCHOLARSHIP

Upon signing up for Potential Magazine's free weekly eNewsletter, students will be entered to win a $1,000 scholarship. The eNewsletter offers information on ACT/SAT prep tips, college prep info, scholarship opportunities, and more. Your entry also allows you access to the latest eBook from our Countdown to College ebook series, containing advice on financial aid, scholarships and college admissions. Upon submission of this form you will be redirected to the pdf of the eBook. This scholarship is for college-bound teens in grades 9th-12th. The scholarship does not require specific test scores, GPA, or class ranking. Parents can also register but will need to designate a student to receive the award. In order to be awarded the scholarship, you must be a current C2C eNews subscriber at the time of the drawing. Deadline: May 1, 2017. The winner of the $1,000 "Countdown to College" nationwide scholarship will be notified via email on May 5, 2017 and given 48 hours to respond after being contacted. Failure to respond will result in the selection of another winner. The winner will be announced on social media and in our "Countdown to College" (C2C) newsletter one week after being selected.

Award: Scholarship for use in freshman year; not renewable. *Number:* 1. *Amount:* $1000.

Eligibility Requirements: Applicant must be high school student; planning to enroll or expecting to enroll full- or part-time at a two-year or four-year institution or university; resident of Alabama and studying in Alabama. Available to U.S. citizens.

Application Requirements: Application form. *Deadline:* January 31.

Contact: Editor
Potential Magazine
61 Market Place E
Montgomery, AL 36117
E-mail: editor@potentialmagazine.com

"DON'T WAIT TO REACH YOUR POTENTIAL" SCHOLARSHIP

Upon signing up for Potential Magazine's free weekly "Countdown to College" (C2C) eNewsletter, Alabama students will be entered to Win a $1,000 scholarship. The eNewsletter offers information on ACT/SAT prep tips, college prep info, scholarship opportunities, and more. Your entry also allows you access to the latest eBook from our Countdown to College ebook series, containing advice on financial aid, scholarships and college admissions. Upon submission of this form you will be redirected to the pdf of the eBook. This scholarship is for college-bound teens in grades 9th-12th residing in the state of Alabama. The scholarship does not require specific test scores, GPA, or class ranking. Parents can also register but will need to designate a student to receive the scholarship. In order to be awarded the scholarship, you must be a current C2C eNews subscriber at the time of the drawing. Deadline: January 31, 2017. The winner of the $1,000 "Don't Wait to Reach Your Potential" scholarship for Alabama residents will be notified via email around February 1, 2017 and given 48 hours to respond after being contacted. Failure to respond will result in the selection of another winner. The winner will be announced on social media and in our "Countdown to College" (C2C) newsletter one week after being selected.

Award: Scholarship for use in freshman year; not renewable. *Number:* 1. *Amount:* $1000.

Eligibility Requirements: Applicant must be high school student; planning to enroll or expecting to enroll full- or part-time at a two-year or four-year institution or university and resident of Alabama. Available to U.S. citizens.

Application Requirements: Application form. *Deadline:* May 1.

Contact: Editor
Potential Magazine
61 Market Place E
Montgomery, AL 36117
E-mail: editor@potentialmagazine.com

PRESCOTT AUDUBON SOCIETY

http://prescottaudubon.org

ENVIRONMENTAL SCHOLARSHIP

A $1000 scholarship awarded to a degree-seeking, continuing college student who is passionate about the environment and/or conservation. Must be from Mohave or Yavapai County (home residence), and/or enrolled at a college operating in Yavapai or Mohave County, Arizona.

Award: Scholarship for use in freshman, sophomore, junior, or senior years; not renewable. *Number:* 1. *Amount:* $1000.

Eligibility Requirements: Applicant must be enrolled or expecting to enroll full- or part-time at a two-year or four-year institution or university and resident of Arizona. Available to U.S. citizens.

Application Requirements: Application form, essay. *Deadline:* December 9.

Contact: Scholarship Committee
E-mail: scholarship@prescottaudubon.org

PRIDE FOUNDATION

http://www.PrideFoundation.org/

PRIDE FOUNDATION SCHOLARSHIP PROGRAM

Pride Foundation provides scholarships to current and future lesbian, gay, bisexual, transgender and straight-ally student leaders from Alaska, Idaho, Montana, Oregon, and Washington. Our scholarships cover most accredited post-secondary schools, including community colleges; 4-year public or private colleges and universities; trade or certificate programs; and graduate, medical, or law school.

Award: Scholarship for use in freshman, sophomore, junior, senior, graduate, or postgraduate years; not renewable. *Number:* 85–125. *Amount:* $1000–$20,000.

Eligibility Requirements: Applicant must be enrolled or expecting to enroll full- or part-time at a two-year or four-year or technical institution or university; resident of Alaska, Idaho, Montana, Oregon, Washington and must have an interest in LGBT issues. Available to U.S. and non-U.S. citizens.

Application Requirements: Application form, application form may be submitted online (http://www.PrideFoundationScholar.org), community service, essay, interview, recommendations or references, transcript. *Deadline:* January 31.

Contact: Anthony Papini, Director of Educational Leadership
Pride Foundation
1122 East Pike Street
PMB 1001
Seattle, WA 98122
Phone: 206-323-3318 Ext. 110
Fax: 206-323-1017
E-mail: scholarships@pridefoundation.org

PROJECT BEST SCHOLARSHIP FUND

http://www.projectbest.com/

PROJECT BEST SCHOLARSHIP
• *See page 555*

PUEBLO OF SAN JUAN, DEPARTMENT OF EDUCATION

OHKAY OWINGEH TRIBAL SCHOLARSHIP OF THE PUEBLO OF SAN JUAN
• *See page 614*

POP'AY SCHOLARSHIP
• *See page 614*

REACH HIGHER MONTANA

http://www.ReachHigherMontana.org

REACH HIGHER MONTANA SCHOLARSHIPS
• *See page 614*

RENEE B. FISHER FOUNDATION

http://www.rbffoundation.org/

MILTON FISHER SCHOLARSHIP FOR INNOVATION AND CREATIVITY
Renewable scholarship for exceptionally innovative and creative high school juniors, seniors, and college freshmen who are graduating or have graduated from a Connecticut or New York City metro area high school (and plan to attend or are attending college anywhere in the U.S.) or are graduating or have graduated from any high school in the U.S. who plan to attend (or are attending) college in CT or NYC. You must graduate from a high school in the U.S. and complete an exceptionally innovative and creative project: solved artistic, scientific, or technical problems in new or unusual ways, come up with a distinctive solution to problems faced by your school, community or family or created a new group, organization, or institution that serves an important need. For more information, please contact http://www.rbffoundation.org

Award: Scholarship for use in freshman, sophomore, junior, or senior years; renewable. *Number:* 1–8. *Amount:* $250–$20,000.

Eligibility Requirements: Applicant must be enrolled or expecting to enroll full-time at a four-year or technical institution or university; resident of Alabama, Alaska, Arizona, Arkansas, California, Colorado, Connecticut, Delaware, District of Columbia, Florida, Georgia, Hawaii, Idaho, Illinois, Indiana, Iowa, Kansas, Kentucky, Louisiana, Maine, Maryland, Massachusetts, Michigan, Minnesota, Mississippi, Missouri, Montana, Nebraska, Nevada, New Hampshire, New Jersey, New Mexico, New York, North Carolina, North Dakota, Ohio, Oklahoma, Oregon, Pennsylvania, Rhode Island, South Carolina, South Dakota, Tennessee, Texas, Utah, Vermont, Virginia, Washington, West Virginia, Wisconsin, Wyoming and studying in Alabama, Alaska, Arizona, Arkansas, California, Colorado, Connecticut, Delaware, District of Columbia, Florida, Georgia, Hawaii, Idaho, Illinois, Indiana, Iowa, Kansas, Kentucky, Louisiana, Maine, Maryland, Massachusetts, Michigan, Minnesota, Mississippi, Missouri, Montana, Nebraska, Nevada, New Hampshire, New Jersey, New Mexico, New York, North Carolina, North Dakota, Ohio, Oklahoma, Oregon, Pennsylvania, Rhode Island, South Carolina, South Dakota, Tennessee, Texas, Utah, Vermont, Virginia, Washington, West Virginia, Wisconsin, Wyoming. Available to U.S. and non-U.S. citizens.

Application Requirements: Application form, essay. *Deadline:* April 30.

Contact: Milton Fisher Scholarship Liaison
Renee B. Fisher Foundation
70 Audubon Street
New Haven, CT 06510
Phone: 203-777-2386
E-mail: mfscholarship@gmail.com

RHODE ISLAND FOUNDATION

http://www.rifoundation.org/

ALDO FREDA LEGISLATIVE PAGES SCHOLARSHIP
Awarded to support Rhode Island Legislative Pages enrolled in a college or university. Must show scholastic achievement and good citizenship. Must be accepted into a full-time accredited postsecondary institution or graduate program. Must be a Rhode Island resident and a citizen of the United States.

Award: Scholarship for use in freshman, sophomore, junior, senior, or graduate years; not renewable. *Number:* 2–3. *Amount:* $1000–$1500.

Eligibility Requirements: Applicant must be enrolled or expecting to enroll full- or part-time at a two-year or four-year institution or university and resident of Rhode Island. Available to U.S. citizens.

Application Requirements: Application form, essay, financial need analysis, recommendations or references, transcript. *Deadline:* June 3.

Contact: Libby Monahan, Funds Administrator
Phone: 401-274-4564 Ext. 3117
E-mail: libbym@rifoundation.org

ANDREW BELL SCHOLARSHIP
Scholarships to high school graduates pursuing a post-secondary education. Must demonstrate financial need.

Award: Scholarship for use in freshman, sophomore, junior, or senior years; not renewable.

Eligibility Requirements: Applicant must be enrolled or expecting to enroll full-time at a two-year or four-year or technical institution or university and resident of Rhode Island. Available to U.S. citizens.

Application Requirements: Application form, financial need analysis. *Deadline:* continuous.

Contact: Urban League of Rhode Island
Phone: 401-351-5000

A.T. CROSS SCHOLARSHIP
• *See page 571*

BRUCE AND MARJORIE SUNDLUN SCHOLARSHIP
Scholarships for low-income single parents seeking to upgrade their career skills. Preference given to single parents previously receiving state support, and also for those previously incarcerated. Must be a Rhode Island resident and must attend school in the state.

Award: Scholarship for use in freshman, sophomore, junior, or senior years; not renewable. *Amount:* up to $1500.

Eligibility Requirements: Applicant must be enrolled or expecting to enroll full- or part-time at a two-year or four-year or technical institution or university; single; resident of Rhode Island and studying in Rhode Island. Available to U.S. and non-U.S. citizens.

Application Requirements: Application form, essay, financial need analysis, recommendations or references, self-addressed stamped envelope with application, transcript. *Deadline:* June 14.

Contact: Libby Monahan, Funds Administrator
Phone: 401-274-4564 Ext. 3117
E-mail: libbym@rifoundation.org

LILY AND CATELLO SORRENTINO MEMORIAL SCHOLARSHIP
Scholarships for Rhode Island residents. Applicant must be 25 years or older wishing to attend college or university in Rhode Island (only students attending non-parochial schools). Must demonstrate financial need. Preference given to first-time applicants. Financial need must be demonstrated.

Award: Scholarship for use in freshman, sophomore, junior, or senior years; not renewable. *Amount:* $500–$1000.

Eligibility Requirements: Applicant must be enrolled or expecting to enroll full- or part-time at a four-year institution or university; resident of Rhode Island and studying in Rhode Island. Available to U.S. citizens.

Application Requirements: Application form, financial need analysis, self-addressed stamped envelope with application, transcript. *Deadline:* May 1.

Contact: Libby Monahan, Funds Administrator
Phone: 401-274-4564 Ext. 3117
E-mail: libbym@rifoundation.org

NONDRAS HURST VOLL SCHOLARSHIP

Scholarship for single mothers transitioning off public assistance who are enrolled or planning to enroll in college certificate or degree program. Must be a Rhode Island resident and demonstrate financial need.

Award: Scholarship for use in freshman, sophomore, junior, or senior years; not renewable.

Eligibility Requirements: Applicant must be enrolled or expecting to enroll full- or part-time at a two-year or four-year institution or university; single female and resident of Rhode Island. Available to U.S. citizens.

Application Requirements: Application form, copy of U.S. income tax return, list of dependent children, copy of financial aid award letter if applicable, essay, financial need analysis, transcript. *Deadline:* April 19.

Contact: Fund for Community Progress, Nondas Hurst Voll Scholarship
    Committee
    Rhode Island Foundation
    90 Jefferson Boulevard
    Suite B
    Warwick, RI 02888
    Phone: 401-941-7100

PATTY & MELVIN ALPERIN FIRST GENERATION SCHOLARSHIP

Renewable scholarship for Rhode Island high school seniors whose parents did not graduate from college. Must be accepted or enrolled in an accredited two- or four-year college and demonstrate financial need.

Award: Scholarship for use in freshman year; renewable. *Amount:* $1000.

Eligibility Requirements: Applicant must be high school student; planning to enroll or expecting to enroll full- or part-time at a two-year or four-year institution or university and resident of Rhode Island. Available to U.S. citizens.

Application Requirements: Application form, financial need analysis, transcript. *Deadline:* May 1.

Contact: Libby Monahan, Funds Administrator
    Phone: 401-274-4564 Ext. 3117
    E-mail: libbym@rifoundation.org

RHODE ISLAND ASSOCIATION OF FORMER LEGISLATORS SCHOLARSHIP

One-time award of $1500 for graduating high school seniors who are Rhode Island residents. Must have a history of substantial voluntary involvement in community service. Must be accepted into an accredited post-secondary institution and should be able to demonstrate financial need.

Award: Scholarship for use in freshman year; not renewable. *Number:* 4–5. *Amount:* $1500.

Eligibility Requirements: Applicant must be high school student; planning to enroll or expecting to enroll full-time at a four-year institution or university and resident of Rhode Island. Available to U.S. citizens.

Application Requirements: Application form, essay, financial need analysis, recommendations or references, self-addressed stamped envelope with application, test scores, transcript. *Deadline:* May 1.

Contact: Libby Monahan, Funds Administrator
    Phone: 401-274-4564 Ext. 3117
    E-mail: libbym@rifoundation.org

RHODE ISLAND COMMISSION ON WOMEN/FREDA GOLDMAN EDUCATION AWARD

Scholarship to assist women with transportation, child-care, tutoring, educational materials, and/or other support services. Must be pursuing education or job training beyond high school. Preference given to highly motivated, self-supporting, low-income women completing a first undergraduate degree or certificate program.

Award: Scholarship for use in freshman, sophomore, junior, or senior years; not renewable. *Amount:* $500–$1000.

Eligibility Requirements: Applicant must be enrolled or expecting to enroll full- or part-time at a four-year institution or university; female and resident of Rhode Island. Available to U.S. citizens.

Application Requirements: Application form, essay, recommendations or references, self-addressed stamped envelope with application, transcript. *Deadline:* June 14.

Contact: Libby Monahan, Funds Administrator
    Phone: 401-274-4564 Ext. 3117
    E-mail: libbym@rifoundation.org

UNITED ITALIAN AMERICAN INC. SCHOLARSHIP

For Rhode Island residents with financial need who wish to attend a two- or four-year college or university. Scholarship is based on merit as evidenced by superior achievement and leadership in school and/or community.

Award: Scholarship for use in freshman, sophomore, junior, or senior years; not renewable.

Eligibility Requirements: Applicant must be enrolled or expecting to enroll full-time at a two-year or four-year institution or university; resident of Rhode Island and must have an interest in leadership. Available to U.S. citizens.

Application Requirements: Application form, community service, financial need analysis, transcript. *Deadline:* June 3.

Contact: Libby Monahan, Funds Administrator
    Phone: 401-274-4564 Ext. 3117
    E-mail: libbym@rifoundation.org

ROBERT H. MOLLOHAN FAMILY CHARITABLE FOUNDATION, INC.

http://www.mollohanfoundation.org/

CARL R. MORRIS MEMORIAL SCHOLARSHIP

The Carl. R. Morris Memorial Scholarship is a $1000 scholarship that will be awarded to a resident of Calhoun County that best emulates Mr. Morris' commitment to community and education. The student must be enrolled, or planning to enroll, at Alderson-Broaddus College, Glenville State College, or West Virginia University, must have at least a 3.0 GPA, and must have demonstrated financial need.

Award: Scholarship for use in freshman, sophomore, junior, or senior years; not renewable. *Number:* 1–60. *Amount:* $1000.

Eligibility Requirements: Applicant must be enrolled or expecting to enroll full-time at a four-year institution or university; resident of West Virginia and studying in West Virginia. Applicant must have 3.0 GPA or higher. Available to U.S. citizens.

Application Requirements: Application form, essay, recommendations or references, resume, test scores, transcript.

Contact: Aime Shaffer, Program Manager
    Phone: 304-333-6783
    E-mail: ashaffer@wvhtf.org

DR. ROBERTO F. CUNANAN MEMORIAL SCHOLARSHIP

The Dr. Roberto F. Cunanan Memorial Scholarship was created to honor Dr. Cunanan's energetic spirit and loving heart. This $1000 scholarship is awarded to a Bridgeport High School student who is enrolled or planning to enroll at a West Virginia college or university, and who is an active participant in both academics and athletics.

Award: Scholarship for use in freshman, sophomore, junior, or senior years; not renewable. *Number:* 1–60. *Amount:* $1000.

Eligibility Requirements: Applicant must be high school student; planning to enroll or expecting to enroll full-time at a four-year institution or university; resident of West Virginia and must have an interest in athletics/sports. Available to U.S. citizens.

Application Requirements: Application form, essay, recommendations or references, resume, test scores, transcript.

Contact: Aime Shaffer, Program Manager
    Phone: 304-333-6783
    E-mail: ashaffer@wvhtf.org

HELEN HOLT MOLLOHAN SCHOLARSHIP

The Helen Holt Mollohan Scholarship is a $1000 scholarship that is awarded to a West Virginia female who is enrolled, or planning to enroll, at Glenville State College. This young woman should exhibit strong character, integrity, service to community, concern for others, and high standards of scholarship, like the late Mrs. Mollohan herself.

Award: Scholarship for use in freshman, sophomore, junior, or senior years; renewable. *Amount:* $1000.

Eligibility Requirements: Applicant must be high school student; planning to enroll or expecting to enroll full-time at a four-year institution or university; female; resident of West Virginia and studying in West Virginia. Available to U.S. citizens.

Application Requirements: Application form, essay, recommendations or references, resume, transcript.

Contact: Aime Shaffer, Program Manager
Phone: 304-333-6783
E-mail: ashaffer@wvhtf.org

ROOTHBERT FUND INC.

http://www.roothbertfund.org/

ROOTHBERT FUND INC. SCHOLARSHIP

Scholarships are open to all in the United States regardless of sex, age, color, nationality or religious background. The award must be used in the following states: CT, DC, DE, MA, MD, ME, NC, NH, NJ, NY, OH, PA, RI, VA, VT, or WV. Preference will be given to those who can satisfy high scholastic requirements and are considering careers in education. The Fund seeks candidates who are motivated by spiritual values, and works to foster fellowship among them.

Award: Scholarship for use in freshman, sophomore, junior, senior, or graduate years; renewable. *Number:* 50–60. *Amount:* $2000–$3000.

Eligibility Requirements: Applicant must be enrolled or expecting to enroll full-time at a two-year or four-year or technical institution or university; resident of Connecticut, Delaware, District of Columbia, Maine, Maryland, Massachusetts, New Hampshire, New Jersey, New York, North Carolina, Ohio, Pennsylvania, Rhode Island, Virginia, West Virginia and studying in Connecticut, Delaware, District of Columbia, Maryland, Massachusetts, New Hampshire, New Jersey, New York, Ohio, Pennsylvania, Rhode Island, Vermont, Virginia, West Virginia. Available to U.S. and non-U.S. citizens.

Application Requirements: Application form, essay, financial need analysis, interview, personal photograph. *Deadline:* February 1.

Contact: Percy Preston, Office Manager
Roothbert Fund Inc.
475 Riverside Drive, Room 1622
New York, NY 10115
Phone: 212-870-3116
E-mail: office@roothbertfund.org

RYU FAMILY FOUNDATION, INC.

SEOL BONG SCHOLARSHIP
• *See page 637*

SACHS FOUNDATION

http://www.sachsfoundation.org/

SACHS FOUNDATION SCHOLARSHIPS
• *See page 698*

ST. ANDREW'S SOCIETY OF WASHINGTON, DC

http://www.saintandrewssociety.org/

DONALD MALCOLM MACARTHUR SCHOLARSHIP
• *See page 698*

ST. CLAIRE REGIONAL MEDICAL CENTER

http://www.st-claire.org/

SR. MARY JEANNETTE WESS, S.N.D. SCHOLARSHIP
• *See page 615*

SALT RIVER ELECTRIC COOPERATIVE CORPORATION

http://www.srelectric.com/

SALT RIVER ELECTRIC SCHOLARSHIP PROGRAM

Scholarships available to Kentucky high school seniors who reside in Salt River Electric Service area or the primary residence of their parents/guardian is in the service area. Must be enrolled or plan to enroll in a postsecondary institution. Minimum GPA of 2.5 required. Must demonstrate financial need. Must submit a 500-word essay on a topic chosen from the list on the website. Application and additional information available on website http://www.srelectric.com.

Award: Scholarship for use in freshman year; not renewable. *Number:* 4. *Amount:* $1000.

Eligibility Requirements: Applicant must be high school student; planning to enroll or expecting to enroll full- or part-time at a two-year or four-year or technical institution or university and resident of Kentucky. Applicant must have 2.5 GPA or higher. Available to U.S. citizens.

Application Requirements: Application form, community service, essay, financial need analysis, personal photograph, transcript. *Deadline:* April 4.

Contact: Nicky Rapier, Scholarship Coordinator
Phone: 502-348-3931
Fax: 502-348-1993
E-mail: nickyr@srelectric.com

SALVADORAN AMERICAN LEADERSHIP AND EDUCATIONAL FUND

http://www.salef.org/

FULFILLING OUR DREAMS SCHOLARSHIP FUND
• *See page 698*

THE SAN DIEGO FOUNDATION

http://www.sdfoundation.org/

COMMON SCHOLARSHIP APPLICATION

The Common Scholarship Application uses one online form to access more than 100 scholarships. Scholarships are available for graduating high school seniors, undergraduates, graduate students and adult re-entry students who are attending 2-year colleges, 4-year universities, trade/vocational schools, graduate, medical and professional schools and teaching credential programs. Scholarships range from $500 to more than $5,000 and, depending on the scholarship, can pay for tuition, room and board, books, fees and other related expenses. Note that almost all of our scholarships require San Diego County residency.

Award: Scholarship for use in freshman, sophomore, junior, senior, or graduate years; renewable. *Number:* 95–110. *Amount:* $500–$5000.

Eligibility Requirements: Applicant must be enrolled or expecting to enroll full- or part-time at a two-year or four-year or technical institution or university and resident of California. Applicant must have 2.5 GPA or higher. Available to U.S. citizens.

Application Requirements: Application form, essay. *Deadline:* February 1.

Contact: Daniel Stigall, Scholarships Coordinator
E-mail: scholarships@sdfoundation.org

SCHOLARSHIPOWL.COM

http://www.scholarshipowl.com

YOU DESERVE IT! SCHOLARSHIP

Everyone 16 years of age or older is eligible to apply who is enrolled or plans to be enrolled next semester to college. The scholarship renews every month and expires on the 29th of each month. See website for details. For an application, please go to https://scholarshipowl.com/awards/you-deserve-it-scholarship.

Award: Scholarship for use in freshman, sophomore, junior, senior, graduate, or postgraduate years; not renewable. *Number:* 10. *Amount:* $1000.

Eligibility Requirements: Applicant must be enrolled or expecting to enroll full- or part-time at a two-year or four-year or technical institution or university; resident of Alabama, Alaska, Alberta, Arizona, Arkansas, British Columbia, California, Colorado, Connecticut, Delaware, District of Columbia, Florida, Georgia, Guam, Hawaii, Idaho, Illinois, Indiana, Iowa, Kansas, Kentucky, Louisiana, Maine, Manitoba, Maryland, Massachusetts, Michigan, Minnesota, Mississippi, Missouri, Montana, Nebraska, Nevada, New Brunswick, Newfoundland, New Hampshire, New Jersey, New Mexico, New York, North Carolina, North Dakota, Northwest Territories, Nova Scotia, Ohio, Oklahoma, Ontario, Oregon,

Pennsylvania, Prince Edward Island, Puerto Rico, Quebec, Saskatchewan, South Carolina, South Dakota, Tennessee, Texas, Utah, Vermont, Virginia, Washington, West Virginia, Wisconsin, Wyoming, Yukon and studying in Alabama, Alaska, Alberta, Arizona, Arkansas, British Columbia, California, Colorado, Connecticut, Delaware, District of Columbia, Florida, Georgia, Guam, Hawaii, Idaho, Illinois, Indiana, Iowa, Kansas, Kentucky, Louisiana, Maine, Manitoba, Maryland, Massachusetts, Michigan, Minnesota, Mississippi, Missouri, Montana, Nebraska, Nevada, New Brunswick, Newfoundland, New Hampshire, New Jersey, New Mexico, New York, North Carolina, North Dakota, Northwest Territories, Nova Scotia, Ohio, Oklahoma, Ontario, Oregon, Pennsylvania, Prince Edward Island, Puerto Rico, Quebec, Saskatchewan, South Carolina, South Dakota, Tennessee, Texas, Utah, Vermont, Virginia, Washington, West Virginia, Wisconsin, Wyoming, Yukon. Available to U.S. citizens.

Application Requirements: Application form. *Deadline:* continuous.

Contact: Mr. Mark Galea
ScholarshipOwl.com
210/2, Manwel Dimech Street
Slimena slm1050
MLT
E-mail: contact@scholarshipowl.com

SHELBY ENERGY COOPERATIVE

http://www.shelbyenergy.com/

SHELBY ENERGY COOPERATIVE SCHOLARSHIPS

Scholarships for high school seniors in Kentucky, whose parents or guardians are Shelby Energy members. Award based on financial need, academic excellence, community and school involvement, and essay.

Award: Scholarship for use in freshman year; not renewable. *Number:* 6. *Amount:* $1000.

Eligibility Requirements: Applicant must be high school student; planning to enroll or expecting to enroll full-time at a four-year institution or university and resident of Kentucky. Available to U.S. citizens.

Application Requirements: Application form, community service, financial need analysis. *Deadline:* March 10.

Contact: Ms. Candi Waford, Manager, Member Services
Shelby Energy Cooperative
620 Old Finchville Road
Shelbyville, KY 40065
Phone: 502-633-4420
Fax: 502-633-2387
E-mail: candi@shelbyenergy.com

SILICON VALLEY COMMUNITY FOUNDATION

www.siliconvalleycf.org

ABBY SOBRATO SCHOLARSHIP
• *See page 616*

BOBETTE BIBO GUGLIOTTA MEMORIAL SCHOLARSHIP FOR CREATIVE WRITING
• *See page 616*

CRAIN EDUCATIONAL GRANTS PROGRAM

Scholarship applicant must have demonstrated community involvement over a period of several years; have a minimum cumulative grade point average of 3.5 on a 4.0 scale; and must have demonstrated financial hardship. Must be a current graduating senior, or graduate of a public or private high school in San Mateo County or Santa Clara County. Must be planning to enroll or enrolled in a four-year college or university as a full-time student. United States citizenship required. See website for more information, http://www.siliconvalleycf.org/scholarships

Award: Scholarship for use in freshman year; not renewable. *Number:* 10. *Amount:* $1000–$5000.

Eligibility Requirements: Applicant must be high school student; planning to enroll or expecting to enroll full-time at a four-year institution or university and resident of California. Applicant must have 3.5 GPA or higher. Available to U.S. citizens.

Application Requirements: Application form, community service, essay, financial need analysis. *Deadline:* February 22.

CURRY AWARD FOR GIRLS AND YOUNG WOMEN
• *See page 616*

HAROLD JOHNSON LAW ENFORCEMENT SCHOLARSHIP
• *See page 616*

HAZEL REED BAUMEISTER SCHOLARSHIP PROGRAM
• *See page 616*

JUNIPER NETWORKS ENGINEERING SCHOLARSHIP

Established in 2012, The Juniper Networks Engineering Scholarship program provides support to residents of California, Virginia, Massachusetts, New Jersey and Canada who intend to major in engineering. The committee seeks to identify young leaders with the potential to take on the toughest challenges facing our communities, to connect and empower people everywhere, and make a meaningful difference in our communities. Must have demonstrated success in STEM education courses (science, technology, engineering and math) and be planning to major in engineering. Preference will be given to students pursuing majors in computer science, computer engineering, electrical engineering and computer networking. Graduating high school senior residing in San Mateo County and Santa Clara County in California; Fairfax County, Loudoun County, and Prince Williams County in Virginia; Middlesex County and Worcester County in Massachusetts, New Jersey and Ottawa West (Kanata, Nepean, Bell's Corners, Stittsville, Dunrobin, Richmond, Fitzroy) in Ontario, Canada. Minimum cumulative high school grade point average of 3.5 on a 4.0 U.S. scale or 70% on Ontario, Canada grading scale. Intention to enroll full-time in four-year university or college. Demonstrated community involvement over a period of several years. Must be a United States or Canadian citizen or legal resident.

Award: Scholarship for use in freshman, sophomore, junior, or senior years; not renewable. *Number:* 1–10. *Amount:* $1000–$5000.

Eligibility Requirements: Applicant must be high school student; planning to enroll or expecting to enroll full-time at a four-year institution or university and resident of California, Massachusetts, New Jersey, Ontario, Virginia. Applicant must have 3.5 GPA or higher. Available to U.S. and Canadian citizens.

Application Requirements: Application form, community service, essay, financial need analysis. *Deadline:* February 22.

KRISHNAN-SHAH FAMILY SCHOLARSHIP

The Krishnan-Shah Family Scholarship was established by Ajay Shah, Lata Krishnan and their family. This scholarship program seeks to support financially needy students with academic potential and demonstrated community involvement, and provide meaningful and ongoing financial support to ensure that students complete their undergraduate degree. Must be graduating high school senior residing in the greater Silicon Valley Region (includes Santa Clara County, San Mateo County, San Francisco County, Alameda County and Santa Cruz County) or current community college student who graduated from a high school within the five listed counties; first generation college student (neither parent earned a four-year college degree), pursuing first undergraduate degree; planning to enroll in a four-year college or university on a full-time basis in the upcoming fall session; have a maximum cumulative grade point average of 3.75 on a 4.0 scale; demonstrated involvement in activities (extracurricular, volunteer, paid, etc.); and demonstrated financial need or hardship.

Award: Scholarship for use in freshman, sophomore, junior, or senior years; not renewable. *Number:* 1–5. *Amount:* $1000–$10,000.

Eligibility Requirements: Applicant must be enrolled or expecting to enroll full-time at a four-year institution or university and resident of California. Available to U.S. and non-U.S. citizens.

Application Requirements: Application form, financial need analysis. *Deadline:* February 22.

Contact: Anamika Patel
E-mail: apatel@siliconvalleycf.org

LATINOS IN TECHNOLOGY SCHOLARSHIP
• *See page 617*

MARIE A. CALDERILLA SCHOLARSHIP

This program was established in 2007 through a generous gift from Marie A. Calderilla, pictured, who believed deeply in the importance of education. The purpose of this scholarship is to enable women to pursue courses of study that they would otherwise be unable to follow due to limited financial means. The selection committee looks for academic promise, women who have demonstrated a commitment to completing a degree or certificate program or to increasing their work skills, and personal characteristics such as honesty, good judgment and perseverance. Recipients are eligible for up to three years of funding; however, students must meet renewal requirements to continue to receive the award. Students enrolled in a four-year degree program at a San Mateo County Community College District college are eligible for up to four years of funding. Must be a female student, pursuing first undergraduate degree or certificate program; graduating high school senior or re-entry student planning to attend a college in the San Mateo County Community College District (Cañada College, College of San Mateo and Skyline Community College); demonstrate financial hardship; serious about improving her life through education; and a United States citizen or eligible non-citizen (eligible non-citizens include United States legal residents and A.B. 540 students).

Award: Scholarship for use in freshman, sophomore, junior, or senior years; renewable. *Number:* 1–30. *Amount:* $1000–$5000.

Eligibility Requirements: Applicant must be enrolled or expecting to enroll full- or part-time at a four-year institution or university; female; resident of California and studying in California. Available to U.S. and Canadian citizens.

Application Requirements: Application form, financial need analysis. *Deadline:* March 15.

Contact: Anamika Patel
E-mail: APatel@siliconvalleycf.org

PENINSULA REGENT CHARITABLE FOUNDATION EDUCATIONAL GRANT PROGRAM

This program is made possible through the generous contributions of the residents of The Peninsula Regent. Educational grants between $1,000 and $10,000 each will be awarded annually. The program has been created to help employees and/or their dependents with the costs of higher education or the costs of attending courses, including those offered at community colleges and vocational schools. Must be a current employee of TPR for at least 90 days as of the application deadline, or a dependent of an employee who has worked at the TPR for at least 90 days as of the application deadline, or past TPR scholarship recipient and employee of the TPR who was employed for at least 90 days. Preference will be given to applicants with strong educational motivation, perseverance and involvement outside the classroom, and personal characteristics such as honesty and good judgment. The selection committee will also strongly consider applicants who have dropped out of school for reasons beyond their control or have undergone unusual hardships to remain in school. Must demonstrate financial hardship and be a United States citizen or legal resident.

Award: Grant for use in freshman year; not renewable. *Number:* 1–30. *Amount:* $1000–$10,000.

Eligibility Requirements: Applicant must be enrolled or expecting to enroll full- or part-time at a two-year or four-year or technical institution or university and resident of California. Available to U.S. citizens.

Application Requirements: Application form, financial need analysis. *Deadline:* March 22.

Contact: Anamika Patel
E-mail: APatel@siliconvalleycf.org

RALPH HALE AND MARTHA L. RUPPERT EDUCATIONAL SCHOLARSHIP

The Ruppert Educational Grant Program was established through a trust and bequest agreement by Ralph Hale Ruppert and Lenore Martha Ruppert in memory of their mothers, Nellie Hale Ruppert and Amanda Miller Edwards. The program is designed to assist young people who have financial need and are willing to help themselves. Scholarships are awarded to "late bloomers"—those students who show academic promise and improvement during the last years of high school or in the first few years of college, but are unlikely to receive other scholarships because of their low GPAs. Applicant must be a "late bloomer" who demonstrates academic promise and continuous grade point average improvement during high school or college; must demonstrate community involvement; have a maximum cumulative grade point average of 3.3 on a 4.0 scale; demonstrate financial hardship; be a graduating high school senior or graduate of a public or private high school in San Mateo County, San Francisco County, or Santa Clara County; planning to enroll or enrolled in two- or four-year college, university, or vocational school as a full-time student; and be a United States citizen or eligible non-citizen (eligible non-citizens include United States legal residents and A.B. 540 students).

Award: Scholarship for use in freshman, sophomore, junior, or senior years; not renewable. *Number:* 1–30. *Amount:* $1000–$10,000.

Eligibility Requirements: Applicant must be enrolled or expecting to enroll full-time at a two-year or four-year or technical institution or university and resident of California. Available to U.S. citizens.

Application Requirements: Application form, community service, essay, financial need analysis. *Deadline:* February 22.

SAND HILL SCHOLARS PROGRAM

The Sand Hill Scholars Program was created by Thomas W. Ford and Susan B. Ford, and is underwritten by the Sand Hill Foundation. This program provides scholarships for promising students whose educational opportunities and success will be increased by financial assistance, mentoring, college and career success training, and summer internship opportunities. Special considerations are given to students who graduated from the Ravenswood City School District. The selection committee looks for students who have shown leadership in educational and community or job-related activities outside the school environment, and have overcome hardships to remain in school. Award recipients must be willing to participate actively in workshop and mentoring activities throughout their undergraduate careers. Must be a graduating high school senior attending a high school in San Mateo County; have a cumulative grade point average between 3.0 to 3.8 on a 4.0 scale; planning to enroll in a four-year college or university as a full-time student; have demonstrated financial hardship; and be a United States citizen or eligible non-citizen (eligible non-citizens include United States legal residents and A.B. 540 students).

Award: Scholarship for use in freshman year; renewable. *Number:* 1–2. *Amount:* $1000–$12,000.

Eligibility Requirements: Applicant must be high school student; planning to enroll or expecting to enroll full-time at a four-year institution or university and resident of California. Applicant must have 3.0 GPA or higher.

Application Requirements: Application form, community service, essay, financial need analysis. *Deadline:* February 22.

SIMON FOUNDATION FOR EDUCATION AND HOUSING

http://www.sfeh.org/

SIMON SCHOLARS PROGRAM

Scholarships are given to high school seniors at qualified high schools in Atlanta, GA, Santa Fe and Albuquerque, NM, and Anaheim, Santa Ana, Oceanside, or Garden Grove, CA. Deadlines vary for each region. For more details visit website http://www.simonscholars.org.

Award: Scholarship for use in freshman year; not renewable. *Number:* 100. *Amount:* $16,000.

Eligibility Requirements: Applicant must be high school student; planning to enroll or expecting to enroll full-time at a two-year or four-year institution or university and resident of California, Georgia, New Mexico. Applicant must have 3.0 GPA or higher. Available to U.S. citizens.

Application Requirements: Application form, community service, essay, financial need analysis, interview, recommendations or references, test scores, transcript. *Deadline:* varies.

Contact: Dr. Heather Huntley, Director of Partnerships and Development
Phone: 949-270-3622
Fax: 949-729-8072
E-mail: heatherh@simonscholars.org

SOUTH CAROLINA COMMISSION ON HIGHER EDUCATION

http://www.che.sc.gov/

PALMETTO FELLOWS SCHOLARSHIP PROGRAM

Renewable award for qualified high school seniors in South Carolina to attend a four-year South Carolina institution. The scholarship must be applied directly towards the cost of attendance, less any other gift aid received.

Award: Scholarship for use in freshman year; renewable. *Number:* 4846. *Amount:* $6700–$7500.

Eligibility Requirements: Applicant must be high school student; planning to enroll or expecting to enroll full-time at a four-year institution or university; resident of South Carolina and studying in South Carolina. Applicant must have 3.5 GPA or higher. Available to U.S. citizens.

Application Requirements: Application form, test scores, transcript. *Deadline:* December 15.

Contact: Dr. Karen Woodfaulk, Director of Student Services
South Carolina Commission on Higher Education
1333 Main Street, Suite 200
Columbia, SC 29201
Phone: 803-737-2244
Fax: 803-737-3610
E-mail: kwoodfaulk@che.sc.gov

SOUTH CAROLINA HOPE SCHOLARSHIP

A merit-based scholarship for eligible first-time entering freshman attending a four-year South Carolina institution. Minimum GPA of 3.0 required. Must be a resident of South Carolina.

Award: Scholarship for use in freshman year; not renewable. *Number:* 2605. *Amount:* $2800.

Eligibility Requirements: Applicant must be high school student; planning to enroll or expecting to enroll full-time at a four-year institution or university; resident of South Carolina and studying in South Carolina. Applicant must have 3.0 GPA or higher. Available to U.S. citizens.

Application Requirements: Transcript. *Deadline:* continuous.

Contact: Gerrick Hampton, Scholarship Coordinator
South Carolina Commission on Higher Education
1333 Main Street, Suite 200
Columbia, SC 29201
Phone: 803-737-4544
Fax: 803-737-3610
E-mail: ghampton@che.sc.gov

SOUTH CAROLINA NEED-BASED GRANTS PROGRAM

Award based on FAFSA. A student may receive up to $2500 annually for full-time and up to $1250 annually for part-time study. The grant must be applied directly towards the cost of college attendance for a maximum of eight full-time equivalent terms.

Award: Grant for use in freshman, sophomore, junior, senior, or graduate years; renewable. *Number:* 1–26,730. *Amount:* $1250–$2500.

Eligibility Requirements: Applicant must be enrolled or expecting to enroll full- or part-time at a two-year or four-year or technical institution or university; resident of South Carolina and studying in South Carolina. Available to U.S. citizens.

Application Requirements: Application form, financial need analysis. *Deadline:* continuous.

Contact: Dr. Karen Woodfaulk, Director of Student Service
South Carolina Commission on Higher Education
1333 Main Street, Suite 200
Columbia, SC 29201
Phone: 803-737-2244
Fax: 803-737-2297
E-mail: kwoodfaulk@che.sc.gov

SOUTH CAROLINA DIVISION OF VETERANS AFFAIRS

http://www.govoepp.state.sc.us/vetaff.htm

EDUCATIONAL ASSISTANCE FOR CERTAIN WAR VETERANS DEPENDENTS SCHOLARSHIP-SOUTH CAROLINA

• *See page 662*

SOUTH CAROLINA STATE EMPLOYEES ASSOCIATION

http://www.scsea.com/

ANNE A. AGNEW SCHOLARSHIP

• *See page 559*

RICHLAND/LEXINGTON SCSEA SCHOLARSHIP

• *See page 559*

SOUTH CAROLINA TUITION GRANTS COMMISSION

http://www.sctuitiongrants.org/

SOUTH CAROLINA TUITION GRANTS PROGRAM

• *See page 617*

SOUTH DAKOTA BOARD OF REGENTS

http://www.sdbor.edu/

SOUTH DAKOTA BOARD OF REGENTS MARLIN R. SCARBOROUGH MEMORIAL SCHOLARSHIP

One-time merit-based award for a student who is a junior at a South Dakota university. Must be nominated by the university and must have community service and leadership experience. Minimum 3.5 GPA required. Application deadline varies.

Award: Scholarship for use in junior year; not renewable. *Number:* 1. *Amount:* $1000.

Eligibility Requirements: Applicant must be enrolled or expecting to enroll full-time at an institution or university; resident of South Dakota; studying in South Dakota and must have an interest in leadership. Applicant must have 3.5 GPA or higher. Available to U.S. citizens.

Application Requirements: Application form, essay. *Deadline:* varies.

Contact: Dr. Paul Turman, System Vice President for Research and Economic Development
South Dakota Board of Regents
301 East Capital Avenue, Suite 200
Pierre, SD 57501
Phone: 605-773-3455
Fax: 605-773-2422
E-mail: paul.turman@sdbor.edu

SOUTH DAKOTA OPPORTUNITY SCHOLARSHIP

Renewable scholarship may be worth up to $5000 over four years to students who take a rigorous college-prep curriculum while in high school and stay in the state for their postsecondary education.

Award: Scholarship for use in freshman, sophomore, junior, or senior years; renewable. *Number:* 1000. *Amount:* $1000.

Eligibility Requirements: Applicant must be high school student; planning to enroll or expecting to enroll full-time at a two-year or four-year or technical institution or university; resident of South Dakota and studying in South Dakota. Applicant must have 3.0 GPA or higher. Available to U.S. citizens.

Application Requirements: Application form, test scores, transcript. *Deadline:* September 1.

Contact: Janelle Toman, Scholarship Committee
South Dakota Board of Regents
306 East Capitol, Suite 200
Pierre, SD 57501-2545
Phone: 605-773-3455
Fax: 605-773-2422
E-mail: info@sdbor.edu

SOUTH FLORIDA FAIR AND PALM BEACH COUNTY EXPOSITIONS INC.

http://www.southfloridafair.com/

SOUTH FLORIDA FAIR COLLEGE SCHOLARSHIP

Renewable award of up to $4000 for students who might not otherwise have an opportunity to pursue a college education. Must be a permanent resident of Florida.

Award: Scholarship for use in freshman, sophomore, junior, or senior years; renewable. *Number:* 10. *Amount:* $1000–$4000.

Eligibility Requirements: Applicant must be enrolled or expecting to enroll full- or part-time at a four-year institution or university and resident of Florida. Available to U.S. and non-U.S. citizens.

Application Requirements: Application form, community service, essay, recommendations or references, self-addressed stamped envelope with application, test scores, transcript. *Deadline:* October 15.

Contact: Scholarship Committee
South Florida Fair and Palm Beach County Expositions Inc.
PO Box 210367
West Palm Beach, FL 33421-0367
Phone: 561-790-5245

STATE EMPLOYEES ASSOCIATION OF NORTH CAROLINA (SEANC)

http://www.seanc.org/

STATE EMPLOYEES ASSOCIATION OF NORTH CAROLINA (SEANC) SCHOLARSHIPS

• *See page 700*

STATE STUDENT ASSISTANCE COMMISSION OF INDIANA (SSACI)

http://www.in.gov/ssaci

FRANK O'BANNON GRANT PROGRAM

A need-based, tuition-restricted program for students attending Indiana public, private, or proprietary institutions seeking a first undergraduate degree. Students (and parents of dependent students) who are U.S. citizens and Indiana residents must file the FAFSA yearly by the March 10 deadline.

Award: Grant for use in freshman, sophomore, junior, or senior years; not renewable. *Amount:* $200–$10,992.

Eligibility Requirements: Applicant must be enrolled or expecting to enroll full-time at a two-year or four-year or technical institution or university; resident of Indiana and studying in Indiana. Available to U.S. citizens.

Application Requirements: Application form, FAFSA, financial need analysis. *Deadline:* March 10.

Contact: Grants Counselor
State Student Assistance Commission of Indiana (SSACI)
150 West Market Street, Suite 500
Indianapolis, IN 46204-2805
Phone: 317-232-2350
Fax: 317-232-3260
E-mail: grants@ssaci.state.in.us

HOOSIER SCHOLAR AWARD

A $500 nonrenewable award. Based on the size of the senior class, one to three scholars are selected by the guidance counselors of each accredited high school in Indiana. The award is based on academic merit and may be used for any educational expense at an eligible Indiana institution of higher education.

Award: Scholarship for use in freshman year; not renewable. *Number:* 666–840. *Amount:* $500.

Eligibility Requirements: Applicant must be high school student; planning to enroll or expecting to enroll full-time at a two-year or four-year institution or university; resident of Indiana and studying in Indiana. Applicant must have 3.5 GPA or higher. Available to U.S. citizens.

Application Requirements: Application form, recommendations or references. *Deadline:* March 10.

Contact: Ada Sparkman, Program Coordinator
State Student Assistance Commission of Indiana (SSACI)
150 West Market Street, Suite 500
Indianapolis, IN 46204-2805
Phone: 317-232-2350
Fax: 317-232-3260

INDIANA NATIONAL GUARD SUPPLEMENTAL GRANT

• *See page 644*

PART-TIME GRANT PROGRAM

Program is designed to encourage part-time undergraduates to start and complete their Associate or Baccalaureate degrees or certificates by subsidizing part-time tuition costs. It is a term-based award that is based on need. State residency requirements must be met and a FAFSA must be filed. Eligibility is determined at the institutional level subject to approval by SSACI.

Award: Grant for use in freshman, sophomore, junior, or senior years; not renewable. *Number:* 4680–6700. *Amount:* $20–$4000.

Eligibility Requirements: Applicant must be enrolled or expecting to enroll part-time at a two-year or four-year or technical institution or university; resident of Indiana and studying in Indiana. Available to U.S. citizens.

Application Requirements: Application form, financial need analysis. *Deadline:* continuous.

Contact: Grants Counselor
State Student Assistance Commission of Indiana (SSACI)
150 West Market Street, Suite 500
Indianapolis, IN 46204-2805
Phone: 317-232-2350
Fax: 317-232-3260
E-mail: grants@ssaci.state.in.us

TWENTY-FIRST CENTURY SCHOLARS GEAR UP SUMMER SCHOLARSHIP

Grant of up to $3000 that pays for summer school tuition and regularly assessed course fees (does not cover other costs such as textbooks or room and board).

Award: Scholarship for use in freshman, sophomore, junior, or senior years; not renewable. *Number:* 1. *Amount:* up to $3000.

Eligibility Requirements: Applicant must be enrolled or expecting to enroll full-time at a two-year or four-year institution or university; resident of Indiana and studying in Indiana. Available to U.S. citizens.

Application Requirements: Application form, must be in twenty-first century scholars program, high school diploma. *Deadline:* varies.

Contact: Coordinator, Office of Twenty-First Century Scholars
State Student Assistance Commission of Indiana (SSACI)
150 West Market Street, Suite 500
Indianapolis, IN 46204
Phone: 317-234-1394
E-mail: 21stscholars@ssaci.in.gov

STEPHEN PHILLIPS MEMORIAL SCHOLARSHIP FUND, INC.

http://www.phillips-scholarship.org/

STEPHEN PHILLIPS MEMORIAL SCHOLARSHIP FUND, INC.

A renewable award open to full-time undergraduate students with financial need who display academic achievement, a commitment to serving others (in school, in the community or at home,) a strong work ethic, and leadership qualities. A US citizen or noncitizen who has a current lawful presence in the United States and has a work permit, and is a permanent resident of a New England state. Qualifying students may attend college anywhere in the U.S. For more details see website www.phillips-scholarship.org.

Award: Scholarship for use in freshman, sophomore, junior, or senior years; renewable. *Number:* 130–140. *Amount:* $3000–$18,000.

Eligibility Requirements: Applicant must be enrolled or expecting to enroll full-time at a four-year institution or university and resident of Connecticut, Maine, Massachusetts, New Hampshire, Rhode Island, Vermont. Applicant must have 3.0 GPA or higher. Available to U.S. citizens.

Application Requirements: Application form, community service, essay, financial need analysis. *Deadline:* May 1.

Contact: Ms. Barbara Iler, Executive Director
Stephen Phillips Memorial Scholarship Fund, Inc.
PO Box 870
Salem, MA 01970
Phone: 978-744-2111
E-mail: staff@spscholars.org

STEPHEN T. MARCHELLO SCHOLARSHIP FOUNDATION

http://www.stmfoundation.org/

A LEGACY OF HOPE SCHOLARSHIPS FOR SURVIVORS OF CHILDHOOD CANCER

Scholarship of up to $2,000 of a one time grant for postsecondary undergraduate education. Applicant must be a survivor of childhood cancer. Must submit a letter from doctor, clinic, or hospital where cancer treatment was received. Residents of CO and MT are eligible. Must be U.S. citizen. Minimum 2.5 GPA required.

Award: Scholarship for use in freshman year; not renewable. *Number:* 1–10. *Amount:* $200–$1500.

Eligibility Requirements: Applicant must be high school student; age 17–20; planning to enroll or expecting to enroll full- or part-time at a two-year or four-year or technical institution or university and resident of Colorado, Montana. Applicant must have 3.5 GPA or higher. Available to U.S. citizens.

Application Requirements: Application form, essay. *Deadline:* March 15.

Contact: Mr. Mario Marchello, Secretary
Stephen T. Marchello Scholarship Foundation
1170 East Long Place
Centennial, CO 80122
Phone: 303-886-5018
E-mail: stmfoundation@hotmail.com

SWISS BENEVOLENT SOCIETY

http://www.sbssf.com/

WILLY ISLER SCHOLARSHIPS
• *See page 700*

SWISS BENEVOLENT SOCIETY OF CHICAGO

http://www.sbschicago.org/

SWISS BENEVOLENT SOCIETY OF CHICAGO SCHOLARSHIPS
• *See page 701*

SWISS BENEVOLENT SOCIETY OF NEW YORK

http://www.sbsny.org/

PELLEGRINI SCHOLARSHIP GRANTS
• *See page 701*

TAMPA BAY TIMES FUND, INC.

http://www.tampabay.com/fund

BARNES SCHOLARSHIP

The Barnes Scholarships were established in 1999 to help college-bound teens who are high academic achievers, who have overcome significant obstacles in their lives and who have financial need. Each of the four winners is eligible to receive up to $15,000 per year for four years to attend any nationally accredited college or university. The scholarship may be used to pay for expenses related to the cost of college attendance. The students must be enrolled full-time and remain in good academic standing to continue to receive the scholarship. High school seniors from these Florida counties are eligible to apply: Hernando, Pasco, Pinellas, Hillsborough. Application period: August 1 to October 21. On-line applications only.

Award: Scholarship for use in freshman, sophomore, junior, or senior years; renewable. *Number:* 1–4. *Amount:* $1000–$15,000.

Eligibility Requirements: Applicant must be high school student; age 17–19; planning to enroll or expecting to enroll full-time at a four-year institution or university; single and resident of Florida. Applicant must have 3.0 GPA or higher. Available to U.S. citizens.

Application Requirements: Application form, community service, essay, interview. *Deadline:* October 20.

Contact: Ms. Nancy Waclawek, Scholarship administrator
Tampa Bay Times Fund, Inc.
PO Box 1121
St. Petersburg, FL 33731-1121
E-mail: tbtschls@gmail.com

TAMPA BAY TIMES FUND BARNES SCHOLARSHIP

Four high school seniors from the Tampa Bay Times' audience area are selected each year and each are awarded up to $15,000 annually for four years to attend any nationally accredited college or university. Criteria for the scholarship include high academic achievement, financial need, evidence of having overcome significant obstacles in life, and community service.

Award: Scholarship for use in freshman, sophomore, junior, or senior years; renewable. *Number:* 4. *Amount:* $15,000.

Eligibility Requirements: Applicant must be high school student; age 18–22; planning to enroll or expecting to enroll full-time at a four-year institution or university; single and resident of Florida. Applicant must have 3.0 GPA or higher. Available to U.S. citizens.

Application Requirements: Application form, community service, essay, financial need analysis, interview. *Deadline:* October 15.

Contact: Nancy Waclawek, Scholarship Administrator
Phone: 813-340-4125
E-mail: tbtschls@gmail.com

TENNESSEE STUDENT ASSISTANCE CORPORATION

http://www.tn.gov/collegepays

DEPENDENT CHILDREN SCHOLARSHIP PROGRAM
• *See page 619*

HELPING HEROES GRANT
• *See page 619*

HOPE WITH ASPIRE
• *See page 619*

NED MCWHERTER SCHOLARS PROGRAM
• *See page 620*

TELS HOPE ACCESS GRANT
• *See page 620*

TELS -HOPE WITH GENERAL ASSEMBLY MERIT SCHOLARSHIP (GAMS)
• *See page 620*

TELS - TENNESSEE HOPE SCHOLARSHIP
• *See page 620*

TENNESSEE DUAL ENROLLMENT GRANT
• *See page 620*

TENNESSEE EDUCATION LOTTERY SCHOLARSHIP PROGRAM WILDER-NAIFEH TECHNICAL SKILLS GRANT
• *See page 620*

TENNESSEE HOPE FOSTER CHILD TUITION GRANT
• *See page 620*

TENNESSEE STEP UP SCHOLARSHIP
• *See page 621*

TENNESSEE STUDENT ASSISTANCE AWARD
• *See page 621*

TERRY FOUNDATION
http://www.terryfoundation.org/

TERRY FOUNDATION SCHOLARSHIP
Scholarships to Texas high school seniors who have been admitted to: University of Texas at Austin; Texas A&M University at College Station; University of Houston; Texas State University; University of Texas at San Antonio; University of Texas at Dallas; University of North Texas; Texas Tech University; Texas Woman's University; Texas A&M at Galveston; Sam Houston State University; University of Texas at El Paso; or University of Texas at Arlington. Scholarship is based upon leadership potential and character; scholastic record and ability; and financial need.

Award: Scholarship for use in freshman, sophomore, junior, or senior years; renewable. *Number:* 253.

Eligibility Requirements: Applicant must be high school student; planning to enroll or expecting to enroll full-time at a four-year institution or university; resident of Texas; studying in Texas and must have an interest in leadership. Applicant must have 3.0 GPA or higher. Available to U.S. citizens.

Application Requirements: Application form, essay, financial need analysis, interview.

Contact: Jodie Koszegi, Scholarship Program Director
Terry Foundation
3104 Edloe, Suite 205
Houston, TX 77027
Phone: 713-552-0002
Fax: 713-622-6352
E-mail: jkoszegi@terryfoundation.org

TERRY FOUNDATION TRANSFER SCHOLARSHIP
Scholarships to Texas high school seniors who have been admitted to: University of Texas at Austin; Texas A&M University at College Station; University of Houston; Texas State University; University of Texas at San Antonio; University of Texas at Dallas; University of North Texas; Texas Tech University; Texas Woman's University; Texas A&M University at Galveston; Sam Houston State University; University of Texas at El Paso; University of Texas at Arlington. Scholarship is based upon leadership potential and character; scholastic record and ability; and financial need.

Award: Scholarship for use in sophomore, junior, or senior years; renewable. *Number:* 120. *Amount:* $13,500.

Eligibility Requirements: Applicant must be enrolled or expecting to enroll full-time at a four-year institution or university; resident of Texas; studying in Texas and must have an interest in leadership. Applicant must have 2.5 GPA or higher. Available to U.S. citizens.

Application Requirements: Application form, essay, financial need analysis, interview.

Contact: Jodie Koszegi, Scholarship Program Director
Terry Foundation
3104 Edloe, Suite 205
Houston, TX 77027
Phone: 713-552-0002
Fax: 713-622-6352
E-mail: jkoszegi@terryfoundation.org

TEXAS 4-H YOUTH DEVELOPMENT FOUNDATION
http://texas4hfoundation.org/

TEXAS 4-H OPPORTUNITY SCHOLARSHIP
Renewable award for Texas 4-H members to attend a Texas college or university. Minimum GPA of 2.5 required. Must attend full-time.

Award: Scholarship for use in freshman, sophomore, junior, or senior years; renewable. *Number:* 225. *Amount:* $1500–$15,000.

Eligibility Requirements: Applicant must be enrolled or expecting to enroll full-time at a two-year or four-year or technical institution; resident of Texas; studying in Texas and must have an interest in animal/agricultural competition. Applicant must have 2.5 GPA or higher. Available to U.S. citizens.

Application Requirements: Application form, essay, financial need analysis, interview, recommendations or references, test scores, transcript. *Deadline:* varies.

Contact: Jim Reeves, Executive Director
Phone: 979-845-1213
Fax: 979-845-6495
E-mail: jereeves@ag.tamu.edu

TEXAS AFL-CIO
http://www.texasaflcio.org/

TEXAS AFL-CIO SCHOLARSHIP PROGRAM
• *See page 559*

TEXAS ASSOCIATION OF DEVELOPING COLLEGES
http://www.txadc.org

THE URBAN SCHOLARSHIPS FUND
• *See page 622*

TEXAS BLACK BAPTIST SCHOLARSHIP COMMITTEE
http://www.bgct.org/

TEXAS BLACK BAPTIST SCHOLARSHIP
• *See page 702*

TEXAS HIGHER EDUCATION COORDINATING BOARD
http://www.collegeforalltexans.com/

TEXAS EDUCATIONAL OPPORTUNITY GRANT (TEOG)
Provides grant aid to students with financial need attending public two-year colleges. For initial award, student must be enrolled at least half-time and awarded in the first 30 hours (or its equivalent) of an associate's degree or certificate program (excluding credits for dual enrollment or by examination). For renewal award, student must also maintain a minimum overall GPA of 2.50 and successfully complete a minimum of 75% of classes attempted during the school year.

Award: Grant for use in freshman, sophomore, junior, or senior years; not renewable. *Amount:* $1–$8000.

Eligibility Requirements: Applicant must be enrolled or expecting to enroll full- or part-time at a two-year institution; resident of Texas and studying in Texas. Available to U.S. citizens.

Application Requirements: FAFSA, financial need analysis.
Contact: Financial Aid Office of relevant institution.

TOP 10% SCHOLARSHIP PROGRAM
Encourage outstanding high school students who graduate within the top 10 percent of their high school graduating class to attend a public college or university in Texas. Students must demonstrate financial need and complete the FAFSA by the state priority deadline of March 15. Renewal

award students must also maintain a minimum overall GPA of 3.25, successfully complete at least 30 SCH each year, and successfully complete at least 75% of the hours attempted each year.

Award: Scholarship for use in freshman, sophomore, junior, or senior years; renewable. *Amount:* $1–$600.

Eligibility Requirements: Applicant must be enrolled or expecting to enroll full-time at a two-year or four-year or technical institution or university; resident of Texas and studying in Texas. Available to U.S. citizens.

Application Requirements: FAFSA, financial need analysis.

Contact: Financial Aid Office of relevant institution.

TOWARD EXCELLENCE, ACCESS, AND SUCCESS (TEXAS) GRANT

Renewable aid for students enrolled at least three-quarter time in a public four-year college or university in Texas within sixteen months of graduation from high school. Must demonstrate financial need and have completed the Foundation, Recommended, or DAP Curriculum in high school. For renewal awards, must also maintain a minimum GPA of 2.5 and complete a minimum of 24 SCH's each year. Amount of award is determined by the financial aid office of each school. Priority FAFSA completion deadline is March 15. Contact the college/university financial aid office for additional eligibility information.

Award: Grant for use in freshman, sophomore, junior, or senior years; renewable. *Amount:* $1–$8000.

Eligibility Requirements: Applicant must be enrolled or expecting to enroll full- or part-time at a four-year institution or university; resident of Texas and studying in Texas. Available to U.S. citizens.

Application Requirements: Financial need analysis, transcript.

Contact: Financial Aid Office of relevant school.

TEXAS OUTDOOR WRITERS ASSOCIATION

http://www.towa.org/

TEXAS OUTDOOR WRITERS ASSOCIATION SCHOLARSHIP

Annual merit award available to students attending an accredited Texas college or university preparing for a career which would incorporate communications skills about the outdoors, environmental conservation, or resource management. Minimum 2.5 GPA required. Submit writing/photo samples.

Award: Scholarship for use in freshman, sophomore, junior, senior, or graduate years; not renewable. *Number:* 1–2. *Amount:* $2000.

Eligibility Requirements: Applicant must be enrolled or expecting to enroll full- or part-time at a two-year or four-year institution or university; resident of Texas; studying in Texas and must have an interest in writing. Applicant must have 2.5 GPA or higher. Available to U.S. citizens.

Application Requirements: Application form. *Deadline:* February 1.

Contact: Judy Mills, Scholarship Co-Chair
Texas Outdoor Writers Association
14871 Estrellita
Houston, TX 77060
Phone: 281-448-5811
E-mail: offtheroad.mills@earthlink.net

TEXAS SOCIETY, MILITARY ORDER OF THE STARS AND BARS

http://www.texasmosb.com/

TEXAS SOCIETY, MILITARY ORDER OF THE STARS AND BARS SCHOLARSHIP

The award is given on the basis of scholastics, extracurricular activities, recommendations, and financial need. Applicants must prove genealogical descent or blood relationship to a Confederate Officer, or government official of the Confederacy. Application and complete rules may be found on the Texas Society, Military Order of the Stars and Bars website.

Award: Scholarship for use in freshman, sophomore, junior, or senior years; not renewable. *Number:* 1. *Amount:* $500–$500.

Eligibility Requirements: Applicant must be enrolled or expecting to enroll full- or part-time at a two-year or four-year or technical institution or university and resident of Texas. Available to U.S. citizens.

Application Requirements: Application form, community service, essay, financial need analysis, genealogical proof, recommendations or references, transcript. *Deadline:* March 1.

Contact: Mr. James Templin, Texas Society Scholarship Chairman
Texas Society, Military Order of the Stars and Bars
2500 Woodlawn Drive
Ennis, TX 75119-7644
Phone: 972-878-2752
E-mail: hjtemp@sbcglobal.net

TEXAS TENNIS FOUNDATION

http://www.texastennisfoundation.com/

TEXAS TENNIS FOUNDATION SCHOLARSHIPS AND ENDOWMENTS

College scholarships for highly recommended students residing in Texas, with an interest in tennis. Financial need is considered. Must be between the ages of 17 and 19. Refer to website for details http://www.texastennisfoundation.com

Award: Scholarship for use in freshman, sophomore, junior, or senior years; not renewable. *Number:* 10. *Amount:* $1000.

Eligibility Requirements: Applicant must be age 17-19; enrolled or expecting to enroll full-time at a two-year or four-year or technical institution or university; resident of Texas and must have an interest in athletics/sports. Available to U.S. citizens.

Application Requirements: Application form, copy of parent or guardian's federal tax return, essay, financial need analysis, personal photograph, recommendations or references, test scores, transcript. *Deadline:* April 15.

Contact: Van Barry, Executive Director
Phone: 512-443-1334 Ext. 201
Fax: 512-443-4748
E-mail: vbarry@texas.usta.com

THEODORE R. AND VIVIAN M. JOHNSON SCHOLARSHIP FOUNDATION INC.

http://www.jsf.bz/

THEODORE R. AND VIVIAN M. JOHNSON SCHOLARSHIP PROGRAM FOR CHILDREN OF UPS EMPLOYEES OR UPS RETIREES

• See page 571

TIDEWATER SCHOLARSHIP FOUNDATION

http://www.accesscollege.org/

ACCESS SCHOLARSHIP/LAST DOLLAR AWARD

A renewable scholarship of $500 to $1000 for the undergraduates participating in Norfolk, Portsmouth, and Virginia Beach, Virginia secure scholarships and financial aid for college.

Award: Scholarship for use in freshman year; renewable. *Amount:* $500–$1000.

Eligibility Requirements: Applicant must be high school student; planning to enroll or expecting to enroll full-time at a two-year or four-year institution or university and resident of Virginia. Applicant must have 2.5 GPA or higher. Available to U.S. citizens.

Application Requirements: Application form, financial need analysis. *Deadline:* May 1.

Contact: Bonnie Sutton, President and Chief Executive Officer
Phone: 757-962-6113
Fax: 757-962-7314
E-mail: bsutton@accesscollege.org

TIGER WOODS FOUNDATION
http://www.tigerwoodsfoundation.org/

ALFRED "TUP" HOLMES MEMORIAL SCHOLARSHIP
Given yearly to one worthy Atlanta metropolitan area graduating high school senior who has displayed high moral character while demonstrating leadership potential and academic excellence. Must be U.S. citizen. Minimum 3.0 GPA required.

Award: Scholarship for use in freshman year; not renewable. *Number:* 1. *Amount:* $2500.

Eligibility Requirements: Applicant must be high school student; planning to enroll or expecting to enroll full-time at a two-year or four-year institution or university and resident of Georgia. Applicant must have 3.0 GPA or higher. Available to U.S. citizens.

Application Requirements: Application form, community service, essay, recommendations or references, test scores, transcript. *Deadline:* April 1.

Contact: Michelle Kim, Scholarship and Grant Coordinator
Phone: 949-725-3003
Fax: 949-725-3002
E-mail: grants@tigerwoodsfoundation.org

TKE EDUCATIONAL FOUNDATION
http://www.tke.org/

DORIS AND ELMER H. SCHMITZ, SR. MEMORIAL SCHOLARSHIP
• *See page 560*

TORTOISE CAPITAL ADVISORS, LLC
http://www.tortoiseadvisors.com

TORTOISE YOUNG ENTREPRENEURS SCHOLARSHIP
The program is designed to give deserving students a leg up in their academic endeavors. In turn, we hope their educational experience will help them mold an entrepreneurial mindset that helps them conceive or support firms that create innovative products, processes and solutions. To be eligible, applicants must: be a permanent resident of Kansas or Missouri who is enrolled or plans to enroll in a full-time undergraduate course of study towards a Bachelor's degree, or; be a non-resident of either state who is enrolled or plans to enroll as a full-time student in a four-year Bachelor's program at a Kansas or Missouri accredited university or college, and; have a minimum 3.3 grade-point average (on a 4.0 scale or equivalent) and a minimum ACT score of 24 or minimum SAT score of 1680 (includes writing section).

Award: Scholarship for use in freshman, sophomore, junior, or senior years; not renewable. *Number:* 3. *Amount:* $1000–$3000.

Eligibility Requirements: Applicant must be enrolled or expecting to enroll full-time at a four-year institution or university; resident of Kansas, Missouri and studying in Kansas, Missouri. Applicant must have 3.0 GPA or higher. Available to U.S. citizens.

Application Requirements: Application form, application form may be submitted online (http://www.tortoiseadvisors.com/scholarship), community service, essay, recommendations or references, test scores, transcript. *Deadline:* February 28.

Contact: Ben Fraser, Scholarship Coordinator
E-mail: scholarship@tortoiseadvisors.com

TOWNSHIP OFFICIALS OF ILLINOIS
http://www.toi.org/

TOWNSHIP OFFICIALS OF ILLINOIS SCHOLARSHIP PROGRAM
The scholarships are awarded to graduating Illinois high school seniors who have a B average or above, have demonstrated an active interest in school activities, who have submitted an essay on "The Importance of Township Government", high school transcript, and letters of recommendation. Students must attend Illinois institutions, either four-year or junior colleges. Must be full-time student. Must complete an interview with a current township official.

Award: Scholarship for use in freshman year; not renewable. *Number:* 7. *Amount:* $1500.

Eligibility Requirements: Applicant must be high school student; planning to enroll or expecting to enroll full-time at a two-year or four-year institution or university; resident of Illinois and studying in Illinois. Applicant must have 3.0 GPA or higher. Available to U.S. citizens.

Application Requirements: Application form, essay, interview. *Deadline:* March 1.

Contact: Amy Rourke, Associate Editor
Township Officials of Illinois
3217 Northfield Dr
Springfield, IL 62701-1804
Phone: 217-744-2212
E-mail: amy@toi.org

TRIANGLE COMMUNITY FOUNDATION
http://www.trianglecf.org

GEORGE AND MARY NEWTON SCHOLARSHIP
• *See page 571*

TWO TEN FOOTWEAR FOUNDATION
http://www.twoten.org/

CLASSIC SCHOLARSHIPS
• *See page 622*

TWO TEN FOOTWEAR FOUNDATION SCHOLARSHIP
• *See page 622*

TWO TEN FOUNDATION FOOTWEAR DESIGN SCHOLARSHIP
Unlike our traditional college scholarships, the Footwear Design Scholarship is available to any student who is studying design with a focus on footwear. This program was created in 2003 to assist students with a demonstrated interest and skill in pursuing a career in footwear design. Applicants are evaluated by design potential and financial need. Awards of up to $3,000 annually are renewable for up to four years of undergraduate study.

Award: Scholarship for use in freshman, sophomore, junior, or senior years; renewable. *Number:* 5. *Amount:* $3000.

Eligibility Requirements: Applicant must be enrolled or expecting to enroll full- or part-time at a two-year or four-year or technical institution or university; resident of Alabama, Alaska, Arizona, Arkansas, California, Colorado, Connecticut, Delaware, Florida, Georgia, Hawaii, Idaho, Illinois, Indiana, Iowa, Kansas, Kentucky, Louisiana, Maine, Maryland, Massachusetts, Michigan, Minnesota, Mississippi, Missouri, Montana, Nebraska, Nevada, New Hampshire, New Jersey, New Mexico, New York, North Carolina, North Dakota, Ohio, Oklahoma, Oregon, Pennsylvania, Puerto Rico, Rhode Island, South Carolina, South Dakota, Tennessee, Texas, Utah, Vermont, Virginia, Washington, West Virginia, Wisconsin, Wyoming and studying in Alabama, Alaska, Arizona, Arkansas, California, Colorado, Connecticut, Delaware, Florida, Georgia, Hawaii, Idaho, Illinois, Indiana, Iowa, Kansas, Kentucky, Louisiana, Maine, Maryland, Massachusetts, Michigan, Minnesota, Mississippi, Missouri, Montana, Nebraska, Nevada, New Hampshire, New Jersey, New Mexico, New York, North Carolina, North Dakota, Nova Scotia, Ohio, Oklahoma, Oregon, Pennsylvania, Puerto Rico, Rhode Island, South Carolina, South Dakota, Tennessee, Texas, Utah, Vermont, Virginia, Washington, West Virginia, Wisconsin, Wyoming. Applicant must have 2.5 GPA or higher. Available to U.S. citizens.

Application Requirements: Application form, essay, financial need analysis, portfolio. *Deadline:* April 15.

Contact: Liz Watson, Scholarship Coordinator
Phone: 781-736-1510
E-mail: scholarship@twoten.org

ULMAN CANCER FUND FOR YOUNG ADULTS

http://www.ulmanfund.org/scholarships

JACQUELINE SHEARER MEMORIAL SCHOLARSHIP
• *See page 623*

LISA HIGGINS-HUSSMAN FOUNDATION SCHOLARSHIP
• *See page 623*

MARILYN YETSO MEMORIAL SCHOLARSHIP
• *See page 624*

OLIVIA M. MARQUART SCHOLARSHIP
• *See page 624*

PERLITA LIWANAG MEMORIAL SCHOLARSHIP
• *See page 624*

VERA YIP MEMORIAL SCHOLARSHIP
• *See page 624*

UNITED DAUGHTERS OF THE CONFEDERACY

http://www.hqudc.org/

CHARLOTTE M. F. BENTLEY/NEW YORK CHAPTER 103 SCHOLARSHIP
• *See page 564*

GERTRUDE BOTTS-SAUCIER SCHOLARSHIP
• *See page 564*

LOLA B. CURRY SCHOLARSHIP
• *See page 565*

UNITED NEGRO COLLEGE FUND

http://www.uncf.org/

DEBORAH L. VINCENT FAHRO EDUCATION SCHOLARSHIP AWARD
• *See page 704*

FOUR PROMISES SCHOLARSHIP
• *See page 704*

HAUSMAN FAMILY CHARITABLE TRUST SCHOLARSHIP
• *See page 704*

KROGER MICHIGAN SCHOLARSHIP
• *See page 704*

MINNESOTA STUDENT AID SCHOLARSHIP
• *See page 704*

MUTUAL SAVINGS LIFE COMPANY SCHOLARSHIP (KEMPER)
• *See page 705*

PENNSYLVANIA STATE EMPLOYEES COMBINED CAMPAIGN SCHOLARSHIP (SECA)
• *See page 705*

RELIABLE LIFE INSURANCE COMPANY SCHOLARSHIP (KEMPER)
• *See page 705*

ROLLIN M. GERSTACKER FOUNDATION SCHOLARSHIP
• *See page 705*

RONALD MCDONALD HOUSE OF CHARITIES FOR CENTRAL INDIANA SCHOLARSHIP
• *See page 705*

UNCF HONDA MANUFACTURING OF INDIANA SCHOLARSHIP
• *See page 706*

UNION NATIONAL LIFE INSURANCE COMPANY SCHOLARSHIP (KEMPER)
• *See page 706*

UNITED INSURANCE COMPANY SCHOLARSHIP (KEMPER)
• *See page 706*

USA FUNDS SCHOLARSHIP
• *See page 706*

UNIVERSITY OF WYOMING

http://www.uwyo.edu/scholarships

VIETNAM VETERANS AWARD-WYOMING
• *See page 662*

UTAH HIGHER EDUCATION ASSISTANCE AUTHORITY

http://www.uheaa.org/

HIGHER EDUCATION SUCCESS STIPEND PROGRAM
Award available to students with substantial financial need for use at any of the participating Utah institutions. The student must be a Utah resident. Contact the financial aid office of the participating institution for requirements and deadlines.

Award: Grant for use in freshman, sophomore, junior, or senior years; not renewable. *Number:* 495–8243. *Amount:* $300–$5000.

Eligibility Requirements: Applicant must be enrolled or expecting to enroll full- or part-time at a two-year or four-year or technical institution or university; resident of Utah and studying in Utah. Available to U.S. citizens.

Application Requirements: Financial need analysis. *Deadline:* continuous.

Contact: Mr. Ronell Crossley
Utah Higher Education Assistance Authority
60 S 400 W
Salt Lake City, UT 84101-1284
Phone: 801-321-7291
Fax: 801-366-8470
E-mail: rcrossley@utahsbr.edu

VERMONT STUDENT ASSISTANCE CORPORATION

http://www.vsac.org/

VERMONT INCENTIVE GRANTS
Renewable grants for Vermont residents based on financial need. Must meet needs test. Must be college undergraduate or graduate student enrolled full-time at an approved post secondary institution. Only available to Vermont residents.

Award: Grant for use in freshman, sophomore, junior, or senior years; renewable. *Amount:* $500–$10,800.

Eligibility Requirements: Applicant must be enrolled or expecting to enroll full-time at a two-year or four-year or technical institution or university and resident of Vermont. Available to U.S. citizens.

Application Requirements: Application form, FAFSA, financial need analysis. *Deadline:* continuous.

Contact: Grant Program
Vermont Student Assistance Corporation
PO Box 2000
Winooski, VT 05404-2000
Phone: 802-655-9602
Fax: 802-654-3765

VERMONT NON-DEGREE STUDENT GRANT PROGRAM

Need-based, renewable grants for Vermont residents enrolled in non-degree programs in a college, vocational school, or high school adult program, that will improve employability or encourage further study. Award amounts vary.

Award: Grant for use in freshman, sophomore, junior, or senior years; renewable.

Eligibility Requirements: Applicant must be enrolled or expecting to enroll full- or part-time at a two-year or four-year or technical institution or university and resident of Vermont. Available to U.S. citizens.

Application Requirements: Application form, financial need analysis. *Deadline:* continuous.

Contact: Grant Program Department
Phone: 802-655-9602

VERMONT PART-TIME STUDENT GRANTS

For undergraduates carrying less than twelve credits per semester who have not received a Bachelor's degree. Must be a Vermont resident. Based on financial need. Complete Vermont Financial Aid Packet to apply. May be used at any approved post-secondary institution.

Award: Grant for use in freshman, sophomore, junior, or senior years; renewable. *Amount:* $250–$8100.

Eligibility Requirements: Applicant must be enrolled or expecting to enroll part-time at a four-year institution or university and resident of Vermont. Available to U.S. citizens.

Application Requirements: Application form, financial need analysis. *Deadline:* continuous.

Contact: Grant Program
Vermont Student Assistance Corporation
PO Box 2000
Winooski, VT 05404-2000
Phone: 802-655-9602
Fax: 802-654-3765

VIRGINIA DEPARTMENT OF EDUCATION

http://www.doe.virginia.gov

GRANVILLE P. MEADE SCHOLARSHIP

High school seniors only are eligible to apply for scholarship. Students are selected based upon GPA, standardized test scores, letters of recommendations, extra curricular activities, and financial need.

Award: Scholarship for use in freshman year; renewable. *Number:* 5. *Amount:* $2000.

Eligibility Requirements: Applicant must be high school student; planning to enroll or expecting to enroll full-time at a two-year or four-year institution or university and resident of Virginia. Available to U.S. citizens.

Application Requirements: Application form, essay, financial need analysis, recommendations or references, test scores, transcript. *Deadline:* March 16.

Contact: Joseph Wharff, School Counseling Connections Specialist
Phone: 804-225-3370
E-mail: joseph.wharff@doe.virginia.gov

VIRGINIA DEPARTMENT OF VETERANS SERVICES

http://www.dvs.virginia.gov/

VIRGINIA MILITARY SURVIVORS AND DEPENDENTS EDUCATION PROGRAM

• *See page 663*

VIRGINIA STATE COUNCIL OF HIGHER EDUCATION

http://www.schev.edu/

VIRGINIA COMMONWEALTH AWARD

Need-based award for undergraduate or graduate study at a Virginia public two- or four-year college, or university. Undergraduates must be Virginia residents. The application and awards process are administered by the financial aid office at the Virginia public institution where the student is enrolled. Dollar value of each award varies. Contact college financial aid office for application and deadlines.

Award: Grant for use in freshman, sophomore, junior, or senior years; not renewable.

Eligibility Requirements: Applicant must be enrolled or expecting to enroll full- or part-time at a two-year or four-year institution or university; resident of Virginia and studying in Virginia. Available to U.S. citizens.

Application Requirements: Financial need analysis.

Contact: Contact the financial aid office of participating Virginia public college.

VIRGINIA GUARANTEED ASSISTANCE PROGRAM

Awards to undergraduate students proportional to their need, up to full tuition, fees and book allowance. Must be a graduate of a Virginia high school. High school GPA of 2.5 required. Must be enrolled full-time in a public Virginia two- or four-year institution and demonstrate financial need. Must maintain minimum college GPA of 2.0 for renewal awards.

Award: Grant for use in freshman, sophomore, junior, or senior years; not renewable.

Eligibility Requirements: Applicant must be enrolled or expecting to enroll full-time at a two-year or four-year institution or university; resident of Virginia and studying in Virginia. Available to U.S. citizens.

Application Requirements: Financial need analysis.

Contact: Contact the financial aid office of participating Virginia public college.

VIRGINIA TUITION ASSISTANCE GRANT PROGRAM (PRIVATE INSTITUTIONS)

Awards for undergraduate students. Also available to graduate and first professional degree students pursuing a health-related degree program. Not to be used for religious study. Must be US citizen or eligible non-citizen, Virginia domiciled, and enrolled full-time at an approved private, nonprofit college within Virginia. Information and application available from participating Virginia colleges financial aid office. Visit http://www.schev.edu and click on Financial Aid.

Award: Grant for use in freshman, sophomore, junior, senior, or graduate years; renewable. *Amount:* $775–$3100.

Eligibility Requirements: Applicant must be enrolled or expecting to enroll full-time at a four-year institution or university; resident of Virginia and studying in Virginia. Available to U.S. citizens.

Application Requirements: Application form. *Deadline:* July 31.

Contact: Contact the financial aid office of the participating private nonprofit Virginia college or university.

WASHINGTON HOSPITAL HEALTHCARE SYSTEM

http://www.whhs.com/

WASHINGTON HOSPITAL EMPLOYEE ASSOCIATION SCHOLARSHIP

Scholarship for a dependent of a Washington Hospital Employee. Must be a graduating senior, community college student, transferring community college student, or a student attending a four-year institution.

Award: Scholarship for use in freshman, sophomore, junior, or senior years; not renewable. *Number:* 1. *Amount:* $2000.

Eligibility Requirements: Applicant must be enrolled or expecting to enroll full- or part-time at a two-year or four-year or technical institution or university and resident of California. Available to U.S. citizens.

Application Requirements: Application form, driver's license, essay, recommendations or references, test scores, transcript. *Deadline:* March 5.

Contact: Scholarship Chair, c/o Personnel Department
Washington Hospital Healthcare System
2500 Mowry Avenue
Fremont, CA 94538
Phone: 510-818-6220

WASHINGTON STATE PARENT TEACHER ASSOCIATION SCHOLARSHIP PROGRAM

http://www.wastatepta.org/

WASHINGTON STATE PARENT TEACHER ASSOCIATION SCHOLARSHIPS FOUNDATION

One-time scholarships for students who have graduated from a public high school in the state of Washington, and who greatly need financial help to begin full-time postsecondary education.

Award: Scholarship for use in freshman year; not renewable. *Number:* 60–80. *Amount:* $1000–$2000.

Eligibility Requirements: Applicant must be high school student; planning to enroll or expecting to enroll full-time at a four-year institution or university and resident of Washington. Available to U.S. citizens.

Application Requirements: Application form, community service, essay, financial need analysis, recommendations or references, transcript. *Deadline:* March 31.

Contact: Mr. Bill Williams, Executive Director
Phone: 253-565-2153
Fax: 253-565-7753
E-mail: jcarpenter@wastatepta.org

WASHINGTON STUDENT ACHIEVEMENT COUNCIL

COLLEGE BOUND SCHOLARSHIP

This program provides financial assistance to low-income students who want to achieve the dream of a college education. The application is a two-step process. Eligible students should complete an application during their 7th or 8th grade year via www.collegebound.wa.gov. The second step requires students to submit a financial aid application their senior year of high school and every year of college for income verification. Additional scholarship pledge requirements can be found at www.collegebound.wa.gov.

Award: Scholarship for use in freshman, sophomore, junior, or senior years; renewable.

Eligibility Requirements: Applicant must be enrolled or expecting to enroll full- or part-time at a two-year or four-year or technical institution or university; resident of Washington and studying in Washington.

Application Requirements: Application form. *Deadline:* June 30.

Contact: Sarah Weiss, Associate Director
Washington Student Achievement Council
917 Lakeridge Way SW
Olympia, WA 98502
Phone: 888-535-0747
E-mail: collegebound@wsac.wa.gov

WATSON-BROWN FOUNDATION INC.

http://www.watson-brown.org/

WATSON-BROWN FOUNDATION SCHOLARSHIP

Scholarships are awarded based on academic merit and financial need. Students must be from designated counties in Georgia or South Carolina and may attend any four- year, accredited, non-profit U.S. college or university. Renewable scholarships are awarded on two levels: $3000 and $5000.

Award: Scholarship for use in freshman, sophomore, junior, or senior years; renewable. *Number:* 200. *Amount:* $3000–$5000.

Eligibility Requirements: Applicant must be enrolled or expecting to enroll full-time at a four-year institution or university and resident of Georgia, South Carolina. Applicant must have 3.0 GPA or higher. Available to U.S. citizens.

Application Requirements: Application form, essay, financial need analysis, IRS Form 1040, recommendations or references, test scores, transcript. *Deadline:* February 15.

Contact: Sarah Drury, Director, Scholarships and Alumni Relations
Watson-Brown Foundation Inc.
310 Tom Watson Way
Thomson, GA 30824
Phone: 706-595-8886
E-mail: skdrury@watson-brown.org

WESTERN FRATERNAL LIFE ASSOCIATION

http://www.wflains.org/

WESTERN FRATERNAL LIFE ASSOCIATION NATIONAL SCHOLARSHIP

• *See page 566*

WESTERN FRATERNAL LIFE NATIONAL SCHOLARSHIP

• *See page 567*

WESTERN INTERSTATE COMMISSION FOR HIGHER EDUCATION

http://www.wiche.edu/

WICHE'S WESTERN UNDERGRADUATE EXCHANGE (WUE)

Students from designated states can enroll in two- and four-year undergraduate programs at more than 150 public institutions in participating Western states and pay 150 percent of resident tuition. Applicants apply directly to the admissions office at participating institution. Applicants must indicate that they want to be considered for the WUE tuition discount. Participating institutions and the majors available at the WUE rate are listed at http://wiche.edu/wue.

Award: Scholarship for use in freshman, sophomore, junior, or senior years; renewable.

Eligibility Requirements: Applicant must be enrolled or expecting to enroll full-time at a two-year or four-year institution or university; resident of Alaska, Arizona, California, Colorado, Hawaii, Idaho, Montana, Nevada, New Mexico, North Dakota, Oregon, South Dakota, Utah, Washington, Wyoming and studying in Alaska, Arizona, California, Colorado, Hawaii, Idaho, Montana, Nevada, New Mexico, North Dakota, Oregon, South Dakota, Utah, Washington, Wyoming. Available to U.S. citizens.

Application Requirements: Application form, driver's license, must demonstrate residency of a WICHE member states (Western U.S.), test scores, transcript.

Contact: Ms. Kim Nawrocki, Administrative Assistant, Student Exchange
Western Interstate Commission for Higher Education
3035 Center Green Drive
Boulder, CO 80301
Phone: 303-541-0270
E-mail: knawrocki@wiche.edu

WEST VIRGINIA HIGHER EDUCATION POLICY COMMISSION-STUDENT SERVICES

http://www.wvhepc.edu

WEST VIRGINIA HIGHER EDUCATION GRANT PROGRAM

Award available for West Virginia resident for one year immediately preceding the date of application, high school graduate or the equivalent, demonstrate financial need, and enroll as a full-time undergraduate at an approved university or college located in West Virginia or Pennsylvania.

Award: Grant for use in freshman, sophomore, junior, or senior years; not renewable. *Number:* 18,000–21,000. *Amount:* $300–$2700.

Eligibility Requirements: Applicant must be enrolled or expecting to enroll full-time at a two-year or four-year institution or university;

resident of West Virginia and studying in Pennsylvania, West Virginia. Available to U.S. citizens.

Application Requirements: Financial need analysis. *Deadline:* April 15.

Contact: Judy Smith, Senior Project Coordinator
West Virginia Higher Education Policy Commission-Student Services
1018 Kanawha Boulevard East, Suite 700
Charleston, WV 25301-2827
Phone: 304-558-4618
E-mail: judy.kee@wvhepc.edu

WILLIAM D. SQUIRES EDUCATIONAL FOUNDATION INC.

http://www.wmdsquiresfoundation.org/

WILLIAM D. SQUIRES SCHOLARSHIP
• *See page 627*

WILLIAM F. COOPER SCHOLARSHIP TRUST

WILLIAM F. COOPER SCHOLARSHIP

Scholarship to provide financial assistance to women living within the state of Georgia for undergraduate studies. Cannot be used for law, theology or medicine fields of study. Nursing is an approved area of study. For more details visit website http://www.wachoviascholars.com.

Award: Scholarship for use in freshman, sophomore, junior, or senior years; renewable. *Amount:* $1000.

Eligibility Requirements: Applicant must be enrolled or expecting to enroll full- or part-time at a four-year institution or university; female and resident of Georgia. Available to U.S. citizens.

Application Requirements: Application form, federal tax form 1040, W-2 forms, financial need analysis, recommendations or references, test scores, transcript. *Deadline:* April 1.

Contact: Sally King, Program Coordinator
Phone: 800-576-5135
Fax: 864-268-7160
E-mail: sallyking@bellsouth.net

WILLIAM G. AND MARIE SELBY FOUNDATION

http://www.selbyfdn.org/

SELBY SCHOLAR PROGRAM

Must be a resident of Sarasota, Manatee, Charlotte, or Desoto counties in Florida. Scholarships awarded up to $7,000 annually, not to exceed 1/3 of individual's financial need. Renewable for four years if student is full-time undergraduate at accredited college or university and maintains 3.0 GPA. Must demonstrate financial need and values of leadership and service to the community. STUDENTS WHO ARE ALREADY ATTENDING A 4-YEAR COLLEGE ARE NOT ELIGIBLE TO APPLY.

Award: Scholarship for use in freshman, sophomore, junior, or senior years; renewable. *Number:* 40. *Amount:* $1000–$7000.

Eligibility Requirements: Applicant must be enrolled or expecting to enroll full-time at a four-year institution or university; resident of Florida and must have an interest in leadership. Applicant must have 3.0 GPA or higher. Available to U.S. citizens.

Application Requirements: Application form, essay, financial need analysis, interview. *Deadline:* April 1.

Contact: Evan Jones, Grants and Scholarships Manager
William G. and Marie Selby Foundation
1800 Second Street, Suite 954
Sarasota, FL 34236
Phone: 941-957-0442
E-mail: ejones@selbyfdn.org

WISCONSIN DEPARTMENT OF VETERANS AFFAIRS (WDVA)

http://www.dva.state.wi.us/

VETERANS EDUCATION (VETED) REIMBURSEMENT GRANT
• *See page 639*

WISCONSIN HIGHER EDUCATIONAL AID BOARD

http://www.heab.wi.gov/

HANDICAPPED STUDENT GRANT-WISCONSIN
• *See page 639*

MINORITY UNDERGRADUATE RETENTION GRANT-WISCONSIN
• *See page 708*

TALENT INCENTIVE PROGRAM GRANT

Grant assists residents of Wisconsin who are attending a nonprofit institution in Wisconsin, and who have substantial financial need. Must meet income criteria, be considered economically and educationally disadvantaged, and be enrolled at least half-time. Refer to website for further details http://www.heab.state.wi.us.

Award: Grant for use in freshman, sophomore, junior, or senior years; renewable. *Amount:* $250–$1800.

Eligibility Requirements: Applicant must be enrolled or expecting to enroll full- or part-time at a two-year or four-year or technical institution or university; resident of Wisconsin and studying in Wisconsin. Available to U.S. citizens.

Application Requirements: Application form, financial need analysis, nomination by financial aid office. *Deadline:* continuous.

Contact: Colette Brown, Program Coordinator
Wisconsin Higher Educational Aid Board
PO Box 7885
Madison, WI 53707-7885
Phone: 608-266-1665
Fax: 608-267-2808
E-mail: colette.brown@wi.gov

WISCONSIN ACADEMIC EXCELLENCE SCHOLARSHIP

Renewable award for high school seniors with the highest GPA in graduating class. Must be a Wisconsin resident attending a nonprofit Wisconsin institution full-time. Scholarship value is $2250 toward tuition each year for up to four years. Must maintain 3.0 GPA for renewal. Refer to your high school counselor for more details.

Award: Scholarship for use in freshman year; renewable. *Amount:* up to $2250.

Eligibility Requirements: Applicant must be high school student; planning to enroll or expecting to enroll full-time at a two-year or four-year or technical institution or university; resident of Wisconsin and studying in Wisconsin. Applicant must have 3.0 GPA or higher. Available to U.S. citizens.

Application Requirements: Application form, test scores, transcript. *Deadline:* continuous.

Contact: Nancy Wilkison, Program Coordinator
Wisconsin Higher Educational Aid Board
PO Box 7885
Madison, WI 53707-7885
Phone: 608-267-2213
Fax: 608-267-2808
E-mail: nancy.wilkison@wi.gov

WISCONSIN HIGHER EDUCATION GRANTS (WHEG)

Grants for residents of Wisconsin enrolled at least half-time in degree or certificate programs at a University of Wisconsin Institution, Wisconsin Technical College or an approved Tribal College. Must show financial need. Refer to website for further details http://www.heab.wi.gov.

Award: Grant for use in freshman, sophomore, junior, or senior years; not renewable. *Amount:* $250–$3000.

Eligibility Requirements: Applicant must be enrolled or expecting to enroll full- or part-time at a two-year or four-year or technical institution or university; resident of Wisconsin and studying in Wisconsin. Available to U.S. citizens.

Application Requirements: Application form, financial need analysis. *Deadline:* continuous.

Contact: Sandra Thomas, Program Coordinator
Wisconsin Higher Educational Aid Board
PO Box 7885
Madison, WI 53707-7885
Phone: 608-266-0888
Fax: 608-267-2808
E-mail: sandy.thomas@heab.state.wi.us

WISCONSIN NATIVE AMERICAN/INDIAN STUDENT ASSISTANCE GRANT
• *See page 708*

WISCONSIN SCHOOL COUNSELOR ASSOCIATION
http://www.wscaweb.org/

WISCONSIN SCHOOL COUNSELOR ASSOCIATION HIGH SCHOOL SCHOLARSHIP

Scholarship is available to high school seniors in Wisconsin who plan to attend a two-year or four-year postsecondary institution in the fall. Students are asked to submit an essay that describes how a school counselor or school counseling program has impacted their life.

Award: Scholarship for use in freshman year; not renewable. *Number:* 2–4. *Amount:* $1000.

Eligibility Requirements: Applicant must be high school student; planning to enroll or expecting to enroll full-time at a two-year or four-year institution or university and resident of Wisconsin. Available to U.S. citizens.

Application Requirements: Application form, essay. *Deadline:* November 1.

Contact: Katie Nechodom, WSCA Professional Recognition and Scholarship Coordinator
E-mail: nechodomk@gmail.com

WOMEN IN DEFENSE MICHIGAN
http://wid-mi.org/

WOMEN IN DEFENSE HORIZONS-MICHIGAN SCHOLARSHIP

The program focuses on the following preferred fields of study: security studies, military history, government relations, engineering, computer science, physics, mathematics, business (as it relates to national security or defense), law (as it relates to national security or defense), international relations, political science, economics. Others will be considered if the applicant can successfully demonstrate relevance to a career in the areas of national security or defense. Awards are based on academic achievement, participation in defense and national security activities, field of study, work experience, statements of objectives, recommendations, and financial need. Awards are made without regard to race, creed, color, or religion. HORIZONS-Michigan reserves the right to revise, suspend or discontinue this program without notice.

Award: Scholarship for use in junior, senior, graduate, or postgraduate years; not renewable. *Number:* 1–4. *Amount:* $1500–$5000.

Eligibility Requirements: Applicant must be enrolled or expecting to enroll full- or part-time at a two-year or four-year or technical institution or university; female; resident of Michigan and studying in Michigan. Applicant must have 3.0 GPA or higher. Available to U.S. citizens.

Application Requirements: Application form, driver's license, essay, financial need analysis. *Deadline:* May 12.

Contact: Melanie Stager, Director of Scholarships
E-mail: scholarships@wid-mi.org

WYOMING DEPARTMENT OF EDUCATION
http://edu.wyoming.gov/

DOUVAS MEMORIAL SCHOLARSHIP

Available to Wyoming residents who are first-generation Americans. Must be between 18 and 22 years old. Must be used at any Wyoming public institution of higher education for study in freshman year.

Award: Scholarship for use in freshman year; not renewable. *Number:* 2. *Amount:* $500.

Eligibility Requirements: Applicant must be age 18-22; enrolled or expecting to enroll full- or part-time at a two-year or four-year institution or university; resident of Wyoming and studying in Wyoming. Available to U.S. citizens.

Application Requirements: Application form. *Deadline:* April 30.

Contact: Stephanie Brady, Social Studies Consultant
Wyoming Department of Education
2300 Capitol Avenue
Hathaway Building, 2nd Floor
Cheyenne, WY 82002
Phone: 307-777-3793
Fax: 307-777-6234
E-mail: stephanie.brady@wyo.gov

HATHAWAY SCHOLARSHIP

Scholarship for Wyoming students to pursue postsecondary education within the state. Award ranges from $840 to $1680 per semester. Deadline varies.

Award: Scholarship for use in freshman, sophomore, junior, senior, or graduate years; renewable. *Amount:* $840–$1680.

Eligibility Requirements: Applicant must be enrolled or expecting to enroll full- or part-time at a two-year or four-year institution or university; resident of Wyoming and studying in Wyoming. Applicant must have 2.5 GPA or higher. Available to U.S. citizens.

Application Requirements: Application form. *Deadline:* continuous.

Contact: Mr. Bradley Barker III, Hathaway Scholarship Consultant
Wyoming Department of Education
2300 Capitol Avenue
Hathaway Building, 2nd Floor
Cheyenne, WY 82002
Phone: 307-777-6226
E-mail: hathawayscholarship@wyo.gov

WYOMING FARM BUREAU FEDERATION
http://www.wyfb.org/

LIVINGSTON FAMILY - H.J. KING MEMORIAL SCHOLARSHIP
• *See page 567*

WYOMING FARM BUREAU CONTINUING EDUCATION SCHOLARSHIPS
• *See page 567*

WYOMING FARM BUREAU FEDERATION SCHOLARSHIPS
• *See page 567*

YOUTH FOUNDATION INC.
http://fdnweb.org/youthfdn

ALEXANDER AND MAUDE HADDEN SCHOLARSHIP
• *See page 627*

TALENT/INTEREST AREA

1-800-HANSONS

www.hansons.com

I-800-HANSONS SCHOLARSHIP PROGRAM
• *See page 572*

A-1 AUTO TRANSPORT, INC.

https://www.a1autotransport.com/a-1-auto-transport-scholarship/

A-I AUTO TRANSPORT SCHOLARSHIP
• *See page 572*

ABBVIE INC.

https://www.abbvie.com/

ABBVIE IMMUNOLOGY SCHOLARSHIP
• *See page 572*

ACTORS THEATRE OF LOUISVILLE

http://www.actorstheatre.org/

NATIONAL TEN-MINUTE PLAY CONTEST
Writers submit short plays (10 pages or less) that have not received an Equity production, which are considered for the $1000 Heideman Award, as well as for production with the Apprentice/Intern Company (to be eligible, characters in the play must be appropriate for actors aged 20 to 30) and the Humana Festival of new American plays. Must be a citizen or permanent resident of the U.S.

Award: Prize for use in freshman, sophomore, junior, senior, graduate, or postgraduate years; not renewable. *Number:* 1. *Amount:* $1000.

Eligibility Requirements: Applicant must be enrolled or expecting to enroll full- or part-time at a two-year or four-year or technical institution or university and must have an interest in theater or writing. Available to U.S. citizens.

Application Requirements: *Deadline:* September 1.

Contact: Ms. Jenni Page-White, Literary Manager
Actors Theatre of Louisville
316 West Main Street
Louisville, KY 40202-4218
E-mail: JPage-White@actorstheatre.org

AIR TRAFFIC CONTROL ASSOCIATION INC.

http://www.atca.org/

AIR TRAFFIC CONTROL ASSOCIATION SCHOLARSHIP
• *See page 573*

BUCKINGHAM MEMORIAL SCHOLARSHIP
• *See page 573*

LAWRENCE C. FORTIER MEMORIAL SCHOLARSHIP
• *See page 573*

ALBERTA HERITAGE SCHOLARSHIP FUND

http://www.alis.alberta.ca/

CHARLES S. NOBLE JUNIOR FOOTBALL SCHOLARSHIPS
• *See page 667*

CHARLES S. NOBLE JUNIOR HOCKEY SCHOLARSHIPS
• *See page 667*

JIMMIE CONDON ATHLETIC SCHOLARSHIPS
• *See page 667*

LAURENCE DECORE AWARDS FOR STUDENT LEADERSHIP
• *See page 668*

PRAIRIE BASEBALL ACADEMY SCHOLARSHIPS
• *See page 726*

ALERTONE SERVICES LLC

https://www.alert-1.com/

ALERTI STUDENT FOR SENIORS SCHOLARSHIP
• *See page 573*

ALERT SCHOLARSHIP

http://www.alertmagazine.org/

ALERT SCHOLARSHIP
• *See page 727*

THE ALEXANDER FOUNDATION

http://www.thealexanderfoundation.org/

THE ALEXANDER FOUNDATION SCHOLARSHIP PROGRAM
• *See page 727*

ALGAECAL INC.

https://www.algaecal.com/

ALGAECAL SCHOLARSHIP
• *See page 573*

ALLIANCE FOR YOUNG ARTISTS AND WRITERS INC.

http://www.artandwriting.org/

SCHOLASTIC ART AND WRITING AWARDS
• *See page 574*

ALLTHEROOMS

http://alltherooms.com

ROOM TO TRAVEL - STUDY ABROAD SCHOLARSHIP
• *See page 574*

AMERICAN ASSOCIATION OF TEACHERS OF JAPANESE BRIDGING CLEARINGHOUSE FOR STUDY ABROAD IN JAPAN

http://www.aatj.org

BRIDGING SCHOLARSHIP FOR STUDY ABROAD IN JAPAN
• *See page 574*

AMERICAN COUNCIL OF THE BLIND

http://www.acb.org/

AMERICAN COUNCIL OF THE BLIND SCHOLARSHIPS
• See page 574

AMERICAN INDIAN GRADUATE CENTER

http://www.aigcs.org/

GATES MILLENNIUM SCHOLARS PROGRAM
• See page 669

AMERICAN INSTITUTE FOR FOREIGN STUDY

http://www.aifsabroad.com/

AIFS AFFILIATE SCHOLARSHIPS

Students from colleges and universities that participate in the AIFS Affiliates program are eligible. Application fee: $95. For more details, visit http://www.aifsabroad.com/scholarships.asp.

Award: Scholarship for use in freshman, sophomore, junior, or senior years; not renewable.

Eligibility Requirements: Applicant must be enrolled or expecting to enroll full-time at a two-year or four-year institution or university and must have an interest in international exchange. Available to U.S. and non-U.S. citizens.

Application Requirements: Application form, essay, personal photograph, recommendations or references, transcript. *Fee:* $95. *Deadline:* varies.

Contact: David Mauro, Admissions Counselor
American Institute for Foreign Study
River Plaza, 9 West Broad Street
Stamford, CT 06902-3788
Phone: 800-727-2437 Ext. 5163
Fax: 203-399-5463
E-mail: dmauro@aifs.com

AIFS DIVERSITYABROAD.COM SCHOLARSHIP
• See page 669

AIFS GENERATION STUDY ABROAD SCHOLARSHIPS

Awards available to undergraduates on an AIFS study abroad program. Applicants must demonstrate leadership potential, have a minimum 3.0 cumulative GPA, and meet program requirements. The program application fee is $95. Deadlines: April 15 for fall, October 1 for spring, and March 1 for summer.

Award: Scholarship for use in freshman, sophomore, junior, or senior years; not renewable. *Number:* up to 130. *Amount:* $500–$1000.

Eligibility Requirements: Applicant must be enrolled or expecting to enroll full-time at a two-year or four-year institution or university and must have an interest in international exchange or leadership. Applicant must have 3.0 GPA or higher. Available to U.S. and non-U.S. citizens.

Application Requirements: Application form, essay, personal photograph, recommendations or references, transcript. *Fee:* $95. *Deadline:* varies.

Contact: David Mauro, Admissions Counselor
American Institute for Foreign Study
1 High Ridge Park
Stamford, CT 06905
Phone: 800-727-2437 Ext. 5163
Fax: 203-399-5463
E-mail: dmauro@aifs.com

AIFS GILMAN SCHOLARSHIP BONUS-$500 SCHOLARSHIPS

Award of $500 available to each undergraduate recipient for use toward an AIFS program. More information is available at http://www.iie.org/gilman.

Award: Scholarship for use in freshman, sophomore, junior, or senior years; not renewable. *Amount:* $500.

Eligibility Requirements: Applicant must be enrolled or expecting to enroll full-time at a four-year institution or university and must have an interest in international exchange. Available to U.S. and non-U.S. citizens.

Application Requirements: Application form, essay, personal photograph, recommendations or references, transcript. *Fee:* $95. *Deadline:* varies.

Contact: David Mauro, Admissions Counselor
American Institute for Foreign Study
1 High Ridge Park
Stamford, CT 06905
Phone: 800-727-2437 Ext. 5163
Fax: 203-399-5463
E-mail: dmauro@aifs.com

AIFS-HACU SCHOLARSHIPS
• See page 669

AIFS STUDY AGAIN SCHOLARSHIPS

Students who studied abroad on an AIFS summer program will receive a $1000 scholarship to study abroad on an AIFS semester or academic year catalog program or a $500 scholarship toward a summer catalog program. Students who studied abroad on an AIFS semester or academic year program will receive a $500 scholarship toward a summer catalog program or a $1000 scholarship toward a semester program in a different academic year. Deadlines: April 15 for fall, October 15 for spring, and March 1 for summer.

Award: Scholarship for use in freshman, sophomore, junior, or senior years; not renewable. *Amount:* $500–$1000.

Eligibility Requirements: Applicant must be enrolled or expecting to enroll full-time at a two-year or four-year institution or university and must have an interest in international exchange. Applicant must have 2.5 GPA or higher. Available to U.S. and non-U.S. citizens.

Application Requirements: Application form, essay, personal photograph, recommendations or references, transcript. *Fee:* $95. *Deadline:* varies.

Contact: David Mauro, Admissions Counselor
American Institute for Foreign Study
1 High Ridge Park
Stamford, CT 06905
Phone: 800-727-2437 Ext. 5163
Fax: 203-399-5463
E-mail: dmauro@aifs.com

AMERICAN JEWISH LEAGUE FOR ISRAEL

http://www.americanjewishleague.org/

AMERICAN JEWISH LEAGUE FOR ISRAEL SCHOLARSHIP PROGRAM

Scholarship provides support with tuition for a full year of study (September to May) at one of seven Israeli universities, Bar Ilan, Ben Gurion, Haifa, Hebrew, Tel Aviv, Technion, and Weizmann, Interdisciplinary Center at Herzliya. Additional information is available on website http://www.americanjewishleague.org/ScholarshipInformation.html.

Award: Scholarship for use in freshman, sophomore, junior, or senior years; not renewable. *Number:* 3–15. *Amount:* $2000.

Eligibility Requirements: Applicant must be enrolled or expecting to enroll full-time at a four-year institution or university and must have an interest in Jewish culture. Available to U.S. citizens.

Application Requirements: Application form, essay, personal and academic aspirations, recommendations or references, transcript. *Deadline:* May 1.

Contact: Mr. Karl Zukerman, University Scholarship Fund
American Jewish League for Israel
4485 Hazleton Lane
Wellington, FL 33449
Fax: 561-963-2923
E-mail: kdzwork@aol.com

AMERICAN LEGION AUXILIARY DEPARTMENT OF WISCONSIN

http://www.amlegionauxwi.org/

AMERICAN LEGION AUXILIARY DEPARTMENT OF WISCONSIN DELLA VAN DEUREN MEMORIAL SCHOLARSHIP
• *See page 531*

AMERICAN LEGION AUXILIARY DEPARTMENT OF WISCONSIN H.S. AND ANGELINE LEWIS SCHOLARSHIPS
• *See page 531*

AMERICAN LEGION AUXILIARY DEPARTMENT OF WISCONSIN MERIT AND MEMORIAL SCHOLARSHIPS
• *See page 531*

AMERICAN LEGION AUXILIARY DEPARTMENT OF WISCONSIN PAST PRESIDENTS' PARLEY HEALTH CAREER SCHOLARSHIPS
• *See page 531*

AMERICAN LEGION AUXILIARY DEPARTMENT OF WISCONSIN PRESIDENT'S SCHOLARSHIPS
• *See page 531*

AMERICAN LEGION AUXILIARY NATIONAL HEADQUARTERS

http://www.ALAforVeterans.org

AMERICAN LEGION AUXILIARY CHILDREN OF WARRIORS NATIONAL PRESIDENTS' SCHOLARSHIP
• *See page 575*

AMERICAN LEGION BASEBALL

http://www.legion.org/baseball

AMERICAN LEGION BASEBALL SCHOLARSHIP
Awarded to graduated seniors who were nominated by American Legion Baseball coach who demonstrate outstanding academics, citizenship, community spirit, leadership and financial need.

Award: Scholarship for use in freshman, sophomore, junior, senior, graduate, or postgraduate years; not renewable. *Number:* 1–51. *Amount:* $500–$2500.

Eligibility Requirements: Applicant must be high school student; planning to enroll or expecting to enroll full-time at a two-year or four-year or technical institution or university and must have an interest in athletics/sports. Applicant must have 2.5 GPA or higher. Available to U.S. and non-Canadian citizens.

Application Requirements: Application form, personal photograph. *Deadline:* July 15.

Contact: Mr. Steve Cloud, Assistant National Program Coordinator
American Legion Baseball
PO Box 1055
Indianapolis, IN 46206
Phone: 317-630-1213
E-mail: baseball@legion.org

AMERICAN LEGION DEPARTMENT OF ARIZONA

http://www.azlegion.org/programs

AMERICAN LEGION DEPARTMENT OF ARIZONA HIGH SCHOOL ORATORICAL CONTEST
• *See page 730*

AMERICAN LEGION DEPARTMENT OF ARKANSAS

http://www.arklegion.homestead.com/

AMERICAN LEGION DEPARTMENT OF ARKANSAS HIGH SCHOOL ORATORICAL CONTEST
• *See page 730*

AMERICAN LEGION DEPARTMENT OF ILLINOIS

http://www.illegion.org/

AMERICAN ESSAY CONTEST SCHOLARSHIP
• *See page 532*

AMERICAN LEGION DEPARTMENT OF ILLINOIS HIGH SCHOOL ORATORICAL CONTEST
• *See page 731*

AMERICAN LEGION DEPARTMENT OF INDIANA

http://www.indianalegion.org

AMERICAN LEGION DEPARTMENT OF INDIANA HIGH SCHOOL ORATORICAL CONTEST
• *See page 731*

FRANK W. MCHALE MEMORIAL SCHOLARSHIPS
• *See page 731*

AMERICAN LEGION DEPARTMENT OF IOWA

http://www.ialegion.org/

AMERICAN LEGION DEPARTMENT OF IOWA HIGH SCHOOL ORATORICAL CONTEST
• *See page 731*

AMERICAN LEGION DEPARTMENT OF IOWA OUTSTANDING SENIOR BASEBALL PLAYER
• *See page 731*

AMERICAN LEGION DEPARTMENT OF KANSAS

http://www.ksamlegion.org/

AMERICAN LEGION DEPARTMENT OF KANSAS HIGH SCHOOL ORATORICAL CONTEST
• *See page 732*

DR. CLICK COWGER BASEBALL SCHOLARSHIP
• *See page 732*

PAUL FLAHERTY ATHLETIC SCHOLARSHIP
• *See page 732*

AMERICAN LEGION DEPARTMENT OF MICHIGAN

http://www.michiganlegion.org/

AMERICAN LEGION DEPARTMENT OF MICHIGAN ORATORICAL SCHOLARSHIP PROGRAM
• *See page 732*

THE AMERICAN LEGION, DEPARTMENT OF MINNESOTA

http://www.mnlegion.org/

AMERICAN LEGION DEPARTMENT OF MINNESOTA HIGH SCHOOL ORATORICAL CONTEST
• *See page 733*

AMERICAN LEGION DEPARTMENT OF MONTANA

http://www.mtlegion.org/

AMERICAN LEGION DEPARTMENT OF MONTANA HIGH SCHOOL ORATORICAL CONTEST
• *See page 733*

AMERICAN LEGION DEPARTMENT OF NEBRASKA

http://www.nebraskalegion.net/

AMERICAN LEGION DEPARTMENT OF NEBRASKA HIGH SCHOOL ORATORICAL CONTEST
• *See page 733*

AMERICAN LEGION DEPARTMENT OF NEBRASKA JIM HURLBERT MEMORIAL BASEBALL SCHOLARSHIP
• *See page 733*

AMERICAN LEGION DEPARTMENT OF NEW YORK

http://www.ny.legion.org/

AMERICAN LEGION DEPARTMENT OF NEW YORK HIGH SCHOOL ORATORICAL CONTEST
• *See page 734*

AMERICAN LEGION DEPARTMENT OF NORTH CAROLINA

http://www.nclegion.org/

AMERICAN LEGION DEPARTMENT OF NORTH CAROLINA HIGH SCHOOL ORATORICAL CONTEST
• *See page 734*

AMERICAN LEGION DEPARTMENT OF NORTH DAKOTA

http://www.ndlegion.org/

AMERICAN LEGION DEPARTMENT OF NORTH DAKOTA NATIONAL HIGH SCHOOL ORATORICAL CONTEST
• *See page 734*

AMERICAN LEGION DEPARTMENT OF OREGON

http://www.orlegion.org/

AMERICAN LEGION DEPARTMENT OF OREGON HIGH SCHOOL ORATORICAL CONTEST
• *See page 734*

AMERICAN LEGION DEPARTMENT OF PENNSYLVANIA

http://www.pa-legion.com/

AMERICAN LEGION DEPARTMENT OF PENNSYLVANIA HIGH SCHOOL ORATORICAL CONTEST
• *See page 735*

AMERICAN LEGION DEPARTMENT OF SOUTH DAKOTA

http://www.sdlegion.org/

AMERICAN LEGION DEPARTMENT OF SOUTH DAKOTA HIGH SCHOOL ORATORICAL CONTEST
• *See page 735*

AMERICAN LEGION DEPARTMENT OF TENNESSEE

http://www.tennesseelegion.org/

AMERICAN LEGION DEPARTMENT OF TENNESSEE HIGH SCHOOL ORATORICAL CONTEST
• *See page 735*

AMERICAN LEGION DEPARTMENT OF TEXAS

http://www.txlegion.org/

AMERICAN LEGION DEPARTMENT OF TEXAS HIGH SCHOOL ORATORICAL CONTEST
• *See page 735*

AMERICAN LEGION DEPARTMENT OF VERMONT

http://www.vtlegion.org

AMERICAN LEGION DEPARTMENT OF VERMONT HIGH SCHOOL ORATORICAL CONTEST
• *See page 735*

AMERICAN LEGION DEPARTMENT OF WASHINGTON

http://www.walegion.org/

AMERICAN LEGION DEPARTMENT OF WASHINGTON CHILDREN AND YOUTH SCHOLARSHIPS
• *See page 536*

AMERICAN LEGION DEPARTMENT OF WEST VIRGINIA

http://www.wvlegion.org/

AMERICAN LEGION DEPARTMENT OF WEST VIRGINIA BOARD OF REGENTS SCHOLARSHIP
• *See page 736*

AMERICAN LEGION DEPARTMENT OF WEST VIRGINIA HIGH SCHOOL ORATORICAL CONTEST
• *See page 736*

AMERICAN MUSEUM OF NATURAL HISTORY

http://www.amnh.org/

YOUNG NATURALIST AWARDS

Essay contest open to students in grades 7-12 who are currently enrolled in a public, private, parochial, or home school in the United States, Canada, the U.S. territories, or a U.S.-sponsored school abroad. Essays must be based on an original scientific investigation conducted by the student. See website for guidelines http://www.amnh.org/nationalcenter/youngnaturalistawards/read.html.

Award: Prize for use in freshman year; not renewable. *Number:* 1.

Eligibility Requirements: Applicant must be high school student; planning to enroll or expecting to enroll part-time at a four-year institution or university and must have an interest in writing. Available to Canadian citizens.

Application Requirements: Application form, essay, personal photograph. *Deadline:* March 1.

Contact: Maria Rios, Assistant Director, Fellowships and Student Affairs
Phone: 212-769-5017
E-mail: fellowships-rggs@amnh.org

AMERICAN QUARTER HORSE FOUNDATION (AQHF)

http://www.aqha.com/foundation

ARIZONA QUARTER RACING SCHOLARSHIP
• *See page 537*

DR. GERALD O'CONNOR MICHIGAN QHY SCHOLARSHIP
• *See page 537*

SWAYZE WOODRUFF MEMORIAL MID-SOUTH SCHOLARSHIP
• *See page 539*

AMERICAN SAVINGS FOUNDATION

http://www.asfdn.org/

ROBERT T. KENNEY SCHOLARSHIP PROGRAM AT THE AMERICAN SAVINGS FOUNDATION
• *See page 576*

AMERICAN STRING TEACHERS ASSOCIATION

http://www.astaweb.com/

NATIONAL SOLO COMPETITION

Twenty-six individual awards. Instrument categories are violin, viola, cello, double bass, classical guitar, and harp. Applicants competing in Junior Division must be under age 19. Senior Division competitors must be ages 19 to 25. Application fee is $75. Visit website for application forms. Applicant must be a member of ASTA.

Award: Prize for use in freshman, sophomore, junior, senior, or graduate years; not renewable. *Number:* 26.

Eligibility Requirements: Applicant must be age 19-25; enrolled or expecting to enroll full- or part-time at a two-year or four-year or technical institution or university and must have an interest in music. Available to U.S. and Canadian citizens.

Application Requirements: Application form, entry in a contest, proof of age, proof of membership. *Fee:* $75. *Deadline:* varies.

Contact: Laura Kobayashi, Committee Chair
American String Teachers Association
4153 Chain Bridge Road
Fairfax, VA 22030
Phone: 703-279-2113
Fax: 703-279-2114
E-mail: lkobayas@myway.com

ANKIN LAW

http://ankinlaw.com

ANKIN LAW OFFICE COLLEGE SCHOLARSHIP
• *See page 576*

ANTHONY MUNOZ FOUNDATION

www.munozfoundation.org

ANTHONY MUNOZ SCHOLARSHIPS
• *See page 577*

ANY INTERN

http://www.anyintern.com

$1,000 5 MINUTE SCHOLARSHIP
• *See page 577*

APPALOOSA HORSE CLUB-APPALOOSA YOUTH PROGRAM

http://www.appaloosayouth.com/

APPALOOSA YOUTH EDUCATIONAL SCHOLARSHIPS
• *See page 539*

ARKANSAS SINGLE PARENT SCHOLARSHIP FUND

http://www.aspsf.org/

ARKANSAS SINGLE PARENT SCHOLARSHIP FUND
• *See page 577*

ARMENIAN RELIEF SOCIETY OF EASTERN USA INC.-REGIONAL OFFICE

http://www.arseastusa.org/

ARMENIAN RELIEF SOCIETY UNDERGRADUATE SCHOLARSHIP
• *See page 670*

ARRL FOUNDATION INC.

http://www.arrl.org/

ALAN G. THORPE, K1TMW, MEMORIAL SCHOLARSHIP FUND

One $1000 scholarship for a student with active Amateur Radio license who is studying at any accredited 4-year college or university.

Award: Scholarship for use in freshman, sophomore, junior, or senior years; not renewable. *Number:* 1. *Amount:* $1000.

Eligibility Requirements: Applicant must be enrolled or expecting to enroll full- or part-time at a two-year or four-year or technical institution or university and must have an interest in amateur radio. Available to U.S. citizens.

Application Requirements: Application form. *Deadline:* January 31.

Contact: Ms. Mary Hobart, Secretary
Phone: 860-594-0397
E-mail: k1mmh@arrl.org

ALBERT H. HIX, W8AH, MEMORIAL SCHOLARSHIP
• *See page 738*

ARRL ROCKY MOUNTAIN DIVISION SCHOLARSHIP
• *See page 738*

ATLANTA RADIO CLUB SCHOLARSHIP
• *See page 738*

BILL, W2ONV, AND ANN SALERNO MEMORIAL SCHOLARSHIP

Two, one-time $1000 awards are available to students who possess any amateur radio license. Must have a 3.7 GPA or higher. Aggregate annual income of the family household should not exceed $100,000. Must attend an accredited four year college or university.

Award: Scholarship for use in freshman, sophomore, junior, senior, or graduate years; not renewable. *Number:* 2. *Amount:* $1000.

Eligibility Requirements: Applicant must be enrolled or expecting to enroll full-time at a four-year institution or university and must have an interest in amateur radio. Available to U.S. citizens.

Application Requirements: Application form, financial need analysis. *Deadline:* January 31.

Contact: Ms. Mary Hobart, Secretary
    Phone: 860-594-0397
    E-mail: k1mmh@arrl.org

BYRON BLANCHARD, N1EKV, MEMORIAL SCHOLARSHIP
• *See page 738*

CENTRAL ARIZONA DX ASSOCIATION SCHOLARSHIP
• *See page 738*

CHALLENGE MET SCHOLARSHIP
• *See page 628*

CHICAGO FM CLUB SCHOLARSHIP FUND
• *See page 738*

DAVID KNAUS MEMORIAL SCHOLARSHIP
• *See page 739*

DAYTON AMATEUR RADIO ASSOCIATION SCHOLARSHIPS

Four $1000 awards are available to students with any active amateur radio license. Must attend an accredited four-year college or university.

Award: Scholarship for use in freshman, sophomore, junior, or senior years; not renewable. *Number:* 4. *Amount:* $1000.

Eligibility Requirements: Applicant must be enrolled or expecting to enroll full- or part-time at a four-year institution or university and must have an interest in amateur radio. Available to U.S. citizens.

Application Requirements: Application form. *Deadline:* January 31.

Contact: Ms. Mary Hobart, Secretary
    Phone: 860-594-0397
    E-mail: k1mmh@arrl.org

ERNEST L. BAULCH, W2TX, AND MARCIA E. BAULCH, WA2AKJ, SCHOLARSHIP

$3500 scholarship for a student with any active Amateur Radio License Class license who is studying at a four-year college or university.

Award: Scholarship for use in freshman, sophomore, junior, or senior years; not renewable. *Number:* 1. *Amount:* $3500.

Eligibility Requirements: Applicant must be enrolled or expecting to enroll full-time at a four-year institution or university and must have an interest in amateur radio. Available to U.S. citizens.

Application Requirements: Application form. *Deadline:* January 31.

Contact: Ms. Mary Hobart, Secretary
    Phone: 860-594-0397
    E-mail: k1mmh@arrl.org

GENERAL FUND SCHOLARSHIPS

Available to students who are amateur radio operators. Students can be licensed in any class of operators. Nonrenewable award for use in undergraduate years. Multiple awards per year.

Award: Scholarship for use in freshman, sophomore, junior, or senior years; not renewable. *Amount:* $2000.

Eligibility Requirements: Applicant must be enrolled or expecting to enroll full-time at a four-year institution or university and must have an interest in amateur radio. Available to U.S. citizens.

Application Requirements: Application form. *Deadline:* January 31.

Contact: Ms. Mary Hobart, Secretary
    Phone: 860-594-0397
    E-mail: k1mmh@arrl.org

GWINNETT AMATEUR RADIO SOCIETY SCHOLARSHIP
• *See page 739*

HELEN LAUGHLIN AM MODE MEMORIAL SCHOLARSHIP

One $1000 scholarship for a student with active General Class amateur radio license who is studying at any accredited 4-year college or university. Preference is given to residents of Texas, If no qualified applicant is identified, preference will be given to residents of Arkansas. If no qualified applicant is identified, preference will be given to residents of the ARRL West Gulf (Texas, Oklahoma) or Delta (Arkansas, Louisiana, Mississippi, Tennessee) Divisions. Preference is given to women Amateur Radio operators who are performing at a high academic level. Preference is given to applicants who have made a contact in the AM mode, but is not required.

Award: Scholarship for use in freshman, sophomore, junior, or senior years; not renewable. *Number:* 1. *Amount:* $1000.

Eligibility Requirements: Applicant must be enrolled or expecting to enroll full-time at a four-year institution or university and must have an interest in amateur radio. Available to U.S. citizens.

Application Requirements: Application form. *Deadline:* January 31.

Contact: Ms. Mary Hobart, Secretary
    Phone: 860-594-0397
    E-mail: k1mmh@arrl.org

JACKSON COUNTY ARA SCHOLARSHIP
• *See page 739*

JAMES COTHRAN, KD3NI, SCHOLARSHIP
• *See page 739*

K2TEO MARTIN J. GREEN SR. MEMORIAL SCHOLARSHIP

Available to students with a general amateur license for radio operation. Preference given to students from a ham family. Nonrenewable award for use in undergraduate years.

Award: Scholarship for use in freshman, sophomore, junior, or senior years; not renewable. *Number:* 1. *Amount:* $1000.

Eligibility Requirements: Applicant must be enrolled or expecting to enroll full-time at a four-year institution or university and must have an interest in amateur radio. Available to U.S. citizens.

Application Requirements: Application form. *Deadline:* January 31.

Contact: Ms. Mary Hobart, Secretary
    Phone: 860-594-0397
    E-mail: k1mmh@arrl.org

L.B. CEBIK, W4RNL, AND JEAN CEBIK, N4TZP, MEMORIAL SCHOLARSHIP

One $1000 award is available to a student with a Technician class or higher radio license. Must attend a four-year college or university.

Award: Scholarship for use in freshman, sophomore, junior, or senior years; not renewable. *Number:* 1. *Amount:* $1000.

Eligibility Requirements: Applicant must be enrolled or expecting to enroll full- or part-time at a four-year institution or university and must have an interest in amateur radio. Available to U.S. citizens.

Application Requirements: Application form. *Deadline:* January 31.

Contact: Ms. Mary Hobart, Secretary
    Phone: 860-594-0397
    E-mail: k1mmh@arrl.org

LOUISIANA MEMORIAL SCHOLARSHIP

One $750 award is available to a resident of Louisiana or a student studying in Louisiana who possesses a technician class or higher amateur radio license. Must be studying at a four-year college or university and maintain a minimum 3.0 GPA.

Award: Scholarship for use in freshman, sophomore, junior, or senior years; not renewable. *Number:* 1. *Amount:* $750.

Eligibility Requirements: Applicant must be enrolled or expecting to enroll full- or part-time at a four-year institution or university and must have an interest in amateur radio. Applicant must have 3.0 GPA or higher. Available to U.S. citizens.

Application Requirements: Application form. *Deadline:* January 31.

Contact: Ms. Mary Hobart, Secretary
Phone: 860-594-0397
E-mail: k1mmh@arrl.org

MARY LOU BROWN SCHOLARSHIP

• See page 739

NEW ENGLAND FEMARA SCHOLARSHIPS

• See page 739

NORMAN E. STROHMEIER, W2VRS, MEMORIAL SCHOLARSHIP

• See page 739

PEORIA AREA AMATEUR RADIO CLUB SCHOLARSHIP

• See page 739

RICHARD W. BENDICKSEN, N7ZL, MEMORIAL SCHOLARSHIP

One $2000 award available to a student with any active amateur radio license attending a four-year college or university.

Award: Scholarship for use in freshman, sophomore, junior, or senior years; not renewable. *Number:* 1. *Amount:* $2000.

Eligibility Requirements: Applicant must be enrolled or expecting to enroll full- or part-time at a four-year institution or university and must have an interest in amateur radio. Available to U.S. citizens.

Application Requirements: Application form. *Deadline:* January 31.

Contact: Ms. Mary Hobart, Secretary
Phone: 860-594-0397
E-mail: k1mmh@arrl.org

SCHOLARSHIP OF THE MORRIS RADIO CLUB OF NEW JERSEY

One $1000 award available to a student who possesses a technician class or higher amateur radio license and attends a four-year college or university.

Award: Scholarship for use in freshman, sophomore, junior, or senior years; not renewable. *Number:* 1. *Amount:* $1000.

Eligibility Requirements: Applicant must be enrolled or expecting to enroll full- or part-time at a four-year institution or university and must have an interest in amateur radio. Available to U.S. citizens.

Application Requirements: Application form. *Deadline:* January 31.

Contact: Ms. Mary Hobart, Secretary
Phone: 860-594-0397
E-mail: k1mmh@arrl.org

SIX METER CLUB OF CHICAGO SCHOLARSHIP

• See page 740

TED, W4VHF, AND ITICE, K4LVV, GOLDTHORPE SCHOLARSHIP

• See page 577

THOMAS W. PORTER, W8KYZ, SCHOLARSHIP HONORING MICHAEL DAUGHERTY, W8LSE

• See page 740

TOM AND JUDITH COMSTOCK SCHOLARSHIP

• See page 740

WAYNE NELSON, KB4UT, MEMORIAL SCHOLARSHIP

• See page 740

WILLIAM BENNETT, W7PHO, MEMORIAL SCHOLARSHIP

• See page 740

YANKEE CLIPPER CONTEST CLUB YOUTH SCHOLARSHIP

• See page 740

YOU'VE GOT A FRIEND IN PENNSYLVANIA SCHOLARSHIP

• See page 540

ZACHARY TAYLOR STEVENS SCHOLARSHIP

• See page 740

ASIAN PACIFIC COMMUNITY FUND

http://www.apcf.org/

ROYAL BUSINESS BANK SCHOLARSHIP PROGRAM

• See page 577

ASIAN REPORTER

http://www.arfoundation.net/

ASIAN REPORTER SCHOLARSHIP

• See page 577

ASSURED LIFE ASSOCIATION

http://assuredlife.org

ASSURED LIFE ASSOCIATION ENDOWMENT SCHOLARSHIP PROGRAM

• See page 540

AUTHOR SERVICES, INC.

http://www.writersofthefuture.com/

L. RON HUBBARD'S ILLUSTRATORS OF THE FUTURE CONTEST

An ongoing competition for new and amateur artists judged by professional artists. Eligible submissions consist of three science fiction or fantasy illustrations. Prize amount ranges from $500 to $5000. Quarterly deadlines: December 31, March 31, June 30 and September 30. All entrants retain rights to artwork.

Award: Prize for use in freshman, sophomore, junior, senior, graduate, or postgraduate years; not renewable. *Number:* 12. *Amount:* $500–$5000.

Eligibility Requirements: Applicant must be enrolled or expecting to enroll full- or part-time at a two-year or four-year or technical institution or university and must have an interest in art. Available to U.S. and non-U.S. citizens.

Application Requirements: *Deadline:* continuous.

Contact: Joni Labaqui, Contest Administrator
Author Services, Inc.
7051 Hollywood Blvd.
Los Angeles, CA 90028
Phone: 323-466-3310
E-mail: contests@authorservicesinc.com

L. RON HUBBARD'S WRITERS OF THE FUTURE CONTEST

An ongoing competition for new and amateur writers judged by professional writers. Eligible submissions are short stories and novelettes of science fiction or fantasy. Deadline varies and prize amount ranges from $500 to $5000.

Award: Prize for use in freshman, sophomore, junior, senior, graduate, or postgraduate years; not renewable. *Number:* 12. *Amount:* $500–$5000.

Eligibility Requirements: Applicant must be enrolled or expecting to enroll full- or part-time at a two-year or four-year or technical institution or university and must have an interest in writing. Available to U.S. and non-U.S. citizens.

Application Requirements: *Deadline:* continuous.

Contact: Joni Labaqui, Contest Administrator
Author Services, Inc.
7051 Hollywood Blvd.
Los Angeles, CA 90028
Phone: 323-466-3310
E-mail: contests@authorservicesinc.com

AUTOMOTIVE HALL OF FAME
http://www.automotivehalloffame.org/

AUTOMOTIVE HALL OF FAME EDUCATIONAL FUNDS

Award for full-time undergraduate and graduate students pursuing studies in automotive and related technologies. Must submit two letters of recommendation supporting automotive interests. Minimum 3.0 cumulative GPA required. Student must study in the United States and either be a United States citizen or on a student visa.

Award: Scholarship for use in freshman, sophomore, junior, senior, or graduate years; renewable. *Number:* 20. *Amount:* $500–$2000.

Eligibility Requirements: Applicant must be enrolled or expecting to enroll full-time at a two-year or four-year or technical institution or university and must have an interest in automotive. Applicant must have 3.0 GPA or higher. Available to U.S. and non-U.S. citizens.

Application Requirements: Application form, essay, financial need analysis, recommendations or references, self-addressed stamped envelope with application, transcript. *Deadline:* June 30.

Contact: Sue Lauster
Automotive Hall of Fame
21400 Oakwood Boulevard
Dearborn, MI 48124-4078
Phone: 313-240-4000
Fax: 313-240-8641

AWEBER COMMUNICATIONS
http://www.aweber.com/

AWEBER DEVELOPING FUTURES SCHOLARSHIP
• *See page 672*

BABE RUTH LEAGUE INC.
http://www.baberuthleague.org/

BABE RUTH SCHOLARSHIP PROGRAM

Program to provide assistance to individuals (former Babe Ruth Baseball, Cal Ripken Baseball or Babe Ruth Softball players) who plan on furthering their education beyond high school. Outstanding student athletes will receive $1000 each towards their college tuition.

Award: Scholarship for use in freshman year; not renewable. *Number:* 1–10. *Amount:* $1000.

Eligibility Requirements: Applicant must be high school student; planning to enroll or expecting to enroll full- or part-time at a two-year or four-year institution or university and must have an interest in athletics/sports. Available to U.S. citizens.

Application Requirements: Application form, application form may be submitted online (http://www.baberuthleague.org), recommendations or references, transcript. *Deadline:* September 1.

Contact: Mr. Joseph Smiegocki, Scholarship Committee
Phone: 800-880-3142
Fax: 609-695-2505
E-mail: info@baberuthleague.org

BARONE DEFENSE FIRM
http://baronedefensefirm.com/

BARONE DEFENSE FIRM WIN BACK YOUR LIFE SCHOLARSHIP
• *See page 578*

BMI FOUNDATION, INC.
http://www.bmifoundation.org/

JOHN LENNON SCHOLARSHIPS

Scholarships available to songwriters and composers age 17 to 24 currently attending a U.S. college or university. The submitted work must be an original song with lyrics accompanied by whatever instrumentation is chosen by the applicant.

Award: Scholarship for use in freshman, sophomore, junior, senior, graduate, or postgraduate years; not renewable. *Number:* 3. *Amount:* $5000–$10,000.

Eligibility Requirements: Applicant must be age 17-24; enrolled or expecting to enroll full- or part-time at a two-year or four-year or technical institution or university and must have an interest in music. Available to U.S. citizens.

Application Requirements: Application form. *Deadline:* February 1.

Contact: Ms. Samantha Cox, Director
BMI Foundation, Inc.
7 World Trade Center
250 Greenwich Street
New York, NY 10007-0030
Phone: 212-220-3103
E-mail: info@bmifoundation.org

NASHVILLE SONGWRITING SCHOLARSHIP

The Nashville Songwriting Scholarship is an annual competition established in 2015 to encourage and support aspiring country music songwriters nationwide. The award commemorates Broadcast Music, Inc. (BMI)'s 75th Anniversary year and pays homage to musical epicenter and "Songwriting Capital of the World," Nashville, Tennessee. A $5,000 scholarship is awarded for the best original song entry in any of the following genres: Americana, blues, bluegrass, contemporary Christian, country, folk, and roots. GRAMMY-winning recording artist and BMI songwriter Kacey Musgraves has endorsed the competition.

Award: Scholarship for use in freshman, sophomore, junior, senior, graduate, or postgraduate years; not renewable. *Number:* 1. *Amount:* $5000.

Eligibility Requirements: Applicant must be enrolled or expecting to enroll full- or part-time at a two-year or four-year or technical institution or university and must have an interest in music. Available to U.S. and non-U.S. citizens.

Application Requirements: Application form. *Deadline:* February 1.

Contact: Clay Bradley
BMI Foundation, Inc.
7 World Trade Center
250 Greenwich Street
New York, NY 10007
Phone: 212-220-3103
E-mail: info@bmifoundation.org

PEERMUSIC LATIN SCHOLARSHIP

Award for the best song or instrumental work in any Latin genre. The competition is open to songwriters and composers between the ages of 17 and 24 who are current students at colleges and universities in the United States or Puerto Rico. Must submit an original work. Applicants must not have had any musical work commercially recorded or distributed.

Award: Scholarship for use in freshman, sophomore, junior, senior, graduate, or postgraduate years; not renewable. *Number:* 1. *Amount:* $5000.

Eligibility Requirements: Applicant must be age 17-24; enrolled or expecting to enroll full- or part-time at a two-year or four-year or technical institution or university and must have an interest in music. Available to U.S. citizens.

Application Requirements: Application form. *Deadline:* February 1.

Contact: Carolina Arenas, Director
BMI Foundation, Inc.
7 World Trade Center
250 Greenwich Street
New York, NY 10007-0030
Phone: 212-220-3103
E-mail: info@bmifoundation.org

BOETTCHER FOUNDATION

http://www.boettcherfoundation.org/

BOETTCHER FOUNDATION SCHOLARSHIP
• *See page 741*

BOUNCE ENERGY

http://www.bounceenergy.com

BE MORE SCHOLARSHIP
• *See page 578*

BRAINLY, INC.

http://www.brainly.com

BRAINLY EVERYONE KNOWS SOMETHING SCHOLARSHIP
• *See page 578*

BRANDES INVESTMENT PARTNERS L.P.

https://www.brandes.com

BRANDES SCHOLARSHIP PROGRAM
• *See page 578*

BREYER LAW OFFICES PC

http://www.breyerlaw.com/

2017 HUSBAND AND WIFE LAW TEAM ARIZONA SCHOLARSHIP
• *See page 578*

BY KIDS FOR KIDS, CO.

http://bkfkeducation.com

CTIA WIRELESS FOUNDATION DRIVE SMART DIGITAL SHORT CONTEST
• *See page 579*

SALLIE MAE® MAKE COLLEGE HAPPEN CHALLENGE
• *See page 579*

CALIFORNIA INTERSCHOLASTIC FEDERATION

http://www.cifstate.org/

CIF SCHOLAR-ATHLETE OF THE YEAR
• *See page 742*

CIF SPIRIT OF SPORT AWARD
• *See page 742*

CALIFORNIA JUNIOR MISS SCHOLARSHIP PROGRAM

http://www.ajm.org/

CALIFORNIA JUNIOR MISS SCHOLARSHIP PROGRAM
• *See page 742*

CAMP NETWORK

https://www.campnetwork.com/

CAMP COUNSELOR APPRECIATION SCHOLARSHIP
• *See page 580*

CANADA ICELAND FOUNDATION INC. SCHOLARSHIPS

http://www.canadaicelandfoundation.com/

CANADA ICELAND FOUNDATION SCHOLARSHIP PROGRAM
One scholarship of $500, to be awarded annually. To be offered to a university student studying towards a degree in any Canadian university.

Award: Scholarship for use in freshman, sophomore, junior, senior, or graduate years; not renewable. *Number:* 1. *Amount:* $500.

Eligibility Requirements: Applicant must be enrolled or expecting to enroll full-time at an institution or university; studying in Alberta, British Columbia, Manitoba, New Brunswick, Newfoundland, Nova Scotia, Ontario, Quebec, Saskatchewan and must have an interest in leadership. Available to Canadian citizens.

Application Requirements: Application form, community service, recommendations or references, test scores, transcript. *Deadline:* varies.

Contact: Karen Bowman, Administrative Assistant
　　　Phone: 204-284-5686
　　　Fax: 204-284-7099
　　　E-mail: karen@lh-inc.ca

CARING.COM

http://caring.com

CARING.COM STUDENT-CAREGIVER BI-ANNUAL SCHOLARSHIP
• *See page 580*

CENTER FOR REINTEGRATION

www.reintegration.com

BAER REINTEGRATION SCHOLARSHIP
• *See page 580*

CGTRADER

https://www.cgtrader.com/

ANNUAL CGTRADER SCHOLARSHIP
• *See page 580*

CHRISTINE GERTSCH ATTORNEY AT LAW

https://www.ctdomesticviolencehelp.com/

CONNECTICUT DOMESTIC VIOLENCE 2017 LEGISLATION REFORM SCHOLARSHIP
• *See page 581*

CHRISTOPHERS

http://www.christophers.org/

POSTER CONTEST FOR HIGH SCHOOL STUDENTS
Contest invites students in grades nine through twelve to interpret the theme "You can make a difference." Posters must include this statement and illustrate the idea that one person can change the world for the better. Judging is based on overall impact, content, originality, and artistic merit. More information can be found at http://www.christophers.org.

Award: Prize for use in freshman, sophomore, junior, or senior years; not renewable. *Number:* up to 8. *Amount:* $100–$1000.

Eligibility Requirements: Applicant must be high school student; planning to enroll or expecting to enroll full-time at a four-year institution or university and must have an interest in art. Available to U.S. citizens.

Application Requirements: Application form, entry in a contest, poster. *Deadline:* February 13.

Contact: Sarah Holinski, Youth Coordinator
Christophers
5 Hanover Square, 22nd Floor
New York, NY 10004
Phone: 212-759-4050 Ext. 240
Fax: 212-838-5073
E-mail: youth@christophers.org

VIDEO CONTEST FOR COLLEGE STUDENTS

Contest requires college students to use any style or format to express the following theme "One person can make a difference." Entries can be up to 5 minutes in length and must be submitted in standard, full-sized DVD format. Entries will be judged on content, artistic and technical proficiency, and adherence to contest rules. More information is available at http://www.christophers.org.

Award: Prize for use in freshman, sophomore, junior, senior, graduate, or postgraduate years; not renewable. *Number:* 2–6. *Amount:* $1000–$2000.

Eligibility Requirements: Applicant must be enrolled or expecting to enroll full- or part-time at a two-year or four-year or technical institution or university and must have an interest in art. Available to U.S. citizens.

Application Requirements: Application form, DVD, entry in a contest. *Deadline:* February 13.

Contact: Sarah Holinski, Youth Coordinator
Christophers
5 Hanover Square, 22nd Floor
New York, NY 10004
Phone: 212-759-4050 Ext. 240
Fax: 212-838-5073
E-mail: s.holinski@christophers.org

CHURCH HILL CLASSICS

http://www.diplomaframe.com/

FRAME MY FUTURE SCHOLARSHIP CONTEST
• *See page 581*

CLAGS: CENTER FOR LGBTQ STUDIES

http://www.clags.org/

SYLVIA RIVERA AWARD IN TRANSGENDER STUDIES

This award, which honors the memory of Rivera, a transgender activist, will be given for the best book or article to appear in transgender studies this year (2015). Applications may be submitted by the author of the work or by nomination.

Award: Prize for use in freshman, sophomore, junior, senior, graduate, or postgraduate years; not renewable. *Number:* 1. *Amount:* $1000.

Eligibility Requirements: Applicant must be enrolled or expecting to enroll full- or part-time at a two-year or four-year institution or university and must have an interest in LGBT issues or writing. Available to U.S. and non-U.S. citizens.

Application Requirements: Application form. *Deadline:* June 1.

Contact: Noam Parness, Membership and Fellowships Coordinator
Phone: 212-817-1958
E-mail: clagsfellowships@gmail.com

UNDERGRADUATE STUDENT PAPER AWARD

Each year, CLAGS sponsors a student paper competition open to all undergraduate students enrolled in the CUNY or SUNY system. A cash prize of $250 awarded to the best paper written in a City University of New York or State University of New York undergraduate class on a topic related to gay, lesbian, bisexual, queer, or transgender experiences. Essays should be between 12 and 30 pages, well thought-out, and fully realized.

Award: Prize for use in freshman, sophomore, junior, or senior years; not renewable. *Number:* 1. *Amount:* $250.

Eligibility Requirements: Applicant must be enrolled or expecting to enroll full- or part-time at a four-year institution or university and must have an interest in LGBT issues. Available to U.S. and non-U.S. citizens.

Application Requirements: Essay. *Deadline:* June 1.

Contact: Noam Parness, Membership and Fellowships Coordinator
Phone: 212-817-1958
E-mail: clagsfellowships@gmail.com

CODA INTERNATIONAL

http://www.coda-international.org

MILLIE BROTHER SCHOLARSHIP FOR CHILDREN OF DEAF ADULTS
• *See page 581*

COGBURN LAW OFFICES

http://cogburnlaw.com/

$5,000 ADVERSITY SCHOLARSHIP
• *See page 581*

COLLEGE ASSISTANCE MIGRANT PROGRAM

https://www.stedwards.edu

COLLEGE ASSISTANCE MIGRANT PROG.
• *See page 581*

COLLEGEBOUND FOUNDATION

http://www.collegeboundfoundation.org/

HY ZOLET STUDENT ATHLETE SCHOLARSHIP
• *See page 745*

COLLEGEWEEKLIVE

http://www.collegeweeklive.com/

COLLEGEWEEKLIVE.COM SCHOLARSHIP

$1000 to $5000 scholarship to students for visiting colleges on CollegeWeekLive. Students must submit an online registration and visit 5 schools on the site. For more information, see website http://www.collegeweeklive.com/sign-up?refcode=PAR_PETERSONS_SCHOLARSHIP

Award: Scholarship for use in freshman year; not renewable. *Number:* 1–15. *Amount:* $1000–$5000.

Eligibility Requirements: Applicant must be enrolled or expecting to enroll full- or part-time at a two-year or four-year or technical institution or university and must have an interest in writing. Available to U.S. and non-U.S. citizens.

Application Requirements: Application form, application form may be submitted online(collegeweeklive.com/sign-up?refcode=PAR_PETERSONS_SCHOLARSHIP). *Deadline:* varies.

Contact: Melissa King, Vice President, Marketing
CollegeWeekLive
100 Crescent Road
Needham, MA 02494
Phone: 617-938-6018
E-mail: info@collegeweeklive.com

COLORADO MASONS BENEVOLENT FUND ASSOCIATION

http://www.cmbfa.org/scholarship

COLORADO MASONS BENEVOLENT FUND SCHOLARSHIPS
• *See page 581*

COLUMBUS CITIZENS FOUNDATION

http://www.columbuscitizensfd.org/scholarships/scholarships.html

COLUMBUS CITIZENS FOUNDATION COLLEGE SCHOLARSHIP PROGRAM
• *See page 582*

COMMUNITY BANKERS ASSOCIATION OF ILLINOIS

http://www.cbai.com/

COMMUNITY BANKERS ASSOC OF IL CHILD OF A BANKER SCHOLARSHIP
• *See page 541*

COMMUNITY BANKERS ASSOC. OF IL ESSAY CONTEST
• *See page 582*

COMMUNITY FOUNDATION FOR GREATER ATLANTA, INC.

http://cfgreateratlanta.org/

DREAMS SQUARED SCHOLARSHIP
• *See page 582*

CONTEMPORARY RECORD SOCIETY

http://www.crsnews.org/

CONTEMPORARY RECORD SOCIETY NATIONAL COMPETITION FOR PERFORMING ARTISTS

There are no age restrictions to participate. Applicant may submit one performance tape of varied length including music of any period of music with each application. The applicant may use any number of instrumentalists and voices. First prize is a commercial distribution of the winner's recording. Application fee is $50 for each recording submitted. Submit self-addressed stamped envelope with the application for returns. The winning applicant will participate in a CD recording released by CRS. (This prize is not applicable toward tuition.)

Award: Prize for use in freshman, sophomore, junior, senior, graduate, or postgraduate years; not renewable. *Number:* 1. *Amount:* $2000–$6000.

Eligibility Requirements: Applicant must be enrolled or expecting to enroll full- or part-time at a two-year or four-year or technical institution or university and must have an interest in music/singing. Available to U.S. and non-U.S. citizens.

Application Requirements: Application form. *Fee:* $50. *Deadline:* March 30.

Contact: Ms. Caroline Hunt, Administrator
Contemporary Record Society
724 Winchester Rd
Broomall, PA 19008
Phone: 610-2059897
E-mail: crsnews@verizon.net

NATIONAL COMPETITION FOR COMPOSERS' RECORDINGS

First prize is a CD recording grant (not tuition). Limited to nine performers and twenty-five minutes duration. Works with additional performers will be accepted provided there is a release of the original recorded master for CD reproduction. Must submit a musical composition that is non-published and not commercially recorded. Limit of 5 works per applicant.

Award: Prize for use in freshman, sophomore, junior, senior, graduate, or postgraduate years; not renewable. *Number:* 1. *Amount:* $2000–$6000.

Eligibility Requirements: Applicant must be enrolled or expecting to enroll full- or part-time at a two-year or four-year or technical institution or university and must have an interest in music/singing. Available to U.S. and non-U.S. citizens.

Application Requirements: Application form. *Fee:* $50. *Deadline:* March 30.

Contact: Ms. Caroline Hunt, Administrator
Contemporary Record Society
724 Winchester Rd
Broomall, PA 19008
Phone: 610-2059897
E-mail: crsnews@verizon.net

COUNCIL OF CITIZENS WITH LOW VISION INTERNATIONAL C/O AMERICAN COUNCIL OF THE BLIND

http://www.cclvi.org/

FRED SCHEIGERT SCHOLARSHIP
• *See page 582*

CROSSLITES

http://www.crosslites.com/

CROSSLITES SCHOLARSHIP AWARD

Scholarship contest is open to high school, college and graduate school students. There are no minimum GPA, SAT, ACT, GMAT, GRE, or any other test score requirements.

Award: Prize for use in freshman, sophomore, junior, senior, or graduate years; not renewable. *Number:* 33. *Amount:* $100–$2500.

Eligibility Requirements: Applicant must be enrolled or expecting to enroll full- or part-time at a two-year or four-year or technical institution or university and must have an interest in writing. Available to U.S. and non-U.S. citizens.

Application Requirements: Application form, entry in a contest, essay. *Deadline:* December 15.

Contact: Samuel Certo, Scholarship Committee
CrossLites
1000 Holt Avenue
Winter Park, FL 32789

CSA MEDICAL SUPPLY

https://csamedicalsupply.com

CSA MEDICAL SUPPLY COLLEGE SCHOLARSHIP
• *See page 583*

THE DALLAS FOUNDATION

http://www.dallasfoundation.org/

THE LANDON RUSNAK SCHOLARSHIP
• *See page 750*

DEMAS LAW GROUP, P.C.

http://www.injury-attorneys.com/

DEMAS LAW GROUP SCHOLARSHIP
• *See page 583*

DIAMANTE, INC.

http://www.diamanteinc.org/

LATINO DIAMANTE SCHOLARSHIP FUND
• *See page 583*

DIBELLA LAW OFFICES, P.C.

http://www.dibellalawoffice.com

2017 DIBELLA LAW OFFICES, P.C. SCHOLARSHIP
• *See page 583*

DIRECT ENERGY

https://www.directenergy.com/

DIRECT ENERGY LIVE BRIGHTER SCHOLARSHIP
• *See page 584*

DIRECTTEXTBOOK.COM

http://www.DirectTextbook.com

DIRECTTEXTBOOK.COM 2016 HAIKU SCHOLARSHIP CONTEST
• *See page 584*

DIRECTTEXTBOOK.COM "SHINE" PHOTO ESSAY CONTEST
• *See page 584*

DISABLEDPERSON INC. COLLEGE SCHOLARSHIP

http://www.disabledperson.com/

DISABLEDPERSON INC. NATIONAL COLLEGE SCHOLARSHIP AWARD FOR COLLEGE STUDENTS WITH DISABILITIES
• *See page 584*

DIXIE BOYS BASEBALL

http://www.dixie.org/boys

DIXIE BOYS BASEBALL BERNIE VARNADORE SCHOLARSHIP PROGRAM
• *See page 752*

DIXIE YOUTH SCHOLARSHIP PROGRAM
• *See page 752*

DOLLARS 4 TIC SCHOLARS

http://www.dollars4ticscholars.org/

DOLLARS 4 TIC SCHOLARS TOURETTE SYNDROME SCHOLARSHIP
• *See page 585*

DOLPHIN SCHOLARSHIP FOUNDATION

http://www.dolphinscholarship.org/

DOLPHIN SCHOLARSHIPS
• *See page 585*

DUDLEY DEBOSIER INJURY LAWYERS

http://www.dudleydebosier.com/home

DUDLEY DEBOSIER SCHOLARSHIP PROGRAM
• *See page 585*

DUKE ENERGY CORPORATION

http://www.duke-energy.com/

DUKE ENERGY SCHOLARS PROGRAM
• *See page 568*

ELEARNERS.COM

http://www.elearners.com

ELEARNERS ONLINE STUDENT SCHOLARSHIP
• *See page 585*

ELIE WIESEL FOUNDATION FOR HUMANITY

http://www.eliewieselfoundation.org/

ELIE WIESEL PRIZE IN ETHICS ESSAY CONTEST
Scholarship for full-time junior or senior at a four-year accredited college or university in the United States. Up to five awards are granted.
Award: Prize for use in junior or senior years; not renewable. *Number:* up to 5. *Amount:* $500–$5000.

Eligibility Requirements: Applicant must be enrolled or expecting to enroll full-time at a four-year institution or university and must have an interest in writing. Available to U.S. and non-U.S. citizens.

Application Requirements: Application form, entry in a contest, essay, self-addressed stamped envelope with application, student entry form, faculty sponsor form. *Deadline:* December 3.

Contact: Ms. Chelsea Friedman, Essay Contest Coordinator
Elie Wiesel Foundation for Humanity
555 Madison Avenue, 20th Floor
New York, NY 10022
Phone: 212-490-7788
Fax: 212-490-6006
E-mail: chelsea@eliewieselfoundation.org

ELIZABETH GREENSHIELDS FOUNDATION

http://www.elizabethgreenshieldsfoundation.org

THE ELIZABETH GREENSHIELDS FOUNDATION GRANT
• *See page 586*

ELKS NATIONAL FOUNDATION

http://www.elks.org/enf

ELKS NATIONAL FOUNDATION MOST VALUABLE STUDENT SCHOLARSHIP CONTEST
Five hundred awards ranging from $1,000 to $12,500 per year, renewable for four years, are allocated nationally by state quota for graduating high school seniors. Based on scholarship, leadership, and financial need. Must be a U.S. citizen pursuing a 4-year degree full-time at an accredited, degree granting U.S. college or university. For more information, visit http://www.elks.org/scholars.

Award: Scholarship for use in freshman, sophomore, junior, or senior years; renewable. *Number:* 500. *Amount:* $4000–$50,000.

Eligibility Requirements: Applicant must be high school student; planning to enroll or expecting to enroll full-time at a four-year institution or university and must have an interest in leadership. Available to U.S. citizens.

Application Requirements: Application form, community service, essay, financial need analysis. *Deadline:* November 27.

Contact: Elks National Foundation Scholarship Office
Elks National Foundation
2750 North Lakeview Avenue
Chicago, IL 60614-2256
Phone: 773-755-4732
E-mail: scholarship@elks.org

ENVIRONMENTAL LITIGATION GROUP P.C.

https://www.elglaw.com/

ENVIRONMENTAL LITIGATION GROUP, P.C. ASBESTOS SCHOLARSHIP
• *See page 586*

EQUALITY SCHOLARSHIP COLLABORATIVE

http://www.equalityscholarship.org

EQUALITY SCHOLARSHIPS FOR COMMUNITY COLLEGE TRANSFER STUDENTS
• *See page 586*

SCHOLARSHIPS FOR HIGH SCHOOL GRADUATES
• *See page 586*

ESSAYHUB

https://essayhub.com/

ESSAY WRITING CONTEST BY ESSAYHUB
• *See page 587*

ESSAYJOLT.COM

http://www.essayjolt.com/

ESSAYJOLT SCHOLARSHIP
• *See page 753*

FARAH & FARAH

http://www.farahandfarah.com/

FARAH & FARAH SCHOLARSHIP
• *See page 587*

FELDMAN & ROYLE, ATTORNEYS AT LAW

http://www.feldmanroyle.com/

AUTISM SCHOLARSHIPS
• *See page 587*

FELDMAN LAW FIRM PLLC

http://www.afphoenixcriminalattorney.com/

DISABLED VETERANS SCHOLARSHIP
• *See page 587*

FLORIDA PTA/PTSA

http://www.floridapta.org/

FLORIDA PTA/PTSA ANNUAL SCHOLARSHIP
• *See page 588*

FLORIDA WOMEN'S STATE GOLF ASSOCIATION

CLUB EMPLOYEES AND DEPENDENTS SCHOLARSHIP
• *See page 756*

FSGA SCHOLARS
• *See page 756*

SARAH E. HUNEYCUTT SCHOLARSHIP
• *See page 756*

FOREST ROBERTS THEATRE

http://www.nmu.edu/

MILDRED AND ALBERT PANOWSKI PLAYWRITING AWARD
Prize designed to encourage and stimulate artistic growth among playwrights. Winner receives a cash prize and a world premiere of their play.

Award: Prize for use in freshman, sophomore, junior, senior, graduate, or postgraduate years; not renewable. *Number:* 1. *Amount:* $2000.

Eligibility Requirements: Applicant must be enrolled or expecting to enroll full- or part-time at a two-year or four-year or technical institution or university and must have an interest in theater or writing. Available to U.S. and non-U.S. citizens.

Application Requirements: Application form, entry in a contest, manuscript in English, self-addressed stamped envelope with application. *Deadline:* October 31.

Contact: Matt Hudson, Playwriting Award Coordinator
Forest Roberts Theatre
Northern Michigan University
1401 Presque Isle Avenue
Marquette, MI 49855-5364
Phone: 906-227-2559
Fax: 906-227-2567

FOUNDATION FOR CHRISTIAN COLLEGE LEADERS

http://www.collegechristianleader.com/

FOUNDATION FOR COLLEGE CHRISTIAN LEADERS SCHOLARSHIP
• *See page 714*

FREEDOM ALLIANCE

https://freedomalliance.org

FREEDOM ALLIANCE SCHOLARSHIP FUND
• *See page 588*

FREEDOM FROM RELIGION FOUNDATION

http://www.ffrf.org/

FREEDOM FROM RELIGION FOUNDATION MICHAEL HAKEEM MEMORIAL ONGOING COLLEGE ESSAY COMPETITION
• *See page 714*

FREEDOM FROM RELIGION FOUNDATION WILLIAM J. SCHULZ MEMORIAL COLLEGE-BOUND HIGH SCHOOL SENIOR ESSAY COMPETITION
• *See page 714*

FUNNEWJERSEY.COM INC.

www.funnewjersey.com

FUNNEWJERSEY.COM SCHOLARSHIP
• *See page 588*

GAY ASIAN PACIFIC ALLIANCE FOUNDATION

http://gapafoundation.org/

GAPA SCHOLARSHIPS

The purpose of the Gay Asian Pacific Alliance (GAPA) Foundation Scholarship is to provide financial assistance to students in high school; undergraduate, graduate or professional school; or trade or vocational school who express activism in the Asian and Pacific Islander (API) and/or lesbian, gay, bisexual, transgender, and queer (LGBTQ) communities.

Award: Scholarship for use in freshman, sophomore, junior, senior, graduate, or postgraduate years; not renewable. *Number:* 3–5. *Amount:* $1000–$3000.

Eligibility Requirements: Applicant must be enrolled or expecting to enroll full- or part-time at a two-year or four-year or technical institution or university and must have an interest in leadership or LGBT issues. Available to U.S. and non-U.S. citizens.

Application Requirements: Application form, essay. *Deadline:* June 30.

Contact: Mr. Drew Ho, Philanthropy Co-Chair
    E-mail: programs@gapafoundation.org

GENERAL BOARD OF HIGHER EDUCATION AND MINISTRY

http://www.gbhem.org

THE REV. DR. KAREN LAYMAN GIFT OF HOPE: 21ST CENTURY SCHOLARS PROGRAM
• *See page 715*

GENERAL FEDERATION OF WOMEN'S CLUBS OF MASSACHUSETTS

http://www.gfwcma.org/

GENERAL FEDERATION OF WOMEN'S CLUBS OF MASSACHUSETTS NICKEL FOR NOTES MUSIC SCHOLARSHIP
• *See page 589*

GENERAL FEDERATION OF WOMEN'S CLUBS OF MASSACHUSETTS PENNIES FOR ART SCHOLARSHIP
• *See page 589*

GIFT BASKETS PLUS

www.giftbasketsplus.com

2017 HIGH SCHOOL GRADUATE SCHOLARSHIP CONTEST
• *See page 589*

GLAMOUR

http://www.glamour.com/

TOP 10 COLLEGE WOMEN COMPETITION

Female students with leadership experience on and off campus, excellence in field of study, and inspiring goals can apply for this competition. Winners will be awarded $3000 along with a trip to New York City. Must be a junior studying full-time with a minimum GPA of 3.0. in either the United States or Canada. Non-U.S. citizens may apply if attending U.S. postsecondary institutions.

Award: Prize for use in junior year; not renewable. *Number:* 10. *Amount:* $3000.

Eligibility Requirements: Applicant must be enrolled or expecting to enroll full-time at a four-year institution or university; female and must have an interest in leadership. Applicant must have 3.0 GPA or higher. Available to U.S. and non-U.S. citizens.

Application Requirements: Application form, essay, personal photograph, recommendations or references, transcript. *Deadline:* February 2.

Contact: Lynda Laux-Bachand, Reader Services Editor
    Glamour
    Four Times Square, 16th Floor
    New York, NY 10036-6593
    Phone: 212-286-6667
    Fax: 212-286-6922

GLENN MILLER BIRTHPLACE SOCIETY

http://www.glennmiller.org/

GLENN MILLER INSTRUMENTAL SCHOLARSHIP

One-time awards for high school seniors and college freshmen. Scholarships are awarded as competition prizes and must be used for any education-related expenses. Must submit 10-minute, high-quality audio tape of pieces selected for competition or those of similar style. Applicant is responsible for travel to and lodging during the competition.

Award: Scholarship for use in freshman year; not renewable. *Number:* 3. *Amount:* $1000–$4500.

Eligibility Requirements: Applicant must be high school student; planning to enroll or expecting to enroll full-time at a four-year institution or university and must have an interest in music/singing. Available to U.S. and non-U.S. citizens.

Application Requirements: Application form, entry in a contest, essay, performance tape or CD. *Deadline:* March 15.

Contact: Arlene Leonard, Secretary
    Glenn Miller Birthplace Society
    107 East Main Street, PO Box 61
    Clarinda, IA 51632-0061
    Phone: 712-542-2461
    Fax: 712-542-2461
    E-mail: gmbs@heartland.net

JACK PULLAN MEMORIAL SCHOLARSHIP

One scholarship for a male or female vocalist, awarded as competition prize and, to be used for any education-related expenses. Must submit 10 minute, high-quality audio tape of pieces selected for competition or those of similar style. Applicant is responsible for travel to and lodging during the competition. One-time award for high school seniors and college freshmen. More information on http://www.glennmiller.org/scholar.htm.

Award: Scholarship for use in freshman year; not renewable. *Number:* 1. *Amount:* $1000.

Eligibility Requirements: Applicant must be high school student; planning to enroll or expecting to enroll full-time at a four-year institution or university and must have an interest in music/singing. Available to U.S. and non-U.S. citizens.

Application Requirements: Application form, entry in a contest, essay, performance tape or CD. *Deadline:* March 15.

Contact: Arlene Leonard, Secretary
    Glenn Miller Birthplace Society
    107 East Main Street, PO Box 61
    Clarinda, IA 51632-0061
    Phone: 712-542-2461
    Fax: 712-542-2461
    E-mail: gmbs@heartland.net

RALPH BREWSTER VOCAL SCHOLARSHIP

One scholarship for a male or female vocalist, awarded as competition prize and, to be used for any education-related expenses. Must submit 10 minute, high-quality audio tape of pieces selected for competition or those of similar style. Applicant is responsible for travel to and lodging during the competition. One-time award for high school seniors and college freshmen.

Award: Scholarship for use in freshman year; not renewable. *Number:* 1. *Amount:* $2000.

Eligibility Requirements: Applicant must be high school student; planning to enroll or expecting to enroll full-time at a four-year institution or university and must have an interest in music/singing. Available to U.S. and non-U.S. citizens.

Application Requirements: Application form, entry in a contest, essay, performance tape of competition or concert quality (up to 5 minutes duration). *Deadline:* March 15.

Contact: Arlene Leonard, Secretary
Glenn Miller Birthplace Society
107 East Main Street, PO Box 61
Clarinda, IA 51632-0061
Phone: 712-542-2461
Fax: 712-542-2461
E-mail: gmbs@heartland.net

GLORIA BARRON PRIZE FOR YOUNG HEROES

http://www.barronprize.org/

GLORIA BARRON PRIZE FOR YOUNG HEROES

Award honors young people ages 8 to 18 who have shown leadership and courage in public service to people or to the planet. Award celebrates 25 young heroes each year, and the top fifteen winners each receive $5,000 to support their service work or higher education. For further information and to apply, see website at http://www.barronprize.org.

Award: Prize for use in freshman year; not renewable. *Number:* 1–15. *Amount:* $1–$5000.

Eligibility Requirements: Applicant must be age 8-18; enrolled or expecting to enroll full- or part-time at a two-year or four-year or technical institution or university and must have an interest in leadership. Available to U.S. and Canadian citizens.

Application Requirements: Application form, community service, essay, personal photograph. *Deadline:* April 15.

Contact: Barbara Ann Richman, Executive Director
Gloria Barron Prize for Young Heroes
PO Box 1470
Boulder, CO 80306
E-mail: director@barronprize.org

GOENNOUNCE, LLC

http://GoEnnounce.com/about

GOENNOUNCE YOURSELF $500 MONTHLY SCHOLARSHIP

• See page 589

GOLF COURSE SUPERINTENDENTS ASSOCIATION OF AMERICA

http://www.eifg.org/

GOLF COURSE SUPERINTENDENTS ASSOCIATION OF AMERICA LEGACY AWARD

• See page 544

JOSEPH S. GARSKE COLLEGIATE GRANT PROGRAM

• See page 544

GORDON LAW GROUP

https://www.gordonlawltd.com

GORDON LAW GROUP NEED-BASED SCHOLARSHIP

• See page 589

GRACO INC.

http://www.graco.com/

GRACO EXCELLENCE SCHOLARSHIP

• See page 569

GREATER KANAWHA VALLEY FOUNDATION

http://www.tgkvf.org/

KID'S CHANCE OF WEST VIRGINIA SCHOLARSHIP

• See page 759

WEST VIRGINIA GOLF ASSOCIATION FUND

• See page 761

GREATER SEATTLE BUSINESS ASSOCIATION

http://thegsba.org/

GSBA SCHOLARSHIP FUND

• See page 761

GREENHOUSE SCHOLARS

http://greenhousescholars.org/our-scholars/become-a-scholar/

GREENHOUSE SCHOLARS

• See page 590

GRUNGO COLARULO

https://gcinjurylaw.com/

GRUNGO COLARULO GIVING BACK TO THE COMMUNITY SCHOLARSHIP

• See page 590

HARNESS HORSE YOUTH FOUNDATION

http://www.hhyf.org/

CURT GREENE MEMORIAL SCHOLARSHIP

• See page 590

HARRINGTON FAMILY FOUNDATION

http://harringtonfamilyfoundation.org

OREGON COMMUNITY QUARTERBACK SCHOLARSHIP

• See page 590

HELEN DILLER FAMILY FOUNDATION

http://www.dillerteenawards.org

DILLER TEEN TIKKUN OLAM AWARDS

• See page 591

HENKEL CONSUMER ADHESIVES INC.

http://www.ducktapeclub.com/

DUCK BRAND DUCT TAPE "STUCK AT PROM" SCHOLARSHIP CONTEST

• See page 591

HISPANIC METROPOLITAN CHAMBER SCHOLARSHIPS

http://www.hmccoregon.com/

HISPANIC METROPOLITAN CHAMBER SCHOLARSHIPS
• *See page 592*

HORIZONS FOUNDATION

http://www.horizonsfoundation.org/

MARKOWSKI-LEACH SCHOLARSHIP

Scholarship of $1250 awarded to a student who attends San Francisco State University, Stanford University, or University of California, and self-identifies as lesbian, gay, bisexual, transgender, or queer. Recipient is chosen based on demonstrated promise for becoming a positive role model for other LGBTQ people. All prospective undergraduate and graduate students may apply. Students transferring to one of these universities are also encouraged to apply.

Award: Scholarship for use in freshman, sophomore, junior, or senior years; renewable. *Number:* 1. *Amount:* $1250.

Eligibility Requirements: Applicant must be enrolled or expecting to enroll full-time at a two-year or four-year or technical institution or university; studying in California and must have an interest in LGBT issues. Applicant must have 2.5 GPA or higher. Available to U.S. and Canadian citizens.

Application Requirements: Application form, essay, recommendations or references. *Deadline:* April 1.

Contact: Markowski-Leach Scholarship Committee
Horizons Foundation
PO Box 13315, PMB #206
Oakland, CA 94661-0315
E-mail: MLScholarships@gmail.com

HOSTESS COMMITTEE SCHOLARSHIPS/MISS AMERICA PAGEANT

http://www.missamerica.org/

MISS AMERICA COMMUNITY SERVICE SCHOLARSHIPS
• *See page 592*

MISS AMERICA ORGANIZATION COMPETITION SCHOLARSHIPS

Scholarship competition open to 70 contestants, each serving as state representative. Women will be judged in Private Interview, Swimsuit, Evening Wear and Talent competition. Other awards may be based on points assessed by judges during competitions. Upon reaching the National level, award values range from $2000 to $50,000. Additional awards not affecting the competition can be won with values from $1000 to $10,000.

Award: Prize for use in freshman, sophomore, junior, senior, or graduate years; not renewable. *Number:* 70. *Amount:* $2000–$50,000.

Eligibility Requirements: Applicant must be age 17-24; enrolled or expecting to enroll full- or part-time at a two-year or four-year or technical institution or university; female and must have an interest in beauty pageant. Available to U.S. citizens.

Application Requirements: Application form, entry in a contest. *Deadline:* varies.

Contact: Doreen Lindell Gordon, Controller and Scholarship Administrator
Phone: 609-345-7571 Ext. 27
Fax: 609-347-6079
E-mail: doreen@missamerica.org

MISS AMERICA SCHOLAR AWARD

$1000 award offered to one woman in each state, District of Columbia and U.S. Virgin Islands, competing at the state level, for academic excellence. Competition is opened only to those competing at the state level. Must submit official transcripts of the immediate prior two years (4 semesters) of academic study, along with application.

Award: Scholarship for use in freshman, sophomore, junior, senior, graduate, or postgraduate years; not renewable.

Eligibility Requirements: Applicant must be enrolled or expecting to enroll full- or part-time at a four-year institution or university; female and must have an interest in beauty pageant. Available to U.S. citizens.

Application Requirements: Application form, transcript. *Deadline:* varies.

Contact: Doreen Lindell Gordon, Controller and Scholarship Administrator
Phone: 609-345-7571 Ext. 27
Fax: 609-347-6079
E-mail: doreen@missamerica.org

HOUSTON COMMUNITY SERVICES

AZTECA SCHOLARSHIP
• *See page 592*

HOW TO WIN COLLEGE SCHOLARSHIPS

https://how2winscholarships.com

SAVOR SUMMER COLLEGE SCHOLARSHIP
• *See page 592*

HUBSHOUT

http://hubshout.com/

HUBSHOUT INTERNET MARKETING SCHOLARSHIP
• *See page 592*

HUMANA FOUNDATION

http://www.humanafoundation.org/

HUMANA FOUNDATION SCHOLARSHIP PROGRAM
• *See page 593*

INSTITUTE FOR JUSTICE

http://www.ij.org

LIBERTY IN ACTION ESSAY CONTEST: REMOVING BARRIERS TO ENTREPRENEURSHIP
• *See page 593*

INTERNATIONAL BOWLING CAMPUS YOUTH DEVELOPMENT

http://www.bowl.com/

GIFT FOR LIFE SCHOLARSHIP
• *See page 545*

USBC ALBERTA E. CROWE STAR OF TOMORROW AWARD

Award annually recognizes star qualities in a female USBC Youth member who competes in the sport of bowling. Star qualities include distinguished certified bowling performances on the local, state and national level, academic achievement and extra-curricular activities.

Award: Scholarship for use in freshman, sophomore, junior, or senior years; not renewable. *Number:* 1. *Amount:* $6000.

Eligibility Requirements: Applicant must be enrolled or expecting to enroll full-time at a two-year or four-year institution or university; female and must have an interest in bowling. Applicant must have 3.0 GPA or higher. Available to U.S. citizens.

Application Requirements: Application form, entry in a contest, recommendations or references, transcript. *Deadline:* December 1.

Contact: Roger Noordhoek, Senior Director Youth Marketing
International Bowling Campus Youth Development
621 Six Flags Dr.
Arlington, TX 76011
Phone: 800-514-2695 Ext. 8308
E-mail: contactus@ibcyouth.com

USBC ANNUAL ZEB SCHOLARSHIP
• *See page 593*

USBC CHUCK HALL STAR OF TOMORROW SCHOLARSHIP

Scholarship annually recognizes star qualities in a male USBC Youth member who competes in the sport of bowling. Award is given to a male high school senior or college student and must be a current USBC Youth or USBC member in good standing.

Award: Scholarship for use in freshman, sophomore, junior, or senior years; renewable. *Number:* 1. *Amount:* $6000.

Eligibility Requirements: Applicant must be enrolled or expecting to enroll full-time at a two-year or four-year institution or university; male and must have an interest in bowling. Applicant must have 3.0 GPA or higher. Available to U.S. citizens.

Application Requirements: Application form, recommendations or references, transcript. *Deadline:* December 1.

Contact: Roger Noordhoek, Senior Director Youth Marketing
International Bowling Campus Youth Development
621 Six Flags Dr.
Arlington, TX 76011
Phone: 800-514-2695 Ext. 8308
E-mail: contactus@ibcyouth.com

USBC EARL ANTHONY MEMORIAL SCHOLARSHIP
• *See page 545*

USBC YOUTH AMBASSADOR OF THE YEAR (M/F)

Annually recognizes one male and one female USBC Youth bowler for his/her exemplary contributions to the sport of bowling, academic accomplishments and community involvement.

Award: Scholarship for use in freshman year; not renewable. *Number:* 2. *Amount:* $1500.

Eligibility Requirements: Applicant must be high school student; planning to enroll or expecting to enroll full- or part-time at a four-year institution or university and must have an interest in bowling. Available to U.S. citizens.

Application Requirements: Application form, recommendations or references, transcript. *Deadline:* December 1.

Contact: Roger Noordhoek, Senior Director Youth Marketing
International Bowling Campus Youth Development
621 Six Flags Dr.
Arlington, TX 76011
Phone: 800-514-2695 Ext. 8308
E-mail: contactus@ibcyouth.com

INTERNATIONAL COLLEGE COUNSELORS

www.internationalcollegecounselors.com

INTERNATIONAL COLLEGE COUNSELORS SCHOLARSHIP
• *See page 593*

INTERNATIONAL DAIRY DELI BAKERY ASSOCIATION

http://www.iddba.org

INTERNATIONAL DAIRY DELI BAKERY ASSOCIATION'S SCHOLARSHIP FOR GROWING THE FUTURE
• *See page 594*

INTERNATIONAL FLIGHT SERVICES ASSOCIATION

http://www.ifsanet.com

AMI SCHOLARSHIP AWARD
• *See page 594*

INTERNATIONAL VOLUNTEER HQ

https://www.volunteerhq.org/

VOLUNTEER OF THE YEAR SCHOLARSHIP
• *See page 595*

IOWA STUDENT LOAN

http://www.IowaStudentLoan.org/

IOWA FINANCIAL KNOW-HOW CHALLENGE: SENIOR SCHOLARSHIP
• *See page 596*

ISEECARS.COM

http://www.iseecars.com/

ANNUAL ISEECARS FUTURE ENTREPRENEURS SCHOLARSHIP

iSeeCars.com will award $1,000 to a college student who has a demonstrated interest in entrepreneurship or has plans to become an entrepreneur. The scholarship will be awarded based on the application materials submitted by students.

Award: Scholarship for use in freshman, sophomore, junior, senior, graduate, or postgraduate years; not renewable. *Number:* 1. *Amount:* $1000.

Eligibility Requirements: Applicant must be enrolled or expecting to enroll full-time at a four-year institution or university; studying in Alabama, Alaska, Alberta, Arizona, Arkansas, California, Colorado, Connecticut, Delaware, District of Columbia, Florida, Georgia, Guam, Hawaii, Idaho, Illinois, Indiana, Iowa, Kansas, Kentucky, Louisiana, Maine, Maryland, Massachusetts, Michigan, Minnesota, Mississippi, Missouri, Montana, Nebraska, Nevada, New Hampshire, New Jersey, New Mexico, New York, North Carolina, North Dakota, Ohio, Oklahoma, Oregon, Pennsylvania, Puerto Rico, Rhode Island, South Carolina, South Dakota, Tennessee, Texas, Utah, Vermont, Virginia, Washington, West Virginia, Wisconsin, Wyoming and must have an interest in entrepreneurship. Available to U.S. and non-U.S. citizens.

Application Requirements: Application form, essay, personal photograph. *Deadline:* December 31.

Contact: Scholarship Coordinator
E-mail: team@iseecars.com

JACKIE ROBINSON FOUNDATION

http://www.jackierobinson.org/

JACKIE ROBINSON SCHOLARSHIP
• *See page 596*

JASON KALAFAT ATTORNEY AT LAW

https://criminallawyerwashingtondc.com/

JASON KALAFAT MAKE A DIFFERENCE SCHOLARSHIP
• *See page 596*

JOHN B. FABRIELE, III, LLC

https://www.fabrielelaw.com/

FABRIELE DISABILITY AWARENESS SCHOLARSHIP
• *See page 596*

JOHN F. AND ANNA LEE STACEY SCHOLARSHIP FUND

http://www.nationalcowboymuseum.org/

JOHN F. AND ANNA LEE STACEY SCHOLARSHIP FUND

Scholarships for artists who are high school graduates between the ages of 18 and 35, who are U.S. citizens, and whose work is devoted to the classical or conservative tradition of Western culture. Awards are for drawing or painting only. Must submit no more than six color digital images of work.

Award: Scholarship for use in freshman, sophomore, junior, senior, graduate, or postgraduate years; not renewable. *Number:* 3–5. *Amount:* $1000–$4000.

Eligibility Requirements: Applicant must be age 18-35; enrolled or expecting to enroll full- or part-time at a two-year or four-year or technical institution or university and must have an interest in art. Available to U.S. citizens.

Application Requirements: Application form. *Deadline:* February 1.

Contact: Ms. Melissa Owens, Registrar & Exhibits Coordinator
John F. and Anna Lee Stacey Scholarship Fund
National Cowboy and Western Heritage Museum
1700 NE 63rd Street
Oklahoma City, OK 73111
Phone: 405-478-2250 Ext. 220
Fax: 405-478-4714
E-mail: registrar@nationalcowboymuseum.org

JUNIOR ACHIEVEMENT

http://www.ja.org/

JOE FRANCOMANO SCHOLARSHIP
• See page 546

JUREWITZ LAW GROUP

http://www.jurewitz.com/

JUREWITZ LAW GROUP SCHOLARSHIP
• See page 596

KAUFMAN & STIGGER, PLLC

http://www.getthetiger.com/

THE ALBERTA C. KAUFMAN SCHOLARSHIP
• See page 597

KELLER LAW OFFICES

http://www.kellerlawoffices.com/

KELLER LAW OFFICES SCHOLARSHIP FOR HIGHER EDUCATION
• See page 597

KELLY & SOTO LAW

http://www.1800lawguys.com

KELLY & SOTO LAW SCHOLARSHIP PROGRAM
• See page 597

KELLY LAW TEAM

http://www.jkphoenixpersonalinjuryattorney.com/

DOWN SYNDROME SCHOLARSHIP
• See page 597

KIDGUARD

http://www.kidguard.com/

KIDGUARD FOR EDUCATION ESSAY SCHOLARSHIP FOR HIGH SCHOOL
• See page 598

KITCHEN GUIDES

http://www.kitchensguides.com/

SMART KITCHEN IMPROVEMENT SCHOLARSHIP BY KITCHEN GUIDES
• See page 598

KNIGHTS OF PYTHIAS

http://www.pythias.org/

KNIGHTS OF PYTHIAS POSTER CONTEST

Poster contest open to all high school students in the U.S. and Canada. Contestants must submit an original drawing. Eight winners are chosen. The winners are not required to attend institution of higher education.

Award: Prize for use in freshman year; not renewable. *Number:* 8. *Amount:* $100–$1000.

Eligibility Requirements: Applicant must be high school student; planning to enroll or expecting to enroll full- or part-time at a four-year institution or university and must have an interest in art. Available to U.S. and Canadian citizens.

Application Requirements: Entry in a contest. *Deadline:* April 30.

Contact: Alfred Saltzman, Supreme Secretary
Phone: 617-472-8800
Fax: 617-376-0363
E-mail: kop@earthlink.net

LADIES AUXILIARY TO THE VETERANS OF FOREIGN WARS

http://www.ladiesauxvfw.org/

YOUNG AMERICAN CREATIVE PATRIOTIC ART AWARDS PROGRAM

One-time awards for high school students in grades 9 through 12. Must submit an original work of art expressing their patriotism. First place state-level winners go on to national competition. Eight awards of varying amounts. Must reside in same state as sponsoring organization.

Award: Scholarship for use in freshman, sophomore, junior, or senior years; not renewable. *Number:* up to 8. *Amount:* $500–$10,000.

Eligibility Requirements: Applicant must be high school student; planning to enroll or expecting to enroll full-time at a two-year or four-year or technical institution or university; single and must have an interest in art. Available to U.S. citizens.

Application Requirements: Application form, artwork, entry in a contest. *Deadline:* March 31.

Contact: Connie Wahlen, Programs Coordinator
Phone: 816-561-8655
E-mail: cwahlen@ladiesauxvfw.org

LARSON JEWELERS

www.larsonjewelers.com

BAND WITH SUCCESS SCHOLARSHIP
• See page 598

LATIN AMERICAN EDUCATIONAL FOUNDATION

http://www.laef.org/

LATIN AMERICAN EDUCATIONAL FOUNDATION SCHOLARSHIPS
• See page 598

LAW OFFICE OF DAVID D. WHITE, PLLC

http://www.wm-attorneys.com/

ANNUAL TRAUMATIC BRAIN INJURY SCHOLARSHIPS
• See page 598

LAW OFFICE OF MATTHEW L. SHARP

https://mattsharplaw.com/

LAW OFFICE OF MATTHEW L. SHARP NEED-BASED SCHOLARSHIP
• See page 599

LAW OFFICE OF MATTHEW SHRUM

http://www.shrumlawoffice.com/

ANNUAL SINGLE MOTHERS SCHOLARSHIP
• See page 599

LAW OFFICES OF DAVID A. BLACK

http://www.dbphoenixcriminallawyer.com

ANNUAL HEARING IMPAIRED SCHOLARSHIP
• See page 599

LAW OFFICES OF JUDD S. NEMIRO, PLLC

http://www.jnphoenixfamilylawyer.com/

ANNUAL DYSLEXIA SCHOLARSHIP
• See page 599

LAW OFFICES OF RYAN J. TEGNELIA

http://www.sandiegocriminallawyerrt.com/

ANNUAL VETERANS WITH POST-TRAUMATIC STRESS SCHOLARSHIP
• See page 599

LAW OFFICES OF SHERYL R. RENTZ, P.C.

http://www.srrentzlaw.com/

2017 LAW OFFICES OF SHERYL R. RENTZ SCHOLARSHIP
• See page 600

LAW OFFICES OF THOMAS J. LAVIN

http://www.lawlavinflorida.com/

THOMAS J. LAVIN SCHOLARSHIP
• See page 600

LAW OFFICES OF TRAGOS, SARTES & TRAGOS

https://tragoslaw.com/

TRAGOS WRITE YOUR OWN LAW SCHOLARSHIP
• See page 600

LEAGUE FOUNDATION

http://www.leaguefoundation.org/

LEAGUE FOUNDATION ACADEMIC SCHOLARSHIP

The LEAGUE Foundation provides financial resources for America's Gay, Lesbian, Bisexual, and Transgender high school seniors entering their first year of institutions of higher learning. The scholarship application opens annually in January and closes in April with awards distributed in the summer of each year. For scholarship criteria: www.leaguefoundation.org.

Award: Scholarship for use in freshman year; not renewable. *Number:* 4–8. *Amount:* $1500–$2500.

Eligibility Requirements: Applicant must be high school student; planning to enroll or expecting to enroll full-time at a two-year or four-year or technical institution or university and must have an interest in LGBT issues. Applicant must have 3.0 GPA or higher. Available to U.S. and Canadian citizens.

Application Requirements: Application form, application form may be submitted online (http://www.leaguefoundation.org/scholarships/), college or university acceptance letter, community service, essay, personal photograph, recommendations or references, test scores, transcript. *Deadline:* April 30.

Contact: Mr. Jason Forsyth, Executive Director
LEAGUE Foundation
208 South Akard Street
Room 251012
Dallas, TX 75202
Phone: 214-757-3013
E-mail: info@leaguefoundation.org

LEE-JACKSON EDUCATIONAL FOUNDATION

http://www.lee-jackson.org/

LEE-JACKSON EDUCATIONAL FOUNDATION SCHOLARSHIP COMPETITION
• See page 768

LEPENDORF & SILVERSTEIN, P.C.

http://www.lependorf.com/

LEPENDORF & SILVERSTEIN, P.C. 2017 NEW JERSEY SCHOLARSHIP
• See page 600

LEP FOUNDATION FOR YOUTH EDUCATION

http://www.lepfoundation.org/applications

CURE—CANCER SUPPORT SCHOLARSHIP
• See page 600

JOHN LEPPING MEMORIAL SCHOLARSHIP
• See page 600

LIBERTY GRAPHICS INC.

http://www.lgtees.com

ANNUAL LIBERTY GRAPHICS ART CONTEST
• See page 768

THE LINCOLN FORUM

http://www.thelincolnforum.org/

PLATT FAMILY SCHOLARSHIP PRIZE ESSAY CONTEST

The Platt Family Scholarship Prize Essay Contest is designed for students who are full-time students in an American college or university. You do not have to be an American citizen, but you do need to be attending an AMERICAN COLLEGE OR UNIVERSITY during the eligibility period. For details, refer to website http://thelincolnforum.org/scholarship-essay-contest.php

Award: Prize for use in freshman, sophomore, junior, or senior years; not renewable. *Number:* 3. *Amount:* $500–$1500.

Eligibility Requirements: Applicant must be enrolled or expecting to enroll full-time at a two-year or four-year institution or university and must have an interest in writing. Available to U.S. and non-U.S. citizens.

Application Requirements: Entry in a contest, essay. *Deadline:* July 31.

Contact: Don McCue, Director
> *Phone:* 909-798-7632
> *E-mail:* archives@akspl.org

LIVE POETS SOCIETY AND JUST POETRY!!! MAGAZINE

http://www.highschoolpoetrycontest.com/

NATIONAL HIGH SCHOOL POETRY CONTEST
• *See page 601*

MAINE STATE SOCIETY FOUNDATION OF WASHINGTON, DC INC.

http://mainestatesociety.org/foundation/

MAINE STATE SOCIETY FOUNDATION SCHOLARSHIP
• *See page 601*

MAINOR WORTH INJURY LAWYERS

https://mainorwirth.com/

MAINOR WIRTH INJURY LAWYERS NEED-BASED SCHOLARSHIP
• *See page 601*

MANA DE SAN DIEGO

http://www.manasd.org/

MANA DE SAN DIEGO SYLVIA CHAVEZ MEMORIAL SCHOLARSHIP
• *See page 601*

MARTIN D. ANDREWS SCHOLARSHIP

http://www.mdascholarship.tripod.com/

MARTIN D. ANDREWS MEMORIAL SCHOLARSHIP FUND

One-time award for student seeking undergraduate or graduate degree. Recipient must have been in a Drum Corp for at least three years. Must submit essay and two recommendations. Must be U.S. citizen.

Award: Scholarship for use in freshman, sophomore, junior, senior, or graduate years; not renewable. *Number:* 2–5. *Amount:* $300–$1000.

Eligibility Requirements: Applicant must be enrolled or expecting to enroll full- or part-time at a two-year or four-year institution or university and must have an interest in drum corps. Available to U.S. citizens.

Application Requirements: Application form, essay. *Deadline:* June 1.

Contact: Peter Andrews, Scholarship Committee
Martin D. Andrews Scholarship
2069 Perkins Street
Bristol, CT 06010
Phone: 860-250-4757
E-mail: psandrews@charter.net

MARYLAND ASSOCIATION OF PRIVATE COLLEGES AND CAREER SCHOOLS

http://www.mapccs.org/

MARYLAND ASSOCIATION OF PRIVATE COLLEGES AND CAREER SCHOOLS SCHOLARSHIP
• *See page 602*

MATRIX HEALTH GROUP

http://www.matrixhealthgroup.com

JOE HOLIBAUGH MEMORIAL SCHOLARSHIP
• *See page 602*

MARK COATS MEMORIAL SCHOLARSHIP
• *See page 602*

RON NIEDERMAN MEMORIAL SCHOLARSHIP
• *See page 603*

TIM KENNEDY MEMORIAL SCHOLARSHIP
• *See page 603*

MCCURRY FOUNDATION INC.

http://www.mccurryfoundation.org/

MCCURRY FOUNDATION SCHOLARSHIP
• *See page 773*

MENSA FOUNDATION

http://mensafoundation.org

U.S. SCHOLARSHIP PROGRAM
• *See page 603*

MES FOUNDATION

http://www.mesfoundation.org

RICHARD H. PIERCE MEMORIAL SCHOLARSHIP
• *See page 603*

MINDSUMO

http://www.mindsumo.com

MINDSUMO 15-MINUTE SCHOLARSHIP
• *See page 603*

MINNESOTA MASONIC CHARITIES

http://www.mnmasoniccharities.org

MINNESOTA MASONIC CHARITIES SIGNATURE SCHOLARSHIP
• *See page 604*

MINNESOTA MASONIC CHARITIES UNDERGRADUATE SCHOLARSHIP
• *See page 604*

MITCHELL INSTITUTE
http://www.mitchellinstitute.org/

THE SENATOR GEORGE J. MITCHELL SCHOLARSHIP RESEARCH INSTITUTE
• *See page 604*

MLD WEALTH MANAGEMENT GROUP
http://mywealthmanagement.ca/

ANNUAL MLD SCHOLASTIC SCHOLARSHIP
• *See page 604*

NATIONAL AIDS MEMORIAL GROVE
http://www.aidsmemorial.org

PEDRO ZAMORA YOUNG LEADERS SCHOLARSHIP
• *See page 605*

NATIONAL AMATEUR BASEBALL FEDERATION (NABF)
http://www.nabf.com/

NATIONAL AMATEUR BASEBALL FEDERATION SCHOLARSHIP FUND
Scholarships are awarded to candidates who are enrolled in an accredited college or university. Applicant must be a bona fide participant in a federation event and be sponsored by an NABF-franchised member association. Self-nominated candidates are not eligible for this scholarship award.

Award: Scholarship for use in freshman, sophomore, junior, or senior years; not renewable.

Eligibility Requirements: Applicant must be enrolled or expecting to enroll full-time at a two-year or four-year or technical institution or university and must have an interest in athletics/sports. Available to U.S. citizens.

Application Requirements: Application form, community service, essay, letter of acceptance, recommendations or references, transcript. *Deadline:* November 15.

Contact: Awards Committee Chairman
National Amateur Baseball Federation (NABF)
PO Box 705
Bowie, MD 20718

NATIONAL ASSOCIATION FOR CAMPUS ACTIVITIES
http://www.naca.org/

JOHN ZAGUNIS STUDENT LEADER SCHOLARSHIP
Scholarships will be awarded to undergraduate or graduate students maintaining a cumulative GPA of 3.0 or better at the time of the application and during the academic term in which the scholarship is awarded. Applicants should demonstrate leadership skills and abilities while holding a significant leadership position on campus. Applicants must submit two letters of recommendation and a description of the applicant's leadership activities, skills, abilities and accomplishments. Must be enrolled in a college/university in the NACA Great Lakes Region.

Award: Scholarship for use in freshman, sophomore, junior, senior, or graduate years; not renewable. *Number:* 1. *Amount:* $300.

Eligibility Requirements: Applicant must be enrolled or expecting to enroll full-time at a two-year or four-year institution or university; studying in Delaware, Illinois, Indiana, Kentucky, Maryland, Michigan, New Jersey, New York, Ohio, Pennsylvania, West Virginia and must have an interest in leadership. Applicant must have 3.0 GPA or higher. Available to U.S. citizens.

Application Requirements: Application form, essay. *Deadline:* November 1.

Contact: Kayla Brennan, Education and Development Coordinator
Phone: 803-217-3471
Fax: 803-749-1047
E-mail: kaylab@naca.org

LORI RHETT MEMORIAL SCHOLARSHIP
• *See page 605*

NATIONAL ASSOCIATION FOR CAMPUS ACTIVITIES MID ATLANTIC UNDERGRADUATE SCHOLARSHIP FOR STUDENT LEADERS
• *See page 605*

NATIONAL ASSOCIATION FOR CAMPUS ACTIVITIES NORTHERN PLAINS REGION STUDENT LEADERSHIP SCHOLARSHIP
• *See page 605*

NATIONAL ASSOCIATION FOR CAMPUS ACTIVITIES SOUTH REGION STUDENT LEADER SCHOLARSHIP
• *See page 606*

SCHOLARSHIPS FOR STUDENT LEADERS
• *See page 606*

TESE CALDARELLI MEMORIAL SCHOLARSHIP
Scholarship available to undergraduate or graduate students with a minimum 3.0 GPA. Must demonstrate significant leadership skills and hold a significant position on campus. Must attend school in the NACA Mid Atlantic or Mid America Regions. The scholarship is to be used for educational purposes, such as tuition, fees and books or for professional development purposes.

Award: Scholarship for use in freshman, sophomore, junior, senior, or graduate years; not renewable. *Amount:* $300.

Eligibility Requirements: Applicant must be enrolled or expecting to enroll full-time at a two-year or four-year institution or university; studying in Delaware, Illinois, Indiana, Kentucky, Maryland, Michigan, New Jersey, New York, Ohio, Pennsylvania, West Virginia and must have an interest in leadership. Applicant must have 3.0 GPA or higher. Available to U.S. citizens.

Application Requirements: Application form, essay. *Deadline:* November 1.

Contact: Kayla Brennan, Education and Development Coordinator
Phone: 803-217-3471
Fax: 803-749-1047
E-mail: kaylab@naca.org

NATIONAL ASSOCIATION FOR THE SELF-EMPLOYED
http://www.NASE.org/

NASE SCHOLARSHIPS
• *See page 549*

NATIONAL COSTUMERS ASSOCIATION SCHOLARSHIPS
http://www.costumers.org

NATIONAL COSTUMERS ASSOCIATION SCHOLARSHIPS
The National Costumers Association offers two types of scholarships. The Memorial scholarship is an annual scholarship based on a brief bio and essay and GPA. The Creative scholarship is offered in odd number years is and consists of a hands on project submitted for judging.

Award: Scholarship for use in freshman, sophomore, junior, senior, graduate, or postgraduate years; not renewable. *Number:* 1–5. *Amount:* $250–$1000.

Eligibility Requirements: Applicant must be enrolled or expecting to enroll full-time at a two-year or four-year institution or university and must have an interest in museum/preservation work, sewing, or theater.

Applicant must have 2.5 GPA or higher. Available to U.S. and non-U.S. citizens.

Application Requirements: Application form, autobiography, essay, personal photograph. *Deadline:* April 1.

Contact: Linda Adams Foat, Past President
National Costumers Association Scholarships
1321 S Demeter Dr
Freeport, IL 61032
Phone: 815-233 1861
E-mail: ipp@costumers.org

NATIONAL COUNCIL OF JEWISH WOMEN LOS ANGELES (NCJW L LA)

http://ncjwla.org/

DODELL WOMEN'S EMPOWERMENT SCHOLARSHIP
• *See page 606*

SOPHIE GREENSTADT SCHOLARSHIP FOR MID-LIFE WOMEN
• *See page 606*

STEPHEN L. TELLER & RICHARD HOTSON TV, CINEMA, AND THEATER SCHOLARSHIP
• *See page 606*

SUSAN SCHULMAN BEGLEY MEMORIAL SCHOLARSHIP
• *See page 606*

NATIONAL FEDERATION OF STATE POETRY SOCIETIES (NFSPS)

http://www.nfsps.com/

NATIONAL FEDERATION OF STATE POETRY SOCIETIES' COLLEGE UNDERGRADUATE POETRY (CUP) COMPETITION

Open to students enrolled in a degree program at an accredited U.S. college or university. Awards $500 plus publication and 75 complimentary chapbooks marketed on Amazon.com. Winners get invitation, travel stipend of $300, and convention perks to read their work at NFSPS Annual Convention. Online submission of titled manuscript containing exactly ten original poems. For more information, visit NFSPS website, www.nfsps.com, Poetry Contests tab.

Award: Prize for use in freshman, sophomore, junior, or senior years; not renewable. *Number:* 2. *Amount:* $500.

Eligibility Requirements: Applicant must be enrolled or expecting to enroll full-time at a two-year or four-year institution or university and must have an interest in writing. Available to U.S. and non-U.S. citizens.

Application Requirements: Application form. *Deadline:* January 31.

Contact: Shirley Blackwell, Chairman
National Federation of State Poetry Societies (NFSPS)
PO Box 1352
Los Lunas, NM 87031
E-mail: sonneteer@earthlink.net

NATIONAL FEDERATION OF THE BLIND (NFB)

http://www.nfb.org/scholarships

AAF KENNETH JERNIGAN SCHOLARSHIP FOR $12,000
• *See page 607*

CHARLES AND MELVA T. OWEN SCHOLARSHIP FOR $10,000
• *See page 607*

NATIONAL MULTIPLE SCLEROSIS SOCIETY

http://www.nmss.org/

NATIONAL MULTIPLE SCLEROSIS SOCIETY SCHOLARSHIP PROGRAM
• *See page 607*

NATIONAL ORDER OF OMEGA

http://www.orderofomega.org/

FOUNDERS SCHOLARSHIP
• *See page 550*

NATIONAL PRESS FOUNDATION

http://www.nationalpress.org/

EVERT CLARK/SETH PAYNE AWARD
• *See page 607*

NATIONAL SOCIETY OF COLLEGIATE SCHOLARS (NSCS)

http://www.nscs.org/

NSCS EXEMPLARY SCHOLAR AWARD
• *See page 551*

NATIONAL SOCIETY OF HIGH SCHOOL SCHOLARS

www.nshss.org

CLAES NOBEL ACADEMIC SCHOLARSHIPS
• *See page 551*

NATIONAL SCHOLAR AWARDS FOR NSHSS MEMBERS
• *See page 552*

ROBERT P. SHEPPARD LEADERSHIP AWARD FOR NSHSS MEMBERS
• *See page 552*

NATIONAL SOCIETY OF THE SONS OF THE AMERICAN REVOLUTION

http://www.sar.org/

JOSEPH S. RUMBAUGH HISTORICAL ORATION CONTEST

Prize ranging from $1000 to $3000 is awarded to a sophomore, junior, or senior. The oration must be original and not less than five minutes or more than six minutes in length.

Award: Prize for use in sophomore, junior, or senior years; not renewable. *Number:* 1–3. *Amount:* $1000–$3000.

Eligibility Requirements: Applicant must be enrolled or expecting to enroll full-time at a two-year or four-year or technical institution or university and must have an interest in public speaking. Available to U.S. and non-U.S. citizens.

Application Requirements: Application form, entry in a contest. *Deadline:* June 15.

Contact: Lawrence Mckinley, National Chairman
National Society of the Sons of the American Revolution
12158 Holly Knoll Circle
Great Fall, VA 22066
E-mail: dustoff@bellatlantic.net

NEBRASKA'S COORDINATING COMMISSION FOR POSTSECONDARY EDUCATION

https://ccpe.nebraska.gov/

NEBRASKA OPPORTUNITY GRANT
• *See page 608*

NFIB YOUNG ENTREPRENEUR FOUNDATION

http://www.nfib.com/yef

YOUNG ENTREPRENEUR AWARDS

The Young Entrepreneur Awards program was designed to identify and reward students who have demonstrated entrepreneurial spirit and initiative by running their own entrepreneurial venture. Since 2003, YEF has awarded over 2,500 scholarships worth more than $2.5 million to graduating high school seniors. We award students who have demonstrated entrepreneurial talent by owning and/or operating their own business. Young Entrepreneur Awards range from $2,000 to $25,000 and enable students to further their studies in a two-year or four-year institution of higher learning while encouraging them to consider joining the ranks of America's independent business owners. For more information visit www.nfib.com/yea.

Award: Scholarship for use in freshman year; not renewable. *Number:* 100. *Amount:* $2000–$25,000.

Eligibility Requirements: Applicant must be high school student; planning to enroll or expecting to enroll full- or part-time at a two-year or four-year or technical institution or university and must have an interest in entrepreneurship. Available to U.S. citizens.

Application Requirements: Application form, essay, interview.

Contact: Molly young, Director, Young Entrepreneur Foundation
NFIB Young Entrepreneur Foundation
1201 F Street NW
Suite 200
Washington, DC 20004
Phone: 202-314-2042
E-mail: yef@nfib.org

NICODEMUS WILDERNESS PROJECT

http://www.wildernessproject.org/

APPRENTICE ECOLOGIST SCHOLARSHIP
• *See page 608*

NIKKO COSMETIC SURGERY CENTER

http://www.drnikko.com/

BREAST CANCER SURVIVOR SCHOLARSHIPS
• *See page 608*

NIMROD INTERNATIONAL JOURNAL

http://www.utulsa.edu/nimrod

THE KATHERINE ANNE PORTER PRIZE FOR FICTION

The Katherine Ann Porter Prize is given for a single extraordinary short story of less than 7,500 words.

Award: Prize for use in freshman, sophomore, junior, senior, graduate, or postgraduate years; not renewable. *Number:* 2. *Amount:* $1000–$2000.

Eligibility Requirements: Applicant must be enrolled or expecting to enroll full- or part-time at a two-year or four-year or technical institution or university and must have an interest in writing. Available to U.S. citizens.

Application Requirements: *Fee:* $20. *Deadline:* April 30.

Contact: Ellis O'Neal, Editor-in-Chief
Nimrod International Journal
The University of Tulsa, 800 South Tucker Drive
Phone: 918-631-3080
Fax: 918-631-3033
E-mail: nimrod@utulsa.edu

NISEI STUDENT RELOCATION COMMEMORATIVE FUND

http://www.nsrcfund.org/

NISEI STUDENT RELOCATION COMMEMORATIVE FUND
• *See page 608*

NO BULL SPORTS

http://nobullsports.org/

NO BULL SPORTS SCHOLARSHIP
• *See page 609*

NOPLAG PLAGIARISM CHECKER

http://noplag.com/

NOPLAG SCHOLARSHIP ESSAY CONTEST
• *See page 609*

NORTH CAROLINA DIVISION OF VOCATIONAL REHABILITATION SERVICES

http://www.dhhs.state.nc.us/

TRAINING SUPPORT FOR YOUTH WITH DISABILITIES
• *See page 609*

NORTH CAROLINA VIETNAM VETERANS, INC.

http://www.ncvvi.org

NC VIETNAM VETERANS, INC., SCHOLARSHIP PROGRAM
• *See page 609*

OHIO DEPARTMENT OF HIGHER EDUCATION

www.ohiohighered.org

OHIO COLLEGE OPPORTUNITY GRANT
• *See page 609*

OHIO SAFETY OFFICERS COLLEGE MEMORIAL FUND
• *See page 609*

OHIO WAR ORPHANS SCHOLARSHIP
• *See page 610*

ONE LOVE FOUNDATION

www.joinonelove.org

ONE LOVE FOUNDATION PETS VS. PARTNERS SCHOLARSHIP
• *See page 610*

OPTIMIST INTERNATIONAL FOUNDATION

http://www.optimist.org/

OPTIMIST INTERNATIONAL ESSAY CONTEST

Essay contest for youth under the age of 19 who have not graduated high school or its equivalent. U.S. students attending school on a military installation outside the United States are eligible to enter in their last U.S. home of record. Club winners advance to the District contest to compete for a college scholarship.

Award: Scholarship for use in freshman, sophomore, junior, or senior years; not renewable. *Number:* 40–49. *Amount:* up to $2500.

Eligibility Requirements: Applicant must be enrolled or expecting to enroll full- or part-time at a two-year or four-year or technical institution or university and must have an interest in writing. Available to U.S. and non-U.S. citizens.

Application Requirements: Application form, birth certificate or passport, entry in a contest, essay, self-addressed stamped envelope with application. *Deadline:* varies.

Contact: Danielle Baugher, Director of International Programs
Optimist International Foundation
4494 Lindell Boulevard
St. Louis, MO 63108
Phone: 800-500-8130
Fax: 314-371-6006
E-mail: programs@optimist.org

OPTIMIST INTERNATIONAL ORATORICAL CONTEST

Contest for youth to gain experience in public speaking and to provide them with the opportunity to compete for college scholarships. The contest is open to youth under the age of 19 before graduating high school or the equivalent. Students must first compete at the Club level. Club winners are then entered into the Zone contest and those winners compete in the District contest. District winners are awarded scholarships. District winners will be able to compete in a Regional Contest then be able to compete in the World Championships at St. Louis University in St. Louis, Missouri USA.

Award: Scholarship for use in freshman, sophomore, junior, or senior years; not renewable. *Number:* 90–115. *Amount:* $1000–$2500.

Eligibility Requirements: Applicant must be enrolled or expecting to enroll full- or part-time at a two-year or four-year or technical institution or university and must have an interest in public speaking. Available to U.S. and non-U.S. citizens.

Application Requirements: Application form, birth certificate or passport, speech, entry in a contest, self-addressed stamped envelope with application. *Deadline:* varies.

Contact: Dana Thomas, Director of International Programs
Optimist International Foundation
4494 Lindell Boulevard
St. Louis, MO 63108
Phone: 800-500-8130
Fax: 314-371-6006
E-mail: programs@optimist.org

OREGON COMMUNITY FOUNDATION

http://www.oregoncf.org/

DOROTHY S. CAMPBELL MEMORIAL SCHOLARSHIP FUND

Scholarship for female graduates of Oregon high schools with a strong and continuing interest in the game of golf. For use in the pursuit of a postsecondary education at a four-year college or university in Oregon.

Award: Scholarship for use in freshman, sophomore, junior, or senior years; renewable. *Number:* 9. *Amount:* $1000.

Eligibility Requirements: Applicant must be enrolled or expecting to enroll full-time at a four-year institution or university; female and must have an interest in golf. Available to U.S. citizens.

Application Requirements: Application form, recommendations or references. *Deadline:* March 1.

Contact: Dianne Causey, Program Associate for Scholarships and Grants
Phone: 503-227-6846 Ext. 1418
E-mail: dcausey@oregoncf.org

OREGON STUDENT ASSISTANCE COMMISSION

http://www.GetCollegeFunds.org/

DOROTHY CAMPBELL MEMORIAL SCHOLARSHIP
• *See page 786*

ORGANIZATION FOR AUTISM RESEARCH

www.researchautism.org

LISA HIGGINS HUSSMAN SCHOLARSHIP
• *See page 610*

SCHWALLIE FAMILY SCHOLARSHIP
• *See page 610*

OUR WORLD UNDERWATER SCHOLARSHIP SOCIETY

http://www.owuscholarship.org/

OUR WORLD UNDERWATER SCHOLARSHIPS

Annual award for individual planning to pursue a career in a water-related discipline through practical exposure to various fields and leaders of underwater endeavors. Scuba experience required. Must be at least 21 but not yet 26. Scholarship value is $25,000 for the North American Rolex Scholar, open to North American citizens only. The European Rolex Scholarship is open to European citizens and the Australasian Rolex Scholarship is open to citizens of the Australasian region.

Award: Scholarship for use in freshman, sophomore, junior, or senior years; not renewable. *Number:* 3. *Amount:* $25,000.

Eligibility Requirements: Applicant must be age 21-26; enrolled or expecting to enroll full- or part-time at a two-year or four-year or technical institution or university and must have an interest in scuba diving. Available to U.S. and non-U.S. citizens.

Application Requirements: Application form, autobiography, community service, driver's license, essay, interview. *Fee:* $50. *Deadline:* December 31.

Contact: Roberta Flanders, Scholarship Application Coordinator
Our World Underwater Scholarship Society
PO Box 6157
Woodridge, IL 60517
Phone: 630-969-6690
E-mail: info@owuscholarship.org

OUTRIGGER DUKE KAHANAMOKU FOUNDATION

http://www.dukefoundation.org

ODKF GENERAL SCHOLARSHIP AWARD
• *See page 611*

PANHELLENIC SCHOLARSHIP FOUNDATION

http://www.panhellenicscholarships.org/

PANHELLENIC SCHOLARSHIP AWARDS
• *See page 611*

PAPERCHECK

https://www.papercheck.com/

PAPERCHECK, LLC—CHARLES SHAFAE' SCHOLARSHIP FUND
• *See page 611*

PENGUIN GROUP

http://www.penguin.com/services-academic/essayhome/

SIGNET CLASSIC SCHOLARSHIP ESSAY CONTEST

Open to 11th and 12th grade full-time matriculated students who are attending high schools located in the fifty United States and the District of Columbia, or home-schooled students between the ages of 16 to 18 who are residents of the fifty United States and the District of Columbia. Students should submit four copies of a two- to three-page double-spaced essay answering one of three possible questions on a designated novel. Entries must be submitted by a high school English teacher.

Award: Scholarship for use in freshman year; not renewable. *Number:* 5. *Amount:* $1000.

Eligibility Requirements: Applicant must be high school student; planning to enroll or expecting to enroll full-time at a four-year institution or university and must have an interest in writing. Available to U.S. citizens.

Application Requirements: Entry in a contest, essay, recommendations or references. *Deadline:* April 15.

Contact: Kym Giacoppe, Academic Marketing Assistant
Phone: 212-366-2377
E-mail: academic@penguin.com

PENNSYLVANIA FEDERATION OF DEMOCRATIC WOMEN INC.

www.pafedofdemwomen.org

PENNSYLVANIA FEDERATION OF DEMOCRATIC WOMEN INC. ANNUAL SCHOLARSHIP AWARDS
• *See page 554*

PENNSYLVANIA HIGHER EDUCATION ASSISTANCE AGENCY

http://www.pheaa.org/

BLIND OR DEAF BENEFICIARY GRANT PROGRAM
• *See page 612*

PHI SIGMA PI NATIONAL HONOR FRATERNITY

http://www.phisigmapi.org/

RICHARD CECIL TODD AND CLAUDA PENNOCK TODD TRIPOD SCHOLARSHIP
• *See page 555*

PILOT INTERNATIONAL FOUNDATION

http://www.pilotinternational.org/

BECKY BURROWS MEMORIAL SCHOLARSHIP
• *See page 612*

PLAINTIFF RELIEF

http://plaintiffrelief.com/

PLAINTIFF RELIEF SCHOLARSHIP
• *See page 612*

POLSON & POLSON, P.C.

https://www.polsonlawfirm.com/

POLSON & POLSON, P.C. CONQUERING ADVERSITY SCHOLARSHIP
• *See page 612*

PONY OF THE AMERICAS CLUB INC.

http://www.poac.org/

POAC NATIONAL SCHOLARSHIP
• *See page 555*

PRICE BENOWITZ LLP

http://pricebenowitz.com/

AMATO SANITA BRIGHTER FUTURE SCHOLARSHIP
• *See page 613*

ANGIE DIPIETRO WOMEN IN BUSINESS SCHOLARSHIP
• *See page 613*

APRIL COCKERHAM DREAM ACT SCHOLARSHIP
• *See page 613*

KAREN RILEY PORTER GOOD WORKS SCHOLARSHIP
• *See page 613*

KERRI CASTELLINI WOMEN'S LEADERSHIP SCHOLARSHIP
• *See page 613*

KUSH ARORA FEDERAL CRIMINAL JUSTICE REFORM SCHOLARSHIP
• *See page 613*

PRICE BENOWITZ SOCIAL JUSTICE SCHOLARSHIP
• *See page 613*

SETH OKIN GOOD DEEDS SCHOLARSHIP
• *See page 613*

THOMAS SOLDAN HEALTHY COMMUNITIES SCHOLARSHIP
• *See page 614*

PRIDE FOUNDATION

http://www.PrideFoundation.org/

PRIDE FOUNDATION SCHOLARSHIP PROGRAM
• *See page 790*

PRIVATE AID TEST SURVEY

A TEST PROGRAM NAME
• *See page 614*

PRO BOWLERS ASSOCIATION

http://www.pba.com/

BILLY WELU BOWLING SCHOLARSHIP

Scholarship awarded annually, recognizing exemplary qualities in male and female college students who compete in the sport of bowling. Winner will receive $1000. Candidates must be amateur bowlers who are currently in college (preceding the application deadline) and maintain at least a 2.5 GPA or equivalent.

Award: Scholarship for use in freshman, sophomore, junior, or senior years; not renewable. *Number:* 1. *Amount:* $1000.

Eligibility Requirements: Applicant must be enrolled or expecting to enroll full-time at a two-year or four-year institution or university and must have an interest in bowling. Applicant must have 2.5 GPA or higher. Available to U.S. citizens.

Application Requirements: Application form, essay, transcript. *Deadline:* May 31.

Contact: Karen Day, Controller
Phone: 206-332-9688
Fax: 206-332-9722
E-mail: karen.day@pba.com

PROMPT
http://prompt.com

PROMPT'S $20,000 SCHOLARSHIP
• *See page 614*

REACH HIGHER MONTANA
http://www.ReachHigherMontana.org

REACH HIGHER MONTANA SCHOLARSHIPS
• *See page 614*

THE RESERVE OFFICERS ASSOCIATION
http://www.roa.org/

HENRY J. REILLY MEMORIAL SCHOLARSHIP-HIGH SCHOOL SENIORS AND FIRST YEAR FRESHMEN
• *See page 557*

RHINE LAW FIRM, P.C.
http://www.carolinaaccidentattorneys.com/

2017 RHINE LAW FIRM, P.C. SCHOLARSHIP
• *See page 615*

RHODE ISLAND FOUNDATION
http://www.rifoundation.org/

UNITED ITALIAN AMERICAN INC. SCHOLARSHIP
• *See page 792*

ROBERT H. MOLLOHAN FAMILY CHARITABLE FOUNDATION, INC.
http://www.mollohanfoundation.org/

DR. ROBERTO F. CUNANAN MEMORIAL SCHOLARSHIP
• *See page 792*

RON BROWN SCHOLAR FUND
http://www.ronbrown.org/

RON BROWN SCHOLAR PROGRAM
• *See page 697*

ROSENGREN KOHLMEYER, LAW OFFICE CHTD.
http://rokolaw.com

ROSENGREN KOHLMEYER LAW OFFICE SCHOLARSHIP
• *See page 615*

ST. CLAIRE REGIONAL MEDICAL CENTER
http://www.st-claire.org/

SR. MARY JEANNETTE WESS, S.N.D. SCHOLARSHIP
• *See page 615*

SALLIE MAE FUND
http://www.thesalliemaefund.org/

$1,000 PLAN FOR COLLEGE SWEEPSTAKES
• *See page 615*

SCHOLARSHIPOWL.COM
http://www.scholarshipowl.com

YOU DESERVE IT! SCHOLARSHIP
• *See page 793*

SCHOLARSHIP WORKSHOP LLC
http://www.scholarshipworkshop.com/

LEADING THE FUTURE II SCHOLARSHIP
The scholarship is designed to elevate students' consciousness about their future and their role in helping others. Open to high school seniors and college students who are U.S. citizens. Students must visit http://www.scholarshipworkshop.com (see scholarships) to apply. Scholarship is sponsored by Marianne Ragins, $400,000 scholarship winner. Learn more at www.scholarshipworkshop.com/movie.

Award: Scholarship for use in freshman, sophomore, junior, or senior years; not renewable. *Number:* 1–3. *Amount:* $100–$300.

Eligibility Requirements: Applicant must be enrolled or expecting to enroll full-time at a four-year institution or university and must have an interest in leadership. Available to U.S. citizens.

Application Requirements: Application form, essay. *Deadline:* March 1.

Contact: Scholarship Coordinator
Phone: 703-579-4245
E-mail: scholars@scholarshipworkshop.com

SELECTBLINDS.COM
http://www.selectblinds.com

SELECTBLINDS.COM $1000 COLLEGE SCHOLARSHIP
• *See page 615*

SEXNER & ASSOCIATES LLC
http://www.sexner.com/personal-injury/

MITCHELL S. SEXNER & ASSOCIATES LLC SCHOLARSHIP
• *See page 616*

SHAWN SUKUMAR ATTORNEY AT LAW
https://www.washingtondccriminallawyer.net/

SHAWN SUKUMAR CRIMINAL JUSTICE REFORM SCHOLARSHIP
• *See page 616*

SILICON VALLEY COMMUNITY FOUNDATION
www.siliconvalleycf.org

ABBY SOBRATO SCHOLARSHIP
• *See page 616*

BOBETTE BIBO GUGLIOTTA MEMORIAL SCHOLARSHIP FOR CREATIVE WRITING
• *See page 616*

CURRY AWARD FOR GIRLS AND YOUNG WOMEN
• *See page 616*

HAZEL REED BAUMEISTER SCHOLARSHIP PROGRAM
• *See page 616*

HUANG LEADERSHIP DEVELOPMENT SCHOLARSHIP
• *See page 617*

LATINOS IN TECHNOLOGY SCHOLARSHIP
• *See page 617*

SISTER KENNY REHABILITATION INSTITUTE

http://www.allina.com/ahs/ski.nsf

INTERNATIONAL ART SHOW FOR ARTISTS WITH DISABILITIES
• *See page 637*

SOCIETY FOR APPLIED ANTHROPOLOGY

http://www.sfaa.net/

ANNUAL SFAA STUDENT ENDOWED AWARD
• *See page 617*

TOURISM AND HERITAGE STUDENT PAPER COMPETITION
• *See page 617*

SOCIETY OF DAUGHTERS OF THE UNITED STATES ARMY

SOCIETY OF DAUGHTERS OF THE UNITED STATES ARMY SCHOLARSHIPS
• *See page 617*

SOCIETY OF SATELLITE PROFESSIONALS INTERNATIONAL

http://www.sspi.org/

SSPI NORTHEAST CHAPTER SCHOLARSHIP
Students from or studying in the Northeast US region.
Award: Scholarship for use in freshman, sophomore, junior, senior, or graduate years; not renewable. *Number:* 1. *Amount:* $2500.
Eligibility Requirements: Applicant must be enrolled or expecting to enroll full-time at a two-year or four-year institution or university. Available to U.S. and non-U.S. citizens.
Application Requirements: Essay, financial need analysis. *Deadline:* April 15.
Contact: Ms. Tamara Bond-Williams, Membership Director
Society of Satellite Professionals International
250 Park Avenue, 7th Floor
New York, NY 10177
Phone: 212-809-5199 Ext. 103
Fax: 212-825-0075
E-mail: tbond-williams@sspi.org

SOUTH CAROLINA TUITION GRANTS COMMISSION

http://www.sctuitiongrants.org/

SOUTH CAROLINA TUITION GRANTS PROGRAM
• *See page 617*

SOUTH DAKOTA BOARD OF REGENTS

http://www.sdbor.edu/

SOUTH DAKOTA BOARD OF REGENTS MARLIN R. SCARBOROUGH MEMORIAL SCHOLARSHIP
• *See page 796*

SPANISHDICT

www.spanishdict.com/traductor

BECA #TRADUCTOR
• *See page 618*

SPINE SURGEON DR. VICTOR HAYES

https://tampabaybackpaindoctor.com/

TAMPA BAY SPINE CENTER ROAD TO RECOVERY SCHOLARSHIP
• *See page 618*

STATE EMPLOYEES ASSOCIATION OF NORTH CAROLINA (SEANC)

http://www.seanc.org/

STATE EMPLOYEES ASSOCIATION OF NORTH CAROLINA (SEANC) SCHOLARSHIPS
• *See page 700*

STONEWALL COMMUNITY FOUNDATION

http://www.stonewallfoundation.org/

GENE AND JOHN ATHLETIC FUND SCHOLARSHIP
Scholarship of $2500 to $5000 for LGBT student athletes looking to continue their education while pursuing athletics.
Award: Scholarship for use in freshman, sophomore, junior, senior, graduate, or postgraduate years; not renewable. *Number:* 1–3. *Amount:* $2500–$5000.
Eligibility Requirements: Applicant must be enrolled or expecting to enroll full-time at a two-year or four-year or technical institution or university and must have an interest in athletics/sports or LGBT issues. Available to U.S. and Canadian citizens.
Application Requirements: Application form, essay. *Deadline:* June 31.
Contact: Carlie Steen, Program Manager
Stonewall Community Foundation
446 West 33rd Street
New York, NY 10001
Phone: 212-367-1537
E-mail: grants@stonewallfoundation.org

HARRY BARTEL MEMORIAL SCHOLARSHIP
• *See page 618*

LEVIN-GOFFE SCHOLARSHIP FOR LGBTQI IMMIGRANTS
The Levin-Goffe Scholarship Fund was established to cover up to two years of schooling for immigrants here in New York City who identify as LGBTQI. Scholarships from this fund are intended to provide a measure of economic stability for those who stand at the intersection of marginalization that can be created by being both LGBTQI and an immigrant.
Award: Scholarship for use in sophomore, junior, senior, graduate, or postgraduate years; not renewable. *Number:* 1. *Amount:* $25,000.
Eligibility Requirements: Applicant must be enrolled or expecting to enroll full-time at a four-year institution or university; studying in New York and must have an interest in LGBT issues. Available to U.S. and non-Canadian citizens.
Application Requirements: Application form.

Contact: Carlie Steen, Program Manager
Stonewall Community Foundation
446 West 33rd Street
New York, NY 10001
Phone: 212-457.1349
E-mail: grants@stonewallfoundation.org

NEW YORK RAMBLERS SCHOLARSHIP FOR STUDENT ATHLETES
• *See page 618*

TRAUB-DICKER RAINBOW SCHOLARSHIP
• *See page 618*

STROM & ASSOCIATES

https://stromlawyers.com

STROM & ASSOCIATES NEED-BASED SCHOLARSHIP
• *See page 619*

SUPERCOLLEGE.COM

http://www.supercollege.com/

$1,500 SUPERCOLLEGE.COM SCHOLARSHIP

An award for outstanding high school, college or graduate students. Based on academic and extracurricular achievement, leadership, and integrity. May study any major and attend or plan to attend any accredited college or university in the United States. No paper applications accepted. Applications are only available online at http://www.supercollege.com/scholarship/.

Award: Scholarship for use in freshman, sophomore, junior, senior, or graduate years; not renewable. *Number:* 1–5. *Amount:* $500–$1500.

Eligibility Requirements: Applicant must be enrolled or expecting to enroll full-time at a two-year or four-year or technical institution or university and must have an interest in leadership. Available to U.S. citizens.

Application Requirements: Application form. *Deadline:* continuous.

Contact: Scholarship Coordinator
Phone: 650-618-2221
E-mail: supercollege@supercollege.com

SWISS BENEVOLENT SOCIETY OF NEW YORK

http://www.sbsny.org/

MEDICUS STUDENT EXCHANGE
• *See page 701*

TARADASH LAW FIRM

https://taradashlaw.com/

TARADASH LAW FIRM SCHOLARSHIP
• *See page 619*

TELEVISION ACADEMY FOUNDATION

http://www.televisionacademy.com/foundation

TELEVISION ACADEMY FOUNDATION
• *See page 619*

TENNESSEE STUDENT ASSISTANCE CORPORATION

http://www.tn.gov/collegepays

HELPING HEROES GRANT
• *See page 619*

HOPE WITH ASPIRE
• *See page 619*

NED MCWHERTER SCHOLARS PROGRAM
• *See page 620*

TELS HOPE ACCESS GRANT
• *See page 620*

TELS -HOPE WITH GENERAL ASSEMBLY MERIT SCHOLARSHIP (GAMS)
• *See page 620*

TELS - TENNESSEE HOPE SCHOLARSHIP
• *See page 620*

TENNESSEE DUAL ENROLLMENT GRANT
• *See page 620*

TENNESSEE EDUCATION LOTTERY SCHOLARSHIP PROGRAM WILDER-NAIFEH TECHNICAL SKILLS GRANT
• *See page 620*

TENNESSEE HOPE FOSTER CHILD TUITION GRANT
• *See page 620*

TENNESSEE STEP UP SCHOLARSHIP
• *See page 621*

TENNESSEE STUDENT ASSISTANCE AWARD
• *See page 621*

TERRY FOUNDATION

http://www.terryfoundation.org/

TERRY FOUNDATION SCHOLARSHIP
• *See page 799*

TERRY FOUNDATION TRANSFER SCHOLARSHIP
• *See page 799*

TERRY FOX HUMANITARIAN AWARD

http://terryfoxawards.ca/

TERRY FOX HUMANITARIAN AWARD
• *See page 621*

TETHERBOX

http://www.tetherbox.com/

$1,000 CREATIVE VIDEO CHALLENGE COLLEGE SCHOLARSHIP
• *See page 621*

TEXAS 4-H YOUTH DEVELOPMENT FOUNDATION

http://texas4hfoundation.org/

TEXAS 4-H OPPORTUNITY SCHOLARSHIP
• *See page 799*

TEXAS ASSOCIATION OF DEVELOPING COLLEGES

http://www.txadc.org

THE URBAN SCHOLARSHIPS FUND
• *See page 622*

TEXAS MUTUAL INSURANCE COMPANY

http://www.texasmutual.com/

TEXAS MUTUAL INSURANCE COMPANY SCHOLARSHIP PROGRAM
• *See page 622*

TEXAS OUTDOOR WRITERS ASSOCIATION

http://www.towa.org/

TEXAS OUTDOOR WRITERS ASSOCIATION SCHOLARSHIP
• *See page 800*

TEXAS TENNIS FOUNDATION

http://www.texastennisfoundation.com/

TEXAS TENNIS FOUNDATION SCHOLARSHIPS AND ENDOWMENTS
• *See page 800*

TKE EDUCATIONAL FOUNDATION

http://www.tke.org/

CHARLES J. TRABOLD SCHOLARSHIP
• *See page 560*

CHARLES R. WALGREEN, JR. LEADERSHIP AWARD
• *See page 560*

CHARLES R. WALGREEN, JR. SCHOLARSHIP AWARD
• *See page 560*

CHRISTOPHER GRASSO SCHOLARSHIP
• *See page 560*

DONALD A. AND JOHN R. FISHER MEMORIAL SCHOLARSHIP
• *See page 560*

DORIS AND ELMER H. SCHMITZ, SR. MEMORIAL SCHOLARSHIP
• *See page 560*

DWAYNE R. WOERPEL MEMORIAL LEADERSHIP SCHOLARSHIP
• *See page 561*

EUGENE C. BEACH MEMORIAL SCHOLARSHIP
• *See page 561*

FATHER TIMOTHY VAKOC MEMORIAL SCHOLARSHIP
• *See page 561*

GABE ANAYA SCHOLARSHIP
• *See page 561*

J.D. WILLIAMS SCHOLARSHIP
• *See page 561*

JOHN A. COURSON SCHOLARSHIP
• *See page 561*

J. RUSSEL SALSBURY MEMORIAL SCHOLARSHIP
• *See page 562*

KENNETH L. DUKE, SR. MEMORIAL SCHOLARSHIP
• *See page 562*

LENWOOD S. COCHRAN SCHOLARSHIP
• *See page 562*

LON G. JUSTICE SCHOLARSHIP
• *See page 562*

MICHAEL CERUSSI LEADERSHIP SCHOLARSHIP
• *See page 562*

MICHAEL J. MORIN MEMORIAL SCHOLARSHIP
• *See page 562*

MILES GRAY MEMORIAL SCHOLARSHIP
• *See page 562*

RONALD REAGAN LEADERSHIP AWARD
• *See page 563*

T.J. SCHMITZ SCHOLARSHIP
• *See page 563*

TKE SERVANT LEADERSHIP SCHOLARSHIP
• *See page 563*

WALLACE MCCAULEY MEMORIAL SCHOLARSHIP
• *See page 563*

WILLIAM V. MUSE SCHOLARSHIP
• *See page 563*

WILLIAM WILSON MEMORIAL SCHOLARSHIP
• *See page 564*

TOSHIBA/NSTA

http://www.exploravision.org/

EXPLORAVISION SCIENCE COMPETITION

Competition for students in grades K-12 who enter as small teams by grade level and work on a science project. In each group, first place team members are each awarded a savings bond worth $10,000 at maturity, second place, a $5000 savings bond. Deadline varies.

Award: Prize for use in freshman year; not renewable. *Amount:* $5000–$10,000.

Eligibility Requirements: Applicant must be enrolled or expecting to enroll full- or part-time at a four-year institution or university and must have an interest in science. Available to U.S. citizens.

Application Requirements: Application form, entry in a contest. *Deadline:* varies.

Contact: Paloma Olbes, Media Contact
    Phone: 212-388-1400
    E-mail: polbes@dba-pr.com

TOURO SYNAGOGUE FOUNDATION

http://www.tourosynagogue.org/

AARON AND RITA SLOM SCHOLARSHIP FUND FOR FREEDOM AND DIVERSITY

Scholarship available for high school seniors who plan to enroll in an institute of higher learning for a minimum of 6 credits. Entries should include an interpretative work focusing on the historic "George Washington Letter to the Congregation" in context with the present time. Text of the letter is available on the website. Submissions may be in the form of an essay, story, poem, film, video, or computer presentation. Applications, guidelines, resource materials are available on website http://www.tourosynagogue.org

Award: Scholarship for use in freshman year; not renewable. *Number:* 2–4. *Amount:* $500–$1000.

Eligibility Requirements: Applicant must be high school student; planning to enroll or expecting to enroll full- or part-time at a two-year or four-year institution or university and must have an interest in writing. Available to U.S. citizens.

Application Requirements: Application form. *Deadline:* April 24.

Contact: Meryle Cawley
Touro Synagogue Foundation
85 Touro Street
Newport, RI 02840
Phone: 401-847-4794 Ext. 207
E-mail: tours@tourosynagogue.org

TWO TEN FOOTWEAR FOUNDATION

http://www.twoten.org/

CLASSIC SCHOLARSHIPS
• See page 622

ULMAN CANCER FUND FOR YOUNG ADULTS

http://www.ulmanfund.org/scholarships

JACQUELINE SHEARER MEMORIAL SCHOLARSHIP
• See page 623

JAMIE L. ROBERTS MEMORIAL SCHOLARSHIP AWARD
• See page 623

JEFFREY P. MEYER MEMORIAL SCHOLARSHIP
• See page 623

JILL WEAVER STARKMAN SCHOLARSHIP
• See page 623

JOHN HANLEY MEMORIAL SCHOLARSHIP
• See page 623

LISA HIGGINS-HUSSMAN FOUNDATION SCHOLARSHIP
• See page 623

MARILYN YETSO MEMORIAL SCHOLARSHIP
• See page 624

OLIVIA M. MARQUART SCHOLARSHIP
• See page 624

PERLITA LIWANAG MEMORIAL SCHOLARSHIP
• See page 624

SATOLA FAMILY SCHOLARSHIP
• See page 624

SEAN SILVER MEMORIAL SCHOLARSHIP AWARD
• See page 624

VERA YIP MEMORIAL SCHOLARSHIP
• See page 624

VITTORIA DIANNA RICARDO MEMORIAL SCHOLARSHIP
• See page 625

UNION PLUS SCHOLARSHIP PROGRAM

http://www.unionplus.org/

UNION PLUS EDUCATION FOUNDATION SCHOLARSHIP PROGRAM
• See page 564

UNITED NEGRO COLLEGE FUND

http://www.uncf.org/

NATIONAL BLACK MBA ASSOCIATION UNDERGRADUATE SCHOLARSHIP
• See page 705

UNITED STATES JUNIOR CHAMBER OF COMMERCE

http://www.usjaycees.org/

JAYCEE WAR MEMORIAL FUND SCHOLARSHIP

$1000 scholarship for students who are U.S. citizens, possess academic potential and leadership qualities, and show financial need. Minimum 2.5 GPA required. To receive an application, send $10 application fee and stamped, self-addressed envelope by February 1.

Award: Scholarship for use in freshman, sophomore, junior, or senior years; not renewable. *Number:* 10. *Amount:* $1000.

Eligibility Requirements: Applicant must be enrolled or expecting to enroll full-time at a two-year or four-year or technical institution or university and must have an interest in leadership. Applicant must have 2.5 GPA or higher. Available to U.S. citizens.

Application Requirements: Application form, financial need analysis, self-addressed stamped envelope with application, transcript. *Fee:* $10. *Deadline:* February 1.

Contact: Karen Fitzgerald, Customer Service and Data Processing
Phone: 918-584-2481
E-mail: customerservice@usjaycees.org

UNITED TRANSPORTATION UNION INSURANCE ASSOCIATION

http://www.utuia.org/

UTUIA SCHOLARSHIP
• See page 625

UNIVERSITY CONSORTIUM FOR LIBERIA

http://ucliberia.com/

JOSEPH N. BOAKAI SR. HIGHER EDUCATION SCHOLARSHIP
• See page 625

U.S. COAST GUARD

www.gocoastguard/cspi

COLLEGE STUDENT PRE-COMMISSIONING INITIATIVE (CSPI)
• See page 625

VALUEPENGUIN

http://www.valuepenguin.com

VALUEPENGUIN SCHOLARSHIP
• See page 626

VETERANS OF FOREIGN WARS OF THE UNITED STATES

http://www.vfw.org/

VOICE OF DEMOCRACY PROGRAM

Student must be sponsored by a local VFW Post. Student submits a three to five minute audio essay on a contest theme (changes each year). Open to high school students (9th to 12th grade). Award available for all levels of postsecondary study in an American institution. Open to permanent U.S. residents only. Competition starts at local level. No entries are to be submitted to the National Headquarters. Visit website https://www.vfw.org/VOD/ for more information.

Award: Scholarship for use in freshman, sophomore, junior, senior, graduate, or postgraduate years; not renewable. *Number:* 54. *Amount:* $1000–$30,000.

Eligibility Requirements: Applicant must be high school student; age 14-19; planning to enroll or expecting to enroll full- or part-time at a two-year or four-year or technical institution or university and must have an interest in public speaking or writing. Available to U.S. citizens.

Application Requirements: Application form, essay. *Deadline:* October 31.

Contact: Kris Harmer, Program Coordinator
Veterans of Foreign Wars of the United States
406 West 34th Street
Kansas City, MO 64111
Phone: 816-968-1117
Fax: 816-968-1149
E-mail: kharmer@vfw.org

VSA

http://www.kennedy-center.org/education/vsa/

VSA PLAYWRIGHT DISCOVERY AWARD

Young writers with disabilities and collaborative groups that include students with disabilities, in U.S. grades 6-12 (or equivalents) or ages 11-18 for non-U.S. students, are invited to explore the disability experience through the art of writing for performance: plays, screenplays, spoken word poetry (for single performer or a group), or music theater. Writers are encouraged to craft short works from their own experiences and observations, create fictional characters and settings, or choose to write metaphorically or abstractly about the disability experience.

Award: Prize for use in freshman year; not renewable. *Number:* 1.

Eligibility Requirements: Applicant must be high school student; age 11-18; planning to enroll or expecting to enroll full- or part-time at an institution or university and must have an interest in theater or writing. Available to U.S. citizens.

Application Requirements: Application form. *Deadline:* February 1.

Contact: Megan Bailey, Administrative Assistant
VSA
2700 F St NW
Washington, DC 20566
Phone: 202-416-8822
E-mail: vsainfo@kennedy-center.org

WALTER W. NAUMBURG FOUNDATION

http://www.naumburg.org/

INTERNATIONAL VIOLONCELLO COMPETITION

Prizes of $2500 to $7500 awarded to violoncellists between the ages of 17 and 31. Application fee is $125.

Award: Prize for use in freshman, sophomore, junior, senior, graduate, or postgraduate years; not renewable. *Number:* 3. *Amount:* $2500–$7500.

Eligibility Requirements: Applicant must be age 17-31; enrolled or expecting to enroll full- or part-time at a two-year or four-year or technical institution or university and must have an interest in music. Available to U.S. and non-U.S. citizens.

Application Requirements: Applicant's audio track (CD) of no less than 30 minutes, application form, entry in a contest, recommendations or references, self-addressed stamped envelope with application. *Fee:* $125. *Deadline:* March 1.

Contact: Lucy Mann, Executive Director
Phone: 212-362-9877
Fax: 212-362-9877
E-mail: luciamann@aol.com

WARD LAW GROUP, PL

http://thecoveragelawyer.com/

WARD LAW GROUP BETTER FUTURE SCHOLARSHIP

• See page 626

WASHINGTON SOCIETY OF CERTIFIED PUBLIC ACCOUNTANTS

http://www.wscpa.org/

WSCPA FOUNDATION SCHOLARSHIPS

• See page 626

WILLIAM D. SQUIRES EDUCATIONAL FOUNDATION INC.

http://www.wmdsquiresfoundation.org/

WILLIAM D. SQUIRES SCHOLARSHIP

• See page 627

WILLIAM G. AND MARIE SELBY FOUNDATION

http://www.selbyfdn.org/

SELBY SCHOLAR PROGRAM

• See page 805

WILLIAM RANDOLPH HEARST FOUNDATION

http://www.hearstfdn.org/

UNITED STATES SENATE YOUTH PROGRAM

Scholarship for high school juniors and seniors holding elected student offices. Two students selected from each state. Selection process will vary by state. Contact school principal or state department of education for information. Deadlines: early fall of each year for most states, but specific date will vary by state (see website www.ussenateyouth.org). Program is open to citizens and permanent residents of the United States Department of Defense schools overseas and the District of Columbia (not the territories).

Award: Scholarship for use in freshman, sophomore, junior, or senior years; not renewable. *Number:* 104. *Amount:* $10,000.

Eligibility Requirements: Applicant must be high school student; planning to enroll or expecting to enroll full-time at a two-year or four-year institution or university; single; studying in Alabama, Alaska, Arizona, Arkansas, California, Colorado, Connecticut, Delaware, District of Columbia, Florida, Georgia, Hawaii, Idaho, Illinois, Indiana, Iowa, Kansas, Kentucky, Louisiana, Maine, Maryland, Massachusetts, Michigan, Minnesota, Mississippi, Missouri, Montana, Nebraska, Nevada, New Hampshire, New Jersey, New Mexico, New York, North Carolina, North Dakota, Ohio, Oklahoma, Oregon, Pennsylvania, Rhode Island, South Carolina, South Dakota, Tennessee, Texas, Utah, Vermont, Virginia, Washington, West Virginia, Wisconsin, Wyoming and must have an interest in leadership or public speaking. Applicant must have 3.5 GPA or higher. Available to U.S. citizens.

Application Requirements: Application form, essay, interview.

Contact: Lynn DeSmet, Deputy Program Director
William Randolph Hearst Foundation
90 New Montgomery Street
Suite 1212
San Francisco, CA 94105
Phone: 415-908-4540
E-mail: ussyp@hearstfdn.org

WOMEN'S BASKETBALL COACHES ASSOCIATION

http://www.wbca.org/

WBCA SCHOLARSHIP AWARD

One-time award for two women's basketball players who have demonstrated outstanding commitment to the sport of women's basketball and to academic excellence. Minimum 3.5 GPA required. Must be nominated by the head coach of women's basketball who is WBCA member.

Award: Scholarship for use in freshman, sophomore, junior, senior, or graduate years; not renewable. *Number:* up to 2. *Amount:* up to $1000.

Eligibility Requirements: Applicant must be enrolled or expecting to enroll full- or part-time at a four-year institution or university; female and must have an interest in athletics/sports. Applicant must have 3.5 GPA or higher. Available to U.S. and non-U.S. citizens.

Application Requirements: Application form, recommendations or references, statistics. *Deadline:* February 15.

Contact: Betty Jaynes, Consultant
Phone: 770-279-8027 Ext. 102
Fax: 770-279-6290
E-mail: bettyj@wbca.org

WOMEN'S JEWELRY ASSOCIATION

http://www.womensjewelryassociation.com

MEMBER GRANTS
• *See page 627*

WOMEN'S JEWELRY ASSOCIATIONS VETERANS GRANT
• *See page 627*

WOMEN'S SPORTS FOUNDATION

http://www.womenssportsfoundation.org/

LINDA RIDDLE/SGMA ENDOWED SCHOLARSHIP
• *See page 627*

WOMEN'S WESTERN GOLF FOUNDATION

http://www.wwga.org/foundation.htm

WOMEN'S WESTERN GOLF FOUNDATION SCHOLARSHIP

Scholarships for female high school seniors for use at a four-year college or university. Based on academic record, financial need, character, and involvement in golf. Golf skill not a criteria. Must continue to have financial need. Award is $2000 per student per year. Must be 17 to 18 years of age.

Award: Scholarship for use in freshman year; renewable. *Number:* 20–70. *Amount:* $2000.

Eligibility Requirements: Applicant must be high school student; age 17-18; planning to enroll or expecting to enroll full-time at a four-year institution or university; female and must have an interest in golf. Applicant must have 3.0 GPA or higher. Available to U.S. citizens.

Application Requirements: Application form. *Deadline:* March 1.

Contact: David Grady, President
Phone: 817-265-4074
E-mail: grady@orderofomega.org

WRITER'S DIGEST

http://www.writersdigest.com/

WRITER'S DIGEST ANNUAL WRITING COMPETITION

Annual writing competition. Only original, unpublished entries in any of the ten categories accepted. Visit http://www.writersdigest.com/competitions/writers-digest-annual-competition for guidelines and entry form. Application fee.

Award: Prize for use in freshman, sophomore, junior, senior, or graduate years; not renewable. *Number:* 501. *Amount:* $100–$3000.

Eligibility Requirements: Applicant must be enrolled or expecting to enroll full- or part-time at a two-year or four-year or technical institution or university and must have an interest in writing. Available to U.S. and non-U.S. citizens.

Application Requirements: Application form, application form may be submitted online, entry in a contest. *Deadline:* May 1.

Contact: Nicole Howard, Customer Service Representative
Phone: 715-445-4612
Fax: 513-531-0798
E-mail: writing-competitions@fwmedia.com

WRITER'S DIGEST POPULAR FICTION AWARDS

Writing contest accepts as many manuscripts as the applicant likes in each of the following categories: romance, mystery/crime fiction, sci-fi/fantasy, thriller/suspense and horror. Manuscripts must not be more than 4,000 words. http://www.writersdigest.com/popularfictionawards

Award: Prize for use in freshman, sophomore, junior, senior, graduate, or postgraduate years; not renewable. *Number:* 7. *Amount:* $500–$2500.

Eligibility Requirements: Applicant must be enrolled or expecting to enroll full- or part-time at a two-year or four-year or technical institution or university and must have an interest in writing. Available to U.S. and non-U.S. citizens.

Application Requirements: Application form, entry in a contest, manuscript. *Fee:* $20. *Deadline:* September 1.

Contact: Nicole Howard, Customer Service Representative
Phone: 715-445-4612 Ext. 13430
Fax: 513-531-0798
E-mail: writing-competitions@fwmedia.com

WRITER'S DIGEST SELF-PUBLISHED BOOK AWARDS

Awards open to self-published books for which the author has paid full cost. Visit http://www.writersdigest.com/competitions/selfpublished/ for guidelines and entry form. Application fee: $99.

Award: Prize for use in freshman, sophomore, junior, senior, graduate, or postgraduate years; not renewable. *Number:* 45. *Amount:* $1000–$3000.

Eligibility Requirements: Applicant must be enrolled or expecting to enroll full- or part-time at a two-year or four-year or technical institution or university and must have an interest in writing. Available to U.S. and non-U.S. citizens.

Application Requirements: Application form, entry in a contest. *Fee:* $99. *Deadline:* April 1.

Contact: Nicole Howard, Customer Service Representative
Phone: 715-445-4612 Ext. 13430
Fax: 513-531-0798
E-mail: writing-competitions@fwmedia.com

YORKVILLE GOODS LLC

http://yorkvilleblankets.com/

YORKVILLE BLANKETS ASD SCHOLARSHIP
• *See page 627*

Miscellaneous Criteria

101ST AIRBORNE DIVISION ASSOCIATION

http://www.screamingeaglefoundation.org/

101ST AIRBORNE DIVISION ASSOCIATION CHAPPIE HALL SCHOLARSHIP PROGRAM

Scholarship to provide financial assistance to students who have the potential to become assets to our nation. The major factors to be considered in the evaluation and rating of applicants are eligibility, career objectives, academic record, financial need, and insight gained from the letter and/or essay requesting consideration, and letters of recommendation. Applicant's parents, grandparents, or spouse, living or deceased must be/had been a regular member with 101st Airborne Division Association in good standing. Dollar amount and total number of awards varies.

Award: Scholarship for use in freshman, sophomore, junior, or senior years; not renewable. *Number:* 15–30. *Amount:* $1000–$2000.

Eligibility Requirements: Applicant must be enrolled or expecting to enroll full-time at a two-year or four-year or technical institution or university. Available to U.S. and non-U.S. citizens.

Application Requirements: Application form, community service, essay, personal photograph. *Deadline:* April 11.

Contact: Mr. Randal Underhill, Executive Director
101st Airborne Division Association
PO Box 929
Fort Campbell, KY 42223-0929
Phone: 931-431-0199 Ext. 35
E-mail: 101exec@comcast.net

1800WHEELCHAIR.COM

http://www.1800wheelchair.com/

1800WHEELCHAIR.COM SCHOLARSHIP

Established in 2006, the 1800wheelchair scholarship fund now bestows two $500 awards each year. We are going to repeat our visual contest. Please submit a visual poem, in a style of your choosing, on the theme of overcoming a personal challenge. Limit your visual poem to an 8.5in x 11in piece of paper. You can choose to represent words, images, or both. It can abstract or representational. Please include a personal statement that gives us an idea of who you are and how your poem relates to a challenge you've faced. The poem and essay (combined) should be between 500 and 1,000 words, but feel free to write a little more or less. See website for more information, http://www.1800wheelchair.com/scholarship/

Award: Prize for use in freshman, sophomore, junior, or senior years; renewable. *Number:* 2. *Amount:* $500.

Eligibility Requirements: Applicant must be enrolled or expecting to enroll full-time at a two-year or four-year or technical institution or university. Applicant must have 3.0 GPA or higher. Available to U.S. citizens.

Application Requirements: Personal photograph, portfolio. *Deadline:* December 30.

Contact: Mr. Joseph Piekarski, President
1800Wheelchair.com
320 Roebling Street
Suite 515
Brooklyn, NY 11211
E-mail: scholarship@1800wheelchair.com

1 ON 1 LESSONS

http://www.1on1lessons.com

MYFAVORITETEACHER SCHOLARSHIP

Education is beyond important as it creates a foundation on which we develop as individuals. Teachers deserve proper acknowledgment for their contributions and dedication to education. The My Favorite Teacher Scholarship aims to make students reflect upon the teachers and professors who have had a positive impact on their education. Applicants are also encouraged to share their reflections with the teachers themselves to give them the proper acknowledgement and praise they deserve. More information available at http://www.1on1lessons.com/scholarship/

Award: Scholarship for use in freshman, sophomore, junior, senior, graduate, or postgraduate years; not renewable. *Number:* 2. *Amount:* $500.

Eligibility Requirements: Applicant must be enrolled or expecting to enroll full- or part-time at a two-year or four-year institution or university. Applicant must have 2.5 GPA or higher. Available to U.S. citizens.

Application Requirements: Application form, essay. *Deadline:* December 31.

Contact: Mr. James McQuillin, Owner
Naples, FL
Phone: 239-877-7867
E-mail: scholarship@1on1lessons.com

37TH DIVISION VETERANS ASSOCIATION

http://www.37thdva.org/

37TH DIVISION VETERANS ASSOCIATION SCHOLARSHIP GRANT PROGRAM

Must be a current member of the organization in good standing or be the direct lineal descendant (to the third generation) of such a member. Please visit http://www.37thdva.org to see a copy of the application and to determine eligibility. Please note that the 37th Infantry Division was part of the U.S. Army.

Award: Scholarship for use in freshman, sophomore, junior, senior, graduate, or postgraduate years; not renewable.

Eligibility Requirements: Applicant must be enrolled or expecting to enroll full-time at a two-year or four-year or technical institution or university. Available to U.S. citizens.

Application Requirements: Application form, community service, essay. *Deadline:* May 1.

Contact: Mandy Oberyszyn, Executive Director
37th Division Veterans Association
35 East Chestnut Street, Suite 512
Columbus, OH 43215
Phone: 614-228-3788
E-mail: mandy@37thdva.org

A1 GARAGE DOOR SERVICE

www.phoenixazgaragedoorrepair.com/

A1 GARAGE DOOR SERVICE COLLEGE SCHOLARSHIP

Ongoing scholarship for $1000, that will be awarded twice annually. In addition to the online application, the applicant must submit a an essay (600 words or more) or video which shows a students best idea for a marketing campaign in the service industry. One submission, per student, per semester. Essays/Videos may be features on our website, Facebook page, blog or other social media accounts.

Award: Scholarship for use in freshman, sophomore, junior, or senior years; not renewable. *Number:* 1. *Amount:* $1000.

Eligibility Requirements: Applicant must be enrolled or expecting to enroll full-time at a four-year institution. Applicant must have 2.5 GPA or higher. Available to U.S. citizens.

Application Requirements: Application form, essay. *Deadline:* continuous.

Contact: Tommy Mello
E-mail: tommy.mello.social@gmail.com

ACTIVIA TRAINING

https://www.activia.co.uk/

ACTIVIA TRAINING US SCHOLARSHIP

Activia Training are pleased to offer a $1,500 annual scholarship for college, university, high school or trade school students in the US. There are two scholarship awards of $750 each year, awarded in November and May, and there is no specific course of study required in order to enter.

Award: Scholarship for use in freshman, sophomore, junior, senior, graduate, or postgraduate years; not renewable. *Number:* 4. *Amount:* $250–$500.

Eligibility Requirements: Applicant must be enrolled or expecting to enroll full- or part-time at a two-year or four-year or technical institution or university. Available to U.S. and non-U.S. citizens.

Application Requirements: Application form. *Deadline:* continuous.

Contact: Ashley Andrews
    E-mail: ashleyandrews@activia.co.uk

ACUITY TRAINING LIMITED

http://www.acuitytraining.co.uk

ACUITY TRAINING SCHOLARSHIP FOR OUTSTANDING LEADERSHIP AWARD

You have a chance to win a scholarship for $1000. Your video entry should ideally be three to four minutes in length. We want you to include some of the following ideas: A) What is leadership? Why is it valuable and how can it be developed? What is the difference between leadership, management and assertiveness?, B) Examples of how and when you have shown leadership and the benefits that have flowed from that, and C) The importance of leadership qualities in the 21st century workplace? The best submission will be awarded $1000 that can be used to further their education. This award is only available to students that are currently enrolled at a college, university, high school or trade school.

Award: Scholarship for use in freshman, sophomore, junior, senior, graduate, or postgraduate years; not renewable. *Number:* 1. *Amount:* $1000.

Eligibility Requirements: Applicant must be enrolled or expecting to enroll full- or part-time at a two-year or four-year or technical institution or university. Available to U.S. and non-U.S. citizens.

Application Requirements: Application form may be submitted online (http://www.acuitytraining.co.uk/scholarships/), video. *Deadline:* December 31.

Contact: Ben Richardson
    Phone: +44-1483688488
    E-mail: scholarships@acuitytraining.co.uk

ALFRED G. AND ELMA M. MILOTTE SCHOLARSHIP FUND

http://www.milotte.org/

ALFRED G. AND ELMA M. MILOTTE SCHOLARSHIP

Grant of up to $4000 to high school graduate or students holding the GED. Applicants must have been accepted at a trade school, art school, two-year or four-year college or university for undergraduate or graduate studies.

Award: Scholarship for use in freshman, sophomore, junior, senior, or graduate years; not renewable. *Amount:* up to $4000.

Eligibility Requirements: Applicant must be enrolled or expecting to enroll full- or part-time at a two-year or four-year or technical institution or university. Applicant must have 3.0 GPA or higher. Available to U.S. citizens.

Application Requirements: Application form, recommendations or references, samples of work expressing applicant's observations of the natural world, transcript. *Deadline:* March 1.

Contact: Sean Ferguson, Assistant Vice President
    Phone: 800-832-9071
    Fax: 800-552-3182
    E-mail: info@milotte.org

ALL-INK.COM PRINTER SUPPLIES ONLINE

ALL-INK.COM COLLEGE SCHOLARSHIP PROGRAM

One-time award for any level of postsecondary education. Minimum 2.5 GPA. Must apply online only at website http://www.all-ink.com. Recipients selected annually.

Award: Scholarship for use in freshman, sophomore, junior, senior, graduate, or postgraduate years; not renewable. *Number:* 5–10. *Amount:* $1000–$5000.

Eligibility Requirements: Applicant must be enrolled or expecting to enroll full-time at a two-year or four-year or technical institution or university. Applicant must have 2.5 GPA or higher. Available to U.S. and non-U.S. citizens.

Application Requirements: Application form, entry in a contest, essay. *Deadline:* December 31.

Contact: Aaron Gale, President
    All-Ink.com Printer Supplies Online
    1460 North Main Street, Suite 2
    Spanish Fork, UT 84660
    Phone: 801-794-0123
    Fax: 801-794-0124
    E-mail: scholarship@all-ink.com

ALPHA KAPPA ALPHA

http://www.akaeaf.org

AKA EDUCATIONAL ADVANCEMENT FOUNDATION, INC. FINANCIAL NEEDS SCHOLARSHIP

Financial needs scholarships are for students who have completed a minimum of one year in a degree-granting institution and have a financial burden that is preventing them from continuing their studies. Students must have a minimum GPA of 2.5 and show evidence of leadership by participating in community or campus activities.

Award: Scholarship for use in sophomore, junior, senior, or graduate years; not renewable.

Eligibility Requirements: Applicant must be enrolled or expecting to enroll full-time at a four-year institution or university. Applicant must have 3.5 GPA or higher. Available to U.S. and non-U.S. citizens.

Application Requirements: Application form, essay, financial need analysis. *Deadline:* April 15.

Contact: Ms. Erika Everett, Executive Director
    Alpha Kappa Alpha
    5656 South Stony Island
    3rd Floor
    Chicago, IL 60637
    Phone: 773-947-0026
    E-mail: eeverett@akaeaf.net

AKA EDUCATIONAL ADVANCEMENT FOUNDATION, INC. MERIT SCHOLARSHIP

Scholarships are for students demonstrating exceptional academic achievements. Applicants must have completed a minimum of one year in a degree-granting institution and will be continuing their program in that institution. Students must have a GPA of 3.0 or higher and show evidence of leadership by participating in community or campus activities.

Award: Scholarship for use in sophomore, junior, senior, or graduate years; not renewable.

Eligibility Requirements: Applicant must be enrolled or expecting to enroll full-time at a four-year institution or university. Applicant must have 3.0 GPA or higher. Available to U.S. and non-U.S. citizens.

Application Requirements: Application form, essay. *Deadline:* April 15.

Contact: Erika Everett, Executive Director
    Phone: 773-947-0026
    E-mail: akaeaf@akaeaf.net

AKA EDUCATIONAL ADVANCEMENT FOUNDATION, INC. YOUTH PARTNERS ACCESSING CAPITAL SCHOLARSHIP

Youth-PAC awards are for undergraduate members of Alpha Kappa Alpha Sorority, Inc. with at least a sophomore status. Members must have a minimum GPA of 3.0 and participate in leadership, volunteer, civic, or campus activities, as well as demonstrate academic achievements or have a financial need.

Award: Scholarship for use in sophomore, junior, or senior years; not renewable.

Eligibility Requirements: Applicant must be enrolled or expecting to enroll full-time at a four-year institution or university. Applicant must have 3.0 GPA or higher. Available to U.S. and non-U.S. citizens.

Application Requirements: Application form, essay. *Deadline:* April 15.

Contact: Erika Everett, Executive Director
Phone: 773-947-0026
E-mail: akaeaf@akaeaf.net

ALPHA LAMBDA DELTA
http://www.nationalald.org/

JO ANNE J. TROW SCHOLARSHIPS
One-time award for initiated members of Alpha Lambda Delta. Minimum 3.5 GPA required. Must be nominated by chapter.

Award: Scholarship for use in junior year; not renewable. *Number:* 1–36. *Amount:* $1000–$6000.

Eligibility Requirements: Applicant must be enrolled or expecting to enroll full-time at a four-year institution or university. Applicant must have 3.5 GPA or higher. Available to U.S. and non-U.S. citizens.

Application Requirements: Application form, essay. *Deadline:* April 1.

Contact: Eileen Merberg, Executive Director
Alpha Lambda Delta
PO Box 444
fairport, NY 14450
Phone: 585-364-0840
E-mail: eileen@nationalald.org

AMBROSIA TREATMENT CENTER
https://www.ambrosiatc.com/?ambTRK=PR

WE DO RECOVER SCHOLARSHIP
Every accomplishment starts with a decision to try. Have you been affected by drug addiction or alcoholism looking to better yourself by continuing your education? Share a positive story of your recovery or the recovery of your loved one. Your story will be featured like the ones above, so use those as an example, but be unique and creative. Then, share on social media! The winner will be selected July 31, 2017, based on the most shares on Facebook or Linkedin. Please submit the following: a 1,000 word written story, 1-2.5 minute video, and 2+ images of yourself to the survey on our We Do Recover webpage.

Award: Scholarship for use in freshman, sophomore, junior, senior, graduate, or postgraduate years; not renewable. *Number:* 1–3. *Amount:* $500.

Eligibility Requirements: Applicant must be enrolled or expecting to enroll full- or part-time at a two-year or four-year institution or university. Available to U.S. citizens.

Application Requirements: Application form, essay, personal photograph. *Deadline:* July 31.

Contact: Parker Horveath, Digital Marketing Coordinator
E-mail: phorveath@ambrosiatc.com

AMERICAN ASSOCIATION OF COLLEGES OF NURSING
http://aacn.nche.edu

AFTERCOLLEGE/AACN NURSING SCHOLARSHIP PROGRAM
The AfterCollege-AACN Scholarship Fund supports students who are seeking a baccalaureate, Master's or doctoral degree in nursing. Special consideration will be given to students in a graduate program with the goal of becoming a nurse educator; students completing an RN-to-BSN or RN-to-MSN program; and those enrolled in an accelerated program. One scholarship in the amount of $2,500 will be awarded each quarter. Nursing Scholarship Deadlines: March 31, June 30, September 30, December 31. Please note that all applicants must already be enrolled (not just accepted) at an AACN member institution. To check if your school is a member, see AACN Members. Only finalists are contacted and may be asked to submit letters of recommendation, published articles, awards/honors, etc. to the selection committee. Recipients will be announced within one month of each deadline and contacted to redeem the award. Check out this list of past scholarship recipients. Have questions about this scholarship? You can reach us at scholarships@aftercollege.com, and visit our Official Scholarship Rules for full details!

Award: Scholarship for use in freshman, sophomore, junior, senior, graduate, or postgraduate years; not renewable. *Number:* 1. *Amount:* $2500.

Eligibility Requirements: Applicant must be enrolled or expecting to enroll full-time at a four-year institution or university. Available to U.S. and non-U.S. citizens.

Application Requirements: Application form. *Deadline:* continuous.

Contact: Sonja Bradfield, Communications Coordinator
American Association of Colleges of Nursing
1 Dupont Circle NW
Washington, DC 20036
Phone: 202-463-6930 Ext. 260
E-mail: sbradfield@aacn.nche.edu

AMERICAN BULLION, INC.
http://www.americanbullion.com

AMERICAN BULLION SCHOLARSHIP
The American Bullion Scholarship is offered to current college students. Applicants are asked to write a 500-1,000 word essay answering a question regarding precious metals ownership. Winning submissions are selected by a team of executives at American Bullion.

Award: Scholarship for use in freshman, sophomore, junior, senior, graduate, or postgraduate years; not renewable. *Number:* 5. *Amount:* $500.

Eligibility Requirements: Applicant must be enrolled or expecting to enroll full- or part-time at a four-year institution or university. Available to U.S. citizens.

Application Requirements: Application form, application form may be submitted online (https://www.americanbullion.com/scholarship/), essay. *Deadline:* October 31.

Contact: Orkan Ozkan, Chief Executive Officer
American Bullion, Inc.
12301 Wilshire Boulevard, #650
Los Angeles, CA 90025
Phone: 310-689-7720
E-mail: scholarship@americanbullion.com

AMERICAN COPY EDITORS SOCIETY
http://www.copydesk.org/

ACES EDUCATION FUND SCHOLARSHIP
Scholarships available to undergraduate students entering their junior or senior year, graduate students, and just-graduating students. Students should be aspiring to be professional editors.

Award: Scholarship for use in junior, senior, or graduate years; not renewable. *Number:* 5. *Amount:* $1500–$2500.

Eligibility Requirements: Applicant must be enrolled or expecting to enroll full-time at a four-year institution or university. Available to U.S. and non-U.S. citizens.

Application Requirements: Application form, essay. *Deadline:* November 15.

Contact: Alex Cruden
E-mail: alex@copydesk.org

AMERICAN FIRE SPRINKLER ASSOCIATION
http://www.afsascholarship.org/

AFSA HIGH SCHOOL SCHOLARSHIP CONTEST
One-time award for high school seniors. This scholarship essay contest requires applicants to go online to http://www.afsascholarship.org, and read a short essay about sprinklers and fire safety. After finishing, they complete a ten-question quiz on what they just read. Each correct answer

gives the student a chance at winning one of ten $2,000 scholarships (maximum 10 chances per entrant).

Award: Scholarship for use in freshman year; not renewable. *Number:* 10. *Amount:* $2000.

Eligibility Requirements: Applicant must be high school student and planning to enroll or expecting to enroll full-time at a two-year or four-year or technical institution or university. Available to U.S. citizens.

Application Requirements: Application form. *Deadline:* April 7.

Contact: Darcy Montalvo, Public Relations Manager
American Fire Sprinkler Association
12750 Merit Drive, Suite 350
Dallas, TX 75251
Phone: 214-349-5965
E-mail: dmontalvo@firesprinkler.org

AFSA SECOND CHANCE SCHOLARSHIP CONTEST

Online entries only. Enter at www.afsascholarship.org/ and click on Second Chance Contest; U.S. citizens or legal residents who graduated from U.S. high school may enter. University/trade school/college must be accredited using link provided on Website. No phone calls or emails. Entrants read an online essay and then take online quiz for up to 10 entries into drawing to win.

Award: Scholarship for use in freshman, sophomore, junior, senior, graduate, or postgraduate years; not renewable. *Number:* 5. *Amount:* $1000.

Eligibility Requirements: Applicant must be enrolled or expecting to enroll full-time at a two-year or four-year or technical institution or university. Available to U.S. citizens.

Application Requirements: Application form. *Deadline:* August 30.

Contact: Mrs. Darcy Montalvo, PR Manager
American Fire Sprinkler Association
12750 Merit Drive, Suite 350
Dallas, TX 75251
Phone: 214-349-5965
E-mail: dmontalvo@firesprinkler.org

AMERICAN LEGION AUXILIARY DEPARTMENT OF COLORADO

http://www.alacolorado.com

AMERICAN LEGION AUXILIARY DEPARTMENT OF COLORADO DEPARTMENT PRESIDENT'S SCHOLARSHIP AND SCHOLARSHIP FOR JUNIOR MEMBER

Open to children, spouses, grandchildren, and great-grandchildren of veterans, and veterans who served in the Armed Forces during eligibility dates for membership in the American Legion. Applicants must have been accepted by an accredited school.

Award: Scholarship for use in freshman year; not renewable. *Number:* 2–5. *Amount:* $500–$1000.

Eligibility Requirements: Applicant must be high school student and planning to enroll or expecting to enroll full- or part-time at a two-year or four-year institution or university. Available to U.S. citizens.

Application Requirements: Application form, essay. *Deadline:* March 15.

Contact: Rhonda Larkowski, Department Secretary and Treasurer
American Legion Auxiliary Department of Colorado
7465 East First Avenue, Suite D
Denver, CO 80230
Phone: 303-367-5388
E-mail: www.dept-sec@alacolorado.com

AMERICAN LEGION DEPARTMENT OF MARYLAND

http://www.mdlegion.org/

AMERICAN LEGION, DEPARTMENT OF MARYLAND, HIGH SCHOOL ORATORICAL SCHOLARSHIP CONTEST

Scholarship awarded to winner of the Department of MD High School Oratorical Contest. Applicants must apply at their local Posts and compete in and win their Post, County, and District level competitions for eligibility. The winner of this contest goes on to compete at Nationals for a chance at $18,000 first prize scholarship. For details http://www.legion.org/oratorical

Award: Scholarship for use in freshman, sophomore, junior, or senior years; not renewable. *Number:* 1–7. *Amount:* $500–$2000.

Eligibility Requirements: Applicant must be high school student and planning to enroll or expecting to enroll full-time at a two-year or four-year institution or university. Available to U.S. citizens.

Application Requirements: Entry in a contest, must win post, county, and district contests. *Deadline:* varies.

Contact: Russell Myers, Department Adjutant
American Legion Department of Maryland
101 North Gay Street
Room E
Baltimore, MD 21202
Phone: 410-752-1405
Fax: 410-752-3822
E-mail: russell@mdlegion.org

AMERICAN MILITARY RETIREES ASSOCIATION

http://amra1973.org/

BERNARD E. DILLON VOCATIONAL SKILLS SCHOLARSHIP

Five $1,000 scholarships available to students for vocational/technical training. Applicant or sponsor must be a current member of our association.

Award: Scholarship for use in freshman, sophomore, junior, or senior years; not renewable. *Number:* 1–5. *Amount:* $1000.

Eligibility Requirements: Applicant must be enrolled or expecting to enroll full-time at a technical institution. Available to U.S. citizens.

Application Requirements: Application form, community service, essay. *Deadline:* March 8.

Contact: Ms. Crystal Mang, Office Manager
Phone: 800-424-2969
Fax: 518-324-5204
E-mail: info@amra1973.org

SERGEANT MAJOR DOUGLAS R. DRUM MEMORIAL SCHOLARSHIP

One-time award for college undergraduate students. Qualified applicants may reapply each year. The AMRA Scholarship Fund was developed to honor the Founder and first National President of The American Military Retirees Association (AMRA). Applicant or their sponsor must be a current member of our association.

Award: Scholarship for use in freshman, sophomore, junior, or senior years; not renewable. *Number:* 1–24. *Amount:* $1000–$5000.

Eligibility Requirements: Applicant must be enrolled or expecting to enroll full-time at a two-year or four-year institution or university. Available to U.S. citizens.

Application Requirements: Application form, community service, essay. *Deadline:* March 8.

Contact: Ms. Crystal Mang, Office Manager
Phone: 800-424-2969
Fax: 518-324-5204
E-mail: info@amra1973.org

AMERICAN SCHOOL OF CLASSICAL STUDIES AT ATHENS

http://www.ascsa.edu.gr/

CHARLES M. EDWARDS SCHOLARSHIP

Edwards scholarship is for participation in the ASCSA Summer Sessions program only. It is not for funding at the student's home institution.

Award: Scholarship for use in senior year; not renewable. *Number:* 1. *Amount:* $500.

Eligibility Requirements: Applicant must be enrolled or expecting to enroll part-time at a four-year institution. Available to U.S. and non-U.S. citizens.

Application Requirements: Application form. *Fee:* $25. *Deadline:* January 15.

Contact: ASCSA Committee on the Summer Sessions
American School of Classical Studies at Athens
6-8 Charlton Street
Princeton, NJ 08540
E-mail: ssapplication@ascsa.org

AMERICAN SOCIETY FOR NONDESTRUCTIVE TESTING

http://www.asnt.org

ROBERT B. OLIVER ASNT SCHOLARSHIPS

The Robert B. Oliver Scholarship is granted to the student(s) who submit the most outstanding paper about NDT research, investigation, or development.

Award: Scholarship for use in freshman, sophomore, junior, or senior years; not renewable. *Number:* 3. *Amount:* $2500.

Eligibility Requirements: Applicant must be enrolled or expecting to enroll full-time at a two-year or four-year or technical institution or university. Available to U.S. citizens.

Application Requirements: Application form, essay. *Deadline:* February 15.

Contact: Jessica VanDervort, Program Coordinator
E-mail: jvandervort@asnt.org

AMERICAN SOCIETY OF MECHANICAL ENGINEERS AUXILIARY INC.

http://www.asme.org/

LUCY AND CHARLES W.E. CLARKE SCHOLARSHIP

Scholarship for high school seniors on a FIRST Robotics Team only.

Award: Scholarship for use in freshman year; not renewable. *Number:* 5–12. *Amount:* $5000.

Eligibility Requirements: Applicant must be high school student and planning to enroll or expecting to enroll full-time at a four-year institution or university.

Contact: RuthAnn Bigley, ASME Auxiliary Staff Coordinator
American Society of Mechanical Engineers Auxiliary Inc.
Two Park Avenue
Mailstop RB
New York, NY 10016
Phone: 212-591-7650
E-mail: bigleyr@asme.org

AMERICAN WELDING SOCIETY

http://www.aws.org/

BARBARA AND RICHARD COUCH HYPERTHERM SCHOLARSHIP

Student pursuing a two or four year degree in an engineering or technical major in the welding or cutting field (applicable areas of mechanical, software, process, electrical engineering). Priority will be given to sons and daughters of Hypertherm associates. Applicant must have a 2.8 minimum overall GPA. Proof of financial need is not required but would be a priority.

Award: Scholarship for use in freshman, sophomore, junior, or senior years; not renewable.

Eligibility Requirements: Applicant must be enrolled or expecting to enroll full- or part-time at a two-year or four-year institution. Applicant must have 2.5 GPA or higher. Available to U.S. and non-U.S. citizens.

Application Requirements: Application form, financial need analysis. *Deadline:* February 15.

Contact: Vicki Pinsky, Associate Director, Scholarships, AWS Foundation
American Welding Society
8669 NW 36 Street, Suite 130
Miami, FL 33166
Phone: 800-443-9353 Ext. 212
E-mail: vpinsky@aws.org

D. FRED AND MARIAN L. BOVIE TECHNICAL SCHOLARSHIP

Awarded to a student pursuing an Associates degree in welding. Applicant must have a minimum 2.8 overall GPA and may be enrolled full or part time. Proof of Financial need is required.

Award: Scholarship for use in freshman or sophomore years; not renewable.

Eligibility Requirements: Applicant must be enrolled or expecting to enroll full- or part-time at a two-year institution. Available to U.S. citizens.

Application Requirements: Application form, financial need analysis. *Deadline:* February 15.

Contact: Vicki Pinsky, Associate Director, Scholarships, AWS Foundation
American Welding Society
8669 NW 36 Street, #130
Miami, FL 33166
Phone: 800-443-9353 Ext. 212
E-mail: vpinsky@aws.org

GLENN W. OYLER MEMORIAL TECHNICAL SCHOLARSHIP

Awarded to a student pursuing a certificate or associates degree in welding or related. The student must be a US citizen with a 2.5 overall GPA, and have proof of financial need. Students in New Mexico and Pennsylvania only.

Award: Scholarship for use in freshman or sophomore years; not renewable.

Eligibility Requirements: Applicant must be enrolled or expecting to enroll full- or part-time at a two-year or technical institution. Applicant must have 2.5 GPA or higher. Available to U.S. citizens.

Application Requirements: Application form, financial need analysis. *Deadline:* February 15.

Contact: Vicki Pinsky, Associate Director, Scholarship, AWS Foundation
American Welding Society
8669 NW 36 Street, Suite 130
Miami, FL 33166
Phone: 800-443-9353 Ext. 212
E-mail: vpinsky@aws.org

JOHN DEERE COMPANY SCHOLARSHIP

Two scholarships available. One will be awarded to a mid-west student pursuing a Bachelor's degree in welding engineering, welding engineering technology, manufacturing or mechanical engineering with a welding emphasis. High school attendance or permanent address in states of Iowa, Illinois, Minnesota, Wisconsin or Missouri, with a 3.0 overall GPA and full time school attendance. Proof of financial need not required. One awarded to a female or minority student with the same business degree as above. High school attendance or, with a 3.0 overall GPA and full time. Must be a permanent resident of Iowa, Illinois, Minnesota, Wisconsin, Missouri, Nebraska, Kansas or North or South Dakota. Proof of financial need not required.

Award: Scholarship for use in sophomore, junior, or senior years; not renewable.

Eligibility Requirements: Applicant must be enrolled or expecting to enroll full- or part-time at a four-year institution. Applicant must have 3.0 GPA or higher. Available to U.S. citizens.

Application Requirements: Application form, financial need analysis. *Deadline:* February 15.

Contact: Vicki Pinsky, Associate Director, Scholarships, AWS Foundation
American Welding Society
8669 NW 36 Street
Miami, FL 33166
Phone: 800-443-9353 Ext. 212
E-mail: vpinsky@aws.org

ANDY GREEN, ATTORNEY AT LAW, P.C.

http://www.andygreenlaw.com

PERSONS IN OR AFFECTED BY RECOVERY SCHOLARSHIP

The Persons in or Affected by Recovery Scholarship was created to acknowledge the powerful journey that accompanies addiction recovery. As somebody who is personally in recovery, I wanted to make this scholarship available to help those who are working to help themselves. The Persons in or Affected by Recovery Scholarship is open to all qualifying students enrolled in a 2-year, 4-year, graduate level or certification program. Andy Green Law will award one $1,000 scholarship to the student who writes the best response to the following question: Explain your road to recovery (or a loved one's road to recovery), and how it has impacted your desire to pursue your future goals. All entries must be a minimum of 500 and maximum of 1000 words. Diagrams, schematics, illustrations and photographs may be included as supporting documents.

Award: Scholarship for use in freshman, sophomore, junior, senior, or graduate years; not renewable. *Number:* 1. *Amount:* $1000.

Eligibility Requirements: Applicant must be enrolled or expecting to enroll full- or part-time at a two-year or four-year or technical institution or university. Available to U.S. and non-U.S. citizens.

Application Requirements: Application form, essay. *Deadline:* July 1.

Contact: Mr. Andy Green, Attorney
Andy Green, Attorney at Law, P.C.
121 SW Salmon Street, Suite 1100
Portland, OR 97204
Phone: 503-471-1385
E-mail: andygreenlawpdx@gmail.com

APPALACHIAN STUDIES ASSOCIATION

http://www.appalachianstudies.org/

CARL A. ROSS STUDENT PAPER AWARD

All papers must adhere to guidelines for scholarly research. Middle/high school papers should be 8–15 pages in length. Undergraduate/graduate papers should be 15–30 pages in length. Nominations should be submitted by emailing a Microsoft Word copy of the paper to the chair of the selection committee before January 15. Papers submitted to the undergraduate/graduate competition must have been completed during the current or previous academic year. Submissions must include proof of student status during the current or previous academic year; documentation may consist of a copy of a schedule of classes or (unofficial or official) transcript or a letter from a faculty advisor (which should include the faculty advisor's e-mail address, phone number, and mailing address). Students who wish to present their papers at the conference must also submit a proposal for participation by the submission deadline (generally in October). Costs of attending the conference are the winner's responsibility.

Award: Prize for use in freshman, sophomore, junior, senior, or graduate years; not renewable. *Number:* 2. *Amount:* $100.

Eligibility Requirements: Applicant must be enrolled or expecting to enroll full- or part-time at a two-year or four-year institution or university. Available to U.S. and non-U.S. citizens.

Application Requirements: Essay. *Deadline:* January 15.

Contact: Casey LaFrance
E-mail: TC-Lafrance@wiu.edu

APPLYKIT

http://applykit.com

APPLYKIT SCHOLARSHIP $500 NO ESSAY!

The $500 ApplyKit Scholarship is awarded to one user who registers for free at ApplyKit.com. Registration is available at the following website: http://www.applykit.com/user/registration/?partner=petersons. Open to undergraduate students pursuing both full and part-time studies.

Award: Scholarship for use in freshman, sophomore, junior, or senior years; not renewable. *Number:* 1. *Amount:* $500.

Eligibility Requirements: Applicant must be age 15-19 and enrolled or expecting to enroll full- or part-time at a two-year or four-year or technical institution or university. Available to U.S. and non-U.S. citizens.

Application Requirements: Application form may be submitted online (http://www.applykit.com/user/registration/?partner=petersons). *Deadline:* December 1.

Contact: Alex Hollis, Chief Marketing Officer
ApplyKit
844 Elm Street
Manchester, NH 03101
E-mail: alex@applykit.com

ARMY EMERGENCY RELIEF (AER)

http://www.aerhq.org/

OVERSEAS SPOUSE EDUCATION ASSISTANCE PROGRAM

The Overseas Spouse Education Assistance Program (OSEAP) is a need-based education assistance program designed to provide spouses with financial assistance to pursue educational goals. Spouses must physically reside at overseas residence, and be enrolled, accepted, or pending acceptance as students for the entire term in postsecondary or vocational institutions under contract at the education office and approved by the U.S. Department of Education.

Award: Scholarship for use in freshman, sophomore, or junior years; renewable. *Amount:* $500–$2500.

Eligibility Requirements: Applicant must be enrolled or expecting to enroll full- or part-time at an institution or university and married. Available to U.S. citizens.

Application Requirements: *Deadline:* continuous.

Contact: Mrs. Angie Pratt
Army Emergency Relief (AER)
Headquarters, Army Emergency Relief, Attention: Overseas Spouse Education Assistance
200 Stovall Street
Stovall, VA 22332-0600
Phone: 703-325-0313
E-mail: Overseas@aerhq.org

ASM MATERIALS EDUCATION FOUNDATION

http://www.asmfoundation.org/

LADISH CO. FOUNDATION SCHOLARSHIPS

Two scholarships of $2,500 each. Student must be a Wisconsin resident and must attend a Wisconsin university to qualify.

Award: Scholarship for use in junior or senior years; not renewable. *Number:* 1–2. *Amount:* $2500.

Eligibility Requirements: Applicant must be enrolled or expecting to enroll full-time at an institution or university. Available to U.S. and Canadian citizens.

Application Requirements: Essay, financial need analysis, interview, personal photograph. *Deadline:* May 1.

Contact: Pergentina Deatherage, Administrator, Foundation Programs
ASM Materials Education Foundation
ASM Materials Education Foundation
9639 Kinsman Road
Materials Park, OH 44073
Phone: 440-338-5151 Ext. 5533
E-mail: scholarshipsUG@asminternational.org

LUCILLE & CHARLES A. WERT SCHOLARSHIP

One year full tuition of up to $10,000. Established in 2006 through a generous bequest by Dr. & Mrs. Charles Wert.

Award: Scholarship for use in junior or senior years; not renewable. *Number:* 1. *Amount:* $10,000.

Eligibility Requirements: Applicant must be enrolled or expecting to enroll full-time at an institution or university. Available to U.S. and Canadian citizens.

Application Requirements: Essay, financial need analysis, personal photograph. *Deadline:* May 1.

Contact: Pergentina Deatherage, Administrator, Foundation Programs
ASM Materials Education Foundation
ASM Materials Education Foundation
9639 Kinsman Road
Materials Park, OH 44073
Phone: 440-338-5151 Ext. 5533
E-mail: scholarshipsUG@asminternational.org

WILLIAM & MARY DYRKACZ SCHOLARSHIPS

Four scholarships of $6,000 each. Established in 2011 through a generous contribution by Mr. & Mrs. William Dyrkacz as an expression of their commitment to education and the materials science and engineering community.

Award: Scholarship for use in junior or senior years; not renewable. *Number:* 1–4. *Amount:* $6000.

Eligibility Requirements: Applicant must be enrolled or expecting to enroll full-time at a four-year institution or university. Available to U.S. and Canadian citizens.

Application Requirements: Essay, financial need analysis. *Deadline:* May 1.

Contact: Pergentina Deatherage, Administrator, Foundation Programs
ASM Materials Education Foundation
ASM Materials Education Foundation
9639 Kinsman Road
Materials Park, OH 44073
Phone: 440-338-5151 Ext. 5533
E-mail: scholarshipsUG@asminternational.org

ASSOCIATED MEDICAL SERVICES INC.

http://www.ams-inc.on.ca/

AMS HISTORY OF MEDICINE HANNAH SUMMER STUDENTSHIPS

The Hannah Summer Studentship offers four undergraduate students each summer an opportunity to learn the techniques of historical research and to encourage their serious future study of medical history. The studentships are jointly administered with the Canadian Society for the History of Medicine.

Award: Scholarship for use in freshman, sophomore, junior, senior, or graduate years; not renewable. *Number:* 4. *Amount:* $5500.

Eligibility Requirements: Applicant must be enrolled or expecting to enroll full- or part-time at an institution or university. Available to Canadian citizens.

Contact: Anne Avery, Director of Communications
Phone: 416-924-3368
Fax: 416-323-3338
E-mail: anne.avery@ams-inc.on.ca

ASSOCIATION OF SIKH PROFESSIONALS

http://www.sikhprofessionals.org/

SIKH EDUCATION AID FUND

This fund has been set up to support financially deserving Sikh students, to recognize Sikh students of outstanding academic abilities, and to support those individuals doing research in the Sikh religion or engaged in Sikh studies. Awards are in the form of scholarships, grants through endowments, and interest-free loans for which repayment is expected after graduation.

Award: Scholarship for use in freshman, sophomore, junior, or senior years. *Amount:* $400–$4000.

Eligibility Requirements: Applicant must be enrolled or expecting to enroll full- or part-time at an institution or university. Available to U.S. citizens.

Application Requirements: *Deadline:* June 1.

AVERMEDIA INFORMATION, INC.

http://www.averusa.com/

AVERVISION SCHOLARSHIP PROGRAM

The AVerMedia scholarship will be awarded to two 2011 graduating high school seniors entering an accredited four year college. Applicants must submit a one-page essay answering: Explain how classroom technology has changed throughout your educational path. How has classroom technology impacted your learning?

Award: Scholarship for use in freshman year. *Number:* 2. *Amount:* $2500.

Eligibility Requirements: Applicant must be high school student and planning to enroll or expecting to enroll full-time at a four-year institution or university. Applicant must have 2.5 GPA or higher. Available to U.S. and Canadian citizens.

Application Requirements: *Deadline:* May 31.

AYN RAND INSTITUTE

https://www.aynrand.org

ATLAS SHRUGGED ESSAY CONTEST

Annual Essay Contest on Ayn Rand's novel, Atlas Shrugged, for college/university and 12th grade students. Essays will be judged on whether the student is able to argue for and justify his or her view, not on whether the Institute agrees with the view the student expresses. Judges will look for writing that is clear, articulate and logically organized. Winning essays must demonstrate an outstanding grasp of the philosophic meaning of Atlas Shrugged. For complete rules and guidelines, visit https://www.aynrand.org/students/essay-contests#atlasshrugged-1

Award: Prize for use in freshman, sophomore, junior, senior, graduate, or postgraduate years; not renewable. *Number:* 84. *Amount:* $50–$20,000.

Eligibility Requirements: Applicant must be enrolled or expecting to enroll full- or part-time at a two-year or four-year or technical institution or university. Available to U.S. and non-U.S. citizens.

Application Requirements: Essay. *Deadline:* April 28.

Contact: Anthony Loy, Student Outreach Coordinator
Ayn Rand Institute
2121 Alton Parkway, Suite 250
Irvine, CA 92606
Phone: 949-222-6550 Ext. 269
Fax: 949-222-6558
E-mail: essays@aynrand.org

BAPTIST JOINT COMMITTEE FOR RELIGIOUS LIBERTY

http://www.BJConline.org/

RELIGIOUS LIBERTY ESSAY SCHOLARSHIP CONTEST

To enter, students submit an essay based on the year's topic. All high school juniors and seniors are eligible, and they must have an essay adviser (a teacher or church staff member) to verify that the student's work is his or her own. http://www.BJConline.org/contest.

Award: Scholarship for use in freshman year; not renewable. *Number:* 1–3. *Amount:* $250–$2000.

Eligibility Requirements: Applicant must be high school student and planning to enroll or expecting to enroll full- or part-time at a two-year or four-year or technical institution or university. Available to U.S. citizens.

Application Requirements: Application form, essay. *Deadline:* March 4.

Contact: Charles Watson, Education and Outreach Specialist
Phone: 202-544-4226
Fax: 202-544-2094
E-mail: cwatson@BJConline.org

BARBIZON INTERNATIONAL LLC

http://www.barbizonmodeling.com/scholarships/

BARBIZON COLLEGE TUITION SCHOLARSHIP

The Barbizon International scholarship offers $100,000 college tuition awarded every other year by random drawing. Entry forms are available at high schools throughout the United States. For more details, visit www.barbizonmodeling.com/scholarships.

Award: Scholarship for use in freshman, sophomore, junior, or senior years; not renewable. *Number:* 1. *Amount:* $100,000.

Eligibility Requirements: Applicant must be enrolled or expecting to enroll full-time at a four-year institution or university. Available to U.S. citizens.

Application Requirements: Application form. *Deadline:* December 1.

Contact: Kristina Anderson, Marketing Specialist
Phone: 888-999-9404

BERKSHIRE HATHAWAY HOMESERVICES OF GEORGIA

http://www.bhhsgeorgia.com/

AMERICAN DREAM SCHOLARSHIP

$1000 scholarship for college freshmen. To apply, students must submit a 500-1000 word essay based on one of the three essay questions about their personal experience with homeownership. Send a Word doc attachment to scholarship@bhhsgeorgia.com with essay submission. The file name should be student's full name, state, and date of birth. For example, Chipper-Jones-GA-4-24-1972. All submission emails must contain the student's full name, date of birth, email address, postal address, high school they are currently enrolled in, and a phone number to contact. For more information, visit http://www.bhhsgeorgia.com/american-dream-scholarship.aspx.

Award: Scholarship for use in freshman year; not renewable. *Number:* 1. *Amount:* $1000.

Eligibility Requirements: Applicant must be high school student and planning to enroll or expecting to enroll full-time at a two-year or four-year or technical institution or university. Available to U.S. citizens.

Application Requirements: Essay. *Deadline:* May 30.

Contact: Tony Floyd
Phone: 770-992-4100
E-mail: scholarship@bhhsgeorgia.com

BLINDED VETERANS ASSOCIATION

http://www.bva.org/

KATHERN F. GRUBER SCHOLARSHIP

Award for undergraduate or graduate study is available to dependent children, grandchildren and spouses of legally blind veterans to include Active Duty legally blinded Armed Forces members. The veteran's blindness may be either service or non-service connected. High school seniors may apply. Applicant must be enrolled or accepted for admission as a full-time student in an accredited institution of higher learning, business, secretarial, or vocational school. Six awards of $2000 each are given.

Award: Scholarship for use in freshman, sophomore, junior, senior, or graduate years; not renewable. *Number:* 6. *Amount:* $2000.

Eligibility Requirements: Applicant must be enrolled or expecting to enroll full-time at a two-year or four-year or technical institution or university. Available to U.S. citizens.

Application Requirements: Application form, essay. *Deadline:* April 21.

Contact: Scholarship Coordinator
Blinded Veterans Association
125 N. West St.
Suite 300
Alexandria, VA 22314
Phone: 202-371-8880
E-mail: bva@bva.org

BMI FOUNDATION, INC.

http://www.bmifoundation.org/

BMI FUTURE JAZZ MASTER SCHOLARSHIP

The BMI Future Jazz Master Scholarship competition is open to jazz performers age 17-24 attending colleges and universities nationwide. The $5,000 award was established in 2015 in honor of the National Endowment for the Arts Jazz Masters Fellowship. A panel of Jazz Masters will select the winner based on evidence of talent and potential as a jazz performer. BMI writer and NEA Jazz Master Nancy Wilson lends her support as the honorary spokesperson for this year's competition.

Award: Scholarship for use in freshman, sophomore, junior, senior, graduate, or postgraduate years; not renewable. *Number:* 1. *Amount:* $5000.

Eligibility Requirements: Applicant must be age 17-24 and enrolled or expecting to enroll full- or part-time at a two-year or four-year or technical institution or university. Available to U.S. and non-U.S. citizens.

Application Requirements: Application form. *Deadline:* February 1.

Contact: Pat Cook, Director
BMI Foundation, Inc.
7 World Trade Center
250 Greenwich Street
New York, NY 10007
Phone: 212-220-3103
E-mail: info@bmifoundation.org

BMW OF FREEPORT

http://www.bmwoffreeport.com

BIANNUAL SCHOLARSHIP PROGRAM

BMW of Freeport values higher education and is proud to announce the start of our biannual scholarship worth $500. Submit your 1,000 to 1,500 word entry on the topic below to scholarship@bmwoffreeport.com along with proof of enrollment and grade point average. Deadline is August 3rd, 2017 with the winner to be announced August 25th, 2017 via email. BMW is considered The Ultimate Driving Machine and BMW of Freeport wants to know what drives you to succeed. In 1,000 to 1,500 words, write about what motivates you to succeed. In order to enter into BMW of Freeport's scholarship, applicants must meet the following criteria: Senior in high school or freshman in college located in the United States Must be currently attending or planning to attend an accredited college or university during the fall 2017 academic year and have at least a 3.0 GPA. Must be in good academic standing with your current educational institution. Applicants under 18 must have permission from a parent or legal guardian. Must apply to the scholarship via email and provide your name, address, and the name of the institution you are attending or plan to attend, along with your current transcript. Must provide your written essay (PDF format preferred) by August 3rd, 2017.

Award: Scholarship for use in freshman year; not renewable. *Number:* 1. *Amount:* $500.

Eligibility Requirements: Applicant must be enrolled or expecting to enroll full-time at a four-year institution or university. Applicant must have 3.0 GPA or higher. Available to U.S. citizens.

Application Requirements: Essay. *Deadline:* August 3.

Contact: Jeff Kovacich
E-mail: Scholarship@bmwoffreeport.com

BRADLEY CORBETT LAW

http://www.bradleycorbettlaw.com/scholarship

LAW OFFICE OF BRADLEY R. CORBETT SCHOLARSHIP

$2000 award for a college or university student in the United States. Scholarship will be awarded to the student who submits the best overall essay; details are available at the website http://www.bradleycorbettlaw.com/scholarship/. Must be a U.S. citizen and submit proof of college enrollment.

Award: Scholarship for use in freshman, sophomore, junior, senior, graduate, or postgraduate years; not renewable. *Number:* 1. *Amount:* $2000.

Eligibility Requirements: Applicant must be enrolled or expecting to enroll full-time at a two-year or four-year or technical institution or university. Available to U.S. citizens.

Application Requirements: Essay, proof of enrollment. *Deadline:* July 15.

Contact: Mr. Cameron Cox, Scholarship Outreach Manager
Bradley Corbett Law
620 South Melrose
Suite 101
Vista, CA 92081
Phone: 619-800-4449
E-mail: ccox@scholarassociation.org

BRITISH COLUMBIA MINISTRY OF ADVANCED EDUCATION

http://www.studentaidbc.ca/

IRVING K. BARBER BRITISH COLUMBIA SCHOLARSHIP PROGRAM (FOR STUDY IN BRITISH COLUMBIA)

Scholarship to students who, after completing two years at a British Columbia public community college, university college or institute, must transfer to another public postsecondary institution in British Columbia to complete their degree. Students must demonstrate merit as well as exceptional involvement in their institution and community. Must have a GPA of at least 3.5. For more details, visit http://www.aved.gov.bc.ca/studentaidbc/specialprograms/irvingkbarber/bc_scholarship.htm.

Award: Scholarship for use in junior or senior years; not renewable. *Number:* up to 150. *Amount:* up to $5000.

Eligibility Requirements: Applicant must be enrolled or expecting to enroll full-time at a four-year institution or university and studying in British Columbia. Applicant must have 3.5 GPA or higher. Available to Canadian citizens.

Application Requirements: Application form, community service, essay, recommendations or references, test scores, transcript. *Deadline:* March 31.

Contact: Victoria Thibeau, Loan Remission and Management Unit
Phone: 250-387-6100
E-mail: victoria.thibeau@gov.bc.ca

BURGER KING MCLAMORE FOUNDATION

https://bkmclamorefoundation.org/

BURGER KING SCHOLARS PROGRAM

Created in memory of BURGER KING® Co-founder James W. McLamore, the BURGER KING Scholars program has awarded $28.3 million in scholarships to more than 26,800 high school students, BK® employees and their families across the U.S., Canada and Puerto Rico since 2000. In 2016 alone, the Foundation awarded $3 million to more than 2,800 students in North America. Scholarship grants range from $1,000 to $50,000 and are intended to help students offset the cost of attending college or post-secondary vocational/technical school. Recipients are selected based on their grade point average (GPA), work experience, extracurricular activities and community service. Primarily funded by the BURGER KING® system and guests through annual fundraising activities, scholarships are awarded in the spring of each year. Our ultimate goal? To provide one $1,000 scholarship for every BURGER KING® restaurant in North America that's more than $7 million each year! The application period for the 2018-2019 school year begins on Oct. 15, 2017 and closes Dec. 15, 2017.

Award: Scholarship for use in freshman year; not renewable. *Amount:* $1000–$5000.

Eligibility Requirements: Applicant must be high school student and planning to enroll or expecting to enroll full-time at a two-year or four-year or technical institution or university. Applicant must have 2.5 GPA or higher. Available to U.S. and Canadian citizens.

Application Requirements: Application form, community service, personal photograph. *Deadline:* December 15.

Contact: Scholarship Management Services
Phone: 507-931-1682
E-mail: burgerkingscholars@scholarshipamerica.org

CALVIN COOLIDGE PRESIDENTIAL FOUNDATION, INC.

http://www.coolidgefoundation.org

COOLIDGE SCHOLARSHIP

The Coolidge Scholarship is a full-ride presidential scholarship that covers a student's tuition, room, board, and expenses for four years of undergraduate study and leadership training. The Coolidge may be used by recipients at any American university. Anyone of any background, pursuing any academic discipline of study, may apply to this non-partisan, need-blind, program. ONLY current high school juniors are eligible to apply.

Award: Scholarship for use in freshman, sophomore, junior, or senior years; renewable. *Number:* 2.

Eligibility Requirements: Applicant must be high school student and planning to enroll or expecting to enroll full-time at a four-year institution or university. Available to U.S. citizens.

Application Requirements: Application form, essay. *Deadline:* February 13.

Contact: Mr. Rob Hammer, Program Associate
Calvin Coolidge Presidential Foundation, Inc.
Calvin Coolidge Presidential Foundation
PO Box 97
Plymouth, VT 05056
Phone: 802-672-3389
E-mail: coolidgescholars@coolidgefoundation.org

CASUALTY ACTUARIES OF THE SOUTHEAST

http://www.casact.org/community/affiliates/case/

CASUALTY ACTUARIES OF THE SOUTHEAST SCHOLARSHIP PROGRAM

Scholarships available for undergraduate students in the southeastern states for the study of actuarial science. Must be studying in Alabama, Arkansas, Florida, Georgia, Kentucky, Louisiana, Mississippi, North Carolina, South Carolina, Tennessee, or Virginia. Incoming freshmen/first-year students are not eligible for the scholarship. Must have demonstrated strong interest in mathematics or mathematics-related field and high scholastic achievement. Applicants should demonstrate interest in the actuarial profession, mathematical aptitude, and communication skills.

Award: Scholarship for use in sophomore, junior, or senior years; not renewable. *Number:* 2–4. *Amount:* $1000–$1500.

Eligibility Requirements: Applicant must be enrolled or expecting to enroll full-time at a four-year institution or university and studying in Alabama, Arkansas, Florida, Georgia, Kentucky, Louisiana, Mississippi, North Carolina, South Carolina, Tennessee, Virginia. Available to U.S. and Canadian citizens.

Application Requirements: Application form, essay, recommendations or references, transcript. *Deadline:* May 1.

Contact: Karen Jordan
Casualty Actuaries of the Southeast
3274 Medlock Bridge Road
Peachtree Corners, GA 30092
Phone: 678-684-4877
E-mail: kjordan@merlinosinc.com

CENTRAL NATIONAL BANK & TRUST COMPANY OF ENID TRUSTEE

http://cnb-ok.com/

MAY T. HENRY SCHOLARSHIP FOUNDATION

A $1000 scholarship renewed annually for four years. Awarded to any student enrolled in an Oklahoma state-supported college, university or tech school. Based on need, scholastic performance and personal traits valued by May T. Henry. Minimum 3.0 GPA required.

Award: Scholarship for use in freshman, sophomore, junior, senior, graduate, or postgraduate years; renewable. *Amount:* $1000.

Eligibility Requirements: Applicant must be enrolled or expecting to enroll full-time at a two-year or four-year or technical institution or university and studying in Oklahoma. Applicant must have 3.0 GPA or higher. Available to U.S. and non-U.S. citizens.

Application Requirements: Application form, essay, financial need analysis, recommendations or references, test scores, transcript. *Deadline:* April 1.

Contact: Trust Department
Central National Bank & Trust Company of Enid Trustee
PO Box 3448
Enid, OK 73702-3448
Phone: 580-213-1700
Fax: 580-249-5911
E-mail: cfelix@cnb-enid.com

CHAMELEONJOHN.COM

http://www.chameleonjohn.com/

$3,000 USA UNIVERSITY STUDENT SCHOLARSHIP

Our mission at ChameleonJohn.com is to help people save money on their online purchases. That is why we get the best coupon codes from hundreds of online stores around the United States. After having saved money for thousands of consumers, we decided to give a hand to students who are struggling financially and thus established an annual University Student Scholarship with which we give away $3,000 every year to one student in the United States.

Award: Scholarship for use in freshman, sophomore, junior, senior, or graduate years; renewable. *Number:* 1. *Amount:* $3000.

Eligibility Requirements: Applicant must be enrolled or expecting to enroll full- or part-time at a two-year or four-year or technical institution or university. Available to U.S. and non-U.S. citizens.

Application Requirements: Essay. *Deadline:* continuous.

Contact: Alan Trapulionis
E-mail: scholarships@chameleonjohn.com

CHEGG

http://www.chegg.com/scholarships

$1,000 MONTHLY SCHOLARSHIP

$1000 monthly scholarship for full-time students planning on attending accredited colleges or universities. Must be a student currently enrolled in a U.S. high school.

Award: Scholarship for use in freshman, sophomore, junior, or senior years; not renewable. *Number:* 1. *Amount:* $1000.

Eligibility Requirements: Applicant must be high school student and planning to enroll or expecting to enroll full-time at a four-year institution or university. Available to U.S. citizens.

Application Requirements: Application form. *Deadline:* continuous.

Contact: Renee Campbell
E-mail: scholarships@chegg.com

CLARICODE

http://www.claricode.com/

CLARICODE MEDICAL SOFTWARE SCHOLARSHIP ESSAY

One awards of $1250 available to full-time undergraduate or graduate students attending a U.S. accredited college or university. Must be at least 18 years old at time of entry and submit a 500 to 1000-word essay on the topic chosen by Claricode (and listed on the website). All majors/concentrations are welcome to apply. For additional information visit website http://www.claricode.com/scholarship.

Award: Scholarship for use in freshman, sophomore, junior, senior, graduate, or postgraduate years; not renewable. *Number:* 1. *Amount:* $1250.

Eligibility Requirements: Applicant must be enrolled or expecting to enroll full-time at a two-year or four-year or technical institution or university. Available to U.S. citizens.

Application Requirements: Application form, application form may be submitted online (http://www.claricode.com/scholarship/), essay. *Deadline:* October 31.

Contact: Chief Executive Officer
E-mail: scholarship@claricode.com

COCA-COLA SCHOLARS FOUNDATION INC.

http://www.coca-colascholars.org/

COCA-COLA SCHOLARS PROGRAM

Renewable scholarship for graduating high school seniors enrolled either full-time or part-time in accredited colleges or universities. Minimum 3.0 GPA required. 252 awards are granted annually.

Award: Scholarship for use in freshman, sophomore, junior, senior, or graduate years; renewable. *Number:* 250. *Amount:* $10,000–$20,000.

Eligibility Requirements: Applicant must be high school student and planning to enroll or expecting to enroll full- or part-time at a two-year or four-year or technical institution or university. Applicant must have 3.0 GPA or higher. Available to U.S. citizens.

Application Requirements: Application form, application form may be submitted online (http://www.coca-colascholars.org), community service, essay, interview, recommendations or references, test scores, transcript. *Deadline:* October 31.

Contact: Mark Davis, President
Coca-Cola Scholars Foundation Inc.
PO Box 442
Atlanta, GA 30301-0442
Phone: 800-306-2653
Fax: 404-733-5439
E-mail: scholars@na.ko.com

COLLEGE INSIDER RESOURCES

http://www.ezcir.com/

COLLEGE INSIDER SCHOLARSHIP PROGRAM

Scholarship offered to undergraduate students with a minimum GPA of 2.5. International students attending college in the United States are also eligible. Refer to website for additional information, http://www.ezcir.com/college_request.asp.

Award: Scholarship for use in freshman, sophomore, junior, or senior years; renewable. *Number:* 1. *Amount:* $1000.

Eligibility Requirements: Applicant must be enrolled or expecting to enroll full-time at a two-year or four-year or technical institution or university. Available to U.S. and non-U.S. citizens.

Application Requirements: Application form. *Deadline:* varies.

Contact: Mr. Cliff deQuilettes, CEO
Phone: 406-652-8900
E-mail: cliff@ezcir.com

COLLEGE JUMPSTART SCHOLARSHIP FUND

http://www.jumpstart-scholarship.net

COLLEGE JUMPSTART SCHOLARSHIP

The College JumpStart Scholarship is an annual, merit-based competition—financial need is not considered—that is open to 10th-12th graders, college students and non-traditional students. The main requirement is that you are committed to going to school and can express your goals for getting a higher education.

Award: Scholarship for use in freshman, sophomore, junior, senior, or graduate years; not renewable. *Number:* 6. *Amount:* $750–$1500.

Eligibility Requirements: Applicant must be high school student and planning to enroll or expecting to enroll full- or part-time at a two-year or four-year or technical institution or university. Available to U.S. citizens.

Application Requirements: Application form, essay. *Deadline:* October 17.

Contact: Scholarship Administrator
E-mail: admin@jumpstart-scholarship.net

COLLEGETOOLKIT.COM

http://www.collegetoolkit.com/

COLLEGE TOOLKIT SCHOLARSHIP CONTEST FOR COLLEGE STUDENTS

College Toolkit is giving away a $1000 scholarship to a college student. We want you to hear your thoughts about the college you attend. The award is open to anyone who will be an undergraduate college student this upcoming fall. You must be attending an accredited 2-year or 4-year college and a U.S. resident to enter.

Award: Scholarship for use in sophomore, junior, or senior years; not renewable. *Number:* 1. *Amount:* $1000.

Eligibility Requirements: Applicant must be enrolled or expecting to enroll full- or part-time at a two-year or four-year institution or university. Available to U.S. citizens.

Application Requirements: Application form. *Deadline:* September 30.

Contact: Scholarship Committee
Phone: 800-265-0179
E-mail: services@CollegeToolkit.com

COLLEGE TOOLKIT SCHOLARSHIP CONTEST FOR HIGH SCHOOL STUDENTS

College Toolkit is giving away a $1000 scholarship to a high school student. We want you to share with us what colleges you are most interested in. The award is open to anyone who will be a high school student this upcoming fall. You must be 14 years of age or older and a U.S. resident to enter.

Award: Scholarship for use in freshman year; not renewable. *Number:* 1. *Amount:* $1000.

Eligibility Requirements: Applicant must be high school student and planning to enroll or expecting to enroll full- or part-time at a two-year or four-year institution. Available to U.S. citizens.

Application Requirements: Application form.

Contact: Scholarship Committee
Phone: 800-265-0179
E-mail: services@CollegeToolkit.com

COMEDY DEFENSIVE DRIVING

http://comedydefensivedriving.com/

GETTING REAL ABOUT DISTRACTED DRIVING SCHOLARSHIP

At Comedy Defensive Driving, we believe that quality education is too damn expensive for many students and should be obtainable for everyone. If you are up for trying something meaningful to help achieve your goal of a college education, then design an advertisement against distracted driving. You will be judged based on the quality of the content in terms of marketability, and how it effectively convinces drivers to stay focused on the road. To qualify, you must like the Comedy Defensive Driving Facebook fan page, take the pledge to not use your phone while driving, and definitely not to drive while you're buzzed. And definitely don't use your phone if driving. All forms of ads are accepted including PSA, music, billboards, media, graphics, etc. No time restraints, however, keep in mind that you are making an advertisement, not a Ridley Scott movie. Overt profanity, and nudity of any kind will not be allowed. Plagiarism automatically disqualified. There is no GPA requirement, financial requirement, or any other kind of requirement—just knowing you are making the effort to get out of bed and do something positive before noon qualifies. Please submit files (all formats accepted) to scholarships@comedydefensivedriving.com only. We will not be judging based on anything other than the advertisement, so don't sweat over an introductory email; just give us your name, and the best way to reach you if you win. Submission deadline is 4/30/16 and the recipient will be announced by 5/31/16.

Award: Scholarship for use in freshman, sophomore, junior, or senior years; not renewable. *Number:* 1. *Amount:* $1000.

Eligibility Requirements: Applicant must be enrolled or expecting to enroll full- or part-time at a two-year or four-year or technical institution or university. Available to U.S. and Canadian citizens.

Application Requirements: Application form. *Deadline:* May 31.

Contact: Richard Schiller
Comedy Defensive Driving
1825 W. Walnut Hill Lane
Suite 101
Irving, TX 75038
E-mail: scholarships@comedydefensivedriving.com

COMMON KNOWLEDGE SCHOLARSHIP FOUNDATION

http://www.cksf.org/

COMMON KNOWLEDGE SCHOLARSHIP

The Common Knowledge Scholarship Foundation (CKSF) is a 501(c)(3) nonprofit organization that creates Internet-based quiz competition for students of all ages. There is no essay, long application, or GPA requirement. A single CKSF registration is good from high school all the way through college and graduate school.

Award: Scholarship for use in freshman, sophomore, junior, senior, graduate, or postgraduate years; renewable. *Number:* 1–15. *Amount:* $250–$1000.

Eligibility Requirements: Applicant must be enrolled or expecting to enroll full- or part-time at a two-year or four-year or technical institution or university. Available to U.S. and non-U.S. citizens.

Application Requirements: Application form may be submitted online (http://www.cksf.org), online registration and quiz competition, portfolio. *Deadline:* continuous.

Contact: Daryl Hulce, President
Phone: 954-262-8553

COMPARECARDS.COM

http://www.comparecards.com

EDU SCHOLARSHIP AWARD

Each month, CompareCards will award $2500 to any qualifying college (or college bound) student in need who can answer a tricky trivia question. Using their best pop culture and math skills, and probably a bit of help from Professor Google, students should be able to answer a series of questions to arrive at a final answer in no time. After the submission deadline, CompareCards will gather all the correct answers and a tiebreaker question will be emailed with a link to submit the answer. Students who submit the correct tiebreaker answer will be entered into a random drawing and one winner will be selected.

Award: Scholarship for use in freshman, sophomore, junior, senior, graduate, or postgraduate years; not renewable. *Number:* 1–12. *Amount:* $2500.

Eligibility Requirements: Applicant must be enrolled or expecting to enroll full- or part-time at a two-year or four-year or technical institution or university. Available to U.S. citizens.

Application Requirements: Application form may be submitted online (http://www.comparecards.com/scholarship-award). *Deadline:* continuous.

Contact: Sarah Meyer
E-mail: sarah@comparecards.com

CONCERT ARTISTS GUILD

http://www.concertartists.org/

CONCERT ARTISTS GUILD COMPETITION

The Concert Artists Guild Victor Elmaleh Competition is an annual competition open to instrumentalists and chamber ensembles performing classical and non-traditional repertoire.

Award: Prize for use in freshman, sophomore, junior, senior, graduate, or postgraduate years; not renewable.

Eligibility Requirements: Applicant must be enrolled or expecting to enroll at an institution or university. Available to U.S. and non-U.S. citizens.

Application Requirements: Application form. *Deadline:* April 14.

Contact: Jessica Lightfoot, Administrator, Programs and Development
E-mail: info@concertartists.org

CONNECTHER

http://www.connecther.org/

GIRLS IMPACT THE WORLD SCHOLARSHIP PROGRAM

The Girls Impact the World Film Festival, presented by Connecther, is a film festival and scholarship program in which high school and undergraduate college students submit 3-6 minute short films that focus on a variety of global women's issues, including maternal health, misrepresentation of beauty, athletes against assault of women, violence against women, child-marriage, sex-trafficking, poverty alleviation, environmental issues, etc.

Award: Scholarship for use in freshman, sophomore, junior, or senior years; renewable. *Number:* 12. *Amount:* $1000–$5000.

Eligibility Requirements: Applicant must be age 13-25 and enrolled or expecting to enroll full- or part-time at a two-year or four-year or technical institution or university. Available to U.S. and non-U.S. citizens.

Application Requirements: Application form. *Deadline:* January 20.

Contact: Lila Igram
Connecther
12301 Zeller Lane
Austin, TX 78753
E-mail: filmfest@connecther.org

CONSTITUTING AMERICA

http://www.constitutingamerica.org

WE THE FUTURE CONTEST

We The Future Contest offers a $1000 scholarship for high school students, $2000 scholarship for college students plus a mentoring trip. Contest information about how to enter, and prizes including scholarships, may be found at http://www.constitutingamerica.org/downloads.php. Entry topics are based on the U.S. Constitution.

Award: Scholarship for use in freshman, sophomore, junior, senior, or graduate years; not renewable. *Number:* 12–12. *Amount:* $1000–$2000.

Eligibility Requirements: Applicant must be enrolled or expecting to enroll full- or part-time at a two-year or four-year institution or university. Available to U.S. citizens.

Application Requirements: Application form may be submitted online (http://www.constitutingamerica.org/docs/WeTheFutureContestPermissi on.pdf), contest entry form, entry in a contest. *Deadline:* September 17.

Contact: Ms. Amanda Hughes, Outreach Director
Constituting America
PO Box 1988
Colleyville, TX 76034
Phone: 888-937-0917
E-mail: wethepeople917@yahoo.com

CORELLA AND BERTRAM F. BONNER FOUNDATION

http://www.bonner.org

BONNER SCHOLARS PROGRAM

Student apply directly to the colleges and universities sponsoring the program. It is a four year scholarship program, in return students are required to complete 10-12 hours of community service per week and two summers of service at 300 hours each.

Award: Scholarship for use in freshman, sophomore, junior, or senior years; renewable. *Number:* 1560–1600. *Amount:* $4500.

Eligibility Requirements: Applicant must be enrolled or expecting to enroll full-time at a four-year institution or university. Available to U.S. and non-U.S. citizens.

Application Requirements: Application form. *Deadline:* continuous.

Contact: Ms. Annie Pasqua, National Program Director
Corella and Bertram F. Bonner Foundation
10 Mercer Street
Princeton, NJ 08540
Phone: 609-924-6663
Fax: 609-683-4626
E-mail: apasqua@bonner.org

COUPONCHIEF.COM

https://www.couponchief.com/

COUPONCHIEF.COM SCHOLARSHIP PROGRAM

We at CouponChief.com want to support young leaders that understand frugality and saving money, and how the skills and knowledge of using coupons can contribute to that end. We will award 1 scholarship winner with $1000 to put towards education every year.

Award: Scholarship for use in freshman, sophomore, junior, senior, graduate, or postgraduate years; not renewable. *Number:* 1. *Amount:* $1000.

Eligibility Requirements: Applicant must be enrolled or expecting to enroll full- or part-time at a two-year or four-year or technical institution or university. Available to U.S. citizens.

Application Requirements: *Deadline:* July 31.

Contact: Angela Thompson
CouponChief.com
774 Mays Blvd #10-528
Incline Village, NV 89451
Incline Village, NV 89451
Phone: 858-342-5970
E-mail: angela@couponchief.com

COURAGE TO GROW SCHOLARSHIP PROGRAM

http://couragetogrowscholarship.com/

COURAGE TO GROW SCHOLARSHIP

High school juniors and seniors or college students with a minimum GPA of 2.5 or better are eligible. U.S. citizens only please. An essay of 250 words or less is required. One award of $500 will be given out per month. Applicants can reapply each month throughout the year.

Award: Scholarship for use in freshman, sophomore, junior, senior, graduate, or postgraduate years; not renewable. *Number:* 1–12. *Amount:* $500.

Eligibility Requirements: Applicant must be enrolled or expecting to enroll full- or part-time at a two-year or four-year or technical institution or university. Applicant must have 2.5 GPA or higher. Available to U.S. citizens.

Application Requirements: Application form, essay. *Deadline:* continuous.

Contact: Kimberly Johnson, Founder
Courage to Grow Scholarship Program
PO Box 2507
Chelan, WA 98816
Phone: 509-731-3056
E-mail: support@couragetogrowscholarship.com

COURSE HERO, INC.

http://www.coursehero.com

COURSE HERO $5,000 MONTHLY SCHOLARSHIP

While Course Hero can help you study smarter, we can also help you pay for school with a $5,000 monthly scholarship. It only takes a few minutes to apply! Just sign up for a free account and respond to our creative short-answer question

Award: Scholarship for use in freshman, sophomore, junior, senior, graduate, or postgraduate years; not renewable. *Number:* 1. *Amount:* $1000–$5000.

Eligibility Requirements: Applicant must be enrolled or expecting to enroll full- or part-time at a two-year or four-year institution or university. Available to U.S. citizens.

Application Requirements: *Deadline:* continuous.

Contact: Sura Hussain, Marketing Manager
Course Hero, Inc.
1400B Seaport Boulevard, Floor 2
Redwood City, CA 94063
Phone: 888-634-9397
E-mail: scholarships@coursehero.com

CRESCENT ELECTRIC SUPPLY COMPANY

http://www.cesco.com/

CRESCENT ELECTRIC SUPPLY COMPANY'S ENERGY EFFICIENT SCHOLARSHIP

If you are currently enrolled in college or headed there in 2017 and want to win a $1000 scholarship to help cover expenses, consider entering the Crescent Electric College Scholarship Contest. Crescent Electric Supply Company will award a $1000 scholarship to a highly motivated student who can thoughtfully share a photo of their effort to minimize energy usage on social media.

Award: Scholarship for use in freshman, sophomore, or junior years; not renewable. *Number:* 1. *Amount:* $1000.

Eligibility Requirements: Applicant must be age 16-22 and enrolled or expecting to enroll full-time at a two-year or four-year or technical institution or university. Available to U.S. and Canadian citizens.

Application Requirements: Personal photograph. *Deadline:* August 8.

Contact: Scholarship Director
E-mail: jessie@elitefixtures.com

CRIMINAL DEFENSE INCORPORATED
http://criminaldefenseinc.com/

CRIMINAL DEFENSE INCORPORATED 2016 SCHOLARSHIP
Criminal Defense Incorporated will be awarding $500 to a qualifying student who has demonstrated a meaningful commitment to not only building their own future, but improving the local community as well. The legal team at Criminal Defense Incorporated values education, and we're glad to offer this scholarship to students shaping both our present and future.

Award: Scholarship for use in freshman, sophomore, junior, or senior years; not renewable. *Number:* 1. *Amount:* $500.

Eligibility Requirements: Applicant must be enrolled or expecting to enroll full-time at a four-year institution or university. Applicant must have 3.0 GPA or higher. Available to U.S. citizens.

Application Requirements: Application form, driver's license, essay. *Deadline:* April 15.

Contact: Chad Lewin
E-mail: lewin@criminaldefenseinc.com

CRUSH THE CPA EXAM
http://crushthecpaexam.com

CRUSH THE GMAT SCHOLARSHIP PROGRAM
One Grand Prize Winner will receive a $250 reimbursement of GMAT fees plus free access to a Magoosh review course that is valued at $399! This is an annual scholarship for potential business school students. Applicants must enter prior to May 31st, 2017, when the winner will be chosen and announced by our staff.

Award: Scholarship for use in junior, senior, or graduate years; not renewable. *Number:* 1. *Amount:* $600–$649.

Eligibility Requirements: Applicant must be enrolled or expecting to enroll full-time at a four-year institution or university. Applicant must have 3.0 GPA or higher. Available to U.S. and non-U.S. citizens.

Application Requirements: Application form, essay. *Deadline:* May 31.

Contact: Ms. Stephanie Murguia, Outreach Coordinator
Crush The CPA Exam
10505 Roselle St
San Diego, CA 92121
E-mail: stephanie@crushempire.com

CRUSH THE GRE SCHOLARSHIP PROGRAM
One Grand Prize Winner will receive a $160 reimbursement of GRE fees plus a Magoosh review course that is valued at $399! This is an annual scholarship for potential graduate school students. Applicants must enter prior to May 31st, 2017, when the winner will be chosen and announced.

Award: Scholarship for use in junior, senior, or graduate years; not renewable. *Number:* 1. *Amount:* $500–$559.

Eligibility Requirements: Applicant must be enrolled or expecting to enroll full-time at a four-year institution or university. Applicant must have 3.0 GPA or higher. Available to U.S. and non-U.S. citizens.

Application Requirements: Application form, essay. *Deadline:* May 31.

Contact: Bryce Welker, CEO
Crush The CPA Exam
10505 Roselle St
San Diego, CA 92121
Phone: 858-858-888-9063
E-mail: crushthecpaexam@gmail.com

CRUSH THE USMLE SCHOLARSHIP PROGRAM
One Grand Prize Winner will receive $605 to cover the cost of Step 1 of the USMLE and access to a Graduate review course that is valued at $289! This is an annual scholarship for medical professionals who need to obtain licensure. Applicants must enter prior to May 31st, 2017, when the winner will be chosen and announced by our staff.

Award: Scholarship for use in junior, senior, or graduate years; not renewable. *Number:* 1. *Amount:* $800–$894.

Eligibility Requirements: Applicant must be enrolled or expecting to enroll full- or part-time at a four-year institution or university. Applicant must have 3.0 GPA or higher. Available to U.S. and non-U.S. citizens.

Application Requirements: Application form, essay. *Deadline:* May 31.

Contact: Stephanie Murguia
E-mail: stephanie@crushempire.com

THE DALLAS FOUNDATION
http://www.dallasfoundation.org/

BROOK HOLLOW GOLF CLUB SCHOLARSHIP
Established in 2007 to benefit children or grandchildren of full- or part-time employees of Brook Hollow Golf Club. Applicants must be a child or grandchild of an active employee in good standing of Brook Hollow Golf Club and a graduating high school senior who has been accepted in, or a student already enrolled in, an undergraduate program of study in pursuit of a degree from a public or private, regionally accredited community college, college, university, or vocational or trade institute. Applicants must demonstrate financial need.

Award: Scholarship for use in freshman or sophomore years; renewable. *Amount:* $2000–$4500.

Eligibility Requirements: Applicant must be high school student and planning to enroll or expecting to enroll full-time at a two-year or four-year or technical institution or university.

Application Requirements: Application form, financial need analysis, transcript. *Deadline:* April 1.

Contact: Rachel Lasseter, Program Associate
Phone: 214-741-9898
E-mail: scholarships@dallasfoundation.org

THE HIRSCH FAMILY SCHOLARSHIP
The Hirsch Family Scholarship was established as a scholarship fund in 2009 to benefit dependent children of active employees of Eagle Materials, Performance Chemicals and Ingredients, Martin Fletcher, Hadlock Plastics, Highlander Partners and any of their majority-owned subsidiaries.

Award: Scholarship for use in freshman, sophomore, junior, or senior years; not renewable. *Amount:* $2000–$10,000.

Eligibility Requirements: Applicant must be enrolled or expecting to enroll full-time at a two-year or four-year or technical institution or university.

Application Requirements: Application form, transcript. *Deadline:* March 15.

Contact: Rachel Lasseter, Program Associate
Phone: 214-741-9898
E-mail: scholarships@dallasfoundation.org

KRISTOPHER KASPER MEMORIAL SCHOLARSHIP
Award for a child of a Centex Homes Texas Region employee. Based on the eligibility criteria, one scholarship of at least $1000 will be awarded annually. The scholarship may be used for tuition, fees, or books, and will be paid directly to the school. There will be an opportunity for renewal if renewal requirements are met.

Award: Scholarship for use in freshman, sophomore, junior, or senior years; renewable. *Number:* 1. *Amount:* $1000.

Eligibility Requirements: Applicant must be high school student and planning to enroll or expecting to enroll full-time at a two-year or four-year or technical institution or university. Applicant must have 2.5 GPA or higher.

Application Requirements: Application form, community service, recommendations or references, resume, transcript. *Deadline:* April 15.

Contact: Rachel Lasseter, Program Associate
Phone: 214-741-9898
E-mail: scholarships@dallasfoundation.org

DAUGHTERS OF THE CINCINNATI
http://www.daughters1894.org/

DAUGHTERS OF THE CINCINNATI SCHOLARSHIP
Need and merit-based award available to graduating high school seniors. Minimum GPA of 3.0 required. Must be daughter of commissioned officer in regular Army, Navy, Coast Guard, Air Force, Marines (active,

retired, or deceased). Must submit parent's rank and branch of service. Application can be completed and downloaded from website, http://www.daughters1894.org.

Award: Scholarship for use in freshman year; renewable. *Number:* 4–5. *Amount:* $3000–$5000.

Eligibility Requirements: Applicant must be high school student; planning to enroll or expecting to enroll full-time at a four-year institution or university and female. Applicant must have 3.0 GPA or higher. Available to U.S. citizens.

Application Requirements: Application form, essay, financial need analysis. *Deadline:* March 15.

Contact: Mrs. Evelyn Donatelli, Scholarship Administrator
Phone: 212-991-9945
E-mail: scholarships@daughters1894.org

THE DAVID & DOVETTA WILSON SCHOLARSHIP FUND

http://www.wilsonfund.org/

THE DAVID & DOVETTA WILSON SCHOLARSHIP FUND

The purpose of The David and Dovetta Wilson Scholarship Fund (DDWSF) is to provide deserving high school seniors across the nation with financial assistance to pursue their academic goals.

Award: Scholarship for use in freshman year; not renewable. *Number:* 9. *Amount:* $300–$1000.

Eligibility Requirements: Applicant must be enrolled or expecting to enroll full-time at a two-year or four-year institution or university. Available to U.S. citizens.

Application Requirements: Application form, community service, essay, financial need analysis, personal photograph. *Fee:* $20. *Deadline:* March 31.

Contact: Timothy Wilson, Treasurer
The David & Dovetta Wilson Scholarship Fund
115-67 237th Street
Elmont, NY 11003
Phone: 516-643-5762
E-mail: ddwsf4@aol.com

DEFENSIVEDRIVING.COM

http://defensivedriving.com

DEFENSIVEDRIVING.COM SCHOLARSHIP

This award will be given to the high school senior or college student who submits the most unique video following the prompt under the Make A Video tab on https://www.defensivedriving.com/scholarship. Applicants are also required to like DefensiveDriving.com's Facebook page to be considered. See detailed instructions here: https://www.defensivedriving.com/scholarship

Award: Scholarship for use in freshman, sophomore, junior, or senior years; not renewable. *Number:* 1. *Amount:* $1000.

Eligibility Requirements: Applicant must be enrolled or expecting to enroll full- or part-time at a two-year or four-year or technical institution or university. Available to U.S. citizens.

Application Requirements: *Deadline:* May 30.

DELAWARE HIGHER EDUCATION OFFICE

http://www.doe.k12.de.us

GOVERNOR'S EDUCATION GRANT FOR UNEMPLOYED ADULTS

Grants for unemployed part-time undergraduate students attending Delaware College of Art and Design, Delaware State University, Delaware Technical and Community College, Goldey-Beacom College, University of Delaware, Wesley College, Widener University (Delaware Campus), or PolyTech Adult division, Sussex Tech Adult division, or Wilmington College. Must be at least 18 years old, and a resident of Delaware.

Award: Grant for use in freshman, sophomore, junior, or senior years; not renewable. *Number:* up to 1000. *Amount:* $2000.

Eligibility Requirements: Applicant must be enrolled or expecting to enroll part-time at a two-year or four-year or technical institution or university. Available to U.S. citizens.

Application Requirements: Application form. *Deadline:* continuous.

Contact: Ms. Carylin Brinkley, Program Administrator
Delaware Higher Education Office
401 Federal Street
Suite 2
Dover, DE 19901
Phone: 302-735-4120
Fax: 302-739-5894
E-mail: cbrinkley@doe.k12.de.us

DELETE CYBERBULLYING

http://www.deletecyberbullying.org

DELETE CYBERBULLYING SCHOLARSHIP

The application form is only available online. The purpose of this scholarship is to get students committed to the cause of deleting cyberbullying.

Award: Scholarship for use in freshman, sophomore, junior, senior, or graduate years; not renewable. *Number:* 2. *Amount:* $1500.

Eligibility Requirements: Applicant must be enrolled or expecting to enroll full- or part-time at a two-year or four-year or technical institution or university. Available to U.S. citizens.

Application Requirements: Application form, essay. *Deadline:* June 30.

Contact: Scholarship Coordinator
E-mail: help@deletecyberbullying.org

DENTAL INSURANCE SHOP

https://www.dentalinsuranceshop.com/index.html

DENTAL INSURANCE SHOP MERIT SCHOLARSHIP

We know saving up for school can be tough. At The Dental Insurance Shop, we believe that scholarships can give ambitious students the opportunity to focus on his or her studies instead of worrying about the cost of books and tuition. With that little extra help, we believe you can achieve greatness. The Dental Insurance Shop is offering a $1,000 non-renewable scholarship to enable one student chosen from all entries to pursue his or her education. All entries must be made by using the application on https://www.dentalinsuranceshop.com/scholarship.html.

Award: Scholarship for use in freshman year; not renewable. *Number:* 1. *Amount:* $1000.

Eligibility Requirements: Applicant must be high school student and planning to enroll or expecting to enroll full-time at a two-year or four-year institution or university. Applicant must have 3.5 GPA or higher. Available to U.S. citizens.

Application Requirements: Application form. *Deadline:* June 30.

Contact: Kevin Knutson
Dental Insurance Shop
12280 Nicollet Ave
Suite #104
Burnsville, MN 55306
Phone: 855-871-2242
E-mail: scholarship@dentalinsuranceshop.com

DIGITAL RESPONSIBILITY

http://www.digitalresponsibility.org

DIGITAL PRIVACY SCHOLARSHIP

The purpose of this scholarship is to help you understand why you should be cautious about what you post on the Internet. You must be a high school freshman, sophomore, junior, or senior or a current or entering college or graduate school student of any level. Home schooled students are also eligible. There is no age limit. Complete the application form including a 140-character message about digital privacy. The top 10 applications will be selected as finalists. The finalists will be asked to write a full length 500- to 1,000-word essay about digital privacy.

Award: Scholarship for use in freshman, sophomore, junior, senior, graduate, or postgraduate years; not renewable. *Number:* up to 2. *Amount:* $500–$1500.

Eligibility Requirements: Applicant must be enrolled or expecting to enroll full- or part-time at a two-year or four-year or technical institution or university. Available to U.S. citizens.

Application Requirements: Application form, application form may be submitted online (http://www.digitalresponsibility.org/digital-privacy-scholarship/), essay. *Deadline:* June 30.

Contact: Scholarship Coordinator
E-mail: scholarship@digitalresponsibility.org

DON'T TEXT AND DRIVE SCHOLARSHIP

The purpose of this scholarship is to help you understand the risks of texting while driving. You must be a high school freshman, sophomore, junior, or senior or a current or entering college or graduate school student of any level. Home schooled students are also eligible. There is no age limit. Complete the application form including a 140-character message about texting while driving. The top 10 applications will be selected as finalists. The finalists will be asked to write a full length 500- to 1,000-word essay about texting while driving.

Award: Scholarship for use in freshman, sophomore, junior, senior, graduate, or postgraduate years; not renewable. *Number:* up to 2. *Amount:* $500–$1500.

Eligibility Requirements: Applicant must be enrolled or expecting to enroll full- or part-time at a two-year or four-year or technical institution or university. Available to U.S. citizens.

Application Requirements: Application form, application form may be submitted online (http://www.digitalresponsibility.org/dont-text-and-drive-scholarship/), essay. *Deadline:* September 30.

Contact: Scholarship Coordinator
E-mail: scholarship@digitalresponsibility.org

E-WASTE SCHOLARSHIP

The purpose of this scholarship is to help you understand the impact of e-waste and what can be done to reduce e-waste. You must be a high school freshman, sophomore, junior, or senior or a current or entering college or graduate school student of any level. Home schooled students are also eligible. There is no age limit. Complete the application form below including a 140-character message about e-waste. The top 10 applications will be selected as finalists. The finalists will be asked to write a full length 500- to 1,000-word essay about e-waste.

Award: Scholarship for use in freshman, sophomore, junior, senior, graduate, or postgraduate years; not renewable. *Number:* up to 2. *Amount:* $500–$1500.

Eligibility Requirements: Applicant must be enrolled or expecting to enroll full- or part-time at a two-year or four-year or technical institution or university. Available to U.S. citizens.

Application Requirements: Application form, application form may be submitted online (http://www.digitalresponsibility.org/ewaste-scholarship/), essay. *Deadline:* April 30.

Contact: Scholarship Coordinator
E-mail: scholarship@digitalresponsibility.org

TECHNOLOGY ADDICTION AWARENESS SCHOLARSHIP

With technology always at the ready at your fingertips, it can be a challenge to unplug. But taking a break from technology is healthy for both the mind and body. The purpose of this scholarship is to help you understand the negative effects of too much screen time. You must be a high school freshman, sophomore, junior, or senior or a current or entering college or graduate school student of any level. Home schooled students are also eligible. There is no age limit. Complete the application form below including a 140-character message about technology addiction. The top 10 applications will be selected as finalists. The finalists will be asked to write a full length 500- to 1,000-word essay about technology addiction.

Award: Scholarship for use in freshman, sophomore, junior, senior, graduate, or postgraduate years; not renewable. *Number:* up to 2. *Amount:* $500–$1500.

Eligibility Requirements: Applicant must be enrolled or expecting to enroll full- or part-time at a two-year or four-year or technical institution or university. Available to U.S. citizens.

Application Requirements: Application form, application form may be submitted online (http://www.digitalresponsibility.org/technology-addiction-awareness-scholarship/), essay. *Deadline:* January 30.

Contact: Scholarship Coordinator
E-mail: scholarship@digitalresponsibility.org

DIRECTTEXTBOOK.COM

http://www.DirectTextbook.com

2016 HIGH SCHOOL SENIOR SCHOLARSHIP ESSAY CONTEST

Complete an essay of 500 words or less that answers the questions: What does self-responsibility mean to you? How does living self-responsibly affect your life? How does avoiding self-responsibility affect your life? Applications will no longer be accepted after May 4th, 2016. Once the contest is closed, all essays will be reviewed. The winners of each award will be notified by e-mail on or before May 8th, 2016.

Award: Scholarship for use in freshman year; not renewable. *Number:* 3. *Amount:* $500–$3000.

Eligibility Requirements: Applicant must be high school student and planning to enroll or expecting to enroll full- or part-time at a two-year or four-year institution or university. Available to U.S. citizens.

Application Requirements: Essay. *Deadline:* May 4.

Contact: Hanna Robin
DirectTextbook.com
1525 Chemeketa Street, NE
Salem, OR 97301
Phone: 503-930-4568
Fax: 503-210-0716
E-mail: hann@directtextbook.com

DIRECTTEXTBOOK.COM 2017 HIGH SCHOOL SENIOR SCHOLARSHIP ESSAY CONTEST

Scholarship award amount: $3000 to first place, $1000 to second place, $500 to third place. Scholarship opening date: March 14th, 2017. Application deadline date: May 4th, 2017. Awards available: 3. In 500 words or less write a response to a friend that has just asked you this question "I have all these options in life, how do I choose the ones that create the life I want?" Applications will no longer be accepted after May 4th, 2017. Once the contest is closed, all essays will be reviewed. The winners of each award will be notified by email on or before June 8th, 2017. Applicant must be a current U.S. citizen, a current high school senior and have a most recent GPA of 2.0 or higher. See website for more details and to apply, http://www.directtextbook.com/scholarship.php

Award: Scholarship for use in freshman year; not renewable. *Number:* 3. *Amount:* $500–$3000.

Eligibility Requirements: Applicant must be high school student and planning to enroll or expecting to enroll full- or part-time at a two-year or four-year or technical institution or university. Available to U.S. citizens.

Application Requirements: Application form, essay. *Deadline:* May 4.

Contact: Hanna Wharton
Phone: 503-791-2414
E-mail: hanna@directtextbook.com

DISTINGUISHED YOUNG WOMEN

http://www.distinguishedyw.org

DISTINGUISHED YOUNG WOMEN

We are a non-profit organization that offers Life Skills Workshops to prepare young women for life after high school and over $1 billion in college scholarships opportunities plus it's free to participate. Awards are given to participants in the local, state, and national levels of competition. Must be female, high school juniors or seniors, U.S. citizens, and legal residents of the county and state of competition. Participants are evaluated on scholastic achievement, interview, talent, fitness, and public speaking. The number of awards and their amount vary from year to year.

Award: Scholarship for use in freshman, sophomore, junior, senior, or graduate years; not renewable.

Eligibility Requirements: Applicant must be high school student; age 15-19; planning to enroll or expecting to enroll full-time at a two-year or four-year or technical institution or university and single female. Available to U.S. citizens.

Application Requirements: Application form, interview, personal photograph. *Deadline:* continuous.

Contact: Lisa Lawley Burnette, National Field Director
Phone: 251-438-3621
E-mail: lisa@distinguishedyw.org

E-COLLEGEDEGREE.COM

http://www.e-collegedegree.com/

E-COLLEGEDEGREE.COM ONLINE EDUCATION SCHOLARSHIP AWARD

The award is to be used for online education. Application must be submitted online. Visit website for more information and application, http://www.e-collegedegree.com.

Award: Scholarship for use in freshman, sophomore, junior, senior, graduate, or postgraduate years; renewable. *Number:* 1. *Amount:* $1000.

Eligibility Requirements: Applicant must be enrolled or expecting to enroll full- or part-time at a two-year or four-year or technical institution or university. Available to U.S. citizens.

Application Requirements: Application form, entry in a contest, essay. *Deadline:* December 31.

Contact: Chris Lee, Site Manager
e-CollegeDegree.com
9109 West 101st Terrace
Overland Park, KS 66212
Phone: 913-341-6949
E-mail: scholarship@e-collegedegree.com

EDSOUTH SERVICES

http://www.edsouthservices.com

ECAMPUSTOURS SCHOLARSHIP DRAWING

Two $1000 awards are available.

Award: Scholarship for use in freshman, sophomore, junior, senior, or graduate years; not renewable. *Number:* 2. *Amount:* $1000.

Eligibility Requirements: Applicant must be enrolled or expecting to enroll full- or part-time at a two-year or four-year or technical institution or university. Available to U.S. citizens.

Application Requirements: *Deadline:* March 31.

Contact: Online Marketing Manager
E-mail: info@edsouthservices.com

EVERIPEDIA INC.

https://www.everipedia.com

2017 INTERNATIONAL WOMEN IN MEDIA SCHOLARSHIP

The International Women in Media Scholarship was established by Everipedia, Inc. in 2017. It aims to increase awareness of women in journalism and the media, along with the challenges they face around the world. Applicants, instead of writing an essay, will create a Wikipedia-style biography page for a woman of their choice. A sample list of women will be provided, but applicants are free to chose their own. Our scholarship offers an award of $500 and is open to all incoming and current college students.

Award: Scholarship for use in freshman, sophomore, junior, senior, graduate, or postgraduate years; renewable. *Number:* 1. *Amount:* $500.

Eligibility Requirements: Applicant must be enrolled or expecting to enroll full- or part-time at a two-year or four-year or technical institution or university. Available to U.S. and non-U.S. citizens.

Application Requirements: Essay. *Deadline:* July 1.

Contact: Mr. Travis Moore, CTO
Everipedia Inc.
972 Hilgard Ave, PH2
Los Angeles, CA 90024
Phone: 702-723-6417
E-mail: scholarships@everipedia.com

EXECUTIVE WOMEN INTERNATIONAL

http://www.ewiconnect.com/

ADULT STUDENTS IN SCHOLASTIC TRANSITION

Scholarship for adult students at transitional points in their lives. Applicants may be single parents, individuals just entering the workforce, or displaced homemakers. Applications are available on the organization's website, http://www.ewiconnect.com.

Award: Scholarship for use in freshman, sophomore, junior, or senior years; not renewable. *Number:* 100–150. *Amount:* $250–$2500.

Eligibility Requirements: Applicant must be enrolled or expecting to enroll full-time at a two-year or four-year or technical institution or university. Available to U.S. and non-U.S. citizens.

Application Requirements: Application form, essay, financial need analysis, interview, personal photograph, recommendations or references, self-addressed stamped envelope with application, tax information, transcript.

EXECUTIVE WOMEN INTERNATIONAL SCHOLARSHIP PROGRAM

Competitive award to high school juniors planning careers in any business or professional field of study which requires a four-year college degree. Award is renewable based on continuing eligibility. All awards are given through local Chapters of the EWI. Applicant must apply through nearest Chapter and live within the Chapter's boundaries. Student must have a sponsoring teacher and school to be considered, and only one applicant per school. For more details visit http://www.ewiconnect.com.

Award: Scholarship for use in freshman, sophomore, junior, or senior years; renewable. *Number:* 75–100. *Amount:* $1000–$10,000.

Eligibility Requirements: Applicant must be high school student; age 15-17 and planning to enroll or expecting to enroll full-time at a four-year institution or university. Available to U.S. and non-U.S. citizens.

Application Requirements: Application form, community service, essay, interview, personal photograph, recommendations or references, self-addressed stamped envelope with application, transcript.

Contact: Mr. James Pollan, Executive Director and Trustee
E-mail: stuhrstudents@earthlink.net

EXPERTS EXCHANGE

http://www.experts-exchange.com/

EXPERTS EXCHANGE SCHOLARSHIP CONTEST

At Experts Exchange, we believe in creativity that sparks innovation and makes this a better world to live in. We know that creativity and innovation are within each of us. Some express it through art, some through technology, some through social work, and some find original ways to solve problems in their public and private spheres. We are passionate about supporting the creative genius in all of those in technology, including students, and would love to commend those outstanding students who have a made a difference in the lives of others in some innovative or technological fashion. Students will submit an original piece of work via an article or video on a technology topic of their choosing to the Experts Exchange website. The work must be helpful in nature, describing and/or solving a specific problem.

Award: Scholarship for use in freshman, sophomore, junior, senior, graduate, or postgraduate years; not renewable. *Number:* 3. *Amount:* $500–$1500.

Eligibility Requirements: Applicant must be enrolled or expecting to enroll full- or part-time at a two-year or four-year or technical institution or university. Available to U.S. and non-U.S. citizens.

Application Requirements: Application form. *Deadline:* June 30.

Contact: Scholarship Committee
Phone: 805-787-0603
E-mail: scholarship@experts-exchange.com

FEDERAL EMPLOYEE EDUCATION AND ASSISTANCE FUND

http://www.feea.org/

FEDERAL EMPLOYEE EDUCATION AND ASSISTANCE FUND SCHOLARSHIP PROGRAM

The FEEA Scholarship Program is for current civilian federal employees and their dependent family members (spouse/child). The applicant or the applicant's sponsoring federal employee must have at least three (3) years of civilian federal service by application deadline. The applicant must be at least a college freshman by the fall semester. All applicants must have at least a 3.0 cumulative grade point average (CGPA) unweighted on a 4.0 scale. All applicants must be current high school seniors or college students working towards an accredited degree or enrolled in a two- or four-year undergraduate, graduate or postgraduate program.

Award: Scholarship for use in freshman, sophomore, junior, senior, graduate, or postgraduate years; not renewable. *Number:* 350–450. *Amount:* $1000.

Eligibility Requirements: Applicant must be enrolled or expecting to enroll full- or part-time at a two-year or four-year institution or university. Applicant must have 3.0 GPA or higher. Available to U.S. citizens.

Application Requirements: Application form, community service, essay. *Deadline:* March 27.

Contact: Niki Gleason, Sr Program and Operations Manager
Federal Employee Education and Assistance Fund
1641 Prince St
Alexandria, VA 22314
Phone: 202-554-0007 Ext. 102
E-mail: ngleason@feea.org

NATIONAL ACTIVE AND RETIRED FEDERAL EMPLOYEE SCHOLARSHIP PROGRAM

Children, grandchildren, great-grandchildren and step-children of all current NARFE members are eligible. Applicant must be a high school senior planning to attend college full time in the fall of the application year. Must have a GPA of at least 3.0 on an unweighted 4.0 scale.

Award: Scholarship for use in freshman year; not renewable. *Number:* 60. *Amount:* $1000.

Eligibility Requirements: Applicant must be high school student and planning to enroll or expecting to enroll full-time at a two-year or four-year institution or university. Applicant must have 3.0 GPA or higher. Available to U.S. citizens.

Application Requirements: Application form, community service, essay. *Deadline:* April 28.

Contact: Niki Gleason, Sr Program and Operations Manager
Federal Employee Education and Assistance Fund
1641 Prince St
Alexandria, VA 22314
Phone: 202-554-0007 Ext. 102
E-mail: ngleason@feea.org

FEDERATION OF AMERICAN CONSUMERS AND TRAVELERS

http://www.usafact.org

FEDERATION OF AMERICAN CONSUMERS AND TRAVELERS IN-SCHOOL SCHOLARSHIP

FACT scholarships are offered in four categories for current high school seniors, persons who graduated from high school, four or more years ago and now plan to go to a university or college, for students currently enrolled in a college or university, and for trade or technical school aspirants. Scholarships range in amount from $2500 to $10,000. Members of FACT, their children and grandchildren are eligible to apply.

Award: Scholarship for use in freshman, sophomore, junior, or senior years; not renewable. *Number:* 2. *Amount:* $2500–$10,000.

Eligibility Requirements: Applicant must be enrolled or expecting to enroll full-time at a two-year or four-year institution or university. Available to U.S. citizens.

Application Requirements: Application form, community service, entry in a contest, essay, recommendations or references, test scores, transcript. *Deadline:* January 15.

Contact: Vicki Rolens, Managing Director
Federation of American Consumers and Travelers
PO Box 104
318 Hillsboro Avenue
Edwardsville, IL 62025
Phone: 800-872-3228
Fax: 618-656-5369
E-mail: vrolens@usafact.org

FEDERATION OF AMERICAN CONSUMERS AND TRAVELERS SECOND CHANCE SCHOLARSHIP

The FACT Second Chance Scholarship is for persons who graduated from high school four or more years ago and now plan to go to a university or college. It is designed for those individuals who did not have the opportunity to go to college immediately after graduating from high school. Scholarships range in size from $2500 to $10,000.

Award: Scholarship for use in freshman, sophomore, junior, or senior years; not renewable. *Number:* 2. *Amount:* $2500–$10,000.

Eligibility Requirements: Applicant must be enrolled or expecting to enroll full- or part-time at a two-year or four-year institution or university. Available to U.S. citizens.

Application Requirements: Application form, community service, entry in a contest, essay, recommendations or references, test scores, transcript. *Deadline:* January 15.

Contact: Vicki Rolens, Managing Director
Federation of American Consumers and Travelers
PO Box 104
318 Hillsboro Avenue
Edwardsville, IL 62025
Phone: 800-872-3228
Fax: 618-656-5369
E-mail: vrolens@usafact.org

FELDCO WINDOWS, SIDING AND DOORS

http://www.4feldco.com

FELDCO WINDOWS, SIDING AND DOORS SCHOLARSHIP

Acceptable essays will be between 700-1,000 words long that answer the question: How has your family contributed to who you are today? All entries should be sent to scholarship@4feldco.com. Send your entry to us as an email attachment and include your full name, a headshot of yourself (.png or.jpg format), mobile phone number and address in the email. The scholarship will be awarded to the applicant that best demonstrates in their own words, how their family has contributed to who they are today. Please use the full word limit (700-1,000 words) to best describe how your family has shaped your life. The winner of the scholarship will be notified by phone, email and/or U.S. mail by July 5th, 2017. Your emailed entry must be received by June, 15th 2017. Applications received after the deadline will not be considered. Proof of enrollment must be provided with your email submission. This can include a digital scan of your unofficial transcript, letter from admissions or acceptance letter on a school letterhead.

Award: Scholarship for use in freshman, sophomore, junior, or senior years; renewable. *Number:* 1. *Amount:* $1000.

Eligibility Requirements: Applicant must be enrolled or expecting to enroll full-time at a four-year institution or university. Available to U.S. citizens.

Application Requirements: Essay, personal photograph. *Deadline:* June 15.

Contact: Carl Krzeczkowski
E-mail: carlk@4feldco.com

FIRST CHOICE COLLEGE PLACEMENT LLC

http://www.firstchoicecollege.com/

ADMISSIONHOOK.COM ESSAY CONTEST

This award is part of our ongoing mission to help students get into and pay for the college of their dreams. There are two ways to win the scholarship. First, you can create an account and submit your essay. If your essay is one of the top 5 vote recipients, your essay will be reviewed by a committee and the winner will be notified within 14 days of the close of the scholarship contest. Second, you can create an account and vote on other student's essays (you can also vote on your own). The registered user who votes on the most essays as of the scholarship deadline will receive a $500 scholarship.

Award: Prize for use in freshman, sophomore, junior, or senior years; not renewable. *Number:* 2–4. *Amount:* $500–$1000.

Eligibility Requirements: Applicant must be enrolled or expecting to enroll full-time at a two-year or four-year institution or university. Available to U.S. citizens.

Application Requirements: Application form, essay.

Contact: Mr. James Maroney, Managing Member
First Choice College Placement LLC
50 Cherry Street
Milford, CT 06460
Phone: 203-878-7998
Fax: 203-878-6087
E-mail: james@admissionhook.com

FLORIDA STATE DEPARTMENT OF EDUCATION

http://www.floridastudentfinancialaid.org/

ROSEWOOD FAMILY SCHOLARSHIP FUND

Renewable award for eligible direct descendants of African-American Rosewood families affected by the incident of January 1923. Must not have previously received a baccalaureate degree. For more details, visit the website at http://www.FloridaStudentFinancialAid.org/SSFAD/home/uamain.htm.

Award: Scholarship for use in freshman, sophomore, junior, or senior years; renewable. *Number:* up to 50. *Amount:* up to $6100.

Eligibility Requirements: Applicant must be enrolled or expecting to enroll full- or part-time at a two-year or four-year or technical institution or university and studying in Florida. Available to U.S. citizens.

Application Requirements: Application form, documentation of Rosewood ancestry, financial need analysis. *Deadline:* April 1.

Contact: Florida Department of Education, Office of Student Financial Assistance, Customer Service
Florida State Department of Education
325 West Gaines Street
Tallahassee, FL 32399
Phone: 888-827-2004
E-mail: osfa@fldoe.org

FORECLOSURE.COM

http://www.foreclosure.com/

FORECLOSURE.COM SCHOLARSHIP PROGRAM

The Foreclosure.com Scholarship Program encourages students to offer innovative ideas and solutions to "solve the foreclosure crisis" in the form of an essay. Essay submissions must be between 1000 and 2500 words and all accepted freshman and enrolled under-graduate and graduate-students are eligible to apply. First place prize is $5000 and second through fifth place will be awarded $1,000 each. Checks will be made out to the college or university attended in the form of a non-renewable scholarship grant.

Award: Scholarship for use in freshman, sophomore, junior, or senior years; not renewable. *Number:* 5. *Amount:* $1000–$5000.

Eligibility Requirements: Applicant must be enrolled or expecting to enroll full- or part-time at a two-year or four-year or technical institution or university. Available to U.S. citizens.

Application Requirements: Application form, application form may be submitted online (http://www.foreclosure.com/scholarship), essay. *Deadline:* December 15.

Contact: Mrs. Jacquelyn Marks
Foreclosure.com
1095 Broken Sound Parkway NW
Suite 200
Boca Raton, FL 33435
Phone: 561-988-9669 Ext. 7387

FOSTER CARE TO SUCCESS

http://www.fc2success.org/

FOSTER CARE TO SUCCESS SCHOLARSHIP PROGRAM

Award of up to $6000 to young people under the age of 25 who spent the 12 consecutive months prior to their 18th birthday in foster care or who were adopted or placed into legal guardianship from foster care after their 16th birthday. Scholarships are awarded for the pursuit of postsecondary education, including vocational/technical training, and are renewable for up to five years based on satisfactory progress and financial need.

Award: Scholarship for use in freshman, sophomore, junior, or senior years; not renewable. *Number:* 100. *Amount:* $1000–$6000.

Eligibility Requirements: Applicant must be enrolled or expecting to enroll full- or part-time at a two-year or four-year or technical institution or university. Available to U.S. citizens.

Application Requirements: Application form, essay, financial need analysis. *Deadline:* March 31.

Contact: Ms. Tina Raheem, Scholarship Director
Phone: 571-203-0270 Ext. 102
Fax: 571-203-0273
E-mail: tinar@fc2success.org

FOUNDATION FOR INDEPENDENT HIGHER EDUCATION

http://www.fihe.org/

HSBC FIRST OPPORTUNITY PARTNERS SCHOLARSHIPS

Award targets the students with multiple at-risk factors as identified by financial aid officers in FIHE colleges. For undergraduate students with at least 2.4 GPA after the first semester of the freshman year. Deadline varies.

Award: Scholarship for use in sophomore or junior years; renewable. *Amount:* $5000.

Eligibility Requirements: Applicant must be enrolled or expecting to enroll full-time at a four-year institution or university. Available to U.S. citizens.

Application Requirements: Application form, essay, financial need analysis, transcript. *Deadline:* varies.

Contact: Ms. Jacalyn Cox, Program Manager
E-mail: jcox@fihe.org

UPS SCHOLARSHIP PROGRAM

Scholarship program for undergraduate students attending FIHE-affiliated colleges. Deadline varies.

Award: Scholarship for use in freshman, sophomore, junior, or senior years; not renewable. *Amount:* $2700.

Eligibility Requirements: Applicant must be enrolled or expecting to enroll full- or part-time at a four-year institution or university. Available to U.S. and non-U.S. citizens.

Application Requirements: *Deadline:* varies.

Contact: Dr. Myrvin Christopherson, Acting President
Phone: 202-367-0333
E-mail: info@fihe.org

FOUNDATION FOR OUTDOOR ADVERTISING RESEARCH AND EDUCATION (FOARE)

http://www.oaaa.org/

FOARE SCHOLARSHIP PROGRAM

One-time award of $2000 for 6 students. High school seniors, undergraduates, and graduate students enrolled in or accepted to an accredited institution are eligible to apply. Selections are based on financial need, academic performance, and career goals.

Award: Scholarship for use in freshman, sophomore, junior, senior, or graduate years; not renewable. *Number:* 6. *Amount:* $2000.

Eligibility Requirements: Applicant must be enrolled or expecting to enroll full-time at a four-year institution or university. Available to U.S. citizens.

Application Requirements: Application form, essay, financial need analysis, transcript. *Deadline:* June 15.

Contact: Scholarship Program
Foundation for Outdoor Advertising Research and Education (FOARE)
c/o Thomas M. Smith & Associates
4601 Tilden Street, NW
Washington, DC 20016
Phone: 202-364-7130
E-mail: tmfsmith@starpower.net

THE FRANK M. AND GERTRUDE R. DOYLE FOUNDATION INC.

http://www.frankmdoyle.org/

THE FRANK M. AND GERTRUDE R. DOYLE FOUNDATION, INC.

Eligible applicants for this scholarship must be graduating seniors or graduates (GED is acceptable) of the Huntington Beach Union High School District, Huntington Beach, California; Washoe County Unified High School District, Reno, Nevada; students or graduates of the Huntington Beach Adult High School; students or graduates of the Washoe County Adult High School; graduates or current/previous students of the following community colleges in Southern California: Orange Coast, Golden West, Coastline, Irvine Valley, Fullerton, Cypress, Santa Ana, Saddleback, or Santiago Canyon. Age is not a factor. Applications may be downloaded from the foundations website, http//www.frankmdoyle.org, anytime after 1 December. See website for details.

Award: Scholarship for use in freshman, sophomore, junior, senior, graduate, or postgraduate years; not renewable. *Amount:* $500–$30,000.

Eligibility Requirements: Applicant must be age 17-99 and enrolled or expecting to enroll full- or part-time at a two-year or four-year or technical institution or university. Available to U.S. citizens.

Application Requirements: Application form, essay, recommendations or references, Student Aid Report (SAR), transcript. *Deadline:* March 1.

GEORGE T. BOCHANIS LAW OFFICES

http://lvaccident.com/

GEORGE T. BOCHANIS LAW OFFICES COLLEGE SCHOLARSHIP

George T. Bochanis Law Offices is offering a $5,000 need-based scholarship to the applicant whose essay best addresses how to make driving safer in our community. This scholarship is open to any U.S. citizen or permanent U.S. resident who will be enrolled full-time as a freshman, sophomore, or junior student in an accredited community college or four-year college or university in the fall of 2017.The scholarship must be applied toward full-time tuition costs incurred during the 2017–2018 school year and will be sent directly to the university or college. The student must complete the online application by June 1, 2017. Applications submitted via any other channel will not be considered. The applicant must write an essay (maximum 400 words) on the community safety topic below. The winning student must submit FAFSA results to verify need and must provide proof of enrollment should his or her essay be selected. The winner must consent to using his or her picture and other basic information on the winner page of the lvaccident.com website. There are roughly 55,000 auto collisions every year in Nevada, about half of which result in injury. Our Las Vegas collision attorneys know that all too often, these incidents occur because of a negligent driver, a negligent company or bad road design. Submit an original essay that discusses how you would make driving safer in your community.

Award: Scholarship for use in freshman, sophomore, or junior years; not renewable. *Number:* 1. *Amount:* $5000.

Eligibility Requirements: Applicant must be enrolled or expecting to enroll full-time at a two-year or four-year institution or university. Available to U.S. citizens.

Application Requirements: Application form, essay, financial need analysis. *Deadline:* June 1.

Contact: Rafi Arbel
George T. Bochanis Law Offices
620B Academy Drive
Northbrook, IL 60065
Phone: 847-940-4000
E-mail: rarbel@marketjd.com

GERMAN ACADEMIC EXCHANGE SERVICE (DAAD)

http://www.daad.org/

DAAD GROUP STUDY VISITS

Grants are available for an information visit of seven to twelve days to groups of 10 to 15 students, accompanied by a faculty member. They are intended to encourage contact with academic institutions, groups and individuals in Germany, and offer insight into current issues in the academic, scientific, economic, political and cultural realms. All departments/disciplines are eligible, preference is given to groups with a homogeneous academic background and may be drawn from more than one institution. Applications must reach DAAD New York at least six months before the beginning date of the planned visit. Groups will not be eligible for funding in successive years.

Award: Grant for use in junior, senior, or graduate years; not renewable.

Eligibility Requirements: Applicant must be enrolled or expecting to enroll full-time at a four-year institution or university. Available to U.S. and non-U.S. citizens.

Application Requirements: Application form.

Contact: DAAD New York
German Academic Exchange Service (DAAD)
871 UN Plaza
New York, NY 10017
Phone: 212-758-3223
E-mail: daadny@daad.org

DAAD STUDY SCHOLARSHIP

DAAD's flagship competitive scholarship awarded for study at all public universities in Germany. Open to all fields. Study Scholarships are granted for one academic year (10 months) with the possibility of a one-year extension for students completing a full degree program in Germany.

Award: Scholarship for use in senior, graduate, or postgraduate years; renewable.

Eligibility Requirements: Applicant must be enrolled or expecting to enroll full-time at a four-year institution or university. Available to U.S. and non-U.S. citizens.

Application Requirements: Application form. *Deadline:* November 4.

Contact: DAAD New York
German Academic Exchange Service (DAAD)
871 UN Plaza
New York, NY 10017
Phone: 212-758-3223
E-mail: daadny@daad.org

DAAD UNDERGRADUATE SCHOLARSHIP

Highly qualified undergraduate students are invited to apply for scholarships to fund study, thesis research or internships in Germany. Preference is given to students whose enroll independently at German universities or participate in a project or program based at and organized by a German university. Scholarships may also be applied toward participation in an organized study abroad program, such as those organized by their school that are at least one semester long. It must take place during the German academic year, from October to July, either one semester (four months) or an academic year (10 months) in duration.

Award: Scholarship for use in junior or senior years; not renewable.

Eligibility Requirements: Applicant must be enrolled or expecting to enroll full-time at a four-year institution or university. Available to U.S. and non-U.S. citizens.

Application Requirements: Application form. *Deadline:* January 31.

Contact: DAAD New York
German Academic Exchange Service (DAAD)
871 UN Plaza
New York, NY 10017
Phone: 212-758-3223
E-mail: daadny@daad.org

GETEDUCATED.COM

https://www.geteducated.com/

$1,000 EXCELLENCE IN ONLINE EDUCATION SCHOLARSHIP

Scholarships for distance education available only to U.S. citizens enrolled in a CHEA-accredited online degree program located in the USA with a minimum cumulative GPA of 3.0. Provide a copy of your most recent grade transcripts, completed application, a copy of your most recent FAFSA or 1040 tax return, and submit a 500-word essay: "What a College Degree Means to Me."

Award: Scholarship for use in freshman, sophomore, junior, senior, or graduate years; not renewable. *Number:* 1–6. *Amount:* $1000.

Eligibility Requirements: Applicant must be enrolled or expecting to enroll full- or part-time at a two-year or four-year institution or university. Applicant must have 3.0 GPA or higher. Available to U.S. citizens.

Application Requirements: Application form, essay, financial need analysis. *Deadline:* March 15.

Contact: Tony Huffman, CEO of GetEducated.com
GetEducated.com
PO Box 458
Monterey, VA 24465
Phone: 802-899-4866
E-mail: thuffman@perdiaeducation.com

GIRLTEREST ONLINE MAGAZINE

http://girlterest.com/

GIRLTEREST SCHOLARSHIP PROGRAM FOR YOUNG WOMEN

Girlterest Online Magazine is offering an annual scholarship to undergraduate and postgraduate female students. As strong advocates for higher learning and women's empowerment, we are proud to give back to aspiring women through the Girlterest Yearly Scholarship. This scholarship is merit based, requires an essay submission, and the winning student will receive $1,000 towards their costs of education. All of the application details and terms, as well as the 2017 essay topics are available on our website at girlterest.com/scholarship/.

Award: Scholarship for use in freshman, sophomore, junior, senior, graduate, or postgraduate years; renewable. *Number:* 1. *Amount:* $1000.

Eligibility Requirements: Applicant must be enrolled or expecting to enroll full- or part-time at a two-year or four-year or technical institution or university and female. Available to U.S. and non-U.S. citizens.

Application Requirements: Essay, personal photograph. *Deadline:* December 30.

Contact: Mrs. Maureen Mizrahi, Co-Founder
Girlterest Online Magazine
33 Burla street 75736
Israel
Rishon leZion
Phone: 66-958570634
E-mail: scholarships@girlterest.com

GOLDEN KEY INTERNATIONAL HONOUR SOCIETY

http://www.goldenkey.org/

GOLDEN KEY SERVICE AWARD

One award totaling $500, disbursed as $250 to the recipient and $250 to the charity of the recipient's choice. Undergraduate and graduate members who were enrolled as students during the previous academic year are eligible.

Award: Scholarship for use in sophomore, junior, senior, or graduate years; not renewable. *Number:* 1. *Amount:* $500.

Eligibility Requirements: Applicant must be enrolled or expecting to enroll full- or part-time at a four-year institution or university. Available to Canadian and non-U.S. citizens.

Application Requirements: Application form, community service, cover page from the online registration, statement of project, essay, recommendations or references. *Deadline:* March 3.

Contact: Crystal Hunter, Program Manager
Phone: 800-377-2401
E-mail: awards@goldenkey.org

GOODCALL LLC

http://www.goodcall.com

GOODCALL BEST DECISION SCHOLARSHIP

At GoodCall, we try to help people make smarter decisions by giving them access to important data. We want to know about a great decision you've made in your life. Write an essay between 400 and 500 words detailing one of the most important decisions you've made in your life. What information did you rely on? What decision did you make? How did you know it was the right choice? Please apply through our website; do not email.

Award: Scholarship for use in freshman, sophomore, or senior years; not renewable. *Number:* 1. *Amount:* $2500.

Eligibility Requirements: Applicant must be enrolled or expecting to enroll full-time at a two-year or four-year or technical institution or university. Available to U.S. citizens.

Application Requirements: Essay. *Deadline:* July 31.

GOTCHOSEN

https://gotchosen.com/home

THE SOCIAL NETWORK SCHOLARSHIP

$500 scholarship open to all fields if study in the U.S. and internationally. No purchase is required. Entrants must be 18 years or older and have been accepted to a post-secondary program or college. A valid email address must be entered in your GotChosen's Registration page for prize notification. Participants have the opportunity to win a US $5000 scholarship by posting on any channel. The participant's post with the highest number of votes at the end of the month will win the scholarship. Make interesting on-topic posts so the community will vote for them, and ask everyone you know to vote for your post. This is a monthly contest. Starting on the first day of each month and completing on the last day of each month.

Award: Scholarship for use in freshman, sophomore, junior, or senior years; not renewable. *Amount:* $5000.

Eligibility Requirements: Applicant must be enrolled or expecting to enroll full- or part-time at a two-year or four-year institution or university. Available to U.S. citizens.

Application Requirements: *Deadline:* continuous.

Contact: Ms. Trish Niedergeses, Project Administrator
Phone: 407-284-1242
E-mail: info@gotchosen.com

GRADUATEPROGRAMS.COM

http://graduateprograms.com

BECAUSE COLLEGE IS EXPENSIVE SCHOLARSHIP

Super easy, fast and anyone can win! Simply register online and you could be the next winner! The $500 Because College is Expensive Scholarship is open to all students and those planning on enrolling within 12 months. The winner will be determined by random drawing and then contacted directly and announced on the Scholarship Winners page. One entry per person is all that is necessary. Read the official rules for additional information. Please see our website at cedaredlending.com for more details and the application.

Award: Scholarship for use in freshman, sophomore, junior, senior, graduate, or postgraduate years; not renewable. *Number:* 1. *Amount:* $500.

Eligibility Requirements: Applicant must be enrolled or expecting to enroll full- or part-time at a four-year institution or university. Available to U.S. citizens.

Application Requirements: Application form. *Deadline:* June 30.

Contact: Mr. Harvey Berkey, President
GraduatePrograms.com
25 Hidden Ledge Road
Englewood, NJ 7631
Phone: 201-615-5981
E-mail: harvey@graduateprograms.com

GRADUATE PROGRAMS FOUNDATION PRE-GRAD SCHOLARSHIP

Applicant must a current junior or senior undergraduate at an accredited institution or recent college graduate who is thinking of applying to graduate school. The applicant is required to enter the basic information and include your Statement of Purpose. To register, please go to http://www.graduateprograms.com/pre-grad-registration/.

Award: Scholarship for use in junior or senior years; not renewable. *Number:* 4. *Amount:* $1000.

Eligibility Requirements: Applicant must be enrolled or expecting to enroll full- or part-time at a four-year institution or university. Available to U.S. and non-U.S. citizens.

Application Requirements: Application form, essay.

Contact: Mr. Harvey Berkey, President
GraduatePrograms.com
25 Hidden Ledge Road
Englewood, NJ 07631
Phone: 201-615-5981
E-mail: harvey@graduateprograms.com

GUARDIAN DEBT RELIEF

https://www.guardiandebtrelief.com/

GUARDIAN DEBT RELIEF SCHOLARSHIP

Guardian Debt Relief is offering a scholarship for students entering into or already enrolled in college. Guardian Debt Relief realizes the importance of higher education and wants to lend our aid to those who pursue a degree. We will award five (5) scholarships of $1000 each to impressive college students who qualify. Eligible applicants will be required to submit a 2,000 word essay based on one of the three essay topics listed below. The five (5) most impressive and informative essays will be selected for the awards. The applicants must be enrolled in an accredited 4-year university or college located in the United States. Open to both graduate and undergraduate students. Graduating high school seniors with a GPA of 3.0 or higher are eligible to apply for the scholarship. You must have a cumulative GPA of 3.0 if you are already enrolled in college. You must successfully complete the application form and written essay. The essay must be double spaced and submitted through email. Word Documents and PDF (.doc,.docx,.pdf) formats will be accepted. All other formats will not be considered. All essays must be at least 2000 words in length and must include a heading with your full name and date on the first page. Essays totaling less than 2000 words will not be considered. See website https://www.guardiandebtrelief.com/guardian-debt-relief-scholarship

Award: Scholarship for use in freshman, sophomore, junior, senior, or graduate years; not renewable. *Number:* 1–5. *Amount:* $1–$1000.

Eligibility Requirements: Applicant must be enrolled or expecting to enroll full- or part-time at a two-year or four-year or technical institution or university. Applicant must have 3.0 GPA or higher. Available to U.S. citizens.

Application Requirements: Application form, essay. *Deadline:* December 31.

Contact: Michael Milington
Phone: 212-5920300
E-mail: scholarships@guardiandebtrelief.com

G.W. NETWORKS INC.

http://mmanuts.com

PRINT IT SCHOLARSHIP FOR ASPIRING CONTENT CREATORS

Please contact us to submit your entry or with any questions you may have by sending an email to scholarships@mmanuts.com with Scholarship Inquiry in the subject line. You may also reach us at our main office at (773) 599-1662.

Award: Scholarship for use in freshman, sophomore, junior, or senior years; not renewable. *Number:* 1. *Amount:* $250.

Eligibility Requirements: Applicant must be age 18-50 and enrolled or expecting to enroll full- or part-time at a two-year or four-year or technical institution or university. Available to U.S. citizens.

Application Requirements: Application form. *Deadline:* March 8.

Contact: Mr. Ingo Weigold, President and Owner
G.W. Networks Inc.
112 E Sunset
Lombard, IL 60148
Phone: 630-379 Ext. 7673
E-mail: ingo.weigold@mmanuts.com

HARVARD TRAVELLERS CLUB PERMANENT FUND

http://www.travellersfund.org/

HARVARD TRAVELLERS CLUB PERMANENT FUND

From one to three grants made each year to persons with projects that involve intelligent travel and exploration. The travel must be intimately involved with research and/or exploration. Prefer applications from persons working on advanced degrees.

Award: Grant for use in freshman, sophomore, junior, senior, graduate, or postgraduate years; not renewable. *Number:* 1–4. *Amount:* $1000–$4000.

Eligibility Requirements: Applicant must be enrolled or expecting to enroll full- or part-time at a four-year institution or university. Available to U.S. and non-U.S. citizens.

Application Requirements: Application form, financial need analysis. *Deadline:* continuous.

Contact: Mr. George Bates, Trustee
Harvard Travellers Club Permanent Fund
PO Box 190
Canton, MA 02021
Phone: 781-821-0400
E-mail: gpbates@shieldpackaging.com

THE HIGGINS FIRM

https://www.thehigginsfirm.com

JUDGE BILL HIGGINS PUBLIC SERVICE SCHOLARSHIP

The applicant must be currently enrolled in an accredited community college, undergraduate, or graduate program. This also includes incoming first- year college students who are high school graduates or possess a GED. For more information visit https://www.thehigginsfirm.com/#scholarship

Award: Scholarship for use in freshman, sophomore, junior, senior, graduate, or postgraduate years; not renewable. *Number:* 1. *Amount:* $500.

Eligibility Requirements: Applicant must be enrolled or expecting to enroll full- or part-time at a two-year or four-year or technical institution or university. Applicant must have 3.0 GPA or higher. Available to U.S. and non-U.S. citizens.

Application Requirements: Application form, community service, essay. *Deadline:* July 21.

Contact: Jim Higgins
E-mail: info@higginsfirm.com

HISPANIC ASSOCIATION OF COLLEGES AND UNIVERSITIES (HACU)

http://www.hacu.net/

HISPANIC ASSOCIATION OF COLLEGES AND UNIVERSITIES SCHOLARSHIP PROGRAMS

The scholarship programs are sponsored by corporate organizations. To be eligible, students must attend a HACU member college or university and meet all additional criteria. Visit website, http//www.hacu.net, for details.

Award: Scholarship for use in freshman, sophomore, junior, senior, or graduate years; not renewable. *Number:* up to 200. *Amount:* up to $2000.

Eligibility Requirements: Applicant must be enrolled or expecting to enroll full- or part-time at a two-year or four-year institution or university. Applicant must have 3.0 GPA or higher. Available to U.S. citizens.

Application Requirements: Application form, enrollment certification form, essay, financial need analysis, resume, transcript. *Deadline:* May 27.

Contact: Scholarship Department
Phone: 210-692-3805
Fax: 210-692-0823
E-mail: scholarship@hacu.net

HONOR SOCIETY OF PHI KAPPA PHI

http://www.PhiKappaPhi.org/

STUDY ABROAD GRANT COMPETITION

Grants up to $1000 awarded to undergraduates as support for seeking knowledge and experience by studying abroad. Must have 3.75+ cumulative GPA and attend a school with an Active Phi Kappa Phi chapter. Travel cannot begin prior to May 1.

Award: Grant for use in freshman, sophomore, junior, or senior years; not renewable. *Number:* 50. *Amount:* $1000.

Eligibility Requirements: Applicant must be enrolled or expecting to enroll full-time at a four-year institution or university. Available to U.S. and non-U.S. citizens.

Application Requirements: Application form, community service, essay, letter of acceptance into a study abroad program, recommendations or references, transcript. *Deadline:* April 1.

Contact: Mrs. Kelli Partin, Awards and Benefits Manager
Honor Society of Phi Kappa Phi
7576 Goodwood Boulevard
Baton Rouge, LA 70806
Phone: 225-388-4917 Ext. 35
Fax: 225-388-4900
E-mail: kpartin@phikappaphi.org

HORATIO ALGER ASSOCIATION OF DISTINGUISHED AMERICANS

https://scholars.horatioalger.org/

HORATIO ALGER ASSOCIATION SCHOLARSHIP PROGRAMS

The Association provides financial assistance to high school seniors (U.S citizens only) who have faced adversity, have financial need (family adjusted gross income under $55,000), and are pursuing higher education. Recipients must pursue a bachelor's degree, however, students may start their studies at a 2 year school and then transfer to a 4 year university. Minimum 2.0 GPA required.

Award: Scholarship for use in freshman, sophomore, junior, or senior years; renewable. *Number:* 1009. *Amount:* $7000–$25,000.

Eligibility Requirements: Applicant must be high school student and planning to enroll or expecting to enroll full-time at a four-year institution or university. Available to U.S. and Canadian citizens.

Application Requirements: Application form, community service, essay, financial need analysis. *Deadline:* October 25.

Contact: Ms. Colin Dixon, Educational Programs Assistant
Horatio Alger Association of Distinguished Americans
99 Canal Center Plaza, Suite 320
Alexandria, VA 22314
Phone: 703-684-9444
E-mail: programs@horatioalger.org

HORATIO ALGER NATIONAL CAREER & TECHNICAL SCHOLARSHIP PROGRAM

Must have completed high school or plan to complete high school by spring 2016 with plans to enroll at a non-profit post-secondary institution by fall 2016; exhibit a strong commitment to pursue and complete a career or technical program at an accredited non-profit postsecondary institution in the United States; demonstrated critical financial need (must be eligible to receive the Federal Pell grant as determined by completion of the FAFSA); demonstrated perseverance in overcoming adversity; be involved in community service activities; be younger than 30 years old, and a United States citizen. The application will be open with a rolling deadline until all awards have been given out. Applications will be reviewed monthly.

Award: Scholarship for use in freshman or sophomore years; not renewable. *Number:* 510. *Amount:* $2500.

Eligibility Requirements: Applicant must be high school student and planning to enroll or expecting to enroll full-time at a technical institution. Available to U.S. citizens.

Application Requirements: Application form, essay, financial need analysis. *Deadline:* continuous.

Contact: Mr. Colin Dixon, Educational Programs Administrator
Horatio Alger Association of Distinguished Americans
99 Canal Center Plaza, Suite 320
Alexandria, VA 22314
Phone: 703-684-9444
E-mail: scholarships@horatioalger.org

IMAGINE AMERICA FOUNDATION

www.imagine-america.org

ADULT SKILLS EDUCATION PROGRAM (ASEP)

The Adult Skills Education Program (ASEP) offers scholarships to non-traditional students who decide to pursue career college training. This $1,000 award is available to any qualified adult student for attendance at a participating career college.

Award: Scholarship for use in freshman, sophomore, junior, or senior years; not renewable. *Number:* 10,000. *Amount:* $1000.

Eligibility Requirements: Applicant must be enrolled or expecting to enroll full-time at a two-year or four-year or technical institution. Available to U.S. citizens.

Application Requirements: Application form. *Deadline:* continuous.

Contact: Lee Doubleday, Student Services Representative
Imagine America Foundation
12001 Sunrise Valley Drive, Suite 203
Reston, VA 20191
Phone: 571-267-3015
E-mail: leroyd@imagine-america.org

IMAGINE AMERICA HIGH SCHOOL SCHOLARSHIP

Imagine America, sponsored by the Imagine America Foundation (IAF), is a $1,000 career education award that is available to recent high school graduates who are pursuing postsecondary education at participating career colleges across the United States. Only recent high school graduates who meet the following recommended guidelines should apply: likelihood of successful completion of postsecondary education; high school grade point average of 2.5 or greater; financial need; demonstrated voluntary community service during senior year.

Award: Scholarship for use in freshman, sophomore, junior, or senior years; not renewable. *Number:* 15,000. *Amount:* $1000.

Eligibility Requirements: Applicant must be age 16-19 and enrolled or expecting to enroll full- or part-time at a two-year or four-year or technical institution. Applicant must have 2.5 GPA or higher. Available to U.S. citizens.

Application Requirements: Application form. *Deadline:* December 31.

Contact: Lee Doubleday, Student Services Representative
Imagine America Foundation
12001 Sunrise Valley Drive, Suite 203
Reston, VA 20191
Phone: 571-267-3015
E-mail: leroyd@imagine-america.org

INSUREON

http://www.insureon.com

INSUREON SMALL BUSINESS SCHOLARSHIP

Two scholarships of $2500 for full-time students at four-year colleges. Complete application form and essay.

Award: Scholarship for use in freshman, sophomore, junior, or senior years; renewable. *Number:* 2. *Amount:* $2500.

Eligibility Requirements: Applicant must be enrolled or expecting to enroll full-time at a four-year institution. Available to U.S. and non-U.S. citizens.

Application Requirements: Application form, application form may be submitted online (http://www.insureon.com/insureonu/small-business-scholarship). *Deadline:* April 30.

Contact: Mr. Alexander Williamson, Business Analyst
E-mail: alex@insureon.com

INTER-COUNTY ENERGY

http://www.intercountyenergy.net/

KENTUCKY WOMEN IN RURAL ELECTRIFICATION SCHOL.

WIRE scholarships are open to any eligible student whose family is served by a Kentucky electric cooperative and has at least 60 hours of credit at a Kentucky college or university by the start of the fall term.

Award: Scholarship for use in junior, senior, graduate, or postgraduate years; not renewable. *Number:* 3. *Amount:* $1000.

Eligibility Requirements: Applicant must be enrolled or expecting to enroll full- or part-time at a four-year institution or university. Available to U.S. citizens.

Application Requirements: Application form, essay, financial need analysis. *Deadline:* June 9.

Contact: Mary Dennis
Inter-County Energy
P.O. Box 32170
Louisville, KY 40232

INTEREXCHANGE FOUNDATION

http://www.interexchange.org/foundation/

CHRISTIANSON GRANT

The Christianson Grant is awarded to U.S. citizens between 18 and 28 who have arranged their own service project abroad programs. Proposed programs must be at least six months in length and emphasize a work component. The grant program does not support independent research projects or academic study abroad programs. Application deadlines: March 15, July 15, and October 15

Award: Grant for use in sophomore, junior, senior, graduate, or postgraduate years; not renewable. *Number:* 8. *Amount:* $2500–$10,000.

Eligibility Requirements: Applicant must be age 18-28 and enrolled or expecting to enroll full- or part-time at a four-year institution or university. Available to U.S. citizens.

Application Requirements: Application form, essay, interview. *Fee:* $50.

Contact: Ashley Lulling, Senior Program Coordinator
InterExchange Foundation
100 Wall Street
Suite 301
New York, NY 10005
Phone: 917-305-5404
E-mail: grants@interexchange.org

THE INTERNATIONAL ASSOCIATION OF ASSESSING OFFICERS

http://www.iaao.org

IAAO ACADEMIC PARTNERSHIP PROGRAM

IAAO provides financial support for students to complete research in areas related to property appraisal, assessment administration, and property tax policy. The grant carries with it an obligation to submit a satisfactory report for publication by the editor of any IAAO publication and/or a presentation at an IAAO conference.

Award: Grant for use in junior, senior, graduate, or postgraduate years; not renewable. *Number:* 1–5. *Amount:* $1000–$5000.

Eligibility Requirements: Applicant must be enrolled or expecting to enroll full- or part-time at a four-year institution or university. Available to U.S. and non-U.S. citizens.

Application Requirements: Application form, application form may be submitted online (http://www.iaao.org/APPGrant), essay, recommendations or references. *Deadline:* February 15.

Contact: Tami Knight, Director of Research
The International Association of Assessing Officers
314 West 10th Street
Kansas City, MO 64105
Phone: 816-701-8132
Fax: 816-701-8149
E-mail: knight@iaao.org

INTERNATIONAL FLIGHT SERVICES ASSOCIATION

http://www.ifsanet.com

GOURMET FOODS SCHOLARSHIP AWARD

Individuals are selected to receive the award based on scholastic merit and dedication to an advanced education. Must be an employee of a current IFSA member company in good standing, or a relative of an employee of a current IFSA member company. Please address financial need within essay.

Award: Scholarship for use in freshman, sophomore, junior, or senior years; not renewable. *Number:* 1. *Amount:* $5000.

Eligibility Requirements: Applicant must be enrolled or expecting to enroll full- or part-time at an institution or university. Applicant must have 3.0 GPA or higher. Available to U.S. and non-U.S. citizens.

Application Requirements: Application form, essay, recommendations or references, transcript. *Deadline:* May 14.

Contact: Ms. Kelly McLendon, Programs Manager
International Flight Services Association
1100 Johnson Ferry Road, NE
Suite 300
Atlanta, GA 30342
Phone: 678-303-3042
E-mail: kmclendon@kellencompany.com

HARVEY & LAURA ALPERT SCHOLARSHIP AWARD

Individuals are selected to receive this award based on scholastic merit and dedication to pursuing a career in onboard services operations. Must be an employee of a current IFSA member company in good standing, or a relative of an IFSA member company employee.

Award: Scholarship for use in freshman, sophomore, junior, or senior years; not renewable. *Number:* 1. *Amount:* $5000.

Eligibility Requirements: Applicant must be enrolled or expecting to enroll full-time at an institution or university. Available to U.S. and non-U.S. citizens.

Application Requirements: Application form, essay, recommendations or references, transcript. *Deadline:* May 14.

Contact: Ms. Kelly McLendon, Programs Manager
International Flight Services Association
1100 Johnson Ferry Road, NE
Suite 300
Atlanta, GA 30342
Phone: 678-303-3042
E-mail: kmclendon@kellencompany.com

INTERNATIONAL FRANCHISE ASSOCIATION FRANCHISE EDUCATION AND RESEARCH FOUNDATION

www.franchise.org

DON DEBOLT FRANCHISING SCHOLARSHIP PROGRAM

Scholarship award to students with a focus on law, marketing, business and franchise management.

Award: Scholarship for use in junior, senior, graduate, or postgraduate years; not renewable. *Number:* 1. *Amount:* $2500.

Eligibility Requirements: Applicant must be enrolled or expecting to enroll full-time at a two-year or four-year institution or university. Applicant must have 3.0 GPA or higher. Available to U.S. and non-U.S. citizens.

Application Requirements: Application form, essay. *Deadline:* continuous.

Contact: Miriam Brewer, Senior Director
International Franchise Association Franchise Education and Research Foundation
1900 K Street, NW Suite 700
Washington, DC 20006
Phone: 202-662-0784
E-mail: mbrewer@franchise.org

JACK KENT COOKE FOUNDATION

http://www.jackkentcookefoundation.org/

COLLEGE SCHOLARSHIP PROGRAM

Scholarships to high-performing high school seniors with financial need who seek to attend and graduate from the nation's best accredited four-year colleges/universities. Candidates are selected based on academic achievement, financial need, persistence, leadership, and desire to help others. Awards vary by individual.

Award: Scholarship for use in freshman, sophomore, junior, or senior years; renewable. *Number:* 40. *Amount:* up to $40,000.

Eligibility Requirements: Applicant must be high school student and planning to enroll or expecting to enroll full-time at a four-year institution or university. Applicant must have 3.5 GPA or higher. Available to U.S. and non-U.S. citizens.

Application Requirements: Application form, application form may be submitted online, essay, financial need analysis, recommendations or references, test scores, transcript.

Contact: Gaby Ruess, Scholarship Committee
Phone: 800-498-6478
Fax: 319-337-1204
E-mail: jkc-g@act.org

JACK KENT COOKE FOUNDATION UNDERGRADUATE TRANSFER SCHOLARSHIP PROGRAM

Scholarships to students and recent alumni from community colleges to complete Bachelor's degrees at accredited four-year colleges/universities in the United States. Candidates are selected based on academic achievement, financial need, persistence, leadership, and desire to help others. Minimum 3.5 GPA required.

Award: Scholarship for use in sophomore, junior, or senior years; renewable. *Number:* 85. *Amount:* up to $40,000.

Eligibility Requirements: Applicant must be enrolled or expecting to enroll full-time at a four-year institution or university. Applicant must have 3.5 GPA or higher. Available to U.S. and non-U.S. citizens.

Application Requirements: Application form, application form may be submitted online (http://www.jkcf.org/scholarship-programs/undergraduate-transfer/), essay, financial need analysis, recommendations or references, resume, transcript.

Contact: Gaby Ruess, Scholarship Committee
Phone: 800-498-6478
Fax: 319-337-1204
E-mail: jkc-g@act.org

JACKSONWHITE ATTORNEYS AT LAW

http://www.jacksonwhitelaw.com/

JACKSONWHITE BI-ANNUAL LABOR LAW SCHOLARSHIP

JacksonWhite seeks to encourage personal and professional growth through higher education. The JacksonWhite Labor Law Bi-Annual Scholarship has been established to support hardworking individuals of any educational background. Education is essential to a successful future and JacksonWhite Law is proud to support determined students. Please visit our website for scholarship details.

Award: Scholarship for use in freshman, sophomore, junior, senior, graduate, or postgraduate years; not renewable. *Number:* 1–2. *Amount:* $1000–$2000.

Eligibility Requirements: Applicant must be enrolled or expecting to enroll full-time at a two-year or four-year or technical institution or university. Applicant must have 2.5 GPA or higher. Available to U.S. and non-U.S. citizens.

Application Requirements: Essay. *Deadline:* April 30.

Contact: Ms. DeAnna Alvarez, Client Services Coordinator
JacksonWhite Attorneys at Law
40 N. Center Street
Mesa, AZ 85201

JACKSONWHITE CRIMINAL LAW BI-ANNUAL SCHOLARSHIP

JacksonWhite understands the financial burden that comes with pursuing your goals in higher education. The JacksonWhite Criminal Law Bi-Annual Scholarship has been established in hopes of contributing to the

investment of students and future leaders. Education is essential to a successful future and JacksonWhite Law is proud to support determined students. No application is required to apply for this scholarship. Please visit our website for scholarship details.

Award: Scholarship for use in freshman, sophomore, junior, senior, graduate, or postgraduate years; not renewable. *Number:* 1. *Amount:* $1000.

Eligibility Requirements: Applicant must be enrolled or expecting to enroll full-time at a two-year or four-year or technical institution or university. Applicant must have 2.5 GPA or higher. Available to U.S. and non-U.S. citizens.

Application Requirements: Essay. *Deadline:* April 30.

Contact: Ms. DeAnna Alvarez, Client Services Coordinator
JacksonWhite Attorneys at Law
40 N. Center Street
Mesa, AZ 85201

JACKSONWHITE FAMILY LAW BI-ANNUAL SCHOLARSHIP

Attorney Tim Durkin of JacksonWhite Attorneys at Law is offering the Family Law Bi-Annual Scholarship to honor the importance of higher education. In spite of rising costs to receive a college education, JacksonWhite believes in its value and is proud to support students in their pursuits. Please visit our website for scholarship details.

Award: Scholarship for use in freshman, sophomore, junior, senior, graduate, or postgraduate years; not renewable. *Number:* 1–2. *Amount:* $1000–$2000.

Eligibility Requirements: Applicant must be enrolled or expecting to enroll full-time at a two-year or four-year or technical institution or university. Applicant must have 2.5 GPA or higher. Available to U.S. citizens.

Application Requirements: Essay. *Deadline:* April 30.

Contact: Ms. DeAnna Alvarez, Client Services Coordinator
JacksonWhite Attorneys at Law
40 N. Center Street
Mesa, AZ 85201

JACKSONWHITE PERSONAL INJURY BI-ANNUAL SCHOLARSHIP

Aspiring professionals should all have access to higher education. With the increasing costs of universities, this is has become more difficult. JacksonWhite Attorneys at Law believes in the importance of education and is proud to support students in hopes of enriching their future.

Award: Scholarship for use in freshman, sophomore, junior, senior, graduate, or postgraduate years; not renewable.

Eligibility Requirements: Applicant must be enrolled or expecting to enroll full-time at a two-year or four-year or technical institution or university. Applicant must have 2.5 GPA or higher. Available to U.S. and non-U.S. citizens.

Application Requirements: Essay. *Deadline:* April 30.

Contact: DeAnna Alvarez, Client Services Coordinator
JacksonWhite Attorneys at Law
40 N Center Street
Mesa, AZ 85201
Phone: 480-464 1111
E-mail: scholarship@jacksonwhitelaw.com

JEANNETTE RANKIN WOMEN'S SCHOLARSHIP FUND

http://www.rankinfoundation.org/

JEANNETTE RANKIN WOMEN'S SCHOLARSHIP FUND

Applicants must be low-income women, age 35 or older, who are U.S. citizens or permanent residents of the U.S. pursuing a technical/vocational education, an associate degree, or a first bachelor's degree at a regionally or ACICS accredited college. Applications are available on our website http://www.rankinfoundation.org/students/application/ from November through March.

Award: Scholarship for use in freshman, sophomore, junior, or senior years; renewable. *Number:* 25–50. *Amount:* $2000.

Eligibility Requirements: Applicant must be enrolled or expecting to enroll full- or part-time at a two-year or four-year or technical institution or university and female. Available to U.S. citizens.

Application Requirements: Application form, essay, financial need analysis. *Deadline:* March 17.

Contact: LaTrena Stokes, Program Scholarship Manager
Jeannette Rankin Women's Scholarship Fund
1 Huntington Road, #701
Athens, GA 30606
Phone: 706-208-1211
E-mail: info@rankinfoundation.org

JOHN F. KENNEDY LIBRARY FOUNDATION
http://www.jfklibrary.org/

PROFILE IN COURAGE ESSAY CONTEST

Essay contest open to all high school students, grades nine to twelve. Students in U.S. territories and U.S. citizens attending schools overseas may also apply. All essays will be judged on the overall originality of topic and the clear communication of ideas through language. Winner and their nominating teacher are invited to Kennedy Library to accept award. Winner receives $3000, nomination teacher receives grant of $500; second place receives $1000 and five finalists receive $500.

Award: Prize for use in freshman year; not renewable. *Number:* 7. *Amount:* $500–$10,000.

Eligibility Requirements: Applicant must be high school student and planning to enroll or expecting to enroll full-time at a four-year institution. Available to U.S. citizens.

Application Requirements: Application form, essay. *Deadline:* continuous.

Contact: Esther Kohn, Essay Contest Coordinator
John F. Kennedy Library Foundation
Columbia Point
Boston, MA 02125
Phone: 617-514-1649
E-mail: profiles@nara.gov

JONATHAN DE ARAUJO REAL ESTATE
www.searchmasshomes.com

REAL ESTATE SCHOLARSHIP

Lexington MA Realtor Jonathan de Araujo at Century 21 Commonwealth is committed to continuing efforts to help students who have the ambition and drive to succeed. He is sponsoring an annual scholarship of $1,000 to award one College student with the financial assistance to accomplish their educational goals and prepare for future potential career aspirations related to Real Estate.

Award: Scholarship for use in freshman, sophomore, junior, senior, graduate, or postgraduate years; not renewable. *Number:* 1. *Amount:* $1000.

Eligibility Requirements: Applicant must be enrolled or expecting to enroll full-time at a two-year or four-year institution or university. Applicant must have 2.5 GPA or higher. Available to U.S. citizens.

Application Requirements: Application form, essay. *Deadline:* November 1.

Contact: Jonathan de Araujo, Principal
E-mail: jonathan@searchmasshomes.com

JOURNALISM EDUCATION ASSOCIATION
http://www.jea.org/

NATIONAL HIGH SCHOOL JOURNALIST OF THE YEAR/SISTER RITA JEANNE SCHOLARSHIPS

One-time award recognizes the nation's top high school journalists. Open to graduating high school seniors who have worked at least two years on school media. Applicants must have JEA member as adviser. Minimum 3.0 GPA required. Submit digital portfolio to state contest coordinator by the deadline set by the state organization (usually between Feb. 1 and March 1).

Award: Scholarship for use in freshman year; not renewable. *Number:* 1–7. *Amount:* $850–$3000.

Eligibility Requirements: Applicant must be high school student; age 17-19 and planning to enroll or expecting to enroll full-time at a four-year institution or university. Applicant must have 3.0 GPA or higher. Available to U.S. citizens.

Application Requirements: Application form, essay, personal photograph, portfolio. *Deadline:* February 1.

Contact: Connie Fulkerson, Administrative Assistant
Journalism Education Association
105 Kedzie Hall
828 Mid-Campus Dr S
Manhattan, KS 66506-1500
Phone: 785-532-5532
E-mail: staff@jea.org

JRC INSURANCE GROUP
http://www.jrcinsurancegroup.com/scholarship/

JRC INSURANCE GROUP SCHOLARSHIP

The JRC Insurance Group Scholarship awards one $1,000 prize each semester to the high school senior or college student who best explains why the family breadwinner's income should be protected by life insurance, and the characteristics displayed by those who put their family first. The winner will be the person who best demonstrates the need for life insurance in U.S. households. Two $1,000 cash scholarships will be awarded. One scholarship will be awarded in the fall, and another in the spring. Essays will be reviewed by a selection committee made up of members of the JRC Insurance Group executive team. The winning essay will be selected based on originality and quality of writing. Submission deadlines: October 15, 2016 (fall) and February 1, 2017 (spring). See website for further details, http://www.jrcinsurancegroup.com/scholarship/

Award: Scholarship for use in freshman, sophomore, junior, senior, graduate, or postgraduate years; not renewable. *Number:* 2. *Amount:* $1000.

Eligibility Requirements: Applicant must be age 18-25 and enrolled or expecting to enroll full-time at a four-year institution or university. Available to U.S. citizens.

Application Requirements: Essay. *Deadline:* October 15.

Contact: Mr. Cliff Pendell, Vice President of Marketing and Operations
JRC Insurance Group
3914 Murphy Canyon Rd
Suite A236
San Diego, CA 92123
Phone: 855-247-9555
E-mail: Info@jrcinsurancegroup.com

J. WALTER THOMPSON
https://www.jwt.com/en/

HELEN LANSDOWNE RESOR SCHOLARSHIP

The Helen Lansdowne Resor Scholarship is an international opportunity that addresses the lack of female creative leadership in the ad industry by empowering female college students with the support they need to join advertising's creative ranks. Named after Helen Lansdowne Resor, our and the industry's first female copywriter, the Scholarship was established in partnership with the 4A's in 2014. Each year, it awards five individual scholarships up to USD 10,000. Additionally, each recipient will be offered a paid summer internship with a JWT office in her respective region; a JWT mentor, and a first look placement consideration upon graduation. Since 2014, 10 young women from diverse academic backgrounds and across six regions have been named recipients of the HLR Scholarship. To be eligible, an applicant must be female; be registered as a student at a participating undergraduate and/or portfolio school and be no less than 12 months from completion of their degree at May 14, 2017; show creative talent and promise; and maintain satisfactory academic and creative progress as determined by their school.

Award: Scholarship for use in freshman, graduate, or postgraduate years; not renewable. *Number:* 5. *Amount:* $10,000.

Eligibility Requirements: Applicant must be enrolled or expecting to enroll full- or part-time at a two-year or four-year or technical institution or university and female. Applicant must have 2.5 GPA or higher. Available to U.S. and non-U.S. citizens.

Application Requirements: Application form. *Deadline:* May 14.

Contact: Jessica Watson
E-mail: hlrscholarship@jwt.com

KAHN ROVEN, LLP

http://www.kahnroven.com/

KAHN ROVEN, LLP SCHOLARSHIP

What does post-secondary education mean to you? How is it going to help you achieve your future goals? Application needs to be mailed in, but can be found at the following website: http://www.kahnroven.com/scholarship.html

Award: Scholarship for use in freshman year; not renewable. *Number:* 1. *Amount:* $500.

Eligibility Requirements: Applicant must be high school student and planning to enroll or expecting to enroll full-time at a four-year institution or university. Applicant must have 3.0 GPA or higher. Available to U.S. citizens.

Application Requirements: Application form, essay. *Deadline:* April 15.

Contact: Mr. Johnathan Roven
E-mail: kahnroven@gmail.com

KENNEDY FOUNDATION

http://uskennedyfoundation.org/scholarships/kennedy-foundation-scholarship/

KENNEDY FOUNDATION SCHOLARSHIPS

Renewable scholarships for current high school students for up to four years of undergraduate study. Renewal contingent upon academic performance. Must maintain a GPA of 2.5. Send self-addressed stamped envelope for application. See website for details http://www.columbinecorp.com/kennedyfoundation to download an application.

Award: Scholarship for use in freshman year; renewable. *Number:* 8–14. *Amount:* $2000.

Eligibility Requirements: Applicant must be high school student and planning to enroll or expecting to enroll full-time at a two-year or four-year institution or university. Applicant must have 2.5 GPA or higher. Available to U.S. citizens.

Application Requirements: Application form, self-addressed stamped envelope with application, test scores, transcript. *Deadline:* June 30.

Contact: Jonathan Kennedy, Vice President

KENTUCKY OFFICE OF VOCATIONAL REHABILITATION

http://www.ovr.ky.gov/

KENTUCKY OFFICE OF VOCATIONAL REHABILITATION

Grant provides services necessary to secure employment. Eligible individual must possess physical or mental impairment that results in a substantial impediment to employment; benefit from vocational rehabilitation services in terms of an employment outcome; and require vocational rehabilitation services to prepare for, enter, or retain employment.

Award: Grant for use in freshman, sophomore, junior, senior, graduate, or postgraduate years; renewable.

Eligibility Requirements: Applicant must be enrolled or expecting to enroll full- or part-time at a two-year or four-year or technical institution or university.

Application Requirements: Application form, eligibility for OVR services and in proper priority category, financial need analysis, interview, transcript. *Deadline:* continuous.

Contact: Charles Puckett, Program Administrator
Kentucky Office of Vocational Rehabilitation
600 West Cedar Street, Suite 2E
Louisville, KY 40202
Phone: 502-595-4173
Fax: 502-564-2358
E-mail: marianu.spencer@mail.state.ky.us

KIM AND HAROLD LOUIE FAMILY FOUNDATION

http://www.louiefamilyfoundation.org

LOUIE FAMILY FOUNDATION SCHOLARSHIP

Please visit www.louiefamilyfoundation.org

Award: Scholarship for use in freshman year; not renewable. *Number:* 25–35. *Amount:* $1000–$10,000.

Eligibility Requirements: Applicant must be enrolled or expecting to enroll full-time at a two-year or four-year or technical institution or university. Applicant must have 3.0 GPA or higher. Available to U.S. and non-U.S. citizens.

Application Requirements: Application form, essay, personal photograph. *Deadline:* March 31.

Contact: Stan Sze, Director
Kim and Harold Louie Family Foundation
1325 Howard Ave., #949
Burlingame, CA 94010
Phone: 650-491-3434
E-mail: louiefoundation@gmail.com

KNOWLEDGE IS KEY, INC.

http://www.knowledgeiskeyinc.org/

KNOWLEDGE IS KEY, INC. SCHOLARSHIP AWARD

The mission of Knowledge Is Key, Inc. (K.I.K) is to educate, encourage and support the general public by providing free educational resources and yearly academic scholarships. Each year, we award a scholarship based on the applicant's academic achievement, writing ability and community involvement. K.I.K's philanthropic efforts focus heavily on enlightening and cultivating communities and thus, scholarship recipients must also demonstrate an active commitment to community elevation. Open to all candidates attending institutions within the U.S. only. The Knowledge Is Key, Inc. Scholarship is available to any individual of any generation who has been accepted to and at time of receipt can prove enrollment in an accredited college, university or trade school.

Award: Scholarship for use in freshman, sophomore, junior, senior, graduate, or postgraduate years; not renewable. *Number:* 1. *Amount:* $1000.

Eligibility Requirements: Applicant must be enrolled or expecting to enroll full- or part-time at a two-year or four-year or technical institution or university. Available to U.S. and non-U.S. citizens.

Application Requirements: Application form, community service, essay. *Deadline:* March 30.

Contact: Candice Chin, Scholarship Committee Chair
Knowledge Is Key, Inc.
29 Marvin Ave.
Uniondale, NY 11553
Phone: 516-610-0214
E-mail: info@knowledgeiskeyinc.org

LANCE SURETY BOND ASSOCIATES, INC.

https://www.suretybonds.org

LANCE SURETY'S $1,500 COLLEGE SCHOLARSHIP

Lance Surety Bonds Associates is offering an annual $1,500 scholarship available to all students enrolled in an undergraduate or graduate degree program at any accredited college, university, or trade school in the U.S. To apply for our scholarship, you have to submit an essay of minimum 500 words on one of the following topics: 1. What would be your motivation to start a small business, if you could launch it right now? 2. How does the U.S. economy benefit from surety bonds? Please make sure the topic you select covers a major aspect of the industry such as starting a business, the current state of the field, and the perks of the job.

Award: Scholarship for use in freshman, sophomore, junior, senior, graduate, or postgraduate years; not renewable. *Number:* 1. *Amount:* $1500.

Eligibility Requirements: Applicant must be enrolled or expecting to enroll full- or part-time at a two-year or four-year or technical institution or university. Available to U.S. and non-U.S. citizens.

Application Requirements: Essay. *Deadline:* December 15.

Contact: Mr. Vic Lance
Lance Surety Bond Associates, Inc.
4387 Swamp Road, #287
Doylestown, PA 18902
Phone: 877-514-5146
Fax: 267-362-4817
E-mail: scholarship@suretybonds.org

LA TUTORS

www.latutors123.com

INNOVATION IN EDUCATION SCHOLARSHIP

We at LA Tutors are passionate about sparking the creative genius in students and would love to commend those outstanding students who have a made a difference in the lives of others in some innovative or technological fashion. In order to achieve this, we have established a scholarship for students who meet certain criteria.

Award: Scholarship for use in freshman, sophomore, junior, senior, graduate, or postgraduate years; not renewable. *Number:* 1. *Amount:* $500.

Eligibility Requirements: Applicant must be enrolled or expecting to enroll full- or part-time at a two-year or four-year or technical institution or university. Applicant must have 3.0 GPA or higher. Available to U.S. and Canadian citizens.

Application Requirements: Application form, essay, personal photograph.

Contact: Arash Fayz, Director
LA Tutors
9454 Wilshire Blvd. Suite 600
Beverly Hills, CA 90212
Phone: 424-335-0035
Fax: 866-666-9426
E-mail: arash@latutors123.com

THE LAW OFFICES OF MICHAEL L. GUISTI

http://www.topcalifornialawyer.com/our-firm.html

THE LAW OFFICES OF MICHAEL L. GUISTI 2016 SCHOLARSHIP

At The Law Offices of Michael L. Guisti, our dedication to the community goes beyond our criminal defense legal work. With 15 years helping people throughout Orange County, CA, to defend against criminal accusations, we are proud of our many achievements for those we represent. Mr. Guisti has made the decision to offer a scholarship to either graduating high school students or current two-year college or four-year university students. The young students of today will shape the society of tomorrow, and gaining post-secondary education is a powerful tool for making positive changes.

Award: Scholarship for use in freshman, sophomore, junior, or senior years; not renewable. *Number:* 1. *Amount:* $500.

Eligibility Requirements: Applicant must be enrolled or expecting to enroll full- or part-time at a two-year or four-year institution or university. Applicant must have 3.0 GPA or higher. Available to U.S. citizens.

Application Requirements: Application form, essay. *Deadline:* May 30.

Contact: Mr. Michael Guisti, Head Attorney
The Law Offices of Michael L. Guisti
2030 Main Street, Suite 1300
Irvine, CA 92614
Phone: 949-342-8508
E-mail: michael@guistilaw.com

LEMBERG LAW

http://www.lemberglaw.com

$1,000 LEMBERG LAW LEMON JUSTICE SCHOLARSHIP

An insightful, original creative work about the impact that lemons–defective products that are protected by consumer laws–and/or lemon laws have on consumers. (Do a bit of research and you'll see the variety of lemon laws on the books). Your work can be sent as a Word document (for an essay or a poem) or a.jpg or.pdf (for visual art). If you want to submit a video or audio file, send us a link where we can download it.

Award: Scholarship for use in freshman, sophomore, junior, or senior years; not renewable. *Number:* up to 1. *Amount:* $1000–$1000.

Eligibility Requirements: Applicant must be enrolled or expecting to enroll full-time at a two-year or four-year institution. Available to U.S. and non-U.S. citizens.

Application Requirements: Application form may be submitted online(www.lemonjustice.com/i/1000-lemberg-law-lemon-justice-scholarship/), Creative Work (writing, art, video, or audio). *Deadline:* November 30.

Contact: Ms. Sally Smith, Scholarship Manager
Lemberg Law
43 Danbury Road
Wilton, CT 06897
Phone: 203-653-2250
E-mail: scholar@lembergjustice.com

$1,000 LEMBERG LAW STOP DEBT COLLECTION HARASSMENT SCHOLARSHIP

Applications for the Stop Debt Collection Harassment Scholarship are due by 11:59 p.m. EDT on May 31, 2016. Apply now! Who are we looking for? Students who want to educate the public about their rights under the Fair Debt Collection Practices Act, and a high school senior who plans to enroll full-time in an accredited two-year or four-year college or university in the U.S. during the 2016-2017 school year; or an undergraduate student who will be enrolled full-time in an accredited two-year or four-year college or university in the U.S. during the 2016-2017 school year. Send an email to scholar (at) lembergjustice.com that includes your name, mailing address, phone number, email address, and the name of the university you plan to or hope to attend. Include an insightful, original public service announcement about consumer rights under the Fair Debt Collection Practices Act (FDCPA). Your work can be attached as a Word document (for a poem) or a.jpg or.pdf (for visual art). If you want to submit a video or audio file, send us a link where we can download it, a statement saying that your submission is your own work, and that you understand the scholarship rules.

Award: Scholarship for use in freshman, sophomore, junior, or senior years; not renewable. *Number:* 1. *Amount:* $1000.

Eligibility Requirements: Applicant must be enrolled or expecting to enroll full-time at a two-year or four-year institution or university. Available to U.S. and non-U.S. citizens.

Application Requirements: *Deadline:* May 31.

Contact: Ms. Sally Smith, Scholarship Manager
Lemberg Law
43 Danbury Road
Wilton, CT 06897
Phone: 203-653-2250
E-mail: scholar@lembergjustice.com

$1,000 STOP SPAM TEXTS SCHOLARSHIP

Submit a download link to a one- to three-minute original video about unwanted spam text messages. The student must be attending (or planning to attend) a U.S. college/university.

Award: Scholarship for use in freshman, sophomore, or junior years; not renewable. *Number:* 1. *Amount:* $1000.

Eligibility Requirements: Applicant must be enrolled or expecting to enroll full-time at a two-year or four-year institution or university. Available to U.S. and non-U.S. citizens.

Application Requirements: *Deadline:* January 31.

Contact: Ms. Sally Smith, Scholarship Manager
Lemberg Law
43 Danbury Road
Wilton, CT 06897
Phone: 203-653-2250
E-mail: scholar@lembergjustice.com

LEMBERG LAW DO-NOT-CALL-COMPLAINTS.COM SCHOLARSHIP

Inspired to learn more about consumer law? Creatively express your viewpoint, in video format, on do-not-call complaints. Videos must be between one and three minutes long, and be submitted in one of the following file formats:.m4v,.wmv,.mp4, or.mov

Award: Scholarship for use in freshman, sophomore, junior, or senior years; not renewable. *Number:* up to 1. *Amount:* $1000–$1000.

Eligibility Requirements: Applicant must be enrolled or expecting to enroll full-time at a two-year or four-year institution or university. Available to U.S. and non-U.S. citizens.

Application Requirements: Video. *Deadline:* July 31.

Contact: Ms. Sally Smith, Scholarship Manager
Lemberg Law
43 Danbury Road
Wilton, CT 06897
Phone: 203-653-2250
E-mail: scholar@lembergjustice.com

LEMBERG LAW STOPCOLLECTOR.COM SCHOLARSHIP

A $1,000 scholarship will be awarded to the student who writes the best 400- to 600-word essay on one aspect of debt collection.

Award: Scholarship for use in freshman, sophomore, junior, or senior years; not renewable. *Number:* up to 1. *Amount:* $1000–$1000.

Eligibility Requirements: Applicant must be enrolled or expecting to enroll full-time at a two-year or four-year institution or university. Available to U.S. and non-U.S. citizens.

Application Requirements: Application form may be submitted online(www.stopcollector.com/i/2015/06/27/lemberg-law-stopcollector-com-scholarship/), Contact information, name of college/university, essay. *Deadline:* September 30.

Contact: Ms. Sally Smith, Scholarship Manager
Lemberg Law
43 Danbury Road
Wilton, CT 06897
Phone: 203-653-2250
E-mail: scholar@lembergjustice.com

STOP CELL PHONE ROBOCALLS $1,000 SCHOLARSHIP

Applicants to submit a 140-character statement that completes this sentence: "Cell phone robocalls need to be regulated because..." Applicants with top 10 submissions invited to submit a 500-word essay. Scholarship awarded based on originality and creativity in essay's information about cell phone robocalls.

Award: Scholarship for use in freshman, sophomore, junior, or senior years; not renewable. *Number:* 1. *Amount:* $1000.

Eligibility Requirements: Applicant must be enrolled or expecting to enroll full-time at a four-year institution or university. Available to U.S. and non-U.S. citizens.

Application Requirements: *Deadline:* March 31.

Contact: Ms. Sally Smith, Scholarship Manager
Lemberg Law
43 Danbury Road
Wilton, CT 06897
Phone: 203-653-2250
E-mail: scholar@lembergjustice.com

LENDINGTREE

https://www.lendingtree.com

LENDINGTREE $2,500 SCHOLARSHIP

The LendingTree Scholarship is available to all high school seniors that will be starting college in 2016. Applicants must be US citizens and have a minimum 3.5 GPA. To apply, simply fill out the online application at https://www.lendingtree.com/about/scholarship and then submit a video no longer than 30 seconds that respond to the question - What is your plan for paying for college?

Award: Scholarship for use in freshman year; not renewable. *Number:* 1. *Amount:* $2500.

Eligibility Requirements: Applicant must be high school student and planning to enroll or expecting to enroll full-time at a two-year or four-year or technical institution or university. Applicant must have 3.5 GPA or higher. Available to U.S. citizens.

Application Requirements: Application form. *Deadline:* July 15.

Contact: Mr. Thomas Sumrak, Content Specialist
LendingTree
11115 Rushmore Dr
Charlotte, NC 28277
E-mail: thomas.sumrakjr@lendingtree.com

LEOPOLD SCHEPP FOUNDATION

http://www.scheppfoundation.org/

LEOPOLD SCHEPP SCHOLARSHIP

Scholarship for undergraduates under 30 years of age and graduate students under 40 years of age at the time of application. Applicants must have a minimum GPA of 3.0. High school seniors are not eligible. All applicants must either be enrolled in college or have completed at least one year of college at the time of issuing the application. Must be citizens or permanent residents of the United States. Deadline varies.

Award: Scholarship for use in sophomore, junior, senior, or graduate years; renewable. *Number:* 1–30. *Amount:* up to $8500.

Eligibility Requirements: Applicant must be enrolled or expecting to enroll full-time at a four-year institution or university. Applicant must have 3.0 GPA or higher. Available to U.S. citizens.

Application Requirements: Application form, financial need analysis, interview, recommendations or references, transcript. *Deadline:* varies.

Contact: Scholarship Committee
Leopold Schepp Foundation
551 Fifth Avenue, Suite 3000
New York, NY 10176
Phone: 212-692-0191

LIFE HAPPENS

http://www.lifehappens.org

LIFE LESSONS SCHOLARSHIP PROGRAM

The Life Lessons Scholarship Program is for college students and college-bound high school seniors who have experienced the death of a parent or legal guardian. To apply students must complete and submit an online application (www.lifehappens.org/scholarship), including an essay of no more than 500 words or a 3 minutes video discussing how the death of a parent or guardian affected his or her life financially and emotionally. Applicants must explain how the lack of adequate life insurance coverage (or no coverage at all) impacted their family's financial situation. Please make sure to review the Scholarship Program rules at www.lifehappens.org/scholarship-program-rules.

Award: Scholarship for use in freshman, sophomore, junior, senior, or graduate years; not renewable. *Number:* 20–50. *Amount:* $5000–$15,000.

Eligibility Requirements: Applicant must be age 17-24 and enrolled or expecting to enroll full- or part-time at a two-year or four-year or technical institution or university. Available to U.S. citizens.

Application Requirements: Application form, essay. *Deadline:* March 1.

Contact: Julie Holsinger, Manager of Programs
Life Happens
1530 Wison Blvd
Suite 1060
Arlington, VA 22209
Phone: 703-888-5000 Ext. 4446
E-mail: scholarship@lifehappens.org

MAINE COMMUNITY FOUNDATION, INC.

http://www.mainecf.org/

JOSEPH W. MAYO ALS SCHOLARSHIP FUND

Scholarship available to assist men and women who are children, stepchildren, grandchildren, spouses, domestic partners, or the primary care givers of ALS patients. Must be attending a post-secondary educational institution, including both four-year colleges and two-year Associate programs. The recipient must be a graduate of a Maine high school or GED program.

Award: Scholarship for use in freshman, sophomore, junior, or senior years; not renewable.

Eligibility Requirements: Applicant must be enrolled or expecting to enroll full-time at a two-year or four-year institution or university. Available to U.S. citizens.

Application Requirements: Application form. *Deadline:* May 1.

Contact: Ms. Amy Pollien, Grants Administration
Phone: 207-667-9735 Ext. 1109
E-mail: apollien@mainecf.org

MALESENSE PRO

https://www.malesensepro.com

MALESENSE PRO INTERNET MARKETING SCHOLARSHIP

We created the MaleSensePro E-Marketing Scholarship for Undergraduate or Postgraduate students with the passion of Internet Marketing to receive a $1000 award.

Award: Scholarship for use in freshman, sophomore, junior, senior, graduate, or postgraduate years; renewable. *Number:* 1–10. *Amount:* $1000–$10,000.

Eligibility Requirements: Applicant must be enrolled or expecting to enroll full- or part-time at a two-year or four-year institution or university. Applicant must have 2.5 GPA or higher. Available to U.S. and non-U.S. citizens.

Application Requirements: *Deadline:* December 31.

Contact: Support. Eric White, Support Team
E-mail: eric@malesensepro.com

MARGARET MCNAMARA MEMORIAL FUND

http://www.mmmf-grants.org/

MARGARET MCNAMARA MEMORIAL FUND FELLOWSHIPS

One-time award for female students from developing countries enrolled in accredited graduate programs relating to women and children. Must be attending an accredited institution in the United States. Candidates must plan to return to their countries or a developing country within two years. Must be over 25 years of age. U.S. citizens are not eligible.

Award: Grant for use in sophomore, junior, senior, graduate, or postgraduate years; not renewable. *Number:* 6–12. *Amount:* $12,000.

Eligibility Requirements: Applicant must be enrolled or expecting to enroll full-time at a four-year institution or university and female. Available to citizens of countries other than the U.S. or Canada.

Application Requirements: Application form, application form may be submitted online (http://www.mmmf-grants.org/grants-us-application-process.html), autobiography, copy of visa, I20 and DS2019, essay, financial need analysis, interview, personal photograph, recommendations or references, transcript. *Deadline:* January 15.

Contact: Chairman, Selection Committee
Margaret McNamara Memorial Fund
MSN-J2-202, 1818 H Street, NW
Washington, DC 20433
Phone: 202-458-2436
Fax: 202-522-3142
E-mail: mmmf@worldbank.org

MATINÉE MULTILINGUAL

http://www.matinee.co.uk/

MATINÉE VOICE-OVER SCHOLARSHIP

This Matinée Scholarship opportunity is open to any student enrolled in an accredited college or university in the USA, Canada or the United Kingdom. To apply for this scholarship, each applicant must submit a 250–500 word blog post on the following topic: How does video enhance the user experience on a webpage? Discuss your ideas on the subject with regard to the user experience and level of engagement. You may want to discuss the benefits for non-English speak audiences and for users with learning difficulties. What are the benefits of hearing information as opposed to reading information on a screen?

Award: Scholarship for use in freshman, sophomore, junior, senior, or postgraduate years; not renewable. *Number:* 1. *Amount:* $1000.

Eligibility Requirements: Applicant must be enrolled or expecting to enroll full-time at a four-year or technical institution or university. Available to U.S. and non-U.S. citizens.

Application Requirements: Application form. *Deadline:* January 5.

MCNEELY STEPHENSON

http://www.indianapilaw.com/

COMMUNITY INVOLVEMENT SCHOLARSHIP AWARD

This scholarship is designed to encourage and reward dedication of an exemplary individual who is deeply involved in the community that surrounds them. McNeely Stephenson believes in good citizenship and recognition for those who support their local communities through direct involvement, meaningful commitment and generosity of their time and efforts. Scholarship applicants must submit a detailed report of their community service efforts during their high school careers. This should be submitted in the form of an essay describing the involvement and how they feel this award will further both their college career and their continued dedication to helping others.

Award: Scholarship for use in freshman year; not renewable. *Amount:* $1000.

Eligibility Requirements: Applicant must be high school student and planning to enroll or expecting to enroll full- or part-time at a four-year institution or university. Available to U.S. citizens.

Application Requirements: Application form, essay. *Deadline:* May 1.

Contact: Ellie Blair
Phone: 859-4571224
E-mail: ellie@gladiatorlawmarketing.com

MICHAEL AND SUSAN DELL FOUNDATION

http://www.msdf.org/

DELL SCHOLARS PROGRAM

250 scholarships offered annually to high school students participating in approved college readiness programs. Must have a minimum 2.4 GPA and should be participating in a MSDF-approved college readiness program for a minimum of two years prior to application.

Award: Scholarship for use in freshman year; not renewable. *Number:* 250.

Eligibility Requirements: Applicant must be high school student and planning to enroll or expecting to enroll full- or part-time at a two-year or four-year or technical institution or university. Available to U.S. citizens.

Application Requirements: Application form, recommendations or references, transcript. *Deadline:* January 15.

Contact: Scholarship Committee
Phone: 512-329-0799

MICHIGAN CONSUMER CREDIT LAWYERS

http://www.micreditlawyer.com/

MCCL THOUGHT LEADERSHIP SCHOLARSHIP

The scholarship is an essay writing competition. Students are to write on the topic of the student loan debt crisis and what possible solutions there might be to fixing the issue. When the student's application is written and submitted, it is immediately received and reviewed.

Award: Scholarship for use in freshman, sophomore, junior, senior, graduate, or postgraduate years; renewable. *Number:* 1–3. *Amount:* $250–$1000.

Eligibility Requirements: Applicant must be enrolled or expecting to enroll full-time at a four-year institution or university. Applicant must have 2.5 GPA or higher. Available to U.S. citizens.

Application Requirements: Application form may be submitted online (http://www.micreditlawyer.com/mccl-thought-leadership-scholarship/), entry in a contest, essay, transcript. *Deadline:* continuous.

Contact: Philip Rudy, Webmaster
Michigan Consumer Credit Lawyers
211 East 9 Mile Road
Ferndale, MI 48220
Phone: 616-238-3838
E-mail: philip@beshapeless.com

MILITARY OFFICERS ASSOCIATION OF AMERICA (MOAA) SCHOLARSHIP FUND

http://www.moaa.org/scholarshipfund

GENERAL JOHN RATAY EDUCATIONAL FUND GRANTS

Grants available to the children of the surviving spouse of retired officers. Must be under 24 years old and the child of a deceased retired officer who was a member of MOAA. For more details and an application go to website http://www.moaa.org/education.

Award: Grant for use in freshman, sophomore, junior, or senior years; renewable. *Number:* 1–5. *Amount:* $4000–$5000.

Eligibility Requirements: Applicant must be enrolled or expecting to enroll full-time at a two-year or four-year institution or university. Applicant must have 3.0 GPA or higher. Available to U.S. citizens.

Application Requirements: Application form, financial need analysis. *Deadline:* March 1.

Contact: Program Director
Phone: 800-234-6622
E-mail: edassist@moaa.org

MOAA AMERICAN PATRIOT SCHOLARSHIP

Students under the age of 24 and who are children of MOAA members and children of active-duty, reserve, National Guard, or enlisted personnel whose military parent has died on active service or whose military parent is severely wounded (as defined as Traumatic SGLI) are eligible to apply. For more information and to access the online application go to website http://www.moaa.org/education.

Award: Grant for use in freshman, sophomore, junior, or senior years; renewable. *Number:* 1–60. *Amount:* $2500–$5000.

Eligibility Requirements: Applicant must be enrolled or expecting to enroll full-time at a two-year or four-year institution or university. Applicant must have 3.0 GPA or higher. Available to U.S. citizens.

Application Requirements: Application form, financial need analysis. *Deadline:* March 1.

Contact: Program Director
Phone: 800-234-6622
E-mail: edassist@moaa.org

MILITARY ORDER OF THE STARS AND BARS

http://www.militaryorderofthestarsandbars.org/

MILITARY ORDER OF THE STARS AND BARS SCHOLARSHIPS

Applicants must be accepted to a degree-granting junior college or four-year college or university or already enrolled in such a facility. Awards shall be made annually, and the total amount of the scholarship money to be awarded each year to each recipient shall not exceed $1000. Applicants must be sponsored by a local MOS&B Chapter or MOS&B State Society. Applicants must be able to prove they are a descendant of a commissioned officer or civil servant of the Confederate States of America. Preference is given to relatives of currently active MOS&B members. All application information is found on the MOS&B website.

Award: Scholarship for use in freshman, sophomore, junior, senior, graduate, or postgraduate years; not renewable. *Number:* 3–6. *Amount:* $1000.

Eligibility Requirements: Applicant must be enrolled or expecting to enroll full-time at a two-year or four-year institution or university. Applicant must have 3.0 GPA or higher. Available to U.S. and non-U.S. citizens.

Application Requirements: Application form, personal photograph. *Deadline:* March 1.

Contact: Dr. Gary Loudermilk, Scholarship Chairman
Military Order of the Stars and Bars
2801 14th Street
Brownwood, TX 76801
E-mail: gmldhl@harrisbb.com

MINNESOTA MASONIC CHARITIES

http://www.mnmasoniccharities.org

MINNESOTA MASONIC CHARITIES HERITAGE SCHOLARSHIP

Heritage Scholarships are provided each year to Minnesota high school students with a GPA of 3.0-3.59. Applicants must plan to enroll in a four-year college program.

Award: Scholarship for use in freshman, sophomore, junior, or senior years; renewable. *Number:* 20. *Amount:* $2500.

Eligibility Requirements: Applicant must be high school student and planning to enroll or expecting to enroll full-time at a four-year institution. Applicant must have 3.0 GPA or higher. Available to U.S. citizens.

Application Requirements: Application form, essay. *Deadline:* March 1.

Contact: Ms. Kim Ramaker, Scholarships Manager
Minnesota Masonic Charities
11501 Masonic Home Drive
Bloomington, MN 55437
Phone: 952-948-6227
E-mail: kim.ramaker@mnmasonic.org

THE MORRIS K. UDALL AND STEWART L. UDALL FOUNDATION

http://www.udall.gov/

UDALL UNDERGRADUATE SCHOLARSHIP

Fifty one-time scholarships and fifty one-time honorable mention awards to full-time college sophomores or juniors with demonstrated commitment to careers related to the environment, tribal public policy (Native American/Alaska Native students only), or Native American health care (Native American/Alaska Native students only). Students from all fields and disciplines are encouraged to apply. Students must be nominated by their college or university. Visit http://www.udall.gov for additional information.

Award: Scholarship for use in junior or senior years; not renewable. *Number:* 50. *Amount:* $1–$5000.

Eligibility Requirements: Applicant must be enrolled or expecting to enroll full-time at a two-year or four-year institution or university. Available to U.S. and Canadian citizens.

Application Requirements: Application form, application form may be submitted online (http://udall.gov), essay, nomination by campus faculty representative, recommendations or references, transcript. *Deadline:* March 4.

Contact: Paula Randler, Scholarship Program Manager
Phone: 520-901-8564
Fax: 520-901-8570
E-mail: randler@udall.gov

MULLEN & MULLEN LAW FIRM

http://www.mullenandmullen.com

REGIS L. MULLEN $2,500 ACCIDENT INJURY SCHOLARSHIP

Students must apply each year to qualify to compete for that year's award. Only one scholarship will be awarded per year.

Award: Scholarship for use in freshman, sophomore, junior, senior, graduate, or postgraduate years; not renewable. *Number:* 1. *Amount:* $2500.

Eligibility Requirements: Applicant must be enrolled or expecting to enroll full- or part-time at a two-year or four-year institution or university. Applicant must have 3.0 GPA or higher. Available to U.S. citizens.

Application Requirements: Essay. *Deadline:* March 1.

Contact: Shelley Cates, Director of Marketing
Mullen & Mullen Law Firm
1825 Market Center Blvd #200
Dallas, TX 75207
Phone: 214-747-5240
E-mail: scholarships@mullenandmullen.com

NATIONAL ASSOCIATION OF RAILWAY BUSINESS WOMEN

http://www.narbw.org/

NARBW SCHOLARSHIP

Scholarship awarded to the members of NARBW and their relatives. The number of awards varies every year. Applications are judged on scholastic ability, ambition and potential, and financial need.

Award: Scholarship for use in freshman, sophomore, junior, or senior years; not renewable. *Amount:* $500–$1000.

Eligibility Requirements: Applicant must be enrolled or expecting to enroll full-time at a two-year or four-year or technical institution or university and female. Available to U.S. citizens.

Application Requirements: Application form, financial need analysis. *Deadline:* varies.

Contact: Scholarship Chairman
E-mail: narbwinfo@narbw.org

NATIONAL BLACK MBA ASSOCIATION

http://www.nbmbaa.org/

NATIONAL BLACK MBA ASSOCIATION GRADUATE SCHOLARSHIP PROGRAM

Program's mission is to identify and increase the pool of Black talent for business, public, private and non-profit sectors.

Award: Scholarship for use in freshman, sophomore, junior, or senior years; not renewable. *Number:* 10–25. *Amount:* $2500–$15,000.

Eligibility Requirements: Applicant must be enrolled or expecting to enroll full-time at a four-year institution or university. Available to U.S. and non-U.S. citizens.

Application Requirements: Application form, community service, essay, interview, resume, transcript. *Deadline:* April 17.

Contact: Ms. Lori Johnson, Program Administrator, University
Relations
National Black MBA Association
180 North Michigan Avenue, Suite 1400
Chicago, IL 60601
Phone: 312-580-8086
E-mail: scholarship@nbmbaa.org

NATIONAL CENTER FOR POLICY ANALYSIS

http://www.ncpa.org

YOUNG PATRIOTS ESSAY CONTEST

The Young Patriots Essay Contest is designed to challenge high school students to creatively solve problems in the realm of economics and public policy through the art of writing. The current prompt is "Drawing on the readings, discuss the relationship between individual freedom and social/economic prosperity. Feel free to incorporate outside research. " The short required readings are available for free on the contest main page.

Award: Scholarship for use in freshman year; not renewable. *Number:* 3. *Amount:* $2000–$5000.

Eligibility Requirements: Applicant must be high school student and planning to enroll or expecting to enroll full- or part-time at a two-year or four-year or technical institution or university. Available to U.S. and non-U.S. citizens.

Application Requirements: Application form may be submitted online (http://debate-central.ncpa.org/yp14/), entry in a contest, essay. *Deadline:* January 5.

Contact: Ms. Rachel Stevens, Director of Youth Programs
National Center for Policy Analysis
14180 Dallas Parkway
Suite 350
Dallas, TX 75254
Phone: 972-308-6487
Fax: 972-239-9823
E-mail: Rachel.Stevens@NCPA.org

NATIONAL COLLEGIATE CANCER FOUNDATION

http://collegiatecancer.org/

NATIONAL COLLEGIATE CANCER FOUNDATION SCHOLARSHIPS

The National Collegiate Cancer Foundation was established to provide services and support to young adults whose lives have been impacted by cancer and who have continued with their education throughout treatment or after their treatment. The NCCF Survivor Scholarship Program awards are $1,000 competitive awards, to be judged based on the criteria listed below. Applicants must meet all of the requirements listed below: 1. must be a cancer survivor or current patient, 2. must be between the ages of 18-35. An exception will be made if you are 17 and entering college in the fall following application; 3. must be a U.S. citizen or permanent resident; 4. must be attending or planning to attend an accredited college, university, or vocational institution in pursuit of an Associate, Bachelor, Master's, doctorate or certificate. Applicants will be evaluated based on six criteria--displaying a "Will Win" attitude with respect to his or her cancer experience, quality of essays, financial need, overall story of cancer survivorship, commitment to education, and quality of recommendations. Legacy Scholarship Program awards provide financial assistance to young adults pursuing their education who have lost a parent or guardian to cancer. These $1,000 competitive awards will be judged based on the criteria listed below. Applicants must meet all of the requirements listed below: 1. must have lost a parent or guardian to cancer; 2. must be between the ages of 18-35. An exception will be made if you are 17 and entering college; 3. must be a U.S. citizen or permanent resident; 4. Must be attending or planning to attend an accredited college, university, or vocational institution in pursuit of an Associate, Bachelor, Master's, doctorate or certificate. Applicants will be evaluated based on the following criteria: journey, encouragement, financial need, notable accomplishments, and quality of recommendations.

Award: Scholarship for use in freshman, sophomore, junior, senior, graduate, or postgraduate years; not renewable. *Number:* 50. *Amount:* $1000.

Eligibility Requirements: Applicant must be age 17-35 and enrolled or expecting to enroll full- or part-time at a two-year or four-year or technical institution or university. Available to U.S. citizens.

Application Requirements: Application form, essay, financial need analysis. *Deadline:* May 15.

Contact: Meghan Rodgers
National Collegiate Cancer Foundation
4858 Battery Lane #216
Bethesda, MD 20814
Phone: 240-5156262
E-mail: info@collegiatecancer.org

NATIONAL HEMOPHILIA FOUNDATION

http://www.hemophilia.org/

KEVIN CHILD SCHOLARSHIP

Scholarship applicants must be individuals diagnosed with either hemophilia A or B, and a high school senior with aspirations of attending an institute of higher education (college, university or vocational-technical school), a college student already pursuing a post-secondary education, or a student in a graduate-level program. Interested students need to submit an application along with a current official transcript of their grades and one letter of recommendation from a person familiar with their personal and academic achievements (ex. teacher, mentor). The Kevin Child Scholarship recipient will be chosen on the basis of their academic performance, participation in school or community activities and the personal application essay detailing their educational and career goals.

Award: Scholarship for use in freshman, sophomore, junior, senior, or graduate years; not renewable. *Number:* 1. *Amount:* up to $1000.

Eligibility Requirements: Applicant must be enrolled or expecting to enroll full- or part-time at a two-year or four-year or technical institution or university. Available to U.S. citizens.

Application Requirements: Application form, community service, essay, recommendations or references, transcript. *Deadline:* June 3.

Contact: NHF/HANDI
National Hemophilia Foundation
116 West 32nd Street, 11th Floor
New York, NY 10001-3212
Phone: 212-328-3700 Ext. 2
E-mail: handi@hemophilia.org

NATIONAL INSTITUTE OF GENERAL MEDICAL SCIENCES, NATIONAL INSTITUTE OF HEALTH

www.nigms.nih.gov

MARC UNDERGRADUATE STUDENT TRAINING IN ACADEMIC RESEARCH (U-STAR) AWARDS

Maximizing Access to Research Careers (MARC) U-STAR awards provide support for undergraduate students who are underrepresented in the biomedical sciences to improve their preparation for high-caliber graduate training at the Ph.D. level. Institutions with significant enrollments of college students from underrepresented groups may be eligible to apply. Awards are made to colleges and universities that offer the baccalaureate degree. Only one grant per eligible institution is awarded. MARC institutions select the trainees to be supported. Trainees must be honors students majoring in the biomedical sciences who have expressed interest in pursuing postgraduate education leading to the Ph.D., M.D.-Ph.D. or other combined professional degree-Ph.D. in these fields upon completing their baccalaureate degree.

Award: Grant for use in junior or senior years; renewable.

Eligibility Requirements: Applicant must be enrolled or expecting to enroll at a four-year institution or university. Available to U.S. citizens.

Application Requirements: Application form.

Contact: Dr. Sailaja Koduri
National Institute of General Medical Sciences, National
Institute of Health
45 Center Drive, MSC6200
Bethesda, MD 20892
Phone: 301-594-3900
E-mail: sailaja.koduri@nih.gov

NATIONAL JUNIOR ANGUS ASSOCIATION

http://www.angus.org/njaa/

AMERICAN ANGUS AUXILIARY SCHOLARSHIP

Scholarship available to graduating high school senior. May apply only in one state. Any unmarried girl or unmarried boy recommended by a state or regional Auxiliary is eligible.

Award: Scholarship for use in freshman year; not renewable. *Number:* 10. *Amount:* $1000–$14,000.

Eligibility Requirements: Applicant must be high school student; planning to enroll or expecting to enroll full-time at a two-year or four-year or technical institution or university and single. Available to U.S. and Canadian citizens.

Application Requirements: Application form, entry in a contest, personal photograph, recommendations or references, test scores, transcript. *Deadline:* May 1.

Contact: Mrs. Anne Lampe, American Angus Auxiliary Scholarship
Chairman
National Junior Angus Association
5201 East Road 110
Scott City, KS 67871
Phone: 620-872-3915

NAVAL SERVICE TRAINING COMMAND/NROTC

http://www.nrotc.navy.mil/

NROTC SCHOLARSHIP PROGRAM

Scholarships are based on merit and are awarded through a highly competitive national selection process. NROTC scholarships pay for college tuition, fees, uniforms, a book stipend, a monthly allowance and other financial benefits. Room and board expenses are not covered. Scholarship nominees must be medically qualified. Upon graduation scholarship recipients have an obligation of eight years commissioned

service, five of which must be active duty. For more information, visit our website at https://www.nrotc.navy.mil.

Award: Scholarship for use in freshman, sophomore, junior, or senior years; renewable. *Number:* 2400–2900.

Eligibility Requirements: Applicant must be age 17-23 and enrolled or expecting to enroll full-time at a four-year institution or university. Available to U.S. citizens.

Application Requirements: Application form, essay, interview, recommendations or references, test scores, transcript. *Deadline:* January 31.

Contact: NROTC Scholarship Selection Office (OD2)
Phone: 800-628-7682
E-mail: pnsc_nrotc.scholarship@navy.mil

NAVY COUNSELORS ASSOCIATION

http://www.usnca.org/

NAVY COUNSELORS ASSOCIATION EDUCATIONAL SCHOLARSHIP

The program awards at least one scholarship to a deserving student who is currently enrolled in, or accepted to, an undergraduate-level college, university or vocational tech program. Scholarship nominations must be from immediate family members of NCA members.

Award: Scholarship for use in freshman, sophomore, junior, or senior years; not renewable. *Number:* 1–4.

Eligibility Requirements: Applicant must be enrolled or expecting to enroll full- or part-time at a four-year institution or university. Applicant must have 3.0 GPA or higher. Available to U.S. citizens.

Application Requirements: Application form, essay, recommendations or references, transcript. *Deadline:* April 30.

Contact: Joseph Mack, President
Phone: 901-874-3194
Fax: 901-874-2055
E-mail: president@usnca.org

NAVY-MARINE CORPS RELIEF SOCIETY

http://www.nmcrs.org/education

NMCRS EDUCATION ASSISTANCE PROGRAM

Scholarship and/or zero interest loan for full-time undergraduate students enrolled in accredited colleges or universities. Must be a spouse or child of a Sailor or Marine who is: active duty, retired, or deceased on active duty or after retirement. Must be 23 years of age or younger. Must have minimum 2.0 GPA.

Award: Scholarship for use in freshman, sophomore, junior, or senior years; not renewable. *Number:* 1–300. *Amount:* $500–$3000.

Eligibility Requirements: Applicant must be enrolled or expecting to enroll full-time at a two-year or four-year or technical institution or university. Applicant must have 2.5 GPA or higher. Available to U.S. citizens.

Application Requirements: Application form, financial need analysis. *Deadline:* May 1.

Contact: Mrs. Beverly Langdon, Education, Program Manager
Navy-Marine Corps Relief Society
875 North Randolph Street, Suite 225
Arlington, VA 22203
Phone: 703-696-4960
E-mail: education@nmcrs.org

NEEDHAM AND COMPANY WTC SCHOLARSHIP FUND

http://www.needhamco.com/

NEEDHAM AND COMPANY SEPTEMBER 11TH SCHOLARSHIP FUND

Scholarship going to those individuals who had a pre-September 11th gross income of less than $125,000. Must be currently accepted or attending an accredited university or college. Recipients decided on a case-by-case basis. Fund designed to benefit the children of the victims who lost their lives at the World Trade Center.

Award: Scholarship for use in freshman, sophomore, junior, or senior years; not renewable. *Number:* 8–15. *Amount:* $7000–$10,000.

Eligibility Requirements: Applicant must be enrolled or expecting to enroll full-time at a four-year institution or university. Available to U.S. citizens.

Application Requirements: Application form, financial need analysis. *Deadline:* continuous.

Contact: Joseph Turano, Secretary and Treasurer
Needham and Company WTC Scholarship Fund
445 Park Avenue
New York, NY 10022
Phone: 212-705-0314
E-mail: jturano@needhamco.com

NEW MEXICO COMMISSION ON HIGHER EDUCATION

http://www.hed.state.nm.us/

NEW MEXICO COMPETITIVE SCHOLARSHIP

Scholarships for non-residents or non-citizens of the United States to encourage out-of-state students who have demonstrated high academic achievement in high school to enroll in public four-year universities in New Mexico. Renewable for up to four years. For details visit http://fin.hed.state.nm.us.

Award: Scholarship for use in freshman year; renewable.

Eligibility Requirements: Applicant must be high school student; planning to enroll or expecting to enroll full-time at a four-year institution or university and studying in New Mexico. Available to Canadian and non-U.S. citizens.

Application Requirements: Application form, essay, recommendations or references, test scores. *Deadline:* varies.

Contact: Tashina Moore, Director of Financial Aid
New Mexico Commission on Higher Education
1068 Cerrillos Road
Santa Fe, NM 87505
Phone: 505-476-6549
Fax: 505-476-6511
E-mail: tashina.banks-moore@state.nm.us

NEW YORK STATE HIGHER EDUCATION SERVICES CORPORATION

https://www.hesc.ny.gov/

WORLD TRADE CENTER MEMORIAL SCHOLARSHIP

Renewable awards of up to the cost of educational expenses at a State University of New York four-year college. Available to the children, spouses and financial dependents of victims who died or were severely disabled as a result of the September 11, 2001 terrorist attacks on the U.S. and the rescue and recovery efforts.

Award: Scholarship for use in freshman, sophomore, junior, or senior years; renewable.

Eligibility Requirements: Applicant must be enrolled or expecting to enroll full-time at a four-year institution or university and studying in New York. Available to U.S. and non-U.S. citizens.

Application Requirements: Application form, financial need analysis, recommendations or references, transcript. *Deadline:* May 1.

Contact: Scholarship Unit
New York State Higher Education Services Corporation
99 Washington Avenue, Room 1320
Albany, NY 12255
Phone: 888-697-4372

NEXTSTEPU

http://www.nextstepu.com/

WIN FREE COLLEGE TUITION GIVEAWAY

NextStepU.com will award one $2,500 scholarship to one randomly selected winner twice a year. Applicants must enter online at http://www.nextstepu.com/winfreetuition. Winner must be enrolled in college within 3 years of when the prize is awarded. DEADLINE (1): June 30 DEADLINE (2): December 31.

Award: Scholarship for use in freshman, sophomore, junior, senior, graduate, or postgraduate years; not renewable. *Number:* 2. *Amount:* $2500.

Eligibility Requirements: Applicant must be enrolled or expecting to enroll full- or part-time at a two-year or four-year or technical institution or university. Available to U.S. and Canadian citizens.

Application Requirements: Application form. *Deadline:* continuous.

Contact: Web Department
E-mail: webcopy@nextstepu.com

NICHE

http://www.niche.com

$2,000 NO ESSAY SCHOLARSHIP

Scholarships don't get easier than this. Simply complete the form (found here https://colleges.niche.com/scholarship/no-essay-scholarship/), and you could be the next winner! No GPA, no essay—apply in minutes! The scholarship is awarded monthly, so make sure you apply every month!

Award: Scholarship for use in freshman, sophomore, junior, senior, graduate, or postgraduate years; not renewable. *Number:* 12. *Amount:* $2000.

Eligibility Requirements: Applicant must be enrolled or expecting to enroll full- or part-time at a two-year or four-year or technical institution or university. Available to U.S. citizens.

Application Requirements: Application form. *Deadline:* continuous.

Contact: Omid Gahari, Chief Operating Officer
Niche
5830 Ellsworth Avenue
Suite 101
Pittsburgh, PA 15232
Phone: 412-361-5080

NITRO COLLEGE

https://www.nitrocollege.com/

$5,000 NITRO COLLEGE SCHOLARSHIP

Nitro cares about providing you the resources you need to successfully navigate financing college. That's why we are offering you the opportunity to earn a $5,000 scholarship from Nitro. We know that college is a big step forward in achieving your goals and we want to help you get there using all the tools Nitro has to offer. As an added bonus, you have another chance to earn a $1,000 scholarship by recommending your friends after you apply. If your friend includes your name in their application and wins, you also get a $1,000 scholarship. There is no limit. Invite as many friends as you wish.

Award: Scholarship for use in freshman, sophomore, junior, senior, or graduate years; not renewable. *Number:* 1–2. *Amount:* $1000–$5000.

Eligibility Requirements: Applicant must be enrolled or expecting to enroll full-time at a two-year or four-year institution or university. Available to U.S. citizens.

Application Requirements: Application form. *Deadline:* March 31.

Contact: Mike Brown
Nitro College
1105 North Market Street, Suite 1600
Wilmington 19801
E-mail: mike@nitrocollege.com

NORTH CAROLINA STATE DEPARTMENT OF HEALTH AND HUMAN SERVICES/DIVISION OF SOCIAL SERVICES

http://www.ncdhhs.gov/dss

NORTH CAROLINA EDUCATION AND TRAINING VOUCHER PROGRAM

Four-year scholarship for NC foster youth and former foster youth. Must have been accepted into or be enrolled in a degree, certificate or other accredited program at a college, university, technical or vocational school and show progress towards a degree or certificate. Must be a U.S. citizen or qualified non-citizen. Applications available at: www.statevoucher.org.

Award: Grant for use in freshman, sophomore, junior, or senior years; renewable. *Amount:* $1–$5000.

Eligibility Requirements: Applicant must be age 18-23 and enrolled or expecting to enroll part-time at a two-year or four-year or technical institution or university. Available to U.S. citizens.

Application Requirements: Application form, essay. *Deadline:* continuous.

Contact: Ms. Danielle McConaga, NC DSS LINKS Independent Living Coordinator
North Carolina State Department of Health and Human Services/Division of Social Services
820 South Boylan Drive
Raleigh, NC 27603
Phone: 919-527-6343
E-mail: Danielle.McConaga@dhhs.nc.gov

NOVOSECURE

https://www.mynovosecure.com/

SEVENSECURE ADULT EDUCATION GRANT

Provides grants to adults aged 23 and over with either hemophilia with inhibitors or FVII deficiency who would are continuing their education in pursuit of a degree/certificate, either to improve their career or transition to a new one, as well as primary caregivers of minor enrollees. Applications are accepted throughout the year. One award per eligible patient per year (up to four awards lifetime).

Award: Grant for use in freshman, sophomore, junior, senior, graduate, or postgraduate years; not renewable. *Amount:* up to $2500.

Eligibility Requirements: Applicant must be enrolled or expecting to enroll full- or part-time at a two-year or four-year or technical institution or university. Available to U.S. citizens.

Application Requirements: Application form.

Contact: NovoSecure Specialist
Phone: 844-668-6732
Fax: 866-488-6576
E-mail: mynovosecuresupervisor@mynovosecure.com

OKLAHOMA STATE REGENTS FOR HIGHER EDUCATION

http://www.okhighered.org/

ACADEMIC SCHOLARS PROGRAM

Awards for students of high academic ability to attend institutions in Oklahoma. Renewable up to four years. ACT or SAT scores must fall between 99.5 and 100th percentiles, or applicant must be designated as a National Merit scholar or finalist. Oklahoma public institutions can also select institutional nominees.

Award: Scholarship for use in freshman, sophomore, junior, senior, or graduate years; renewable. *Amount:* $1800–$5500.

Eligibility Requirements: Applicant must be high school student; planning to enroll or expecting to enroll full-time at a two-year or four-year institution or university and studying in Oklahoma. Available to U.S. citizens.

Application Requirements: Application form.

Contact: Scholarship Programs Coordinator
Oklahoma State Regents for Higher Education
PO Box 108850
Oklahoma City, OK 73101-8850
Phone: 800-858-1840
E-mail: studentinfo@osrhe.edu

ONLINECOLLEGEPLANNING.COM

http://onlinecollegeplanning.com

ONLINECOLLEGEPLANNINGSCHOLARSHIP.COM

This scholarship is part of our mission to make college accessible to students. We give two scholarships a year. The scholarship requires a 250 word essay on the biggest influence in making you want to go to college.

Value of the scholarship is $1,000. Applications are only accepted online and can be submitted at http://onlinecollegeplanningscholarship.com/

Award: Scholarship for use in freshman year; not renewable. *Number:* 2. *Amount:* $1000.

Eligibility Requirements: Applicant must be high school student; age 13-21 and planning to enroll or expecting to enroll full-time at a four-year institution or university. Applicant must have 2.5 GPA or higher. Available to U.S. citizens.

Application Requirements: Application form, essay. *Deadline:* June 30.

Contact: Mr. James Maroney
OnlineCollegePlanning.com
56 Payne Road
Lebanon, NJ 08833
E-mail: james@onlinecollegeplanningscholarship.com

OREGON STUDENT ASSISTANCE COMMISSION

http://www.GetCollegeFunds.org/

ALICE AND MASON WHITE MEMORIAL SCHOLARSHIP

One-time award for graduates of Oregon high schools planning to enroll as college juniors or above for fall term/semester in undergraduate study. Minimum 3.0 GPA and FAFSA required. Evidence in activities chart of at least one extracurricular school activity preferred.

Award: Scholarship for use in junior or senior years; not renewable.

Eligibility Requirements: Applicant must be enrolled or expecting to enroll full-time at a four-year institution or university and studying in Oregon. Applicant must have 3.0 GPA or higher. Available to U.S. citizens.

Application Requirements: Application form, essay, financial need analysis. *Deadline:* March 1.

Contact: Melissa Adams, Scholarship Processing Coordinator
Phone: 541-687-7409
E-mail: melissa.adams@hecc.oregon.gov

ALLCOTT/HUNT SHARE IT NOW II SCHOLARSHIP, HONORING EMORY S. AND ELIZABETH BURKETT HUNT

Award for first or second generation immigrants to the United States. Eligible applicants must provide an answer to the citizenship status question in Item 4 of the Scholarship Application. Recipients must enroll at least half-time in college in the United States.

Award: Scholarship for use in freshman, sophomore, junior, or senior years; not renewable.

Eligibility Requirements: Applicant must be enrolled or expecting to enroll full- or part-time at a two-year or four-year institution or university. Available to U.S. and non-U.S. citizens.

Application Requirements: Application form, essay. *Deadline:* March 1.

Contact: Melissa Adams, Scholarship Processing Coordinator
Phone: 541-687-7409
E-mail: melissa.adams@hecc.oregon.gov

BARTOO/MOSHINSKY SCHOLARSHIP

Award is available to dependents of eligible employees of credit unions affiliated with, current clients of, or past clients of Merger Solution Group, The Watch Reports, and any other division of Bartoo Associates, LLC. Oregon residency is not required. Recipient must enroll at least half-time in a college or university in the United States. Apply/compete annually.

Award: Scholarship for use in freshman, sophomore, junior, or senior years; not renewable.

Eligibility Requirements: Applicant must be enrolled or expecting to enroll full- or part-time at a two-year or four-year institution or university. Available to U.S. citizens.

Application Requirements: Application form. *Deadline:* March 1.

Contact: Melissa Adams, Scholarship Processing Coordinator
Phone: 541-687-7409
E-mail: melissa.adams@hecc.oregon.gov

BETTER A LIFE SCHOLARSHIP

Scholarship award available to single parents age 17-25. High schools seniors must have at least 3.0 GPA and college students must have at least

872 Peterson's® Scholarships, Grants & Prizes 2018

a 2.5 GPA or GED equivalent. For use at Oregon public and nonprofit colleges and universities. Applicants may not already possess a Bachelor's degree. May reapply for one additional year of funding.

Award: Scholarship for use in freshman, sophomore, junior, or senior years; not renewable.

Eligibility Requirements: Applicant must be age 17–25; enrolled or expecting to enroll full- or part-time at a two-year or four-year institution or university; single and studying in Oregon. Applicant must have 3.0 GPA or higher. Available to U.S. citizens.

Application Requirements: Application form, financial need analysis. *Deadline:* March 1.

Contact: Melissa Adams, Scholarship Processing Coordinator
   Phone: 541-687-7409
   E-mail: melissa.adams@hecc.oregon.gov

BRUCE AND KARIN BAILEY SCHOLARSHIP

Award is for dependents of eligible employees of Bend Garbage & Recycling, Deschutes Recycling, Deschutes Transfer, High Country Disposal, and Mid Oregon Recycling. Eligible employees must have been employed by one of these companies two or more years as of the March scholarship deadline. High school seniors must have at least a 3.25 GPA. Apply/compete annually.

Award: Scholarship for use in freshman, sophomore, junior, or senior years; not renewable.

Eligibility Requirements: Applicant must be enrolled or expecting to enroll full-time at a two-year or four-year institution or university. Available to U.S. citizens.

Application Requirements: Application form, financial need analysis. *Deadline:* March 1.

Contact: Melissa Adams, Scholarship Processing Coordinator
   Phone: 541-687-7409
   E-mail: melissa.adams@hecc.oregon.gov

CENTRAL CITY CONCERN SCHOLARSHIP

Scholarship for current employees of Central City Concern who have been employed by the company for two + continuous years as of the March scholarship deadline. FAFSA is recommended. Oregon residency is not required. Apply/compete annually.

Award: Scholarship for use in freshman, sophomore, junior, or senior years; not renewable.

Eligibility Requirements: Applicant must be enrolled or expecting to enroll full-time at a four-year institution or university. Available to U.S. and non-U.S. citizens.

Application Requirements: Application form, financial need analysis. *Deadline:* March 1.

Contact: Melissa Adams, Scholarship Processing Coordinator
   Phone: 541-687-7409
   E-mail: melissa.adams@hecc.oregon.gov

CHILDREN OF INSITU SCHOLARSHIP

Award available to dependents of eligible employees or former employees of Insitu, Inc. Oregon residency is not required. Recipients must enroll at least half-time in a college or university in the United States. FAFSA is required.

Award: Scholarship for use in freshman, sophomore, junior, or senior years; not renewable.

Eligibility Requirements: Applicant must be enrolled or expecting to enroll full- or part-time at a four-year institution or university. Available to U.S. citizens.

Application Requirements: Application form, financial need analysis. *Deadline:* March 1.

Contact: Melissa Adams, Scholarship Processing Coordinator
   Phone: 541-687-7409
   E-mail: melissa.adams@hecc.oregon.gov

CORNELIA VALENTINE MURPHY MEMORIAL SCHOLARSHIP

Award for undergraduate study to Oregon AFSCME Council #75 members (active, laid-off, retired, or disabled) in good standing, and their dependents, grandchildren, and spouses. Member must have been active in the Oregon Council 1+ year as of the March scholarship deadline or

have been a member 1+ year preceding the date of layoff, death, disability, or retirement. Part-time enrollment (minimum six credit hours) will be considered for active members, their spouses (or life partners), or laid-off members. Essay and FAFSA are required.

Award: Scholarship for use in freshman, sophomore, junior, or senior years; not renewable.

Eligibility Requirements: Applicant must be enrolled or expecting to enroll full- or part-time at a four-year institution or university. Available to U.S. citizens.

Application Requirements: Application form, essay, financial need analysis. *Deadline:* March 1.

Contact: Melissa Adams, Scholarship Processing Coordinator
   Phone: 541-687-7409
   E-mail: melissa.adams@hecc.oregon.gov

DREAM FORMER FOSTER YOUTH SCHOLARSHIP

Award for first-time freshman, undergraduate, or graduate student who meets one of the following criteria: applies for and qualifies for the Chafee Education and Training Grant, was adopted from foster care between the ages of 14 and 16, is a former Chafee awardee now over age 23 and currently enrolled in a degree-seeking program, or is a Chafee-eligible youth who did not receive Chafee funds before age 21. Apply/compete annually. Must be enrolled at least half-time. FAFSA is required.

Award: Scholarship for use in freshman, sophomore, junior, senior, or graduate years; not renewable.

Eligibility Requirements: Applicant must be enrolled or expecting to enroll full- or part-time at a four-year institution or university. Available to U.S. citizens.

Application Requirements: Application form, financial need analysis. *Deadline:* March 1.

Contact: Melissa Adams, Scholarship Processing Coordinator
   Phone: 541-687-7409
   E-mail: melissa.adams@hecc.oregon.gov

ERIK NIELSEN SCHOLARSHIP

Award for at least half-time study at Oregon public and nonprofit colleges. Applicants must have or recently had at least a three-year gap in their education. First preference given to GED recipients, then those with a high school diploma, then undergraduates who have been out of college for at least three years. Not for applicants with an existing Bachelor's degree. FAFSA is required.

Award: Scholarship for use in freshman, sophomore, junior, or senior years; not renewable.

Eligibility Requirements: Applicant must be enrolled or expecting to enroll full- or part-time at a two-year or four-year institution or university and studying in Oregon. Available to U.S. citizens.

Application Requirements: Application form, financial need analysis. *Deadline:* March 1.

Contact: Melissa Adams, Scholarship Processing Coordinator
   Phone: 541-687-7409
   E-mail: melissa.adams@hecc.oregon.gov

ERNEST ALAN AND BARBARA PARK MEYER SCHOLARSHIP

Award for graduates of Oregon high schools and have transferred (or will be transferring during the same calendar year as the application year) from a community college to a four-year college in Oregon. Minimum 3.5 GPA and FAFSA are required. Preference to first-generation college attendees. Apply/compete annually.

Award: Scholarship for use in freshman, sophomore, junior, or senior years; not renewable.

Eligibility Requirements: Applicant must be enrolled or expecting to enroll full-time at a four-year institution or university and studying in Oregon. Applicant must have 3.5 GPA or higher. Available to U.S. citizens.

Application Requirements: Application form, financial need analysis. *Deadline:* March 1.

Contact: Melissa Adams, Scholarship Processing Coordinator
   Phone: 541-687-7409
   E-mail: melissa.adams@hecc.oregon.gov

FORD SONS AND DAUGHTERS OF EMPLOYEES OF ROSEBURG FOREST PRODUCTS COMPANY SCHOLARSHIP

Renewable award for dependents of eligible employees of Roseburg Forest Products Company. Parent must have been a full-time employee a minimum of 18 months prior to the March scholarship application deadline. Must enroll full-time, on campus, in the fall of the application year and be 21 years of age or younger. Not for applicants with existing Bachelor's degrees. May attend any eligible U.S. technical, 2- or 4-year school or college.

Award: Scholarship for use in freshman, sophomore, junior, or senior years; renewable.

Eligibility Requirements: Applicant must be enrolled or expecting to enroll full-time at a two-year or four-year or technical institution. Available to U.S. citizens.

Application Requirements: Application form, interview. *Deadline:* March 1.

Contact: Scholarship Coordinator
Oregon Student Assistance Commission
44 Club Road, Suite 100
Eugene, OR 97401
Phone: 877-864-2872
E-mail: fordscholarships@tfff.org

FRANZ STENZEL M.D. AND KATHRYN STENZEL SCHOLARSHIP

One award for graduates (including GED recipients and home-schooled graduates) of Oregon high schools and one award for nontraditional students, first-generation college students, and students approaching the final year of their programs. Students applying for first award must be majoring in medicine (pre-med and graduate-level), nursing, or physician assistant studies. Second award is not open to graduating high school seniors, medical, nursing, or physician assistant students. For both awards, high school seniors must have minimum 2.75 GPA and college students a minimum 2.5 GPA. Both awards are automatically renewable if renewal criteria is met.

Award: Scholarship for use in freshman, sophomore, junior, senior, or graduate years; renewable.

Eligibility Requirements: Applicant must be enrolled or expecting to enroll full- or part-time at a four-year institution or university. Available to U.S. citizens.

Application Requirements: Application form, financial need analysis. *Deadline:* March 1.

Contact: Melissa Adams, Scholarship Processing Coordinator
Phone: 541-687-7409
E-mail: melissa.adams@hecc.oregon.gov

GEORGIA HARRIS MEMORIAL SCHOLARSHIP

Award for employees and dependents of eligible employees of Papa's Pizza. Eligible employees must have been employed by Papa's Pizza 1+ year as of the March scholarship deadline. Oregon residency is not required. Must submit essay and apply/compete annually.

Award: Scholarship for use in freshman, sophomore, junior, senior, or graduate years; not renewable.

Eligibility Requirements: Applicant must be enrolled or expecting to enroll full-time at a two-year or four-year or technical institution or university. Available to U.S. citizens.

Application Requirements: Application form, essay. *Deadline:* March 1.

Contact: Melissa Adams, Scholarship Processing Coordinator
Phone: 541-687-7409
E-mail: melissa.adams@hecc.oregon.gov

LYNDA PILGER MEMORIAL SCHOLARSHIP

One-time award available to graduating seniors (including home-schooled seniors) of Oregon high schools. Minimum GPA of 2.75. Award must be used at a four-year public college or university in the United States. Must submit an essay describing work in the area of animal rights or animal welfare and how a college education will enhance efforts in these areas.

Award: Scholarship for use in freshman year; not renewable.

Eligibility Requirements: Applicant must be high school student and planning to enroll or expecting to enroll full-time at a four-year institution or university. Available to U.S. citizens.

Application Requirements: Application form, essay. *Deadline:* March 1.

Contact: Melissa Adams, Scholarship Processing Coordinator
Phone: 541-687-7409
E-mail: melissa.adams@hecc.oregon.gov

MAY TRUCKING COMPANY SCHOLARSHIP

One-time award for dependents of eligible employees of May Trucking Company. Eligible employees must have been employed by May Trucking Company 3+ years as of the March 1 scholarship deadline. Preferred GPA of 3.4 and 1400+ combined SAT scores.

Award: Scholarship for use in freshman, sophomore, junior, or senior years; not renewable.

Eligibility Requirements: Applicant must be enrolled or expecting to enroll full-time at a four-year institution or university. Available to U.S. citizens.

Application Requirements: Application form. *Deadline:* March 1.

Contact: Melissa Adams, Scholarship Processing Coordinator
Phone: 541-687-7409
E-mail: melissa.adams@hecc.oregon.gov

MIRABELLA EMPLOYEE-YES PROJECT SCHOLARSHIP

One-time award for hourly employees of Mirabella Portland. Oregon residency is not required. May attend school less than half time. Must specify dates of employment.

Award: Scholarship for use in freshman, sophomore, junior, senior, or graduate years; not renewable.

Eligibility Requirements: Applicant must be enrolled or expecting to enroll full- or part-time at a two-year or four-year or technical institution or university. Available to U.S. and non-U.S. citizens.

Application Requirements: Application form. *Deadline:* March 1.

Contact: Melissa Adams, Scholarship Processing Coordinator
Phone: 541-687-7409
E-mail: melissa.adams@hecc.oregon.gov

MY PATH, OUR FUTURE: HSE SCHOLARS OF OREGON

Annual award for GED graduates or students who will complete their GED. Must enroll at least part time. Oregon residency is preferred.

Award: Scholarship for use in freshman, sophomore, junior, or senior years; not renewable.

Eligibility Requirements: Applicant must be enrolled or expecting to enroll full- or part-time at a four-year institution or university. Available to U.S. citizens.

Application Requirements: Application form. *Deadline:* March 1.

Contact: Melissa Adams, Scholarship Processing Coordinator
Phone: 541-687-7409
E-mail: melissa.adams@hecc.oregon.gov

NECA OREGON-COLUMBIA CHAPTER SCHOLARSHIP

Award for graduating high school seniors who are either children or grandchildren of members of NECA Oregon-Columbia Chapter, or dependents of employees of NECA Oregon-Columbia Chapter. Scholarship is automatically renewable if renewal criteria met.

Award: Scholarship for use in freshman year; renewable.

Eligibility Requirements: Applicant must be high school student and planning to enroll or expecting to enroll full-time at a two-year or four-year or technical institution or university. Available to U.S. citizens.

Application Requirements: Application form. *Deadline:* March 1.

Contact: Melissa Adams, Scholarship Processing Coordinator
Phone: 541-687-7409
E-mail: melissa.adams@hecc.oregon.gov

OREGON ALBACORE COMMISSION SCHOLARSHIP

One-time award for first-time freshmen or undergraduates enrolled at least half-time at any college or university in the U.S. Open to Oregon commercially licensed albacore tuna landing permit holders, their captains, and their children and dependents who have paid assessments to the Oregon Albacore Commission within the past year; and processors, employees and their children and dependents where the business has purchased Oregon albacore tuna and paid assessments to the Oregon Albacore Commission within the past year. FAFSA is required. Apply/compete for additional year of funding.

Award: Scholarship for use in freshman, sophomore, junior, or senior years; not renewable.

Eligibility Requirements: Applicant must be enrolled or expecting to enroll full- or part-time at a two-year or four-year institution or university. Available to U.S. citizens.

Application Requirements: Application form. *Deadline:* March 1.

Contact: Melissa Adams, Scholarship Processing Coordinator
Phone: 541-687-7409
E-mail: melissa.adams@hecc.oregon.gov

OREGON MOVING AND STORAGE ASSOCIATION JACK L. STEWART SCHOLARSHIP

Award for eligible members of Oregon Moving and Storage Association and their dependents and grandchildren or dependents and grandchildren of employees of members of Oregon Moving and Storage Association. Apply/compete annually.

Award: Scholarship for use in freshman, sophomore, junior, or senior years; not renewable.

Eligibility Requirements: Applicant must be enrolled or expecting to enroll full-time at a four-year institution or university and studying in Oregon. Available to U.S. citizens.

Application Requirements: Application form. *Deadline:* March 1.

Contact: Melissa Adams, Scholarship Processing Coordinator
Phone: 541-687-7409
E-mail: melissa.adams@hecc.oregon.gov

OREGON OCCUPATIONAL SAFETY AND HEALTH DIVISION WORKERS MEMORIAL SCHOLARSHIP

One-time award for Oregon high school graduates or GED recipients who are either (1) dependents or spouses of an Oregon worker who has incurred permanent total disability on the job while working for an Oregon employer; or (2) receiving, or have received, fatality benefits as dependents or spouses of an Oregon worker fatally injured on the job while working for an Oregon employer. Requires information about the worker's injury and relationship.

Award: Scholarship for use in freshman, sophomore, junior, or senior years; not renewable.

Eligibility Requirements: Applicant must be enrolled or expecting to enroll full- or part-time at a four-year institution or university. Available to U.S. citizens.

Application Requirements: Application form, essay. *Deadline:* March 1.

Contact: Melissa Adams, Scholarship Processing Coordinator
Phone: 541-687-7409
E-mail: melissa.adams@hecc.oregon.gov

OREGON SALMON COMMISSION SCOTT BOLEY MEMORIAL SCHOLARSHIP

Award for dependents of licensed commercial Oregon troll salmon permit fishermen and/or captains of the vessels of licensed commercial Oregon troll salmon permit fishermen who have paid assessments to the Oregon Salmon Commission within the past three years. Preference given to graduating high school seniors.

Award: Scholarship for use in freshman, sophomore, junior, or senior years; not renewable.

Eligibility Requirements: Applicant must be enrolled or expecting to enroll full-time at a four-year institution or university. Available to U.S. citizens.

Application Requirements: Application form, financial need analysis. *Deadline:* March 1.

Contact: Melissa Adams, Scholarship Processing Coordinator
Phone: 541-687-7409
E-mail: melissa.adams@hecc.oregon.gov

OREGON SCHOLARSHIP FUND COMMUNITY COLLEGE STUDENT AWARD

Scholarship open to students enrolled or planning to enroll at least half time in Oregon community college programs. Recipients may reapply for one additional year.

Award: Scholarship for use in freshman or sophomore years; renewable.

Eligibility Requirements: Applicant must be enrolled or expecting to enroll full- or part-time at a two-year institution and studying in Oregon. Available to U.S. citizens.

Application Requirements: Application form, financial need analysis. *Deadline:* March 1.

Contact: Melissa Adams, Scholarship Processing Coordinator
Phone: 541-687-7409
E-mail: melissa.adams@hecc.oregon.gov

OREGON SCHOLARSHIP FUND TRANSFER STUDENT AWARD

Award open to students who are currently enrolled in their second year at a community college and are planning to transfer to a four-year college in Oregon. Must enroll at least half-time.

Award: Scholarship for use in junior or senior years; renewable.

Eligibility Requirements: Applicant must be enrolled or expecting to enroll full- or part-time at a four-year institution or university and studying in Oregon. Available to U.S. citizens.

Application Requirements: Application form, financial need analysis. *Deadline:* March 1.

Contact: Melissa Adams, Scholarship Processing Coordinator
Phone: 541-687-7409
E-mail: melissa.adams@hecc.oregon.gov

PETER CONNACHER MEMORIAL SCHOLARSHIP

Renewable award for American prisoners-of-war and their descendants. Written proof of prisoner-of-war status and discharge papers from the U.S. Armed Forces must accompany application. Statement of relationship between applicant and former prisoner-of-war is required. Oregon residency preferred but not required.

Award: Scholarship for use in freshman, sophomore, junior, senior, or graduate years; renewable.

Eligibility Requirements: Applicant must be enrolled or expecting to enroll full-time at a two-year or four-year institution. Available to U.S. citizens.

Application Requirements: Application form. *Deadline:* March 1.

Contact: Melissa Adams, Scholarship Processing Coordinator
Phone: 541-687-7409
E-mail: melissa.adams@hecc.oregon.gov

PITB TRANSPORTATION SCHOLARSHIP

One-time award for high school graduates (including home schooled graduates) who are dependents of PITB Transportation employees or dependents of PITB Transportation members. Must be enrolled in college at least half-time and have a minimum 3.0 GPA.

Award: Scholarship for use in freshman, sophomore, junior, or senior years; not renewable.

Eligibility Requirements: Applicant must be enrolled or expecting to enroll full- or part-time at a four-year institution or university. Applicant must have 3.0 GPA or higher. Available to U.S. citizens.

Application Requirements: Application form. *Deadline:* March 1.

Contact: Melissa Adams, Scholarship Processing Coordinator
Phone: 541-687-7409
E-mail: melissa.adams@hecc.oregon.gov

REGISTER-GUARD FEDERAL CREDIT UNION SCHOLARSHIP

Award is available to current members of the Register-Guard Federal Credit Union, or those eligible for membership, with preference in the following order: (1) current employees, independent contractors of The Register-Guard including members of their immediate families or households, (2) retired persons as pensioners or annuitants, (3) spouses of persons who died within membership, (4) organizations of such persons, (5) members of the Confederated Tribes of Grande Ronde or their immediate family members, and (6) employees or contracted employees of the law office of Donald Slayton and Alan Seglison or their immediate family members. Minimum 2.5 GPA, or GED of 2500+.

Award: Scholarship for use in freshman, sophomore, junior, senior, or graduate years; not renewable.

Eligibility Requirements: Applicant must be enrolled or expecting to enroll full-time at a two-year institution or university. Applicant must have 2.5 GPA or higher. Available to U.S. citizens.

Application Requirements: Application form, essay. *Deadline:* March 1.

Contact: Melissa Adams, Scholarship Processing Coordinator
Phone: 541-687-7409
E-mail: melissa.adams@hecc.oregon.gov

SP FIBER TECHNOLOGIES DEPENDENTS SCHOLARSHIP

Renewable award for dependents of eligible employees of WestRock, formerly SP Fiber Technologies. Eligible employees must have been employed 1+ year as of the March scholarship deadline.

Award: Scholarship for use in freshman, sophomore, junior, or senior years; renewable.

Eligibility Requirements: Applicant must be enrolled or expecting to enroll full-time at a two-year or four-year institution or university. Applicant must have 3.0 GPA or higher. Available to U.S. citizens.

Application Requirements: Application form. *Deadline:* March 1.

Contact: Melissa Adams, Scholarship Processing Coordinator
Phone: 541-687-7409
E-mail: melissa.adams@hecc.oregon.gov

UNIVERSITY CLUB OF PORTLAND SCHOLARSHIP

Award available to eligible employees and dependents of eligible employees of the University Club of Portland. Eligible employees must be in good standing and must have been employed by University Club of Portland one or more years as of the March scholarship deadline. College applicants must have a minimum 2.5 GPA. Apply/compete annually; prior recipients must be currently enrolled to reapply.

Award: Scholarship for use in freshman, sophomore, junior, senior, or graduate years; not renewable.

Eligibility Requirements: Applicant must be enrolled or expecting to enroll full- or part-time at a four-year institution or university. Available to U.S. citizens.

Application Requirements: Application form. *Deadline:* March 1.

Contact: Melissa Adams, Scholarship Processing Coordinator
Phone: 541-687-7409
E-mail: melissa.adams@hecc.oregon.gov

WAYNE MORSE LEGACY SCHOLARSHIP

Award for graduates (including GED recipients and home-schooled graduates) of Oregon high schools who are enrolled or planning to enroll at least half-time at Oregon public and nonprofit institutions. Must be a U.S. citizen and have a minimum 2.8 GPA. Can reapply for 1 additional year.

Award: Scholarship for use in freshman, sophomore, junior, senior, or graduate years; not renewable.

Eligibility Requirements: Applicant must be enrolled or expecting to enroll full- or part-time at a two-year or four-year institution or university and studying in Oregon. Applicant must have 2.5 GPA or higher. Available to U.S. citizens.

Application Requirements: Application form, essay. *Deadline:* March 1.

Contact: Melissa Adams, Scholarship Processing Coordinator
Phone: 541-687-7409
E-mail: melissa.adams@hecc.oregon.gov

OTA GUIDE

http://occupational-therapy-assistant.org/

COTA SCHOLARSHIP FOR OCCUPATIONAL THERAPY ASSISTANTS

The Occupational Therapy profession is experiencing a huge increase in demand. In an effort to encourage more bright students down the path to becoming a COTA to help serve this increase in demand, we created this scholarship for COTA students. Each year we will award one COTA student with a $500 scholarship.

Award: Scholarship for use in freshman, sophomore, junior, senior, graduate, or postgraduate years; not renewable. *Number:* 1–2. *Amount:* $1–$500.

Eligibility Requirements: Applicant must be enrolled or expecting to enroll full- or part-time at a two-year or four-year or technical institution or university. Available to U.S. and non-U.S. citizens.

Application Requirements: Essay. *Deadline:* December 1.

Contact: Kelly Clark
OTA Guide
2801 Oak Crest Avenue
Austin, TX 78704

OUTSTANDING STUDENTS OF AMERICA

OUTSTANDING STUDENTS OF AMERICA SCHOLARSHIP

Awards of $1000 each are payable to the college of the recipient's choice. Students must be high school seniors, participate in community/school activities, and maintain a minimum GPA of 3.0. For details refer to website, http://www.outstandingstudentsofamerica.com/.

Award: Scholarship for use in freshman year; not renewable. *Amount:* $1000.

Eligibility Requirements: Applicant must be high school student and planning to enroll or expecting to enroll full- or part-time at a four-year institution or university. Applicant must have 3.0 GPA or higher. Available to U.S. citizens.

Application Requirements: Application form, community service, self-addressed stamped envelope with application. *Deadline:* October 1.

Contact: Michael Layson, President
Phone: 205-344-6322
Fax: 205-344-6322
E-mail: info@outstandingstudentsofamerica.com

PATIENT ADVOCATE FOUNDATION

http://www.patientadvocate.org/

SCHOLARSHIP FOR SURVIVORS

Four years after Patient Advocate Foundation's inception, founder Nancy Davenport-Ennis created Patient Advocate Foundation's Scholarship for Survivors program after witnessing multiple recurring counts of patients whose post-secondary education had been impacted due to their life-threatening, chronic or debilitating illness. Despite their condition, these students excelled academically, served the community, and demonstrated the drive and desire to attend college. The purpose of our scholarship program is to provide support to individuals, under the age of 25, who have been diagnosed with or treated for cancer and/or a chronic/life threatening disease within the past five years.

Award: Scholarship for use in freshman, sophomore, junior, senior, or graduate years; renewable. *Number:* 12. *Amount:* $3000.

Eligibility Requirements: Applicant must be enrolled or expecting to enroll full-time at a two-year or four-year institution or university. Applicant must have 3.0 GPA or higher. Available to U.S. citizens.

Application Requirements: Application form, essay, financial need analysis. *Deadline:* February 25.

Contact: Ms. Shawn Nason, Director, Events, Travel, Admin Services
Patient Advocate Foundation
421 Butler Farm road
Hampton, VA 23666
Phone: 800-532-5274
E-mail: scholarship@patientadvocate.org

PHI BETA SIGMA FRATERNITY INC.

http://www.pbs1914.org/

PHI BETA SIGMA FRATERNITY NATIONAL PROGRAM OF EDUCATION

Scholarships are awarded to both graduate and undergraduate students. Applicants must have minimum 3.0 GPA.

Award: Scholarship for use in freshman, sophomore, junior, senior, or graduate years; not renewable.

Eligibility Requirements: Applicant must be enrolled or expecting to enroll full-time at a four-year institution or university and male. Applicant must have 3.0 GPA or higher. Available to U.S. citizens.

Application Requirements: Application form, essay, personal photograph, recommendations or references, resume, transcript. *Deadline:* June 15.

Contact: Emile Pitre, Chairman
Phi Beta Sigma Fraternity Inc.
2 Belmonte Circle, SW
Atlanta, GA 30311
Phone: 404-759-6827
E-mail: mikewhines@aol.com

P.L.A.Y.

http://www.petplay.com/

P.L.A.Y. SCHOLARSHIP

$1000 scholarship for incoming college freshmen. To apply, students must submit a 500-1000 word essay with 2-3 photos of their volunteer efforts to help animals in need and how that involvement has changed their lives or shaped their perceptions on the importance of animal welfare. Send a Word doc attachment to scholarship@petplay.com with essay submission. The file name should be student's full name, state, and date of birth. For example, Chipper-Jones-GA-4-24-1972. All submission emails must contain the student's full name, date of birth, email address, postal address, high school they are currently enrolled in, and a phone number to contact. For more information on how to apply, visit http://www.petplay.com/scholarship/.

Award: Scholarship for use in freshman year; not renewable. *Number:* 1. *Amount:* $1000.

Eligibility Requirements: Applicant must be high school student and planning to enroll or expecting to enroll full-time at a two-year or four-year or technical institution or university. Available to U.S. citizens.

Application Requirements: Community service, essay, personal photograph. *Deadline:* December 3.

Contact: Sarah Lively
Phone: 404-220-8448
E-mail: scholarship@petplay.com

PRETTY LIGHTROOM PRESETS

https://www.lightroompresets.com/

PRETTY LIGHTROOM PRESETS BI-ANNUAL SCHOLARSHIP

The Pretty Lightroom Presets $500 biannual scholarship (awarded twice per year) provides college and university students an opportunity to earn money to further their education. The deadline for scholarship entries is biannually on June 15 and December 15. The winning entry will be published on Pretty Presets Blog. The winner will be notified by e-mail three weeks after the deadline. Scholarship entries will be carefully reviewed by a team of judges at LightroomPresets.com. The scholarship will be paid out in amounts of $500 (U.S.) to each winner biannually, twice each year, in the form of a co-payable check that will be mailed to the college or university attended by the winning student. Carefully research and compose an essay style Adobe Lightroom tutorial of 800 to 1,000 words, with screenshots and photos included to illustrate your points on one of the following topics. Use proper grammar and punctuation.

Award: Scholarship for use in freshman, sophomore, junior, senior, graduate, or postgraduate years; not renewable. *Number:* 2. *Amount:* $500.

Eligibility Requirements: Applicant must be enrolled or expecting to enroll full- or part-time at a two-year or four-year institution or university. Available to U.S. and Canadian citizens.

Application Requirements: Essay, personal photograph. *Deadline:* June 15.

Contact: Karlen Kleinkopf
E-mail: scholarship@lightroompresets.com

PRETTY PHOTOSHOP ACTIONS

https://www.photoshopactions.com/

PRETTY PHOTOSHOP ACTIONS BI-ANNUAL SCHOLARSHIP

The Pretty Photoshop Actions $500 biannual scholarship (awarded twice per year) provides college and university students an opportunity to earn money to further their education. The deadline for scholarship entries is biannually on April 15 and October 15. The winning entry will be published on Pretty Actions Blog. The winner will be notified by e-mail three weeks after the deadline. Scholarship entries will be carefully reviewed by a team of judges at PhotoshopActions.com. The scholarship will be paid out in amounts of $500 (U.S.) to each winner biannually, twice each year, in the form of a co-payable check that will be mailed to the college or university attended by the winning student.

Award: Scholarship for use in freshman, sophomore, junior, senior, graduate, or postgraduate years; not renewable. *Number:* 2. *Amount:* $500.

Eligibility Requirements: Applicant must be enrolled or expecting to enroll full- or part-time at a two-year or four-year institution or university. Available to U.S. and Canadian citizens.

Application Requirements: Essay, personal photograph. *Deadline:* April 15.

Contact: Karlen Kleinkopf
E-mail: scholarship@photoshopactions.com

PRICE BENOWITZ LLP

http://pricebenowitz.com/

ED TAYTER OUTSTANDING CITIZEN SCHOLARSHIP

The Edward Tayter Outstanding Citizen Scholarship aims to give demonstrated community leaders and dedicated citizens an opportunity to pursue the education that will inform and better their causes.

Award: Scholarship for use in freshman, sophomore, junior, senior, or graduate years; not renewable.

Eligibility Requirements: Applicant must be enrolled or expecting to enroll full- or part-time at a two-year or four-year institution or university. Applicant must have 3.0 GPA or higher. Available to U.S. citizens.

Application Requirements: Essay. *Deadline:* May 1.

Contact: Price Benowitz
Price Benowitz LLP
409 7th Street NW
Washington, DC 20004
Phone: 202-417-6013
E-mail: info@pricebenowitz.com

MICHAEL KIELY STRONG ROOTS SCHOLARSHIP AND ESSAY CONTEST

Michael Kiely is proud to sponsor the Strong Roots Scholarship and Essay Contest as a way to promote discussion about the meaning of community in the digital age and as a way to sponsor educational opportunities for individuals who are dedicated to building strong communities where passions and careers can take root.

Award: Scholarship for use in freshman, sophomore, junior, senior, or graduate years; not renewable.

Eligibility Requirements: Applicant must be enrolled or expecting to enroll full- or part-time at a two-year or four-year institution or university. Applicant must have 3.0 GPA or higher. Available to U.S. and non-U.S. citizens.

Application Requirements: Essay. *Deadline:* May 1.

Contact: Price Benowitz
Price Benowitz LLP
409 7th Street NW
Washington, DC 20004
Phone: 202-417-6013
E-mail: info@pricebenowitz.com

TATIANA MENDEZ FUTURE RESOURCES SCHOLARSHIP

Ms. Mendez is proud to sponsor conversation on the topic of natural preservation, as well as to aid in the educational goals of those who wish to achieve positive change through stewardship.

Award: Scholarship for use in freshman, sophomore, junior, senior, graduate, or postgraduate years; not renewable.

Eligibility Requirements: Applicant must be enrolled or expecting to enroll full- or part-time at a four-year institution or university. Applicant must have 3.0 GPA or higher. Available to U.S. citizens.

Application Requirements: Essay. *Deadline:* May 1.

Contact: Price Benowitz
Price Benowitz LLP
409 7th Street NW
Washington, DC 20004
Phone: 202-417-6013
E-mail: info@pricebenowitz.com

PROOF READING, LLC

http://www.proof-reading.com/

PROOF READING, LLC SCHOLARSHIP PROGRAM

Applicants must write an essay that satisfies the question found on the organization website. The minimum word count is 1,500 words. Focus will be on grammar and ability to present ideas clearly. Include a Works Cited page, with a minimum of three sources. The essay must follow MLA writing guidelines. For more information, visit website http://www.proof-reading.com/proof-reading_scholarship_program.asp.

Award: Scholarship for use in freshman, sophomore, junior, or senior years; not renewable. *Number:* 1. *Amount:* $1500.

Eligibility Requirements: Applicant must be enrolled or expecting to enroll full-time at a four-year institution or university. Applicant must have 3.5 GPA or higher. Available to U.S. citizens.

Application Requirements: Application form, essay. *Deadline:* January 23.

Contact: Mr. Mike Williams, Scholarship Coordinator
Proof Reading, LLC
664 Natoma Street
San Francisco, CA 94103
Phone: 866-433-4867
E-mail: scholarships@proof-reading.com

PROOFREADINGSERVICES.COM

http://www.proofreadingservices.com/

HIGH SCHOOL AND UNIVERSITY WRITING SCHOLARSHIPS

Applicants must respond to the following writing prompt: Write about a defining moment in your life in the style of your favorite children's author. Three scholarships will be awarded to high school seniors and three will be awarded to university students. See more at: http://www.proofreadingservices.com/pages/scholarship#sthash.A7Jv5CsH.dpuf.

Award: Scholarship for use in freshman, sophomore, junior, senior, or graduate years; not renewable. *Number:* 6. *Amount:* $100–$500.

Eligibility Requirements: Applicant must be enrolled or expecting to enroll full- or part-time at a two-year or four-year or technical institution or university. Applicant must have 3.0 GPA or higher. Available to U.S. and non-U.S. citizens.

Application Requirements: Application form, essay. *Deadline:* June 1.

Contact: Mr. Luke Palder, CEO
ProofreadingServices.com
1 Broadway
14th Floor
Cambridge, MA 02142
Phone: 800-492-6773
E-mail: scholarship@proofreadingservices.com

PRUDENT PUBLISHING COMPANY INC.

http://www.gallerycollection.com/

10TH ANNUAL CREATE-A-GREETING-CARD $10,000 SCHOLARSHIP CONTEST

Students must submit an original photo, piece of artwork, or computer graphic for the front of a greeting card. The student with the best design will win a $10,000 scholarship and have his or her entry made into an actual greeting card to be sold in The Gallery Collection's line. The winning student's school will also receive a $1000 prize for helping to promote the contest. For complete details visit http://www.gallerycollection.com/greeting-cards-scholarship.htm.

Award: Scholarship for use in freshman, sophomore, junior, senior, or graduate years; not renewable. *Number:* 1. *Amount:* $10,000.

Eligibility Requirements: Applicant must be enrolled or expecting to enroll full- or part-time at a two-year or four-year or technical institution or university. Available to U.S. citizens.

Application Requirements: Application form, entry in a contest, greeting card design. *Deadline:* December 31.

Contact: Scholarship Administrator
Prudent Publishing Company Inc.
65 Challenger Road
Ridgefield Park, NJ 07660
Phone: 201-641-7900
E-mail: scholarshipadmin@gallerycollection.com

PUSH FOR EXCELLENCE

http://www.pushexcel.org/

ORA LEE SANDERS SCHOLARSHIP

U.S. citizens who will be freshmen, sophomores, juniors, or seniors are eligible. The scholarship is renewable up to 4 years based upon GPA. Full time study with minimum 2.5 GPA.

Award: Scholarship for use in freshman, sophomore, junior, or senior years; renewable. *Amount:* $1000.

Eligibility Requirements: Applicant must be enrolled or expecting to enroll full-time at a four-year institution or university. Applicant must have 2.5 GPA or higher. Available to U.S. citizens.

Application Requirements: Application form, essay, proof of current enrollment or acceptance in a college or university, recommendations or references, self-addressed stamped envelope with application, transcript. *Deadline:* April 30.

Contact: Scholarship Committee
Push for Excellence
930 East 50th Street
Chicago, IL 60615
Phone: 773-373-3366
E-mail: info@pushexcel.org

RADIO TELEVISION DIGITAL NEWS ASSOCIATION

www.rtdna.org

PRESIDENTS SCHOLARSHIP

Two $1,000 awards are given each year to aspiring journalists in honor of former RTDNA Presidents Theodore Koop, Bruce Dennis, James McCulla, John Salisbury, Bruce Palmer, Dick Cheverton, Jim Byron, Ben Chatfield and John Hogan.

Award: Scholarship for use in sophomore, junior, or senior years; not renewable. *Number:* 2. *Amount:* $1000.

Eligibility Requirements: Applicant must be enrolled or expecting to enroll full-time at a four-year institution or university. Available to U.S. and non-U.S. citizens.

Application Requirements: Application form, essay, portfolio. *Deadline:* May 31.

Contact: Ms. Karen Hansen, Membership and Program Manager
Radio Television Digital News Association
529 14th Street, NW
Suite 1240
Washington, DC 20045
Phone: 202-662-7257
E-mail: karenh@rtdna.org

RENTHOP

www.renthop.com

RENTHOP: COLLEGE AND UNIVERSITY SCHOLARSHIP PROGRAM

To apply, send an essay under 500 words that follows the following prompt: Technology is changing every aspects of our daily lives, from searching for real estate to phones in our pocket that are more powerful than anyone would have imaged a generation prior. In the next 5 years, what do you feel will be the most profound changes that impact college graduates, their careers, and their personal lives? How are your those changes aligned with the RentHop values and those of your school and degree program? Apply today at college-scholarship@renthop.com. You must apply using your school email address. There are two deadlines for the scholarship, April 30th and August 31st. The two deadlines for the scholarship will be available year after year. You must be a current student in an eligible undergraduate program or a graduating high school senior, working towards a Bachelor's degree or Associate's degree. A total of two students will be chosen as finalists for the $1000 scholarship each year. More scholarships of lesser amounts may be awarded for additional students.

Award: Scholarship for use in freshman, sophomore, junior, or senior years; not renewable. *Number:* 1–5. *Amount:* $250–$1000.

Eligibility Requirements: Applicant must be age 15-26 and enrolled or expecting to enroll full- or part-time at a four-year institution or university. Available to U.S. and non-U.S. citizens.

Application Requirements: Essay. *Deadline:* continuous.

Contact: Faye Chou, Statistical Analyst
RentHop
335 Madison Avenue
4th Floor (GCT Hub)
New York, NY 10017
Phone: 913-982-6682
E-mail: faye@renthop.com

REPLACE MY CONTACTS

http://www.replacemycontacts.com

REPLACE MY CONTACTS ACADEMIC SCHOLARSHIP

$1000 scholarship for college freshmen, sophomores, or juniors or high school seniors. Student must complete survey on sponsor's website and also an essay on a topic listed in order to participate. Only one entry permitted per student. The top eligible essays will be determined by a panel of chosen judges and the public will be encouraged to help select the winner(s) through online visiting. The winning essay(s) will have received the most votes from online voters. Information may be found on the website, http://www.replacemycontacts.com/topics/6276/1000-scholarship-essay-contest.mvc.

Award: Scholarship for use in freshman, sophomore, or junior years; not renewable. *Number:* 1. *Amount:* $1000.

Eligibility Requirements: Applicant must be enrolled or expecting to enroll full-time at a four-year institution or university. Available to U.S. citizens.

Application Requirements: Application form may be submitted online (http://www.replacemycontacts.com/topics/6276/1000-scholarship-essay-contest.mvc), complete website survey, essay. *Deadline:* April 15.

Contact: Todd Messinger, President of Replace My Contacts
Replace My Contacts
4119 Mauch Chunk Road
Coplay, PA 18037
E-mail: scholarship@ReplaceMyContacts.com

RHODE ISLAND FOUNDATION

http://www.rifoundation.org/

BEACON BRIGHTER TOMORROWS SCHOLARSHIP

Scholarship for a dependent child whose parent sustained a work related injury with an employer who had workers compensation insurance with Beacon Mutual Insurance Company. Must have been accepted into an accredited post-secondary institution (including an academic, trade, or vocational program) on a full-time or part-time basis. Must have maintained a grade point average of C or better for the past two years, be a U.S. citizen or legal resident, and demonstrate financial need.

Award: Scholarship for use in freshman, sophomore, junior, or senior years; renewable.

Eligibility Requirements: Applicant must be high school student and planning to enroll or expecting to enroll full- or part-time at a two-year or four-year or technical institution or university. Available to U.S. citizens.

Application Requirements: Application form, copy of student aid report calculated upon completion of the FAFSA, proof of acceptance to an accredited institution, financial need analysis, recommendations or references, transcript. *Deadline:* June 15.

Contact: Libby Monahan, Funds Administrator
Phone: 401-274-4564 Ext. 3117
E-mail: libbym@rifoundation.org

RONALD REAGAN PRESIDENTIAL FOUNDATION & INSTITUTE

http://www.reaganfoundation.org

GE-REAGAN FOUNDATION SCHOLARSHIP PROGRAM

Honoring the legacy and character of our nation's 40th President, the GE-Reagan Foundation Scholarship Program rewards college-bound students who demonstrate exemplary leadership, drive, integrity, and citizenship with financial assistance to pursue higher education. Each year, the program selects numerous recipients to receive a $10,000 scholarship renewable for up to an additional three years—up to $40,000 total per recipient. Awards are for undergraduate and graduate study, and may be used for education-related expenses, including tuition, fees, books, supplies, room, and board. In addition, scholars are invited to participate in a special awards program. To be eligible for this award, applicants must demonstrate at school, at the workplace, and within the community the attributes of leadership, drive, integrity, and citizenship; demonstrate strong academic performance (minimum 3.0 grade point average/4.0 scale or equivalent); be citizens of the United States of America; be current high school seniors attending high school in the United States (students living on U.S. Armed Forces base and homeschooled students are also eligible); and plan to enroll in a full-time undergraduate course of study toward a Bachelor's degree at an accredited four-year college or university in the United States for the entire upcoming academic year. In addition, semifinalists must be nominated by an eligible community leader, such as a high school principal, elected official or executive director of a nonprofit organization, and must provide documentation to certify academic performance and financial need. Finalists will be interviewed via Skype or telephone by a member of the selection committee.

Award: Scholarship for use in freshman year; renewable. *Number:* 20. *Amount:* $10,000.

Eligibility Requirements: Applicant must be high school student and planning to enroll or expecting to enroll full-time at a four-year institution or university. Applicant must have 3.0 GPA or higher. Available to U.S. citizens.

Application Requirements: Application form, community service, essay, financial need analysis, interview. *Deadline:* January 5.

SAMUEL HUNTINGTON FUND

http://www.nationalgridus.com/huntington.asp

SAMUEL HUNTINGTON PUBLIC SERVICE AWARD

Award provides a $15,000 stipend to a graduating college senior to undertake a one-year public service project anywhere in the world immediately following graduation. Written proposals of 1000 words or less are required with application. Project may encompass any activity that furthers the public good. Awards will be based on quality of proposal, academic record, and other personal achievements. Finalists will be interviewed.

Award: Grant for use in senior year; not renewable. *Number:* 1–3. *Amount:* $15,000.

Eligibility Requirements: Applicant must be enrolled or expecting to enroll full-time at a four-year institution or university. Available to U.S. and non-U.S. citizens.

Application Requirements: Application form, essay, financial need analysis. *Deadline:* January 18.

Contact: Amy Stacy, Executive Assistant
Samuel Huntington Fund
National Grid
40 Sylvan Road
Waltham, MA 02451
Phone: 781-907-3358
E-mail: amy.stacy@nationalgrid.com

SCHOLARSHIP AMERICA

www.scholarshipamerica.org

BRISTOL-MYERS SQUIBB SCHOLARSHIP FOR CANCER SURVIVORS

The Bristol-Myers Squibb Scholarship for Cancer Survivors program was created to assist cancer survivors who plan to continue their education in college or vocational school programs. Scholarships of up to $10,000 will be awarded to up to 50 qualified students. Applicants must be cancer survivors (diagnosed by a physician as having treatment of cancer and survived), age 25 and under, who are high school seniors or graduates or postsecondary undergraduates. Qualified applicants must plan to enroll in a full-time undergraduate study at an accredited two- or four-year college, university, or vocational-technical school for the entire 2017-18 academic year. They must have a minimum grade point average of 3.5 on a 4.0 scale (or the equivalent). Scholarships will be awarded based on applicant's academic record, demonstrated leadership and participation in school and community activities, honors, work experience, statement of goals and aspirations, personal impact statement and an outside appraisal. Financial need is not considered. Students may reapply to the program each year they meet eligibility requirements.

Award: Scholarship for use in freshman, sophomore, or junior years; not renewable. *Number:* 50. *Amount:* $10,000.

Eligibility Requirements: Applicant must be enrolled or expecting to enroll full-time at a two-year or four-year or technical institution or university. Applicant must have 3.5 GPA or higher. Available to U.S. citizens.

Application Requirements: Application form. *Deadline:* March 31.

Contact: Ms. Patricia Halter, Executive Assistant, Operations
Scholarship America
One Scholarship Way
Saint Peter, MN 56082
Phone: 800-537-4180 Ext. 437
E-mail: phalter@scholarshipamerica.org

SCHOLARSHIP AMERICA DREAM AWARD

Scholarship America's Dream Award is to assist students across the nation entering their second year or higher of education beyond high school. Renewable scholarships are offered for full-time study at an accredited institution of the student's choice with the awards growing in amount each year, allowing students to receive aid throughout their college careers. To qualify, students must be U.S. citizens, U.S. permanent residents (holders of a Permanent Resident Card), or individuals granted deferred action status under the Deferred Action for Childhood Arrivals program (DACA), have received a high school diploma or equivalent from a U.S. school, and be planning to complete a minimum of one full year of postsecondary education by the end of the 2016-17 academic year. Applicants must plan to enroll in full-time undergraduate study at the sophomore-year level or higher at an accredited two- or four-year college, university or vocational-technical school in the United States for the entire 2017-18 academic year, and must have a minimum cumulative grade point average of 3.0 on a 4.0 scale (or its equivalent). Applicants must demonstrate financial need. In addition to the general awards, a portion of the funds has been designated for students majoring in a STEM field (science, technology, engineering or math) and a portion has been designated the World Journal Award for Chinese-American students.

Award: Scholarship for use in sophomore, junior, or senior years; renewable. *Amount:* $5000–$15,000.

Eligibility Requirements: Applicant must be enrolled or expecting to enroll full-time at a two-year or four-year or technical institution or university. Applicant must have 3.0 GPA or higher. Available to U.S. citizens.

Application Requirements: Application form. *Deadline:* December 15.

Contact: Program Manager
Scholarship America
Scholarship America
One Scholarship Way
Saint Peter, MN 56082
Phone: 800-537-4180
E-mail: dreamaward@scholarshipamerica.org

SCHOLARSHIP WORKSHOP LLC

http://www.scholarshipworkshop.com/

RAGINS/BRASWELL NATIONAL SCHOLARSHIP

Scholarship available to high school seniors, undergraduate, and graduate students who attend The Scholarship Workshop presentation or an online class given by Marianne Ragins, $400,000 scholarship winner. Award is based on application, essay, leadership, extracurricular activities, achievements, and community responsibility. Scholarship amounts vary. Learn more at www.scholarshipworkshop.com/movie.

Award: Scholarship for use in freshman, sophomore, junior, or senior years; not renewable. *Number:* 1–3. *Amount:* $100–$500.

Eligibility Requirements: Applicant must be enrolled or expecting to enroll full-time at a four-year institution or university. Available to U.S. citizens.

Application Requirements: Application form, essay. *Deadline:* April 30.

Contact: Scholarship Coordinator
Phone: 703-579-4245
E-mail: scholars@scholarshipworkshop.com

SCREEN ACTORS' GUILD FOUNDATION

http://www.sagfoundation.org/

JOHN L. DALES SCHOLARSHIP PROGRAM

Applicant must have ten vested years of pension credits with the SAG AFTRA union or lifetime earnings of $150,000. Must be U.S. citizen. Scholarship amount ranges between $1000 and $5000. Consult office or website for more information.

Award: Scholarship for use in freshman, sophomore, junior, senior, graduate, or postgraduate years; not renewable. *Number:* 1–16. *Amount:* $1000–$5000.

Eligibility Requirements: Applicant must be enrolled or expecting to enroll full- or part-time at a two-year or four-year institution or university. Available to U.S. citizens.

Application Requirements: Application form, community service, essay, financial need analysis, recommendations or references, resume, test scores, transcript. *Deadline:* March 15.

Contact: Davidson Lloyd, Director of Assistance Programs
Screen Actors' Guild Foundation
5757 Wilshire Boulevard
Suite 124
Los Angeles, CA 90036
Phone: 323-549-6649
Fax: 323-549-6710
E-mail: dlloyd@sagfoundation.org

SCREEN ACTORS GUILD FOUNDATION/JOHN L. DALES SCHOLARSHIP FUND (STANDARD)

Applicant must be a member of SAG AFTRA Union or the child of a member of SAG AFTRA Union. Member under the age of twenty-one must have been a member of AFTRA SAG Union for five years and have a lifetime earnings of $30,000. Parent of an applicant must have ten vested years of pension credits OR lifetime earnings of $150,000. Consult office or website for more information. Number and amount of awards vary.

Award: Scholarship for use in freshman, sophomore, junior, senior, graduate, or postgraduate years; not renewable. *Number:* 100–135. *Amount:* $1000–$5000.

Eligibility Requirements: Applicant must be enrolled or expecting to enroll full-time at a two-year or four-year or technical institution or university. Available to U.S. citizens.

Application Requirements: Application form, community service, essay, financial need analysis, recommendations or references, resume, test scores, transcript. *Deadline:* March 15.

Contact: Davidson Lloyd, Director of Assistance Programs
Screen Actors' Guild Foundation
5757 Wilshire Boulevard
Suite 124
Los Angeles, CA 90036
Phone: 323-549-6649
Fax: 323-549-6710
E-mail: dlloyd@sagfoundation.org

SEABEE MEMORIAL SCHOLARSHIP ASSOCIATION, INC.

http://www.seabee.org/

SEABEE MEMORIAL ASSOCIATION SCHOLARSHIP

Award available to children or grandchildren of current or former members of the Naval Construction Force (Seabees) or Naval Civil Engineer Corps. Not available for graduate study or for great-grandchildren of Seabees.

Award: Scholarship for use in freshman, sophomore, junior, or senior years; renewable. *Number:* 127. *Amount:* $3200.

Eligibility Requirements: Applicant must be enrolled or expecting to enroll full-time at a two-year or four-year institution or university. Available to U.S. citizens.

Application Requirements: Application form, essay, financial need analysis. *Deadline:* April 15.

Contact: Sheryl Chiogioji, Administrative Assistant
Seabee Memorial Scholarship Association, Inc.
PO Box 6574
Silver Spring, MD 20916
Phone: 301-570-2850
E-mail: smsa@seabee.org

SGM LAW GROUP PLLC

http://www.immi-usa.com/

SGM LAW GROUP BI-ANNUAL SCHOLARSHIP

This award recognizes outstanding achievements in academics and as a law firm, we seek to reward a passionate and determined student interested in the field of law. As attorneys, we have all benefited from scholarships throughout our academic careers and now we hope to play a small role in helping a deserving student realize his or her academic goals. This scholarship is open to students who are currently enrolled in an accredited university, college or law school within the U.S. Must have a cumulative GPA of 3.0 or higher and must be a full time student enrolled in classes for spring 2017. Students will have the opportunity to earn $1,000 towards their education by submitting a 500–1000 word essay, which can be written on any of the topics listed below. Please be aware that anything over 1000 words will not be considered. Once the winner of this award is chosen, a check for $1,000 will be made to the scholarship recipient's school of choice to help cover education expenses. 1. What hardship did you conquer to achieve your goal of pursuing law studies? 2. Explain your motivation for becoming a lawyer and what about the law inspires you. 3. Discuss the impact of employment immigration on U.S. economy, including the effects of related immigration reforms. 4. What field of law are you interested in and how will you help others with your earned law degree?

Award: Scholarship for use in freshman, sophomore, junior, senior, or graduate years; not renewable. *Number:* 1–2. *Amount:* $1000.

Eligibility Requirements: Applicant must be enrolled or expecting to enroll full- or part-time at a two-year or four-year or technical institution or university. Applicant must have 3.0 GPA or higher. Available to U.S. and non-U.S. citizens.

Application Requirements: Essay. *Deadline:* December 15.

SILICON VALLEY COMMUNITY FOUNDATION

www.siliconvalleycf.org

WINE GROUP SCHOLARSHIPS

The Wine Group Scholarship Fund was established in 2009 by a group of owners of The Wine Group LLC (TWG). Its mission is to provide the children, grandchildren or legal dependents of TWG's employees with financial assistance to pursue or continue postsecondary education in any area of study. Must be a child, legal dependent or grandchild of a full-time employee of TWG. Employee must have at least one year of continuous, full-time service with TWG as of Feb. 1 of the year in which the scholarship will be awarded. Employee must be employed with TWG at the time scholarship award selections are made. Children, legal dependents, and grandchildren of current and former owners of TWG are not eligible The Wine Group Merit Scholarship Requirements: scholarship winners of TWG Merit Scholarship will demonstrate a desirable mix of a high level of academic performance, strong communication and leadership skills, and participation in extra-curricular activities. Current graduating high school senior planning to attend a two- or four-year college/university program on a full-time (12 or more units/credits per quarter/semester) or part-time (a minimum of 6 to a maximum of 11 units/credits per quarter/semester) basis or current full-time or part-time college student. Minimum cumulative grade point average of 3.0 on a 4.0 scale. The Wine Group Opportunity Scholarship Requirements: scholarship winners of TWG Opportunity Scholarship

will demonstrate a desirable mix of educational motivation, perseverance and demonstrated financial need or hardship. Applicant must be planning to enroll or currently enrolled in a two- or four-year college or vocational school on a part-time or full-time basis (as defined by the school of attendance). Must have demonstrated financial need or hardship with a maximum family income of $150,000.

Award: Scholarship for use in freshman, sophomore, junior, or senior years; not renewable. *Number:* 1–10. *Amount:* $1000–$5000.

Eligibility Requirements: Applicant must be enrolled or expecting to enroll full- or part-time at a two-year or four-year or technical institution. Applicant must have 3.0 GPA or higher.

Application Requirements: Application form, financial need analysis. *Deadline:* March 22.

Contact: Anamika Patel
E-mail: APatel@siliconvalleycf.org

SIMON YOUTH FOUNDATION

http://www.sms.scholarshipamerica.org/simonyouth

SIMON YOUTH FOUNDATION COMMUNITY SCHOLARSHIP PROGRAM

Scholarships available to high school seniors attending school and living in close proximity of a Simon Property Mall or Community Center. Recipients should reside within 50 miles of a Simon Mall. Must be planning to enroll in a full-time undergraduate course of study at an accredited two- or four-year college, university, or vocational/technical school.

Award: Scholarship for use in freshman year; not renewable. *Number:* 100–200. *Amount:* $1400–$2500.

Eligibility Requirements: Applicant must be high school student and planning to enroll or expecting to enroll full-time at a two-year or four-year or technical institution or university. Available to U.S. citizens.

Application Requirements: Application form, community service, copy of page 1 of parent's tax Form 1040, financial need analysis, test scores, transcript. *Deadline:* March 1.

Contact: Casey Rubischko, Program Manager
Phone: 507-931-1682

SIMPLILEARN AMERICAS LLC

https://www.simplilearn.com/

SIMPLILEARN STUDENT AMBASSADOR SCHOLARSHIP

Getting a college degree is a huge accomplishment, but it does not necessarily prepare you for the best jobs in today's digital economy. That is where Simplilearn comes in. We provide online training in today's hottest careers--from digital marketing, to cyber security, to cloud computing. As a Simplilearn Ambassador, you can help us spread the word and help your classmates launch their careers. Participation is free. For every visitor you bring to Simplilearn.com, via your unique referral URL, you will get another entry to our $1,000 cash Ambassador Scholarship. Simply fill out the brief form below, select the skills training that you are most interested in, get your unique link to Simplilearn, along with some tips on how to promote us, and start racking up entries to our $1,000 payout. See https://www.simplilearn.com/student-ambassador-scholarship-program for more details.

Award: Scholarship for use in freshman, sophomore, junior, senior, graduate, or postgraduate years; not renewable. *Number:* 1–3. *Amount:* $1000–$3000.

Eligibility Requirements: Applicant must be enrolled or expecting to enroll full- or part-time at a two-year or four-year institution or university. Available to U.S. citizens.

Application Requirements: Application form, personal photograph. *Deadline:* March 17.

Contact: Mr. Nirmal Kumar, Simplilearn Americas LLC
Simplilearn Americas LLC
201 Spear Street
Suite 1100
San Francisco, CA 94105
Phone: 844-532-7688 Ext. 1025
E-mail: scholarship@simplilearn.com

SLOTOZILLA

http://www.slotozilla.com/

INTERNET MARKETING SCHOLARSHIP

Slotozilla is interested in attracting our players as well as helping future marketing experts. Just like ads on the internet, you never know when and where the next marketing genius will pop-out. That is why we created an annual Internet Marketing Scholarship. This scholarship is available for full-time students doing Bachelor or Master course at any accredited college or university. See website for more information, http://www.slotozilla.com/

Award: Scholarship for use in freshman, sophomore, junior, senior, graduate, or postgraduate years; not renewable. *Number:* 1. *Amount:* $500.

Eligibility Requirements: Applicant must be enrolled or expecting to enroll full- or part-time at a two-year or four-year or technical institution or university. Available to U.S. and Canadian citizens.

Application Requirements: Essay. *Deadline:* August 31.

Contact: Vanessa Skadi
E-mail: scholarship@slotozilla.com

SLS CONSULTING

http://www.legalinternetmarketing.com/

SLS CONSULTING MARKETING SCHOLARSHIP

Our company is offering this award as a way to help fund a student's secondary education. We run an Internet marketing company and our goal is to help someone who might be interested in a field that relates, in any way, to the work we do at SLS Consulting.

Award: Scholarship for use in freshman, sophomore, junior, senior, graduate, or postgraduate years; not renewable. *Number:* 1. *Amount:* $500.

Eligibility Requirements: Applicant must be enrolled or expecting to enroll full- or part-time at a two-year or four-year or technical institution or university. Applicant must have 3.0 GPA or higher. Available to U.S. citizens.

Application Requirements: Application form, application form may be submitted online (http://www.legalinternetmarketing.com/scholarship.html), driver's license, essay, transcript. *Deadline:* April 15.

Contact: Mr. Scott Simpson, Department Manager, Social Media and Local Search
Phone: 323-254-1510 Ext. 114
Fax: 323-254-1588
E-mail: scholarships@slsconsulting.com

SMARTPAPERHELP

http://www.smartpaperhelp.com/

SMART PAPER HELP SCHOLARSHIP

SmartPaperHelp invites students to participate in our Smart Scholarship program. All you have to do is to show off your writing skills and write an essay on one of the given topics: 1. Problems Of Modern Educational System And Their Solutions; 2. Difficulties We Face In College; 3. What Problems Do You See In Your College And How Do They Affect You Personally? Participate and win cash prizes. Full guidelines you can find on the following page: http://www.smartpaperhelp.com/blog/scholarship-program-for-students

Award: Scholarship for use in freshman, sophomore, junior, senior, graduate, or postgraduate years; not renewable. *Number:* 1–3. *Amount:* $400–$1000.

Eligibility Requirements: Applicant must be enrolled or expecting to enroll full- or part-time at a two-year or four-year institution or university. Available to U.S. citizens.

Application Requirements: Application form, essay. *Deadline:* February 29.

Contact: Sheri Aldridge, Contest
E-mail: contest@smartpaperhelp.com

SNOW, CARPIO & WEEKLEY, PLC

http://workinjuryaz.com

SCW ACADEMIC SCHOLARSHIP

Video submissions required. High school senior or recent graduate seeking a degree with a 3.0 GPA. To be awarded the fall semester of 2016. Applications must be submitted on our website http://workinjuryaz.com/tucson-workers-compensation-lawyers/#academic See all requirement and info on our website as well.

Award: Scholarship for use in freshman or sophomore years; not renewable. *Number:* 2. *Amount:* $2500.

Eligibility Requirements: Applicant must be enrolled or expecting to enroll full- or part-time at a two-year or four-year or technical institution or university. Applicant must have 3.0 GPA or higher. Available to U.S. citizens.

Application Requirements: Application form. *Deadline:* May 31.

Contact: April Snow
E-mail: snowcarpioaz@gmail.com

SOCIETY FOR APPLIED ANTHROPOLOGY

http://www.sfaa.net/

BEATRICE MEDICINE AWARDS

Two awards ($500 each) will be made to attend the Annual Meeting of the SfAA.

Award: Prize for use in freshman, sophomore, junior, senior, graduate, or postgraduate years; not renewable. *Number:* 2. *Amount:* $500.

Eligibility Requirements: Applicant must be enrolled or expecting to enroll full- or part-time at a two-year or four-year institution or university. Available to U.S. and non-U.S. citizens.

Application Requirements: Application form. *Deadline:* December 20.

Contact: Dr. Trish Colvin, Office Manager
Phone: 405-843-5113
Fax: 405-843-8553
E-mail: info@sfaa.net

DEL JONES AWARD

This Fund supports two travel grants of $500 for a student to attend the annual meeting of the Society.

Award: Prize for use in freshman, sophomore, junior, senior, graduate, or postgraduate years; not renewable. *Number:* 2–500.

Eligibility Requirements: Applicant must be enrolled or expecting to enroll full- or part-time at a two-year or four-year institution or university. Available to U.S. and non-U.S. citizens.

Application Requirements: Essay. *Deadline:* December 20.

Contact: Dr. Trish Colvin, Office Manager
Phone: 405-843-5113
Fax: 405-843-8553
E-mail: info@sfaa.net

EDWARD H. AND ROSAMOND B. SPICER TRAVEL AWARDS

The Awards commemorate the lifelong concern of Edward H. and Rosamond B. Spicer in furthering the maturation of students in the social sciences, both intellectually and practically, and their lifelong interest in the nature of community as both cause of, and solution to, problems in the human condition.

Award: Prize for use in freshman, sophomore, junior, senior, graduate, or postgraduate years; not renewable. *Number:* 2. *Amount:* $500.

Eligibility Requirements: Applicant must be enrolled or expecting to enroll full- or part-time at a two-year or four-year institution or university. Available to U.S. and non-U.S. citizens.

Application Requirements: Essay. *Deadline:* December 20.

Contact: Dr. Trish Colvin, Office Manager
Phone: 405-843-5113
Fax: 405-843-8553
E-mail: info@sfaa.net

GIL KUSHNER MEMORIAL TRAVEL AWARD

Scholarship of $500 to attend the SfAA annual meeting. Abstracts (paper or poster) should be concerned with the persistence of cultural groups.

Award: Prize for use in freshman, sophomore, junior, senior, graduate, or postgraduate years; not renewable. *Number:* 2. *Amount:* $500.

Eligibility Requirements: Applicant must be enrolled or expecting to enroll full- or part-time at a two-year or four-year institution or university. Available to U.S. and non-U.S. citizens.

Application Requirements: Essay. *Deadline:* December 20.

Contact: Dr. Trish Colvin, Office Manager
  Phone: 405-843-5113
  Fax: 405-843-8553
  E-mail: info@sfaa.net

HUMAN RIGHTS DEFENDER STUDENT AWARD

This annual award recognizes the recipient's commitment to the resolution of human rights issues.

Award: Prize for use in freshman, sophomore, junior, senior, graduate, or postgraduate years; not renewable. *Number:* 1. *Amount:* $500.

Eligibility Requirements: Applicant must be enrolled or expecting to enroll full- or part-time at a two-year or four-year institution or university. Available to U.S. and non-U.S. citizens.

Application Requirements: Essay. *Deadline:* December 20.

Contact: Dr. Trish Colvin, Office Manager
  Phone: 405-843-5113
  Fax: 405-843-8553
  E-mail: info@sfaa.net

PETER KONG-MING NEW STUDENT PRIZE

Prize awarded for SFAA's annual student research competition in the applied social and behavioral sciences. The issue of research question should be in the domain of health care or human services (broadly construed). The winner of the competition will receive a cash prize of $3000, a crystal trophy, and travel funds to attend the annual meeting of the SFAA. For more details, see website at http://www.sfaa.net.

Award: Prize for use in freshman, sophomore, junior, senior, or graduate years; not renewable. *Number:* 3. *Amount:* $500–$3350.

Eligibility Requirements: Applicant must be enrolled or expecting to enroll full- or part-time at a two-year or four-year institution or university. Available to U.S. and non-U.S. citizens.

Application Requirements: Essay. *Deadline:* December 31.

Contact: Dr. Trish Colvin, Office Manager
  Phone: 405-843-5113
  Fax: 405-843-8553
  E-mail: info@sfaa.net

VALENE SMITH PRIZE

The posters which are submitted for the Valene Smith Competition will be set up and exhibited with all other posters at the Annual Meeting of the Society for Applied Anthropology and should be concerned in some way with the applied social science of tourism.

Award: Prize for use in freshman, sophomore, junior, senior, graduate, or postgraduate years; not renewable. *Number:* 3. *Amount:* $250–$500.

Eligibility Requirements: Applicant must be enrolled or expecting to enroll full- or part-time at a two-year or four-year institution or university. Available to U.S. and non-U.S. citizens.

Application Requirements: *Deadline:* October 15.

Contact: Dr. Trish Colvin, Office Manager
  Phone: 405-843-5113
  Fax: 405-843-8553
  E-mail: info@sfaa.net

SOCIETY FOR SCIENCE & THE PUBLIC

http://societyforscience.org

INTEL INTERNATIONAL SCIENCE AND ENGINEERING FAIR

The Intel International Science and Engineering Fair (ISEF) is the culminating event in a series of local, regional, state and international science fairs. Students, grades 9 - 12, who compete successfully at an Intel ISEF-affiliated fair can advance and ultimately participate at the Intel ISEF.

Award: Prize for use in freshman, sophomore, junior, or senior years; not renewable. *Number:* 1–600. *Amount:* $500–$75,000.

Eligibility Requirements: Applicant must be high school student; age 12-20 and planning to enroll or expecting to enroll full- or part-time at a two-year or four-year institution or university. Available to U.S. and non-U.S. citizens.

Application Requirements: Application form, interview. *Deadline:* continuous.

Contact: Lisa Icenroad, Program Manager
  Society for Science & the Public
  1719 N Street, NW
  Washington, DC 20036
  Phone: 202-785-2255 Ext. 152
  E-mail: licenroad@societyforscience.org

REGENERON SCIENCE TALENT SEARCH

The Regeneron Science Talent Search (STS), a program of Society for Science & the Public, is the nation's most prestigious pre-college science competition. Alumni of STS have made extraordinary contributions to science and hold more than 100 of the world's most distinguished science and math honors, including the Nobel Prize and the National Medal of Science. Each year, 300 Regeneron STS Scholars and their schools are recognized. From the select pool of scholars, 40 student finalists are invited to Washington, DC in March to participate in final judging, display their work to the public, meet with notable scientists, and compete for the top award of $250,000.

Award: Prize for use in freshman, sophomore, junior, senior, or graduate years; not renewable. *Number:* 40. *Amount:* $25,000–$250,000.

Eligibility Requirements: Applicant must be high school student and planning to enroll or expecting to enroll full- or part-time at a two-year or four-year institution or university. Available to U.S. citizens.

Application Requirements: Application form, essay.

Contact: Allison Stifel, Regeneron Science Talent Search
  Society for Science & the Public
  1719 N Street, NW
  Washington, DC 20036
  Phone: 202-785-2255 Ext. 140
  E-mail: astifel@societyforscience.org

SOROPTIMIST INTERNATIONAL OF THE AMERICAS

http://www.soroptimist.org/

THE SOROPTIMIST LIVE YOUR DREAM: EDUCATION AND TRAINING AWARDS FOR WOMEN

Applicants must be a woman who is the head of her household, the primary financial provider for her family, pursuing a vocational or undergraduate degree and show financial need. To be eligible, applicants must live in one of Soroptimist's 20 member countries. For full eligibility requirements and application instructions go to: www.soroptimist.org/awards/eligibility.html

Award: Grant for use in freshman, sophomore, junior, or senior years; not renewable. *Amount:* $500–$15,000.

Eligibility Requirements: Applicant must be enrolled or expecting to enroll full- or part-time at a two-year or four-year or technical institution or university and female. Available to U.S. and non-U.S. citizens.

Application Requirements: Application form, essay, financial need analysis. *Deadline:* November 15.

Contact: Program Assistant
  E-mail: lydawards@soroptimist.org

SOUND MONEY DEFENSE LEAGUE

http://soundmoneydefense.org

MONEY METALS EXCHANGE SCHOLARSHIP PROGRAM

Money Metals Exchange, a national precious dealer recently ranked Best in the USA, has teamed up with the Sound Money Defense League to help qualified students pay for the ever-rising costs of higher education. These groups have just introduced the first gold-backed scholarship of the modern era, setting aside 100 oz. of physical gold for scholarships to outstanding undergraduate and graduate students who display deep understanding of economics and monetary policy. Money Metals Exchange and the Sound Money Defense League will be awarding this scholarship to two incoming or current undergraduate students and two graduate students each year. Judged Scholarship Award: Undergraduate Student First Place: $2,000, Undergraduate Student Runner Up: $1,000, Graduate Student First Place: $2,000Graduate Student Runner Up: $1,000, People's Choice Award: First Place: $500. Application, resume, and essay must be submitted by September 30, 2017. For more information, visit moneymetals.com/scholarship

Award: Scholarship for use in freshman, sophomore, junior, senior, or graduate years; not renewable. *Number:* 1–5. *Amount:* $500–$2000.

Eligibility Requirements: Applicant must be enrolled or expecting to enroll full-time at a two-year or four-year institution or university. Available to U.S. and non-U.S. citizens.

Application Requirements: Application form, essay. *Deadline:* September 30.

Contact: Mr. Jp Cortez, Assistant Director
Sound Money Defense League
15720 Brixham Hill Avenue
Charlotte, NC 28277
E-mail: jp.cortez@soundmoneydefense.org

SOUTHWESTERN RUGS DEPOT

https://www.southwesternrugsdepot.com/

SOUTHWESTERN RUGS DEPOT SCHOLARSHIP

Minimum 300 word essay on why decor matters to you. Open to all college students. Deadline Jan. 2nd 2018. Apply here: https://www.southwesternrugsdepot.com/scholarship/

Award: Scholarship for use in freshman, sophomore, junior, senior, or graduate years; not renewable. *Number:* 1. *Amount:* $500.

Eligibility Requirements: Applicant must be enrolled or expecting to enroll full- or part-time at a two-year or four-year or technical institution or university. Available to U.S. and non-U.S. citizens.

Application Requirements: Essay. *Deadline:* January 2.

Contact: Mr. Connor Butterworth
Phone: 770-7736416
E-mail: contact@southwesternrugsdepot.com

SR EDUCATION GROUP

http://www.sreducationgroup.org

COMMUNITY COLLEGE SCHOLARSHIP

Community college can be one of the most cost-effective options for people looking to start or change their careers; however, tuition can still be a large burden for many individuals. To help those with high financial need, SR Education Group is awarding $2,500 community college scholarships. To provide our judges with a true understanding of each applicant, he or she must answer two open-ended, personal, and thought-provoking questions. The students whose responses are the most persuasive, compelling, and well-written, as judged by our panel, will be considered finalists.

Award: Scholarship for use in freshman, sophomore, junior, senior, graduate, or postgraduate years; not renewable. *Number:* 2–6. *Amount:* $2500.

Eligibility Requirements: Applicant must be enrolled or expecting to enroll full- or part-time at a two-year or technical institution. Available to U.S. citizens.

Application Requirements: Application form. *Deadline:* continuous.

SR EDUCATION GROUP $5K SCHOLARSHIPS

SR Education Group is awarding two need-based scholarships of $5,000 each quarter. The scholarships will rotate to help target under-served populations. Graduate Scholarship for Teachers: March 2017 (one $5,000 winner). Students enrolled in a graduate program through an accredited college or university may apply. Military Scholarships: June 2017 (two $5,000 winners). Veterans/active military, their sons, daughters, or spouses may apply; spouses, sons, and daughters of deceased veterans or deceased active duty members are also eligible. Children of service members/veterans must be under the age of 21, or if full-time students, under the age of 23. Scholarship for Women: September 2017 (two $5,000 winners). Female students enrolled at a private or public educational institution, and working towards a certificate, diploma, or degree may apply. Scholarship for Minorities: December 2017 (two $5,000 winners). Minority students (Hispanic, African-American, Asian,

or Native American ethnicity) enrolled at a private or public educational institution, and working towards a certificate, diploma, or degree may apply. A child is a military dependent through age 21, or through age 23, if enrolled as a full time college student

Award: Scholarship for use in freshman, sophomore, junior, senior, graduate, or postgraduate years; not renewable. *Number:* 1–2. *Amount:* $5000.

Eligibility Requirements: Applicant must be enrolled or expecting to enroll full- or part-time at a two-year or four-year or technical institution or university. Available to U.S. citizens.

Application Requirements: Application form. *Deadline:* continuous.

STATE DEPARTMENT FEDERAL CREDIT UNION ANNUAL SCHOLARSHIP PROGRAM

http://www.sdfcu.org/

STATE DEPARTMENT FEDERAL CREDIT UNION ANNUAL SCHOLARSHIP PROGRAM

Scholarships available to members who are currently enrolled in a degree program and have completed 12 credit hours of coursework at an accredited college or university. Must have own account in good standing with SDFCU, have a minimum 2.5 GPA, submit official cumulative transcripts, and describe need for financial assistance to continue their education. Scholarship only open to members of State Department Federal Credit Union.

Award: Scholarship for use in sophomore, junior, senior, or graduate years; not renewable. *Amount:* $2500.

Eligibility Requirements: Applicant must be enrolled or expecting to enroll full-time at a four-year institution or university. Applicant must have 2.5 GPA or higher. Available to U.S. and non-U.S. citizens.

Application Requirements: Application form, financial need analysis. *Deadline:* April 29.

Contact: Scholarship Coordinator
Phone: 703-706-5000
E-mail: sdfcu@sdfcu.org

STRAIGHTFORWARD MEDIA

http://www.straightforwardmedia.com/

DALE E. FRIDELL MEMORIAL SCHOLARSHIP

Scholarships are open to anyone aspiring to attend a university, college, trade school, technical institute, vocational training, or other postsecondary education program. Eligible students may not have already been awarded a full tuition scholarship or waiver from another source. International students are welcome to apply. For more information, visit website http://www.straightforwardmedia.com/fridell/form.php.

Award: Scholarship for use in freshman, sophomore, junior, or senior years; not renewable. *Number:* 2. *Amount:* $1000.

Eligibility Requirements: Applicant must be enrolled or expecting to enroll full- or part-time at a two-year or four-year or technical institution or university. Available to U.S. and non-U.S. citizens.

Application Requirements: Essay. *Deadline:* varies.

Contact: Scholarship Committee
Phone: 605-348-3042

HELPING HAND SCHOLARSHIP

Annual award to help students hampered by debt to continue their studies. Must be attending or planning to attend a college, trade school, technical institute, vocational program or other postsecondary education program. For more information, see web http://www.straightforwardmedia.com/debt2/debt-apply.html.

Award: Scholarship for use in freshman, sophomore, junior, or senior years; not renewable. *Number:* 4. *Amount:* $500.

Eligibility Requirements: Applicant must be enrolled or expecting to enroll full- or part-time at a two-year or four-year or technical institution or university. Available to U.S. and non-U.S. citizens.

Application Requirements: Essay. *Deadline:* varies.

Contact: Scholarship Committee
Phone: 605-348-3042

MESOTHELIOMA MEMORIAL SCHOLARSHIP

Open to all students attending or planning to attend a postsecondary educational program, including 2- or 4-year college or university, vocational school, continuing education, ministry training, and job skills training. Refer to website for details http://www.straightforwardmedia.com/meso/.

Award: Scholarship for use in freshman, sophomore, junior, or senior years; not renewable. *Number:* 4. *Amount:* $500.

Eligibility Requirements: Applicant must be enrolled or expecting to enroll full- or part-time at a two-year or four-year or technical institution or university. Available to U.S. and non-U.S. citizens.

Application Requirements: Essay. *Deadline:* varies.

Contact: Scholarship Committee
　　　　Phone: 605-348-3042

STUDENT INSIGHTS

http://www.studentinsights.com

STUDENT-VIEW SCHOLARSHIP PROGRAM

Scholarship available by random drawing from the pool of entrants who respond to an online survey from Student Insights marketing organization. Parental permission to participate required for applicants under age 18.

Award: Scholarship for use in freshman year; not renewable. *Number:* 13. *Amount:* $500–$4000.

Eligibility Requirements: Applicant must be high school student and planning to enroll or expecting to enroll full-time at a two-year or four-year or technical institution or university. Available to U.S. citizens.

Application Requirements: Application form. *Deadline:* April 22.

Contact: Mr. John Becker, Program Coordinator
　　　　Student Insights
　　　　136 Justice Drive
　　　　Valencia, PA 16059
　　　　Phone: 724-903-0439
　　　　E-mail: contact@studentinsights.com

STUDYPORTALS

http://www.studyportals.eu/

GLOBAL STUDY AWARDS

We want to ultimately encourage young people to study abroad as part of their tertiary studies in order to experience and explore new countries, cultures and languages. The Global Study Awards recognizes studying abroad as a positively life changing experience for many students, opening their minds to alternative ways of personal life and professional career, as well as promoting intercultural understanding and tolerance. The Award prize will be applied toward the cost of tuition fees in the first instance, paid directly to the Higher Education Institution that the successful candidate will attend. If tuition fees are below the maximum individual award fund of €10,000, the remaining funds may be allocated per diem for living costs for a maximum of 52 weeks starting from when the student first registered at the higher education institution.

Award: Scholarship for use in freshman, sophomore, junior, senior, graduate, or postgraduate years; not renewable. *Number:* 1–9. *Amount:* $11,215–$11,215.

Eligibility Requirements: Applicant must be enrolled or expecting to enroll full- or part-time at a two-year or four-year institution or university. Available to U.S. and non-U.S. citizens.

Application Requirements: Application form, application form may be submitted online(www.studyportals.com/scholarship), essay, transcript. *Deadline:* varies.

Contact: Ms. Sissy Bottcher, Community Manager
　　　　StudyPortals
　　　　Torenallee 45 - 4.02
　　　　Eindhoven 5617 BA
　　　　NLD
　　　　Phone: 3-140 218 0238
　　　　Fax: 3-140 292 0075
　　　　E-mail: students@studyportals.com

SUNTRUST BANK

http://www.suntrusteducation.com/

OFF TO COLLEGE SCHOLARSHIP SWEEPSTAKES AWARD

Award of $1000 to a high school senior planning to attend college in the fall. Must complete an online entry form by accessing the website, http://www.offtocollege.info. Scholarship sweepstakes drawings are random and occur every other week from October 31 to May 15.

Award: Scholarship for use in freshman year; not renewable. *Number:* 15. *Amount:* $1000.

Eligibility Requirements: Applicant must be high school student and planning to enroll or expecting to enroll full- or part-time at a two-year or four-year or technical institution or university. Available to U.S. citizens.

Application Requirements: Application form. *Deadline:* continuous.

Contact: Joy Blauvelt, Scholarship Coordinator
　　　　Phone: 800-552-3006

TALL CLUBS INTERNATIONAL FOUNDATION, INC.

http://www.tall.org

KAE SUMNER EINFELDT SCHOLARSHIP

Females 5'10",or males 6'2" (minimum heights), are eligible to apply for the scholarship. Interested individuals should contact their local Tall Clubs Chapter. Canadian and U.S. winners are selected from finalists submitted by each local chapter.'

Award: Scholarship for use in freshman year; not renewable. *Number:* 2–6. *Amount:* $1000.

Eligibility Requirements: Applicant must be age 17-21 and enrolled or expecting to enroll full- or part-time at a two-year or four-year institution or university. Available to U.S. and Canadian citizens.

Application Requirements: Application form, essay, personal photograph, recommendations or references, transcript, verification of height. *Deadline:* March 1.

Contact: Carolyn Goldstein, TCI Foundation Scholarship Contact
　　　　E-mail: tcischolarships@hotmail.com

TECHNICAL ASSOCIATION OF THE PULP & PAPER INDUSTRY (TAPPI)

http://www.tappi.org/

TAPPI PLACE (POLYMERS, LAMINATIONS, ADHESIVES, COATINGS AND EXTRUSIONS) SCHOLARSHIP

Awarded only in even numbered years, the TAPPI PLACE (Polymers, Laminations, Adhesives, Coatings and Extrusions) Scholarship is designed to encourage talented science and engineering students to pursue careers in the packaging industry and to develop awareness of the industry, and of the TAPPI Polymers, Laminations, Adhesives, Coatings, and Extrusions (PLACE) Division. Membership in a TAPPI Student Chapter is required.

Award: Scholarship for use in freshman, sophomore, junior, or senior years; not renewable. *Number:* 1. *Amount:* $4000.

Eligibility Requirements: Applicant must be enrolled or expecting to enroll full-time at a two-year or four-year institution or university. Available to U.S. and non-U.S. citizens.

Application Requirements: Application form. *Deadline:* February 14.

Contact: Mr. Laurence Womack, Director of Standards and Awards
　　　　Technical Association of the Pulp & Paper Industry (TAPPI)
　　　　15 Technology Parkway South
　　　　Suite 115
　　　　Peachtree Corners, GA 30092
　　　　Phone: 770-209-7276
　　　　E-mail: standards@tappi.org

TEXAS FEDERATION OF BUSINESS AND PROFESSIONAL WOMEN'S FOUNDATION

GILDA MURRAY SCHOLARSHIP

Scholarship of $500 awarded to members of BPW/Texas, age 25 or older, to obtain education or training at an accredited college or university, technology institution, or training center. The number of awards varies.

Award: Scholarship for use in freshman, sophomore, junior, or senior years; not renewable. *Amount:* $500.

Eligibility Requirements: Applicant must be enrolled or expecting to enroll full- or part-time at a four-year or technical institution or university. Available to U.S. citizens.

Application Requirements: Application form, essay, recommendations or references, regular attendance at LO meetings, active participation on at least one BPW committee. *Deadline:* May 1.

Contact: Nancy Jackson, Chair
　　　Phone: 817-283-0862
　　　E-mail: bpwtx@sbcglobal.net

TEXAS GUARANTEED STUDENT LOAN CORPORATION

http://www.tgslc.org/

CHARLEY WOOTAN GRANT PROGRAM

Provides assistance to students who have difficulties pursuing their higher education dreams because of financial need. Deadline for Texas residents, 4-year school-May 15; Deadline for Texas residents, 2-year school-May 2; Deadline for non-Texas residents-April 29.

Award: Scholarship for use in freshman, sophomore, junior, or senior years; not renewable. *Amount:* $1000–$4394.

Eligibility Requirements: Applicant must be enrolled or expecting to enroll full- or part-time at a two-year or four-year or technical institution or university. Available to U.S. citizens.

TEXAS HIGHER EDUCATION COORDINATING BOARD

http://www.collegeforalltexans.com/

GOOD NEIGHBOR SCHOLARSHIP PROGRAM

Provides assistance for tuition to students from other nations of the Western Hemisphere (other than Cuba). Students must have lived for at least five years in the Western Hemisphere, scholastically qualify for admission, and must intend to return to their country upon completion of their program of study. Students that apply for Permanent Resident status or have dual citizenship are not eligible. Renewal awards require student meet the institution's minimum GPA requirement. Contact your institution for more information.

Award: Scholarship for use in freshman, sophomore, junior, senior, or graduate years; not renewable.

Eligibility Requirements: Applicant must be enrolled or expecting to enroll full- or part-time at a two-year or four-year institution or university and studying in Texas. Available to Canadian and non-U.S. citizens.

Application Requirements: Application form.

Contact: Student Financial Aid Office at the institution

TUITION EQUALIZATION GRANT (TEG) PROGRAM

Renewable award for Texas residents enrolled at least three-quarter time at an independent college or university in Texas in a degree program that does not lead to ordination or licensure to preach. Non-residents who are National Merit Finalists and are receiving at least $1,000 in scholarships may also receive awards. Awards are based on financial need. Renewal awards also require the student to maintain a minimum overall college GPA of at least 2.5, complete at least 24 SCH's each year (18 SCH's for students in graduate programs), and complete a minimum of 75% of classes attempted each year. Priority deadline to complete the FAFSA is March 15. Must not be receiving athletic scholarship concurrently. Contact college/university financial aid office for application information.

Award: Grant for use in freshman, sophomore, junior, senior, or graduate years; not renewable. *Amount:* $1–$4875.

Eligibility Requirements: Applicant must be enrolled or expecting to enroll full- or part-time at a two-year or four-year institution or university and studying in Texas. Available to U.S. citizens.

Application Requirements: Financial need analysis.

Contact: Financial Aid Office of relevant institution.

THEPENNYHOARDER.COM

http://www.thepennyhoarder.com/

FRUGAL STUDENT

You just need to tell us in 150 words or less the craziest, funniest, most interesting, unique, or creative way you've ever saved or made extra money.

Award: Scholarship for use in freshman, sophomore, junior, or senior years; renewable. *Number:* 1. *Amount:* $2000.

Eligibility Requirements: Applicant must be enrolled or expecting to enroll full- or part-time at a two-year or four-year institution or university. Available to U.S. citizens.

Application Requirements: Application form, application form may be submitted online (http://www.thepennyhoarder.com/frugal-student-scholarship/), entry in a contest, essay. *Deadline:* December 31.

Contact: Cynthia Moll
　　　E-mail: scholarships@thepennyhoarder.com

THETA DELTA CHI EDUCATIONAL FOUNDATION INC.

http://www.tdx.org/

THETA DELTA CHI EDUCATIONAL FOUNDATION INC. SCHOLARSHIP

Scholarships for undergraduate or graduate students enrolled in an accredited institution. Awards are based on candidate's history of service to the fraternity, scholastic achievement, and need. See website for application and additional information http://www.tdx.org/scholarship/scholarship.html.

Award: Scholarship for use in freshman, sophomore, junior, senior, or graduate years; renewable. *Number:* 15. *Amount:* $1000–$5000.

Eligibility Requirements: Applicant must be enrolled or expecting to enroll full-time at a four-year institution or university. Available to U.S. and non-U.S. citizens.

Application Requirements: Application form, financial need analysis, recommendations or references, transcript. *Deadline:* May 15.

Contact: William McClung, Executive Director
　　　Phone: 617-742-8886
　　　Fax: 617-742-8868
　　　E-mail: execdir@tdx.org

THIRD MARINE DIVISION ASSOCIATION, INC.

http://www.caltrap.com/

THIRD MARINE DIVISION ASSOCIATION MEMORIAL SCHOLARSHIP FUND

Scholarship assistance for children and grandchildren of qualified Third Marine Division Association members (Marine or Navy), or qualified service-connected deceased 3rd Marine Division veterans. For further details visit website http://www.caltrap.com. Total number of awards varies.

Award: Scholarship for use in freshman, sophomore, junior, or senior years; renewable. *Number:* 5–25. *Amount:* $500–$1500.

Eligibility Requirements: Applicant must be age 16-23 and enrolled or expecting to enroll full-time at a two-year or four-year or technical institution or university. Available to U.S. citizens.

Application Requirements: Application form, financial need analysis, personal photograph. *Deadline:* April 15.

Contact: Patrick Conroy, Secretary, Memorial Scholarship Fund
Third Marine Division Association, Inc.
3454 Stillwood Blvd.
Stow, OH 44224-4684
Phone: 330-322-9952
E-mail: conroypj11@aol.com

THURGOOD MARSHALL SCHOLARSHIP FUND

http://www.tmcf.org/

THURGOOD MARSHALL SCHOLARSHIP

Merit scholarships for students attending one of 45 member HBCUs (historically black colleges, universities) including 5 member law schools. Must maintain an average GPA of 3.0 to renew, demonstrate financial need, and be a U.S. citizen. Apply through member HBCU's campus scholarship coordinator. For further details refer to website, http://www.thurgoodmarshallfund.org.

Award: Scholarship for use in freshman, sophomore, junior, senior, or graduate years; renewable. *Amount:* up to $4400.

Eligibility Requirements: Applicant must be enrolled or expecting to enroll full-time at a four-year institution or university. Applicant must have 3.0 GPA or higher. Available to U.S. citizens.

Application Requirements: Application form, essay, financial need analysis, interview, personal photograph, recommendations or references, resume, test scores, transcript. *Deadline:* July 15.

Contact: Deshuandra Walker, Senior Manager of Scholarships
Thurgood Marshall Scholarship Fund
1770 Saint James Place Suite 414
Houston, TX 77056
Phone: 713-955-1073
Fax: 202-448-1017
E-mail: deshuandra.walker@tmcf.org

TWIN TOWERS ORPHAN FUND

http://www.ttof.org/

TWIN TOWERS ORPHAN FUND

Fund offers assistance to children who lost one or both parents in the terrorist attacks on September 11, 2001. Long-term education program established to provide higher education needs to children until they complete their uninterrupted studies, or reach age of majority. Visit website for additional information http://www.ttof.org.

Award: Scholarship for use in freshman, sophomore, junior, or senior years; not renewable. *Amount:* $1500–$6000.

Eligibility Requirements: Applicant must be enrolled or expecting to enroll full- or part-time at a two-year or four-year or technical institution or university. Available to U.S. citizens.

Application Requirements: Application form, financial need analysis. *Deadline:* continuous.

Contact: Karlene Boss, Case Manager
Phone: 661-633-9076
E-mail: ttof2@ttof.org

ULMAN CANCER FUND FOR YOUNG ADULTS

http://www.ulmanfund.org/scholarships

BERNICE MCNAMARA MEMORIAL SCHOLARSHIP

The Ulman Cancer Fund for Young Adults is committed to helping young adults continue their education after being affected by cancer through their own diagnosis or the diagnosis of a loved one. Many scholarships offered by UCF share similar applicant criteria. Applicants need only submit one application, which will be considered for any and all scholarships for which the student applies and is eligible.

Award: Scholarship for use in freshman, sophomore, junior, senior, or graduate years; not renewable. *Number:* 1. *Amount:* $2500.

Eligibility Requirements: Applicant must be age 15-39 and enrolled or expecting to enroll full-time at a two-year or four-year institution or university. Available to U.S. citizens.

Application Requirements: Application form, essay. *Deadline:* March 1.

Contact: Lauriann Parker, Scholarship Coordinator
Ulman Cancer Fund for Young Adults
1215 E. Fort Ave.
Ste. 104
Baltimore, MD 21230
Phone: 410-964-0202 Ext. 105
E-mail: scholarship@ulmanfund.org

UNICO FOUNDATION INC.

http://www.unico.org/

GUGLIELMO MARCONI ENGINEERING SCHOLARSHIP

An applicant must be a United States citizen of Italian heritage, currently enrolled full time in an accredited campus based college/university, pursuing an Engineering Degree. A candidate must reside in the home state of an active UNICO Chapter. Applications may be acquired from and submitted through a Chapter, the District Governor, or the UNICO National Office. Preference is given to candidates demonstrating financial need.

Award: Scholarship for use in sophomore, junior, senior, or graduate years; not renewable. *Number:* 1. *Amount:* $1250.

Eligibility Requirements: Applicant must be enrolled or expecting to enroll full-time at a four-year institution or university. Applicant must have 3.0 GPA or higher. Available to U.S. citizens.

Application Requirements: Application form, essay, financial need analysis. *Deadline:* April 15.

Contact: Joan Tidona, Scholarship Director
Phone: 973-808-0035
Fax: 973-808-0043
E-mail: uniconational@unico.org

LOUISE TORRACO MEMORIAL SCHOLARSHIP FOR SCIENCE

The UNICO Foundation will grant two scholarships valued at $2,500 each, to students enrolled full-time in an accredited college/university program in the United States pursuing study of the Physical Sciences or Life Sciences. A nominee must hold United States citizenship. This program is open to applicants of all ethnicities. Candidates must reside in the home state of an active UNICO Chapter. Applications may be acquired from and submitted through a State Chapter, the District Governor or the UNICO National Office.

Award: Scholarship for use in sophomore, junior, senior, or graduate years; not renewable. *Number:* 2. *Amount:* $2500.

Eligibility Requirements: Applicant must be enrolled or expecting to enroll full-time at a four-year institution or university. Applicant must have 3.0 GPA or higher. Available to U.S. citizens.

Application Requirements: Application form, essay. *Deadline:* April 15.

Contact: Joan Tidona, Scholarship Director
Phone: 973-808-0035
Fax: 973-808-0043
E-mail: uniconational@unico.org

MARIA AND PAOLO ALESSIO SOUTHERN ITALY SCHOLARSHIP

The UNICO Foundation will provide a scholarship, valued at $1,000, to a student enrolled full-time, in an accredited college/university program in the United States pursuing a degree. An applicant must be a United States citizen of Southern Italian heritage, specifically the regions of Abruzzo, Basilicata, Campania, Calabria, Latium, Molise, Puglia, Sardinia, or Sicilia.

Award: Scholarship for use in sophomore, junior, or senior years; not renewable. *Number:* 1. *Amount:* $1000.

Eligibility Requirements: Applicant must be enrolled or expecting to enroll full-time at a four-year institution or university. Applicant must have 3.0 GPA or higher. Available to U.S. citizens.

Application Requirements: Application form. *Deadline:* April 15.

Contact: Joan Tidona, Scholarship Director
Phone: 973-808-0035
Fax: 973-808-0043
E-mail: uniconational@unico.org

RALPH J. TORRACO FINE ARTS SCHOLARSHIP

The UNICO Foundation will grant two scholarships valued at $2,500 each, to students enrolled full-time in an accredited college/university program in the United States pursuing a degree in Fine Arts. A nominee must hold United States citizenship. This program is open to applicants of all ethnicities. Candidates must reside in the home state of an active UNICO Chapter. Applications may be acquired from and submitted through a State Chapter, the District Governor or the UNICO National Office.

Award: Scholarship for use in sophomore, junior, senior, or graduate years; not renewable. *Number:* 2. *Amount:* $2500.

Eligibility Requirements: Applicant must be enrolled or expecting to enroll full-time at a four-year institution or university. Applicant must have 3.0 GPA or higher. Available to U.S. citizens.

Application Requirements: Application form, essay, financial need analysis. *Deadline:* April 15.

Contact: Joan Tidona, Scholarship Director
 Phone: 973-808-0035
 Fax: 973-808-0043
 E-mail: uniconational@unico.org

RALPH J. TORRACO SCHOLARSHIP

The UNICO Foundation will grant two scholarships valued at $2,500 each, to students enrolled full-time, in an accredited college/university program in the United States pursuing a degree. A nominee must hold United States citizenship. This program is open to applicants of all ethnicities. Candidates must reside in the home state of an active UNICO Chapter. Applications may be acquired from and submitted through a State Chapter, the District Governor or the UNICO National Office.

Award: Scholarship for use in sophomore, junior, senior, or graduate years; not renewable. *Number:* 2. *Amount:* $2500.

Eligibility Requirements: Applicant must be enrolled or expecting to enroll full-time at a four-year institution or university. Applicant must have 3.0 GPA or higher. Available to U.S. citizens.

Application Requirements: Application form, essay, financial need analysis. *Deadline:* April 15.

Contact: Joan Tidona, Scholarship Director
 Phone: 973-808-0035
 Fax: 973-808-0043
 E-mail: uniconational@unico.org

ROBERT J. TARTE SCHOLARSHIP FOR ITALIAN STUDIES

An applicant must be a United States citizen, currently enrolled full time in an accredited campus based college/university, pursuing a major or minor in Italian Studies or Italian Language. A candidate must reside in the home state of an active UNICO Chapter. Applications may be acquired from and submitted through a Chapter, the District Governor, or the UNICO National Office. Preference is given to candidates demonstrating financial need. This program is open to applicants of all ethnicities.

Award: Scholarship for use in sophomore, junior, senior, or graduate years; not renewable. *Number:* 1. *Amount:* $1000.

Eligibility Requirements: Applicant must be enrolled or expecting to enroll full-time at a four-year institution or university. Applicant must have 3.0 GPA or higher. Available to U.S. citizens.

Application Requirements: Application form, essay, financial need analysis. *Deadline:* April 15.

Contact: Joan Tidona, Scholarship Director
 Phone: 973-808-0035
 Fax: 973-808-0043
 E-mail: uniconational@unico.org

UNIGO

https://www.scholarshipexperts.com

ALL ABOUT EDUCATION SCHOLARSHIP

Applicants must complete a profile on the scholarshipexperts.com website, be thirteen years of age or older at the time of application, be legal residents of the 50 United States or the District of Columbia, be currently enrolled (or enroll no later than the fall of 2021) in an accredited post-secondary institution of higher education. Submit an online short written response (250 words or less) for the topic: 'How will a $3,000 scholarship for education make a difference in your life?'

Award: Scholarship for use in freshman, sophomore, junior, senior, graduate, or postgraduate years; not renewable. *Number:* 1. *Amount:* $3000.

Eligibility Requirements: Applicant must be enrolled or expecting to enroll full- or part-time at a two-year or four-year or technical institution or university. Available to U.S. citizens.

Application Requirements: Application form, essay. *Deadline:* April 30.

Contact: Scholarship Committee
 Unigo
 10751 Deerwood Park Boulevard, #125
 Jacksonville, FL 32256
 Phone: 904-483-2939
 Fax: 904-483-2934
 E-mail: info@scholarshipexperts.com

DO-OVER SCHOLARSHIP

Applicants must be thirteen years of age or older at the time of application, be legal residents of the 50 United States or the District of Columbia, be currently enrolled (or enroll no later than the fall of 2021) in an accredited post-secondary institution of higher education. Submit an online short written response (250 words or less) for the question: "If you could get one 'do over' in life, what would it be and why?"

Award: Scholarship for use in freshman, sophomore, junior, senior, graduate, or postgraduate years; not renewable. *Number:* 1. *Amount:* $1500.

Eligibility Requirements: Applicant must be enrolled or expecting to enroll full- or part-time at a two-year or four-year or technical institution or university. Available to U.S. citizens.

Application Requirements: Application form, essay. *Deadline:* June 30.

Contact: Scholarship Committee
 Unigo
 10751 Deerwood Park Boulevard, #125
 Jacksonville, FL 32256
 Phone: 904-483-2939
 Fax: 904-483-2934
 E-mail: info@scholarshipexperts.com

EDUCATION MATTERS SCHOLARSHIP

Applicants must: Complete a profile on the ScholarshipExperts.com website. Be thirteen years of age or older at the time of application. Be legal residents of the fifty United States or the District of Columbia. Be currently enrolled (or enroll no later than the fall of 2021) in an accredited post-secondary institution of higher education. Submit an online short written response (250 words or less) for the question: 'What would you say to someone who thinks education doesn't matter, or that college is a waste of time and money?'

Award: Scholarship for use in freshman, sophomore, junior, senior, graduate, or postgraduate years; not renewable. *Number:* 1. *Amount:* $5000.

Eligibility Requirements: Applicant must be enrolled or expecting to enroll full- or part-time at a two-year or four-year or technical institution or university. Available to U.S. citizens.

Application Requirements: Application form, essay. *Deadline:* November 30.

Contact: Scholarship Committee
 Unigo
 10751 Deerwood Park Boulevard, #125
 Jacksonville, FL 32256
 Phone: 904-483-2939
 Fax: 904-483-2934
 E-mail: info@scholarshipexperts.com

FIFTH MONTH SCHOLARSHIP

Applicants must: Be thirteen years of age or older at the time of application. Be legal residents of the fifty United States or the District of Columbia. Be currently enrolled (or enroll no later than the fall of 2021) in an accredited post-secondary institution of higher education and submit an online short written response (250 words or less) for the topic: "May is the fifth month of the year. Write a letter to the number five explaining why five is important. Be serious or be funny. Either way, here's a high five to you just for being original."

Award: Scholarship for use in freshman, sophomore, junior, senior, graduate, or postgraduate years; not renewable. *Number:* 1. *Amount:* $1500.

Eligibility Requirements: Applicant must be enrolled or expecting to enroll full- or part-time at a two-year or four-year or technical institution or university. Available to U.S. citizens.

Application Requirements: Application form, essay. *Deadline:* May 31.

Contact: Scholarship Committee
Unigo
10751 Deerwood Park Boulevard, #125
Jacksonville, FL 32256
Phone: 904-483-2939
Fax: 904-483-2934
E-mail: info@scholarshipexperts.com

I HAVE A DREAM SCHOLARSHIP

Applicants must: Be thirteen years of age or older at the time of application. Be legal residents of the fifty United States or the District of Columbia. Be currently enrolled (or enroll no later than the fall of 2021) in an accredited post-secondary institution of higher education and submit an online short written response (250 words or less) for the topic: "We want to know, what do you dream about? Whether it's some bizarre dream from last week, or your hopes for the future, share your dreams with us for a chance to win $1,500 for college."

Award: Scholarship for use in freshman, sophomore, junior, senior, graduate, or postgraduate years; not renewable. *Number:* 1. *Amount:* $1500.

Eligibility Requirements: Applicant must be enrolled or expecting to enroll full- or part-time at a two-year or four-year or technical institution or university. Available to U.S. citizens.

Application Requirements: Application form, essay. *Deadline:* January 31.

Contact: Scholarship Committee
Unigo
10751 Deerwood Park Boulevard, #125
Jacksonville, FL 32256
Phone: 904-483-2939
Fax: 904-483-2934
E-mail: info@scholarshipexperts.com

SHOUT IT OUT SCHOLARSHIP

Applicants must be thirteen years of age or older at the time of application, be legal residents of the 50 United States or the District of Columbia, and be currently enrolled (or enroll no later than the fall of 2021) in an accredited post-secondary institution of higher education and submit an online short written response (250 words or less) for the topic: 'If you could say one thing to the entire world at once, what would it be and why?'

Award: Scholarship for use in freshman, sophomore, junior, senior, graduate, or postgraduate years; not renewable. *Number:* 1. *Amount:* $1500.

Eligibility Requirements: Applicant must be enrolled or expecting to enroll full- or part-time at a two-year or four-year or technical institution or university. Available to U.S. citizens.

Application Requirements: Application form, essay. *Deadline:* September 30.

Contact: Scholarship Committee
Unigo
10751 Deerwood Park Boulevard, #125
Jacksonville, FL 32256
Phone: 904-483-2939
Fax: 904-483-2934
E-mail: info@scholarshipexperts.com

SUPERPOWER SCHOLARSHIP

Applicants must be thirteen years of age or older at the time of application, be legal residents of the 50 United States or the District of Columbia, be currently enrolled (or enroll no later than the fall of 2021) in an accredited post-secondary institution of higher education. Submit an online short written response (250 words or less) for the question: 'Which superhero or villain would you want to changes places with for a day and why?'

Award: Scholarship for use in freshman, sophomore, junior, or senior years; not renewable. *Number:* 1. *Amount:* $2500.

Eligibility Requirements: Applicant must be enrolled or expecting to enroll full- or part-time at a two-year or four-year or technical institution or university. Available to U.S. citizens.

Application Requirements: Application form, essay. *Deadline:* March 31.

Contact: Scholarship Committee
Unigo
10751 Deerwood Park Boulevard, #125
Jacksonville, FL 32256
Phone: 904-483-2939
Fax: 904-483-2934
E-mail: info@scholarshipexperts.com

SWEET & SIMPLE SCHOLARSHIP

Applicants must be thirteen years of age or older at the time of application, be legal residents of the 50 United States or the District of Columbia, and be currently enrolled (or enroll no later than the fall of 2020) in an accredited post-secondary institution of higher education and submit an online short written response (250 words or less) for the topic: "Not every gift has to be expensive or extravagant. In fact, sometimes it's the sweet and simple things that make a real difference in our lives. Think back and tell us about something you received as a gift and why it meant so much to you."

Award: Scholarship for use in freshman, sophomore, junior, senior, graduate, or postgraduate years; not renewable. *Number:* 1. *Amount:* $1500.

Eligibility Requirements: Applicant must be enrolled or expecting to enroll full- or part-time at a two-year or four-year or technical institution or university. Available to U.S. citizens.

Application Requirements: Application form, application form may be submitted online (https://www.scholarshipexperts.com/scholarships/our-scholarships/sweet-and-simple-scholarship), essay. *Deadline:* February 28.

Contact: Scholarship Committee
Unigo
10751 Deerwood Park Boulevard, #125
Jacksonville, FL 32256
Phone: 904-483-2939
Fax: 904-483-2934
E-mail: info@scholarshipexperts.com

TOP TEN LIST SCHOLARSHIP

Applicants must: Be thirteen years of age or older at the time of application. Be legal residents of the fifty United States or the District of Columbia. Be currently enrolled (or enroll no later than the fall of 2021) in an accredited post-secondary institution of higher education. Submit an online short written response (250 words or less) for the topic: 'Create a Top Ten List of the top ten reasons you should get this scholarship.'

Award: Scholarship for use in freshman, sophomore, junior, senior, graduate, or postgraduate years; not renewable. *Number:* 1. *Amount:* $1500.

Eligibility Requirements: Applicant must be enrolled or expecting to enroll full- or part-time at a two-year or four-year or technical institution or university. Available to U.S. citizens.

Application Requirements: Application form, essay. *Deadline:* December 31.

Contact: Scholarship Committee
Unigo
10751 Deerwood Park Boulevard, #125
Jacksonville, FL 32256
Phone: 904-483-2939
Fax: 904-483-2934
E-mail: info@scholarshipexperts.com

UNITED NEGRO COLLEGE FUND

http://www.uncf.org/

VOYA SCHOLARS

Award for current juniors who are enrolled full-time at a UNCF member college or university in a restricted major in accounting, actuarial science, business/business management, finance/investment, marketing, mathematics, or quants/quantitative. Preference will be given to students with a home residence in Atlanta, GA; Hartford, CT; Jackson, Mississippi; Minneapolis, MN New York City; and Philadelphia, PA.

Award: Scholarship for use in junior year; not renewable.

Eligibility Requirements: Applicant must be enrolled or expecting to enroll full-time at a four-year institution or university. Applicant must have 3.0 GPA or higher. Available to U.S. citizens.

Application Requirements: Application form, essay, financial need analysis. *Deadline:* December 12.

Contact: Mary Williams, Director of Outreach and Recruitment
Phone: 800-331-2244

UNITED STATES ACHIEVEMENT ACADEMY

http://www.usaa-academy.com/

DR. GEORGE A. STEVENS FOUNDER'S AWARD

One $10,000 scholarship cash grant to enhance the intellectual and personal growth of students who demonstrate a genuine interest in learning. Award must be used for educational purposes. Must maintain a minimum GPA of 3.0.

Award: Grant for use in freshman year; not renewable. *Number:* 1. *Amount:* $10,000.

Eligibility Requirements: Applicant must be high school student and planning to enroll or expecting to enroll full-time at a four-year institution or university. Applicant must have 3.0 GPA or higher. Available to U.S. and non-U.S. citizens.

Application Requirements: Application form.

Contact: Scholarship Committee
Phone: 859-269-5674
Fax: 859-268-9068
E-mail: usaa@usaa-academy.com

NATIONAL SCHOLARSHIP CASH GRANT

The Foundation awards 400 national scholarship cash grants of $1500. All scholarship winners are determined by an independent selection committee. Winners are selected based on GPA, school activities, SAT scores (if applicable), honors and awards. All students in grades 6 to 12 are eligible.

Award: Grant for use in freshman year; not renewable. *Number:* 400. *Amount:* $1500.

Eligibility Requirements: Applicant must be high school student and planning to enroll or expecting to enroll full-time at a four-year institution or university. Applicant must have 3.0 GPA or higher. Available to U.S. and non-U.S. citizens.

Application Requirements: Application form, application form may be submitted online (http://www.fs22.formsite.com/USAA/form23/index.html). *Deadline:* June 1.

Contact: Scholarship Committee
Phone: 859-269-5674
Fax: 859-268-9068
E-mail: usaa@usaa-academy.com

UNITED STATES-INDONESIA SOCIETY

http://www.usindo.org/

UNITED STATES-INDONESIA SOCIETY TRAVEL GRANTS

Grants are provided to fund travel to Indonesia or the United States for American and Indonesian students and professors to conduct research, language training or other independent study/research. Must have a minimum 3.0 GPA.

Award: Grant for use in freshman, sophomore, junior, senior, graduate, or postgraduate years; not renewable. *Number:* 1–15. *Amount:* $1000–$2000.

Eligibility Requirements: Applicant must be enrolled or expecting to enroll full- or part-time at a four-year institution or university. Applicant must have 3.0 GPA or higher. Available to U.S. and non-Canadian citizens.

Application Requirements: Application form, basic budget, recommendations or references, resume, transcript. *Deadline:* continuous.

Contact: Thomas Spooner, Educational Officer
Phone: 202-232-1400
Fax: 202-232-7300
E-mail: tspooner@usindo.org

UNPAKT LLC

https://www.unpakt.com/

UNPAKT COLLEGE SCHOLARSHIP

Dream big and tell us where you see yourself moving to start your professional life after college. Dreaming of startups in Redwood City or helping urban development in Buffalo? Focusing on intelligence and politics in Washington, D.C. or educating Bostonian minds? Whether you are planning on moving out of state or staying local, we want to know about it. In no more than 500 words, let us know where you plan to move once you finish your education and why. Winners will be chosen by committee review. Judges will be looking for passion and commitment to the dream. Applicant must be a current college student or recent college graduate (within one year) at time of award announcement on December 31, 2017. Apply online. www.unpakt.com/scholarship

Award: Prize for use in freshman, sophomore, junior, or senior years; not renewable. *Number:* 1. *Amount:* $1000.

Eligibility Requirements: Applicant must be enrolled or expecting to enroll full-time at a four-year institution or university. Available to U.S. citizens.

Application Requirements: Application form, essay. *Deadline:* December 15.

Contact: Scholarship Coordinator
Phone: 212-677-5333 Ext. 107
E-mail: scholarship@unpakt.com

U.S. BANK INTERNET SCHOLARSHIP PROGRAM

http://www.usbank.com/

U.S. BANK INTERNET SCHOLARSHIP PROGRAM

A high school senior planning to enroll or a current college freshmen, sophomore or junior at an eligible four-year college or university participating in the U.S. Bank No Fee Education Loan Program. Apply online at usbank.com/studentbanking from October through March. No paper applications accepted.

Award: Scholarship for use in freshman, sophomore, or junior years; not renewable. *Number:* up to 40. *Amount:* up to $1000.

Eligibility Requirements: Applicant must be enrolled or expecting to enroll full- or part-time at a four-year institution or university. Available to U.S. and non-U.S. citizens.

Application Requirements: Application form. *Deadline:* March 31.

Contact: Mary Ennis, Scholarship Coordinator
Phone: 800-242-1200
E-mail: mary.ennis@usbank.com

US PAN ASIAN AMERICAN CHAMBER OF COMMERCE EDUCATION FOUNDATION

http://www.uspaacc.com/

BRUCE LEE SCHOLARSHIP

The applicant should demonstrate academic achievement of 3.3 GPA or higher, leadership in extracurricular activities involvement in community service, and financial need. The amount of the scholarship depends on the sponsors' contributions and varies between $2000 and $5000.

Award: Scholarship for use in freshman year; renewable. *Number:* 1. *Amount:* $2000–$5000.

Eligibility Requirements: Applicant must be high school student and planning to enroll or expecting to enroll full-time at an institution or university. Available to U.S. citizens.

Application Requirements: Application form. *Deadline:* March 17.

Contact: Diana Yee
US Pan Asian American Chamber of Commerce Education
Foundation
1329 18th Street N.W.
Washington D.C. 20036
Phone: 202-3781121
E-mail: diana@uspaacc.com

VALEANT PHARMACEUTICALS NORTH AMERICA, LLC

http://www.valeant.com

ASPIRE HIGHER SCHOLARSHIP PROGRAM

Valeant Dermatology ASPIRE HIGHER Scholarship Program will award scholarships of up to $10,000 each to nine individual students who will be attending an undergraduate or graduate education program during the 2016 to 2017 school year. The scholarships recognize students who have been diagnosed and treated for a dermatologic condition and are pursuing a higher education degree. Applicants need not have used a Valeant dermatologic prescription medication to be eligible, and use of a Valeant product will not increase an applicant's chance of being awarded a scholarship. Three scholarships will be awarded in three different categories: Undergraduate Scholar Awards for students pursuing an undergraduate degree, Graduate Scholar Awards for students pursuing a graduate degree and Today's Woman Scholar Awards for students who are mothers pursuing either a graduate or undergraduate degree.

Award: Scholarship for use in freshman, sophomore, junior, senior, or graduate years; not renewable. *Number:* 9. *Amount:* $10,000.

Eligibility Requirements: Applicant must be enrolled or expecting to enroll full- or part-time at a four-year institution or university. Available to U.S. citizens.

Application Requirements: Essay. *Deadline:* April 30.

Contact: Christopher Vancheri
Phone: 973-588-2043
E-mail: cvancheri@coynepr.com

THE VEGETARIAN RESOURCE GROUP

http://www.vrg.org/

THE VEGETARIAN RESOURCE GROUP SCHOLARSHIP

Three scholarships (one $10,000; two $5,000) will be awarded to graduating U.S. high school students who promoted vegetarianism (includes veganism) in their schools and/or communities. Vegetarians do not eat meat, fish, or fowl. Applicants will be judged on a strong commitment to promoting a peaceful world through a vegetarian diet/lifestyle.

Award: Scholarship for use in freshman year; not renewable. *Amount:* $5000–$10,000.

Eligibility Requirements: Applicant must be high school student and planning to enroll or expecting to enroll full- or part-time at a two-year or four-year institution or university. Available to U.S. citizens.

Application Requirements: Application form, essay. *Deadline:* February 20.

Contact: Scholarship Coordinator
Phone: 410-366-8343
Fax: 410-366-8804
E-mail: vrg@vrg.org

VELVETJOBS LLC

http://www.velvetjobs.com

RESUME TEMPLATE DESIGN SCHOLARSHIP

VelvetJobs is proud to announce a $1000 scholarship for students studying in the USA or overseas. The Employee Morale Scholarship aims to get students thinking about their own potential future management position and how their decisions can affect employee morale. Through our own outplacement services we've dealt with thousands of employers on the issues that affect them most when it comes to retaining employees and keeping them happy. We're looking for students to write about their favorite idea on how to boost and maintain employee morale. Open to USA or international students. Entrants must

18 years or older. No GPA requirement. Submit an essay that includes a headline of a morale boosting idea and then should include at least 500 words on how to effectively deploy the strategy. Email your essay to scholarship@velvetjobs.com. Please include the following information: full name, phone number, college or university where you are enrolled or plan to attend, current school year. We will be judging the strategy on both it's uniqueness and it's practicality. That means the idea should stand out from the crowd but also be easily implemented into the workforce. The idea does not have to be overarching to all types of workforce but can be individualized to a specific workforce such as (office based, manufacturing, mobile workers, etc.).Deadline is December 16th, 2017

Award: Scholarship for use in freshman, sophomore, junior, senior, graduate, or postgraduate years; renewable. *Number:* 1. *Amount:* $1000.

Eligibility Requirements: Applicant must be enrolled or expecting to enroll full- or part-time at a two-year or four-year or technical institution or university. Available to U.S. and non-U.S. citizens.

Application Requirements: *Deadline:* December 16.

Contact: Christina Murphy, Scholarship Coordinator
VelvetJobs LLC
1400 North Martel Avenue, Suite 108
Los Angeles, CA 90046
Phone: 877-370-7552
E-mail: scholarship@velvetjobs.com

WISCONSIN LIBRARY ASSOCIATION

http://www.wla.wisconsinlibraries.org/

WAAL SCHOLARSHIP

The WAAL Professional Development Committee has created three scholarship application forms for individuals wanting to apply for a scholarship to attend the annual WAAL conference.

Award: Scholarship for use in sophomore, junior, senior, or graduate years; not renewable.

Eligibility Requirements: Applicant must be enrolled or expecting to enroll full- or part-time at a four-year institution or university.

Application Requirements: Application form, essay. *Deadline:* March 4.

Contact: Brigitte Rupp Vacha, WLA Conference Liaison
Wisconsin Library Association
4610 S Biltmore Lane
Suite 100
Madison, WI 53718
Phone: 608-245-3640
Fax: 608-245-3646
E-mail: ruppvacha@wisconsinlibraries.org

WOMEN'S INDEPENDENCE SCHOLARSHIP PROGRAM, INC.

http://www.wispinc.org/

WOMEN'S INDEPENDENCE SCHOLARSHIP PROGRAM

Scholarship for female survivors of intimate partner abuse, separated from their abusive partner a minimum of one year but not more than seven years, and sponsored by a domestic violence service agency they have worked with for a minimum of six months. Funding is available for those attending an accredited course of study at a U.S. institution. The application is only available online and must be submitted electronically.

Award: Scholarship for use in freshman, sophomore, junior, senior, or graduate years; renewable. *Number:* 350–500. *Amount:* $500–$3000.

Eligibility Requirements: Applicant must be enrolled or expecting to enroll full- or part-time at a two-year or four-year or technical institution or university and female. Available to U.S. citizens.

Application Requirements: Application form, essay, financial need analysis. *Deadline:* continuous.

Contact: Nancy Soward, Executive Director
Women's Independence Scholarship Program, Inc.
4900 Randall Parkway, Suite H
Wilmington, NC 28403
Phone: 910-397-7742 Ext. 101
Fax: 910-397-0023
E-mail: nancy@wispinc.org

WOMEN'S OVERSEAS SERVICE LEAGUE

http://www.wosl.org/

WOMEN'S OVERSEAS SERVICE LEAGUE SCHOLARSHIPS FOR WOMEN

Awarded to women committed to careers in public service who have completed 12 semester or 18 quarter units in any higher education institution with a 2.5 GPA, are admitted to an institution in a program leading to an Associate's Degree or higher and enrolled for a minimum of 6 semester or 9 quarter hours.

Award: Scholarship for use in sophomore, junior, senior, graduate, or postgraduate years; renewable. *Number:* 10–20. *Amount:* $1000–$2000.

Eligibility Requirements: Applicant must be enrolled or expecting to enroll full- or part-time at a two-year or four-year or technical institution or university and female. Applicant must have 2.5 GPA or higher. Available to U.S. citizens.

Application Requirements: Application form, community service, essay, financial need analysis. *Deadline:* March 1.

Contact: Ms. Ann Kelsey, Scholarship Committee Chair
E-mail: kelsey@openix.com

WYZANT INC.

WYZANT COLLEGE SCHOLARSHIPS

Each individual who applies (Applicant) will be required to write an essay in English of no more than 300 words answering the question: "Who has been most important tutor, teacher or coach in my life and why?" As part of the application, Applicant may use tools and services provided by WyzAnt to promote the essay to friends and family. Contest runs from October 1 through May 1 each year.

Award: Scholarship for use in freshman, sophomore, junior, or senior years; not renewable.

Eligibility Requirements: Applicant must be enrolled or expecting to enroll full- or part-time at a four-year institution or university. Available to U.S. citizens.

Application Requirements: Essay. *Deadline:* May 1.

ZELUS RECOVERY

http://zelusrecovery.com/

ZELUS RECOVERY $1000 COLLEGE SCHOLARSHIP

Zelus Recovery specializes in treating adolescents and young adults with substance abuse problems. Our goal is to help young people find their way back to health and happiness so they can become contributing members of society. We have created the Zelus Recovery Scholarship for undergraduate and postgraduates students to further that message.

Award: Scholarship for use in freshman, sophomore, junior, senior, graduate, or postgraduate years; not renewable. *Number:* 1. *Amount:* $1000.

Eligibility Requirements: Applicant must be enrolled or expecting to enroll full- or part-time at a two-year or four-year or technical institution or university. Available to U.S. citizens.

Application Requirements: Essay. *Deadline:* August 1.

Contact: Jason Zelus, Director
Zelus Recovery
1965 S. Eagle Road Suite 140
Meridian, ID 83642
Phone: 208-957-6514
Fax: 208-957-6506
E-mail: info@zelusrecovery.com

ZOOMITA

http://zoomita.com

$1,000 NOT AN ESSAY SCHOLARSHIP

Application essays are hard. Zoomita makes them easier. Create a free account and respond to the mystery question for a chance to win $1,000 toward your college expenses!

Award: Scholarship for use in freshman year; not renewable. *Number:* up to 1. *Amount:* up to $1000.

Eligibility Requirements: Applicant must be high school student; age 15-19 and planning to enroll or expecting to enroll full- or part-time at a four-year or technical institution or university. Available to U.S. and non-U.S. citizens.

Application Requirements: Application form may be submitted online (http://zoomita.com/VGhpc1NIb3VkbEJFSGlkZGVu), response to mystery question. *Deadline:* December 31.

Contact: Sandeep Chauhan
Zoomita
1440 Broadway
Oakland, CA 94612
E-mail: info@edswell.com

INDEXES

Award Name

Alan G. Thorpe, K1TMW, Memorial Scholarship Fund *811*

Alan Lucas Memorial Educational Scholarship *122*

Alan R. Epstein Scholarship *773*

Alaska Chapter Scholarship *463*

AlaskAdvantage Education Grant *725*

Alaska Geological Society Scholarship *240*

Alaskan Aviation Safety Foundation Memorial Scholarship Fund *136*

Alaska Performance Scholarship *725*

Al-Ben Scholarship for Academic Incentive *179*

Al-Ben Scholarship for Professional Merit *179*

Al-Ben Scholarship for Scholastic Achievement *179*

Alberta Agriculture Food and Rural Development 4-H Scholarship Program *528*

Alberta Apprenticeship and Industry Training Scholarships *726*

Alberta Barley Commission-Eugene Boyko Memorial Scholarship *96*

Alberta Centennial Scholarships-Alberta *666*

The Alberta C. Kaufman Scholarship *597*

Alberta Pre-Apprenticeship Scholarships *726*

Albert E. and Florence W. Newton Nurse Scholarship *460*

Albert E. Wischmeyer Memorial Scholarship Award *306*

Albert H. Hix, W8AH, Memorial Scholarship *738*

Albert M. Lappin Scholarship *533*

Albina Fuel Company Scholarship *569*

Al Conklin and Bill de Decker Business Aviation Management Scholarship *145*

Aldo Freda Legislative Pages Scholarship *791*

A Legacy of Hope Scholarships for Survivors of Childhood Cancer *798*

Alert1 Student for Seniors Scholarship *573*

Alert Scholarship *727*

Alexander and Maude Hadden Scholarship *627*

The Alexander Foundation Scholarship Program *727*

Alexander Rutherford Scholarships for High School Achievement *667*

Alexander Scholarship Loan Fund *171*

Alfred E. Friend Jr., W4CF, Memorial Scholarship *177*

Alfred G. and Elma M. Milotte Scholarship *840*

Alfred Steele Engineering Scholarship *293*

Alfred "Tup" Holmes Memorial Scholarship *801*

AlgaeCal Scholarship *573*

Alice and Mason White Memorial Scholarship *872*

Alice Glaisyer Warfield Memorial Scholarship *517*

Alice L. Haltom Educational Fund *160*

Alice T. Schafer Mathematics Prize for Excellence in Mathematics by an Undergraduate Woman *414*

All About Education Scholarship *888*

Allcott/Hunt Share It Now II Scholarship, Honoring Emory S. and Elizabeth Burkett Hunt *872*

Allegheny Mountain Section Air & Waste Management Association Scholarship *317*

Allen and Bertha Watson Memorial Scholarship *294*

Allen J. Baldwin Scholarship *418*

Allied Healthcare Scholarship Program *151*

All-Ink.com College Scholarship Program *840*

Allison Fisher Scholarship *383*

Allogan Slagle Memorial Scholarship *671*

Al Neuharth Free Spirit and Journalism Conference Program *380*

Alpha Omega Scholarship In Memory Of Peter Agris *201*

Alphonse A. Miele Scholarship *703*

Alphonso Deal Scholarship Award *226*

Alumni Student Assistance Program *673*

Alvin E. Heaps Memorial Scholarship *557*

Alwin B. Newton Scholarship *264*

AMACESP Student Scholarships *136*

Amato Sanita Brighter Future Scholarship *613*

AMBUCS Scholars-Scholarships for Therapists *134*

Amelia Kemp Scholarship *709*

American Angus Auxiliary Scholarship *870*

American Association for Geodetic Surveying Joseph F. Dracup Scholarship Award *507*

American Association of Family & Consumer Sciences National Undergraduate Scholarship *362*

American Baptist Financial Aid Program *710*

American Board of Funeral Service Education Scholarships *340*

American Bullion Scholarship *841*

American Chemical Society, Rubber Division Undergraduate Scholarship *109*

American Chemical Society Scholars Program *172*

American College of Musicians/National Guild of Piano Teachers $200 Scholarships *427*

American Council of the Blind Scholarships *574*

American Criminal Justice Association-Lambda Alpha Epsilon National Scholarship *224*

American Dental Association Foundation Dental Hygiene Scholarship Program *234*

American Dental Association Foundation Dental Student Scholarship Program *234*

American Dream Scholarship *846*

American Essay Contest Scholarship *532*

American Express Scholarship Program *367*

American Express Travel Scholarship *519*

American Federation of State, County, and Municipal Employees Oregon Council # 75 Scholarship *553*

American Federation of State, County, and Municipal Employees Scholarship Program *528*

American Ground Water Trust-AMTROL Inc. Scholarship *240*

American Ground Water Trust-Baroid Scholarship *241*

American Ground Water Trust-Thomas Stetson Scholarship *241*

American Hotel & Lodging Educational Foundation Pepsi Scholarship *228*

American Indian Education Foundation Scholarship *669*

American Indian Nurse Scholarship Program *346*

American Jewish League for Israel Scholarship Program *808*

American Legion Auxiliary Children of Warriors National Presidents' Scholarship *575*

American Legion Auxiliary Department of Alabama Scholarship Program *650*

American Legion Auxiliary Department of Arizona Health Care Occupation Scholarships *347*

American Legion Auxiliary Department of Arizona Nurses' Scholarships *445*

American Legion Auxiliary Department of Arizona Wilma Hoyal-Maxine Chilton Memorial Scholarship *488*

American Legion Auxiliary Department of California General Scholarship *650*

American Legion Auxiliary Department of California Past Presidents' Parley Nursing Scholarships *445*

American Legion Auxiliary Department of Colorado Department President's Scholarship and Scholarship for Junior Member *842*

American Legion Auxiliary Department of Colorado Past Presidents' Parley Health Care Professional ScholarshipNurses Scholarship *133*

American Legion Auxiliary Department of Connecticut Memorial Educational Grant *529*

American Legion Auxiliary Department of Connecticut Past Presidents' Parley Memorial Education Grant *529*

American Legion Auxiliary Department of Idaho Nursing Scholarship *445*

American Legion Auxiliary Department of Iowa Children of Veterans Merit Award *650*

American Legion Auxiliary Department of Iowa Harriet Hoffman Memorial Merit Award for Teacher Training *248*

American Legion Auxiliary Department of Iowa M.V. McCrae Memorial Nurses Merit Award *445*

American Legion Auxiliary Department of Kentucky Laura Blackburn Memorial Scholarship *645*

American Legion Auxiliary Department of Kentucky Mary Barrett Marshall Scholarship *650*

American Legion Auxiliary Department of Maine Daniel E. Lambert Memorial Scholarship *650*

American Legion Auxiliary Department of Maine Past Presidents' Parley Nurses Scholarship *347*

American Legion Auxiliary Department of Massachusetts Department President's Scholarship *574*

American Legion Auxiliary Department of Massachusetts Past Presidents' Parley Scholarship *651*

American Legion Auxiliary Department of Michigan Medical Career Scholarship *347*

American Legion Auxiliary Department of Michigan Memorial Scholarship *651*

American Legion Auxiliary Department of Michigan Scholarship for Non-Traditional Student *651*

American Legion Auxiliary Department of Minnesota Past Presidents' Parley Health Care Scholarship *347*

American Legion Auxiliary Department of Minnesota Scholarships *652*

American Legion Auxiliary Department of Missouri Lela Murphy Scholarship *529*

American Legion Auxiliary Department of Missouri National President's Scholarship *529*

American Legion Auxiliary Department of Missouri Past Presidents' Parley Scholarship *446*

American Legion Auxiliary Department of Nebraska Ruby Paul Campaign Fund Scholarship *530*

Mario Cugia Italian Studies Scholarship Program *683*

Marion A. and Eva S. Peeples Scholarships *455*

Marion A. Lindeman Scholarship *354*

Marion Barr Stanfield Art Scholarship *131*

Marion Huber Learning Through Listening Awards *548*

Mark Coats Memorial Scholarship *602*

Market Inspector $1,000 Scholarship In Support of Those Under the Revised U.S. Travel Ban *688*

Markley Scholarship *171*

Markowski-Leach Scholarship *822*

Marshall E. McCullough-National Dairy Shrine Scholarships *100*

Martha Ann Stark Memorial Scholarship *262*

Martha R. Dudley LVN/LPN Scholarship *456*

Martin D. Andrews Memorial Scholarship Fund *826*

Martin Duffy Adult Learner Scholarship Award *548*

Martin Luther King, Jr. Memorial Scholarship *250*

Marvin Mundel Memorial Scholarship *301*

Mary E. Horstkotte Scholarship Fund *785*

Mary Elizabeth Guest Scholarship *505*

Mary Gunther Memorial Scholarship *311*

Mary Jo Young Scholarship *768*

Maryland Association of Private Colleges and Career Schools Scholarship *602*

Maryland Boys State Scholarship *732*

Maryland SPJ Pro Chapter College Scholarship *388*

Mary Lou Brown Scholarship *739*

Mary Macey Scholarship *103*

Mary Marshall Practical Nursing Scholarship (LPN) *462*

Mary Marshall Registered Nursing Scholarships *462*

Mary McLeod Bethune Scholarship *755*

Mary McMillan Scholarship Award *249*

Mary Morrow-Edna Richards Scholarship *256*

Mary Olive Eddy Jones Art Scholarship *126*

Mary P. Oenslager Scholastic Achievement Awards *548*

Mary Quon Moy Ing Memorial Scholarship Award *379*

Mary Serra Gili Scholarship Award *450*

Mary T. Carothers Summer Environmental Studies Scholarship *321*

Mary V. Munger Scholarship *185*

Mary York Scholarship Fund *450*

Mas Family Scholarship Award *165*

Masonic Range Science Scholarship *94*

Massachusetts AFL-CIO Scholarship *772*

Massachusetts Assistance for Student Success Program *772*

Massachusetts Cash Grant Program *772*

Massachusetts Federation of Polish Women's Clubs Scholarships *686*

Massachusetts Gilbert Matching Student Grant Program *773*

Massachusetts Part-Time Grant Program *773*

Massachusetts Public Service Grant Program *602*

Master's Scholarship Program *181*

MASWE Scholarship *186*

Materials Processing & Manufacturing Division Scholarship *283*

Math and Science Scholarship *156*

Math, Engineering, Science, Business, Education, Computers Scholarships *162*

Matinée Voice-over Scholarship *867*

Matsuo Bridge Company Ltd. of Japan Scholarship *193*

Maureen L. and Howard N. Blitman, PE Scholarship to Promote Diversity in Engineering *180*

Maynard Jensen American Legion Memorial Scholarship *535*

Mayo Foundations Scholarship *457*

The Mayor's Chesapeake Energy Scholarship *750*

Mayors Educational Assistance Program *777*

May T. Henry Scholarship Foundation *847*

May Trucking Company Scholarship *874*

MCCL Thought Leadership Scholarship *867*

McCurry Foundation Scholarship *773*

M.D. "Jack" Murphy Memorial Scholarship *447*

Medical/Health Services Education Scholarship *631*

Medical Scrubs Collection Scholarship *106*

Medicus Student Exchange *701*

Melville H. Cohee Student Leader Conservation Scholarship *558*

Member grants *627*

Menominee Indian Tribe Adult Vocational Training Program *689*

Menominee Indian Tribe of Wisconsin Higher Education Grants *689*

Meredith Thoms Memorial Scholarships *287*

Mesothelioma Memorial Scholarship *885*

MIA/POW Scholarship *657*

Michael Cerussi Leadership Scholarship *562*

Michael Jackson Scholarship *212*

Michael J. Morin Memorial Scholarship *562*

Michael J. Powell High School Journalist of the Year *382*

Michael Kiely Strong Roots Scholarship and Essay Contest *877*

Michael Moody Fitness Scholarship *255*

Michael P. Anderson Scholarship in Space Science *486*

Michael S. Libretti Scholarship *206*

Michele L. McDonald Scholarship *76*

Michigan Competitive Scholarship *773*

Michigan Tuition Grant *774*

Mid-Atlantic Aerospace Scholarship *146*

Mid-Continent Instrument Scholarship *136*

Mike Hylton Memorial Scholarship *633*

Mike Reynolds Journalism Scholarship *209*

Mike Wallace Memorial Scholarship *205*

Mildred and Albert Panowski Playwriting Award *819*

Miles Gray Memorial Scholarship *562*

Military Award Program (MAP) *641*

Military Dependent's Scholarship Program *655*

Military Order of the Purple Heart Scholarship *658*

Military Order of the Stars and Bars Scholarships *868*

Miljenko "Mike" Grgich's American Dream Scholarship *231*

Miller Electric International World Skills Competition Scholarship *278*

Miller Electric Mfg. Co. Scholarship *278*

Millie Brother Scholarship for Children of Deaf Adults *581*

Millie Gonzalez Memorial Scholarship *633*

Millie Snyder Scholarship *760*

Milton Fisher Scholarship for Innovation and Creativity *791*

MindSumo 15-Minute Scholarship *603*

Minnesota AFL-CIO Scholarships *548*

Minnesota GI Bill Program *774*

Minnesota Indian Scholarship *690*

Minnesota Legionnaires Insurance Trust Scholarship *534*

Minnesota Masonic Charities Heritage Scholarship *868*

Minnesota Masonic Charities Legacy Scholarship *774*

Minnesota Masonic Charities Signature Scholarship *604*

Minnesota Masonic Charities Undergraduate Scholarship *604*

Minnesota Space Grant Consortium Scholarship Program *142*

Minnesota State Grant Program *774*

Minnesota State Veterans' Dependents Assistance Program *775*

Minnesota Student Aid Scholarship *704*

Minorities in Government Finance Scholarship *78*

Minority Affairs Committee Award for Outstanding Scholastic Achievement *174*

Minority Scholarship Awards for College Students *174*

Minority Scholarship Awards for Incoming College Freshmen *174*

Minority Scholarship Program *155*

Minority Student Summer Scholarship *118*

Minority Teacher Incentive Grant Program *251*

Minority Teachers of Illinois Scholarship Program *253*

Minority Undergraduate Retention Grant-Wisconsin *708*

Mirabella Employee-YES Project Scholarship *874*

Miriam Schaefer Scholarship *415*

Miss America Community Service Scholarships *592*

Miss America Organization Competition Scholarships *822*

Miss America Scholar Award *822*

Mississippi Association of Broadcasters Scholarship *382*

Mississippi Eminent Scholars Grant *775*

Mississippi Nurses' Association Foundation Scholarship *455*

Mississippi Press Association Education Foundation Scholarship *382*

Mississippi Resident Tuition Assistance Grant *775*

Mississippi Scholarship *111*

Missouri Broadcasters Association Scholarship *524*

Missouri Conservation Agents Association Scholarship *776*

Missouri Funeral Directors Association Scholarships *340*

Missouri Higher Education Academic Scholarship (Bright Flight) *776*

Missouri Insurance Education Foundation Scholarship *375*

Mitchell S. Sexner & Associates LLC Scholarship *616*

MJSA Education Foundation Jewelry Scholarship *131*

MOAA American Patriot Scholarship *868*

Top 10% Scholarship Program *799*
Top Ten List Scholarship *889*
Tortoise Young Entrepreneurs Scholarship *801*
Touchmark Foundation Nursing Scholarship *461*
Touchstone Energy All "A" Classic Scholarship *768*
Tourism and Heritage Student Paper Competition *617*
Toward EXcellence, Access, and Success (TEXAS) Grant *800*
Township Officials of Illinois Scholarship Program *801*
TPA Scholarship Trust for the Hearing Impaired *638*
Traditional Marching Band Extravaganza Scholarship Award *429*
Tragos Write Your Own Law Scholarship *600*
Training Support for Youth with Disabilities *609*
Transit Hall of Fame Scholarship Award Program *191*
Transportation Clubs International Charlotte Woods Scholarship *518*
Transportation Clubs International Fred A. Hooper Memorial Scholarship *282*
Transportation Clubs International Ginger and Fred Deines Canada Scholarship *518*
Transportation Clubs International Ginger and Fred Deines Mexico Scholarship *518*
Transtutors Scholarship 2015-16 *85*
Traub-Dicker Rainbow Scholarship *618*
Treadwell/Pringle Scholarships *647*
Tribal Business Management Program (TBM) *74*
Tribal Priority Award *682*
Trimmer Education Foundation Scholarships for Construction Management *223*
Tri-State Surveying and Photogrammetry Kris M. Kunze Memorial Scholarship *161*
TruckerToTrucker.com College Scholarship *622*
Trucker to Trucker Scholarship *515*
Truckload Carriers Association Scholarship Fund *168*
Truman D. Picard Scholarship *93*
Tuition Aid Grant *779*
Tuition and Fee Remission for Children and Spouses of National Guard Members *643*
Tuition Equalization Grant (TEG) Program *886*
Tuition Exchange Scholarships *622*
Tuition Incentive Program *774*
Tuition Reduction for Non-Resident Nursing Students *455*
Tuition Waiver for Foster Care Recipients *771*
Tuition Waiver Programs *588*
Turf and Ornamental Communicators Association Scholarship Program *102*
Turner Construction Scholarship *188*
Tuskegee Airmen Scholarship *147*
Twenty-first Century Scholars Gear Up Summer Scholarship *797*
Twin Towers Orphan Fund *887*
Two Ten Footwear Foundation Scholarship *622*
Two Ten Foundation Footwear Design Scholarship *801*
UCB Family Epilepsy Scholarship *638*
Udall Undergraduate Scholarship *868*
UDT-SEAL Scholarship *665*
UL Scholarship *469*
UltrasoundTechnicianSchools.com Scholarship *356*
UNCF/Alliance Data Scholarship and Internship Program *91*
UNCF/Anthem Corporate Scholars Program *170*

UNCF/Carnival Corporate Scholars Program *170*
UNCF General Scholarship Program *705*
UNCF Honda Manufacturing of Indiana Scholarship *706*
UNCF/Koch Scholars Program for Undergraduates *87*
UNCF/Nissan Scholarship *170*
UNCF Northrop Grumman Scholarship *220*
UNCF STEM Scholars Program *159*
UNCF/Travelers Insurance Scholarship *170*
Undergraduate Achievement Awards *558*
Undergraduate Diversity Student Awards *159*
Undergraduate Marketing Education Merit Scholarships *162*
Undergraduate Research Award Program *143*
Undergraduate Scholarship Award *330*
Undergraduate STEM Research Scholarships *114*
Undergraduate Student Paper Award *816*
Undergraduate Texas Broadcast Education Foundation Scholarship *211*
Undine Sams and Friends Scholarship Fund *451*
Union National Life Insurance Company Scholarship (Kemper) *706*
Union Plus Credit Card Scholarship Program *528*
Union Plus Education Foundation Scholarship Program *564*
Union Plus Scholarship Program *549*
United Daughters of the Confederacy Undergraduate Scholarships *565*
United Health Foundation Diverse Scholars Initiative *152*
United Insurance Company Scholarship (Kemper) *706*
United Italian American Inc. Scholarship *792*
United Nations Association of Connecticut Scholarship *133*
United Parcel Service Diversity Scholarship Program *470*
United South and Eastern Tribes Scholarship Fund *706*
United States-Indonesia Society Travel Grants *890*
United States Senate Youth Program *837*
United States Society on Dams Scholarship Award *199*
United States Submarine Veterans Inc. National Scholarship Program *566*
Universities Space Research Association Scholarship Award Program *116*
University Club of Portland Scholarship *876*
University Film and Video Association Carole Fielding Student Grants *327*
University of North Carolina Need-Based Grant *783*
Unmet NEED Grant Program *692*
Unpakt College Scholarship *890*
UPS Hallmark Scholarships *707*
UPS Scholarship for Female Students *301*
UPS Scholarship for Minority Students *301*
UPS Scholarship Program *856*
The Urban Scholarships Fund *622*
URS Safety Scholarship *470*
USAA Scholarship *642*
USA Funds Scholarship *706*
U.S. Army ROTC Four-Year College Scholarship *645*
U.S. Army ROTC Four-Year Historically Black College/University Scholarship *645*

U.S. Army ROTC Four-Year Nursing Scholarship *449*
U.S. Army ROTC Guaranteed Reserve Forces Duty (GRFD), (ARNG/USAR) and Dedicated ARNG Scholarships *647*
U.S. Army ROTC Military Junior College (MJC) Scholarship *646*
U.S. Bank Internet Scholarship Program *890*
U.S. Bates Scholarship Program *546*
USBC Alberta E. Crowe Star of Tomorrow Award *822*
USBC Annual Zeb Scholarship *593*
USBC Chuck Hall Star of Tomorrow Scholarship *823*
USBC Earl Anthony Memorial Scholarship *545*
USBC Youth Ambassador of the Year (M/F) *823*
USDA/1994 Tribal Scholars Program *102*
USDA/Public Service Leader Scholars (PSLS) *706*
U.S. News Path to College Scholarship Program *707*
U. S. Public Health Service-Health Resources and Services Administration, Bureau of Health Professions Scholarships for Disadvantaged Students *239*
Usrey Family Scholarship *315*
U.S. Scholarship Program *603*
Utah Chapter ASSE Scholarship *470*
Utility Workers Union of America Scholarship Awards Program *566*
UTUIA Scholarship *625*
VADM Samuel L. Gravely, Jr., USN(Ret.) Memorial Scholarship *111*
Valene Smith Prize *883*
Valley Press Club Scholarships, The Republican Scholarship, Channel 22 Scholarship *213*
ValuePenguin Scholarship *626*
Vann Kennedy Texas Broadcast Education Foundation Scholarship *211*
Varian Radiation Therapy Advancement Scholarship *349*
VASWCD Educational Foundation Inc. Scholarship Awards Program *437*
Vectorworks Design Scholarship *124*
The Vegetarian Resource Group Scholarship *891*
Vera Yip Memorial Scholarship *624*
Vermont Incentive Grants *802*
Vermont-NEA/Maida F. Townsend Scholarship *260*
Vermont Non-Degree Student Grant Program *803*
Vermont Part-Time Student Grants *803*
Vermont Space Grant Consortium *96*
Vertical Flight Foundation Scholarship *134*
Veterans' Children Educational Opportunities *657*
Veterans Dependents Educational Benefits-Maine *658*
Veterans Education (VetEd) Reimbursement Grant *639*
Veterans of Enduring Freedom (Afghanistan) and Iraqi Freedom Scholarship *214*
Veterans of the Afghanistan and Iraq Conflicts Scholarship Program *658*
Veterans Tuition Credit Program-New Jersey *659*
Veterans United Foundation Scholarship *662*
Victor Poor, W5SMM, Memorial Scholarship *266*
Victor Technologies Award for Excellence in Cutting and Welding *279*

Sponsor

101st Airborne Division Association *233, 346, 482, 493, 509, 839*

1-800-HANSONS *572, 666, 709, 807*

1800Wheelchair.com *839*

180 Medical, Inc. *724*

1 on 1 Lessons *839*

280 Group *160, 245, 406*

37th Division Veterans Association *839*

4MyCash.com, LLC *572, 666, 709*

The 5 Strong Scholarship Foundation, Inc. *666, 725*

A-1 Auto Transport, Inc. *572, 666, 709, 807*

A1 Garage Door Service *840*

AACC International *330*

AACE International *118, 134, 160, 172, 191, 221, 262, 275, 289, 417*

Abbie Sargent Memorial Scholarship Inc. *91, 96, 105, 317, 362, 363*

AbbVie Inc. *573, 666, 709, 725, 807*

Academy Foundation of the Academy of Motion Picture Arts and Sciences *325*

Academy of Nutrition and Dietetics *330*

ACL/NJCL National Latin Exam *200, 338*

Activia Training *840*

Actors Theatre of Louisville *807*

The Actuarial Foundation *160, 245, 327, 375, 413, 506*

Acuity Training Limited *840*

ADC Research Institute *200, 326, 379, 522*

Adelante! U.S. Education Leadership Fund *160, 498*

AEG Foundation *240, 289, 498*

AHIMA Foundation *357*

AHS International—The Vertical Flight Technical Society *134, 262, 275, 289, 417*

AIA New Jersey Scholarship Foundation, Inc. *118*

Air & Waste Management Association, Allegheny Mountain Section *317, 424*

Air & Waste Management Association–Coastal Plains Chapter *318, 482*

Aircraft Electronics Association Educational Foundation *134, 512*

Air Force Aid Society *640, 642*

Air Force Reserve Officer Training Corps *444, 640, 642, 666*

Air Line Pilots Association, International *528*

Airmen Memorial Foundation/Air Force Sergeants Association *640, 642*

Airport Minority Advisory Council Educational and Scholarship Program *136*

Air Traffic Control Association Inc. *136, 573, 666, 709, 807*

AIST Foundation *153, 172, 191, 214, 262, 275, 289, 318, 373, 408, 417, 482*

Alabama Broadcasters Association *522*

Alabama Commission on Higher Education *642, 647, 725*

Alabama Department of Veterans Affairs *725*

Alabama Funeral Directors Association Inc. *340*

Alabama Golf Course Superintendents Association *96, 363*

Alabama Society of Certified Public Accountants *73*

Alaska Commission on Postsecondary Education *725*

Alaska Geological Society Inc. *240*

Alaskan Aviation Safety Foundation *136*

Alaska Society of Certified Public Accountants *73*

Alberta Agriculture Food and Rural Development 4-H Branch *528, 726*

Alberta Heritage Scholarship Fund *96, 153, 233, 247, 291, 338, 344, 346, 392, 444, 478, 503, 504, 509, 512, 522, 667, 726, 807*

Albuquerque Community Foundation *727*

AlertOne Services LLC *573, 669, 710, 807*

Alert Scholarship *727, 807*

The Alexander Foundation *727, 808*

Alexander Graham Bell Association for the Deaf and Hard of Hearing *628*

Alfred G. and Elma M. Milotte Scholarship Fund *840*

AlgaeCal Inc. *574, 669, 710, 808*

Alice L. Haltom Educational Fund *160, 214, 344, 357, 397*

Alliance for Young Artists and Writers Inc. *127, 399, 574, 669, 710, 808*

All-Ink.com Printer Supplies Online *840*

AllTheRooms *574, 669, 710, 808*

Alpena Regional Medical Center *346*

Alpha Kappa Alpha *840*

Alpha Lambda Delta *841*

Alpha Mu Gamma, The National Collegiate Foreign Language Society *338*

Alpha Omega Council of New England *201, 379*

ALS Association *728*

Amarillo Area Foundation *444*

Ambrosia Treatment Center *841*

American Academy of Oral and Maxillofacial Radiology *234*

American Alliance for Health, Physical Education, Recreation and Dance *496, 505*

American Alpine Club *153, 240, 318, 341, 372, 408, 433, 437, 482, 491, 496*

American Association of Airport Executives-Southwest Chapter *136*

American Association of Blood Banks-SBB Scholarship Awards *153*

American Association of Colleges of Nursing *841*

American Association of Family & Consumer Services *362*

American Association of Geographers *341*

American Association of Physics Teachers *247, 483*

American Association of Teachers of Japanese Bridging Clearinghouse for Study Abroad in Japan *574, 669, 710, 808*

American Baptist Financial Aid Program *710*

American Board of Funeral Service Education *340*

American Bullion, Inc. *841*

American Bus Association *516, 519*

American Chemical Society *172, 318, 408, 437, 474, 512*

American Chemical Society, Rubber Division *109, 137, 173, 263, 272, 275, 291, 408, 417, 441*

American Classical League/National Junior Classical League *200, 338, 370*

American College of Musicians/National Guild of Piano Teachers *427*

American Congress on Surveying and Mapping *161, 507*

American Copy Editors Society *842*

American Council of Engineering Companies of Pennsylvania (ACEC/PA) *173, 191, 221, 263, 272, 275, 291, 318, 403, 408, 417, 508, 517*

American Council of the Blind *574, 628, 669, 710, 808*

American Criminal Justice Association-Lambda Alpha Epsilon *224, 392, 501*

American Dental Assistants Association *234*

American Dental Association (ADA) Foundation *234*

American Dental Hygienists' Association (ADHA) Institute For Oral Health *235*

American Federation of State, County, and Municipal Employees *103, 108, 359, 488, 490, 501, 503, 527, 528*

American Federation of Teachers *247, 529, 574*

American Fire Sprinkler Association *842*

American Foundation for the Blind *214, 247, 263, 291, 399, 427, 437, 483, 510, 628*

American Foundation for Translation and Interpretation *338*

American Ground Water Trust *240, 372, 433*

American Hotel and Lodging Educational Foundation *227, 334, 367, 496, 519*

American Indian Education Foundation *669*

American Indian Graduate Center *669, 808*

American Indian Science and Engineering Society *109, 153, 161, 173, 191, 214, 221, 236, 241, 264, 272, 275, 291, 314, 315, 318, 330, 341, 347, 358, 363, 372, 400, 403, 408, 413, 418, 424, 433, 437, 441, 442, 445, 463, 471, 472, 473, 474, 475, 478, 483, 493, 498, 501, 505, 506, 508, 510, 517*

American Institute for Foreign Study *670, 808*

American Institute of Aeronautics and Astronautics *110, 137, 264, 275, 291, 408, 418, 483, 498*

American Institute of Architects *118*

American Institute of Certified Public Accountants *73*

American Institute of Chemical Engineers *173, 318, 373*

American Institute of Polish Culture Inc. *127, 201, 248, 338, 379, 492*

American Institute of Wine and Food-Pacific Northwest Chapter *331, 335, 368*

American Jewish League for Israel *809*

American Legion Auxiliary Department of Alabama *650, 728*

American Legion Auxiliary Department of Arizona *347, 445, 488, 493, 503, 504*

American Legion Auxiliary Department of California *445, 650, 728*

American Legion Auxiliary Department of Colorado *133, 236, 344, 347, 357, 445, 472, 473, 474, 478, 510, 842*

American Legion Auxiliary Department of Connecticut *529, 650, 728*

American Legion Auxiliary Department of Idaho *445*

American Legion Auxiliary Department of Iowa *248, 445, 651, 728*

American Legion Auxiliary Department of Kentucky *645, 651, 728*

American Legion Auxiliary Department of Maine *347, 446, 651, 728*

American Legion Auxiliary Department of Massachusetts *575, 651, 728*

American Legion Auxiliary Department of Michigan *347, 446, 510, 651, 728*

American Legion Auxiliary Department of Minnesota *347, 652, 728*

American Legion Auxiliary Department of Missouri *446, 529, 652, 729*

American Legion Auxiliary Department of Nebraska *530, 652, 729*

American Legion Auxiliary Department of North Dakota *446, 575, 652, 729*

American Legion Auxiliary Department of Ohio *446, 653, 729*

American Legion Auxiliary Department of Oregon *446, 530, 729*

American Legion Auxiliary Department of Pennsylvania *447, 575, 729*

American Legion Auxiliary Department of South Dakota *530, 653, 730*

American Legion Auxiliary Department of Texas *348, 653, 730*

American Legion Auxiliary Department of Utah *530, 653, 730*

American Legion Auxiliary Department of Wisconsin *447, 531, 575, 653, 670, 710, 730, 809*

American Legion Auxiliary National Headquarters *532, 575, 653, 670, 710, 809*

American Legion Baseball *809*

American Legion Department of Arizona *730, 809*

American Legion Department of Arkansas *730, 809*

American Legion Department of Hawaii *730*

American Legion Department of Idaho *532, 654, 731*

American Legion Department of Illinois *532, 731, 809*

American Legion Department of Indiana *533, 731, 809*

American Legion Department of Iowa *533, 731, 810*

American Legion Department of Kansas *427, 447, 477, 533, 732, 810*

American Legion Department of Maine *534, 654, 732*

American Legion Department of Maryland *413, 483, 654, 732, 842*

American Legion Department of Michigan *654, 733, 810*

The American Legion, Department of Minnesota *534, 655, 733, 810*

American Legion Department of Missouri *248, 447, 534, 655, 733*

American Legion Department of Montana *733, 810*

American Legion Department of Nebraska *535, 733, 810*

American Legion Department of New York *734, 810*

American Legion Department of North Carolina *734, 810*

American Legion Department of North Dakota *96, 236, 331, 344, 348, 479, 734, 810*

American Legion Department of Ohio *535, 655*

American Legion Department of Oregon *734, 810*

American Legion Department of Pennsylvania *512, 535, 735, 810*

American Legion Department of South Dakota *735, 810*

American Legion Department of Tennessee *498, 535, 735, 810*

American Legion Department of Texas *735, 811*

American Legion Department of Vermont *535, 576, 735, 811*

American Legion Department of Virginia *736*

American Legion Department of Washington *536, 670, 710, 736, 811*

American Legion Department of West Virginia *536, 655, 736, 811*

American Mathematical Association of Two Year Colleges *414*

American Meteorological Society *424*

American Military Retirees Association *842*

American Montessori Society *248*

American Museum of Natural History *811*

American National Cattle Women Inc. *406*

American Nuclear Society *272, 442*

American Occupational Therapy Foundation Inc. *348, 510*

American Oil Chemists' Society *97, 175, 331*

American Optometric Foundation *473*

American Physical Therapy Association *249, 348, 510*

American Physiological Society *105, 153, 318, 348, 400, 437, 441, 505*

American Planning Association *526*

American Postal Workers Union *536, 576*

American Public Power Association *176, 191, 221, 264, 272, 276, 291, 318, 418, 433*

American Public Transportation Foundation *161, 191, 264, 276, 291, 418, 517*

American Quarter Horse Foundation (AQHF) *105, 201, 379, 480, 510, 536, 576, 736, 811*

American Railway Engineering and Maintenance of Way Association *191, 214, 221, 264, 276, 291, 418*

American Respiratory Care Foundation *348, 510*

American Road & Transportation Builders Association-Transportation Development Foundation (ARTBA-TDF) *576*

American Savings Foundation *576, 670, 710, 737, 811*

American-Scandinavian Foundation *399*

American School of Classical Studies at Athens *108, 116, 118, 126, 127, 200, 359, 370, 426, 480, 497, 843*

American Sephardi Foundation *710*

American Sheep Industry Association *325*

American Society for Engineering Education *110, 276, 291, 414, 483*

American Society for Enology and Viticulture *97, 176, 331, 363*

American Society for Information Science and Technology *214, 397*

American Society for Nondestructive Testing *276, 843*

American Society of Agricultural and Biological Engineers *97, 154, 291*

American Society of Agronomy, Crop Science Society of America, Soil Science Society of America *97, 241, 314, 318, 433, 437*

American Society of Certified Engineering Technicians *176, 192, 221, 239, 264, 272, 276, 292, 328, 389, 403, 409, 418, 508, 513, 517*

American Society of Civil Engineers *192*

American Society of Civil Engineers-Maine Section *193*

American Society of Criminology *225, 391, 392, 501*

American Society of Heating, Refrigerating, and Air Conditioning Engineers, Inc. *119, 176, 221, 264, 272, 276, 292, 358, 418, 475, 513*

American Society of Ichthyologists and Herpetologists *154*

American Society of Interior Designers (ASID) Education Foundation Inc. *376*

American Society of Mechanical Engineers Auxiliary Inc. *292, 418, 843*

American Society of Naval Engineers *110, 137, 193, 265, 272, 293, 403, 409, 419, 443, 483*

American Society of Plumbing Engineers *293, 373*

American Society of Safety Engineers (ASSE) Foundation *463*

American Society of Travel Agents (ASTA) Foundation *520*

American Society of Women Accountants *73*

American String Teachers Association *811*

American Traffic Safety Services Foundation *576*

American Water Resources Association *433*

American Water Ski Educational Foundation *539*

American Welding Society *161, 193, 249, 277, 293, 409, 419, 513, 843*

American Wholesale Marketers Association *161*

AMVETS Auxiliary *539, 655*

Anchor Scholarship Foundation *664*

Andy Green, Attorney at Law, P.C. *844*

Ankin Law *576, 670, 711, 811*

Anthony Munoz Foundation *577, 670, 711, 737, 811*

Any Intern *577, 670, 711, 811*

Appalachian Studies Association *844*

Appaloosa Horse Club-Appaloosa Youth Program *105, 539, 811*

ApplyKit *844*

Appraisal Institute Education Trust *494*

Arab American Scholarship Foundation *201, 488*

Archaeological Institute of America *116*

Architectural Precast Association *119*

ARC of Washington Trust Fund *504*

Arctic Institute of North America *249, 318, 434, 437*

Arizona Business Education Association *249*

Arizona Commission for Postsecondary Education *737*

Arizona Hydrological Society *241, 372, 434, 443, 498*

Arizona Nursery Association *363*

Arizona Private School Association *737*

Arizona Professional Chapter of AISES *294, 349, 434, 483*

Arkansas Department of Higher Education *655, 737*

Arkansas Single Parent Scholarship Fund *577, 670, 711, 738, 812*

Arkansas Student Loan Authority *738*

Armed Forces Communications and Electronics Association, Educational Foundation *110, 137, 154, 214, 241, 249, 265, 280, 294, 409, 414, 426, 437, 483, 495, 506*

Armenian Relief Society of Eastern USA Inc.-Regional Office *670, 711, 812*

Armenian Students Association of America Inc. *671*

Army Emergency Relief (AER) *844*

Army Officers' Wives Club of Greater Washington Area *645*

ARRL Foundation Inc. *111, 154, 162, 177, 193, 201, 215, 221, 236, 249, 265, 272, 280, 294, 318, 349, 363, 378, 379, 403, 410, 414, 419, 437, 443, 447, 472, 473, 474, 475, 483, 498, 510, 522, 540, 577, 628, 738, 812*

Asian American Journalists Association *202, 379*

Academic Fields/Career Goals

Alabama Golf Course Superintendent's
  Association's Donnie Arthur Memorial
  Scholarship 96
Alberta Barley Commission-Eugene Boyko
  Memorial Scholarship 96
American Society for Enology and Viticulture
  Scholarships 97
AOCS Biotechnology Student
  Excellence Award 97
Calcot-Seitz Scholarship 98
CHS Foundation High School Scholarships 91
CHS Foundation Two-Year College
  Scholarships 92
CHS Foundation University Scholarships 92
CME Beef Industry Scholarship 93
Donald A. Williams Scholarship Soil Conservation
  Scholarship 95
Edward R. Hall Scholarship 95
Elizabeth and Sherman Asche Memorial
  Scholarship Fund 98
Elizabeth Gardner Norweb Summer
  Environmental Studies Scholarship 98
Evan Turek Memorial Scholarship 98
Evan Turek Memorial Scholarship and
  Internship 98
Howard F. DeNise Scholarship 101
J. Fielding Reed Scholarship 97
Joseph Fitcher Scholarship Contest 101
Kildee Scholarships 100
Klussendorf / McKown Scholarship 100
Kraft Heinz Research Scholarship 99
Les Dames d'Escoffier International, Colorado
  Chapter Scholarship 93
Maine Rural Rehabilitation Fund Scholarship
  Program 93
Marshall E. McCullough-National Dairy Shrine
  Scholarships 100
Mary Macey Scholarship 103
Masonic Range Science Scholarship 94
MO Show-Me Chapter SWCS Scholarship 95
National Council of State Garden Clubs Inc.
  Scholarship 99
National Dairy Shrine/Dairy Marketing Inc. Milk
  Marketing Scholarships 100
National Dairy Shrine/Iager Dairy
  Scholarship 100
National Dairy Shrine/Maurice E. Core
  Scholarship 93
National Garden Clubs Inc.
  Scholarship Program 100
National JACL Headquarters Scholarship 99
National Poultry and Food Distributors
  Association Scholarship Foundation 94
NDS Student Recognition Award 94
New York State Association of Agricultural Fairs
  and New York State Showpeople's Association
  Annual Scholarship 94
O. Nesheim Memorial Scholarship 96
Oregon Horticulture Society Scholarship 101
Oregon Sheep Growers Association Memorial
  Scholarship 94
Risk Management Association Foundation
  Scholarship Program 83
Russell W. Myers Scholarship 99
Scholarship for Students Pursuing a Business or
  STEM Degree 84
Sigma Xi Grants-In-Aid of Research 101
South Dakota Board of Regents Bjugstad
  Scholarship 95
South Florida Fair Agricultural College
  Scholarship 102
Truman D. Picard Scholarship 93
Turf and Ornamental Communicators Association
  Scholarship Program 102
USDA/1994 Tribal Scholars Program 102

Virgil Thompson Memorial Scholarship
  Contest 94
Walter J. Clore Scholarship 103
William Helms Scholarship Program
  (WHSP) 103
William J. Adams, Jr. and
  Marijane E. Adams Scholarship 97

American Studies
AFIO Undergraduate and Graduate
  Scholarships 103
AFSCME/UNCF Union Scholars Program 103
B. Phinizy Spalding, Hubert B. Owens, and The
  National Society of the Colonial Dames of
  America in the State of Georgia Academic
  Scholarships 104
Lynn E. May Jr. Study Grant 104
Moody Research Grants 104
Teaching Assistant Program in France 104

Animal/Veterinary Sciences
$1,500 STEM Scholarship 106
Abbie Sargent Memorial Scholarship 91
AvaCare Medical Scholarship 105
David S. Bruce Awards for Excellence in
  Undergraduate Research 105
Edward R. Hall Scholarship 95
Elizabeth and Sherman Asche Memorial
  Scholarship Fund 98
George A. Hall/Harold F. Mayfield Award 108
Hispanic Engineer National Achievement Awards
  Corporation Scholarship Program 106
Jay Pumphrey Animal Sciences Scholarship 105
Kildee Scholarships 100
Klussendorf / McKown Scholarship 100
Lew and JoAnn Eklund Educational
  Scholarship 105
Maine Rural Rehabilitation Fund Scholarship
  Program 93
Masonic Range Science Scholarship 94
Medical Scrubs Collection Scholarship 106
National Poultry and Food Distributors
  Association Scholarship Foundation 94
NDS Student Recognition Award 94
Oregon Sheep Growers Association Memorial
  Scholarship 94
Paul A. Stewart Awards 108
Platinum Educational Group Scholarships Program
  for EMS, Nursing, and Allied Health 107
Saul T. Wilson, Jr., Scholarship Program
  (STWJS) 107
Scholarship for Students Pursuing a Business or
  STEM Degree 84
Sigma Xi Grants-In-Aid of Research 101
StraightForward Media Vocational-Technical
  School Scholarship 107
Western Veterinary Scholarship 107

Anthropology
$1,500 STEM Scholarship 106
AFSCME/UNCF Union Scholars Program 103
ASCSA Summer Sessions Scholarships 108
ISF National Scholarship 108
Medical Scrubs Collection Scholarship 106
Sigma Xi Grants-In-Aid of Research 101
The Society for the Scientific Study of Sexuality
  Student Research Grant 109
Student Design Competition 108

Applied Sciences
$1,500 STEM Scholarship 106
1B USD Worldwide Venture Capital 116
AIAA Foundation Undergraduate
  Scholarships 110
American Chemical Society, Rubber Division
  Undergraduate Scholarship 109

American Society of Naval Engineers
  Scholarship 110
Andy Aitkenhead Scholarship 115
Association of California Water Agencies
  Scholarships 112
Astronaut Scholarship Foundation 112
A.T. Anderson Memorial
  Scholarship Program 109
AWG Undergraduate Excellence in
  Paleontology Award 112
Barry M. Goldwater Scholarship and Excellence in
  Education Program 112
BHW Women in STEM Scholarship 74
Blue Cross Blue Shield of Illinois and Blue Cross
  Blue Shield of Texas Scholarship 115
Carrol C. Hall Memorial Scholarship 115
Charles N. Fisher Memorial Scholarship 111
Clair A. Hill Scholarship 112
Community College STEM Scholarships 114
Davidson Fellows Scholarship Program 113
Grants for Disabled Graduate
  Students in the Sciences 113
H.H. Dow Memorial Student Achievement Award
  of the Industrial Electrolysis and
  Electrochemical Engineering Division of the
  Electrochemical Society Inc. 113
Indian Health Service Health Professions Pre-
  graduate Scholarships 114
Leatrice Gregory Pendray Scholarship 110
Medical Scrubs Collection Scholarship 106
Mississippi Scholarship 111
National Space Grant College and Fellowship
  Program 114
Paul and Helen L. Grauer Scholarship 111
Procter & Gamble STEM Scholarship 116
SAPA Scholarship and Excellence in Education
  Program 115
Scholarship for Students Pursuing a Business or
  STEM Degree 84
Science, Mathematics, and Research for
  Transformation Defense Scholarship for
  Service Program 110
Sehar Saleha Ahmad and Abrahim Ekramullah
  Zafar Foundation Scholarship 115
SPIE Educational Scholarships in Optical Science
  and Engineering 114
STEM Majors Scholarships for Undergraduate
  Students 110
STEM Teachers Scholarship 111
Student Research Awards of the Battery Division
  of the Electrochemical Society Inc. 113
Undergraduate STEM Research
  Scholarships 114
Universities Space Research Association
  Scholarship Award Program 116
VADM Samuel L. Gravely, Jr., USN(Ret.)
  Memorial Scholarship 111
Vermont Space Grant Consortium 96
W1FDR Scholarship 112

Archaeology
ASCSA Summer Sessions Scholarships 108
AWG Maria Luisa Crawford Field Camp
  Scholarship 117
AWG Salt Lake Chapter (SLC) Research
  Scholarship 117
AWG Undergraduate Excellence in Paleontology
  Award 112
BHW Women in STEM Scholarship 74
Jane C. Waldbaum Archaeological Field School
  Scholarship 116
Janet Cullen Tanaka Geosciences Undergraduate
  Scholarship 117
Medical Scrubs Collection Scholarship 106
Minority Student Summer Scholarship 118

Osage Chapter Undergraduate Service
Scholarship *117*
Scholarship for Students Pursuing a Business or
STEM Degree *84*

Architecture

$1,500 STEM Scholarship *106*
AACE International Competitive
Scholarship *118*
AIA/F Diversity Advancement Scholarship *118*
AIA New Jersey Scholarship Program *118*
AIA West Virginia Scholarship *124*
Alan Lucas Memorial Educational
Scholarship *122*
ASCSA Summer Sessions Scholarships *108*
ASHRAE Region IV Benny Bootle
Scholarship *119*
Association for Women in Architecture
Foundation Scholarship *119*
BHW Women in STEM Scholarship *74*
CBC Spouses Visual Arts Scholarship *120*
Center for Architecture Design Scholarship *119*
Center for Architecture, Douglas Haskell Award
for Student Journals *119*
Center for Architecture, Women's Auxiliary
Eleanor Allwork Scholarship *120*
Dallas Center for Architecture Foundation—HKS/
John Humphries Scholarship *120*
Dimitri J. Ververelli Memorial Scholarship for
Architecture and/or Engineering *121*
FEFPA Assistantship *121*
GCA Award in Desert Studies *121*
Green/Sustainable Scholarship *121*
Hispanic Engineer National Achievement Awards
Corporation Scholarship Program *106*
Home Builders Foundation Jim Irvine Statewide
Scholarship *123*
IFMA Foundation Scholarships *122*
J. Neel Reid Prize *121*
MRCA Foundation Scholarship Program *122*
NAWIC Undergraduate Scholarships *122*
Norton E. Salk Scholarship *123*
Odebrecht Award for Sustainable
Development *119*
Plan New Hampshire Scholarship and
Program *123*
QualityBath.com Scholarship Program *123*
Robert W. Thunen Memorial Scholarships *122*
Scholarship for Students Pursuing a
Business or STEM Degree *84*
Southern Oregon Chapter of the American Institute
of Architects Scholarship *123*
Support Creativity Scholarship *124*
Tom Cory Memorial Scholarships *119*
Vectorworks Design Scholarship *124*
The Walter A. Hunt, Jr. Scholarship *120*
Whitley Place Scholarship *120*
YouthForce 2020 Scholarship Program *124*

Area/Ethnic Studies

Adele Filene Student Presenter Grant *125*
Canadian Institute of Ukrainian Studies Research
Grants *124*
King Olav V Norwegian-American
Heritage Fund *126*
Leo J. Krysa Undergraduate Scholarship *125*
National Italian American Foundation Category II
Scholarship *125*
National Security Education Program (NSEP)
David L. Boren Undergraduate
Scholarships *126*
Stella Blum Student Research Grant *125*
StraightForward Media Liberal Arts
Scholarship *126*
Year Abroad Program in Poland *125*

Art History

Adele Filene Student Presenter Grant *125*
ASCSA Summer Sessions Scholarships *108*
Catherine W. Pierce Scholarship *127*
Mary Olive Eddy Jones Art Scholarship *126*
QualityBath.com Scholarship Program *123*
Stella Blum Student Research Grant *125*
StraightForward Media Liberal Arts
Scholarship *126*
Support Creativity Scholarship *124*
Teaching Assistant Program in France *104*

Arts

Adele Filene Student Presenter Grant *125*
Arts Council of Greater Grand Rapids Minority
Scholarship *128*
ASCSA Summer Sessions Scholarships *108*
BMI Student Composer Awards *127*
Catherine W. Pierce Scholarship *127*
CBC Spouses Visual Arts Scholarship *120*
Douglas W. Mummert Scholarship *129*
Florida PTA/PTSA Fine Arts Scholarship *128*
Harriet Irsay Scholarship Grant *127*
Jack J. Isgur Foundation Scholarship *129*
James M. and Virginia M. Smyth
Scholarship *128*
Kerdragon Scholarship *130*
Kirchhoff Family Fine Arts Scholarship *130*
Marion Barr Stanfield Art Scholarship *131*
Mary Olive Eddy Jones Art Scholarship *126*
Minority Student Summer Scholarship *118*
MJSA Education Foundation Jewelry
Scholarship *131*
Moss Endowed Scholarship *130*
NOA Vocal Competition/Legacy Award
Program *129*
Office Supply Scholarship *128*
OLM Malala Yousafzai Scholarship
2017-2018 *129*
Ossie Davis Endowment Scholarship
Program *132*
Patricia W. Edwards Memorial Art
Scholarship *131*
Pauly D'Orlando Memorial Art Scholarship *132*
Polish Arts Club of Buffalo Scholarship
Foundation Trust *130*
QualityBath.com Scholarship Program *123*
Rhythm Nation/Janet Jackson Scholarship *132*
Ruth Clark Furniture Design Scholarship *129*
Scholastic Art and Writing Awards-Writing
Section Scholarship *127*
SEIU Moe Foner Scholarship Program for Visual
and Performing Arts *131*
Stanfield and D'Orlando Art Scholarship *132*
Stella Blum Student Research Grant *125*
StraightForward Media Art School
Scholarship *131*
Support Creativity Scholarship *124*
Technical Training Fund Scholarship *130*
Teletoon Animation Scholarship *131*
Vectorworks Design Scholarship *124*
Visual and Performing Arts
Achievement Awards *128*
Warner Bros. Animation/Hanna-Barbera
Honorship *132*
Women's Jewelry Association Student
Scholarship *132*
Worldstudio AIGA Scholarships *133*

Asian Studies

Japan Studies Scholarship *133*
United Nations Association of Connecticut
Scholarship *133*

Audiology

AMBUCS Scholars-Scholarships for
Therapists *134*
American Legion Auxiliary Department of
Colorado Past Presidents' Parley Health Care
Professional ScholarshipNurses
Scholarship *133*
Caroline Kark Award *134*
Hispanic Engineer National Achievement Awards
Corporation Scholarship Program *106*
Medical Scrubs Collection Scholarship *106*
Scholarship for Students Pursuing a Business or
STEM Degree *84*

Aviation/Aerospace

$1,500 STEM Scholarship *106*
1B USD Worldwide Venture Capital *116*
AACE International Competitive
Scholarship *118*
ADMA Scholarship *137*
AFIO Undergraduate and Graduate
Scholarships *103*
AIAA Foundation Undergraduate
Scholarships *110*
Airbus Leadership Grant *149*
Alaskan Aviation Safety Foundation Memorial
Scholarship Fund *136*
Al Conklin and Bill de Decker Business Aviation
Management Scholarship *145*
AMACESP Student Scholarships *136*
American Chemical Society, Rubber Division
Undergraduate Scholarship *109*
American Society of Naval Engineers
Scholarship *110*
Armed Forces Communications and Electronics
Association ROTC Scholarship Program *137*
Astronaut Scholarship Foundation *112*
Aviation Council of Pennsylvania Scholarship
Program *137*
BHW Women in STEM Scholarship *74*
BMW/SAE Engineering Scholarship *146*
Boeing Company Career Enhancement
Scholarship *149*
CABAA/FlightSafety Citation Excel Professional
Pilot Training Award *138*
CABAA/FlightSafety Corporate Scheduler and
Dispatcher Training Award *138*
CABAA/FlightSafety Maintenance Professional
Training Award *138*
CABAA Maintenance Committee Financial
Award *138*
CABAA Scholarship *139*
CAE SimuFlite Citation Type Rating
Scholarship *147*
Charlie Wells Memorial Aviation
Scholarship *138*
Chicago Area Business Aviation Association
Scholarship *147*
Chuck Peacock Memorial Scholarship *134*
Daedalian Foundation Matching Scholarship
Program *139*
Dan L. Meisinger, Sr. Memorial Learn to Fly
Scholarship *144*
Dassault Falcon Jet Corporation Scholarship *149*
David Arver Memorial Scholarship *134*
Delta Air Lines Aircraft Maintenance
Technology Scholarship *149*
Delta Air Lines Engineering Scholarship *149*
Delta Air Lines Maintenance Management/
Aviation Business Management
Scholarship *150*
Dutch and Ginger Arver Scholarship *135*
Edward D. Hendrickson/SAE Engineering
Scholarship *146*
Edward W. Stimpson "Aviation Excellence"
Award *140*

Behavioral Science

Biology

Business/Consumer Services

Campus Activities

Canadian Studies

Chemical Engineering

High Technology Scholars Program *158*

Hispanic Engineer National Achievement Awards Corporation Scholarship Program *106*

Honeywell Scholarship *184*

Hubertus W.V. Wellems Scholarship for Male Students *180*

IBM Linda Sanford Women's Technical Advancement Scholarship *185*

Independent Laboratories Institute Scholarship Alliance *156*

Intel Scholarship Program *190*

Jill S. Tietjen P.E. Scholarship *185*

John J. McKetta Undergraduate Scholarship *174*

Joseph A. Levendusky Memorial Scholarship *178*

Kellogg Scholarship *185*

Koch Discovery Scholarship *185*

Kurt H. and Donna M. Schuler Small Grant *176*

Lillian Moller Gilbreth Memorial Scholarship *185*

Mary V. Munger Scholarship *185*

Mas Family Scholarship Award *165*

Master's Scholarship Program *181*

MASWE Scholarship *186*

Maureen L. and Howard N. Blitman, PE Scholarship to Promote Diversity in Engineering *180*

Medical Scrubs Collection Scholarship *106*

Minority Affairs Committee Award for Outstanding Scholastic Achievement *174*

Minority Scholarship Awards for College Students *174*

Minority Scholarship Awards for Incoming College Freshmen *174*

Minority Scholarship Program *155*

Montana Space Grant Scholarship Program *142*

Nancy Lorraine Jensen Memorial Scholarship *189*

NASA Idaho Space Grant Consortium Scholarship Program *157*

NASA Maryland Space Grant Consortium Undergraduate Scholarships *142*

National Association of Water Companies-New Jersey Chapter Scholarship *80*

National Board Technical Scholarship *180*

National Space Grant College and Fellowship Program *114*

National Student Design Competition-Individual *174*

National Student Paper Competition *174*

Odebrecht Award for Sustainable Development *119*

Olive Lynn Salembier Memorial Reentry Scholarship *186*

Outstanding Student Chapter Advisor Award *174*

Paula Loring Simon Scholarship *186*

Paul H. Robbins Honorary Scholarship *180*

Plastics Pioneers Association Scholarships *182*

Process Development Division Student Paper Award *175*

Procter & Gamble STEM Scholarship *116*

Professional Engineers in Industry Scholarship *180*

Regional Student Paper Competition *175*

Roberta Banaszak Gleiter Engineering Endeavor Scholarship *186*

Rochelle Perry Memorial Scholarship *186*

Safety and Chemical Engineering Education (SACHE) Student Essay Award For Safety *175*

Safety and Health National Student Design Competition Award for Safety *175*

Scholarship for Students Pursuing a Business or STEM Degree *84*

Sigma Xi Grants-In-Aid of Research *101*

Society of American Military Engineers Portland Post Scholarship *181*

Society of Plastics Engineers Scholarship Program *182*

Society of Women Engineers-Rocky Mountain Section Scholarship Program *188*

SPIE Educational Scholarships in Optical Science and Engineering *114*

Steven Engineering Scholarship *178*

StraightForward Media Engineering Scholarship *189*

Student Research Awards of the Battery Division of the Electrochemical Society Inc. *113*

Susan Miszkowicz Memorial Scholarship *186*

SWE Baltimore-Washington Section Scholarship *186*

SWE Central New Mexico Pioneers Scholarship *187*

SWE Central New Mexico Reentry Scholarship *187*

SWE Mid-Hudson Section Scholarship *187*

SWE Phoenix Section Scholarship *187*

SWE Region E Scholarship *187*

SWE Region G Judy Simmons Memorial Scholarship *188*

SWE Region H Scholarships *188*

SWE Region J Scholarship *188*

Tau Beta Pi Scholarship Program *189*

Technical Minority Scholarship *190*

TMC/SAE Donald D. Dawson Technical Scholarship *147*

Transtutors Scholarship 2015-16 *85*

Turner Construction Scholarship *188*

Undergraduate STEM Research Scholarships *114*

Universities Space Research Association Scholarship Award Program *116*

W1FDR Scholarship *112*

Wanda Munn Scholarship *188*

Child and Family Studies

Alexander Scholarship Loan Fund *171*

Child Development Teacher and Supervisor Grant Program *190*

CompHealth Medical Scholarship *151*

Society of Pediatric Nurses Educational Scholarship *190*

Civil Engineering

$1,500 STEM Scholarship *106*

AACE International Competitive Scholarship *118*

AGC Education and Research Foundation Undergraduate Scholarships *193*

Al-Ben Scholarship for Academic Incentive *179*

Al-Ben Scholarship for Professional Merit *179*

Al-Ben Scholarship for Scholastic Achievement *179*

Alfred E. Friend Jr., W4CF, Memorial Scholarship *177*

American Society of Civil Engineers-Maine High School Scholarship *193*

American Society of Naval Engineers Scholarship *110*

American Transmission Co. Scholarship *182*

Anne Shen Smith Endowed Scholarship *182*

AREMA Graduate and Undergraduate Scholarships *191*

Arsham Amirikian Engineering Scholarship *193*

Associated General Contractors NYS Scholarship Program *194*

Association for Iron and Steel Technology David H. Samson Canadian Scholarship *172*

Association of California Water Agencies Scholarships *112*

A.T. Anderson Memorial Scholarship Program *109*

Bayer Scholarship *183*

Betty Lou Bailey SWE Region F Scholarship *183*

BHW Women in STEM Scholarship *74*

B.J. Harrod Scholarship *183*

Carol Stephens SWE Region F Scholarship *183*

Center for Architecture Design Scholarship *119*

Clair A. Hill Scholarship *112*

College and Trade/Technical School Scholarships *178*

Conditional Grant Program *199*

David F. Ludovici Scholarship *178*

DEED Educational Scholarship *176*

DEED Student Internship *176*

DEED Student Research Grants *191*

DEED Technical Design Project *176*

Dr. Ivy M. Parker Memorial Scholarship *184*

Dorothy Lemke Howarth Memorial Scholarship *184*

Dorothy P. Morris Scholarship *184*

Eckenfelder Scholarship *155*

Elizabeth McLean Memorial Scholarship *198*

Elson T. Killam Memorial Scholarship *196*

Environmental Protection Scholarship *157*

Eric J. Gennuso and LeRoy D. (Bud) Loy, Jr. Scholarship Program *173*

Eugene C. Figg Jr. Civil Engineering Scholarship *192*

Exelon Corporation Scholarship *184*

FECON Scholarship *195*

Francis X. Crowley Scholarship *166*

Gary Wagner, K3OMI, Scholarship *177*

General Electric Women's Network Scholarship *198*

Grants for Disabled Graduate Students in the Sciences *113*

Hispanic Engineer National Achievement Awards Corporation Scholarship Program *106*

Home Builders Foundation Jim Irvine Statewide Scholarship *123*

IBM Linda Sanford Women's Technical Advancement Scholarship *185*

Independent Laboratories Institute Scholarship Alliance *156*

James L. Allhands Essay Competition *194*

Jere W. Thompson, Jr., Scholarship Fund *194*

Jill S. Tietjen P.E. Scholarship *185*

John Lenard Civil Engineering Scholarship *192*

Joseph Murphy Scholarship *196*

Kentucky Transportation Cabinet Civil Engineering Scholarship Program *195*

Koch Discovery Scholarship *185*

Kurt H. and Donna M. Schuler Small Grant *176*

Lawrence W. and Francis W. Cox Scholarship *192*

Lillian Moller Gilbreth Memorial Scholarship *185*

Lois Manley, K7LMZ, and Randall Pitchford, WW7ZZ, Scholarship *193*

Mary V. Munger Scholarship *185*

Mas Family Scholarship Award *165*

MASWE Scholarship *186*

Matsuo Bridge Company Ltd. of Japan Scholarship *193*

Maureen L. and Howard N. Blitman, PE Scholarship to Promote Diversity in Engineering *180*

Minority Scholarship Program *155*

Montana Space Grant Scholarship Program *142*

MRCA Foundation Scholarship Program *122*

NASA Idaho Space Grant Consortium Scholarship Program *157*

National Asphalt Pavement Association Research and Education Foundation Scholarship Program *196*

Classics

Communications

Wisconsin Broadcasters Association Foundation Scholarship *213*

Wyoming Trucking Association Scholarship Trust Fund *87*

Computer Science/Data Processing

$1,500 STEM Scholarship *106*

1B USD Worldwide Venture Capital *116*

Admiral Grace Murray Hopper Scholarship *218*

AFIO Undergraduate and Graduate Scholarships *103*

Al-Ben Scholarship for Academic Incentive *179*

Al-Ben Scholarship for Professional Merit *179*

Al-Ben Scholarship for Scholastic Achievement *179*

Alice L. Haltom Educational Fund *160*

Androscoggin Amateur Radio Club Scholarship *215*

Anheuser-Busch Legends of the Crown Scholarship Program *86*

AREMA Graduate and Undergraduate Scholarships *191*

Armed Forces Communications and Electronics Association ROTC Scholarship Program *137*

Association for Iron and Steel Technology Ohio Valley Chapter Scholarship *153*

Association for Iron and Steel Technology Willy Korf Memorial Scholarship *172*

Astronaut Scholarship Foundation *112*

A.T. Anderson Memorial Scholarship Program *109*

Automotive Women's Alliance Foundation Scholarships *74*

Barry M. Goldwater Scholarship and Excellence in Education Program *112*

BASF/Alfred Chisholm Endowed Memorial Scholarship *86*

BHW Women in STEM Scholarship *74*

Blue Cross Blue Shield of Illinois and Blue Cross Blue Shield of Texas Scholarship *115*

Colgate–Palmolive Corporate Scholars Program *86*

Community College STEM Scholarships *114*

Conditional Grant Program *199*

Cummins Scholarship *183*

Dallas SWE Annie Colaço Collegiate Leader Scholarship *218*

Davis Scholarship for Women in STEM *189*

Dell Corporate Scholars Program *169*

Eric D. Dunning Scholarship *219*

Galactic Unite Bytheway Scholarship *190*

Grants for Disabled Graduate Students in the Sciences *113*

High Technology Scholars Program *158*

Hispanic Engineer National Achievement Awards Corporation Scholarship Program *106*

Honeywell Scholarship *184*

ICIF Scholarship for Employees and Dependents of Member Organizations *204*

Indianapolis Amateur Radio Association Scholarship *215*

Intel Scholarship Program *190*

International Communications Industries Foundation AV Scholarship *204*

Jake McClain Driver, KC5WXA, Scholarship *215*

Jill S. Tietjen P.E. Scholarship *185*

John Wiley & Sons Best JASIST Paper Award *214*

Koch Discovery Scholarship *185*

Lillian Moller Gilbreth Memorial Scholarship *185*

Lockheed Martin Corporation Scholarship *218*

Lynda Baboyian Memorial Scholarship *163*

Magnolia DX Association Scholarship *202*

Master's Scholarship Program *181*

Math, Engineering, Science, Business, Education, Computers Scholarships *162*

Minnesota Space Grant Consortium Scholarship Program *142*

Montana Space Grant Scholarship Program *142*

NANOG Scholarship Program *217*

NASA Idaho Space Grant Consortium Scholarship Program *157*

NASA Maryland Space Grant Consortium Undergraduate Scholarships *142*

NASCAR Black History Month Awards *86*

National Association of Water Companies-New Jersey Chapter Scholarship *80*

National Security Agency Stokes Educational Scholarship Program *217*

National Space Grant College and Fellowship Program *114*

North Fulton Amateur Radio League Scholarship *215*

Oracle Corporate Scholars Program *169*

Paul W. Ruckes Scholarship *214*

PHD Scholarship *215*

Procter & Gamble General Scholarship *91*

Ray, N0RP, & Katie, W0KTE, Pautz Scholarship *215*

Roberta Banaszak Gleiter Engineering Endeavor Scholarship *186*

Robert V. McKenna Scholarships *219*

Rochelle Perry Memorial Scholarship *186*

Rockwell Collins Scholarship *218*

Rolf S. Jaehnigen Family Scholarship *79*

Scholarship for Students Pursuing a Business or STEM Degree *84*

SEMA Memorial Scholarship Fund *85*

Sigma Xi Grants-In-Aid of Research *101*

Social Entrepreneurship Scholarship *218*

Society of Women Engineers-Rocky Mountain Section Scholarship Program *188*

Society of Women Engineers-Twin Tiers Section Scholarship *219*

Southeastern DX Club Scholarship *215*

STEM Majors Scholarships for Undergraduate Students *110*

SUEZ Corporate Scholars Program *87*

SWE Region E Scholarship *187*

SWE Region G Judy Simmons Memorial Scholarship *188*

Technical Minority Scholarship *190*

Transtutors Scholarship 2015-16 *85*

Tribal Business Management Program (TBM) *74*

UNCF/Alliance Data Scholarship and Internship Program *91*

UNCF/Anthem Corporate Scholars Program *170*

UNCF Northrop Grumman Scholarship *220*

UNCF STEM Scholars Program *159*

Undergraduate STEM Research Scholarships *114*

Universities Space Research Association Scholarship Award Program *116*

VADM Samuel L. Gravely, Jr., USN(Ret.) Memorial Scholarship *111*

Vermont Space Grant Consortium *96*

Veterans of Enduring Freedom (Afghanistan) and Iraqi Freedom Scholarship *214*

Walter Reed Smith Scholarship *168*

Women in Technology Scholarship (WITS) *220*

Wyoming Trucking Association Scholarship Trust Fund *87*

You Can Make a Difference Scholarship *216*

Construction Engineering/Management

$1,500 STEM Scholarship *106*

AACE International Competitive Scholarship *118*

Ada I. Pressman Memorial Scholarship *182*

AGC Education and Research Foundation Undergraduate Scholarships *193*

Alfred E. Friend Jr., W4CF, Memorial Scholarship *177*

American Transmission Co. Scholarship *182*

Anne Maureen Whitney Barrow Memorial Scholarship *182*

Anne Shen Smith Endowed Scholarship *182*

AREMA Graduate and Undergraduate Scholarships *191*

ASHRAE Region III Boggarm Setty Scholarship *176*

Associated General Contractors NYS Scholarship Program *194*

A.T. Anderson Memorial Scholarship Program *109*

Bayer Scholarship *183*

Betty Lou Bailey SWE Region F Scholarship *183*

BHW Women in STEM Scholarship *74*

B.J. Harrod Scholarship *183*

BK Krenzer Memorial Reentry Scholarship *183*

Carol Stephens SWE Region F Scholarship *183*

Colorado Contractors Association Scholarship Program *222*

Community College STEM Scholarships *114*

Darooge Family Scholarship for Construction Trades *222*

David F. Ludovici Scholarship *178*

DEED Educational Scholarship *176*

DEED Student Internship *176*

DEED Student Research Grants *191*

DEED Technical Design Project *176*

Dr. Ivy M. Parker Memorial Scholarship *184*

Dorothy P. Morris Scholarship *184*

Eckenfelder Scholarship *155*

Eric J. Gennuso and LeRoy D. (Bud) Loy, Jr. Scholarship Program *173*

Exelon Corporation Scholarship *184*

FCA Women in Engineering Scholarship *184*

FECON Scholarship *195*

FEFPA Assistantship *121*

Gary Wagner, K3OMI, Scholarship *177*

Hispanic Engineer National Achievement Awards Corporation Scholarship Program *106*

IBM Linda Sanford Women's Technical Advancement Scholarship *185*

IFMA Foundation Scholarships *122*

James L. Allhands Essay Competition *194*

Koch Discovery Scholarship *185*

Kurt H. and Donna M. Schuler Small Grant *176*

Lillian Moller Gilbreth Memorial Scholarship *185*

Mary V. Munger Scholarship *185*

MASWE Scholarship *186*

Minority Scholarship Program *155*

MRCA Foundation Scholarship Program *122*

National Asphalt Pavement Association Research and Education Foundation Scholarship Program *196*

National Association of Water Companies-New Jersey Chapter Scholarship *80*

Odebrecht Award for Sustainable Development *119*

Olive Lynn Salembier Memorial Reentry Scholarship *186*

Roberta Banaszak Gleiter Engineering Endeavor Scholarship *186*

Rochelle Perry Memorial Scholarship *186*

Society of Women Engineers-Rocky Mountain Section Scholarship Program *188*

Steven Engineering Scholarship *178*

Susan Miszkowicz Memorial Scholarship *186*

SWE Baltimore-Washington Section Scholarship *186*

AWG Undergraduate Excellence in Paleontology Award *112*

Barry M. Goldwater Scholarship and Excellence in Education Program *112*

BHW Women in STEM Scholarship *74*

B.O.G. Pest Control Scholarship Fund *155*

Carrol C. Hall Memorial Scholarship *115*

Donald A. Williams Scholarship Soil Conservation Scholarship *95*

Eckenfelder Scholarship *155*

Edward R. Hall Scholarship *95*

Elizabeth and Sherman Asche Memorial Scholarship Fund *98*

Elizabeth Gardner Norweb Summer Environmental Studies Scholarship *98*

Environmental Protection Scholarship *157*

Eric D. Dunning Scholarship *219*

Florida Space Research Program *142*

Hispanic Engineer National Achievement Awards Corporation Scholarship Program *106*

Independent Laboratories Institute Scholarship Alliance *156*

Janet Cullen Tanaka Geosciences Undergraduate Scholarship *117*

J. Fielding Reed Scholarship *97*

Life Member Montana Federation of Garden Clubs Scholarship *243*

Lone Star Rising Career Scholarship *242*

Medical Scrubs Collection Scholarship *106*

Minnesota Space Grant Consortium Scholarship Program *142*

Minority Scholarship Program *155*

MO Show-Me Chapter SWCS Scholarship *95*

NASA Idaho Space Grant Consortium Scholarship Program *157*

NASA Maryland Space Grant Consortium Undergraduate Scholarships *142*

National Association of Geoscience Teachers-Far Western Section scholarship *243*

National Association of Water Companies-New Jersey Chapter Scholarship *80*

National Garden Clubs Inc. Scholarship Program *100*

National Space Grant College and Fellowship Program *114*

NGWA Foundation's Len Assante Scholarship *244*

Osage Chapter Undergraduate Service Scholarship *117*

Rocky Mountain Coal Mining Institute Scholarship *197*

Rogers Family Scholarship *243*

Scholarship for Students Pursuing a Business or STEM Degree *84*

Sehar Saleha Ahmad and Abrahim Ekramullah Zafar Foundation Scholarship *115*

Sigma Xi Grants-In-Aid of Research *101*

STEM Teachers Scholarship *111*

Susan Ekdale Memorial Field Camp Scholarship *242*

Tilford Field Studies Scholarship *240*

Undergraduate Research Award Program *143*

Universities Space Research Association Scholarship Award Program *116*

Vermont Space Grant Consortium *96*

Women in Technology Scholarship (WITS) *220*

Economics

280 Group Product Management Scholarship *160*

Actuary of Tomorrow—Stuart A. Robertson Memorial Scholarship *160*

Automotive Women's Alliance Foundation Scholarships *74*

Colgate–Palmolive Corporate Scholars Program *86*

Curtis E. Huntington Memorial Scholarship (Formerly The John Culver Wooddy Scholarship) *245*

Fukunaga Scholarship Foundation *77*

Humane Studies Fellowships *204*

John Kelly Labor Studies Scholarship Fund *246*

Julianne Malveaux Scholarship *245*

Mas Family Scholarship Award *165*

Minorities in Government Finance Scholarship *78*

National Association of Water Companies-New Jersey Chapter Scholarship *80*

National Security Education Program (NSEP) David L. Boren Undergraduate Scholarships *126*

National Society Daughters of the American Revolution Enid Hall Griswold Memorial Scholarship *246*

New England Employee Benefits Council Scholarship Program *81*

Oregon State Fiscal Association Scholarship *246*

Risk Management Association Foundation Scholarship Program *83*

Scholarship for Students Pursuing a Business or STEM Degree *84*

Society of Automotive Analysts Scholarship *84*

StraightForward Media Business School Scholarship *90*

StraightForward Media Liberal Arts Scholarship *126*

Transtutors Scholarship 2015-16 *85*

Tribal Business Management Program (TBM) *74*

UNCF/Koch Scholars Program for Undergraduates *87*

Education

ABEA Student Teacher Scholarships *249*

Alexander Scholarship Loan Fund *171*

American Legion Auxiliary Department of Iowa Harriet Hoffman Memorial Merit Award for Teacher Training *248*

American Montessori Society Teacher Education Scholarship Fund *248*

Anna and John Kolesar Memorial Scholarships *247*

Applegate/Jackson/Parks Future Teacher Scholarship *255*

Arne Engebretsen Wisconsin Mathematics Council Scholarship *261*

ARTC Glen Moon Scholarship *250*

AWG Ethnic Minority Scholarship *241*

AWG Maria Luisa Crawford Field Camp Scholarship *117*

AWG Salt Lake Chapter (SLC) Research Scholarship *117*

Barbara Lotze Scholarships for Future Teachers *247*

Bill Mason Scholarship Fund *257*

Brookmire-Hastings Scholarships *261*

Carrol C. Hall Memorial Scholarship *115*

Charlotte Plummer Owen Memorial Scholarship *262*

Child Development Teacher and Supervisor Grant Program *190*

Christa McAuliffe Scholarship Program *259*

Continental Society, Daughters of Indian Wars Scholarship *251*

CTRI/Chris Seeber, KA1GEU, Memorial Scholarship *249*

Delta Gamma Foundation Florence Margaret Harvey Memorial Scholarship *247*

Developmental Disabilities Scholastic Achievement Scholarship for College Students who are Lutheran *236*

Distinguished Student Scholar Award *257*

Dorothea Deitz Endowed Memorial Scholarship *262*

Early Childhood Educators Scholarship Program *254*

Edith M. Allen Scholarship *252*

Education Achievement Awards *252*

Erman W. Taylor Memorial Scholarship *248*

Ethel A. Neijahr Wisconsin Mathematics Council Scholarship *261*

Francis J. Flynn Memorial Scholarship *260*

Frieda L. Koontz Scholarship *261*

Future Teacher Scholarship-Oklahoma *256*

GAE GFIE Scholarship for Aspiring Teachers *252*

Gates Millennium Scholars (GMS) Program *260*

General Scholarships *261*

Golden Apple Scholars of Illinois *252*

Graduate Student Scholar Award *257*

Haines Memorial Scholarship *258*

Harriet A. Simmons Scholarship *256*

Harriet Irsay Scholarship Grant *127*

Harry A. Applegate Scholarship *75*

Hawaii Education Association Student Teacher Scholarship *253*

Hiroshi Barbara Kim Yamashita HEA Scholarship *253*

Illinois PTA Scholarship *253*

Indiana Retired Teachers Foundation Scholarship *253*

"Inspire Our Future" $2,500 Scholarship *259*

International Technology Education Association Undergraduate Scholarship in Technology Education *254*

Jack J. Isgur Foundation Scholarship *129*

James and Patricia Sood Scholarship *260*

James Carlson Memorial Scholarship *256*

Janet L. Hoffmann Loan Assistance Repayment Program *254*

Jeanne S. Chall Research Fellowship *254*

Jim Bourque Scholarship *249*

John M. Stropki STEM Scholarship *249*

Joseph C. Basile, II Memorial Scholarship Fund *253*

Kansas Teacher Service Scholarship *254*

Languages in Teacher Education Scholarships *247*

Leo J. Krysa Undergraduate Scholarship *125*

L. Gordon Bittle Memorial Scholarship *250*

Lone Star Rising Career Scholarship *242*

Margie H. Verbal Emergency Scholarship Fund *260*

Martha Ann Stark Memorial Scholarship *262*

Martin Luther King, Jr. Memorial Scholarship *250*

Mary McMillan Scholarship Award *249*

Mary Morrow-Edna Richards Scholarship *256*

Math, Engineering, Science, Business, Education, Computers Scholarships *162*

Michael Moody Fitness Scholarship *255*

Minority Teacher Incentive Grant Program *251*

Minority Teachers of Illinois Scholarship Program *253*

Nadeen Burkeholder Williams Music Scholarship *257*

NASA RISGC Summer Scholarship for Undergraduate Students *143*

National Association for Campus Activities Mid Atlantic Higher Education Research Scholarship *171*

Native American Leadership in Education (NALE) *163*

Newtonville Woman's Club Scholarship *252*

Northern Alberta Development Council Bursary *234*

Office Supply Scholarship *128*

Energy and Power Engineering

Engineering-Related Technologies

Engineering/Technology

Alfred E. Friend Jr., W4CF, Memorial
    Scholarship *177*
Alfred Steele Engineering Scholarship *293*
Allen and Bertha Watson Memorial
    Scholarship *294*
Alwin B. Newton Scholarship *264*
American Chemical Society, Rubber Division
    Undergraduate Scholarship *109*
American Society of Naval Engineers
    Scholarship *110*
American Transmission Co. Scholarship *182*
American Welding Society International
    Scholarship *277*
Andy Aitkenhead Scholarship *115*
Anheuser-Busch Legends of the Crown
    Scholarship Program *86*
Anne Maureen Whitney Barrow Memorial
    Scholarship *182*
Anne Shen Smith Endowed Scholarship *182*
A.O. Putnam Memorial Scholarship *299*
AREMA Graduate and Undergraduate
    Scholarships *191*
Arizona Professional Chapter of AISES
    Scholarship *294*
Armed Forces Communications and Electronics
    Association ROTC Scholarship Program *137*
Arthur and Gladys Cervenka Scholarship
    Award *306*
ASABE Foundation Scholarship *291*
ASHRAE General Scholarships *276*
ASHRAE Region III Boggarm Setty
    Scholarship *176*
ASHRAE Region IV Benny Bootle
    Scholarship *119*
ASHRAE Region VIII Scholarship *276*
ASME Auxiliary Undergraduate Scholarship
    Charles B. Sharp *292*
ASM Outstanding Scholars Awards *295*
Association for Iron and Steel Technology
    Baltimore Chapter Scholarship *275*
Association for Iron and Steel Technology David
    H. Samson Canadian Scholarship *172*
Association for Iron and Steel Technology
    Midwest Chapter Betty McKern
    Scholarship *289*
Association for Iron and Steel Technology
    Midwest Chapter Don Nelson
    Scholarship *289*
Association for Iron and Steel Technology
    Midwest Chapter Engineering
    Scholarship *289*
Association for Iron and Steel Technology
    Midwest Chapter Jack Gill Scholarship *289*
Association for Iron and Steel Technology
    Midwest Chapter Mel Nickel
    Scholarship *290*
Association for Iron and Steel Technology
    Midwest Chapter Non-Engineering
    Scholarship *290*
Association for Iron and Steel Technology
    Midwest Chapter Western States
    Scholarship *290*
Association for Iron and Steel Technology
    Northwest Member Chapter Scholarship *290*
Association for Iron and Steel Technology Ohio
    Valley Chapter Scholarship *153*
Association for Iron and Steel Technology
    Pittsburgh Chapter Scholarship *290*
Association for Iron and Steel Technology
    Southeast Member Chapter Scholarship *290*
A.T. Anderson Memorial Scholarship
    Program *109*
Automotive Women's Alliance Foundation
    Scholarships *74*
Barry M. Goldwater Scholarship and Excellence in
    Education Program *112*

BASF/Alfred Chisholm Endowed Memorial
    Scholarship *86*
Bayer Scholarship *183*
Bechtel Corporation Scholarship *310*
Betty Lou Bailey SWE Region F
    Scholarship *183*
Betty Weatherford, KQ6RE, Memorial
    Scholarship *266*
BHW Women in STEM Scholarship *74*
B.J. Harrod Scholarship *183*
BK Krenzer Memorial Reentry Scholarship *183*
Blue Cross Blue Shield of Illinois and Blue Cross
    Blue Shield of Texas Scholarship *115*
BMW/SAE Engineering Scholarship *146*
Brill Family Scholarship *310*
Carol Stephens SWE Region F Scholarship *183*
Caterpillar Scholars Award Fund *306*
C.B. Gambrell Undergraduate Scholarship *300*
Center for Architecture, Douglas Haskell Award
    for Student Journals *119*
Chapter 17-St. Louis Scholarship *307*
Chapter 198-Downriver Detroit Scholarship *307*
Chapter 23-Quad Cities Iowa/Illinois
    Scholarship *307*
Chapter 31-Tri City Scholarship *307*
Chapter 3-Peoria Endowed Scholarship *307*
Chapter 4-Lawrence A. Wacker Memorial
    Scholarship *307*
Chapter 63-Portland James E. Morrow
    Scholarship *307*
Chapter 63-Portland Uncle Bud Smith
    Scholarship *307*
Chapter 67-Phoenix Scholarship *307*
Chapter 6-Fairfield County Scholarship *308*
Chapter 93-Albuquerque Scholarship *308*
Charles N. Fisher Memorial Scholarship *111*
CIE Undergraduate Scholarship *300*
Clarence and Josephine Myers Scholarship *308*
Clinton J. Helton Manufacturing Scholarship
    Award Fund *308*
Colgate–Palmolive Corporate Scholars
    Program *86*
College and Trade/Technical School
    Scholarships *178*
Community College STEM Scholarships *114*
Connie and Robert T. Gunter Scholarship *308*
Cooper Industries *169*
CTRI/Chris Seeber, KA1GEU, Memorial
    Scholarship *249*
Cummins Scholarship *183*
Dallas SWE Annie Colaço Collegiate Leader
    Scholarship *218*
Dallas SWE High School Senior Scholarship *312*
Dan Huettl, WZ7U, Memorial Scholarship *280*
David F. Ludovici Scholarship *178*
Davidson Fellows Scholarship Program *113*
Davis Scholarship for Women in STEM *189*
DEED Educational Scholarship *176*
DEED Student Internship *176*
DEED Student Research Grants *191*
DEED Technical Design Project *176*
Dell Corporate Scholars Program *169*
Delta Faucet Company Scholarship Program *167*
Detroit Chapter One-Founding Chapter
    Scholarship *308*
Detroit Section SAE Technical Scholarship *286*
D. Fred and Marian L. Bovie National
    Scholarship *293*
Dimitri J. Ververelli Memorial Scholarship for
    Architecture and/or Engineering *121*
Director's Scholarship Award *308*
Dr. Ivy M. Parker Memorial Scholarship *184*
Donald and Shirley Hastings Scholarship *293*
Donald F. Hastings Scholarship *277*
Dorothy Lemke Howarth Memorial
    Scholarship *184*

Dorothy P. Morris Scholarship *184*
Duane Hanson Scholarship *264*
DuPont Company Scholarship *184*
Dwight D. Gardner Scholarship *300*
Eckenfelder Scholarship *155*
Edward D. Hendrickson/SAE Engineering
    Scholarship *146*
Edward J. Brady Memorial Scholarship *278*
Edward J. Dulis Scholarship *295*
Edward S. Roth Manufacturing Engineering
    Scholarship *308*
Elizabeth McLean Memorial Scholarship *198*
Ellen Hippeli Memorial Scholarship *311*
Engineering/Technology Achievement
    Award *299*
Eric D. Dunning Scholarship *219*
Eric J. Gennuso and LeRoy D. (Bud) Loy, Jr.
    Scholarship Program *173*
Eric Primavera Memorial Scholarship *298*
E. Wayne Kay Community College Scholarship
    Award *308*
E. Wayne Kay Co-op Scholarship *309*
E. Wayne Kay High School Scholarship *309*
E. Wayne Kay Scholarship *309*
Exelon Corporation Scholarship *184*
FCA Women in Engineering Scholarship *184*
Fleming/Baszcak Scholarship *181*
Ford Motor Company Scholarship *270*
Fort Wayne Chapter 56 Scholarship *309*
Francis H. Moffitt Memorial Scholarship *296*
Frank M. Coda Scholarship *264*
Fred M. Young Sr./SAE Engineering
    Scholarship *306*
Galactic Unite Bytheway Scholarship *190*
Gary Wagner, K3OMI, Scholarship *177*
Gates Millennium Scholars (GMS) Program *260*
GE/LULAC Scholarship *166*
General Electric Women's Network
    Scholarship *198*
George A. Roberts Scholarship *295*
Georgia Engineering Foundation Scholarship
    Program *298*
GM/LULAC Scholarship *302*
Grants for Disabled Graduate Students in the
    Sciences *113*
Guiliano Mazzetti Scholarship Award *309*
Gulf Coast Hurricane Scholarship *181*
Gus Archie Memorial Scholarships *310*
Harold and Inge Marcus Scholarship *300*
Henry Adams Scholarship *265*
Henry Broughton, K2AE, Memorial
    Scholarship *280*
H.H. Dow Memorial Student Achievement Award
    of the Industrial Electrolysis and
    Electrochemical Engineering Division of the
    Electrochemical Society Inc. *113*
High School Scholarship *298*
High Technology Scholars Program *158*
Hispanic Engineer National Achievement Awards
    Corporation Scholarship Program *106*
Home Builders Foundation Jim Irvine Statewide
    Scholarship *123*
Honda Scholarship *311*
Honeywell Scholarship *184*
Howard E. and Wilma J. Adkins Memorial
    Scholarship *278*
Hubertus W.V. Wellems Scholarship for Male
    Students *180*
IBM Linda Sanford Women's Technical
    Advancement Scholarship *185*
IFMA Foundation Scholarships *122*
IIE Council of Fellows Undergraduate
    Scholarship *300*
Illinois Society of Professional Engineers/Melvin
    E. Amstutz Memorial Award *299*

Les Dames d'Escoffier International, Colorado
Chapter Scholarship *93*
Stella Blum Student Research Grant *125*
Walter Reed Smith Scholarship *168*

Horticulture/Floriculture

Abbie Sargent Memorial Scholarship *91*
Alabama Golf Course Superintendent's
Association's Donnie Arthur Memorial
Scholarship *96*
American Society for Enology and Viticulture
Scholarships *97*
Arizona Nursery Association Foundation
Scholarship *363*
A.T. Anderson Memorial Scholarship
Program *109*
BHW Women in STEM Scholarship *74*
Bryan A. Champion Memorial Scholarship *92*
CANERS Foundation Endowment
Scholarship *363*
Carville M. Akehurst Memorial Scholarship *315*
CHS Foundation High School Scholarships *91*
CHS Foundation Two-Year College
Scholarships *92*
Corliss Knapp Engle Scholarship in
Horticulture *364*
ECA Scholarship *363*
Edward R. Hall Scholarship *95*
Federated Garden Clubs of Connecticut Inc.
Scholarships *156*
Francis Sylvia Zverina Scholarship *365*
GCA Award in Desert Studies *121*
GCA Summer Scholarship in Field Botany *364*
GCSAA Scholars Competition *365*
Horticulture Scholarships *365*
Idaho Nursery and Landscape Association
Scholarships *366*
Joan K. Hunt and Rachel M. Hunt Summer
Scholarship in Field Botany *364*
Joseph Shinoda Memorial Scholarship *366*
Katharine M. Grosscup Scholarships in
Horticulture *364*
Life Member Montana Federation of Garden Clubs
Scholarship *243*
Loy McCandless Marks Scholarship in Tropical
Horticulture *364*
Muggets Scholarship *366*
National Council of State Garden Clubs Inc.
Scholarship *99*
National Garden Clubs Inc. Scholarship
Program *100*
National Garden Clubs Scholarship *367*
Rain Bird Intelligent Use of Water
Scholarship *366*
Robert D., W8ST, and Donna J., W9DJS, Streeter
Scholarship *318*
Robert Lewis Baker Scholarship *364*
Rogers Family Scholarship *243*
Russell W. Myers Scholarship *99*
Sara Shallenberger Brown GCA National Parks
Conservation Scholarship *365*
Sidney B. Meadows Scholarship Endowment
Fund *367*
Spring Meadow Nursery Scholarship *366*
Timothy and Palmer W. Bigelow Jr.,
Scholarship *92*
Turf and Ornamental Communicators
Association Scholarship Program *102*
Usrey Family Scholarship *315*
Western Reserve Herb Society Scholarship *365*
Zeller Summer Scholarship in
Medicinal Botany *352*

Hospitality Management

AH&LEF Annual Scholarship Grant
Program *227*
American Express Scholarship Program *367*

American Hotel & Lodging Educational
Foundation Pepsi Scholarship *228*
Bern Laxer Memorial Scholarship *230*
Bill Schwartz Memorial Scholarship *369*
Bob Smith Tourism Scholarship *336*
Careers Through Culinary Arts Program Cooking
Competition for Scholarships *229*
Clem Judd, Jr. Memorial Scholarship *368*
Costa Rican Vacations Scholarship *320*
Culinary, Vinifera, and Hospitality
Scholarship *331*
Ecolab Scholarship Program *228*
Fukunaga Scholarship Foundation *77*
Golden Gate Restaurant Association Scholarship
Foundation *229*
Harry A. Applegate Scholarship *75*
Hometeam Homecare Scholarship *369*
Hyatt Hotels Fund for Minority Lodging
Management *228*
IATAN Ronald A Santana Scholarship *369*
Illinois Restaurant Association Educational
Foundation Scholarships *229*
Incoming Freshman Scholarships *228*
International Foodservice Editorial Council
Communications Scholarship *88*
Joe Perdue Scholarship Program *368*
Maine Restaurant Association Education
Foundation Scholarship Fund *232*
National Black McDonald's Owners Association
Hospitality Scholars Program *86*
National Restaurant Association Educational
Foundation Undergraduate Scholarships for
College Students *336*
National Restaurant Association Educational
Foundation Undergraduate Scholarships for
High School Seniors and General Education
Diploma (GED) Graduate s *337*
New Horizons Kathy LeTarte Scholarship *337*
Oregon Wine Brotherhood Scholarship *232*
Pat and Jim Host Scholarship *370*
Rama Scholarship for the American Dream *228*
R.W. "Bob" Holden Scholarship *368*
Scholarship for Students Pursuing a Business or
STEM Degree *84*
South Carolina Tourism and Hospitality
Educational Foundation Scholarships *232*
UNCF/Carnival Corporate Scholars Program *170*

Humanities

ASCSA Summer Sessions Scholarships *108*
Developmental Disabilities Scholastic
Achievement Scholarship for College Students
who are Lutheran *236*
Frances L. Booth Medical Scholarship sponsored
by LAVFW Department of Maine *353*
Humane Studies Fellowships *204*
Jack J. Isgur Foundation Scholarship *129*
James M. and Virginia M. Smyth
Scholarship *128*
Leo J. Krysa Undergraduate Scholarship *125*
Math, Engineering, Science, Business, Education,
Computers Scholarships *162*
National Junior Classical League
Scholarship *200*
Native American Leadership in Education
(NALE) *163*
Noet Humanities Scholarship *371*
Ossie Davis Endowment Scholarship
Program *132*
Phi Alpha Theta World History Association Paper
Prize *361*
Polish Arts Club of Buffalo Scholarship
Foundation Trust *130*
StraightForward Media Liberal Arts
Scholarship *126*
Teaching Assistant Program in France *104*

Human Resources

Alexander Scholarship Loan Fund *171*
Automotive Women's Alliance Foundation
Scholarships *74*
CVS Pharmacy, Inc. Business Scholarships *86*
Fukunaga Scholarship Foundation *77*
New England Employee Benefits Council
Scholarship Program *81*
Oracle Corporate Scholars Program *169*
Scholarship for Students Pursuing a Business or
STEM Degree *84*
SHRM Foundation Student Scholarships *371*
SUEZ Corporate Scholars Program *87*

Hydrology

AAC Research Grants *153*
American Ground Water Trust-AMTROL Inc.
Scholarship *240*
American Ground Water Trust-Baroid
Scholarship *241*
American Ground Water Trust-Thomas Stetson
Scholarship *241*
Arizona Hydrological Society Scholarship *241*
Association of California Water Agencies
Scholarships *112*
A.T. Anderson Memorial Scholarship
Program *109*
AWG Ethnic Minority Scholarship *241*
AWG Maria Luisa Crawford Field Camp
Scholarship *117*
AWG Salt Lake Chapter (SLC) Research
Scholarship *117*
Barry M. Goldwater Scholarship and Excellence in
Education Program *112*
BHW Women in STEM Scholarship *74*
California Groundwater Association
Scholarship *372*
Clair A. Hill Scholarship *112*
Donald A. Williams Scholarship Soil Conservation
Scholarship *95*
Eckenfelder Scholarship *155*
Environmental Protection Scholarship *157*
Hispanic Engineer National Achievement Awards
Corporation Scholarship Program *106*
Janet Cullen Tanaka Geosciences Undergraduate
Scholarship *117*
Lone Star Rising Career Scholarship *242*
Minority Scholarship Program *155*
MO Show-Me Chapter SWCS Scholarship *95*
NGWA Foundation's Len Assante
Scholarship *244*
Osage Chapter Undergraduate Service
Scholarship *117*
Sigma Xi Grants-In-Aid of Research *101*
Susan Ekdale Memorial Field Camp
Scholarship *242*
United States Society on Dams Scholarship
Award *199*

Industrial Design

1B USD Worldwide Venture Capital *116*
Alfred Steele Engineering Scholarship *293*
Association for Iron and Steel Technology Willy
Korf Memorial Scholarship *172*
Automotive Women's Alliance Foundation
Scholarships *74*
BHW Women in STEM Scholarship *74*
Center for Architecture Design Scholarship *119*
Chapter 198-Downriver Detroit Scholarship *307*
Chapter 67-Phoenix Scholarship *307*
Community College STEM Scholarships *114*
Fleming/Baszcak Scholarship *181*
Fort Wayne Chapter 56 Scholarship *309*
Gulf Coast Hurricane Scholarship *181*
Hispanic Engineer National Achievement Awards
Corporation Scholarship Program *106*

Industrial Designers Society of America Undergraduate Scholarship *374*

James J. Burns and C. A. Haynes Scholarship *374*

Maine Manufacturing Career and Training Foundation Scholarship *142*

MRCA Foundation Scholarship Program *122*

North Central Region 9 Scholarship *309*

OLM Malala Yousafzai Scholarship 2017-2018 *129*

Ruth Clark Furniture Design Scholarship *129*

Safety and Health National Student Design Competition Award for Safety *175*

Simple Solutions Design Competition *286*

Society of Plastics Engineers Scholarship Program *182*

Support Creativity Scholarship *124*

TiMOTION Engineering and Excellence Scholarship *199*

Transtutors Scholarship 2015-16 *85*

Vectorworks Design Scholarship *124*

Wichita Chapter 52 Scholarship *310*

Insurance and Actuarial Science

Actuarial Diversity Scholarship *375*

Actuary of Tomorrow—Stuart A. Robertson Memorial Scholarship *160*

BHW Women in STEM Scholarship *74*

Curtis E. Huntington Memorial Scholarship (Formerly The John Culver Wooddy Scholarship) *245*

D.W. Simpson Actuarial Science Scholarship *375*

Liberty Mutual Scholarship *169*

Missouri Insurance Education Foundation Scholarship *375*

New England Employee Benefits Council Scholarship Program *81*

Scholarship for Students Pursuing a Business or STEM Degree *84*

Spencer Educational Foundation Scholarship *375*

UNCF/Travelers Insurance Scholarship *170*

Interior Design

Alan Lucas Memorial Educational Scholarship *122*

ASID Foundation Legacy Scholarship for Undergraduates *376*

Center for Architecture Design Scholarship *119*

Green/Sustainable Scholarship *121*

Home Builders Foundation Jim Irvine Statewide Scholarship *123*

IFDA Leaders Commemorative Scholarship *376*

IFDA Student Member Scholarship *376*

IFMA Foundation Scholarships *122*

NAWIC Undergraduate Scholarships *122*

OLM Malala Yousafzai Scholarship 2017-2018 *129*

Part Time Student Scholarship *376*

Plan New Hampshire Scholarship and Program *123*

QualityBath.com Scholarship Program *123*

Robert W. Thunen Memorial Scholarships *122*

Rug & Home Scholars Program *377*

Ruth Clark Furniture Design Scholarship *129*

Support Creativity Scholarship *124*

Vectorworks Design Scholarship *124*

YouthForce 2020 Scholarship Program *124*

International Migration

United Nations Association of Connecticut Scholarship *133*

International Studies

AFIO Undergraduate and Graduate Scholarships *103*

Automotive Women's Alliance Foundation Scholarships *74*

Don Riebhoff Memorial Scholarship *378*

ISF National Scholarship *108*

Mas Family Scholarship Award *165*

Moody Research Grants *104*

National Security Education Program (NSEP) David L. Boren Undergraduate Scholarships *126*

Phi Alpha Theta World History Association Paper Prize *361*

Teaching Assistant Program in France *104*

United Nations Association of Connecticut Scholarship *133*

WIIT Charitable Trust Scholarship Program *378*

Journalism

Allison Fisher Scholarship *383*

Al Neuharth Free Spirit and Journalism Conference Program *380*

Alpha Omega Scholarship In Memory Of Peter Agris *201*

AQHF Journalism or Communications Scholarship *201*

Associated Press Television/Radio Association-Clete Roberts Journalism Scholarship Awards *379*

Bernard Kilgore Memorial Scholarship for the NJ High School Journalist of the Year *385*

Betty Endicott/NTA-NCCB Student Scholarship *383*

Bill Farr Scholarship *387*

BMI Founders Award for Radio Broadcasting *203*

Career Journalism Scholarship *210*

Carl Greenberg Scholarship *387*

Carole Simpson Scholarship *208*

CCNMA Scholarships *203*

CIC/Anna Chennault Scholarship *202*

Connecticut SPJ Bob Eddy Scholarship Program *203*

David J. Clarke Memorial Scholarship *205*

Dr. Lynne Boyle/John Schimpf Undergraduate Scholarship *89*

Douglas W. Mummert Scholarship *129*

Dow Jones News Fund High School Journalism Workshops Writing, Photography and Multimedia Competition *380*

Durwood McAlister Scholarship *381*

Ed Bradley Scholarship *208*

Edward J. Nell Memorial Scholarship in Journalism *386*

George Foreman Tribute to Lyndon B. Johnson Scholarship *208*

Georgia Press Educational Foundation Scholarships *381*

Gerald Boyd/Robin Stone Non-Sustaining Scholarship *383*

Geraldo Rivera Scholarship *384*

Guy P. Gannett Scholarship Fund *382*

Harold K. Douthit Scholarship *89*

Harriet Irsay Scholarship Grant *127*

Harry C. Hamm Family Scholarship *209*

Helen Johnson Scholarship *387*

Indiana Broadcasters Foundation Scholarship *381*

International Foodservice Editorial Council Communications Scholarship *88*

ISF National Scholarship *108*

Jack Shaheen Mass Communications Scholarship Award *200*

Jackson Foundation Journalism Scholarship *386*

Jackson Foundation Journalism Scholarship Fund *385*

Jake McClain Driver, KC5WXA, Scholarship *215*

Jim McKay Memorial Scholarship *205*

John Bayliss Broadcast Radio Scholarship *204*

Julianne Malveaux Scholarship *245*

Kathryn Dettman Memorial Journalism Scholarship *380*

Ken Inouye Scholarship *387*

Kirk Sutlive Scholarship *381*

Lee Thornton Scholarship *208*

Leonard M. Perryman Communications Scholarship for Ethnic Minority Students *212*

Lou and Carole Prato Sports Reporting Scholarship *208*

Maria Elena Salinas Scholarship *339*

Marshall E. McCullough-National Dairy Shrine Scholarships *100*

Maryland SPJ Pro Chapter College Scholarship *388*

Mary Quon Moy Ing Memorial Scholarship Award *379*

Mas Family Scholarship Award *165*

Michael J. Powell High School Journalist of the Year *382*

Michael S. Libretti Scholarship *206*

Mike Reynolds Journalism Scholarship *209*

Mike Wallace Memorial Scholarship *205*

Mississippi Association of Broadcasters Scholarship *382*

Mississippi Press Association Education Foundation Scholarship *382*

Morris Newspaper Corporation Scholarship *381*

NABJ Scholarship *205*

National Academy of Television Arts and Sciences Trustees Scholarship *205*

National Association of Black Journalists and Newhouse Foundation Scholarship *383*

National Association of Black Journalists Non-Sustaining Scholarship Awards *384*

National Association of Broadcasters Grants for Research in Broadcasting *206*

National Association of Hispanic Journalists Scholarship *206*

National Institute for Labor Relations Research William B. Ruggles Journalism Scholarship *206*

National JACL Headquarters Scholarship *99*

National Press Club Scholarship for Journalism Diversity *384*

National Writers Association Foundation Scholarships *385*

Native American Journalists Association Scholarships *89*

Nebraska Press Association Foundation Scholarship *89*

Newhouse Scholarship Program *343*

Northwest Journalists of Color Scholarship *88*

NSPA Journalism Honor Roll Scholarship *384*

OAB Foundation Scholarship *207*

Ohio Newspapers Foundation Minority Scholarship *89*

Ohio Newspapers Foundation University Journalism Scholarship *90*

ONWA Annual Scholarship *90*

Outdoor Writers Association of America - Bodie McDowell Scholarship Award *207*

Overseas Press Club Foundation Scholar Awards *386*

Palm Beach Association of Black Journalists Scholarship *386*

Pete Wilson Scholarship *209*

PHD Scholarship *215*

Philadelphia Association of Black Journalists Scholarship *386*

Printing Industry Midwest Education Foundation Scholarship Fund *207*

Randy Falco Scholarship *205*

Mathematics

Occupational Safety and Health

American Society of Naval Engineers
Scholarship *110*

Andy Aitkenhead Scholarship *115*

Anheuser-Busch Legends of the Crown
Scholarship Program *86*

Arizona Professional Chapter of AISES
Scholarship *294*

Armed Forces Communications and Electronics
Association ROTC Scholarship Program *137*

Association for Iron and Steel Technology Ohio
Valley Chapter Scholarship *153*

A.T. Anderson Memorial Scholarship
Program *109*

AWG Ethnic Minority Scholarship *241*

AWG Maria Luisa Crawford Field Camp
Scholarship *117*

AWG Salt Lake Chapter (SLC) Research
Scholarship *117*

Barbara Lotze Scholarships for Future
Teachers *247*

Barry M. Goldwater Scholarship and Excellence in
Education Program *112*

BASF/Alfred Chisholm Endowed Memorial
Scholarship *86*

BHW Women in STEM Scholarship *74*

Blue Cross Blue Shield of Illinois and Blue Cross
Blue Shield of Texas Scholarship *115*

Carrol C. Hall Memorial Scholarship *115*

Charles S. Brown Scholarship in Physics *485*

Coastal Plains Chapter of the Air and Waste
Management Association Environmental
Steward Scholarship *318*

CompHealth Medical Scholarship *151*

CTRI/Chris Seeber, KA1GEU, Memorial
Scholarship *249*

Dan Huettl, WZ7U, Memorial Scholarship *280*

Elizabeth and Sherman Asche Memorial
Scholarship Fund *98*

Elmer S. Imes Scholarship in Physics *485*

Eric D. Dunning Scholarship *219*

Gates Millennium Scholars (GMS) Program *260*

Grants for Disabled Graduate Students in the
Sciences *113*

Harvey Washington Banks Scholarship in
Astronomy *486*

H.H. Dow Memorial Student Achievement Award
of the Industrial Electrolysis and
Electrochemical Engineering Division of the
Electrochemical Society Inc. *113*

High Technology Scholars Program *158*

Hispanic Engineer National Achievement Awards
Corporation Scholarship Program *106*

Hubertus W.V. Wellems Scholarship for Male
Students *180*

Independent Laboratories Institute Scholarship
Alliance *156*

James M. and Virginia M. Smyth
Scholarship *128*

Janet Cullen Tanaka Geosciences Undergraduate
Scholarship *117*

Leatrice Gregory Pendray Scholarship *110*

Lois Manley, K7LMZ, and Randall Pitchford,
WW7ZZ, Scholarship *193*

Lone Star Rising Career Scholarship *242*

Math and Science Scholarship *156*

Math, Engineering, Science, Business, Education,
Computers Scholarships *162*

Medical Scrubs Collection Scholarship *106*

Michael P. Anderson Scholarship in Space
Science *486*

Minnesota Space Grant Consortium Scholarship
Program *142*

NASA Idaho Space Grant Consortium Scholarship
Program *157*

NASA Maryland Space Grant Consortium
Undergraduate Scholarships *142*

National Association of Water Companies-New
Jersey Chapter Scholarship *80*

National Society of Black Physicists and Lawrence
Livermore National Library Undergraduate
Scholarship *486*

National Space Grant College and Fellowship
Program *114*

Native American Leadership in Education
(NALE) *163*

Osage Chapter Undergraduate Service
Scholarship *117*

Paul W. Ruckes Scholarship *214*

Payzer Scholarship *140*

PepsiCo Scholarship and Internship *333*

Ronald E. McNair Scholarship in Space and
Optical Physics *486*

Scholarship for Students Pursuing a Business or
STEM Degree *84*

Science, Mathematics, and Research for
Transformation Defense Scholarship for
Service Program *110*

Sehar Saleha Ahmad and Abrahim Ekramullah
Zafar Foundation Scholarship *115*

Sigma Xi Grants-In-Aid of Research *101*

Society of Physics Students Leadership
Scholarships *487*

Society of Physics Students Outstanding Student in
Research *487*

Society of Physics Students Peggy Dixon Two-
Year College Scholarship *487*

STEM Majors Scholarships for Undergraduate
Students *110*

STEM Teachers Scholarship *111*

Student Research Awards of the Battery Division
of the Electrochemical Society Inc. *113*

Susan Ekdale Memorial Field Camp
Scholarship *242*

Tech High School Alumni Association/W.O.
Cheney Merit Scholarship Fund *297*

Technical Minority Scholarship *190*

UNCF STEM Scholars Program *159*

Undergraduate STEM Research
Scholarships *114*

Universities Space Research Association
Scholarship Award Program *116*

VADM Samuel L. Gravely, Jr., USN(Ret.)
Memorial Scholarship *111*

Vermont Space Grant Consortium *96*

Veterans of Enduring Freedom (Afghanistan) and
Iraqi Freedom Scholarship *214*

W1FDR Scholarship *112*

Walter Samuel McAfee Scholarship in Space
Physics *486*

Whitley Place Scholarship *120*

Willie Hobbs Moore, Harry L. Morrison, and
Arthur B.C. Walker Physics
Scholarships *486*

Political Science

AFIO Undergraduate and Graduate
Scholarships *103*

AFSCME/UNCF Union Scholars Program *103*

American Legion Auxiliary Department of
Arizona Wilma Hoyal-Maxine Chilton
Memorial Scholarship *488*

Bruce B. Melchert Scholarship *489*

Harry S. Truman Scholarship *488*

Humane Studies Fellowships *204*

Jerry Clark Memorial Scholarship *488*

Kansas Federation of Republican Women
Scholarship *360*

Lebanese American Heritage Club's Scholarship
Fund *201*

Minorities in Government Finance
Scholarship *78*

Moody Research Grants *104*

Naqvi Law Scholarship *226*

National Society Daughters of the American
Revolution Dr. Aura-Lee A. Pittenger and
James Hobbs Pittenger American History
Scholarship *360*

National Society Daughters of the American
Revolution Enid Hall Griswold Memorial
Scholarship *246*

Ossie Davis Endowment Scholarship
Program *132*

Spence Reese Scholarship *297*

StraightForward Media Liberal Arts
Scholarship *126*

SUEZ Corporate Scholars Program *87*

Teaching Assistant Program in France *104*

UNCF/Koch Scholars Program for
Undergraduates *87*

United Nations Association of Connecticut
Scholarship *133*

Washington Crossing Foundation
Scholarship *489*

Washington State Association for Justice
American Justice Essay & Video
Scholarship *227*

Psychology

AFSCME/UNCF Union Scholars Program *103*

Allied Healthcare Scholarship Program *151*

AvaCare Medical Scholarship *105*

BHW Women in STEM Scholarship *74*

CompHealth Medical Scholarship *151*

Cynthia E. Morgan Memorial Scholarship Fund,
Inc. *316*

Health Professions Preparatory Scholarship
Program *152*

Ketamine Clinics of Los Angeles Scholarship
Program *152*

Medical Scrubs Collection Scholarship *106*

OnlinePsychologyDegrees.com Education
Scholarships *490*

Pacific Mental Health Work Force Award *346*

Pilot International Scholarship *355*

Recovery Village Healthcare Scholarship *238*

Ruby Newhall Memorial Scholarship *355*

Sigma Xi Grants-In-Aid of Research *101*

The Society for the Scientific Study of Sexuality
Student Research Grant *109*

StraightForward Media Liberal Arts
Scholarship *126*

Virtuous Prom Peace Scholarship *491*

Public Health

AAC Research Grants *153*

Annual Healthcare and Life Sciences
Scholarship *156*

AvaCare Medical Scholarship *105*

Catherine E. Philbin Scholarship *491*

CompHealth Medical Scholarship *151*

Elizabeth and Sherman Asche Memorial
Scholarship Fund *98*

Florida Environmental Health Association
Educational Scholarship Awards *316*

Gates Millennium Scholars (GMS) Program *260*

Laurence R. Foster Memorial Scholarship *492*

Medical Scrubs Collection Scholarship *106*

Michael Moody Fitness Scholarship *255*

National Environmental Health Association/
American Academy of Sanitarians
Scholarship *316*

New England Employee Benefits Council
Scholarship Program *81*

Platinum Educational Group Scholarships Program
for EMS, Nursing, and Allied Health *107*

Teaching Assistant Program in France   *104*
Washington State Association for Justice
    American Justice Essay & Video
    Scholarship   *227*
WIFLE Scholarship   *227*

Social Services

AFSCME/UNCF Union Scholars Program   *103*
Alexander Scholarship Loan Fund   *171*
Allied Healthcare Scholarship Program   *151*
Alphonso Deal Scholarship Award   *226*
American Legion Auxiliary Department of
    Arizona Wilma Hoyal-Maxine Chilton
    Memorial Scholarship   *488*
CompHealth Medical Scholarship   *151*
Continental Society, Daughters of Indian Wars
    Scholarship   *251*
Developmental Disabilities Scholastic
    Achievement Scholarship for College Students
    who are Lutheran   *236*
Edith M. Allen Scholarship   *252*
Graduate and Professional Scholarship Program-
    Maryland   *238*
Helen Hamilton Scholarship Fund   *503*
Janet L. Hoffmann Loan Assistance Repayment
    Program   *254*
Northern Alberta Development Council
    Bursary   *234*
Ruby Newhall Memorial Scholarship   *355*
Steve Dearduff Scholarship   *351*
Student Opportunity Scholarship   *258*
Ted Bricker Scholarship   *504*

Special Education

American Legion Auxiliary Department of
    Arizona Wilma Hoyal-Maxine Chilton
    Memorial Scholarship   *488*
Anna and John Kolesar Memorial
    Scholarships   *247*
Applegate/Jackson/Parks Future Teacher
    Scholarship   *255*
ARC of Washington Trust Fund Stipend
    Program   *504*
Brookmire-Hastings Scholarships   *261*
Developmental Disabilities Scholastic
    Achievement Scholarship for College Students
    who are Lutheran   *236*
Illinois Special Education Teacher Tuition
    Waiver   *504*
James Carlson Memorial Scholarship   *256*
Jeanne S. Chall Research Fellowship   *254*
Judith Cary Memorial Scholarship   *505*
Mary Elizabeth Guest Scholarship   *505*
Pilot International Scholarship   *355*
Ruby Newhall Memorial Scholarship   *355*
StraightForward Media Teacher Scholarship   *258*

Sports-Related/Exercise Science

$1,500 STEM Scholarship   *106*
Alexander Scholarship Loan Fund   *171*
A.T. Anderson Memorial Scholarship
    Program   *109*
Bill Mason Scholarship Fund   *257*
CANFIT Nutrition, Physical Education and
    Culinary Arts Scholarship   *229*
CompHealth Medical Scholarship   *151*
David S. Bruce Awards for Excellence in
    Undergraduate Research   *105*
Linda Craig Memorial Scholarship presented by
    St. Vincent Sports Medicine   *355*
Lou and Carole Prato Sports Reporting
    Scholarship   *208*
Michael Moody Fitness Scholarship   *255*
National Athletic Trainers' Association Research
    and Education Foundation Scholarship
    Program   *354*

Ruth Abernathy Presidential Scholarship   *496*
Scholarship for Students Pursuing a Business or
    STEM Degree   *84*
StraightForward Media Vocational-Technical
    School Scholarship   *107*
Tobin Sorenson Physical Education
    Scholarship   *257*
The Walter J. Travis Memorial Scholarship   *388*

Statistics

$1,500 STEM Scholarship   *106*
Actuary of Tomorrow—Stuart A. Robertson
    Memorial Scholarship   *160*
A.T. Anderson Memorial Scholarship
    Program   *109*
Automotive Women's Alliance Foundation
    Scholarships   *74*
Colgate–Palmolive Corporate Scholars
    Program   *86*
Curtis E. Huntington Memorial Scholarship
    (Formerly The John Culver Wooddy
    Scholarship)   *245*
Hispanic Engineer National Achievement Awards
    Corporation Scholarship Program   *106*
STEM Majors Scholarships for Undergraduate
    Students   *110*
STEM Teachers Scholarship   *111*
Transtutors Scholarship 2015-16   *85*
VADM Samuel L. Gravely, Jr., USN(Ret.)
    Memorial Scholarship   *111*

Surveying, Surveying Technology, Cartography, or Geographic Information Science

$1,500 STEM Scholarship   *106*
Abraham Anson Memorial Scholarship   *296*
ACEC/Florida Scholarship   *298*
ACSM Fellows Scholarship   *507*
ACSM Lowell H. and Dorothy Loving
    Undergraduate Scholarship   *507*
American Association for Geodetic Surveying
    Joseph F. Dracup Scholarship Award   *507*
Associated General Contractors NYS Scholarship
    Program   *194*
Association of California Water Agencies
    Scholarships   *112*
A.T. Anderson Memorial Scholarship
    Program   *109*
Berntsen International Scholarship in
    Surveying   *507*
Berntsen International Scholarship in Surveying
    Technology   *508*
Cady McDonnell Memorial Scholarship   *508*
Clair A. Hill Scholarship   *112*
Eckenfelder Scholarship   *155*
Eric J. Gennuso and LeRoy D. (Bud) Loy, Jr.
    Scholarship Program   *173*
Francis H. Moffitt Memorial Scholarship   *296*
John O. Behrens Institute for Land Information
    Memorial Scholarship   *296*
Kenneth J. Osborn Memorial Scholarship   *296*
Kurt H. and Donna M. Schuler Small Grant   *176*
MALSE Scholarships   *302*
Minority Scholarship Program   *155*
MO Show-Me Chapter SWCS Scholarship   *95*
Nettie Dracup Memorial Scholarship   *508*
Pierre H. Guillemette Scholarship   *509*
Professional Land Surveyors of Oregon
    Scholarship   *509*
Robert E. Altenhofen Memorial Scholarship   *296*
Schonstedt Scholarship in Surveying   *508*
Ted G. Wilson Memorial Scholarship
    Foundation   *197*
Tri-State Surveying and Photogrammetry Kris M.
    Kunze Memorial Scholarship   *161*

Therapy/Rehabilitation

Aboriginal Health Careers Bursary   *153*
Al & Williamary Viste Scholarship   *233*
Allied Healthcare Scholarship Program   *151*
AMBUCS Scholars-Scholarships for
    Therapists   *134*
American Legion Auxiliary Department of
    Colorado Past Presidents' Parley Health Care
    Professional ScholarshipNurses
    Scholarship   *133*
American Legion Auxiliary Department of
    Michigan Medical Career Scholarship   *347*
Annual Healthcare and Life Sciences
    Scholarship   *156*
A.T. Anderson Memorial Scholarship
    Program   *109*
AvaCare Medical Scholarship   *105*
Carlotta Welles Scholarship   *348*
Carole J. Streeter, KB9JBR, Scholarship   *236*
CompHealth Medical Scholarship   *151*
Cynthia E. Morgan Memorial Scholarship Fund,
    Inc.   *316*
Delta Gamma Foundation Florence Margaret
    Harvey Memorial Scholarship   *247*
Developmental Disabilities Scholastic
    Achievement Scholarship for College Students
    who are Lutheran   *236*
EAAT Hippotherapy Scholarship   *510*
Frances L. Booth Medical Scholarship sponsored
    by LAVFW Department of Maine   *353*
Health Careers Scholarship   *238*
Janet L. Hoffmann Loan Assistance Repayment
    Program   *254*
Jimmy A. Young Memorial Education Recognition
    Award   *348*
Ketamine Clinics of Los Angeles Scholarship
    Program   *152*
Linda Craig Memorial Scholarship presented by
    St. Vincent Sports Medicine   *355*
Marion A. Lindeman Scholarship   *354*
Mary McMillan Scholarship Award   *249*
Medical Scrubs Collection Scholarship   *106*
Michael Moody Fitness Scholarship   *255*
Morton B. Duggan, Jr. Memorial Education
    Recognition Award   *348*
National Athletic Trainers' Association Research
    and Education Foundation Scholarship
    Program   *354*
National Society Daughters of the American
    Revolution Occupational Therapy
    Scholarship   *511*
Pilot International Scholarship   *355*
Recovery Village Healthcare Scholarship   *238*
Ruby Newhall Memorial Scholarship   *355*
Rudolph Dillman Memorial Scholarship   *248*
Scholarship for Students Pursuing a Business or
    STEM Degree   *84*
Sepracor Achievement Award for Excellence in
    Pulmonary Disease State Management   *348*
StraightForward Media Medical Professions
    Scholarship   *239*
Tobin Sorenson Physical Education
    Scholarship   *257*
U. S. Public Health Service-Health Resources and
    Services Administration, Bureau of Health
    Professions Scholarships for Disadvantaged
    Students   *239*
William and Dorothy Ferrell Scholarship   *250*

Trade/Technical Specialties

$1,500 STEM Scholarship   *106*
Alwin B. Newton Scholarship   *264*
American Chemical Society Scholars
    Program   *172*
American Welding Society District Scholarship
    Program   *277*

American Welding Society International
Scholarship *277*

Arsham Amirikian Engineering Scholarship *193*

ASHRAE General Scholarships *276*

Automotive Aftermarket Scholarship
Central *164*

Bradford White Corporation Scholarship *358*

Chapter 198-Downriver Detroit Scholarship *307*

Chapter 67-Phoenix Scholarship *307*

Charles W. Riley Fire and Emergency Medical
Services Tuition Reimbursement
Program *329*

Clinton J. Helton Manufacturing Scholarship
Award Fund *308*

College and Trade/Technical School
Scholarships *178*

David L. Massee Education Scholarship *514*

Delta Faucet Company Scholarship Program *167*

Donald F. Hastings Scholarship *277*

Duane Hanson Scholarship *264*

Dutch and Ginger Arver Scholarship *135*

ECA Scholarship *363*

Edward J. Brady Memorial Scholarship *278*

E. Wayne Kay Community College Scholarship
Award *308*

E. Wayne Kay Scholarship *309*

Fleming/Baszcak Scholarship *181*

Fort Wayne Chapter 56 Scholarship *309*

Frank M. Coda Scholarship *264*

GARMIN-Jerry Smith Memorial
Scholarship *135*

GARMIN Scholarship *135*

Gulf Coast Hurricane Scholarship *181*

Henry Adams Scholarship *265*

Howard E. and Wilma J. Adkins Memorial
Scholarship *278*

IFDA Student Member Scholarship *376*

International Executive Housekeepers Educational
Foundation *336*

Jim and Dianna Murphy Scholarship *514*

Kurt H. and Donna M. Schuler Small Grant *176*

Lee Tarbox Memorial Scholarship *135*

Lowell Gaylor Memorial Scholarship *135*

Lynn G. Bellenger Scholarship *265*

Maine Manufacturing Career and Training
Foundation Scholarship *142*

Mid-Continent Instrument Scholarship *136*

Miller Electric International World Skills
Competition Scholarship *278*

Miller Electric Mfg. Co. Scholarship *278*

MRCA Foundation Scholarship Program *122*

National Association of Water Companies-New
Jersey Chapter Scholarship *80*

NAWIC Construction Trades Scholarship *514*

NAWIC Undergraduate Scholarships *122*

Norm Manly—YMTA Maritime Educational
Scholarships *402*

North Central Region 9 Scholarship *309*

PHCC Educational Foundation Need-Based
Scholarship *167*

PHCC Educational Foundation Scholarship
Program *167*

Registered Apprenticeship Program/Career and
Technologies Studies (RAPS/CTS)
Scholarships *512*

Reuben Trane Scholarship *265*

Robert W. Valimont Endowment Fund Scholarship
(Part II) *512*

Rocky Mountain Coal Mining Institute Technical
Scholarship *515*

Ronald Lorah Memorial Scholarship *516*

SEMA Memorial Scholarship Fund *85*

Singerman/Nosseck Memorial Scholarship *514*

Society of Plastics Engineers Scholarship
Program *182*

StraightForward Media Vocational-Technical
School Scholarship *107*

Technical Training Fund Scholarship *130*

Ted G. Wilson Memorial Scholarship
Foundation *197*

Trucker to Trucker Scholarship *516*

Vermont Space Grant Consortium *96*

Wachovia Technical Scholarship Program *514*

Wichita Chapter 52 Scholarship *310*

William E. Weisel Scholarship Fund *269*

Women in Logistics Scholarship *170*

Women's jewelry association student
scholarship *132*

Workforce Development Scholarship *221*

Wyoming Trucking Association Scholarship Trust
Fund *87*

Transportation

ABA Academic Merit Scholarships *516*

ABA Diversity Scholarships *516*

Alice Glaisyer Warfield Memorial
Scholarship *518*

Associated General Contractors NYS Scholarship
Program *194*

A.T. Anderson Memorial Scholarship
Program *109*

Automotive Women's Alliance Foundation
Scholarships *74*

Dan Reichard Jr. Scholarship *161*

Denny Lydic Scholarship *518*

Dr. George M. Smerk Scholarship *517*

Donald C. Hyde Essay Program *517*

Eric J. Gennuso and LeRoy D. (Bud) Loy, Jr.
Scholarship Program *173*

Jack Gilstrap Scholarship *291*

Kurt H. and Donna M. Schuler Small Grant *176*

National Customs Brokers and Forwarders
Association of America Scholarship
Award *518*

Parsons Brinckerhoff-Jim Lammie
Scholarship *517*

Plan New Hampshire Scholarship and
Program *123*

SEMA Memorial Scholarship Fund *85*

TAC Foundation Scholarships *519*

Texas Transportation Scholarship *518*

Transit Hall of Fame Scholarship Award
Program *191*

Transportation Clubs International Charlotte
Woods Scholarship *518*

Transportation Clubs International Fred A. Hooper
Memorial Scholarship *282*

Transportation Clubs International Ginger and
Fred Deines Canada Scholarship *518*

Transportation Clubs International Ginger and
Fred Deines Mexico Scholarship *518*

Truckload Carriers Association Scholarship
Fund *168*

Western Association of State Highway and
Transportation Officials Scholarship *519*

Women in Logistics Scholarship *170*

Wyoming Trucking Association Scholarship Trust
Fund *87*

Travel/Tourism

ABA Academic Merit Scholarships *516*

ABA Diversity Scholarships *516*

AH&LEF Annual Scholarship Grant
Program *227*

American Express Travel Scholarship *520*

American Hotel & Lodging Educational
Foundation Pepsi Scholarship *228*

Arizona Chapter Gold Scholarship *520*

Avis Scholarship *520*

Bill Schwartz Memorial Scholarship *369*

Bob Smith Tourism Scholarship *336*

Costa Rican Vacations Scholarship *320*

Ecolab Scholarship Program *228*

George Reinke Scholarships *520*

Holland-America Line Westours
Scholarships *520*

Hyatt Hotels Fund for Minority Lodging
Management *228*

IATAN Ronald A Santana Scholarship *369*

Incoming Freshman Scholarships *228*

Joseph R. Stone Scholarships *520*

New Horizons Kathy LeTarte Scholarship *337*

Northern California Chapter Richard Epping
Scholarship *521*

Pacific Northwest Chapter-William Hunt
Scholarship Fund *521*

Pat and Jim Host Scholarship *370*

Princess Cruises and Princess Tours
Scholarship *521*

Rama Scholarship for the American Dream *228*

R.W. "Bob" Holden Scholarship *368*

Share Your Story with Homekitchenary *331*

Southern California Chapter/Pleasant Hawaiian
Holidays Scholarship *521*

Stan and Leone Pollard Scholarships *521*

UNCF/Carnival Corporate Scholars
Program *170*

TV/Radio Broadcasting

Alabama Broadcasters Association
Scholarship *522*

Androscoggin Amateur Radio Club
Scholarship *215*

Associated Press Television/Radio Association-
Clete Roberts Journalism Scholarship
Awards *379*

Belo Texas Broadcast Education Foundation
Scholarship *211*

Betty Endicott/NTA-NCCB Student
Scholarship *383*

Bonner McLane Texas Broadcast Education
Foundation Scholarship *211*

Broadcast Scholarship Program *523*

California Broadcasters Foundation Intern
Scholarship *522*

Career Journalism Scholarship *210*

Carole Simpson Scholarship *208*

CCNMA Scholarships *203*

Charles and Lucille King Family Foundation
Scholarships *203*

David J. Clarke Memorial Scholarship *205*

Dr. Lynne Boyle/John Schimpf Undergraduate
Scholarship *89*

Douglas W. Mummert Scholarship *129*

Ed Bradley Scholarship *208*

George Foreman Tribute to Lyndon B. Johnson
Scholarship *208*

Geraldo Rivera Scholarship *384*

Great Falls Broadcasters Association
Scholarship *524*

Hawaii Association of Broadcasters
Scholarship *523*

Helen Johnson Scholarship *387*

Indiana Broadcasters Foundation
Scholarship *381*

ISF National Scholarship *108*

Jack Shaheen Mass Communications Scholarship
Award *200*

J. D. Edsal Scholarship *90*

Jim McKay Memorial Scholarship *205*

John Bayliss Broadcast Radio Scholarship *204*

Kathryn Dettman Memorial Journalism
Scholarship *380*

Leonard M. Perryman Communications
Scholarship for Ethnic Minority Students *212*

Lou and Carole Prato Sports Reporting
Scholarship *208*

Louis F. Wolf Jr. Memorial Scholarship *210*

Civic, Professional, Social, or Union Affiliation

Dr. Gerald O'Connor Michigan QHY
Scholarship *537*
Dogwood Scholarship *537*
EAAT Hippotherapy Scholarship *510*
Excellence in Equine & Agricultural Involvement
Scholarship *538*
Farm and Ranch Heritage Scholarship *538*
Guy Stoops Professional Horsemen's Family
Scholarship *538*
Indiana Quarter Horse Youth Scholarship *538*
James F. and Doris M. Barton Scholarship *538*
Jay Pumphrey Animal Sciences
Scholarship *105*
Joan Cain Florida Quarter Horse Youth
Scholarship *538*
Joyce Wyatt Pennsylvania Quarter Horse Youth
Scholarship *538*
Nebraska Quarter Horse Youth Scholarship *539*
Scoop Vessels Scholarship *539*
Swayze Woodruff Memorial Mid-South
Scholarship *539*

American Radio Relay League
Don Riebhoff Memorial Scholarship *378*
Edmond A. Metzger Scholarship *266*
IRARC Memorial, Joseph P. Rubino,
WA4MMD, Scholarship *266*
Mississippi Scholarship *111*
North Fulton Amateur Radio League
Scholarship *215*
PHD Scholarship *215*
Ray, N0RP, & Katie, W0KTE, Pautz
Scholarship *215*
You've Got a Friend in Pennsylvania
Scholarship *540*

**American Society for Photogrammetry and
Remote Sensing**
Robert E. Altenhofen Memorial
Scholarship *296*

American Society of Civil Engineers
Eugene C. Figg Jr. Civil Engineering
Scholarship *192*
John Lenard Civil Engineering Scholarship *192*
Lawrence W. and Francis W. Cox
Scholarship *192*
Robert B.B. and Josephine N. Moorman
Scholarship *192*
Samuel Fletcher Tapman ASCE Student Chapter
Scholarship *192*
Y.C. Yang Civil Engineering Scholarship *192*

**American Society of Ichthyologists and
Herpetologists**
Gaige Fund Award *154*
Raney Fund Award *154*

American Society of Mechanical Engineers
ASME Auxiliary Undergraduate Scholarship
Charles B. Sharp *292*

**American Society of Radiologic
Technologists**
Elekta Radiation Therapy Scholarship *349*
Professional Advancement Scholarship *344*
Siemens Clinical Advancement
Scholarship *349*

American Society of Safety Engineers
Alaska Chapter Scholarship *463*
America Responds Memorial Scholarship *463*
ASSE-Gulf Coast Past Presidents
Scholarship *463*
ASSE Member Get A Member Scholarship *464*
ASSE-United Parcel Service Scholarship *464*
Central Florida Chapter Scholarship *464*

FabEnCo-LaCook Investment for Excellence in
Occupational Safety & Health
Scholarship *465*
Georgia Chapter Scholarship *465*
Greater Baton Rouge Chapter Don Jones
Excellence in Safety Scholarship *466*
Great Plaines Chapter Scholarship *466*
Harold F. Polston Scholarship *466*
Harry Taback 9/11 Memorial Scholarship *466*
James Joseph Davis Scholarship *467*
Lancaster County Industrial Safety Council
Scholarship in Honor of Craig Schroll & Jan
Getz *467*
Liberty Mutual Scholarship *467*
Northeastern Illinois Chapter Scholarship *468*
Northern Ohio Chapter Scholarship *468*
Region II Scholarship *469*
Scott Dominguez-Craters of the Moon Chapter
Scholarship *469*
United Parcel Service Diversity Scholarship
Program *470*

American Society of Travel Agents
Pacific Northwest Chapter-William Hunt
Scholarship Fund *521*

AMVETS Auxiliary
AMVETS National Ladies Auxiliary
Scholarship *539*

**Appaloosa Horse Club/Appaloosa Youth
Association**
Appaloosa Youth Educational Scholarships *539*
Lew and JoAnn Eklund Educational
Scholarship *105*

Arizona Business Education Association
ABEA Student Teacher Scholarships *249*

ASM International
ASM Outstanding Scholars Awards *295*
Edward J. Dulis Scholarship *295*
George A. Roberts Scholarship *295*
John M. Haniak Scholarship *295*
William P. Woodside Founder's
Scholarship *295*

Association for Iron and Steel Technology
AIST Alfred B. Glossbrenner and John Klusch
Scholarships *289*
Association for Iron and Steel Technology
Baltimore Chapter Scholarship *275*
Association for Iron and Steel Technology
Midwest Chapter Betty McKern
Scholarship *289*
Association for Iron and Steel Technology
Midwest Chapter Don Nelson
Scholarship *289*
Association for Iron and Steel Technology
Midwest Chapter Engineering
Scholarship *289*
Association for Iron and Steel Technology
Midwest Chapter Jack Gill Scholarship *289*
Association for Iron and Steel Technology
Midwest Chapter Mel Nickel
Scholarship *290*
Association for Iron and Steel Technology
Midwest Chapter Non-Engineering
Scholarship *290*
Association for Iron and Steel Technology
Midwest Chapter Western States
Scholarship *290*
Association for Iron and Steel Technology
Northwest Member Chapter
Scholarship *290*
Association for Iron and Steel Technology Ohio
Valley Chapter Scholarship *153*

Association for Iron and Steel Technology
Pittsburgh Chapter Scholarship *290*
Association for Iron and Steel Technology
Southeast Member Chapter Scholarship *290*

Association of Energy Service Companies
Association of Energy Service Companies
Scholarship Program *549*

Association of Engineering Geologists
Tilford Field Studies Scholarship *240*

Automotive Recyclers Association
Automotive Recyclers Association Scholarship
Foundation Scholarship *540*

Boy Scouts
American Legion Department of Illinois Boy
Scout/Explorer Scholarship *532*
American Legion Department of Iowa Eagle
Scout of the Year Scholarship *533*
American Legion Department of Tennessee Eagle
Scout of the Year *535*
American Legion Eagle Scout of the Year *535*
Eastern Orthodox Committee on Scouting
Scholarships *541*
Royden M. Bodley Scholarship *323*

California Teachers Association
California Teachers Association Scholarship for
Dependent Children *541*
California Teachers Association Scholarship for
Members *541*
L. Gordon Bittle Memorial Scholarship *250*
Martin Luther King, Jr. Memorial
Scholarship *250*

**Canadian Society for Medical Laboratory
Science**
Canadian Society for Medical Laboratory Science
Founders Fund Awards *350*
Canadian Society of Laboratory Technologists
Student Scholarship Program *350*
E.V. Booth Scholarship Award *345*

Children of the Confederacy
Charlotte M. F. Bentley/New York Chapter 103
Scholarship *564*
Elizabeth and Wallace Kingsbury
Scholarship *564*
Helen James Brewer Scholarship *361*
Winnie Davis-Children of the Confederacy
Scholarship *565*

Civil Air Patrol
Civil Air Patrol Academic Scholarships *541*
Major General Lucas V. Beau Flight Scholarships
Sponsored by the Order of Daedalians *139*

Columbian Squires
Fourth Degree Pro Deo and Pro Patria
Scholarships *547*

Community Banker Association of Illinois
Community Bankers Assoc of IL Child of a
Banker Scholarship *541*

Costume Society of America
Adele Filene Student Presenter Grant *125*
Stella Blum Student Research Grant *125*

Daughters of the American Revolution
National Society Daughters of the American
Revolution Lillian and Arthur Dunn
Scholarship *551*
National Society Daughters of the American
Revolution Madeline Pickett (Halbert)
Cogswell Nursing Scholarship *458*

Democratic Party
Pennsylvania Federation of Democratic Women
Inc. Annual Scholarship Awards *554*

Dermatology Nurses' Association
Career Mobility Scholarship *449*

Distribution Ed Club or Future Business Leaders of America
Harry A. Applegate Scholarship *75*
Nebraska DECA Leadership Scholarship *166*

Eastern Surfing Association
ESA Marsh Scholarship Program *542*

Elks Club
Elks Emergency Educational Grants *542*
Elks National Foundation Legacy Awards *542*

Experimental Aircraft Association
Hansen Scholarship *139*
Payzer Scholarship *140*

Explorer Program/Learning for Life
Captain James J. Regan Scholarship *392*
International Associations of Fire Chiefs
Foundation Scholarship *329*
Sheryl A. Horak Memorial Scholarship *392*

Family, Career and Community Leaders of America
C.J. Davidson Scholarship for FCCLA *362*
FCCLA Regional Scholarships *164*
FCCLA Texas Farm Bureau Scholarship *164*
Oklahoma Alumni & Associates of FHA, HERO,
and FCCLA Inc. Scholarship *553*

Federation of American Consumers and Travelers
Federation of American Consumers and Travelers
Educational Grant Program *542*
Federation of American Consumers and Travelers
Trade/Technical School Scholarship *542*

First Catholic Slovak Ladies Association
First Catholic Slovak Ladies Association High
School Scholarships *542*

Fleet Reserve Association/Auxiliary
Colonel Hazel Elizabeth Benn U.S.M.C.
Scholarship *543*
Doran/Blair Scholarships *543*
Ladies Auxiliary of the Fleet Reserve Association
Scholarship *547*
Sam Rose Memorial Scholarship *548*

Florida Environmental Health Association
Florida Environmental Health Association
Educational Scholarship Awards *316*

Freemasons
Edward Leon Duhamel Freemasons
Scholarship *557*
Pennsylvania Masonic Youth Foundation
Educational Endowment Fund
Scholarships *554*

Future Farmers of America
National FFA Collegiate Scholarship
Program *550*

Gamma Theta Upsilon
Buzzard-Maxfield-Richason and Rechlin
Scholarship *342*

Girl Scouts
Eastern Orthodox Committee on Scouting
Scholarships *541*
Emily Chaison Gold Award Scholarship *543*

Glass, Molders, Pottery, Plastics and Allied Workers International Union
GMP Memorial Scholarship Program *543*

Golden Key National Honor Society
GEICO Life Scholarship *543*
Golden Key Study Abroad Scholarships *543*

Golden State Bonsai Federation
Horticulture Scholarships *365*

Golf Course Superintendents Association of America
GCSAA Scholars Competition *365*
Golf Course Superintendents Association of
America Legacy Award *544*
Joseph S. Garske Collegiate Grant Program *544*

Grange Association
California Grange Foundation Scholarship *540*
Caroline Kark Award *134*
June Gill Nursing Scholarship *458*
Susan W. Freestone Education Award *552*

Greek Organization
Delta Sigma Pi Undergraduate Scholarship *163*
Kappa Alpha Theta Foundation Non-Degree
Educational Grant Program *546*
Kappa Alpha Theta Foundation Scholarship
Program *547*
Richard Cecil Todd and Clauda Pennock Todd
Tripod Scholarship *555*
Student Support Scholarship *257*

Hawaii Education Association
Hawaii Education Association High School
Student Scholarship *544*
Hawaii Education Association Student Teacher
Scholarship *253*
Hawaii Education Association Undergraduate
College Student Scholarship *544*

Healthcare Information and Management Systems Society
HIMSS Foundation Scholarship Program *345*

Hellenic University Club of Pennsylvania
Paideia Scholarship *544*

Ice Skating Institute
Higher Education Supplemental Scholarship
Isleta Pueblo Higher Education
Department *556*

Idaho Library Association
Idaho Library Association Gardner Hanks
Scholarship *398*

Independent Office Products and Furniture Dealers Association
NOPA and OFDA Scholarship Award *545*

Indiana Sheriffs' Association
Indiana Sheriffs' Association Scholarship
Program *225*

Institute of Industrial Engineers
A.O. Putnam Memorial Scholarship *299*
C.B. Gambrell Undergraduate Scholarship *300*
Dwight D. Gardner Scholarship *300*
IIE Council of Fellows Undergraduate
Scholarship *300*
Lisa Zaken Award For Excellence *300*
Marvin Mundel Memorial Scholarship *301*
Presidents Scholarship *301*
UPS Scholarship for Female Students *301*
UPS Scholarship for Minority Students *301*

International Brotherhood of Electrical Workers
International Brotherhood of Electrical Workers
Local 280 Scholarship *553*

International Brotherhood of Teamsters
James R. Hoffa Memorial Scholarship
Fund *545*

International Chemical Workers Union
Walter L. Mitchell Memorial Awards *545*

International Executive Housekeepers Association
International Executive Housekeepers
Association Educational Foundation Spartan
Scholarship *546*
International Executive Housekeepers
Educational Foundation *336*

International Technology Education Association
International Technology Education Association
Undergraduate Scholarship in Technology
Education *254*

International Union of Bricklayers and Allied Craftworkers
Canadian Bates Scholarship Program *546*
U.S. Bates Scholarship Program *546*

International Union of Operating Engineers
International Union of Operating Engineers Local
701 Scholarship *553*

Italian Catholic Federation
Italian Catholic Federation First Year
Scholarship *546*

Jaycees
Charles R. Ford Scholarship *565*
Thomas Wood Baldridge Scholarship *565*

Jobs Daughters
Grotto Scholarship *239*
Supreme Guardian Council Scholarship *559*
Susie Holmes Memorial Scholarship *559*

Junior Achievement
Joe Francomano Scholarship *546*

Junior Classical League
National Junior Classical League
Scholarship *200*

Knights of Columbus
Fourth Degree Pro Deo and Pro Patria
(Canada) *547*
Fourth Degree Pro Deo and Pro Patria
Scholarships *547*
Francis P. Matthews and John E. Swift
Educational Trust Scholarships *547*
John W. McDevitt (Fourth Degree)
Scholarships *547*
Percy J. Johnson Endowed Scholarships *547*

Learning Ally
Marion Huber Learning Through Listening
Awards *548*
Mary P. Oenslager Scholastic Achievement
Awards *548*

Marine Technology Society
Charles H. Bussman Undergraduate
Scholarship *401*
John C. Bajus Scholarship *401*

Ralph K. Hillquist Honorary SAE
Scholarship 286
SAE Long Term Member Sponsored
Scholarship 306

Society of Motion Picture and Television Engineers
Louis F. Wolf Jr. Memorial Scholarship 210
Student Paper Award 210

Society of Pediatric Nurses
Society of Pediatric Nurses Educational
Scholarship 190

Society of Physics Students
Society of Physics Students Leadership
Scholarships 487
Society of Physics Students Outstanding Student
in Research 487
Society of Physics Students Peggy Dixon Two-
Year College Scholarship 487

Society of Women Engineers
Bechtel Corporation Scholarship 310
Betty Lou Bailey SWE Region F
Scholarship 183
Carol Stephens SWE Region F Scholarship 183
Cummins Scholarship 183
Dr. Ivy M. Parker Memorial Scholarship 184
Dorothy Lemke Howarth Memorial
Scholarship 184
Dorothy P. Morris Scholarship 184
DuPont Company Scholarship 184
Elizabeth McLean Memorial Scholarship 198
Ellen Hippeli Memorial Scholarship 311
Exelon Corporation Scholarship 184
FCA Women in Engineering Scholarship 184
Ford Motor Company Scholarship 270
General Electric Women's Network
Scholarship 198
Honda Scholarship 311
Honeywell Scholarship 184
Judith Resnick Memorial Scholarship 311
Kellogg Scholarship 185
Mary V. Munger Scholarship 185
Roberta Banaszak Gleiter Engineering Endeavor
Scholarship 186
Rochelle Perry Memorial Scholarship 186
Rockwell Collins Scholarship 218
SWE Baltimore-Washington Section
Scholarship 186
SWE Central New Mexico Pioneers
Scholarship 187
SWE Central New Mexico Reentry
Scholarship 187
SWE Phoenix Section Scholarship 187
SWE Region E Scholarship 187
SWE Region G Judy Simmons Memorial
Scholarship 188
SWE Region H Scholarships 188
SWE Region J Scholarship 188
Turner Construction Scholarship 188

Soil and Water Conservation Society
Donald A. Williams Scholarship Soil
Conservation Scholarship 95
Melville H. Cohee Student Leader Conservation
Scholarship 558
Walt Bartram Memorial Education Award 309

SOKOL, USA
Slovak Gymnastic Union SOKOL, USA/Milan
Getting Scholarship 558

South Carolina State Employees Association
Anne A. Agnew Scholarship 559

Springfield Newspaper 25-Year Club
Horace Hill Scholarship 541

Tau Beta Pi Association
Tau Beta Pi Scholarship Program 189

Tau Kappa Epsilon
Bruce B. Melchert Scholarship 489
Carrol C. Hall Memorial Scholarship 115
Charles J. Trabold Scholarship 560
Charles R. Walgreen, Jr. Leadership Award 560
Charles R. Walgreen, Jr. Scholarship Award 560
Christopher Grasso Scholarship 560
Donald A. and John R. Fisher Memorial
Scholarship 560
Doris and Elmer H. Schmitz, Sr.
Memorial Scholarship 560
Dwayne R. Woerpel Memorial Leadership
Scholarship 561
Eric D. Dunning Scholarship 219
Eugene C. Beach Memorial Scholarship 561
Father Timothy Vakoc Memorial
Scholarship 561
Francis J. Flynn Memorial Scholarship 260
Gabe Anaya Scholarship 561
George W. Woolery Memorial Scholarship 212
Harry J. Donnelly Memorial Scholarship 85
J.D. Williams Scholarship 561
John A. Courson Scholarship 561
John C. Fitzgerald, Jr. Scholarship 168
J. Russel Salsbury Memorial Scholarship 562
Kenneth L. Duke, Sr. Memorial
Scholarship 562
Lenwood S. Cochran Scholarship 562
Lon G. Justice Scholarship 562
Michael Cerussi Leadership Scholarship 562
Michael J. Morin Memorial Scholarship 562
Miles Gray Memorial Scholarship 562
Robert D. Planck Scholarship 563
Ronald Reagan Leadership Award 563
T.J. Schmitz Scholarship 563
TKE Servant Leadership Scholarship 563
Wallace McCauley Memorial Scholarship 563
William V. Muse Scholarship 563
William Wilson Memorial Scholarship 564

Teamsters
Clyde C. Crosby/Joseph M. Edgar and Thomas J.
Malloy Memorial Scholarship 553
Josh Hieter Memorial/Teamsters Local 223
Scholarship 554
Teamsters Council 37 Federal Credit
Union Scholarship 554
Teamsters Local 305 Scholarship 554

Tennessee Education Association
TEA Don Sahli-Kathy Woodall Sons and
Daughters Scholarship 259

Texas Association of Broadcasters
Belo Texas Broadcast Education Foundation
Scholarship 211
Bonner McLane Texas Broadcast Education
Foundation Scholarship 211
Student Texas Broadcast Education Foundation
Scholarship 211
Tom Reiff Texas Broadcast Education
Foundation Scholarship 211
Undergraduate Texas Broadcast Education
Foundation Scholarship 211
Vann Kennedy Texas Broadcast Education
Foundation Scholarship 211

Transportation Club International
Alice Glaisyer Warfield Memorial
Scholarship 518
Denny Lydic Scholarship 518
Texas Transportation Scholarship 518
Transportation Clubs International Charlotte
Woods Scholarship 518
Transportation Clubs International Ginger and
Fred Deines Canada Scholarship 518
Transportation Clubs International Ginger and
Fred Deines Mexico Scholarship 518

United Daughters of the Confederacy
Barbara Jackson Sichel Memorial
Scholarship 564
Charlotte M. F. Bentley/New York Chapter 103
Scholarship 564
Gertrude Botts-Saucier Scholarship 564
Helen James Brewer Scholarship 361
Lola B. Curry Scholarship 565
Phoebe Pember Memorial Scholarship 461
United Daughters of the Confederacy
Undergraduate Scholarships 565
Walter Reed Smith Scholarship 168

United Food and Commercial Workers
James A. Suffridge United Food and Commercial
Workers Scholarship Program 565

United States Society on Dams
United States Society on Dams Scholarship
Award 199

USA Water Ski
American Water Ski Educational Foundation
Scholarship 539

Utility Workers Union of America
Utility Workers Union of America Scholarship
Awards Program 566

Vermont-NEA
Vermont-NEA/Maida F. Townsend
Scholarship 260

Veterans of Foreign Wars or Auxiliary
Frances L. Booth Medical Scholarship sponsored
by LAVFW Department of Maine 353
United States Submarine Veterans Inc. National
Scholarship Program 566

VietNow
VietNow National Scholarship 566

Western Fraternal Life Association
Western Fraternal Life Association National
Scholarship 566
Western Fraternal Life National
Scholarship 567

Wisconsin Association for Food Protection
WAFP Memorial Scholarship 567

Women in Aviation, International
Airbus Leadership Grant 149
Boeing Company Career Enhancement
Scholarship 149
Dassault Falcon Jet Corporation
Scholarship 149
Delta Air Lines Aircraft Maintenance
Technology Scholarship 149
Delta Air Lines Engineering Scholarship 149
Delta Air Lines Maintenance Management/
Aviation Business Management
Scholarship 150
Keep Flying Scholarship 150
Women in Aviation, International Achievement
Awards 150

Corporate Affiliation

Employment/Volunteer Experience

Agriculture
Abbie Sargent Memorial Scholarship   *91*
Benson & Bingham First Annual
    Scholarship   *393*
California Table Grape Farm Workers Scholarship
    Program   *580*
Collegiate Beef Advocacy Program   *406*
Donald A. Williams Scholarship Soil
    Conservation Scholarship   *95*
Excellence in Equine & Agricultural Involvement
    Scholarship   *538*
Farm and Ranch Heritage Scholarship   *538*
Fruits Industries Scholarships   *603*
International Dairy Deli Bakery Association's
    Scholarship for Growing the Future   *594*
Jay Pumphrey Animal Sciences Scholarship   *105*

Air Traffic Control
Air Traffic Control Association Scholarship   *573*
Buckingham Memorial Scholarship   *573*
CABAA/FlightSafety Maintenance Professional
    Training Award   *138*

Banking
Community Bankers Assoc of IL Child of a
    Banker Scholarship   *541*

Community Service
Alexander and Maude Hadden Scholarship   *627*
American Legion Auxiliary Department of Maine
    Past Presidents' Parley Nurses
    Scholarship   *347*
American Legion Auxiliary Department of
    Massachusetts Department President's
    Scholarship   *574*
American Legion Auxiliary Department of North
    Dakota National President's
    Scholarship   *575*
American Legion Eagle Scout of the Year   *535*
ARC of Washington Trust Fund Stipend
    Program   *504*
Comcast Leaders and Achievers
    Scholarship   *582*
Continuing Education-PTA Volunteers
    Scholarship   *540*
Delaware Solid Waste Authority John P. "Pat"
    Healy Scholarship   *281*
Distinguished Student Scholar Award   *257*
Dr. Hilda Richards Scholarship   *456*
eQuality Scholarships for Community College
    Transfer Students   *586*
Georgia Engineering Foundation Scholarship
    Program   *298*
Graduate Student Scholar Award   *257*
Graduating High School Senior Scholarship   *579*
Greenhouse Scholars   *590*
Harris Wofford Awards   *618*
Harry Bartel Memorial Scholarship   *618*
Helen Hamilton Scholarship Fund   *503*
Hispanic Annual Salute Scholarship   *591*
Hospital Central Services Student Volunteer
    Scholarship   *592*
Idaho Governor's Cup Scholarship   *593*
Jackie Robinson Scholarship   *596*
Jeffrey P. Meyer Memorial Scholarship   *623*

Jesse Brown Memorial Youth Scholarship
    Program   *584*
J. Fielding Reed Scholarship   *97*
Jill Weaver Starkman Scholarship   *623*
Latino Diamante Scholarship Fund   *583*
Lori Rhett Memorial Scholarship   *605*
MANA de San Diego Sylvia Chavez Memorial
    Scholarship   *601*
Markley Scholarship   *171*
Martha R. Dudley LVN/LPN Scholarship   *456*
Miss America Community Service
    Scholarships   *592*
National Association for Campus Activities Mid
    Atlantic Undergraduate Scholarship for
    Student Leaders   *605*
National Association for Campus Activities
    Northern Plains Region Student Leadership
    Scholarship   *605*
National Association for Campus Activities South
    Region Student Leader Scholarship   *606*
NBNA Board of Directors Scholarship   *457*
NGPA Education Fund, Inc.   *145*
Nursing Scholarship   *449*
Ohkay Owingeh Tribal Scholarship of the Pueblo
    of San Juan   *614*
Pacers TeamUp Scholarship   *611*
PoP'ay Scholarship   *614*
Safeway/Greater Washington Urban League
    Scholarship   *590*
SAR Family Emergency Scholarship   *625*
Scholarships for High School Graduates   *586*
Scholarships for Student Leaders   *606*
Sr. Mary Jeannette Wess, S.N.D.
    Scholarship   *615*
Taylor Michaels Scholarship Fund   *601*
Ted, W4VHF, and Itice, K4LVV, Goldthorpe
    Scholarship   *577*
Terry Fox Humanitarian Award   *621*
USBC Annual Zeb Scholarship   *593*
Washington State Association for Justice Past
    Presidents' Scholarship   *397*

Construction
ARTBA-TDF Lanford Family Highway Workers
    Memorial Scholarship Program   *576*
MRCA Foundation Scholarship Program   *122*
Project BEST Scholarship   *555*
Roadway Worker Memorial Scholarship
    Program   *576*

Designated Career Field
AQHF Racing Scholarships   *536*
Arizona Quarter Racing Scholarship   *537*
EAAT Hippotherapy Scholarship   *510*

Engineering/Technology
ASNT Engineering Undergraduate
    Scholarship   *276*
Association for Iron and Steel Technology Willy
    Korf Memorial Scholarship   *172*
High School Scholarship   *298*
Kaufman CALPHAD Scholarship   *268*
Materials Processing & Manufacturing Division
    Scholarship   *283*
TMS/EPD Scholarship   *283*

TMS/International Symposium on Superalloys
    Scholarship Program   *283*
TMS/Light Metals Division Scholarship
    Program   *284*
TMS Outstanding Student Paper Contest-
    Undergraduate   *284*

Environmental-Related Field
Donald A. Williams Scholarship Soil
    Conservation Scholarship   *95*
Steve Duckett Conservation Scholarship   *323*

Explosive Ordnance Disposal
Explosive Ordnance Disposal Memorial
    Scholarship   *586*

Farming
College Assistance Migrant Prog.   *581*
Collegiate Beef Advocacy Program   *406*
Farm and Ranch Heritage Scholarship   *538*
Jay Pumphrey Animal Sciences Scholarship   *105*

Federal/Postal Service
E.C. Hallbeck Scholarship Fund   *536*
Vocational Scholarship Program   *536*

Fine Arts
Women's jewelry association student
    scholarship   *132*

Food Service
Collegiate Beef Advocacy Program   *406*
Illinois Restaurant Association Educational
    Foundation Scholarships   *229*
International Dairy Deli Bakery Association's
    Scholarship for Growing the Future   *594*
Nancy Curry Scholarship   *333*
National Restaurant Association Educational
    Foundation Undergraduate Scholarships for
    College Students   *336*
National Restaurant Association Educational
    Foundation Undergraduate Scholarships for
    High School Seniors and General Education
    Diploma (GED) Graduate s   *337*
Professional Growth Scholarship   *334*
Schwan's Food Service Scholarship   *334*
W. Price, Jr. Memorial Scholarship   *232*

Government/Politics
Friends of Bill Rutherford Education
    Scholarship   *610*
Janet L. Hoffmann Loan Assistance Repayment
    Program   *254*

Harness Racing
AQHF Racing Scholarships   *536*
Arizona Quarter Racing Scholarship   *537*
Curt Greene Memorial Scholarship   *590*
HTA/Harold Snyder Memorial
    Scholarships   *590*

Helping Handicapped
ARC of Washington Trust Fund Stipend
    Program   *504*
EAAT Hippotherapy Scholarship   *510*
Jesse Brown Memorial Youth Scholarship
    Program   *584*

Impairment

Location of Study

UNITED STATES

Alabama

Alaska

Arizona

Arkansas

California

Two Ten Foundation Footwear Design
Scholarship *801*
United States Senate Youth Program *837*
ValuePenguin Scholarship *626*
Women in Rural Electrification (WIRE)
Scholarships *767*
You Deserve It! Scholarship *793*

Louisiana

AbbVie Immunology Scholarship *572*
Annual CGTrader Scholarship *580*
Annual iSeeCars Future Entrepreneurs
Scholarship *823*
ASHRAE Region VIII Scholarship *276*
Benson & Bingham First Annual
Scholarship *393*
Brainly Everyone Knows Something
Scholarship *578*
Broadcast Scholarship Program *523*
Casualty Actuaries of the Southeast Scholarship
Program *847*
CBC Spouses Education Scholarship *676*
CBC Spouses Heineken USA Performing Arts
Scholarship *428*
CBC Spouses Visual Arts Scholarship *120*
Classic Scholarships *622*
Costa Rican Vacations Scholarship *320*
Greenhouse Scholars *590*
Gulf Coast Hurricane Scholarship *181*
Jules Cohen Scholarship *266*
Korean-American Scholarship Foundation
Southern Region Scholarships *686*
Louisiana Department of Veterans Affairs State
Educational Aid Program *658*
Louisiana National Guard State Tuition Exemption
Program *644*
Markley Scholarship *171*
Milton Fisher Scholarship for Innovation and
Creativity *791*
Morrow & Sheppard College Scholarship *395*
National Make It With Wool Competition *325*
Pedro Zamora Young Leaders Scholarship *605*
Rockefeller State Wildlife Scholarship *157*
Society of Louisiana CPAs Scholarships *84*
Taylor Opportunity Program for Students Honors
Level *769*
Taylor Opportunity Program for Students
Opportunity Level *769*
Taylor Opportunity Program for Students
Performance Level *769*
Taylor Opportunity Program for Students Tech
Level *770*
Two Ten Footwear Foundation Scholarship *622*
Two Ten Foundation Footwear Design
Scholarship *801*
United States Senate Youth Program *837*
ValuePenguin Scholarship *626*
You Deserve It! Scholarship *793*

Maine

AbbVie Immunology Scholarship *572*
Annual CGTrader Scholarship *580*
Annual iSeeCars Future Entrepreneurs
Scholarship *823*
Benson & Bingham First Annual
Scholarship *393*
Brainly Everyone Knows Something
Scholarship *578*
CBC Spouses Education Scholarship *676*
CBC Spouses Heineken USA Performing Arts
Scholarship *428*
CBC Spouses Visual Arts Scholarship *120*
Classic Scholarships *622*
Costa Rican Vacations Scholarship *320*
Dr. James L. Lawson Memorial Scholarship *202*
Early College for ME *770*
Greenhouse Scholars *590*

Jules Cohen Scholarship *266*
Korean-American Scholarship Foundation
Northeastern Region Scholarships *686*
Maine Manufacturing Career and Training
Foundation Scholarship *142*
Maine Society of Professional Engineers Vernon
T. Swaine-Robert E. Chute Scholarship *283*
Maine State Society Foundation Scholarship *601*
Massachusetts Assistance for Student Success
Program *772*
Milton Fisher Scholarship for Innovation and
Creativity *791*
Morrow & Sheppard College Scholarship *395*
National Make It With Wool Competition *325*
New England Employee Benefits Council
Scholarship Program *81*
New England Regional Student Program-Tuition
Break *778*
Odd Fellows and Rebekahs Ellen F. Washburn
Nurses Training Award *458*
Patriot Education Scholarship Fund *166*
Pedro Zamora Young Leaders Scholarship *605*
Seol Bong Scholarship *637*
State of Maine Grant Program *753*
Tuition Waiver Programs *588*
Two Ten Footwear Foundation Scholarship *622*
Two Ten Foundation Footwear Design
Scholarship *801*
United States Senate Youth Program *837*
ValuePenguin Scholarship *626*
Veterans Dependents Educational Benefits-
Maine *658*
You Deserve It! Scholarship *793*

Maryland

AbbVie Immunology Scholarship *572*
Annual CGTrader Scholarship *580*
Annual iSeeCars Future Entrepreneurs
Scholarship *823*
ASHRAE Region III Boggarm Setty
Scholarship *176*
Benson & Bingham First Annual
Scholarship *393*
Betty Endicott/NTA-NCCB Student
Scholarship *383*
Brainly Everyone Knows Something
Scholarship *578*
Carmen V. D'Anna Memorial Scholarship of the
Mars Supermarket Educational Fund *744*
CBC Spouses Education Scholarship *676*
CBC Spouses Heineken USA Performing Arts
Scholarship *428*
CBC Spouses Visual Arts Scholarship *120*
Charles W. Riley Fire and Emergency Medical
Services Tuition Reimbursement
Program *329*
Classic Scholarships *622*
Costa Rican Vacations Scholarship *320*
Cynthia E. Morgan Memorial Scholarship Fund,
Inc. *316*
Delegate Scholarship Program-Maryland *770*
Direct Energy Live Brighter Scholarship *584*
Edward T. Conroy Memorial Scholarship
Program *602*
Graduate and Professional Scholarship Program-
Maryland *238*
Greenhouse Scholars *590*
Howard P. Rawlings Educational Excellence
Awards Educational Assistance Grant *771*
Howard P. Rawlings Educational Excellence
Awards Guaranteed Access Grant *771*
Janet L. Hoffmann Loan Assistance Repayment
Program *254*
J.F. Tolbert Memorial Student Grant
Program *771*
John Zagunis Student Leader Scholarship *827*

Jules Cohen Scholarship *266*
Korean-American Scholarship Foundation Eastern
Region Scholarships *685*
Lee Thornton Scholarship *208*
MACPA Educational Foundation Scholarship
Award *79*
Maryland Association of Private Colleges and
Career Schools Scholarship *602*
Maryland SPJ Pro Chapter College
Scholarship *388*
Milton Fisher Scholarship for Innovation and
Creativity *791*
Morrow & Sheppard College Scholarship *395*
NASA Maryland Space Grant Consortium
Undergraduate Scholarships *142*
National Association for Campus Activities Mid
Atlantic Higher Education Research
Scholarship *171*
National Association for Campus Activities Mid
Atlantic Undergraduate Scholarship for
Student Leaders *605*
National Make It With Wool Competition *325*
Part-Time Grant Program-Maryland *771*
Pedro Zamora Young Leaders Scholarship *605*
Roothbert Fund Inc. Scholarship *793*
Senatorial Scholarships-Maryland *771*
Sigma Delta Chi Scholarships *387*
SWE Baltimore-Washington Section
Scholarship *186*
SWE Region E Scholarship *187*
Tese Caldarelli Memorial Scholarship *827*
Tuition Reduction for Non-Resident Nursing
Students *455*
Tuition Waiver for Foster Care Recipients *771*
Two Ten Footwear Foundation Scholarship *622*
Two Ten Foundation Footwear Design
Scholarship *801*
Undergraduate Marketing Education Merit
Scholarships *162*
United States Senate Youth Program *837*
ValuePenguin Scholarship *626*
Vera Yip Memorial Scholarship *624*
Veterans of the Afghanistan and Iraq Conflicts
Scholarship Program *658*
Workforce Shortage Student Assistance Grant
Program *771*
You Deserve It! Scholarship *793*

Massachusetts

AbbVie Immunology Scholarship *572*
Agnes M. Lindsay Scholarship *772*
American Legion Auxiliary Department of
Massachusetts Department President's
Scholarship *574*
American Legion Auxiliary Department of
Massachusetts Past Presidents' Parley
Scholarship *651*
Annual CGTrader Scholarship *580*
Annual iSeeCars Future Entrepreneurs
Scholarship *823*
Benson & Bingham First Annual
Scholarship *393*
Brainly Everyone Knows Something
Scholarship *578*
CBC Spouses Education Scholarship *676*
CBC Spouses Heineken USA Performing Arts
Scholarship *428*
CBC Spouses Visual Arts Scholarship *120*
Classic Scholarships *622*
Costa Rican Vacations Scholarship *320*
Direct Energy Live Brighter Scholarship *584*
Dr. James L. Lawson Memorial Scholarship *202*
Edward S. Roth Manufacturing Engineering
Scholarship *308*
John and Abigail Adams Scholarship *772*

Military Service

Air Force

Air Force National Guard

Army

Army National Guard

Coast Guard

General

Nationality or Ethnic Heritage

African

American Meteorological Society Minority
    Scholarships   *426*
CANFIT Nutrition, Physical Education and
    Culinary Arts Scholarship   *229*
Joseph N. Boakai Sr. Higher Education
    Scholarship   *628*
Market Inspector $1,000 Scholarship In Support
    of Those Under the Revised U.S. Travel
    Ban   *692*
Northwest Journalists of Color Scholarship   *88*
OLM Malala Yousafzai Scholarship
    2017-2018   *129*

Albanian

OLM Malala Yousafzai Scholarship
    2017-2018   *129*

American Indian/Alaska Native

2017 Nurture for Nature Scholarship   *640*
5 Strong Scholars Scholarship   *669*
Aboriginal Health Careers Bursary   *153*
Accenture American Indian Scholarship   *672*
Actuarial Diversity Scholarship   *376*
Adolph Van Pelt Special Fund for Indian
    Scholarships   *674*
AFSCME/UNCF Union Scholars Program   *103*
Agnes Jones Jackson Scholarship   *551*
AIA/F Diversity Advancement Scholarship   *118*
AIET Minorities and Women Educational
    Scholarship   *496*
AIFS DiversityAbroad.com Scholarship   *673*
Al-Ben Scholarship for Academic Incentive   *179*
Al-Ben Scholarship for Professional Merit   *179*
Al-Ben Scholarship for Scholastic
    Achievement   *179*
Allogan Slagle Memorial Scholarship   *674*
Alumni Student Assistance Program   *677*
Amelia Kemp Scholarship   *712*
American Chemical Society Scholars
    Program   *173*
American Indian Education Foundation
    Scholarship   *672*
American Indian Nurse Scholarship
    Program   *347*
American Meteorological Society Minority
    Scholarships   *426*
American Physical Society Corporate-Sponsored
    Scholarship for Minority Undergraduate
    Students Who Major in Physics   *487*
Amy Hunter-Wilson, MD Scholarship   *358*
APEX Scholarship   *674*
Arizona Professional Chapter of AISES
    Scholarship   *295*
Arts Council of Greater Grand Rapids Minority
    Scholarship   *128*
A.T. Anderson Memorial Scholarship
    Program   *109*
AWG Ethnic Minority Scholarship   *242*
BHP Billiton University Scholarships   *705*
BIA Higher Education Grant   *685*
Blackfeet Nation Higher Education Grant   *675*
Breakthrough to Nursing Scholarships for Racial/
    Ethnic Minorities   *453*
Bureau of Indian Education Grant Program   *676*
CANFIT Nutrition, Physical Education and
    Culinary Arts Scholarship   *229*
Carole Simpson Scholarship   *208*
Catherine W. Pierce Scholarship   *127*

Cherokee Nation Higher Education
    Scholarship   *677*
Chief Manuelito Scholarship Program   *697*
Citizen Potawatomi Nation Tribal
    Scholarship   *678*
Colgate "Bright Smiles, Bright Futures" Minority
    Scholarship   *235*
College Student Assistance Program   *677*
College Student Pre-Commissioning Initiative
    (CSPI)   *629*
Continental Society, Daughters of Indian Wars
    Scholarship   *252*
David Risling Emergency Aid Scholarship   *675*
Dell Corporate Scholars Program   *169*
Diavik Diamonds Inc. Scholarships for College
    Students   *705*
Displaced Homemaker Scholarship   *675*
Ed Bradley Scholarship   *208*
EDSA Minority Scholarship   *391*
Elizabeth and Sherman Asche Memorial
    Scholarship Fund   *98*
Epsilon Sigma Alpha Foundation
    Scholarships   *682*
Essay Writing Contest by EssayHub   *590*
#FortOnFleek Challenge Scholarship   *681*
Gates Millennium Scholars (GMS) Program   *261*
Gates Millennium Scholars Program   *672*
GE/LULAC Scholarship   *166*
GM/LULAC Scholarship   *302*
Goldia.com Scholarship   *633*
HBCUConnect.com Minority Scholarship
    Program   *683*
Health Professions Preparatory Scholarship
    Program   *152*
Higher Education Scholarship Program   *696*
Higher Education Supplemental Scholarship Isleta
    Pueblo Higher Education Department   *558*
Hopi Education Award   *685*
Hubertus W.V. Wellems Scholarship for Male
    Students   *180*
Hyatt Hotels Fund for Minority Lodging
    Management   *228*
Indian Health Service Health Professions Pre-
    graduate Scholarships   *114*
International Order of the King's Daughters and
    Sons North American Indian
    Scholarship   *686*
Jackie Robinson Scholarship   *599*
Jim Bourque Scholarship   *249*
Judith McManus Price Scholarship   *529*
Kansas Ethnic Minority Scholarship   *688*
Ken Inouye Scholarship   *389*
LAGRANT Foundation Scholarship for
    Undergraduates   *88*
Leonard M. Perryman Communications
    Scholarship for Ethnic Minority
    Students   *212*
Mae Lassley Osage Scholarship   *700*
Martin Luther King, Jr. Memorial
    Scholarship   *251*
Master's Scholarship Program   *181*
Math, Engineering, Science, Business, Education,
    Computers Scholarships   *162*
Maureen L. and Howard N. Blitman, PE
    Scholarship to Promote Diversity in
    Engineering   *180*
Menominee Indian Tribe Adult Vocational
    Training Program   *692*
Menominee Indian Tribe of Wisconsin Higher
    Education Grants   *692*

Minnesota Indian Scholarship   *693*
Minorities in Government Finance
    Scholarship   *78*
Minority Affairs Committee Award for
    Outstanding Scholastic Achievement   *174*
Minority Scholarship Awards for College
    Students   *174*
Minority Scholarship Awards for Incoming
    College Freshmen   *174*
Minority Scholarship Program   *155*
Minority Student Summer Scholarship   *118*
Minority Teacher Incentive Grant Program   *252*
Minority Teachers of Illinois Scholarship
    Program   *254*
Minority Undergraduate Retention Grant-
    Wisconsin   *712*
Multicultural Scholarship Program   *171*
NACME Pre-Engineering Scholarship
    Program   *304*
NACME Scholars Program   *304*
National Dental Association Foundation Colgate-
    Palmolive Scholarship Program
    (Undergraduates)   *238*
National Press Club Scholarship for Journalism
    Diversity   *386*
National Society Daughters of the American
    Revolution American Indian
    Scholarship   *695*
National Society Daughters of the American
    Revolution Frances Crawford Marvin
    American Indian Scholarship   *695*
Native American Journalists Association
    Scholarships   *89*
Native American Leadership in Education
    (NALE)   *163*
Native American Natural Resource Research
    Scholarship   *436*
Native American Supplemental Grant   *700*
NativeVision   *695*
Navajo Generating Station Navajo
    Scholarship   *306*
New York State Aid to Native Americans   *695*
North Dakota Indian Scholarship Program   *696*
Northwest Journalists of Color Scholarship   *88*
Ohio Newspapers Foundation Minority
    Scholarship   *89*
Ohkay Owingeh Tribal Scholarship of the Pueblo
    of San Juan   *617*
OLM Malala Yousafzai Scholarship
    2017-2018   *129*
Oneida Higher Education Scholarship
    Program   *698*
Oregon Native American Chamber of Commerce
    Scholarship   *698*
Osage Nation Higher Education
    Scholarship   *613*
Owanah Anderson Scholarship   *675*
Peter Doctor Memorial Indian Scholarship
    Foundation Inc.   *699*
PoP'ay Scholarship   *617*
Public Relations Society of America Multicultural
    Affairs Scholarship   *90*
Rama Scholarship for the American Dream   *229*
RDW Group Inc. Minority Scholarship for
    Communications   *209*
Richard S. Smith Scholarship   *681*
Robert Aqqaluk Newlin Sr. Memorial Trust
    Scholarship   *694*
Robert Dole Scholarship for Disabled
    Students   *641*

UNCF/Anthem Corporate Scholars Program *170*
UNCF/Carnival Corporate Scholars Program *170*
United Parcel Service Diversity Scholarship Program *472*
UPS Hallmark Scholarships *711*
UPS Scholarship for Minority Students *302*
Vincent Chin Memorial Scholarship *381*
Warner Norcross and Judd LLP Scholarship for Students of Color *395*
WinWin Products, Inc. Scholarship *711*
YouthForce 2020 Scholarship Program *124*

Australian
OLM Malala Yousafzai Scholarship 2017-2018 *129*

Belgian
OLM Malala Yousafzai Scholarship 2017-2018 *129*

Black, Non-Hispanic
1040K Run/Walk Scholarships *77*
2017 Nurture for Nature Scholarship *640*
5 Strong Scholars Scholarship *669*
Actuarial Diversity Scholarship *376*
AFROTC HBCU Scholarship Program *642*
AFSCME/UNCF Union Scholars Program *103*
Agnes Jones Jackson Scholarship *551*
AIA/F Diversity Advancement Scholarship *118*
AIET Minorities and Women Educational Scholarship *496*
AIFS DiversityAbroad.com Scholarship *673*
Al-Ben Scholarship for Academic Incentive *179*
Al-Ben Scholarship for Professional Merit *179*
Al-Ben Scholarship for Scholastic Achievement *179*
Amelia Kemp Scholarship *712*
American Chemical Society Scholars Program *173*
American Meteorological Society Minority Scholarships *426*
American Physical Society Corporate-Sponsored Scholarship for Minority Undergraduate Students Who Major in Physics *487*
Anheuser-Busch Legends of the Crown Scholarship Program *86*
Arts Council of Greater Grand Rapids Minority Scholarship *128*
Ashley Stewart Scholarship *169*
AWG Ethnic Minority Scholarship *242*
BASF/Alfred Chisholm Endowed Memorial Scholarship *86*
Bishop Joseph B. Bethea Scholarship *683*
Blacks in Safety Engineering Scholarship *466*
Blue Cross Blue Shield of Illinois and Blue Cross Blue Shield of Texas Scholarship *116*
Breakthrough to Nursing Scholarships for Racial/Ethnic Minorities *453*
CANFIT Nutrition, Physical Education and Culinary Arts Scholarship *229*
Carole Simpson Scholarship *208*
Catherine W. Pierce Scholarship *127*
CBC Spouses Education Scholarship *679*
CBC Spouses Heineken USA Performing Arts Scholarship *429*
Charles S. Brown Scholarship in Physics *488*
City of Chicago Scholarship *707*
Colgate–Palmolive Corporate Scholars Program *86*
Colgate "Bright Smiles, Bright Futures" Minority Scholarship *235*
College Student Pre-Commissioning Initiative (CSPI) *629*
Cooper Industries *169*
CVS Pharmacy, Inc. Business Scholarships *86*

CVS Pharmacy, Inc. Pharmacy Scholarship *482*
Davis Scholarship for Women in STEM *190*
Deborah L. Vincent FAHRO Education Scholarship Award *707*
Dell Corporate Scholars Program *169*
Dr. Dan J. and Patricia S. Pickard Scholarship *680*
Ed Bradley Scholarship *208*
Edith M. Allen Scholarship *252*
EDSA Minority Scholarship *391*
Epsilon Sigma Alpha Foundation Scholarships *682*
Essay Writing Contest by EssayHub *590*
FedEx/UNCF Scholarship Program *707*
Foot Locker Foundation, Inc./UNCF Scholarship *707*
#FortOnFleek Challenge Scholarship *681*
Four Promises Scholarship *707*
Galactic Unite Bytheway Scholarship *190*
Gates Millennium Scholars (GMS) Program *261*
GE/LULAC Scholarship *166*
GM/LULAC Scholarship *302*
Goldia.com Scholarship *633*
Hallie Q. Brown Scholarship *694*
Harvey Washington Banks Scholarship in Astronomy *488*
Hausman Family Charitable Trust Scholarship *707*
HBCUConnect.com Minority Scholarship Program *683*
Herbert Lehman Scholarship Program *693*
Hubertus W.V. Wellems Scholarship for Male Students *180*
Hyatt Hotels Fund for Minority Lodging Management *228*
IABA Scholarship *686*
Intel Scholarship Program *190*
Jack and Jill of America Foundation Scholarship *707*
Jackie Robinson Scholarship *599*
John Lennon Endowed Scholarship Program *212*
Joseph A. Towles African Study Abroad Scholarship *707*
Joseph N. Boakai Sr. Higher Education Scholarship *628*
Judith McManus Price Scholarship *529*
Julianne Malveaux Scholarship *246*
Kansas Ethnic Minority Scholarship *688*
Ken Inouye Scholarship *389*
Kroger Michigan Scholarship *708*
LAGRANT Foundation Scholarship for Undergraduates *88*
Leonard M. Perryman Communications Scholarship for Ethnic Minority Students *212*
Liberty Mutual Scholarship *169*
Lorenzo Felder Scholarship *678*
Margie H. Verbal Emergency Scholarship Fund *261*
Martha R. Dudley LVN/LPN Scholarship *458*
Martin Luther King, Jr. Memorial Scholarship *251*
Master's Scholarship Program *181*
Maureen L. and Howard N. Blitman, PE Scholarship to Promote Diversity in Engineering *180*
Michael Jackson Scholarship *213*
Michael P. Anderson Scholarship in Space Science *488*
Minnesota Student Aid Scholarship *708*
Minorities in Government Finance Scholarship *78*
Minority Affairs Committee Award for Outstanding Scholastic Achievement *174*
Minority Scholarship Awards for College Students *174*

Minority Scholarship Awards for Incoming College Freshmen *174*
Minority Scholarship Program *155*
Minority Student Summer Scholarship *118*
Minority Teacher Incentive Grant Program *252*
Minority Teachers of Illinois Scholarship Program *254*
Minority Undergraduate Retention Grant-Wisconsin *712*
Multicultural Scholarship Program *171*
Mutual Savings Life Company Scholarship (Kemper) *708*
NACME Pre-Engineering Scholarship Program *304*
NACME Scholars Program *304*
NASCAR Black History Month Awards *86*
National Black MBA Association Undergraduate Scholarship *708*
National Black McDonald's Owners Association Hospitality Scholars Program *86*
National Dental Association Foundation Colgate-Palmolive Scholarship Program (Undergraduates) *238*
National Press Club Scholarship for Journalism Diversity *386*
National Scholarship *694*
National Society of Black Physicists and Lawrence Livermore National Library Undergraduate Scholarship *488*
Northwest Journalists of Color Scholarship *88*
NSBE O-I Corporate Scholarship Program *285*
Ohio Newspapers Foundation Minority Scholarship *89*
OLM Malala Yousafzai Scholarship 2017-2018 *129*
Oracle Corporate Scholars Program *170*
Ossie Davis Endowment Scholarship Program *132*
Palm Beach Association of Black Journalists Scholarship *388*
Pennsylvania State Employees Combined Campaign Scholarship (SECA) *708*
Pepsico Foundation-UNCF Last Dollar Scholarship *708*
Philadelphia Association of Black Journalists Scholarship *388*
Procter & Gamble General Scholarship *91*
Procter & Gamble STEM Scholarship *116*
Public Relations Society of America Multicultural Affairs Scholarship *90*
Rama Scholarship for the American Dream *229*
RDW Group Inc. Minority Scholarship for Communications *209*
Reliable Life Insurance Company Scholarship (Kemper) *708*
Retha M. Ford Scholarship for English Majors *402*
Rhythm Nation/Janet Jackson Scholarship *132*
Richard S. Smith Scholarship *681*
Ricoh Scholarship Program *87*
Robert Dole Scholarship for Disabled Students *641*
Rodney Thaxton/Martin E. Segal Scholarship *693*
Rollin M. Gerstacker Foundation Scholarship *708*
Ronald E. McNair Scholarship in Space and Optical Physics *488*
Ronald McDonald House of Charities for Central Indiana Scholarship *709*
Ron Brown Scholar Program *701*
Rowling, Dold & Associates LLP Scholarship *76*
Royce Osborn Minority Student Scholarship *350*
Sachs Foundation Scholarships *701*
SAR Family Emergency Scholarship *628*

Scholarship for the Visually Impaired to Study in Japan *632*

Teri and Art Iwasaki Scholarship *687*

Jewish
Diller Teen Tikkun Olam Awards *594*

Jewish Federation of Metropolitan Chicago Academic Scholarship Program *688*

JVS Scholarship Program *687*

Lessans Family Scholarship *677*

OLM Malala Yousafzai Scholarship 2017-2018 *129*

Sara and Max Goldsammler Scholarship Fund *698*

Korean
1B USD Worldwide Venture Capital *116*

Kimbo Foundation Scholarship *688*

Korean-American Scholarship Foundation Eastern Region Scholarships *689*

Korean-American Scholarship Foundation Northeastern Region Scholarships *689*

Korean-American Scholarship Foundation Southern Region Scholarships *689*

Korean-American Scholarship Foundation Western Region Scholarships *689*

Northwest Journalists of Color Scholarship *88*

OLM Malala Yousafzai Scholarship 2017-2018 *129*

Seol Bong Scholarship *640*

Lao/Hmong
Distinguished Raven FAC Memorial Scholarship *681*

Nisei Student Relocation Commemorative Fund *612*

Northwest Journalists of Color Scholarship *88*

OLM Malala Yousafzai Scholarship 2017-2018 *129*

Latin American/Caribbean
American Meteorological Society Minority Scholarships *426*

CCNMA Scholarships *203*

Fulfilling Our Dreams Scholarship Fund *701*

Mas Family Scholarship Award *166*

Northwest Journalists of Color Scholarship *88*

OLM Malala Yousafzai Scholarship 2017-2018 *129*

Second Chance Scholarships *691*

Latvian
OLM Malala Yousafzai Scholarship 2017-2018 *129*

Lebanese
Northwest Journalists of Color Scholarship *88*

OLM Malala Yousafzai Scholarship 2017-2018 *129*

Lithuanian
OLM Malala Yousafzai Scholarship 2017-2018 *129*

Mexican
Automotive Women's Alliance Foundation Scholarships *74*

Fleming/Baszcak Scholarship *182*

Latinos in Technology Scholarship *620*

Northwest Journalists of Color Scholarship *88*

OLM Malala Yousafzai Scholarship 2017-2018 *129*

Transportation Clubs International Ginger and Fred Deines Mexico Scholarship *521*

Mongolian
Northwest Journalists of Color Scholarship *88*

OLM Malala Yousafzai Scholarship 2017-2018 *129*

New Zealander
OLM Malala Yousafzai Scholarship 2017-2018 *129*

Pacific Health Workforce Award *347*

Pacific Mental Health Work Force Award *347*

Nicaraguan
OLM Malala Yousafzai Scholarship 2017-2018 *129*

Norwegian
King Olav V Norwegian-American Heritage Fund *126*

Nancy Lorraine Jensen Memorial Scholarship *189*

OLM Malala Yousafzai Scholarship 2017-2018 *129*

Polish
Massachusetts Federation of Polish Women's Clubs Scholarships *689*

OLM Malala Yousafzai Scholarship 2017-2018 *129*

Polish American Club of North Jersey Scholarships *690*

Polish Arts Club of Buffalo Scholarship Foundation Trust *130*

Polish Heritage Scholarship *699*

Polish National Alliance of Brooklyn USA Inc. Scholarships *690*

Polish Women's Alliance Academic College Undergraduate Scholarships *699*

Tomaszkiewicz-Florio Scholarship *690*

Portuguese
Cabrillo Civic Clubs of California Scholarship *676*

OLM Malala Yousafzai Scholarship 2017-2018 *129*

Portuguese Foundation Scholarship Program *616*

Rumanian
OLM Malala Yousafzai Scholarship 2017-2018 *129*

Russian
OLM Malala Yousafzai Scholarship 2017-2018 *129*

Scandinavian
OLM Malala Yousafzai Scholarship 2017-2018 *129*

Scottish
Donald Malcolm MacArthur Scholarship *701*

OLM Malala Yousafzai Scholarship 2017-2018 *129*

St. Andrews Scholarship *701*

Slavic/Czech
First Catholic Slovak Ladies Association Fraternal Scholarship Award *682*

OLM Malala Yousafzai Scholarship 2017-2018 *129*

Spanish
American Meteorological Society Minority Scholarships *426*

OLM Malala Yousafzai Scholarship 2017-2018 *129*

Sub-Saharan African
Northwest Journalists of Color Scholarship *88*

OLM Malala Yousafzai Scholarship 2017-2018 *129*

Swedish
OLM Malala Yousafzai Scholarship 2017-2018 *129*

Swiss
Medicus Student Exchange *704*

OLM Malala Yousafzai Scholarship 2017-2018 *129*

Pellegrini Scholarship Grants *704*

Swiss Benevolent Society of Chicago Scholarships *704*

Willy Isler Scholarships *704*

Syrian
Market Inspector $1,000 Scholarship In Support of Those Under the Revised U.S. Travel Ban *692*

Northwest Journalists of Color Scholarship *88*

OLM Malala Yousafzai Scholarship 2017-2018 *129*

Turkish
Northwest Journalists of Color Scholarship *88*

OLM Malala Yousafzai Scholarship 2017-2018 *129*

Ukrainian
International Education Awards-Ukraine *670*

OLM Malala Yousafzai Scholarship 2017-2018 *129*

Roberta B. Willis Scholarship Program—Need-Based Grant *680*

Vietnamese
Nisei Student Relocation Commemorative Fund *612*

Northwest Journalists of Color Scholarship *88*

OLM Malala Yousafzai Scholarship 2017-2018 *129*

Welsh
OLM Malala Yousafzai Scholarship 2017-2018 *129*

Yemeni
Afghanistan and Iraq War Veterans Scholarship *497*

Market Inspector $1,000 Scholarship In Support of Those Under the Revised U.S. Travel Ban *692*

Northwest Journalists of Color Scholarship *88*

OLM Malala Yousafzai Scholarship 2017-2018 *129*

Religious Affiliation

Baha'i Faith
OLM Malala Yousafzai Scholarship
2017-2018 *129*

Baptist
American Baptist Financial Aid Program *710*
OLM Malala Yousafzai Scholarship
2017-2018 *129*
Texas Black Baptist Scholarship *702*

Brethren
OLM Malala Yousafzai Scholarship
2017-2018 *129*

Buddhist Faith
OLM Malala Yousafzai Scholarship
2017-2018 *129*

Christian
Foundation For College Christian Leaders
Scholarship *714*
OLM Malala Yousafzai Scholarship
2017-2018 *129*
Young Christian Leaders Scholarship *712*

Disciple of Christ
OLM Malala Yousafzai Scholarship
2017-2018 *129*

Eastern Orthodox
Alpha Omega Scholarship In Memory Of Peter
Agris *201*
Eastern Orthodox Committee on Scouting
Scholarships *541*
OLM Malala Yousafzai Scholarship
2017-2018 *129*

Episcopalian
OLM Malala Yousafzai Scholarship
2017-2018 *129*
Stuart & Lucille Armstrong Scholarship *716*

Friends
OLM Malala Yousafzai Scholarship
2017-2018 *129*

Hindu Faith
OLM Malala Yousafzai Scholarship
2017-2018 *129*

Jewish
Broome and Allen Boys Camp and Scholarship
Fund *710*
Diller Teen Tikkun Olam Awards *591*
Jewish Federation of Metropolitan Chicago
Academic Scholarship Program *684*
JVS Scholarship Program *684*
Lessans Family Scholarship *674*
OLM Malala Yousafzai Scholarship
2017-2018 *129*
Sara and Max Goldsammler Scholarship
Fund *695*

Latter-Day Saints
OLM Malala Yousafzai Scholarship
2017-2018 *129*

Lutheran
Amelia Kemp Scholarship *709*
Belmer/Flora Prince Scholarship *724*
Developmental Disabilities Scholastic
Achievement Scholarship for College
Students who are Lutheran *236*
OLM Malala Yousafzai Scholarship
2017-2018 *129*

Methodist
Bishop Joseph B. Bethea Scholarship *679*
David W. Self Scholarship *713*
E. Craig Brandenburg Graduate Award *715*
Edith M. Allen Scholarship *252*
Helen and Allen Brown Scholarship *715*
Leonard M. Perryman Communications
Scholarship for Ethnic Minority
Students *212*
OLM Malala Yousafzai Scholarship
2017-2018 *129*
The Rev. Dr. Karen Layman Gift of Hope: 21st
Century Scholars Program *715*
Richard S. Smith Scholarship *677*

Muslim Faith
Annual Award Program *714*
ISF National Scholarship *108*
Jack J. Isgur Foundation Scholarship *129*
OLM Malala Yousafzai Scholarship
2017-2018 *129*

Pentecostal
OLM Malala Yousafzai Scholarship
2017-2018 *129*

Presbyterian
National Presbyterian College Scholarship *720*
Native American Supplemental Grant *697*
OLM Malala Yousafzai Scholarship
2017-2018 *129*
Samuel Robinson Award *721*
Student Opportunity Scholarship *258*

Protestant
Ed E. and Gladys Hurley Foundation
Scholarship *497*
OLM Malala Yousafzai Scholarship
2017-2018 *129*

Roman Catholic
Fourth Degree Pro Deo and Pro Patria
(Canada) *547*
Fourth Degree Pro Deo and Pro Patria
Scholarships *547*
Francis P. Matthews and John E. Swift
Educational Trust Scholarships *547*
Italian Catholic Federation First Year
Scholarship *546*
John W. McDevitt (Fourth Degree)
Scholarships *547*
Mae Lassley Osage Scholarship *697*
Mario Cugia Italian Studies Scholarship
Program *683*
OLM Malala Yousafzai Scholarship
2017-2018 *129*
Percy J. Johnson Endowed Scholarships *547*
Post High School Tuition Scholarships *711*

Seventh-Day Adventist
OLM Malala Yousafzai Scholarship
2017-2018 *129*

Unitarian Universalist
Children of Unitarian Universalist Ministers *723*
Joseph Sumner Smith Scholarship *723*
Marion Barr Stanfield Art Scholarship *131*
OLM Malala Yousafzai Scholarship
2017-2018 *129*
Pauly D'Orlando Memorial Art Scholarship *132*
Roy H. Pollack Scholarship *498*
Stanfield and D'Orlando Art Scholarship *132*

Residence

Wisconsin

Wyoming

Talent/Interest Area

Automotive

Automotive Aftermarket Scholarship Central *164*
Automotive Hall of Fame Educational Funds *814*
Automotive Women's Alliance Foundation Scholarships *74*
SEMA Memorial Scholarship Fund *85*

Aviation

ADMA Scholarship *137*
Air Traffic Control Association Scholarship *573*
Alaskan Aviation Safety Foundation Memorial Scholarship Fund *136*
Aviation Council of Pennsylvania Scholarship Program *137*
CAE SimuFlite Citation Type Rating Scholarship *147*
Edward W. Stimpson "Aviation Excellence" Award *140*
Gabriel A. Hartl Scholarship *136*
Illinois Pilots Association Memorial Scholarship *140*
International Society of Women Airline Pilots Grace McAdams Harris Scholarship *141*
John R. Lillard Virginia Airport Operators Council Scholarship Program *148*
Joseph Frasca Excellence in Aviation Scholarship *148*
Joshua Esch Mitchell Aviation Scholarship *140*
Lawrence C. Fortier Memorial Scholarship *573*
Major General Lucas V. Beau Flight Scholarships Sponsored by the Order of Daedalians *139*
National Aviation Explorer Scholarships *141*
NGPA Education Fund, Inc. *145*
PAPA Scholarship & Safety Foundation *146*
Paul A. Whelan Aviation Scholarship *148*
Rhode Island Pilots Association Scholarship *146*
Vertical Flight Foundation Scholarship *134*
Willard G. Plentl Aviation Scholarship Program *148*

Beauty Pageant

California Junior Miss Scholarship Program *742*
Eugenia Vellner Fischer Award for Performing Arts *477*
Miss America Community Service Scholarships *592*
Miss America Organization Competition Scholarships *822*
Miss America Scholar Award *822*

Bowling

Billy Welu Bowling Scholarship *831*
Gift for Life Scholarship *545*
USBC Alberta E. Crowe Star of Tomorrow Award *822*
USBC Annual Zeb Scholarship *593*
USBC Chuck Hall Star of Tomorrow Scholarship *823*
USBC Earl Anthony Memorial Scholarship *545*
USBC Youth Ambassador of the Year (M/F) *823*

Drum Corps

Martin D. Andrews Memorial Scholarship Fund *826*

English Language

American Legion Department of Illinois High School Oratorical Contest *731*
Teaching Assistant Program in France *104*
William Faulkner-William Wisdom Creative Writing Competition *416*

Entrepreneurship

1B USD Worldwide Venture Capital *116*
Al Neuharth Free Spirit and Journalism Conference Program *380*
Annual iSeeCars Future Entrepreneurs Scholarship *823*
Young Entrepreneur Awards *829*

Foreign Language

1B USD Worldwide Venture Capital *116*
Medicus Student Exchange *701*
National Junior Classical League Scholarship *200*
Teaching Assistant Program in France *104*

French Language

Fellowships for Full-Time Studies in French *338*
Teaching Assistant Program in France *104*

German Language/Culture

DAAD University Summer Course Grant *339*

Golf

Club Employees and Dependents Scholarship *756*
Dorothy Campbell Memorial Scholarship *786*
Dorothy S. Campbell Memorial Scholarship Fund *830*
FSGA Scholars *756*
Sarah E. Huneycutt Scholarship *756*
The Walter J. Travis Memorial Scholarship *388*
West Virginia Golf Association Fund *761*
Women's Western Golf Foundation Scholarship *838*

Greek Language

National Latin Exam Scholarship *200*

International Exchange

1B USD Worldwide Venture Capital *116*
AIFS Affiliate Scholarships *808*
AIFS DiversityAbroad.com Scholarship *669*
AIFS Generation Study Abroad Scholarships *808*
AIFS Gilman Scholarship Bonus-$500 Scholarships *808*
AIFS-HACU Scholarships *669*
AIFS Study Again Scholarships *808*
Teaching Assistant Program in France *104*

Italian Language

National Italian American Foundation Category II Scholarship *125*

Jewish Culture

American Jewish League for Israel Scholarship Program *808*

Latin Language

National Latin Exam Scholarship *200*

Leadership

$1,500 SuperCollege.com Scholarship *834*
Adelante Fund Scholarships *160*
AIFS Generation Study Abroad Scholarships *808*
Airbus Leadership Grant *149*
Al Neuharth Free Spirit and Journalism Conference Program *380*
American Society of Women Accountants Undergraduate Scholarship *73*
Anheuser-Busch Legends of the Crown Scholarship Program *86*
Appaloosa Youth Educational Scholarships *539*
ASHRAE General Scholarships *276*
Berna Lou Cartwright Scholarship *418*

Boettcher Foundation Scholarship *741*
Bruce B. Melchert Scholarship *489*
California Junior Miss Scholarship Program *742*
Canada Iceland Foundation Scholarship Program *815*
Carrol C. Hall Memorial Scholarship *115*
Charles J. Trabold Scholarship *560*
Charles R. Walgreen, Jr. Leadership Award *560*
Charles R. Walgreen, Jr. Scholarship Award *560*
Christopher Grasso Scholarship *560*
Claes Nobel Academic Scholarships *551*
Delaware Solid Waste Authority John P. "Pat" Healy Scholarship *281*
Director's Scholarship Award *308*
Distinguished Student Scholar Award *257*
Donald A. and John R. Fisher Memorial Scholarship *560*
Doris and Elmer H. Schmitz, Sr. Memorial Scholarship *560*
Dwayne R. Woerpel Memorial Leadership Scholarship *561*
Elks National Foundation Most Valuable Student Scholarship Contest *818*
Eric D. Dunning Scholarship *219*
Eugene C. Beach Memorial Scholarship *561*
Father Timothy Vakoc Memorial Scholarship *561*
Ford Motor Company Scholarship *270*
Foundation For College Christian Leaders Scholarship *714*
Founders Scholarship *550*
Francis J. Flynn Memorial Scholarship *260*
Frank M. Coda Scholarship *264*
Frank W. McHale Memorial Scholarships *731*
Gabe Anaya Scholarship *561*
GAPA Scholarships *820*
Gates Millennium Scholars (GMS) Program *260*
Gates Millennium Scholars Program *669*
General Electric Women's Network Scholarship *198*
George W. Woolery Memorial Scholarship *212*
Gloria Barron Prize for Young Heroes *821*
Graduate Student Scholar Award *257*
Greenhouse Scholars *590*
Harry J. Donnelly Memorial Scholarship *85*
Harry S. Truman Scholarship *488*
Henry Adams Scholarship *265*
Henry J. Reilly Memorial Scholarship-High School Seniors and First Year Freshmen *557*
Jackie Robinson Scholarship *596*
Jaycee War Memorial Fund Scholarship *836*
J.D. Williams Scholarship *561*
J. Fielding Reed Scholarship *97*
Joe Francomano Scholarship *546*
John A. Courson Scholarship *561*
John C. Fitzgerald, Jr. Scholarship *168*
John J. McKetta Undergraduate Scholarship *174*
John Zagunis Student Leader Scholarship *827*
J. Russel Salsbury Memorial Scholarship *562*
Juliette A. Southard Scholarship *234*
Kenneth L. Duke, Sr. Memorial Scholarship *562*
Kid's Chance of West Virginia Scholarship *759*
Latino Diamante Scholarship Fund *583*
Laurence Decore Awards for Student Leadership *668*
Leading the Future II Scholarship *832*
Lenwood S. Cochran Scholarship *562*
Lon G. Justice Scholarship *562*
Lori Rhett Memorial Scholarship *605*
Lynn G. Bellenger Scholarship *265*

American Legion Department of Tennessee High
School Oratorical Contest 735
American Legion Department of Texas High
School Oratorical Contest 735
American Legion Department of Vermont High
School Oratorical Contest 735
American Legion Department of West Virginia
Board of Regents Scholarship 736
American Legion Department of West Virginia
High School Oratorical Contest 736
California Junior Miss Scholarship Program 742
Joseph S. Rumbaugh Historical Oration
Contest 828
Optimist International Oratorical Contest 830
United States Senate Youth Program 837
Voice of Democracy Program 837

Scandinavian Language
American-Scandinavian Foundation Translation
Prize 399

Science
ExploraVision Science Competition 835
Nancy Lorraine Jensen Memorial
Scholarship 189
Undergraduate Diversity Student Awards 159

Scuba Diving
Our World Underwater Scholarships 830

Sewing
National Costumers Association
Scholarships 827
National Make It With Wool Competition 325

Spanish Language
Maria Elena Salinas Scholarship 339
NoJEF Travel Grants 339

Theater
CBC Spouses Heineken USA Performing Arts
Scholarship 428
Mildred and Albert Panowski Playwriting
Award 819
National Costumers Association
Scholarships 827
National Ten-Minute Play Contest 807
VSA Playwright Discovery Award 837

Wildlife Conservation/Animal Rescue
Wildlife Leadership Awards 436

Writing
Aaron and Rita Slom Scholarship Fund for
Freedom and Diversity 835
Alert Scholarship 727
Al Neuharth Free Spirit and Journalism
Conference Program 380
American Essay Contest Scholarship 532
American Society of Criminology Gene Carte
Student Paper Competition 225
AQHF Journalism or Communications
Scholarship 201
Bernard Kilgore Memorial Scholarship for the NJ
High School Journalist of the Year 385
Bobette Bibo Gugliotta Memorial Scholarship for
Creative Writing 616
Center for Architecture, Douglas Haskell Award
for Student Journals 119
CollegeWeekLive.com Scholarship 816
Connecticut SPJ Bob Eddy Scholarship
Program 203
CrossLites Scholarship Award 817
Edward J. Nell Memorial Scholarship in
Journalism 386
Elie Wiesel Prize in Ethics Essay Contest 818
EssayJolt Scholarship 753
Essay Writing Contest by EssayHub 587
Freedom From Religion Foundation Michael
Hakeem Memorial Ongoing College Essay
Competition 714
Freedom From Religion Foundation William J.
Schulz Memorial College-bound High School
Senior Essay Competition 714
International Foodservice Editorial Council
Communications Scholarship 88
The Katherine Anne Porter Prize for Fiction 829
Law in Society Award Competition 396
Lee-Jackson Educational Foundation Scholarship
Competition 768
Literary Achievement Awards 399
L. Ron Hubbard's Writers of the Future
Contest 813
Michael J. Powell High School Journalist of the
Year 382
Mildred and Albert Panowski Playwriting
Award 819

National Association of Black Journalists and
Newhouse Foundation Scholarship 383
National Association of Black Journalists Non-
Sustaining Scholarship Awards 384
National Association of Hispanic Journalists
Scholarship 206
National Federation of State Poetry Societies'
College Undergraduate Poetry (CUP)
Competition 828
National Institute for Labor Relations Research
William B. Ruggles Journalism
Scholarship 206
National Ten-Minute Play Contest 807
National Writers Association Foundation
Scholarships 385
Native American Journalists Association
Scholarships 89
Optimist International Essay Contest 830
Outdoor Writers Association of America - Bodie
McDowell Scholarship Award 207
Overseas Press Club Foundation Scholar
Awards 386
Phi Alpha Theta/Western Front Association Paper
Prize 361
Philadelphia Association of Black Journalists
Scholarship 386
Platt Family Scholarship Prize Essay
Contest 826
Scholastic Art and Writing Awards-Writing
Section Scholarship 127
Signet Classic Scholarship Essay Contest 831
Sylvia Rivera Award in Transgender Studies 816
Texas Outdoor Writers Association
Scholarship 800
Valley Press Club Scholarships, The Republican
Scholarship, Channel 22 Scholarship 213
Voice of Democracy Program 837
VSA Playwright Discovery Award 837
William C. Rogers Scholarship 381
William Faulkner-William Wisdom Creative
Writing Competition 416
Writer's Digest Annual Writing Competition 838
Writer's Digest Popular Fiction Awards 838
Writer's Digest Self-Published Book
Awards 838
Young Naturalist Awards 811

NOTES

NOTES

NOTES

NOTES

NOTES

NOTES

NOTES

NOTES

NOTES

NOTES

NOTES

NOTES

NOTES

NOTES

NOTES

NOTES

NOTES

NOTES

NOTES

NOTES

NOTES

NOTES